Contents

How to Use This Guidebook ■ 3
Alaska Highway Rendezvous '92 ■ 5
Key to Highways Map ■ 8
Traveling the North Country ■ 9
How to Read a Highway Log ■ 12
Welcome to the North Country ■ 13
General Information ■ 630
Mileage Chart ■ back of Plan-A-Trip Map

Highways

Alaska Highway ■ 68
Dawson Creek, BC, to Fairbanks AK

Alaska Highway via East Access Route ■ 22
Great Falls, MT, to Dawson Creek, BC

Alaska Highway via West Access Route ■ 42
Seattle, WA, to Dawson Creek, BC

Atlin Road ■ 604
Alaska Highway, YT, to Atlin, BC

Campbell Highway ■ 610
Watson Lake to Carmacks, YT

Canol Road ■ 615
Alaska Highway, YT, to NWT Border

Cassiar Highway ■ 223
Yellowhead Highway, BC, to Alaska Highway, YT

Copper River Highway ■ 517
Cordova, AK, to the Million Dollar Bridge

Dalton Highway ■ 624
Elliott Highway to Deadhorse, AK

Dempster Highway ■ 619
Klondike Highway 2, YT, to Inuvik, NWT

Denali Highway ■ 392
Paxson to Cantwell, AK

Edgerton Highway ■ 520
Richardson Highway to McCarthy, AK

Elliott Highway ■ 406
Fox to Manley Hot Springs, AK

George Parks Highway ■ 316
Anchorage to Fairbanks, AK

Glenn Highway/Tok Cutoff ■ 256
Tok to Anchorage, AK

Haines Highway ■ 596
Haines, AK, to Haines Junction, YT

Hudson's Hope Loop ■ 65
Alaska Highway to Chetwynd, BC

Klondike Highway 2 ■ 600
Skagway, AK, to Alaska Highway, YT

Klondike Loop ■ 237
Whitehorse, YT, to Taylor Highway, AK

Liard Highway ■ 180
Alaska Highway, BC, to Mackenzie Highway, NWT

Mackenzie Highway ■ 183
Edmonton, AB, to Yellowknife, NWT

Nahanni Range Road ■ 614
Campbell Highway, YT, to Tungsten, NWT

Richardson Highway ■ 506
Valdez to Delta Junction, AK

Seward Highway ■ 411
Anchorage to Seward, AK

Silver Trail Highway ■ 608
Klondike Highway to Keno City, YT

Steese Highway ■ 398
Fairbanks to Circle, AK

Sterling Highway ■ 434
Seward Highway to Homer, AK

Tagish Road ■ 607
Alaska Highway to Carcross, YT

Taylor Highway ■ 252
Tetlin Junction to Eagle, AK

Yellowhead Highway 16 ■ 197
Edmonton, AB, to Prince Rupert, BC

Railroads

Alaska Railroad ■ 397
White Pass & Yukon Route ■ 495

Marine Access Routes

Alaska State Ferries, BC Ferries and Cruise Ships ■ 524

Major Attractions

Anchorage ■ 285
Denali National Park and Preserve ■ 380
(formerly Mount McKinley National Park)
Fairbanks ■ 350
Kenai Peninsula ■ 410
Kodiak Island ■ 484
Prince William Sound ■ 489
Columbia Glacier, Whittier, Valdez, Cordova

Southeastern Alaska

Angoon ■ 566
Glacier Bay National Park and Preserve ■ 574
Gustavus ■ 578
Haines ■ 579
Hoonah ■ 567
Juneau ■ 568
Kake ■ 566
Ketchikan ■ 548
Metlakatla ■ 552
Pelican ■ 567
Petersburg ■ 560
Prince of Wales Island ■ 553
Sitka ■ 562
Skagway ■ 587
Tenakee Springs ■ 567
Wrangell ■ 557
Yakutat ■ 578

A straight stretch of the Alaska Highway along the Tanana River in Alaska.

DISCOVER THE PRINCESS DIFFERENCE

WHEN YOU LOOK INTO PRINCESS ...YOU SEE ALASKA

At Princess®, we pioneered luxury Alaska vacations more than 25 years ago... and today we offer more ways than ever to see the Great Land.

ALASKA UP CLOSE. The ultimate in Alaska rail travel is Princess' Midnight Sun Express®. Our private ULTRA DOME® rail cars offer 360° views from windows that are more than twice as large as any other dome cars.

DENALI, PRINCESS STYLE. Just a mile from the entrance to Denali National Park, Harper Lodge Princess® provides the ideal vantage point for exploring both towering Mt. McKinley and the park itself.

GO OUT AND PLAY. The fabulous Kenai Princess Lodge℠ is in the heart of Alaska's playground - fish, go river rafting, or simply relax in style. Or settle in at the Kenai Princess RV Park.

NORTH TO PRUDHOE. Travel with us along the Dalton Highway from Fairbanks to Prudhoe Bay and we'll show a land filled with fantastic wildlife, including the largest migratory caribou herd in North America.

AND THERE'S MORE. Princess also offers Arctic, Yukon, and Soviet Far East tours. Plus, sightseeing excursions from Anchorage and Fairbanks.

LOOK INTO PRINCESS. For more information and reservations, call (800) 835-8907. Or write: Princess Alaska, Dept. MPST, P.O. Box 19575, Seattle WA 98109-1575.

PRINCESS ALASKA
CRUISES & TOURS

General Manager, Anthony J. Robinson
Operations Director, Carolyn J. Threadgill
Managing Editor, Kris Valencia Graef
Copy Editor, Fay Bartels
Editorial Assistance: Camilla Newell, Billie Greenhalgh
Field Editors: Earl L. Brown, Lynn Lausterer, Jerrianne Lowther, Judy Parkin, Rollo and Chris Pool
Advertising Traffic Manager, Victoria Snyder
Production Manager, Nancy Deahl
Production Supervisor, Louise Helmick
Production Staff: David Berger, Brita Gilthvedt, Victoria Hall, Brenda Potts, David Ranta, Pamela Smith
Art Director, Kate Thompson
Designer, Cameron Mason
Fulfillment Manager, Cherryl Benson
Fulfillment Supervisor, Georgia Boyd

Copyright © 1992 GTE Discovery Publications, Inc. All rights reserved. No part of this book may be reproduced or transmitted in any form or by any means, electronic or mechanical, including photocopying, recording or by any information storage and retrieval system, without written permission of the publisher.

ISSN 0361-1361   ISBN 0-88240-216-1
Key title: The Milepost
Printed in U.S.A.

Alaska Northwest Books™
A Division of GTE Discovery Publications, Inc.
22026 20th Ave. S.E., Bothell, WA 98021
1-800-331-3510

Publishers of:
The MILEPOST®
The ALASKA WILDERNESS MILEPOST®
NORTHWEST MILEPOSTS®
Books about the North Country

COVER: Today's Alaska Highway winds along Kluane Lake. (Alissa Crandall)
INSET: The Alaska Highway in the 1940s. (William A. Wallace)

The gold stamp is the logo of the Alaska Highway Rendezvous '92 Society, which coordinated and sponsored many of the special events celebrating the highway's anniversary this year. The MILEPOST® is an official gold sponsor of Alaska Highway Rendezvous '92.

How to Use This Guidebook

STEP 1—Pull out the Plan-A-Trip map for an overview of the North Country and the access routes north.

STEP 2—Read "Traveling the North Country with *The MILEPOST®*" on page 9 for basic information on planning your trip North and using *The MILEPOST®* on the road. The Key to Highways map on page 8 will familiarize you with the routes covered in *The MILEPOST®*.

STEP 3—Read "Welcome to the North Country" on page 13 for highlights of highways and destinations covered in *The MILEPOST®*. Begin a list of places you want to include on your trip.

STEP 4—Look at the Contents on page 1. Information in *The MILEPOST®* is organized into sections: Highways, Major Attractions, Railroads, Marine Access Routes, and Southeastern Alaska. You may also find specific places by checking the Index in the back of the book.

STEP 5—Look through General Information in the back of the book. This section will answer many of your questions about traveling to Alaska.

STEP 6—Choose one of the Highways listed on the Contents page and turn to that section. Read the brief description of the highway on the first page of the section; look at the highway strip map; and try reading the highway log. If it seems confusing, go back to page 12 and review "How to Read a Highway Log."

STEP 7—Start planning your itinerary, referring to appropriate sections in *The MILEPOST®*. If you are driving the Alaska Highway, consult one of the two Access Routes to the Alaska Highway logged in *The MILEPOST®* and the Alaska Highway section. If you are taking the water route to Alaska, refer to the Marine Access Routes section for cruise ship and ferry information; read the descriptions of communities accessible by ferry in the Southeastern Alaska section; and refer to the Haines Highway and Klondike Highway 2 logs for road connections for ferry travelers.

Which MILEPOST to use?

Map Key (below left) indicates area covered by each book.

The MILEPOST® covers all highways and roads in Alaska, Yukon Territory,

western Northwest Territories and northern British Columbia and Alberta. (*Highlighted in red on map.*)

NORTHWEST MILEPOSTS® covers all interstate, U.S. and provincial highways, and some scenic routes, in Idaho, Oregon, Washington, western Montana and southern British Columbia and Alberta. (*Area shaded green on map.*)

The ALASKA WILDERNESS MILEPOST® covers only Alaska, and only off-the-road Alaska, except for a few key communities accessible by road that are jumping-off points for Bush destinations. (*Area shaded gold on map.*)

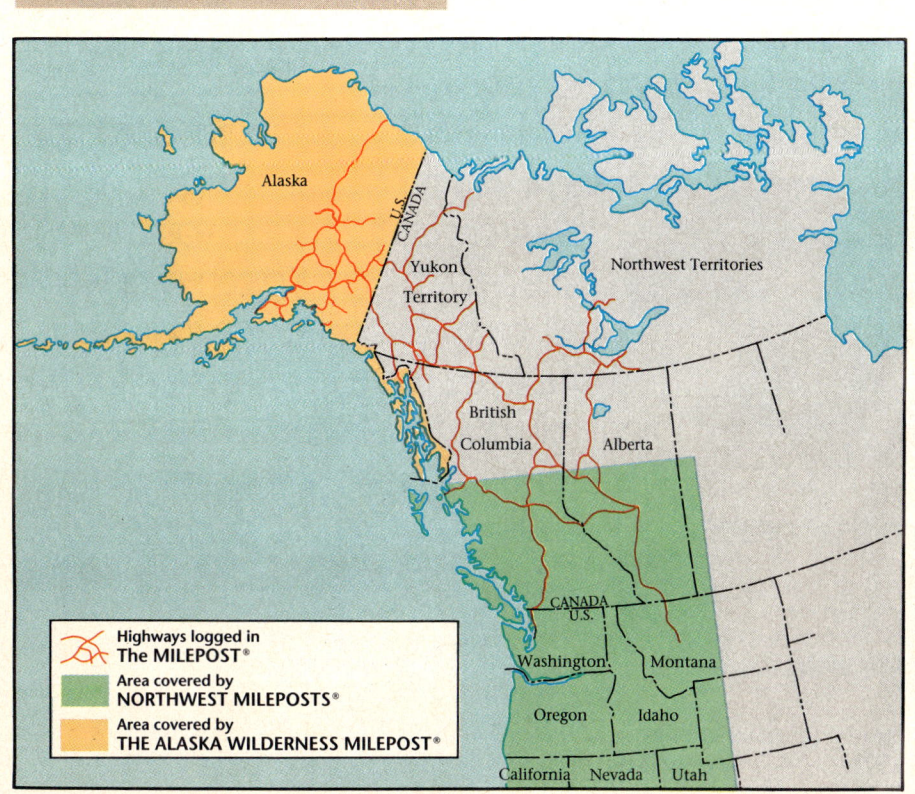

COME SEE WHAT'S BEEN ATTRACTING VISITORS TO THE ARCTIC FOR MORE THAN 14,000 YEARS.

The Eskimo people first set foot on the American continent over 14,000 years ago along the Arctic coast.

Today, you can meet their direct descendents in Kotzebue, sixty miles north of the Arctic circle. Watch the dances, listen to the haunting music, shop for finely-carved jade, talk to the people.

See how native traditions are still handed down.

Gaze across hundreds of square miles of tundra stretching as far as your imagination with completely unique wildlife and vegetation untouched by man's presence. All bathed in the glow of a midnight sun that never sets throughout the summer.

Buy your souvenir from the artist who made it.

Feel the still-fresh excitement of rough-and-tumble Gold Rush days in legendary Nome. See a sled dog demonstration and try your hand at gold-panning.

With an Alaska Airlines Arctic tour, you'll see it all. Our two day, one night packages include roundtrip airfare, accommodations and sightseeing.

ARCTIC TOURS $419
2 DAYS / 1 NIGHT INCLUDING AIRFARE FROM ANCHORAGE

It's two days you won't regret or forget. And if you don't have all night, which in the Arctic is a long time, you can still take a day tour of Kotzebue or Nome, and return to Anchorage that evening. For a free brochure or more information, call your travel agent or Alaska Airlines Vacations at 1-800-468-2248.

Alaska Airlines VACATIONS

Voted "Best U.S. Airline" by the readers of *Condé Nast Traveler* magazine.

Price shown is roundtrip from Anchorage. Price is per person based on double occupancy and includes roundtrip airfare, accommodations, transfers, taxes and sightseeing as outlined in the brochure. Seats and accommodations are limited. Changes and cancellations may be subject to a fee. Prices are subject to change without notice. Other restrictions may apply.

Alaska Highway Rendezvous '92 Society

March, 1992

Dear Alaska Highway Traveller:

As Chair of the Alaska Highway Rendezvous '92 Society, I wish to personally invite you to join us in 1992 to commemorate the 50th anniversary of the construction of the Alaska Highway.

This great event involves British Columbia, the Yukon and Alaska. For several years we have been working together to create what has become the largest single event of its kind ever to take place in the northern reaches of Canada and the United States.

There are literally hundreds of new historic and cultural events and attractions that will be happening in communities all along the highway in 1992 - the scope of which has already captured the imagination of northern residents and visitors alike.

I am especially proud to welcome GTE Discovery Publications, Inc. and The MILEPOST to a distinguished group of Gold Sponsors. Their generosity has made possible the unique calendar of ceremonies and events that will take place in communities all along "Rendezvous Road".

Since 1949 The MILEPOST has evolved along with the Alaska Highway. Published annually, it is the most comprehensive travel guide to services and attractions along the highway.

Mile by mile - and kilometre by kilometre - The MILEPOST is loaded with historic and vital information that has earned its reputation as a valued companion of highway travellers.

Let The MILEPOST by your guide in 1992, and share with us the adventure and nostalgia that awaits you with Alaska Highway Rendezvous '92.

Sincerely,

Ken McKinnon
Commissioner of the Yukon
Chair, AHR '92

KM:jdg

CHAIRMAN
Commissioner Ken McKinnon
Yukon Government
211 Hawkins Street
Whitehorse, Yukon Y1A 1X3
Telephone: (403) 667-5121
Fax: (403) 667-4153

EXECUTIVE DIRECTOR
Terence R. Thompson
14 - 9223 - 100th Street
Fort St. John, B.C. V1J 3X3
Telephone: (604) 787-1992
Fax: (604) 787-7613

Rendezvous '92
Celebrating the 50th Anniversary of the Alaska Highway

In 1942, the United States and Canada joined together to build the Alaska Highway. Construction of the pioneer road began in March 1942, and was completed less than 9 months later. Alaska and Canada will again join together in 1992 to commemorate the 50th anniversary of the construction of this historic road, considered one of the greatest engineering feats of the 20th century. The official celebration is called "Alaska Highway Rendezvous '92," and it is sponsored by the governments of the U.S. and Canada.

Special Events

A year-long calendar of events and attractions has been planned by the Alaska Highway Rendezvous '92 Society. Major international events along the highway include:

Opening Ceremonies. Scheduled for Feb. 15-16 in Dawson Creek, BC.

Airmada '92. An international air event involving military aircraft reenacting the historic ferrying of aircraft along the Northwest Staging Route from Great Falls, MT, to Fairbanks, AK. The Airmada will begin at Great Falls on July 4, 1992, and land at Fairbanks July 11-12, making stops at other communities along the way. Phone (604) 478-4144 for more information.

International Air Shows. Flying and ground displays will be featured at airshows throughout July in Great Falls, MT; Fort St. John, BC; Whitehorse, YT; and Fairbanks, AK. Phone (604) 478-4144 for more information.

Alaska Highway Trailblazers. A month-long horse and wagon trek along the Alaska Highway begins at Pouce Coupe, BC, June 13, 1992. Phone (604) 786-5794 for more information.

Army Motors Convoy. Vintage military vehicles depart Edmonton, AB, June 10, 1992, en route to Fairbanks, AK. A tribute to the Army Engineering Corps, some 74 military vehicles will take part in the 20-day return trip. The convoy will stop at communities along the highway to take part in local parades and special displays.

Floatplane Competition. In recognition of the key role floatplanes have played in development of the North, this Alaska Highway Rendezvous '92 event tests the flying and maneuvering skills of some 60 planes. The floatplanes depart Dawson Creek, BC, on their way to Fairbanks, AK, on June 21, 1992. Stops are made at communities along the way. Phone (604) 478-4144 for more information.

Rallye Alaska Highway '92. This event starts in Dawson Creek, BC, Sept. 17, 1992, and ends in Fairbanks, AK, Sept. 27, 1992. Professional race car drivers, truck drivers, tourists and senior citizens are welcome to compete in one of several categories of vehicle, including antique, passenger, motorhome, commercial and competition classes. Phone (604) 583-1197 for more information.

North West Staging Route Commemoration and Gala. Ladd Field in Fairbanks will be the stage for a gala affair on July 11, 1992, to commemorate the North West Staging Route. Veterans of the Lend–Lease program are invited to attend the ceremony, along with U.S., Canadian and Russian dignitaries. Phone (604) 787-1992 for more information.

Rededication Ceremonies. The dedication ceremony of the Alaska Highway on Nov. 10, 1942, will be reenacted Nov. 20, 1992, at Soldier's Summit near Kluane Lake. Phone (604) 787-1992 for more information.

Top—Contact Creek bridge, circa 1943. The bridge, located south of the Yukon Territory border, marks where Alaska Highway construction crews working west from Fort Nelson and east from Whitehorse met on Sept. 25, 1942. *(Edwin Bonde)*

Above—Commemorative Alaska Highway stamp issued for 1992 was designed by artist Byron Birdsall, the first Alaskan to design a postage stamp.

Top—*Cover of the first edition of* The MILEPOST®. *Published in 1949, it was the first guidebook to the Alaska Highway. The 72-page book included logs of the Alaska Highway; the Glenn Highway/Slana–Tok Cutoff; the Richardson Highway; and the Steese Highway.*

Above—*Two MILEPOST field editors, Jerrianne Lowther and Earl Brown (pictured here at the Tok Public Lands Information Center), cover today's Alaska Highway.* (Jerrianne Lowther, staff)

Reunions. U.S. Army Regiments, Canadian and U.S. contractors, U.S. Public Roads Administration, Soviet and U.S. pilots and others who worked and lived along the Alaska Highway in 1942, are planning reunions during 1992. For information on reunions you may like to attend or sponsor, contact any of the organizing offices of Rendezvous '92. Reunion centres have been set up in Northeastern British Columbia Tourist Infocentres.

A busy calendar of events and attractions is also planned at the local level by highway communities. Check the events calendars in the Alaska Highway log in *The MILEPOST*® and also check with community visitor information centers along the way to find out what's happening locally.

Visitors should see quite a parade of people and vehicles along the Alaska Highway in 1992, as individuals and organizations walk, run, dogsled, wagon train and ski from Milepost 0 to Alaska. Adventurer Charles E. Kux Kardos plans to drive his Rolls Royce up the highway.

For more information

To make your plans to participate in Rendezvous '92, and for more information on scheduled events, contact the following organizations:

Great Alaska Highways Society, P.O. Box 74250, Fairbanks, AK 99707, phone (907) 452-8000

Rendezvous '92, Suite 14, 9223 100th St., Fort St. John, BC V1J 3X3, phone (604) 787-1992

Yukon Anniversaries Commission, Bag 1992, Whitehorse, YT Y1A 5L9, phone (403) 668-1992

A Brief History of the Alaska Highway

Construction of the Alaska Highway officially began on March 8, 1942, and ended 8 months and 12 days later on Oct. 25, 1942. But an overland link between Alaska and the Lower 48 had been studied as early as 1930 under President Herbert Hoover's authorization. It was not until the bombing of Pearl Harbor in December 1941 that construction of the highway was deemed a military necessity. Alaska was considered vulnerable to a Japanese invasion. On Feb. 6, 1942, approval for the Alaska Highway was given by the Chief of Staff, U.S. Army. On Feb. 11, President Roosevelt authorized construction of the pioneer road.

The general route of the highway, determined by the War Department, was along a line of existing airfields from Edmonton, AB, to Fairbanks, AK. This chain of airfields was known as the Northwest Staging Route, and was used to ferry more than 8,000 war planes from Great Falls, MT, to Ladd Air Force Base in Fairbanks, AK, as part of the Russian-American Lend Lease Program. The planes were flown from Fairbanks to Nome, then on to Russia.

In March 1942, rights-of-way through Canada were secured by formal agreement between the 2 countries. The Americans agreed to pay for construction and turn over the Canadian portion of the highway to the Canadian government after the war ended. Canada furnished the right-of-way, and waived import duties, sales taxes, income taxes and immigration regulations, and provided construction materials along the route.

A massive mobilization of men and equipment began. Regiments of the U.S. Army Corps of Engineers were moved north to work on the highway. By June, more than 10,000 American troops had poured into the Canadian North. The Public Roads Administration tackled the task of organizing civilian engineers and equipment. Trucks, road-building equipment, office furniture, food, tents and other supplies all had to be located and then shipped north.

Road work began in April, with crews working out of the 2 largest construction camps, Whitehorse and Fort St. John. The highway followed existing winter roads, old Indian trails, rivers and, on occasion, "sight" engineering.

For the soldiers and civilian workers, it was a hard life. Working 8-hour shifts, 7 days a week, they endured mosquitoes and black flies in summer, and below zero temperatures in winter. Weeks would pass with no communication between headquarters and field parties. According to one senior officer with the Public Roads Administration, "equipment was always a critical problem. There never was enough."

In June 1942, the Japanese invaded Attu and Kiska islands in the Aleutians, adding a new sense of urgency to completion of the road. Crews working from east and west connected at Contact Creek on Sept. 25. By October, it was possible for vehicles to travel the entire length of the highway. The official opening of the Alaska Highway was a ribbon-cutting ceremony held Nov. 20, 1942, on Soldier's Summit at Kluane Lake.

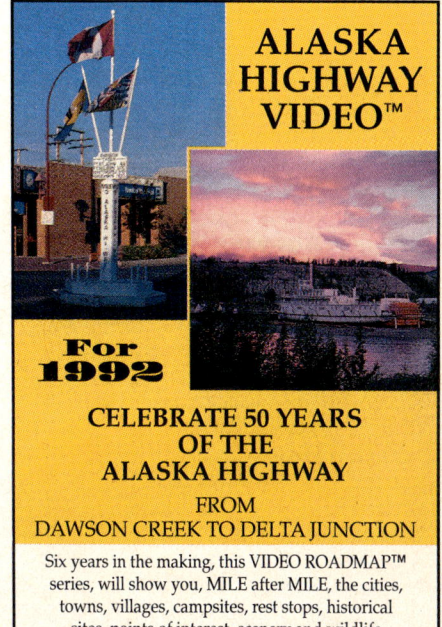

ALASKA HIGHWAY VIDEO™

For 1992

CELEBRATE 50 YEARS OF THE ALASKA HIGHWAY
FROM
DAWSON CREEK TO DELTA JUNCTION

Six years in the making, this VIDEO ROADMAP™ series, will show you, MILE after MILE, the cities, towns, villages, campsites, rest stops, historical sites, points of interest, scenery and wildlife along the ALASKA HIGHWAY in less than two hours. For just $19.92 plus $3 postage and handling, you can see it before you drive it.

Please write to: BeauMonde Production Co. PO Box 110931, Anchorage, Alaska 99511-0931

Traveling the North Country with The MILEPOST®

The MILEPOST® has been designed to help you get the most out of your travels in the North. It will help you plan your trip North, and guide you mile-by-mile through the country once you get there. The Key to Highways map in this section will show you what highways are covered in *The MILEPOST®*. How to Read a Highway Log (page 12) gives a detailed explanation of the highway logging system.

The first thing to think about in planning your trip North is how you wish to travel—by highway, by ferry, by cruise ship, by airplane, on your own or with a tour. You may want to use more than one form of transportation, such as driving the Alaska Highway one way and taking the Alaska Marine Highway (the state ferry system) the other way.

Regardless of how you travel, *The MILEPOST®* works the same way. Information in *The MILEPOST®* is organized into sections: Highways, Major Attractions, Railroads, Marine Access Routes, Southeastern Alaska and General Information. All sections are listed on the Contents page. If you are driving from Anchorage to Denali National Park, for example, turn to the George Parks Highway section for the log of the highway and the Denali National Park section for a description of the park and its facilities. Pertinent sections are always cross-referenced in capital letters in the log at the appropriate junction. For example, when you reach the turnoff for Denali National Park on the George Parks Highway, the log entry reads "see DENALI NATIONAL PARK section for details."

The quickest way to find another section is to refer back to the Contents page. Place-names and highways are also indexed in the back of the book.

By Highway

For highway travelers, there are mile-by-mile logs and detailed maps of all highways in Alaska and northwestern Canada. The highway logs include campgrounds, businesses offering food, gas, lodging and other services, attractions, fishing spots, and the geography and history of the land. Descriptions of highway communities are included in the highway logs. Highway communities are also indexed in the back of the book.

Whether you are an independent traveler in your own vehicle, or part of a motorcoach tour, you can follow along with these logs. (See How to Read a Highway Log page 12.)

A general description of the highway, including type of surfacing and length in miles, is included in the introduction to each highway section. Mileages are also keyed on the highway strip maps which accompany each highway section.

By Water

Travel to and within Alaska by water is described in *The MILEPOST®*. Major water

Sightseeing southeastern Alaska by cruise ship and helicopter. Flightseeing trips are offered in many communities.

Alissa Crandall

The Alaska Railroad, connecting Seward, Anchorage and Fairbanks, was built in 1923. (John W. Warden)

carriers are the Alaska state ferries, British Columbia ferries and cruise ships. These are covered in detail in the Marine Access Routes section. There are also numerous charter boat services, private tour boats and some government-operated ferries along the highways; details on these appear in the highway logs.

The Alaska state ferry's Southeastern system connects Bellingham, WA, and Prince Rupert, BC, with southeastern Alaska cities from Ketchikan to Skagway. These communities are covered in detail in the Southeastern Alaska section.

The Alaska state ferry's Southwestern system connects Seldovia, Homer, Seward, Whittier, Cordova, Valdez and Kodiak. Homer, Seward and Valdez are accessible by highway. Whittier is accessible by the Alaska Railroad. Seward is covered in the Seward Highway section; Homer and Seldovia in the Sterling Highway section; and Cordova, Valdez and Whittier in the Prince William Sound section. The Southwestern system also has limited summer service to Aleutian Chain communities.

Check the descriptions of attractions along the highways and in the communities for other water carriers. The Prince William Sound community of Valdez, for example, has a number of tour boat operators with sightseeing trips out to see Columbia Glacier. Fishing charter services are also available in Prince William Sound, as well as in Kenai Peninsula communities and Southeastern Alaska communities.

By Air

Air travel is one of the most common forms of transportation in the North. A list of scheduled air operators to and within the North Country is found in Air Travel in the General Information section. Also read the information on air transportation included in each community. There is a vast network of scheduled flights to small communities. These flights, combined with the numerous air charter services, make it possible to visit virtually any spot, no matter how remote.

Check the advertisements in the communities and along the highways for air charter operators offering fly-in hunting and fishing trips, flightseeing and transportation. You may, for instance, take a flightseeing trip out of Anchorage or Talkeetna for a spectacular view of Mount McKinley. From Fairbanks you may fly out to Fort Yukon or Prudhoe Bay for the day, or take an overnight trip to Point Barrow. There are scheduled flights to Glacier Bay out of Juneau which include accommodations; charter planes available by the hour for sightseeing Glacier Bay; and helicopters offering close-up views of Juneau Icefield. These are just a few examples of the variety of air travel available in the North and described in The MILEPOST®.

Pilots of private planes can refer to The MILEPOST® highway logs which include the location of airstrips along highways in Alaska and northwestern Canada.

By Rail

No railroads connect Alaska or the Yukon with the Lower 48, but 2 railroads do operate in the North: the historic White Pass & Yukon Route and the Alaska Railroad.

The White Pass & Yukon Route offers an excursion rail trip to White Pass out of Skagway and through-service to Whitehorse by motorcoach. See the White Pass & Yukon Route section for details.

The Alaska Railroad offers year-round service between Anchorage, Denali Park and Fairbanks, and summer service to Seward. The Alaska Railroad also runs a shuttle service from the Seward Highway to Whittier, port for Alaska state ferries crossing Prince William Sound. See the Alaska Railroad section for more information.

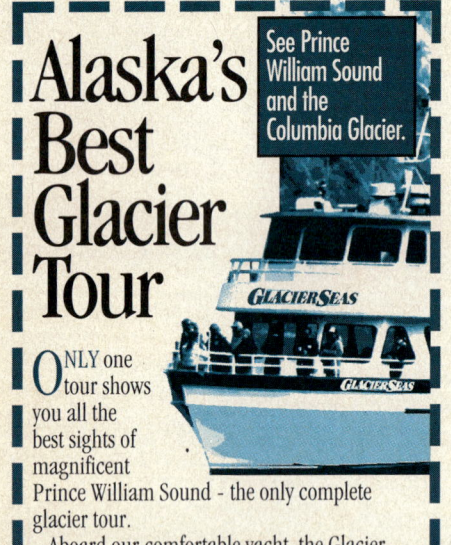

Alaska's Best Glacier Tour

See Prince William Sound and the Columbia Glacier.

ONLY one tour shows you all the best sights of magnificent Prince William Sound - the only complete glacier tour.

Aboard our comfortable yacht, the Glacier Seas, you'll see the incredible glaciers of Barry Arm - up close. View Harriman Fjord, Esther Passage. And the biggest of them all, Columbia Glacier.

We also offer Denali Park, Fairbanks, the Arctic and more.

See us across the street from the Log Cabin Visitor's Center!

Alaska Sightseeing CruiseWest
513 West 4th Ave., Anchorage AK 99501

Outside Alaska: (800) 426-7702
In Anchorage: (907) 276-1305

Experience the Last Frontier again—with these titles from Alaska Northwest Books™

TAKE ALASKA HOME WITH YOU

The MILEPOST® 1992

The bible of North Country travel is updated every year to provide the best information available. This year, you'll find a celebration of the highway's 50th anniversary, a mile-by-mile log of the Alaska Highway and 27 other roads within Canada and Alaska, detailed strip maps and a pull out Plan-A-Trip map, plus ferry, railroad, and accommodation information. Beautiful color photographs complete the package.
$16.95, 600 pp., 8 3/8" x 10 7/8"

The Alaska Wilderness MILEPOST® Sixth Edition

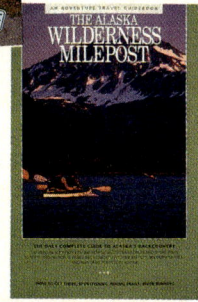

Much of Alaska's majestic beauty is off the road. Now you can find it all easily with The ALASKA WILDERNESS MILEPOST®. Thorough information on access and visitor services in 250 remote villages, 50 national and state parks, wildlife refuges, public use cabins, tips on finding the right guide and more make this the most comprehensive guide to backcountry travel available.
$14.95, 480 pp., 6" x 9"

The MILEPOST® Souvenir Log Book

Historical photos and lively captions about the early days of the Alaska Highway highlight this practical logbook. It's an easy way to keep track of trip expenses, create a diary, and record your gas, mileage, food, lodging, and wildlife sightings.
$4.95, 64 pp., 5 3/8" x 8 1/4"

Northwest MILEPOSTS® Fourth Edition

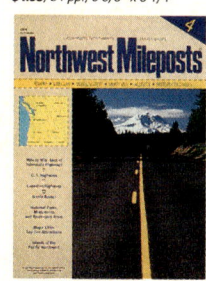

The most complete guide to travel in the region—with mile-by-mile logs of the key highways in Oregon, Washington, Idaho, western Montana and southwestern Canada, plus helpful maps, detailed information on major cities, islands, parks and more.
$14.95, 328 pp., 8 3/8" x 10 7/8"

Discover Alaska: An Introduction to America's Last Frontier

A wonderful souvenir of your trip or a gift for those you left behind, DISCOVER ALASKA presents this enormous state in breathtaking color photos and lively, informative text. Learn of the people, the land, the wildlife, the history, and the future of this land of spectacular contrasts.
$8.95, 64 pp., 8 3/8" x 10 7/8"

Facts about Alaska Fifteenth Edition

FACTS ABOUT ALASKA covers every Northern topic imaginable, from the location of the northernmost supermarket in the U.S. to the fact that Alaska actually grew 4,592 miles in 1984. You'll find the latest data, drawings, and maps to answer your every question.
$8.95, 232 pp., 5 3/8" x 8 3/8"

Jeff Gnass/WestStock

Beautiful Glacier Bay, Alaska. From Discover Alaska

Along the Alaska Highway

A perfect companion to our MILEPOST and just in time to celebrate the highway's 50th anniversary. Award-winning photos and engaging text take you through the history of this epic road, a 1,422 mile path through the dense forests of British Columbia to the raw wilderness of the Yukon Territory and across Alaska.
$16.95, 96 pp., 8 3/8" x 10 7/8"

The Alaska-Yukon Wild Flowers Guide

Wild flower lovers will appreciate this book's large color photos and black and white drawings plus handy reference indexes and take-along size.
$16.95, 224 pp., 5 3/8" x 8 3/8"

Guide to the Birds of Alaska, Revised Edition

This book, recognized as the authority on Alaska birds, features 437 species of birds with color photos and paintings and a useful map of the biogeographic regions.
$19.95, 349 pp., 6" x 9"

Alaska Wild Berry Guide and Cookbook

Identify Alaska's multitude of berries through color photos, detailed drawings and descriptive text and then proceed to the kitchen and use the recipes for enjoyable eating experiences.
$14.95, 212 pp., 6" x 9"

TO ORDER, CALL TOLL FREE (800) 331-3510

Or mail in this handy order form

QUANTITY	BOOK TITLE	COST	SUBTOTAL

TOTAL _____

Enclosed is my ☐ check ☐ money order
Charge it to my ☐ VISA ☐ MasterCard
Account # _____
Signature (Required): _____
Send my books to:
NAME _____
ADDRESS _____
CITY/STATE/ZIP _____
PHONE (required for credit card orders) _____
☐ Please send me a free catalog of all of Alaska Northwest Books' titles.

Floatplanes are a popular form of transport. From Along the Alaska Highway.

Alissa Crandall

How to Read a Highway Log

Seward Highway Log

ALASKA ROUTE 1
Distance from Seward (S) is followed by distance from Anchorage (A). Physical mileposts show distance from Seward.

S 17.7 (28.5 km) **A 109.3** (175.9 km) Bridge over center channel of Snow River.
S 17 (27 km) **A 110** (177 km) Turn west for Primrose USFS campground, 1 mile/1.6 km from the highway, overlooking Kenai Lake; 10 sites, toilets, dumpsters, tables, firepits, boat ramp, water.
Bridge over south channel Snow River.
S 15 (24.1 km) **A 112** (180.2 km) Watch for moose in ponds and meadows in this area.
S 14 (22.5 km) **A 113** (181.9 km) CAUTION: Railroad crossing.
S 11.6 (18.6 km) **A 115.4** (185.7 km) Paved parking area and USFS trail No. 6 to **Golden Fin Lake**, Dolly Varden averaging 8 inches.
S 6.6 (10.6 km) **A 120.4** (193.7 km) **Bear Creek RV and Mobile Home Park.** Good Sam Park has full and partial hookups, dump station, restrooms, showers, cable TV in travelers lounge, propane, laundry, convenience store. Leave your trailer/RV with us, have it serviced or repaired in our RV garage while you explore Seward. [ADVERTISEMENT]
S 3.7 (6 km) **A 123.3** (198.4 km) Turnoff for Exit Glacier Road. This 9-mile/14.5-km dirt road ends at a parking lot at Exit Glacier ranger station. A nature trail leads to base of glacier.
S 3.2 (5.1 km) **A 123.8** (199.2 km) Nash Road.
The White House B&B. See display ad this section.
S 0 A 127 (203.2 km) **Seward**, located on Resurrection Bay.

Above is an abbreviated version of part of the Seward Highway log, illustrated to show you how the written log reflects what you will see along the highway. In reading the log, it will help you to know 3 things: the boldface letters represent beginning and ending destinations (as explained in the opening boldface paragraph in each log); that the boldface numbers represent the distance in miles from those places, the lightface numbers the metric equivalent in kilometres; and that most highways in *The MILEPOST* are logged either south to north or east to west. (Exceptions to this rule include the Seward Highway in our example above.) If you are traveling the opposite direction of the log, you will read the log back to front.

It may also help you to know *how* our field editors log the highways. *The MILE-POST* field editors drive each highway, taking notes on facilities, features and attractions along the way and noting the mile at which they appear. Mileages are measured from the beginning of the highway, which is generally at a junction or the city limits, to the end of the highway, also usually a junction or city limits.

Physical mileposts (usually steel rods with a mileage flag at the top) are found on most highways in Alaska. Kilometreposts are up along most highways in Canada.

Advertising also appears in the highway logs, either as a display advertisement or as a "log" advertisement. Display advertisers are keyed in the log by a boldface entry at their location, followed by the words "see display ad this section." Log advertisements are identified by the boldface name of the business at the beginning of the entry and "[ADVERTISEMENT]" at the end. These log entries are written by the advertiser.

Finally, to determine driving distance between 2 points, simply subtract the first mileage figures. For example, the distance from the Primrose Campground turnoff at **Milepost S 17** to the trailhead at **Milepost S 11.6** is 5.4 miles.

12 The MILEPOST® ■ 1992

Welcome to the North Country

Visitors have an excellent chance of seeing wildlife, like these moose, at Denali National Park and Preserve.

The North Country is the land north of 51°16′ latitude. Geographically, it encompasses Alaska, Yukon Territory, western Northwest Territories, northern British Columbia and Alberta. *The MILEPOST®* covers this immense region by exploring its highway system.

Following is an introduction to the highways of the North Country, and some of the sights visitors will see along the way. Highways and destinations covered in *The MILEPOST®* are keyed in **boldface type**; see Contents for page number. We've highlighted here only a few of the top attractions in each area. Read through the individual highway sections in the book for a more complete listing of both attractions and services.

Alaska

Alaska is the most sparsely populated state in the Union. The state's population is 550,043, and its area is 586,412 square miles. That translates into about 1.07 square miles for every person. It became the 49th state in 1959.

Two mountain systems span the Alaskan mainland, and 17 of the 20 highest mountains in the United States are in the 49th state. Above the Arctic Circle is the Brooks Range, a northern extension of the Rocky Mountains and the last major mountain system in North America to be mapped and explored. More massive than the Brooks Range is the Alaska Range, which curves around southcentral Alaska and continues south through southeastern Alaska and Canada as the Pacific Coast ranges. Crowning the Alaska Range is Mount McKinley (also known as Denali), the highest peak in North America.

Roughly 6 distinct natural regions make up the state of Alaska: the Interior, the Arctic, Southcentral, Southeastern, the Bering Sea coast, and the Alaska Peninsula and Aleutian Chain. Each has its own climate, geography, history and industries.

Interior Alaska lies cradled between the Brooks Range to the north and the Alaska Range to the south, a vast area of approximately 166,000 square miles/431,600 square km that drains the Yukon River and its tributaries. It is a climate of extremes, with -40°F temperatures in winter and 90°F days in summer.

Fairbanks is the hub of the Interior, jumping-off point for bush communities in both the Interior and Arctic, and the crossroads of several Interior highways. It is also home to the excellent University of Alaska Museum, Alaskaland and the sternwheeler *Discovery*.

The **George Parks Highway** connects Fairbanks and Anchorage. This critical link between the 2 cities also provides access to **Denali National Park**, site of Mount McKinley (Denali), one of Alaska's top attractions. The **Steese Highway** out of Fairbanks provides access to 2 hot springs (Chena Hot Springs and Arctic Circle Hot Springs), Gold Dredge Number

Discover easier shopping.

When you're discovering Alaska, discover the store with more of your vacation needs in one fast, easy stop. Fred Meyer. With 29 stores under one roof, you can get all your shopping done in no time and have more time to spend exploring the Great North.

You'll find:

- **Outdoor Gear:** Camping, fishing and hunting supplies, fishing and hunting licenses.
- **Shoes and Clothing:** Hiking boots, running shoes, rain gear, sweaters and jeans.
- **Photo needs:** Cameras, film, batteries, film processing.
- **Pharmacy:** Have prescriptions filled while you shop.
- **Fred Meyer Music Market:** Get tapes, CD's, radios, tape players, batteries and supplies.
- **Snacks and Beverages:** Stock up before you head out. Pop, crackers, cheese, meats and more, at reasonable prices.

Fred Meyer Coupon

Variety Department

SAVE 10%
From Reg. Prices*
WITH THIS COUPON

All Alaska souvenirs in stock.

Cash value 1/20 of 1¢. Prices good at Alaska Fred Meyer Stores only.

FAIRBANKS
19 College Road
New Fred Meyer store at 3755 Airport Way.
Open 8AM to 10PM. Complete Grocery Store with Bakery and Deli

JUNEAU
8181 Glacier Hwy.

ANCHORAGE
1000 E. Northern Lights Blvd.
2000 W. Dimond Blvd

KENAI
11312 Kenai Spur Hwy.
at Carrs Mall
Clothing & Apparel only
Mon. through Fri. 9AM - 9PM
Sat. and Sun. 9AM - 7PM

Unless otherwise stated above, Fred Meyer Stores are open from 9AM to 10PM daily for your convenience.

Fred Meyer

8, the old F.E. Co. Gold Camp at Chatanika, and Circle City on the Yukon River. The **Elliott Highway** also leads to a hot springs (Manley) and a gold camp (Little Eldorado), and provides access to the Dalton Highway.

The **Alaska Highway** traverses the eastern edge of the Interior, following the Tanana River north from Tok through Delta Junction to Fairbanks. (Although the 98-mile section of road between Delta Junction and Fairbanks is officially designated as part of the Richardson Highway, it is logged in *The MILEPOST* as a natural extension of the Alaska Highway.) Visitors get their first taste of Alaska in Tok, a bustling community offering traveler services, dog mushing demonstrations and gift shops. Visitors get their first glimpse of the trans-Alaska pipeline at Delta Junction, and a look at Alaska's agriculture. The **Taylor Highway**, which junctions with the Alaska Highway near Tok, leads north past gold mining claims on the Fortymile River to the pioneer community of Eagle on the Yukon River.

Arctic Alaska lies above the Arctic Circle, between the Brooks Range to the south and the Arctic sea coast to the north, and from the Canadian border to the east westward to Kotzebue. Flightseeing trips to 2 Arctic destinations—Kotzebue and Prudhoe Bay—are popular sightseeing packages offered out of both Anchorage and Fairbanks. The only highway in the region, the **Dalton Highway**, forms a lonely ribbon of road stretching from Fairbanks to Prudhoe Bay on the North Slope. Built in conjunction with the trans-Alaska pipeline, this gravel road is open to public travel as far as Dietrich Camp. Beyond the checkpoint the highway is restricted to pipeline-related traffic.

The Southcentral region of Alaska curves 650 miles/1046 km north and west from the Gulf of Alaska coast to the Alaska Range. This region has tremendous geographic variety: fertile river valleys, rugged mountain ranges, glaciers, forests, and coastal waters rich in sea life.

Highways in Southcentral reflect this variety. The **Glenn Highway** cuts diagonally across the region. Highlights include magnificent views of the Wrangell and Chugach mountains, Matanuska Glacier, musk oxen and flower gardens at Palmer, and access to Independence Mine State Park. The **Denali Highway**, noted for its scenery and geography, follows the south flank of the Alaska Range to Denali National Park. The **Richardson Highway** offers spectacular views (of Thompson Pass and Worthington Glacier) and access to Valdez, location of the trans-Alaska pipeline terminal and gateway to **Prince William Sound** and Columbia Glacier. The state ferry from Valdez to Cordova is the only way to reach the **Copper River Highway** to the Million Dollar Bridge. The **Edgerton Highway** branches off the Richardson Highway and connects with the McCarthy Road to the historic mining town of Kennicott.

Southcentral includes the **Kenai Peninsula**, a popular spot for sport fishermen and outdoorsmen. The **Seward Highway**, 1 of 2 major routes on the Kenai, provides access to Alyeska ski resort, Portage Glacier, the Hope Highway, and to Seward, gateway to Kenai Fjords National Park. The **Sterling Highway** follows the Kenai River west to Cook Inlet (waters famous for salmon and halibut), then winds south along the peninsula's west coast to scenic Homer.

Anchorage, Alaska's largest city, is the hub of Southcentral. Anchorage began as a tent city of railroad workers at the head of Cook Inlet during the construction of the **Alaska Railroad** (1915–23). Today, the railroad provides passenger service between Fairbanks, Denali Park, Anchorage and Seward, with a branch line to Whittier, port for cruise ships and the state ferry to Prince William Sound communities. Anchorage offers first-class hotels, shopping, the excellent Anchorage Museum of History and Art, and a variety of other cultural and recreational attractions.

Less than an hour's flight from Anchorage, and about 10 hours by ferry from Homer, is **Kodiak**, the largest island in Alaska and the second largest island in the U.S. Kodiak is known for its brown bears, fishing, Russian heritage and WWII historical sites.

Southeastern Alaska is a moist, luxuriantly forested panhandle extending some 500 miles/805 km from Icy Bay on the Gulf of Alaska coast to Dixon Entrance south of Ketchikan. Southeast encompasses both the narrow strip of coast separated from the mainland (and Canada) by the Coast Mountains, and the hundreds of islands that make up the Alexander Archipelago.

The geography of this region prohibits road building, and southeastern communities (with the exception of Haines, Skagway and Hyder) are not connected to any highway system. Transportation is by air or by water, with **Alaska state ferries** providing transport for people and vehicles to more than a dozen communities. Cruise ships also call at mainline ports in Southeast, as well as cruising the waters of Glacier Bay National Park and Preserve. The all-weather **Haines Highway** connects Haines to the Alaska Highway, and also provides access to eagle-viewing areas along the Chilkat River. Scenic **Klondike Highway 2** connects Skagway to the Alaska Highway, cresting the Coast Range at White Pass summit.

Indian art, Russian architecture, the gold rush, and the lumber and fishing industries make up the sights and sounds of communities in Southeast. A few of the major attractions and events are: the historic **White Pass & Yukon Route** railway at Skagway, the state capitol in Juneau, Sitka National Historic Park, Totem Bight outside Ketchikan, the Little Norway Festival in Petersburg, and the Southeast Alaska State Fair in Haines.

Two of Alaska's regions—the Bering

A tidewater glacier in Holgate Arm, Kenai Fjords National Park. The park is accessible by tour boat from Seward. (George Wuerthner)

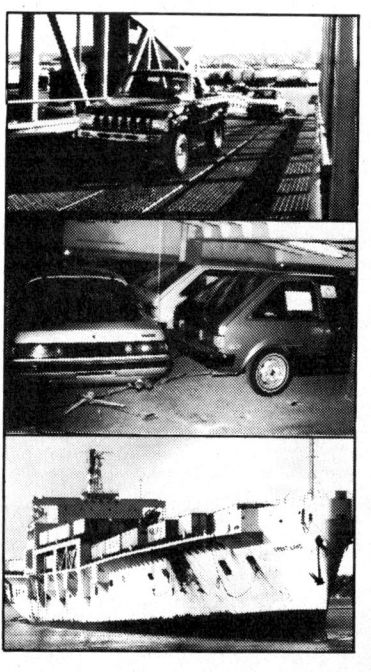

EASY ALCAN RETURN

Let TOTEM ship your vehicle to Anchorage or Seattle/Tacoma. We leave twice a week and our short-cut takes only 2½ days.

- DEPARTS SEATTLE/TACOMA EVERY THURSDAY AND SATURDAY
- DEPARTS ANCHORAGE EVERY SUNDAY AND TUESDAY

SEATTLE/TACOMA
(206) 628-4343
(800) 426-0074

ANCHORAGE
(907) 276-5868

TOTEM OCEAN TRAILER EXPRESS, INC.

FISHING ALASKA ON DOLLAR$ A DAY

"An excellent book that is essential for anyone considering making the trip to Alaska."
Tom Stienstra, San Francisco Examiner

In this 352-page guide you receive:
- Details on nearly 200 wilderness cabins that are **free or rent for dollars a day**. These cabins are located on streams and lakes that offer excellent fishing for trophy salmon, steelhead, trout and char.
- Exact locations, how to get there, boats for your personal use.
- Fish-catching advice on tackle, flies and equipment.
- Over 150 topographical maps, charts and photographs that direct you to hundreds of additional fishing hotspots. **$23.95 postpaid.**

Order NOW by calling **1-907-455-8000** *or write:*
ALASKA ANGLER PUBLICATIONS
P.O. Box 83550-M • Fairbanks, Alaska 99708

The majority of Alaska's Native people are Eskimo, Indian and Aleut. This young man is with the Chilkat Dancers in Haines. (Philip and Karen Smith)

Sea Coast and the Alaska Peninsula/Aleutians—are covered in detail in our companion guide *The ALASKA WILDERNESS MILEPOST®*. The Bering Sea coast, often called western Alaska, stretches from the head of Bristol Bay north along the coast to the Seward Peninsula near the Arctic Circle and extends inland about 200 miles/322 km from the coast, encompassing the Yukon–Kuskokwim Delta. Probably the region's most popular destination with out-of-state visitors is Nome, with its Native culture and gold rush relics.

The Alaska Peninsula and Aleutian Chain make up southwestern Alaska. The Alaska Peninsula extends 550 miles/885 km southwest from Mount Iliamna, on the west shore of Cook Inlet, to its tip at False Pass. The Aleutian Islands chain reaches another 1,100 miles/1770 km toward Asia. The volcanic Aleutian Range forms the spine of the peninsula, and the Aleutian Islands are actually crests of an arc of submarine volcanoes. Perhaps one of the best known attractions of this region is Katmai National Park and Preserve, accessible by air from Anchorage to King Salmon.

Yukon Territory

Yukon Territory, shaped somewhat like a right triangle, is bordered on the west by Alaska at 141° longitude and on the south by British Columbia at latitude 60°. The northern boundary is the Beaufort Sea in the Arctic Ocean and the eastern boundary the Mackenzie Mountains that separate Yukon Territory from Northwest Territories.

Yukon Territory is larger than all the New England states combined. It has an area of 186,300 square miles/482,573 square km and a population of only 25,000.

The **Alaska Highway** crosses the 60th parallel north into Yukon Territory just south of Watson Lake, YT, and travels through the territory for about 580 miles/935 km before reaching the Alaska border. Scenic and historic attractions abound along this pioneer highway: the Watson Lake sign forest, historic Silver City, huge Kluane Lake. The Alaska Highway also provides access to Whitehorse, the territorial capital, home to the SS *Klondike* National Historic Site, the Frantic Follies, Miles Canyon and other attractions.

The **Klondike Loop**, which junctions with the Alaska Highway near Whitehorse, leads north along the Yukon River to the territory's first capital, Dawson City. Yukon's modern history dates from the great Klondike gold rush of 1898, which brought thousands of gold seekers to the Yukon and Alaska. Dawson City, which grew out of that gold rush, is a living history lesson for visitors to the North. The Klondike Loop continues west via the Top of the World Highway to Alaska.

Branching off the Klondike Loop are 3 Yukon highways: the Silver Trail (High-

View of Dawson City and the Yukon and Klondike rivers. (Philip and Karen Smith)

way 11) and the all-gravel **Dempster** (Highway 5) and **Campbell** (Highway 4). The **Silver Trail** leads to the mining communities of Mayo, Elsa and Keno City. The remote **Dempster Highway** starts just south of Dawson City and heads 461 miles/742 km north through magnificent untouched wilderness to Inuvik, NWT. The **Campbell Highway** heads north from Watson Lake through Pelly River country, past the silver–lead–zinc mines at Faro, to Carmack.

Other Yukon routes for the adventurous to explore are: the old **Canol Road**, with its relics from the WWII oil pipeline; the short but scenic **Tagish Road**; and the lonely Nahanni Range Road.

Portions of the **Atlin Road, Haines Highway** and **Klondike Highway 2** are also within the Yukon Territory, as are some of the main attractions found along these roads. The Yukon portion of the Haines Highway skirts the eastern boundary of Kluane National Park, and provides access to Kathleen Lake, the only established campground within the park. Klondike Highway 2 passes by Rainbow Lake, one of Yukon's most colorful lakes, and the Carcross desert.

Northwest Territories

Nearly twice the size of Alaska, with less than half the population of Anchorage, Canada's Northwest Territories is a vast arctic and subarctic wilderness with only 1,300 miles/2000 km of highway. Its 46,000 inhabitants are spread over 1,304,903 square miles/3,376,698 square km.

Even its national parks are immense. Wood Buffalo National Park, on Highway 5, is the second largest park in the world with 17,300 square miles/44,980 square

NAPA AUTO PARTS

WITH 23 STORES FROM FAIRBANKS TO SEWARD NAPA IS TRULY YOUR ALASKA AUTO PARTS PIPELINE

All NAPA stores are Alaskan Owned and Operated

NAPA AUTO PARTS stores receive shipments daily to keep the parts you need in stock and available. If having the right part in a hurry is important to your business, check with your closest **NAPA AUTO PARTS** store. Quality parts, great service, and competitive prices make NAPA the place to call for automotive, marine, heavy duty parts and supplies.

Anchorage Dowling 563-3637	Anchorage East 5th 276-3996	Anchorage Huffman 345-5122	Anchorage W. International 248-5858	Anchorage Muldoon 337-6622	Anchorage E. International 563-3052	Anchorage Spenard 277-3546	Big Lake Quality Auto 852-8000	Cordova Anchor Parts 892-7433	Delta Junction Buffalo Center 895-4251
Eagle River Quality Auto 694-2110	Fairbanks College Road 456-7312	Fairbanks Gaffney 456-8863	Glennallen Valley Center 822-3686	Homer Parts, Inc. 235-8663	Kenai Parts, Inc. 283-3513	North Pole Brown & Sons 488-6272	Palmer Quality Auto 745-2181	Seward Parts, Inc. 224-8048	
		Soldotna Parts, Inc. 262-6233	Tok Junction Toklat Auto 883-5858	Valdez Parts, Inc. 835-4350	Wasilla Quality Auto 376-5204				

For The NAPA Auto Parts Store Nearest You Call 1-800-LET-NAPA

All the Right Parts in All the Right Places

km. Nahanni National Park, accessible by air, is 1,840 square miles/4765 square km and has one of the world's deepest canyons.

The majority of the population is Native—Dene (Indian), Inuit (Eskimo), Metis (mixed ancestry)—and the remainder of other extraction. Their unique stone sculpture, carvings, garments and artwork are sold at retail outlets in most cities.

In the southern region of the Northwest Territories, daylight lasts 20 hours in summer, giving visitors long days for driving, fishing, hunting and camping. Average temperature from June to September is 55°F/13°C.

Access to Northwest Territories is from Alberta via the Mackenzie Highway to Fort Simpson. All-weather gravel highways branch off this central highway to Yellowknife, Fort Resolution and Fort Smith. Northwest Territories highways are all covered in the **Mackenzie Highway** section of *The MILEPOST*. Three other highways cross into Northwest Territories: the Dempster Highway to Inuvik; the Nahanni Range Road to Tungsten; and the territory's newest highway, the **Liard Highway**, connecting the Alaska Highway and Mackenzie Highway via Fort Liard.

British Columbia

British Columbia, population about 3,000,000, is Canada's most westerly province. It stretches 813 miles/1300 km from its southern border with the United States to the north boundary with Yukon Territory. It is 438 miles/700 km wide, bounded on the east by Alberta and on the west by the Pacific Ocean. Victoria, the capital city, is located on Vancouver Island and is accessible from the mainland by ferry and by air.

British Columbia is where the **Alaska Highway** begins. Mile 0 is at Dawson Creek, BC (not to be confused with Dawson City, YT). The highway crosses the Rocky Mountains at Summit Lake, highest point on the Alaska Highway, before reaching the Yukon Territory border some 600 miles/960 km north of Dawson Creek. Two highlights of the drive are the Stone sheep in Stone Mountain Provincial Park and Muncho Lake Provincial Park.

The **West Access Route** to the Alaska Highway follows Trans-Canada Highway 1 and Provincial Highway 97 from the U.S.-Canada border north along the Fraser and Thompson rivers to Prince George and the junction with Yellowhead Highway 16. There, travelers have a choice: follow the Hart Highway over Pine Pass to Dawson Creek, or go west on **Yellowhead Highway 16** to Prince Rupert, departure point for British Columbia and Alaska state ferries.

Yellowhead Highway 16 also provides access to another scenic road north, the **Cassiar Highway.** This spectacular route follows the Coast Mountains north to the Alaska Highway. There are worthwhile side trips along the way to Stewart, Hyder and Telegraph Creek.

Other scenic side trips include: the **Hudson's Hope Loop** to W.A.C. Bennett Dam, Peace Canyon Dam and Moberly Lake; and **Atlin Road** to Atlin, the province's most northwesterly town in one of its most memorable settings.

Portions of the Liard Highway, Haines Highway and Klondike Highway 2 also cross into British Columbia.

Alberta

The province of Alberta is known for its great geographical diversity, from the Canadian Rockies which mark the western border of the province to the vast wilderness region of lakes, rivers and forests of the northern half of the province. Rolling prairie—and the agricultural heartland of Alberta—stretches from the U.S. border north to Edmonton. Routes west from Edmonton to Dawson Creek, BC, and the start of the Alaska Highway, pass through an area known as the "parkland"—broad valleys, wide ridges, lakes, streams and timberland.

The **East Access Route** to the Alaska Highway crosses both prairie and parkland in its 750-mile/1207-km journey from the southern border of Alberta to Dawson Creek, BC. The Provincial Highway 2 portion of this route, which has served Alaska-bound travelers since the 1940s, also provides access to Calgary and Edmonton. Calgary is perhaps best known for the Calgary Stampede in July, while Edmonton's most famous attraction might be the West Edmonton Mall.

At Edmonton, travelers may turn west on the transprovincial **Yellowhead Highway 16**, which crosses into British Columbia at Yellowhead Pass in the Canadian Rockies. Follow Highway 16 west from Edmonton 906 miles/1,458 km to its end at Prince Rupert, BC, departure point for British Columbia and Alaska state ferries.

Alberta is also the gateway to Northwest Territories. Mile 0 of the Mackenzie Highway to Fort Simpson, NWT, is located at Grimshaw, AB, in Peace River country.

Cairn in downtown Dawson Creek, BC, marks start of the famous Alaska Highway. (Alissa Crandall)

TRAVELING THE ALASKA HIGHWAY?
YOU MUST HAVE THIS TAPE!
"Going to the End of the World",
an exclusive 50th Anniversary audio cassette tape featuring songs, poems and stories of *The Greatest Highway on Earth*.
Available in select highway gift shops . . . BUT DON'T WAIT!
Order now and receive at no extra charge, a Special Collector's Edition
By Bernhardt-Stancliff Productions
BE READY FOR YOUR WORLD CLASS® ADVENTURE
$9.95 includes Postage & Handling
Bernhardt, Box 110, Tok, Alaska 99780

20 GREAT ALASKA FISHING ADVENTURES

"A Travel-Planning Guide for Those Who Want The Best in Alaska Sportfishing"
— The Alaska Angler

- This 223-page book by Chris Batin provides you with specific travel details that reveal Alaska's best fishing hotspots. Do-it-yourself budget and guided trips for trophy salmon, trout, halibut and more. Over 150 photos and maps show the best rivers, road-access routes, fish, and adventure you can experience NOW!
- Free guide with addresses and phone numbers for lodges, charter pilots, and contacts for do-it-yourself trips. **$23.95 ppd.**

Order NOW by calling 1-907-455-8000 or write:
ALASKA ANGLER PUBLICATIONS
P.O. Box 83550-M • Fairbanks, Alaska 99708

Write for our **FREE Resource Guide** to Alaska fishing and hunting books and periodicals.

Pure gold, no rush.

This year the road north is full of opportunities. Some as golden as the sun in Alberta and the Canadian Rockies. Winding your way through soaring peaks astride deep blue lakes, you may find a one hour rest stop becoming a day. Or longer. For this is a land whose heavenly beauty is matched only by the earthly comforts she affords you. Like modern highways, alpine resorts, splendid campgrounds and a very warm welcome. So why rush? Call us toll-free today at 1-800-661-8888. We'll help you plan a leisurely tour.

Alberta, in all her majesty.
Canada

WEST EDMONTON MALL ♦ WATERTON LAKES ♦ KLONDIKE DAYS ♦ PEACE COUNTRY ♦ 1-800-661-8888

Alaska Highway via
EAST ACCESS ROUTE

**Great Falls, Montana, to Dawson Creek, British Columbia
via Calgary and Edmonton, Alberta
Interstate Highway 15 and Provincial Highways 4, 3, 2, 43, and 34**
(See maps, pages 23–24)

When the Alaska Highway opened to civilian traffic in 1948, there was only one access route to Dawson Creek, BC, start of the highway, and that was through Edmonton, AB. First referred to as the East Access Route in the 1949 edition of *The MILEPOST®*, this route led from Great Falls, MT, through Calgary to Edmonton. From Edmonton, the route continued north to Clyde and from there to Athabasca via Highway 2 or Smith via Highway 44. From Smith, the next sizable town was High Prairie, 115 miles away. At Triangle, the junction of Highways 2 and 2A (then Highway 34), motorists either headed north to McLennan and Peace River, or south via Valleyview to Grande Prairie, another 110 miles. Total driving distance from Edmonton to Dawson Creek was 454 miles over lightly graveled dirt roads that became "exceedingly muddy in wet weather, at times almost impassable," according to early editions of *The MILEPOST®*. In late 1955, Highway 43 was completed connecting Edmonton and Valleyview via Whitecourt.

Highways on this route are all paved primary routes, with visitor services readily available along the way.

The East Access Route is logged in *The MILEPOST®* as one of the 2 major access routes (the other is the West Access Route following) to the Alaska Highway, although several major highways cross the international border now. A glance at the Plan-A-Trip map shows a number of choices for routing through southern Alberta and British Columbia. Motorists wishing to use any of these other routes, such as U.S. Highway 95 and Provincial Highways 95/93, or U.S. Highway 97 and Yellowhead Highway 5, should consult our companion guide—*NORTHWEST MILEPOSTS®*—for detailed logs of U.S. highways, interstates and all provincial highways in southwestern Canada and the northwestern U.S.

---

*Spend your first night
in Canada with us.*

**High Country
Bed & Breakfast Bureau**

P.O. Box 61, Millarville, ALTA T0L 1K0

Phone (403) 931-3514
or
(403) 625-4389

Over 20 B&Bs to Choose From
Free Brochure

A threshing demonstration is part of the festivities during Pioneer Day in July at the South Peace Centennial Museum near Beaverlodge. (Earl L. Brown, staff)

INTERSTATE HIGHWAY 15
The East Access Route begins in **GREAT FALLS** (pop. 57,310; elev. 3,333 feet/1,016m), Montana's second largest city. Head north through northcentral Montana on Interstate 15. From Great Falls to the Canadian border it is 117 miles/188.3 km. *The MILEPOST®* log begins at the Canadian border. (A detailed log of Interstate 15 is included in *NORTHWEST MILEPOSTS®*, which also covers Glacier and Waterton national parks.)

East Access Route Log

HIGHWAY 4
The East Access Route log is divided into 2 sections: Canadian border to Edmonton, and Edmonton to Dawson Creek.
This section of the log shows distance from the Canadian border (CB) followed by distance from Edmonton (E).

CB 0   E 382.2 (615 km) U.S.–Canada border, customs and immigration open 24 hours a day. Food, gas and lodging at border.

CB 13 (21 km) E 369.2 (594.1 km) **MILK RIVER** (pop. 900) has food, gas, stores, lodging and a small public campground (6 sites). Grain elevators are on the west side of the highway, services are on the east side. The Travel Alberta information centre here has 8 flags flying over it (7 represent countries and 1 the Hudson's Bay Co., all of which once laid claim to this area). ▲

CB 13.5 (21.7 km) E 368.7 (593.3 km) **Junction** with Secondary Road 501 east to Writing-on-Stone Provincial Park, 26 miles/42 km; camping, Indian petroglyphs.

CB 16.3 (26.3 km) E 365.9 (588.8 km) Stop of interest sign about Milk River Ridge.

CB 24.4 (39.2 km) E 357.8 (575.8 km) Road west to community of **WARNER** (pop. 434); store, gas, restaurant.

CB 24.6 (39.6 km) E 357.6 (575.5 km) **Junction** with Highway 36A north to Taber, centre of Alberta's sugar beet industry.

CB 36.8 (59.2 km) E 345.4 (555.8 km) Small community of New Dayton; 1 hotel.

CB 41.5 (66.8 km) E 340.7 (548.3 km) **Junction** at Craddock elevators with Highway 52 west to McGrath.

CB 46.1 (74.2 km) E 336.1 (540.9 km) Small community of Stirling to west; grain elevators and rail yards alongside highway.

CB 46.6 (75 km) E 335.6 (540 km) **Junction** with Highway 61 east to Cypress Hills.

CB 57.2 (92.1 km) E 325 (523 km) Stop of interest sign describing how large scale irrigation began in this area in 1901.

CB 61.1 (98.4 km) E 321.1 (516.7 km) **LETHBRIDGE** (pop. 60,000), Alberta's third largest city, has complete facilities; department stores, shopping malls, a wide choice

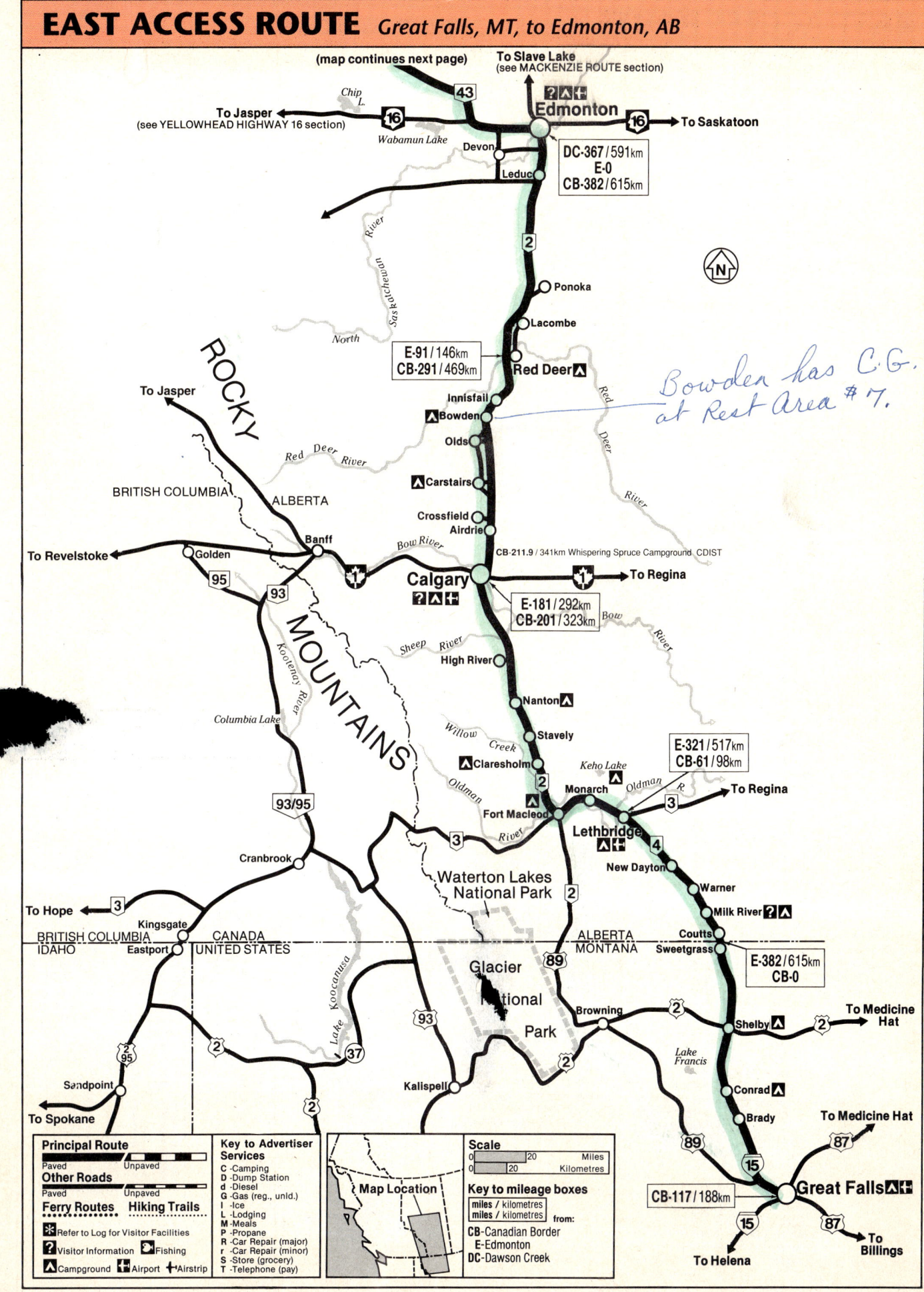

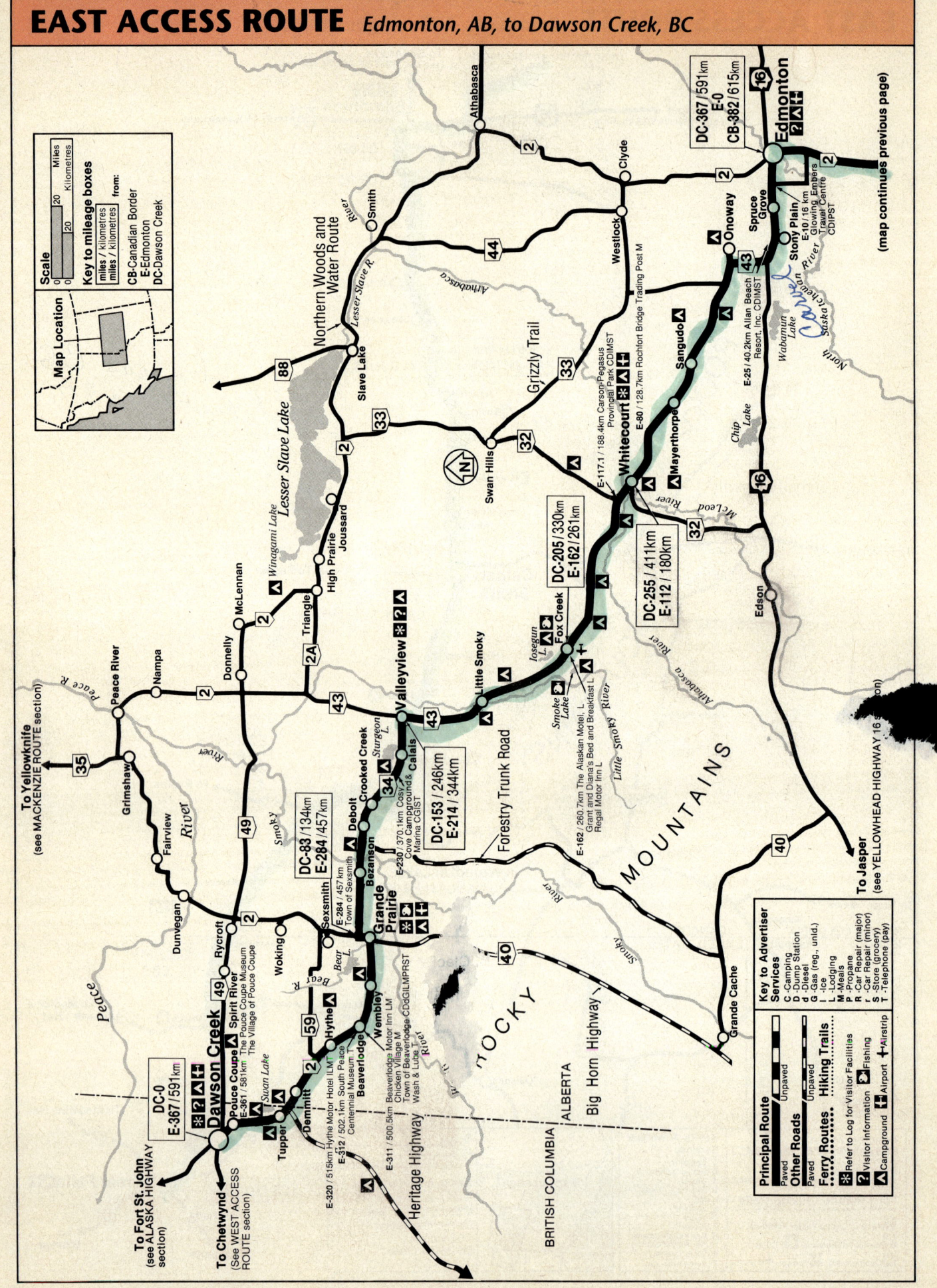

of hotel/motel accommodations and restaurants.

Founded in 1870 on the wealth of nearby coal mines, its economy today is based upon grain, livestock, sugar beets, oil and gas. It is home to Canada's largest agricultural research station. Attractions include Indian Battle Park (exit west on Whoop-up Drive from Highway 4), which contains a replica of Fort Whoop-Up, one of the whiskey-trading posts instrumental in bringing the North West Mounted Police to the west.

Camping at Henderson Lake Park (exit on Mayor McGrath Drive from highway); picnic area, tent and full hookup campsites. Nikka Yuko Japanese Gardens, west end of Henderson Lake, has authentic Oriental gardens. ▲

CB 62.9 (101.3 km) **E 319.3** (513.8 km) **Junction** with Highway 5 south to Cardston and Waterton Park. Mayor McGrath Drive to east provides access to motels, hotels and Henderson Lake Park.

Tourist information office and rest area just north of junction with picnic facilities, dump station and play area; open year-round.

CB 66.6 (107.2 km) **E 315.6** (507.9 km) Tourist information centre beside Brewery Gardens.

Highway 4 ends northbound. Route now follows Highway 3 (Crowsnest) West.

HIGHWAY 3

CB 69.5 (111.8 km) **E 312.7** (503.2 km) **Junction** with Highway 25. Access to Park Lake Provincial Park (9 miles/14 km north); 53 campsites, swimming, boat launch, fishing, playground. ▲

CB 72 (115.9 km) **E 310.2** (499.2 km) Community of Coalhurst just north of highway; gas station.

CB 73.5 (118.3 km) **E 308.7** (496.8 km) CPR marshalling yards at Kipp.

CB 80.3 (129.2 km) **E 301.9** (485.8 km) **Junction** with Highway 23 north. Continue west on Highway 3 for Fort Macleod.

CB 81.5 (131.2 km) **E 300.7** (483.9 km) Community of Monarch; hotel, gas.

Westbound, the highway enters Oldman River valley. Good view west of the Rockies on a clear day.

CB 96.1 (154.7 km) **E 286.1** (460.4 km) **Junction** with Highway 2 south to the U.S. border and access to Waterton Lakes and Glacier national parks. Highway 3 continues through **FORT MACLEOD** (pop. 3,100; elev. 3,300 feet/1,006m). There are several hotels and motels, restaurants, shopping facilities and gas stations. The main attraction in Fort Macleod is the Fort Museum, a replica of the original fort built in 1874, the first outpost of the North West Mounted Police (later the RCMP) in western Canada. Open daily from May to September.

CB 99 (159.4 km) **E 283.2** (455.8 km) **Junction** with Highway 2 north to Calgary and Edmonton. Highway 3 (Crowsnest) continues west to Hope, BC. (The Crowsnest Highway 3 log to Hope appears in *NORTHWEST MILEPOSTS®*.) Travel Alberta information office west side of junction; open May to September.

HIGHWAY 2

CB 100 (160.8 km) **E 282.2** (454.1 km) Oldman River bridge. Alberta government campground to southwest with 10 campsites, dump station, playgrounds, fishing and swimming. North of the river is the largest turkey farm in Alberta. ▲

CB 100.4 (161.6 km) **E 281.8** (453.5 km) Side road leads 10 miles/16 km to Head-Smashed-In Buffalo Jump, a World Heritage Site; open 9 A.M. to 8 P.M., May 15 to Labour Day, 9 A.M. to 5 P.M., the remainder of the year.

CB 111.2 (179 km) **E 271** (436.1 km) Road east to Granum, a small settlement dominated by grain elevators. Recreation park in town with 41 campsites. ▲

CB 116.2 (187 km) **E 266** (428 km) Community of Woodhouse.

CB 121.8 (196 km) **E 260.4** (419.1 km) **CLARESHOLM** (pop. 3,500), a prosperous ranching centre with all visitor facilities. The old railway station houses a museum. Camping at Centennial Park; 16 sites, dump station, playground. ▲

CB 125.9 (202.6 km) **E 256.3** (412.5 km) Stop of interest sign commemorating The Leavings, a stopping place on the Fort Macleod-Calgary trail in 1870.

CB 131.3 (211.3 km) **E 250.9** (403.8 km) Community of Stavely to the east.

CB 132.1 (212.6 km) **E 250.1** (402.5 km) Access road west to Willow Creek Provincial Park; 150 campsites, swimming, fishing. ▲

CB 138.4 (222.8 km) **E 243.8** (392.3 km) Small settlement of Parkland.

CB 145.9 (234.8 km) **E 236.3** (380.3 km) Nanton free campground (20 sites) at junction with Secondary Road 533 west to Chain Lakes Provincial Park. ▲

CB 146.8 (236.3 km) **E 235.4** (378.8 km) **NANTON** (pop. 1,700); all visitor facilities. Nanton is famous for its springwater, which is piped from the Big Spring in the Porcupine Hills, 6 miles/10 km west of town, to a large tap located in town centre. Springwater tap operates mid-May to September. WWII Lancaster bomber on display at Centennial Park.

CB 151.1 (243.2 km) **E 231.1** (371.9 km) **Junction** with Highway 2A, which parallels Highway 2 northbound.

CB 162.8 (262 km) **E 219.4** (353.1 km) **Junction** with Highway 23 west to **HIGH RIVER** (pop. 5,000) located on Highway 2A. All visitor facilities.

CB 164 (264 km) **E 218.2** (351.1 km) Stop of interest commemorating Spitzee Post, built in 1869.

CB 170 (273.6 km) **E 212.2** (341.5 km) Stop of interest sign about cattle brands.

CB 171.6 (276.1 km) **E 210.6** (338.9 km) **Junction** with Highways 2A and 7. Stop of interest commemorating the Turner Valley oil fields.

CB 173.3 (278.9 km) **E 208.9** (336.2 km) Sheep Creek bridge. Sheep Creek Provincial Park has a picnic area, playground, swimming and fishing.

CB 188.6 (303.5 km) **E 193.6** (311.6 km) Calgary southern city limits.

CB 196.5 (316.2 km) **E 185.7** (298.8 km) Exit for Glenmore Trail, the southwest bypass route that connects with Trans-Canada Highway 1 west to Banff and Vancouver, BC. (The log of Trans-Canada Highway 1 appears in *NORTHWEST MILEPOSTS®*.)

Calgary

CB 200.8 (323.1 km) **E 181.4** (291.9 km) Located at the confluence of the Bow and Elbow rivers. **Population:** 620,000. **Elevation:** 3,440 feet/1,049m. **Emergency Services:** Phone 911 for emergency services. **Hospitals:** Calgary General, 841 Centre Ave. NE; Holy Cross, 2210 2nd St. SW; Foothills, 1403 29th St. NW; Rockyview, 7007 14th St. SW.

Visitor Information: In the downtown area at 237 8th Ave. SE and at the base of Calgary Tower; both are open year-round. Other centres (open summer only) are located on major access routes into the city. Or call Calgary Convention & Visitors Bureau at 262-2766.

This flat, sprawling city is one of Alberta's 2 major population and business centres. The great influx of homesteaders to Calgary came with completion of the Canadian Pacific Railway in 1883. It grew as a trading centre for surrounding farms and ranches. Oil and gas discovered south of the city in 1914 contributed more growth.

Perhaps the city's best known attraction is the annual Calgary Stampede, which takes place at the Exhibition Grounds, July 3-12, 1992. The week-long event includes a parade

View of distinctive Calgary Tower from Olympic Square. (Philip and Karen Smith)

1992 ■ The MILEPOST® 25

ALASKA HIGHWAY VIA EAST ACCESS

and rodeo; phone 1-800-661-1260 for Stampede information and tickets.

Some other major attractions are: Calgary Centennial Planetarium and Aero-Space Museum, 11th Street and 7th Avenue; the Energeum, at the Energy Resources Bldg., 640 5th Ave. SW; Fort Calgary interpretive centre, 750 9th Ave. SE; Calgary Zoo, off Memorial Drive, has a prehistoric park with life-sized replicas of dinosaurs; and Heritage Park, west of 14th Street and Heritage Drive SW, a re-creation of Calgary's pioneer eras. Visitors may recognize the distinctive Saddledome, located at the Exhibition Grounds, which was the site of the 1988 Winter Olympics skating and hockey events. Olympic Park (site of ski jumping, luge and bobsled) is on Trans-Canada Highway 1, west of Sarcee Trail.

Calgary has large shopping malls, department stores, restaurants and a wide range of hotels and motels. Most of the hotels and motels are downtown or on Highway 2 south (Macleod Trail), Trans-Canada Highway 1 north (16th Avenue) and Alternate 1A (Motel Village). There are several campgrounds in and around the city. ▲

East Access Route Log

(continued)

CB 211.3 (340 km) **E 170.9** (275 km) Calgary northern city limits.

Highway 2 from Calgary to Edmonton bypasses most communities. Except for a few service centres built specially for freeway traffic, motorists must exit the freeway for communities and gas, food or lodging.

CB 211.9 (341 km) **E 170.3** (273 km) Exit to community of Balzac.

Whispering Spruce Campground. See display ad this section.

CB 217.9 (350.7 km) **E 164.3** (264.4 km) Road west to **AIRDRIE** (pop. 10,500). All visitor facilities available.

CB 225 (362 km) **E 157.2** (253 km) Dickson-Stephensson Stopping House on Old Calgary Trail; rest area, tourist information.

CB 232.2 (373.6 km) **E 150** (241.4 km) **Junction** with Highway 2A west to Crossfield and Highway 72 east to Drumheller, 60 miles/97 km, site of Alberta's Badlands. The Badlands are famous for the dinosaur fossils found there. Fossil displays at world-renowned Tyrrell Museum of Paleontology in Drumheller.

CB 232.6 (374.4 km) **E 149.6** (240.7 km) Stop of interest sign about the buffalo which once darkened the prairies here. Gas and restaurant at turnout.

CB 235.1 (378.3 km) **E 147.1** (236.7 km) Exit to **CROSSFIELD**; gas, hotel, food.

CB 243.1 (391.2 km) **E 139.1** (223.9 km) Exit west for **CARSTAIRS** (pop. 1,725), a farm and service community with tourist information centre and campground. The campground has 28 sites, electric hookups, hot showers and dump station. Services here include groceries, liquor store, banks, a motel, propane and gas stations. ▲

CB 252.7 (406.6 km) **E 129.5** (208.4 km) **Junction** with Highway 27 west to **OLDS** (pop. 4,888); all visitor facilities, museum and information booth.

CB 268.8 (432.5 km) **E 113.4** (182.5 km) **Junction** with highway west to Bowden and Red Lodge Provincial Park (8.5 miles/14 km); 110 campsites, playground, swimming and fishing. **BOWDEN** (pop. 1,000) is the site of a large oil refinery. ▲

Heritage rest area with tourist information booth at highway junction.

CB 276 (444 km) **E 106.2** (171 km) **Junction** with Highway 54 west to **INNISFAIL** (pop. 5,500); all visitor facilities. South of Innisfail 3 miles/5 km is the RCMP Dog Training Centre, the only one in Canada; open to the public daily year-round from 9 A.M. to 4 P.M.

CB 278.8 (448.7 km) **E 103.4** (166.4 km) Stop of interest sign about explorer Anthony Henday.

CB 285.6 (459.6 km) **E 96.6** (155.4 km) **Junction** with Highway 42 west to Penhold, a service community for the nearby air force base.

CB 290 (466.8 km) **E 92.2** (148.3 km) Tourist service area with gas stations and restaurants.

CB 290.5 (467.5 km) **E 91.7** (147.6 km) Tourist information booth.

CB 291.4 (468.9 km) **E 90.8** (146.1 km) **Junction** with Highway 2A east to **RED DEER** (pop. 55,000), in the centre of cattle ranching and grain growing, with a burgeoning oil and gas industry and nearby ethylene plants. All visitor facilities available. Camping at Lions Municipal Campground on Riverside Drive; 62 sites, dump station, laundry, picnic area, playground. ▲

CB 298 (479.6 km) **E 84.2** (135.5 km) **Junction** with Highway 11 to Sylvan Lake (10 miles/16 km) and Rocky Mountain House (51 miles/82 km). Sylvan Lake Provincial Park has picnicking and swimming. Private campgrounds and waterslide nearby.

CB 302.5 (486.8 km) **E 80.2** (129.1 km) Access road east to community of **BLACKFALDS** (pop. 1,500). Tourist services and accommodations.

CB 309.1 (497.4 km) **E 73.1** (117.6 km) **Junction** with Highway 12. Exit east for **LACOMBE** (pop. 6,000); all visitor facilities. Camping at Michener Park; 21 sites. Site of the Federal Agricultural Research Station; open to the public weekdays, 8 A.M. to 4:30 P.M.

Exit west on Highway 12 for Aspen Beach Provincial Park at Gull Lake (6 miles/10 km); camping, swimming. ▲

CB 325 (524.7 km) **E 56.2** (90.4 km) **Junction** with Highway 53 east to **PONOKA** (pop. 5,000); all visitor facilities. Camping at Ponoka Stampede Trailer Park, May to October. Ponoka's Stampede is held July 1 at Stampede Park. ▲

CB 340.7 (548.3 km) **E 41.5** (66.8 km) Northbound-only access to Wetaskiwin rest area with picnic tables and information centre (open May to September); restrooms, gas service and groceries.

Whispering Spruce CAMPGROUND

One mile north of Calgary city limits on Highway 2

(403) 226-0097

- 30-amp Full Serviced Pull-throughs
- Free Hot Showers • Laundry
- Groceries • Dump Station • RV Supplies
- Game Room & T.V. • Pay Phone

CLEAN AND SECURE

CB 345.3 (555.7 km) **E 36.9** (59.4 km) **Junction** of Highway 13 east to Wetaskiwin.

CB 356 (572.9 km) **E 26.2** (42.2 km) Turnout to east with litter barrels and pay phone.

CB 366 (589 km) **E 16.2** (26.1 km) Exit for Edmonton bypass route (see NOTE) and access to **LEDUC** (pop. 12,500), founded and named for the Leduc oil well, which blew in on Feb. 13, 1947; all visitor facilities.

NOTE: Northbound motorists wishing to avoid heavy traffic through Edmonton may exit west on Highway 39 for Devon Bypass. Drive 6.8 miles/11 km west on Highway 39, then 20 miles/32 km north on Highway 60 to junction with Yellowhead Highway 16, 10 miles/16 km west of Edmonton (see Milepost E 10 this section).

CB 372 (598.6 km) **E 10.2** (16.4 km) **Junction** with Highway 19 west to community of Devon, Devon Bypass and University of Alberta Devonian Botanic Garden, open daily May through September, 10 A.M. to 6 P.M. From Devon continue north on Highway 60 to bypass Edmonton and rejoin this route at **Milepost E 10** on Yellowhead Highway 16 West.

CB 382.2 (615 km) **E 0** Whitemud Drive. Turn east for Highway 16 East, turn west for Highway 16 West (see YELLOWHEAD HIGHWAY 16 section). Continue north for Edmonton city centre (description follows).

Whitemud Drive west continues as Highway 2, crossing the Saskatchewan River, then turns north to become 170 Street. Access to West Edmonton Mall on 170 Street.

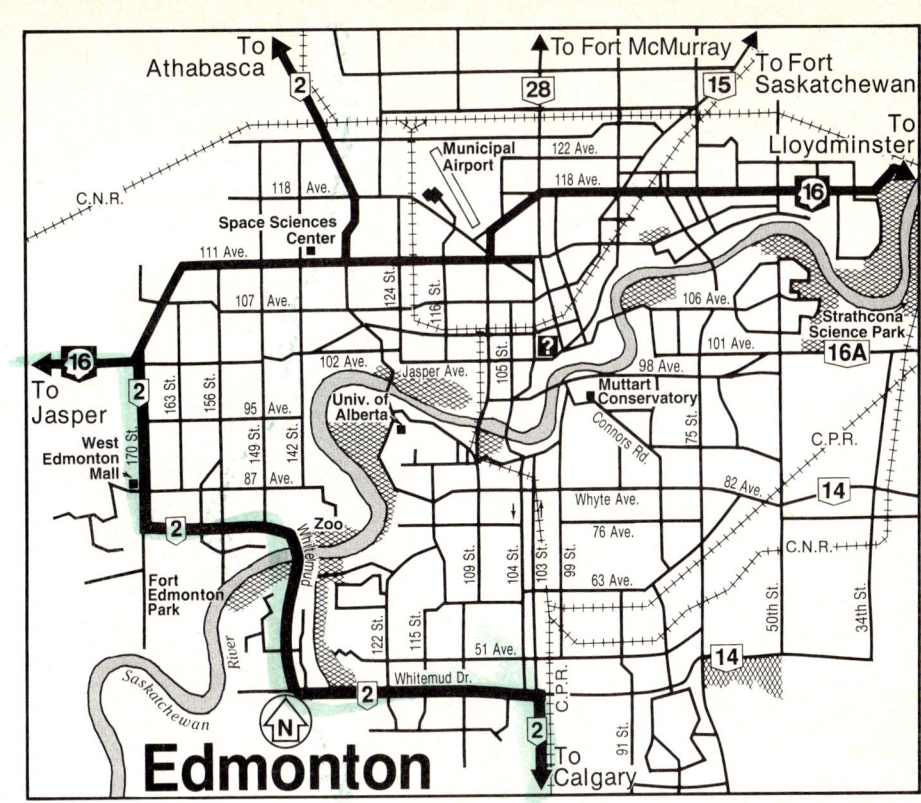

Edmonton

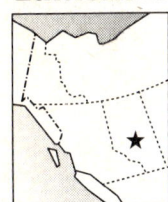

E 0 DC 367 (590.6 km) Capital of Alberta, 1,853 miles/2982 km from Fairbanks, AK. **Population:** 605,538; area 785,500. **Elevation:** 2,182 feet/665m. **Emergency Services:** Phone 911 for all emergency services. **Five hospitals:** Charles Camsell, 12815 115th Ave.; General, 11111 Jasper Ave.; Misericordia, 16940 87th Ave.; Royal Alexandra, 10240 Kingsway Ave.; University, 84th Avenue and 112th Street.

Visitor Information: Edmonton Tourism operates 4 visitor information centres within the city—Downtown, Highway 2 south, Highway 16 East and Highway 16 West. Hours vary. Write, Edmonton Tourism, 9797 Jasper Ave. N. 104, Edmonton, AB T5J 1N9; phone 422-5505.

The North Saskatchewan River winds through the centre of Edmonton, its banks lined with public parks. Major attractions include the Edmonton Space Sciences Centre, Fort Edmonton Par, Muttart Conservatory, Strathcona Science Park and the Provincial Museum. A shopping centre is also on the list of major attractions for visitors: West Edmonton Mall, dubbed "the world's largest mall," features some 800 stores and services. The mall also has a waterpark, ice arena, aquariums, aviaries, and some 100 restaurants. Located on 170 Street, the shopping mall is open 7 days a week.

Known as the festival city, Edmonton hosts a number of events throughout the year. These include: Children's Festival (May 19-27, 1992); Teen Festival of the Arts (April 28-May 2, 1992); Jazz City International Festival (June 26-July 8, 1992); Street Performers Festival (July 10-19, 1992); Klondike Days (July 16-25, 1992); Heritage Festival (Aug. 2-3, 1992); Edmonton Folk Music Festival (Aug. 7-9, 1992); and Fringe Theatre (Aug. 15-23, 1992).

There are 80 hotels and motels in Edmonton and hundreds of restaurants. Within the city limits there are 2 campgrounds. Rainbow Valley public campground has 80 sites, electrical hookups and showers; from Highway 2 drive west 2 miles/3.2 km on Whitemud Drive. A private campground on Highway 2 at Ellerslie Road has 200 sites for both tents and RVs. Just west of the city limits off Highway 16 West at the Devon Overpass there is a private campground with 300 sites and all facilities. ▲

East Access Route Log

(continued)

HIGHWAY 16 WEST
This section of the log shows distance from Edmonton (E) followed by distance from Dawson Creek (DC).

E 0 DC 367 (590.6 km) Downtown Edmonton. Take Jasper Avenue westbound (becomes 16A then Yellowhead 16 at city limits).

E 10 (16 km) **DC 357** (574.5 km) **Junction** of Highways 16 West and 60 (Devon Overpass); access to private campground. ▲

NOTE: Southbound travelers may bypass Edmonton by taking Highway 60 south, then either Highway 19 or 39 east Highway 2.

Glowing Embers Travel Centre. See display ad this section.

E 18 (29 km) **DC 349** (561.6 km) **SPRUCE GROVE** (pop. 11,343). All visitor

---

Glowing Embers Travel Centre
Ultra Modern Campground Facilities

- 300 FULLY SERVICED SITES
- SHOWERS • LAUNDROMAT
- PRIVATE MEETING ROOM
- PROPANE & RV ACCESSORIES
- GROCERY STORE
- COIN-OP CAR & TRAILER WASH
- YEAR-ROUND STORAGE FACILITIES

Good Sampark • MasterCard • VISA

Located just **five minutes** from the city of Edmonton on the S.W. corner of the Devon Overpass — junction Highway 16 West and Highway 60.

Mailing address: **(403) 962-8100**
26309 Highway 16, Spruce Grove, ALTA T7X 3H1

ALLAN BEACH RESORT, INC.

Sandy Beach – Fishing – Spring-fed Lake
88 FULL HOOKUPS
36 Water/Power Sites – Pull-Throughs
49 Tenting Sites
Day Use Picnic Area with BB-Q Pits
CONCESSION
New Playground • Boat Rentals
Coin Laundromat and Showers
ICE - GROCERIES - Sani-Station
Supervised Grounds

Box 37, Site 5, RR #2
Stony Plain, AB T0E 2G0

20 minutes to West Edmonton Mall

MasterCard • VISA **(403) 963-6362**

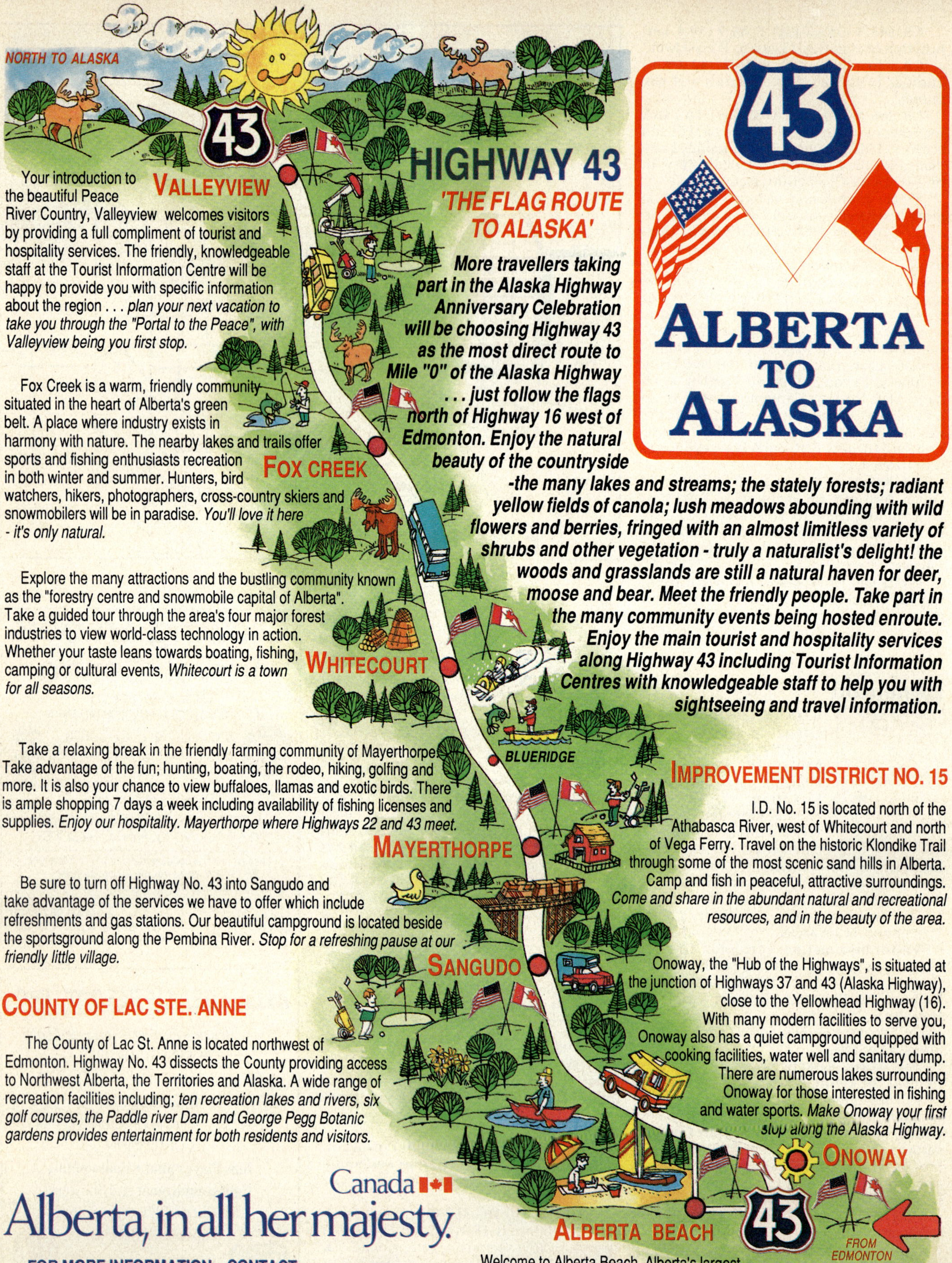

HIGHWAY 43
'THE FLAG ROUTE TO ALASKA'

NORTH TO ALASKA

VALLEYVIEW
Your introduction to the beautiful Peace River Country, Valleyview welcomes visitors by providing a full compliment of tourist and hospitality services. The friendly, knowledgeable staff at the Tourist Information Centre will be happy to provide you with specific information about the region . . . plan your next vacation to take you through the "Portal to the Peace", with Valleyview being you first stop.

FOX CREEK
Fox Creek is a warm, friendly community situated in the heart of Alberta's green belt. A place where industry exists in harmony with nature. The nearby lakes and trails offer sports and fishing enthusiasts recreation in both winter and summer. Hunters, bird watchers, hikers, photographers, cross-country skiers and snowmobilers will be in paradise. *You'll love it here - it's only natural.*

WHITECOURT
Explore the many attractions and the bustling community known as the "forestry centre and snowmobile capital of Alberta". Take a guided tour through the area's four major forest industries to view world-class technology in action. Whether your taste leans towards boating, fishing, camping or cultural events, *Whitecourt is a town for all seasons.*

MAYERTHORPE
Take a relaxing break in the friendly farming community of Mayerthorpe. Take advantage of the fun; hunting, boating, the rodeo, hiking, golfing and more. It is also your chance to view buffaloes, llamas and exotic birds. There is ample shopping 7 days a week including availability of fishing licenses and supplies. *Enjoy our hospitality. Mayerthorpe where Highways 22 and 43 meet.*

SANGUDO
Be sure to turn off Highway No. 43 into Sangudo and take advantage of the services we have to offer which include refreshments and gas stations. Our beautiful campground is located beside the sportsground along the Pembina River. *Stop for a refreshing pause at our friendly little village.*

COUNTY OF LAC STE. ANNE
The County of Lac St. Anne is located northwest of Edmonton. Highway No. 43 dissects the County providing access to Northwest Alberta, the Territories and Alaska. A wide range of recreation facilities including; ten recreation lakes and rivers, six golf courses, the Paddle river Dam and George Pegg Botanic gardens provides entertainment for both residents and visitors.

More travellers taking part in the Alaska Highway Anniversary Celebration will be choosing Highway 43 as the most direct route to Mile "0" of the Alaska Highway . . . just follow the flags north of Highway 16 west of Edmonton. Enjoy the natural beauty of the countryside -the many lakes and streams; the stately forests; radiant yellow fields of canola; lush meadows abounding with wild flowers and berries, fringed with an almost limitless variety of shrubs and other vegetation - truly a naturalist's delight! the woods and grasslands are still a natural haven for deer, moose and bear. Meet the friendly people. Take part in the many community events being hosted enroute. Enjoy the main tourist and hospitality services along Highway 43 including Tourist Information Centres with knowledgeable staff to help you with sightseeing and travel information.

BLUERIDGE

IMPROVEMENT DISTRICT NO. 15
I.D. No. 15 is located north of the Athabasca River, west of Whitecourt and north of Vega Ferry. Travel on the historic Klondike Trail through some of the most scenic sand hills in Alberta. Camp and fish in peaceful, attractive surroundings. *Come and share in the abundant natural and recreational resources, and in the beauty of the area.*

Onoway, the "Hub of the Highways", is situated at the junction of Highways 37 and 43 (Alaska Highway), close to the Yellowhead Highway (16). With many modern facilities to serve you, Onoway also has a quiet campground equipped with cooking facilities, water well and sanitary dump. There are numerous lakes surrounding Onoway for those interested in fishing and water sports. *Make Onoway your first stop along the Alaska Highway.*

ONOWAY

ALBERTA BEACH — FROM EDMONTON

Welcome to Alberta Beach, Alberta's largest summer village. Fully equipped campground and clean sandy beaches promise fun in the sun. Our beautiful lake allows exhilarating windsurfing, sailboating, canoeing, fishing and swimming. Farmers market, boat rental, mini-golf and overnight accomodations with dining at its best. *Information on the many facilities is available at the tourist booth for your daily or weekly visits.*

Alberta, in all her majesty.

FOR MORE INFORMATION CONTACT:
Highway 43 Promotion Committee
c/o Box 1011, Whitecourt, Alberta, Canada
T0E 2L0
(403) 778-5363

facilities including motels, restaurants, grocery stores and gas stations. Large public park in city centre.

E 22 (35.4 km) **DC 345** (555.2 km) **STONY PLAIN** (pop. 4,442). All visitor facilities including hotels, restaurants, supermarket, shopping mall and gas stations with major repair service; RCMP and hospital; swimming pool and golf course. The Multicultural Heritage Centre here has a living museum, art gallery and archives, and serves pioneer food. Open daily 10 A.M. to 4 P.M. Information available at the Old Caboose by the railroad.

Tours of Andrew Wolf Wine Cellars, located along the north side of Highway 16, available Monday through Saturday, 10 A.M. to 6 P.M.; phone (403) 963-7717. Lions campground with 26 sites located nearby. ▲

E 25 (40.2 km) **DC 34** (550.4 km) Turnoff north for Allan Beach recreation area.

Allan Beach Resort. See display ad on page 27. ▲

E 25.6 (41.2 km) **DC 341.4** (549.4 km) Edmonton Beach turnoff to south.

E 26.1 (42 km) **DC 340.9** (548.6 km) Hubbles Lake turnoff to north.

E 27.2 (43.8 km) **DC 339.8** (546.8 km) Restaurant, gas station and store to north.

E 28.4 (45.7 km) **DC 338.6** (544.9 km) Lake Eden Recreation Area to north.

E 31 (49.9 km) **DC 336** (540.7 km) **Junction** of Yellowhead Highway 16 and Highway 43. Turn north onto Highway 43. (If you are continuing west on Yellowhead Highway 16 for Prince George or Prince Rupert, BC, turn to the YELLOWHEAD HIGHWAY section.)

HIGHWAY 43

E 36.9 (59.4 km) **DC 330** (531.2 km) **Junction** of Highways 43 and 33. Continue on Highway 43.

E 37.3 (60 km) **DC 329.7** (530.6 km) Turnout to east with litter barrel and historical information sign about construction of the Alaska Highway.

E 38.7 (62.3 km) **DC 328.3** (528.3 km) Gas station to east.

E 39.2 (63.1 km) **DC 327.8** (527.5 km) Highway 633 west to Alberta Beach Recreation Area on Lac Ste. Anne.

E 41.6 (66.9 km) **DC 325.4** (523.7 km) **ONOWAY** (pop. 669). Gas, laundromat, restaurants, motel, car wash, post office and other facilities. Information booth and Elks campground with 8 sites. Devil's Lake Corral, an entertainment centre, is east of Onoway. ▲

E 45.4 (73.2 km) **DC 321.5** (517.4 km) Alberta government campground with dump station, water, toilets and stoves. ▲

E 45.9 (73.9 km) **DC 321.1** (516.7 km) Restaurant and gas station.

E 48 (77.2 km) **DC 318.9** (513.2 km) **Lessard Lake** county campground; water, stoves, boat launch, fishing for pike and perch. Golf course to west. ◄▲

E 63.7 (102.5 km) **DC 303.3** (488.1 km) Gas station.

E 72 (115.8 km) **DC 295** (474.8 km) **SANGUDO** (pop. 401) is on a 0.3-mile/0.4-km side road. Restaurant, motel and gas station with garage open 7 days a week; grocery store, banks, post office, laundromat and car wash. Public campground at sportsground. ▲

E 74.4 (119.7 km) **DC 292.6** (470.9 km) Pembina River bridge.

E 75.4 (121.3 km) **DC 291.6** (469.3 km) Gas station and restaurant to south.

E 79.5 (128 km) **DC 287.5** (462.7 km)

The Vibrant Community of
WHITECOURT
Welcomes You
"Forestry Centre and Snowmobile Capital of Alberta'

THE HUB OF ACTIVITY IS THE

TOURIST INFORMATION CENTRE
On Highway 43

● Stop in to check for daily activities such as: Schedules of **Industrial and Nature Tours,** rodeo, river boat races, sports events, cultural activities, golfing, swimming, horseback riding, corn roast or pitch fork barbecues.

● A community well worth stopping for with a complete and attractive business district which includes 2 malls, 5 major banks, large liquor vendor, convenient parking and much, much more.

● Choose from over 600 competitively priced hotel and motel rooms and over 275 shaded campsites.

● Enjoy the relaxing atmosphere in our community with open spaces and surrounding forests and rivers.

Lions Campground

Business District Entrance

1992 ■ The MILEPOST® 29

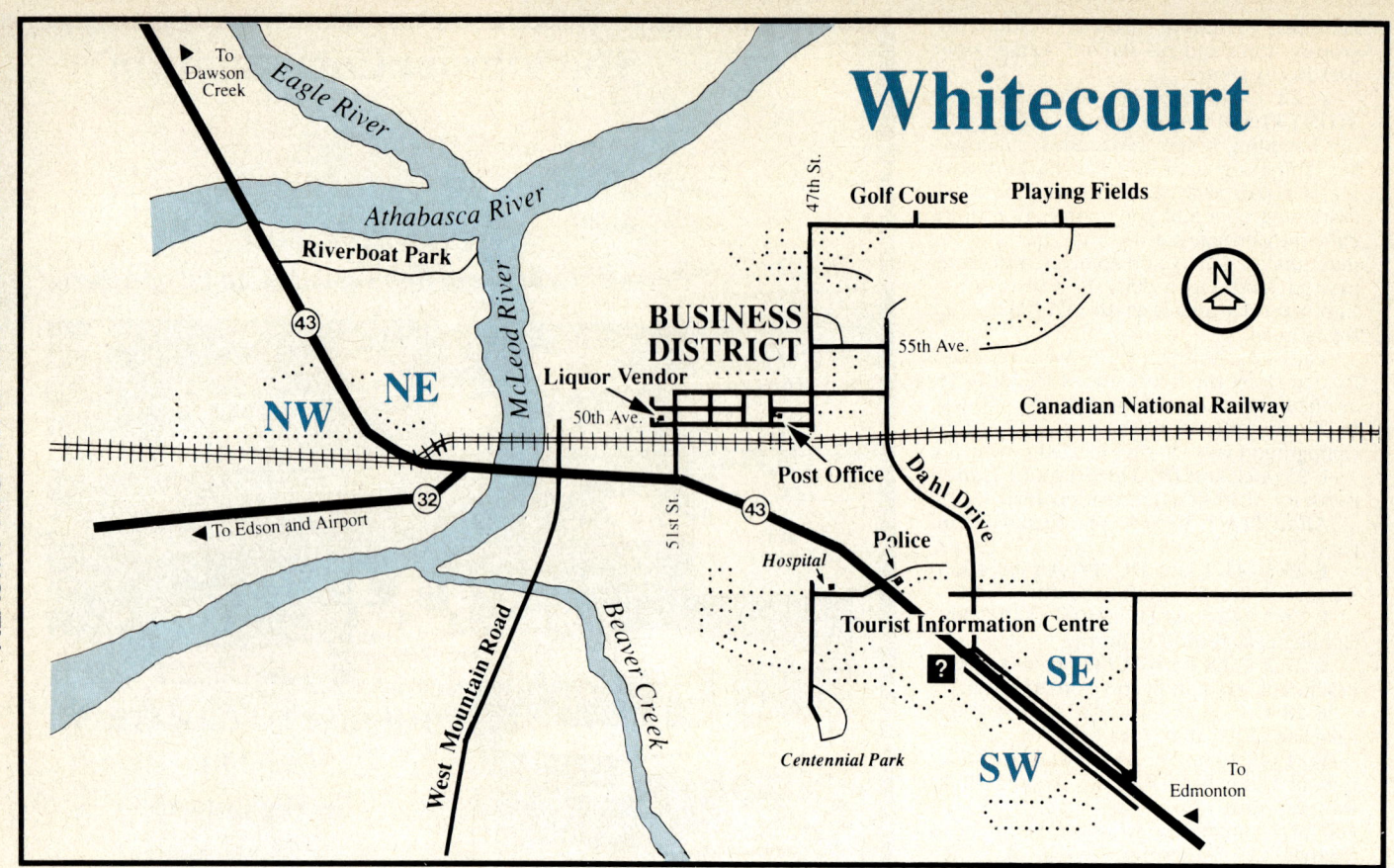

Whitecourt

ALASKA HIGHWAY VIA EAST ACCESS ROUTE

CAR/TRUCK TRAILER SERVICES GUIDE

Business	Operating Hours	Visa	Master Card	American Exp	Others	Full Service	Self Service	Gasoline	Diesel	Propane	Franchise Car	Mechanic	Car Wash	Tire Service	Exhaust Repair	Alignment	Towing	Welding	Auto Parts	Auto Rental	Conv. Store	Laundromat	Bank Machine	Wheel Chair	Fast Food	Bakery	Restaurant
EVERGREEN AUTO SUPPLY (UAP, NAPA) 38 Ave. North Hwy. 43 SE (403) 778-6116	8 am – 5:30 pm	•	•																•								
FAS GAS HILLTOP SERVICE Hwy 43 SE (403) 778-5541	24 HR	•	•			•	•		•	•	•										•				•	•	•
GASLAND Hwy 43 NE (403) 778-2655	6 am – 11 pm	•	•			•	•	•	•	•											•				•	•	
GATEWAY ESSO SERVICE Hwy 43 NW (403) 778-3776	24 HR	•	•	•	•	•	•	•	•										•								•
HB AUTOMOTIVE REPAIRS 37 Ave. North Hwy 43 SE (403) 778-5755	7am - 5 pm	•	•									•															
HILLTOP TAGS FOOD & GAS HUSKY Hwy 43 SW (403) 778-6088	24 HR	•	•			•	•	•	•	•											•				•	•	•
KAMMEC MECHANICAL Hwy 43 SW (37 Ave.) (403) 778-3184	7am - 6pm	•	•									•							•								
MALJO AUTO AND RV SUPPLIES Bus. Dist., 50 Ave. & 49 St. (403) 778-3834	8:30 am – 6 pm	•	•																•								
MOHAWK SERVICE Hwy 43 SE (403) 778-3377	6am – 11pm	•	•			•	•	•	•												•				•		
RAM TOWING Hwy 43 NW (403) 778-2715	24 HR																•										
SMYL CHEV OLDS GM DEALER (403) 778-2202	8am – 5pm	•	•								•	•		•	•												
TAGS DOWNTOWN FOOD & GAS HUSKY Bus. Dist., 49 St. & 52 Ave. (403) 778-4447	6 am – 12 pm	•	•																		•				•	•	
TIMBER TIRE Hwy 43 SE (403) 778-3863	7 am – 8 pm	•	•									•		•													
TURBO Hwy 43 NW Hwy 32 (403) 778-6698	6 am – 10 pm	•	•				•	•												•							
WESTWIND FORD Hwy 43 NE, 54 St. (403) 778-4777	8 am – 5 pm	•	•								•								•								
WHITECOURT CHRYSLER-JEEP Hwy 43 SW (403) 778-4411	9 am – 7 pm	•	•								•	•															
WHITECOURT SHELL SERVICE Hwy 43 SE (403) 778-2665	7 am – 11 pm	•	•			•	•	•	•	•		•							•								

ATTRACTIVE & COMPLETE BUSINESS DISTRICT — 2 blocks north of HWY. 43 with plenty of convenient parking and much, much more...

(Paid Advertisement)

Whitecourt RESTAURANT GUIDE

A & W RESTAURANT Hwy 43 SW	(403) 778-6611
DAIRY QUEEN Hwy 43 SW	(403) 778-4633
FIFTH WHEEL RESTAURANT (Northside Esso) Hwy 43 NE	(403) 778-4939
GREEN GABLES RESTAURANT Hwy 43 SW	(403) 778-3142
KG'S SANDWICH BAR Bus. Dist. 5011-51 Ave.	(403) 778-5286
KENTUCKY FRIED CHICKEN Hwy 43 SE	(403) 778-4700
MILL RESTAURANT Hwy. 43 SE	(403) 778-2898
MOUNTAIN PIZZA AND STEAK HOUSE Hwy 43 SW	(403) 778-3600
PETER'S PIZZA, PASTA & BONES Hwy 43 SE	(403) 778-4444
RENFORD INN Hwy 43 SW 1 (800) 661-6498 FAX (403) 778-3764	(403) 778-3133
RIVERS MOTOR HOTEL Hwy. 43 NE (Along McLeod) Fax (403) 778-6933	(403) 778-3951
ROYAL OAK HOTEL RESTAURANT Hwy 43 SW	(403) 778-4443
SMITTY'S INN Hwy 43 NW	(403) 778-5055
SPORTSMAN RESTAURANT (Midtown Mall) Bus. Dist. 5145 - 49 St.	(403) 778-4648

ALASKA HIGHWAY VIA EAST ACCESS ROUTE

Restaurant Details Table

Operating Hours	Seating Capacity	Visa	Master Card	American Exp.	Others	Fast Food	Take Out	Drive Thru	Restaurant	Licensed Dining	Lounge	Tavern	Entertainment	Banquet Room	Meeting Room	Tour Buses (Ph. Ahead)	Delivery	Hotel	Motel	Service Station	Retail Business
6 am - 11 pm	96					●	●	●												●	
10 am - 10:30 pm	60	●				●	●		●												
5:30 am - 11 pm	66	●	●	●		●	●		●											●	
6 am - 11 pm	110	●	●						●	●									●		
8 am - 4 pm	50																				●
10 am - 10 pm	76					●	●	●												●	
24 Hr	112																			●	
11 am - 10:30 pm	146	●	●				●		●												
4 pm - 2 am	70	●	●				●		●	●			●								
6:30 am	316	●	●	●	●				●	●	●			●	●	●		●			
5:30 am - 12:00 am	198	●	●	●					●	●	●	●	●	●		●		●			
5:30 am - 12:00 am	200	●	●						●	●	●	●	●	●		●		●			
6 am - 10 pm	230	●	●				●		●	●				●		●			●		
9 am - 12 am	150	●	●	●					●	●	●										●

WHITECOURT ACCOMMODATION GUIDE
HOTELS, MOTELS, CAMPSITES
Over 600 rooms & 275 campsites to choose from

ALASKA HIGHWAY MOTEL & CAMPSITE Hwy 43 SW	(403) 778-4156
CARSON-PEGASUS PROVINCIAL PARK & CAMPGROUND 12 miles NW of Whitecourt on Lake	(403) 778-2664
CASCADE MOTOR INN Hwy 43 SW	(403) 778-4545
GLENVIEW MOTEL Hwy 43 SW	(403) 778-2276
GREEN GABLES INN Hwy 43 SE	(403) 778-4537
JACKPINE MOTEL Hwy 43 SE	(403) 778-2241
LIONS CLUB CAMPGROUND 1 mile east on Hwy. 43 S.W.	(403) 778-6782
RENFORD INN Hwy 43 SW 1 (800) 661-6498 Fax (403) 778-3764	(403) 778-3133
RIVERS MOTOR HOTEL Hwy 43 NE (Along McLeod) Fax (403) 778-6933	(403) 778-3951
ROYAL OAK INN HOTEL Hwy. 43 S.W.	(403) 778-4443
SMITTY'S INN Hwy 43 NW	(403) 778-5055
THE CATCHEM CENTRE SPORTING GOODS Hwy 43 NW	(403) 778-4040
WHITE-KAPS MOTEL Hwy 43 SW	(403) 778-2246

Accommodation Details Table

Number of Rooms	Under 30	30-60	Over 60	Visa	Master Card	American Exp	Others	Cable TV	Satelite TV	Home Movies	Kitchenettes	Laundromat	Waterbed	Indoor Pool	Meeting Rooms	Wheel Chair Access	Pets Accepted	Free Parking	Restaurant (See Chart)	Number of Stalls	Power	Showers	Shelter	Tables	Firewood	Boat Rental	Store
36		●		●	●			●			●							●		22	●	●	●	●	●		
		●	●	●	●						●				●		●			182	●	●	●	●	●		●
64		●		●	●		●	●		●		●	●					●									
31		●		●	●			●		●	●					●											
49		●		●	●		●	●			●							●	●								
27	●			●				●								●				4							
				●																74	●	●	●	●	●		
111		●		●	●	●	●	●		●		●		●	●			●	●								
70		●	●	●	●	●		●	●		●	●		●	●			●	●								
40		●		●	●	●		●			●				●	●		●	●								
28		●		●	●			●								●		●									
19	●			●	●						●							●									●
20		●		●	●			●								●		●		10	●		●				

"Your low cost Supermarket"
4807-50th Ave

Drug Mart
People Helping People
Corner of 50th st. & 50th Ave.

SAGITAWAH
SPORTS
HUNTING, FISHING, BIKES ETC.
"THE BEST LITTLE LURE HOUSE IN WHITECOURT"
4911-51 AVE.

Super Market Fresh Bakery & Deli
Centre Valley Mall

WHITECOURT

A Community well worth stopping in! Only a 2 hour drive from West Edmonton Mall

Plan to stay and enjoy the things you long for in ideal surroundings

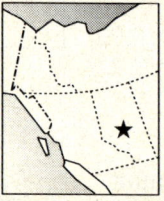

Guided Industrial and Nature Tours
River Fishing
Horseback Riding
Hunting
Lake Fishing
Golf

Alberta, in all her majesty.
Canada

Take a Rest in Whitecourt
"Where Even The Rivers Meet"

Second longest wooden railway trestle in the world crosses highway and Paddle River.

E 80 (128.7 km) **DC 287** (461.9 km) Gas, convenience store, gift shop, restaurant, and Lac St. Anne Pioneer Museum.

Rochfort Bridge Trading Post. See display ad this section.

E 83.1 (133.7 km) **DC 283.9** (456.1 km) Paved turnouts with litter barrels both sides of highway.

E 85 (136.8 km) **DC 282** (453.8 km) **MAYERTHORPE** (pop. 1,475). One mile/1.6 km from the highway on a paved access road. Hotel, motel, restaurant, grocery store, gas stations with repair service, car wash, hospital, laundromat, post office, RCMP and banks. A free public campground with 30 sites (no hookups, pit toilets) and 9-hole golf course are located 1 mile/1.6 km south of town. Airstrip located 2 miles/3.2 km southwest of town. ▲

E 87 (140 km) **DC 280** (450.6 km) Gas station and restaurant at junction with Highway 658 north to Goose Lake.

E 109 (175.4 km) **DC 258** (415.2 km) Lions Club Campground; 50 sites, pit toilets, water, tables and firepits. Fee charged. ▲

Whitecourt

E 111.8 (179.9 km) **DC 255.2** (410.7 km). Located 2 hours from Edmonton. **Population:** 7,000. **Emergency Services: Police,** phone 778-5454. **Fire Department,** phone 778-2311. **Hospital** located on Hilltop, phone 778-2285. Ambulance service.

Visitor Information: Tourist information booth on Highway 43 west at the traffic lights. The helpful staff will assist with travel plans and directions to Whitecourt sights and activities. The booth is fully stocked with pamphlets and brochures. Open daily, 8 A.M. to 7 P.M., May 1 to Sept. 1; weekdays only, 9 A.M. to 5 P.M., September through April. Free dump station and freshwater fill-up, Bigway Grocery and Deli with fresh bakery and banking machine, adjacent tourist booth.

Information is also available from the Chamber of Commerce, P.O. Box 1011, Whitecourt, AB T7S 1N9; phone 778-5363.

Elevation: 2,567 feet/782m. **Radio:** 1400 CJYR-AM, 107.5 SKUA-FM. **Television:** 10 channels. **Newspaper:** *Whitecourt Star* (weekly).

Transportation: Air–Whitecourt Airport, 4 miles/6.4 km south on Highway 32, has a 5,800-foot/1,768-m paved runway; all-weather facility, 24-hour flight service

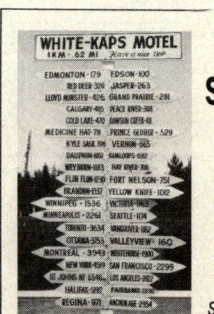

S**TO**P at the
WHITE-KAPS MOTEL & RV PARKING
• Air Conditioned
• Kitchenettes
• Color TV • Clean
Next to the Hill Top Shopping Center...
Swimming Pool & Tennis nearby

12 miles to famous Carson Lake for trout fishing
Your Hosts: Garry & Darlene Pearce (403) 778-2246
Box 1586   Whitecourt, ALTA T7S 1P4

WHITECOURT ADVERTISERS

Gateway Esso .... On Hwy. 43
Highway 43 Promotion
  Committee .... Ph. (403) 778-5363
White-Kaps Motel &
  RV Parking .... Next to Hill Top
                                    Shopping Center
Whitecourt Chamber of
  Commerce .... Ph. (403) 778-5363

---

station. AV gas and jet fuel, aircraft maintenance, available. Local charter air service available; helicopter and fixed-wing aircraft. **Bus**–Greyhound service to Edmonton, Grande Prairie, Peace River and points north.

Located at the junction of Highways 43 and 32, Whitecourt dubs itself the "Gateway to the Alaska Highway and the fabulous North." Established as a small trading, trapping and forestry centre, Whitecourt became an important stop for Alaska Highway travelers when a 106-mile section of Highway 43 connecting Whitecourt and Valleyview was completed in October 1955. This new route was 72 miles shorter than the old Edmonton to Dawson Creek route via Slave Lake.

Several major forest industries operating in and around Whitecourt offer visitors an opportunity to observe state-of-the-art technologies at sawmills, medium density fiberboard production and pulp and paper manufacturing plants. The Eric S. Huestis Demonstration Forest, northwest of town on Highway 32, has 4.3 miles/7 km of self-guided trails with interpretive sites and information signs describing forest management techniques and the forest life-cycle; phone 778-7165.

The Whitecourt Chamber of Commerce has a program of guided industrial tours that are available for visitors. Tours vary from 1½ to 2 hours in length and reservations are advised; phone 778-5362.

Recreational activities include an excellent 18-hole public golf course and fishing in area creeks, rivers and lakes (boat rentals at Carson Pegasus Provincial Park). Swimming, rollerskating, mini-golf, tennis and gold panning are also enjoyed in summer. Other attractions available: an exotic animal farm; a guest ranch with arts and crafts; horseback riding; and river boating. In the fall, big game hunting is very popular. During the winter there is ice fishing, snowmobiling and cross-country skiing on area trails, downhill skiing at a local facility, skating and curling, bowling, and swimming at the indoor pool.

There are 14 hotels/motels, 20 restaurants, 14 gas stations, several laundromats, 2 malls, a liquor vendor and 5 banks. Most services are located on the highway or 2 blocks north in the downtown business district. Some gas stations and restaurants are open 24 hours. House Mountain Gallery and Artists' Center, at the corner of Whitecourt Avenue and Sunset Boulevard, features exhibits by local artists.

This full-service community also supports a library and 7 churches. The Legion, located in the business district, is open year-round. Service clubs (Lions, Kinsmen) and community organizations (Masons, Knights of Columbus) meet on a regular basis and welcome visitors.

A popular wilderness area nearby is Carson-Pegasus Provincial Park, located 14.6 miles/23.5 km west and north of town on Highway 32 (paved). The park has 182 campsites, electrical hookups, dump station, boat launch, boat rentals, concession, convenience store, hot showers and laundry facilities; open year-round. There are 2 lakes at the park: McLeod (Carson) Lake, stocked with rainbow trout, has a speed limit of 12 kmph for boaters; Little McLeod (Pegasus) Lake has northern pike and whitefish, electric motors and canoes only.

East Access Route Log

(continued)

E 111.9 (808 km) **DC 255.1** (410.5 km) Beaver Creek bridge.

E 112.4 (180.9 km) **DC 254.6** (409.7 km) McLeod River.

E 112.6 (181.2 km) **DC 254.4** (409.4 km) Railroad crossing.

E 112.7 (181.4 km) **DC 254.3** (409.2 km) **Junction** with Highway 32 south.

E 112.9 (181.7 km) **DC 254.1** (408.9 km) Gas station.

E 113.4 (182.5 km) **DC 253.6** (408.1 km) Riverboat Park to north with boat launch, picnic area and toilets, located at the confluence of the McLeod and Athabasca rivers.

E 113.6 (182.8 km) **DC 253.4** (407.8 km) Athabasca River bridge.

E 115.6 (186 km) **DC 251.4** (404.6 km) Vehicle inspection station to north.

E 117.1 (188.4 km) **DC 249.9** (402.2 km) **Junction** with Highway 32 north. Turn off for Carson-Pegasus Provincial Park 9.3 miles/15 km north via paved highway, open year-round; 182 campsites, electrical hookups, group camping area, tables, flush toilets, showers, water, dump station, firewood, store, laundromat, playground, boat launch, boat rentals and rainbow trout fishing.

Carson-Pegasus Provincial Park. See display ad this section.

E 117.6 (189.2 km) **DC 249.4** (401.4 km) Alberta Newsprint Co. to south.

E 122 (196.3 km) **DC 245** (394.3 km) Turnout with litter barrel.

E 122.5 (197.1 km) **DC 244.5** (393.5 km) Chickadee Creek government campground; 7 sites, pit toilets, water, tables and firepits.

E 124.3 (200 km) **DC 242.7** (390.6 km) Chickadee Creek.

E 131.8 (212.1 km) **DC 235.2** (378.5 km) Turnouts with litter barrels both sides of highway.

E 140.5 (226.1 km) **DC 226.5** (364.5 km) Two Creeks government campground; 8 sites, pit toilets, water, tables and firepits.

E 142.5 (229.3 km) **DC 224.5** (361.3 km) Turnout with litter barrel to south.

E 143 (230.1 km) **DC 224** (360.5 km) Turnout with litter barrel to north.

E 152 (244.6 km) **DC 215** (346 km)

ROCHFORT BRIDGE TRADING POST

Enjoy the friendly western atmosphere at our

Gift Shop and Restaurant

Fully Licensed • Home-Style Cooking
Large Veranda Dining Area

Unique All-Canadian Gifts and Crafts
Tourist Information

**Lac St. Anne Pioneer Museum
Donkeys and Mules • Carriage Rides**

RV Parking and Picnic Area *(not serviced)*
Outdoor Washrooms

Open Year-Round
9 a.m. to 9 p.m. • 7 days a week

Phone (403) 785-3467
Box 120, Rochfort Bridge
Alberta, Canada T0E 1Y0
Mile E 80 on Highway #43

CARSON — PEGASUS PROVINCIAL PARK

182 Supervised Sites
(including 27 pull-through 30-amp power hookups)
20 site group area

• Free showers • Free firewood
Store • Laundromat • Ice • Pay Phone
Beach

Stocked Rainbow Trout lake

Camping and fishing supplies
Boat rentals • Sani-station

Reservations available (403) 778-2664
Your hosts — Bruce and Sandy Russell

Just 10 minutes
off Highway 43—
completely
paved access

P.O. Box 305
Whitecourt, ALTA T7S 1N5

GATEWAY ESSO

24-HOUR FULL SERVICE
Auto and Bottled Propane
Gas · Diesel · Parts

24-Hour Towing and Mobile Tire Service

(403) 778-ESSO
(403) 778-2463

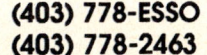

**RESTAURANT
GROCERY STORE**
WHITECOURT, ALBERTA

ALASKA HIGHWAY VIA EAST ACCESS ROUTE

ALASKA HIGHWAY VIA EAST ACCESS

Iosegun Creek government campground; 15 sites, pit toilets, water, tables and firepits. ▲

E 159 (255.9 km) **DC 208** (334.7 km) Fox Creek airport; paved runway.

E 162 (260.7 km) **DC 205** (329.9 km) **FOX CREEK** (pop. 2,063; elev. 2,800 feet/853m). **Emergency Services: RCMP,** phone 622-3740. **Hospital,** phone 622-3545. All visitor facilities including a hotel, 3 motels, gas stations with repair service, a grocery and deli, pharmacy, bank, hospital and medical clinic, and a 9-hole golf course with artificial greens. Municipal campground with 16 sites, full hookups. Dump station located at north end of town. Visitor information booth open in summer; phone 622-3624. Shops open Friday evening, closed Sunday.

Centre of oil and gas exploration and production, North America's largest known natural gas field is here. There are 4 major gas plants in the area (Amoco, Chevron, Dome, Petro-Canada) and a full range of related industrial services.

Fox Creek is in the heart of big game country, and hunting guides are available. Two local lakes popular with residents and visitors are Iosegun and Smoke. Camping, boat launch and fishing at **Iosegun Lake**, 6.8 miles/11 km north on good gravel road; northern pike and perch. Camping, boat launch and fishing at **Smoke Lake**, 8 miles/13 km southwest; northern pike, perch and pickerel.

The Alaskan Motel. See display ad this section.

Grant and Diana's Bed and Breakfast. See display ad this section.

Regal Motor Inn. See display ad this section.

E 167 (268.7 km) **DC 200** (321.9 km) Turnout with litter barrel.

E 169.5 (272.8 km) **DC 197.5** (317.8 km) Turnouts with litter barrels both sides of highway.

E 172 (276.8 km) **DC 195** (313.8 km) Pines government campground; 40 sites, shelter, firewood, pump water, tables and pit toilets. ▲

E 182.1 (293 km) **DC 184.9** (297.6 km) Turnout with litter barrel.

E 192 (309 km) **DC 175** (281.6 km) **LITTLE SMOKY** (pop. about 50). Motel, pay phone, propane, grocery store, service station and post office.

E 192.2 (309.3 km) **DC 174.8** (281.3 km) Little Smoky River bridge.

E 193.5 (311.4 km) **DC 173.5** (279.2 km) Waskahigan (House) River bridge at confluence with Smoky River. Government campground with pit toilets, water, tables and firepits. ▲

Regal MOTOR INN
Modern Units • Kitchenettes
Complimentary Coffee
Satellite & Cable TV
Direct Dial Phones – Plug-ins
Auto Wake Up Service
Air Conditioning
Box 539, Fox Creek, ALTA T0H 1P0
(403) 622-3333

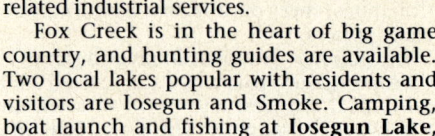

The Alaskan Motel
61 Modern Units • Colour TV
Direct Dial Phones
Free In-Room Coffee
Box 700 • Fox Creek, Alberta • T0H 1P0
PHONE (403) 622-3073

Grant and Diana's BED and BREAKFAST
Come share our forest wilderness
Grant and Diana Deans
Box 466, Fox Creek, Alberta T0H 1P0
(403) 622-3930 Adult Accommodation

"The Lion's Den"
TRAILER PARK and CAMPGROUND
SHOWERS, POWER and WATER
Reasonable Rates... PHONE (403) 524-3536
Valleyview, Alberta T0H 3N0

HORIZON MOTEL & RESTAURANT
✴ 62 APPROVED MODERN GUEST ROOMS
✴ 24-Hour Desk and Direct Dial Phones
✴ Kitchenettes Available
✴ Air-Conditioning
✴ Satellite Movie & Sports Channels
FULLY LICENSED DINING
Box 1590, Valleyview, AB T0H 3N0
(403) 524-3904

PORTAL TO THE PEACE
Valleyview, Alberta

Located on scenic Highway 43 en route to the Alaska Highway, Valleyview offers many opportunities to tourists
*camping *water sports
*regional parks *fishing

*over 400 in-town and rural business services.

TOURIST INFORMATION CENTRE
(open from May to September)
1-403-524-4129

Alberta, in all her majesty.
Canada
GAME COUNTRY

Information about community amenities can be obtained year 'round by calling
1-403-524-5150 or 524-3942
TOWN OF VALLEYVIEW
BOX 270, VALLEYVIEW, ALBERTA T0H 3N0 524-5150

VALLEYVIEW ESSO SERVICE
— 24 Hour Service —
Gas • Diesel
Confectionery • Ice
RESTAURANT

(403) 524-3504
Junction Hwy. 43 and Hwy. 34

Visa • MasterCard • American Express

E 197 (317 km) DC 170 (273.6 km) Turnout.

E 204.7 (329.4 km) DC 162.3 (261.2 km) Gas station, restaurant and grocery; pay phone.

E 206.7 (332.6 km) DC 160.3 (258 km) Turnout with litter barrel.

E 208.5 (335.5 km) DC 158.5 (255.1 km) Peace pipeline storage tanks.

E 210.8 (339.2 km) DC 156.2 (251.4 km) Valleyview Riverside golf course.

E 213.2 (343.1 km) DC 153.8 (247.5 km) Valleyview tourist information centre; pay phone, picnic tables, flush toilets. Open daily in summer, 8 A.M. to 8 P.M.

E 213.4 (343.4 km) DC 153.6 (247.2 km) Valleyview airport to west.

Valleyview

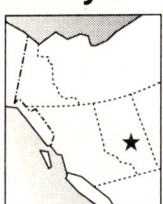

E 214.1 (344.4 km) DC 152.9 (246.1 km) **Population:** 2,218. **Emergency Services:** RCMP, phone 524-3343. **Fire Department,** 524-3211. **Ambulance,** phone 524-3916. **Hospital,** Valleyview General, 35 beds, phone 524-3356. **Visitor Information:** Major tourist information centre and rest stop located 0.9 mile/1.5 km south of Valleyview on Highway 43. Open 8 A.M. to 8 P.M. May 1 through Labour Day; helpful staff and well stocked with travel information. Phone 524-4129.

Elevation: 2,400 feet/732m. **Newspaper:** *Valley Views* (weekly).

Transportation: Air–Airport 0.7 mile/1.1 km south; length 3,000 feet/914m; paved. **Bus**–Greyhound.

Valleyview, the "Portal to the Peace," is at the junction of Highways 43 and 34.

VALLEYVIEW ADVERTISERS

Hi Valley Motor Inn .... Hwy. 43
Horizon Motel
   & Restaurant .... Ph. (403) 524-3904
Lion's Den, The .... W. edge of town
Town of Valleyview .... Ph. (403) 524-3924
Valleyview Esso
   Service .... Ph. (403) 524-3504

Hi Valley Motor Inn
(403) 524-3324
- 60 Modern Rooms
- Family Restaurant
- Nightly Entertainment
- Dining Lounge
- Cocktail Lounge
- 170-Seat Tavern

Alberta Accommodation
★ *Recommended* ★
Valleyview, Alberta

Cosy Cove Campground & Marina
Boat Rentals - Camping - Supplies
Groceries - Ice - Fishing Tackle, Bait & Licences
Proposed for '92: Shower, Laundry, Dump Station.
Located on the shores of Sturgeon Lake (23km west of Valleyview)
CALL **(403) 957-2400** for information

Sturgeon Lake west of Valleyview offers fishing, boating, camping. (Earl L. Brown, staff)

Highway 34 leads west to Grande Prairie and Dawson Creek. Highway 43 continues north to Peace River and the Mackenzie Highway to Northwest Territories (see MACKENZIE ROUTE section). Highway 43 also connects with Highway 2 east to Athabasca, the Slave Lake route from Edmonton used by Alaska Highway travelers until 1955, when Highway 43 was completed to Whitecourt.

Originally called Red Willow Creek when it was homesteaded in 1916, Valleyview was a village with a small hotel, gas station and a cafe during the first years of public travel on the Alaska Highway. But the community boomed with the discovery of oil and gas in the 1950s, and services grew along with the population. Today, Valleyview's economy is based on both oil and gas and agriculture. Farming consists of grain, oilseed, beef cattle and forage production.

The community has a full range of services, including a library, banks, swimming pool, schools and several churches. The area boasts abundant wildlife, including moose and bear.

All visitor facilities including 5 motels and hotels, restaurants, gas stations (many with major repair service), laundromat, grocery stores, liquor store and a golf course. Some gas stations and restaurants open 24 hours a day.

Lions Den Campground, west end of town, has 19 sites with hookups, tables, showers and toilets. ▲

East Access Route Log

(continued)

E 216 (347.6 km) DC 151 (243 km) Highway 43 continues north. Highway 34 begins westbound; continue west on Highway 34.

E 222.6 (358.2 km) DC 144.4 (232.4 km) 24-hour convenience store.

E 224.7 (361.6 km) DC 142.3 (229 km) Access north to Sturgeon Lake; fishing and camping. Williamson Provincial Park (1.2 miles/2 km) has 62 campsites, boat launch, showers and dump station. Sturgeon Lake Campground has 106 sites, some hookups, tables, showers, laundry, dump station and store. Fishing for perch, pickerel, northern pike and whitefish. ⌕▲

Heritage Park Campground
— SEXSMITH —
A family oriented Community

Photos by Brian Calkins

13 Sites, tap water, public phone, showers, sewage disposal, fishing and mini-golf.

Be sure to visit our historic Blacksmith Shop and N.A.R. Station.

Town of Sexsmith
P.O. Box 420, Sexsmith, AB T0H 3C0, Ph: 568-3681

ALASKA HIGHWAY VIA EAST ACCESS ROUTE

HIGHWAY 34

E 227 (365.3 km) DC 140 (225.3 km) CALAIS (pop. about 550); post office and grocery store.

E 230 (370.1 km) DC 137 (220.5 km) Private campground and marina on **Sturgeon Lake**; fishing, boat rentals.

Cosy Cove Concession & Marina. See display ad on page 35.

E 232 (373.3 km) DC 135 (217.3 km) Sturgeon Heights. Turnoff for Youngs Point Provincial Park, 6 miles/10 km northeast; 72 campsites, dump station, boat launch, fishing in Sturgeon Lake.

E 235 (378.2 km) DC 132 (212.4 km) Turnouts both sides of highway.

E 240 (386.2 km) DC 127 (204.4 km) CROOKED CREEK (pop. 10); gas station, grocery, post office and pay phone.

E 246 (395.9 km) DC 121 (194.7 km) DeBOLT, a small farming community north of highway with a general store and district museum. Garage with gas on highway. Adjacent restaurant serves buffalo burgers.

E 253.8 (408.7 km) DC 113.2 (181.9 km) **Junction.** Forestry Trunk Road leads 632 miles/1017 km south, intersecting Yellowhead Highway 16 and Trans-Canada Highway 1, to Highway 3.

E 255.2 (410.7 km) DC 111.8 (179.9 km) Microwave towers to east.

E 259.5 (417.6 km) DC 107.5 (173 km) Smoky River bridge and government campground; 30 sites, shelter, firepits, firewood, tables, pit toilets, water pump and boat launch.

E 264 (424.9 km) DC 103 (165.7 km) BEZANSON. Post office, gas station with minor repair service, grocery, general store, propane.

E 269 (432.9 km) DC 98 (157.7 km) Kleskun Hills Park to north 3 miles/5 km. The park features an ancient sea bottom with fossils of dinosaurs and marine life.

E 270.6 (435.5 km) DC 96.4 (155.1 km) Turnout to north with historical sign about the Kleskun Hills.

E 283.5 (456.2 km) DC 83.5 (134.4 km) Weigh scales to north.

E 283.8 (456.7 km) DC 83.2 (133.9 km) Railroad crossing.

E 284 (457 km) DC 83 (133.6 km) **Junction**, Highways 34 and 2. Westbound travelers turn south for Grande Prairie and Highway 2 to Dawson Creek (log follows). Turn north on Highway 2 for Sexsmith, 8.5 miles/13.7 km north and for Grimshaw, 105 miles/169 km north, Mile 0 of the Mackenzie Highway (see MACKENZIE ROUTE section). SEXSMITH has a hotel, restaurants, 13-site campground, banks, gas station and golf course. Its economy is based on agriculture, petroleum and the Northern Alberta Rapeseed Processing plant. Known for its upland game hunting, attractions in Sexsmith also include a restored working 1916 blacksmith shop and the 1928 Northern Alberta Railway Station (currently under restoration).

Town of Sexsmith. See display ad on page 35.

HIGHWAY 2

From its junction with Highway 34, Highway 2 leads south into Grande Prairie (description follows). To reach Grande Prairie city centre, keep straight ahead on Highway 2 (Clairmont Road) as it becomes 100th Street and follow it downtown. To skirt the downtown area, take the Highway 2 Bypass. Highway 2 becomes 100th Avenue (Richmond Avenue) on the west side of Grande Prairie. See the city map on page 38.

NOTE: Bighorn Highway 40 connects Grande Prairie with Grande Cache and Yellowhead Highway 16. To reach the Bighorn Highway, follow Wapiti Road (108th Street) south from Highway 2 on the west side of Grande Prairie. See BIGHORN HIGHWAY log below.

Bighorn Highway 40 Log

This 206.6-mile/332.5-km highway connects Yellowhead Highway 16 and Highway 2, and the communities of Grande Cache and Grande Prairie. It opened in 1987. The highway is paved from its junction with Yellowhead Highway 16 to just beyond Grande Cache. It is gravel, and there are no services between Grande Cache and Grande Prairie, a distance of 114 miles/183 km. **Distance from Yellowhead Highway 16 junction (J) is shown.**

J 0 **Junction** of Bighorn Highway 40 and Yellowhead Highway 16. (See **Milepost E 178** in the YELLOWHEAD HIGHWAY 16 section.)

J 12 (19 km) William A. Switzer Provincial Park; 195 campsites, swimming, boat launch and fishing.

J 68.4 (110 km) Pierre Grey government campground; 65 sites, fireplaces, firewood, and water pumps.

J 80.2 (129 km) Mason Creek day-use area; picnic facilities and trail to Muskeg River.

J 87 (140 km) Grande Cache Lake; picnic area, swimming, boat launch.

J 88.9 (143 km) Victor Lake; canoeing and fishing.

J 90 (145 km) GRANDE CACHE (pop. 4,618; elev. 3,602 feet/1098m). A planned community, built in the early 1970s with the development of a coal mine. Grande Cache also has a major sawmill. There are 2 banks, laundromats, 2 hotels, 4 motels, restaurants, recreational centre, a tourist information centre, post office and gas stations. Shopping facilities include 2 supermarkets, a bakery, sporting goods store and department store. There is scheduled air and bus service to Grande Prairie and Edmonton.

Camping at Marv Moore municipal campground, located at the north edge of town past the golf course. There are 26 sites (gravel pads), full hookups, dump station, showers and laundry facilities. Camping fee is $10.

J 91.9 (147.9 km) Highway 40 descends toward the Smoky River northbound. *NOTE: No services next 114.3 miles/184 km northbound.*

J 93 (149.6 km) Blue Bridge government campground; 22 sites, shelters, firewood, firepits, water pump, tables and pit toilets. No camping fee. Trail access to Willmore Wilderness Park. **Smoky River**, fishing for arctic grayling, Dolly Varden and whitefish; boat launch.

J 93.2 (150 km) Smoky River bridge.

J 94 (151.3 km) Turnoff to south for Willmore Wilderness Park; parking area 5 miles/6.4 km.

J 98.2 (158 km) Grande Cache gun range to east. Northbound, Highway 40 parallels the Northern Alberta Resource railroad and the Smoky River.

J 101.5 (163.4 km) Pavement ends, gravel begins, northbound.

J 102.2 (164.5 km) Turnout to east overlooks the industry of this area: Smoky River Coal Ltd. and H.R. Milner Generating Station.

J 108.5 (174.6 km) Turnoff to east for Sheep Creek day-use area; shaded picnic tables, firewood, firepits, water pump, litter barrels, outhouses and gravel parking area. Boat launch on Smoky River.

J 108.9 (175.2 km) Sheep Creek bridge.

J 111.7 (179.8 km) Wayandie Road. Highway climbs northbound; some sections of 7 percent grade.

J 126.3 (203.3 km) Southview recreation area to east; gravel parking area, shaded picnic tables, litter barrels and outhouses. Highbush cranberries in season.

J 131.5 (211.7 km) 16th Baseline sign marks north-south hunting boundary.

J 143 (230.2 km) Distance marker indicates Grande Prairie 62 miles/100 km. *CAUTION: Watch for soft spots on road between here and Grande Prairie.*

J 146.5 (235.9 km) Kakwa River bridge.

J 146.8 (236.3 km) Turnoff for **Kakwa River** day-use area; picnic tables, firewood, firepits, water pump, litter barrels, outhouses and gravel parking area. Fishing for arctic grayling.

J 159.9 (257.4 km) Side road leads east 3.7 miles/6 km to **Musreau Lake** day-use area and campground. There are 50 picnic sites and 30 campsites; tables, firewood, firepits, water pumps, litter barrels and outhouses. Boat launch and fishing.

J 162 (260.8 km) Chuck's Coulee.

J 162.5 (261.6 km) Steep Creek.

J 165.1 (265.7 km) Cutbank River bridge. River access at north end of bridge.

J 166.3 (267.7 km) Elk Creek.

J 172.9 (278.2 km) Distance marker indicates Grande Prairie 31 miles/50 km.

J 181.5 (292.1 km) Big Mountain Creek.

J 183.4 (295.1 km) Bald Mountain Creek.

J 191.4 (308.1 km) Bent Pipe Creek.

J 199.6 (321.2 km) Gravel ends, pavement begins, northbound.

J 199.8 (321.6 km) Wapiti River bridge.

J 206.6 (332.5 km) **Junction** with Highway 2 at Grande Prairie.

**Return to Milepost E 284
East Access Route**

DRIVE
THE BIGHORN ROUTE

"THE WORLD'S MOST SCENIC INTERNATIONAL TOURIST ROUTE"

Alberta, in all her majesty.
Canada

For complete information contact...
Game Country Tourism Association
9928 - 111 Avenue
Grande Prairie, Alberta T8V 4C3
Phone 403-539-4300

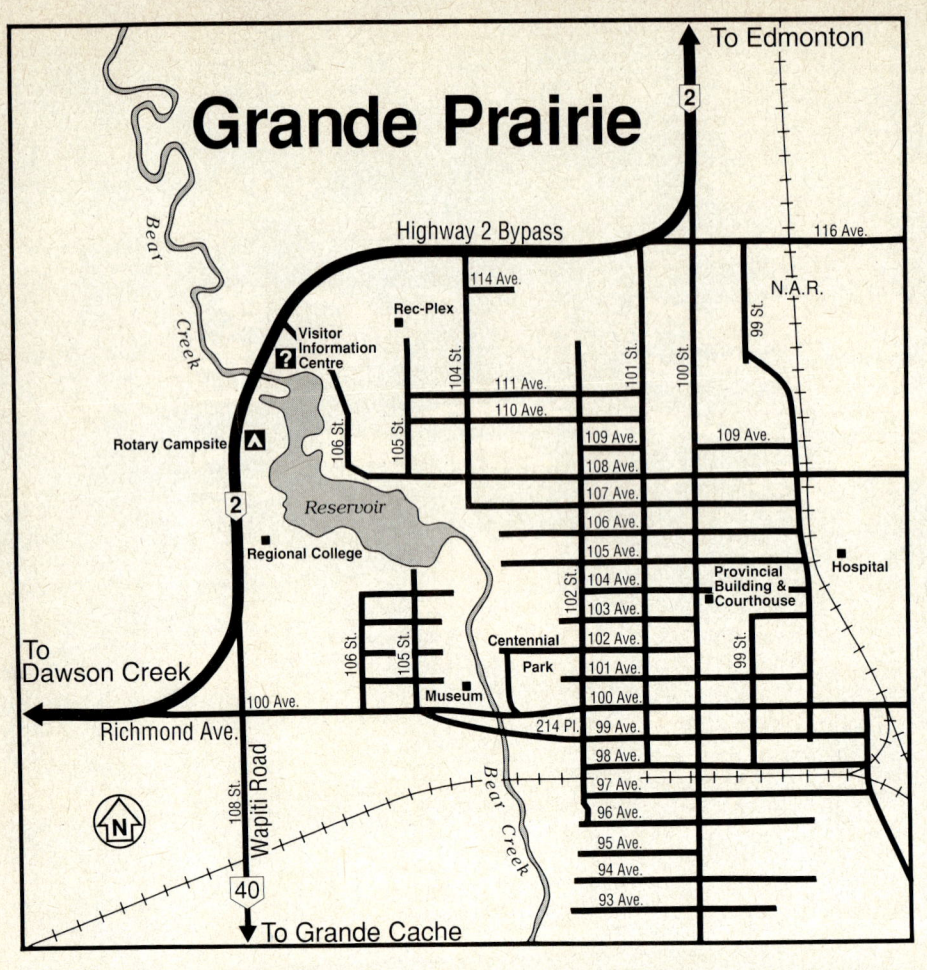

ALASKA HIGHWAY VIA EAST ACCESS

Grande Prairie

Elevation: 2,198 feet/670m. **Climate:** A mild climate with a mean average in summer of 58°F/15°C, and in winter dropping to 10°F/-12°C, with an average of 116 frost-free days annually. Average annual rainfall is 11 inches and snowfall 69 inches.

Radio: CFGP 1050, CJXX 1430, CKYL 610, CBC-FM 102.5, CKUA-FM 100.9. **Newspaper:** *Herald-Tribune* (Monday through Friday).

Transportation: Air–Scheduled air service to Vancouver, BC, Edmonton, Calgary, and points north. All-weather 6,500-foot/1,981-m paved runway. **Bus**–Greyhound.

Grande Prairie was first incorporated as a village in 1914, as a town in 1919, and as a city in 1958, by which time its population had reached nearly 8,000. In 1949 the population was 3,500 and Grande Prairie was described in the first edition of *The MILEPOST* as the most sizable town between Edmonton and Dawson Creek on the Alaska Highway East Access Route via Slave Lake. At that time it had "telegraph offices, good stores and two recently completed auto courts." Today, there are dozens of hotels, motels and restaurants and 2 indoor shopping malls.

Called "The Commerce Center of the Peace Country," Grande Prairie's economy is based on agriculture (canola, wheat, barley, oats, rye, fescue), forestry (a bleached kraft pulp mill and sawmill are located here), mining, government services, petroleum and natural gas.

There are 2 municipal swimming pools, an 18-hole golf course, skiing, hockey, skating, broom-ball, curling and tennis facilities, an art gallery and public library, plus theatrical and musical groups and events. Grande Prairie also has many churches, elementary and high schools, and a regional college designed by Douglas Cardinal. The Provincial Bldg. and courthouse are located at Jubilee Park on 100th Street.

Muskoseepi Park encompasses 5 units along the Bear Creek corridor in town, each offering a variety of facilities and connected by trail. Easiest access is via 106th Street off the Highway 2 Bypass to Bear Creek Reservoir, which offers bicycling, camping, picnicking, canoeing and tourist information services. Nearby Centennial Park has tennis courts, a playground, lawn bowling and is the site of the Pioneer Museum and Village. Open daily in summer from 10 A.M. to 6 P.M., Pioneer Museum (532-5482) features a log church built in 1911, a 1-room schoolhouse

Grande Prairie

E 288 (463.5 km) DC 79 (127.1 km). Located at junction of Highways 2 and 34. **Population:** 27,208. **Emergency Services: RCMP,** phone 538-5700. **Fire Department,** phone 532-2100. **Ambulance,** phone 532-9511. **Hospital,** Queen Elizabeth, 10409 98th St., phone 538-7100.

Visitor Information: Chamber of Commerce office at 10011 103rd Ave., and a visitor information centre off Highway 2 Bypass on 106th Street at Bear Creek Reservoir, open 9 A.M. to 9 P.M. in July and August, shorter hours in June.

GRANDE PRAIRIE ADVERTISERS

Econolodge Motor Inn .....Ph. (403) 539-4700
Game Country Tourism
 Association...................Ph. (403) 539-4300
Trumpeter Motor Inn ....Ph. (403) 539-5561

ECONOLODGE MOTOR INN

★ 24-HOUR CHECK-IN ★

50 MOTEL UNITS
CABLE T.V.
TANNING STUDIO
HEATED OUTDOOR POOL
(May through September)
24-HOUR PHONE
(Restaurant Adjacent)

10909 — 100th Avenue
(Highway 2 West)
Grande Prairie, ALTA T8V 3J9

(403) 539-4700
FAX (403) 539-4700

1-800-661-7874 (Reservations only)
in BC & Alberta

MasterCard • American Express • VISA

TRUMPETER MOTOR INN

- Swany's Bar
- Dave's Saloon
- Cygnet Dining Room
- Trump's Game Room
- Wheatsheaf Coffee Garden
- 124 Luxurious Rooms
- Executive Suites
- Meeting Rooms
- Whirlpool
- Pool

— Fully Air-conditioned —

(403) 539-5561 • 1-800-661-9435 • FAX (403) 538-4636

12102 - 100 Street, Grand Prairie, ALTA T8V 5P1

David and Elizabeth Chomik — Your Hosts

VISA • MasterCard • American Express

GATEWAY TO ALASKA

Welcome back! Back to 50 years ago, when we provided supplies and services to our American friends during the construction of that everlasting monument to the cooperation of two great nations, **THE ALCAN HIGHWAY**. Share special memories with us as you travel through our area! In addition to a summer full of good times, we've planned special commemorative events to ensure that your perceptions of the wonderful north become total reality. Be sure your travel plans include visits to several of the attractions and festivals in the Trumpeter Region. **Experience the warmth of the North—it comes from the heart!**

GRANDE PRAIRIE

The greatest place to be! For the ultimate in fun and enjoyment, let this thoroughly modern city entertain you as you journey up to the famous Alaska Highway. From the joining of cultures in a multicultural festival, to a visit to a world class art gallery to camping in the wilds, you're only minutes away from your favorite activity hosted as only the northerners know how—whole heartedly!

BEAVERLODGE

South Peace Centennial Museum: one of the largest operating museums in Alberta—it's a walk through history! Open daily during the summer, don't miss "Pioneer Day", July 19. Located on Highway #2, just 2 km north of Beaverlodge.

HYTHE

"Volunteer Capital of Alberta". Still going strong with the pioneer spirit that settled and built this thriving community. Enquire about Staggs Bison Ranch, Driftwood Exotic Ranch & Wildlife Haven and Windy Ridge Nursery.

WEMBLEY

"Wheat King of the World". Take in our rodeo, visit our summer fair, or just stop and visit. Centrally located to Pipestone Creek and Lake Saskatoon Provincial Park and Pipestone Putters golf course. Home of the rare Pachyrhinosaurus dinosaur.

'92 CALENDAR OF EVENTS

June 5-7	Stompede
June 6	G.P. Highland Games
June 10	Vintage Car Rally
June 13	Sexsmith Chautaugua Day -old fashioned family fair
July 1	Canada Day Muskoseepi Park
July 5-6	Airmada
July 18-19	Heritage Days
July 26	Great Peace Country Duck Race
July 28- Aug 4	Pacific Rim Balloon Championships
Aug 22-23	Dinosaur Festival

ON-GOING SUMMER ACTIVITIES

- "Buffalo Burger & Saskatoon Pie" nights in Hythe, during summer of '92
- Second Street Theatre
- People in the Park
- Pioneer Museum
- Entire summer of country rodeos, fairs, farmers' markets, festivals and reunions

Contact the Tourism office for complete schedule and detailed information on these events and more!

SEXSMITH

Let us present our unique heritage and spirit to you—take a walk down our "1930's" main street. Our park and main street projects make Sexsmith a fun people place to be, with special theme events taking place throughout the year.

COUNTY OF GRANDE PRAIRIE

Enjoy some of the finest scenery in Canada as you relax in one of the several parks operated by the County. Well-stocked lakes, birdwatching, zoos and game farms... Every weekend is festive with a fair, rodeo or reunion in at least one location, and **always** lots of friendly residents to make you welcome!

For complete information contact:

Game Country Tourism Association

9928 - 111 Avenue
Grande Prairie, Alberta T8V 4C3
Telephone: (403) 539-4300
Fax: (403) 532-3380

Alberta, in all her majesty.
Canada

ALASKA HIGHWAY VIA EAST ACCESS

and rural post office, and collections of fossils, rocks, mounted wildlife and implements and tools used by Peace River pioneers. Admission fee charged.

Rotary Park public campground with 39 sites, hookups and dump station, is located off Highway 2 Bypass at the northwest edge of town next to the college. A private campground is located at the south edge of town. ▲

Wee Links Golf & Campground. Campground, Pitch & Putt Golf Course (grass greens) and driving range at a secluded setting within Grande Prairie city limits. Clean washrooms, hot showers, pay phone, water and power at sites, firepits, snacks, hiking/biking trails. 68 Avenue and 100 Street. VISA and MasterCard. Reservations (403) 538-4501. [ADVERTISEMENT] ▲

East Access Route Log

(continued)
HIGHWAY 2 WEST

E 298 (479.6 km) DC 69 (111 km) Saskatoon Island Provincial Park is 1.9 miles/3 km north; 96 campsites, dump station, boat launch, swimming, playground. ▲

E 299 (481.2 km) DC 68 (109.4 km) WEMBLEY (pop. 1,209), hotel, banking service at hotel, post office, government liquor store, grocery, gas stop, car wash and restaurant. Picnicking at Sunset Lake Park in town. Camping May 1 to Oct. 15 at Pipestone Creek County Park, 9 miles/14.5 km south; 99 sites, showers, flush toilets, dump station, boat launch, fishing, playground.

E 311 (500.5 km) DC 56 (90.1 km) **Town of Beaverlodge.** Driving? Plan to stay at Pioneer Campsite. In town, on the highway. Showers, water, dump station, daily rates. Visitor information: local, Alberta and British Columbia, Yukon and Alaska. Opera–

tor: Town of Beaverlodge. Or Flying? Beaverlodge DeWit Airpark. Camping, on-site security, tie-downs, power, transportation available. Showers and radio beacon in 1989. ARCAL radio control lights (123.2 Mhz), rotating beacon, 3,000-foot paved runway. Report Grande Prairie Airport (126.7 Mhz). [ADVERTISEMENT]

BEAVERLODGE (pop. 1,808; elev. 2,419 feet/737m). **Emergency Services: RCMP,** phone 354-2485. **Ambulance,** phone 354-2154. **Hospital,** phone 354-2136. Visitor information located in the restored Lower Beaver Lodge School on the north side of Highway 2 at the west end of town.

Beaverlodge is a service centre for the area with a provincial courthouse, RCMP, hospital, medical and dental clinic. There are 9 churches, schools, a swimming pool and tennis courts.

Visitor services include 2 motels, 8 restaurants and gas stations. There are supermarkets, banks, a drugstore, car wash and sporting goods store. The Beaverlodge Hotel and Museum Tavern here features quite a collection of stuffed animals, antiques, guns and other memorabilia. Camping is available at the municipal Pioneer Campsite (19 sites, showers, dump station, tourist information). The Beaverlodge Airpark, 2 miles/3.2 km south of town, is becoming a popular stopover on the flying route to Alaska. The Airpark has a paved runway and directional beacon. ▲

Beaverlodge is also home to Canada's most northerly Agricultural Research Station (open to the public), and serves as regional centre for grain transportation, seed cleaning and seed production. Cereal grains, such as wheat, barley and oats, are the main crops in the area.

Beaverlodge Motor Inn. See display ad this section.

Chicken Village. See display ad this section.

Wash & Lube. See display ad this section.

E 312 (502.1 km) DC 55 (88.5 km) South Peace Centennial Museum to east, open daily in summer; phone 354-8869. The museum features 15 display buildings and working steam-powered farm equipment from the early 1900s. Open 10 A.M. to 8 P.M., mid-May through mid-October. The annual Pioneer Day celebration, held here the third Sunday in July, attracts several thousand visitors.

South Peace Centennial Museum. See display ad this section.

E 314.3 (505.8 km) DC 52.6 (84.8 km) Golf course. This joint project of Hythe and Beaverlodge residents has a clubhouse that was once a NAR station. The 9-hole par 35

CHICKEN VILLAGE
BEAVERLODGE
– PHONE (403) 354-8350
Next to the Pioneer Campsite on the highway
- Burgers • Ice Cream
- Salads • Chicken
- Pleasant Eating Area

VISA MasterCard

BEAVERLODGE HOTEL
Museum Tavern
Featuring Buffalo Steaks & Burgers

Taxidermy Display
Gun Collection — Antiques — etc.
LIVE ENTERTAINMENT NIGHTLY
Dance til 2:00 a.m.
— Games Room —
(403) 354-2059
VISA MasterCard AMERICAN EXPRESS

"The BMI" Beaverlodge Motor Inn
(and auxiliary BEAVER INN)

- Deluxe Rooms • Kitchenettes • Cable & Satellite TV
- Direct Dial Phones • *Room Service*
- Valet Service • Paved Parking • Bus Tours Welcome
- Sunday Brunch • Banquet Facilities • Licensed Dining Room
- Licensed Restaurant • Open 6 a.m. - 11 p.m. Daily

Bus Depot • *Limo Service to Airpark*

Lounge — Outdoor Patio
Good Motorhome Parking – Plug-ins Available
Walking Distance to the Museum Tavern

Open 24 Hours
Phone (403) 354-2291 • FAX (403) 354-2225
608-6A Street, Highway 2, Beaverlodge, Alberta

WASH & LUBE
Full Time Attendant

CAR, TRUCK AND R.V. WASH
FOAM BRUSH WASH
OIL CHANGE

SHOWER • SOFT WATER
FULL LAUNDRY FACILITIES

Local Souvenirs
Confectionery • Tourist Information
VISA **(403) 354-3555** MasterCard
Your Hosts — Norm and Ruth Isley
Highway 2, Beaverlodge

South Peace Centennial Museum
Featuring: PIONEER VILLAGE — 14 Display Buildings 
Steamers, Tractors, Sawmill, Planer
All Equipment Operational
Open daily mid-May to Sept. 30; 10:00 a.m. - 6:00 p.m.
Pioneer Day — 3rd Sunday in July
Box 493, Beaverlodge, ALTA T0H 0C0 • (403) 354-8869

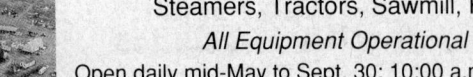

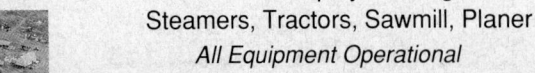

Bright yellow flowers are canola, grown as a low cholesterol oil seed. (Earl L. Brown, staff)

course has grass greens. Visitors are welcome; rentals available.

E 320 (515 km) DC 47 (75.6 km) **HYTHE** (pop. 681) is an agricultural service community and processing center for fruit and berry crops, especially saskatoon berries. Canola is also a major crop. The town has a motel, restaurant, laundromat, gas station, tire repair, car wash, outdoor covered heated swimming pool, complete shopping facilities and a hospital. Municipal campground in town with 20 sites, showers, dump station and playground. The information centre is housed in the Tags Food and Gas store. ▲

Hythe Motor Hotel. See display ad this section.

E 329 (529.4 km) DC 38 (61.1 km) **Junction** with Highway 59 east to Sexsmith.

E 337 (542.3 km) DC 30 (48.3 km) **DEMMITT**, an older settlement, site of 2 sawmills, has a general store with postal service and gas.

E 340 (547.2 km) DC 27 (43.4 km) Railway crossing.

E 341 (548.8 km) DC 26 (41.8 km) Public campground to east; 15 sites, shelter, firewood, tables, pit toilets, pump water and playground. ▲

E 341.3 (549.2 km) DC 25.7 (41.3 km) Vehicle inspection station to west.

E 342 (550.4 km) DC 25 (40.2 km) Gas station and convenience store.

E 343.3 (552.5 km) DC 23.7 (38.1 km) Alberta-British Columbia border. Turnout with litter barrels and pay phone.

TIME ZONE CHANGE: Alberta is on Mountain time; most of British Columbia is on Pacific time.

E 345.1 (555.4 km) DC 21.9 (35.2 km) **Junction** with Heritage Highway 52 (gravel surface) which leads 18.5 miles/30 km south to One Island Lake Park (30 campsites, fee charged, excellent rainbow fishing) and 92 miles/148 km southwest from Highway 2 to Tumbler Ridge townsite, built in conjunction with the North East Coal development. Heritage Highway loops north 59.5 miles/96 km from Tumbler Ridge to join Highway 97 just west of Dawson Creek (see **Milepost PG 237.7** in the WEST ACCESS ROUTE section).

E 345.7 (556.3 km) DC 21.3 (34.3 km) Tupper Creek bridge.

E 347 (558.5 km) DC 20 (32.1 km) Swan Lake Provincial Park, with 41 campsites, picnic area, playground and boat launch, is 1.2 miles/2 km north of the tiny hamlet of TUPPER which has a general store. ▲

E 347.9 (559.9 km) DC 19.1 (30.7 km) Sudeten Provincial Park; 15 campsites, 8 picnic tables. Plaque tells of immigration to this valley of displaced residents of Sudetenland in 1938-39. ▲

E 348.9 (561.5 km) DC 18.1 (29.1 km) Tate Creek bridge.

E 349.7 (562.7 km) DC 17.3 (27.8 km) Side road west to community of Tomslake.

E 356.3 (573.4 km) DC 10.7 (17.2 km) Turnout to east with litter barrel.

E 358 (576.1 km) DC 9 (14.5 km) Historic sign tells of Pouce Coupe Prairie.

E 359.4 (578.4 km) 7.6 (12.2 km) Railway crossing.

E 360 (579.3 km) DC 7 (11.2 km) Weigh scales to east.

E 360.4 (580 km) DC 6.6 (10.6 km) Bissett Creek bridge. Regional park located at south end of bridge.

E 361 (581 km) DC 6 (9.6 km) **POUCE COUPE** (pop. 1,200; elev. 2,118 feet/646m). **Visitor Information:** Tourist Bureau Office on Highway 2, open 9 A.M. to 5 P.M., May 15 to Sept. 15.

The Pouce Coupe area was first settled in 1898 by a French Canadian, who set up a trading post in 1908. The Edson Trail, completed in 1911, brought in the main influx of settlers from Edmonton in 1912. Historical artifacts are displayed at the Pouce Coupe Museum, located in the old NAR railroad station, 1 block south of Highway 2; open 8 A.M. to 5 P.M. The museum is also the site of a pancake breakfast on May 17 and July 1; the Harvest Tea and Bake, Sept. 19; and a smorgasbord for Road Rally, Sept. 21.

Pouce Coupe is the starting point for the Alaska Highway trailblazers 1992 horse and wagon trek to Fairbanks along the Trail of '42. The trip commemorates the 50th anniversary of the construction of the Alaska Highway, and is scheduled to depart June 13. Other special events in 1992 include: June 11, coffee break for Alcan Convoy; July 1, Canada Day Parade, Homecoming Weekend and Pouce Coupe Park Hospital Barbecue. For more information contact P.O. Box 1992, Pouce Coupe, BC V0C 2C0.

The village has 2 motels, a hotel, restaurant, post office, gas station, dump station, car wash, garage and food store. Camping at Regional Park, open mid-May to mid-September; hookups. ▲

The Pouce Coupe Museum. See display ad this section.

The Village of Pouce Coupe. See display ad this section.

E 364.5 (586.6 km) DC 2.5 (4 km) Dawson Creek airport.

E 367 (590.6 km) DC 0 **DAWSON CREEK**, the beginning of the Alaska Highway. For details turn to the ALASKA HIGHWAY section.

ALASKA HIGHWAY VIA EAST ACCESS ROUTE

The Pouce Coupe Museum

Box 293, Pouce Coupe, BC
Tourist Infocentre
8 a.m. – 5 p.m. – 7 Days a Week
Located on Highway 2 • Seasonal
Souvenirs • **Local Pioneer Artifacts**
Museum Hours • 8 a.m. – 5 p.m. – Monday – Friday
Located 1 block south of Highway 2
Summer (604) 786-5555

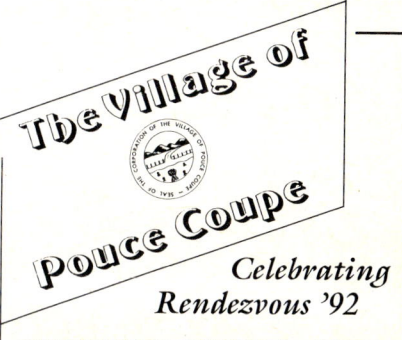

Super, Natural Scenic Adventure

The Village of Pouce Coupe

Celebrating Rendezvous '92

SCHEDULED EVENTS for 1992:

June 11 – Alcan Convoy Coffee Break
June 12 – Send-off of Alaska Highway Trailblazers
July 1 – Canada Day Parade and Bar-B-Que
60th Anniversary Homecoming Weekend
Sept. 19 – Museum's Harvest Tea
Sept. 21 – Road Rally Smorg and many more events!

VILLAGE OF POUCE COUPE
Box 190, Pouce Coupe, B.C. V0C 2C0
Phone (604) 786-5183
FAX (604) 786-5257

Super, Natural Scenic Adventure

HYTHE MOTOR HOTEL

Rooms at Reasonable Rates
RESTAURANT – LICENSED
Air-Conditioning - Private Telephones
Satellite T.V. - Tavern

Right on Highway 2
HYTHE • (403) 356-2151

Alaska Highway via
WEST ACCESS ROUTE

**Seattle, Washington, to Dawson Creek, British Columbia
via Cache Creek and Prince George, British Columbia
Interstate Highway 5, Trans-Canada Highway 1 and BC Highway 97
(See maps, pages 43–44)**

The West Access Route links Interstate 5, Trans-Canada Highway 1 and B.C. Highway 97 form the most direct route to Dawson Creek, BC, for West Coast motorists.

This has been the major western route to the start of the Alaska Highway since 1952, when the John Hart Highway connecting Prince George and Dawson Creek was completed. Heralded in the 1953 edition of *The MILEPOST*® as a "link between the Alaska Highway at Dawson Creek and the highway system of the Pacific Coast," the 250-mile section of Highway 97 known today as the John Hart-Peace River Highway brought Seattle about 535 miles closer to Dawson Creek by eliminating the long drive east to Calgary then north through Edmonton. It is 817 miles from Seattle to Dawson Creek via the West Access Route.

The West Access Route junctions with Yellowhead Highway 16 at Prince George. This east-west highway connects with the Alaska State Ferry System and BC Ferries at Prince Rupert, and with the East Access Route to the Alaska Highway at Edmonton. Turn to the YELLOWHEAD HIGHWAY 16 section for a complete log of that route.

Other major highways connecting with the West Access Route and covered in detail in our companion travel guide, *NORTHWEST MILEPOSTS*®, are: Interstate 5, Crowsnest Highway 3, Trans-Canada Highway 1 to Calgary, AB, the Coquihalla Highway, Highway 20 to Bella Coola and Highway 26 to Barkerville. Motorists driving north from Wenatchee, WA, will also find mile-by-mile logs of U.S. Highway 97, B.C. Highway 97 and Yellowhead Highway 5 in *NORTHWEST MILEPOSTS*®.

INTERSTATE HIGHWAY 5

The West Access Route begins in **SEATTLE, WA** (pop. 493,846), the largest city in the Pacific Northwest. Seattle has been called the Alaska gateway city since the Klondike gold rush days, when it became the major staging and departure point for most of the gold seekers. Seattle was also southern terminus of the Alaska Marine Highway System until 1989, when the Alaska state ferries moved to the Fairhaven Terminal at Bellingham, WA (Interstate 5, Exit 250). Seattle-Tacoma International Airport is the departure point for jet flights to Alaska. The air terminal is located 10 miles/16 km south of city center via Interstate 5 (Exit 154).

Like most interstate routes in the United States, Interstate 5 has physical mileposts along its route and corresponding numbered exits. From Seattle, drive 92 miles north on Interstate 5 to Bellingham and turn off onto Highway 539 north (Exit 256), which goes north 12 miles to Highway 546, which will take you another 13 miles to Sumas, WA, and the U.S.-Canada border (customs open 24 hours a day). *The MILEPOST*® log begins on Trans-Canada Highway 1 near Abbotsford.

From Seattle to Abbotsford via Sumas it is 120 miles. From Abbotsford to Cache Creek, it is 170 miles; from Cache Creek to Prince George, 277 miles; and from Prince George to Dawson Creek it is 250 miles.

West Access Route Log

TRANS-CANADA HIGHWAY 1
The West Access Route log is divided into 3 sections: Abbotsford to Cache Creek; Cache Creek to Prince George; and Prince George to Dawson Creek.
This section of the log shows distance from Abbotsford (A) followed by distance from Cache Creek (CC).

A 0 CC 170 (273.6 km) **Junction** of Trans-Canada Highway 1 and Highway 11 south to the international border crossing at Sumas-Huntingdon. Highway 11 north to **ABBOTSFORD** (pop. 60,400), all visitor services. Abbotsford is the "Raspberry Capital of Canada" and is the home of the Abbotsford International Airshow.

Bridge over the Fraser River to Mission and Highway 7 to Harrison Hot Springs.

A 1.9 (3 km) CC 168.1 (270.5 km) Exit 95 to Watcom Road and westbound exit to Sumas River rest area. Access to Sumas Mountain Provincial Park; hiking.

A 5.3 (8.5 km) CC 164.7 (265.1 km) Exit 99 to Sumas River rest area (eastbound only); tables, toilet, pay phones.

A 8.8 (14.2 km) CC 161.2 (259.4 km) Exit 104 to small farming community of Yarrow and road to Cultus Lake. The Lower Fraser River Valley is prime agricultural land.

CAUTION: Watch for farm vehicles crossing freeway.

A 15 (24.1 km) CC 155 (249.4 km) Exit 116 to Lickman Road; access to tourist infocentre, open daily in summer. Chilliwack Antique Powerland museum located behind infocentre.

A 16.8 (27.1 km) CC 153.2 (246.5 km) Highway 119B to Chilliwack Airport.

A 17 (27.4 km) CC 153 (246.2 km) Exit

Beautiful Azouzetta Lake near Pine Pass, Milepost PG 119.3, on the John Hart Highway. The Hart Highway opened in 1952. (Earl L. Brown, staff)

**CRUISE
Bellingham to Victoria**
See ad in
"Marine Access Routes" section
**Gray Line Cruises
800-443-4552**

WEST ACCESS ROUTE — Seattle, WA, to Lac La Hache, BC

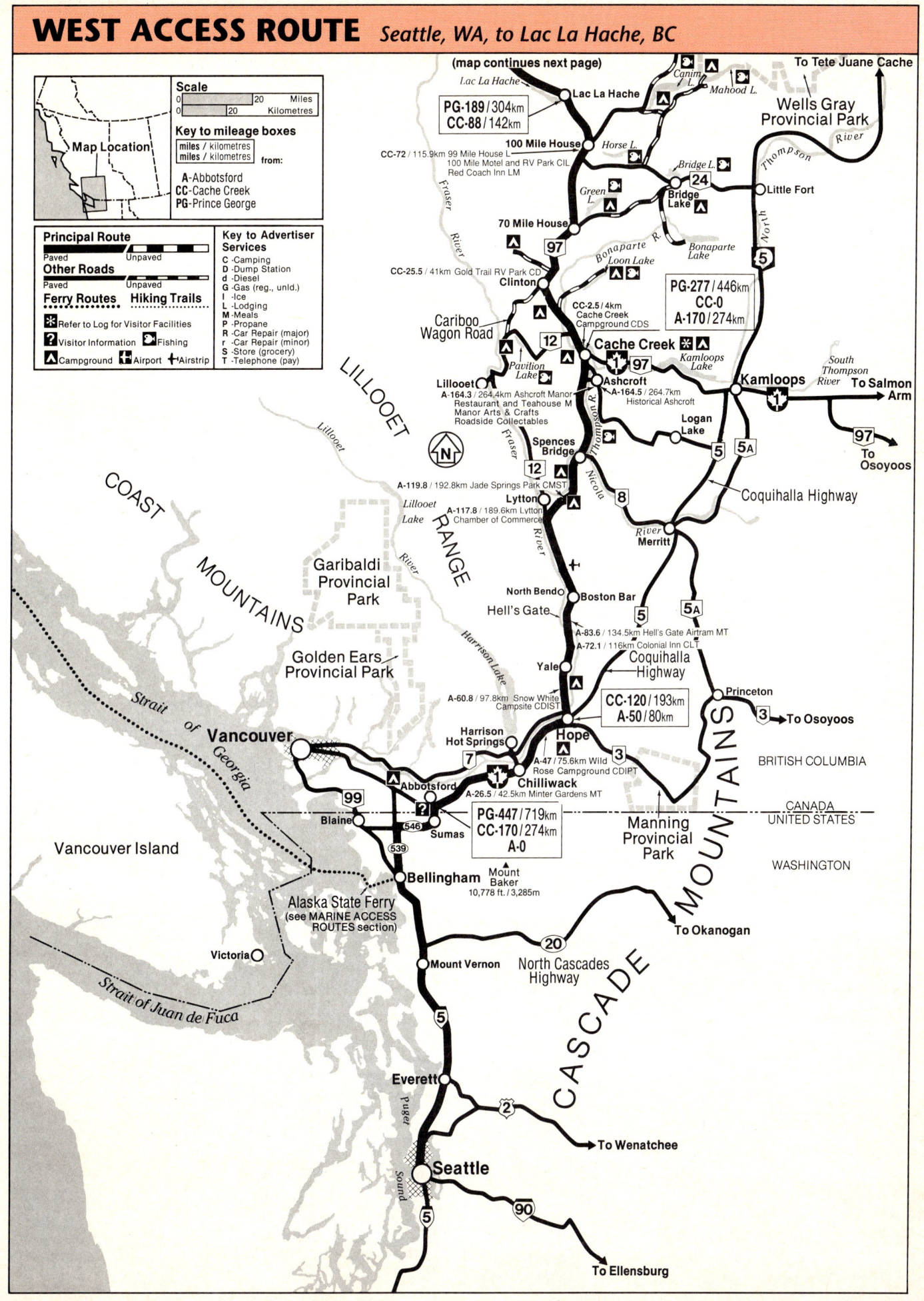

ALASKA HIGHWAY VIA WEST ACCESS ROUTE

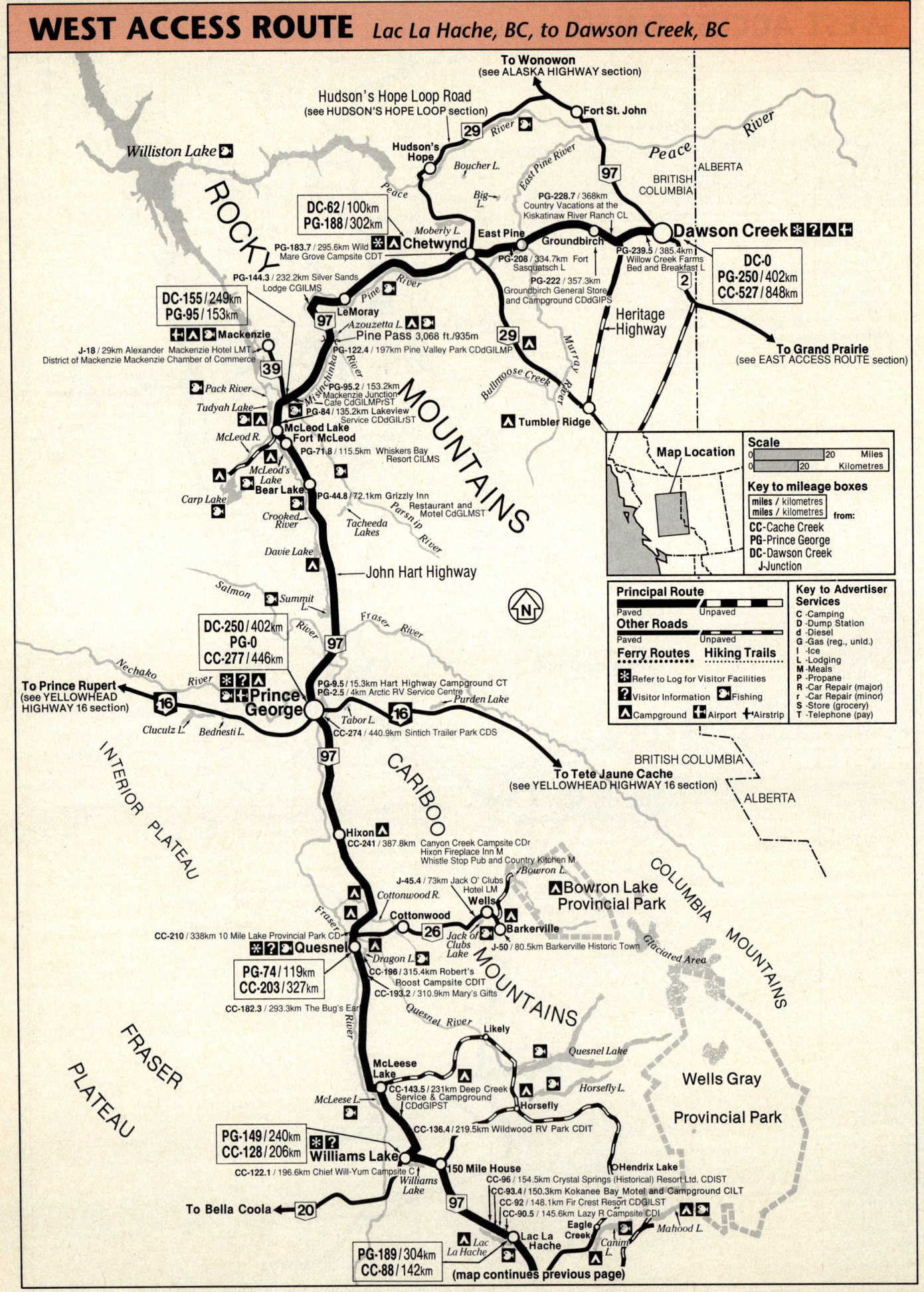

WEST ACCESS ROUTE — Lac La Hache, BC, to Dawson Creek, BC

119 (Vedder Road) south to Sardis and Vedder Crossing, north to Chilliwack and airport.

A 18 (29 km) **CC 152** (244.6 km) Exit 123 Prest Road north to Rosedale, south to Ryder Lake.

A 26.5 (42.5 km) **CC 143.5** (230.9 km) Exit 135 to Highway 9 east to Harrison Hot Springs and alternate route Highway 7 to Hope and Vancouver. Westbound exit for Bridal Veil Falls. Also exit here for access to Minter Gardens, which rivals Victoria's famous Butchart Gardens for beauty. Open daily mid-June to mid-September, weekends only late May to mid-June.

Minter Gardens. See display ad this section.

A 27.3 (43.9 km) **CC 142.7** (229.6 km) Exit 138 to Popkum Road. Eastbound access to Bridal Veil Falls Provincial Park to south; picnicking, trail to base of falls. Also access to small community of Popkum and various roadside attractions, including waterslide, Sandstone Gallery rock and gem museum, and Flintstones amusement park. Food, gas and lodging.

A 34.5 (55.5 km) **CC 135.5** (218.1 km) Exit 146 for Herrling Island. Eastbound traffic exit center lane.

A 40.5 (65.2 km) **CC 129.5** (208.4 km) Exit 153 to small community of Laidlaw and Jones Lake.

A 42.5 (65.6 km) **CC 127.5** (205.2 km) Truck weigh scales; public phone.

A 44.7 (71.9 km) **CC 125.3** (201.6 km) Exit 160 to Hunter Creek rest area; tables, toilet, pay phone and tourist information trailer.

A 45.5 (73.2 km) **CC 124.5** (200.4 km) Exit 165 to Flood/Hope Road, business route to Hope (eastbound) and Hope airport.

A 47 (75.6 km) **CC 123** (197.9 km) **Wild Rose Campground** (Good Sam). On Highway 1 east (from Vancouver) 4.8 km (3 miles) west of Hope take Flood-Hope Road exit 165. On Highway 1 west (from Hope) take Flood-Hope Road exit 168. Full hookups, 15-30 amps, separate tenting area, level grassy sites in parklike setting, 18 maximum (60 feet) pull-throughs, free cable TV, free hot showers, laundry, playground, horseshoes, firepits, picnic tables, a limited store. Ice, wood, pay phone, sani-station, near restaurant. Senior citizen discount, weekly rates, CB Channel 13, MasterCard, VISA. Small pets. Cancellation policy—2 days. Phone (604) 869-9842. [ADVERTISEMENT] ▲

A 48.5 (78.1 km) **CC 121.5** (195.5 km) Exit 168 to Silverhope Creek (eastbound only).

A 48.7 (78.4 km) **CC 121.3** (195.2 km) Silver Creek, Flood-Hope Road exit.

A 50 (80.5 km) **CC 120** (193.1 km) **Junction** of Trans-Canada Highway 1 and Highway 3 (Crowsnest Highway). Turn north on Trans-Canada Highway 1 for Hope.

Hope

A 50.2 (80.8 km) **CC 119.8** (192.8 km) **Population:** 5,000. **Elevation:** 140 feet/43m. **Emergency Services:** RCMP, phone 869-5644. **Fire Department,** phone 869-5500. **Ambulance,** phone 869-5112. **Hospital,** 1275 7th Ave., phone 869-5656.

Visitor Information: Travel Infocentre and museum building, corner of Hudson and Water streets, on the right northbound as you enter town. Open 8 A.M. to 8 P.M. daily in summer.

Hope is on a bend of the Fraser River where it flows through a picturesque gap in the forested Coast Mountains near Mount Hope (elev. 6,000 feet/1,289m). It is a popular tourist stop with complete services. About 20 motels and resorts are in Hope or just outside town on Trans-Canada Highway 1 and on Highway 3. Other facilities include auto body shops, service stations, department stores, restaurants and grocery stores.

The museum, connected to the Travel Infocentre on the corner of Hudson and Water streets, displays an unusual collection of relics which traces the development of the Hope area; open June to September.

The major attraction in the Hope area is the Coquihalla Canyon Provincial Recreation Area, the focus of which is the Othello Quintette Tunnels. The 5 rock tunnels which cut through the tortuous canyon were part of the Kettle Valley Railway. This stretch of railway has been restored as a walking trail through 3 of the tunnels and across bridges. The tunnels are accessible from downtown Hope via Kawakawa Lake Road, about a 10-minute drive.

The Coquihalla Highway, completed in 1987, connects Hope with the Trans-Canada Highway just west of Kamloops, a distance of 118 miles/190 km. This is a 4-lane divided highway which travels through the Cascade Range by way of the Coquihalla and Coldwater river valleys. The Hope to Merritt section is a toll road; $10 (Canadian) for cars, RVs and light trucks.

There are private campgrounds on all roads into town. A town-operated campground on Kawakawa Lake Road has 95 RV sites, 22 tent sites, coin showers and sani-station. ▲

West Access Route Log

(continued)

A 50.7 (81.6 km) **CC 119.3** (191.9 km) Bridge over Fraser River. Turnout at north end, access to pedestrian bridge across the Fraser.

A 51.5 (82.8 km) **CC 118.5** (190.7 km) **Junction** with Highway 7, which leads west to Harrison Hot Springs and Vancouver.

A 53.1 (85.5 km) **CC 116.9** (188.1 km) Rest area (westbound access only) with picnic tables to west by Lake of the Woods.

A 60.8 (97.8 km) **CC 109.2** (175.7 km) Easy-to-miss turnoff (watch for sign 400m before turn) for Emory Creek Provincial Park east of highway. Level gravel sites in trees, water, fire rings, picnic tables, firewood, outhouses and litter barrels. Camping fee May to October. Gold panning in Fraser River. ▲

Very much in evidence between Hope and Cache Creek are the tracks of the Canadian National and Canadian Pacific railways. Construction of the CPR—Canada's first transcontinental railway—played a significant role in the history of the Fraser and Thompson river valleys. Begun in 1880, the CPR line between Kamloops and Port Moody was contracted to Andrew Onderdonk.

A 64.8 (104.3 km) **CC 105.2** (169.3 km) **YALE** (pop. 500; elev. 250 feet/76m). **Police,** phone 869-6544. **Ambulance,** phone 869-5656. Visitor facilities include motels, stores, gas stations and restaurants. Travel Infocentre located at the north edge of town, open June 1 to Labour Day; pay phone.

Yale was the head of navigation for the Lower Fraser River and the beginning of the overland gold rush trail to British Columbia's goldfields. The Anglican Church of Saint John the Divine here was built for the miners in 1859 and is the oldest church still on its original foundation in mainland British Columbia. Next to the church is Yale Museum and a bronze plaque honouring Chinese construction workers who helped build the Canadian Pacific Railway. Walking around town, look for the several plaques relating Yale's history.

A 65.6 (105.5 km) **CC 104.5** (168.2 km) Entering Fraser Canyon northbound. The Fraser River and canyon were named for Simon Fraser (1776–1862), the first white man to descend the river in 1808. This is the dry forest region of British Columbia, and it can be a hot drive in summer. The scenic Fraser Canyon travelers drive through today was a formidable obstacle for railroad engineers in 1881.

A 66 (106.2 km) **CC 104** (167.4 km) Yale Tunnel, first of several northbound through the Fraser Canyon.

A 67.3 (108.3 km) **CC 102.7** (165.2 km) Turnout to east with plaque about the Cariboo Wagon Road, which connected Yale with the Cariboo goldfields near Barkerville. Built between 1861 and 1863 by the Royal Engineers, it replaced an earlier route to the goldfields—also called the Cariboo Wagon Road—which started from Lillooet.

A 68.4 (110.1 km) **CC 101.6** (163.5 km) Saddle Rock Tunnel. This 480-foot-/146-m-long tunnel was constructed in 1957-58.

A 72.1 (116 km) **CC 97.9** (157.5 km) **Colonial Inn.** In scenic Fraser Canyon. Cabin-style sleeping and kitchen units with showers and satellite TV. Pay phones. Picnic area with barbecues. Mountain views. Campground with full hookups and showers. For reservations call (604) 863-2277 or write RR #1, Yale, BC V0K 2S0. [ADVERTISEMENT] ▲

A 72.3 (116.3 km) **CC 97.7** (157.2 km) Sailor Bar Tunnel. There were dozens of bar claims along the Fraser River in the 1850s bearing colourful names like Sailor Bar.

A 75 (120.8 km) **CC 95** (152.9 km) 24-hour truck stop.

ALASKA HIGHWAY VIA WEST ACCESS ROUTE

A 76.5 (123.1 km) **CC 93.5** (150.5 km) Spuzzum (unincorporated), gas station and food.

A 77.1 (124.1 km) **CC 92.9** (149.5 km) Stop of interest at south end of Alexandra Bridge, the second largest fixed arch span in the world at more than 1,640 feet/500m in length.

A 77.5 (124.8 km) **CC 92.5** (148.9 km) Alexandra Bridge Provincial Park, picnic areas and interpretive displays on both sides of highway. Hiking trail down to the old Alexandra Bridge, still intact. This suspension bridge was built in 1926, replacing the original built in 1863.

A 77.8 (125.2 km) **CC 92.2** (148.4 km) Historic Alexandra Lodge is the last surviving original roadhouse on the Cariboo Wagon Road.

A 79.5 (128 km) **CC 90.5** (145.6 km) Alexandra Tunnel.

A 80.5 (129.5 km) **CC 89.5** (144 km) Rest area by Copper Creek to east.

A 82.6 (133 km) **CC 87.4** (140.7 km) Hells Gate Tunnel.

A 83.3 (134 km) **CC 86.7** (139.5 km) Ferrabee Tunnel.

A 83.6 (134.5 km) **CC 86.4** (139 km) Hells Gate, the narrowest point on the Fraser River and a popular attraction. (Northbound traffic park at lot immediately south of attraction on east side of road; southbound traffic park on west side of road at attraction.)

Two 28-passenger aerial trams take visitors 500 feet down across the river to a restaurant and shops. Footbridge across river to view fish ladders built in 1913-14 where some 2 million sockeye salmon pass through each year. Trams operate daily, April to September. There is also a steep trail down to the fish ladders; strenuous hike.

Hells Gate was well named. It was by far the most difficult terrain for construction of both the highway and the railway and many workers lost their lives here. To haul supplies for the railway upstream of Hells Gate, Andrew Onderdonk built the stern-wheel steamer *Skuzzy*. The *Skuzzy* made its way upstream through Hells Gate in 1882, hauled by ropes attached to the canyon walls by bolts.

Hell's Gate Airtram. See display ad this section.

A 85.7 (137.9 km) **CC 84.3** (135.7 km)

---

hell's gate airtram

- Salmon House Restaurant
- Gold Panner Gift Shop
- Christmas Shop
- Fudge Factory
- Observation Deck
- Suspension Bridge

• Located in the Scenic Fraser Canyon on the Trans-Canada Highway #1, between Cache Creek and Hope.

Phone (604) 867-9277 FAX (604) 867-9279
PO Box 129, Hope, BC, Canada V0X 1L0

Snake rail fence is typical of the Cariboo region. (Philip Smith)

China Bar Tunnel, built in 1960. It is almost 2,300 feet/700m long, one of the longest tunnels in North America. Point of interest sign at south end about Simon Fraser.

A 91 (146.5 km) **CC 79** (127.1 km) **BOSTON BAR** (pop. 1,000; elev. 400 feet/122m), site of a large mill, has gas stations, cafes, grocery stores and a motel. Boston Bar was the southern landing for the steamer *Skuzzy*, which plied the Fraser River between here and Lytton during construction of the CPR.

A 108.5 (174.6 km) **CC 61.5** (99 km) Gas station and restaurant.

A 112.8 (181.5 km) **CC 57.2** (92.1 km) Viewpoint to west overlooking the Fraser River.

A 114.6 (184.5 km) **CC 55.4** (89.2 km) Skupper rest area (northbound only); toilets, tables, litter barrels.

A 117.8 (189.6 km) **CC 52.2** (84 km) **Junction** with Highway 12. Turn west here for **LYTTON** (pop. 400); all visitor facilities.

Lytton. Rafting capital of British Columbia in the scenic Fraser Canyon. Full visitor services. Whitewater rafting on the Thompson River with raft rides through Hells Gate on the Fraser during August and September. Hiker access to the Stein and Botannie valleys. Many other natural attractions from Spence's Bridge to Yale. Visit the Infocentre: view the "jellyroll"—a rare geological formation, get highway and local travel information, arrange for woods and sawmills. At the confluence of the Thompson and Fraser rivers. Pan for gold at water's edge. Infocentre, 400 Fraser St., phone (604) 455-2523. [ADVERTISEMENT]

Continue north on Trans-Canada Highway 1, which swings away from the Fraser River to parallel the Thompson River. There are some narrow winding stretches along here.

A 119.8 (192.8 km) **CC 50.2** (80.8 km) **Jade Springs Park.** On Trans-Canada Highway 1. Write: Box 488, Lytton, BC V0K 1Z0. Campground, RV park (May-October) 2 km (1.2 miles) east of Lytton on Highway 1. Forest setting, complete washrooms, hot showers, laundry, full and partial hookups, some pull-throughs. Licensed restaurant, horseshoe pits, phone, fishing, river rafting, grocery store, pets. (604) 455-2420. [ADVERTISEMENT] ▲

A 122.8 (197.6 km) **CC 47.2** (76 km) Skihist Provincial Park to east; 68 campsites. Picnic area on west side of highway. ▲

A 134.7 (216.8 km) **CC 35.3** (56.8 km) Goldpan Provincial Park to west alongside river; 14 campsites, picnic area, fishing. ▲

A 140 (225.3 km) **CC 30** (48.3 km) **Junction** with Highway 8 to Merritt and south access to Spences Bridge. Plaque here about the great landslide of 1905.

A 141.2 (227.2 km) **CC 28.8** (46.3 km) North access to **SPENCES BRIDGE** (pop. 300; elev. 760 feet/231m) located at the confluence of the Thompson and Nicola rivers. A record 30-lb., 5-oz. steelhead was caught in the Thompson River in 1984.

A 153.4 (246.9 km) **CC 16.6** (26.7 km) Viewpoint overlooking Thompson River with plaque about the Canadian Northern Pacific (now the Canadian National Railway), Canada's third transcontinental railway, completed in 1915.

A 158.4 (255 km) **CC 11.6** (18.7 km) Red Hill rest area to east; tables, toilets, litter barrels, pay phone.

A 164.3 (264.4 km) **CC 5.7** (9.2 km) Stop of interest sign to east describes Ashcroft Manor, a roadhouse on the Cariboo Wagon Road. Today, this 19th century roadhouse houses a museum, antique and gift shops, and restaurant. Well worth a stop.

Ashcroft Manor Restaurant and Teahouse. See display ad this section.

Manor Arts and Crafts. See display ad this section.

Roadside Collectables. See display ad this section.

A 164.5 (264.7 km) **CC 5.5** (8.9 km) **Junction** with road to **ASHCROFT**, a small village with full tourist facilities just east of

---

46   The MILEPOST® ■ 1992

3 Minute "Detour It!" Through
HISTORICAL ASHCROFT

ALASKA HIGHWAY VIA WEST ACCESS ROUTE

Experience a drive through the true Old West - HISTORICAL ASHCROFT, a MUSEUM - a VILLAGE that was the major wagon team centre of transportation activity on the "Gold Rush Trail". (A downtown revitalization is in the process to revert this town to its Historical Past of the 1885 - 1915 era in time - including board sidewalks.)

By any other name...Ashcroft has undergone many name changes in the past. The native Indians called the area Tuk Tuk Chim. The first pioneers referred to it as Harper's Mill. The CPR's Mr. Van Horne noted it as St. Cloud in his records, although freighters and prospectors called it Barnes Station. The name that finally stayed with the town was "Ashcroft", a name used by the Cornwall brothers for their nearby home, and which recalled an estate in England.

The Cornwalls established Ashcroft Manor in 1858 and Ashcroft's first industries. Then Mr. Clement Cornwall became B.C.'s first Lieutenant Governor in 1881.

Ashcroft as we know it began with the construction of the Thompson River Hotel in 1883. Today there is a new Hotel on the Thompson River, Ashcroft's River Inn. As well, the first bridge was built in 1883. Today we see the newly constructed bridge, opened in August 1991.

The great fire of 1916 saw the large Chinese Community become very prosperous, building several General Stores, Restaurants and new Hotels to replace those lost in the fire. They were so successful that Dr. Sun Yat Sen spent an entire week in Ashcroft when travelling Canada to raise money to overthrow the Man Chu Dynasty in China. (Chinatown, now lost to age and time, is currently in the plan for rebuilding as a memorial and an active business opportunity through the Chinese Benevolent Society) Their graveyard, still intact, is a reminder of their deep rooted history here of which many were responsible for the building of the great canadian railways - by which both Canadian National and Canadian Pacific Railways travel.

Ashcroft became famous for its crops of delicious tomatoes and potatoes, grown and produced by the Chinese. Its excellent Canada-wide reputation lead to the nick name of "Spud City". However, tomatoes soon became the most lucrative crop and the Cannery of 1924 became Canada's largest. By 1930 Canadian Canners marketed Ashcroft grown Aylmer Brand tomatoes, shipping 30,000 cases per season, each season attracting 100's of Chinese from Vancouver to cultivate and harvest the crops. (We are in the process of investigating an opportunity to put back this historical cannery for tourist interests)

The first newspaper, The Journal, established in 1885, continues to serve Ashcroft and area today. Pick up your copy of the historical publication "Out of the Sagebrush" or "Bittersweet Oasis" a book that tells it all!! Historical Ashcroft is on its way to becoming a #1 attraction - "NOT TO BE MISSED!"

Sand and sage and the magical moods of the desert hills create a healthy sunshine location where the oasis named Ashcroft, with the Thompson River flowing thru, becomes a place to discover and spend time at the full facility LEGACY PARK CAMPSITE. Near Ashcroft are some of the best fishing lakes in B.C. - including the Thompson River's Steelhead fishing, grouse hunting, bird watching, and horseback riding across the vast lands of some of the largest Cattle Ranches in B.C.

> For further information,
> come and visit the
> **TRAVEL INFOCENTRE**
> at the junction of Hwys. #1 and 97c
> (seasonal operation)

SOME EVENTS & ATTRACTIONS NOT TO MISS...

* NL'AKAPXM EAGLE MOTORPLEX holds 15 drag races a season. Among them are the Oldtime Drag Races in June with classic cars & the Winston Cup in September with over $100,000.00 in prize money.
* CANADA DAY CELEBRATIONS July 1st with family fun day at old fashioned prices.
* ASHCROFT & DISTRICT RODEO & PARADE 2nd week in May.
* SUN COUNTRY RODEO in August.
* ASHCROFT MUSEUM at the corner of 4th & Brink streets, open daily in summer.

SPONSORED BY: Argon Group Ltd., Ashcroft & District Chamber of Commerce, Ashcroft Apartment Motel, Ashcroft Cycle & Saw, Ashcroft Dental Clinic, Ashcroft Medical Clinic, Ashcroft River Inn, Associated Electrical Services, Barton, Black & Robertson, Cariboo Travel Services, Copper Valley Cablevision, Foodmaster, Frank's New & Used, Fulton & Co., Home Hardware, Joe Rieck Construction, J.P. Thiessen & Co., The Journal, Morelli Chertkow, Murray Kane Ltd., Nl'akapxm Eagle Motorplex, People's Drug Mart, Quality Glass & Upholstery, Railway Shell Service, Royal LePage, Safety Mart, Superior Propane, The Toggery, Uniglobe Travel, and The Village Of Ashcroft.

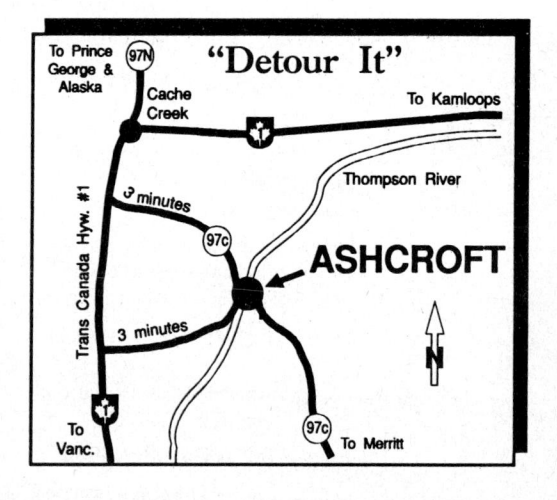

1992 ■ The MILEPOST® 47

ALASKA HIGHWAY VIA WEST ACCESS ROUTE

HIGH COUNTRY
YOUR HIGHWAY TO ALASKA '92

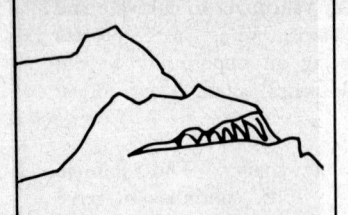

British Columbia's Interior
The spectacular **Fraser Canyon** is one of **High Country Highways** to Alaska '92. On your **Highway Home** explore the **Yellowhead** and **Trans Canada Highways** that carve through a picture perfect paradise. Allow plenty of time to enjoy the **Breathtaking Scenery, Exhilarating Adventure** and **High Country Hospitality!**

For FREE information on exploring the High Country, contact High Country Tourism Association, #2 - 1490 (MP) Pearson Place, Kamloops, B.C. V1S 1J9; Phone: (604) 372-7770, Fax: (604) 828-4656

SUNDANCE GUEST RANCH
The Western Experience Deluxe

100 happy horses and air conditioned accommodation. Heated pool, new tennis court, great meals and all-inclusive rates.

Write: Box 489
Ashcroft, B.C. V0K IA0
(Just 4 hours north of Vancouver)
Tel. (604) 453-2554/2422

Desert Motel
Your Hosts
Fred & Margaret Robertson

CACHE CREEK'S
FINEST ACCOMMODATION

Write or call collect for Reservations
Box 339
Cache Creek, B.C. V0K 1H0
In B.C. call 1-800-663-0212
Tel: (604) 457-6226

Cariboo Jade & Gifts
Free Gem-Cutting Demonstrations
B.C. Jade • B.C. Rhodonite
Alaska Black Diamond
Handcrafted Gifts & Souvenirs

Hours:
7 Days a Week in Summer
8 a.m. - 10 p.m.

1093 Todd Road
on the junction
Box 280,
Cache Creek, B.C. V0K 1H0
Fax (604) 457-9669
Tel: (604) 457-9566

Manor Arts and Crafts
Featuring B.C. Handicrafts
B.C. Jade and Rhodonite
Unique Jewelery

Madeline Saunders
Box 927, Ashcroft, B.C.
Tel: (604) 453-2438

BONAPARTE MOTEL
• Whirlpool • Summer Pool •
• TV: 22 Channels •
CAA/AAA APPROVED

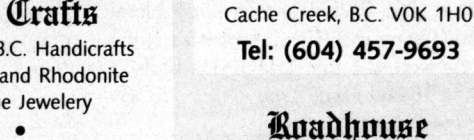

Box 487
Cache Creek, B.C. V0K 1H0
Tel: (604) 457-9693

Roadhouse Collectables
Antiques
Collectables

Dora Baycroft
Box 1388, Ashcroft, B.C.
Tel: (604) 453-2438

Wander-Inn RESTAURANT
Chinese & Western Cuisine - Sizzling Steaks
Dining and Cocktail Lounges
Coffee Shop • Banquet Room

Open Daily - Mon - Sat 7a.m. to 12:30 a.m. • Sunday 7 a.m. to 11 p.m.

Junction of Trans-Canada Highway and Cariboo Highway
Cache Creek, B.C.
Tel: (604) 457-6511

Ashcroft Manor Restaurant and Teahouse
We provide fine dining in an historic setting.
Enjoy your meal inside or on the shaded patio. Choose from an extensive menu at reasonable prices.
Fully licensed / 9 a.m. - 9 p.m.

Reservations
Tel: (604) 453-9983

SUPER NATURAL BRITISH COLUMBIA

the highway, and to the mining community of Logan Lake. Copper mine tours are available at Logan Lake, site of the second largest open-pit copper mine in North America.

Historic Ashcroft supplanted Yale as gateway to the Cariboo with the arrival of the Canadian Pacific Railway in 1885.

Historical Ashcroft. See display ad on page 47.

A 168.2 (270.7 km) **CC 1.8** (2.9 km) Second turnoff northbound for Ashcroft and road to Logan Lake. Travel Infocentre at junction.

Cache Creek

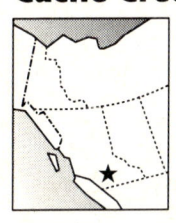

A 170 (273.6 km) **PG 277** (445.8 km) Located at the junction of Trans-Canada Highway 1 and Highway 97. **Population:** 3,000. **Elevation:** 1,508 feet/460m. **Emergency Services: RCMP,** phone 453-2216. **Ambulance,** phone 1-374-5937. **Hospital,** phone 453-5306 or 457-9668.

Visitor Information: Tourist Infocentre located on the west side of Highway 97. Write Box 460, Cache Creek, BC V0K 1H0; phone 457-9118.

Cache Creek has ample facilities for the traveler (most located on or just off the main highways), including motels, restaurants, department store, service stations and grocery store. Private campgrounds are available east of Cache Creek on Trans-Canada Highway 1 (across from the golf course) and just north of town on Highway 97.

A post office and bus depot are on Todd Road. Nearby, a jade shop offers free stone-cutting demonstrations in summer. Public park and swimming pool on the Bonaparte River, east off Highway 97 at the north edge of town.

The settlement grew up around the confluence of the creek and the Bonaparte River. The Hudson's Bay Co. opened a store here, and Cache Creek became a major supply point on the Cariboo Wagon Road. Today, hay and cattle ranching, mining, logging and tourism support the community.

From the junction, Highway 97 leads north 277 miles/445.8 km to Prince George. Kamloops is 52 miles/83.7 km east via Trans-Canada Highway 1. Traveling north from Cache Creek the highway generally follows the historic route to the Cariboo goldfields.

Brookside Campsite. 1 km east of Cache Creek on Highway 1, full (30 amp) and partial hookups, pull-throughs, tent sites, super clean wash and laundry rooms, sani-stations, store, playground, horseshoes, nature path and fishing, golf course adjacent, pets on leash, pay phone. VISA, MasterCard, C.P. 2 days. Proposed pool completion 1992. Good Sam. Box 737, Cache Creek, BC V0K 1H0. Phone: (604) 457-6633. [ADVERTISEMENT] ▲

CACHE CREEK ADVERTISERS

Bonaparte Motel ....Ph. (604) 457-9693
Brookside Campsite ....1 km E. of jct.
Cariboo Jade & Gifts.........Ph. (604) 457-9566
Desert Motel....................Ph. (604) 457-6226
Wander-Inn
 Restaurant ....Ph. (604) 457-6511

West Access Route Log

(continued)
HIGHWAY 97
From Cache Creek, continue north on BC Highway 97 for Dawson Creek. Highway 97 between Cache Creek and Prince George is called the Cariboo Highway.
This section of the log shows distance from Cache Creek (CC) followed by distance from Prince George (PG).

CC 2.5 (4 km) **PG 274.5** (441.8 km) **Cache Creek Campground,** 3 km north of Cache Creek on Highway 97 north. Full hookups, pull-throughs and tenting, sani-station, store, country kitchen, laundromat, coin showers, heated washrooms. Outdoor pool and whirlpool (no charge). 18-hole mini-golf, seasonal river swimming and fishing. P.O. Box 127, Cache Creek, BC V0K 1H0. For reservations, phone (604) 457-6414. [ADVERTISEMENT] ▲

CC 7 (11.3 km) **PG 270** (434.5 km) **Junction** with Highway 12 west to Lillooet (46.5 miles/75 km). Drive 0.4 mile/0.7 km west on Highway 12 for Hat Creek House, one of the largest of the Cariboo Trail roadhouses, now restored and managed by BC Heritage Trust. Hours are 9:30 A.M. to 6 P.M.

Marble Canyon Provincial Park, 17.5 miles/28 km west on Highway 12, has 34 campsites, picnicking and hiking trails. ▲

CC 10 (16 km) **PG 267** (430 km) Plaque about the BX stagecoaches that once served Barkerville. Formally known as the BC Express Company, the BX served the Cariboo for 50 years.

CC 13.6 (21.9 km) **PG 263.4** (423.9 km) Gravel road leads east to **Loon Lake,** rainbow fishing, boat launch. Camping at Loon Lake Provincial Park (16 miles/26 km); 14 sites. ⬥▲

CC 16.6 (26.7 km) **PG 260.4** (419.1 km) Rest area.

CC 25 (40.2 km) **PG 252** (405.5 km) **Junction** with road west to Pavilion via Kelly Lake. Camping at Downing Provincial Park (11 miles/18 km); 25 sites, swimming, fishing. ▲

CC 25.5 (41 km) **PG 251.5** (404.7 km) **CLINTON** (pop. 900, area 4,000; elev. 2,911 feet/887m). All visitor facilities. Originally the site of 47 Mile Roadhouse, a gold rush settlement on the Cariboo Wagon Road from Lillooet. The museum, housed in a red brick building that once served as a courthouse, has fine displays of pioneer tools and items from the gold rush days, and a scale model of the Clinton Hotel. Clinton pioneer cemetery just north of town. Clinton boasts the oldest continuously held event in the province, the Clinton Ball (in May the weekend following Victoria Day), an annual event since 1868.

Gold Trail RV Park. Brand new! 30 fully serviced sites with 30-amp power. Pull-throughs. Immaculate. Washrooms with flush toilets, handicap-equipped. Free hot showers for guests. TV. On highway in town; easy walking to all amenities. Well-lit level sites. Grassed and landscaped. Sani-station. Complimentary RV U-wash. 1620 Cariboo Highway North, Clinton, BC V0K 1K0. (604) 459-2519. [ADVERTISEMENT]

CC 31 (49.9 km) **PG 246** (395.9 km) Dirt and gravel road leads 21 miles/34 km west to Big Bar Lake Provincial Park; 33 campsites, fishing, boat launch. ▲

Rest area to east just north of Big Bar Lake turnoff; toilets, tables, litter barrels.

CC 35 (56.3 km) **PG 242** (389.5 km) Loop road leads east 3 miles/5 km to Painted Chasm geological site and Chasm Provincial Park picnic area.

CC 45 (72.4 km) **PG 232** (373.4 km) **70 MILE HOUSE** (unincorporated), originally a stage stop named for its distance from Lillooet, Mile 0. General store, post office, restaurant, motel, gas station with diesel and bus depot.

A paved road leads east 7.5 miles/12 km to Green Lake Provincial Recreation Area; 3 campgrounds, boat launch. Rainbow and kokanee fishing at **Green Lake.** Gravel roads lead north to Watch Lake, east to Bonaparte Lake, and northeast to join Highway 24 at Bridge Lake. ⬥▲

CC 66 (106.2 km) **PG 211** (339.6 km) **Junction** with Highway 24 East to Bridge Lake and Little Fort (60 miles/96.5 km) on Yellowhead Highway 5. Highway 24 provides access to numerous fishing lakes and resorts, including Bridge Lake Provincial Park (31 miles/50 km east) with 19 campsites. ⬥▲

100 Mile House

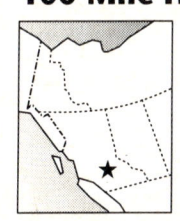

CC 72 (115.9 km) **PG 205** (329.9 km) **Population:** 1,692. **Elevation:** 3,050 feet/930m. **Emergency Services: Police,** phone 395-2456. **Ambulance,** phone 1-374-5937. **Hospital,** phone 395-2202. **Visitor Information:** At the log cabin by 100 Mile House Marsh, a bird sanctuary at the north edge of town. Look for the 39-foot-/12-m-long skis!

This large bustling town was once a stop for fur traders and later a post house on the Cariboo Wagon Road to the goldfields. In 1930, the Marquis of Exeter established the 15,000-acre Bridge Creek Ranch here. Today, 100 Mile House is the site of 2 lumber mills, and an extensive log home building industry.

Visitor services include restaurants,

Welcome!
RED COACH INN

- Adventure Packages
- 48 Comfortable Guest Rooms
- Fine Dining Room/Restaurant
- Cozy Lounge
- Conference Facilities
- Sauna, Whirlpool

Discover the wide open spaces... or the great indoors.
1-800-663-8432   Highway 97, 100 Mile House, BC V0K 2E0

ALASKA HIGHWAY VIA WEST ACCESS ROUTE

For Family Fun and Adventure follow the Goldrush TRAIL

The Best Route to Rendezvous '92

to Williams Lake

Home of the Famous 66th ANNUAL WILLIAMS LAKE STAMPEDE July 1, 2, 3 & 4

WILLIAMS LAKE "WILLY" (Cowboy Extraordinaire)

Something for Everyone!

- Hunting
- Fishing: over 8,000 holes
- Horseback Riding
- Rodeos
- Nature Center
- Historical Museum
- Wildlife Viewing
- Camping, Golfing, Hiking
- Skiing: X-Country & Downhill
- Local Art Galleries & Gift Shops

WILLIAMS LAKE SUPER 8 MOTEL
We offer: 24 hour desk, guest laundry, suites, jacuzzi suite, continental breakfast, free local calls, remote control cable TV, in room VCR, outside outlets.
Located on Hwy. 97 just south of town next to the Laughing Loon Pub.
1712 South Broadway
Williams Lake, B.C. V2G 2W4
(604) 398-8684 or 1-800-800-8000

The Laughing Loon PUB
- PATIO DINING
- HOME COOKED MEALS
- COLD BEER & WINE STORE
- OPEN 7 DAYS A WEEK & HOLIDAYS
- GREAT, FRIENDLY SERVICE
2 miles South Highway 97
398-LOON

the Overlander MOTOR INN
Conveniently located at jct. Hwy. 97/Hwy. 20.
Excellent dining. Pub, Beer & Wine Store. Spacious, air conditioned rooms. Fresh coffee in units. Room service.
1118 Lakeview Crescent, Williams Lake, BC V2G 1A3
(604) 392-3321 or 1-800-663-6898 (BC only) FAX 392-3963

CAESARS INN
102 air conditioned rooms. Easy access with ample parking. Family restaurant, pub, beauty salon. Within walking distance of downtown. Attractively priced.
55 South 6th Ave. Williams Lake, BC V2G 1K8
Tel. (604) 392-7747   Fax (604) 392-4852

SPRINGHOUSE TRAILS RANCH
Summer resort. 20 km from Williams Lake on Dog Creek Rd. Camping facilities, serviced RV sites, licensed premises, rooms, laundry, trail rides, restaurant.
Box 2, RR1, Springhouse Trails, Williams Lake, B.C. V2G 2P1.
Telephone/Fax (604) 392-4780

THE Fraser Inn HOTEL
THE BILLY MINER SALOON • THE GREAT CARIBOO STEAK CO.
- 76 rooms • cable TV
- room service • catering
- saunas • whirlpool
- Franny's Treasures
- Breakfast, lunch, dinner
- 12 noon - 2 a.m.
285 Donald Road, Williams Lake, BC V2G 4K4
398-7055 Fax 398-8269

CHEMO RV SALES & SERVICE
Easy access. Adjacent to main hwy. RV parts, sales, service. Open 6 days a week. City selection with hometown friendliness.
Williams Lake   Quesnel
(604) 392-4451   747-4451

By the Lakeside
Drummond Lodge Motel
"The Motel With a View"
Affordable air conditioned rooms & kitchen units
Phone 392-5334
Toll Free: 1-800-667-4555
1405 Cariboo Hwy. Williams Lake, BC V2G 2W3

Hearth Restaurant & Native Arts & Crafts Shop
Cariboo Friendship Society
99 S. Third Ave. Williams Lake B.C. V2G 1J1
(604) 398-6831 Fax (604) 398-6115

For further information write:
WILLIAMS LAKE & DISTRICT CHAMBER OF COMMERCE
Box "C"
1148 S. Broadway, Williams Lake, B.C. V2G 1A2
Phone: Travel Infocentre (604) 392-5025 or USA and B.C. Phone: 800-663-5885.

motels, gas stations with repair service, stores, a post office and a golf course. Government liquor store, supermarket, and bank at Cariboo Mall on east side of highway. A second shopping mall is located across from the Red Coach Inn. Birch Avenue, 1 block east of the highway, offers more shopping and 2 banks.

100 Mile House is a popular destination for snowmobiling and cross-country skiing in winter. It is also the jumping-off point for fishermen headed for Canim Lake and Mahood Lake in Wells Gray Provincial Park.

Horse Lake Road leads east from 100 Mile house to **Horse Lake** (kokanee) and other fishing lakes of the high plateau.

Red Coach Inn. See display ad this section.

99 Mile Motel. Air-conditioned sleeping and housekeeping units. Fridges in all units, housekeeping units with microwave ovens. DD touchtone phones, remote control cable TV, super channel and TSN, courtesy in-room coffee and tea. Carports, winter plug-ins, freezer available for guests, bowling, legion supermarket and cross-country ski trails. Senior citizens discount, commercial rates, wheelchair accessible, small pets. Highway 97, 100 Mile House, BC V0K 2E0. (604) 395-2255. [ADVERTISEMENT]

100 Mile Motel and RV Park. 310 Highway 97. Downtown. Ground level sleeping and housekeeping units. DD phones, cable TV, seniors' rates, campground and RV park with hookups, showers, flush toilets, hiking trail, shopping and restaurants nearby. P.O. Box 112, 100 Mile House, BC V0K 2E0. (604) 395-2234. [ADVERTISEMENT]

West Access Route Log

(continued)

CC 74 (119 km) **PG 203** (326.7 km) **Junction** with road east to **Ruth, Canim** and **Mahood lakes.** Resorts and fishing at all lakes. Camping at Canim Beach Provincial Park (27 miles/43 km); 16 sites. Access to spectacular Canim Falls.

CC 78.2 (125.8 km) **PG 198.8** (319.9 km) 108 Mile Ranch, a recreational community built in the 1970s, was once a cattle ranch. Motel and golf course.

CC 80.5 (129.5 km) **PG 196.5** (316.2 km) Rest area to west beside 108 Mile Lake. Alongside is Heritage Centre with some of the original log buildings from 108 Mile Ranch, and others relocated from 105 Mile.

CC 88 (141.6 km) **PG 189** (304.2 km) LAC LA HACHE (pop. 800; elev. 2,749 feet/838m), unincorporated. Motels, stores, gas stations and a museum with visitor information. Playground adjacent museum. The community holds a fishing derby in July and a winter carnival in mid-February. Lac La Hache is French for "Ax Lake." There are many stories of how the lake got its name, but Molly Forbes, local historian, says it was named by a French-Canadian *coureur de bois* (voyaguer) "because of a small ax he found on its shores."

Lac La Hache, lake char, rainbow and kokanee; good fishing summer and winter (great ice fishing).

CC 90.5 (145.6 km) **PG 186.5** (300.1 km) **Lazy R Campsite.** 24 lovely sites right on Lac La Hache. Full and partial hookups. 20-amp service. Shaded tent sites with tables.

Free hot showers for campers. Children's playground. Boat launch. Sani-dump. Good fishing in May/June for kokanee, char and rainbow. Box 57, Lac La Hache, BC V0K 1T0. (604) 396-7368. [ADVERTISEMENT]

CC 92 (148.1 km) **PG 185** (297.7 km) **Fir Crest Resort** (Good Sam). Quiet parklike setting just 2 minutes from Highway 97, but away from traffic noise. Full hookups including pull-throughs, camping and cabins on the lakeshore. Sandy beach, swimming, games room, groceries, sani-dump. Full marina with boat, motor, canoe and tackle rentals. Your hosts, Jim and Virginia Wilson. Phone (604) 396-7337. [ADVERTISEMENT]

CC 93.4 (150.3 km) **PG 183.6** (295.4 km) **Kokanee Bay Motel and Campground.** Relaxation at its finest right on the lakeshore. Fish for kokanee and char or take a refreshing dip. We have a modern, comfortable motel, cabins. Full trailer hookups, grassy tenting area, hot showers, laundromat. Aquabike, boat and canoe rentals. Fishing tackle and ice. Phone (604) 396-7345. [ADVERTISEMENT]

CC 96 (154.5 km) **PG 181** (291.3 km) **Crystal Springs Campsite (Historical) Resort Ltd.** (Good Sam), 8 miles north of Lac La Hache. Parklike setting on lakeshore. Showers, flush toilets, laundromat, full (20 and 30 amp pull-throughs) and partial hookups, boat rentals. Groceries, tackle, camping supplies. Games room, playground. Pets on leash. Public beach and boat launch adjacent, fishing. BCAA/AAA. Your hosts, Doug and Lorraine Whitesell. Phone (604) 396-4497. [ADVERTISEMENT]

CC 96 (154.5 km) **PG 181** (291.3 km) Lac La Hache Provincial Park; 83 campsites, boat launch, swimming, picnic tables, hiking trail, fishing and sani-station.

CC 104.4 (168 km) **PG 172.6** (277.7 km) Plaque about the Cariboo gold rush to west.

CC 118.5 (190.7 km) **PG 158.5** (255.1 km) 150 MILE HOUSE, so named because it was 150 miles from Lillooet on the old Cariboo Wagon Road. The post office, which serves about 1,200 people in the area, was established in 1871. Hotel, restaurant, pub, gas station with repair service and a store open daily. Hunting and fishing licenses available at the store.

CC 119.1 (191.7 km) **PG 157.9** (254.1 km) **Junction** with road to **Quesnel** and **Horsefly lakes**. Horsefly Lake Provincial Park (40 miles/65 km) has 22 campsites. Fishing for rainbow and lake trout.

CC 122.1 (196.6 km) **PG 154.9** (249.3 km) **Chief Will-Yum Campsite.** 32 full hookups. Tenting. Tepees. Large covered cooking area. Some treed sites. Coin-operated showers. Flush toilets. 5 km to shopping. Children's play area. Quiet. Fully

WILLIAMS LAKE ADVERTISERS

Lakeside Resort Motel ..... Ph. 1-800-663-4938
Williams Lake & District Chamber
 of Commerce .... See ad for locations

Lakeside Resort Motel
Williams Lake - Highway 97
• Quiet Parklike Setting •
Toll Free in BC 1-800-663-4938

supervised. General Delivery, 150 Mile House, BC V0K 2G0. (604) 296-4544. Reservations accepted. We cater to large groups. [ADVERTISEMENT]

Williams Lake

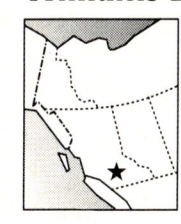

CC 128 (206 km) **PG 149** (239.8 km) Located at the junction of Highway 97 and Highway 20 to Bella Coola. **Population:** 11,000. **Elevation:** 1,964 feet/599m. **Emergency Services: Police,** phone 392-6211. **Hospital,** phone 392-4411.

Visitor Information: Travel Infocentre located on east side of highway just south of the junction of Highways 97 and 20; phone 392-5025. Open year-round.

The administrative and transportation hub of the Cariboo-Chilcotin region, Williams Lake has complete services, including hotels/motels, restaurants, and an 18-hole golf course. The airport, 7 miles/11 km north of town on Highway 97, is served by daily flights to Vancouver and other interior communities.

Located on the shore of the lake of the same name, it was named for Shuswap Indian Chief Willyum. The town grew rapidly with the advent of the Pacific Great Eastern Railway (now B.C. Railway) in 1919, to become a major cattle marketing and shipping centre for the Cariboo-Chilcotin. Today the city has the largest and most active cattleyards in the province. Lumber and mining for copper-molybdenum are the mainstays of the economy.

The famous Williams Lake Stampede, British Columbia's premier rodeo, is held here annually on the July 1 holiday. The 4-day event draws contestants from all over Canada and the U.S. The rodeo grounds are located in the city.

Highway 20 travels west from Williams Lake 288 miles/449 km to Bella Coola, giving access to the Chilcotin country's excellent freshwater fishing, Tweedsmuir Provincial Park, and the remote central coast. The highway is paved for the first 112.5 miles/181 km. At Heckman Pass (elev. 5,000 feet/1,524m), 217 miles/349 km west of Williams Lake, the highway descends a section of narrow, switchbacked road with an 18 percent grade for about 12 miles/19 km. Beyond "the hill" the road is paved to Bella Coola. Highway 20 is logged in *NORTHWEST MILEPOSTS*.

West Access Route Log

(continued)

CC 136.4 (219.5 km) **PG 140.6** (226.3 km) Wildwood Road; gas station, store, access to private campground.

ALASKA HIGHWAY VIA WEST ACCESS ROUTE

The official route to the Alaska Highway in 1992...

Goldrush TRAIL

Quesnel

· BRITISH COLUMBIA · CANADA ·

Quesnel Airport Inn Motel and RV Park
• Conveniently located on Highway 97, a half-mile south of the Barkerville and Airport junction. • Our clean quiet rooms provide affordable comfort. • DD phones, color cablevision with sports and movie channels. • RV Park has level pull-through spaces with 30 amp full hook-ups. • Also tent sites, showers, washrooms, laundry facilities, sani-station, lawn parking. Your friendly hosts Stella and Fred Bartels guarantee you will be pleased or your money refunded.
Box 4422, Quesnel, BC, Canada V2J 3J4 • Telephone (604) 992-5942

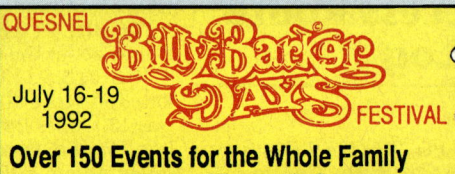

QUESNEL Billy Barker DAYS FESTIVAL
July 16-19 1992
Over 150 Events for the Whole Family
For your Free Program of Events, write Box 4441, Quesnel, BC, V2J 3J4 or phone (604) 992-1234

Dragon Lake Golf Course & Campsite
9 Hole Course and Driving Range
Situated on edge of Dragon Lake at $5/night
• Flush toilets • Showers • Sani-Dump • Wharf • Trout Fishing • Snack Bar • Lounge • Located off Highway 97 just 10 minutes south of City Centre
1692 Flint Ave, Quesnel BC Canada • (604) 747-1358

FOUNTAIN MOTOR MOTEL
(604) 992-7071 - Quesnel, BC
• 34 Modern Units • Heated Indoor Pool • Sauna • Color Cable TV • Phones • Air Conditioned • FREE coffee and ice
AAA   CAA
One Block from Downtown

Mary's Gift Shop
CANADIAN HANDCRAFTED GIFTS
• Gold, Silver and Jade Jewelry • Native Art and Moccasins • Weaving • Pottery
Shop located 100 yds off Hwy. 97 S on Dragon Lake Road
MAILING ADDRESS
Box 32, RR1
Quesnel, BC, V2J 3H5

SYLVAN MOTEL
(604) 992-5611 - Quesnel, BC
• 26 Kitchen and Sleeping Units
• Super Channel • Free Coffee
• River Views • Restaurant Nearby

FOR YOUR FREE CALENDAR OF EVENTS AND NORTH CARIBOO ACTIVITY MAP, WRITE 405 BARLOW AVENUE, QUESNEL, BC, V2J 2C3

Super, Natural, British Columbia.

Wildwood RV Park. See display ad this section. ▲

CC 141.3 (227.3 km) PG 135.7 (218.4 km) Turnout with litter barrel.

CC 145.3 (233.9 km) PG 131.7 (211.9 km) Turnout with litter barrel.

CC 147.8 (237.9 km) PG 129.2 (207.9 km) Replica of a turn-of-the-century roadhouse (food and beverage service only) at junction with side road to settlement of Soda Creek. Soda Creek was the transfer point from wagon road to steamboat for miners bound for Quesnel.

CC 155 (249.4 km) PG 122 (196.4 km) **McLEESE LAKE**, small community with gas stations, cafe, post office, store, pub, private campground and motel on McLeese Lake. The lake was named for a Fraser River steamboat skipper. Mining and logging are the chief industries here. Public tours of Gibraltar Copper Mine, 11 miles/17.7 km east of the highway (watch for sign just north of here), from June to September. ▲

McLeese Lake, rainbow to 2 lbs., troll using a flasher, worms, or flatfish lure. ⊙

CC 155.3 (250 km) PG 121.7 (195.8 km) Turnoff to Horsefly and Likely; resorts and active mining area.

CC 155.5 (250.2 km) PG 121.5 (195.5 km) Rest area to west overlooking McLeese Lake.

CC 160 (257.5 km) PG 117 (188.3 km) Turnout with litter barrel to west with plaque about Fraser River paddle-wheelers.

CC 167 (268.8 km) PG 110 (177 km) Free reaction ferry across the Fraser River at Marguerite.

CC 169.8 (273.2 km) PG 107.2 (172.5 km) Stone cairn commemorates Fort Alexandria, the last North West Co. fur-trading post established west of the Rockies, built in 1821.

CC 180 (289.7 km) PG 97 (156.1 km) Australian rest area to west with toilets, tables and litter barrels. Private campground to east. ▲

CC 182.3 (293.3 km) PG 94.7 (152.4 km) **The Bug's Ear.** See display ad this section.

CC 188.5 (303.4 km) PG 88.5 (142.4 km) Kersley (unincorporated), gas and food.

CC 193.2 (310.9 km) PG 83.8 (134.9 km) **Mary's Gifts**, located 100 yards east of Highway 97 on Dragon Lake Road. Exciting wonderland of Canadian handcrafted gifts. Moccasins, Indian crafts, jade, gold and silver jewellery, wood crafts, paintings and prints, linens, cards and candles, pottery, souvenirs. Open daily 9 A.M. to 5 P.M. Easy RV access. Mail orders. Box 32, Dragon Lake Road, RR 1, Quesnel, BC V2J 3H5. (604) 747-2993. [ADVERTISEMENT]

CC 196 (315.4 km) PG 81 (130.4 km) Loop road east to **Dragon Lake**, a small shallow lake popular with Quesnel families. Camping and fishing for rainbow. ⊙

CC 196 (315.4 km) PG 81 (130.4 km) **Robert's Roost Campsite** located 6 km south of Quesnel and 2 km east of Highway 97 in a parklike setting on beautiful Dragon Lake. Grass sites, both partial and fully serviced. 15- and 30-amp service. Sanidump, fishing, boat rental, swimming, horseshoes, playground, hot showers, flush toilets and laundromat. Can accommodate any length unit. Limited accommodation. Approved by Good Sam and Tourism BC. Hosts: Bob and Vivian Wurm, 3121 Gook Road, Quesnel, BC V2J 4K7. Phone (604) 747-2015. [ADVERTISEMENT] ▲

Quesnel

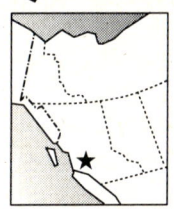

CC 203 (326.7 km) PG 74 (119.1 km). **Population:** 8,790. **Elevation:** 1,789 feet/545m. **Emergency Services:** RCMP, phone 992-9211. **Hospital**, phone 992-2181. **Visitor Information:** At the museum, located on the east side of the highway just north of Quesnel

QUESNEL ADVERTISERS

Dragon Lake Golf Course
 & Campsite .... Ph. (604) 747-1358
Fountain Motor Motel ...... Ph. (604) 992-7071
Mary's Gift Shop .... Dragon Lk. Rd.
Quesnel Airport Inn
 Motel and RV Park .... Ph. (604) 992-5942
Sylvan Motel .... Ph. (604) 992-5611

River bridge, in Le Bourdais Park. Open daily May to mid-September. Or write Quesnel and District Tourist Bureau, 703 Carson Ave., Quesnel, BC V2J 2B6; phone 992-8716.

Quesnel (kwe NEL) is a prospering lumber centre with motels, shopping centres and gas stations with diesel. This large city stretches along the highway for several miles south and north of the Quesnel River bridge. City centre is north of the bridge. At the confluence of the Fraser and Quesnel rivers, the town began as a supply point for miners. There are some interesting eroded pillars at Pinnacles Park, a few miles west of town. Picnicking and swimming at Puntchesakut Lake, 25 miles/40 km west on Nazko Road (paved), and at Ten Mile Lake, 7 miles/11.2 km north on Highway 97.

A worthwhile side trip is Highway 26, which intersects Highway 97 at Milepost CC 206. This 50-mile/80.5-km paved highway leads to Barkerville Provincial Historic Park, a reconstructed and restored Cariboo gold rush town. (See HIGHWAY 26 side road log on page 54.)

Billy Barker Days, a 4-day event held in mid-July in Quesnel, commemorates the discovery of gold at Barkerville in 1858. For more information, write Box 4441, Quesnel, BC V2J 3J4.

West Access Route Log

(continued)

CC 206 (331.5 km) PG 71 (114.3 km) Quesnel airport. Junction with Highway 26 to Barkerville and Bowron Lake. See HIGHWAY 26 side road log this section.

CC 210 (338 km) PG 67 (107.8 km) Ten Mile Lake Provincial Park; 142 campsites, picnic area, boat launch, good swimming beach. ▲

10 Mile Lake Provincial Park. See display ad this section.

CC 214.2 (344.7 km) PG 62.8 (101.1 km) Cottonwood River bridge. Turnout with litter barrels and stop of interest sign at

ALASKA HIGHWAY VIA WEST ACCESS ROUTE

Wildwood RV Park
(604) 989-4711
Free Hot Showers • Some Pull-throughs
Laundromat • 30-amp. Hookups • Cable TV
Box 50, RR #4, Site 6
Williams Lake, BC V2G 4M8

The Bug's Ear
A Country Doll & Gift Shop
Come in and see our extensive collection of porcelain and soft dolls of every description. Dolls to collect and dolls to love.
28 km south of Quesnel
Box 46, Yendryas, R.R. #1, Quesnel, BC V2J 3H5
(604) 993-4592

---

10 MILE LAKE Provincial Park
142 Sites
• 2 Camping Areas
• Pull-Through Sites
• Sani-Station

• 2 SANDY BEACH AREAS • EXCELLENT SWIMMING
• BOAT LAUNCH • BOAT RENTALS • FISHING
• 10 KM OF WALKING TRAILS
• SELF-GUIDED NATUREWALK
• 2 GRASS PLAYING AREAS
• KID'S ACTIVITY CENTRE
• COVERED PICNIC SHELTER

BC Parks

Mile CC 210 West Access Route

1992 ■ The MILEPOST® 53

Highway 26 Log

This 50-mile/80.5-km paved road leads to Barkerville Provincial Historic Park. **Distance from Highway 97 junction (J) is shown.**

J 0 Junction with Highway 97 at **Milepost CC 206**. Highway 26 climbs steeply up through the jackpine forests of Mouse Mountain, then descends to the Cottonwood River.

J 9.3 (15 km) Good example of caribou bull or snake fence, on the west side.

J 15.8 (25.5 km) Cottonwood House Provincial Park, a restored and furnished log roadhouse built in 1864. Picnicking and guided tours by costumed docents; open May to September.

J 21.1 (34 km) Viewpoint to south.

J 24.5 (39.5 km) Highway descends steep hill to Lightning Creek.

J 26 (42 km) Rest area to north.

J 26.7 (43 km) Historical stop of interest marker for Charles Morgan Blessing's grave. Blessing, from Ohio, was murdered on his way to Barkerville in 1866. His killer was caught when he gave Blessing's keepsake gold nugget stickpin, in the shape of an angel, to a Barkerville dance hall girl. His murderer, John Barry, was the only white man hanged in the Cariboo during the gold rush.

J 27 (43.5 km) Troll's Ski Resort; cross-country and downhill.

J 36.6 (59 km) Stanley Road to north; gold rush cemetery.

J 39.5 (63.5 km) Gravel turnout at start of Devil's Canyon, a narrow winding stretch of road above Chisholm Creek.

J 42 (67.5 km) Rest area at Slough Creek.

J 43.8 (70.5 km) North shore of **Jack of Clubs Lake**; fishing for rainbows, lake trout and Dolly Varden. Picnic tables and boat launch.

J 45.4 (73 km) **WELLS** (pop. 300) offers all visitor facilities. A museum with displays of local mining history is open daily from June to September. Wells dates to the 1930s when the Cariboo Gold Quartz Mine, promoted and developed by Fred Wells, brought hundreds of workers to this valley. The mine closed in 1967.

Jack O'Clubs Hotel. See display ad this section.

White Caps Motor Inn. See display ad this section.

St. George's Gallery and Marie Nagel Art Studio. Located in the former Anglican church in historic uptown Wells. Original oils, watercolors and acrylics by Marie Nagel, hand-painted shirts, handmade paper, pottery. Candles, soaps, stained glass, art books, and other quality gift items. Open 10 A.M. to 6 P.M. June to Labour Day. Box 84, Wells, BC V0K 2R0. (604) 994-3492. [ADVERTISEMENT]

J 48.5 (78 km) Barkerville Provincial Park Forest Rose Campground to north. Lowhee Campground to south; 170 campsites, picnic areas and dump stations.

J 49 (79 km) Gravel road leads north 11 miles/18 km to Bowron Lakes Provincial Park, noted for its interconnecting chain of lakes and the resulting 72-mile/116-km canoe circuit, which takes from 7 to 10 days to complete.

Visitor information available at registration center next to main parking lot where canoeists must register and pay circuit fees. Groups are limited to 6 people.

There are 2 private lodges at the north end of the lake with restaurants and canoe rentals. Provincial park campground has 25 sites and a boat launch.

J 49.7 (80 km) Road to Barkerville cemetery and access to Government Hill provincial campground.

J 50 (80.5 km) **BARKERVILLE**, a provincial historic park; open year-round. Visitor information available at Barkerville museum.

Barkerville was named for miner Billy Barker, who staked a claim on Williams Creek, dug down 52 feet/16m, and struck gold. The resulting gold rush in 1862 created Barkerville. Burned down and rebuilt in 1888, Barkerville was virtually a ghost town when the provincial government began restoration in 1958.

Today, Barkerville's buildings and boardwalks are faithful restorations or reconstructions from the town's heyday. Visitors can pan for gold, shop at the old-time general store, watch a blacksmith at work, have a drink in the saloon, or take in a show at the Theatre Royal. It is best to visit between mid-June and Labour Day, when the Theatre Royal offers daily performances and all exhibits are open.

Beyond Barkerville's main street, the Cariboo Wagon Road leads on (for pedestrians only) to Richfield, 1.5 miles/2 km, to the courthouse where "Hanging" Judge Begbie still holds court.

Barkerville Historic Town. See display ad this section.

Return to Milepost CC 206 West Access Route

Costumed docents lead guided tours of Cottonwood House. (Tom Parkin)

White Caps Motor Inn

32 UNITS, some with kitchens
all with private bath and showers
Satellite TV

Public Laundromat and Pay Showers
RV PARK
Full and Partial Hookups and Tent Sites

Reservations: (604) 994-3489
Box 153, Wells, BC V0K 2R0

VISA and MasterCard Accepted

JACK O' CLUBS HOTEL

PREMIER HISTORIC HOTEL
Where Liquid Gold Flows All Day
Restaurant • Pub • Arcade

CLEAN COMFORTABLE ROOMS
From $22 - $32
— Wells, BC —
For Reservations Call
(604) 994-3412

WE COME FROM A LONG LINE OF SHOW PEOPLE.

Whether you're coming from or going to Rendezvous '92, be sure you stop at Barkerville.

Stroll along the main street of our authentic 1870's gold rush town. Get into the act with costumed characters playing out lively scenes of Barkerville life.

Hear Judge Begbie lay down the majesty of British law. Grab a front row seat at the Theatre Royal for rollicking musical comedy—just as the miners did over 100 years ago. Pan for gold on the Eldorado claim. Take a ride on the Barnard Express Stage Coach. Or meander through over 90 authentic and reconstructed buildings.

Spend a day or two in Barkerville this summer, and see some of the best shows in history. For more information, call us at (604) 994-3332.

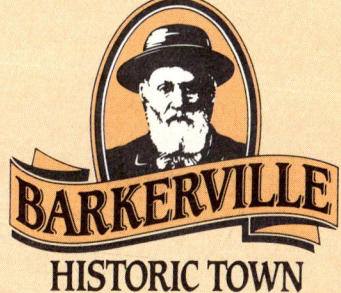

BARKERVILLE
HISTORIC TOWN

Barkerville is on Highway 26, just 89 km east of Quesnel, B.C.

Heritage Attraction
BRITISH COLUMBIA

Ministry of Municipal Affairs, Recreation and Culture

ALASKA HIGHWAY VIA WEST ACCESS ROUTE

The Fort George Railway tours Fort George Park. The park also offers playgrounds, picnicking and a museum. (Earl L. Brown, staff)

south end of bridge describes railway bridge seen upriver.

CC 218.7 (352 km) **PG 58.3** (93.8 km) Hush Lake rest area to west; toilets, tables, litter barrels.

CC 229.6 (369.5 km) **PG 47.4** (76.3 km) Strathnaver (unincorporated), no services.

CC 241 (387.8 km) **PG 36** (58 km) **HIXON** (pop. 1,500) has a post office, 2 motels, gas stations, grocery stores, 2 restaurants (1 with licensed premises), a pub and private campground. Hixon is the Cariboo's most northerly community. Southbound drivers watch for roadside display about points of interest in the Cariboo region located just north of Hixon. ▲

Hixon Fireplace Inn. See display ad this section.

Canyon Creek Campsite (Good Sam/CAA). Very long pull-through sites (100 feet) with 30 amps and water. Full hookups. Tent spaces in the trees with firepits. Modern restroom, hot showers, laundromat, sanistation, children's playground. Grocery stores, restaurant and pub within easy walking distance. Nature trail by the creek. Swimming hole and fishing pools (in season). Pets welcome, even horses. Aussi Tim welcomes you. (604) 998-4307. Box 390, Hixon, BC V0K 1S0. [ADVERTISEMENT] ▲

CC 247.6 (398.5 km) **PG 29.4** (47.3 km) Woodpecker rest area to west; toilets, tables, litter barrels.

CC 257.7 (414.7 km) **PG 19.3** (31 km) Stoner (unincorporated), no services.

CC 261.8 (421.3 km) **PG 15.2** (24.5 km) Red Rock (unincorporated), gas station with diesel; pay phone.

CC 270.6 (435.5 km) **PG 6.4** (10.3 km) Junction with bypass road to Yellowhead 16 East. Keep left for Prince George; continue straight ahead for Jasper and Edmonton. If you are headed east on Yellowhead Highway 16 for Jasper or Edmonton, turn to **Milepost E 450** in the YELLOWHEAD HIGHWAY 16 section and read the log back to front.

CC 273.4 (440 km) **PG 3.6** (5.8 km) Access to Prince George airport to east.

CC 274 (440.9 km) **PG 3** (4.8 km) **Sintich Trailer Park.** See display ad this section. ▲

CC 275.2 (442.8 km) **PG 1.8** (2.8 km) Bridge over the Fraser River. Turn right at north end of bridge then left at stop sign for city centre via Queensway. This is the easiest access for Fort George Park; follow Queensway to 20th Avenue and turn east.

Continue straight ahead for Highway 16 entrance to city.

CC 276 (444.1 km) **PG 1** (1.6 km) **Junction** of Highway 97 with Yellowhead 16 West. Description of Prince George follows. If you are headed west on Yellowhead Highway 16 for Prince Rupert, turn to **Milepost PG 0** in the YELLOWHEAD HIGHWAY 16 section.

Prince George

CC 277 (445.8 km) **Population:** 71,000, area 160,000. **Emergency Services:** RCMP, phone 562-3371, emergency only, phone 563-1111. **Fire Department**, phone 563-1261. **Ambulance**, 24-hour service, phone 564-4558. **Poison Control Centre**, phone 565-2442. **Hospital**, Prince George Regional, phone 565-2000; emergency, phone 565-2444.

Visitor Information: Tourism Prince George, 1198 Victoria St., phone 562-3700 or fax 563-3584. Open year-round, 8:30 A.M. to 5 P.M. weekdays September to June, daily in July and August. Visitor centre, junction Yellowhead 16 and Highway 97; open daily mid-May to Labour Day, 9 A.M. to 8 P.M., phone 563-5493.

Elevation: 1,868 feet/569m. **Climate:** The inland location is tempered by the protection of mountains. The average annual frost-free period is 78 days, with 1,865 hours of bright sunshine. Dry in summer; chinooks off and on during winter which, accompanied by a western flow of air, break up the cold weather. Summer temperatures average 72°F/22°C with lows to 46°F/8°C.

Welcome to the North Country.

SINTICH TRAILER PARK
"AN ADULT COMMUNITY"
Pull-throughs • Large RV Lots • 30 amp Service
Showers and Laundromat • RV Storage
GROCERY STORE • SERVICE STATION
South of Prince George on 97
Good Sampark
Box 1022, Prince George, BC V2L 4V1
For reservations: **Phone (604) 963-9862**
Super, Natural North by Northwest   CAA • VISA • MasterCard

Fully Licensed • Excellent Cuisine
PHONE (604) 998-4518 • Ample Parking • Your Hosts, Fran and David Krieger
HIXON FIREPLACE INN
Monday to Saturday 7 a.m. to 8 p.m. • Sunday noon to 8 p.m.
Food is Our Business, International is Our Cuisine
Most Major Card Accepted   Hixon, BC

Grama's Inn
An Annex of Ester's Inn
62 Air-Conditioned Units
Family Restaurant
24-hour desk service • Cable TV • Sauna
(604) 563-7174
901 Central Avenue, Prince George, BC
Super, Natural North by Northwest

SPRUCELAND INN MOTEL
1391 Central - 97 Highway at 15th Ave.

"WE WELCOME YOU"
Newly Renovated
82 Deluxe Units • 23 Kitchen Units
HEATED SWIMMING POOL • SAUNAS
GAME ROOM • CABLE TV • HOT TUB

RESTAURANT

Ph: (604) 563-0102
1-800-663-3295
FAX (604) 663-3295
Prince George

Super, Natural North by Northwest

Radio: CKPG 550, CJCI 620, BC-FM 94.3, CBC-FM 91.5, C-101 FM. **Television:** 11 channels via cable. **Newspaper:** *The Citizen* (daily except Sunday).

Prince George is located at the confluence of the Nechako and Fraser rivers, near the geographical centre of British Columbia. It is the hub of the trade and travel routes of the province, located at the junction of Yellowhead Highway 16—linking Prince Rupert on the west coast with the Interior of Canada—and Highway 97, which runs south to Vancouver and north to Dawson Creek.

In the early 1800s, Simon Fraser of the North West Trading Co. erected a post here which he named Fort George in honour of the reigning English monarch. In 1906, survey parties for the transcontinental Grand Trunk Pacific Railway (later Canadian National Railways) passed through the area, and with the building of the railroad a great land boom took place. The city was incorporated in 1915 under the name Prince George. Old Fort George is now a park and picnic spot and the site of Fort George Museum.

PRINCE GEORGE ADVERTISERS

Big John's
  R.V. Clinic .... 888 Lower Patricia Blvd.
Downtown Motel .... 650 Dominion St.
Esther's Inn .... 10th Ave. & Commercial
Goldcap Motor Inn .... 1458 7th Ave.
Grama's Inn .... 901 Central Ave.
Inland Spring and
  Axle Ltd. .... 1852 Quinn St.
Log House Restaurant and
  RV Park, The .... Tabor Lake
P.G. Hi-Way Motel .... 1737 20th Ave.
Prince George KOA
  Campground .3 miles W. on Yellowhead 16
Spruceland Inn
  Motel .... Hwy. 97 & 15th Ave.
Tourism Prince George .... 1198 Victoria St.

ALASKA HIGHWAY VIA WEST ACCESS ROUTE

Newest Motel in Prince George.
Enclosed Tropical Polynesian Garden
With Pool and Coffee Terrace.

ESTHER'S INN

LOUNGE • DINING ROOM
COLOUR TV
SWIMMING POOL
Jacuzzis • Sauna • Waterslides
132 AIR CONDITIONED UNITS
Ample Parking

Write: 1151 Commercial Drive
Prince George, BC V2M 6W6
Phone: (604) 562-4131
Toll Free 1-800-663-6844

Located at 10th Avenue off Highway 97N

ESTHER'S INN

Super, Natural North by Northwest

FULL SERVICE SHOP

INLAND SPRING and AXLE LTD.
562-9090
1852 QUINN ST., PRINCE GEORGE, B.C.
HITCHES • SPRING REBUILDING • AXLES • WELDING

Motorhomes
Travel Trailers

Trucks
Cars • Vans

Springs • Axles • Hitches • Parts • Service • Repairs • Welding

Owner-operated for fast, personal service   Open Monday - Saturday 8 a.m. - 5 p.m.
1852 Quinn Street, Prince George, BC (604) 562-9090
VISA   **For faster service and directions to the shop call 1-800-663-3228**   MasterCard

---

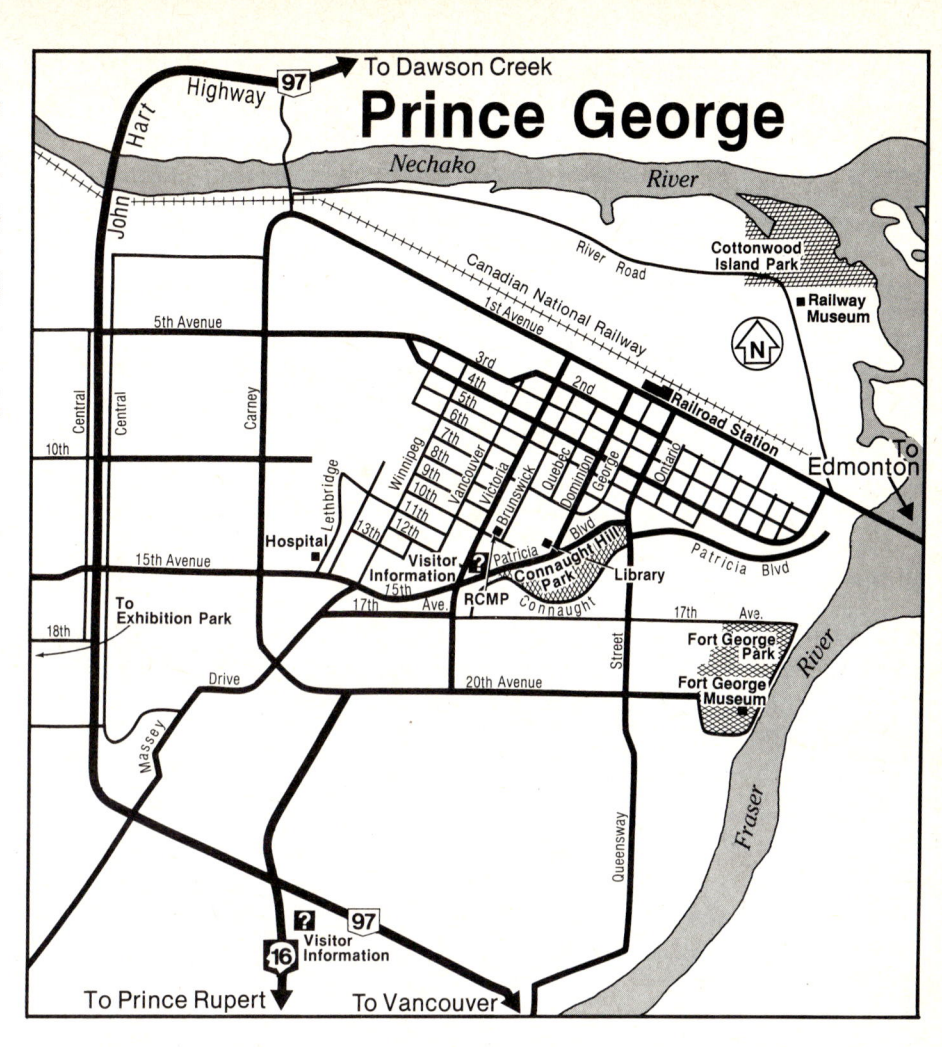

A Guide to the Queen Charlotte Islands (revised 10th edition). Learn about British Columbia's remote and beautiful islands from longtime resident and author Neil Carey. To order from Alaska Northwest Books™ call toll free 1-800-343-4567.

BIG JOHN'S
R.V. CLINIC

(604) 562-JOHN (5646)
Service Is Our Business

★ Major appliance repairs
★ Hitch repairs and Installations
★ Service and repairs to all RV models

Insurance repairs welcome

888 Lower Patricia Blvd., Prince George, BC, V2L 5K5

Super, Natural North by Northwest

1992 ■ The MILEPOST® 57

ALASKA HIGHWAY VIA WEST ACCESS ROUTE

Prince George is primarily an industrial centre, fairly dependent on the lumber industry, with 3 pulp mills, sawmills, planers, dry kilns, a plywood plant and 2 chemical plants to serve the pulp mills. Oil refining, mining and heavy construction are other major area industries. The Prince George Forest Region is the largest in the province.

Prince George is the focal point of the central Interior for financial and professional services, equipment and wholesale firms, machine shops and many services for the timber industry.

Agriculture in central British Columbia is basically a forage-livestock business, for which the climate and soils are well suited. Dairying and beef are the major livestock enterprises, with minor production in sheep and poultry.

ACCOMMODATIONS

Prince George offers 5 hotels, 17 motels and 8 trailer parks, as well as 6 bed and breakfasts. Most accommodations are within easy reach of the business district and the more than 80 restaurants in the downtown area. Most stores are open 7 days a week. The usual hours of operation are: Sunday, noon to 5 P.M.; Saturday and Monday through Wednesday, 9:30 A.M. to 6 P.M.; Thursday and Friday, 9:30 A.M. to 9 P.M.

The city campground at 18th Avenue, across from Exhibition Grounds, open mid-May to mid-September, provides trailer spaces, tenting, showers, washrooms and dump station. RV parks are also located just south and north of town on Highway 97, and west and east of town on Yellowhead Highway 16.

TRANSPORTATION

Air: Prince George airport is southeast of the city, serviced by Canadian Airlines International and Air BC. Limousine service to and from the airport.

B.C. Gov't. Approved
CAA AAA

Highway 16 – West entrance Prince George
P.G. HI–WAY MOTEL
B.C. STYLE HOSPITALITY

33 Units • 11 with Kitchens • Family Accommodations • Electric Heat
Cable Colour TV • Phones in all Rooms • Plug-ins • Some Units Air-conditioned

Avy and Thomas Tang have worked hard to provide a pleasant home-away-from-home atmosphere for all their guests in the P.G. HI–WAY MOTEL. FAX (604) 562-5687

1737 20th Avenue, Prince George, BC V2L 4B9 • Phone (604) 564-6869

MasterCard VISA AMERICAN EXPRESS

Ferry Information | Super, Natural North by Northwest

Goldcap MOTOR INN

The Place to Stay
CABLE TV
IN-HOUSE MOVIES
AIR CONDITIONED
WINTER PLUG-INS

MasterCard VISA AMERICAN EXPRESS
GOLDCAP MOTOR INN CAA AAA

75 ROOMS – EFFICIENCY UNITS
Licensed Restaurant • Lounge
Conveniently Located Downtown
1458 7th Avenue, Prince George
(604) 563-0666
Within BC, Call Toll Free
1-800-663-8239 • FAX (604) 563-5775

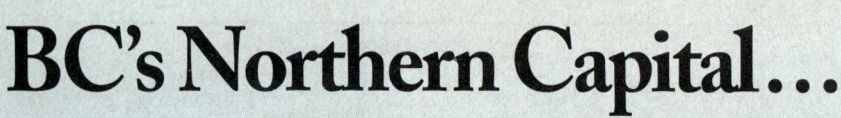

Super, Natural North by Northwest

BC's Northern Capital...
...where people make the difference.

Enjoy Northern Hospitality at its best!

Located in the heart of BC's beautiful interior, Prince George offers the quality services you might expect from a modern city of 71,000 — accommodations, campgrounds, restaurants, museums, art galleries, shopping, RV services and more.

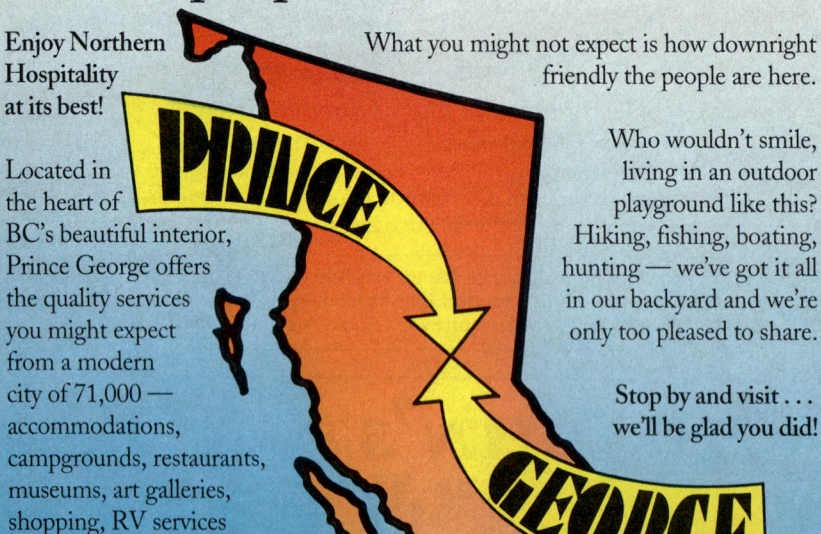

What you might not expect is how downright friendly the people are here.

Who wouldn't smile, living in an outdoor playground like this? Hiking, fishing, boating, hunting — we've got it all in our backyard and we're only too pleased to share.

Stop by and visit... we'll be glad you did!

Just five hours to Alaska Highway Mile "0"

For more information:
TOURISM PRINCE GEORGE, 1198(MP) Victoria St., Prince George, BC V2L 2L2
Phone: (604) 562-3700 • FAX: (604) 563-3584 | Super, Natural North by Northwest

---

PRINCE GEORGE KOA CAMPGROUND
YOUR FAMILY CAMPGROUND
STORE • ICE • HEATED POOL • MINI-GOLF
95 sites — Long pull-throughs — Full hookups
Camping cabins — Grassy tenting — Laundromat
Recreation building — Playground — Pay phone
• Box 2434, Prince George, BC V2N 2S6

3 miles west of Highway 97 on Yellowhead Highway
Phone (604) 964-7272

DOWNTOWN MOTEL

• 45 Sleeping Units
• Air Conditioning
• Cable TV
• Movie Channel

Close to downtown facilities (dining adjacent)

(604) 563-9241
1-800-663-5729 (B.C. only)
650 Dominion Street, Prince George
VISA, MasterCard, American Express

THE LOG HOUSE RESTAURANT AND R.V. PARK

We feature an outstanding collection of big game trophies in our unique restaurant.
Power and Water Hookups
Showers ▲ Laundromat
Boat Rental ▲ Float Plane Base
Enjoy the only lakeshore park in the area — along with its excellent trout fishing.
Located 9 miles east of Prince George on alternate Highway 16A East (Giscome Road) (604) 963-9515

Railroad: VIA Rail connects Prince George with Prince Rupert and Jasper, AB. Daily passenger service south to Vancouver via British Columbia Railway.

Bus: Greyhound. City bus service is provided by Prince George Transit & Charter Ltd.

ATTRACTIONS

City View: Follow Connaught Drive to the viewpoint at Connaught Hill Park for a panoramic view of the city.

City Landmarks: Centennial Fountain at the corner of 7th Avenue and Dominion Street depicts the early history of Prince George in mosaic tile. A cairn at Fort George Park commemorates Sir Alexander Mackenzie.

Prince George Art Gallery on 15th Avenue features regional, national and international artists.

Fort George Park is the largest park in Prince George and a good stop for travelers with its playgrounds, picnic tables, barbecue facilities and museum. The Fort George Regional Museum displays artifacts from the pioneer days through 1920. The museum is open daily in summer from 10 A.M. to 5 P.M.; phone 562-1612. The Fort George Railway operates on weekends and holidays at the park from a railway building patterned after the original Grand Trunk Pacific stations.

Cottonwood Island Park, located on the Nechako River (see city map), has picnic facilities and extensive nature trails.

Giscome Portage Regional Park contains the historic Huble Homestead. Tour the Huble House, built in 1912, and the other carefully reconstructed farm buildings in this beautiful setting. Located north of Prince George on Highway 97; see **Milepost PG 26.9.**

Prince George Railway Museum, located adjacent Cottonwood Island Park, has an excellent selection of antique rail stock. Attractions include a 1914 Grand Trunk Railway station and restored dining car.

Golf Courses: Aspen Grove Golf Club is 9 miles/14.5 km south of the city; Yellowhead Grove Golf Club, Pine Valley Golf Club and Prince George Golf and Curling Club are on Yellowhead Highway 16 West.

Swimming: Four Seasons Swimming Pool at the corner of 7th Avenue and Dominion Street has a pool, waterslide, diving tank and fitness centre. Open to the public afternoons and evenings.

Rockhounding: The hills and river valleys in the area provide abundant caches of Omineca agate and Schmoos. For more information, contact Prince George Rock and Gem Club, phone 562-4526; or Spruce City Rock and Gem Club, phone 562-1013.

Tennis Courts: A total of 20 courts currently available to the public at 3 places—20th Avenue near the entrance to Fort George Park, at Massey Drive in Carrie Jane Gray Park, and on Ospika Boulevard in the Lakewood Secondary School complex.

Industrial Tours are available from mid-May through August by contacting Tourism Prince George at 562-3700. Tours, which are on weekdays only, include Northwood Pulp and Timber and North Central Plywoods. Tours of Prince George Pulp and Intercon Pulp are available on request.

Special Events: Elks May Day celebration and the Prince George Regional Forest Exhibition in May; Folkfest on July 1, Canada Day; live theatre through July and August; Simon Fraser Days in late July-early August includes raft races, International Food Festival; Annual Sandblast Skiing in August; Prince George Exhibition in August; Oktoberfest in October; and the winter Mardi Gras Festival in mid-February. Details on these and other events are available from Tourism Prince George.

Side Trips: Prince George is the starting point for some of the finest holiday country in the province. There are numerous lakes and resorts nearby, among them: Bednesti Lake, 30 miles/48 km west of Prince George; Cluculz Lake, 44 miles/71 km west; Purden Lake, 42 miles/68 km east; and Tabor Lake, 6 miles/10 km east. Day-use only sandy beaches are found at Bear Lake, 40 miles/66 km north, and West Lake, 15 miles/25 km west.

AREA FISHING: Highways 16 and 97 are the ideal routes for the sportsman, with year-round fishing and easy access to lakes and rivers. Hunters and fishermen stop over in Prince George as the jumping-off place for some of North America's finest big game hunting and fishing. For information regarding hunting and fishing contact: Rod & Gun Club, P.O. Box 924, Prince George; Spruce City Wildlife Assoc., in Prince George, phone 564-6859; or Tourism Prince George, phone 562-3700. A comprehensive fishing guide booklet is available from Tourism Prince George.

West Access Route Log

(continued)

HIGHWAY 97/HART HIGHWAY
The John Hart Highway, completed in 1952, was named for the former B.C. premier who sponsored its construction. The highway is a 2-lane paved highway with both straight stretches and winding stretches.

This section of the log shows distance from Prince George (PG) followed by distance from Dawson Creek (DC).

PG 0 DC 250 (402.3 km) John Hart Bridge over the Nechako River. The 4-lane highway extends approximately 6.5 miles/10.5 km northbound through the commercial and residential suburbs of Prince George.

PG 1.5 (2.4 km) DC 248.5 (399.9 km) Truck weigh scales to west.

PG 2.5 (4 km) DC 247.5 (398.3 km) Arctic RV Service Centre. See display ad this section.

PG 6.5 (10.5 km) DC 243.5 (391.9 km) Two-lane highway (with passing lanes) begins abruptly northbound.

PG 9.5 (15.3 km) DC 240.5 (387 km) Hart Highway Campground. See display ad this section.

PG 14.6 (23.5 km) DC 235.4 (378.8 km) Salmon River bridge. Litter barrel and river access to west at north end of bridge.

PG 16.4 (26.4 km) DC 233.6 (357.9 km) Highway overpass crosses railroad tracks.

PG 22 (35.4 km) DC 228 (366.9 km) Gravel turnouts both sides of highway.

PG 26.5 (42.6 km) DC 223.5 (359.7 km) Paved turnout to east with litter barrels and point of interest sign about Crooked River Forest Recreation Area.

PG 26.9 (43.3 km) DC 223.1 (359 km) Access west to Giscome Portage regional park via Mitchell Road; narrow road. Site of Huble Farm, a 1912 homestead.

PG 28.2 (45.4 km) DC 221.8 (356.9 km) Turnoff to west for **Summit Lake,** a resort area popular with Prince George residents; lake char and rainbow fishing spring and fall.

PG 29.3 (47.2 km) DC 220.7 (355.2 km) Westcoast Energy station.

PG 30.7 (49.4 km) DC 219.3 (352.9 km) Second turnoff to west for Summit Lake.

PG 36.6 (58.9 km) DC 213.4 (343.4 km) Cottonwood Creek.

PG 38.8 (62.4 km) DC 211.2 (339.9 km) Paved turnout with litter barrel.

PG 42 (67.6 km) DC 208 (334.7 km) Slow down for sharp turn across railroad tracks.

PG 43.3 (69.7 km) DC 206.7 (332.6 km) Turnoff to west for Bear Lake Campground in Crooked River Provincial Park; 90 campsites, flush toilets, tables, firepits, dump station. Also horseshoe pits, volleyball, playground, trails and swimming. Powerboats prohibited. Picnic shelter with wood stove. Fee is $7. **Crooked River** and area lakes have fair fishing for rainbow, Dolly Varden, grayling and whitefish.

PG 43.9 (70.6 km) DC 206.1 (331.7 km) Turnoff to west for Bear Lake picnic area in Crooked River Provincial Park; fishing and swimming. Highway 97 follows the Crooked River north to McLeod Lake.

PG 44.8 (72.1 km) DC 205.2 (330.1 km) Bear Lake (unincorporated); gas, grocery, restaurant, motel, gift shop, post office and ambulance station. Highway maintenance camp.

Hart Highway Campground

30 FULLY-SERVICED SITES • TENTING
PULL-THROUGHS • HOT SHOWERS • GRASS
FLUSH TOILETS • PLAYGROUND • PHONE
(604) 962-5010
R.R. #2, Site 9, Comp. 1, Prince George, BC V2N 2H9

Arctic RV SERVICE CENTRE

Mile 2.5 John Hart Highway

Service — Parts — Accessories For
Trailers — Motorhomes — Campers — Vans
5th Wheels — Boat Trailers

Fibreglass Boat Repairs • Hitches • Awnings • Wiring
Axles • Brakes • Drums • Springs • Spray Foam Insulation

All I.C.B.C. or private insurance claims handled promptly

(604) 962-9631   PRINCE GEORGE, BC V2K 1M8   • DIV. OF AUTOBODY LTD.

ALASKA HIGHWAY VIA WEST ACCESS ROUTE

Bijoux Falls at Milepost PG 115.3 makes a pleasant stop. (Earl L. Brown, staff)

PG 50.7 (81.6 km) **DC 199.3** (320.7 km) Angusmac Creek.

PG 54.2 (87.2 km) **DC 195.8** (315.1 km) Tumbler Ridge branch line British Columbia Railway connects Tumbler Ridge with the B.C. Railway and Canadian National Railway, allowing for shipments of coal from Tumbler Ridge to Ridley Island near Prince Rupert.

PG 55.6 (89.5 km) **DC 194.4** (312.8 km) Large gravel turnout with litter barrel to west.

PG 56.1 (90.3 km) **DC 193.9** (312 km) Large gravel turnout with litter barrel to west.

PG 57 (91.7 km) **DC 193** (310.6 km) Large gravel turnout with litter barrel to west.

PG 60.8 (97.8 km) **DC 189.2** (304.5 km) Turnout with litter barrel to east.

PG 62.4 (100.4 km) **DC 187.6** (301.9 km) Large gravel turnout with litter barrel to east.

PG 65.2 (104.9 km) **DC 184.8** (297.4 km) Lomas Creek.

PG 71.8 (115.5 km) **DC 178.2** (286.8 km) Cafe, cabins and camping.

Whiskers Bay Resort. See display ad this section.

PG 76.6 (123.3 km) **DC 173.4** (279.1 km) First view northbound of McLeod Lake and view of Whisker's Point.

PG 77.7 (125 km) **DC 172.3** (277.3 km) Turnoff to west for Whisker's Point Provincial Park on McLeod Lake. This is an exceptionally nice campground with a paved loop road, 69 level gravel sites, a dump station, tap water, flush toilets, boat ramp, fire rings, firewood and picnic tables. Also horseshoe pits, volleyball, playground and picnic shelter. Camping fee is $7. Boat launch, swimming, changehouse, sandy beach and fishing. ▲

McLeod Lake has fair fishing for rainbow, lake char and Dolly Varden, spring and fall, trolling is best.

PG 84 (135.2 km) **DC 166** (267.1 km) **Lakeview Service**, just north of Whisker's Point. Shell station, regular and unleaded gas, tire sales and repairs, tow truck and welding. Headlight, radiator rock screens put on $15. Store, snacks, ice, good fishing advice and worms. Eight motel units (single $28, double $38 and up), cooking available. Camping sites with firewood. Power hookups. Showers. Your hosts, K.G. Wheeler and the mop squeezer. (604) 750-4472. [ADVERTISEMENT] ▲

PG 84.5 (136 km) **DC 165.5** (266.3 km) Fort McLeod (unincorporated) has a gas station, grocery, motel and cafe. A monument here commemorates the founding of Fort McLeod, oldest permanent settlement west of the Rockies and north of San Francisco. Founded in 1805 by Simon Fraser as a trading post for the North West Trading Co., the post was named by Fraser for Archie McLeod.

PG 84.7 (136.3 km) **DC 165.3** (266 km) McLeod Lake (unincorporated), post office, store and lodging.

PG 85 (136.8 km) **DC 165** (265.5 km) Turnoff for Carp Lake Provincial Park, 20 miles/32 km west via a gravel road; 105 campsites on Carp and War lakes, picnic tables, firepits, boat launch, fishing and swimming. Also horseshoe pits, playground and picnic shelter with wood stove. Fee is $7. Park access road follows the McLeod River to Carp Lake. ▲

Carp Lake, rainbow June through September; special restrictions in effect, check current posted information. **McLeod River**, rainbow from July, fly-fishing only.

PG 85.6 (137.8 km) **DC 164.4** (264.6 km) Gravel turnout with litter barrel to west.

PG 87.6 (141 km) **DC 162.4** (261.4 km) Westcoast Energy station and McLeod Lake school.

PG 89.8 (144.5 km) **DC 160.2** (257.8 km) Turnoff to west for Tudyah Lake Provincial Park; 36 campsites, tables, firerings, firewood, pit toilets, drinking water. Also swimming, sandy beach, boat ramp, fishing. Fee is $5. ▲

Tudyah Lake, shore access, rainbow, Dolly Varden and some grayling in summer and late fall. **Pack River** (flows into Tudyah Lake), fishing for grayling, June 1 to July 1; rainbow, June 10 to November; large Dolly Varden, Sept. 15 to Oct. 10, spinning.

PG 89.9 (144.7 km) **DC 160.1** (257.6 km) Bear Creek bridge.

PG 93.9 (151.1 km) **DC 156.1** (251.2 km) Gas, food and lodging.

PG 94.7 (152.4 km) **DC 155.3** (249.9 km) Parsnip River bridge. This is the Rocky Mountain Trench, marking the western boundary of the Rocky Mountains. Northbound motorists begin gradual climb through the Misinchinka then Hart ranges of the Rocky Mountains.

Parsnip River, good fishing for grayling and Dolly Varden, some rainbow, best from August to October; a boat is necessary.

PG 95.2 (153.2 km) **DC 154.8** (249.1 km) Junction with Highway 39 (paved), which leads 18 miles/29 km to Mackenzie (description follows). Food, gas, lodging, camping and tourist information at junction.

Signed trailheads along Highway 39 are part of the Mackenzie Demonstration Forest. There are 8 self-guiding trails in the demonstration forest, each focusing on an aspect of forest management. Interpretive signs are posted along each of the trails.

Mackenzie Junction Cafe. See display ad this section. ▲

Mackenzie

Located 18 miles/29 km northwest of the John Hart Highway 97 via Highway 39. **Population:** 5,550. **Emergency Services:** RCMP, phone 997-3288. **Hospital,** 12 beds. **Ambulance,** phone 1-563-5433. **Visitor Information:** At the railway caboose located at the junction of Highways 97 and 39. Or write the Chamber of Commerce, Box 880, Mackenzie, BC V0J 2C0.

Elevation: 2,300 feet/701m. **Radio:** CKMK 1240, CKPG 1240; CBC-FM 990. **Television:** Channels 6, 9 and cable.

A large, modern, planned community, Mackenzie was built in 1965. It lies at the south end of Williston Lake, the largest manmade reservoir on the continent. Construction of the new town in what had been just wilderness was sparked by the Peace River Dam project and the need to attract skilled employees for industrial growth. Mackenzie was incorporated in May 1966 under "instant town" legislation; the first residents moved here in July 1966. Industry

---

Whiskers Bay Resort
Cabins – Lakeside Camping
Cafe – Store
Fishing – Swimming
On Headwaters of McLeod Lake, BC

Mackenzie Junction Cafe
Licensed Premises
Convenience Store • Take-out Chicken
Motel • Ice • Propane
❖ 24-HOUR TOWING ❖
Camping • Full Hookups • Showers
Fishing & Hunting Licenses & Supplies
(604) 750-4454
Super, Natural Scenic Adventures
TEXACO

While in Mackenzie,
Stop at the . . .
ALEXANDER MACKENZIE HOTEL
Sauna and Whirlpool
Restaurant
Suites • Lounge • Pub
(604) 997-3266
1-800-663-2964
On Mackenzie Boulevard
P.O. Box 40, Mackenzie, BC V0J 2C0
Super, Natural Scenic Adventure

here includes mining and forestry, with 5 sawmills, a paper mill and 2 pulp mills.

On display in Mackenzie is the "world's largest tree crusher." The 56-foot-long electrically powered Le Tourneau G175 tree crusher was used in clearing land at the Peace River Power Project in the mid-1960s.

Attractions include swimming, waterskiing and boating at Morfee Lake, a 10-minute walk from town. There are boat launches on both Morfee Lake and Williston Lake reservoir. Good view of Mackenzie and Williston Lake reservoir from the top of Morfee Mountain (elev. 5,961 feet/1,817m). The big summer event here is the Blue Grass Festival, held in August.

Mackenzie has all visitor facilities, including motels, restaurants, shopping, gas stations, swimming pool, tennis courts, 9-hole golf course and other recreation facilities. There is also a paved 5,000-foot/1,524-m airstrip.

There is a free municipal RV park with 20 sites, flush toilets, showers and sani-dump. Fishing for rainbow, Dolly Varden, arctic char and grayling in **Williston Lake**.

Alexander Mackenzie Hotel. See display ad this section.

District of Mackenzie. See display ad this section.

West Access Route Log

(continued)

PG 95.2 (153.2 km) **DC 154.8** (249.1 km) Junction with Highway 39 to Mackenzie; food, gas, lodging and tourist booth at junction.

PG 95.5 (153.7 km) **DC 154.5** (248.6 km) Highway crosses railroad tracks.

PG 98.9 (158.2 km) **DC 151.1** (243.2 km) Gravel turnout with litter barrel to east.

PG 106 (170.6 km) **DC 144** (231.7 km) Turnout with litter barrel to east.

PG 108.4 (174.4 km) **DC 141.6** (227.9 km) Highway maintenance yard.

PG 108.5 (174.6 km) **DC 141.5** (227.7 km) Bridge over Honeymoon Creek.

PG 109.6 (176.4 km) **DC 140.4** (225.9 km) Powerlines crossing highway carry electricity south from hydro dams in the Hudson Hope area. (See HUDSON'S HOPE LOOP section.)

PG 110.5 (177.8 km) **DC 139.5** (224.5 km) Slow down for sharp curve across railroad tracks.

PG 112.3 (180.7 km) **DC 137.7** (221.6 km) Bridge over Rolston Creek; dirt turnout by small falls to west.

PG 115.3 (185.6 km) **DC 134.7** (216.8 km) Bijoux Falls Provincial Park; pleasant picnic area adjacent falls on west side of highway. This day-use area has paved parking for 50 cars, pit toilets and picnic tables. Good photo opportunity.

Misinchinka River, southeast of the highway; fishing for grayling, whitefish and Dolly Varden.

PG 116.3 (187.2 km) **DC 133.7** (215.2 km) Highway crosses under railroad.

PG 119.3 (191.8 km) **DC 130.8** (210.5 km) Crossing Pine Pass (elev. 3,068 feet/935m), the highest point on the John Hart-Peace River Highway. Beautiful view of the Rockies to the northeast. Good highway over pass; steep grade southbound.

PG 119.4 (192.2 km) **DC 130.6** (210.2

Mackenzie, B.C.

Restaurants, shopping, golf course, recreation centre, great fishing
**LOTS TO SEE AND DO!
COME VISIT US.**

Glen Dick

FREE Municipal RV Park, washroom/shower facilities and sani-dump.

Come visit the Home of the World's Largest Tree Crusher

Just 18 miles off of Highway 97 on Highway 39

For more information contact:
Mackenzie Chamber of Commerce
P.O. Box 880, Mackenzie, BC V0J 2C0
Telephone: (604) 997-5459

Super, Natural Scenic Adventure

PINE VALLEY PARK
(Halfway between Prince George and Dawson Creek)
Located at the Edge of Beautiful Azouzetta Lake

OPEN YEAR-ROUND

LODGE & LICENSED RESTAURANT

CAMPGROUND   Partial Hookups
Hot Showers • Sani-Station
Free Boat Launch

MasterCard   **(604) 565-9284**   VISA

Mailing Address:
BOX 1189, MACKENZIE, BC V0J 2C0

GAS • OIL • PROPANE

TEMPO

Super, Natural Scenic Adventure

ALASKA HIGHWAY VIA WEST ACCESS ROUTE

1992 ■ The MILEPOST® 61

ALASKA HIGHWAY VIA WEST ACCESS ROUTE

Chetwynd's Little Giant statue at town centre. (Earl L. Brown, staff)

km) Turnoff to Powder King ski resort. This area receives over 30 feet/9m of snow in winter.
 PG 121.4 (195.4 km) **DC 128.6** (207 km) Viewpoint to east with point of interest sign about Pine Pass and view of Azouzetta Lake. Pit toilet and litter barrels.
 PG 122.4 (197 km) **DC 127.6** (205.3 km) Pine Valley Park; gas station, propane, diesel, cafe, lodge, campground on **Azouzetta Lake.** Very scenic spot. Spectacular hiking on Murray Mountain Trail; inquire at lodge for details. A scuba diving school operates at Azouzetta Lake in summer. Fishing for rainbow (stocked lake) to 1½ lbs., flies or lures, July to October. Boat launch.
 Pine Valley Park. See display ad on page 61.
 PG 125.7 (202.3 km) **DC 124.3** (200 km) Westcoast Energy station.
 PG 127 (204.4 km) **DC 123** (198.1 km) West Pine rest area beside Pine River; large gravel turnout with tables, pit toilets and garbage containers.
 PG 131.1 (211 km) **DC 118.9** (191.3 km) Turnout with litter barrel.
 PG 140.6 (226.3 km) **DC 109.4** (176.1 km) Bridge over Link Creek.

PG 141.4 (227.5 km) **DC 108.6** (174.8 km) Gravel turnout with litter barrels.
 PG 143 (230.1 km) **DC 107** (172.2 km) Rest area with litter barrel beside Pine River.
 PG 143.4 (230.8 km) **DC 106.6** (171.6 km) Bridge over Pine River, B.C. Railway overpass.
 PG 143.9 (231.6 km) **DC 106.1** (170.7 km) Abandoned buildings north of highway.
 PG 144.3 (232.2 km) **DC 105.7** (170.1 km) Food, gas, towing, lodging and camping.
 Silver Sands Lodge. See display ad this section.
 PG 146.1 (235.1 km) **DC 103.9** (167.2 km) Cairns Creek.
 PG 146.9 (236.4 km) **DC 103.1** (165.9 km) Gravel access road to Pine River to south.
 PG 148.2 (238.5 km) **DC 101.8** (163.8 km) LeMoray (unincorporated). Lodge to north of highway (status of services unknown).
 PG 148.3 (238.7 km) **DC 101.7** (163.7 km) Gravel turnout to south.
 PG 148.8 (239.5 km) **DC 101.2** (162.9 km) Lillico Creek.
 PG 149.7 (240.9 km) **DC 100.3** (161.4 km) Marten Creek.
 PG 150.4 (242 km) **DC 99.6** (160.3 km) Big Boulder Creek.
 PG 156.2 (251.4 km) **DC 93.8** (151 km) Fisher Creek.
 PG 156.9 (252.5 km) **DC 93.1** (149.8 km) Large gravel turnout with litter barrel to south beside Pine River.
 PG 159.9 (257.3 km) **DC 90.1** (145 km) Crassier Creek.
 PG 161.7 (260.2 km) **DC 88.3** (142.1 km) Westcoast Energy station.

PG 163.6 (263.3 km) **DC 86.4** (139 km) Pine Valley rest areas, both sides of highway, with picnic tables. Pine River to south.
 PG 166.6 (268.1 km) **DC 83.4** (134.2 km) Antique shop.
 PG 169.5 (272.8 km) **DC 80.5** (129.5 km) Turnout with litter barrel to south overlooking the beautiful Pine River valley.
 PG 172.4 (277.4 km) **DC 77.6** (124.9 km) Westcoast Energy, Pine River plant. View of the Rocky Mountain foothills to the south and west.
 PG 177.4 (285.5 km) **DC 72.6** (116.8 km) Turnout with litter barrel.
 PG 181.9 (292.7 km) **DC 68.1** (109.6 km) Bissett Creek.
 PG 183.6 (295.5 km) **DC 66.4** (106.9 km) Turnout with litter barrels at Wildmare Creek.
 PG 183.7 (295.6 km) **DC 66.3** (106.7 km) **Wild Mare Grove Campsite.** 50 extra wide and long spaces. Beautifully treed with easy access to and from the highway. A quiet well-drained area. Pull-through spaces, some with full hookups, barbecues and picnic tables. Showers, sani-station, pay phone, good drinking water. Pets welcome. 4 miles west of Chetwynd on Highway 97. Phone (604) 788-2747. Box 42, Chetwynd, BC V0C 1J0. [ADVERTISEMENT] ▲
 PG 184 (296.1 km) **DC 66** (106.2 km) Gas station.
 PG 186.1 (299.5 km) **DC 63.9** (102.8 km) Welcome to Chetwynd sign.

Chetwynd

PG 187.6 (301.9 km) **DC 62.4** (100.4 km) Located on Highway 97 at the junction with Highway 29 north to the Alaska Highway via Hudson's Hope, and south to Tumbler Ridge. **Population:** 3,000, area 7,000. **Emergency Services:** RCMP, phone 788-9221. **Hospital, Poison Control Centre** and **Ambulance,** phone 1-562-7241. **Fire Department,** phone 788-2345.
 Visitor Information: Chamber of Commerce, open 8 A.M. to 8 P.M. May 24 to Sept. 2; open 9 A.M. to 4 P.M. rest of year. Write Box 1000, Chetwynd V0C 1J0, or phone 788-3345 or 788-3655. Chetwynd Infocentre is located on Highway 97 near the town's Little Giant statue. Free caboose museum adjacent the infocentre displays railway artifacts. The Little Prairie Heritage Museum, located on Highway 97 at the west end of town, features the region's pioneer days; inquire at infocentre for directions.
 Elevation: 2,017 feet/615m. **Radio:** CFGP 105, CISN-FM 102, CJDC 890, CKNL 560, CBC 1170, CFMI-FM 103.9. **Television:** 7 channels (includes CBC, BCTV, ABC, CBS and NBC) plus pay cable.

SILVER SANDS LODGE
Mile 147 — PINE PASS, B.C.

Open 7 Days A Week
Gas • Oil
Groceries • Coffee • Liquor Agency
Rooms & Cabins
Campground • Showers
Fishing & Hunting Supplies
and Licenses

Radio Phone: N698406
Pine Valley Channel   VISA

43 Miles West of Chetwynd on Highway 97
Mile 147, Box 628, Chetwynd, BC V0C 1J0

CHETWYND ESSO (Esso)
CONVENIENCE STORE
• Full Service • Diesel • Propane
• Tires and Tire Repairs • Licensed Mechanics
• Fishing Supplies and Information
Bug Screens and Headlight Protectors Installed

Junction of Highway 97 and
Highway 29 at the lights.

Chetwynd, BC
(604) 788-2320

62   The MILEPOST® ■ 1992

The town was formerly known as Little Prairie and is a division point on the British Columbia Railway. The name was changed to honour the late British Columbia Minister of Railways Ralph Chetwynd, who was instrumental in the northward extension of the province-owned railway.

Chetwynd lies at the northern end of one of the largest known coal deposits on earth. Access from Chetwynd south to Tumbler Ridge and the resource development known as the North East Coal is via Highway 29 south, a 66-mile/106-km paved road. Gwillim Lake Provincial Park, with 49 campsites, fishing, boating, hiking and picnicking, is 32 miles/52 km south of Chetwynd on this road. Forestry, mining, natural gas processing, ranching and farming are the main industries in Chetwynd. Louisiana Pacific has a modern nonpolluting pulp mill here. Free guided industrial tours.

Chetwynd has several large motels, restaurants, banks, post office, laundromat, gas stations, supermarkets, art gallery and golf course. Good traveler's stop with easy access to all services. Chetwynd has a leisure centre with a wave pool; open daily 6 A.M. to 10 P.M., visitors welcome. A big annual event here is the Bluegrass Festival held in July. Chetwynd also hosts the annual National Rodeo Assoc. finals in its indoor rodeo arena.

Free municipal campground in town with 20 sites and dump station. There's also a dump station at the car/truck wash. There are also private tent and trailer parks in town and at Moberly Lake. Moberly Lake Provincial Park is 12 miles/19.3 km north of Chetwynd via Highway 29 north (see Milepost PG 187.9) and 1.9 miles/3 km west via a gravel road. The park has 109 campsites, beach, picnic area, playground, nature trail, boat launch and a private marina next door with boat rental and concession. There's good swimming at huge Moberly Lake on a warm summer day. Worth the drive. ▲

Chetwynd is 1 of 8 northeastern British Columbia communities taking part in the Alaska Highway Rendezvous '92, the 50th anniversary of the construction of the Alaska Highway. Chetwynd is also celebrating the 40th anniversary of the Hart Highway and its own 30th anniversary. Declared the 1992 Forestry Capital of Canada, Chetwynd has decorated the community with unique chain saw wildlife sculptures. Scheduled events in 1992 include the Canada-U.S. Summer Curling Bonspiel (June 28 to July 5) and the 10th annual Bluegrass Music Festival (July 4-6). For more information about Alaska Highway Rendezvous '92 events in Chetwynd, contact the AHR '92 committee, Box 1880, Chetwynd, BC V0C 1J0, or phone 788-2992.

West Access Route Log

(continued)

PG 187.8 (302.2 km) **DC 62.2** (100.1 km) Highway crosses railroad tracks.

PG 187.9 (302.4 km) **DC 62.1** (99.9 km) **Junction** with Highway 29 north, which leads 12 miles/19.3 km to Moberly Lake, 36.5 miles/58.7 km to Peace River Provincial Recreation Area and Peace Canyon dam, and 40.4 miles/64.9 km to community of Hudson's Hope and access to W.A.C. Bennett Dam; Highway 29 connects with the Alaska Highway 53.7 miles/86.4 km north of Dawson Creek. (See HUDSON'S HOPE LOOP section for details.)

Highway climbs next 12 miles/19 km for Dawson Creek-bound motorists.

PG 189.4 (304.8 km) **DC 60.6** (97.5 km) **Junction** with Highway 29 (paved) south to Sukunka Falls, Gwillim Lake and **TUMBLER RIDGE** (description follows). Tumbler Ridge is also accessible from **Milepost PG 237.7** via the Heritage Highway.

The townsite was built in conjunction with development of the North East Coal resource and is British Columbia's newest community. Tumbler Ridge has a motel, shopping facilities, and a distinctive town hall. Camping facilities include the Lion's Campground (28 sites, showers) and a RV park with hookups. Tours of the open-pit coal mines (Canada's largest) are available during the summer; phone the chamber of commerce at 242-4702 for booking information. Special events in Tumbler Ridge include the Arts and Crafts Fair (June 27-29, 1992) and the annual Grizzly Valley Days Fair and Rodeo (Aug. 14-16, 1992). Snowmobiling is a popular winter sport here, and the local Ridge Riders Snowmobile Club sponsored the Alaska Challenge Snowmobile Safari as part of the 50th anniversary of the Alaska Highway. For more information

---

CHETWYND ADVERTISERS

Chetwynd Esso.................At the traffic lights
District of Chetwynd........Ph. (604) 788-2281
Pine Cone Motor Inn.......Ph. 1-800-663-8082
Robert's Auto Repair........Ph. (604) 788-9194
Swiss Inn
   Restaurant, The.....0.5 mile E of traffic light

The Swiss Inn RESTAURANT

SEAFOOD • PIZZA • SALAD BAR
SCHNITZEL • LUNCH BUFFET

VISA MasterCard AMERICAN EXPRESS

Chetwynd, BC – (604) 788-2566

Super, Natural Scenic Adventure

Welcome to the Heart of Northeast Coal Country
... Chetwynd's Finest
LICENSED RESTAURANT
(6 a.m. to 10:30 p.m.)
54 UNITS • 13 with Kitchenettes
Air Conditioning

PINE CONE motor inn
RESERVATIONS ARRANGED NO CHARGE
Box 686, Chetwynd, BC V0C 1J0
Phone (604) 788-3311 • 1-800-663-8082

Robert's Auto Repair   Chevron

BCAA AUTHORIZED ROAD SERVICE

Regular • Unleaded • Supreme Unleaded
Licensed Mechanic • 24-Hour Towing
(604) 788-9194   Chetwynd, BC
MasterCard VISA

CHETWYND British Columbia
Forestry Capital of Canada 1992

1992 FORESTRY CAPITAL OF CANADA

A **FOUR SEASON** recreation and tourism community offers clean, fresh mountain air, some of the best camping, hunting and fishing to be found in **BEAUTIFUL BRITISH COLUMBIA. Home** to a natural playground for all types of wildlife including deer, elk, Canada geese, ptarmigan, moose and black bear. You are invited to visit our **Leisure (WAVE) Pool Center**, soak up the sunshine, hospitality and experience a trip into **Canada's last true frontier!**

Your **SUPER, NATURAL SCENIC ADVENTURE** into the Peace River Country begins here.

Sponsors: District of Chetwynd (788-2281)
Econ. Dev. Commission (788-2281)

Chetwynd — Little Giant of the Peace

about Alaska Highway Rendezvous '92 events in Tumbler Ridge, contact the AHR '92 committee, Box 100, Tumbler Ridge, BC V0C 2W0, or phone 242-4242. For information on Tumbler Ridge, write the Chamber of Commerce, Box 606, Tumbler Ridge, BC V0C 2W0.

Monkman Provincial Park, site of spectacular 225-foot/69m Kinuseo (Keh-NEW-see-oh) Falls, lies south of Tumbler Ridge. A new (1991) 40-site campground is accessible via a 25-mile/40-km road from Tumbler Ridge. Viewing platform of falls at campground; backcountry hiking. Monkman Park is also accessible by jet boat trip up the Murray River, fly-in or by horseback trip. Contact BC Parks in Prince George (565-6270), Fort St. John or Tumbler Ridge for more information. ▲

PG 199.3 (320.7 km) **DC 50.7** (81.6 km) Gravel turnouts with litter barrels both sides of highway.

PG 201.2 (323.8 km) **DC 48.8** (78.5 km) Slow down for sharp curve across railroad tracks.

PG 205.6 (330.9 km) **DC 44.4** (71.5 km) Turnout with litter barrel and a commanding view of the East Pine River valley to the south.

PG 206.5 (332.3 km) **DC 43.5** (70 km) Sharp curves approximately next 2 miles/3.2 km as highway descends toward Dawson Creek. View of Table Mountain.

PG 207.9 (334.6 km) **DC 42.1** (67.7 km) Highway crosses under railroad.

PG 208 (334.7 km) **DC 42** (67.6 km) **Fort Sasquatsch**, Box 133, Groundbirch, BC V0C 1T0. Phone (604) 788-9671, fax (604) 785-4424. Soft adventure lodge, A-frame cabins, kitchen and bathroom, American plan available. Guided canoeing, rafting, horseback riding, hiking at scenic East Pine, where Pine and Murray rivers meet. Ask Wolfgang about local gold deposits. Smokers, nonsmokers, kids and pets welcome. Enjoy Super, Natural Scenic Adventure. [ADVERTISEMENT]

PG 208.1 (334.9 km) **DC 41.9** (67.4 km) Sharp turn to south at west end of bridge for East Pine Provincial Park (0.5 mile on gravel road); picnicking and boat launch on Pine River. Turnout with litter barrel at park entrance.

From East Pine Provincial Park, canoeists may make a 2-day canoe trip down the Pine River to the Peace River; take-out at Taylor Landing Provincial Park (at **Milepost DC 34** on the Alaska Highway). Check with Fort Sasquatsch for current river conditions.

PG 208.2 (335.1 km) **DC 41.8** (67.3 km) Bridge across East Pine River. Railroad also crosses river here.

PG 208.3 (335.2 km) **DC 41.7** (67.1 km) Turnout with litter barrel to south.

PG 209.8 (337.6 km) **DC 40.2** (64.7 km) East Pine (unincorporated) has a store, gas station and distinctive treehouse.

PG 211.7 (340.7 km) **DC 38.3** (61.6 km) Turnout with litter barrel to north.

PG 217.4 (349.8 km) **DC 32.6** (52.5 km) Gas station and store.

PG 221.5 (356.5 km) **DC 28.5** (45.9 km) Turnouts with litter barrels both sides of highway.

PG 222 (357.3 km) **DC 28** (45 km) **GROUNDBIRCH** (unincorporated), gas station with diesel, store, laundromat and campground. ▲

Groundbirch General Store and Campground. See display ad this section.

PG 228.7 (368 km) **DC 21.3** (34.3 km) **Country Vacations At The Kiskatinaw River Ranch.** Turn north, proceed 7 miles/1 km, located junction of Sunset Creek Kiskatinaw River between John Hart Highway and Alaska Highway. Interested in "life in the slow lanes"? Please try our guest ranch atmosphere! Rural, remote, peaceful, pastoral. 3-, 5- or 7-night bookings. 2 cabins. Fresh air and room to roam. Also group barbecues on the river with travel by team and wagon. Some space for overnight camping and RV units. Your hosts: The Nimitzes, Box 908, Dawson Creek, BC V1G 1L6. (604) 843-7108. Enjoy Super, Natural Scenic Adventure. [ADVERTISEMENT]

PG 230.7 (371.3 km) **DC 19.3** (31.1 km) Progress (unincorporated), highway maintenance yard, cairn and pay phone.

PG 234.4 (377.2 km) **DC 15.6** (25.1 km) Turnout with litter barrels to north.

PG 237.7 (382.5 km) **DC 12.3** (19.8 km) **Junction** with Heritage Highway, which leads 59.5 miles/96 km south to the community of Tumbler Ridge and access roads to the North East Coal Development. (Tumbler Ridge is also accessible via Highway 29 south from Chetwynd. See description of Tumbler Ridge at **Milepost PG 189.4**.) This stretch of the Heritage Highway is paved to Mile 18/29 km, then gravel surfaced to Mile 55/89 km.

From Tumbler Ridge, the Heritage Highway continues 92 miles/148 km east and north to connect with Highway 2 southeast of Dawson Creek. Inquire locally about road conditions.

PG 238 (383 km) **DC 12** (19.3 km) Kiskatinaw River bridge.

PG 239.5 (385.4 km) **DC 10.5** (16.9 km) **Willow Creek Farms Bed and Breakfast.** Located east of Heritage Highway junction on Hart Highway. Turn south on Road 239; drive 1.63 miles (2.6 km). Enjoy quiet, friendly atmosphere. Two large bedrooms, shared bath in modern, colonial farmhouse, 15 minutes from Dawson Creek. Hearty, homemade breakfasts. See our display ad in Dawson Creek section. $55 double, $45 single. Your hosts: Dan and Sharon Bell. (604) 843-7253. Box 2121, Dawson Creek, BC V1G 4K9. [ADVERTISEMENT]

PG 240.7 (387.4 km) **DC 9.3** (15 km) Arras (unincorporated), cafe and gas station.

PG 247.9 (398.9 km) **DC 2.1** (3.4 km) Small turnout with litter barrel and point of interest sign to south.

PG 249.9 (402.2 km) **DC 0.1** (0.2 km) Entering Dawson Creek. Private campground on south side of highway; Rotary Lake Park and camping on north side of highway. ▲

PG 250 (402.3 km) **DC 0** **Junction** of the Hart Highway and Alaska Highway; turn right for downtown Dawson Creek. See description of Dawson Creek in the ALASKA HIGHWAY section.

COUNTRY VACATIONS AT THE KISKATINAW RIVER RANCH
FEATURING
"Life in the Slow Lanes"
Located at the junction of Sunset Creek and Kiskatinaw River
(604) 843-7108
Box 908, Dawson Creek, BC V1G 1L6
Super, Natural Scenic Adventure

GROUNDBIRCH GENERAL STORE AND CAMPGROUND

- GROCERIES
- LIQUOR AGENCY
- COLD BEER • ICE
- GAS
- PROPANE
- DIESEL
- POST OFFICE

- LAUNDROMAT
- SHOWERS
- VIDEO RENTALS
- WELL WATER
- HUNTING AND FISHING LICENSES
- EASY ACCESS

- PULL-THROUGHS
- HOOKUPS
- SANI-DUMP
- LARGE CAMPSITES
- FIRE PITS
- PICNIC TABLES
- PLAY AREAS

VISA / MasterCard
Visit our local Reindeer Farm

Discounts For Seniors
PHONE (604) 780-2334

Super, Natural Scenic Adventure

HUDSON'S HOPE LOOP

**Chetwynd, British Columbia, to the Alaska Highway
BC Highway 29**
(See map page 66)

The Hudson's Hope Loop Road links the John Hart Highway (Highway 97) with the Alaska Highway (also Highway 97). This 86.9-mile/139.8-km paved loop road provides year-round access to the town of Hudson's Hope, W.A.C. Bennett Dam, Peace Canyon Dam and Moberly Lake. Highway 29 is a good 2-lane road but steep and winding in places.

A popular side trip with Alaska Highway travelers today, and an alternate access route to the Alaska Highway, Highway 29 was only a 53-mile side road to the Hudson Hope Coal Mines in the 1950s. In the 1960s, with construction of the W.A.C. Bennett Dam under way, Alaska Highway travelers drove the side road to see the Peace River dam site. The highway was completed to Chetwynd in 1968.

Hudson's Hope Loop Road Log

Distance from Chetwynd (C) is followed by distance from Alaska Highway Junction (AH).

C 0 AH 86.9 (139.8 km) Junction of Highways 29 and 97 at Chetwynd (see **Milepost PG 187.6** in the WEST ACCESS ROUTE section for description of Chetwynd).

C 0.5 (0.8 km) AH 86.4 (139 km) Truck weigh scales to west.

C 2.3 (3.7 km) AH 84.6 (136.1 km) Jackfish Road to east.

C 5 (8 km) AH 81.9 (131.8 km) Turnout with litter barrel to west.

C 12 (19.3 km) AH 74.9 (120.5 km) Gravel access road leads 2 miles/3.2 km west to **Moberly Lake** Provincial Park on south shore; 109 campsites, swimming, waterskiing, picnicking, drinking water, dump station, boat launch, $7 camping fee. Moberly Marina adjacent park. This beautiful 9-mile-/14.5-km-long lake drains at its south end into Moberly River, which in turn runs into the Peace River. Fishing for lake trout, Dolly Varden and whitefish.

C 12.2 (19.6 km) AH 74.7 (120.2 km) Moberly River bridge; parking area with litter barrel at south end.

C 15.9 (25.6 km) AH 71 (114.3 km) Highway cairn is memorial to John Moberly, fur trader and explorer who first landed here in 1865.

C 16.4 (26.4 km) AH 70.5 (113.5 km) Spencer Tuck Provincial Park; picnic tables, swimming, fishing and boat launch.

C 17.4 (28 km) AH 69.5 (111.8 km) **Harv's Resort**, on the north shore of beautiful Moberly Lake. Treed picnic sites, large grass picnic field, cabins and campsites, hookups. Swimming, fishing, pay phone and showers. Store, restaurant, and licensed dining room. Gas, oils, propane, hunting and fishing licenses. Boat launch and golf course nearby. Your hosts, Harve and Darlene Evans. Open till 10 P.M. daily. (604) 788-9145. [ADVERTISEMENT]

C 18.3 (29.4 km) AH 68.6 (110.4 km) **MOBERLY LAKE.** Post office, cafe, store and pay phone.

C 18.5 (29.8 km) AH 68.4 (110.1 km) Moberly Lake and District Golf Club, 0.7 mile/1.1 km from highway; 9 holes, grass greens, rentals, clubhouse, licensed lounge. Open May to September.

C 25.4 (40.9 km) AH 61.5 (99 km) Cameron Lake camping area; tables, water, toilets, firewood, playground, horseshoe pits, boat launch and swimming. Camping fee $8.

C 30.7 (49.4 km) AH 56.2 (90.4 km) Gravel turnout with litter barrel to east. Highway descends northbound to Hudson's Hope.

C 35.9 (57.8 km) AH 51 (82.1 km) Bridge over Peace River; paved turnouts at both ends of bridge with concrete totem pole sculptures. View of Peace Canyon dam.

C 36.5 (58.7 km) AH 50.4 (81.1 km) Turnoff to west for Dinosaur Lake Campground and B.C. Hydro Peace Canyon dam. The visitor centre, 0.6 mile/1 km in on paved access road, is open from 8 A.M. to 4 P.M. daily from late May through Labor Day; Monday through Friday the rest of the year (closed holidays). Self-guided tour includes models of dinosaurs, a tableau portraying Alexander Mackenzie's discovery of the Peace River canyon, and a scale model of a steamboat. A pictorial display traces the construction of the Peace Canyon dam. You may view the dam spillway from the visitor centre. Get permission before walking across top of dam.

Dinosaur Lake Campground, on Dinosaur Lake, has 30 campsites with firepits, water, toilets and tables. Boat launch and swimming area. Camping fee $8.

C 38.3 (61.6 km) AH 48.6 (78.2 km) Alwin Holland Memorial Park (0.5 mile/0.8 km east of highway) is named for the first teacher in Hudson's Hope, who willed his property, known locally as The Glen, to be used as a public park. There are 17 campsites, picnic grounds, barbecues and water. Camping fee $8.

C 38.9 (62.6 km) AH 48 (77.2 km) Welcome to Hudson's Hope sign.

C 39 (62.8 km) AH 47.9 (77.1 km) King Gething Park; small campground with 15 grassy sites, picnic tables, cookhouse, toilets

Information on Hudson's Hope is available at the museum. (Earl L. Brown, staff)

HUDSON'S HOPE LOOP Chetwynd, BC, to Milepost DC 53.7 Alaska Highway

and dump station east side of highway. Camping fee $8.

Hudson's Hope

C 40.4 (65 km) AH 46.5 (74.8 km) **Population:** 1,158. **Emergency Services: RCMP,** phone 783-5241. **Fire Department,** phone 783-5700. **Ambulance,** phone 112-562-7241. **Medical Clinic,** phone 783-9991.

Visitor Information: A log building houses the tourist information booth at Beattie Park, across from the museum and St. Peter's Anglican United Church. Open daily mid-May to mid-September, hours are 8 A.M. to 8 P.M. mid-May to August, 9 A.M. to 5 P.M. in September. Phone 783-9154 or write Box 330, Hudson's Hope, BC V0C 1V0. (Off-season, phone the district office at 783-9901.)

Elevation: 1,707 feet/520m. **Climate:** Summer temperatures range from 60°F/16°C to 90°F/32°C, with an average of 135 frost-free days annually. **Radio:** CBC, CKNL 560, CJDC 870. **Television:** Channels 2, 5, 8, 11 and cable.

Private Aircraft: Hudson's Hope airstrip, 3.7 miles/6 km west; elev. 2,200 feet/671m; length 5,200 feet/1,585m; asphalt.

Hudson's Hope is the third oldest permanently settled community in British Columbia. The site was first visited in 1793 by Alexander Mackenzie. In 1805 a Hudson's Bay trading post was established here by Simon Fraser. In 1916, after the fur-trading days were over, a major influx of settlers arrived in the area. It was the head of navigation for steamboats on the lower Peace River until 1936, the year of the last scheduled steamboat run. Area coal mines supplied Alaska Highway maintenance camps during the 1940s.

Modern development of Hudson's Hope was spurred by construction of the Peace Power project in the 1960s. Today the area's principal claim to fame is the 600-foot-/183-m-high W.A.C. Bennett Dam at the upper end of the Peace River canyon, 15 miles/24 km west of Hudson's Hope. The 100-million-ton dam is one of the largest earth-fill struc-

BChydro — BChydro

FREE DAM TOURS

W.A.C BENNETT DAM
(604) 783-5211

Located 15 miles West of Hudson's Hope. Visitor center, complete with snack shop. Hands-on displays describe the history of electricity, what it is, how it is produced and the B.C. Hydro system. A short film is shown and then a bus takes visitors 500 feet underground into one of the largest powerhouses in the world.

PEACE CANYON
(604) 783-9943

Located 5 miles South of Hudson's Hope. This is a self-guided tour of one of B.C. Hydro's newest dams. Displays describe the construction of the dam and the history of the Peace from the time that the dinosaurs roamed the area.

HUDSON'S HOPE ADVERTISERS

B.C. Hydro ....Ph. (604) 783-5211 or 9943
District of
  Hudson's Hope ....Ph. (604) 783-9901
Hudson's Hope
  Gourmet Pizza ......Across from Beattie Park
Hudson's Hope Tempo .....Ph. (604) 783-5256
Kyllo Bros. ....Ph. (604) 783-5248

66 The MILEPOST® ■ 1992

tures in the world and Williston Lake, behind it, is the largest body of fresh water in British Columbia. Tours of the Gordon M. Shrum generating station are available daily from mid-May through Thanksgiving weekend, weekdays only the remainder of the year (closed holidays). Check with the visitor bureau for tour schedule.

Also of interest is the Hudson's Hope Museum on Highway 29 in town. The museum has a fine collection of artifacts and dinosaur fossils from the Peace District. Souvenir shop in the museum. Next door to the museum is the log St. Peter's Anglican United Church (still in use).

Visitor services in Hudson's Hope include a motel, hotel, 3 restaurants, 3 service stations, a laundromat, supermarket, and convenience and hardware stores. There are also a bank, post office, liquor store, community hall, library, swimming pool, tennis courts, and numerous parks and playgrounds. Sightseeing and flightseeing tours are available locally. The main business district is along Highway 29 and adjoining streets. The RCMP office is at the corner of 100th Street and 100th Avenue.

Special Events. The W.A.C. Bennett Dam celebrates its 25th anniversary in 1992 and reunions for dam workers will be held 3 weekends in August. The Hudson's Hope High School Reunion will be on the last weekend in July and the first and third weekends in August. The annual Demolition Derby is held on Father's Day weekend. The Portage Mountain Yacht Club Fishing Derby is at Williston Lake the first weekend in August. For more information about Alaska Highway Rendezvous '92 events in Hudson's Hope, contact AHR '92 Committee, Box 492, Hudson's Hope, BC V0C 1V0, or phone 783-9901.

Hudson's Hope Loop Road Log

(continued)

C 41.2 (66.3 km) AH 45.7 (73.5 km) Turnout to north with Hudson's Hope visitor map.

C 44 (70.8 km) AH 42.9 (69 km) Lynx Creek bridge.

C 48.3 (77.7 km) AH 38.6 (62.1 km) Pay phone, north side of road.

C 48.4 (77.9 km) AH 38.5 (62 km) Turnout to north for view of the Peace River.

C 50.9 (81.9 km) AH 36 (57.9 km) Farrell Creek bridge and picnic site.

C 56.6 (91.1 km) AH 30.3 (48.8 km) Pull-through turnout with litter barrels. View of Peace River valley.

C 57.1 (91.9 km) AH 29.8 (48 km) Turnout to south with litter barrels and view of Peace River valley.

C 59.3 (95.4 km) AH 27.6 (44.4 km) Turnout to south with litter barrels.

C 64.7 (104.1 km) AH 22.2 (35.7 km) Halfway River.

C 67.2 (108.1 km) AH 19.7 (31.7 km) Rest area to south with point of interest sign, litter barrel and toilet. A slide occurred here on May 26, 1973, involving an estimated 10 million to 15 million cubic yards of overburden. Slide debris completely blocked the river channel for some 12 hours, backing up the river an estimated 24 feet/7m above normal level.

C 68.4 (110.1 km) AH 18.5 (29.8 km) Milepost 19.

C 71.1 (114.4 km) AH 15.8 (25.4 km) Turnout to north.

C 71.4 (114.9 km) AH 15.5 (24.9 km) Milepost 16.

C 73.5 (118.3 km) AH 13.4 (21.6 km) Beaver dam to north.

C 74.6 (120.1 km) AH 12.3 (19.8 km) Cache Creek 1-lane bridge. Turnout to north at east end of bridge for picnic area with litter barrels.

C 76.6 (123.3 km) AH 10.3 (16.6 km) Turnout with litter barrel to north overlooking Bear Flat in the Peace River valley. Highway begins climb eastbound.

C 78.1 (125.6 km) AH 8.8 (14.2 km) Highest point on Highway 29 (2,750 feet/838m) overlooking Peace River Plateau. Highway descends 10 percent grade westbound.

C 86.9 (139.8 km) AH 0 Junction with the Alaska Highway, 6.7 miles/10.8 km north of Fort St. John (see **Milepost DC 53.7** in the ALASKA HIGHWAY section).

One of two concrete sculptures at the Peace River Bridge. (Earl L. Brown, staff)

HUDSON'S HOPE — TEMPO
GAS • OIL • DIESEL • PROPANE
Open Daily 7:00 a.m. — 8:00 p.m.
≡ 783-5256 ≡
MARGS MINI MART
GROCERIES • ICE • HOT COFFEE
MacKeigan Enterprises Ltd.
Box 540 Hwy. 29
Hudson's Hope, B.C. V0C 1V0

FLY SPECTACULAR ROCKY MTN. Trench To WILDERNESS FT. GRAHAM LODGE

AFFORDABLE Custom Tours – 3 hours to 30 days. **EXCITING** Trophy Fishing, Trail Rides, Hiking, Gold Panning, Fossils, Riverboat Tours, Indian Villages, or just **RELAXING** scenic Flight to FT. GRAHAM LODGE for brunch.

DON'T MISS OUT – CALL NOW!   *special group packages*

Phone (604) 783-5248 • FAX (604) 783-9125
KYLLO BROS.
Box 238, Hudson's Hope, B.C. V0C 1V0
Super, Natural Scenic Adventure

HUDSON'S HOPE
GOURMET PIZZA
The Ultimate Taste
Licensed Dining Lounge & Restaurant
Open 7 days a week
(Summer hours 6:00 a.m. — 10:00 p.m.)
At Peace Glen Coffee Shop & Hotel
Laundromat adjacent
Across from Beattie Park, Hudson's Hope
(604) 783-9966
Super, Natural Scenic Adventure

Home of Dudley Dinosaur — WELCOME!

VISIT THE LAND OF DINOSAURS AND DAMS
HUDSON'S HOPE, BC
"The Playground of the Peace"

Phone (604) 783-9901
Box 330
Hudson's Hope, BC V0C 1V0

Super, Natural Scenic Adventure

ALASKA HIGHWAY

Dawson Creek, British Columbia, to Fairbanks, Alaska
BC Highway 97, Yukon Highway 1 and Alaska Route 2
(See maps, pages 69–73)

The Alaska Highway stretches in a northwesterly direction from Mile 0 at Dawson Creek, BC, through Yukon Territory to Mile 1520 at Fairbanks, AK. Although the Alaska Highway does not compare with highways in the Lower 48, it is no longer a wilderness road but rather a road through the wilderness. The Alaska Highway is driven by thousands of people each year in all sorts of vehicles. The highway is open and maintained year-round.

The Alaska Highway was built in 1942. For more on the history of the highway and on the 50th anniversary celebration in 1992, see the INTRODUCTION section. Historical highlights and special events in highway communities are included in the ALASKA HIGHWAY log following.

Road conditions

Almost all of the Alaska Highway between Dawson Creek, BC, and Fairbanks, AK, is asphalt-surfaced. Repaving and highway improvement continue. Surfacing of the Alaska Highway ranges from poor to excellent.

There are stretches of poor surfacing with many chuckholes, gravel breaks (sections of gravel ranging from a few feet to several miles), hardtop with loose gravel, deteriorated shoulders and bumps. On the Alaska portion of the highway, watch for frost heaves. This rippling effect in the pavement is caused by the freezing and thawing of the ground. Drive slowly in sections of frost heaves to avoid breaking an axle or trailer hitch.

Surfacing on much of the highway is fair, with older patched pavement and a minimum of gravel breaks and chuckholes. There are also sections of excellent surfacing where highway maintenance crews have recently upgraded the road.

Travelers should keep in mind that road conditions are subject to change! Weather and traffic may cause deterioration of newer pavement, while construction may improve older sections. Always be alert for bumps and holes in the road and for abrupt changes in highway surfacing.

Always watch for construction crews along the Alaska Highway. Extensive road construction may require a detour or travelers may be delayed while waiting for a pilot car to guide them through the construction. Motorists may also encounter some muddy roadway at construction areas if there are heavy rains while the roadbed is torn up.

For current road conditions from Dawson Creek to the BC-YT border, phone the Peace River Alaska Highway Tourist Assoc. in Fort St. John at (604) 785-2544, or the Dawson Creek Tourist Infocentre at (604) 782-9595.

The Alaska Highway winds along Muncho Lake. (Philip and Karen Smith)

Driving Information

The Alaska Highway is a 2-lane highway that winds and rolls across the wilderness. There are sections of road with no centerline and stretches of narrow highway with little or no shoulder. The best advice is to take your time; drive with your headlights on at all times; keep to the right on hills and corners; and—as you would on any highway anywhere else—drive defensively.

Dust and mud may be a problem in construction areas and on some stretches of the highway. Gravel road is treated with calcium chloride to keep the dust down. This substance corrodes paint and metal: wash your vehicle as soon as possible. In heavy rains, calcium chloride and mud combine to make a very slippery road surface; drive carefully! There are relatively few steep grades. The most mountainous section of highway is between Fort Nelson and Watson Lake, as the highway crosses the Rocky Mountains. Flying gravel—which may damage headlights, radiators, gas tanks, windshields and paint—is still a problem. There are many sections of hardtop with loose gravel and gravel breaks along the highway. Side roads and access roads to campgrounds and other destinations are generally not paved. Keep in mind that many highways in the Yukon and some highways in Alaska are gravel.

Gas, food, and lodging are found along the Alaska Highway on an average of every 20 to 50 miles. (The longest stretch without services is about 100 miles.) Not all businesses are open year-round, nor are most services available 24 hours a day. There are dozens of government and private campgrounds along the highway.

Remember that you will be driving in 2 different countries which use 2 different currencies: For the best rate, exchange your money at a bank. There are several banks in Dawson Creek, Fort St. John, Whitehorse and Fairbanks. There are 2 banks in Fort Nelson, 1 in Watson Lake and 1 in Delta Junction. Haines Junction has banking service at the general store.

Read the following sections in GENERAL INFORMATION in the back of the book: Customs Requirements, Driving Information, Holidays and Money/Credit Cards.

(Continues on page 74)

ALASKA HIGHWAY Dawson Creek, BC, to Milepost DC 409

ALASKA HIGHWAY — Milepost DC 409 to Teslin, YT

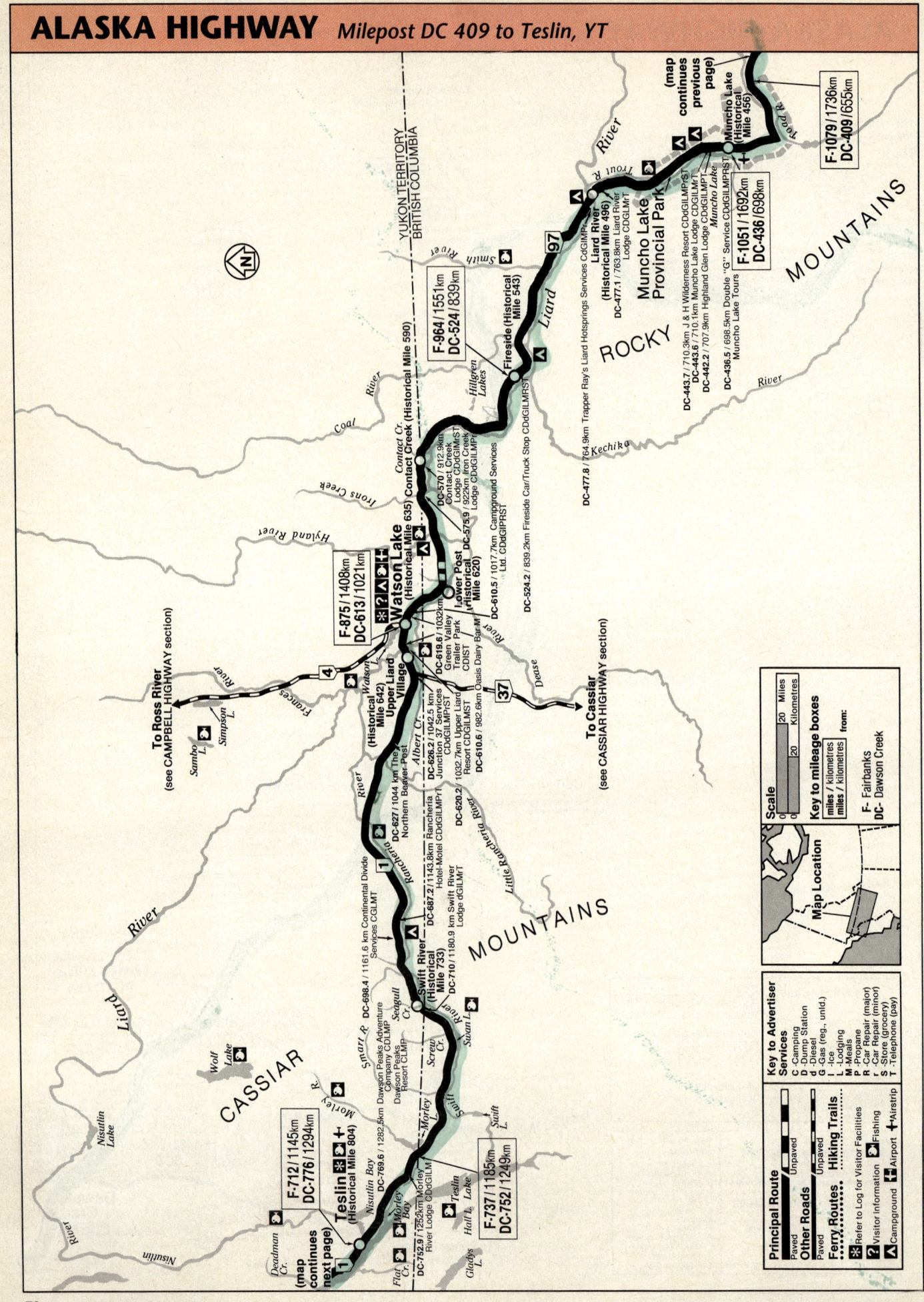

ALASKA HIGHWAY — Teslin, YT, to Milepost DC 1136

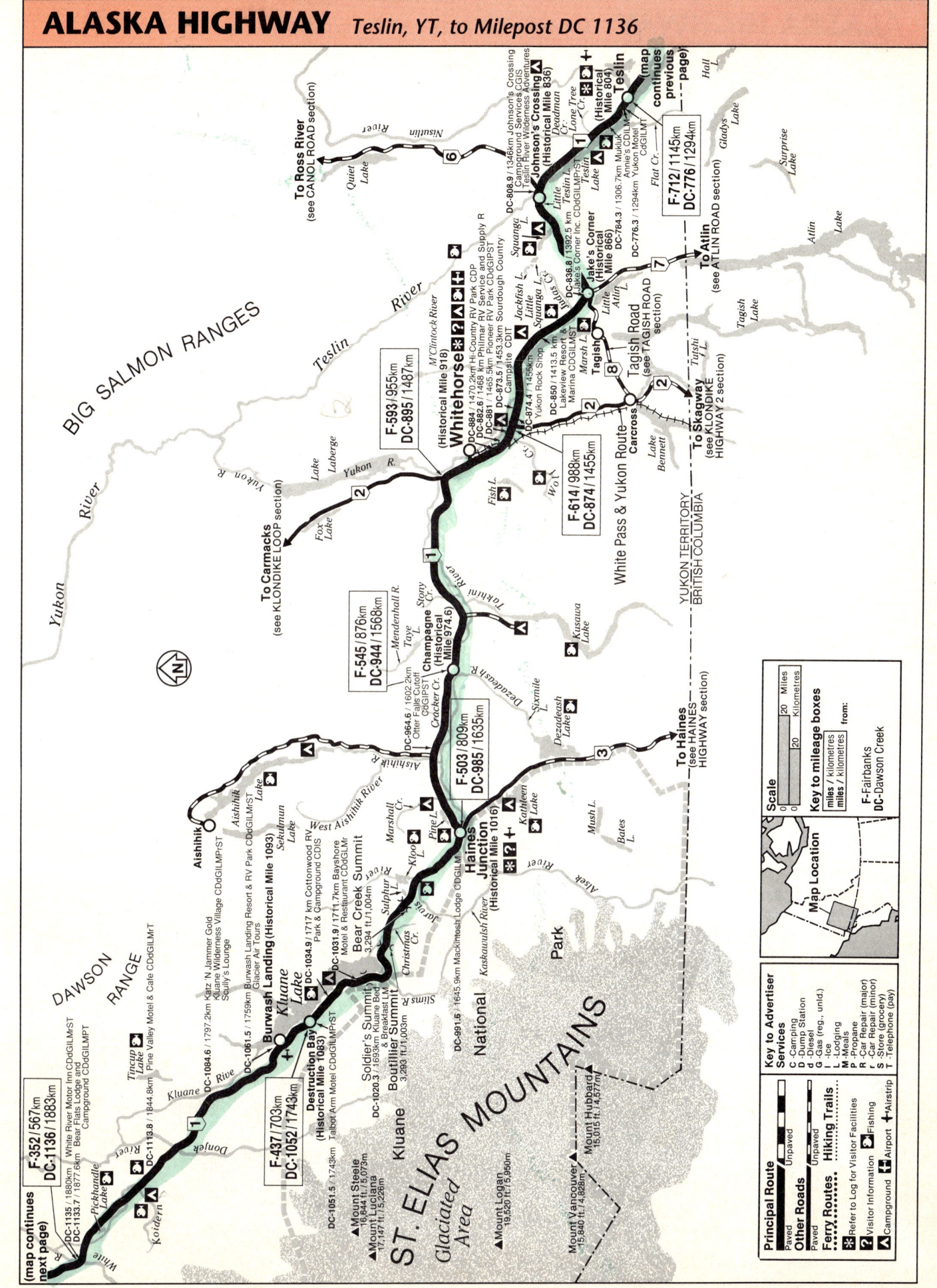

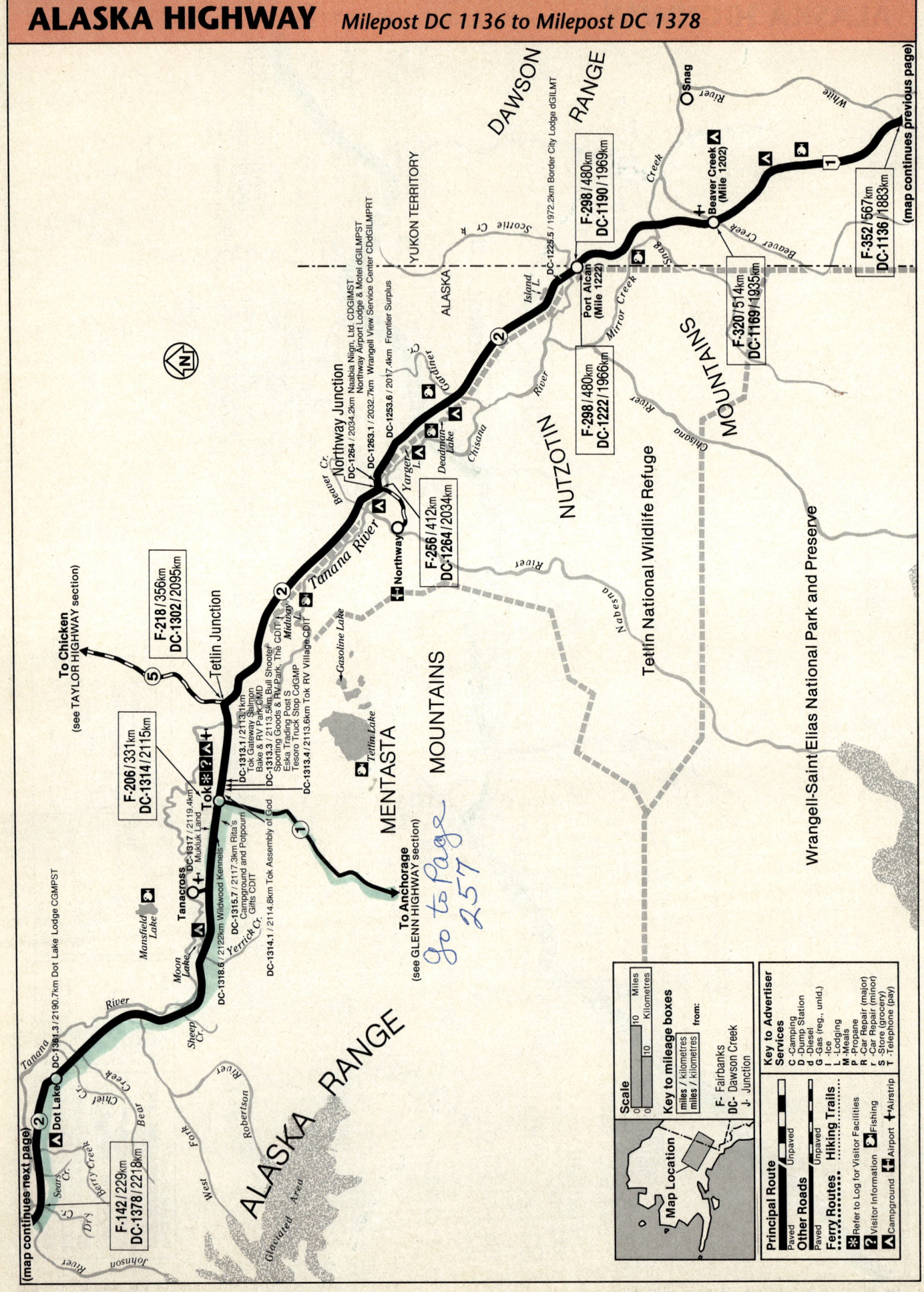

ALASKA HIGHWAY — Milepost DC 1136 to Milepost DC 1378

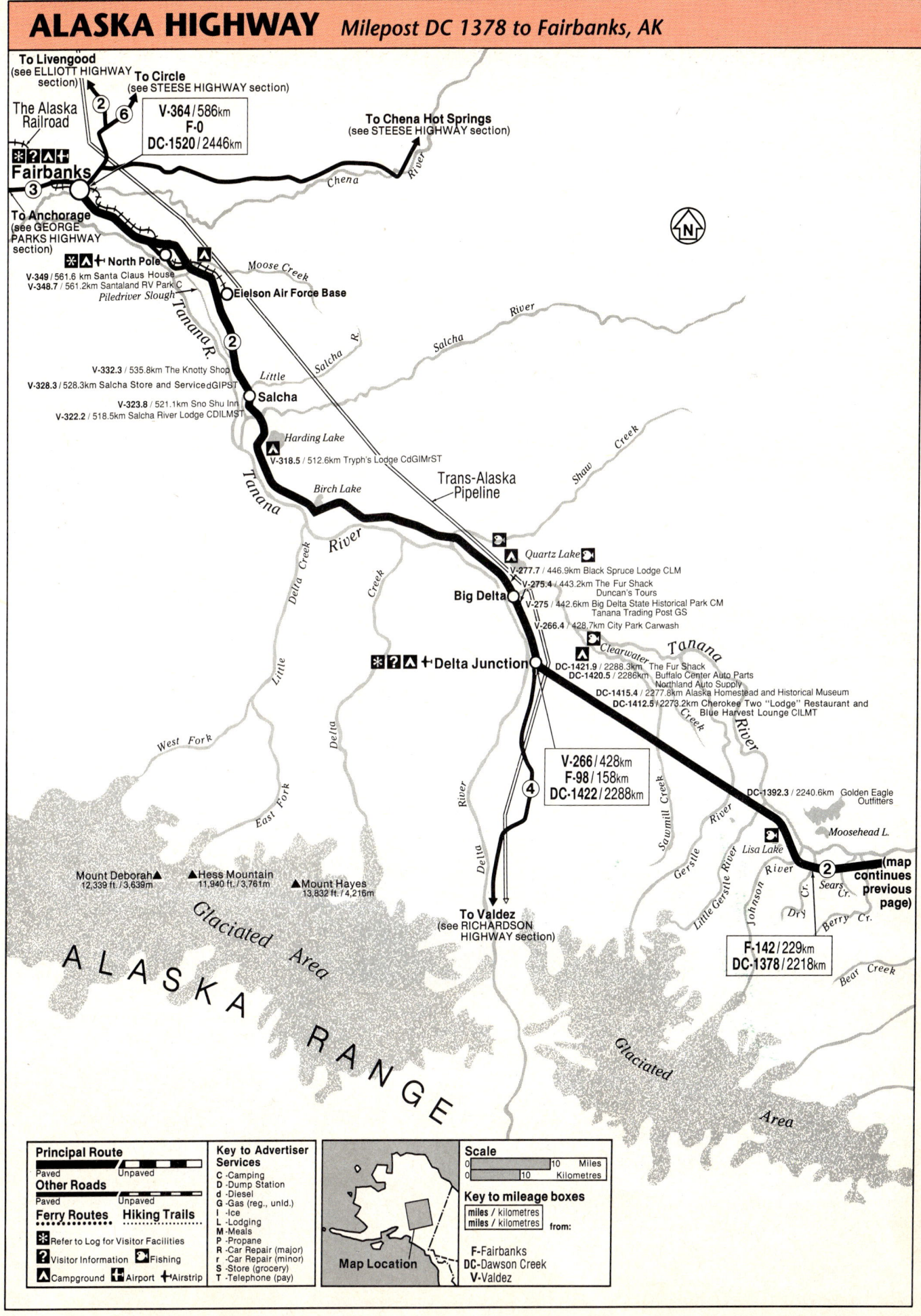

ALASKA HIGHWAY Milepost DC 1378 to Fairbanks, AK

Mileposts and Kilometreposts

Mileposts were first put up at communities and lodges along the Alaska Highway in the 1940s to help motorists know where they were in this vast wilderness. Today, those original mileposts remain a tradition with communities and businesses on the highway and are still used as mailing addresses and reference points, although the figures no longer accurately reflect driving distance.

When Canada switched to the metric system in the mid-1970s, the mileposts were replaced by kilometreposts. These posts are located on the right-hand side of the highway (Alaska-bound). Kilometreposts are up along the British Columbia portion of the Alaska Highway every 3 miles/5 km; reflective white numerals on green signs. In Yukon Territory, white posts with black numerals are up along the highway every 1.2 miles/2 km. In addition, the Yukon government installed 83 historic highway mileposts along the Yukon portion of the Alaska Highway in late 1991. These mileposts reflect the original or traditional mileage and do not reflect actual driving distance.

The kilometerage of the British Columbia portion of the Alaska Highway was recalibrated by the government in the fall of 1990, with kilometreposts corrected to reflect current driving distances. As of our press time, kilometreposts along the Yukon Territory portion of the Alaska Highway still reflected the metric equivalent of the historical mileposts. Thus, at the BC/YT border (historical Mile 627) the kilometerage from Dawson Creek is given as 967.6 km on the BC side and 1009 km on the YT side.

The MILEPOST® log of the Alaska Highway gives distance from Dawson Creek to the AK-YT border as actual driving distance in miles from Dawson Creek followed by kilometre distance based on the kilometreposts. Use our mileage figure from Dawson Creek to figure correct distance between points on the Alaska Highway in Canada. Use our kilometre figure from Dawson Creek to pinpoint location in reference to physical kilometreposts on the Alaska Highway in Canada. Traditional milepost figures in Canada are indicated in the text as **Historical Mile.** In Yukon Territory, where the government has installed historical mileposts, the text reads **Historical Milepost** at those locations that could be confirmed at our press time.

On the Alaska portion of the highway, mileposts are based on historical miles, so distance from Dawson Creek in the log is given according to the mileposts up along the road. This figure is followed by the metric equivalent in kilometres.

How Long is the Alaska Highway?

The answer to that question depends on when, to where, and how it was measured. The distance of the Alaska Highway is measured from Mile 0 at Dawson Creek. But is it measured to Fairbanks or to Delta Junction?

Emergency Medical Services

Milepost DC 0 Dawson Creek to DC 47 Fort St. John. Dawson Creek ambulance 782-2211; RCMP 782-5211.

Milepost DC 47 Fort St. John to DC 101 Wonowon. Fort St. John ambulance 785-2079; RCMP 785-6617.

Milepost DC 101 Wonowon to DC 222.3 Bougie Creek bridge. Pink Mountain ambulance 772-3234.

Milepost DC 222.3 Bougie Creek bridge to DC 373.3 Summit Lake Lodge. Fort Nelson ambulance 774-2344; RCMP 774-2777.

Milepost DC 373.3 Summit Lake Lodge to DC 605.1 BC-YT border. Toad River ambulance 232-5351.

Milepost DC 605.1 BC-YT border to DC 710 Swift River. Watson Lake ambulance 536-2541; RCMP 536-7443.

Milepost DC 710 Swift River to DC 821 Squanga Lake. Teslin ambulance 390-2510; RCMP 390-2500.

Milepost DC 821 Squanga Lake to DC 936.8 Mendenhall River bridge. Whitehorse ambulance 668-9333; RCMP 667-5555.

Milepost DC 936.8 Mendenhall River bridge to DC 1023.7 Kluane Lake Lodge. Haines Junction ambulance 634-2213; RCMP 634-2221.

Milepost DC 1023.7 Kluane Lake Lodge to DC 1122.7 Longs Creek. Destruction Bay ambulance 841-5331; RCMP 643-2221.

Milepost DC 1122.7 Longs Creek to DC 1189.8 YT-AK border. Beaver Creek RCMP 862-7300; Health Centre 863-7225; Ambulance 862-7333.

Milepost DC 1221.8 YT-AK border to DC 1314.2 Tok. Northway EMS 778-2211. Port Alcan Rescue Team (Alaska Customs) 774-2252.

Milepost DC 1314.2 Tok to DC 1361.3 Dot Lake. Tok ambulance 883-2300 or 911.

Milepost DC 1361.3 to DC 1422 Delta Junction. Delta Rescue Squad phone 911 or 895-4600; Alaska State Troopers 895-4800.

Milepost DC 1422 Delta Junction to DC 1520 Fairbanks. Dial 911.

COME TO NORTHEASTERN BRITISH COLUMBIA
Scenic Adventure for All Season Recreation

Enjoy our parks, campgrounds, wilderness and cities. An area steeped in history and surrounded by some of British Columbia's most beautiful country!

Peace River Alaska Highway Tourist Assoc.
Box 6850-M, Fort St. John, B.C. Canada V1J 4J3
Phone (604) 785-2544 • FAX (604) 785-4424

Please send me more information on the Peace River Alaska Highway Tourist Region.

NAME: _____
ADDRESS: _____
CITY: _____
PROV/STATE: _____ POSTAL/ZIP: _____

Super, Natural Scenic Adventure

We look after you at Husky along the Alaska Highway, and on your way there too!

Here on the Alaska Highway it's Husky

Ask your dealer for an Alaska Highway Husky Buck — it's good for $1 off your next Husky fill-up.

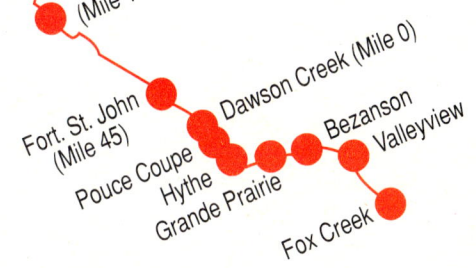

We accept Husky, Visa, Mastercard, Unocal credit cards.

OUTLET NAME	SERVICES
Husky Car/Truck Stop, Fox Creek	D/G/P/R/T
Southside Service, Valleyview	D/G/P/R/T
Bezanson General Service Centre	G/P/S
Husky Grande Prairie	D/G/P/R/T
TAGS Food & Gas, Hythe	D/G/P/S
Redwood Husky Food Store, Pouce Coupe	G/LA/P/S

ALASKA HIGHWAY BEGINS

Redwood Husky Food Store, Dawson Creek (0)	D/G/S
Fort St. John Car/Truck Wash (45)	D/G/P
Mae's Kitchen, Pink Mountain (147)	G/L/M/R/T
Husky 5th Wheel Truck Stop, Muskwa Heights (293)	C/D/G/LA/M/P/R/RV/S/T
Downtown Husky, Fort Nelson (300)	D/G/P/R/T
Steamboat Mtn. Husky (351)	C/D/G/M/R/T
Toad River Lodge (422)	C/D/G/L/M/P/R/S/T
Highland Glen Lodge, Muncho Lake (462)	C/D/G/L/M
Coal River Husky (533)	C/D/G/LA/L/P/RV
Camp-Ground Services, Watson Lake (632)	C/D/G/LA/P/R/RV/S/T
Carcross Corner Husky (904)	D/G/M/P/T
Tags Food & Gas, Whitehorse (918)	D/G/S
Ida's Motel & Cafe, Beaver Creek (1202)	D/G/L/M

LEGEND

CAMPING
DIESEL
GASOLINE
LAUNDROMAT
LODGING
MEALS
PROPANE
REPAIR
RECREATIONAL **V**EHICLE
STORE
TIRE SALES/REPAIR

Map locations:
- Beaver Creek Alaska Border (Mile 1202)
- Whitehorse (Mile 918)
- Carcross Corner (Mile 904)
- Watson Lake (Mile 632)
- Coal River (Mile 533)
- Muncho Lake (Mile 462)
- Toad River (Mile 422)
- Steamboat Mtn. (Mile 351)
- Fort Nelson (Mile 300)
- Muskwa Heights (Mile 293)
- Pink Mountain (Mile 147)
- Fort St. John (Mile 45)
- Dawson Creek (Mile 0)
- Pouce Coupe
- Hythe
- Grande Prairie
- Bezanson
- Valleyview
- Fox Creek

Shell helps!
1-800-661-1600

MILE	OUTLET NAME		SERVICES
ALASKA HIGHWAY 97			
MILE 0	HARV'S SHELL		G/NL/R/P/CW/D
	CIRCLE K FOOD STORE		G/SUPER NL/S/NL
	NOMAX HOLDINGS	(CL)	D/NL
MILE 40	BALDDONNELL		G/NL/S
MILE 47	CIRCLE K FOOD STORE		G/NL/SUPER NL/S
	CRAIG FUEL	(CL)	D/R
MILE 54	SHELL TRUCK STOP		G/SUPER/NL/S/CL/P/M/D/R
MILE 147	DANNY'S SHELL		G/D/NL/C/M/L
MILE 293	STREEPER PETROLEUMS	(CL)	G/D/NL
MILE 300	FT. NELSON SHELL		G/D/NL/R
MILE 426	POPLARS SHELL		G/D/NL/P/C/T/L/S/M
MILE 463	J & H WILDERNESS		G/D/NL/M/S/C/L/R
MILE 477	LIARD RIVER		G/D/NL/C/M
MILE 596	IRON CREEK		G/D/NL/C/M/S/L
MILE 612	WATSON LAKE		G/NL/D/R
ALASKA HIGHWAY 1			
MILE 804	HALSTEADS		G/NL/D/M/L/S/RV/B
MILE 913	WHITEHORSE		G/NL/D/S
	WHITEHORSE	(CL)	D/S
MILE 1167	BEAR FLATS LODGE		G/NL/D/RV/M/L/C/R
LIARD HIGHWAY 77			
MILE 142	LIARD VALLEY DEVELOPMENT		G/NL
CASSIAR HIGHWAY 37			
MILE 147	DEASE LAKE SHELL		G/NL/D/R/S
	DEASE LAKE SHELL	(CL)	G/NL/D/P/TW/R
KLONDIKE HIGHWAY 2			
MILE 522	BONANZA SHELL		G/NL/D/S

LEGEND
- CL — CARD LOCK
- C — CAMPING
- D — DIESEL
- G — GASOLINE
- L — LODGING
- NL — NO LEAD
- P — PROPANE
- R — REPAIRS
- S — STORE
- T — TIRE SERVICE
- RV — RECREATIONAL VEHICLE PARK
- TW — TRUCK WASH
- M — MEALS
- B — BOAT RENTALS
- CW — CAR WASH

Map locations: DAWSON CITY 522, BEAVER CREEK 1167, WHITEHORSE 913, TESLIN 804, WATSON LAKE 612, IRON CREEK 596, FORT LIARD 142, LIARD RIVER 477, MUNCHO LAKE 463, DEASE LAKE 147, TOAD RIVER 426, FORT NELSON 300, PINK MOUNTAIN 147, FORT ST JOHN 47, BALDONNELL 40, DAWSON CREEK 0

Delta Junction, at the traditional milepost figure of 1422, is the official end of the Alaska Highway. Delta Junction is connected to Fairbanks by the Richardson Highway.

The Richardson Highway, which begins in Valdez, was built by the Alaska Road Commission in the early 1900s. During construction of the Alaska Highway and during the war years, the portion of the Richardson Highway north of its junction with the Alaska Highway (from Delta Junction to Fairbanks), became part of the army road.

Today, this stretch of road is designated the Richardson Highway, with mileposts reflecting distance from Valdez, and the Alaska Highway ends in Delta Junction. But as often as not, the distance of the Alaska Highway is given as 1,500 odd miles, which is the distance to Fairbanks.

What is the distance to Fairbanks? In a 1945 government report on the Alaska Highway, a summary of mileages based on odometer readings at that time showed Delta Junction at Mile 1420 and Fairbanks at Mile 1519. But the Mile Zero post erected in downtown Dawson Creek in 1946 used 1,523 miles distance to Fairbanks.

The 1949 edition of The MILEPOST® logged Delta at Mile 1420 and Fairbanks at Mile 1523. In later editions, Delta appeared at Mile 1422 and Fairbanks at Mile 1520, changes probably reflecting a change in the location of the mileposts, junction or city limit.

Because odometers differ, and because reconstruction and rerouting continue to shorten the Alaska Highway, it is difficult to give an accurate mileage. The MILEPOST® uses the traditional 1,422 miles to Delta Junction and 1,520 miles to Fairbanks, but notes that by the time you reach the Yukon-Alaska border, the Alaska Highway is already 32 miles/51 km shorter than the historical mileposts reflect.

Dawson Creek

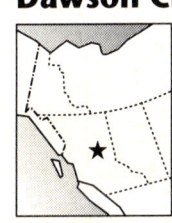

Milepost 0 of the Alaska Highway. **Population:** 12,000, area 66,500. **Emergency Services: RCMP,** phone 782-5211. **Fire Department,** phone 782-5000. **Ambulance,** phone 782-2211. **Hospital and Poison Centre,** Dawson Creek and District Hospital, 11000 13th St., phone 782-8501.

Visitor Information: At NAR (Northern Alberta Railway) Park on Alaska Avenue at 10th Street (1 block west of the traffic circle), in the building behind the railway car. Open year-round, 8 A.M. to 8 P.M. daily in summer, 9 A.M. to 5 P.M. Tuesday through Saturday in winter. Phone 782-9595. Plenty of public parking in front of the refurbished grain elevator which houses the Dawson Creek Art Gallery.

Elevation: 2,186 feet/666m. **Climate:** Average temperature in January is 0°F/-18°C; in July it is 60°F/15°C. The average annual snowfall is 72 inches with the average depth of snow in midwinter at 19.7 inches. Frost-free days total 97, with the first frost of the year occurring about the first week of September. **Radio:** CJDC 890. **Television:** 13 channels via cable including pay TV. **Newspapers:** Peace River Block News (daily); The Mirror (biweekly).

Private Aircraft: Dawson Creek airport, 2 miles/3.2 km southeast; elev. 2,148 feet/

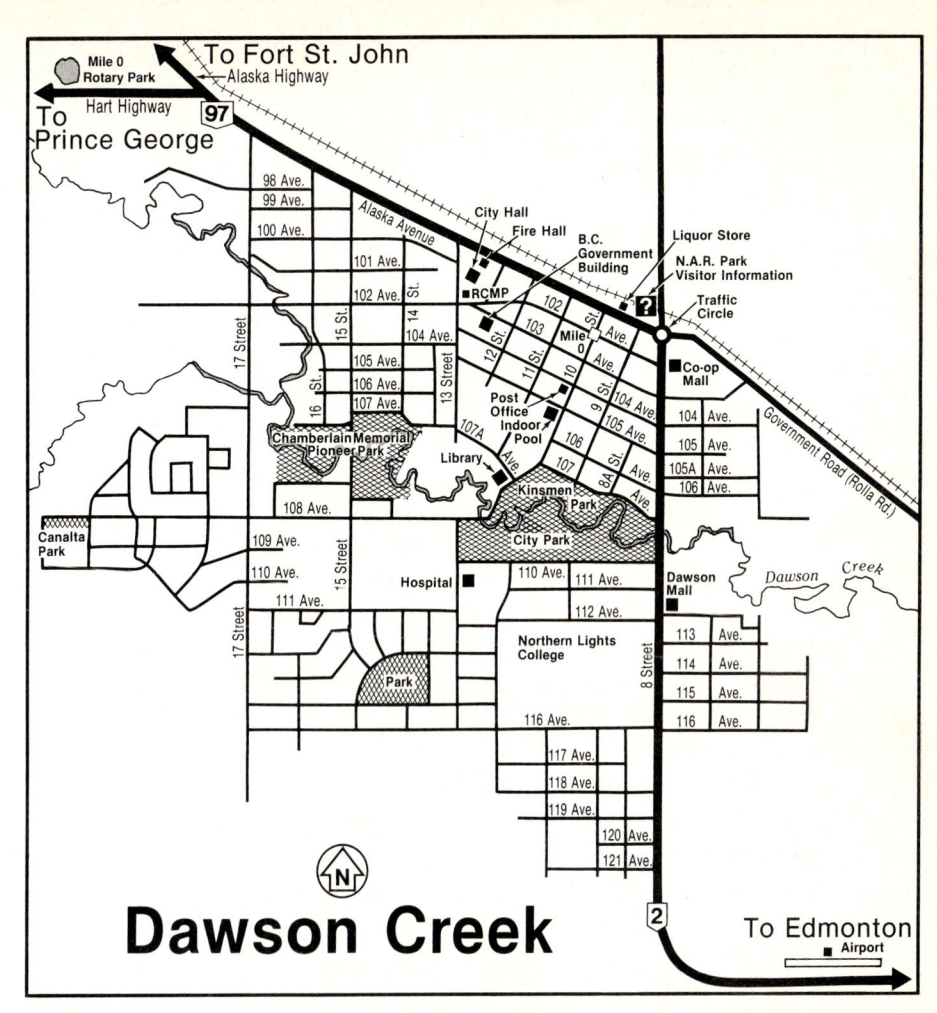

ALASKA HIGHWAY ▪ DAWSON CREEK

TLC Car Wash
11601 - 8th Street, Dawson Creek, BC
(604) 782-5773
Across from Northern Lights Collage

Timed Wand Wash • Confectionery
Car Wash Supplies
7 Inside Bays • 1 RV Bay
VISA   MasterCard

Dawson Mall

• **ACRES OF PARKING SPACE**
(overnighters welcome)

• **AIR-CONDITIONED**

• **OVER 25 STORES TO SERVE ALL YOUR TRAVELLING NEEDS**

Right along Highway 2, just 3/4 of a mile from the Traffic Circle.

Super, Natural Scenic Adventure

1992 ▪ The MILEPOST®

ALASKA HIGHWAY • DAWSON CREEK

MILE 0 CAMPSITE

- **BEAUTIFUL TREED SITES**
- **ELECTRICAL HOOKUPS**
- **FREE SHOWERS • LAUNDRY**
- **SANI DUMP • PAY PHONE**

Located 1 Mile West of Junction of Hart and Alaska Highways

Adjacent to Rotary Lake and Walter Wright Pioneer Village

PHONE:
(604) 782-9595
FAX (604) 782-9538

900 ALASKA AVENUE
DAWSON CREEK, BC V1G 4T6

Super, Natural Scenic Adventure

JOY PROPANE LTD.

DAWSON CREEK LOCATIONS:
Main: 724 - 114th Avenue
West: 1901 - Hart Highway
(604) 782-6000

- Auto Propane
- Cylinder Refills
- Propane Carburetion

FORT ST. JOHN LOCATION:
10304 Alaska Road
(604) 785-5000

VISA MasterCard

655m; length 5,000 feet/1,524m; asphalt; fuel 100, jet. Floatplane base parallels runway.

Dawson Creek lies 367 miles/591 km northwest of Edmonton, AB, and 250 miles/402 km northeast of Prince George, BC.

Dawson Creek (like Dawson City in the Yukon Territory) was named for George Mercer Dawson of the Geological Survey of Canada, whose geodetic surveys of this region in 1879 helped lead to its development as an agricultural settlement. The open level townsite is surrounded by rolling farmland, part of the government-designated Peace River Block.

The Peace River Block consists of 3.5 million acres of arable land in northeastern British Columbia which the province gave to the Dominion Government in 1883 in return for financial aid toward construction of the Canadian Pacific Railway. (While a route through the Peace River country was surveyed by CPR in 1878, the railroad was eventually routed west from Calgary through Kicking Horse Pass.) The Peace River Block was held in reserve by the Dominion Government until 1912, when some of the land was opened for homesteading. The federal government restored the Peace River Block to the province of British Columbia in 1930.

Today, agriculture is an important part of this area's economy. The fields of bright yellow flowers (in season) in the area are canola, a hybrid of rapeseed which was developed as a low cholesterol oil seed. Raw seed is processed in Alberta and Japan. The Peace River region also produces most of the province's cereal grain, along with fodder,

WALTER WRIGHT PIONEER VILLAGE, DAWSON CREEK

Super, Natural Scenic Adventure

ALASKA HIGHWAY • DAWSON CREEK

1. Shangri-La Service — (403) 836-3312
2. Courtesy Corner — (403) 765-3630
3. Prairie Mall Service — (403) 532-0066
4. Southside Service — (403) 532-6210
5. Petro-Canada Farm Center — (403) 532-2010
6. Manor Service & Restaurant — (403) 782-8400
7. Peace Country Automotive — (604) 782-5020
8. C & G Service — (604) 789-3444
9. Select Gas — (604) 787-0090
10. Dodd's Truck Stop — (604) 787-2302
11. Chetwynd Service — (604) 788-9920
12. Muskwa Service — (604) 774-6374
13. Blue Bell Motel — (604) 774-6961
14. Wye-Tech. Service — (403) 536-2555
15. Junction 37 Service — (403) 536-7794
16. Don Acorn Service — (403) 667-4003
17. Northland Service — (403) 668-2257
18. Kopper King Services — (403) 668-2422
19. North Country Service — (403) 634-2505
20. Kluane Wilderness Village — (403) 841-4141
21. Farwest Service — (403) 862-7220

THINGS TO SEE IN DAWSON CREEK:
Art Gallery, N.A.R. Park, Tourist Info,
Museum, Mile "0" Post, Alaska Highway
Cairn, Walter Wright Pioneer Village.

They sure know how to throw a party in Dawson Creek! The Rendezvous 92 excitement all starts here at Mile "O". It's a year long celebration and you still have time to join us. Dawson Creek is the place to visit!

Elizabeth

50 Years Alaska Highway
1942 - 1992

FOR INFORMATION:
DAWSON CREEK TOURISM INFORMATION BUREAU
900 ALASKA AVENUE, DAWSON CREEK, B.C. V1G 4T6
OR CALL (604) 782-9595 FAX: (604) 782-9538

Super, Natural Scenic Adventure

cattle and dairy cattle. Other industries include the production of honey, hogs, eggs and poultry. Some potato and vegetable farming is also done here.

On the British Columbia Railway line and the western terminus of the Northern Alberta Railway (now Canadian National Railway), Dawson Creek is also the hub of 4 major highways; the John Hart Highway (Highway 97 South) to Prince George; the Alaska Highway (Highway 97 North); Highway 2, which leads east to Grande Prairie, AB; and Highway 49, which leads east to Spirit River and Donnelly.

The Northern Alberta Railway reached Dawson Creek in 1930. As a railhead, Dawson Creek was an important funnel for supplies and equipment during construction of the Alaska Highway in 1942. Some 600 carloads arrived by rail within a period of 5 weeks in preparation for the construction program, according to a report by the Public Roads Administration in 1942. A "rutted provincial road" linked Dawson Creek with Fort St. John, affording the only approach to the southern base of operations. Field headquarters were established at Fort St. John and Whitehorse. Meanwhile, men and machines continued to arrive at Dawson Creek. By May of 1942, 4,720 carloads of equipment had arrived by rail at Dawson Creek for dispersement to troops and civilian engineers to the north.

With the completion of the Alaska Highway in 1942 (and opening to the public in 1948) and the John Hart Highway in 1952, Dawson Creek expanded both as a distribution centre and tourist destination. Dawson Creek was incorporated as a city in 1958.

Alaska Hwy. Campgrounds and R.V. Park

A PEACEFUL SETTING JUST 2 MILES OFF THE ALASKA HIGHWAY

Turn Off At MILE 17
Kilometrepost 28

- Adult Oriented
- A 73-Acre Natural Paradise
- Full Hookups to Tenting
- Level Pull-Throughs
- Clean Washrooms
- Hot Showers • Laundromat
- Dump Station • Pay Phone
- Vehicle Storage
- Convenience Store
- Walking Trails
- Fishing — No License Required

(604) 843-7464
Your Hosts: Flemming & Anita Nielsen

P.O. Box 749
DAWSON CREEK, B.C.
CANADA V1G 4H7

Super, Natural Scenic Adventure

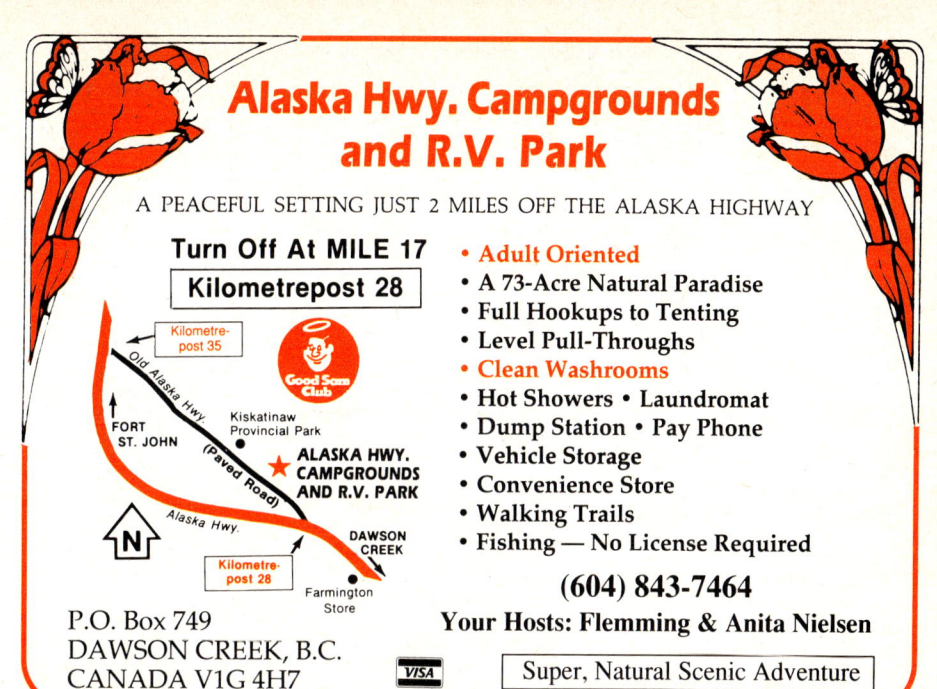

DAWSON CREEK COIN LAUNDRY LTD.
• WASHERS • DRYERS • SHOWERS •
Ample Parking Area
800 - 106th Ave.   (604) 782-9389
(Five blocks south of the Traffic Circle)

NORTHERN LIGHTS RV PARK LTD.
(604) 782-9433 • All New for '92
OPEN 24 HOURS • Pull-Through Parking
30-amp Hookups • FREE Hot Showers
Laundry • Car Wash
Highway 97, Box 2476, Dawson Creek, BC V1G 4T9

Boston Pizza
We're not just pizza anymore.

Ribs   Pasta   Salads   Sandwiches   Steaks   Pasta   Ribs

LICENSED PREMISES • TAKE OUT ORDERS • 24 VARIETIES OF PIZZA PLUS...

Spaghetti • The "Boston Brute" • Baked Lasagna • Other Pasta Selections
Bar-B-Que Pork Spareribs • Steaks • Soups • Salads

HOURS: Open at 11:00 a.m. Daily 7 Days a Week

1525 ALASKA AVENUE • DAWSON CREEK, B.C.
(604) 782-8585

Super, Natural Scenic Adventure

Ribs   Pasta   Salads   Sandwiches   Steaks   Pasta   Ribs

THE "ALASKA" EXPERIENCE!

The ALASKA Cafe & Pub

PEACE COUNTRY CUISINE

55 PACES SOUTH OF MILEPOST "0"

Deluxe Evolutionary

Reservations
(604) 782-7040

*Featured in
"Where to Eat in Canada"*

VISA, MasterCard, American Express Welcome

"READ ABOUT US IN THE ACCOMMODATION SECTION"

Super, Natural Scenic Adventure

WILLOW CREEK FARMS
Bed and Breakfast

10 miles west of Dawson Creek
on Hart Highway

LARGE, COMFORTABLE ROOMS
HEARTY BREAKFASTS
QUIET FARM SETTING

Hosts: Dan and Sharon Bell
(604) 843-7253
Box 2121, Dawson Creek, BC V1G 4K9

TUBBY'S TENT and TRAILER PARK

...on Hwy. 97 South (Hart Hwy.) toward Prince George
1,000 feet from the junction with the Alaska Hwy.

ACRES OF CAMPING
97 FULL HOOKUPS
Picnic Tables • Ice
Coin Showers and Laundromat
Clean, Modern Rest Rooms
5 Bay Truck and Car Wash
Adjacent to Swimming Pool

Write: Comp 29, 1725 Alaska Ave.
Dawson Creek, B.C. V1G 1P5

PHONE (604) 782-2584
1913 Hart Highway, Dawson Creek, BC

USB — UNITED SPRING & BRAKE LTD.
"THE SPECIALISTS"

Largest R.V. Running Gear & Chassis Parts in the North

CERTIFIED MECHANICS

Brakes • Suspensions • Axels • Hitches
Wheel Alignment Service

COMPLETE SHOP FACILITIES

All Chassis Repairs — Including the Largest Motorhomes

11634 - 7th Street, Dawson Creek, BC
Phone (604) 782-1136 • FAX (604) 782-7888
Directly Behind McDonald's

VISA   MasterCard

The development of oil and natural gas exploration in northeastern British Columbia, and related industries such as pipeline construction and oil storage, have contributed to the economic expansion of Dawson Creek. The city is also one of the major supply centres for the massive resource development known as North East Coal, southwest of Dawson Creek. Access to the coal development and the town of Tumbler Ridge is via the Heritage Highway,

DAWSON CREEK ADVERTISERS

**Alaska Cafe &
  Pub, The** ....Half-block S. of Mile 0 post
**Alaska Hwy. Campgrounds
  and R.V. Park**............Mile 17.3 Alaska Hwy.
Boston Pizza........................1525 Alaska Ave.
Central Motel & RV Park.......1301 Alaska Ave.
Dawson Creek Art Gallery ....NAR Park
**Dawson Creek Coin
  Laundry Ltd.**.........5 blocks S. of traffic circle
Dawson Creek Lodge............1317 Alaska Ave.
**Dawson Creek Tourist
  Information Bureau**.....Ph. (604) 782-9595
Dawson Mall ....On Hwy. 2, 0.75 mile
                                              from traffic circle
Econo-Lodge.............................632 103rd Ave.
Expert Automotive Ltd......................1 blk. W.
                                               of liquor store
Fas Gas Oil Ltd. ....3 locations—See ad
Joy Propane Ltd. ....2 locations—See ad
King Koin Laundromat..................Across from
                                               BC Government Bldg.
**Kinuseo Falls Wilderness
  Tours**...........................Ph. (604) 782-4996
Law's "1 Hr." Photo Variety..........Co-Op Mall
Mile Zero Campsite.............Mile 0 Rotary Park
Mile Zero Esso............................10532 8th St.
**Northern Lights
  RV Park Ltd.**..................Hart Hwy., 0.5 mile
                                            from Alaska Hwy. Jct.
"North to Alaska" ....Bookstores
**"This Was No
  %YX#H Picnic"**............See ad for locations
TLC Carwash ....Across from Northern
                                               Lights College
Trail Motel............................1748 Alaska Ave.
Treasure House Imports ....10109 10th St.
**Tubby's Tent &
  Trailer Park** ....1913 Hart Hwy.
**United Spring &
  Brake Ltd.**.........Directly behind McDonald's
**Voyaguer Motor
  Inn** ....Across from Dawson Mall
**Walter Wright
  Pioneer Village** ....Mile 0 Rotary Park
**Willow Creek Farms
  Bed and Breakfast** ....Ph. (604) 843-7253
Windsor Hotel ....1 blk. W. Mile 0 post
Yarn Barn, The ....Across from Provincial Bldgs.

Private Truck & Semi-trailer Parking

• CABLE COLOUR TV
• FREE LOCAL CALLS
• ECONOMY RATES
• COFFEE • PHONES
• KITCHENETTES

ECONO- Lodge
BEST $ VALUE

VISA   MasterCard   American Express

Phone (604) 782-9181
1-800-665-1759 (B.C. and Alberta)
Located East of the Co-op Mall
632 103rd Ave.
Dawson Creek, B.C. Canada V1G 2E8

which branches off the John Hart Highway just west of Dawson Creek and also branches off Highway 2 southeast of the city. Highway 29 extends south from Chetwynd to Tumbler Ridge.

Louisiana Pacific's waferboard plant, located on the Alaska Highway on the north edge of town, uses aspen and poplar logs to make sheets of waferboard, which is touted to be stronger than plywood. The use of poplar has been beneficial to local farmers: long considered a weed, farmers now earn extra income by selling off cleared trees.

Provincial government offices and social services for the South Peace region are located in Dawson Creek. The city has a modern 100-bed hospital, a public library, a college (Northern Lights) and a 600-seat concert hall (Unchagah Hall). There are also an indoor swimming pool, 2 skating arenas, a curling arena, bowling alley, golf course, art gallery, museum, tennis and racquetball courts. There are numerous churches in Dawson Creek (check at the visitor infocentre for location and hours of worship).

ACCOMMODATIONS

There are 13 hotels/motels and dozens of restaurants. Department stores, banks, grocery, drug and hardware stores and many specialty shops are located both downtown and in the 2 shopping centres, Co-op Mall and Dawson Mall. Dawson Mall is considered to be the most modern shopping complex in the Peace River region. Visitors will also find laundromats, car washes, gas stations and automotive repair shops. The liquor store is adjacent the NAR visitor information centre on Alaska Avenue.

The Alaska Cafe and Pub combine the spirit of northern adventure with Old World charm. *Where to Eat in Canada*, which lists the 500 top restaurants in Canada, suggests that "it is a good idea to start out on the Alaska Highway with a good meal under your belt and there's no better place than the Alaska Cafe." The Cafe also holds membership in World Famous Restaurants International; a definite must when in Dawson Creek. In the old days the Hotel Alaska advertised that "when you drop in to Dawson Creek, do drop in to the Dew Drop Inn." The pub features live entertainment 6 nights per week and is a hot spot in town. At The Alaska the philosophy is Deluxe Evolutionary, which means "always changing for the better." Gearing up for the year-long celebration of the building of the Alaska Highway in 1992, the hotel is being refurbished to provide theme bed and breakfast. AMEX, VISA, MasterCard and Diners Club credit cards accepted. Open 7 days for brunch, lunch, dinner and snacks. Located off Mile Zero Plaza 55 paces south of the Mile Zero Post. Phone (604) 782-7040 for reservations and information. Enjoy Super, Natural Scenic Adventure. [ADVERTISEMENT]

There are 4 campgrounds in Dawson Creek, 2 are located on either side of the Hart Highway at its junction with the Alaska Highway and 2 are located on Alaska Avenue. There are also a private campground and provincial park campground 17 miles/28 km north of Dawson Creek on the Alaska Highway.

Tubby's Tent and Trailer Park. On

TRAIL MOTEL

Junction of Alaska Highway and Hart Highway 97

40 Modern Units All With Private Baths
Air Conditioned • Cable TV • Direct Dial Phones • Sauna

Reasonable Rates
Complimentary Coffee
Plug-ins

(604) 782-8595
1-800-663-2749 (B.C. & Alberta)
1748 Alaska Ave., P.O. Box 667, Dawson Creek, B.C. V1G 4H7

EXPERT AUTOMOTIVE LTD.

ONE STOP PARTS AND SERVICE

BUMPER TO BUMPER. Auto Parts Professionals

Certified mechanics on duty
R.V. SPECIALISTS
Mufflers • Brakes • Tune ups
Wheel Alignment

★ Propane conversions
★ Bug and rock screens ★ Headlight protectors

COMPLETE MAJOR and MINOR REPAIRS

The Peace country's most complete automotive care clinic

(604) 782-6200 • FAX (604) 782-6161

1101 Alaska Ave., Dawson Creek, B.C.
(one block west from the Liquor Store)

MINUTE MUFFLER

NORTH TO ALASKA!

Fifty Years on the World's Most Remarkable Highway

KEN COATES

In 1992, Canadians and Americans will celebrate fifty years of the Alaska Highway. Starting in Dawson Creek, B.C., this historically rich route leads north for 1,500 miles, crossing muskeg and permafrost, forest, lakes, and massive rivers, over the mountains, on through pristine sub-Arctic wilderness, to Fairbanks, Alaska. Ken Coates has mined a rich vein of history based on encounters with more than 700 Alaska Highway veterans in this lavishly illustrated commemorative volume.

304 pages • 100 b&w photos

Published by
McClelland & Stewart
and **University of Alaska Press**
Available in Bookstores Everywhere

DAWSON CREEK
South Entrance
MILE Esso ZERO

10532 - 8th Street
PH. (604) 782-2228
SPECIAL LUBE PIT FOR ALL RV's

Good Drinking Water
Atlas Tires • Bug Screens
Headlight Protectors
Diesel • Propane
LICENSED MECHANICS
OPEN 7 a.m. — 11 p.m. DAILY

Super, Natural Scenic Adventure

KING KOIN LAUNDROMAT
Directly Across from the B.C. Government Building
1220 - 103rd Ave.   Dawson Creek, B.C.
Dry-Cleaning Service

SOFT WATER   SHOWER
Attendant   Welcome Visitors
8 a.m. – 9 p.m.   (604) 782-2395

Super, Natural Scenic Adventure

I DROVE THE ALASKA HIWAY

ALASKA HIGHWAY T-SHIRTS
IN FULL COLOUR
AND BEAUTIFUL WILDLIFE DESIGNS

We have a large selection of souvenirs. Eskimo soapstone carvings and totem poles. B.C. Jade, Indian and Eskimo dolls, moccasins, gold nugget jewelry and Alaska Black Diamond jewelry and carvings. You'll also enjoy our beautiful gifts, which we import from many countries. Come in & browse; you'll like our low prices.

10109 - 10th Street
Dawson Creek, BC
Located between tourist information and the Mile "0" Post
Phone (604) 782-5955

Treasure House Imports

Super, Natural Scenic Adventure

1992 Events

MARCH
9-13   Peace Country Arts Festival
13-14 Dawson Creek Symphonette & Choir Opera

APRIL
3   Spas Art Auction
24-26 Kiwanis Club Annual Trade & Sports Show
30-5/2 North Central Municipal Assoc. Conference

MAY
1-2   Municipal Assoc. Conference continues
5-7   Aircraft Maintenance Engineering Convention
14-16 Northern BC Truck & Equipment Show
21-24 Rotary Convention
28-31 Mile 0 Days
29-31 BC Chamber Convention
30   Grand Opening Mile Zero Rotary Park/Pioneer Village
30-6/1 Mile 0 Barbecue
31   Military Reunion

JUNE
1   Mile 0 Barbecue continues
1-8/31 Muskeg North Musical Revue
1-31   Spas First Summer Show
5   Vintage Car Rally
9-12   140th Truck Company Reunion
11   Army Motors Convoy Welcoming Celebration
13   Alaska Highway Trailblazers Grand Opening
21-24 Float Plane Race (overnight)
27-28 Army Motors Convoy overnight

JULY
1-8/31 Muskeg Musical continues
1-31   Spas Second Summer Show
7-8   Airmada

AUGUST
1-31   Muskeg Musical continues
7-9   Annual Fall Fair & Rodeo
27-30 BC Seniors Summer Games

SEPTEMBER
6   341st and 1776th Engineers Regiment Reunion
18-27 Rallye Alaska Highway '92

NOVEMBER
16   Emeralds Dance
28-30 Dawson Creek Cash Spiel

DECEMBER
3-5   BC Figure Skating

Highway 97 South (Hart Highway) toward Prince George, 1,000 feet from the junction with the Alaska Highway. Clean, modern restrooms, easy access, full hookups, all level. Picnic tables, laundromat, coin hot showers, lots of grass for camping. Adjacent to swimming pool, 5-bay truck and car wash. Full rig-up needs for the Alaska Highway. [ADVERTISEMENT] ▲

TRANSPORTATION

Air: Scheduled service from Dawson Creek airport to Prince George, Vancouver, Edmonton, Grande Prairie and Calgary via Air BC. The airport is located 3 miles/4.8 km south of the Alaska Avenue traffic circle via 8th Street/Highway 2; there is a small terminal at the airport. There is also a floatplane base.

Railroad: Northern Alberta Railway (now CNR) and British Columbia Railway provide freight service only. B.C. Railway provides passenger service from Vancouver to Prince George.

Bus: Coachways service to Prince George and Vancouver, BC; Edmonton, AB; and Whitehorse, YT. Dawson Creek also has a city bus transit system.

ATTRACTIONS

NAR Park, on Alaska Avenue at 10th Street (near the traffic circle), is the site of the Tourist Information Bureau which is housed in a restored railway station. The tourist bureau offers a self-guided historical walking tour with descriptions of Dawson Creek in the early 1940s during construction of the Alaska Highway.

Also at the station is the Dawson Creek Station Museum, operated by the South Peace Historical Society, which contains pioneer artifacts and wildlife displays.

In front of the station is a 1933 railway car. Adjacent the station is a huge wooden

GIFTS & SOUVENIRS
LAW'S "1 HR." PHOTO VARIETY
(604) 782-9851
Co-op Mall, Dawson Creek

The Yarn Barn — Browsers Welcome
WOOL, NEEDLEWORK and CRAFT SUPPLIES
Across from the Provincial buildings
1224 - 103rd Avenue, Dawson Creek • (604) 782-8994

In Downtown Dawson Creek
CENTRAL MOTEL & RV PARK

KITCHENETTES • CABLE TV
PETS WELCOME
FULL HOOKUPS / 10 SITES *(sorry – no pull throughs)*

Walking distance from — Laundromat • Showers • Shopping • Information Centre
Liquor Store • Restaurants • Garages • Post Office • Banking

1301 Alaska Avenue, Dawson Creek, BC V1G 1Z4   **(604) 782-8525**

VISA   MasterCard

MILEPOST field editor Earl Brown at Milepost 0. The original post was erected in 1946.

grain elevator which has been refurbished; its annex now houses an art gallery which features art shows throughout the summer. The last of Dawson Creek's old elevators, it was bought and moved to its present location by the art society in 1982.

Recreational facilities in Dawson Creek include a bowling alley, indoor pool, 2 ice arenas, curling rink, 18-hole golf course, tennis courts, and an outdoor pool at Rotary Lake Park.

Walter Wright Pioneer Village and **Mile 0 Rotary Park** are a must see attraction. The pioneer village contains an impressive collection of local pioneer buildings, including a teahouse, photo studio, artist's studio and store. Adjacent the village is Toms Lake Hall, which offers dinner theatre every evening from May 30 to Aug. 31. The dinner show's theme is the 1940s, when the building of the Alaska Highway forever changed Dawson Creek. The village and hall share the same site as Rotary Lake, an outdoor swimming pool.

Tumbler Ridge Side Trip. To reach Tumbler Ridge, drive west from Dawson Creek 12 miles/20 km on Highway 97 to junction with the Heritage Highway (see **Milepost PG 237.7** in the WEST ACCESS ROUTE section), or drive west 60.6 miles/97.5 km to junction with Highway 29 South (see **Milepost PG 189.4** in the WEST ACCESS ROUTE section). Heritage Highway 5 (paved and gravel) leads south 59.5 miles/96 km to the community of Tumbler Ridge. Highway 29 South is paved maintained road all the way to Tumbler Ridge. Tumbler Ridge is the townsite for Quintette Coal Limited's large-scale surface mines, and also serves workers of the Bullmoose Mine. Tours of Quintette and Bullmoose mines are available; inquire at the information centre in Tumbler Ridge. The huge coal processing plant and overhead conveyor are visible from the road. Monkman Provincial Park, site of spectacular 225-foot/69-m Kinuseo (Keh-NEW-see-oh) Falls, lies south of Tumbler Ridge. A new (1991) 40-site campground is accessible via a 25-mile/40-km road from Tumbler Ridge. Viewing platform of falls at campground; backcountry hiking. Monkman Park is also accessible by jet boat trip up the Murray River, fly-in or by horseback trip. Contact BC Parks in Prince George (565-6270), Fort St. John or Tumbler Ridge for more information.

At Tumbler Ridge, motorists have a choice: return to Highway 97 via Highway 5; return to Highway 97 via Highway 29 South to Chetwynd; or continue on the Heritage Highway loop 92 miles/148 km via all-gravel road to Highway 2 southeast of Dawson Creek. There are no services on the Heritage Highway except at Tumbler Ridge, which has a motel, campground, bank and shopping. On gravel stretches of the road, watch for poor road conditions in wet weather.

Special Events. In addition to the events listed in the 1992 calendar this section, Dawson Creek hosts a number of special interest benefits, dances, tournaments and exhibits. Check locally for details and dates on all events in the community.

Alaska Highway Log

BC HIGHWAY 97
Distance* from Dawson Creek (DC) is followed by distance from Fairbanks (F). Original mileposts are indicated in the text as Historical Mile.

*Mileages from Dawson Creek are based on actual driving distance. Kilometres from Dawson Creek are based on physical kilometreposts. Please read Mileposts and Kilometreposts in the introduction on page 74 for an explanation of how this highway is logged.

DC 0 F 1488 (2394.6 km) Mile 0 marker of the Alaska Highway on 10th Street in downtown Dawson Creek.

Northbound: Good pavement approximately next 284 miles/457 km (through Fort

INTERESTED IN THE ALASKA HIGHWAY?

Then you'll want to read...

"THIS WAS NO PICNIC"
BY JOHN SCHMIDT

A well-written collection of Alaska Highway stories

Available at Book Stores, Retail Outlets and Info Centres

"Save a buck when you buy this book!
$1.00 Off
at the Dawson Creek Tourist Info Centre when you show this ad.

The Trading Post
Mile 3 Alaska Highway

INDIAN AND ESKIMO HANDCRAFTS
Ivory • Jade • Antler Carvings and Jewelry
Moose Hair Tuftings • Yukon Parkas
Dania Down Quilts (The best quilt available)
Indian Made Sweaters

VISA   U.S. EXCHANGE   VISA

Many local and Native handcrafts too numerous to mention. For futher information please write:

THE TRADING POST
Box 2058
Dawson Creek, BC, V1G 4K8
Phone (604) 782-4974

Windsor Hotel

"FULL FACILITIES"

RENDEZVOUS FAMILY RESTAURANT
Banquet Facilities • Castle Dining Lounge
Checkers Cabaret • Sportsman Pub

63 ROOMS

Inquire about special arrangements for tour buses

1101 - 102 AVENUE
DAWSON CREEK, BC V1G 2C1
(one block from the Mile "0" post)

PHONE (604) 782-3301 • FAX (604) 782-3331

Super, Natural Scenic Adventure

1992 ■ The MILEPOST® 85

A highway is born

Traffic along the Alaska-Canada Military Highway—the "Alcan." Construction of the Alaska Highway began in April 1942, a combined effort of the U.S. Army Corps of Engineers, the Public Roads Administration, and civil engineers. Reconstruction, bridge building and relocation of much of the highway took place in 1943, as the pioneer road was upgraded for increased military traffic. The highway was opened to the public in 1948.

Nelson). Watch for road construction and surface changes from Pink Mountain north.

DC 1.2 (1.9 km) F 1486.8 (2392.7 km) **Junction** of the Alaska Highway and John Hart Highway.

Prince George-bound travelers turn to the end of the WEST ACCESS ROUTE section and read log back to front. Alaska-bound travelers continue with this log.

DC 1.5 (2.4 km) F 1486.5 (2392.2 km) Mile 0 Rotary Park, Walter Wright Pioneer Village and campground to west. ▲

DC 2 (3.2 km) F 1486 (2391.4 km) Recreation centre and golf course to west. Louisiana Pacific's waferboard plant to east.

DC 2.7 (4.3 km) F 1485.3 (2390.3 km) Truck scales and public phone to east.

DC 2.9 (4.7 km) F 1485.1 (2390 km) Northern Alberta Railway (NAR) tracks.

DC 3.3 (5.3 km) F 1484.7 (2389.3 km) Turnout with litter barrel to east.

DC 3.4 (5.5 km) F 1484.6 (2389.2 km) **Mile 3. The Trading Post** to east. See display ad on page 85.

DC 11.2 (18 km) F 1476.8 (2376.6 km) Turnout with litter barrels to west.

DC 11.5 (18.5 km) F 1476.5 (2376.1 km) Turnout with litter barrels to east.

DC 14.8 (24 km) F 1473.2 (2370.8 km) Farmington (unincorporated).

DC 15.2 (24.5 km) F 1472.8 (2370.2 km) Farmington store to west; gas, groceries, phone.

DC 17.3 (27.8 km) F 1470.7 (2366.8 km) **Alaska Hwy. Campgrounds and R.V. Park.** Turnoff 17 miles north of Dawson Creek onto the Kiskatinaw Provincial Park road (old Alaska Highway, paved). A short 2 miles to a peaceful setting on green grass, surrounded by trees and flowers. A spot for every need and something for every interest. We know you'll enjoy this supervised campground, just minutes away from the hectic highway. Enjoy Super, Natural Scenic Adventure. [ADVERTISEMENT] ▲

DC 17.3 (27.8 km) F 1470.7 (2366.8 km) Exit east for loop road to private campground and Kiskatinaw Provincial Park. Follow good 2-lane paved road (old Alaska Highway) 2 miles/3.2 km for Alaska Hwy. Campgrounds, 2.5 miles/4 km for Kiskatinaw Provincial Park. This side road gives travelers the opportunity to drive the original old Alaska Highway and to cross the historic curved wooden Kiskatinaw River bridge. The provincial park has 28 campsites, drinking water, firewood, picnic tables, fire rings, outhouses, garbage containers and grayling and Dolly Varden fishing in the **Kiskatinaw River.** Camping fee $6 to $12. ▲

DC 17.5 (28.2 km) F 1470.5 (2366.5 km) Distance marker indicates Fort St. John 29 miles/47 km.

DC 19.4 (31.2 km) F 1468.6 (2363.4 km) Large turnout to east.

DC 19.8 (31.9 km) F 1468.2 (2362.8 km) Highway descends northbound to Kiskatinaw River.

DC 20.9 (33.6 km) F 1467.1 (2361 km) Kiskatinaw River bridge. *CAUTION: Strong crosswinds on bridge.* Turnout with litter barrel and picnic tables to east at north end of bridge. View of unique bridge support.

DC 21.6 (34.5 km) F 1466.4 (2359 km) Loop road to Kiskatinaw Provincial Park, Kiskatinaw River bridge and private campground (see **Milepost DC 17.3**).

DC 22 (35.4 km) F 1466 (2359.2 km) **Country Vacations At The Kiskatinaw River Ranch.** Turn west, proceed 13 miles/21 km. Located at the junction of Sunset Creek Kiskatinaw River between the Alaska Highway and John Hart Highway. Interested in life in the slow lanes? Please try our guest ranch atmosphere! Rural, remote, peaceful, pastoral. Your hosts: The Nimitzes, Box 908, Dawson Creek, BC V1G 1L6. Phone (604) 843-7108. Enjoy Super, Natural Scenic Adventure. [ADVERTISEMENT]

DC 25.4 (41 km) F 1462.6 (2353.8 km) NorthwesTel microwave tower to east. Alaska Highway travelers will be seeing many of these towers as they drive north. The Northwest Communications System was constructed by the U.S. Army in 1942-43. This land line was replaced in 1963 with the

---

10% DISCOUNT ON HONEY AND POLLEN IF YOU GIVE US THIS AD

the HONEY PLACE

SEE THE WORLD'S LARGEST GLASS BEEHIVE
OPEN 9:00 A.M. to 5:30 P.M.
CLOSED SUNDAY AND HOLIDAYS

HONEY, POLLEN, LEATHERCRAFT KNITTING YARNS
Largest selection in the Peace River Country

Mile DC 42.3, KM 66.5 Alaska Highway • R.R. 1, Fort St. John, BC V1J 4M6 • (604) 785-4808

Redwood ESSO

GAS • AUTO & BOTTLED PROPANE • CAR WASH BAYS
SHOWERS • LAUNDROMAT
COMPLETE CONVENIENCE STORE
Film • Block & Cube Ice • Magazines • Souvenirs • Fast Food • Health & Beauty Items
Automotive Department and much more

Open 6 a.m. to 11 p.m.
Next to the RV Park

TAYLOR B.C.

TAYLOR LODGE
• Kitchenettes • Cable T.V.

construction of 42 microwave relay stations by Canadian National Telecommunications (CNT)—now NorthwesTel—between Grande Prairie, AB, and the YT-AK border.

DC 30.5 (49.1 km) **F 1457.5** (2345.5 km) Turnout to east with litter barrels. Turnout to west with litter barrels, pit toilet and historical marker about explorer Alexander MacKenzie.

Highway begins steep winding descent northbound to the Peace River bridge. Good views to northeast of Peace River valley and industrial community of Taylor. Some wide gravel shoulder next 4 miles/6.4 km for northbound traffic to pull off.

DC 33.8 (54.4 km) **F 1454.2** (2340.2 km) Pingle Creek.

DC 34 (54.7 km) **F 1454** (2339.9 km) Access to Taylor Landing Provincial Park; boat launch, parking, fishing. Also access to Peace Island Regional Park, 0.5 mile/0.8 km west of the highway, situated on an island in the Peace River connected to the south shore by a causeway. Peace Island has 19 shaded campsites with gravel pads, firewood, fire rings, picnic tables, picnic shelter, toilets, pump water and playground. There are also 4 large picnic areas and a tenting area. Camping fee. Nature trail, good bird watching and good fishing in clear water. Boaters should use caution on the Peace River since both parks are downstream from the W.A.C. Bennett and Peace Canyon dams and water levels may fluctuate rapidly.

DC 34.4 (55.4 km) **F 1453.6** (2339.3 km) Peace River bridge. Gas pipeline bridge visible to east.

Bridging the Peace was one of the first goals of Alaska Highway engineers in 1942. Traffic moving north from Dawson Creek was limited by the Peace River crossing, where 2 ferries with a capacity of 10 trucks per hour were operating in May. Three different pile trestles were constructed across the Peace River, only to be washed out by high water. Work on the permanent 2,130-foot suspension bridge began in December 1942 and was completed in July 1943. One of 2 suspension bridges on the Alaska Highway, the Peace River bridge collapsed in 1957 after erosion undermined the north anchor block of the bridge. The cantilever and truss type bridge that crosses the Peace River today was completed in 1960.

DC 35 (56.3 km) **F 1453** (2338.3 km) **TAYLOR** (pop. 711, elev. 1,804 feet/550m), on the north bank of the Peace River, is an industrial community clustered around a Westcoast Energy Inc. gas-processing plant and large sawmill. Established in 1955 with the discovery and development of a natural gas field in the area, Taylor is the site of a pulp mill and plants which handle sulfur processing, gas compressing, high-octane aviation gas production and other byproducts of natural gas. The Westcoast Energy natural gas pipeline reaches from here to Vancouver, BC, with a branch to western Washington.

The fertile Taylor Flats area has several market gardens and roadside stands in summer. A hotel, motels, cafes, grocery store, gas station and post office are located here. Free municipal dump station located behind the hotel. Taylor holds an annual Class A World Gold Panning Championship in August.

Redwood Esso. See display ad this section.

DC 36.3 (58.4 km) **F 1451.7** (2336.2 km) Railroad tracks.

DC 40 (64.5 km) **F 1448** (2330.3 km) **Historical Mile 41.** Gas station, convenience store and post office. Private campground. ▲

Alcan Store & Service Station. See display ad this section.

DC 40.3 (65 km) **F 1447.7** (2329.8 km) Exit east for Fort St. John airport.

DC 40.4 (65 km) **F 1447.6** (2329.6 km) B.C. Railway overhead tracks.

DC 41.3 (66.5 km) **F 1446.7** (2328.2 km) **Historical Mile 42.3. The Honey Place** to west. See display ad this section.

DC 45.8 (73.7 km) **F 1442.2** (2320.9 km) South access to Fort St. John via 100th Street. Exit east for visitor information and downtown Fort St. John.

DC 47 (75.6 km) **F 1441** (2319 km) **Historical Mile 48.** North access to Fort St. John via 100th Avenue to downtown. Truck stop with 24-hour gas and food.

Fort St. John

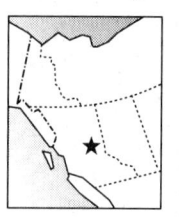

DC 47 (75.6 km) **F 1441** (2319 km) Located approximately 236 miles/380 km south of Fort Nelson. **Population:** 14,000; area 40,000. **Emergency Services:** RCMP, phone 785-6617. **Fire Department:** phone 785-2323. **Ambulance**, phone 785-2079. **Hospital**, on Centre (100th) Avenue and 96th Street, phone 785-6611.

Visitor Information: Located behind the 150-foot oil derrick in the museum, at 9323 100th St. (Fort St. John, BC V1J 4N4); phone 785-3033. Open year-round: 8 A.M. to 8 P.M. in summer, 8:30 A.M. to 5 P.M. the rest of the year. While here, visitors may also contact the Ministry of Environment & Parks, Parks and Outdoor Recreation Division, regarding wilderness hiking opportunities along the Alaska Highway. The Ministry is located across the street from the museum at 9512 100th St.; phone 787-3407.

Elevation: 2,275 feet/693m. **Radio:** CKNL 560. **Television:** Cable. **Newspaper:** *Alaska Highway News* (daily), *The Northerner* (weekly).

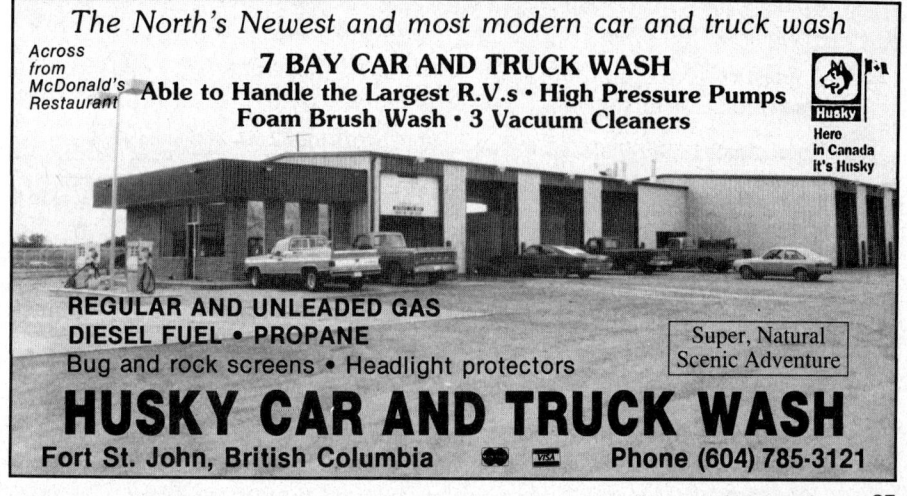

ALCAN STORE & SERVICE STATION
Post Office • Ice • Ice Cream • Cold Pop
Mile 41 Alaska Highway, BC V0C 1C0
Phone (604) 785-4861

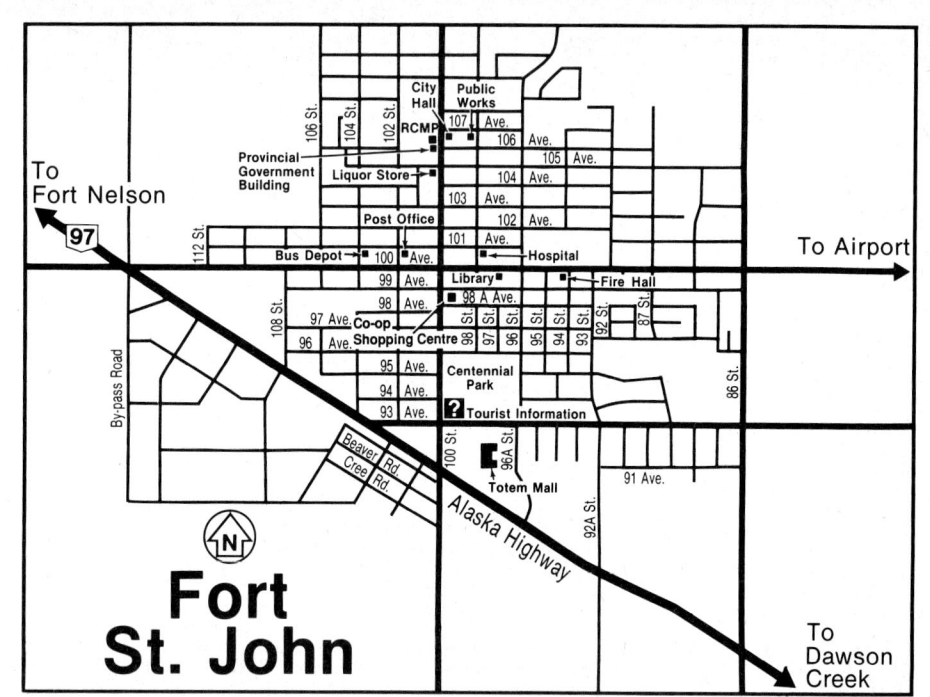

The North's Newest and most modern car and truck wash
Across from McDonald's Restaurant
7 BAY CAR AND TRUCK WASH
Able to Handle the Largest R.V.s • High Pressure Pumps
Foam Brush Wash • 3 Vacuum Cleaners

Husky — Here in Canada it's Husky

REGULAR AND UNLEADED GAS
DIESEL FUEL • PROPANE
Bug and rock screens • Headlight protectors

Super, Natural Scenic Adventure

HUSKY CAR AND TRUCK WASH
Fort St. John, British Columbia   Phone (604) 785-3121

Private Aircraft: Fort St. John airport, 3.8 miles/6.1 km east; elev. 2,280 feet/695m; length 6,900 feet/2,103m and 6,700 feet/2,042m; asphalt; fuel 80, 100. Charlie Lake airstrip, 6.7 miles/10.8 km northwest; elev. 2,680 feet/817m; length 1,800 feet/549m; gravel; fuel 80, 100.

Visitor services are located just off the Alaska Highway and in the town centre, a few blocks north of the highway. Fort St. John is a large modern city with all services available.

Fort St. John is set in the low, rolling hills of the Peace River Valley. The original Fort St. John was established in 1806 on the muddy banks of the Peace River, about 10 miles south of the present townsite, as a trading post for the Sikanni and Beaver Indians. The Rocky Mountain Fort site, near the mouth of the Moberly River, dates from 1794 and is currently being excavated. A granite monument, located on Mackenzie Street (100th Street) in Fort St. John's Centennial Park, is inscribed to Sir Alexander Mackenzie, who journeyed west to the Pacific Ocean along the old Indian route and camped here in 1793.

In 1942, Fort St. John became field headquarters for U.S. Army troops and civilian engineers working on construction of the Alaska Highway in the eastern sector. It was the largest camp, along with Whitehorse (headquarters for the western sector), of the dozen or so construction camps along the highway. Much of the field housing, road building equipment and even office supplies were scrounged from old Civilian Conservation Corps camps and the Work Projects Administration.

As reported by Theodore A. Huntley of the Public Roads Administration, "A narrow winter road from Fort St. John to Fort Nelson, 256 miles north, provided the only access to the forest itself. From Fort St. John north and west for almost 1,500 miles the wilderness was broken only by dog and pack trails or short stretches of winter road, serviceable only until made impassable by the spring thaw.

"But men and machines were arriving by the thousands for its final conquest. Within six months the first vehicle to travel overland to Alaska would roll into Fairbanks.

"Thus was a Highway born."

The Alaska Highway was opened to the traveling public in 1948, attracting vacationers and homesteaders. An immense natural oil and gas field discovered in 1955 made Fort St. John the oil capital of British Columbia. Land of the New Totems, referring to the many oil rigs, became the slogan for the region.

An extension of the Pacific Great Eastern Railway, now called British Columbia Railway, from Prince George in 1958 (continued to Fort Nelson in 1971), gave Fort St. John a

FORT ST. JOHN ADVERTISERS

Alexander MacKenzie Inn........9223 100th St.
Boston Pizza............................9824 100th St.
Caravan Motel ....Ph. (604) 787-1191
City of Fort St. John ....Ph. (604) 785-6037
Dodds Truck Stop
  and Restaurant............Mile 48 Alaska Hwy.
Fort St. John Motor Inn ....10707 102nd St.
Fort St. John-
  North Peace Museum.........9323 100th St.
Four Seasons Motor Inn ....9810 100th St.
Husky Car and Truck
  Wash.....................Across from McDonald's
Joy Propane Ltd. ....2 locations—See ad
Peace Coaches Inc. ....Ph. (604) 785-5945
Totem Mall......................................Alaska Hwy.

City of Fort St. John invites you to visit...

The ENERGY CAPITAL of BRITISH COLUMBIA

Population 14,000
Over 800 businesses to serve you

Mile 45 Alaska Highway

For your convenience:
➤ **RV Park** with water and power hookups, sani-dump, showers, laundromat
  RV Park open May - October
  Clean and friendly!
➤ **Tourist Information Centre**
  Open 8:00 a.m. to 8:00 p.m.
➤ Centennial Nature Park
➤ Tennis Courts
➤ Horseshoe Pits
➤ Indoor Public Pool
➤ Playground

Come and catch the
"SPIRIT OF THE NORTH"
right here in
FORT St. JOHN

BUSINESS INFO CENTRE

Near downtown and mall shopping, all located in surrounding area.

9323 - 100 Street
Fort St. John, BC
V1J 4N4

Phone (604) 785-6037
FAX (604) 785-7181

FORT ST. JOHN CHAMBER OF COMMERCE — LAND OF NEW TOTEMS

Super, Natural Scenic Adventure

Boston Pizza
We're not just pizza anymore.

Family Restaurant

OPEN 11:00 a.m. DAILY

MasterCard VISA AMERICAN EXPRESS

9824 - 100 St.
Fort St. John, BC
(604) 787-0455

link with the rail yards and docks at North Vancouver.

Today, Fort St. John is a centre for oil and gas exploration, forestry and agriculture. Farms in the North Peace region raise grain and livestock, such as sheep and cattle. Bison are also raised locally. The fields of clover and alfalfa have also attracted bees, and honey is produced for both local markets and export.

TRANSPORTATION

Air: Canadian Airlines International, Time Air and Air BC; to Fort Nelson, Watson Lake, Whitehorse, Vancouver, Grande Prairie, Edmonton and Prince George. **Bus:** Coachways service to Prince George, Vancouver, Edmonton and Whitehorse; depot at 10355 101st Ave., phone 785-6695. Peace Coaches Inc. service to Hudson's Hope and Chetwynd, phone 785-5945.

ACCOMMODATIONS

Numerous major motels, hotels, restaurants and full-service gas stations are located on the Alaska Highway and in town. Other services include laundromat, car wash and shops. A large shopping mall is located on the Alaska Highway. Fresh water fill-up and dump station located at the northwest corner of 86th Street and the Alaska Highway.

The Alexander MacKenzie Inn. The management and staff of the MacKenzie Inn invite you to stay at our hotel when you are in town. Our rates are great. Our meals are out of this world. The coffee shop is open from 6 A.M. to 8 P.M. and can be opened earlier for groups of 10 or more. Every lunch hour Monday-Friday, enjoy our buffet in the dining room from 11:30 A.M. to 2 P.M. The dining room is open from 5-10 P.M. daily for supper and on Sundays 10 A.M. to 2 P.M. is our Dixieland Buffet Extravaganza. This is a must if you are in town. For those who want a quiet drink, we have the Log Cabin Lounge

1992 Events

MARCH
7-8 Ice Carnival
9-11 Men's Curling Bonspiel

APRIL
24-26 CKNL Trade Show
26-27 Northern Dance Extravaganza
29 Ice Breaker Softball Tournament

MAY
16-18 Annual Championship Dog Show
28-30 BC Cattlemen's Convention

JUNE
11-12 Army Motors Convoy overnight
18-20 Children's Festival
20-21 Slowpitch Midseason Tournament
27 Annual North Peace Horse Show

JULY
7-8 Airmada
10-12 Fort St. John Rodeo
11-12 Remote Control Club War Bird Fun Fly
19 International Airshow
31-8/3 Firefighters Homecoming 50th Anniversary
31-8/3 Trapper's Rendezvous

AUGUST
1-3 Firefighters Anniversary continues
1-3 Trapper's Rendezvous continues
8-9 North Peace Fall Fair
8-9 Antique Car Show
30 Scavenger Hunt

SEPTEMBER
3-5 Shrine Club Ceremonial
19-22 Rallye Alaska Highway '92

NOVEMBER
20-21 Stage North Dinner Theatre
26-
12/24 Fall Art Show

DECEMBER
1-24 Fall Art Show continues
2 Museum Christmas Tea

PEACE COACHES INC.

SCHEDULED SERVICE: Daily
Fort St. John — Hudson's Hope
Chetwynd and Return

TOURS AND CHARTERS:
W.A.C. Bennett Dam
Liard Hotsprings

Super, Natural Scenic Adventure

P.O. Box 6730
Fort St. John, B.C.
V1J 2B0
(604) 785-5945

Fort St. John Motor Inn
10707 - 102 Street, Fort St. John
British Columbia, Canada V1J 2E8
Behind Courthouse
Easy Walking Distance to Downtown Shopping
FULL-SERVICE DINING • COCKTAIL LOUNGE
96 Quiet Air-conditioned Rooms with Queen-size Beds
Cable Color TV • Direct Dial Phones
Coin-operated Laundry • Wheelchair Accessibility
Ample Parking for Large Vehicles • Plug-ins
Bus Tours & Groups Welcome
Phone (604) 787-0411

Super, Natural Scenic Adventure

Four Seasons Motor Inn
(FORMERLY FORT ST. JOHN TRAVELODGE)

TELEPHONE
(604) 785-6647

9810 - 100th St.
Fort St. John, BC
V1J 3Y1
Canada

CARAVAN MOTEL

(604) 787-1191
FAX (604) 785-5488

*Centrally Located
Across from Totem Mall*

• Air Conditioned Motel Units
• Cable TV • Coin Laundry
• Direct Dial Phone

9711 Alaska Road • Fort St. John, BC

YOU'RE WELCOME AT...

TOTEM MALL

"Heart of the North"   Fort St. John, BC

Visit British Columbia's Largest Fully Enclosed Shopping Mall on the Alaska Highway

Climate Controlled Shopping • Acres of Parking
RV Park located just across the street

"SUPERHOST BUSINESSES"

33 STORES FOR ALL YOUR SHOPPING CONVENIENCE
Including: Gas Bar • Food Store • Pharmacy • Restaurants • Postal Service and more...

American Money Exchanged at Bank Rates — Banking Machine at Safeway

... WE LOOK FORWARD TO SERVING YOU!

Super, Natural Scenic Adventure

Fort St. John — North Peace MUSEUM

- Gift Shop • Souvenirs
- Tourist Information Centre located within
- Local Pioneer Artifacts
- 10,500-year-old Archaeological Artifacts from Charlie Lake Cave

Located 1 block north of Alaska Highway
9323 - 100th Street (604) 787 0430
Fort St. John, British Columbia
"A visit to our museum is a must!"
Summer Hours: 8 a.m.-8 p.m. 7 days a week
Winter Hours: 11 a.m.-4 p.m. Mon.-Sat.

Super, Natural Scenic Adventure

JOY PROPANE LTD.
- Auto Propane
- Cylinder Refills
- Propane Carburetion

DAWSON CREEK LOCATIONS:
Main: 724 - 114th Avenue
West: 1901 - Hart Highway
(604) 782-6000

FORT ST. JOHN LOCATION:
10304 Alaska Road
(604) 785-5000

DODDS TRUCK STOP and RESTAURANT

OPEN 24 HOURS
MILE 48 KM 77 Alaska Highway
FORT ST. JOHN, BC
8 ACRES OF PARKING • Car & RV Wash
Convenience Store • Shower
RV Servicing • Air Conditioner Service

PETRO-CANADA
GAS DIESEL PROPANE

Licensed Mechanic on Duty 16 Hours a Day — 7 DAYS a WEEK
Major and Minor Repairs • Tire Sales and Repair

We accept all Petro-Canada affiliated Credit Cards

— TOURIST INFORMATION AVAILABLE —
INTERSECTION OF
100TH AVENUE AND ALASKA HIGHWAY
PHONE (604) 787-2302

WE ACCEPT:
Cummings Check
Com Chek, Fast Track

Super, Natural Scenic Adventure

ROTARY R.V. PARK
On Beautiful Charlie Lake

"Best 'Walleye' Fishing in B.C."
40 SERVICED R.V. SITES
Electricity, Washrooms, Showers,
Laundry, Sani-Staion,
Security Fenced, Public Phone
Some Sites with Water and Sewer

— Boat Ramp and Dock —
Ample Lighted Parking
Next to Convenience Store and
Service Station and
Landmark 'Red Barn' Pub

(604) 785-1700
Only 6 KM north of full services in FORT ST. JOHN

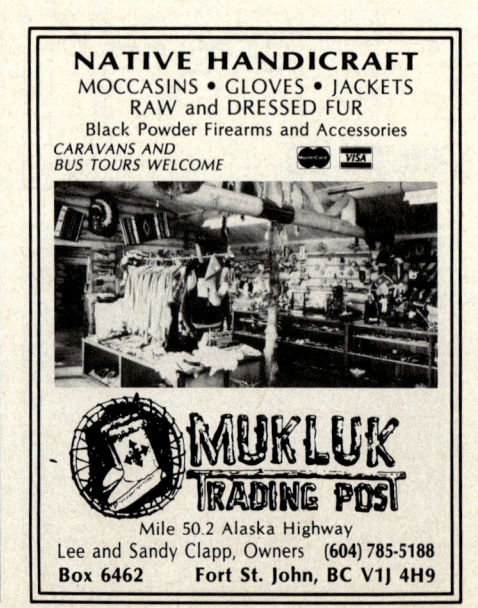

— ENJOY —
Super, Natural Scenic Adventure

---

which is open from noon to 1 A.M. daily. The roadhouse saloon is open daily from noon to 2 A.M. featuring live country music. Our rooms are designed to fill everyone's needs from singles to suites and even a jacuzzi for that special stay. (604) 785-8364 or 1-800-663-8313, fax 1-604-785-7547. Enjoy Super, Natural Scenic Adventure.

[ADVERTISEMENT]

Fort St. John RV Park, located at the east end of Centennial Park behind the museum, has 39 sites, showers, a laundry, dump station and hookups; senior citizen rates. Also camping north of the city at Beatton and Charlie Lake provincial parks, and at private and Rotary campgrounds at Charlie Lake. ▲

ATTRACTIONS

Centennial Park, located on 100th Street, has a museum, Chamber of Commerce, visitor information and the RV park. Fort St. John's North Peace Museum has artifacts from the region and from an 1806 Fort St. John post, a trapper's cabin and re-creation of an early-day schoolroom. Directly in front of the tourist centre is a 150-foot oil derrick, presented to the North Peace Historical Society and the people of Fort St. John. The derrick is especially resplendent in winter when it is decorated with Christmas lights, making it the tallest Christmas tree in northern British Columbia.

Check with the North Peace Museum (787-0430) about summer entertainment at the derrick.

W.A.C. Bennett Dam is a major attraction in the area. For an interesting side trip, drive north from Fort St. John on the Alaska Highway to **Milepost DC 53.7** and take Highway 29 west 46.5 miles/74.8 km to Hudson's Hope. Highway 29 follows the original Canadian government telegraph trail of 1918. Hudson's Hope, formerly a pioneer community established in 1805 by explorer Simon Fraser, grew with construction of the W.A.C. Bennett Dam, which is located 13.5 miles/21.7 km west of town. B.C. Hydro's Peace Canyon dam is located approximately 4 miles/6.4 km south of Hudson's Hope. Turn to the HUDSON'S HOPE LOOP section for more information.

Special Events. In addition to the events listed in the 1992 calendar this section, Fort St. John hosts a number of special interest benefits, dances, tournaments and exhibits. Check locally for details and dates on all events in the community. Fort St. John is also headquarters for Rendezvous '92, the 50th anniversary celebration of the Alaska Highway. Contact them at Suite 14, 9223 100 St., Fort St. John, BC V1J 3X3, phone (604) 787-1992, for more information on this 1992 event.

Alaska Highway Log

(continued)
Distance* from Dawson Creek (DC) is followed by distance from Fairbanks (F). Original mileposts are indicated in the text as Historical Mile.

*Mileages from Dawson Creek are based on

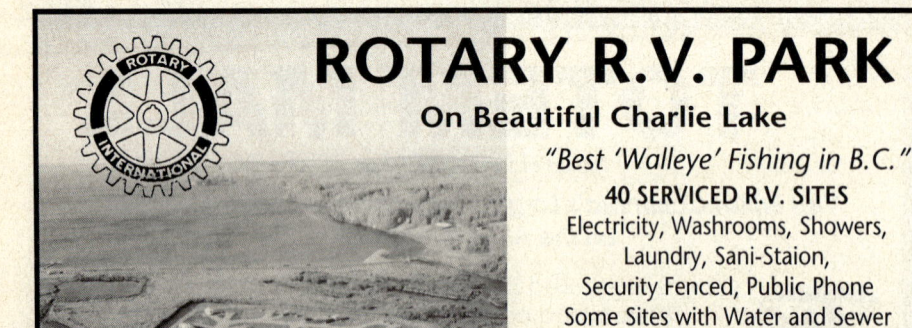

NATIVE HANDICRAFT
MOCCASINS • GLOVES • JACKETS
RAW and DRESSED FUR
Black Powder Firearms and Accessories
CARAVANS AND BUS TOURS WELCOME

MUKLUK TRADING POST
Mile 50.2 Alaska Highway
Lee and Sandy Clapp, Owners   (604) 785-5188
Box 6462   Fort St. John, BC V1J 4H9

actual driving distance. Kilometres from Dawson Creek are based on physical kilometreposts. Please read Mileposts and Kilometreposts in the introduction for an explanation of how this highway is logged.

DC 45.8 (73.7 km) **F 1442.2** (2320.9 km) South access to Fort St. John via 100th Street.

DC 47 (75.6 km) **F 1441** (2319 km) **Historical Mile 48.** North access to Fort St. John via 100th Avenue. Dodds Truck Stop with 24-hour gas and food.

DC 49.5 (79.6 km) **F 1438.5** (2315 km) Exit for Beatton Provincial Park, 5 miles/8 km east via paved road; 37 campsites, picnic shelter, wood stove, horseshoe pits, volleyball net, playground, baseball field, sandy beach, swimming and boat launch. Camping fee $6 to $12. Fishing for northern pike, walleye (July best) and yellow perch in **Charlie Lake.**

DC 50.2 (80.8 km) **F 1437.8** (2313.9 km) **Mukluk Trading Post.** See display ad this section.

DC 50.6 (81.4 km) **F 1437.4** (2313.2 km) **CHARLIE LAKE** (unincorporated), gas station, grocery, pub, private RV park and Ministry of Energy, Mines and Petroleum. Access to lakeshore east side of highway; boat launch, no parking.

At one time during construction of the Alaska Highway, Charlie Lake was designated Mile 0, as there was already a road between the railhead at Dawson Creek and Fort St. John, the headquarters for troops and engineers working in the eastern sector.

Charlie Lake General Store. See display ad this section.

Rotary RV Park, Charlie Lake. New park on south end of beautiful Charlie Lake, 6 km north of Fort St. John. 40 serviced sites. Electricity, washrooms, showers, laundry, sani-station, security fenced, public phone. Some sites with water and sewer. Boat ramp and dock, ample lighted parking. Next to convenience store, service station and landmark Red Barn Pub. Charlie Lake is noted for some of the best walleye fishing in British Columbia. Phone (604) 785-1700. Enjoy Super, Natural Scenic Adventure. [ADVERTISEMENT]

DC 50.8 (81.7 km) **F 1437.2** (2312.9 km) **Ron's R.V. Park. Historical Mile 52** Alaska Highway, 8 km/5 miles north of Fort St. John. Treed sites with complete RV hookups, shaded lawned tenting areas, picnic tables, firepits, firewood provided. Walking trails, playground, flush toilets, large molded vanity sinks, hot showers, laundromat, pay phone, ice, mini-variety store (gift shop). Coffee shop, small outdoor patio seating, lakefront sites, shaded beach area, shaded full-hookup pull-throughs, good drinking water, on-site phone hookup available. Large boat launching facilities nearby. Small boat launching from park, aluminum outboards, canoes, pedal boats, fishing gear, charter fishing boat (14-foot fiberglass with canopy, "leave the driving to us"), rent wet suit floating fish suit. Customer boat tie available. Fishing rods, net rentals. Quiet location away from hectic city confusion. Post office, golf course, Red Barn Pub nearby. Short scenic drive to W.A.C. Bennett Dam. Lakeshore parking on the shores of Charlie Lake, world famous for walleye and northern pike fishing. Phone (604) 787-1569. [ADVERTISEMENT]

DC 52 (83.7 km) **F 1436** (2311 km) Exit east on Charlie Lake Road for lakeshore picnicking.

DC 53.6 (86.3 km) **F 1434.4** (2308.4 km) Truck weigh scales east side of highway.

DC 53.7 (86.4 km) **F 1434.3** (2308.2 km) **Junction** with Highway 29, which leads west to Hudson's Hope and the W.A.C. Bennett Dam, then south to connect with the Hart Highway (97) at Chetwynd. (See HUDSON'S HOPE LOOP section.) Truck stop to west.

Turn east for Charlie Lake Provincial Park, just off highway: paved loop road (with speed bumps) leads through campground. There are 58 shaded sites, picnic tables, kitchen shelter with wood stove, firepits, firewood, outhouses, dump station, water and garbage. Level gravel sites, some will accommodate 2 large RVs. Camping fee $6 to $12. Playfield, playground horseshoe pits, volleyball net and a 1.2-mile/2-km hiking trail down to lake. Fishing in **Charlie Lake** for walleye, northern pike and yellow perch. Access to the lake for vehicles and boats is from the Alaska Highway just east of the park entrance. Boat launch and picnic area at lake.

DC 63.6 (102 km) **F 1424.4** (2292.3 km) Microwave tower to east.

DC 65.4 (105 km) **F 1422.6** (2289.4 km) Turnout with litter barrel to west.

DC 71.7 (115.4 km) **F 1416.3** (2279.3 km) **Historical Mile 72.** Food, gas, camping, lodging and crafts store.

Northern Expressions Gift Shop. See display ad this section.

The Shepherd's Inn. We specialize in making folks at home, offering regular and breakfast specials, complete lunch and dinner menu. Our specialties: homemade soups, home-baked sweet rolls, cinnamon rolls, blueberry and bran muffins, bread, biscuits and trappers bannock. Strawberry-rhubarb and Dutch apple pie. Hard ice cream. Specialty coffees: Norwegian Mint, Swiss Almond, Cafe Valencia. Refreshing fruit drinks from local fruits: blueberry and raspberry coolers. Full RV hookups, motel service 24 hours. Phone (604) 827-3676. An oasis on the Alcan at Mile 72. [ADVERTISEMENT]

DC 72.7 (117 km) **F 1415.3** (2277.6 km) **Historical Mile 73.** Gas and food to west (current status unknown).

DC 72.8 (117.1 km) **F 1415.2** (227.5 km) Road to Prespetu and Buick Creek.

DC 79.1 (127.3 km) **F 1408.9** (2267.5 km) **Historical Mile 80** rest area to west with litter barrels, picnic tables and pit toilets.

DC 91.4 (147.1 km) **F 1396.6** (2247.5 km) **Historical Mile 92.** Gas well to west.

Northern Expressions Gift Shop

Jewelry, Cards
Handcrafted Quilts
Unique Kid's Corner
Fresh Confectionery

A QUAINT SHOP WITH SOMETHING FOR EVERYONE!
Extension of The Shepherd's Inn
MILE 72, ALASKA HIGHWAY
Box 446, Charlie Lake, BC V0C 1H0 • (604) 827-3834

The Shepherd's Inn

MILE 72
Alaska Highway

LOCAL CRAFTS AND GIFTS

7 am - 9 pm Mon.-Sat.
Closed Sunday

"An Oasis on the Alaska Highway"

LIVE INSPIRATIONAL DINING MUSIC EVERY FRIDAY EVENING (tapes available)
RESTAURANT and DINING ROOM ... *A Dining Treat*
Delicious fresh-baked goods • Special coffee blends and cool fruit drinks
Fine Home Cooking • Reservations Recommended
Clean Air Concept • No Smoking Please
23 CLEAN, MODERN ROOMS • TV • Ideal for Families
Motel Open 24 Hours • Reasonable Rates
FULL RV PULL-THROUGH HOOKUPS • In-house Showers

Phone (604) 827-3676 FAX (604) 785-4759
Box 6425, Fort St. John, BC V1J 4H8, Canada
Your Hosts – Don and Dorothy Rutherford

Bus Tours and RV Caravans Welcome
GAS and PROPANE
Super, Natural Scenic Adventure

Charlie Lake General Store
POST OFFICE

Gas • Diesel • Propane
Groceries • Confectionary
Books • Ice
Take-out Food, Chicken & Ribs
Sporting Goods
Hunting and Fishing Licenses
Your Hosts — Albert & Barb Hockney
Mile 50.6 Alaska Highway • (604) 787-0655

Blueberry Esso Food Store & Motel

OPEN YEAR-ROUND

"YOUR ONE STOP SERVICE"

RESTAURANT
Home-Cooked Meals and Pastries

GROCERY STORE • LIQUOR AGENCY
Full line of Groceries • Fresh Meat and Produce
Ice • Soft Ice Cream • Paperbacks • Souvenirs

MOTEL
21 Fully Modern Units • Colour Television
Family Rooms & Family Rates • Reasonable Rates
Hunting and Fishing Licenses Available

VISA, EXXON, MasterCard, MARATHON, AMERICAN EXPRESS, Mobil, DINERS CLUB, PHILLIPS 66, SOHIO, BP

ESSO
Regular
Unleaded
Diesel
Propane
Tire Sales & Tire Repairs
Laundromat
CAMPGROUND
Free Parking

Box 28, Wonowon, British Columbia, Canada V0C 2N0
Mile 101 Alaska Highway
Phone: (604) 772-3322
(604) 772-3363

Super, Natural Scenic Adventure

PINK MOUNTAIN CAMPSITE

MILE 143 ALASKA HIGHWAY

Gas • Propane • Diesel • Groceries • Liquor Store
Post Office • Gifts & Souvenirs • Fishing Licenses
Showers • Laundromat • Shaded Campsite

VISA   MasterCard

(604) 774-1033

BOX 43, PINK MOUNTAIN, BC V0C 2B0

Super, Natural Scenic Adventure

Pink Mountain Motor Inn

MILE 143 KM 225
OPEN YEAR-ROUND
Esso

Write: Pink Mountain, BC, V0C 2B0
Walter, Donalda, Scott and Stewart Karpiuk
Phone (604) 772-3234

We Hope You Enjoy Your Alaska Highway Adventure!

Super, Natural Scenic Adventure   VISA

FULLY MODERN
34 Comfortable Units

FULLY LICENSED RESTAURANT
Fresh Baked Pies and Pastries
Home Cooked Meals

Tow Truck

ELECTRIC HOOKUPS FOR RVS

STORE AND GIFT SHOP
Souvenirs

Regular, Unleaded, Diesel and Propane

BUS TOURS WELCOME
Lunch - Written Reservations Required

— **NEW FOR 1992** —
Treed Camp Sites
with Good Gravel Parking
Picnic Tables • Water • Hot Showers
Laundromat and Dump Station

CARAVANS WELCOME
Reservations Recommended

DC 94.6 (152.2 km) F 1393.4 (2242.4 km) Oil pump east of highway behind trees.

DC 101 (161.7 km) F 1387 (2232.1 km) Historical Mile 101. WONOWON (pop. 150), unincorporated, has 3 gas stations, 3 restaurants, 2 motels, camping, a food store, pub and post office. Formerly known as Blueberry, Wonowon was the site of an official traffic control gate during WWII. Wonowon Horse Club holds an annual race meet and gymkhana at the track beside the highway, where the community club holds its annual snowmobile rally in February. ▲

The Alaska Highway follows the Blueberry and Prophet river drainages north to Fort Nelson. The Blueberry River, not visible from the highway, lies a few miles east of Wonowon.

Blueberry Esso, Food Store & Motel. See display ad this section.

DC 101.5 (163.3 km) F 1386.5 (2231.3 km) Food, gas, camping and lodging to east.

Nomadic Services. See display ad this section.

Pine Hill Motels. See display ad this section.

DC 114 (183.2 km) F 1374 (2211.2 km) Paved turnout with litter barrel to east.

DC 124.3 (200 km) F 1363.7 (2194.6 km) The Cut (highway goes through a small rock cut). Relatively few rock cuts were necessary during construction of the Alaska Highway in 1942-43. However, rock excavation was often made outside of the roadway to obtain gravel fill for the new roadbed.

DC 135.3 (217.7 km) F 1352.7 (2176.9 km) Gravel turnout to east.

DC 140.4 (225.9 km) F 1347.6 (2168.7 km) **Historical Mile 143. PINK MOUNTAIN** (pop. 99, area 300; elev. 3,600 feet/1,097m). Post office, grocery, motels, restaurant, campground, gas stations with minor repair service. Bus depot and ambulance service at Pink Mountain Motor Inn east side of highway.

Pink Mountain Motor Inn. Mile 143, a welcome stopping point for all travelers. 34

fully modern rooms, Get and Go groceries, gift shop, and licensed restaurant with fresh baked pies and pastries (our famed butter tarts) and home-cooked meals. The perfect lunch break stop for bus tours. Ample parking space, picnic tables. For RVs, electric hookups, gravel sites. New for 1992: treed camping sites with good gravel parking. Picnic tables. Water, hot showers, laundromat. Dump station. Caravans welcome, reservations recommended. Full line of Esso products. We hope you're enjoying your Alaska Highway adventure! Your hosts: The Karpiuk Family. (604) 772-3234. [ADVERTISEMENT]

Pink Mountain Campsite, on left northbound. Unleaded gas, diesel, metered propane for RVs and auto. Post office, general store, souvenirs, liquor store, fishing and hunting licenses. Shaded campsites, tents and RVs welcome. Coin laundromat and showers. Open year-round. VISA and MasterCard. (604) 774-1033. Enjoy Super, Natural Scenic Adventure. [ADVERTISEMENT] ▲

DC 144.1 (231.9 km) F 1343.9 (2162.7 km) Historical Mile 147. Sportsman Inn to east. See display ad this section. ▲

DC 144.5 (232.5 km) F 1343.5 (2162.1 km) Historical Mile 147. Mae's Kitchen and Ed's Garage to east. See display ad this section.

DC 144.7 (232.9 km) F 1343.3 (2161.8 km) Beatton River bridge. The Beatton River was named for Frank Beatton, a Hudson's Bay Co. employee. The Beatton River flows east and then south into the Peace River system.

DC 146 (234 km) F 1342 (2159.7 km) Private Aircraft: Sikanni Chief flight strip to east; elev. 3,258 feet/993m; length, 6,000 feet/1,829m; gravel; not maintained in winter, soft in spring.

DC 156.6 (252 km) F 1331.4 (2142.6 km) Sikanni Hill.

DC 159.2 (256.2 km) F 1328.8 (2138.4 km) Sikanni Chief River bridge (elev. 2,662 feet/811m). To the west you can see the old wooden bridge this bridge replaced. The timber truss bridge built across the Sikanni Chief River in the spring of 1943 was the first permanent structure completed on the Alaska Highway. Highway construction crews rerouted much of the pioneer road built in 1942 and replaced temporary bridges with permanent structures in 1943.

The Sikanni Chief River flows east and then north into the Fort Nelson River, which flows into the Liard River and on to the Mackenzie River which empties into the Arctic Ocean. Check at the park for information on Sikanni River Falls (see **Milepost DC 168.5**).

Sikanni Chief River, fair fishing at mouth of tributaries in summer for pike; grayling to 2½ pounds; whitefish to 2 pounds.

DC 159.4 (256.5 km) F 1328.6 (2138.1 km) Historical Mile 162. SIKANNI CHIEF. Food, gas, lodging and camping. ▲

Sikanni River RV Park. See display ad on page 94.

MOTEL • CAMPGROUND • RV HOOKUPS
9 MODERN CABINS

Housekeeping and sleeping units with bath or shower
24 RV Full Hookups Sites • Tent Sites
Cable TV in Motel and Campground

Showers • Laundromat
Winter Plug-ins

PINE HILL MOTELS

MILE 101.5 ALASKA HIGHWAY
P.O. Box 30, Wonowon, BC V0C 2N0
(604) 772-3340

VISA Super, Natural Scenic Adventure

SPORTSMAN INN

Homecooked Meals • Rooms • Ice   Open 7 Days A Week

DANNY'S
Gas • Diesel
(competitive prices)
VISA, MasterCard,
American Express, and Shell Accepted
FREE RV PARKING including hookups with fill-up

RV PARKING
Over 100 Sites (2 locations)
• Full Hookups
• Partial Hookups
• Dry Sites
• Dump Stations

MILE 147, ALASKA HIGHWAY • PINK MOUNTAIN, BC V0C 2B0
(604) 772-3220

Super, Natural Scenic Adventure

Nomadic Services

Mile 102 — Alaska Highway

✻ **24-Hour Restaurant** ✻
Fine home cooking
Fresh bread and pastries

Bus Tours Welcome (Please call ahead)

✻ **Rooms** ✻
34 clean rooms
Satellite TV • Phones
Reasonable rates year round

✻ **Fuel — 24 Hours** ✻
Gas • Diesel • Propane

— Credit Cards Accepted —

Snowbird Arts & Crafts
Traditional Native handicrafts
Beaded mukluks and moccasins
Pottery, handcrafted furniture
Original pieces, souvenirs

Box 89, Wonowon, BC
Phone (604) 772-3288

Super, Natural Scenic Adventure

❖ **BUS TOURS WELCOME** ❖
(Please call ahead)

❖ **RESTAURANT** ❖
Well prepared foods served with fresh baked breads and pastries.
Take our souvenir cookbook home

❖ **LOCAL CRAFTS** ❖
Postcards and T-Shirts

❖ **MOTEL** ❖
With clean, modern rooms
Reasonable Rates

Mae's Kitchen
AND
Ed's Garage
Div. of Headwaters Ranch Ltd.

OPEN YEAR-ROUND
FULL SERVICE
GARAGE
and Towing
Unleaded Gas and Diesel

Mile 147, Alaska Hwy.
Pink Mountain, BC   (604) 772-3215

Husky
Here on the Alaska Highway It's Husky

Super, Natural Scenic Adventure

Sikanni River RV Park. Come and enjoy the only riverside RV park in the area. A peaceful, scenic setting to a natural playground for birds and wildlife. 50 sites, picnic tables, fire rings. Free firewood. Water and dump complimentary for guests. Store, souvenirs, ice, fishing and camping supplies. Munchies. Reasonable rates. Resident owners. Clean, safe and secure. Open 7 A.M. to 10 P.M. daily. Inspected by Trailer Life. See display ad this section. [ADVERTISEMENT] ▲

DC 160.4 (258.1 km) F 1327.6 (2136.5 km) Section of the old Alaska Highway is visible to east; no access.

DC 168.5 (271.2 km) F 1319.5 (2123.5 km) Gravel road west to Sikanni River Falls. This private road is signed "Travel at own risk." Drive in 10.5 miles/16.9 km to parking area with picnic tables at B.C. Forest Service trailhead; 10-minute hike in on well-marked trail to view falls. Gravel access road has some steep hills and a single-lane bridge. *CAUTION: Do not travel in wet weather. Not recommended for vehicles with trailers.*

DC 172.5 (277.6 km) F 1315.5 (2117 km) Polka Dot Creek.

DC 173.1 (278 km0 F 1314.9 (2116.9 km) Buckinghorse River bridge; access to river at north end of bridge.

DC 173.2 (278.2 km) F 1314.8 (2115.9 km) **Historical Mile 175.** Inn with gas and camping to east at north end of bridge. Also turnoff east for Buckinghorse River Provincial Park. Follow the narrow gravel road past the gravel pit 0.7 mile/1.1 km along river to camping and picnic area. Camping fee $6 to $12. The provincial park has 30 picnic tables, side-by-side camper parking, firewood, fire rings, water pump, outhouses and garbage containers. Poor fishing for grayling in **Buckinghorse River.** Swimming in downstream pools. ▲

Today's Alaska Highway in winter.
(Earl L. Brown, staff)

DC 173.4 (278.5 km) F 1314.6 (2115.6 km) **Historical Mile 175. Buckinghorse River Lodge**, on left northbound. Motel, cafe, licensed dining room with home cooking and a friendly atmosphere. Service station, large parking area, camping. Picnic tables and beautiful scenery. A good spot to take a break to go fishing or walking. Enjoy Super, Natural Scenic Adventure. (604) 773-6468. [ADVERTISEMENT] ▲

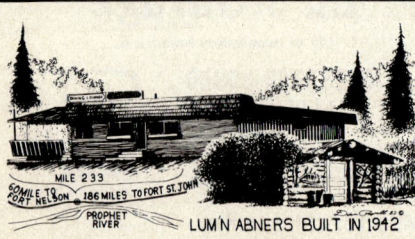

DC 176 (283.2 km) F 1312 (2111.4 km) South end of 28-mile/45-km Trutch Mountain bypass. Completed in 1987, this section of road rerouted the Alaska Highway around Trutch Mountain, eliminating the steep, winding climb up to Trutch Summit (and the views). Named for Joseph W. Trutch, civil engineer and first governor of British Columbia, Trutch Mountain was the second-highest summit on the Alaska Highway with an elevation of 4,134 feet/1,260m. The new roadbed cuts a wide swath through the flat Minaker River valley. The river, not visible to motorists, is west of the highway; Trutch Mountain is to the east. Motorists can see part of the old highway on Trutch Mountain. Part of the old Trutch summit route may be reopened to travelers this year for the 50th anniversary of the highway.

DC 182.8 (294.2 km) F 1305.2 (2100.4 km) Gravel turnout with litter barrel to west.

DC 204.2 (328 km) F 1283.8 (2066 km) Beaver Creek. North end of Trutch Mountain bypass.

DC 217.2 (349.3 km) F 1270.8 (2045.1 km) Turnoff to west for Prophet River Provincial Park, 0.4 mile/0.6 km via gravel road. The park access road crosses an airstrip (originally an emergency airstrip on the Northwest Air Staging Route) and part of the old Alaska Highway (the Alcan). Side-by-side camper parking (36 sites), picnic tables, firewood, fire rings, water pump, outhouses and garbage containers. Camping fee $6 to $12. ▲

Private Aircraft: Prophet River emergency airstrip; elev. 1,954 feet/596m; length 6,000 feet/1,829m; gravel.

DC 218.2 (350.7 km) F 1269.8 (2043.5 km) View of Prophet River to west.

DC 222.3 (357.2 km) F 1265.7 (2036.9 km) Bougie Creek bridge; turnout with litter barrel beside creek at south end of bridge.

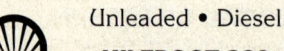

DC 224.8 (360.6 km) F 1263.2 (2032.8 km) Microwave tower to east.

DC 226.2 (363.4 km) F 1261.8 (2030.6 km) Prophet River Indian Reserve to east.

DC 226.5 (363.9 km) F 1261.5 (2030.1 km) St. Paul's Roman Catholic Church.

DC 227 (364.7 km) F 1261 (2029.3 km) **Historical Mile 233. PROPHET RIVER**, gas, food, camping and lodging. Southbound travelers note: Next service 68 miles/109 km. ▲

Prophet River Services. See display ad this section.

DC 227.7 (365.9 km) F 1260.3 (2028.2 km) Adsett Creek.

DC 230.7 (370.7 km) F 1257.3 (2023.3 km) Natural gas pipeline crosses beneath highway.

DC 235.5 (378.4 km) F 1252.5 (2015.6 km) Mesalike topography to the east is Mount Yakatchie.

DC 241.5 (388 km) F 1246.5 (2006 km) Parker Creek.

DC 264.6 (425.2 km) F 1223.4 (1968.8 km) Jackfish Creek bridge.

DC 265.5 (426.5 km) F 1222.5 (1967.4 km) Turnoff to east for Andy Bailey Lake Provincial Park via 6.8-mile/11-km dirt and gravel access road. (Large RVs and trailers note: only turnaround space on access road is approximately halfway in.) The park is located on **Andy Bailey Lake** (formerly Jackfish Lake); side-by-side camper parking (35 sites), tenting and picnic area, picnic tables, fire rings, firewood, water, outhouses, garbage containers, boat launch (no powerboats), swimming and fair fishing for northern pike. Camping fee $6 to $12. Bring insect repellent! ⛺▲

DC 270.8 (435.1 km) F 1217.2 (1958.8 km) Gas pipeline crosses highway overhead.

DC 271 (435.4 km) F 1217 (1958.5 km) Westcoast Energy gas processing plant to east. Petrosul (sulfur processing) to west.

DC 276.2 (443.8 km) F 1211.8 (1950 km) Rodeo grounds to west.

DC 276.7 (444.6 km) F 1211.3 (1949.3 km) Railroad tracks. Microwave tower at Muskwa Heights.

DC 277.5 (446.2 km) F 1210.5 (1948 km) Muskwa Heights (unincorporated), an industrial area with rail yard, plywood plant, sawmill and bulk fuel outlet. Truck stop with gas, restaurant and RV campground. ▲

Husky 5th Wheel Truck Stop and R.V. Park. See display ad this section.

DC 278 (446.8 km) F 1210 (1947.3 km) Truck scales to west. Chopstick manufacturing plant.

DC 279.5 (449.8 km) F 1208.5 (1944.8 km) Klahanie Trailer and RV Park. ▲

DC 281 (451.4 km) F 1207 (1942.4 km) Muskwa River bridge, lowest point on the Alaska Highway (elev. 1,000 feet/305m).

The **Muskwa River** flows northeast to the Fort Nelson River. Fair fishing at the mouth of tributaries for northern pike; some goldeye. The Fort Nelson River is too muddy for fishing. 🐟

The Alaska Highway swings west at Fort Nelson above the Muskwa River, winding southwest then northwest through the Canadian Rockies.

DC 283 (454.3 km) F 1205 (1939.2 km) Entering Fort Nelson northbound. Fort Nelson's central business district extends along the highway from the private campground at the east end of the city to the private campground at the west end. Businesses and services are located both north and south of the highway.

Winter on the pioneer road

An Army truck stuck in an icy culvert along the Alaska Highway in 1943. Construction and traffic along the highway were severely hampered by subzero temperatures. Concrete bridge deckings could not be poured in cold weather. Steel became brittle and grease in bearings and gear boxes hardened. Experienced drivers left their motors idling while they napped or ate their meals. But winter actually made some sections of the pioneer road easier to travel by freezing stretches of swampy ground.

Edwin Bonde

Husky 5th Wheel
Truck Stop and RV Park

OPEN 24 HOURS

5 miles south of downtown Fort Nelson on Alaska Highway

RESTAURANT
- Home-cooked meals

GROCERY STORE
- Full line of groceries
- Magazines and paperbacks

GAS • DIESEL • PROPANE

Husky — Here in Canada it's Husky   UNOCAL

Minor & Major Mechanical
TIRE SALES AND REPAIRS
• FIRESTONE • BRIDGESTONE

CAMPGROUND (Good Sam Club)
We Cater to Caravans
74 Fully Serviced Sites
- Dump Station • Propane
- Ice • Showers • Laundromat
- Rec Hall Facilities with Spa

VISA   MasterCard

(604) 774-7270
FAX (604) 774-7200
R.R. #1, Fort Nelson, BC V0C 1R0

Super, Natural Scenic Adventure

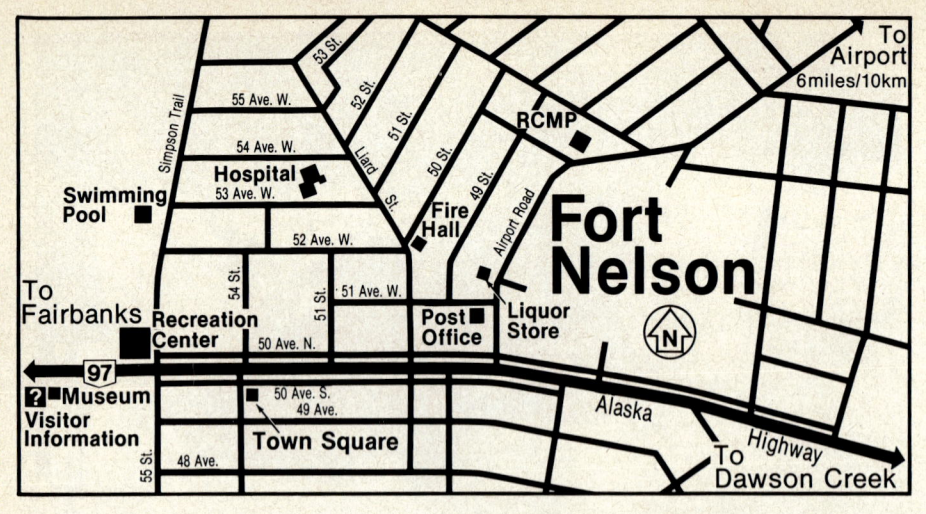

Fort Nelson

DC 283 (454.3 km) F 1205 (1939.2 km) Historical Mile 300. Population: 3,729; area 5,300. Emergency Services: RCMP, phone 774-2777. Fire Department, phone 774-2222. Hospital, 41 beds, phone 774-6916. Ambulance, phone 774-2344. Medical, dental and optometric clinics. Visiting veterinarians and chiropractors.

Visitor Information: At the blue chalet travel infocentre on the Alaska Highway at the west end of town, open 8 A.M. to 8 P.M. Inquire here about road conditions on the Liard Highway. Fort Nelson Heritage Museum adjacent infocentre. Contact the Town of Fort Nelson by writing Bag Service 399, Fort Nelson, BC V0C 1R0; phone (604) 774-6400 (seasonal) or 774-2541 (all year).

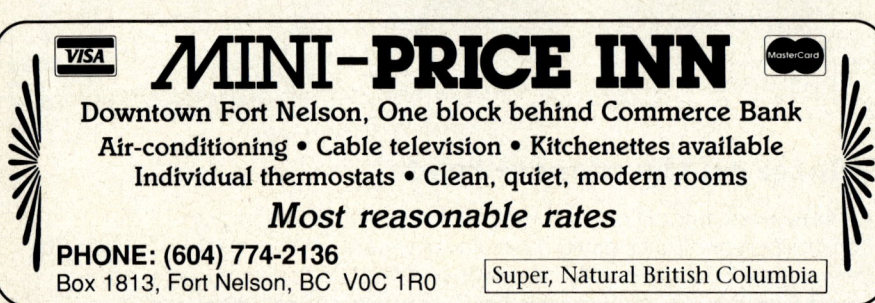

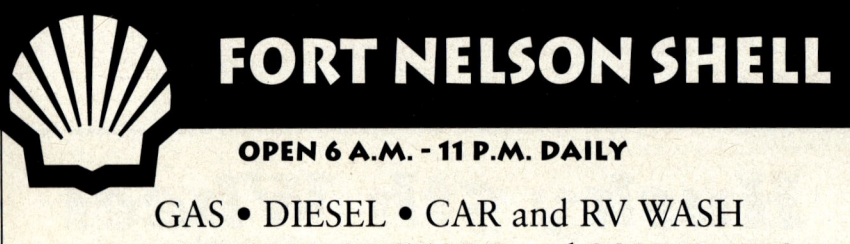

Elevation: 1,383 feet/422m. **Climate:** Winters are cold with short days. Summers are hot and the days are long. In mid-June (summer solstice), twilight continues throughout the night. The average number of frost-free days annually is 116. Last frost occurs about May 11, and the first frost Sept. 21. Average annual precipitation of 16.3 inches. **Radio:** CFNL 590, CBC 1610. **Television:** Channels 8, 13 and cable. **Newspaper:** *Fort Nelson News* (weekly).

Transportation: Air—Scheduled service to Edmonton, Grande Prairie and Watson Lake, and to Prince George and Vancouver via Time Air and Canadian Airlines International. Charter service available. **Bus**—Greyhound service daily except Sunday. **Railroad**—B.C. Railway (freight service only).

Private Aircraft: Fort Nelson airport, 3.8 air miles/6.1 km east northeast; elev. 1,253 feet/382m; length 6,400 feet/1,950m; asphalt; fuel 80, 100, jet B. Gordon Field, 4 miles/6.4 km west; elev. 1,625 feet/495m

MINI-PRICE INN
Downtown Fort Nelson, One block behind Commerce Bank
Air-conditioning • Cable television • Kitchenettes available
Individual thermostats • Clean, quiet, modern rooms
Most reasonable rates
PHONE: (604) 774-2136
Box 1813, Fort Nelson, BC V0C 1R0
VISA MasterCard
Super, Natural British Columbia

FORT NELSON SHELL
OPEN 6 A.M. - 11 P.M. DAILY
GAS • DIESEL • CAR and RV WASH
CONVENIENCE STORE and SOUVENIRS
ICE • DUMP STATION • U-HAUL AGENT
(604) 774-3945
Premier Propane Inc.
BOTTLED AND AUTO PROPANE
AMERICAN EXPRESS MasterCard VISA

Provincial Motel
Restaurant and Dining Room Adjacent
37 Fully Modern Units • 13 with Kitchenettes
Phones • Cable Television • Extra-Long Beds

South End of Fort Nelson
Box 690, Fort Nelson, B.C., Canada V0C 1R0
Phone (604) 774-6901 • FAX (604) 774-4208
MasterCard VISA
Super, Natural Scenic Adventure

BLUE BELL MOTEL
FAMILY RESTAURANT
MODERN QUIET ROOMS
and Kitchenettes
Full RV and Campground Facilities
Showers • Laundromat • Convenience Store

PETRO-CANADA
SELF-SERVICE
OPEN 24 HOURS
GASOLINE
Unleaded, Super Unleaded, Diesel and Oil Products
MasterCard VISA

South End of Fort Nelson
(604) 774-6961
Box 873, Fort Nelson, BC Canada V0C 1R0

Super, Natural Scenic Adventure

approximately; length 2,000 feet/610m; turf; fuel 80.

Fort Nelson is located in the lee of the Rocky Mountains, surrounded by the Muskwa, Nelson and Prophet rivers. The area is heavily forested with white spruce, poplar and aspen. Geographically, the town is located about 59° north latitude and 122° west longitude.

Flowing east and north, the Muskwa, Prophet and Sikanni Chief rivers converge to form the Fort Nelson River, which flows into the Liard River, then on to the Mackenzie River which empties into the Arctic Ocean. Rivers provided the only means of transportation in both summer and winter in this isolated region until 1922, when the Godsell Trail opened, connecting Fort Nelson with Fort St. John. The Alaska Highway linked Fort Nelson with the Outside in 1942.

In the spring, the Muskwa River frequently floods the low country around Fort Nelson and can rise more than 20 feet/6m. At an elevation of 1,000 feet/305m, the Muskwa (which means "bear") is the lowest point on the Alaska Highway. There was a danger of the Muskwa River bridge washing out every June during spring runoff until 1970, when a higher bridge—with piers arranged to prevent log jams—was built.

Fort Nelson's existence was originally based on the fur trade. In the 1920s, trapping was the main business in this isolated pioneer community populated with less than 200 Indians and a few white men. Trappers still harvest beaver, wolverine, weasel, wolf, fox, lynx, mink, muskrat and marten. Other area wildlife includes black bears, which are plentiful, some deer, caribou and a few grizzly bears. Moose remains an important food source for the Indians.

Fort Nelson Indians are mostly Slave (slay-vee), who arrived here about 1775 from the Great Slave Lake area and speak an Athabascan dialect.

Fort Nelson was first established in 1805 by the North West Fur Trading Co. The post,

FORT NELSON ADVERTISERS

Bennetts Travel
   Time Inc. ....Ph. (604) 774-6144
Blue Bell Motel ....S. end of town
Coachouse Inn ....4711 50th Ave. S.
Fort Nelson Esso...........Across from post office
Fort Nelson Heritage
   Museum..............Adjacent travel infocentre
Fort Nelson Hotel ....Ph. (604) 774-6971
Fort Nelson Shell ....S. end of town
Gra-lin Burger Barn.....51st Ave. W. & Liard St.
KaCee's Koin Kleaners.............Landmark Plaza
Klahanie Trailer and
   R.V. Park ....3 miles S. of town
Miki's Books............................Landmark Plaza
Mini-Price Inn ....Ph. (604) 774-2136
Mr. Milkshare ....1 blk. W. of Town Square
Northern Husky..............................Downtown
Northern Lights Deli ....Landmark Plaza
Peter's Place ....Next to Bank of Commerce
Pioneer Motel ....Ph. (604) 774-6459
Poplar Hills Golf and
   Country Club.............Mile 304 Alaska Hwy.
Provincial Motel ....S. end of town
Red Rose Convenience
   Store ....S. end of town
Shannon Motel ....N. end of town
Town of Fort Nelson ....Town Square
Trapper's Den ....4 miles S. of town
Westend Campground............N. end of town

TAKE-OUT or EAT-IN   **PHONE 774-4442**

GRA-LIN BURGER BARN

99 flavours — The Yogurt and Ice Cream Shoppe   10 a.m. - 10 p.m. daily
Shakes • Sundaes • Banana Splits . . .   Liard St. and 51st Ave. W.
100% Lean Homemade Hamburgers   (Behind the Saan Store)

KLAHANIE TRAILER AND R.V. PARK

(Just 3 Miles South of Fort Nelson)

◆ Spacious Full Hookup Sites
◆ Coin Laundry
◆ Picnic Tables
◆ Fire Pits

(604) 774-7013
P.O. Box 1, Fort Nelson, BC V0C 1R0

PETER'S PLACE
"Fort Nelson's Finest Dining"
An intimate dining atmosphere with a select choice of food and gracious service

Licensed

Home of the Peter Pappas Perfect Pizza

MAIN STREET   774-6633
Next to The Bank of Commerce

Fort Nelson Esso

UNLEADED • PREMIUM • DIESEL

Licensed Mechanics
Air Conditioning Service
Front End Alignment

Ice • Accessories • Cold Pop

Auto and Bottled Propane
B.F. Goodrich Tires
Sani-Dump • 24 Hour Towing

BCAA AUTHORIZED ROAD SERVICE   Good Sam Emergency Road Service

Tilden Car and Truck Rentals

Alaska Highway and Airport Road, opposite the Post Office

(604) 774-2627
Box 2221, Fort Nelson, BC V0C 1R0

Super, Natural Scenic Adventure

FORT NELSON HOTEL (Bus Tour Specialists)

145 modern rooms, some with kitchenettes – all with private baths. Cable colour TV and phones in every room. Ample hard surface parking. Licensed dining rooms and cocktail lounge. Air conditioned. Courtesy airport limousine.

New Deluxe Units • Indoor Pool • Saunas
Cable Colour TV • Telephones • Coffee Shop
Gift Shop • Tiki Dining Room • Nightly Entertainment and Dancing
For Reservations (604) 774-6971 • 1-800-663-5225 • FAX (604) 774-6711

Super, Natural Scenic Adventure   FORT NELSON HOTEL, BOX 240, FORT NELSON V0C 1R0

believed to have been located about 80 miles/129 km south of Nelson Forks, was named for Lord Horatio Nelson, the English admiral who won the Battle of Trafalgar.

A second Fort Nelson was later located south of the first fort, but was destroyed by fire in 1813 after Indians massacred its 8 residents. A third Fort Nelson was established in 1865 on the Nelson River's west bank (1 mile from the present Fort Nelson airport) by W. Cornwallis King, a Hudson's Bay Co. clerk. This trading post was built to keep out the free traders who were filtering in from the Mackenzie River and Fort St. John areas.

The free traders' higher fur prices were a threat to the Hudson's Bay Co., which in 1821 had absorbed the rival North West Fur Trading Co. and gained a monopoly on the fur trade in Canada.

This Hudson's Bay Co. trading post was destroyed by a flood in 1890 and a fourth Fort Nelson was established on higher ground upstream and across the river, which is now known as Old Fort Nelson. The present town of Fort Nelson is the fifth site.

Fort Nelson saw its first mail service in 1936. Scheduled air service to Fort Nelson—by ski- and floatplane—also was begun in the 1930s by Yukon Southern Air (which was later absorbed by CPAir, now Canadian Airlines International). The Canadian government began construction of an airport in 1941 as part of the Northwest Air Staging Route, and this was followed by perhaps the biggest boom to Fort Nelson—the construction of the Alaska Highway in 1942. About 2,000 soldiers were bivouacked in Fort Nelson, which they referred to as Zero, as it was the beginning of a road to Whitehorse and another road to Fort Simpson. Later Dawson Creek became Mile 0 and Fort Nelson Mile 300.

Fort Nelson expanded in the 1940s and 1950s as people came here to work for the government or to start their own small businesses: trucking, barging, aviation, construction, garages, stores, cafes, motels and sawmills. It is surprising to consider that as recently as the 1950s, Fort Nelson was still a

Fort Nelson
(604) 774-3911
FAX (604) 774-3730

COACHOUSE INN
RESTAURANT • SAUNA

72 Modern Rooms • Individual Heat / Air Conditioning • Direct Dial Phones • Cable TV • Licensed Lounge & Dining • Whirlpool & Saunas Wheelchair Access • Winter Plug-ins
♦ **Reasonable Rates** ♦
(Military / AAA / Corporate Discounts)

Super, Natural Scenic Adventure

Bennetts TRAVEL TIME Inc

TRAVEL TIME
FULL SERVICE TRAVEL AGENCY

PHONE (604) 774-6144
FAX (604) 774-2133

—Plus—
Information and Reservations for
ADVENTURE VACATIONS, ACCOMMODATIONS and ATTRACTIONS
in
Super Natural Northern British Columbia

BOX 800, DEPT. M92
FORT NELSON, BC V0C 1R0

PIONEER MOTEL
(Centrally Located • Reasonable Rates)
12 Units — Kitchenettes Available

Cable TV
Pets Welcome
Coin-op Laundry Facilities

Your Hosts — Rocky and Carola Lynch

Box 1944, Fort Nelson B.C.
VISA **(604) 774-6459** MasterCard

Super, Natural Scenic Adventure

Fort Nelson Heritage Museum

**PIONEER ARTIFACTS
HIGHWAY CONSTRUCTION DISPLAY
SPRUCE BARK CANOE
SOUVENIRS ... and more**
Run by a nonprofit society—admission charged

Located next to Visitors Information Centre
Fort Nelson Historical Society
Box 716, Fort Nelson, BC, V0C 1R0 • (604) 774-3536

Super, Natural Scenic Adventure

NORTHERN HUSKY

Open 7 Days A Week, 7 a.m. – 11 p.m.   **Downtown Fort Nelson**
★ FULL SERVICE ★ Licenced Mechanic
★ Tire Sales and Tire Repairs
– 10% discount for senior citizens on parts and labour –
★ DUMPING STATON ★ ICE
WE GIVE EXCHANGE ON AMERICAN CURRENCY

Unleaded
Diesel
Propane

Husky
Here in Canada it's Husky

Box 3267, Fort Nelson, BC
V0C 1R0 (604) 774-2376

Super, Natural Scenic Adventure

LAUNDROMAT
KaCee's Koin Kleaners

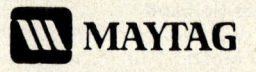

MAYTAG

"Drop Off Service"

LANDMARK PLAZA   Phone 774-2911
On the right going North   Fort Nelson

Super, Natural Scenic Adventure

pioneer community without power, phones, running water, refrigerators or doctors. Interesting recollections of Fort Nelson's early days may be found in Gerri Young's book *The Fort Nelson Story;* available at the museum.

Fort Nelson was an unorganized territory until 1957 when it was declared an Improvement District. Fort Nelson took on village status in 1971 and town status in 1987.

Forestry is a major industry here with a veneer plant, plywood plant and sawmill. Chopsticks are manufactured at a local plant here for export to Asian markets.

Forestry products are shipped south by truck and by rail. Fort Nelson became a railhead in 1971 with the completion of a 250-mile extension of the Pacific Great Eastern Railway (now British Columbia Railway) from Fort St. John.

Agriculture is under development here with the recent establishment of the 55,000-acre McConachie Creek agricultural subdivision. A local honey farm produces excellent honey.

Northeastern British Columbia is the only sedimentary area in the province currently producing oil and gas. Oil seeps in the Fort Nelson area were noted by early residents. Major gas discoveries were made in the 1960s when the Clarke Lake, Yoyo/Kotcho, Beaver River and Pointed Mountain gas reserves were developed. The Westcoast Energy natural gas processing plant at Fort Nelson was constructed in 1964. This plant purifies the gas before sending it south through the 800-mile-long pipeline which connects the Fort Nelson area with the British Columbia lower mainland. Sulfur, a

Mr. Milkshake FAST-FOOD

Just one block west of Town Square

SPECIALIZING IN . . .
- Tender Fried Chicken
- Honey and Garlic Ribs
- Homemade Hamburgers
- Thick Crust Pizzas
- Soup and Sandwiches
- Seafood • JoJo Potatoes
- SALADS (serveral varieties)
- Homemade Pies

**MILKSHAKES - 20 Flavours
HARD and SOFT ICE CREAM
Sundaes and Banana Splits**

(604) 774-2526

Open 10 a.m. - 11 p.m. daily

**80-Seat Restaurant
♦ AIR CONDITIONED ♦**

Bus Tours and Caravans Welcome

Super, Natural Scenic Adventure

WELCOME TO RESOURCE-FULL FORT NELSON-LIARD

ALASKA HIGHWAY Rendezvous '92

RENDEZVOUS '92 EVENTS:

x GRAND OPENING PHOENIX THEATRE	JANUARY
x NORTHERN B.C. WINTER GAMES	FEBRUARY
x SNOWMOBILE SAFARI '92	FEBRUARY
x ALASKA HIGHWAY TRAILBLAZERS	JUNE
x ARMY MOTORS CONVOY	JUNE
x FLOAT PLANE COMPETITION	JUNE
x AIRMADA	JULY
x RALLY ALASKA HIGHWAY '92	SEPTEMBER
x CANADIAN OPEN SLED DOG RACES	DECEMBER

YOU ARE INVITED TO ATTEND THE
ORIGINAL WELCOME VISITOR PROGRAM
MID-MAY THROUGH AUGUST

VISIT OUR
**TRAVEL INFOCENTRE
AND
HISTORICAL MUSEUM**

**TOWN OF FORT NELSON
FORT NELSON-LIARD REGIONAL DISTRICT**
TOWN SQUARE, 5319 50TH AVE. SOUTH
BAG SERVICE 399 M92
FORT NELSON, BC CANADA V0C 1R0
PHONE: (604) 774-2541 FAX: (604) 774-6794

Super, Natural Scenic Adventure

ALASKA HIGHWAY • FORT NELSON

WESTEND CAMPGROUND

Over 120 Sites • Pull-throughs • Tent Sites • Full Hookups
Laundromat • Dump Station • Hot Showers • Ice • Groceries
FREE Car Wash • Gifts and Souvenirs

Your Hosts: Chris and Sandra Brown
Box 398, Fort Nelson, BC V0C 1R0
Phone (604) 774-2340 • FAX (604) 774-3104
VISA
Easy Walking Distance to Museum and Info Centre

New for '92 — Alaska Highway Mini-Golf

Good Sam Club

Super, Natural Scenic Adventure

Tell our advertisers you saw their advertisement in *The MILEPOST*®.

Virginia Falls
and
Nahanni National Park
A Unesco World Heritage Site

• Sightseeing, day trips, hiking and camping tours
• Canoe trips to various points in Nahanni Park • Rentals available

From: FORT LIARD, NWT, CANADA

"Cheapest Fares to Virginia Falls"

Alaska-bound travellers!!! Fort Liard, NWT is only 2-1/2 hours by road from Fort Nelson, BC on the Liard Highway — a nice sidetrip.

• You can say that you have been to the Northwest Territory
• Handmade Native Crafts Available
• Campers Welcome (Facilities Available)

Call or Write:
DEH CHO AIR LTD.
General Delivery
Fort Liard, NWT X0G 0A0
Phone (403) 770-4103
FAX (403) 770-3555

DEH CHO AIR LTD.
PHONE 770-4103
FORT LIARD, N.W.T.

VISA

Personalized Trophy Fishing Trips Available
"WE GO THE EXTRA MILE"

Loading sulfur at Fort Nelson's gas processing plant. (Earl L. Brown, staff)

byproduct of natural gas processing, is processed in a recovery plant and shipped to Outside markets in pellet form.

ACCOMMODATIONS
Fort Nelson has 9 hotels/motels, several gas stations and restaurants, a pub, an auto supply store, department stores and other services, most located north and south just off the Alaska Highway. The post office and liquor store are on Airport Drive. There are 2 banks on the business frontage road north of the highway. Fresh water fill-up and free municipal dump station adjacent the blue chalet travel infocentre. Inquire at the infocentre for location of local churches and their hours of worship.

Trapper's Den. Owned and operated by a local trapping family. Moose horns, diamond willow, northern novelties and books, postcards, souvenirs and professionally tanned furs. Located 300 yards north of Husky 5th Wheel RV Park on the Alaska Highway. Open 10 A.M. to 8 P.M. daily. John and Cindy Wells. Box 1164, Fort Nelson, BC V0C 1R0. [ADVERTISEMENT]

Red Rose Convenience Store/Bi-Lo Gas Station. Open 6 A.M. to 11 P.M. daily. Groceries, fresh produce and dairy, ice and ice cream, take-out deli—subs and sandwiches, coffee to go. Magazines, Lotto ticket centre. Motorhomes and caravans—save 2¢/litre on volume gasoline purchase (250 or more litres). Located south end of town (watch for the big Bi-Lo canopy). Your hosts, Michael and Lorna Cooper. (604) 774-3737.
[ADVERTISEMENT]

Westend Campground. Overnight parking. Over 120 large individual gravelled sites, full hookups. Pull-throughs. Dump station. Campfires and free firewood. Drinking water, coin-op hot showers, laundromat, free car wash. Good Sam Park. Groceries, ice, souvenirs and gift shop. Pay phone. New for 1992—Alaska Highway mini golf. Handicap facilities. North end of town. Caters to caravans. Your new hosts, Chris and Sandra

---

100   The MILEPOST® ▪ 1992

Brown. Box 398, Fort Nelson, BC V0C 1R0. Phone 774-2340. Super, Natural Scenic Adventure. [ADVERTISEMENT] ▲

Fort Nelson has 4 campgrounds: one is located at the north (or west) end of town adjacent the travel infocentre; one is at the south (or east) end of town; and the others are in the Muskwa Heights area south of Fort Nelson. ▲

ATTRACTIONS

Fort Nelson offers travelers a free "Welcome Visitors Program" on summer evenings. These interesting and entertaining presentations are put on by local residents and range from slide shows to talks on items of local interest. Check with the travel infocentre or at the Town Square for details.

The Fort Nelson Heritage Museum, adjacent the travel infocentre, has displays of pioneer artifacts, Alaska Highway history, a spruce bark canoe and souvenirs and books for sale. Native crafts are displayed at the Fort Nelson-Liard Native Friendship Centre, located on 49th Avenue.

The recreation centre, across from the blue chalet, has tennis courts; hockey and curling arena for winter sports. Swimming pool, swirl pool, sauna and gym located in the Aqua Centre on Simpson Trail. For golfers, there is the Poplar Hills Golf and Country Club, just north of town. The course has grass greens and is open daily until dark.

Fort Nelson is also the gateway to the Liard Highway, which junctions with the Alaska Highway 17 miles/27 km north of town. The Liard opened in 1984, providing access to Fort Liard, NWT, and the Mackenzie Highway.

Special Events. In addition to the events listed in the 1992 calendar this section, Fort Nelson hosts a number of special interest benefits, dances, tournaments and exhibits. Check locally for details and dates on all events in the community.

1992 Events

MARCH
2-8 Trapper's Rendezvous

APRIL
29-5/3 Tourism North Conference

MAY
1-3 Tourism Conference continues
2 Boy Scouts Talent Show
19-8/28 Welcome Visitor Program

JUNE
1-8/28 Visitor Program continues
6 Alaska Highway Trailblazers stop
12-13 Army Motors Convoy overnight
21-23 Float Plane Race overnight
26-27 Army Motors Convoy overnight

JULY
1-8/28 Visitor Program continues
1 Canada Day Parade
4-5 Toad River Reunion
9-10 Airmada
10-12 843rd Signal Service Battalion Annual Reunion

AUGUST
1-28 Visitor Program continues
11-13 Alaska Highway Square Dancers
14-16 Fort Nelson Rodeo
22 Fall Fair

SEPTEMBER
13 BC Fire Training Officers Assoc. Conference
20-22 Rallye Alaska Highway '92 stop

OCTOBER
1-4 Alaska Highway Assoc. Inaugural Conference
31 Spookerama

NOVEMBER
26-28 Broken Stick Hockey Tournament

DECEMBER
5 Christmas Craft Fair
12-13 Canadian Open Sled Dog Races

Alaska Highway Log

(continued)

Distance* from Dawson Creek (DC) is followed by distance from Fairbanks (F). Original mileposts are indicated in the text as Historical Mile.

*Mileages from Dawson Creek are based on actual driving distance. Kilometres from Dawson Creek are based on physical kilometreposts. Please read Mileposts and Kilometreposts in the introduction for an explanation of how this highway is logged.

DC 284 (456.4 km) F 1204 (1937.6 km) West end of Fort Nelson. Visitor information and log museum south side of highway, private campground adjacent. ▲

Northbound: Watch for sections of rough, narrow, winding road and breaks in surfacing between Fort Nelson and the BC-YT border (approximately next 321 miles/516.5 km). Muskwa Valley bypass planned between Mile 301 and Mile 308.

Southbound: Good pavement, wider road, next 284 miles/457 km (to Dawson Creek).

DC 284.5 (457.5 km) F 1203.5 (1936.8 km) Fort Nelson District Forestry Office.

DC 287.9 (462.6 km) F 1200.1 (1931.3 km) **Historical Mile 304.** Exit north on 1.5-mile/2.4-km access road for Poplar Hills

---

MIKI'S BOOKS
(Located in Landmark Plaza)

— BOOKS ON THE NORTH —
Historical – Flora and Fauna
Fiction and Non-Fiction – Maps

SOUVENIRS — Made in Fort Nelson
T-Shirts, Sweats, Hats (ALL Canadian made)
Spoons – Spoon Racks – Clocks – Flags
Bumper Stickers – Decals . . . and much more!

VISA Map Agent for Maps B.C. MasterCard

Phone (604) 774-2631 • FAX (604) 774-3301

Shannon Motel
• 56 modern units
• Kitchenettes available
• Cable color television
• Direct dial phones

Phone: (604) 774-6000
North End of Fort Nelson
Box 480, Fort Nelson, BC
Canada V0C 1R0
Super, Natural Scenic Adventure

All Rentals Available   *Open 8:00 till dark daily*
Poplar Hills Golf and Country Club
9 holes • Par 35 • Pro Shop   Grass Greens • Driving Range
Snack Bar • Licensed Premises
Visitors Welcome
4 miles west of Fort Nelson • (604) 774-3862

NORTHERN LIGHTS DELI
FORMERLY SMITTY'S DELI

We will help make your trip a happier one.

• Submarine Sandwiches
• Salads • Pizza • Homefrys
and much, much more

**50 varieties of EUROPEAN MEATS AND SAUSAGES
IMPORTED CHEESES**

☞ **HARD ICE CREAM**   Bus Tour Box Lunches
(on advance notice)

• Ice • Groceries
• Magazines and Paperbacks

VISA

Fort Nelson, BC
Near laundromat in Landmark Plaza
Super, Natural Scenic Adventure

Open 7 Days a Week 6:30 a.m. to 11 p.m.
Phone (604) 774-3311 • FAX (604) 774-2710

Digging culverts

C Company 35th Engineers building a culvert. A total of more than 8,000 culverts—an average of 6 per mile—were required in construction of the pioneer road. Runoff from steep slopes, sporadic heavy rainfall, and large volumes of water during spring thaw had to be drained off the road.

Edwin Bonde

9-hole golf course; driving range, grass greens, clubhouse (licensed), golf club rentals. Open 8 A.M. to dusk, May to October.

DC 289.1 (464.6 km) **F 1198.9** (1929.4 km) Welcome to Fort Nelson sign for southbound travelers.

DC 291 (467.6 km) **F 1197** (1926.3 km) Parker Lake Road.

DC 301 (483.5 km) **F 1187** (1910.2 km) Turnoff north for Liard Highway (BC Highway 77) to Fort Liard, Fort Simpson and other Northwest Territories destinations. See LIARD HIGHWAY section.

DC 308.2 (495.3 km) **F 1179.8** (1898.7 km) Raspberry Creek. Turnout with garbage barrels to south.

DC 316.6 (506.2 km) **F 1171.4** (1885.1 km) Turnout with litter barrel to south.

DC 318.4 (509.1 km) **F 1169.6** (1882.2 km) Kledo Creek bridge.

DC 318.7 (509.5 km) **F 1169.3** (1881.8 km) Kledo Creek wayside rest area to north (unmaintained).

DC 322.7 (516 km) **F 1165.3** (1875.3 km) Steamboat Creek bridge. Highway begins climb northbound up Steamboat Mountain; some 10 percent grades.

DC 329 (526.1 km) **F 1159** (1865.2 km) Pull-through turnout with litter barrel to south.

DC 333 (532.5 km) **F 1155** (1858.7 km) **Historical Mile 351. STEAMBOAT** (unincorporated), lodge with food and gas (diesel) to south; open year-round.

Steamboat. See display ad this section.

DC 333.7 (533.5 km) **F 1154.3** (1857.6 km) Winding road ascends Steamboat Mountain westbound. Views of the Muskwa River valley and Rocky Mountains to the southwest from summit of 3,500-foot/1,067-m Steamboat Mountain, named because of its resemblance to a steamship. Narrow winding road; watch for sharp curves and rough spots.

DC 334.3 (534.5 km) **F 1153.7** (1856.6 km) Turnout with view and litter barrel to south.

DC 336.7 (538.5 km) **F 1151.3** (1852.8 km) Turnout to south with litter barrels and pit toilets. Highway descends for westbound travelers.

DC 339.1 (542.5 km) **F 1148.9** (1848.9 km) Drinking water to north. *CAUTION: Hairpin curve!*

DC 342.8 (548 km) **F 1145.2** (1843 km) View of Indian Head Mountain, a high crag resembling the classic Indian profile.

DC 343.4 (549 km) **F 1144.6** (1842 km) Turnout with litter barrel, outhouse and point of interest sign to south.

DC 345 (551.5 km) **F 1143** (1839.4 km) Scenic Teetering Rock viewpoint with litter barrel and outhouses to north. Teetering Rock is in the distance on the horizon. Stay on well-marked trails, keep pets on leash; it is easy to get lost in this country.

DC 346.4 (553.9 km) **F 1141.6** (1837.2 km) Mill Creek, which flows into the Tetsa River. The highway follows the Tetsa River westbound. The Tetsa heads near Summit Lake in the northern Canadian Rockies.

Tetsa River, good fishing for grayling to 4 lbs., average 1 1/2 lbs., flies or spin cast with lures; Dolly Varden to 7 lbs., average 3 lbs., spin cast or black gnat, coachman, Red Devils, flies; whitefish, small but plentiful, use flies or eggs, summer.

DC 346.5 (554 km) **F 1141.5** (1837 km) Turnoff to south for Tetsa River Provincial Park, 1.2 miles/1.9 km via gravel road. Grass tenting area, 25 level gravel sites in trees, picnic tables, fire rings, firewood, outhouses, water and garbage containers. Camping fee $6 to $12. ▲

DC 351 (561.2 km) **F 1137** (1829.8 km) *CAUTION: Slow down, dangerous curve!*

DC 357.5 (571.5 km) **F 1130.5** (1819.3 km) **Historical Mile 375.** Gas, store and private campground. ▲

Tetsa River Outfitters. See display ad this section.

DC 358.6 (573.3 km) **F 1129.4** (1817.5 km) Highway follows Tetsa River westbound. Turnouts next 0.2 mile/0.3 km south to river.

DC 360.2 (575.9 km) **F 1127.8** (1815 km) Turnout with litter barrel, picnic site.

DC 364.4 (582.6 km) **F 1123.6** (1808.2 km) Gravel turnout to south.

DC 365.6 (584.6 km) **F 1122.4** (1806.3 km) Tetsa River bridge No. 1, clearance 17 feet/5.2m.

DC 366 (585.4 km) **F 1122** (1805.6 km) Pull-through turnout with litter barrel to north.

STEAMBOAT
Mile 351

Hosts – Willa & Ken MacRae

- GAS • DIESEL
- TIRE REPAIR
- CAFE with Home cooked Meals
- FRESH BAKED BREAD, PIES & PASTRY

AND AFFILIATES Along the Alaska Highway it's Husky

(604) 774-1010

Overnight Parking • Picnic Area
Open Year-Round

Super, Natural Scenic Adventure

TETSA RIVER OUTFITTERS

BIG GAME GUIDE OUTFITTERS

- ◆ HOMEMADE BREAD ◆ Store
- ◆ Souvenirs ◆ Camping - $5
- ◆ Dump Station ◆ Ice ◆ Showers
- ◆ CABINS ◆ Bed & Breakfast
- ◆ Fishing Licenses ◆ Photo Safaris
- ◆ Wildlife Display ◆ Fur Hats
- ◆ Stained Glass ◆ Beadwork

HISTORICAL MILE 375, ALASKA HIGHWAY V1G 4J8

UNLEADED GAS

- ◆ Minor Repairs
- ◆ Welding

Rocky Mountain Wilderness Horseback Adventures and Working Guest Ranch
(by reservation only)

Your Hosts: Cliff & Lori Andrews
(604) 774-1005

Super, Natural Scenic Adventure

DC 367.3 (587.3 km) **F 1120.7** (1803.5 km) Tetsa River bridge No. 2.

The high bare peaks of the central Canadian Rockies are visible ahead westbound.

DC 371.5 (594.2 km) **F 1116.5** (1796.8 km) South boundary of Stone Mountain Provincial Park.

CAUTION: Northbound, watch for caribou along the highway. Stone sheep on the highway. Stone sheep are indigenous to the mountains of northern British Columbia and southern Yukon Territory. They are darker and somewhat slighter than the bighorn sheep found in the Rocky Mountains. Dall or white sheep are found in the mountains of Yukon, Alaska and Northwest Territories. *DO NOT FEED WILDLIFE. Do not stop vehicles on the highway to take photos; use shoulders or turnouts.*

DC 372.7 (596 km) **F 1115.3** (1794.9 km) Pull-through turnout with litter barrel to north.

DC 373.3 (597 km) **F 1114.7** (1793.9 km) **Historical Mile 392. SUMMIT LAKE** (unincorporated), lodge with cafe, grocery, gas, food and lodging. Open year-round. The peak behind Summit Lake is Mount St. George (elev. 7,419 feet/2,261m) in the Stone Mountain range. The Summit area is known for dramatic and sudden weather changes.

DC 373.5 (597.4 km) **F 1114.5** (1793.5 km) Rough gravel side road leads 1.5 miles/2.5 km to Flower Springs Lake trailhead, 4.3 miles/7 km to microwave tower viewpoint. Not suitable for motorhomes, trailers or low clearance vehicles.

DC 373.6 (597.6 km) **F 1114.4** (1793.4 km) Gravel turnout and campground to south at east end of Summit Lake. This is the highest summit on the Alaska Highway (elev. 4,250 feet/1,295m) and a very beautiful area of bare rocky peaks (which can be snow-covered anytime of the year). Summit Lake provincial campground has 28 level gravel sites; picnic tables; water and garbage containers; information shelter; boat launch. Camping fee $6 to $12. Hiking trails to Flower Springs Lake and Summit Peak. Fair fishing for lake trout, whitefish and rainbows in **Summit Lake**.

DC 375.6 (600.8 km) **F 1112.4** (1790.2 km) Turnout to north.

DC 375.9 (601.3 km) **F 1112.1** (1789.7 km) Picnic site to south with tables and litter barrel on Rocky Crest Lake.

DC 376 (601.5 km) **F 1112** (1789.5 km) Erosion pillars north of highway (0.6-mile/1-km hike north). Northbound, the highway winds through a rocky limestone gorge, before descending into the wide and picturesque MacDonald River valley. Turnouts next 2.5 miles/4 km northbound with views of the valley. Watch for Stone sheep along rock cut.

DC 378.6 (605.7 km) **F 1109.4** (1785.4 km) **Historical Mile 397.** Rocky Mountain Lodge to south; gas, lodging, store and camping. Open year-round.

Rocky Mountain Lodge. See display ad this section.

DC 379.7 (607.4 km) **F 1108.3** (1783.6 km) Turnout to south.

DC 380.7 (609 km) **F 1107.3** (1782 km) North boundary of Stone Mountain Provincial Park. *CAUTION: Southbound, watch for wildlife alongside and on the road. DO NOT FEED WILDLIFE.*

DC 381.2 (611.2 km) **F 1106.8** (1781.2 km) Highway winds along above the wide rocky valley of MacDonald Creek.

DC 382.2 (612.8 km) **F 1105.8** (1779.5 km) Trail access via abandoned Churchill Mines Road (4-wheel drive only beyond river) to Wokkpash Recreation Area, located 12 miles/20 km south of the highway. B.C. Parks is developing hiking trails in this remote area, which adjoins the southwest boundary of Stone Mountain Provincial Park. The area features extensive hoodoos (erosion pillars) in Wokkpash Gorge, and the scenic Forlorn Gorge and Stepped Lakes. Contact the Parks District Office in Fort St. John before venturing into this area; phone (604) 787-3407.

DC 383.3 (614.6 km) **F 1104.7** (1777.8 km) 113 Creek. The creek was named during construction of the Alaska Highway for its distance from Mile 0 at Fort Nelson. While Dawson Creek was to become Mile 0 on the completed pioneer road, clearing crews began their work at Fort Nelson, since a rough winter road already existed between Dawson Creek and Fort Nelson. Stone Range to the northeast and Muskwa Ranges of the Rocky Mountains to the west.

DC 384.2 (615.4 km) **F 1103.8** (1776.3 km) 115 Creek Provincial campground to southwest, adjacent highway; double-ended entrance. Side-by-side camper parking (8 sites), water, garbage containers, picnic tables. Camping fee $6 to $12. Access to the rocky riverbank of 115 Creek and **MacDonald Creek**. Beaver dams nearby. Fishing for grayling and Dolly Varden.

DC 385.4 (615.6 km) **F 1102.6** (1774.4 km) 115 Creek bridge. Turnout to south at east end of bridge with tables and litter barrels. Like 113 Creek, 115 Creek was named during construction of the pioneer road for its distance from Fort Nelson, Mile 0 for clearing crews.

DC 390.5 (624.8 km) **F 1097.5** (1766.2 km) **Historical Mile 408.** MacDonald River Services (current status unknown).

DC 392.5 (627.8 km) **F 1095.5** (1763 km) MacDonald River bridge, clearance 17 feet/5.2m. Highway winds through narrow valley.

MacDonald River, fair fishing from May to July for Dolly Varden and grayling.

DC 394.8 (631.8 km) **F 1093.2** (1759.3 km) Turnout with litter barrel to east.

DC 396.1 (633.8 km) **F 1091.9** (1757.2 km) Folding rock formations on mountain face to west. The Racing River forms the boundary between the Sentinel Range and the Stone Range, both of which are composed of folded and sedimentary rock.

DC 399.1 (638.6 km) **F 1088.9** (1752.4 km) Stringer Creek.

DC 400.7 (641.1 km) **F 1087.3** (1749.8 km) Racing River bridge, clearance 17 feet/5.2m. River access to north at east end of bridge.

Racing River, grayling to 16 inches; Dolly Varden to 2 lbs., use flies, July through September.

DC 404.6 (647.4 km) **F 1083.4** (1743.5 km) **Historical Mile 422. TOAD RIVER** (unincorporated), situated in a picturesque valley. Highway maintenance camp, school and private residences on north side of highway. Lodge on south side of highway with cafe, gas, propane, camping and lodging. Ambulance service. Toad River Lodge is known for its hat collection. Also, inquire at the lodge about good wildlife viewing locations nearby.

Toad River Lodge. See display ad this section.

Private Aircraft: Emergency gravel

Stone Mountain Park
Gateway to the New Wokkpash Park

Rocky Mountain Lodge

Motel Rooms
Satellite Color TV
Groceries • Ice
Deli-Style Takeout Food
"Try our famous cinnamon buns"
Campground
Gas at Town Prices
Minor Mechanical Repairs

U.S. Exchange at Bank Rates

MasterCard — VISA

New for 1991 Packhorses for Rent Daily Trail Rides

We offer the best water on the Alaska Highway

Mile 397 Alaska Highway
Open Year-Round
Phone and FAX (604) 232-5000
British Columbia, Canada

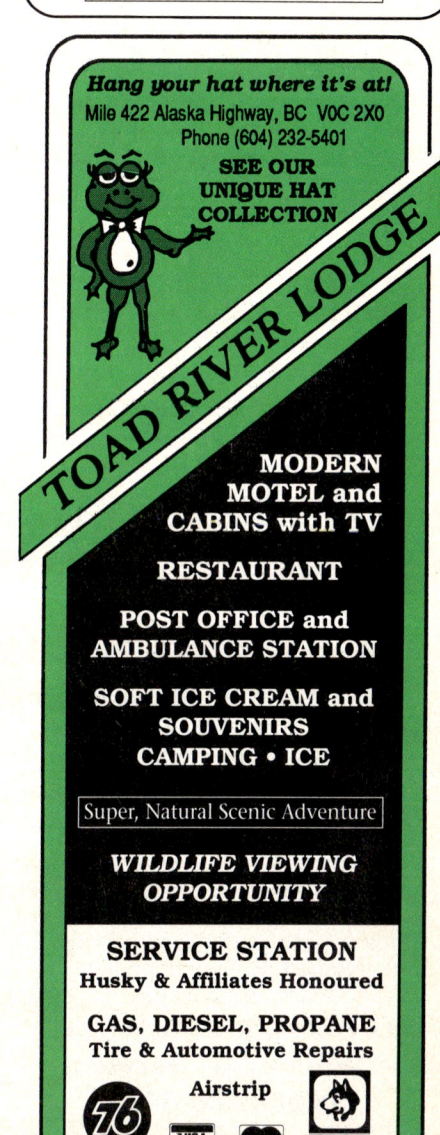

Super, Natural Scenic Adventure

Hang your hat where it's at!
Mile 422 Alaska Highway, BC V0C 2X0
Phone (604) 232-5401

SEE OUR UNIQUE HAT COLLECTION

TOAD RIVER LODGE

MODERN MOTEL and CABINS with TV

RESTAURANT

POST OFFICE and AMBULANCE STATION

SOFT ICE CREAM and SOUVENIRS
CAMPING • ICE

Super, Natural Scenic Adventure

WILDLIFE VIEWING OPPORTUNITY

SERVICE STATION
Husky & Affiliates Honoured

GAS, DIESEL, PROPANE
Tire & Automotive Repairs

Airstrip

76 — VISA — MasterCard — Husky

airstrip; elev. 2,400 feet/732m; length 2,300 feet/701m.

DC 406.3 (650.1 km) **F 1081.7** (1740.8 km) Turnout with litter barrels to north.

DC 407.5 (652 km) **F 1080.5** (1738.8 km) **Historical Mile 426.** Food, gas and camping south side of highway.

The Poplars Campground. See display ad this section.

DC 409.2 (654.6 km) **F 1078.8** (1736.1 km) South boundary of Muncho Lake Provincial Park.

DC 410.6 (656.8 km) **F 1077.4** (1733.9 km) Impressive rock folding formation on mountain face, known as Folded Mountain.

DC 411 (657.4 km) **F 1077** (1733.2 km) Beautiful turquoise-coloured Toad River to north. The highway now follows the Toad River westbound.

Toad River, grayling to 16 inches; Dolly Varden to 10 lbs. use flies, July through September.

DC 415.5 (664.7 km) **F 1072.5** (1726 km) 150 Creek bridge. Creek access to south at east end of bridge.

DC 417.6 (668.2 km) **F 1070.4** (1722.6 km) Centennial Falls to south.

DC 419.8 (671.7 km) **F 1068.2** (1719 km) Toad River bridge. Turnout with litter barrel to south at west end of bridge.

DC 422.6 (676.2 km) **F 1065.4** (1714.5 km) Watch for moose in pond to north; morning or evening best.

DC 423 (676.8 km) **F 1065** (1713.9 km) Turnout with litter barrel to north.

CAUTION: Watch for Stone sheep along the highway (or standing in the middle of the highway). DO NOT FEED WILDLIFE. Do not stop vehicles on the highway to take photos; use shoulders or turnouts.

DC 423.1 (677 km) **F 1064.9** (1713.7 km) The highway swings north for Alaska-bound travelers. For Dawson Creek-bound travelers, the highway follows an easterly direction.

DC 424.1 (678.7 km) **F 1063.9** (1712.1 km) Peterson Creek No. 1 bridge. The creek was named for local trapper Pete Peterson, who helped Alaska Highway construction crews select a route through this area.

DC 429.5 (688.9 km) **F 1058.5** (1703.4 km) Viewpoint to east with information shelter and litter barrels.

DC 436.5 (698.5 km) **F 1051.5** (1692.6 km) **Historical Mile 456.** Entering MUNCHO LAKE (pop. 24; elev. 2,700 feet/823m). Muncho Lake businesses extend from here north along the east shore of Muncho Lake to approximately **Milepost DC 443.7**. Businesses in Muncho Lake include 4 lodges, gas stations with towing and repair, restaurants, cafes and campgrounds. The post office is located at Double G Service.

The Muncho Lake area offers hiking in the summer and cross-country skiing in the winter. Narrated boat tours of Muncho Lake are available in summer; check with Double G Service. This highly recommended tour highlights the history and geography of the area. Boat rentals are available from J&H Wilderness Resort and Highland Glen Lodge. An annual lake trout derby is held in June; inquire locally for dates of this event.

CAUTION: Watch for Stone sheep and moose on the highway north of here. Please DO NOT FEED WILDLIFE. Please do not stop on the highway to take photos; use shoulders or turnouts.

Double G Service, located at the south end of beautiful Muncho Lake, offers you "one stop" service. Have your vehicle repaired in our mechanic's shop or stay for the night in the campground or motel. Our cozy cafe has delicious homemade bread and pastries to go, or stay in and try our hearty soups, stews and chili. Your children will enjoy our playground and there is excellent hiking just out the back door. For a more relaxed outing, pick up your tickets for the Muncho Lake boat tour aboard the MV *Sandpiper*. Your hosts, The Gunness Family, invite you to stop and check the cleanliness, comfort and friendliness yourself. Enjoy Super, Natural Scenic Adventure.
[ADVERTISEMENT]

Muncho Lake Tours. See display ad this section.

DC 436.9 (699.2 km) **F 1051.1** (1691.5 km) Gravel airstrip to west; length 1,200 feet/366m. View of Muncho Lake ahead northbound. The highway along Muncho Lake required considerable rock excavation by the Army in 1942. The original route went along the top of the cliffs, which proved particularly hazardous. The Army relocated the road by benching into the cliffs a few feet above lake level.

Muncho Lake, known for its beautiful deep green and blue waters, is 7 miles/11 km in length, and 1 mile/1.6 km in width; elevation of the lake is 2,680 feet/817m. The colours are attributed to copper oxide leaching into the lake. Deepest point has been reported to be 730 feet/223m, although recent government tests have not located

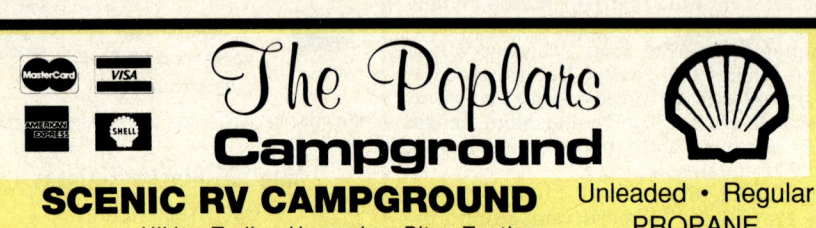

The Poplars Campground

SCENIC RV CAMPGROUND

Hiking Trails • Horseshoe Pits • Tenting
Hot Showers • Good Water • Electric
Dump Station • Lodging • Ice
Fresh Baking • Clean Cafe • Ice Cream & Shakes
FOOT-LONG HOT DOGS • Souvenirs
Jade & Gold Gifts • T-Shirts

Mile 426 Alaska Highway, BC
Phone (604) 232-5465

Unleaded • Regular
PROPANE
Tire Sales & Repair
Welding
✓Free coffee with gas fill-up

Dan & Vicky Clements

Home of the foot-long HOT DOGS

Super, Natural Scenic Adventure

DOUBLE "G" SERVICE

Mile 456 KM 727.4
MUNCHO LAKE
ALASKA HIGHWAY
Esso

RV REPAIRS • LICENSED MECHANIC
24-HOUR TOWING • WELDING • DIESEL
MODERN MOTEL (Seniors' Discount) **POST OFFICE**
CAFE • Fresh Baking Daily • Hard Ice Cream
Campground • Playground • Showers • Ice • Auto Propane

Super, Natural Scenic Adventure

Phone **(604) 776-3411**
THE GUNNESS FAMILY

MUNCHO LAKE TOURS

... cordially invite you to join them for a personally guided and narrated **one-hour tour** on picturesque Muncho Lake.

FAMILY ORIENTED RATES
NO RESERVATIONS REQUIRED — JUNE TILL SEPTEMBER

Our comfortable 32-foot, 20-passenger MV SANDPIPER has an all-enclosed cabin with 360° visibility ... Bring your camera!

Four departure docks to serve you.
Schedule posted locally
and at dockside.
CALL FOR MORE INFORMATION AT
Double "G" Service
(604) 776-3411

Super, Natural Scenic Adventure

any point deeper than 400 feet/122m. The lake drains the Sentinel Range to the east and the Terminal Range to the west, feeding the raging Trout River in its 1,000-foot/305-m drop to the mighty Liard River. The mountains surrounding the lake are approximately 7,000 feet/2,134m high.

Muncho Lake, fishing for Dolly Varden; some grayling; whitefish to 12 inches; lake trout (record to 50 lbs.), use spoons, spinners, diving plug or weighted spoons, June and July best. The lake trout quota is 3 trout per person; minimum size 15^3/$_4$ inches. Make sure you have a current British Columbia fishing license and a copy of the current regulations. Also rainbow trout.

DC 437.7 (700.5 km) **F 1050.3** (1690.2 km) Strawberry Flats campground, Muncho Lake Provincial Park; 15 sites on rocky lakeshore, picnic tables, outhouses, garbage containers. Camping fee $6 to $12. ▲

CAUTION: Watch for bears in area.

DC 442.2 (707.9 km) **F 1045.8** (1683 km) **Historical Mile 462**. Highland Glen Lodge with cabins, restaurant, gas and camping west side of highway. ▲

Highland Glen Lodge, Mile 462, Muncho Lake, BC, (604) 776-3481. Individual chalets, licensed dining room, stone-oven bakery, RV hookups, campground, showers, washrooms, laundromat, Husky service station. Liard Air/Liard Tours offers fly-in fishing trips for arctic grayling, Dolly Varden, rainbow and lake trout, walleye, northern pike, whitefish. Air charter service to Kwadacha and Stone Mountain provincial parks, Virginia Falls and Headless Valley in famous Nahanni National Park—a world heritage site. Bush Pilot Film Festival at Highland Glen Lodge! Free nightly presentations for guests. [ADVERTISEMENT] ▲

DC 442.9 (709 km) **F 1045.1** (1681.9 km) Turnoff to west for MacDonald campground, Muncho Lake Provincial Park; 15 level gravel sites, firewood, picnic tables, outhouses, boat launch, information shelter, pump water, on Muncho Lake. Camping fee $6 to $12. ▲

A moose feeds in a pond at Milepost DC 422.6. (Earl L. Brown, staff)

CAUTION: Watch for bears in area.

DC 443.6 (710.1 km) **F 1044.4** (1680.8 km) **Historical Mile 463**. Muncho Lake Lodge; gas, propane, food, camping and lodging.

Muncho Lake Lodge. See display ad on page 106.

DC 443.7 (710.3 km) **F 1044.3** (1680.6 km) **Historical Mile 463.1**. J&H Wilderness

ALASKA HIGHWAY • BRITISH COLUMBIA

Highland Glen
LODGE
MOTEL and LICENSED DINING ROOM
(604) 776-3481

Mile 462, Alaska Highway – Muncho Lake, B.C. • (604) 776-3481

★ ★ BUS TOURS WELCOME ★ ★

To avoid disappointment, please make reservations by phoning ahead.
Owned and operated by "bush-pilot" Urs and wife Marianne

Restaurant — Chalets and Motel Rooms — Stone-Oven Bakery — Sauna — RV Hookups — Campground
Showers — Clean Washrooms — Laundromat — Barbecue Pit

On beautiful Muncho Lake Highland Glen Lodge offers modern facilities in a natural setting with INDIVIDUAL CHALETS. In Highland Glen's rustic style LICENSED DINING ROOM, try our famous specialties: bratwurst with sauerkraut, cold plate of European sausages, wiener schnitzel or a great-tasting pizza.

BUSH PILOT FILM FESTIVAL — Free nightly presentation for guests.

LIARD AIR LTD.
- Nahanni National Park excursions
- Fly-in Fishing Trips
- Air Taxi Service to remote mountain lakes in northeastern B.C.

Husky
Here in Canada it's Husky

QUALITY GASOLINE AT DISCOUNT PRICES

Year-round address: **LIARD TOURS LTD.**
P.O. Box 3190-M, Fort Nelson, B.C. V0C 1R0 Canada
Phone: (604) 774-2909 • FAX: (604) 774-2908

Super, Natural Scenic Adventure

Resort; food, gas, store, boat rentals, tackle, lodging and camping. Open year-round. Muncho Lake businesses extend south to **Milepost DC 436.5.** ▲

J&H Wilderness Resort. See display ad this section.

DC 444.9 (712.2 km) **F 1043.1** (1678.7 km) Muncho Lake viewpoint to west with litter barrels and outhouses.

NOTE: Watch for Stone sheep on highway next 10 miles/16 km northbound.

DC 453.3 (725.6 km) **F 1034.7** (1665.1 km) Turnout with litter barrel to east.

DC 454 (726.7 km) **F 1034** (1664 km) Mineral lick; watch for Stone sheep. There is a trailhead 0.2 mile/0.3 km off the highway; a 5- to 10-minute loop hike takes you to viewpoints overlooking the Trout River valley and the steep mineral-laden banks frequented by sheep, goats, caribou and elk. Good photo opportunities, early morning best. *CAUTION: Steep banks, slippery when wet. Bring insect repellent. Watch for bears.*

NOTE: Watch for Stone sheep on highway next 10 miles/16 km southbound.

DC 455.5 (729.2 km) **F 1032.5** (1661.6 km) Turnout with litter barrel and message board to west.

DC 457.7 (732.7 km) **F 1030.3** (1658.1 km) Trout River bridge. The Trout River drains into the Liard River. The highway follows the Trout River north for several miles.

Trout River, grayling to 18 inches; whitefish to 12 inches, flies, spinners, May, June and August best.

DC 458.9 (734.6 km) **F 1029.1** (1656.1 km) Gravel turnout to east.

DC 460.7 (737.4 km) **F 1027.3** (1653.2 km) Prochniak Creek bridge. North boundary of Muncho Lake Provincial Park.

DC 463.3 (741.6 km) **F 1024.7** (1649 km) Watch for curves next 0.6 mile/1 km northbound.

DC 465.6 (745.3 km) **F 1022.4** (1645.6 km) Turnout with litter barrel to east.

DC 466.3 (746.3 km) **F 1021.7** (1644.2 km) *CAUTION: Dangerous curves next 3 miles/ 5 km northbound.*

DC 468.9 (749.5 km) **F 1019.1** (1640 km) Pull-through turnout with litter barrel to east.

DC 471 (754.1 km) **F 1017** (1636.7 km) First glimpse of the mighty Liard River for northbound travelers. Named by French-Canadian voyageurs for the poplar ("liard") which line the banks of the lower river. The Alaska Highway parallels the Liard River from here north to Watson Lake. The river offered engineers a natural line to follow during routing and construction of the Alaska Highway in 1942.

DC 472.2 (756 km) **F 1015.8** (1634.7 km) Washout Creek.

DC 474.3 (759.5 km) **F 1013.7** (1631.3 km) Turnout with litter barrel to west.

DC 476.7 (763 km) **F 1011.3** (1627.5 km) Lower Liard River bridge. This is the only suspension bridge on the Alaska Highway. (The Peace River suspension bridge collapsed in October 1957. It was replaced by a cantilever and truss type bridge, completed in 1960.)

The **Liard River** flows eastward toward the Fort Nelson River and parallels the Alaska Highway from the Lower Liard River bridge to the BC-YT border. The scenic Grand Canyon of the Liard is to the east and not visible from the highway. Good fishing for Dolly Varden, grayling, northern pike and whitefish.

DC 477.1 (763.8 km) **F 1010.9** (1626.8 km) **Historical Mile 496. LIARD RIVER** (unincorporated), lodge with gas, store, pay phone, food, camping and lodging to west. ▲

Liard River Lodge. See display ad this section.

DC 477.7 (764.7 km) **F 1010.3** (1625.9 km) Turnoff to north for Liard River Hotsprings Provincial Park, long a favorite stop for Alaska Highway travelers. (The park has become so popular in recent years that the campground fills up very early each day in summer.) The park is open year-round. This well-developed provincial park has 53 large, shaded, level gravel sites (some will accommodate 2 RVs); picnic tables, picnic shelter, water, garbage containers, firewood, fire rings, playground and outhouses. Camping

MUNCHO LAKE LODGE

Friendly Gas — **GAS FOR LESS**

Mile 463 — *Caravans Welcome*

Hotel Accommodations – Modern Cabins with Kitchenettes
Cafe and Restuarant – Licensed Dining Lounge
— Featuring Home Cooking and Baking —
32-Space Trailer Park with All Hookups plus Additional Overnight Parking
Just $10 – $12 a Night, Showers Included

Group Discounts — VISA, MasterCard

- 10% Discount to Senior Citizens and Reservations on Motel or Trailer Park.
- Laundromat and Showers
- Sanitary Disposal Station
- Complete Car, Light Truck and RV Tire Sales and Service

Your Hosts: Mary Tauers & David Nishio

Phone: (604) 776-3456
Box 10
Muncho Lake, BC V0C 1Z0

Open May to September

Super, Natural Scenic Adventure

J & H WILDERNESS RESORT

ON BEAUTIFUL MUNCHO LAKE

Open Year-Round
MILE 463.3 Alaska Highway

Licensed Restaurant • Modern Motel Units
Grocery Store and Souvenirs

- GAS
- DIESEL
- PROPANE
- TIRE SERVICE • ICE

RV CARAVAN SPECIALISTS — Bus Tours Welcome (*Reservations Please*)

Pull-through RV Hookups by the Lake
55 Level Serviced Sites • Dump Station • Hot Showers
Laundromat • Recreation Hall
Fire Pits and Firewood • Horseshoe Pits

VISA • MasterCard • American Express

— Boat Rentals • Fishing Tackle & Licenses —

*"FOR SERVICE, HOSPITALITY AND REASONABLE RATES...
VISIT US, THE LAST RESORT NORTHBOUND ALONG MUNCHO LAKE"*

P.O. Box 38, Muncho Lake, BC V0C 1Z0   (604) 776-3453
Your Hosts: Dennis and Joey Froese

Super, Natural Scenic Adventure

fee $6 to $12. Pay phone at park entrance. ▲

A boardwalk leads to the pools, crossing a wetlands environment that supports more than 250 boreal forest plants, including 14 orchid species and 14 plants that survive at this latitude because of the hot springs. Also watch for moose feeding in the pools. There are 2 hot springs pools. Nearest is the Alpha pool with a children's wading area. Beyond the Alpha pool is Beta pool, which is larger and deeper. Both have changing rooms. Beta pool is about a 0.4-mile/0.6-km walk. Plenty of parking at trailhead.

Excellent interpretive programs and nature walks in summer; check schedule posted at park entrance and at information shelter near trailhead. Emergency phone at park headquarters.

DC 477.8 (764.9 km) F 1010.2 (1625.7 km) Historical Mile 497. Food, gas, lodging and camping. ▲

Trapper Ray's Liard Hotsprings Services. See display ad this section.

DC 482.8 (772.9 km) F 1005.2 (1617.7 km) Teeter Creek. A footpath leads upstream (10-minute walk) to falls. Grayling fishing.

DC 486.6 (779 km) F 1001.4 (1611.6 km) NOTE: Northbound travelers watch for road construction and rough road! Rough surface, gravel breaks and loose gravel next 118.5 miles/190.7 km (to BC-YT border).

DC 489 (783.6 km) F 999 (1607.7 km) Private Aircraft: Liard River airstrip; elev. 1,400 feet/427m; length 4,000 feet/1,219m; gravel.

DC 495 (792.3 km) F 993 (1598 km) Smith River bridge, clearance 17 feet/5.2m. Access to river via 1.6-mile/2.6-km gravel road; not recommended for large RVs or trailers or in wet weather. Hiking trail down to 2-tiered Smith River Falls from parking area. Grayling fishing.

DC 509.4 (815.6 km) F 978.6 (1574.9 km) Large turnout with litter barrel to east.

DC 513.9 (822.8 km) F 974.1 (1567.6 km) Historical Mile 533. COAL RIVER, lodge with gas, food, camping and lodging. ▲

DC 514.2 (823.2 km) F 973.8 (1567.1 km) Historical Mile 533.2. Coal River bridge. The Coal River flows into the Liard River south of the bridge.

DC 514.6 (823.7 km) F 973.4 (1566.5 km) Steep grades northbound next 3.7 miles/6 km.

DC 519.5 (831.4 km) F 968.5 (1558.6 km) Sharp easy-to-miss turnoff to west for undeveloped "do-it-yourself campsite" (watch for sign). Small gravel parking area with outhouse and litter barrels. Beautiful view from here of the Liard River and Whirlpool Canyon (not visible from the highway). ▲

DC 524.2 (839.2 km) F 963.8 (1551 km) Historical Mile 543. FIRESIDE (unincorporated). Gas station with diesel and major repair, and cafe. This community was partially destroyed by fire in the summer of 1982. Evidence of the fire can be seen from south of Fireside north to Lower Post. The 1982 burn, known as the Eg fire, was the second largest fire in British Columbia history, destroying more than 400,000 acres.

Fireside Car/Truck Stop. See display ad this section.

DC 527.4 (844.3 km) F 960.6 (1545.9 km) Good view of Liard River to west.

DC 534.8 (856.3 km) F 953.2 (1534 km) NorthwesTel microwave tower to east.

DC 535.6 (857.6 km) F 952.4 (1532.7 km) Large pull-through turnout with litter barrel to east. Northbound trucks stop here and check brakes before descending steep grade.

DC 536.9 (859.7 km) F 951.1 (1530.6 km) CAUTION: Slow down! Dangerous curves next 4.4 miles/7.1 km northbound. Watch for loose gravel.

DC 539 (863 km) F 949 (1527.2 km) Turnout with litter barrel to west. LeQuil Creek.

DC 540 (864.6 km) F 948 (1525.6 km) Large pull-through turnout with litter barrel to west.

Alaska Highway travelers relax at Liard Hot Springs pool. (Earl L. Brown, staff)

MILE 496 ALASKA HIGHWAY, BC, V1G 4J8
Overlooking the Liard Suspension Bridge . . . Only ½ mile from the Liard Hot Springs

Liard River Lodge
(LIARD HOT SPRINGS REGION)
An ideal spot for a four-season holiday
Make Liard River Lodge your base for enjoying the Hot Springs, hiking or exploring many miles of cross-country trails. Afterward enjoy a hearty home-cooked meal.

A SUMMER OASIS, A WINTER FAIRYLAND
Motorcades and Tour Buses Welcome (please call ahead)
LODGING • CAFE with HOME COOKING • LICENSED DINING
RV PARKING • DUMP STATION • CAMPING • GOOD WATER • SHOWERS
UNLEADED GAS • TIRE REPAIRS • ICE
GREYHOUND BUS STOP • SOUVENIRS • GAME ROOM • HELIPORT

Your Hosts: Gene & Anne Beitz
Monitoring CB Channel 19
PHONE (604) 776-3341

Pickup service from Liard Airstrip upon request

Super, Natural Scenic Adventure

TRAPPER RAY'S
LIARD HOTSPRINGS SERVICES

CAFE
Home Baking • Ice Cream • Ice
Souvenirs • Snacks for Bus Tours

Ask about the local fur spiders

Open May – October   6 a.m. – 11 p.m.

Unleaded • Diesel • Propane

CABINS • CAMPING
Over 40 RV Pull Through Sites

Radiophone JJ 36252
Mould Creek Channel (via Fort Nelson)

Mile 497 KM 801
Across from Liard River Hot Springs

Super, Natural Scenic Adventure

ALASKA HIGHWAY • BRITISH COLUMBIA

DC 541.3 (866.7 km) **F 946.7** (1523.5 km) Southbound travelers: *Slow down! Dangerous curves next 4.4 miles/7.1 km.*

DC 545.9 (874.2 km) **F 942.1** (1516.1 km) Turnout with litter barrel to west overlooking the Liard River.

DC 550.9 (882.2 km) **F 937.1** (1508 km) **Historical Mile 570.** Allen's Lookout; pull-through turnout with outhouse and litter barrel to west overlooking the Liard River. Goat Mountain to west. Legend has it that a band of outlaws took advantage of this sweeping view of the Liard River to attack and rob riverboats of furs and supplies.

ALASKA HIGHWAY
Fireside Car / Truck Stop
Mile 543, Alaska Highway

Cafe • Ice
Home Cooking
Ice Cream
Regular
Unleaded
Diesel

LICENSED MECHANIC • RV REPAIRS
TIRE SALES AND REPAIRS

Your hosts: Omer and Bev Leveque

• Open Year-Round •

Fireside, BC   Phone (604) 776-3302

Super, Natural Scenic Adventure

Bridge building

Crews test a just-completed bridge across the Coal River. Responsibility for bridge building along the Alaska Highway in 1942 was shared by the U.S. Army Corps of Engineers and Public Roads Administration engineers. In all, 133 bridges of 20 feet or more in length were required along the highway. Most of the bridges built in 1942 were timber truss and timber trestle bridges. Sawmills operated at full capacity producing timber for bridges. But these temporary wooden structures were frequently washed out by floods or knocked out by ice and debris. Permanent steel bridges were planned for all major streams on the highway by 1943.

Edwin Bonde

First stop in the Yukon...
MILE 590, ALASKA HIGHWAY

Contact Creek Lodge

Open Year-Round   **Town Prices**

— *Caravan Fuel Discounts* —

Gas • Diesel • Tires
Minor Repairs • Welding

TEMPO

PRESSURE WASH

WRECKER SERVICE (24 HOURS)

FULL HOOKUPS • DUMP STATION • SPRING WATER
Camping • Showers • Ice • Pay Phone
Souvenirs • BC and Yukon Fishing Licenses

Bus Tours Welcome   **(403) 536-2262**

Your Hosts: Richard and Dennie Hair

DC 555 (888.8 km) **F 933** (1501.5 km) Good berry picking in July among roadside raspberry bushes; watch for bears.

DC 556 (890.4 km) **F 932** (1499.9 km) Highway swings west Alaska-bound.

DC 562.5 (900.8 km) **F 925.5** (1489.4 km) Large gravel turnout with litter barrel.

DC 567.9 (909.4 km) **F 920.1** (1480.7 km) **Historical Mile 588.** Contact Creek bridge. Turnout to south at east end of bridge with tables, toilets, litter barrels and information shelter. This bridge marks the location of the contact of highway construction crews working west from Fort Nelson and east from Whitehorse on Sept. 25, 1942.

DC 568.3 (910.2 km) **F 919.7** (1480.1 km) First of 9 crossings of the BC-YT border. Large gravel turnout to north with point of interest sign about the Yukon Territory. "The Yukon Territory takes its name from the Indian word *Youcon,* meaning 'big river.' It was first explored in the 1840s by the Hudson's Bay Co., which established several trading posts. The territory, which was then considered a district of the Northwest Territories, remained largely untouched until the Klondike gold rush, when thousands of people flooded into the country and communities sprang up almost overnight. This sudden expansion led to the official formation of the Yukon Territory on June 13, 1898."

DC 570 (912.9 km) **F 918** (1477.3 km) **Historical Mile 590.** CONTACT CREEK, lodge open year-round with camping, food, gas, car repair and pay phone. ▲

Contact Creek Lodge. See display ad this section.

DC 573.9 (918.9 km) **F 914.1** (1471.1 km) Iron Creek bridge. Turnout with litter barrel to south at east end of bridge.

DC 575.9 (922 km) F 912.1 (1467.8 km) **Historical Mile 596.** Iron Creek Lodge; food, gas, lodging and camping.

Iron Creek Lodge. See display ad this section.

DC 582 (931.8 km) F 906 (1458 km) NorthwesTel microwave tower.

DC 585 (937 km) F 903 (1453.2 km) **Hyland River** bridge; good fishing for rainbow, Dolly Varden and grayling.

NOTE: Watch for logging trucks northbound to Watson Lake. Gravel and potholes next 13.7 miles/22 km northbound.

DC 585.3 (937.2 km) F 902.7 (1452.7 km) **Historical Mile 605.9.** Hyland River bridge. The Hyland River is a tributary of the Liard River. The river was named for Frank Hyland, an early-day trader at Telegraph Creek on the Stikine River. Hyland operated trading posts throughout northern British Columbia, competing successfully with the Hudson's Bay Co., and at one time printing his own currency.

DC 598.7 (957.5 km) F 889.3 (1431.2 km) Access to **LOWER POST** (unincorporated), at **Historical Mile 620**, via short gravel road; cafe and store. A B.C. Forest Service field office is located here. This British Columbia settlement is a historic Hudson's Bay Co. trading post and the site of an Indian village. The Liard and Dease rivers meet near here. The Dease River, named for Peter Warren Dease, a fur trader for the Hudson's Bay Co., heads in Dease Lake to the southwest on the Cassiar Highway.

DC 605.1 (967.6 km) F 882.9 (1420.8 km) **Historical Milepost 627.** BC-YT border; Welcome to the Yukon sign. Monitor CB Channel 9 for police. The Alaska Highway dips back into British Columbia several times before making its final crossing into the Yukon Territory near Morley Lake (**Milepost DC 751.5**).

NOTE: Kmposts on the Yukon portion of the highway reflect historical mileposts. Kmposts on the British Columbia portion of the highway reflect actual driving distance. There is approximately a 40-km difference at the BC-YT border between these measurements.

Northbound: Good paved highway with wide shoulders next 380 miles/611.5 km to Haines Junction, with the exception of some short sections of narrow road and occasional gravel breaks.

Southbound: Watch for rough, narrow, winding road and breaks in surfacing between border and Fort Nelson (approximately 321 miles/516.6 km).

DC 606.9 (1011.9 km) F 881.1 (1418 km) Lucky Lake picnic area to south. **Lucky Lake** is a popular local swimming hole for Watson Lake residents, who installed a water slide here. Relatively shallow, the lake warms up quickly in summer, making it one of the few area lakes where swimming is possible. Stocked with rainbow trout.

DC 609.2 (1015.5 km) F 878.8 (1414.3 km) Rest area with litter barrel and outhouses to north.

DC 610.4 (1017.5 km) F 877.6 (1412.3 km) Weigh station.

DC 610.5 (1017.7 km) F 877.5 (1412.2 km) **Mile 632.5. Campground Services** at **Mile 632.5** is the largest and best equipped RV park in Watson Lake, the gateway to the Yukon. The park features full or partial hookups and pull-throughs, tent sites, showers, a laundry, car wash and playground, firepits and a screened kitchen. Good Sam Park. A food market stocks groceries, convenience items, fishing tackle, licenses and ice. Husky gasoline and diesel and ICG propane are available at the self-serve pumps. A licensed mechanic is available for repairs, alignments, tire changes, etc. Agents for Western Union money transfers. Open for business 12 months a year. Call (403) 536-7448. [ADVERTISEMENT]

DC 610.6 (982.6 km) F 877.4 (1412 km) **Oasis Dairy Bar.** See display ad this section.

Watson Lake

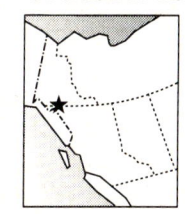

DC 612.9 (1021 km) F 875.1 (1408.3 km). **Historical Milepost 635.** "Gateway to the Yukon," located 329 miles/529 km from Fort Nelson, 274 miles/441 km from Whitehorse. **Population:** 1,700. **Emergency Services: RCMP,** phone 536-7443 or 536-7444. **Fire Department,** phone 536-2222. **Hospital,** phone 536-2541.

Visitor Information: The visitor information centre is located directly behind the sign forest, north of the Alaska Highway; access to the centre is from the Campbell Highway.

Elevation: 2,265 feet/690m. **Climate:** Average temperature in January is -15°F/-26°C, in July 57°F/14°C. Record high

---

BEN'S AUTO REPAIRS
- Licensed Mechanic
- Welding
- RV and Tire Repair
- 24 Hour Towing

MAJOR AND MINOR REPAIRS
Open 6 Days a Week
VISA   MasterCard
"LOOK FOR THE BIG BLUE QUONSET BUILDING"
(403) 536-2720 • Watson Lake, Yukon

IRON CREEK Lodge
Mile 596
- Gas • Diesel
- Welding • Propane
♦ MOTEL ♦
RV PARK • Tentsites
Fishing from your Campsite
SHOWERS • LAUNDROMAT
DUMP STATION
(Good Sam Discount)

Licensed CAFE
Home Cooking
Baked Goodies • Ice Cream
YOUR HOSTS: VERN AND DEE HINSON
(403) 536-2266

Oasis Dairy Bar
- Ice Cream
- Milkshakes
- Sundaes
- Mouthwatering Burgers
- Fries

Bus Tours Welcome — Easy Highway Access
(Next to Campground Services/Gateway to Yukon RV Park) Watson Lake

---

Campground Services Ltd.
Gateway to Yukon RV Park
- Full and partial Hook-Ups and pull-throughs
- Complete Food Market
- Husky Self Serve Gas

Husky
Here in Watson Lake it's Husky

Mile 632.5, Watson Lake
Box 345, Watson Lake, Yukon Territory
(403) 536-7448

ALASKA HIGHWAY • WATSON LAKE

Chevron

KLONDIKE PassPORT
Chevron • WHITE PASS & YUKON ROUTE

VENTURE NORTH TO THE KLONDIKE WITH CONFIDENCE

Be on the lookout for the sign of the Chevron as you travel Yukon and Northern B.C. highways and receive your free Klondike Passport. It's your passport to quality Chevron products and services; and to the scenic and historic White Pass and Yukon Route Railway.

Pick up your free souvenir KLONDIKE PassPORT at any Chevron Dealer, select RV Parks, or at the White Pass & Yukon Railway Offices in Skagway and Whitehorse.

Have your PassPORT stamped each time you purchase fuel at our participating Chevron Dealers. Collect stamps to receive valuable discounts and prizes that will leave you with an unforgettable memory of your Klondike Adventure.

Chevron — your guarantee of quality products and friendly service.

Most major credit cards accepted

VISA   MasterCard   Chevron

CHEVRON PRODUCTS DISTRIBUTED BY
White Pass Petroleum Services

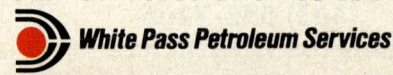

110   The MILEPOST® ■ 1992

93°F/34°C in June 1950, record low -74°F/-59°C in January 1947. Annual snowfall is 90.6 inches. Driest month is April, wettest month is September. Average date of last spring frost is June 2; average date of first fall frost is Sept. 14. **Radio:** CBC 990, CKYN-FM 96.1 (Visitor Radio CKYN is broadcast from the visitor information centre from mid-May to mid-September). **Television:** Channel 8 and cable.

Private Aircraft: Watson Lake airport, 8 miles/12.9 km north of Campbell Highway; elev. 2,262 feet/689m; length 5,500 feet/1,676m and 3,530 feet/1,076m; asphalt; fuel 80, 100, jet B. Heliport and floatplane bases also located here. The Watson Lake airport terminal building was built in 1942. The log structure has been designated a Heritage Building.

In the late 1800s, Watson Lake was known as Fish Lake. According to one source, the lake was renamed Watson for Frank Watson of Yorkshire, England, who gave up on the gold rush in 1898 to settle here on its shores with his Indian wife. Another source states that Watson Lake was named for Bob Watson, who opened a trading post here in 1936. Whatever its derivation, today Watson Lake is an important service stop on the Alaska and Campbell highways (Campbell Highway travelers fill your gas tanks here!); a communication and distribution centre for the southern Yukon; and a base for prospectors, trappers, hunters and fishermen.

Watson Lake businesses are located along either side of the Alaska Highway. The lake itself is not visible from the Alaska Highway. Access to the lake, airport and hospital is via the Campbell Highway (locally referred to as Airport Road). About 4 miles/6.4 km out the Campbell Highway is Mount Maichen ski hill.

Watson Lake airport, constructed in 1941, and the Alaska Highway, built in 1942, helped bring both people and commerce to this once isolated settlement. A post office opened here in July 1942. The economy of Watson Lake is based on services and also the forest products industry. White spruce and lodgepole pine are the 2 principal trees of the Yukon and provide a forest industry for the territory. White spruce grows straight and fast wherever adequate water is available, and it will grow to extreme old age without showing decay. The lodgepole pine developed from the northern pine and can withstand extreme cold, grow at high elevations and take full advantage of the almost 24-hour summer sunlight of a short growing season.

ACCOMMODATIONS

There are several hotels/motels, restaurants, and gas stations with regular, unleaded, diesel and propane, automotive and tire repair. There are also department, variety, grocery and hardware stores. A complex on the north side of the highway contains the post office, library, fire hall and government liquor store. The RCMP office is east of town centre on the Alaska Highway. There is 1 bank in Watson Lake, open Monday through Thursday from 10 A.M. to 3 P.M., Friday 10 A.M. to 6 P.M.; closed holidays. Check at the visitor information centre for locations of local churches. Watson Lake's public swimming pool is open daily in summer; admission fee.

Belvedere Motor Hotel, located in the centre of town, is Watson Lake's newest and finest hotel. It offers such luxuries as jacuzzi tubs in the rooms, waterbeds, and cable TV, and all at competitive prices. Dining is excellent, whether you decide to try the superb Dining Room Menu, or the Coffee Shop Menu, for those of us on a budget. Phone (403) 536-7712. [ADVERTISEMENT]

The turnoff for Watson Lake Yukon government campground is 2.4 miles/3.9 km west of the sign forest via the Alaska Highway; see description at **Milepost DC 615.3**. There is a private campground at **Milepost DC 619.6**, 4.3 miles/6.9 km past the turnoff for the government campground; a private campground 2.4 miles/3.9 km east of the sign forest on the Alaska Highway (see Mile-

Watson Lake sign forest had almost 13,000 signs in 1991. (Gilbert E. Nelson Jr.)

WATSON LAKE ADVERTISERS

Belvedere Motor Hotel.....Ph. (403) 536-7712
Ben's Auto Repairs............Ph. (403) 536-2720
Campground Services Ltd. .....E. edge of town
Canteen Show, The..............Next to signposts
Cedar Lodge Motel...........Ph. (403) 536-7406
Downtown RV Park.......................Downtown
Gateway Motor Inn ....Ph. (403) 536-7744
Greenway's Greens .....Mile 620.3 Alaska Hwy.
Grunow Motors ....Ph. (403) 536-2272
Heritage House Wildlife & Historic
   Museum......Across from Watson Lake Hotel
Kal Tire..............................Ph. (403) 536-2585
Napa Auto Parts ....Ph. (403) 536-2521
Shopping Unlimited.......................Downtown
Signpost Services ....Across from signposts
Town of Watson Lake.......Ph. (403) 536-7778
Watson Lake Esso ....Ph. (403) 536-2545
Watson Lake Hotel ....Ph. (403) 536-7781
Wye Tech Services ....Ph. (403) 536-2555

CEDAR LODGE MOTEL
8 Rooms with Complete Baths
Complimentary Coffee, Tea in Rooms
Box 243, Watson Lake, Yukon Y0A 1C0
Phone (403) 536-7406
Peter and Terri Skerget

Shopping Unlimited
Authorized
RADIO SHACK
Sales & Service Centre
* **Jade Souvenirs** *
Toys • Silk Plants • Furniture
Photo Finishing by Pix-A-Color
VISA
In the Strip Mall - Near the Bank of Commerce
Downtown Watson Lake   (403) 536-2721

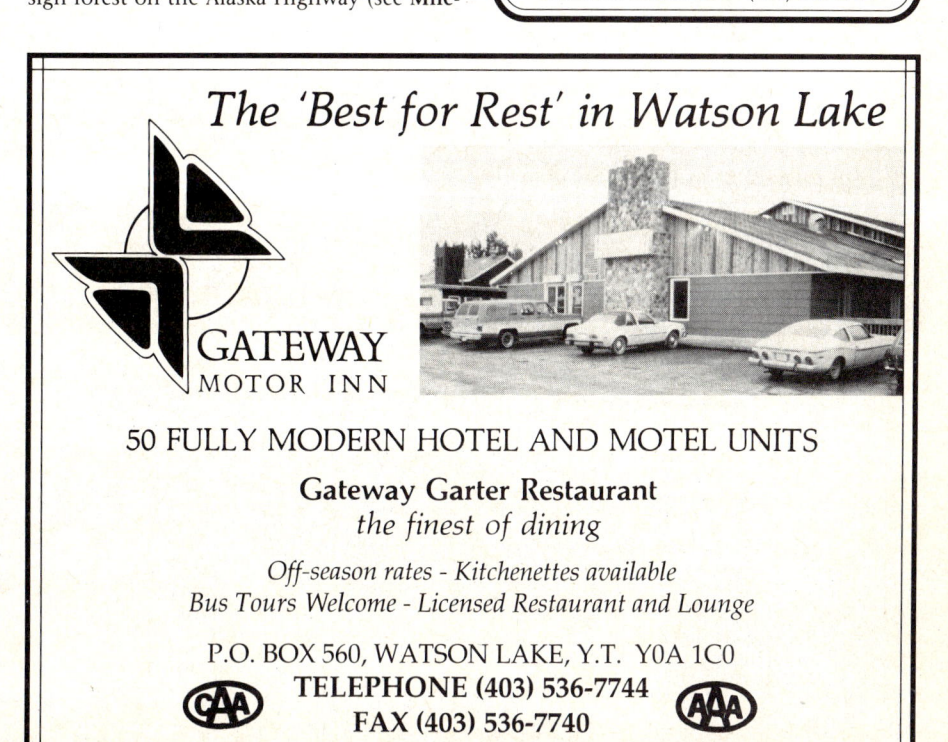

The 'Best for Rest' in Watson Lake

GATEWAY MOTOR INN

50 FULLY MODERN HOTEL AND MOTEL UNITS

Gateway Garter Restaurant
the finest of dining

Off-season rates - Kitchenettes available
Bus Tours Welcome - Licensed Restaurant and Lounge

P.O. BOX 560, WATSON LAKE, Y.T. Y0A 1C0
TELEPHONE (403) 536-7744
FAX (403) 536-7740
CAA   AAA

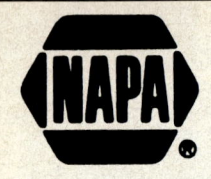

NAPA AUTO PARTS
Cars • Trucks • RV's • Parts and Accessories
Call (403) 536-2521   After Hours (403) 536-7541
Or write Box 371, Watson Lake, Yukon Y0A 1C0

ICG PROPANE INC.

SERVING THE YUKON WITH 28 DEALERS AND 2 BRANCH OUTLETS:

- BOTTLED GAS
- AUTO-PROPANE
- SALES
- SERVICE
- PARTS

ICG Propane
Mile 635, Alaska Highway
Watson Lake, Yukon
403-536-2531

ICG Propane
106 Galena Road
Whitehorse, Yukon
403-667-6723

---

post DC 610.5); and an RV park located downtown. ▲

Downtown RV Park, situated in the centre of town. 71 full hookup stalls, 19 with pull-through parking; showers; laundromat. Free truck/trailer, motorhome wash with overnight stay. Easy walking distance to stores, garages, hotels, restaurants, liquor store, banking, churches, information centre and the world-famous signpost forest. Phone (403) 536-2646 or 536-2224. [ADVERTISEMENT] ▲

TRANSPORTATION

Air: Scheduled service to Fort Nelson, Fort St. John, Edmonton and Calgary via Time Air. Service to Whitehorse via Air North. Helicopter and fixed-wing aircraft charters available. **Bus:** Scheduled service to Edmonton and Whitehorse via Coachways. **Taxi** and **Car Rental:** Available.

ATTRACTIONS

The **Alaska Highway Interpretive Centre** here is well worth a visit. Excellent slide presentation and displays, including photographs taken in the mid-1940s showing the construction of the Alaska Highway in this area, and a brief Alaska Highway video. Visitor information and campground permits are available at the Interpretive Centre, which is located behind the sign forest, north of the Alaska Highway. Open 9 A.M. to 9 P.M., May to mid-September. Free admission.

Special Events. In addition to the events listed in the 1992 calendar for Watson Lake this section, check with the visitor information centre for details and dates of ongoing displays and other events celebrating the 50th anniversary of the Alaska Highway.

WELCOME TO WATSON LAKE
YUKON'S GATEWAY
GATEWAY TO THE YUKON

TOWN OF WATSON LAKE
Box 590, Watson Lake, Yukon Y0A 1C0 (403) 536-7778 Fax (403) 536-7522

1992 Events

MAY
22-25 First School Reunion

JUNE
14-15 Army Motors Convoy overnight
22-26 Float Plane Race overnight
24-25 Army Motors Convoy overnight
28-29 Alaska Highway Trailblazers

JULY
9-10 Airmada

AUGUST
19 Peter Gzowski Invitational Golf Tournament

SEPTEMBER
11-13 Homecoming Reunion for Troops and Civilians
13 Ceremony at Contact Creek, BC
21-23 Rallye Alaska Highway '92

The Watson Lake sign forest seen at the north end of town at the junction of the Alaska and Robert Campbell highways, was started by Carl K. Lindley of Danville, IL, a U.S. Army soldier in Company D, 341st Engineers, working on the construction of the Alaska Highway in 1942. (Carl Lindley is expected to visit Watson Lake in 1992 as part of the Alaska Highway anniversary.) Travelers are still adding signs to the collection, which reached almost 13,000 in number in 1991.

Heritage House, built in 1948 by the late G.C.F. Dalziel, is the oldest house in Watson Lake and now a wildlife and historic museum. It is located 1 block north of the sign forest. Dalziel came to this region as a trapper in the 1920s. His heirs opened Heritage House in 1987. Goldsmith on premises. Open daily in summer. Free admission.

The Canteen Show. Starting its 5th

Welcome to Yukon

Wye Tech Services

SELF SERVE
PETRO-CANADA

Gasoline – Diesel – Oils

PETRO-CANADA STORE
ICE • VIDEO RENTAL

P.O. Box 128 • Watson Lake, YT
(403) 536-2555

...Also **McWANK'S**
Gourmet Take-out
Ice Cream • Burgers
Fish & Chips
(Summer Months Only)

WATSON LAKE ESSO
Esso Gas & Oil • Unleaded • Diesel Fuel
Cylinder & Auto Propane
Laundromat • Car Wash
Dump Station • Water
– TOW TRUCK –

(403) 536-2545 • Watson Lake, Yukon

KAL TIRE
ASSOCIATE DEALER
— Now in our 18th year of business —
COMPLETE TIRE SERVICE
Passenger – R.V. – Truck & Offroad
Phone (403) 536-2585

DOWNTOWN R.V. PARK
Center of Watson Lake

FULL HOOKUPS — PULL-THROUGH PARKING
LAUNDRY — SHOWERS
FREE R.V. WASH WITH OVERNIGHT STAY

WALKING DISTANCE FROM: Shopping, garages, hotels, restaurants, post office, banking, churches, liquor store, information centre.

Box 609, Watson Lake, Yukon, Y0A 1C0
Phone (403) 536-2646 or (403) 536-2224

VISA

K-Fuels Diesel • Gas
Car Wash • Tires

Automotive Parts Store • 24 Hour Wrecker Service

(403) 536-2272

GRUNOW MOTORS
Look for the large blue garage
IN WATSON LAKE
* MECHANICS & WELDING *
Specializing in Diesel, Gas and Propane Engines

VISA • MasterCard

SIGNPOST SERVICES
(Across from the Interpretive Center and Famous Watson Lake Signposts)

Chevron TAGS CONVENIENCE STORES

24-Hours
June-July-August
Ample Parking • Pay Phone

Gas Bar • Diesel • Car Wash • Souvenirs • Propane
Convenience Store • Laundromat • Showers • Ice • Stamps

Restaurant & Pizzaria
...offering Pizza, Fried Chicken, Sandwiches & Dairy Bar
• Take Out, Eat In or Delivery •
Off-Sales Wine, Liquor & Beer (Until 2 a.m.)

PHONE (403) 536-7422
Bus Tours Welcome (please call ahead)

MasterCard VISA

ALASKA HIGHWAY • WATSON LAKE

season of morale-boosting entertainment for all ages. This 1940s USO camp show is unique, differing from other summer productions throughout British Columbia, Yukon and Alaska, as it relates to the building of the "Alcan," rather than the gold rush. The Canteen Show is hilarious and upbeat. A must see while on your northern holiday. Live shows 8 P.M. nightly. Adults $12, children $6. Located under the big top next to the signpost forest. [ADVERTISEMENT]

Play golf at Upper Liard, 6 miles/9.6 km north of Watson Lake on the Alaska Highway. The 9-hole, par 35 course has grass greens and is open daily May through September. Phone 536-2477.

Wilderness Trips. Outfitters in the area offer guided fishing trips to area lakes. Trips can be arranged by the day or by the week. Check with the visitor information centre.

Wye Lake, 0.3 mile/0.4 km from town, is regularly stocked with rainbow. (Trail improvement and day-use area development are scheduled for Wye Lake.) **Watson Lake** has grayling, trout and pike. **McKinnon Lake** (walk-in only), 20 miles/32 km west of Watson Lake, pike 5 to 10 lbs. **Toobally Lake** and string of lakes 14 miles/23 km long, 90 air miles/145 km east, lake trout 8 to 10 lbs.; pike 5 to 10 lbs.; grayling 1 to 3 lbs. **Stewart Lake**, 45 air miles/72 km north northeast; lake trout, grayling.

WATSON LAKE HOTEL

Reservations
(403) 536-7781
FAX (403) 536-2724

Suites, Deluxe & Standard Rooms
Lounge, Dining Room
Coffee Shop, Banquet Facilities
Airline Office
Free Laundry & Sauna

48 HOTEL/MOTEL ROOMS

"Where Northern Hospitality Begins"

Box 370, Watson Lake, Yukon Y0A 1C0
Conveniently Located Beside the "Signpost Forest" and Visitor Centre

---

HERITAGE HOUSE WILDLIFE & HISTORIC MUSEUM

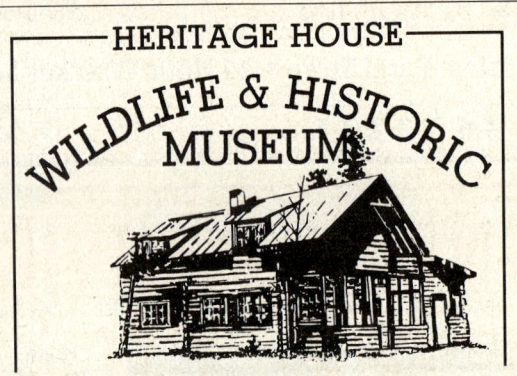

OLDEST HOUSE in WATSON LAKE

Home of the World's 2nd Largest Stone Sheep

"ENTER FREE DRAWING"
Gold Nugget Pendant
Drawing held Oct. 15

OPEN
9-9 Daily June 1-Aug. 31
9-5 Daily Sept. 1-Oct. 15

FREE ADMISSION

Souvenirs • Native Arts and Crafts • Gold Nugget Jewelry (handcrafted on the premises)
ACROSS FROM THE WATSON LAKE HOTEL
Box 392, Watson Lake, Yukon, Y0A 1C0   Phone (403) 536-2400 or 536-2291

"Do Your Thing in Watson Lake, Then Overnight Where it's Nice and Quiet at..."

Green Valley Trailer Park

KM 1032 ALASKA HIGHWAY

GOLD PANNING

◄ SERVICED and UNSERVICED SITES ►

PARK IT IN A PARK

Dump Station — Laundry — Showers — Groceries — Ice — Souvenirs — Pay Phone
Fishing Licenses • Boat Ramp • Fish from Our River Shore
SHADED RIVERSIDE CAMPING – TENTING – KITCHEN SHELTER
Country Setting   Caravans Welcome   Your Hosts: Ralph and Marion Bjorkman
P.O. Box 191, WATSON LAKE, YT   PHONE (403) 536-2276

Alaska Highway Log

(continued)

Distance* from Dawson Creek (DC) is followed by distance from Fairbanks (F). Original mileposts are indicated in the text as Historical Mile.

*Mileages from Dawson Creek are based on actual driving distance. Kilometres from Dawson Creek are based on physical kilometreposts. Please read Mileposts and Kilometreposts in the introduction for an explanation of how this highway is logged.

DC 612.9 (1021 km) **F 875.1** (1408.3 km) Watson Lake sign forest at the **junction** of the Campbell Highway (Yukon Route 4) and Alaska Highway. The Campbell Highway leads north to Ross River and Faro (see CAMPBELL HIGHWAY section). Campbell Highway travelers should fill gas tanks in Watson Lake. The first 6 miles/9.7 km of the Campbell Highway is known locally as Airport Road; turn here for access to visitor information (in the Alaska Highway Interpretive Centre), airport, hospital and ski hill. *CAUTION: Watch for large ore trucks.*

DC 615.3 (1025 km) **F 872.7** (1404.4 km) Turnoff to north for Watson Lake Recreation Park. Drive in approximately 2 miles/3 km for Watson Lake Yukon government campground; 50 gravel sites, most level, some pull-through, drinking water, kitchen shelters, outhouses, firepits, firewood and litter barrels. Camping fee $8.

There is a separate group camping area and also a day-use area (boat launch, swimming, picnicking at Watson Lake). Follow signs at fork in access road. Trails connect all areas.

DC 618.5 (1030 km) **F 869.5** (1399.3 km) Watch for livestock.

DC 619.6 (1032 km) **F 868.4** (1397.5 km) **Green Valley Trailer Park.** See display ad this section.

DC 620 (1032.4 km) **F 868** (1396.9 km) Upper Liard River bridge. The Liard River heads in the St. Cyr Range in southcentral Yukon Territory and flows southeast into British Columbia, then turns east and north to join the Mackenzie River at Fort Simpson, NWT.

Liard River, grayling, lake trout, whitefish and northern pike.

DC 620.2 (1032.7 km) **F 867.8** (1396.5 km) Historical Mile 642. UPPER LIARD VILLAGE, site of Our Lady of the Yukon Church. Gas, food, lodging and camping; open year-round.

Upper Liard Resort, Mile 642, Alaska Highway. Open year-round. A welcome

---

GREENWAY'S GREENS

9 HOLE   PAR 35
GRASS GREENS

Box 42, Watson Lake, Yukon Y0A 1C0
KM 1033
Open Daily From 6 a.m. – 10 p.m.
SPECIAL RATES FOR SENIORS
Phone (403) 536-2477

114   The MILEPOST® ■ 1992

stopping point for all travelers on the mighty Liard River. Gas, general store, souvenirs, motel, TV, cabins, RV park, camping, showers, laundromat, restaurant, lounge. Canadian and European cuisine. Good fishing, hunting and boating. Enjoy the magic in the Land of Midnight Sun. Phone (403) 536-2271. [ADVERTISEMENT] ▲

DC 620.3 (1033 km) F 867.7 (1396.4 km) Greenway's Greens golf course to south with 9 holes, par 35, grass greens, open daily in summer.

DC 620.8 (1033.7 km) F 867.2 (1395.6 km) Albert Creek bridge. Turnout with litter barrel to north at east end of bridge.

DC 626.2 (1042.5 km) F 861.8 (1386.9 km) **Historical Milepost 649. Junction** with the Cassiar Highway, which leads south to Yellowhead Highway 16 (see CASSIAR HIGHWAY section). Services here include gas, store, propane, car repair, car wash, cafe, camping and lodging. ▲

Junction 37 Services. See display ad this section.

DC 627 (1044 km) F 861 (1385.6 km) **The Northern Beaver Post.** As with trading posts of the past, The Northern Beaver Post is an essential stop for any traveler. Here you will find unique, quality items which are often as useful as they are decorative. In the friendly atmosphere of the Post, discover a fine selection of Native crafts, jewellery, gold, jade, authentic Eskimo carvings, furs, woolens, northern art, tufting, sweatshirts and tees, cards, gifts, and more. Open 8 A.M. to 9 P.M. 7 days a week, May through September. Free overnight RV parking. Phone (403) 536-2307. [ADVERTISEMENT]

DC 633 (1055.6 km) F 855 (1376 km) Turnout to north.

DC 637.8 (1063.3 km) F 850.2 (1368.2 km) NorthwesTel microwave tower access road to north.

DC 639.8 (1066.5 km) F 848.2 (1365 km) Hill and sharp curve.

DC 647.2 (1078.5 km) F 840.8 (1353.1 km) Turnout with litter barrel on Little Rancheria Creek to north.

DC 647.4 (1079 km) F 840.6 (1352.8 km) Little Rancheria Creek bridge. Sign reads: Northbound winter travelers put on chains here.

DC 650.6 (1084 km) F 837.4 (1347.6 km) Highway descends westbound to Big Creek.

DC 651.1 (1084.8 km) F 836.9 (1346.8 km) Big Creek bridge, clearance 17.7 feet/ 5.4m. Turnout at east end of bridge.

DC 651.2 (1085 km) F 836.8 (1346.7 km) Turnoff to north for Big Creek Yukon government day-use area, adjacent highway on Big Creek; gravel loop road, outhouses, firewood, kitchen shelter, litter barrels, picnic tables, drinking water.

DC 652.5 (1087.3 km) F 835.5 (1344.6 km) Sign reads: Northbound winter travelers chains may be removed.

DC 658.4 (1096.7 km) F 829.6 (1335.1 km) Pull-through turnout south side of highway.

DC 662.3 (1102.9 km) F 825.7 (1328.8 km) NorthwesTel microwave tower road to north.

DC 664.1 (1105.8 km) F 823.9 (1325.9 km) Turnout to north to Lower Rancheria River.

DC 664.3 (1106.2 km) F 823.7 (1325.6 km) Bridge over Lower Rancheria River. For northbound travelers, the highway closely follows the Rancheria River west from here to the Swift River.

Rancheria River, fishing for Dolly

The Northern Beaver Post

Specializing in Quality Yukon and Canadian Handcrafts

* Gold and Jade Jewelry
* Native Moccasins and Crafts
* Sweatshirts and Teeshirts
* Local Art
* Northern Books
* And More!...

On the Alaska Highway, 1/2 mile west of Junction 37
(403) 536-2307

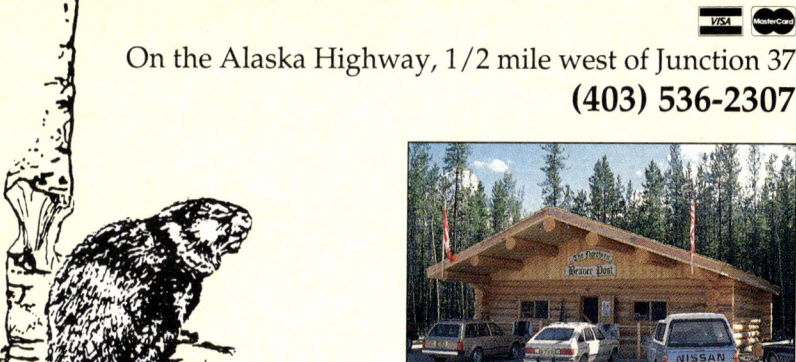

See Log Ad for More!

Chevron **JUNCTION 37 SERVICES** **PETRO-CANADA**
(403) 536-2794 Mile 649

- UNLEADED • DIESEL • PROPANE BOTTLE FILLING
- WELDING • TOWING • METERED PROPANE
- Tires • Mechanical Repair • Car Wash
- Ice • Free RV Dumping

Good Sam Club

CAFE • CAMPGROUND WITH FULL HOOKUPS • MOTEL
LAUNDROMAT • STORE WITH GROCERIES AND SOUVENIRS
SHOWERS • BEER OFF SALES • LICENSED DINING AND BAR
Fishing Licenses For Sale

ALASKA HIGHWAY • YUKON

1992 ■ The MILEPOST® 115

The winding road

Speed of construction was the primary consideration in construction of the pioneer road. The Alaska Highway was literally bulldozed through the wilderness in 1942. Ninety-degree turns and 25 percent grades were not uncommon. Construction of a better highway to support the movement of military vehicles in all weather conditions was to follow. In early 1943, a directive on road standards called for a 24-foot surfaced roadway, maximum grades of 7 percent, curves no sharper than 8 degrees, a minimum sight distance of 600 feet, and at least 12 inches of well-graded crushed or screened gravel. But standards changed often in the early years, as engineers came up against the constraints of time and terrain.

U.S. Army

RANCHERIA HOTEL-MOTEL

KM 1143.8 • Mile 710
Licensed Dining Room
Cocktail Lounge
Modern Rooms
RV Park
Tires, Minor Repairs, Towing
Regular, Diesel and Unleaded Gas
Propane • Camping • Showers
Ice • Cold Beer • Telephone
OPEN 24 HOURS
PHONE (403) 851-6456 or (403) 667-1016

CONTINENTAL DIVIDE
MILE 721

Shell Gas • Licensed Restaurant • Pub
Nightly Roast • Salad Bar • Kids Menu
Home Baking • Sourdough Bread
RV Parking • Clean Budget Rooms

Bus Tours Welcome (Please phone ahead)
OPEN 7 A.M. 'TIL WEE SMALL HOURS

(403) 851-6451
Mail Bag, Swift River, Yukon Y0A 1A0

Varden and grayling.

DC 665.1 (1110.4 km) F 822.9 (1324.3 km) Scenic viewpoint.

DC 667.2 (1113.7 km) F 820.8 (1320.9 km) Turnout to south.

DC 667.6 (1114.3 km) F 820.4 (1320.2 km) Turnout with litter barrel to south.

DC 671.9 (1118.7 km) F 816.1 (1313.3 km) Spencer Creek.

DC 673.4 (1121 km) F 814.6 (1310.9 km) Steep grade as highway descends westbound. Road narrows. Cassiar Mountains visible ahead for westbound travelers.

In November of 1942, the month the Alaska Highway was officially "finished," the most difficult stretch for movement of traffic proved to be from Summit Lake to Teslin Lake. One Public Roads Administration officer described the section between Watson Lake and Teslin as "the worst," with heavy grades, narrow widths and sharp curves.

DC 677 (1126.9 km) F 811 (1305.1 km) Turnout with litter barrel to south overlooking the Rancheria River. Trail down to river.

According to R.C. Coutts, author of *Yukon: Places & Names*, the Rancheria River was named by Cassiar miners working Sayyea Creek in 1875, site of a minor gold rush at the time. Rancheria is an old Californian or Mexican miners' term from the Spanish, meaning a native village or settlement. It is pronounced Ran-che-RI-ah.

DC 678.5 (1129.3 km) F 809.5 (1302.7 km) George's Gorge, culvert.

DC 683.2 (1137 km) F 804.8 (1295.2 km) NorthwesTel microwave tower to south.

DC 684 (1138.4 km) F 804 (1293.9 km) Turnout with litter barrel overlooking Rancheria River. *CAUTION: Watch for livestock on or near highway in this area.*

DC 687.2 (1143.8 km) F 800.8 (1288.7 km) **Historical Milepost 710.** Rancheria Hotel-Motel to south; gas, food, camping and lodging. Open year-round. ▲

Rancheria Hotel-Motel. See display ad this section.

DC 687.4 (1143.9 km) F 800.6 (1288.4 km) Turnoff to south for Rancheria Yukon government campground, adjacent highway overlooking Rancheria River; gravel loop road, 12 level sites, outhouses, kitchen shelter, litter barrels, water pump, picnic tables, firepits and firewood. Camping fee $8. ▲

DC 689.2 (1146.6 km) F 798.8 (1285.5 km) Canyon Creek.

DC 690 (1148 km) F 798 (1284.2 km) Highway follows the Rancheria River, which is to the south of the road. The Rancheria is a tributary of the Liard River.

DC 692.5 (1152 km) F 795.5 (1280.2 km) Young Creek.

DC 694.2 (1155 km) F 793.8 (1277.5 km) **Historical Mile 717.5.** Abandoned building.

DC 695.2 (1156.5 km) F 792.8 (1275.8 km) Rancheria Falls recreation site has a good gravel and boardwalk trail to the falls; easy 10-minute walk. Parking area with toilets and litter barrels at trailhead.

DC 697.4 (1160 km) F 790.6 (1272.3 km) Beautiful view of the Cassiar Mountains.

DC 698.4 (1161.6 km) F 789.6 (1270.7 km) **Historical Mile 721.** Continental Divide; gas, food, camping and lodging. ▲

Continental Divide. See display ad this section.

DC 698.7 (1162 km) F 789.3 (1270.2 km) Upper Rancheria River bridge, clearance 17.7 feet/5.4m. For northbound travelers, the highway leaves the Rancheria River.

DC 699.1 (1162.8 km) F 788.9 (1269.6 km) Continental Divide turnout with point of interest sign to north; litter barrels. This marks the water divide between rivers that drain into the Arctic Ocean via the Mackenzie River system and those that drain into the Pacific Ocean via the Yukon River system. All rivers crossed by the Alaska Highway between here and Fairbanks, AK, drain into the Yukon River.

DC 699.6 (1163.3 km) F 788.4 (1268.8 km) **Historical Milepost 722.** Pine Lake airstrip to north (status unknown).

DC 702.2 (1168 km) F 785.8 (1264.6 km) Swift River bridge. For northbound travelers, the highway now follows the Swift River west to the Morley River.

DC 706.2 (1174.5 km) F 781.8 (1258.2 km) Steep hill for westbound travelers.

DC 709.7 (1180 km) F 778.3 (1252.5 km) Seagull Creek.

DC 710 (1180.9 km) F 778 (1252 km) **Historical Milepost 733, SWIFT RIVER.** Lodge with food, gas, lodging, car repair, pay phone and highway maintenance camp. Open year-round.

Swift River Lodge. Friendly haven in a beautiful mountain valley. Tasty cooking with a plentiful supply of coffee. Rest and talk with the Breeden family. Comfortable modern rooms with reasonable rates. Wrecker service, welding and repairs. Tempo gas and diesel at the best prices on the highway. Clean restrooms, gifts and public phone. Southern hospitality. [ADVERTISEMENT]

DC 710.5 (1181.5 km) F 777.5 (1251.2 km) **Historical Mile 733.5.** The highway reenters British Columbia for approximately 42 miles/68 km northbound.

DC 712.7 (1185 km) F 775.3 (1247.7 km) Partridge Creek.

Alaska Highway winds through Rancheria River Valley. (Earl L. Brown, staff)

DC 719.6 (1196 km) F 768.4 (1236.6 km) **Historical Mile 743.** Turnout with litter barrel to south on **Swan Lake.** Fishing for trout and whitefish. The pyramid-shaped mountain to south is Simpson Peak.

DC 724.2 (1203.7 km) F 763.8 (1229.2 km) Pull-through turnout to south.

DC 727.9 (1209.5 km) F 760.1 (1223.2 km) Logjam Creek. Litter barrel.

DC 735.8 (1222.5 km) F 752.2 (1210.5 km) Smart River bridge. The Smart River flows south into the Cassiar Mountains in British Columbia. The river was originally called Smarch, after an Indian family of that name who lived and trapped in this area.

DC 741.4 (1231.7 km) F 746.6 (1201.5

SWIFT RIVER LODGE

Mile 733 Alaska Highway
Swift River, Yukon Y0A 1A0

**Motel • Restaurant • Souvenirs • Welding
Wrecker Service • Repairs • Gas • Diesel • Tires**

Need R.V. Water? Tire Repair?
Rest Rooms? . . . or just a break?
Stop with us for home cooking and Southern Hospitality!

Reasonable Prices

OPEN YEAR ROUND
THE BREEDEN FAMILY

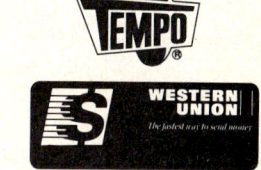

TEMPO
WESTERN UNION

(403) 851-6401 • FAX Service (403) 851-6400

km) Microwave tower access road to north.

DC 744.1 (1236 km) **F 743.9** (1197.2 km) Upper Hazel Creek.

DC 745.2 (1238 km) **F 742.8** (1195.4 km) Lower Hazel Creek.

DC 746.9 (1240.7 km) **F 741.1** (1192.6 km) Turnouts both sides of highway; litter barrel at south turnout.

DC 749 (1245 km) **F 739** (1189.3 km) Andrew Creek.

DC 751.5 (1249.2 km) **F 736.5** (1185.2 km) Morley Lake to north. The Alaska Highway reenters the Yukon Territory northbound. This is the last of 9 crossings of the YT-BC border.

DC 752 (1250 km) **F 736** (1184.4 km) Sharp turnoff to north for **Morley River** Yukon government day-use area; large gravel parking area, picnic tables, kitchen shelter, water, litter barrels and outhouses. Fishing.

DC 752.3 (1251 km) **F 735.7** (1184 km) Morley River bridge; turnout with litter barrel to north at east end of bridge. Morley River flows into the southeast corner of Teslin Lake. The river, lake and Morley Bay (on Teslin Lake) were named for W. Morley Ogilvie, assistant to Arthur St. Cyr on the 1897 survey of the Telegraph Creek-Teslin Lake route.

Morley Bay and **River**, good fishing near mouth of river for northern pike 6 to 8 lbs., best June to August, use small Red Devils; grayling 3 to 5 lbs., in May and August, use small spinner; lake trout 6 to 8 lbs., June to August, use large spoon.

DC 752.9 (1252 km) **F 735.1** (1183 km) **Historical Mile 777.** Morley River Lodge, food, gas, diesel, camping and lodging. ▲

Morley River Lodge. See display ad this section.

DC 754.8 (1256 km) **F 733.2** (1179.9 km) *CAUTION: Watch for livestock on highway.*

DC 757.9 (1261 km) **F 730.1** (1174.9 km) Small marker to south (no turnout) reads: "In memory of Max Richardson 39163467, Corporal Co. F 340th Eng. Army of the United States; born Oct. 10, 1918, died Oct. 17, 1942. Faith is the victory."

DC 761.5 (1267.9 km) **F 726.5** (1169.1 km) Strawberry Creek.

DC 764.1 (1273.7 km) **F 723.9** (1165 km) Hayes Creek.

DC 769.6 (1282.5 km) **F 718.4** (1156.1 km) **Historical Mile 797.** Food, lodging and camping. ▲

Dawson Peaks Resort. Slow down folks! No need to drive any farther. Fishing's good, coffee's on, camping is easy and the rhubarb pie can't be beat. Couple that with our renowned Yukon hospitality and you'll have one of the best experiences on your trip. We're looking forward to seeing you this summer. [ADVERTISEMENT]

DC 776 (1292 km) **F 712** (1145.8 km) Nisutlin Bay (Nisutlin River) bridge, longest water span on the Alaska Highway at 1,917 feet/584m. The Nisutlin River flows into Teslin Lake here. Good view northbound of the village of Teslin and Teslin Lake. Teslin Lake straddles the BC-YT border; it is 86 miles/138 km long, averages 2 miles/3.2 km across, and has an average depth of 194 feet/59m. The name is taken from the Indian name for the lake—Teslintoo ("long, narrow water").

Turnout with litter barrel and point of interest sign at south end of bridge, east side of highway.

At the north end of the bridge, west side of the highway, is a summer information pavilion, parking area, marina and day-use area with picnic tables and boat ramp. Start of the "Walk Around a Northern Block" tour; stop by the information pavilion for details. Turn west on side road here for access to Teslin village (description follows).

DC 776.3 (1294 km) **F 711.7** (1145.3 km) Entering Teslin (**Historical Mile 804**) at north end of bridge. Gas, food and lodging along highway.

Yukon Motel, just right (northbound) on the north side of Nisutlin Bridge. An excellent stop for a fresh lake trout dinner (or full menu), accompanied by good and friendly service topped off with a piece of fantastic rhubarb and strawberry pie (lots of fresh baking). Soft ice cream. Recently renovated. 3 satellite TV channels. Open year-round, summer hours 6-11. A real home away from home on the shore of beautiful Nisutlin Bay. (403) 390-2575. [ADVERTISEMENT]

MORLEY RIVER LODGE

Mile 777.7 KM 1252 ALASKA HIGHWAY

GAS • Diesel • Towing   Licensed Restaurant   Souvenirs
Fully Modern Motel Units • Laundromat
Riverside Camping • Plug-ins
Dump Station • Boat Launch — *GREAT FISHING!*
Off-sales: liquor, wine and beer

Phone (403) 390-2639

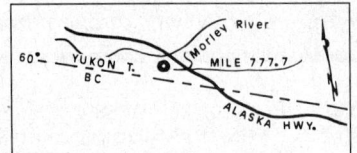

VISA   MasterCard

DAWSON PEAKS RESORT

"FRIENDLY SERVICE IN AN AUTHENTIC COOKTENT ATMOSPHERE"

LOCATED 7 MILES SOUTH OF TESLIN

CAMPGROUND - From Tents to RVs
Rustic Lakeview Cabins
Home Cooking and Baking

Showers • Sauna • Propane • Guided Fishing • Canoe and Boat Rentals
Giftshop and Northern Bookstore • Fishing Licenses Sold

▶ Drop-off and pick-up shuttle service for Teslin, Nisutlin and Big Salmon Rivers
▶ Wilderness Expediting
▶ Bus Tours Welcome (Please call in advance)

Your Hosts: David Hett and Carolyn Allen

KM 1282, Alaska Highway, Teslin, Yukon Y0A 1B0
(403) 390-2310 Answering Service • FAX (403) 390-2682 • Mobile 2M3169 Teslin Channel

---

YUKON MOTEL

14 Modern Units
Phone (403) 390-2575

Licensed Cafe Seats 56 • Satellite TV
We Cater to Bus Tours (please phone ahead)
Soft Ice Cream • Souvenirs • Ice
Laundromat and Showers • Ample Parking
Cocktail Bar, Liquor and Beer Off Sales
Self-serve Unleaded Gas and Diesel

R.V. Park Ready for 1991 Season
On the Shore of Beautiful Nisutlin Bay
Mile 804 KM 1293.9, Teslin, Yukon... Free Transportation from local airport

VISA   MasterCard

Teslin

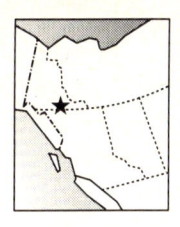

Located at **Historical Milepost 804**, 111 miles/179 km southeast of Whitehorse, 163 miles/263 km northwest of Watson Lake. **Population:** 465. **Emergency Services:** RCMP, phone 390-2500. **Fire Department**, phone 390-2538. **Nurse**, phone 390-2510.

Elevation: 2,239 feet/682.4m. **Climate:** Average temperature in January, -7°F/-22°C, in July 57°F/14°C. Annual snowfall 66.2 inches/168.2cm. Driest month April, wettest month July. Average date of last spring frost is June 19; first fall frost Aug. 19. **Radio:** CBC 940. **Television:** Channel 13.

The village of Teslin, situated on a point of land at the confluence of the Nisutlin River and Teslin Lake, began as a trading post in 1903. Today the community consists of log, clapboard and trailer homes, a trading post, Catholic church, health centre and post office. There is a 3-sheet regulation curling rink, skating rink and swimming pool.

Teslin has one of the largest Native populations in Yukon Territory and much of the community's livelihood revolves around traditional hunting, trapping and fishing. In addition, some Tlingit residents are involved in the development of Native woodworking craft (canoes, snowshoes and sleds) in a local factory; traditional sewn art and craft items (moccasins, mitts, moose hair tufting, gun cases); and the tanning of moose hides.

George Johnston Museum, renovated in 1991, is located on the right on the way into the village. The museum, run by the Teslin Historical Society, is open daily, 9 A.M. to 7 P.M. in summer; minimal admission fee. The museum displays items from gold rush days and the pioneer mode of living, Indian artifacts and many items of Tlingit culture. A Tlingit Indian, George Johnston (1884-1972) was an innovative individual, known for his trapping as well as his photography. With his camera he captured the life of the inland Tlingit people of Teslin and Atlin between 1910 and 1940. Johnston also brought the first car to Teslin, a 1928 Chevrolet. Since the Alaska Highway had not been built yet, George built a 3-mile road for his "Teslin taxi." In winter, he put chains on the car and drove it on frozen Tetlin Lake. The '28 Chevy has been restored and is on display at Taylor Chevrolet Oldsmobile Ltd. in Whitehorse.

Teslin is located west of the Alaska Highway, accessible via a short side road from the north end of Nisutlin Bay bridge. Nisutlin Trading Post in the village has groceries and general merchandise. Gas, diesel and propane, car repair, gift shop, restaurants and motels are found along the Alaska Highway. There is 1 bank, located in the Teslin Village office building; open Wednesday afternoons only in summer. The Teslin area has an air charter service, boat rentals and houseboat tours.

1992 Anniversary. Plan to stop at Mile 804. Take a break with us. Teslin's 1992 Anniversary Society welcomes all travelers.

1992 Events

JUNE
23-24 Army Motors Convoy overnight

JULY
16-20 Festival of First Nations

SEPTEMBER
23 Rallye Alaska Highway '92

TESLIN ADVERTISERS

Halsteads' ....Mile 807 Alaska Hwy.
1992 Anniversary Society ......N. end of bridge
Nisutlin Trading Post........Ph. (403) 390-2521
Northlake Motel
  and Cafe ....Ph. (403) 390-2571
Teslin Lake Motors............Ph. (403) 390-2551
Totem Pole Craft
  Shop ....Next to Chevron station
Yukon Motel ....Ph. (403) 390-2575

TESLIN LAKE MOTORS
CHEVRON PRODUCTS
(Discounts over 100 liters)

WELDING • MECHANIC • WRECKER
FREE WATER FOR CUSTOMERS
PROPANE FOR BOTTLES AND MOTOR FUEL

Chargex, MasterCard & Affiliated Cards Accepted
Mile 804, Teslin, Yukon • Phone (403) 390-2551

Totem Pole Craft Shop
◆ *Specializing in local Tlingit and Yukon Indian Crafts* ◆

Unique Gifts — Souvenirs — Collectibles
Northern Books and Magazines
Silver and Turquoise • Yukon Gold Nugget Jewelry

Fishing Licenses — Smoked Salmon — Film — Confections

Come and see our pictorial display on Alaska Highway construction

Lots of Parking Area   Teslin, Yukon • (403) 390-2206

HALSTEADS'
Located on beautiful Teslin Lake
(3 miles west of bridge)

GAS — Dependable quality SHELL products
 • *Free* water and dump with fill-up

CAFE — Yukon rhubarb pie • *Famous* 6 oz. all-beef hamburgers
 • Fried chicken • Bakery • Take-outs available

SOUVENIRS — CHECK US OUT! Best and largest shop on the highway • Furs • Yukon sweats and Tees • Carvings
 • Jewelry and Eskimo dolls

MOTEL — Modern, clean rooms • Satellite TV, refrigerators, private baths and non-smoking rooms

RV PARK — Hookups • Pull-throughs • Satellite TV • Tables
 • Grills • Showers
 Quiet park-like setting with trees and sandy beach

ICE CREAM (7 *flavors*) • COLD BEER • ICE
LAUNDROMAT • MAIL DROP • STAMPS • TELEPHONE

YES! We're the "inside tip" written up and recommended in Ron Dalby's book ALASKA HIGHWAY...AN INSIDERS GUIDE

The Place Everybody's Talking About   Clean and Friendly
Dale and Mary Halstead   **Teslin, Yukon Y0A 1B0**
Over 20 years serving the public   **(403) 390-2608**

ALASKA HIGHWAY • TESLIN

You're invited to experience the sights of our northern community, and go for a "Walk Around a Northern Block." Stop by our information pavilion at the north end of the bridge and discover what Teslin is all about. [ADVERTISEMENT]

Nisutlin Trading Post, on short loop road, left northbound in Teslin Village. A pioneer store established in 1928, and located on the shore of Nisutlin Bay, an "arm" of Teslin Lake. This store handles a complete line of groceries, general merchandise including clothing, hardware, fishing tackle and licenses. Open all year 9 A.M. to 5:30 P.M. Closed Sunday. Founded by the late R. McCleery, Teslin pioneer, the trading post is now operated by Mr. and Mrs. Bob Hassard. Phone 390-2521. FAX 390-2103. [ADVERTISEMENT]

Teslin Lake, fishing for trout, grayling, pike and whitefish. Guides and boats available locally.

NORTHLAKE MOTEL AND CAFE

MILE 804/km 1294
Alaska Highway
Teslin, YT
OPEN YEAR-ROUND

MOTEL UNITS
Reasonable Rates
Winter Plug-ins
Satellite TV • Pets Welcome

LICENSED RESTAURANT
Good Home Cooking
Fresh Baked Goods

COCKTAIL LOUNGE
Cold Draught on Tap
Off Sales
Liquor, Wine & Beer

ICE FOR SALE

LOCAL NATIVE HANDICRAFTS
Yukon Gold Jewellery
FREE TRANSPORTATION FROM LOCAL AIRPORT
BUS TOURS — Coffee, Lunch or Dinner Stop
Phone ahead (48 hours minimum)
Phone (403) 390-2571 / 390-2411 / 390-2553

VISA MasterCard

Alaska Highway Log

(continued)

Distance* from Dawson Creek (DC) is followed by distance from Fairbanks (F). Original mileposts are indicated in the text as Historical Mile.

*Mileages from Dawson Creek are based on actual driving distance. Kilometres from Dawson Creek are based on physical kilometreposts. Please read Mileposts and Kilometreposts in the introduction for an explanation of how this highway is logged.

DC 777 (1295 km) **F 711** (1144.2 km) **Historical Milepost 805. Private Aircraft:** Teslin airstrip to east; elev. 2,313 feet/705m; length 5,500 feet/1,676m; gravel; fuel 80, 100.

DC 779.1 (1298.5 km) **F 708.9** (1140.8 km) **Historical Mile 807.** Halsteads' gas, food, camping and lodging. Microwave tower on hillside to northwest. ▲

DC 779.5 (1299 km) **F 708.5** (1140.2 km) Fox Creek.

DC 784.3 (1306.7 km) **F 703.7** (1132.5 km) Mukluk Annie's; food, lodging and camping. ▲

Mukluk Annie's. See display ad this section.

DC 785.2 (1308 km) **F 702.8** (1131 km) **Historical Mile 813.** Teslin Lake Yukon government campground to west; 19 sites (some level) in trees on **Teslin Lake**, water pump, litter barrels, kitchen shelter, firewood, firepits, picnic tables. Camping fee $8. Fishing. Boat launch 0.3 mile/0.5 km north of campground.

DC 785.3 (1308.2 km) **F 702.7** (1130.8 km) Tenmile Creek.

DC 788.9 (1314 km) **F 699.1** (1125 km) Lone Tree Creek.

DC 794.6 (1323 km) **F 693.4** (1115.9 km) Deadman's Creek.

DC 800.8 (1333.3 km) **F 687.2** (1105.9 km) Robertson Creek.

DC 801.6 (1334.4 km) **F 686.4** (1104.6 km) **Historical Milepost 829.** Brooks' Brook. According to R.C. Coutts in *Yukon: Places & Names*, this stream was named by black Army engineers who completed this section of road in 1942, for their company officer, Lieutenant Brooks.

"JESUS IS LORD"

JUST 9 MILES NORTHBOUND FROM TESLIN

Free Camping for All At...

MUKLUK ANNIE'S SALMON BAKE

Featuring:
- Pacific Salmon
- Bar-B-Que Ribs,
  Bar-B-Que Steaks and
  Bar-B-Que Pork Chops
- Salad Bar

CAFE with complete menu • Open from 8 a.m. to 11 p.m.
SALMON BAKE SERVING FROM 11 a.m. to 9 p.m. DAILY

Caravans and Bus Tours Welcome – Special Rates
Call Collect for Rates and Information

Motel with Low Rates	Gift Shop	Hookups • Ice
Smoked Salmon	Boats	Tenting Area
Fresh Donuts	Currency Exchange	Hot Showers
Free R.V. Parking	Free Dump Station	Free Water

VISA **Phone (403) 667-1200** MasterCard
Mile 812 Alaska Highway – KM 1306 Alaska Highway

Mile 836 KM 1346 Alaska Highway, Yukon
Phone 390-2607

GROCERIES • HOME BAKING

Johnson's Crossing Campground Services

1992 — Our 45th Year!

GIFTS AND SOUVENIRS
WOODED CAMPSITES *(Some with electricity)*
SERVICE STATION • LAUNDROMAT
OFF-SALES BEER • HOT SHOWERS

OPEN MAY 1 TO SEPT. 30

DC 808.2 (1345 km) **F 679.8** (1094 km) **Junction** with the Canol Road (Yukon Highway 6) which leads northeast to the Campbell Highway.

The Canol (Canadian Oil) Road was built in 1942–44 to provide access to oil fields at Norman Wells, NWT. Conceived by the U.S. War Dept., the $134 million project was abandoned soon after the war ended in 1945. (See the CANOL ROAD section for details.)

DC 808.6 (1345.6 km) **F 679.4** (1093.3 km) Teslin River bridge, third longest water span on the highway (1,770 feet/539m), was constructed with a very high clearance above the river to permit steamers of the British Yukon Navigation Co. to pass under it en route from Whitehorse to Teslin. River steamers ceased operation on the Teslin River in 1942. Before the construction of the Alaska Highway, all freight and supplies for Teslin traveled this water route from Whitehorse.

DC 808.9 (1346 km) **F 679.1** (1092.9 km) **Historical Milepost 836. JOHNSON'S CROSSING** to east at north end of bridge; store, food and camping. Ellen Davignon of Johnson's Crossing Services is the author of *The Cinnamon Mine,* about her life growing up on the Alaska Highway. This is the family's 45th year in business at this location. Access to Teslin River; boat launch, no camping on riverbank. ▲

Johnson's Crossing Campground Services. See display ad this section.

Teslin River Wilderness Adventures. See display ad this section.

Teslin River, excellent grayling fishing from spring to late fall, 10 to 15 inches, use spinner or red-and-white spoons for spinning or black gnat for fly-fishing. King salmon in August.

Canoeists report that the Teslin River is wide and slow, but with gravel, rocks and weeds. Adequate camping sites on numerous sand bars; boil drinking water. Abundant wildlife—muskrat, porcupine, moose, eagles and wolves—also bugs and rain. Watch for bear. The Teslin enters the Yukon River at Hootalinqua, an old steamboat landing and supply point (under restoration). Roaring Bull rapids: choppy water. Pull out at Carmacks. Inquire locally about river conditions before setting out.

DC 809.1 (1346.5 km) **F 678.9** (1092.5 km) Access road east to the Teslin River. The Big Salmon Range, also to the east, parallels the Teslin. For Alaska-bound travelers, the highway now swings west.

DC 812.8 (1352.5 km) **F 675.2** (1086.6 km) Little Teslin Lake on south side of highway.

DC 819.8 (1364 km) **F 668.2** (1075.3 km) In mid-June, the roadside is a profusion of purple Jacob's ladder and yellow dandelions.

DC 820.3 (1364.8 km) **F 667.7** (1074.5 km) Seaforth Creek bridge.

DC 820.4 (1365 km) **F 667.6** (1074.4 km) Large turnout to south; picnic area.

DC 820.6 (1365.3 km) **F 667.4** (1074 km) Squanga Lake to northwest. Named Squanga by Indians for a type of whitefish of the same name found in the lake. Watch for **Historical Milepost 843**, Squanga Lake flightstrip.

DC 821 (1366 km) **F 667** (1073.4 km) Turnoff to northwest to **Squanga Lake** Yukon government campground: 13 sites, kitchen shelter, drinking water. Small boat launch. Fishing for northern pike, grayling, whitefish, rainbow and burbot. ▲

DC 827.5 (1376.8 km) **F 660.5** (1062.9 km) White Mountain, to the southeast, was named by William Ogilvie during his 1887 survey, for Thomas White, then Minister of the Interior. The Yukon government intro-

Teslin River bridge was constructed to permit clearance of river steamers. (Earl L. Brown, staff)

ALASKA HIGHWAY • YUKON

Teslin River Wilderness Adventures
(Pick up at Johnson's Crossing)
- River Tours
- Hiking Trails
- Fishing Guide
- Rustic Riverfront Cabins

Bring your camera!

Your Hosts: Bob and Ida McCormick
General Delivery
Teslin, Yukon Y0A 1B0
Radio Phone 2M3121 Teslin Channel via: Whitehorse

Visit ATLIN

It's been called... Utopia... Shangri-La... Switzerland... inspirational, tranquil, spectacular, timeless...

DISCOVER FOR YOURSELF.

Full services available; see Atlin section

Super, Natural North by Northwest

Atlin Visitors Association
Box 365-M
Atlin, BC V0W 1A0
FAX (604) 651-7696

1992 ■ The MILEPOST® 121

duced mountain goats to this area in 1981.

DC 836.8 (1392.5 km) **F 651.2** (1048 km) **Historical Milepost 866. Junction**, commonly known as **JAKE'S CORNER**; gas, food and lodging. The Alaska Highway junctions here with Yukon Highway 7 south to Atlin, a very scenic spot that is well worth a side trip (see ATLIN ROAD section). This turnoff also provides access to Yukon Highway 8 to Carcross and Klondike Highway 2 to Skagway, AK. (Klondike Highway 2 junctions with the Alaska Highway at **Milepost DC 874.4.**) Yukon Highway 8 is a scenic alternative to driving the Carcross-Alaska Highway portion of Klondike Highway 2 (see TAGISH ROAD and KLONDIKE HIGHWAY 2 sections for details).

Jake's Corner Inc. See display ad this section.

There are 2 versions of how Jake's Corner got its name. In 1942, the U.S. Army Corps of Engineers set up a construction camp here to build this section of the Alcan Highway and the Tagish Road cutoff to Carcross for the Canol pipeline. (The highway south to Atlin, BC, was not constructed until 1949–50.) The camp was under the command of Captain Jacobson, thus Jake's Corner. However, another version that predates the Alcan construction is that Jake's Corner was named for Jake Jackson, a Teslin Indian who camped in this area on his way to Carcross.

DC 843.2 (1402.7 km) **F 644.8** (1037.6 km) Judas Creek bridge.

DC 850 (1413.5 km) **F 638** (1026.7 km) Turnoff to west for Lakeview Resort on Marsh Lake; camping, lodging, boat launch. ▲

Lakeview Resort & Marina. See display ad this section.

DC 851.6 (1416 km) **F 636.4** (1024.1 km) Several access roads along here which lead to summer cottages. Marsh Lake is a popular recreation area for Whitehorse residents.

DC 852.7 (1417.8 km) **F 635.3** (1022.4 km) Good view of Marsh Lake to west. The highway parallels this beautiful lake for several miles. Marsh Lake (elev. 2,152 feet/656m) is part of the Yukon River system. It is approximately 20 miles/32 km long and was named in 1883 by Lt. Frederick Schwatka, U.S. Army, for Yale professor Othniel Charles Marsh.

Marsh Lake, excellent fishing for grayling and northern pike.

DC 854.4 (1421 km) **F 633.6** (1019.6 km) **Historical Milepost 883.** Marsh Lake Camp. The plaque here is one of dozens of such signs put up along the Alaska Highway at the sites of old highway construction camps to commemorate the 50th anniversary of the highway. Boat ramp turnoff to west.

DC 854.8 (1421.2 km) **F 633.2** (1019 km) Caribou Road leads northwest to Airplane Lake; hiking trail, good skiing and snowmachining in winter. This road was bulldozed out to get men and equipment into a small lake where an airplane had made an emergency landing.

DC 859.9 (1432 km) **F 628.1** (1010.8 km) **Historical Mile 890.** Turnoff to west for Marsh Lake Yukon government campground via 0.4-mile/0.6-km gravel loop road: 47 sites, most level, some pull-through; outhouses, firewood, firepits, litter barrels, picnic tables, kitchen shelter, water pump. Camping fee $8. ▲

For group camping and day-use area, follow signs near campground entrance. Day-use area includes sandy beach, change house, picnic area, playground, kitchen shelter and boat launch.

DC 861.1 (1431.8 km) **F 626.9** (1008.9 km) M'Clintock River, named by Lieutenant Schwatka for Arctic explorer Sir Francis M'Clintock. This river flows into the north end of Marsh Lake. Boat ramp turnoff to west at north end of bridge. M'Clintock River is narrow, winding and silty with thick brush along shoreline. However, it is a good river for boat trips, especially in late fall.

DC 864.3 (1437 km) **F 623.7** (1003.7 km) Bridge over Kettley's Canyon.

DC 867.3 (1441.8 km) **F 620.7** (998.9 km) **Historical Milepost 897.** Yukon River bridge. Turnout to north for day-use area and boat launch on **Yukon River** at Marsh Lake bridge near Northern Canada Power Commission (NCPC) control gate. Point of interest sign and litter barrels. From here (elev. 2,150 feet/645m) the Yukon River flows 1,980 miles/3,186 km to the Bering Sea. Good fishing for grayling and some trout.

DC 873.5 (1453.3 km) **F 614.5** (988.9 km) **Historical Mile 904.** Sourdough Country Campsite to east. ▲

Sourdough Country Campsite. See display ad this section.

DC 874.1 (1455 km) **F 613.6** (987.5 km) **Historical Mile 905. Junction** with Klondike Highway 2 (Carcross Road) which leads south to Carcross and Skagway. (See KLONDIKE HIGHWAY 2 section.) Food, gas, car repair and rock shop here.

Yukon Rock Shop. See display ad this section.

DC 874.6 (1455.3 km) **F 613.4** (987.1 km) Whitehorse city limits. Incorporated June 1, 1950, Whitehorse expanded in 1974 from its original 2.7 square miles/6.9 square kilometres to 162 square miles/421 square kilometres.

DC 875.6 (1456.9 km) **F 612.4** (985.5 km) Kara Speedway to west.

DC 875.9 (1457.4 km) **F 612.1** (985 km) Cowley Creek.

DC 876.8 (1459 km) **F 611.2** (983.6 km) **Historical Mile 906.** Wolf Creek Yukon government campground to east. An 0.8-mile/1.3-km gravel loop road leads through this campground: 49 sites, most level, some pull-through; kitchen shelters, water pumps, picnic tables, firepits, firewood, outhouses, litter barrels, playground. Camping fee $8.

JAKE'S CORNER INC

Gas • Diesel • Propane
MOTEL • RESTAURANT • LOUNGE
Home-style Cooking and Baked Goodies
Your Hosts: Dave & Laureen Gilbert

Mile 866, Alaska Highway
Yukon Territory Y1A 4S8
(403) 668-2727

STOP — DON'T MISS THE TURN TO...
FRONTIERLAND
(2 miles north of Carcross on the South Klondike Highway)

Access from Alaska Highway via Tagish/Carcross Loop   (See ad — Klondike Highway #2)

LAKEVIEW RESORT & MARINA

1 Hour South of Whitehorse
4 Hours North of Watson Lake

Box 4759, Whitehorse, YT Y1A 4N6   Phone (403) 399-4567

NEW FULLY LICENSED RESTAURANT • Dining Room & Lounge • Outside Beer Patio
RV PARK -- 34 spaces (18 fully serviced) • Dump Station • Tent Spaces • RV Full Hookup $7.50
10 FULLY MODERN CABINS with Kitchens • 10 MOTEL ROOMS -- Rooms from $37
Good Fishing • Good Hiking & Ski Trails
Windsurfer Rental • Mountain Bike Rentals • Boat & Motor Rentals
Store • Showers • Laundromat • Ice
Situated at Kilometre 1414 • 2 Km off Alaska Highway in a quiet, relaxed setting on scenic Marsh Lake

---

YUKON ROCK SHOP
MINING AND MINERAL DISPLAY
Souvenirs
Operated by The Wrays... Open 7 days a week
VISA accepted... Bank rate on U.S. funds
Mile 905, Alaska Highway at Junction of Klondike Highway (Carcross Road)

MacKenzie's RV PARK
Just 6 miles north of city centre
FULL SERVICE and CAMPING SITES AVAILABLE
(403) 633-2337
(See our ad north end of Whitehorse section.)

SOURDOUGH COUNTRY CAMPSITE
Electrical & Water Hookups • Tent Sites • Firepits • Showers • Laundromat • Dump Station
Wir Sprechen Deutsch, Nous Parlons Francais
"FRIENDLINESS AND CLEANLINESS IS OUR MOTTO"
11 Miles South of Whitehorse on Alaska Highway
Phone (403) 668-2961 • Box 4543, Whitehorse Y1A 2R8

Fishing in **Wolf Creek** for grayling.

DC 879.4 (1463 km) **F 608.6** (979.4 km) Highway crosses railroad tracks.

DC 879.6 (1463.3 km) **F 608.4** (979.1 km) Point of interest sign about 135th meridian to east; small turnout. Gas station.

DC 879.8 (1463.7 km) **F 608.2** (978.8 km) **Historical Milepost 910.** McCrae truck stop to east.

DC 880.4 (1464.5 km) **F 607.6** (977.8 km) Turnoff to west for Whitehorse Copper Mines (closed). Road to east leads to Yukon River.

DC 881 (1465.5 km) **F 607** (976.8 km) **Historical Milepost 911.** Site of Utah Construction Camp. Pioneer RV Park, store and self-serve gas to east.

Pioneer R.V. Park celebrates 40 years of service! We will be honouring the 50 states, 10 provinces, 2 territories and global travelers in 1992 by offering special discounts. All you have to do is show up the day your state, province or country is being honoured and you win!! As well, your name automatically will be entered in a draw to win a genuine Yukon gold nugget. Pioneer R.V. Park thanks you for your patronage. (403) 668-5944. [ADVERTISEMENT]

DC 881.3 (1466 km) **F 606.7** (976.4 km) White Pass & Yukon Route's Utah siding to east. (WP&YR ceased operation in 1982, but started limited service again in 1988 between Skagway and Fraser. See WHITE PASS & YUKON ROUTE section.) This was also the site of an Army camp where thousands of soldiers were stationed during construction of the Alaska Highway.

DC 881.7 (1466.6 km) **F 606.3** (975.7 km) Sharp turnoff to east (watch for camera viewpoint sign) to see Miles Canyon. Drive down side road 0.3 mile/0.5 km to fork. The right fork leads to Miles Canyon parking lot. From the parking area it is a short walk to the Miles Canyon bridge; good photo spot. Cross bridge for easy hiking trails overlooking Yukon River. The left fork leads to Schwatka Lake Road, which follows the lake and intersects the South Access Road into Whitehorse. Turnouts along road overlook Miles Canyon.

DC 882.6 (1468 km) **F 605.4** (974.3 km) Historical Mile 912. RV service and supply.

Philmar RV Service and Supply. See display ad this section.

DC 883.7 (1469.7 km) **F 604.3** (972.5 km) Turnout to east with litter barrel, outhouses, pay phone and information sign.

DC 884 (1470.2 km) **F 604** (972 km) **Hi-Country R.V. Park.** Good Sam. New facilities to serve the traveler. Large wooded sites, electric and water hookups, dump station, hot showers. Picnic tables and firepits, gift shop with wildlife display. Propane. Conveniently located on the highway at the south access to Whitehorse, next to beautiful Yukon Gardens. (403) 667-7445, fax (403) 668-7432. [ADVERTISEMENT]

DC 884 (1470.2 km) **F 604** (972 km) Exit east for South Access Road to Whitehorse via 4th Avenue and 2nd Avenue. At the turnoff is Yukon Gardens botanical exhibit. At Mile 1.4/2.3 km on this access road is the side road to Miles Canyon and Schwatka Lake; at Mile 1.6/2.6 km is Robert Service Campground (tent camping only) with a picnic area for day use; at Mile 2.6/4.2 km is the SS *Klondike,* turn left for downtown Whitehorse. The new (1992) Visitor Reception Centre is located on the Alaska Highway 1.7 miles/2.7 km north of this turnoff (see **DC 885.7**).

Alaska Highway log continues on page 137. Description of Whitehorse follows.

The SS Klondike *in Whitehorse is open for tours in summer.* (Earl L. Brown, staff)

PHILMAR RV SERVICE AND SUPPLY

COMPLETE RV REPAIRS PARTS AND WELDING

Mile 912, KM 1468 Alaska Highway

(403) 668-6129
FAX (403) 668-4927

HOURS Monday — Saturday
8:30 a.m. – 5 p.m.

Garry and Mary-Anne Phillips
Box 4147, Whitehorse, YT Y1A 3S9

PIONEER RV PARK

5 Miles South of Downtown Whitehorse On Alaska Highway

134 SITES • 53 FULL HOOKUP PULL-THROUGHS
20 Full Hookups • 16 Partial Hookups
36 Wooded Tent Sites with Firepits • *No Charge for Additional People*

Hot Showers • Laundromat • Grocery Store
Clean Restrooms

Car Wash with Lots of Hot Soapy Water
Rec Hall has Nightly Live Entertainment
Tickets and Reservations Available for Local Attractions
Handicap Accessible

RR1, Site 8, Comp. 4, Whitehorse, YT Y1A 4Z6
Phone: (403) 668-5944   Mile 911 Km 1465

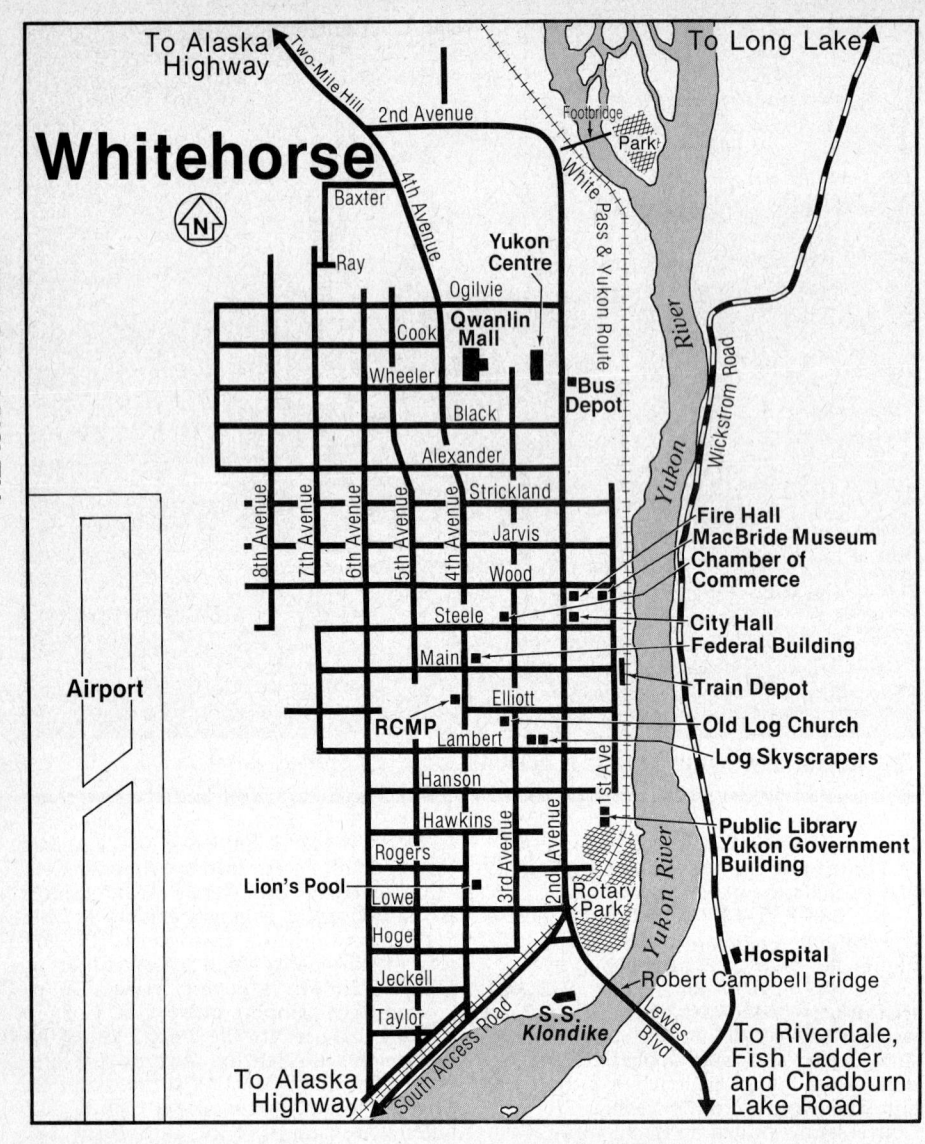

Whitehorse

Historical Milepost 918. Located on the upper reaches of the Yukon River in Canada's subarctic at latitude 61°N. Whitehorse is 100 miles/160 km from Haines Junction; 109 miles/175 km from Skagway, AK; 250 miles/ 241 km from Haines, AK; and 396 miles/637 km from Tok, AK. **Population:** 20,721. **Emergency Services:** RCMP, 4100 4th Ave., phone 667-5555. **Fire Department**, 2nd Avenue at Wood Street, phone 667-2222. **Ambulance/Inhalator**, phone 668-9333. **Hospital**, Whitehorse General, phone 668-9444.

Visitor Information: The new (1992) Visitor Reception Centre is located on the Alaska Highway at **Milepost DC 885.7**, adjacent the Transportation Museum. A multi-image slide presentation on Yukon National Parks and historical sites is presented at the centre, and Yukon attractions can be previewed on a laser disc player. Radio CKYN "Yukon Gold," 96.1-FM, is broadcast from the centre. The centre is open from mid-May to mid-September, 8 A.M. to 8 P.M.; phone 667-2915. Young people dressed in bright 1898 uniforms of the North West Mounted Police are in downtown Whitehorse in summer to answer questions. For additional visitor information contact: Whitehorse Chamber of Commerce, Suite 101, 302 Steele St., Whitehorse, YT Y1A 2C5, phone 667-7545, or Tourism Yukon, Box 2703, Whitehorse, YT Y1A 2C6. Canadian government topographic maps are available at Jim's Toy and Gift on Main Street. The Canadian Parks Service is located in the Federal Bldg. at 4th and Main; phone 668-2116.

Elevation: 2,305 feet/703m. **Climate:** Wide variations are the theme here with no 2 winters alike. The lowest recorded temperature is -62°F/-52°C and the warmest 94°F/35°C. Mean temperature for month of January is -6°F/-21°C and for July 57°F/14°C. Annual precipitation is 10.3 inches, equal parts snow and rain. On June 21 Whitehorse enjoys 19 hours, 11 minutes of daylight and on Dec. 21 only 5 hours, 37 minutes. **Radio:** CFWH 570, CBC network with repeaters throughout territory; CKRW 610, local; CKYN-FM 96.1, summer visitor information

---

A Hearty Welcome to Travellers

THE DRIFTERS
Bed & Breakfast

44 Cedar Crescent   (403) 633-5419
Whitehorse (Porter Creek), Yukon Y1A 4P3
Free Airport and Downtown Pickup

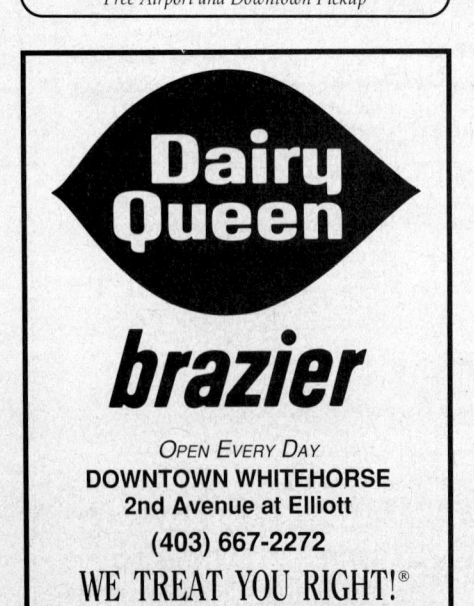

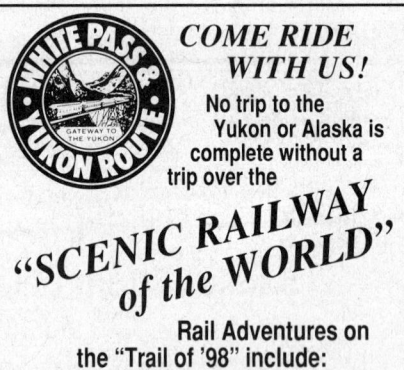

Dairy Queen
brazier

OPEN EVERY DAY
DOWNTOWN WHITEHORSE
2nd Avenue at Elliott
(403) 667-2272

WE TREAT YOU RIGHT!®

COME RIDE WITH US!

No trip to the Yukon or Alaska is complete without a trip over the

"SCENIC RAILWAY of the WORLD"

Rail Adventures on the "Trail of '98" include:

- Daily scheduled summer "Through" Motorcoach/Rail Service between Whitehorse, Y.T. and Skagway, AK.
- Chilkoot Trailhead Service to and from Fraser Station and Lake Bennett, BC.
- Morning and afternoon Rail Excursions to the Summit of White Pass and return to Skagway

TICKETS available in Whitehorse from Atlas Tours at the Westmark Whitehorse Mall, 2nd Avenue between Steele & Wood streets.

For reservations (locally call 668-RAIL), dial 1-800-343-7373 or (907) 983-2217. **Write:** White Pass & Yukon Route, P.O. Box 435, Skagway, Alaska 99840.

When in Whitehorse, visit...

THE ART FACTORY

AUTHENTIC YUKON PRODUCTS
Ceramics • Pottery • Carvings
Paintings and Prints
Dolls and Knitted Wear

Discuss special orders with the artists in their studio. We can mail anywhere.

THE ART FACTORY
(403) 668-6768 • 667-7331
211 Hanson St., Whitehorse, Yukon Y1A 1Y3

station, "Yukon Gold," broadcasts mid-May to mid-September. **Television:** CBC-TV live, colour via ANIK satellite, Canadian network; WHTV, local cable; CanCom stations via satellite, many channels. **Newspapers:** *Whitehorse Star* (weekdays); *Yukon News* (twice-weekly); *Yukon Indian News* (monthly).

Private Aircraft: Whitehorse International Airport, 3 runways; has approach over city and an abrupt escarpment; elev. 2,305 feet/703m; main runway length 7,200 feet/2,195m; surfaced; fuel 80/87, 100/130, jet fuel available; AOE.

WHITEHORSE ADVERTISERS

Airline Inn Hotel
   (Yukon) Ltd..................Across from airport
Art Factory, The.......................211 Hanson St.
Atlas Tours.............Westmark Whitehorse Mall
Baker's Bed & Breakfast....Ph. (403) 633-2308
Barb's Bed & Breakfast.....Ph. (403) 667-4104
Bill's Sporting Goods..........Yukon Centre Mall
Budget Car and
   Truck Rental..................Ph. (403) 667-6200
Coffee • Tea & Spice..................Qwanlin Mall
Dairy Queen........................2nd Ave. at Elliott
Deli, The...................................203 Hanson St.
Designers North.................1st Ave. & Main St.
Drifters Bed &
   Breakfast, The...............Ph. (403) 633-5419
Fort Yukon Hotel........................2163 2nd Ave.
Fourth Avenue Residence..........4051 4th Ave.
Frantic Follies.......Westmark Whitehorse Hotel
Hi-Country R.V. Park...Next to Yukon Gardens
Hougen Centre, The.....................305 Main St.
Indian Craft Shop Ltd...................504 Main St.
International House
   Bed & Breakfast............Ph. (403) 633-5490
Jim Robb Series, The....................Retail outlets
Klondike Recreational
   Rentals Ltd....................Ph. (403) 668-2200
Kopper King...............Mile 918.3 Alaska Hwy.
Lapis Art & Artefacts.................3123 3rd Ave.
Lost Moose Publishing....................Bookstores
MacKenzie's RV Park......Km 1484 Alaska Hwy.
MV *Anna Maria*, The..........Ph. (403) 667-4155
"Oregon Boy in the Yukon—
   An Alaska Highway Story".....Retail outlets
Pioneer RV Park..................Ph. (403) 668-5944
Pot O' Gold............................4th Ave. & Wood
Qwanlin Mall..4th Ave.
Regina Hotel...............................102 Wood St.
Roadhouse Saloon.....................2163 2nd Ave.
Sky High Wilderness
   Ranches..........................Ph. (403) 667-4321
Sourdough Bed and
   Breakfast........................Ph. (403) 667-2087
Special Discoveries.....................206B Main St.
Takhini Hot Springs....Takhini Hot Springs Rd.
Tire Town.................................2283 2nd Ave.
Trail of '98 R.V. Park..........Ph. (403) 668-3768
Westmark Klondike Inn.......Ph. 800-999-2570
Westmark Whitehorse..........Ph. 800-999-2570
White Pass & Yukon
   Route..............................Ph. (403) 668-RAIL
Whitehorse Center Motor Inn....206 Jarvis St.
Whitehorse Chamber of
   Commerce....................101-302 Steele St.
Whitehorse Performance
   Centre..................................4th Ave. at Jarvis
Wishes Gifts................................206A Main St.
Yukon Inn..................................4220 4th Ave.
Yukon Native Products..............4230 4th Ave.
Yukon Radiator....................108 Industrial Rd.
Yukon Tire Center Ltd.........107 Industrial Rd.
Yukon Transportation
   Museum, The...........................At the airport

Cousins flight strip, 8 miles/12.8 km northwest; elev. 2,180 feet/665m; length 3,000 feet/914m; sand and gravel. Summer or emergency only; fuel available at Whitehorse airport. Floatplane base on Schwatka Lake above Whitehorse Dam (take the South Access Road from Alaska Highway and turn on road by the railroad tracks).

DESCRIPTION

Whitehorse has been the capital of Yukon Territory since 1953, and serves as the centre for transportation, communications and supplies for Yukon Territory and the Northwest Territories.

The downtown business section of Whitehorse lies on the west bank of the Yukon River. The Riverdale subdivision is on the east side. The low mountains rising behind Riverdale are dominated by Canyon Mountain, known locally as Grey Mountain. Wolf Creek and Hillcrest subdivisions lie south of the city; Porter Creek, Takhini and Crestview subdivisions are north of the city. The Takhini area is the location of the Yukon College campus, which offers 1- and 2-year programs in business, applied arts, trades and technology.

Downtown Whitehorse is flat and marked at its western limit by a rising escarpment dominated by the Whitehorse International Airport. Originally a woodcutter's lot, the airstrip was first cleared in 1920 to accommodate 4 U.S. Army planes on a test flight from New York to Nome. Access to the city is by Two-Mile Hill from the north and by access road from the south; both connect with the Alaska Highway.

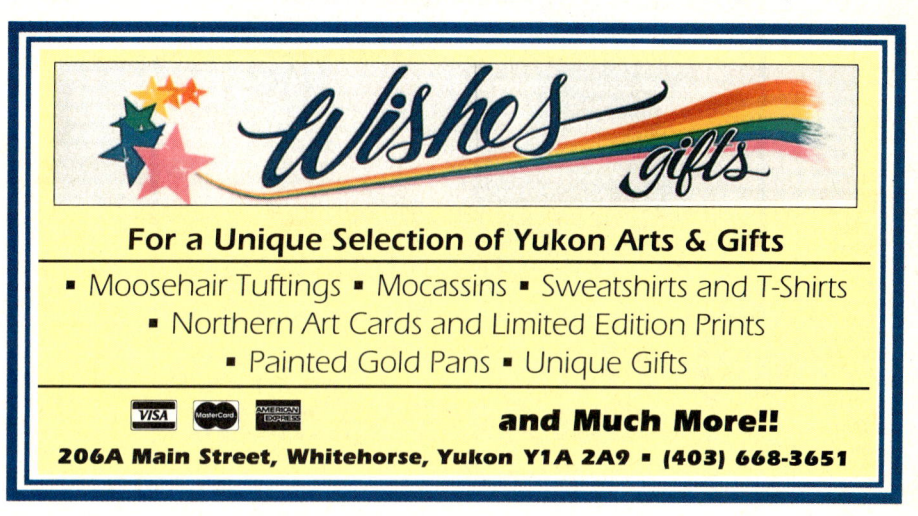

Wishes gifts

For a Unique Selection of Yukon Arts & Gifts

- Moosehair Tuftings • Mocassins • Sweatshirts and T-Shirts
- Northern Art Cards and Limited Edition Prints
- Painted Gold Pans • Unique Gifts

VISA • MasterCard • American Express

and Much More!!

206A Main Street, Whitehorse, Yukon Y1A 2A9 • (403) 668-3651

International House
BED & BREAKFAST

OPEN YEAR ROUND

Welcomes Alaska Highway Travellers

Refreshments Served at Night

Hosts: Al and Ann Dibbs

Lions and Lionesses Welcome

Reservations Recommended
(403) 633-5490

17 - 14th Ave.
Whitehorse, Yukon
Y1A 5A7

PICK UP AVAILABLE   VISA

In Porter Creek, 2 blocks off Alaska Highway, behind Mohawk gas station.

SKY HIGH WILDERNESS RANCHES

World-class TRUE wilderness adventures by horse and dog team. High adventure *or* gentle ventures.
Wildlife Viewing Treks - 3-5-7-10 days. Wildlife photography and nature appreciation retreats
FREE lakeside campsites • restaurant • boat and canoe rentals • camp and fishing supplies
spectacular fishing • casual riding (hour/day) with or without a guide

Just 15 miles from downtown Whitehorse   ***WE NEVER CLOSE!***

*Experience the Yukon Wilderness with knowlegable 40-year residents.
We travelled the Alaska Highway by covered wagon.*

write for free brochure: Ian and Sylvia McDougall
Box 4482, Whitehorse, Yukon, Canada Y1A 2R8

Phone (403) 667-4321 • FAX (403) 668-7953
Mobile Radio YS39074 Whitehorse Channel

YUKON NATIVE PRODUCTS
An Indian Arts and Crafts Co-op

Yukon's Largest Selection Of Indian Arts & Crafts

- beaded moccasins & mukluks
- moose hair tufting • northern souvenirs
- birch bark & porcupine quill baskets
- exclusive distributor of the Original Yukon Parka, Kluane Anorak & new Whitehorse Parkas

4230 – 4th Avenue, Whitehorse, Yukon Y1A 1K1
(across from McDonald's)

(403) 668-5935
FAX (403) 668-6466

In 1974, the city limits of Whitehorse were expanded from the original 2.7 square miles/6.9 square kilometres to 162 square miles/421 square kilometres making Whitehorse at one time the largest metropolitan area in Canada. More than two-thirds of the population of Yukon Territory live in the city.

Today, Whitehorse is the hub of a network of about 2,664 miles/4287 km of all-weather roads now serving Yukon Territory and is becoming a popular year-round convention centre. A major attraction in winter is the Sourdough Rendezvous, held the last week in February. During this annual event local citizens wear the garb of trappers, miners and saloon hall girls, and menus feature moose stew and sourdough pancakes. Among the many activities are dogsled races, a beard-judging contest and a flour-packing competition.

Whitehorse is also the start and/or finish of the annual Yukon Quest Sled Dog Race in February. This 1,000-mile race between Whitehorse and Fairbanks, AK, takes mushers from 10 to 14 days, with a mandatory 36-hour layover at Dawson City.

Whitehorse is the territorial headquarters for the world-famous Royal Canadian Mounted Police. Their office is located at 4th Avenue and Elliott. Responsible for law and order in the Yukon since 1894, today the force relies more on the airplane and automobile than the romantic dog teams that carried mail and the law as far north as Herschel Island off the Yukon's Arctic coast, and across southern Yukon into northern British Columbia.

HISTORY, ECONOMY

When the White Pass & Yukon Route railway was completed in July 1900, connecting Skagway with the Yukon River, Whitehorse came into being as the northern terminus. Here the famed river steamers connected the railhead to Dawson City, and some of these boats made the trip all the way to St. Michael, a small outfitting point on Alaska's Bering Sea coast.

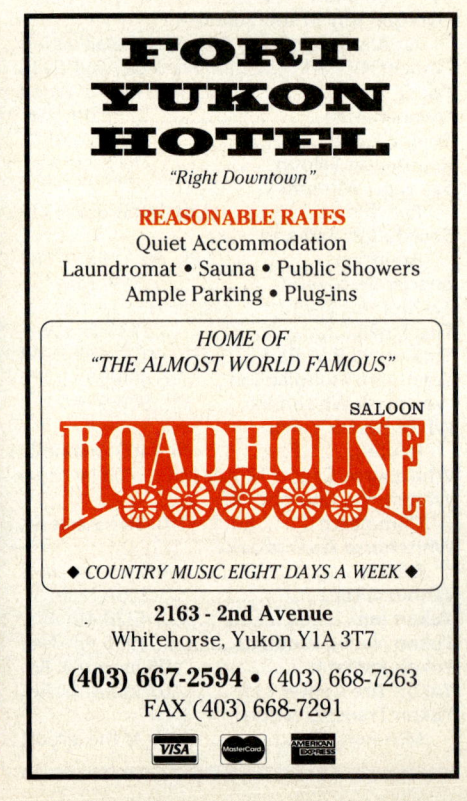

GOLD RUSH VARIETY ENTERTAINMENT
FRANTIC FOLLIES
The Yukon's Only Legal Cure For Cabin Fever

Shows nightly at the Westmark Whitehorse Hotel

June through mid-September

BOX OFFICE:
(located in the Westmark Whitehorse Hotel 2nd and Wood St.)
Frantic Follies
P.O. Box 4609
Whitehorse, Yukon, Canada Y1A 2R8
PHONE (403) 668-2042
FAX (403) 633-4363

FORT YUKON HOTEL
"Right Downtown"

REASONABLE RATES
Quiet Accommodation
Laundromat • Sauna • Public Showers
Ample Parking • Plug-ins

HOME OF
"THE ALMOST WORLD FAMOUS"
SALOON
ROADHOUSE

◆ COUNTRY MUSIC EIGHT DAYS A WEEK ◆

2163 - 2nd Avenue
Whitehorse, Yukon Y1A 3T7

(403) 667-2594 • (403) 668-7263
FAX (403) 668-7291

Klondike stampeders landed at Whitehorse to dry out and repack their supplies after running the famous Whitehorse Rapids. (The name Whitehorse was in common use by the late 1800s; it is believed that the first miners in the area thought that the foaming rapids resembled white horses' manes and so named the river rapids.) The rapids are no longer visible since construction of the Yukon Energy Corporation's hydroelectric dam on the river. This dam created man-made Schwatka Lake, named in honour of U.S. Army Lt. Frederick Schwatka, who named many of the points along the Yukon River during his 1883 exploration of the region.

The gold rush brought stampeders and the railroad. The community grew as a transportation centre and transshipment point for freight from the Skagway-Whitehorse railroad and the stern-wheelers plying the Yukon River to Dawson City. The river was the only highway until WWII, when military expediency built the Alaska Highway in 1942.

Whitehorse was headquarters for the western sector during construction of the Alaska Highway. Fort St. John was headquarters for the eastern sector. Both were the largest construction camps along the highway.

The first survey parties of U.S. Army engineers reached Whitehorse in April of 1942. By the end of August, they had constructed a pioneer road from Whitehorse west to White River, largely by following an existing winter trail between Whitehorse and Kluane Lake. November brought the final breakthrough on the western end of the highway, marking completion of the pioneer road.

During the height of the construction of the Alaska Highway, thousands of American military and civilian workers were employed in the Canadian North. It was the second boom period for Whitehorse.

There was an economic lull following the war, but the new highway was then opened to civilian travel, encouraging new development. Mineral exploration and the development of new mines had a profound effect on the economy of the region as did the steady growth of tourism. The Whitehorse Copper Mine, located a few miles south of the city in the historic Whitehorse copper belt, is now closed. Curragh Resources Mine, located in Faro, produces lead-silver and zinc

---

COMPLETE TIRE SERVICE
RADIAL TIRE SPECIALISTS

NORTHERN METALIC SALES
TIRE TOWN®
PHONE (403) 667-4251 • FAX (403) 667-2742

FULL AUTO GLASS SERVICE

2ND AT 4TH AVE.
For Campers, Pick Ups, Motor Homes & Cars

Across from the Klondike Inn   2283 2nd Avenue, Whitehorse

QWANLIN MALL

14 STORES TO SERVE YOU

Your friendly One Stop Shopping Mall

At Fourth Avenue and Ogilvie

Whitehorse, Yukon   (403) 667-4584

Ample Parking

Extended Summer Hours

Welcome to

THE HOUGEN CENTRE

Serving Yukoners and Visitors Since 1944

HOUGEN'S ONE HOUR PHOTO
★ Enlargements up to 11" x 14"
★ Prints from slides

Kodak Colorwatch System
Member 1986

COMPLETE PHOTO CENTRE
FILM • CAMERAS • PHOTO PRODUCTS

THE GOLD PANNER GIFT SHOP
SOUVENIRS • GOLD NUGGET JEWELRY
SOUVENIR SHIRTS

The Sports Lodge

Where the fun begins!
FISHING and HUNTING LICENSES
Everything for the Yukon outdoors!

Fishing • Hunting • Camping
Information on the best places to fish

Sourdough Pancake Breakfast
THE BEST!
Served Daily 'til 11:00 a.m.

3 FLOORS OF ENDLESS SELECTION
Hardware • Fashions
Shoes • Sound • Appliances

...and Access to Over 30 Stores and Services

305 Main Street
Whitehorse, Yukon Y1A 2B4
Phone (403) 667-4222 • FAX (403) 668-6328

EXPLORE THE OPTIONS!

Do More On Your Trip North!

Every northern community has its own unique attractions. At Atlas, we can arrange all the 'extras' that turn your vacation into special, lasting memories!

- ➤ Frantic Follies
- ➤ MV *Schwatka* River Cruise
- ➤ *Anna Maria* River Cruise
- ➤ Pt. Barrow / Prudhoe Bay
- ➤ Nome / Kotzebue
- ➤ Columbia Glacier Cruise
- ➤ Glacier Bay Excursions
- ➤ White Pass & Yukon Rail

atlas tours
(403) 668-3161

RELAX ON YOUR TRIP SOUTH!

Plan your trip home now, and avoid disappointment of finding no space available for an . . .

INSIDE PASSAGE — CRUISE — Via

ALASKA STATE FERRY

B.C. FERRIES

atlas travel
(403) 667-7823

Write for more information or visit us in the
WESTMARK WHITEHORSE MALL
P.O. Box 4340, Whitehorse
Yukon, Canada Y1A 3T5

The Coast of British Columbia, explores more than 17,000 miles along British Columbia's pristine and majestic coastline. Available at bookstores and Alaska Northwest Books™.

---

concentrates. Gold mining activity has been taking place southwest of Whitehorse in the last few years. Stop by the Yukon Chamber of Mines office on Main Street for information on mining and rockhounding in Yukon Territory. The Chamber of Mines log building also houses a mineral display.

Because of its accessibility, Whitehorse became capital of the Yukon Territory (replacing Dawson City in that role) on March 31, 1953.

Bridges built along the highway to Dawson City, after Whitehorse became capital of the territory, were too low to accommodate the old river steamers, and by 1955 all steamers had been beached. After her last run in 1960, the SS *Keno* was berthed on the riverbank in Dawson City where she became a national historic site in 1962. The SS *Klondike* was moved through the streets of Whitehorse in 1968 to its final resting place as a riverboat museum beside the Robert Campbell bridge.

ACCOMMODATIONS

Whitehorse offers 22 hotels and motels for a total of about 840 rooms. Several hotels include conference facilities; most have cocktail lounges, licensed dining rooms and taverns. Rates range from $40 to $120 for a double room with bath. Bed-and-breakfast accommodations are also available.

The city has a reputation for gourmet dining. The 31 restaurants serve meals ranging from French cuisine to fast food; 14 have liquor licenses.

Whitehorse has a downtown shopping district stretching 6 blocks along Main Street. The Qwanlin Mall at 4th Avenue and Ogilvie has a supermarket and a variety of shops. The Riverdale Mall is located on the east side of the river in the Riverdale subdivision. Another shopping mall is located in the Porter Creek subdivision north of the city on the Alaska Highway.

In addition to numerous supermarkets, garages and service stations, there are churches, banks, movie houses, beauty salons and a covered swimming pool.

NOTE: There is no central post office in Whitehorse. Inquire locally for downtown location of the authorized Canadian Post agency. Postal services are available in Qwanlin Mall at Coffee, Tea & Spice. General delivery pickup at corner of 3rd Avenue and Wood Street.

Specialty stores include gold nugget and ivory shops where distinctive jewelry is

Takhini hot springs

TURN AT SIGN ON KLONDIKE LOOP ROAD AT MILE 3.6 (KM 5.8) AND DRIVE 6 MILES

Concrete pool • Odorless mineral water at 100°F (38°C). Campground with tables, firewood. Horseback riding. Cross-country ski trails. Modern facilities, hot showers. Reasonable rates for all-day swimming. Suit and towel rentals. Coffee Shop. Relaxing and refreshing for the travel weary. Some electrical hookups. Laundromat. 100 sites.

OPEN YEAR-ROUND . . . Just 17 miles north of Whitehorse
For information write:
R.R. 2, SITE 19, COMPARTMENT 4
WHITEHORSE, Y.T. Y1A 5A5 • PHONE (403) 633-2706

HI–COUNTRY R.V. PARK

- Electric & Water Hookups • Pull-Through Sites
- Showers Included • Pay Phone • Laundromat • Dump Station
- Picnic Tables • Fire Pits • Propane • Auto Propane
- Gold Panning • Gold Nugget Jewellry

✹ **LOTS OF TREES!** ✹
Gift Shop with Yukon Wildlife Display

FOR RESERVATIONS:
411 Main St., Whitehorse, Yukon Y1A 2B6
(403) 667-7445 • FAX (403) 668-7432

Located 5 minutes from downtown
along the Alaska Highway
at the south access to Whitehorse
next to beautiful Yukon Gardens

manufactured, and Indian craft shops specializing in moose hide jackets, parkas, vests, moccasins, slippers, mukluks and gauntlets. Inuit and Indian handicrafts from Canada's Arctic regions are featured in some stores.

Baker's Bed & Breakfast. Make Baker's Bed & Breakfast your home away from home. Hosts are longtime residents of Yukon. Friendly, cozy home, decorated with country crafts, and located in quiet area. Enjoy large yard and fireplace. Hearty, variety breakfasts served with fresh fruit. We look forward to sharing our home with you. Phone (403) 633-2308. 84 - 11th Ave., Whitehorse, YT Y1A 4J2. [ADVERTISEMENT]

The Drifters Bed & Breakfast. While experiencing Whitehorse and Yukon attractions you will be welcome in our quiet and comfortable home. Hearty and wholesome breakfasts are served. We look forward to your company. Open all year. Free pickup from airport or downtown. 44 Cedar Crescent, Whitehorse, YT Y1A 4P3. (403) 633-5419. [ADVERTISEMENT]

Fourth Avenue Residence offers the highway traveler full facilities at reasonable prices. Open year-round, located next to Lions Pool and on city bus route. Short walk to downtown. Single and shared rooms with kitchen and laundry facilities, as well as fully equipped family units. Public showers for campers. Ample parking. VISA, MasterCard. Reservations recommended. 4051 4th Ave. (403) 667-4471, fax (403) 667-6457. [ADVERTISEMENT]

Sourdough Bed and Breakfast. Enjoy cozy, comfortable charm in a quiet neighbourhood close to tourist attractions and hiking trails. Nutritious homemade breakfast and evening snack. Satellite TV. Make our Yukon home your Yukon home. Brochure available. Ralph and Barb Zaccarelli, 83 Teslin Road, Whitehorse, YT Y1A 3M7. (403) 667-2087. [ADVERTISEMENT]

There is a private RV park on the north access road (Two Mile Hill). Tent camping only is available at Robert Service Park on the South Access Road. There are 3 private campgrounds south of downtown Whitehorse on the Alaska Highway (see **Mileposts DC 873.5, 881** and **883.7** in the highway log), and 1 private campground 6 miles/9.6 km north of the city on the highway (see **Milepost DC 891.9**). Wolf Creek Yukon government campground is 7 miles/11 km south of Whitehorse on the Alaska Highway. A private campground and Yukon govern-

---

Pot O' Gold

"The Yukon Jewellery Store Where Service and Quality Count"

4129 4th Avenue Corner of 4th and Wood
Whitehorse, Yukon Territory Phone: 668-2058

FINE YUKON GOLD NUGGET JEWELLERY
YUKON-MADE QUALITY CRAFTS
Designers and Manufacturers of
NATURAL GOLD NUGGET JEWELLERY
Open Year-Round — 7 Days a Week
For your convenience extended summer hours
We are happy to work with your nuggets

WHITEHORSE!

Please let us help you plan your visit to the...

YUKON'S CAPITAL!

We have information to meet your every need. Sights to see, facts and figures about **Whitehorse**, a detailed City map and the answers to all your questions on how you can enjoy your stay.

The Whitehorse Chamber of Commerce
101-302 Steele Street
Whitehorse, Yukon Y1A 2C5
Phone (403) 667-7545 or FAX (403) 667-4507

FOURTH AVENUE RESIDENCE

Family Units with Kitchen
Single & Shared Accommodation

*Kitchen and Laundry Facilities
Public Showers
Walk to Downtown*

4051 4th Avenue
(Next to Lions Pool)

Whitehorse, Yukon Y1A 1H1
(403) 667-4471
FAX (403) 667-6457

Airline Inn Hotel

Mile 916 Alaska Highway, 16 Burns Road, Whitehorse Y1A 4Y9

RUDY'S DINING ROOM
"Where We Really Care"
German Specialties
Breakfast, Lunch & Dinner Daily
Banquet & Catering Services
Friendly Cosy Atmosphere
Licensed
Dinner Reservations Suggested
Lizz & Rudy Welcome You
(403) 668-4330

30 MODERN ROOMS
Colour Cable TV
Telephone
Lounge with Panoramic View
(403) 668-4400
FAX (403) 668-2641

CONVENIENCE STORE & Self-Serve MOHAWK GAS BAR
Open 24 Hrs. - 7 Days a Week
Lotto Centre - Ice - Magazines
Groceries - Lubricants, Air & Water
Diesel & Propane
(403) 668-4440

GUESSEPPI'S
Take-out Pizza
(403) 667-6776

ALASKA HIGHWAY • WHITEHORSE

Northern Lights ...

Northern Nights ...

YUKON INN

Come stay in one of our 98 newly renovated rooms, ranging from kitchenettes to jacuzzi suites. Visit our lounges, restaurant, beauty salon, and gift shop - all the comforts that make you feel you're at "your home away from home". We're just across the street from recreational facilities and the largest shopping complex in town. Fully equipped banquet and conference facilities accommodating 10 to 300 people will meet your every need.

True Northern Hospitality in the Hotel that *is* the Yukon

For Reservations
403-667-2527 or 1-800-661-0454 in Western Canada   FAX 403-668-7643
4220 - 4th Avenue, Whitehorse, Yukon Y1A 1K1

ment campground are located at Marsh Lake.

IMPORTANT: RV caravans should contact private campground operators well in advance of arrival regarding camping arrangements. At our press time, there was no designated RV parking in downtown Whitehorse.

Pioneer R.V. Park celebrates 40 years of service! We will be honouring the 50 states, 10 provinces, 2 territories and global travelers in 1992 by offering special discounts. All you have to do is show up the day your state, province or country is being honoured and you win!! As well, your name automatically will be entered in a draw to win a genuine Yukon gold nugget. Located just 5 miles south of downtown Whitehorse on the Alaska Highway, Pioneer R.V. Park thanks you for your patronage. (403) 668-5944. [ADVERTISEMENT]

TRANSPORTATION
Air: Service by Canadian Airlines Interna-

New Attraction!

THE YUKON TRANSPORTATION MUSEUM

Open May to September

Mile 917, at the Airport, Whitehorse
(403) 663-4792

Need Fishing Equipment?
Our prices are competitive, our advice is free!

At Bill's Sporting Goods you'll get more than what you're fishing for. Not only will we provide you with quality fishing equipment at competitive prices, we'll give you free advice on what lures to use, when to fish, and where to catch the big ones. We also sell fishing and hunting licences, and detailed maps.

Check out the complete line of fishing, camping and hunting equipment at Bill's.

Mail orders available

Bill's SPORTING GOODS

YUKON CENTRE MALL
2190 2nd Ave., Whitehorse, Yukon Y1A 1C7
Phone (403) 668-6111   Fax: (403) 668-5605

tional and Alkan Air daily to major cities and Yukon communities. Air North to Dawson City, Watson Lake, Juneau and Fairbanks, AK. Whitehorse International Airport is reached from the Alaska Highway.

Seaplane dock on Schwatka Lake just above the Whitehorse Dam (take the South Access Road from Alaska Highway and turn right on road by the railroad tracks to reach the base).

Trans North Air offers helicopter sightseeing tours from the airport.

Bus: Coachways service to Watson Lake, Dawson Creek, Prince George and other points in southern Canada. Norline serves Mayo and Dawson City. Alaska-Yukon Motorcoaches serves Skagway, Haines, Tok, Anchorage and Fairbanks. Alaska Direct to Anchorage, Skagway and Haines, phone 1-800-288-1305 or contact office at 4th Avenue Residence. North West Stage Lines to Haines Junction, Beaver Creek, Faro, Carmacks and Ross River. See Bus Lines in the GENERAL INFORMATION section.

Whitehorse Transit Commission operates bus service around city and suburbs from Qwanlin Mall.

Railroad: Arrangements for White Pass & Yukon Route service between Skagway, AK, and Bennett, BC (with bus service between Bennett and Whitehorse), can be made locally with Atlas Tours at the Westmark Whitehorse Mall, or phone 668-RAIL. (See WHITE PASS & YUKON ROUTE section for more details.)

Taxi: 5 taxi companies operate in Whitehorse.

Car, Truck and Camper Rentals: Several local and national agencies are located in Whitehorse.

ATTRACTIONS

The **SS Klondike** National Historic Site is hard to miss. This grand old stern-wheeler sits beside the Yukon River near the Robert Campbell bridge. After carrying cargo and passengers between Whitehorse and Dawson City from 1937 until the 1950s, the SS Klondike went into permanent retirement on the bank of the Yukon River. Refurbished by Parks Canada, the stern-wheeler is open to the public. Built by British Yukon Navigation Co., the SS Klondike is 210 feet/64m long and 41.9 feet/12.5m wide. Visitor information centre and public parking at the site.

AN OREGON BOY IN THE YUKON
An Alaska Highway Story
By Willis Grafe (Friesen Printers)

Join a survey crew in 1942 and be one of the pathfinders of the Alaska-Canada highway in the Western Yukon.

Land on the ice in April, stay in the bush until September, then winter in Haines.

Be there to finish the job in 1943 so the original pioneer road can finally be called a HIGHWAY.

A first person account by a PRA surveyor and later career engineer who was there from start to finish, with more than fifty pictures by the author.

Mr. Grafe has included a concise history of the construction as well, pinpointing the location of Army regiments and contractors along much of the line and a listing of many of the engineers who were there.

Find it at bookstores, information centers and gift shops.

Capital Accommodations

Capital of the Yukon Territory and popular overnight stay for visitors traveling the Alaska Highway, Whitehorse offers a wealth of Klondike lore and warm hospitality. The Westmark Whitehorse provides modern full-service accommodations, personalized service and a convenient downtown location.

- 181 Rooms • No Smoking Rooms
- Free Parking • Gallery and Gift Shop
- Dining Room and Lounge
- Beauty Salon/Barber Shop

Special Summer Value Rates from $49

Rooms at lower rates are capacity controlled and good on selected rooms & dates only. Call for complete information. Subject to change without notice.

Westmark
WHITEHORSE

2nd and Wood Streets
P.O. Box 4250, Whitehorse
Yukon Territory, Y1A 3T3

Central Reservations
1-800-544-0970 (U.S.)
1-800-999-2570 (Canada)

Westmark Hotels covers the north with hotels and inns throughout Alaska and the Yukon. Come be our guest.

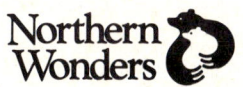

Northern Wonders
The finest northern gifts & handicrafts at very reasonable prices.
Located at Westmark Hotels

A classic adventure tale of the Royal Northwest Mounted Police is found in *The Lost Patrol*.

The JIM ROBB Series
of Yukon Landmarks

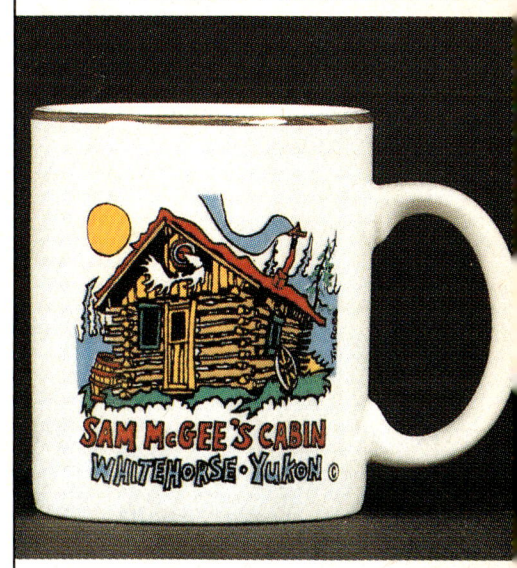

Seven choices of Jim Robb's original drawings carefully reproduced are now available on delightful ironstone coffee mugs with a 24 kt gold rim and Enamel Brass Pins with a safety clasp.

The JIM ROBB Series of Yukon Landmarks

Log Skyscaper, *Whitehorse*

The Duchess, *Carcross*

Old Post Office, *Dawson City*

Our Lady of the Way, *Haines Junction*

Horn Rack, *Old Crow*

Signposts, *Watson Lake*

Available Throughout The Yukon At Retail Outlets

In search of the perfect Yukon souvenir
ANOTHER LOST WHOLE MOOSE CATALOGUE

"Editor's choice...a welcome tonic in tough times." GLOBE AND MAIL
"Lost Moose captures Yukon soul." VANCOUVER COURIER
"Good browsing for cold winter nights." ANCHORAGE TIMES
156 BIG pages. $19.95. Ask for it where you buy books.
Lost Moose Publishing • (403) 668-5076 • fax (403) 668-6223
58 Kluane Crescent • Whitehorse, Yukon • Y1A 3G7

Regina Hotel
53 spacious units — all with color TV.
Featuring the only heated underground parking in the Yukon.
Dining Room and cocktail lounge. Banquet room.
American Express, VISA, MasterCard cards honored.
RESERVATIONS: Phone (403) 667-7801 • Fax (403) 668-6075
102 Wood Street, Downtown Whitehorse Y1A 2E3
Across From the MacBride Museum

TRAIL of '98 RV PARK

100 LEVEL FULL-SERVICE SITES • Clean, Modern Restrooms
Showers - lots of hot pressurized water • Laundromat

1898 THEME GIFT SHOP
A large selection of unique northern and locally made gifts,
Indian slippers and gold nugget jewelry

RV Wash • Pet Walk • Marked Hiking Trails • Pay Phones
Gold Panning • Horseshoe Pit
Transportation and tickets available for local attractions

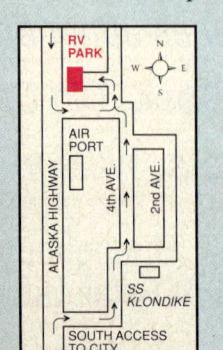

DAILY - SOURDOUGH PANCAKE BREAKFAST
An old family favorite from the Days of '98
SALMON BAR-B-Q
Pacific salmon, ribs or steak grilled to perfection,
plus all-you-can-eat salad bar, baked beans, rolls and coffee.

*Indoor or outdoor dining with a
spectacular view of the Yukon River valley.*
EVERYONE WELCOME

MODERN FACILITIES... OLD-FASHIONED SERVICE
Box 4145, Whitehorse, Yukon Y1A 3S9
(403) 668-3768 • FAX (403) 667-7553

A film on the history of riverboats is shown continuously in a tent theatre adjacent the boat. The visitor centre and stern-wheeler are open mid-May to mid-September. Free tours of the stern-wheeler leave on the half hour. The free 20-minute film is shown prior to each tour.

Frantic Follies, a very popular vaudeville stage show held nightly June through mid-September at the Westmark Whitehorse Hotel. 1992 marks the 25th season for this almost 2-hour show which features entertainers, a high-kicking chorus line, rousing music, hilarious skits from Robert W. Service ballads and plenty of laughs for the whole family. Visitors are advised to get tickets well ahead of time (tickets available at the box office in the Westmark). Be early to get good seats.

Take a hike with the Yukon Conservation Society. Every summer the society offers free guided nature walks, ranging in difficulty from easy to strenuous, from July to late August. Trips are 1 to 6 hours in length and informative guides explain the local flora, fauna, geology and history along the trails. For a schedule of hikes, contact the Yukon Conservation Society, at 302 Hawkins St.; phone 668-5678.

World's largest weathervane. Whitehorse International Airport boasts the world's largest weathervane—a Douglas DC-3. This vintage plane (registration number CF-CPY) flew for several Yukon airlines from 1946 until 1970, when it blew an engine on takeoff. The plane was restored by Joe Muff with the help of the Yukon Flying Club and the Whitehorse community. The restored

---

COME SEE.... SANTA'S Reindeer at NORTHERN SPLENDOR REINDEER FARM
MILE 10.5 Klondike Highway #2
FEEDING AND PETTING
Cameras and Videos Welcome
Open 8:30 a.m. - 9 p.m. — Tourist Season
Admission Charge   Complimentary Coffee
Come a stranger... Leave a friend
Box 5137
Whitehorse, Yukon Y1A 4S3   (403) 633-2996

LAPIS
ART & ARTEFACTS
Jewellery
Antiques
3123 – 3rd Avenue
Whitehorse, Yukon
Canada Y1A 1E6
(403) 668-5728

plane was mounted on a rotating pedestal in 1981 and now acts as a weathervane, pointing its nose into the wind.

The Yukon Transportation Museum, located on the Alaska Highway adjacent to the Whitehorse Airport, features exhibits on all forms of transportation in the North. Housed in a renovated gymnasium, the museum opened in 1990. Displays include the full-size replica of the *Queen of the Yukon* Ryan monoplane, sister ship to Lindbergh's *Spirit of St. Louis;* railway rolling stock; Alaska Highway vintage vehicles, dogsleds and stagecoaches. The museum includes a theatre and small gift shop. Plenty of parking. Admission charged. Open May to September. Write P.O. Box 5867, Whitehorse, YT Y1A 5L6 or phone (403) 668-4792.

Historical walking tours of Whitehorse are conducted by the Yukon Historical & Museums Assoc. These free walks take in the city's heritage buildings. Meet at the Donnenworth House, 3126 3rd Ave.; phone 667-4704. There are tours daily from July to the end of August. For self-guided tours, *A Walking Tour of Yukon's Capital* is available from local stores or from the Yukon Historical & Museums Assoc., Box 4357, Whitehorse, YT Y1A 3T5.

MacBride Museum, on 1st Avenue between Steele and Wood streets, features all aspects of Yukon history, wild animal displays, gold rush and riverboat exhibits housed in an attractive sod-roofed log complex facing the Yukon River. Its grounds display many larger exhibits of railway equipment, stagecoach era and mining machinery. Added attractions are Sam McGee's cabin, a cache and telegraph office. Admission charged. Open daily May 15 to Sept. 30. Phone (403) 667-2709 or write Box 4037, Whitehorse, YT Y1A 3S9.

Old Log Church, 1 block off Main on Elliott at 3rd. Built in 1900 by Rev. R.J. Bowen for the Church of England, this log structure and the log rectory next to it have been declared the first territorial historic

YUKON TIRE CENTRE LIMITED
ALIGNMENT & MECHANICAL

107 INDUSTRIAL ROAD • WHITEHORSE, YUKON
PHONE (403) 667-6102 • FAX (403) 668-6483
On Two Mile Hill (North Access Road to Whitehorse)

Chevron
Bridgestone
MICHELIN
UNIROYAL
BFGoodrich

- ICG Propane • Dump Station • Water and Free Cubed Ice
- Tires & Wheels: Car, RVs, Truck & Trailer
- Computerized Alignment Centre
- DISCOUNT GAS • Service Truck

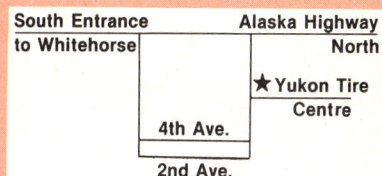

The Deli — The World of Fine Foods

HOMEMADE MEALS
Home Baking

Welcome Willkommen Bien Venue

Cured and Smoked Meats
Smoked Fish • Custom Work
Canadian and Imported Cheese and Bread
European Style Sausage
Wild Game Processing
EAT IN or TAKE OUT

VISA

Phone (403) 667-7583 • 203 Hanson St., Whitehorse, YT

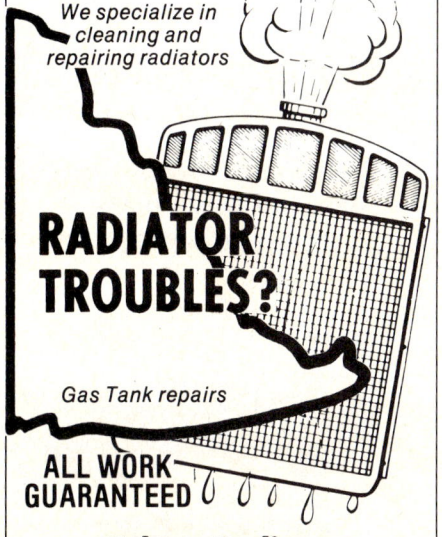

WHITEHORSE CENTER MOTOR INN
SHANNON LOUNGE

MasterCard VISA
Proprietor: Doug Hogan
Phone: **(403) 668-4567**
FAX: **(403) 667-6154**

30 Quiet Hotel and Motel Units • Colour TV, Phone, Baths
Off-street parking • Winter plug-ins • Coin-Laundromat
Downtown Central Location • Rates – $55 Single; $65 Double; +Tax

PETS WELCOME   TRACY'S RESTAURANT
Whitehorse Center Motor Inn   **206 Jarvis Street, Whitehorse, Y.T. Y1A 2H1**

We specialize in cleaning and repairing radiators

RADIATOR TROUBLES?

Gas Tank repairs

ALL WORK GUARANTEED

Yukon Radiator
108 Industrial Road

668-4902

Big or Small We Fix Em All

sites in the Yukon and are to be gradually restored. An ecumenical church museum in the log church displays relics of pioneer northern missions; open to the public June to September. Admission fee. Anglican (Episcopal) services held Sunday evenings at 7 P.M.

Yukon Government Building, 2nd Avenue and Hawkins, open 9 A.M. to 5 P.M. Administrative and Legislative headquarters of Yukon Territory, the building contains some notable artworks. On the main floor mall is an acrylic resin mural, 120 feet/37m long, which portrays the historical evolution of the Yukon. The 24 panels, each measuring 4 by 5 feet/1.2 by 1.5m, highlight events such as the arrival of Sir John Franklin at Herschel Island in 1825, the Klondike gold rush, and the coming of the automobile. The mural was created by Vancouver, BC, artist David MacLagen.

In the Legislative Chamber, an 18-by-12-foot/5-by-4-m tapestry is an abstraction of the fireweed plant, Yukon's floral emblem. The Yukon Women's Tapestry, 5 panels each 7 by 13 feet/2 by 4m, hangs in the legislative library lounge. The wool panels portray the role of women in the development of the territory, depicting the 5 seasons of the North; spring, summer, autumn, winter and "survival," the cold gray season between winter and spring and fall and winter. Begun by the Whitehorse Branch of the Canadian Federation of Business and Professional Women in 1976 to mark International Women's Year, the wall hangings were stitched by some 2,500 Yukoners.

Yukon Gardens, located at the junction of the Alaska Highway and South Access Road, is the only formal northern botanical garden. The 22-acre site features more than 100,000 wild and domestic flowers; vegetables, herbs and fruits; scenic pathways and floral displays; a children's "Old MacDonald's farm"; gift shop; and fresh produce in summer. Open daily in summer. Admission charged.

Whitehorse Rapids Fishway. The fish ladder was built in 1959 to provide access for chinook (king) salmon and other species above the Yukon Energy Corporation hydroelectric dam. Located at the end of Nisutlin Drive in the Riverdale suburb. Open daily, 8 A.M. to 10 P.M., from mid-July to mid-September. Interpretive displays and viewing decks.

The Sarsparilla Sisters is a musical review journey through 100 years of Sarsparilla family history, from the gold rush through the building of the Alaska Highway. Performed nightly, mid-May to mid-August, at Pioneer Trailer Park on the Alaska Highway, 2 miles/3.2 km south of Whitehorse turnoff (South Access Road). Admission charged.

Mountainview Public Golf Course,

Fly & Drive

Travel the Yukon and Alaska in the comfort of a Motorhome or Truck with Camper.

Over 60 Units to choose from.
BOOK EARLY

Minimum Rental is one week.
SUPER SAVERS: May – June
One-Way Specials with RV pick-up in Kamloops or Vancouver, British Columbia, and drop-off in Whitehorse, Yukon,
with 2000 FREE km and low off-season rates.

Klondike Recreational Rentals, Ltd.
Serving the RV traveler since 1978

108 Industrial Road
Box 5156(A), Whitehorse, YT Y1A 4S3
FAX (403) 668-6567
Phone (403) 668-2200 • Telex 036-8-483
RESERVATONS:
Phone (604) 675-4911 Collect
FAX (604) 675-4944

YUKON RIVER CRUISE
M.V. Anna Maria

Enjoy history, scenery, delicious food, entertainment in a 60' river cruiser.

Departs daily from downtown Whitehorse.

Fully licensed, heated and modern.

M.V. ANNA MARIA
6208 - 6th Avenue
Whitehorse, Yukon Y1A 1P2
(403) 667-4155 • FAX (403) 668-4288

Barb's Bed & Breakfast
Welcome to Yukon Hospitality Whitehorse Style

- Clean, cozy, quiet rooms with PRIVATE BATHROOMS
- 5 minute drive from downtown in the Riverdale Area
- Spacious sitting room with color TV
- Serving fresh fruits, cereals, homemade scones & muffins
- Reasonable rates

Your Hosts: Barb & Blaine McFarlane
64 Boswell Cresent
Whitehorse, Yukon Y1A 4T3
Phone: (403) 667-4104

WE RENT
- CAMPERS •
- 4X4's •
- BRONCOS •
- TRUCKS
- CARS • VANS

Best to book early
(403) 667-6200

Rent By the Day or the Week or the Month

Budget
car and truck rental

Mail: 4178 4th, Whitehorse, YT Y1A 1J6
FAX (403) 667-6246

WHITEHORSE PERFORMANCE CENTRE
Auto Repair & Parts Centre
Phone 667-7231

• Tune-Ups • Oil Changes • Transmission Rebuilding & Servicing
• Mufflers • Complete Exhaust Systems • Brakes & Wheels
AND A FULL LINE OF
DOMESTIC & IMPORT AUTO PARTS & ACCESSORIES
4th Avenue at Jarvis, Whitehorse, Yukon Y1A 1J1

Hillside view of downtown Whitehorse. (Philip and Karen Smith)

located in Porter Creek subdivision on the Yukon River, is accessible via the Porter Creek exit off the Alaska Highway or from Range Road. Eighteen holes, grass greens; green fees.

Picnic in a park. Picnicking on a small island in the Yukon River, accessible via footbridge from 2nd Avenue, north of the railroad tracks. Picnic facilities are also available at Robert Service Campground, located on the South Access Road into Whitehorse. Rotary Park is central to downtown and a popular picnic spot.

Whitehorse Public Library, part of the Yukon Government Bldg. on 2nd Avenue, has a room with art displays and books about the Yukon and the gold rush. It features a large double stone and copper fireplace, comfortable chairs, tables and helpful staff. Open noon to 9 P.M. weekdays, 10 A.M. to 6 P.M. Saturday, 1-9 P.M. Sunday and closed holidays.

Yukon Archives is located adjacent Yukon College at Yukon Place. The archives was established in 1972 to acquire, preserve and make available the documented history of the Yukon. The holdings, dating from 1845, include government records, private manuscripts, corporate records, photographs, maps, newspapers (most are on microfilm), sound recordings, university theses, books, pamphlets and periodicals.

206B Main Street
Whitehorse
Yukon Y1A 2A9
Phone (403) 667-6765

Special Discoveries

- For exceptional handcrafts from Yukon and across Canada
- For fine imports and collectibles

MasterCard • VISA • American Express

GREAT NORTH
BED & BREAKFAST

5 minutes to downtown tourist attractions, restaurants and shopping
Children welcome — any age
Adjacent to hiking, walking and x-country ski trails. 1/2 mile to Chadburn Lake
Spacious sitting room with colour TV (with Super Channel)
Hearty all-you-can-eat breakfast
Reasonable rates • Non-smoking home
Your Hostess: Trina Schaus
31 Boswell Crescent
Whitehorse, Yukon Y1A 4T2
Phone (403) 668-7659
VISA

MacKenzie's RV PARK

54 Large Full-Service Sites
22 Camping Sites
Reasonable Rates

Good Sampark

• **FREE GOLD PANNING** •

Horseshoe Pit
HOT CLEAN SHOWERS
LAUNDROMAT • STORE • CABLE TV

City Bus Stops Here
Handicap Accessible

— **OPEN YEAR ROUND** —

Just 6 miles north of City Centre
Phone (403) 633-2337

301-922.5 Alaska Highway
Whitehorse, Yukon Y1A 3Y9

MILE 922.5 / KM 1484

DESIGNERS NORTH

HORWOODS MALL

a truly unique and friendly store specializing in natural gold nugget jewellry, designer T-shirts and sweat tops and limited edition art.

• Exclusively featuring the art of eminent Yukon artist **TED HARRISON** on porcelain.
• Gold plated collector spoons

•••

Across from the old White Pass & Yukon Route station

DESIGNERS NORTH
1ST AND MAIN
P.O. BOX 5360, WHITEHORSE,
YUKON, CANADA Y1A 4Z2
PHONE (403) 668-7700
FAX (403) 668-2388

AMBASSADOR
Motorhome and Recreational Services Ltd.

WHITEHORSE • VANCOUVER • TERRACE

Discover Yukon/Alaska and British Columbia in the Comfort of a motorhome, camperhome, car or 4x4. Also one way rentals between these stations. **BOOK EARLY.**

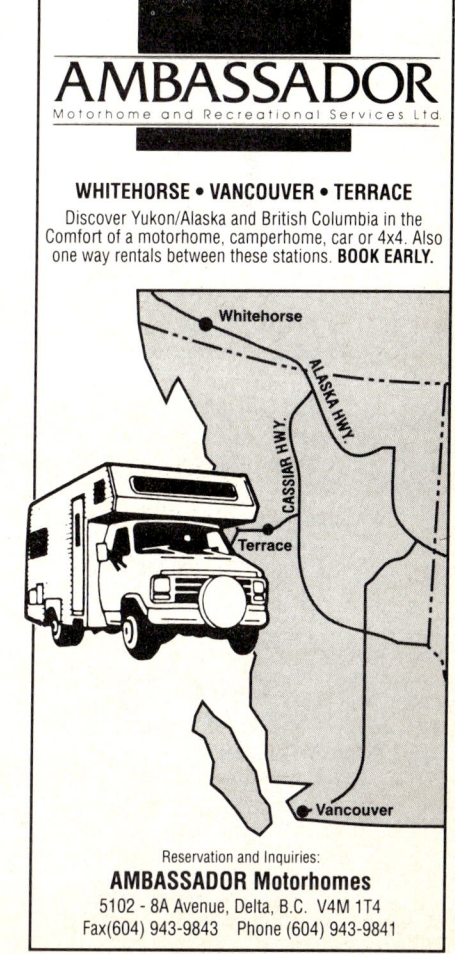

Reservation and Inquiries:
AMBASSADOR Motorhomes
5102 - 8A Avenue, Delta, B.C. V4M 1T4
Fax (604) 943-9843   Phone (604) 943-9841

Visitors are welcome. Phone (403) 667-5321 for hours, or write Box 2703, Whitehorse, YT Y1A 2C6, for more information.

Special Events. Whitehorse hosts a number of special events throughout the year. Many of these major events are listed in the 1992 calendar this page. In addition, there are a number of ongoing displays and special exhibits planned to help celebrate the 50th anniversary of the Alaska Highway in 1992. For details and up-to-the-minute information on dates, write the Yukon Anniversaries Commission, Bag 1992, Whitehorse, YT Y1A 5L9, or phone 668-1992.

Perhaps the major winter event in Whitehorse is the Yukon Quest International Sled Dog Race in February. This 1,000-mile sled dog race is a grueling 10- to 14-day course between Whitehorse and Fairbanks, AK. The race alternates starting points between the 2 cities. In 1992, the Yukon Quest starts in Fairbanks Feb. 9 and finishes in Whitehorse.

Boat Tours. The MV *Anna Maria* offers a 2-hour noon tour and a 4-hour dinner cruise daily in summer. The 60-foot river cruiser cruises down the Yukon River to Lake Laberge. Phone 667-4155 for more information.

Boat tours of scenic Miles Canyon aboard the MV *Schwatka* depart from the dock on Schwatka Lake and cruise up the Yukon River through Miles Canyon and back in about 2 hours. Phone 668-3161 for more information. Miles Canyon is also accessible by road: take Schwatka Lake Road off the South Access Road into Whitehorse, or turn off the Alaska Highway (see **Milepost DC 881.7**); follow signs.

Day trips from Whitehorse. Marsh Lake, 24 miles/39 km south of Whitehorse on the Alaska Highway, and Takhini Hot Springs, 17 miles/27 km north of town via the Alaska and Klondike highways, are within easy driving distance of Whitehorse. The Yukon government day-use area at Marsh Lake offers an excellent sandy beach, picnic area,

The Yukon's favorite place to stay.

The Yukon's most popular gathering place, the Westmark Klondike Inn is an area landmark. When you stay with us you'll find newly remodeled rooms, a choice of dining options, including an elegant dining experience at Charlie's Restaurant and true Yukon hospitality.

- 96 rooms and suites •
- Dining room, coffee shop and lounge •
- Gift shop • Hair salon •
- Free parking •

Special Summer Value Rates from $49

Rooms at lower rates are capacity controlled and good on selected rooms & dates only. Call for complete information. Subject to change without notice.

Westmark
KLONDIKE INN

2288 Second Avenue
Whitehorse, Yukon Territory
Y1A 1C8

Central Reservations
1-800-544-0970 (U.S.)
1-800-999-2570 (Canada)

Westmark Hotels covers the north with hotels and inns throughout Alaska and the Yukon. Come be our guest.

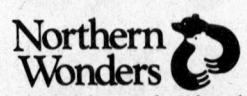

Northern Wonders
The finest northern gifts & handicrafts at very reasonable prices.
Located at Westmark Hotels

The Hidden Coast: Kayak Explorations from Alaska to Mexico, 168 pages of adventure by Joel W. Rogers.

KOPPER KING
Top of the Town on the Alaska Highway
Mile 918.3 · KM 1477.5
Open 7 Days a Week
Phone (403) 668-2347

MOTEL
Cable TV • Good Rates
Kitchenettes

G & P PIZZA HOUSE
Dine In or Take Out
For Delivery Call 668-4708

TAVERN & LOUNGE
Featuring a Miniature Railroad
Chinese Food and Steaks
Live Entertainment
Off-Sales Liquor and Beer

MINI-MARK • GAS
Self-Serve at the Best Price
Cold Beer to Go • Water
Ice • Maps • Fishing Licenses
Tourist Information
Hours 6:00 a.m. to 11:00 p.m.

1992 Events

MARCH
26-29 — 40th International Anniversary Bonspiel

APRIL
3 — Invasion Day

MAY
15-17 — Alaska Highway Symposium
15-24 — Alcan Festival
17 — Milepost Day Celebration

JUNE
12-15 — Northern Storytelling Festival's Highway Stories Tent
15-17 — Army Motors Convoy overnight
23-27 — Float Plane Race overnight

JULY
1 — Experience Our Traditional Ways, Cultural Show
2 — Northwest Highway Systems: Rangers Rifle Shoot
4-5 — Cycling Race Series
10-11 — Airmada
17-19 — Run for the Midnight Sun: Harley (Davidson motorcycles) Owners Group Rush '92
26 — International Airshow
27 — Senior Golf Tournament
31-8/2 — Old Time Fiddle Contest & Festival

AUGUST
1-2 — Fiddle Contest continues
7-10 — Alcan Highway International Scouts Jamboree at Congdon Creek Campground
8-9 — Yukon First Nation's Trade & Cultural Show
14 — Military Festival of Bands
20-21 — Peter Gzowski Invitational Golf Tournament
22 — 1942 Homecoming Exhibition Basketball Game
28-30 — Whitehorse Public School Commemorative Reunion

SEPTEMBER
TBA — Klondike Trail of '98 Road Relay 110-mile Race (Skagway, AK, to Whitehorse)
22-24 — Rallye Alaska Highway '92

NOVEMBER
5-8 — Takhini Highway Anniversary Bonspiel

change house and boat launch. Lakeview Resort at Marsh Lake offers boat rentals. Takhini Hot Springs offers all-day swimming and horseback riding. Beyond Takhini Hot Springs about 7 miles/11 km on the Klondike Loop is a commercial reindeer farm. The farm is open daily in summer, 8 A.M. to 8 P.M., and children may pet and feed the reindeer. Admission charged.

Longer trips (which you may want to extend to an overnight) are to Atlin, about 2½ hours by car, and Skagway, 3 hours by car. Visitors heading for Skagway should call ahead for accommodations if they expect to overnight. You may make a circle tour, driving down to Skagway then turning off onto the Tagish Road on your way back and continuing on to Atlin via the Atlin Road.

Rockhounding. A wide variety of copper

Camps constructed

Tent housing for workers at Whitehorse in 1942. Prefabricated barracks, warehouses and maintenance shops had to be constructed, along with sewer and water systems, for thousands of workers arriving to work on the highway. A postal worker in Whitehorse, which along with Fort St. John was one of the largest construction camps along the Alaska Highway, recalled that one day he was handling mail for 350 people, the next day for 10,000. As headquarters for the Western Sector, the camp at Whitehorse had its own hospital, steam laundry, central heating plant and service club. Workers in the line camps had few of these amenities.

minerals can be found in the Whitehorse area. The following location is suggested by Fred Dorward of the Whitehorse Gem & Mineral Club (26 Sunset Dr. N., Whitehorse, YT Y1A 4M8). Other sources of information for rock hounds include the Yukon Rock Shop, junction of the Alaska Highway and Klondike Highway 2 (Carcross Road), and the Yukon Chamber of Mines on Main Street.

Drive north on the Alaska Highway to the Fish Lake Road turnoff (**Milepost DC 889.4**), located 2 miles/3.2 km from the north entrance to Whitehorse. About 0.5 mile/0.8 km in on Fish Lake Road, park and walk across McIntyre Creek to the old Copper King mine workings. Excellent but small specimens of brown garnet, also serpentine. IMPORTANT: Rock hounds should exercise extreme caution when exploring. Do not enter old mine workings. Please respect No Trespassing signs.

Canoe, Raft or Boat to Dawson City. Canoe rentals by the day, week or month, and guide services are available in Whitehorse. From the Yukon River's outlet at Marsh Lake south of Whitehorse to the Alaska border it is 530 river miles/853 km; from Whitehorse to Dawson City it is 410 river miles/660 km. There is a boat launch at Rotary Park, behind the Yukon Government Bldg. You may also launch at Deep Creek Campground on Lake Laberge.

NOTE: Before leaving on any river or other wilderness trip, for your own protection, report

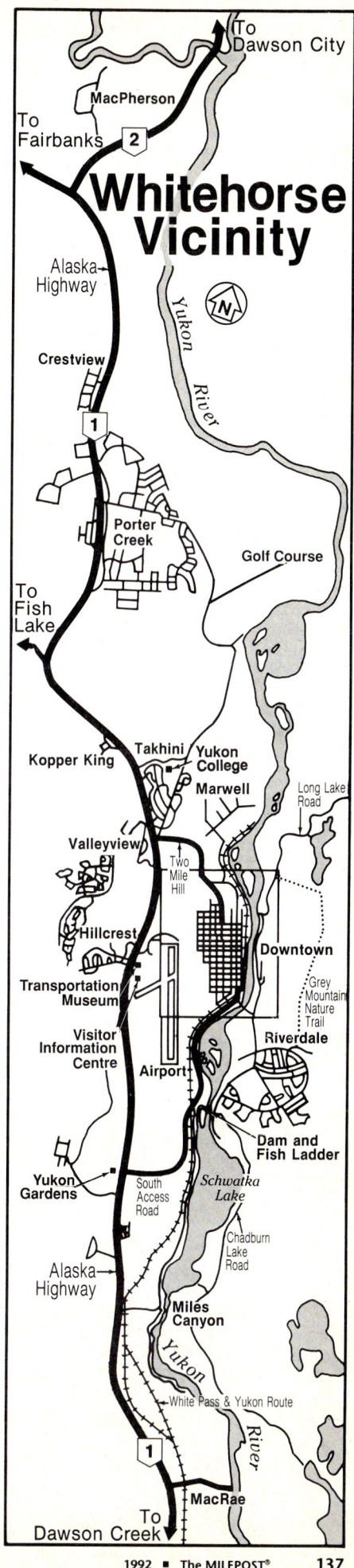

CANADA POST SUB POST OFFICE
MAIL DROP AND STAMPS
Gourmet Coffees and Teas

COFFEE·TEA & SPICE

EDNA DOUCET   JOHN RUSSELL
Proprietors

Qwanlin Mall, 4th Avenue & Ogilvie
Whitehorse, Yukon Territory

INDIAN CRAFT SHOP LTD.

Indian Crafts and Souvenirs
Made Locally and Across Canada

Parkas • Mukluks • Moccasins
Gold and Silver Jewelry
Indian Craft Supplies • Hides • Furs
Large and Small Souvenirs

**Now at 504 Main Street
Whitehorse, Yukon**
(403) 667-7216

your plans and itinerary to the RCMP. Do not attempt the Five Finger Rapids on the Yukon River without qualified advice. For more information on wilderness travel, contact Tourism Yukon office, located between 2nd and 3rd on Hawkins; phone 667-5340. Hikers planning to do the Chilkoot Trail should check with Canadian Parks Service, in the Federal Bldg. at 4th and Main; phone 668-2116.

Mt. McIntyre Recreation Centre, 0.9 mile/1.5 km west of the Alaska Highway (see **Milepost DC 887.6**), has 70 kilometres of groomed cross-country ski trails (open for hiking, running and mountain biking in summer). Contact Whitehorse Cross-Country Ski Club, P.O. Box 4639, Whitehorse, YT Y1A 3Y7.

Sportsmen can obtain complete information on fishing and hunting in the Whitehorse area by writing Tourism Yukon, Box 2703, Whitehorse, YT Y1A 2C6. They will provide lists of guides, advise what licenses are required and assist you in making plans.

Alaska Highway Log

(continued)
Distance* from Dawson Creek (DC) is followed by distance from Fairbanks (F). Original mileposts are indicated in the text as Historical Mile.
*Mileages from Dawson Creek are based on actual driving distance. Kilometres from Dawson Creek are based on physical kilometreposts. Please read Mileposts and Kilometreposts in the introduction for an explanation of how this highway is logged.

DC 885.7 (1425.4 km) **F 602.3** (969.3 km) Yukon Visitors Reception Centre, open mid-May to mid-September, 8 A.M. to 8 P.M. daily; phone 667-2915. Preview Yukon attractions on laser disc player. Enjoy a multi-image slide presentation on Yukon National Parks and historic sites. Radio CKYN "Yukon Gold," 96.1-FM, broadcasts from the centre.

DC 885.8 (1425.5 km) **F 602.2** (969.1 km) Yukon Transportation Museum features exhibits on all forms of transportation in the North, with special exhibits and displays celebrating the 50th anniversary of the Alaska Highway in 1992. Open May to September. Admission charged.

DC 886.2 (1473.8 km) **F 601.8** (968.5 km) Turnoff to east for Whitehorse International Airport. Built for and used by both U.S. and Canadian forces during WWII. DC-3 weathervane.

DC 887.1 (1475.2 km) **F 600.9** (967 km)

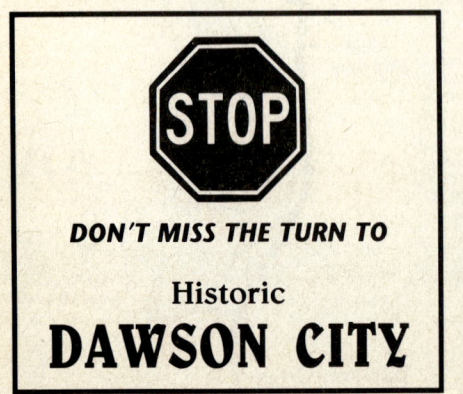

To east, in front of NorthwesTel's maintenance complex, are cairns commemorating 18 years of service on the Alaska Highway (1946–64) by the Corps of Royal Canadian Engineers. At this site, on April 1, 1946, the U.S. Army officially handed over the Alaska Highway to the Canadian Army.

DC 887.4 (1475.6 km) **F 600.6** (966.5 km) North access road to Whitehorse (exit east) via Two-Mile Hill and 4th Avenue. Access to private RV park. At Mile 1.2/1.9 km on this access road is Qwanlin Mall.

DC 887.6 (1476 km) **F 600.4** (966.2 km) Turnoff to west on Hamilton Boulevard for Mt. McIntyre Recreation Centre (0.9 mile/1.5 km); 70 kilometres of cross-country ski trails (summer hiking and biking), chalet for indoor waxing, curling and bonspiels. Truck weigh scales west side of highway.

DC 888.6 (1477.5 km) **F 599.4** (964.6 km) **Mile 918.3.** Turnoff for Kopper King restaurant, grocery and gas.

DC 889.3 (1478.6 km) **F 598.7** (963.5 km) McIntyre Creek.

DC 889.4 (1478.8 km) **F 598.6** (963.3 km) Turnoff to west for Fish Lake Road. Follow paved road west 2.5 miles/4 km to historic information sign about copper mining in this area. Road continues 10.5 miles/17 km (winding gravel) to Jackson Lakes (named Franklin and Louise).

DC 889.8 (1479.4 km) **F 598.2** (962.7 km) Turnoff to west to municipal dump.

DC 890.1 (1479.9 km) **F 597.9** (962.2 km) Rabbit's Foot Canyon.

DC 890.5 (1480.6 km) **F 597.5** (961.6 km) Turnoff to Porter Creek to east.

DC 891 (1481.4 km) **F 597** (960.8 km) Porter Creek grocery.

DC 891.3 (1482 km) **F 596.7** (960.3 km) **Historical Mile 921**, laundromat, gas and other businesses.

DC 891.5 (1482.3 km) **F 596.5** (959.9 km) Clyde Wann Road. Access to Range Road and Mountain View Golf Course (18 holes).

DC 891.6 (1482.2 km) **F 596.4** (959.8 km) Truck stop to west.

DC 891.8 (1482.5 km) **F 596.2** (959.5 km) MacDonald Road to north; auto repair.

DC 891.9 (1484 km) **F 596.1** (959.3 km) **Historical Mile 922.5.** Access to MacKenzie's RV Park. Azure Road. ▲

DC 894.3 (1486.4 km) **F 593.7** (955.4 km) Turnoff east to Cousins dirt airstrip.

DC 894.5 (1486.7 km) **F 593.5** (955.1 km) Rest area to west with litter barrels, outhouses, information sign and pay phone.

DC 894.8 (1487.2 km) **F 593.2** (954.6 km) **Junction** with Klondike Highway 2 to Dawson City. (See KLONDIKE LOOP section.) Turn off on Klondike Highway 2 for Takhini Hot Springs and reindeer farm. For Alaska-bound travelers, the highway now swings west.

DC 895.5 (1488.3 km) **F 592.5** (953.5 km) Turnoff to south for Haeckel Hill. Not recommended for hiking as this area is used for target practice.

DC 899.1 (1495.4 km) **F 588.9** (947.7 km) Turnoff for 3-mile/4.8-km loop drive

Reconstructed Canyon Creek bridge at Milepost DC 965.6. (Earl L. Brown, staff)

on old section of Alaska Highway.

DC 901.6 (1499.3 km) **F 586.4** (943.7 km) Turnoff to north to sled dog track.

DC 905.4 (1507.1 km) **F 582.6** (937.6 km) **Historical Milepost 937**. Camera viewpoint turnout to north with point of interest sign about the old Dawson Trail. There were at least 50 stopping places along the old Dawson Trail winter stagecoach route between Whitehorse and Dawson City, and from 1 to 3 roadhouses at each stop. At this point, the stagecoach route crossed the Takhini River. This route was discontinued in 1950 when the Mayo-Dawson Road (now Klondike Highway 2) was constructed.

DC 908.7 (1512.4 km) **F 579.3** (932.3 km) Private farm and windmill; good example of Yukon agriculture. Facilities for overnighting large livestock.

DC 914.7 (1525 km) **F 573.3** (922.6 km) Takhini River bridge. According to R. Coutts in *Yukon: Places & Names*, the name Takhini derives from the Tagish Indian *tahk*, meaning mosquito, and *heena*, meaning river.

DC 922.7 (1535 km) **F 565.3** (909.7 km) Watch for horses and other livestock grazing on open range near highway.

DC 924.5 (1538.4 km) **F 563.5** (906.8 km) Stoney Creek.

DC 924.7 (1538.7 km) **F 563.3** (906.5 km) View of Mount Bratnober.

DC 926 (1540.8 km) **F 562** (904.4 km) Turnout to south with point of interest sign about 1958 burns. More than 1.5 million acres/629,058 hectares of Yukon forest lands were burned in 1958. Campfires were responsible for most of these fires.

IMPORTANT: Northbound motorists WATCH FOR BUFFALO on road between Kusawa Lake turnoff and Haines Junction. A free-roaming herd of wood bison was released in this area in 1988, and collisions between vehicles and buffalo have occurred. DRIVE CAREFULLY, especially from dusk through dark, when it is difficult to see these animals. Buffalo are *extremely* unpredictable and should never be approached.

DC 927.3 (1542.9 km) **F 560.7** (902.3 km) Turnoff to south for viewpoint (1.9 miles/3 km) and Kusawa Lake Yukon government campground (15 miles/24 km). Access road to campground is a narrow, winding gravel road, very slippery when wet;

not recommended for long trailers or heavily loaded vehicles. ▲

Day-use area with sandy beach, boat dock, kitchen shelter and drinking water; boat launch 0.6 mile/1 km south. Campground at north end of lake has 32 sites, kitchen shelter, firepits and drinking water. Camping fee $8.

Kusawa Lake (formerly Arkell Lake), located in the Coast Mountains, is 45 miles/72 km long and averages 2 miles/3.2 km wide, with a shoreline perimeter of 125 miles/200 km. An access road to the lake was first constructed by the U.S. Army in 1945 to obtain bridge timbers for Alaska Highway construction.

Kusawa Lake, lake trout to 20 lbs, good to excellent; also grayling and pike.

DC 936.8 (1558 km) F 551.2 (887 km) Mendenhall River bridge. A tributary of the Takhini River, the Mendenhall River—like the Mendenhall Glacier outside Juneau, AK—was named for Thomas Corwin Mendenhall (1841-1924), superintendent of the U.S. Coast & Geodetic Survey.

DC 939.5 (1562.3 km) F 548.5 (882.7 km) View of 3 prominent mountains northbound (from left to right): Mount Kelvin; center mountain unnamed; and Mount Bratnober.

DC 942.8 (1567.6 km) F 545.2 (877.4 km) NorthwesTel microwave tower to south.

DC 943.5 (1568.5 km) F 544.5 (876.3 km) **Historical Milepost 974, CHAMPAGNE.** Originally a camping spot on the Dalton Trail to Dawson City, established by Jack Dalton in the late 1800s. In 1902, Harlow "Shorty" Chambers built a roadhouse and trading post here, and it became a supply centre for first the Bullion Creek rush and later the Burwash Creek gold rush in 1904. The origin of the name is uncertain, although one account is that Dalton's men—after successfully negotiating a herd of cattle through the first part of the trail—celebrated here with a bottle of French champagne. Today, it is home to members of the Champagne Indian Band. There is an Indian cemetery on right northbound, just past the log cabin homes; a sign there reads: "This cemetery is not a tourist attraction. Please respect our privacy as we respect yours."

For northbound travelers, the Alaska Highway parallels the Dezadeash River (out of view to the south) from here west to Haines Junction. The Dezadeash Range is to the south.

DC 955.8 (1588 km) F 532.2 (856.5 km) First glimpse northbound of Kluane Range.

DC 957 (1590 km) F 531 (854.5 km) **Historical Milepost 987.** Cracker Creek.

DC 964.6 (1602.2 km) F 523.4 (842.3 km) **Historical Mile 995.** Otter Falls Cutoff, junction with Aishihik Road. Gas station and store to south, Aishihik Road turnoff to north.

Otter Falls Cutoff. See display ad this section.

Aishihik Road leads 84 miles/135 km north to the old Indian village of Aishihik (AYSH-ee-ak, means high place). Northern Canada Power Commission built a 32-megawatt dam at the foot of Aishihik Lake in 1976 to supply power principally to the mining industry. Flow hours for the Otter Falls hydro project are given at the start of Aishihik Road. This is a narrow, gravel road, maintained for summer travel only to the government campground. Aishihik Road is not recommended for large RVs and trailers.

The Northwest Highway System

On April 1, 1946, a handshake between Major Bernard Zhon, 6th Service Cmd. (left) and Lt. Col. J.R.B. Jones, RCE, signifies transfer of the Alaska Highway to the Canadian Army. In an agreement between the 2 countries in 1942, the U.S. agreed to survey and construct the pioneer road, and then maintain the completed highway until "termination of the present war and for 6 months thereafter unless the Government of Canada prefers to assume responsibility at an earlier date for the maintenance of so much of it as lies in Canada." The Northwest Highway System, the branch of the Canadian Army responsible for maintenance of the Alaska Highway, was later handed over to the federal Dept. of Public Works.

There is a day-use recreation site at Otter Falls, 12.6 miles/20.3 km distance; picnic shelter, tables, outhouses and boat ramp.

The Yukon government Aishihik Lake campground is located at the south end of Aishihik Lake, approximately 27 miles/43 km distance; 13 sites, drinking water, picnic tables, firepits, kitchen shelter, boat launch and playground. Camping fee $8. ▲

Aishihik Lake, fishing for lake trout and grayling. As with most large Yukon lakes, ice is not out until late June. Low water levels may make boat launching difficult. **Pole Cat Lake,** just before the Aishihik weather station; fishing for pike.

CAUTION: Bears in area. Other wildlife includes eagles, moose and caribou.

DC 965.6 (1603.8 km) F 522.4 (840.7 km) **Historical Milepost 996.** Turnoff to north at east end of Aishihik River bridge (watch for camera viewpoint sign) to see Canyon Creek bridge. The original bridge was built about 1920 by the Jacquot brothers to move freight and passengers across the Aishihik River to Silver City on Kluane Lake, and from there by boat to Burwash Landing. The bridge was reconstructed in 1942 by Army Corps of Engineers during construction of the Alaska Highway. It was rebuilt again in 1987.

DC 965.7 (1604 km) F 522.3 (840.5 km) Aishihik River bridge.

DC 966.3 (1605 km) F 521.7 (839.6 km) View of impressive Kluane Range ice fields straight ahead northbound between Kilometreposts 1604 and 1616.

DC 974.9 (1619 km) F 513.1 (825.7 km) Turnout to south on Marshall Creek.

DC 977.1 (1622.4 km) F 510.9 (822.2 km) Turnout to north with information plaques about the Kluane Ranges. The rugged snowcapped peaks of the Kluane Icefield Ranges and the outer portion of the St. Elias Mountains are visible to the west, straight ahead northbound.

The Kluane National Park Icefield Ranges are Canada's highest and the world's largest nonpolar alpine ice field, forming the interior wilderness of the park. In clear weather, Mount Kennedy and Mount Hubbard, 2 peaks that are twice as high as the front ranges seen before you, are visible from here.

DC 979.3 (1626 km) F 508.7 (818.6 km) Between Kilometreposts 1626 and 1628, look for the NorthwesTel microwave

---

At Mile 995
OTTER FALLS CUTOFF

- **GAS STATION – STORE**
  "Cheapest Gas From Here to Alaska"
- **GENERAL STORE** (New for 1991)
  Free Animal Exhibit Inside
  (As partially seen in "National Geographic")
- **GUIDED FISHING TRIPS**
  Hunting Trips Arranged

Tent Camping and Camper Parking Area
Free Picnic Area and Playground
for Our Customers

Your Hosts Leonard & Brenda Beecher
(403) 634-2812

Area wildlife is depicted in Haines Junction sculpture. (Earl L. Brown, staff)

repeater station on top of Paint Mountain. The station was installed with the aid of helicopters and supplied by the tramline carried by high towers which is also visible from here.

DC 980.9 (1628.7 km) **F 507.1** (816.1 km) Turnoff to north for Yukon government Pine Lake recreation park and campground. Day-use area has sandy beach, boat launch and dock, group firepits, drinking water and 7 tent sites near beach. The campground, adjacent **Pine Lake** with a view of the St. Elias Mountains, has 33 sites, outhouses, firewood, litter barrels, kitchen shelter, playground and drinking water. Camping fee $8. Fishing is good for lake trout, northern pike and grayling.

DC 982.2 (1630.8 km) **F 505.8** (814 km) Turnoff to north for Haines Junction airport. **Private Aircraft:** Haines Junction airstrip; elev. 2,150 feet/655m; length 6,000 feet/1,839m; gravel.

Highway swings to south for last few miles into Haines Junction offering a panoramic, close-up view of the Auriol Range straight ahead.

DC 984.8 (1635 km) **F 503.2** (809.8 km) Northbound travelers turn right (southbound travelers turn left) on Kluane Street for Kluane National Park Visitor Centre.

DC 985 (1635.3 km) **F 503** (809.5 km) **Historical Mile 1016, junction** of Alaska Highway and Haines Highway (Haines Road).

IMPORTANT: This junction can be confusing; choose your route carefully! Fairbanks-bound travelers TURN RIGHT at this junction for continuation of Alaska Highway (Yukon Highway 1); highway log follows description of Haines Junction, YT. Continue straight ahead (south) on the Haines Highway (Yukon Highway 3) for port of Haines, AK; see HAINES HIGHWAY section. (Haines-bound motorists note: Next gas 119 miles/191.5 km.)

Haines Junction

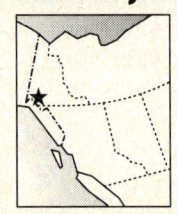

DC 985 (1635.3 km) **F 503** (809.5 km) **Historical Milepost 1016**, at the junction of the Alaska Highway (Yukon Highway 1) and the Haines Highway (Yukon Highway 3, also known as the Haines Road). Driving distance to Whitehorse, 100 miles/161 km; YT-AK border, 205 miles/330 km; Tok, 296 miles/476 km; and Haines, 150.5 miles/242 km. **Population:** 536. **Elevation:** 1,956 feet/596m. **Emergency Services:** RCMP, phone 634-2221. **Nursing Centre**, phone 634-2213. **Radio:** 890.

Visitor Information: At the Kluane National Park and Yukon government visitor information centre, 0.2 mile/0.3 km east of the junction just off the Alaska Highway. Interpretive exhibits, displays and a slide show are featured. The centre is open 8:30 A.M. to 9 P.M., daily from May to September.

Haines Junction camp was established in 1942 during construction of the Alaska Highway. The first buildings here were Army barracks for the U.S. Army Corps of Engineers. The engineers were to build a new branch road connecting the Alaska Highway with the port of Haines on Lynn Canal. The branch road—today's Haines Highway—was completed in 1943.

Haines Junction will be participating in the Alaska Highway 50th anniversary celebration in 1992. Some of the special 1992 events are listed in the calendar this section. In addition, Haines Junction hosts bingo games (April 24, May 22, June 19, July 24 and Aug. 21, 1992) and coffee houses every Wednesday from May 27. A summer-long historic photo exhibit and art display is also planned.

The Our Lady of the Way Catholic mission in Haines Junction was built in 1954, using parts from an old Army hut left from highway construction days.

Haines Junction is still an important stop for travelers on the Alaska and Haines highways. Services are located along both highways, and clustered around Village Square at the junction, where a 24-foot

HAINES JUNCTION ADVERTISERS

Alcan Fuels	Ph. (403) 634-2268
Cabin Crafts	Across from visitor centre
Chù Chäda Hovercraft Tours	Ph. (403) 633-5030
Cozy Corner Motel & Restaurant	Ph. (403) 634-2511
Gateway Motel	Ph. (403) 634-2371
Gerry's Fishing Charters	Ph. (403) 634-2654
Haines Junction Self Serve	Ph. (403) 634-2246
Kluane Park Inn Ltd.	Ph. (403) 634-2261
Kluane RV Kampground	Mile 985.3 Alaska Hwy.
Kruda Ché Rentals	Ph. (403) 634-2378
Madley's General Store	Ph. (403) 634-2200
Mountain View Motor Inn	Ph. (403) 634-2646
North Country Service Centre	Ph. (403) 634-2505
Village Bakery	Next to visitor centre

Val Drummond (Proprietor)

CABIN CRAFTS

Unique Handcrafted Yukon Gifts & Souvenirs

Interesting Display of Antiques – Fossils – Animal Mounts

Open Daily — Located across from Kluane Park Visitors Information Centre

General Delivery: Haines Junction, Yukon Y0B 1L0

(403) 634-2683

VISA / MasterCard

NORTH COUNTRY SERVICE CENTRE

- Quality Gas, Diesel and Oil Products
- Friendly Full Service • **Clean** Restrooms
- FREE Coffee with fill up
- Cold Beverages • Snacks • Ice Cream
- Video Rentals • Ice • Souvenirs

SAVE ON RV SERVICES
- RV Hookups (electricity and water) Only $10
- Self contained? – FREE Dry Camping
- FREE RV Water Fill and Dump Station with fill up

VISA • MasterCard • American Express • PETRO-CANADA

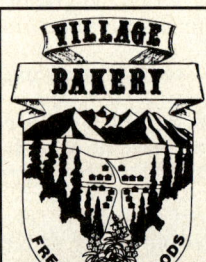

(403) 634-2505
Summer Hours: 7:00 a.m.–12:00 p.m.
First service station entering Haines Junction from Whitehorse

---

VILLAGE BAKERY

LOCATED NEXT TO THE KLUANE VISITOR CENTRE IN THE VILLAGE OF HAINES JUNCTION, YUKON MILE 1016 ALASKA HWY.

- Bread • Buns • Muffins
- Cookies • Ice Cream
- Refreshments
- Specialties • Ice
- Deli Sandwiches

Sourdough is our Specialty!
Phone (403) 634-BUNS!

1992 Events

MAY
30 Trail of '42 Road Race

JUNE
13 Alsek June Bug Music Festival
22-23 Army Motors Convoy

SEPTEMBER
24-25 Rallye Alaska Highway '92

NOVEMBER
20 Rededication Ceremony at Soldiers' Summit

---

monument depicts area wildlife.

Visitor facilities in Haines Junction include motels, restaurants, a bakery, gas stations, a campground, garage services, groceries and souvenirs. There is an indoor public swimming pool with showers available; open daily, fee charged. Also here are a RCMP office, Lands and Forest District Office and health centre. The post office and bank are located in Madley's General Store. (Banking service weekdays, 12:30-3:30 P.M.; extended hours on Fridays.) The weigh sta-

---

GROCERIES HARDWARE

BANKING FACILITIES

◆ IN STORE ◆
Bakery and Deli Products
Fresh Fruit and Vegetables
Full Meat and Dairy Counter

FISHING TACKLE
CAMPING SUPPLIES
MAGAZINES AND SOUVENIRS

CUBE and BLOCK ICE

Phone (403) 634-2200
Box 5371, Haines Junction, YT

POST OFFICE

MADLEY'S General Store

Gateway Motel

Rooms Available 24 Hours

• All rooms with private bath
• Lounge • Satellite colour TV
• Public Laundromat • Showers
• RV Park – Complete hookups

Box 5460, Haines Junction, Yukon Y0B 1L0
(403) 634-2371

Mile 1016/KM 1635
Alaska Highway
Haines Junction
(403) 634-2261
FAX (403) 634-2273

Come in and see us ... we'd like to get to know you and give you lots of tips on what to see and do while you are here.

FOUNDED IN 1946   OPEN YEAR-ROUND

KLUANE PARK INN LTD.
HOME OF THE KLUANE NATIONAL PARK

20 FULLY MODERN HOTEL-MOTEL UNITS • Reasonable Rates
Available 24 Hours • Color TV • Individual Thermostats
Free Plug-ins • Cocktail Lounge • Cube Ice

OPEN YEAR ROUND

Mountain View Motor Inn

60-SEAT RESTAURANT and **LICENSED DINING ROOM**
with Delicious
Home Cooking & Baking
Daily Specials

MODERN MOTEL
with Satellite TV

CAR WASH
SERVICE STATION with
COMPLETE TIRE REPAIR

RV PARKING • Full Facilities
Free Dump Station and Water
Laundromat • Public Showers
Cube Ice
Souvenirs • Fishing Licenses

U.S. Exchange

(403) 634-2646
Box 5479, Haines Junction, YT Y0B 1L0 Canada

CHÙ CHÄDA HOVERCRAFT TOURS

Leaving Haines Junction Daily   New for 1992

EXPERIENCE THE ADVENTURE OF EXPLORING THE ALSEK VALLEY
INTO THE KLUANE NATIONAL PARK

Breathtaking Photo Opportunities   — Tours to Lowell Glacier
Wildlife Viewing   — Gold Seeking and Cultural Interpretation

Comfortable 18-passenger, fully enclosed all-weather air-cushioned vehicle
(Coast Guard Approved) Dutch Manufactured

Washroom equipped • Handicap accessible
Environmentally Sensitive
(Charters Available)

Information and Reservations: Phone/FAX (403) 633-5030 • (403) 633-5924
Additional Information From —
VISITOR INFORMATION CENTRE AND KLUANE RV KAMPGROUND
MAILING ADDRESS: P.O. BOX 5554, WHITEHORSE, YUKON Y1A 5H4

ALASKA HIGHWAY • HAINES JUNCTION

tion is located on the Haines Highway (Kilometre 255.6 Haines Road), 0.2 mile/0.3 km south from the Alaska Highway junction. Across from the weigh station is the Commissioner James Smith Administration Bldg., which contains the government liquor store and public library. The airport is located on the Alaska Highway just east of town (see **Milepost DC 982.2**).

Haines Junction is on the eastern boundary of Kluane National Park. Administration offices and the visitor centre for the park are located in town; the park warden and general works station is located just north of town. Kluane (pronounced kloo-WA-nee) National Park encompasses extensive ice fields, mountains and wilderness. It is virtually undeveloped, with only 1 campground (Kathleen Lake on the Haines Highway) and some hiking trails. Flightseeing the park (by helicopter from Haines Junction; by small plane from Whitehorse and Burwash Landing) is a popular way to see Kluane's magnificent scenery. A local tour operator offers hovercraft trips up the Alsek River into the park daily in summer.

The park was first suggested in 1942, and in 1943 land was set aside and designated the Kluane Game Sanctuary. A formal park region was established in 1972 and the national park boundaries were official in 1976. In 1980, Kluane National Park, along with Wrangell-St. Elias National Park in Alaska, became a joint UNESCO World Heritage Site.

For more information on Kluane National Park, stop by the excellent visitor centre and see the exhibits and the award-winning multi-image slide presentation. Also check at the visitor centre for a schedule of guided activities and nature programs. Contact Kluane National Park at Box 5495, Haines Junction, YT Y0B 1L0, or phone (403) 634-2251.

Picnicking available at day-use area on the Dezadeash River, located at the west edge of town on the Haines Highway. Other outdoor recreation available locally includes guided fishing and boating (canoe and boat rentals available).

A private campground with dump station is located just north of the junction at **Milepost DC 985.3**. Yukon government campground located 4.1 miles/6.6 km east of junction on the Alaska Highway at Pine Lake. ▲

Alaska Highway Log

(continued)

Distance* from Dawson Creek (DC) is followed by distance from Fairbanks (F). Original mileposts are indicated in the text as Historical Mile.
*Mileages from Dawson Creek are based on actual driving distance. Kilometres from Dawson Creek are based on physical kilometreposts. Please read Mileposts and Kilometreposts in the introduction for an explanation of how this highway is logged.

DC 985 (1635.3 km) **F 503** (809.5 km) **Junction** of the Alaska Highway (Yukon Highway 1) and the Haines Highway (Yukon Highway 3). Markers indicate distance to Destruction Bay 67 miles/108 km, Beaver Creek 186 miles/299 km.

Northbound: From Haines Junction to

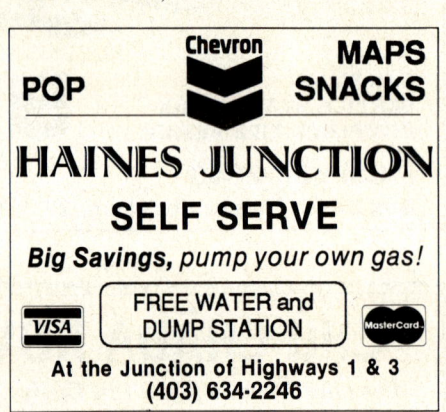

ALCAN FUELS
Serving Kluane Country
Mile 1017
Open Year-Round 7 Days A Week
Competitive Prices
✻ Free Coffee ✻
GAS • DIESEL
Auto and Bottled Propane
Auto Repairs • Towing

Bob and Sue Burton   Phone (403) 634-2268
Box 5327   FAX (403) 634-2420
Haines Junction, Yukon
Y0B 1L0

Chevron
POP MAPS SNACKS
HAINES JUNCTION
SELF SERVE
Big Savings, pump your own gas!
FREE WATER and DUMP STATION
At the Junction of Highways 1 & 3
(403) 634-2246

KRUDA CHÉ (Otter) RENTALS
CANOES
Inflatable Boats
Motors
Gear
(403) 634-2378
or (403) 634-2709
Box 5358, Haines Junction, Yukon Y0B 1L0

Good Food and Old Fashion Hospitality!
12 FULLY MODERN MOTEL UNITS . . .
Satellite Colour TV • Full Baths
Licensed Dining
OPEN YEAR ROUND
Cozy Corner Motel & Restaurant
Mile 1016 KM 1635 • Phone (403) 634-2511 • HAINES JUNCTION, Y.T.

GERRY'S FISHING CHARTERS
• Full and Half-Day Charters •

CHARTER INCLUDES:
GUIDE • LIFE JACKETS
FISHING RODS • TACKLE
Overnight charters require advanced booking
Box 5379, Haines Junction, Yukon Y0B 1L0
Phone (403) 634-2654

KLUANE R.V. KAMPGROUND
NEW
(403) 634-2709
RV CARAVANS AND TOUR GROUPS WELCOME
Owned and Operated by Yukoners
Reasonable Rates
✓Clean Modern Restrooms   ✓30 Wooded Campsites   ✓Laundromat — Showers
✓Pull-throughs   ✓Dump Station   ✓Tent Sites
✓50 Full Hookups   ✓Pay Phones — TV   ✓BBQ – Picnic Tables
✓Power — Water   ✓Store – Ice   ✓Hiking Trail
Box 5496, Haines Junction, YT Canada Y0B 1L0
At KM 1635.9 on the Alaska Highway, in the Heart of Kluane National Park

the YT-AK border, the Alaska Highway is in fair to good condition but narrow, often without shoulders. Watch for frost heaves north from Destruction Bay.

Southbound: Good paved highway with wide shoulders next 380 miles/611.5 km (from here to Watson Lake) with the exception of some short sections of narrow road and occasional gravel breaks. *NOTE: This junction can be confusing; choose your route carefully!* Whitehorse-bound travelers TURN LEFT at junction for continuation of Alaska Highway (Yukon Highway 1); highway log follows description of Haines Junction. TURN RIGHT for the Haines Highway (Yukon Highway 3) to the port of Haines, AK; see HAINES HIGHWAY section for log. (Haines-bound motorists note: Next gas 119 miles/191.5 km.)

CAUTION: Southbound motorists WATCH FOR BUFFALO on road south to Kusawa Lake turnoff.

DC 985.3 (1635.9 km) F 502.7 (809 km) Kluane RV Kampground.

DC 985.8 (1636.5 km) F 502.2 (808.2 km) **Historical Mile 1017.** Alcan Fuels; gas, diesel, propane, auto repair and towing. Open daily. Open year-round.

DC 986.6 (1637.8 km) F 501.4 (806.9 km) Highway follows the Kluane Ranges which are to the west. Livestock open range in this area: Watch for horses and cattle!

DC 987.8 (1639.8 km) F 500.2 (805 km) **Historical Mile 1019.** Kluane National Park warden headquarters. (Visitor information in Haines Junction at the visitor centre.)

DC 988.3 (1640.6 km) F 499.7 (804.1 km) Rest area to west with pit toilets.

DC 991.4 (1645.6 km) F 496.6 (799.1 km) Photo stop on right northbound. A short hike up hill leads to lookout and information sign about ancient lakes in the area.

DC 991.6 (1645.9 km) F 496.4 (798.9 km) **Historical Milepost 1022.** Mackintosh Lodge to east; food, gas, lodging and camping. Trailhead to west for Alsek Pass trail; 18 miles/29 km long, suitable for shorter day hikes, mountain bikes permitted.

Mackintosh Lodge. See display ad this section.

DC 1000.1 (1660 km) F 487.9 (785.2 km) Bear Creek Summit (elev. 3,294 feet/1,004m), highest point on the Alaska Highway between Whitehorse and Fairbanks.

Glimpse of Kloo Lake to north of highway between Kilometreposts 1660 and 1662.

DC 1003.5 (1665.4 km) F 484.5 (779.7 km) Jarvis Creek.

DC 1003.6 (1665.6 km) F 484.4 (779.5 km) **Historical Mile 1035.** Turnout to west next to Jarvis Creek. Pretty spot for a picnic. Trail rides may be available here.

Jarvis Creek, grayling 8 to 16 inches, good all summer; Dolly Varden 8 to 10 inches, best in early summer.

DC 1013.6 (1682 km) F 474.4 (763.5 km) Beautiful view to west of the snow-covered Kluane Ranges. For northbound travelers, the Alaska Highway parallels the Kluane Ranges from Haines Junction to Koidern, presenting a nearly unbroken chain of 8,000-foot/2,438-m summits interrupted only by a few large valleys cut by glacier-fed rivers and streams. West of the Kluane Ranges is the Duke Depression, a narrow trough separating the Kluane Ranges from the St. Elias Mountains. Major peaks in the St. Elias (not visible from the highway) are: Mount Logan, Canada's highest peak, at 19,520 feet/5,950m; Mount St. Elias, 18,008 feet/5,489m; Mount Lucania, 17,147 feet/5,226m; King Peak, 16,971 feet/5,173m; Mount Steele, Mount Wood, Mount Vancouver and Mount Hubbard, all over 15,000 feet/4,572m.

DC 1016.5 (1686.7 km) F 471.5 (758.8 km) Turnout to west with view of Kluane Ranges.

DC 1017.2 (1687.8 km) F 470.8 (757.7 km) Christmas Creek.

DC 1019.8 (1692 km) F 468.2 (753.5 km) First glimpse of Kluane Lake for northbound travelers at Boutillier Summit (elev. 3,293 feet/1,003m), second highest point on the highway between Whitehorse and Fairbanks.

DC 1020 (1692.5 km) F 468 (753.2 km) Turnout to east with information plaques on area history and geography.

DC 1020.3 (1693 km) F 467.7 (752.7 km) **Historical Milepost 1053.** Turn off to east at camera viewpoint sign for Silver City and bed and breakfast. Follow dirt and gravel road 3.1 miles/5 km to ruins of Silver City. This old trading post, with roadhouse and North West Mounted Police barracks, was on the wagon road from Whitehorse to the placer goldfields of Kluane Lake (1904-24). Good photo opportunities.

Kluane Bed and Breakfast. Just 3 miles off the highway at historical Silver City on the shore of Kluane Lake. Private heated A-frame cabins with mountain view, cooking and shower facilities, full family-style

Historic Silver City at Milepost DC 1020.3. (Earl L. Brown, staff)

KLUANE BED & BREAKFAST

Km 1693 - Mile 1055

"3 miles off Alaska Highway at Historic Silver City on the shore of Kluane Lake"

• Private Heated A-Frame Cabins
• Full Family Style Breakfast
• Cooking and Shower Facilities

Reservations Recommended

Mobile Operator 2M 3924
Destruction Bay Channel

General Delivery
Destruction Bay
Yukon Y0B 1H0

Mile 1022 Alaska Highway
MODERN MOTEL AND R.V. PARK

145 Seat Licensed Restaurant
Gift Shop • Coin-op Laundry

TOUR GROUPS WELCOME
(please phone ahead)

Beer and Liquor To Go
Ice

SKIERS WELCOME

Showers and Tubs • Ample Parking • Full Pull-through Hookups
Scenic, Natural Camping Area
Winter Rates and Ski Packages Available • Relax By The Fire In Our Cocktail Lounge

Mackintosh Lodge

Phone (403) 634-2301   Unleaded Gas

1992 ■ The MILEPOST® 143

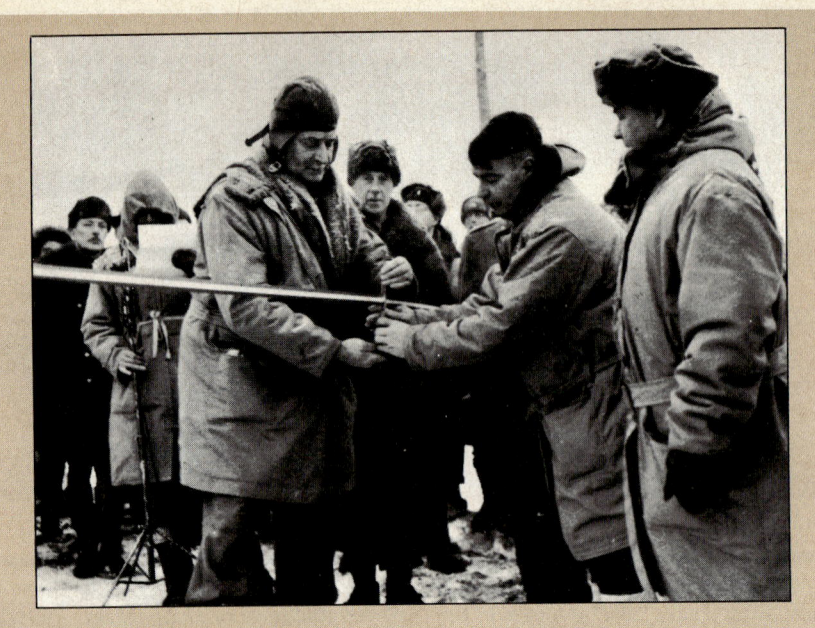

Soldiers Summit

On a blizzardy Nov. 20, 1942, the Alaska Highway was officially opened with a ribbon-cutting ceremony at Soldiers Summit, Mile 1061. A red, white and blue ribbon was stretched across the road and 5 U.S. soldiers and 8 RCMP constables in dress uniform lined up facing the ribbon. The ribbon was cut by E.L. Bartlett, then Alaska's voteless delegate to Congress and later senator, and Canada's Ian MacKenzie, MP from Ottawa, while the 18th Engineers band played "God Save the King" and "The Star Spangled Banner."

The Alaska Highway winds along Kluane Lake. (John W. Warden)

breakfast. Your hosts—The Sias Family, a sixth generation Yukon family. Contact mobile operator, 2M 3924, Destruction Bay channel. Reservations recommended. General Delivery, Destruction Bay, Yukon Y0B 1H0. [ADVERTISEMENT]

DC 1020.9 (1694 km) **F 467.1** (751.7 km) Silver Creek.

DC 1022.5 (1696.5 km) **F 465.5** (749.1 km) Turnoff to east for Kluane Lake Research Station; station and airstrip are 0.9 mile/1.4 km via a straight gravel road. This research station is sponsored by the Arctic Institute of North America, University of Calgary.

Highway follows west shore of Kluane Lake next 39 miles/63 km northbound to Burwash Landing.

DC 1023.7 (1698.5 km) **F 464.3** (747.2 km) **Historical Milepost 1056.** Kluane Camp commemorative plaque. Kluane Lake Lodge (current status unknown).

DC 1026.8 (1703.4 km) **F 461.2** (742.2 km) Slim's River East trail; parking at trailhead.

DC 1027.8 (1705 km) **F 460.2** (740.6 km) Slim's River bridge (clearance 17.7 feet/ 5.4m). Sheep Mountain is directly ahead for northbound travelers. The highway winds along Kluane Lake: Drive carefully!

DC 1029 (1706.8 km) **F 459** (738.7 km) Sheep Mountain visitor information centre; excellent interpretive programs, parking, outhouses. Open mid-May to mid-September, hours are 9 A.M. to 7 P.M. in summer (10 A.M. to 6 P.M. spring and fall). Stop here for information on Kluane National Park's flora and fauna. A viewing telescope is set up to look for sheep on Sheep Mountain. This is the sheep's winter range; best chance to see them is late August and September, good chance in late May to early June. Slim's River West trail; trailhead adjacent visitor information centre.

DC 1030.7 (1709.5 km) **F 457.3** (735.9 km) **Historical Milepost 1061.** Soldier's Summit. A sign on the lake side of the highway commemorates the official opening of the Alaska Highway held here on Nov. 20, 1942. A rededication ceremony is planned for Nov. 20, 1992, at Soldier's Summit.

Across the highway from the commemorative sign is an old cabin. The small white cross on the side of Sheep Mountain marks the grave of Alexander Clark Fisher, a prospector who came into this area about 1906. Several turnouts overlooking Kluane Lake next mile northbound. This beautiful lake is the largest in Yukon Territory, covering approximately 154 square miles/400 square km. The Ruby Range lies on the east side of the lake. Boat rentals are available at Destruction Bay and Burwash Landing.

Kluane Lake, excellent fishing for lake trout, northern pike and grayling.

DC 1031.9 (1711.7 km) **F 456.1** (734 km) **Historical Mile 1064. Bayshore Motel and Restaurant.** Located on the shores of beautiful Kluane Lake just 3 miles north of Sheep Mountain. Enjoy the friendly down-home atmosphere and cooking. Souvenirs, local handicrafts, art work and gold jewelry for sale. 6 units with showers. Totem oil products, unleaded and diesel. Dump station. Minor repairs. RV sites and tent camping. Affordable family-sized lakeshore straight-walled tent accommodations. Everyone welcome! Your hosts, Jim and Gaile Lewis. (403) 841-4551. [ADVERTISEMENT]

DC 1034.5 (1715.8 km) **F 453.5** (729.8 km) Williscroft Creek. Trailhead to west; 1 mile/1.6 km hike to Williscroft Canyon.

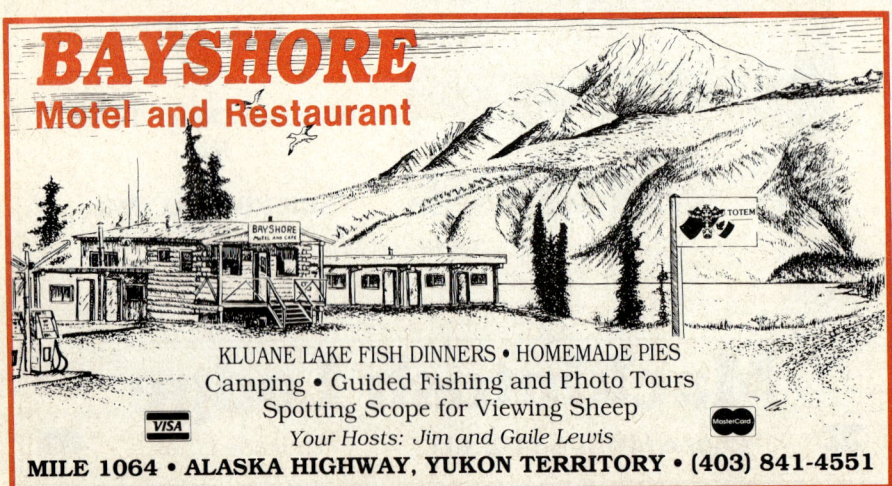

BAYSHORE Motel and Restaurant

KLUANE LAKE FISH DINNERS • HOMEMADE PIES
Camping • Guided Fishing and Photo Tours
Spotting Scope for Viewing Sheep
Your Hosts: Jim and Gaile Lewis
MILE 1064 • ALASKA HIGHWAY, YUKON TERRITORY • (403) 841-4551

DC 1034.9 (1717 km) F 453.1 (729.2 km) **Historical Mile 1067.** Cottonwood campground to east. ▲

Cottonwood RV Park and Campground. See display ad this section.

DC 1039.7 (1724.7 km) F 448.3 (721.4 km) Congdon Creek trailhead to west; 16-mile/26-km hike to Sheep Mountain.

DC 1039.9 (1725 km) F 448.1 (721.1 km) **Historical Mile 1072.** Turnoff to east for Congdon Creek Yukon government campground on Kluane Lake. Drive in 0.4 mile/0.6 km via gravel loop road; tenting area, 77 level sites (some pull-through), outhouses, kitchen shelters, water pump, firewood, firepits, picnic tables, sandy beach, interpretive talks, playground, boat launch. Camping fee $8. ▲

DC 1040.4 (1725.6 km) F 447.6 (720.3 km) Congdon Creek. According to R. Coutts, *Yukon: Places & Names*, Congdon Creek is believed to have been named by a miner after Frederick Tennyson Congdon. A lawyer from Nova Scotia, Congdon came to the Yukon in 1898 and held various political posts until 1911.

DC 1046.9 (1735.3 km) F 441.1 (709.9 km) Nines Creek. Turnout to east.

DC 1047.3 (1736.2 km) F 440.7 (709.2 km) Mines Creek.

DC 1048.9 (1739 km) F 439.1 (706.6 km) Bock's Brook.

DC 1051.5 (1743 km) F 436.5 (702.5 km) **Historical Milepost 1083. DESTRUCTION BAY** (pop. less than 100). **Emergency Services: Health clinic**, phone 841-4151; **Ambulance**, phone 841-5331. Located on the shore of Kluane Lake, Destruction Bay is one of several towns which grew out of the building of the Alaska Highway. It earned its name when a storm destroyed buildings and materials here. A highway maintenance camp is located here. Destruction Bay has camping, boat launch, boat rentals and guided fishing tours. The Phil Temple Memorial Rodeo and Fair is scheduled to take place here July 31 to Aug. 2, 1992. Food, gas and lodging at the Talbot Arm, west side of highway; open year-round. ◆◀▲

Talbot Arm Motel. See display ad this section.

DC 1051.9 (1743.6 km) F 436.1 (701.8 km) Rest area.

DC 1055.1 (1748.8 km) F 432.9 (696.7 km) Lewes Creek.

DC 1058.3 (1753.9 km) F 429.7 (691.5 km) Halfbreed Creek trailhead.

DC 1061.5 (1759 km) F 426.5 (686.4 km) **Historical Milepost 1093.** Turnoff to east for **BURWASH LANDING**, a resort with gas, food, camping and lodging on Kluane Lake. Boat rentals and Kluane Lake fishing trips available. Flightseeing trips of Kluane National Park are available out of Burwash Landing.

Burwash Landing was settled in 1904 by the Jacquot brothers, Louis and Eugene, as a supply centre for local miners. The log mission here, Our Lady of the Holy Rosary, was built in 1944.

The highly recommended Kluane Museum of Natural History is located on the east side of highway at the turnoff; open 9 A.M. to 9 P.M. in summer. Wildlife, minerals and other natural history exhibits, and a craft shop. Admission charged.

Special events in the community for the Alaska Highway Rendezvous '92 include Kluane Kapers, a Native cultural display and Native cultural performances. The Floatplane Rally and Competition is scheduled

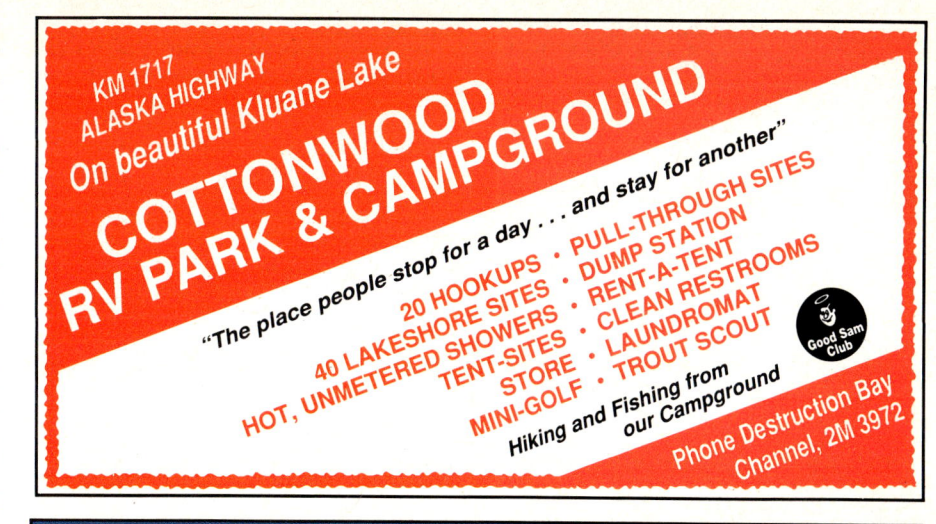

KM 1717 ALASKA HIGHWAY
On beautiful Kluane Lake

COTTONWOOD RV PARK & CAMPGROUND

"The place people stop for a day . . . and stay for another"

- 20 HOOKUPS
- PULL-THROUGH SITES
- 40 LAKESHORE SITES
- DUMP STATION
- HOT, UNMETERED SHOWERS
- RENT-A-TENT
- TENT-SITES
- CLEAN RESTROOMS
- STORE
- LAUNDROMAT
- MINI-GOLF
- TROUT SCOUT

Hiking and Fishing from our Campground

Phone Destruction Bay Channel, 2M 3972

Good Sam Club

TALBOT ARM MOTEL

Rebuilt in 1987 and Ready to Serve All Alaska Highway Travellers Year-Round

WITH

- **32 MODERN SPACIOUS CLEAN ROOMS**
  Complimented with Satellite TV and Laundromat

- **90-SEAT CAFETERIA**
  Good Food Already Prepared for Tour Groups and Others

- **FULL SERVE DINING ROOM**
  Friendly, Efficient Waitered Service for Families, Truckers, and Small Groups

- **INTIMATE LOUNGE**
  Relaxing . . . Drinks also served in the Dining Room

- **CHEVRON SERVICE STATION**
  Gasoline, Diesel, Oils and Other Automotive Necessities including Towing, Tire Repairs, Propane, etc.

- **GENERAL STORE**
  Local and Canadian-made Souvenirs, T-Shirts, Sunglasses, Fresh, Frozen and Canned Goods, Cigarettes, *Film*, Toiletries and Some Drug Store Remedies, *Post Cards, Souvenir Pins*

- **CAMPERS and MOTORHOMES • RV Park**
  Propane, Dump Station, Electric Hookups, Drinking Water, Store, Showers, Laundromat, Large Clean Restrooms • ICE

FREE PARKING • WINTER PLUG-INS

—FOR RESERVATIONS—CALL: (403) 841-4461
WRITE: Box M, Destruction Bay, Yukon, Y0B 1H0

DEDICATED SERVICE TO TRAVELLERS SINCE 1967
Garry and Sheree Van der Veen, Your Hosts

for June 25-26 in Burwash Landing.
Burwash Landing Resort & R.V. Park. See display ad this section.
Glacier Air Tours. See display ad this section.
DC 1062.7 (1761 km) **F 425.3** (684.4 km) **Historical Milepost 1094. Private Aircraft:** Burwash Yukon government airstrip to north; elev. 2,643 feet/806m; length 6,000 feet/1,829m; gravel.
DC 1067 (1768.8 km) **F 421** (677.5 km) Duke River bridge (clearance 17.7 feet/5.4m). The Duke River flows into Kluane Lake; named for George Duke, an early prospector.
DC 1071.9 (1776.5 km) **F 416.1** (669.6 km) Turnout to north. Burwash Creek, named for Lachlin Taylor Burwash, a mining recorder at Silver City in 1903.
DC 1076.7 (1784.1 km) **F 411.3** (661.9 km) Sakiw Creek.
DC 1078.5 (1787 km) **F 409.5** (659 km) Buildings to west belong to Hudson Bay Mining and Smelting Co.'s Wellgreen Nickel Mines, named for Wellington Bridgeman Green, the prospector who discovered the mineral showing in 1952. During the mine's operation, from May 1972 to July 1973, 3 shiploads of concentrates (averaging 13,000 tons each) were trucked to Haines, AK. The material proved to be too insufficient to be economical. No facilities or services.
DC 1079.4 (1788.5 km) **F 408.6** (657.6 km) Quill Creek.
DC 1080.9 (1791 km) **F 407.1** (655.1 km) Glacier Creek. Kluane River to east of highway.
DC 1083.5 (1795.5 km) **F 404.5** (651 km) Monument to U.S. Army lieutenant who lost his life during construction of the Alaska Highway.
DC 1084.6 (1797.2 km) **F 403.4** (649.2 km) **Historical Mile 1118** Kluane Wilderness Village; gas, restaurant, camping and lodging. Open year-round. Viewing platform of: Mount Kennedy, Mount Logan and Mount Lucania. Halfway mark between Whitehorse and Tok. ▲
Katz 'N Jammer Gold. See display ad this section.
Kluane Wilderness Village. See display ad this section.
Scully's Lounge. See display ad this section.
DC 1086.6 (1799.5 km) **F 401.4** (646 km) Swede Johnson Creek. Turnout to east.
DC 1087.4 (1801.7 km) **F 400.6** (644.7 km) *CAUTION: Rough road northbound next 168 km (104 miles), maximum 70 kmph (about 45 mph), some gravel patches, some winding sections. Drive carefully, especially vehicles with trailers. Road surface can be particularly hard on trailer hitches.*
DC 1091.3 (1808 km) **F 396.7** (638.4 km) Buildings to east are a dormant pump station once used to pressure up fuel being transferred from Haines to Fairbanks.
DC 1095 (1814 km) **F 393** (632.4 km) NorthwesTel microwave tower visible ahead northbound.
DC 1095.4 (1814.6 km) **F 392.6** (631.8 km) Abandoned Mountain View Lodge. View of Donjek River Valley.
Alaska Highway workers faced one of their toughest construction jobs during completion of the Alaska Highway in 1943 from the Donjek River to the Alaska border. Swampy ground underlain by permafrost, numerous creeks, lakes and rivers, plus a thick insulating ground cover made this section particularly difficult for road builders.
DC 1096.3 (1816 km) **F 391.7** (630.4 km) Turnout to west with view of Donjek River Valley and the Icefield Ranges of the St. Elias Mountains. Interpretive display.
DC 1100 (1820 km) **F 388** (624.4 km) Donjek River bridge (clearance 17.4 feet/5.3m). Access to river at north end of bridge on west side of highway. This wide silty river is a major tributary of the White River. According to R. Coutts *Yukon: Places & Names*, the Donjek is believed to have been named by Charles Willard Hayes in 1891 from the Indian word for a peavine that grows in the area.
Watch for breaks in surfacing next several miles northbound.
DC 1113.5 (1844.4 km) **F 374.5** (602.7 km) **Edith Creek** bridge, turnout to west. Try your hand at gold panning here, "colours" have been found. Grayling fishing, June through September.
DC 1113.8 (1844.8 km) **F 374.2** (602.2

Glacier AIR TOURS

See spectacular Mount Logan — Canada's highest peak — and view the largest expanse of nonpolar permanent ice in the world

Those who have flown with us have said:
"It was the highlight of our northern vacation."

Departs from the Burwash Landing Resort
(403) 841-5171
Mile 1093 Alaska Highway, Yukon

---

32 UNITS • $25 AND UP • 24-HOUR ACCOMMODATIONS
135-SEAT LICENSED DINING ROOM AND LOUNGE
Full Service Station — Open 24 Hours

Overlooking Beautiful Kluane Lake

BURWASH LANDING RESORT & RV Park

MILE 1093 KM 1759
ALASKA HIGHWAY

OPEN 6:30 A.M.
TO MIDNIGHT

BUS TOURS WELCOME
Over 100 Shaded Sites

PHONE (403) 841-4441
FAX (403) 841-4444

Glacier flights over the vast ice fields of Kluane National Park.
Fishing Trips, Boat Rentals, Gold Panning, Lakeshore RV Parking, Tenting, Hiking, Camping

VISA "YOUR PLACE" — Self-serve Bus Service for 350 MasterCard

Katz 'N Jammer Gold
REASONABLE PRICES
– Gold Nugget Jewelry
– Local Native Crafts and Beadwork
– Gifts
– Painting and Sketches by Local Artists
– Original Work by Artist Brent Kieser

Ask for your FREE Copper Nugget

Mile 1118 Alaska Highway, Yukon Y1A 3V4
Adjacent to service station

JOIN US FOR THE PARTY
JUNE - SEPTEMBER 1992
CELEBRATING THE
50TH ANNIVERSARY
OF THE ALASKA HIGHWAY

Live entertainment nightly in Scully's Lounge at Kluane Wilderness Village

EASY LISTENING TUNES OF
LORNE AND IKE McKEARNEY

Old-time Favourites
Bluegrass and Country Western
Rockabilly Classics

THEY'LL PLAY YOUR REQUESTS
Relax and enjoy some good old-fashioned fun!

km) **Historical Mile 1147. Pine Valley Motel and Cafe.** Thanks to all our customers for your patronage from your hosts Carmen and Wayne. Add your card to our collection. The largest collection of business cards in western Canada. We have unleaded and diesel available (seniors gas discount). Tire repairs, towing, minor repairs and welding. Ready for 1992—RV park and campground, pull-throughs, water and power hookups, showers included, dump station, picnic tables, firepits and horseshoe pits. Good Sam and caravan discounts. Gold panning and good fishing at Edith Creek. Motel units, cabins with colour TV, mini-rooms and rent-a-tent available. Licensed cafe with full menu and bakery, featuring hearty soups, homemade bread, pies and pastries. Ask about occasional salmon and game barbecues (reservations required). Off-sales for beer, wine and spirits. Pay phone, block ice, fishing license and tackle, souvenirs. Second

Road-building machinery

A D-8 cat stuck in swampy ground. Crews often used "swamp cats" on difficult sections of the pioneer road. Spare tractor treads were split down the middle with one of the resulting halves then welded onto the normal width of tread on the tractor, thus increasing the bearing area. Although, as Senior Highway Engineer R.E. Royall pointed out, the "greatest array of road-building machinery ever assembled on a single project in the history of American road building" was strung out along the Alaska Highway, lack of spare parts idled many machines and resourceful mechanics did what they could to keep the equipment going. Much of the government machinery was scrounged from the C.C.C. and W.P.A. Contractors had to transport their equipment an average of 2,700 miles to the job site.

MILE 1147   KM 1845

PINE VALLEY MOTEL

cafe WITH HOME BAKING

KLUANE WILDERNESS VILLAGE

The Most Reasons To Stop, Year-Around

MILE 1118

MOTOR COACH STOP
- Self-serve Dining Room
  Newly renovated — Seats 150
- Lunch, coffee, overnight
- **We cater to overnight buses**

RESTAURANT
- Full Service
  Homemade pies and pastries —
  our specialty

"SCULLY'S" LOUNGE
- *See the world-famous "Burl Bar"*
- Package Liquor

SOUVENIRS • GROCERIES
- Unique BURL Gifts —
  See Scully at work
- **24-Hour** One-stop Grocery Shop

24-HR. SERVICE STATION
- Towing • Tires
- Welding • Repairs
- Gas • Diesel
- Propane
- Gulf, Petro-Canada, Mobil Travel cards accepted
- U-Haul Repair Depot

ACCOMMODATIONS
- 25 Log Cabins (May - October)
  Each with electric heat and bath
- 6 Motel Units
  Year-Around
  Satellite TV   **NEW**

All beds with Beautyrest Mattresses

RVs & CAMPERS
- Full-service and
  Pull-through Hook-ups
- Campsites
- BBQ Pit • Cookhouse
- Showers • Bag Ice • Propane
- Laundromat • Public Phone

RAINBOW TROUT FISHING!
- Stocked Lake
- *No fishing license required*
- Boat and Tackle Rentals

LOCATION
WHITEHORSE
TOK, ALASKA   200 MILES

BEAVER CREEK
HAINES JUNCTION   100 MILES

YOUR HOSTS LIZ AND JOHN TROUT
Phone ahead for reservations — Year-Around: (403) 841-4141
Or Write: Mile 1118 Alaska Highway, Yukon Territory Y1A 3V4

BEAR FLATS LODGE AT KOIDERN

RV PARK • CAFE • MOTEL
Camping • Showers
Welding • Minor Repairs

MILE 1167, ALASKA HIGHWAY
Yukon, Canada Y1A 3V4   (403) 862-7401

Ida's MOTEL & CAFE
Husky

"IN CANADA'S MOST WESTERLY COMMUNITY"

MILE 1202 KM 1934.4   OPEN YEAR-ROUND

14 Comfortable MOTEL UNITS • Rooms with Private Baths and TV

CAFE featuring Homemade Pastries and Homestlye Cooking

Licensed CAFE and DINING ROOM — 7 a.m. - 10 p.m. May-August
7 a.m. - 9 p.m. Sept.-April
LOUNGE and POOL ROOM — 5 p.m. - 2 a.m.
Liquor • Off Sales — 12 Noon - 1 a.m.

Ask about our BBQ Pit – Fry your own steak with salad bar

HOMEY ATMOSPHERE   *Piano for entertainment*

DIESEL and UNLEADED GAS — 7 a.m. - 2 a.m.
Pay Telephone • Lots of FREE RV Parking

VISA   MasterCard

"Our clocks are one hour ahead of Alaska Time"

Beaver Creek, Yukon Y0B 1A0   Phone (403) 862-7223

KM 1882 ◆ Mile 1169
ALASKA HIGHWAY

OPEN YEAR AROUND
PHONE: (403) 862-7408

WHITE RIVER MOTOR INN
SERVING OUR CUSTOMERS FOR 35 YEARS

Chevron Products ◆ Unleaded Gas ◆ Propane ◆ Diesel Fuel ◆ Jet B Aviation Fuel

Chevron
Warm car storage for sure winter starts ◆ Windshield cleaned ◆ Chevron, VISA, MasterCard, and affiliated cards honored

Liquor and Cold Beer to go ◆ All Homemade Foods, Soups and Baking
Log Cabins with Private Bath ◆ Rooms in Main Lodge ◆ Television ◆ Pay Phone
Good Water ◆ Tenting, Camping and RV Hookups ◆ Dump Station
Laundromat and Showers ◆ Modern, Clean Rest Rooms ◆ Fishing Licenses
Hunting and Fishing Information ◆ Trail Rides and Old Mine Tours
Salmon Bakes and Horse Drawn Wagon Rides Daily ◆ Overnight Livestock Corrals

---

annual spring opener on May 24th long weekend. Harleys welcome. Free cup of coffee in the morning to get you going with your overnight stay. MasterCard and VISA. Phone (403) 862-7407. In winter, contact (403) 633-6478. [ADVERTISEMENT] ▲

DC 1118.3 (1852.2 km) **F 369.7** (595 km) Koidern River bridge No. 1.

DC 1118.8 (1853 km) **F 369.2** (594.2 km) **Historical Mile 1152.** Lake Creek Yukon government campground just west of highway; 30 large level sites (6 pull-through), water pump, litter barrels, firewood, firepits, picnic tables, kitchen shelter and outhouses. Camping fee $8. ▲

DC 1122.7 (1859.5 km) **F 365.3** (587.9 km) **Historical Milepost 1156.** Longs Creek.

DC 1125 (1863.5 km) **F 363** (584.2 km) Turnout to east with litter barrel.

DC 1125.7 (1864.7 km) **F 362.3** (583 km) **Pickhandle Lake** to west, good fishing from boat for northern pike all summer; also grayling, whitefish and lingcod.

DC 1128 (1868.4 km) **F 360** (579.3 km) Aptly named Reflection Lake to west mirrors the Kluane Ranges. The highway parallels this range between Koidern and Haines Junction.

DC 1130.6 (1872.6 km) **F 357.4** (575.2 km) **Historical Mile 1164.** Lodge. There are 2 "lodges" at Koidern; continue north past Koidern River bridge No. 2 for Bear Flats Lodge at Koidern.

DC 1130.7 (1872.8 km) **F 357.3** (575 km) Koidern River bridge No. 2.

DC 1133.7 (1877.6 km) **F 354.3** (570.2 km) **Historical Milepost 1167.** Bear Flats Lodge; gas, food, camping and lodging.

Bear Flats Lodge and Campgrounds. On left side northbound, 3 miles past Koidern River bridge No. 2. RV park with electric and water hookups and central dumps. A large grassy tenting area with firepits. Excellent well water, hot showers and flush toilet for our serviced sites, and 10 acres of free unserviced camping, which sure beats a gravel pit or roadside. Our motel units each have full private baths and TV. Rates begin at $40 for a single and they are clean. We also offer discounts to all active duty and retired military. Advance motel reservations are almost a must during June through August. There is a use-at-your-own-risk airstrip 60 feet by 1,400 feet with 500-foot clear approach on either end, and field elevation of 2,500 ASL. We serve complete meals in our restaurant which has been rated by the Yukon Liquor Corp. as "One of the cleanest and a credit to the highway." Our salads are mostly from our greenhouse and "Shari's" soups, cinnamon rolls and homemade pies are known from Miami to Nome and Melbourne to Rome and we can serve beer and wine with meals. The gold pan paintings are Shari's and she plans to have some canvas paintings this year. Each painting is an original. We also have a trade-a-book shelf in the cafe. We have diesel, gas and propane sales and accept VISA or MasterCard. For the 50th anniversary of the building of the Alcan and in honour of our veterans we will be flying the 50 state, 10 provincial, 2 territorial and national flags of the U.S. and Canada. The history of the origin of each flag will be displayed in our main building. This should be a must photograph for our tourists and we are planning a free wild game barbecue for July 4 and invite all to stop by. Bring your own "trimmin's" and the meat is free. We will open on May 1 and close sometime in September. Your hosts are Shari and Noland Hallman (Sgt. Major, U.S. Army, Retired). Phone (403) 862-7401. [ADVERTISEMENT] ▲

DC 1135 (1880 km) **F 353** (568 km) **Historical Mile 1169.** White River Motor Inn; food, gas, lodging and camping. Open year-round. ▲

White River Motor Inn. See display ad this section.

DC 1135.6 (1881 km) **F 352.4** (567.1 km) White River bridge, clearance 17.1 feet/5.2m. The White River, a major tributary of the Yukon River, was named by Hudson's Bay Co. explorer Robert Campbell for its white colour, caused by the volcanic ash in the water. *This river is considered very dangerous; not recommended for boating.*

CAUTION: *Slow down for sharp turn in*

148   The MILEPOST® ■ 1992

road at north end of bridge.

DC 1141.5 (1890.5 km) F 346.5 (557.6 km) **Moose Lake** to west, grayling to 18 inches, use dry flies and small spinners, midsummer. Boat needed for lake.

DC 1144.3 (1895 km) F 343.7 (553.1 km) Sanpete Creek, named by an early prospector after Sanpete County in Utah.

DC 1147.5 (1900.3 km) F 340.5 (548 km) Dry Creek No. 1. Turnout to east.

DC 1149.8 (1904 km) F 338.2 (544.3 km) CAUTION: Slow down for bumpy banked descent to Dry Creek No. 2.

DC 1150.3 (1904.5 km) F 337.7 (543.5 km) **Historical Mile 1184.** Dry Creek No. 2. Historical marker to west about the Chrisna gold rush.

DC 1155 (1911.8 km) F 333 (535.9 km) Small Lake to east.

DC 1155.2 (1913 km) F 332.8 (535.6 km) **Historical Milepost 1188.** Turnoff for Snag Junction Yukon government campground, 0.4 mile/0.6 km in on gravel loop road. There are 15 tent and vehicle sites (some level), a kitchen shelter, outhouses, picnic tables, firewood, firepits and litter barrels. Camping fee $8. Small-boat launch. Swimming in Small Lake. A dirt road (status unknown) connects the Alaska Highway here with the abandoned airfield and Indian village at Snag to the northeast.

DC 1162.1 (1924.5 km) F 325.9 (524.5 km) Inger Creek.

DC 1165.7 (1930 km) F 322.3 (518.7 km) View of Nutzotin Mountains to northwest, Kluane Ranges to southwest. On a clear day you should be able to see the snow-clad Wrangell Mountains in the distance to the west.

DC 1167.2 (1932.4 km) F 320.8 (516.3 km) Beaver Creek plank bridge, clearance 17.1 feet/5.2m.

Beaver Creek

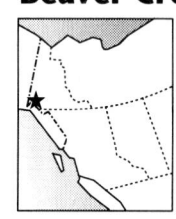

DC 1168.5 (1934.5 km) F 319.5 (514.2 km) **Historical Milepost 1202.** Driving distance to Haines Junction, 184 miles/295 km; to Tok, 113 miles/182 km; to Haines, 334 miles/537.5 km. **Population:** 106. **Emergency Services:** RCMP, phone 862-7300. **Visitor Information:** Yukon government visitor information centre open daily 9 A.M. to 9 P.M. late May through mid-September.

Site of the old Canadian customs station. Local residents were pleased to see customs relocated north of town in 1983, having long endured the flashing lights and screaming sirens set off whenever a tourist forgot to stop.

Beaver Creek is 1 of 2 sites where Alaska Highway construction crews working from opposite directions connected the highway. In October 1942, Alaska Highway construction operations were being rushed to conclusion as winter set in. Eastern and western sector construction crews pushed through to meet at a junction on Beaver Creek, thus making it possible for the first time for

BEAVER CREEK ADVERTISERS

Far West Service Centre ...Ph. (403) 862-7220
Ida's Motel & Cafe............Ph. (403) 862-7223
Westmark Inn.....................Ph. 800-478-1111

FAR WEST

Canada's Most Westerly Service Centre

Gas • Diesel • Propane • Repairs • Welding • Mechanic • 24-Hour Towing
RV Parking • Hookups • Water • Ice • Coffee • Pop • Candy • Ice Cream
Souvenirs • T-Shirts

Mile 1202 Alaska Highway, Beaver Creek, Yukon, Canada • (403) 862-7220

Award-winning photos by Alaskan photographer Alissa Crandall and engaging text written by Gloria Maschmeyer combine to reveal the people and landscape of the North in all seasons in ALONG THE ALASKA HIGHWAY—a perfect companion to *The MILEPOST*®. Available from bookstores or call toll free 1-800-343-4567, ext. 571.

We've got you covered at the border.

The highway traveler will find comfort and convenience at our modern rendition of the traditional roadhouse.

• 174 Rooms •
• Dining Room and Lounge •
• Guest Laundry • Wildlife Display •

Special Summer Value Rates from $49

Rooms at lower rates are capacity controlled and good on selected rooms & dates only. Call for complete information. Subject to change without notice.

Add a little spice to your visit with our
Trapper's Rendezvous Party
A spectacular barbecue feast and live stage show held evenings during the summer at the Inn.

Westmark Inn

BEAVER CREEK

MP 1202 Alaska Highway, Beaver Creek, YT, Canada • **OPEN SEASONALLY**
Central Reservations: **1-800-544-0970** (U.S.), **1-800-999-2570** (Canada)
Westmark Hotels covers the north with hotels and inns throughout Alaska and the Yukon. Come be our guest.

Northern Wonders
The finest northern gifts and handicrafts at very reasonable prices
Located at the Westmark Hotel

BORDER CITY LODGE

2ND GAS STOP in Alaska

Located 3 1/2 miles north of U.S. Customs

A **TEXACO** SUPER VOLUME PUMPER using 12 Gas & Diesel Pumps

RV PARKING, EASY IN-OUT

Everyday low fuel prices and clean indoor restrooms

CAFE
Specializing in Homemade Pies & Rolls

OPEN LONG HOURS
OPEN YEAR AROUND
Large, clean **ROOMS** with private baths

BEAUTY SHOP

For Information and reservations, call (907) 774-2211
Ask for Wilma or Louis

Largest Selection on the Alcan of Postcards, Caps, Sweat and T-Shirts

Tour Buses Welcome With Advance Calls

Stop, Shop, Sleep, Eat and Fuel Up at the FRIENDLIEST STOP on the Alcan Highway.

1992 Events

MAY
20-10/20 Horseshoe Pits & Tournament
23 50th Anniversary Contact Point Monument and Reunion

JUNE
1-10/20 Horseshoe Tournament continues
17-18 Army Motors Convoy

JULY
1-10/20 Horseshoe Tournament continues

SEPTEMBER
23-24 Rallye Alaska Highway '92

OCTOBER
1-20 Horseshoe Tournament continues

---

vehicles to travel the entire length of the highway. East-west crews had connected at Contact Creek on Sept. 25, 1942.

Motels, gas stations with repair service, a post office, and licensed restaurants are located here. Beaver Creek is also an overnight stop for bus travelers. Private RV park with hookups, hot showers, store, laundry and dump station. ▲

The interesting looking church here is Our Lady of Grace mission. Built in 1961, it is 1 of 3 Catholic missions on the north Alaska Highway (the others are in Burwash Landing and Haines Junction). Services from the last Sunday of May to first Sunday of September. There is a public swimming pool beside the community club. Check with the information centre about the live stage show at the Westmark Inn, evenings in summer; admission charged.

Ida's Motel & Cafe, a welcome stopping spot on the highway offering the traveler licensed cafe and dining room with home-style cooking and pastries, open daily from 7 A.M. Regular rooms from $50, larger rooms from $60 (+ $5 per additional person). Private baths and TV. Deposit required for pets. Soft ice cream, souvenirs, sweaters and hats. Husky oil products available 7 A.M. to 2 A.M. Open year-round. Reservations, Mile 1202, Alaska Highway, Beaver Creek, YT Y0B 1A0. (403) 862-7223. Enjoy your Alaska Highway adventure! [ADVERTISEMENT]

Alaska Highway Log

(continued)
Distance* from Dawson Creek (DC) is followed by distance from Fairbanks (F). Original mileposts are indicated in the text as Historical Mile.
*Mileages from Dawson Creek are based on actual driving distance. Kilometres from Dawson Creek are based on physical kilometreposts. Please read Mileposts and Kilometreposts in the introduction for an explanation of how this highway is logged.

DC 1169.7 (1936.3 km) **F 318.3** (512.2 km) Rest area to west with litter barrels and outhouses.
DC 1170.3 (1937.3 km) **F 317.7** (511.3 km) **Private Aircraft:** Beaver Creek airstrip; elev. 2,129 feet/649m; length 3,740 feet/1,140m; gravel; fuel 100. Airport of entry for Canada customs.
DC 1170.5 (1937.6 km) **F 317.5** (511 km) Beaver Creek Canada customs station. Open 24 hours a day year-round. All traffic entering Canada must stop here for clearance.

Narrow winding road from here to border northbound (next 19.4 miles/31.2 km). Watch for bad corners and rough spots in road surface. Watch for construction crews summer 1992.
DC 1175.4 (1945.5 km) **F 312.6** (503.1 km) Snag Creek plank bridge.
DC 1176.3 (1946.9 km) **F 311.7** (501.6 km) Mirror Creek.
DC 1178.3 (1952 km) **F 309.7** (498.4 km) Lake to east, turnout to west.
DC 1186 (1963 km) **F 302** (486 km) Little Scottie Creek.
DC 1189.5 (1967.5 km) **F 298.5** (480.4 km) Historical Mile 1221.4. Turnout with plaque and other markers at Canada-U.S. international border. From the viewing decks, note the narrow clearing marking the border. This is part of the 20-foot-/6-m-wide swath cut by surveyors from 1904 to 1920 along the 141st meridian (from Demarcation Point on the Arctic Ocean south 600 miles/966 km to Mount St. Elias in the Wrangell Mountains) to mark the Alaska-Canada border. This swath continues south to mark the boundary between southeastern Alaska and Canada. Portions of the swath are cleared periodically by the International Boundary Commission.

TIME ZONE CHANGE: Alaska observes Alaska time; Yukon Territory observes Pacific time. See Time Zones in the GENERAL INFORMATION section for details.
DC 1189.8 (1968 km) **F 298.2** (479.9 km) **Mile 1221.8.** U.S. customs border station.

IMPORTANT: The MILEPOST® log now switches to physical mileposts for northbound travelers. For southbound travelers, the log is based on actual driving distance. The Alaska Highway is approximately 32 miles/51 km shorter than the traditional figure of 1,221.8 miles between Dawson Creek and the YT-AK border. Please read the information on Mileposts and Kilometreposts in the introduction to the Alaska Highway.

Northbound: Fair to good pavement to Fairbanks. Watch for frost heaves, potholes and pavement breaks next 40 miles/64 km.

A bicyclist from Holland stops to read an interpretive sign. (Jerrianne Lowther, staff)

Expect road construction.

Southbound: Narrow, winding road to Haines Junction. Fair to good pavement. Watch for frost heaves and rough spots.

ALASKA ROUTE 2
Distance* from Dawson Creek (DC) is followed by distance from Fairbanks (F).
*Mileages from Dawson Creek and Fairbanks are based on physical mileposts in Alaska. Kilometres given are the metric equivalents of these mileages.

DC 1221.8 (1966.3 km) **F 298.2** (479.9 km) Port Alcan U.S. Customs and Immigration Service border station, open 24 hours a day year-round; pay phone (credit card and collect calls only) and restrooms. All traffic entering Alaska must stop for clearance. Phone (907) 774-2242; emergencies, 774-2252.

Read through the GENERAL INFORMATION section for details on alcoholic beverages, holidays, customs requirements, fishing regulations, driving and other aspects of travel-in Alaska and Canada.

DC 1222.5 (1967.4 km) **F 297.5** (478.8 km) Tetlin National Wildlife Refuge boundary sign to west.

DC 1222.7 (1967.7 km) **F 297.3** (478.4 km) Gas station. Border Branch U.S. post office located here; open limited hours.

DC 1223.4 (1968.9 km) **F 296.6** (477.3 km) Scotty Creek bridge.

DC 1224.6 (1970.7 km) **F 295.4** (475.4 km) Double-ended gravel turnout to southwest with USF&WS interpretive signs on wetlands and peoples. Beaver lodges southwest side of highway.

DC 1225.4 (1972 km) **F 294.6** (474.1 km) Gravel turnout to southwest. Access to Desper Creek, canoe launch.

DC 1225.5 (1972.2 km) **F 294.5** (473.9 km) **Border City Lodge**, 3.5 miles north of U.S. customs; second gas stop in Alaska. Low U.S. discount prices, using 12 self-serve pumps for Texaco gas and diesel. Cafe. Homemade pies and rolls daily. Largest selection of Alaska gifts, T-shirts, sweatshirts, caps, souvenirs. Overnight RV parking. Large sleeping rooms with private baths in lodge. Credit cards accepted. Open long hours 7 days a week. Phone (907) 774-2211. See display ad this section. [ADVERTISEMENT] ▲

DC 1227.8 (1975.9 km) **F 292.2** (470.2 km) Large double-ended parking area to southwest with litter barrels and USF&WS interpretive sign on migratory birds and area geography. View to south of lakes in Chisana (SHOE-sanna) River valley along Scotty Creek and west to the Wrangell Mountains. The Chisana gold rush took place in 1913. A mining camp was established on Cross Creek near the Chisana River, 38 miles southeast of Nabesna in the Wrangell Mountains. The settlement's population peaked at 148 in 1920.

DC 1229 (1977.8 km) **F 291** (468.3 km) USF&WS log cabin visitor center to south. Viewing deck and outdoor displays on wildlife and other subjects. Indoor wildlife displays and mounts. Restrooms. Open 7 A.M. to 7 P.M. Memorial Day to mid-September. Current highway conditions and fishing information posted on bulletin board.

DC 1230.9 (1980.9 km) **F 289.1** (465.3 km) View of Island Lake.

DC 1233.3 (1984.7 km) **F 286.7** (461.4 km) Large paved double-ended parking area to northeast on old alignment; litter barrels. Watch for bears.

Watch for frost heaves, patches and potholes northbound and southbound.

DC 1240.3 (1996 km) **F 279.7** (450.1 km) Vertical culverts on either side of highway are an experiment to keep ground from thawing and thus prevent frost heaves.

DC 1243.6 (2001.3 km) **F 276.4** (444.8 km) Paved turnout. Scenic viewpoint to south on loop road has a litter barrel and USF&WS interpretive signs on fire management and the effects of forest fires on the natural history of area. Highway passes through gray sand dunes with occasional outcrops of granite or old metamorphosed rock northbound to Tetlin Junction.

DC 1246.6 (2006.1 km) **F 273.4** (440 km) **Gardiner Creek** bridge; parking to west at south end of bridge. Grayling fishing.

DC 1247.6 (2007.8 km) **F 272.4** (438.4 km) Paved double-ended viewpoint to east with litter barrels.

DC 1249.3 (2010.5 km) **F 270.7** (435.6 km) **Deadman Lake** USF&WS campground, 1.5 miles/2.4 km in on dirt road. Good picnic site with table at entrance to campground access road. The campground has 15 sites on long loop road, some pull-throughs for large RVs and trailers, firepits, toilets, picnic tables, no drinking water, boat ramp and self-guided nature trail. Scenic spot. Swimming and fishing. Northern pike average 2 feet, but skinny (local residents call them "snakes"); use wobbling lures or spinners.

Pavement patches next mile northbound.

DC 1250.1 (2011.8 km) **F 269.9** (434.3 km) Rest area to west. Double-ended paved parking area, 4 picnic tables, litter barrels, concrete fireplaces, toilets, no water.

DC 1252.2 (2015.2 km) **F 267.8** (431 km) Double-ended gravel turnout to south with USF&WS interpretive sign on solar basins (warm ponds and shallow marshes).

DC 1253 (2016.5 km) **F 267** (429.7 km) Views of lakes and muskeg in Chisana River valley.

DC 1253.6 (2017.4 km) **F 266.4** (428.7 km) **Frontier Surplus.** Military surplus goods. Clothing, sleeping bags, extreme cold weather "bunny boots," military tents, ammunition, fishing lures, tanned furs, Alaska T-shirts and caps. Local crafts, shed moose and caribou antlers. Antler products, belt buckles, earrings, bolo ties, hat racks, handmade ulus. "Moosquitoes," diamond willow lamps and canes, finished or unfinished. Used Alaska license plates, cold pop. Open late every day. Motorhome and RV loop. Phone (907) 778-2274. [ADVERTISEMENT]

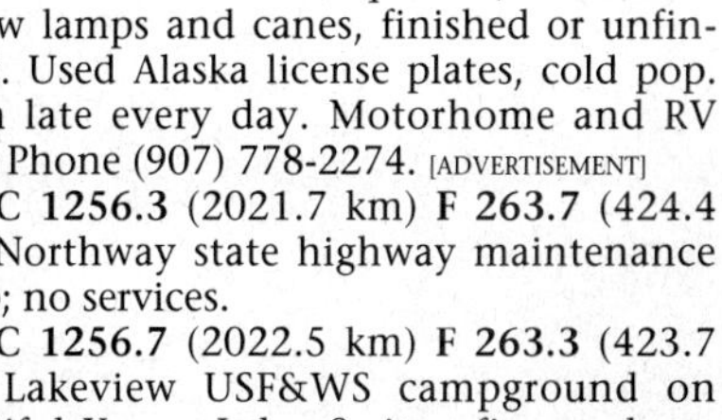

DC 1256.3 (2021.7 km) **F 263.7** (424.4 km) Northway state highway maintenance camp; no services.

DC 1256.7 (2022.5 km) **F 263.3** (423.7 km) Lakeview USF&WS campground on beautiful Yarger Lake; 8 sites, firewood, no drinking water. *NOTE: No turnaround space. Not recommended for trailers, 5th wheelers or large RVs (use Deadman Lake Campground).* ▲

This is a good place to view ducks and loons. Look for the St. Elias Range to the south, Wrangell Mountains to the southwest, and Mentasta Mountains to the west.

Stuck in the mud

Heavy truck traffic, rain and poor drainage turned sections of the pioneer road into an impassable mire. Worst were stretches of swampy ground underlain by permafrost. These sections of road could only be traveled when the ground was frozen. Vehicles trying to cross after the spring thaw sank into the muck and remained there all summer. Men and equipment could advance only after crews scraped away ground cover and backfilled with gravel and rock.

NAABIA NIIGN CAMPGROUND

Full and Partial Hookups • Dump Station
Phone • Laundromat • Showers

COFFEE SHOP
Coffee • Soup • Sandwiches
Hamburgers • Cheeseburgers

TESORO GAS • GROCERIES
Ice Cream • Produce

Phone (907) 778-2297
Mile 1264 Alaska Highway at Northway Junction

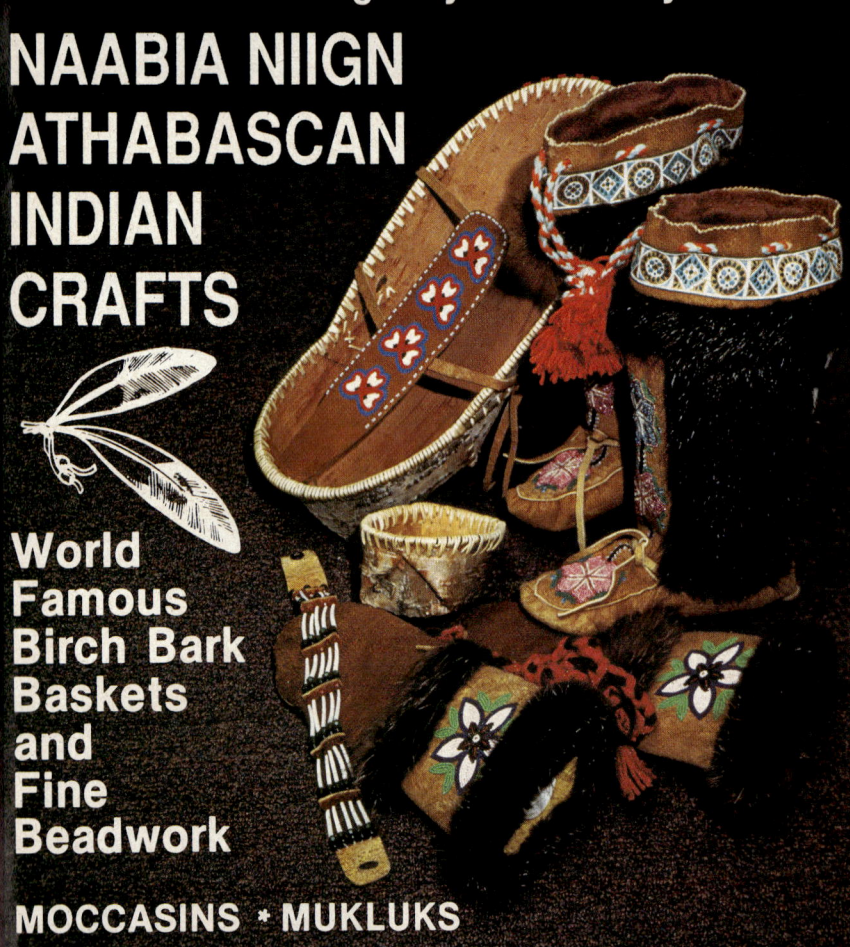

NAABIA NIIGN ATHABASCAN INDIAN CRAFTS

World Famous Birch Bark Baskets and Fine Beadwork

MOCCASINS • MUKLUKS

NAABIA NIIGN, LTD.
ARTS AND CRAFTS SHOP

P.O. BOX 476 • Northway
Alaska 99764

(907) 778-2297

VISA & MASTERCARD ACCEPTED

EXTENDED SUMMER HOURS

MILEPOST 1264 ALASKA HIGHWAY

Roadside wildflowers include sweet pea, pale yellow Indian paintbrush, yarrow and Labrador tea.

DC 1258 (2024.5 km) **F 262** (421.6 km) Watch for rough patches in pavement.

DC 1260.2 (2028 km) **F 259.8** (418.1 km) 1260 Inn roadhouse (current status unknown).

Southbound: Watch for frost heaves, potholes and pavement breaks next 40 miles/64 km to border.

DC 1263.1 (2032.7 km) **F 256.9** (413.4 km) **Wrangell View Service Center.** See display ad this section.

DC 1263.5 (2033.4 km) **F 256.5** (412.8 km) Chisana River parallels the highway to the southwest. This is the land of a thousand ponds, most unnamed. Good trapping country. In early June, travelers may note numerous cottony white seeds blowing in the wind; these seeds are from a species of willow.

DC 1264 (2034.2 km) **F 256** (412 km) **Northway Junction.** Campground, gas, laundromat, store, cafe and Native arts and crafts shop located at junction. An Alaska State Trooper is also stationed here. ▲

Naabia Niign, Ltd. See display ad this section.

A 7-mile/11.3-km side road leads south across the Chisana River bridge to the community of Northway (description follows). A boat launch at Chisana River bridge is 1 of 3 boat access points to Tetlin National Wildlife Refuge.

Northway

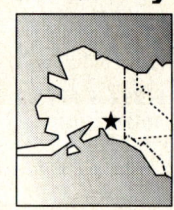

Located 7 miles/11.3 km south of the Alaska Highway via a side road. **Population:** 364 (area). **Emergency Services: Alaska State Troopers,** phone 778-2245. **EMS,** phone 778-2211. **Fire Department,** Clinic.

Elevation: 1,710 feet/521m. **Climate:** Mean monthly temperature in July, 58.5°F/15°C. In January, -21°F/-30°C. Record high 91°F/33°C in June 1969; record low -72°F/-58°C in January 1952.

Private Aircraft: Northway airport, adjacent south; elev. 1,716 feet/523m; length 5,147 feet/1,569m; asphalt; fuel 80, 100, jet; customs available.

Northway has a community hall, post office and modern school. FAA station and customs office are at the airport. Visitor services include motels, grocery, liquor store, propane, gas stations and air taxi service.

Northway Airport Lodge & Motel. See display ad this section.

Historically occupied by Athabascan Indians, Northway was named to honor the village chief who adopted the name of a river boat captain in the early 1900s. The rich Athabascan tradition of dancing, crafts, and hunting and trapping continue today in Northway Village. Local Athabascan handicrafts available for purchase include birch-bark baskets, beadwork accessories, and moose hide and fur items such as moccasins, mukluks, mittens and hats.

Northway's airport was built in the 1940s as part of the Northwest Staging Route. This cooperative project of the United States and Canada was a chain of air bases from Edmonton, AB, through Whitehorse, YT, to Fairbanks. This chain of air bases helped build up and supply Alaska defense during

WWII and also was used during construction of the Alcan and the Canol project. Lend-lease aircraft bound for Russia were flown up this route to Ladd Field (now Fort Wainwright) in Fairbanks. Northway is still an important port of entry for air traffic to Alaska, and a busy one.

Northway is located within Tetlin National Wildlife Refuge. Established in 1980, the 950,000-acre refuge stretches south from the Alaska Highway and west from the Canadian border. The major physical features include rolling hills, hundreds of small lakes and 2 glacial rivers (the Nabesna and Chisana) which combine to form the Tanana River. The refuge has a very high density of nesting waterfowl. Annual duck production in favorable years exceeds 90,000. Among the larger birds using the refuge are sandhill cranes, Pacific and common loons, osprey, bald eagles and ptarmigan. Other wildlife includes moose, black and grizzly bear, wolf, coyote, beaver and red fox. Activities allowed on the refuge include wildlife observation, hunting, fishing, camping, hiking and trapping. Check with refuge personnel at the USF&WS office in Tok prior to your visit for more detailed information. Write Refuge Manager, Tetlin National Wildlife Refuge, Box 155, Tok, AK 99780; or phone (907) 883-5312. Information on the refuge is also available at the USF&WS visitor center at **Milepost DC 1229** on the Alaska Highway.

Confluence of Moose Creek and Chisana River, about 0.8 mile/1.3 km downstream from Chisana River bridge on Northway Road, south side of river, northern pike to 15 lbs., use red-and-white spoon, spring or fall. **Chisana River**, downstream from bridge, lingcod (burbot) to 8 lbs., use chunks of liver or meat, spring. **Nabesna Slough**, south end of runway, grayling to 3 lbs., use spinner or gold flies, late May.

NORTHWAY AIRPORT LODGE & MOTEL

5 MODERN ROOMS WITH BATH & TV
Snack Bar ♦ Package Store ♦ Grocery Store
Auto & AV Gas   Picnic Area ♦ Information

P.O. Box 410, Northway, AK 99764   Lud Larson   (907) 778-2266

Turn off Alaska Highway at MILEPOST 1264
7 miles to Northway Airport

The Year Around Gateway to Alaska

WRANGELL VIEW SERVICE CENTER

Overlooking the Upper Tanana Valley and spectacular Wrangell Mountains, WRANGELL VIEW offers full, modern, facilities to all travelers.

TRUCK STOP   TOUR BUSES WELCOME   RV HOOKUPS and DUMP

RESTAURANT
• Breakfast, Lunch, Dinner Menu
• Salad Bar
• Homemade Soups and Pastries

LOUNGE
• Beers • Wines
• Cocktails
• Ice • Pay Phone

MOTEL
• Modern Rooms with Private Bath, Phone & Color TV
• Economy Rooms
• Rustic Cabins
• Laundromat

GARAGE
• Full Service Gas, Diesel and Propane
• Heated Repair Facilities for All Sizes of Vehicles
• Tire Sales and Service
• Heavy and Light Wreckers

VISA MasterCard DISCOVER AMERICAN EXPRESS U-HAUL

MILE 1263

P.O. Box 395M
Northway, AK 99764

(907) 778-2261

Good Sam Club

FAIRBANKS 255 — WRANGELL ★ VIEW — 350 WHITEHORSE
380 — 400
ANCHORAGE   HAINES

Alaska Highway Log

(continued)

DC 1267.4 (2039.6 km) **F 252.6** (406.5 km) *CAUTION: Slow down for a big bump in the road known as "Beaver Slide." Watch for road construction here by summer of 1993.*
Wonderful view of the Tanana River.

DC 1268.1 (2040.8 km) **F 251.9** (405.4 km) Beaver Creek bridge. The tea-colored water flowing in the creek is the result of tanins absorbed by the water as it flows through muskeg. This phenomenon may be observed in other Northern creeks.

DC 1269 (2042.2 km) **F 251** (403.9 km) Scenic viewpoint. Double-ended gravel turnout to west has a litter barrel and USF&WS interpretive sign about the Tanana River, largest tributary of the Yukon River.

DC 1269.1 (2042.4 km) **F 250.9** (403.8 km) Slow down for bad pavement break.

DC 1272.7 (2048.2 km) **F 247.3** (398 km) Scenic viewpoint. Double-ended paved turnout to west with litter barrels. USF&WS interpretive sign on pond ecology and mosquitoes.

To the northwest the Tanana River flows near the highway; beyond, the Kalutna River snakes its way through plain and marshland. Mentasta Mountains are visible to the southwest.

DC 1273.9 (2050.1 km) **F 246.1** (396 km) Paved parking area with litter barrel to west by Tanana River.

In June, wild sweet peas create thick borders along the highway. This is rolling country, with aspen, birch, cottonwood, willow and white spruce.

DC 1275.5 (2052.7 km) **F 244.5** (393.5 km) Slide area next 0.3 mile/0.5 km northbound.

DC 1279 (2058.3 km) **F 241** (387.8 km) Highway cuts through sand dune stabilized by aspen and spruce trees.

DC 1281 (2061.5 km) **F 239** (384.6 km) Rough road, pavement cracks.

DC 1284.2 (2066.7 km) **F 235.8** (379.5 km) Tetlin National Wildlife Refuge boundary sign.

DC 1284.6 (2067.3 km) **F 235.4** (378.8 km) Large double-ended paved turnout to east.

DC 1285.7 (2069.1 km) **F 234.3** (377.1 km) Granite intrusion in older metamorphosed rock is exposed by road cut.

DC 1289 (2074.4 km) **F 231** (371.7 km) Midway Lake. Tetlin Indian village lies hidden in the flats about 10 miles/16 km southwest of Midway Lake and is not accessible by road. The waterways have long been the highways of this bush country. The lakes and ponds bear colorful names such as Long Fred, Gasoline and Grass.

DC 1289.4 (2075 km) **F 230.6** (371.1 km) Turnout uphill on east side of highway with litter barrels, view of Midway Lake and USF&WS interpretive signs on Wrangell-St. Elias National Park and Native peoples. *NOTE: Difficult access for large vehicles and trailers, easier access from southbound lane.*

DC 1290 (2076 km) **F 230** (370.1 km) Beautiful view of Midway Lake southbound.

DC 1292.4 (2079.8 km) **F 277.6** (366.3 km) Paved turnout west side.

DC 1293.7 (2081.9 km) **F 266.3** (364.2 km) Paved turnout west side.

DC 1301.7 (2094.8 km) **F 218.3** (351.3 km) **Tetlin Junction**, Alaska Highway and Taylor Highway (Alaska Route 5) junction. The Taylor Highway (gravel, open summer only) heads northeast via Jack Wade Junction to Eagle (see TAYLOR HIGHWAY section) and to Yukon Highway 9 (Top of the World Highway) to Dawson City. (See KLONDIKE LOOP section for log of Yukon Highway 9 and description of Dawson City.)

NOTE: If you are traveling to Dawson City, keep in mind that both the Canada and U.S. customs stations are closed at night; you CANNOT cross the border unless customs stations are open. Customs hours in summer 1991 were 8 A.M. to 8 P.M. Alaska time, 9 A.M. to 9 P.M. Pacific time on the Canadian side.

DC 1302.7 (2096.4 km) **F 217.3** (349.7 km) Scenic viewpoint at paved turnout with litter barrel to southwest.

DC 1303.4 (2097.5 km) **F 216.6** (348.6 km) Tanana River bridge. Informal parking area and boat launch to east at north end of bridge. Tanana (TAN-uh-naw), an Indian name, was first reported by the Western Union Telegraph Expedition of 1886. According to William Henry Dall, chief scientist of the expedition, the name means "mountain river." The Tanana is the largest tributary in Alaska of the Yukon River. From here the highway parallels the Tanana to Fairbanks. The Alaska Range looms in the distance.

DC 1304.6 (2099.5 km) **F 215.4** (346.6 km) Evidence of 1990 burn from here north to Tok. The Tok River fire occurred in July of 1990 and burned 97,352 acres. The fire closed the Alaska and Glenn highways at times and threatened the town of Tok. One result of the fire was a brief but bountiful crop of morel mushrooms in 1991 which were harvested and sold commercially.

DC 1306.6 (2102.7 km) **F 213.4** (343.4 km) Road east to lake.

DC 1308.5 (2105.7 km) **F 211.5** (340.4 km) Weigh station and turnoff to U.S. Coast Guard loran-C station and signal towers.

This loran (long range navigation) station is 1 of 7 in Alaska. A series of 4 700-foot/213-m towers suspends a multi-element wire antenna used to transmit navigation signals. These signals may be used by air, land and sea navigators as an aid in determining their position. This station is located here as necessary for good geometry with 2 Gulf of Alaska loran transmitting stations.

DC 1308.8 (2106.3 km) **F 211.2** (339.9 km) Paved turnout with litter barrels to west.

DC 1309.2 (2106.9 km) **F 210.8** (339.2 km) Tok River state recreation site; 25 campsites, overflow parking, tables, firepits, toilets (wheelchair accessible), litter barrels, nature trail and boat launch. Check bulletin board for schedule of interpretive programs. Camping fee $8/night or annual pass. *CAUTION: Swift water.* ▲

Annual passes good for unlimited camping at all Alaska state parks within a calendar year are available for $60 residents, $75 non-residents. Passes may be purchased at the Alaska Public Lands Information Center in Tok.

DC 1309.4 (2107.2 km) **F 210.6** (338.9 km) Tok River bridge.

DC 1312.7 (2112.5 km) **F 207.3** (333.6 km) Tok community limits. Mountain views ahead northbound. Motel.

TESORO TRUCKSTOP at NORTHSTAR

Mile 1313.3 Alaska Highway
Tok, Alaska 99780
1-800-645-4167
or (907) 883-4502

OPEN 24 HOURS
Serving Your Needs With
GAS • DIESEL • PROPANE
CAR WASH • RV CAMPING
LAUNDRY • SHOWERS
SNACK BAR • GROCERIES
GIFTS

FULL RESTAURANT
Breakfast • Lunch • Dinner
Homemade Pies

Other Services To Meet Your Needs
WESTERN UNION OFFICE
Send and Recieve Money

Bus Stop for
Alaska Direct Bus Lines

We Take VISA, MasterCard,
American Express, Discover, Tesoro

OPEN YEAR AROUND
by PCA Partnership

When you arrive in Tok, A MUST stop is
RITA'S CAMPGROUND
AND **POTPOURRI GIFTS**
An experience you will long remember
See ad at Mile 1315.7 Alaska Highway

STOP
DON'T MISS THE TURN TO
Historic
DAWSON CITY

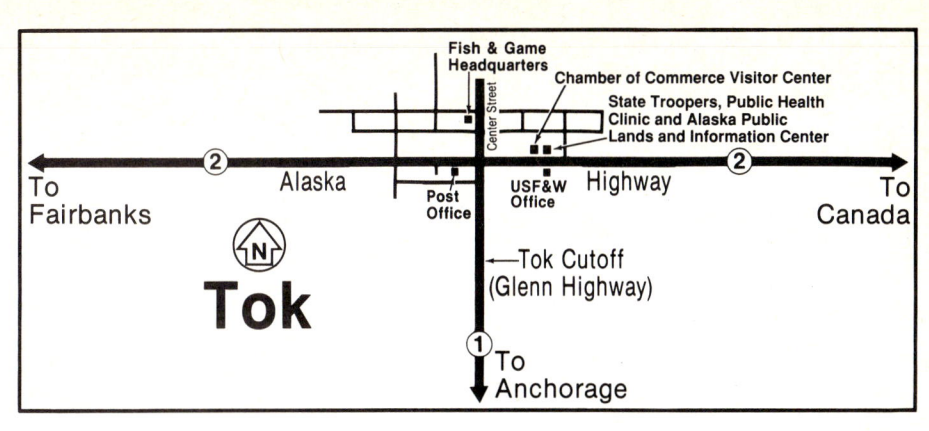

DC 1312.8 (2112.7 km) **F 207.2** (333.4 km) Tok Dog Mushers Assoc. track and buildings. Paved bike trail from Tok ends here.

DC 1313 (2113 km) **F 207** (333.1 km) Airstrip. See Private Aircraft information in Tok section. Entering Tok (northbound), description follows. Tok is located at the junction of the Alaska Highway and Tok Cutoff (Glenn Highway). Anchorage-bound travelers turn west on the Tok Cutoff (see the GLENN HIGHWAY section). Fairbanks-bound travelers continue north on the Alaska Highway.

Southbound travelers: Driving distance from Tok to Beaver Creek is 113 miles/182 km; Haines Junction 296 miles/476 km; Haines (departure point for Alaska state ferries) 446.5 miles/718.5 km; and Whitehorse 396 miles/637 km.

DC 1313.1 (2113.1 km) **F 206.9** (332.9 km) **Tok Gateway Salmon Bake and RV Park.** Vacationers should not miss Tok's Gateway Salmon Bake, featuring outdoor flame-grilled Alaska king salmon, halibut, ribs and reindeer sausage. Buffalo and salmon burgers. Good food, friendly people; casual dining at its best. Open daily 11 A.M. to 9 P.M. Wooded RV and tent sites with tables, clean restrooms, dump station and water. [ADVERTISEMENT]

DC 1313.3 (2113.5 km) **F 206.7** (332.7 km) **The Bull Shooter Sporting Goods & RV Park**, Tok, Alaska. Fishing and hunting licenses and information. Sporting goods. Large selection of fishing gear and tackle. Camping supplies. Guns and ammo. Plan to stay at the Bull Shooter's nice, quiet, wooded RV park. 49 spaces, 37 pull-throughs, some tent spaces. Water and electric, dump station, good drinking water. Some sewer hookups, showers, restrooms, ice and phone. We accept VISA and MasterCard. Welcome to Alaska! We are on the left as you come into Tok. P.O. Box 553, Tok, AK 99780. Call (907) 883-5625. See display ad in Tok section. [ADVERTISEMENT]

DC 1313.3 (2113.5 km) **F 206.7** (332.6 km) **Tesoro Truck Stop at Northstar.** Open 24 hours in summer for gas, diesel, propane, car wash, RV campground with hookups, dump station, laundry, showers, snackbar, gifts. Restaurant open for breakfast, lunch, dinner. Homemade pies. Western Union office. VISA, MasterCard, American Express accepted. Canadian money exchanged. Open year-round. See display ad this section. [ADVERTISEMENT]

DC 1313.3 (2113.5 km) **F 206.7** (332.6 km) **Eska Trading Post**, on the left northbound, home of premium quality hand-dipped ice cream, an Alaska-made gourmet treat. Frozen yogurt. Video and Nintendo rentals. Alaska crafts and souvenirs and a large selection of Alaska books. Snacks, cold pop, ice. "Hex" tanning unit. See display ad this section. [ADVERTISEMENT]

DC 1313.4 (2113.6 km) **F 206.6** (332.5 km) **Tok RV Village.** Alaska's finest. Good Sam or KOA cards honored. Convenient pull-through spaces with 30 amp power. Full and partial hookups, clean restrooms and showers, dump station, laundry, car wash, picnic tables, public phones. Gift shop. RV supplies, ice. Located next door to shopping area with gas, diesel, propane, liquor store, restaurant, nightclub, hardware store and video rentals. MasterCard and VISA. See display ad in Tok section. [ADVERTISEMENT]

DC 1314.1 (2114.8 km) **F 205.9** (311.4 km) **Tok Assembly of God** cares about your family! Start your travel day off right with a spiritually refreshing half-hour devotional offered daily, 7 A.M. Everyone is welcome! Regular service schedule: Sunday school 10 A.M.; Morning worship 11 A.M.; Evening worship 6 P.M.; Wednesday bible study 7 P.M. Located 1 block behind information center. (907) 883-2171. [ADVERTISEMENT]

Tok

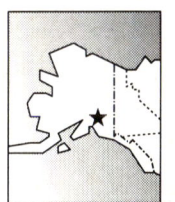

DC 1314.2 (2115 km) **F 205.8** (331.2 km) At the junction of the Alaska Highway and Tok Cutoff (Glenn Highway) between the Tanana River to the north and the Alaska Range to the southwest. **Population:** 1,200; area 3,600. **Emergency Services: Alaska State Troopers**, phone 883-5111. **Fire Department**, phone 883-2333. **Community Clinic**, across from the fire hall on the Tok Cutoff, phone 883-5855 during business hours. **Public Health Clinic**, next to the Alaska

Read the *"Tent In Tok"* books side-busting, tongue-in-cheek, Alaskan poetry by Tok's Poet Laureate, Donna Bernhardt. Just $5.95. Pick them up while visiting Tok. Autographed! Available in many local shops and at Mukluk Land. Mail orders: PO Box 110, Tok, Alaska 99780.

Meet Donna Bernhardt, author of the "Tent In Tok" books, Sunday, 7 p.m. at Mukluk Land, Mile 1317 Alaska Hwy. Live entertainment featuring Donna reading her poetry and telling about life in the tent when temperatures dropped to 69 degrees below zero.

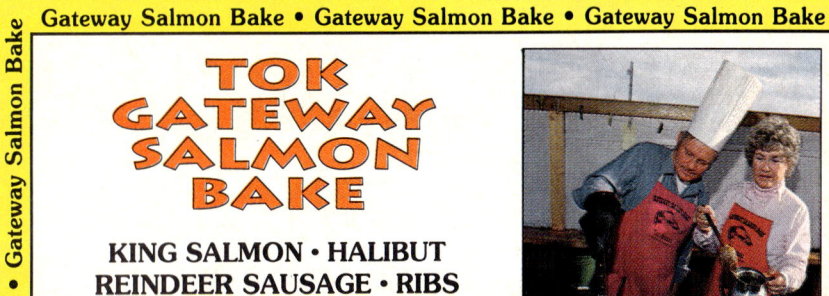

TOK'S MINI-MALL
Video and Nintendo Rentals

"HEX" Tanning System

Postcards • Books
Souvenirs

Hand-dipped
Premium Ice Cream
and
Frozen Yogurt

Snacks • Pop • Ice

ESKA TRADING POST
(907) 883-5343   Mile 1313.3

TOK GATEWAY SALMON BAKE

KING SALMON • HALIBUT
REINDEER SAUSAGE • RIBS
Flame-grilled to perfection • Buffalo Burgers

RV Park (no hookups) • (907) 883-5555
Buses and Caravans Welcome
Reservations Appreciated (not required)

Clean Restrooms • Tent Sites • Picnic Area
• Dump Station • Water Available

Come, enjoy a taste of Alaska with us

See Log Ad — Mile 1313.1 ALASKA HIGHWAY

PO Box 577, Tok, Alaska 99780

State Troopers at **Milepost 1314.1**, phone 883-4101.

Visitor Information: The state-operated Alaska Public Lands Information Center at **Milepost DC 1314.1** offers free coffee and has a public phone and message board. Alaska State Park annual passes may be purchased here. Open 8 A.M. to 8 P.M. daily May through September. Winter hours (Oct. 1 through May 15) are 8 A.M. to 4:30 P.M., weekdays. Write: Box 359, Tok, AK 99780. Phone (907) 883-5667.

The Tok Chamber of Commerce operates a visitor center adjacent to the Public Lands Information Center. A sign in front of the visitor center shows the temperature extremes in Tok during the year.

The U.S. Fish & Wildlife Service office is located directly across the highway from the Public Lands Information Center. Visitors are welcome. Check with them regarding Tetlin National Wildlife Refuge. Office hours are 8 A.M. to noon and 1-4:30 P.M., weekdays. Write Box 155, Tok, AK 99780, or phone (907) 883-5312.

Elevation: 1,635 feet/498m. **Climate:** Mean monthly temperature in January, -19°F/-29°C; in July 59°F/14°C. Record low was -71°F/-57°C in January 1965; record high, 96°F/36°C in June 1969. **Radio:** FM stations are 90.5, 91.1 (KUAC-FM, University of Alaska Fairbanks) and 101.5. **Television:** Satellite channel 13. **Newspaper:** *Mukluk News* (twice monthly).

Private Aircraft: Tok airstrip, **Milepost DC 1313.2** Alaska Highway; elev. 1,670 feet/509m; length 2,700 feet/823m; asphalt; fuel 80, 100; unattended. Tok NR 2 airstrip; elev. 1,630 feet/497m; length 2,000 feet/609m; asphalt; fuel 80, 100; unattended.

Tok had its beginnings as a construction camp on the Alcan Highway in 1942. The community celebrates its anniversary in 1992 along with the Alaska Highway. Highway engineer C.G. Polk was sent to Fairbanks in May of 1942 to take charge of Alaskan construction, and start work on the road between Tok Junction and Big Delta. Work was also under way on the Gulkana-Slana-Tok Junction road (now the Tok Cutoff on the Glenn Highway to Anchorage). But on June 7, 1942, a Japanese task force invaded Attu and Kiska islands in the Aleutians, and the Alcan took priority over the Slana cutoff.

The name Tok is believed to be derived from Tokyo Camp, patriotically shortened during WWII to Tok. But there exist at least 3 other versions of how Tok (pronounced to rhyme with poke) got its name.

Because Tok is the major overland point of entry to Alaska, it is primarily a trade and

TOK ADVERTISERS

"A Tent in Tok" .........................P.O. Box 110
Bull Shooter Sporting Goods &
   RV Park, The.........Mile 1313.3 Alaska Hwy.
Burnt Paw ....Adjacent post office
Cleft of the Rock
   Bed and Breakfast ....Ph. (907) 883-4219
Empire on Ice ...............................P.O. Box 252
Eska Trading Post......Mile 1313.3 Alaska Hwy.
Fast Eddie's
   Restaurant............Mile 1313.3 Alaska Hwy.
First Baptist Church ....Downtown
First Gallery ....Mile 1313.6 Alaska Hwy.
Frontier Foods ....Across from visitor center
Golden Bear Motel
   & Restaurant ....Mile 0.3 Tok Cutoff
Golden Bear RV Park ....Ph. (907) 883-2561
Grizzly Auto Repair...........Ph. (907) 883-5514
Hayner's Trading Post.......Mile 1.7 Tok Cutoff
Jacqueline's
   Boutique................Mile 1313.8 Alaska Hwy.
Kuebler's Husky
   Lounge & Liquor..........Ph. (907) 883-2381
Lois's Bed & Breakfast ......Ph. (907) 883-5647
Mukluk Land................Mile 1317 Alaska Hwy.
Northern Energy
   Corp. ....Mile 1314.8 Alaska Hwy.
Quail's Nest, The ....Mile 1313.8 Alaska Hwy.
Shamrock Hardware ....Ph. (907) 883-2161
Snowshoe Fine Arts
   and Gifts..............Across from visitor center
Snowshoe Gateway
   Motel ....Across from visitor center
Sourdough Campground ..Mile 1.7 Tok Cutoff
Sourdough Pancake
   Breakfast ....Mile 1.7 Tok Cutoff
Stage Stop, The ....Ph. (907) 883-5338
Texaco Truck Stop and
   Restaurant............Mile 1313.8 Alaska Hwy.
Tok Assembly of God.......Behind visitor center
Tok Chamber of Commerce ....Next to
                    Public Lands info center
Tok Gateway Salmon
   Bake & RV Park ....Mile 1313.1 Alaska Hwy.
Tok Liquor & Mini-Mart ...Adjacent Tok Lodge
Tok Lodge ....Ph. (907) 883-2853
Tok RV Village ....Mile 1313.4 Alaska Hwy.
Tok Saveway Motel, RV Park,
   Groceries & Gas...........Ph. (907) 883-5389
Ulu Factory, The................Ph. (907) 276-3119
Westmark Tok ....At jct. Alaska Hwy. &
                                       Tok Cutoff
Wildwood Kennels ....Mile 1318.6 Alaska Hwy.
Young's Chevron
   Service ....Ph. (907) 883-2821
Young's Motel ....Ph. (907) 883-4411

Welcome to Tok, Alaska
Don't Miss Tok's Highlight
Mukluk Land -- Mile 1317
A trip highlight for all ages
Senior Citizen Discounts
See our display ad

Enjoy Alaskan Hospitality at
Kuebler's HUSKY LOUNGE & Liquor
Mile 1313.2 Alaska Highway in Tok
Phone: (907) 883-2381 or 883-2382

Friendly...
Comfortable Atmosphere

Breakfast • Lunch • Daily Specials
Mixed Drinks • Ice Cold Beer
PACKAGE STORE

Near Motel, Laundry and Mini-Mart
LeeRoy and Betty Kuebler welcome you to Tok

THE BULL SHOOTER Sporting Goods
• One Stop Shopping for All Your Hunting,
  Fishing and Camping Needs
• Fishing and Hunting Licenses and Tags

P.O. Box 553, Tok, Alaska 99780 • (907) 883-5625
On your left coming into Tok

THE BULL SHOOTER RV Park
• Level Wooded Spaces • Hookups
• Tent Sites • Water • Dump Station • Showers
• Restrooms • Pay Phone

See log ad Mile 1313.3 Alaska Highway

SHAMROCK HARDWARE

– 0.8 mile from
the junction toward Canada

True Value   *TRU-TEST PAINTS*

CAMPER & TRAILER SUPPLIES
For the Do-It-Yourselfer

Summer hours 8 a.m. – 6 p.m.

MP 1313.3 Alaska Hwy. – Open 9 a.m. – 6 p.m. Mon. – Sat. • (907) 883-2161 service center for all types of transportation, especially for summer travelers coming up the Alaska Highway. A stopover here is a good opportunity to meet other travelers and swap experiences.

Tok's central business district is at the junction of the Alaska Highway and Tok Cutoff (Glenn Highway). From the junction, homes and businesses spread out along both highways on flat terrain dotted with densely timbered stands of black spruce.

Tok has 13 churches, a library, a large state of Alaska highway maintenance shop, elementary school, a 4-year accredited high school and a University of Alaska extension program.

ACCOMMODATIONS

There are several motels, restaurants and gas stations. Also here are grocery, hardware and sporting goods stores, bakery, beauty shop, gift shops, liquor stores, auto repair and auto parts stores, wrecker service, laundromats and a post office. The nearest bank is in Delta Junction or Glennallen.

Cleft of the Rock Bed and Breakfast. Warm, friendly Christian hospitality. Newly finished guest rooms, private apartment and an Alaskan log cabin for your comfort. Comfortable, clean, private. Open year-round. Mile 1316.6 Alaska Highway; 0.5 mile north

The Quail's Nest

Fabrics and Yarns
Craft Kits and Supplies
Patterns and Notions
Handcrafted Gifts

— Special Orders Welcome —

(907) 883-4353

P.O. Box 480, Tok, Alaska 99780
MILE 1313.8 ALASKA HIGHWAY

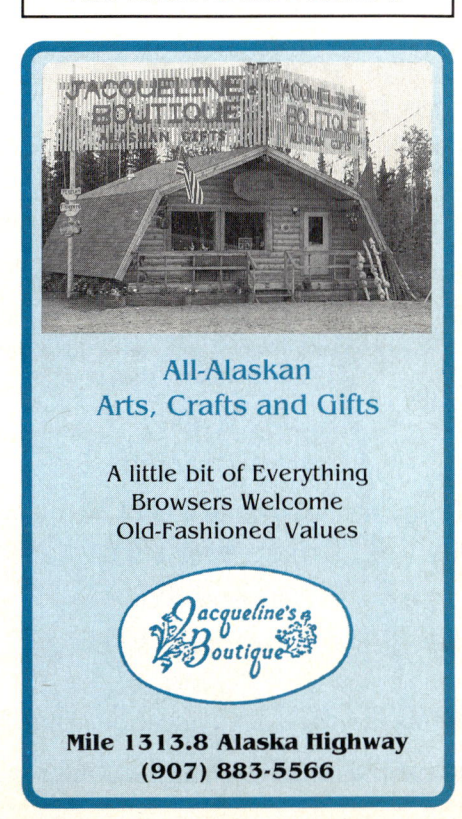

Jacqueline's Boutique

All-Alaskan
Arts, Crafts and Gifts

A little bit of Everything
Browsers Welcome
Old-Fashioned Values

Mile 1313.8 Alaska Highway
(907) 883-5566

When You Visit Tok, Enjoy The Comfort of...

YOUNG'S MOTEL

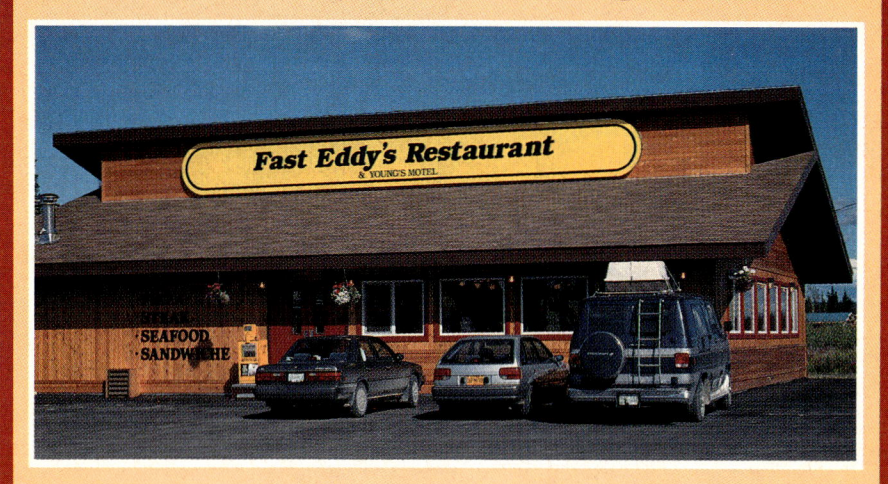

- Modern Accommodations
- Large Rooms
- Private Baths
- Tubs and Showers
- Color TV

Motel office in Fast Eddy's Restaurant
Write: Box 482, Tok, Alaska 99780
(907) 883-4411

FAST EDDY'S RESTAURANT

Pizza ■ Steaks ■ Sandwiches
Open for Breakfast in the Summer
■ Sunday Brunch ■

Open Year-Round
■ Summer hours 6 a.m. to midnight ■

Mile 1313.3 Alaska Highway
3/4 mile from the Junction
Write: Box 482, Tok, Alaska 99780
(907) 883-4411

ALASKA HIGHWAY • TOK

TOK RV VILLAGE

Alaska's Finest

Good Sampark

MILE 1313.4 ALASKA HIGHWAY

FEATURING:

95 SPACES • FULL and PARTIAL HOOKUPS
61 Pull-thru Spaces to 70-Feet
DRY CAMPSITES • TENT SITES
30-AMP. POWER • DUMP STATION
★ **VEHICLE WASH FACILITY**
★ **LAUNDRY**

CLEAN RESTROOMS and SHOWERS
Handicap Accessible
NON-METERED SHOWERS
PRIVATE DRESSING ROOMS
★ **GOOD SAM OR KOA DISCOUNTS**
★ **RV SUPPLIES • ICE**

MAIL FORWARDING • PHOTOCOPY and FAX SERVICE • PAY PHONES
HUNTING and FISHING LICENSES • TOURIST INFORMATION and LITERATURE
Walking Distance to Shopping Area

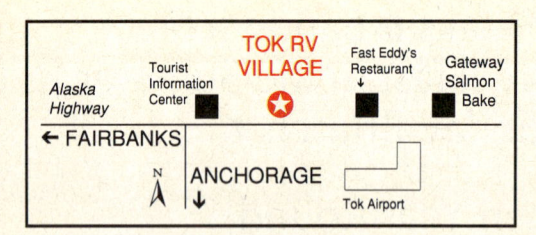

Map: Alaska Highway ← FAIRBANKS — Tourist Information Center — **TOK RV VILLAGE** ★ — Fast Eddy's Restaurant — Gateway Salmon Bake — ANCHORAGE — Tok Airport

TOK RV VILLAGE GIFT SHOP

A small gift shop full of surprises

T-Shirts • Sweatshirts
Film • Videos • Postcards
Alaskan Made Crafts
Jewelry

Quality Gifts at Reasonable Prices

VISA   MasterCard

Reservations Accepted
Phone (907) 883-5877
FAX (907) 883-5878
1-800-478-5878 (Toll-free within Alaska)

P.O. Box 741, Tok, Alaska 99780

See our log ad at Mile 1313.4 Alaska Highway

*We wish to thank all of you wonderful customers who have made our business such a great success.
Thanks!
The Jernigan Family*

on Sundog Trail. John and Jill Rusyniak. (907) 883-4219; in Alaska 1-800-478-5646. See display ad this section. [ADVERTISEMENT]

The Stage Stop, Bed and breakfast for people and horses. Private cabin and 2 large rooms with king and queen beds plus full breakfast. Quiet location Mile 2.1 Tok Cutoff highway. New barn and corrals for horses. Reasonable rates from $35. Open all year. Mary Underwood, Box 69, Tok, AK 99780. Phone (907) 883-5338. [ADVERTISEMENT]

Tok Lodge. Bud and Pam Johnson welcome you to Alaska. We invite you to share in our famous hospitality and congenial atmosphere. Tok Lodge, located on the Glenn Highway, 1 block from the junction, is one of a vanishing breed of Alaskan lodges. We can handle buses for meals in our Alcan Room while leaving the dining room free for highway traffic, 36 new motel units (total of 48 rooms). Enjoy our comfortable Alaskan cocktail lounge. New mini-mart

Tok Assembly of God
"We Care About Your Family"
Daily Devotional 7:00 a.m.
(May 24 - August 2)
Mile 1314.1 behind Information Center

Welcome to the North Country.

Across the Alaska Highway from the Tok Information Center

AUTHENTIC ALASKAN GIFTS
Walrus & Mastodon Ivory • Birch & Grass Baskets

Many gifts to choose from for your shopping pleasure.

SNOWSHOE FINE ARTS AND GIFTS

Paul and LuV Smith welcome you to Tok

P.O. Box 559   (907) 883-4181
Tok, Alaska 99780

Buses and tour groups welcome • Free shuttle service available locally

SNOWSHOE GATEWAY MOTEL

Rooms from $25 • Economy & Deluxe Units • Clean & Comfortable • Families Welcome
Write Box 559, Tok, Alaska 99780 • Phone (907) 883-4511
Toll Free In Alaska, Yukon and Northern British Columbia 1-800-478-4511

TEXACO TRUCK STOP AND RESTAURANT
Located on the Alaska Highway — Tok, Alaska
A SELF-SERVE STATION   Phone (907) 883-5833
24-Hour Wrecker Service on ANY size vehicle
A ONE-STOP CENTER FOR TRAVELERS

LOW GAS PRICES • PROPANE
Diesel • Free Water • Rest Rooms
MECHANIC ON DUTY
Prompt Quality Tire Repair • Welding
Firestone Tires • Lubrication
COIN CAR WASH
Heated Water • High Pressure Spray
AUTOMOTIVE / TRUCK PARTS
AND EQUIPMENT

A Mexican-American-Italian RESTAURANT
On the Alaska Highway in Tok, Alaska

Specializing in Authentic
MEXICAN FOOD
Delicious Lunch & Dinner Buffet
Salad Bar & **PIZZA!**
Beer & Wine

International CABAÑA

VISIT AN OLD-FASHIONED AND UNUSUAL ALASKAN DEPARTMENT STORE
WADSWORTH'S DEPARTMENT STORE

CAMPER SUPPLIES • SPORTING GOODS
HARDWARE and BUILDING SUPPLIES
CLOTHING • TOILETRIES • SOUVENIRS
Just about anything you can imagine you might need!
COURTEOUS SERVICE ALWAYS
Located on the Alaska Highway — Tok, Alaska

1992 ■ The MILEPOST®

and liquor store. Known for our friendliness and fine food since 1971. See display ad this section. [ADVERTISEMENT]

Grizzly Auto Repair, offering a complete range of repairs and adjustments for your vehicle. From electrical to mechanical along with welding. We have excellent equipment for wheel alignments and brake care. We also offer Goodyear tires. Plenty of room to park. Motorhomes welcome. The finest professional service, reasonable shop rates. See display ad this section. [ADVERTISEMENT]

Sourdough Campground's Pancake Breakfast, served 7-11 A.M. Genuine "Sourdough"! Full and partial RV hookups. Dry campsites. Showers included in price. High-pressure car wash. Browse through open-air museum with gold rush era memorabilia. Evening slide show. Located 1.7 miles from the junction toward Anchorage on the Tok Cutoff (Glenn Highway). See display ad this section. [ADVERTISEMENT] ▲

There are several private campgrounds in Tok. Tok AYH youth hostel is located on Pringle Road, 0.8 mile/1.3 km south of **Milepost DC 1322.6.** There is no phone at the hostel. Several state campgrounds are nearby: Tok River State Recreation Site at **Milepost DC 1309.3** and Moon Lake State Recreation Site at **Milepost DC 1331.9** Alaska Highway; and Eagle Trail State Recreation Site at **Milepost GJ 109.3** Tok Cutoff

VEHICLE REPAIRS AND SERVICE IN TOK ALASKA

Grizzly Auto Repair

FEATURING:

- **VEHICLE REPAIRS**
  Engines, Transmissions, Drive Trains, Brake Systems, Electrical Systems, Exhaust Systems.
- **VEHICLE SERVICES**
  Lube and Oil Change, Belts, Hoses, Engine Tune-Ups, Batteries.
- **GOODYEAR TIRES**
- **COMPUTERIZED WHEEL ALIGNMENT SYSTEM**
- **SHOP AND FIELD WELDING**
- **MOTOR HOMES WELCOME**
- **TOWING SERVICE AVAILABLE**
- **TBI FUEL INJECTION SERVICE**

Grizzly Auto Repair

BOX 248
TOK, ALASKA 99780

Full Service Center

907-883-5514

MasterCard   VISA

Located One Mile South of Tok Junction on Glenn Highway

FRONTIER FOODS

Directly across from Tok's Visitor Information Center

Quality Meats
Garden Fresh Produce
Full Grocery Line
Deli and Salad Bar
In-Store Bakery
Film and Photo Supplies
Block and Cube Ice

YOUNG'S CHEVRON SERVICE

Major Credit Cards

GAS • REGULAR AND UNLEADED • **DIESEL**
SELF-SERVE AND FULL SERVE AVAILABLE
FREE RV DUMP WITH FILL-UP • TIRE REPAIR
PROPANE • ICE • WATER
• 24-HOUR WRECKER SERVICE •

Lubrication and Minor Repairs

**CAFE • BBQ RIBS & CHICKEN
BREAKFAST ALL DAY • SOURDOUGH HOTCAKES**

Box 167, Tok, Alaska 99780
PHONE (907) 883-2821   LOCATED AT THE JUNCTION

ALASKA HIGHWAY • TOK

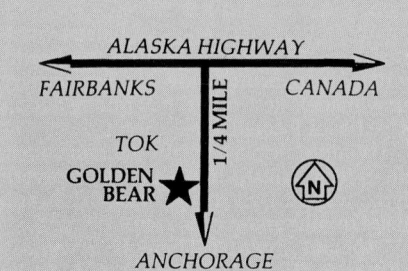

GOLDEN BEAR RV PARK

ALASKA HIGHWAY
FAIRBANKS ← → CANADA
TOK
GOLDEN BEAR ★ | 1/4 MILE
↓
ANCHORAGE

Box 276, TOK, ALASKA 99780   **(907) 883-2561**

New Heated Bathhouse

New Pull-through Campsites

Showers included in price

ICE

All **New** Washers and Dryers

Tent Site $10
Water and Electric $14
Full Hookup $16
Based on 2-person Occupancy

— SHOW THIS AD AND RECEIVE 10% OFF CAMPSITE —

GOLDEN BEAR MOTEL & RESTAURANT

62 DELUXE UNITS
...including homelike log suites, beautiful new rooms with or without kitchens, handicap access

All units have firm beds, tub/shower, thermostatically controlled heat, satellite TV

QUIET LOCATION near groceries, car wash, garage.

FOR MOTEL RESERVATION
Call **1-800-874-5248**
FAX (907) 883-4341

CHECK OUR REASONABLE RATES!

FINE DINING
6 a.m. - 10 p.m.
Enjoy our warm, friendly atmosphere while you delight in our homemade pie, soup, bread.
Our menu includes:
Alaskan Seafood, salad bar, sandwiches
Senior & Children's Meals Available

GIFT Shop

Open daily summers 7 a.m. to 10 p.m.
One of the finest selections of Alaskana in the state. Reasonable prices. Masks, baskets, jade, ivory, and soapstone carvings, totems, dolls, slippers, ceramics. Jade, hematite, ivory and gold nugget jewelry and much, much more! *You are cordially invited to browse and compare.*

Credit Cards welcome

(Glenn Highway) 16 miles/25 km west.

TRANSPORTATION

Air: Charter air service available; inquire at Tok state airstrip (**Milepost DC 1313.2**). Charter flightseeing and fly-in fishing trips available. Scheduled passenger and freight service between Tok, Delta Junction and Fairbanks 4 days a week via 40-Mile Air.

Bus: See Bus Lines in the GENERAL INFORMATION section for scheduled service to other communities. Local tour service via the Red Bus.

ATTRACTIONS

Alaska Public Lands Information Center has a large floor map, trip-planning center, and a historical timeline room. Also on display are examples of baleen (part of the food-filtering apparatus of the bowhead whale, from which fine Alaskan jewelry is now made). Restrooms, pay phone and message board located here.

Wildlife displays at the museum include an 8-foot grizzly bear, a wolf, wolverine, lynx, walrus, Dall sheep, musk-ox, a caribou head mount and moose rack.

Special Events: There is a variety of things to do in Tok, thanks to local businesses and clubs. Local campgrounds offer slide shows, movies, gold panning, a salmon bake, miniature golf and sourdough pancake breakfasts. Burnt Pass gift shop puts on a sled dog demonstration. There's also live entertainment and a presentation by Donna Bernhardt at Mukluk Land.

Special events in 1992 (see calendar this section) include the Tok "Mainstreet Alaska" Sourdough Potlatch. Inspired by the Athabascan Indian tradition, this monthly summer celebration offers storytelling, games and a meal of Alaska caribou stew

---

Whether on business, or vacation in Tok, enjoy...

Lois's Bed & Breakfast

Friendly atmosphere • Queen-size bed with firm Sealy mattress
Convenient location, but away from the center of town

Open Year-round   Brochure Available, or call for directions
(907) 883-LOIS • In Alaska 1-800-478-LOIS • P.O. Box 527, Tok, Alaska 99780

HAYNER'S TRADING POST   (907) 883-5536

Alaskan Handmade Jewelry and Gifts • Beads and Supplies • Sporting Goods
Greeting and Note Cards • Custom Leather Work and Repairs
— Free Coffee and Tea —

Open Year Around   Summer Hours: Monday-Saturday 10 a.m. - 8 p.m.
Mile 123.3 Glenn Highway (1.7 mile from Tok Junction on Tok Cutoff)

SOURDOUGH CAMPGROUND
Established 1966

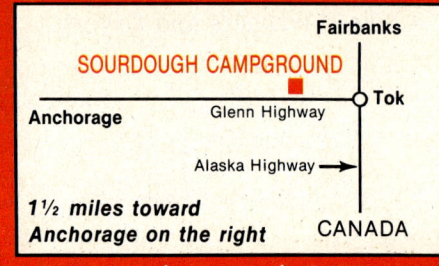

1½ miles toward Anchorage on the right

and SOURDOUGH PANCAKE BREAKFAST
Don and Joyce Farris • Box 47, Tok, Alaska 99780 • (907) 883-5543

SOUVENIR GIFT SHOP
Unique Alaska Gifts by Alaska Artists
Gold Rush Era Memorabilia —
Articles & photos from early days at Dawson, Eagle & the 40-Mile Country

Guaranteed CLEAN REST ROOMS

FULL SERVICE CAMPGROUND
- FULL HOOKUPS (Water, Electricity, Sewer)
- Pull-through Spaces – 70'
- Natural Wooded Area
- Tent Sites
- Picnic Tables
- Dump Station
- Laundromat
- Showers and Clean Rest Rooms

High Pressure Car Wash Vacuum

Free Sourdough Slide Show ... Shown Nightly
A historical adventure that will take you back to the gold rush days and lead you right up to the present day pipeline construction, with stops along the way to look at Alaskan wildlife, Mount McKinley and things to do and see in Alaska.

Good Sam "or" Senior Citizen Discount
Large, tree-shaded sites
LOCATED AT MILE 122.8 GLENN HIGHWAY

SOURDOUGH PANCAKE BREAKFAST
Start your morning the true *Alaskan* way with our
Genuine Sourdough Pancakes!
REINDEER SAUSAGE
Open 7 a.m.
Where good friends and friendly strangers meet

Wander through our OPEN AIR MUSEUM.
Gold Rush era Memorabilia and Alaskana
Bike and Jogging Trail to Tok
SEE OUR LOG AD UNDER ACCOMMODATIONS

1992 Events

MARCH
28-29 Tok Race of Champions

APRIL
18 12th Annual Tok Trot

JUNE
14 Tok "Mainstreet Alaska" Sourdough Potlatch
18 Army Motors Convoy stop
26-27 Floatplane Race

JULY
26 Tok "Mainstreet Alaska" Sourdough Potlatch

AUGUST
23 Tok "Mainstreet Alaska" Sourdough Potlatch

and Alaska cabbage cole slaw.

Other local events include twice-weekly bingo games (Tuesday and Thursday), square dancing with the T-Squares and softball games at the local field. Visitors are welcome at the senior citizens center ("a lot of old-timers meet here"). The Alaska Sports Car Club holds races at Tanacross airfield Memorial Day and Labor Day weekends. There are 3 boat races held annually. The Tanana 100, between Tanacross and the Tanana River bridge, is held on Memorial Day and Labor Day weekends. The Tanana 300, a 2-day boat race between Tanacross and Northway, is held in July. Fourth of July is also a big event here, with a parade and picnic. Check with the visitor information center about these local events.

Bike Trail: A wide paved bike trail extends southeast from Tok on the Alaska Highway as far east as the Dog Mushers Assoc. track, and as far west as Tanacross Junction; approximate length is 13.2 miles/21.2 km. You may also bike out the Tok Cutoff (Glenn Highway) past Sourdough Campground. Travelers may park their vehicles in and around Tok and find a bike trail nearby leading into or out of Tok.

Native Crafts: Tok is a trade center for the Athabascan Native villages of Tanacross, Northway, Tetlin, Mentasta, Dot Lake and Eagle. Several of the Native women make birch baskets, beaded moccasins, boots and beaded necklaces. Examples of Native work may be seen at the Native-operated gift shop at Northway junction and at several gift

---

THE STAGE STOP

Bed & Breakfast FOR People & Horses

Private Cabin or Master Bedroom
New Barn & Corrals for your horse

Open All Year (907) 883-5338

P.O. Box 69, Tok, Alaska 99780
Mile 122.9 Glenn Highway
(1.7 miles from Tok Junction)

TOK LODGE
Box 135, Tok, Alaska 99780

MOTEL • DINING ROOM • COCKTAILS
TOUR BUSES WELCOME
Phone (907) 883-2851
— SEE OUR LOG AD UNDER ACCOMMODATIONS —

TOK LIQUOR & MINI-MART
Cold Beer • Fine Wines
FULL LINE LIQUOR STORE • ICE
Grocery and Convenience Items
Video Rental
Phone (907) 883-2852

ALASKA HIGHWAY • TOK

shops and other outlets in Tok.

The state of Alaska has a crafts identification program which identifies authentic Native and Alaskan handicrafts. This symbol is of a polar bear.

Birch baskets were once used in the Native camps and villages. Traditionally they had folded corners, would hold water, and were even used for cooking by dropping heated stones into the liquid in the baskets. The baskets are made by peeling the bark from the birch trees, usually in the early summer months. The bark is easiest to work with when moist and pliable. It is cut into shape and sewn together with strips of spruce root dug out of the ground and split. If the root is too dry it is soaked until it is manageable. Holes are put in the birch bark with a punch or screwdriver and the spruce root is laced in and out. Native women dye the spruce root with food coloring, watercolors or berry juice. A few Natives also make birch canoes and birch baby carriers.

Many of the moccasins and mukluks for sale in Tok are made with moose hide that has the "Native tan." This means moose hide tanned by the Native. First the excess fat and meat is scraped off the hide, then it is soaked in a soap solution (some use a mixture of brains and ashes). After soaking, all the moisture is taken out by constant scraping with a dull knife or scraper. The hide is then scraped again and rubbed together to soften it. Next it is often smoke-cured in rotted spruce wood smoke. The tanning process takes from a few days to a week.

Beading can be a slow and tedious process. Most women say if they work steadily all day they can put the beading on 1 moccasin, but usually they do their beadwork over a period of several days, alternating it with other activities.

Snowshoe Fine Arts and Gifts suggests you use their free local shuttle bus service (call 883-4181) to visit their art gallery, which features Alaskan artists. Art books,

Tok's Finest Lodging

You'll find comfortable lodging, personalized service and fine dining at the Westmark Tok

- 72 Rooms •
- Dining Room and Lounge •
- Adjacent to Visitor's Center •

Special Summer Value Rates from $49

Rooms at lower rates are capacity controlled and good on selected rooms & dates only. Call for complete information. Subject to change without notice.

Westmark TOK

Junction of the Alaska and Glenn Highways
P.O. Box 130, Tok Alaska 99780

Central Reservations
1-800-544-0970 (U.S.)
1-800-999-2570 (Canada)

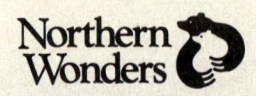

Northern Wonders FACTORY OUTLET

The finest selection of gifts and native handicrafts can be found at our factory outlet store located at the Westmark Tok. You'll find some of the region's best values and a wide selection.

Cleft of the Rock
BED & BREAKFAST
Warm, friendly Christian hospitality
P.O. Box 122-MP, Tok, Alaska 99780
(907) 883-4219 • 1-800-478-5646 in Alaska
See log ad under Accommodations

TOK SAVEWAY MOTEL
RV PARK, GROCERIES & GAS

9 MODERN ROOMS with BATH, TV, PHONES
Self-Service Alaskan Refined Gasoline at Low Prices
OPEN 24 HOURS YEAR-ROUND

P.O. Box 539, Tok, Alaska 99780   (907) 883-5389

Located 2 blocks south of Tok Junction on the Glenn Highway, across from Tok Lodge

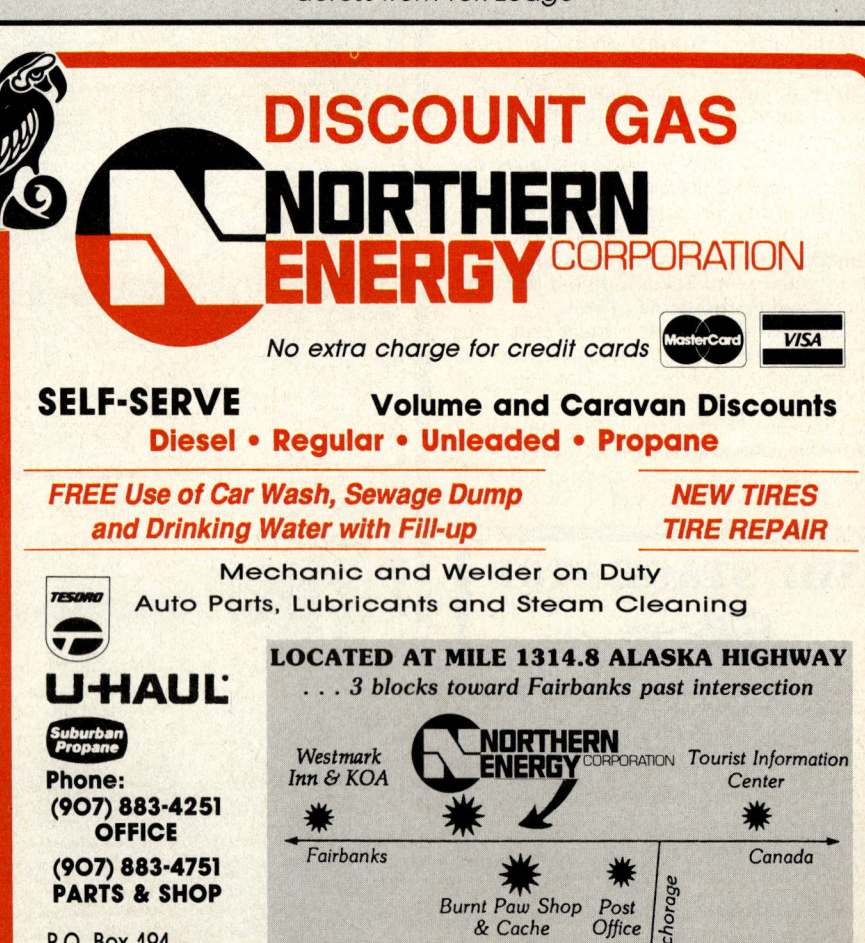

DISCOUNT GAS
NORTHERN ENERGY CORPORATION

No extra charge for credit cards   MasterCard   VISA

SELF-SERVE   **Volume and Caravan Discounts**
Diesel • Regular • Unleaded • Propane

FREE Use of Car Wash, Sewage Dump and Drinking Water with Fill-up   **NEW TIRES / TIRE REPAIR**

Mechanic and Welder on Duty
Auto Parts, Lubricants and Steam Cleaning

TESORO
U-HAUL
Suburban Propane

Phone:
(907) 883-4251 OFFICE
(907) 883-4751 PARTS & SHOP

P.O. Box 194
Tok, Alaska 99780

LOCATED AT MILE 1314.8 ALASKA HIGHWAY
...3 blocks toward Fairbanks past intersection

Westmark Inn & KOA — NORTHERN ENERGY CORPORATION — Tourist Information Center
Fairbanks — Burnt Paw Shop & Cache — Post Office — Anchorage — Canada

note cards and prints by Doug and Patti Lindstrand. Also, C. Alan Johnson art prints, figurines, and Christmas ornaments. Alaska Native-made soapstone carvings, birch-bark baskets and beadwork. Gold nugget, ivory, jade and Alaska black diamond jewelry. Fur hats and earmuffs by Sue Entsminger. Bronzes by Frank Entsminger. Complete portfolio of Entsminger's wilderness creations on display. Souvenir items to fit almost any budget. See display ad this section. [ADVERTISEMENT]

A Mukluk Special. Live entertainment at Mukluk Land every Sunday, 7 P.M., June 15-Aug. 15, featuring Native dancers and "Tent-in-Tok" lady, Donna Bernhardt. Free with Mukluk Land admission. Don't forget your camera! Mile 1317 Alaska Highway. See our display ads. [ADVERTISEMENT]

Sled Dog Breeding and Training: Dog mushing is Alaska's official state sport, and Tok has become known as the "Sled Dog Capital of Alaska," with at least 1 out of every 3 people in town involved in some way with raising dogs. Kennels range in size from 100 dogs to a single family pet. Visitors who come to Tok seeking either a pet or a racing sled dog will probably find what they are looking for here.

Got Kids?
Mukluk Land Is A Must!

Skee Ball, Igloo, Dog Sled Ride, Golf
FREE With Admission
$5 Adults, $2 Kids
Mile 1317, Open 1-9, June - August

First Baptist Church
SBC

WELCOME VISITORS

Sunday School 10:00 a.m.
Morning Worship 11:00 a.m.
Evening Worship 7:00 p.m.
Wednesday Prayer Meeting
7:00 p.m.

PHONE: (907) 883-2911

On Alaska Highway, just past the Junction Fairbanks-bound, next to Burnt Paw

TOK CHAMBER OF COMMERCE
WELCOMES YOU TO ALASKA.
Tok, the **"Mainstreet"** to Alaska, where there's plenty of things to do and real Alaskan hospitality.
RENEW YOUR ENERGY, ENTHUSIASM AND EXCITEMENT!
Let us educate you to the splendors of Alaska awaiting you. Stop in at the Chamber visitors center, right at the junction for free literature or *write* Box 389, Tok Alaska 99780.
Plan to attend our "1992 Sourdough Potlaches"

Add to the beauty of your trip with THE ALASKA-YUKON WILD FLOWERS GUIDE (includes 188 color photographs and 161 drawings). To order, phone 1-800-343-4567, Ext. 571.

FREE . . .
Dog Team Demonstration
7:30 p.m. nightly, except Sunday

BURNT PAW
Northland Specialties

WIN A RIDE IN A DOG SLED
See SLED DOGS
AND EQUIPMENT DISPLAY
LOG GIFT SHOP AND CACHE

FEATURING
Northland Gifts, Ulus, Summer Parkas, Jade, Hematite and Gold Nugget Jewelry, Native Crafts. Best Selection of Alaska T-Shirts and Sweatshirts. Sled Dog Equipment and Sled Dog Pups.

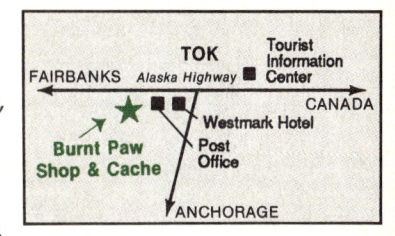

Bill and Nancy Arpino
Write P.O. Box 7, Tok, AK 99780 • Phone (907) 883-4121 or 451-8256

RITA'S CAMPGROUND AND POTPOURRI GIFTS

Clean, Modern Restrooms with Hot Showers • Excellent Water
Picnic Tables • Firepits with Free Wood • Sewer Disposal
Electric and Dry Parking • Quiet, Shaded, Level Sites
Located Beside Paved Bike and Walking Path
1.7 Miles Northwest of Tok Junction • Reasonable Rates
GIFTS • PAY PHONE • ICE • SOFT DRINKS
Pioneers Rita and Doug Euers welcome you and provide a relaxing Alaska camping and parking experience
(907) 883-4342 • Mile 1315.7 Alaska Highway • Box 599, Tok, AK 99780

ALASKA HIGHWAY • TOK

Qwik Lube

PENNZOIL 10 MINUTE OIL CHANGE lube oil filter

FAIRBANKS
1780 Peger Road
Next to Norlite Camper Park
(2 Blocks from Alaskaland)

(907) 479-5655

FAIRBANKS OR ANCHORAGE
We are your RV Service Headquarters!

"We don't give you time to miss your car!"

We offer fast, dependable service so you won't spend your vacation wishing you were on the road!!

COMPLETE LUBE SERVICE PLUS...

BF GOODRICH TIRES

- ★ Tune-ups
- ★ I/M Tests
- ★ Tire Repair
- ★ Brake Service
- ★ U-Joint Repair
- ★ Gear Lube Change
- ★ Repack Wheel Bearings
- ★ Transmission Service
- ★ Fuel Injection Cleaning
- ★ Cooling System Flush
- ★ Seal Replacement
- ★ Lights
- ★ Belts
- ★ Air Conditioning
- ★ Generator Service

MECHANIC ON DUTY

Restrictions may apply to some services.
MONDAY-SATURDAY 8 A.M. to 6 P.M.

Sled dog puppies from a Tok kennel.
(Jerrianne Lowther, staff)

The Siberian husky is the most popular sled dog and often times has distinctive blue eyes. The Alaskan malamute is much larger than the Siberian and is used for hauling heavy loads at a slower pace. Both breeds are AKC recognized. The Alaskan husky (or husky) is a catchall term for any of the arctic breeds or northern types of dogs and is usually a cross. Sled dogs may be any registered breed or crossbreed, since mushers look for conformation, attitude and speed when putting together a working team rather than pedigrees. Common strains in racing dogs have included Irish setter, Labrador and wolf, among others.

Wildwood Kennels, authentic racing kennels, established 1964. AKC Siberian and Alaskan Huskies. AKC Chesapeake Bay Retrievers. Puppies and breeding stock for sale. Winter sled dog tours by reservation only, meals and lodging included. Ask about dogsled rides. Anthony and Susann Vanderbloom. (907) 883-5866. See display ad at Mile 1318.6 Alaska Highway. [ADVERTISEMENT]

Sled Dog Trails and Races: Tok boasts a well-known and long-established dog mushing trail, which draws many world-class and recreational mushers. The 20.5-mile/33-km trail begins at the rustic log Tok Dog Mushers Assoc. building at **Milepost DC 1312.7** on the Alaska Highway. The trail is a favorite with spectators because it affords many miles of viewing from along the Alaska Highway.

Racing begins in late November and extends through the end of March. Junior mushers include 1-, 2-, 3- and 5-dog classes; junior adult mushers include 5- and 8-dog classes. Open (unlimited) classes can run as many as 16 dogs.

The biggest race of the season in Tok is the Race of Champions, held in late March, which also has the largest entry of any sprint race in Alaska. Begun in 1954 as a bet between 2 roadhouse proprietors, today the Race of Champions includes over 100 teams in 3 classes competing for prize money and trophies. It is considered to be the third leg of sled dog racing's "triple crown," following the Fur Rendezvous in Anchorage and the Fairbanks North American Championship. Visitors are also welcome to attend the Tok Native Assoc.'s potlatch, held the same weekend as the race, in the Tok school gym.

AREA FISHING: Fly-in fishing to area lakes for northern pike, grayling and lake trout; inquire at Tok state airstrip. There are at least 14 lakes stocked with rainbow trout in the Delta-Tok area. Most easily accessible are **North Twin**, **South Twin** and **Mark Lake**. There is a trailhead 0.5 mile/0.8 km east of the Gerstle River bridge for **Big Donna Lake** (3.5-mile/5.6-km hike) and **Little Donna Lake** (4.5 miles/7.2 km). **Quartz Lake**, north of Delta Junction, is a popular spot for rainbow trout and silver salmon.

Alaska Highway Log

(continued)

DC 1315.7 (2117.3 km) **F 204.3** (328.8 km) Rita's Campground and Potpourri Gifts. See display ad this section.

DC 1316.6 (2118.8 km) **F 203.4** (327.3 km) Scoby Road, Sundog Trail. Access to bed and breakfast.

DC 1317 (2122 km) **F 201.4** (324.1 km) Mukluk Land. See display ad this section.

DC 1318.6 (2112.7 km) **F 207.2** (333.4 km) **Wildwood Kennels**. See display ad this section.

DC 1322.6 (2128.5 km) **F 197.4** (317.7 km) Pringle Road. Tok youth hostel, housed in a wall tent, is located 0.8 mile/1.3 km south; 10 beds, tent space available.

DC 1324.6 (2131.7 km) **F 195.4** (314.5 km) Tanacross fireguard station.

DC 1324.7 (2131.8 km) **F 195.3** (314.3 km) Gravel access road to Tanacross airstrip. (See also next milepost.)

DC 1325.7 (2133.4 km) **F 194.3** (312.7 km) **Tanacross Junction**. End of paved bike trail from Tok and access to Tanacross.

Drive in 1.2 miles/1.9 km on gravel road to junction, turn left for village of **TANACROSS** (pop. 117), home of the once numerous branch of the Tanah, or Tinneh, Indians. This village of colorful modern houses is built on a short 0.7-mile-/1.1-km-loop road. Turn right at junction and drive 0.2 mile/0.3 km for access road to airstrip, or 0.3 mile/0.5 km to reach Tanana River and view across river of the white church steeple in the old village of Tanacross which burned down in 1979. Road eventually dead ends in residential area.

Private Aircraft: Tanacross airstrip; elev. 1,549 feet/472m; 2 runways, length 5,000 feet/1,524m and 5,100 feet/1,554m; asphalt; fuel 80, 100 and jet A, B.

DC 1327.3 (2136 km) **F 192.7** (310.1 km) Road access south to small lake.

DC 1327.4 (2136.2 km) **F 192.6** (310 km) Parking area at lake to north.

DC 1328 (2137.2 km) **F 192** (309 km) Watch for sections of patched pavement and frost heaves northbound to Dot Lake.

DC 1330.1 (2140.5 km) **F 189.9** (305.6 km) Paved turnout with litter container to east. View of Alaska Range to the west.

DC 1330.7 (2141.5 km) **F 189.3** (304.6 km) Paved turnout with litter barrels to east.

DC 1331.9 (2143.5 km) **F 188.1** (302.7 km) Moon Lake State Recreation Site, 0.2 mile/0.3 km north off highway; 15 campsites, toilets, tables, water, firepits, swimming (watch for floatplanes). Camping fee $8/night or annual pass. ▲

DC 1333.6 (2146.2 km) **F 186.4** (300 km) Yerrick Creek bridge.

DC 1335 (2148.4 km) **F 185** (297.7 km) Watch for moose.

DC 1338.2 (2153.5 km) **F 181.8** (292.6 km) Highway crosses Cathedral Creeks 3 times between here and **Milepost DC 1339**.

DC 1342.2 (2160 km) **F 177.8** (286.1 km) Sheep Creek culvert.

DC 1344.5 (2163.8 km) **F 175.5** (282.4 km) Double-ended paved parking area with litter barrels to east. Mentasta Mountains to the south. Good photo stop.

DC 1347.3 (2168.2 km) **F 172.7** (277.9 km) Entering Game Management Unit 20D northbound, Unit 12 southbound.

DC 1347.5 (2168.5 km) **F 172.5** (277.6 km) Robertson River bridge. The river was named by Lt. Henry T. Allen for a member of his 1885 expedition.

DC 1348 (2169.3 km) **F 172** (276.8 km) Bad frost heaves.

DC 1348.1 (2169.5 km) **F 171.9** (276.6 km) Side road west to parking lot at old

---

A Trip Highlight for Every Age!

MUKLUK LAND

Mile 1317 AK. HWY., 3 miles west of Tok Junction, (907) 883-2571
Alaska Garden, Pipeline Video and Display, Golf,
Indoor-Outdoor Museum, Northern Lights Video, Tent-in-Tok,
Large Mosquito, Skee Ball, Dog Sled Ride, Igloo . . .
& More — All FREE with Admission

LIVE ENTERTAINMENT

Native Dancers   Tent-in-Tok Lady Donna Bernhardt
Every Sunday, 7 p.m., June 15 - August 15 — *FREE with Admission*
Adults $5, Senior Citizens $4.50, Kids $2 — Open 1-9 Daily, June 1 - August 31
GOLD PANNING — *Gold Guaranteed* **— $5/ Pan with admission**

Wildwood Kennels

AUTHENTIC RACING KENNELS
Established 1964
**AKC Siberian & Alaskan Huskies
AKC Chesapeake Bay Retrievers
Puppies • Breeding Stock**
— WINTER SLED DOG TOURS —
Meals & Lodging Included
By Reservation Only **(907) 883-5866**
Anthony and Susann Vanderbloom
P.O. Box 21
Tok, AK 99780
Mile 1318.6
Alaska Highway

The Perfect ALASKA Gift

the ALASKA ULU

THE LEGENDARY KNIFE OF THE PEOPLE OF THE ARCTIC, is still the north's most popular knife. Our skilled craftsmen make them here in Alaska using a high quality heat treated stainless steel blade. Keeping in the Eskimo tradition our ULUs come in a variety of sizes and styles. You can choose one of our ULUs with handles of walnut, cultured ivory or ALASKAN JADE. Every one of our knives comes gift boxed with a walnut display stand, history, instructions and suggested uses. ASK FOR AN ULU FROM THE ULU FACTORY WE'RE SURE YOU'll SEE THE DIFFERENCE

Send self addressed stamped envelope for our free catalog

THE ULU FACTORY
298 Warehouse Ave., Anchorage, AK 99501

AVAILABLE AT HOTELS, GIFT SHOPS, AND CUTLERY STORES THROUGHOUT ALASKA

Haines pipeline right-of-way. Hike in 0.3 mile/0.5 km for **Robertson No. 2 Lake**; rainbow fishing.

DC 1350.5 (2173.3 km) **F 169.5** (272.8 km) Double-ended paved turnout with litter barrels to west.

DC 1350.9 (2174 km) **F 169.1** (272.1 km) Rough road next mile northbound.

DC 1353.7 (2178.5 km) **F 166.3** (267.6 km) Jan Lake Road. Drive in 0.5 mile/0.8 km to parking area with boat launch and toilets. No overnight camping, carry out garbage. **Jan Lake** is stocked with rainbow, use spinners, flies, or salmon eggs with bobber. Dot Lake Native Corp. land, limited public access.

DC 1357.3 (2184.4 km) **F 162.7** (261.8 km) Bear Creek bridge. Paved turnout with litter barrel to west.

DC 1358.7 (2186.6 km) **F 161.3** (259.6 km) Chief Creek bridge. Paved turnout with litter barrel to west at north end of bridge.

DC 1361.3 (2190.7 km) **F 158.7** (255.4 km) **DOT LAKE** (pop. 80). Gas, groceries, lodge restaurant, car wash, camping and post office. Headquarters for the Dot Lake (Athabascan) Indian Corp. Homesteaded in the 1940s, a school was established here in 1952. Dot Lake's historic chapel was built in 1949. ▲

Dot Lake Lodge. See display ad this section.

DC 1361.5 (2191 km) **F 158.5** (255.1 km) Gravel turnout by lake to east. Rough narrow road northbound.

DC 1370.2 (2205.1 km) **F 149.8** (241.1 km) Double-ended gravel parking area with litter barrels to west.

DC 1371.5 (2207.2 km) **F 148.5** (239 km) Berry Creek bridge.

DC 1374.2 (2211.5 km) **F 145.8** (234.5 km) Sears Creek bridge.

DC 1378 (2217.7 km) **F 142** (228.5 km) Bridge over Dry Creek.

DC 1379 (2219.2 km) **F 141** (226.9 km) Double-ended paved turnout to west with mountain views.

DC 1380.5 (2221.6 km) **F 139.5** (224.5 km) Johnson River bridge. A tributary of the Tanana River, the Johnson River was named by Lt. Henry T. Allen in 1887 for Peder Johnson, a Swedish miner and member of his party. Road narrows northbound.

DC 1381.1 (2222.6 km) **F 138.9** (223.5 km) Bumpy paved turnout to west. Access road to **Lisa Lake** (stocked). Watch for patches of rough pavement northbound.

DC 1383.9 (2227.1 km) **F 136.1** (219 km) **Craig Lake** access west side of highway via 0.5-mile/0.8-km trail; rainbow trout fishing.

DC 1388.4 (2234.4 km) **F 131.6** (211.8 km) Little Gerstle River bridge.

DC 1391.9 (2240 km) **F 128.1** (206.2 km) Trailhead to **Big Donna Lake**, 3.5 miles/5.6 km, and **Little Donna Lake**, 4.5 miles/7.2 km; stocked with rainbow.

DC 1392.3 (2240.6 km) **F 127.7** (205.5 km) Cummings Road through Delta barley project. Access to wilderness outfitter. *CAUTION:* Watch for buffalo (bison) on highway between here and Delta Junction.

Golden Eagle Outfitters. See display ad this section.

DC 1392.7 (2241.3 km) **F 127.3** (204.9 km) Gerstle River bridge. The river was named for Lewis Gerstle, president of the Alaska Commercial Co., by Lt. Henry T. Allen, whose 1885 expedition explored the Copper, Tanana and Koyukuk river regions for the U.S. Army Dept. of the Columbia.

DC 1393 (2241.8 km) **F 127** (204.4 km) Gerstle River Wayside; rest area with covered picnic tables, firepits, toilets and litter barrels.

DC 1396.9 (2248 km) **F 123.1** (198.1 km)

GOLDEN EAGLE OUTFITTERS

GUIDED OR UNGUIDED WILDERNESS EXPERIENCES

Fly-in Fishing • Secluded Cabins and Camps • Wildlife and Scenic Tours

Moose • Sheep • Caribou • Bear • Bison
Boat and Plane Trips

Dean and Jim Cummings

At Mile 1392.3 Alaska Highway
Turn on Cummings Road
Drive 5.7 miles, follow signs

Box 737 or Box 692, Delta Junction, AK 99737
Phone (907) 895-1010

Buffalo Center Auto Parts
Mile 1420.5 Alaska Highway
Delta Junction, Alaska 99737
907 - 895-4251

Owner Operated

Troxell Hebert   Glenda Hebert

DOT LAKE LODGE

Home of Alaska's Bigger Burger
Ice Cream Cones • Pie • Coffee
CAFE – CRAFTS – VEHICLE WASH

GAS – PROPANE – GROCERIES – GAME LICENSES
Lakeside Overnight Camping • Post Office
Open Year-round • About midway between Delta Junction and Tok
A PLEASANT PLACE TO STOP
Phone (907) 882-2691 • Sallie Ostrander, Owner
Box 2255, Dot Lake, Alaska 99737   Mile 1361.3 Alaska Highway

---

ALASKA HOMESTEAD & HISTORICAL MUSEUM
Guided Tours of an Authentic Alaska Homestead Farm

- Large collection of historical farming, logging, mining equipment
- Operating sawmill barns, corrals, salmon drying racks

(907) 895-4627

- Log home, gardens greenhouse, root cellar, hayfields
- Meet a real Alaska freight sled dog team, farm animals, pack horses

Picnic Shelter • Large Parking Area for RV's and Tour Buses
Open 10 a.m. to 7 p.m. June 1 - Sept. 15   Admission Fee for Tours
Write: Larry Dorshorst, P.O. Box 389, Delta Junction, Alaska 99737
Turn South on Dorshorst Road at Mile 1415.4 Alaska Highway

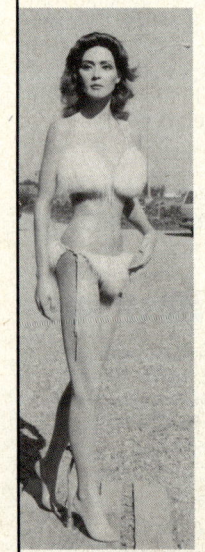

THE FUR SHACK

Furs and Fur Products
from
Alaska's Interior

Custom Orders

Have your picture taken with Ethel, wearing her famous Arctic fur bikini

— **TWO LOCATIONS** —
Delta Junction Visitor Center
and
Tanana River Pipeline Crossing

Mile V 275.4
Richardson/Alaska Highway

DRL ENTERPRISES
1714 Pine Lane, Delta Junction, AK 99737
(907) 895-4714   *(Year Around)*

Delta Burn (1979), now overgrown, to north for next mile.

On the south side of the Alaska Highway (on left northbound), not visible because of the trees, is the Bison Range. This range provides the bison herd with autumn and winter grazing on over 3,000 acres of grassland. It was developed to reduce agricultural crop depredation by bison.

DC 1401 (2254.7 km) **F 119** (191.5 km) Double-ended gravel turnout to northeast.

DC 1403.6 (2258.8 km) **F 116.4** (187.3 km) Sawmill Creek Road to northeast. This rough gravel road goes through the heart of the Delta barley fields. A sign just off the highway explains the barley project. Visiting farmers are welcome to talk with local farmers along the road, except during planting (May) and harvesting (August or September) when they are too busy.

DC 1403.9 (2259.3 km) **F 116.1** (186.8 km) Sawmill Creek bridge.

DC 1408 (2265.9 km) **F 112** (180.2 km) Entrance to University of Alaska Agricultural and Forestry Experiment Station. Major research at this facility concentrates on agricultural cropping, fertilization and tillage management.

DC 1410 (2269.1 km) **F 110** (177 km) Access road north to Delta barley project.

DC 1411.7 (2271.8 km) **F 108.3** (174.3 km) Double-ended gravel turnout with litter barrels. Scenic view of Alaska Range to south.

DC 1412.5 (2273.2 km) **F 107.5** (173 km) **Cherokee Two "Lodge" Restaurant & Blue Harvest Lounge.** See display ad this section. ▲

DC 1413.3 (2274.4 km) **F 106.7** (171.7 km) Grain storage facility.

DC 1414.9 (2277 km) **F 105.1** (169.1 km) Clearwater Road leads north past farmlands to Clearwater State Recreation Site campground and junctions with Remington Road. Stay on pavement leading to Jack Warren Road, which goes west to the Richardson Highway at **Milepost DC 1424.4 (V 268.4)**. Good opportunity to see area agriculture; see Delta Vicinity map this section.

To reach the state campground, follow Clearwater Road 5.2 miles/8.4 km north to junction with Remington Road; turn right and drive 2.8 miles/4.5 km east for Clearwater state campground on bank of stream. There are 15 campsites, toilets, tables, firepits, water and boat ramp. Camping fee $6/night or annual pass. Grocery, gas and lodge nearby. ▲

Delta–Clearwater River (boat needed for best fishing), beautiful spring-fed stream, grayling and whitefish; silver salmon spawn here in October. **Goodpaster River**, accessible by boat via Delta–Clearwater and Tanana rivers; excellent grayling fishing.

DC 1415.4 (2277.8 km) **F 104.6** (168.3 km) Dorshorst Road; access to homestead farm and private museum, open to public June 1 to Sept. 15, admission charged. **Alaska Homestead & Historical Museum.** See display ad this section.

DC 1419.1 (2283.7 km) **F 100.9** (162.4 km) Berm piles are debris from clearing of agricultural land.

DC 1420.2 (2285.5 km) **F 99.8** (160.6 km) Restaurant.

DC 1420.5 (2286 km) **F 99.5** (160.1 km) **Buffalo Center Auto Parts.** See display ad this section.

DC 1420.5 (2286 km) **F 99.5** (160.1 km) **Northland Auto Supply.** See display ad this section.

DC 1420.7 (2286.3 km) **F 99.3** (159.8 km) Alaska State Troopers.

DC 1420.9 (2286.7 km) **F 99.1** (159.5 km) Private RV park. ▲

DC 1421.9 (2288.3 km) **F 98.1** (157.9 km) **The Fur Shack.** See display ad this section.

Delta Junction

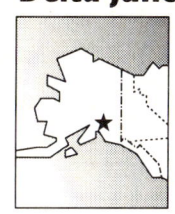

DC 1422 (2288.4 km) **F 98** (157.7 km) **V 266** (428.1 km). Located at the junction of the Alaska and Richardson highways. **Population:** 1,228; area 4,292. **Emergency Services:** Emergencies only phone 911. **Alaska State Troopers**, in the Jarvis Office Center at Milepost DC 1420.5, phone 895-4800. **Fire Department** and **Ambulance Service**, phone 895-4600 (emergency only). **Clinics.** One doctor in private practice.

Visitor Information: Junction of Alaska and Richardson highways. Open daily 8:30 A.M. to 7:30 P.M., mid-May to mid-September, phone 895-9941 for information.

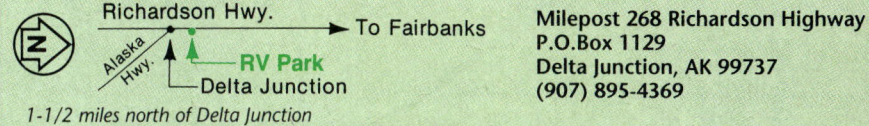

SMITH'S GREEN ACRES RV PARK
Richardson Hwy. → To Fairbanks
Alaska Hwy. — RV Park
— Delta Junction
1-1/2 miles north of Delta Junction
Milepost 268 Richardson Highway
P.O. Box 1129
Delta Junction, AK 99737
(907) 895-4369
ELECTRICITY • SEWER • DUMP STATION • WATER • SHOWERS • CAMPING
Featuring
Tree-shaded Pull-thru Sites • Nice Level Lots   Lawn Games • Miniature Golf
Free Showing of Trans-Alaska Pipeline Video

Northland Auto Supply
Delta Junction
COMPLETE LINE AUTO PARTS
Phone (907) 895-4479
1420.5 ALASKA HIGHWAY

Cherokee Two "LODGE" Restaurant & Blue Harvest Lounge
Homemade Pies & Good Home Cooking
Homemade Chili Daily
Camping • Showers • "Laundry Matt"
Rooms • Package Store • Scenic Flights
OPEN 6:00 A.M.
Bed & Breakfast — $18.50 per person
Kathy Scott • Phone: (907) 895-4814
Mile 1412.5 Alaska Highway
Left side northbound

---

visit Delta Junction in 1992

END OF THE ALASKA HIGHWAY — MILE 1422 — DELTA JUNCTION, ALASKA

End of the Alaska Highway certificates available

ALASKA • CANADA HIGHWAY 1942–1992 50 years

1992 marks the 50th Anniversary of the construction of the Alaska Highway

Alaska's Friendly Frontier

- Delta Agricultural Project
- Memorial Day Buffalo Wallow Square Dance Jamboree
- Largest free-roaming bison herd in Alaska
- Deltana Fair, July 31-August 1-2, 1992
- Big Delta State Historical Park
- Two state camping grounds, several private RV parks with full hookups
- Fine dining and major hotels and motels
- Great fishing, hunting in season, and hiking throughout the season
- Farmer's Market open 10-5 in season
- Local crafts and furs available at Visitor Center, open 8:30 a.m. to 7:30 p.m. daily
- Buffalo Barbeque on July 4, 1992
- Quartz Lake: fishing, hiking, camping, picnics
- Pipeline viewing area and bridge

For futher information contact the Delta Chamber of Commerce (907) 895-5068 or the Delta Visitor Center (907) 895-9941 Box 987, Delta Junction, Alaska 99737

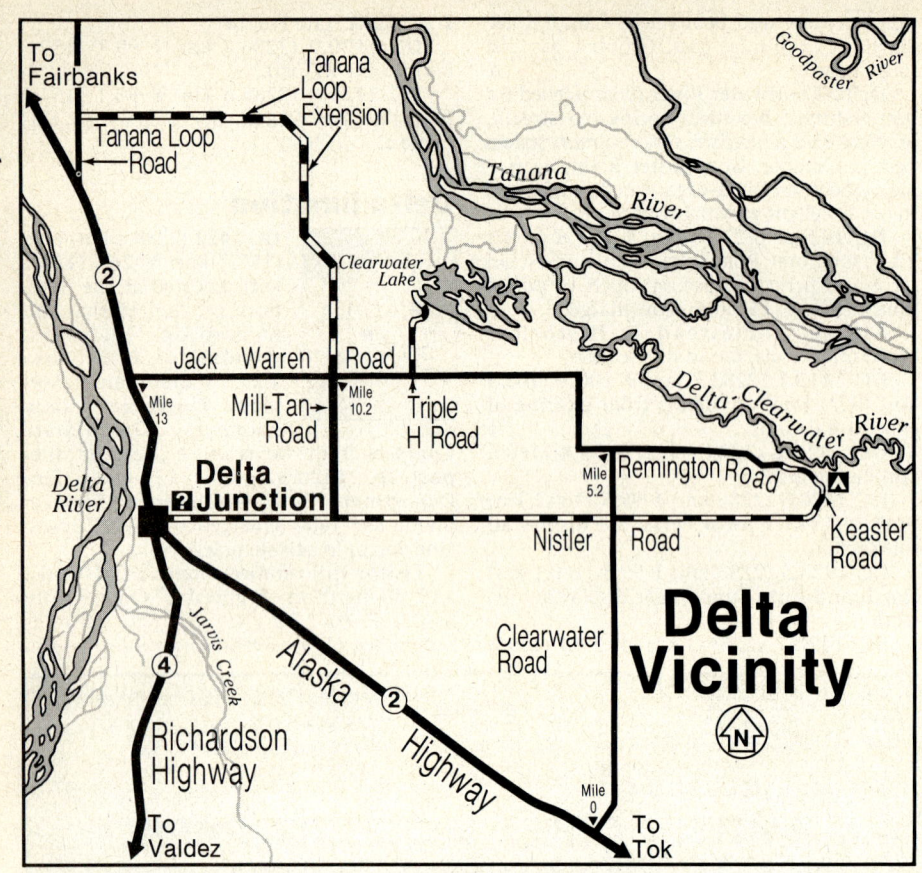

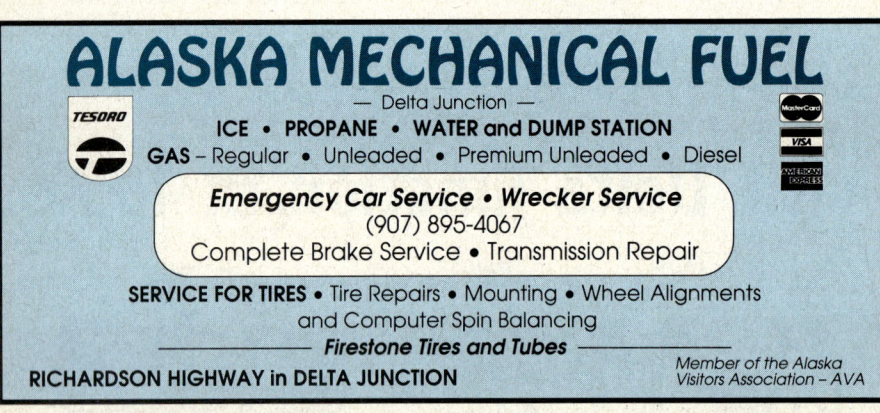

Visitor center garden with local grains, flowers and vegetables. Pay phone located here. Highway information, phone 451-2207. Dept. of Fish and Game at north edge of town, **Milepost DC 1422.8**; phone 895-4632.

Elevation: 1,180 feet/360m. **Climate:** Mean monthly temperature in January, -15°F/-26°C; in July 58°F/14°C. Record low was -66°F/-54°C in January 1989; record high was 88°F/31°C in August 1990. Mean monthly precipitation in July, 2.57 inches/6.5cm. **Radio:** KUAC-FM 91.7 broadcasts from University of Alaska Fairbanks. **Television:** 3 channels from Fairbanks. **Newspaper:** *The Delta Paper* (biweekly).

Private Aircraft: Delta Junction airstrip, 1 mile/1.6 km north; elev. 1,190 feet/363m; length 2,400 feet/731m; gravel. Allen Army Airfield, 3 miles/4.8 km south; elev. 1,277 feet/389m; 3 asphalt-surfaced runways available, length to 7,500 feet/2,286m; joint-use

DELTA JUNCTION ADVERTISERS

Alaska Mechanical Fuel.....Ph. (907) 895-4067
Alaska 7 Motel .....Mile 270.3 Richardson Hwy.
Alaskan Outback
 Expeditions.........................6369 Nistler Rd.
Bed & Breakfast at
 the Home of Alys.........Ph. (907) 895-4128
Bergstad's Travel and
 Trailer Court.........Mile 1420.9 Alaska Hwy.
City Park Carwash ....Behind post office
Delta Self-Service Laundry and
 Cleaners ....Mile 267.5 Richardson Hwy.
Delta Shop-Rite .....0.5 mile N. of visitor center
Delta Visitor Information
 Center ....Mile 1422 Alaska Hwy.
Diehl's Shopping
 Center.....................0.5 N. of visitor center
Jack's Chevron and Jack's Liquor
 Store ....Mile 265.8 Richardson Hwy.
Kelly's Country
 Inn Motel.....................Ph. (907) 895-4667
Kountry Korner Store ....2395 Kimball St.
Pizza Bella Family
 Restaurant...........Across from visitor center
Smith's Green Acres RV
 Park ....Mile 268 Richardson Hwy.
Talbott's Bed &
 Breakfast.....................Ph. (907) 895-5025

ALASKA MECHANICAL FUEL
— Delta Junction —

ICE • PROPANE • WATER and DUMP STATION
GAS – Regular • Unleaded • Premium Unleaded • Diesel

Emergency Car Service • Wrecker Service
(907) 895-4067
Complete Brake Service • Transmission Repair

SERVICE FOR TIRES • Tire Repairs • Mounting • Wheel Alignments
and Computer Spin Balancing

— Firestone Tires and Tubes —

RICHARDSON HIGHWAY in DELTA JUNCTION

Member of the Alaska Visitors Association – AVA

DIEHL'S SHOPPING CENTER

ONE STOP SHOPPING

Junior Department Store • Clothing • Souvenirs
Hunting & Fishing Licenses • Camping Equipment & Supplies
Photo Supplies • Bank services in building

Diehl's Delights in our mall

POPCORN • Caramel and Flavored
ESPRESSO • Coffee Beans
ICE CREAM • CHOCOLATES
GIFTS • GIFTS • GIFTS

Neil & Joanne Heitman, Owners since 1961

HOURS: Monday-Saturday 10 a.m.- 7 p.m.
(907) 895-4651   0.5 miles north of Visitors Center   P.O. Box 669, Delta Junction, Alaska 99737

military/civil airport (prior permission required).

Delta Junction is at the actual end of the Alaska Highway. From here, the Richardson Highway leads to Fairbanks. (*The MILEPOST®* logs this stretch of highway as a continuation of the Alaska Highway.) Have your picture taken with the monument in front of the visitor center that marks the highway's end. The chamber of commerce visitor center also has free brochures and displays of Alaska wildflowers, mounted animals, and furs to touch. Travelers may also purchase certificates here, certifying that they have reached the end of the Alaska Highway.

Delta Junction is also the first view of the trans-Alaska pipeline for travelers coming up the Alaska Highway from Canada. A good spot to see and photograph the pipeline is at **Milepost V 275.4**, just north of town, where the pipeline crosses the Tanana River. There is an interesting display of pipe used in 3 Alaska pipeline projects outside the visitor center.

Named after the nearby Delta River, Delta Junction began as a construction camp on the Richardson Highway in 1919. (It was first known as Buffalo Center because of the American bison that were transplanted here in the 1920s.)

The Richardson Highway, connecting Valdez at tidewater with Fairbanks in the Interior, predates the Alaska Highway by 20 years. The Richardson was already a wagon road in 1910, and was updated to automobile standards in the 1920s by the Alaska Road Commission (ARC).

In the last decade, the state has encouraged development of the agricultural industry in the Delta area. In 1978, the state began Delta Agricultural Project I, disposing of 60,000 acres and creating 22 farms averaging approximately 2,700 acres each. In 1982, the Delta II project disposed of 25,000 acres, creating 15 farms averaging more than 1,600 acres each.

In 1991, nearly 40,000 acres were in some form of agricultural use (including production of barley, oats, wheat, forage, pasture, grass seed, canola, potatoes, field peas, forage brassicas) and conservation use. Barley is the major feed grain grown in Delta. It is an excellent energy feed for cattle, hogs and sheep. Production acreages are determined by the in-state demand for barley.

Delta barley is stored on farms or in a local co-op elevator, sold on the open market, or used to feed livestock. Small-scale farming of vegetables, 2 commercial potato farms, 3 active dairies, a dairy processing center, 6 beef producers, 3 swine producers, a bison ranch and 2 commercial greenhouses all contribute to Delta Junction's agriculture. Recently, a reindeer ranch for meat and breeding stock has begun development.

ACCOMMODATIONS

Delta Junction has motels, restaurants, gas stations, a laundromat and dry cleaners, a shopping center, post office, bank and other businesses. There are several churches. Delta Community Park, on Kimball Street 1 block off the highway, has softball and soccer fields. There is also a car wash on Kimball.

Alaska 7 Motel, 16 large, clean, comfortable rooms with full bath and showers. Color TV and courtesy coffee in each room. Kitchenettes and phone available. Comfort at a comfortable price. Open year-round. Major credit cards accepted. Mile 270.3 Richardson-Alaska Highway. (907) 895-4848. See display ad this section. [ADVERTISEMENT]

Delta international hostel north of town: turn at **Milepost V 271.7** (Tanana Loop Road), drive 1 mile/1.6 km and turn right on Tanana Loop Extension then left on a gravel road named Main Street, USA (follow signs). Sleeping bags are required. Fee: $5 per night.

Jack's Chevron
- Chevron and related products
- Specializing in automotive tune-ups, tire repair, tire balancing and wheel alignments

CLEAN REST ROOMS
(907) 895-9994 • Delta Junction, Alaska
DOWNTOWN, 1,000 FT. PAST VISITORS CENTER ON RIGHT SIDE NORTHBOUND

Jack's Liquor Store
COLD BEER • WINE • PACKAGED LIQUOR
"Next door to Jack's Chevron"

CITY PARK CARWASH
On Kimball Street, 2 blocks behind Delta Diner
Delta Junction, Alaska   (907) 895-4306
THOUSANDS OF SATISFIED USERS — LOOK FOR THE SIGN!

OPEN 24 Hours 7 DAYS

High Pressure • Coin-Operated • R.V. Bay • Bubble Brush

Richard Miller, Owner

DELTA SHOP-RITE

YOUR FULL-SERVICE SUPERMARKET

A Large Selection of Groceries and Fresh Produce at Competitive Prices
FRESH MEAT • DAIRY PRODUCTS • FROZEN FOODS • ICE CREAM
BULK FOODS • HEALTH & BEAUTY PRODUCTS
COMPLETE DELI • FRIED CHICKEN • FAST FOODS
DAILY HOMECOOKED SPECIALS • FOUNTAIN DRINKS
IN-STORE BAKERY, BAKED FRESH DAILY
BAGGED and BLOCK ICE

Great Prices and Values — Come In and See for Yourself!

P.O. Box 829, Delta Junction, Alaska 99737

SUMMER HOURS: 6:30 a.m. - 11 p.m. Daily
ACROSS FROM POST OFFICE • In Downtown Delta Junction   (907) 895-4653

ALASKA HIGHWAY • DELTA JUNCTION

Spectacular Alaska Range as seen across Delta River valley. (Jerrianne Lowther, staff)

1992 Events

MAY
21-25 Alaska Square and Round Dance Festival
22-26 Buffalo Wallow

JUNE
18 Army Motors Convoy stop

JULY
4 Buffalo Barbecue
31-8/2 Deltana Fair

AUGUST
1-2 Deltana Fair continues

ATTRACTIONS

Buffalo Herd: American bison were transplanted into the Delta Junction area in the 1920s. Because the bison have become costly pests to many farmers in the Delta area, the 70,000-acre Delta Bison Range was created south of the Alaska Highway in 1980. However, keeping the bison on their refuge and out of the barley fields is a continuing problem. Summer visitors who wish to look at the bison are advised to visit the viewpoint at **Milepost V 241.3** on the Richardson Highway; use binoculars. The herd contained 300 bison in 1988 when the last census was taken by the ADF&G.

Special Events: As the official end of the Alaska Highway, Delta Junction will be celebrating the 50th anniversary of the highway throughout the year. In addition to this special event, Delta Junction celebrates a traditional Fourth of July with a Buffalo Barbecue, sponsored by the Pioneers.

Buffalo Wallow, a 4-day square dance festival hosted by Buffalo Squares, is held every Memorial Day weekend. This year, the Alaska State Square and Round Dance

Hostel open Memorial Day through Labor Day; phone 895-5074.

There are private RV parks just south and just north of town. Two public campgrounds are located nearby: Delta state campground at **Milepost V 267.1**, and Clearwater state campground on Remington Road (see **Milepost DC 1414.9** and **V 268.3**). ▲

TRANSPORTATION

Air: Scheduled service via 40-Mile Air from Tok to Fairbanks; Delta stop on request. Local air service available. **Bus:** See Bus Lines in the GENERAL INFORMATION section for scheduled service to other communities.

Talbott's Bed & Breakfast
Clean, Comfortable Rooms in New Log Home
Country Breakfast 
3 miles east of Delta in a beautiful Birch grove
Please call for reservations
(907) 895-5025
Your Hosts: Larry and Monica Talbott
P.O. Box 857, Delta Junction, AK 99737

Bergstad's TRAVEL and TRAILER COURT
Located One Mile Southeast of Delta Junction on Alaska Highway
Large — Camper • Trailer • Tent Spaces in a wooded area, with water, electricity, dump station, car wash and sewer treatment plant
Clean Showers, Laundry and Rest Rooms
104 Full Hookups
Phone (907) 895-4856
Mile 1420.9 Alaska Highway in Delta Junction

In Delta Junction
delta SELF SERVICE LAUNDRY and CLEANERS
Hours: 9 a.m. to 10 p.m. Daily
Two blocks north of Public Campground at Milepost 267.5 Richardson Hwy. Left Side Northbound
INDIVIDUAL SHOWER UNITS•STOP! RELAX! CLEAN UP!
Owner: Theta Musgrove — Attendant on duty

KELLY'S COUNTRY INN MOTEL
MODERN UNITS • PRIVATE BATHS • KITCHENETTES AVAILABLE
TELEVISION • TELEPHONES • PHONE (907) 895-4667 or 895-4973
Box 849, Delta Junction 99737 Chaddie Kelly, Owner
Downtown Delta Junction
Right Side Northbound

♥ **KOUNTRY KORNER STORE** ♥
Specialty and Handicraft Gifts
Mon. - Sat. 10 - 6 p.m. • (907) 895-4224
Downtown – Turn on Kimball Street
Across highway from Diehl's and Shop-Rite
(street alongside Interior Building Supply)

NEW, SPACIOUS COMFORTABLE DINING ROOM • QUICK TABLE SERVICE

PIZZA BELLA FAMILY RESTAURANT

FULL MENU • ITALIAN & AMERICAN CUISINE
Homemade Soups • Salads • Pizza • Hot Sandwiches
Steaks • Prime Rib • Seafood • Orders To Go
Wines and Cold Beer • Satisfaction Guaranteed

TOUR BUSES WELCOME
Reservations Appreciated *(not required)*
Open 7 Days 10 a.m. to Midnight
(907) 895-4841 or 895-4524

Across from Visitor Information Center in Delta Junction

ALASKAN OUTBACK EXPEDITIONS 
• Float Trips on Wild & Scenic Rivers
• Fly-In Fishing for Rainbow Trout or Northern Pike
• Big Game Photography for Sheep, Moose & Bear
• Hiking & Camping to Explore Glaciers & Glacial Geology

EXPLORE ALASKA'S INTERIOR
1-800-676-5963 or (907) 895-4886
Alaskan Outback Expeditions
P.O. Box 80281
Fairbanks, Alaska 99708
For Information and Free Color Brochure Call or Write

Festival will be held in Delta Junction May 21-25, 1992. The Buffalo Squares also sponsor a campout and dance at Delta state campground the second Saturday in July.

The Deltana Fair is held the first Friday, Saturday and Sunday in August. The fair includes a barbecue, Lions' pancake breakfast, local handicrafts, displays and games, concessions, contests and a parade. A highlight of the fair is the Great Alaska Outhouse Race, held on Sunday, in which 4 pushers and 1 sitter compete for the coveted "Golden Throne" award.

Tour the agriculture of the area by driving Sawmill Creek Road (turn off at **Milepost DC 1403.6** Alaska Highway) and Clearwater Road (see **Milepost DC 1414.9**). Sawmill Creek Road goes through the heart of the grain-producing Delta Ag Project and local farmers welcome visiting farmers' questions in between planting and harvesting. Along Clearwater and Remington roads you may view the older farms, which produce forage crops and livestock. The Clearwater-Remington Road area has some of the older homesteads which were the prime movers behind the current agricultural expansion. Tanana Loop Road (**Milepost V 271.7**), Tanana Loop Extension and Mill-Tan Road go past many new farms which have been developed in the last few years. The visitor information center in downtown Delta Junction can answer many questions on local agriculture.

AREA FISHING: **Delta-Clearwater River**, grayling and whitefish; silver salmon spawn here in October. Access via Clearwater Road or Jack Warren Road (see Delta Vicinity map). (Although USGS topographic maps show this tributary of the Tanana River as Clearwater Creek, local residents refer to the stream as the Delta-Clearwater River.) **Goodpaster River**, accessible by boat via Delta-Clearwater and Tanana rivers; excellent grayling fishing.

Richardson–Alaska Highway Log

(continued)
Although logged as a natural extension of the Alaska Highway, the highway between Delta Junction and Fairbanks is designated as part of the Richardson Highway, with existing mileposts showing distance from Valdez.

Distance from Valdez (V) is followed by distance from Dawson Creek (DC) and distance from Fairbanks (F).

V 266 (428 km) DC 1422 (2288.5 km) F 98 (157.7 km) Delta Junction visitor information center sits at the junction of the Alaska and Richardson highways. Turn south for Valdez (see RICHARDSON HIGHWAY section). Continue north for Fairbanks.

V 266.3 (428.6 km) DC 1422.3 (2289 km) F 97.7 (157.2 km) Delta Junction post office.

V 266.4 (428.7 km) DC 1422.4 (2289.1 km) F 97.6 (157.1 km) **City Park Carwash.** New high-pressure coin-operated car wash with 7 special wash selections. Extra-tall RV bay. Change machine and vendors. Our bubble brush is famous for removing that Alcan Highway mud. Open 24 hours, 7 days. Turn on Kimball Street. We're 2 blocks off Richardson-Alaska Highway behind Delta Diner. Watch for our sign. (907) 895-4306.
[ADVERTISEMENT]

V 266.5 (428.9 km) DC 1422.5 (2289.2 km) F 97.5 (156.9 km) Delta Junction library and city hall.

V 266.8 (429.4 km) DC 1422.8 (2289.7 km) F 97.2 (156.4 km) Alaska Dept. of Fish and Game office.

V 267.1 (430 km) DC 1423.1 (2290.2 km) F 96.9 (155.9 km) Delta state campground to east; 24 sites, water, tables, shelter with covered tables, toilets, $6 nightly fee or annual pass. Large turnout at campground entrance. Turnout on west side of highway on bank of the Delta River offers excellent views of the Alaska Range.

V 267.2 (430 km) DC 1423.2 (2290.4 km) F 96.8 (155.7 km) Alaska Division of Forestry office.

V 267.5 (430.5 km) DC 1423.5 (2290.9 km) F 96.5 (155.3 km) Laundromat (showers).

V 267.9 (431.1 km) DC 1423.9 (2291.5 km) F 96.1 (154.7 km) Private RV park.

V 268.3 (431.7 km) DC 1424.3 (2292.1 km) F 95.7 (154 km) **Junction** with Jack Warren Road (see Delta Vicinity map this section). Turn here for access to Clearwater state campground (10.5 miles/16.9 km). Clearwater campground has toilets, tables, water and boat launch; pleasant campsites on bank of river. Camping fee $6/night or annual pass.

Driving this loop is a good opportunity to see local homesteads. Gas station on Clearwater Road near Mile 5.2; gas, grocery and lodge on Remington Road near campground. Note that mileposts on these paved side roads run backward from Mile 13 at this junction to Mile 0 at the junction of Clearwater Road and the Alaska Highway.

V 270.3 (435 km) DC 1426.3 (2295.3 km) F 93.7 (150.8 km) Motel.

V 271 (436.1 km) DC 1427 (2296.5 km) F 93 (149.7 km) Medical clinic.

V 271.7 (437.2 km) DC 1427.7 (2297.6 km) F 92.3 (148.5 km) Tanana Loop Road. Turn here for Delta Junction youth hostel. To make a loop drive through farmlands, follow Tanana Loop Road approximately 1 mile/1.6 km, turn right on Tanana Loop Extension, which connects with Jack Warren Road. Turn west on Jack Warren Road to return to highway.

V 272.1 (437.9 km) DC 1428 (2298 km) F 92 (148 km) Fire station.

V 275 (442.6 km) DC 1431 (2303.9 km) F 89 (143.2 km) **The Tanana Trading Post.** See display ad this section.

V 275 (442.6 km) DC 1431 (2303.9 km) F 89 (143.2 km) **Rika's Roadhouse at Big Delta State Historical Park.** Turn northeast at Rika's Road for Rika's Roadhouse and Landing on the banks of the Tanana River. Tour buses welcome. Parking areas with restrooms at both park entrances. The newly renovated Rika's Roadhouse offers worldwide postal service and gift shop specializing

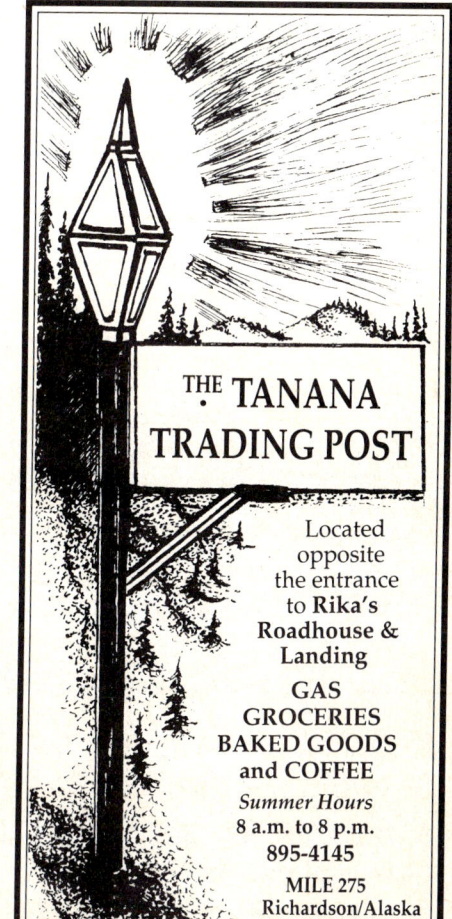

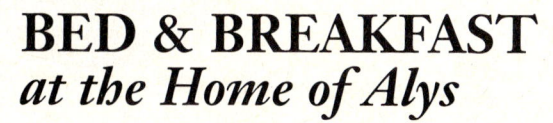

BED & BREAKFAST at the Home of Alys
Queen-Size Beds • TV
Sauna • Spacious Rooms
Quiet Garden Setting
(907) 895-4128
P.O. Box 317, Delta Junction, Alaska 99737
Mile 267.8 Richardson-Alaska Highway / Brewis Subdivision • Follow signs
Hosts: Hank & Alys Brewis

ALASKA 7 MOTEL
(907) 895-4848
Daily and Weekly Rates
CLEAN ECONOMICAL
COLOR TVs
FULL BATHS WITH SHOWERS
Kitchenettes Available
OPEN YEAR-ROUND
Major Credit Cards Accepted
Mile 270.3 Richardson Highway
Write: Box 1115, Delta Junction, Alaska 99737

THE TANANA TRADING POST
Located opposite the entrance to Rika's Roadhouse & Landing
GAS
GROCERIES
BAKED GOODS
and COFFEE
Summer Hours
8 a.m. to 8 p.m.
895-4145
MILE 275
RICHARDSON/ALASKA Highway

On the banks of the Tanana River at *BIG DELTA STATE HISTORICAL PARK*, enjoy

RIKA'S ROADHOUSE & LANDING

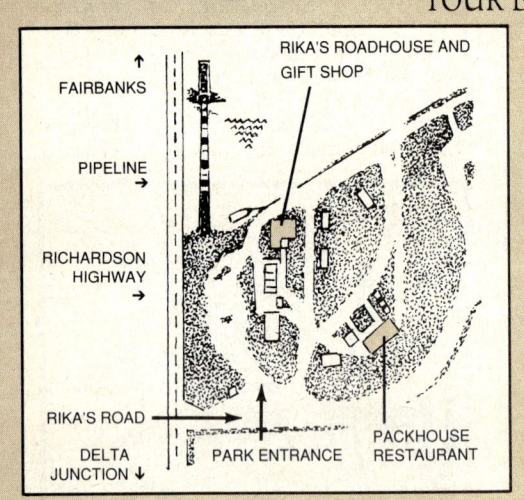

Rated #1 on the Alaska Highway by Major Tour Companies

Roadhouse & Historical Buildings clustered in 10-acre Park
TOUR BUSES WELCOME • FREE ADMISSION, PARKING AND TOURS

Boat and Fishing Trips Available
Staff Attired in Period Costumes

THE ROADHOUSE GIFT SHOP
Specializing in Alaskan-made gifts of
Gold Nugget Jewelry, Fossil Ivory,
Finished Fur Apparel & Diamond Willow,
Souvenir Shirts, Cards & Postcards

WORLDWIDE POSTAL SERVICE

ALASKAN RANCH-RAISED FURS
from **Whitestone Furs of Alaska**
featured in The Roadhouse Gift Shop
Coats, Jackets, Stoles,
Flings, Clings & Collars,
Hats, Hand Muffs & Ear Muffs
Fur Items Made To Order

PACKHOUSE RESTAURANT
• Seating for over 150
for Breakfast and Lunch
(Dinners for Special Functions)
• Homemade Soups
• Fresh Salads & Sandwiches
• Fresh Baked Pies, Breads & Cookies
from **The Alaska Baking Company**

Park Hours 8–8 Daily
Restaurant 9–5 Daily

Mile 275 Richardson/Alaska Highway
Just upstream from the Trans-Alaska Pipeline Tanana River Crossing

Call (907) 895-4201 or (907) 895-4938 Anytime
P.O. Box 1229, Delta Junction, Alaska 99737
See our log ad at Mile 275 Richardson/Alaska Highway • Brochure Available

ALASKA STATE PARKS

in fox furs, gold and diamond willow. Visit the sod-roofed museum, barn, Signal Corp station and other historic structures. Local artisans at work. Live farm animals. Guides in period costumes are available to walk with you through the history of this important crossroads on the Valdez–Fairbanks trail. Meals served 8 A.M. to 5 P.M. in our Packhouse Restaurant, home of the Alaska Baking Co. Breakfast served 8-9:30 A.M. Try out famous bear claws and homemade muffins. The Packhouse Restaurant also offers homemade soups, fresh salads and sandwiches. Guests rave about our homemade pies, featuring strawberry-rhubarb, pecan, chocolate truffle and gourmet silk pies. Overnight RV parking; breakfast available from 8 A.M. RV dump station planned for 1992. After the dust of the highway, the green gardens of the 10-acre park are a welcome haven. Inquire about boat tours and fishing trips. Brochure available. P.O. Box 1229, Delta Junction, AK 99737. Phone (907) 895-4201 or 895-4938 anytime. Free admission. Handicapped access. See display ad this section. [ADVERTISEMENT]

Rika's Roadhouse, which reopened in 1986 after extensive restoration, was built in 1910 by John Hajdukovich. In 1923, Hajdukovich sold it to Rika Wallen, a Swedish immigrant who had managed the roadhouse since 1917. Rika ran the roadhouse into the late 1940s and lived there until her death in 1969.

V 275.4 (443.2 km) **DC 1431.4** (2303.6 km) **F 88.6** (142.6 km) Big Delta Bridge across the Tanana River; spectacular view of pipeline suspended across river. Slow down for parking area at south end of bridge with litter barrels and interpretive sign about pipeline.

The Fur Shack at the pipeline viewpoint features furs and fur products from Alaska's Interior. Large selection of Made-In-Alaska gifts. Alaska pipeline information cards available. Have your picture taken with Ethel, wearing her famous arctic fur bikini. See Ethel also at the Delta Junction Visitor Center. See display ad in Delta Junction section. [ADVERTISEMENT]

From here to Fairbanks there are views of the Tanana River and the Alaska Range to the south. Farming community of **BIG DELTA** (pop. 285); gas, store, 2 bars, a church, Kenner Sawmill and Tanana River boat landing.

V 277.7 (446.9 km) **DC 1433.7** (2307.2 km) **F 86.3** (138.9 km) Turnoff to east for Quartz Lake Recreation Area. Drive in 2.5 miles/4 km on gravel road to intersection: turn left for Lost Lake, continue straight ahead for Quartz Lake (another 0.3 mile/ 0.5 km). Lost Lake, 0.2 mile/0.3 km from intersection, has 8 campsites with picnic tables, toilet and a large parking area with tables and litter barrels. A shallow, picturesque lake with no fish. Quartz Lake has more developed campsites on good loop road, firepits, water, tables, toilet and 2 boat launches. Boat launch fee $3 or annual boat launch pass. Camping fees at both campgrounds: $6/night or annual pass. A trail connects Lost Lake and Quartz Lake camping areas. Excellent fishing for rainbow and silver salmon in **Quartz Lake**. Boat and motor rentals available from Black Spruce Lodge.

Black Spruce Lodge. See display ad this section.

V 277.9 (447.2 km) **DC 1242.1** (1998.9 km) **F 86.1** (138.6 km) Former U.S. Army petroleum station, now closed.

V 278.2 (447.7 km) **DC 1434.2** (2308 km) **F 85.8** (138.1 km) South end of long double-ended turnout to west. Several of these long turnouts northbound are old sections of the Alaska Highway.

V 280.3 (451.1 km) **DC 1436.3** (2311.4 km) **F 83.7** (134.7 km) Gravel turnout to east.

V 284 (457 km) **DC 1440** (2317.4 km) **F 80** (128.7 km) Watch for moose.

V 286 (461.2 km) **DC 1442.6** (2321.6 km) **F 77.4** (124.6 km) Shaw Creek bridge.

V 286.7 (461.4 km) **DC 1442.7** (2321.7 km) **F 77.3** (124.4 km) **Shaw Creek** road. Good to excellent early spring and fall grayling fishing; subject to closure (check locally). Good view northbound of Tanana River which parallels the highway. Fireweed and pale oxytrope along roadsides in summer.

V 287.2 (462.2 km) **DC 1443.2** (2322.5 km) **F 76.8** (123.6 km) Turnout and road to slough to east. Birch trees are thick along this stretch of highway.

V 288 (463.5 km) **DC 1444** (2323.8 km) **F 76** (122.3 km) Panoramic view to the south with vistas of 3 great peaks of the Alaska Range: Mount Hayes, elev. 13,832 feet/4,216m, almost due south; Hess Mountain, elev. 11,940 feet/3,639m, to the west (right) of Mount Hayes; and Mount Deborah, elev. 12,339 feet/3,761m, to the west (right) of Hess Mountain. Mount Hayes is named for Charles Hayes, an early member of the U.S. Geological Survey. Mount Deborah was named in 1907 by the famous Alaskan Judge Wickersham for his wife.

NOTE: Watch for road construction (repaving) next 22 miles/35 km northbound in summer 1992.

V 289.8 (466.4 km) **DC 1445.8** (2326.7 km) **F 74.2** (119.4 km) Paved double-ended turnout with litter barrels to east.

V 291.8 (469.6 km) **DC 1447.8** (2329.9 km) **F 72.2** (116.2 km) Northbound truck lane begins.

V 292.8 (471.2 km) **DC 1448.8** (2331.5 km) **F 71.2** (114.6 km) Truck lanes end. View of Tanana River valley.

V 294 (473.1 km) **DC 1450** (2333.5 km)

The first convoy

The first truck convoy from Whitehorse to Fairbanks, Nov. 20, 1942. The Richardson Highway connecting Valdez, Delta Junction and Fairbanks had been constructed by the Alaska Road Commission in the early 1900s, first as a trail, then a wagon road, and updated to automobile standards in the 1920s. The actual end of the Alaska Highway was—and is—Delta Junction, although most of the early military traffic was bound for Fairbanks or for Anchorage via the Tok Cutoff (built by the Army) and Glenn Highway (built by the Alaska Road Commission). To these existing roads, engineers built the pioneer road south from Tok across the Alaska–Canada border, meeting the Whitehorse forces at Beaver Creek in October 1942.

The BLACK SPRUCE LODGE *on beautiful* **Quartz Lake**
Mile V 277.7 Richardson Hwy. • 24-hour Boat and Lakeside Cabin Rentals
Boat tours of Lake to observe MOOSE feeding
Best RAINBOW TROUT and SILVER SALMON fishing
Food and Beverages • Bar • Boat Rental in parking area
Call (907) 895-4668 or write 2740 Old Richardson Hwy., Delta Junction, AK 99737

F 70 (112.7 km) Paved double-ended turnout.

V 294.2 (473.5 km) **DC 1450.2** (2333.8 km) **F 69.8** (112.3 km) Southbound truck lane begins.

V 294.9 (474.6 km) **DC 1450.9** (2334.9 km) **F 69.1** (111.2 km) Game Management Unit boundary between 20B and 20D. Entering Fairbanks North Star borough northbound.

V 295 (474.7 km) **DC 1451** (2355.1 km) **F 69** (111 km) Site of the original old Richardson Roadhouse which burned down in December 1982.

V 295.4 (475.4 km) **DC 1451.4** (2335.7 km) **F 68.6** (110.4 km) Banner Creek bridge; historic placer gold stream.

V 296.4 (477 km) **DC 1452.4** (2337.3 km) **F 67.6** (108.8 km) Paved turnout with litter barrel to west; view of Alaska Range and Tanana River to south.

V 297.7 (479.1 km) **DC 1453.7** (2339.4 km) **F 66.3** (106.7 km) Large gravel parking area to west below highway; good scenic viewpoint. Paved access road to Tanana River.

V 298.2 (479.9 km) **DC 1454.2** (2340.2 km) **F 65.8** (105.9 km) Scenic viewpoint; paved double-ended turnout with litter barrel to west.

V 301.7 (485.5 km) **DC 1457.5** (2345.9 km) **F 62.3** (100.3 km) South end of long double-ended turnout to west.

V 304.3 (489.7 km) **DC 1460.3** (2350 km) **F 59.7** (96.1 km) Small paved turnout to east.

V 305.2 (491.2 km) **DC 1461.2** (2351.5 km) **F 58.8** (94.6 km) Birch Lake Road to east.

V 306 (492.4 km) **DC 1462** (2352.8 km) **F 58** (93.3 km) Large parking area with toilet to east overlooking **Birch Lake**; unimproved gravel boat launch and beach; fish from shore in spring, from boat in summer, for rainbow and silver salmon. Birch Lake is the site of summer homes of many Fairbanks residents.

V 306.1 (492.6 km) **DC 1462.1** (2352.9 km) **F 57.9** (93.2 km) Turnoff to west for **Lost Lake**. Drive in 0.7 mile/1.1 km on dirt road; silver salmon fishing.

V 307.2 (494.3 km) **DC 1463.2** (2354.7 km) **F 56.8** (91.4 km) Birch Lake highway maintenance station.

V 308.4 (496.3 km) **DC 1464.4** (2356.6 km) **F 55.6** (89.5 km) South end of long double-ended turnout to east.

V 310 (498.9 km) **DC 1466** (2359.2 km) **F 54** (86.9 km) Parking area with litter barrel to west.

NOTE: *Watch for road construction (repaving) next 22 miles/35 km southbound in summer 1992.*

V 313 (503.7 km) **DC 1469** (2364 km) **F 51** (82.1 km) Paved double-ended turnout with litter barrels to west.

V 314.8 (506.6 km) **DC 1470.8** (2366.9 km) **F 49.2** (79.2 km) Midway Lodge.

V 317.9 (511.6 km) **DC 1473.9** (2371.9 km) **F 45.4** (73.1 km) Double-ended gravel turnout.

V 318.5 (512.6 km) **DC 1474.5** (2372.9 km) **F 45.5** (73.2 km) **Tryph's Lodge.** See display ad this section.

V 319.3 (513.8 km) **DC 1475.3** (2374.2 km) **F 44.7** (71.9 km) Access road to Harding Lake summer homes.

V 319.8 (514.7 km) **DC 1475.8** (2375 km) **F 44.2** (71.1 km) Second access road northbound to Harding Lake summer homes. Access to **Little Harding Lake**, king salmon fishing.

V 321.5 (517.4 km) **DC 1477.5** (2377.8 km) **F 42.5** (68.4 km) **Harding Lake** State Recreation Area turnoff; drive east 1.5 miles/2.4 km on paved road to campground. Park headquarters, drinking water fill-up and dump station ($3 charge) at campground entrance. Picnic grounds on lakeshore, swimming, boat ramp ($3 launch fee or annual boat launch pass), ball fields and about 80 campsites. Camping fee $6/night or annual pass. Fishing for lake trout, arctic char, burbot, northern pike, salmon and trout. Lake is reported to be "hard to fish." Worth the drive! Bring your insect repellent. You may need it!

V 322.2 (518.5 km) **DC 1478.2** (2378.9 km) **F 41.8** (67.3 km) Salcha post office. **Salcha River Lodge.** See display ad this section.

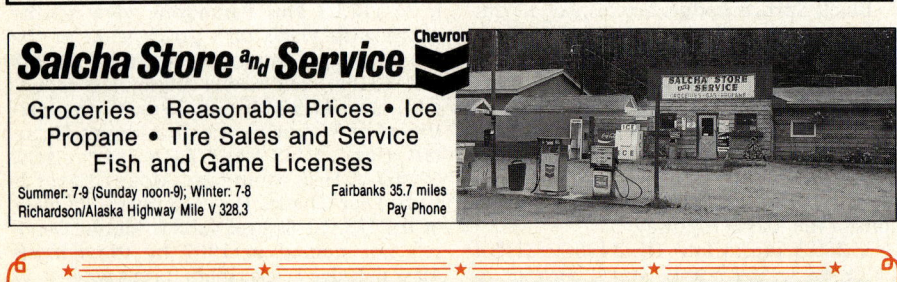

V 323.1 (520 km) **DC 1479.1** (2380.3 km) **F 40.9** (65.8 km) **Salcha River** State Recreation Site; large parking area with 75 sites, boat ramp ($3 launch fee or annual boat launch pass), picnic area, toilets and water. Camping fee $6/night or annual pass. Fishing for king and chum salmon, grayling, sheefish, northern pike and burbot.

V 323.3 (520.3 km) DC 1479.3 (2380.6 km) F 40.7 (65.5 km) Salcha River bridge.

V 323.8 (521.1 km) DC 1479.8 (2381.4 km) F 40.2 (64.7 km) **Sno Shu Inn.** Pan for gold. We supply gold pan and tailings from an operating Alaskan gold mine. Keep all the gold you are sure to find. See Alaskan artifacts collected by 3 generations of a pioneer Alaska family. Bar with sandwiches and snacks. Package liquor store. Cold beverages. [ADVERTISEMENT]

V 324 (521.4 km) DC 1480 (2381.7 km) F 40 (64.4 km) Clear Creek bridge.

V 324.6 (522.4 km) DC 1480.6 (2382.7 km) F 39.4 (63.4 km) Double-ended gravel turnout to east.

V 324.8 (522.7 km) DC 1480.8 (2383 km) F 39.2 (63.1 km) Munsons Slough bridge.

V 325.5 (523.8 km) DC 1481.5 (2384.2 km) F 38.5 (62 km) The community of **SALCHA** (pop. 533) stretches along the highway in both directions. The elementary school is located here. The post office (Zip 99714) is at **Milepost V 322.2**.

V 326.4 (525.3 km) DC 1482.4 (2385.6 km) F 37.6 (60.5 km) Salcha Baptist church to west.

V 327 (526.2 km) DC 1483 (2386.6 km) F 37 (59.5 km) Picturesque log home to west.

V 327.7 (527.4 km) DC 1483.7 (2387.7 km) F 36.3 (58.4 km) Little Salcha River bridge.

V 328.3 (528.3 km) DC 1484.3 (2388.7 km) F 35.7 (57.4 km) **Salcha Store and Service.** See display ad this section.

V 332.3 (535.8 km) DC 1488.3 (2395.1 km) F 31.7 (51 km) **The Knotty Shop.** Stop and be impressed by a truly unique Alaskan gift shop and wildlife museum. Jim and Paula have attempted to maintain a genuine Alaskan flavor—from the unusual burl construction to the Alaskan wildlife displayed in a natural setting to the handcrafted Alaskan gifts. Don't miss the opportunity to stop and browse. See display ad this section. Show us *The MILEPOST®* advertisement for a free small ice cream cone. [ADVERTISEMENT]

V 334.7 (538.6 km) DC 1490.7 (2399 km) F 29.3 (47.2 km) South boundary of Eielson AFB.

V 340.7 (548.3 km) DC 1496.7 (2308.6 km) F 23.3 (37.5 km) Divided highway begins for northbound traffic.

V 341 (548.8 km) DC 1497 (2409.1 km) F 23 (37 km) Entrance to **EIELSON AIR FORCE BASE**, constructed in 1943 and named for Carl Ben Eielson, a famous Alaskan bush pilot. A weekly tour of the base is offered. Phone the Public Affairs office at (907) 377-1410 for reservations and more information.

V 343.7 (553.1 km) DC 1499.7 (2413.5 km) F 20.3 (32.7 km) Moose Creek Road and general store.

Piledriver Slough parallels the highway from here north, flowing into the Tanana River. It is stocked with rainbow trout.

Boaters and floatplanes use Harding Lake at Milepost V 321.5. (Jerrianne Lowther, staff)

Check with general store for access and fishing information.

V 344.7 (554.7 km) DC 1500.7 (2415 km) F 19.3 (31.1 km) Moose Creek bridge.

V 345.5 (556 km) DC 1501.5 (2416.4 km) F 18.5 (29.8 km) *CAUTION: Highway crosses Alaska Railroad tracks.*

V 346 (556.8 km) DC 1502 (2417.2 km) F 17.9 (28.8 km) Chena Flood Channel bridge. Upstream dam is part of flood control project initiated after the Chena River left its banks and flooded Fairbanks in 1967.

V 346.7 (558 km) DC 1502.7 (2418.4 km) F 17.3 (27.8 km) Laurance Road. Turn right northbound for Chena Lakes Recreation Area (follow signs, 2.2 miles/3.5 km to entrance). Constructed by the Army Corps of Engineers and run by Fairbanks North Star Borough, the recreation area has 80 campsites, 92 picnic sites (some with handicap access), pump water, volleyball courts, and a 250-acre lake with swimming beach. **Chena Lake** is stocked with silver salmon and rainbow trout. Nonmotorized boats may be rented from a concessionaire. The **Chena River** flows through part of the recreation area and offers good grayling fishing and also northern pike, whitefish and burbot. Hiking and self-guiding nature trails. Open year-round. Fee charged Memorial Day to Labor Day; day use $3 per vehicle, camping $6 per day.

V 347.1 (558.6 km) DC 1503.1 (2419 km) F 16.9 (27.2 km) Newby Road.

V 347.7 (559.6 km) DC 1503.7 (2419.9 km) F 16.3 (26.2 km) Exit west for St. Nicholas Drive, east for Dawson Road. St. Nicholas Drive is a frontage road that crosses 5th Avenue and ends at Santa Claus Lane. Access to several businesses.

V 348.7 (561.2 km) DC 1504.7 (2421.5 km) F 15.3 (24.6 km) North Pole Visitor Information Center. Turn right on Mission Road for radio station KJNP, turn left northbound for 5th Avenue businesses. North Pole businesses are located along the highway and also along 5th Avenue, which loops back to the highway (becoming Santa Claus Lane) at **Milepost V 349.5**. North Pole is a fast-growing area, with several Fairbanks businesses opening branches here; see description following.

Santaland RV Park. Located in the center of the North Pole business area. Construction on 150 sites started in August 1991, to be completed by May 1992. Facilities for handicapped. Within easy walking to most of the North Pole businesses and churches. Daily shuttle bus to Fairbanks points of interest. North Pole's newest and finest. See display ad this section. [ADVERTISEMENT]

V 349 (561.6 km) DC 1505 (2422 km) F 15 (24.1 km) **Santa Claus House.** In 1949, Con Miller began wearing a Santa Claus suit on business trips throughout the territory, bringing the spirit of St. Nicholas to hundreds of children for the first time. Here the Miller family continues this tradition. Ask about Santa's Christmas letter. Enjoy the unique gift shop and exhibits. See display ad this section. [ADVERTISEMENT]

V 349.5 (562.3 km) DC 1505.5 (2422.8 km) F 14.5 (23.3 km) North Pole and North Pole Plaza to the left northbound via Santa Claus Lane; Badger Road to the right. The Jolly Acres Motel, a truck stop with diesel, 2 small shopping malls and other businesses are located on Badger Road. Santa Claus Lane has several businesses along it, and connects with 5th Avenue, which loops back to the highway at **Milepost V 348.6**. Badger Road is a loop road leading 12 miles/19.3 km along Badger Slough. It reenters the Alaska Highway 7 miles/11.3 km outside of Fairbanks.

JOLLY ACRES MOTEL
— *Quiet & Restful* —

Close to Downtown North Pole
With Kitchens • Continental Breakfast

3068 Badger Road
North Pole, Alaska 99705

For Reservations
(907) 488-9339

North Pole

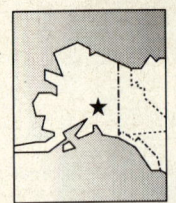

V 349.5 (562.3 km) DC 1505.5 (2422.8 km) F 14.5 (23.3 km) West of the Alaska Highway. **Population:** 1,620; area 15,000. **Emergency Services:** Emergencies only phone 911. **Police**, phone 488-6902. **Alaska State Troopers**, phone 452-2114. **Fire Department**, phone 488-2232.

Visitor Information: At Milepost V 348.6. Open June through August.

Elevation: 500 feet/152m. **Radio:** KJNP-AM 1170, KJNP-FM 100.3; also Fairbanks stations.

Private Aircraft: Bradley Sky Ranch, 0.9 mile/1.4 km northwest; elev. 483 feet/147m; length 4,100 feet/1,250m; gravel; fuel 100.

North Pole has most visitor facilities including restaurants, a motel, laundromats, car wash, grocery and gas stops, gift stores, library, churches, a public park, pharmacy and supermarket. The post office is on 5th Avenue.

North Pole has an annual Winter Carnival with sled dog races, carnival games, food booths and other activities. In summer there's a big Fourth of July celebration.

In 1944 Bon V. Davis homesteaded this area. Dahl and Gaske Development Co. bought the Davis homestead, subdivided it, and named it North Pole, hoping to attract a toy manufacturer who could advertise products as being made in North Pole.

North Pole is the home of many Fairbanks commuters. It has an oil refinery that produces heating fuel, jet fuel and other products. Eielson and Wainwright military bases are nearby.

Radio station KJNP, operated by Calvary's Northern Lights Mission, broadcasts music and religious programs on 1170 AM and 100.3 FM. They also operate television station KJNP Channel 4. Visitors are welcome between 8 A.M. and 10 P.M.; tours may be arranged. KJNP is located on Mission Road about 0.6 mile/1 km northeast of the Alaska Highway. The missionary project includes a

---

AM 1170 KJNP FM 100.3 RADIO
AM 50,000 W
FM 25,000 W

BOX 0 NORTH POLE

All are welcome...
Log Cabins • Sod Roofs
The True Alaskan Motif
... to our community

Channel 4 • TV
9:00 p.m. Live
"CLOSING COMMENTS"

ALASKA 99705

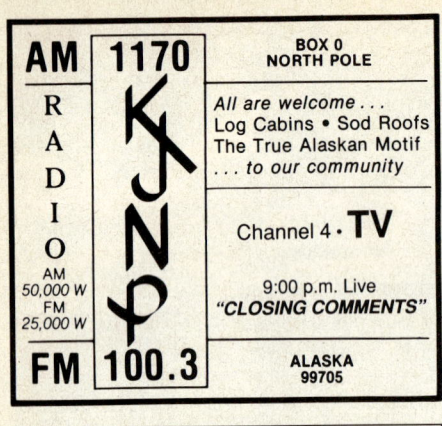

Travelers of the Cold—Sled Dogs of the Far North. A dramatic history of man and dog thriving in harsh winter climates. To order from Alaska Northwest Books™, call 1-800-343-4567.

Beaver Lake Resort Motel
First left off Mission Road • Near Visitor Center
Kitchens • Laundry Facilities • Saunas
EXCEPTIONAL LAKE SETTING
(907) 488-9600 • VISA & MasterCard Accepted
P.O. Box 56137, North Pole, Alaska 99705

BO'S LOGOS
• T'S • SWEATS • CAPS •
LARGEST SELECTION OF ALASKAN AND NORTH POLE DESIGNS
See Our Life-Size Mounted Musk Ox
Bus Tours Welcome
VISA • MasterCard
(907) 488-8280
North Pole Plaza Mall

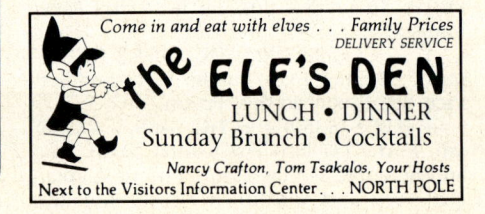

NORTH POLE ADVERTISERS

Beaver Lake Resort .... Ph. (907) 488-9600
Bo's Logos .... North Pole Plaza
Elf's Den, The .... Next to visitor center
Jolly Acres Motel .... 3068 Badger Rd.
KJNP .... Mission Rd.
Prospector Apparel & Sporting
    Goods, The .... North Pole Plaza
Santa Claus House .... St. Nicholas Dr.
Santaland RV Park .... St. Nicholas Dr.

---

the ELF'S DEN
Come in and eat with elves... Family Prices
DELIVERY SERVICE
LUNCH • DINNER
Sunday Brunch • Cocktails
Nancy Crafton, Tom Tsakalos, Your Hosts
Next to the Visitors Information Center... NORTH POLE

Santa Claus House
Alaska's Most Unique GIFT SHOP

ALASKAN GIFTS AND JEWELRY
Pick up a FREE BROCHURE

"Be sure to ask about our
CHRISTMAS LETTER
from Santa to children."

TOYS • CHRISTMAS ORNAMENTS
See our SANTA ROOM... a unique collection
SOFT DRINKS AVAILABLE

Between Both North Pole Exits...
ALASKA-RICHARDSON HIGHWAY MILE V 349
Phone (907) 488-2200... or write... SANTA CLAUS HOUSE, NORTH POLE, AK 99705

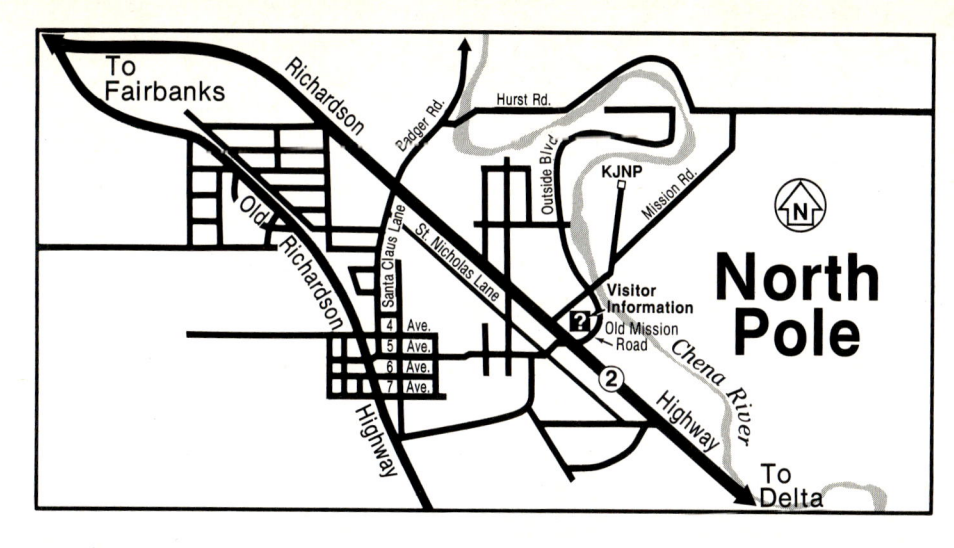

dozen hand-hewn, sod-roofed homes and other buildings constructed of spruce logs.

North Pole Public Park, on 5th Avenue, has a small paved parking area for RVs and trailers; tent sites in trees along narrow dirt road, no camping fee. Santaland RV Park located in downtown. Dump station available at North Pole Plaza. ▲

Richardson–Alaska Highway Log

(continued)

V 350.6 (564.2 km) DC 1506.6 (2424.6 km) F 13.4 (21.6 km) CAUTION: Highway crosses Alaska Railroad tracks.

V 351 (564.9 km) DC 1507 (2425.3 km) F 13 (20.9 km) Twelvemile Village exit.

V 351.7 (566 km) DC 1507.7 (2426.3 km) F 12.3 (19.8 km) Supper club.

V 354.4 (570.3 km) DC 1510.4 (2430.7 km) F 9.6 (15.4 km) Old Richardson Highway exit.

V 356 (572.9 km) DC 1512 (2433.3 km) F 8 (12.9 km) Private RV park.

V 357.1 (574.7 km) DC 1513.1 (2435 km) F 6.9 (11.1 km) Badger Road. This loop road connects with the Alaska Highway again at North Pole. A motel and other businesses are located on Badger Road.

V 357.6 (575.5 km) DC 1513.6 (2435.8 km) F 6.4 (10.3 km) Weigh stations both sides of highway.

V 358.6 (577.1 km) DC 1514.6 (2437.4 km) F 5.4 (8.7 km) Entrance to Fort Wainwright.

V 359.2 (578.1 km) DC 1515.2 (2438.4 km) F 4.8 (7.7 km) CAUTION: Highway crosses Alaska Railroad tracks.

V 359.6 (578.7 km) DC 1515.6 (2439.1 km) F 4.4 (7.1 km) West truck route (Old Richardson Highway) exit for westbound traffic only. Access to motels, restaurants, and Cushman Street business area.

V 360.6 (580.3 km) DC 1516.6 (2440.7 km) F 3.4 (5.5 km) Denali Park/Parks Highway (Alaska Route 3) exit northbound to bypass Fairbanks via the Robert J. Mitchell expressway. Hospital this exit.

V 361 (581 km) DC 1517 (2441.4 km) F 3 (4.8 km) Exit via 30th Avenue to Big Bend business area for east and westbound traffic. Access to motels, restaurants, Old Richardson Highway, Van Horn Road, Cushman Street and downtown Fairbanks.

V 361.3 (581.4 km) DC 1517.3 (2441.8 km) F 2.7 (4.3 km) 30th Avenue overpass; exits both sides of highway.

V 363 (584.2 km) DC 1519 (2444.6 km) F 1 (1.6 km) Turn right on Gaffney Road for Fort Wainwright; left on Airport Way for downtown Fairbanks, University of Alaska, Alaskaland and George Parks Highway (Alaska Route 3). Follow city center signs to downtown Fairbanks and visitor information center. Go straight ahead on the Steese Expressway for Gavora Mall, Bentley Mall, Fox, Steese and Elliott highways and Chena Hot Springs Road.

V 363.3 (584.7 km) DC 1519.3 (2445 km) F 0.7 (1.1 km) 10th Avenue exit to Fairbanks.

V 363.6 (585.1 km) DC 1519.6 (2445.6 km) F 0.4 (0.6 km) Steese Expressway crosses Chena River.

V 363.9 (585.6 km) DC 1519.9 (2446 km) F 0.1 (0.2 km) 3rd Street exit. Gavora Mall.

V 364 (585.8 km) DC 1520 (2446.2 km) F 0 FAIRBANKS. College Road exit route to University of Alaska, Bentley Mall and city center (turn left). For details see FAIRBANKS section.

The PROSPECTOR — APPAREL & SPORTING GOODS

Hunting • Fishing • Camping Equipment • Hunting and Fishing Licenses
Sport • Work • Western Wear • Shoes • Boots
ALASKAN T-SHIRTS

OPEN 7 DAYS • (907) 488-7372   VISA • MASTERCARD
301 N. SANTA CLAUS LANE • NORTH POLE PLAZA MALL

Santaland RV Park

NORTH POLE'S FINEST
Completion date May 1992

* Level Sites Surrounded by Christmas Trees
* Full Service Hookups * Pull Throughs * Hot Showers
* Separate Island for Tents * Laundry Facilities
* Covered Picnic and Bar-B-Que Area

Open May thru September

Between both North Pole exits — *Caravans Welcome*
P.O. Box 55317, North Pole, Alaska 99705

Phone (907) 488-9123   *See log ad at Mile 348.7*

NEXT DOOR TO SANTA CLAUS HOUSE

LIARD HIGHWAY

**Junction with Alaska Highway to Mackenzie Highway junction
BC Highway 77, NWT Highway 7**

The Liard Highway (known locally as 317 Road, also called the Fort Simpson Highway, BC Highway 77 and NWT Highway 7) is named for the Liard River Valley through which it runs for most of its length. The Liard Highway begins about 17 miles/27 km north of Fort Nelson on the Alaska Highway and leads northeast through British Columbia and Northwest Territories for 244.4 miles/393.4 km to junction with the Mackenzie Highway (NWT Highway 1).

The Liard is a relatively straight 2-lane gravel road through boreal forest and muskeg. In French, Liard means "black poplar," and this wilderness highway (officially opened in June 1984) is a corridor through a forest of white and black spruce, trembling aspen and balsam poplar.

The road can be dusty when dry and very muddy when wet. Travelers should check current road conditions by phoning 1-800-661-0750 or (403) 873-0157. Or inquire locally at the visitor information centres in Fort Nelson, BC, or Fort Simpson, NWT. Travel information for the Northwest Territories is also available from the Arctic Hotline; phone toll free weekdays 1-800-661-0788. Visitor facilities are available at Fort Liard.

Although the Liard Highway parallels the Liard River on the Northwest Territories portion of the highway, the road allows few access points to the river. Travelers may enhance their trip by visiting Blackstone Territorial Park and exploring Nahanni National Park by air charter out of Fort Liard, Fort Simpson or Fort Nelson. Blackstone Territorial Park is accessible by road. Along the highway, travelers may walk the cut lines, drive to abandoned construction camps, swim in the borrow pits and bird watch at the barge landings. Remember to bring along lots of insect repellent! (Black flies are worst in September.)

Fishing the highway streams is only fair, but watch for wildlife such as moose, black bear, wood bison, grouse and red-tailed hawks.

NOTE: Gas and limited services are available at Fort Liard, and gas is available at the junction with the Mackenzie Highway. It is a good idea to fill up with gas at Fort Nelson.

Liard Highway Log

Physical kilometreposts are up on the British Columbia portion of the highway about every 5 kilometres, starting with Km 0 at the Alaska Highway junction and ending at the BC–NWT border. Kilometreposts are up about every 2 kilometres on the Northwest Territories portion of the highway, starting with Km 0 at the BC–NWT border and ending at the junction with the Mackenzie Highway.

Distance from the junction with the Alaska Highway (A) is followed by distance from the Mackenzie Highway junction (M).

A 0 M 244.44 (393.4 km) Junction with the Alaska Highway.

A 6.2 (10.1 km) **M 238.2** (383.3 km) Beaver Creek.

A 6.4 (10.3 km) **M 238** (383.1 km) Short side road east to Beaver Lake recreation site; 2 picnic tables, litter barrels, pit toilets, firewood, turnaround space. Short hike downhill through brush to floating dock; limited lake access.

A 14.3 (23.1 km) **M 230.1** (370.3 km) Stanolind Creek. Beaver dams to west.

A 15.6 (25.2 km) **M 228.8** (368.2 km) Gravel pit to west.

A 17.5 (28.2 km) **M 226.9** (365.2 km) Pond to west and cut line through trees shows Cat access in summer, ice road in winter.

A 21.1 (34 km) **M 223.3** (359.4 km) Westcoast Transmission Pipeline crossing. Pipeline transports natural gas from Pointed Mountain near Fort Liard to the company's gas plant on the Alaska Highway just south of Fort Nelson.

A 23.9 (38.4 km) **M 220.5** (355 km) Gravel pit to west.

A 24.2 (38.9 km) **M 220.2** (354.5 km) Road begins descent northbound to Fort Nelson River.

A 26.4 (42.5 km) **M 218** (350.9 km) Fort Nelson River bridge, single lane, reduce speed. The Nelson bridge is the longest Acrow bridge in the world at 1,410 feet/430m. It is 14 feet/4m wide, with a span of 230 feet/70m from pier to pier. The Acrow bridge, formerly called the Bailey bridge after its designer Sir Donald Bailey, is designed of interchangeable steel panels coupled with pins for rapid construction.

A 26.6 (42.9 km) **M 217.8** (350.5 km) Turnout at north end of bridge with pit toilet, table and garbage container. View of the Fort Nelson River.

A 39.7 (63.9 km) **M 204.7** (329.5 km) Tsinhia Creek, grayling run for about 2 weeks in spring.

A 43.4 (69.8 km) **M 201** (323.5 km) Trappers cabin to east.

A 51.8 (83.3 km) **M 192.6** (310.1 km) Side road leads west 1.9 miles/3 km to Tsinhia Lake and dead ends in soft sandy track. A recreation site is planned at Tsinhia Lake.

A 59.2 (95.3 km) **M 185.2** (298.1 km) Concrete beams on west side of highway were dropped from a truck during construction of the Petitot River bridge, setting completion of the bridge back a year. Known locally as the "million dollar garbage heap."

There are several winter roads in this area used by the forest, oil and gas industries. To most summer travelers these roads look like long cut lines or corridors through the Bush.

Floatplane above Virginia Falls will take visitors back to Fort Liard. (Earl L. Brown, staff)

LIARD HIGHWAY
Alaska Highway Junction to Mackenzie Highway Junction

The Liard Highway has replaced the old Fort Simpson winter road which joined Fort Nelson and Fort Simpson.

A 69.4 (111.7 km) **M 175** (281.7 km) Bridge over d'Easum Creek. Good bird-watching area.

A 71.4 (115 km) **M 173** (278.4 km) Access to Maxhamish Lake via 8-mile/13-km winter road accessible in summer by all-terrain vehicles only. A recreation site is planned for Maxhamish Lake.

A 74 (119.1 km) **M 170.4** (274.3 km) Wide unnamed creek flows into Emile Creek to east. Good bird-watching area, beaver pond.

A 75.4 (121.4 km) **M 169** (272 km) Highway emerges from trees northbound; view west of Mount Martin (elev. 4,460 feet/1,360m) and the Kotaneelee Range.

A 80.6 (129.7 km) **M 163.8** (263.7 km) View northwest of mountain ranges in Northwest Territories.

A 81.2 (130.7 km) **M 163.2** (262.6 km) Highway begins descent (7 percent grade) northbound to Petitot River.

A 82.8 (133.2 km) **M 161.6** (260.2 km) Petitot River bridge. The **Petitot River** is reputed to have the warmest swimming water in British Columbia (70°F/21°C). A 9-hour canoe trip to Fort Liard is possible from here (some sheer rock canyons and rapids en route). Good bird-watching area. Also freshwater clams, pike and pickerel; short grayling run in spring.

The Petitot River was named for Father Petitot, an Oblate missionary who came to this area from France in the 1860s.

The Petitot River bridge was the site of the official opening of the Liard Highway on June 23, 1984. The ceremony was marked by an unusual ribbon cutting: A 1926 Model T Ford, carrying dignitaries, was driven through the ribbon (which stretched for about 20 feet before snapping) while a guard of kilted pipers from Yellowknife played on. The Model T Ford, driven by Marl Brown of Fort Nelson, had been across this route in March 1975 just weeks after the bush road had been punched through by Cats and seismic equipment. This earlier trip, in which Mr. Brown was accompanied by Mickey Hempler, took 44 hours from Fort Nelson to Fort Simpson.

A 84.1 (135.4 km) **M 160.3** (258 km) Crest of Petitot River hill (10 percent grade).

A 85 (136.8 km) **M 159.4** (256.6 km) BC-NWT border. TIME ZONE CHANGE: British Columbia observes Pacific time, Northwest Territories observes Mountain time.

Northwest Territories restricts liquor importation as follows: 1 40-oz. hard liquor or 1 40-oz. wine or 1 dozen bottles of beer per person.

A 85.2 (137.1 km) **M 159.2** (256.2 km) Turnout to east with litter barrels.

A 107 (172.2 km) **M 137.4** (221.1 km) Vehicle inspection station and weigh scales to east.

A 108.6 (174.8 km) **M 135.8** (218.5 km) **Junction** with side road which leads 4 miles/6.4 km to Fort Liard (description follows). Pointed Mountain Highway Services Ltd., located at junction, has gas, diesel, propane, restaurant, lodging, craft shop, showers, laundromat, car repair and visitor information.

Views from road into Fort Liard across the Liard River of Mount Coty (elev. 2,715 feet/830m) and Pointed Mountain (elev. 4,610 feet/1,405m) at the southern tip of the Liard Range.

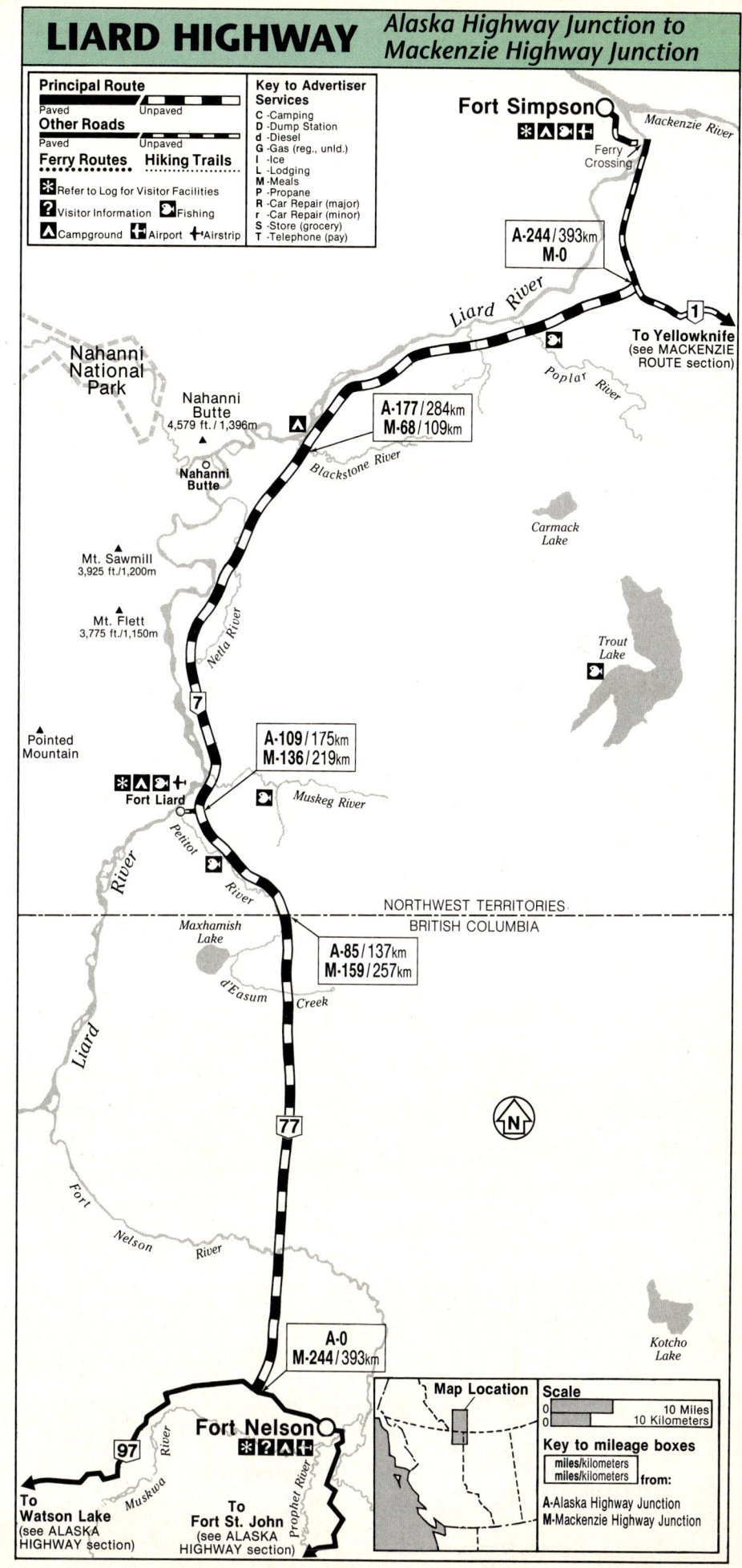

Fort Liard

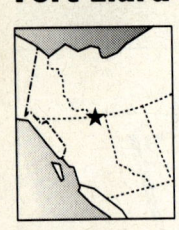

Located on the south bank of the Liard River near its confluence with the Petitot River (known locally as Black River because of its colour), about 50 miles/80 km south of Nahanni Butte. **Population:** 396. **Emergency Services: RCMP**, phone 770-4221. **Fire Department**, phone 770-4241. **Nursing Station**, phone 770-4301.

Elevation: 700 feet/213m. **Climate:** There is no permafrost here. Good soil and water, a long summer season with long hours of daylight, and comparatively mild climate considering Fort Liard's geographical location. Luxuriant local gardens. The Liard River here is approximately 1,500 feet/450m wide, fairly swift, and subject to occasional flooding. **Radio and Television:** CBC radio (microwave), a Native language station from Yellowknife and a community radio station; 4 channels plus CBC Television (Anik) and private satellite receivers.

Private Aircraft: Fort Liard airstrip; elev. 700 feet/213m; length 2,950 feet/899m; gravel; fuel 100/130 (obtain from Deh Cho Air Ltd.).

Transportation: Air–Charter service year-round via Deh Cho Air. **Barge**–Non-scheduled barge service in summer from Fort Nelson and Hay River.

This small, well-laid-out settlement of log cabins and homes is located among tall poplar, spruce and birch trees on the south bank of the Liard River. The shy but friendly residents live a comparatively traditional life of hunting, trapping, fishing and making handicrafts. Fort Liard residents are well known for the high quality of their birch-bark baskets and porcupine quill workmanship.

Recreation and sightseeing in the area include swimming and fishing (for pike, pickerel, goldeye and spring grayling) at the confluence of the Liard and Petitot rivers; air charter or canoe trip to Trout Lake, Bovie Lake, Fisherman's Lake, 300-foot-/91-m-high Virginia Falls in Nahanni National Park, Tlogotsho Plateau, or scenic Liard and Kotaneelee mountain ranges. Good viewing for Dall sheep, grizzly bear and caribou. Canoe rentals available from Deh Cho Air Ltd.

The North West Co. established a trading post near here at the confluence of the Liard and Petitot rivers called Riviere aux Liards in 1805. The post was abandoned after the massacre of more than a dozen residents by Indians. It was reestablished in 1820, then taken over by the Hudson's Bay Co. in 1821 when the 2 companies merged. The well-known geologist Charles Camsell was born at Fort Liard in 1876.

Facilities here include a hotel with 8 rooms, 6 with kitchenettes (reservations suggested), 2 general stores, playground, outdoor rink, curling rink, craft shop (open 1-5 P.M. weekdays) and a Roman Catholic mission. There is no bank in Fort Liard. The community centre has a snack bar which operates irregularly. There is a motel/service station complex with laundromat and coffee shop at the highway junction.

Community-run Hay Lake Campground located just off the access road into Fort Liard; campsites, picnic tables, toilets and floating dock. Campground road may be slippery when wet. ▲

FORT LIARD ADVERTISERS

Acho-Dene Native
  Crafts ....Ph. (403) 770-4161
Deh Cho Air Ltd................Ph. (403) 770-4103

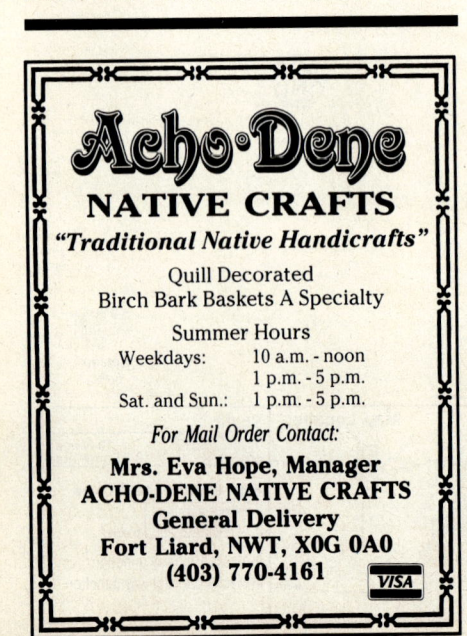

Liard Highway Log

(continued)

A 113.3 (182.4 km) **M 131.1** (211 km) Muskeg River bridge; turnout at north end. Gravel bars on the river make a good rest stop. Trapper's cabin on left. Fishing for pike, pickerel and freshwater clams. The Muskeg River is the local swimming hole for Fort Liard residents.

A 124.9 (201 km) **M 119.5** (192.4 km) Rabbit Creek bridge. Highway now runs close to the Liard River with good views of Liard Range to the west and northwest for the next 13 miles/21 km northbound.

A 128 (206 km) **M 116.4** (187.4 km) Kilometrepost 70.

A 131.1 (211 km) **M 113.3** (182.4 km) Good view of Mount Flett (elev. 3,775 feet/1,150m) ahead northbound.

A 136.7 (220 km) **M 107.7** (173.4 km) Access to Liard River (15-minute hike) via Paramount Mine winter road, an abandoned exploration road across the Liard River into the Liard Range. Watch for wolf and wood bison tracks.

A 146.9 (236.4 km) **M 97.5** (157 km) Short road west to locally named Whissel Landing on the Liard River, where road construction materials were brought in by barge during construction of the Liard Highway.

A 147.3 (237 km) **M 97.1** (156.4 km) Road widens for an emergency airstrip.

A 157.8 (253.9 km) **M 86.6** (139.5 km) Bridge over Netla River. The Netla River Delta is an important waterfowl breeding habitat and a significant Indian fishing and hunting area.

A 163.7 (263.4 km) **M 80.7** (130 km) Road widens for an emergency airstrip.

A 165.9 (267 km) **M 78.5** (126.4 km) Turnoff to west for winter road to Nahanni Butte (no summer access).

A 171.8 (276.5 km) **M 72.6** (116.8 km) Creek Bridge, once called Scotty's Creek after an old trapper who had a cabin upstream. There are many such cabins in this area that once belonged (and still do) to prospectors and trappers, but they are not visible to the motorist. Stands of white spruce, white birch and balsam poplar along highway.

A 176.3 (283.7 km) **M 68.1** (109.7 km) Bridge over Upper Blackstone River. Picnic area on riverbank with tables, firewood, firepits and garbage containers.

A 176.6 (284.2 km) **M 67.8** (109.2 km) Blackstone River bridge.

A 179.1 (288.3 km) **M 65.3** (105.1 km) Entrance to Blackstone Territorial Park; 19 campsites with tables and firepits; firewood, water and garbage containers, outhouses and boat dock. The boat launch here is usable only in high water early in the season; use boat launch at Cadillac Landing, Milepost A 182.9, during low water. The visitor information building, built with local logs, is located on the bank of the Liard River with superb views of Nahanni Butte (elev. 4,579 feet/1,396m). The centre is open mid-May to mid-September. ▲

A 180.9 (291.2 km) **M 63.5** (102.2 km) Entrance to Lindberg Landing, the homestead of Liard River pioneers Edwin and Sue Lindberg. The Lindbergs offer overnight accommodations in self-contained units, canoe and ATV rentals, boat launch and river tours.

A 182.9 (294.3 km) **M 61.5** (99.1 km) Barge landing once used to service Cadillac Mine and bring in construction materials. Access to river via 0.6-mile/0.9-km road (muddy when wet).

Air charter service operates floatplane flightseeing trips of Nahanni National Park from Cadillac Landing.

A 192.8 (310.3 km) **M 51.6** (83.1 km) Road widens for emergency airstrip.

A 197.8 (318.4 km) **M 46.6** (75 km) Kilometrepost 180.

A 211.3 (340.1 km) **M 33.1** (53.3 km) Bridge over Birch River.

A 216.7 (348.8 km) **M 27.7** (44.6 km) Kilometrepost 210.

A 222.8 (358.5 km) **M 21.6** (34.9 km) Good grayling and pike fishing in **Poplar River** culverts.

A 223 (358.8 km) **M 21.4** (34.6 km) Dirt road on left northbound leads 4 miles/6.4 km to Liard River; 4-wheel drive recommended. Wide beach, good spot for viewing wildlife.

A 228.1 (367.1 km) **M 16.3** (26.3 km) Microwave tower to east. Vegetation changes northbound to muskeg with black spruce, tamarack and jackpine.

A 235.6 (379.2 km) **M 8.8** (14.2 km) Kilometrepost 240.

A 244.2 (393 km) **M 0.2** (0.4 km) Road maintenance camp.

A 244.4 (393.4 km) **M 0 Junction** with the Mackenzie Highway (NWT 1). Turn right (south) for Hay River and Yellowknife; turn left (north) for Fort Simpson. See MACKENZIE ROUTE section for details.

Restaurant and gas station with regular, unleaded and diesel located at junction, operated by the Fort Simpson Indian Band.

Acho·Dene NATIVE CRAFTS
"Traditional Native Handicrafts"

Quill Decorated
Birch Bark Baskets A Specialty

Summer Hours
Weekdays: 10 a.m. - noon
    1 p.m. - 5 p.m.
Sat. and Sun.: 1 p.m. - 5 p.m.

For Mail Order Contact:
**Mrs. Eva Hope, Manager
ACHO-DENE NATIVE CRAFTS
General Delivery
Fort Liard, NWT, X0G 0A0
(403) 770-4161**
VISA

DEH CHO AIR LTD.
TOURS TO NAHANNI PARK

See our display ad in the Fort Nelson section

MACKENZIE HIGHWAY

Edmonton, Alberta, to Yellowknife, Northwest Territories
Alberta Highway 35, NWT Highways 1, 2, 3, 4, 5 and 6
(See maps, pages 184–185)

Named for explorer Alexander Mackenzie, who in 1779 navigated Great Slave Lake and sailed to the mouth of the Mackenzie River seeking a trade route for the Hudson's Bay Co., the Mackenzie Route is an adventure for modern explorers. It is not a trip for the impulsive. While there are accommodations, gas stations and other services in cities and settlements along the highways, long distances and some rough roads require motorists to plan in advance.

The Mackenzie Route covers the following highways: Alberta Highway 35 and NWT Highway 1 to Fort Simpson (Mackenzie Highway); Highway 2 to Hay River; Highway 3 to Yellowknife; Highway 4 (Ingraham Trail); Highway 5 to Fort Smith; and Highway 6 to Fort Resolution. NWT Highway 7, the Liard Highway, connecting the Mackenzie Highway with the Alaska Highway north of Fort Nelson, is covered in the LIARD HIGHWAY section.

Allow at least 2 weeks to travel the entire route. For general information on travel in the Northwest Territories, phone the Arctic Hotline toll free 1-800-661-0788 during business hours on weekdays.

Highway maintenance crews are continually graveling the roads and treating them for dust, but you may find the roads dusty in dry weather and muddy in wet. You will also find mosquitoes, so take along repellent. Most Northwest Territories highways are gravel; see Driving Information in the GENERAL INFORMATION section for tips on driving gravel roads. For road conditions call the Arctic Hotline 1-800-661-0750.

In summer, the Northwest Territories government provides free ferry service for cars and passengers across the Mackenzie River to Fort Providence and across the Liard River to Fort Simpson. In winter, traffic crosses on the ice. For current ferry information call (403) 873-7799 in Yellowknife, or 1-800-661-0751.

The Mackenzie Highway begins at Grimshaw, AB. There are several routes to Grimshaw to choose from. *The MILEPOST* logs the Valleyview route from Edmonton to Grimshaw via Highways 16, 43 and 2, and Highway 2 north from Grande Prairie through Dunvegan and Fairview to Grimshaw (logs follow). You may also reach Grimshaw via Highway 2 or 33 north from Edmonton through Slave Lake and via Highways 2 and 49.

LOG OF THE DUNVEGAN-FAIRVIEW ROUTE TO THE MACKENZIE HIGHWAY
Distance from Grande Prairie (GP) is shown.

GP 0 GRANDE PRAIRIE; turn to the EAST ACCESS ROUTE section for details on Grande Prairie.

GP 3.7 (6 km) **Junction** of Highways 2 and 34. Continue north on Highway 2 for Fairview and Grimshaw.

GP 5.9 (9.5 km) Town of Clairmont to east.

GP 12.2 (19.7 km) **SEXSMITH**, sometimes called the "Grain Capital of Alberta" because of its agricultural industry. Campground with 13 RV sites, tent sites, picnic shelters, restrooms, showers, dump station and playground. ▲

GP 14.3 (23 km) **Junction** with Highway 59 west.

GP 35.3 (56.8 km) **WOKING** (pop. 150), an agricultural community. Free provincial park campground with 20 sites, picnic shelter, firewood, fireplaces, tables, pit toilets and pump water. ▲

GP 43.2 (69.5 km) **Junction** with Highway 49. Town of **RYCROFT** (pop. 734) to west.

GP 43.5 (70.1 km) Paved turnout with litter barrels.

GP 46.1 (74.3 km) Spirit River bridge.

GP 56.2 (90.5 km) Dunvegan Bridge, Alberta's only motor vehicle suspension bridge, and the agricultural community of **DUNVEGAN**. Site of Fort Dunvegan, a Hudson's Bay Co. post, and St. Charles Mission, the first permanent Roman Catholic mission established in the Peace River district. A cairn commemorating the mission is located at the provincial park at the north end of Dunvegan Bridge, where some of the old buildings of both the mission and post have been restored. There are several market gardens in the Dunvegan area.

Provincial campground at north end of Dunvegan Bridge has 20 tent and RV sites, shelter, firewood, fireplaces, tables, pit toilets, pump water and public phone. No camping fee. ▲

GP 59.4 (95.7 km) Turnout to east with litter barrels and historical marker about the Peace River.

GP 64.3 (103.5 km) **Junction** with Highway 64 north.

GP 71.2 (114.7 km) **FAIRVIEW** (pop. 3,281), an agricultural centre for the northwest Peace River region. **Emergency Services:** RCMP, phone 835-2211, and **Hospital.** Visitor information centre located at the south end of town. Fairview has 6 hotels/motels (2 with dining), 3 fast-food outlets, and a free Lions campground with 20 sites, tables, firewood, shelter, pit toilets, tap water and playground. ▲

GP 78.9 (127 km) Settlement of Bluesky; grain elevators.

GP 101.3 (163 km) Settlement of Berwyn; Bissell Memorial United Church located here.

GP 108.7 (175 km) Grimshaw; see description at Mile 0 of the Mackenzie Highway log this section.

Alexandra Falls, at Milepost G 338.8, plunges 109 feet. (Earl L. Brown, staff)

MACKENZIE ROUTE Grimshaw, AB, to Steen River, AB

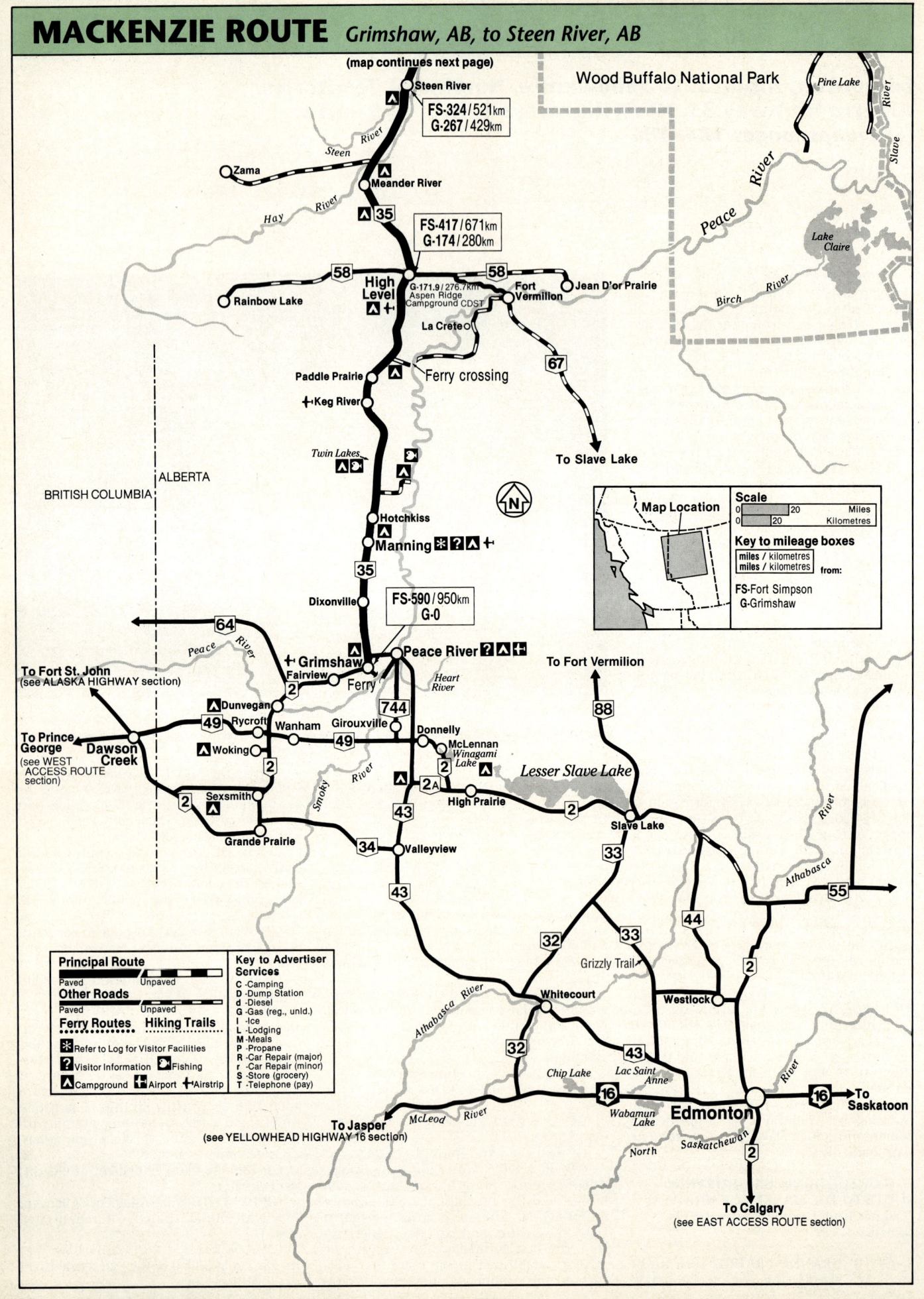

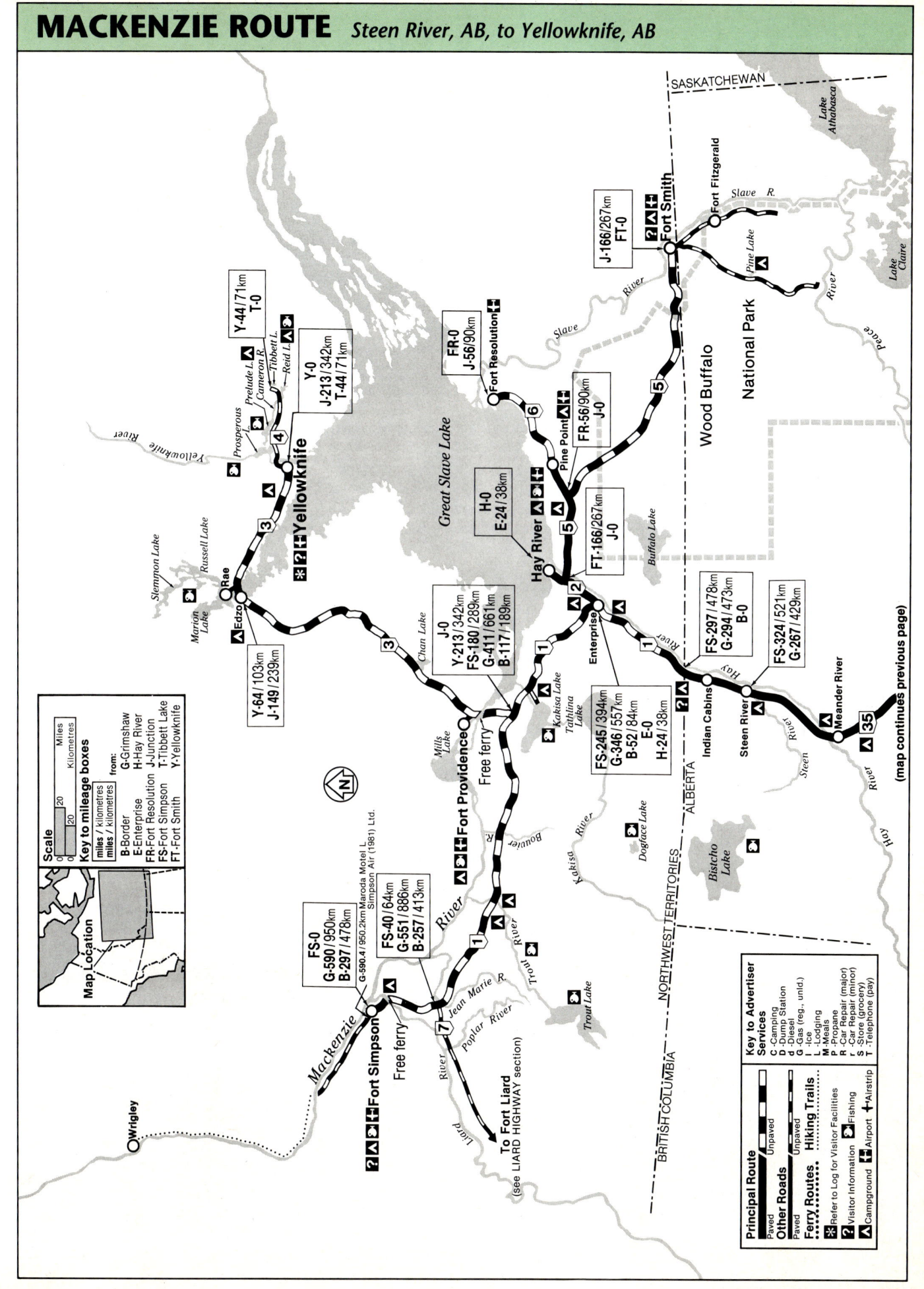

MACKENZIE ROUTE
Steen River, AB, to Yellowknife, AB

MACKENZIE CONNECTION CIRCLE TOUR

Hwy. 49, part of the original supply route to Alaska, extends a warm invitation to visit while travelling the Mackenzie Connection.

Heading west from Donnelly Corner, the junction of Hwy. 2 and 49, there is plenty to see and do. The museum at Girouxville, is renowned for it's vast collection of artifacts relating to the fur trade and pioneer days. The Lakeside Golf and Country Club, a beautiful nine hole course with overnight camping available, boarders several square miles of marshland that has been designated as a wild bird sanctuary. Wanham hosts the annual Provincial Plowing match. 1992 will see them hosting the Canadian Plowing Championships. Wanham invites you to attend this exciting and fun filled 4 day event in late June.

Courtesy Corner Tourist Service, located at the junction of Hwy. 49 and 2 is open 24 hrs. a day and is proud of their huge teepee. From here you can continue west to Dawson Creek or north on Hwy. 2.

You will long remember the magnificence of the Peace River valley as you come over the crest and begin your decent. The Dunvegan suspension bridge is the fourth largest suspension bridge in Canada and nestled along the river is Historic Fort Dunvegan. This old Fort has been restored and has many stories to tell.

Wanham will host the 1992 Canadian Plowing Championships.

Go back in time and take a ferry ride across the Mighty Peace River.

Make your first stop in High Level - Mackenzie Crossroads Museum and Visitors Centre.

THE TEN BIGGEST DAYS IN THE NORTH! Peace River Alberta.

Grimshaw is mile zero on the Mackenzie Hwy. Take Hwy. 684 just south of Grimshaw and enjoy one of the most beautiful drives in all of Alberta. This road will bring you back down into the valley.

Slip into the past - take a ferry ride across the Peace, before continuing on the Peace River town.

Peace River is planning a celebration. August 29th, 1992, voyageurs re-tracing Mackenzie's route (students from Lakehead University) will arrive in Peace River. This will kickoff TEN days of events, ceremonies, celebration and fun. From Grimshaw the Mackenzie Hwy. stretches north, forming Alberta's link to Canada's north. There is plenty to do, from golfing to hunting and birdwatching. Manning is home to the Mighty Moose and also has one of the best Agricultural Museums in northern Alberta. By taking Hwy. 697 you can again cross the Peace River by ferry. After a visit to LaCrete and Fort Vermilion you can take Hwy. 58 back to High Level.

High Level's new Mackenzie Crossroads Museum and Visitors centre is you first point of interest as you arrive in this community. The museum has over 1600 artifacts and is designed to depict the typical general store of the old days. Several beautiful murals on the buildings of the downtown area depict different aspects of life in this area.

Continuing north, you pass out of Alberta and can enjoy the unique offerings of the NWT. The Liard Hwy. is a well graded gravel road with services open only through the summer months. This is your connection to the Alaska Hwy. and the loop of your Mackenzie Connection Circle Tour.

Historic Fort Dunvegan and the fourth largest suspension bridge in Canada.

Grimshaw - Mile 0 on the Mackenzie Highway.

LOG OF THE VALLEYVIEW ROUTE TO THE MACKENZIE HIGHWAY
Distance from Edmonton (E) is shown.

E 0 EDMONTON. Head west on Yellowhead Highway 16. For details on facilities along the highway to Valleyview, turn to the EAST ACCESS ROUTE section.

E 31 (49.9 km) **Junction** of Yellowhead Highway 16 and Highway 43. Turn north on Highway 43.

E 216 (347.6 km) **VALLEYVIEW**; all visitor facilities. Continue north on Highway 43.

E 245 (393.6 km) **Junction** of Highways 43 and 2A; continue north on Highway 43. Little Smoky River Campground, just west of junction, has 50 sites. ▲

E 263 (422.6 km) **Junction** of Highways 43, 2 and 49 at Donnelly Corner. **DONNELLY** (pop. 362), just east of the junction, has a motel and 24-hour service station. Continue north on Highway 2.

E 302 (486 km) **PEACE RIVER** (pop. 6,690; elev. 1,050 feet/320m) is on the banks of the Peace River, 15 miles/24 km northeast of Grimshaw (Mile 0 of the Mackenzie Highway).

Visitor Information: Available at the visitor centre. Peace River Centennial Museum, open daily 2-5 P.M., offers a video on local history of water transportation on the Peace River. The largest town in the region, Peace River has a hotel, 3 motels, 20 restaurants, 8 gas stations (4 with repair service), a hospital, golf course and indoor swimming pool.

Lion's Club Park in town has 75 campsites with full hookups, showers and phone; $7 camping fee. A second public campground located on the outskirts of town has 15 sites. ▲

Private Aircraft: Peace River airport, 7 miles/11.2 km west; elev. 1,873 feet/571m; length 5,000 feet/1,524m; asphalt; fuel 80, 100, jet B.

A view of the Peace River valley and the Twelve-Foot Davis Historical Site are 2 miles/3.2 km east of town on 100th Avenue. A statue marks the grave of Davis, who joined the Cariboo gold rush of the 1840s but arrived after the best land had been staked. Davis filed a claim on a 12-foot strip between 2 larger claims, which eventually earned him $15,000 in gold and the nickname 12-foot Davis. He died in 1900 and was buried here as he had wished.

E 309.5 (498 km) **Junction** with Highway 2 to Grimshaw.

E 314.4 (506 km) **Junction** with Highway 35 (Mackenzie Highway) at **Milepost G 3** (log follows). Grimshaw (description follows) is 3 miles/4.8 km south of this junction.

Mackenzie Highway Log

ALBERTA HIGHWAY 35
Distance from Grimshaw (G) is followed by distance from Fort Simpson (FS).

G 0 FS 590.4 (950.2 km) **GRIMSHAW**, Mile 0 of the Mackenzie Highway. **Population:** 2,645. **Emergency Services:** RCMP, phone 332-4666. **Hospital** and **Ambulance**, phone 332-1155. **Fire Department**, phone 332-4430. **Visitor Information:** In the NAR

MACKENZIE CONNECTION Circle Tour

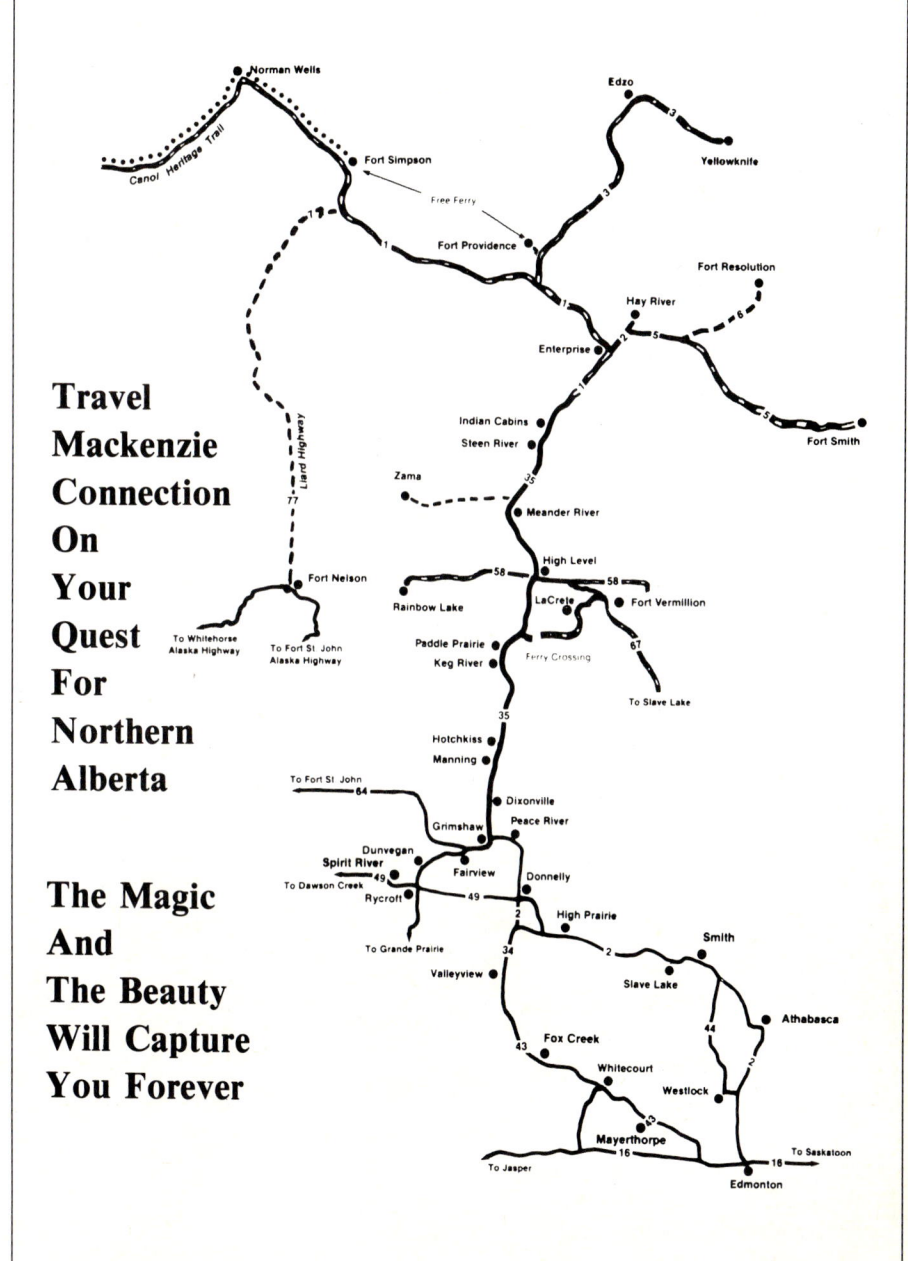

Travel Mackenzie Connection On Your Quest For Northern Alberta

The Magic And The Beauty Will Capture You Forever

For more information contact
The Mighty Peace Tourist Association
Box 6627
Peace River, AB T8S 1S4
Phone (403) 624-4042

——— Mackenzie Highway
- - - - - - Gravel
• • • • • • Winter Road

Alberta, in all her majesty.
Canada

MACKENZIE HIGHWAY

railway car located adjacent the centennial monument marking Mile 0 of the Mackenzie Highway.

Named for pioneer doctor M.E. Grimshaw, who established a practice at Peace River Crossing in 1914, Grimshaw developed as a community centre for area farmers and as a shipping point with the arrival of the railroad in 1921. Scheduled air service from Edmonton and High Level to Peace River airport, 8 miles/12.8 km east.

Grimshaw became a town in February 1953. Local resources are wheat and grains, livestock, gravel, lumber, gas and oil.

Grimshaw has 1 motel, 2 hotels, 5 service stations, a car wash, laundromat and all other visitor facilities. There is a RV dump station and freshwater station located south of the Mile 0 marker and 2 blocks east. Camping just north of town (see **Milepost G 1.9**). There are also an outdoor swimming pool, tennis courts, golf course and seasonal market garden located here.

G 0.2 (0.4 km) **FS 590.2** (949.8 km) **Private Aircraft**: Airstrip to west; elev. 2,050 feet/625m; length, 3,000 feet/914m; turf; fuel 80, 100.

G 1.9 (3 km) **FS 588.5** (947.2 km) Grimshaw provincial campsite and Queen Elizabeth Provincial Park to west. Grimshaw campsite has 20 sites, picnic shelter, firepits, firewood, tables, outhouses, water pump and no camping fee. Queen Elizabeth park (located 3 miles/5 km west) on Lac Cardinal has 56 campsites, picnic shelter, firewood, firepits, toilets, playground and swimming. ▲

G 2.8 (4.6 km) **FS 587.6** (945.6 km) **Junction** of Highways 35 and 2 (east).

G 3.4 (5.5 km) **FS 587** (944.7 km) Sign about construction of the Mackenzie Highway.

G 4.1 (6.6 km) **FS 586.3** (943.6 km) Turnout to east with litter barrels.

G 6.9 (11.1 km) **FS 583.5** (939.1 km) Truck scales to west.

G 20.8 (33.5 km) **FS 569.6** (916.7 km) Chinook Valley to east; cafe, pay phone and 24-hour gas station with tire repair.

G 23.2 (37.3 km) **FS 567.2** (912.9 km) Whitemud River.

G 25.1 (40.4 km) **FS 565.3** (909.8 km) **DIXONVILLE** (pop. 200) has a post office, gas station and souvenir shop. Sulphur Lake provincial campground is located 34 miles/55 km west via Highway 689 (gravel road).

G 28.6 (46.1 km) **FS 561.8** (904.1 km) Pay phone to east.

G 36 (57.9 km) **FS 554.4** (892.3 km) Microwave tower to west.

G 38.4 (61.8 km) **FS 552** (888.4 km) **Junction** with Secondary Road 690 east to Deadwood (6.8 miles/11 km). There is a private exotic bird farm located 2 miles east then 1 mile south. The Bradshaws have geese, peacocks, turkeys, pheasants and other birds; visitors welcome.

G 44.4 (71.5 km) **FS 546** (878.7 km) Buchanan Creek.

G 46.8 (75.4 km) **FS 543.6** (874.8 km) Community of North Star to east.

Manning

G 50.6 (81.4 km) **FS 539.8** (868.8 km) Located on the Notikewin River at the junction of Highways 35 and 691. **Population**: 1,260. **Emergency Services**: RCMP, phone 836-3007. **Hospital and Ambulance**, phone 836-3391. **Fire Department**, phone 836-3000.

Visitor Information: In the information centre. There is a playground adjacent the centre and a dump station across the street.

Named for an Alberta premier, Manning was established in 1947. The railway from Roma, AB, to Pine Point, NWT, reached Manning in September 1962. Today, Manning is a service centre and jumping-off point for hunters and fishermen.

Manning has 5 restaurants, 3 hotel/motels, a pharmacy, food market, golf course, swimming pool and ice rink. Attractions here include the Battle River Pioneer Museum, located on the grounds of the Battle River Agricultural Society, 0.6 mile/1 km east via Highway 691. The museum, which features tools and machinery from the pioneer days, is open daily 1-5 P.M., from June 1 to mid-September.

Turn east at the information centre for Manning municipal campground; 14 sites on the banks of the Notikewin River, fireplaces, tables, water and flush toilets. ▲

NOTE: Last sizable community with all facilities for the next 123 miles/198 km northbound.

Distinctive Manning tourist information centre. (Earl L. Brown, staff)

Mackenzie Highway Log

(continued)

G 52.9 (85.1 km) **FS 537.5** (865.1 km) **Private Aircraft**: Manning airstrip to west; elev. 1,611 feet/491m; length 5,577 feet/1,700m; asphalt; fuel 100/130, jet B.

G 53.2 (85.6 km) **FS 537.2** (864.5 km) Restaurant and service station to west.

G 54.6 (87.8 km) **FS 535.8** (862.4 km) Community of Notikewin to west.

G 59 (94.9 km) **FS 531.4** (355.2 km) Railroad crossing.

G 60.6 (97.6 km) **FS 529.8** (852.6 km) Hotchkiss River bridge.

G 60.8 (97.8 km) **FS 529.6** (852.4 km) Hotchkiss Provincial Park to east; 10 tent and trailer sites, picnic shelter, tables, firepits, fishing, outhouses and water pump. No camping fee. ◄▲

G 61.1 (98.3 km) **FS 529.3** (851.9 km) Microwave tower to east.

G 61.3 (98.6 km) **FS 529.1** (851.6 km) Community of Hotchkiss to east, golf course to west. Hotchkiss has a post office, service station, pay phone, coffee bar, grocery and fuel and propane available. The Condy Meadow Golf Course (0.7 mile/1.2 km west) has 9 holes, sand greens and clubhouse.

G 65.4 (105.3 km) **FS 525** (844.9 km) Chinchaga Forestry Road to west.

G 66.9 (107.6 km) **FS 523.5** (842.6 km) Meikle River bridge.

G 68 (109.4 km) **FS 522.4** (840.7 km) Railroad crossing.

G 68.1 (109.6 km) **FS 522.3** (840.5 km) Hawk Hills to east.

G 71.2 (114.6 km) **FS 519.2** (835.5 km) Turnout with litter barrel to west.

G 74.3 (119.5 km) **FS 516.1** (830.7 km) **Junction** with Highway 692 and access to Notikewin Provincial Park (18.6 miles/30 km) on the Notikewin and Peace rivers. Highway 692 is fairly straight with good gravel surface, although the road narrows and the surfacing may be muddy in wet weather as you approach the park. Just past the entrance to the park is the Top of Hill trailer drop-off site; 10 campsites with tables, toilets, water pump and garbage container. The park road then winds down the hill for 1.4 miles/2.2 km (not recommended for trailers, slippery when wet) to the riverside campground and day-use area; 19 campsites on the **Notikewin River** and 6 picnic sites on the **Peace River**; facilities include tables, water pump, pit toilets, garbage containers, firepits, boat launch and fishing. *CAUTION: Bears in area.* ◄▲

G 88.4 (142.3 km) **FS 502** (807.9 km) Twin Lakes Lodge to east; gas, food, lodging, pay phone and fishing supplies.

G 88.9 (143 km) **FS 501.5** (807.2 km) Twin Lakes Campground to west; 30 shaded sites, picnic shelter, fireplaces, firewood, tables, outhouses, water; beach, boat launch (no gas motors). No camping fee. **Twin Lakes** is stocked with rainbow; good fishing June to September. ◄▲

G 89.3 (143.7 km) **FS 501.1** (806.5 km) Microwave tower to west.

G 95.8 (154.1 km) **FS 494.6** (796.1 km) Turnout to west.

G 96 (154.5 km) **FS 494.4** (795.7 km) Railroad crossing.

G 102.9 (165.6 km) **FS 487.5** (784.6 km) Kemp Creek.

Aspen Ridge Campground

"Opened Spring 1986"

- 30 Campsites — all sizes
- Excellent Water
- Dump Station
- Coin Laundromat
- Hot Showers
- Electrical Hookups
- Children's Playground
- Convenience Store
- Pay Phone

Your Hosts: Pete Bjornson and Family

(403) 926-4540

Box 1796, High Level, Alberta

3 KM South of High Level town centre, Highway 35

G 111.2 (179 km) **FS 479.2** (771.2 km) Gravel road leads east 24 miles/38 km to community of Carcajou.

G 112.3 (180.8 km) **FS 478.1** (769.4 km) Keg River bridge. The community of **KEG RIVER** just north of the bridge has a gas station, post office, grocery, cafe, cabins, pay phone and airstrip.

G 112.4 (180.9 km) **FS 478** (769.3 km) **Private Aircraft**: Keg River airstrip; elev. 1,350 feet/410m; approximate length 2,700 feet/832m; turf; emergency only.

G 123.8 (199.3 km) **FS 466.6** (750.9 km) Microwave tower to east.

G 124 (199.6 km) **FS 466.4** (750.6 km) Boyer River bridge.

G 129.5 (208.4 km) **FS 460.9** (741.8 km) Paddle Prairie, a Metis settlement. The Metis culture, a combination of French and Amerindian, played a key role in the fur trade and development of northwestern Canada.

G 134.2 (216 km) **FS 456.2** (734.2 km) Turnout to west with litter barrels.

G 135.1 (217.4 km) **FS 455.3** (732.7 km) Boyer River provincial campground to east; 8 sites, tables, firewood, firepits, picnic shelter, toilets and water pump. ▲

G 136.2 (219.2 km) **FS 454.2** (731 km) **Junction** with Highway 697, which leads east approximately 53 miles/85 km to the community of LaCrete, then 25 miles/40 km north to Fort Vermilion. Major access to Fort Vermilion is via Highway 58 east from High Level (junction at **Milepost G 174**). See log of Highway 58 East.

G 151.3 (243.5 km) **FS 439.1** (706.7 km) Microwave tower to west.

G 153.5 (247 km) **FS 436.9** (703.2 km) Turnout with litter barrel to west. Watch for waterfowl in small lakes along highway.

G 165.5 (266.3 km) **FS 424.9** (683.9 km) Melito Creek.

G 167.5 (269.6 km) **FS 422.9** (680.6 km) Railroad crossing.

G 170.6 (274.6 km) **FS 419.8** (675.6 km) Turnout with litter barrel to west.

G 171.9 (276.7 km) **FS 418.5** (673.5 km) Private campground with hot showers and electrical hookups.

Aspen Ridge Campground. See display ad this section. ▲

G 173.3 (278.9 km) **FS 417.1** (671.3 km) **Junction** with Highway 58 west, which leads 85 miles/137 km to **RAINBOW LAKE** (pop. 900), a service community for oil and natural gas development in the region. The first well brought in was in 1965 at the Rainbow field. The Zama field was discovered in 1967; see **Milepost G 228.1**.

High Level

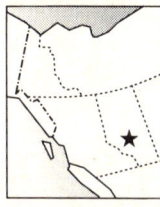

G 173.6 (279.3 km) **FS 416.8** (670.9 km) Located at the junction of Highways 35 and 58. **Population**: 3,004. **Emergency Services**: **RCMP**, phone 926-2226. **Hospital**, 25 beds, 6 doctors, phone 926-3791. **Ambulance**, phone 926-2545. **Fire Department**, phone 926-3141.

Visitor Information: Located at the south end of town; open in summer. A dump station is located here.

Begun as a small settlement on the Mackenzie Highway after WWII, High Level grew with the oil boom of the 1960s and completion of the railroad to Pine Point. High Level has a strong agricultural economy and boasts the most northerly grain elevators in Canada. The community is also supported by a sawmill complex and serves as a transportation centre for the northwestern Peace River region. There is scheduled air service to Edmonton daily.

Visitor facilities include a hotel, 5 motels, restaurants and service stations with major repair. There are also an ice arena and curling rink, golf course, swimming pool, playgrounds, banks, schools and churches. Recreation includes hunting (moose, caribou, deer) and fishing for northern pike, perch, walleye, whitefish, goldeye and grayling.

There is a private campground at the south edge of town. A municipal campground is located just east of town on Highway 58. ▲

Mackenzie Highway Log

(continued)

G 173.3 (278.9 km) **FS 417.1** (671.3 km) **Junction** with Highway 58 west.

Highway 58 East Log

Distance is measured from junction with the Mackenzie Highway (J).

J 0 Junction with Mackenzie Highway at High Level.

J 0.2 (0.4 km) High Level municipal campground to south; 33 sites, no camping fee, picnic shelter, stoves, firewood, tables, toilets, water pump. ▲

J 1.5 (2.5 km) Bushe River bridge.

J 15.3 (24.7 km) Turnoff to south for Machesis Lake Campground, 22 miles/35 km via gravel road; 21 sites, picnic shelter, firepits, firewood, tables, toilets, water. Fishing for rainbows in **Machesis Lake**. ⇌▲

J 20.3 (32.7 km) Turn south for Eleskie Shrine (5 miles/8 km), Native church and burial grounds.

J 27 (43.5 km) Turnout with litter barrels to north.

J 27.4 (44.1 km) Side road leads south 3.7 miles/6 km to Rocky Lane; museum located in school.

J 28 (45 km) Ponton River bridge.

J 35.4 (57 km) **Junction** of Highway 58 and Highway 67. From this junction, Highway 58 turns to gravel road and continues 37 miles/59 km east to Jean D'or Prairie (no services). Highway 67 (Red Earth Road) leads south to Fort Vermilion (log follows) then continues 255 miles/410 km to Slave Lake. Highway 67 is paved to Fort Vermilion; the rest of the road is gravel. There are no services along the road south of Fort Vermilion and travel is not recommended on the gravel portion in wet weather.

HIGHWAY 67

J 40 (64.3 km) Boyer River bridge.

J 43.1 (69.3 km) Historical sign about Fort Vermilion and access to Fort Vermilion provincial campground (0.1 mile/0.2 km east); 16 sites, picnic shelter, fireplace, firewood, tables, toilets, water, no camping fee. ▲

J 43.4 (69.8 km) Fort Vermilion Bridge over the Peace River.

J 45.2 (72.7 km) **Junction** with Highway 697, which leads south 25 miles/40 km to **LA CRETE**, an agricultural community settled by Mennonites. Services there include a motel, restaurant, cafe, laundromat, service stations, bank, grocery, clothing and hardware stores. Highway 697 continues south and west 53 miles/85 km, returning to the Mackenzie Highway at **Milepost G 136.2**.

J 48 (77.2 km) **Junction** with Highway 67 south to Red Earth and Slave Lake. Continue straight ahead for Fort Vermilion (description follows).

J 48.5 (78 km) **FORT VERMILION** (pop. 800), located on the Peace River. **Emergency Services**: **RCMP** and **Hospital**, phone 927-3741. A trading post was established near here by the North West Co. in 1786. By 1831, the Hudson's Bay Co. had established a prosperous trading enterprise at Fort Vermilion. The area's farming potential gained attention when Fort Vermilion's wheat took top prize at the 1893 Chicago World's Fair. Transportation to the community was by riverboat until the Mackenzie Highway was built.

Visitor facilities include a motel, restaurants, service stations, bank and liquor store. The airport is located just south of town. Attractions include good hunting and fishing nearby and some historic old buildings dating back to the 1800s.

Return to Milepost G 174 Mackenzie Highway

G 173.6 (279.3 km) **FS 416.8** (670.9 km) Downtown High Level.

G 174 (280 km) **FS 416.4** (670.2 km) **Junction** with Highway 58 east to Jean D'or Prairie and Highway 67 to Fort Vermilion. See side road log of HIGHWAY 58 EAST this section.

G 174 (280 km) **FS 416.4** (670.2 km) **Junction** of Highways 35 and 58.

G 176.2 (283.5 km) **FS 414.2** (666.7 km) High Level golf and country club to east. Open daily, May 1 to first snow, until midnight. Grass greens and 9 holes.

G 181.1 (291.5 km) **FS 409.3** (658.7 km) **Private Aircraft**: High Level airport; elev. 1,110 feet/338m; length 5,000 feet/1,524m; asphalt; fuel 80, 100, jet B. Floatplane base at Footner Lake, 0.6 mile/1 km west.

G 193.4 (311.2 km) **FS 397** (639 km) Turnoff to west for Hutch Lake Recreation Area; parking, 8 picnic sites with tables and firepits, toilets. Short path leads down to lake. Bring mosquito repellent.

G 196 (315.5 km) **FS 394.4** (634.7 km) Hutch Lake provincial campground, 2.9 miles/4.6 km west; 12 sites, firepits, firewood, tables, toilets, water. Beach and boat launch on Hutch Lake. Hiking trails. Good spot for bird-watchers. No camping fee. ▲

G 196.8 (316.7 km) **FS 393.6** (633.5 km)

1992 ■ The MILEPOST® 189

MACKENZIE HIGHWAY

Turnouts with litter barrels both sides of highway.

G 207.3 (333.6 km) **FS 383.1** (616.6 km) Wooden railway bridge to east.

G 219.3 (352.9 km) **FS 371.1** (597.3 km) **MEANDER RIVER** (pop. 340) has a post office, grocery store and confectionary with pay phone.

G 223.8 (360.1 km) **FS 366.6** (590.1 km) Meander River Campground to east; 8 sites, no camping fee, picnic shelter, tables, firepits, firewood and water. ▲

The Mackenzie Highway crosses the Hay River here and follows it north into Northwest Territories.

G 227 (365.3 km) **FS 363.4** (584.9 km) Microwave tower to east.

G 227.5 (366.2 km) **FS 362.9** (584 km) Railway bridge over Hay River to east. Construction of the Great Slave Lake Railway (now part of Canadian National Railway's Peace River Division) was one of the largest railway construction projects since the boom of the first transcontinental railway lines in the late 1800s and early 1900s in Canada. The line extends 377 miles/607 km from Roma Junction near Peace River, AB, to Hay River, NWT, on the shore of Great Slave Lake. (A 54-mile/87-km branch line extended the line to the now-defunct lead-zinc mine at Pine Point, NWT.) Opened for traffic in 1964, the line carries mining shipments south and supplies north to Hay River.

G 228.1 (367.1 km) **FS 362.3** (583.1 km) Gravel road leads west 39 miles/63 km to **ZAMA** (pop. 200), an oil field community. Drilling and related operations take place at Zama in winter. Zama is the southern terminal of the interprovincial pipeline, carrying Norman Wells crude to Edmonton refineries.

G 241.8 (389.1 km) **FS 348.6** (561.1 km) Railroad crossing.

G 243.5 (391.9 km) **FS 346.9** (558.3 km) Paved turnout with litter barrels to west.

G 256.6 (413 km) **FS 333.8** (537.2 km) Microwave tower to west.

G 263.1 (423.4 km) **FS 327.3** (526.8 km) Steen River campground to west; 11 sites, no camping fee, picnic shelter, fireplaces, firewood, tables, outhouses, water. ▲

G 263.3 (423.7 km) **FS 327.1** (526.5 km) Steen River bridge.

G 266.7 (429.2 km) **FS 323.7** (521 km) **STEEN RIVER** to east has a gas station (unleaded gas available), cafe and pay phone. Tire and minor repairs available.

G 266.9 (429.7 km) **FS 323.5** (520.7 km) Steen River Forestry Tanker Base to west. Grass airstrip.

G 284 (457 km) **FS 306.4** (493.2 km) **INDIAN CABINS** to east has a gas station, cafe, grocery, pay phone and historic log church. The old Indian cabins which gave this settlement its name are gone, but nearby is an Indian cemetery with spirit houses.

NOTE: No services next 61 miles/98 km northbound.

G 287.5 (462.7 km) **FS 302.9** (487.5 km) Microwave tower to east.

G 293.7 (472.7 km) **FS 296.7** (477.5 km) 60th parallel. Border between Alberta and Northwest Territories. The Mackenzie Highway now changes from Alberta Highway 35 to NWT Highway 1.

NWT HIGHWAY 1

Highway 1 begins its own series of kilometre markers, starting with Kilometre 0 at the border, which appear about every 2 kilometres.

Distance from Grimshaw (G) is followed by distance from Fort Simpson (FS) and distance from the AB-NWT border (B).

G 293.7 (472.7 km) **FS 296.7** (477.5 km) **B 0** AB-NWT border, 60th Parallel. A government visitor information centre here has brochures, maps, fishing licenses, camping permits, a dump station and emergency radiophone. Déne (Indian) arts and crafts are on display. Also check here on road and ferry conditions before proceeding. The visitor centre is open May 15 to Sept. 15 from 8 A.M. to midnight.

60th Parallel Campground and picnic area adjacent visitor centre. Facilities include 12 campsites, 5 picnic sites, kitchen shelter and drinking water. The park overlooks the Hay River and canoeists may launch here. ▲

Driving distance from the border to destinations in Northwest Territories are as follows (see individual highway logs this section for details): Hay River 76 miles/122 km; Fort Simpson 297 miles/478 km; Fort Providence 140 miles/225 km; Yellowknife 330 miles/531 km; Fort Smith 238 miles/383 km.

G 295.5 (475.6 km) **FS 294.9** (474.6 km) **B 1.8** (2.9 km) Reindeer Creek.

G 302.1 (486.1 km) **FS 288.3** (464.1 km) **B 8.4** (13.4 km) Pavement ends, gravel road begins northbound, with some short stretches of asphalt surfacing.

G 318.5 (512.6 km) **FS 271.9** (437.6 km) **B 24.8** (39.9 km) Grumbler Rapids, just off highway, is audible during low water periods in late summer.

G 319.1 (513.5 km) **FS 271.3** (436.6 km) **B 25.4** (40.8 km) Swede Creek.

G 334.2 (537.8 km) **FS 256.2** (412.4 km) **B 40.5** (65.1 km) Mink Creek.

G 338.8 (545.3 km) **FS 251.6** (404.9 km) **B 45.1** (72.6 km) Alexandra Falls picnic area to east. Paved parking area and gravel walkway to falls viewpoint, overlooking the Hay River, which plunges 109 feet/33m to form Alexandra Falls. Excellent photo opportunities; easy hike down to top of falls.

G 340.3 (547.6 km) **FS 250.1** (402.6 km) **B 46.6** (74.9 km) Turnoff to east for Louise Falls picnic area and territorial campground; 18 campsites, 6 picnic sites, kitchen shelters, tables, toilets, firepits, firewood, water. Hiking trails to viewpoint overlooking 3-tiered Louise Falls, which drops 50 feet/15m. Steep trail down to the water. Hike along bluff 3 miles/5 km for Alexandra Falls. ▲

G 341.9 (550.2 km) **FS 248.5** (400 km) **B 48.2** (77.5 km) Escarpment Creek picnic area; tables, shelter, toilets, firepits, garbage container, water pump. Spectacular series of waterfalls downstream.

G 342.1 (550.5 km) **FS 248.3** (399.7 km) **B 48.4** (77.8 km) Highway crosses Escarpment Creek.

G 345.4 (555.9 km) **FS 245** (394.3 km) **B 51.7** (83.2 km) Truck weigh scales to east, service station to west. Entering Enterprise northbound.

G 345.8 (556.5 km) **FS 244.6** (393.7 km) **B 52.1** (83.8 km) **Junction** of Highway 1 and Highway 2. Highway 2 leads 23.6 miles/38 km from here to **HAY RIVER** (pop. 2,964), the hub for transportation on Great Slave Lake and a major service centre with all visitor facilities (see Highway 2 log on page 192 for details on Hay River). Continue on Highway 1 for Enterprise (description follows) and Fort Simpson.

ENTERPRISE (pop. 56), a highway community with food, gas (regular, unleaded and diesel) and lodging. Pay phone. It is a good idea to fill up gas tanks here. View of Hay River Gorge just east of the highway.

G 346 (556.8 km) **FS 244.4** (393.3 km) **B 52.3** (84.1 km) Railroad crossing.

G 348.4 (560.7 km) **FS 242** (389.4 km) **B 64.7** (104.1 km) Gravel stock pile to east.

G 350.5 (564 km) **FS 239.9** (386.1 km) **B 66.8** (107.5 km) Microwave tower to east.

G 365.8 (588.7 km) **FS 224.6** (361.4 km) **B 72.1** (116 km) Microwave tower to east.

G 369.3 (594.3 km) **FS 221.1** (355.8 km) **B 75.6** (121.6 km) Turnout to east with view of McNally Creek Falls.

G 374.7 (603 km) **FS 215.7** (347.2 km) **B 81** (130.3 km) Easy-to-miss Hart Lake Fire Tower access road turnoff to east, 0.5 mile/0.8 km to picnic area and forest fire lookout tower. Panoramic view over more than 100 square miles/259 square km of forest to Great Slave Lake and Mackenzie River. Path to ancient coral reef. *CAUTION: Keep the fly repellent handy and stay away from the edge of escarpment.*

G 379.4 (610.5 km) **FS 211** (339.7 km) **B 85.7** (137.8 km) Trapper's cabin to east.

G 391.7 (630.3 km) **FS 198.7** (319.9 km) **B 98** (157.6 km) Turnout with litter barrels.

G 398.7 (641.7 km) **FS 191.7** (308.5 km) **B 105** (169 km) Access road leads south 4.5 miles/7.2 km to Lady Evelyn Falls where the Kakisa River drops 49 feet/15m over an escarpment. Staircase down to viewing platform. Hiking trail to base of falls; swimming and wading. Ample parking, territorial campground with 10 tent sites, 18 RV sites and 5 picnic sites; tables, firepits, firewood, garbage containers, water pump, kitchen shelters. At end of road, 4 miles/6.4 km past campground, is Slavey Indian village and **Kakisa Lake**; good fishing for walleye, pike and grayling. ◆▲

G 399.6 (643.1 km) **FS 190.8** (307.1 km) **B 105.9** (170.4 km) Kakisa River bridge.

G 399.8 (643.4 km) **FS 190.6** (306.8 km) **B 106.1** (170.7 km) Kakisa River bridge picnic area with 10 sites, tables, fireplaces and firewood. Hiking trails along river lead upstream to Lady Evelyn Falls. Good fishing in **Kakisa River** for grayling. ◆

G 410.5 (660.6 km) **FS 179.9** (289.5 km) **B 116.8** (187.9 km) Turnout with litter barrels.

G 410.9 (661.2 km) **FS 179.5** (289 km) **B 117.2** (188.5 km) **Junction** of Highway 1 and Highway 3. Highway 3 leads 212.5 miles/342 km north to Yellowknife, capital of Northwest Territories (see Yellowknife Highway log this section). Continue with this log of Highway 1 for the Liard Highway turnoff and Fort Simpson westbound.

G 438.4 (705.5 km) **FS 152** (244.7 km) **B 144.7** (232.8 km) Emergency survival cabin and turnout with litter barrels and outhouse to south.

G 455.4 (732.8 km) **FS 135** (217.2 km) **B 161.7** (260.2 km) Microwave tower.

G 456.3 (734.5 km) **FS 134.1** (215.8 km) **B 162.6** (261.6 km) Dust-free passing zone.

G 466.2 (750.3 km) **FS 124.2** (199.9 km) **B 172.5** (277.6 km) Bouvier River.

G 467.2 (751.9 km) **FS 123.2** (198.3 km) **B 173.5** (279.2 km) Emergency survival cabin and turnout with litter barrels to south.

The vegetation in this area is coming back after being ravaged by a forest fire a few years ago. A good reminder to be careful with fire.

G 473.9 (762.6 km) **FS 116.5** (187.6 km)

190 The MILEPOST® ■ 1992

B 180.2 (289.9 km) Wallace Creek. Scenic canyon to north.
G 477 (767.6 km) FS 113.4 (182.6 km)
B 183.3 (294.9 km) Highway maintenance camp to south.
G 477.6 (768.6 km) FS 112.8 (181.6 km)
B 183.9 (295.9 km) Redknife River.
G 488.7 (786.4 km) FS 101.7 (163.8 km)
B 195 (313.7 km) Morrissey Creek.
G 495.7 (797.8 km) FS 94.7 (152.4 km)
B 202 (325 km) Whittaker Falls Territorial Park, located on a bluff overlooking the **Trout River**. There are 3 picnic sites, 5 campsites, tables, litter barrels, firepits and firewood. Walk along the river to view large deposits of shale and limestone. Grayling fishing, use dry flies in deep pools. Hike to Coral Falls.
G 523.7 (842.8 km) FS 66.7 (107.3 km)
B 229.9 (370 km) **Ekali Lake** access; pike and pickerel fishing.
G 527.4 (848.7 km) FS 63 (101.4 km)
B 233.6 (376 km) Winter road leads 17 miles/27 km to Jean Marie River, a Slavey community known for its fine handicrafts.
G 530.5 (853.7 km) FS 59.9 (96.5 km)
B 236.8 (381 km) Emergency survival cabin and turnout to north with outhouse and litter barrels.
G 534.8 (860.7 km) FS 55.6 (89.5 km)
B 241.1 (388 km) I.P.L. pipeline camp and pump station to north. Highway crosses pipeline.
G 536.3 (863 km) FS 54.1 (87 km)
B 242.6 (390.4 km) Microwave tower to south.
G 550.4 (885.8 km) FS 40 (64.4 km)
B 256.7 (413.1 km) Jean Marie Creek bridge.
G 550.5 (885.9 km) FS 39.9 (64.3 km)
B 256.8 (413.2 km) Service station and restaurant to east, operated by the Fort Simpson Indian Band.
G 550.6 (886.1 km) FS 39.8 (64.1 km)
B 256.9 (413.4 km) **Junction** with the Liard Highway (NWT Highway 7), which leads south to Fort Liard and junctions with the Alaska Highway near Fort Nelson. See the LIARD HIGHWAY section for details.
G 552 (888.4 km) FS 38.4 (61.8 km)
B 258.3 (415.7 km) Turnout to east.
G 563.7 (907.1 km) FS 26.7 (43.1 km)
B 270 (434.4 km) Emergency survival cabin and turnout with litter barrels and outhouse to west.
G 577.8 (929.8 km) FS 12.6 (20.4 km)
B 284.1 (457.1 km) Highway crests hill; view of Liard River ahead. Ferry landing 3,280 feet/1,000m.
G 578.2 (930.5 km) FS 12.2 (19.7 km)
B 284.5 (457.8 km) Liard River campground to accommodate travelers who miss the last ferry at night, has 5 sites, tables, firepits, outhouse and garbage container.
G 578.5 (930.9 km) FS 11.9 (19.3 km)
B 284.8 (458.2 km) Free government-operated Liard River ferry operates daily May through October from 8 A.M. to 11:40 P.M., 7 days a week. Crossing time is 6 minutes. Capacity is 8 cars or 2 trucks, with a maximum total weight of 130,000 lbs./59,090kg. An ice bridge opens for light vehicles in late November and heavier vehicles as ice thickens. *NOTE: No crossing possible during breakup (about mid-April to mid-May) and freezeup (November).*
G 580.7 (934.6 km) FS 9.7 (15.6 km)
B 287 (461.9 km) Fort Simpson airport. See Private Aircraft information in Fort Simpson.
G 588.1 (946.4 km) FS 2.3 (3.8 km)
B 294.4 (473.7 km) **Junction** with Fort Simpson access road. The Mackenzie Highway extends beyond this junction approximately 52 miles/84 km to Camsell Road on the Mackenzie River, then a rough summer trail (ice road in winter) proceeds north to Wrigley. There are no bridges and ferry service is not available across the river. No gravel surfacing on road. In wet weather the road is muddy, slippery and rutted. Winter road mileages are as follows: Fort Simpson to Wrigley, 143 miles/230 km; Wrigley to Fort Norman, 148 miles/238 km; Fort Norman to Norman Wells, 50 miles/80 km; and Fort Norman to Fort Franklin, 68 miles/110 km.
G 589.7 (949 km) FS 0.7 (1.2 km) B 296 (476.3 km) Causeway to Fort Simpson Island.
G 590.1 (949.6 km) FS 0.3 (0.6 km)
B 296.4 (476.9 km) Turnoff for village campground.

Fort Simpson

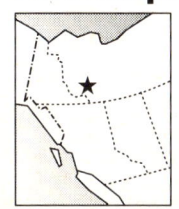

G 590.4 (950.2 km) FS 0
B 296.7 (477.5 km) Located on an island at the confluence of the Mackenzie and Liard rivers. **Population:** 987. **Emergency Services:** RCMP, phone 695-3111. **Hospital** (12 beds), for medical emergency phone 695-2291. **Fire Department** (volunteer), phone 695-2222.

Visitor Information: Village office operates a visitor booth June through August. A new (1991) visitor centre is open till 8 P.M., 7 days a week in summer; closed Sundays in winter. Nahanni National Park information centre on Main Street has a photo exhibit and films. For information on the park you may also write Superintendent, Postal Bag 300, Fort Simpson, NT X0E 0N0.

Television: Channels 2, 4, 6, 7, 9, 11. **Transportation:** Scheduled service to Yellowknife via NWT Airways and Ptarmigan Air. Fixed wing and helicopter charters available. **Rental cars**–Available. **Taxi service**–Available.

Private Aircraft: Fort Simpson airport; elev. 554 feet/169m; length 6,000 feet/1,829m; asphalt; fuel 100, jet B. Fort Simpson Island; elev. 405 feet/123m; length 3,000 feet/914m; gravel; fuel 100, jet B.

Fort Simpson is a full-service community. There is a motel with kitchenettes and a hotel; dining at the hotel (licensed premises) and 3 restaurants in town; gas stations with repair service (unleaded, diesel gas and propane available); 2 grocery stores, department store, hardware store, a bank, laundromat, post office, crafts shop and sports shop. Small engine repair shop and mechanics available. Fort Simpson has grade schools, churches (Anglican, Catholic and Pentecostal) and various territorial and federal offices. Recreational facilities include an arena, curling rink, gym, ball diamond, tennis, small indoor pool and a boat launch at government wharf.

Public campground at edge of town in wooded area has 30 campsites and 4 picnic sites.

Fort Simpson is the oldest continuously occupied site on the Mackenzie River, dating from 1804 when the North West Co. established its Fort of the Forks. There is a historical marker on the bank of the Mackenzie. The Hudson's Bay Co. began its post here in 1821. At that time the fort was renamed after Sir George Simpson, one of the first

Spectacular canyons of the Ram Plateau are located about 100 air miles west of Fort Simpson. (Earl L. Brown, staff)

Simpson Air
(1981) Ltd.

E.J. (Ted) Grant, Owner-Operator
24-hour Charter Service
FLOATS • WHEELS • SKIS

Charter Trips to Nahanni National Park
Licensed Outfitter
Canoe, Raft and Kayak Rentals
• CESSNA 185s • TWIN OTTER
• KING AIR • CESSNA 207 • BEAVER

For our brochure write to:
Simpson Air (1981) Ltd.
Box 260, Fort Simpson, NWT, X0E 0N0
Phone: (403) 695-2505 or 695-3141
FAX: (403) 695-2925

MACKENZIE HIGHWAY

governors of the combined North West Co. and Hudson's Bay Co. Fort Simpson served as the Mackenzie District headquarters for the Hudson's Bay Co. fur-trading operation. Its key location on the Mackenzie River also made Fort Simpson an important transportation centre. Anglican and Catholic missions were established here in 1858 and 1894.

Fort Simpson continues to be an important centre for the Northwest Territories water transport system.

For visitors, Fort Simpson has Slavey crafts, such as birch-bark baskets and beadwork. Fort Simpson is also the jumping-off point for the Mackenzie River and Nahanni National Park.

The 4,766-square-km **NAHANNI NATIONAL PARK**, listed as a unique geological area on the UNESCO world heritage site list, is accessible only by nonpowered boat or aircraft. Located southwest of Fort Simpson near the Yukon border, day trip flightseeing tours of the park may be arranged in Fort Simpson, Fort Liard and Yellowknife, and from Fort Nelson, BC, and Watson Lake, YT. Highlights include spectacular Virginia Falls: At 300 feet/90m, it is twice as high as Niagara Falls. One of the most popular attractions in the park is running the South Nahanni River or its tributary, the Flat River. The South Nahanni River route stretches about 186 miles/300 km from Rabbitkettle Lake to the eastern park boundary. Rabbitkettle Hot Springs, a major feature on the upper section of the river, is reached by trail (restricted access, hikers must be guided by park staff). Near the east park boundary is Kraus Hot Springs, on the remains of the old Kraus homestead. The Flat River route stretches 80 miles/128 km from Seaplane Lake to the confluence with the South Nahanni. Charter air service for canoe drop-offs is available in Fort Simpson. For more information, contact the Park Superintendent by mail or check with the Canadian Parks Service information centre on Main Street. The information centre is open 8:30 A.M. to 5 P.M., 7 days a week in July and August, weekdays the rest of the year.

AREA FISHING: **Willow**, **Dogface** and **Trout lakes** accessible by air. Good fishing for trout and grayling. Inquire locally for details.

Maroda Motel. See display ad this section.

Simpson Air (1981) Ltd. See display ad this section.

Hay River Highway Log

NWT HIGHWAY 2
Highway 2 is paved from Enterprise to Hay River; watch for rough spots in the surfacing. Kilometreposts along the highway reflect distance from Enterprise.
Distance from Enterprise (E) is followed by distance from Hay River (H).

E 0 H 23.6 (38 km) **Junction** of Highways 1 and 2.

E 8.7 (14 km) H 14.9 (24 km) Private campground 0.7 mile/1.1 km east. Market garden in season. ▲

E 11.6 (18.6 km) H 12 (19.4 km) Sawmill Road to east.

E 16 (25.7 km) H 7.6 (12.3 km) Gravel road leads east 0.6 mile/1 km to Hay River Golf and Country Club; large log clubhouse, driving range, 9 holes (par 36), sand greens. Site of the NWT Open every second year in late August.

E 19.2 (30.9 km) H 4.4 (7.1 km) Railroad crossing.

E 20 (32.3 km) H 3.6 (5.7 km) **Junction** with Highway 5 to Fort Smith (see Fort Smith Highway Log this section).

E 22.4 (36 km) H 1.2 (2 km) Chamber of commerce Welcome to Hay River sign. Parking area to east, where the riverboat *Liard River* is on display.

Hay River

E 23.6 (38 km) H 0 Located on the south shore of Great Slave Lake at the mouth of the Hay River, on both the mainland and Vale Island. **Population:** 2,964. **Emergency Services: Police**, phone 874-6555. **Fire Department**, phone 874-2222. **Hospital**, phone 874-2565.

Visitor Information: Visitor information centre, just east of the highway, is housed in a 2-story brown structure. The centre is open mid-June to early September; 10 A.M. to 8 P.M., Monday through Saturday, noon to 8 P.M. on Sunday. There is a dump station located here. Write Chamber of Commerce, Box 1278, Hay River, NT X0E 0R0; phone 874-3277.

Radio: CKHR-FM 107.3; CBC 1490. **Television:** Channels 2, 6, 7, 10 and 12 via satellite. **Newspaper:** *The Hub* (weekly). **Transportation:** Air–Canadian Airlines International, Ptarmigan Airways, Landa Aviation, Carter Air and Buffalo Airways. **Bus**–Coachways. **Rental cars**–Available.

Private Aircraft: Hay River airport; elev. 543 feet/165m; length 6,000 feet/1,830m, paved; 4,000 feet/1,219m, gravel; fuel 100, jet B.

Hay River was established in 1868 with the building of a Hudson's Bay Co. post. Today's economy combines transportation, communications, commercial fishing and service industries. The community is the transfer point from highway and rail to barges on Great Slave Lake bound for arctic and subarctic communities. The airstrip was built in 1942 on Vale Island by the U.S. Corps of Engineers. Vale Island was the townsite until floods in 1951 then 1963 forced evacuation of the population to the mainland townsite, where most of the community is now concentrated. Vale Island, referred to as "Old Town," is bounded by Great Slave Lake and the west and east channels of the Hay River.

The town boasts the tallest building in the Northwest Territories; the 17-story apartment building is a landmark that can be seen for miles around. The ground floor houses some shops and the offices of *The Hub*, Hay River's weekly newspaper. Another unique structure in town is the high school, which is painted purple (the colour was chosen by the students).

There are 10 restaurants, gas stations with unleaded gas, propane and repair service, and grocery stores. Reservations are a must at the town's 5 hotels/motels; lodgings are booked solid in busy summer season by construction and transportation workers. There is also a bed-and-breakfast. Other facilities include 2 banks, a laundromat and a variety of shops.

Hay River has schools, churches, a civic centre with a swimming pool (1 of only 2 year-round swimming pools in Northwest Territories), curling sheets, hockey arena and dance hall. Northwest Territories Centennial Library headquarters is located here. There is a public boat launch at Porritt Landing on Vale Island.

There is a public campground on Vale Island (follow the signs; it is about 6 miles/10 km past the information centre). There are 21 sites (4 with electrical hook-ups), showers, firewood and firepits, picnic area, playground and horseshoe pit. Rates are $5 for tents, $6 for RVs. Open mid-May to mid-September. ▲

Great sportfishing area with fly-in fishing camps (check with the chamber of commerce). Boat rentals on nearby **Great Slave Lake**, where northern pike up to 40 lbs. are not unusual. Inconnu (sheefish), pickerel and grayling also found here.

Yellowknife Highway Log

NWT HIGHWAY 3
Distance from the junction of Highways 1 and 3 (J) is followed by distance from Yellowknife (Y).

J 0 Y 212.5 (342 km) **Junction** of Highways 1 and 3. Turn right northbound for Fort Providence, Rae-Edzo and Yellowknife.

About the first mile of Highway 3 is paved, the remainder of the highway is

---

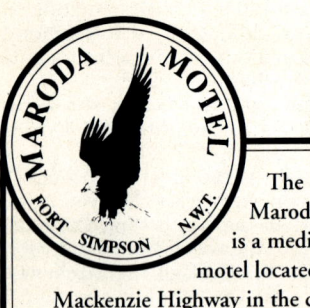

The Maroda Motel is a medium sized motel located on the Mackenzie Highway in the centre of Fort Simpson, N.W.T. and just minutes from shops, restaurants and all government offices.

We have 15 units including 8 fully-equipped air-conditioned kitchenettes complete with microwave ovens.

Each unit is equipped with:
2 Double Beds • Full Bath
Color Television (8 channels)
Direct Dial Phone • Clock Radio
Winter Plug-ins
Ample Free Parking
Seniors' Discounts
Complimentary Airport Limo

Clean - Quiet - Friendly

THE MARODA MOTEL
PO Box 67, Fort Simpson, NWT X0E 0N0
Phone (403) 695-2602
FAX (403) 695-2273
Your Hosts: Rose & Graham Davis

good gravel road to Yellowknife.

J 9.1 (14.7 km) **Y 203.4** (327.3 km) Dory Point maintenance camp to west.

J 13.2 (21.2 km) **Y 199.3** (320.8 km) Dory Point picnic area to east with 5 sites and kitchen shelter, no drinking water; overlooking Mackenzie River with view of passing riverboats.

Campground with hookups, service station with regular, unleaded and diesel, and restaurant. ▲

J 15.1 (24.3 km) **Y 197.4** (317.7 km) Free government-operated Mackenzie River ferry operates daily May through November from 6 A.M. to midnight. Crossing time is 8 minutes. Capacity is 10 cars or 4 trucks, with a maximum total weight of 220,000 lbs./100,000kg. An ice bridge opens for light vehicles in December and heavier vehicles as ice thickens. *NOTE: No crossing possible during breakup (about April to mid-May).* Ice breaking procedures now keep the channel open for the ferry during freezeup while an ice bridge is being constructed. For ferry information phone 873-7799 or 1-800-661-0751.

J 15.9 (25.6 km) **Y 196.6** (316.4 km) Sign indicates Mackenzie Wood Bison Sanctuary. The wood bison are not often seen along the highway, however, sandhill cranes, squirrels, spruce grouse and ptarmigan may be seen in season.

J 19.4 (31.2 km) **Y 193.1** (310.8 km) Motel, restaurant and service station with unleaded, diesel and propane. Pay phone.

J 19.6 (31.6 km) **Y 192.9** (310.4 km) **Junction** with access road which leads 2.8 miles/4.5 km west to Fort Providence (description follows). There is an airstrip located 0.4 mile/0.6 km west on the access road.

NOTE: It is a good idea to fill gas tanks here if you are bound for Yellowknife. Next gas available is in Rae-Edzo.

Fort Providence territorial campground is located 0.7 mile/1.1 km west of the highway on the access road; 30 sites, tables, firewood, kitchen shelter, garbage container, pump water and dump station. Situated on the banks of the Mackenzie River. Rental boats, boat launch and fishing nearby. ▲

Entering MacKenzie Bison Sanctuary northbound.

Fort Providence

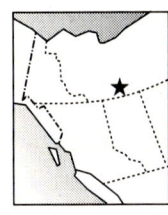

Located on the Mackenzie River, 2.8 miles/4.5 km northwest of Highway 3. **Population:** 688. **Emergency Services: Police,** phone 699-3291. **Fire Department,** phone 699-4222. **Nursing station,** phone 699-4311.

Elevation: 550 feet/168m. **Radio:** 1230. **Television:** Channels 6 and 13 (CBC). **Transportation: Air**–Air Providence and charter service. **Bus**–Coachways.

Private Aircraft: Fort Providence airstrip; elev. 530 feet/162m; length 3,000 feet/915m; gravel; fuel emergency only.

Facilities include 2 motels, 2 restaurants, gas stations with minor repair service, grocery and general stores.

A Roman Catholic mission was established here in 1861. Although noted for its early agricultural endeavors, Fort Providence is traditionally a trapping community. Three historical markers in the community commemorate the roles of the church and explorer Alexander Mackenzie in settling the area.

Unique and popular with northern collectors is the moose hair embroidery found in local gift shops. Local craftswomen are also noted for their porcupine quill work. Along with seeing the crafts, visitors may cruise the Mackenzie River. Spectacular photo opportunities here for sunsets on the Mackenzie.

Good to excellent fishing in **Mackenzie River;** guides and cabins available, also boats and air charter trips. Northern pike to 30 lbs., May 30 to September, use large Red Devils; grayling and pickerel from 1 to 6 lbs., June to September, use anything (small Red Devils will do).

Sunset on Great Slave Lake at Hay River. (Earl L. Brown, staff)

Yellowknife Highway Log

(continued)

J 27.5 (44.3 km) **Y 185** (297.7 km) Bluefish River.

J 31.9 (51.3 km) **Y 180.6** (290.7 km) Dust-free passing zone.

J 42.3 (68.1 km) **Y 170.2** (273.9 km) Turnout to east with litter barrels.

J 58.6 (94.3 km) **Y 153.9** (247.7 km) Microwave tower to east.

J 62.6 (100.8 km) **Y 149.9** (241.2 km) Dust-free passing zone.

J 75.6 (121.6 km) **Y 136.9** (220.4 km) Chan Lake picnic area to east with kitchen shelter, tables, firepits and firewood. No drinking water. Watch for waterfowl.

J 76.1 (122.5 km) **Y 136.4** (219.5 km) Turnout with litter barrels to east.

J 96.1 (154.7 km) **Y 116.4** (187.3 km) Dust-free passing zone.

J 100 (160.9 km) **Y 112.5** (181.1 km) Turnout with litter barrels to east. Watch for buffalo.

J 104.4 (168 km) **Y 108.1** (174 km) Microwave tower to east.

J 109.8 (176.7 km) **Y 102.7** (165.3 km) Dust-free passing zone.

J 129.7 (208.8 km) **Y 82.8** (133.2 km) Turnout with litter barrels to east. Northbound travelers may notice the trees are getting shorter as you move farther north.

J 140.2 (225.7 km) **Y 72.3** (116.3 km) Turnout to east.

Steep downgrade northbound as highway approaches Mosquito Creek.

J 141.2 (227.3 km) **Y 71.3** (114.7 km) Highway crosses **Mosquito Creek.** Fishing for pickerel and whitefish, May and June.

J 144.2 (232 km) **Y 68.3** (110 km) North Arm Territorial Park on the shores of Great Slave Lake. Picnic area with kitchen shelter, tables, toilets, firewood, firepits and boat launch (*Caution: Reefs*). Lowbush cranberries and other berries in area. Beware of bears.

J 148.5 (239 km) **Y 64** (103 km) **Junction** with access road west to community of Edzo (see description at **Milepost J 152.2**).

J 148.8 (239.5 km) **Y 63.7** (102.5 km) Edzo campground and picnic area to west. Pickerel fishing in **West Channel** in spring. ▲

J 149.3 (240.2 km) **Y 63.2** (101.8 km) West Channel.

J 151.5 (243.8 km) **Y 61** (98.2 km) Bridge over Frank Channel, which extends from the head of the North Arm of Great Slave Lake to the Indian village of Rae. Charter air service (floatplane) at south end of bridge, forestry station at north end of bridge.

J 152.2 (245 km) **Y 60.3** (97 km) **Junction** with road which leads west 7 miles/11.2 km to community of Rae (description follows).

RAE-EDZO (pop. about 1,378). **Emergency Services: RCMP,** in Rae, phone 392-6181. **Nursing station** in Edzo, phone 371-3551. The 2 hamlets of Rae and Edzo contain the territories' largest Déne (Indian) community. The Rae area, where most of the community resides, is an old Indian hunting spot and was the site of 2 early trading posts. The Edzo site was developed in 1965 by the government to provide schools and an adequate sanitation system. Rae has grocery stores, a post office, Native crafts shop, 2 hotels, food service and gas stations with regular, unleaded and diesel. Pay phones are located at the community sports centre and at the cafe.

J 159.8 (257.2 km) **Y 52.7** (84.8 km) Stagg River bridge. After crossing the North Arm of Great Slave Lake, the highway swings southeast toward Yellowknife. Winding road to Yellowknife, good opportunities to see waterfowl in the many small lakes.

J 160.4 (258.1 km) **Y 52.1** (83.9 km) Turnout with litter barrels to south.

J 182.1 (293 km) **Y 30.4** (49 km) Dust-free passing zone.

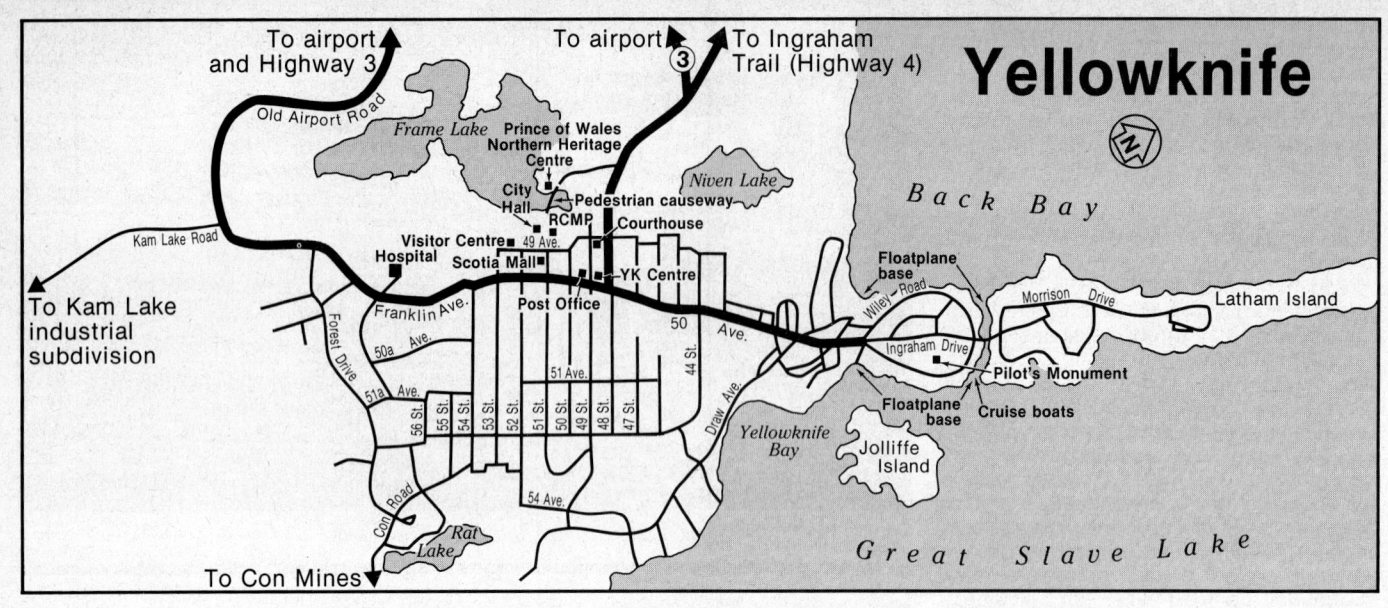

J 189.2 (304.5 km) **Y 23.3** (37.5 km) Turnout with litter barrels to north.

J 189.5 (304.9 km) **Y 23** (37.1 km) Boundary Creek.

J 204.5 (329.1 km) **Y 8** (12.9 km) Microwave tower to south.

J 208.5 (335.5 km) **Y 4** (6.5 km) Gravel ends, pavement begins.

J 208.7 (335.8 km) **Y 3.8** (6.2 km) Yellowknife Golf Club to north; 9 holes, sand greens and course, licensed clubhouse. Site of the June 21 Midnight Tournament. Some modified rules have been adopted by this Far North golf course, among them: "No penalty assessed when ball carried off by raven."

J 209.8 (337.7 km) **Y 2.7** (4.3 km) Yellowknife airport to south.

J 210 (338 km) **Y 2.5** (4 km) Fred Henne Recreational Park on Long Lake. Attractive public campground with 82 sites, water, firewood, firepits, picnic area, boat launch, snack bar, showers and pay phone. Daily and seasonal rates available; open from mid-May to mid-September. Sandy beach and swimming in Long Lake. Interpretive trail. ▲

J 210.5 (338.7 km) **Y 2** (3.3 km) Old Airport Road access to Yellowknife. Just past the turnoff is the Welcome to Yellowknife sign and the hard-to-miss Wardair Bristol freighter to the south. A historical plaque commemorates the Bristol freighter, which was the first wheel-equipped aircraft to land at the North Pole. Picnic sites nearby.

J 211.4 (340.2 km) **Y 1.1** (1.8 km) Stock Lake to south.

J 211.7 (340.7 km) **Y 0.8** (1.3 km) Junction of Highway 3 and Highway 4 (Ingraham Trail); see log this section.

Yellowknife

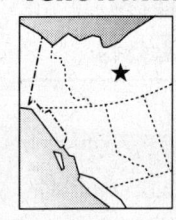

J 212.5 (342 km) **Y 0** On the north shore of Great Slave Lake, approximately 940 miles/1513 km from Edmonton, AB. **Population:** 15,000. **Emergency Services: Police,** phone 920-8311. **Fire Department** and **Ambulance,** phone 873-3434 or 873-2222. **Hospital,** Stanton Yellowknife, phone 920-4111.

Visitor Information: Write Travel-Arctic, Dept. of Economic Development & Tourism, Yellowknife, NT X1A 2L9. Or write the Chamber of Commerce, Box 906, Yellowknife, NT X1A 2N7; phone 920-4944. National Frontier Regional Visitors Centre, showcasing the culture and crafts of the area, is located at 4807 49th St.; phone 873-4262..

Radio: 1240, 1340, 101.1-FM. **Television:** Channel 8; 15 cable channels. **Newspapers:** *News/North* (weekly); *Yellowknifer* (twice weekly); *Native Press* (weekly).

Private Aircraft: Yellowknife airport; elev. 674 feet/205m; length 7,500 feet/2,286m; asphalt; fuel 100/130, jet B. Float-plane bases located at East Bay and West Bay of Latham Island.

Yellowknife, capital of Northwest Territories and considered the only "city" in Northwest Territories, is a relatively new community. White settlers arrived in 1934 with the discovery of gold in the area. Cominco poured its first gold brick in 1938. WWII intervened and gold mining was halted until Giant Yellowknife Mines began milling May 12, 1948. It was not until 1960 that the road was completed connecting the city with the provinces. Yellowknife became capital of the Northwest Territories in 1967.

For 2 to 6 weeks each spring and fall vehicle traffic to Yellowknife is cut off due to ice (breakup or freezeup) on the Mackenzie River crossing near Fort Providence. All fresh meat, produce and urgent supplies must be airlifted during this period, resulting in higher prices.

Yellowknife has continued to develop as a mining, transportation and government administrative centre for the territories.

ACCOMMODATIONS

Accommodations at 6 hotels, 3 motels, 7 bed-and-breakfasts, and the YWCA (co-ed). There are 14 restaurants, 3 dining lounges (no minors), 8 cocktail lounges and several shopping malls. Northern handicraft shops for fur parkas and other Native crafts are a specialty here, and there are shops specializing in Northern art.

TRANSPORTATION

Air: Scheduled air service to Edmonton via NWT Airways and Canadian Airlines International; Winnipeg via NWT Airways. Carriers serving Yellowknife and arctic communities are NWT Airways, Canadian Airlines International, Ptarmigan Airways, Simpson Air, Air Providence and First Air. Charter service available. **Bus:** Greyhound from Edmonton with connections at Enterprise. **Rentals:** Several major car rental agencies; boat and canoe rentals.

ATTRACTIONS

Prince of Wales Northern Heritage Centre. Opened in April 1979, this large museum complex was built to collect, preserve, document, exhibit, study and interpret the North's natural and cultural history. For visitors there are a variety of temporary exhibits ranging from Inuit stone sculpture

---

You haven't seen Yellowknife 'til you've seen **THE YELLOWKNIFE Trading Post**

DENE and INUIT HANDICRAFTS

SOUVENIRS and GIFTS

Send for our mail order brochure: #4 Lessard Drive Yellowknife, NWT X1A 2G5

(403) 873-3020 FAX (403) 920-7310 VISA MasterCard

THE YELLOWKNIFE Book Cellar
Northern Books
• Books for All Ages
• Special Orders • Mail Order Service
• Northern Book List on Request
2 Locations: **Centre Square Mall**
Panda II Mall
(403) 920-2220, FAX (403) 873-6105
Write: Box 1256
Yellowknife, NWT, X1A 2N9

YELLOWKNIFE ADVERTISERS

Yellowknife Book
  Cellar, The..................2 locations—See ad
Yellowknife Trading
  Post, The......................Ph. (403) 873-3020

to historical photographs, and permanent exhibits in the galleries. The orientation gallery gives general background on the Northwest Territories; the south gallery tells the story of the land and the Déne and Inuit people; the north gallery shows the arrival of the Euro-Canadians. The centre is located on Frame Lake, accessible via 48th Street or by way of a pedestrian causeway behind City Hall.

Tours. There are a variety of local tours offered. Visitors may take a 2- or 3-hour tour of the city or a 2-hour cruise on Great Slave Lake. Local tour operators also offer tours out Ingraham Trail (NWT Highway 4), a scenic route which leads some 44 miles/71 km along an almost continual chain of lakes and streams.

Explore Yellowknife. Drive or walk down the hill and around the "Rock" where the original town sprang up on Yellowknife Bay and where there are now barges, fishing boats and a large floatplane base; climb steps to the cairn on top of the rock, a tribute to early-day bush pilots who opened up this country in the 1930s and 1940s. The log Wildcat Cafe (open May to September) at the bottom of the rock is operated by the Old Stope Assoc., which renovated this historic building. Drive out to Old Town on Latham Island to see some of the creative solutions builders have found to the problem of building on solid rock.

Ingraham Trail Log

NWT HIGHWAY 4

NWT Highway 4 begins in Yellowknife and extends 44 miles/71 km along an almost continual chain of lakes and streams, ending at Tibbett Lake. It was named for pioneer prospector and hotelman Vic Ingraham. **Distance from Yellowknife (Y) is followed by distance from Tibbett Lake (T).**

Y 0 T 44.1 (70.9 km) **Junction** of Highways 3 and 4. The first 12 miles/19.2 km of Highway 4 are paved, the remainder of the road is good gravel.

Y 1.9 (3.1 km) **T 42.2** (67.9 km) Giant Yellowknife Mines main office. The mine has been operating since 1947. Tours of the mine may be arranged in Yellowknife.

Y 4.7 (7.5 km) **T 39.4** (63.4 km) Single-lane bridge across the **Yellowknife River**. Historical sign at north end of bridge about the Ingraham Trail. Picnic area with tables and boat launch. Good fishing for northern pike, lake trout and grayling.

Y 6.1 (9.8 km) **T 38** (61.2 km) Turnoff to south by 2 transmission towers for 7-mile/11-km road to Detah Indian village; no services.

Y 11.9 (19.2 km) **T 32.2** (51.7 km) **Prosperous Lake** picnic area and boat launch to north. Fishing for northern pike, whitefish and lake trout.

Y 14.9 (24 km) **T 29.2** (46.9 km) **Madeline Lake** picnic area and boat launch to north. Fishing for northern pike, whitefish, cisco and yellow perch.

Y 16.4 (26.4 km) **T 27.7** (44.5 km) **Pontoon Lake** picnic area and boat launch to south. Fishing for northern pike, whitefish, cisco and suckers.

Y 17.5 (28.2 km) **T 26.6** (42.7 km) Side road leads north 1 mile/1.6 km to Prelude Lake territorial campground with 28 campsites, 20 picnic sites, boat launch and swimming. Prelude Wildlife Trail, which starts from and ends at the campground, is a 1½-hour walk. The trail has 15 interpretive stations showing the adaptations and relationships of wildlife in the North. Boat rentals, cabins and a restaurant located here. Fishing in **Prelude Lake** for lake trout, grayling, whitefish, cisco, burbot, suckers and northern pike.

Good views of Prelude Lake from the highway next 10 miles/16 km eastbound.

Y 28.6 (46 km) **T 15.5** (24.9 km) Powder Point on Prelude Lake to north; parking area. Boat launch for canoeists doing the route into Hidden Lake, Lower Cameron River, or 4-day trip to Yellowknife River bridge.

Y 30.1 (48.4 km) **T 14** (22.5 km) Cameron River Falls trailhead to north; parking. This 0.6-mile/1-km trail leads to cliffs overlooking Cameron River Falls.

Y 35.4 (57 km) **T 8.7** (13.9 km) Single-lane Bailey bridge across Cameron River; parking area, picnicking, canoeing and swimming.

Y 37.9 (61 km) **T 6.2** (9.9 km) **Reid Lake** territorial campground with 27 campsites, 10 picnic sites, kitchen shelter, swimming, hiking trail, boat launch and fishing. Canoe launch point for Upper Cameron River and Jennejohn Lake routes. *CAUTION: Watch for bears.*

Y 44.1 (70.9 km) **T 0** Tibbett Lake. End of road. Launch point for Pensive Lakes canoe route (advanced canoeists only).

Fort Smith Highway Log

NWT HIGHWAY 5
Distance from Highway 2 junction (J) followed by distance from Fort Smith (FT).

J 0 FT 166 (267.2 km) Highway 5 begins its own series of markers giving distances in kilometres.

The first 37.7 miles/60.8 km of Highway 5 are paved. Watch for construction and rough spots in surfacing. There are no services or gas available until Fort Smith.

J 1.3 (2.2 km) **FT 164.7** (265 km) Railroad and auto bridge crosses Hay River.

J 5.4 (8.8 km) **FT 160.6** (258.4 km) Highway crosses Sandy Creek.

J 9.4 (15.2 km) **FT 156.6** (252 km) Railroad crossing.

J 17.3 (27.9 km) **FT 148.7** (239.3 km) Birch Creek bridge.

J 23.7 (38.2 km) **FT 142.3** (229 km) Highway crosses Twin Creek.

J 30.3 (48.8 km) **FT 135.7** (218.4 km) Good gravel road leads 1 mile/1.6 km north to **Polar Lake**. Lake is stocked with rainbow; no motorboats allowed. Good bird watching.

J 33.8 (54.4 km) **FT 132.2** (212.7 km) Buffalo River bridge.

J 34.1 (55 km) **FT 131.9** (212.2 km) Turnout to north with litter barrel.

J 37.3 (60 km) **FT 128.7** (207.1 km) **Junction** with Highway 6 east to Pine Point and Fort Resolution (see log this section). Highway 5 turns south for Fort Smith (continue with this log). Highway maintenance camp.

J 37.6 (60.6 km) **FT 128.4** (206.6 km) Microwave tower to south.

J 37.7 (60.8 km) **FT 128.3** (206.4 km) Pavement ends, gravel begins, southbound.

J 54 (87 km) **FT 112** (180.2 km) Turnoff for **Sandy Lake**, 8 miles/13 km south; swimming, sandy beach, fishing for northern pike.

J 59.6 (96 km) **FT 106.4** (171.2 km) Entrance to Wood Buffalo National Park. Established in 1922 to protect Canada's only remaining herd of wood bison, **WOOD BUFFALO NATIONAL PARK** (a UNESCO world heritage site) is a vast wilderness area of 44,800 square kilometres with the greater portion located in the northeast corner of Alberta. Park headquarters and Visitor Reception Centre are located in Fort Smith and Fort Chipewyan; excellent audio-video presentations, exhibits and visitor information are available. Or write the Superintendent, Wood Buffalo National Park, Box 750, Fort Smith, NT X0E 0P0; or phone (403) 872-2349 Fort Smith or (403) 697-3662 Fort Chipewyan.

The wood bison, a slightly larger and darker northern relative of the Plains bison, numbered about 1,500 in the area, representing the largest free-roaming herd in Canada at the time the park was established. Soon after this more than 6,600 Plains bison were moved from southern Alberta to the park. Today's herd of about 3,500 bison is

This Wardair Bristol freighter welcomes visitors to Yellowknife. (Earl L. Brown, staff)

considered to be mostly hybrids.

Also found within the park are many species of waterfowl and the world's only remaining natural nesting grounds of the endangered whooping crane.

The park is open year-round, with an interpretive program offered from June to September. Check the schedule of events at the park office.

J 63.8 (102.7 km) **FT 102.2** (164.4 km) Dust-free passing zone begins southbound.

Paralleling most of the highway to Fort Smith are hydro transmission power lines carrying power to Fort Smith, Pine Point and Fort Resolution that is generated at the Taltson Dam in the Canadian Shield north of the Slave River.

Much of the flora along this stretch of highway is new growth following the devastating forest fires of 1981. *NOTE: To report a forest fire, call the operator toll free and ask for Zenith 5555.*

J 66 (106.2 km) **FT 100** (160.9 km) Picnic area with tables to north at Angus Fire Tower. The sinkhole seen here is an example of karst topography. Sinkholes are formed when the roofs of caves (formed by underground water dissolving bedrock) collapse.

Buffalo wallow beside highway from here to approximately **Milepost J 98.9.**

J 68 (109.4 km) **FT 98** (157.7 km) Dust-free passing zone ends southbound.

J 70.6 (113.6 km) **FT 95.4** (153.5 km) Gravel stockpile to south.

J 74 (119.2 km) **FT 92** (148 km) Highway crosses Nyarling River, which runs under the dry creekbed.

J 74.2 (119.4 km) **FT 91.8** (147.7 km) Turnout to south with litter barrel.

J 84.7 (136.4 km) **FT 81.3** (130.8 km) Gravel stockpile to south.

J 90.7 (146 km) **FT 75.3** (121.2 km) Dust-free passing zone begins southbound.

J 95.9 (154.3 km) **FT 70.1** (112.8 km) Dust-free passing zone ends southbound.

J 98.9 (159.2 km) **FT 67.1** (108 km) Highway maintenance building to north.

J 110.8 (178.4 km) **FT 55.2** (88.8 km) Highway crosses Sass River. Shallow lakes from here south to Preble Creek provide nesting areas for whooping cranes.

J 116.2 (187 km) **FT 49.8** (80.1 km) Highway crosses Preble Creek.

J 121.1 (195 km) **FT 44.9** (72.2 km) More evidence of the 1981 forest fire. In some cases the fire only burned on one side of the highway with the road acting as a firebreak. Fires in the wilderness of Wood Buffalo National Park are allowed to burn unless they threaten rare plants or animals, human life or property.

J 130.5 (210 km) **FT 35.5** (57.1 km) The highway leaves and reenters Wood Buffalo National Park several times southbound.

J 131 (211 km) **FT 34.9** (56.1 km) Little Buffalo River bridge. Camping and picnic area. ▲

J 142.5 (229.4 km) **FT 23.5** (37.8 km) Turnoff for Parsons Lake Road (narrow gravel) which leads south 8 miles/13 km to Salt Plains overlook. Interpretive exhibit and viewing telescope. Springs at the edge of a high escarpment are bringing salt to the surface and spreading it across the huge flat plain; only plants specially adapted to high salinity can grow here. Fine view of a unique environment. Gravel parking area with tables, firepits and toilets at overlook; hiking trail down to Salt Plains (bring boots). *CAUTION: Parsons Lake Road beyond the overlook may be impassable in wet weather.*

J 147.9 (238 km) **FT 18.1** (29.1 km) Salt River bridge.

J 151.6 (244 km) **FT 14.4** (23.2 km) Thebacha (Salt River) private campground and picnic area 10 miles/16 km north via good gravel road. Located on the **Salt River**; 8 sites, toilets, parking, small-boat launch (cruise down to Slave River), and fishing for pike, walleye, inconnu and goldeye. ↵▲

J 163.4 (263 km) **FT 2.6** (4.2 km) Turnoff to north for Fort Smith airport and Queen Elizabeth Park campground with 19 campsites, 15 picnic sites, water, kitchen shelter, showers and dump station. Short hike from campground to bluff overlooking Rapids of the Drowned on the Slave River; look for pelicans feeding here. ▲

Fort Smith

J 166 (267.2 km) **FT 0 Population:** 2,460. **Emergency Services: Police,** phone 872-2107. **Fire Department,** phone 872-6111. **Hospital,** phone 872-3111. **Visitor Information:** Chamber of commerce information centre in Conibear Park, open June to September. For general information on the area, contact the Economic Development and Tourism Office, Box 390, Fort Smith, NT X0E 0P0.

Climate: Mean high temperature in July 75°F/24°C; mean low 48°F/9°C. **Radio:** 860, 101.9-FM. **Television:** Channels 12 (local) and 5 (CBC) plus 6 cable channels. **Newspaper:** *Slave River Journal.*

Transportation: Air—Canadian Airlines International provides scheduled service; there are also 3 charter air services here. **Bus**—Available. **Rental cars**—Available.

Private Aircraft: Fort Smith airport; elev. 666 feet/203m; length, 6,000 feet/1,829m; asphalt; fuel 80, 100.

Fort Smith began as a trading post at a favorite campsite of the portagers traveling the 1,600-mile/2575-km water passage from Fort McMurray to the Arctic Ocean. The 4 sets of rapids, named (south to north) Cassette, Pelican, Mountain and the Rapids of the Drowned, separate the Northwest Territories from Alberta. In 1874 Hudson's Bay Co. established a permanent post and the Roman Catholic mission was transferred here in 1876. By 1911 the settlement had become a major trading post for the area.

There are a hotel, a motel, 2 groceries, a takeout outlet, 3 bars, 3 convenience stores, and gas stations with unleaded gas and repair service.

Wood Buffalo National Park headquarters is located in the Federal Bldg. on McDougal Road, which also houses the post office. The multi-image presentation here is highly recommended. Exhibit area and trip planning assistance available at the visitor reception area. You can drive from Fort Smith to Peace Point via an all-weather gravel road. There is a picnic area at the Salt River, several hiking trails off the road, and a 36-site campground at Pine Lake, 38 miles/61 km south of Fort Smith. There is also a good opportunity for seeing bison on the road between Pine Lake and Peace Point. Contact the park office, phone 872-2349.

Other attractions in Fort Smith include Northern Life Museum, which features a comprehensive view of the area's Indian culture and life of the white settlers since mid-19th century.

Fort Resolution Highway Log

NWT HIGHWAY 6
Distance from junction with Highway 5 (J) is followed by distance from Fort Resolution (FR).

J 0 FR 55.9 (90 km) **Junction** of Highways 5 and 6.

The first 14.7 miles/23.7 km of the highway is paved; the rest is gravel to Fort Resolution. Narrow shoulders.

J 5 (8 km) **FR 50.9** (81.9 km) Pine Point Gun Club shooting range to south.

J 9.1 (14.6 km) **FR 46.8** (75.3 km) Pine Point mine private haul road (no trespassing).

J 13.2 (21.3 km) **FR 42.7** (68.7 km) Main access road north to **PINE POINT**; no services. A mining town, Pine Point was built in the 1960s by Cominco Ltd. The open-pit lead-zinc mine shut down in 1987. Once a community of almost 2,000 residents, most people moved out in 1988 and houses and structures have been moved or destroyed. The Great Slave Lake Railway (now CNR) was constructed in 1961 from Roma, AB, to Pine Point to transport the lead-zinc ore to market.

J 14.6 (23.6 km) **FR 41.3** (66.4 km) Secondary access road to Pine Point.

J 14.7 (23.7 km) **FR 41.2** (66.3 km) Pavement ends, gravel begins, eastbound.

J 15.8 (25.5 km) **FR 40.1** (64.5 km) Pine Point airport to north, microwave and satellite dish to south.

J 24.6 (39.6 km) **FR 31.3** (50.3 km) Tailing piles from open-pit mining to south.

J 32.3 (52 km) **FR 23.6** (38 km) Turnoff to north for Dawson Landing viewpoint on Great Slave Lake, accessible via a 25-mile/40-km bush road (not recommended in wet weather).

J 36.5 (58.8 km) **FR 19.4** (31.2 km) Turnout to north with litter barrel.

J 37.8 (60.8 km) **FR 18.1** (29.1 km) Glimpse of Great Slave Lake to north.

J 38.4 (61.8 km) **FR 17.5** (28.1 km) Gravel stockpile to south.

J 41.4 (66.7 km) **FR 14.5** (23.3 km) Bridge over **Little Buffalo River.** Good fishing for northern pike and walleye. ↵

J 54.5 (87.7 km) **FR 1.4** (2.2 km) Campground to west; 5 gravel sites, outhouses, tables and firepits. ▲

J 55.9 (90 km) **FR 0 FORT RESOLUTION** (pop. 447), located on the south shore of Great Slave Lake on Resolution Bay. **Emergency Services:** RCMP, phone 394-4111. This historic community grew up around a Hudson's Bay Co. post established in 1786, and was named Fort Resolution in 1821 when the Hudson's Bay Co. and North West Co. united. Missionaries settled in the area in 1852, establishing a school and hospital to serve the largely Chipewyan population. Walking tours through the village to visit the many old log buildings and sites may be arranged. The road connecting Fort Resolution with Pine Point was built in the 1960s.

Today's economy is based on trapping and a logging and sawmill operation. There are a small motel, 2 general stores, a gas station with minor repair service, a post office and cafe. Meals are also available at the community hall.

YELLOWHEAD HIGHWAY

Edmonton, Alberta, to Prince Rupert, British Columbia
(See maps, pages 198–200)

Yellowhead Highway 16 is a paved trans-Canada highway extending from Winnipeg, MB, through Saskatchewan, Alberta, and British Columbia to the coastal city of Prince Rupert. (The highway connecting Masset and Queen Charlotte on Graham Island has also been designated as part of Yellowhead Highway 16.) The MILEPOST® logs Yellowhead Highway 16 from Edmonton, AB, to Prince Rupert, BC, a distance of 906 miles/1,458 km.

Yellowhead Highway 16 terminates at Prince Rupert, BC, where you may connect with the Alaska Marine Highway System to southeastern Alaska cities, and the British Columbia ferry system to Port Hardy on Vancouver Island (see MARINE ACCESS ROUTES section).

This is a major east-west route, providing access to a number of attractions in Alberta and British Columbia. Yellowhead Highway 16 is also a very scenic highway, passing through both forest and farmland. Visitor

Fall colors touch the Bulkley River valley near Smithers. (Hugh B. White)

THE YELLOWHEAD HIGHWAY
A beautiful way to tour Canada's West

More travellers each year are choosing the Yellowhead Highway as the only way to tour Western Canada. More spectacular scenery! And beautiful cities like Edmonton, known as "The Gateway to the North" and "Canada's Festival City", with seven annual summer festivals, the world famous West Edmonton Mall and historic Fort Edmonton.

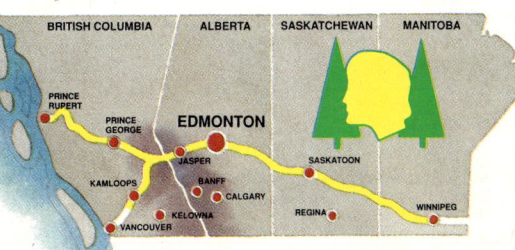

For information, contact:
Edmonton Tourism
9797 Jasper Avenue,
#104, Edmonton, Alberta
Canada T5J 1N9
Phone: (403) 422-5505

YELLOWHEAD IT VIA EDMONTON
'the other Trans Canada Highway'

1992 ■ The MILEPOST® 197

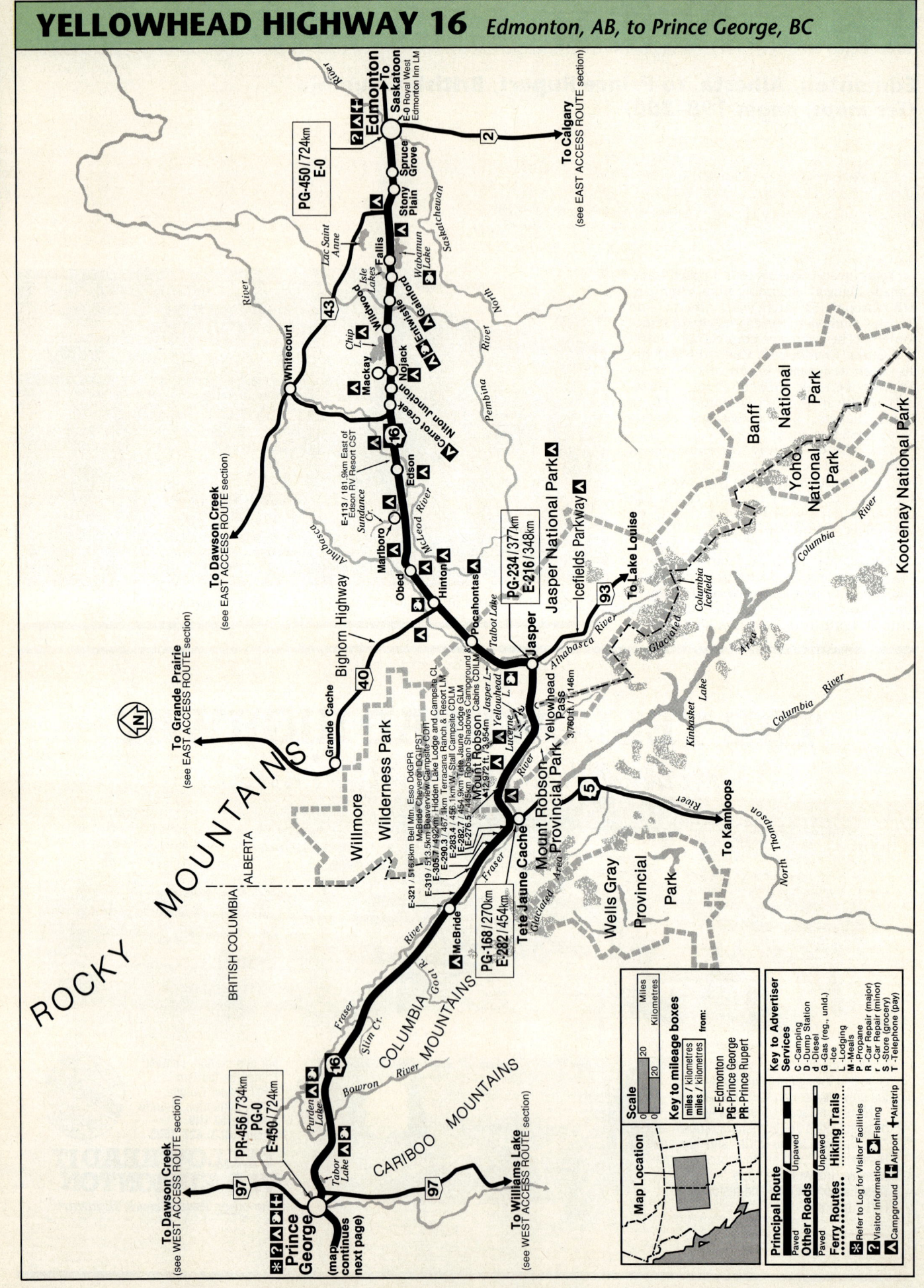

YELLOWHEAD HIGHWAY 16 Edmonton, AB, to Prince George, BC

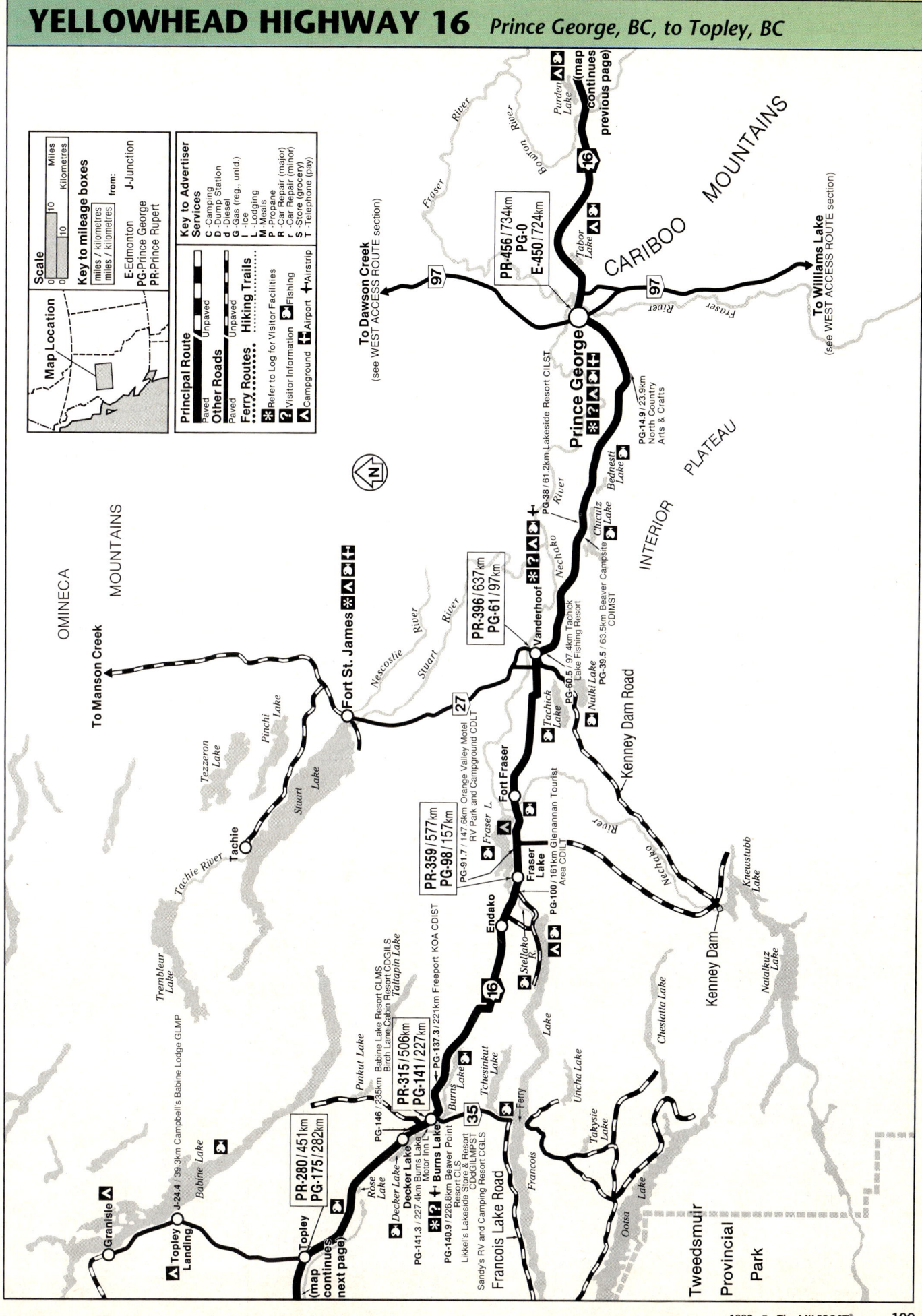

YELLOWHEAD HIGHWAY 16 — Prince George, BC, to Topley, BC

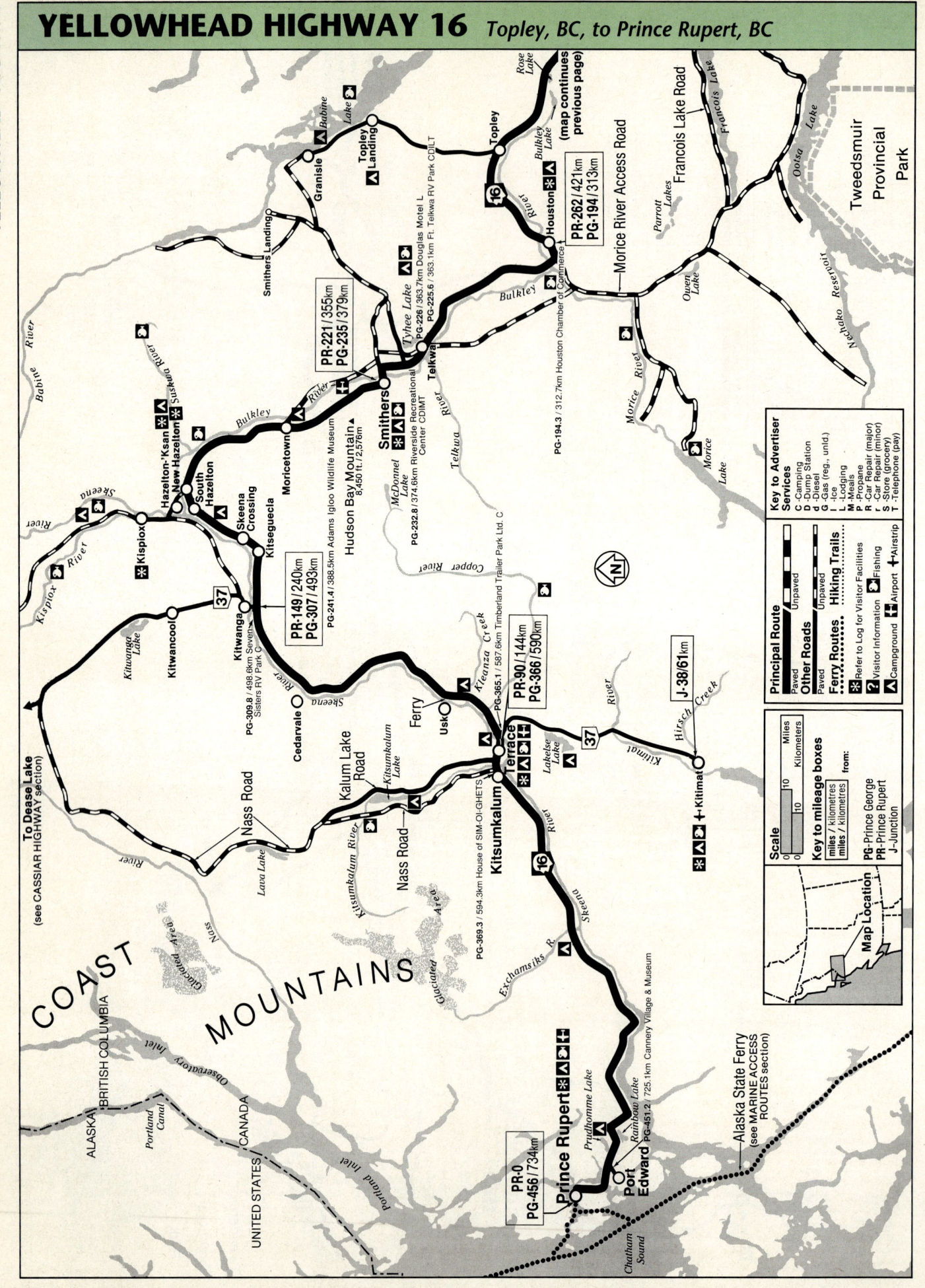

YELLOWHEAD HIGHWAY 16 Topley, BC, to Prince Rupert, BC

services are readily available in towns along the way, and campsites may be found in town and along the highway at both private and provincial park campgrounds. (It is unsafe and illegal to overnight in rest areas.)

Yellowhead Highway 16 Log

The Yellowhead Highway log is divided into 2 sections: Edmonton to Prince George, and Prince George to Prince Rupert.
This section of the log shows distance from Edmonton (E) followed by distance from Prince George (PG).

E 0 PG 450 (724.2 km) **EDMONTON** city limit. See EAST ACCESS ROUTE section for description of city.
Royal West Edmonton Inn. See display ad this section.

E 4 (6.4 km) **PG 446** (717.7 km) **Junction** of Highways 16 West and 60 (Devon Overpass); access to private campground. ▲

E 12 (19.3 km) **PG 438** (704.9 km) **SPRUCE GROVE** (pop. 11,861). All visitor facilities including a motel, restaurants, grocery stores and gas stations.

E 16 (25.7 km) **PG 434** (698.4 km) **STONY PLAIN** (pop. 5,761). All visitor facilities including hotels, restaurants, supermarket, shopping mall and gas stations with major repair service; RCMP and hospital; swimming pool and golf course. The Multicultural Heritage Centre here has a museum serves pioneer food. Open daily 10 A.M. to 4 P.M. Visitor information at the Old Caboose by the railroad.

E 19 (30.6 km) **PG 431** (693.6 km) Allan Beach Resort, 1.9 miles/3 km north; laundromat, campground with full hookups, showers and dump station. Day-use area, boat rental, playground and swimming. Phone (403) 963-6362. ▲

E 19.6 (31.5 km) **PG 430.4** (692.6 km) Edmonton Beach turnoff to south.

E 20.1 (32.3 km) **PG 429.9** (691.8 km) Hubbles Lake turnoff to north.

E 21.2 (34.1 km) **PG 428.8** (690.1 km) Restaurant, gas station and store to north.

E 22.4 (36 km) **PG 427.6** (688.1 km) Lake Eden Recreation Area to north.

E 25 (40.2 km) **PG 425** (684 km) **Junction** with Highway 43. Turn north for access to Alaska Highway (see EAST ACCESS ROUTE section) and Northwest Territories (see MACKENZIE ROUTE section). Continue west for Prince George.

E 33 (53.1 km) **PG 417** (671.1 km) Wabamun Lake Provincial Park, 1 mile/1.6 km south on access road; 288 campsites, fishing, boating and swimming. ◂▲

E 43 (69.2 km) **PG 407** (655 km) **FALLIS** (pop. 190). Cafe, grocery, 2 gas stations (1 with minor repair service).

E 49 (78.9 km) **PG 401** (645.3 km) **GAINFORD** (pop. 205). Cafe, hotel and post office. Free public campground at west end of town with 8 sites, firewood, tables, pit toilets and water.

E 58 (93.3 km) **PG 392** (630.8 km) **ENTWISTLE** (pop. 477). Restaurants, gas station, 2 motels, post office, swimming pool and grocery store. Pembina River Provincial Park, 1.9 miles/3 km north; 129 campsites, fee charged, firewood, tables, pit toilets, water and dump station. Fishing, swimming, playground and phone. ◂▲

E 68 (109.4 km) **PG 382** (614.8 km) **WILDWOOD** (pop. 375), the "Bingo Capital of Canada." Attractive village with post office, motel, hotel, gas station with major repair service, restaurants and shops. There is a farmers market on Friday afternoon. Campground at Chip Lake with 14 sites, tables, firewood, pit toilets, water, fishing, swimming and boat launch. ▲

E 82 (131.9 km) **PG 368** (592.2 km) **NOJACK** and **MACKAY** (pop. 250). Grocery,

---

BC's Northern Capital...
...where people make the difference.

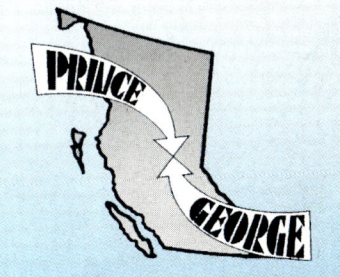

PRINCE GEORGE

See our ad under Prince George
(West Access Route section)
TOURISM PRINCE GEORGE
1198(MP) Victoria St., Prince George, BC V2L 2L2
Phone: (604) 562-3700 • FAX (604) 563-3584

Super, Natural North by Northwest

You're welcome at the new, elegant Royal West Edmonton Inn.

Relax and unwind in one of our deluxe rooms!
You deserve it!
We will meet and exceed your expectations!

ROYAL WEST EDMONTON INN

Our Inn offers you: Plenty of free parking, a health centre with steambath and Jacuzzis, the *Copper Room*, a bistro-style restaurant, *Jade Dining Room*, and *Mirage Lounge* featuring big screen sporting events.

10010 - 178th Street
Edmonton, Alberta T5S 1T3
Telephone (403) 484-6000
1-800-661-4879

YELLOWHEAD HIGHWAY

Summit of Mount Robson is often shrouded in clouds. (Philip and Karen Smith)

post office, restaurant and gas station with towing, diesel and major repair service. Mackay is 1.9 miles/3 km north of Nojack on a gravel road. Campgrounds 1 mile/1.6 km and 3 miles/4.8 km west of town on Highway 16. ▲

E 90 (144.8 km) **PG 360** (579.3 km) **NITON JUNCTION.** Hamlet with gas, groceries and post office.

E 94 (151.3 km) **PG 356** (572.9 km) **CARROT CREEK,** post office, grocery store, gas station and car wash. Campground 1.9 miles/3 km north with 8 sites, tables, pit toilets and water.

E 99 (159.3 km) **PG 351** (564.9 km) **Junction** with Highway 32 which leads to Whitecourt and Highway 43, 42 miles/68 km north on paved road.

E 106.6 (171.6 km) **PG 343.4** (552.6 km) Rest area to south.

E 113 (181.9 km) **PG 337** (542.3 km) **East of Edson RV Resort.** 8 km (5 miles) east of Edson on Highway 16. Full services in the wilderness. Rustic drive-through sites with 30/15-amp service. Coin-op hot showers. Laundromat. Small store. Public phone. Walkways. Recreation activities. Pets welcome. Reservations (403) 723-2287. Box 7378, Edson, AB T7E 1V6. [ADVERTISEMENT] ▲

E 113.6 (182.8 km) **PG 366.4** (541.4 km) McLeod River bridge.

E 118 (189.9 km) **PG 332** (534.4 km) **EDSON** (pop. 7,323). Large highway community with 14 motels, many restaurants and gas stations; 18-hole golf course, indoor pool; hospital and RCMP post. There is camping at Lions Club Campground east of town (42 sites), and at Willmore Recreation Park, 3.7 miles/6 km south of town on the McLeod River. Campground resort, 5 miles/8 km east of Edson, with full hookups; open May to November. Edson's economy is based on coal mining, forestry, oil and natural gas, and manufacturing (Weyerhaeuser oriented strand board plant). ▲

E 122 (196.3 km) **PG 328** (527.9 km) Point of interest sign about Edson-Grande Prairie trail.

E 124 (199.6 km) **PG 326** (524.6 km) Food, gas, lodging.

E 130 (209.2 km) **PG 320** (515 km) Hornbeck Creek public campground; 35 sites. ▲

E 134.7 (216.8 km) **PG 315.3** (507.4 km) Small community of Marlboro to north.

E 140 (225.3 km) **PG 310** (498.9 km) First glimpse of Canadian Rockies westbound.

E 145.1 (233.5 km) **PG 304.9** (490.7 km) Turnout with litter barrel.

E 150.6 (242.4 km) **PG 299.4** (481.8 km) Obed Lake public campground; 13 sites, no fee, firewood, tables, pit toilets and water. ▲

E 152 (244.6 km) **PG 298** (479.6 km) **OBED.** Phone, gas and groceries.

E 158.7 (255.4 km) **PG 291.3** (468.8 km) Highest elevation on the Yellowhead Highway at 3,819 feet/1,164m.

E 159.5 (256.7 km) **PG 290.5** (467.5 km) Roundcroft public campground to south; 9 sites, no fee, firewood, tables, pit toilets and water. ▲

E 170 (273.6 km) **PG 280** (450.6 km) **HINTON** (pop. 8,537). All visitor facilities including hotels and motels, golf course, hospital, dentist, RCMP and recreation complex with indoor pool. Campground with 50 sites, hookups and dump station. Site of St. Regis (Alberta) Ltd. pulp mill; tours of mill complex may be arranged. ▲

E 178 (286.5 km) **PG 272** (437.7 km) **Junction** with Bighorn Highway 40, which leads north 90 miles/145 km (paved) to Grande Cache then another 117 miles/188 km (gravel) to Grande Prairie. (See log of Bighorn Highway 40 in the EAST ACCESS ROUTE section.)

E 181.3 (291.8 km) **PG 268.7** (432.4 km) Picnic area.

E 182.4 (293.5 km) **PG 267.6** (430.6 km) Weigh scales and pay phone.

E 183.7 (295.6 km) **PG 266.3** (428.6 km) Public campground 3.1 miles/5 km north. ▲

E 186.2 (299.6 km) **PG 263.8** (424.5 km) Private campground, pay phone. ▲

E 187.5 (301.7 km) **PG 262.5** (422.4 km) Resort with lodging to north.

E 188 (302.5 km) **PG 262** (421.6 km) Point of interest sign about Athabasca River.

E 190 (305.8 km) **PG 260** (418.4 km) East entrance to Jasper National Park. Motor vehicle license sticker required for all visitors using facilities in Rocky Mountain national parks. Permit fees: 1 day, $3; 4 days, $6; annual permit, $20.

E 193 (310.6 km) **PG 257** (413.6 km) **POCAHONTAS.** Grocery, motel, cafe and gas station with minor repair service. Miette Hot Springs Road leads 0.6 mile/1 km south to Park Service campground with 140 sites, 11 miles/18 km south of Miette Hot Springs and resort. ▲

E 196.1 (315.6 km) **PG 253.9** (408.6 km) Turnout to south with historical marker.

E 196.5 (316.2 km) **PG 253.5** (408 km) Turnout to north.

E 198.1 (318.8 km) **PG 251.9** (405.4 km) Turnout to north with litter barrels and picnic tables.

E 198.3 (319.1 km) **PG 251.7** (405.1 km) Rocky River bridge.

E 198.5 (319.4 km) **PG 251.5** (404.7 km) Turnout to north with historical marker.

E 200.7 (323 km) **PG 249.3** (401.2 km) Talbot Lake to south; picnic tables.

E 202.2 (325.4 km) **PG 247.8** (398.8 km) Turnout to south.

E 203 (326.7 km) **PG 247** (397.5 km) Jasper Lake to north.

E 204.6 (329.3 km) **PG 245.4** (394.9 km) Turnout with litter barrels to south.

E 206.3 (332 km) **PG 243.7** (392.2 km) Turnout to south; trailhead.

E 206.6 (332.5 km) **PG 243.4** (391.7 km) Athabasca River bridge.

E 208.7 (335.9 km) **PG 241.3** (388.3 km) Snaring River bridge.

E 210.2 (338.3 km) **PG 239.8** (385.9 km) Jasper airfield to south.

E 211.3 (340 km) **PG 238.7** (384.1 km) Snaring rest area to south.

E 212.1 (341.3 km) **PG 237.9** (382.9 km) Pallsades rest area to south.

E 213.4 (343.4 km) **PG 236.6** (380.8 km) Turnout to south with litter barrels and view of Mount Edith Cavell.

E 214.5 (345.2 km) **PG 235.5** (379 km) Turnout with litter barrel to south.

E 215 (346 km) **PG 235** (378.2 km) Access road to Jasper Park Lodge.

E 216 (347.6 km) **PG 234** (376.6 km) Access to Jasper and **junction** with Highway 93, the scenic Icefields Parkway, south to Banff past Columbia Icefield.

Many residents in this area maintain hummingbird feeders. The 2 species of hummingbirds found in the Canadian Rockies are the Rufous and the Calliope.

E 216.5 (348.4 km) **PG 233.5** (375.8 km) Miette River.

E 218.3 (351.4 km) **PG 231.7** (372.9 km) Turnout with litter barrels to north.

E 220.7 (355.2 km) **PG 229.3** (369 km) Paved turnout to south with litter barrels and picnic table.

E 221.6 (356.7 km) **PG 228.4** (367.5 km) Paved turnout to north with outhouses, litter barrels and interpretive sign about Yellowhead Pass.

E 222.3 (357.7 km) **PG 227.7** (366.4 km) Meadow Creek.

E 222.7 (358.4 km) **PG 227.3** (365.8 km) Trailhead for: Virl Lake, Dorothy Lake and Christine Lake.

E 225.5 (363 km) **PG 224.5** (361.3 km) Clairvaux Creek.

E 235 (378.2 km) **PG 215** (346 km) West entrance to Jasper National Park; motor vehicle license required for all visitors using facilities in Rocky Mountain national park. Permit fees: 1 day, $3; 4 days, $6; annual permit, $20.

E 235.5 (379 km) **PG 214.5** (345.2 km) Yellowhead Pass (elev. 3,760 feet/1,146m), Alberta-British Columbia border. Named for an Iroquois trapper and guide who worked for the Hudson's Bay Co. in the early 1800s. His light-colored hair earned him the name Tete Jaune ("yellow head") from the French voyageurs.

East entrance to Mount Robson Provincial Park. Portal Lake picnic area with tables, toilets, information board and hiking trail.

TIME ZONE CHANGE: Alberta observes Mountain standard time. Most of British Columbia observes Pacific standard time. Both observe daylight saving time. See Time Zones in the GENERAL INFORMATION section for details.

E 237 (381.4 km) **PG 213** (342.8 km) **Yellowhead Lake**; picnic tables, viewpoint, boat launch and fishing.

E 240 (386.2 km) **PG 210** (338 km) Lucerne Campground; 32 sites, picnic tables, drinking water and swimming. Camping fee $7. ▲

E 241.4 (388.5 km) **PG 208.6** (335.7 km) Fraser Crossing rest area to south; tables, litter barrels and toilets.

E 241.5 (388.6 km) **PG 208.5** (335.6 km) Fraser River bridge No. 1.

E 244.5 (393.5 km) **PG 205.5** (330.7 km)

202 The MILEPOST® • 1992

Fraser River bridge No. 2.

E 248.2 (399.4 km) PG 201.8 (324.8 km) Grant Brook.

E 250.9 (403.8 km) PG 199.1 (320.4 km) Moose Creek bridge.

E 254 (408.2 km) PG 196 (316 km) Turnout at east end of Moose Lake; tables, litter barrels, toilet and boat launch.

E 258.4 (415.8 km) PG 191.6 (308.3 km) Information sign on avalanches and wildlife.

E 262.5 (422.4 km) PG 187.5 (301.7 km) Turnout with litter barrels. Avalanche gates.

E 266.7 (429.2 km) PG 183.9 (296 km) Turnout with litter barrels to south.

E 269.5 (433.7 km) PG 180.5 (290.5 km) Gravel turnout to south.

E 271.1 (436.3 km) PG 178.9 (287.9 km) Overland Falls rest area to south; pit toilets, litter barrels. Hiking trail to Overlander Falls, about 45 minutes round-trip.

E 272 (437.7 km) PG 178 (286.5 km) Viewpoint of Mount Robson (elev. 12,972 feet/3954m), highest peak in the Canadian Rockies, and visitor centre. Parking, picnic tables, restrooms, litter barrels, gas and restaurant. Berg Lake trailhead; hike-in campgrounds. Private campground north of highway. Robson Meadows government campground south of highway with 125 sites, showers, dump station, pay phone, interpretive programs, tables, firewood, pit toilets, water and horseshoe pits. Camping fee is $7. ▲

E 272.5 (438.5 km) PG 177.5 (285.6 km) Robson River government campground to north with 19 sites, tables, firewood, pit toilets, water and horseshoe pits. Camping fee is $8. ▲

E 272.9 (439.2 km) PG 177.1 (285 km) Robson River bridge. Look for Indian paintbrush June through August. The bracts are orange-red while the petals are green.

E 273.4 (440 km) PG 176.6 (284.2 km) West entrance to Mount Robson Provincial Park. Turnout with litter barrels and statue.

E 273.5 (440.2 km) PG 176.5 (284 km) Gravel turnout with litter barrels.

E 274.4 (441.6 km) PG 175.6 (282.6 km) Swift Current Creek.

E 274.7 (442.1 km) PG 175.3 (282.1 km) Turnout with litter barrels.

E 276.5 (445 km) PG 173.5 (279.2 km) **Robson Shadows Campground and Cabins.** See display ad this section. ▲

E 277.6 (446.7 km) PG 172.4 (277.4 km) Mount Terry Fox Provincial Park picnic area with tables, restrooms and viewing telescope. The information board here points out the location of Mount Terry Fox in the Selwyn Range of the Rocky Mountains. The peak was named in 1981 to honour cancer victim Terry Fox, who before his death from the disease, raised some $25 million for cancer research during his attempt to run across Canada.

E 279.4 (449.7 km) PG 170.6 (274.5 km) Gravel turnout to north with Yellowhead Highway information sign.

E 279.5 (449.8 km) PG 170.5 (274.4 km) Rearguard Falls Provincial Park picnic area. Easy half-hour round-trip to falls viewpoint. Upper limit of 800-mile migration of Pacific salmon; look for chinook in late summer.

E 280.5 (451.9 km) PG 169.2 (272.3 km) Gravel turnout. Avalanche gates.

E 281.3 (452.7 km) PG 168.7 (271.5 km) Weigh scales.

E 281.7 (453.3 km) PG 168.3 (270.8 km) Tete Jaune Cache rest area with tables, litter barrels and toilets.

E 282 (453.8 km) PG 168 (270.4 km)

Rearguard Falls is reached by trail from picnic area at Milepost E 279.5. (Earl L. Brown, staff)

Junction with Yellowhead Highway 5 to Tete Jaune Cache and Kamloops, BC. Food, gas and lodging just west of the junction. Yellowhead Highway 5 opened in 1969. A year earlier, construction of the section of the highway east from Prince George to Tete Jaune Cache had connected Highway 16 with a rough road east to Jasper National Park. The final link in Northern Trans-provincial Highway 16 (now Yellowhead Highway 16)—between Prince George and Edmonton—officially opened in 1969.

Tete Jaune Lodge. See display ad this section.

E 282.7 (454.9 km) PG 167.3 (269.2 km) Turnoff for gas and lodging.

E 283.4 (456.1 km) PG 166.6 (268.1 km) **W. Stall Campsite.** See display ad this section. ▲

E 290.3 (467.1 km) PG 159.7 (257 km) **Terracana Ranch & Resort,** luxury in the wilderness. 18 scenic deluxe log cabins for 2 and 4 persons, licensed restaurant and bar, conference room, recreational rooms, guided tours, horseback riding, canoeing, ATVs, mountain bikes, heli-hiking, fishing, riverboating, jet-boat tours, sightseeing tours, car rentals, own trails, 2.5 km river frontage. Phone (604) 968-4304, fax (604) 968-4445. Box 909, Valemount, BC V0E 2Z0. [ADVERTISEMENT]

E 291.2 (468.6 km) PG 158.8 (255.6 km) Small River rest area by stream with tables, toilets and litter barrels.

E 295.5 (475.5 km) PG 154.5 (248.6 km) Horsey Creek.

E 301.9 (485.8 km) PG 148.1 (238.3 km) Turnoff to south for settlement of Dunster; gas and general store.

E 305.6 (491.8 km) PG 144.4 (232.4 km) Holiday Creek.

E 305.7 (492 km) PG 144.3 (232.2 km) **Hidden Lake Lodge and Campsite.** Enjoy our quiet place between the Rocky and Cariboo Mountains. You'll stay in cabins with bathrooms, some with kitchens, or park your RV at the campground. While you canoe the lake and observe wildlife let us prepare your breakfast. Electric hookups, picnic tables, firewood, flush toilets, showers, local crafts. General Delivery, Dunster, BC V0J 1J0. Phone and fax (604) 968-4327 [ADVERTISEMENT] ▲

E 306.1 (492.6 km) PG 143.9 (231.6 km) Baker Creek rest area with tables, litter barrels and toilets.

E 310 (498.9 km) PG 140 (225.3 km) Neven Creek.

E 313 (503.7 km) PG 137 (220.5 km) Turnouts at both ends of Holmes River bridge.

ROBSON SHADOWS CAMPGROUND & CABINS

Panorama View of Mt. Robson — Partial Hookups
Log-sided Housekeeping Cabins — Coffee Shop
Camping by the Fraser River — Fishing Licenses

Phone: (604) 566-4821
Mailing Address: Mt. Robson, c/o PO Box 157
Valemount, BC V0E 2Z0

TETE JAUNE LODGE

Large, comfortable rooms, some with river view
Queen Size Beds • Satellite Colour TV
Licensed Dining in Historical Log Restaurant
Gas Bar • Confectionery

PO BOX 879, VALEMOUNT, BC V0E 2Z0
(604) 566-9815

W. Stall Campsite

TETE JAUNE CACHE, BC
Hot Showers • Restaurant • Cabins
Hookups • Sani-dump

Senior Discount   (604) 566-9810
Box 823, Valemount, BC, V0E 2Z0

E 319 (513.5 km) **PG 131** (210.8 km) **Beaverview Campsite.** See display ad this section. ▲

E 319.6 (514.3 km) **PG 130.4** (209.9 km) Fraser River bridge. A forest fire swept through the Robson Valley in 1912. As you look at the sides of the mountain to the north of the highway it is possible to distinguish the new growth which has taken place in the last 80 years.

E 320.3 (515.4 km) **PG 129.7** (208.7 km) Turnout to north with litter barrels.

E 321 (516.6 km) **PG 129** (207.6 km) **McBRIDE** (pop. 582, elev. 2,369 feet/722m), located in the Robson Valley by the Fraser River. The Park Ranges of the Rocky Mountains are to the northeast. A dirt road leads to Teare Mountain lookout for spectacular view of countryside. The village of McBride was established in 1913 as a divisional point on the railroad and was named for Richard McBride, then premier of British Columbia. Forest products are a major industry today.

Visitor Information: Travel Infocentre located in railcar adjacent south side of Highway 16. Look for the carved grizzly bear family in front.

McBride has all visitor facilities, including 4 hotels/motels, 2 supermarkets, clothing stores, restaurants, pharmacy, hospital and gas stations. There is a private campground just east of town. Dump station located at fire department.

Bell Mtn. Esso. See display ad this section.

McBride Chevron. See display ad this section.

NOTE: *Next gas stop westbound is 91 miles/146.4 km from here (Purden Lake).*

E 324.1 (521.6 km) **PG 125.9** (202.6 km) Dore River bridge.

Beaverview Campsite (604) 569-2513
Good Sampark
Laundry • Sani-Station
FREE HOT SHOWERS
Grassed Pull-thru • Hookups • Jet Boat Rides
Yellowhead Highway East, McBride, BC
Super, Natural North by Northwest

McBride Chevron
Highway 16, McBride B.C.
Chevron Gas & Oil Products
Propane, Store, Ice, Dump Station
(604) 569-3221

BELL MTN. ESSO
Esso
Box 386, McBride, BC V0J 2E0
Gas • Diesel • Propane
Sani-Dump
Licensed Mechanic
Heavy Duty Repairs
Super, Natural North by Northwest

E 329.4 (530.1 km) **PG 120.6** (194.1 km) Macintosh Creek.

E 330.9 (532.5 km) **PG 119.1** (191.7 km) Clyde Creek.

E 339.6 (546.5 km) **PG 110.4** (177.7 km) West Twin Creek bridge.

E 348 (560 km) **PG 102** (164.1 km) Goat River bridge. Rest area to north with tables and litter barrels.

E 354.3 (570.2 km) **PG 95.7** (154 km) Snowshoe Creek.

E 359.3 (578.2 km) **PG 90.7** (146 km) Catfish Creek.

E 365.1 (587.6 km) **PG 84.9** (136.6 km) Ptarmigan Creek bridge.

E 368.2 (592.6 km) **PG 81.8** (131.6 km) Turnout with litter barrel to north.

E 371.5 (597.9 km) **PG 78.5** (126.3 km) Slate quarry to north.

E 373.4 (600.9 km) **PG 76.6** (123.3 km) Dome Creek bridge. Diner.

E 375.7 (604.6 km) **PG 74.3** (119.6 km) Ministry of Highways camp.

E 376.8 (606.4 km) **PG 73.2** (117.8 km) Slim Creek rest area to south with tables, litter barrels and toilets. Watch for bears.

E 377.5 (607.5 km) **PG 72.5** (116.7 km) Slim Creek bridge.

E 388.7 (625.5 km) **PG 61.3** (98.6 km) Driscol Creek.

E 390.8 (628.9 km) **PG 59.2** (95.3 km) Gravel turnout with litter barrel to north.

E 392 (630.8 km) **PG 58** (93.3 km) Lunate Creek.

E 395 (635.7 km) **PG 55** (88.5 km) Hungary Creek. Watch for Ministry of Forests signs indicating the year in which a logged area was replanted. Wildflowers include fireweed, mid-July through August.

E 398.7 (641.6 km) **PG 51.3** (82.6 km) Sugarbowl Creek.

E 403.7 (649.7 km) **PG 46.3** (74.5 km) Paved turnout with litter barrel to north.

E 405 (651.8 km) **PG 45** (72.4 km) Kenneth Creek.

E 411.5 (662.2 km) **PG 38.5** (62 km) Purden Mountain ski resort.

E 412 (663 km) **PG 38** (61.2 km) Resort with gas, lodging and camping. ▲

NOTE: *Next gas stop eastbound is 91 miles/146.4 km from here (McBride).*

E 414 (666.3 km) **PG 36** (57.9 km) Purden Lake Provincial Park; 78 campsites, 48 picnic sites, tables, water, dump station, firewood, playground and horseshoe pits. This recreation area offers a sandy beach, change houses, swimming, hiking trails, waterskiing and boat launch. Good rainbow fishing to 4 lbs., trolling.

E 415.5 (668.6 km) **PG 34.5** (55.5 km) Bowron River bridge. Paved rest area to north on river with toilets, tables and litter barrels.

E 422 (679.2 km) **PG 28** (45.1 km) Vama Vama Creek.

NORTH COUNTRY ARTS & CRAFTS
BC Jade, Indian Crafts, Unique Quality Souvenirs, Wonderful Variety
Hwy #16 West
Prince George, BC (604) 560-5485
Super, Natural North by Northwest

E 425 (684 km) **PG 25** (40.2 km) Wansa Creek.

E 428 (688.8 km) **PG 22** (35.4 km) Willow River bridge. Rest area at west end of bridge beside river; tables, litter barrels, toilets and nature trail. The 1.2-mile-/1.9-km-long Willow River Forest Interpretation Trail is an easy 45-minute walk.

E 430.4 (692.7 km) **PG 19.6** (31.5 km) Bowes Creek.

E 430.5 (692.8 km) **PG 19.5** (31.4 km) Turnout to north with litter barrels and information board on 1961 forest fire and moose habitat. Hiking trails to moose observation site.

E 436 (701.7 km) **PG 14** (22.5 km) Tabor Mountain ski hill.

E 436.2 (702 km) **PG 13.8** (22.2 km) Gravel turnout to north with litter barrels.

E 438.5 (705.7 km) **PG 11.5** (18.5 km) Turnoff for Log House Restaurant and RV Park. Access to **Tabor Lake**; good fishing for rainbow in spring.

E 444 (714.5 km) **PG 6** (9.7 km) Junction, Highway 16B with Highway 97 south bypass.

E 450 (724.2 km) **PG 0 PRINCE GEORGE**, **Junction** with Highway 97, north to Dawson Creek and the beginning of the Alaska Highway.

See **WEST ACCESS ROUTE** section for details on Prince George and the log of Highway 97 north. Continue west for Prince Rupert (log follows).

Yellowhead Highway 16 Log

(continued)

This section of the log shows distance from Prince George (PG) followed by distance from Prince Rupert (PR).

PG 0 PR 456 (733.8 km) From Prince George to Prince Rupert, Highway 16 is a 2-lane highway with 3-lane passing stretches. Fairly straight, with no high summits, the highway follows the valleys of the Nechako, Bulkley and Skeena rivers, paralleling the Canadian National Railway route. There are few services between towns. NOTE: *There are few passing lanes between Prince George and Vanderhoof. Pass with caution.*

PG 3 (4.8 km) **PR 453** (729 km) KOA campground. ▲

PG 4.8 (7.8 km) **PR 451.2** (726.1 km) West Lake Provincial Park 8 miles/13 km south; day-use area with swimming, fishing and boat launch.

PG 14.9 (23.9 km) **PR 441.1** (709.9 km) North Country Arts & Crafts. See display ad this section.

Lakeside Resort & ATTIC PUB
Cabins • Camping • RV Park
Laundromat & Hot Showers • Store
Hookups • Playground • Marine Gas
FISH CLUCULZ LAKE
Record Char, Kokanee and Rainbow
Floatplane and Boat Mooring
Boat Rentals and Ramp • Tackle
(604) 441-3344
Box 881, Vanderhoof, BC V0J 3A0
Super, Natural North by Northwest

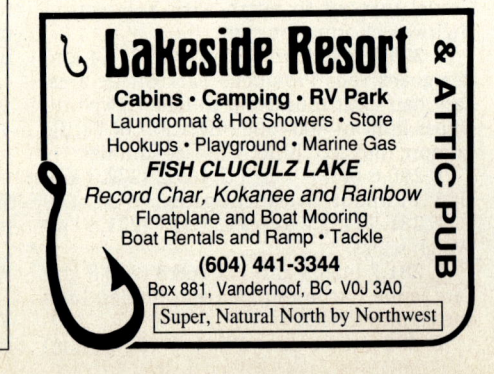

PG 32.1 (51.7 km) **PR 423.9** (682.2 km) Rest area to north with picnic tables, toilets and litter barrels.

PG 38 (61.2 km) **PR 418** (672.7 km) Access to lakeside resort and fishing at **Cluculz Lake** (not visible from highway). Rainbow to 3¾ lbs. by trolling, use snell hook and worms; kokanee to 1½ lbs., troll with snell hook and worms, in spring; arctic char to 57 lbs., use large flatfish, spoons, plugs and weights, early spring and late fall; whitefish to 5 lbs., anytime. Very good fishing in spring; ice goes out about the first week of May. Good ice fishing December to March. In September kokanee are at their peak. *Lake gets rough when windy.*

Lakeside Resort. See display ad this section.

PG 39.1 (62.9 km) **PR 416.9** (670.9 km) Cluculz rest area to south with flush toilets (summer only), picnic tables and litter barrels.

PG 39.5 (63.5 km) **PR 416.5** (670.3 km) **Beaver Campsite & Cafe**, 45 restful sites in quiet pine forest. 8 pull-throughs. Electric hookups, laundromat, hot coin-op showers, sani-station. Ice. Store. Cafe with delicious home cooking. Laundromat. Playground. Water. Your hosts, Ed and Jean Sokoloski. RR 1, Site 17, Comp. 14, Vanderhoof, BC V0J 3A0. (604) 441-3385. [ADVERTISEMENT]

Vanderhoof

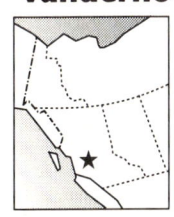

PG 60.5 (97.4 km) **PR 395.5** (636.5 km). **Population:** 3,906; area 12,000. **Emergency Services: Police**, phone 567-2222. **Fire Department**, phone 567-2345. **Ambulance**, phone 112-562-7241. **Hospital**, St. John's, Northside District, phone 567-2211.

Visitor Information: Travel Infocentre downtown on Burrard Street, 1 block off Highway 16. Write Vanderhoof & District Chamber of Commerce, Box 126-MP, Vanderhoof, BC J0V 3A0; phone (604) 567-2124.

Elevation: 2,086 feet/636m. **Radio:** CJCI 620, CFPR-FM 96.7, CKPG 550, CIVH 1340. **Television:** Channels 2, 4, 5, 6, 8. **Newspapers:** *Omineca Express-Bugle* (weekly). **Transportation: Air**—Vanderhoof airport, 2 miles/3.2 km from intersection of Highways 16 and 27; 5,000-foot/1,524-m paved runway. Seaplane landings on Nechako River at corner of View Street and Boundary Avenue. **Railroad**—VIA Rail, station at 2222 Church Ave. **Bus**—Greyhound.

Vanderhoof was named for Chicago publisher Herbert Vanderhoof, who founded the village in 1914 when he was associated with the Grand Trunk Development Co. Today, Vanderhoof is the supply and distribution centre for a large agricultural, lumbering and mining area.

The community's history is preserved at Vanderhoof Heritage Village Museum, just off Highway 16. Relocated pioneer structures furnished with period artifacts recall the early days of the Nechako Valley.

Located on the Nechako River, Vanderhoof is a stopping place in April for thousands of migrating waterfowl. The river flats upstream of the bridge are a bird sanctuary. Pelicans have been spotted feeding at Tachick Lake south of town.

Vanderhoof is also home to the second largest international air show in British Columbia, held in July or August (check with chamber of commerce). Nechako Valley Summer School of the Arts is in session the last week in July, first week in August.

There are 7 hotels and motels and 16 restaurants in the town. All shopping facilities and several gas stations. Dump station at the Esso station at 1st and Fraser. Municipal campground is west of town on Highway 16. Nine hole, par 35, golf course located 1.9 miles/3 km north of town.

Area attractions include Fort St. James (see page 206), Tachick Lake and Kenney Dam. Follow the gravel road southwest from Vanderhoof 60 miles/96 km to Kenney Dam. At the time of its construction, it was North America's largest earth-filled dam. Near the dam site are Cheslatta Falls and Nechako River canyon (good area for rockhounding). Beautiful Tachick Lake (18 miles/29 km south) has a modern log building fishing resort. Also access to Nulki Lake; see fishing information following. Kenney Dam Road turnoff is at the Shell service station on Highway 16.

Nulki Lake, 12 miles/19.3 km south on Kenney Dam Road, rainbow to 6 or 7 lbs., average 2 lbs., use worms, year-round. **Tachick Lake**, 18 miles/29 km south on Kenney Dam Road, rainbow 2 to 7 lbs. year-round, largest fish in the area were taken from this lake; several small lakes in the area abound with rainbow and kokanee. Fishing charters available at Vanderhoof airport.

Tachick Lake Fishing Resort. See display ad this section.

Unusual burl moose stands amidst wildflowers alongside Highway 16. (Earl L. Brown, staff)

Yellowhead Highway 16 Log

(continued)

PG 60.5 (97.4 km) **PR 395.5** (636.5 km) First **junction** westbound with Highway 27, which extends north from Vanderhoof several hundred miles. The 37 miles/59.6 km to Fort St. James are fully paved (see page 206).

PG 61.1 (98.3 km) **PR 394.9** (635.5 km) Vanderhoof Municipal Campground, pleasantly situated on a creek.

PG 62.3 (100.2 km) **PR 393.7** (633.6 km) Family Farm to south has a children's zoo and snack barn.

PG 64.7 (104.2 km) **PR 391.3** (629.7 km) Second **junction** westbound with Highway 27 (see description at **Milepost PG 60.5**). This route skirts Vanderhoof. Truck weigh scales to north.

PG 72.8 (117.2 km) **PR 383.2** (616.7 km) Restaurant with pay phone and RV parking.

PG 73.7 (118.6 km) **PR 392.3** (615.2 km) Westar sawmill to south.

PG 83.8 (134.9 km) **PR 372.2** (599 km) Turnout to south with view of Nechako River. The Grand Trunk Pacific Railroad was completed near this site in 1914. The railroad (later the Canadian National) linked Prince Rupert, a deep-water port, with interior British Columbia.

PG 84.3 (135.7 km) **PR 371.7** (598.2 km) **FORT FRASER** (pop. 600). **Radio:** CBC-FM 102.9. Small community with food, gas,

---

TACHICK LAKE FISHING RESORT

Full Service Campsites overlooking Lake
Free Showers, Laundromat
Fine European Cuisine (weekends only)
Clean and Modern Cabins. Boat Rental

BOX 1112, VANDERHOOF, BC V0J 3A0
(604) 567-4929

Super, Natural North by Northwest

1992 ■ The MILEPOST® 205

Fort St. James

Fort St. James

Located 37 miles/59.6 km north of Vanderhoof on Highway 27. **Population:** 1,983. **Emergency Services: Police,** phone 996-8269. **Ambulance:** phone 1-562-7241. **Elevation:** 2,208 feet/673m. **Radio:** CKPG 550, CBC-FM 1070, CJCI 1480.

Fort St. James is the site of **FORT ST. JAMES NATIONAL HISTORIC PARK**, a federal project which has restored 5 and reconstructed 2 of the more than dozen buildings which were part of the Hudson's Bay Co. post in 1896. Established in 1806 by Simon Fraser as a post for the North West Trading Co., Fort St. James served throughout the 19th century as headquarters for the New Caledonia fur trade district. The general warehouse, fish cache, men's house, officers' dwelling, dairy and trade shop are open to the public. Check with the visitor centre regarding tours and interpretive programs.

From mid-May through June and in September, the park is open from 10 A.M. to 5 P.M. daily. In July and August, hours are 9:30 A.M. to 5:30 P.M. daily. For the remainder of the year, the site is closed.

The historic site and village are located on Stuart Lake. Named for John Stuart, the man who succeeded Simon Fraser as head of the New Caledonia district, the 59-mile-long lake is the southernmost in a 3-lake chain which provides hundreds of miles of boating and fishing. The water course starts in Stuart Lake, then up the Tachie River into Trembleur Lake, then up the Middle River to remote Takla Lake.

Historic Our Lady of Good Hope Church. (Judy Parkin, staff)

The village of Fort St. James serves as a supply centre for fishermen, hunters and prospectors headed for Tachie, Manson Creek and other settlements in the Omineca Mountains. The main industry here is lumber.

Attractions include the Our Lady of Good Hope Catholic Church and the Chief Kwah burial site. The recently renovated church is one of the oldest in British Columbia. Open for services only, check schedule. Chief Kwah was one of the first Carrier Indian chiefs to confront early white explorers. His burial site is located on the Nak'azdli Indian Reserve at the mouth of the Stuart River.

Fort St. James has a hotel, lodge, resort, 3 motels, 2 private campgrounds, 2 government marinas, 2 private marinas and several restaurants. Other services include 3 gas stations and 4 dump stations. The village has 2 shopping centres. Picnicking and swimming at Cottonwood Park on Stuart Lake.

Stuart Lodge, Stones Bay, Fort St. James. On Stuart Lake below the Mount Pope rock. Comfortable, fully supplied cabins, spectacular view, boat rental, sundecks, barbecue. Sorry, no pets. The friendly, quiet and clean place for vacationists, fishermen and business people. $29 (U.S.) and up per night. Phone (604) 996-7917. Enjoy Super, Natural North by Northwest. [ADVERTISEMENT]

Stuart River Campgrounds. Treed sites, tenting to full hookups, showers and laundry, firepits and firewood, pay phone. Playgrounds, horseshoe pits; marina with launching ramp and moorage space. Great fishing! Boat rentals, fishing licenses and tackle. Your hosts, George and Heather Malbeuf, Box 306, Fort St. James, BC V0J 1P0. (604) 996-8690. Enjoy Super, Natural North by Northwest. [ADVERTISEMENT]

Paarens Beach Provincial Park is located 6.8 miles/11 km off Highway 27 on Sowchea Bay Road; 66 campsites, picnic shelter, picnic tables, litter barrels, toilets, water, firepits, boat launch, swimming, $6 camping fee. **Sowchea Bay Provincial Park** is located 10.6 miles/17 km off Highway 27 on Sowchea Bay Road; 30 campsites, $6 camping fee, picnic tables, litter barrels, toilets, water, firepits, boat launch and swimming. Good fishing in **Stuart Lake** for rainbow and char (to trophy size), kokanee and Dolly Varden.

Return to Milepost PG 60.5 or PG 64.7 Yellowhead Highway 16

FORT ST. JAMES ADVERTISERS

Fort St. James Chamber
 of Commerce ....Ph. (604) 996-7023
Jackson Place Creatives ....234 Kwah Rd.
Stuart Lodge.................Ph. (604) 996-7917
Stuart River
 Campgrounds ....Ph. (604) 996-8690

RELIVE THE PAST!

- A National Historic Park where you can experience the fur trade of the 1890s. Admission Free.
- Beautiful Stuart Lake, 80 km of excellent fishing, boating, sailing, swimming and windsurfing.
- Access to 42 Ministry of Forests campsite areas on numerous lakes and rivers in the Fort St. James area.
- Hike to the 1472m peak of Mount Pope for a breathtaking view of surrounding lakes and mountains.
- Good commercial accommodation, boat launches, boat charter and boat services.

Super, Natural North by Northwest

FORT ST. JAMES CHAMBER OF COMMERCE (604) 996-7023

JACKSON PLACE CREATIVES

LICENSED EATING ESTABLISHMENT

Country Home Cookin' and Baked Goodies

Craft Shop—featuring local crafts for that unique gift

Open 7 days a week 10:30 - 6:00
Located next to the Historical Fort

(604) 996-2227

propane, lodging and first-aid station. Gas station with hot showers, convenience store and restaurant. Named for Simon Fraser, who established a trading post here in 1806. Now a supply centre for surrounding farms and sawmills. The last spike of the Grand Trunk Railway was driven here on April 7, 1914.

PG 85.1 (137 km) PR 370.9 (598.2 km) Nechako River bridge. Turnout to south with parking, litter barrels and access to **Nechako River**; fishing for rainbow and Dolly Varden, June to fall. At the east end of Fraser Lake, the Nautley River—less than a mile long—drains into the Nechako River.

PG 87 (140 km) PR 369 (593.8 km) Beaumont Provincial Park, on beautiful **Fraser Lake**, north side of highway; site of original Fort Fraser. Boat launch, swimming, hiking, fishing, 49 campsites, picnic tables, firewood, restrooms, water, playground, horseshoe pits, dump station, $7 camping fee. Park gates closed from 10 P.M. to 7 A.M. Fishing for rainbow and lake trout, burbot, sturgeon and Dolly Varden.

PG 89.2 (143.5 km) PR 366.8 (590.3 km) Private campground to north.

PG 90.7 (146 km) PR 365.3 (587.9 km) Dry William Lake rest area to south with picnic tables, toilets and litter barrels.

PG 91.7 (147.6 km) PR 364.3 (586.3 km) Orange Valley Motel, R.V. Park and Campground. Easy access featuring level sites, large pull-throughs, electricity, water, some with sewer. Free showers, flush toilets, sani-dump, treed shaded sites with picnic tables. Firepits and firewood. Quiet relaxed setting. Pay phone, golf driving range, hiking trails, beaver dam. Phone (604) 699-6350. [ADVERTISEMENT]

PG 93.8 (151 km) PR 362.2 (582.9 km) Fraser Lake sawmill to north.

PG 95.5 (153.7 km) PR 360.5 (580.2 km) Rest area to north. Trail to Fraser Lake.

PG 97.5 (156.9 km) PR 358.5 (576.9 km) FRASER LAKE (pop. 1,400, elev. 2,580 feet/786m). **Visitor Information:** Travel Infocentre and museum in log building at east edge of town. **Radio:** CJCI 1450. Small community with all facilities. Created by Endako Mines Ltd. in 1964 on an older townsite; named after the explorer Simon Fraser. Endako Mines Ltd. began operating in 1965 and was Canada's largest molybdenum mine until production slowed in 1982. Mining resumed in 1986. Mine tours are available on Wednesdays; check with the Travel Infocentre for reservations. Also located here is Fraser Lake Sawmills, the town's largest employer.

PG 100 (161 km) PR 356 (572.9 km) Junction with main access road south to scenic Francois Lake; also accessible via roads from Burns Lake to Houston. Francois Lake Road (gravel) leads south 7 miles/11.2 km to the east end of Francois Lake (where the Stellako River flows from the lake) and back to Highway 16 at Endako. Molyhills golf course and several resorts with camping, cabins and boats are located on this scenic rural road through the Glenannan area.

Glenannan Tourist Area. See display ad this section.

Francois Lake, good fishing for rainbow to 5 lbs., May to October; kokanee to 3/4 lb., use flashers, willow leaf, flashers with worms, flatfish or spinners, August and September; char to 30 lbs., use large flatfish or spoon, June and July. **Stellako River** is considered one of British Columbia's better fly-fishing streams with rainbow over 2 lbs., all summer; whitefish averaging 1 lb., year-round.

PG 100.1 (161.1 km) PR 355.9 (572.7 km) Bridge over Stellako River. Highway passes through the Stellako Indian Reserve.

PG 105.9 (170.4 km) PR 350.1 (563.4 km) ENDAKO. A small highway community with grocery (closed Sunday), post office, pub and gas station with minor repair service. Turnoff for molybdenum mine just east of town. Several private campgrounds are located along Francois Lake Road to the south in the Glenannan area.

PG 107 (172.2 km) PR 349 (561.6 km) Endako River bridge.

PG 110.5 (177.8 km) PR 345.5 (556 km) Savory rest area to north beside Watskin Creek.

PG 113.3 (182.3 km) PR 342.7 (551.5 km) Ross Creek.

PG 122.1 (196.5 km) PR 333.9 (537.3 km) Paved turnout to south.

PG 126.1 (202.9 km) PR 329.9 (530.9 km) Babine Forest Products sawmill to south.

PG 128.7 (207.1 km) PR 327.3 (526.7 km) Food and pay phone to south.

PG 133.7 (215.2 km) PR 322.3 (518.7 km) Rest area to south with toilet, tables, litter barrels and Tintagel Cairn point of interest.

PG 137.3 (221 km) PR 318.7 (512.9 km) Freeport K.O.A., a day's drive from Prince Rupert ferry. Tenting to full hookups, store, heated showers, laundromat, game room, playground. Mini-golf, canoe and boat rentals, lake swimming and horseshoes. Open May 1 to Sept. 30. Pay phone. Your host, Ed Brown, Box 491, Burns Lake, BC V0J 1E0. (604) 692-3105. [ADVERTISEMENT]

PG 139.9 (225.1 km) PR 316.1 (508.7 km) Welcome to Burns Lake sign.

PG 140.9 (226.8 km) PR 315.1 (507.1 km) Junction with scenic Highway 35 (paved) south to Tchesinkut, Francois, Takysie and Ootsa lakes; lodging, camping and fishing. Another of the Yellowhead's popular fishing areas with a variety of family-owned camping and cabin resorts.

Likkel's Lakeside Store and Resort. See display ad this section.

Beaver Point Resort located on Tchesinkut Lake 10 miles south of village of Burns Lake on Highway 35. RV and tent sites with partial hookups. Showers, picnic tables, marina, boat rentals, launching ramp, smokehouse. Snack bar with basic groceries and tackle. 5 housekeeping cabins—no bedding. Trolling best for rainbow, kokanee and char. Family oriented; pets on leashes. Reasonable rates. Hosts: Brenda and Jake Hiebert, Box 587, Burns Lake, BC V0J 1E0; phone (604) 695-6519. (Off-season 698-7665.) [ADVERTISEMENT]

Sandy's RV and Camping Resort, located on Francois Lake. Paved road, 15 miles south of Burns Lake on Highway 35, 4 miles west. 1,500 feet of shoreline; rainbows to 3 lbs., lake trout to 30 lbs. Cabins, boat rentals, launch, docks, gas, store, licenses, laundromat, showers, washrooms, picnic tables, firewood. Great fishing, friendly service. May to Oct. 15. Phone (604) 695-6321. Super, Natural North by Northwest. [ADVERTISEMENT]

Burns Lake

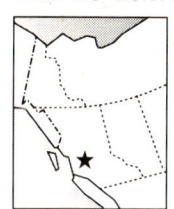

PG 141.3 (227.4 km) PR 314.7 (506 km) Population: 2,300; area 10,000. **Visitor Information:** Government Travel Infocentre at the flashing light (the only one in town) on the west side of the village. The infocentre also houses a museum and art gallery.

Elevation: 2,320 feet/707m. **Radio:** CBC-

LIKKEL'S LAKESIDE STORE & RESORT

30 miles south of Burns Lake via free Francois Lake Ferry

Excellent side trip for rainbow fishing and sightseeing.

STORE • RESTAURANT
GAS • DIESEL • PROPANE
Cabins • Campsites • Sani-dump
Tackle • Boat Rentals
Laundromat

(604) 694-3403
Box 11, Takysie Lake, B.C. V0J 2V0

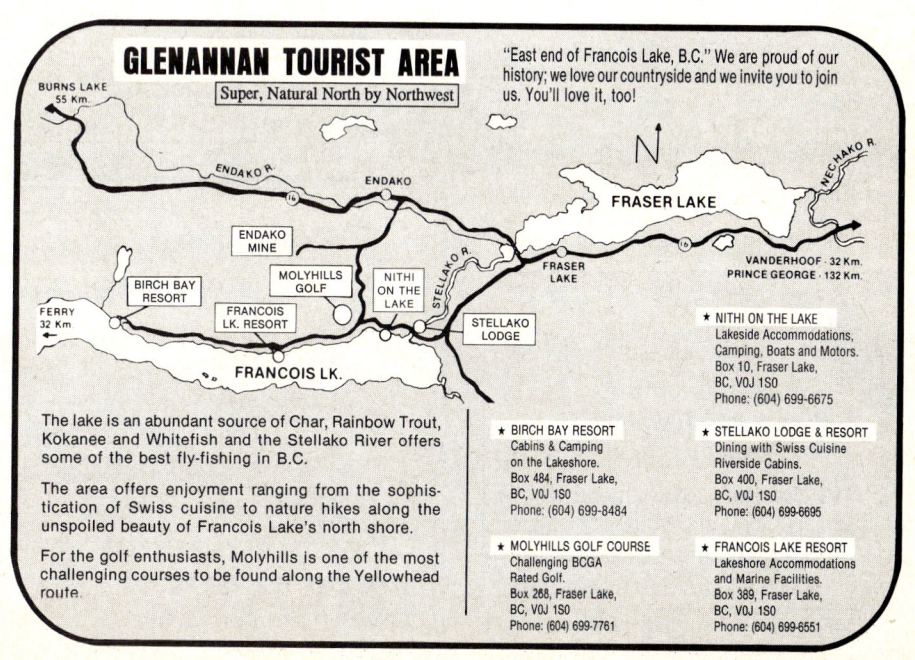

GLENANNAN TOURIST AREA
Super, Natural North by Northwest

"East end of Francois Lake, B.C." We are proud of our history; we love our countryside and we invite you to join us. You'll love it, too!

The lake is an abundant source of Char, Rainbow Trout, Kokanee and Whitefish and the Stellako River offers some of the best fly-fishing in B.C.

The area offers enjoyment ranging from the sophistication of Swiss cuisine to nature hikes along the unspoiled beauty of Francois Lake's north shore.

For the golf enthusiasts, Molyhills is one of the most challenging courses to be found along the Yellowhead route.

★ NITHI ON THE LAKE
Lakeside Accommodations, Camping, Boats and Motors.
Box 10, Fraser Lake, BC, V0J 1S0
Phone: (604) 699-6675

★ BIRCH BAY RESORT
Cabins & Camping on the Lakeshore.
Box 484, Fraser Lake, BC, V0J 1S0
Phone: (604) 699-8484

★ STELLAKO LODGE & RESORT
Dining with Swiss Cuisine Riverside Cabins.
Box 400, Fraser Lake, BC, V0J 1S0
Phone: (604) 699-6695

★ MOLYHILLS GOLF COURSE
Challenging BCGA Rated Golf.
Box 268, Fraser Lake, BC, V0J 1S0
Phone: (604) 699-7761

★ FRANCOIS LAKE RESORT
Lakeshore Accommodations and Marine Facilities.
Box 389, Fraser Lake, BC, V0J 1S0
Phone: (604) 699-6551

YELLOWHEAD HIGHWAY

Huge Babine Lake is popular with boaters. (Judy Parkin, staff)

FM 99.1, CJCI 760. **Transportation:** Greyhouse Bus, VIA Rail.

Burns Lake began about 1911 as a construction camp for the Grand Trunk Pacific Railway. Forestry is the economic mainstay of the area today, with ranching and tourism also important.

Located in the heart of the Lakes District, Burns Lake boasts "3,000 miles of fishing." Species include rainbow trout, char and salmon. Small family-owned fishing resorts offering lodging and camping are tucked along these lakes offering quality vacation experiences.

Burns Lake is also the gateway to Tweedsmuir Provincial Park, 50 miles/80 km south. This huge wilderness park is accessible by boat, trail and air.

Rock hounds can visit Eagle Creek opal deposits, a short drive south of Burns Lake (not recommended for motorhomes).

There are 6 gas stations (1 with a dump station), 5 hotels/motels, 7 restaurants, several gift shops—many of which feature local crafts and artists—and shopping malls.

Burns Lake Motor Inn. See display ac this section.

The Burns Lake Municipal Park, located next to the civic centre, offers a pleasant setting for a picnic. On the north shore of the lake, the park has picnic tables and a small pier.

From Burns Lake, Highway 35 (paved) extends south 18 miles/29 km past **Tchesinkut Lake** to **Francois Lake** ferry landing. A free 36-car ferry departs from the south shore on the hour, from the north shore on the half-hour. From the south shore of Francois Lake, Highway 35 continues to **Takysie Lake** and **Ootsa Lake**, with access to a number of other fishing lakes. There are several resorts along Highway 35 offering camping and lodging. Gas stations, stores and food service are also available.

Yellowhead Highway 16 Log

(continued)

PG 146 (235 km) **PR 310** (498.9 km) Side road leads north to Babine Lake, the longest natural lake in the province. One of British Columbia's most important salmon producing lakes, Babine Lake drains into the Skeena River. At Mile 15/24 km on this road is Ethel F. Wilson Provincial Park on Pinkut Lake; 10 campsites, fishing, swimming, picnic tables, boat launch. Pendleton Bay Provincial Park on Babine Lake offers 12 campsites, picnic tables, fishing, swimming and boat launch. Resorts with cabins and camping on Babine Lake.

Birch Lane Cabin Resort. See display ad this section.

Babine Lake Resort, 48 km from Burns Lake. British Columbia's largest natural body of water. Good fishing. Photographer's dream. Self-contained cabins, power, water hookups, showers, tenting, boats, smokehouses, store, licensed dining. Ausserdem sprechen wir deutsch. Accepting VISA. Bill and Traude Hoff welcome you. Box 528, Burns Lake. JK-H-496674. [ADVERTISEMENT]

PG 150 (241.4 km) **PR 306** (492.4 km) Small community of **DECKER LAKE**.

Decker Lake, good char and trout fishing; fly-fishing in **Endako River**, which joins Decker and Burns lakes.

PG 153.3 (246.7 km) **PR 302.7** (487.1 km) Palling rest area with picnic tables, toilets and litter barrels.

PG 157.1 (252.8 km) **PR 298.9** (481 km) Baker Lake airstrip to south is used by fire-fighting tankers. Weather station.

PG 160.2 (257.8 km) **PR 295.8** (476 km) Rose Lake to south.

PG 165.2 (265.9 km) **PR 290.8** (468 km) **Broman Lake,** rainbow and char to 4 lbs., use white-winged flies, spring and summer.

PG 169.1 (272.1 km) **PR 286.9** (461.7 km) China Nose Mountain Summit (elev. 4,669 feet/1,423m) to west.

PG 175.5 (282.4 km) **PR 280.5** (451.4 km) **TOPLEY** (pop. 300). Grocery, post office, cafe, motel and gas station. Turn north here for Babine Lake Recreation Area. This paved side road leads north to Topley Landing and Granisle on Babine Lake (descriptions follow). From its junction with the highway at Topley, mileages are as follows: Mile 4.3/7 km, Findlay Fall rest area; Mile 23.6/38 km, private lodge; Mile 24.4/39.3 km, turnoff to village of Topley Landing; Mile 28.8/46.3 km, Fulton River spawning channel; Mile 28/45 km, Red Bluff Provincial Park; Mile 31.4/50.5 km, Granisle; Mile 33.4/53.8 km, begin 16-mile/26-km gravel road to Smithers Landing Road, which connects Smithers Landing and Smithers.

TOPLEY LANDING has several resorts and a provincial park for picnicking, swimming and fishing. The government-operated Fulton River spawning channel has 2 major spawning channels on the river, which connects Fulton Lake and Babine Lake. Babine Lake, which flows into the Skeena River, is

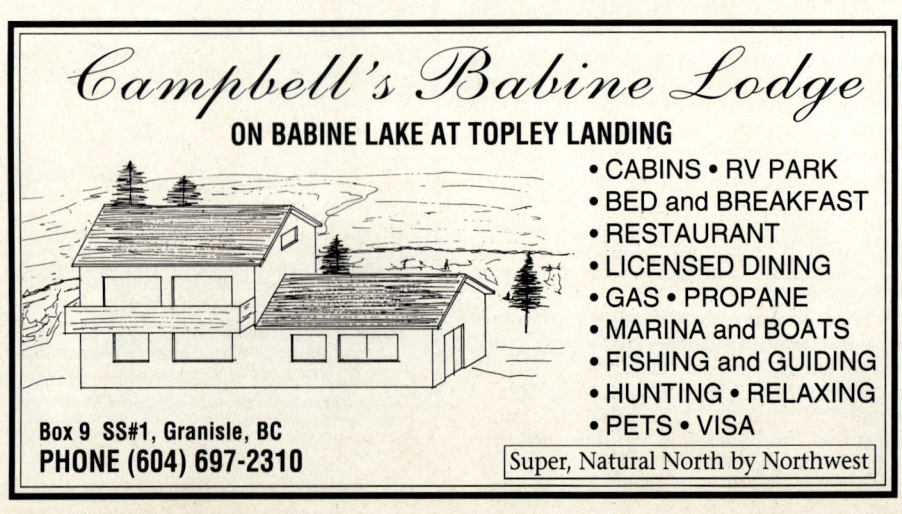

BIRCH LANE CABIN RESORT
ON BABINE LAKE
Happiness is Having You Back
HOUSEKEEPING CABINS
Boats & Motors • Store • Showers • RV Sites
Licenses & Tackle • Ice • Smokehouse
Box 622   Radiophone: Birch Lane
Burns Lake, BC V0J 1E0   N692559

BURNS LAKE MOTOR INN
Some Non-Smoking Rooms

Quiet Rooms
Where the Commercial Travellers Stay!

Reservations Recommended
(604) 692-7545 • FAX (604) 692-7683
1-800-663-2968 (BC only)
Box 1135, Burns Lake, B.C. V0J 1E0

Super, Natural North by Northwest

Campbell's Babine Lodge
ON BABINE LAKE AT TOPLEY LANDING

- CABINS • RV PARK
- BED and BREAKFAST
- RESTAURANT
- LICENSED DINING
- GAS • PROPANE
- MARINA and BOATS
- FISHING and GUIDING
- HUNTING • RELAXING
- PETS • VISA

Box 9 SS#1, Granisle, BC
PHONE (604) 697-2310

Super, Natural North by Northwest

one of the largest freshwater habitats for sockeye salmon. The salmon enhancement project at Fulton River produces about 95 million sockeye fry annually. The sockeye run takes place in August and September. Tours available at hatchery office. ▲

Campbell's Babine Lodge. See display ad this section.

GRANISLE (pop. 800) **Visitor Information:** Travel Infocentre is in the 2-story log building which also has a museum, ice, public showers and laundry facilities; open daily in summer, weekdays in winter. **Radio:** CBC 920, CFBV 870, CHLD 1480. This village was established in 1966 as a company town for the Granisle Copper Mine. In 1972, Noranda Mines Bell Copper Division went into operation. Today, Granisle is a resort area for fishing and boating on Babine Lake. Facilities at Granisle include wilderness resorts, a gas station, grocery store, shopping centre, an inn with restaurant and lounge, post office, health clinic, boat launch, tennis courts and library. Camping at Lions Beach, close to town. Red Bluff Provincial Park, south of Granisle on Babine Lake, has 64 campsites, 20 picnic tables, boat launch and swimming beach. Free bus/barge tours are available weekly in summer, weather permitting, of Noranda's copper mine across Babine Lake; inquire at the visitor centre.

Babine Lake, rainbow 6 to 8 lbs.; lake trout to 40 lbs., use spoons, flashers, and red-and-white spoons, May through November. When fishing for either early in the year, use a short troll. ◂

PG 175.8 (282.9 km) **PR 280.2** (450.9 km) Rest area to south with view of coastal mountains.

Houston

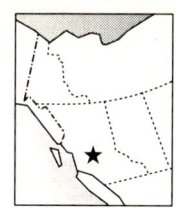

PG 194.3 (312.7 km) **PR 261.7** (421.2 km) **Population:** 3,960. **Emergency Services:** Police, phone 845-2204. Ambulance, phone 112-562-7241. **Visitor Information:** Travel Infocentre in log building on Highway 16 across from the mall; open year-round. Write Houston Travel Infocentre, Box 396, Houston, BC V0J 1Z0, or phone (604) 845-7640.

Elevation: 1,949 feet/594m. **Radio:** CJFW 105.5, CFBV 1450, CFPR-FM 102.1. **Transportation:** Greyhound bus, VIA Rail.

Established in the early 1900s, Houston was a tie-cutting centre during construction of the Grand Trunk Pacific Railway in 1912. It was named for Prince Rupert newspaperman John Houston, the former mayor of Nelson, BC. Logging continued to support the local economy with the rapid growth of mills and planer mills in the 1940s and 1950s. Houston was incorporated as a village in 1957.

Today, the main industry in Houston is forest products. The Equity Silver Mine, which began production in 1980, is scheduled to close in October 1992. There are 2 large sawmills here. Forestry awareness tours (a joint effort of Houston Forest Products, Northwood Pulp and Timber, and the chamber of commerce) are offered at the Nature Interpretation Centre located in the renovated train station behind the Infocentre.

Sportfishing is a major attraction here with the Bulkley River and nearby Morice River. Look for the World's Largest Fly Fishing Rod on display at the Travel Infocentre. The 60-foot-long anodized aluminum fly rod was built by local volunteers. (The 21-inch fly is a fluorescent "Skykomish Sunrise.") Near the Infocentre is a salmon enhancement project with fish fence and trap, tables and toilet.

Houston has all visitor facilities, including motels, campgrounds, restaurants, gas stations and a shopping centre. ▲

Houston Chamber of Commerce. See display ad this section.

Yellowhead Highway 16 Log

(continued)

PG 197.4 (317.7 km) **PR 258.6** (416.1 km) **Junction** with the Morice River access road which extends 52 miles/84 km south to Morice Lake. Approximately 20 miles/32 km along the Morice River Road you can turn east on a gravel road which leads past Owen Lake and Nadina River Road to Francois Lake. From Francois Lake ferry landing Highway 35 leads north to Burns Lake.

The 2 famous salmon and steelhead streams, **Morice** and **Bulkley**, unite near Houston and it is possible to fish scores of pools all along the Morice River. *NOTE: Special requirements apply to fishing these streams; check with Fish and Game officer.*

PG 198.5 (319.4 km) **PR 257.5** (414.4 km) Bulkley River bridge; picnic spot with tables, litter barrel and toilets.

HOUSTON

Where the welcome is warm, and the wilderness beckons...

FOR MORE INFORMATION CONTACT:
Houston & District Chamber of Commerce
P.O. Box 396, Houston, B.C. V0J 1Z0
(604) 845-7640 • FAX (604) 845-3682

PHOTO CREDIT: GEORGE RHOADES PHOTOS

HOME OF THE WORLD'S LARGEST FLY ROD
On display by the Travel InfoCentre

PLEASANT VALLEY DAYS
Rodeo, Pony and Chariot Races, Logger Sports, Parade, Ball Tournament, Dance ... and much more
Mid-May

DISCOVER HOUSTON TRADE SHOW
Home, Recreation and Information Show
Mid-September
Claude L. Parish Memorial Arena

FORESTRY TOURS
"All things considered"

FISHING
Home of the world famous Morice and Bulkley River systems for steelhead, spring and coho salmon
Numerous great producing lakes
See the Salmon Enhancement Project – fish fence and trap on the Bulkley River

INDUSTRIAL TOURS
Tour Canada's largest primary producer of silver;
Tour a modern high-tech sawmill

MORICE MOUNTAIN CROSS-COUNTRY SKI TRAILS
25 km of skiing – from gentle to Alpine
Groomed and natural trails, 2 cabins

FULL FACILITIES FOR THE TRAVELLER
Accommodation and restaurants
Excellent camping; 2 nine-hole golf courses

YELLOWHEAD HIGHWAY

PG 202.5 (325.9 km) PR 253.5 (407.9 km) View of Morice River valley eastbound. Westbound travelers are in the Bulkley River valley.

PG 205.3 (330.4 km) PR 250.7 (403.5 km) Hungry Hill Summit (elev. 2,769 feet/844m). To the north are the snow-capped peaks of the Babine Mountains, to the west is the Hudson Bay Range.

PG 222.8 (358.6 km) PR 233.2 (375.3 km) Bulkley View paved rest area with picnic tables, toilets and litter barrels.

PG 225.6 (363.1 km) PR 230.4 (370.8 km) Ft. Telkwa RV Park. See display ad this section. ▲

PG 226 (363.7 km) PR 230 (370.1 km) TELKWA (pop. 863). A pleasant village on the Bulkley River (you can fish the river from Main Street). Travel Infocentre at the museum in the old schoolhouse. Facilities include a grocery, post office, motel, cafe, a delicatessen, pub and gas station with auto repair. A unique shop found here is Horsfield Harness and Leather which specializes in handmade fishing rod cases, leather water bottles and other leather goods. Fishing and hunting information, licenses and supplies available at the general store. Kinsmen Barbecue is held over Labour Day weekend; games, contests and demolition derby. Eddy Park, on the western edge of town beside the Bulkley River, is a good spot for picnicking (look for the wishing well). St. Stephen's Anglican Church here was built in 1911 and the bell and English gate added in 1921. Other quaint old buildings here date back to 1908 and are designated Heritage Buildings.

Douglas Motel beside beautiful Bulkley River. River view units, cabins in relaxing resort atmosphere. Hot pool, sauna complex, kitchens, cablevision, queen beds, electric heat, picnic area, firepit, barbecues, horseshoe pitch. Salmon and steelhead fishing. Walking distance to stores and lake. VISA and MasterCard. Douglas Family, (604) 846-5679. Member, Super, Natural North by Northwest. [ADVERTISEMENT]

PG 226.5 (364.5 km) PR 229.5 (369.3 km) Turnoff to north for Tyhee Lake Provincial Park; 55 campsites, 20 picnic tables, dump station, hiking trails, fishing, swimming, boat launch. Seaplane base at lake; charter fly-in fishing. ▲

Also turnoff here on the Telkwa High Road which intersects with Babine Lake access road (gravel) which leads 46 miles/ 74 km north to Smithers Landing on Babine Lake and 56 miles/90 km to Granisle.

Tyhee Lake, rainbow and lake trout to 2 lbs., use tee-spinners, spoons, worms, June through August; Kamloops trout to 2 lbs. Boat launching facilities available. **Babine River**, steelhead to 40 lbs., use winged bobbers, Kitamats and weighted spoons in late fall; can be reached by road or water. **Telkwa River**, spring and coho salmon to 24 lbs., summer to fall. ◄

PG 231.5 (372.6 km) PR 224.5 (361.3 km) Second turnoff westbound for Babine Lake.

PG 232.8 (374.6 km) PR 223.2 (359.2 km) Riverside Recreational Center. See display ad this section. ▲

PG 233.1 (375.1 km) PR 222.9 (358.7 km) Turnoff to north on gravel road for Driftwood Canyon Provincial Park; picnic area and fossil beds in shale outcroppings along creekbank. This gravel side road continues north to Smithers Landing.

PG 233.7 (376.1 km) PR 222.3 (357.7 km) Bridge over Bulkley River.

Smithers

PG 235.4 (378.8 km) PR 220.6 (355 km). Population: 5,000; area 19,000. **Emergency Services: Police,** phone 847-3233. **Hospital and Poison Centre,** 3950 8th Ave., phone 847-2611. **Ambulance,** phone 112-562-7241. **Visitor Information:** Travel Infocentre at the intersection of Highway 16 and Main Street, east side of highway, in the rail car adjacent to the museum; open daily in summer.

Elevation: 1,621 feet/494m. **Climate:** Relatively warmer and drier than mountainous areas to the west, average temperature in July is 58°F/15°C, in January 14°F/-10°C; annual precipitation, 13 inches. **Radio:** CFBV 1230, CFPR-FM 97.5. **Television:** Channels 5, 13 and cable. **Newspaper:** *Interior News* (weekly).

Transportation: Air–Scheduled service to Vancouver and Terrace via Canadian Airlines International. Daily flights to Prince George, Terrace and Burns Lake via Central Mountain Air. **Railroad**–VIA Rail. **Bus**–Greyhound. **Car Rentals**–Available.

Sitting amidst rugged mountains, the alpine flavour of the town has been enhanced by Swiss-style storefronts that

---

"BEST ROUTE TO ALASKA"
OPEN ALL YEAR
JUST EAST OF TELKWA ON HWY. 16

FT. TELKWA R.V. PARK

- DELUXE ADULT FACILITIES
- RIVERFRONT SITES • GLACIER VIEW
- FULL HOOKUPS • LAUNDRY
- FREE PRIVATE DELUXE SHOWER ROOMS
- CABLE TV • SAUNA
- FREE RV HIGH-PRESSURE WASH

RESERVATIONS (604) 846-5012

GROUPS ARE WELCOME

Super, Natural North by Northwest

RIVERSIDE Recreation Centre

PAR 3 GOLF and driving range

- 30 Sites – Easy Pull-throughs
- 30-amp Electric Service • Water
- Sani-station • Showers
- LICENSED
- RESTAURANT
- Groups Welcome

SHADED   RIVER FISHING

Box 4314, Smithers, BC V0J 2N0
2 miles east of Smithers
(604) 847-3229

Super, Natural North by Northwest

Strategically Located
SORENTO MOTEL
► Midway between Prince Rupert and Prince George ◄

Housekeeping and sleeping units. Complimentary coffee, colour TV and telephones. Ample parking. Families welcome. Close to the downtown. BRAND NEW ROOMS affordably priced.

Situated on Highway 16 close to the city centre.

Your hosts: Rocco & Gilda Schina

P.O. Box 444, Smithers, B.C. V0J 2N0
(604) 847-2601

FLORENCE MOTEL

Rates as low as $33.00

- 21 Units • Owner Operated
- Colour Cable TV
- Complimentary Coffee
- Direct Dial Phones
- Queen, Double & Twin Beds
- Tub Showers • Kitchen Units

Near Civic Centre and Town Swimming Pool

Super, Natural North by Northwest

P.O. Box 516, Smithers, BC V0J 2N0
Highway 16 W., Smithers   (604) 847-2678

have been added to many of the buildings. Reconstructed in 1979, Main Street offers many shops and restaurants. Incorporated as a village in 1921, Smithers officially became a town in Canada's centennial year, 1967. The original site was chosen in 1913 by construction crews working on the Grand Trunk Pacific Railroad (the town was named for one-time chairman of the railway A.W. Smithers). Today it is a distribution and supply centre for farms, mills and mines in the area.

Smithers is the largest town in the Bulkley Valley and the site of Hudson Bay Mountain, a popular ski area (skiing from November to mid-April).

ACCOMMODATIONS

Smithers has several motels, gas stations, restaurants and good shopping. Government liquor store located on Queen Street at Broadway Avenue. There are 2 golf courses (9- and 18-hole).

Driftwood Lodge. Enjoy relaxed country accommodation in our large log home, overlooking Hudson Bay Mountain and the beautiful Bulkley Valley. Lodge atmosphere with comfortable rooms and private baths; great room with large stone fireplace; recreation room, hot tub. Country walks, guided hiking and fishing. Cross-country skiing. Downhill ski packages. Bed and breakfast, American plan. Weekly packages available. VISA and MasterCard. Comp. 11, Site 53, RR 2, Smithers, BC V0J 2N0. (604) 847-5016.
[ADVERTISEMENT]

There is a public campground (no facilities) at Riverside Park on the Bulkley River; turn north at the museum across from Main Street and drive up the hill about a mile and watch for sign. There are private campgrounds located east and west of town; see highway log. A dump station is located across the street from the Travel Infocentre.

ATTRACTIONS

The Art Gallery and Museum, in the Central Park Bldg. at the corner of Main Street and Highway 16, displays both local and traveling art shows in addition to artifacts from the early days of the Bulkley Valley.

Bulkley Valley Fall Fair is held on the last weekend in August each year, and is one of the largest agricultural exhibitions in the province.

Area Attractions. Smithers offers a

SMITHERS ADVERTISERS

Aspen Motor Inn	Ph. (604) 847-4551
Driftwood Lodge	Ph. (604) 847-5016
Esso Gas and Groceries	Ph. (604) 847-5031
Florence Motel	Ph. (604) 847-2678
Hilltop Inn	Ph. (604) 847-4481
Hudson Bay Lodge	Ph. (604) 847-4581
Juniper Berry, The	1215 Main St.
Savala's Steak House	1338 Main St.
Smithers Chamber of Commerce	Central Park Bldg.
Sorento Motel	Ph. (604) 847-2601
Wash The Works	On the Access Rd.

ESSO Self-Service **GAS AND GROCERIES**

Coffee and Submarines
Groceries
Meat
Produce • Ice
Hunting and Fishing Licenses
Postage Stamp Sales

OPEN 24 HOURS
Lottery Ticket Centre

Super, Natural North by Northwest

HIGHWAY 16 WEST, SMITHERS, BC • (604) 847-5031

SMITHERS
A Town for All Seasons
Short Route to Alaska

PHOTO BY HAIDE

- **SKI SMITHERS**
  3 LIFTS, 1750' Vertical, 19 Runs, Ski School, Pro-shop, Full Facilities

- **BULKLEY VALLEY DAYS**
  LAST WEEKEND OF AUGUST TO LABOUR DAY WEEKEND IN SEPTEMBER
  Parade, Fair, BBQ, Numerous Special Events, Heavy Horse Pulls, Demolition Derby

- **GOLFING**
  LUSH, 18-HOLE COURSE, Rentals, Lounge, Club House; Picturesque 9-Hole, Par 3, Rentals Lounge Club House, Full Service R.V. Park

- **WINTERFEST**
  A FOUR DAY WINTER FESTIVAL HELD IN FEBRUARY, Torchlight Parade Down Hudson Bay Mountain, Winter Wonderland Parade, Fireworks, Fun Events For The Whole Family

- **MIDSUMMER FESTIVAL**
  END OF JUNE. Concerts, Workshops, Dances, Arts & Crafts, Entertainment

- **RIVERSIDE MUNICIPAL CAMPGROUND**
  CLOSE TO TOWN, Fishing at your doorstep, Cookhouse, Firepits, Walking Trail

- **FISHING**
  WORLD-RENOWNED Steelhead, Coho & Spring Salmon, River & Lake Fishing

For More Information Contact:
SMITHERS CHAMBER OF COMMERCE
P.O. Box 2379
Smithers, BC, V0J 2N0
(604) 847-5072 • 847-9854

Super, Natural North by Northwest

number of scenic drives. Hudson Bay Mountain (elev. 8,700 feet/ 2,652m) is a 14-mile/ 22-km drive from Highway 16; the plateau above timberline at the ski area is a good spot for summer hikes.

Fossil hunters should drive to Driftwood Canyon Provincial Park; turn off Highway 16 just east of the Bulkley River bridge (travelers are advised to stop at the visitor information centre in town first for a map and directions). A display at the park illustrates the fossils, such as metasequoia, a type of redwood that occurs in the shale formation.

Adams Igloo Wildlife Museum, just west of town on Highway 16, has an excellent display of mammals found in British Columbia.

A beautiful spot not to be missed is Twin Falls and Glacier Gulch. Take the 4-mile-/ 6.4-km-long gravel road (steep in places) from Highway 16 on the western edge of town. Detailed maps of the area showing all hiking trails are available at the information centre.

Fishing: An extensive list of lakes in the area with information on boat launches, boat rentals, fishing, and angling regulations is available from the Smithers District Chamber of Commerce, Box 2379, Smithers, BC V0J 2N0, phone 847-9854, or ask at the Travel Infocentre.

Hunting: Moose, mule deer, grizzly, black bear, mountain goat and caribou are found in the area, and guides and outfitters are available locally. All species of grouse can be hunted in the Bulkley Valley during the fall. Information is available from the Fish and Wildlife Branch office in Smithers.

Yellowhead Highway 16 Log

(continued)

PG 237.8 (382.7 km) PR 218.2 (351.1 km) Paved access road to Lake Kathlyn. There is a municipal park with small beach and boat launch located here. Powerboats not permitted. Closed to waterfowl hunting. Side road continues 4 miles/6.4 km (gravel)

Wash The Works

Wash Your Car
- 1 High-clearance automatic rollover
- 3 High-clearance coin-op bays
- 4 Vacuums with lots of power

Wash Your Clothes
- Clean spacious laundromat
- Full-time attendant
- A table at every dryer to fold your clothes

Wash Your Back
- We have clean, spacious shower facilities
- Full-time attendant
- Towels optional

Wash The Works
Open 7 Days a Week
Daily 8 a.m. to 10 p.m.
Full-time Attendant
(604) 847-4177
On the access road next to A&W

Free Overnight Parking For RVs and Trucks

Easy-in, easy-out parking

Super, Natural North by Northwest

A Touch of Fine Dining

Air Conditioned. No-smoking Section Available

Try Our Salad Bar

OPEN 7 DAYS A WEEK
Monday-Saturday 11 a.m.-11 p.m.
Sundays and Holidays, 4 p.m.-10 p.m.

1338 MAIN STREET
SMITHERS
(604) 847-4567

Lunch Buffet Monday Thru Saturday
11:30 a.m. – 2:30 p.m.

Pastas	Pizza
Steaks	Chicken
Seafood	Ribs

—Salad Bar—

Savala's STEAK HOUSE
PIZZA - SPARERIBS
ITALIAN DISHES

Lunch Specials
Monday to Friday
11 a.m. to 2:30 p.m.

Other Locations

SAVALA'S NO. 1	SAVALA'S NO. 2	SAVALA'S NO. 3	SAVALA'S NO. 5
36 N. 3rd	240 Reid St.	4644 Lazelle	1310 5th Ave.
WILLIAMS LAKE	QUESNEL	TERRACE	PRINCE GEORGE
398-8246	992-9453	635-5944	563-1452

Super, Natural North by Northwest

ASPEN Motor Inn

Indoor Swimming Pool
Hot Tub • Saunas
Non-Smoking Rooms
60 Full Facility Rooms

Dining Room • Coffee Shop
Specialize In
SEAFOOD and BAVARIAN
• Salad Bar •

No Smoking section available in restaurant

For Reservations Call
(604) 847-4551
In BC: (800) 663-7676
FAX (604) 847-4492

4268 Highway 16 West
Smithers, BC V0J 2N0

Next door to laundromat, pressure wash, and RV dump station

Super, Natural North by Northwest

Hudson Bay Lodge

Full facility hotel complex - Smithers, BC

If you come to northcentral British Columbia to lose yourself in the peaceful slopes of the majestic mountains and the forested slopes, you'll fall in love with Smithers.

There's no place better to enjoy the scenery than at our 100-room inn. We offer 18-channel colour TV, Twin Falls dining room, Fireside Lounge, restaurant, meeting/banquet rooms. Hiking, fishing, skiing on Hudson Bay Mountain. Whirlpool and saunas to help you relax.

Courtesy limousine to and from the airport.

HUDSON BAY LODGE
P.O. Box 3636 • Smithers BC V0J 2N0
3251 E. Highway 16
(604) 847-4581 • FAX (604) 847-4878
BC/Alberta only: 1-800-663-5040

Photo courtesy Smithers Interior News

Super, Natural North by Northwest

to Twin Falls and Glacier Gulch.

PG 238.9 (384.5 km) **PR 217.1** (349.4 km) Road to north leads to Smithers airport.

PG 241.4 (388.5 km) **PR 214.6** (345.3 km) **Adams Igloo Wildlife Museum.** The finest collection of big game animals, furbearers and birds native to British Columbia. Mounted life-size and displayed in their natural habitat. The inside mural, painted by leading wildlife artist Tom Sander, gives a 3-dimensional impression for realism. Stop at the White Dome 6 miles west of Smithers beside one of the highway's most beautiful viewpoints. Fur rugs and souvenirs for sale. Jack Adams, Curator. [ADVERTISEMENT]

PG 241.5 (388.6 km) **PR 214.5** (345.2 km) Hudson Bay rest area to west with picnic tables, toilets and litter barrels. Beautiful view of Hudson Bay Mountain.

PG 249.5 (401.6 km) **PR 206.5** (332.3 km) Trout Creek bridge. Store with groceries, post office and phone; fishing licenses available.

PG 255.5 (411.2 km) **PR 200.5** (322.7 km) Turnout to north with picnic tables and view of Bulkley River and Moricetown Canyon; good photo stop.

PG 255.7 (411.4 km) **PR 200.3** (322.3 km) Short side road on the north side of the highway leads to Moricetown Canyon and Falls on the Bulkley River and Moricetown campground. For centuries a famous Indian fishing spot, Indians may still be seen here gaffing, jigging and netting salmon in July and August. A worthwhile stop. ▲

NOTE: The sale and barter of salmon by Natives is illegal and both seller and buyer are liable to heavy fines.

PG 257.9 (415 km) **PR 198.1** (318.8 km) **MORICETOWN** (pop. 680; elev. 1,341 feet/408m). **Radio:** CBC-FM 96.5. Moricetown has a gas station with minor repair service and diesel fuel. There is a handicraft store. A campground is located in Moricetown Canyon (turnoff at **Milepost PG 255.7**). Moricetown is an Indian reserve and village, the oldest settlement in the Bulkley Valley. The centuries-old Indian settlement ('Kyah Wiget) is named after Father A.G. Morice, a Roman Catholic missionary. Born in France, Father Morice came to British Columbia in 1880 and worked with the Indians of northern British Columbia from 1885 to 1904. He achieved world recognition for his authoritative writings in anthropology, ethnology and history.

Traditionally, the native people (Wet'suwet'en) took advantage of the narrow canyon to trap salmon. Today, gaffing is used in place of the traps and baskets which were banned by the government.

PG 271.5 (436.9 km) **PR 184.5** (296.9 km) Turnoff to north for Forest Service campsite (7.5 miles/12 km) with pit toilets, tables and litter barrels. Fishing in **Suskwa River;** coho salmon to 10 lbs., use tee-spinners in July; steelhead to 20 lbs., use Kitamat #32 and soft bobbers in late fall. ◄▲

PG 276.5 (445 km) **PR 179.5** (288.9 km) Turnoff to north for Ross Lake Provincial Park; 25 picnic sites, boat launch (no powerboats), swimming. Fishing at **Ross Lake** for rainbow to 4 lbs. ◄

PG 278.5 (448.2 km) **PR 177.5** (285.6 km) Turnout with litter barrel and Hazelton area map.

PG 278.8 (448.6 km) **PR 177.2** (285.2 km) Entering New Hazelton, the first of 3 communities westbound sharing the name Hazelton; the others are Hazelton and South Hazelton.

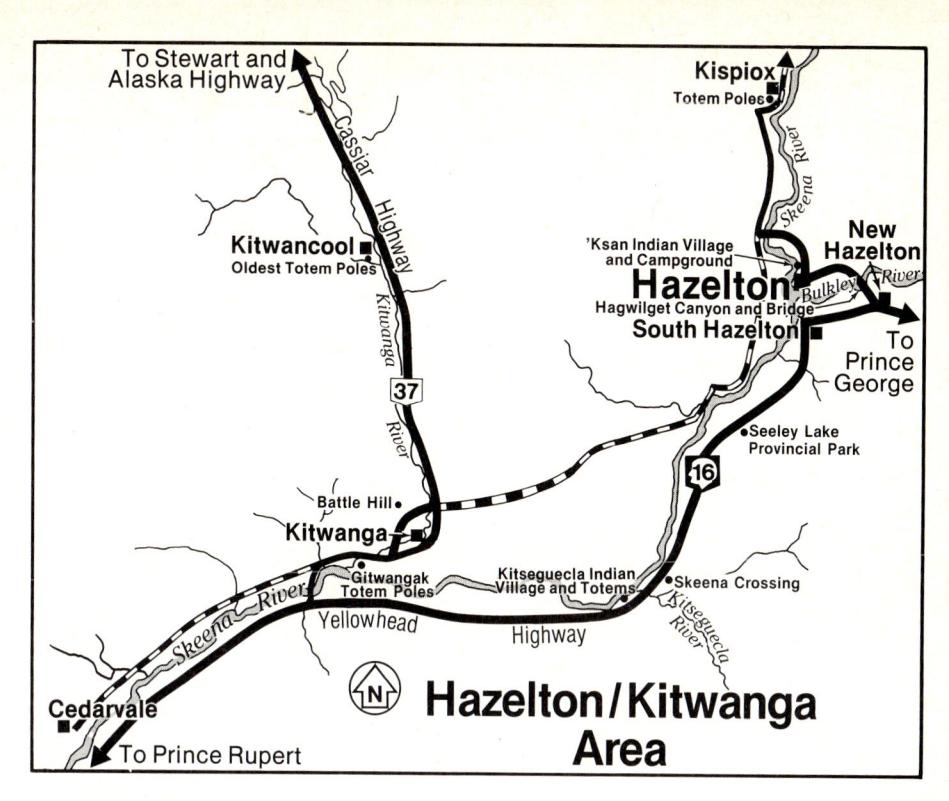

Hazelton/Kitwanga Area

New Hazelton

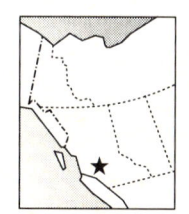

PG 279 (449 km) **PR 177** (284.8 km) **Junction** of Highway 16 and Highway 62 to Hazelton, 'Ksan and Kispiox. **Population:** area 1,300. **Emergency Services: Police,** phone 842-5244. **Visitor Information:** Travel Infocentre in 2-story log building at the junction. Look for the 3 statues representing the gold rush packer Cataline, the Northwest miner, and the Upper Skeena logger. Museum located in Infocentre.

Elevation: 1,150 feet/350m. **Radio:** CBC 1170. **Transportation:** VIA Rail. Greyhound bus.

HAZELTON ADVERTISERS

Bulkley Valley Motel	Hwy. 16
Hazeltons Travel Info Centre	Hwy. 16
Hummingbird, The	Ph. (604) 842-5628
Kispiox River Resort & Campground	Kispiox Valley Rd.
Kispiox Steelhead Camp	Kispiox
'Ksan Campground	Hwy. 16
Robber's Roost Lodge	Ph. (604) 842-6916
28 Inn	Ph. (604) 842-6006

This small highway community has gas stations, major auto repair, restaurants, cafes, post office, general store, a hotel and motel. Laundromat, propane, sporting goods and hunting and fishing licenses available in town. Mount Rocher Deboule towers 8,000 feet/2,438m behind the town.

Attractions here include historic Hazelton, the Indian village of 'Ksan and sportfishing the Bulkley and Kispiox rivers. Descriptions follow.

HAZELTON. Situated at the confluence

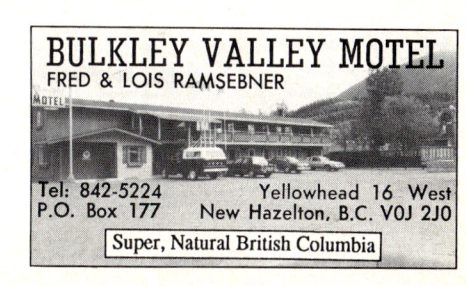

BULKLEY VALLEY MOTEL
FRED & LOIS RAMSEBNER

Tel: 842-5224   Yellowhead 16 West
P.O. Box 177   New Hazelton, B.C. V0J 2J0

Super, Natural British Columbia

Robber's ▲ Roost ▲ Lodge

TV • DD Phone • Fridge Every Room
Kitchenettes • Paved Parking
Adjacent Restaurant

Highway 16

Box 555   (604) 842-6916
NEW HAZELTON, BC V0J 2J0

Super, Natural North by Northwest

---

28 INN

Highway 16, New Hazelton

Brand new rooms with remote control TVs,
fridges or kitchenettes. Restaurant.
Complimentary coffee.
Paved, well-lit parking lot.
Stores and laundry across the street.

We're the logical stop before or after Hwy. 37

Box 358, New Hazelton, BC Canada V0J 2J0
(604) 842-6006 • FAX (604) 842-6340

VISA, MasterCard, Diners Card

Super, Natural North by Northwest

of the Skeena and Bulkley rivers, Hazelton grew up at "The Forks" as a transshipping point at the head of navigation on the Skeena and a wintering place for miners and prospectors from the rigorous Interior. Thomas Hankin established a Hudson's Bay Co. trading post in 1868. The name Hazelton comes from the numerous hazelnut bushes growing on the flats.

Cataline, famous pioneer packer and traveler, is buried near here. Jean Caux (his real name) was a Basque who, from 1852 to 1912, with loaded mules plodding 12 miles/19 km a day, supplied mining and construction camps from Yale and Ashcroft northward through Hazelton, where he often wintered. His mule trails became roads, his exploits legends.

For some years, before the arrival of railroad and highways, supplies for trading posts at Bear and Babine lakes and the Omineca goldfields moved by riverboat from the coast to Hazelton and from there over trails to the backcountry. Some of the Yukon gold rushers passed through Hazelton on their way to the Klondike, pack trains having made the trip from Hazelton to Telegraph Creek over the old Telegraph Trail as early as 1874.

This community has reconstructed the town in the 1800s period. Look for the antique machinery downtown. The history of the Hazelton area can be traced by car on the Hand of History tour. Pick up a brochure from local businesses showing the location of the 19 historic sites on the driving tour. There is a hotel here and a campground near 'Ksan village.

'KSAN, a replica Gitksan Indian village, is 4.5 miles/7.2 km from Highway 16. It was constructed at the junction of the Bulkley and Skeena rivers by the 'Ksan Assoc. with the assistance of the governments of Canada and British Columbia. There are 6 communal houses, totem poles and dugout canoes. At the Carving House of All Times master carvers produce Indian arts and crafts which can be purchased in the Today House of the Arts.

For a nominal charge from May to September, you can join a guided tour of the communal houses. Performances of traditional dancing and singing are presented every Friday evening during July and August in the Wolf House.

A well-maintained full-service trailer park and campground on the banks of the Skeena and Bulkley rivers is operated by the Hazelton Band of Gitksan adjacent to 'Ksan village. ▲

KISPIOX (pop. 825) Indian village and 3 fishing resorts are 20 miles/32 km north on a good paved road at the confluence of the Skeena and Kispiox rivers. Kispiox is noted for its stand of totems. There is a market garden (fresh vegetables) located approximately 7 miles/11.3 km north on the Kispiox Road (about 2 miles/ 3.2 km before the Kispiox totem poles). Camping, cabins and fishing at lodges and campgrounds in the valley.

Kispiox River Resort & Campground. Beautiful location on banks of Kispiox River in peaceful valley setting. Excellent fishing throughout the year including spring salmon, cutthroat and rainbow trout, Dolly Varden and steelhead. Campground. Housekeeping cabins. Showers. Tenters welcome. Fishing licenses. Guides. Tackle. 26 miles from Highway 16. Kispiox Valley Road. RR 1, Hazelton, BC V0J 1Y0. (604) 842-6182.

[ADVERTISEMENT] ▲

Detail of a totem at 'Ksan Indian village. (George Wuerthner)

'KSAN CAMPGROUND
Campground, Trailer Park
(May 1-October 31)
Complete Trailer Hookups, Showers, Flush Toilets
Adjacent to Indian Village, Museum, Indian Craft Shop
BOX 440   PHONE 842-5940
HAZELTON, B.C.   1-800-663-4590
Prices Subject to Change

Welcome to . . .
The Hummingbird
HAZELTON'S FINEST DINING
Open 11 a.m. to 10 p.m.
**PRIME RIB
GOURMET BURGERS
SOUP & SALAD BAR
TACO SALAD**
FULLY LICENSED   OUTDOOR EATING DECK
Reservations: (604) 842-5628
En route to 'Ksan

Kispiox Steelhead Camp
World's record steelhead 36.5 lbs. Trout Salmon Steelhead July 1st through November 30th. Excellent fly fishing. 7 housekeeping cabins. RV hook-ups & sani-station. Campsites. Smoking & freezing facilities. Raft trips & guiding arranged. Hiking trails & lots more. 20 miles north of Hazelton near K'SAN. Contact Mrs. Olga Walker R.R. 1, Hazelton, BC V0J 1Y0. 842-5435

Owner retiring: For private sale

Super, Natural North by Northwest

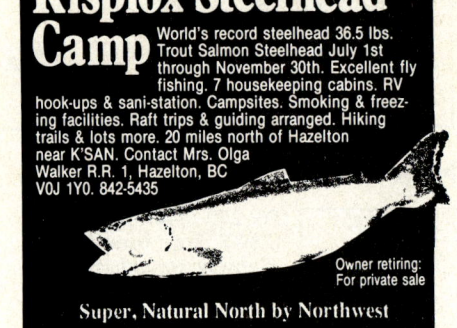

The Hazeltons
Historic Heartland of Northwest British Columbia

PHOTO BY HAROLD DEMETZER

☐ Totem Pole Capital of the World
☐ Trophy Salmon & Steelhead
☐ 'Ksan Historic Indian Village & Museum
☐ Historic "Old Town" Hazelton
☐ Full Visitor Services

For a free brochure write:
Hazeltons Travel Info Centre
Box 340Z
New Hazelton, B.C.
Canada V0J 2J0

Bulkley River, Dolly Varden to 5 lbs.; spring salmon, mid-July to mid-August; coho salmon 4 to 12 lbs., Aug. 15 through September, flies, spoons and spinners; steelhead to 20 lbs., July through November, flies, Kitamats, weighted spoons and soft bobbers. **Kispiox River** is famous for its trophy-sized steelhead. Check on regulations and obtain a fishing license before your arrival. Fishing is done with single-hook only, with catch-release for steelhead between Aug. 15 and Sept. 30. Season is July 1 to Nov. 30 for salmon, trout and steelhead. Excellent fly-fishing waters. Sizable Dolly Vardens and cutthroat. Steelhead average 20 lbs., with some catches over 30 lbs.

Yellowhead Highway 16 Log

(continued)

PG 281.4 (452.8 km) PR 174.6 (281 km) Motel adjacent highway. Turnoff to north for 2-mile/3.2-km loop road through small community of **SOUTH HAZELTON**; restaurant, general store, gas station with minor repair, lodging.

PG 285 (458.6 km) PR 171 (275.2 km) Seeley Lake Provincial Park; 20 campsites, water pump, day-use area with picnic tables, swimming, fishing. Camping fee $8.

PG 290.5 (467.5 km) PR 165.5 (266.3 km) *CAUTION: Highway turns sharply to cross Canadian National Railway tracks.*

PG 294.7 (474.2 km) PR 161.3 (259.6 km) Skeena Crossing. Historic CNR bridge (see plaque at Kitseguecla). *CAUTION: Blind sharp corner under bridge.*

PG 295.9 (476.2 km) PR 160.1 (257.6 km) **KITSEGUECLA**, Indian village. Totem poles throughout village are classic examples, still in original locations. Historical plaque about Skeena Crossing.

PG 306.6 (493.4 km) PR 149.4 (240.4 km) Gas station and cafe at **junction** with Cassiar Highway. Bridge across Skeena River to Kitwanga and Cassiar Highway to Stewart, Hyder and Alaska Highway. This is the principal access to the Cassiar Highway. Alternate access via Nass Road at **Milepost PG 379.9**. See CASSIAR HIGHWAY section.

Highway passes Seven Sisters peaks, the highest is 9,140 feet/2,786m.

PG 309.8 (498.6 km) PR 146.2 (235.3 km) **Seven Sisters RV Park**, located 3 miles west of Junction 37 on Highway 16, offers sewage dump, water, bathroom facilities, picnic tables, firepits with wood, all for $5. It has a better view of the Seven Sisters mountains than can be seen from Highway 16. Phone (604) 849-5489 for reservations.
[ADVERTISEMENT]

PG 312.4 (502.8 km) PR 143.6 (231.1 km) Boulder Creek rest area; parking for large vehicles, toilets, litter barrels and picnic tables.

PG 316.5 (509.4 km) PR 139.5 (224.5 km) Gravel turnout to north with litter barrel.

PG 318.2 (512.1 km) PR 137.8 (221.8 km) **CEDARVALE** and **junction** with loop road through rural setting. Historical plaque about Holy City.

PG 322.9 (519.6 km) PR 133.1 (214.2 km) Gravel turnout to north on Skeena River.

PG 324.8 (522.7 km) PR 131.2 (211.1 km) Paved turnout with historical plaque on Skeena riverboats. Watch for bears fishing the river for salmon in late July and early August.

PG 329.3 (530 km) PR 126.7 (203.9 km) Gravel turnout to north with litter barrel.

PG 335.8 (540.4 km) PR 120.2 (193.4 km) Watch for fallen rock on this stretch of highway.

PG 345.2 (555.6 km) PR 110.8 (178.3 km) Paved rest area on riverbank with water pump, picnic tables, toilets and litter barrels. Historical plaque about Skeena River steamboats.

PG 345.5 (556.1 km) PR 110.5 (177.8 km) Skeena Cellulose private bridge across Skeena River to access tree farms on north side.

PG 352.6 (567.4 km) PR 103.4 (166.4 km) Tiny chapel to south serves small community of **USK**; the village is reached via the reaction ferry seen to north. The nondenominational chapel is a replica of the pioneer church that stood in Usk until 1936, when the Skeena River flooded, sweeping away the village and the church. The only item from the church to survive was the Bible, which was found floating atop a small pine table.

PG 354.9 (571.1 km) PR 101.1 (162.7 km) Side road leads 0.5 mile/0.8 km south to Kleanza Creek Provincial Park; 23 campsites, 12 picnic sites, fishing. Short trail to remains from Cassiar Hydraulic Mining Co. gold sluicing operations here (1911-14).

PG 360.7 (580.4 km) PR 95.3 (153.4 km) **Copper (Zymoetz) River**, can be fished from Highway 16 or follow local maps. Coho salmon to 10 lbs., use tee-spinners in July; steelhead to 20 lbs., check locally for season and restrictions.

PG 362.4 (583.2 km) PR 93.6 (150.6 km) Turnout to north with tourist information sign and area map.

PG 364.5 (586.6 km) PR 91.5 (147.2 km) Northern Motor Inn.

PG 365.1 (587.6 km) PR 90.9 (146.3 km) 4-way stop; east access to Terrace and **junction** with Highway 37 south to Kitimat. For access to downtown Terrace, turn north here and continue over 1-lane bridge. For west access to Terrace and continuation of Yellowhead Highway 16 westbound, go straight at intersection. Turn south for Kitimat (see log of HIGHWAY 37 SOUTH on page 218).

PG 365.1 (587.6 km) PR 90.9 (146.3 km) **Timberland Trailer Park, Ltd.**, 4619 Queensway Dr., Terrace. Phone (604) 635-7411. Follow signs at junction of Highways 16 and 37 south. Sixteen spaces including 12 pull-throughs. Full hookups. Cablevision. Landscaped with shade trees in quiet surroundings. Garbage service, laundry, coin showers, clubhouse. Your hosts, Ron and Ginny Lowrie. CB XM148513, Channel 7. Super, Natural North by Northwest.
[ADVERTISEMENT]

PG 365.6 (588.3 km) PR 90.4 (145.5 km) Bridge over Skeena River. Ferry Island municipal campground; 68 sites, some electrical hookups. Covered picnic shelters, barbecues, walking trails and a fishing bar are also available.

Westbound, highway crosses railway overpass.

PG 366.2 (589.3 km) PR 89.8 (144.5 km) Terrace Chamber of Commerce Travel Infocentre.

PG 366.3 (589.5 km) PR 89.7 (144.4 km) Stoplight; west access to Terrace. Turn north at intersection for downtown (description of Terrace follows). Continue through intersection westbound for Prince Rupert, eastbound for Prince George.

CAUTION: No gas or services available between Terrace and Prince Rupert.

Terrace

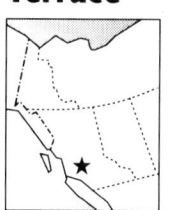

Located on the Skeena River. City centre is located north of Highway 16: Exit at overpass (PG 366.3) or at Highway 37 junction (PG 365.1). **Population:** 12,000; area 17,000. **Emergency Services:** Police, fire and ambulance located at intersection of Eby Street and Highway 16. Police, phone 635-4911. **Fire Department**, phone 638-8121. **Ambulance**, phone 638-1102. **Hospital**, 2711 Tetrault St., phone 635-2211.

Visitor Information: Travel Infocentre

TERRACE ADVERTISERS

City of Terrace	3215 Eby St.
Don Diego's Restaurant	3212 Kalum St.
Kermodei Trading Co.	Ph. (604) 638-1808
Northern Light Studio	4820 Halliwell Ave.
Northern Motor Inn	Ph. (604) 635-6375
RV Parks & Repair	Ph. (604) 635-5432
Terrace Inn Bed and Breakfast, The	Ph. (604) 635-6630
Timberland Trailer Park Ltd.	4619 Queensway Dr.

THE TERRACE INN
Bed and Breakfast
4551 Greig Avenue, Terrace, BC V8G 1M7
(604) 635-6630 • FAX (604) 635-2788
1-800-663-8156 (In Canada)
Super, Natural North by Northwest

RV PARTS & REPAIR
Parts and Service for most RV's
Open Monday - Saturday 8:30 - 6:00
CHINOOK SALES - 5506 Hwy. 16 W., Terrace
Located right on the highway • (604) 635-5432

Super, Natural North By Northwest

NORTHERN MOTOR INN
RESTAURANT • LOUNGE
PUB • COLD BEER STORE

3086 YELLOWHEAD HWY 16
TERRACE, BC V8G 3N5
NORTHERN MOTOR INN, LTD

- RESTAURANT & DINING ROOM
- HIDEAWAY LOUNGE
- GEORGE'S PUB (ENTERTAINMENT NIGHTLY)
- GUESTS ROOMS

(604) 635-6375

- CLEAN & COMFORTABLE • NEWLY RENOVATED
- AIR CONDITIONED
- WATER & QUEEN SIZE BEDS AVAILABLE
- TRUCK & RV PLUG INS
- TV SATELLITE (COLOUR)

located in the chamber of commerce log building at **Milepost PG 366.2.** Open in summer Sunday through Saturday, 9 A.M. to 8 P.M.; in winter, Monday through Friday, 9 A.M. to 5 P.M. Write Box 107, Terrace, BC V8G 4A2; phone (604) 635-2063. Information also available from Municipal Hall, #5-3215 Eby St.; open weekdays, phone 635-6311.

Elevation: 220 feet/67m. **Climate:** Average summer temperature is 69°F/20°C; yearly rainfall 36 inches, snowfall 71.5 inches. **Radio:** CFPR-FM 95.3; CFTK 590, CJFW-FM 103.9. **Television:** 8 channels (cable). **Newspapers:** *Terrace Review* (weekly), *Terrace Standard* (weekly).

Transportation: Air–Canadian Airlines International, Air BC and Central Mountain Air from Terrace-Kitimat airport on Highway 37 South. **Railroad**–VIA Rail, 4531 Railway Ave. **Bus**–Farwest Bus Lines and Greyhound. **Car Rentals**–Available.

Terrace has become an important service stop for motorists heading up the Cassiar Highway to the Alaska Highway. It is the last large retail-commercial centre for travelers until they reach the similar-sized community of Whitehorse, YT.

Tom Thornhill, the first white settler, found an Indian village just east of the present location of Terrace in 1892. When stern-wheelers were plying the Skeena, the first farmer in the area, George Little, gave land to the community that became a port of call and post office in 1905. Originally it was known as Little Town, and later was named Terrace because of the natural terraces cut by the river. The village site was laid out in 1910 and the Grand Trunk Pacific Railroad reached Terrace in 1914. The municipality was incorporated in 1927.

Terrace is a regional centre for trade, entertainment and government, with ties to the forestry industry.

ACCOMMODATIONS

There are 14 motels/hotels, 20 restaurants and 2 shopping centres. The government liquor store is at 4721 Lakelse Ave. There are 4 laundromats. The community has a library and art gallery, indoor swimming pool, tennis courts, and a 9-hole golf course.

Public campgrounds are located at Ferry Island, turn off at Skeena River bridge (**Milepost PG 365.6**); Kleanza Creek, 10 miles/16 km east of Terrace; and Lakelse Lake, 11.7 miles/18.8 km south. There are 2 private campgrounds, one on the Skeena River and the other at the east edge of the city (follow signs at junction of Highways 16 and 37). Fisherman's Park on the east side of the Kalum River, at its junction with the Skeena, provides picnic facilities.

ATTRACTIONS

Heritage Park is a collection of original log buildings from this region. Chosen to represent both the different aspects of pioneer life, as well as different log building techniques, the structures include a trapper's cabin, miner's cabin and lineman's cabin. The 9 structures also house artifacts from the period. Managed by the Terrace Regional Museum Society; guided tours available in summer, admission charged.

Lakelse Lake Provincial Park at Furlong Bay, 11 miles/18 km south of Terrace on Highway 37, offers a huge camping area, picnicking, washrooms and showers, sandy beaches, swimming, nature trails and interpretive programs.

Hiking trails in the Terrace area range from easy to moderate. Terrace Mountain Nature Trail is a 3.2-mile/5-km uphill hike which offers good views of the area; it begins at Halliwell and Anderson streets. Check with the Travel Infocentre for details on other area trails.

Special events in Terrace include the Skeena Valley Fall Fair, Labour Day weekend; and River Boat Days, B.C. Day weekend.

Lava Beds, Extinct Volcano and Indian Rock Painting. The lava beds, 48 miles/77 km north of Terrace, are only 220 years old. Much of the valley looks like the surface of the moon.

Sportfishing. Fish on the banks of the province's second largest river, the **Skeena**. Terrace is ideally situated for sportfishing, with easy access to the **Copper, Kalum, Kitimat** and **Lakelse rivers.** Cutthroat, Dolly Varden and rainbow are found in all lakes and streams; salmon (spring, king and coho) from May to late autumn. Chinooks average 40 to 70 lbs.; coho 14 to 20 lbs. Check locally for season and restrictions on steelhead. Information and fishing licenses are available from B.C. Government Bldg., 4506 Lakelse Ave., Terrace (phone 635-5423), and at most sporting goods stores.

Yellowhead Highway 16 Log

(continued)

PG 366.3 (589.5 km) **PR 89.7** (144.4 km) Stoplight; west access to Terrace. Turn north at intersection for downtown. Continue through intersection eastbound for Prince George, westbound for Prince Rupert.

PG 366.5 (589.8 km) **PR 89.5** (144 km) **Junction** with Kalum Lake Road which joins the Nass Road alternate route to Cranberry Junction on the Cassiar Highway. The paved Kalum Lake Road is recommended over the lower portion of Nass Road, which is a gravel logging road.

PG 367.9 (592.1 km) **PR 88.1** (141.7 km) Access road to boat launch (fee charged) on the Kitsumkalum River downstream from Highway 16 bridge; RV parking.

Leaving Terrace, Highway 16 is in good condition westbound although the few straightaways are interrupted by some amazing 70-degree zigzags as the highway crosses the railroad tracks. The section of highway along the Skeena River is spectacular, with waterfalls cascading down the steep rock faces.

PG 369.3 (594.3 km) **PR 86.7** (139.5 km) **KITSUMKALUM.** Grocery store and craft center. This Native enterprise on reserve land handles only authentic arts and crafts such as totem poles, leather goods and local carvings. This is also the **junction** with Nass Road which leads north 15 miles/24 km to

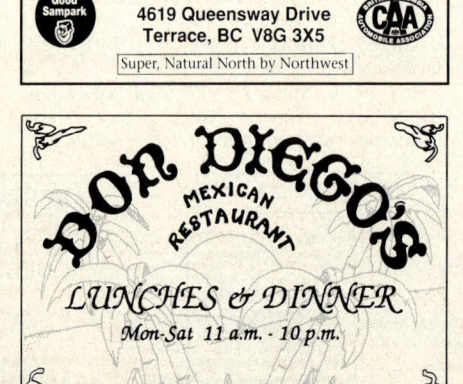

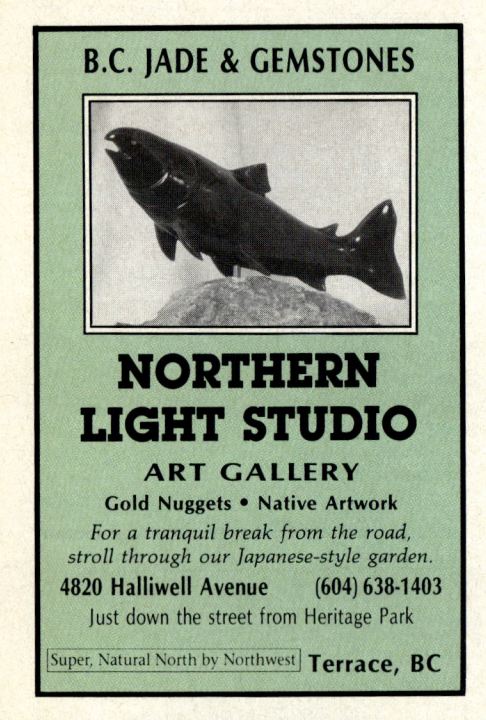

DAY 10 — TERRACE, B.C.
AND WE MAY NEVER REACH ALASKA

Spent yesterday visiting Heritage Park. I saw a stove just like my Grandma's in one of the buildings (brought back HAPPY memories). The kids ran around the grounds. Lots of equipment to climb on and play with. Bob's going golfing (of course) and I'm spending the day (with the kids glued to me) in Terrace shopping. They sure have a great selection of stores and malls to choose from. Off to the hotsprings tonight! They have water slides, a pool for the kids and a natural spring hot pool for us to soak in. Then dinner at one of Terrace's great restaurants. The area around Terrace has some of the most beautiful scenery and wildlife in the world. We saw a lot of eagles on the way into town and Bob and the kids saw a bear. (I was driving and missed it)! I think we will be going fishing on the Skeena River tomorrow. (Skeena — a local native word mean "River of Mists"). Bob saw a kid pull in a 30 pound salmon last night, and the kid said they use that for bait around here!
Maybe I'll just curl up in our room and finish my book — let Bob take the kids fishing for the day (HA! HA!)

TERRACE
A Whole Lot In Store For You

CITY OF TERRACE
Tourism & Economic Development Dept.
3215 Eby Street, Terrace, B.C. Canada V8G 2X8
Tel: (604) 635-6311 Fax: (604) 635-4744

CHAMBER OF COMMERCE
P.O. Box 107, Terrace, B.C. Canada V8G 4A2
Tel: (604) 635-2063

Highway 37 South Log

Distance is measured from the junction with Yellowhead Highway 16 (J).

J 0.9 (1.5 km) Krumm Road. Turn east for golf course.

J 3.1 (5 km) Terrace-Kitimat airport access road. Daily jet flights to Vancouver.

J 7.9 (12.7 km) Lakelse Lake Provincial Park parking area and trail to Gruchy's Beach.

J 8.7 (14 km) Lakelse Lake Provincial Park parking areas and picnic area; tables, toilets, changehouses and beach. Park headquarters located here.

J 11.4 (18.3 km) Lakelse Lake Provincial Park Furlong Bay Campground and picnic area; 156 campsites, nature trail, swimming beach, flush toilets, dump station and boat launch. ▲

J 19.3 (31 km) Highway passes through forest of western hemlock planted in 1972.

J 20.6 (33.2 km) Access to Kitimat River.

J 27.4 (44.1 km) Kitimat Airpark landing strip for small planes.

J 34.8 (56 km) Hirsch Creek Park to west; picnic area, camping, fishing and hiking. ▲

J 35 (56.3 km) Hirsch Creek bridge.

J 35.8 (57.6 km) Kitimat Travel Infocentre to east.

J 36.2 (58.3 km) Minette Bay Road leads east to MK Bay Marina and salmon viewing area near Kitamaat Village.

J 36.6 (58.9 km) Viewpoint of Douglas Channel and city map. Picnic tables, garden.

Kitimat

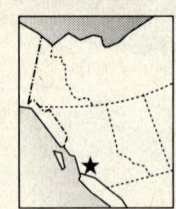

J 37.6 (60.5 km) Located at the head of Douglas Channel. **Population:** 12,000. **Emergency Services: RCMP,** phone 632-7111. **Fire Department,** phone 639-9111. **Ambulance,** phone 632-5433. **Hospital,** phone 632-2121. **Radio:** CBC-FM 101.1, CKTK 1230, CJFW-FM 103.1. **Newspaper:** *The News Advertiser* (weekly); *Northern Sentinel* (weekly).

This community was planned and built in the early 1950s when the B.C. government attracted Alcan (Aluminum Co. of Canada) to establish a smelter here. Today, Kitimat is a major port and home to several industries. Tours are available (reservations recommended) at Alcan, phone 639-8259; Eurocan Pulp and Paper, phone 632-6111; Ocelot Chemicals Inc., phone 639-9292; and Kitimat fish hatchery, phone 639-9616.

Kitimat's location at the head of Douglas Channel makes it a popular boating and fishing destination. There are several charter operators.

Attractions in Kitimat include extensive hiking trails with views of surrounding mountains. MK Bay Marina offers full facilities for boaters and fishermen. Alcan Beach south of Alcan, has a day-use area with sandy beach, boat ramp and restrooms; and there are several area hiking trails.

Kitimat has all visitor facilities, including a modern shopping mall, restaurants and motels; library, theatre, swimming pool and gym; and an 18-hole golf course. The Centennial Museum is located at city centre. For further information contact the Chamber of Commerce, Box 214, Kitimat, BC V8C 2G7; phone (604) 632-6294.

There is camping at Radley Park in town; electrical hookups, showers, toilets, playground and dump station. (Radley Park is also the site of a 165-foot/50-m Sitka spruce, largest of its kind in the province.) There is also camping at Hirsch Creek Park on the edge of town. ▲

Local fishermen line the banks of the **Kitimat River** in May for the steelhead run. Chinook salmon run in June and July. Coho run in August and into September.

Return to Milepost PG 365.1 Yellowhead Highway 16

KITIMAT ADVERTISERS

City Centre Motel........Ph. (604) 632-4848
Kitimat Chamber
   of Commerce ....Ph. (604) 632-6294

For that warm northern hospitality Kitimat has it all

Centred in one of Canada's last Wilderness areas
See nature at its best –
Mountains, Fishing, Sightseeing, Industrial Tours
Kitimat truly does – HAVE IT ALL!

COME VISIT our planned community located at the head of Douglas Channel. **Enjoy** fresh- and saltwater fishing (charters available). **GOLF** at the modern Hirsch Creek Golf Course. **HIKE** on peaceful trails suited to people of all ages. **RELAX** at Radley Park on the Kitimat River with its campsites, electric hook-ups, hot showers and even a fish smokehouse! **UNWIND** at our modern recreation centre with its sauna, whirl and swimming pools. **TAKE IN FREE** tours at the Alcan Smelter, Eurocan Pulp & Paper Mill, Ocelot Chemicals Plant and the Kitimat River Fish Hatchery. **JOIN US** for July 1st Festivities and our Annual Fish Derby on the Labour Day Weekend. We are only 30 minutes from Mt. Layton Hot Springs Resort.

For futher information contact the Travel Infocentre at:

KITIMAT CHAMBER OF COMMERCE
Box 214, Kitimat, B.C. V8C 2G7
Phone: (604) 632-6294

Super, Natural North by Northwest

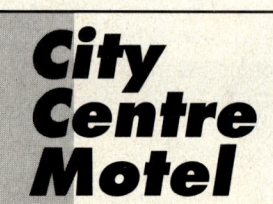

City Centre Motel

New Modern Units
Color Cable TVs
Direct Dial Phones
Kitchen Units

Reservations
1-800-663-3391
in B.C. Only

480 City Centre
Kitimat, BC, Canada
(604) 632-4848

Super, Natural British Columbia

Kitsumkalum Provincial Park with 20 campsites. This narrow gravel logging road joins the Cassiar Highway. (Kalum Lake Road from Terrace, past the community college, joins the Nass Road; it is paved to the junction.)

The Nass Road is a narrow gravel and pavement road used by logging trucks. The best route to the Cassiar Highway is from Kitwanga, Milepost PG 306.6. For details, see CASSIAR HIGHWAY section.

House of SIM-OI-GHETS. See display ad on page 216.

PG 380.2 (611.9 km) PR 75.8 (122 km) Paved turnout with litter barrels to south alongside the Skeena River; views of fishermen in salmon season.

PG 387.2 (623.1 km) PR 68.8 (110.8 km) Rest area on left westbound with picnic tables and toilets.

PG 393.1 (632.6 km) PR 62.9 (101.3 km) CAUTION! Highway turns sharply across railroad tracks.

PG 395.5 (636.5 km) PR 60.5 (97.4 km) Sharp curves and falling rocks approximately next mile westbound.

PG 397.2 (639.2 km) PR 58.8 (94.6 km) CAUTION: Slow down for sharp curve and steep grade.

PG 400.6 (644.7 km) PR 55.4 (89.2 km) Exchamsiks River Provincial Park; 18 campsites and 20 picnic sites among old-growth Sitka spruce. Open May to October, camping fee, water and pit toilets. Good salmon fishing in **Exchamsiks River.** Access to Gitnadoix River canoeing area across Skeena River.

PG 401.1 (645.5 km) PR 54.9 (88.4 km) Very pleasant rest area north side of road at west end of bridge; boat launch on Exchamsiks River.

PG 402.4 (647.6 km) PR 53.6 (86.3 km) Conspicuous example of Sitka spruce on north side of highway. As you travel west, the vegetation becomes increasingly influenced by the maritime climate.

PG 406 (653.4 km) PR 50 (80.5 km) Kasiks River; boat launch.

PG 416.4 (670.1 km) PR 39.6 (63.8 km) Kwinitsa River bridge and boat launch. No public moorage.

PG 421.1 (677.7 km) PR 34.9 (56.1 km) Telegraph Point rest area to south on bank of Skeena River; paved turnout with outhouses, picnic tables, litter barrels and water pump.

PG 427.8 (688.5 km) PR 28.2 (45.4 km) Basalt Creek rest area to south with picnic tables and toilets.

PG 432.5 (696 km) PR 23.5 (37.8 km) Turnout to south.

PG 435 (700 km) PR 21 (33.8 km) Watch for pictograph, visible from the road for eastbound traffic only, which was discovered in the early 1950s by Dan Lippett of Prince Rupert.

PG 435.5 (700.9 km) PR 20.5 (33 km) Scenic viewpoint to south with litter barrels and historical plaque about Skeena River. Highway leaves Skeena River westbound.

PG 440.5 (708.9 km) PR 15.5 (24.9 km) Rainbow Summit, elev. 528 feet/161m.

PG 442.8 (712.6 km) PR 13.2 (21.3 km) Side road south to Rainbow Lake Reservoir; boat launch. The reservoir water is used by the pulp mill on Watson Island.

PG 445.4 (716.8 km) PR 10.6 (17.1 km) Prudhomme Lake Provincial Park; 24 campsites, well water.

PG 446.3 (718.2 km) PR 9.7 (15.6 km) Turnoff for Diana Lake Provincial Park, 1.5 miles/2.4 km south via single-lane gravel road (use turnouts). Very pleasant grassy picnic area on lakeshore with 50 picnic tables, kitchen shelter, firewood, grills, outhouses, water pump and garbage cans. Parking for 229 vehicles. The only freshwater swimming beach in the Prince Rupert area. Fish viewing at Diana Creek on the way into the lake.

PG 451.2 (725.1 km) PR 4.8 (7.7 km) Junction. Turnoff for **PORT EDWARD**, pulp mill, historic canneries and Wolf Creek Hatchery (tour hours posted). The North Pacific Cannery Village and Fishing Museum at Port Edward is open daily in summer. This is the oldest cannery village on the north coast.

Cannery Village & Museum. See display ad this section.

PG 451.3 (726.3 km) PR 4.7 (7.6 km) Bridge. Prince Rupert is located on Kaien Island.

PG 451.5 (726.6 km) PR 4.5 (7.2 km) Galloway Rapids rest area to south with litter barrels, picnic tables and visitor information sign. View of Watson Island pulp mill.

PG 453 (729 km) PR 3 (4.8 km) Ridley Island access road. Ridley Island is the site of grain and coal terminals used for the transfer of coal from the North East Coal resource near Dawson Creek, and grain from Canada's prairies, to ships.

PG 453.4 (729.7 km) PR 2.6 (4.2 km) Oliver Lake rest area to south just off highway; picnic tables, grills, firewood. Point of interest sign about bogs.

PG 455.4 (732.9 km) PR 0.6 (0.9 km) Turnoff to north for viewpoint of Butze Rapids, a series of reversing rapids. The action of the tidal waters creates quantities of foam as the waters flow through the rapids. It is from these "foaming waters" that the island takes its Indian name *Kaien*.

PG 456 (733.8 km) PR 0 Prince Rupert industrial park on the outskirts of Prince Rupert. Continue straight ahead 3 miles/4.8 km for the Travel Infocentre in downtown Prince Rupert. Yellowhead Highway 16 becomes McBride Street as you enter the city centre.

Prince Rupert

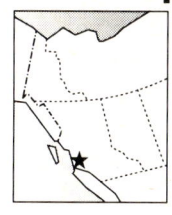

Located on Kaien Island near the mouth of the Skeena River, 90 miles/145 km by air or water south of Ketchikan, AK. **Population:** 17,500; area 25,000. **Emergency Services: RCMP**, 6th Avenue and McBride Street, phone 624-2136. **Fire Department**, phone 911. **Hospital**, Prince Rupert Regional, phone 624-2171.

Visitor Information: Travel Infocentre at 1st Avenue and McBride Street. Open in summer Monday through Saturday, 9 A.M. to 9 P.M., Sunday 9 A.M. to 5 P.M. Open in winter Monday through Saturday, 10 A.M. to 5 P.M. Travel information is also available at the Park Avenue Campground; open daily in summer, 9 A.M. to 9 P.M., and until midnight for B.C. Ferry arrivals. Write Box 669-MP, Prince Rupert, BC V8J 3S1, phone (604) 624-5637.

Elevation: Sea level. **Climate:** Temperate with mild winters. Annual precipitation 95.4 inches. **Radio:** CBC 860, CHTK 560, CJFW-FM 101.9. **Television:** 12 channels, cable. **Newspaper:** *The Prince Rupert Daily News*, *Prince Rupert This Week* (weekly).

Prince Rupert, "Gateway to Alaska," was surveyed prior to 1905 by the Grand Trunk Pacific Railway (later Canadian National

Visit B.C.'s oldest Cannery Village
Built 1889 — Restoration Project Ongoing

Relive the story of the northcoast cannery in the oldest cannery village on the northcoast. The only one of its kind, the village was built in 1889 and is undergoing restoration.

Visit the manager's house, the cannery store, the mess house and living quarters of the workers, the cannery buildings and exhibits on the northcoast fishery.

A daily heritage show animates important events and people.

Open mid-May — mid-September
1889 SKEENA DRIVE, PORT EDWARD, B.C.

Are you heading...
- North to Alaska?
- South to Vancouver Island?
- East to Stewart/Cassiar or further?

Come discover Prince Rupert.

Contact our InfoCentre and get your free information on...

- Attractions
- Accommodations
- Transportation Schedules
- Fishing and Adventure Tours
- Special Events

PRINCE RUPERT
BRITISH COLUMBIA, CANADA
Experience our Island!

FOR MORE INFORMATION,
CALL 1/800.667.1994

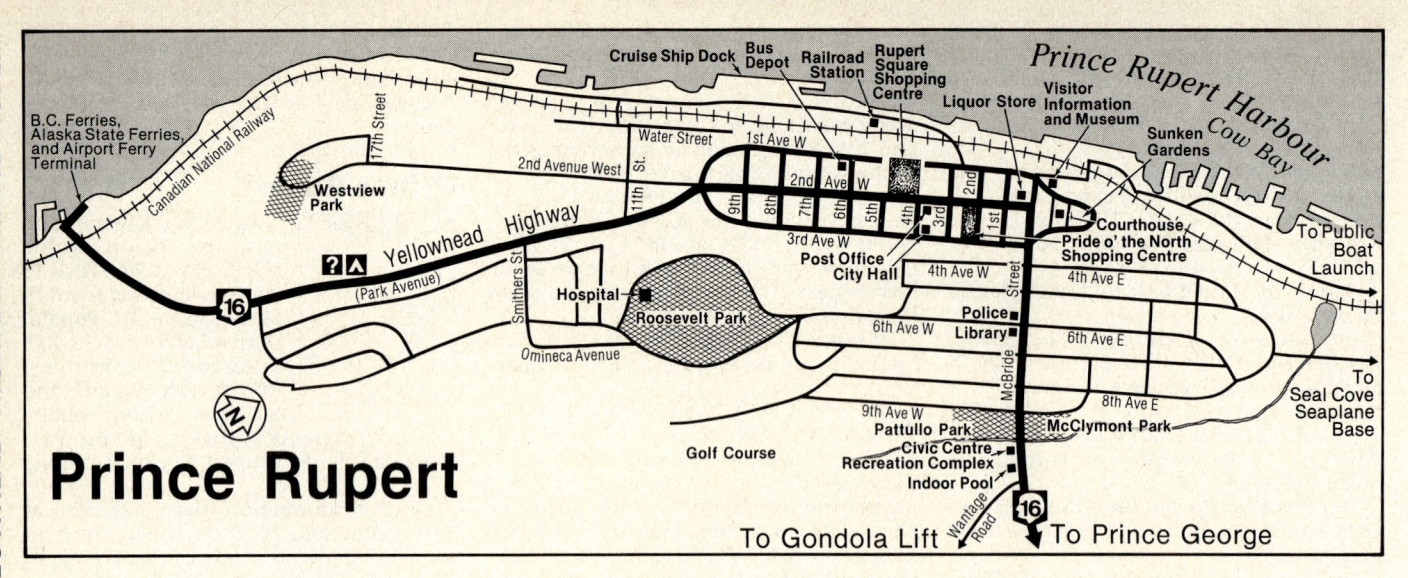

Railway) as the terminus for Canada's second transcontinental railroad.

Twelve thousand miles/19,312 km of survey lines were studied before a final route along the Skeena River was chosen. Some 833 miles/1340.6 km had to be blasted from solid rock, 50 men drowned, and costs went to $105,000 a mile (the final cost of $300 million comparable to Panama Canal construction) before the last spike was driven near Fraser Lake on April 7, 1914. Financial problems continued to plague the company, forcing it to amalgamate to become part of the Canadian National Railway system in 1923.

PRINCE RUPERT ADVERTISERS

Cow Bay Gift Galley	25 Cow Bay Rd.
Crest Motor Hotel	222 1st Ave. W.
Inn On The Harbour	Ph. (604) 624-9107
Moby Dick Inn	935 2nd Ave. W.
Park Avenue Campground	1750 Park Ave.
Philpott Evitt	Rupert Square
Prince Rupert Charter Operators	Ph. (800) 667-1994
Prince Rupert Convention & Visitors Bureau	1750 Park Ave.
Rose's Bed & Breakfast	Ph. (604) 624-5539
Totem Lodge Motel	1335 Park Ave.

Charles M. Hays, president of the company, was an enthusiastic promoter of the new terminus, which was named by competition from 12,000 entries. While "Port Rupert" had been submitted by 2 contestants, "Prince Rupert" (from Miss Eleanor M. Macdonald of Winnipeg) called to mind the dashing soldier-explorer, cousin to Charles II of England and first governor of the Hudson's Bay Co. which had traded on the coast rivers for years. Three first prizes of $250 were awarded and Prince Rupert was officially named in 1906.

Prince Rupert's proposed port and adjacent waters were surveyed by G. Blanchard Dodge of the Hydrographic branch of the Marine Dept. in 1906, and in May the little steamer *Constance* carried settlers from the village of Metlakatla to clear the first ground on Kaien Island. Its post office opened Nov. 23, 1906, and Prince Rupert, with a tent-town population of 200, began an association with communities on the Queen Charlotte Islands, with Stewart served by Union steamships and CPR boats, and with Hazelton 200 miles/321.9 km up the Skeena River on which the stern-wheelers of the Grand Trunk Pacific and the Hudson's Bay Co. traveled.

Incorporated as a city March 10, 1910, Prince Rupert attracted settlers responding to the enthusiasm of Hays, with his dreams of a population of 50,000 and world markets supplied by his railroad. Both the city and the railway suffered a great loss with the death of Charles M. Hays when the *Titanic* went down in April 1912. Even so, work went ahead on the Grand Trunk Pacific and 2 years later the first train arrived at Prince Rupert, linking the western port with the rest of Canada. Since then, the city has progressed through 2 world wars and economic ups and downs to its present period of growth and expansion, not only as a busy port but as a visitor centre.

During WWII, more than a million tons of freight and 73,000 persons, both military and civilian, passed through Prince Rupert on their way to military operations in Alaska and the South Pacific.

Construction of the pulp operations on Watson Island in 1951 greatly increased the economic and industrial potential of the area. The operations include a pulp mill and a kraft mill.

With the start of the Alaska State Ferry System in 1963, and the British Columbia Ferry System in 1966, Prince Rupert's place as an important visitor centre and terminal point for highway, rail and marine transportation was assured.

Prince Rupert is the second major deep-sea port on Canada's west coast, exporting grain, pulp, lumber and other resources to Europe and the Orient. The port of Prince Rupert has also become a major coal and grain port with facilities on Ridley Island. Other industries include fishing and fish processing and the manufacture of forest products.

Prince Rupert is built on a layer of

Moby Dick Inn

* 63 spacious guest rooms
* Satellite and cable TV
* Restaurant open 24 hours
* Complimentary parking
* Vehicle storage
* Whirlpool and sauna
* Lounge open noon -- 2 a.m.
* Entertainment from 8:30 nightly for live music
* Fair exchange on U.S. dollars

935 2nd Avenue West
Prince Rupert, BC
For reservations:
(604) 624-6961
Within BC call toll free 1-800-772-0822

Super, Natural North by Northwest

Fish Prince Rupert

Variety of boats and options
• Deep-sea Saltwater Fishing
• Harbour Tours
• Adventure Excursions
1/2 day, full day, overnight
— *Favourable Prices* —

Prince Rupert Charter Operators
Box 669-MP, Prince Rupert, BC V8J 3S1
Ph. (604) 624-5637 • 1-800-667-1994 toll free

Super, Natural North by Northwest

Reproductions of original totems are found throughout the city. (Rollo Pool, staff)

muskeg (unstable organic matter) on solid rock which makes a difficult foundation to build on. Many sites are economically unfeasible for development as they would require pilings 70 feet/21m or more into the muskeg to provide a firm foundation. Some of the older buildings have sagged slightly as a result of unstable foundations.

ACCOMMODATIONS

More than a dozen hotels and motels accommodate the influx of ferry passengers each summer. Many restaurants feature fresh local seafood in season.

Inn On The Harbour. Combine the convenience of a modern motor inn with the warmth and comfort of a traditional hotel. Situated downtown overlooking Prince Rupert harbour. 50 deluxe units. Cablevision, complimentary coffee. Phone (604) 624-9107, fax (604) 627-8232. Toll free in British Columbia and Alberta 1-800-663-8155. Write: 720 W. 1st Ave., Prince Rupert, BC V8J 3P9. Super, Natural North by Northwest. [ADVERTISEMENT]

Modern supermarkets, shopping centres and a hospital are available. Government liquor store is at the corner of 2nd Avenue and Highway 16. There are 5 main banks, the Civic Centre Recreation Complex, 18-hole golf course, racquet centre, bowling alley, a swimming pool and tennis courts.

Park Avenue Campground on Highway 16 in the city has 87 campsites with hookups, unserviced sites, restrooms with hot showers, children's play area and picnic shelters. There are 24 campsites at Prudhomme Lake Park, 12.5 miles/20 km east on Highway 16. A private RV park on McBride Street offers camper and trailer parking. ▲

TRANSPORTATION

Air: Trans-Provincial Airlines to Stewart and Ketchikan; North Coast Air Services and Trans-Provincial to Queen Charlotte Islands; Canadian Airlines International daily jet service to Terrace and Vancouver; and Air BC to Vancouver and Victoria.

Prince Rupert airport is located on Digby Island, which is connected by city-operated ferry to Prince Rupert. There is a small terminal at the airport. The airport ferry leaves from the Fairview dock, next to the Alaska State ferry dock; cost is $9 one way for the 20-minute ferry ride. Check with the Canadian Airlines International office at the downtown Rupert Mall (office is open for passenger check-in only when planes are arriving or departing). Air BC check-in at corner of 6th Street and 1st Avenue West.

Park Avenue Campground
1750 PARK AVE, PRINCE RUPERT, B.C.

Conveniently located 1/2 mile from BC and Alaska ferries and close to convenience store and propane/gas bar.

77 Sites fully serviced with water, sewer, 30-amp electricity • Unserviced sites • Overflow parking • Laundry room • Tenting • 2 Washroom facilities with free showers • Firewood • Playground • 10-minute walk from downtown
Open year-round • Reservations accepted • VISA and MasterCard

Super, Natural North By Northwest

1750 Park Avenue, P.O. Box 612-MP
(604) 624-5861   Prince Rupert, BC V8J 3R5

YELLOWHEAD HIGHWAY • PRINCE RUPERT

How long has it been since you talked about where you stayed, instead of just how many miles you covered?

PRINCE RUPERT'S
Crest
MOTOR HOTEL

Super, Natural North by Northwest

Prince Rupert's finest accommodations and dining at affordable rates

222 1st Ave. West
P.O. Box 277
Prince Rupert, BC, V8J 3P6
(604) 624-6771   Telex 047-89145
Toll Free in B.C. and Alberta
1-800-663-8150   FAX (604) 627-ROOM

AAA FOUR DIAMOND AWARD

Bus service to airport from airline check-in areas.

There is a seaplane base at Seal Cove with airline and helicopter charter services.

Ferries: British Columbia Ferry System, Fairview dock, phone 624-9627, provides automobile and passenger service from Prince Rupert to Port Hardy, and between Prince Rupert and Skidegate in the Queen Charlotte Islands. For details, see MARINE ACCESS ROUTES section.

Alaska Marine Highway System, Fairview dock, phone 627-1744, provides automobile and passenger service to southeastern Alaska. See MARINE ACCESS ROUTES section.

NOTE: Vehicle storage is available. See advertisements this section.

Car Rentals: Tilden (624-5318) and Budget.

Railroad: VIA Rail, in British Columbia, phone 1-800-665-8630.

Bus: Greyhound, phone 624-5090. Farwest Bus Lines, phone 624-6400. Charter sightseeing tours available.

ATTRACTIONS

Take a Tour. Tour the city's historic and scenic points of interest. Maps are available at the Travel Infocentre. Scattered throughout the city are 18 large cedar totem poles, each with its own story. Most are reproductions by Native craftsmen of the original Tsimshian (SHIM shian) poles from the mainland and the Haida (HI duh) carvings from the Queen Charlotte Islands. The originals are now in the British Columbia Provincial Museum in Victoria. Several totem poles may be seen at Service Park, near 3rd Avenue W. and Fulton.

Check with the Museum of Northern British Columbia (1st and McBride) about tours of area archaeological sites. Included is a stop at "Old" Metlakatla in Prince Rupert harbour ("new" Metlakatla is located on Annette Island near Ketchikan, AK; see METLAKATLA section).

Prince Rupert Grain on Ridley Island (turn off Highway 16 at **Milepost PG 453**) offers a look at Canada's most advanced cleaning grain terminal. Tours may be arranged through the Travel Infocentre.

"Photographs and Memories" is a well done multi-media production on Prince Rupert's history. Plays daily in the Crest Motor Hotel. Admission charged.

Watch the Seaplanes. From McBride Street, head north on 6th Avenue East (watch for signs to seaplane base); drive a few miles to Solly's Pub, then turn right to Seal Cove seaplane base. Visitors can spend a fascinating hour here watching seaplanes loading, taking off and landing. Helicopter tours of the area are available at Seal Cove.

Swim at Diana Lake. This provincial park, about 13 miles/21 km from downtown on Highway 16, offers the only freshwater swimming in the Prince Rupert area. Picnic tables, kitchen shelter, parking and beach.

Swim at Earl Mah Aquatic Centre, located next to the Civic Centre Recreation Complex. There are an indoor swimming pool, weight room, saunas, showers and whirlpool, slides and diving boards. Access for handicapped. Phone 627-7946. Admission charged.

Museum of Northern British Columbia/Art Gallery displays an outstanding collection of artifacts depicting the settlement history of British Columbia's north coast. Traveling art collections are displayed in the gallery, and works by local artists are available for purchase. Centrally located at 1st Avenue and McBride Street, marked by several tall totem poles. Summer hours 9 A.M. to 9 P.M. Monday through Saturday, 9 A.M. to 5 P.M. Sunday; winter hours 10 A.M. to 5 P.M. Monday through Saturday.

Archaeology Tours. Prince Rupert's inner harbour shelters more than 150 archaeological sites dating back 5,000 years. This fascinating harbour tour visits these sites and offers full descriptions of early inhabitants. The tour stops at the historic Indian village of Metlakatla for snacks and souvenirs. Guided by knowledgeable museum staff you'll travel in an enclosed ferry with ample window seating. Regular departures. Reserve with Museum of Northern British Columbia, Box 669, Prince Rupert, BC V8J 3S1. (604) 624-3207. [ADVERTISEMENT]

Mount Hays Gondola Lift travels 1,850 feet/564m to the top of Mount Hays for an overview of Prince Rupert, the harbour, surrounding mountains and the Queen Charlotte Islands. Enjoy mountain wildflowers in the summer. Lift operates seasonally. Restaurant in chalet. Drive east on McBride Street and turn right on Wantage Road; continue on gravel road past golf course to base of gondola. Phone 624-5637 for additional information. Admission charged.

Cannery Tour. North Pacific Cannery Village and Fishing Museum at Port Edward (turn off Highway 16 at **Milepost PG 451.2**). Built in 1889, this restored heritage site has dozens of displays on this once major industry of the region. A live performance highlighting the history of the cannery is given twice daily. Open daily in summer, admission charged.

Numerous freshwater fishing areas are available near Prince Rupert. For information on bait, locations, regulations and licensing, contact local sporting goods stores or the Travel Infocentre. This area abounds in all species of salmon, steelhead, crab, shrimp and abalone. Public boat launch facility is located at Rushbrook Public Floats at the north end of the waterfront. Public floats are also available at Fairview, past the Alaska state ferry terminal near the breakwater.

Harbour Tours and Fishing Charters are available. For information, contact the Prince Rupert charter operators, phone 624-5637.

The Civic Centre Recreation Complex located on McBride Street (Highway 16) welcomes visitors. Activities include fitness gym, squash, basketball and volleyball. Supervised children's activities during summer. Ice skating and roller skating rinks also located at the centre. Phone 624-6707 for more information.

Performing Arts Centre offers both professional and amateur theatre, with productions for children, and classical and contemporary plays presented. The 700-seat facility may be toured in summer; phone 627-8888.

Golf Course includes 18-hole course, resident pro, equipment rental, clubhouse and restaurant. Entrance on 9th Avenue W.

Special Events. Seafest is a 4-day celebration held the second weekend in June that includes a parade and water-jousting competition. Indian Culture Days, a 2-day event held during Seafest, features Native food, traditional dance, and arts and crafts. The All Native Basketball Tournament, held in February, draws spectators and players from hundreds of miles away and is the largest event of its kind in Canada.

Visit the Queen Charlotte Islands. British Columbia ferry service is available between Prince Rupert and Skidegate on Graham Island, largest of the 150 islands and islets that form Queen Charlotte Islands. Located 100 miles/160 km west of Prince Rupert (an 8-hour ferry ride), Graham Island's paved road system connects Skidegate with Masset, largest town in the Queen Charlottes. Trans-Provincial Airlines has daily scheduled flights from Prince Rupert to Sandspit and Masset. Major attractions include the virgin forest, Indian culture and wildlife. *A Guide to Queen Charlotte Islands* by Neil Carey is available from Alaska Northwest Books™ and in local bookstores.

Rose's Bed & Breakfast
Quiet, Comfortable Suites
Cooking Facilities and TV Rooms
Located Downtown

(604) 624-5539   943 1st Ave. West
Teresa "Rose"   Prince Rupert, BC
Hostess   Canada V8J 1B4

COW BAY GIFT GALLEY
- Native Art
- Wood Carvings
- T-Shirts

Plus A complete Selection of Kitchen and Bath Products

25 Cow Bay Road, Prince Rupert, B.C.
Open 7 Days a Week

CAR · BOAT · TRAILER STORAGE
Daily and Monthly Rates
PHILPOTT EVITT   (604) 624-2101
Lower Level, Rupert Square
Box 370   Prince Rupert, BC V8J 3P9

Super, Natural North by Northwest

TOTEM LODGE MOTEL
31 Quiet Comfortable Rooms with Kitchenettes
Non-Smoking Rooms • Laundry Facilities
Satellite and Cable TV • Vehicle Storage
Closest to Alaska / BC Ferries

Phone (604) 624-6761
1335 Park Ave., Prince Rupert, BC V8J 1K3

Super, Natural North by Northwest

CASSIAR HIGHWAY

Junction with the Yellowhead Highway, British Columbia, to Junction with the Alaska Highway
BC Highway 37
(See map, page 224)

The Cassiar Highway junctions with Yellowhead Highway 16 at the Skeena River bridge (**Milepost PG 306.6** in the YELLOWHEAD HIGHWAY 16 section) and travels north to the Stewart, BC–Hyder, AK, access road, Dease Lake, and Cassiar, ending at the Alaska Highway about 14 miles/22 km west of Watson Lake, YT. Total driving distance is 455.6 miles/733.2 km. It offers a most enjoyable adventure drive with outstanding and varied scenery.

Completed in 1972, much of the Cassiar has been leveled, straightened, and brought up to all-weather standards. The highway is paved from **Milepost J 0** to Meziadin junction. From Meziadin junction to the Alaska Highway, the highway is surfaced (pavement or seal coat) with the exception of 3 gravel sections. On gravel stretches watch for washboard and potholes. Gravel road may be dusty in dry weather and muddy in wet weather. Seal coat is subject to deterioration from weather and traffic. A few bridges are still single lane. Watch for potholes at bridge ends and slippery bridge decks. Resurfacing and other improvements may be expected in 1992. Drive with your headlights on. The Cassiar Highway is the route of commercial truckers headed north of 60°; it is several hours shorter than the alternative Alaska Highway route.

Watch for logging trucks on the lower Cassiar Highway, asbestos trucks south from Cassiar and freight trucks anywhere on the highway. *WARNING: Exercise extreme caution when passing or being passed by these trucks; reduce speed and allow trucks adequate clearance.*

Increasingly popular with motorists in recent years, both because of its savings in travel time and its scenery, the Cassiar also provides access to Hyder and Stewart. These 2 communities are described in detail in this section.

Food, gas and lodging are available along the Cassiar Highway but check the highway log for distances between services. Be sure your vehicle is mechanically sound with good tires. It is a good idea to carry a spare tire and extra fuel, especially in winter. In case of emergency, motorists are advised to flag down trucks to radio for help. It is unlawful to camp overnight in turnouts and rest areas unless otherwise posted. Camp at private campgrounds or in provincial park campgrounds.

Bear Glacier on the Stewart–Hyder access road. (Joe Prax)

Cassiar Highway Log

BC HIGHWAY 37
Kilometreposts are up along the Cassiar Highway about every 5 to 10 kms, but the posts do not always accurately reflect driving distance nor are they measured from a single starting point. *The MILEPOST®* log indicates the physical location of kilometreposts as they occurred in summer 1991.
Distance from junction with the Yellowhead Highway (J) is followed by distance from Alaska Highway (AH).

J 0 AH 455.6 (733.2 km) Junction with Yellowhead Highway 16 (see **Milepost PG 306.6** in the YELLOWHEAD HIGHWAY 16 section). Gas station. Bridge across Skeena River from Yellowhead Highway 16 to start of Cassiar Highway.

N&V Johnson Services Ltd. See display ad this section.

J 0.3 (0.5 km) **AH 455.3** (732.7 km) Turn on side road to view totem poles and church of Gitwangak. The Native reserve of Gitwangak was renamed after sharing the name Kitwanga with the adjacent white settlement. Gitwangak has some of the finest authentic totem poles in the area. Also here is St. Paul's Anglican Church; the original old

---

N & V Johnson Services Ltd.
Petro Canada Dealer

**Specializing
in Wheel Alignment
Complete Brake Service
Pronto Muffler Systems**

*Also – Lottery Tickets
Groceries &
Restaurant on Premises*

Summer Hours:
7 a.m. to 10 p.m. Daily
Winter Hours:
8 a.m. to 9 p.m.

1992 ■ The MILEPOST® 223

CASSIAR HIGHWAY

Yellowhead Highway Junction to Alaska Highway Junction

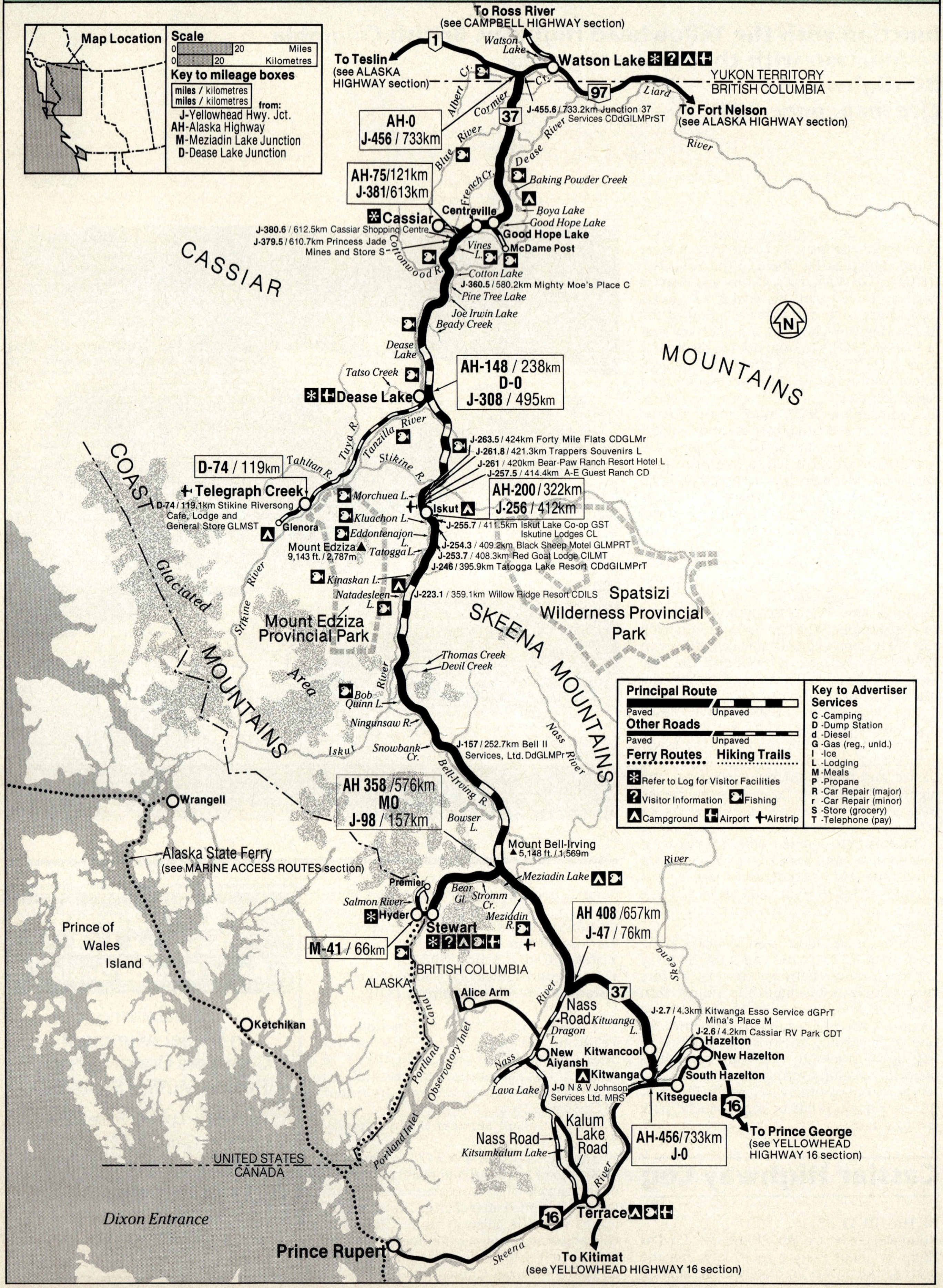

bell tower standing beside the church dates back to 1893.

J 2.6 (4.2 km) **AH 453** (729 km) Kitwanga post office and a private RV park. ▲

Cassiar RV Park. See display ad this section.

J 2.7 (4.3 km) **AH 452.9** (728.9 km) South end of 1.6-mile/2.5-km loop access road which leads to **KITWANGA** (pop. 1,200). **Radio:** CBC 630 AM. **Emergency Services:** Ambulance. The business area of Kitwanga has a visitor information booth (open June to August, local crafts for sale), gas station, car wash, a general store and small restaurant. There is a free public campground. ▲

Kitwanga is at the crossroads of the old upper Skeena "grease trail" trade. The "grease" was eulachon (candlefish) oil, which was a trading staple among tribes of the Coast and Interior. The grease trails are believed to have extended north to the Bering Sea.

A paved turnout with litter barrel and sign on the Kitwanga access road mark Kitwanga Fort National Historic Site, where a wooden fortress and palisade once crowned the large rounded hill here. Seven interpretive panels along the trail up Battle Hill explain the history of the site. Kitwanga Fort was the first major western Canadian native site commemorated by Parks Canada.

Kitwanga Esso Service. See display ad this section.

Mina's Place. See display ad this section.

J 4.2 (6.8 km) **AH 451.4** (726.4 km) North end of 1.6-mile/2.5-km loop access road (Kitwanga North Road) to Kitwanga; see description preceding milepost.

J 4.3 (6.9 km) **AH 451.3** (726.3 km) **Junction** with alternate access route (signed Hazelton–Kitwanga Road) from Hazelton to the Cassiar Highway via the north side of the Skeena River.

J 6.2 (10 km) **AH 449.4** (723.2 km) Between Kilometreposts 10 and 15, the mountain chain of Seven Sisters is visible to west (weather permitting).

J 13 (21 km) **AH 442.6** (712.3 km) Highway follows Kitwanga River and former grease trail route.

J 13.4 (21.6 km) **AH 442.2** (711.6 km) South access to **KITWANCOOL**, a small Indian village with many fine old recently restored totems, among them the famous Hole-in-the-Ice pole. A Native craft shop in the village sells local art. The village of Kitwancool was originally called Gitanyow, meaning place of many people, but was renamed Kitwancool, meaning place of reduced number, after many of its inhabitants were killed in raids.

J 16.5 (26.5 km) **AH 439.1** (706.6 km) North access to Kitwancool.

J 19.2 (30.9 km) **AH 436.4** (702.3 km) Bridge over Moon Lit Creek.

J 19.3 (31.1 km) **AH 436.3** (702.1 km) Road east to rest area by creek with tables, toilets and litter barrels. Road west is the old highway and access to Kitwanga Lake. Fishing, camping, and boat launch spots on lake. Old highway may be in poor condition; drive carefully. It rejoins the main highway at Kilometrepost 40.3. Access to the lake is strictly from the old highway.

J 20.2 (32.5 km) **AH 435.4** (700.7 km) Access to Kitwanga Lake.

J 21.7 (34.9 km) **AH 433.9** (698.3 km) Good views of Kitwanga Lake to west; old highway visible, below west, winding along lakeshore.

J 26.3 (42.4 km) **AH 429.3** (690.9 km) Kitwancool Forest Road to west.

J 39.2 (63.1 km) **AH 416.4** (670.1 km) **Cranberry River** bridge No. 1. A favorite salmon stream in summer; consult fishing regulations.

J 47 (75.6 km) **AH 408.6** (657.5 km) Paved turnout to west.

J 47.3 (77.1 km) **AH 408.3** (657.1 km) **Junction** with Nass Road from Terrace.

J 47.6 (76.6 km) **AH 408** (656.6 km) Cranberry River bridge No. 2. Turnout with toilets, tables and litter barrels.

J 53.6 (86.2 km) **AH 402** (646.9 km) BC Hydro power line crosses and parallels highway. Completed in 1990, this line links Stewart to the BC Hydro power grid. Previously, Stewart's power was generated by diesel fuel, as is the power in all other communities along the highway.

J 59.3 (95.4 km) **AH 396.3** (637.8 km) Small lake with rest area at north end. First view northbound of Nass River.

J 64.7 (104.1 km) **AH 390.9** (629.1 km) Paved turnout.

J 66.3 (106.7 km) **AH 389.3** (626.5 km) View of Nass River to west. The Nass River is one of the province's prime producers of sockeye salmon.

J 67.1 (108 km) **AH 388.5** (625.2 km) Views northbound (weather permitting) of the Coast Mountains to the west. Watch for Cambrian ice field to west.

J 70.8 (114 km) **AH 384.8** (619.2 km) Paved turnout to west.

J 76.7 (123.5 km) **AH 378.9** (609.8 km) Road widens and serves as emergency airstrip; pull over for any approaching aircraft.

J 85.7 (137.9 km) **AH 369.9** (595.3 km) Paved turnout with litter barrels to west.

J 86.6 (139.3 km) **AH 369** (593.8 km) Elsworth logging camp; open to public; fuel, groceries, emergency phone, 7 A.M. to 10 P.M. daily. Private airstrip.

J 88.7 (142.8 km) **AH 366.9** (590.4 km)

RESTAURANT
Mina's Place KITWANGA, BC
Breakfast Served All Day
Light Lunches, Dinner, Chinese Food
VISA   (604) 849-5744

"En Route To Alaska"
CASSIAR RV PARK

25 FULL SERVICE SITES
Large Pull-throughs • Sani-Station
Free Hot Showers • Laundry Facilities
Public Phone • RV Pressure Washer

Kitwanga, B.C.
(604) 849-5488

Super, Natural North by Northwest

Nass River 1-lane bridge. Paved rest area with picnic tables, toilets and litter barrel to east at south end of bridge. A plaque at the north end commemorates bridge opening. The gorge is almost 400 feet/122m wide; main span of bridge is 186 feet/57m. Steel reinforcement supports loads up to 90 tons. Bridge decking is 130 feet/40m above the riverbed.

J 94.1 (151.5 km) **AH 361.5** (581.8 km) Tintina Creek. Along with Hanna Creek, this stream produces 40 percent of the sockeye salmon spawning in the Meziadin Lake watershed.

KITWANGA
Esso
SERVICE

On Kitwanga Access Loop

AUTOMOTIVE AND RV SERVICE AND REPAIRS

Diesel • Auto Propane
Pressure Car Wash • Towing

(604) 849-5521

FAIR U.S. EXCHANGE

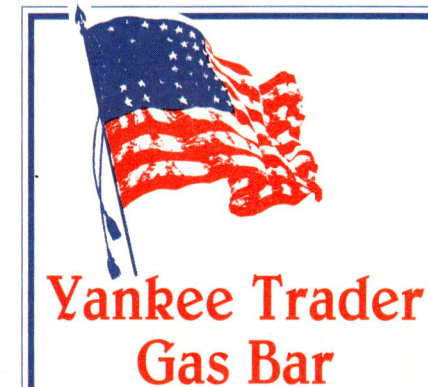

Yankee Trader Gas Bar

Hyder, Alaska

Friendliest Ghost Town in Alaska
5 minutes from Stewart, BC

FILL UP AT U.S. PRICES

Hyder: *Unforgetable*
• Visit Salmon Glacier
• See Fish Creek
Salmon and Bears

BEST OF ALL!!!
Gasoline at Yankee Prices!

Meziadin Lake has good fishing for trout, whitefish and Dolly Varden. (Judy Parkin, staff)

J 95.6 (153.8 km) **AH 360 (579.3 km)**
Hanna Creek. Sockeye salmon spawn here in autumn. It is illegal to fish for or harass these fish. CAUTION: Watch for bears.

J 96.7 (155.7 km) **AH 358.9** (577.6 km)
Meziadin Lake Provincial Park; 42 campsites (many on lake), drinking water, firewood, garbage containers, boat launch. The lake has a significant fish population, including rainbow trout, mountain whitefish, and Dolly Varden. Fishing is especially good at the mouths of small streams draining into Meziadin Lake. CAUTION: Watch for bears. The hills around the lake are prime bear habitat.

J 97.5 (157 km) **AH 358.1** (576.3 km)
Meziadin Lake Junction (Mezy-AD-in); Cassiar Highway junctions with the access road to Stewart, BC, and Hyder, AK. Motel, cafe and gas station at junction. *(NOTE: Status of gas availability unknown at press time.)* A visitor information cabin is located here, open daily in summer. See STEWART, BC–HYDER, AK, ACCESS ROAD this section.
NOTE: This junction can be confusing. Choose your route carefully.

Bell II Services Ltd.
MILE J 157

REGULAR AND SUPREME UNLEADED
DIESEL ★ TIRE and MINOR REPAIRS
PROPANE

Home Cooking ★ Cabins
Sani-Station ★ Drinking Water

Proposed for 1992:
Serviced and Unserviced RV Sites

Radiophone H49-5845
Bell Irving Channel

OPEN YEAR-ROUND
7 a.m. - 9 p.m. Summer
7 a.m. - 7 p.m. Winter

MasterCard   VISA

Super, Natural North by Northwest

J 100.3 (161.4 km) **AH 355.3** (571.8 km)
Kilometrepost 160.

J 103.2 (166.1 km) **AH 352.4** (567.1 km)
Hanna Creek river and bridge.
Northbound: Pavement ends, gravel begins. Construction under way in 1991. Watch for upgrading and possible paving in 1992.
Southbound: Pavement begins, gravel ends.

J 116.6 (187.6 km) **AH 339** (545.5 km)
Pleasant view of Mount Bell–Irving across pond. Watch for bears along this stretch of highway.
Travelers will notice large areas of clear-cut along the southern half of the Cassiar Highway. Bark beetle infestation necessitated the harvest of timber along this particular stretch of highway. After logging, it was burned off and reforested. CAUTION: Watch for logging trucks.

J 118.8 (191.2 km) **AH 336.8** (542 km)
Bell II rest area at north end of Bell–Irving bridge; picnic tables, pit toilets, litter barrels.

J 121.1 (194.9 km) **AH 334.5** (538.3 km)
Spruce Creek bridge.

J 125.6 (202.1 km) **AH 330** (531.1 km)
Bell–Irving River parallels highway.

J 128 (206 km) **AH 327.6** (527.2 km)
Cousins Creek.

J 129.7 (208.7 km) **AH 325.9** (524.5 km)
Ritchie Creek bridge.

J 133.5 (214.8 km) **AH 322.1** (518.3 km)
Taft Creek.

J 134.8 (216.9 km) **AH 320.8** (516.3 km)
Kilometrepost 215.

J 139.2 (224 km) **AH 316.4** (509.2 km)
Deltaic Creek.

J 144.7 (232.9 km) **AH 310.9** (500.3 km)
Glacier Creek.

J 146.9 (236.4 km) **AH 308.7** (496.8 km)
Skowill Creek bridge. The old 1-lane bridge is visible to the east.

J 151.4 (243.6 km) **AH 304.2** (489.5 km)
Oweegee Creek.

J 155.5 (250.2 km) **AH 300.1** (483 km)
Nice picnic site by **Hodder Lake**; tables, litter barrels, boat launch. Fly or troll for small rainbows.
Northbound: Gravel ends, seal coat begins.

Southbound: Seal coat ends, gravel begins.

J 157 (252.7 km) **AH 298.6** (480.5 km)
Food, gas (unleaded and diesel), propane and lodging.
Bell II Services Ltd. See display ad this section.

J 157.3 (253.1 km) **AH 298.3** (480 km)
Second crossing northbound of Bell–Irving River.

J 162.9 (262.1 km) **AH 292.7** (471 km)
Snowbank Creek.

J 163.3 (262.8 km) **AH 292.3** (470.4 km)
Avalanche area: No stopping in winter or spring. Avalanche chutes are visible on slopes to west in summer.

J 165.2 (265.9 km) **AH 290.4** (467.3 km)
Redflat Creek.

J 165.4 (266.2 km) **AH 290.2** (467 km)
Highway serves as emergency airstrip. Watch for aircraft landing or taking off; keep to side of road! End avalanche area northbound.

J 167.9 (270.3 km) **AH 287.7** (463 km)
Revision Creek.

J 170.6 (274.5 km) **AH 285** (458.6 km)
Kilometrepot 115 reflects distance from Meziadin Lake junction.

J 173.7 (279.5 km) **AH 281.9** (453.7 km)
Turnout with litter barrels to east overlooking large moose pasture, beaver ponds.

J 174 (280 km) **AH 281.6** (453.2 km) Liz Creek.

J 174.5 (281 km) **AH 281.1** (452.4 km)
Ningunsaw Pass (elev. 1,530 feet/466m). Nass–Stikine water divide; turnout with litter barrels to west beside **Ningunsaw River**. Mountain whitefish and Dolly Varden. The highway parallels the Ningunsaw northbound. Watch for fallen rock on road through the canyon. The Ningunsaw is a tributary of the Stikine watershed.

J 176.5 (284 km) **AH 279.1** (449.2 km)
Alger Creek. The massive piles of logs and debris in this creek are from a 1989 avalanche.

J 177.4 (285.5 km) **AH 278.2** (447.7 km)
Ogilvie Creek.

J 181.8 (292.6 km) **AH 273.8** (440.6 km)
Point of interest sign about Yukon Telegraph line. The 1,900-mile Dominion Telegraph line linked Dawson City with Vancouver. Built in 1899–1901, the line was a route for prospectors and trappers headed to Atlin; it was replaced by radio in the 1930s.

J 182.1 (293.1 km) **AH 273.5** (440.1 km)
Echo Lake. Flooded telegraph cabins are visible in the lake below. Good view of Coast Mountains to west. Spectacular cliffs to the east are part of the Skeena Mountains (Bowser Basin).

J 185.1 (297.9 km) **AH 270.5** (435.3 km)
Bob Quinn Forest Service Road, under construction as the Iskut Mining Road (1991) will provide year-round access to goldfields west of Ningunsaw River. The road will follow the Iskut River Valley toward the Stikine River, with a side branch to Eskay Creek gold deposit.

J 185.7 (298.8 km) **AH 269.9** (434.3 km)
Little Bob Quinn Lake, rainbow and Dolly Varden, summer and fall. Access to Bob Quinn Lake at **Milepost J 187.5**.

J 186 (299.3 km) **AH 269.6** (433.9 km)
Bob Quinn flight airstrip. This is a staging site for supplies headed for the Stikine/Iskut goldfields.

J 187.5 (301.7 km) **AH 268.1** (431.4 km)
Bob Quinn highway maintenance camp; meals, lodging, helicopter base. Access to Bob Quinn Lake; toilet, picnic table,
(Continues on page 231)

Stewart, BC-Hyder, AK, Access Road Log

HIGHWAY 37A
Distance is measured from Meziadin Lake Junction (M).

M 0 **Junction** with Cassiar Highway at **Milepost J 98.5**. Visitor information cabin open daily in summer.

M 7.7 (12.4 km) Surprise Creek bridge.

M 10.1 (16.3 km) Turnout to south with view of hanging glaciers.

M 11.5 (18.5 km) Windy Point bridge.

M 13 (20.9 km) Cornice Creek bridge.

M 13.5 (21.7 km) Strohn Creek bridge.

M 14.7 (23.7 km) Rest area with litter barrels, view of Bear Glacier.

M 15.8 (25.4 km) Turnouts along lake into which Bear River Glacier calves its icebergs. Watch for falling rock from slopes above road in spring. Morning light is best for photographing spectacular Bear River Glacier. At one time the glacier reached this side of the valley; the old highway can be seen hundreds of feet above the present road.

M 18.4 (29.6 km) Cullen River bridge.

M 18.9 (30.4 km) Huge delta of accumulated avalanche snow. Narrow road with little shoulder; no stopping.

M 21.5 (34.6 km) Argyle Creek.

M 23.2 (37.3 km) Narrow, steep-walled Bear River canyon. Watch for rocks on road.

M 24.5 (39.4 km) Turnout with litter barrel to north.

M 24.8 (39.9 km) Bear River bridge.

M 30.1 (48.4 km) Bitter Creek bridge.

M 32.5 (52.3 km) Wards Pass cemetery. The straight stretch of road along here is the former railbed from Stewart.

M 36.9 (59.4 km) Bear River bridge and welcome portal to Stewart.

M 38.5 (62 km) Highway joins main street of Stewart (description follows).

M 40.9 (65.8 km) U.S.–Canada border. Hyder (description follows).

TIME ZONE CHANGE: Stewart observes Pacific time, Hyder observes Alaska time. See Time Zones in the GENERAL INFORMATION section.

Stewart, BC–Hyder, AK

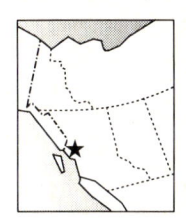

Stewart is at the head of Portland Canal on the AK–BC border. **Hyder** is 2.3 miles/3.7 km beyond Stewart. **Population:** Stewart about 2,200; Hyder 85. **Emergency Services:** In Stewart, RCMP, phone 636-2233. EMS personnel and Medivac helicopter in Hyder. **Fire Department**, phone 636-2345. **Hospital** and **Ambulance**, Stewart General (10 beds), phone 636-2221.

Visitor Information: Stewart Historical Society (Box 402, Stewart, BC V0T 1W0), museum and information centre in the old fire hall at 6th and Columbia streets; phone 636-2568.

Elevation: Sea level. **Climate:** Maritime, with warm winters and cool rainy summers. Summer temperatures range from 41°F/5°C to 57°F/14°C; winter temperatures range 25°F/-4°C to 43°F/6°C. Average temperature in January is 27°F/-3°C; in July, 67°F/19°C. Reported record high 89°F/32°C, record low -18°F/-28°C. Slightly less summer rain than other Northwest communities, but heavy snowfall in winter. **Radio:** CFPR 1450, CFMI-FM 101. **Television:** 4 channels.

Private Aircraft: Stewart airport, on 5th Street; elev. 24 feet/7m; length 3,900

STEWART ADVERTISERS

Brother's Bakery .... 5th Ave.
Hub's Pharmacy .... 5th Ave.
King Edward Motel/
    Hotel .... 5th & Columbia
Shoreline Cleaners Ltd. .... Downtown
Stewart Lions Campground &
    RV Park .... Ph. (604) 636-2537
Stewart Tourist
    Information .... Ph. (604) 636-2568

Historic mining building in downtown Stewart. (Philip and Karen Smith)

STOP at HUB'S PHARMACY
Your Health Care Centre
Complete Prescription Services
Sporting Goods & Sundries
(604) 636-2484
HOURS: Monday – Saturday
9 am - 5:30 pm / 7 pm - 9 pm
Sunday
12 noon - 4 pm
Lotto 649   Stewart, B.C.

Super, Natural North by Northwest

STEWART LIONS CAMPGROUND & RV PARK
MAY - OCTOBER
62 shaded, gravelled sites, each with firepit and picnic table • 35 sites with electrical hookup
Flush toilets, coin showers, sani-dump, public phone, horseshoe pits, tennis courts, and nature walk. Also, grass tent area, each site with picnic table and firepit.
Five minute walk from downtown.
Reservations
P.O. Box 431, Stewart, BC V0T 1W0
(604) 636-2537

STEWART, BC - GLACIER COUNTRY
Super, Natural North by Northwest
On The Alaska Border

- Campground with sani-dump and showers
- Boat launch and fishing
- Sightseeing charters
- Full visitor services
- International Days celebrations

Stewart Tourist Information
Box 402, Stewart, BC, V0T 1W0
Ph. (604) 636-2568 or 636-2251

Free Colour Brochure

Stewart, BC-Hyder, AK, Access Road Log (continued)

Thousands of pilings visible at tidewater in Hyder bear testimony to the once large size of the community. (Judy Parkin, staff)

feet/1,189m; asphalt; fuel 80, 100.

Stewart and Hyder are on a spur of the Cassiar Highway, at the head of Portland Canal, a narrow saltwater fjord approximately 90 miles/145 km long. The fjord forms a natural boundary between Alaska and Canada. Stewart has a deep harbor and boasts of being Canada's most northerly ice-free port.

The area economy has always been linked to mining, and has boomed and waned several times. The surrounding mountains and river valleys have yielded gold, silver, copper, lead, zinc and tungsten.

Prior to the coming of the white man, Nass River Indians knew the head of Portland Canal as *Skam-A-Kounst*, meaning safe place, probably referring to the place as a retreat from the harassment of the coastal Haidas. The Nass annually came here to hunt birds and pick berries. Little evidence of their presence remains.

In 1896, Captain D.D. Gaillard (after whom the Gaillard Cut in the Panama Canal was later named) explored Portland Canal for the U.S. Army Corps of Engineers. Two years after Gaillard's visit, the first prospectors and settlers arrived. Among them was D.J. Raine, for whom a creek and mountain in the area were named. The Stewart brothers arrived in 1902 and in 1905 Robert M. Stewart, the first postmaster, named the town Stewart. Hyder was first called Portland City, then renamed Hyder after a Canadian mining engineer Frederick B. Hyder, when the U.S. Postal Authority told residents there were already too many cities named Portland.

Gold and silver mining dominated the early economy. Hyder boomed with the discovery of rich silver veins in the upper Salmon River basin in 1917–18. Hundreds of pilings, which supported structures during this boom period, are visible on the tidal flats at Hyder.

Hyder became an access and supply point for the mines, while Stewart served as the centre for Canadian mining activity. Mining ceased in 1956, with the exception of the Granduc copper mine, which operated until 1984. Currently, Westmin Resources Ltd. operates a gold and silver mine.

ACCOMMODATIONS

Stewart: 3 hotels/motels, 3 restaurants, 2 grocery stores, 2 churches, service stations, dry cleaners with laundromat, pharmacy, post office, a bank (open 10 A.M. to 3 P.M. Monday through Thursday, Fridays until 6 P.M.), liquor store and other shops. Camping at Stewart Lion's Campground and RV Park; this park has washrooms with showers, 35 sites with electrical hookups, a dump station and picnic tables. ▲

Hyder: a grocery, 3 gift shops, a post office, 3 cafes, a Baptist church, a motel and 2 bars. There is no bank in Hyder.

TRANSPORTATION

Air: Ketchikan Air Service (charter) from Hyder to Ketchikan. **Bus:** Limousine service to Terrace. **Ferry:** See the Alaska state ferry schedules (Southern Panhandle) in the MARINE ACCESS ROUTES section for service between Ketchikan and Hyder. *IMPORTANT: Check ferry departure times carefully!*

ATTRACTIONS

Historic Buildings: In Stewart, the former fire hall at 6th and Columbia streets built in 1910, which now houses the Historical Society Museum and visitor

---

Shoreline Cleaners Ltd.   OPEN DAILY
CLEAN UP in our Coin-op Laundromat
Downtown Location
STEWART, BC   PHONE (604) 636-2322

BROTHERS' BAKERY
Deli • Coffee Shop • Courtyard
Full Line of Breads and Pastries
Fresh Daily • *No Preservatives*
(604) 636-2435   Stewart, BC

King Edward Motel / King Edward Hotel
70 MODERN UNITS • COFFEE SHOP • DINING ROOM
Kitchenettes • Reasonable Rates
Television • Automatic Phones
PHONE (604) 636-2244
5th & COLUMBIA STS.
BOX 86, STEWART, BC V0T 1W0
Super, Natural North by Northwest

HYDER R.V. PARKING
WATER and ELECTRIC HOOKUPS
HOT SHOWERS
Reasonable Rates   (604) 636-2708

Portland City Dining Emporium — HYDER, AK
FEATURING
Local Alaskan Seafood
Salmon ★ Halibut
Generous Portions ★ Low Prices

The GRAND VIEW INN
Hyder's Newest and Quietest
Daily and Weekly Rates • Three Kitchenettes
For Reservations and Information:
Call (604) 636-9174   or Write Box 49, Hyder, AK 99923

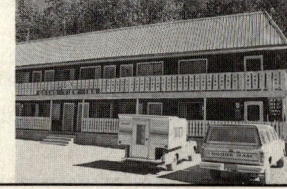

HYDER ADVERTISERS

Canal Trading Post............International St.
Grand View Inn, The ...Ph. (604) 636-9174
Hyder RV Parking ....Ph. (604) 636-2708
Mom's This-N-That Shop ..International St.
Portland City
  Dining Emporium...Ph. (604) 636-2708
Sealaska Inn ....Premier & Nevada Ave.
Yankee Trader Gas Bar ....Downtown

Place *Your* Mark in Alaska

THE SEALASKA INN OFFERS YOU THE UNIQUE OPPORTUNITY TO BECOME A PERMANENT PART OF HISTORIC HYDER, "THE FRIENDLIEST LITTLE GHOST TOWN IN ALASKA"

Order your personalized tile, professionally engraved with your NAME, TOWN, and COUNTRY – optional month/date/year. Each tile will be tastefully displayed within the Sealaska Inn complex. Your name will then be recorded in the annals of Hyder history. So whether you have been to Alaska or plan to visit, we invite you to take advantage of this offer today. A certificate of authenticity will be issued to each participant. Keep in mind these engraved tiles make novel gifts for family and friends.

Please clip and mail this order form to:

Sealaska Inn
P.O. Box 91
Hyder, AK 99923
USA

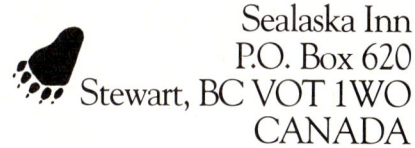

OR

Sealaska Inn
P.O. Box 620
Stewart, BC V0T 1W0
CANADA

- -

NAME	DAY PHONE	EVENING PHONE
ADDRESS		
CITY STATE	COUNTRY	ZIP
ENCLOSED IS MY CHECK FOR $ ___ U.S.	OFFICE USE ONLY	TILE NUMBER	BATCH NUMBER

PLEASE PRINT IN UPPERCASE BLOCK LETTERS. EACH SPACE COUNTS AS ONE LETTER.

TWO-LINE INSCRIPTION ❏ 6" x 6" **$45.00**   ❏ 12" x 12" **$135.00**

LINE 1
LINE 2

THREE-LINE INSCRIPTION ❏ 6" x 6" **$55.00**   ❏ 12" x 12" **$165.00**

LINE 1
LINE 2
LINE 3

Please make your check payable to Sealaska Inn drawn on U.S. funds.

CASSIAR HIGHWAY • STEWART–HYDER

Stewart, BC-Hyder, AK, Access Road Log (continued)

information centre; the Empress Hotel (now occupied by a hardware store) on 4th Street; and St. Mark's Church (built in 1910) on 9th Street at Columbia. On the border at Eagle Point is the stone storehouse built by Captain D.D. Gaillard of the U.S. Army Corps of Engineers in 1896. This is the oldest masonry building in Alaska. Originally 4 of these buildings were built to hold exploration supplies. This one was subsequently used as a cobbler shop and jail. Storehouse Nos. 3 and 4 are included on the (U.S.) National Register of Historic Places.

Stewart Historical Society Museum, in the fire hall, has a wildlife exhibit on the main floor and an exhibit of historical items on the top floor. Included is a display on movies filmed here: *Bear Island* (1978), John Carpenter's *The Thing* (1981), and *The Ice Man* (1982).

Hyder's night life is popular, and has helped Hyder earn the reputation and town motto of "The Friendliest Little Ghost Town in Alaska."

Recreation in Stewart includes winter sports at the indoor skating rink; swimming in the Paddy McNeil Memorial Swimming Pool (indoor); an outdoor tennis court; ball parks; and hiking trails.

Sightseeing tours of the area include active and abandoned mine sites and mills and spectacular glaciers. Receding glaciers have revealed old adits (mine entrances) in some areas. Also included on tours is a visit to Summit Lake at the toe of Salmon Glacier. Once a year, usually in August, the ice dam holding back the water breaks, and the force of the meltwater from Summit Lake carries ice, logs, tree stumps and other debris down the Salmon River, flooding the river valley at Hyder.

Visit the old mines. A 30-mile-long road leads to movie locations and former mine sites. *Caution is advised: The road is narrow and winding.* Access to Premier Mine, Big Missouri Mine and Salmon Glacier. Inquire at the museum in Stewart for more information.

International Days. Fourth of July begins July 1 as Stewart and Hyder celebrate Canada Day and Independence Day. There are a parade and fireworks.

Charter trips by small boat on Portland Canal and vicinity available for sightseeing and fishing. Multicolored chum or dog salmon are seen in their spawning colors in Fish Creek during August; they ascend the streams and rivers in great numbers to spawn. Visitors may photograph feeding bald eagles and black bears which are drawn to the streams by the salmon.

AREA FISHING: Portland Canal, salmon to 50 lbs., use herring, spring and late fall; coho to 12 lbs. in fall, fly-fishing. (NOTE: Alaska or British Columbia fishing license required, depending on whether you fish U.S. or Canadian waters in Portland Canal.) **Fish Creek**, up the Salmon River road from Hyder, Dolly Varden 2 to 3 lbs. on salmon eggs and lures, best in summer. Fish Creek is a fall spawning ground for some of the world's largest chum salmon; it is illegal to kill chum in fresh water in British Columbia. It is legal to harvest chum at both salt and fresh water in Alaska.

Return to Milepost J 98.5 on the Cassiar Highway

View of glacier from old mining road out of Hyder. (Joe Prax)

Yankee Trader Gas Bar
Hyder, Alaska

Friendliest Ghost Town in Alaska
5 minutes from Stewart, BC

FILL UP AT U.S. PRICES

Hyder: *Unforgetable*
- Visit Salmon Glacier
- See Fish Creek
- **Salmon and Bears**

BEST OF ALL!!!
Gasoline at Yankee Prices!

SEALASKA INN
Restaurant • Saloon
Hotel • Gift Shop
— RV PRESSURE WASHER —

Premier Ave., Hyder Alaska

P.O. Box 91
Hyder, Alaska
U.S.A. 99923

P.O. Box 620
Stewart, B.C.
Canada V0T 1W0

(604) 636-9001
FAX (604) 636-9003

GIFTS • JEWELRY • HYDER T-SHIRTS • CARDS
SCULPTURES & MACRAME SUPPLIES
SOUVENIRS • FISHING TACKLE & LICENSES
NOTARY PUBLIC

uptown hyder
Mom's THIS-N-THAT Shop
Owner Dorothy Gutierrez, Box 30, Hyder, Alaska 99923 Phone (604) 636-2449

We're not just another beautiful gift shop!
- Sporting Goods • Fishing Licenses •
- Alaska Ferry Tickets and Reservations •
- Souvenirs • Jewelry • Gold • Etc.
- Come browse and get acquainted •
- Come and see the World Record Class Walrus on display!

P.O. Box 1896 Hyder, Alaska 99923

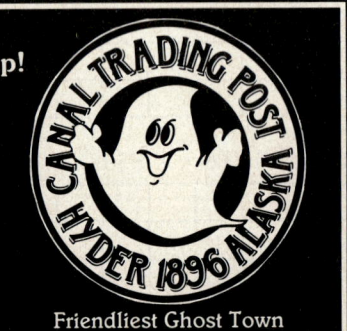

CANAL TRADING POST HYDER 1896 ALASKA

Friendliest Ghost Town in Alaska

Cassiar Highway Log

(continued from page 226)
cartop boat launch.

J 189.4 (304.8 km) **AH 266.2** (428.4 km) Kilometrepost 145.

J 194.6 (313.2 km) **AH 261** (420 km) Devil Creek Canyon bridge.

J 198 (318.6 km) **AH 257.6** (414.6 km) Highway passes through Iskut burn, where fire destroyed 78,000 acres in 1958. This is also British Columbia's largest huckleberry patch.

Northbound, the vegetation begins to change from inland valley western hemlock forest to northern boreal white and black spruce.

J 204.3 (328.8 km) **AH 251.3** (404.4 km) Durham Creek.

Northbound: Gravel begins, pavement ends.

Southbound: Gravel ends, pavement begins.

J 209.7 (337.5 km) **AH 245.9** (395.7 km) Single-lane crosses Burrage River. Note the rock pinnacle upstream.

J 210.5 (338.7 km) **AH 245.1** (394.4 km) Iskut River to west.

J 211.3 (340 km) **AH 244.3** (393.2 km) Kilometrepost 180.

J 212.5 (342 km) **AH 243.1** (391.2 km) Emergency airstrip crosses road; no stopping, watch for aircraft.

J 217.8 (350.5 km) **AH 237.8** (382.7 km) Rest area by Eastman Creek; picnic tables, outhouses, litter barrels and information sign with map and list of services in Iskut Lakes Recreation Area. The creek was named for George Eastman (of Eastman Kodak fame) who hunted big game in this area before the highway was built.

J 220.8 (355.3 km) **AH 234.8** (377.9 km) Slow down for 1-lane bridge across Rescue Creek.

J 223.1 (359.1 km) **AH 232.5** (374.2 km) **Willow Ridge Resort.** See display ad this section. ▲

J 223.4 (359.6 km) **AH 232.2** (373.7 km) Slow down for 1-lane bridge over Willow Creek.

J 226 (363.7 km) **Ah 229.6** (369.5 km) Natadesleen Lake trailhead; toilets and litter barrel. Hike 0.6 mile/1 km west to lake.

J 227.4 (366 km) **Ah 228.2** (367.2 km) Kilometrepost 205.

J 229.2 (368.9 km) **AH 226.4** (364.3 km) Snapper Creek.

J 230.5 (371 km) **AH 225.1** (362.2 km) Kilometrepost 210 reflects distance from Meziadin junction. Entrance to Kinaskan campground with 36 sites, outhouses, firewood, picnic area, drinking water and boat launch on **Kinaskan Lake**; rainbow fishing, July and August. Campground attendant on duty during summer. Start of 15-mile/24-km hiking trail to Mowdade Lake in Mount Edziza Provincial Park.

Northbound: Seal coat surfacing begins, gravel ends.

Southbound: Gravel begins, seal coat surfacing ends.

J 235.2 (378.5 km) **AH 220.4** (354.7 km) Turnout with litter barrel and view of Kinaskan Lake.

J 236.1 (380 km) **AH 219.5** (353.2 km) Small lake to east.

J 236.3 (380.3 km) **AH 219.3** (352.9 km) Kilometrepost 220.

J 238.6 (384 km) **AH 217** (349.2 km) Todagin Creek 1-lane bridge.

J 246 (395.9 km) **AH 209.6** (337.3 km) **Tatogga Lake Resort.** See display ad this section. ▲

J 246.6 (396.8 km) **AH 209** (336.3 km) Coyote Creek.

J 247.2 (397.8 km) **AH 208.4** (335.4 km) Ealue Lake (EE-lu-eh) turnoff.

J 247.3 (397.9 km) **AH 208.3** (335.2 km) Spatsizi trailhead to east.

J 248.9 (400.5 km) **Ah 206.7** (332.6 km) Kilometrepost 240.

J 249.9 (402.2 km) **AH 205.7** (331 km) Turnout beside **Eddontenajon Lake** (Eddon-TEN-ajon). Breakup in late May; freezeup early November. Rainbow fishing July and August.

J 250 (402.3 km) **AH 205.6** (330.9 km) Turnout with litter barrel.

J 252.2 (405.9 km) **AH 203.4** (327.3 km) **Iskutine Lodges**—adventure and environmental center. Specializing in low-impact wilderness use. We offer clean cabins (includes canoe use), nightly steambath,

Floatplane on Eddontenajon Lake at Milepost J 246. (Judy Parkin, staff)

WILLOW RIDGE RESORT

Long RV Pull-Throughs • Sani-Station
Water and Sewer Hookups
Picnic Table, Fire Ring • Tenting Sites
Free Dry Firewood with Every Site
Camp Cabins • Base Rate $7

MOTEL UNIT WITH KITCHENETTE
BATH, SHOWERS • CONVENIENCE STORE
LAUNDRY • SPORTING LICENSES

Horse Shoe Recreation Area
Good Sam Park - BC Approved
FM Radio - Country Western

Visa and MasterCard Accepted
Emergency Radiophone and Electricity Available
Radiophone: JJ3-7280 Meehaus/Iskut Channel
Fort Nelson Operator
Location: 52 km south of Iskut,
56 km north of Bob Quinn Highway Camp
Jack & Pearl Taylor
General Delivery, Iskut, BC V0J 1K0

TATOGGA LAKE RESORT

Esso MILE J 246 / KM 395.9

Gas • Diesel • Restaurant
Minor Repairs • Cabins
Camping • Sani-Dump
RV Park • Hookups • Pay Phone
Boat Rentals • Vehicle Shuttle
Custom Jet Boat
and Fly-in Fishing
Hunting and Sightseeing Tours

"Home of the famous
TATOGGA BURGER"

Phone:
(604) 234-3526
Write: General Delivery
Iskut, BC V0J 1K0

Super, Natural North by Northwest

rustic outhouses, beautiful campsites, excellent dock fishing, charter floatplane base, guide/outfitting services, kayaking, photographic hunting safaris. Box 39, Iskut, BC V0J 1K0. (604) 234-3456. Bicycling? First night camping free! [ADVERTISEMENT] ▲

J 253.7 (408.3 km) AH 201.9 (324.9 km) **Red Goat Lodge**, formerly High Watermark Campsite. Featuring low-density lakeshore RV sites and pull-throughs in a beautiful parklike setting. $8. Excellent rainbow trout fishing. Licenses available. Canoe rentals. $7/day for guests. Ice. In our unique lakeshore lodge we also offer a choice of bed and breakfast at $35 or European-style hostel accommodation from $10. Common kitchen and lounge with fireplace. Deluxe hot showers, laundry, flush toilets. Experience northern hospitality at its very best in immaculate surroundings. Tony and Doreen Shaw, Iskut, BC. Phone (604) 234-3261. Off-season address P.O. Box 8749, Victoria, BC V8W 3S3. Phone (604) 383-1805. [ADVERTISEMENT]

J 253.8 (408.4 km) AH 201.8 (324.8 km) **The Black Sheep Motel.** 24 modern units. Baths or showers. Discount for senior citizens. Dining room. Home-cooked meals, take-outs. Satellite TV, public phones. Gas, propane, tire and minor repairs, autoplan. Permits, hunting and fishing licenses. Agent: Trans-Provincial Airlines sightseeing tours. Fly-in hunting and fishing arrangements. Agent: Kluachon Guide Outfitters. Local guides fully licensed and experienced. Trail rides. Fishing, hunting, wilderness trips. Vehicle shuttle service. Rafters or canoeist. Expediting services. Take a rest—stay with the best. Tom and Robin Black. P.O. Box 120, Iskut, BC V0J 1K0. Phone (604) 234-3141. Super, Natural North by Northwest. [ADVERTISEMENT]

J 255.5 (411.2 km) AH 200.1 (322 km) B.C. Hydro generating plant, supplies power for Iskut area.

J 255.7 (411.5 km) AH 199.9 (321.7 km) ISKUT (pop. 300). Small Tahltan Indian community with post office, grocery store, motel and gas station. Quality beaded moccasins available locally. Camping and cabins available locally. Horse trips and river rafting may be available; inquire locally. Clinic open 1-3 p.m., 5 days a week. For a brochure on the area, write Northern Wilderness Travel Assoc., General Delivery, Iskut, BC V0J 1K0. ▲

Iskut Lake Co-op. See display ad this section.

Private Aircraft: Eddontenajon airstrip, 0.6 mile/1 km north of Iskut; elev. 3,100 feet/945m; length 3,000 feet/914m; gravel; fuel available at Trans-Provincial Airlines base south of here on Eddontenajon Lake.

J 257.5 (414.4 km) AH 198.1 (318.8 km) **A-E Guest Ranch.** Campground and RV sites in secluded parklike setting on Iskut Lake in the Cassiar Mountains with lovely glacier views. Some streamside campsites. Group parking. All sites on crushed gravel pads. Sani-dump, water and power. Excellent lake fishing. See display ad for contact information. [ADVERTISEMENT] ▲

J 258.2 (415.6 km) AH 197.4 (317.7 km) Kilometrepost 255 reflects distance from Meziadin junction.

J 261 (420 km) AH 194.6 (313.2 km) **Bear-Paw Ranch Resort Hotel.** See display ad this section.

J 261.6 (421 km) AH 194 (312.2 km) Kilometrepost 260 reflects distance from Meziadin junction.

J 261.8 (421.3 km) AH 193.8 (311.9 km) **Trappers Souvenirs.** See display ad this section.

J 263.5 (424 km) AH 192.1 (309.1 km) **Forty Mile Flats.** See display ad this section. ▲

J 266.7 (429.2 km) AH 188.9 (304 km) Turnout with litter barrels to west. From here the dormant volcano of Mount Edziza (elev. 9,143 feet/2,787m) and its adjunct cinder cone can be seen to the southwest. The park, not accessible by road, is a rugged wilderness with cinder cones, craters and lava flows. Panoramic view of Skeena and Cassiar mountains for next several miles northbound.

J 269 (433 km) AH 186.6 (300.3 km) Northbound: Gravel begins, seal coat ends.
Southbound: Gravel ends, seal coat begins.

J 271.8 (438.4 km) AH 183.8 (295.8 km) Turnout with litter barrel to west. Wild raspberry patch beside rest area.

J 273.8 (440.6 km) AH 181.8 (292.6 km) Hairpin turn: Keep to right.

J 275.2 (442.9 km) AH 180.4 (290.3 km) Turnout with litter barrels and toilets to west. Tourist map and services directory for Iskut Lakes Recreation Area located here.

J 275.6 (443.5 km) AH 180 (289.7 km) Stikine River bridge.

J 277.2 (446.1 km) AH 178.4 (287.1 km) Kilometrepost 285 reflects distance from Meziadin junction.

J 277.4 (446.4 km) AH 178.2 (286.8 km) Turnout to east with litter barrel.

J 286.6 (461.2 km) AH 169 (272 km) Kilometrepost 300 reflects distance from Meziadin junction.

J 290.1 (466.9 km) AH 165.5 (266.3 km) Northbound: Seal coat begins, gravel ends.
Southbound: Gravel begins, seal coat ends.

J 290.7 (476.8 km) AH 164.9 (265.4 km) Turnout on Upper Gnat Lake; tables, toilets, litter barrels. Long scar across Gnat Pass valley to the east is grading preparation for B.C. Railway's proposed Dease Lake exten-

---

A-E GUEST RANCH

CAMPGROUND • HOT SHOWERS INCLUDED
Government Approved
RV Parking • Modern Cabins • Tenting
Sani-Station • Quality Fishing • Corral Rental
Your Hosts
Al & Elaine Adams
Highway 37, Iskut, BC, V0J 1K0
Radiophone YJ37445 (Fort Nelson operator)
Ask for Mehaus channel

Iskut Lake Co-op

GROCERIES • DRY GOODS • GAS

Summer Hours: Mon.-Sat. 8 a.m.-9 p.m.
Sunday 9 a.m.-5 p.m.
Winter Hours: Mon.-Fri. 9 a.m.-12 noon
1 p.m.-5 p.m.
Saturday 1 p.m.-5 p.m.

(604) 234-3241
Iskut, BC V0J 1K0

BEAR-PAW RANCH

Boat Tours • Hiking
Photography • Fishing
Gold Panning • Trails Rides

RESORT HOTEL

Guest Cabins from $35
Bear Paw Ranch
General Delivery, Iskut, BC V0J 1K0
Radio Tele: 2M3-858   Meehous Ch.
Super, Natural Scenic Adventure

RED GOAT LODGE

Bed & Breakfast Hostel Accommodations
CAMPING • RV SITES • FULLY APPROVED
Showers • Laundry • Fishing Licenses • Ice • Canoe Rentals
(604) 234-3261   VISA Accepted

TRAPPERS SOUVENIRS - ISKUT
Reasonable Prices
Gold Nugget & Jade Jewelry
Wild Furs • Fur Hats & Mitts
Antlers • Wood Clocks
TRAPPERS CABINS FOR RENT $28

Stop In and Chat with Trapper Lorraine Charette

Cafe • Campground • Cabins
Hot Showers • Sani-Dump
Power Hookups • Water on Tap
Car Wash
DIESEL and UNLEADED GAS • Towing
Tire Repair • Welding • Mechanic

Phone MOBILE RADIO YJ36205
Registered in Fort Nelson
Mehaus Channel

The Frocklage Family

FORTY MILE FLATS

sion from Prince George. Construction was halted in 1977. Railway grade is visible for several miles northbound.

J 292.3 (470.4 km) **AH 163.3** (262.8 km) Turnout overlooking **Lower Gnat Lake**, abundant rainbow.

J 292.8 (471.2 km) **AH 162.8** (262 km) Kilometrepost 310 reflects distance from Meziadin junction.

J 295.3 (475.3 km) **AH 160.3** (258 km) Gnat Pass Summit.

J 296 (476.3 km) **AH 159.6** (256.8 km) Kilometrepost 315 reflects distances from Meziadin junction.

J 301.9 (485.8 km) **AH 153.7** (247.3 km) One-lane bridge across **Tanzilla River**. Pleasant rest area with picnic tables and outhouses at south end of bridge beside river. Fishing for grayling to 16 inches, June and July, use flies.

J 303.2 (487.9 km) **AH 152.4** (245.3 km) Dalby Creek.

J 305.3 (491.3 km) **AH 150.3** (241.9 km) Kilometrepost 330 reflects distance from Meziadin junction.

J 306.9 (493.9 km) **AH 148.7** (239.3 km) Divide (elev. 2,690 feet/820m) between Pacific and Arctic ocean watersheds.

J 307.7 (495.2 km) **AH 147.9** (238 km) **Junction** with Telegraph Creek Road and access to Dease Lake (description follows). See TELEGRAPH CREEK ROAD log on page 234.

Dease Lake

Located just west of the Cassiar Highway. **Emergency Services:** RCMP detachment. **Private Aircraft:** Dease Lake airstrip, 1.5 miles/2.4 km south; elev. 2,600 feet/793m; length 6,000 feet/1,829m; asphalt; fuel JP4, 100.

Dease Lake has motels, gas stations (with regular, unleaded, diesel, propane and minor repairs), food stores, restaurant, a post office, highway maintenance centre and government offices. There are charter flights and regular air connections to Terrace and Smithers.

A Hudson's Bay Co. post was established by Robert Campbell at Dease Lake in 1838, but abandoned a year later. The lake was named in 1834 by John McLeod of the Hudson's Bay Co. for Chief Factor Peter Warren Dease. Laketon, on the west side of the lake (see Milepost J 334.6), was a centre for boat building during the Cassiar gold rush of 1872-80. In 1874, William Moore, following an old Indian trail, cut a trail from Telegraph Creek on the Stikine River to the gold rush settlement on Dease Lake. This trail became Telegraph Creek Road, which was used in 1941 to haul supplies for Alaska Highway construction to Dease Lake, where they were ferried down the Dease River to U.S. troops working on the highway.

DEASE LAKE ADVERTISERS

Bonnie & Clyde's Hideout .Ph. (604) 771-4242
Dease Lake Esso............Dease Lake Access Rd.
Food Master Store............Ph. (604) 771-4381
Northway Motor Inn ....Ph. (604) 771-5341
South Dease Service Ltd...Ph. (604) 771-4381
The Trapper's Den
   Gift Shoppe ....Ph. (604) 771-3224

BONNIE AND CLYDE'S HIDEOUT
CAFE, COIN LAUNDRY AND FEED STORE

We're small...not fancy...But we're good.

One block from main highway. Easy access and parking for RVs.
Your hosts, Bonnie and Clyde Dion

OPEN DAILY
(604) 771-4242

South Dease Service, Ltd.
(604) 771-4381
FOOD MASTER STORE

FULL LINE GROCERY PRODUCTS including:
Fresh Produce, Dairy, Deli
Fresh Meats, In-store Bakery

Open 7 Days a Week   9 a.m. - 9 p.m. Summer
                     9 a.m. - 7 p.m. Winter
                     10 a.m. - 7 p.m. Sundays and Holidays

PETRO-CANADA
REGULAR
UNLEADED
DIESEL

Dease Lake Esso
Operating under D.J. Phillips Services (1989)

Gas • Diesel • Minor Repairs • Welding • Mechanic

*Can arrange towing
Also fly-in-fishing, hunting and flightseeing*

General Delivery,
Dease Lake V0C 1L0   **(604) 771-3810**

Super, Natural North by Northwest

NORTHWAY MOTOR INN

VISA MasterCard

We are Cassiar Highway 37's NEWEST Accommodation

Clean and Modern Rooms   **Satellite TV**
Phones in Every Room   **Winter Plug-Ins**
Vehicle Storage   **Kitchenettes**

Your base for some great wilderness recreation

(604) 771-5341 — Or Write:

Super, Natural North by Northwest

Dease Lake, BC, V0C 1L0

1992 ■ The MILEPOST®

Today, Dease Lake is a government centre and supply point for the district. The community has dubbed itself the "jade capital of the province." Jade is available locally. It is a popular point from which to fly in to Mount Edziza and Spatsizi wilderness parks or pack in by horse.

The Trapper's Den Gift Shoppe. Canadian and British Columbia gift items ranging from fine jade and rhodonite to locally crafted Indian moccasins and quality BC cottage crafts. Visit "The Trapper" in "his cabin" in the store, surrounded by his collection of local furs. Just off the highway at the turnoff for Telegraph Creek. VISA accepted. General Delivery, Dease Lake, BC V0C 1L0. (604) 771-3224. [ADVERTISEMENT]

Cassiar Highway Log

(continued)

J 307.7 (495.2 km) **AH 147.9** (238 km) **Dease Lake Junction.** Junction with access road to Dease Lake and Telegraph Creek Road (see log this page).

J 308.2 (496 km) **AH 147.4** (237.2 km) Turnout with interpretive signs on Telegraph Creek and Stikine Recreation Area.

J 310.9 (500.3 km) **AH 144.7** (232.9 km) Kilometrepost 5 reflects distance from Dease Lake junction.

J 314 (505.3 km) **AH 141.6** (227.9 km) Kilometrepost 10 reflects distance from Dease Lake junction.

J 315.8 (508.2 km) **AH 139.8** (225 km) Turnout with litter barrel.

J 316.6 (509.5 km) **AH 139** (223.7 km) Serpentine Creek.

J 317.1 (510.3 km) **AH 138.5** (222.9 km) Seal coat ends northbound, gravel begins and extends 16.4 miles/26.4 km. Seal coat begins southbound and extends to Iskut.

J 323.4 (520.4 km) **AH 132.2** (212.7 km)

Telegraph Creek Road Log

Built in 1922, this was the first road in the vast Cassiar area of northern British Columbia. The scenery is remarkable and the town of Telegraph Creek is a picture from the turn of the century. *CAUTION: Telegraph Creek Road has some steep narrow sections and several sets of steep switchbacks; it is not recommended for trailers or large RVs. However, people in cars and campers who are familiar with mountain driving should have no difficulty. DRIVE CAREFULLY! Use caution when road is wet or icy. Very slippery when wet. Watch for rocks and mud.* There are no visitor facilities en route. Allow about 2 hours driving time with good conditions. Check road conditions at highway maintenance camp or RCMP office in Dease Lake before starting the 74 miles/119 km to Telegraph Creek. According to a Telegraph Creek resident, weather varies considerably: It may be raining in Dease Lake, but clear and sunny in Telegraph Creek. You may phone the Riversong Cafe (235-3196) for weather and road conditions.

Distance from Dease Lake junction (D) on the Cassiar Highway is shown.

D 0 **Dease Lake junction, Milepost J 307.7** Cassiar Highway.

D 0.9 (1.4 km) **Junction** with road to Dease Lake. Turn left for Telegraph Creek.

D 1.1 (1.7 km) Entrance to airport.

D 3.4 (5.4 km) Pavement ends, gravel begins westbound.

D 5 (8 km) Entering Tanzilla Plateau.

D 8 (12.9 km) Tatsho Creek (Eightmile).

D 17.4 (28 km) Augustchilde Creek, 1-lane bridge.

D 19.1 (30.7 km) 19 Mile Creek.

D 19.7 (31.7 km) 22 Mile Creek.

D 36 (57.9 km) Cariboo Meadows. Entering old burn area for 12 miles/19.3 km.

D 37 (59.5 km) Halfway point to Telegraph Creek from Dease Lake. Old road diverges left to follow Tanzilla River and rejoins at **Milepost D 48**.

D 39 (62.8 km) To the southwest the cone of Mount Edziza is visible.

D 48 (77.2 km) End of burn. Old road joins from left.

D 49 (78.9 km) Road enters small canyon,

D 52 (83.7 km) Tuya River bridge.

D 55 (88.5 km) Day's Ranch on left.

D 58 (93.3 km) Road runs through lava beds, on narrow promontory about 50 feet/15m wide, dropping 400 feet/122m on each side to Tahltan and Stikine rivers. Sudden 180-degree right turn begins steep descent to Tahltan River and Indian fishing camps. Excellent views of Grand Canyon of the Stikine and Tahltan Canyon can be seen by walking a short distance across lava beds to promontory point. Best views of the river canyon are by flightseeing trip. The Stikine River canyon is only 8 feet/2.5m wide at its narrowest point.

D 60 (96.6 km) Tahltan River bridge. Traditional communal Indian smokehouses adjacent road at bridge. Smokehouse on north side of bridge is operated by a commercial fisherman; fresh and smoked salmon sold. There is a commercial inland fishery on the Stikine River, one of only a few such licensed operations in Canada.

D 61 (98.2 km) Start of very narrow road on ledge rising steeply up the wall of the Stikine Canyon for 3 miles/4.8 km, rising to 400 feet/122m above the river.

D 64 (102 km) Old Tahltan Indian community above road. Private property: No trespassing! Former home of Tahltan bear dogs. The Tahltan bear dog, believed to be extinct, was only about a foot high and weighed about 15 pounds. Shorthaired, with oversize ears and shaving-brush tail, the breed was recognized by the Canadian Kennel Club. First seen by explorer Samuel Black in 1824, the dogs were used to hunt bears; barking persistently and darting in and out too fast to be hurt by the bear, the dogs would keep the bear at bay until the hunter arrived.

D 65 (104.6 km) Ninemile homestead cabins.

D 66 (106.2 km) Eightmile Creek bridge. Spectacular falls into canyon on left below. Opposite the gravel pit at the top of the hill there is a trailhead and parking.

D 73 (117.5 km) Indian community. Road follows steep winding descent into old town, crossing a deep narrow canyon via a short bridge. Excellent picture spot 0.2 mile/0.3 km from bridge. Glenora Road **junction** on right.

D 74 (119.1 km) **TELEGRAPH CREEK** (pop. 300; elev. 1,100 feet/335m). Former head of navigation on the Stikine and once a telegraph communication terminal. An important centre during the gold rush days on the Telegraph trail to the Atlin and Klondike goldfields, and also during construction of the Alaska Highway.

There are a cafe, lodge, general store, post office, and a public school and nursing station here. Gas is available. Stikine River trips and charter flights are available.

Residents here make their living fishing commercially for salmon, doing local construction work and guiding visitors on hunting, fishing and river trips. Telegraph Creek is becoming a jumping-off point for wilderness hikers headed for Mount Edziza Provincial Park. This is also a significant agricultural area with extensive ranches. Surplus hay is exported from the valley.

The scenic view along the main street bordering the river has scarcely changed since gold rush days. The turn-of-the-century Hudson's Bay post, which now houses the Riversong Cafe, is a designated Heritage building. Historic St. Aidan's Church (Anglican) is also located here.

A 12-mile/19-km road continues west to Glenora, site of attempted railroad route to the Yukon and limit of larger riverboat navigation. There are 2 primitive B.C. Forest Service campsites on the road to Glenora. Several spur roads lead to the Stikine River and to Native fish camps. ▲

Stikine Riversong Cafe, Lodge and General Store. Located in lower town on the riverbank. Former Hudson's Bay store from turn of the century now a renovated B.C. Heritage building. Open 7 days a week all year long, 11 A.M. until 7 P.M. Delicious home-cooked meals, rooms, groceries, hardware, camping supplies, gas and petroleum supplies. Centre for river trips and information. Boat charters to Wrangell and Petersburg, AK. Contact Stikine Riversong, Telegraph Creek, BC V0J 2W0. Phone (604) 235-3196. Super, Natural North by Northwest. [ADVERTISEMENT]

Return to Milepost J 307.7 Cassiar Highway

View of the Stikine River about midway point on Telegraph Creek Road. (Rollo Pool, staff)

Halfmoon Creek. Kilometrepost 25 reflects distance from Dease Lake junction.

J 326 (524.6 km) **AH 129.6** (208.6 km) Rest area with picnic tables, litter barrels and outhouses. View of Dease Lake.

J 326.5 (525.4 km) **AH 129.1** (207.8 km) Kilometrepost 30 reflects distance from Dease Lake junction.

J 329.6 (530.4 km) **AH 126** (202.8 km) Kilometrepost 35 reflects distance from Dease Lake junction.

J 330.2 (531.4 km) **AH 125.4** (201.8 km) Turnout with litter barrels to west.

J 331.4 (533.4 km) **AH 124.2** (199.9 km) Black Creek.

J 332.7 (535.4 km) **AH 122.9** (197.8 km) Kilometrepost 40 reflects distance from Dease Lake junction.

J 333.5 (536.7 km) **AH 122.1** (196.5 km) Pavement begins northbound and extends to end of highway at Alaska Highway junction; watch for gravel breaks and new road construction. Pavement ends southbound, gravel begins and extends 16.4 miles/26.4 km.

J 333.6 (536.9 km) **AH 122** (196.3 km) Side road leads west to **Dease Lake** for fishing. Lake trout to 30 lbs., use spoons, plugs, spinners, June to October, deep trolling in summer, spin casting in fall.

J 334.6 (538.5 km) **AH 121** (194.7 km) The site of the ghost town, Laketon, lies across the lake at the mouth of Dease Creek. Laketon was the administrative centre for the district during the Cassiar gold rush (1872-80). Boat building was a major activity along the lake during the gold rush years, with miners heading up various creeks and rivers off the lake in search of gold.

J 335.3 (539.6 km) **AH 120.3** (193.6 km) Dorothy Creek.

J 336.5 (541.5 km) **AH 119.1** (191.7 km) Kilometrepost 45 reflects distance from Dease Lake junction.

J 337.6 (543.3 km) **AH 118** (189.9 km) Beady Creek. Entering the Cassiar Mountains northbound.

J 339 (545.5 km) **AH 116.6** (187.6 km) Kilometrepost 50 reflects distance from Dease Lake junction.

J 339.2 (545.8 km) **AH 116.4** (187.3 km) Turnout to west with litter barrels.

J 340.9 (548.6 km) **AH 114.7** (184.6 km) Turnout with litter barrel to west. **Dease River** parallels the highway. Grayling to 17 inches; Dolly Varden and lake trout to 15 lbs.; northern pike 8 to 10 lbs., May through September.

J 341.9 (550.2 km) **AH 113.7** (183 km) Packer Tom Creek, named for a well-known Indian who lived in this area.

J 342.1 (550.5 km) **AH 113.5** (182.7 km) Kilometrepost 55 reflects distance from Dease Lake junction.

J 343.6 (552.9 km) **AH 112** (180.2 km) Elbow Lake.

J 345.2 (555.6 km) **AH 110.4** (177.7 km) Kilometrepost 60 reflects distance from Dease Lake junction.

J 349.4 (562.3 km) **AH 106.2** (170.9 km) Grassy turnout beside Pyramid Creek.

J 350 (563.3 km) **AH 105.6** (169.9 km) Dease River 1-lane wooden deck bridge.

J 351.4 (565.5 km) **Ah 104.2** (167.7 km) Beale Creek and Kilometrepost 70.

J 353.7 (569.2 km) **AH 101.9** (164 km) Look for an eagle's nest in a cottonwood tree to the east.

J 354.5 (570.5 km) **AH 101.1** (162.7 km) Turnout beside **Pine Tree Lake**. Good grayling and lake char fishing.

J 355 (571.3 km) **AH 100.6** (161.9 km) Turnout with litter barrels beside Pine Tree Lake.

J 357.8 (575.8 km) **AH 97.8** (157.4 km) Kilometrepost 80 reflects distance from Dease Lake junction.

J 359.1 (577.9 km) **AH 96.5** (155.3 km) Burn area. An abandoned campfire started the fire in July 1982.

J 360.5 (580.2 km) **AH 95.1** (153 km) **Mighty Moe's Place.** Home of the world famous "five minute—one hour show" and listen to the tall tales of Mighty Moe. Rustic campground $7 per night. Free showers and coffee for guests. Boats, motors and canoes for rent. Fishing tackle, some confections and convenience foods for sale. Fishing and canoe trips arranged from 6 miles to 180 miles on the historic Dease River, between Dease Lake and Lower Post. Come as a stranger, leave as a friend. Home is where you hang your hat. For information and reservations, write to Mighty Moe at Box 212, Cassiar, BC, Canada V0C 1E0. [ADVERTISEMENT]

J 366 (589 km) **AH 89.6** (144.2 km) **Cottonwood River** bridge; rest area 0.4 mile/0.6 km west on old highway on south side of river. Fishing for grayling and whitefish. Early summer runs of Dolly Varden.

J 366.2 (589.3 km) **AH 89.4** (143.9 km) Cottonwood River rest area No. 2 is 0.5 mile/0.9 km west on old highway on north side of river.

J 371.7 (598.2 km) **AH 83.9** (135 km) Turnout to west beside **Simmons Lake**; picnic tables, picnic shelter, toilets, small beach and dock. Fishing for lake trout.

J 373.4 (600.9 km) **AH 82.2** (132.3 km) Road runs on causeway between Twin Lakes.

J 375 (603.5 km) **AH 80.6** (129.7 km) Lang Lake and creek. Needlepoint Mountain visible straight ahead southbound.

J 375.6 (604.4 km) **AH 80** (128.7 km) **Vines Lake**, named for bush pilot Lionel Vines; fishing for lake trout.

J 376.6 (606 km) **AH 79** (127.1 km) Kilometrepost 110.

J 378.2 (608.6 km) **AH 77.4** (124.6 km) Erickson gold mine visible on slopes to east. The mine is closed and reclamation is under way.

J 378.7 (609.4 km) **AH 76.9** (123.8 km) Side road east leads down to McDame Lake.

J 379.1 (610.1 km) **AH 76.5** (123.1 km) Trout Line Creek.

J 379.3 (610.4 km) **AH 76.3** (122.8 km) **JADE CITY** (pop. 12), named for the jade deposits found to the east of the highway community. The huge jade boulders visitors can see being cut here are from the Princess Jade Mine, 82 miles/132 km east, one of the largest jade claims in the world.

J 379.5 (610.7 km) **AH 76.1** (122.5 km) **Princess Jade Mines and Store.** See display ad this section.

J 380.6 (612.5 km) **AH 75** (120.7 km) **Cassiar junction.** Take a sharp turn to west for the Cassiar Road which leads 9.7 miles/15.7 km to the Cassiar Asbestos Mine and community of Cassiar. Continue straight ahead for Alaska Highway.

Cassiar

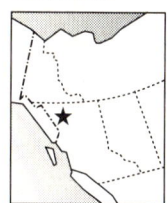

9.7 miles/15.7 km west of junction at **Milepost J 380.6** on the Cassiar Highway. **Population:** 1,000. **Emergency Services: RCMP** and public **hospital. Elevation:** 3,500 feet/1,067m. **Radio:** CBC 1340; Toronto, Edmonton and Vancouver FM stations via cable. **Television:** Channel 7; Channels 2, 3, 4, 5, 6, 9 and 10 via cable.

A company town of Cassiar Mining Corp., Cassiar has a gas station with regular

Jade City

PRINCESS JADE MINES AND STORE

Watch boulder cutting on property
Huge selection of jade gifts
Raw jade sold by pound or ton
Gold nuggets and local crafts

40 level unserviced RV sites on crushed gravel.
Free water and sani-dump for patrons.

1 mile south of junction to Cassiar
Phone (604) 2M3536 (Cassiar Channel)
Box 208, CASSIAR, BC V0C 1E0

Super, Natural North by Northwest

and unleaded gas and repair service; post office, bank (open weekdays), liquor store, video store, Sears, travel service, government agent's office, a curling rink and other sports facilities for town and area residents. Fishing licenses are sold locally. Private businesses in town include 2 restaurants, a lounge, motel and grocery. The nearest campground is at Boya Lake Provincial Park at **Milepost J 402.2** on the Cassiar Highway.

There is bus service 3 times weekly from Cassiar to Watson Lake, connecting with daily jet flights to Whitehorse, YT, or Edmonton, AB, and Vancouver, BC.

Look up the tramline to see the asbestos mine, 3 miles/4.8 km away at the 6,500-foot/1,981-m level on McDame Mountain. Recent investment in development here will move the mining operations underground. The large grass-covered mine waste pile at the entrance to town will eventually be re-milled to recover any remaining asbestos. Much of the world's high-grade chrysotile asbestos comes from Cassiar. It is shipped by container truck south on the Cassiar Highway to the port of Stewart, and from there to Vancouver. The yellow Arrow container trucks also transport fuel from Stewart to Cassiar, hauling the asbestos on the return trip.

The Cassiar Shopping Centre is located 14 km west of the junction of the Stewart–Cassiar Highway and the Cassiar Road. The shopping centre has a full selection of fresh meats and produce. It stocks groceries, a selection of hardware, sporting goods and camping gear. The store carries a good selection of souvenirs and gifts. It serves as the primary general store in Cassiar and the surrounding area. Store hours: Monday to Friday, 10 A.M. to 6 P.M., Saturday 10 A.M. to 1 P.M. (604) 778-7668. [ADVERTISEMENT]

JUNCTION 37 SERVICES
Mile 649 Alaska Hwy.   Phone (403) 536-2794

GAS — DIESEL — PROPANE
Mechanical Repairs • Welding • Towing • Tires

MOTEL • CAFE
STORE with Groceries & Souvenirs

RV PARK • Full Hookups • FREE RV Dumping
Camping - Showers - Laundromat - Car Wash - Ice

B.C. and Yukon Fishing Licenses For Sale
OPEN YEAR ROUND
See Our Full Color Ad on the Alaska Highway Section

The Management and Staff of the

CASSIAR SHOPPING CENTRE

Wish you a safe and enjoyable journey through the North.

For an experience in Northern Shopping, visit us in Cassiar.

Monday to Friday: 10 a.m. to 6 p.m.
Saturday: 10 a.m. to 1 p.m.
Phone: (604) 778-7668

Cassiar Highway Log

(continued)

J 380.6 (612.5 km) **AH 75** (120.7 km) Cassiar junction. *CAUTION: Watch for asbestos trucks.*

J 380.8 (612.8 km) **AH 74.8** (120.4 km) Snow Creek. Gravel turnout with litter barrel to east.

J 381.6 (614.1 km) **AH 74** (119.1 km) Deep Creek.

J 382.8 (616.1 km) **AH 72.8** (117.2 km) Kilometrepost 120 reflects distance from Dease Lake junction.

J 385 (619.6 km) **AH 70.6** (113.6 km) No. 3 North Fork Creek. Placer gold mining operation visible east of highway.

J 386.4 (621.9 km) **AH 69.2** (111.4 km) No. 2 North Fork Creek.

J 388.9 (625.9 km) **AH 66.7** (107.3 km) Settling ponds from placer operation visible on east side of highway.

J 389.3 (626.5 km) **AH 66.3** (106.7 km) Historic plaque about Cassiar gold.

J 389.5 (626.8 km) **AH 66.1** (106.4 km) **CENTREVILLE** (pop. 2; elev. 2,600 feet/792m), a former gold rush town of 3,000, was founded and named by miners for its central location between Sylvester's Landing (later McDame Post) at the junction of McDame Creek with the Dease River, and Quartzrock Creek, the upstream limit of pay gravel on McDame Creek. A miner named Alfred Freeman washed out the biggest all gold (no quartz) nugget ever found in British Columbia on a claim near Centreville in 1877; it weighed 72 ounces. Active mining in area.

J 393.9 (633.9 km) **AH 61.7** (99.3 km) **GOOD HOPE LAKE** (pop. 100), Indian village with grocery store and gas pump.

Turn east on Bush Road and drive 9 miles/14.5 km for **McDAME POST**, an early Hudson's Bay post, at the **confluence of Dease River and McDame Creek**. Good fishing and hunting here.

J 395.4 (636.3 km) **AH 60.2** (96.9 km) Turnout to east alongside Aeroplane Lake.

J 396.3 (637.7 km) **AH 59.3** (95.4 km) Dry Creek.

J 398 (640.5 km) **AH 57.6** (92.7 km) Mud Lake to east.

J 402.2 (647.3 km) **AH 53.4** (85.9 km) Turnout with litter barrels at entrance to **Boya Lake** Provincial Park. The park is 1.6 miles/2.5 km east of highway; 45 campsites, picnic area on lakeshore, boat launch, drinking water, firewood and swimming. Fishing for lake char, whitefish, grayling and burbot. Attendant on duty during summer.

J 402.3 (647.4 km) **AH 53.3** (85.8 km) Turnout. Horseranch Range may be seen on the eastern horizon northbound. These mountains date back to the Cambrian period, or earlier, and are the oldest in northern British Columbia. According to the Canadian Geological Survey, this area contains numerous permatites with crystals of tourmaline, garnet, feldspar, quartz and beryl. Road crosses Baking Powder Creek and then follows Dease River.

J 402.5 (647.7 km) **AH 53.1** (85.5 km) Kilometrepost 150.

J 408 (656.6 km) **AH 47.6** (76.6 km) Beaverdam Creek.

J 409 (658.2 km) **AH 46.6** (75 km) Rest area with visitor information sign to west.

J 410 (659.8 km) **AH 45.6** (73.4 km) Leaving Cassiar Mountains, entering Yukon Plateau, northbound.

J 411.7 (662.5 km) **AH 43.9** (70.6 km) Baking Powder Creek. Kilometrepost 165.

J 414.8 (667.5 km) **AH 40.8** (65.6 km) Kilometrepost 170 reflects distance from Dease Lake junction.

J 419.7 (675.4 km) **AH 35.9** (57.8 km) Side road leads east down to lake.

J 420.1 (676 km) **AH 35.5** (57.1 km) French Creek 1-lane wooden deck bridge.

J 426.4 (686.2 km) **AH 29.2** (47.1 km) Twentyeight Mile Creek. Cassiar Mountains rise to the south.

J 429.3 (690.9 km) **AH 26.3** (42.3 km) Wheeler Lake to west.

J 429.9 (691.9 km) **AH 25.7** (41.3 km) Kilometrepost 195 reflects distance from Dease Lake junction.

J 434.5 (699.3 km) **AH 21.1** (34 km) Begin construction of rerouted road northbound (1991).

J 435.3 (700.5 km) **AH 20.3** (32.7 km) Blue River 2-lane concrete bridge.

J 435.5 (700.9 km) **AH 20.1** (32.3 km) End road construction northbound.

J 438.7 (706 km) **AH 16.9** (27.2 km) Turnout at **Blue Lakes**; picnicking and fishing for pike and grayling.

J 449.6 (723.5 km) **AH 6.2** (10 km) Turnout with litter barrels beside Cormier Creek.

J 451.2 (726.1 km) **AH 4.4** (7.1 km) Begin construction of rerouted road northbound (1991).

J 453.5 (729.8 km) **AH 2** (3.2 km) Informal turnout to west at BC–YT border, 60th parallel.

End of road construction northbound.

J 454.9 (732.1 km) **AH 0.7** (1.2 km) **Albert Creek**. Good grayling fishing. Yukon Territory fishing license required.

J 455 (732.3 km) **Ah 0.6** (1 km) High Lake to east.

J 455.6 (733.2 km) **AH 0** Junction of Cassiar Highway with Alaska Highway. Gas, store, campground, propane, towing and car repair at junction. Turn left for Whitehorse, right for Watson Lake, 13.6 miles/21.9 km southeast. Watson Lake is the nearest major community.

Junction 37 Services. See display ad this section.

Turn to **Milepost DC 626.2** in the ALASKA HIGHWAY section for log of Alaska Highway from this junction.

Southbound travelers on the Cassiar note: Pavement extends south to Dease Lake junction, but watch for gravel breaks and road construction.

KLONDIKE LOOP

Alaska Highway Junction to Taylor Highway Junction via Dawson City, Yukon Territory
Yukon Highways 2 and 9
(See maps, pages 238–239)

The Klondike Loop refers to the 327-mile-/526-km-long stretch of the Klondike Highway (Yukon Highway 2) from its junction with the Alaska Highway north of Whitehorse to Dawson City; the 65-mile/105-km Top of the World Highway; and 109 miles/175 km of the Taylor Highway.

All of the Klondike Highway between the Alaska Highway junction and Dawson City is asphalt-surfaced, although there may be a few short sections undergoing improvement and repaving. Watch for road construction.

CAUTION: Watch for ore trucks south from Carmacks. Yukon Alaska Transport trucks, each carrying up to 50 tons of lead-zinc concentrates, operate between Faro on the Campbell Highway and the port of Skagway on the south Klondike Highway. Depending on production levels at the Faro mine, these 8-axle vehicles may travel the highway at the rate of one every 40 minutes. The trucks are 8½ feet wide and 85 feet long. Drive with your headlights on.

The Top of the World Highway (Yukon Highway 9) is a gravel road with some hills; a truly scenic route, but slippery in wet weather with some steep grades and winding sections. Drive with your headlights on. The Taylor Highway (Alaska Route 5) is a narrow, gravel road with some steep, winding sections and washboard. (For a detailed log of the Taylor Highway, see the TAYLOR HIGHWAY section.) Both the Taylor and Top of the World highways are closed in winter. Klondike Highway 2 is open year-round.

Alaska-bound motorists may turn off the Alaska Highway north of Whitehorse; follow the Klondike Highway to Dawson City; ferry across the Yukon River at Dawson; drive west via the Top of the World Highway into Alaska; then take the Taylor Highway south back to the Alaska Highway near Tok. Total driving distance is 502 miles/807 km. (Driving distance from Whitehorse to Tok via the Alaska Highway is approximately 396 miles/637 km.)

Travelers planning to make this loop should be aware that the Top of the World Highway (reached by ferry from Dawson City) may not open until late spring. Also, customs stations are open in summer only, 12 hours a day: 8 A.M. to 8 P.M., Alaska time, and 9 A.M. to 9 P.M. Pacific time. Travelers should also keep in mind the currency exchange when they cross the border. Exchange your money at a bank.

The highway between Skagway and the Alaska Highway, sometimes referred to as the South Klondike, is also designated Klondike Highway 2 (see KLONDIKE HIGHWAY 2 section for log of that road).

Kilometreposts along the highway to Dawson City reflect distance from Skagway. Driving distance was measured in miles from the junction of the Alaska Highway to Dawson City by our field editor. These mileages were converted into kilometres with the exception of the kilometre distance following Skagway (S). That figure reflects the physical location of the kilometrepost and is not necessarily an accurate conversion of the mileage figure.

The route from Whitehorse to Dawson City began as a trail used by miners and trappers at the turn of the century. Steamships also provided passenger service between Whitehorse and Dawson City. A road was built connecting the Alaska Highway with the United Keno Hill Mine at Mayo in 1950. By 1955, the Mayo Road had been upgraded for automobile traffic and extended to Dawson City. In 1960, the last of 3 steel bridges was completed, crossing the Yukon, Pelly and Stewart rivers. The only ferry crossing remaining is the Yukon River crossing at Dawson City. Mayo Road (Yukon Highway 11) from Stewart Crossing to Mayo, Elsa and Keno was redesignated the Silver Trail in 1985 (see SILVER TRAIL section for road log).

Emergency medical services: Available at Whitehorse, Carmacks, Mayo and Dawson City on the Yukon portion of the highway.

Klondike Loop Log

YUKON HIGHWAY 2
This section of the log shows distance from junction with the Alaska Highway (J) followed by distance from Dawson City (D) and distance from Skagway (S). Physical kilometreposts show distance from Skagway.

J 0 D 327.2 (526.5 km) S 119.2 (191.8 km) Junction with the Alaska Highway.

J 0.6 (1 km) D 326.6 (525.5 km) S 119.8 (192.8 km) Road west to McPherson subdivision.

J 1 (1.6 km) D 326.2 (525 km) S 120.2 (193.4 km) Ranches, farms and livestock next 20 miles/32 km northbound.

J 2.3 (3.7 km) D 324.9 (522.9 km) S 121.5 (195.5 km) Takhini River bridge. The Takhini flows into the Yukon River.

J 3.8 (6.1 km) D 323.4 (520.4 km) S 123 (197.9 km) Takhini Hot Springs Road. Drive west 6 miles/10 km via paved road for Takhini Hot Springs; camping, cafe, trail rides, ski trails in winter. The source of the springs is a constant 117°F/47°C temperature and flows at 86 gallons a minute. The hot springs pool averages 100°F/38°C year-round. The water contains no sulfur. The chief minerals present are calcium, magnesium and iron.

Takhini Hot Springs. See display ad in Whitehorse in ALASKA HIGHWAY section.

Trappers and Indians used these springs around the turn of the century, arriving by way of the Takhini River or the old Dawson Trail. During construction of the Alaska Highway in the early 1940s, the U.S. Army maintained greenhouses in the area and reported remarkable growth regardless of the season.

Scenic Fox Lake at Milepost J 34.8 offers camping and fishing. (Earl L. Brown, staff)

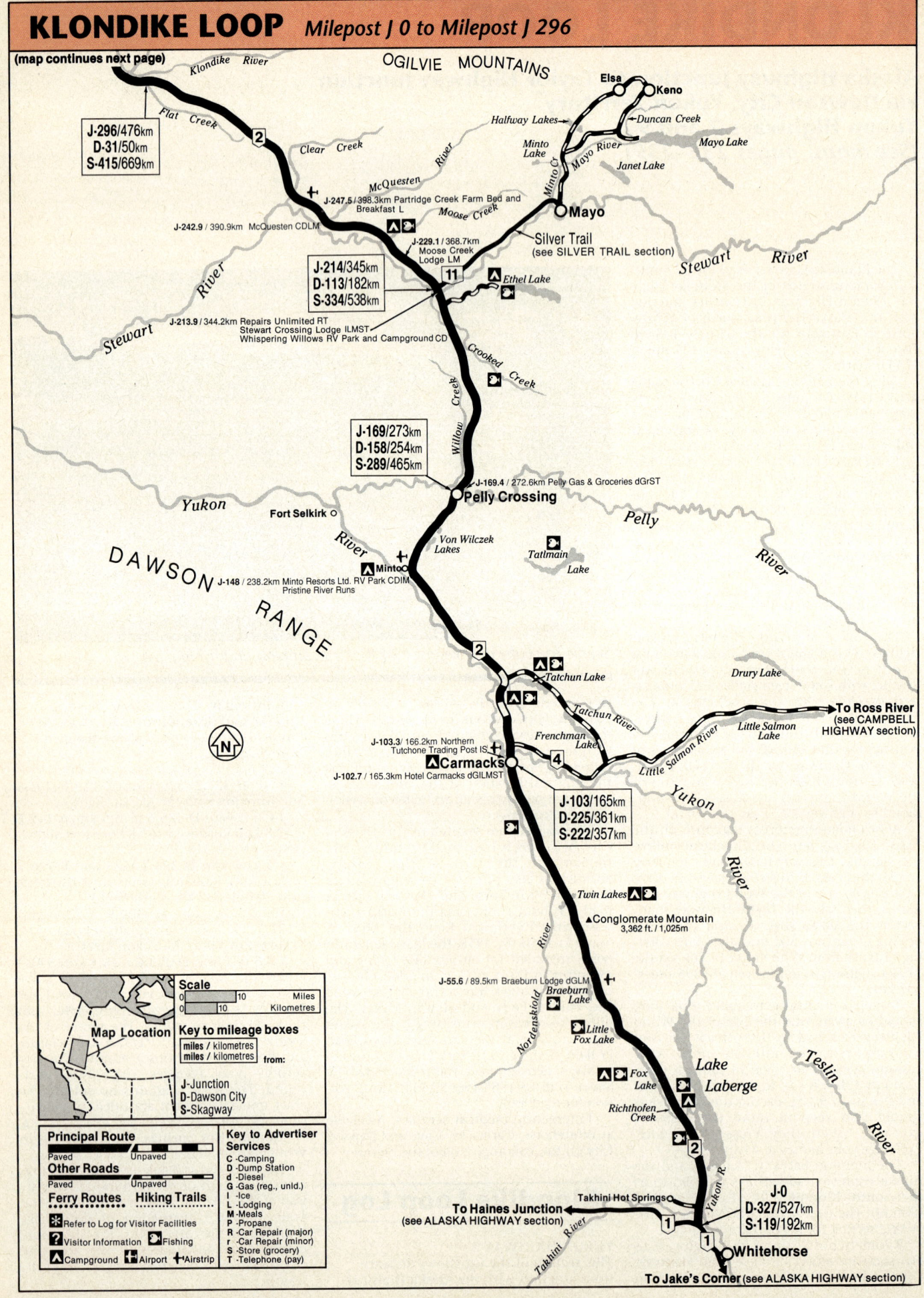

KLONDIKE LOOP — Milepost J 0 to Milepost J 296

KLONDIKE LOOP
Milepost J 296 to Tetlin Junction, Alaska Highway (includes Taylor Highway)

J 9.4 (15.1 km) **D 317.8** (511.4 km) **S 128.6** (207 km) Sawmill to west.

J 10.7 (17.2 km) **D 316.5** (509.3 km) **S 129.9** (209 km) Shallow Bay Road. Access to Northern Splendor Reindeer Farm. This commercial reindeer farm is 0.8 mile/1.3 km east. Reindeer antlers from the farm are sold for export. The farm is open to visitors in summer; there is an admission charge.

Northern Splendor Reindeer Farm. See display ad in Whitehorse in ALASKA HIGHWAY section.

J 12.7 (20.4 km) **D 314.5** (506.1 km) **S 131.9** (212.2 km) Horse Creek Road leads east to Lower Laberge Indian village and lakeshore cottages. **Horse Creek**; good grayling fishing from road.

J 15.8 (25.4 km) **D 311.4** (501.5 km) **S 135** (217.2 km) Microwave site near road.

J 16.8 (27 km) **D 310.4** (499.5 km) **S 136.1** (219.1 km) Large turnout to west.

J 17.4 (27.9 km) **D 309.8** (498.6 km) **S 136.7** (220 km) Lake Laberge to east. The Yukon River widens to form this 40-mile-/64-km-long lake. Lake Laberge was made famous by Robert W. Service with the lines: "The Northern Lights have seen queer sights, but the queerest they ever did see, was that night on the marge of Lake Lebarge I cremated Sam McGee," (from his poem *The Cremation of Sam McGee*).

J 18.2 (29.3 km) **D 309** (497.3 km) **S 137.4** (221.1 km) Gravel pit turnout to east.

J 20.3 (32.7 km) **D 306.9** (493.9 km) **S 139.5** (224.5 km) Deep Creek.

J 20.4 (32.8 km) **D 306.8** (493.7 km) **S 139.6** (224.6 km) Historical marker at turnoff for **Lake Laberge** Yukon government campground. Bakery on campground access road has an emergency phone and message post. The campground is situated 1.8 miles/2.9 km east on Lake Laberge next to Deep Creek; 28 sites, group camping area, kitchen shelter, drinking water, boat launch, and fishing for lake trout, grayling and northern pike.

CAUTION: Storms can blow up quickly and without warning on Lake Laberge as on other northern lakes. Canoeists and other small craft should stay to the west side of the lake, where the shoreline affords safe refuges should a storm come up. The east side of the lake is lined with high, rocky bluffs, and there are few places to pull out. Small craft should not navigate the middle of the lake.

J 20.9 (33.6 km) **D 306.3** (492.9 km) **S 140.1** (225.5 km) View of Lake Laberge for southbound travelers.

J 21.2 (34.1 km) **D 306** (492.4 km) **S 140.4** (225.9 km) Northbound the highway now enters the Miners Range, plateau country of the Yukon, an immense wilderness of forested dome-shaped mountains and high ridges, dotted with lakes and traversed by tributaries of the Yukon River. To the west, Pilot Mountain in the Miners Range (elev. 6,739 feet/2,054m) is visible.

J 22.8 (36.7 km) **D 304.4** (489.9 km) **S 142** (228.5 km) **Fox Creek**; grayling, excellent in June and July.

J 23.5 (37.8 km) **D 303.7** (488.7 km) **S 142.7** (229.8 km) Marker shows distance to Dawson City 486 km.

J 26.9 (43.3 km) **D 300.3** (483.3 km) **S 146.1** (235.1 km) Gravel pit turnout to east.

J 28.8 (46.3 km) **D 298.4** (480.2 km) **S 148** (238.2 km) Highway now follows the east shoreline of Fox Lake northbound.

J 29.4 (47.3 km) **D 297.8** (479.2 km) **S 148.6** (239.1 km) Turnout to west on Fox Lake. Historic sign here reads: "In 1883, U.S. Army Lt. Frederick Schwatka completed a survey of the entire length of the Yukon River. One of many geographical features that he named was Fox Lake, which he called Richthofen Lake, after geographer Freiherr Von Richthofen. Known locally as Fox Lake, the name was adopted in 1957. The Miners Range to the west was named by geologist/explorer George Mercer Dawson in 1887 'for the miners met by us along the river.' "

J 34.8 (56 km) **D 292.4** (470.5 km) **S 154** (247.8 km) Turnoff west for **Fox Lake** Yukon government campground; 30 sites, kitchen shelter, drinking water and boat launch. Good fishing for lake trout and burbot from the shore at the campground; excellent grayling year-round.

J 35.2 (56.6 km) **D 292** (469.9 km) **S 154.4** (248.5 km) Turnout with view of Fox Lake.

J 39.8 (64 km) **D 287.4** (462.5 km) **S 159** (255.8 km) North end of Fox Lake.

J 42 (67.6 km) **D 285.2** (459 km) **S 161.2** (259.4 km) **Little Fox Lake** to west; lake trout 3 to 8 lbs., fish the islands.

J 43.8 (70.5 km) **D 283.4** (456 km) **S 163** (262.1 km) Turnout with litter barrel to west beside Little Fox Lake. Small boat launch.

J 49.5 (79.7 km) **D 277.7** (446.9 km) **S 168.7** (271.5 km) Large turnout to west.

J 50.1 (80.6 km) **D 277.1** (445.9 km) **S 169.3** (272.4 km) First glimpse of Braeburn Lake for northbound travelers.

1992 ■ The MILEPOST® 239

Only Yukon River crossing on highway is at Carmacks. (Alissa Crandall)

J 52.5 (84.5 km) D 274.7 (442.1 km) S 171.7 (276.3 km) Gravel pit turnout to east.

J 55.6 (89.5 km) D 271.6 (437.1 km) S 174.9 (281.5 km) Braeburn Lodge to west; food (especially well known for huge cinnamon buns), gas, lodging and minor car repairs.

Braeburn Lodge. See display ad this section.

Private Aircraft: Braeburn airstrip to east, dubbed Cinnamon Bun Strip; elev. 2,350 feet/716m; length 3,000 feet/914m; dirt strip; wind sock.

J 66.3 (106.7 km) D 260.9 (419.8 km) S 185.5 (298.5 km) Photo stop; pull-through turnout on east side of highway with information sign about Conglomerate Mountain (elev. 3,361 feet/1,024m). Sign reads: "The Laberge Series was formed at the leading edge of volcanic mud flows some 185 million years ago (Early Jurassic). These flows solidified into sheets several kilometres long and about 1 km wide and 100m thick. This particular series of sheets stretches from Atlin, BC, to north of Carmacks, a distance of about 350 km. Other conglomerates of this series form Five Finger Rapids."

Rock hounds can find pieces of conglomerate in almost any borrow pit along this stretch of highway. The rock can be cut and polished.

J 71.6 (115.2 km) D 255.6 (411.3 km) S 190.8 (307 km) Turnouts on both sides of highway between Twin Lakes. These 2 small lakes, one on either side of the road, are known for their beauty and colour.

J 72.3 (116.3 km) D 254.9 (410.2 km) S 191.5 (308.2 km) Turnoff to west for **Twin Lakes** Yukon government campground; 8 sites, drinking water, boat launch. Lake is stocked. Enjoyable fishing for lake trout, grayling and pike. Good swimming for the hardy!

J 81.4 (131 km) D 245.8 (395.5 km) S 200.6 (323 km) Large turnout with litter barrel to east at remains of Montague House, a typical early-day roadhouse which offered lodging and meals on the stagecoach route between Whitehorse and Dawson City. A total of 52 stopping places along this route were listed in the Jan. 16, 1901, edition of the *Whitehorse Star* under "On the Winter Trail between White Horse and Dawson Good Accommodations for Travellers." Montague House was listed at Mile 99.

J 87.4 (140.6 km) D 239.8 (385.9 km) S 206.6 (332.5 km) Small lake to west.

J 101.3 (163 km) D 225.9 (363.5 km) S 220.5 (354.8 km) **Nordenskiold River** to west was named by Lt. Frederick Schwatka, U.S. Army, for Swedish arctic explorer Erik Nordenskiold. Good grayling and pike fishing all summer. This river, which parallels the highway for several miles, flows into the Yukon River at Carmacks.

J 101.5 (163.3 km) D 225.7 (363.2 km) S 220.7 (355.2 km) Pull-through rest area to east.

Carmacks

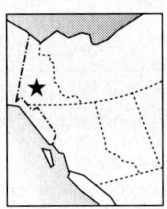

J 102.7 (165.3 km) D 224.5 (361.3 km) S 221.9 (357.1 km). Located on the banks of the Yukon River, Carmacks is the only highway crossing of the Yukon River between Whitehorse and Dawson City. **Population:** 424. **Emergency Services: RCMP,** phone 863-5251. **Ambulance,** phone 863-5501.

Private Aircraft: Carmacks airstrip; elev. 1,770 feet/539m; length 5,200 feet/1,585m; gravel; no fuel.

Carmacks was once an important stop for Yukon River steamers traveling between Dawson City and Whitehorse, and it continues as a supply point today for modern river travelers, although Carmacks has survived—while other river ports have not—as a service centre for highway traffic and mining interests. Carmacks was also a main stopping point on the old Whitehorse to Dawson Trail. It was named for George Carmack, whose gold discovery started the Klondike gold rush, and whose roadhouse and coal mining interests here helped establish this settlement.

Traveler facilities include a hotel, motel, cafes, grocery stores, laundromat and gas stations. Post office and bank (open 3 hours a week in summer) are located at the trading post at the north end of the bridge. A visitor information tent at the trading post has some Native crafts for sale. There are churches, a school and community library.

Carmacks Yukon government campground is situated on the banks of the Yukon River; 16 sites, kitchen shelter, drinking water and boat launch. Put in and take-out point for Yukon River travelers.

Hotel Carmacks. See display ad this section.

Braeburn Lodge

Diesel — Gas — Meals — Rooms

Home Baking for
"THE"
LARGEST CINNAMON BUNS
AND SANDWICHES
IN THE YUKON

Your Home Away From Home

Mile 55.6, KM 281.5 Klondike Highway
Phone 2M-3987 Fox Channel
YOUR HOSTS: CONNY & RAINER

Northern Tutchone Trading Post

(Located at north end of the bridge)

- Native Crafts
- Fishing Tackle & Licenses
- General Store • Post Office
- Ice • Friendly Service
- Tourist Information Tent

Open Year-round — 8 a.m. to 10 p.m.

(403) 863-5381

General Delivery, Carmacks, Yukon

(Owned and operated by the Little Salmon Carmacks Indian Band)

Hotel Carmacks

UNLEADED • DIESEL (Esso)

- Hotel and Motel Units
- Restaurant • Cocktail Lounge
- Laundromat • Showers
- Public Telephone
- Block and Cube Ice

GENERAL STORE
- Groceries • In-store Bakery
- Fishing Tackle • Hardware
- Camping Supplies
- Fishing and Hunting Licenses

Box 160, Carmacks, Yukon Y0B 1C0   Phone (403) 863-5221 • FAX (403) 863-5605

Klondike Loop Log

(continued)

J 103.2 (166.1 km) D 224 (360.5 km)
S 222.4 (357.9 km) Yukon River bridge.

J 103.3 (166.2 km) D 223.9 (360.3 km)
S 222.5 (358.1 km) Trading post with store and post office at north end of Yukon River bridge.

Northern Tutchone Trading Post. See display ad this section.

J 104.4 (168 km) D 222.8 (358.5 km)
S 223.6 (359.8 km) **Junction** with Campbell Highway (Yukon Highway 4), also known as Watson Lake-Carmacks Road, which leads east and south to Faro, Ross River and Watson Lake. See CAMPBELL HIGHWAY section.

J 105.1 (169.1 km) D 222.1 (357.4 km)
S 224.3 (361 km) Side road east to Tantalus Butte Coal Mine; the coal was used in Cyprus Anvil Mine's mill near Faro for drying concentrates. The butte was named by Lt. Frederick Schwatka because it is seen many times before it is actually reached.

J 105.4 (169.6 km) D 221.8 (356.9 km)
S 224.6 (361.4 km) Turnout to west with view of Yukon River Valley.

J 108 (173.8 km) D 219.2 (352.7 km)
S 227.2 (365.3 km) Side road west to agate site for rock hounds.

J 110 (177 km) D 217.2 (349.5 km)
S 229.2 (368.8 km) Small lake to west.

J 117.5 (189.1 km) D 209.7 (337.5 km)
S 236.7 (378.5 km) Pull-through rest area to west with toilets, litter barrels and view of Five Finger Rapids. Information sign here reads: "Five Finger Rapids named by early miners for the 5 channels, or fingers, formed by the rock pillars. They are a navigational hazard. The safest passage is through the nearest, or east, passage." Stairs (219 steps) lead down to a closer view of the rapids.

J 118.9 (191.3 km) D 208.3 (335.2 km)
S 238.1 (380.6 km) Tatchun Creek. Side road to Five Finger Rapids boat tour operator (current status unknown).

J 119 (191.5 km) D 208.2 (335 km)
S 238.2 (380.8 km) First turnoff (northbound) to east for **Tatchun Creek** Yukon government campground; 13 sites, kitchen shelter and drinking water. Good fishing for grayling, June through September; salmon, July through August.

J 119.1 (191.6 km) D 208.1 (334.9 km)
S 238.3 (380.9 km) Second turnoff (northbound) east for Tatchun Creek Yukon government campground.

J 119.6 (192.5 km) D 207.6 (334.1 km)
S 238.8 (381.8 km) Side road leads east to **Tatchun Lake.** Follow side road 4.3 miles/7 km east to boat launch and pit toilets. Continue past boat launch 1.1 miles/1.8 km for Tatchun Lake Yukon government campground with 20 sites, pit toilets, firewood, litter barrels and picnic tables. Fishing for northern pike, best in spring or fall.

This maintained side road continues east past Tatchun Lake to Frenchman Lake, then loops south to the Campbell Highway, approximately 25 miles/40 km distance. The main access to Frenchman Lake is from the Campbell Highway.

J 121.8 (196 km) D 205.4 (330.6 km)
S 241 (388 km) Tatchun Hill.

J 126.6 (203.7 km) D 200.6 (322.8 km)
S 245.8 (395.8 km) Large turnout overlooking Yukon River.

J 126.9 (204.2 km) D 200.3 (322.3 km)
S 246.1 (396.3 km) Highway descends hill, northbound. Watch for falling rocks.

J 132 (212.4 km) D 195.2 (314.1 km)
S 251.2 (404.5 km) McGregor Creek.

J 136.6 (219.8 km) D 190.6 (306.7 km)
S 255.8 (411.9 km) Good representation of White River ash layer for approximately next mile northbound. Some 1,250 years ago a layer of white volcanic ash coated a third of the southern Yukon, or some 125,000 square miles, and it is easily visible along many roadcuts. This distinct line conveniently provides a division used by archaeologists for dating artifacts: materials found below this major stratigraphic marker are considered to have been deposited before A.D. 700, while those found above the ash layer are postdated A.D. 700. The small amount of data available does not support volcanic activity in the White River area during the same period. One theory is that the ash could have spewn forth from one violent volcanic eruption. The source may be buried under the Klutlan Glacier in the St. Elias Mountains in eastern Alaska.

J 144 (231.7 km) D 183.2 (294.8 km)
S 263.2 (423.8 km) McCabe Creek.

J 144.1 (231.9 km) D 183.1 (294.7 km)
S 263.4 (424 km) Midway Lodge (current status unknown).

J 148 (238.2 km) D 179.2 (288.4 km)
S 267.2 (430.4 km) **Minto Resorts Ltd. RV Park.** 1,400-foot Yukon River frontage. Halfway between Whitehorse and Dawson City on the Old Stage Road, Minto was once a steamboat landing and trading post. 27 sites, wide easy access, picnic tables, firepits, souvenirs, fishing licenses, ice, snacks, pop. Coin-op showers and laundry, clean restrooms, dump station, and water. Bus tour buffet, reservation only. Caravans welcome. Wildlife viewing opportunities. Try fishing the river. Owned and operated by Yukoners. Come and visit us! See display ad this section. [ADVERTISEMENT]

J 148 (238.2 km) D 179.2 (288.4 km)
S 267.2 (430.4 km) **Pristine River Runs.** See display ad this section.

J 148.6 (239.1 km) D 178.6 (287.4 km)
S 267.8 (431.4 km) Minto Road, a short loop road, leads west to location of the former riverboat landing and trading post of **MINTO.** Drive in 1.2 miles/2 km for Minto Landing Yukon government campground situated on the scenic, grassy banks of the Yukon River; 10 sites, kitchen shelter and drinking water. Large flat grassy area may be used for parking. This campground is used as a put in and takeout site by river travelers. Check with Pristine River Runs about river tours to Sheep Mountain and Fort Selkirk leaving daily from Minto Resorts. ▲

Fort Selkirk, 22 river miles/35 km from here, was established by Robert Campbell in 1848 for the Hudson's Bay Co. In 1852, the fort was destroyed by Chilkat Indians, who had dominated the fur trade of central Yukon until the arrival of the Hudson's Bay Co. The site was occupied sporadically by traders and missionaries until 1950.

Private Aircraft: Minto airstrip; elev. 1,550 feet/472m; length 5,000 feet/1,524m; gravel.

J 160.3 (258 km) D 166.9 (268.6 km)
S 279.5 (450.5 km) Side road east to Von Wilczek Lakes.

J 163.4 (262.9 km) D 163.8 (263.6 km)
S 282.6 (455.5 km) Rock Island Lake to east.

J 164.2 (264.2 km) D 163 (262.3 km)
S 283.4 (456.8 km) Turnout. Small lake to west.

J 168.7 (271.5 km) D 158.5 (255.1 km)
S 287.9 (464 km) Road west to garbage dump.

J 169.4 (272.6 km) D 157.8 (253.9 km)
S 288.6 (465 km) Side road to **PELLY CROSSING** (pop. about 230). RCMP, phone 537-3311. There are a nursing station, post office and trading post here, general store with phone, and gas station with unleaded, diesel and tire repair.

Pelly Gas & Groceries. See display ad this section.

BOAT TOURS

Explore the Yukon River through unspoiled wilderness to Historic Fort Selkirk

• 6 Hour Trip leaving MINTO RESORTS 10 a.m. Daily
• Evening Trips to Sheep Mountain
(Maximum 6 passengers)

Call
PRISTINE RIVER RUNS
for reservations
at 2M3210 Minto Channel (5 - 9 p.m.)

MINTO RESORTS LTD.

R.V. PARK
CAMPGROUND ❖ SNACKS
SHOWERS ❖ LAUNDRY
TENTING

MILE 148 KLONDIKE HIGHWAY

Pat & Geraldine Van Bibber
(403) 633-5251
Mobile: 2M 8419 Minto Channel

4 - 12th Avenue
WHITEHORSE, YT Y1A 4J4

PELLY GAS & GROCERIES

• Unleaded Gas • Diesel
• Tire and Minor Repairs
• Groceries • Produce
• Frozen Meat
• Film and Souvenirs
• Drug Store Items

✷ OPEN 7 DAYS A WEEK — May 15-September 1 ✷

VISA (403) 537-3710 • FAX (403) 537-3010 MasterCard

This Selkirk Indian community attracted residents from Minto when the highway to Dawson City was built. School, mission and sawmill located near the big bridge. The local economy is based on hunting, trapping, fishing and guiding. The Selkirk Indian Band has erected signs near the bridge on the history and culture of the Selkirk people.

J 169.7 (273.1 km) **D 157.5** (253.5 km) **S 288.9** (465.5 km) Pelly River bridge.

J 170.4 (274.2 km) **D 156.8** (252.3 km) **S 289.6** (467 km) Turnout with litter barrel to east. View of Pelly Crossing and river valley. A historical marker here honours the Canadian Centennial (1867–1967). The Pelly River was named in 1840 by explorer Robert Campbell for Sir John Henry Pelly, governor of the Hudson's Bay Co. The Pelly River heads near the Northwest Territories border and flows approximately 375 miles/600 km to the Yukon River.

J 171.5 (276 km) **D 155.7** (250.5 km) **S 290.7** (468.6 km) **Private Aircraft:** Airstrip to east; elev. 1,870 feet/570m; length 3,000 feet/914m; gravel. No services.

J 179.6 (289 km) **D 147.6** (237.5 km) **S 298.8** (481.7 km) Pull-through turnout to east.

J 180.9 (291.1 km) **D 146.3** (235.4 km) **S 300.1** (483.8 km) Small lake to west.

J 183.8 (295.8 km) **D 143.4** (230.8 km) **S 303** (488.6 km) Large turnout to west. Bridge over Willow Creek.

J 185.5 (298.5 km) **D 141.7** (228 km) **S 304.7** (491.3 km) Side road west to Jackfish Lake.

J 195.6 (314.8 km) **D 131.6** (211.8 km) **S 314.8** (506.6 km) Access road west to **Wrong Lake** (stocked); fishing.

J 197.4 (317.7 km) **D 129.8** (208.9 km) **S 316.6** (511 km) Turnout with litter barrel to west. Winding descent begins for northbound traffic.

J 203.6 (327.6 km) **D 123.6** (198.9 km) **S 322.8** (521 km) Pull-through turnout to east.

J 205.9 (331.3 km) **D 121.3** (195.2 km) **S 325.1** (524.6 km) **Crooked Creek**; pike; grayling, use flies, summer best.

J 207.2 (333.4 km) **D 120** (193.1 km) **S 326.4** (526.7 km) Pull-through turnout with litter barrel to east at turnoff for **Ethel Lake** Yukon government campground. Drive in 16.6 miles/26.7 km on narrow and winding side road (not recommended for large RVs) for government campground; 15 sites, boat launch, good fishing.

J 213.8 (344 km) **D 113.4** (182.5 km) **S 333** (537.3 km) Stewart Crossing government maintenance camp to east.

J 213.9 (344.2 km) **D 113.3** (182.3 km) **S 333.1** (537.5 km) Stewart Crossing Lodge (camping, food, lodging) and auto repair/gas station east side of highway, turnout with information sign west side of highway. Silver Trail information booth (summer phone 996-2926).

Stewart Crossing Lodge. See display ad this section.

Whispering Willows RV Park and Campground. See display ad this section.

Repairs Unlimited. See display ad this section.

In 1886 Stewart Crossing was the site of a trading post established by Arthur Harper, Jack McQuesten and Alfred Mayo to support gold mining in the area. Later a roadhouse was built here as part of the Whitehorse to Dawson overland stage route. Stewart Crossing also functioned as a fuel stop for the riverboats and during the 1930s was a transfer point for the silver ore barges from Mayo.

Harper, Mayo and McQuesten are 3 prominent names in Yukon history. Harper, an Irish immigrant, was one of the first white men to prospect in the Yukon, although he never struck it rich. He died in 1898 in Arizona. (His son, Walter Harper, was on the first complete ascent of Mount McKinley in 1913. Walter died in 1918 in the SS *Princess Sophia* disaster off Juneau.)

Mayo, a native of Maine, explored, prospected and traded in the Yukon until his death in 1924. McQuesten, like Harper, worked his way north from the California goldfields. Often referred to as the "Father of the Yukon," Jack Leroy Napoleon McQuesten ended his trading and prospecting days in 1898 when he moved to California. He died in 1909 while in Seattle for the Alaska-Yukon-Pacific Exposition.

J 214.3 (344.9 km) **D 112.9** (181.7 km) **S 333.5** (538 km) Stewart River bridge. The Stewart River flows into the Yukon River upstream from Dawson City.

J 214.4 (345 km) **D 112.8** (181.5 km) **S 333.6** (538.2 km) **Silver Trail (Stewart Crossing) Junction** at north end of Stewart River bridge. Marker shows distance to Dawson 182 km. The Silver Trail (Yukon Highway 11) leads northeast to Mayo, Elsa and Keno; see SILVER TRAIL section.

J 214.8 (345.6 km) **D 112.4** (180.9 km) **S 334** (538.8 km) View to west of Stewart River and mountains as highway climbs northbound.

J 220.8 (355.3 km) **D 106.4** (171.2 km) **S 340** (545.1 km) Dry Creek.

J 224.4 (361.1 km) **D 102.8** (165.4 km) **S 343.6** (556.2 km) Access to Stewart River to west. Historical information sign about Stewart River. A major tributary of the Yukon River, the Stewart River was named for James G. Stewart who discovered it in 1849. Stewart was at the time assistant to Robert Campbell of the Hudson's Bay Co.

J 229.1 (368.7 km) **D 98.1** (157.7 km) **S 348.3** (561.9 km) **Moose Creek Lodge.** A must for Yukon travelers! Dine in an authentic trapper's cabin featuring sourdough pancakes, delicious meals, homemade soups and scrumptious baked goods. Meet Max the Mosquito and Murray the Moose! Native tepee. Smokehouse. Local crafts and unique gifts. Gold nugget jewellery. Cozy log cabins. For reservations, dial 1311 and ask for JL3-9570 on Stewart Channel or write, General Delivery, Mayo, YT Y0B 1M0. Moose Creek is also serving group tours in their beautiful open-air gazebo, reservations suggested. VISA and MasterCard. [ADVERTISEMENT]

J 229.2 (368.8 km) **D 98** (157.7 km) **S 348.4** (562 km) Moose Creek bridge.

J 229.5 (369.3 km) **D 97.7** (157.2 km) **S 348.7** (562.4 km) Turnout to west at turnoff for Moose Creek Yukon government

---

REPAIRS UNLIMITED

Chevron (403) 996-2904

COMPLETE MECHANICAL REPAIRS
TIRE SALES and REPAIRS
• TOWING •

"A friendly full-service stop with competitive prices"

Hours: 8 a.m. to 11 p.m. (summer) 8 a.m. to 10 p.m. (winter)
Located at Stewart Crossing Lodge, Mile 213

Open Year-Round

Regular, Unleaded, Diesel Fuel

Credit Cards Honored

KM 538 Klondike Highway

STEWART CROSSING LODGE

GROCERY STORE • ICE

Licensed Restaurant • Home cooking
Fresh baked bread and pastries
Hotel Rooms • Open Year-Round

Located at the junction of the Klondike Highway and the Silver Trail

Phone (403) 996-2501

◆ Quiet, Scenic, Country Spot

WHISPERING WILLOWS RV PARK AND CAMPGROUND

• SHOWERS • LAUNDROMAT
• FRESH WELL WATER
• 32 WATER, POWER HOOKUPS
• DUMP STATION

Next to Stewart Crossing Lodge
Caravans Welcome (please call ahead)
Good fishing in the area (403) 996-2411

∽ McQUESTEN ∽
Spruce Grove R.V.
KM 584

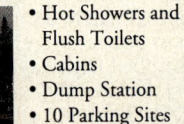

Old House Cafe

• Hot Showers and Flush Toilets
• Cabins
• Dump Station
• 10 Parking Sites *(water and sewer)*
• Picnic Tables and Firepits

campground adjacent **Moose Creek** and Stewart River; good picnic spot. There are 30 campsites, tenting sites, kitchen shelter, playground and playfield. Short trail to Stewart River. Good fishing for grayling, 1 to 1¼ lbs.

J 242.7 (390.5 km) **D 84.5** (136 km) **S 361.9** (583.7 km) **McQuesten River**, a tributary of the Stewart River, named for Jack (Leroy Napoleon) McQuesten.

J 242.9 (390.9 km) **D 84.3** (135.6 km) **S 362.1** (584 km) McQuesten, a lodge with cafe, cabins and RV sites. Site of Old McQuesten River Lodge to east.

McQuesten. See display ad this section.

J 247.5 (398.3 km) **D 79.7** (128.3 km) **S 366.7** (591 km) **Partridge Creek Farm Bed and Breakfast** (nonsmoking) is NOT your usual farm or bed and breakfast. Experience yesterday's hospitality and quality of life. Full farm breakfast. (Suppers by appointment). Spring and fall waterfowl refuge, beaver ponds, fishing, hiking gold panning.

Organic vegetables available. Rooms $55 to $80 (includes tax). VISA. Closed Saturday nights. Hosts: Del and Virginia Buerge. Mailbag 450, Dawson City, YT Y0B 1G0. Phone (403) 993-5772. [ADVERTISEMENT]

J 249.3 (401.2 km) **D 77.9** (125.4 km) **S 368.5** (594 km) **Private Aircraft:** McQuesten airstrip 1.2 miles/1.9 km west; elev. 1,500 feet/457m; length 5,000 feet/1524m; gravel and turf. No services.

J 251.3 (404.4 km) **D 75.9** (122.1 km) **S 370.5** (596.5 km) Clear Creek, access via side road west.

J 260.4 (419.1 km) **D 66.8** (107.5 km) **S 379.6** (612 km) Barlow Lake, access via 0.6-mile-/1-km-long side road west.

J 263.7 (424.4 km) **D 63.5** (102.2 km) **S 382.9** (617.2 km) Beaver Dam Creek.

J 266 (428 km) **D 61.2** (98.5 km) **S 385.2** (621 km) Willow Creek.

J 268.5 (432.1 km) **D 58.7** (94.5 km) **S 387.7** (625 km) Flat Hill.

J 268.8 (432.5 km) **D 58.4** (94 km) **S 388** (625.5 km) Gravel Lake to east.

J 272.1 (437.9 km) **D 55.1** (88.6 km) **S 391.3** (630.8 km) Meadow Creek.

J 272.5 (438.5 km) **D 54.7** (88 km) **S 391.7** (631.4 km) Rest area with litter barrel to south.

J 276.5 (445 km) **D 50.7** (81.6 km) **S 395.7** (637.9 km) French Creek.

J 279.7 (450.1 km) **D 47.5** (76.4 km) **S 398.9** (643.1 km) Stone Boat Swamp.

J 288.9 (464.9 km) **D 38.3** (61.6 km) **S 408.1** (657.9 km) Rest area.

J 289.3 (465.5 km) **D 37.9** (61 km) **S 408.5** (658.5 km) Geologic point of interest turnout to east overlooking Tintina Trench. This geologic feature, which extends hundreds of miles across Yukon and Alaska, provides visible proof of plate tectonics.

J 295.1 (474.9 km) **D 32.1** (51.6 km) **S 414.3** (667.8 km) Flat Creek.

J 295.9 (476.2 km) **D 31.3** (50.4 km) **S 415.1** (669 km) Klondike River to east.

J 297.6 (478.9 km) **D 29.6** (47.6 km) **S 416.8** (671.9 km) Large turnout to east with historic sign about Klondike River and information sign on Dempster Highway.

J 298 (479.5 km) **D 29.2** (47 km) **S 417.2** (672.5 km) Watch for livestock.

J 301.6 (485.3 km) **D 25.6** (41.2 km) **S 420.8** (678.5 km) **Junction** of Klondike Highway and the Dempster Highway (Dempster Corner). Klondike River Lodge east side of highway just north of the junction; food, gas and lodging. The Dempster Highway leads northeast to Inuvik, NWT. See DEMPSTER HIGHWAY section for log of that road. (Details on the Dempster are also available from the Western Arctic Information Centre in Dawson City.)

Klondike River Lodge. See display ad this section.

J 307.3 (494.5 km) **D 19.9** (32 km) **S 426.5** (687.4 km) Goring Creek.

J 308.4 (496.3 km) **D 18.8** (30.2 km) **S 427.6** (689.2 km) Turnout to north with access to the Klondike River.

J 312.1 (502.2 km) **D 15.1** (24.3 km) **S 431.3** (695.1 km) Log cabin east side of highway is flanked by fireweed in July.

J 315.2 (507.2 km) **D 12** (19.3 km) **S 434** (700 km) Turnoff to north for Klondike River Yukon government campground, located on Rock Creek near the Klondike River; 28 sites, kitchen shelter, drinking water.

J 315.7 (508 km) **D 11.5** (18.5 km) **S 434.9** (700.8 km) Dawson City airport to south. **Private Aircraft:** Runway 02-20; elev. 1,211 feet/369m; length 5,000 feet/1,524m; gravel; fuel 80 (in drums at Dawson City), 100, JP4.

J 317.1 (510.3 km) **D 10.1** (16.3 km) **S 436.3** (703.6 km) Hunker Creek Road to south.

J 318.4 (512.4 km) **D 8.8** (14.2 km) **S 437.6** (705.4 km) Turnout to south with point of interest sign about Hunker Creek. Albert Hunker staked the first claim on Hunker Creek Sept. 11, 1896. George Carmack made the big discovery on Bonanza Creek on Aug. 17, 1896. Hunker Creek is 16 miles/26 km long, of which 13 miles/21 km

was dredged between 1906 and 1966.

J 318.9 (513.2 km) **D 8.3** (13.4 km) **S 438.1** (706.1 km) Bear Creek Road to south.

J 319.6 (514.3 km) **D 7.6** (12.2 km) **S 438.8** (707.2 km) Turnout with historic sign about the Yukon Ditch and tailings to north. To the south is Bear Creek historical site. Open 9:30 A.M. to 5 P.M. daily in summer. This 62-acre compound of the Yukon Consolidated Gold Corp. features a complete blacksmith shop, machinery shop and gold room.

J 324.5 (522.2 km) **D 2.7** (4.3 km) **S 443.7** (715 km) Bonanza Creek Road to Discovery Claim and historic Dredge No. 4, largest wooden hull dredge in North America. Restoration and preparation for refloating the dredge is under way. No tours, but well worth the drive out to see this huge dredge. Bonanza Creek Road is maintained for 10 miles/16 km. Commercial RV park and gold panning at junction.

GuggieVille. Good Sam. This clean, attractive campground is built on dredge tailings at the former site of the Guggenheim's mining camp. 60 RV sites with water and electricity ($13), 15 unserviced sites ($8.75), public showers ($2.25 each). Rates include tax. Car wash, dump station and laundromat are available. A mining display features gas diggers, a hand-built bulldozer, wagons and ore cars are open to the public free of charge. Gold panning discount for those staying at GuggieVille. Owners sell gold from their placer mine. [ADVERTISEMENT]

J 324.6 (522.4 km) **D 2.6** (4.2 km) **S 443.8** (714.2 km) **Trail of '98 Mini-Golf.** Cabins, RV parking, tent sites, gift shop, cafe and ice cream. Rustic log cabins, quiet and homey. Sleep 4. Very reasonable rates. Reservations recommended. Home-style cafe

features local dishes, homemade bread, daily specials, friendly service and economical prices. Also offering souvenirs, crafts and gold; a challenging 9-hole mini-golf course with historic gold rush theme; free picnic, playground and games area. Open daily 7 A.M. to 11 P.M. Write Box 653, Dawson City, YT Y0B 1G0. Phone (403) 993-5664. Fax (403) 993-5943. VISA, MasterCard. [ADVERTISEMENT]

J 324.7 (522.5 km) **D 2.5** (4 km) **S 443.9**

Moose Creek Lodge 
- DELICIOUS MEALS
- FRESH BAKED GOODS
- HANDMADE CRAFTS
- RUSTIC LOG CABINS

RADIOPHONE: JL3 9570 STEWART CHANNEL
OPEN 7 A.M. DAILY • KM 561.8 • TOUR GROUPS WELCOMED

---

25 Miles South of Dawson City At Dempster Corner
MILE 0 DEMPSTER HIGHWAY
Esso **Klondike River Lodge** Good Sam Club
(This Business For Sale) (403) 993-6892
Open All Year 7 a.m. to Midnight
Reasonable Prices
Restaurant • Motel • Grocery Store
Gas & Diesel • Propane • Towing
Tires & Repairs • Licensed Mechanic
RV Parking • Dump Station • Car Wash

(715.3 km) Gas station, store and campground.

Bonanza Shell. See display ad this section.

J 324.8 (522.7 km) **D** 2.4 (3.9 km) **S** 444 (715.5 km) Klondike River bridge.

J 325.3 (523.5 km) **D** 1.9 (3.1 km) **S 444.5** (716.4 km) Large turnout with information sign and map.

J 325.8 (524.3 km) **D** 1.4 (2.3 km) **S** 445 (717.2 km) Dome Road to north leads 5.7 miles/9.2 km to Dome Mountain (elev. 2,592 feet/790m), which offers panoramic views of the Yukon and Klondike rivers, Bonanza Creek and the Ogilvie Mountains.

J 326.1 (524.8 km) **D** 1.1 (1.8 km) **S 445.3** (717.7 km) Fifth Avenue. Turnout with sign about the Klondike River to south: "With headwaters in the Ogilvie Mountains, the Klondike River and its tributaries gave birth to the world's greatest gold rush—the Klondike Gold Rush of '98."

J 327.2 (526.5 km) **D** 0 **S** 446.4 (719.5 km) Dawson City, ferry at Yukon River. *Description of Dawson City follows. Log of Klondike Loop continues page 251.*

Dawson City

J 327.2 (526.5 km) **D 0 S** 446.4 (719.5 km) Located 165 miles/266 km south of the Arctic Circle on the Yukon River at its junction with the Klondike River. **Population:** 1,852. **Emergency Services: RCMP,** 1st Avenue S., phone 993-5444. **Fire Department,** phone 993-5555. **Nursing station** and **Ambulance,** phone 993-5333.

Visitor Information: At Front and King streets, in a replica of a Northern Commercial Co. store. Yukon information and a Dawson City street map are available. Video disks on a variety of subjects. Walking tours are part of the daily schedule. Open 9 A.M. to 9 P.M. daily, mid-May to mid-September, phone 993-5566.

Western Arctic Information Centre is located in the B.Y.N. (British Yukon Navigation) Bldg. on Front Street, across from the Yukon visitor centre; open 9 A.M. to 9 P.M., June to September. Information on Northwest Territories and the Dempster Highway. Phone 993-6506.

Elevation: 1,050 feet/320m. **Climate:** There are 20.9 hours of daylight June 21, 3.8 hours of daylight on Dec. 21. Mean high in July, 72°F/22.2°C. Mean low in January, -30.5°F/-31.1°C. First fall frost end of August, last spring frost end of May. Annual snowfall 59.8 inches/151.8 cm. **Radio:** CBC 560; CFYT-FM 106, CKYN-FM 96.1 (summer visitor station). **Television:** CBC Anik Channel 7 and 4 other channels. **Newspaper:** *Klondike Sun* (monthly).

Private Aircraft: Dawson City airport located 11.5 miles/18.5 km southeast (see Milepost J 315.7). Customs clearance available.

Originally laid out to serve 30,000 people, Dawson City today still occupies much of the original townsite but with only a fraction of the buildings and people, although in the summer the city is crowded with visitors and with miners headed for the goldfields. Dawson City has lost 47 historic buildings to fires, flood and demolition in the past years. There was a surge of reconstruction after the May 1979 flood when the ice-jammed Yukon River overflowed its banks. A dike was built along Front Street in 1987–88 to protect the downtown area.

Historically, Dawson City dates from the discovery of gold on a Klondike River tributary (Rabbit Creek, renamed Bonanza Creek) in 1896. There were several hundred prospectors in the region before the big strike, and most of them swarmed over the creeks staking claims long before the stampeders began trickling into the country the following year.

Of the several routes followed by the hordes of gold seekers, most famous was the Trail of '98: by ship from Seattle to Skagway,

---

GuggieVille

CLEAN AND QUIET CAMPGROUND ON FAMOUS BONANZA CREEK

3 Minutes From City Center on Bonanza Road

★ HOOKUPS
★ GOLD PANNING
★ GIFT SHOP
★ SHOWERS
★ CAR WASH
★ LAUNDROMAT

Box 311, Dawson City, Yukon Territory Y0B 1G0
Gordon and Brenda Caley   Phone (403) 993-5008

BONANZA SHELL
Gas • Diesel • Propane • Tires • Repairs
Mini Food Store • Ice • Snacks

R.V. PARK & CAMPGROUND
Hookups • Laundromat • Rest Rooms • Showers
Gold Panning • Car Wash
Open Daily 7 – 11
Box 957, Dawson City, Yukon • (403) 993-5142

When in town visit the . . .

DAWSON CITY MUSEUM

Open 10 a.m. - 6 p.m. June 1 - Labour Day

KINGS OF THE KLONDIKE GALLERY
AV Shows — City Life Gallery
Gift Shop
Resource Library
Historic Train Collection

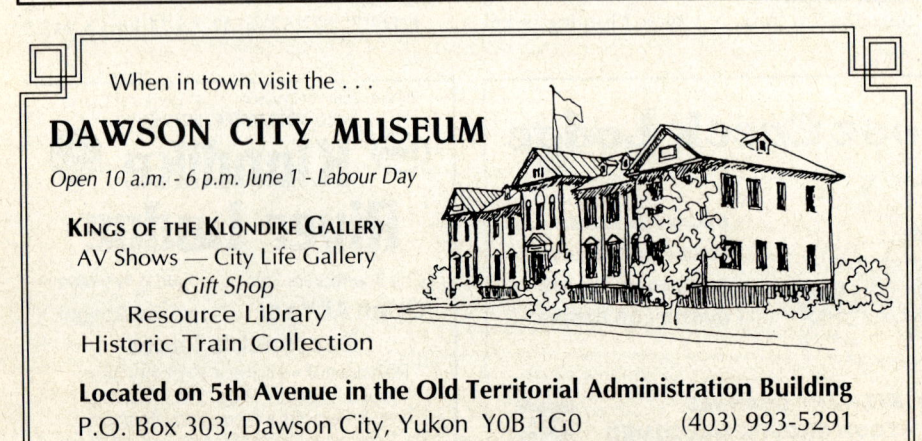

Located on 5th Avenue in the Old Territorial Administration Building
P.O. Box 303, Dawson City, Yukon Y0B 1G0   (403) 993-5291

Hair and Skin Care

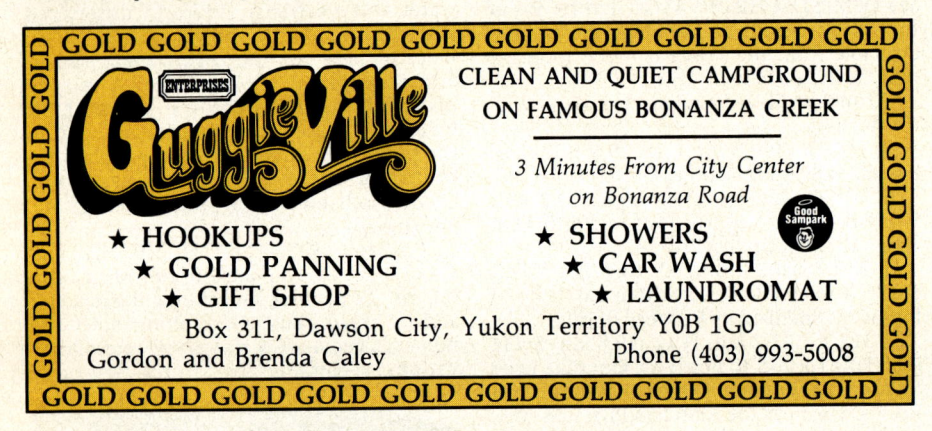

HAIR CABARÉT

MEN and WOMEN
CUTS • PERMS • TINTS
— Latest Styles —
Sculptured Nails, Electrolysis, etc.

MASSAGE   2nd & Queen
OPEN DAILY   (403) 993-5222

SOURDOUGH PANCAKES
HOMEMADE SOUPS
ICE CREAM • BAKERY
SOURDOUGH PIZZA

Nancy's
FRONT STREET

AK, then over the ice and snow of Chilkoot Pass or White Pass to Lakes Lindeman and Bennett, then down the Yukon River to Dawson City by boat.

There were other routes as difficult. The longest was the all-water route by ocean steamer around Alaska's west coast to the port of St. Michael at the mouth of the 2,000-mile-/3219-km-long Yukon River, followed by the long voyage upriver by stern-wheeler to Dawson.

The townsite was prepared by Joe Ladue, a trader and sawmill operator, and surveyed by William Ogilvie. The town was named for George Mercer Dawson of the Geological Survey of Canada. Trading companies moved to Dawson City from Forty Mile and Circle City and established warehouses along the waterfront. Food and mining supplies sufficient for their normal trade with Indian trappers and the 200 white men in the watershed at the time were not enough for the masses of people who had arrived by winter 1897. While additional steamers did start for Dawson City from St. Michael with extra cargo, at least 3 were frozen into the ice 200 miles/322 km before reaching their goal and forced to remain until the ice went out in May 1898. Men who said that gold would buy anything had not reckoned with Dawson City in 1897—which had nothing to sell.

The next summer, when the great rush to the Klondike got into full swing, there was sufficient shipping to move the freight required to create a city in a wilderness

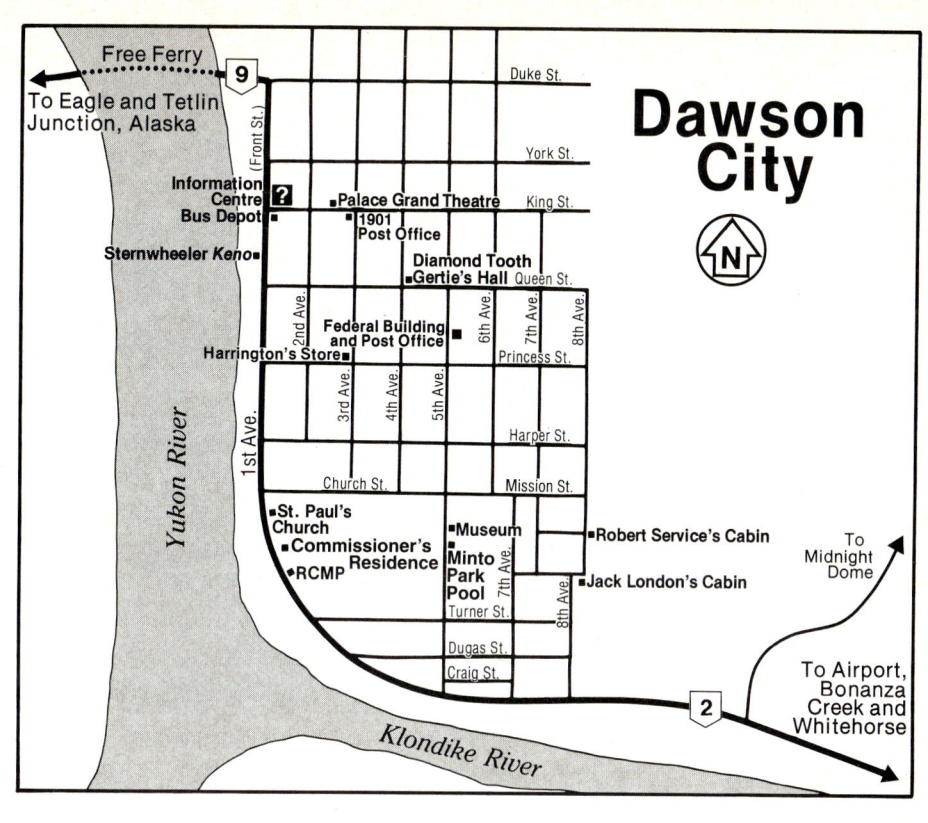

DAWSON CITY ADVERTISERS

Arctic Cotton	Front St.
Bonanza Aviation	Airport
Capt. Dick's Sour Toe Cocktail	Keno Lounge, Westmark Inn
Dawson City Bed & Breakfast	Ph. (403) 993-5649
Dawson City Museum	5th Ave. & Church St.
Dawson Trading Post	5th Ave. & Harper St.
Downtown Hotel	2nd Ave. & Queen St.
Eldorado Hotel, The	3rd Ave. & Princess St.
5th Avenue Bed and Breakfast	Adjacent museum
Gas Shack	5th Ave. & Princess St.
Gold City Tours	Ph. (403) 993-5175
Gold Rush Campground	5th Ave. & York St.
GuggieVille	Jct. of Klondike Hwy. & Bonanza Creek Rd.
Hair Cabaret	2nd Ave. & Queen St.
Klondike Kate's Motel	3rd Ave. & King St.
Klondike Nugget & Ivory Shop	Front St. at Queen St.
Klondike Visitors Assoc.	Front & King sts.
Maximilian's Gold Rush Emporium	Front St. at Queen St.
Midnight Sun Hotel, The	3rd Ave. & Queen St.
Nancy's	S. end of Front St.
'98 Drive-In	Front St.
Northern Comfort Bed & Breakfast	6th Ave. & Church St.
Paradise Alley Emporium & Atelier	2nd Ave.
Peabody's Photo Parlor	Front St. at Queen St.
Raven's Nook & Loft, The	2nd & Queen St.
Triple "J" Hotel	5th Ave. & Queen St.
Westmark Inn Dawson City	5th Ave. & Harper St.
White Ram Manor Bed & Breakfast	7th Ave. & Harper St.
Yukon Native Products	Front & Princess sts.

Dawson City

(map showing Yukon River, Klondike River, streets and landmarks including Free Ferry to Eagle and Tetlin Junction, Alaska; Information Centre/Bus Depot; Sternwheeler Keno; Palace Grand Theatre; 1901 Post Office; Diamond Tooth Gertie's Hall; Federal Building and Post Office; Harrington's Store; St. Paul's Church; Commissioner's Residence; RCMP; Museum; Minto Park Pool; Robert Service's Cabin; Jack London's Cabin; to Midnight Dome; to Airport, Bonanza Creek and Whitehorse)

YUKON NATIVE PRODUCTS
An Indian Arts and Crafts Co-op

Front & Princess Street
Dawson City, Yukon Y0B 1G0
(403) 993-5115   FAX (403) 993-6114

YUKON'S LARGEST SELECTION OF INDIAN ARTS & CRAFTS

- beaded moccasins & mukluks
- moose hair tufting • northern souvenirs
- birch-bark & porcupine quill baskets
- exclusive distributor of the Original Yukon Parka, Kluane Anorak & new Whitehorse Parkas

KLONDIKE KATE'S
Motel & Full Service Restaurant
T.V. In Every Cabin
3rd and King Street

P.O. Box 777, Dawson City,
Yukon Y0B 1G0
(403) 993-5491

Also – Mary's Rooms
– Reasonable Rates
(403) 993-6013

Gold Rush Campground
R·V P·A·R·K

Offering the traveler full facilities in a convenient downtown location

Car wash • Store • Laundromat
Hookups • Showers • Ice

Block of 5th & York streets
Dawson City, YT • (403) 993-5247

'98 DRIVE-IN

FRONT STREET, DAWSON CITY ... Opposite steamer Keno

Open every day 11 a.m. to 9 p.m.
Homemade Fries and Hamburgers
Hot Dogs • Hard and Soft Ice Cream
Sundaes • Shakes • Banana Splits

Dawson City   Yukon Territory   (403) 993-5226

VISIT HISTORIC
Coming or Going!!
DAWSON CITY
YUKON
HEART OF THE KLONDIKE

TOK JUNCTION ALASKA — TOP OF THE WORLD HIGHWAY — **DAWSON CITY YUKON**

ALASKA HIGHWAY / KLONDIKE HIGHWAY

WHITEHORSE

YOU'VE COME THIS FAR!!
DON'T MISS
THE MOST HISTORIC PLACE NORTH OF 60!!

THE SITE OF THE GREATEST GOLD RUSH EVER!!
RELIVE THE ERA ON DAWSON'S BOARD
SIDEWALKS, BUILDINGS AS THEY WERE!
SEE DREDGE #4
NORTH AMERICA'S LARGEST WOODEN HULLED DREDGE
TRY YOUR LUCK OR TAKE IN THE SHOW
AT DIAMOND TOOTH GERTIES GAMBLING HALL
THE ONLY ONE OF ITS KIND IN CANADA
ATTEND THE GASLIGHT FOLLIES
IN THE BEAUTIFUL PALACE GRAND THEATRE
(FORMERLY THE DAWSON OPERA HOUSE)
HAVE YOUR MAIL HAND STAMPED
AT THE OLD POST OFFICE
PAN FOR GOLD
VISIT THE CABINS OF JACK LONDON
AND ROBERT SERVICE
SEE PIERRE BERTON'S
CHILDHOOD HOME.

DAWSON CITY THROUGH THE VISITOR SEASON OFFERS WIDE AND DIVERSIFIED ACTIVITIES THAT YOU CAN TAKE PART IN.

Klondike Dart Tournament
SEPT. 11-13, 1992

Commissioners Ball
JUNE 13, 1992

Midnight Dome Race
JULY 18, 1992

Gold Panning Championships
JULY 1, 1992

Klondike Outhouse Race
SEPT. 6, 1992

Discovery Days Events
AUGUST 14-17, 1992

KLONDIKE VISITORS ASSOCIATION P.O. Box 389 Dawson City, Y.T. Y0B 1G0 (403) 993-5575

where every stick, nail and scrap of paper had to be brought in. By 1900 Dawson City was the largest city west of Winnipeg and north of San Francisco.

These were the conditions and the days that built Dawson City. They prevailed until 1903, when stampedes to Nome and other Alaska points drew off the froth from Dawson society, leaving a sturdy government-cum-mining fraternity that maintained an aura of big city worldliness until WWI.

In later years, Dawson City nearly became a ghost town. Each year a few more buildings were abandoned by owners. They did, however, keep possession by paying their taxes. With the tenacity of Yukoners "keen to find the gold," some still maintain their ownership today, allowing the buildings to deteriorate to shabbiness. Since they were privately owned, no one could use, repair or maintain them. Until recently the city of Dawson could not protect them. Fire and vandals destroyed many; neglect and permafrost have caused others to topple.

By 1953, Whitehorse—on the railway, the highway and with a large airport—was so much the hub of activity that the federal government moved the capital from Dawson City, along with 800 civil servants, and years of tradition and pride. Some recompense was offered in the form of a road linking Whitehorse with the mining at Mayo and Dawson City. With its completion, White Pass trucks replaced White Pass steamers and that great highway, the Yukon River.

New government buildings were built in Dawson, including a fire hall. In 1962 the federal government reconstructed the Palace Grand Theatre for a gold rush festival that featured the Broadway musical, *Foxy*, with Bert Lahr. A museum was established in the Administration Bldg. and tours and entertainments were begun, which continue today.

Dawson City was declared a national historic site in the early 1960s. Canadian Parks Service is currently involved with 35 properties in Dawson City. Many buildings will be restored, some reconstructed and others stabilized. Canadian Parks Service offers a full interpretive program each summer for visitors to this historic city.

ACCOMMODATIONS

Accustomed to a summer influx of visitors, Dawson has modern hotels and motels (rates average $75 and up) and several bed and breakfasts. The community has a bank, restaurants, 5 laundromats (4 with showers), 2 grocery stores (with bakeries), general stores, souvenir shops, churches, post office, government offices, government liquor store, information centre, swimming pool and plenty of entertainment. However, its several hotels and motels cannot accommodate all the visitors that come to Dawson City for the Discovery Day celebrations, held in mid-August; make your reservations early.

Old tailings near Dawson still yield gold. (Earl L. Brown, staff)

KLONDIKE LOOP • DAWSON CITY

YOUR PLACE IN THE SUN

The Midnight Sun Hotel

• DELUXE ACCOMMODATIONS •
CONVENIENTLY LOCATED
ON THE CORNER
OF THIRD & QUEEN

FULL RANGE OF SERVICES

FROM MAY TO OCTOBER
Telephone: (403) 993-5495
Fax: (403) 993-6425
Box 840
Dawson City, Y.T. Y0B 1G0

FROM NOVEMBER TO APRIL
Telephone: (604) 291-2652
Fax: (604) 291-2652
1645 Kensington Avenue
Burnaby, B.C. V5B 4C7

CAPT. DICK'S
World Famous

Sourtoe Cocktail

"NIGHTLY"

Keno Lounge —
Westmark Hotel
Dawson City, Yukon

Information: Capt. Dick, Box 1,
Dawson City, Yukon Y0B 1G0

The Raven's Nook & Loft

Unique
Gold Nugget Jewellery
T-Shirts • Gifts • Fine China
Rhodonite • Ivory • Crystal
• Film •
Ladies' Clothing, Shoes and Accessories
Petite – Regular – Oversize

(403) 993-5530 • 993-5591
2nd Avenue and Queen Street

THE ELDORADO HOTEL

Phone (403) 993-5451
FAX (403) 993-5256

In Yukon and Northern BC
1-800-661-0518

In Alaska
1-800-764-ELDO

OPEN YEAR ROUND
ALL MODERN ROOMS • SUITES • KITCHENETTES
PHONES • COLOR TV • LAUNDRY • WINTER PLUG-INS

★ SLUICE BOX LOUNGE
Air Conditioned

★ BONANZA DINING ROOM
Featuring Northern Specialties
Pleasant surroundings and excellent service

3rd Avenue and Princess Street • P.O. Box 338, Dawson City, Yukon Y0B 1G0

Complimentary Airport Transfers for Registered Guests

WE ARE NORTHERN HOSPITALITY!

After the Gold Rush

Dawson still retains the gold rush charm which fascinated a generation at the turn of the century. Today the Westmark Inn, situated near famed Diamond Tooth Gertie's, offers visitors the opportunity to relive some of the excitement of that era. As our guest you'll find comfortable rooms, a memorable dining experience and our famous Westmark service.

- 131 Rooms
- Dining Room and Lounge
- Gift Shop • No-smoking Rooms

Special Summer Value Rates from $49

Rooms at lower rates are capacity controlled and good on selected rooms & dates only. Call for complete information. Subject to change without notice.

Westmark Inn

DAWSON CITY

Fifth & Harper Streets
P.O. Box 420, Dawson City
Yukon Territory Y0B 1G0

OPEN SEASONALLY

Central Reservations
1-800-544-0970 (U.S.)
1-800-999-2570 (Canada)

Westmark Hotels covers the north with hotels and inns throughout Alaska and the Yukon. Come be our guest.

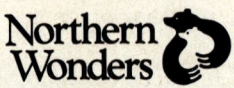

Northern Wonders

The finest northern gifts & handicrafts at very reasonable prices.
Located at Westmark Hotels

Welcome to the North Country.

Reservations are a must anytime from June through August.

Dawson City Bed & Breakfast. Located in a quiet setting at the junction of the Klondike and Yukon rivers. Northern hospitality with an Oriental theme. Walking distance to downtown attractions. Complimentary airport, bus and waterfront transportation provided. Open year-round. Reservations recommended. Single $59, double $69, queen with private bathroom $79. (10 percent discount for seniors with reservations). VISA and MasterCard. Includes full continental breakfast. Send for free brochure package. Box 954, 451 Craig St., Dawson City, YT Y0B 1G0. Phone (403) 993-5649, Fax (403) 993-5648. [ADVERTISEMENT]

5th Avenue Bed and Breakfast. Located next to the museum in downtown Dawson City, a modern home with an emphasis on comfort, serving a hearty, healthy breakfast. Need information, stay with us, 19-year area resident. Mom and dad, no charge for children under 12 years. VISA. Call or write Larry and Pat Vezina, Box 722, Dawson City, YT Y0B 1G0. Phone (403) 993-5941. [ADVERTISEMENT]

Northern Comfort Bed & Breakfast. Enjoy Northern comfort and hospitality within easy walking distance of all major Dawson City attractions. The Hunston family welcomes you. We have a separate 3-room suite, complete with private bathroom, for your convenience. Reservations recommended. Families welcome. Box 135, Dawson City, YT Y0B 1G0. Phone (403) 993-5271. [ADVERTISEMENT]

White Ram Manor Bed & Breakfast, at 7th and Harper. (Look for the "pink" house.) Come stay with us while you take in Dawson's many attractions. Meet other guests and share your Northern experiences. Laundry facilities. Reservations recommended. VISA, MasterCard. Call or write John/Gail Hendley, Box 302, Dawson City, YT, Y0B 1G0. (403) 993-5772. Fax (403) 993-6509. [ADVERTISEMENT]

Arctic Cotton. Known throughout the Yukon for being the "best T-shirt shop" and offering the most unusual gifts. Exclusive designs by local artist Merlin M. Grade silkscreened on superior quality shirts. Located in a beautiful turn-of-the-century building on 2nd Avenue, between Queen and King streets. Open 7 days a week. 10 A.M. to 8 P.M. Phone (403) 993-5549, Fax (403) 993-6620. [ADVERTISEMENT]

Nancy's. If you're looking for delicious food at reasonable prices, then Nancy's will be your favorite eating place in Dawson. In fact, some visitors claim to eat most of their meals in this well-run eatery. Nancy's opens at 6 A.M. for sourdough pancakes, fresh cinnamon buns and their own fresh ground coffee! For lunch, homemade soup and belt-bustin' sandwiches are served, along with a wide selection of pies, cakes, pastries and cheesecakes, fresh from Nancy's bakery. Evening fare includes scrumptious salads, quiches, pot pies, all-you-can-eat salmon, and tasty sourdough pizza. Nancy's is also Dawson's favorite ice cream spot, serving Haagen-Dazs premium ice cream. Nancy's is located at Front and Princess streets. [ADVERTISEMENT]

Paradise Alley Emporium & Atelier, the "purple house" located on 2nd Avenue in historic Dawson City. Specializes in original artwork by local artists. Many T-shirts and sweatshirts, all with unique designs. Yukon gold nuggets and jewelry. Other gift items. Yukon wildflowers abound in the flower garden. (403) 993-6507. [ADVERTISEMENT]

There are 2 Yukon government (YTG) campgrounds in the Dawson area. Yukon River YTG campground is across the Yukon River (by ferry) from town, adjacent the west side ferry approach. Klondike River YTG campground is southeast of town near the airport (see **Milepost J 315.2**). Private RV parks in the Dawson area include Gold Rush Campground, downtown at 5th and York; GuggieVille, east of town at **Milepost**

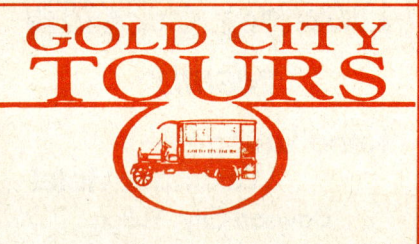

GOLD CITY TOURS

Located on Front Street across from the riverboat "KENO"

SIGHTSEEING TOURS
of Dawson City and
The Klondike Gold Fields
AND
The Midnight Dome
Gold Panning & Gold Mining Tours
Step-on Guide Service

DEMPSTER HIGHWAY BUS SERVICE
Scheduled Service Dawson to Inuvik,
Crossing the Arctic Circle

*Special Tours Arranged on Request
Limo & Charter Service Also Available*
FULL SERVICE TRAVEL AGENCY
Reservations for B.C. and Alaska State Ferries

**P.O. Box 960, Dawson City, Yukon Y0B 1G0
Phone (403) 993-5175 • FAX (403) 993-5261**

David H. (Buffalo) Taylor, Proprietor
Member-Dawson City C. of C., K.V.A., T.I.A.Y., I.A.T.A.

Locally owned and operated year-round

Dawson Trading Post

Box 889, Dawson City
Yukon Y0B 1G0
(403) 993-5316

YOUR OUTDOOR SUPPLIER
Camping, Hunting, Hiking, Trapping, Fishing
Equipment, Furs & Antlers

Gold Panning — Raw GOLD NUGGETS For Sale

Experience the Yukon Wilderness

Canoe Rentals
Pickup & Delivery Available

MasterCard — VISA

J 324.5; Trail of '98 Mini-Golf at **Milepost J 324.5**; and Bonanza Shell at **Milepost J 324.7**.

TRANSPORTATION

Air: Dawson City airport is 11.5 miles/18.5 km southeast of the city. Alkan Air provides scheduled service to Inuvik, NWT, Old Crow, Mayo and Whitehorse. Air North connects Dawson with Old Crow, Fairbanks and Whitehorse (daily service in summer), and with Watson Lake and Juneau (3 times weekly in summer). Charter and flightseeing tours available from Bonanza Aviation. Helicopter tours from Trans North Air.

Ferry: The Yukon government operates a free 24-hour ferry, the *George Black,* across the Yukon River from about the 3rd week in May to mid-October (depending upon breakup and freezeup); ferry departs Dawson City on demand. The ferry carries vehicles and passengers across to the public campground and is the only connection to Yukon Highway 9.

Taxi: Airport taxi service available from downtown hotels. Scheduled and charter limo service available from Gold City Tours.

Bus: Service between Whitehorse and Dawson City, and to Inuvik, NWT (check with Gold City Tours).

Boat: Service to Eagle, AK, on the *Yukon Queen*. Canoe rentals available from Dawson Trading Post.

ATTRACTIONS

Take a Walking Tour. Town core tours leave the visitor reception centre several times daily in summer. The Fort Herchmer walking tour starts at the Commissioner's Residence on Front Street. This handsome building was once the residence of Hon. George Black, M.P., Speakers of the House of Commons, and his famous wife Martha Louise, who walked in over the Trail of '98 and stayed to become the First Lady of the Yukon. (For the complete and fascinating story of Martha Louise Black, read *Martha Black*; available in bookstores or from Alaska Northwest Books™.) Pick up a schedule of daily events at the visitor reception centre.

Take a Bus Tour. Motorcoach and van tours of Klondike creeks, goldfields and Dawson City are available; inquire at Gold City Tours. For a panoramic view of Dawson City, the Klondike, Bonanza Creek and Yukon River, take the bus or drive your vehicle the 5 miles/8 km up to Midnight Dome mountain (elev. 3,050 feet/930m).

Take a River Tour: Tours aboard the miniature stern-wheeler launch *Yukon Lou* leave the dock below SS *Keno* at 1 P.M. daily in summer and travel to Pleasure Island and the stern-wheeler graveyard. Westours operates the *Yukon Queen* between Dawson and Eagle; check with the Westmark Inn about tickets. One-way and round-trip passage is sold on a space-available basis. The trip takes 4 hours downstream to Eagle, 6 hours back to Dawson.

Visit the Palace Grand Theatre. This magnificently reconstructed theatre, now a national historic site, is home to the "Gaslight Follies," a turn-of-the-century entertainment. Performances nightly except

---

5th Avenue
Bed & Breakfast
NEXT TO THE MUSEUM

- Comfortable Modern Home
- Rooms with Private or Shared Washroom
- Kitchen Facilities

Mom & Dad — No charge for children under 12 years

Write Larry & Pat Vezina
Box 722, Dawson City, Yukon Y0B 1G0
Phone (403) 993-5941

Reasonable Rates
VISA

DOWNTOWN HOTEL

- VIP Suites
- 60 Modern Comfortable Rooms
- Jacuzzi
- Telephones • Cable TV
- Airport Limousine • Plug-ins
- Jack London Grill
- Sourdough Saloon
- Banquet and Meeting Facilities

Located on the corner of 2nd and Queen, one block from Diamond Tooth Gertie's and the Palace Grand Theatre.

Box 780, Dawson City, Yukon, Canada Y0B 1G0
Major Credit Cards Accepted
FOR RESERVATIONS CALL: 1-800-661-0514 (YK & BC)   1-800-764-GOLD (AK)
(403) 993-5346 FAX (403) 993-5076
Operated Year-Round by Yukoners

BONANZA AVIATION LTD.
DAWSON CITY YUKON

Aircraft Charter Sightseeing Flights

SEE DAWSON CITY BY AIR
Spectacular Tombstone Mountains
Klondike Gold Fields
Yukon River

FLY
Across the Arctic Circle
to the Beaufort Sea
(Inuvik and Tuktoyaktuk)

CALL: (403) 993-6904

Box 284, Dawson City
Yukon Territory Y0B 1G0
VISA MasterCard

On The Corner Of Front & Queen Streets

Dawson City
Yukon Y0B 1G0

VISA, MasterCard, American Express taken by all shops

KLONDIKE NUGGET & IVORY SHOP
Dawsons City's oldest establishment. Nugget jewelry handcrafted on premises, Gifts – Fine China – Jade – Mammoth Ivory jewelry. See our gold nugget display.
Phone: (403) 993-5432   P.O. Box 250

PEABODY'S PHOTO-PORTRAIT PARLOUR
Capture summer memories with a unique Klondike photo. Same day film processing. Yukon artwork, film, spoons, plush toys and one of the largest selections of postcards in the Yukon.
Phone: (403) 993-5209   Bag 7040

MAXIMILLIANS GOLD RUSH EMPORIUM
Complete selection of Yukon and Northern books, magazines, cassettes and CDs, gifts and souvenirs, T-shirt boutique, film, caps, postcards, paperbacks, pins and glassware.
Phone: (403) 993-5486   P.O. Box 304

Tuesday, from late May to early September. Arizona Charlie Meadows opened the Palace Grand in 1899 and today's visitors, sitting in the curtained boxes around the balcony, will succumb to the charm of this beautiful theatre. Tours of the building are conducted daily by Canadian Parks Service, June through September. There are daily interpretive programs during July and August. The excellent film *City of Gold* is shown here daily in summer.

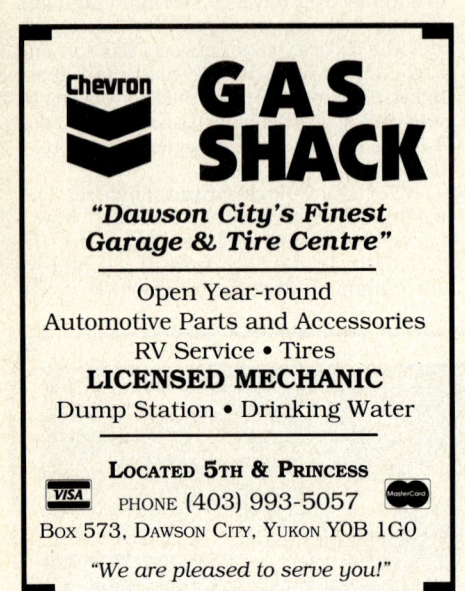

Gamble. Klondike Visitors Assoc. (a nonprofit community organization) operates Diamond Tooth Gertie's gambling hall, open nightly (except Sunday). There are Klondike gambling tables (specially licensed in Yukon), bar service and 4 floor shows nightly. Have a soft drink if you prefer, and still see the cancan girls present their floor show. Persons under 19 not admitted.

Visit the Dawson City Museum. Housed in the renovated Territorial Administration Bldg. on 5th Avenue, the museum is open daily from 10 A.M. to 6 P.M., June through Labour Day; by appointment the rest of the year. Featured are the Kings of the Klondike and City Life Galleries, daily audiovisual shows and the museum's collection of narrow-gauge locomotives, including a Vauclain-type Baldwin engine, the last one in existence. New exhibits in 1992 include a Yukon Ditch photo display and "Dawson City at -40°" slide show.

The audiovisual shows include slide shows on the Dempster Highway and Yukon Ditch, and the film *The Yukoner*. A selection of silent film serials, news and documentary reels from 1903 to 1929, is also shown.

The museum has a gift shop, resource library, genealogy service and an extensive photography collection. A nominal admission fee is charged.

SS *Keno* National Historic Site. The SS *Keno* was the last steamer to run the Yukon River when she sailed from Whitehorse in 1960 to her present berth on the riverbank next to the bank. Although closed to the public while under restoration, an interpretive display is set up beside the site.

Historic Harrington's Store, 3rd Avenue and Princess Street, houses a photographic exhibit entitled *Dawson As They Saw It*. Open daily; no admission charged.

Visit Robert Service's Cabin: On the hillside on 8th Avenue, Robert Service's cabin has been restored by Canadian Parks Service. Stories and poetry recitals (by actor Tom Byrne) are offered daily in summer at 10 A.M. and 3 P.M. Visitors come from every part of the world to sign the guest book on the rickety desk where the bank clerk-author wrote his famous poems, which include *The Shooting of Dan McGrew* and *The Cremation of Sam McGee*. Open 9 A.M. to noon and 1-5 P.M. daily. No admission charged.

Visit the Historic Post Office, where you may buy stamps and all first-class mail receives the old hand cancellation stamp. Open daily.

Visit Jack London's Cabin: Along 8th Avenue and past Service's home is Jack London's cabin, built from one-half of the logs saved from its original site in the Bush where the famous northern writer stayed on his way to the Klondike. (The rest of the logs were used to build an identical cabin in Jack London Square in Oakland, CA.) Interpretation daily at 1 P.M. No admission charged. Dick North, author of *The Lost Patrol* (Alaska Northwest Books™), is curator and consultant at Jack London's Cabin.

Special Events. Dawson City hosts a number of unique and unusual celebrations during the year. The Dawson City International Gold Show is scheduled for May 30 to June 1, 1992. The Commissioner's Ball follows on June 13, 1992. The Yukon Gold Panning Championship is held July 1 each year in Dawson City. (For long-range planners, the World Gold Panning competition is scheduled to return to Dawson City in 1996.) Then on July 18 of this year it's the international Midnight Dome Race. Held the third Saturday in July, this race attracts over 100 runners each year from all over the world. The 4.6-mile/7.4-km course rises a total elevation of 1,850 feet/564m.

The 14th Annual Dawson City Museum Festival, scheduled for July 19-21, 1992, features entertainers and artists from Canada and the U.S., free workshops, dances and dinners. Tickets and information in advance from the Music Festival Assoc., Box 456, Dawson City, YT Y0B 1G0. Phone (403) 993-5584.

If you are near Dawson Aug. 14-17, 1992, be sure to join the Discovery Day fun when Yukon Order of Pioneers stage their annual parade and the town is packed with Yukoners for ball games and dances and a rare old time. This event is a Yukon holiday commemorating the Klondike gold discovery of Aug. 17, 1896. A Military Festival of Bands is scheduled for Aug. 15.

The Great Klondike International Outhouse Race, held the Sunday of Labour Day weekend (Sept. 6, 1992), is a race of outhouses (on wheels) over a 3-km course through the streets of Dawson City.

See the Midnight Sun: If you are in Dawson on June 21, be sure to make it to the top of the Dome by midnight, when the sun barely dips behind the 6,000-foot/1,829-m Ogilvie Mountains to the north—the picture of a lifetime. There's quite a local celebration up on the Dome June 21, so for those who don't like crowds, a visit before or after summer solstice will also afford fine views and photos. Turnoff for Midnight Dome mountain is at **Milepost J 325.8**; it's about a 5-mile/8-km drive.

Chevron GAS SHACK
"Dawson City's Finest Garage & Tire Centre"
Open Year-round
Automotive Parts and Accessories
RV Service • Tires
LICENSED MECHANIC
Dump Station • Drinking Water
LOCATED 5TH & PRINCESS
PHONE (403) 993-5057
Box 573, DAWSON CITY, YUKON Y0B 1G0
"We are pleased to serve you!"

TRIPLE J HOTEL
5th and QUEEN DAWSON CITY
P.O. BOX 359 Y0B 1G0
YUKON TERRITORY
NEXT TO DIAMOND TOOTH GERTIE'S
Motel / Hotel rooms • Executive suite
Cabins with kitchenettes and full bath
Phone, colour TV, coin laundry
Air-conditioned lounge and restaurant
Conference room
Airport taxi service
(403) 993-5323 FAX 993-5030

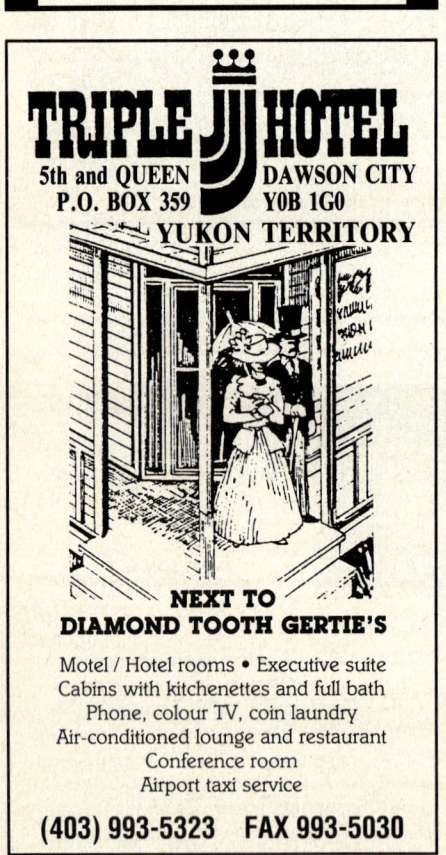

WHITE RAM MANOR
Bed & Breakfast
DAWSON CITY, YUKON
SPACIOUS HOME AT 7TH & HARPER
"A Travellers Delight"
Within Walking Distance of Dawson's many attractions
Full Breakfast Laundry and Kitchen Facilities
Waterfront and Bus Pickup Available
Ask for information on
NORTHERN NETWORK B&B
BC – Yukon – Alaska
Write – John & Gail Hendley
Box 302, Dawson City, Yukon Y0B 1G0
Phone (403) 993-5772 • FAX (403) 993-6509

DAWSON CITY BED & BREAKFAST
• Single • Double • Triple • Queen with Private Bathroom
Seniors Reservations – 10% Discount
"Send for our brochure package"
Phone (403) 993-5649
FAX (403) 993-5648
Box 954, 451 Craig St.
Dawson City, Yukon Y0B 1G0
Open All Year

Pan for Gold: The chief attraction for most visitors is panning for gold. There are several mining operations set up to permit you to actually pan for your own "colours" under friendly guidance. Take Bonanza Creek Road from **Milepost J 324.5** up famous Bonanza Creek, past No. 4 Dredge, Discovery Claim and miles of gravel tailings worked over 2 and 3 times in the continuing search for gold. The Klondike Visitors Assoc. sponsors a public panning area at No. 6 above Discovery, 13 miles/21 km from Dawson City on Bonanza Creek Road.

Bear Creek Camp, about 7 miles/11 km southeast of the city on the Klondike Highway, was operated by Yukon Consolidated Gold Corp. until 1966, when the dredges shut down. Tours are conducted by Canadian Parks Service interpreters; check with the information centre for current tour schedule. The compound features the Gold Room, where the gold was melted and poured into bricks, complete blacksmith and machinery shops, and other well-preserved structures. Open 9:30 A.M. to 5 P.M. from mid-June to late August. No admission charged.

Klondike Loop Log

(continued)
YUKON HIGHWAY 9
The Top of the World Highway (Yukon Highway 9) connects Dawson City with the Taylor Highway in Alaska. A free ferry carries passengers and vehicles from Dawson City across the Yukon River to the beginning of the Top of the World Highway. The Alaska Highway is 176.6 miles/284.2 km from here; Eagle, AK, is 146.2 miles/235.3 km from here. Allow plenty of time for this drive; average speed for this road is 25 to 40 mph/ 40 to 64 kmph. DRIVE WITH YOUR HEADLIGHTS ON! Yukon Highway 9 and the Taylor Highway (Alaska Route 5) in Alaska are closed from fall freezeup to spring breakup.

IMPORTANT: U.S. and Canada customs are open from about May 15 to Sept. 15 for 12 hours a day. (1991 hours were 9 A.M. to 9 P.M. Pacific time on the Canadian side; 8 A.M. to 8 P.M. Alaska time.) Check with the RCMP or visitor information centre in Dawson City to make certain the border crossing at Milepost D 67 will be open. Serious fines are levied for crossing the border without clearing customs!

This section of the log shows distance from Dawson City (D) followed by distance from junction with the Taylor Highway (T) at Jack Wade Junction. Physical kilometreposts show distance from Dawson City.

D 0 T 78.8 (126.9 km) **DAWSON CITY.** Free ferry crosses the Yukon River daily in summer.

D 0.2 (0.3 km) **T 78.6** (126.5 km) Yukon River government campground on riverbank opposite Dawson City; 76 sites, 20 tent sites, 2 kitchen shelters, playground and drinking water. Put-in and takeout spot for Yukon River travelers. ▲

D 2.9 (4.6 km) **T 75.9** (122.1 km) Turnout for viewpoint overlooking Dawson City and the Yukon and Klondike rivers.

D 3.2 (5 km) **T 75.6** (121.7 km) Turnout with good view of Yukon River and river valley farms.

D 9 (12.4 km) **T 69.8** (112.3 km) Rest

U.S.–Canada border. (Philip and Karen Smith)

area with pit toilets, picnic tables, litter barrels and information sign.

D 11 (15.6 km) **T 67.8** (109.1 km) "Top of the World" view as highway climbs above tree line.

D 16.4 (26.2 km) **T 62.4** (100.4 km) Snow fence along highway next 8 miles/13 km westbound.

D 18.4 (29.4 km) **T 60.4** (97.2 km) Large turnout on left.

D 29.2 (47 km) **T 49.6** (79.8 km) Evidence of 1989 burn.

D 32.1 (51.2 km) **T 46.7** (75.1 km) First outcropping (westbound) of Castle Rock. Turnout to south with panoramic view of countryside.

D 33.1 (52.8 km) **T 45.7** (73.5 km) Distance marker shows customs 52 km, Dawson City 53 km.

D 35.2 (56 km) **T 43.6** (70.2 km) Main outcropping of Castle Rock; lesser formations are also found along this stretch. Centuries of erosion have created these formations. Turnout on left westbound.

D 37.4 (59 km) **T 41.8** (67.3 km) Unmaintained road leads 25 miles/40.2 km to the former settlement of Clinton Creek, which served the Cassiar Asbestos Mine from 1967–79. There are no facilities or services available there. Distance marker shows U.S. border 43 km.

The confluence of the Yukon and Fortymile rivers is 3 miles/4.8 km below the former townsite of Clinton Creek. Clinton Creek bridge is an access point on the Fortymile National Wild and Scenic River system, managed by the Bureau of Land Management. The Fortymile River offers intermediate and advanced canoeists over 100 miles/160 km of challenging water.

Yukon River, near Clinton Creek, grayling to 3 lbs. in April; chum salmon to 12 lbs. in August; king salmon to 40 lbs., July and August. **Fortymile River,** near Clinton Creek, grayling to 3 lbs. during ice breakup and fall freezeup; inconnu (sheefish) to 10 lbs. in July and August.◆

D 54 (85.6 km) **T 24.8** (39.9 km) Old sod-roofed prospector's cabin on right westbound.

D 54.3 (86.1 km) **T 24.5** (39.4 km) Road forks left westbound to old mine workings at Sixtymile which have been reactivated by Cogasa Mining Co. Keep to right for Alaska. The road winds above timberline for many miles. The lack of fuel for warmth and shelter made this a perilous trip for the early sourdoughs.

D 65.2 (103.7 km) **T 13.6** (21.9 km) Pull-through rest stop with toilet. Good viewpoint.

D 66.1 (105.1 km) **T 13.2** (21.2 km)

U.S.–Canada border (elev. 4,127 feet/ 1,258m). Canada Customs and Immigration Little Gold Creek office is open 9 A.M. to 9 P.M. (Pacific time) from about May 15 to Sept. 15. All traffic entering Canada must stop here. The U.S. border station Poker Creek office, just past the Canadian station, is open 8 A.M. to 8 P.M. (Alaska time) from about May 15 to Sept. 15. All traffic entering the U.S. must stop here. Both stations are closed in winter.

TIME ZONE CHANGE: Alaska observes Alaska time; Yukon Territory observes Pacific time. See Time Zones in GENERAL INFORMATION section for details.

D 67.1 (108 km) **T 12** (19.3 km) Turnout to north with view of mountains.

Poker Creek Gold will be your first (or last!) stop in Alaska and one you will always remember. It is a scenic overlook offering updates about current road and weather conditions, maps, history and points of interest sheets (Alaska and the Yukon), mining and artifacts and wildflower display. Locally mined gold nuggets and Alaskan handmade gold jewelry at unbelievably low prices. Coffee, picnic tables and a view from the top of the world! It's the perfect stop to rest at the top! See display ad this section.
[ADVERTISEMENT]

D 69.2 (111.4 km) **T 9.4** (15.1 km) **BOUNDARY.** Boundary Lodge was one of the first roadhouses in Alaska; food and gas (current status unknown). Watch your gas supply. Between here and Tetlin Junction on the Alaska Highway, gas is available again only at Chicken, **Milepost TJ 66.6**. From here to Eagle, gas may be available at O'Brien Creek Lodge, **Milepost TJ 125.3**. Gas is available in Eagle. Emergency phone at roadhouse for contacting Alaska State Troopers.

Private Aircraft: Boundary airstrip; elev. 2,940 feet/896m; length 2,100 feet/640m; earth and gravel; fuel 80; unattended.

D 78 (125.6 km) **T 0.8** (1.3 km) Viewpoint.

D 78.8 (126.9 km) **T 0 Jack Wade Junction, Milepost TJ 95.7** on the Taylor Highway. The Taylor Highway (Alaska Route 5), also known as the Eagle Road or Eagle Cutoff, leads north 65.3 miles/105 km to Eagle, AK, or south 95.7 miles/154 km to Tetlin Junction, just east of Tok, on the Alaska Highway. The Taylor Highway is a narrow, winding, mountain road: Drive carefully!

NOTE: Eagle-bound and Alaska Highway-bound travelers turn to **Milepost TJ 95.7** on page 254 in the TAYLOR HIGHWAY section to continue log. Eagle-bound travelers continue with log forward from **Milepost TJ 95.7**. Alaska Highway-bound travelers read log backward from **Milepost TJ 95.7**.

POKER CREEK GOLD

Unique Alaskan Gold Jewelry
Locally mined — Locally made
— Road and Weather Info —
**Between the Border and Boundary
Mile 12, Top of the World Highway**
See log ad at Mile 67.1

1992 ■ The MILEPOST® 251

TAYLOR HIGHWAY

Tetlin Junction to Eagle, Alaska
Alaska Route 5
(See map, page 239)

Autumn display of birch and aspen along Fortymile River. (George Wuerthner)

The 161-mile/259-km Taylor Highway (Alaska Route 5) begins at Tetlin Junction on the Alaska Highway and ends at the small town of Eagle on the Yukon River. This is a beautiful "top of the world" drive and Eagle is well worth a visit.

The highway also provides access to river runners for the Fortymile River National Wild and Scenic River system. A brochure on access points and float times is available from the Bureau of Land Management, 1150 University Ave., Fairbanks, AK 99709-3844; phone 474-2350.

The Taylor Highway is a narrow, winding, dusty mountain road with many steep hills and some hairpin curves. Allow plenty of time to drive its length. The road surface is gravel, with sporadic soft spots during breakup or after heavy rains. Road surface ranges from poor to good depending on maintenance. Large RVs and trailers especially should use caution in driving this road. The highway is not maintained in winter (from about Oct. 10 to April).

The Taylor is the shortest route to Dawson City, YT, from Alaska. Drive 95.7 miles/154 km north on the Taylor Highway to Jack Wade Junction and turn east on the Top of the World Highway (Yukon Highway 9) for Dawson City. (See end of KLONDIKE LOOP section for log of Yukon Highway 9.) Dawson-bound travelers keep in mind that gas is available only at Chicken and perhaps at Boundary Lodge (current status unknown). Also, the U.S. and Canada customs offices at the border are open 12 hours a day from about mid-May to mid-September. In summer 1991, customs hours were 8 A.M. to 8 P.M. Alaska time, 9 A.M. to 9 P.M. Pacific time on the Canadian side. IMPORTANT: You cannot cross the border unless the customs office for the country you are entering is open. Severe fines are levied for crossing without clearing customs. There are no traveler facilities at the border.

NOTE: All gold-bearing ground in area is claimed. Do not pan in streams.

Emergency medical services: Between Tetlin Junction and O'Brien Creek bridge at **Milepost TJ 113.2**, phone the Tok ambulance, 911 or 883-2300. Between O'Brien Creek bridge and Eagle phone the Eagle EMS, 547-2230 or 547-2211. Use CB channel 21.

Taylor Highway Log

Distance from Tetlin Junction (TJ) is followed by distance from Eagle (E).

TJ 0 E 161 (259 km) **Tetlin Junction.** Junction of the Alaska and Taylor highways. Forty Mile Roadhouse (closed in 1991; current status unknown).

Begin 9 miles/14.5 km of winding road up out of the Tanana River valley. Highway traverses stabilized sand dunes first 5 miles/8 km.

TJ 4.5 (7.2 km) **E 156.5** (251.9 km) Gravel turnout to east. An 0.7-mile/1.1-km trail leads to **Four Mile Lake**; rainbow and sheefish.

TJ 5.4 (8.7 km) **E 155.6** (250.4 km) Evidence of 1990 forest fire known as the Porcupine burn.

TJ 5.9 (9.5 km) **E 155.1** (249.6 km) Entering Tok Management Area, Tanana Valley State Forest, northbound.

TJ 6 (9.7 km) **E 155** (249.4 km) Double-ended turnout to east, easy for trailers but can be soft or bumpy.

Winding road northbound. Watch for ruts and soft spots, and for loose gravel on curves. Wildflowers along the highway include arnica, chiming bells, wild roses and Labrador tea. As the name suggests, Labrador tea leaves (and flowers) may be steeped in boiling water to make tea. However, according to Janice Scofield, author of *Discovering Wild Plants* (Alaska Northwest Books™), Labrador tea contains a narcotic toxin that can cause ill effects if used too frequently or in high concentrations.

TJ 9.4 (15.1 km) **E 151.6** (244 km) Entering Game Management Unit 20E northbound; entering GMU 12 southbound. Road begins gradual climb of Mount Fairplay for northbound travelers.

TJ 12.1 (19.5 km) **E 148.9** (239.6 km) Entering Tok Management Area, Tanana State Forest, southbound.

TJ 14.6 (23.5 km) **E 146.4** (235.6 km) Blueberries in season.

TJ 21.2 (34.1 km) **E 139.8** (225 km) Long descent northbound.

TJ 28.3 (45.5 km) **E 132.7** (213.6 km) Turnout with view to west.

TJ 34.4 (55.4 km) **E 126.6** (203.7 km) Double-ended turnout with view to west.

TJ 35.1 (56.5 km) **E 125.9** (202.6 km) Entering Fortymile Mining District northbound. Double-ended turnout near summit of Mount Fairplay (elev. 5,541 feet/1,689m). Interpretive sign here reads: "The Taylor Highway leads through some of the earliest and richest gold mining country in Alaska to the city of Eagle on the Yukon River. Gold was discovered by Franklin in 1886 and the old town of Fortymile was located on the Yukon River at the mouth of the Fortymile River. A riverboat trip from Eagle will take you to this historic town. The Chicken Creek area was also a rich gold mining area at about the same time. Wade Creek was another rich area and the remains of an old dredge still stand along the road. The old horse and wagon trail used by the early-day miners and freighters is still visible in many places and the present highway often parallels this trail. The largest herd of caribou in Alaska crosses the Taylor Highway each fall on its annual migration. This is truly a sportsman's paradise with an abundance of fish and game."

Highway descends a 9-percent grade northbound. Southbound, the road descends for the next 25 miles/40 km from Mount Fairplay's summit, winding down through heavily forested terrain. Panoramic views of valleys of the forks of the Fortymile River. Views of the Alaska Range to the southwest.

TJ 39.1 (62.9 km) **E 121.9** (196.2 km) Large turnout to west.

TJ 43 (69.2 km) **E 118** (189.9 km) Logging Cabin Creek bridge; small turnout to west at south end of bridge. Side road to creek. This is the south end of the Fortymile National Wild and Scenic River system managed by BLM.

TJ 49 (78.8 km) **E 112** (180.2 km) Loop roads through BLM West Fork recreation site; 25 sites (7 pull-through sites), tables, firepits, no water, covered tables, toilets, dumpsters. Access point of Fortymile River canoe trail. Improved campground. ▲

TJ 49.3 (79.3 km) **E 111.7** (179.7 km) Bridge over West Fork of the Dennison Fork of the Fortymile River. Access point for Fortymile River National Wild and Scenic River system.

TJ 50.5 (81.3 km) **E 110.5** (177.8 km) Taylor Creek bridge. All-terrain vehicle trail to Taylor and Kechumstuk mountains; heavily used in hunting season.

TJ 57 (91.7 km) **E 104** (167.4 km) Scenic viewpoint turnout to east.

TJ 54 (86.9 km) **E 107** (172.2 km) Turnout to east. Drive in, no easy turnaround.

TJ 58.9 (94.8 km) **E 102.1** (164.3 km) Scenic viewpoint turnout with litter barrels to east. Drive in, no easy turnaround.

TJ 63.7 (102.5 km) **E 97.3** (156.6 km) Steep descent northbound to Mosquito Fork.

TJ 64.1 (103.1 km) **E 96.9** (155.9 km) Well-traveled road leads to private buildings, not into Chicken.

TJ 64.3 (103.5 km) **E 96.7** (155.6 km) Bridge over Mosquito Fork of the Fortymile River; day-use area with table, toilet and litter barrel at north end of bridge. The Mosquito Fork is a favorite access point for the Fortymile National Wild and Scenic River system, according to the BLM.

TJ 66 (106.2 km) **E 95** (152.9 km) Entering CHICKEN (pop. 37), northbound. *(NOTE: Driving distance between **Milepost 66** and **67** is 0.7 mile.)* This is the newer commercial settlement of Chicken. The original mining camp (abandoned, private property) is north of Chicken Creek (see **Milepost TJ 67**). Chicken is a common name in the North for ptarmigan. One story has it that the early miners wanted to name their camp ptarmigan, but were unable to spell it and settled for Chicken. Access point for the Fortymile River canoe trail is below Chicken airstrip.

TJ 66.3 (106.7 km) **E 94.7** (152.4 km) Chicken post office (Zip code 99732) located on hill beside the road. The late Ann Purdy lived in this area. The book *Tisha* is based on her experiences as a young schoolteacher in the Alaska Bush.

TJ 66.4 (106.9 km) **E 94.6** (152.2 km) Airport Road. Access to Chicken airstrip. Combination grocery store, restaurant, bar and gas station located here.

Private Aircraft: Chicken airstrip, adjacent southwest; elev. 1,640 feet/500m; length 2,500 feet/762m; gravel; maintained year-round.

Chicken Mercantile Emporium, Chicken Creek Cafe, Saloon and Gas. Unfortunately, as too often happens, the main road bypasses the most interesting part of Chicken. If it's modern facilities you are looking for, original Chicken is not for you. The Chicken Creek Saloon and Cafe are some of the last remnants of the old frontier Alaska. It is a trading post where local miners (some straight out of Jack London) trade gold for supplies and drink. While in Chicken, be sure and try a slice of bread made by "Tisha's" daughter Lynn. And pick up an autographed copy of *Tisha*. Tisha's schoolhouse and other historic buildings may be seen on the walking tour of old Chicken, meeting daily at the Chicken Creek Cafe. A wealth of gifts abound in the Chicken Mercantile Emporium and the cafe is famous throughout Alaska for its excellent food, homemade pies, pastries and cinnamon buns. Chicken Creek Saloon, Cafe and Mercantile Emporium are a rare treat for those with the courage to stray just a few hundred yards from the beaten path.

CHICKEN, AK. TURN HERE...
STORE • LQ • BAR • CAFE
GAS • GIFTS • FOOD
Famous CHICKEN CREEK SALOON
MOTORCOACHES & CARAVANS WELCOME / AIRPORT RD.
MAJOR CREDIT CARDS ACCEPTED

CHICKEN MERCANTILE EMPORIUM
World Famous Chicken T-Shirts • Chicken Hats and Chicken Pins
Lots of Chicken Souvenirs • Local Gold for Sale
Original Chicken Cross-Stitch Designs • Tisha Books

CHICKEN CREEK CAFE
GREAT HOMEMADE FOOD!
Hamburgers
Pies — Pastries and Cinnamon Buns

ALWAYS Low Priced Gas, Friendly Service and Propane in CHICKEN

AIRPORT ROAD   CHICKEN, AK.

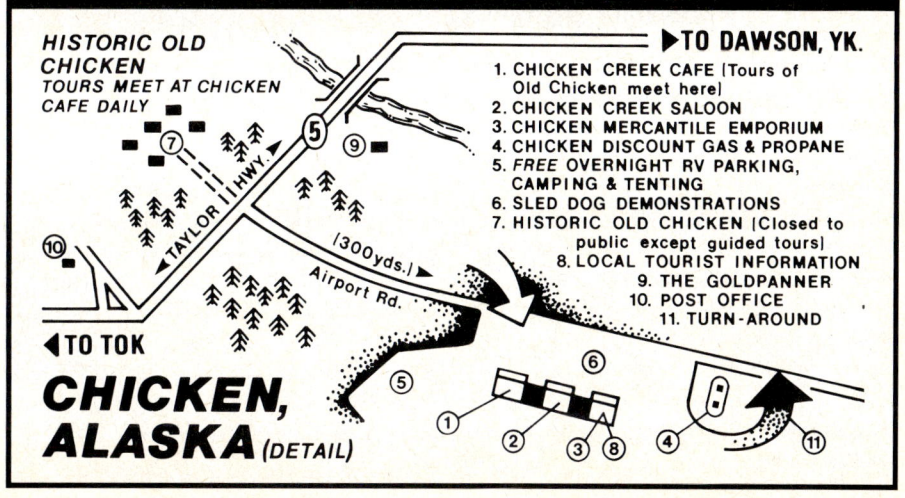

CHICKEN, ALASKA (DETAIL)

HISTORIC OLD CHICKEN TOURS MEET AT CHICKEN CAFE DAILY
▶TO DAWSON, YK.
◀TO TOK

1. CHICKEN CREEK CAFE (Tours of Old Chicken meet here)
2. CHICKEN CREEK SALOON
3. CHICKEN MERCANTILE EMPORIUM
4. CHICKEN DISCOUNT GAS & PROPANE
5. *FREE* OVERNIGHT RV PARKING, CAMPING & TENTING
6. SLED DOG DEMONSTRATIONS
7. HISTORIC OLD CHICKEN (Closed to public except guided tours)
8. LOCAL TOURIST INFORMATION
9. THE GOLDPANNER
10. POST OFFICE
11. TURN-AROUND

TJ 66.5 (107 km) **E 94.5** (152.1 km) **The Goldpanner.** Owners, Bill, Mary, Grant and Dana Morris welcome you to Chicken. We have lots of parking and turnaround space. Our station has gas, diesel, tire repair and minor repairs. The store carries some groceries, staples, snacks, cold pop, canned meats and souvenirs. Chicken souvenirs include T-shirts, sweatshirts, hats, spoons, cups, patches, magnets, bumper stickers, postcards and hatpins. We also carry many other articles including the book *Tisha.* Try your hand at our FREE gold panning or get your local gold already in vials, nuggets, or jewelry. For the sportsman, hunting and fishing licenses are available. For those interested in local history, old bones, rocks and mining artifacts are on display on the porch and throughout the store. There is no charge for our dry RV overnight parking. Buses and caravans are always welcome. [ADVERTISEMENT] ▲

TJ 66.6 (107.2 km) **E 94.4** (151.9 km) Chicken Creek bridge.

TJ 67 (107.8 km) **E 94** (151.3 km) View of abandoned old townsite of Chicken. The road in is blocked off and the dozen or so old buildings are owned by a mining company. Private property, do not trespass. Look upstream (northwest) on Chicken Creek to see the old gold dredge which was shut down in the 1960s.

Mining claims cover several popular stretches of the Fortymile River and virtually all of the bed of the South Fork is claimed. (Although the Fortymile River is a National Wild and Scenic River, the riverbed belongs to the state, which allows underwater mining claims.) Travelers may see some hydraulic mining, suction dredging and sluicing operations along the Fortymile.

TJ 68.2 (109.8 km) **E 92.8** (149.3 km) BLM Chicken field station; information and emergency communications. Trailhead for Mosquito Fork Dredge trail (3 miles round-trip).

TJ 68.9 (110.9 km) **E 92.1** (148.2 km) Lost Chicken Creek. Site of Lost Chicken Hill Mine, established in 1895. Mining was under way in this area several years before the Klondike gold rush of 1897–98. The first major placer gold strike was in 1886 at Franklin Gulch, a tributary of the Fortymile. Watch for hydraulic mining operations in the creek.

TJ 70 (112.7 km) **E 91** (146.4 km) Turnouts at gravel pits on both sides of road.

TJ 71.7 (115.4 km) **E 89.3** (143.7 km) Steep descent northbound as road winds down to South Fork.

TJ 74.4 (119.7 km) **E 86.6** (139.4 km) South Fork River access road.

TJ 74.5 (119.9 km) **E 86.5** (139.2 km) South Fork DOT/PF state highway maintenance station.

TJ 75.3 (121.2 km) **E 85.7** (137.9 km) South Fork bridge. Day-use area with toilet and litter barrels at south end of bridge, west side of road. Access point for the Fortymile River National Wild and Scenic River system. The muddy, bumpy road leading into the brush is used by miners.

TJ 76.8 (123.6 km) **E 84.2** (135.5 km) Turnout with litter barrels to west. View of Oxbow lakes in South Fork valley.

TJ 78.5 (126.3 km) **E 82.5** (132.8 km) Views of Fortymile River valley northbound to **Milepost TJ 82.**

TJ 78.8 (126.8 km) **E 82.2** (132.3 km) Steep descent northbound.

TJ 81.9 (131.8 km) **E 79.1** (127.3 km) Walker Fork bridge.

TJ 82.1 (132.1 km) **E 78.9** (127 km) Walker Fork BLM campground with 16 sites; 2 picnic sites with covered tables. Access point for Fortymile River National Wild and Scenic River system. An old Alaska Road Commission road grader is on display here. ▲

TJ 86.1 (138.5 km) **E 74.9** (120.5 km) Old Jack Wade No. 1 dredge in creek next to road. Turnout to east. This is actually the Butte Creek Dredge, installed in 1934 below the mouth of Butte Creek, and eventually moved to Wade Creek. This was one of the first bucketline dredges used in the area, according to the BLM.

CAUTION: Rough road next 5 miles/8 km northbound; roadbed has been mined. Slow down!

TJ 90 (144.8 km) **E 71** (114.2 km) Jack Wade, an old mining camp which operated until 1940. Active mining is under way in this area. *Do not trespass on mining claims!*

TJ 91.9 (147.9 km) **E 69.1** (111.2 km) Turnout to east.

TJ 93.5 (150.5 km) **E 67.5** (108.6 km) *Slow down for hairpin curve!* Road climbs northbound. *NOTE: Large vehicles use turnouts when meeting oncoming vehicles.*

TJ 95.7 (154 km) **E 65.3** (105.1 km) **Jack Wade Junction.** Continue north on the Taylor Highway for Eagle. Turn east for Boundary Lodge and Alaska–Canada border. Dawson City is 78.8 miles/126.9 km east via the Top of the World Highway. The Top of the World Highway (Yukon Highway 9) is a winding gravel road with some steep grades. Slippery in wet weather. Drive carefully!

Dawson City-bound travelers turn to the end of the KLONDIKE LOOP section and read the Top of the World Highway log back to front. Eagle-bound travelers continue with this log.

TJ 96 (154.5 km) **E 65** (104.6 km) Turnout. View to the north-northeast of Canada's Ogilvie Mountains in the distance.

TJ 99.5 (160.1 km) **E 61.5** (99 km) Road winds around the summit of Steele Creek Dome (elev. 4,015 feet/1,224m) visible directly above the road to the east. *CAUTION: Road is slippery when wet.*

TJ 99.6 (160.3 km) **E 61.4** (98.8 km) *CAUTION: Slow down for hairpin curve!*

TJ 105.1 (169.1 km) **E 55.9** (90 km) Scenic viewpoint with litter barrel to east. The road descends next 7 miles/11.3 km northbound to the valley of the Fortymile River, so named because its mouth was 40 miles below Fort Reliance, an old trading post near the confluence of the Yukon and Klondike. Along the road are abandoned cabins, tailings and dredges.

TJ 108.7 (174.9 km) **E 52.3** (84.2 km) *Slow down for hairpin curve!*

TJ 109 (175.4 km) **E 52** (83.7 km) *CAUTION: Steep, narrow, winding road northbound. Slow down!* Frequent small turnouts and breathtaking views to north and west.

TJ 112.4 (180.9 km) **E 48.6** (78.2 km) Fortymile River bridge; parking area, toilet. No camping. Active mining in area. Nearly vertical beds of white marble can be seen on the northeast side of the river. Access to the Fortymile River National Wild and Scenic River system.

TJ 112.6 (181.2 km) **E 48.4** (77.9 km) Private home and mining camp.

TJ 113.1 (182 km) **E 47.9** (77.1 km) Highway maintenance camp located here.

TJ 113.2 (182.2 km) **E 47.8** (76.9 km) O'Brien Creek bridge. Access to creek.

TJ 113.7 (183 km) **E 47.3** (76.1 km) Winding road northbound, highway parallels O'Brien Creek to Liberty Fork; several turnouts. *CAUTION: Watch for small aircraft using road as runway.*

TJ 117.1 (188.5 km) **E 43.9** (70.7 km) Alder Creek bridge.

TJ 118.3 (190.4 km) **E 42.7** (68.7 km) Road narrows northbound; Watch for falling rock next 1.5 miles/2.4 km northbound.

TJ 122 (196.3 km) **E 39** (62.6 km) Slide area, watch for rocks.

TJ 124.5 (200.3 km) **E 36.5** (58.7 km) Columbia Creek bridge.

TJ 125.3 (201.6 km) **E 35.7** (57.5 km) Lodge with gas.

TJ 128 (206 km) **E 33** (53.1 km) Mileposts between Mile 129 and 160 are 1 to 2 miles off from actual driving distance. This section may be re-signed in 1992.

TJ 134 (215.6 km) **E 27** (43.4 km) King Solomon Creek bridge. Primitive camping (no facilities) at south end of bridge, east side of road, at site of former BLM campground. Highway follows King Solomon Creek next 0.5 mile/0.8 km northbound. Physical milepost 134 (1991).

TJ 137 (220.5 km) **E 24** (38.6 km) *CAUTION: Slow down for hairpin curve.*

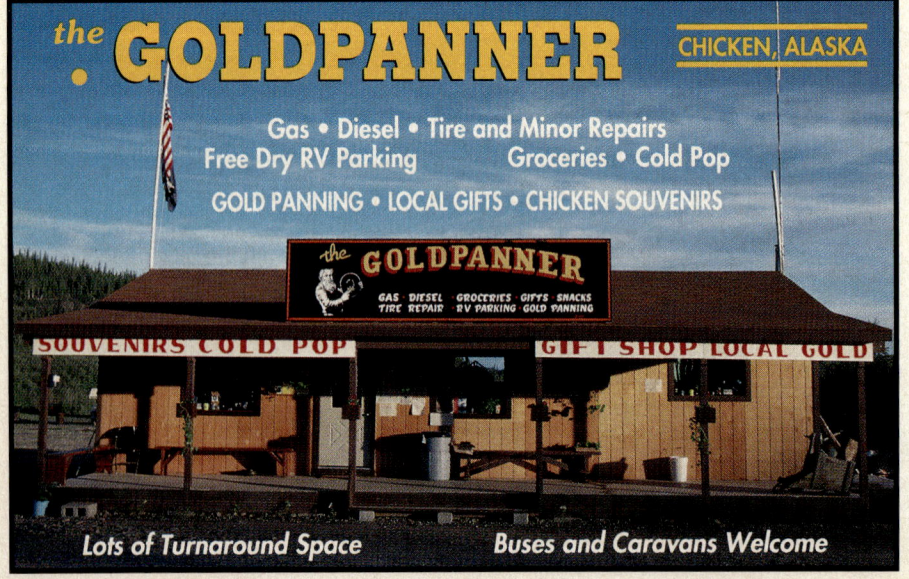

TJ 137.8 (221.8 km) **E 23.2** (37.3 km)

North Fork Solomon Creek bridge.

TJ 142 (228.5 km) **E 19** (30.6 km) Glacier Mountain management area; walk-in hunting only.

TJ 144.7 (232.9 km) **E 16.3** (26.2 km) Turnout on summit. Top of the world views.

TJ 147 (236.6 km) **E 14** (22.5 km) Road begins winding descent northbound to Yukon River.

TJ 150.1 (241.5 km) **E 10.9** (17.5 km) Bridge over Discovery Fork.

TJ 151.7 (244.1 km) **E 9.3** (15 km) Old cabin by creek to west is a local landmark. Private property.

TJ 152.5 (245.4 km) **E 8.5** (13.7 km) American Creek bridge No. 1. "Colors" may occasionally be found when panning for gold on this creek. Outcroppings of asbestos, greenish or gray with bits of white, and serpentine along creekbank.

TJ 153.1 (246.4 km) **E 7.9** (12.7 km) Bridge No. 2 over American Creek.

TJ 160.1 (257.6 km) **E 0.9** (1.4 km) Turnout with historical sign about the settlement of Eagle.

TJ 160.3 (258 km) **E 0.7** (1.1 km) Fourth Avenue. Eagle school to east. Side road to west leads 1 mile/1.6 km to Fort Egbert mule barn, officers' quarters and parade ground (occasionally used as a runway, watch for aircraft). From here a road leads 0.8 mile/1.3 km to Eagle campground; 13 sites. ▲

Eagle

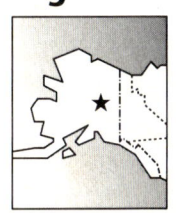

TJ 161 (259 km) **E 0** Population: 168. **Emergency Services:** Eagle health clinic. **Visitor Information:** The Eagle Historical Society conducts an informative tour of Eagle, at 10 A.M. daily Memorial Day through Labor Day; meet at the courthouse. The tour includes the Wickersham courthouse, Waterfront Customs House and the mule barn, water wagon shed and NCO quarters at Fort Egbert; cost is $2 per person, members of Eagle Historical Society and children under 12 years free (annual society membership, $5). Special tours may be arranged. Books, maps and gifts available at the museum store in the courthouse. For more information contact the Eagle Historical Society, Box 23, Eagle City, AK 99738. Fort Egbert, renovated and restored by the BLM, has an interpretive exhibit and a photo display showing the stages of reconstruction.

The National Park Service office, headquarters for Yukon–Charley Rivers National Preserve, is located on the banks of the Yukon River at the base of Fort Egbert. Reference library available to the public. Office hours are 8 A.M. to 5 P.M. weekdays. The National Park Service Visitor Center offers maps and books for sale. Also a video on the preserve is shown on request. Informal talks and interpretive programs available. Visitor center hours are 8 A.M. to 5 P.M. daily in summer (Memorial Day weekend through Labor Day weekend). Check at the visitor center for information on the Yukon River, Yukon–Charley Rivers National Preserve, and other parklands in Alaska. (Write them at Box 167, Eagle 99738, or phone 547-2233.) The visitor center was temporarily located adjacent the headquarters in 1991.

Elevation: 820 feet/250m. **Climate:** Mean monthly temperature in July 59°F/15°C; in January -13°F/-25°C. Record low -71°F/-57°C in January 1952; record high 95°F/35°C in July 1925. July also has the greatest mean number of days (21) with temperatures above 70°F/21°C. Mean precipitation in July 1.94 inches; in December 10.1 inches. Record snow depth 42 inches in April 1948.

Transportation: By road via the Taylor Highway (closed by snow October to April); air taxi, scheduled air service; dog team and snow machine in winter. Eagle is also accessible via the Yukon River. U.S. customs available at post office for persons entering Alaska via the Yukon River or by air.

Private Aircraft: Eagle airstrip, 2 miles/3.2 km east; elev. 880 feet/268m; length 3,500 feet/1,067m; gravel; unattended.

This small community was once the supply and transportation center for miners working the upper Yukon and its tributaries. In the center of town stands a windmill and wellhouse (built in 1909); both still provide water for over half the town's population. There are gas stations, restaurants, gift shops, museum store, post office, showers, laundromat, hardware store and mechanic shop with tire repair. Groceries and sundries are available. Overnight accommodations at motels and rental cabins. RV parking with hookups is available or stay at Eagle BLM campground just outside town (turn left on 4th Avenue and left again along airstrip at Fort Egbert). Eagle Village, an Athabascan settlement, is 3 miles/4.8 km from Eagle.

Eagle had its beginnings in the early 1880s, when Francois Mercier, one of Alaska Commercial Co.'s first upriver fur traders, established his Belle Isle trading post here. Fur traders were followed by gold seekers, and by 1898 Eagle's population was 1,700. The town population included missionaries, the U.S. Army (which established Fort Egbert), and Judge James Wickersham, who presided over the federal court.

By 1910, Eagle's population had dwindled to 178. Gold strikes in Fairbanks and Nome had lured away many miners. Judge Wickersham, and the district court, moved to Fairbanks in 1904. Fort Egbert was abandoned in 1911.

Historically an important riverboat landing, Eagle is still a popular jumping-off point for Yukon River travelers. Most popular is a summer float trip from Eagle downriver through the **YUKON–CHARLEY RIVERS NATIONAL PRESERVE** to Circle. Length of the Eagle–Circle trip is 154 river miles, with most trips averaging 5 to 10 days. Boaters also often float the Fortymile to the Yukon River, then continue to the boat landing at Eagle to take out. Commercial boat trips are also available. Breakup on the Yukon is in May; freezeup in October. For details on weather, clothing, gear and precautions, contact the National Park Service, Box 167, Eagle 99738; phone 547-2233.

Westours (Gray Line of Alaska) operates the *Yukon Queen* boat service between Eagle and Dawson City, YT. Check locally about tickets. Round-trip and one-way passage is sold on a space available basis. The trip to Dawson City takes 6 hours, return trip is 4 hours.

Eagle Trading Co. See display ad this section.

The Village Store and Gallery. See display ad this section.

THE VILLAGE STORE AND GALLERY

Locally handcrafted Alaskan gifts and art gallery featuring Alaskan artists

GROCERIES • GAS • PROPANE
VIDEO ARCADE • HOT SANDWICHES
Hunting and fishing licenses available
• ROOMS •

Bed & Breakfast
Major and Government credit cards accepted

(907) 547-2270
P.O. Box 111 • Eagle, Alaska 99738

EAGLE TRADING CO.

Groceries • Cafe • Lodging
Ice • Propane • Tire Repair
Gas • Diesel • AV Gas
Coin-op Laundry • Gifts
RV Hookups • Public Showers
Hunting & Fishing Licenses
Airport Shuttle

EAGLE'S NEWEST AND MOST COMPLETE FACILITY

We guarantee the lowest gas prices in town

End of the Taylor Highway on the Banks of the Yukon

For Information & Motel Reservations:
Box 36, Eagle, Alaska 99738 • (907) 547-2220 • FAX (907) 547-2202

GLENN HIGHWAY

**Includes Tok Cutoff
Tok, Alaska, to Anchorage, Alaska
Alaska Route 1
(See maps, pages 257–258)**

Magnificent Matanuska Glacier seen from the Glenn Highway. (Hugh B. White)

The Glenn Highway (Alaska Route 1) is the principal access route from the Alaska Highway west to Anchorage and southcentral Alaska. It includes the original 189-mile/304-km road of this name between Anchorage and the Richardson Highway, a 14-mile/22.5-km link via the Richardson Highway and the 125-mile/201-km Tok–Slana Cutoff (referred to as the Tok Cutoff), first built in 1942 as a shortcut for Army convoys en route to Anchorage.

It is a full day's drive between Tok and Anchorage on this paved all-weather highway. Areas to watch for road construction in 1992 are from **Milepost GJ 52 to GJ 38**; **Milepost A 141.2 to A 118**; and **Milepost A 56 to A 26.5**. The highway between Tok and Glennallen has some very narrow sections with no shoulders. Also watch for frost heaves and pavement breaks along the entire highway. Slow down at signs saying Bump—they mean it!

Four side roads are logged in this section: the Nabesna Road to the old Nabesna Mine, which also provides access to Wrangell-St. Elias National Park and Preserve; Lake Louise Road, which leads to Lake Louise Recreation Area; the Hatcher Pass Road, connecting the Glenn and George Parks highways to Independence Mine State Historical Park; and the Old Glenn Highway, an alternate route between Palmer and Anchorage.

Emergency medical services: Between Tok and Duffy's Roadhouse at **Milepost GJ 63**, phone the Tok ambulance at 883-2300 or 911. Between Duffy's and Gakona Junction, phone the Glennallen EMS at 822-3203 or 911. From Gakona Junction to Anchorage phone 911. CB channel 9 between **Milepost A 30.8** and Anchorage.

Glenn Highway Log

TOK CUTOFF
On the first section of the Glenn Highway, the physical mileposts read from **Milepost 125** at Tok to **Milepost 0** at Gakona Junction, the north junction with the Richardson Highway. From Glennallen to Anchorage the mileposts show distance to Anchorage.
Distance from Gakona Junction (GJ) is followed by distance from Anchorage (A) and distance from Tok (T).

GJ 125 (201.2 km) **A 328** (527.8 km) **T 0** Tok (see description in the ALASKA HIGHWAY section).

GJ 124.2 (199.9 km) **A 327.2** (526.6 km) **T 0.8** (1.3 km) Tok Community Center.

GJ 124.1 (199.7 km) **A 327.1** (526.4 km) **T 0.9** (1.4 km) Tok Community Clinic, Tok Fire Station.

GJ 124 (199.6 km) **A 327** (526.2 km) **T 1** (1.6 km) Dept. of Natural Resources.

GJ 123.9 (199.4 km) **A 326.9** (526.1 km) **T 1.1** (1.8 km) Dept. of Transportation and Public Facilities, Tok Station.

GJ 123.7 (199.1 km) **A 326.7** (525.8 km) **T 1.3** (2.1 km) Borealis Avenue.
  Grizzly Auto Repair, offering a complete range of repairs and adjustments for your vehicle. From electrical to mechanical along with welding. We have excellent equipment for wheel alignments and brake care. We also offer Goodyear tires. Plenty of room to park. Motorhomes welcome. The finest professional service, reasonable shop rates. See display ad in Tok in the ALASKA HIGHWAY section. [ADVERTISEMENT]

GJ 123.3 (198.4 km) **A 326.3** (525.1 km) **T 1.7** (2.7 km) **Hayner's Trading Post.** Alaskan handmade jewelry and gifts, beads and supplies, greeting and note cards. Sporting goods and black powder supplies. Custom leather work and repairs. Free coffee and tea. Open year-round. Summer hours 10 A.M. to 8 P.M. Rocky and Sue Hayner, owners. (907) 883-5536. See display ad in Tok in the ALASKA HIGHWAY section. [ADVERTISEMENT]

GJ 122.8 (197.6 km) **A 325.8** (524.3 km) **T 2.2** (3.5 km) **Sourdough Campground's Pancake Breakfast** served 7-11 A.M. Genuine "Sourdoughs." Full and partial RV hookups. Dry campsites. Showers included in price. High-pressure car wash with brush. Open-air museum. Evening slide show. Located 1.7 miles from the junction toward Anchorage on Tok Cutoff (Glenn Highway). See display ad in Tok in the ALASKA HIGHWAY section. [ADVERTISEMENT] ▲

GJ 122.6 (197.3 km) **A 325.6** (524 km) **T 2.4** (3.9 km) Bayless and Roberts Airport. Paved bike trail from Tok ends here.

GJ 116.7 (187.8 km) **A 319.7** (514.5 km) **T 8.3** (13.4 km) Entering Tok Management Area, Tanana Valley State Forest, westbound.

GJ 113 (181.9 km) **A 316** (508.5 km) **T 12** (19.3 km) Beautiful mountain views westbound.

GJ 110 (177 km) **A 313** (503.7 km) **T 15** (24.1 km) Flashing lights are from U.S. Coast Guard loran station at **Milepost DC 1308.5** on the Alaska Highway. Watch for frost heaves westbound.

GJ 109.3 (175.9 km) **A 312.3** (502.6 km) **T 15.7** (25.3 km) Eagle Trail State Recreation Site; 40 campsites, 15-day limit, 4 picnic sites, water, toilets, firepits, rain shelter, hiking trail, Clearwater Creek. Camping fee $8/night or annual pass. The access road is designed with several loops to aid larger vehicles. A 0.9-mile/1.4-km section of the pioneer trail to Eagle is signed for hikers; trailhead near covered picnic tables. The historic Tok-Slana Cutoff road goes through this campground. ▲

GJ 106 (170.6 km) **A 309** (497.3 km) **T 19** (30.6 km) Beautiful mountain views westbound.

GJ 104.5 (168.2 km) **A 307.5** (494.9 km)

256 The MILEPOST® ■ 1992

GLENN HIGHWAY *Tok Cutoff (GJ-125 to GJ-0) to Milepost A 160*

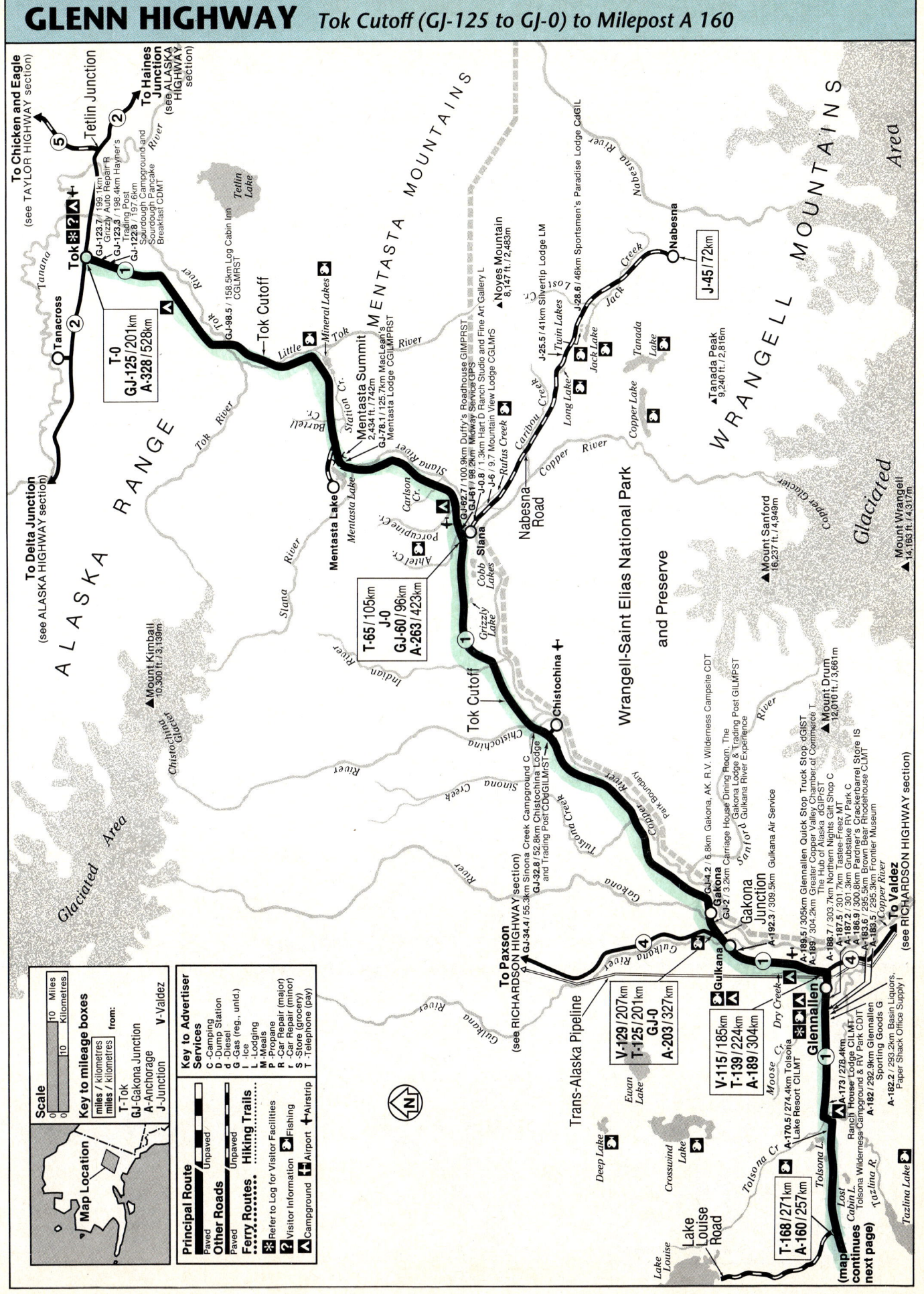

GLENN HIGHWAY — Milepost A 160 to Anchorage, AK

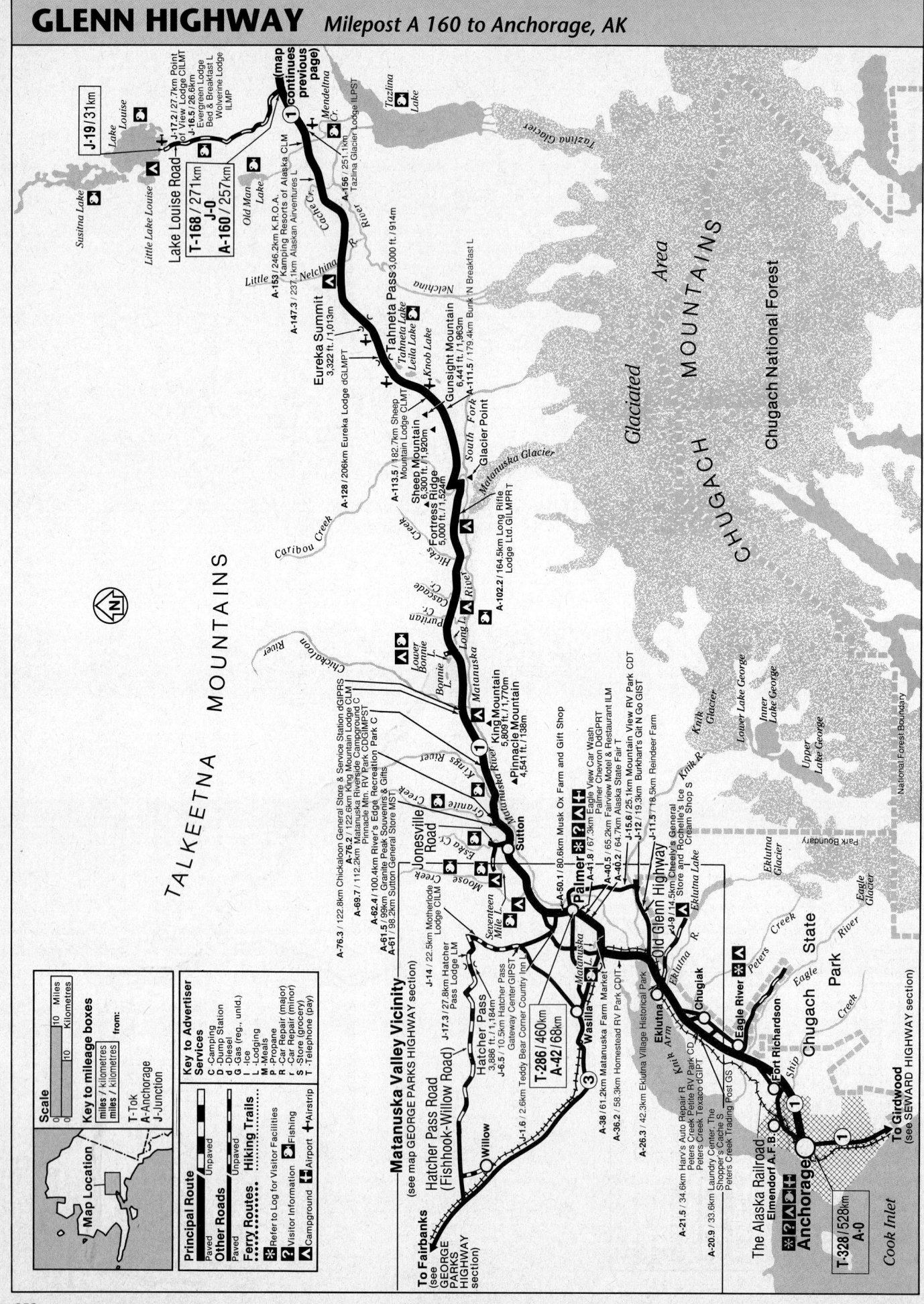

T 20.5 (33 km) Small paved turnout with litter barrels to north. Stream runs under highway in culvert.

GJ 104.1 (167.5 km) A 307.1 (494.2 km) T 20.9 (33.6 km) Bridge over Tok River, side road north to riverbank and boat launch.

Wildlife is abundant from here west to Mentasta Summit. Watch for moose in roadside ponds, bears on gravel bars, and Dall sheep on mountainsides. For best wildlife viewing, stop at turnouts and use good binoculars. Wildflowers include sweet peas, chiming bells, arnica, oxytrope and lupine.

GJ 103.5 (166.6 km) A 306.5 (493.3 km) T 21.5 (34.6 km) Paved turnout with litter barrels to north.

GJ 102.4 (164.8 km) A 305.4 (491.5 km) T 22.6 (36.4 km) Entering Tok Management Area, Tanana Valley State Forest, eastbound.

GJ 99.3 (159.8 km) A 302.3 (486.5 km) T 25.7 (41.4 km) Rest area; paved double-ended turnout with litter barrels to north. Cranberries in late summer.

GJ 98.5 (158.5 km) A 229.5 (369.3 km) T 26.5 (42.6 km) **Log Cabin Inn.** See display ad this section. ▲

GJ 98 (157.7 km) A 301 (484.4 km) T 27 (43.5 km) Bridge over Little Tok River, which parallels highway. Parking at end of bridge.

GJ 97.7 (157.2 km) A 300.7 (483.9 km) T 27.3 (43.9 km) *NOTE:* Westbound travelers watch for sections of narrow highway (no shoulders); some gravel patches, bumps, dips and pavement breaks; and frost heaves.

GJ 95.2 (153.2 km) A 298.2 (479.9 km) T 29.8 (48 km) Rest area; paved turnout with litter barrels to south.

GJ 91 (146.4 km) A 294 (473.1 km) T 34 (54.7 km) Gravel turnout with dumpster to north. Side road with bridge (weight limit 20 tons) across **Little Tok River;** good fishing for grayling, 12 to 14 inches, use small spinner. ⊶

GJ 90 (144.8 km) A 293 (471.5 km) T 35 (56.3 km) Small paved turnout to south.

GJ 89.5 (144 km) A 292.5 (470.7 km) T 35.5 (57.1 km) **Mineral Lakes.** These are sloughs of the Little Tok River and provide both moose habitat and a breeding place for waterfowl. Good fishing for northern pike and grayling. ⊶

GJ 89 (143.2 km) A 292 (469.9 km) T 36 (57.9 km) Small paved turnout to south.

GJ 86.7 (139.5 km) A 289.7 (466.2 km) T 38.3 (61.6 km) Good place to spot moose.

GJ 83.2 (133.9 km) A 286.2 (460.6 km) T 41.8 (67.3 km) Bridge over Bartell Creek. Just beyond is the divide between the drainage of the Tanana River, tributary of the Yukon River system flowing into the Bering Sea, and the Copper River system, emptying into the North Pacific near Cordova.

GJ 81 (130.4 km) A 284 (457 km) T 44 (70.8 km) Access road to **MENTASTA LAKE** (pop. 72), a Native village.

GJ 79.4 (127.8 km) A 282.4 (454.5 km) T 45.6 (73.4 km) Mentasta Summit (elev. 2,434 feet/742m). Watch for Dall sheep on mountainsides. Boundary between Game Management Units 12 and 13C and Sportfish Management Units 8 and 2.

GJ 78.1 (125.7 km) A 281.1 (452.4 km) T 46.9 (75.5 km) **MacLean's Mentasta Lodge.** See display ad this section. ▲

GJ 78 (125.5 km) A 281 (452.2 km) T 47 (75.6 km) View for westbound traffic of snow-covered Mount Sanford (elev. 16,237 feet/4,949m).

GJ 77.9 (125.4 km) A 280.9 (452.1 km) T 47.1 (75.8 km) Paved turnout to north by Slana Slough; salmon spawning area in August. Watch for beavers.

GJ 76.3 (122.8 km) A 279.3 (449.5 km) T 48.7 (78.4 km) Bridge over Mabel Creek. Mastodon flowers (marsh fleabane) in late July; very large (to 4 feet) with showy seed heads.

GJ 76 (122.3 km) A 279 (449 km) T 49 (78.8 km) Bridge over Slana Slough.

GJ 75.6 (121.7 km) A 278.6 (448.3 km) T 49.4 (79.5 km) Bridge over Slana River. Rest area to south with large paved parking area, dumpsters, toilets and picnic tables along the river. This river flows from its source glaciers some 55 miles/88.5 km to the Copper River.

GJ 74 (119.1 km) A 277 (445.8 km) T 51 (82.1 km) Large paved turnout to south overlooking Slana River.

GJ 68 (109.4 km) A 271 (436.1 km) T 57 (91.7 km) Carlson Creek bridge. Paved turnout to south at west end of bridge.

GJ 65.5 (105.4 km) A 268.5 (432.1 km) T 59.5 (95.8 km) Paved turnout to south; viewpoint.

GJ 64.2 (103.3 km) A 267.2 (430 km) T 60.8 (97.8 km) Bridge over Porcupine Creek. State Recreation Site 0.2 mile/0.3 km from highway; 12 campsites, 15-day limit, $6 nightly fee or annual pass, drinking water, firepits, toilets, picnic tables and dumpster. Lowbush cranberries in fall. *CAUTION: Watch for bears.*

GJ 63 (101.4 km) A 266 (428 km) T 62 (99.8 km) Scenic viewpoint with view of Wrangell Mountains. The dominant peak to the southwest is Mount Sanford, a dormant volcano; the pinnacles of Capital Mountain can be seen against its lower slopes. Mount Jarvis (elev. 13,421 feet/4,091m) is visible to the south behind Mount Sanford; Tanada Peak (elev. 9,240 feet/2,816m) is more to the south. (Tanada Peak is sometimes mistaken for Noyes Mountain.)

Walk up the gravel hill behind the sign to view Noyes Mountain (elev. 8,147 feet/2,483m), named for U.S. Army Brig. Gen. John Rutherford Noyes, a one-time commissioner of roads in the territory of Alaska. Appointed adjutant general of the Alaska National Guard in 1953, he died in 1956 from injuries and frostbite after his plane crashed near Nome.

GJ 62.7 (100.9 km) A 265.7 (427.6 km) T 62.3 (100.3 km) **Duffy's Roadhouse.** See display ad this section.

Private Aircraft: Duffy's Tavern airstrip; elev. 2,420 feet/737m; length 1,800 feet/548m; silt and gravel; unmaintained.

LOG CABIN INN
EST. 1954

Experience the real Alaska Bush and hospitality in remote, unspoiled splendor...like it used to be.

Private RV Spaces	Hunting & Fishing
EZ Turn-around	Hiking & Scenery
Tent Camping	Abundant Wildlife
Cabins	Nature Lore
Cafe & Grocery	Horseshoe Court
Gas & Garage	Picnic Area

Turn east at Milepost 98.5 of the Tok Cutoff (Glenn Highway). Proceed 2 miles.

Reservations Accepted

MasterCard   HC-01 Box 650
VISA Welcome   Gakona, AK 99586

(907) 883-4236

MACLEAN'S MENTASTA LODGE

- Cafe
- Bar
- Motel
- Free Overnight Parking
- Gas / Garage
- Groceries
- 24-Hour Towing
- Propane
- Laundromat
- Liquor Store
- Pets Welcome
- U-Haul Service
- Pawn Shop
- Showers
- *Senior Discount: 20% off Motel*

TERI & DUNCAN MACLEAN   (907) 291-2324

MILE 78 TOK CUTOFF

GAKONA, ALASKA 99586

Duffy's ROADHOUSE

Chevron

RESTAURANT
GAS • Groceries
Bar • Package Store
Propane • Welding
Mechanic • Auto Parts
Gift Shop • Pay Phone
Fishing & Hunting Licenses

NAPA

Mile 62.7 Tok Cutoff
Buses Welcome

Open Year Around - 7 Days A Week
Summer Hours: 6 a.m. - 10 p.m.

(907) 822-3888 (Cafe)
(907) 822-3133 (Bar)

MAJOR CREDIT CARDS ACCEPTED

Nabesna Road Log

The Nabesna Road leads 45 miles/72.4 km southeast from **Milepost GJ 59.8** Glenn Highway (Tok Cutoff) to the mining community of Nabesna. The first 4 miles/6.4 km of road is chip seal surface, the remainder is gravel. Beyond **Milepost J 28.6** the road becomes rough and crosses several creeks which may be difficult to ford; inquire about current road conditions at Sportsmen's Paradise Lodge. This side trip can be enjoyable for campers; there are no formal campgrounds but there are plenty of beautiful spots to camp. The area also offers good fishing.

Distance is measured from the junction with the Glenn Highway (J).

J 0.1 (0.2 km) Highway maintenance station.

J 0.2 (0.3 km) Slana NPS ranger station; information on road conditions and on Wrangell–St. Elias National Park and Preserve. Open 8 A.M. to 5 P.M. daily, June 1 through September. Pay phone.

J 0.8 (1.3 km) The Slana post office is located at the picturesque Hart D Ranch, home of artist Mary Frances DeHart.

Hart D Ranch Studio and Fine Art Gallery. See display ad this section.

J 1 (1.6 km) **SLANA** (pop. 39), once an Indian village on the north bank of the Slana River, now refers to this general area. Besides the Indian settlement, Slana boasted a popular roadhouse, now a private home. Slana elementary school is located here.

J 1.5 (2.4 km) Slana River bridge; undeveloped camping area. Boundary between Game Management Units 11 and 13C.

J 2 (3.2 km) BLM homestead area next 2 miles/3.2 km southbound. Blueberries in the fall; grouse are seen in this area.

J 3.9 (6.2 km) Entering Wrangell–St. Elias National Park and Preserve. The Glenn Highway follows the northern boundary of the preserve between Slana and Gakona Junction; Nabesna Road provides access to the park.

J 4 (6.4 km) Turnouts. Hard surface ends, gravel begins, southbound.

J 4.7 (7.6 km) Double-ended turnout to north.

J 6 (9.7 km) **Mountain View Lodge.** See display ad this section.

J 7 (11.3 km) Road crosses **Rufus Creek** culvert. Dolly Varden to 8 inches, June to October. Watch out for bears, especially during berry season.

J 8.9 (14.3 km) Rough turnout.

J 9.1 (14.6 km) Batzulnetas trail leads to a fish camp on the Copper River; working fish wheel during salmon runs. Check with the NPS ranger station about trail condition.

J 11 (17.7 km) Suslota Lake trailhead No. 1 to north.

J 11.4 (18.3 km) Gravel pit, room to park or camp.

J 12.2 (19.6 km) Road crosses Caribou Creek culvert.

J 12.5 (20.1 km) Turnout to southeast; Copper Lake trailhead.

J 13 (20.9 km) Suslota Lake trailhead No. 2 to north.

J 15 (24.1 km) Turnout.

J 15.4 (24.8 km) Beautiful views of Mount Sanford and Tanada Peak in the Wrangell Mountains, across the great plain of the Copper River.

J 16 (25.7 km) Turnout to northeast.

J 16.6 (26.7 km) Turnout to southwest.

J 16.9 (27.2 km) Turnout by large lake which reflects Mount Sanford.

J 18 (29 km) Pond to northeast. The highly mineralized Mentasta Mountains are visible to the north. This is sparsely timbered high country.

J 18.8 (30.3 km) Caribou Creek culvert.

J 19.3 (31.1 km) Turnout at gravel pit to northwest. Look for poppies, lupine, arnica and chiming bells in season.

J 21.2 (34.1 km) Turnout at gravel pit to northwest.

J 21.8 (35.1 km) Rock Creek culvert.

J 22.3 (35.9 km) Rock Lake; turnouts both sides of road.

J 22.9 (36.8 km) Long Lake; no turnouts. Good place for floatplane landings.

J 23.4 (37.7 km) Turnout. Floatplane landing.

J 24.4 (39.3 km) Turnout to southwest with view of Wrangell Mountains. Tanada Lake trail.

J 25.2 (40.6 km) Boundary between Sportfish Areas C and K, and Game Management Areas 11 and 12.

J 25.5 (41 km) Glimpse of Tanada Lake beneath Tanada Peak to the south.

J 25.5 (41 km) **Silvertip Lodge.** See display ad this section.

J 25.9 (41.7 km) Little Jack Creek.

J 26.1 (42 km) Turnoff for Jack Lake, 2 miles/3.2 km. Road crosses private property.

J 27 (43.5 km) Turnout to north.

J 28.2 (45.4 km) Turnouts at Twin Lakes; primitive campsite, good place to observe waterfowl. Wildflowers in June include Lapland rosebay, lupine and 8-petalled avens.

AREA FISHING: Twin Lakes, grayling 10 to 18 inches, mid-May to October, flies or small spinner; also burbot. **Copper Lake** (fly in from Jack Lake), lake trout 10 to 12 lbs., mid-June to September, use red-and-white spoon; kokanee 10 to 12 inches, mid-June to July, use small spinner; grayling 12 to 20 inches, July through September; also burbot. **Long** and **Jack lakes,** grayling fishing. **Tanada Lake** (fly in from Long Lake), grayling and lake trout.

J 28.6 (46 km) **Sportsmen's Paradise**

Floatplane docked on lake near Sportsmen's Paradise Lodge. (Sharon Paul Nault)

Silvertip Lodge & Air Service
Backpacking, Fishing, Float Trips
Hunting, Food, Lodging
Mile 25.5 Nabesna Road
Write: SRA Box 1260, Slana, AK 99586
or call Anchorage (907) 337-2065

HART D RANCH STUDIO AND FINE ART GALLERY
Studio and Art Gallery of Western and Wildlife bronze sculptor,
Mary Frances DeHart
See the Art Display and Working Studio
Mile 0.8 Nabesna Road
Rustic Housekeeping Cabin / B&B
Write: HART D RANCH
Slana, Alaska 99586
Phone: (907) 822-3973
SLANA U.S. POST OFFICE

Mountain View Lodge
Mile 6 Nabesna Road • (907) 822-3119
Completely surrounded by National Park Land
Easy access to Wrangell-St. Elias National Park and Hiking Trails
Motel • Restaurant • Laundry
Groceries • Liquor • Lounge • Videos
Gas • Auto Repair • Dry RV Parking
FLY-IN FISHING AVAILABLE
SRA Box 1190, Slana, AK 99586

Lodge is located 28.6 miles from the Glenn Highway on the Nabesna Gold Mine Road. Miles of magnificent views on this old road to the former Nabesna Gold Mine. Free camper parking, sandwiches, bar, gas, air taxi service, fishing, boating, hunting. A side trip not to miss. Fly-in fishing to Copper Lake, boats, motors, light-housekeeping cabins available. Dick and Lucille Frederick, your hosts. [ADVERTISEMENT] ▲

J 28.6 (46 km) The road deteriorates beyond this point and you will have to ford several creeks. If you are going on, inquire at lodge here about road conditions.

J 29.6 (47.6 km) Trail Creek crosses road; no culvert but road has gravel base here. Easy to drive through creek, especially in fall.

J 31.4 (50.5 km) Road crosses Lost Creek, a very wide expanse of water in spring and may remain difficult to cross well into summer. Loose gravel makes it easy to get stuck in creek if you spin your wheels. Scout it out first. If you hesitate once in the creek, wheels may dig in. The road crosses several more creeks beyond here; these may also be difficult to ford.

J 31.6 (50.9 km) Creek (must ford).
J 32.4 (52.1 km) Chalk Creek culvert.
J 33 (53.1 km) Big Grayling Lake trailhead.
J 34.1 (54.9 km) Radiator Creek culvert.
J 35 (56.3 km) Creek (must ford).
J 36 (57.9 km) Jack Creek bridge.
J 36.1 (58.1 km) Informal campsite. The road crosses 5 creeks the next 4.3 miles/6.9 km southbound. Watch for loose gravel in creekbeds.

J 41 (66 km) An unmarked trail, approximately 5 miles/8 km long, leads to Nabesna River and Reeves Field. Devils Mountain is to the left of the trail. The trail on the river also leads to the old Indian village of Khiltat.

J 41.4 (66.6 km) Creek (must ford).
J 42 (67.6 km) Devil's Mountain Lodge. Four-wheel-drive vehicles only beyond this point.

J 45 (72.4 km) **NABESNA** (area pop. less than 25; elev. 3,000 feet/914m). Primitive area with no facilities. This region has copper reserves, as well as gold in the streams and rivers, silver, molybdenum and iron ore deposits. Gold mining has only recently resumed here. Area residents subsist on caribou, Dall sheep, moose, bear, fish and small game. Fire fighting and trapping also provide some income. Big game hunting is popular in this area and several outfitters have headquarters along Nabesna Road.

Return to Milepost GJ 59.8 Glenn Highway (Tok Cutoff)

Glenn Highway Log

(continued)

GJ 61 (98.2 km) **A 264** (424.9 km) **T 64** (103 km) **Midway Service.** See display ad this section.

GJ 60.8 (97.8 km) **A 263.8** (424.6 km) **T 64.2** (103.3 km) Bridge over **Ahtell Creek**; grayling. Parking area to south at east end of bridge. This stream drains a mountain area of igneous rock, where several gold and silver-lead claims are located. ◆

GJ 59.8 (96.2 km) **A 262.8** (422.9 km) **T 65.2** (104.9 km) **Junction** with Nabesna Road. See NABESNA ROAD log this section.

GJ 59.7 (96.1 km) **A 262.7** (422.8 km) **T 65.3** (105.1 km) Gravel turnout to south. View of Tanada Peak, Mount Sanford, Mount Blackburn and Mount Drum to the south and southwest. The Mentasta Mountains are to the east.

GJ 59.2 (95.3 km) **A 262.2** (422 km) **T 65.8** (105.9 km) Gravel turnout to south with view of Tanana Peak and Mount Sanford.

GJ 56.5 (90.9 km) **A 259.5** (417.6 km) **T 68.5** (110.2 km) Cobb Lakes.

GJ 55.2 (88.8 km) **A 258.2** (415.5 km) **T 69.8** (112.3 km) Viewpoint; gravel turnout to south.

GJ 53 (85.3 km) **A 256** (412 km) **T 72** (115.9 km) Grizzly Lake. Watch for horses on road.

GJ 51.6 (83 km) **A 254.6** (409.7 km) **T 73.4** (118.1 km) Road narrows. Watch for possible road construction westbound to **Milepost GJ 38** in 1992.

GJ 44.6 (71.8 km) **A 247.6** (398.5 km) **T 80.4** (129.4 km) Turnout to north. Eagle Trail access (not marked).

GJ 43.8 (70.5 km) **A 246.8** (397.1 km) **T 81.2** (130.6 km) Bridge over Indian River. This is a salmon spawning stream, usually late June through July. Picnic site to south at west end of bridge with tables, 2 firepits, litter barrels, toilets.

GJ 43.4 (69.8 km) **A 246.4** (396.5 km) **T 81.6** (131.3 km) Double-ended gravel turnout to south.

GJ 40.1 (64.5 km) **A 243.1** (391.2 km) **T 84.9** (136.6 km) Small paved turnout to south.

GJ 39 (62.8 km) **A 242** (389.5 km) **T 86** (138.4 km) Views of the Copper River valley and Wrangell Mountains. Looking south, peak on left is Mount Sanford and on right is Mount Drum (elev. 12,010 feet/3,661m).

Look for cottongrass and mastodon flowers in late July and August.

GJ 38.7 (62.2 km) **A 241.7** (389 km) **T 86.3** (138.8 km) Paved turnout to north. Mankomen Lake trail.

GJ 35.5 (57.1 km) **A 238.5** (383.8 km) **T 89.5** (144 km) Chistochina River bridge No. 2. Mount Sanford is first large mountain to the southeast, then Mount Drum.

GJ 35.4 (57 km) **A 238.4** (383.7 km) **T 89.6** (144.2 km) Chistochina River bridge No. 1; parking at west end. Chistochina River trailhead. This river heads in the Chistochina Glacier on Mount Kimball (elev. 10,300 feet/3,139m). Chistochina is thought to mean marmot creek.

GJ 34.7 (55.8 km) **A 237.7** (382.5 km) **T 90.3** (145.3 km) Posty's Sinona Creek Trading Post (current status unknown).

GJ 34.6 (55.7 km) **A 237.6** (382.4 km) **T 90.4** (145.5 km) Bridge over Sinona Creek. Sinona is said to mean place of the many burls, and there are indeed many burls on area spruce trees.

GJ 34.4 (55.3 km) **A 237.4** (382 km) **T 90.6** (145.8 km) **Sinona Creek Campground.** See display ad this section. ▲

GJ 34.1 (54.9 km) **A 237.1** (381.6 km) **T 90.9** (146.3 km) Chistochina ball fields.

GJ 32.9 (52.9 km) **A 235.9** (379.6 km) **T 92.1** (148.2 km) Road access to **CHISTOCHINA** (pop. 43), a Native village.

Private Aircraft: Barnhart airstrip, 3 miles/4.8 km north; elev. 1,930 feet/588m;

MIDWAY SERVICE
Full Line Groceries
Hardware & Automotive
Ammunition &
Fishing Supplies
Hunting & Fishing Licenses
Big Game Tags
Laundry & Showers
Propane
Open Year Round
9 a.m. to 8 p.m.
7 Days a Week
(907) 822-5877
Mile 61 Tok Cutoff

SINONA CREEK CAMPGROUND
MILE 34.4
TOK CUTOFF

**WOODED SITES
FULL HOOKUPS**
Wide Gravel Roads & Pads
Near Historic Chistochina
Tents & Camping Vehicles Welcome

*Grayling Fishing in Sinona Creek
Gift Shop • Horses for Trail Rides*

(907) 822-3914
CHISTOCHINA, ALASKA

KC am 790

Part of the family!

Box 249, Glennallen, Alaska 99588
(907) 822-3434
Music – News – Road Conditions

GLENN HIGHWAY

GULKANA RIVER EXPERIENCE
WORLD CLASS KING SALMON CHARTERS
All Inclusive Full & Half Day Trips
June 1 – July 20
Based at Gakona Lodge
822-3482
P.O. Box 1307
Fairbanks, AK 99707

GAKONA LODGE & TRADING POST

the CARRIAGE HOUSE
...The most unique
DINING ROOM
in the Copper River Basin...
Rustic Log... Over 60 years old
LUNCH and DINNER
Featuring Seafood
Charcoal Grilled Steaks
Homemade Soups and Pies
Overlooking the Gakona River

CHEVRON GAS & PRODUCTS
CLOSED WINTERS

Enjoy Old-Time Lodging in a Rustic Alaskan Lodge
NAMED IN THE NATIONAL REGISTER OF HISTORIC PLACES

TRAPPER'S DEN BAR • GROCERY & NATURAL FOOD STORE
LIQUORS—HARDWARE—SPORTING GOODS—CLOTHING—PROPANE—ICE
HUNTING AND FISHING LICENSES—GUNS AND AMMO—PAY PHONE

PHONE (907) 822-3482
Box 285, Gakona, Alaska 99586

BARB, JERRY AND JOHN STRANG
(Mile 2-Tok Cutoff) A 205 Glenn Highway

A UNIQUE EXPERIENCE   MP 32.8 TOK-SLANA

CHISTOCHINA LODGE and TRADING POST

Quiet FAMILY Atmosphere
Clean and Friendly
Open Year-Round
Sarah Endres, Your Host

Groceries • Ice • Cafe
• Rustic Saloon
Homemade Pies and Cinnamon Rolls
Sarah's Oldtyme Sourdough Pancakes
Alaska Berry Products

Visit Gold Panner Gifts
& Ice Cream Parlor

GAS • UNLEADED • DIESEL

Full Service RV Park Opening 1992
FREE Tent Camping & Picnic Area • Dump Station • Public Sauna • Showers

PAN FOR GOLD!

Comfortable Private Rooms • Some Private Baths • TV

Set of Locked Horns on Display • Fish Wheel
Aircraft Charter Available • Fly-in Fishing • Moose Hunting Headquarters
Public Phone • Hunting/Fishing Information • River Trip Info

WRITE   — MasterCard and VISA accepted —   CALL
MP 32.8 Tok-Slana Highway via Gakona, Alaska 99586   (907) 822-3366

---

length 2,500 feet/762m; earth; unattended. Chistochina airstrip, adjacent southwest; elev. 1,850 feet/564m; length 2,000 feet/610m; gravel; fuel 80, 100. Posty's airstrip, 1.7 miles/2.7 km north; elev. 1,900 feet/579m; length 1,300 feet/396m; turf and gravel; unattended.

GJ 32.8 (52.8 km) **A 235.8** (379.5 km) **T 92.2** (148.4 km) Chistochina Lodge and Trading Post. See display ad this section. ▲

GJ 30.1 (48.4 km) **A 233.1** (375.1 km) **T 94.9** (152.7 km) Paved turnout to south. Road narrows eastbound; no shoulders. Watch for frost heaves.

GJ 28.1 (45.2 km) **A 231.1** (371.9 km) **T 96.9** (155.9 km) Double-ended paved parking area to south with a marker on the Alaska Road Commission. The ARC was established in 1905, the same year the first automobile arrived in Alaska at Skagway. The ARC operated for 51 years, building roads, airfields, trails, and other transportation facilities. It was replaced by the Bureau of Public Roads (referred to by some Alaskans at the time as the Bureau of Parallel Ruts) in 1956. In 1960 the Bureau of Public Roads was replaced by the Dept. of Public Works.

GJ 24 (38.6 km) **A 227** (365.3 km) **T 101** (162.5 km) Large rest area to south with paved double-ended parking area, toilets, picnic tables and firepits on grass under trees; paths lead to Copper River. Mount Sanford is to the southeast, Mount Drum to the south.

GJ 21.3 (34.3 km) **A 224.3** (361 km) **T 103.7** (166.9 km) Buster Gene trailhead to south.

GJ 20.9 (33.6 km) **A 223.9** (360.3 km) **T 104.1** (167.5 km) Turnout to south.

GJ 17.8 (28.6 km) **A 220.8** (355.3 km) **T 107.2** (172.5 km) Tulsona Creek bridge. Good grayling fishing.

GJ 11.6 (18.7 km) **A 214.6** (345.4 km) **T 113.4** (182.5 km) Yellow pond lily (*Nuphar polysepalum*) in ponds along highway.

GJ 9.4 (15.1 km) **A 212.4** (341.8 km) **T 115.6** (186 km) Paved turnout to north.

GJ 9.2 (14.8 km) **A 212.2** (341.5 km) **T 115.8** (186.4 km) Paved turnout to north. BLM trailhead.

GJ 6.3 (10.1 km) **A 209.3** (336.8 km) **T 118.7** (191 km) Paved turnout to southeast.

GJ 4.2 (6.8 km) **A 207.2** (333.4 km) **T 120.8** (194.4 km) Gakona, A.K., R.V.

GAKONA, AK. R.V. WILDERNESS CAMPSITE RECREATIONAL FACILITIES

48 SPACES • 24 PULL-THROUGHS
FULL & PARTIAL HOOKUPS
DUMP STATION • SHOWERS • LAUNDRY
CONCESSIONS • PHONE
ALASKAN ADVENTURES

COPPER RIVER ACCESS
Chipping & Putting Green • Large Recreational Area
Wrangell Mountain Views
Close to two good restaurants,
excellent fishing, rafting, and hiking opportunities.

Watch & photograph working Indian-made fish wheels.

Information & Reservations:
(907) 822-3550
P.O. Box 160, Gakona, Alaska 99586

Wilderness Campsite. See display ad this section. ▲

GJ 2.7 (4.3 km) A 205.7 (331 km) T 122.3 (196.8 km) **GAKONA** (area pop. 200). The village of Gakona lies between the Gakona and Copper rivers (Gakona is Athabascan for "rabbit"). Originally Gakona was a Native wood and fish camp, and fish wheels are still common. The post office is located on the highway here.

GJ 2 (3.2 km) A 205 (330 km) T 123 (198 km) Gakona Lodge, entered on the National Register of Historic Places in 1977. Originally one of several roadhouses providing essential food and lodging for travelers, it opened in 1905 and was first called Doyle's Ranch. The original carriage house is now a restaurant.

Gakona Lodge & Trading Post and **The Carriage House Dining Room.** See display ad this section.

Gulkana River Experience. See display ad this section.

GJ 1.8 (2.9 km) A 204.8 (329.6 km) T 123.2 (198.3 km) Bridge over Gakona River. Entering Game Management Unit 13B westbound and 13C eastbound. The highway climbs a short hill and joins the Richardson Highway 1.8 miles/2.9 km from this bridge. From the hill there is a fine view of the many channels where the Gakona and Copper rivers join.

GJ 1 (1.6 km) A 204 (328.3 km) T 124 (200 km) Rest area to south has paved turnout overlooking the valley of the Gakona and Copper rivers; picnic tables and litter barrels. View of Mount Drum and Mount Sanford. Good photo stop.

GJ 0 A 203 (326.7 km) T 125 (201.2 km) **Gakona Junction.** North junction of the Glenn Highway with the Richardson Highway from Delta Junction; the 2 roads share a common alignment for the next 14 miles/22.5 km westbound. Travelers may turn north here for Delta Junction via the Richardson Highway. Continue on the Glenn Highway southwest for Anchorage, northeast for Tok via the Tok Cutoff. NOTE: THIS JUNCTION CAN BE CONFUSING. CHOOSE YOUR ROUTE CAREFULLY.

Eastbound travelers note: The highway between Gakona Junction and Tok is referred to as the Tok Cutoff or Slana–Tok Cutoff. Physical mileposts show distance from Gakona Junction (GJ in our log). Watch for sections of narrow highway (no shoulders), some gravel patches, bumps, dips and pavement breaks, frost heaves and possible road construction between **Milepost GJ 38 and 52** in 1992.

Delta Junction-bound travelers turn to **Milepost V 128.6** in the RICHARDSON HIGHWAY section. Tok- or Anchorage-bound travelers continue with this log.

Physical mileposts for the next 14 miles/22.5 km westbound give distance from Valdez and are added to this log.

Distance from Anchorage (A) is followed by distance from Tok (T) and distance from Valdez (V).

A 203 (326.7 km) T 125 (201.2 km) V 128.6 (207 km) North junction of the Glenn Highway with the Richardson Highway at Gakona Junction. Watch for frost heaves between here and **Milepost V 124.**

A 201 (323.5 km) T 127 (204.4 km) V 126.9 (204.2 km) Access road to **GULKANA** (pop. 82) on the bank of the Gulkana River. Camping is permitted along the river by the bridge; signs posted tell where to pay camping fee. Excellent grayling fishing and good king and sockeye salmon fishing (June and July) in the **Gulkana River.** Most of the Gulkana River frontage in this area is owned by Gulkana village and managed by Ahtna, Inc. Access permits to fish on Ahtna lands are sold at the Ahtna Corp. building at **Milepost V 104** Richardson Highway. In summer, there is often someone selling these permits along the highway. Permits are $10 and good for season; children under 18 years of age are not required to buy a permit. ◆▲

A 200.9 (323.3 km) T 127.1 (204.5 km) V 126.8 (204 km) Gulkana River bridge. Entering Game Management Unit 13B eastbound, 13A westbound.

A 200.1 (322 km) T 127.9 (205.8 km) V 126 (202.8 km) Paved double-ended turnout to north.

A 197.3 (317.5 km) T 130.7 (210.3 km) V 123.2 (198.3 km) Large paved turnout to south.

A 192.3 (309.5 km) T 135.7 (218.4 km) V 118.3 (190.4 km) **Gulkana Air Service.** See display ad this section.

A 192.1 (309.1 km) T 135.9 (218.7 km) V 118.1 (190 km) **Private Aircraft:** Gulkana airstrip; elev. 1,578 feet/481m; length 4,200 feet/1,280m; asphalt; fuel 80, 100. Flying service located here.

A 192 (309 km) T 136 (218.9 km) V 118 (189.9 km) Dry Creek State Recreation Site; 58 campsites, 15-day limit, $6 nightly fee or annual pass, 4 picnic sites, toilets, picnic shelter. Bring mosquito repellent! ▲

A 189.5 (305 km) T 138.5 (222.9 km) V 115.5 (185.9 km) **Glennallen Quick Stop Truck Stop.** Stop for friendly family service and gas and diesel prices that are hard to beat. A well-stocked convenience store contains ice, pop, snacks, postcards, ice cream, specialty items, a phone, and free coffee. Several interesting items are on display, including an authentic Native Alaskan fish wheel. [ADVERTISEMENT]

Mount Drum dominates the Glennallen skyline. (Jerrianne Lowther, staff)

GULKANA AIR SERVICE
WRANGELL · CHUGACH · ST ELIAS, ALASKA

✈ **FLIGHTSEEING ADVENTURE TOURS**
Closeup views of majestic snow-capped peaks and ice fields

✈ Fly-in fishing, rafting, mountaineering, and glacier landings

✈ Special rates on trips to McCarthy when combined with accommodations

(907) 822-5532
Gulkana Airport
Mile 118 Richardson Highway
PO Box 342, Glennallen, Alaska 99588

The perfect companion book to *The MILEPOST* is *FACTS ABOUT ALASKA: THE ALASKA ALMANAC*. Fascinating information about every Alaska subject imaginable. Order from Alaska Northwest Books™ at 1-800-343-4567, Ext. 571.

Northern Nights Campground and "No Frills" RV Park

- A full line of gift items
- Native-made handicrafts
- Free coffee and ice water
- Restroom facilities
- Freezer available
- Tenters & RVs always welcome
- Electric hook-ups
- Competitive rates
- Caravans welcome
- RV pull-thrus
- Friendly
- Wooded, natural setting
- Firepits, firewood available

Visit the Greater Copper Valley!

The Greater Copper Valley Chamber of Commerce invites you to visit our visitor information center at the junction of the Glenn and the Richardson highways in Glennallen. Our log cabin boasts a warm, friendly atmosphere complete with free hot coffee.

The Copper River Valley hosts the nation's largest national park, **Wrangell-St. Elias** — six times the size of Yellowstone National Park. Unlimited recreational activities abound in the valley including fishing, hiking, backpacking, photography, mountain climbing, rafting, bird watching, wild flowers, flightseeing, to name but a few.

For more information, please call:
(907) 822-5555
Write: P.O. Box 469, Glennallen, AK 99588
Or better yet, STOP BY!
Visitor Center open Mid-May through Labor Day

NO ROOM FOR BEARS, by Frank Dufresne, offers a narrative for all readers who love the outdoors and marvel at learning more about bears. Woven among personal adventure tales are sketches of the evolution, varieties and folklore of this extraordinary animal. Available from Alaska Northwest Books™. To order, call toll free 1-800-343-4567, Ext. 571.

THE HUB OF ALASKA
COPPER BASIN VISITORS CENTER LOCATED HERE
OPEN 24 HOURS

TWO 40' BAYS FOR ALL YOUR SERVICE NEEDS
RV Repair • Tire Sales & Service • Batteries
TEXACO GASOLINES • DIESEL FUEL
Propane • Oil • Mechanic On Duty • Towing Service
Large Gift Shop • Full Line of Groceries • Snacks • Ice

TEXACO We Accept All Major Credit Cards

(907) 822-3555

SENIORS DISCOUNT ✹ CARAVAN DISCOUNTS
Junction of Richardson-Glenn Highways at Glennallen

A 189 (304.2 km) T 139 (223.7 km) V 115 (185.1 km) **Greater Copper Valley Chamber of Commerce.** See display ad this section.

The Hub of Alaska. See display ad this section.

A 189 (304.2 km) T 139 (223.7 km) V 115 (185.1 km) **South junction** of the Glenn Highway with the Richardson Highway from Valdez. Turn south here on the Richardson Highway for Valdez. Continue west on the Glenn Highway for Anchorage, east for Tok. *NOTE: This junction can be confusing. Choose your route carefully.* Copper River Valley Visitor Information Center in log cabin; open 9 A.M. to 7 P.M. daily in summer. There's also a convenience grocery and a gas station (with diesel) at junction.

Eastbound travelers note: Physical mileposts next 14 miles/22.5 km eastbound show distance from Valdez as the Glenn and Richardson share a common alignment to **Milepost V 128.6.**

Valdez-bound travelers turn to **Milepost V 115** *in the RICHARDSON HIGHWAY section. Anchorage- or Tok-bound travelers continue with this log.*

A 188.7 (303.7 km) T 139.3 (224.2 km) **Northern Nights Gift Shop.** See display ad this section.

A 188.3 (303 km) T 139.7 (224.8 km) Trans-Alaska pipeline passes under the highway.

A 187.5 (301.7 km) T 140.5 (226.1 km) **Tastee-Freez.** This popular spot features an excellent menu of fast food with the lowest prices on the highway. Appetites of all sizes are satisfied, from a quick taco to double cheeseburgers, if you dare! On display in the comfortable dining room is a selection of the finest original drawings and paintings available in Alaska's "bush." Plan to stop! [ADVERTISEMENT]

A 187.2 (301.3 km) T 140.8 (226.6 km) **Grubstake RV Park** offers secluded overnight camping in the heart of Glennallen. Take advantage of water and electric hookups at low rates and enjoy a variety of local gift shops, restaurants and services within walking distance of the Grubstake RV Park! Located between Last Frontier Pizza and Tastee-Freez. [ADVERTISEMENT] ▲

A 187.2 (301.3 km) T 140.8 (226.6 km) Post office a block north of highway. Description of Glennallen follows.

Glennallen

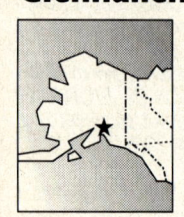

A 187 (300.9 km) T 141 (226.9 km) Near the south junction of Glenn and Richardson highways. **Population:** 928. **Emergency Services:** Alaska State Troopers, Milepost A 186.2, phone 822-3263 (if no answer call Anchorage 272-1524 collect). **Fire Department,** phone 911. **Ambulance,** Copper River EMS, phone 822-3671 or 911. **Clinic,** Milepost A 186.6, phone 822-3203. **Road Conditions,** phone 822-5511.

Visitor Information: Copper River Valley Visitor Information Center is located in the log cabin at the junction of the Glenn and Richardson highways. **Milepost A 189;** open 10 A.M. to 6 P.M. daily in summer. The Alaska Dept. of Fish and Game office is located at **Milepost A 186.2** on the Glenn Highway; phone 822-3309.

Elevation: 1,460 feet/445m. **Climate:**

Mean monthly temperature in January -10°F/-23°C; in July, 56°F/13°C. Record low was -61°F/-52°C in January 1975; record high, 90°F/32°C in June 1969. Mean precipitation in July, 1.53 inches/3.9cm. Mean precipitation (snow/sleet) in December, 11.4 inches/29cm. **Radio:** KCAM 790, KUAC-FM 92.1. **Television:** Rural Alaska Television Network and Wrangell Mountain TV Club via satellite; Public Broadcasting System.

Private Aircraft: Gulkana airstrip, 4.3 miles/6.9 km northeast of Glennallen at **Milepost A 192.1**; elev. 1,578 feet/481m; length 4,200 feet/1,280m; asphalt; fuel 80, 100. Flight service station open 16 hours daily. Parking with tie downs. Mechanic available.

The name Glennallen is derived from the combined last names of Capt. Edwin F. Glenn and Lt. Henry T. Allen, both leaders in the early exploration of the Copper River region.

Glennallen lies at the western edge of the huge Wrangell–St. Elias National Park and

GLENNALLEN ADVERTISERS

Bishop's RV Park & Car Wash	Downtown
Caribou Cafe Family Restaurant	Downtown
Glennallen Chevron	Ph. (907) 822-3303
KCAM Radio	Ph. (907) 822-3434
Last Frontier Pizza	Ph. (907) 822-3030
Mechanix Warehouse Auto Parts	Ph. (907) 822-3444
New Caribou Hotel, Gift Shop and Restaurant	Ph. (907) 822-3302
Old Post Office Gallery II	Adjacent Tastee-Freez
Pardner's Crackerbarrel Store	Mile A 186.9 Glenn Hwy.
Park's Place Supermarket	Ph. (907) 822-3334
Tastee-Freez	Downtown
Tolsona Wilderness Campground	Mile 173 Glenn Hwy.

TOLSONA WILDERNESS CAMPGROUND

Mile 173 Glenn Highway • 14 miles west of Glennallen

Hot Showers • Laundromat
RV Hookups • Tent Sites
Dump Station • Ice
Fishing • Phone

P.O. Box 23, Glennallen, Alaska 99588 • (907) 822-3865

AAA • Good Sampark

Caribou Cafe Family Restaurant

LUNCHEON AND DINNER SPECIALS DAILY

Come in and let Dennis Petty and family treat you to the finest service, food and atmosphere in the Interior.

Buses Welcome

Banquet Facilities

Open 7 days a week year around

(907) 822-3656

Downtown Glennallen

---

tastee-freez

Open year around   Glennallen, Mile 187   (907) 822-3923

RELAX AND ENJOY ORIGINAL ARTWORK IN OUR COMFORTABLE DINING ROOM

Summer Hours: **10:00** a.m. to **11:00** p.m. daily
Memorial Day through Labour Day

Preserve. It is a gateway to the Wrangell Mountains and the service center for the Copper River basin. Glennallen is also a fly-in base for several guides and outfitters.

Four prominent peaks of the majestic Wrangell Mountains are to the east; from left they are Mounts Sanford, Drum, Wrangell and Blackburn. The best views are on crisp winter days at sunset. The rest of the countryside is relatively flat with small lakes and streams.

The main business district is 1.5 miles/2.4 km west of the south junction of the Glenn and Richardson highways. There are also several businesses located at the south junction. About two-thirds of the area's residents are employed by trade/service firms; the balance hold various government positions. Offices for the Bureau of Land Management, the Alaska State Troopers and Dept. of Fish and Game are located here. There are several small farms in the area.

There is a substantial Native population in the area and the Native-owned Ahtna Corp. has its headquarters near Glennallen at **Milepost V 104** Richardson Highway.

Also headquartered here is KCAM radio, which broadcasts on station 790. KCAM broadcasts area road condition reports daily and also airs the popular "Caribou Clatter," which will broadcast personal messages. Radio messages are still a popular form of communication in Alaska and a necessary one in the Bush. Similar programs throughout the state are KJNP's "Trapline Chatter"; KYAK's "Bush Pipeline"; KHAR's "Northwinds"; and KIAK's "Pipeline of the North." KFAR in Fairbanks broadcast "Tundra Topics" for 37 years; it was taken off the air in 1980.

ACCOMMODATIONS

Because of its strategic location, most traveler services are available. During summer months reservations are advised for visitor accommodations. Glennallen has several lodges and motels, fast-food outlets and restaurants. Auto parts, groceries, gifts, clothing, propane, sporting goods and other supplies are available at local stores. Services include a bank, a dentist, several churches, a

Willow ptarmigan, Alaska's state bird, in summer phase. (Steve D. Lackie)

A real Alaskan store that sells everything

Meats • Groceries
Fresh Produce
Drugs • Gifts
Toys • Souvenirs
Postcards • Film
Newsstand
Housewares • Ice
Clothing

PARDNER'S
Crackerbarrel

Historic Alaska Photographs Display
Ammo • Hunting and Fishing Supplies
MILE 186.9 GLENN HIGHWAY
Long a favorite stop for many.

New
CARIBOU HOTEL, GIFT SHOP AND RESTAURANT

45 NEW ROOMS • 6 Rooms with Whirlpool Bath • Alaskan Decor
3 Suites with Full Kitchens • Handicap Room • FAX Lines
Also Pipeline Annex Economy Accommodations
(See our log ad under Accommodations)

Caribou Restaurant next door - Seats 135 • Private Dining Room for Tour Buses
(See related ad)

Log Cabin Gift Shop filled with Alaskan Gifts and Souvenirs
Authentic Turn-of-the-Century Setting • Alaskan-made Items • Jewelry
Gold • Jade • Ivory • Scrimshaw • Ornaments • Art • Beadwork • Figurines
Furs • Knives • Gag Gifts • T-Shirts and Sweatshirts • Postcards and much more

Reservations: (907) 822-3302, FAX (907) 822-3711
Write: New Caribou Hotel, P.O. Box 329, Glennallen, AK 99588
Downtown Glennallen • Mile 186.9 Glenn Highway

KCam 790

Part of the family!

Box 249, Glennallen, Alaska 99588
(907) 822-3434
Music – News – Road Conditions

Mechanix WAREHOUSE
AUTO PARTS

(907) 822-3444
1 (800) 478-8822
GATES BELTS and HOSES
FRAM FILTERS • GAS CAPS
Champion Plugs
Standard Blue Streak Ignition
— Open 6 Days A Week —
DOWNTOWN GLENNALLEN

chiropractic center, a laundromat, gas stations and major auto repair.

New Caribou Hotel, Gift Shop and Restaurant. The New Caribou Hotel in downtown Glennallen, on the edge of the largest national park in America, was completed fall of 1990. This 45-unit modern facility features custom built furniture, state-of-the-art color coordinated Alaskan decor, 6 rooms with 2-person whirlpool baths, 2-bedroom fully furnished suites with kitchens and cooking facilities. Alaskan art, handicap facilities, conference rooms, phones and Fax lines, remote control color TVs. Large full menu restaurant with banquet room, unique Alaskan gift shop (a must stop in your travels). Tour buses welcome. Airport transportation. Ask us for travel and visitor information. Open year-round. Phone (907) 822-3302. [ADVERTISEMENT]

There are 2 private campgrounds west of town on the Glenn Highway (see **Milepost A 173** and **A 170.5**) and Tolsona Creek state campground at **Milepost A 172.9**. East of Glennallen 5 miles/8 km is Dry Creek state campground (see **Milepost A 192**). ▲

TRANSPORTATION

Bus: Scheduled service between Valdez and Anchorage, and between Glennallen and McCarthy via Copper Center and Chitina.

ATTRACTIONS

According to the ADF&G, approximately 50 lakes in the Glennallen area are stocked with grayling, rainbow trout and coho salmon. (A complete list of lakes, locations and species is available at the Copper River Valley Visitor Center.) Locally, there's good grayling fishing in **Moose Creek**, **Tulsona Creek** to the east at Milepost GJ 17.5, and west on the Glenn Highway at **Tolsona Creek, Milepost A 173**, and **Mendeltna Creek, Milepost A 152.8**. Lake Louise, approximately 27 miles/43 km west and 19 miles/30.5 km north from Glennallen, offers

---

BISHOP'S RV PARK & CAR WASH

Full or Partial Hookups
Good Water • Dump Station
Self-Service Car and Truck Wash

Centrally located in downtown Glennallen
Next to supermarket and laundromat

The Friendly Place

PARK'S PLACE SUPERMARKET

A quarter-mile west of the trans-Alaska pipeline
Mile 187.8 Glenn Highway – Downtown Glennallen

Interior Alaska's Finest Mini-Mall

Film • Post Cards • Souvenirs

Hours:
Daily 8 a.m. to 9 p.m.
Sunday 10 a.m. to 7 p.m.

Phone: (907) 822-3334

Full Line of Groceries • Produce
Fresh Meats • Copy Machine
Fill Your Propane Tanks Nearby
Ice • Snacks • Sundries • Laundromat
Barber & Beauty Shop • Flowers & Gifts

Downtown Glennallen

GLENNALLEN CHEVRON

Complete Mechanical Service • Custom Welding

GAS • DIESEL • PROPANE • PUBLIC PHONE
SOFT DRINKS • CLEAN REST ROOMS
(907) 822-3303 • 24-Hour Wrecker Service
ATLAS Tires, Batteries and Accessories

All authorized Standard credit cards plus VISA and MasterCard honored

Last Frontier PIZZA

PIZZA • SALAD BAR
DAILY all-you-can-eat specials

HARD ICE CREAM
Submarine Sandwiches

ORDERS TO GO
(907) 822-3030

Next to Mechanix Warehouse
Downtown Glennallen

OLD POST OFFICE

GALLERY II

IN GLENNALLEN
Next to Tastee Freeze

ORIGINAL ALASKAN AND NATIVE ART
Watercolors By Jean Rene' • Oils
Limited Edition Prints

Native Beadwork • Baskets • Dolls • Slippers

Alaskan Books • Art Supplies • Beading Supplies

Specializing in Custom Framing
Needlework • Photos • Prints • Original Art

WE MAIL — (907) 822-3694 — BROWSERS WELCOME
P.O. Box 379, Copper Center, Alaska 99573

excellent grayling and lake trout fishing.

Many fly-in lakes are located in the Copper River basin and Chugach Mountains near Glennallen. **Crosswind Lake**, large lake trout, whitefish and grayling, early June to early July. **Deep Lake**, all summer for lake trout to 30 inches. **High Lake**, lake trout to 22 inches, June and early July with small spoons; some rainbow, fly-fishing; cabin, boats and motors rental. **Tebay Lakes**, excellent rainbow fishing, 12 to 15 inches, all summer, small spinners; cabin, boats and motors rental. **Jans Lake**, 12- to 14-inch silver salmon, June, spinners; also rainbow. **Hanagita Lake**, excellent grayling fishing all summer; also lake trout and steelhead in September. **Minnesota Lake**, lake trout to 30 inches, all summer; boat only, no cabins.

The Alaska Dept. of Fish and Game is located at **Milepost A 186.2**; phone 822-3309.

Glenn Highway Log

(continued)

Physical mileposts between Glennallen and Anchorage show distance from Anchorage. **Distance from Anchorage (A) is followed by distance from Tok (T).**

A 186.9 (300.8 km) T 141.1 (227.1 km) **Pardner's Crackerbarrel Store.** The oldest Alaskan store between Anchorage and Valdez expanded to carry almost everything found in supermarkets, plus many uniquely Alaskan items. See the display of old photographs and take pictures of the beautiful view of the Wrangell Mountains. Owned and operated by Georgia Strunk and Drucilla Allain. [ADVERTISEMENT]

A 186.6 (300.3 km) T 141.4 (227.6 km) Clinic and community college.

A 186.4 (300 km) T 141.6 (227.9 km) Bureau of Land Management district office.

A 186.2 (229.7 km) T 141.8 (228.2 km) Alaska State Troopers and Alaska State Dept. of Fish and Game.

A 186 (299.3 km) T 142 (228.5 km) **Moose Creek** culvert; good grayling fishing in spring. From here westbound, the highway knifes across the southern rim of a vast tableland that reaches from the Alaska Range, 80 miles/129 km north, to the Chugach Mountains, 15 miles/24 km south.

A 183.6 (295.5 km) T 144.4 (232.4 km) **Brown Bear Rhodehouse.** Because of the excellent food, reasonable prices and Alaskan hospitality, this famous old lodge is a favorite eating and gathering place for local people and travelers alike. If eating in the Glennallen area, we recommend stopping here, and if coming from south it is well worth the extra few minutes wait. Superb steaks and seafood are the specialties, along with broasted chicken and the widest sandwich selection in the area. Your hosts, Doug and Cindy Rhodes, have managed to take one of the largest grizzly-brown bear photograph collections anywhere. So, if not dining, you will enjoy just stopping and looking at the many photographs that cover the walls or listening to a few bear tales in the lounge. This is also the only place on the highway to get a bucket of golden brown broasted chicken to go. Phone (907) 822-3663. [ADVERTISEMENT]

A 183.5 (295.3 km) T 144.5 (232.5 km) **Frontier Museum.** See the relics and tools of the gold rush and WWII. Learn about frontier life and nature. Many large fossils and minerals are also displayed in our new facility. Gifts, relics, fossils, minerals, diamond willow, outdoor and mining supplies on sale. Gold mining and panning. Free picnic area, volcano view. Money back guarantee. Open daily summers. Tour buses by appointment anytime. (907) 822-3548. [ADVERTISEMENT]

A 182.2 (293.2 km) T 145.8 (234.6 km) **Basin Liquors, Paper Shack Office Supply.** Liquor store opens 8 A.M., 7 days a week, 365 days a year. Liquor, snacks, ice, cigarettes. We invite you to take a break; walk around in one of the most beautiful yards on the Glenn Highway, longtime home of pioneer resident "Gramma Ole" Hanson. [ADVERTISEMENT]

A 182 (292.9 km) T 146 (235 km) **Glennallen Sporting Goods.** See display ad this section.

A 176.6 (284.2 km) T 151.4 (243.6 km) Paved turnout to south with interpretive sign about the Wrangell Mountains and view east across the Copper River valley to Mount Drum. Northeast of Mount Drum is Mount Sanford and southeast is Mount Wrangell (elev. 14,163 feet/4,317m), a semi-active volcano. Mount Wrangell last erupted in 1912 when lava flowed to its base and ash fell as far west as this point.

Wildflowers growing along the roadside include cinquefoil, oxytrope, Jacob's ladder and sweet pea.

A 174.7 (281.1 km) T 153.3 (246.7 km) Double-ended paved turnout to south.

A 173 (278.4 km) T 155 (249.4 km) **Tolsona Wilderness Campground & RV Park.** AAA approved, Good Sam Park. This beautiful campground, located three-quarter mile north of the highway, is surrounded on 3 sides by untouched wilderness. Each shady campsite is situated beside sparkling Tolsona Creek and is complete with table, litter barrel and fireplace. It is a full-service campground with tent sites, restrooms, dump

---

BROWN BEAR RHODEHOUSE
Alaskan Hospitality Year Around
-80° to +90°
4 Miles from Glennallen toward Anchorage
Restaurant • Bar • Cabins
Unique Alaskan Gifts
Steaks • Fresh Seafood • Pizza

Broasted Chicken By the Bucket

Widest Variety of Sandwiches in the Area
Phone (907) **822-FOOD**

RV Parking   Picnic Sites
A Favorite Mushers' Checkpoint in the Copper Basin 300 Sled Dog Race
Caravan and Bus Tours Please Call Ahead
Unbelievable Grizzly/Brown Bear Photo Collection

Mile 183.6 Glenn Highway • Your Hosts: Doug & Cindy Rhodes
P.O. Box 110, Glennallen, Alaska 99588 • (907) 822-3663

GLENNALLEN SPORTING GOODS
Complete Fishing & Hunting Equipment

GUIDED KING SALMON FISHING TRIPS

Licenses • Supplies
Gas • Guns • Ammo

Mile 182 Glenn Highway

P.O. BOX 28 • GLENNALLEN • PH: (907) 822-3780

station, coin-op showers, laundromat, water and electric hookups for RVs. Public phone.

Open from May 20 through Sept. 10. $8 to $15 per night. Phone (907) 822-3865. [ADVERTISEMENT]

Tolsona Creek, grayling to 16 inches, use mosquito flies in still, clear pools behind obstructions, June, July and August. Best fishing 1.5 miles/2.4 km upstream from highway. Tolsona and Moose lakes, rainbow trout, grayling to 16 inches, all summer; boats, food and lodging.

A 173 (278.4 km) T 155 (249.4 km) Ranch House Lodge. Enjoy friendly hospitality in an authentic rustic atmosphere in Alaska's most beautiful log lodge. Superb steaks and seafood. Our Ranchburgers are built on custom-made buns and are famous statewide. Cocktails over solid log bar. Dancing. Rustic log cabins. Liquor store. Ice. Alaskan gifts. Camping available. Located on beautiful Tolsona Creek. Phone (907) 822-3882 or write HC-01 Box 1980, Glennallen, AK 99588. [ADVERTISEMENT]

A 172.9 (278.2 km) T 155.1 (249.6 km) Tolsona Creek State Recreation Site; 10 campsites, 15-day limit, no camping fee, no drinking water, toilets.

A 170.5 (274.4 km) T 157.5 (253.5 km) Tolsona Lake, grayling to 16 inches. Crosswind Lake, 18 miles/29 km north by floatplane, excellent fishing for lake trout, grayling and whitefish.

A 170.5 (274.4 km) T 157.5 (253.5 km) Tolsona Lake Resort. See display ad this section.

A 169.3 (272.3 km) T 158.7 (255.4 km) Mae West Lake trail. Paved double-ended turnout and litter disposal to south. The long narrow lake, fed by Little Woods Creek, is a little less than 1 mile/1.6 km away.

A 168 (270.4 km) T 160 (257.5 km) Rough road, patched pavement and frost heaves westbound. Soup Lake. Trumpeter swans can sometimes be seen in lakes and ponds along this section of highway. In June and July look for wildflowers such as sweet pea, fireweed, lupine, cinquefoil, oxytrope, Jacob's ladder and milk vetch.

A 166.1 (267.3 km) T 161.9 (260.5 km) Atlasta House, a local landmark, was named by the homesteader who was happy to have a real house at last.

A 166 (267.2 km) T 162 (260.7 km) Tolsona Mountain (elev. 2,974 feet/906m), a prominent ridge just north of highway, is a landmark for miles in both directions. This area is popular with berry-pickers in late summer and early fall. Varieties of wild berries include blueberries, lowbush cranberries and raspberries.

A 165.9 (267 km) T 162.1 (260.9 km) Paved double-ended turnout to south and 2-mile/3.2-km trail to Lost Cabin Lake.

A 162.3 (261.2 km) T 165.7 (266.7 km) Paved turnout to south.

A 162 (260.7 km) T 166 (267.1 km) Tex Smith Lake to north.

A 159.8 (257.2 km) T 168.2 (270.7 km) Little Junction Lake, 0.3-mile/0.4-km hike south; grayling and rainbow.

A 159.8 (257.2 km) T 168.2 (270.7 km) Junction with Lake Louise Road to Lake Louise Recreation Area. See LAKE LOUISE ROAD log on page 270.

A 159 (255.8 km) T 169 (272 km) Watch for bumps in pavement and frost heaves westbound to Milepost A 133.

A 156 (251.1 km) T 172 (276.8 km) Tazlina Glacier, seen to the east, feeds into 20-mile-/32-km-long Tazlina Lake situated at its foot.

Tazlina Glacier Lodge & Tazlina Glacier Air. Visit a historic, all-log lodge built on the banks of Smokey Lake in 1943. Stay in one of the original rustic cabins and relive the history of bygone days. Enjoy the "Tazlina Tourist Trap," full of Alaska-made souvenirs, furs, fine gifts and candies. Plus film, batteries, groceries, ice cream, snacks, ice and propane. We have a good selection of bait and fishing tackle, plus hunting and fishing licenses and tags. Your Alaska adventure can start at Tazlina! Hunting, fishing, air photography and flightseeing trips are available—guides on request. And don't forget to pick up one of our free fishing maps of local good fishing areas. We are located across from 1,600-foot Tazlina airstrip and have a floatplane lake in our backyard, so if you can't drive to see us, fly in! Art and Bonny Wikle and their Smokey Lake Gang hope to see you soon. HC01 Box 1862, Glennallen, AK 99588. Phone (907) 822-3061. [ADVERTISEMENT]

A 155.8 (250.7 km) T 172.2 (277.1 km) Private Aircraft: Tazlina airstrip; elev. 2,450 feet/747m; length 1,400 feet/427m; gravel.

A 155.7 (250.6 km) T 172.3 (277.3 km) Arizona Lake to south; fishing for

GLENN HIGHWAY

Tolsona Lake Resort
MILE 170.5 • OPEN YEAR-ROUND
(907) 822-3433 • 1-800 245-3342
MODERN MOTEL ROOMS
Also rustic cabins for rent • Boat and canoe rentals
Cafe • Dining room • Cocktail Lounge
CAMPER PARKING FOR SELF-CONTAINED RVs
FLOAT POND AVIATION GAS  
Open Year-round *(Closed the month of October)*
WINTER SPORTS: snow machine racing, cross country skiing ice fishing, nice big fireplace.
A variety of wild game trophies on display
WALK-IN FREEZER FOR FISH AND MEAT STORAGE

Close to the highway on beautiful Tolsona Lake...
KIRK AND JULIE WILSON INVITE YOU TO COME AND ENJOY OUR BEAUTIFUL LAKE RESORT

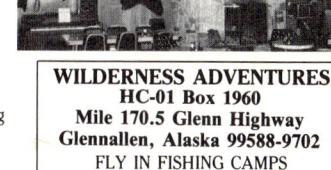

WILDERNESS ADVENTURES
HC-01 Box 1960
Mile 170.5 Glenn Highway
Glennallen, Alaska 99588-9702
FLY IN FISHING CAMPS
Fully accommodated
Mile A 170.5 Glenn Hwy.

KAMPING RESORTS OF ALASKA
Mile 153 Glenn Highway • (35 miles southwest of Glennallen)
Half-way point: Anchorage - Valdez and Tok - Anchorage

All Modern Facilities
Over 90% Graveled Pull-Throughs

Special Rates for Caravans (2 or more)
We can handle any size - over 100 sites

RESTAURANT EXTRAORDINAIRE - New Log Cathedral Restaurant
Visit King Salmon Observation Deck
Fresh Dough Brick Oven Pizzas and Giant Cinnamon Rolls are
AN ALASKAN TRADITION at K.R.O.A.
Large, Handmade Hamburgers • 15 Varieties of Pancakes
Buses Welcome - Large Dining Area - Quick Service

MUSEUM OF ALASKA'S DRUNKEN FOREST - Free
HC 03, Box 8795 (Mendeltna) via Palmer, AK 99645

Carol & Vern Adkins of Miami, Florida
(907) 822-3346

1992 ■ The MILEPOST® 269

Lake Louise Road Log

This 19.3-mile-/31-km-long scenic gravel road from the Glenn Highway north to Lake Louise Recreation Area is open year-round. Lake Louise is known for its good lake trout fishing; ice fishing in winter. Excellent cross-country skiing. Many turnouts and parking areas along the road; views of Tazlina Glacier and Lake; berry picking for wild strawberries and blueberries (July and August), and cranberries (September).

Distance is measured from the junction with the Glenn Highway (J).

J 0.2 (0.3 km) **Junction Lake** to east; grayling fishing.

J 1.1 (1.8 km) Turnout with view of Tazlina Glacier and Crater Lake.

J 1.2 (1.9 km) Double-ended turnout to west. Just north is the road west to **Crater Lake**. There are a number of small lakes along the road with good fishing for grayling, rainbow and silver salmon.

J 9.4 (15.1 km) Beautiful pothole lakes. First view of Lake Louise northbound.

J 11 (17.7 km) Good view on clear days of the Alaska Range and Susitna River valley.

J 11.5 (18.5 km) Road west to **Caribou Lake**; silver salmon fishing. Turnout to east by Elbow Lake.

J 14 (22.5 km) Boundary of Matanuska–Susitna Borough.

J 15.4 (24.8 km) Gas station, public dumpster.

J 16.1 (25.9 km) Turnoff to lodge.

J 16.5 (26.6 km) Turnoff to lakeside accommodations. **Evergreen Lodge Bed & Breakfast on Lake Louise.** See display ad this section.

Wolverine Lodge. See display ad this section.

J 16.8 (27 km) **Conner Lake**, grayling fishing.

J 17.2 (27.7 km) Side road to lodge and Lake Louise State Recreation Area's Army Point and Lake Louise campgrounds; 52 campsites on 2 loop roads, firepits, toilets (handicap accessible), covered picnic tables at lakeshore and a boat launch. Well water. Camping fee $6/night or annual pass. Swimming in Lake Louise. Winter ski trail access. ▲

J 17.2 (27.7 km) **Point of View Lodge.** See display ad this section.

J 17.6 (28.3 km) Turnout to west. Winter ski trail access.

J 18.8 (30.3 km) Airport road to west. **Private Aircraft:** Lake Louise airstrip; elev. 2,450 feet/747m; length 2,200 feet/670m; gravel; fuel 80. Seaplane base adjacent.

J 19.3 (31 km) Road ends at Lake Louise rest area; picnic tables, fireplaces, toilets, parking, boat launch.

Lake Louise, excellent grayling and lake trout fishing; lake trout 20 to 30 lbs., average 10 lbs., good year-round, best spring through July, then again in late September; early season use herring or whitefish bait, cast from boat; later (warmer water) troll with #16 red-and-white spoon, silver Alaskan plug or large silver flatfish; grayling 10 to 12 inches, casting flies or small spinners, June, July and August; in winter set lines with herring-baited hook through ice holes or jig for lake trout.

Susitna Lake can be reached by boat across Lake Louise; excellent lake trout and grayling fishing. Both lakes can be rough; underpowered boats not recommended.

Return to Milepost A 159.8 Glenn Highway

A quiet pond along scenic Lake Louise Road. (Jerrianne Lowther, staff)

Evergreen Lodge Bed & Breakfast on Lake Louise

CABINS
BOAT RENTAL • SKI TRAILS
Guided Fly-in Fishing by Reservation Only
Remote Fly-in Cabins

Your Host: Jack Hansen   HC 01 BOX 1709, GLENNALLEN, ALASKA 99588 • (907) 822-3250
Turn off Glenn Highway at Mile 159.8 — See log ad at Mile 16.5 Lake Louise Road

---

POINT OF VIEW LODGE
Mile 17.2 Lake Louise Road   (907) 822-5566

- Modern Rooms
- Dining
- Fishing
- Boating
- Cross Country Ski Trails
- Fly-out Guided Fishing

Panoramic Lake View

Reservations Advised
HC 01 Box 1706
Glennallen, AK 99588

WOLVERINE LODGE

- Record Lake Trout
- Charter Fishing Trips
- Boat Gas • Docking
- Repair Shop
- Hunting & Fishing Licenses
- Restaurant
- Cocktail Lounge
- Modern Rooms
- Showers • Ice
- Propane

OPEN YEAR AROUND
"Friendly Atmosphere"

HC-01 Box 1704, Glennallen, Alaska 99588
Phone: (907) 822-3988
TURN OFF GLENN HIGHWAY MILE 159.8

Located on Beautiful Lake Louise

grayling and burbot.

A **155.5** (250.2 km) T **172.5** (277.6 km) Paved turnout to south.

A **153** (246.2 km) T **175** (281.6 km) **K.R.O.A. Kamping Resorts of Alaska** on the Little Mendeltna, a natural spring-fed stream. Excellent fishing for grayling, whitefish and others. Many lakes nearby. Fishing, hunting guides available. Gateway to Tazlina Lake and Glacier. Ski, hiking, snow machine trails. Modern hookups. Pull-throughs. Laundromat. Hot showers. Can handle any size caravan. Rustic cabins. Brick oven fresh dough pizza. Homemade cinnamon rolls. Museum of Alaska's Drunken Forest, a large collection of unusual and artistic natural designs of trees. Minerals. Artifacts of Alaska's drunken forest. Free. [ADVERTISEMENT] ▲

A **152.8** (245.9 km) T **175.2** (282 km) Mendeltna Creek bridge.

AREA FISHING: Mendeltna Creek, good fishing north to Old Man Lake; watch for bears. (The Mendeltna Creek drainage is closed to the taking of salmon.) Excellent fishing for grayling to 17 1/2 inches, May to November, use spinners and flies; whitefish to 16 inches; small Dolly Varden; burbot to 30 inches, May to November, use spinners or flies; rainbow, from May to November, use spinners or flies. Walk or boat away from the bridge.

A **152.7** (245.7 km) T **175.3** (282.1 km) Paved double-ended rest area to north with picnic tables, dumpster and toilets.

A **147.3** (237.1 km) T **180.7** (290.8 km) **Alaskan Airventures.** See display ad this section.

A **147.3** (237.1 km) T **180.7** (290.8 km) **Cache Creek** culvert. Grayling in late May and June. Trail leading from parking area to lake, approximately 0.5 mile/0.8 km. Small picnic area on east side of highway. Steep approach.

A **147** (236.6 km) T **181** (291.3 km) Very bad frost heaves.

A **144.9** (233.2 km) T **183.1** (294.7 km) Lottie Sparks (Nelchina) Elementary School.

A **143.2** (230.4 km) T **184.8** (297.4 km) Nelchina Lodge (closed 1991, current status unknown).

A **141.2** (227.2 km) T **186.8** (300.6 km) Nelchina state highway maintenance station. Slide Mountain trailhead located behind station.

NOTE: Watch for major road construction to **Milepost A 118** in 1992.

A **137.6** (221.4 km) T **190.4** (306.4 km) Little Nelchina State Recreation Site 0.3 mile/0.5 km from highway; 11 campsites, 15-day limit, no camping fee, no drinking water, tables, firepits, toilet. Watch for moose and bear. ▲

A **137.5** (221.3 km) T **190.5** (306.6 km) Little Nelchina River bridge.

A **137** (220.5 km) T **191** (307.4 km) Boundary of Matanuska–Susitna Borough.

A **135.7** (218.4 km) T **192.3** (309.5 km) Small paved turnout. Highway widens eastbound.

A **134.8** (216.9 km) T **193.2** (310.9 km) Watch for loose livestock on highway.

A **132.1** (212.6 km) T **195.9** (315.2 km) Caribou crossing. Gravel turnout to north. View of Mount Sanford eastbound. Caribou and moose seen in this area in winter. The Nelchina caribou herd passes through here in October–November.

A **131** (210.8 km) T **197** (317 km) View west to the notch of Gunsight Mountain. From here to Eureka Summit there are views of the Wrangell and Chugach mountains.

A **130.3** (209.7 km) T **197.7** (318.2 km) Old Man Creek trailhead parking to north. Old Man Creek 2 miles/3 km; Crooked Creek 9 miles/14.5 km; Nelchina Town 14.5 miles/23 km. Established trails west from here to Palmer are part of the Chickaloon–Knik–Nelchina trail system.

A **129.3** (208.1 km) T **198.7** (319.8 km) Eureka Summit (elev. 3,322 feet/1,013m). Highest point on the Glenn Highway, near timberline, with unobstructed views south toward the Chugach Mountains. The Nelchina Glacier winds downward through a cleft in the mountains. To the northwest are the peaks of the Talkeetnas, and to the west the highway descends through river valleys which separate these 2 mountain ranges. This is the divide of 3 big river systems: Susitna, Matanuska and Copper.

A **128** (206 km) T **200** (321.9 km) Site of the first lodge on the Glenn Highway, the Eureka Roadhouse, which was opened in 1937 by Paul Waverly and has operated continuously ever since. The original log building is next to Eureka Lodge.

A **128** (206 km) T **200** (321.9 km) **Eureka Lodge.** See display ad this section.

Private Aircraft: Eureka airstrip; elev. 3,289 feet/1,002m; length 2,400 feet/732m; gravel; fuel 80.

A **127** (204.4 km) T **201** (323.4 km) Gravel turnout to south.

A **126.4** (203.4 km) T **201.6** (324.4 km) Watch closely for turnout to Belanger Creek–Nelchina River trailhead parking to south. Eureka Creek 1.5 miles/2.4 km; Goober Lake 8 miles/13 km; Nelchina River 9 miles/14.5 km.

A **125** (201.2 km) T **203** (326.7 km) Gunsight Mountain (elev. 6,441 feet/1,963m) is visible for the next few miles to those approaching from Glennallen. The notch or "gunsight" is plain if one looks closely.

A **123.3** (198.4 km) T **204.7** (329.4 km) Belanger Pass trailhead: Belanger Pass 3 miles/5 km; Albert Creek 6.5 miles/10.5 km; Albert Creek 8 miles/13 km.

A **123.1** (198.1 km) T **204.9** (329.8 km) Tahneta Inn (closed 1991, current status unknown).

Private Aircraft: Tahneta airstrip; elev. 2,960 feet/902m; length 1,800 feet/549m; gravel/dirt. Fuel available. Floatplanes land on Tahneta Lake.

A **122.9** (197.8 km) T **205.1** (330 km) Gunsight Mountain Lodge (closed 1991, current status unknown).

A **122** (196.3 km) T **206** (333.5 km) Tahneta Pass (elev. 3,000 feet/914m). Double-ended paved turnout to north. **Leila Lake** trailhead (unsigned) on old alignment to north; grayling 8 to 14 inches abundant through summer, best fishing June and July. Burbot, success spotty for 12 to 18 inches in fall and winter.

A **120.8** (194.4 km) T **207.2** (333.4 km) Boundary of Sportfish Management Area 2 and Sheep Mountain Closed Area.

A **120.3** (193.6 km) T **207.7** (334.3 km) View eastbound overlooks Tahneta Pass. The largest lake is Leila Lake; in the distance is Tahneta Lake. Drive carefully along the southern part of Tahneta Pass. The road is narrow with frost heaves and little shoulder space.

A **118.6** (190.9 km) T **209.4** (337 km) Gravel turnout to south.

A **118.5** (190.7 km) T **209.5** (337.1 km) FAA road south to communication towers.

A **118.3** (190.4 km) T **209.7** (337.5 km) Large gravel turnout to south.

NOTE: Watch for major road construction eastbound to **Milepost A 141.2** in 1992.

A **117.8** (189.5 km) T **210.2** (338.2 km) Turnout with viewpoint. Looking southeast of the highway, a tip of a glacier can be seen coming down South Fork Canyon. Knob Lake and the "knob" (elev. 3,000 feet/914m) can be seen to the northeast.

A **117.6** (189.3 km) T **210.4** (338.6 km) Squaw Creek trailhead: Squaw Creek 3.5 miles/5.6 km; Caribou Creek 9.5 miles/15 km; Alfred Creek 13 miles/21 km; Sheep Creek 15 miles/24 km.

A **115** (185 km) T **213** (342.8 km) Between **Milepost A 115** and **A 116** there are 3 turnouts with views of mineralized Sheep Mountain and the Matanuska Glacier area.

A **114.5** (184.3 km) T **213.5** (343.6 km) In season, on slopes adjacent the highway and along old creek beds back from the road, are many kinds of flowers, including lupine, Labrador tea, bluebells, fireweed, chiming bells and large patches of forget-me-nots, Alaska's state flower.

A **114.3** (183.9 km) T **213.7** (343.9 km) For Anchorage-bound travelers a vista of incomparable beauty as the road descends in a long straightaway toward Glacier Point, also known as the Lion Head, an oddly formed rocky dome. No turnouts for 1 mile/1.6 km.

A **114** (183.5 km) T **214** (344.4 km) Winding road, long stretches without shoulders, watch for rocks and frost heaves west-

ALASKAN AIRVENTURES

AIR TAXI CHARTERS • BED & BREAKFAST
Photo and Scenic Flights • Drop Off and Pickup for Hunting, Fishing, Backpack and Float Trips

C.P. and Rosemary Bartley
HC 03 Box 8758
Palmer, Alaska 99645

(907) 822-3905
Snowshoe Lake
Mile 147.3 Glenn Highway

Tom & Mary Ann Berkley

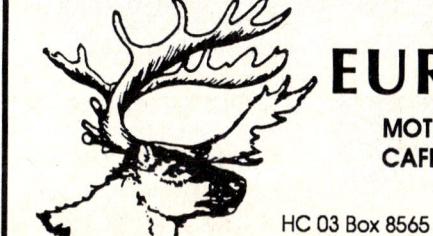

EUREKA LODGE

MOTEL
CAFE

Chevron Gas

YAMAHA

HC 03 Box 8565
Palmer, Alaska

Mile 128 Glenn Highway
(907) 822-3808

bound between here and Palmer.

A 113.5 (182.7 km) **T 214.5** (345.2 km) **Sheep Mountain Lodge.** Operated since 1946. Home-cooked meals and desserts, bar, liquor store, Alaskan gifts and souvenirs. Cozy log cabins, campsites, RV hookups. Hot tub, sauna, telescope to view Dall sheep. Good hiking. Cross-country ski trails. Open year-round. HCO3 Box 8490, Palmer, AK 99645. (907) 745-5121. [ADVERTISEMENT] ▲

Private Aircraft: Sheep Mountain airstrip; elev. 2,750 feet/838m; length 2,200 feet/670m; gravel; unattended.

A 113.5 (182.7 km) **T 214.5** (345.2 km) As the highway descends westbound into the valley of the Matanuska River, there is a view of the great glacier which is the main headwater source and gives the water its milky color.

A 113 (181.9 km) **T 215** (346 km) Gravel turnout.

A 112.5 (181.1 km) **T 215.5** (346.8 km) View to north of Sheep Mountain (elev. 6,300 feet/1,920m) for 11 miles/17.7 km between Tahneta Pass and Caribou Creek. Sheep are often seen high up these slopes. The area surrounding Sheep Mountain is closed to the taking of mountain sheep.

A 112 (180.2 km) **T 216** (347.6 km) Gravel turnout by creek. View westbound of Lion Head and first view of Matanuska Glacier.

A 111.5 (179.4 km) **T 216.5** (348.4 km) **Bunk 'N Breakfast.** Rustic homestead accommodations below Sheep Mountain Preserve. Bring sleeping bag. Sleeps 6. Summer $10.50, winter $12.60/person. Family rates. Complimentary coffee, tea and juice. Within 10 miles of Matanuska Glacier, hiking, fishing, flightseeing, horseback tours, cross-country skiing and snowmobiling. Dee Larson, HC 03, Box 8488A, Palmer, AK 99645. (907) 745-5143. [ADVERTISEMENT]

A 111 (178.6 km) **T 217** (349.2 km) Sharp curves and falling rocks for the next mile westbound.

A 110.3 (177.5 km) **T 217.7** (350.3 km) Watch for mountain sheep.

A 109.7 (176.5 km) **T 218.3** (351.3 km) Paved turnout to south.

A 109.5 (176.2 km) **T 218.5** (351.6 km) Paved turnout to south.

A 108.4 (174.4 km) **T 219.6** (353.4 km) Large gravel turnout to south.

A 107.8 (173.5 km) **T 220.2** (354.4 km) Turnout with view of Glacier Point (Lion Head) and Matanuska Glacier. Exceptional picture stop.

A 107.1 (172.4 km) **T 220.9** (355.5 km) Large gravel turnouts to south, viewpoint.

A 106.8 (171.9 km) **T 221.2** (356 km) Caribou Creek bridge and Caribou Creek trailhead. Hiking distances: Squaw Creek 9 miles/14.5 km; Alfred Creek 13 miles/21 km; Sheep Creek 15 miles/24 km; and Squaw Creek trailhead 18.5 miles/30 km. Caribou Creek trail zigzags up the mountainside between the highway and the creek and leads back behind Sheep Mountain. A pleasant hike for good walkers.

Highway makes a steep descent (from both directions) down to Caribou Creek. The banks of this stream provide good rockhounding, particularly after mountain storms. There are turnouts on both sides of the highway here. Fortress Ridge (elev. 5,000 feet/1,524m) above the highway to the north. Sheep Mountain reserve boundary.

A 106 (170.6 km) **T 222** (357.3 km) Large gravel turnout overlooking Caribou Creek canyon. Steep descent eastbound.

A 105.8 (170.3 km) **T 222.2** (357.6 km) Road (closed to public) to FAA station on flank of Glacier Point. Mountain sheep occasionally are seen on the upper slopes.

A 105.5 (169.8 km) **T 222.5** (358.1 km) Gravel turnout to south.

A 105.3 (169.4 km) **T 222.7** (358.4 km) Turnout with views of Matanuska Glacier and the FAA station on Glacier Point.

A 104.1 (167.5 km) **T 223.9** (360.3 km) Access to Glacier View School, which overlooks Matanuska Glacier.

A 104 (167.4 km) **T 224** (360.5 km) From here to **Milepost A 98** several kinds of wild orchids and other wildflowers may be found along the trails into the roadside brush.

A 102.8 (165.4 km) **T 225.2** (362.4 km) Gravel turnout to south with view of Matanuska Glacier.

A 102.2 (164.5 km) **T 225.8** (363.4 km) **Long Rifle Lodge Ltd.** See display ad this section.

A 102 (164.2 km) **T 226** (363.7 km) Access to foot of Matanuska Glacier via Glacier Park Resort. Admission fee charged.

A 101.7 (163.7 km) **T 227.7** (366.4 km) Paved turnout with good view of Matanuska Glacier, which heads in the Chugach Mountains and trends northwest 27 miles/43.5 km. Some 18,000 years ago the glacier reached all the way to the Palmer area. The glacier's average width is 2 miles/3.2 km; at its terminus it is 4 miles/6.4 km wide. The glacier has remained fairly stable the past 400 years. At the glacier terminus meltwater drains into a stream which flows into the Matanuska River.

A 101 (162.5 km) **T 227** (365.3 km) Matanuska Glacier State Recreation Site; 12 campsites on loop drive, 3-day limit, $6 nightly fee or annual pass, water and toilets. Excellent views of the glacier and good vantages for photographs from hiking trails along the bluff. (Use caution when walking near edge of bluff.) Wildflowers here in late July include fireweed, yarrow and sweet peas. ▲

A 100.8 (162.2 km) **T 227.2** (365.6 km) Large gravel turnout to south.

A 99.2 (159.6 km) **T 228.8** (368.2 km) Gravel turnout to south, viewpoint. Pinochle–Hicks Creek trail.

A 97.8 (157.4 km) **T 230.2** (370.5 km) Gravel turnout to west, viewpoint.

Winding road with steep grades westbound.

A 97 (156 km) **T 231** (371.7 km) Gravel turnout to north.

A 96.6 (155.5 km) **T 231.4** (372.4 km) Hicks Creek, named by Captain Glenn in 1898 for H.H. Hicks, the guide of his expedition. Ridges back from here, right side Anchorage-bound, are good rockhound areas. Anthracite Ridge has jasper, rosy-banded agate, petrified wood and rock crystal. Difficult to reach on foot.

A 96.4 (155.1 km) T 231.6 (372.7 km) Small gravel turnout to south.

A 94.9 (152.7 km) T 233.1 (375.1 km) Victory Road. Slide area. Look for lupine and wild sweet pea.

A 93.4 (150.3 km) T 234.6 (377.5 km) Cascade state highway maintenance camp.

A 93 (149.7 km) T 235 (378.2 km) Gravel turnouts both sides of highway. Views of Amulet Peak and Monument Glacier and Valley.

A 91.3 (146.9 km) T 236.7 (380.9 km) Cascade Creek culvert.

A 91 146.4 km) T 237 (381.4 km) First view eastbound of Matanuska Glacier.

A 90.6 (145.8 km) T 237.4 (382 km) Paved turnout to south.

A 90.1 (145 km) T 237.9 (382.9 km) Turnout to south.

A 89 (143.2 km) T 239 (384.6 km) Puritan Creek trailhead. Bridge over Puritan Creek. (Although signed Puritan, the stream is officially named Purinton Creek.) Good blueberry patches in season if you can beat the bears to them. The stream heads on Anthracite Ridge and flows into the Matanuska River. Westbound, watch for coal seams along the highway.

A 87.8 (141.3 km) T 240.2 (386.5 km) Two small gravel turnouts to south.

A 87.6 (141 km) T 240.4 (386.9 km) Large gravel turnout above Weiner Lake.

A 87.4 (140.6 km) T 240.6 (387.2 km) Weiner Lake access.

A 87.3 (140.5 km) T 240.7 (387.4 km) Turnout. Highway descends eastbound.

A 86.8 (139.7 km) T 241.2 (388.2 km) Slide area: Watch for falling rock.

A 86.5 (139.2 km) T 241.5 (388.6 km) Good gravel turnout overlooking Long Lake to south.

A 85.3 (137.3 km) T 242.7 (390.6 km) **Long Lake**, in a narrow canyon below the highway, is a favorite fishing spot for Anchorage residents. Fair for grayling to 18 inches, spring through fall; fish deeper as the water warms in summer. Good ice fishing in winter for burbot, average 12 inches. Long Lake State Recreation Site has 9 campsites, 15-day limit, $6 nightly fee or annual pass, tables, water pump, firepits and toilets. Wildflowers include roses, sweet pea, paintbrush and lupine. Long upgrade begins eastbound.

A 84.6 (136.1 km) T 243.4 (391.7 km) There are several gravel turnouts westbound.

A 84.3 (135.7 km) T 243.7 (392.2 km) Large double-ended turnout. View of Matanuska River and unnamed mountains.

A 84.1 (135.3 km) T 243.9 (392.5 km) Large double-ended gravel turnout.

CAUTION: Watch for road equipment in slide areas next 4 miles/6.4 km eastbound.

A 83.2 (133.9 km) T 244.8 (394 km) Narrow gravel road to Ravine and Lower Bonnie lakes. (Side road not signed.) Drive in 0.8 mile/1.3 km on side road to reach **Ravine Lake**; fishing from shore for rainbows. **Lower Bonnie Lake** is a 2-mile/3.2-km drive from the highway; Bonnie Lake State Recreation Site has 8 campsites, 15-day limit, no camping fee, toilets and boat launch. Fishing for grayling and rainbow.

Steep and winding road beyond Ravine Lake is not recommended for large vehicles or trailers; during rainy season this road is not recommended for any vehicle.

A 82 (132 km) T 246 (395.9 km) Pyramid-shaped King Mountain is to the right (westbound) of the milepost as you look across the canyon. Several small gravel turnouts westbound.

A 80.8 (130 km) T 247.2 (397.8 km) Entering Matanuska Valley Moose Range westbound. Large gravel turnout to south.

A 79.5 (127.9 km) T 248.5 (399.9 km) Views of King Mountain (elev. 5,809 feet/1,770m).

A 79.1 (127.3 km) T 248.9 (400.6 km) Gravel turnout to south.

A 78.2 (125.8 km) T 249.8 (402 km) Gravel turnout with view of King Mountain and Matanuska River.

A 77.7 (125 km) T 250.3 (402.8 km) Chickaloon River bridge. Boundary between Game Management Units 13 and 14. There are some picnic spots along the old Chickaloon Road, which winds upstream to an abandoned oil well and a coal mine. Trails here lead into big game country in the rugged Talkeetna Mountains, habitat of sheep, moose, caribou, black and grizzly bear. Gravel turnout.

A 77.5 (124.7 km) T 250.5 (403.1 km) Gravel turnout to south. Steep ascent eastbound. Highway parallels Matanuska River.

A 76.5 (123.1 km) T 251.5 (404.7 km) Gravel turnout by river.

A 76.3 (122.8 km) T 251.7 (405.1 km) **Chickaloon General Store & Service Station.** See display ad this section.

A 76.2 (122.6 km) T 251.8 (405.2 km) **King Mountain Lodge.** See display ad this section.

A 76.1 (122.5 km) T 251.9 (405.4 km) King Mountain State Recreation Site. Pleasant campground on the banks of the Matanuska River with 22 campsites, 2 picnic sites, fireplaces, picnic tables, water, toilets. Camping fee $6/night or annual pass; 15-day limit. King Mountain to the southeast.

CAUTION: Watch for road equipment in slide areas westbound to **Milepost A 60.**

A 73 (117.5 km) T 255 (410.4 km) Ida Lake/Fish Lake subdivision. Chickaloon River loop road.

A 72.5 (116.4 km) T 255.7 (411.5 km) Ida Lake is visible to the west.

A 71.2 (114.6 km) T 256.8 (413.3 km) End slide area. Beaver pond to north.

A 71 (114.3 km) T 257 (413.6 km) Turnouts to south by Matanuska River.

A 70.6 (113.6 km) T 257.4 (414.2 km) Access to Matanuska River to south.

A 70 (112.7 km) T 258 (415.2 km) Double-ended gravel turnout.

A 69.7 (112.2 km) T 258.3 (415.7 km) Chickaloon post office (Zip code 99674), 2 private campgrounds.

Pinnacle Mtn. RV Park. All new full-service nonmembership family campground. 42 sites on 26 acres, plus tent sites. Full and partial hookups. 4 restrooms, large private showers, dump station, laundry, good water. Cafe with good home-cooking, gas, propane, country store, ice, video rentals, gift shop. Post office. Forward your vacation mail here and we will hold it until you arrive. Good

CHICKALOON
General Store & Service Station
24-Hour Wrecker   Mechanic on Duty   Phone 745-4520
GROCERIES • LAUNDROMAT • ALASKA GIFT SHOP
Full Service Station   GAS   PROPANE • ICE

Good Area Information   "The Moose Stops Here"
Mike and Debbie Pietrok Welcome You   Mile 76.3 Glenn Hwy.

KING MOUNTAIN LODGE
Food — Lodging — Bar
Liquor Store — Showers
Electrical Hookups

Your Hosts
Gordon and Karen Romriell
and Frank Foster

(907) 745-4280   MILE 76.2 Glenn Highway

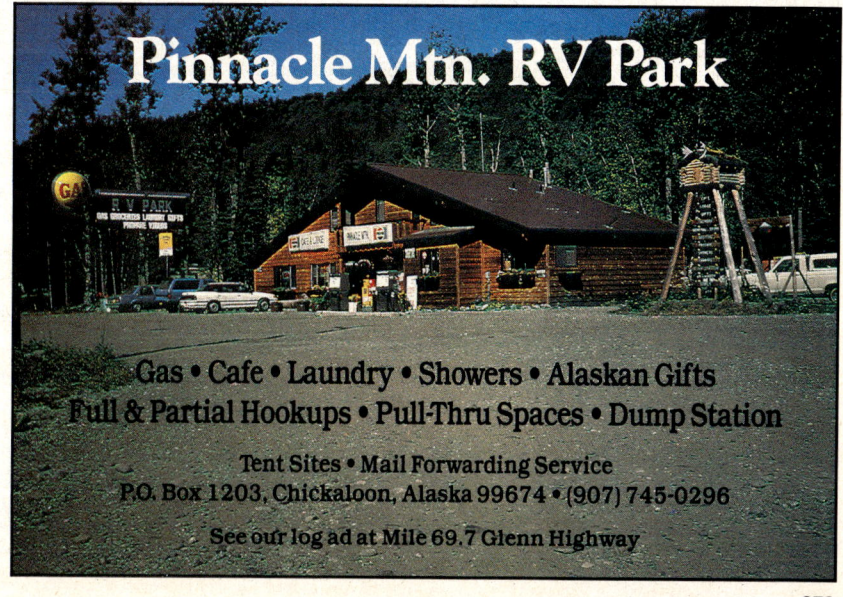

Pinnacle Mtn. RV Park
Gas • Cafe • Laundry • Showers • Alaskan Gifts
Full & Partial Hookups • Pull-Thru Spaces • Dump Station

Tent Sites • Mail Forwarding Service
P.O. Box 1203, Chickaloon, Alaska 99674 • (907) 745-0296

See our log ad at Mile 69.7 Glenn Highway

Hatcher Pass Road Log

The 49-mile-/79-km-long Hatcher Pass (Fishhook–Willow) Road leads north and west from **Milepost A 49.5** on the Glenn Highway to **Milepost A 71.2** on the George Parks Highway, providing access to Independence Mine State Historical Park. (See Matanuska Valley Vicinity map this section.) It is a mostly gravel road, not recommended for large RVs or trailers beyond **Milepost J 13.9**. The road usually does not open until late June and snow may close the pass in September. The road stays open to the historical park and to Hatcher Pass Lodge in winter, a popular winter sports area for snowmobiling and cross-country skiing.

Distance from junction with the Glenn Highway (J) is followed by distance from junction with the George Parks Highway (GP).

J 0 (GP 49.1) (79 km) **Junction** with the Glenn Highway at **Milepost A 49.5**. Fishhook–Willow Road heads west through farm country.

J 1.4 (2.3 km) **GP 47.7** (76.8 km) **Junction** with Farm Loop Road.

J 1.6 (2.6 km) **GP 47.4** (76.3 km) **Teddy Bear Corner Country Inn.** See display ad this section.

J 2.4 (3.9 km) **GP 46.7** (75.2 km) **Junction** with Trunk Road.

J 6.5 (10.5 km) **GP 42.5** (68.4 km) **Hatcher Pass Gateway Center.** See display ad this section.

J 6.6 (10.6 km) **GP 42.4** (68.2 km) Turner Drive.

J 6.8 (10.9 km) **GP 42.3** (68.1 km) **Junction** with Wasilla–Fishhook Road. This road leads south to connect with the George Parks Highway at Wasilla.

J 7.2 (11.6 km) **GP 41.9** (67.4 km) Pavement ends, gravel begins, northbound.

J 8.5 (13.7 km) **GP 40.6** (65.3 km) Little Susitna River bridge. Road parallels river. Several turnouts westbound.

J 9 (14.5 km) **GP 40.1** (64.5 km) Entering Hatcher Pass public-use area westbound. No flower picking or plant removal without a permit in public-use area.

J 12.7 (20.4 km) **GP 36.4** (58.6 km) Beaver pond.

J 14 (22.5 km) **GP 35.1** (56.5 km) Motherlodge Lodge. Side "road" (4-wheel-drive vehicle recommended) to mine and trails parallels Little Susitna River. Trailhead parking for Gold Mint trail and Arkose Ridge trail. Snowmobile trail. Hatcher Pass Road begins climb to Hatcher Pass via a series of switchbacks. There are several turnouts the next 2.4 miles/3.9 km westbound.

Motherlode Lodge. See display ad this section.

J 14.6 (23.5 km) **GP 34.5** (55.5 km) Archangel Valley Road to Mabel and Fern mines and Reed Lakes. Road crosses private property (do not trespass). Winter trails (snowmobiles prohibited east of Archangel Road).

J 16.4 (26.4 km) **GP 32.7** (52.6 km) Parking lot to east, snowmobile trail to west.

J 17.3 (27.8 km) **GP 31.8** (51.2 km) Gold Cord Road provides year-round access to lodge and Independence Mine State Historical Park (1.5 miles/2.4 km). The 271-acre **INDEPENDENCE MINE STATE HISTORICAL PARK** includes several buildings and old mining machinery. Park visitor center is housed in the red-roofed building, which was built in 1939 to house the mine manager. In 1991, the visitor center and assay office were open from 11 A.M. to 6 P.M., Friday through Monday, from June through Labor Day; weekends the rest of the year. Guided tours of the bunkhouse, mess hall and warehouse are given from June to Labor Day (weather permitting) for a nominal fee; phone visitor center at 745-2827 or phone 745-3975 in Palmer for current information. Groups of 20 or more call ahead for tours. Office hours and tour times may vary, but visitors are always welcome to explore on their own.

Alaska Pacific Consolidated Mine Co., one of the largest gold producers in the Willow Creek mining district, operated here from 1938 through 1941. The Gold Cord Mine buildings (private property) are visible on the hill above and to the north of Independence Mine.

Recreational gold panning is permitted in the park. Some pans are available for loan at the visitor center.

Motherlode Lodge
Hatcher Pass
Beautiful Scenery & Historic Sights

Independence Gold Mine

**New Hotel Rooms
Super Special at $65.00**
Popular Restaurant & Bar

- KAYAKING
- NATURE TRAILS
- HIKING
- WILD BERRY PICKING
- GOLD PANNING
- PARASAILING
- FREE CAMPING
- SKIING
- SLEDDING

Only 60 miles from Anchorage!

Mile 14, Fishhook Rd. Palmer, AK

Phone 907 746•1464

Gateway To Hatcher Pass
HATCHER PASS GATEWAY CENTER

Self-service Gas — Chevron
Unleaded and Regular
Chevron Products
Propane • Air

Grocery • Convenience Store, Ice

Liquor Store • Cold Beer, Wine
Package Liquor

Laundromat • Clean and Modern
Front-load Washers • **Hot Showers**

Clean Rest Rooms • Water • Phone

**MILE 6.5 HATCHER PASS ROAD
(907) 745-6161**

RELAX IN THE MOUNTAINS FOR THE DAY OR OVERNIGHT

- 90 minutes north of Anchorage, four hours to Denali National Park
- Modern Guest Cabins • Outdoor Sauna
- Gourmet Restaurant and Bar
- Lodge situated within the 761 acre Independence Mine State Historical Park — Nearby museum and historic gold mining village
- Hiking trails

HATCHER PASS LODGE

P.O. Box 763
Palmer, Alaska 99645
(907) 745-5897

Snowmobiling is prohibited in the park.

Hatcher Pass Lodge. See display ad this section.

J 18.9 (30.4 km) **GP 30.1** (48.4 km) Hatcher Pass Summit (elev. 3,886 feet/1,184m). Several turnouts westbound.

J 19.2 (30.9 km) **GP 29.8** (48 km) Summit Lake, headwaters of Willow Creek. Summit Lake State Recreation Site under development. The road follows Willow Creek from here to the George Parks Highway. There are several old and new mines in the area.

J 20.4 (32.8 km) **GP 28.6** (46 km) Upper Willow Creek Valley Road to mine.

J 23.8 (38.3 km) **GP 25.3** (40.7 km) Craigie Creek Road (very rough) leads to mine sites. Remains of historic Lucky Shot and War Baby mines on hillside are visible on hillside ahead westbound.

J 24.3 (39.1 km) **GP 24.8** (39.9 km) Beaver lodges and dams; watch for others along road.

J 25.6 (41.2 km) **GP 23.5** (37.8 km) View of Beaver Ponds to west; mine site visible to south below road. Road begins descent westbound into Little Willow Creek valley; numerous turnouts.

J 30.3 (48.8 km) **GP 18.7** (30.1 km) Leaving Hatcher Pass public-use area westbound.

J 34.2 (55 km) **GP 14.9** (24 km) Little Willow Creek bridge; large parking area.

J 38.9 (62.6 km) **GP 10.2** (16.4 km) Gravel ends, pavement begins, westbound.

J 47.9 (77.1 km) **GP 1.2** (1.9 km) Willow Creek State Recreation Area Deception Creek Campground; 7 campsites, 15-day limit, $6 nightly fee or annual pass, covered picnic tables, water, toilets (handicap accessible). ▲

J 48 (77.2 km) **GP 1.1** (1.8 km) Deception Creek bridge.

J 48.2 (77.5 km) **GP 0.9** (1.4 km) Deception Creek picnic area. Back road into Willow from here.

J 48.5 (78.1 km) **GP 0.6** (1 km) Road crosses Alaska Railroad tracks.

J 49.1 (79 km) **GP 0 Junction** with George Parks Highway at **Milepost A 71.2.** (Turn to the GEORGE PARKS HIGHWAY section.)

Return to Milepost A 49.5 Glenn Highway

Teddy Bear Corner Country Inn
Bed and Breakfast

Hostesses: Peg Rogers and Diane Marble
OPEN YEAR AROUND
Reservations (907) 745-4156
P.O. Box 1151, Palmer, AK 99645
Mile 1.6 Hatcher Pass Road

Glenn Highway Log

(continued from page 273)
Sam park. Caravan discounts. Separate caravan corral for 30 units, some with electric. Wooded sites, picnic tables. Guest lodge with TV, entertainment, social activities, games. Or just relax with a book. Volleyball, badminton, horseshoes. Rates from $8 for 2, includes showers. Stay 6 days, get 7th free. See display ad this section. [ADVERTISEMENT] ▲

Matanuska Riverside Campground and Alaska Visitor Gardens. See famous Matanuska vegetables and brilliant Alaska-grown flowers. Gravel walkways, wooded riverside campsites. Beautiful views; no hookups. Watch salmon spawning in our spring-fed stream. $5/night. See Pinnacle Mtn. RV Park ad for additional services. Plan to stay and enjoy our hiking trails. [ADVERTISEMENT] ▲

A 68.6 (110.4 km) **T 259.4** (417.5 km) Slide areas. Several gravel turnouts; watch for soft shoulders along highway.

A 68 (109.4 km) **T 260** (418.4 km) Pinnacle Mountain (elev. 4,541 feet/138m) rises directly southeast of the highway—easy to identify by its unusual top. Cottonwoods and aspen along the highway. Talkeetna Mountains to the north.

A 66.5 (107 km) **T 261.5** (420.8 km) King River bridge. Turnouts both sides of highway.

AREA FISHING: King River (Milepost A 66.5), trout, early summer best, use eggs. **Granite Creek (Milepost A 62.4)**, small Dolly Varden and trout, spring or early summer, use flies or single eggs. **Seventeenmile Lake (Milepost A 57.9 or 60.9)**, small grayling, early spring, use flies or spinners; trout, early spring, use eggs. **Eska Creek (Milepost A 60.8)**, small Dolly Varden, spring, use flies or single eggs; silver salmon, August or September, use eggs. **Moose Creek (Milepost A 54.6)**, trout and Dolly Varden, summer, use eggs. 🐟

A 66.4 (106.8 km) **T 261.6** (421 km) King River trailhead: King River Crossing 5 miles/8 km.

A 62.7 (100.9 km) **T 265.3** (426.9 km) Large gravel turnout to south along Matanuska River. Dwarf fireweed and sweet pea in June.

A 62.4 (100.4 km) **T 265.6** (427.4 km) Granite Creek bridge and access to private campground. ▲

River's Edge Recreation Park. Our park offers secluded campsites for RVs and tents. We have fresh well water, restrooms and electric hookups. While camping or visiting for the day, play volleyball or horseshoes and enjoy the beauty of the Sutton area. Spawning salmon, bald eagles, wildflowers and plenty of firewood. (907) 746-CAMP. [ADVERTISEMENT] ▲

A 62.2 (100.1 km) **T 265.8** (427.7 km) Sutton post office. Sign in at their guest book.

A 61.6 (99.1 km) **T 267.6** (430.6 km) Alpine Heritage and Cultural Center operates an open-air museum here featuring the concrete ruins of the Sutton Coal Washery, built between 1920 and 1922. The park also has the Chickaloon Bunkhouse (circa 1917) and the first Sutton post office (1948). Access via Elementary School Road. The museum is still under development. No admission charged.

A 61.5 (99 km) **T 267.5** (430.5 km) Granite Peak Souvenirs & Gifts. Beautiful view of the Matanuska River. Free coffee and nice, clean restrooms. Circular driveway to accommodate motorhomes. Postcards, ulus, jewelry, T-shirts, S/Y ceramics, gold pans, film, stamps, pop, candy and much more. Quality at a decent price. We specialize in Alaskan Made. Fishing and hunting licenses and tags. See the "Eska Coal Washer," coal dryer, coal cars, antique engines, hoists, steam engines, boilers and authentic "Spirit Houses." Open daily 10 A.M. to 8 P.M. VISA, MasterCard. [ADVERTISEMENT]

A 61 (98.2 km) **T 267** (429.7 km) SUTTON (pop. 340) was established as a railroad siding about 1918 for the once-flourishing coal industry and is now a small highway community. Sutton has a fire department, general store, post office and 2 gas stations with major and minor repairs. Fossilized shells and leaves can be found in this area 1.7 miles/2.7 km up the Jonesville Road. Inquire locally for directions.

Sutton General Store. Same location for 20 years. All your grocery needs. Hardware, hunting and fishing licenses and tags. Clean restrooms, phone. Hot snacks, coffee, relaxing seating. Full line of Doug Lindstrand notecards, prints, calendars. Local arts and crafts. Junction Jonesville Road and Glenn Highway. Scheduled opening 1992: Jonesville Diner. [ADVERTISEMENT]

A 60.9 (98 km) **T 267.1** (429.8 km) Jonesville Road. Access to Coyote Lake Recreation Area (3 miles/4.8 km); day-use area with pavilion, covered picnic tables, toilets, fireplaces, trails and swimming. Also access to Seventeenmile Lake (for recommended access see **Milepost A 57.9**). Drive north 1.7 miles/2.7 km to end of pavement; continue straight ahead for residential area and old Jonesville and Eska coal mines; turn left where pavement ends for Seventeenmile Lake. From the turnoff on Jonesville Road it is 3.1 miles/5 km via a rough dirt road (may be muddy) to **Seventeenmile Lake**; undeveloped parking area on lakeshore, boat launch, good grayling fishing. Inquire at local businesses about road conditions. ◆▲

A 60.8 (97.8 km) **T 267.2** (430 km) Eska Creek bridge.

A 60.7 (97.7 km) **T 267.3** (430.2 km) Paved double-ended turnout to south; pavement break.

A 60 (96.6 km) **T 268** (431.3 km) Long winding descent eastbound. *CAUTION: Watch for road equipment in slide areas eastbound to Milepost A 76.*

A 59.5 (95.7 km) **T 267.5** (430.5 km) Gas station (status unknown).

A 58.6 (94.3 km) **T 269.4** (433.5 km) Small gravel turnout to south. View of Matanuska River.

Celebrate Highway '92 While Camping Alaskan Style at

RIVER'S EDGE RECREATION PARK

Photos and Information
MILE 62.4 Glenn Highway

1992 ■ The MILEPOST® 275

A 57.9 (93.2 km) **T 270.1** (434.7 km) 58 Mile Road. Access to Palmer Correctional Center. Alternate access (see also **A 60.9**) to Seventeenmile Lake. Drive north 0.5 mile/0.8 km; turn right and drive 1.7 miles/2.7 km; turn left, drive 0.3 mile/0.5 km; turn right, drive 0.2 mile/0.3 km; turn right again and drive 0.2 mile/0.3 km to lake. Undeveloped camping on lakeshore.

A 56.7 (91.2 km) **T 271.3** (436.6 km) Entering Matanuska Valley Moose Range eastbound.

A 56 (90.1 km) **T 272** (437.7 km) *NOTE: Watch for major road construction and/or resurfacing westbound to* **Milepost A 26.5** *in 1992.*

A 54.6 (87.9 km) **T 273.4** (440 km) Bridge over Moose Creek. Highway ascends steeply from creek in both directions. Moose Creek State Recreation Site; 12 campsites, 7-day limit, $6 nightly fee or annual pass, 4 picnic sites, water, covered tables, firepits and toilets (wheelchair accessible). Look for fossils in the road bank on the west side of the highway. ▲

A 53 (85.3 km) **T 275** (442.6 km) Side road to Buffalo Coal Mine. Wild rose, geranium and chiming bells bloom along this section of highway.

A 52.3 (84.2 km) **T 275.7** (443.7 km) Soapstone Road.

A 51.2 (82.4 km) **T 276.8** (445.5 km) Fire station.

A 50.9 (81.9 km) **T 277.1** (445.9 km) Farm Loop Road, a 3-mile/4.8-km loop road connecting with Fishhook–Willow Road.

A 50.1 (80.6 km) **T 277.9** (447.2 km) Turn here for the Musk Ox Farm.

Musk Ox Farm and Gift Shop. The world's only domestic musk-ox farm. The animals are combed for the precious qiviut, which is then hand-knit by Eskimos in isolated villages, aiding the Arctic economy. During the farm tours in the summer, you can see these shaggy ice age survivors romping in beautiful pastures with Pioneer Peak as a backdrop. Open May to September. Phone (907) 745-4151 or 745-2353.
[ADVERTISEMENT]

A 49.5 (79.7 km) **T 278.5** (448.2 km) **Junction** with Hatcher Pass (Fishhook–Willow) Road which leads west and north over Hatcher Pass to connect with the George Parks Highway at **Milepost A 71.2** north of Willow. See HATCHER PASS ROAD log on page 274.

A 49 (78.9 km) **T 279** (449 km) Entering Palmer, which extends to Milepost **A 41**. Actual driving distance between **Milepost 49** and **42** is 1 mile/1.6 km. Just beyond here the highway emerges on a hill overlooking the Matanuska Valley, a view of the farms and homes of one of Alaska's agricultural areas, and the business center of Palmer.

A 42.1 (67.8 km) **T 285.9** (460.1 km) Arctic Avenue leads east through Palmer to the Old Glenn Highway, a scenic alternate route to Anchorage that rejoins the highway at **Milepost A 29.6**. A recommended route if road construction is under way between Palmer and Anchorage. Highlights of this route include the original Matanuska Colony Farms, commercial reindeer farm, U-pick vegetable farms, camping and salmon spawning viewing areas. See OLD GLENN HIGHWAY log on page 280 (Anchorage-bound travelers read log back to front).

Access to Palmer High School west at this junction.

Palmer

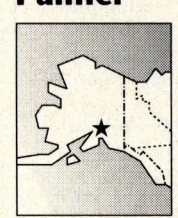

A 42 (67.6 km) **T 286** (460.3 km). In the Matanuska Valley northeast of Anchorage. The city extends from about **Milepost A 49** to **A 41**, an actual driving distance of 2.1 miles/3.4 km. **Population:** 3,016. **Emergency Services:** Phone 911. **Alaska State Troopers**, phone 745-2131. **City Police**, phone 745-4811. **Fire Department** and **Ambulance**, phone 745-2105. **Valley Hospital**, 515 E. Dahlia, phone 745-4813.

Visitor Information: Visitor center in log cabin across the railroad tracks on South Valley Way at East Fireweed Avenue. Pick up a brochure and map of downtown Palmer's historic buildings. Open daily 9 A.M. to 6 P.M. May to Sept. 15; limited hours Sept. 16 to December. Pay phone. Small museum in basement; local crafts may be for sale on main floor. Mailing address: Chamber of Commerce, P.O. Box 45, Palmer, AK 99645. Matanuska Valley Agricultural Showcase adjacent visitor center features flower and vegetable gardens.

Excellent local library, located at 655 S. Valley Way; open noon to 8 P.M. Monday through Thursday, 9 A.M. to 5 P.M. Friday and Saturday.

Elevation: 240 feet/74m. **Climate:** Temperatures range from 4° to 21°F/-16° to -6°C in January and December, with a mean monthly snowfall of 8 to 10 inches. Record low was -40°F/-40°C in January 1975. Temperatures range from 44° to 68°F/7° to 20°C in June and July, with a mean monthly precipitation of 2 inches. Record high was 89°F/32°C in June 1969. Mean annual rainfall is 15.5 inches, with 50.7 inches of snow. **Radio:** Anchorage stations; KABN (Big Lake); KMBQ (Wasilla). **Television:** Anchorage

MUSK OX FARM & Gift Shop
Mile 50.1 Glenn Highway
Open May – September
Phone (907) 745-4151 or 245-2353

Church of a thousand trees
United Protestant Church
(Presbyterian)
South Denali and Elmwood Streets
Worship 11 a.m., Church School 9:30 a.m.
Listed in the National Register of Historic Places
Palmer, Alaska 99645

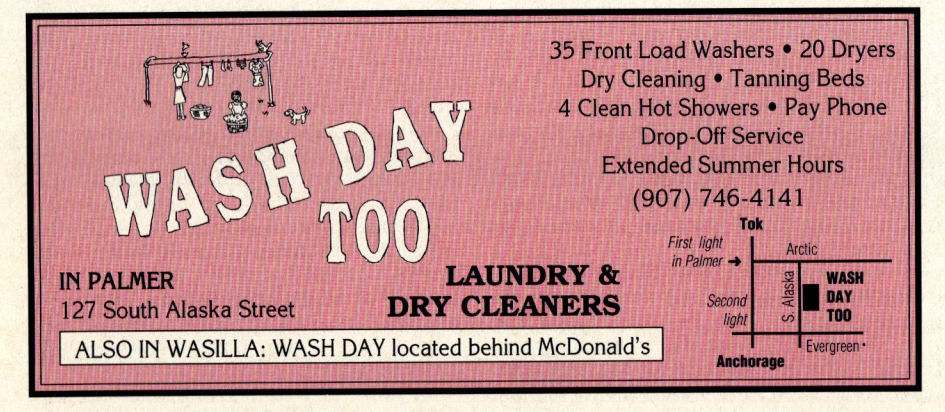

WASH DAY TOO
LAUNDRY & DRY CLEANERS
IN PALMER
127 South Alaska Street
35 Front Load Washers • 20 Dryers
Dry Cleaning • Tanning Beds
4 Clean Hot Showers • Pay Phone
Drop-Off Service
Extended Summer Hours
(907) 746-4141
ALSO IN WASILLA: WASH DAY located behind McDonald's

PALMER 
18-Hole — Par 72 Municipal Golf Course & Driving Range
Campground with R.V. Park
Visitor Center & Agricultural Showcase
Colony Days Celebration 6/19 -20 -21
Alaska State Fair 8/28 - 9/7
231 WEST EVERGREEN AVENUE, PALMER, ALASKA 99645

PALMER ADVERTISERS

Ace Hardware	421 S. Alaska Way
City of Palmer	231 W. Evergreen Ave.
Finger Lake Bed & Breakfast	Ph. (907) 376-6132
Hatcher Pass Bed & Breakfast	Ph. (907) 745-4210
Mountain View RV Park	Old Glenn Hwy.
Musk Ox Farm and Gift Shop	Mile 50.1 Glenn Hwy.
Pioneer Motel & Apt.	Ph. (907) 745-3425
Reindeer Farm	Mile J 11.5 Old Glenn Hwy.
Tern Inn-On The Lake-B&B	Ph. (907) 745-1984
United Protestant Church	S. Denali & Elmwood
Valley Hospital	515 E. Dahlia
Valley Hotel	606 S. Alaska St.
Wash Day Too	127 S. Alaska St.

A baby musk-ox at the Musk Ox Farm outside of Palmer. (George Wuerthner)

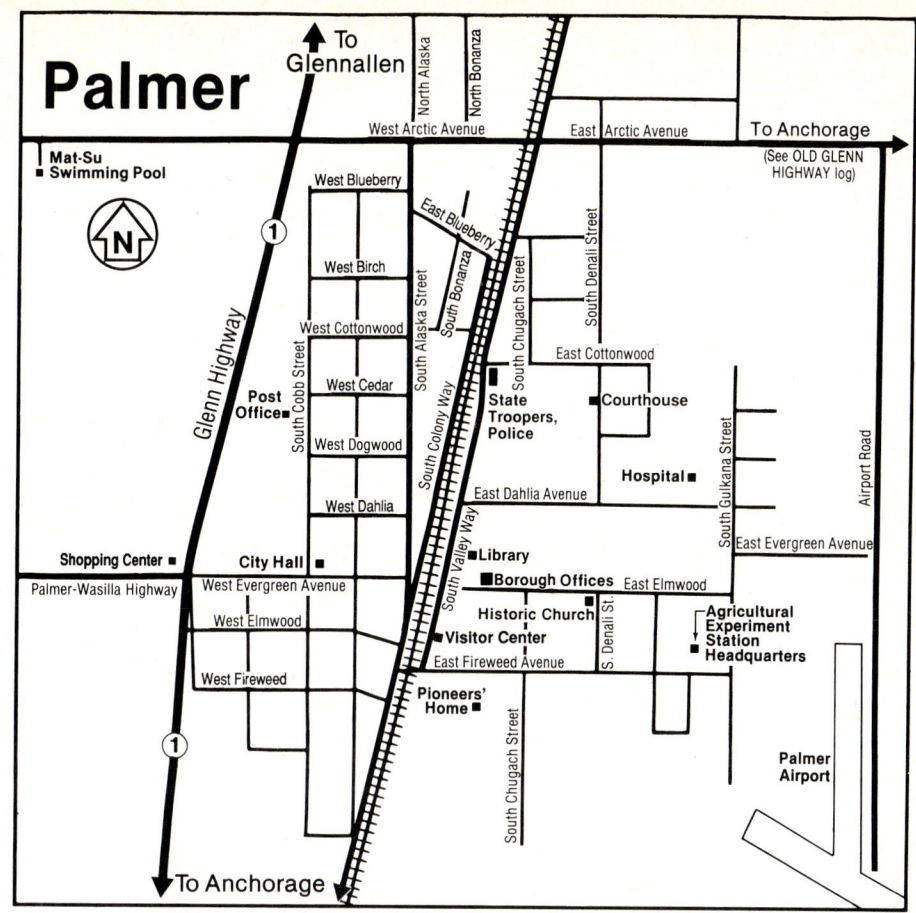

channels and cable. **Newspaper:** *The Frontiersman* (twice weekly).

Private Aircraft: Palmer Municipal Airport, adjacent southeast; elev. 232 feet/71m; length 5,500 feet/1,676m; asphalt; fuel 80, 100. Butte Municipal, 6 miles/9.7 km southeast; elev. 64 feet/19m; length 2,000 feet/609m; gravel; unattended. Seaplane base on Finger Lake.

Palmer is a commercial center for the Matanuska and Susitna valleys (collectively referred to as the Mat–Su valleys). The town was established about 1916 as a railway station on the Matanuska branch of the Alaska Railroad.

In 1935, Palmer became the site of one of the most unusual experiments in American history: the Matanuska Valley Colony. The Federal Emergency Relief Administration, one of the many New Deal relief agencies created during Franklin Roosevelt's first year in office, planned an agricultural colony in Alaska to utilize the great agricultural potential in the Matanuska–Susitna valleys, and to get some American farm families—struck by first the dust bowl then the Great Depression—off the dole. Social workers picked 203 families, mostly from the northern counties of Michigan, Wisconsin and Minnesota, to join the colony, because it was thought that the many hardy farmers of Scandinavian descent in those 3 states would have a natural advantage over other ethnic groups. The colonists arrived in Palmer in the early summer of 1935, and though the failure rate was high, many of their descendants still live in the Matanuska Valley. Palmer gradually became the unofficial capital of the Matanuska Valley, acting as headquarters for a farmers cooperative marketing organization and as the business and social center for the state's most productive farming region.

Palmer is Alaska's only community which developed primarily from an agricultural economy. (Real estate now takes a close second to agriculture.) The growing season averages 80 to 110 days a year, with long hours of sunshine. The University of Alaska–Fairbanks has an Agricultural and Forestry Experiment Station Office and a district Cooperative Extension Service Office here. The university also operates their Matanuska Research Farm, located on Trunk Road off the George Parks Highway, about a 7-mile/11.3-km drive from Palmer. The university farm conducts research in agronomy, horticulture and animal science.

The community has a hospital, the Mat–Su Community College (University of Alaska), a library, banks and several state and federal agency offices. Palmer has churches representing most denominations. The United Protestant Church in Palmer, the "church of a thousand logs," dates from Matanuska Colony days and is one of the oldest churches in Alaska still holding services. It is included in the National Register of Historic Places.

ACCOMMODATIONS

Palmer has all visitor facilities including a

Tern Inn - On The Lake - B&B
In the Heart of the Matanuska Valley
Firm Queen Beds
Clean Private Baths
Smoke-Free Environs 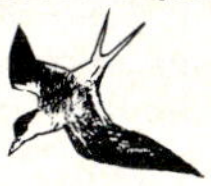
Sumptuous Breakfast
Lakeside Solarium
Modern Victorian Decor
Hosts: Connie and Gordon Kler
Box 1105, Palmer, AK 99645 • (907) 745-1984

VALLEY HOTEL
34 Rooms with Bath & Cable TV
Coffee Shop - Open 24 hours
Caboose Lounge & Ironhorse Liquor Store
606 S. ALASKA STREET
(907) 745-3330   Toll free within Alaska
Palmer, AK 99645   1-800-478-ROOM

Hatcher Pass Bed & Breakfast
(907) 745-4210
Very reasonable • Breakfast included
- OPEN YEAR ROUND - 
Visit beautiful Hatcher Pass and enjoy a cozy log cabin.
THE MEMORABLE CHOICE
8 miles outside of Palmer at the base of Hatcher Pass
Mile 6.8 Hatcher Pass Road
Hosts: Dick & Roxy Anderson
HC 01 Box 6797-D, Palmer, Alaska 99645

hotel, 3 motels, gas stations, grocery stores, laundromat, auto repair and parts, and shopping. The Matanuska Valley region has several lake resorts offering boat rentals, golf, fly-in fishing, hunting and horseback riding. Palmer 18-hole golf course; par 72, rental golf carts and clubs, driving range, green fees $20 weekends, $18 weekdays.

Valley Hospital is a 36-bed, full-service, modern hospital serving the Matanuska-Susitna Valley. Services include a 24-hour physician-staffed Emergency Department, intensive care and coronary care units, same-day surgery, CT full-body scanner, laboratory and imaging, including diagnostic ultrasound. HMR medical weight loss program, physician referral line (746-1556), home care program. Convenient location, 515 E. Dahlia. Phone (907) 745-4813. [ADVERTISEMENT]

Finger Lake Bed & Breakfast. Retired couple has the time and room to operate a bed and breakfast. Meeting folks who enjoy a leisurely home-cooked breakfast and time to visit. Home located on lake with view of mountains and lake from every window. Located on Palmer-Wasilla Highway. Phone (907) 376-6132; P.O. Box 1593, Palmer, AK 99645. [ADVERTISEMENT]

There is a private RV park on Smith Road off the Old Glenn Highway. There are also private campgrounds on the Glenn Highway a few miles west of Palmer. The Mat-Su Borough operates Matanuska River Park, located 1.1 miles/1.8 km south of town at Mile 17.5 Old Glenn Highway; 51 campsites, picnic area, some pull-through sites, water, dump station (fee charged), firewood for sale, flush toilets, hot showers, camping fee. Finger Lakes State Recreation Site, about 6 miles/9.7 km northwest of Palmer just off Bogard Road, has 69 campsites, 7-day limit, toilets, water, trails, boating and fishing. Camping fee $6/night or annual pass. To reach Finger Lake, take Palmer–Wasilla Highway north 4 miles/6.4 km from **Milepost A 41.8** to Trunk Road, then follow Trunk Road to Bogard Road. ▲

Mountain View RV Park offers breathtaking views of the Matanuska mountains. Watch wildlife from your door. Full hookups, hot showers included. New bathrooms and laundromat, dump station. Good Sam Park. Call (907) 745-5747 for reservations. Mail forwarding. Write P.O. Box 2521, Palmer, AK 99745. From Mile A 42.1 Glenn Highway (Arctic), follow Old Glenn Highway 2.8 miles. Turn east on Smith Road, drive 0.6 mile, turn right (0.3 mile). We're 3.7 miles from the Glenn Highway. See display ad this section. [ADVERTISEMENT] ▲

TRANSPORTATION

Air: No scheduled service, but the local airport has a number of charter operators.
Bus: Scheduled and charter service.

ATTRACTIONS

Go Swimming: The 25-m Mat–Su swimming pool is open to the public 7 days a week—$2 for adults and showers are available. The pool is located at Palmer High School; phone 376-4222.

Get Acquainted: Stop at the visitor information center, a log building just off the "main drag" (across the railroad tracks near the intersection of East Fireweed Avenue and South Valley Way). The center includes a museum, artifacts and a gift shop.

Visit the Musk Ox Farm. Located 8.1 miles/13 km east of Palmer on the Glenn Highway at **Milepost 50.1**, the Musk Ox Farm is the only place in the world these exotic animals are raised domestically. Hunted to near extinction in Alaska in 1865, the species was reintroduced in the 1930s. The farm is open May to September; admission is charged.

Visit a Reindeer Farm, located 8.1 miles/11.5 km south of Palmer via the Old Glenn Highway to Bodenburg Butte Loop Road. This commercial reindeer farm is open daily in summer; admission is charged.

Enjoy Water Sports. Fishing, boating, waterskiing and other water sports are popular in summer at Finger Lake west of Palmer. Kepler–Bradley Lakes State Recreation Area on Matanuska Lake has canoe rentals; turn off the Glenn Highway at **Milepost A 36.4**.

Visit a Museum. The Museum of Alaska Transportation and Industry relocated from Palmer to Wasilla. The transportation museum, now located at **Milepost A 46.5** George Parks Highway, features rare railroad and aviation artifacts. Colony Village, located at the state fairgrounds at **Milepost A 40.2** Glenn Highway, preserves some of the buildings from Palmer's early days. Included are 2 houses, a barn and a church from the Matanuska Valley Colony of 1935. The Hesse House is used as a post office during the Alaska State Fair.

Alaska State Fair (Aug. 28–Sept. 7, 1992): The Alaska State Fair, an 11-day annual event ending on Labor Day, has agricultural and mechanical exhibits from farms throughout Alaska. There are also food booths, games and rides. This is a very popular event, and fairgoers from Anchorage can tie up traffic. But it's worth the drive just to see the vegetables: the winning cabbage in 1990 weighed 98 pounds.

Visit Scenic Hatcher Pass: A 6- to 8-hour drive from **Milepost A 49.5** near Palmer that climbs through the beautiful Hatcher Pass Recreation Area and connects with the George Parks Highway at **Milepost A 71.2**. Access to Independence Mine State

---

REINDEER FARM
Palmer, Alaska

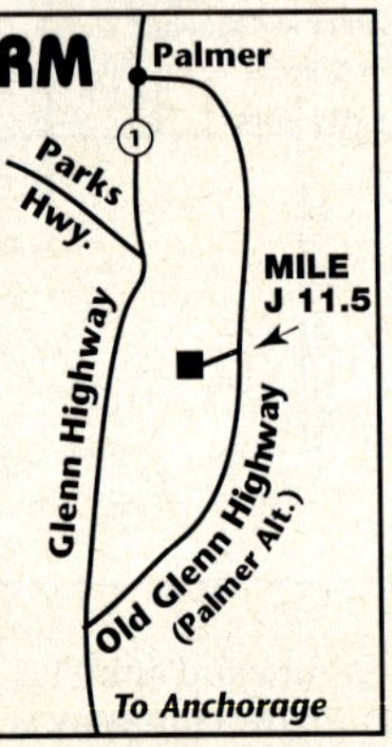

See our ad in the Old Glenn Hwy. (Palmer Alt.) Section

MILE J 11.5

ACE HARDWARE
When in downtown Palmer... stop and see us for all your hardware needs.
ELECTRONICS • SPORTING GOODS • TOOLS
Phone (907) 745-4100 - 6 days a week

See Alaska's Famous and Beautiful MATANUSKA VALLEY
New Units, Cable TV, Apartments – daily or weekly $35 and up
PIONEER MOTEL & APT.
124 W. Arctic
Palmer, AK 99645
Turn off the Glenn Highway toward Palmer at the Tesoro Station (Arctic Avenue)
Across from Mom & Pops Grocery & Donut Shop
Telephone
(907) 745-3825

PALMER CHEVRON
PHONE 746-6363 — OPEN 24 HOURS
GLENN HIGHWAY and EVERGREEN • PALMER, ALASKA
Chevron GAS
► Complete Mechanical Service ► Towing Service Available
► Complete Tire Service ► Atlas Tires, Batteries and Accessories
► Dump Station ► Propane ► Water ► Public Phone
► Soft Drinks ► Clean Rest Rooms ► Traveler Information
All authorized Chevron credit cards, plus VISA, MasterCard, American Express and Discover honored
Chevron DIESEL

FAIRVIEW MOTEL & RESTAURANT
Fine Dining
Queen-Size Beds
TV • Phone
Coin-op Laundry
R.A. (Bob) Rehus
Phone (907) 745-1505 • PO Box 745, Palmer, Alaska 99645
Mile 40.5 Glenn Highway • Across from State Fairgrounds

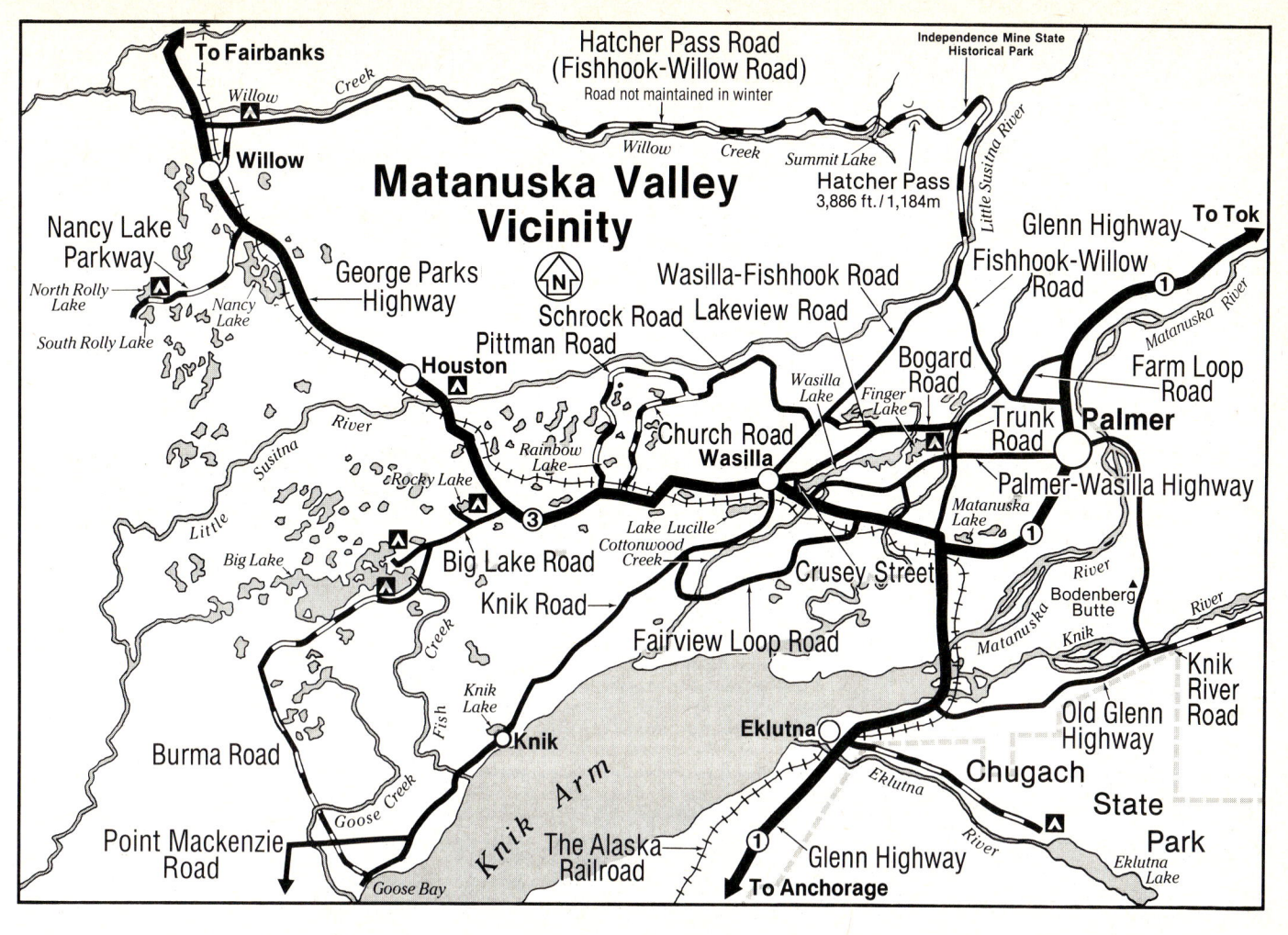

Historical Park. See HATCHER PASS ROAD log this section.

See the Matanuska Glacier: Drive 59 miles/95 km east on the Glenn Highway from Palmer to visit this spectacular 27-mile-/43.5-km-long glacier, one of the few you can drive to and explore on foot. Access to the foot of the glacier is through a private campground at **Milepost A 102**; admission charged. If you're not interested in getting close, there are several vantage points along the highway and from trails at Matanuska Glacier Campground, **Milepost A 101**.

Glenn Highway Log

(continued)

A 41.8 (67.3 km) T 286.2 (460.6 km) Junction with Palmer–Wasilla Highway. Gas station and shopping mall. West Evergreen Avenue access to downtown Palmer.

Palmer–Wasilla Highway leads northwest 10 miles/16 km to the George Parks Highway. It provides access to a car wash, several other businesses, Mat–Su Community College, Finger Lake State Recreation Site (via Trunk and Bogard roads) and Wolf Lake State Recreation Site. At Mile 1.9 on the Palmer–Wasilla Highway is the Crevasse Moraine trailhead; parking, picnic tables, fireplaces and access to 5 loop hiking trails.

Carrs Pioneer Square shopping mall, located at this junction, is the site of a bronze sculpture by Jacques and Mary Regat dedicated to the Matanuska Valley pioneers.

Eagle View Car Wash. See display ad this section.

Palmer Chevron. See display ad this section.

A 41.2 (66.3 km) T 286.8 (461.5 km) First access road to Palmer business district for eastbound travelers.

A 40.5 (65.2 km) T 287.5 (462.7 km) Fairview Motel & Restaurant. See display ad this section.

A 40.2 (64.7 km) T 287.8 (463.2 km) Main entrance to fairgrounds (site of Alaska State Fair), Herman Field (home of the Mat–Su Miners baseball team), and Colony Village. Colony Village preserves some of Palmer's buildings from the days of the Matanuska Valley Colony, and houses a collection of historic photographs and artifacts. Colony

DRIVE IN DIRTY ...

LEAVE CLEAN!

Modern large and open bays, perfect for motorhomes. Vacuums, fresh softened hot water on all cycles.

Located 2.5 miles west of Palmer on the Palmer-Wasilla Highway

All modern equipment to serve the Matanuska Valley.

EAGLE VIEW CAR WASH
SELF-SERVE

Bring in your dirty car, boat, trailer, motorhome, RV, truck!

OPEN
7 a.m. to 11 p.m.
7 days a week

Old Glenn Highway (Palmer Alternate) Log

This 18.6-mile/29.9-km paved road is a scenic alternate route between Palmer and Anchorage, intersecting the Glenn Highway near Anchorage at **Milepost A 29.6** and rejoining the Glenn Highway at **Milepost A 42.1** via Arctic Avenue in Palmer. The Old Glenn Highway gives access to Knik River Road and Bodenburg Butte Loop Road through the heart of the original Matanuska Colony agricultural lands.

Distance from south junction with the Glenn Highway (J) is followed by distance from Palmer (P).

J 0 P 18.6 (29.9 km) Junction with Glenn Highway at **Milepost A 29.6**. Paved parking area.

J 6.1 (9.8 km) P 12.3 (19.8 km) Goat Creek bridge.

J 7.2 (11.6 km) P 11.4 (18.3 km) View of Bodenburg Butte across Knik River.

J 8.6 (13.8 km) P 10 (16.1 km) Junction with Knik River Road, a gravel side road which leads to view of Knik Glacier. Pioneer Ridge/Knik River trailhead 3.6 miles/5.8 km from bridge. Knik River Road dead ends 11.4 miles/18.3 km from here.

J 8.7 (14 km) P 9.9 (15.9 km) Knik River bridge; parking at east end of bridge.

J 11.4 (18.3 km) P 7.2 (11.6 km) Butte branch U.S. post office. Pioneer Peak dominates the skyline for southbound travelers.

J 11.5 (18.5 km) P 7.1 (11.4 km) South **junction** with Bodenburg Butte Loop Road which leads west (see description following), and **junction** with Plumley Road to east. Plumley Road provides access to wolf kennels (open to the public) and to **Jim Creek** trail off Caudill Road; fishing for Dolly Varden, silver and red salmon.

The 5.8-mile/9.3-km Bodenburg Butte Road rejoins the Old Glenn Highway at Dack Acres Road (**Milepost J 12.6**). The **BODENBURG BUTTE** area (pop. 1,232) has original Matanuska Colony farms and a commercial reindeer farm (visitors welcome, fee charged).

Measuring mileages from the south junction, look for these attractions: Mile 0.6/1 km, Matanuska Colony log house and Bodenburg trailhead; Mile 0.8/1.3 km, reindeer farm; Mile 1.3/2.1 km, a world-class woodpile; Mile 2.4/3.9 km, spur road to Alaska Division of Agriculture Plant Materials Center.

The road circumnavigates Bodenburg Butte, a geological formation known as a monadnock (residual mountain) on a peneplain (an area eroded almost to a plain).

Reindeer Farm. Commercial reindeer farm on Bodenburg Butte Loop Road 0.8 mile off Old Glenn Highway (turn at Mile J 11.5 opposite Butte Quick Shop.) View tame reindeer and famous Pioneer Peak. Hand feed reindeer. Bring camera. Hours 10 A.M.-6 P.M. daily. Families with children welcome. Large parties please phone ahead. (907) 745-4000. Fee charged.
[ADVERTISEMENT]

J 12 (19.3 km) P 6.5 (10.5 km) Burkhart's Git N Go. See display ad this section.

J 12.6 (20.3 km) P 6 (9.7 km) Junction with Dack Acres Road, north end of Bodenburg Butte Loop Road (see **Milepost J 11.5**).

J 13.3 (21.4 km) P 5.3 (8.5 km) Turnout to west. Bodenburg Creek parallels highway next 0.7 mile/1.1 km northbound; red and pink salmon spawn here from late August through September. Eagles nest across the creek. *CAUTION: Use turnouts and watch for heavy traffic.*

J 14.5 (23.3 km) P 4.1 (6.6 km) Maud Road. Access to **Mud Lake** (4 miles/6.4 km); fishing for Dolly Varden.

J 15.6 (25.1 km) P 3 (4.8 km) Junction with Smith Road. Access to private campground. Trail rides available at a nearby ranch.

Mountain View RV Park. See display ad this section.

J 16.1 (25.9 km) P 2.5 (4 km) Clark-Wolverine Road; access to Lazy Mountain recreation area hiking trails. Drive in 0.7 mile/1.1 km; turn right on Huntly Road at T; drive 1 mile/1.6 km on gravel road and take right fork to recreation area and overlook. Picnic tables, toilets, good berry picking.

J 16.8 (27 km) P 1.8 (2.9 km) Matanuska River bridge. Access to river.

J 17.5 (28.2 km) P 1.1 (1.8 km) Matanuska River Park; 51 campsites, picnic area, some pull-through sites, water, dump station, flush toilets, hot showers. Camping and dump station fees charged.

J 17.6 (28.3 km) P 1 (1.6 km) Airport Road. View of Pioneer Peak southbound.

J 18.6 (29.9 km) P 0 Junction of Old Glenn Highway (Arctic Avenue) at **Milepost A 42.1** Glenn Highway.

Return to Milepost A 42.1 or A 29.6 Glenn Highway

BURKHART'S GIT N GO

GAS • GROCERIES • RV PARK
TRAIL RIDES • GLACIER VIEW

(907) 745-8707

Show this ad for $1 off any grocery purchase over $10, or 10% off on haircuts or perms, or trail rides.

Beauty Salon — 745-8706   Video Rentals • Glacier Ice

For information on trail rides, RV park and glacier tours write to: Wayne Burkhart, P.O. Box 660, Palmer, Alaska 99645

MOUNTAIN VIEW RV PARK

Full or Partial Hookups • Some Pull-throughs
Hot Showers Included • Pay Phone
New Bathrooms and Laundromat

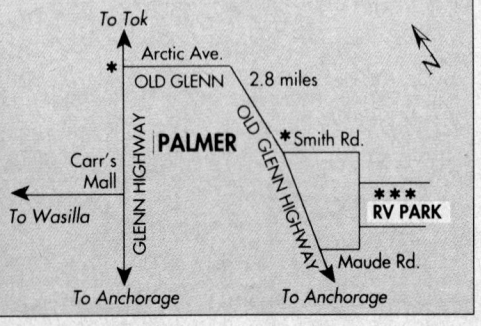

CARAVANS WELCOME
OPEN YEAR AROUND

Reservations (907) 745-5747

Forward your mail for pickup when you arrive

Write: P.O. BOX 2521, PALMER, ALASKA 99645

See log ad in Palmer section under Accommodations

Off Old Glenn Highway on Smith Road • 3.7 miles from Palmer

Glenn Highway Log

(continued from page 279)
Days is held June 19-21, 1992. Alaska State Fair is held Aug. 28–Sept. 7, 1992.

Alaska State Fair. See display ad this section.

A 39.2 (63.1 km) **T 288.8** (464.8 km) Outer Springer Loop. Short trail to Meiers Lake.

A 38 (61.2 km) **T 290** (466.7 km) **Matanuska Farm Market.** See display ad this section.

A 37.4 (60.2 km) **T 290.6** (467.7 km) Kepler Drive; access to private campground and lake.

A 37 (59.5 km) **T 291** (468.3 km) Echo Lake Road.

A 36.4 (58.6 km) **T 291.6** (469.3 km) Kepler–Bradley Lakes State Recreation Area on Matanuska Lake; day-use area with water, toilets, parking, picnic tables, canoe rentals, fishing and hiking. The lakes are Matanuska Lake, Canoe Lake, Irene Lake and Long Lake.

A 36.2 (58.3 km) **T 291.8** (469.6 km) **The Homestead RV Park.** Wooded pull-throughs to 70 feet, tent sites. Very clean rest rooms and showers. Electric and water hookups; dump station. Laundry. Firewood, picnic tables, firepits, pay phone. Fireside chats. Heated, enclosed pavilion. Walking and jogging trails, trout fishing nearby. Good Sam park. 60 sites. Handicap access. Beautiful view. Commuting distance to Anchorage. Caravans welcome. Phone (907) 745-6005. See display ad this section. [ADVERTISEMENT]

A 35.3 (56.8 km) **T 292.7** (471.1 km) *CAUTION: Traffic signal at busy* **junction** *of the Glenn Highway and George Parks Highway (Alaska Route 3), which form a common highway into Anchorage.* If headed for Fairbanks or Mount McKinley turn north on the George Parks Highway. See **Milepost A 35** GEORGE PARKS HIGHWAY section for details.

A 34.9 (56.2 km) **T 293.1** (471.7 km) *CAUTION: Highway crosses the Alaska Railroad tracks.*

A 34 (54.7 km) **T 294** (473.1 km) Paved double-ended turnout west side of highway. Rabbit Slough.

A 32.4 (52.1 km) **T 295.6** (475.7 km) Palmer Hay Flats state game refuge. According to the ADF&G, this is the most heavily utilized waterfowl hunting area in Alaska. Access to the refuge is via Fairview Loop Road off the George Parks Highway.

A 31.5 (50.7 km) **T 296.5** (477.2 km) Bridge over the Matanuska River, which is fed by the Matanuska Glacier.

A 30.8 (49.6 km) **T 297.5** (478.8 km) There are 3 Knik River bridges; parking areas below highway at south end of the 2 most southern bridges. The Knik River comes down from the Knik Glacier to the east and splits into several branches as it approaches Knik Arm. Game Management Unit 14C boundary. Also boundary of Matanuska–Susitna Borough.

Moose winter in this area and the cows and calves may be seen early in the morning and in the evening as late as early July. In winter, watch for moose on the road between here and Anchorage.

A 29.6 (47.6 km) **T 298.4** (480.2 km) **Junction** with the Old Glenn Highway (Palmer Alternate). See OLD GLENN HIGHWAY log opposite page. A recommended alternate route if major road construction is under way between Anchorage and Palmer.

A 27.6 (44.4 km) **T 300.4** (483.4 km) Divided highway from here to Anchorage.

A 27.3 (43.9 km) **T 300.7** (483.9 km) The highway crosses a swampy area known locally as Eklutna Flats. These flats are a protected wildflower area (picking flowers is strictly prohibited). Look for wild iris, shooting star, chocolate lily and wild rose in early June.

A 26.8 (43.1 km) **T 301.2** (484.7 km) Highway crosses Alaska Railroad via overpass.

NOTE: Watch for major road construction from here to **Milepost A 56** *in 1992.*

A 26.3 (42.3 km) **T 301.7** (485.5 km) Eklutna overpass, exits both sides of highway. Access to Eklutna Road (description follows), the village of Eklutna and also access to Thunderbird Falls (see **Milepost A 25.3**) for Anchorage-bound travelers. West of the highway is the Indian village of **EKLUTNA** (pop. 25), site of Eklutna Village Historical Park, which preserves the heritage and traditions of the Athabascan Alaska Natives. Attractions include the historic St. Nicholas Russian Orthodox Church and a hand-built Siberian prayer chapel. Admission fee charged. The bright little grave houses or spirit houses in the cemetery are painted in the family's traditional colors.

Eklutna Village Historical Park. Learn about 350 years of Athabascan culture on half-hour tours of this authentic Native cultural center. See Russian Orthodox churches, Anchorage's oldest building, colorful "Spirit Houses" and historical displays depicting Native lifestyles. Alaska Native and Russian gifts for sale. Open daily mid-May to mid-September. [ADVERTISEMENT]

Eklutna Road leads east 10 miles/16.1 km to Eklutna Lake Recreation Area in Chugach State Park. General store at Mile 9. The recreation area has a campground, picnic area and hiking trails. The campground has 50 sites, drinking water, pit toilets and a 15-day limit. Camping fee $6/night or annual pass. The 32-unit picnic area is located at the trailhead parking lot, which will accommodate

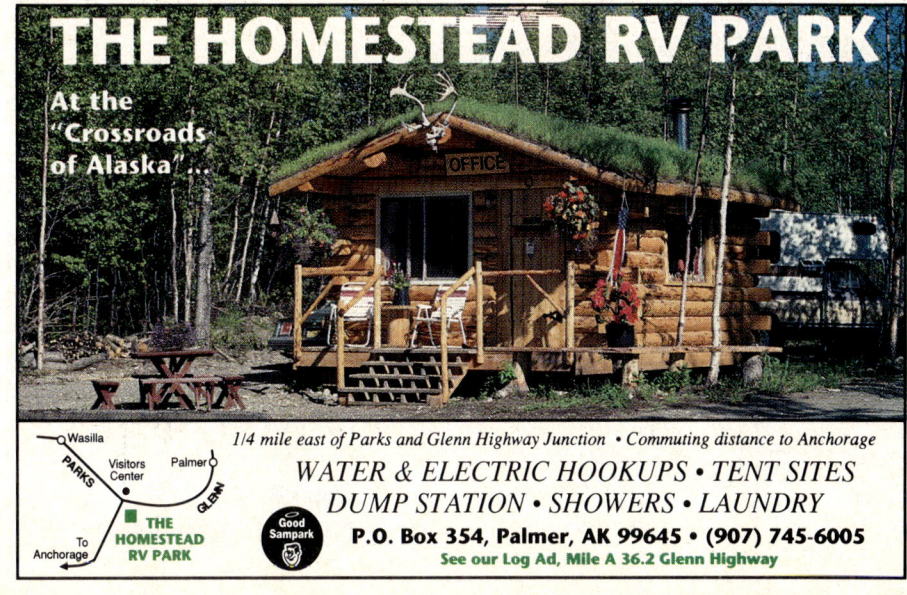

Matanuska Farm Market
FRESH LOCALLY GROWN VEGETABLES
We feature the finest Alaska-grown produce
Highest quality • Fair prices • Friendly service
Cold drinks and ice
Myron & Helen Marcey welcome you
Summer Hours 10 a.m. to 6 p.m.
MILE 38 GLENN HIGHWAY

ALASKA STATE FAIR
11 DAYS, ending on
Labor Day, every summer
Mile 40.2 Glenn Hwy.

(907) 745-4827
WRITE
2075 Glenn Highway
Palmer, Alaska 99645

THE HOMESTEAD RV PARK
At the "Crossroads of Alaska"...

1/4 mile east of Parks and Glenn Highway Junction • Commuting distance to Anchorage
WATER & ELECTRIC HOOKUPS • TENT SITES
DUMP STATION • SHOWERS • LAUNDRY
P.O. Box 354, Palmer, AK 99645 • (907) 745-6005
See our Log Ad, Mile A 36.2 Glenn Highway

GLENN HIGHWAY

CHEELY'S GENERAL STORE and ROCHELLE'S ICE CREAM STOP
Great Old-Fashioned Banana Splits
13 Flavors of Hard Ice Cream

Mile 9 Eklutna Lake Road
Located near Eklutna Lake & Glacier
Within Chugach State Park

Groceries • Ice • Picnic & Camping Supplies
Fishing Licenses • Souvenirs • Postcards
Propane • Mountain Bicycle Rentals

PETERS CREEK PETITE RV PARK
Full and Partial Hookups ■ Dump Station
(Behind the Greenhouse; across from Texaco)
Mile 21.5 Old Glenn Highway
(907) 688-2487

HARV'S AUTO REPAIR
Complete AUTO - TRUCK - R.V.
Service & Repair
Towing Available • Certified Mechanic
ALL WORK GUARANTEED
VISA MasterCard
Senior Citizen Discount
Mile 21.5 South Peters Creek Exit

PETERS CREEK TRADING POST
Groceries • Gas • Laundry Facilities
and Auto Parts all at one stop

Granny's Grocery
The Laundry
Chevron Gas
(907) 688-2121

Peters Creek Auto Parts
(907) 688-6000
MILE 21.5 Old Glenn Highway

THE LAUNDRY CENTER
Coin-Op • Clean Showers

THE SHOPPER'S CACHE
Groceries • Liquor
FREE COFFEE

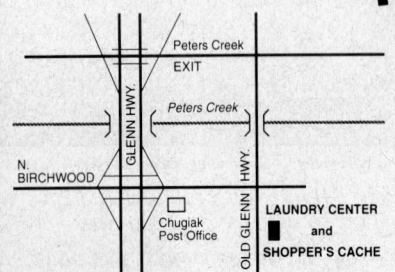

• • ONE STOP CONVENIENCE • •
6:30 a.m. to 10 p.m.
(907) 688-0260

MILE 20.5
OLD GLENN HIGHWAY

GAS • DIESEL • PROPANE • WATER • AIR • SNACKS • ICE

TEXACO
Peters Creek Texaco
MILE 21 GLENN HIWAY
JUST OFF SOUTH PETERS CREEK EXIT
(907) 688-2333

Summer Hours: Mon.-Sat. 6 a.m. to 10 p.m.
Sunday 7 a.m. to 10 p.m.

TIPS BAR & CAFE
LIVE MUSIC
FRIDAY & SATURDAY
Alaskan Hospitality
Downtown Eagle River
(on old Glenn Highway)

ALASKA Limited Editions

Art Publishers - Distributors
• IDITAROD POSTER SERIES
• ALASKA POSTER SERIES
• ALASKA ARTIST POSTER SERIES
• FUR RONDY POSTER SERIES
&
Studio of
JON VAN ZYLE
Call for directions and appointment
(907) 688-3627
Write for brochure
P.O. Box 770746
Eagle River, Alaska 99577

---

80 cars and has a boat launch for hand-carried boats. Three trails branch off the trailhead: Twin Peaks, Lakeside and Bold Ridge. The Lakeside trail skirts Eklutna Lake and gives access to Eklutna Glacier (12.7 miles/20.4 km). **Eklutna Lake** is the largest lake in Chugach State Park, measuring approximately 7 miles long by a mile wide. Fed by Eklutna Glacier, it offers fair fishing for Dolly Varden. *CAUTION: Afternoon winds can make the lake dangerous for boaters.* Interpretive displays on wildlife and a public telescope for viewing Dall sheep, eagles and other wildlife are located at the trailhead.

Cheely's General Store and Rochelle's Ice Cream Stop. See display ad this section.

A 25.7 (41.3 km) T 302.3 (486.5 km) Highway crosses Eklutna River.

A 25.3 (40.7 km) T 302.7 (487.1 km) Thunderbird Falls exit (northbound traffic only) and northbound access to Eklutna Road (see **Milepost A 26.3** for description). Drive about 0.3 mile/0.5 km to parking area. Thunderbird Falls is about 1 mile/1.6 km from the highway. The scenic trail to the falls winds through private property on a 25-foot right-of-way and follows a hillside down to Thunderbird Creek. The falls are just upstream. *CAUTION: Do not climb the steep cliffs overhanging the falls!*

A 24.5 (39.4 km) T 303.5 (488.4 km) Southbound exit to Edmonds Lake residential area and Mirror Lake picnic wayside. The shallow, 73-acre Mirror Lake is located at the foot of Mount Eklutna.

A 23.6 (38 km) T 304.4 (489.9 km) Access to Mirror Lake picnic wayside for northbound traffic only.

A 23 (37 km) T 305 (490.8 km) North Peters Creek overpass, exits both sides of highway.

A 21.5 (34.6 km) T 306.5 (493.3 km) South Peters Creek underpass, exits both sides of highway. Access to Peters Creek and portion of the Old Glenn Highway, which parallels the newer highway south to Eagle River, and provides access to a number of local services. **PETERS CREEK** services include gas stations, grocery, car wash, body repair shop and restaurant.

Harv's Auto Repair. See display ad this section.

Peters Creek Petite RV Park. See display ad this section.

Peters Creek Texaco. See display ad this section.

A 21.2 (34.1 km) T 306.8 (493.7 km) Peters Creek bridge.

A 20.9 (33.6 km) T 306.9 (493.9 km) North Birchwood Loop Road underpass, exits both sides of highway; turn east for community of **CHUGIAK** and for portion of Old Glenn Highway, which leads south to Eagle River and north to Peters Creek. There are many services and attractions in the Peters Creek–Chugiak–Eagle River area.

The Laundry Center. See display ad this section.

Peters Creek Trading Post. See display ad this section.

The Shopper's Cache. See display ad this section.

A 17.2 (27.7 km) T 310.8 (500.2 km) South Birchwood Loop Road underpass, exits both sides of highway. Access to Chugiak High School, Gruening Junior High School and Old Glenn Highway.

A 15.3 (24.6 km) T 312.7 (503.2 km) Exits for Fire Lake residential area, Old Glenn Highway and Eagle River.

A 13.4 (21.6 km) T 314.6 (506.3 km) Eagle River overpass. Exit east for community of Eagle River (all visitor services), the North Anchorage Visitor Information Center (located at Valley River Mall in Eagle River) and Eagle River Road to Chugach State Park visitor center (a highly recommended stop); descriptions follow.

Eagle River

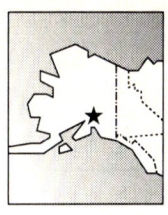

A 13.4 (21.6 km) T 314.6 (506.3 km) **Population:** Area 9,000. **Emergency Services:** Clinic, phone 694-2807. **Visitor Information:** The Anchorage Convention and Visitors Bureau North Anchorage Visitor Information Center is located at the Valley River Mall in Eagle River. Stop by for information on Anchorage events, parking maps and brochures. For information on Eagle River, contact the Chugiak–Eagle River Chamber of Commerce, P.O. Box 770353, Eagle River, AK 99577; phone 694-4702.

The Chugiak–Eagle River area was homesteaded after WWII when the new Glenn Highway opened this rural area northeast of Anchorage. Today, Eagle River community offers a full range of businesses, most located near or on Business Boulevard and the Old Glenn Highway east off the Glenn Highway. There are a motel, restaurants, supermarket, laundromat, post office, gas stations and shopping center. Eagle River also has several churches, schools, a library and recreation center. Artist Jon Van Zyle's studio is located in Eagle River. Boondock Sporting Goods store here has an antique gun display.

From downtown Eagle River, follow scenic Eagle River Road (paved) 12.7 miles/20.4 km to reach the Chugach State Park Visitor Center. Beautiful views of the Chugach Mountains from the center's veranda; telescopes are set up for viewing Dall sheep and other wildlife. The center has a pay phone and restrooms. Trailhead for the Old Iditarod–Crow Pass trail. There are also short hiking trails from the center and scheduled ranger-led hikes and naturalist

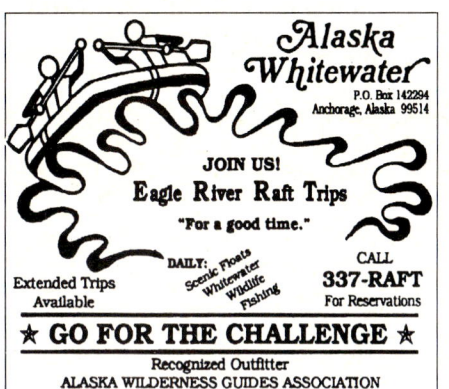

EAGLE RIVER ADVERTISERS

- **Alaska Limited Editions**.....Ph. (907) 688-3627
- **Alaska Whitewater**............Ph. (907) 337-RAFT
- **Anchorage Convention & Visitors Bureau**...................Valley River Mall
- **Boondock Sporting Goods & Outfitters**.....................Eagle River Loop Rd.
- **Chugiak-Eagle River Chamber of Commerce**...............Ph. (907) 694-4702
- **Eagle River Car Wash and Duck Pond**.........................Old Glenn Hwy.
- **Eagle River Motel/Hotel**...Ph. (907) 694-5000
- **Laundry Basket, The**..................Business Blvd.
- **Merrill's Ltd**................................Eagle Plaza Mall
- **Picture This Art Gallery**............Eagle River Shopping Center
- **Tips Bar & Cafe**.......................Old Glenn Hwy.
- **Valley River Center**.........12001 Business Blvd.

COIN-OP LAUNDRY and DRY CLEANERS

THE LAUNDRY BASKET

694-8670

Open 7-10 Daily
Very Clean
Free Coffee
Full-time Attendant

12110 Business Blvd., Eagle River, AK
Across from Pay 'n Save and Safeway Mall

EAGLE RIVER Motel/Hotel

Rooms with Phone and Cable TV

Kitchenettes

Quiet Location, off Glenn Highway on Lynn Drive

Phone: (907) 694-5000

Alaska Whitewater
P.O. Box 142294
Anchorage, Alaska 99514

JOIN US!
Eagle River Raft Trips
"For a good time."

DAILY: Scenic Floats, Whitewater, Wildlife, Fishing

Extended Trips Available

CALL **337-RAFT** For Reservations

★ GO FOR THE CHALLENGE ★

Recognized Outfitter
ALASKA WILDERNESS GUIDES ASSOCIATION

Eagle River Car Wash & Duck Pond

CAR WASH & DUCK POND ENTRANCE 24 HRS

OPEN 24 HOURS

Duck Pond on premises open to public to observe wild Alaskan waterfowl in their natural habitat.

MILE 15 OLD GLENN HWY.
See Log Ad This Section.

Chugiak-Eagle River Chamber of Commerce
VISITOR INFORMATION

12110 Business Boulevard (Next to TCBY)
P.O. Box 770353, Eagle River, Alaska 99577

(907) 694-4702

July 3rd — Fireworks and Festivities at Lions Park
July 4th — Chugiak Community Parade
July 9-12 — BEAR PAW FESTIVAL and Community Parade

Come Celebrate the 50th Anniversary of the Alaska Highway with Us!

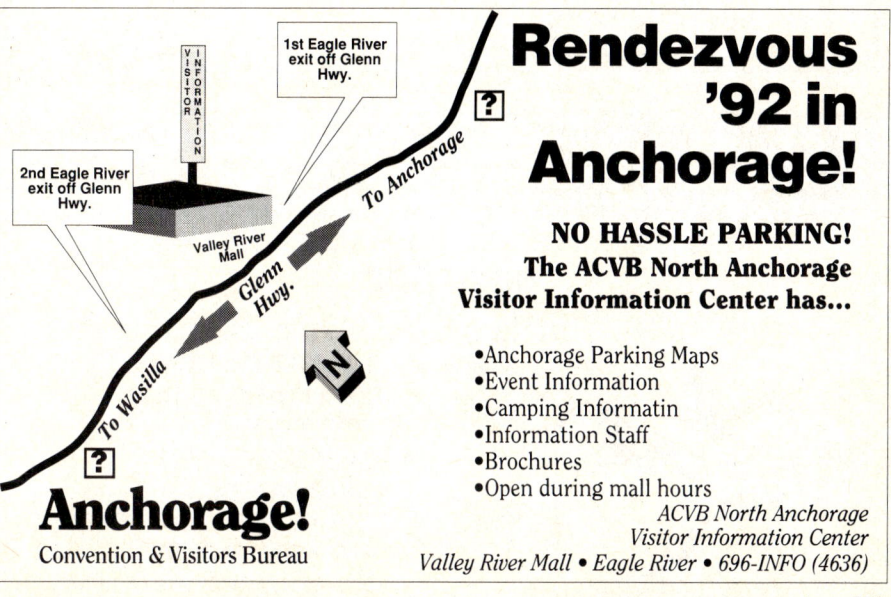

Rendezvous '92 in Anchorage!

1st Eagle River exit off Glenn Hwy.
2nd Eagle River exit off Glenn Hwy.
Valley River Mall
To Anchorage
Glenn Hwy.
To Wasilla

Anchorage! Convention & Visitors Bureau

NO HASSLE PARKING!
The ACVB North Anchorage Visitor Information Center has...

- Anchorage Parking Maps
- Event Information
- Camping Informatin
- Information Staff
- Brochures
- Open during mall hours

ACVB North Anchorage Visitor Information Center
Valley River Mall • Eagle River • 696-INFO (4636)

A female moose with calves near Anchorage. (Bruce M. Herman)

programs. The center is open year-round. Phone 694-2108 for hours.

Kayaks, rafts and canoes can put in at Mile 7.5 Eagle River Road at the **North Fork Eagle River** access/day-use area with paved parking, toilets, fishing for rainbow trout and Dolly Varden, and cross-country skiing and snowmachining in winter. Additional river access for nonmotorized craft is available at Mile 9 Eagle River Road. The Eagle River offers class II, III and IV float trips. Check with rangers at Chugach State Park for information on river conditions.

Eagle River Car Wash and Duck Pond. Facilities available for washing cars, campers, trucks, boats and travel homes. Vacuums available. A duck pond on the premises is open to the public and features cedar viewing decks for observing some of the natural wild Alaskan waterfowl in their natural habitat. Mile 15.5 Old Glenn Highway. Ask anyone in Eagle River for directions. See display ad this section. [ADVERTISEMENT]

Glenn Highway Log

(continued)

A 12.8 (20.6 km) **T 315.2** (507.3 km) Eagle River bridge.

A 11.6 (18.7 km) **T 316.4** (509.2 km) Hiland Road exit. Access to Alaska State Forest Nursery and Eagle River Campground in Chugach State Park. The nursery welcomes visitors; phone 694-5880 for tours. Eagle River Campground, 1.4 miles/2.3 km from the highway, has 50 campsites, a 4-day camping limit, 12 picnic sites, flush toilets and drinking water. Camping fee $12/night or annual pass. This is one of the most popular campgrounds in the state. ▲

A 10.6 (17.1 km) **T 317.4** (510.8 km) Truck weigh stations on both sides of highway. Pay phones.

The last 9 miles/14.5 km of the Glenn Highway has been designated the Veterans' Memorial Parkway.

A 7.5 (12.1 km) **T 320.5** (515.8 km) Southbound exit to **FORT RICHARDSON** and Arctic Valley road.

CAUTION: Watch for moose. Dozens of moose are hit and killed by automobile traffic each year.

A 6.1 (9.8 km) **T 321.9** (518 km) Northbound exit to Fort Richardson and Arctic Valley Road. Road to Arctic Valley Ski Area is steep and winding but offers spectacular views of Anchorage and Cook Inlet. It is approximately 7.5 miles/12 km to the ski area. Good berry picking in summer. Not recommended for large vehicles.

A 6 (9.7 km) **T 322** (518.2 km) Ship Creek.

A 4.4 (7.1 km) **T 323.6** (520.8 km) Muldoon Road overpass. (Exit here to connect with Seward Highway via Muldoon and Tudor roads bypass.) U.S. Air Force Hospital and Bartlett High School to the north, Muldoon Road to the south. Exit south on Muldoon for Centennial Park municipal campground. To reach the campground, go south on Muldoon to first left (Boundary); go about 100 yards then make a second left; continue about quarter-mile to campground entrance. There is a bicycle trail from Muldoon Road to Mirror Lake, **Milepost A 23.6**. ▲

A 3 (4.8 km) **T 325** (523 km) Boniface Parkway; access to hotel, private campground and other businesses. Russian Jack Springs city campground is located south of the Glenn Highway on Boniface Parkway just north of DeBarr. Turn north for Elmendorf AFB.

A 1.8 (2.9 km) **T 326.2** (525 km) Bragaw Street.

A 0.7 (1.1 km) **T 327.3** (526.7 km) Reeve Boulevard; access to **ELMENDORF AFB**.

A 0.3 (0.5 km) **T 327.7** (527.4 km) Concrete Street. Access to Elmendorf AFB.

A 0 T 328 (527.9 km) The Glenn Highway ends at Medfra Street. Continue straight ahead on 5th Avenue (one-way westbound) to downtown Anchorage. Turn left at Gambell Street (one-way southbound) for the Seward Highway and Kenai Peninsula. See ANCHORAGE section following for description of city.

Alaska's Finest Gun Store
BOONDOCK
SPORTING GOODS & OUTFITTERS
Quality Hunting Gear & Fishing Tackle
ANTIQUE GUN DISPLAY
Rod & Reel Rentals
(907) 694-2229
Eagle River Loop Rd., Eagle River, AK 99577

Merrill's Ltd.
Native Made Handicrafts • Ivory • Baskets • Native Dolls
(907) 694-6800 Located in the Eagle Plaza
11823 Old Glenn Highway, Suite 108, Eagle River, AK 99577

Attention Alaskana and Wildlife Art Collectors
We feature originals, limited edition prints, photography, carvings, decoys, jewelry, pottery, and gift items by Alaskan and nationally known artists.

A beautiful FREE "We ♥ Eagle River" poster to our out-of-state visitors

Picture This Art Gallery
11401 OLD GLENN HIGHWAY, SUITE 107, EAGLE RIVER, ALASKA 99577
EAGLE RIVER SHOPPING CENTER
(907) 694-5475

Valley River Center

• 12001 BUSINESS BLVD. • EAGLE RIVER •
694-1822

VISTA OPTICAL • TUNDRA CHOCOLATES
D'VONS SALON • EARTH TREASURES
HIS & HER SPORTS CARDS
PHOTO EXPRESS
FASHION DIRECTION
PACIFIC FABRICS
GARCIA'S CANTINA • FESTIVAL THEATERS
SAFEWAY • PAY N SAVE

ANCHORAGE

(See maps, pages 286–287)

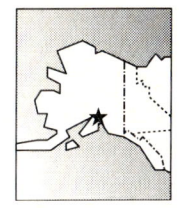

Located on the upper shores of Cook Inlet, at 61° north latitude and 150° west longitude, Anchorage is in the heart of Alaska's southcentral gulf coast. The townsite is on a low-lying alluvial plain bordered by mountains, dense forests of spruce, birch and aspen, and water. Cook Inlet's Turnagain Arm and Knik Arm define the broad peninsula on which the city lies. Anchorage is situated 358 miles/576 km south of Fairbanks via the George Parks Highway; 304 miles/489 km from Valdez, southern terminus of the trans-Alaska pipeline, via the Glenn and Richardson highways; 2,435 driving miles/3919 km, 1,644 nautical miles, and 3 hours flying time from Seattle. Anchorage has been called "Air Crossroads of the World." In terms of nonstop air mileages, Anchorage is the following distances from these cities: Amsterdam, 4,475/7202 km; Chicago, 2,839/4569 km; Copenhagen, 4,313/6941 km; Hamburg, 4,430/7129 km; Honolulu, 2,780/4474 km; London, 4,487/7221 km; Paris, 4,683/7536 km; San Francisco, 2,015/3243 km; Seattle, 1,445/2325 km; Tokyo, 3,460/5568 km.

Population: Anchorage Municipality 237,907. **Emergency Services: Police, Fire Department, Ambulance** and **Search & Rescue,** phone 911. **Police,** phone 786-8500. **Alaska State Troopers,** phone 269-5511. **Hospitals:** Humana Hospital, phone 276-1131; Alaska Native Medical Center, phone 279-6661; Providence, phone 562-2211; U.S. Air Force, phone 552-5555. **Dental emergencies,** phone 279-9144 (24-hour service). **Civil Defense,** phone 786-8449. **Crisis Line,** phone 562-4048 or 563-3200. **Rape & Assault,** phone 276-7273. **Battered Women,** phone 272-0100. **Pet Emergency,** phone 274-5636. **Poison Control,** phone 261-3193. **Road Conditions** (in winter), phone 243-7675.

Visitor Information: Log Cabin Visitor Information Center, operated by the Anchorage Convention and Visitors Bureau, is at 4th Avenue and F Street; open daily, year-round. Hours are 7:30 A.M. to 7 P.M. June through August; 8:30 A.M. to 6 P.M. in May and September; and 9 A.M. to 4 P.M. the remainder of the year. The cabin offers a wide assortment of free brochures and maps. Mailing address is 1600 A St., Suite 200, Anchorage 99501; phone 274-3531. The bureau also operates a year-round visitor information phone with a recorded message of the day's special events and attractions, including films, plays, sports events and gallery openings; phone 276-3200. Additional visitor information centers are open daily at Anchorage International Airport, one on the lower level for passengers

Aponés T-Shirt Cache has the **biggest** and **best** selection of **T-Shirts** & Sweatshirts in Alaska
LOWEST PRICES
(907) 272-1007
SEARS MALL • ANCHORAGE, AK

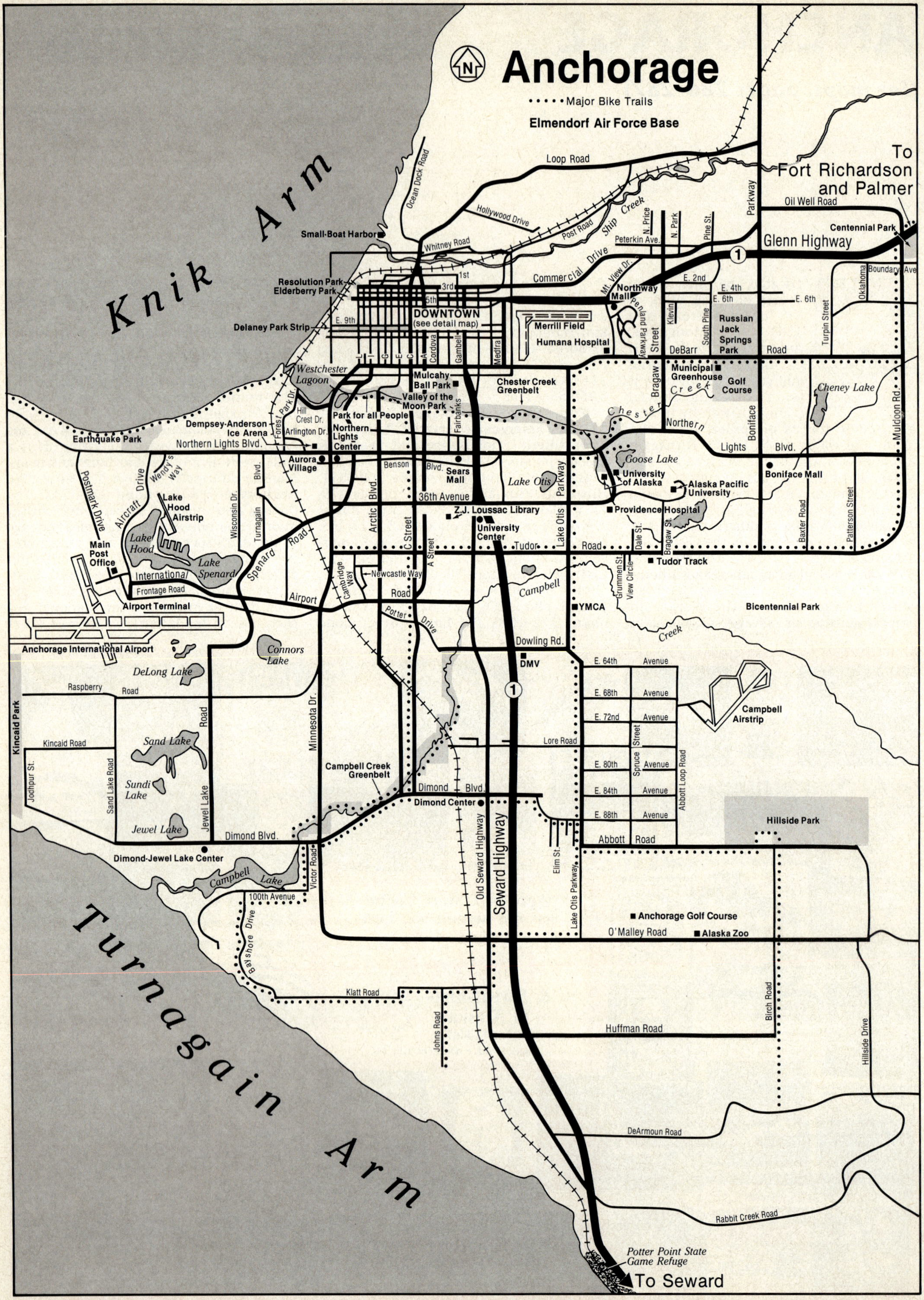
Anchorage
Major Bike Trails
Elmendorf Air Force Base
Knik Arm
Turnagain Arm
To Fort Richardson and Palmer
To Seward
Loop Road
Ocean Dock Road
Hollywood Drive
Post Road
Ship Creek
Small-Boat Harbor
Whitney Road
Oil Well Road
Centennial Park
Glenn Highway
Parkway
Pine St.
N. Park
N. Price
Peterkin Ave.
Commercial Drive
Mt. View Dr.
Resolution Park
Elderberry Park
1st
3rd
5th
E. 2nd
E. 4th
E. 6th
Boundary Ave
Oklahoma
Northway Mall
Penland Parkway
DOWNTOWN (see detail map)
E. 9th
Delaney Park Strip
Merrill Field
Humana Hospital
Klevin
South Pine
Russian Jack Springs Park
Turpin Street
Bragaw
Street
DeBarr
Road
Westchester Lagoon
Cordova
Gambell
Medfra
Mulcahy Ball Park
Valley of the Moon Park
Chester Creek Greenbelt
Municipal Greenhouse
Golf Course
Cheney Lake
Chester Creek
Northern
Lights
Blvd.
Boniface
Muldoon Rd.
Dempsey-Anderson Ice Arena
Forest Park Dr.
Hill Crest Dr.
Arlington Dr.
Park for all People
Northern Lights Center
Fairbanks
Earthquake Park
Northern Lights Blvd.
Aurora Village
Benson Blvd.
Sears Mall
Goose Lake
University of Alaska
Alaska Pacific University
Boniface Mall
Lake Otis
Parkway
Postmark Drive
Aircraft Drive
Wendy's Way
Lake Hood Airstrip
Lake Hood
Wisconsin Dr.
Turnagain Blvd.
Arctic Blvd.
C Street
A Street
36th Avenue
Z.J. Loussac Library
University Center
Providence Hospital
Baxter Road
Patterson Street
Main Post Office
Lake Spenard
Spenard Road
Tudor Road
Dale St.
Bragaw St.
Tudor Track
International
Frontage Road
Airport Terminal
Airport
Cambridge Way
Newcastle Way
Road
Campbell
Grummen St.
View Circle
YMCA
Bicentennial Park
Potter Drive
Creek
Anchorage International Airport
Connors Lake
Dowling Rd.
DMV
E. 64th Avenue
E. 68th Avenue
E. 72nd Avenue
DeLong Lake
Raspberry Road
Campbell Airstrip
Kincaid Park
Kincaid Road
Jodhpur St.
Sand Lake Road
Sand Lake
Jewel Lake Road
Minnesota Dr.
Lore Road
Spruce Street
Abbott Loop Road
E. 80th Avenue
E. 84th Avenue
E. 88th Avenue
Sundi Lake
Campbell Creek Greenbelt
Dimond Blvd.
Dimond Center
Hillside Park
Jewel Lake
Dimond Blvd.
Dimond-Jewel Lake Center
Old Seward Highway
Seward Highway
Elm St.
Lake Otis Parkway
Abbott Road
Campbell Lake
Victor Road
100th Avenue
Bayshore Drive
Anchorage Golf Course
O'Malley Road
Alaska Zoo
Klatt Road
Johns Road
Huffman Road
Birch Road
Hillside Drive
DeArmoun Road
Rabbit Creek Road
Potter Point State Game Refuge

Downtown Anchorage

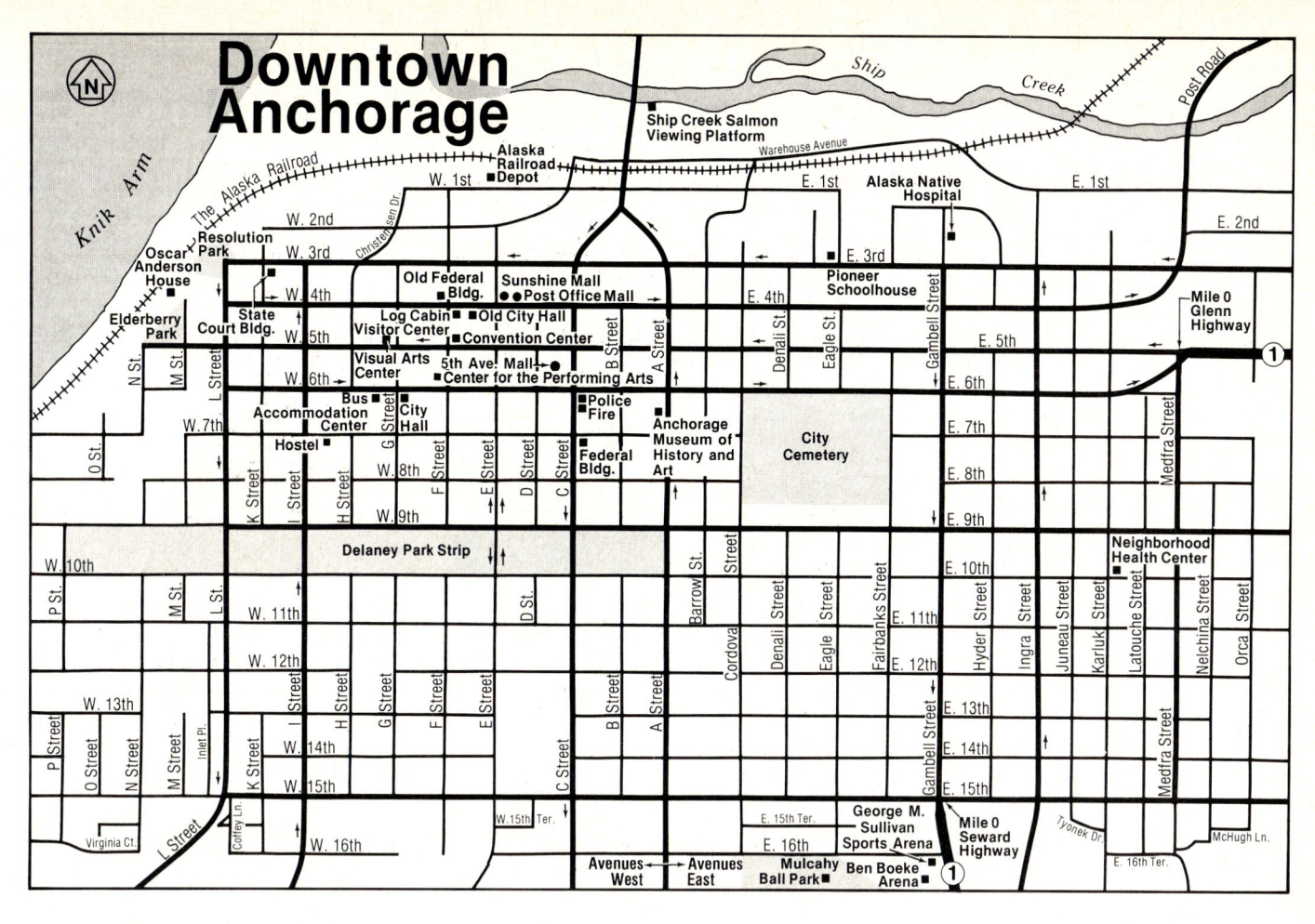

arriving on domestic flights; the other in the customs-secured area of the international concourse. The North Anchorage visitor information center is located at Valley River Mall in Eagle River, just off the Glenn Highway. The Community Calendar Services of the Anchorage Convention and Visitors Bureau offers information on community events, phone 276-4118.

The Alaska Public Lands Information Center, in the historic Federal Bldg. on 4th Avenue and F Street, has extensive displays and information on outdoor recreation lands in Alaska; phone 271-2737. (See detailed description of the center under Attractions this section.)

Elevation: 38 to 120 feet/16 to 37m, with terrain nearly flat throughout the bowl area.

Climate: Anchorage has a climate closely resembling that of the Rocky Mountains area. Shielded from excess Pacific moisture by the Kenai Mountains to the south, the city has an annual average of only 15 inches of precipitation. Winter snowfall averages about 70 inches per year, with snow on the ground typically from October to April. Anchorage is in a transition zone, between the moderating influence of the Pacific Ocean and the extreme temperatures found in interior Alaska. The average temperature in January (coldest month) is 13°F/-11°C; in July (warmest month), 58°F/14°C. Record high was 85°F/29°C in June 1969. Record low was -34°F/-37°C in January 1975. The growing season in the area is 100 to 120 days and typically extends from late May to early September. Anchorage has a daily maximum of 19 hours, 21 minutes of daylight in summer, and 5 hours, 28 minutes in winter.

The Maps Place
3545 Arctic Blvd.
(Olympic Center)
Anchorage, Alaska 99503
(907) 562-MAPS (562-6277)

Valarian Visit
Home Away From in Anchorage
Proprietor: Kitty Evans
FULLY FURNISHED APARTMENTS ON DAILY,
WEEKLY OR MONTHLY BASIS
CAN SLEEP UP TO SIX COMFORTABLY
1536 Valarian St., Anchorage, AK 99508 • (907) 274-5760

Discover Alaska in our motorhomes!

The ideal way to see Alaska— at your own pace!

- Comfortable, convenient, clean self-contained units
- 20' - 31' motorhomes
- Sleeps up to 8 people
- Housekeeping and fishing packages available
- Free airport pickup in Anchorage

MAKE RESERVATIONS EARLY!
(907) 562-7051
(800) 421-3456
Telex: 25147 Attn: Clippership
FAX (907) 562-7053

Clippership Motorhome Rentals
5401 Old Seward Highway
Anchorage, Alaska 99518

ANCHORAGE

Anchorage is situated on a low-lying alluvial plain. (Bruce M. Herman)

Prevailing wind direction is north at a mean speed of 6.6 mph/10.6 kmph.

Radio: KENI 550, KHAR 590, KYAK 650, KBYR 700, KFQD 750, KPXR-FM 102, KLEF 98.1, KKSD 1080, KATB-FM 89.3, KSKA-FM 91.1, KEAG-FM 97.3, KYMG-FM 98.9, KBFX-FM 100.5, KGOT-FM 101.3, KPXR-FM 102.1, KKLV-FM 104.1, KNIK-FM 105.3, KWHL-FM 106.5, KASH-FM 107.5. **Television:** KTUU (NBC), Channel 2; KTBY (independent), Channel 4; KYES (independent) Channel 5; KAKM (PBS), Channel 7; KTVA (CBS), Channel 11; KIMO (ABC), Channel 13; and UHF channels. Pay cable television is also available. **Newspapers:** *Anchorage Daily News* (daily); *The Anchorage Times* (daily); *Alaska Journal of Commerce and Pacific Rim Reporter* (weekly); *Chugiak-Eagle River Star* (weekly); *Tundra Times* (weekly).

Private Aircraft: Anchorage airports provide facilities and services to accommodate all types of aircraft. See the *Alaska Supplement*, the U.S. government's flight information publication, for the following airports: Anchorage International, Merrill Field, Birchwood, Campbell airstrip, Providence Hospital heliport, Elmendorf Hospital heliport, Elmendorf AFB, Bryant Field (Fort Richardson) and Lake Hood floatplane base. For more information call the Anchorage Flight Service station at 278-3322.

ALASKA PANORAMA R.V. RENTALS Inc.

"The Only Way to Really See ALASKA"

Reserve Yours Now!

Motorhomes 20' – 33'
Sleep up to 6 people

Pickup Campers

Completely Self-Contained Housekeeping Packages

Canoe and Fishing Gear Rental Available

Transportation Available to and from Airport or Hotel

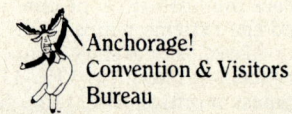

REPAIR AND SERVICE ON ALL RV'S
- Insurance Work • Complete Rebuild Facility • All Appliance Repairs
- Hitches and Welding Fabrication • Awnings, Pods, Air Conditioners
- Holding Tanks – Repairs and Replacement

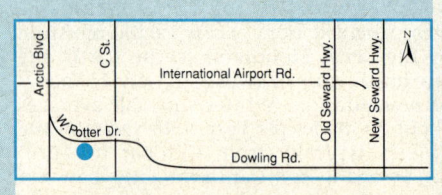

AUTHORIZED WARRANTY STATION

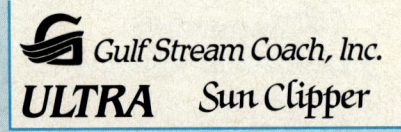

Gulf Stream Coach, Inc. • ULTRA • Sun Clipper • Bounder NEW FOR 1992's BY FLEETWOOD • FLEETWOOD • SOUTHWIND BY FLEETWOOD

Anchorage! Convention & Visitors Bureau

MEMBER Travel Industry Association of America • BBB BETTER BUSINESS BUREAU • AVA ALASKA VISITORS ASSOCIATION

Write or call for details:
712 W. POTTER DRIVE • ANCHORAGE, ALASKA 99518
PHONE (907) 562-1401 • TELEX 981-061 • FAX (907) 561-8762

HISTORY AND ECONOMY

In 1914 Congress authorized the building of a railroad linking an ocean port with the interior river shipping routes. The anchorage at the mouth of Ship Creek was chosen as the construction camp and headquarters for the Alaskan Engineering Commission. By the summer of 1915 the camp's population, housed mainly in tents, had grown to about 2,000.

The name Anchorage (earlier names included Woodrow, Ship Creek, Ship Creek Landing and Knik Anchorage) was chosen by the federal government when the first post office opened in May 1915. A few months later the bluff south of the creek was cleared and surveyed and 655 lots, on 347 acres, were auctioned off by the General Land Office for $148,000. The intersection of 4th Avenue and C Street was regarded as the center of the business district, and by late summer about 100 wooden structures had been built. Anchorage continued to prosper and was incorporated in 1920.

Anchorage's growth has been in spurts, propelled by: (1) construction of the Alaska Railroad and the transfer of its headquarters from Seward to Anchorage in 1917; (2) colonization of the Matanuska Valley, a farming region 45 miles/72 km to the north, in 1935; (3) construction of Fort Richardson and Elmendorf Field in 1940; (4) oil discoveries between 1957 and 1961 in Cook Inlet; and (5) the development of North Slope oil fields and the construction of the trans-Alaska pipeline—all since 1968.

The earthquake of March 27, 1964, which caused millions of dollars in damage, resulted in a flurry of new construction. Government relief funds (in the form of Small Business Administration loans) were offered to those who wished to rebuild. Most did, and a distinctly new Anchorage began to emerge.

In the 1970s and 80s, Anchorage underwent a population and construction boom tied to oil production. The decline in oil prices in recent years has brought about a slower economy than was enjoyed in those "boom" years.

Today, Anchorage is a center of commerce and distribution for the rest of Alaska. Mainstays of the economy are government agencies (federal and state), tourism, the oil industry, military bases and transportation facilities including an expanding port and international airport.

DESCRIPTION

Anchorage is a sprawling city, bordered on the east by the stunningly beautiful Chugach Mountain Range and on the west by Knik Arm of Cook Inlet. On a clear day, you can catch a tantalizing glimpse of Mount McKinley, 135 miles/217 km to the north.

ANCHORAGE ADVERTISERS

ABC Motor Home
  Rentals .... 2360 Commerical Dr.
Accommodations Alaska
  Style .... Ph. (907) 278-8800
Alaska Aviation Heritage
  Museum .... 4721 Aircraft Dr.
Alaska Camera Exchange
  and Repair .... 701 W. 36th Ave.
Alaska Experience Center .... Downtown
Alaska Fur Exchange .... 4417 Old Seward Hwy.
Alaska Fur Gallery .... 4 locations—See ad
Alaska Private Lodgings .... Ph. (907) 248-2292
Alaska Railroad .... Ph. 1-800-544-0552
Alaska Sourdough
  Bed & Breakfast .... Ph. (907) 563-6244
Alaska Spring .... Ph. (907) 563-3802
Alaska State Parks .... Ph. (907) 762-2617
Alaska State Parks
  Volunteers .... Ph. (907) 762-2655
Alaska Towing and
  Wrecking .... Ph. (907) 272-2438
Alaska Wild Berry
  Products .... Dimond Center Mall
Alaska Wilderness
  Gourmet .... 219 E. Intl. Airport Rd.
Alaska Wilderness Travel .... 715 W. Fireweed
Alaskan Adventures
  R.V. Rentals .... Ph. 1-800-676-8911
Alaskan Frontier Gardens
  Bed & Breakfast .... Ph. (907) 561-1514
Alaska's B&B Gazette .... Ph. (907) 345-4761
Alaska's Tudor Motel ...... 4423 Lake Otis Pkwy.
Alaska-Yukon RV
  Caravans .... Ph. 1-800-426-9865
Allstar Rent-A-Car .... 2 locations—See ad
All the Comforts
  of Home .... Ph. (907) 345-4279
All Ways Travel Inc. .... Ph. (907) 276-3644
Alpine Apartments .... 5210 Mockingbird Dr.
Anchorage Alternative
  Lodgings .... Ph. (907) 522-1922
Anchorage Eagle
  Nest Hotel .... 4110 Spenard Rd.
Anchorage Fur Factory .... 105 W. 4th Ave.
Anchorage Historic
  Properties .... Ph. (907) 274-3600
Anchorage Parking Authority .... Downtown
Apones Treasure Cache .... Sears Mall
Arctic Images .... 145 W. 6th Ave.
Arctic Poppy Bed &
  Breakfast .... Ph. (907) 258-7795
Arctic Tern Inn .... Ph. (907) 337-1544
Associated Brokers Inc. ...... Ph. (907) 563-3333

Big Bear Bed & Breakfast . Ph. (907) 277-8189
Black Angus Inn .... 1430 Gambell St.
Bonanza Lodge .... Ph. (907) 563-3590
Book Cache, The .... 6 locations—See ad
Brewster's Department
  Store .... 2 locations—See ad
B.T. Service & Supply .... 4440 View Circle
Castleton's .... 3340 Mt. View Dr.
Centennial Camper Park .... Boundary Ave.
Cleaning World Self-Service
  Co-Op Laundry .... 1120 Huffman Rd.
Clippership Motorhome
  Rentals .... 5401 Old Seward Hwy.
David Green
  Master Furrier .... 2 locations—See ad
Denny's .... 3 locations—See ad
DeVeaux's
  Contemporary B&B ..... Ph. (907) 349-8910
Downtown Bicycle
  Rental .... Ph. (907) 279-5293
Downtown Deli and Cafe ...... 525 W. 4th Ave.
8th Avenue Hotel .... Ph. (907) 274-6213
Eklutna Village Historical
  Park .... 2331 Scarborough Dr.
Era Helicopters .... Ph. (907) 266-8351
Far North Bed &
  Breakfast .... 4001 Galactica Dr.
5th Ave. RV & Auto
  Center .... Ph. (907) 277-1526
Gallery Bed and Breakfast .... 1229 G St.
Gingham House .... 841 I St.
Golden Nuggett
  Camper Park .... 4100 DeBarr Rd.
Gray Line of Alaska .... Ph. (907) 277-5581
Great Alaskan Holidays ..... Ph. (907) 248-7777
Hegedus & Sons Inc. .... Ph. (907) 274-6602
HeliTour Alaska .... 6400 S. Airpark Dr.
Highlander Camper Park .... 2704 Fairbanks St.
Hillside Motel &
  Camper Park .... 2150 Gambell St.
Historic Fourth Avenue
  Theatre .... Ph. (907) 279-3557
John's Motel .... 3543 Mt. View Dr.
John's RV Park &
  Consignment .... 3543 Mt. View Dr.
Katmailand Inc. .... 4700 Aircraft Dr.
Kodiak Furs .... 425 D St.
Lake Shore Motel .... Ph. (907) 248-3485
Laura Wright Alaskan
  Parkys .... 343 W. 5th Ave.
Longs Drugs .... 200 E. Northern Lights Blvd.
Lynn's Pine Point
  Bed and Breakfast .... Ph. (907) 333-2244

Mall at Sears,
  The .... 700 E. Northern Lights Blvd.
Mapco Express .... 13 locations—See ad
Maps Place, The .... 3555 Arctic Blvd.
Michael's Jewelers .... 4th & E St.
Mobile Trailer Supply, Inc. . 3150 Mt. View Dr.
Mountain View Carwash,
  Inc. .... 3433 Commercial Dr.
Municipality of Anchorage Parks
  & Recreation .... 3 locations—See ad
Murphy's RV Sales &
  Rentals .... Ph. 1-800-582-5123
Mush-Inn Motel .... 333 Concrete St.
New Hope Baptist Church ...... 333 N. Price St.
Northwoods Guest
  House .... Ph. (907) 243-3249
OK Bed & Breakfast .... Ph. (907) 243-1914
Old Anchorage Salmon Bake .... 3rd & K
Oomingmak, Musk Ox Producers'
  Co-operative .... 604 H St.
Phillips' Cruises .... Ph. (907) 276-8023
Photo Express .... 7 locations—See ad
Pia's Scandinavian Wool .... 345 E St.
Pines Club .... Tudor & Laurel
Potters and Charters
  Bed and Breakfast .... 7423 Pamela Pl.
Puffin Inn .... 4400 Spenard Rd.
Richard's Bunka Art ..... 6242 W. Dimond Blvd.
Ride 'n Shine .... 1341 S. Bragaw
Royal Suite Lodge .... 3811 Minnesota Dr.
R.V. Electric .... 1418 E. Dimond Blvd.
6 Bar E Ranch
  Bed & Breakfast .... Ph. (907) 279-9907
Six Robblee's, Inc. .... 3 locations—See ad
Sixth & B Bed & Breakfast .... 6th & B
Sourdough Camper
  Rentals .... 5773 Old Seward Hwy.
Sourdough Motel .... Ph. (907) 279-4148
Sport Fishing Alaska .... 1401 Shore Dr.
Stephan Fine Art .... 5 locations—See ad
Stewart's Photo Shop .... 531 W. 4th Ave.
Super 8 Motel .... Ph. 1-800-800-8000
Sweet Retreat Motorhome
  Rentals .... 6820 Arctic Blvd.
Taheta Arts and Cultural
  Group .... Ph. (907) 272-5829
10th & M Seafoods .... 2 locations—See ad
Tesoro Alaska .... Downtown
Tookalook Sales .... 322 Concrete St.
Trapper Jack's Trading Post ... 701 W. 4th Ave.
Tudor Coin Laundry &
  Dry Cleaning .... 2494 E. Tudor Rd.
Valarian Visit .... Ph. (907) 274-5760

350 Years of Athabascan Culture
30 Minutes from Downtown Anchorage

Come see our colorful "Spirit Houses" and Russian Orthodox Churches. Learn about our history and traditions on half-hour tours.

- Historical photos and displays
- Native arts and crafts

Call for details:
(907) 276-5701
or 688-6026

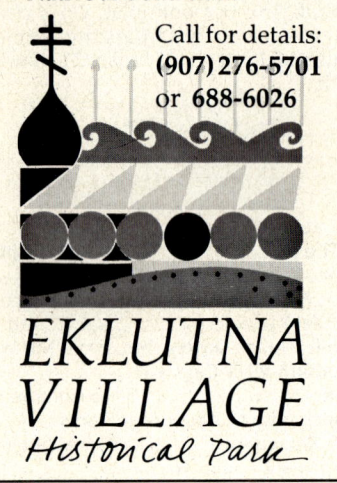

EKLUTNA VILLAGE
Historical Park

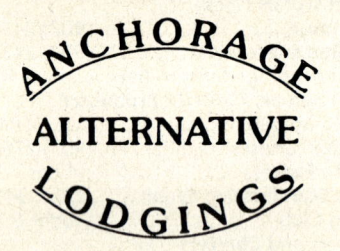

SOURDOUGH VISITORS LODGE MOTEL

PRICED LOWER THAN MOST MOTEL ROOMS

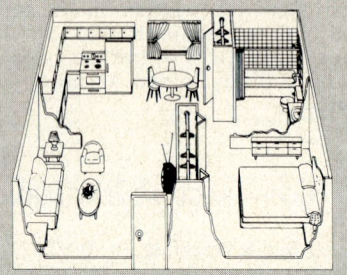

1 BEDROOM SUITE

- Suites with kitchen, coffee pots, toasters
- Clean, quiet, and comfortable
- Free local calls
- Major credit cards

801 Erickson St., Anchorage, AK 99501
On Gov't Hill 1 block from Elmendorf AFB
(907) 279-4148   FAX (907) 257-9738
In Alaska (800) 478-3030
Outside AK (800) 777-3716

ANCHORAGE ALTERNATIVE LODGINGS

BED and BREAKFAST APARTMENT

We invite you to enjoy our Alaskan hospitality in a 1,000 square foot clean, quiet, comfortable two-bedroom apartment, located in the lower level of our South Anchorage home.

* Private Bath, semi-private entrance, off-street driveway parking.
* Fully eqipped modern kitchen, dining and family room area with colored T.V., stereo, tape deck and microwave.
* Located 15 minutes from the airport, downtown, railroad depot and seaport.
* Close to malls, laundromat, zoo, swimming, hiking and mountains.
* Send for free picture brochure

Member
Bed & Breakfast Association of Alaska

ANCHORAGE ALTERNATIVE LODGINGS
P.O. Box 231154, Anchorage, AK 99523
(907) 522-1922   Open all year

Bed & Breakfast

Guest accomodations provided for a memorable Alaska stay!
ALSO Business and weekend getaways
South Central Alaska – Fairbanks to Homer

ALASKA PRIVATE LODGINGS

Send $3.00 for descriptive directory
P.O. Box 200047-MP, Anchorage, Alaska 99520-0047

We take major credit cards
(907) 248-2292 • FAX (907) 248-2602

Best Motel Value in Anchorage...
ALASKA'S TUDOR MOTEL
— SPEND A NIGHT NOT A FORTUNE —

- One-bedroom apartments with 380 sq. ft.
- Color TV with Multivisions • Direct dial phones
- Full kitchen with utensils • Laundry nearby
- Shopping centers and restaurants nearby
- *Military, airline and senior citizen discounts*
- CONVENIENT TO DOWNTOWN AND AIRPORTS

4423 Lake Otis Parkway, Anchorage, Alaska 99507

(907) 561-2234
Southeast corner of Lake Otis Parkway & Tudor Road

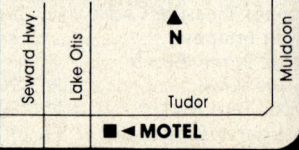

Many new buildings dot the Anchorage skyline. Millions of dollars were allocated by the legislature for Project 80s, the largest construction program in Anchorage's history. Perhaps best known is the Alaska Center for the Performing Arts, located at the corner of 5th Avenue and F Street. Construction costs on the center grew from an original estimate of $22 million to more than $70 million. Visitors may notice the fences on the center's roof: these had to be added to prevent snow from sliding off the steep pitch of the roof and onto pedestrians below. Other completed projects include the George M. Sullivan Sports Arena, William A. Egan Civic and Convention Center, Z.J. Loussac Public Library, and a major expansion and renovation of the Anchorage Museum of History and Art.

With its curious mixture of the old frontier and the jet age, Anchorage is truly a unique place. In profile, the town has:

- About 80 schools, including special education and alternative programs. University of Alaska, Alaska Pacific University and Alaska Business College.
- More than 160 churches and temples.
- Z.J. Loussac Public Library, plus 4 branch libraries, National Bank of Alaska Heritage Library Museum, Dept. of the Interior's Alaska Resource Library, and the University of Alaska Library.
- Municipal bus service: 4 taxi services.
- In the arts—**Dance:** Alaska Center for Performing Arts; Alaska Dance Theatre; Anchorage Concert Assoc.; Anchorage Opera; Ballet Alaska. **Music:** Alaska Airlines Winter Classics; Anchorage Community Chorus; Anchorage Community Concert Band; Anchorage Concert Assoc.; Anchorage Girls and Boys Choir; Alaska Stage Company; Anchorage Symphony Orchestra; Anchorage Youth Symphony; Anchorage Festival of Music; Sweet Adelines (Cheechako and Sourdough chapters); University

of Alaska–Anchorage Singers; Young People's Concerts. **Theater:** Out North Theater Company; Alaska Junior Theater; Alaska Theatre of Youth; Anchorage Community Theatre; Alaska Stage Company; Theatre Guild; Valley Performing Arts. **Art:** Visual Arts Center of Alaska; and about 35 commercial art galleries.

ACCOMMODATIONS

There are more than 50 motels and hotels in the Anchorage area with prices for a double room ranging from $50 to $70 and up. Reservations are a must. Bed-and-breakfast accommodations are also available in more than 100 private residences.

Anchorage International Hostel is located at 700 H St., 1 block from the People Mover Transit Center in downtown Anchorage. The hostel is open 8-10 A.M. and 5-12 P.M.; cost for members is $10 per night, nonmembers $13. American Youth Hostel cards available at the hostel or by mail. The hostel is open year-round and has kitchen facilities, common rooms, laundry room and TV room. For information phone 276-3635. Write for reservations (prepayment required): 700 H St., Anchorage 99501.

Restaurants number more than 300, with many major fast-food chains, formal dining rooms and specialty establishments including Cantonese, Italian, Japanese, Korean, Chinese, Mandarin, Mexican, Polynesian, Greek, German, Sicilian, soul food, seafood, smorgasbord and vegetarian.

Accommodations Alaska Style/Stay With A Friend. A bed-and-breakfast reservation service offering rooms in private homes and lodges personally inspected for

---

Plan Your Great Alaska Get Away

Rent a Motorhome!

- Several sizes (20' to 34')
- Sleep up to 8 people
- Fully self-contained
- Airport & Hotel pick-up

Get away from everything but comfort in your Sweet Retreat motorhome. We provide everything you need to explore the "Great Land." Go where you want, at your own pace!

SWEET RETREAT
MOTORHOME RENTALS

6820 Arctic Blvd., Anchorage, AK 99518
Phone (907) 344-9155 • (800) 759-4861
FAX (907) 344-8279

"Your Home Away From Home"

ALASKAN FRONTIER GARDENS

Bed and Breakfast

1011 E. Tudor Road, #160
Anchorage, Alaska 99503

(907) 561-1514 or (907) 345-6562

DeVeaux's Contemporary B&B

- Located Lower Hillside
- 10 Minutes from Downtown & airport
- Elegant Rooms w/View & Separate Sitting Room
- Smoke-free Environment

(907) 349-8910   4011 Iona Circle Anchorage, AK 99507

MAGNIFICENT KATMAI And "ANGLER'S PARADISE"
Remote... Yet easily Accessible

BROOKS LODGE
- Located in the heart of Katmai National Park
- Brooks River Falls, the Valley of 10,000 Smokes, Fishing and Hiking
- The most accessible spot to view the Alaska brown bear

ANGLER'S PARADISE
Get away from the highway and crowds...

KULIK LODGE
- Alaska's premier flyout sportfishing lodge

GROSVENOR LODGE
- Superb sportfishing and ideal for small groups or families

KATMAI/BRISTOL BAY FISHING FLOAT TRIPS
- Guided or Unguided

Angler's Paradise Lodges
Katmailand Inc.

4700 Aircraft Dr., Anchorage, AK 99502
1-800-544-0551 • (907) 243-5448 • FAX (907) 243-0649
In Alaska 1-800-478-5448

MUSH-INN Motel

- REASONABLE RATES
- JACUZZIS • KITCHENS
- KIDS, PETS WELCOME
- CONVENIENTLY LOCATED
- OFF-STREET PARKING
- LAUNDRY FACILITIES

333 Concrete Street, Anchorage, AK 99501
(907) 277-4554 • 1-800-478-4554 In State
(Pilots: We're across from Merrill Field)

Laura Wright Alaskan Parkys

WEARABLE ALASKAN ART
Since 1947

Beautiful Eskimo Style Summer & Winter Parkas

343 West 5th Ave.
(on 5th Ave. between "C" & "D" St.)
Anchorage, AK 99501
(907) 274-4215

Gingham House

Downtown Bed & Breakfast
2 BLKS. FROM CENTER OF CITY

Your own private cottage tastefully furnished in antiques. Maximum 4 guests. Proprietors next door.

841 "I" St.
Anchorage, Alaska 99501
(907) 276-0407

No Smoking
RV Parking
Open All Year
MC/VISA

NORTHWOODS GUEST HOUSE

3 Bedroom Suites
with Fully Equipped Kitchen, Dining Room and Living Room

Located near the airport in a quiet area bordering a municipal park and bike path

2300 West Tudor
Anchorage, Alaska 99517

(907) 243-3249

BIG BEAR Bed & Breakfast

Old Fashioned Alaskan Hospitality — Lifelong Alaskan

Alaskan Art & Artifacts • Wildberry Specialties • Antiques

3-BEDROOMS • SMOKE-FREE ENVIRONMENT • SITTING ROOM WITH VCR
10 minutes from Downtown / 10 minutes from Railroad Depot

3401 Richmond Ave., Anchorage, Alaska 99508   **(907) 277-8189**

Highlander CAMPER PARK

We're Your Home Away from Home in Anchorage!

Movie Theatres, Restaurants, Beauty Salons and More, All Within a Short Walking Distance!

- ALL HOOK-UPS INCLUDED
- BATHOUSE
- LAUNDRY FACILITIES AVAILABLE

• Monthly • Weekly • Daily Rates

CONVENIENTLY LOCATED ACROSS FROM THE SEARS MALL

2704 Fairbanks St., Anchorage

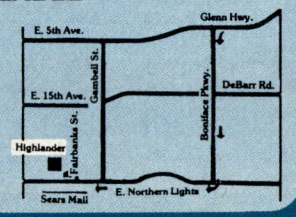

VISA / MasterCard   **(907) 277-2407**

---

cleanliness, comfort, safety and friendly service at reasonable rates. Locations: Anchorage, Anchor Point, Denali Park/Healy, Fairbanks, Glennallen, Girdwood, Homer, Juneau, Kenai/Soldotna, Palmer, Seward, Sitka, Talkeetna, Valdez, Wasilla, Willow. Phone (907) 278-8000; Fax (907) 272-8800 or write 3605 Arctic Blvd. #173, Anchorage, AK 99503 for free brochure. $2 for descriptive directory. [ADVERTISEMENT]

Alaskan Frontier Gardens Bed and Breakfast. Elegant accommodations on a scenic 3-acre wooded setting. Come enjoy our Alaskan hospitality with 27-year resident. Located in Anchorage's peaceful "hillside" area near the Chugach State Park, 20

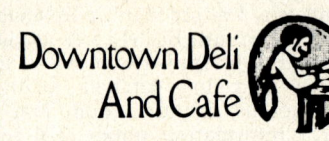

Downtown Deli And Cafe

For breakfast, lunch or dinner, reasonably priced Alaska sized breakfasts, hearty soups and sandwiches, healthy salads, wholesome dinners, fresh ground coffee and tempting sweets.

A tradition of good tastes!

summer hours - 6 am to 11 pm daily
winter hours - 7 am to 10 pm Mon.- Sat
9 am to 4 pm Sunday

**525 West Fourth Avenue
Anchorage, Alaska
276-7116
Across from the Log Cabin
Visitors Center**

LAKE SHORE MOTEL

Economy Rates

* Close to International Airport and Lake Hood
* Color Television & Telephones
* Laundry Room & Fish Freezers
* Singles, Doubles, & Kitchenettes

3009 Lake Shore Drive
Anchorage, Alaska 99517

248-3485

* Free Airport Shuttle
* VISA/MC/DINERS CLUB
* Family Rooms with Kitchenettes

Located 1/2 block west of Spenard Rd. on Lake Shore Drive

minutes from downtown. Spacious rooms, luxury suite with jacuzzi, sauna and fireplace. Great for honeymooners. Year-round. Full breakfast. Laundry service. 1011 Tudor Road, Suite 160, Anchorage, AK 99503. (907) 561-1514 or 345-6562. Fax (907) 562-2923. [ADVERTISEMENT]

The Downtown Deli and Cafe, 525 W. 4th Ave. Located in the heart of downtown Anchorage across the street from the Log Cabin Visitor Center. The Deli is known locally for giant sweet rolls, huge omelettes, hearty sandwiches, healthy salads and a dinner menu featuring Alaska seafood. Beer and wine. Summer hours 6 A.M. to 11 P.M. daily. Winter hours 7 A.M. to 10 P.M. Monday–Saturday, 9 A.M. to 4 P.M. Sunday. [ADVERTISEMENT]

Lynn's Pine Point Bed and Breakfast. Quiet, comfortable lodging in our beautiful cedar retreat located near the Chugach Mountains. Enjoy a large room with private shower, TV, VCR, microwave and queen bed. Continental or traditional breakfast, many other extras. Business travelers welcome. VISA and MasterCard accepted. The comforts of home only minutes from all of Alaska. 3333 Creekside Dr., Anchorage, AK 99504. Phone (907) 333-2244. [ADVERTISEMENT]

Puffin Inn. Perfect for the business or pleasure traveler looking for a comfortable room and moderate price. Located 5 minutes from the airport with courtesy shuttle transportation. Complimentary coffee, muffins, and newspaper served daily. Cable TV and freezer space. Seasonal packages available October through April. Kitchenette units available at our off-site location. Phone (907) 243-4044, or Fax (907) 248-6853. [ADVERTISEMENT]

Sixth & B Bed & Breakfast. Prime downtown location. Complimentary bicycles. Low winter rates. Call or write for brochure, 145 W. 6th Ave., Anchorage, AK 99501. (907) 279-5293. 7 blocks from railroad station. Near all major downtown hotels. 1 block from Federal Building. Across the street from

---

Far North Bed & Breakfast

(907) 248-3393

We welcome the business traveler

Call night or day
4001 Galactica Dr., Anchorage, AK 99517

• A Full Alaskan Breakfast • Rooms are Neat and Clean • TV Room with Snacks and Cable TV • Close to Airport / Airport Pickup • Easy Access by City Bus • Room with Private Bath and TV Available • Close to Bike Trails

Have a quiet, restful stay while in Anchorage

5TH AVE. RV & AUTO CENTER

COMPLETE RV/AUTO
SALES • SERVICE • PARTS • BODY REPAIR
★ RV RENTALS ★
277-1526 --- 272-0544
1801 E. 5th Avenue • Anchorage, Alaska 99501

Hillside Motel & Camper Park

MOTEL — Reservations Accepted
26 Units w/wo Kitchenettes • In-Room Coffee
Off-Street Parking
Individual Heat • Combination Tub-Showers
Cable TV • Radios • Direct Dial Phones

CAMPER PARK
59 Units • Full Hookups
Hot Showers • Laundromat
LP Gas Available
Daily and Weekly Rates

CONVENIENTLY LOCATED IN MID-TOWN
Nearby: Supermarkets, restaurants, service stations, etc.

2150 Gambell (same as Seward Highway), **Anchorage, Alaska 99503**
(907) 258-6006 • 1-800-478-6008

John's RV Park

3543 Mountain View Drive
ANCHORAGE, ALASKA 99508
(907) 277-4332 • FAX (907) 272-0739
800-478-4332

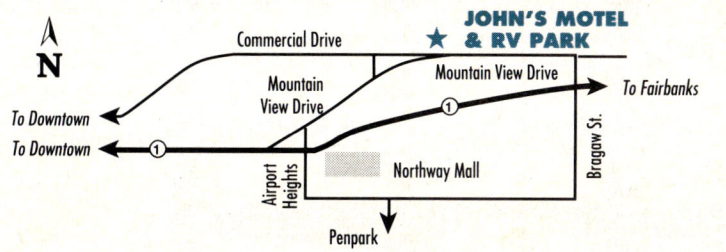

Good Sam Club

- FULL HOOKUPS
- FREE SHOWERS
- CONCRETE PADS
- LAUNDROMAT
- DUMP STATION
- GIFT SHOP
- TOUR INFORMATION & TICKET SALES

2.5 Miles from Downtown on Bus Line
ADULT RV PARK ONLY   PETS WELCOME

John's Motel

3543 Mountain View Drive
Anchorage, Alaska 99508
(907) 277-4332 • FAX (907) 272-0739
800-478-4332

Singles • Doubles • Kitchenettes
Individual Heat Control
Color TV with Radios • Direct Dial Phones
Combination Tub/ Shower
Off-Street Parking

DAILY & WEEKLY RATES

John's R.V. & Auto Consignment

Located at John's Motel and RV Park
3543 Mountain View Drive
Anchorage, Alaska 99508
(907) 278-1227
FAX (907) 272-0739

CASH BUYER ON LOT

RV CAMPERS!

Shop in Downtown Anchorage and have someone else make your bed for a day or two.

For a quick trip through Alaska's largest city use this map to locate your convenient parking place for only $5.00 per day.

Then, if you decide to recuperate overnight at the Anchorage Hilton Hotel, the hotel will give you a free parking pass.

THE ANCHORAGE HILTON

Camp in Alaska's wilderness, then enjoy the best of Alaskan accommodations !

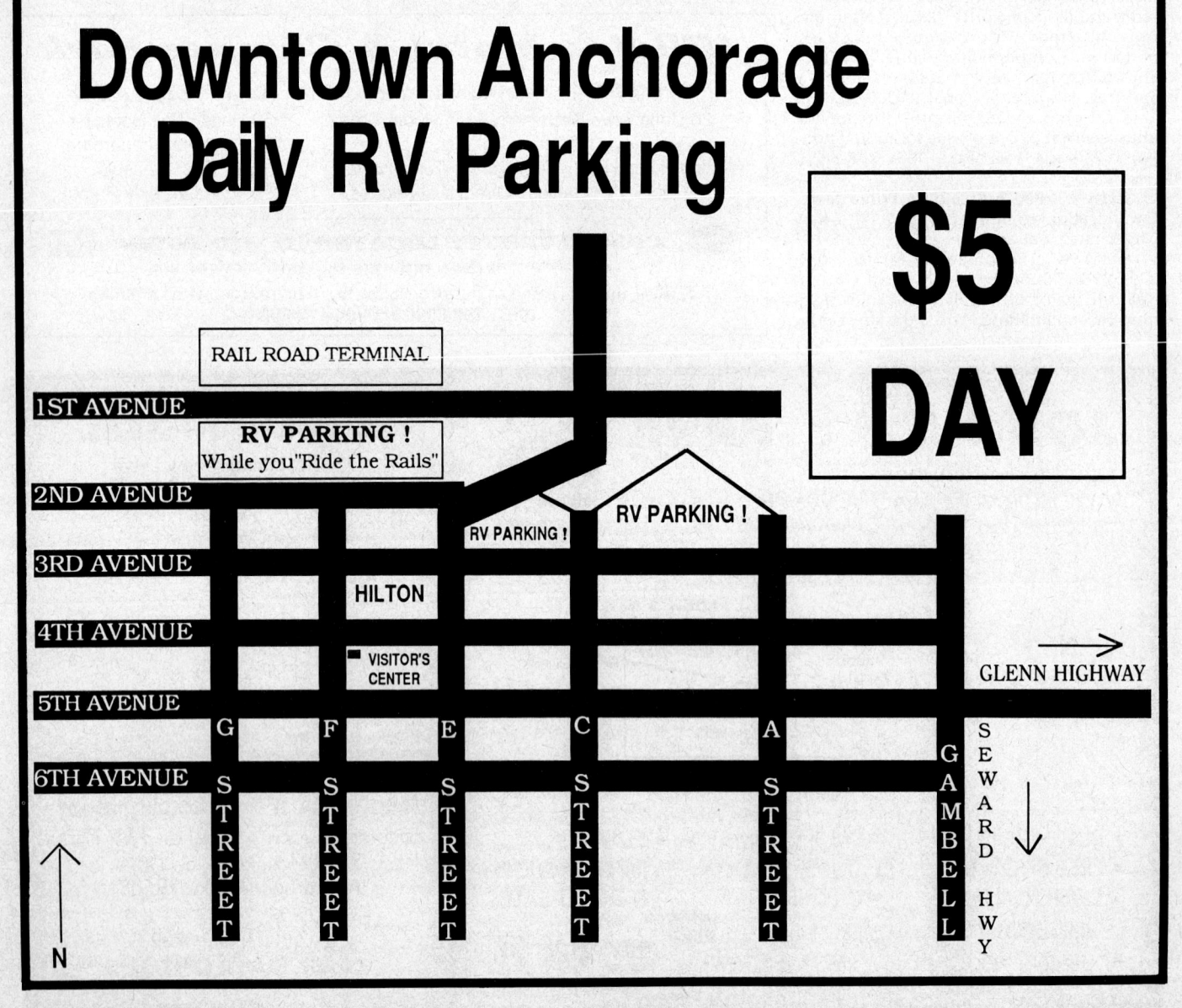

ANCHORAGE PARKING AUTHORITY

Downtown Anchorage
Daily RV Parking

$5 DAY

RAIL ROAD TERMINAL

1ST AVENUE

RV PARKING !
While you "Ride the Rails"

2ND AVENUE

RV PARKING !   RV PARKING !

3RD AVENUE

HILTON

4TH AVENUE

VISITOR'S CENTER

→ GLENN HIGHWAY

5TH AVENUE

6TH AVENUE

G STREET   F STREET   E STREET   C STREET   A STREET   GAMBELL   SEWARD HWY ↓

N ↑

museum. Summer rates are $45, $55 and $80. Winter rates are $33, $43 and $45.

[ADVERTISEMENT]

Sourdough Motel. 1 mile north of downtown Anchorage on A Street—go across the bridge to the top of the hill. Free parking, pets OK, laundromat, several parks and restaurants within walking distance. We have suites with fully equipped kitchens, full bath, and color TV. Priced lower than a regular room downtown. (907) 279-4148 or (800) 777-3716 (Outside Alaska) or (800) 478-3030 (Alaska only). [ADVERTISEMENT]

Anchorage has 1 public campground, Centennial Park, open from May through October. Fees are $12 for non-Alaskans; $10 for Alaska residents; and $8 for seniors. To reach Centennial Park, take the Muldoon Road exit south off the Glenn Highway and take the first left (Boundary); take the next first left and follow the signs. Centennial, recommended for large RVs, has barracks-type showers, flush toilets and a dump station. Call 333-9711 for details.

Chugach State Park has campgrounds located near Anchorage at Bird Creek (Seward Highway), and at Eagle River and Eklutna Lake (Glenn Highway). Anchorage also has several private campgrounds.

TRANSPORTATION

Air: More than a dozen international and domestic air carriers and numerous intrastate airlines serve Anchorage; see Air Travel in the GENERAL INFORMATION section for details.

Anchorage International Airport is located 6.5 miles/10.5 km from downtown.

ALASKA Sourdough Bed & Breakfast ASSOCIATION, LTD.

More than a place to stay.

Guest rooms & suites in private homes & cabins. From $30.

A European tradition with a warm Alaskan touch.

Write: 889 Cardigan Circle
Anchorage, Alaska 99503
or call (907) 563-6244.

Member ACVB
AMEX/VISA/MC Accepted

BONANZA LODGE

There's NO Place Like HOME Except BONANZA!!

— 48 SPACIOUS SUITES —
Your Home Away From Home

In the Heart of Anchorage
$59.95/night & up *(plus tax)*
1 or 2 people

For Reservations Call:
(907) 563-3590

4455 Juneau Street, Anchorage, AK 99503

Ann Boudreaux, General Partner
John K. Neill, General Manager

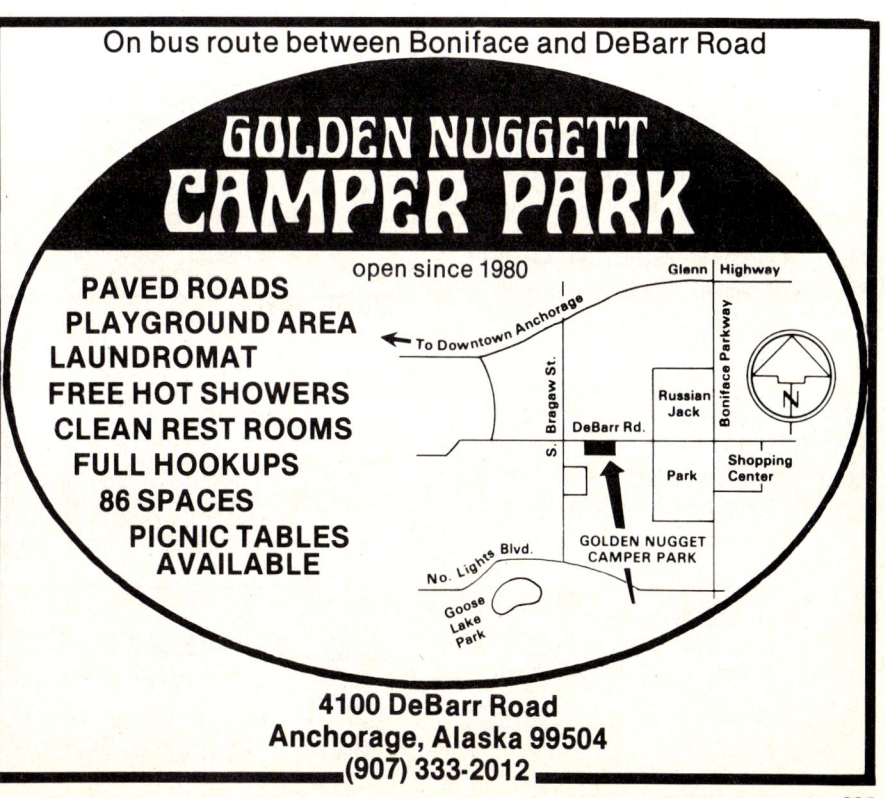

Alpine Apartments

◆ INTRIGUING VIEWS OF MOUNTAINS, CITY LIGHTS, AND SUNSETS ◆
◆ 1 AND 2 BEDROOM AND STUDIOS ◆
◆ FULLY FURNISHED SHORT TERM SUITES ALSO ◆
◆ COMPLETE FITNESS CENTER – JACUZZI – SAUNA ◆
◆ PLEASANT, WELL MAINTAINED ENVIRONMENT ◆

5210 Mockingbird Drive
Anchorage, Alaska 99507

Telephone
(907) 561-2930

ARCTIC TERN INN *(Your home in Alaska)*

- 3 Minutes to downtown • Close to military bases
- Cable TV and direct dial phones
- Rooms with complete kitchens • Laundry facilities
- Singles • Doubles • Family suites
- Sauna / Jacuzzi exercise room
- Complimentary breakfast
- Free airport pick-up

MasterCard • VISA

Phone (907) 337-1544 • FAX (907) 337-2288
5000 Taku Drive, Anchorage AK 99508

Anchorage Eagle Nest Hotel

4110 Spenard Road (MP) Anchorage, AK 99517

LARGE 1 AND 2 BEDROOM SUITES
COMPLETE WITH FULL KITCHENS
40-channel cable TV • Laundromat
Restaurants nearby
Deli food service items

Convenient to airport, downtown and shopping
On bus route • Children welcome
Airport pickup • Major credit cards
WE NEVER OVERBOOK

FAX (907) 248-9258 • 1-800-848-7852
For reservations Call (907) 243-2957 or Write

GOLDEN NUGGETT CAMPER PARK

On bus route between Boniface and DeBarr Road

open since 1980

PAVED ROADS
PLAYGROUND AREA
LAUNDROMAT
FREE HOT SHOWERS
CLEAN REST ROOMS
FULL HOOKUPS
86 SPACES
PICNIC TABLES
AVAILABLE

**4100 DeBarr Road
Anchorage, Alaska 99504
(907) 333-2012**

ANCHORAGE

Limousine service to and from major downtown hotels is available. Bus service to downtown is via People Mover (follow signs for city bus from baggage claim area to bus stop).

Ferry: There is no ferry service to Anchorage. The nearest port is Whittier on Prince William Sound, served by Alaska state ferry from Cordova and Valdez. Whittier is accessible by train from either Anchorage or Portage on the Seward Highway. See the Southwestern Ferry Schedules in the MARINE ACCESS ROUTES section for details.

Cruise Ships: See Cruise Ships in the MARINE ACCESS ROUTES section for ships making Anchorage a port of call.

Railroad: The Alaska Railroad offers daily passenger service in summer from Anchorage to Seward, to Denali National Park (Mount McKinley) and to Fairbanks. In addition, a shuttle train for both foot passengers and vehicles operates between Portage and Whittier from May 10 to Sept. 27. The Whittier Shuttle, operating 6 trips a day, 7 days a week, provides connections with the Alaska Marine Highway to Valdez and Cordova on Prince William Sound. *NOTE: Rail transportation is NOT available between Anchorage and Portage.*

See the ALASKA RAILROAD section for

8th Avenue Hotel

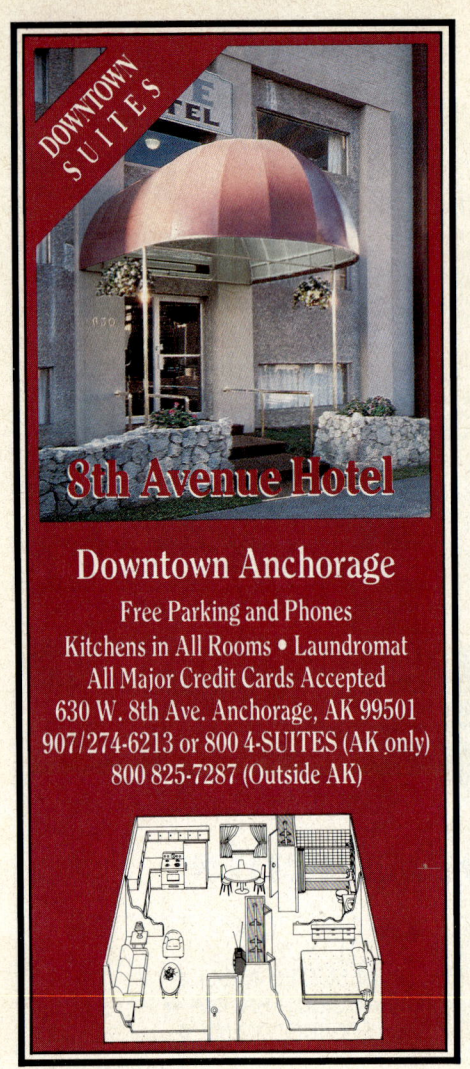

Downtown Anchorage

Free Parking and Phones
Kitchens in All Rooms • Laundromat
All Major Credit Cards Accepted
630 W. 8th Ave. Anchorage, AK 99501
907/274-6213 or 800 4-SUITES (AK only)
800 825-7287 (Outside AK)

ROYAL SUITE LODGE

- Excellent Location • Newly Remodeled
- Apartment-Style Units
- Daily & Weely Rates
- Parking in Carport • Full Kitchen

Free Airport Shuttle
Non-Smoking Suites Available
Free Local Phone
Cable T.V. with HBO

(907) 563-3114 (Phone & FAX No.)

3811 Minnesota Drive, Anchorage, AK 99503

Alaska Center for the Performing Arts on 5th Avenue and F Street. (John W. Warden)

Where the WORLD meets!!
6 BAR E RANCH BED AND BREAKFAST

Unique Alaskan Experience
Multilingual Professionals

For information and B & B reservations:
Earth Tours Inc.
705 West 6th Ave, Anchorage, Ak 99501
Ph. (907) 279-9907 FAX: (907) 279-9862

CAMPING
Just 5 miles from downtown Anchorage
Close to stores, gas stations and bus stop

CENTENNIAL CAMPER PARK
90 Spaces
Showers • Dump Station
Picnic Tables • 40 Tent Spaces
50-meter Pool 1/2 mile away

Turn south off Glenn Highway onto Muldoon Road, then turn east on Boundary Avenue.

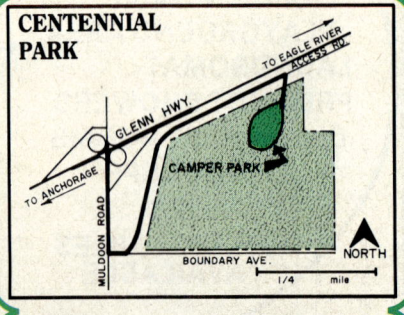

WATCH FOR THE SIGNS!
Parks are open May-September
"MUNICIPALITY OF ANCHORAGE"

POTTERS and CHARTERS BED and BREAKFAST

A modern suburban Bed and Breakfast
Hosts: Mary and Jerry Eidem
331 Pamela Place, Anchorage, Alaska 99504
(907) 333-7056 • (907) 338-5905
Call or send for brochure

BLACK ANGUS INN
Steak House & Lounge

- Free Limo Service to & from Airport & Train Station
- Cable TV & HBO
- Close to main shopping malls
- One block from Sullivan Arena & Carrs

FOR RESERVATIONS CALL 272-7503
1430 Gambell St. Anchorage, AK 99501

CLEANING WORLD
COIN-OP LAUNDROMAT

We have the largest coin-op washer in Alaska
Dry Cleaning • Alterations • Extractor
Drop-off laundry service
CLEAN MODERN FACILITIES
Owner Operated
Open 8 a.m. - 9 p.m. 7 days a week

(907) 345-2311
1120 Huffman Road
(Huffman Square at Old Seward Highway)

passenger schedules. For more information, write the railroad at P.O. Box 107500, Anchorage 99510; phone 1-800-544-0552 or (907) 265-2494.

The Alaska Railroad depot is located on 1st Avenue, within easy walking distance of downtown.

Bus: Local service via People Mover, which serves most of the Anchorage bowl from Peters Creek to Oceanview. Fares are 80¢ for adults, 40¢ for youth 5-18, 25¢ for senior citizens and disabled citizens with transit identification. Monthly passes are sold at the Transit Center (6th and H Street), the Penney Mall Transit Center, the Dimond Transit Center, municipal libraries, Book Cache outlets and several other locations. For bus route information, phone Rideline 343-6543.

Taxi: There are 4 taxi companies.

Car and Camper Rentals: There are more than 20 car rental agencies located at the airport and downtown. There are also several RV rental agencies (see advertisements this section).

RV Parking: The Anchorage Parking Authority's long-range plan is to have in operation spaces for oversized vehicles (motorcoaches, campers, large trucks). The first of these lots is located at 3rd Avenue,

All the Comforts of Home

Twelve room cedar home with quiet adult atmosphere overlooks Anchorage from 1100' elevation. Five peaceful acres. Hot tub and sauna. Pioneer hostess serves hearty breakfasts. Smoke free. Double occupancy $85 – $125.

12531 Turk's Turn
Anchorage, AK 99516-3309
(907) 345-4279   FAX (907) 345-4761

Beautiful Mornings Begin At 8.

SUPER 8 MOTEL

Toll-Free Reservations:
1-800-800-8000

Four Convenient Alaska Locations

ANCHORAGE
Fairbanks • Juneau • Ketchikan

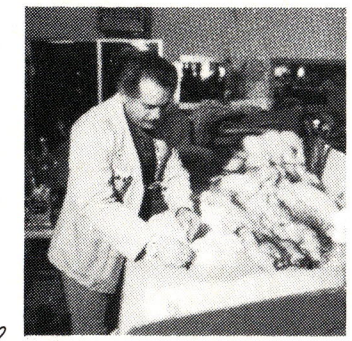

ANCHORAGE FUR FACTORY
Wholesale & Retail

Visit Our Factory

We Manufacture
Fur Coats • Parkas
Mukluks • Souvenirs

Free Tours Every Hour
On The Hour
(907) 277-8414
FAX 274-3474

105 West 4th Avenue
Anchorage, Alaska 99501

-THE BOOK CACHE-
Alaska's Bookseller

ANCHORAGE • EAGLE RIVER • KENAI
WASILLA • FAIRBANKS • SOLDOTNA

Atop Mt. McKinley

Telephone (907) 277-2723

Photo • Robert S. Thompson

Day Trips From Anchorage

Several interesting and memorable sights may be taken in on a day's drive from Anchorage by heading either south of downtown on the Seward Highway or north on the Glenn or George Parks highways. Following are some of the points of interest along these roads. Follow the mile-by-mile logs given in the related highway sections in *The MILEPOST*. Keep in mind that several companies offer motorcoach tours to many of these same attractions and that you can see a great many attractions in a short amount of time by taking a flightseeing trip out of Anchorage; there's even a 1-day trip to Kotzebue from Anchorage.

South from Anchorage, the Seward Highway offers some spectacular views of Turnagain Arm less than 10 miles/16 km from downtown. Stop at one of the scenic viewpoints for photos. Other stops close-in to Anchorage include Potter Marsh for bird watching and the Potter Section House, which serves as the Chugach State Park Visitor Center and features displays of railroad history.

Continue south to **Milepost S 90** (37 miles/59.5 km from Anchorage) for the Girdwood/Alyeska Road turnoff. About 2 miles/3.2 km up this road a gravel road forks to the left and leads 3.1 miles/5 km to Crow Creek Mine, a historic 1898 mining camp where visitors can pan for gold and tour the camp's old buildings. Returning from the mine to the main road, continue about another mile for Alyeska resort and recreation area. In summer, visitors can take the chair lift up Mount Alyeska for some spectacular views of Turnagain Arm.

Back out on the Seward Highway, continue south 11 miles/17.7 km to **Milepost S 79.1** and the Portage Glacier Access Road. On the 5-mile/8-km drive to the glacier, watch for salmon spawning at Williwaw Creek and look for the hanging Explorer Glacier. The Begich, Boggs Visitor Center at Portage Glacier has interpretive displays on glaciers and Forest Service naturalists are available to answer your questions. You can stand on the shore of Portage Lake for a close-up view of the fantastically shaped blue and white icebergs calved by Portage Glacier.

Return to the Seward Highway. Depending on your time, you may wish to head back up the highway to Anchorage (which would add up to about 114 miles/183.5 km total driving distance), or extend your trip farther south to take in the old gold mining town of Hope on the Hope Highway (another 39 miles/63 km, 1 way). You can drive to Seward, Homer and other communities and attractions on the Kenai Peninsula in a day, but you'll have time to see and do more if you allow for an overnight trip.

North from Anchorage, the Glenn and George Parks highways offer many attractions. Drive out the Glenn Highway from downtown Anchorage to Palmer, 42 miles/67.6 km. Heart of the Matanuska–Susitna Valley, the Palmer–Wasilla area has the Alaska State Fair (Aug. 28–Sept. 7, 1992), Colony Village, a herd of muskoxen, Knik Museum and Mushers' Hall of Fame, Wasilla Museum and Frontier Village, and the Iditarod Trail headquarters visitor center. Drive 59 miles/95 km east on the Glenn Highway from Palmer to see the spectacular Matanuska Glacier. Several lakes in the area offer picnicking and water sports. Largest is Big Lake, a year-round recreation area accessible from Big Lake Road off the George Parks Highway, 52 miles/84 km from Anchorage. Kepler–Bradley state recreation area on Matanuska Lake, at **Milepost A 36.4** Glenn Highway, has canoe rentals.

You may wish to stop off at Eklutna Lake or the Eagle River Visitor Center. Also, take the Eklutna Road exit for Eklutna Village Historical Park, which features 350 years of Athabascan culture. The park includes St. Nicholas Russian Orthodox Church and spirit houses. It is open daily, 9 A.M. to 9 P.M., from the end of May to mid-September; admission charged.

GOLD STAR ENERGY

■ Alaska's Petroleum Products From Tesoro.

As you travel around our state, you'll see a lot of our eight stars of gold. Those stars give Alaskans a special spirit, an energy all their own. And that special spirit, that Gold Star Energy, goes into every petroleum product that Tesoro makes, whether it's gasoline or diesel fuel. Because it's all made here in Alaska, by Alaskans.

So, as you're seeing the sights, stop in at one of the 113 independent Tesoro dealers around Alaska. We'll fill you up with some Gold Star Energy all your own.

Tesoro dealers accept Tesoro, Visa and MasterCard credit cards.

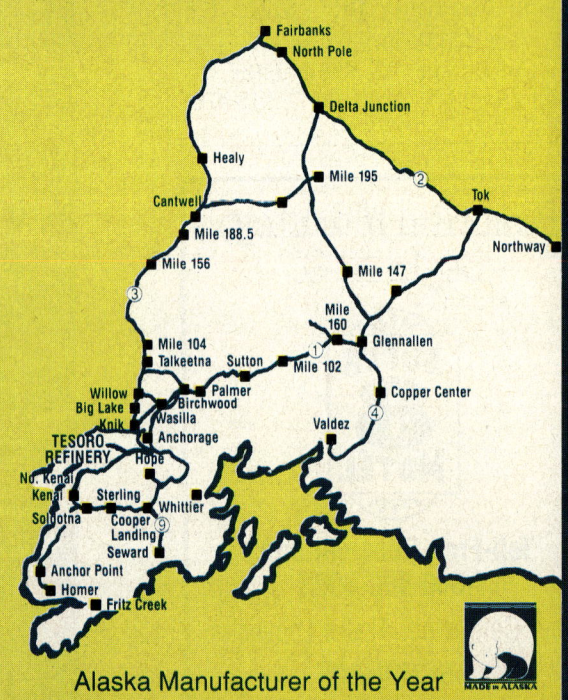

Alaska Manufacturer of the Year

north of the Holiday Inn, between A and C streets. Parking is $5 per space, per day. For more information, phone 276-8970.

Highway: Anchorage can be reached via the Glenn Highway and the Seward Highway.

ATTRACTIONS

Get Acquainted: Start at the Log Cabin Visitor Information Center at 4th Avenue and F Street, open 7:30 A.M. to 7 P.M. June through August; 8:30 A.M. to 6 P.M. in May and September; and 9 A.M. to 4 P.M. the remainder of the year; phone 274-3531. Free visitor guidebooks.

Take a Historic Walking Tour: Start at the Log Cabin Visitor Information Center at 4th Avenue and F Street. The Anchorage Convention and Visitors Bureau's *Anchorage Visitors Guide* has an excellent guide for a downtown walking tour.

Take a Tour: Several tour operators offer local and area sightseeing tours. These range from a 3-hour narrated motorcoach tour of Anchorage to full-day tours of area attractions such as Portage Glacier and Alyeska resort and ski area. Two-day or

---

Sport Fishing Alaska

If you're planning a fishing trip to Alaska, make sure you really PLAN IT!

Call us today at
(907) 344-8674
FAX (907) 349-4330

Russ and Donna Redick
Owners

✓ We're not a guide service: our job is to PLAN YOUR TRIP FOR YOU.
✓ YOU don't need to be an expert on Alaska sportfishing; we've done that for you with 25 years of experience with Alaska Department of Fish & Game.
✓ Guide service or solo; accommodations, connections, advice on gear and optimum times; we do it all for you BEFORE YOU LEAVE FOR ALASKA!

Sport Fishing Alaska — Alaska's only sportfisherman's planning service.
1401-M Shore Drive, Anchorage, Alaska 99515

STEWART'S PHOTO SHOP

ACROSS FROM THE TOURIST LOG CABIN
531 West Fourth Ave. • Anchorage • Phone 272-8581
ALASKA'S LARGEST PHOTO SHOP   Open 9-9 Mon.-Sat., 10-6 Sun.
Photograph our live reindeer!
Over 50 years' collection of Alaska color slides, movies, photos, and postcards.
Alaskan jade for sale by the pound or ton!

PORTAGE GLACIER.
DON'T LEAVE UNTIL YOU'VE SEEN IT.

And unless you see Portage Glacier with us, you'll probably be looking at it from miles away. Because only Gray Line's cruise on the mv Ptarmigan can give you a close-up view of this icy-blue giant. So close you'll want to reach out and touch it. Here is magnificence and antiquity and beauty—seen not from the shore, but from the deck of our vessel that brings you face to face with it. It's truly an experience you'll not forget.

Just an hour's drive from Anchorage, Gray Line has ample RV parking and cruises leaving every ninety minutes. Call or stop by our Anchorage office or the Portage Glacier Cruise Center for information or reservations.

ADULTS $19.50
$9.75 children under 12

Bring this ad to the Portage Glacier Cruise Center to receive $2 off each adult fare.

GRAY LINE Gray Line of Alaska
745 West 4th Avenue, Anchorage, AK 99501 (907) 277-5581
Portage Glacier Cruise Center at Portage Lake (907) 783-2983

Portage Glacier Cruises operates on National Forest System Lands of the Chugach National Forest and is operated under a special use permit from the U.S.D.A. Forest Service.

ANCHORAGE

longer excursions by motorcoach, rail, ferry and air travel to nearby attractions such as Prince William Sound or remote areas are also available. Inquire at your hotel, see ads this section or contact a travel agent.

The Alaska Public Lands Information Center, located in the historic Federal Bldg. on 4th Avenue and F Street, offers a wide variety of information on all of Alaska's state and federal parks, forests and wildlife refuges. Displays, video programs and computers permit self-help trip-planning. Expert staff provide additional assistance and supply maps, brochures and other aids. Federal passports (Golden Age, Eagle and Access) and state park passes are available. Reservations may be made here (in person or by mail only) for U.S. Forest Service cabins throughout the state. Receive up-to-date public lands news by touch-tone phone by calling 258-PARK for recorded information. The center is open year-round. Summer hours are 9 A.M. to 7 P.M. daily. Open in winter 10 A.M. to 5:30 P.M. Monday through Saturday. Closed holidays. Phone 271-2737

ALASKA'S MOST SPECTACULAR VISITOR ATTRACTION

ALASKA EXPERIENCE CENTER

Two unforgettable Alaskan Attractions

See Alaska come alive on our giant 180° domed screen in the OMNI THEATER and relive the Great Alaska Earthquake in o unique Alaskan Earthquake Exhibit!

Located in Downtown Anchorage
24-hr. recorded message 276-3730

Alaska's Favorite Gift Store

Over 4,000 square feet of Alaskan souvenirs, gifts and **friendly service.**

Featuring the largest selection of **Alaskana** Sweatshirts and T-shirts.

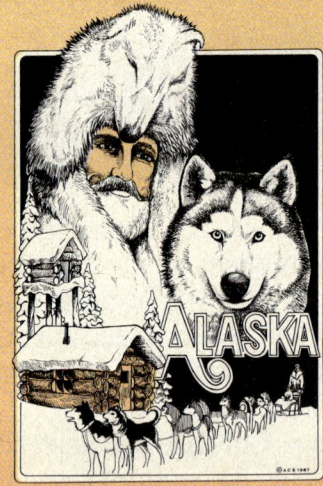

TRAPPER JACK'S TRADING POST

701 West Fourth Avenue
Anchorage, Alaska 99501
(907) 272-6110
WE MAIL

FREE Alaskan Tote Bag

"RV ALASKA" with "THE ORIGINAL"

ALL RIGS GO! SINCE 1983

ALASKA-YUKON RV CARAVANS

VANS, MOTOR HOMES   TRAILERS, 5TH-WHEELS

"Join us for Rendezvous '92"
A 1500-mile long extravaganza!

SPECIAL ALASKAN RV ADVENTURES

- 39 day "ESCORTED" ALASKA TOUR
- FLY / DRIVE / CRUISE TOURS
- INDEPENDENT RV TOURS
- RV RENTALS AVAILABLE
- SPECIAL ADD-ON ADVENTURES
- FISHING / FLIGHTSEEING / RAFTING

FREE 16 PAGE COLOR BROCHURE

1-800-426-9865

CALL TOLL FREE OR WRITE
ALASKA-YUKON RV CARAVANS
400 "D" Street, Suite 210
Anchorage, Alaska 99501

Denny's

ALWAYS OPEN

Three locations in ANCHORAGE
- DeBarr & Bragaw
- Benson & Denali St.
- Dimond Blvd. & New Seward Hwy.

FAIRBANKS - Airport Road

Children's Menu   No Smoking Section

Chugach State Park

This 495,000-acre park flanking Anchorage to the north, east and south, offers wilderness opportunities for all seasons: hiking, wildlife viewing, camping, berry picking, skiing and snowmobiling. Information about the park is available from Chugach State Park, H.C. 52, Box 8999, Indian, AK 99540; phone 345-5014. The Chugach State Park office, located in Potter Section House on the Seward Highway, has maps showing access to the park's recreation areas.

Between June and September, park staff offer guided nature walks and more strenuous hikes on the weekends to various points of interest in the park. The nature walks, which last about 2 hours, focus on some aspect of natural history, such as wildflower identification or bird watching. The more strenuous hikes last approximately 4 hours. Phone 694-6391 for a recorded message.

There are several access points to Chugach State Park attractions from Anchorage. North from downtown on the Glenn Highway take the Eklutna Road exit (**Milepost A 26.3**) and drive in 10 miles/16 km to reach Eklutna Lake Recreation Area. Eklutna Lake is the largest lake in Chugach State Park. The recreation area has a campground, picnic area and hiking trails. Cross-country skiing and snowmobiling in winter.

You may also reach the park's Eagle River Visitor Center by driving north on the Glenn Highway and taking the Eagle River exit (**Milepost A 13.4**). Follow Eagle River Road 12.7 miles/20.4 km to reach this beautifully situated visitor center, with its views of the Chugach Mountains. Excellent wildlife displays, a nature trail, Dall sheep viewing and other summer activities make this a worthwhile stop. Cross-country skiing and snowmobiling in winter. Phone 694-2108 for more information.

Another easily accessible park area from downtown is Arctic Valley. Turn off the Glenn Highway at Arctic Valley Road, **Milepost A 6.1**, and drive in 7.5 miles/12 km. Spectacular views of Anchorage and Cook Inlet. Good berry picking and hiking in summer; downhill and cross-country skiing in winter.

The park's hillside trailheads may be reached by driving south from downtown to the O'Malley Road exit at **Milepost S 120.8** on the Seward Highway. Follow O'Malley Road east for 4 miles/6.4 km until Hillside Drive enters from the right; turn on Hillside and proceed about 1.5 miles/2.4 km to the intersection of Upper Huffman Road and Hillside Drive. Turn left on Upper Huffman Road and continue 4 miles/6.4 km to the trailhead. Hiking in summer, cross-country skiing and snowmobiling in winter.

The Seward Highway south from Anchorage gives access to several Chugach State Park hiking trails.

See Part of Alaska No One Else Can Show You!

Take a ride on the Alaska Railroad and see the heart of Alaska. From Seward, past majestic Mt. McKinley to Fairbanks, explore the same route as our pioneers onboard the **NEWEST** passenger cars traveling the railroad. Call 800-544-0552 for information and reservations for both independent excursions and package tours. Group rates are also available.

ALASKA RAILROAD CORPORATION
Anchorage, Alaska
Call Toll Free 800-544-0552

---

or write the center at 605 W. 4th Ave., Suite 105, Anchorage, AK 99501, for more information.

The Anchorage Museum of History and Art, located at 121 W. 7th Ave., is a must stop. One of the most visited attractions in Anchorage, the museum features permanent displays of Alaska's cultural heritage and artifacts from its history. The 15,000-square-foot Alaska Gallery on the second floor is the Museum's showcase, presenting Alaska Native cultures—Aleut, Eskimo and Indian—and their encounters with the Russians, New England whalers and gold rush prospectors. Displays include full-scale dwellings and detailed miniature dioramas. The gallery contains some 300 photographs, more than 1,000 artifacts, 33 maps and specially made ship and aircraft models. The main floor of the museum consists of 6 connecting

Alaska's Largest Selection of Fine Furs

Parkas • Coats • Jackets • Skins
Custom Design Factory & Fur Service on Premises

2 Locations to Serve You

130 West 4th Avenue
Between A & B streets
Anchorage, Alaska 99501

423 West 5th Avenue
Across from Penney's
Phone (907) 277-9595

David Green Master Furrier
Alaska's most recommended furrier
serving Alaska since 1922

Wouldn't you rather be dancing at the

PINES CLUB
Dining • Dancing • Cocktails

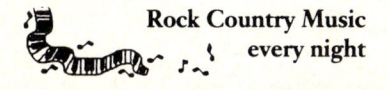

Rock Country Music every night

Corner Tudor & Laurel   (907) 563-0001

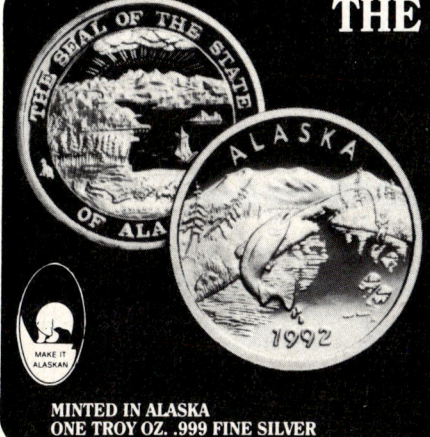

THE ANCHORAGE MINT presents

The 1992 ALASKA SILVER MEDALLION

ONLY $9.95
(subject to silver market)

445 W. 4th Ave. Anchorage, AK 99501
(907) 278-8414 • FAX (907) 278-8415
MAIL ORDERS WELCOME
(add $2.00 ea. for shipping & handling)

SEE COMPLETE COIN DISPLAY
at MICHAEL'S JEWELERS 4th & E St.

MINTED IN ALASKA
ONE TROY OZ. .999 FINE SILVER

ANCHORAGE

GRAY LINE OF ALASKA

FOR ALL OF YOUR SIGHTSEEING NEEDS.

Take one of our many tours, cruises or let us help with your independent arrangements. In addition to daily flights to the Arctic from Anchorage, or to Barrow from Fairbanks, Gray Line offers popular options such as these.

PORTAGE GLACIER.
Don't miss Gray Line's cruise on the mv Ptarmigan for a close-up view of this icy-blue giant. Bring this ad to the Portage Cruise Center and receive $2.00 off each adult ticket. Ample RV parking available.

ADULTS $19.50 / $9.75 children under 12

ALASKON EXPRESS. *Scheduled Motorcoach Service.* From the Marine Highway, at Haines and Skagway, board our motorcoach to Whitehorse, Anchorage or Fairbanks and all the stops in between.

COLUMBIA GLACIER. Alaska's best Columbia Glacier tour. Cruise on our Valdez Special to the face of this magnificent glacier on the Glacier Queen II for only $79 per person.*

For a *free* brochure or to pre-book, call 1-800-544-2206.

Gray Line Offices:

Anchorage	(907) 277-5581
Juneau	(907) 586-3773
Valdez	(907) 835-2357
Ketchikan	(907) 225-5930
Fairbanks	(907) 452-2843
Whitehorse	(403) 668-3225
Skagway	(907) 983-2241
Portage Glacier Cruise Center	(907) 783-2983

GRAY LINE Gray Line of Alaska

*Limited space for roundtrip cruise.
Portage Glacier Cruises operates on National Forest System Lands of the Chugach National Forest and is operated under a special use permit from the U.S.D.A. Forest Service.

---

galleries displaying early Alaskan art through contemporary Alaskan artists, such as Sydney Laurence. The museum also hosts special temporary exhibits. From May 17 to Sept. 6, 1992, the museum will present "Gifts from the Great Land: The Ehtholen Collection," an array of more than 700 Aleut, Eskimo and Athabascan objects collected by a Russian-Alaska governor from 1818 to 1845 and now part of a traveling exhibit from the National Museum of Finland. Of special interest to the younger visitors is "The House That Jack Built," an exhibit of innovative children's furniture in a participatory "crazy house" setting. The museum also has a reference library and archives, a free film series (daily in summer), the Museum Shop, and a cafe in the atrium. Admission is $3 for adults, $2.50 for seniors 65 and older, under 18 free. Open 9 A.M. to 6 P.M. daily. May 15 to Sept. 15; 10 A.M. to 6 P.M. Tuesday through Saturday, and 1-5 P.M. Sunday, in winter (closed Monday and holidays). Phone 343-6173 for recorded information about special shows, or 343-4326 during business hours for more information.

Visit the Oscar Anderson House: The city's first wood-frame house, now on the National Register of Historic Places, has been beautifully restored and is well worth a visit. Located in the north corner of Elderberry Park, at the west end of 5th Avenue. Summer hours are 1-4 P.M. weekdays May 15-31 and Sept. 1-15, and from 10 A.M. to 4 P.M. weekdays and 1-4 P.M. weekends from June 1 to Aug. 31. Also open in mid-December for Hearthside Tours. Adults, $2; children 6 to 12 and seniors, $1. Group tours may be arranged in advance from Sept. 15 to May 15. Phone 274-2336.

Alaska Wild Berry Products invites you to stop by our Anchorage gift shop for delicious wild berry jams, jellies and chocolates. We also offer a unique selection of gifts, souvenirs, mail order gift packs and much more. Located in Dimond Center near Kay-Bee Toys, overlooking the ice rink. (907) 349-5984. See our full-page display ad in Homer, Alaska, in the STERLING HIGHWAY section.
[ADVERTISEMENT]

Arctic Images. Waging war on the tacky tee since 1986. See Alaska's best T-shirt at 2 downtown Anchorage locations. Shop corner 6th and B, summer vending cart at

HeliTourAlaska

adventures for uncommon people

6400 S. Airpark Dr.
Anchorage, AK 99502
(907) 243-1466 or 243-3404

---

302 The MILEPOST® ■ 1992

4th and F. Artistic Alaskan designs, 100 percent cotton beefy tees, reasonable prices, quantity discounts. (907) 279-5293. Summer hours 9 A.M. to 10 P.M. [ADVERTISEMENT]

Tour Elmendorf AFB. Free bus tours of the base are offered every Wednesday from June 1 to Aug. 30. Contact the Public Affairs office in advance by phoning (907) 552-5755. Groups of 10 or more persons call ahead for special arrangements. Elmendorf has a base population of approximately 7,000 military personnel.

Alaska Wilderness Gourmet. Family owned and operated manufacturer of jams, jellies, sauces, syrups and vinegars. Gourmet food products made on-site from wild Alaskan berries. Taste our samples. Tour our facility. Gift packs, custom packing, and mail-order available. (907) 563-1997. 219 E. International Airport Road, Suite 101, Anchorage, AK 99518. [ADVERTISEMENT]

Laura Wright Alaskan Parkys. Known worldwide for beautiful Eskimo-style summer and winter parkas. Off the rack or custom made. Started by Laura Wright in Fairbanks in 1947 and continuing the tradition is granddaughter Sheila. Purchase "wearable Alaskan art" for the whole family at 343 W. 5th Ave., Anchorage, AK 99501. Phone (907) 274-4215. Bank cards welcome. Mail and phone orders accepted. We airmail everywhere. [ADVERTISEMENT]

Exercise Your Imagination: Visit the Imaginarium, 725 W. 5th Ave., a hands-on science discovery center offering unique insights into the wonders of nature, science and technology. Open daily year-round. Adults, $4; seniors, $3; children 2 to 12, $2. Phone 276-3179.

Take in an Art Exhibit: The gallery at the Visual Arts Center of Alaska, 713 W. 5th

Mountain View Car Wash, Inc.

3433 Commercial Drive

(907) 279-4819

▶ Glenn Highway westbound, turn right at Bragaw, then turn left 3 blocks on Mt. View Drive

OPEN 24 HOURS

- Large Stalls for Trucks & R.V.s
- High Pressure
- R.V. DUMP STATION (newly added)
- Vacuums
- Rug & Upholstery Shampooer
- Foam-n-Brush
- Hot Wax
- Tire Cleaner
- Engine Degreaser
- Tar Remover
- Fragrance Centers (5 scents)
- Power Dryer
- Two Bill Changers Available
- FULL-TIME ATTENDANT

COIN-OPERATED

TAHETA
Arts and Cultural Group

Eskimo, Indian & Aleut
Non-Profit Coop

Authentic Native Handicrafts

See Artists at Work

Custom Orders

(907) 272-5829

Located across from the museum

605 A Street, Anchorage, Alaska 99501

4th Avenue

Coming this summer to Anchorage's
Historic Fourth Avenue Theatre:

The Best of Alaska

Starring:

Alaska's scenic splendor on the theatre's full size movie screen

A wide assortment of gifts and Alaskan craft items

Great meals and snacks from our 4th Avenue Cafe

Souvenirs, Cafe, Free Alaskan Movies, Sightseeing Info

Located on Fourth Avenue between F and G Streets

Downtown Anchorage (907) 279-3557

ANCHORAGE

We Have a Better Way to See Alaska!

5% Discount With Ad

- Largest Fleet Selection
- Cars, Vans, Trailers, Boats
- Completely Self-Contained
- Free Airport Transportation

Call Now! 1-800-421-7456

ABC MOTORHOME RENTAL
(907) 279-2000
2360-M Commercial Drive • Anchorage, Alaska 99501

Arctic Poppy Bed & Breakfast

307 E. 15th Terrace
Anchorage, Alaska 99501
Telephone: (907) 258-7795

Private Bathrooms
Close to Downtown
Open Year Round
Children Welcome
R.V. Parking

STATE OF THE ART WHEEL LIFTS

24 HR. TOWING

MOTORHOME HAULING STATEWIDE

AUTO & TRUCK HAULING

LICENSED • BONDED INSURED

USED & REBUILT AUTO PARTS
276-6417

ATW — **ALASKA TOWING and WRECKING**

MasterCard   VISA

(907) 272-2438
401 CHIPPERFIELD DRIVE
ANCHORAGE, ALASKA 99501

— SERVING ALASKANS FOR OVER 30 YEARS —

Ave., exhibits contemporary works of local and national artists. Open year-round, Tuesday through Saturday, noon til 6 P.M.; Sunday noon to 5 P.M., $2 admission. Phone 274-9641.

Stephan Fine Arts. Visit Alaska through its arts at 5 locations of Stephan Fine Arts in Anchorage. Alaskan to international art. Paintings, prints, sculpture, ivory and Native arts along with gifts unique to Alaska. 600 W. 6th Ave., Captain Cook Hotel lobby, Hilton Hotel lobby, Fifth Avenue Mall, and 4007 Old Seward Highway. Phone (907) 278-9555. Open 7 days. Toll free 800-544-0779.
[ADVERTISEMENT]

Taheta Arts and Cultural Group, at 6th and A Street in Anchorage, where Alaskan Native artists can be seen and met in person, while working on crafts. Open 9:30 A.M. to 6:30 P.M. Monday-Saturday, noon to 6 P.M. Sunday. Off-season, 10 A.M. to 6 P.M., closed Sunday. Phone (907) 272-5829. (Eskimo, Indian and Aleut nonprofit co-op.) Observe and purchase: ivory, stone, wood and bone carvings; grass, birch-bark and baleen baskets; slippers, moccasins and mukluks; bead, porcupine quill, silver, ivory, mastadon, and baleen jewelry; Eskimo yo-yo's, dance fans, parkas, kuspuks, masks, etchings, drawings and prints. Special orders accepted.
[ADVERTISEMENT]

Tour a Campus: Two colleges are located in Anchorage: the University of Alaska-Anchorage, at 3211 Providence Dr. and Alaska Pacific (formerly Alaska Methodist) University at 4101 University Dr.

Special for Seniors: Every Friday night the Anchorage Senior Center at 1300 E. 19th Ave., hosts a big band dance. On Sunday the center holds a senior drop-in from 11 A.M. to 3 P.M. All seniors are welcome to come for games and refreshments. Lunch is served from 11 A.M. to 2 P.M. weekdays with a daily special offered for $4. Call 258-7823 for more information.

Go to the Zoo: The Alaska Zoo is located on 25 acres of wooded land and displays more than 50 species of Alaskan wildlife, including glacier bears, polar bears, brown and black bears, reindeer, moose, Dall sheep, otters, wolves, foxes, musk-oxen and marmots. Be sure to stop in at the gift shop, located on your right as you enter. The zoo is open 9 A.M. to 6 P.M. daily from May 1 to Oct. 1; 10 A.M. to 5 P.M. the remainder of the year (closed Tuesday from Oct. 1 to May 1). Drive south from the downtown area on the Seward Highway to **Milepost S 120.8.** Take O'Malley exit, turn left on O'Malley Road and proceed 2 miles/3.2 km to the zoo, which will be on your left. Admission $5 for adults, $4 for seniors, $3 students 13 to 18, and $2 for children 3 to 12. Free admission for children under 3. Phone 346-3242 for details.

See Alaskan Wildlife: Fort Richardson Alaskan Fish and Wildlife Center, located in Bldg. 600 on Fort Richardson Military Reservation, has a display of approximately 250 mounts and trophies of Alaskan sport fish, birds and mammals. Open year-round, free admission. Phone 384-0431 for hours.

Elmendorf Air Force Base Wildlife Museum is open weekdays year-round from noon to 5 P.M. Displays include more than 200 native Alaskan species from big game to small birds and fish. Enter the base from the intersection of Boniface Parkway and the Glenn Highway. Ask guards for directions to Bldg. 4-803. Phone 552-2282 for details.

See an Old Schoolhouse: The Pioneer

Schoolhouse at 3rd Avenue and Eagle Street is a 2-story memorial to the late Ben Crawford, Anchorage banker. It was the first school in Anchorage.

Visit the Library, City Hall, Federal Building, Post Office: If you need to do some local research or talk to a city official or mail a postcard, the city hall offices are in the Hill Building at 6th Avenue and G Street, the large Z.J. Loussac Public Library is located at 36th Avenue and Denali Street. The Federal Building, located at 7th Avenue and C Street, is one of the largest and most modern office buildings in Anchorage. The lobby features a multimedia collection of artwork, and the cafeteria is open to the public. In downtown Anchorage, the U.S. Post Office is located on the lower level of the Post Office Mall on 4th Avenue. The main post office, located near the airport, offers all services, 24 hours a day. Smaller postal stations are located throughout the city.

Visit the Port of Anchorage: The Anchorage waterfront, with its huge cargo cranes offloading supplies from container ships, makes an interesting stop, especially in winter when ice floes drift eerily past the dock on the fast-moving tide. Visitors may watch activity on the dock from a viewing platform on the 3rd floor of the port office building. To get there, drive north from the downtown area on A Street, take the Port off-ramp and follow Ocean Dock Road to the office; about 1.5 miles/2.4 km from downtown.

A good viewpoint of the port for downtown walkers is at the northeast corner of 3rd Avenue and Christensen Road.

Heritage Library Museum, in the National Bank of Alaska, Northern Lights Boulevard and C Street, has an excellent collection of historical artifacts, Native tools, costumes and weapons and a research library. Free admission. Open weekdays noon to 5 P.M. between Memorial Day and Labor Day, noon to 4 P.M. at other times of the year.

Charter a Plane: Dozens of air taxi operators are based in Anchorage. Fixed-wheel (skis in winter) or floatplanes may be chartered for flightseeing trips to attractions such as Mount McKinley and Prince William Sound, for fly-in hunting and fishing, or just for transportation. Scheduled flightseeing trips by helicopter are also available.

Watch Small Planes: Drive out to Merrill Field, Lake Hood or Lake Spenard for an afternoon of plane watching. On a busy weekend, hundreds of small planes take off and land at Merrill Field, and Lakes Hood and Spenard are crowded with floatplanes in summer.

Alaska Aviation Heritage Museum, located on the south shore of Lake Hood at 4721 Aircraft Dr., preserves the colorful history of Alaska's pioneer bush pilots. Included are rare historical films of Alaska's pioneer aviators as well as an extensive photo exhibit of pioneer pilot memorabilia.

A floatplane prepares for takeoff at Lake Hood. (Bruce M. Herman)

The museum features a rare collection of Alaskan bush planes. Open year-round, phone 248-5325. Admission fee charged.

Era Helicopters. Experience a panoramic view of the Anchorage Bowl area and the unspoiled wilderness and wildlife of the Chugach Mountains. Soar through the picturesque mountains, valleys and glaciers, minutes away from Alaska's largest city. 1- and 2-hour tours. Phone (907) 266-8351 or outside Alaska 800-843-1947. Tours available

ALASKA SPRING 563-3802

SINCE 1965

TOLL FREE 800-478-3802
FAX # 561-6888

600 W. 48th Ave.
Anchorage
Alaska
99503

"More Than Repairs...We Solve Problems"

COMPLETE SPRING SERVICE CUSTOM FABRICATION

- ★ LEAF SPRINGS
- ★ COIL SPRINGS
- FOREIGN & DOMESTIC
- ★ OVERLOAD KITS
- ★ OVERLOAD KITS FOR CAMPERS & RV'S

- ★ SHOCKS & MacPHERSON STRUTS
- ★ CUSTOM U-BOLTS
- ★ LIFT KITS
- ★ CUSTOM RE-ARCHING
- ★ WALKING BEAMS REBUSHED

TRUCK & TRAILER
SUSPENSION, PARTS & SERVICE
- HENDRICKSON
- HUTCH
- RAYCO
- MACK
- WHITE
- PETERBILT

WHEEL ALIGNMENT • COMPLETE FRONT END REPAIR
• 4 W.D. SERVICE • COMPLETE BRAKE SERVICE

Member: Spring Service Association & Chamber Of Commerce
mor/ryde Rubber Suspension Systems

Qiviut Handknits

QIVIUT

FOR THE DISCERNING VISITOR

The finest and warmest of the rare wools, from the domestic Arctic Musk Ox. Take home exquisite garments hand-knitted in traditional patterns by Alaskan villagers.

Visit the Musk Ox Farm in Palmer
June 1 — September 15

Brochure available. See or order from:
OOMINGMAK,
MUSK OX PRODUCERS CO-OP
604 H Street — Dept MP
Anchorage, Alaska 99501
Phone (907) 272-9225

ANCHORAGE

YOUR ONE-STOP RV SHOP

- RV SUPPLIES
- RENTALS
- SALES
  - PACE ARROW
  - PROWLER
  - JAMBOREE
  - FLAIR
  - Coleman FOLDING TRAILERS

Outside Alaska 1-800-888-4313

Complete RV service, most makes and models. Dump Station.

(907) 279-9234
Tookalook Sales
322 Concrete Street, Anchorage, AK 99501

NEW HOPE BAPTIST CHURCH

SUNDAY
Morning Worship .... 10:30 a.m.
Evening Worship .... 6:30 a.m.
Sunday School .... 9:00 a.m.
Bus Service Available

WEDNESDAY Prayer Meeting .... 7:30 p.m.

(907) 272-9315
333 North Price St., Anchorage

---

in Juneau, Mount McKinley and Valdez.
[ADVERTISEMENT]

Columbia Glacier Cruises. Join Gray Line for Alaska's best Columbia Glacier tour. Cruise on the *Glacier Queen II* to the face of Columbia Glacier, then tour the Matanuska Valley, Palmer, Valdez and the Chugach Mountains. 2 days, 1 night for as low as $189 per person. Tours depart daily from Anchorage. Call (907) 277-5581. [ADVERTISEMENT]

Take in an Alaska Film: Alaska films can be seen at the Anchorage Museum of History and Art, 121 W. 7th, at 3 P.M., 7 days a week during summer. Alaska Experience Theatre, located at 6th and G Street, offers *Alaska the Great Land*, a 70mm film presented on a 180-degree domed screen, and a film on the 1964 earthquake. Admission fee charged; open year-round. Call 276-3730 for recorded information.

Watch the Tide Come In: With frequent tidal ranges of 30 feet/9m within 6 hours, and some approaching 40 feet/12m, one of Anchorage's best nature shows is the rise and fall of the tides in both the Knik and Turnagain arms of upper Cook Inlet. Among the better vantage points along Knik Arm are Earthquake Park, Elderberry Park (at the west end of 5th Avenue), Resolution Park (near the corner of 3rd Avenue and L Street) and the Anchorage small-boat harbor.

A good overlook for the tides in Turnagain Arm is Bird Creek state campground south of Anchorage at **Milepost S 101.2** on the Seward Highway. With good timing you just might see a tidal bore, an interesting phenomenon you probably won't see elsewhere. A bore tide is a foaming wall of tidal water, up to 6 feet/2m in height, formed by

---

26 GLACIER CRUISE *In One Day!*

CRUISE PRINCE WILLIAM SOUND

Most people won't see even one glacier in a lifetime - we'll show you the world's most breathtaking glaciers in just one glorious day! Daily cruise from mid-May through mid–September. Transportation to Whittier available.

- Majestic Glacier–filled fjords
- Luxurious cruising
- Narrated 110-mile voyage
- Awesome wildlife
- Complimentary hot meal
- Saloon & snack bar
- Professional, friendly crew

$119.00 plus tax
Cruise only from Whittier

Phillips'
26 GLACIER CRUISE

(907) 276-8023
1-(800)-544-0529

509 West 4th Avenue
Anchorage, Alaska 99501

---

306 The MILEPOST® ■ 1992

a flood tide surging into a constricted inlet, such as Knik and Turnagain arms.

CAUTION: In many places the mud flats of Turnagain and Knik arms are like quicksand. Don't go wading!

Play Golf: The municipality of Anchorage maintains 2 golf courses: Anchorage Golf Course, 3561 O'Malley Road, is an all-grass, 18-hole course which opened in 1987. The course is open from mid-May through mid-September; phone 522-3363 for more information. The 9-hole course at Russian Jack Springs, Debarr Road and Boniface Parkway, features artificial turf greens and is open from mid-May through mid-September. Phone 333-8338 or 343-4474 for details. Two military courses are open to civilians. Elmendorf Golf Course, an 18-hole, par 72 course, is located on Elmendorf Air Force Base, near the Post Road gate. Open mid-May through September. Call 552-2773 for tee times; rentals available. Fort Richardson's 18-hole Moose Run Golf Course is the oldest golf course in Alaska. The course is accessible from Arctic Valley Road (Milepost A 6.1 Glenn Highway) and is open May through September. Rentals available. Call 428-0056 for tee times.

Play Tennis: The municipality of Anchorage maintains 54 tennis courts throughout the city. In addition, private clubs offer year-round indoor courts.

Picnic at a Park. Anchorage has several parks for picnicking. Chester Creek Green Belt, which stretches from Westchester Lagoon to Goose Lake, has a number of public parks along it and a paved bike trail (also popular with joggers) runs the length of the greenbelt. The greenbelt is accessible

Alaska State Parks

Alaska's state parks offer the best of the Great Land!
132 parks, 3 million acres, 2,000 camp sites, visitor centers, rental cabins, mountains, glaciers, wildlife, fishing, camping, hiking, and more. For information, and to order an annual pass for unlimited camping in state campgrounds ($60 Alaska residents, $75 non-residents) write: Alaska State Parks, P.O. Box 107001, Anchorage, AK 99510. Phone 907-762-2617. (Photo: Eagle River Visitor Center, Chugach State Park)

Old Anchorage Salmon Bake
Mention this ad for FREE Gold Panning
4 to 10 p.m. Daily
3rd & K Streets   279-8790

CASTLETON'S
CUSTOM FILM PROCESSING
Ph: 274-3017 SAME DAY SERVICE
Ph: 274-4368 ON EKTACHROME SLIDES
3340 Mt. View Drive, Anchorage, AK 99501

Why wait to have your film developed?

PHOTO EXPRESS Image Centers

7 Locations to serve you.

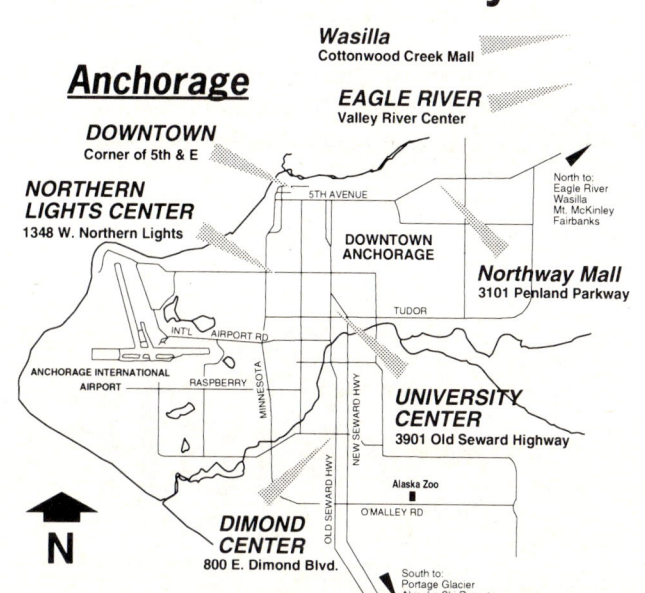

Anchorage
- DOWNTOWN — Corner of 5th & E
- NORTHERN LIGHTS CENTER — 1348 W. Northern Lights
- Northway Mall — 3101 Penland Parkway
- UNIVERSITY CENTER — 3901 Old Seward Highway
- DIMOND CENTER — 800 E. Dimond Blvd.

Wasilla — Cottonwood Creek Mall
EAGLE RIVER — Valley River Center

At PhotoExpress, our professionals will develop your film as quickly and as inexpensively as back home.

Make sure your photos turn out!

For many, a trip to Alaska is a once in a lifetime adventure.

Don't wait until you get home to find out that your precious memories didn't turn out. Have them developed while you are still here. Our prices are comparable to those charged in your home town, and we can have your photos professionally developed in as little as one hour.

Get an additional set of Prints FREE!

As our way of welcoming you to Alaska, bring this ad and your film for developing into any PhotoExpress and receive a second set of prints free!

Get a set for friends & family.

Not good with any other discount.
Limit 3 rolls. One coupn per customer.

PHOTO EXPRESS Image Centers

from several streets; Spenard Road leads to Westchester Lagoon and E Street to Valley of the Moon Park.

Elderberry Park, at the foot of 5th Avenue, overlooks Knik Arm. Nearby Resolution Park, at 3rd Avenue and L Street, where a statue of Capt. James Cook stands, has terraced decks overlooking Knik Arm. The Capt. James Cook statue was dedicated in 1976 as a Bicentennial project.

Tour Anchorage by Bicycle: The municipality has about 120 miles of paved bike trails (including trails in Eagle River and Girdwood) paralleling many major traffic arteries and also passing through some of the city's most beautiful greenbelt areas. Offering an especially unique experience is the 11-mile/17.7-km Coastal Trail from Elderberry Park around Point Woronzof to Point Campbell and Kincaid Park. Bicyclists, joggers and walkers are afforded close-up views of Knik Arm (watch for beluga whales) and on clear days a beautiful view of the Alaska Range.

Downtown Bicycle Rental. Convenient downtown bicycle base at corner of 6th and B. Daily rental rates of $10 to $14 depending on number of speeds. Open 9 A.M. to 10 P.M. during the long days of summer. 4-hour rental $10. Call (907) 279-5293 with questions or to receive flyer. [ADVERTISEMENT]

Watch Birds: There are some surprisingly good bird-watching spots within the city limits. Lakes Hood and Spenard, for instance, are teeming with seaplanes but also, during the summer, are nesting areas for grebes and arctic loons. Also seen are wigeons, arctic terns, mew gulls, green-winged teals, spotted and least sandpipers.

Another great spot is Potter Point State Game Refuge, known locally as Potter Marsh, south of downtown on the Seward Highway at **Milepost S 117.4**. Early July evenings are best, according to local bird watchers. Forests surrounding Anchorage also are good for warblers, juncos, robins, white-crowned sparrows, varied thrushes and other species.

The Park for All People in the Chester Creek Green Belt on W. 19th Avenue near Spenard Road has a nature trail through a

---

Ride 'n Shine Car Wash
AUTO SERVICE CENTER

ALASKA'S MOTORHOME SERVICE PROFESSIONALS!

- Lube, Oil, Filter Change
- Exterior Hand Washing by Appointment

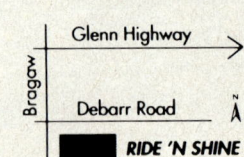

(907) 338-3932
1341 S. Bragaw, Anchorage

ALASKA FUR GALLERY

Alaska's Largest Fur Manufacturer
Wholesale to the public
Master Furriers since 1935
Visit our factory and receive a free souvenir

4 LOCATIONS THROUGHOUT ALASKA TO SERVE YOU

ANCHORAGE
428 W. 4th
(907) 274-3877

SITKA
108 Lincoln St.

JUNEAU
175 S. Franklin St.   289 Marine Way
(907) 463-5588   Juneau, AK 99801

Complete Arrangements to, from & within Alaska!
GROUP OR INDIVIDUAL

Contact Us for Your Alaskan Adventure

ALL WAYS TRAVEL INC

BACKPACKING • BALLOONING • FISHING • RIVER EXPEDITIONS
WILDERNESS TREKS • ARCTIC ADVENTURES

302 G STREET, DEPT. MP, (one block west of the Hilton) ANCHORAGE, AK 99501
(907) 276-3644 or FAX (907) 258-2211

One Stop Shopping in Anchorage

Located in the center of Anchorage, the Mall at Sears offers you a complete variety of one-of-a-kind and national retail stores, including Sears! Of special interest to visitors, we offer film processing, dining and snacks, parcel service, beauty and barber shops, groceries, and even an extended hour pharmacy.

Special Visitors Offer

Check the Mall Directory and present this ad to the store listed to receive a Mall at Sears Gift Bag filled with over $10 worth of discounts and free merchandise!

The Mall at Sears

On the corner of Northern Lights and Seward Highway

bird nesting area.

For a prerecorded message of local bird sightings and field trips, call the Anchorage Audubon Society's hot line at 248-2473.

Go Backpacking: Wilderness experiences are available for all visitors with or without their own equipment. Several guide services specialize in hiking, mountaineering, ski touring and backpacking. A list of guides is found in the free *Anchorage Visitors Guide,* available at the Log Cabin Visitor Information Center.

Backcountry travel information for visitors planning to backpack on their own is available from the Alaska Public Lands Information Center in the old Federal Bldg., at 605 W. 4th Ave., phone 271-2737.

Summer Solstice. Alaskans celebrate the longest day of the year with a variety of special events. In Anchorage, there's the annual Mayor's Midnight Sun Marathon, a 26-mile, 385-yard run through the city. This event is usually scheduled on the Saturday nearest summer solstice (June 20 or 21).

See a Baseball Game: Some fine semi-pro baseball is played in Anchorage. Every summer some of the nation's top college players play for the Anchorage Glacier Pilots and Anchorage Bucs, the Peninsula Oilers, the Mat-su Miners and the Fairbanks Goldpanners. Anchorage games are played at Mulcahy Ball Park, Cordova and E. 16th Avenue. Check local newspapers for schedules.

Watch a Salmon: King, coho, pink and a few chum salmon swim up Ship Creek and can be seen jumping a spillway in the dam just east of Ocean Dock Road. Watch for kings from early June until mid-July, and for

---

ALASKA AVIATION HERITAGE MUSEUM
located at
The Lake Hood Seaplane Base
4721 Aircraft Drive
(Lake Hood Exit off Int'l Airport Rd.)
VISIT THE ALASKAN AVIATION GIFT SHOP

- 15 Historical Alaskan Bush Planes and Military Aircraft on Display.
- Oldtime Alaskan Theatre w/15 Titles Shown Continuous Daily
- Exhibit Galleries Depicting Pioneer, Commercial & Military Air History in Alaska-Hundreds of Photos, Memorabilia & Scale Models

ADMISSION $5.00 • 1/2 PRICE FOR CHILDREN UNDER 12
DISCOUNT COUPONS AVAILABLE AT VISITOR CENTER
Guided Tours Available
Open 7 Days a Week, 9 am - 6 pm Summer Months
(907) 248-5325
"Presenting the History of Alaskan Aviation"

Gifts & Souvenirs
Dimond Center

Our unique store is located above the Ice Skating Rink *next to Kay-Bee-Toys*. We have Alaska's finest selection of souvenirs, jams, jellies, candies and mail order gifts.
Call (907) 349-5984.

Also visit our factory & Gift shop in Homer, Alaska. *(see display ad in Homer section).* Tour Groups are welcome.
Call (907) 235-8858.

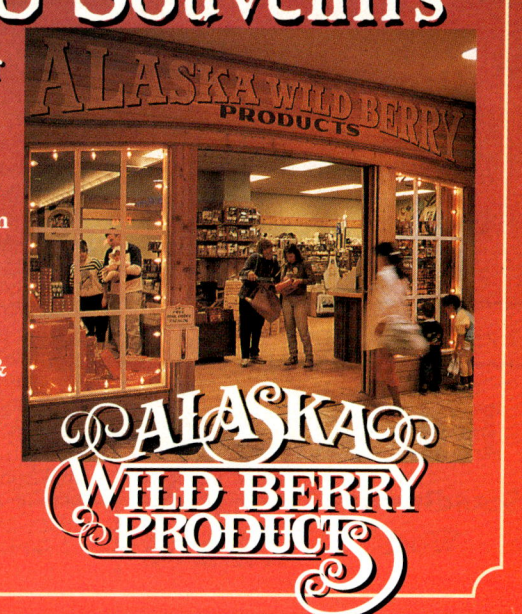

ALASKA WILD BERRY PRODUCTS

R.V. • MOTOR HOME TRAILER REPAIRS

WE DO WARRANTY WORK FOR
- Dometic
- Duo-therm
- Coleman
- Atwood
- Norcold
- Mor-Flo • Elixir
- Mansfield
- Suburban
- Instamatic
- Monogram
- Hydro Flame
- Wedgewood
- Shurflo's

MOTORHOME RENTALS
4440 View Circle
Anchorage, AK 99507
(907) 561-1645

B.T. Service & Supply
Monday - Friday 8-5

WE REPAIR AND INSTALL
- Ranges
- Ovens
- Water Heaters
- Furnaces
- Trailer Wiring
- Electric 12V & 110V
- Brake Service & Repair
- Sheet Metal
- Refrigerators

AMERICAN EXPRESS • VISA • MasterCard

WE MAIL ORDER PARTS

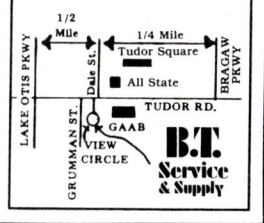

---

* Come see us for all your photo needs!
* Largest full service camera store in Alaska
* Dealers for Ricoh, Nikon, Minolta, Kodak, Pentax, Canon, Olympus
* Fuji professional film stock house
* Full on-site repair facilities
* Olympus Pro-Tech Center

The Camera People

ALASKA CAMERA EXCHANGE AND REPAIR

OLYMPIC CENTER, 701 W. 36th, Suite A-7   (907) 562-7801   (800) 478-2725

Why Pay More?
New & Used Cars & Vans
- Low Rates – Daily – Weekly or Monthly
- Cash Deposits Welcome
- Airport Pick-up

ALLSTAR Rent-A-Car
Toll-Free 1-800-426-5243

FAIRBANKS
(907) 479-4229 • 1-800-478-4229
4415 Airport Way
Fairbanks, Alaska 99709

ANCHORAGE
(907) 561-0350 • 1-800-437-3303
512 W. International Airport Way
Anchorage, Alaska 99518

Fast Courteous Service   **Major Credit Cards Accepted**

OK Bed & Breakfast

Near Airport
Quiet Neighborhood
Fresh Baked Goods
Fresh Ground Coffee

Call For Reservations
2003 West 46th Avenue
Anchorage, AK 99517-3160
243-1914

Pia's Scandinavian Wool

Sweaters, caps, socks, mittens for Alaskan outdoors . . . from Norway and New Zealand

**Factory Outlet Sales
Always Discount Prices
Open Every Day**

Downtown Anchorage
Corner of 4th & E St.

345 E Street   Anchorage, Alaska 99501
(907) 277-7964

BREWSTER'S DEPARTMENT STORE
Anchorage Alaska

Your 'One Stop' Clothing/Footwear Store

MasterCard   VISA

Raingear Boots
Socks   Gloves

Levi's   Carhartts
Shirts   Rubber Boots

Hats   Woolrich
Pendleton Walls

Warm Clothing for your Alaskan visit at **20% DISCOUNT** if you mention this ad or... take advantage of our Senior Citizen Discounts

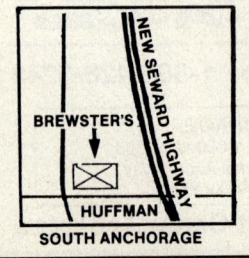

- Brewster's Coupons
- Gift Certificates
- Alterations
- Free Gift Wrap Table provided for your convenience
- Bush Orders Welcome
- Layaway plan 20% down with monthly payments
- Senior Citizen Rate

1320 Huffman Park Drive
Anchorage, AK 99515
(907) 345-4598
800-478-4598

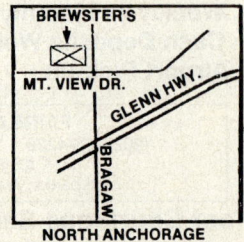

3825 Mt. View Drive
Anchorage, AK 99508
(907) 279-0533
800-478-0533

---

other species from mid-August until September. A fine wooden viewing platform has been built to make salmon watching easy.

Kayaking, Canoeing, Rafting: All are available in or near Anchorage. Guided tours from 1 to 14 days run on several rivers within 100 miles/160 km of Anchorage, including the Chulitna, Susitna, Little Susitna, Matanuska and Kenai rivers and Glacier and Portage creeks. Information on guided raft and canoe trips is available through travel agencies, local sporting goods stores and in the free *Visitors Guide* available from the Log Cabin Visitor Information Center.

Several flying services provide unguided float trips. The service flies customers to a remote river, then picks them up at a predetermined time and place downriver.

Several streams in the area make excellent canoeing and kayaking paths. Information on the Swanson River and Swan Lake canoe trails on the Kenai Peninsula is available from the Kenai National Wildlife Refuge Manager, P.O. Box 2139, Soldotna, AK 99669-2139; phone 262-7021.

Sailing in the Anchorage area is limited to freshwater lakes and lagoons (usually ice free by May). A popular sailing area in the city is Jewel Lake *(CAUTION: low-flying aircraft).*

Big Lake, 52 miles/84 km north of Anchorage on the George Parks Highway, is also a popular spot for small sailboats.

Motorboating: Big Lake and Lake Lucille along the George Parks Highway offer motorboating. Several rivers, including the Susitna, offer riverboating, but the shallowness and shifting bottoms of most of Alaska's rivers mean a jet-equipped, flat-bottom boat is almost required.

Cruises on larger boats are available from Whittier into Prince William Sound, and from Homer Spit into Kachemak Bay and Cook Inlet. Venturing into those areas in small boats without a guide who has local knowledge of the area can be dangerous.

Cook Inlet waters around Anchorage are only for the experienced because of powerful bore tides, unpredictable weather, dangerous mud flats and icy, silty waters. Turnagain Arm is strictly off-limits for any boats and Knik Arm and most of the north end of Cook Inlet is the domain of large ships and experienced skiff and dory operators.

Swimming: Anchorage Parks and Recreation can answer questions about aquatics, phone 343-4474.

Goose Lake is open daily, June through Labor Day, from 9:30 A.M. to 5:30 P.M.; lifeguards, bathhouse and picnic area. Located 3 miles/4.8 km east from downtown Anchorage on UAA Drive.

Jewel Lake, 6.5 miles/10.4 km from downtown Anchorage on W. 88th off Jewel Lake Road, is open daily June through Labor Day, from 9:30 A.M. to 5:30 P.M.; lifeguards, restrooms and covered picnic area.

Spenard Lake is open daily, June through Labor Day, from 9:30 A.M. to 5:30 P.M.; lifeguards, restrooms, picnic area. Located 3 miles/4.8 km from downtown Anchorage on Spenard Road, then west on Wisconsin to Lakeshore Drive.

CAUTION: Do not even consider swimming in Cook Inlet! Soft mud and swift tides—not to mention the muddy, icy water—make this extremely dangerous!

The YMCA, 5353 Lake Otis Parkway, offers discounts to outside members with YMCA identification. Call 563-3211 for pool schedule and information on other facilities.

The following pools are also open to the public: Service High School Pool, 5577 Abbott Road, phone 346-3040; Bartlett High School Pool, 2525 Muldoon Road, phone

THE 'EXTRAS' AREN'T EXTRA

With your deluxe late model Winnebago Motorhome rental, you get **F R E E**: housekeeping and linen package, insurance coverage, airport pickup...and when you return the motorhome **WE** do the cleaning! Travel the elegant route with GREAT ALASKAN HOLIDAYS.

Great Alaskan Holidays

Located at Anchorage International Airport

Our unequaled service starts with this **FREE** number. Call now for information.

800/642-6462

3901 W. International Airport Rd., Anchorage, AK 99502
907/248-7777

337-6375; West High School Pool, 1700 Hillcrest Dr., phone 274-5161; East High School Pool, 4025 E. 24th Ave., phone 278-9761; Dimond High School Pool, 2909 W. 88th Ave., phone 249-0355; Chugiak High School Pool, Birchwood Loop Road, off the Glenn Highway north of Anchorage, phone 696-2010; and University of Alaska Pool, Providence Drive, phone 786-1233.

Charter Boats: Visitors must drive south to the Kenai Peninsula for charter boats. Sightseeing and fishing charters are available at Whittier, Seward and Homer.

Fishing: The Alaska Dept. of Fish and Game annually stocks about 30 lakes in the Anchorage area with rainbow trout, landlocked chinook (king) salmon, grayling and arctic char. Nearly 135,000 6- to 8-inch rainbow trout are released each year along with about 50,000 salmon. All lakes, except those on Elmendorf Air Force Base, are open to the public. In addition, salmon-viewing areas and limited salmon fishing are available in the immediate Anchorage area. For specific information, check the Alaska fishing regulations book, call the agency at 267-2218, or phone 349-4687 for a recorded message.

Within a day's drive of Anchorage are several excellent fishing spots. The Kenai Peninsula offers streams where king, red, silver, pink and chum salmon may be caught during the season. Dolly Varden and steelhead also run in peninsula streams. Several lakes contain trout and landlocked salmon. Saltwater fishing for halibut, rockfish and several species of salmon is excellent in season at many spots along the peninsula and out of Whittier, Homer and Seward. For specific fishing spots both north and south of Anchorage see the Seward, Sterling, Glenn and George Parks highways sections. Because of the importance of fishing to Alaska both commercially and for sport, regulations are strictly enforced. Regulations are updated yearly by the state, often after *The MILEPOST®* deadline, so it is wise to obtain a current regulations book.

MOBILE TRAILER SUPPLY, INC.

Complete
PARTS & ACCESSORIES
for ALL makes & models
of MOTOR HOMES,
TRAVEL TRAILERS
& CAMPERS

Free Dump Station · RV Storage

3150 MT. VIEW DRIVE
Ph: (907) 277-1811 · 277-1818

ALASKAN ADVENTURES RV Rentals

See Alaska at your Leisure!

- Deluxe 22'-31' Motorhomes
- Housekeeping Packages Available
- Fishing Packages Available
- Free Airport and Hotel Pickup
- Boat Rentals

Early Reservations Recommended

ALASKAN ADVENTURES RV RENTALS
6924 Foothill Dr.-MP Anchorage, AK 99504

(907) 333-7997
1-800-676-8911

ALASKA WILDERNESS TRAVEL

LET US BRING YOU TO ALASKA AND PLAN YOUR TRIP
Fly-out Fishing Packages • Denali-Columbia Glacier Tours • Dog Sleds and Ski Treks

(907) 277-7671 • FAX (907) 277-4197 • U.S. Toll-Free 1-800-544-2236
— Lower Airfares with Packages — 715 W. Fireweed, Suite E, Anchorage, AK 99503

SOMETHING FOR EVERYONE

★ Racquetball ★ Aerobics ★
★ Weightroom ★ Dance ★ Ceramics ★
★ Badminton ★ Martial Arts ★ *Room Rentals* ★
Kitchen Facilities & *MUCH MUCH MORE!!*

We invite you to visit your 3 Community Recreation Centers or call to see which center offers the program for you.

- *Fairview Community Rec. Ctr.*
  1121 E. 10th Ave., 279-7555
- *Mt View Community Rec. Ctr.*
  315 Price St., 274-8851
- *Spenard Community Rec. Ctr.*
  2020 W. 48th, 248-5868

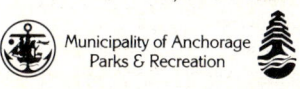

Municipality of Anchorage
Parks & Recreation

Flying Fish?

▶ You bet! **10th & M Seafoods** will ship your seafood or theirs air freight almost anywhere. Overnight **FED-EX** service is available door-to-door to most U.S. cities.

▶ If you're traveling, 10th & M Seafoods offers special packaging for hand-carrying your seafood purchase.

▶ 10th & M Seafoods, Alaska's premiere retail seafood store, carries an excellent selection of the finest fresh or frozen seafood from Alaska and from around the world.

▶ Custom game and fish processing and fish smoking available.

Major credit cards accepted.

Seafood Gift Packs
- King Crab
- Salmon
- Halibut
- Shrimp
- Canned Salmon
- Lox
- Squaw Candy
- Kippered Salmon
- Scallops

272-FISH

Original Location:
1020 M St., Anchorage, AK 99501
Hours: 8-6 Mon.-Fri.,
9-6 Sat. Closed Sun. (907) **272-3474**

Branch Store:
301 Muldoon Rd., Anchorage, AK 99504
Hours: 11-7 Tues.-Sat.
12-6 Sun. Closed Mon. (907) **337-8831**

10th and M Seafoods
Serving Alaskans since 1943

1992 ■ The MILEPOST® 311

ANCHORAGE

OPEN 24 HOURS

MAPCO Express
for people on the go

— GASOLINE
— GROCERIES
— CONVENIENCE ITEMS

ANCHORAGE [map]

Traveler's checks welcome

Cash or credit same low price

Mastercard — Visa
American Express
Discover

MAPCO Express

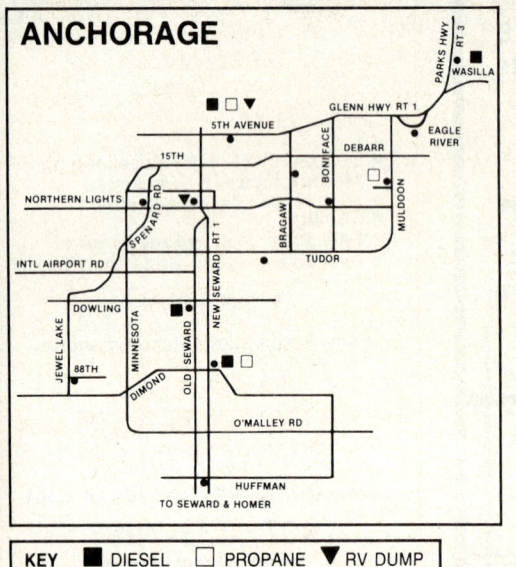

KEY: ■ DIESEL □ PROPANE ▼ RV DUMP

WINTERTIME ATTRACTIONS

Alyeska Resort and Ski Area: Mount Alyeska, about 40 miles/65 km southeast of downtown Anchorage via the Seward Highway, is Alaska's major ski resort, with snow from mid-November to the end of April. Snow-making equipment will guarantee snow at the base of the mountain throughout the season. Ski facilities include 1 high-speed detachable bubble quad and 4 chair lifts, a poma lift and 2 rope tows. The resort area, which includes a lodge, rental condominiums, restaurants, ski school and rental shop, is located near sea level, but the upper ski slopes are above timberline. Two lighted chair lifts extend to the mountaintop skyride restaurant with views of Turnagain Arm. In ski season, shuttle bus service is available between Anchorage and the resort. For information, phone 783-2222.

Alpenglow at Arctic Valley: East of downtown Anchorage in the Chugach Mountains, Arctic Valley ski area has a 4,500-foot/1,372-m double chair lift, a 2,200-foot/671-m double chair lift, and a 2,800-foot/873-m T-bar platter lift combination. Three 700-foot/213-m rope tows are situated on gentle slopes for beginners. A day lodge with soup and sandwich bar is located nearby. Cross-country skiing is available, but trails are not maintained. The ski area operates weekends and holidays only mid-November to the end of April. Drive northeast from downtown on the Glenn Highway. Just beyond Ship Creek, turn right on Arctic Valley Road and follow the main road 7.5 miles/12 km to the ski area. For more information, phone 428-1208.

Chugach State Park: Although the entire

HEGEDUS & SONS INC

- FOREIGN CAR SPECIALIST
- TUNE-UPS
- FRONT END ALIGNMENT
- TRANSMISSIONS
- BRAKES
- BATTERIES

MasterCard VISA DISCOVER American Express Firestone

90 Days Same As Cash. Instant Credit.

Firestone TIRES

COMPLETE AUTO REPAIR & TIRE CENTER

[map: A ST. / CORDOVA / Firestone / NORTHERN LIGHTS / SEWARD HWY. / SEARS MALL]

274-6602

301 E. NORTHERN LIGHTS BLVD.
ACROSS FROM SEARS MALL

- MOTORHOME-TRAVEL TRAILER SPECIALIST
- COMPLETE SERVICE
- ALIGNMENTS
- LUBE, OIL, FILTER
- TIRES / BRAKES
- SHOCKS / STRUTS

park is open to cross-country skiers, most maintained ski trails are found in the Hillside Trail System/Campbell Creek area, accessible via Upper Huffman Road and Upper O'Malley Road. Skiers are encouraged to use established trails as most of Chugach State Park is prime avalanche country.

Four major areas in the park are open to snowmobiling when snow levels are deep enough: Eklutna Valley, reached from the Glenn Highway via Eklutna Road; Eagle River valley, also accessible from the Glenn Highway; Bird Creek, **Milepost S 101.2** Seward Highway; and portions of the Hillside/Campbell Creek area, accessible from Upper Huffman Road.

Ski trail maps and snowmobiling information are available at the trailheads or from the park office, phone 345-5014. Chugach State Park offers winter programs, held on weekends, which include winter survival, winter camping, avalanche awareness, safety and how to select proper outdoor gear. To find out the current programs, call 694-6391 for a recorded message.

Ski Touring: Popular unmaintained trails include Beach Lake Park, Campbell Creek Green Belt, Earthquake Park, Edmonds Lake Park, Muldoon Park, O'Malley Park, Alaska Pacific University, University of Alaska and backcountry areas of Chugach National Forest and Chugach State Park.

Russian Jack Springs: Located at DeBarr Road and Boniface Parkway. This ski area has a chalet, a ski rope tow and almost 6.8 miles/11 km of cross-country ski trails, 3 miles/5 km of which are lighted. The ski area is maintained by the Municipality of Anchorage.

Far North Bicentennial Park (Campbell Creek Resource Land): Best access to this 5,000-acre tract in the eastern portion of the Anchorage bowl is via Tudor Road or Abbott Road. Cross-country skiing is allowed anywhere in the area except on dogsled trails. For further information, contact the Municipality of Anchorage, Division of Parks and Recreation, P.O. Box 196650, Anchorage 99519; phone 343-4474.

Centennial Park: 3.1 miles/5 km of wooded cross-country ski trails over some hilly terrain. Maintained by the Municipality of Anchorage and located near Glenn Highway and Muldoon Road.

Chester Creek Green Belt: Located in the heart of Anchorage, the municipality maintains more than 6.2 miles/10 km of cross-country ski trails.

Hillside Park: The Municipality of Anchorage maintains more than 5 miles/8 km of cross-country ski trails located just off Abbott Road; 1.6 miles/2.5 km are lighted trails.

Kincaid Park: 15 miles/24 km of cross-country ski trails are marked and maintained for novice, intermediate and expert skiers by the municipality. There are 1.6 miles/2.5 km of lighted trails and a warm-up chalet. Access is from the west end of Raspberry Road.

Turnagain Pass: On the Seward Highway, about 59 miles/95 km south of downtown Anchorage. Turnagain Pass (elev. 988 feet/301m) is a popular winter recreation area in the Chugach National Forest. The west side of the pass is open to snowmobiling as soon as snow cover permits; the east side is reserved for skiers. Snow depths in this pass often exceed 12 feet/4m.

State game refuge south of city offers good bird watching. (Alissa Crandall)

A Unique & Very Special Place to Visit

KODIAK FURS
425 D Street Anchorage, AK 99501
(907) 279-3644

Furs • Ivory • Soapstone • Bone Carvings • Native Arts
Artifacts • Hats • Mukluks • Mittens • Parkas • Coats
And Much More

STOP IN AND SEE ALASKA NATIVE ARTIST AT WORK!
LEARN ABOUT SOAPSTONE & IVORY CARVING!
SEE HOW FURS ARE MADE!

We can custom make almost anything! Individual Art Pieces Commissioned!

Items to fit any price range & taste. Alaskan Arts & Crafts for gifts or "one of a kind" pieces for the discriminating collector.

Volunteers in Parks

Alaska State Parks

Opportunities include:
- Campground hosts
- Ranger assistants
- Information services
- Trail crews
- Historic park guides
- College internships

Volunteer season: May ~ September, with a minimum 4-week commitment

For more information please contact:
Volunteer Coordinator
Alaska State Parks
P.O. Box 107001
Anchorage, AK 99510-7001
(907) 762-2655

ANCHORAGE IS NOT OLD BY TRADITIONAL STANDARDS, BUT ITS HISTORY IS RICH AND VARIED. Once called Ship Creek Landing, Anchorage was founded as a railroad town. Learn more about Anchorage's history by taking a tour guided by our enthusiastic and knowledgable guides.

Oscar Anderson House — 420 "M" Street
Built in 1915, by Oscar Anderson who reportedly was the 18th person to set foot in "Tent City". Open Monday - Friday 10 a.m. - 4 p.m., Saturday and Sunday 1 p.m. - 4 p.m.

Guided Walking Tours
Visit a number of historic properties in downtown Anchorage. Tour takes approximately 1 1/2 hours of easy walking. Tours are given Monday, Wednesday and Friday at 1 p.m., beginning at Old City Hall, 524 W. 4th Avenue.

For more information call (907) 274-3600

ANCHORAGE HISTORIC PROPERTIES INCORPORATED

ANCHORAGE

Dog Mushing begins in December. Dog mushing organizations in the Montana Creek area, Knik, Chugiak, Palmer and Anchorage sponsor races every weekend. Anchorage races usually begin in January at the Tudor Track and continue through the end of February. In addition, some of the clubs offer instruction in the sport. Several of the races are considered preliminaries to the World Championship races held during the Anchorage Fur Rendezvous.

The annual Iditarod Trail Sled Dog Race, 1,049 miles/1688.2 km to Nome, takes place in March. The race begins on 4th Avenue in downtown Anchorage and mushers on the trail can be seen along the Glenn Highway, in the Knik Bridge area about 30 miles/48.2 km north of Anchorage and at Knik on the west side of Knik Arm.

To find a race, watch local newspapers for times, dates and places.

Anchorage Fur Rendezvous: Major event of the winter season is the Anchorage Fur Rendezvous. Billed as the "Mardi Gras of the North," this elaborate winter festival, held in February, attracts thousands of celebrants annually.

The week-long celebration dates from 1936 when it began primarily as a fur auction where trappers could bring their pelts to town and make a few extra dollars selling them to buyers from around the world. Trappers still bring their pelts to town, and the fur auction, held downtown, still attracts many buyers.

Alaskans shake off cabin fever during "Rondy" (the local term for the Fur Rendezvous). There are arts and crafts exhibits, a parade, the Miners' and Trappers' Ball, a blanket toss, a carnival and pet shows. Past Rondy competitions have been unique: a beard-growing contest, a waiter and waitress race, an ice and snow sculpturing contest and a home-brew competition, to name a few.

During the first weekend of the Fur Rendezvous, the Annual World Championship Dog Weight Pulling Contest attracts several thousand spectators at Mulcahy Park, located at E. 16th and Cordova streets.

The highlight of the Fur Rendezvous, however, is dog mushing. The World Championship Sled Dog Race, held during the last 3 days, attracts dozens of mushers from Alaska, Canada and the Lower 48. Thousands of spectators line the 25-mile/40-km race course, which begins and ends on 4th Avenue in downtown Anchorage. *(CAUTION: Leave pets and flashbulbs home, as they'll distract the dog teams.)* The musher with the best total elapsed time in 3 heats over 3 days is declared the winner. The women's and junior world championship sled dog races are held at Tudor Track the first weekend of Fur Rendezvous. For more

HAVE YOU READ ALASKA'S B&B GAZETTE

RECEIVE YOUR FREE COPY CONTAINING LOCATIONS, AMENITIES, PRICES, ALASKA FACTS, MILEAGES AND MAP ACCOMMODATIONS IN ALASKA
A B&B REFERRAL SERVICE OPERATED BY PIONEER ALASKANS TRADITIONAL "HOMESTAYS" IN 20 FRIENDLY COMMUNITIES
P.O. BOX 110624
ANCHORAGE, AK 99511-0624
(907) 345-4761 PHONE AND FAX

Richard's Bunka Art
Embroidery Lessons • Alaska or Japanese Scenes
"Do it yourself"
Country Flowers — Silk Flower Kits and Supplies
6242 W. Dimond Blvd.
Anchorage, AK 99502 • (907) 561-1246

SOURDOUGH CAMPER RENTALS

To get the feel and flavor of this mighty land, flying is not enough! In the comfort of our motorhomes, experiencing Alaska firsthand can be a once in a lifetime thrill! Our self-contained motorhomes range from 20' Class C units to 30' Class A units. Housekeeping packages and convenience items available.

Free airport transportation also available.

FREE BROCHURE
SOURDOUGH Camper Rentals
P.O. Box 92440, Anchorage, AK 99509
(907) 563-3268
FAX (907) 563-8817 • Telex: 25-147

ALASKA FUR EXCHANGE

Not just furs, but a truly Alaskan store!

The state's largest selection of genuine Native-made arts and crafts.

S.E. Corner Old Seward Hwy & Tudor Rd. Anchorage

(907) 563-3877

R.V. ELECTRIC
We'll Fix You In A Day Or Camp You For A Night

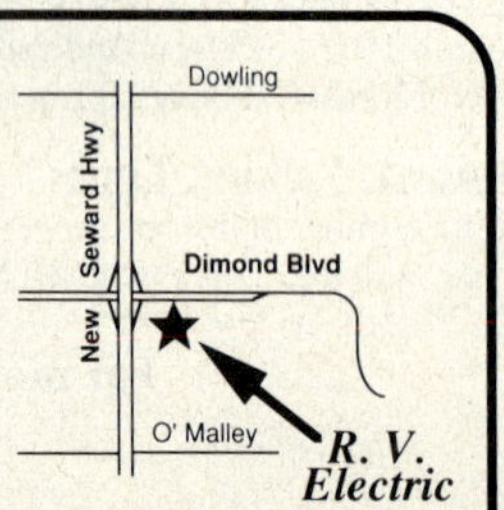

MOTORHOMES
TRAVEL TRAILERS & CAMPERS

NORCOLD
DOMETIC
DUO-THERM
COLEMAN
ATWOOD
SUBURBAN
HYDRO FLAME

SERVICE
PARTS
ACCESSORIES

REFRIGERATORS
FURNACES
WATER HEATERS
CONVERTERS
ALTERNATORS
PLUMBING
HOLDING TANKS
TRAILER BRAKES
GENERATORS

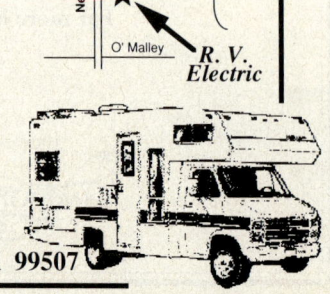

PH. (907) 349-1808
1418 E. DIMOND BLVD. ANCHORAGE, AK 99507

TUDOR COIN-LAUNDRY & DRY CLEANING

2494 E. Tudor Road
(Across from The Pines)
(907) 561-7406
Open 7 Days, 9 a.m. – 9 p.m.

- Drop Laundry Service
- Professional Dry Cleaning
- Alterations & Repairs
- 36 Washers – 21 Dryers
- Free Parking – Plenty of RV Parking
- Free Coffee
- Attendant on Duty
- Movie Rentals

---

314 The MILEPOST® ■ 1992

information, phone 277-8615.

Ice-skating: 3 municipal facilities, Ben Boeke Ice Arena (334 E. 16th Ave., phone 274-2767), Dempsey-Anderson Ice Arena (1741 W. Northern Lights, phone 277-7571) and Firelake Recreation Center (13701 Old Glenn Highway in Eagle River, phone 696-0051) offer a total of 4 indoor rinks for spectator as well as participatory uses. The University of Alaska also has 1 indoor rink. Outdoor ice-skating areas include Cheney Lake, DeLong Lake, Delaney Community Center, Goose Lake, Jewel Lake Park, Mountain View Community Center, Spenard Lake, Tikishla Park and Westchester Lagoon. In addition, about 40 Anchorage schools maintain outdoor hockey rinks.

Sledding: Popular sledding hills are at Centennial Park, Nunaka Valley Park, Sitka Street Park, Service High School and Alaska Pacific University.

Snowshoeing: Muldoon Park, Far North Bicentennial Park and Campbell Creek Green Belt are used for snowshoeing, as are backcountry areas of Chugach National Forest and Chugach State Park.

Winter Basketball. Anchorage hosts 2 major collegiate basketball events. The Great Alaska Shoot-Out, held every Thanksgiving weekend, features 8 major college basketball teams in this well-known invitational tournament. The Northern Lights Invitational showcases women's collegiate basketball with 8 teams in a 3-day playoff the last weekend in February.

Ice Fishing: Countless lakes in the Anchorage and the Matanuska-Susitna Valley areas offer excellent ice fishing. Ice fishing is especially good in the early winter in Southcentral. Some Anchorage lakes are stocked each year with silver salmon or rainbow trout. Among them: **Jewel Lake, Little Campbell Lake** in Kincaid Park, **Beach Lake, Cheney Lake** and the lake on C Street in the Taku/Campbell Park. For more information contact the Alaska Dept. of Fish and Game at 344-0541; for a recorded message on fishing and ice conditions, phone 349-4687.

WHEELS

8" to 24.5"

Axle Assemblies
Axels, Brakes, Hubs, Bearings,
Fenders, Electrical Connectors,
Couplers, Overload Springs.

Tire & Tube Patches
Tire Chains and much, much more

VISA - MasterCard

Six Robblees' Inc.

3000 Commercial Drive, **Anchorage**
(907) 276-5171

201 E. Dimond, **Anchorage**
(907) 344-7497

3060 S. Cushman, **Fairbanks**
(907) 452-6160

Travel Alaska in Comfort

* Prices To Fit Every Budget
* Deluxe Late Model Units
* Fully Equipped
* Year Round Rentals
* Custom Travel Plans
* Off Season Rates
* Special Discounts
* Airport Pickup

"Dreams Do Come True"
MURPHY'S RV
SALES & RENTALS
800-582-5123
FAX (907) 258-4510

PO Box 202063 MP, Anchorage, AK 99520

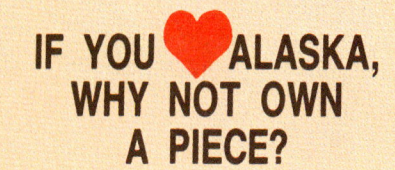

IF YOU ♥ ALASKA, WHY NOT OWN A PIECE?

ASSOCIATED BROKERS INC.

Lou Campbell and Eric Dyrud, or one of their real estate professionals, can assist you or your firm in becoming a part of Alaska.

640 W. 36th Ave. Ste. #1
Anchorage, AK
99503-5807

(907) 563-3333
FAX 562-3808

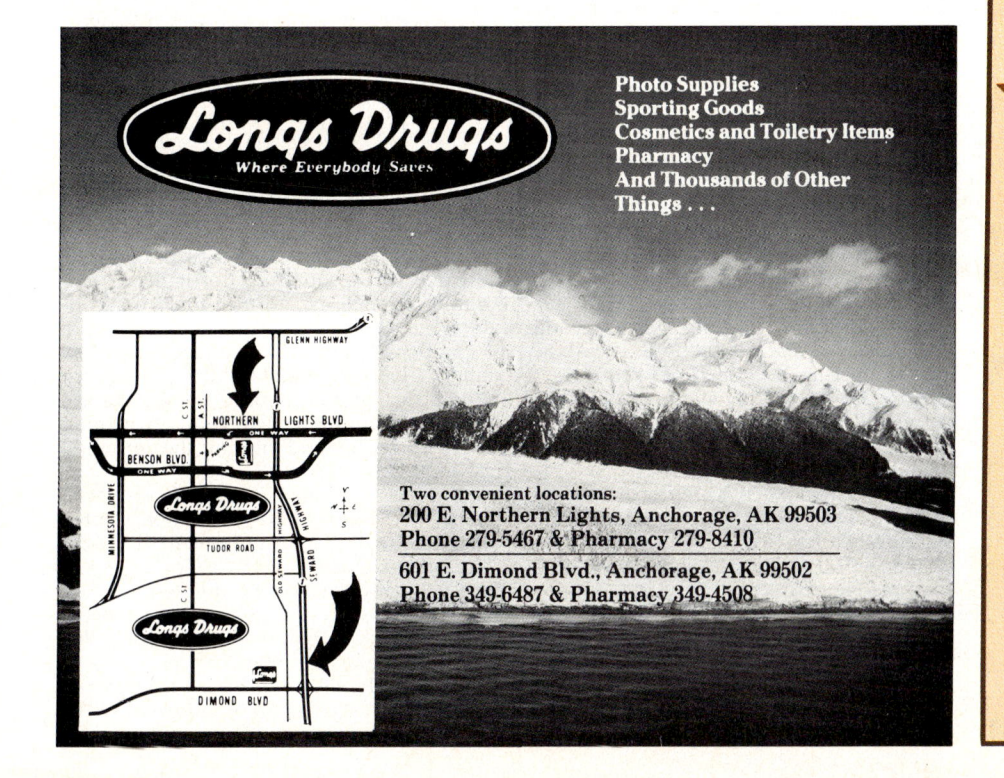

Longs Drugs
Where Everybody Saves

Photo Supplies
Sporting Goods
Cosmetics and Toiletry Items
Pharmacy
And Thousands of Other Things...

Two convenient locations:
200 E. Northern Lights, Anchorage, AK 99503
Phone 279-5467 & Pharmacy 279-8410

601 E. Dimond Blvd., Anchorage, AK 99502
Phone 349-6487 & Pharmacy 349-4508

GEORGE PARKS HIGHWAY

Anchorage to Fairbanks, Alaska
Alaska Route 3
(See maps, pages 317–318)

The George Parks Highway provides access to Denali National Park. (Jerrianne Lowther)

The George Parks Highway connects Anchorage and Fairbanks, Alaska's largest population centers. The route, called the Anchorage–Fairbanks Highway after its completion in 1971, was renamed in July 1975, in honor of George A. Parks (1883–1984), the territorial governor from 1925 to 1933.

The highway runs 358 miles/576.1 km through some of the grandest and most rugged land that Alaska has to offer. The road is a modern paved highway, maintained year-round. The highway is mostly in good condition with some pavement breaks and frost heaves. Watch for road construction at the Chulitna River bridge (**Milepost A 132.8**) and resurfacing between **Mileposts A 215.7** and **231.3** in 1992.

Motorists who plan to drive the highway during the winter (roughly from Oct. 1 to June 1) should check highway conditions before proceeding. Severe winter storms and extremely low temperatures can create hazardous driving conditions. Contact the Alaska Dept. of Transportation or the Alaska State Troopers in Anchorage or Fairbanks.

Some facilities along the highway north of the Talkeetna turnoff (**Milepost A 98.7**) and south of Nenana (**Milepost A 304.5**) are open in summer only.

From approximately **Milepost A 70** north of Anchorage there are many places where Mount McKinley—also called Denali—(elev. 20,320 feet/6,194m) is visible from the highway, weather permitting.

The George Parks Highway provides the most direct highway access to Denali National Park and Preserve (formerly Mount McKinley National Park) from either Anchorage or Fairbanks. Driving distance to the park entrance is 237.3 miles/381.9 km from Anchorage and 120.7 miles/194.2 km from Fairbanks. See DENALI NATIONAL PARK section for details.

Emergency medical services: Between the Glenn Highway junction and **Milepost A 202.1**, phone 911. Between **Milepost A 174** at Hurricane Gulch bridge and **Milepost A 224** at Carlo Creek bridge, phone the Cantwell ambulance at 768-2982 or the state troopers at 768-2202. Between **Milepost A 224** and Fairbanks, phone 911.

George Parks Highway Log

ALASKA ROUTE 1
Distance from Anchorage (A) is followed by distance from Fairbanks (F).

A 0 F 358 (576.1 km) ANCHORAGE. Follow the Glenn Highway (Alaska Route 1) north 35 miles/56.3 km to junction with the George Parks Highway. (Turn to the end of the GLENN HIGHWAY section and read log back to front from Anchorage to junction with the George Parks Highway.)

ALASKA ROUTE 3
A 35 (56.3 km) **F 323** (519.8 km) Traffic light at **junction** of the George Parks Highway (Alaska Route 3) and the Glenn Highway (Alaska Route 1). Produce stand just north of junction.

Bushes Bunches Stand. See display ad this section.

A 35.4 (57 km) **F 322.6** (519.2 km) Trunk Road. Turn right, northbound, for a guest ranch with riding stables, Mat-Su Community College and the University of Alaska–Fairbanks' Matanuska Research Farm.

The Matanuska Research Farm conducts research in agronomy, horticulture and animal science. No formal tours are conducted.

Mat-Su Community College has a 1.5-mile/2.4-km nature trail featuring the plants, soil and wildlife of Alaska. The well-marked woodchip path has benches and observation decks for resting and viewing the surrounding mountains.

A 35.5 (57.1 km) **F 322.5** (519 km) Welcome Way; access to Mat-Su Visitors Center, operated by the Mat-Su Convention & Visitors Bureau. Open May 15 to Sept. 15, 8 A.M. to 6 P.M. daily. This large center offers a wide variety of displays and information on the Mat-Su Valley; pay phone. Write HC01, Box 6616J21, Palmer, AK 99645; or phone (907) 746-5002. The visitors bureau also operates an Events Line year-round; phone 745-8001 for the current events and attractions.

Bushes Bunches Stand
Specializing in Alaska Grown Produce
The largest selection of fruits and vegetables in the State
• Also Smoked Salmon
Alaskan Made Ice Cream • Bedding Plants

Stop in and see our famous Giant Cabbages and tour our Gardens and Greenhouse

Hours 10 a.m. – 8p.m. – 7 Days A Week

Mile 35 Parks Highway – Junction of Parks & Glenn Highway

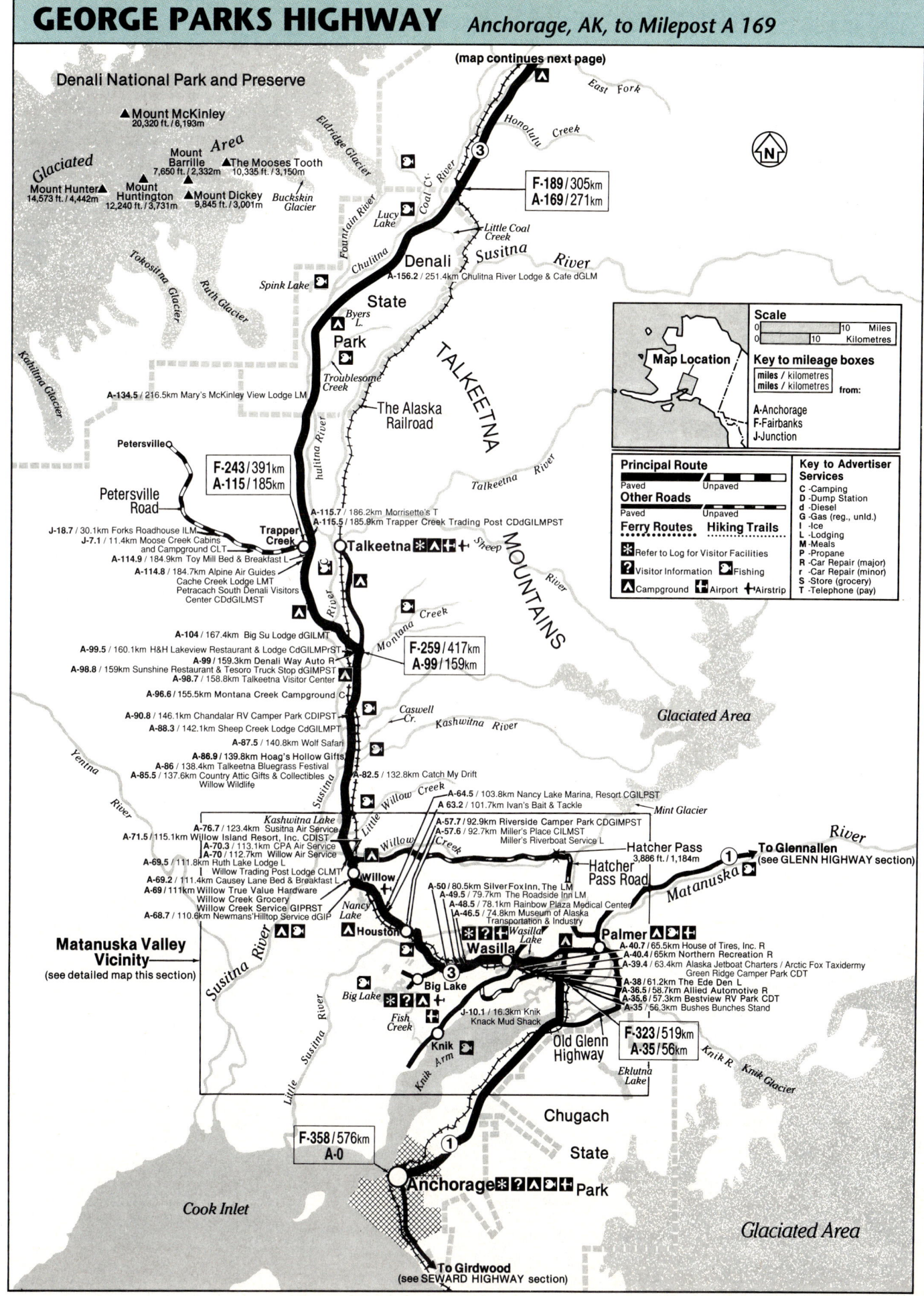

GEORGE PARKS HIGHWAY — Anchorage, AK, to Milepost A 169

GEORGE PARKS HIGHWAY *Milepost A 169 to Fairbanks, AK*

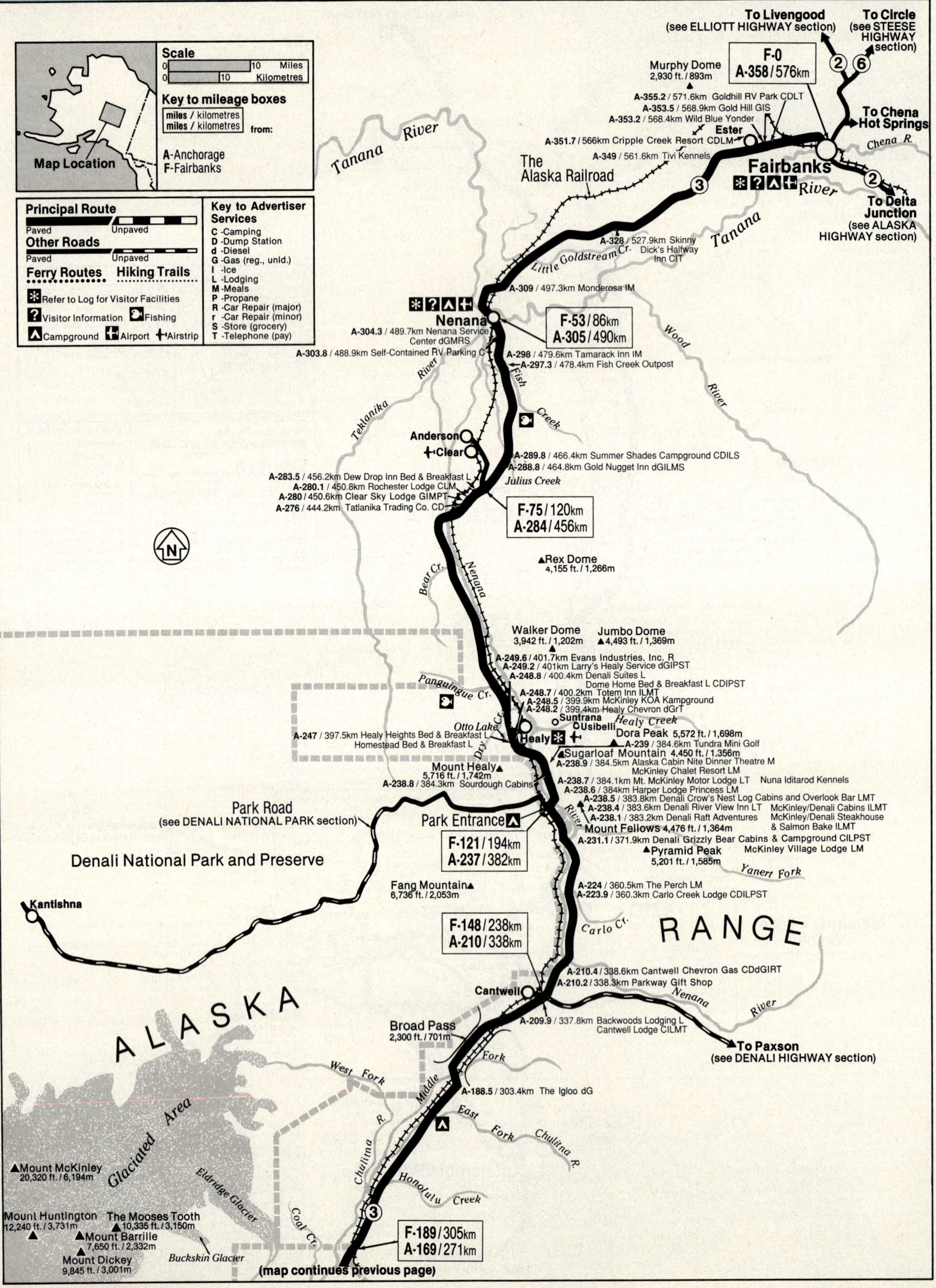

A 35.6 (57.3 km) F 322.4 (518.8 km) **Best View RV Park.** See display ad this section. ▲

A 36.2 (58.3 km) F 321.8 (517.9 km) Highway narrows to 2 lanes northbound.

A 36.5 (58.7 km) F 321.5 (517.4 km) **Allied Automotive.** See display ad this section.

A 37.4 (60.2 km) F 320.6 (515.9 km) Updraft Road; road to airstrip.

A 37.8 (60.8 km) F 320.2 (515.3 km) Hyer Road. Wasilla Creek bridge.

A 38 (61.2 km) F 320 (515 km) Fairview Loop Road to west leads 11 miles/17.7 km to connect with Knik Road. Access to state game refuge.

The Ede Den. See display ad this section.

A 39.4 (63.4 km) F 318.6 (512.7 km) **Alaska Jetboat Charters, Arctic Fox Taxidermy.** Fishing charters, taxidermy shop, Alaska Jetboat Charters (907) 376-4776. Offers guided full day or half-day fishing trips for king salmon May 25 to July 14. Silver, red, pink and chum salmon July 15 to September. Arctic Fox Taxidermy, a full service taxidermy shop, specializes in Alaskan fish and big game mounts. (907) 376-4776. [ADVERTISEMENT]

A 39.4 (63.4 km) F 318.6 (512.7 km) **Green Ridge Camper Park.** Modern—35 complete hookups, showers included in price, washers and dryers, pay phone; 2.5 miles/4 km from Wasilla, close to lakes. Lovely parklike setting, scenic view. Close to Palmer. Carl and Vicky Fritzler welcome you to the beautiful Matanuska Valley. Phone (907) 376-5899. [ADVERTISEMENT] ▲

A 39.4 (63.4 km) F 318.6 (512.7 km) Seward Meridian Road, which junctions with the Palmer–Wasilla Highway (see **Milepost A 41.1**). Shopping center.

A 39.5 (63.6 km) F 318.5 (512.6 km) Wasilla city limits; medical clinic (376-1276). Wasilla shopping, services and attractions are located along the highway (from here north to **Milepost A 45**) and at Main Street in Wasilla city center.

A 40 (64.4 km) F 318 (511.8 km) Veterinary clinic.

A 40.4 (65 km) F 317.6 (511.1 km) **Northern Recreation.** Complete parts, accessories, service and repairs for campers, travel trailers, motorhomes and fifth-wheelers. We stock parts and do repair work on all major appliances, water systems, waste systems and running gear. Open Monday-Friday 8 A.M. to 6 P.M., Saturday 9 A.M. to 5 P.M. Phone (907) 376-8087. [ADVERTISEMENT]

A 40.7 (65.5 km) 317.3 (510.6 km) **House of Tires, Inc.** See display ad this section.

A 40.8 (65.7 km) F 317.2 (510.5 km) Cottonwood Creek bridge.

A 41.1 (66.1 km) F 316.9 (510 km) Junction with Palmer–Wasilla Highway, which leads east 10 miles/16 km to the Glenn Highway at Palmer. It provides access to several businesses, Finger Lake state recreation site and a day-use area with picnic sites and playground.

A 41.7 (67 km) F 316.3 (509 km) Park with picnic shelter, restrooms, playground and swimming beach on Wasilla Lake; limited parking. Monument to George Parks.

A 41.8 (67.3 km) F 316.2 (508.9 km) Crusey Street, access to Bogard Road, Mat–Su Resort (motel and dining on Wasilla Lake) and Finger Lake state recreation site. Turn right (northbound) and drive 3.7 miles/6 km via Crusey Street and Bogard Road to reach Finger Lake. (The recreation site is also accessible from Palmer–Wasilla Highway, or turn east at **Milepost A 42.2** and drive 0.3 mile/0.5 km to intersection of Wasilla–Fishhook and Bogard roads, then follow Bogard Road 4.1 miles/6.6 km to Finger Lake.) Finger Lake has picnic tables, campsites, water, toilets and a boat launch. Also access to Wolf Lake state recreation site, off

The Ede Den — James Ede, Julia Ede
Open Daily
Antiques
Bed & Breakfast
On Davis Road
Box 870365, Wasilla 99687
(907) 376-2162

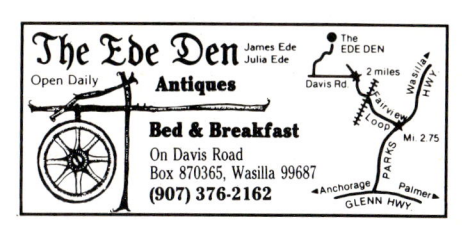

THE HOMESTEAD RV PARK
At the "Crossroads of Alaska"... 1 mile from the Visitors Center
1/4 mile east of Parks and Glenn Highway Junction • Commuting distance to Anchorage
WATER & ELECTRIC HOOKUPS • DUMP STATION • SHOWERS • LAUNDRY
P.O. Box 354, Palmer, AK 99645 • (907) 745-6005
See our Log Ad, Mile A 36.2 Glenn Highway

ALLIED AUTOMOTIVE
Motorhomes Chassis Repaired and Serviced
We're here to help! All work guaranteed
Same Day Service (in most cases)
CERTIFIED MECHANICS ON DUTY
IMPORT AND DOMESTIC CAR AND LIGHT TRUCK REPAIR
TIRES AND TIRE SERVICE
Hours: Monday-Friday 8-6 • Saturday 9-5
(907) 745-3500
MILE 36.5 PARKS HIGHWAY
1 mile west from Parks/Glenn Jct.
WASILLA

HOUSE OF TIRES, INC. AAA Allstate Motor Club
• Front End Alignments
• Shocks, Brakes, Tune-ups
• Motorhomes & Camper Repairs
• 24-Hour Wrecker Service
GOODYEAR
Complete line of auto, truck, camper & farm tires
Mile 40.5 Parks Hwy. (907) 376-5279

Best View RV Park
LOCATED AT THE GATEWAY TO THE MAT-SU VALLEY
Good Sampark
• Beautiful Log Visitor's Center
• Museum of Alaska Transportation & Industry
• Iditarod Headquarters • Musk Ox Farm
• Mushers Hall of Fame Museum
• Wasilla Museum / Frontier Village
• Scenic Beauty • Excellent Location
• Paved Streets • Common Areas

Park with the Best
Mile 35.6 George Parks Highway
Best View
P.O. Box 872001, Wasilla, AK 99687
(907) 745-7400
1-800-478-6600 (Toll Free in Alaska)

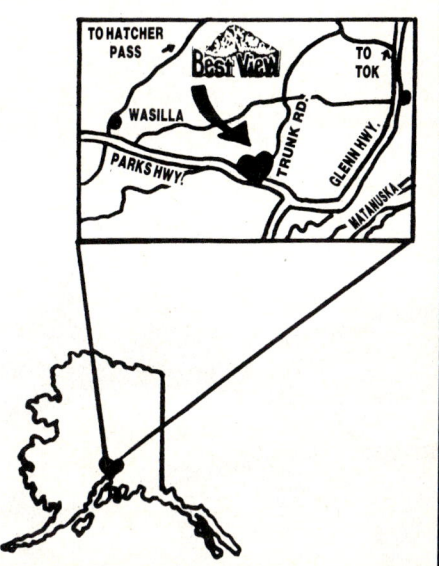

Knik Road Log

Distance is measured from the junction (J) with George Parks Highway.

J 0.1 (.2 km) CAUTION: Road crosses railroad tracks.

J 0.7 (1.1 km) Glenwood Avenue, Senior center.

J 1.5 (2.4 km) Gas station.

J 2.2 (3.5 km) Smith ball fields.

J 2.2 (3.5 km) Iditarod Trail Committee headquarters and visitor center; historical displays, souvenir shop. Open 8 A.M. to 5 P.M., daily in summer, weekdays the rest of the year.

J 2.3 (3.7 km) **Lake Lucille** Mat–Su Borough Park Campground and day-use area 0.6 mile/1 km north via gravel road; 60 campsites, pavilion with covered picnic tables, firepits, parking. Camping fee charged. Fishing for landlocked silver salmon.

J 4.1 (6.6 km) **Junction** with Fairview Loop Road, which joins the Parks Highway at **Milepost A 38**; access to state game refuge. Shopping center with gas and groceries at this junction.

J 7 (11.3 km) Knik fire hall.

J 8 (12.9 km) Settlers Bay, a housing development built around a lodge; golf course and stables.

J 10.1 (16.3 km) Turnoff for Homestead Museum, with a large collection of early Alaskan memorabilia, and gift shop.

Knik Knack Mud Shack. See display ad this section.

J 11.1 (17.9 km) Laurence airport.

J 13.3 (21.4 km) **KNIK** on **Knik Lake.** There is a bar here with a pay phone, also a liquor store, gas station and private campground. Lake fishing for rainbow; inquire at the Knik Bar. Knik is a checkpoint on the Iditarod Trail Sled Dog Race route and is often called the "Dog Mushing Center of the World"; many famous Alaskan dog mushers live in this area.

J 14 (22.5 km) Knik Museum and Sled Dog Mushers Hall of Fame, open noon to 6 P.M. Wednesday through Sunday, from June 1 through Labor Day. The museum is housed in 1 of 2 buildings remaining from old Knik (1898–1919). Regional memorabilia, a Canine Hall of Fame (featuring famous sled dogs), and historical displays on the Iditarod Trail and Alaskan mushers. Admission fee $1 for adults, 50¢ for children. Phone (907) 376-7755 or 376-2005.

Traditional Athabascan graveyard with fenced graves and spirit houses south of Knik Museum.

J 16.1 (25.9 km) **Fish Creek** bridge; parking, fishing for silver salmon.

J 17.2 (27.7 km) Goose Bay Point Road to Little Susitna River public-use facility at state game refuge (12 miles/19.3 km); 83 parking spaces, 65 campsites, boat ramps, dump station, water, tables, toilets. Also access to Point Mackenzie state dairy project.

J 18.5 (29.8 km) Pavement ends at small bar beside road. Road continues into rural area.

**Return to Milepost A 42.2
George Parks Highway**

Knik Knack Mud Shack

Bud & Mary Longenecker & family welcome you to the Knik Knack Mud Shack   **Mile 10 Knik Road**
(2 miles in on Knik Knack Mud Shack Road)

ALASKA'S FINEST NATIVE CLAY
• A gift for every occasion

• Visit the Homestead Museum
One of the most outstanding private museums in Alaska

P.O. Box 87-7550, Wasilla, AK 99687
(907) 376-5793

Bogard Road, which has picnic sites, toilets and hiking trail.

A 42 (67.6 km) F 316 (508.5 km) Art gallery and food market.

A 42.1 (67.8 km) F 315.9 (508.4 km) Boundary Street, gas station.

A 42.2 (67.9 km) F 315.8 (508.2 km) Wasilla's Main Street; visitor center and museum 1 block north; post office 2 blocks north (Zip code 99687). Access to Hatcher Pass and Knik from this intersection. Turn south across railroad tracks for Knik Road (see KNIK ROAD log this page). Turn north on Wasilla's Main Street for downtown Wasilla and Hatcher Pass. Description of Wasilla follows.

Wasilla–Fishhook Road leads northeast about 10 miles/16 km to junction with Hatcher Pass (Fishhook–Willow) Road; turn to the Hatcher Pass side road log in the GLENN HIGHWAY section, page 274, for a description of the road to Hatcher Pass from this junction (J 6.8 in that log). See also the Matanuska Valley Vicinity map this section. Hatcher Pass Road junctions with the George Parks Highway at **Milepost A 71.2**.

Wasilla

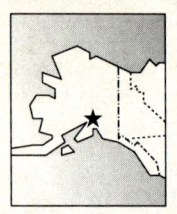

A 42.2 (67.9 km) F 315.8 (508.2 km). Located between Wasilla and Lucille lakes in the Susitna Valley, about an hour's drive from Anchorage. **Population:** 3,666. **Emergency Services: State Police**, phone 745-2131, emergency only phone 911. **Fire Department** and **Ambulance**, phone 376-5320, emergency only phone 911. **Hospital**, in Palmer. **Doctor** on Seward Meridian Road, **Milepost A 39.5**, phone 376-1276, and at West Valley Medical Center, E. Bogard Road, phone 376-5028. Chiropractic clinics on Main Street.

Visitor Information: At the Dorothy G. Page Museum and Historical Park on Main Street just off the George Parks Highway, phone 376-2005. Or contact the chamber of commerce, P.O. Box 871826, Wasilla 99687, phone 376-1299.

ATTEND THE MAT-SU SUMMER SCHOOL

School's in session all summer long, access is easy and the lessons, challenging. With over 3,000 lakes, rivers and streams to choose from, you're bound to make the grade when you fish the Mat-Su Valley.

MATANUSKA-SUSITNA
CONVENTION & VISITORS BUREAU
HC01 Box 6166J21, Palmer, Alaska 99645
(907) 746-5000   Events Line 745-8001

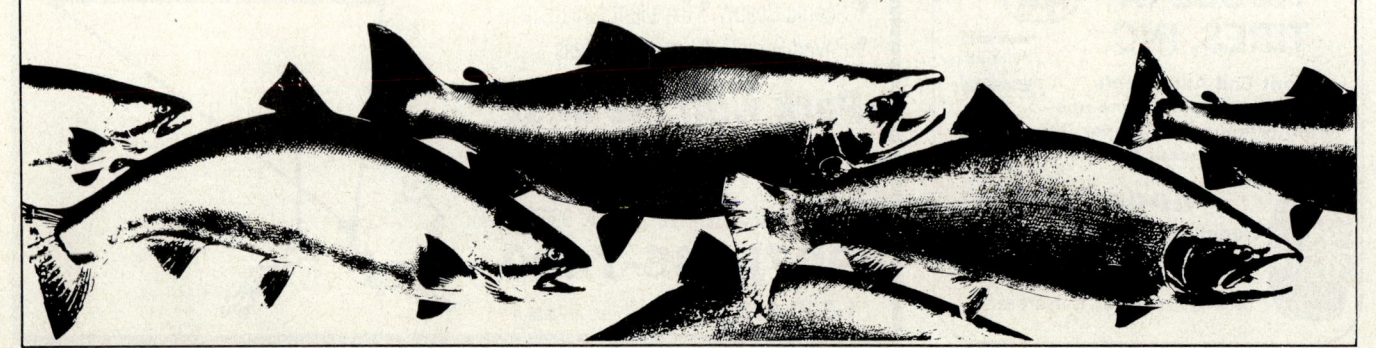

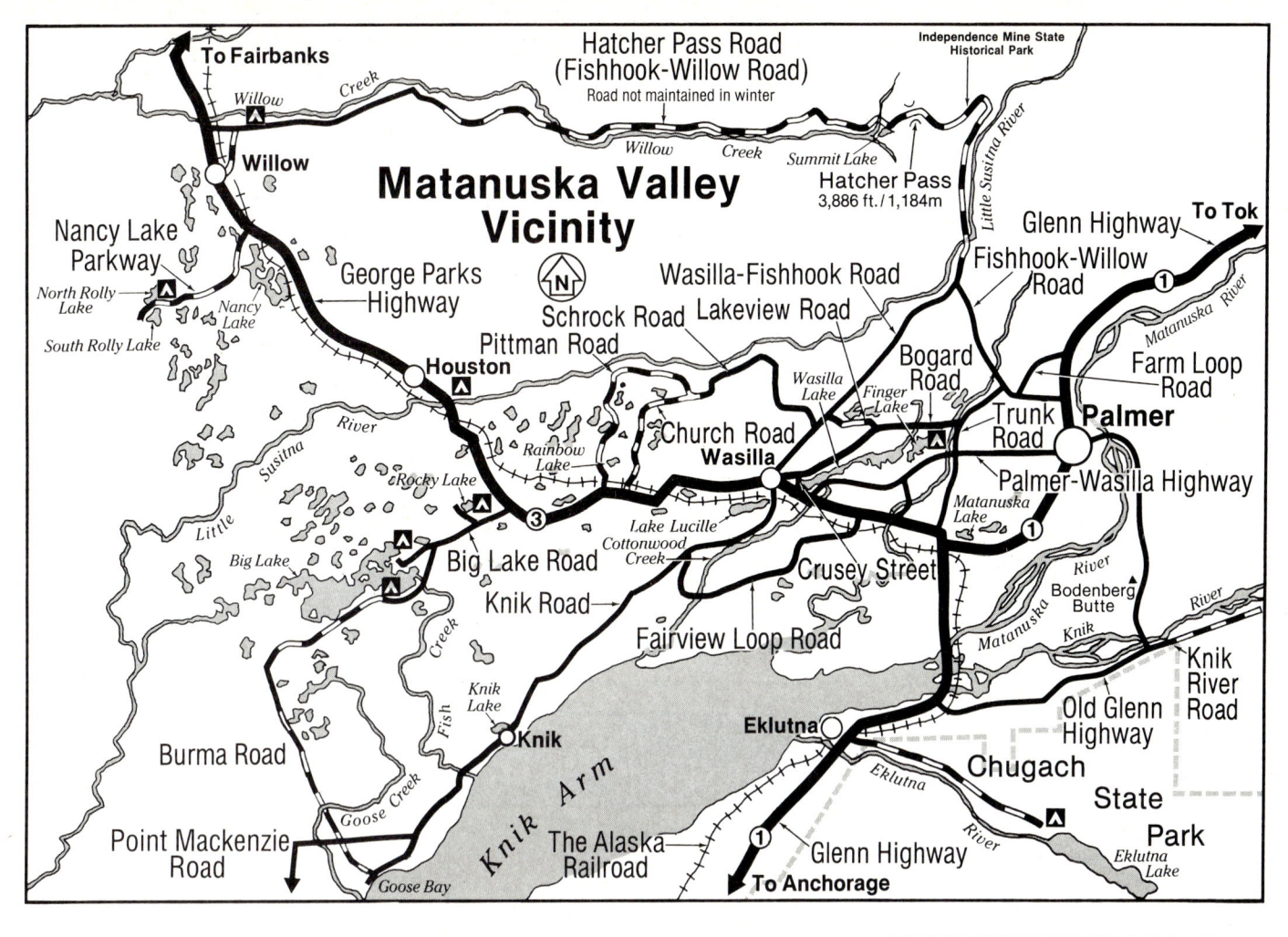

Radio and Television via Anchorage stations; KNBZ-FM 99.7. **Newspaper:** *The Valley Sun* (weekly); *The Frontiersman* (semiweekly). **Transportation: Air**–Charter service available. **Railroad**–Alaska Railroad. **Bus**–Matanuska Valley commuter to Anchorage.

Private Aircraft: Wasilla airstrip, 0.9 mile/1.4 km northwest; elev. 370 feet/113m; length 2,100 feet/640m; gravel; fuel 80, 100. Wasilla Lake seaplane base, 0.9 mile/1.4 km east; elev. 330 feet/100m.

Wasilla is one of the Matanuska–Susitna Valley's pioneer communities. Long before the George Parks Highway was built, local residents and visitors bound for Lake Lucille, Wasilla Lake, Big Lake and Knik, drove over the valley roads from Palmer to the village of Wasilla. Wasilla became a station on the Alaska Railroad about 1916.

Today, Wasilla is the largest community on the George Parks Highway between Anchorage and Fairbanks. Shopping malls and businesses here offer a wide assortment of services.

ACCOMMODATIONS

All visitor facilities are available here, including sporting goods stores, post office, gas stations, tire and RV repair, and other services. Mat–Su Ice Arena, at Bogard Road and Crusey Street, has ice skating, picnic area and fitness court. Swimming and showers are available at Wasilla High School.

Valley Chiropractic Clinic, 24-hour emergency service. Phone (907) 373-2022. Gentle, effective, family health care. Located at 400 N. Main. Turn north at 7-11 on Main Street. Located across from post office. [ADVERTISEMENT]

WASILLA ADVERTISERS

Chimo Guns	Next to Carr's
Country Lakes FlyingService Bed & Breakfast	Ph. (907) 376-5868
Dorothy G. Page Museum and Historical Park	323 Main St.
Family Medicine of Alaska, Inc.	Mile 39.5 Parks Hwy.
Fly-in Hyena Lodge	Ph. (907) 892-8903
Gallery, The	290 N. Yenlo
Glacier Mountain Adventures	Ph. (907) 376-1699
Iditarod Trail Committee, Inc.	Mile 2.2 Knik Rd.
Knik Museum and Sled Dog Musher's Hall of Fame	Mile 14 Knik Rd.
Lakeshore Bed and Breakfast	Ph. (907) 376-1380
Larson Chiropractic	501 N. Main
Matanuska-Susitna Convention & Visitors Bureau	Ph. (907) 746-5002
Mat–Su Resort	Mile 1.3 Bogard Rd.
Northern Recreation	Mile 40.4 Parks Hwy.
Snowbird Inn Bed & Breakfast	Ph. (907) 376-7048
Town Square Art Gallery	Land Co. Bldg.
Valley Chiropractic Clinic	400 N. Main St.
Wash Day Laundry & Dry Cleaners	Behind McDonald's
Wasilla Home Style Laundry	Wasilla Shopping Mall
Wasilla One-Hour Photo	Wasilla Shopping Mall
Windbreak Hotel Cafe and Lounge	Mile 40.5 Parks Hwy.

SNOWBIRD INN
Bed & Breakfast
1½ miles from downtown Wasilla
— Private Country Setting —
Wholesome Breakfasts
(907) 376-7048

KNIK MUSEUM and Sled Dog Mushers' Hall of Fame
MILE 14 KNIK ROAD

• *Turn of the century furniture and household equipment* • *Native artifacts* • *Dog mushing equipment* • *Iditarod Trail Race Memorabilia*

Open June 1-Labor Day • 12 p.m.-6 p.m. Wed.-Sunday
Phone (907) 376-7755 or Wasilla Museum 376-2005

The Wasilla Museum and Historical Park and The Knik Museum and Sled Dog Mushers' Hall of Fame are operated by the Wasilla-Knik-Willow Creek Historical Society.

Larson CHIROPRACTIC

Better Health for the Whole Family

DR. DANIEL W. LARSON
Chiropractic Physician

501 N. Main
Suite 130
Wasilla, Alaska 99687

Clinic: 376-2225
FAX: 376-9225

GEORGE PARKS HIGHWAY • WASILLA

Mat-Su Resort

Lakeside Motel and Cabins
with full Kitchenettes, phones and Cable TV

Fine Continental Cuisine Menu
- Paddleboat and Rowboat Rentals
- Excellent trout fishing year round
- Big Game mounts on display
- Beautiful Alaskan Flowers on display

Directions to Mat-Su Resort:
At McDonalds in Wasilla, turn onto Crusey St.
Turn right onto Bogard Road
Watch for Mat-Su Resort on your right
1.2 mi. up Crusey • .5 mi. from Bogard to Mat-Su

Cruise on the Diamond Willow
Daily lunch cruises
Dinner cruises and parties by reservation

Reservations and information 1-800-376-3229

WASILLA HOME STYLE LAUNDRY
SELF-SERVICE LAUNDRY
- Maytag Washers
  Single & Triple Loaders
- Drop-off Service
- Showers
- Dry Cleaning
- Fully Attended

**Wasilla Shopping Center
Parks Highway**

Country Lakes Flying Service
Bed & Breakfast
- Spectacular seaplane glacier tours!
- Quiet waterfront accommodations

VISA / MasterCard   (907) 376-5868
2651 E. Palmer-Wasilla Hwy., Wasilla, AK 99654

LAKESHORE BED AND BREAKFAST
- Rooms with private bath
- Paddleboat and Canoe available
- On Lake Lucille, 3-1/2 hours from Denali Park

Access from Mile 43.3 Parks Highway
1701 W. Tillicum Ave.
Wasilla, Alaska 99654   (907) 376-1380

Wasilla One Hour Photo

- Photofinishing
- Film ■ Frames
- Low Everyday Prices
- Friendly Service

(907) 376-FILM
Wasilla Shopping Center
469 W. Parks Highway, Wasilla

Kodak ROYAL PAPER

Flowers at Wasilla visitor center flourish during long summer days. (Ruth Fairall)

Glacier Mountain Adventures. Camping, hiking, fishing, backpack on good trails in the habitat of Dall sheep, moose, caribou and bear. Take a mountain bike trip into the backcountry. Winter camping and cross-country skiing. Contact Dick Stoffel at (907) 376-1699. 1352 Pioneer Peak Dr., Wasilla, AK 99687. [ADVERTISEMENT] ▲

See the Alaska you missed! ...Visit The
Dorothy G. Page Museum and Historical Park

Wildlife Diorama • "Flying Dentist's" Office • Eskimo Artifacts
Gold Mining Display • Early Day Household Equipment

ROB STAPLETON

HISTORIC PARK — *Adjacent to The Wasilla Museum*

Herning/Teeland/Mead House	Blacksmith Shop	Walter Trensch Cabin
Paddy Marion Cabin	Log Sauna	Capital Site Cabin
1917 Schoolhouse	Smokehouse	

Open 7 days a week 10 a.m. - 6 p.m. • Admission: Adults $3.00, Senior Citizen $2.50
323 MAIN STREET, WASILLA   (907) 376-2005   Under 18 FREE

WINDBREAK HOTEL CAFE and LOUNGE

Low Weekly & Monthly Rates on Rooms
● Ask about our Winter Rates

GREAT FOOD
Guided & Unguided Fishing Trips
Rainbow Trout/Salmon/Lake Trout our Specialty
● Let us help you plan your fishing trips to all areas

(907) 376-4209 • 376-4484
40 miles north of Anchorage
MILE 40.5 PARKS HIGHWAY, Wasilla

NORTHERN RECREATION
RV Headquarters in Alaska . . .

Full line of parts and accessories.
Repair for campers, motorhomes, fifth-wheels and travel trailers.
We carry everything from toilet chemicals to brake parts.

*Hours Monday through Friday 8:00 a.m. to 6:00 p.m. • Saturday 9:00 a.m. to 5:00 p.m.

(907) 376-8087
Mile 40, Parks Highway   Wasilla, Alaska

TOWN SQUARE ART GALLERY

COLLECTORS' FINE ART — CUSTOM FRAMING

Wildlife • Western
Indian • Alaskan

We welcome all credit cards
Packing and shipping available

(907) 376-0123
701 E. Parks Highway #105, Wasilla, AK 99687
Located in Land Co. Bldg., Carr's Center

ATTRACTIONS

On the town's Main Street, north of the Parks Highway, are the Wasilla museum, library and post office. The museum is open daily year-round, 10 A.M. to 6 P.M.; admission fees are $3 adults, $2.50 senior citizens; under 18 years free. Included in the price of admission to the museum is entrance to Frontier Village. This historical park has renovated buildings from the pioneer days, including a smokehouse; the first public sauna in Alaska; an early ferris wheel; Teeland's General Store (1914); Wasilla's first schoolhouse (built in 1917); and the Herning/Teeland/Mead House. The schoolhouse, Teeland's, the museum and the railroad depot in Wasilla are on the National Register of Historic Sites.

Wasilla is home to the Iditarod Trail Committee, the organization which stages the famous 1,049-mile Iditarod Trail Sled Dog Race from Anchorage to Nome. The Iditarod headquarters and visitors center is located at Mile 2.2 Knik Road. The center features historical displays on the Iditarod and has a gift shop with unique souvenirs. Open daily in summer, weekdays in winter, from 8 A.M. to 5 P.M. Historical displays on

---

WASH DAY
LAUNDRY & DRY CLEANERS

- Coin-op 36 WASHERS • Coin-op 25 DRYERS
- Drop-Off Service
- Clean Hot Showers
- Handicapped Shower
- Pay Phone
- RV Dump Station

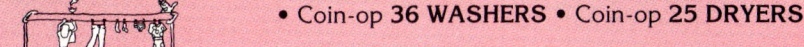

745 East West Point Avenue, Wasilla, Alaska
Turn on Crusey Street — We're behind McDonald's
Also: Look for WASH DAY TOO in Palmer

Phone (907) 376-4141
Open 24 hours June 1 - Labor Day

IDITAROD: The Great Race to Nome, by Bill Sherwonit; photographs by Jeff Schultz, the official race photographer. Sherwonit chronicles the origins of the trail, the struggles of the mushers and their dogs and Schultz offers a powerful graphic accompaniment. From Alaska Northwest Books™, call 1-800-343-4567, Ext. 571.

CHIMO GUNS
SPORTING GOODS

We carry a complete line of camping & fishing equipment

(current hunting & fishing information)

Canoe Rentals

VISA   (907) 376-5261   Next to Carr's in Wasilla
505 E. Herning, Wasilla, AK 99687   MasterCard

FLY-IN HYENA LODGE

OFFERING
BED AND BREAKFAST AND
FLOAT PLANE TIE DOWN
ON BIG LAKE
YEAR-ROUND
(907) 892-8903
OR LOMA GOOD ENTERPRISES
PO BOX 872147
WASILLA, ALASKA 99687

Family Medicine of Alaska, Inc.

M. E. KIRKPATRICK, PA-C
(907) 376-1276
Mile 39.5 George Parks Highway

---

the Gallery
YOUR AUTHORIZED DEALER FOR
Mill Pond Press

S/N - ORIGINALS - CUSTOM FRAMING
FEATURING
- MACHETANZ
- BATEMAN
- DOOLITTLE
- REN
- CALLE
- SEERY LESTER
- FREDERICK
- LYMAN
- LARSON
- GLAZIER

373-2350   745-1420
290 N. YEN LO, META ROSE SQ. WASILLA   1500 S. COLONY WY. PALMER

In Wasilla... Don't Miss
Iditarod Headquarters
Home of the Last Great Race

Photo by Jim Brown

• **Historical Displays** • **Souvenir Shop**
Open 8 to 5 — 5 days a week, year around
Additional Summer Hours: June 1 through Mid-September
Saturday 8 - 4 • Sunday 8 - 12

Iditarod Trail Committee, Inc.
Mile 2.2 Knik Road, Wasilla
(907) 376-5155 • FAX (907) 373-6998

1992 ■ The MILEPOST®

Wasilla Lake beach playground attracts youngsters on sunny days. (Jerrianne Lowther, staff)

the Iditarod Trail and Alaskan mushers can be found at the Knik Museum and Sled Dog Mushers Hall of Fame at Mile 14 Knik Road (see Knik Road log this section).

The Wasilla Water Festival is held the Fourth of July weekend. Iditarod Days is held in conjunction with the Iditarod Race, usually the first week in March. Other area winter events include ice golf at Mat–Su Resort and ice bowling at Big Lake.

George Parks Highway Log

(continued)

A **42.7** (68.7 km) F **315.3** (507.4 km) Airport Drive; food and shopping.

A **43.3** (69.7 km) F **314.7** (506.4 km) Lucas Road; access to Lake Lucille.

A **43.5** (70 km) F **314.5** (506.1 km) Divided highway ends northbound.

A **44.4** (71.4 km) F **313.6** (504.7 km) Church Road.

A **45** (72.4 km) F **313** (503.7 km) Wasilla city limits. Shopping and services are located along the highway to **Milepost A 39.5** and at Main Street in Wasilla city center.

A **46.4** (74.7 km) F **311.6** (501.5 km) CAUTION: Railroad crossing.

A **46.5** (74.8 km) F **311.5** (501.3 km) Rocky Ridge Road. The Museum of Alaska Transportation and Industry, open 10 A.M. to 4 P.M. Tuesday–Saturday. Admission fee charged.

Museum of Alaska Transportation & Industry. See display ad this section.

A **48.5** (78.1 km) F **309.5** (498 km) Turnoff on Pittman Road to Rainbow Lake. Medical center (373-1065), convenience store, gas station, cafe and Meadow Lakes post office.

Rainbow Plaza Medical Center. See display ad this section.

A **49.5** (79.7 km) F **308.5** (496.5 km) **The Roadside Inn.** See display ad this section.

A **50** (80.5 km) F **308** (495.7 km) **The Silver Fox Inn.** See display ad this section.

A **52.3** (84.2 km) F **305.7** (492 km) **Junction** with Big Lake Road. Meadowood shopping mall located here with a service station, hardware store, grocery and emergency phone (dial 911). See BIG LAKE ROAD log on opposite page.

A **53.3** (85.8 km) F **304.7** (490.4 km) Houston High School and Wasilla Senior Center. Turnout to west with map and information sign.

A **56.1** (90.3 km) F **301.9** (485.8 km) Miller's Reach Road.

A **56.4** (90.8 km) F **301.6** (485.4 km) CAUTION: Railroad crossing.

A **57.1** (91.9 km) F **300.9** (484.2 km) Bridge over the Little Susitna River; turnouts either side. This river heads at Mint Glacier in the Talkeetna Mountains to the northeast and flows 110 miles/177 km into Upper Cook Inlet.

A **57.4** (92.4 km) F **300.6** (483.8 km) Turnoff to Houston city-operated Little Susitna River Campground. Large, well-maintained campground with 86 sites (many wide, level gravel sites); camping fee, water, restrooms, covered picnic area, 10-day limit. Off-road parking lot near river with access to river. Follow signs to camping and river. Day-use area with water and toilets west side of highway. ▲

The **Little Susitna River** has a tremendous king salmon run and one of the largest silver salmon runs in southcentral Alaska. Kings to 30 lbs. enter the river in late May and June, use large red spinners or salmon eggs. Silvers to 15 lbs., come in July and August, with the biggest run in late July, use small weighted spoons or fresh salmon roe. Also red salmon to 10 lbs., in mid-July, use coho flies or salmon eggs. Charter boats nearby.

A **57.5** (92.5 km) F **300.5** (483.6 km) 🐟 **HOUSTON** (pop. 725) has a grocery store, restaurant (open daily), laundromat, gift shop, inn with food, lodging and pay

VALLEY CHIROPRACTIC CLINIC
"Gentle, Effective Family Health Care"
400 N. MAIN
WASILLA, ALASKA 99654
Telephone (907) 373-2022 (24 Hours)
Dr. James D. Martin

RUMELY OIL-PULL TRACTOR

Tues.-Sat., 10 a.m. - 4 p.m.
ADMISSION CHARGE

MUSEUM OF ALASKA TRANSPORTATION & INDUSTRY
Mile 46.5 Parks Highway
(FOLLOW SIGNS / .8 MI)
P.O. Box 870646, WASILLA, AK 99687
(907) 745-4493 • (907) 376-1211

THE ROADSIDE INN
MILE 49.5 Parks Highway

For Reservations Call (907) 373-4646

RESTAURANT — 8:00 til 10:00
MOTEL ✸ LOUNGE — 8:00 til 12:00

Quality Rooms at Economy Prices

Kings • Queens • Singles
With TV
Showers or Tubs
Close to Grocery and Laundry

RAINBOW PLAZA MEDICAL CENTER

Mile 48.5 Parks Highway
(907) 373-1065
Family Medicine
Minor Emergency   Ken Wilcox, PA-C

Located next to 7-11

The Silver Fox Inn
Motel • Lounge • Cafe
Hank & Wanda Dunnaway   Mile 50 Parks Highway
Owner-Operators   Wasilla, Alaska 99687
(907) 892-6179

Big Lake Road Log

The 6.5-mile/10.5-km Big Lake Road leads south from the George Parks Highway junction at **Milepost A 52.3** to **BIG LAKE** (pop. 2,333), a recreation area with swimming, camping, boating, waterskiing, fishing, jet skiing, tour boat rides and water taxi service in summer; snow machine racing, ice skating, cross-country skiing and sled dog races in winter. There are motels and lodges, campgrounds, marinas, picnic areas, boat rentals, restaurants and shopping malls. Big Lake airport is a 15-minute flight from Anchorage. The Big Lake Regatta and Triathalon are held here in July. The Big Lake 500 snow machine race is held here in winter. Businesses are found along Big Lake Road and along North Shore Drive, which forks off Big Lake Road at Mile J 3.6.
Distance is measured from the junction (J) with the George Parks Highway.

J 0 Junction with George Parks Highway. Meadowood Mall and gas station.

J 3.4 (5.5 km) Beaver Lake Road turnoff. Lions Club dump station at gas station located at intersection. Turn right here for public and private campgrounds and fish hatchery. Drive 0.5 mile/0.8 km on Beaver Lake Road (gravel) for Rocky Lake state recreation site; 10 campsites, $6 nightly fee or annual pass, toilets, firepits, water and boat launch. Drive 0.9 mile/1.4 km on Beaver Lake Road for state salmon hatchery; open 8 A.M. to 4 P.M. ▲

J 3.6 (5.8 km) Fisher's Y; gas station and Big Lake post office (Zip code 99652). Big Lake Road forks here: Go straight ahead for North Shore Drive (description follows); keep to left for south Big Lake Road businesses and Big Lake South state recreation site (continue with this log).

North Shore Drive provides access to Sail "N" Fun Campground (1.2 miles/1.9 km), Klondike Inn and restaurant (1.4 miles/2.3 km) and Big Lake East state recreation site (1.6 miles/2.6 km), which has parking for 120 vehicles, overnight RV parking, tent sites, $6 nightly fee or annual pass, covered picnic tables, water, toilets, dumpsters, boat launch and sandy beach. ▲

The Klondike Inn is nestled on the shore of beautiful Big Lake just 60 paved miles from Anchorage. At the Klondike Inn you will find a full-service resort complete with hotel, saunas, restaurant, lounge, marina and boat launch. Floatplane landing and mooring. 20- to 30- person party barge rental. Fly-in fishing or sightseeing trips available. An ideal location to headquarter your stay in Alaska. Phone (907) 892-6261, fax (907) 892-6445. P.O. Box 521020, Big Lake, AK 99652. [ADVERTISEMENT]

J 3.7 (6 km) Shopping mall.

J 3.9 (6.3 km) Big Lake fire station.

J 4 (6.4 km) East Lake Mall; visitor information center, restaurant, Big Lake Barbers and grocery.

J 4.1 (6.6 km) Turnoff for Islander paddlewheel tour boat dock, dining and picnic area on Long Island.

J 4.7 (7.6 km) Aero Drive and Big Lake airport. Big Lake is a 15-minute flight from Anchorage.

Private Aircraft: 1 mile/1.6 km southeast; elev. 150 feet/46m; length 2,800 feet/853m; gravel; fuel 80, 100.

J 4.9 (7.9 km) Big Lake Motel.

J 5 (8 km) Bridge over Fish Creek. Fish Creek park picnic area; fish weir with salmon spawning view area. Fishing prohibited.

J 5.2 (8.4 km) Big Lake South state recreation site; 13 campsites, 6 picnic sites, toilets, water, dumpsters, boat ramp. Camping fee $6/night or annual pass. ▲

J 5.3 (8.5 km) Double-ended turnout with picnic tables and water.

J 5.7 (9.2 km) Gravel turnout, Echo Lake Road. Dog mushers' race track.

J 6.5 (10.5 km) Pavement ends. Burma Road continues into rural area, providing access to Point MacKenzie dairy project and Little Susitna River public-use facility at state game refuge (also accessible via Knik Road); parking, camping, boat ramps.

Big Lake is connected with smaller lakes by dredged waterways. It is possible to boat for several miles in the complex. Fish in Big Lake include lake trout, Dolly Varden, rainbow, red and coho salmon, and burbot.

Return to Milepost A 52.3
George Parks Highway

A boater returns to shore at sunset on Big Lake. (Jerrianne Lowther, staff)

BIG LAKE ADVERTISERS

Big Lake Barbers .... East Lake Mall
Big Lake Motel .... Mile 4.9 Big Lake Rd.
Islander & Big Lake
 Tours .... Ph. (907) 892-7144
Klondike Inn, The .... North Shore Dr.
Sail "N" Fun
 Campground .... North Shore Dr.

BIG LAKE BARBERS — Personal Family Hair Care
In East Lake Mall • (907) 892-7878
Tuesday-Saturday 9 a.m.-5:30 p.m.
Owners: Steve and Sandy Broughten

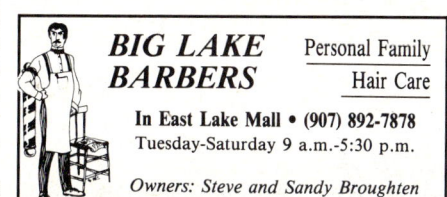

BIG LAKE MOTEL
Come Enjoy Flying • Water Sport • Winter Sport
New, Spacious Clean Rooms
(907) 892-7976
Across from Airport • Mile 5 South Big Lake Road
Owners: Ralph & LaRae Eldridge
P.O. Box 520728, Big Lake, Alaska 99652

Islander & Big Lake Tours
Paddle Wheel Cruises on Beautiful Big Lake, Alaska
LOCATED ON LONG ISLAND
Fine Dining and Cocktails • Picnic Area
Phone (907) 892-7144
Box 520148   Big Lake, Alaska 99652

KLONDIKE INN LAKE FRONT HOTEL
Hotel, Restaurant, Lounge, Marina, Rentals
Floatplane Trips - Landing and Mooring at the Lodge
View of Beautiful Mt. McKinley

Summer	ACTIVITIES	Winter
• Fishing		• Ice Fishing
• Water Skiing		• X-C Skiing
• Boating		• Snow Machining
• Party Barge Rental 20-30 persons		• Saunas

MEETINGS • RETREATS • PARTIES
P.O. Box 521020, Big Lake, Alaska 99652
(907) 892-6261

SAIL "N" FUN CAMPGROUND
5 ACRES OF FUN ON BIG LAKE
Overnight spaces for self-contained units or tents

• **WE RENT:** Motorboats, Paddleboats, Rowboats, Canoes, Sailboats

Your hosts: Jim & Camille Carlson

• CAMPING
• DOCK FISHING
• PICNIC FACILITIES (covered & open)
• MINIATURE GOLF
• VOLLEYBALL • BADMINTON • HORSESHOES

LOCATION: from Mile A 52.3 on the Parks Highway, turn west on Big Lake Road. Drive 3.5 miles to Fisher's Y. Turn right, drive 1.2 miles and watch for our signs.

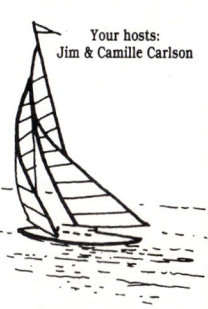

George Parks Highway Log

(continued)

phone, a campground and gas station. Post office located in the grocery store. Fishing charter operators and marine service are located here. Emergency phone at Houston fire station. ▲

Homesteaded in the 1950s, incorporated as a city in 1966. Houston is a popular fishing center for anglers on the Little Susitna River.

A 57.6 (92.7 km) **F 300.4** (483.4 km) **Miller's Place.** Don't miss this stop! Groceries, post office, laundry, RV parking, cabin rentals, tenting on riverbank. Gift shop, fishing tackle and licenses, fresh salmon eggs. Ice, sporting goods sales and rental, pay phone. Fishing charters available; full day only $40. Probably the best soft ice cream and hamburgers in Alaska. Clean restrooms. Visitor information experts. Family-run Christian business. Gary and Debbie Miller. (907) 892-6129.
[ADVERTISEMENT]

A 57.7 (92.9 km) **F 300.3** (483.3 km) **Riverside Camper Park.** See display ad this section.

A 63.2 (101.7 km) **F 294.8** (474.4 km) **Ivan's Bait & Tackle.** See display ad this section.

A 64.5 (103.8 km) **F 293.5** (472.3 km) **Nancy Lake Marina, Resort.** See display ad this section. ▲

A 66.5 (107 km) **F 291.5** (469.1 km) Highway crosses Alaska Railroad tracks. Turnoff (not well marked) for Nancy Lake state recreation site; 30 campsites, 30 picnic sites, toilets, boat launch. Camping fee $6/night or annual pass. ▲

A 67.2 (108.1 km) **F 290.8** (468 km) Wide gravel road into Nancy Lake Recreation Area in the mixed birch and spruce forest of the Susitna River valley (good mushroom hunting area). At Mile 2.5/4 km on the access road there is a well-marked nature trail, toilets and parking area. At Mile 4.7/7.6 km there is a canoe launch, toilet and parking area. At Mile 5.7/9.2 km a hiking trail leads 3 miles/4.8 km to Chicken Lake, 5.5 miles/8.9 km to Red Shirt Lake. At Mile 6.2/10 km is South Rolly Lake overlook (day use only) with barbecues, 11 picnic tables, litter barrels and toilets. There are 106 campsites at South Rolly Lake Campground, at Mile 6.6/10.6 km, with firepits, toilets, water and boat launch; firewood sometimes is provided. Camping fee $6/night or annual pass. ▲

South Rolly Lake, small population of rainbow, 12 to 14 inches.

A 68.7 (110.6 km) **F 289.3** (465.6 km) **Newman's Hilltop Service.** See display ad this section.

A 69 (111 km) **F 289** (465.1 km) **WILLOW** (pop. 494). Visitor facilities include 2 gas stations, grocery, hardware and notions store, air taxi service, lodges, RV parks, video rental and restaurants. The Willow civic organization sponsors an annual Winter Carnival in January.

Willow extends about 2.5 miles/4 km north along the George Parks Highway. The community is also a stop on the Alaska Railroad. Willow had its start about 1897, when gold was discovered in the area. In the early 1940s, mining in the nearby Talkeetna Mountains slacked off, leaving Willow a virtual ghost town. The community made a comeback upon completion of the Parks Highway in 1972.

In 1976, Alaska voters selected the Willow area for their new capital site. However, funding for the capital move from Juneau to Willow was defeated in the November 1982 election.

Willow True Value Hardware, Willow Creek Grocery and Willow Creek Service. See display ad this section.

A 69.2 (111.4 km) **F 288.8** (464.8 km) Long Lake Road. Alternate access to Deshka Landing.

Causey Lane Bed & Breakfast. See display ad this section.

HOUSTON
Little Susitna River
Mile 57.5 Parks Highway
(907) 892-6129
THE #1 STOP

MILLER'S RIVERBOAT SERVICE
Drop-offs ONLY $40
CABIN RENTALS $35 - $75
892-6872

Licenses • Tackle • Grocery • Gifts
Laundry • Showers • Post Office
Fast Food
RV PARKING

IVAN'S BAIT & TACKLE
FISHING INFORMATION

Salmon Roe • Nightcrawlers
FISHING AND HUNTING LICENSES AND TAGS

OPEN YEAR AROUND
MILE 63.2 PARKS HIGHWAY

• VISA and MasterCard Accepted

Nancy Lake Marina, Resort
Mile 64.5 Parks Highway
Cabins • Camping • Fishing
Boat & Canoe Rentals
Camp Store • Fuel • Propane

Phone (907) 495-6284
P.O. Box 114
Willow, AK 99688

RIVERSIDE CAMPER PARK
ON THE
LITTLE SUSITNA RIVER
CARAVANS WELCOME
Mile 57.7 Parks Hwy.   (907) 892-9020

56 FULL HOOKUPS
30 amp electricity
30x40 RV spaces
DUMP STATION
LAUNDROMAT
FREE SHOWERS
with plenty of hot water for guests

ICE • PROPANE
WASH your RV ... FREE
King and Silver Salmon
BANK FISHING in park
RIVERBOAT CHARTER
service available locally
Long Distance Phone In Park

VISA/MasterCard accepted

Post Office, Grocery Store, Service Station,
Restaurant & Bar within walking distance

P.O. Box 87, HOUSTON, ALASKA 99694

Good Sam Club

Enjoy ... ONE STOP SHOPPING — in Willow
MILE A 69 PARKS HIGHWAY

WILLOW TRUE VALUE HARDWARE
For all your lumber & hardware supplies
Film • Fishing Tackle • Toys
(907) 495-6275   Fishing Licenses • Housewares
Open 7 days a week   Doyle and Judy Holmes

Groceries • Soft Ice Cream
Ice • Dairy Products • Picnic Supplies
willow creek GROCERY
BILL and JOSIE LORENTZEN

WILLOW CREEK SERVICE
Mechanic on Duty
Batteries & Accessories
Parts • Towing
PROPANE • FUEL OIL
Water Fill-up • Tires
Full Service Station
Gas — Unleaded
495-6336

A 69.4 (111.7 km) F 288.6 (464.4 km) Willow library.

A 69.5 (111.8 km) 288.5 (464.3 km) Short road to Willow post office, trading post with cabins and camper spaces, and Alaska Railroad depot. ▲

Ruth Lake Lodge. See display ad this section.

Willow Trading Post Lodge. Open all year. Just follow the geese to this historic lodge. It's a great place to have a meal, a drink, meet the local folks, and stay the night. Incredible flower displays make this a must-see summer attraction. Variety of lodging available from cozy cabins for 2 to a large furnished home with full kitchen. Well-stocked bar and liquor store, laundry facilities, bathhouse and sauna help make your visit comfortable and relaxing. Excellent private RV park with picnic pavilion and hookups. Stop in for a real taste of Alaska. Catering available for parties, weddings, meetings, etc., as well as assistance with fishing charters, flightseeing trips and local events. Other favorite summer activities include fishing, hiking and berry picking. Winter activities include snow machining, dog mushing, cross-country skiing and ice fishing. See display ad for more information. [ADVERTISEMENT]

A 69.6 (112 km) F 288.4 (464.1 km) Willow elementary school.

A 69.7 (112.2 km) F 288.3 (464 km) Willow Community Center, open daily; covered picnic pavilion, grills, ball court, boat launch and pay phone.

A 69.9 (112.5 km) F 288.1 (463.6 km) Fire station.

A 70 (112.7 km) F 288 (463.5 km) **Private Aircraft:** Willow airport; elev. 220 feet/67m; length 4,600 feet/740m; gravel; fuel 80, 100, B.

A 70 (112.7 km) F 288 (463.5 km) **Willow Air Service Inc.** See display ad this section.

A 70.3 (113.1 km) F 287.7 (463 km) **CPA Air Service.** See spectacular Alaska every day, every season. Let CPA Air help you discover Alaska: meadows of moose and bear, mile-high rock walls, cascading glaciers, salmon filled rivers, hillsides of caribou and sheep. Most reasonable rates per hour for McKinley flights. CPA offers: experienced McKinley pilot, fly-in fishing and hunting, scenic flights, headphones for every passenger. Main office: Willow Airport. Mailing address: CPA Air Service, Box 207, Willow, AK 99688. Call (907) 495-6785 or 892-9182. [ADVERTISEMENT]

A 70.8 (113.9 km) F 287.2 (462.2 km) Willow Creek Parkway (**Susitna River** access road) to Willow Creek state recreation area (4 miles/6.4 km); parking, litter barrels, trail to mouth of creek. Deshka Landing boat launch. Fishing for king and silver salmon, rainbow trout.

A 71 (114.3 km) F 287 (461.9 km) Willow DOT/PF highway maintenance station.

A 71.2 (114.6 km) F 286.8 (461.5 km) **Junction** with Hatcher Pass (Fishhook–Willow) Road. This road leads east and south across Hatcher Pass 49 miles/79 km to junction with the Glenn Highway. Independence Mine State Historical Park is 31.8 miles/51.2 km from here. Turn to the Hatcher Pass side road in the GLENN HIGHWAY section, page 274, for log of this road. (Parks Highway travelers should read that log back to front.) See also the Matanuska Valley Vicinity map this section. Hatcher Pass Road is mostly gravel with some steep, narrow, winding sections; it is not recommended for large RVs or trailers.

Access to Willow Creek state recreation area via Hatcher Pass Road. Deception Creek main campground, with 17 campsites, is located 1.2 miles/1.9 km from this junction via Hatcher Pass Road. Additional campsites and a picnic area are located 0.8 mile/1.3 km east. Both sites have tables, firepits and toilets. Camping fee $6/ night or annual pass. ▲

A 71.4 (114.9 km) F 286.4 (461.2 km) Lodge (current status unknown). Bridge over **Willow Creek.** This stream heads in Summit Lake, west of Hatcher Pass on the Hatcher Pass Road, and is a favorite launch site for airboat enthusiasts. Excellent king salmon fishing; also silvers, rainbows. Inquire at Willow Island Resort for information. Enter-

CAUSEY LANE BED & BREAKFAST

Country lakeside setting for the perfect vacation
Summer salmon fishing • Northern lights
Winter fun • Cross-country skiing
Hosts: Bill & Liz Causey • Open All Year
PO Box 1034, Willow, Alaska 99688
Mile 69.2 Parks Highway • (907) 495-6534

RUTH LAKE LODGE

Elegant Accommodations
Meal Packages Available

World Class Salmon Fishing
Charter Service Available
X-C Skiing
on Set Trails

Mile 69.5 Parks Highway
P.O. Box 87
Willow, Alaska 99688
(907) 495-6428

MILE 68.8 PARKS HIGHWAY PHONE: 495-6479
Newmans' HILLTOP Service
GAS — Regular & Unleaded — DIESEL
Propane — Tool Rental — 24-Hour Wrecker Service
Candy — Popcorn — Free Coffee
Alaskan GIFTS . . . many locally made
Pat and Gene Welcome you

Visit HILL TOP VARIETY and GIFTS

Willow Trading Post Lodge

Lodging
RV Park
Laundry
Showers

Bar & Cafe
Gift Nook
Liquor Store
. . . and more!

See our incredible flower displays!
Mile 69.5 Parks Highway • P.O. Box 69, Willow, AK 99688 • (907) 495-6457

WILLOW AIR SERVICE INC.

Specializing in:
Float Plane Flying
Fly-in
King & Silver Salmon
Trout & Pike Fishing
Drop-offs & Pickups
Canoe & Raft Trips
Unguided Big Game Hunting

70 miles north of Anchorage on the way to or from Denali National Park
(907) 495-6370 • P.O. Box 42, Willow, Alaska 99688
MILE 70 PARKS HIGHWAY

ing Game Management Subunit 14B northbound, 14A southbound.

From here to Denali National Park and Preserve watch for views of the Alaska Range to the east of the highway.

A 71.5 (115.1 km) F 286.5 (461.1 km) **Willow Island Resort, Inc.** Scenic riverside RV park and campground. Great salmon and trout fishing from the banks of crystal clear Willow Creek. Full hookups on level riverbank sites. Hot showers, laundry, dump station, tackle, mini-grocery, good water. Excellent king and silver salmon fishing. Rainbows to 10 lbs. Fly-in, boat-in, scenic fishing and hunting charters. Guide services available. Gold panning. Close to Hatcher Pass; 3 hours from Denali National Park. Plan to stay awhile. Write: P.O. Box 85, Willow, AK 99688 or call (907) 495-6343. See display ad this section. [ADVERTISEMENT]

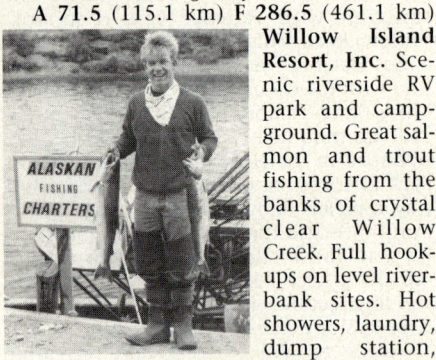

A 74.7 (120.2 km) F 283.3 (455.9 km) Bridge over Little Willow Creek. Large undeveloped parking areas below highway on either side of creek.

A 76.4 (122.9 km) F 281.6 (453.2 km) Paved double-ended turnout to west by Kashwitna Lake. Small planes land on lake. Good camera viewpoints of lake and Mount McKinley (weather permitting).

A 76.7 (123.4 km) F 281.3 (452.7 km) **Susitna Air Service.** Floatplane base located at Kashwitna Lake, Mile 76.5 Parks Highway. Relax in our remote cabins featuring salmon, rainbow or pike fishing. Fly-in camping, hiking or nature trips. 20 years flying experience in the Susitna Valley. Phone (907) 495-6789 or write P.O. Box 521206, Big Lake, AK 99652. [ADVERTISEMENT]

A 81.3 (130.8 km) F 276.7 (445.3 km) Grey's Creek, gravel turnouts both sides of highway.

A 82.5 (132.8 km) F 275.5 (443.4 km) Susitna Landing boat launch on Susitna River, 1 mile/1.6 km on side road; operated by state park concessionaire.

"Catch My Drift" Raft Tour. A leisurely and scenic 4- to 5-hour rafting tour, including an all-you-can-eat salmon bake and a live Alaskana show performed for you from the banks of the Big Su! For reservations call 373-6360 or 1-800-478-6360. A reasonably priced Alaskana experience. [ADVERTISEMENT]

The Susitna River heads at Susitna Glacier in the Alaska Range to the northeast and flows west then south for 260 miles/418 km to Cook Inlet.

A 83.2 (133.9 km) F 274.8 (442.2 km) Bridge over Kashwitna River; parking areas at both ends of bridge. River heads in a glacier in the Talkeetna Mountains and flows westward 60 miles/96.5 km to enter the Susitna River 12 miles/19 km north of Willow.

A 84.3 (135.7 km) F 273.7 (440.5 km) Large paved turnout to west. Walk-in for fishing at **Caswell Creek**; kings, silvers, pinks and rainbow.

A 85.1 (137 km) F 272.9 (439.2 km) Caswell Creek, large gravel turnout.

A 85.5 (137.6 km) F 272.5 (438.5 km) **Country Attic Gifts & Collectibles.** See display ad this section.

Birch "conks," a type of tree fungus. Like burls, conks are used in arts and crafts. (Sharon Nault)

Willow Wildlife
Art & Framing Gallery
Featuring Alaskan Wildlife Art
by *David Totten*
Mile 85.5 Parks Highway
HC 89, Box 351, Willow, Alaska 99688 • (907) 495-1090

COUNTRY ATTIC
Gifts & Collectibles
Olive Bibeau and Jackie Cerra   (907) 495-6718
HC 89, Box 364, Willow, Alaska 99688
MILE 85.5 PARKS HIGHWAY

Willow Island Resort, Inc.
KINGS!   SILVERS!   RAINBOWS!
Excellent Bank Fishing • Charter Service
RV Park • Camping • Laundry
Mini-grocery • Tackle • Ice
Full Hookups • Showers • Dump Station
(907) 495-6343
SEE LOG AD AT MILE A 71.5 PARKS HIGHWAY

Hoag's Hollow Gifts
Jim & Polly Hoag Welcome You to The Something Different Place

VISA – MasterCard Accepted

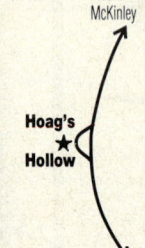

- Native Clay Ceramics
- Workshop Tours
- Quality Gifts at Wholesale Prices
- Custom Orders
- We Mail Anywhere
- Easy Trailer Access
- *Free Coffee*

Mount McKinley ↑ Hoag's Hollow ★ ↓ Anchorage

Box 1006, Willow, Alaska 99688   (907) 495-6214
Hoag's Hollow Gifts – See our log ad at Mile 86.9 Parks Highway

Willow Wildlife. See display ad this section.

A 86 (138.4 km) F 272 (437.7 km) Public access road leads 1.3 miles/2.1 km to mouth of Sheep Creek public boat launch and Bluffs on Susitna. Sheep Creek has parking, toilets, dumpster, and wheelchair accessible trail to mouth of creek; fishing for kings, silvers, pinks and rainbow. Bluffs on Susitna is the site of the annual Talkeetna Bluegrass Festival.

Talkeetna Blue Grass Festival, "dirty Ernie style," Aug. 7-9, 1992, on the bluffs of the Susitna. Mile 86 Park Highway—not in Talkeetna. Alaska's greatest musicians, handcrafts, food, best variety, good roads, outhouses, RV parking, no hookups. Great family weekend camping. Bring camping gear and cushions. $15 weekend, seniors and children 12 and under, free. No carry in alcohol, please. Phone (907) 495-6718.
[ADVERTISEMENT]

A 86.9 (139.8 km) F 271.1 (436.3 km) Hoag's Hollow Gifts. The something different place with easy trailer access. The ceramics, macrame and crafts are made on site by Jim and Polly. Workshop tours. See the originality in pouring of Alaska native clay and quality craftsmanship, in combination with fine macrame and bead art, gives an outstanding display inside our unique hand-peeled log cabin showroom. All of this framed in a pleasant birch and spruce forest, makes for a relaxing stop. Quality and lower prices guaranteed along with free coffee.
[ADVERTISEMENT]

A 87.5 (140.8 km) F 270.5 (435.3 km) Wolf Safari. See display ad this section.

A 88.3 (142.1 km) F 269.7 (434 km) Sheep Creek Lodge. See display ad this section.

A 88.6 (142.6 km) F 269.4 (433.5 km) Bridge over Sheep Creek. Unimproved picnic area on west side below bridge by creek.

A 90.8 (146.1 km) F 267.2 (430 km) Chandalar RV Camper Park. See display ad this section. ▲

"You Getta Pettum"

WOLF SAFARI
9 a.m. - 8 p.m. Daily
(907) 495-5874
Home of the Kissing Wolves
Memento Shop
20 Pettable Adult Animals
Low Priced Tours • Cubs For Sale
Planned for 1992:
Picnic Area • RV Parking
Mile 87 Parks Highway

CHANDALAR RV CAMPER PARK
MILE 90.8 PARKS HIGHWAY • 1 Block Off Highway • **QUIET**
Full or Partial Hook-ups (30 amp) • Large Spaces • Pull-throughs • Level • Easy Turnaround Tent Sites • Dump Station • Clean Restrooms • Tub and Showers • Laundromat • Propane
GROCERY STORE OPEN YEAR AROUND • Ice • Gifts • Pay Phone
Fishing Tackle & Licenses • Excellent Fishing at nearby Montana or Sheep Creek
Caravans Welcome   HC 89 Box 408, Willow, Alaska 99688   (907) 495-6700

SHEEP CREEK LODGE

GATEWAY TO DENALI
Mile 88.2 Parks Highway • (907) 495-6227

Chevron Fuel & Propane
Long Summer Hours

A Modern Alaskan Log Lodge
★ Mt. McKinley View
★ Fine Dining & Cocktail Lounge
★ Breakfast, Lunch, Dinner
★ Warm, Cozy Cabins
★ Creekside RV Parking & Camping
★ Package Liquor Store, Ice, Phone
★ Gift Shop, Unique Alaskan Gifts
★ Many Alaskan Wildlife Mounts, Including Moose & Polar Bear
★ Excellent Salmon & Trout Fishing Within Walking Distance
★ Visitor Information & Reservations for all Local Activities
★ Raft Trips, Fishing Guides, Flightseeing

Have your picture taken with our 10 ft. Kodiak bear.

Visa • MaterCard • American Express
Large Caravans & Tour Groups Welcome with Reservations
HC 89 Box 406 • Willow, AK 99688 • (907) 495-6227

GEORGE PARKS HIGHWAY

GEORGE PARKS HIGHWAY

Common loons nest on large lakes. Loons and other waterfowl may be observed at Christianson Lake on the Talkeetna Spur Road. (Steve Lackie)

A 91.7 (147.6 km) F 266.3 (428.5 km) CAUTION: Railroad crossing.
A 92 (148.1 km) F 266 (428.1 km) Turnouts.
A 92.3 (148.5 km) F 265.7 (427.6 km) Beaver dam.
A 93 (149.7 km) F 265 (426.5 km) Gravel turnout to west.
A 93.4 (150.3 km) F 264.6 (425.8 km) Gravel turnouts both sides of highway.
A 93.5 (150.5 km) F 264.5 (425.7 km) Goose Creek culvert; gravel turnout. Fishing.
A 93.6 (150.6 km) F 264.4 (425.5 km) Goose Creek community center; park pavilion, picnic tables, grills, litter barrels.

A 95.1 (153 km) F 262.9 (423.1 km) Private Aircraft: Montana Creek airstrip; elev. 250 feet/76m; length 2,400 feet/731m; gravel; fuel 80, 100.
A 96.5 (155.3 km) F 261.5 (420.8 km) Montana Creek state recreation site with campsites, tables, firepits, toilets, water and trails (wheelchair accessible). Parking and access to Susitna River. Interpretive signs about salmon. Camping fee $6/night or annual pass.
A 96.6 (155.5 km) F 261.4 (420.7 km) Bridge over Montana Creek. Homesteaders settled in the area surrounding this creek in the 1950s. Today, about 200 families live in the Montana Creek area. In winter, the Montana Creek Dog Mushers Club holds races and maintains trails. Camping and picnic areas on both sides of **Montana Creek**; excellent king salmon fishing, also silvers, pinks (even-numbered years), grayling, rainbow and Dolly Varden.
A 96.6 (155.5 km) F 261.4 (420.7 km) **Montana Creek Campground.** Located on the north side of Montana Creek, all campsites in this private campground are scenic, with many overlooking one of Alaska's best salmon and trout fishing streams. Picnic tables, campfires, toilets. Only a short walk to the Susitna River. Conveniently located within 3 miles of grocery store, cafe, laundromat, and showers. [ADVERTISEMENT]
A 97.8 (157.4 km) F 260.2 (418.7 km) Sunshine Community Health Center (medical clinic) and Alaska State Troopers post (phone 733-2556 or 911 for emergencies).
A 98 (157.7 km) F 260 (418.4 km) For weather information, tune your radio to 830-AM (99.7-FM).
A 98.3 (158.2 km) F 259.7 (417.9 km) Large gravel turnout to east.
A 98.4 (58.3 km) F 259.6 (417.8 km) Susitna Valley High School. Five-kilometer trail for running in summer, cross-country skiing in winter.
A 98.7 (158.8 km) F 259.3 (417.3 km) **Junction** with Talkeetna Spur Road; visitor information cabin. Turn right northbound on paved spur road which leads 14.5 miles/23.3 km to Talkeetna (description begins on opposite page). See TALKEETNA SPUR ROAD log on opposite page. Continue straight ahead on the George Parks Highway for Fairbanks (continue with this log). Restaurant and gas station just north of junction.
Talkeetna Visitor Center. This quaint log cabin located at the junction of the Talkeetna Spur Road and the Parks Highway offers information on local fishing areas, flightseeing around Mount McKinley and other area attractions. Tackle shop and gift store. Large picnic area and public restrooms available. [ADVERTISEMENT]
A 98.8 (159 km) F 259.2 (417.1 km) **Sunshine Restaurant & Tesoro Truck Stop.** See display ad this section.
A 99 (159.3 km) F 259 (416.8 km) **Denali Way Auto.** See display ad this section.
A 99.3 (159.8 km) F 258.7 (416.3 km) Lakes both sides of highway; watch for floatplanes.

SUNSHINE RESTAURANT & TESORO TRUCK STOP

AT THE TALKEETNA "Y"

Open 24 Hours 7 Days A Week

Good Home Cooking • Daily Specials • Homemade Pies

Pay Phone

Phone (907) 733-1371 or 733-3835

SUNSHINE ONE STOP

Gas • Diesel • Propane • Wrecker Service
Convenience Store • Package Liquor • Ice
RV Parking

MILE 98.8 PARKS HIGHWAY

DENALI WAY AUTO

Mile 99 Parks Highway

◄ AUTOMOTIVE PARTS HOUSE ►
MAJOR NAME BRANDS
FOR REPLACEMENT PARTS

Darrell & Judy Bowersox • (907) 733-2797

◄ INDEPENDENT MECHANICS ►
TIRES, TUNEUPS, MAJOR REPAIRS

Glen & Roger   (907) 733-2562

Talkeetna Spur Road

Distance from George Parks Highway junction (J) at Milepost A 98.7 is shown.

J 3.1 (5 km) Turn east on Yoder Road (gravel) for **Benka Lake**. Drive in 0.6 mile/1 km on the gravel road, turn left and drive 0.7 mile/1.1 km to lake. Small turnaround space at lake (room for 1 self-contained RV) and a steep boat launch; fishing for silvers and Dolly Varden.

J 5.3 (8.5 km) Answer Creek.
J 7.1 (11.4 km) Question Lake.
J 7.8 (12.6 km) Lodge.
J 9.2 (14.8 km) Fish Lake private floatplane base.
J 11.5 (18.5 km) Bed and breakfast.
J 12 (19.3 km) Turn east on paved Comsat Road (unmarked) for **Christianson Lake**; drive in 0.7 mile/1.1 km on Comsat Road, turn left at Christianson Lake Road sign onto gravel road and drive 0.7 mile/1.1 km, turn right and follow signs to floatplane base. Fishing for silvers and rainbow. Good place to observe loons and waterfowl.
J 13 (20.9 km) Large gravel double-ended turnout with interpretive sign and viewpoint at crest of hill. Splendid views of Mount McKinley, Mount Foraker and the Alaska Range above the Susitna River. A must photo stop when the mountains are out. CAUTION: Watch for traffic.
J 13.3 (21.4 km) CAUTION: Alaska Railroad crossing.
J 13.5 (21.7 km) Talkeetna public library.
J 13.7 (22 km) Gas station.
J 13.8 (22.2 km) Restaurant and motel.
J 14 (22.5 km) East Talkeetna Road leads to state airport, municipal campground, boat launch on Susitna River and businesses.
J 14.2 (22.9 km) Talkeetna post office (Zip code 99676).
J 14.3 (23 km) Welcome to Beautiful Downtown Talkeetna sign and Talkeetna Historical Society visitor center log cabin; walking tour brochures available. (Description of Talkeetna follows.)
J 14.5 (23.3 km) Talkeetna Spur Road ends at Talkeetna River Park Campground.

Talkeetna

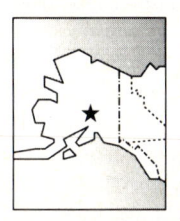

Located on a spur road, north of **Milepost A 98.7** George Parks Highway. **Population:** 441. **Emergency Services:** Alaska State Troopers, Fire Department and Ambulance, phone 911 or 733-2556. **Doctor,** phone 733-2708.

Visitor Information: Stop by the Little Red Schoolhouse Museum 1 block off Main Street behind the National Park Service ranger station. Visitor information also available at log cabin at junction of Parks Highway and spur road. Or, write Talkeetna Chamber of Commerce, P.O. Box 334, Talkeetna 99676.

The National Park Service maintains a ranger station that is staffed full time from mid-April through mid-September and intermittently during the winter. Mountaineering rangers provide information on Denali National Park and climbing within the Alaska Range. A reference library and video program are available to climbers. All climbers must register for climbs of Mount McKinley and Mount Foraker. Mountaineering information may be obtained from Talkeetna Ranger Station, P.O. Box 588, Talkeetna, AK 99676; phone (907) 733-2231.

Elevation: 346 feet/105m. **Radio:** KSKA-FM (PBS). **Television:** Channels 4, 6, 9.

Private Aircraft: Talkeetna airstrip (state airport), adjacent east; elev. 358 feet/109m; length 4,000 feet/1,219m; paved; fuel 80, 100, B. Talkeetna village airstrip on Main Street; elev. 346 feet/105m; length 1,200 feet/366m; gravel;

Talkeetna Riverboat Service
FISHING. Excellent fishing May to October. 5 species of salmon, trout and grayling. Day fishing. Reasonable rates. Drop-off or full & half-day guided fishing charters. See us at VILLAGE ARTS and CRAFTS GIFT SHOP Downtown Talkeetna
Phone (907) 733-2281
Mac A. Stevens • P.O. Box 74 • Talkeetna, Alaska 99676

VILLAGE ARTS & CRAFTS 
Unique Alaskan Gift Shop
Featuring: Furs • Ivory • Gold
Plus Maps • Books • Cards
Fishing Tackle • Licenses
Local Alaskan Handicraft
NANCY TRUMP
P.O. Box 395
Talkeetna, AK 99676
(907) 733-2281

LATITUDE 62° LODGE / MOTEL
Fine Dining — Cocktails
Modern Rooms with Private Baths
Alaskan Decor • Fireplace • Player Piano
P.O. Box 478
Talkeetna, Alaska 99676
Phone (907) 733-2262
OPEN YEAR-ROUND
• Fishing Charters for Salmon — Trout — Grayling
• Maintained cross-country skiing/hiking trails
• Mt. McKinley Scenic Flights
• Dogsled and Snowmobile Rides available

Swiss-Alaska Inn
• RESTAURANT — Complete Menu
  Fresh Halibut and Salmon Dinners
• COCKTAIL LOUNGE
• MOTEL — All Modern Rooms with Bath
  Reasonable Prices • PAY PHONE
EAST TALKEETNA BY BOAT LAUNCH—watch for sign
P.O Box 565, Talkeetna, AK 99676   Phone (907) 733-2424
OPEN YEAR-ROUND   Please contact: Werner Rauchenstein

MAHAY'S Riverboat Service 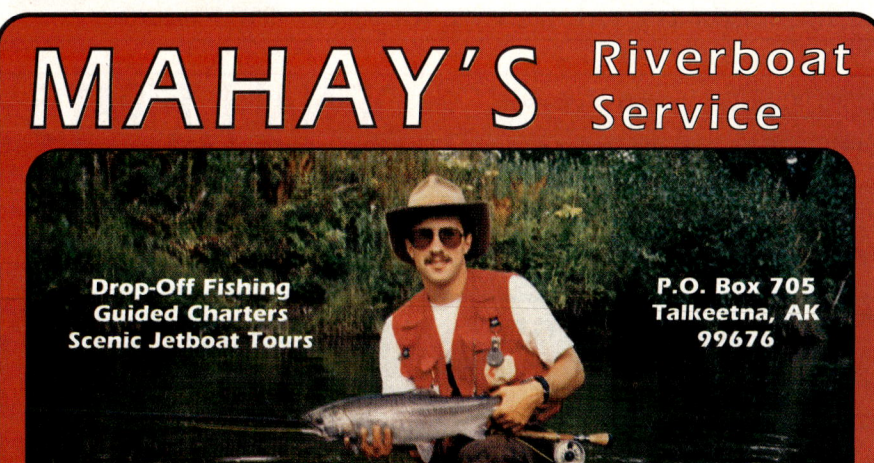
Drop-Off Fishing
Guided Charters
Scenic Jetboat Tours
P.O. Box 705
Talkeetna, AK 99676
(907) 733-2223

Talkeetna Spur Road (continued)

village airstrip not recommended for transient aircraft or helicopters (watch for closures and poor conditions).

A Welcome to Beautiful Downtown Talkeetna sign is posted at the town park as you enter Talkeetna's old-fashioned Main Street, the only paved street in town. Log cabins and clapboard homes and businesses line Main Street, which dead ends at the Susitna River. Walk or drive down to the riverside park at the end of Main Street, where there is parking, picnicking and sometimes a volleyball game in progress. There are also fishing and picnicking on the gravel bars of the Susitna.

Talkeetna was one of the pioneer mining and trapping settlements in the upper Susitna River valley. The first settlers came via the Susitna River about 1901 and built roads into the coal, gold and silver mines to the east in the Talkeetna Mountains.

The town reportedly gets its name from an Indian word meaning "where the rivers meet"; the Talkeetna and Chulitna rivers join the Susitna River here. The upper Susitna and Talkeetna rivers are popular with big game hunters, guides and river runners.

Talkeetna is the jumping-off point for many climbing expeditions to Mount McKinley, and in summer it's not unusual to find an international collection of visitors getting ready to climb, or coming back from a climb, on Mount McKinley and other peaks. Most climbing expeditions use the West Buttress route, pioneered by Bradford Washburn, flying in in specially equipped ski-wheel aircraft from Talkeetna to Kahiltna Glacier. The actual climb on Mount McKinley is made from about 7,000 feet/2,134m (where the planes land) to the summit of the South Peak (elev. 20,320 feet/6,193m). Talkeetna is also headquarters for a private guide service which guides climbing expeditions on Mount McKinley and other peaks.

ACCOMMODATIONS

Talkeetna has 5 motels/hotels, several bed and breakfasts, 6 restaurants, 2 gas stations, laundromats, gift and clothing shops, grocery and general stores. Dump station located at Three Rivers Tesoro.

There is a municipal campground with toilets and shelters at the public boat launch (fee charged) just beyond the Swiss Alaska Inn; take East Talkeetna Road (a right turn at Mile 14 on the Spur Road as you approach Talkeetna). There is also camping at Talkeetna River Park

TALKEETNA ADVERTISERS

Alaska Log Cabin
  B & B .... Ph. (907) 733-2668
Bays Bed and
  Breakfast .... Ph. (907) 733-1342
Denali Dry Goods .... Main St.
Denali Floats .... Ph. (907) 733-2384
Doug Geeting
  Aviation .... Ph. (907) 733-2366
Hudson Air Service, Inc. .... Main St.
K2 Aviation .... Ph. (907) 733-2291
Latitude 62° Lodge/
  Motel .... Ph. (907) 733-2262
Mahay's Riverboat
  Service .... Ph. (907) 733-2223
Mountain Gift Shop and Visitor
  Information Center, The .... Main St.
Mt. McKinley
  Flight Tours .... Ph. (907) 733-2366
Paradise Lodge .... Ph. (907) 733-1471
River Beauty Bed &
  Breakfast .... Ph. (907) 733-2741
Swiss–Alaska Inn .... Ph. (907) 733-2424
Talkeetna Air Taxi .... Ph. (907) 733-2218
Talkeetna Camp and
  Canoe .... Ph. (907) 733-2267
Talkeetna Gift and Collectables .... Main St.
Talkeetna Motel, Restaurant
  and Lounge .... Ph. (907) 733-2323
Talkeetna Riverboat Service .... Main St.
Talkeetna Roadhouse .. Ph. (907) 733-1351
Tri-River Charters .... Ph. (907) 733-2400
Village Arts & Crafts .... Main St.
Wax Museum of the North .... Main St.

HEROES OF THE HORIZON, by Gerry Bruder, relates the true stories of 28 veteran bush pilots who flew in Alaska's golden age of aviation. From Alaska Northwest Books™.

TRI-RIVER CHARTERS
Guided Fishing • Drop Off Fishing
(May – October)
All species salmon, trout, grayling
Early Reservations Recommended
DISCOUNT FOR GROUPS OF SIX OR MORE

Phone (907) 733-2400 – In Alaska 1(800) 487-2620
Next to Talkeetna Post Office   P.O. Box 312, Talkeetna, Alaska 99676

TALKEETNA MOTEL
In Picturesque Talkeetna

25 MODERN ROOMS
UNIQUE RESTAURANT and COCKTAIL LOUNGE
OPEN YEAR AROUND

BOX 115, TALKEETNA, AK 99676 • (907) 733-2323

Ivory • Soapstone
Native Handicrafts • Books
Health Foods • Woolens
An "Old Alaska" community store
SIBERIAN IMPORTS!

DENALI FLOATS
• Scenic Day Trips • Whitewater Rafting
• Wilderness Expeditions • Remote Fishing

Brochure: Box 330, Talkeetna, Alaska 99676 • (907) 733-2384

TALKEETNA GIFTS & COLLECTABLES
Pan for GOLD — GOLD Guaranteed!
NEW LOG BUILDING   2 FLOORS OF TREASURES

★ Native Arts & Gifts
★ Handmade Dolls
★ Plush Toys ★ Jewelry

Alaskan counted cross-stitch patterns

Alaskan Foods ★
Sweaters ★ Books ★
Souvenirs ★

Summer: 9-7 Daily • Winter 10-5:30 • Closed some Mondays and Tuesdays
Box 101, Main Street, Talkeetna, Alaska 99676 • (907) 733-2710

WAX MUSEUM of the North
• Life-sized waxed figures
• 3-D dioramas of historic northern events and characters
• Plus a collection of fascinating tidbits about the far North
(See log ad under Attractions)
MAIN STREET • Groups Welcome
Box 101, Talkeetna, Alaska 99676
(907) 733-2710
Mention this ad for discount

located at the end of the Talkeetna Spur Road (Mile 14.5). ▲

Alaska Log Cabin B & B. Lodging and cooking facilities in custom-crafted cabin on quiet, wooded acre. A leisurely quarter-mile walk from shops, restaurants, museums, parks, riverboats, Alaska Railroad and post office. Families welcome. Showers in town. Outhouse only. Double $45; each additional person $5. P.O. Box 19, Talkeetna, AK 99676. Phone (907) 733-2668. [ADVERTISEMENT]

Bays Bed and Breakfast. 11.5 miles on Talkeetna Spur Road. New modern log home, 3 large rooms, 1.5 miles from downtown Talkeetna. Enjoy flightseeing, riverboating, fishing—view Mount McKinley. Call (907) 733-1342. Write P.O. Box 527, Talkeetna, AK 99676 for reservations. Open year-round. [ADVERTISEMENT]

Talkeetna Motel, Restaurant and Lounge. Owned since 1979 by Al Sousa, the motel was originally built by "Evil" Alice and Sherm Powell. The "Tee-Pee" (as affectionately nicknamed by locals) has been a favorite with Alaskans for many years. Come try our famous burgers, homemade pies, char-broiled steaks, as well as nightly specials plus full menu. Open year-round. [ADVERTISEMENT]

Talkeetna Roadhouse. Authentic "Old Alaska" roadhouse providing comfortable lodging and delicious home-cooked meals since 1944. Full breakfast and lunch menus with family-style dinners—a tasty change from ordinary restaurants! Warm, friendly atmosphere. Reasonable rates. Open year-round. Home of Alaska's Homestead B-B-Q Sauce, available throughout the state. (907) 733-1351. See display ad this section. [ADVERTISEMENT]

TRANSPORTATION

Air: There are 4 air taxi services in Talkeetna. Charter service, flightseeing and glacier landings are available. **Railroad:** The Alaska Railroad. **Limousine:** From Anchorage airport and Denali National Park.

ATTRACTIONS

Talkeetna's Little Red Schoolhouse Museum is located 1 block off Main Street behind the Park Service ranger station. The schoolhouse, built in 1936, houses displays of historical items, local art and a historical library. The museum has a history of mountain climbing display which includes background on the late Ray Genet (who climbed Mount McKinley 25 times) and the late Don Sheldon, a famous Alaskan bush pilot. The museum also has an impressive 12-foot-by-12-foot scale model of Mount McKinley (Denali). Donations accepted. Pick up a walking tour map of Talkeetna's historical sites here. The Talkeetna Historical Society is restoring several old structures in town and many have identifying signs. The first cabin in Talkeetna—the Miner–Trappers cabin—is located on the museum ground. Picnic area adjacent museum. The museum is open 10 A.M. to 6 P.M. daily in summer.

Miners Day. Held the weekend before Memorial Day, this family-oriented event has a trade and craft fair, local cancan dancers, softball tournament, pie auction, a thrilling outhouse race, street dance and parade.

Annual Moose Dropping Festival is held second Saturday in July as a fund-raising project for the museum. Activities include a parade, barbecue, food and game booths, and, of course, a moose dropping throwing contest.

Riverboat tours up Talkeetna Canyon, Devils Canyon, Chulitna River and Tokositna River are available. Several guides also offer riverboat fishing trips from Talkeetna. Inquire locally for details.

Mahay's Riverboat Service. Fish clear-water streams for all 5 species of Pacific salmon and trout. Custom-designed jet boats allow access to over 200 miles of prime fishing territory. Guided fishing charters include all equipment needed. Fishing packages are available that include fishing, accommodations, meals and all the "extras." Spend the day exploring an authentic trapper's cabin, panning for gold and viewing nesting bald eagles on a Talkeetna or

Talkeetna's welcome sign.
(Jerrianne Lowther, staff)

HUDSON AIR SERVICE, INC.
CLIFF, OLLIE & SONS
SINCE 1948

Freight For The Bush
Glacier Flights & Landings
Scenic Trips • Prospecting
Charter Trips • Kayakers
Rafting & Hunting

(907) 733-2321
P.O. Box 82, Talkeetna, Alaska 99676

TALKEETNA CAMP AND CANOE

A Wilderness Experience

Heated fully-furnished tent cabins
Canoe rental • Guided fishing and canoe adventures • Ice fishing
Dog mushing • X-country Skiing

Open Year-Round

PO Box 378
Talkeetna, Alaska 99676

(907) 733-CAMP

Doug Geeting Aviation's McKinley Flight Tours & Glacier Landings

Turbocharged, ski-equipped, 5-6 seat aircraft with oxygen and intercom
• Over-the-Summit Flights •
• Glacier Landings, our specialty •

1. Visit the Kahiltna Base Camp where the expeditions start.
2. Land at Little Switzerland or at the Don Sheldon Mountain House and Circle Denali.
3. Wildlife-Glacier tour with Landing in Denali National Park.
4. Aerial Photo Platforming.
5. Enjoy our 6-passenger Cessna 207 turbocharged, with oxygen.

PRICES START AT $65 PER SEAT!

"It's a small price to pay for the treasures at the top of Mt. McKinley and the man who can get you there." —Erma Bombeck, columnist and author

"Barbara and I fly with DGA because they provide an excellent platform for mountain photography." —Galen Rowell, Mountain Light Photography, Inc.

For more information and reservations:
Call us collect at (907) 733-2366
or FAX us at (907) 733-1000
or write to:
DOUG GEETING AVIATION
Box 42MP, Talkeetna, Alaska 99676

Talkeetna Spur Road (continued)

Devils Canyon Tour. Drop-off fishing locations are also available at reasonable rates. We accept all major credit cards. (907) 733-2223, fax (907) 733-2712. [ADVERTISEMENT]

Talkeetna Gifts and Collectables. "One of the nicest and most complete gift shops in Alaska." Located in a spacious, new log building with 2 floors of handmade keepsakes, souvenirs, jewelry, books, Alaskana, antiques, quilts and other treasures. Also sealskin slippers, fur accessories, beautiful sweatshirts and Norwegian sweaters. For the kids, plush toys, puppets, huggable Eskimo dolls and locally made wooden toys. Alaskan foods and sourdough mix. We carry Alaska counted cross-stitch patterns featuring Suzy's exclusive "Alaska Map Sampler." We strive for quality with friendly service. Pan for gold, too. Gold guaranteed. Open year-round. See display ad this section. [ADVERTISEMENT]

Wax Museum of The North (and other things of interest), featuring life-size waxed figures depicting historical facts and fables of Alaska and the Far North. Entertaining, educational and exciting for all age groups. Meander through the historic railroad building experiencing Alaskana at every turn. Also home of the "Talkeetna Puppechanics." Gift shop too! Open daily mid-May through Labor Day. Special winter openings by appointment. Admission fee. Groups welcome. Mention this ad and get a discount. Main Street, Box 101, Talkeetna, AK 99676. Phone (907) 733-2710. [ADVERTISEMENT]

The Mountain Gift Shop and Visitor Information Center. Located in historic log cabin by the famous Welcome to Beautiful Downtown Talkeetna sign. View of Mount McKinley from porch. A fun place to shop with mountain, railroad and moose theme items: books, maps, posters, T-shirts, flags, hand-painted gold pans plus much more. Moose nugget items our specialty! Open 10 A.M. to 5:30 P.M. from May 15 to Labor Day. Free town map with list of attractions. [ADVERTISEMENT]

K2 Aviation. Always something to see—every day, every season. Let K2 help you discover hidden Alaska: mile-high rock walls, icy peaks, twisting glaciers, salmon-filled rivers, hillsides of bear, caribou and sheep, meadows of moose and wildflowers, clear winter days, sunny summer nights. All in the shadow of Mount McKinley. Jim Okonek's K2 offers: experienced McKinley pilots, glacier landings, fly-in fishing and hunting, climbing expedition air support, scenic flights, headphones for every passenger, natural history and local lore. For a really complete tour, circle Mount McKinley. Denali National Park overnight tours, statewide Explore Air tours. Office at Talkeetna airport. P.O. Box 545, Talkeetna, AK 99676. Phone (907) 733-2291, fax (907) 733-1221. [ADVERTISEMENT]

The ALASCOM Earth Station can be reached by driving 2.5 miles/4 km south of Talkeetna to Mile 12 Talkeetna Spur Road, then 3.4 miles/5.5 km east on a paved side road. The station provides interstate communications between Alaska and the other 49 states by processing signals sent and received via a satellite in synchronous orbit 22,000 miles/35,405 km above the equator. The dish-shaped antenna stands 98 feet/32m and can be rotated 1 degree per second and precisely track the movements of the satellite to within 0.02 of a degree. No tours of the facility.

Talkeetna Air Taxi. Fly Mount McKinley with Talkeetna Air Taxi. An awe-inspiring, memorable experience. Tour this vast glimmering world of towering peaks, glaciers and snow. Watch for animals—climbers—and take pictures. Satisfaction guaranteed. Glacier landings available. Sportfishing and hunting flights, aerial photography. Climbing expedition support. Office at state airport coming into Talkeetna. Follow our signs. Write Box 73-MP, Talkeetna, AK 99676. (907) 733-2218. See large ad in the DENALI NATIONAL PARK section. [ADVERTISEMENT]

Mt. McKinley Flight Tours. Experience a flight with renowned glacier and flying expert Doug Geeting, who knows the climbers and all the lore and legend of Denali (the great one). You can experience a glacier landing and look up at 5,000-foot walls of ice and rock that will astound the most world-weary traveler. This flight will definitely be the high point of all your Alaska adventures! Intercom-equipped. Group rates available. Guest house available, $65 per night. Fly-in fishing cabins. Open year-round. For reservations and prices write or call Doug Geeting Aviation, Box 42 MP, Talkeetna, AK 99676; (907) 733-2366. See display ad in the Denali National Park section. [ADVERTISEMENT]

Fishing. A Calico (chum) Salmon Derby is held the first 3 weeks of August. The **Susitna River** basin offers many top fishing streams and lakes, either accessible by road, plane or riverboat.

Return to Milepost A 98.7 George Parks Highway

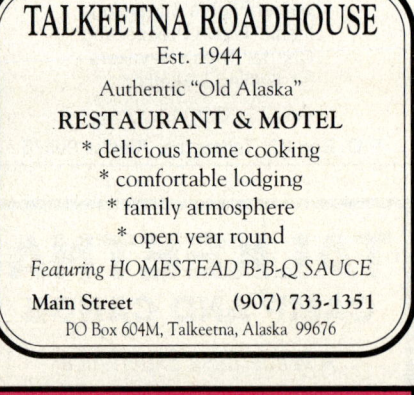

Experience McKinley
K2 aviation
(907) 733-2291
See log ad under Attractions

TALKEETNA ROADHOUSE
Est. 1944
Authentic "Old Alaska"
RESTAURANT & MOTEL
* delicious home cooking
* comfortable lodging
* family atmosphere
* open year round

Featuring HOMESTEAD B-B-Q SAUCE

Main Street   (907) 733-1351
PO Box 604M, Talkeetna, Alaska 99676

Paradise Lodge
Enjoy peace and serenity in a unique log lodge (Bed & Breakfast) or in a cozy log cabin.

SPECTACULAR MT. McKINLEY VIEW
Guided Salmon & Trout Fishing
Horseback Riding • Canoeing
Ice Fishing • Sleigh Rides • Skiing
Dog Mushing • Snowmobiling
(907) 733-1471 or 349-7747 *Open Year Around*
PO Box 203, Talkeetna, Alaska 99676

River Beauty
Bed & Breakfast

Office at Twister Creek Fuel
P.O. Box 525MP   (907) 733-2741
Talkeetna, Alaska 99676

George Parks Highway Log

(continued from page 330)

A 99.5 (160.1 km) **F 258.5** (416 km) **H & H Lakeview Restaurant & Lodge.** See display ad this section. ▲

A 99.8 (160.6 km) **F 258.2** (415.5 km) Access road to YMCA camp on Peggy Lake.

A 100.4 (161.6 km) **F 257.6** (414.6 km) CAUTION: Railroad crossing.

A 102.2 (164.5 km) **F 255.8** (411.7 km) Paved double-ended turnout to east opposite lake.

A 102.4 (164.8 km) **F 255.6** (411.3 km) Turnout at Sunshine Road; access to **Sunshine Creek** for fishing via dirt road.

A 104 (167.4 km) **F 254** (408.8 km) **Big Su Lodge.** See display ad this section.

A 104.2 (167.7 km) **F 253.8** (408.4 km) Entering Game Management Unit 16A, northbound, Unit 14B southbound.

A 104.3 (167.8 km) **F 253.7** (408.3 km) Bridge over Big Susitna River. State rest area to west on south bank of river; loop road, parking area, tables, firepits, toilets, no drinking water. ▲

Some of the finest stands of white birch in Alaska may be seen for several miles on both sides of the river. This area is also noted for its fiddlehead ferns, much prized by gourmets. The ferns (lady fern, ostrich fern and shield fern) are harvested in the spring, when their young shoots are tightly coiled, resembling a fiddle's head. The fiddleheads should be picked clean of the brown flakes which coat them. (Of the 3 ferns, ostrich fern is favored because it has the least amount of this coating.) Fiddleheads should be cooked before consumption. For physical descriptions of the ferns

BIG SU LODGE
GAS • MOTEL
CAFE • BAR
MILE 104 PARKS HIGHWAY
HC 89, Box 701   Willow, AK 99688
Troy and Barbara Jones
Summer – 24 hours   (907) 733-2464

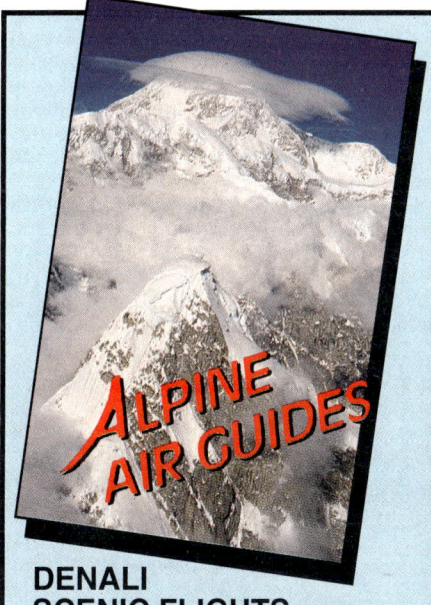

ALPINE AIR GUIDES

DENALI SCENIC FLIGHTS
GLACIER LANDINGS on Mt. McKinley
STATEWIDE AIR CHARTERS

MILE 114.8 PARKS HIGHWAY at Petracach

(907) 733-2302 or 733-2000

WRITE
PO Box 746, Talkeetna, Alaska 99676

TOY MILL (907) 733-2220
A Shop of Unique Handcrafted Alaskan Toys
Bed & Breakfast
A Memorable Refreshing Pause
Mile 1/3 Petersville Rd., Box 13068, Trapper Creek, AK 99683

A feast for the senses...

LAKEVIEW DINING IN A RUSTIC ALASKAN SETTING

OPEN 7 DAYS A WEEK

H & H Lakeview Restaurant & Lodge

COMFORTABLE ATMOSPHERE
FRIENDLY SERVICE

OMELETTES • HAMBURGERS • STEAK AND SEAFOOD
"OUR BREAD PUDDING IS FAMOUS STATEWIDE"

LODGING • LAKESIDE RV PARKING and CAMPING
GAS • DIESEL • PROPANE   LAUNDRY • SHOWERS
Groceries • Gift Shop • Fishing Licenses & Supplies
MAJOR CREDIT CARS ACCEPTED
TEXACO
Caravans and Tour Groups Welcome (Please call ahead)
(907) 733-2415 • HC 89 Box 616, Willow, AK 99688
MILE 99.5 PARKS HIGHWAY • 1/2 mile north of Talkeetna turnoff

GEORGE PARKS HIGHWAY

Cache Creek Lodge, Inc.

★ RESTAURANT ★ BAR
★ MOTEL ★ GIFT SHOP

Motorcoaches Are Our Specialty

★ BUFFET ★ LIVE MUSIC
★ PARK SETTING
★ Live Animal Friends

Turn in at the Chevron Station
Mile 114.8 Parks Highway

P.O. Box 13-132
Trapper Creek, Alaska 99683
(907) 733-2401

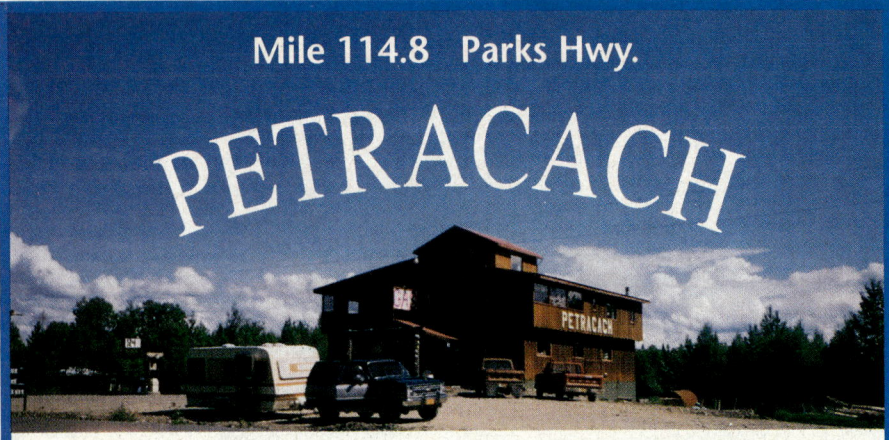

PETRACACH
Mile 114.8 Parks Hwy.

SOUTH DENALI VISITORS CENTER

LARGE RV PARK
Hook-ups & Dump Station
Large Gazebo

FISHING CHARTERS
Licenses • Supplies
Information

LAUNDROMAT (13 machines)
Restrooms • Showers • Sunbed

DELUXE LODGING
View of Mt. McKinley

P.O. Box 13209 • Trapper Creek, AK 99683
Phone (907) 733-2302 • FAX (907) 733-1002
Reservations Accepted   VISA • MasterCard

CHARTER FLIGHTS
Flightseeing south side or north side of Mt. McKinley
Fly-in Fishing & Hunting • 3,000-foot Runway
Raft Trips & Horseback Trips arranged • Dog Sled Tours

TRAVELERS' SUPPLIES
Cold Pop • Ice Cream • Snacks
Hot Sandwiches • Coffee • Ice
Doughnuts • Groceries • Sundries

GAS & OIL, etc.
Discount Prices

GIFT SHOP
Local Gold & Ivory Jewelry
Wooden Burl Bowls
Jade & Soapstone Carvings
Alaskan Motif T-Shirts &
Sweatshirts

Locally owned and operated by the Devon family, life-long Alaskans

---

and recipe, see *Discovering Wild Plants* by Janice Schofield (Alaska Northwest Books™).

A 104.6 (168.3 km) **F 253.4** (407.8 km) Rabideu Creek access; parking, 0.3 mile/0.5 km trail to mouth of creek. Watch for seasonal flooding.

A 104.8 (168.7 km) **F 253.2** (407.5 km) Double-ended turnout to west.

A 105.9 (170.4 km) **F 252.1** (405.7 km) Rabideaux Creek.

A 107.6 (173.2 km) **F 250.4** (403 km) View of Mount McKinley for northbound travelers.

A 114.8 (184.7 km) **F 243.2** (391.4 km) Cluster of businesses (lodges with gift shops, gas and restaurant) serving highway travelers and Trapper Creek the next mile northbound. ▲

Alpine Air Guides. See display ad on page 335.

Cache Creek Lodge, Inc. See display ad this section.

Petracach South Denali Visitors Center. Gas, diesel, travelers' supplies, gift shop. Deluxe lodging. Large Good Sam RV park with full hookups and dump station, restrooms, laundry, pay phone. Caravan fuel discounts. Also, space for 100 RVs without hookups. Deli and mini-grocery, coffee, ice, etc. Flightseeing and fishing charters arranged. VISA and MasterCard accepted. Phone (907) 733-2302. See large display ad in this section. [ADVERTISEMENT]

A 114.9 (184.9 km) **F 243.1** (391.2 km) **TRAPPER CREEK** (area pop. about 700), at **junction** with Petersville Road. Trapper Creek post office (Zip code 99683). Miners built the Petersville Road in the 1920s and federal homesteading began here in 1948, with settlement continuing through the 1950s and 1960s. The George Parks Highway opened as far as Trapper Creek in 1967. Today it is the southern gateway to Denali park and the Alaska Range, with access via the Petersville Road (description follows). Trapper Creek businesses are located along the Parks Highway and up Petersville Road.

Toy Mill Bed & Breakfast. See display ad on page 335.

Petersville Road leads west and north from Trapper Creek approximately 40 miles/64 km (no winter maintenance beyond Mile 14). This scenic gravel road (with excellent views of Mount McKinley) goes through a homestead and gold mining area which also

THE FORKS ROADHOUSE

BAR • MEALS LODGING

Historic Roadhouse
Hunting • Fishing • Winter Sports
Your Hostess: Ginger Jones
(907) 733-1851

Mile 18.7 Petersville Road
PO Box 13109,
Trapper Creek, Alaska 99683

---

336   The MILEPOST® ■ 1992

contains some new subdivisions. At Mile 7.1/11.4 km is Moose Creek Cabins and Campground. At Mile 18.7/30.1 km is The Forks Roadhouse. Turn down the right fork for the abandoned mining camp of Petersville (4-wheel drive recommended). The left fork leads 0.2 mile/0.3 km to Peters Creek stream. The bridge across Peters Creek is impassable. The road to Petersville is rough and used primarily by miners and trappers beyond The Forks Roadhouse. ▲

The Forks Roadhouse. See display ad this section.

Moose Creek Cabins and Campground. Rustic log cabins with bedding—or bring your own sleeping bag. Overnight RV parking and tent sites beside Moose Creek. Bed and breakfast available. Fishing for salmon and grayling. Hiking trails. William and Pauleen Floyd, Box 13463, Trapper Creek, AK 99683. Phone (907) 733-1345.
[ADVERTISEMENT] ▲

A 115.2 (185.4 km) F 242.8 (390.7 km) Trapper Creek community park.

A 115.5 (185.9 km) F 242.5 (390.1 km) **Trapper Creek Trading Post.** See display ad this section. ▲

A 115.6 (186 km) F 242.4 (390.1 km) Highway crosses Trapper Creek.

A 115.7 (186.2 km) F 242.3 (389.8 km) **Morrisette's.** See display ad this section.

A 121.1 (194.9 km) F 236.9 (381.2 km) Chulitna highway maintenance camp.

A 121.5 (195.5 km) F 236.5 (380.6 km) Easy-to-miss large paved double-ended rest area to east with tables, firepits, drinking water, toilet and interpretive bulletin board.

A 123.4 (198.6 km) F 234.6 (377.5 km) Wooded area with many dead trees covered with "conks" (a term applied to a type of bracket fungus).

A 126.6 (203.7 km) F 231.4 (372.4 km) Large paved turnout to east.

A 128.4 (206.6 km) F 229.6 (369.5 km) Undeveloped parking area below highway by creek.

A 132 (212.4 km) F 226 (363.7 km) Boundary of Denali State Park (see description next milepost).

A 132.7 (213.6 km) F 225.3 (362.6 km) Denali State Park entrance sign. This 324,240-acre park has 48 miles/77.2 km of hiking trails. Camping at Troublesome Creek (**Milepost A 137.3**) and at Byers Lake (**Milepost A 147**). Hunting is permitted in the park, but discharge of firearms is prohibited within 0.3 mile of highway or 0.5 mile of a developed facility.

A 132.8 (213.7 km) F 225.2 (362.4 km) **Chulitna River** bridge. *CAUTION: Slow down. Watch for road construction and bridge improvement in 1992.* Fishing for grayling, rainbow. Game Management Unit 13E,

---

TRAPPER CREEK TRADING POST
CAFE • CABINS • PACKAGE LIQUOR
GAS • GROCERY AND GIFT SHOP

MAJOR CREDIT CARDS

TEXACO Gas & Oil Products

24-Hour Wrecker Service

BREAKFAST • LUNCH • DINNER
GROCERIES • ICE • CAMPSITES • LIQUOR
Full Hookups • Showers • Dump Station • Coin-op Laundry
Propane • Fishing and Camping Supplies • Pay Phone

Write: Box 13167 • Trapper Creek, AK 99683 • Phone: (907) 733-2315
Open Year-round   *Bud and Judy Welcome You*
Mile A 115.5 Parks (Anchorage-Fairbanks) Highway

MARY'S McKINLEY VIEW LODGE
(Mary Carey is Back)
Mile 134.5 Parks Highway
Phone (907) 733-1555

Dine in glassed-in comfort with the best highway view of Alaska's stellar attraction, Mt. McKinley

Excellent food, featuring home-baked pies and fiddlehead fern, a gourmet delight

Spacious rooms with private baths, picture windows facing North America's tallest peak • Moderate rates

Mary Carey's Gift Shop
Visit with Lenora Preston, who has 10 years of expertise in dealing with ivory, soapstone, furs, and Alaska Native crafts, to help you select the perfect gift

Alaska's famed author MARY CAREY is present to autograph her books:

A Texas Brat In Alaska (The Cat-Train Kid) $10.95
An Auto Trip To Alaska's Shangri-La 10.00
Bank Robbers Wrote My Diary 12.95
Alaska, Not For A Woman $13.95
Fireweed Philosophy 3.95
Green Gold In Alaska 14.95
Let's Taste Alaska 6.95
Amazing Alaska 6.95
Jane's Texas 13.95
How Long Must I Hide 12.95
A-Lass-Kan Adventure 17.95

Also Available: Frozen & Pickled Fiddlehead Fern

For Mail Orders and Brochures, Write to Mary Carey at
The Fiddlehead Fern Farm, Mile 1 Talkeetna Spur Road
HC 89 Box 8540, Talkeetna, AK 99676-9705 • (907) 733-2428
Please enclose $1.50 postage for each book ordered

Morrisette's
"Friendliest Little Gift Shop In Alaska"
ALASKAN SHIRTS GALORE
Souvenirs   Country Gifts
Free Coffee   Picnic Area
OPEN YEAR-ROUND
Greg & Linda Morrisette
Mile 115.7 Parks Highway

Dramatic Hurricane Gulch Bridge at Milepost A 174. (Jerrianne Lowther, staff)

leaving unit 16A, northbound.

A 134.5 (216.5 km) **F 223.5** (359.7 km) Mary's McKinley View Lodge. See display ad on page 337.

A 135.2 (217.6 km) **F 222.8** (358.6 km) Large paved turnout with litter barrels and view of 20,320-foot/6,194-m Mount McKinley; a display board here points out peaks. From here northbound for many miles there are views of glaciers on the southern slopes of the Alaska Range to the west. Ruth, Buckskin and Eldridge glaciers are the most conspicuous.

Ruth Glacier trends southeast through the Great Gorge for 31 miles/50 km. The glacier was named in 1903 by F.A. Cook for his daughter. The Great Gorge was named by mountain climbers in the late 1940s. Nicknamed the Grand Canyon of Alaska, peaks on either side of the gorge tower up to 5,000 feet/1,500m above Ruth Glacier. The gorge opens into Don Sheldon Amphitheater, at the head of Ruth Glacier, where the Don Sheldon mountain house sits. Donald E. Sheldon (1921–1975) was a well-known bush pilot who helped map, patrol and aid search and rescue efforts in this area.

Flightseeing trips can be arranged which take you close to Mount McKinley, into the Don Sheldon Amphitheater, through the Great Gorge and beneath the peak of The Mooses Tooth. Inquire at Chulitna River Lodge, **Milepost A 156.2**, or with air taxi operators in Talkeetna or in the national park.

Peaks to be sighted, left to right, along the next 20 miles/32.2 km to the west are: Mount Hunter (elev. 14,573 feet/4,442m); Mount Huntington (elev. 12,240 feet/3,731m); Mount Barrille (elev. 7,650 feet/2,332m); and Mount Dickey (elev. 9,845 feet/3,001m).

A 137.3 (221 km) **F 220.7** (355.1 km) Troublesome Creek bridge. Lower Troublesome Creek state recreation site has 10 campsites, $6/night camping fee or annual pass, day-use area with sheltered picnic sites, toilets, water and litter barrels. Lower Troublesome Creek trailhead. This is usually a clear runoff stream, not silted by glacial flour. The stream heads in a lake and flows 14 miles/22.5 km to the Chulitna River. ▲

Troublesome Creek, rainbow, grayling and salmon (king salmon fishing prohibited); June, July, August and September.

A 137.6 (221.4 km) **F 220.4** (354.7 km) Upper Troublesome Creek trailhead and parking area. Trails to Byers Lake (15 miles/24 km) and Tarn Point, elev. 2,881 feet/878m (10.8 miles/17.3 km). Trailhead and trail to Mile 5.5 closed from mid-July through end of season due to the high concentration of bears feeding on spawning salmon.

A 139.9 (225.1 km) **F 218.1** (351 km) Paved turnout with litter barrels to west.

A 143.2 (230.5 km) **F 214.8** (345.7 km) Large double-ended turnout to east.

A 143.9 (231.6 km) **F 214.1** (344.6 km) Bridge over Byers Creek.

A 145.7 (234.5 km) **F 212.3** (341.6 km) Paved turnout to west.

A 147 (236.6 km) **F 211** (339.6 km) **Byers Lake** state campground with 66 sites, $6/night camping fee or annual pass, picnic tables, firepits, water, toilets (wheelchair accessible), and access to Byers Lake (electric motors permitted). Fishing for grayling, burbot, rainbow, lake trout and whitefish. Remote campsite 1.8-mile/2.9-km hike from campground (see directions posted on bulletin board). Hiking trail to Curry Ridge and south to Troublesome Creek. *CAUTION: Black bears frequent campground. Keep a clean camp.* ▲

A 147.2 (236.9 km) **F 210.8** (339.2 km) Alaska Veterans Memorial loop road to rest area with toilets (wheelchair accessible), picnic shelter, drinking water, picnic tables and firepits. There is a unique concrete memorial—5 sculpted upright slabs, statue and flagpole—at this wayside honoring the armed forces. Loop road returns to highway at **Milepost A 147.4**.

A 155.6 (250.4 km) **F 202.4** (325.7 km) For the next mile northbound, there are views of Eldridge Glacier to the left. The snout of the glacier is 6 miles/9.7 km from the road. The Fountain River heads at the terminus of the glacier and flows into the Chulitna.

A 156.2 (251.4 km) **F 201.8** (324.8 km) **Chulitna River Lodge & Cafe.** Located in the center of Denali State Park with easy access to camping, hiking and fishing spots, all with spectacular views of Mount McKinley. Log cabins from $50 to $80. Within 90 minutes (75 miles) of Denali National Park entrance. Open year-round. See display ad this section. [ADVERTISEMENT]

NOTE: No gas available from here north to **Milepost A 188.5**.

AREA FISHING (fly in): Lucy Lake, lake trout and grayling, use spinners and spoons, June and July, 10-minute flight. **Spink Lake**, rainbow, use spinners and spoons, July, August and September, 15-minute flight. **Portage Creek**, rainbow, grayling and salmon, use spoons, spinners, flies, July, August and September, 20-minute flight. **Chulitna Lake**, rainbow, July, August and September, 20-minute flight. **Donut Lake**, Dolly Varden, use spinners, spoons, flies, July and August, 20-minute flight. **Bull Lake**, lake trout and grayling, use spoons, spinners, July and August, 20-minute flight.

A 157.7 (253.8 km) **F 200.3** (322.3 km) Small paved turnout to west.

A 159.4 (256.5 km) **F 198.6** (319.6 km) Double-ended paved turnout to west.

A 159.9 (257.3 km) **F 198.1** (318.8 km) Parking area by Horseshoe Creek.

A 160.8 (258.8 km) **F 197.2** (317.4 km) The highway makes a steep descent northbound with moderate S-curves to Little Coal Creek.

A 161 (259.1 km) **F 197** (317 km) Large gravel turnout to east.

A 162.4 (261.4 km) **F 195.6** (314.8 km) Large paved turnout to west.

A 162.7 (261.8 km) **F 195.3** (314.3 km) Small paved turnout to east. Watch for beaver pond to west northbound.

A 163.1 (262.5 km) **F 194.9** (313.6 km) Double-ended paved turnout to west.

A 163.2 (262.6 km) **F 194.8** (313.5 km) Bridge over Little Coal Creek.

Coal Creek, rainbow, grayling and salmon, July through September.

A 163.8 (263.6 km) **F 194.2** (312.5 km) Little Coal Creek trailhead and parking area. According to park rangers, this trail offers the easiest access (1½-hour hike) to alpine area within Denali State Park.

A 165.6 (266.5 km) **F 192.4** (309.6 km) A small stream passes under the road; paved turnouts on both sides of highway. Good berry picking in the fall.

A 168.5 (271.2 km) **F 189.5** (305 km) Denali State Park sign.

A 169 (272 km) **F 189** (304.2 km) *CAUTION: Railroad crossing.* A solar collector here helps power the warning signals.

Denali State Park boundary (leaving park northbound, entering park southbound).

A 170.3 (274 km) **F 187.7** (302.1 km) Paved viewpoint area with litter barrels to west.

A 171 (275.2 km) **F 187** (300.9 km) There are several small turnouts with litter barrels next 5 miles/8 km northbound.

A 174 (280 km) **F 184** (296.1 km) Bridge over Hurricane Gulch; rest area. From the south end of the bridge, scramble through alders up the east bank of the gulch to find photographers' trail (unmarked). A 0.3-mile/

Chulitna River Lodge & Cafe
OPEN ALL YEAR
LOG CABINS • Fishing Tackle • Gifts
Alaska Gifts and Souvenirs
Great Selection - Come By and See!!
Fly-In Fishing • Whitewater Rafting • Hiking Trips
Snowmobiling • X-C Skiing • Dogsledding • Ski-joring
In Center of Denali State Park, Close to hiking trails, Mt. McKinley scenic views
Send for brochure
Write: PO Box 13317, Trapper Creek, Alaska 99683
See our log ad at Mile 156.2 Parks Highway

DIESEL • GAS
VISA • MasterCard
Tesoro cards accepted
PHONE: (907) 733-2521

0.4-km trail along edge of Hurricane Gulch offers good views of the bridge span and gulch. A pleasant walk, good berry picking in the fall. *Do not go too near the edge.* Parking areas at both ends of bridge.

Construction costs for the bridge were approximately $1.2 million. The 550-foot/168-m deck of the bridge is 260 feet/79m above Hurricane Creek, not as high as the railroad bridge that spans the gulch near the Chulitna River. From this bridge the highway begins a gradual descent northbound to Honolulu Creek.

A 176 (283.2 km) **F 182** (292.9 km) Paved turnout with litter barrel to east. There are several small turnouts next 5 miles/8 km southbound.

A 176.5 (284 km) **F 181.5** (292.1 km) Double-ended gravel turnout to west with view of the Alaska Range. Highway descends long grade northbound.

A 177.8 (286.1 km) **F 180.2** (290 km) Paved turnout with litter barrels and view of eroded bluffs to west.

A 178.1 (286.6 km) **F 179.9** (289.5 km) Bridge over Honolulu Creek. The highway begins a gradual ascent northbound to Broad Pass, the gap in the Alaska Range crossed by both the railroad and highway. Undeveloped parking areas below highway on the creek.

A 179.5 (288.9 km) **F 178.5** (287.3 km) Paved turnout to west with litter barrels by small lake. In early September blueberries are plentiful for the next 25 miles/40 km.

A 180 (289.7 km) **F 178** (286.5 km) Small paved turnout to west with litter barrels by small lake.

A 183.2 (294.8 km) **F 174.8** (281.3 km) Paved turnouts both sides of highway. Look to the west across the Chulitna River for dramatic view of the Alaska Range.

A 184.5 (296.9 km) **F 173.5** (279.2 km) Paved turnout with litter barrels to west.

A 185 (297.7 km) **F 173** (278.4 km) East Fork DOT/PF highway maintenance station.

A 185.1 (297.9 km) **F 172.9** (278.3 km) Bridge over East Fork Chulitna River.

A 185.6 (298.7 km) **F 172.4** (277.4 km) East Fork rest area (no sign at turnoff) on right northbound. A 0.5-mile/0.8-km paved loop gives access to a gravel picnic area with overnight parking, 23 tables, concrete fireplaces, picnic shelter, pit toilets, water pump, dump station, restrooms with hot and cold water and flush toilets. The rest area is in a bend of the East Fork Chulitna River amid a healthy growth of Alaskan spruce and birch. Cut wood is often available. ▲

A 186.4 (300 km) **F 171.6** (276.2 km) Small paved turnout to east.

A 187.5 (301.8 km) **F 170.5** (274.4 km) Paved double-ended turnout with litter barrels to west; small paved turnout east side of highway.

A 188.5 (303.4 km) **F 169.5** (272.8 km) **The Igloo.** 50 miles south of entrance to Denali National Park. Unleaded, regular, diesel fuels. Ask for 5¢ discount for cash fill-up. Caravan discounts. Postcards, candy, soft drinks, snacks. Many quality Alaskan gifts and souvenirs. Specialty T-shirts and sweats. Open May 1 to Sept. 30. (907) 768-2622. Free camper parking with fill-up.
[ADVERTISEMENT]

A 189.9 (305.6 km) **F 168.1** (270.5 km) Gravel double-ended turnout. Watch for beaver dam to east northbound.

A 191.2 (307.7 km) **F 166.8** (268.4 km) Large paved turnout with litter barrels to west. Look for cotton grass.

A 194.3 (312.7 km) **F 163.7** (263.4 km) *CAUTION: Railroad crossing.*

A 194.5 (313 km) **F 163.5** (263.1 km) Bridge over Middle Fork Chulitna River. Undeveloped parking area southwest of bridge below the highway. *CAUTION: Windy area through Broad Pass.*

A 195 (313.8 km) **F 163** (262.3 km) Entering Broad Pass northbound.

A 195.7 (314.9 km) **F 162.3** (261.2 km) Paved parking area to the east. Good views of Broad Pass.

A 200.9 (323.3 km) **F 157.1** (252.8 km) Large paved parking area to east with litter barrels and mountain view.

A 201.3 (324 km) **F 156.7** (252.2 km) Summit of Broad Pass (not signed). Broad Pass is one of the most beautiful areas on the George Parks Highway. A mountain valley, bare in some places, dotted with scrub spruce in others, and surrounded by mountain peaks, there's a top-of-the-world feeling for the traveler, although it is one of the lowest summits along the North American mountain system. Named in 1898 by George Eldridge and Robert Muldrow, the 2,300-foot/701-m pass, sometimes called Caribou Pass, marks the divide between the drainage of rivers and streams that empty into Cook Inlet and those that empty into the Yukon River.

Orange towers of weather service station building west of highway.

A 202.1 (325.2 km) **F 155.9** (250.9 km) Boundary of Matanuska–Susitna Borough.

A 203.1 (326.9 km) **F 154.9** (249.3 km) *CAUTION: Railroad crossing.*

A 203.7 (327.8 km) **F 154.3** (248.3 km) Paved parking area with view to east.

A 208 (334.7 km) **F 150** (241.4 km) Turnout to west at end of bridge over Pass Creek; blueberries in season.

A 209.5 (337.1 km) **F 148.5** (239 km) Bridge over Jack River; paved turnout.

A 209.9 (337.8 km) **F 148.1** (238.3 km) **Junction** of the George Parks Highway with the Denali Highway. **CANTWELL** post office and school, as well as a motel, lodge, restaurant, grocery and gas stations are located here. **Emergency Services: Alaska State Troopers,** phone 768-2202. **Ambulance,** phone 768-2982. The original town of Cantwell, 1.8 miles/2.9 km east of this junction, has a cafe, bar and liquor store. Turn west on the Denali Highway for Cantwell, turn east for Paxson (see DENALI HIGHWAY section for description of Cantwell and Denali Highway log).

Backwoods Lodging. See display ad this section.

Cantwell Lodge. See display ad this section.

A 210 (338 km) **F 148** (238.2 km)

DRIVE THE DENALI
Stay at
PAXSON LODGE
At Junction of Richardson & Denali Highways
See display ad in
Richardson Highway Section — Mile 185.5

The Igloo
SNACKS • GIFTS
T-SHIRTS • SWEATS
Gasoline • Diesel • JP4
Ask for 5¢ discount for cash fillup.
Mile A 188.5 Parks Highway • Denali National Park Area
VISA • MASTERCARD
(907) 768-2622

BACKWOODS LODGING
Open year-a-round . . . . . 30 minutes to Denali Park
VIEW MT. McKINLEY and **FISH GRAYLING NEARBY**
Family-sized units   *Owner-operated*
T.V., Phone, Refrigerator   Homestead Atmosphere
RV HOOKUPS
Phone (907) 768-2232   Box 32, Cantwell, Alaska 99729
0.2 mile east of Parks Highway on the Denali Highway

Mile 135.5 Denali Highway, Box 87, Cantwell, Alaska 99729
CANTWELL LODGE
Old Town Cantwell   (907) 768-2300
On The Railhead   CAFE — BAR — LIQUOR STORE (907) 768-2512
                    "Home of the Longhorned Sheep"
Rooms • Laundromat • Showers • Camping • RV Hookups • Ice • Pay Phone
Complimentary Ice with the Above Services
Located 2 miles west of the Parks and Denali Highway Junction

Keith and Armeda Bulard, longtime Cantwell residents, are your new hosts. We offer you clean, friendly year around service. Enjoy coffee with the locals. There are large turn-around parking spaces for over-sized vehicles. America's largest National Park — Denali — is only 30 minutes away. Extraordinary views of Mt. McKinley within the immediate area.

Cantwell post office (Zip code 99729).

A 210.2 (338.3 km) **F 147.8** (237.9 km) **Parkway Gift Shop.** See display ad this section.

A 210.4 (338.6 km) **F 147.6** (237.5 km) **Cantwell Chevron Gas.** See display ad this section.

A 211.5 (340.4 km) **F 146.5** (235.8 km) Paved parking area to west with litter barrels.

A 212.7 (342.3 km) **F 145.3** (233.8 km) Gravel turnout by Nenana River. Watch for large beaver dam to west southbound.

A 213.9 (344.2 km) **F 144.1** (231.9 km) Paved double-ended turnout with litter barrels to west among tall white spruce and fireweed.

A 215.3 (346.5 km) **F 142.7** (229.6 km) Access road to Nenana River, which parallels the highway northbound.

A 215.7 (347.1 km) **F 142.3** (229 km) First bridge northbound over the Nenana River. Highway narrows northbound.

NOTE: Watch for road construction north to Milepost A 231.3 in 1992.

A 216.2 (347.9 km) **F 141.8** (228.2 km) Entering Game Management Unit 20A and leaving unit 13E northbound.

A 216.3 (348.1 km) **F 141.7** (228 km) Paved double-ended turnout with litter barrels to west. Good spot for photos of Panorama Mountain (elev. 5,778 feet/1,761m), the prominent peak visible to the east.

A 217.6 (350.2 km) **F 140.4** (225.9 km) Small gravel turnout to west.

A 218.6 (351.8 km) **F 139.4** (224.3 km) Double-ended turnout to west with litter barrels and beautiful view of Nenana River.

A 219 (352.4 km) **F 139** (223.7 km) Slide area: Watch for rocks next 0.4 mile/0.6 km northbound.

A 219.8 (353.7 km) **F 138.2** (222.4 km) Paved double-ended turnout with litter barrel to west overlooking Nenana River.

A 220.2 (354.4 km) **F 137.8** (221.8 km) Wide gravel turnout to east.

A 220.6 (355 km) **F 137.4** (221.1 km) Long double-ended gravel turnout.

A 222.2 (357.6 km) **F 135.8** (218.5 km) Large, paved double-ended turnout to west with litter barrels beside Nenana River slough.

A 223.9 (360.3 km) **F 134.1** (215.8 km) **Carlo Creek Lodge.** (907) 683-2576, 683-2573. 12 miles south of Denali Park entrance. 20 wooded acres bordered by beautiful Carlo Creek, the Nenana River and Denali National Park. Cozy log cabins with own bathroom and shower on creek. RV park, dump station, tent sites, large barbecue pit with roof. Public bathrooms with showers. Small general store, propane, gift shop with Alaskan made gifts from fur to lace. Information and pay phone. Walking distance to The Perch Restaurant. See display ad this section. [ADVERTISEMENT] ▲

A 224 (360.5 km) **F 134** (215.7 km) Bridge over Carlo Creek. River runner's (Osprey Expeditions) office located at the bridge.

The Perch. A beautiful new restaurant-bar perched on a private hill. Spectacular dining, specializes in freshly baked bread, seafood and steaks. Also, take-out giant cinnamon rolls for breakfast. Open 5 P.M. to 10 P.M., daily, Memorial Day weekend through September. Sleeping cabins with central bath, 1 with kitchenette, beside Carlo Creek. Owners/operators, Jerry and Elaine Pollock. (907) 683-2523. Denali Route 2, Mile 244, Healy, AK 99743. [ADVERTISEMENT]

A 226 (363.7 km) **F 132** (212.4 km) Fang Mountain (elev. 6,736 feet/2,053m) may be visible to the west through the slash in the mountains.

A 229.7 (369.7 km) **F 128.3** (206.5 km) Paved turnout with litter barrel to west.

A 231.1 (371.9 km) **F 126.9** (204.2 km) **Denali Grizzly Bear Cabins & Campground.** South boundary Denali National Park. AAA approved. Drive directly to your individual kitchen, sleeping, or tent cabin with its old-time Alaskan atmosphere overlooking scenic Nenana River. Two conveniently located buildings with toilets, sinks, coin-operated hot showers. Advance cabin reservations suggested. Tenting and RV campsites also available in peaceful lower wooded area. Hookups. Propane. Caravans welcome! Hot coffee and rolls, ice cream, snacks, groceries, ice, liquor store, Alaskan gifts. Specialty sweatshirts. VISA and MasterCard accepted. Owned and operated by a pioneer Alaskan family. Reservations (907) 683-2696 (summer); (907) 488-3932 (winter). See display ad in DENALI NATIONAL PARK section. [ADVERTISEMENT] ▲

A 231.1 (371.9 km) **F 126.9** (204.2 km) **McKinley Village Lodge.** McKinley Village Lodge is convenient to all Denali National Park activities. This comfortable lodge is located on a quiet stretch of the Nenana River. Lounge with light dining, coffee shop, gift shop, complete tour and raft arrangements and transfers. [ADVERTISEMENT]

A 231.3 (372.2 km) **F 126.7** (203.9 km) Crabb's Crossing, second bridge northbound over the Nenana River.

At the north end of this bridge is the boundary of Denali National Park and Preserve. From here north for 6.8 miles/10.9 km the George Parks Highway is within the boundaries of the park and travelers must abide by park rules. No discharge of firearms permitted.

NOTE: Watch for road construction south to Milepost A 215.7 in 1992.

A 233.1 (375.1 km) **F 124.9** (201 km) Gravel turnout to east.

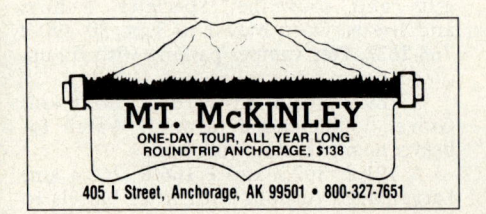

A 234.1 (376.7 km) **F 123.9** (199.4 km) Double-ended turnout with litter barrels to east; scenic viewpoint. No overnight parking or camping. Mount Fellows (elev. 4,476 feet/1,364m) to the east. The constantly changing shadows make this an excellent camera subject. Exceptionally beautiful in the evening. To the southeast stands Pyramid Peak (elev. 5,201 feet/1,585m).

A 235.1 (378.4 km) F 122.9 (197.8 km) CAUTION: Railroad crossing.

A 236.7 (380.9 km) F 121.3 (195.2 km) Alaska Railroad crosses over highway. From this point the highway begins a steep descent northbound to Riley Creek.

A 237.2 (381.7 km) F 120.8 (194.4 km) Riley Creek bridge.

A 237.3 (381.9 km) F 120.7 (194.2 km) Entrance to Denali National Park and Preserve (formerly Mount McKinley National Park) to west. Fresh water fill-up hose and dump station 0.2 mile/0.3 km from junction on Park Road; Visitor Access Center is 0.5 mile/0.8 km from the highway junction. Campsites within the park are available on a first-come, first-served basis; sign up at the Visitor Access Center. You may also pick up schedules for the shuttle bus service at the Visitor Access Center (private vehicle access to the park is restricted). See DENALI NATIONAL PARK section for details. Highway businesses (lodges, cabins, campground, restaurants) serving park visitors are located both south and north of the park entrance between Cantwell and Healy.

A 238 (383 km) F 120 (193.4 km) Third bridge northbound over the Nenana River. The 4.8 miles/7.7 km of road and 7 bridges in the rugged Nenana Canyon cost $7.7 million to build.

Sugarloaf Mountain (elev. 4,450 feet/1,356m), to the east, is closed to the hunting of Dall sheep, which are regularly sighted in the early and late summer months. Mount Healy (elev. 5,716 feet/1,742m) is to the west.

Southbound for 6.8 miles/10.9 km the George Parks Highway is within the boundaries of Denali National Park and Preserve and travelers must abide by park rules. No discharge of firearms.

A 238.1 (383.2 km) F 119.9 (193 km) **Denali Raft Adventures.** Come with the original Nenana River rafters! Paddleboats, too! All ages welcome, 7 departures daily. White water or scenic floats. Get away to untouched wilderness! 2-hour, 4-hour and 6-hour trips. See display ad in DENALI NATIONAL PARK section. Phone (907) 683-2234. VISA, MasterCard accepted. [ADVERTISEMENT]

A 238.3 (383.5 km) F 119.7 (192.6 km) Kingfisher Creek.

A 238.4 (383.6 km) F 119.6 (192.5 km) **Denali River View Inn.** Beautiful clear views of the national park and the sounds of the Nenana River. We have attractive rooms, TVs, excellent service and transportation. Pay phone. Conveniently located. Please visit our shirt shop. Wide selection of T-shirts and sweatshirts. Major credit cards. For reservations and information write P.O. Box 49M, Denali Park, AK 99755 or call winter (206) 384-1078, summer (907) 683-2663. See display ad in the DENALI NATIONAL PARK section. [ADVERTISEMENT]

A 238.5 (383.8 km) F 119.5 (192.3 km) Alaska flag display features a 10-by-15-foot/3-by-5-m state flag and plaques detailing history of flag design and song.

Commercial outfitters offer river-running trips on the Nenana. (Jerrianne Lowther, staff)

A 238.5 (383.3 km) F 119.5 (192.3 km) **McKinley/Denali Steakhouse and Salmon Bake.** Satisfy that hearty Alaskan appetite at a real home-style barbecue restaurant, featuring char-broiled steaks, fresh salmon and halibut, tender beef ribs, barbecued chicken with rice pilaf, burgers and sandwiches, baked beans, extensive salad bar, homemade soups and desserts. Rustic heated indoor seating with majestic view of mountains. Free shuttle from all local hotels. Sourdough breakfasts. Large selection of postcards in our upstairs gift shop. Ice for sale. Pay phone. Open daily 5 A.M. to 10:30 P.M. in summer. Phone (907) 683-2733. See display ad in DENALI NATIONAL PARK section. [ADVERTISEMENT]

A 238.5 (383.3 km) F 119.5 (192.3 km) **McKinley/Denali Cabins.** Economy cabins from $50. Closest full-service facility to park entrance, wildlife shuttles. Close to raft trips, store, gift shop, gas. New beds, linens, blankets. Central showers. Pay phone. Some cabins with private baths. Shuttle to visitor center, railroad depot available. Free visitor information. Call us for reservations on many area activities. Reservations: (907) 683-2258 or 683-2733 or write: Box 90M, Denali Park, AK 99755. See display ad in DENALI NATIONAL PARK section. [ADVERTISEMENT]

A 238.5 (383.8 km) F 119.5 (192.3 km) **Denali Crow's Nest Log Cabins and the Overlook Bar & Grill.** Open mid-May to mid-September, offering the finest view in area. Close to park entrance. Hot tubs, tour bookings. Dine indoors or on the deck. For courtesy shuttle, call (907) 683-2723, fax (907) 683-2323. See display ads in DENALI NATIONAL PARK section. [ADVERTISEMENT]

A 238.6 (384 km) F 119.4 (192.2 km) **Harper Lodge Princess®.** Offering 192 rooms and suites with phones and TVs. Free shuttle to rail depot and park activities. Spas, gift shop, fine dining and deli. Handicap accommodations. Seasonal service mid-May to mid-September. Rates from $145. VISA, MasterCard, American Express. Write Princess Tours®, 2815 2nd Ave., Suite #400, Seattle, WA 98121 or call (800) 426-0500 year-round. [ADVERTISEMENT]

A 238.7 (384.1 km) F 119.3 (192 km km) **Mt. McKinley Motor Lodge.** We specialize in serving the highway traveler. Close to park entrance. Rooms with full bath, color TV, beautiful park view. Front door parking, outdoor barbecue area. Reasonable rates. Central booking for all park activities. Your hosts: Rick and Keri Zarcone. (907) 683-1240 (summer); (907) 683-2567 (anytime). See display ad in the DENALI NATIONAL PARK section. [ADVERTISEMENT]

A 238.7 (384.1 km) F 119.3 (192 km) **Nuna Iditarod Kennels.** Meet Iditarod veteran mushers Dewey and Kathy Halverson. See Alaskan huskies used in the 1,049-mile race from Anchorage to Nome. Pet our

THE SHIRT SHOP at...
Denali
RIVER VIEW INN

Great Selection • The Best Prices

Major Credit Cards
MILE 238.4 PARKS HIGHWAY

GEORGE PARKS HIGHWAY

Northern lights (aurora borealis) near Healy. (Nancy Faville)

husky pups. View our photo collection and displays of the mushers, dogs, country and equipment used in the Last Great Race. Come visit and ask questions. Dogsled demonstrations. Winter dog tours. Unique Alaska gift items. Mail: P.O. Box 13183, Trapper Creek, AK 99683; phone (907) 345-5008. [ADVERTISEMENT]

A 238.8 (384.3 km) **F** 119.2 (191.8 km) **Sourdough Cabins.** Office and front desk are located here, adjacent to Sourdough Gift Shop and the McKinley Raft Tours office. Sourdough offers brand new individual heated cabins, nestled in a spruce forest located below the office, away from the highway noise. (907) 683-2773. VISA, MasterCard accepted. See display ad in the DENALI NATIONAL PARK section. [ADVERTISEMENT]

A 238.9/384.5 km) **F** 119.1/191.7 km) **Alaska Cabin Nite Dinner Theatre.** Located at McKinley Chalet Resort. Sourdough style salmon and ribs dinner served family style in beautiful handcrafted log cabin. Dinner is followed by a rousing 40-minute wilderness revue. Two seatings nightly. See display ad in DENALI NATIONAL PARK section. [ADVERTISEMENT]

A 238.9 (384.5 km) **F** 119.1 (191.7 km)

Homestead Bed & Breakfast

On Otto Lake
Mile 247 Parks Highway
Winter Rates Available
P.O. Box 420 • Healy, Alaska 99743
(907) 683-2575
June James, Proprietor

MOTEL Mile 248.7 • Open 24 Hours Year-round
Breakfast • Lunch • Dinner
STEAKS • SEAFOOD Phone (907) 683-2420
TOTEM INN LOUNGE

McKinley Chalet Resort, 254 2-room mini-suites in chalet-style cedar lodges overlooking the Nenana River. Dining room, deli, lounge, gift shop. Indoor swimming pool, hot tub. Sauna and exercise room. Home of Alaska Cabin Nite Theatre. Phone (907) 276-7234. See display ad in DENALI NATIONAL PARK section. [ADVERTISEMENT]

A 239 (384.6 km) **F** 119 (191.5 km) **Tundra Mini-Golf.** Eighteen holes of golf with an all-Alaskan theme. Driving practice net. Hours are 2-10 P.M. Turn toward the river on Quigley Trail at McKinley Chalets and left at Sourdough Cabins. Fun for the whole family, come on out and join us! (907) 683-GOLF (4653). [ADVERTISEMENT]

A 240.1 (386.4 km) **F** 117.9 (189.7 km) Bridge over Ice Worm Gulch. *CAUTION: Rock slide areas north- and southbound. Slow down.* High winds in the Nenana Canyon can make this stretch of road dangerous for campers and motorhomes.

WARNING: The highway has many sharp curves. Do not park along the highway. Use the many parking areas provided.

A 240.2 (386.6 km) **F** 117.8 (189.6 km) Hornet Creek bridge. Paved double-ended turnout to west beside Nenana River.

A 240.3 (386.7 km) **F** 117.7 (189.4 km) Large gravel parking area with litter barrels to west by river.

A 240.7 (387.4 km) **F** 117.3 (188.8 km) Paved double-ended turnout to west beside river.

A 241 (387.7 km) **F** 117 (188.3 km) Paved turnout with litter barrels to west.

A 241.2 (388.2 km) **F** 116.8 (188 km) Bridge over Fox Creek; gravel road to creek. Large gravel turnout to west. Slide area next 0.4 mile/0.6 km northbound.

A 241.7 (389 km) **F** 116.3 (187.2 km) Large gravel turnout to west.

A 242.3 (389.9 km) **F** 115.7 (186.2 km) Paved double-ended turnout with litter barrels to west.

A 242.4 (390.1 km) **F** 115.6 (186 km) Dragonfly Creek bridge; paved double-ended turnout with litter barrels to west.

A 242.8 (390.7 km) **F** 115.2 (185.4 km) Paved double-ended turnout with litter barrels to west. *CAUTION: Windy area next mile northbound.*

A 242.9 (390.9 km) **F** 115.1 (185.2 km) Moody Bridge. The fourth bridge northbound over the Nenana River. This bridge measures 174 feet/53m from its deck to the bottom of the canyon. Dall sheep can be spotted from the bridge. Entering Game Management Unit 20A northbound, 20C southbound.

A 243.6 (392 km) **F** 114.4 (184.1 km) Bridge over Bison Gulch. Paved viewpoint to east with litter barrels. A steep grade follows northbound, end wind area.

A 244.6 (393.6 km) **F** 113.4 (182.5 km) Bridge over Antler Creek.

A 246.9 (397.3 km) **F** 111.1 (178.8 km) Paved turnout to east with litter barrels and beautiful view of Healy area.

A 247 (397.5 km) **F** 111 (178.6 km) Side road leads 1 mile/1.6 km to Otto Lake, 5 miles/8 km to Black Diamond Coal Mine. Primitive parking area on lakeshore (0.8-mile/1.3-km drive in) with toilet, litter barrels, shallow boat launch. Denali hostel. Access to bed and breakfasts.

Healy Heights Bed & Breakfast. Located 12 miles north of the entrance to Denali National Park. This beautiful rural setting overlooks the Alaska Range. Individual cabins and rooms. Can accommodate small groups. Continental breakfast. Open all year. Call or write: Monte & Shirley Lamer, Box 277, Healy, AK 99743. (907) 683-2639. See display ad in DENALI NATIONAL PARK section. [ADVERTISEMENT]

Homestead Bed & Breakfast. See display ad this section.

A 248.2 (399.4 km) **F** 109.8 (176.7 km) **Healy Chevron.** See display ad this section.

A 248.5 (399.9 km) **F** 109.5 (176.2 km) **McKinley KOA Kampground.** One of the nicest campgrounds around; 88 sites, 13 full hookups, 27 electrical. Only store building is seen from the highway. Laundromat, showers (private), pay phone, ice, groceries. Wooded landscape, picnic tables, grills, firewood and evening program. Dog boarding while you are at the park. Scheduled transportation to Denali National Park. Propane available. Reservations recommended. Write Box 340MP, Healy, AK 99743. Phone (907) 683-2379, fax (907) 683-2281. In Alaska call 1-800-478-AKOA (478-2562). [ADVERTISEMENT]

A 248.5 (399.9 km) **F** 109.5 (176.2 km) Paved turnout with litter barrel to east. Looking south, Mount Healy is visible just west of the highway; first mountain east of the highway is Sugarloaf; to the northeast is Dora Peak (elev. 5,572 feet/1,698m).

A 248.7 (400.2 km) **F** 109.3 (175.9 km) Community of Healy (description follows); food, gas and lodging. Homes and businesses of this growing Alaska community are widely dispersed along the highway, spur road and east of the highway toward the Nenana River.

Totem Inn. See display ad this section.

Denali Suites. Located 15 minutes north of entrance to Denali National Park. Units include 2-bedroom, kitchen, living room, TV and VCR, coin-operated laundry facilities. Open all year. Call (907) 683-2848 or write Box 393, Healy, AK 99743. See display ad in the DENALI NATIONAL PARK section. [ADVERTISEMENT]

Chevron Healy Chevron
Visit our famous Healy Leverite Mine

Regular • Unleaded • Diesel
Complete Camper & Auto
Service & Repair
Pay Phone

(907) 683-2700
Mile 248.2 Park Highway

Dome Home Bed & Breakfast is a 4,500-plus-foot round geodesic home on nearly 3 wooded acres. Just turn off the Parks Highway at Healy at the Dome Home signs. We're across from the community center. The 6-bedroom, 5-bathroom house is owned and operated year-round by the Miller family. Write P.O. Box 262, Healy, AK 99743 or call (907) 683-1239. [ADVERTISEMENT]

Healy

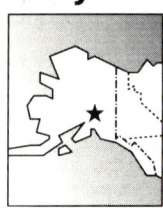

A 248.8 (400.4 km) F 109.2 (175.7 km) Located on a spur road off the George Parks Highway. **Population:** 334. **Emergency Services: Alaska State Troopers**, phone 683-2232. **Fire Department**, Tri-Valley Volunteer Fire Dept., phone 911 or 683-2223. **Clinic**, Healy Clinic, located on 2nd floor of Tri-Valley Community Center at Mile 0.5 Usibelli Spur Road, phone 683-2211 or 911 (open 24 hours). **Radio:** KUAC-FM 101.7.

Visitor Information: Available at the Healy Senior Center, located on Healy Spur Road behind the grocery store. Open 11 A.M. to 7 P.M., year-round; phone 683-1317.

Private Aircraft: Healy River airstrip adjacent north; elev. 1,294 feet/394m; length 2,600 feet/792m; gravel; unattended.

Healy's power plant has the distinction of being the largest coal-fired steam plant in Alaska, as well as the only mine-mouth power plant. This plant is part of the Golden Valley Electric Assoc., which furnishes electric power for Fairbanks and vicinity. The Fairbanks-Tanana Valley area uses primarily coal and also oil to meet its electrical needs.

Across the Nenana River lie the mining settlements of Suntrana and Usibelli. Dry Creek, Healy and Nenana river valleys comprise the area referred to as Tri-Valley. Coal mining began here in 1918 and has grown to become Alaska's largest coal mining operation. Usibelli Coal Mine, the state's only commercial coal mine, mines about 800,000 tons of coal a year, supplying South Korea, the University of Alaska, the military and other Fairbanks-area utilities. The Usibelli Coal Mine began a successful reclamation program in 1971; Dall sheep now graze where there was once only evidence of strip mining.

From the highway, you may see a 33-cubic-yard walking dragline (named Ace in the Hole by local schoolchildren in a contest) removing the soil, or overburden, to expose the coal seams. This 4,275,000-pound machine, erected in 1978, moves an average of 24,000 cubic yards each 24 hours. Private vehicles are not allowed into the mining area and no tours are available.

George Parks Highway Log

(continued)

A 249.1 (400.9 km) F 108.9 (175.3 km) Suntrana Road, post office and Tri-Valley School.

A 249.2 (40 km) F 108.8 (175.1 km) **Larry's Healy Service**. See display ad this section.

A 249.3 (401.2 km) F 108.7 (174.9 km) Dry Creek bridge No. 1.

Morning fog lifts at scenic Otto Lake, Milepost A 247. (Sharon Nault)

A 249.6 (401.7 km) F 108.4 (174.4 km) Evans Industries, Inc. See display ad this section.

A 249.8 (402 km) F 108.2 (174.1 km) Dry Creek bridge No. 2. Good berry picking area first part of August. Watch for commercial bison herd east side of highway northbound.

A 251.1 (404.1 km) F 106.9 (172 km) Stampede Road to west.

A 251.2 (404.3 km) F 106.8 (171.9 km) Turnout with litter barrel to west. Coal seams visible in bluff to east. Cotton grass and lupine along roadside in June, fireweed in July.

A 252.5 (406.4 km) F 105.5 (169.8 km) Bridge over **Panguingue Creek**; turnout at end. Moderate success fishing for grayling. This stream, which flows 8 miles/13 km to the Nenana River, was named for a Philippine card game.

Watch for frost heaves northbound.

A 259.4 (417.5 km) F 98.6 (158.7 km) Large paved turnout with litter barrel to east. Views of Rex Dome to the northeast. Walker and Jumbo domes to the east. Liberty Bell mining area lies between the peaks and highway.

A 261.1 (420.2 km) F 96.9 (155.9 km) Gravel turnout to east. Look for bank swallows, small brown birds that nest in clay and sand banks near streams and along highways.

A 262 (421.6 km) F 96 (154.5 km) Watch for rough patches in pavement and gravel shoulders, northbound. Watch for frost heaves southbound.

A 263 (423.2 km) F 95 (152.9 km) Small gravel turnout to east. Wildflowers include sweet pea and oxytrope.

A 264.5 (425.7 km) F 93.5 (150.5 km) Paved turnout with litter barrel to west.

A 269 (432.9 km) F 89 (143.2 km) June Creek rest area and picnic spot to east; large gravel parking area. Gravel road leads down to lower parking area on June Creek (trailers and large RVs check turnaround space before driving down). Wooden stairs lead up to the picnic spot and a view of the Nenana River. There are picnic tables, fireplaces, toilets, a litter bin and a sheltered

---

Larry's Healy Service

TESORO ALASKA

GAS • DIESEL • PROPANE
TIRE REPAIR • ESSENTIAL GROCERIES • ICE

OPEN 24 HOURS

Major Credit Cards   MILE 249.2 PARKS HIGHWAY • (907) 683-2408

EVANS INDUSTRIES, INC.

Milepost 249.6
(907) 683-2374 • 683-2454

NAPA PARTS and AUTOMOTIVE SERVICE

GOODYEAR Tires

Services
Auto and Truck Repair
Wrecker and Roadside Service
Welding in shop or mobile
Tire Repair

BUCKLE UP

table. Cut wood may be available.

A 269.3 (433.4 km) **F 88.7** (142.8 km) Bridge over Bear Creek. Large paved turnout with litter barrels.

A 271.4 (436.8 km) **F 86.6** (139.4 km) Paved turnout with litter barrels to west. Highway northbound leads through boggy area with few turnouts.

A 275.6 (443.5 km) **F 82.4** (132.6 km) Entering Game Management Unit 20A northbound, 20C southbound.

A 275.8 (443.9 km) **F 82.2** (132.3 km) Rex Bridge over Nenana River.

A 276 (444.2 km) **F 82** (132 km) **Tatlanika Trading Co.** Located in a beautiful pristine wilderness setting. Tent sites and RV parking with electricity, water, dump station, showers, TV. 39 miles from Denali National Park on the Nenana River. Our gift shop features a gathering of handmade art/crafts/artifacts from various villages. Excellent selection of furs at reasonable prices—see the rare Samson fox, along with relics and antiques from Alaska's colorful past in a museum atmosphere with a world-class polar bear. Many historical and educational displays. Nothing sold from overseas. Visitor information. Coffee, pop, juice, snacks. Clean restrooms. This is a must stop. See display ad this section. [ADVERTISEMENT] ▲

A 276.5 (445 km) **F 81.5** (131.2 km) CAUTION: Railroad crossing. Yellow arnica blooms along roadside.

A 280 (450.6 km) **F 78** (125.5 km) **Clear Sky Lodge.** See display ad this section.

A 280.1 (450.8 km) **F 77.9** (125.4 km) **Rochester Lodge.** See display ad this section.

A 280.4 (451.2 km) **F 77.6** (124.9 km) Entering Clear Air Force Station northbound.

A 283.5 (456.2 km) **F 74.5** (119.9 km) **Dew Drop Inn Bed & Breakfast.** See display ad this section.

A 283.5 (456.2 km) **F 74.5** (119.9 km) Access road west to **ANDERSON** (pop. 628) and **CLEAR**. Clear is a military installation (ballistic missile early warning site), and a sign at turnoff states it is unlawful to enter without permission. However, you can drive into Anderson without permission. Located

---

Clear Sky Lodge
MILE 280 PARKS HIGHWAY

Chevron

COCKTAIL LOUNGE • STEAK DINNERS • BURGERS
GAS • PROPANE • LIQUOR STORE • ICE • PHONE

Open year-round 9 a.m. - 2 a.m. 7 days a week
Serving lunch and dinner 11 a.m. - 11:30 p.m.

Phone (907) 582-2251   Clear, Alaska 99704   Carol & Fred Shields, Owners

---

ROCHESTER LODGE
Mile 280 George Parks Highway

◆ Pleasant Comfortable Rooms
◆ Quiet Atmosphere ◆ Showers
◆ Family Style Meals
◆ Breakfast . . . A SPECIALTY
◆ Big Game Trophy Room

Across from Clear Sky Lodge

(907) 582-2354
In Alaska (800) 478-2354
Write for Brochure:
Box 3153
Anderson, AK 99744

MasterCard   VISA

Jay and Karen Reeder, owners

Not just another gift shop, but an experience

- **M**OOSE ANTLER JEWELRY AND HANDMADE ULUS
- **G**ALLERY OF ORIGINAL CRAFTS
- **L**ARGE SELECTION OF ALASKAN FURS
- **M**USEUM ATMOSPHERE, HISTORICAL & EDUCATIONAL DISPLAYS
- **O**VER 70 ALASKAN ARTISTS & CRAFTSMEN REPRESENTED
- **H**ANDCRAFTED TOTEMS, FUR MUKLUKS, TRAPPER HATS
- **S**PRUCE BURLS AND RAW DIAMOND WILLOW
- **L**ARGE PARKING AREA, CLEAN RESTROOMS, PICNIC TABLES

NOTHING SOLD FROM OVERSEAS!!

Full mounted World Class Polar Bear
See our log ad at mile 276

TATLANIKA TRADING CO

39 MILES NORTH OF DENALI NATIONAL PARK AT MILE 276 PARKS HWY
OPEN 9AM TO 6PM   PHONE (907) 582-2341
MAILING ADDRESS: P.O. Box 40179, Clear, Alaska 99704

Come in and MEET George!

6 miles/9.7 km northwest of Clear, Anderson has a city campground with 10 sites on the Tanana River. The community also has churches, a restaurant, softball fields and shooting range. For more information call the city office at 582-2500. Emergency aid is available through the Clear Air Force Site Fire Department; phone 585-6321. ▲

Private Aircraft: Clear airstrip, 2.6 miles/4.2 km southeast; elev. 552 feet/168m; length 4,000 feet/1,219m; gravel; fuel 80; unattended. Clear Sky Lodge airstrip, 4.3 miles/6.9 km south; elev. 650 feet/198m; length 2,600 feet/792m; gravel; fuel 80, 100.

A 285.7 (459.8 km) F 72.3 (116.3 km) Julius Creek bridge.

A 286.3 (460.7 km) F 71.7 (115.4 km) View of Mount McKinley southbound.

A 286.3 (461.5 km) F 71.2 (114.6 km) Double-ended paved parking area with litter barrels to east.

A 288 (463.5 km) F 70 (112.7 km) Entering Clear Military Reservation southbound.

Watch for frost heaves and dip in pavement.

A 288.8 (464.6 km) F 69.2 (111.4 km) **Gold Nugget Inn.** Enjoy a traditional Alaskan meal in a roadhouse atmosphere. Real Alaska "sourdough gold panner cakes" with reindeer sausage. Homemade cinnamon rolls. Preparing blue ribbon quality salmon since 1965. Overnight parking with every meal over $10. Rooms from $50. Gas, diesel, convenience store. No sales tax. VISA, MasterCard accepted. See display ad this section. [ADVERTISEMENT]

A 289.8 (466.4 km) F 68.2 (109.7 km) **Summer Shades Campground.** See display ad this section. ▲

A 293.7 (472.5 km) F 64.3 (103.5 km) Frost heaves northbound to Nenana.

A 296.7 (477.5 km) F 61.3 (98.7 km) Bridge over **Fish Creek.** Small gravel turnout with litter barrels by creek. Access to creek at south end of bridge; moderate success fishing for grayling. ⊸

A 297.3 (478.4 km) F 60.7 (97.7 km) **Fish Creek Outpost.** See display ad this section.

A 298 (479.6 km) F 60 (96.6 km) **Tamarack Inn.** See display ad this section.

A 302.9 (487.4 km) F 55.1 (88.7 km) Nenana municipal rifle range.

A 303.7 (488.7 km) F 54.3 (87.4 km)

Nenana airport (see Private Aircraft information in Nenana).

A 303.8 (488.9 km) F 54.2 (87.2 km) **Self-Contained RV Parking.** See display ad this section.

A 304.3 (489.7 km) F 53.7 (86.4 km) **Nenana Service Center.** See display ad this section.

Sourdough Pancakes • Homemade Pie • Ice Cream
BREAKFAST • LUNCH • DINNER
"Best Salmon in Alaska"

GOLD NUGGET INN

CAFE • ROOMS • BAR • ICE • GAS • DIESEL

Open Daily 6 a.m. – 10 p.m.

No Sales Tax
(907) 582-2113
VISA MasterCard

See log ad — Rt. 2, Mile 288.8 Parks Highway, Nenana, Alaska 99760

SUMMER SHADES CAMPGROUND

75 miles south of Fairbanks on Highway Route 3
Milepost A 289.8 – 54 miles north of Denali National Park

Family Owned and Operated

Our attractions for your enjoyment and relaxation are:

1. The well-stocked Country & Liquor Store with food stuffs, snacks, ice, pop, dairy products, ice cold beer, wine, liquor, etc.
2. Rustic Log Cabins for rent. Hot Showers, a laundromat, and septic dump station for your convenience.
3. Pavilion for barbeque parties, dances, social gatherings, or just plain *"good old-time get-togethers."*
4. Nature trails around 50 wooded acres
5. Use our spacious grounds for camping (water & electric hookups) and picnicking, and then . . .
6. Relax in a cool, refreshing spring-fed lake.
7. Also, a playground for the children, tetherball, volleyball, horseshoes, badminton.

Write: Route 2, Summer Shades
Nenana, Alaska 99760

Hosts: Carolyn & Mike Furrow
Lu & Jim Johnson

Phone: (907) 582-2798

TAMARACK INN

7 Miles South of Nenana
Mile 298 Parks Highway

Dine by soft firelight in a beautiful log setting. . . .

Widely known as one of the best places to eat in Alaska

CHOICEST STEAKS • SEAFOOD

Courteous Service

OPEN YEAR-ROUND

Vic and Pat Rentschler

Phone: (907) 832-5455

Open 5 p.m. to 11 p.m. – Thursday, Friday, Saturday
Sunday 3 p.m. to 11 p.m. – Closed Monday, Tuesday, Wednesday

Dew Drop Inn Bed & Breakfast
Families Welcome • Reasonable Rates
(907) 582-2972 or 582-2856
Hosts: Jeannette & Neil Witte
P.O. Box 3059, Anderson, Alaska 99744
Mile 283.5 PARKS HIGHWAY

FISH CREEK OUTPOST
GIFTS & SOUVENIRS
All Alaskan-made Handicrafts
(907) 832-5826   Lucy & Bill Miller
MILE 297.3 PARKS HIGHWAY

SELF-CONTAINED RV PARKING
10 Complimentary Spaces
Good Fishing • First-Come Basis
Turn west on Cemetery Lane
Mile 303.8 Parks Highway

Nenana Service Center

Truck Stop
Gas & Oil
Diesel & Bulk Fuel
Auto & Truck Parts

Open 24 Hours   **(907) 832-5419**
RV, Auto, Heavy Duty Truck Repairs & Towing Service
Convenience Store
Deli • Fast Foods • Groceries • All Major Credit Cards Accepted
MILE 304.3 PARKS HIGHWAY   Box 270, Nenana, AK 99760

NAPA

Nenana

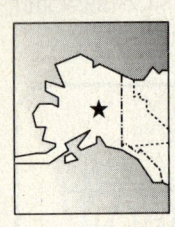

A 304.5 (490 km) F 53.5 (86.1 km) Located at the confluence of the Tanana and Nenana rivers. **Population:** 540. **Emergency Services:** Emergency only (fire, police, ambulance), phone 911. **Alaska State Troopers,** phone 832-5554, at **Milepost A 310** George Parks Highway. **City Police,** phone 832-5632. **Fire Department,** phone 832-5632.

Visitor Information: In a picturesque log cabin with sod roof at junction of the highway and A Street, phone 832-9453. Open 8 A.M. to 6 P.M., 7 days a week, Memorial Day to Labor Day. Pay phone and ice for sale. Ice Classic tickets may be purchased here.

Marge Anderson Senior Citizen Center, located on 3rd Street between Market and B streets, also welcomes visitors.

Elevation: 400 feet/122m. **Radio:** KUAC-FM 91.1. **Transportation: Air**–Nenana maintains an airport with FAA flight services. **Railroad**–The Alaska Railroad.

Private Aircraft: Nenana Municipal Airport, 0.9 mile/1.4 km south; elev. 360 feet/110m; length 5,000 feet/1,524m; asphalt; fuel 80, 100. Floatplane and skiplane strip.

The town got its name from the Indian word Nenana which means "a good place to camp between the rivers." It was first known as Tortella, a white man's interpretation of the Athabascan word *Toghotthele*. In 1902 Jim Duke built a roadhouse and trading post here, trading with Indians and supplying river travelers with goods and lodging.

Nenana boomed as a construction base for the Alaska Railroad. Today, Nenana is home port of the tug and barge fleet that in summer carries tons of freight, fuel and supplies to villages along the Tanana and Yukon rivers. Because the Tanana is a wide, shallow, muddy river, the barges move about 12 mph downstream and 5 mph upstream. The dock area is to the right of the highway northbound. Behind the Nenana visitor information center is the *Taku Chief*: This old tug, which has been renovated, once pushed barges on the Tanana.

On July 15, 1923, Pres. Warren G. Harding drove the golden spike at Nenana, signifying completion of the Alaska Railroad. A monument to the event stands east of the depot here. The Nenana Railroad Depot, located at the end of Main Street, is on the National Register of Historic Places. Built in 1923 and renovated in 1988, the depot has a pressed metal ceiling and houses the state's Alaska Railroad Museum; open 9 A.M. to 6 P.M. daily.

One block from the depot is St. Mark's Mission Church. This Episcopal church was built in 1905 upriver from Nenana; it was moved to its present location in the 1930s when riverbank erosion threatened the structure. A school was located next door to the mission until the 1940s, and pupils were brought in by tug from villages along the river. The recently restored log church has pews with hand-carving and an altar covered with Native beadwork-decorated moosehide.

Nenana is perhaps best known for the Nenana Ice Classic, an annual event which offers cash prizes to the lucky winners who

NENANA ADVERTISERS

A Frame Service ....Mile 304.5 Parks Hwy.
Bed & Maybe Breakfast..................Above Depot Museum
Coghill's General Merchandise......Downtown
Depot Cafe......................1st & A St.
Last Resort ....Next to visitor center
Nenana Inn......................2nd & A St.
Nenana Valley RV Park & Campground................4th St.
Nenana Visitor Center........Parks Hwy. & A St.
Tolovana Lodge ....Ph. (907) 832-5569
Tripod Gift Shop and Mini Mall ....Across from visitor center

---

TRIPOD GIFT SHOP
Across from Nenana Visitor Center

GOLD • NUGGETS
IVORY • HEMATITE
JADE • BALEEN
SCRIMSHAW
ALASKA CLAY
T-SHIRTS • FILM
POST CARDS

**8 a.m. - 7 p.m.
IN THE SUMMER**

Complimentary city tours for buses. By appointment only.

PHONE (907) 832-5272
or 582-2776

We Mail or Ship Anywhere
P.O. BOX 419 — NENANA, ALASKA 99760

COGHILL'S GENERAL MERCHANDISE

9-6 Monday-Saturday
Downtown Nenana

SERVING THE PUBLIC SINCE 1916

GROCERIES • FRESH MEATS & VEGETABLES • CLOTHING
HARDWARE • MAGAZINES • PROPANE GAS
FISHING & HUNTING LICENSES • AREA INFORMATION

PHONE (907) 832-5422   BOX 00100 • NENANA, ALASKA 99760

NENANA VALLEY RV PARK & CAMPGROUND

- 30-amp electrical hookups
- Large pull-through spaces
- Tent campers welcome
- Showers and laundry
- Water available
- City dump station
- Picnic table and firepits
- Pet area • Playground nearby
- Handicap restrooms and showers
- Clean • Day parking available

Centrally located on 4th Street in Nenana • Easy access to everything

Gayle and Charlie Stevens
P.O. Box 00038, Nenana, AK 99760
(907) 832-5431

can guess the exact minute of the ice breakup on the Tanana River. Ice Classic festivities begin the last weekend in February with the Tripod Raising Festival and Nenana Ice Classic Dog Race, and culminate at breakup time (late April or May) when the surging ice on the Tanana River dislodges the tripod. A line attached to the tripod stops a clock, recording the official breakup time.

Nenana celebrates River Daze the first weekend in June. The main event is a raft race down the Tanana River from Fairbanks to Nenana.

Nenana has an auto repair shop, radio station, several churches, a bank, restaurants, a laundromat, gift shops, a grocery and general store. Accommodations at local inn and bed and breakfast; access to wilderness lodge. There are 2 local campgrounds. Picnic tables and rest area beside the restored *Taku Chief* are behind the visitor information center.

Bed & Maybe Breakfast. Step back in time and charm yourself in the atmosphere of the old railroad depot built for President Harding's historic visit in 1923. Oak or brass beds, hardwood floors and braided rugs enhance the decor of these rooms. Overlook the hustling loading dock area of the barge lines on the Tanana River. View the Native cemetery and the historic railroad bridge from your window. Reservations (907) 832-5272 or 582-2776. [ADVERTISEMENT]

Tripod Gift Shop and Mini Mall. "Take

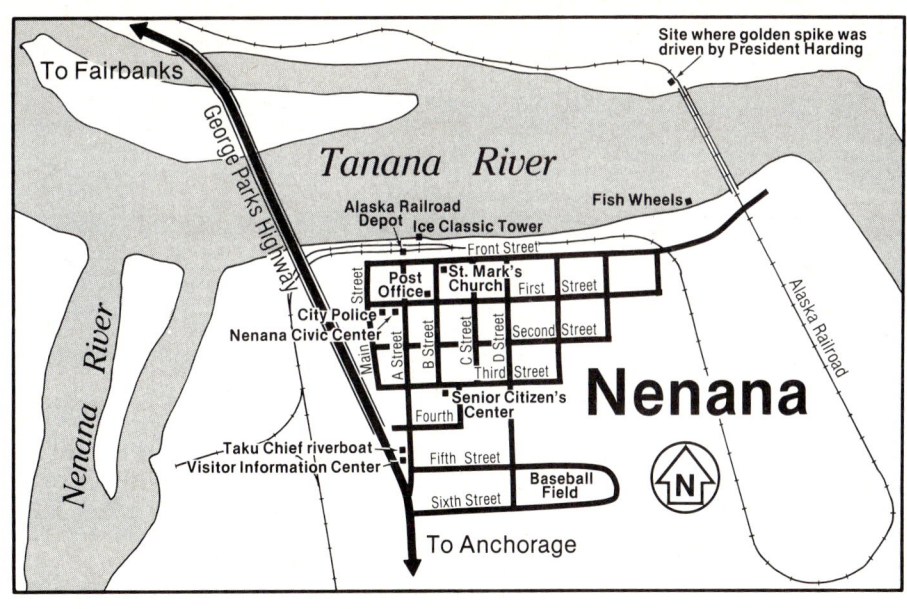

LAST RESORT
RV PARKING
15 spaces for self-contained RVs
(no tents)
Showers
Office at Tripod Gift Shop

tolovana lodge
at the Tanana & Tolovana Rivers
Experience the heart of wild Alaska

Custom first class riverboat tours of Minto Wildlife Refuge.
Coast Guard Licensed

Fishing. Wildlife. Birding. Licenses sold.
Lodge on National Register of Historic Places.

Doug Bowers   PO Box 281
Kathy Lenniger   **(907) 832-5569**   Nenana, Alaska 99760

A FRAME SERVICE
Chevron
Near the "Y" at Nenana
Mi A 304.5 Parks Hwy.
- Chevron Gas
- Diesel • Propane
- Atlas Products
- Coleman — Kerosene
- Sandwiches • Ice
- Essential Groceries

OPEN 24 HOURS SUMMERS
(907) 832-5823

Nenana Inn
Rooms at Reasonable Rates
Open 24 Hours - Year Around
Laundromat
Hot Showers
2nd and A St.
Nenana, Alaska   832-5238

BED & MAYBE BREAKFAST
Above The Nenana Depot Museum
REASONABLE RATES
Reservations (907) 832-5272 or 582-2776
See our log ad under Accommodations

NENANA VISITOR CENTER

Open 8 a.m. - 6 p.m. daily Memorial Day to Labor Day

(907) 832-9953

Sponsored by Nenana Ice Classic

Alaska's Biggest Guessing Game Since 1917

AVERAGE ANNUAL PAYOFF OVER $150,000

Tickets May Be Purchased At The Visitors Information Center In Nenana (No mail orders)

Depot Cafe

1st & A Street, Nenana
Midway between Fairbanks and Mt. McKinley

(907) 832-5601

SALMON or HALIBUT
FISH & CHIPS

Homemade Soups • Daily Specials
Fresh Baked Pies

OPEN DAILY
Breakfast - Lunch - Dinner

A Fourth of July 3-legged race down Nenana's A Street. (Jerrianne Lowther, staff)

time to smell the flowers." Over 12,000 flowers are planted each year to enhance the beauty of one of the loveliest gift shops in Alaska. A fun stop! Enjoy old-time concertina music played by Joanne Hawkins. Take the boardwalk to our Art Lovers' Gallery; Fur Shop stocked with fur hats and a wide selection of local furs; king- and queen-size shirt shop; and Bargain Corner with special prices on T-shirts, hats and mugs. Enjoy ice cream or snacks at our Sweets and Treats Shoppe and purchase our fine locally smoked salmon strips (in season) or canned smoked salmon. Also available: ice, worldwide postcard stamps, assorted camera batteries and wildflower seeds. Complimentary gold panning with $5 purchase in any of these shops. These shops are a must, a highlight of any vacation. Interesting displays include record size moose antlers, Kodiak grizzly bear trap (largest ever manufactured), antique ice saw, working fish wheel, trapper's steam boiler, dog salmon drying rack and authentic 1977 Ice Classic tripod. Be sure to have your picture taken with Sourdough Pete and rub his head for luck. [ADVERTISEMENT]

George Parks Highway Log

(continued)

A **305.1** (491 km) F **52.9** (85.1 km) Tanana River bridge. Large paved turnout with litter barrels to west at north end of bridge. The Tanana is formed by the joining of the Chisana and the Nabesna rivers near Northway and flows 440 miles/708 km westward to the Yukon River. From the bridge, watch for freight-laden river barges bound for the Yukon River. North of this bridge, fish wheels sometimes may be seen in action and occasionally fish may be purchased from the owners of the wheels. Entering Game Management Unit 20B northbound, 20A southbound.

A **305.5** (491.6 km) F **52.5** (84.5 km) Paved turnout to west with litter barrels by Tanana River. There is a Native cemetery 0.6 mile/1 km to east on side road.

A **305.6** (491.8 km) F **52.4** (84.3 km) Paved turnout to west with litter barrel overlooking Tanana River.

A **305.9** (492.3 km) F **52.1** (83.8 km) Double-ended gravel turnout to east.

A **308.9** (497.1 km) F **49.1** (79 km) *CAUTION: Alaska Railroad crossing.*

A **309** (497.3 km) F **49** (78.9 km) **Monderosa.** See display ad this section.

A **314.6** (506.3 km) F **43.4** (69.8 km) Paved double-ended turnout with litter barrels to west.

A **314.8** (506.6 km) F **43.2** (69.5 km) Bridge over Little Goldstream Creek.

A **315.4** (507.6 km) F **42.5** (68.6 km) Truck lane next 2.8 miles/4.5 km northbound.

A **318.8** (513 km) F **39.2** (63.1 km) Paved double-ended turnout to west with scenic view. The view is mostly of bogs, small lakes and creeks, with names like Hard Luck Creek, Fortune Creek, All Hand Help Lake and Wooden Canoe Lake.

Southbound travelers will see the Tanana River on both sides of the highway. It follows a horseshoe-shaped course, the top of the closed end being the bridge at Nenana.

A **321** (516.6 km) F **37** (59.5 km) Fairbanks-bound traffic: Highway climbs a steep grade with sweeping curves next 1 mile/1.6 km; truck lane next mile northbound. Mount McKinley is visible to the southwest on a clear day.

A **323** (519.8 km) F **35** (56.3 km) Tanana River visible to east in valley below highway.

A **323.8** (521.1 km) F **34.2** (55 km) Truck lane next 0.3 mile/0.5 km northbound.

A **324.5** (522.2 km) F **33.5** (53.9 km) Paved double-ended turnout to east with litter barrels and scenic view to south.

A **325** (523 km) F **33** (53.1 km) This stretch of highway is often called Skyline Drive; views to west. Downgrade northbound.

A **325.7** (524.1 km) F **32.3** (52 km) Entering Fairbanks North Star Borough northbound.

A **328** (527.9 km) F **30** (48.3 km) **Skinny Dick's Halfway Inn.** See display ad this section. ▲

A **328.3** (528.3 km) F **29.7** (47.8 km)

For a hamburger you'll write home about

STOP AT THE... **MONDEROSA**

OPEN 10:00 a.m.

Serving: Burgers
Steaks • Chicken
Shrimp • Salad
Nachos • Burritos

OUTDOOR PATIO DINING

Super clean rest rooms

832-5243

Beautiful Alaskan log building
MILE 309 PARKS HIGHWAY • 50 minutes south of Fairbanks

Skinny Dick's HALFWAY INN
SNACKS GIFTS

Phone (907) 452-0304
**Rooms, Camping
Free Parking** and Coffee
No Hookups *"But"* No Charge

Dick and Mable, Hosts

**20 Miles from Fairbanks
Mile 328 Parks Highway
P.O. Box 88, Nenana, Alaska 99760**

Truck lane next 3 miles/4.8 km southbound.

A 329.5 (530.3 km) **F 28.5** (45.9 km) There is a healthy population of black bears in this area. Occasionally a bear may be seen from the highway.

A 331.6 (533.6 km) **F 26.4** (42.5 km) Long paved double-ended turnout to east. Intermittent truck lanes northbound to Fairbanks.

A 338.2 (544.3 km) **F 19.8** (31.9 km) Wide view to east. Look for Murphy Dome (elev. 2,930 feet/893m) with white communication installations on summit to west.

A 339.3 (546 km) **F 19.7** (30.1 km) Viewpoint and sign to east. This is the south end of a 1-mile/1.6-km scenic loop road that rejoins the highway at Milepost A 339.9. Highway begins downgrade northbound.

A 339.9 (547 km) **F 18.1** (29.1 km) Turnoff (unmarked) for Bonanza Experimental Forest via 1-mile/1.6-km loop road east; scenic viewpoint. Established by the Alaska Division of Lands and U.S. Forest Service to study the Interior forest ecosystem. For information contact the Institute of Northern Forestry, U.S. Dept. of Agriculture, in Fairbanks.

A 342.2 (550.7 km) **F 15.8** (25.4 km) Rosie Creek Road.

A 342.4 (551 km) **F 15.6** (25.1 km) Old Nenana Highway.

A 344.2 (553.9 km) **F 13.8** (22.2 km) Monument in honor of George Alexander Parks, former governor of Alaska. Also here is a Blue Star Memorial highway plaque honoring the armed forces. Viewpoint and litter barrels to east. Tanana River can be seen below the Parks monument.

A 348 (560.1 km) **F 10** (16.1 km) Highway passes through forest of aspen.

A 349 (561.6 km) **F 9** (14.5 km) Cripple Creek Road to south (access to TIVI kennels), Park Ridge Road to north. Truck lane next 4.2 miles/6.8 km southbound.

TIVI Kennels. See display ad this section.

A 350 (563.3 km) **F 8** (12.9 km) Alder Creek.

A 351.2 (565.2 km) **F 6.8** (10.9 km) Old dredges visible in the distance.

A 351.7 (566 km) **F 6.3** (10.1 km) Watch for turnoff to west for **ESTER** (pop. 166), a former gold mining camp and current visitor attraction. Drive 0.4 mile/0.6 km in on road, turn right on a second road marked Ester, and drive 0.2 mile/0.3 km to an intersection: Turn left at intersection for Cripple Creek Resort and Malemute Saloon (descriptions follows); turn right for Ester residential area and another saloon. Southbound access to Old Nenana Highway.

Cripple Creek Resort, also known as Ester Gold Camp, is located on the National Register of Historic Places. P.O. Box 109, Ester, AK 99725. (907) 479-2500. Open May 29 through Sept. 7. VISA and MasterCard accepted. Sleep in the historical Cripple Creek Hotel. 22 clean, pleasant rooms with semiprivate bathrooms. Single $45, double $50, triple and quad available. Reservations accepted. Cripple Creek RV Park. Dry camping, no hookups, water and dump station available. $9 per site, showers included. Check-in at hotel desk. Reservations accepted. The Bunkhouse Restaurant. Serving dinner daily from 5-9 P.M. Featuring "all-you-care-to-eat" buffet and Alaskan Dungeness crab. Children's meals (under 12) half price. Reservations advised. Visit the world famous Malemute Saloon. Open daily with food available. *Service With A Smile—* songs, stories of the Gold Rush Days and Robert Service poetry—Monday through Saturday at 9 P.M. (7 P.M. shows Friday and Saturday during July only). Reservations highly recommended. See the Alaskan Photosymphonies at the Firehouse Theatre: *Crown of Light,* 8 P.M. daily (6 and 8 P.M. in July), *Once Around the Sun,* 7 P.M. daily. One show: adults $5, children $3. Both shows: adults $9, children $5. Reservations recommended. Pick and Poke Gift Shop: Alaskan gifts and souvenirs. See display ads in FAIRBANKS section. [ADVERTISEMENT]

A 351.8 (566.2 km) **F 6.2** (10 km) Weigh stations.

A 353.2 (568.4 km) **F 4.8** (7.7 km) **The Wild Blue Yonder.** This is NOT simply another roadside gift shop! We feature a diverse selection of unique Alaskan crafts created by over 30 talented local artisans. Rest on the canopied deck, take a swing on the hammock, chill with a cool drink and then browse at your leisure. Our relaxed, personable atmosphere, quality gifts and reasonable prices will surely please the discerning gift-giver. Open Tuesday-Sunday 10 A.M. to 6 P.M. Special orders welcome; mailing service available. (907) 479-9697. [ADVERTISEMENT]

A 353.5 (568.9 km) **F 4.5** (7.2 km) Gas station and store. Public dumpster.

Gold Hill. See display ad this section.

A 355.2 (571.6 km) **F 2.8** (4.5 km) **Goldhill RV Park.** See display ad this section.

A 355.8 (572.6 km) **F 2.2** (3.5 km) Sheep Creek Road and Tanana Drive. Road to Murphy Dome (a restricted military site).

A 356.8 (574.2 km) **F 1.2** (1.9 km) Turnoff to University of Alaska, Geist Road, Chena Ridge Loop and Chena Pump Road.

A 357.6 (575.5 km) **F 0.4** (0.6 km) Bridge over Chena River.

A 357.7 (575.6 km) **F 0.3** (0.5 km) Fairbanks airport exit.

A 358 (576.1 km) **F 0** Fairbanks exit; George Parks Highway (Robert J. Mitchell Expressway) continues to Richardson Highway, bypassing Fairbanks. Take Fairbanks exit to Airport Way for University Avenue (access to University of Alaska and Chena River state recreation site); Peger Road (access to private campground, flying service and Alaskaland); and Cushman Street turnoff to downtown and to connect with the Richardson Highway and Steese Expressway. (See Fairbanks Vicinity map in the FAIRBANKS section.)

TIVI KENNELS welcomes visitors Monday- Saturday June 15 - Sept. 5, 1992 from 6 - 9 p.m.

TOUR the dog kennels, gardens, small animal pens and fish display.

DINNER-SHOW. Full seafood dinner followed by 40-minute show in the 80-seat arena. Live comedy, skits and touch of magic coordinated with video presentation of Alaska through the seasons and sled dog racing on 10-foot Super Big Screen.

The **ArfMobile RIDE** powered by 10-12 eager sled dogs.

Reservations encouraged. Fee charged for drop-in tours before 5 p.m. Buses welcome with reservations.

Directions: At mile 348.8 Parks Highway, turn south on Cripple Creek Road (right turn if northbound); drive 4.5 miles, turn right on Kallenburg Road; drive 2 miles and park near entrance.

Information: Call **(907) 474-8702.**

Brochures available. Write Ron Tinsley, PO Box 81049, Fairbanks, Alaska 99708. Inquire for group rates, winter visits, including mushing instructions.

RTE. 3, Mile 355.2 Parks Highway
Little Shot Road

GOLDHILL R-V-PARK AND CABINS

30-amp Electric Hookups
Water and Dump Stations
Showers • Laundry • Pay Phones • Gifts • Ice
Cabin Rentals   Tent Campers Welcome
5 Minutes from shopping and entertainment
Reasonable Rates • Tours Available

PO Box 81529   PHONE
Fairbanks, Alaska 99708   (907) 474-8088

FILL UP AT BEST GAS PRICES...
before you get to town... and... as you leave town!
Just 4.5 miles south of Airport Way on the Parks Highway towards Ester

Mile A 353.5 Parks Highway

GOLD HILL

Beer • Ice
Many, many "in-store" specials
Package liquor • Groceries
Union oil products

Open 8 to 10 Sun.-Thurs.
8 to 12 Fri. and Sat.

(907) 479-2333

FAIRBANKS

(See maps, page 352)

Alaskaland Pioneer Park offers small shops, food and entertainment. (John W. Warden)

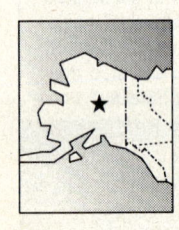

Located in the heart of Alaska's Great Interior country. By highway, Fairbanks is approximately 1,475 miles/2374 km north of Dawson Creek, BC, start of the Alaska Highway (traditional milepost distance is 1,523 miles); 98 miles/158 km from Delta Junction (official end of the Alaska Highway); 358 miles/576 km from Anchorage via the George Parks Highway; and 2,313 miles/3722 km from Seattle.

Population: Fairbanks-North Star Borough, 77,720. **Emergency Services: Alaska State Troopers,** 1979 Peger Road, phone 452-1313 or, for nonemergencies, 452-2114. **Fairbanks Police,** 656 7th Ave., phone 911 or, for nonemergencies, phone 459-6500. **Fire Department** and **Ambulance Service** (within city limits), phone 911. **Hospitals,** Fairbanks Memorial, 1650 Cowles St., phone 452-8181; Bassett Army Hospital, Fort Wainwright, phone 353-5143; Eielson Clinic, Eielson AFB, phone 377-2259. **Crisis Line,** phone 452-4403. **Civil Defense,** phone 459-6500. **Borough Information,** phone 459-1000.

Visitor Information: Fairbanks Convention and Visitors Bureau information center at 550 1st Ave. (1st and Cushman, where a riverside marker shows the distance of Fairbanks from some 75 cities); phone 456-5774 or 1-800-327-5774. Open 8 A.M. to 8 P.M. (subject to change), daily in summer; 8:30 A.M. to 5 P.M., weekdays in winter. Phone 456-INFO for their daily recorded information service.

Visitor information is also available at Fairbanks International Airport in the baggage claim area, at the Alaska Railroad depot and at Alaskaland.

For information on Alaska's state parks, national parks, national forests, wildlife refuges and other outdoor recreational sites, visit the Alaska Public Lands Information Center downstairs in historic Courthouse Square at 250 N. Cushman St. The center is a free museum featuring films on Alaska, interpretive programs, nature walks, lectures, exhibits, artifacts, photographs and short video programs on each region in the state. The exhibit area and information desk are open from 8:30 A.M. to 9 P.M. 7 days a week in summer; 10 A.M. to 6 P.M., Tuesday through Saturday, in winter. Phone 451-7352. For recorded information on Denali National Park, phone 452-PARK. TDD (Telephone Device for the Deaf) information line is 451-7439.

Elevation: 434 feet/132m at Fairbanks International Airport. **Climate:** January temperatures range from -4°F/-20°C to -21°F/-29°C. The lowest temperature ever recorded was -66°/-54°C in January 1934. July temperatures average 62°F/17°C, with a record high of 99°F/37°C in July 1919. In June and early July daylight lasts 21 hours—and the nights are really only twilight. Annual precipitation is 10.4 inches, with an annual average snowfall of 65 inches. **Radio:** KSUA-FM, KFAR, KCBF, KAYY-FM, KWLF-FM, KIAK, KIAK-FM, KJNP-AM and FM (North Pole), KUAC-FM 104.7. **Television:** Channels 2, 4, 9, 11 and cable. **Newspapers:** *Fairbanks Daily News–Miner, Pioneer All-Alaska Weekly.*

Private Aircraft: Facilities for all types of aircraft. Consult the *Alaska Supplement* for information on the following airports: Eielson AFB, Fairbanks International, Fairbanks International Seaplane, Metro Field and Fort Wainwright. For more information phone the Fairbanks Flight Service Station at 474-0137.

HISTORY

In 1901, Captain E.T. Barnette set out from St. Michael by steamer, traveling up the Yukon River with supplies for his trading post, which he proposed to set up at Tanana Crossing (Tanacross), the halfway point on the Valdez to Eagle trail. But the steamer could not navigate the fast moving, shallow Tanana River beyond the mouth of the Chena River. The captain of the steamer finally dropped off the protesting Barnette on the Chena River, near the present site of 1st Avenue and Cushman Street. A year later, Felix Pedro, an Italian prospector, discovered gold about 16 miles/26 km north of Barnette's temporary trading post. The opportunistic Barnette quickly abandoned his plan to continue on to Tanana Crossing.

The ensuing gold rush in 1903–04 established the new gold mining community, which was named at the suggestion of Barnette's friend, Judge James Wickersham, for Sen. Charles Fairbanks. The senator from Indiana later became vice president of the United States under Theodore Roosevelt. The town became an administrative center in 1903 when Judge Wickersham moved the headquarters of his Third Judicial District Court (a district which encompassed 300,000 square miles) from Eagle to Fairbanks.

The new name, Fairbanks, first appeared in the U.S. census in 1910 with a population of 3,541. Miners living beside their claims on creeks north of town brought the area population figure to about 11,000.

Barnette stayed in Fairbanks, wheeling and dealing and serving as mayor, until 1911, when his Washington–Alaska Bank failed. The tale of the "most hated man in Fairbanks" is told in *E.T. Barnette, The Strange Story of the Man Who Founded Fairbanks,* available in bookstores or from Alaska Northwest Books™.

FAIRBANKS' PREMIER ATTRACTION

CRUISE ALASKA'S GOLDEN PAST!

DISCOVERY
STERNWHEELER RIVERBOAT

Board the only authentic operating sternwheelers in Alaska! Cast off for a fabulous, fully-narrated voyage into the interior's historic back country via the Chena/Tanana Rivers. Special features – a bush pilot's airstrip, Indian fishwheels, the "Wedding of the Rivers" and a true dog sledding demonstration by famed author/musher Mary Shields. On board you'll meet our native guides who will accompany you ashore at "Old Chena Village" for a tour of the smokehouse, trapper's cabin, cache, early Athabascan Indian dwellings and more. Your Captain and hosts aboard the deluxe M/V Discovery sternwheeler (complete with snack bar and gift shop) are Jim and Mary Binkley and family, now celebrating 4 generations and 90 years of Alaskan river boating heritage. Welcome aboard your "Golden Past" cruise of a lifetime!

SEND FOR YOUR FREE FULL-COLOR BROCHURE!

MP91F

Name: _____
Address: _____
City: _____
State/Zip: _____

Riverboat Discovery
P.O. Box 80610
Fairbanks, AK 99708

Call (907) **479-6673** or your Travel Agent for reservations on our daily am & pm cruises (mid-May – mid-Sept.).

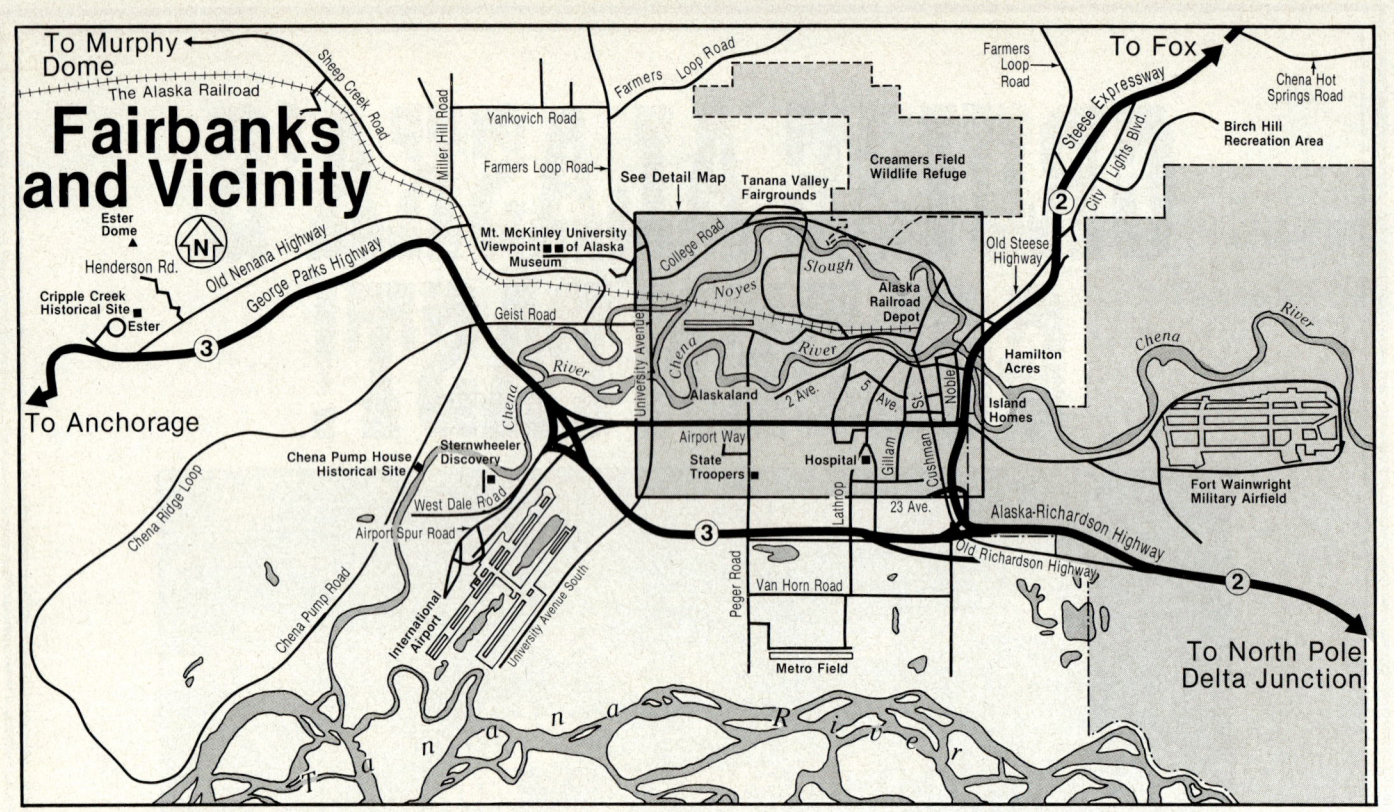

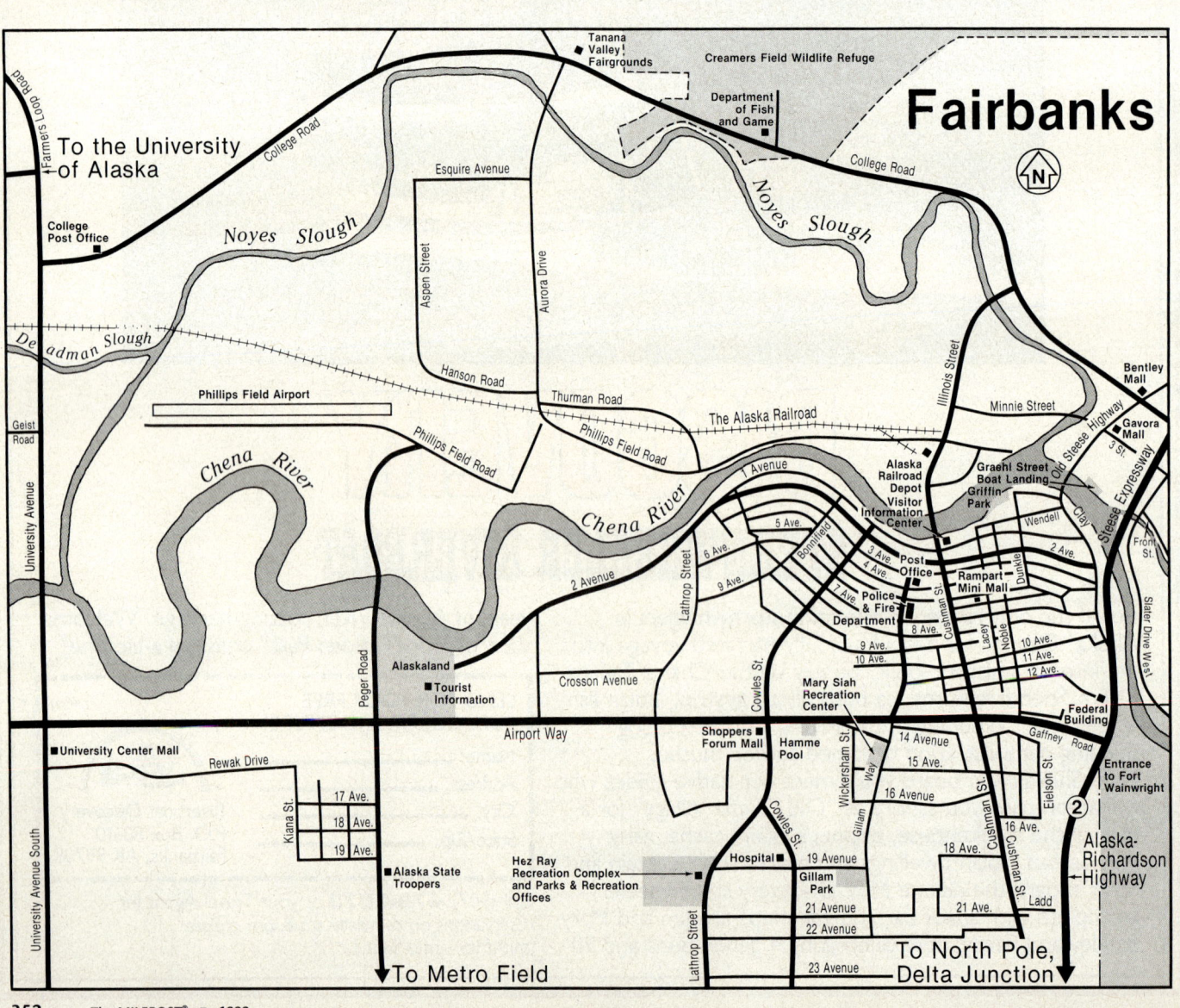

Fairbanks and Vicinity

Fairbanks

ECONOMY

The city's economy is linked to its role as a service and supply point for Interior and Arctic industrial activities. Fairbanks played a key role during construction of the trans-Alaska pipeline in the 1970s. The Dalton Highway (formerly the North Slope Haul Road) to Prudhoe Bay begins about 75 miles/ 121 km north of town.

Government employment—both civilian and military—contributes significantly to the Fairbanks economy. Fort Wainwright plays an important role in both the economy and also in emergency services by assisting with search and rescue operations. (Ladd Field—now Fort Wainwright—was the first Army airfield in Alaska, begun in 1938.) Eielson AFB, located 23 miles/37 km southeast of Fairbanks on the Alaska–Richardson Highway, also has a strong economic impact on the city. Eielson has about 3,600 military personnel and approximately 5,100 dependents assigned, with about 1,700 military personnel and 1,700 family members living off base.

The University of Alaska Fairbanks and tourism are also primary economic factors.

DESCRIPTION

Alaska's second largest city and administrative capital of the Interior, Fairbanks lies on the flat valley floor of the Tanana River on the banks of the Chena River. Good views of the valley are available from Chena Ridge Road to the west and Farmers Loop Road to the north. (Also on Farmers Loop Road, at Mile 5.5, is "the permafrost house." This contemporary home was built on permafrost, which occurs throughout the Interior, causing the foundation to sink and the house to buckle.)

The city is a blend of old and new: modern hotels and shopping malls stand beside log cabins and historic wooden buildings. Fairbanks is bounded to the north, east and west by low rolling hills of birch and white spruce. To the south is the Alaska Range and Denali National Park, about a 2½-hour drive via the George Parks Highway. The Steese and Elliott highways lead north to the White Mountains.

ACCOMMODATIONS

Fairbanks has about 2 dozen hotels and motels and more than 50 bed and breakfasts during the summer. Rates vary widely, from a low of about $40 for a single to a high of $150 for a double. Reservations are suggested during the busy summer months.

The town has at least 100 restaurants ranging from deluxe to fast food.

Ah, Rose Marie Bed and Breakfast. A touch of 1920s Fairbanks in downtown city

R.V. PARKING
$9.00 per site
showers included

Dump Station and Dry Camping
Water

CRIPPLE CREEK RESORT
HOME OF THE WORLD FAMOUS MALEMUTE SALOON
(907) 479-2500
• FOR MORE INFO. SEE LOG AD—Mi. 351.7 GEORGE PARKS HWY. •

SUCH A DEAL Bed & Breakfast
If you like animals, this is the place for you.
HOSPITALITY IN ABUNDANCE
Open year-round   10% Senior discount   Non-smoking household
P.O. BOX 82527, FAIRBANKS, ALASKA 99708   (907) 474-8159

FLY TO REMOTE LAKES FOR THE VERY BEST FISHING — $120
Grayling • Silver Salmon
Northern Pike • Rainbow Trout

BOB ELLIOTT - Licensed Guide - Commercial Pilot
32 years in business

5920 Airport Way, (at Dale Road) Fairbanks, AK 99709 • (907) 479-6323

Adventure into a Gold Camp & KEEP THE GOLD!

DAILY! Morning & Afternoon DEPARTURES

- 2 hour personalized tour of an authentic modern day mining camp in the heart of the historic Fox Gold Fields.
- Ride the narrow gauge railroad and pan for gold.

BROCHURE:
1132 Lakeview Terrace
Fairbanks, AK 99701

Reservations & Info: CALL,

Little El Dorado Gold Camp • 907 / 479-7613

A PIONEER BED & BREAKFAST
Your Own Authentic 1906 Log Cabin
Completely Restored
All Modern Facilities
Very Private
Located – Downtown Fairbanks

1119 2nd Avenue
Fairbanks, AK 99701

(907) 452-5393
452-4628
456-3672

FAIRBANKS' NEWEST RV PARK

River's Edge

4140 BOAT ST. (off Airport Way)
FAIRBANKS, ALASKA
(907) 474-0286

Good Sampark

RIVER'S EDGE
RV PARK & CAMPGROUND

Full and Partial
Hookup Pull-Thrus
30-amp Electric
Dump Station
Dry Sites
Tent Camping
FREE Showers
Laundry
Gift Shop
Pay Phone
Vehicle Wash Facility

Centrally Located • Walking Distance to Major Shopping Centers

RV VISITOR INFORMATION and ACTIVITY CENTER

FREE Shuttle to Sternwheeler *Discovery* and Alaska Salmon Bake

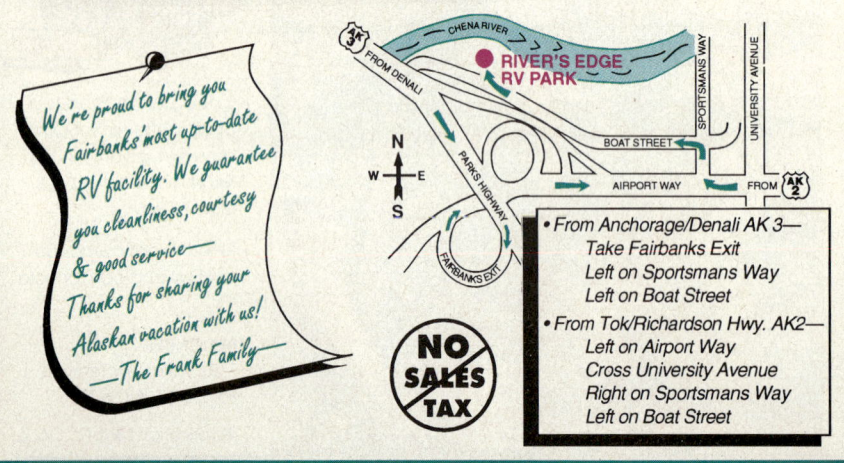

We're proud to bring you Fairbanks' most up-to-date RV facility. We guarantee you cleanliness, courtesy & good service. Thanks for sharing your Alaskan vacation with us!
—The Frank Family

NO SALES TAX

- From Anchorage/Denali AK 3—
  Take Fairbanks Exit
  Left on Sportsmans Way
  Left on Boat Street
- From Tok/Richardson Hwy. AK2—
  Left on Airport Way
  Cross University Avenue
  Right on Sportsmans Way
  Left on Boat Street

FAIRBANKS' TOP RATED CAMPGROUND

Giant cabbages are grown at the UAF experimental gardens. (Bonnie Pickert)

center. Cozy, clean and comfortable. Light or hearty breakfasts on our enclosed front porch. Friendly cat and dog. Open year-round (rates vary with season). Single $40 and up, double $55 and up; plus 8 percent tax. Family room available. John E. Davis, 302 Cowles, Fairbanks, AK 99701. (907) 456-2040. [ADVERTISEMENT]

Alaska's 7 Gables Bed & Breakfast. FAR–B&B Fairbanks, Alaska Reservations Bed & Breakfast. Whether it be a cozy home in the city or a spacious chalet just outside town, we can accommodate your needs. From continental to gourmet breakfasts; canoes to bicycles; individual rooms to private apartments; single to king-sized beds; phones to cable TVs; laundry facilities to jacuzzi; rates $25 to $100 per night. Directions: Geist Road to Fairbanks Street, then south on Fairbanks Street for 1 block and right on Birch Lane to 4312. Write: P.O. Box 80488, Fairbanks, AK 99708, or phone (907) 479-0751. Fax (907) 479-2229. [ADVERTISEMENT]

Beaver Bend Bed and Breakfast. Located on picturesque Chena River close to town with country setting. Rooms are clean and comfortable, shared or private bath. Start the day with a full sourdough breakfast. Hosted

CHENA RIVER BED & BREAKFAST

Elegant RIVERSIDE home on ten peaceful acres

Full sourdough breakfast served family style in our dining room overlooking the river. Minutes from UAF Museum & Riverboat Discovery.

- Non-smoking
- Open year round
- Fly-in fishing trips available
- Laundry facilities • Private bath
- Backpackers & camping families welcome

1001 Dolly Varden, Fairbanks, Alaska 99709
907 • 479 • 2532

by 18-year Alaskans. Rates $55 to $60. Non-smoking. 231 Iditarod, Fairbanks, AK 99701. Phone (907) 452-3240. [ADVERTISEMENT]

(Betty's) Bed & Breakfast. 1-2-3 ABA. Seven quiet, attractively furnished rooms situated near 8 of Fairbanks 11 major attractions. $34 single, $46 double, private suite $85. Shelter & Shower™ accommodations for backpackers, or other travelers on a tight budget. Rates begin at $18. Inexpensive, yet surprisingly comfortable, secure and pleasant. 248 Madcap. Phone (907) 479-5035. [ADVERTISEMENT]

The Chocolate Rush Bed & Breakfast. Open year-round. Comfortable accommodations in lovely remodeled 1940s home, downtown Fairbanks location. A full breakfast served with special coffees. Single $45, double $55, private bath apartment $65, plus 8 percent room tax. For reservations call (907) 474-8633, 10-second voice pager (907) 479-1452, (907) 451-4332. Write P.O. Box 72296, Fairbanks, AK 99707. [ADVERTISEMENT]

Gold Dredge Number 8 Hotel & Bed & Breakfast. Nice accommodations reasonably priced. Acres of safe secure RV parking. Plenty of things to do. See display ad in this section. [ADVERTISEMENT]

Happy Haven Bed and Breakfast. Experience warm Alaskan hospitality and

CRIPPLE CREEK HOTEL

CLEAN, PLEASANT ROOMS AT OLD FASHIONED PRICES

SINGLE $45   DOUBLE $50

National Registry for HISTORICAL PLACES

(Semi-private Bathrooms)

CRIPPLE CREEK RESORT

HOME OF THE WORLD FAMOUS **MALEMUTE SALOON**   (907) 479-2500

• FOR MORE INFO. SEE LOG AD—Mi. 351.7 GEORGE PARKS HWY. •

Kitchenettes available • Pets accepted
Home Box Office movies • Phones
Plug-ins and winter weekly rates available
Free parking • Courtesy coffee
American Express, MasterCard and VISA

ALASKAN MOTOR INN
32 ROOMS
DOWNTOWN MOTEL
Reasonable Rates
PHONE (907) 452-4800
419 Fourth Avenue, Fairbanks, AK 99701

NORLITE CAMPGROUND

- 250 Spaces
- Full, Water, Electric & Tent Spaces
- 2 Dump Stations
- 30-amps Available
- Laundry
- Grocery & Liquor Store
- Truck & RV / Car Wash
- Tour Tickets & Information
- Snack Shop
- Showers (guests only)

Friendly & Caring Staff
Open May 15 thru September 15

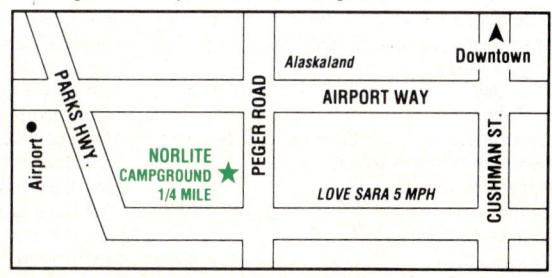

1660 Peger Road, Fairbanks
(907) 474-0206
In State Toll Free 1-800-478-0206
AWARD WINNING CAMPGROUND

FAIRBANKS

enjoy comfort and security in your own suite with private entrance, fully stocked kitchen, private bath, antique furnishings, TV, space for families. On 1½ acres of birch, aspen and fireweed with occasional moose. Just 10 minutes from university, 10 minutes from airport, 15 minutes from downtown Fairbanks. Reasonable rates. (907) 479-2895.
[ADVERTISEMENT]

North Woods Lodge. A rustic, Alaskan log house located in the hills surrounding Fairbanks. Clean, comfortable lodging with queen-sized beds, fully equipped kitchen, laundry facilities, private baths, Jacuzzi hot tub, phone service and TV with VCR. Open year-round. VISA, MasterCard accepted. For reservations and information write: P.O. Box 83615, Fairbanks, AK 99708 or call

FAIRBANKS ADVERTISERS

Affordable Car Rental .... 3101 S. Cushman
Ah, Rose Marie Bed &
    Breakfast .... 302 Cowles St.
Alaska Motel .... 1546 Cushman St.
Alaska Range View
    Bed & Breakfast .... Ph. (907) 479-2082
Alaska Raw Fur Co. .... Ph. (907) 479-2462
Alaska River Charters .... Ph. (907) 455-6827
Alaska Salmon Bake .... Alaskaland
Alaska Spring .... Ph. (907) 563-3802
Alaska Stage Line, Inc. .... Ph. (907) 451-7112
Alaska Trails & Tours .... Ph. (907) 452-8687
Alaska Wildlife Park .... College Rd.
Alaskaland .... Airport Way & Peger Rd.
Alaskan Apparel .... Alaskaland
Alaskan Motor Inn .... 419 4th Ave.
Alaskan Photographic Repair
    Service .... 551½ 2nd Ave.
Alaska's 7 Gables Bed &
    Breakfast .... 4312 Birch Lane
Allstar Rent-A-Car .... Ph. (800) 426-5243
An Alaskan Viewpoint
    Bed & Breakfast .... Ph. (907) 479-7251
Arctic Rent-A-Car .... 2 locations—See ad
Artworks, The .... 3677 College Rd.
Aurora Animal Clinic .... Ph. (907) 452-6055
Aurora Motel .... Ph. (907) 451-1935
Beads & Things .... 2nd Ave.
Bean's Old-Time Photos .... Alaskaland #28
Beaver Bend Bed and
    Breakfast .... Ph. (907) 452-3240
(Betty's) Bed &
    Breakfast .... Ph. (907) 479-5035
Big Ray's All Weather
    Outfitters .... 507 2nd Ave.
Bunkhouse
    Restaurant, The .... Ph. (907) 479-2500
Captain Barlett Inn .... Ph. 1-800-544-7528
Chena Hot Springs
    Resort .... Mile J 56.5 Chena Hot Springs Rd.
Chena River Bed &
    Breakfast .... Ph. (907) 479-2532
Chena River Rafts & Bed &
    Breakfast .... Ph. (907) 479-0007
Chocolate Rush Bed
    & Breakfast, The .... Ph. (907) 474-8633
Chokecherry Inn .... Ph. (907) 474-9381
Circle Hot Springs
    Resort .... Mile 8.3 Circle Hot Springs Rd.
Cookie Jar and Garden
    Cafe, The .... Washington Plaza
Country Setting Bed
    & Breakfast .... Ph. (907) 457-6498
Cripple Creek
    Campground .... Mile 351.7 Parks Hwy.
Cripple Creek Hotel .... Ph. (907) 479-2500
Cripple Creek Resort .... Ph. (907) 479-2500
Cushman Plaza
    Laundry .... 2301 S. Cushman St.
Dog Mushing
    Museum .... Mile 4 Farmers Loop Rd.
Eleanor's Bed & Breakfast .... Downtown
Evergreen Bed and
    Breakfast .... Ph. (907) 451-0139
Fairbanks Bed &
    Breakfast .... Ph. (907) 452-4967

Fairbanks Clinic .... Ph. (907) 452-1761
Fairbanks Convention and
    Visitors Bureau .... 550 1st Ave.
Fairbanks Fast Foto
    and Video .... 2 locations—See ad
Fairbanks Golf and
    Country Club .... Ph. (907) 479-6555
Fairbanks RV Service
    Center .... 2 locations—See ad
Fireweed RV Rentals .... Ph. (907) 479-4229
Frontier Flying
    Service, Inc. .... 3820 University Ave.
G & G Electronics .... Gavora Mall
G & J's Bed and
    Breakfast .... Ph. (907) 479-2564
Gabe's Peger Road
    I/M & Muffler .... Ph.(907) 479-6162
Gene's .... 1804 S. Cushman St.
Gold Dredge
    Number 8 .... Mile 9 Old Steese Hwy.
Golden North Motel .... 4888 Airport Way
Goldhill RV Park .... Mile 355.2 Parks Hwy.
Goldpanner Chevron
    Service, Inc. .... 809 Cushman St.
Great Alaska Bowl
    Company .... 4630 Old Airport Rd.
Great Land Hotel, The .... 723 1st Ave.
Halls With A View .... Ph. (907) 479-6120
Happy Haven Bed and
    Breakfast .... Ph. (907) 479-2895
Hoefler, Vaughan J.,
    D.D.S. .... Ph. (907) 479-4759
Home "Suite" Home .... Ph. (907) 474-9517
Hot Licks Homemade
    Ice Cream .... 3549 College Rd.
Image Alaska's .... Westmark Hotel
Independent Rental .... 2020 S. Cushman St.
Interior Custom Topper .... 604 Hughes
Ivory Jack's .... Ph. (907) 455-6666
Klondike Inn Motel .... 1316 Bedrock St.
Larry's Flying
    Service, Inc. .... Ph. (907) 474-9169
Larson's Fine Jewelers .... 405 Noble St.
Little El Dorado Gold Camp
    Tours .... 1132 Lakeview Terrace
Little Fox Inn .... Ph. (907) 457-6539
L&L RV .... 2751 Davis Rd.
Log Cabin Bed &
    Breakfast .... Ph. (907) 479-2332
Malemute Saloon, The ..... Ph. (907) 479-2500
Mapco Express .... 3 locations—See ad
Marina Air, Inc. .... 1219 Shypoke St.
McCauley's Reprographics .... 721 Gaffney Rd.
Midnight Sun Aviation .... Ph. (907) 452-7039
Mobat Tire .... 3601 S. Cushman St.
Motor Inn Safety Lane .... 2550 Cushman St.
Native Village of Alaskaland .... Alaskaland
New Design Hairstyling .... 3535 College Rd.
Norlite Campground, Inc. ...... 1660 Peger Rd.
North Woods Lodge .... Ph. (907) 479-5300
Northern Alaska Tour
    Company .... Ph. (907) 474-8600
Northern Lights Dolls .... Ph. (907) 488-6149
Northern Lights
    Photosymphony .... Ph. (907) 479-2500
Northwind Group .... Ph. 1-800-759-5154

Novus Windshield Repair .. 229 Forty Mile Ave.
Palace Theatre & Saloon, The .... Alaskaland
Pearl Creek Bed &
    Breakfast .... Ph. (907) 479-8208
Photo Express .... 2 locations—See ad
Pick 'N Poke Gift Shop .... 3175 College Rd.
Pioneer Bed &
    Breakfast, A .... 1119 2nd Ave.
Pioneer R.V. & Trailer
    Court .... 2201 S. Cushman St.
Plane Country Bed &
    Breakfast .... Ph. (907) 479-8130
Plaza Cleaners and
    Laundry .... 3417 Airport Way
Poolside B & B .... Ph. (907) 452-4119
Pump House Restaurant &
    Saloon, The .... Mile 1.3 Chena Pump Rd.
Regency Fairbanks, The .... 95 10th Ave.
River's Edge RV Park
    & Campground .... 4140 Boat St.
Road's End RV Park .... Ph. (907) 488-0295
Rose's Forget-Me-Not
    Bed & Breakfast .... Ph. (907) 456-5734
Santa's Smokehouse .... 2400 Davis Rd.
Sleepy Moose
    Bed & Breakfast .... Ph. (907) 452-4814
Sternwheeler Riverboat
    Discovery, The .... Ph. (907) 479-6673
Such A Deal
    Bed & Breakfast .... Ph. (907) 474-8159
Super 8 Motels .... Ph. 1-800-800-8000
Tamarac Inn Motel .... 252 Minnie St.
Tanana Valley
    Campground .... Mile 2 College Rd.
Tanana Valley Farmers Market ...... College Rd.
Tesoro Alaska ...... Van Horn Rd. & S. Cushman
This Old House
    Bed and Breakfast .... Ph. (907) 452-6343
Tivi Kennels .... Mile 348.8 Parks Hwy.
Totem Chevron, Inc. .... 768 Gaffney Rd.
Touch of Gold, A .... Bentley Mall
Towne House Motel and
    Apartments .... 1010 Cushman St.
Trailer Craft, Inc. .... 2145 Van Horn Rd.
Trident Apartments .... Ph. (907) 479-6313
Turtle Club, The .... Ph. (907) 457-3883
University Avenue Car & Truck
    Wash .... University Ave. & Cameron
University Center
    Mall .... University Ave. & Airport Way
University of Alaska
    Fairbanks .... Ph. (907) 474-7821
University of Alaska
    Museum .... 907 Yukon Dr.
Vango Custom Tours .... Ph. (907) 455-6499
Waltons, The .... Ph. (907) 452-1159
Wet Willy's Automatic
    Car and Truck Wash .... 2 locations—See ad
Wild Iris Inn .... Ph. (907) 474-4747
Wilderness Fishing .... 5920 Airport Way
Woolworth
    Alaska .... 3rd Ave. & Cushman St.
World Eskimo-Indian
    Olympics .... Ph. (907) 452-6646
Wright Air
    Service Inc. .... Fairbanks Int. Airport

(907) 479-5300. [ADVERTISEMENT]

The Wild Iris Inn. This charming country home B&B is nestled in pristine ambiance amidst towering spruce, overlooking a view of the Alaska Range. Spacious, impeccably clean, casual elegance throughout. Smoke-free environment. Separate host quarters. Lavish, 3-course, gourmet breakfasts. Private baths. $75 to $95 (double). P.O. Box 73246, Fairbanks, AK 99707; (907) 474-IRIS (474-4747). [ADVERTISEMENT]

There are several private campgrounds in the Fairbanks area. Chena River recreation site, a state campground, is located on University Avenue by the Chena River bridge; 63 sites, tables, firepits, toilets, water, dump station, $12/nightly camping fee or annual pass, $3 for use of dump station, $3 for use of boat launch. Expect construction in late summer 1992. There is overnight camping for self-contained RVs only at Alaskaland; 5-night limit, $7 fee. City dump station on 2nd Avenue.

Cripple Creek Campground—Located 7 miles west of Fairbanks, Mile 351.7 George Parks Highway in Cripple Creek Resort, Ester. P.O. Box 109, Ester, AK 99725. (907) 479-2500. Dry camping. No hookups. Water

---

COUNTRY SETTING BED & BREAKFAST
"Your Home Away From Home"
- Private apartment lodging (907) 457-6498
- Exceptional view of mountains and town — Send SASE for brochure
- Minutes from town — P.O. Box 80828, Fairbanks, AK 99708

AURORA MOTEL
2016 COLLEGE ROAD
(Near Fairgrounds & University)
- Kitchenettes & Cabins
- RV Parking
- Bed & Breakfast

DAILY & WEEKLY REASONABLE RATES
(907) 451-1935
Peaceful Surroundings

Fairbanks Bed & Breakfast
We are family-run reservation and referral service. We book travelers into bed & breakfast lodging in the Fairbanks area.

GUEST ROOMS, clean and comfortable. Friendly, close to downtown and area attractions.
CAR RENTAL Available; discount to Bed & Breakfast guests; reasonable prices.

CALL (907) 452-4967
Reservations suggested. FREE map included.
Write Fairbanks Bed & Breakfast
Box 74573
Fairbanks, Alaska 99707

"A combination of oldworld tradition and Fairbanks' hospitality at a friendly price."

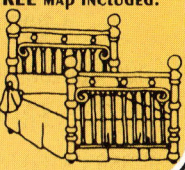

"Northern Lights" PHOTOSYMPHONY SHOW

I could feel the Northern Lights "...ALASKA, I thought"

A show of unparalleled poetry in motion on 28" wide screen.

Call for Reservations

- DAILY Performances in Ester
- One Of-A-Kind Show! STEREO SOUND

CRIPPLE CREEK RESORT
HOME OF THE WORLD FAMOUS **MALEMUTE SALOON** (907) 479-2500
• FOR MORE INFO. SEE LOG AD—Mi. 351.7 GEORGE PARKS HWY. •

THE WALTONS
A Bed & Breakfast Accommodation
Quiet Elegant Residential Setting
Located on the Chena River in Hamilton Acres
201 Iditarod, Fairbanks, Alaska 99701
(907) 452-1159

ROAD'S END RV PARK
V 356 Richardson-Alaska Hwy.
Full Hookups • Showers
Reasonable Prices
Phone **(907) 488-0295**
(Just 6.5 miles south of Fairbanks)
Or Write: 1463 Wescott Lane
North Pole, Alaska 99705

LOG CABIN
BED & BREAKFAST
FAIRBANKS
$25 - $35 - $50
(907) 479-2332

Alaska Range View Bed and Breakfast
Spectacular Million Acre View
Comfort and Luxury
Phone (907) 479-2082
FAX (907) 479-5606
PO Box 82026, Fairbanks, Alaska 99708

KLONDIKE INN

When you're in Fairbanks **STAY WITH US!**
☆ Minutes from the Airport
☆ Modern Kitchen Unit
☆ Television and Phone
☆ Laundry Facilities
☆ On City Transit Route
☆ Park in Front of Your Unit
☆ Liquor Store

Reservations
(907) 479-6241

We're located right next to University Center!
University & Airport Way, 1316 Bedrock Street, Fairbanks, Alaska 99701

Klondike Lounge & Dining Hall
Breakfast • Lunch • Dinner • Cocktails
Outdoor Seating
OPEN 7 DAYS A WEEK   Sunday open at 10 a.m.
Next to Klondike Inn
(907) 479-2224

FAIRBANKS

See the REAL Alaska!
Come to the "Golden Heart" of the Interior!

THE GREAT LAND HOTEL

- Government, Commercial and Union Rates
- 90 Rooms
- Suites
- Lounge
- Full Service Restaurant
- Cable Television

Conveniently located in the Downtown Area!

723 First Ave.
Fairbanks, AK 99701

(907) 452-6661
FAX (907) 452-6126

MasterCard • VISA • American Express

Uniquely Alaskan

CIRCLE HOT SPRINGS RESORT
In the Heart of Gold Country

RV Parking • Restrooms • Showers • State Maintained 3600' Lighted Airstrip
Fishing and Flightseeing trips arranged
Great area to view Northern Lights without artificial light interference September - May.
Ski and Snowmachine trails in winter.
Newly renovated rooms, dining facilities, cabins, saloon and Olympic-size swimming pool

Call (907) 520-5113
or write . . . Circle Hot Springs Resort, Box 254, Central, Alaska 99730
Lodge is open year-round
See our log ad at Circle Hot Springs in the Steese Highway section.

CHENA HOT SPRINGS
Where the Warmth of Alaska is Yours

Relax in our natural hot water pool.
Enjoy the beautiful log atmosphere of our dining room and bar.
Rent a room, cabin or use our spacious free campground.
Picnicking — Badminton
Volleyball
Plenty of woods to stroll through.
Good fishing nearby.
OPEN YEAR-ROUND
Phone: (907) 452-7867

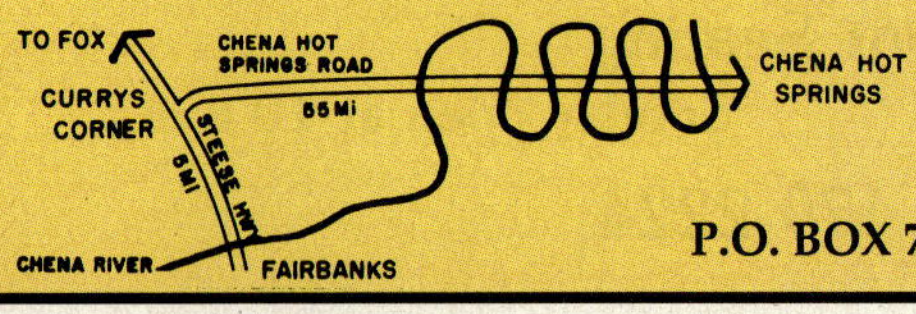

Just 60 scenic miles from Fairbanks up the Chena Hot Springs Road. Just Drive on up!

P.O. BOX 73440, FAIRBANKS, ALASKA 99707

---

and dump station available. $9 per site. Showers included. Check in at hotel desk. Reservations accepted. Hotel, dinner restaurant, saloon, entertainment and gift shop nearby. See log ad **Milepost A 351.7** Parks Highway and display ads in FAIRBANKS section. [ADVERTISEMENT] ▲

Norlite Campground, Inc. Centrally located just 0.3 mile south off Airport Road on Peger Road, Norlite is the most complete of all Fairbanks's campgrounds. City water, sewer and electric hookups, showers, dump station, tour tickets, laundry, liquor store, truck/car wash, snack and ice cream bar and grocery store are all on the grounds. (See ad in this section.) [ADVERTISEMENT] ▲

River's Edge RV Park & Campground. Fairbanks's newest and most modern facility. Centrally located. Only full-service RV park on the Chena River. Pull-through sites, full and partial hookups, 30 amp, dump

---

THE LITTLE FOX INN
A Country Bed & Breakfast

- Clean Spacious Inn
- Private or Shared Bath
- Full Breakfast
- TV • Telephones

For Reservations or Information
Call (907) 457-6539
1351 Little Fox Trail, Fairbanks, AK 99712

G&J's *Bed and Breakfast*

STAY WITH TWO LOCAL TEACHERS
IN THEIR SPACIOUS HOME

LUXURIANT BEDROOMS
• CONTINENTAL BREAKFAST •
EXCELLENT HOSPITALITY
PRIVATE SITTING ROOM WITH TV

(907) 479-2564
73 PEPPERDINE, FAIRBANKS, ALASKA 99708

Beautiful Mornings Begin At 8.

SUPER 8 MOTEL

Toll-Free Reservations:
1-800-800-8000

Four Convenient Alaska Locations

FAIRBANKS
Juneau • Ketchikan • Anchorage

---

358 The MILEPOST® ■ 1992

FAIRBANKS

Immaculate Conception Church.
(Bruce M. Herman)

THE BUNKHOUSE RESTAURANT
For a meal to write home about.

ALL THE Alaska Dungeness Crab YOU CARE TO EAT

Or try our delicious **BUNKHOUSE BUFFET**
Baked Halibut, Reindeer Stew & Country Style Chicken

NIGHTLY 5-9   Reservations Advised

CRIPPLE CREEK RESORT
HOME OF THE WORLD FAMOUS **MALEMUTE SALOON**
(907) 479-2500
• FOR MORE INFO. SEE LOG AD—Mi. 351.7 GEORGE PARKS HWY. •

HOME "SUITE" HOME
Bed & Breakfast

Suite with bath, private entrance

Walking distance to Alaskaland and shopping

Ideal for couples and families

(907) 474-9517

1167 Ivy Drive, Fairbanks, Alaska 99709

HALL'S WITH A VIEW
Bed & Breakfast

Nestled in the hills surrounding Fairbanks

For more information or reservations

call: **(907) 479-6120**
or write: **1443 Holy Cross Drive
Fairbanks, Alaska 99709**

Plane Country
Bed & Breakfast

Situated in rural Fairbanks, just 10 miles from town on a privately owned floatpond and runway. Totally relaxed atmosphere, with the added interest of light aircraft activity. Singles or groups of six can be accomodated in neat, clean apartments, all with private baths and entrys. Do your own thing style! Near the parks highway, University of Alaska, Tanana river campground and the "Pump House" restaurant and saloon. Proprietors: Marge and Tom Kushida
P.O. Box 84458 • Fairbanks, Alaska 99708 • (907) 479-8130

Sleepy Moose Bed & Breakfast
Conveniently Located • Master Suite or Shared Bath • Non-Smoking
Continental Breakfast • Kitchen and Laundry Facilities Available

Reservations (907) 452-4814 • Check-in 5:30 to 9:30 p.m.
Hostess: Teresa Johnson • 820 Joyce Drive, Fairbanks, AK 99701

TAMARAC INN MOTEL

Within Walking Distance to:
City Center • Train Station
Nearly Half the Shopping Malls

252 Minnie Street • Fairbanks
(907) 456-6406
Guest Laundry Facilities • Some Kitchens

The Regency Fairbanks
95 Tenth Avenue, Fairbanks, Alaska 99701   (907) 452-3200

• Dining Room • Cocktail Lounge
• Free Satellite TV • Room Service
• Conference Rooms
• Banquet Rooms
• Handicapped Accommodations

The Newest Most Modern Hotel In Interior Alaska

• Kitchen Units • Laundromat
• Units with Whirlpool Baths
• Air-Conditioned Units
  in all rooms and suites

American Express
VISA / MasterCard
Diners Club Accepted

Limousine service available from Airport & Train Depot

CHOKECHERRY INN
A 4th Generation Alaskan B & B
946 N. Coppet • Fairbanks, Alaska 99709 • (907) 474-9381

• Gracious overnight lodging with a fourth generation Alaskan family
• Within walking distance of Alaskaland.
• 4,000 square feet of Bed & Breakfast area.

• 4 large rooms with TV, telephone, ceiling fans & bath
• Deluxe suite available
• Each room decorated in different themes & colors, created with wicker, brass and country

1992 ■ The MILEPOST® 359

FAIRBANKS

PIONEER R.V. & TRAILER COURT
IN-TOWN LOCATION

☆ Showers ☆ Public Laundromat
☆ Electric ☆ Water ☆ Sewer
☆ 24-Hour Manager
☆ Convenient location for shopping, services, dining

DAILY, WEEKLY, MONTHLY RATES

Cushman & 22nd Avenue
(907) 452-8788   Fairbanks

Pearl Creek Bed & Breakfast
- Comfortable casual country setting
- Continental breakfast
- Open year 'round

(907) 479-8208

Close to the University of Alaska
off Farmers Loop Road
600 Auburn, Fairbanks, AK 99701

CHENA RIVER RAFTS & BED & BREAKFAST
Custom floats & day trips
(907) 479-0007
P.O. Box 60774, Fairbanks, AK 99706

POOLSIDE B & B
Heated Outdoor Pool
Luxury Living - Many Pluses
Hosts Always Present
Tour Assistance
Large Family Rooms
Very Centrally Located
Reasonable Rates

(907) 452-4119

1968 Hilton Avenue, Fairbanks, Alaska 99701

AN ALASKAN VIEWPOINT
BED & BREAKFAST

Panoramic View Overlooking Fairbanks and Alaska Range

Single • Double • Private Apartment

VISA **(907) 479-7251** MasterCard

1244 Viewpoint Drive, Fairbanks, AK 99709

TRIDENT APARTMENTS and BED & BREAKFAST

Enjoy Bed and (cook it yourself) Breakfast in the Privacy of Your Own Apartment

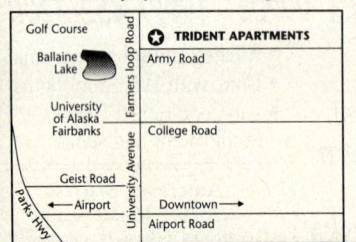

- Cozy, Clean, Quiet
- Tub with Shower in Each Unit
- Reasonable Rates
- Near Golf Course, on Bike and Running Path
- Longtime Alaskan Owners
- Historic Remodeled Pipeline Building
- We'll be glad to pick you up or take you to the train or plane, but our location is best suited to guests that have local transportation.

(907) 479-6313
Box 80304, Fairbanks, Alaska 99708
Toll-free Alaska 1-800-478-6313

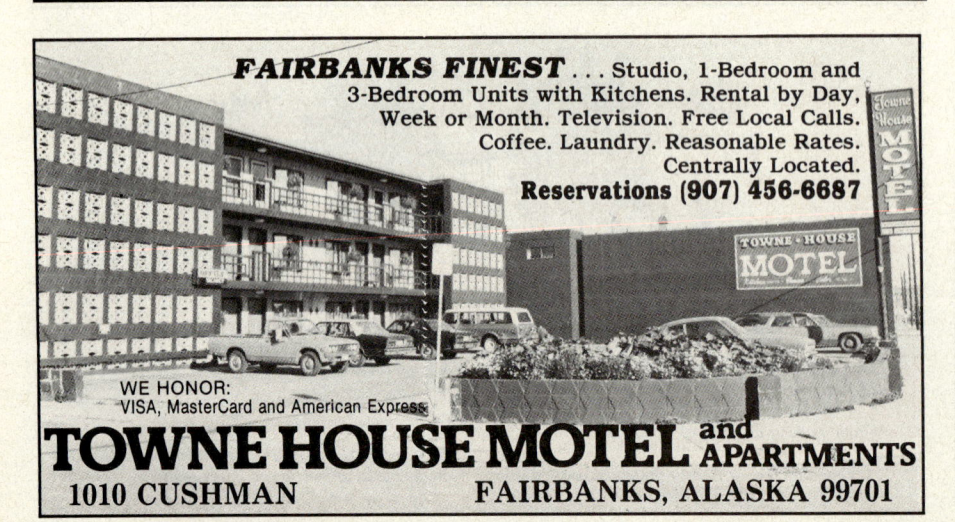

TOWNE HOUSE MOTEL and APARTMENTS

FAIRBANKS FINEST... Studio, 1-Bedroom and 3-Bedroom Units with Kitchens. Rental by Day, Week or Month. Television. Free Local Calls. Coffee. Laundry. Reasonable Rates. Centrally Located.

Reservations **(907) 456-6687**

WE HONOR: VISA, MasterCard and American Express

1010 CUSHMAN   FAIRBANKS, ALASKA 99701

---

station, free showers, laundry. Daily free shuttle to stern-wheeler *Discovery* and Alaska Salmon Bake at Alaskaland. See map in ad. Phone (907) 474-0286. [ADVERTISEMENT] ▲

TRANSPORTATION

Scheduled Air Carriers: Several international, interstate and intra-Alaska air carriers serve Fairbanks; see Air Travel in the GENERAL INFORMATION section for details.

Charter Flights: A large number of air charter services are available for flightseeing, fly-in fishing and hunting trips and trips to bush villages; see ads in this section.

Alaska Railroad: Passenger depot at 280 N. Cushman St. in the downtown area. Daily passenger service in summer between Fairbanks and Anchorage with stopovers at Denali National Park; less frequent service in winter. For details see the ALASKA RAILROAD section, or phone 456-4155.

Bus: Scheduled motorcoach service to Anchorage and points south. Local daily bus service by Metropolitan Area Commuter Service (MACS); no service on weekends and some legal holidays. Drivers do not carry change and exact change or tokens must be

---

ELEANOR'S Northern Lights BED & BREAKFAST

SINGLE $40 • DOUBLE $48-$58
(907) 452-2598
360 STATE STREET, FAIRBANKS, ALASKA 99701
Near downtown • Credit cards accepted

EVERGREEN BED and BREAKFAST

One-room apartments with kitchenette
Two rooms in main house
Kids welcome, large play area

Your Hosts - The Hopple family

For reservations and information call: **(907) 451-0139**
or write: 1514 Evergreen Street
Fairbanks, Alaska 99709

"Your new Alaskan Friends"

4312 Birch Lane • PO Box 80488
Fairbanks, AK 99708

Alaska's 7 Gables Bed & Breakfast
Fairbanks

Excellent Location
Wholesome Gourmet Food
Spacious Tudor Home • Beautiful Floral Gardens
Rooms or Apartments Year Around • Cable TV's
Laundry • Canoes • Bicycles Available • Phone
Separate Smoking Areas • New Mattresses

Rooms $40-$70 • Suites $45-$95

PHONE (907) 479-0751 • FAX (907) 479-2229

used. Fares are: $1 or 1 token. Tokens are available at a variety of shops. Information is available via the Transit Hotline, phone 459-1011, or from MACS offices at 3175 Peger Road, phone 459-1002.

Tours: Local and area sightseeing tours are available.

Alaska Stage Line, Inc. Local transportation. Leave your RV plugged in and enjoy relaxed, personalized service. Create your own itinerary. Join with your friends for reduced rates. Experience the fun and excitement of visiting such landmarks as mining camps, gold dredges, pipeline view, musk-ox farm, University Museum, Alaskaland. Phone (907) 451-7112. [ADVERTISEMENT]

Alaska Trails & Tours. Your "travel agent" for all types of fishing, raft rides, riverboats, Arctic Circle trips, Barrow tours, airline tickets, and much, much more. Reservations, tickets and trip advice. Located summers at Alaskaland from 11 A.M. to 9 P.M.

"This Old House" BED & BREAKFAST

- A historic house with fine new accommodations
- Conveniently located in downtown Fairbanks
- Full Breakfast served

VISA   **(907) 452-6343**   MasterCard
1010 8th Avenue, Fairbanks, AK 99701

The Chocolate Rush Bed & Breakfast

Open Year-Round

Comfortable accommodations in lovely remodeled 1940's downtown Fairbanks location.

A full breakfast served with special coffees.

Single—$45 • Double—$55
Private bath Apt.—$65
Plus 8% room tax

FOR RESERVATIONS CALL
- (907) 474-8633
10-second voice
pager (907) 479-1452
- (907) 451-4332

Write: The Chocolate Rush Bed & Breakfast
P.O. Box 72296
Fairbanks, Alaska 99707

THE MALEMUTE SALOON presents

An Evening of Song, Stories & Robt. Service Poetry with

The SAWDUST STRING BAND
MON.-SAT. at 9 P.M.
Reservations Advised

Saloon Open Daily
◆ Food Served ◆

CRIPPLE CREEK RESORT

HOME OF THE WORLD FAMOUS **MALEMUTE SALOON**   (907) 479-2500

• FOR MORE INFO. SEE LOG AD—Mi. 351.7 GEORGE PARKS HWY. •

Tanana Valley Campground

NATURAL SETTING . . . MODERN

- SHOWERS
- LAUNDRY
- FIREPLACES
- TABLES
- POTABLE WATER
- FIREWOOD
- DUMP STATION
- NO ELECTRIC HOOKUP

Spaces for RV & Motorhomes • On the Bus Route
Tanana Valley State Fairgrounds • 2 Mile College Road
1800 College Road • Fairbanks, Alaska 99709   (907) 456-7956

1-2-3 ABA (Betty's) Bed & Breakfast

Comfortable, Secure & Pleasant, Yet Surprisingly Inexpensive

$34 Single
$46 Double
$18-up Shelter & Shower

(907) 479-5035
248 Madcap Lane
Fairbanks, Alaska 99709

Alaska Motel

REASONABLE RATES!
Senior Citizen Discount • Weekly Rates

- Kitchenettes
- Laundry Facilities
- Cable TV
- Free Parking

Close to Shopping and Restaurants
We accept all major credit cards

**1546 Cushman Street
Fairbanks, Alaska 99701
PHONE (907) 456-6393
FAX (907) 452-4833**

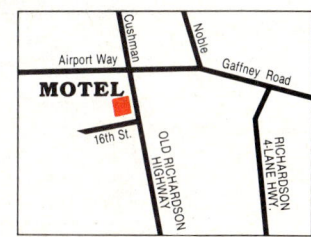

1992 ■ The MILEPOST®   361

FAIRBANKS

Year-round phone (907) 452-TOUR (8687). Call today, we'll help plan your trip.
[ADVERTISEMENT]

VANGO Custom Tours. Take a personalized tour of the Fairbanks area with someone who lives here! Meet the 'locals.' Visit a dog musher's kennel, artist's studio, farms, take a nature walk with Alaskan herbalist, experience the river, gold mining, learn about Native culture, visit museum, and more. VANGO Custom Tours (907) 455-6499. P.O. Box 81914, Fairbanks, AK 99708.
[ADVERTISEMENT]

Taxi Service: 8 cab companies (see phone book).

Car, Camper and Trailer Rentals: Several companies rent cars, campers and trailers; see ads in this section.

ATTRACTIONS

Get Acquainted: A good place to start is at the visitor information center at 550 1st Ave., where you'll find free brochures, maps and tips on what to see and how to get there. Phone 456-5774 or 456-INFO for a recording of current daily events.

Next to the log cabin visitor information center is Golden Heart Park, site of the 18-foot/5-m bronze monument, *Unknown First Family*. The statue, by sculptor Malcolm Alexander, and park were dedicated in July 1986 to celebrate Fairbanks's history and heritage.

The Alaska Public Lands Information Center, located in the lower level of historic Courthouse Square at 3rd Avenue and Cushman Street, is a free museum and information center featuring Alaska's natural history, cultural artifacts and recreational opportunities. In addition to detailed information on outdoor recreation in the state, the center offers films, interpretive programs, lectures, guided nature walks and a museum shop. A must stop.

Tour the University of Alaska–Fairbanks main campus, situated on a 2,250-acre ridge overlooking the city and Tanana River valley. The campus has all the features of a small town, including a fire station, post office, radio and TV station, medical clinic, and a 1,000-seat concert hall.

UAF offers special tours and programs from June through August. These include a tour of the Large Animal Research Station and a show at the Geophysical Institute,

---

Alaskaland
PAID ADVERTISEMENTS

ALASKAN APPAREL
Alaskaland Cabin 31 • Open year-round
Summer & Winter Parkas
KUSPUKS • MUKLUKS • MITTENS • GIFTS
Alaskan Patterns • Custom-Made & Off-the-Racks
Write for brochure: Dorothy Teagarden
Alaskan Apparel Cabin 31   Vernell Thompson
2600 Broadmoore, Fairbanks, AK 99709 (907) 456-4549

ALASKA'S FINEST SALMON BAKE and Fairbanks' Favorite Summertime Entertainment Spot

Alaska Salmon Bake & Palace Theatre

OPEN DAILY • ALASKALAND

Serving OUR SPECIALTY!
KING SALMON Cooked over an open-pit
HALIBUT Deep fried in our special batter
BBQ RIBS Smoked over an alder fire
AND
ALL YOU CAN EAT Baked Beans, Salad Bar, Sourdough Rolls, Blueberry Cake, Ice Tea or Lemonade
Meat Lovers Specialty!
PORTERHOUSE STEAK 16-18oz. grilled over an alder fire

#1 in Quality • #1 in Atmosphere & best of all #1 in TASTE!
Comfortable INDOOR and OUTDOOR seating
DINNER 5 to 9pm Mid-May to Mid-Sept
LUNCH 12 to 2pm Mid-June to Mid-Aug
FREE... Bus Service DAILY from major hotels.

PALACE SHOW
MUSIC • DANCE • FUN
A delightful performance combined into a memorable evening of fun & old-fashioned entertainment.
Located at Alaskaland in the
GOLD RUSH TOWN
Box Office 907 / 456-5960

DINNER and Stage Show at one stop! ☞ **ALASKA SALMON BAKE & PALACE THEATRE & SALOON**
WRITE: Rick Winther, 1028 Aurora, Fairbanks, Alaska 99709 or CALL: (907) 452-7274

ALASKALAND CABIN 28

In less than ten minutes your sepia-toned PHOTO is completely processed for you!!

Now is the time to step into one of our elegant costumes and take your place in Alaska's colorful past.

OPEN daily 11-9 p.m. **Bean's Old Time Photos**

Native Village of Alaskaland

Airport Way & Peger Road
Fairbanks, Alaska 99701

- *Narrated Tours by Native Guides*
- *Special Events Thoughout Summer*
- *Storytelling, Native Singing and Dancing, more*

For Current Information Call (907) 456-3851

*Summer Tourist Information
Phone 459-1095
Airport Way
and Peger Road*

The frontier spirit of Alaska waits for you at Alaskaland. Enter a gold mine; you can almost hear the prospectors' shouts of discovery. Board a paddle wheel riverboat and imagine cruising the Yukon. Feel the spirit of a sourdough at your shoulder.

The Pioneer Museum. A scrumptious salmon bake. The recreated Native Village. A gold rush town. All this and more beckons you to Alaskaland, the only pioneer theme park in all of Alaska. To really understand today's Alaska you've got to visit the Alaska of yesterday.

Concessionaires, cabin curio shops and tourist information center are open 11 a.m. to 9 p.m. daily

Alaskaland

Write: Alaskaland, P.O. Box 71267, Fairbanks, Alaska 99707   RV Parking will be available at a nominal fee.

FAIRBANKS

The Captain Bartlett Inn
Alaskan Charm and Affordable Hospitality

- Authentic Alaskan Architecture
- 197 Rooms
- Plenty of Parking
- Free Cable TV
- Close to Alaskaland
- 1.2 miles West on Airport Way

featuring
Captain's Table Dining Room
Dogsled Saloon

1-800-544-7528 outside Alaska
1-800-478-7900 inside Alaska

1411 Airport Way
Fairbanks, AK 99701

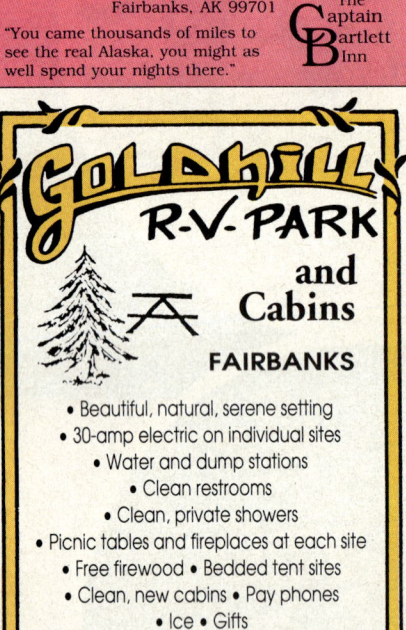

"You came thousands of miles to see the real Alaska, you might as well spend your nights there."

The Captain Bartlett Inn

One of several fine arts displays outside University of Alaska Museum. (Bonnie Pickert)

Owner J.L. Krier
TOTEM Chevron, Inc.
768 GAFFNEY ROAD

SELF SERVE and FULL SERVE ISLANDS
Complete stock of Atlas tires, tubes and batteries • Complete car care service
Tune-ups • Brake jobs • Water fill-up • Good city water
Credit cards accepted • Wrecker service • **456-4606**

*Turn towards Fairbanks at the Gillam Way exit off Airport Road.
Easy access – near shopping and laundry. Friendly, courteous service.*

GOLDEN NORTH MOTEL

"Near the International Airport"

- 1/2 Mile from the Int'l Airport
- Minutes from Downtown
- Color TV
- Tub & Shower in Each Room
- 24-Hour Switchboard
- 62 Attractive Units
- Courtesy Car Available
- Fine Restaurant & Club Nearby
- Open Year-Round
- In-room Coffee
- Continental Breakfast Available
- Summer Rates Start at $69 (No 8% Bed Tax)

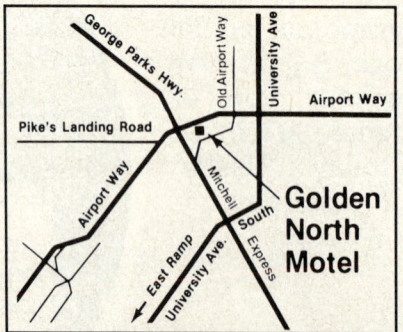

Fairbanks Attractions

Mt. McKinley
Alaskaland
Sternwheeler Riverboat
(Tickets available at Motel)

Major Credit Cards Accepted

Take Airport Way to Old Airport Way and turn south.
We are at the end of the road - just 0.2 miles.

1-800-447-1910

Write: 4888 Old Airport Way, Fairbanks, Alaska 99701

Goldhill R-V-Park and Cabins
FAIRBANKS

- Beautiful, natural, serene setting
- 30-amp electric on individual sites
- Water and dump stations
- Clean restrooms
- Clean, private showers
- Picnic tables and fireplaces at each site
- Free firewood • Bedded tent sites
- Clean, new cabins • Pay phones
- Ice • Gifts
- Tour Information and ticket sales
- 5 Minutes from major shopping and entertainment

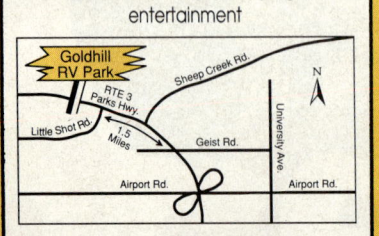

P.O. BOX 81529
Little Shot Road (off Rte. 3-Parks Hwy.)
Fairbanks, Alaska 99708

(907) 474-8088

---

364 The MILEPOST® ■ 1992

where research and study range from the center of the earth to the phenomena of the aurora. Films on mining in Alaska are also shown. Visitors can tour on their own the Agricultural and Forestry Experiment Station's demonstration gardens, which are open to the public. Free guided tours of the campus are provided Monday through Friday at 10 A.M.; tours begin at the UAF Museum. Phone 474-7581 for information.

The **University of Alaska–Fairbanks Museum** is a must stop for visitors to Fairbanks. Displays include prehistoric Alaska; Native Alaskan culture and artifacts, mammals and birds, and the trans-Alaska pipeline story. Highlights include a 36,000-year-old bison mummy recovered from permafrost, the state's largest public gold display, and the aurora borealis (northern lights) shown on a 10-foot video screen. Landscaping around the museum incorporates fine art sculpture, historic structures, and a nature trail identifying boreal vegetation. The museum's 1992 summer exhibit (June–September) celebrates the 50th anniversary of the building of the Alaska Highway, an event that was heralded as one of the great engineering feats of this modern era. WIth the use of artifacts, books, photographs, and personal memorabilia, the exhibit demonstrates the continuing pervasive influence of the highway on Alaska life. The museum is open daily: May to September, 9 A.M. to 5 P.M.; June, July and August, 9 A.M. to 7 P.M.; October through April, noon to 5 P.M. Admission fees: $4 adults, $10 family/household with as many as 4 adults; $3.50 senior citizens and military; children

---

Step into the past, and enjoy the antique setting of the gold days!

THE PUMP HOUSE
RESTAURANT & SALOON
EST. 1933
NATIONAL HISTORICAL SITE

Spend the Day

National Historical Site

We are open for lunch, and do not close our doors again till the wee hours of the morning. You are welcome to spend the day. Enjoy lunch indoors or out, and watch the riverboats and floatplanes come and go. For dinner we specialize in prime, aged beef, *Alaska fresh* seafood — and the farthest north oyster bar in the world. Step into the saloon for some billiards or some easy listening music. We shine Sundays for brunch, 10 a.m.-2 p.m.

OPEN SEVEN DAYS A WEEK
Lunch 11:30 a.m.-2 p.m.
Dinner 5 p.m.-10 p.m.
Saloon 11:30 a.m.-till we close

1.3 Mile Chena Pump Road • Fairbanks • (907) 479-8452

Rose's Forget-Me-Not
BED & BREAKFAST
502 Monroe Street • Fairbanks, Alaska 99701 • (907) 456-5734

ARCTIC CIRCLE
A D V E N T U R E

Original ARCTIC CIRCLE DRIVE
A one day roundtrip guided journey to the heart of Alaska's northland.

★ Cross over the Arctic Circle & recieve an official Arctic Circle Adventure Certificate.

★ Pass over the mighty Yukon River & enjoy a riverside picnic lunch.

★ Walk out on the delicate arctic tundra & feel the frozen ground beneath the surface.

★ Visit a rural Alaskan homestead.

★ View the 800 mile long Trans-Alaska Pipeline.

Arctic Circle FLY / DRIVE
The one day Arctic Circle Fly / Drive adventure includes all the highlights of the driving adventure plus:

★ Cruise the Yukon River & enjoy the majestic beauty of the northland's most famous river.

★ Visit a traditional Athabascan Indian summer fish camp. Meet Alaska's Athabascan people & learn how they harvest & preserve salmon for the long winter ahead.

★ Flightsee back to Fairbanks & receive a spectacular aerial view of the vast Alaska wilderness.

Arctic Ocean PRUDHOE BAY
The first day of your two day Prudhoe Bay adventure includes all the highlights of the fly / drive adventure plus:

★ Overnight in the historic goldmining community of Wiseman. Enjoy a walking tour & sled dog demonstration.

★ Pass through the majestic Brooks Range & cross over the Continental Divide at Atigun Pass.

★ Tour Prudhoe Bay's vast oil fields & feel the frigid Arctic Ocean.

★ Flightsee back to Fairbanks & as an option visit the Inupiat Eskimo village of Anaktuvuk Pass.

Arctic Ocean Prudhoe Bay ESKIMO ADVENTURE
A one day flightseeing journey of Alaska's Interior and Arctic regions.

★ Visit the Inupiat Eskimo village of Anaktuvuk Pass nestled in the heart of the Brooks mountain range.

★ Learn of the local Inupiat Eskimo culture with a tour of the village & a memorable visit to the Simon Paneak Memorial Museum .

★ Tour Prudhoe Bay's vast oil fields & feel the frigid waters of the Arctic Ocean.

All tours are lead by an informative, friendly Alaskan guide in the personalized comfort of our custom vans & coaches.

For General Information and Reservations call or write:

NORTHERN ALASKA TOUR COMPANY • 907 / 474-8600 • PO Box 82991-MP Fairbanks AK 99708

FAIRBANKS

Walk up to Alaska's wildlife

A half-ton polar bear or a ribbon seal. Dazzle at Alaska's largest gold display. Fist-sized nuggets and minted gold coins. Gaze at the aurora. Life-like on a 10-foot screen.

Explore the **Museum Store** for unique Alaskan gifts. Visa and Mastercard accepted. Mail order catalog available.

Daily Hours:

May & Sept.	9AM-5PM
June, July & August	9AM-7PM
October - April	12-5PM

Admission Charge
Closed on Thanksgiving, Christmas, and New Year's Day

university of alaska Museum
907 Yukon Drive
Fairbanks, AK 99775-1200
(907) 474-7505

THE ARTWORKS

Contemporary and Traditional Work by Alaskans

3677 College Road
Campus Corner
Fairbanks, Alaska 99709
(907) 479-2563

- Prints
- Paintings
- Pottery
- Jewelry
- Sculpture
- Fiberwork

WE ARE DIFFERENT

The Northwind Group realizes Alaska's a long way from home. Let us bring it closer to you with our convenient customized service. Call and give us your ideas on what interests you about Alaska. As Alaskans we will explain a variety of places and activities: free and inexpensive to exquisite and luxurious. We will give you the freedom to choose among them and the flexibility to "vary the plan". Our friendly staff will put together the logistics and reservations and have your vacation waiting for your arrival. You set the agenda and we'll get to work.

A Personal Alaskan Experience

THE NORTHWIND GROUP

1-800-478-4669 inside Alaska
1-800-759-5154 outside Alaska
Box 74204 Fairbanks AK 99707-4204

1992 Events

MARCH
- 5-7 Festival of Native Arts
- 13-22 Winter Carnival
- 18 Jeff Studdert Invitational Passenger Sled Dog Race
- 20-22 Alascom Open North American Championship Sled Dog Race

APRIL
- 4-5 Annual International Curling Bonspiel

JUNE
- 6 Great Tanana River Raft Classic
- 20 Midnight Sun Baseball Game
- 20 Midnight Sun Run, Midnight Sun Dance
- 20-21 Yukon 800 Marathon Boat Race

JULY
- 10-19 Golden Days
- 15-18 World Eskimo-Indian Olympics
- 24-8/8 Fairbanks Summer Arts Festival

AUGUST
- 1-8 Summer Arts Festival continues
- 8-16 1942 Heavy Construction Equipment Display
- 8-16 Tanana Valley Fair
- 30 German Thanksgiving

SEPTEMBER
- 19 Equinox Marathon
- 25-26 Oktoberfest

NOVEMBER
- 11-14 10th Annual Athabascan Fiddling Festival
- 27-29 Northern Invitational Curling Bonspiel

DECEMBER
- 6, 20 Preliminary Skijouring and Sled Dog Races

---

under 12 are free. For 24-hour information, call 474-7505.

Take in Some Local Events: Fairbanks has some unique summer celebrations. Late June is a busy time as Fairbanks celebrates the longest day of the year (summer solstice is June 21). The Midnight Sun Baseball Game will be played at 10:45 P.M. on solstice weekend, when no artificial lights are used. The Yukon 800 also gets under way; a marathon outboard boat race of 800 miles/

Northern Lights Dolls, Bears & Surprises

(Personally Crafted Alaska Native Porcelain Dolls)

P.O. Box 10179
Fairbanks, AK 99710
FAX (907) 488-7948
or phone (907) 488-6149

7 inch "Porcelain Baby"
$55.00 Postage Paid
available in blue, pink or lilac
fabric patterns may vary

1287 km on the Chena, Tanana and Yukon rivers to Galena and back. A Midnight Sun 10K Fun Run begins at 10 P.M.

Golden Days, when Fairbanksans turn out in turn-of-the-century dress and celebrate the gold rush, is July 10-19, 1992. Golden Days starts off with a Felix Pedro look-alike taking his gold to the bank and includes a parade and rededication of the Pedro Monument honoring Felix Pedro, the man who started it all when he discovered gold in the Tanana hills. Other events include pancake breakfasts, a dance, canoe and raft races and free outdoor concerts.

The World Eskimo and Indian Olympics, with Native competition in such events as the high kick, greased pole walk, stick pull, fish cutting, parka contest and muktuk eating contest will be held July 15-18, 1992.

The annual Tanana Valley Fair will be held Aug. 8-16, 1992. Alaska's oldest state fair, the Tanana Valley Fair features agricultural exhibits, arts and crafts, food booths, a rodeo and other entertainments.

Fairbanks Summer Arts Festival, 2 weeks of workshops and concerts involving jazz to classics, dance, theater and the visual arts, will be held July 24 to Aug. 8, 1992.

In addition, Fairbanks is an important focal point for an ambitious schedule of activities planned as part of the Alaska Highway Rendezvous '92 celebration marking the 50th anniversary of the Alaska Highway. An assortment of special exhibits, reunions, shows and dedications are scheduled from March to August 1992.

Check with the Fairbanks Convention and Visitors Bureau for more information on local events. Contact the Great Alaska

PICK 'N POKE GIFT SHOP

A Most Unique Gift Shop in Fairbanks, Featuring:
Alaskan Crafts!

- ULUS
- ALASKA BOOKS AND BEST SELLERS
- T-SHIRTS AND CAPS
- CARVINGS
- MASKS
- DOLLS

- BALEEN
- BASKETS
- HAND PAINTED GOLD PANS AND SNOWSHOES
- CLOCKS
- AND MUCH MORE

Also... Gold Nugget Ivory, Jade and Hematite Jewelry

PHONE 479-5880 or 456-1680

3175 College Road

Major Credit Cards accepted

For Your Summer Convenience We Are Also Located at:
The Mining Valley, Alaska Salmon Bake at Alaskaland
Cripple Creek Resort In Ester

Vaughan J. Hoefler, D.D.S.
General Dentistry

EMERGENCIES SEEN PROMPTLY

(907) 479-4759   3535 College Rd., Suite 202
Fairbanks, Alaska 99709

GOLD DREDGE NUMBER 8
National Historic District
▶▶▶ Mile 9 Old Steese Highway ◀◀◀

ALASKA'S GREATEST GOLD MINING ATTRACTION
— ACRES OF RV PARKING —

▶ **BE SURE** to tour the only gold dredge in Alaska open to the public.
▶ **VIEW** our collection of MAMMOTH TUSKS, teeth and other ice age bones. Search for your own on our claims.
▶ **PAN** for gold at your leisure.
▶ **WE SUPPLY** equipment – *you keep your findings.*

Gold Dredge #8 is home to Fairbanks' only coffee roasting operation.

Gold Dredge #8 is a stone's throw away from the Trans-Alaska Pipeline near Fox, Alaska.

DREDGE TOURS & GOLD PANNING
OPEN 9 a.m. – Tours start every 45 minutes
Pan for GOLD as long as you like – Still only $8 • Two for $15
Miner's Club Card with admission – *Return visits for free.*
Children 8 and under free • Group rates available
See log ad under Attractions

Listed in National Register of Historic Sites, National Register of Historic Districts, National Register of Historic Objects, National Historic Mechanical Engineering Records.

P.O. Box 81941, Fairbanks, Alaska 99708   (907)457-6058   FAX (907) 457-8888

FAIRBANKS

UNIVERSITY AVENUE CAR AND TRUCK WASH

Corner of University Avenue and Cameron

Large Bays for Motor Homes, Trailers and Big Trucks with catwalks to reach all areas.

OPEN 24 HOURS

WRIGHT AIR SERVICE INC. BUSH ADVENTURES

EXPERIENCED PILOTS

CHARTER SERVICE AVAILABLE

ANAKTUVUK ARCTIC CIRCLE TOURS
Mt. McKINLEY PHOTO EXCURSIONS
MINTO FISH CAMP
TWIN- AND SINGLE-ENGINE AIRCRAFT

Call: (907) 474-0502 • Write: Box 60142, Fairbanks 99706 • East Ramp Intl. Airport

---

Highway Society (P.O. Box 74250, Fairbanks, AK 99707) for details on the Alaska Highway 50th anniversary celebration events.

Besides these special events, summer visitors can take in a semi-pro baseball game at Growden Park where the Fairbanks Goldpanners take on other Alaska league teams.

Tanana Valley Farmers Market. Visit the Tanana Valley Farmers Market, College Road at the fairgrounds, the only farmers market in the Interior of Alaska. Open seasonally from mid-July through September, Wednesdays 1-5 P.M. and Saturdays 9 A.M. to 4 P.M. We have a great selection of locally grown vegetables and cut flowers. Handmade crafts, baked goods, Alaskan fish products, and pottery are also available. Perennial flowers, shrubs and berry plants ready for transplanting into your garden. Come and visit with us this summer!
[ADVERTISEMENT]

Alaska Wildlife Park is your chance to see up close bears, bison, caribou, porcupine and more in natural setting exhibits. Visit our animal rehab facility. Learn area history on a complimentary horse-drawn wagon ride. Picnicking, petting zoo. Daily 11 A.M. to 7 P.M. Closed Tuesdays. On College Road, 1 mile from University Avenue intersection.
[ADVERTISEMENT]

FAIRBANKS FAST FOTO AND VIDEO

Where Photography is Our Business

1 Hour Photo Processing

3 Hour Ektachrome Slide Processing
Gavora Mall Only

- Custom Quality 4x6 Prints At Both Locations

Technically qualified personnel to help and advise you.
Local phone (907) 456-8896 or 1-800-478-8896

2 Locations:
- Shoppers Forum
  Cowles & Airport
- Gavora Mall
  3rd & Steese

Largest Still and Video Outlet in Fairbanks
Canon ■ Minolta
Kodak ■ Pentax
Olympus ■ Nikon ■ Vivitar
and much more at our Shoppers Forum Location

Large selection of postcards and slides

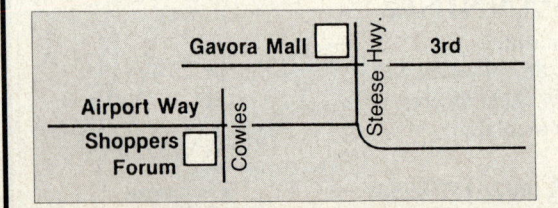

BRING IN THIS AD FOR $1.00 OFF
Each Roll Of Color Print Film Processing

Complete, informative guides to Fairbanks and the Interior
Join us at our riverside
LOG CABIN VISITOR'S CENTER

Welcome

ARCTIC ESKIMO
Join the celebration of the Native culture and experience the beauty of Alaska's northland.

HOT SPRINGS
Soothe traveling bodies in the comfort of natural hot springs pools located throughout the interior. All a leisure drive north from Fairbanks.

Fairbanks, the Golden Heart City

RAILROAD
Wind through striking scenery and travel in comfort on the Alaska Railroad system.

ALL ROADS LEAD to

MILEPOST
The Alaska Highway ends; Milepost 1422 in Delta Jct.

DENALI PARK
Wildlife is abundant within Denali National Park.

Fairbanks
EXTREMELY ALASKA

Fairbanks Convention & Visitors Bureau

550 1st Ave-MP, Fairbanks, AK 99701   **1-800-327-5774**   (907) 456-5774   Fax 452-4190

FAIRBANKS

Interior Alaska Fish Processors, Inc. dba

SANTA'S SMOKEHOUSE

2400 Davis Rd.
FAIRBANKS, Alaska 99701
(907) 456-3885 FAX 456-3889

Experience the flavor of unique salmon products pioneered and developed by Interior Alaska Fish Processors:

- Salmon Breakfast Sausage
- Salmon Hot Dogs
- Smoked Salmon Sausage (3 flavors)
- Salmon Hot Link
- Salmon Bacon (in season)
- Salmon Bratwurst
- Salmon Burger
- Smoked Salmon

Visit Creamer's Field. Follow the flocks of waterfowl to Creamer's Field Migratory Waterfowl Refuge. Located 1 mile from downtown Fairbanks, this 1,800-acre refuge managed by the Alaska Dept. of Fish and Game offers opportunities to observe large concentrations of ducks, geese, shorebirds and cranes in the spring and fall. Throughout the summer, sandhill cranes take advantage of the barley fields planted to provide them with food.

Explore the 2-mile/3.2-km self-guided nature trail and the renovated historic farmhouse that serves as a visitor center. Stop at 1300 College Road to find the trailhead, viewing areas and brochures on Creamer's Field. For more information, phone 452-1531.

Take a Walk. Free guided walking tours of historical downtown Fairbanks are offered by the Fairbanks Convention and Visitors Bureau, weather permitting, twice each day during summer. For tour times, check with the visitor information center at 550 1st Avenue. Or take your own walking tour, beginning at the visitor information center at 1st and Cushman, where Cushman Street crosses the Chena River. Brochures for both self-guided walking and driving tours are available at the log cabin visitor information center.

Chena Pump House National Historic

The Unknown First Family at Golden Heart Park. (John W. Warden)

Woolworth
ALASKA
SOUVENIR HEADQUARTERS IN DOWNTOWN FAIRBANKS

Discover our
HARVEST HOUSE RESTAURANT

VISA & MasterCard Welcome
3rd and Cushman, Fairbanks, Alaska

FLY-IN FISHING

Starting at $110.00 each

MARINA AIR, INC.
Chena Marina Airport & Floatpond
1219 Shypoke
Fairbanks, Alaska 99709
Phone (907) 479-5684

After turning left onto Shypoke I'm at the second driveway

PROVIDED: Boat & Motor, cabin or tent camp

RENT a BOAT!

Inflatable Boats! Canoes!

Tents, Backpacks, Camp Stoves!

Do-It-Yourself Outfitting
(and save your money)

Independent Rental

We Rent Most Everything!
2020 South Cushman Street
Fairbanks, Alaska 99701
(907) 456-6595
1-800-478-1826

THE TURTLE CLUB

For an evening of fine dining

Featuring our famous
PRIME RIB and Prawns •

Lobster Tail • BBQ Ribs
(includes salad bar)

10 Mile Old Steese Highway
Fox, Alaska
For Reservations **(907) 457-3883**

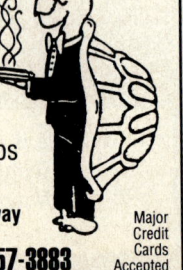

Major Credit Cards Accepted

Site. Built between 1931 and 1933 by the Fairbanks Exploration Co. to pump water from the Chena River to dredging operations at Cripple Creek, the pump house was remodeled in 1978 and now houses a restaurant and saloon. The sheet metal cladding, interior roof and some equipment (such as the intake ditch) are from the original pump house, which shut down in 1958 when the F.E. Co. ceased their Cripple Creek dredging operations. The pump house is located at Mile 1.3 Chena Pump Road.

Sled Dog Racing. The Alaska Dog Mushers' Assoc. hosts a series of dog races beginning in mid-December with preliminary races, and ending in March with the Open North American Championships. The Open is a 3-day event with 3 heats (of 20, 20, and 30 miles) with teams as large as 20 dogs; this race is considered by many to be the "granddaddy of dog races." Fairbanks also hosts the 1,000-mile Yukon Quest Sled Dog Race between Fairbanks and Whitehorse, YT. The Yukon Quest alternates start and finish between the 2 cities: the race will begin in Fairbanks in 1992. For more information, contact the Alaska Dog Musher's Assoc. at 457-MUSH, or the Yukon Quest office at 451-8985.

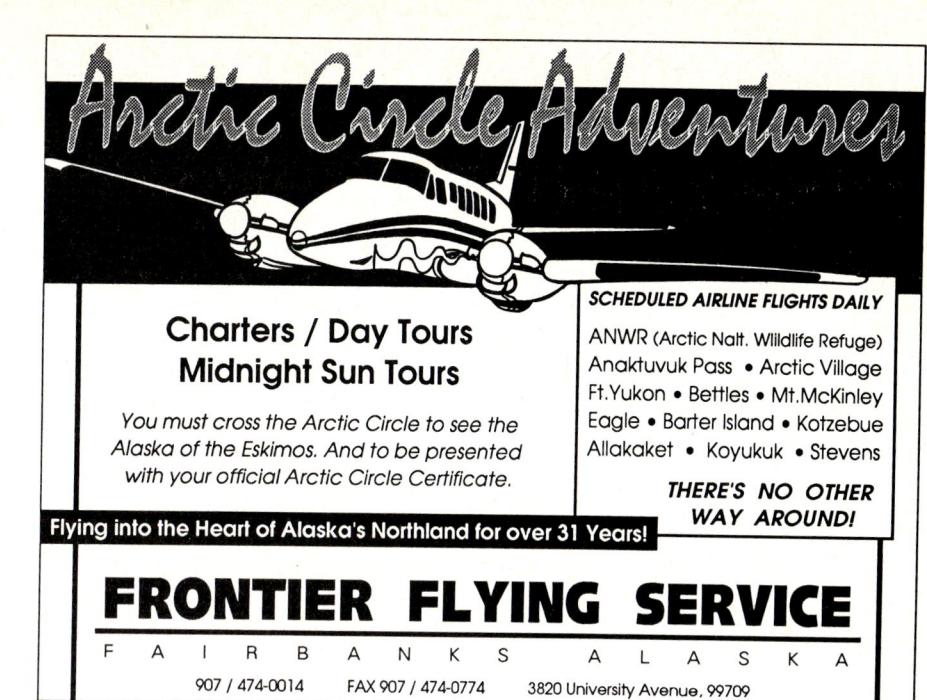

Arctic Circle Adventures

Charters / Day Tours
Midnight Sun Tours

You must cross the Arctic Circle to see the Alaska of the Eskimos. And to be presented with your official Arctic Circle Certificate.

Flying into the Heart of Alaska's Northland for over 31 Years!

SCHEDULED AIRLINE FLIGHTS DAILY
ANWR (Arctic Natl. Wildlife Refuge)
Anaktuvuk Pass • Arctic Village
Ft. Yukon • Bettles • Mt. McKinley
Eagle • Barter Island • Kotzebue
Allakaket • Koyukuk • Stevens

THERE'S NO OTHER WAY AROUND!

FRONTIER FLYING SERVICE
F A I R B A N K S   A L A S K A
907 / 474-0014   FAX 907 / 474-0774   3820 University Avenue, 99709

Big Ray's
ALL WEATHER OUTFITTERS SINCE 1947

Send for FREE catalog

SPORTING GOODS • LEVIS
WORK CLOTHES • FOOTWEAR

Largest selection of outdoor footwear in the Interior • Mosquito Netting • Arctic clothing for men and women

507 2nd Ave.   Phone (907) 452-3458
Fairbanks, Alaska 99701

HOT LICKS
HOMEMADE ICE CREAM

Sun. Noon to 11 p.m.
Mon.-Fri. 7 a.m. to Mid.
Sat. 11 a.m. to Mid.

MAKERS OF ICE CREAM, FROZEN YOGURT, SHERBET, AND SORBET

Also Serving:
Homemade Soup and Bread • Cinnamon Rolls • Brownies
Gourmet Coffee, Espresso and Cappuccino

3549 College Road, Fairbanks — Near University   (907) 479-7813

ALASKAN NATIVE ARTS AND CRAFTS

BEADS & THINGS

Items Handcrafted By Alaskan Natives

• Mittens • Boots • Slippers
• Beadwork • Jewlery
• Soapstone • Ivory • Dolls
• Athabascan Beading Kits

We Do Custom Orders
Located on 2nd Avenue in Downtown Fairbanks

MasterCard   VISA   AMERICAN EXPRESS

(907) 456-2323
537 2nd Ave., Fairbanks, AK 99701

AFFORDABLE CAR RENTAL

• **Courtesy Pick Up & Delivery**
• **4x4's - Vans - Wagons - Cars**
• **Drive Anywhere in Alaska**
• **10% Discount With This Ad**
• **All Major Credit Cards Accepted**

SEE ALASKA THE AFFORDABLE WAY

3101 S. Cushman, Fairbanks
(907) 452-1701

4707 Spenard Rd, Anchorage
(907) 243-3370

FAIRBANKS

PLAZA CLEANERS AND LAUNDRY

LARGEST LAUNDROMAT IN TOWN
❄ NEW • CLEAN • AIR CONDITIONED ❄

SHOWERS
Private rooms with sinks too.
Take your time • One Low Price

COMPLIMENTARY
Coffee • Phone • TV
ONE DAY DRY CLEANING

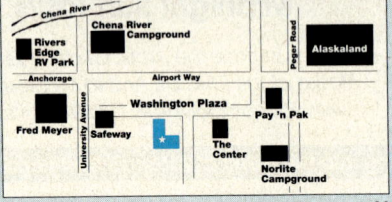

RV Parking
7 a.m. to 11 p.m.
OPEN DAILY
Friendly Attendant On Duty

Washington Plaza
3417 Airport Way
2 Blocks From Alaskaland
2 Blocks From Campgrounds

"Come Clean With Us"

Dog Mushing Museum. Visit the home of the North American championship sled dog race, the oldest continuously run event in the sport! Dog Mushing Museum features the world's most comprehensive exhibit on mushing, and offers sled dog demonstrations, race videos and gifts. See the actual sleds used by the winners of the major races. Located at Mile 4 Farmers Loop Road, it is situated in a beautiful log building with an excellent view of Fairbanks and the mountains. Call (907) 457-MUSH or 455-6528 for schedule, fees. Box 80136, Fairbanks, AK 99707. [ADVERTISEMENT]

TIVI Kennels welcomes visitors to an evening dinner, show and ride in dog-powered ArfMobile, 6-9 P.M., Monday to Saturday, June 7 to Sept. 7. See display ad at **Milepost A 348.8** GEORGE PARKS HIGHWAY section. For reservations, information or transportation, phone (907) 474-8702 or write Dr. Ron Tinsley, P.O. Box 81049,

WET WILLY'S CAR & TRUCK WASH

Corner of Airport Way & (1295) University Avenue
Fairbanks, Alaska • (907) 474-8585

Full Interior and Exterior Cleaning Services
• Specializing in Alaska Highway Vehicles •
Motorhomes by Appointment

"FAST FRIENDLY SERVICE"

SECOND LOCATION Featuring All Chevron Fuels
One Block off Parks Highway, Behind Safeway
Wasilla, Alaska • (907) 376-4446

McCAULEY'S Reprographics
Engineering and Drafting Supplies
CANADIAN MAP DEALER
McCAULEY'S REPROGRAPHICS
721 Gaffney Road
Fairbanks, Alaska 99701
(907) 452-8141

Aurora Animal Clinic
For appointment or emergency (907) 452-6055
1651 College Road, Fairbanks
Open Monday – Saturday

IVORY JACKS

Take the Grand Tour Through Our Menu
Alaska Seafood • Steaks
Prime Rib • Nome Reindeer
Crisp Salads
Grand atmosphere!
Exceptional view and service!
1.5 mile Goldstream Road
Fairbanks   (907) 455-6666

The Cookie Jar's Garden Café

• Breakfast
• Lunch • Dinner
• Muffins
• Soups • Sandwich
• Quiche • Salad
• Divine Desserts
• Gourmet Coffee
• Espresso
• Homemade Pies

Here you'll find a special experience... Enjoy our unique menu of homemade food in a smoke free atmosphere of garden freshness inside our Cafe or at our outdoor tables

Open Monday - Saturday
Washington Plaza, 3415 Airport Way
(907) 479-8319

80' Certified Commercial Scale

We Accept
Cash Control Corporation,
CCIS, ComChek
and Fasttrak

OPEN 24 HRS.
EASY ACCESS AND EXIT

TESORO ALASKA
DISCOUNT TRUCK STOPS

VISA • MasterCard • DISCOVER

DIESEL
HEATING OIL
GAS
GROCERIES

• SNACK BAR
• RV DUMP
• PROPANE
• ICE

S. CUSHMAN / VAN HORN RD.

FAIRBANKS, ALASKA
PHONE (907) 456-1122

Fairbanks, AK 99708. [ADVERTISEMENT]

Play Tennis: There is 1 outdoor plexi-pave court at Hez Ray Recreation Complex, 19th Avenue and Lathrop Street. There are 6 outdoor asphalt courts at the Mary Siah Recreation Center, 1025 14th Ave. No fees or reservations. For more information phone 459-1070.

Play Golf: Maintaining a scenic 9-hole course with artificial greens, the Fairbanks Golf and Country Club (public invited) is west of the downtown area at Farmers Loop and Ballaine Road, phone 479-6555 for information and reservations. The 9-hole Chena Bend Golf Course is located on Fort Wainwright; phone 355-6749.

See Bank Displays: The Key Bank, at 1st Avenue and Cushman Street, has a display of gold nuggets and several trophy animals. Mount McKinley Mutual Savings Bank features a display of McKinley prints and the original cannonball safe used when the bank first opened. The bank is at 531 3rd Ave.

Visit Historic Churches: St. Matthew's Episcopal, 1029 1st Ave., was originally built in 1905, but burned in 1947 and was rebuilt the following year. Of special interest is the church's intricately carved altar, made in 1906 of interior Alaska birch, saved from the fire.

Immaculate Conception Church, on the Chena River at Cushman Street bridge, was moved to its present location by horse in the winter of 1911 from its original site at 1st and Dunkel streets.

Image Alaska's *"The Alaska Wildlife Show."* You'll see wildlife, shimmering northern lights, Mount McKinley in all its splendor, and breathtaking panoramas in this beautifully orchestrated show. Image Alaska blends award-winning wildlife photography, music and narration to bring you a panoramic presentation of the last frontier. Located within walking distance of downtown Fairbanks in the Goldroom of the Westmark Hotel of Fairbanks, 813 Noble St. Showtimes: 5:30 P.M. and 9 P.M. daily. Adults $5, children under 12 free! Dinner show: 7 P.M. daily. For more information call (907) 452-2843 or (907) 455-6988. [ADVERTISEMENT]

See the Pipeline: Drive about 10 miles/16 km north from downtown on the Steese Highway to see the trans-Alaska pipeline. Clearly visible are the thermal devices used to keep the permafrost frozen around the pipeline support columns.

View Mount McKinley: Best spot to see McKinley is from the University of Alaska Fairbanks campus (on Yukon Drive, between Talkeetna and Sheenjek streets) where a turnout and marker define the horizon view of Mount Hayes (elev. 13,832 feet/4,216m); Hess Mountain (elev. 11,940 feet/3,639m); Mount Deborah (elev. 12,339 feet/3,761m); and Mount McKinley (elev. 20,320 feet/6,194m). Distant foothills seen from the viewpoint are part of the Wood River Butte.

Cruise the River Aboard a Sternwheeler: The 160-foot riverboat *Discovery III* offers daily 4-hour voyages down the Chena River and Tanana River from a landing 4.5 miles/7.2 km west of the downtown area (drive west on Airport Way to West Dale Road exit, turn south and follow signs). The tour, with an informative narration by the crew, departs daily at 8:45 A.M. and 2 P.M. It

The Chena River winds through Fairbanks to the Tanana River southwest of town. (Jerrianne Lowther, staff)

Don't Miss the Excitement of the Alaska State Sport!

DOG MUSHING MUSEUM

- World's most comprehensive exhibit on dog mushing history!
- Live sled dog demonstrations!
- Race Videos!
- Gift shop and snacks!
- See the actual sleds which won the major races!

**4 Mile Farmers Loop Road
• Fairbanks •
Call (907) 457-MUSH**
for schedule, programs and fees

MOBAT TIRE
AUTO · TRUCK · RV · MOTOR HOMES

- COMPUTER ALIGNMENT
- COMPUTERIZED WHEEL BALANCE
- COMPLETE BRAKE SERVICE
- COMPLETE FRONT END WORK
- SHOCKS - MONROE & NAPA
- TRANSMISSION SERVICE
- BATTERIES
- LUBE, OIL & FILTER CHANGE

"we're in the people business"
**CORNER OF
CUSHMAN & VAN HORN
452-7131
3601 S. Cushman Street**

VISA   MasterCard   DISCOVER

MICHELIN   DUNLOP

UNIVERSITY OF ALASKA FAIRBANKS
America's University of the North

Consider UAF when you or someone you know is thinking about college.

For details call or write:
Office of Admissions and Records
Suite 102, Signers' Hall
University of Alaska Fairbanks
Fairbanks, Alaska 99775-0060
907/474-7821 (from outside Alaska)
800/478-1UAF (from within the state)

Free campus tours are given each weekday during the summer beginning at 10 a.m. at the UA Museum. Call University Relations at 907/474-7581 for tour information.

UAF is an AA/EO employer and educational institution.

FAIRBANKS

ALASKA SPRING 563-3802
SINCE 1965

600 W. 48th Ave.
Anchorage
Alaska
99503

TOLL FREE 800-478-3802
FAX # 561-6888

"More Than Repairs...We Solve Problems"

COMPLETE SPRING SERVICE CUSTOM FABRICATION

- LEAF SPRINGS
- COIL SPRINGS
  FOREIGN & DOMESTIC
- OVERLOAD KITS
- OVERLOAD KITS FOR CAMPERS & RV'S
- SHOCKS & MacPHERSON STRUTS
- CUSTOM U-BOLTS
- LIFT KITS
- CUSTOM RE-ARCHING
- WALKING BEAMS REBUSHED

TRUCK & TRAILER SUSPENSION, PARTS & SERVICE
- HENDRICKSON
- HUTCH
- RAYCO
- MACK
- WHITE
- PETERBILT

WHEEL ALIGNMENT • COMPLETE FRONT END REPAIR
4 W.D. SERVICE • COMPLETE BRAKE SERVICE

Member: Spring Service Association & Chamber Of Commerce

MOR/ryde Rubber Suspension Systems

Why Pay More?
New & Used Cars & Vans
- Low Rates – Daily – Weekly or Monthly
- Cash Deposits Welcome
- Airport Pick-up

AllSTAR Rent-A-Car
Toll-Free 1-800-426-5243

FAIRBANKS
(907) 479-4229 • 1-800-478-4229
4415 Airport Way
Fairbanks, Alaska 99709

ANCHORAGE
(907) 561-0350 • 1-800-437-3303
512 W. International Airport Way
Anchorage, Alaska 99518

Fast Courteous Service   Major Credit Cards Accepted

Call Us For All Your Motorhome Needs

GABE'S PEGER ROAD I/M & MUFFLER

← River's Edge RV Park

UNIVERSITY AVENUE
PEGER ROAD
Alaskaland
AIRPORT WAY
Norlite RV Park
DMV Troopers
19TH AVE
GABE'S PEGER ROAD I/M & MUFFLER
MITCHELL EXPRESSWAY

COMPLETE REPAIR SERVICE FOR MOTORHOMES

BRAKES • SHOCKS
TUNE-UPS

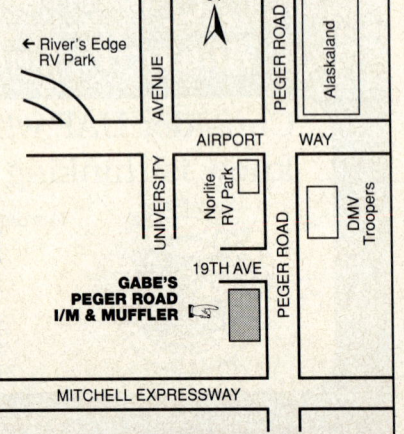

1904 Peger Road • (907) 479-6162

---

includes a look at Indian fish wheels, a trapper's base camp, sled dogs, bush airstrip and an entertaining introduction to sled dogs by well-known author and Interior musher Mary Shields, the first woman to complete the Iditarod Sled Dog Race. Operates mid-May to mid-September, phone 479-6673.

Visit Alaskaland Pioneer Park. Visitors will find a relaxed atmosphere at Alaskaland, a pleasant park with historic buildings, small shops, food, entertainment, playgrounds and 4 covered picnic shelters. The park—which has no admission fee—is open year-round.

The 44-acre historic park was created in 1967 as the Alaska Centennial Park to commemorate the 100th year of American sovereignty. Designed to provide a taste of interior Alaska history, visitors may begin their visit at the information center (inside the newly renovated stern-wheeler *Nenana*). Walk through Gold Rush Town, a narrow winding street of authentic old buildings

FAIRBANKS GOLF AND COUNTRY CLUB

Corner of Farmers Loop and Ballaine Road, Fairbanks

Play the Farthest North Golf Course

• CERTIFICATES AVAILABLE •
OPEN TO THE PUBLIC
PHONE: (907) 479-6555

A Touch of Gold

BENTLEY MALL
College Rd & Steese Exp.

A distinctive selection of
Gold Nugget Jewelry

ALASKAN PLACER MINED

Goldsmith Service and Custom Orders Welcomed

A Touch of Gold

Call or write for color brochure:
907/ 451-7965 • Box 72540
FAIRBANKS ALASKA 99707

that once graced downtown Fairbanks and now house gift shops. Here you will find: the Kitty Hensley and Judge Wickersham houses, furnished with turn-of-the-century items; the First Presbyterian Church, constructed in 1906; and the Pioneers of Alaska Museum, dedicated to those who braved frontier life to found Fairbanks. Free guided historical walking tours take place each evening.

The top level of the Civic Center houses an art gallery, featuring rotating contemporary exhibits and paintings; open year-round, noon to 8 P.M. *Northern Inna,* a show celebrating Native culture is given nightly at 8 P.M. in summer in the Civic Center theater. Admission is $5, or $2.50 for children 5-12. Call 452-6646 for more information.

In the back of the park is the Native Village Museum and Kashims with Native wares, artifacts, crafts and daily exhibitions of Native dancing. Across from the Native Village is Mining Valley, with displays of gold-mining equipment, and daily gold-panning demonstrations. A covered picnic area and the Salmon Bake are also part of Mining Valley. A popular feature, the Salmon Bake is open daily for lunch from noon to 2 P.M. (June 10 to Aug. 15), and for dinner from 5-9 P.M. (end of May to mid-September). Salmon, barbecued ribs and halibut are served, rain or shine. Indoor seating available.

There's entertainment 7 nights a week starting at 8 P.M. at the Palace Theatre & Saloon, featuring a musical comedy review about life in Fairbanks titled *Golden Heart Review* and *Jim Bell's After Hours Show.*

- Factory Trained Technicians
- Parts & Accessory Showroom
- Rental Cars
- Servicing All Makes And Models
- Complete Body Shop
- Quick Service "While You Wait"
- Mobile Service Truck

ANCHORAGE RV SERVICE CENTER
4707 Spenard Rd. Phone 243-3370

FAIRBANKS RV SERVICE CENTER
249 Alta Way Phone 452-4279

FIREWEED R.V. RENTALS

Fully Self-Contained
Housekeeping and Linen Packages Available
Insurance Coverage Optional
Free Airport and Hotel Pickup

(907) 479-4229 • (907) 452-4949
FAX (907) 456-5942
4415 Airport Way

Send for Free Brochure: P.O. Box 61058 Fairbanks, AK 99706

Fairbanks Clinic

Physicians specializing in:
Family Practice • Internal Medicine
Gynecology • Orthopedics • Obstetrics

Quality care... Because we care.
452-1761

REGULAR HOURS:
Monday-Friday 8 - 5 • Saturday 8 - 4

Conveniently Located
1867 Airport Way *(near Super 8 Motel)*

We accept most out of state insurance companies

Alaskan Photographic Repair Service

551½ Second Avenue, Room 221
Lavery Building
Monday-Friday
8-11 a.m. and 12:15-5 p.m.
In Business since 1975
See Us First for
Used Cameras and Lenses
(907) 452-8819

OPEN 24 HOURS
MAPCO Express

—GASOLINE
—GROCERIES
—CONVENIENCE ITEMS

for people on the go

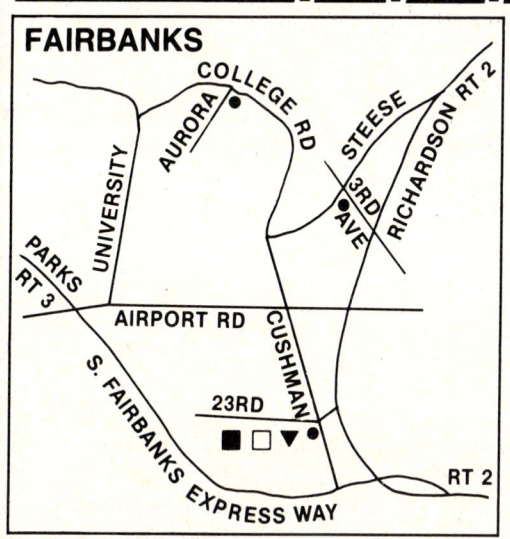

FAIRBANKS

Traveler's checks welcome

Cash or credit same low price

Mastercard — Visa
American Express
Discover

MAPCO Express

KEY ■ DIESEL ☐ PROPANE ▼ RV DUMP

FAIRBANKS

A young visitor tries her hand at gold panning. (Jerrianne Lowther, staff)

Shown throughout the day during summer is *Winter's Light,* an interpretive look at the northern lights through "Surround-sound" music and fast-paced images. The Big Stampede show in Gold Rush Town is a theatre in the round presenting the paintings of Rusty Heurlin depicting the trail of '98; narrative by Ruben Gaines.

The Crooked Creek & Whiskey Island Railroad, a 30-gauge train, takes passengers for a 12-minute ride around the park. Other types of recreational activities available at Alaskaland include miniature golf and an antique carousel. A public dock is located on the Chena River at the rear of the park.

Visitors are welcome to take part in square and round dances year-round at the Alaskaland Dance Center. Square dances are Tuesday at 7:30 P.M., Friday and Saturday at 8 P.M. Round dances are at 7:30 P.M. Thursday. For more information about Alaskaland, call 459-1087.

Gold Dredge Number 8. Turn left on Goldstream Road, then left again on the Old Steese Highway. Drive 0.3 mile to Gold Dredge Number 8 on your right. Guided tour of Dredge Number 8 and gold panning is one of the Interior's top attractions. Visitors receive Miners Club cards enabling return visits without charge. It's so interesting and so authentic that many people come back for more. Families love it. See display ad this section. [ADVERTISEMENT]

Ride Bikes Around Fairbanks: There are many day-touring choices in Fairbanks. A round-trip tour of the city, the University of Alaska and the College area can be made by leaving town on Airport Way and returning on College Road. The Farmers Loop Road or a ride out the highway toward Fox are 2 more easy tours.

Area Attractions: Fairbanks is a good jumping-off point for many attractions in Alaska's Interior. Head out the Steese Highway for swimming at Chena Hot Springs or Circle Hot Springs. At Fox, 11.5 miles/18.5 km north of Fairbanks, the Steese Highway junctions with the Elliott Highway, which leads to the start of the Dalton Highway (formerly the North Slope Haul Road). Popular attractions in this area include Gold Dredge Number 8 (take Goldstream Road exit to Old Steese Highway), a historic 5-deck, 250-foot dredge, and Little El Dorado Gold Camp at Mile 1.2 Elliott Highway, which offers gold mining demonstrations and gold panning. See highway sections for details.

Denali National Park is a 2½-hour drive by bus or car, or a 3½-hour train trip via the Alaska Railroad, from Fairbanks. Once there, take the shuttle bus or guided tour through the park. For area road conditions, phone the Dept. of Transportation at 451-2206.

THE GREAT ALASKAN BOWL COMPANY

- **VISIT** our Showroom & Manufacturing Facility in Fairbanks
- **WATCH** our skilled Bowl Makers create up to 9 one-piece solid wooden bowls ranging from 23" to 7" in diameter... all from a single split log
- **DEMONSTRATIONS** of Bowl Making Monday thru Saturday
- **LEARN** how the rest of the process makes unique one of a kind beautiful bowls

(907) 474-9663
4630 Old Airport Rd. (by New Fred Meyer)

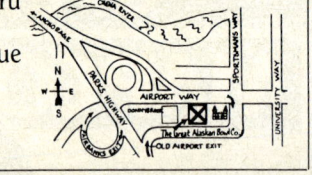

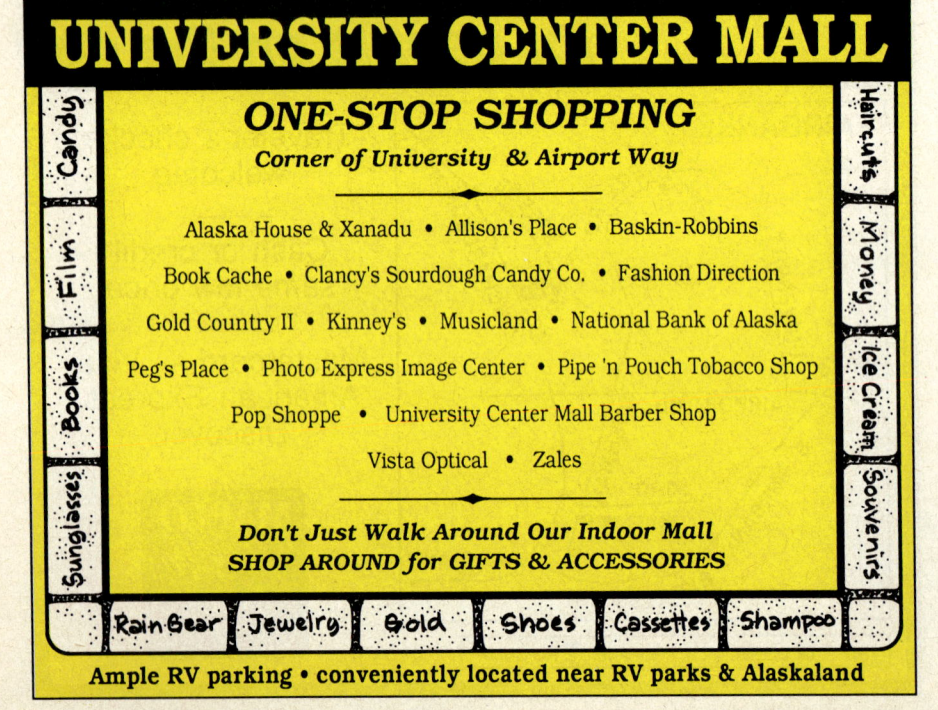

UNIVERSITY CENTER MALL

ONE-STOP SHOPPING
Corner of University & Airport Way

Alaska House & Xanadu • Allison's Place • Baskin-Robbins
Book Cache • Clancy's Sourdough Candy Co. • Fashion Direction
Gold Country II • Kinney's • Musicland • National Bank of Alaska
Peg's Place • Photo Express Image Center • Pipe 'n Pouch Tobacco Shop
Pop Shoppe • University Center Mall Barber Shop
Vista Optical • Zales

Don't Just Walk Around Our Indoor Mall
SHOP AROUND for GIFTS & ACCESSORIES

Ample RV parking • conveniently located near RV parks & Alaskaland

---

New Design HAIRSTYLING and TANNING CENTER

Specializing In
Precision Haircuts and Perms
MEN • WOMEN • CHILDREN
REDKEN
SALON PRESCRIPTION CENTER
Alaskan friendliness in an Alaskan atmosphere at lower 48 prices!

Call (907) 479-HAIR
3535 College Road, Fairbanks, Alaska
Corner of College Road & University Avenue

MOTOR INN SAFETY LANE
CALL US!

Motor Home Alignment and Transmission Work

Motor Home Towing

2550 Cushman
Fairbanks
(907) 456-4721

Eielson AFB, 23 miles/37 km south of Fairbanks on the Richardson–Alaska Highway, was built in 1943. Originally a satellite base to Ladd Field (now Fort Wainwright) and called Mile 26, it served as a storage site for aircraft on their way to the Soviet Union under the WWII Lend-Lease program. Closed after WWII, the base was reactivated in 1948 and renamed Eielson AFB, after Carl Ben Eielson, the first man to fly from Alaska over the North Pole to Greenland. A weekly tour of the base is offered; phone the public affairs office at 377-1410 for reservations and more information.

There are 1-day or longer sightseeing trips to Point Barrow, Prudhoe Bay, Fort Yukon and other bush destinations. See ads in this section or consult local travel services.

Go Skiing: Fairbanks has several downhill ski areas: Cleary Summit, **Milepost F 20.6** Steese Highway; Skiland, **Milepost F 20.9** Steese Highway; Eielson Air Force Base and Fort Wainwright ski hills; and an alpine ski hill at Chena Hot Springs Resort at **Milepost J 56.5** Chena Hot Springs Road.

Cross-country ski trails are at Birch Hill Recreation Area; drive 2.8 miles/4.5 km north of Fairbanks via Steese Expressway to a well-marked turnoff, then drive in 2.3 miles/3.7 km. University of Alaska Fairbanks has 26 miles/42 km of cross-country ski trails. The trail system is quite extensive; you may ski out to Ester Dome.

Go Ice Skating: Hez Ray Recreation Complex, 19th and Lathrop, offers both indoor and outdoor skating rinks; rental skates available. Phone 459-1070 for public skating hours.

Go Swimming. Fairbanks North Star Borough Parks and Recreation Dept. offers 3

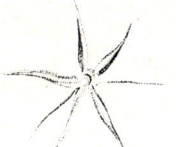

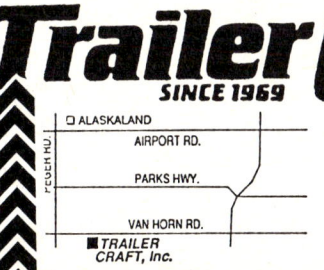

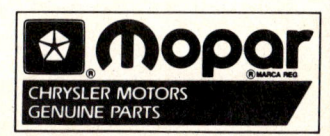

ALASKA RIVER CHARTERS
Fairbanks

Customized Remote Trips by River or Air
Fishing • Wildlife Observation • Hot Springs
Day Trips Available

Call or write for information • **(907) 455-6827**
P.O. Box 81516-MP, Fairbanks, AK 99708
Discover the Outdoors in Interior Alaska

G & G Electronics
Hours 10 – 8 Monday – Saturday

Video Camera and Recorder Accessories • Auxilliary Battery Packs
Bogen Tripods • DC to AC Power Inverters
General Use Cable TV Hardware and Accessories
C.B.s and C.B. Antennas

Alaska Scenic & Wildlife Videos • (907) 456-6225 • 452-3352

Major Credit Cards Accepted

INTERIOR CUSTOM TOPPER AND R V CENTER
Cascade Campers

★ Superior Quality ★
★ RV Parts ★ RV Repair

★ Camper Shells
★ Running Boards

QUICK, RELIABLE SERVICE • INSURANCE WORK WELCOME

Factory Authorized, Certified Repairmen for Dometic & Duo-Therm
604 Hughes • Fairbanks, Alaska 99701
Across From Fairbanks Nissan **(907) 451-8356**

Dometic Duo-Therm

Cushman Plaza Laundry
"Fairbanks Friendliest and Cleanest"

2301 S. Cushman St.   Open 7-11 daily   452-4430

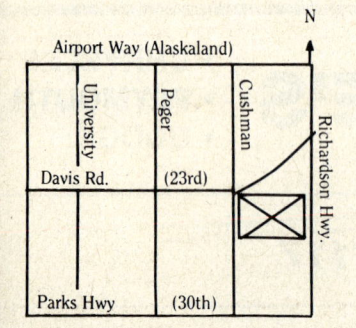

[map: Airport Way (Alaskaland), University, Peger (23rd), Cushman, Davis Rd., Richardson Hwy., Parks Hwy (30th)]

At 23rd St. Exit from Richardson Highway

- Next to Tesoro, Mapco, Petrolane and 7-11
- 1+ acres of free parking
- "Instant" drop-off laundry and dry cleaning
- 60 large, new machines
- Children's lounge/Disney channel
- Non-smoking area
- New wall to wall carpeting

---

pools: Mary Siah Recreation Center, 1025 14th Ave., phone 459-1467; Robert Hamme Memorial Pool, 901 Airport Way, phone 459-1468; and Robert Wescott Memorial Pool, 8th Avenue in North Pole, phone 488-9401. Call for swim hours and fees.

Chena Lakes Recreation Area. This 2,178-acre park, located 17 miles/27 km southeast of Fairbanks on the Richardson Highway, offers a wide assortment of outdoor recreation. There are 80 campsites for both RV and tent camping, including campsites on an island; canoe, sailboat and rowboat rentals; bike paths and trails for nature hikes, skiing, ski-joring and dog mushing; and boat-ramp access to the nearby Chena River ($6 fee charged). Admission to the park, maintained by the Fairbanks North Star Borough, is $3 per vehicle between Memorial Day and Labor Day. No admission is charged the rest of the year.

ARCTIC RENT-A-CAR

- Late Model Cars and Vans
- Very Reasonable Rates

ANCHORAGE 4505 SPENARD ROAD
Courtesy Phone/Baggage Claim Area
3 min. from Airport

(907) 248-1658

FAIRBANKS INT'L. AIRPORT TERMINAL

(907) 479-8044

Mailing Address: P.O. Box 61349
Fairbanks, Alaska 99706-1349

ALASKA RAW FUR CO.

- **Tanned Fur Sales**
  Largest Selection in the Interior
- **Available As Single Fur Skins And Matched Bundles**
- **"Where Alaskans Buy Their Furs"**

(no middle man)
Direct From The Trapper To You

ALASKA RAW FUR CO.

4106 Boat St
Fairbanks, AK

(907) 479-2462

A colorful sunset near Cleary Summit outside Fairbanks. (Joe Prax)

Go Fishing: There are several streams and lakes within driving distance of Fairbanks, and local fishing guides are available. **Chena Lake**, about 20 miles/32 km southeast of the city via the Richardson–Alaska Highway at Chena Lakes Recreation Area, is stocked with rainbow trout, silver salmon and arctic char. The **Chena River** and its tributaries offer good grayling and salmon fishing. The Chena River flows through Fairbanks, where some fishing is available. Chena Hot Springs Road off the Steese Highway provides access to grayling fisheries in the Chena River Recreation Area (see the STEESE HIGHWAY section). The Steese Highway also offers access to the **Chatanika River** for grayling fishing.

Air taxi operators in Fairbanks offer short trips from the city for rainbow trout, grayling, northern pike, lake trout and sheefish in lakes and streams of the Tanana and Yukon river drainages. Some operators have camps set up for overnight trips while others specialize in day trips. The air taxi operators usually provide a boat and motor for their angling visitors. Rates are reasonable, and vary according to the distance from town and type of facilities offered.

Goldpanner Chevron Service, Inc.

Chevron
Off Airport Way on
9th and Cushman
SELF-SERVE and FULL SERVE

Tuneups • Brakes • Atlas Tires
Batteries • Accessories • Towing
FRIENDLY COURTEOUS SERVICE

MasterCard **(907) 456-6964** VISA

Vern Stoner, Dealer
809 Cushman Street
Fairbanks, Alaska 99701

MIDNIGHT SUN AVIATION

SIGHTSEEING FLIGHTS
AS LOW AS **$35** PER SEAT
2 PASSENGER MINIMUM
Rates are Subject to Change

Call for Reservations
(907) 452-7039
P.O. Box 1432, Fairbanks, AK 99707

L&L R.V.
Service and Supply

Quick Reliable Service
Monday-Saturday 9 a.m. - 6 p.m.
Free estimates - All work guaranteed

INCLUDING:
- Complete appliance repair
- Septic system repair
- Brake service and repair
- Plastic tank welding
- Coach wiring

(907) 474-9260
2751 Davis Road
Fairbanks, Alaska

MasterCard   VISA

FAIRBANKS

Why wait to have your film developed?

PHOTO EXPRESS Image Centers

At PhotoExpress, our professionals will develop your film as quickly and as inexpensively as back home.

Make sure your photos turn out!

For many, a trip to Alaska is a once in a lifetime adventure. Don't wait until you get home to find out that your precious memories didn't turn out. Have them developed while you are still here. Our prices are comparable to those charged in your home town, and we can have your photos professionally developed in as little as one hour.

Get an additional set of Prints FREE!

As our way of welcoming you to Alaska, bring this ad and your film for developing into any PhotoExpress and receive a second set of prints free!

Not good with any other discount.
Limit 3 rolls. One coupn per customer.

Bently Mall on College Road
University Mall on AirportWay

2 locations to serve you.

PHOTO EXPRESS Image Centers

DENALI NATIONAL PARK

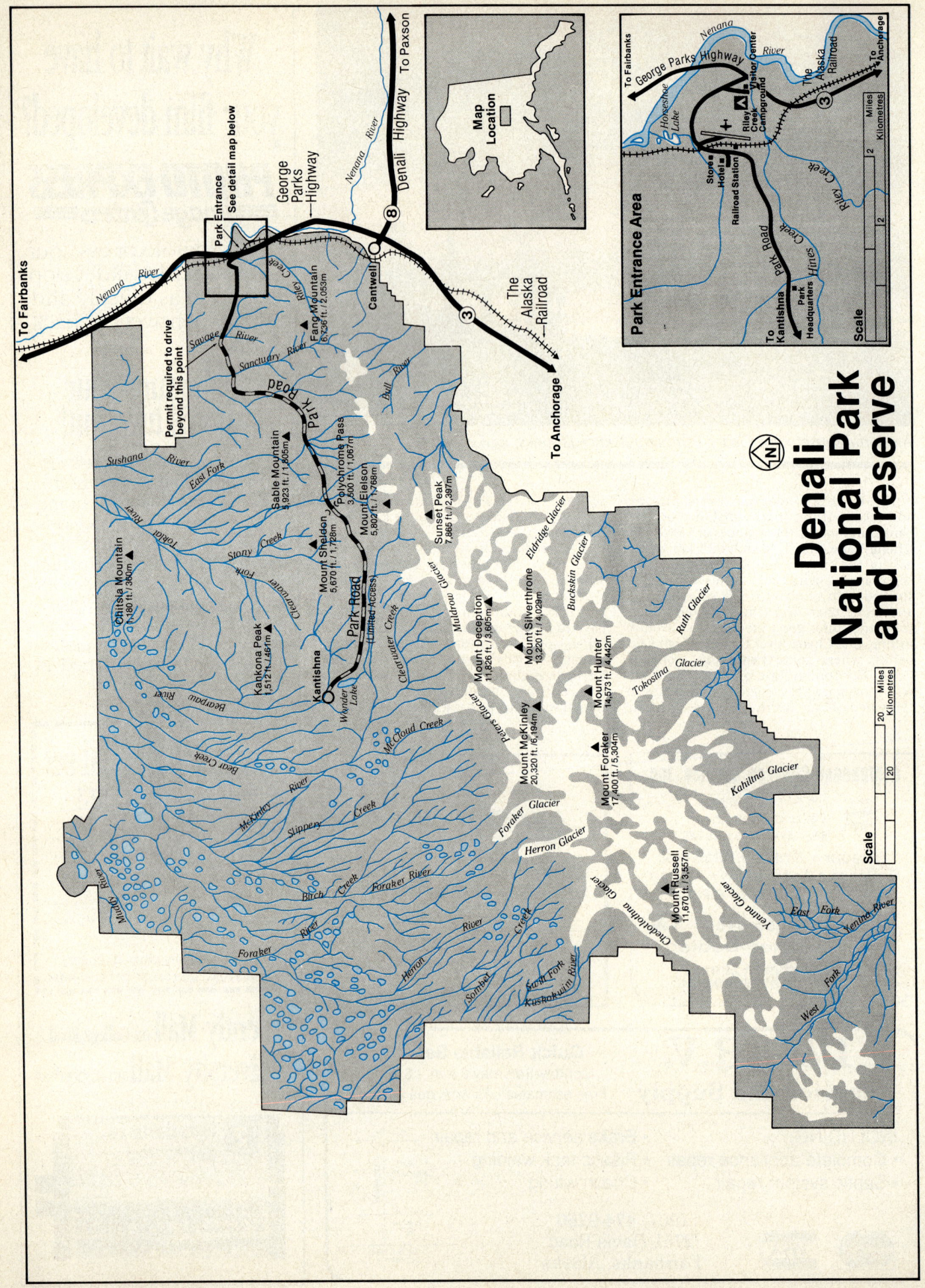

Denali National Park and Preserve

DENALI NATIONAL PARK

(Formerly Mount McKinley National Park)
Includes log of Park Road

Denali National Park and Preserve (formerly Mount McKinley National Park) lies on the north flank of the Alaska Range, 250 miles/402 km south of the Arctic Circle. The park entrance, accessible by highway, railroad and aircraft, is 237 highway miles/382 km north of Anchorage, and about half that distance from Fairbanks.

The park is open year-round to visitors, although the hotel, most campgrounds, gas, food and shuttle bus service within the park are available only from late May or early June to mid-September. (Opening dates for facilities and activities for the summer season are announced in the spring by the Park Service and depend mainly on snow conditions in May.)

During the peak summer season, visitors should allow a minimum of 2 full days in order to obtain bus seats and campground sites within the park. Lodging and camping are available outside the park on the George Parks Highway, and there are a variety of activities—river rafting, hikes and ranger programs—to enjoy. The Denali experience is considered well worth the wait. Check with operators outside the park and with personnel at the Visitor Access Center about programs and activities.

Parking space is limited within the park at the Visitor Access Center. Overflow parking is available at Riley Creek Campground (walk or mini-shuttle to Visitor Access Center).

First-time visitors should be particularly aware of the controlled-access system for Park Road use. Private vehicle traffic on the 91-mile/146-km road into the park is restricted beyond Savage River check station (**Milepost J 14.8**). Campers must register for all campgrounds at the Visitor Access Center; see Accommodations this section. The free shuttle bus system and concession-operated tours are available to allow visitors a means of viewing the park without disturbing the wildlife; see Transportation this section for details on the shuttle service.

An admission fee of $3 per person ($5 per family) is charged to visitors traveling beyond the Savage River checkpoint at Mile 14.8 on the Park Road (see log this section). The fee is collected when visitors obtain shuttle bus tickets and campground permits at the Visitor Access Center. Persons 16 years of age or less, and U.S. citizens 62 years or older, are exempt from the admission fee. (A $15 annual park pass, and the $25 Golden Eagle Pass, are valid for admission.)

For information about the park, write Denali National Park and Preserve, P.O. Box 9, Denali Park, AK 99755; winter phone (907) 683-2294, summer phone (907) 683-1266. Or contact the Alaska Public Lands Information centers in Anchorage at 605 W.

Caribou antlers frame view of Mount McKinley on a rare clear day. (John W. Warden)

4th Ave., 99501, phone (907) 271-2737, and in Fairbanks at 250 Cushman St., 99701, phone (907) 451-7352.

One of the park's best known attractions is Mount McKinley, North America's highest mountain at 20,320 feet/6,194m. (According to the National Park Service, recent measurements of the peak by University of Alaska Fairbanks place its elevation at 20,304 feet.) On a clear day, Mount McKinley is visible from Anchorage. However, cloudy, rainy summer weather frequently obscures the mountain, and travelers have about a 30 percent chance of seeing it.

First mention of Mount McKinley was in 1794, when English explorer Capt. George Vancouver spotted a "stupendous snow mountain" from Cook Inlet. Early Russian explorers and traders called the peak *Bolshaia Gora,* or "Big Mountain." The Tanana Indian name for the mountain is Denali, said to mean the "high one." The mountain was named McKinley in 1896 by a Princeton-educated prospector named William A. Dickey for presidential nominee William McKinley of Ohio. Even today, the mountain has 2 names; Mount McKinley according to USGS maps, and Denali according to the state Geographic Names Board.

The history of climbs on McKinley is as intriguing as its many names. In 1903, Judge James Wickersham and party climbed to an estimated 8,000 feet, while Dr. Frederick A. Cook and party reached the 11,000-foot level. In 1906, Cook returned to the mountain and made 2 attempts at the summit—the first unsuccessful, and the second (according to Cook) successful. Cook's vague description of his ascent route and a questionable summit photo led many to doubt his claim. Tom Lloyd, of the 1910 Sourdough Party (which included Charles McGonagall, Pete Anderson and Billy Taylor) claimed they reached both summits (north and south peaks) but could not provide any photographic evidence. (Much later it was verified that the men had reached the summit of the lower north peak.) The first complete ascent of the true summit of Mount McKinley was made in 1913 by Hudson Stuck, Harry Karstens and Walter Harper.

Today, close to a thousand people attempt to climb Mount McKinley each year between April and June, most flying in to base camp at 7,000 feet. (The first airplane landing on the mountain was flown in 1932 by Joe Crosson.) Geographic features of McKinley and its sister peaks bear the names of many early explorers: Eldridge and Muldrow glaciers, after George Eldridge and Robert Muldrow of the USGS who determined the peak's altitude in 1898; Wickersham Wall; Karstens Ridge; and Mount Carpe and Mount Koven, named for Allen Carpe and Theodore Koven, both killed in a 1932 climb.

Timberline in the park is 2,700 feet/

1992 ■ The MILEPOST® 381

DENALI NATIONAL PARK

SOURDOUGH CABINS

Denali, Alaska

MILE 238.8 PARKS HIGHWAY
ONE MILE NORTH OF
DENALI NATIONAL PARK ENTRANCE

Enjoy "Alaskan Hospitality" and Comfortable Accommodations at Reasonable Rates.

- New Individual Cabins
- Deluxe and Economy Units
- All Services within Walking Distance
- Nestled in a Spruce Forest
- Peaceful and Quiet
- Alaskan Owned and Operated
  VISA and MasterCard Accepted

ADVANCE RESERVATIONS SUGGESTED
Call: (907) 683-2773 or
Write: P.O. Box 118-MP
Denali National Park, AK 99755

Denali Park offers few trails, but plenty of terrain for cross-country hiking. (Rick McIntyre)

823m. The landscape below timberline in this subarctic wilderness is called taiga, or "land of little sticks," a term of Russian origin that describes the scant growth of trees. Black and white spruce, willow, dwarf birch and aspen stand in narrow strips along the lower drainages of the park. The uplands of alpine tundra are carpeted with lichens, mosses, wildflowers and low-growing shrubs. Wildflowers bloom in spring along the steep banks of the passes and in alpine meadows, usually peaking by early July.

The parkland is an ecosystem rich in wildlife. Grizzly bears, caribou, wolves and red fox freely wander over the tundra. Moose wade through streams and lake shallows. A few lynx pursue snowshoe hare in taiga forests. Marmots, pikas and Dall sheep inhabit high, rocky areas. The arctic ground squirrel's sharp warning call is heard throughout the park.

Migratory bird life encompasses species from 6 continents, including waterfowl, shorebirds, songbirds and birds of prey. Ptarmigan, gray jays and magpies are year-round residents.

The park's silted glacial rivers are not an angler's delight, but grayling, Dolly Varden and lake trout are occasionally caught in streams and small lakes.

McKinley / Denali
STEAKHOUSE & SALMON BAKE

Mile 238.5 Parks Highway • One mile north of Park entrance

BREAKFAST: Homemade Blueberry Pancakes, Reindeer Sausage, Fruit, Juice, Eggs, Potatoes

LUNCH: Soup and Sandwiches, Salad Bar, Burgers, Fries

DINNERS: Char-Broiled Steaks, Salmon, Halibut, Ribs, BBQ Chicken, Baked Beans, Rice Pilaf, Sourdough Rolls, Extensive Salad Bar, Homemade Soup, Beer and Wine Bar

FREE VISITOR INFO

PIE & ICE CREAM

Free Shuttle From All Local Hotels
Call (907) 683-2733

Group Rates
Tour Buses Welcome

Visit Our Upstairs
Gift Shop

McKinley / Denali CABINS

- Closest full service facility to Denali National Park entrance
- Close to wildlife shuttles • Close to raft trips

MOST ECONOMICAL LODGING IN AREA • Call for Rates

All new beds, linens, blankets • Central showers
SOME CABINS WITH PRIVATE BATHS
Shuttle available to Park Visitor Center and Railroad Depot

Mile 238.5 Parks Highway • One mile north of Park entrance

Phone (907) 683-2258 or 683-2733   P.O. Box 90M, Denali Park, Alaska 99755

NUNA IDITAROD KENNELS

Mile 238.7 Parks Highway
(1 mile north of Denali National Park entrance)

- Meet Iditarod veteran mushers Dewey and Kathy Halverson
- See Alaskan huskies used in the 1049-mile race from Anchorage to Nome
- Pet our husky pups
- View our photo collection and displays of the mushers, dogs, country and equipment used in the Last Great Race
- Come visit and ask questions
- Dog sled demonstration
- Winter dog tours
- Unique Alaska gift items

Mail: P.O. Box 13183, Trapper Creek, AK 99683
Phone (907) 345-5008

DENALI PARK ADVERTISERS

Backwoods Lodging	Cantwell
Camp Denali	Ph. (907) 683-2290
Carlo Creek Lodge	Mile 224 Parks Hwy.
Denali Crow's Nest Cabins	Mile 238.5 Parks Hwy.
Denali Grizzly Bear Cabins & Campground	Mile 231.1 Parks Hwy.
Denali Hostel	Ph. (907) 683-1295
Denali National Park Hotel	Ph. (907) 276-7234
Denali National Park Central Reservations and Travel	Ph. 1-800-872-2748
Denali Raft Adventures	Ph. (907) 683-2234
Denali Riverview Inn	Mile 238.4 Parks Hwy.
Denali Suites	Mile 248.8 Parks Hwy.
Denali Wilderness Lodge	Ph. 1-800-541-9779
Dome Home Bed & Breakfast	Ph. (907) 683-1239
Doug Geeting Aviation	Ph. (907) 733-2366
Era Helicopters	Ph. (907) 683-2574
Harper Lodge Princess®	Ph. 1-800-426-0500
Healy Heights Bed and Breakfast	Ph. (907) 683-2639
Kantishna Roadhouse	Ph. (907) 733-2535
K2 Aviation	Ph. (907) 733-2291
McKinley Chalet Resort	Ph. (907) 276-7234
McKinley/Denali Cabins	Mile 238.5 Parks Hwy.
McKinley/Denali Steakhouse and Salmon Bake	Mile 238.5 Parks Hwy.
McKinley KOA Kampground	Mile 248.4 Parks Hwy.
McKinley Raft Tours	Mile 238.8 Parks Hwy.
McKinley Wilderness Lodge	Mile 224 Parks Hwy.
Midnight Sun Express®	Ph. 1-800-835-8907
Mt. McKinley Motor Lodge	Mile 238.7 Parks Hwy.
Mt. McKinley Tours	Ph. 1-800-327-7651
Mt. McKinley Village Lodge	Ph. (907) 276-7234
North Face Lodge	Ph. (907) 683-2290
Nuna Iditarod Kennels	Mile 238.7 Parks Hwy.
Osprey Expeditions	Mile 224 Parks Hwy.
Overlook Bar & Grill, The	Mile 238.5 Parks Hwy.
Perch, The	Mile 224 Parks Hwy.
Sourdough Cabins	Mile 238.8 Parks Hwy.
Talkeetna Air Taxi, Inc.	Ph. (907) 733-2218
Waugaman Village	Mile 248.7 Parks Hwy.
Wolf Point Ranch	Ph. (907) 768-2620

When you arrive be sure to stop at the Visitor Access Center, near the park entrance. The center offers information on campgrounds in the park; maps, brochures and schedules of events; details on campfire talks, hikes, nature walks, sled dog demonstrations, wildlife tours; shuttle bus schedules; and other tips on what to see and do in the park. A second source of information is the Eielson Visitor Center at **Milepost J 66**.

Both centers are open daily throughout the summer season. Hours vary, but gener-

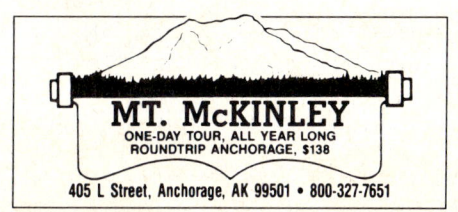

MT. McKINLEY
ONE-DAY TOUR, ALL YEAR LONG
ROUNDTRIP ANCHORAGE, $138
405 L Street, Anchorage, AK 99501 • 800-327-7651

DENALI NATIONAL PARK

MILE 231.1

Denali Grizzly Bear Cabins & Campground

Mile 231.1 Parks Highway, South Boundary Denali National Park, on Nenana River

RV and Tent Sites · Hookups · Tent Cabins · Hot Showers
Alaskan Gifts · Beer · Liquor · Ice · Hot and Cold Snacks
Propane · Phone

Bookings for Local Activities
Kitchen or Sleeping Cabins
Some with Private Baths
Continental Breakfast Available

Early Reservations Suggested
Deposit Required

Summer:
Denali Grizzly Bear, Box 7
Denali National Park, Alaska 99755
(907) 683-2696
Winter:
Denali Grizzly Bear
5845 Old Valdez Trail
Salcha, Alaska 99714
(907) 488-3932

The Overlook BAR & GRILL

Dine with finest view in Denali Park area, inside or out on large sunny deck
Overlooking the Nenana River, Horseshoe Lake, and the ARR Depot
Variations on Steaks, Seafood, Burgers, Chicken, Soups and Salads,
SALMON & HALIBUT
Children's Plates • Box Lunches
Reasonable Prices
45 Varieties of Beer
Fine Wine and Cocktails
Meals 11 a.m. to 10 p.m. • Bar 'til Midnght

Home of the McKinley Margarita

Anywhere in Denali Park Area
COURTESY TRANSPORT
call 683-2723

DENALI NATIONAL PARK

Doug Geeting Aviation's
McKinley Flight Tours & Glacier Landings

- Turbocharged ski-equipped 5-6 passenger aircraft
- Oxygen and intercom
- Wildlife safari
- Circle Denali
- Visit climbers
- Fly over the summit
- Prices start at $65/seat

"It's a small price to pay for the treasure at the foot of Mt. McKinley and the man who can get you there." —Erma Bombeck, columnist and author

Write: Box 42MP, Talkeetna, AK 99676 • Phone: (907) 733-2366 FAX us at: (907) 733-1000

Wolf Point Ranch (907) 768-2620

Alaska's Finest Horseback Adventures ▪ Excellent View of Mt. McKinley

Specializing in:
- 2-hour to full day guided trail rides
- Fully outfitted pack trips of 2-6 days into the wilderness surrounding Denali National Park, with excellent fishing

Just south of Denali Park ▪ Shuttles available from all park establishments
Don't forget your camera ▪ PO BOX 127, CANTWELL, ALASKA 99729

---

ally the centers open early in the morning and remain open into the evening.

NOTE: The following announcement by the National Park Service pertains to the Park Road: "Wildlife sightings along the Denali National Park Road corridor have declined significantly since 1974. This decrease is the result of increased vehicle traffic and the activities associated with private vehicle use. In an effort to preserve the wildlife viewing opportunities for the public, the National Park Service has set road traffic limits. Traffic will be held to the 1984 averages with a 15 percent variance in shuttle and tour buses to allow for daily fluctuations in visitor demand. When planning trips to the park, visitors should plan alternate activities in the entrance area such as attending naturalist programs should there be delays in obtaining a seat on a bus. As private vehicle numbers are reduced, bus numbers will be allowed to increase."

ACCOMMODATIONS

There is only 1 hotel within the park, but several motels will be found outside the park along the George Parks Highway (turn to **Milepost A 237.3** in the GEORGE PARKS HIGHWAY section). Accommodations are also available in the Kantishna area. *NOTE: Visitors should make reservations for lodging far in advance.* The park hotel and area motels are often filled during the summer. Visitors must book their own accommodations.

Camp Denali, begun in 1951, is known as a premier national park wilderness vacation lodge and nature center. Its log cabins dot a hillside looking out onto an expansive view of Mount McKinley and the

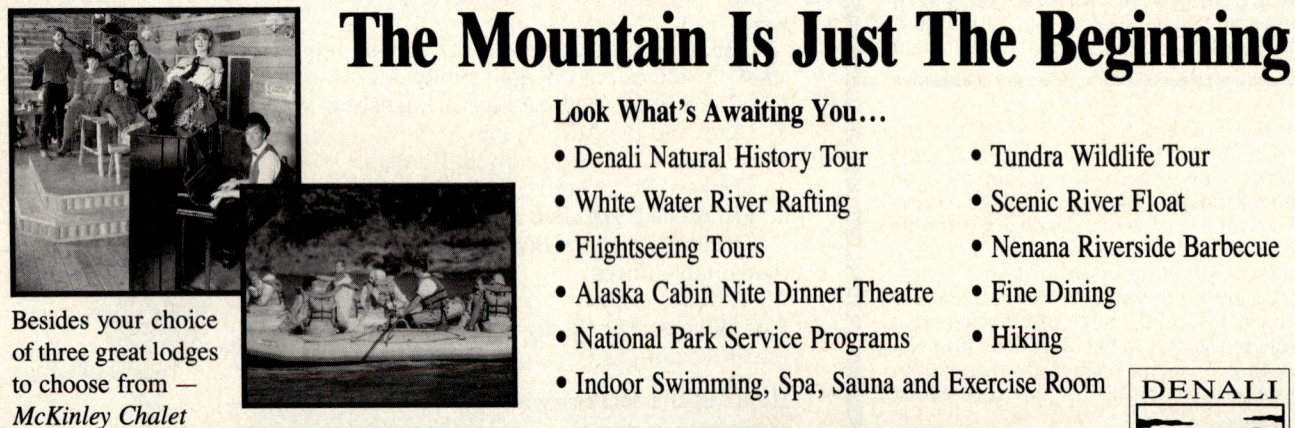

DENALI

The Mountain Is Just The Beginning

Besides your choice of three great lodges to choose from — *McKinley Chalet Resort,* (A 3-Diamond facility), *Denali National Park Hotel* and *Mt. McKinley Village Lodge* — ARA Denali Park Hotels can arrange a variety of activities that will make your visit to Denali National Park a memorable adventure.

Look What's Awaiting You...

- Denali Natural History Tour
- White Water River Rafting
- Flightseeing Tours
- Alaska Cabin Nite Dinner Theatre
- National Park Service Programs
- Indoor Swimming, Spa, Sauna and Exercise Room
- Tundra Wildlife Tour
- Scenic River Float
- Nenana Riverside Barbecue
- Fine Dining
- Hiking

**FOR RESERVATIONS OR INFORMATION:
(907) 276-7234**

Or call (907) 683-2215 within 48 hours of your arrival

DENALI PARK HOTELS
ARA LEISURE SERVICES

ARA Denali Park Hotels, formerly Outdoor World, is an authorized concessioner of the National Park Service.

Alaska Range. Activities focus on guided hiking with experienced naturalists, photography, canoeing, biking, rafting, flightseeing, gold-panning, evening natural history programs and periodic summer seminars. Central dining; 35 to 40 guests; all-expense. See display ad. [ADVERTISEMENT]

Carlo Creek Lodge. (907) 683-2576, 683-2573. Located 12 miles south of Denali Park entrance. 20 wooded acres bordered by beautiful Carlo Creek, the Nenana River and Denali National Park. Cozy log cabins with own bathroom and shower on creek. RV park, dump station, tent sites, large barbecue pit with roof. Public bathrooms with showers. Small general store, gift shop with Alaskan made gifts from fur to lace. Information and pay phone. Walking distance to The Perch Restaurant. See display ad at Mile 224 Parks Highway. [ADVERTISEMENT]

Denali National Park Central Reservations & Travel. Central booking agency for lodging, tours, transportation and wilderness resorts in the Denali Park area. Trip planning for all of Alaska. Year-round service. VISA, MasterCard and American Express accepted. Brochure. Call 1-800-872-2748.

Denali National Park Hotel and **McKinley Chalet Resort** offer the area's finest accommodations, dining and gift shops. Both offer tour desk services to help you reserve wildlife bus tours, rafting and flightseeing. The McKinley Chalet Resort at **Milepost A 238.9** Parks Highway features a health club complete with indoor heated swimming pool, sauna, hot tub and exercise room, and Alaska Cabin Nite dinner theater. The McKinley Village Lodge is convenient to all Denali National Park activities, located nearby at **Milepost 229** Parks Highway. Newly remodeled, it offers friendly service and comfortable accommodations including a lounge, coffee shop, gift shop and complete tour/activity desk. All accommodations, activities and transportation can be arranged with just one call! (907) 276-7234. See display ad this section. [ADVERTISEMENT]

Harper Lodge Princess®. Offering 192 rooms and suites with phones and TVs. Free shuttle to rail depot and park activities. Spas, gift shop, fine dining and deli. Handicap accommodations. Seasonal service mid-May to mid-September. Rates from $145. VISA, MasterCard and American Express. Write

---

denali HOSTEL
Bunk style accommodations $22
Showers • Park pickup/drop-off
Continental breakfast included
Laundry facilities available
(907) 683-1295
P.O. Box 801, Denali National Park, AK 99755

HEALY HEIGHTS
Bed and Breakfast
MINUTES FROM DENALI NATIONAL PARK
Open All Year   (907) 683-2639
Box 277, Healy, Alaska 99743
Mile 247 George Parks Highway

Denali Park's Best Kept Secret...
DENALI WILDERNESS LODGE
- **FLY-IN DINING TOURS DAILY**
- **OVERNIGHT EXCURSIONS**
- **EXTENDED WILDERNESS TRIPS**

Step back into the Gold Rush Days and experience an authentic Alaskan wilderness camp dating back to the early 1900's. Fifteen minutes by air from Denali Park. Flightseeing en route. More than 25 hand-hewn log buildings, guest cabins, wildlife museum, greenhouse, trapper's cabin, sawmill, sauna, barn and main lodge. Daily naturalist tours of historic camp. Over 450 miles of hiking and horse trails. Good food and lots of it! Cozy private accommodations. Evening entertainment and open bar. Uniquely Alaskan. Under same owner-management more than 25 years.

Lodge has been featured on Good Morning America, Eye on L.A., Huntley-Brinkley, ESPN-TV and others.

For Reservations and Information
1-800-541-9779
Phone or Write: P.O. Box 50
Denali Park, Alaska 99755 USA
June thru September 907-683-1287

"Denali's Ultimate Destination in ANY Weather"

DENALI NATIONAL PARK

DISCOVER THE PRINCESS DIFFERENCE

ALASKA UP CLOSE.

There are 356 miles of unbelievable scenery between Anchorage, Denali National Park and Fairbanks that you can only see by rail.

And the ultimate in Alaska rail travel is Princess'® Midnight Sun Express® ULTRA DOME® rail cars. Our one way or round trip packages depart Anchorage or Fairbanks, and can include a night at our own Harper Lodge Princess®.

For details call: (800) 835-8907.

MIDNIGHT SUN EXPRESS

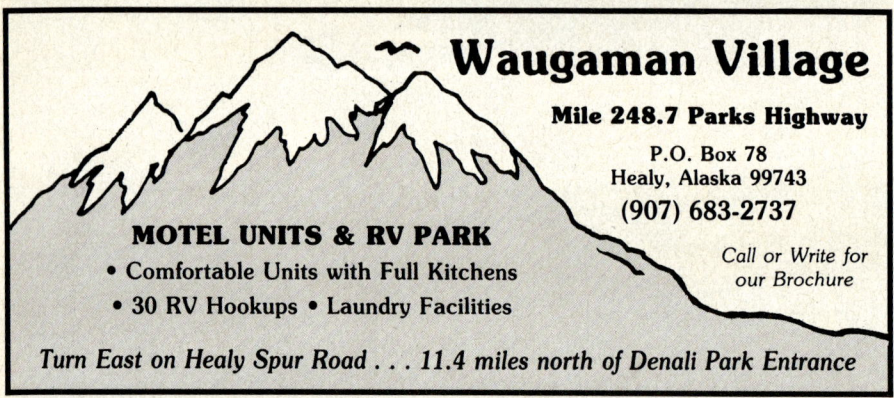

Waugaman Village

Mile 248.7 Parks Highway

P.O. Box 78
Healy, Alaska 99743

(907) 683-2737

Call or Write for our Brochure

MOTEL UNITS & RV PARK
- Comfortable Units with Full Kitchens
- 30 RV Hookups • Laundry Facilities

Turn East on Healy Spur Road . . . 11.4 miles north of Denali Park Entrance

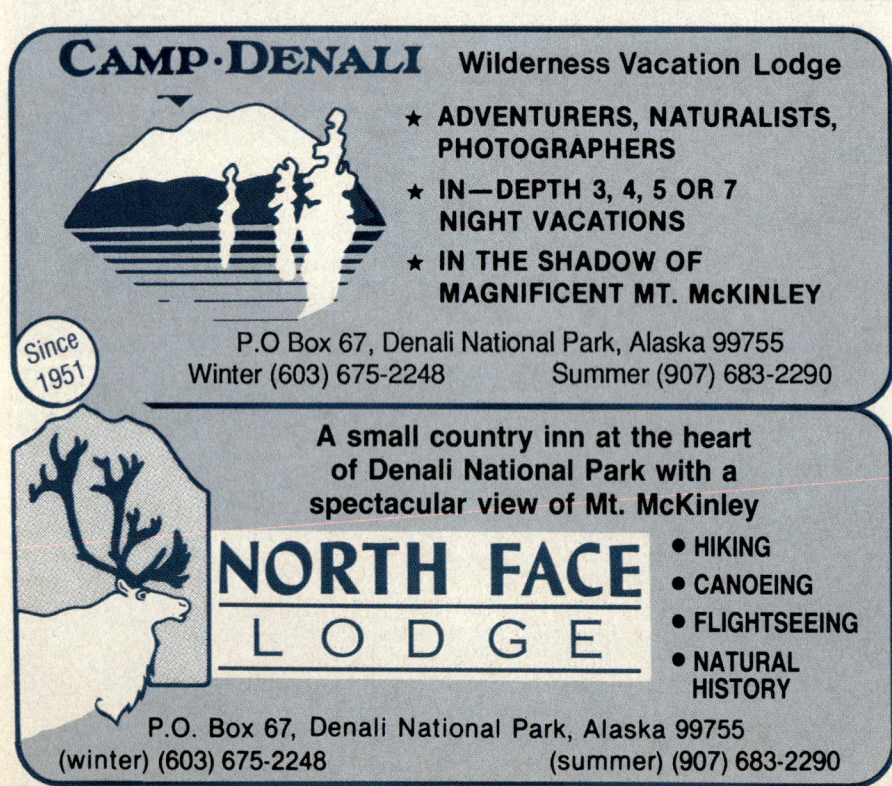

CAMP·DENALI — Wilderness Vacation Lodge

Since 1951

★ ADVENTURERS, NATURALISTS, PHOTOGRAPHERS
★ IN—DEPTH 3, 4, 5 OR 7 NIGHT VACATIONS
★ IN THE SHADOW OF MAGNIFICENT MT. McKINLEY

P.O Box 67, Denali National Park, Alaska 99755
Winter (603) 675-2248   Summer (907) 683-2290

NORTH FACE LODGE

A small country inn at the heart of Denali National Park with a spectacular view of Mt. McKinley

- HIKING
- CANOEING
- FLIGHTSEEING
- NATURAL HISTORY

P.O. Box 67, Denali National Park, Alaska 99755
(winter) (603) 675-2248   (summer) (907) 683-2290

Princess Tours®, 2815 2nd Ave., Suite #400, Seattle, WA 98121 or call 1-800-426-0500 year-round. [ADVERTISEMENT]

Kantishna Roadhouse located at the quiet west end of Denali National Park offers opportunities to view, photograph and explore the park. Packages include lovely, comfortable cabins with private baths, guided hiking, gold panning, horses, fishing, fine meals and Alaskan hospitality. P.O. Box 130, Denali Park, AK 99755. Phone 1-800-942-7420. [ADVERTISEMENT]

North Face Lodge is a small, well-appointed North Country inn in the heart of Denali National Park with a spectacular view of Mount McKinley. It features twin-bedded rooms with private baths, a central dining room and living room. Guest activities include guided hiking with experienced naturalists, canoeing, biking, flightseeing and evening natural history programs. All expense. See display ad. [ADVERTISEMENT]

There are 6 campgrounds in the park along the 87-mile/140-km Park Road (see log of Park Road in this section for locations). Wonder Lake, Sanctuary River and Igloo Creek campgrounds are tent only and accessible only by shuttle bus.

The campgrounds are open from about late May to early September, except for Riley Creek, which is open year-round (snow-covered and no facilities in winter). There is a fee and a 14-day limit at all campgrounds in summer. There is a 3-night minimum stay requirement at Teklanika River Campground, and also a limit of 1 round-trip to this campground for registered campers with vehicles. Additional travel to and from Teklanika is by free shuttle bus. See chart for facilities at each campground.

Campground	Spaces	Tent	Trailer	Pit toilets	Flush toilets	Tap water	Fee
Riley Creek	102	•	•		•	•	$12
Savage River	34	•	•		•	•	$12
Sanctuary River	7	•		•		•	$12
Teklanika River	50	•	•		•	•	$12
Igloo Creek	7	•		•		•	$12
Wonder Lake	28	•			•	•	$12

Several private campgrounds are located outside the park along the George Parks Highway. See display ads this section.

For area accommodations, also turn to pages 340–342 in the GEORGE PARKS HIGHWAY section.

Registration System: Register at the Visitor Access Center at **Milepost J 0.7** Park Road for a campsite. Registration for campsites is in person for same day (if space is available) or 1 day in advance. During peak season, campgrounds typically fill up mid-morning for the following day.

The Alaska Public Lands Information centers in Fairbanks and Anchorage have a limited number of campground permits and shuttle-bus coupons that can be reserved in advance. Reservations must be made in person; no reservations will be accepted by phone. Campground reservations can be made 7 to 21 days in advance only, while shuttle-bus reservations can be made on a next-day basis or up to 21 days in advance. All fees are collected in advance when making reservations. For more information, call the Anchorage center at 271-2737, or the Fairbanks center at 451-7352.

Visitor Services: Available from late May to mid-September, depending on weather. The Denali National Park Hotel has a gift shop, restaurant, snack bar and saloon. Gas and propane *only* are available at the gas station near the hotel, no repair service. A public shower is located behind the gas station; groceries available at gas station. The post office is near the hotel. There is a dump station near Riley Creek Campground.

There are no vehicle or food services after you leave the headquarters entrance area.

Campers should bring a gasoline or propane stove or purchase firewood from concessionaire; a tent or waterproof shelter because of frequent rains; and rain gear for everyone. Camper mail should be addressed in care of General Delivery, Denali National Park, Denali Park, AK 99755.

Talkeetna Ranger Station: The National Park Service maintains a ranger station that is staffed full time from mid-April through mid-September and intermittently during the winter. Mountaineering rangers provide information on Denali National Park and climbing within the Alaska Range. A reference library and slide/tape program are available for climbers. All climbers must register for climbs of Mount McKinley and Mount Foraker. Mountaineering information may be obtained from: Talkeetna Ranger Station, P.O. Box 588, Talkeetna, AK 99676; phone (907) 733-2231.

ATTRACTIONS

The major attraction at Denali National Park is the park itself. Organized activities put on by the Park Service include ranger-led nature hikes; sled dog demonstrations at park headquarters; and campfire programs at Riley Creek, Savage River, Teklanika River and Wonder Lake campgrounds.

Private operators in the park offer flightseeing tours, bus tours, raft tours and wintertime dogsled tours. Cross-country skiing and snowshoeing are also popular in winter.

There are few established trails in the park, but there is plenty of terrain for cross-country hiking. Free permits are required for any overnight hikes.

Permits and information on ranger-led hikes and other activities are available at the Visitor Access Center near the park entrance.

TRANSPORTATION

Highway: Access via the George Parks Highway and the Denali Highway.

The Park Road runs westward 91 miles/ 146.4 km from the park's east boundary to Kantishna. The road is paved only to Savage River (**Milepost J 14.7**). Private vehicle travel is restricted beyond the Savage River checkpoint at Mile 14.8. Mount McKinley is first visible at about **Milepost J 9** Park Road, but the best views begin at about **Milepost J 60** and continue with few interruptions to Wonder Lake. At the closest point, the summit of the mountain is 27 miles/43.5 km from the road. See log this section.

Shuttle bus: The National Park Service provides a free shuttle bus service between the Visitor Access Center and Eielson Visitor Center and between Eielson Visitor Center and Wonder Lake. Boarding coupons are available at the Visitor Access Center for the same day (if space is available) or up to 2

Park visitors may see grizzly bear along the Park Road. Bring binoculars for best wildlife viewing. (Steve Lackie)

Millers'
Dome Home
Bed & Breakfast
(907) 683-1239
137 Healy Spur Road
P.O. Box 262
Healy, AK 99743
Open year round
— clean and economical —
hunting and fishing licenses

DENALI SUITES
OPEN ALL YEAR
2-Bedroom • Kitchen • Living Room • Telephone
TV and VCR • Coin-Operated Laundry
(907) 683-2848 • PO Box 393, Healy, AK 99743
Mile 248.8 Parks Highway
15 minutes north of Denali National Park

KANTISHNA ROADHOUSE
at
Mount McKinley
Located 95 miles inside
Denali National Park
Where the road ends and the trail begins.
P.O. BOX 130, Denali National Park
Kantishna, Alaska 99755
1-800-942-7420

McKinley Wilderness LODGE

Open June 1 - Labor Day

• Park Information
• Tour Assistance
• Large Private Sleeping Cabins
• Continental Breakfast

A Bed and Breakfast at beautiful Carlo Creek
Mile 224 Parks highway

RESERVATIONS & INFORMATION
P.O. Box 89, Denali National Park 99755   907/683-2277

DENALI NATIONAL PARK

Dall sheep are common along rocky mountainsides in the park. (Steve Lackie)

days in advance. During peak season, bus coupons for the next day shuttle are generally gone by midmorning. Shuttle buses pick up and drop off passengers along the Park Road and stop for scenic and wildlife viewing as schedules permit. A round-trip between the Visitor Access Center and Eielson Visitor Center takes about 8 hours. The round-trip between Eielson and Wonder Lake takes another 3 hours. Bring a lunch, camera, binoculars, extra film, warm clothes and rain gear. Buses run daily from the Saturday preceding Memorial Day in May through the second Thursday following Labor Day in September, weather permitting.

Air: Charter flights are available from most nearby towns with airfields, and flightseeing tours of the park are offered by operators from the park area or out of Talkeetna, Anchorage or Fairbanks. A round-trip air tour of the park from Anchorage takes 3 to 4 hours. See display ads this section.

Era Helicopters. Enjoy an eagle-eyed view of the grandeur of Denali National Park with Alaska's oldest and largest helicopter company. Look for moose, sheep and bear in the valleys and mountains below. Located 0.5 mile north of the park entrance, or phone (907) 683-2574 from mid-May to mid-September, or outside Alaska, 1-800-843-1947. [ADVERTISEMENT]

Talkeetna Air Taxi, Inc. Fly Mount McKinley with Talkeetna Air Taxi. An awe-inspiring, memorable experience. Tour this vast glimmering world of towering peaks, glaciers and snow. Watch for animals—climbers—and take pictures. Satisfaction guaranteed. Glacier landings available. Sportfishing and hunting flights, aerial photography. Climbing expedition support. Office at state airport coming into Talkeetna. Follow our signs. Write Box 73-MP, Talkeetna, AK 99676. (907) 733-2218. See large ad this section. [ADVERTISEMENT]

Railroad: The Alaska Railroad offers daily northbound and southbound trains between Anchorage and Fairbanks, with stops at Denali Park Station, during the summer season. For details on schedules and fares see the ALASKA RAILROAD section.

Midnight Sun Express®. Travel aboard the fully domed ULTRA DOME® rail cars between Anchorage, Denali National Park and Fairbanks. Overnight accommodations available at Denali Park. Seasonal service mid-May through mid-September. Brochure. Princess Tours®, 2815 2nd Ave., Suite #400, Seattle, WA 98121 or call 1-800-835-8907 year-round. [ADVERTISEMENT]

Bus: Daily bus service to the park is available from Anchorage and Fairbanks, and special sightseeing tours are offered throughout the summer months. A 6- to 8-hour guided bus tour of the park is offered by the park concessionaire. Tickets and information are available in the hotel lobby at the front desk tour window.

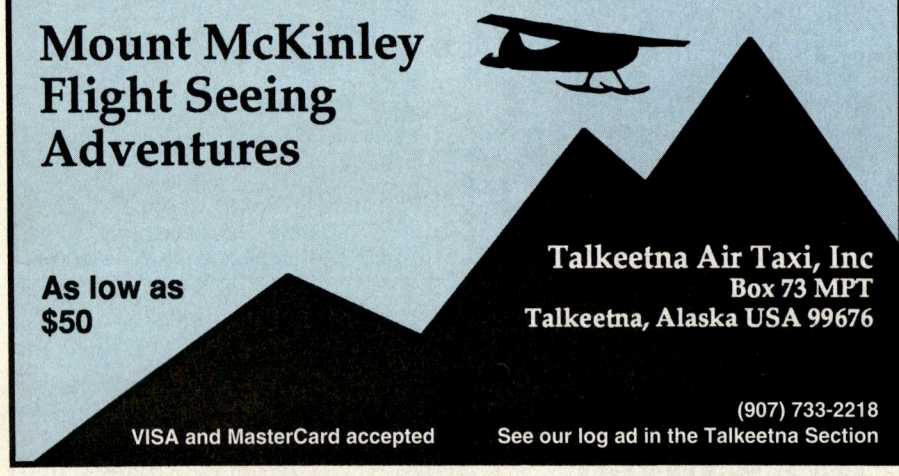

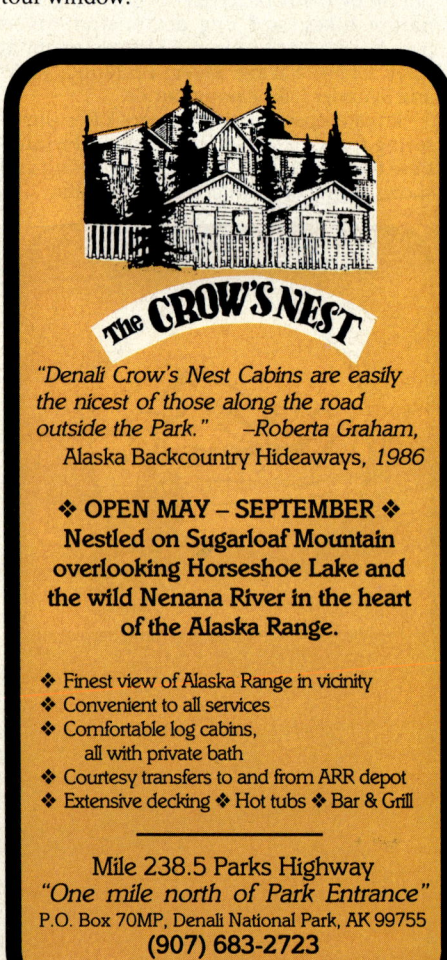

Mount McKinley Flight Seeing Adventures

As low as $50

Talkeetna Air Taxi, Inc
Box 73 MPT
Talkeetna, Alaska USA 99676

(907) 733-2218
See our log ad in the Talkeetna Section

VISA and MasterCard accepted

McKinley KOA Kampground

Grocery - Laundry - Private Showers - Ice
Full Hookups - Reduced Rates for Tent Sites
Picnic Tables - Firepits - Dog Kennels - Pay Phone
Quiet, Hidden Sites - Nightly Recreation Program
Scheduled Transportation available to Denali National Park

(907) 683-2379
(907) 683-2281
or, in Alaska call
1-800-478-AKOA
(478-2562)

Box 340
Healy, AK 99743

**MILE 248.4
George Parks
Highway**

PROPANE SERVICE

THE CROW'S NEST

"Denali Crow's Nest Cabins are easily the nicest of those along the road outside the Park." —Roberta Graham, Alaska Backcountry Hideaways, 1986

❖ **OPEN MAY – SEPTEMBER** ❖
Nestled on Sugarloaf Mountain overlooking Horseshoe Lake and the wild Nenana River in the heart of the Alaska Range.

❖ Finest view of Alaska Range in vicinity
❖ Convenient to all services
❖ Comfortable log cabins, all with private bath
❖ Courtesy transfers to and from ARR depot
❖ Extensive decking ❖ Hot tubs ❖ Bar & Grill

Mile 238.5 Parks Highway
"One mile north of Park Entrance"
P.O. Box 70MP, Denali National Park, AK 99755
**(907) 683-2723
Send for Brochure**

A FEW SPECIAL NOTES FOR VISITORS

The 1980 federal legislation creating a much larger Denali National Park and Preserve also changed some rules and regulations normally followed in most parks. The following list of park rules and regulations apply in the Denali Wilderness Unit—the part of the park that most visitors come to. Contact the Superintendent at Denali (P.O. Box 9, Denali Park, AK 99755) for more information on regulations governing the use of aircraft, firearms, snow machines and motor boats, in the park additions and in the national preserve units.

For those driving: The Park Road was built for scenic enjoyment and not for high speed. Maximum speed is 35 mph except where lower limits are posted. Fast driving is dangerous to you and the wildlife you have come to see.

Your pets and wildlife don't mix. Pets are allowed only on roadways and in campgrounds and must be leashed or under restrictive control at all times. Pets are not allowed on shuttle buses, trails or in the backcountry.

Hikers who stay overnight *must obtain a free backcountry permit* and return it when the trip is completed. Permits available at the Visitor Access Center, **Milepost J 0.5** Park Road.

Mountaineering expeditions are required to register with the superintendent before climbing Mount McKinley or Mount Foraker. At least 2 months' prior notice is recommended. Contact the Talkeetna Ranger Station, P.O. Box 588, Talkeetna, AK 99676; phone (907) 733-2231.

Natural features: The park was established to protect a natural ecosystem. Destroying, defacing or collecting plants, rocks and other features is prohibited. Capturing, molesting or killing any animal is prohibited.

Firearms and hunting are not allowed in the wilderness area.

Fishing licenses are not required in the wilderness area; state law is applicable on all other lands. Limits for each person per day are: lake trout (2 fish); grayling and other fish (10 fish or 10 lbs. and 1 fish). Fishing is poor because most rivers are silty and ponds are shallow.

Motor vehicles of any type, including trail bikes, motorcycles and mopeds, may not leave the Park Road.

Feeding wildlife is prohibited. Wild animals need wild food; your food will not help them.

Park Road Log

Distance from the junction (J) with George Parks Highway is shown.

J 0 (146.4 km) **Junction.** Turn west off the George Parks Highway (Alaska Route 3) at **Milepost A 237.3** onto the Park Road. The Park Road is paved to the Savage River bridge.

J 0.2 (0.3 km) Turnoff for Riley Creek Campground and overflow parking area. A dump station is also located here.

J 0.5 (0.8 km) Visitor Access Center has information on all visitor activities as well as camping and overnight hiking permits. A park orientation program is available in the theater. The center is open 5:45 A.M. to 8 P.M. daily. This is also

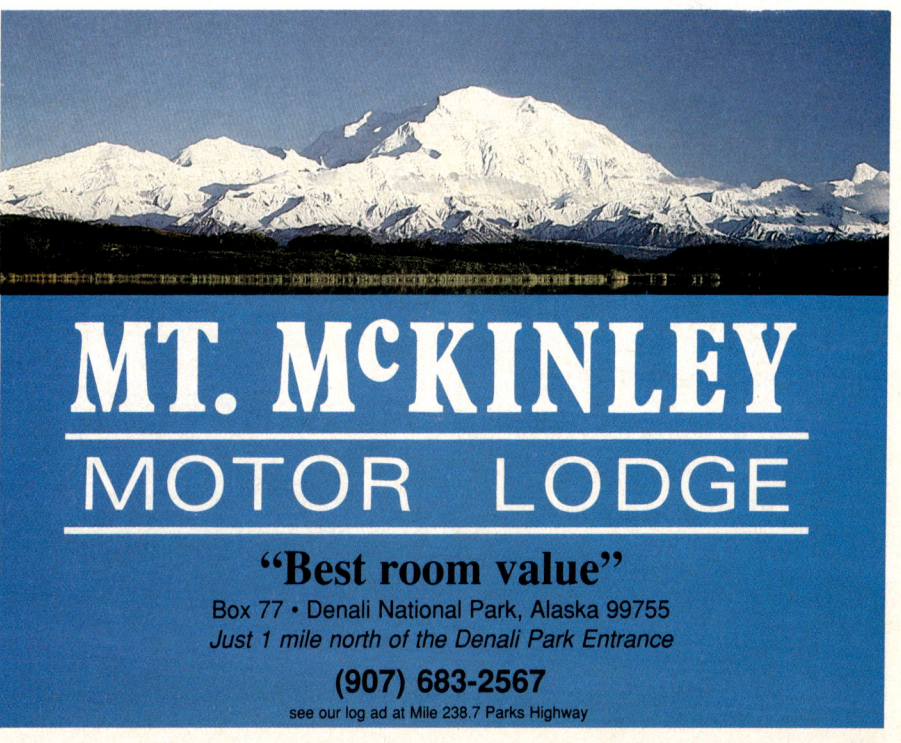

DENALI NATIONAL PARK

DENALI MADE SIMPLE.

If you want to get the most from your visit to Denali, let the travel professionals at Denali National Park Central Reservations & Travel help with all the details.

We can help you plan every part of your trip, from lodging to tours.

And you can contact these expert planners just by calling this toll-free number:
(800) 872-2748.

DENALI NATIONAL PARK
CENTRAL RESERVATIONS AND TRAVEL

---

the PERCH

Fine Dining in a Spectacular Setting

Steaks • Seafood • Full Bar
Fresh Bakery Goods

Open 5-10 p.m. daily (summer)

— CABINS FOR RENT —

See log ad in George Parks Highway Section

Mile 224 Parks Highway • (907) 683-2523

Denali River View Inn

With clear view of the National Park and the sound of the Nenana River.

We have attractive rooms, excellent service & transportation, conveniently located. Please visit us. **MILEPOST 238.4**
907 / 683-2663 • Winter 206 / 384 1078
Box 49M, Denali Park AK 99755
See Log Ad in G.Parks Hwy. Section

MT. McKINLEY MOTOR LODGE

"Best room value"
Box 77 • Denali National Park, Alaska 99755
Just 1 mile north of the Denali Park Entrance

(907) 683-2567
see our log ad at Mile 238.7 Parks Highway

DENALI NATIONAL PARK

Visitors on wildlife tour stop at Mount McKinley viewpoint. (Bruce M. Herman)

the shuttle bus departure point.

J 1.2 (1.9 km) Alaska Railroad crossing. Horseshoe Lake trailhead.

J 1.4 (2.3 km) Gas station, showers and grocery store. No gas available on Park Road beyond this point.

J 1.5 (2.4 km) **Denali National Park Hotel.** Located in Denali National Park, this hotel is the bustling center for visitor activities in the park. Facilities include dining room, snack shop, cocktail lounge, gift shop, grocery store and gas station. The hotel auditorium is the center for national park interpretive services. Wilderness activities include wildlife bus tours, rafting and flightseeing. All arrangements can be made with one call, including accommodations, activities and transportation to and from the park. Phone (907) 276-7234. See display ad this section. [ADVERTISEMENT]

J 1.6 (2.5 km) Denali Park Station (elev. 1,730 feet/527m), the Alaska Railroad station where visitors may make train connections to Anchorage and Fairbanks, daily service during the summer. Denali National Park Hotel is across from the depot. The post office and a flying service office are located in the hotel area.

Private Aircraft: McKinley Park airstrip, 1.7 miles/2.7 km northeast of park headquarters; elev. 1,720 feet/524m; length 3,000 feet/914m; gravel; unattended.

J 3.5 (5.6 km) Park headquarters. This is the administration area for Denali National Park and Preserve. In winter, information on all visitor activities can be obtained here. Parking area for sled dog demonstrations. Report accidents and emergency aid requirements to the chief ranger; phone (907) 683-9100.

J 5.5 (8.9 km) Paved turnout with litter barrel. Sweeping view of countryside. There are numerous small turnouts along the Park Road.

J 12.8 (20.6 km) Savage River Campground (elev. 2,780 feet/847m). Wildlife in the area includes moose, grizzly bear and fox. ▲

J 14.7 (23.7 km) Bridge over the Savage River. Blacktop pavement ends. Access to river, toilet and picnic tables at east end of bridge.

J 14.8 (23.8 km) Savage River check station. PERMIT REQUIRED BEYOND THIS POINT.

NOTE: Road travel permits for access to the Kantishna area are issued at park headquarters only under special conditions.

J 17.3 (27.8 km) Viewpoint of the Alaska Range and tundra.

J 21.3 (34.3 km) Hogan Creek bridge.

J 22 (35.4 km) Sanctuary River bridge, ranger station and campground (tents only). Wildlife: moose, fox, grizzly bear, wolf. ▲

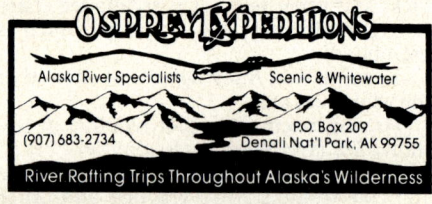

J 29.1 (46.8 km) Teklanika River Campground (elev. 2,580 feet/786m). Grizzly bears may sometimes be seen on the gravel bars nearby. ▲

J 30.7 (49.4 km) Rest stop with chemical toilets.

Denali Raft Adventures
Try it for FUN!

Come with the original Nenana River Rafters

2-, 4- and 6-HOUR TRIPS
Scenic Floats or Whitewater

Prices start at $34
10% off with this ad at our office
Not valid with other discounts

MILE 238.1 Parks Highway
P.O. Drawer 190
Denali National Park, AK 99755
(907) 683-2234
VISA, MasterCard Accepted

BACKWOODS LODGING
See display ad in Cantwell, George Parks Highway section.
Family-sized units • RV hookups
Open Year Around (907) 768-2232
Winter Acitvities' Bookings

OSPREY EXPEDITIONS
Alaska River Specialists — Scenic & Whitewater
(907) 683-2734
P.O. Box 209
Denali Nat'l Park, AK 99755
River Rafting Trips Throughout Alaska's Wilderness

THE VIEW FROM ON TOP OF THE WORLD

There is nowhere on earth like Alaska, and there's no better way to see it than from the safety of an Era Helicopter.

Discover Alaska as the eagles see it. With Era Helicopters, the freedom is yours.

Era Helicopters Flightseeing Tours

Anchorage (907) 248-4422
Juneau (907) 586-2030
Mt. McKinley (907) 683-2574
Valdez (907) 835-2595

J 31.3 (50.4 km) Bridge over Teklanika River.

J 34.1 (54.8 km) Igloo Creek Campground (tents only); accessible by shuttle bus only. Wildlife in the area includes Dall sheep, grizzly bear, moose, fox and wolf. ▲

J 37 (59.5 km) Igloo Creek bridge.

J 39.1 (62.9 km) Sable Pass (elev. 3,900 feet/1,189m). *NOTE: The area within 1 mile/ 1.6 km of each side of the Park Road from Milepost J 38.3 to J 42.9 is closed to all off-road foot travel as a special wildlife protection area.* Toklat grizzlies are often seen in the area.

J 43.4 (69.8 km) Bridge over East Fork Toklat River. Views of Polychrome Mountain, the Alaska Range and several glaciers are visible along the East Fork, from open country south of the road. Wildlife includes Dall sheep, grizzly bear, fox, wolf and caribou.

J 45.9 (73.8 km) Summit of Polychrome Pass (elev. 3,700 feet/1,128m); rest stop with toilets. The broad valley of the Toklat River is visible below to the south. Good hiking in alpine tundra above the road. Wildlife: wolf, grizzly bear, Dall sheep, marmot, pika, eagle and caribou.

J 53.1 (85.4 km) Bridge over the Toklat River. The Toklat and all other streams crossed by the Park Road drain into the Tanana River, a tributary of the Yukon River.

J 53.7 (86.4 km) Ranger station.

J 58.3 (93.8 km) Summit of Highway Pass (elev. 3,980 feet/1,213m). This is the highest point on the Park Road.

J 61 (98.1 km) Stony Hill (elev. 4,508 feet/1,374m). A good view of Mount McKinley and the Alaska Range on clear days. Wildlife: grizzly bear, caribou, fox and birds.

J 62 (99.7 km) Viewpoint.

J 64.5 (103.8 km) Thorofare Pass (elev. 3,900 feet/1,189m).

J 66 (106.2 km) Eielson Visitor Center. Ranger-led hikes, nature programs, displays, restrooms and drinking water. Film, maps and natural history publications for sale. Report accidents and emergencies here.

Excellent Mount McKinley viewpoint. On clear days the north and south peaks of Mount McKinley are visible to the southwest. The impressive glacier, which drops from the mountain and spreads out over the valley floor at this point, is the Muldrow. Wildlife: grizzly bear, wolf, caribou.

For several miles beyond the visitor center the road cut drops about 300 feet/ 91m to the valley below, paralleling the McKinley River.

J 84.6 (136.1 km) Access road leads left, westbound, to Wonder Lake Campground (elev. 2,090 feet/637m). Tents only; campground access by shuttle bus only. An excellent Mount McKinley viewpoint. ▲

The road continues to Wonder Lake, where rafting and canoeing are permitted (no rental boats available). Wildlife: grizzly bear, caribou, moose, beaver, waterfowl.

J 85.6 (137.8 km) Reflection Pond, a kettle lake formed by a glacier.

J 86.6 (139.4 km) Wonder Lake ranger station.

J 87.5 (140.8 km) Picnic area with pit toilets.

J 87.7 (141.1 km) Bridge over Moose Creek.

J 88 (141.6 km) North Face Lodge.

J 88.2 (141.9 km) Camp Denali.

J 91 (146.4 km) **KANTISHNA** (pop. 2 in winter, 135 in summer; elev. 1,750 feet/ 533m). Established in 1905 as a mining camp at the junction of Eureka and Moose creeks. Most of the area around Kantishna is private property and there may be active mining on area creeks in summer. Kantishna Roadhouse, which consists of a dozen log guest cabins and a dining hall, comprises the townsite of Kantishna.

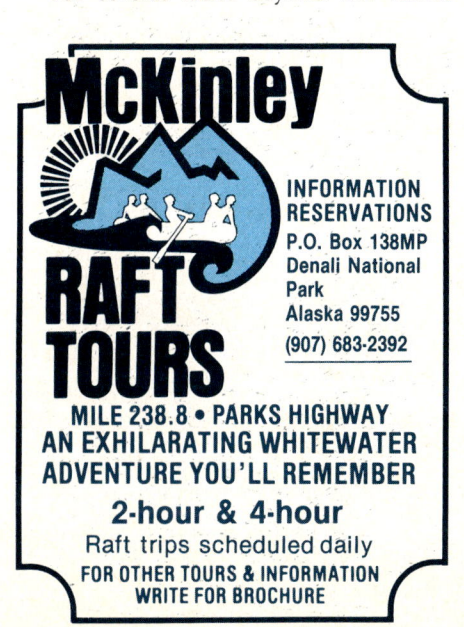

Private Aircraft: Kantishna airstrip, 1.3 miles/2.1 km northwest; elev. 1,575 feet/ 480m; length 1,850 feet/564m; gravel; unscheduled maintenance.

DISCOVER THE PRINCESS DIFFERENCE

DENALI, PRINCESS® STYLE.

Here's the ideal vantage point for exploring Denali National Park; Harper Lodge Princess®, a lodge that combines rustic charm with modern comforts as only Princess can.

It's the perfect starting point for your Denali excursions. And our special packages let you combine a stay at Harper Lodge with a trip on Princess' magnificent Midnight Sun Express®.

To find out more, call:
(800) 426-0500

HARPER LODGE
PRINCESS

McKinley RAFT TOURS

INFORMATION
RESERVATIONS
P.O. Box 138MP
Denali National Park
Alaska 99755
(907) 683-2392

MILE 238.8 • PARKS HIGHWAY
AN EXHILARATING WHITEWATER ADVENTURE YOU'LL REMEMBER

2-hour & 4-hour
Raft trips scheduled daily
FOR OTHER TOURS & INFORMATION
WRITE FOR BROCHURE

Experience McKinley

SCENIC FLIGHTS • GLACIER LANDINGS
FLY-IN HUNTING & FISHING
DENALI OVERNIGHT ADVENTURE TRIANGLE

Jim & Julie Okonek
(907) 733-2291 • FAX (907) 733-1221
See our log ad in the Talkeetna section under Attractions

K2 aviation
Box 545
Talkeetna, Alaska 99676

DENALI HIGHWAY

Paxson, Alaska, to Cantwell, Alaska
Alaska Route 8

Sunset is reflected on mountain and lake near Milepost 82. (Jerrianne Lowther, staff)

The Denali Highway extends 135.5 miles/218.1 km from Paxson at **Milepost V 185.5** on the Richardson Highway to Cantwell, about 2 miles/3.2 km west of **Milepost A 209.9** on the George Parks Highway. The first 21 miles/33.8 km from Paxson are paved and the rest is gravel. The highway is closed from October to mid-May.

The condition of the gravel portion of the highway varies, depending on highway maintenance, weather and the opinion of the driver. The road surface is rough and washboard can develop quickly. Much of the road is in need of gravel, but the roadbed is solid. This can be a dusty and bumpy drive in dry weather. Watch for potholes in wet weather.

There are dozens of informal campsites and turnouts along the highway (heavily used by hunters in the fall). Excellent fishing in lakes and streams accessible on foot or via designated off-road vehicle trails. There are also many unmarked trails leading off into the Bush. Inquire locally and carry a good topographic map before hiking off the highway.

The Denali Highway has very beautiful scenery and some interesting geography. Glacier-formed features visible from the road include: moraines (drift deposited by glaciers); kames (conical hills or terraces of gravel and sand); kettle lakes (holes formed by blocks of ice melting) and eskers (ridges of gravel formed by streams flowing under glaciers).

More than 400 archaeological sites lie in the Tangle Lakes Archeological District between **Mileposts 15** and **45**. To protect this delicate area, the BLM has restricted summer ORV use to 9 signed trails. (Winter use is unrestricted when adequate snow cover exists.) Information and maps are available from the BLM office in Glennallen; phone (907) 822-3219, or write Box 147, Glennallen 99588.

The Denali Highway was the only road link to Denali National Park and Preserve (formerly Mount McKinley National Park) prior to completion of the George Parks Highway in 1972. Before the Denali Highway opened in 1957, Denali National Park was accessible only via the Alaska Railroad.

Emergency medical services: Between Paxson and Milepost P 78 (Susitna Lodge), phone 911 or the state troopers at 822-3263. Between **Milepost P 78** and Cantwell, phone the Cantwell ambulance at 768-2982, the fire department at 768-2240, or the state troopers at 768-2202.

Denali Highway Log

Distance from Paxson (P) is followed by distance from Cantwell (C).

P 0   C 135.5 (218.1 km) **PAXSON** (pop. 33; elev. 2,650 feet/808m). A lodge with restaurant, gas station, post office and small grocery store is located here. Wildlife often seen near here: grizzly bear, moose and porcupine.

Private Aircraft: Paxson airstrip, adjacent south; elev. 2,653 feet/809m; length 2,200 feet/671m; gravel; fuel 80, 100.

P 0   C 135.5 (218.1) **Paxson Lodge.** See display ad this section.

P 0.2 (0.3 km) **C 135.3** (217.7 km) Gulkana River bridge; parking at west end. In season, spawning salmon may be seen here. This portion of the Gulkana River is off-limits to salmon fishing.

P 0.3 (0.5 km) **C 135.2** (217.6 km) Entering Paxson Closed Area westbound. This area is closed to the taking of all big game. Side road leads south to Mud Lake.

Westbound, there are many long steep upgrades and many turnouts the next 13 miles/21 km. Wildflowers carpet the tundra in the spring and summer.

P 1.1 (1.8 km) **C 134.4** (216.3 km) **Mud Lake** below highway; grayling fishing.

P 3.6 (5.8 km) **C 131.9** (212.3 km) Paved turnout to south. Several more turnouts the next 2.5 miles/4 km with views of Summit Lake to the north. Gakona Glacier to the northeast and Icefall Peak to the west of the glacier. West of Icefall Peak is Gulkana Glacier.

P 6.8 (10.9 km) **C 128.7** (207.1 km) Access to **Sevenmile Lake** 0.8 mile/1.3 km north; excellent fishing for lake trout in summer.

P 7.3 (11.7 km) **C 128.2** (206.3 km) Gravel turnout overlooking Sevenmile Lake. Two Bit Lake is the large lake to the north; Summit Lake is to the northeast.

P 7.5 (12.1 km) **C 128** (206 km) Paved turnout overlooking Sevenmile Lake.

P 8.2 (13.2 km) **C 127.3** (204.9 km) Paved turnout overlooking small lakes in Hungry Hollow to the south.

P 9 (14.5 km) **C 126.5** (203.6 km) Gravel turnout. Entering BLM public lands westbound.

P 10.1 (16.3 km) **C 125.4** (201.7 km) Paved turnout to south overlooking **Ten Mile Lake**. Short hike downhill to outlet. Fishing for lake trout, grayling and

---

PAXSON LODGE
ROOMS WITH BATH
CHEVRON • RESTAURANT
GIFTS • LIQUOR
At Jct. of Richardson & Denali
See display ad in Richardson Highway section

DENALI HIGHWAY *Paxson AK, to Cantwell, AK*

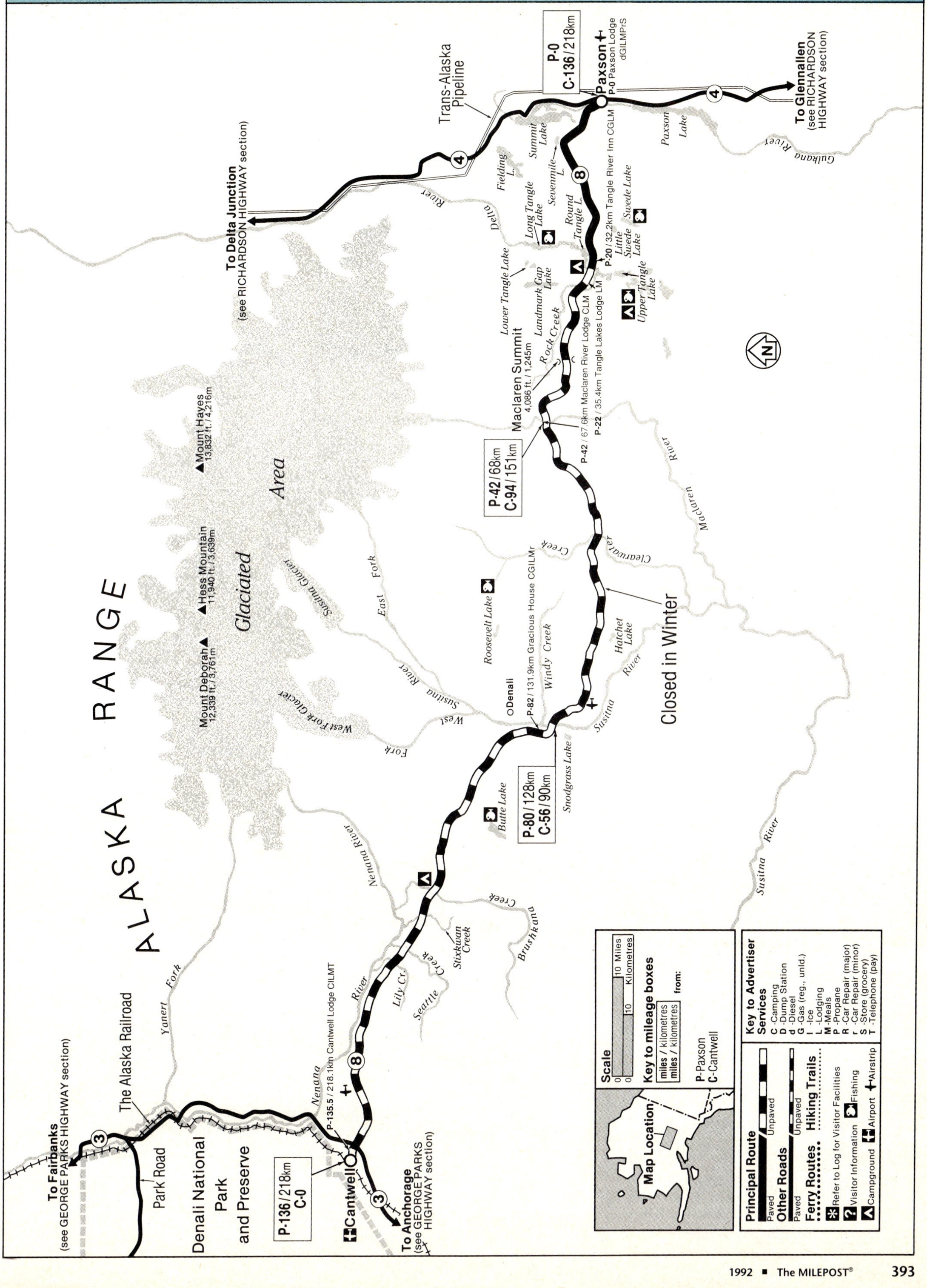

burbot in summer.

P 10.6 (17.1 km) **C 124.9** (201 km) Paved turnout overlooking **Teardrop Lake** to south. Short hike down steep hill to lake; lake trout, grayling and burbot in summer.

For the next 4 miles/6.4 km westbound there are wide-open spaces with magnificent views of the great Denali country.

P 11 (17.7 km) **C 124.5** (200.4 km) Paved turnout and trail to **Octopus Lake** 0.3 mile/0.5 km south; lake trout, grayling.

P 13.1 (21.1 km) **C 122.4** (197 km) Viewpoint at summit. In the spring from this spot a traveler can count at least 40 lakes and potholes. To the southeast are Mount Sanford, Mount Drum and Mount Wrangell in the Wrangell Mountain range.

Highway begins descent westbound to Tangle Lakes area. Lupine blooms alongside the road in late June.

P 15.1 (24.3 km) **C 120.4** (193.8 km) Fourteenmile Lake lies about 1.5 miles/2.4 km north of the highway, beyond 8 smaller ponds.

P 16.8 (27 km) **C 118.7** (191 km) **16.8 Mile Lake** to north (walk up creek 200 yards); lake trout and grayling. **Rusty Lake**, 0.5 mile/0.8 km northwest of 16.8 Mile Lake; lake trout and grayling. Swede Lake trail, 3 miles/4.8 km long, to south; **Little Swede Lake**, 2 miles/3.2 km. This trail connects with the Middle Fork Gulkana River branch trail (access to Dickey Lake and Meier Lake trail) and the Alphabet Hills trail. **Big Swede Lake** has excellent fishing for lake trout, grayling and burbot. Little Swede Lake excellent for lake trout. Inquire at Tangle River Inn for directions.

P 17 (27.4 km) **C 118.5** (190.7 km) **17 Mile Lake** to north, turnout at west end of lake; lake trout and grayling fishing.

P 18.4 (29.6 km) **C 117.1** (188.4 km) Gravel turnout by **Denali–Clearwater Creek**; grayling fishing.

P 20 (32.2 km) **C 115.5** (185.9 km) **Tangle River Inn.** See display ad this section.

P 20.1 (32.3 km) **C 115.4** (185.7 km) Large paved turnout to north overlooking lake.

P 20.6 (33.2 km) **C 114.9** (184.9 km) Paved parking area with toilets to north.

P 21 (33.8 km) **C 114.5** (184.3 km) The Nelchina caribou herd travels through this area, usually around the end of August or early in September.

P 21.3 (34.3 km) **C 114.2** (183.9 km) Pavement ends westbound.

P 21.4 (34.4 km) **C 114.1** (183.6 km) One-lane bridge over Tangle River.

P 21.5 (34.6 km) **C 114** (183.5 km) Tangle Lakes BLM campground and wayside, 0.7 mile/1.1 km north from highway on shore of Round Tangle Lake; 13 sites, toilets, boat launch, picnic area.

Access to Delta River canoe trail, which goes north through Tangle Lakes to the Delta River. The Delta National Wild, Scenic and Recreational River system is managed by the BLM. For details on the trail, contact the Bureau of Land Management, Box 147, Glennallen 99588; phone (907) 822-3217.

Watershed divide. The Gulkana River joins the Copper River, which flows into Prince William Sound. The Delta River joins the Tanana River, which flows into the Yukon River. The Yukon flows into the Bering Sea.

P 21.7 (34.9 km) **C 113.8** (183.1 km) Tangle River BLM campground; toilets, water pump, boat launch. Watch for caribou on surrounding hills.

The name Tangle is a descriptive term for the maze of lakes and feeder streams contained in this drainage system. Access to Upper Tangle Lakes canoe trail, which goes south through Tangle Lakes (portages required) to Dickey Lake, then follows the Middle Fork to the main Gulkana River.

AREA FISHING: Tangle Lakes system north and south of the highway (**Long Tangle, Round Tangle, Upper Tangle** and **Lower Tangle Lake**). Good grayling and lake trout fishing. Fishing begins as soon as the ice goes out, usually about mid-June, and continues into September. Good trolling and some fish are taken from the banks. Inquire locally for information and assistance in getting to where the fish are.

P 22 (35.4 km) **C 113.5** (182.6 km) **Tangle Lakes Lodge.** See display ad this section.

P 24.8 (39.9 km) **C 110.7** (178.2 km) Landmark Gap BLM trail to north. *NOTE: Off-road vehicles prohibited on last mile of trail to protect archaeological sites.* Mountain biking is popular on this trail.

P 24.9 (40 km) **C 110.6** (178 km) **Rock Creek** 1-lane bridge; parking and informal campsites both ends of bridge. Fair grayling fishing. Landmark Gap Lake lies north of highway between the noticeable gap in the mountains (a caribou migration route).

P 28.1 (45.2 km) **C 107.4** (172.8 km) Downwind Lake north side of road.

P 30.6 (49.2 km) **C 104.9** (168.8 km) Cat

Beaver eat succulent plants and the bark of shrubs and trees. (John W. Warden)

Tangle River Inn

Cafe • Bar • Gas • Gifts
Lodging • Liquor • Canoe Rentals
RV Hookups • Showers

Rooms $39 Double

Fishing • Hunting
Hunting and Fishing Licenses
Fishing Equipment

WINTER SUMMER
(907) 895-4022 • (907) 895-4439

Write: Mile 20, Denali Highway
Paxson, Alaska 99737

Tangle Lakes Lodge

Mile 22 Denali Highway

Fine Dining and Cocktails
Cabins • Fly-Fishing Gear
Fishing Trips • Canoe Rentals
Birding and Photography Tours

(907) 688-9173
P.O. Box 670386, Chugiak, Alaska 99567

Maclaren River Lodge Est. 1956

- SIGHT-SEEING
- GLACIER TRIPS
- PHOTOGRAPHY
- BIRD WATCHING

FISHING
RAFT TRIPS

- CAMPING
- HUNTING
- HIKING
- PROSPECTING

Bears • Moose • Caribou • Flowers • Berries • Northern Lights

EXPERIENCE THE REAL ALASKA!
RV/Camping Area • Rustic Cabins • Rooms • Restaurant • Bar

WILDERNESS TRIPS
Complete Tour Packages from Anchorage, Alaska Available
RV Rental Package

Open May 15th through September • Reserve Early - Call (907) 277-2127 for information

Mile 42 Denali Highway • Paxson, Alaska 99737

trail leads 2 miles/3.2 km north to **Glacier Lake**; lake trout, grayling.

P 32 (51.5 km) **C 103.5** (166.6 km) Amphitheater Mountains rise above High Valley to the north. Glacier Lake is visible in the gap in these mountains.

P 35.2 (56.6 km) **C 100.3** (161.4 km) Turnout at Maclaren Summit (elev. 4,086 feet/1,245m). Highest highway pass in Alaska (not including 4,800-foot/1,463-m Atigun Pass on the Dalton Highway, formerly the North Slope Haul Road). A profusion of flowers—notably the various heaths and frigid shooting star.

P 36 (57.9 km) **C 99.5** (160.1 km) **36 Mile Lake** 0.5-mile/0.6-km hike north; lake trout and grayling.

P 36.4 (58.6 km) **C 99.1** (159.5 km) Entering Clearwater Creek controlled-use area westbound. Closed to motorized hunting.

P 37 (59.5 km) **C 98.5** (158.5 km) Turnout with view of Susitna River valley, Mount Hayes and the Alaska Range. Osar Lake trail leads 5 miles/8 km south toward the Alphabet Hills, Maclaren Summit trail leads 3 miles/4.8 km north to good view of Alaska Range; mountain biking. Osar Lake was first named Asar Lake, the Scandinavian word for esker.

P 39.8 (64.1 km) **C 95.7** (154 km) Seven-mile Lake ORV trail to north; 6.5 miles/10.5 km long, parallels Boulder Creek, crosses peat bog.

P 42 (67.6 km) **C 93.5** (150.5 km) Maclaren River and bridge, a 364-foot/111-m multiple span crossing this tributary of the Susitna River. Parking and litter barrels. Maclaren River Lodge west side. Look for cliff swallows nesting under bridge.

Maclaren River Lodge. See display ad this section.

The Maclaren River rises in the glaciers surrounding Mount Hayes (elev. 13,832 feet/4,216m). For the next 60 miles/96.5 km westbound, the highest peaks of this portion of the mighty Alaska Range are visible, weather permitting, to the north. From east to west: Mount Hayes, Hess Mountain (elev. 11,940 feet/3,639m) and Mount Deborah (elev. 12,339 feet/3,761m). Mount Hayes, first climbed in August 1941, is named after Charles Hayes, an early member of the U.S. Geological Survey. Mount Deborah, first climbed in August 1954, was named in 1907 by Judge Wickersham after his wife.

P 43.5 (70 km) **C 92** (148 km) Maclaren River Road leads north 12 miles/17 km to Maclaren Glacier; mountain biking. Maclaren River trailhead to south.

P 44.2 (71.1 km) **C 91.3** (146.9 km) Small turnout to south. Beaver lodge and dam.

P 44.7 (71.9 km) **C 90.8** (146.1 km) Highway crosses Crazy Notch gap.

P 46.9 (75.5 km) **C 88.6** (142.6 km) Road north to **46.9 Mile Lake**; fishing for grayling in lake and outlet stream.

P 47.2 (76 km) **C 88.3** (142.1 km) Beaver dam. Excellent grayling fishing in **Crooked Creek** which parallels the highway.

P 48.4 (77.9 km) **C 87.1** (140.2 km) Informal campsite by small lake.

P 49.5 (79.6 km) **C 86** (138.4 km) The road follows an esker between 4 lakes. Parts of the highway are built on eskers, ridges of sand and gravel that mark the former stream channels of glaciers. Watch for ptarmigan, swans, arctic terns, ducks and beaver.

P 51.6 (83 km) **C 83.9** (135 km) Private hunting camp to south. Trail to north.

P 55.9 (89.9 km) **C 79.6** (128.1 km) **Clearwater Creek** 1-lane bridge and rest area with toilets and litter barrels. Informal camping. Cliff swallows nest under bridge. Grayling fishing in summer.

P 58.2 (93.6 km) **C 77.3** (124.4 km) Clearwater Creek walk-in (no motorized vehicles) hunting area north of highway.

P 58.8 (94.6 km) **C 76.7** (123.4 km) Road winds atop an esker flanked by kames and kettle lakes. Watch for moose.

P 64 (103 km) **C 69.6** (112 km) Road descends westbound into Susitna Valley. Highest elevation of mountains seen to north is 5,670 feet/1,728m.

P 65.7 (105.7 km) **C 69.8** (112.3 km) Waterfall Creek.

P 68.9 (110.9 km) **C 66.6** (107.2 km) Raft Creek. Hatchet Lake lies about 2 miles/3.2 km south of highway. Inquire at Gracious House, **Milepost P 82**, for directions.

P 71.5 (115 km) **C 64** (103 km) Moose often sighted in valley below road.

P 72.2 (116.2 km) **C 63.3** (101.9 km) Nowater Creek.

P 72.8 (117.2 km) **C 62.7** (100.9 km) Swampbuggy Lake.

P 75 (120.7 km) **C 60.5** (97.4 km) Clearwater Mountains to north; watch for bears on slopes. View of Susitna River in valley below.

P 77.5 (124.7 km) **C 58** (93.3 km) Susitna Lodge (status unknown).

Private Aircraft: Susitna Lodge airstrip (private), adjacent west; elev. 2,675 feet/815m; length 2,000 feet/610m; gravel.

P 78.8 (126.8 km) **C 56.7** (91.2 km) Valdez Creek Road. Former mining camp of Denali, about 6 miles/10 km north of the highway via a gravel road, was first established in 1907. Active mining area; watch for large trucks and equipment on road. Do not trespass on private mining claims. Fair fishing reported in **Roosevelt Lake** and area creeks. Watch for bears.

P 79.5 (127.9 km) **C 56** (90.1 km) Susitna River 1-lane bridge, a combination multiple span and deck truss, 1,036 feet/316m long. The Susitna River heads at Susitna Glacier in the Alaska Range (between Mounts Hess and Hayes) and flows southwest 260 miles/418 km to Cook Inlet. Downstream through Devil's Canyon it is considered unfloatable. The river's Tanaina Indian name, said to mean "sandy river," first appeared in 1847 on a Russian chart.

Entering Game Management Unit 13E westbound, leaving unit 13B eastbound.

P 81 (130.3 km) **C 54.5** (87.7 km) Snodgrass Lake (elev. 2,493 feet/760m) is about 2 miles/3.2 km south of the highway. Check with Gracious House, **Milepost P 82**, for directions.

P 82 (131.9 km) **C 53.5** (86.1 km) **Gracious House.** Centrally located on the shortest, most scenic route to Denali National Park. Modern cabins, motel units with private baths, bunkhouse, bar, cafe featuring ice cream and home-baked pies. Chevron products, towing, welding, mechanical repairs, tire service. Air taxi, track vehicles, guide service available in a variety of combinations serving the sportsman, tourist, photographer, families with tours and outings to individual desires, from campouts to guided hunts. Tent sites, parking for self-contained RVs. Restrooms and showers. Bar. Same owners/operators for 34 years. Reasonable rates. For brochure on hunting and fishing trips. Write to the Gracious Family.

THE DENALI HIGHWAY

SEE THE REAL ALASKA

GAS • ROOMS • CAFE • BAR

Nicest rooms on the Denali Highway Complete with or without private baths.

The most direct and scenic route to Denali National Park (a 2-hour drive from the Park)

MILE 82 DENALI HIGHWAY

GRACIOUS HOUSE LODGE & FLYING SERVICE

"BUTCH" AND CAROL GRATIAS
BOX 88, Cantwell, AK 99729
(907) 333-3148

Sail-like dorsal fin distinguishes grayling from other trout. (Joe Prax)

Summer address: P.O. Box 88, Cantwell, AK 99729. Winter address: 859 Elaine Dr., Anchorage, AK 99504. Phone (907) 333-3148. [ADVERTISEMENT] ▲

P 83 (133.5 km) **C 52.5** (84.5 km) Watch for horses. Visible across the Susitna River is Valdez Creek mining camp at the old Denali townsite.

P 84 (135.2 km) **C 51.5** (82.9 km) **Stevenson's Lake** 0.5 mile/0.8 km south; grayling fishing.

P 88.7 (142.7 km) **C 46.8** (75.3 km) Large turnout by pond. Good stop for pictures of the Alaska Range (weather permitting).

P 90.5 (145.6 km) **C 45** (72.4 km) A major water drainage divide occurs near here. East of the divide, the tributary river system of the Susitna flows south to Cook Inlet. West of the divide, the Nenana River system flows north to the Yukon River, which empties into the Bering Sea.

P 91.2 (146.8 km) **C 44.3** (71.3 km) Turnout and access to small lake beside road.

P 93.8 (151 km) **C 41.7** (67.1 km) **Butte Lake**, 5 miles/8 km south of highway. Motorized access by tracked vehicle. Best fishing June through September. Lake trout to 30 lbs., troll with red-and-white spoons or grayling remains; grayling to 20 inches, small flies or spinners; burbot to 12 lbs., use bait on bottom.

P 94.3 (151.8 km) **C 41.2** (66.3 km) Short road leads to parking area above pond. View of Monahan Flat and Alaska Range to the north.

P 94.8 (152.5 km) **C 40.7** (65.5 km) Bridge over Canyon Creek.

P 96.1 (154.6 km) **C 39.4** (63.4 km) Good viewpoint of the West Fork Glacier. Looking north up the face of this glacier, Mount Deborah is to the left and Mount Hess is in the center.

P 97 (156.1 km) **C 38.5** (62 km) Looking at the Alaska Range to the north, Mount Deborah, Mount Hess and Mount Hayes are the highest peaks to your right; to the left are the lower peaks of the Alaska Range and Mount Nenana.

P 99.4 (160 km) **C 34.2** (55 km) Lodge (closed in 1991; current status unknown).

P 100 (160.9 km) **C 35.5** (57.1 km) Residents of this area say it is a wonderful place for picking cranberries and blueberries in August.

P 103 (165.8 km) **C 32.5** (52.3 km) Highway is built on an esker between kettle lakes.

P 104.6 (168.3 km) **C 30.9** (49.7 km) **Brushkana River** bridge and BLM campground; 12 sites beside river, tables, firepits, toilets, litter barrels and water. Fishing for grayling and Dolly Varden. Watch for moose.

P 106.6 (171.6 km) **C 28.9** (46.5 km) **Canyon Creek**, grayling fishing.

P 107.2 (172.5 km) **C 28.3** (45.5 km) Stixkwan Creek flows under highway in culvert.

P 111.2 (179 km) **C 24.3** (39.1 km) **Seattle Creek** 1-lane bridge. Fishing for grayling and Dolly Varden.

P 112 (180.2 km) **C 23.5** (37.8 km) Lily Creek. Matanuska–Susitna Borough boundary.

P 113.2 (182.2 km) **C 22.3** (35.9 km) View to east of the Alaska Range and extensive rolling hills grazed by caribou.

P 115.7 (186.2 km) **C 19.8** (31.9 km) Large gravel turnout with beautiful view of the Nenana River area.

P 117.1 (188.4 km) **C 18.4** (29.6 km) Log cabin beside Nenana River.

P 117.5 (189.1 km) **C 18** (29 km) Leaving BLM public lands westbound.

P 117.7 (189.4 km) **C 17.8** (28.6 km) Highway parallels the Nenana River, which flows into the Tanana River at the town of Nenana.

P 120 (193 km) **C 15.5** (24.9 km) A variety of small water birds, including ducks, snipes and terns, can be observed in the marshy areas along both sides of the road for the next 1 mile/1.6 km westbound.

P 122.3 (196.8 km) **C 11.3** (18.2 km) View (westbound) of Mount McKinley.

P 125.7 (202.3 km) **C 9.8** (15.8 km) **Joe Lake**, about 0.5 mile/0.8 km long (large enough for floatplane), is south of highway. **Jerry Lake** is about 0.2 mile/0.3 km north of the highway. Two small turnouts provide room for campers and fishermen. Both lakes have grayling.

P 128.1 (206.2 km) **C 7.4** (11.9 km) Fish Creek bridge. Access to creek and informal campsite at east end of bridge.

P 128.2 (206.3 km) **C 7.3** (11.7 km) Beautiful view of Talkeetna Mountains to the south.

P 128.6 (206.9 km) **C 6.9** (11.1 km) Small pond just off highway. Good berry picking in the fall. Fishing for grayling in unnamed creek.

P 130.3 (209.7 km) **C 5.2** (8.3 km) The small town of Cantwell, nestled at the foot of the mountains, can be seen across a long, timbered valley dotted with lakes. Excellent view of Mount McKinley, weather permitting.

P 131.5 (211.6 km) **C 4** (6.4 km) **Private Aircraft:** Golden North landing strip 0.5 mile/0.8 km to right of highway; elev. 2,250 feet/686m; length 2,100 feet/640m; gravel; fuel 80, 100.

P 132 (212.4 km) **C 3.5** (5.6 km) Good grayling fishing in stream beside road.

P 133 (214 km) **C 2.4** (4 km) Cantwell Station highway maintenance camp.

P 133.1 (214.2 km) **C 2.4** (3.9 km) Junction with old Anchorage–Fairbanks Highway; turn right westbound for Alaska State Troopers complex located approximately 0.2 mile/0.3 km north on left side of road.

P 133.7 (215.2 km) **C 1.8** (2.9 km) Junction of Denali and George Parks highways. Cantwell post office and school, a lodge, restaurant, mini-grocery, gas stations and gift shop are located here. Continue straight ahead 2 miles/3.2 km for the original town of Cantwell. Turn left (south) for Anchorage or right (north) for Denali National Park and Fairbanks. See **Milepost A 209.9** in the GEORGE PARKS HIGHWAY section for details.

Cantwell

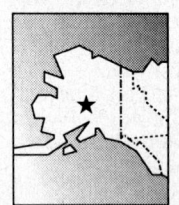

P 135.5 (218.1 km) **C 0** Western terminus of the Denali Highway. **Population:** 91. **Emergency Services: Alaska State Troopers,** phone 768-2202. **Fire,** phone 768-2240. **Ambulance,** phone 768-2982. **Elevation:** 2,190 feet/667m. **Television:** Channels 2 and 9.

Private Aircraft: Cantwell airport, adjacent north; elev. 2,190 feet/667m; length 2,100 feet/640m; gravel; fuel, 80, 100.

Cantwell began as a railroad flag stop between Seward on Prince William Sound and Fairbanks on the Chena River. The Alaska Railroad now serves Cantwell several times a week on its Anchorage to Fairbanks run during summer. The village was named for the Cantwell River, which is the former name of the Nenana River.

Cantwell's newer businesses are located at the intersection of the Denali and George Parks highways. Cantwell Lodge, with cafe, bar and laundry is located in the older section of Cantwell, along the railroad tracks.

Cantwell Lodge. See display ad this section.

Cantwell Lodge
CAFE — BAR — LIQUOR STORE
Rooms with or without baths
At the end of the road
Mile 135.5 Denali Highway
See display ad in George Parks Highway Section

ALASKA RAILROAD

(See maps, pages 317–318 and 412)

The Alaska Railroad operates year-round passenger and freight service between Anchorage and Fairbanks, Portage and Whittier. In summer, passenger service is daily between Anchorage and Fairbanks via Denali Park; Portage and Whittier; and between Anchorage and Seward. Reduced service in winter. For additional information on the Alaska Railroad, write Passenger Services Dept., P.O. Box 107500, Anchorage, AK 99510.

Construction of the railroad began in 1915 under Pres. Woodrow Wilson. On July 15, 1923, Pres. Warren G. Harding drove the golden spike at Nenana, signifying completion of the railroad. The main line extends from Seward to Fairbanks, approximately 470 miles/756 km.

Following are services, schedules and fares available on Alaska Railroad routes. Keep in mind that schedules and fares are subject to change without notice.

ANCHORAGE–DENALI PARK– FAIRBANKS (Express Service)

Passenger service between Anchorage, Denali Park and Fairbanks is offered daily from May 20 to Sept. 20, 1992. The express service operates with a food service car, a vista-dome for all passengers to share, and coaches with comfortable reclining seats. Travel along the 350-mile route between Anchorage and Fairbanks is at a leisurely pace with comfortable window seats and good views of the countryside.

Luxury rail cars are available on the Anchorage–Denali Park–Fairbanks route through Gray Line of Alaska (Holland America Line/Westours) and Princess Tours. These 2 tour companies operate (respectively) the *McKinley Explorer* and *Midnight Sun Express*. Both cars, which are coupled on to the end of the regular Alaska Railroad train, are glass-domed and offer gourmet cuisine along with other amenities. Higher priced than the regular Alaska Railroad cars, tickets are sold on a space-available basis. Packages with a Denali Park overnight are also available. Contact Princess (800-835-8907) or Gray Line (800-544-2206) for details.

The summer schedule is: Northbound express trains depart Anchorage at 8:30 A.M., arrive Denali Park at 3:50 P.M., and arrive Fairbanks at 8:30 P.M. Southbound express trains depart Fairbanks at 8:30 A.M., arrive Denali Park at 12:30 P.M., and arrive Anchorage at 8:30 P.M.

One-way fares are as follows: Anchorage-Denali Park, $85; Fairbanks-Denali Park, $45; Anchorage–Fairbanks, with or without Denali Park stopover, $115. Children aged 2 through 11 ride for approximately half-fare, under 2 ride free.

During fall, winter and spring, weekend-only rail service is provided between Anchorage and Fairbanks, with a self-propelled rail diesel car. The railcar travels from Anchorage to Fairbanks on Saturday and returns on Sunday.

Reservations: Reservations should be made 40 days prior to travel. Write the Alaska Railroad, Passenger Services Dept., P.O. Box 107500, Anchorage, AK 99510; or phone 1-800-544-0552 or (907) 265-2623. Your letter should include the dates you plan to travel, point of departure and destination, the number of people in your party and your home phone number. Tickets may be purchased in advance by mail if you desire.

Baggage: Each adult is allowed 3 pieces of luggage to a maximum weight of 150 lbs. Children are allowed 2 pieces of baggage to a maximum weight of 75 lbs. Excess baggage may be checked for a nominal fee. Bicycles are accepted for a charge of $20 on a space-available basis on the day of travel. Keep in mind that baggage, including backpacks, must be checked before boarding and it is not accessible during the trip. Canoes, motors, motorcycles, items weighing over 150 lbs., etc., are not accepted for transportation on passenger trains. These items are shipped via freight train.

LOCAL SERVICE

Local rural service between Anchorage and Hurricane Gulch operates Wednesday, Saturday and Sunday each week between May 20 and Sept. 20, 1992. This 1-day trip takes you past breathtaking views of Mount McKinley into some remote areas and provides an opportunity to meet local residents who use the train for access. Local service uses self-propelled rail diesel cars and has vending machine snacks available.

PORTAGE–WHITTIER

The Portage–Whittier shuttle train carries passengers and vehicles between Portage on the Seward Highway and Whittier on Prince William Sound. Portage, which has no facilities other than the railroad's vehicle loading ramp, is 47 miles/75 km south of Anchorage at **Milepost S 80.3** Seward Highway. Whittier, on Prince William Sound, is port to the Alaska Marine Highway's ferry MV *Bartlett*, which provides passenger and vehicle service to Cordova and Valdez. The Portage–Whittier railway line is 12.4 miles long, includes 2 tunnels (one 13,090 feet/3,990m long, the other 4,910 feet/1,497m long). Called the Whittier Cutoff, the line was constructed in 1942-43 as a safeguard for the flow of military supplies. It is a 35-minute train ride.

The shuttle makes several round-trips daily between Portage and Whittier, from mid-May through mid-September, connecting with Alaska Marine Highway ferry sailings and other vessels which operate between Whittier and Valdez. (Remember that ferry tickets are purchased separately from train tickets; see MARINE ACCESS ROUTES section, Southwest Ferry System.)

Train tickets for the Whittier shuttle may be purchased from ticket sellers at Portage. Reservations are not accepted for the shuttle train, although passengers with confirmed ferry connections are given priority boarding on the 1:20 P.M. shuttle between Portage and Whittier, if vehicles are at Portage by no later than 12:30 P.M. Standard vehicles under 24 feet in length are charged $70, round-trip between Portage and Whittier; includes driver fare. Other adult passengers in the vehicle are charged $16 round-trip; children (2 to 11 years of age) are $8 round-trip. Vehicle rates are based upon length. Some height and width restrictions apply.

During fall, winter and spring, service to Whittier is provided on Wednesday, Friday, Saturday and Sunday.

ANCHORAGE–SEWARD

Rail passenger service between Anchorage and Seward operates daily between May 22 and Sept. 7, 1992. (Weekend service to Seward is available Sept. 12-13, 19-20 and 26-27, 1992.) The 230-mile excursion follows Turnagain Arm south from Anchorage and passes through some of the most beautiful scenery to be found on the railroad. Travel is aboard self-propelled rail diesel car equipment. Food service is not available. Departs Anchorage at 7 A.M., arrives Seward at 11 A.M. The return trip departs Seward at 6 P.M., arriving Anchorage at 10 P.M. Reservations are required. The round-trip fare is $70 for adults. Overnight tours which include hotel and Resurrection Bay boat excursions are available from the railroad ticket office.

The Alaska Railroad between Anchorage and Fairbanks. (John W. Warden)

STEESE HIGHWAY

Fairbanks, Alaska, to Circle, Alaska
Alaska Routes 2 and 6
Includes logs of Chena Hot Springs Road and Circle Hot Springs Road

Display at Milepost F 8.4 explains history of Alaska pipeline. (Jerrianne Lowther, staff)

The Steese Highway connects Fairbanks with Chena Hot Springs (61.5 miles/99 km) via Chena Hot Springs Road; the town of Central (127.5 miles/205.2 km); Circle Hot Springs (136.1 miles/219 km) via Circle Hot Springs Road; and with Circle, a small settlement 162 miles/260.7 km to the northeast on the Yukon River and 50 miles/80.5 km south of the Arctic Circle. The scenery alone makes this a worthwhile drive.

The first 44 miles/70.8 km of the Steese Highway are paved. Beyond this it is good wide gravel road into Central, where there is a stretch of paved road. From Central to Circle, the highway is a narrow, winding road with good gravel surface. Watch for possible resurfacing between **Milepost F 81** and **126** in 1992-93.

The highway is open year-round; check with the Dept. of Transportation in Fairbanks regarding winter road conditions.

The Steese Highway was completed in 1927 and named for Gen. James G. Steese, U.S. Army, a former president of the Alaska Road Commission.

Among the attractions along the Steese are the sites of old and new mining camps; Eagle Summit, highest pass on the highway, where there is an unobstructed view of the midnight sun at summer solstice (June 21) and great wildflower viewing in June and July; the Chatanika River and Chena River recreation areas; and Chena and Circle hot springs, where early prospectors bathed in comfort and modern visitors can do the same. There are also a number of fine picnic areas and campgrounds along the Steese.

Emergency medical services: Between Fairbanks and Circle, phone the state troopers at 911 or 452-1313. Use CB Channels 2, 19, 22.

Steese Highway Log

ALASKA ROUTE 2
Distance from Fairbanks (F) is followed by distance from Circle (C).

F 0 C 162 (260.7 km) **FAIRBANKS.** Junction of Airport Way, Richardson–Alaska Highway and the Steese Expressway. Follow the 4-lane Steese Expressway north.

F 0.4 (0.6 km) **C 161.6** (260.1 km) Tenth Avenue exit.

F 0.6 (1 km) **C 161.4** (259.7 km) Expressway crosses Chena River.

F 0.9 (1.4 km) **C 161.1** (259.3 km) Third Street exit.

F 1 (1.6 km) **C 161** (259.1 km) College Road exit to west and access to Bentley Mall and University of Alaska.

F 1.4 (2.3 km) **C 160.6** (258.5 km) Trainer Gate Road.

F 2 (3.2 km) **C 160** (257.5 km) Johansen Expressway (Old Steese Highway) to west, City Lights Boulevard to east.

F 2.8 (4.5 km) **C 159.2** (256.2 km) Fairhill Road; access to Birch Hill Recreation Area, 2.3 miles/3.7 km from the highway via a paved road. Access to Farmers Loop Road to the west; residential areas of Birch Hill, Fairhill, Murray Highlands and View Crest to the east.

Birch Hill Recreation Area is mainly for winter use as a ski area; open from 8 A.M. to 10 P.M. There are picnic areas, toilets, firepits and hiking trails. Day use only.

F 4.9 (7.9 km) **C 157.1** (252.8 km) Chena Hot Springs Road underpass, exits both sides of highway. Turn east at exit for Chena Hot Springs Road; see CHENA HOT SPRINGS ROAD log page 400. Turn west for grocery, gas and pay phone at Old Steese Highway.

Curry's Corner. See display ad this section.

F 6.4 (10.3 km) **C 155.6** (250.4 km) Steele Creek Road. Exit for Bennett Road, Hagelbarger Road, Old Steese Highway and Gilmore trail. Exit to left northbound for scenic view of Fairbanks.

F 7 (11.3 km) **C 155** (249.4 km) View of pipeline from top of hill.

F 8 (12.9 km) **C 154** (247.8 km) End 4-lane divided highway, begin 2 lanes, northbound.

F 8.4 (13.5 km) **C 153.6** (247.2 km) Trans–Alaska pipeline viewpoint with interpretive display. Highway parallels the pipeline.

F 9.5 (15.3 km) **C 152.5** (245.4 km) Goldstream Road exit to Old Steese Highway and Gold Dredge Number 8. The dredge, built in 1928, was added to the list of national historic sites in 1984 and designated a National Historical Mechanical Engineering Landmark in 1986. The 5-deck, 250-foot-long dredge operated until 1959; it is now privately owned and open to the public for tours (admission fee).

Gold Dredge Number 8. Turn left on Goldstream Road, then left again on the Old

CURRYS' CORNER
OPEN 7 A.M. TO 11 P.M.
GAS • GROCERIES
LIQUOR
Patrick C. and Jeanne Weaver, Proprietors
Junction of Old Steese and Chena Hot Springs. Turn west (toward Fairbanks) when you leave the expressway at the overpass. We are a block away... Mile F 5.

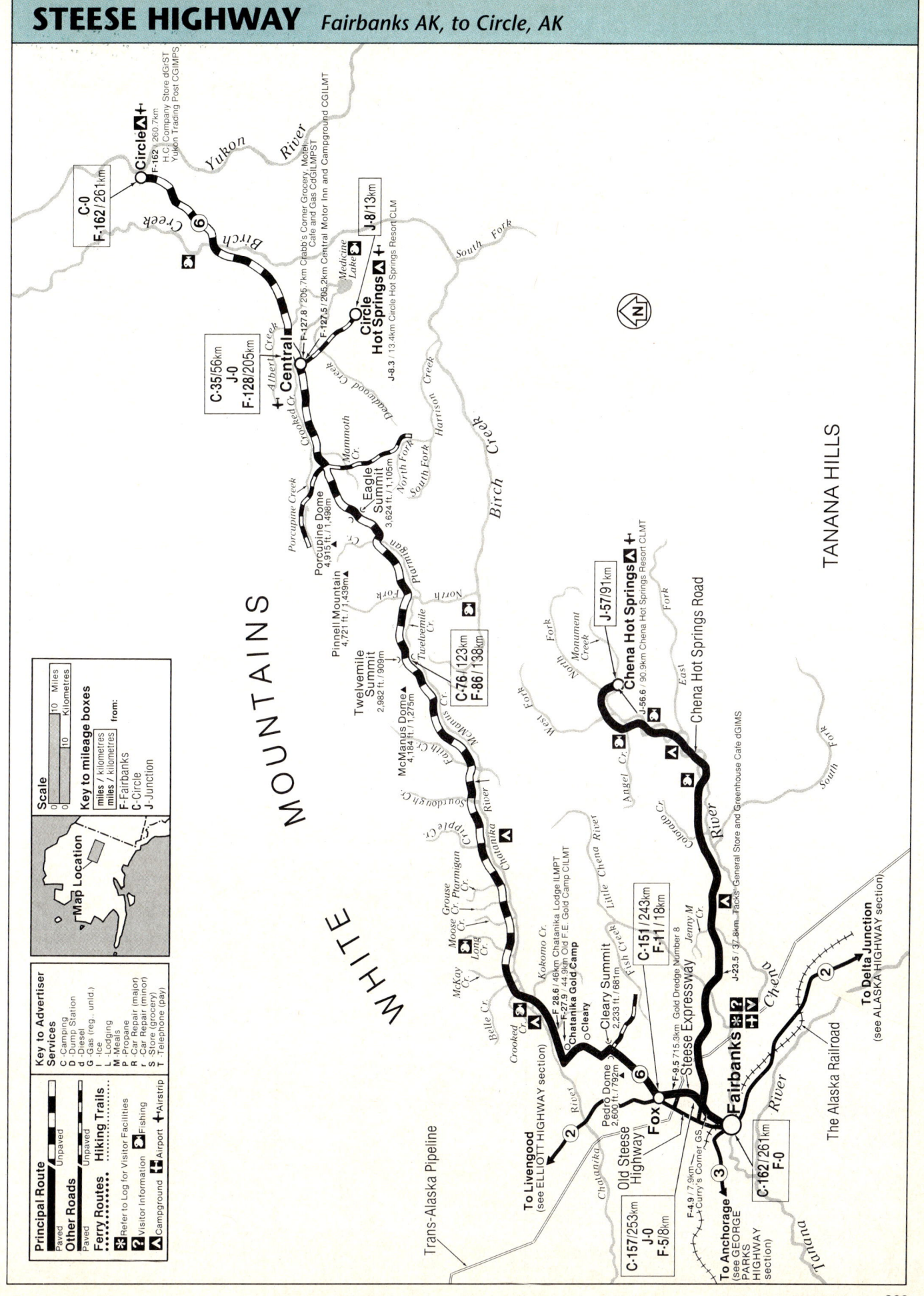

STEESE HIGHWAY — Fairbanks AK, to Circle, AK

STEESE HIGHWAY

Chena Hot Springs Road Log

This paved road, open year-round, leads 56.5 miles/90.9 km east to Chena Hot Springs, a private resort open daily year-round. Chena Hot Springs Road passes through the middle of Chena River Recreation Area, 254,000 acres of mostly undeveloped river bottom and alpine uplands. This is an exceptional recreation area with numerous picnic sites, campgrounds and easy access to the Chena River, one of the most popular grayling fisheries in the state. There's also a whitefish spear fishery (check season and limits). King and chum salmon migrate up the Chena River in July and August. *IMPORTANT: Check current ADF&G regulations regarding the taking of any fish.* Hiking trails include the Colorado Creek trail, Granite Tors trail, Angel Rocks trail and the Chena Dome trail. During winter this area is popular for snow machining, cross-country skiing and dog mushing.

Distance is measured from junction with the Steese Highway (J).

Old auto provides distraction for bathers at Chena Hot Springs. (Jerrianne Lowther, staff)

J 0 Chena Hot Springs Road exit off Steese Highway.
J 1.8 (2.9 km) Bennett Road.
J 3.5 (5.6 km) Steele Creek Road.
J 6.3 (10.1 km) Nordale Road.
J 8.3 (13.4 km) Paved double-ended turnout with litter barrel to south.
J 10.3 (16.6 km) Mini-mart, public dumpster.
J 11.9 (19.2 km) Bridge over Little Chena River. Water gauging station in middle of bridge. The 6 rain gauges and 3 stream-flow meters in the upper Chena River basin help measure the water level in the Chena River. The stations send signals to a master control computer in Anchorage which in turn sends instructions to the Moose Creek dam on the Richardson Highway. This Army Corps of Engineers flood control project, completed in 1979, was designed to prevent floods such as the one which devastated Fairbanks in 1967. The first high-water test of the project was in July 1981, when the floodgates at Moose Creek dam were lowered.
J 14 (22.5 km) Bumpy paved double-ended turnout to south.
J 18 (29 km) Watch for moose.
J 18.6 (29.9 km) Two Rivers Road. Access to Two Rivers School and Two Rivers Recreation Area (maintained by Fairbanks North Star Borough) with cross-country ski and hiking trails.
J 20.1 (32.3 km) Jenny M. Creek. Some 2,000 people reside along the road between here and its junction with the Steese Highway.
J 20.2 (32.5 km) Large, double-ended paved parking area to south.
J 23 (37 km) Double-ended gravel turnout.
J 23.4 (37.7 km) Grocery, public dumpster.
J 23.5 (37.8 km) **Tacks' General Store and Greenhouse Cafe.** See display ad this section.
Two Rivers post office is in store.
J 25.6 (41.2 km) HIPAS Observatory, UCLA Plasma Physics Lab (Geophysical Institute Chena Radio Facility).
J 25.7 (41.4 km) Road passes sloughs and ponds of the Chena River area. Fine place for berry pickers, furred and human.
J 26.1 (42 km) Entering **Chena River** Recreation Area. No shooting except at target range. Grayling fishing (check current regulations).
J 26.5 (42.6 km) Flat Creek.
J 26.7 (43 km) Paved turnout to south for picnic area with tables and toilets.
J 27 (43.5 km) Rosehip state campground to south; 25 sites, picnic tables, firepits, toilets, water, $6 nightly fee or annual pass. Large, flat, gravel pads and an easy 0.7-mile/1.1-km loop road make this a good campground for large RVs and trailers.
Canoe exit point. The Chena is popular with paddlers, but should not be underestimated: The river is cold and the current very strong. Watch for river-wide logjams and sweepers. Secure your gear in waterproof containers. Local paddlers suggest a float from **Milepost J 39.5** to **J 37.9** for easy paddling; **J 44** to **J 37.9** for a longer float; and **J 52.3** to **J 47.3** for paddlers with more skill. Allow about an hour on the river for each road mile traveled.
J 27.5 (44.2 km) Paved turnout to south.
J 27.9 (44.9 km) Toilets and access to river via road to south which leads 0.9 mile/1.4 km to large parking area with picnic tables, dumpster, loop turnaround. Canoe exit point.
J 28.8 (46.3 km) Access road to river, drive 0.7 mile/1.1 km south to canoe launch in brushy area along river; picnic table, toilet, dumpster, parking.
J 29.4 (47.3 km) River access and picnic table to south.
J 29.4 (47.3 km) Pleasant double-ended paved turnout to south on Chena River; picnic table, dumpster.
J 30 (48.3 km) Outdoor education camp (available for rent by groups). Small lake stocked with grayling.
J 30.4 (48.9 km) River access and paved turnout with picnic table. Canoe exit point.
J 31.3 (50.4 km) Bridge over Colorado Creek. River access.
J 31.5 (50.7 km) River access.
J 33.9 (54.6 km) Fourmile Creek flows under the road.
J 35.8 (57.6 km) Paved turnout to south.
J 36.4 (58.5 km) Target shooting

True Value Hardware • Gas • Diesel • White Gas • Ice • Post Office in same building

Tacks' General Store and Greenhouse Cafe

A real old-fashioned general store... well stocked for the traveler and locals. Including fresh milk, cheeses, bread and many basic food items.
Hunting & fishing licenses.
Fishing gear.

has true country charm. Breakfast served till 8 p.m. Burgers and sandwiches anytime. Daily lunch and dinner specials. Real homemade pies and breads.

Take this opportunity to visit our greenhouse full of flowers and hanging baskets
Mile 23.5 Chena Hot Springs Road • (907) 488-3242
8 a.m.–8 p.m. DAILY YEAR-ROUND
One of Alaska's most colorful displays of flowers

Steese Highway Log

range to north. ORV trails, toilets and picnic tables.

J 37.9 (61 km) First bridge over the **North Fork Chena River**. Water gauge in center of bridge (see **Milepost J 11.9**). Grayling fishing (check current regulations).

Side road leaves highway to the south and forks. Left fork is a short road to the river and toilet; right fork leads 0.2 mile/0.3 km to picnic tables by the river. Canoe launch. This road is bordered by dense underbrush which may scratch wide vehicles.

J 39.2 (63.1 km) Paved turnout to south.

J 39.5 (63.5 km) Second bridge over North Fork Chena River. Loop road through Granite Tors trail state campground; 20 large sites among tall spruce trees, parking area, water, toilets, tables, firepits, $6 nightly fee or annual pass. Canoe launch. Picnic area on loop road along river.

Trailhead for Granite Tors trail; follow dike (levee) on west side upstream 0.3 mile/0.4 km to trail sign. It is a 6-mile/9.7-km hike to the nearest tors, 8 miles/12.9 km to the main grouping. Tors are high, isolated pinnacles of jointed granite jutting up from the tundra.

J 39.7 (63.9 km) Dumpster. A 0.2-mile/0.3-km side road leads south to Chena River picnic area with tables, toilets and a riverbank of flat rocks ideal for sunbathing.

J 39.8 (64.1 km) Campground loop road exit; toilet and dumpster beside road.

J 41.8 (67.3 km) Paved turnout to south.

J 42.1 (67.8 km) Large turnout with dumpster south of road. Watch for muskrats and beaver in ponds here.

J 42.8 (68.8 km) Mile 43 Red Squirrel picnic area to north, one of the nicest on this road, with covered tables, firepits, toilets and water. Located on edge of small lake stocked with grayling. Watch for moose.

J 42.9 (69 km) Gravel turnouts to south.

J 43.8 (70.5 km) Small lake to north stocked with grayling.

J 44.1 (71 km) Third bridge over North Fork Chena River. Picnic area with tables and toilets to north at east end of bridge. A favorite place to sunbathe and fish. Canoe launch.

J 45.7 (73.5 km) Fourth bridge over North Fork Chena River.

J 46 (74 km) Paved turnout to south.

J 46.8 (75.3 km) Chena River flows alongside the road; good access point for fishermen. Paved parking to south opposite river.

J 47.3 (76.1 km) Access to river; picnic table north side of road.

J 47.9 (77.1 km) Side road leads 0.1 mile/0.2 km south to **48-Mile Pond**. Stocked with grayling; picnic tables, informal campsites.

J 48.8 (78.5 km) Watch for people and horses next mile eastbound.

J 48.9 (78.7 km) Angel Rocks trailhead; table, toilet, litter barrel. Angel Rocks trail is a 3.5-mile/5.6-km loop trail to spectacular rock outcroppings; strenuous hike.

J 49 (78.9 km) Fifth bridge over **North Fork Chena River**; parking. Excellent fishing from here.

J 49.1 (79 km) Lower Chena Dome trailhead. Side road leads 0.2 mile/0.3 km north to trailhead, parking, water, dumpster and toilets.

J 49.3 (79.3 km) Cathedral Bluffs, an unusual rock formation to southeast.

J 49.9 (80.3 km) Paved turnout to north. **Angel Creek**, grayling 12 to 17 inches.

J 50.5 (81.2 km) Chena Dome trailhead; this 29-mile loop trail exits at **Milepost J 49.1**. Angel Creek Cabin ATV trailhead (6 miles/10 km). Parking, toilets, dumpster. Bring mosquito repellent!

J 50.7 (81.6 km) Chena River Recreation Area boundary.

J 51 (82 km) Access to Chena River.

J 52.3 (84.2 km) Bridge over West Fork Chena River. Gravel side road leads south to parking area along the river.

J 55.3 (89 km) North Fork Chena River bridge. Double-ended paved turnout to south.

J 56.5 (90.9 km) **CHENA HOT SPRINGS:** food, lodging, camping, bar and swimming. To phone ahead, call (907) 452-7867. These mineral hot springs were first reported in 1907 by the U.S. Geological Survey's field teams. The springs take their name from the nearby Chena River, which flows southwest. There is an airstrip at the lodge.

Chena Hot Springs Resort, where the warmth of Alaska is yours. Relax in our hot water pool. Enjoy the beautiful log atmosphere of our dining room and bar. Rent a room, cabin, or use our spacious campground. Picnicking, badminton, volleyball, horseshoes. Plenty of woods to stroll through. Good fishing nearby. Open year-round. Cross-country skiing and dogsled rides in winter. Write: P.O. Box 73440, Fairbanks, AK 99707. Phone (907) 452-7867. Better yet—just drive on up. [ADVERTISEMENT]

Return to Milepost F 4.6 Steese Highway

(continued)
Steese Highway. Drive 0.3 mile to Gold Dredge Number 8 on your right. Guided tour of Dredge Number 8 and gold panning is one of the Interior's top attractions. Visit Gold Dredge Number 8 early on while in Fairbanks. Guests receive Miners Club cards enabling return visits without charge. It's so interesting and so authentic that many people come back again. Families love it. See display ad in the FAIRBANKS section. [ADVERTISEMENT]

F 10.4 (16.7 km) **C 151.6** (244 km) Road to permafrost tunnel to east (research area, not open to public). Excavated in the early 1960s, the tunnel is maintained cooperatively by the University of Alaska-Fairbanks and the U.S. Army Cold Regions Research and Engineering Laboratory.

F 11 (17.7 km) **C 151** (243 km) End of Steese Expressway. Weigh station. Check here for current information on Dalton Highway conditions. Turn east at this junction for continuation of Steese Highway, which now becomes Alaska Route 6 (log follows). Continue straight ahead (north) on Alaska Route 2, which now becomes the Elliott Highway, for access to Dalton Highway and Manley Hot Springs (see ELLIOTT HIGHWAY section for details).

Turn west for Old Steese Highway and for **FOX**, a once famous mining camp established before 1905 and named for nearby Fox Creek. Gas, food and lodging.

ALASKA ROUTE 6

F 13.6 (21.9 km) **C 148.4** (238.8 km) Eisele Road; turnoff on right northbound for NOAA/NESDIS Command and Data Acquisition Station at Gilmore Creek. This facility monitors 2 polar orbiting satellites. Tours of the satellite tracking station are available 9 A.M. to 4 P.M., Monday through Saturday, from June through August. Phone (907) 451-1200 for more information.

F 16.4 (26.4 km) **C 145.6** (234.3 km) Turnout by gold-bearing creek. Now privately claimed; no recreational gold panning permitted.

F 16.5 (26.6 km) **C 145.5** (234.2 km) Gravel turnout to west. Monument to Felix Pedro, the prospector who discovered gold on nearby Pedro Creek in July 1902 and started the rush that resulted in the founding of Fairbanks.

F 17.4 (28 km) **C 144.6** (232.7 km) Gravel turnout to east. Winding ascent northbound to Cleary Summit area.

F 19.6 (31.5 km) **C 142.4** (229.2 km) Large gravel turnout to east.

F 20.6 (33.2 km) **C 141.4** (227.6 km) Cleary Summit (elev. 2,233 feet/681m) has a weekend ski area in winter. Named for early prospector Frank Cleary. On a clear day there are excellent views of the Tanana Valley and Mount McKinley to the south and the White Mountains to the north. Road north to Pedro Dome military site.

Fairbanks Creek Road to the south leads several miles along a ridge crest; access to Fish Creek Road and dirt roads leading to Solo Creek, Bear Creek and Fairbanks Creek.

F 20.9 (33.6 km) **C 141.1** (227 km) Turnout next to ski area buildings; view of current mining operation and old buildings from early mining and dredging on Cleary Creek below.

Old F.E. Co. gold dredge (private property) (Jerrianne Lowther, staff)

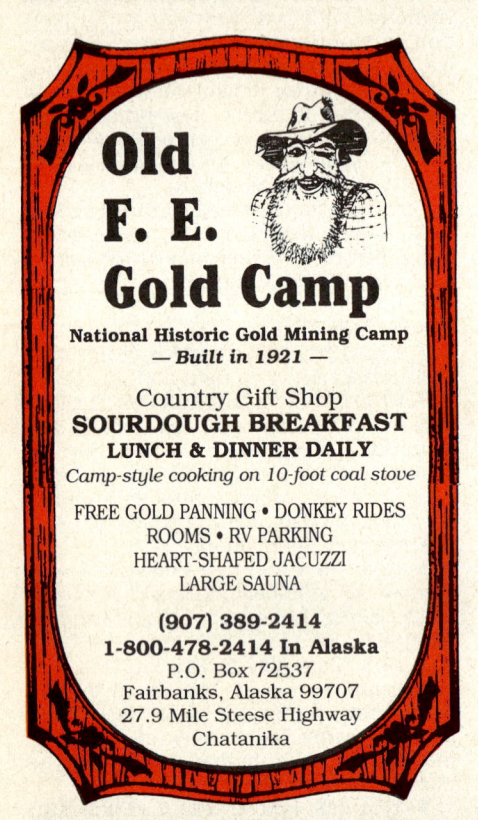

Old F. E. Gold Camp

National Historic Gold Mining Camp
— Built in 1921 —

Country Gift Shop
**SOURDOUGH BREAKFAST
LUNCH & DINNER DAILY**
Camp-style cooking on 10-foot coal stove

FREE GOLD PANNING • DONKEY RIDES
ROOMS • RV PARKING
HEART-SHAPED JACUZZI
LARGE SAUNA

**(907) 389-2414
1-800-478-2414 In Alaska**
P.O. Box 72537
Fairbanks, Alaska 99707
27.9 Mile Steese Highway
Chatanika

Ron & Shirley's CHATANIKA LODGE

Across Highway from 2nd Largest Gold Dredge

Saloon • Country Cooking • Lodging
Package Store • Ice • Propane • Pay Phone

In Alaska, dial 1-389-2164 • 5760 Old Steese Highway North, Chatanika, Alaska 99712
See log ad at Mile 28.6 Steese Highway

F **23.9** (38.4 km) C **138.1** (222.2 km) Gravel turnout to east. Watch for frost heaves.

F **27.6** (44.4 km) C **134.4** (216.3 km) Tailings (gravel and boulders of dredged streambeds) from early mining activity which yielded millions of dollars in gold. There is quite a bit of mining in the Chatanika area now.

F **27.9** (44.9 km) C **134.1** (215.8 km) Sharp right turn up hill for historic Fairbanks Exploration Co. gold camp at CHATANIKA, built in 1925 to support gold dredging operations in the valley. Between 1926 and 1957 the F.E. Co. removed an estimated $70 million in gold. Camp lodge offers meals, lodging, RV parking and gold panning.

Old F.E. Gold Camp. See display ad this section.

F **28.6** (46 km) C **133.4** (214.6 km) Old gold dredge behind tailing piles (private property) to west, lodge to east with meals, lodging and RV parking.

Chatanika Lodge. Cafe open 9 A.M. daily (year-round). Halibut/catfish fry Friday and Saturday, country-fried chicken on Sunday, served family-style, all you can eat. Diamond Willow Lounge. Rustic atmosphere, Alaska artifacts. Historic Alaska gold dredge and aurora borealis videos on big-screen TV. Good grayling fishing. Rooms $30 to $35. RV parking. See display ad this section.
[ADVERTISEMENT]

F **29.5** (47.5 km) C **132.5** (213.2 km) Neal Brown Road to Poker Flat rocket facility; off-limits except to authorized personnel. The Poker Flat rocket range, operated by the Geophysical Institute, University of Alaska, is dedicated to unclassified auroral and upper atmospheric research. It is the only university-owned sounding rocket range in the world and the only high latitude and auroral zone launch facility on U.S. soil. Tours for interested groups may be arranged by calling (907) 474-7634.

Fishing at gravel pit ponds from here north to **Milepost** F **38.5**. Ponds are stocked with grayling.

F **32.3** (52 km) C **129.7** (208.7 km) Captain Creek bridge.

F **32.5** (52.3 km) C **129.5** (208.4 km) CAUTION: *Severe frost heaves and cracks in pavement next 0.2 mile/0.3 km northbound.*

F **34.9** (56.2 km) C **127.1** (204.5 km) Access to Chatanika River. Double-ended paved turnout with litter barrel to west.

F **36.5** (58.7 km) C **125.5** (202 km) Gravel turnout with litter barrel alongside ponds to west. Pond stocked with grayling.

F **37.1** (59.7 km) C **124.9** (201 km) CAUTION: *Severe frost heaves and dips in pavement next 0.1 mile/0.2 km northbound.*

F **37.3** (60 km) C **124.7** (200.7 km) Kokomo Creek bridge.

F **39** (62.8 km) C **123** (197.9 km) Chatanika River bridge. Upper Chatanika River State Recreation Site, just north of the bridge, is a beautiful state campground on the riverbank. There are 25 sites with fireplaces, and a gravel parking area near the bridge. A water pump is at the entrance. Firewood is usually available during the summer. Camping fee $6/night or annual pass. Look for wild roses here in June. ▲

Boats can be launched on the gravel bars by the river. Bring your mosquito repellent. This is an access point to the Chatanika River canoe trail. See **Milepost** F **60** for more information on canoeing this river.

Chatanika River, grayling 8 to 20 inches, use flies or spinners, May to September.

F **39.5** (63.5 km) C **122.5** (197.1 km) Pond stocked with grayling.

F **40.4** (65 km) C **121.6** (195.7 km) Bridge over Crooked Creek.

F **41.5** (66.8 km) C **120.5** (193.9 km) Bridge over Belle Creek. Most homes here are of permanent residents.

F **41.8** (67.3 km) C **120.2** (193.4 km) Trading post.

F **42.9** (69 km) C **119.1** (191.7 km) Bridge over McKay Creek.

F **43.8** (70.5 km) C **118.2** (190.2 km) Pavement ends; it is good gravel road to Circle with the exception of a short stretch of blacktop at Central. Highway parallels the Chatanika River for the next 10 miles/16 km.

F **45.4** (73.1 km) C **116.6** (187.6 km) **Long Creek** bridge. Grayling 8 to 14 inches, use spinners or flies, May to September.

F **49** (78.9 km) C **113** (181.9 km) View down Chatanika River valley to east.

F **53.5** (86.1 km) C **108.5** (174.6 km) Ptarmigan Creek.

F **57.1** (91.9 km) C **104.9** (168.8 km) White Mountains National Recreation Area (BLM managed).

F **57.5** (92.2 km) C **104.7** (168.5 km) U.S. Creek to west. The large pipe near U.S. Creek was part of the Davidson Ditch, built in

1925 by the Fairbanks Exploration Co., to carry water to float gold dredges. The 83-mile-/133.6-km-long ditch, designed and engineered by J.B. Lippincott, begins near **Milepost F 64** on the Steese Highway and ends near Fox. A system of ditches and inverted siphons, the pipeline was capable of carrying 56,100 gallons per minute. After the dredges closed, the water was used for power until 1967, when a flood destroyed a bridge and flattened almost 1,000 feet/305m of pipe.

All-weather road leads 7 miles/11.3 km west to Nome Creek; recreational gold panning. There are some mining claims on Nome Creek. No dredges allowed. The road to Nome Creek is very steep and not recommended for large or underpowered vehicles. Nome Creek is a historic mining area; additional recreational facilities are under development.

F 59 (94.9 km) **C 103** (165.8 km) Wide double-ended gravel parking area to east.

F 60 (96.6 km) **C 102** (164.2 km) Cripple Creek BLM campground (7-day limit), 6 tent, 15 trailer sites; water pumps, fireplaces, toilets, tables, nature trail. Parking for walk-in campers. Firewood is usually available all summer. Recreational gold panning permitted. *Bring mosquito repellent!* ▲

Access to Cripple Creek BLM recreation cabin. Preregister and pay $10 fee at BLM office, 1150 University Ave., Fairbanks 99709; phone 474-2200.

Cripple Creek bridge is the uppermost access point to the Chatanika River canoe trail (follow side road near campground entrance to canoe launch site). *CAUTION: This canoe trail may not be navigable at low water.* The Chatanika River is a clear-water Class II stream. The Steese Highway parallels the river for approximately 28 miles/45 km and there are many access points to the highway downstream from the Cripple Creek bridge. No major obstacles on this canoe trail, but watch for overhanging trees. Downstream pullout points are Perhaps Creek, Long Creek and Chatanika Campground.

F 62.3 (100.2 km) **C 99.7** (160.4 km) Viewpoint to east overlooking Chatanika River.

F 63.4 (102 km) **C 98.6** (158.7 km) View of historic Davidson Ditch pipeline.

F 65 (104.6 km) **C 97** (156.1 km) Side road east to viewpoint.

F 65.6 (105.6 km) **C 96.4** (155.1 km) Sourdough Creek bridge.

F 65.7 (105.7 km) **C 96.3** (155 km) Mile 66. Hendrickson's Miracle Mile Lodge.

F 66 (106.2 km) **C 96** (154.5 km) Sourdough Creek Road to north.

F 69 (111 km) **C 93** (149.7 km) Faith Creek bridge and road. Creek access to east at north end of bridge. Large parking area to west.

F 72 (115.9 km) **C 90** (144.8 km) View ahead for northbound travelers of highway route along mountains, McManus Creek below.

F 73.8 (118.8 km) **C 88.2** (141.9 km) Faith Creek Road to west.

F 79.1 (127.3 km) **C 82.9** (133.4 km) Road widens for parking next 500 feet/152m.

F 80.1 (128.9 km) **C 81.9** (131.8 km) Montana Creek state highway maintenance station. Montana Creek runs under road and into McManus Creek to the east. McManus Dome (elev. 4,184 feet/1,275m) to west.

F 81.2 (130.7 km) **C 80.8** (130 km) Turnout to east. Spring water (untested) piped to roadside. Wide gravel highway begins final ascent to Twelvemile Summit.

F 83 (133.6 km) **C 79** (127.1 km) Watch for the hoary marmot and other small mammals.

F 85.5 (137.6 km) **C 76.5** (123.1 km) Large parking area and viewpoint to east at Twelvemile Summit (elev. 2,982 feet/909m) on the divide of the Yukon and Tanana river drainages. Dozens of species of wildflowers carpet the alpine tundra slopes. Entering Game Management Unit 25C, leaving unit 20B, northbound. Fairbanks North Star Borough limits. This is caribou country; from here to beyond Eagle Summit (**Milepost F 108**) migrating bands of caribou may be seen from late July through mid-September.

Access to Pinnell Mountain national recreation trail (Twelvemile Summit trailhead). The trail is also accessible from **Milepost F 107.1**. Named in honor of Robert Pinnell, who was fatally injured in 1952 while climbing nearby Porcupine Dome. This 27-mile-/43-km-long hiking trail winds through alpine terrain, along mountain ridges and through high passes. Highest elevation point reached is 4,721 feet/1,439m. The trail is marked by rock cairns. Shelter cabins at Mile 10.7 and Mile 17.7. Vantage points along the trail with views of the White Mountains, Tanana Hills, Brooks Range and Alaska Range. Watch for willow ptarmigan, hoary marmot, rock pika, moose, wolf and caribou. Mid-May through July is the prime time for wildflowers with flowers peaking in mid-June. Carry drinking water and insect repellent at all times. Additional information on this trail is available from the Bureau of Land Management, 1150 University Ave., Fairbanks 99708-3844; phone 474-2350.

F 88 (141.6 km) **C 74** (119.1 km) Twelvemile Creek to east below road.

F 88.7 (142.7 km) **C 73.3** (118 km) Bridge over Reed Creek.

F 90.5 (145.6 km) **C 71.5** (115.1 km) Turnout to east.

F 93.4 (150.3 km) **C 68.6** (110.4 km) Bridge over the North Fork Twelvemile Creek. Nice picnic spot to west below bridge.

F 94 (151.3 km) **C 68** (109.4 km) Side road leads 0.2 mile/0.3 km down to north fork of Birch Creek; parking area and canoe launch for Birch Creek canoe trail. This is the main put in point for canoeing Birch Creek, a Wild and Scenic River. Undeveloped campsite by creek. Extensive mining in area. **Birch Creek**, grayling to 12 inches; use flies, June to October.

F 95.6 (153.9 km) **C 66.4** (106.9 km) Bridge over Willow Creek.

Much gold mining activity along this part of the highway. These are private mining claims. *Do not trespass. Do not approach mining equipment without permission.*

F 97.7 (157.2 km) **C 64.3** (103.5 km) Bridge over Bear Creek.

F 98 (157.7 km) **C 64** (103 km) Gold mine and settling ponds in creek valley to east.

F 99.8 (160.8 km) **C 62.2** (100.1 km) Bridge over Fish Creek. Privately owned cabins.

F 100.8 (162.2 km) **C 61.2** (98.5 km) Turnout by stream to east.

F 101.5 (163.3 km) **C 60.5** (97.4 km) Bridge over Ptarmigan Creek (elev. 2,398 feet/731m). Alpine meadows carpeted with wildflowers in spring and summer for next 9 miles/14.5 km.

F 102.3 (164.6 km) **C 59.7** (96.1 km) Ptarmigan Creek access to west.

F 103 (165.8 km) **C 59** (94.9 km) Good view of mining operation next mile northbound.

F 105.4 (169.6 km) **C 56.6** (91 km) Large gravel parking area to west.

The Steese Highway winds along Twelvemile Summit. (Jerrianne Lowther, staff)

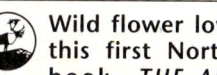

Wild flower lovers will value this first Northland flower book—*THE ALASKA–YUKON WILD FLOWERS GUIDE.* It is the perfect travel companion for *The MILEPOST*. A handy colorful guide with 180 large photographs and 164 black-and-white drawings of every species. Included are handy reference indexes. Available in bookstores and from Alaska Northwest Books™. To order, call toll free 1-800-343-4567, Ext. 571.

Circle Hot Springs Road Log

Distance is measured from junction with Steese Highway (J).

J 0 Pavement extends next 0.3 mile/0.5 km.

J 0.9 (1.4 km) Graveyard Road, 0.5 mile/0.8 km to cemetery.

J 1.9 (3.1 km) Deadwood Creek Road.

J 2.9 (4.7 km) Bridge over Deadwood Creek.

J 5.7 (9.2 km) Bridge over Ketchem Creek. Primitive camping at site of former Ketchem Creek BLM campground on right before bridge; no facilities.

J 8.3 (13.4 km) **CIRCLE HOT SPRINGS**; year-round swimming, lodging, food and RV parking. A popular spot with Alaskans.

According to research done by Patricia Oakes of Central, the hot springs were used as a gathering place by area Athabascans before the gold rush. Local prospectors probably used the springs as early as the 1890s. Cassius Monohan homesteaded the site in 1905, selling out to Frank Leach in 1909. Leach built the airstrip, on which Noel Wien landed in 1924.

Circle Hot Springs Resort, under new management, 4-story hotel with hostel, full meal restaurant, cabins, saloon and Olympic-sized pool fed by the hot springs. RV parking. In the center of Alaska where you can branch out on side trips into the wilderness—winter or summer. State-maintained 3,600-foot lighted airstrip. Heart of many active gold mines. Lodge is open year-round. Call (907) 520-5113 or write Circle Hot Springs Resort, Box 254, Central, AK 99730. [ADVERTISEMENT]

Private Aircraft: Circle Hot Springs state-maintained airstrip; elev. 956 feet/291m; length 3,600 feet/1,097m; gravel; lighted, unattended.

Return to Milepost F 127.8 Steese Highway

F 107.1 (172.4 km) **C 54.9** (88.4 km) Parking area to west. Pinnell Mountain trail access (Eagle Summit trailhead), see description at **Milepost F 85.6**.

F 108 (173.8 km) **C 54** (86.9 km) Eagle Summit (elev. 3,624 feet/1,105m) to the east. Steep, narrow rocky side road leads from the highway 0.8 mile/1.3 km to the summit. This is the third and highest of 3 summits (including Cleary and Twelvemile) along the Steese Highway. Favorite spot for local residents to observe summer solstice (weather permitting) on June 21. Best wildflower viewing on Alaska highway system.

Scalloped waves of soil on hillsides to west are called solifluction lobes. These are formed when meltwater saturates the thawed surface soil, which then flows slowly downhill.

Wildflowers found here include: dwarf forget-me-nots, alpine rhododendron or rosebay, rock jasmine, alpine azalea, arctic bell heather, mountain avens, Jacob's ladder, anemones, wallflowers, Labrador tea, lupine and louseworts. The museum in Central has a display of Eagle Summit alpine flowers to help highway travelers identify the wildflowers of this area.

F 109.2 (175.7 km) **C 52.8** (85 km) Large parking area to east with view down into Miller Creek far below. Highway begins steep descent northbound.

F 114.2 (183.8 km) **C 47.8** (76.9 km) Parking area to east looking down onto the Mastodon and Mammoth creeks area.

F 114.4 (184.1 km) **C 47.6** (76.6 km) Side road to east leads to Mammoth and Mastodon creeks; active gold placer mining areas.

F 116.2 (187 km) **C 45.8** (73.7 km) Road east to creek.

F 116.4 (187.3 km) **C 45.6** (73.4 km) Bridge over Mammoth Creek. Near here fossil remains of many species of preglacial Alaskan mammals have been excavated and may be seen at the University of Alaska museum in Fairbanks and at the museum in Central.

F 117 (188.3 km) **C 45** (72.4 km) Highway crosses over Stack Pup Creek. From here the highway gradually descends to Central.

F 117.6 (189.3 km) **C 44.4** (71.5 km) Parking area to west.

F 119.1 (191.7 km) **C 42.9** (69 km) Bedrock Creek.

F 119.2 (191.8 km) **C 42.8** (68.9 km) Narrow dirt road leads to site of former Bedrock Creek BLM campground; closed.

F 121 (194.7 km) **C 41** (66 km) Bridge over Sawpit Creek.

F 122.5 (197.1 km) **C 39.5** (63.6 km) Road west to parking space by pond.

F 125.4 (201.8 km) **C 36.6** (58.9 km) Bridge over Boulder Creek.

F 126.8 (204.1 km) **C 35.2** (56.6 km) Paved highway begins and continues through Central.

F 127.1 (204.5 km) **C 34.9** (56.2 km) Central elementary school.

F 127.4 (205 km) **C 34.6** (55.7 km) Central post office (Zip code 99730).

F 127.5 (205.2 km) **C 34.5** (55.5 km) **CENTRAL** (pop. approximately 600 in summer, 150 in winter; elev. 965 feet/294m). **Radio**: KUAC-FM 91.7. This small community, formerly called Central House, is situated on Crooked Creek along the Steese Highway. The old 2-story Central House roadhouse is located near **Milepost F 128**. This structure, built in 1926 to replace the 1894 building which burned down, is listed on the National Register of Historic Places.

Central is the central point in the huge Circle Mining District, one of the oldest and still one of the most active districts in the state. The annual Circle Mining District Picnic for local miners and their families is held in August.

Central has many facilities for the visitor: state airstrip (see **Milepost F 128.3**), cafes and bars, motel cabins, laundromat, showers, groceries, gas, tire repair, welding, post office and pay phone. Check with Crabb's Corner for emergency medical services. Report fires to BLM field station at **Milepost F 127.8**. Picnic area at Central Park.

The Circle District Historical Society museum has displays covering the history of the Circle Mining District and its people. Also here are a photo display of wildflowers, fossilized remains of preglacial mammals, a minerals display, library and archives, gift shop and visitor information. Admission is $1 for adults, 50¢ for children under 12; members free. Open daily, Memorial Day through September.

Central Motor Inn and Campground. See display ad this section. ▲

F 127.8 (205.7 km) **C 34.2** (55 km) Junction with Circle Hot Springs Road; see CIRCLE HOT SPRINGS ROAD log this section.

F 127.8 (205.7 km) **C 34.2** (55 km) **Crabb's Corner Grocery, Motel, Cafe and Gas.** Jim and Sandy Crabb offer Chevron gas, oil and diesel. Propane, cafe, bar, package store. Fresh beef hamburgers. RV parking. Fresh water. Laundromat. Complete variety of grocery items including ice and mosquito repellents. Pay phone. Open daily. (907) 520-5115. The place to eat in Central! [ADVERTISEMENT]

F 127.8 (205.7 km) **C 34.2** (55 km) BLM Alaska Fire Services office.

F 127.9 (205.8 km) **C 34.1** (54.9 km) Bridge over Crooked Creek. Old Central House roadhouse (2-story log structure) on south side of bridge.

F 128.1 (206.1 km) **C 33.9** (54.5 km) Central DOT/PF highway maintenance station.

F 128.3 (206.5 km) **C 33.7** (54.2 km) **Private Aircraft**: Central state-maintained

---

CENTRAL MOTOR INN and CAMPGROUND

COCKTAIL LOUNGE • RESTAURANT
Rooms (low rates) • Laundromat • Showers
Parking for RVs & Campers • Tent Campers Welcome
Gasoline • Pay Telephone • Ice
NEVER CLOSED – THE COFFEE POT IS ALWAYS ON

Mile 127.5 Steese Highway ★ Box 24 • Central, Alaska 99730 ★ (907) 520-5228

airstrip, adjacent north; elev. 932 feet/284m; length 3,000 feet/914m; gravel; unattended.

Pavement ends northbound. Watch for soft spots, curves and little or no shoulder between here and Circle; otherwise, the road is in good shape. Wildlife is frequently sighted on the road between Central and Circle.

F **130.5** (210 km) C **31.5** (50.7 km) Pond frequented by a variety of ducks.

F **131.2** (211.1 km) C **30.8** (49.6 km) Albert Creek bridge. Small parking area with litter barrel at end of bridge.

F **133** (214 km) C **29** (46.7 km) Repair shop.

F **147.1** (236.7 km) C **14.9** (24 km) One-lane bridge over Birch Creek; clearance 13 feet, 11 inches. Turnouts with litter barrels, undeveloped campsites, both ends of bridge. Usual takeout point for the Birch Creek canoe trail.

F **147.6** (237.5 km) C **14.4** (23.2 km) Turnout to east.

F **155.9** (250.9 km) C **6.1** (9.8 km) Diamond (Bebb) willow along road.

F **156.7** (252.1 km) C **5.3** (8.5 km) Large turnout opposite gravel pit. Look for bank swallow nests in cliffs.

F **159.6** (256.8 km) C **2.4** (3.9 km) Old Indian cemetery to east.

Residential Circle consists of a few dozen homes, some log with sod-roofs. Two local stores serve the community. (Jerrianne Lowther, staff)

Circle

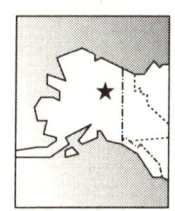

F **162** (260.7 km) C **0**. Located on the banks of the Yukon River, 50 miles/80.5 km south of the Arctic Circle. The Yukon is Alaska's largest river; the 2,000-mile/3219-km river heads in Canada and flows west into Norton Sound on the Bering Sea. **Population:** 94. **Elevation:** 700 feet/213m. **Climate:** Mean monthly temperature in July 61.4°F/16.3°C, in January -10.6°F/-23.7°C. Record high 91°F/32.8°C July 1977, record low -60°F/-51.1°C in December 1961, February 1979 and January 1983. Snow from October (8 inches) through April (2 inches). Precipitation in summer averages 1.45 inches a month.

Private Aircraft: Circle City state-maintained airstrip, adjacent west; elev. 598 feet/182m; length 2,700 feet/823m; gravel; fuel 80, 100, B.

Before the Klondike gold rush of 1898, Circle City was the largest gold mining town on the Yukon River. Prospectors discovered gold on Birch Creek in 1893, and the town of Circle City (so named because the early miners thought it was located on the Arctic Circle) grew up as the nearest supply point to the new diggings on the Yukon River.

Today, Circle serves a small local population and visitors coming in by highway or by river. Gas, groceries, snacks and sundries are available at 2 local stores. The trading post houses the post office, cafe and liquor store. Hunting and fishing licenses are also available at the trading post. There's a lot of summer river traffic here: canoeists put in and take out; the tug *Brainstorm* docks here on its trip from Fort Yukon; Yutana Barge Lines docks here; and floatplanes land on the river.

H.C. Company Store. See display ad this section.

Yukon Trading Post. See display ad this section.

The old Pioneer Cemetery, with its markers dating back to the 1800s, is an interesting spot to visit. Walk a short way upriver (past the old machinery) on the gravel road to a barricade: You will have to cross through a private front yard (please be respectful of property) to get to the trail. Walk straight ahead on the short trail, which goes through dense underbrush (many mosquitoes), for about 10 minutes. Watch for a path on your left to the graves, which are scattered among the thick trees.

Be sure to have your picture taken in front of the sign that welcomes you to Circle. From Dawson Creek, BC, you've driven approximately 1,685 miles/2712 km along the Alaska Highway and the Steese Highway.

Camping on the banks of the Yukon at the end of the road; tables, toilets, parking area. In 1989, when the Yukon flooded, water covered the bottom of the welcome sign at the campground entrance. From the campground you are looking at one channel of the mighty Yukon. ▲

FRIENDLY SERVICE at the END of the HIGHWAY

H.C. COMPANY STORE

• CIRCLE CITY •

TEXACO
Unleaded Gas • Diesel Fuel
Oil Products • Tire Repair
AV Gas

GROCERIES • SNACKS
COLD POP   PHONE
Gold Pans   Handcrafted Gifts

OPEN YEAR AROUND
7 Days a Week (summer)

Dick and Earla Hutchinson Proprietors

MasterCard   VISA

Visit Circle City... 50 miles from the Arctic Circle on the Yukon River. One of the northernmost points you can reach by road in the United States.

On the Mighty Yukon River   **End of the Steese Highway at Mile 162**

YUKON TRADING POST

Finest stop on the Steese Highway

OPEN YEAR AROUND
CAFE · Good Home Cooking
Homemade Pies, Pastries, Cookies
Stop in for Fresh Hot Coffee and Pie

FREE CAMPGROUND... Good Water
Hunting and Fishing Licenses
Ice • Propane • Tire Repair
Showers and Laundromat

Chevron Phone (907) 773-1217
Write: YUKON TRADING POST
Circle, Alaska 99733

VISA MasterCard

Friendly People

**SALOON · LIQUOR STORE
GENERAL STORE**
U.S. Post Office in Store
Souvenirs
Locally Handcrafted Gifts
Chevron Gas and Oil • Aviation Fuel
Owners: Dan and Virginia Pearson

ELLIOTT HIGHWAY

Fox, Alaska, to Manley Hot Springs, Alaska
Alaska Route 2

The historic Manley Roadhouse offers food and lodging. (Jerrianne Lowther, staff)

The Elliott Highway leads 152 miles/ 244.6 km from its junction with the Steese Highway at Fox (11 miles/17.7 km north of Fairbanks) to Manley Hot Springs, a small settlement near the Tanana River with a natural hot springs. The highway was named for Malcolm Elliott, president of the Alaska Road Commission from 1927 to 1932.

The first 28 miles/45.1 km of the Elliott Highway are paved, the remaining 124 miles/200 km are gravel. In 1992, watch for road construction from **Milepost F 7** to **F 28**. The highway is wide, hard-based gravel to the Dalton Highway junction. (It is treated with calcium chloride for dust control; wash your vehicle after travel as it corrodes metal.) From there into Manley, the road is narrower but fairly smooth with some soft spots and a roller-coaster section near Manley. Gas is available at **Milepost F 5.3**, **F 49.5** and at Manley.

Watch for heavy truck traffic. Drivers pulling trailers should be especially cautious when the road is wet. The highway is open year-round; check with the Dept. of Transportation in Fairbanks regarding winter road conditions.

The Elliott Highway also provides access to 4 trailheads in the White Mountains National Recreation Area. These hiking trails are managed by the BLM in Fairbanks.

Emergency medical services: Between Fox and Manley Hot Springs, phone the state troopers at 911 or 452-1313. Use CB channels 9, 14, 19.

Elliott Highway Log

Distance from Fox (F) is followed by distance from Manley Hot Springs (M).

F 0 M 152 (244.6 km) **FOX. Junction** of the Steese Highway with the Elliott Highway. Weigh station.

F 0.4 (0.6 km) **M 151.6** (244 km) Fox Spring picnic area; 2 tables, spring water.

F 1.2 (1.9 km) **M 150.8** (242.7 km) Turnoff for Little Eldorado Gold Mine, a commercial gold mine offering tours and gold panning to the public; admission charged.

F 3.4 (5.5 km) **M 148.6** (239.1 km) Rough side road leads west to Murphy Dome, 28 miles/45 km away; signed "restricted military site."

F 5.3 (8.5 km) **M 146.7** (236.1 km) Gas station and cafe.

F 7.5 (12 km) **M 144.5** (232.5 km) Views to the east of Pedro Dome and Dome Creek. Buildings of Dome and Eldorado camps are in the valley below to the east (best view is southbound).

F 9.2 (14.8 km) **M 142.8** (229.8 km) Olnes, former railroad station of Tanana Valley Railroad and mining camp. Old tailings and abandoned cabins.

F 10.6 (17.1 km) **M 141.4** (227.6 km) Lower Chatanika River State Recreation Area Olnes Creek Campground, 1 mile/1.6 km west of highway on loop road; 50 campsites, toilets, water, tables, group area with campfire ring and benches. Camping fee $6/night or annual pass. ▲

F 11 (17.7 km) **M 141** (226.9 km) Chatanika River bridge. Lower Chatanika State Recreation Area Whitefish Campground at north end of bridge; picnic area (wheelchair accessible) with covered picnic tables, campsites, toilets, firepits, water, litter barrels, river access and boat launch. Camping fee $6/night or annual pass. ▲

F 11.5 (18.5 km) **M 140.5** (226.1 km) General store.

F 12.6 (20.3 km) **M 139.4** (224.3 km) Willow Creek bridge.

F 12.8 (20.6 km) **M 139.2** (224 km) Old log cabin to west is a landmark on the Elliott Highway.

F 18.2 (29.3 km) **M 133.8** (215.3 km) Double-ended paved turnout to west.

F 18.3 (29.5 km) **M 133.7** (215.2 km) Washington Creek. Parking area below bridge east of road; undeveloped campsite.

F 20.2 (32.5 km) **M 131.8** (212.1 km) Beaver pond with dam and lodge to east.

F 20.3 (32.7 km) **M 131.7** (212 km) Cushman Creek Road.

F 23.4 (37.6 km) **M 128.6** (206.9 km) Large double-ended turnout with view of forested valley to west.

F 24.3 (39.1 km) **M 127.7** (205.5 km) Double-ended gravel turnout to east. Snowshoe Creek parallels the road.

F 24.8 (39.9 km) **M 127.2** (204.7 km) Long paved double-ended turnout to east.

F 27.8 (44.7 km) **M 124.2** (199.9 km) Large double-ended paved turnout to west. Highway winds around the base of Wickersham Dome (elev. 3,207 feet/977m). Views of the White Mountains, a range of white limestone mountains (elev. 5,000 feet/ 1,524m). Entering Livengood/Tolovana Mining District northbound, Fairbanks Mining District southbound.

Trailhead for White Mountains–Wickersham Creek trail and White Mountains–Summit trail to Borealis–LeFevre BLM cabin. The Wickersham Creek route is 20 miles/ 32 km in length; ATVs are permitted. The Summit route is 22 miles/35.4 km long and ATVs are prohibited. For more information and cabin registration, contact the BLM office in Fairbanks at 1150 University Ave.; phone 474-2350.

Pipeline access, restricted to ensure public safety and security and to protect the reseeding and restoration of construction areas.

F 28 (45.1 km) **M 124** (199.6 km) Pavement ends.

F 29.1 (46.8 km) **M 122.9** (197.8 km) Sled Dog Rocks ahead northbound.

F 29.5 (47.4 km) **M 122.5** (197.1 km) Double-ended gravel turnout to east.

406 The MILEPOST® ■ 1992

ELLIOTT HIGHWAY — Fox, AK, to Manley Hot Springs, AK

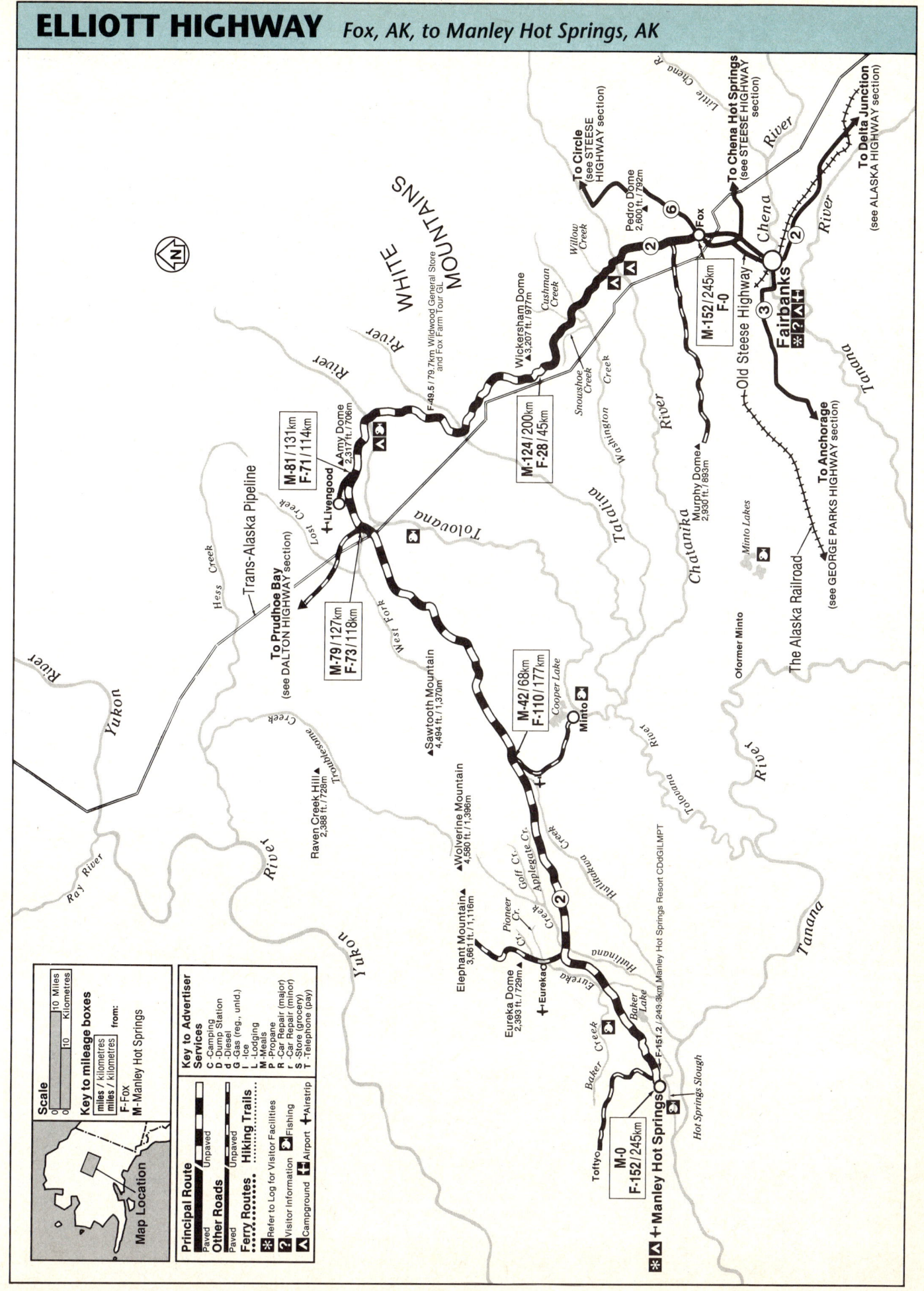

ELLIOTT HIGHWAY

F 29.8 (48 km) **M 122.2** (196.7 km) Turnouts with litter barrel to west. Spring water piped to road.

F 30.3 (48.8 km) **M 121.7** (195.9 km) Rough double-ended turnout to west. Fairbanks/North Star Borough boundary.

F 31 (49.9 km) **M 121** (194.7 km) Long double-ended gravel turnout to east.

F 31.8 (51.2 km) **M 120.2** (193.4 km) Steep, rough double-ended turnout to west.

F 34.7 (55.8 km) **M 117.3** (188.8 km) Good view of pipeline; creek.

F 36.4 (58.6 km) **M 115.6** (186 km) Large double-ended turnout to west.

F 37 (59.5 km) **M 115** (185.1 km) Globe Creek bridge. Steep access road to parking area next to bridge.

F 38 (61.1 km) **M 114** (183.5 km) Highway follows pipeline. View of Globe Creek canyon. Grapefruit Rocks to east.

F 39 (62.8 km) **M 113** (181.9 km) Double-ended turnout to east.

F 39.3 (63.2 km) **M 112.7** (181.4 km) Turnout with litter barrels to west.

F 40.6 (65.3 km) **M 111.4** (179.3 km) Scenic view from double-ended turnout with litter barrel to east.

F 41.2 (66.3 km) **M 110.8** (178.3 km) Drive-in parking area with litter barrel to east; no easy turnaround.

F 42.8 (68.8 km) **M 109.2** (175.7 km) Pipeline pump station No. 7 to west.

F 44.8 (72.1 km) **M 107.2** (172.5 km) Tatalina River bridge; rest area with litter barrel to east at south end of bridge. The Tatalina is a tributary of the Chatanika.

F 47.1 (75.8 km) **M 104.9** (168.8 km) Turnout with litter barrel to east.

F 47.6 (76.6 km) **M 104.4** (168 km) Turnout with litter barrels to east.

F 49.5 (79.7 km) **M 102.5** (165 km) Wildwood General Store. The store began as a lemonade stand run by some of the Carlson's 16 adopted children.

Wildwood General Store. See display ad this section.

F 49.9 (80.3 km) **M 102.1** (164.3 km) Northern Lights School.

F 51.9 (83.5 km) **M 100.1** (161.1 km) Double-ended parking area, water. View of White Mountains to northeast and the Elliott Highway descending slopes of Bridge Creek valley ahead. Bridge Creek flows into the Tolovana River.

F 52 (83.7 km) **M 100** (160.9 km) Grizzly and black bear are sometimes seen in this area.

F 57.1 (91.9 km) **M 94.9** (152.7 km) **Tolovana River** bridge; parking. Recreational gold panning permitted. Grayling to 11 inches; whitefish 12 to 18 inches; northern pike.

Colorado Creek trail to Colorado Creek and Windy Gap BLM cabins. Check with BLM office in Fairbanks for details.

F 58 (93.3 km) **M 94** (151.3 km) Highway winds around Amy Dome (elev. 2,317 feet/706m) to east. The Tolovana River flows in the valley to the southwest, paralleling the road.

F 59.3 (95.4 km) **M 92.7** (149.2 km) Parking area to west by stream.

F 60 (96.6 km) **M 92** (148.1 km) Double-ended turnout to west.

F 62.3 (100.3 km) **M 89.7** (144.4 km) Access to Fred Blixt BLM cabin, east side of road. Preregister at BLM office in Fairbanks.

F 70.1 (112.8 km) **M 81.9** (131.8 km) Livengood Creek, 2-lane bridge. Money Knob to northeast.

F 70.8 (113.9 km) **M 81.2** (130.7 km) Double-ended turnout with litter barrel at **junction** with Livengood access road. Drive 2 miles/3.2 km to **LIVENGOOD** (area pop. about 100); state highway maintenance station, EMT squad and store with liquor and souvenirs.

The settlement of Livengood began in July 1914 with the discovery of gold by Nathaniel R. Hudson and Jay Livengood. A lively mining camp until 1920, some $9.5 million in gold was sluiced out by miners. Large-scale mining was attempted in the late 1930s and again in the 1940s, but both operations were eventually shut down and Livengood became a ghost town.

With the building of the trans-Alaska pipeline and the North Slope Haul Road (now the Dalton Highway) in the 1970s, the town was revitalized as a construction camp. In 1977 a mining corporation acquired much of the gold-rich Livengood Bench. *NO TRESPASSING* on mining claims.

Private Aircraft: Livengood airstrip, adjacent northeast; elev. 730 feet/222m; length 1,000 feet/305m; turf; unattended.

F 70.9 (114.1 km) **M 81.1** (130.5 km) Large double-ended turnout with litter barrel to south.

F 73.1 (117.6 km) **M 78.9** (127 km) **Junction** with the Dalton Highway (see DALTON HIGHWAY section); turn left (west) for Manley Hot Springs.

F 74.1 (119.2 km) **M 77.9** (125.4 km) Alyeska pipeline access road (restricted). Pipeline stretches for miles to the east.

F 74.3 (119.6 km) **M 77.7** (125 km) Site of old Livengood pipeline camp.

F 74.7 (120.2 km) **M 77.3** (124.4 km) Camping spot with litter barrels at west end of **Tolvana River** bridge; grayling to 15 inches, use spinners or flies.

F 76.3 (122.8 km) **M 75.7** (121.8 km) Cascaden Ridge (low hills to north).

F 79 (127.1 km) **M 73** (117.5 km) Travelers should appreciate the abundance of dragonflies seen along the Elliott Highway: their main food is mosquitoes.

F 85.5 (137.6 km) **M 66.5** (107 km) Looking south toward the Tolovana River valley, travelers should be able to see Tolovana Hot Springs Dome (elev. 2,386 feet/727m). (Hot springs are on the other side of dome; no road access.)

F 93.7 (150.8 km) **M 58.3** (93.8 km) Watch for foxes from here to top of hill. Wild rhubarb and fireweed border roadsides for miles.

F 94.5 (152.1 km) **M 57.5** (92.5 km) Long double-ended turnout to south. Good vantage point to view Minto Flats, Tanana River and foothills of the Alaska Range to the south.

F 97 (156.1 km) **M 55** (88.5 km) The mountains to the north are Sawtooth (elev. 4,494 feet/1,370m); Wolverine (elev. 4,580 feet/1,396m); and Elephant (elev. 3,661 feet/1,116m). To the south are Tolovana River flats and Cooper Lake. Wild rhubarb and fireweed grow in old burn area.

F 98.3 (158.2 km) **M 53.7** (86.4 km) Turnout to southwest with view of Minto Lakes.

F 100.4 (161.6 km) **M 51.6** (83 km) Turnout to east in former gravel pit.

F 106.8 (171.9 km) **M 45.2** (72.7 km) Turnout with view of Sawtooth Mountains to north.

F 110 (177 km) **M 42** (67.6 km) **Junction** with Minto Road which leads 11 miles/17.7 km to the Indian village of **MINTO** (pop. 233). The village was moved to its present location from the east bank of the Tanana River in 1971 because of flooding. Minto has a lodge with accommodations and meals and a general store. Most Minto residents make their living by hunting and fishing. Some local people also work in the arts and crafts center, making birch-bark baskets and beaded skin and fur items. Temperatures here range from 55°F to 90°F/13°C to 32°C in summer, and from 32°F to -50°F/0°C to -46°C in winter. Minto Flats is one of the most popular duck hunting spots in Alaska in terms of number of hunters, according to the ADF&G.

Private Aircraft: Minto airstrip 1 mile/1.6 km east; elev. 460 feet/140m; length 2,000 feet/610m; gravel; unattended.

Minto Lakes, pike to 36 inches, use wobblers, bait, red-and-white spoons, good all summer. Also grayling, sheefish and whitefish. Name refers to all lakes in this lowland area. Accessible only by plane or boat; best to fly in.

F 113 (181.9 km) **M 39** (62.8 km) Evidence of 1983 burn.

F 113.5 (182.7 km) **M 38.5** (62 km) West Fork Hutlitakwa Creek.

F 119 (191.5 km) **M 33** (53.1 km) The road travels the ridges and hills, providing a "top of the world" view of hundreds of square miles in all directions.

F 119.5 (192.3 km) **M 32.5** (52.3 km) Eureka Dome (elev. 2,393 feet/729m) to north.

F 121.1 (194.9 km) **M 30.9** (49.7 km) To the north, travelers look down into the draws of Applegate and Goff creeks.

F 123.2 (198.3 km) **M 28.8** (46.3 km) Small turnout to north.

F 123.7 (199.1 km) **M 28.3** (45.5 km) Dugan Hills visible to the south at this point.

F 123.8 (199.2 km) **M 28.2** (45.4 km) Road begins descent into the Eureka area.

F 129.3 (208.1 km) **M 22.7** (36.5 km) Hutlinana Creek bridge.

F 131.3 (211.3 km) **M 20.7** (33.3 km) Eureka Road turnoff; access to private ranch. Active mining is taking place in this area. *NO TRESPASSING* on private claims. A trail leads to the former mining camp of Eureka, at the junction of Pioneer and Eureka creeks, 3 miles/4.8 km south of Eureka Dome.

Private Aircraft: Eureka Creek airstrip; elev. 700 feet/213m; length 1,600 feet/487m; turf; unattended.

F 137.4 (221.1 km) **M 14.6** (23.5 km) One-lane bridge over **Baker Creek.** Grayling 5 to 20 inches, use flies, black gnats, mosquitoes, May 15 to Sept. 30.

Winding road with many ups and downs.

F 138.4 (222.7 km) **M 13.6** (21.9 km) Highway goes over Overland Bluff and through a 1968 burn area. Bracket fungus is growing on the dead birch trees.

F 150 (241.4 km) **M 2** (3.2 km) This part of the road can be extremely slick after heavy rains. Drive with caution.

F 151.1 (243.2 km) **M 0.9** (1.4 km) Manley DOT/PF highway maintenance station.

F 151.2 (243.3 km) **M 0.8** (1.3 km) **Junction** with Tofty Road which leads 16 miles/

Wildwood General Store
and Fox Farm Tour

The Joe & Nancy Carlson family

49.5 ELLIOTT HIGHWAY
JOY, ALASKA

Gas • Tire Repair • Cabins • Snacks • Gifts

25.7 km to former mining area of Tofty, founded in 1908 by pioneer prospector A.F. Tofty, who reportedly took out 376 ounces of gold in 6 weeks. Mining activity in area.

The hot springs is on a hillside on the right before entering the town. One spring runs 35 gallons a minute with a temperature of 136°F/58°C, another runs 110 gallons per minute at 135°F/57°C, for a total of some 208,800 gallons every 24 hours.

F 151.2 (243.3 km) M 0.8 (1.3 km) **Manley Hot Springs Resort.** Open year-round. Swim in hot mineral spring-fed pool. Rooms with half baths, full baths or double jacuzzis; log cabins, restaurant, bar, RV park, dump station, laundromat, showers, gift shop. Gas and diesel, boats available for grayling, northern pike, sheefish. Riverboat charters available. All our tours are to authentic operating fish camps, gold mines. See the real interior Alaska lifestyle. River tours include visits to fish camp (operating fish wheel). Dogsled rides cross-country in winter. Crystal clear winter nights for viewing aurora borealis. Cross-country skiing, snowshoeing, ice skating. We can accommodate up to 65 guests. Write Box 28, Manley Hot Springs Resort, Manley Hot Springs, AK 99756 or phone (907) 672-3611. Fax (907) 672-3461. [ADVERTISEMENT]

Manley Hot Springs

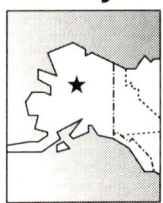

F 152 (244.6 km) M 0 Located at the end of the Elliott Highway on Hot Springs Slough. **Population:** 88. **Elevation:** 330 feet/101m. **Climate:** Mean temperature in July is 59°F/15°C, in January -10.4°F/-23.6°C. Record high 93°F/33.9°C in June 1969, record low -70°F/-56.7°C in January 1934. Precipitation in summer averages 2.53 inches a month. Snow from October through April, with traces in September and May. Greatest mean monthly snowfall in January (11.1 inches). Record snowfall 49 inches in January 1937.

Private Aircraft: Manley Hot Springs civil airstrip (open year-round), adjacent southwest; elev. 270 feet/82m; length 2,700 feet/823m; gravel; fuel 80, 100.

A pocket of "Pioneer Alaska." J.F. Karshner homesteaded here in 1902 about the same time the U.S. Army Signal Corps established a telegraph station nearby. The location soon became known as Baker Hot Springs, after nearby Baker Creek. Frank Manley built a 4-story resort hotel here in 1907. The settlement's name was changed to Manley Hot Springs in 1957. Once a busy trading center during peak activity in the nearby Eureka and Tofty mining districts, Manley Hot Springs is now a quiet settlement with a trading post, roadhouse, airfield and hot springs resort. Many residents are enthusiastic gardeners and visitors may see abundant displays of vegetables and berries growing around homes and businesses. Outstanding display of wild irises at the airstrip in June.

A restaurant, bar and overnight accommodations are at the roadhouse. The post office, gas station and grocery are at the trading post. There is an air taxi service here and scheduled service from Fairbanks.

The Manley Roadhouse. Come visit one of Alaska's oldest original roadhouses from the gold rush era. See the many prehistoric and Alaskana artifacts on display. The Manley Roadhouse is a great place to meet local miners, dog mushers, trappers or fishermen enjoying a cup of coffee. The Manley Roadhouse specializes in traditional Alaska home-style hospitality, fresh-baked pies, giant cinnamon rolls and good food. Largest liquor selection in Alaska. Stop by and see us. See display ad this section. [ADVERTISEMENT]

Manley Hot Springs Park Assoc. maintains a public campground near the bridge in town; fee $2 (pay at roadhouse). The hot springs are a short walk from the campground. There's a nice grassy picnic area on the slough near the campground. A boat launch is also nearby.

Manley Boat Charters. Sightseeing, river tours, pike and sheefishing. Hourly rates for fishing or short scenic trips. Photography. Multi-day trips to Nowitna, Yukon rivers for 3 or more people. Reservations (907) 672-3271 or 672-3321, or write Frank or Dian Gurtler, Box 52, Manley Hot Springs, AK 99756. Fax (907) 672-3461. Frank's Tire Shop. Tire repair, used tires. [ADVERTISEMENT]

Manley Hot Springs Slough, pike 18 to 36 inches, use spinning and trolling lures, May through September. Follow the dirt road from the old Northern Commercial Co. store out of town for 2.5 miles/4 km to reach the Tanana River, king, silver and chum salmon from 7 to 40 lbs., June 15 to Sept. 30. Fish wheels and nets are used.

Boat race on the Tanana River draws a well-prepared competitor. (Jerrianne Lowther, staff)

MANLEY HOT SPRINGS ADVERTISERS

Manley Boat Charters.......Ph. (907) 672-3271
Manley Hot Springs
 Resort.....................Mile 151.2 Elliott Hwy.
Manley Roadhouse, The...Ph. (907) 672-3161
Manley Trading Post.....................Downtown

MANLEY TRADING POST
AVIATION GAS
Bob & Patty Lee

GAS
GIFTS
GROCERIES
LIQUOR
POST OFFICE
Manley Hot Springs, AK

MANLEY ROADHOUSE
SERVING ALASKA SINCE 1906
Historic and Prehistoric Artifacts on display

BAR
GRUB
ROOMS
CABINS

Mile F 152 Elliott Highway
Bob & Patty Lee, Innkeepers • Phone (907) 672-3161

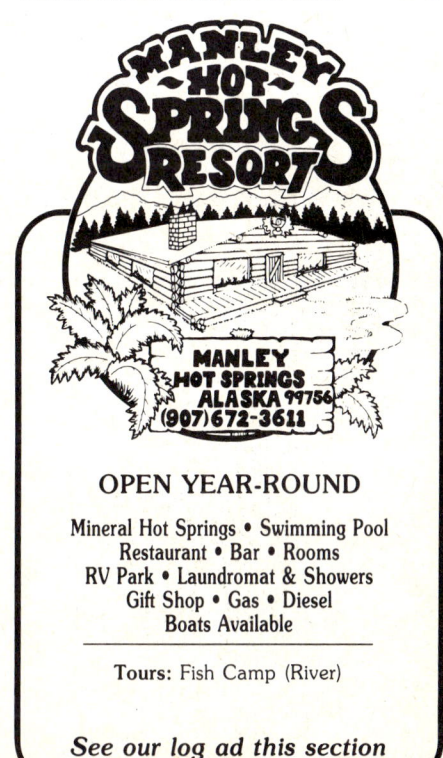

MANLEY HOT SPRINGS RESORT
MANLEY HOT SPRINGS ALASKA 99756
(907) 672-3611

OPEN YEAR-ROUND

Mineral Hot Springs • Swimming Pool
Restaurant • Bar • Rooms
RV Park • Laundromat & Showers
Gift Shop • Gas • Diesel
Boats Available

Tours: Fish Camp (River)

See our log ad this section

KENAI PENINSULA

Includes Sterling, Seward and Hope highway logs and Seldovia
(See maps, pages 412 and 435–436)

The Kenai Peninsula offers spectacular lake and mountain scenery. (John W. Warden)

The Kenai Peninsula lies south of Anchorage, bounded on the north by Turnagain Arm and the Chugach Mountains, on the west by Cook Inlet, and on the south and east by the Gulf of Alaska. The scenery is varied and beautiful. The massive peaks and broad ice fields of the Kenai Mountains form the spine of the peninsula, dropping away to the great forested plateau of the western area. Its many lakes, rivers and streams make the Kenai a prime sportfishing destination.

The Kenai Peninsula section in *The MILEPOST®* is divided into 2 parts: the Seward Highway, Alaska Route 1 to the Sterling Highway junction then Alaska Route 9 to Seward; and the Sterling Highway, Alaska Route 1, from the Seward Highway junction to Homer. Physical mileposts on both highways show distance from Seward. In winter, some sections of the Seward Highway are subject to avalanches. Check Anchorage news sources for winter road conditions.

Several major Kenai Peninsula side roads are logged in the following sections. In the Seward Highway section there are logs of the Hope Highway, Alyeska Access Road and Portage Glacier Road. In the Sterling Highway section there are logs of the following side roads: Skilak Lake Loop Road, Swanson River Road, Kenai Spur Highway, Kalifornsky Beach Road, Cohoe Loop Road and Anchor River Beach Road.

The 127-mile-/204-km-long Seward Highway, connecting Anchorage and Seward, was designated a National Forest Scenic Byway in 1990. The scenic byways program is designed to alert motorists to areas of unique interest, and inform them of the natural history national forest lands.

Leaving Anchorage, the Seward Highway follows the scenic north shore of Turnagain Arm through Chugach State Park and Chugach National Forest, permitting a panoramic view of the south shore and the Kenai Mountains. Pods of beluga whales are sometimes seen in Turnagain Arm. (The only all white whale, belugas are easy to identify.)

Turnagain Arm, an easterly extension of Cook Inlet, was called Return by the Russians. Captain Cook, seeking the fabled Northwest Passage in 1778, called it Turnagain River and Captain Vancouver, doing a better job of surveying in 1794, gave it the present name of Turnagain Arm.

Turnagain Arm is known for having one of the world's remarkably high tides, with a diurnal range of more than 33 feet/10m. Just after low tide, a tidal bore frequently occurs. A bore tide is an abrupt rise of tidal water, moving rapidly landward, formed by a flood tide surging into a constricted inlet such as Turnagain Arm. This foaming wall of water may reach a height of 6 feet/2m and is very dangerous to small craft. To see a bore tide, check the Anchorage-area tide tables for low tide, then add approximately 2 hours and 15 minutes to the Anchorage low tide for the bore to reach points between Miles 32 and 37 on the Seward Highway. *CAUTION: The mud flats of Turnagain Arm are extremely dangerous. Do not walk out on the mud flats.*

There is a bike trail along the Seward Highway between Anchorage and Girdwood. The bike route is marked by signs. Numerous hiking trails branch off both the Seward and Sterling highways. There is mountain biking on many Kenai Peninsula trails, including the 38-mile Resurrection Pass trail.

The Sterling Highway passes through Chugach National Forest and Kenai National Wildlife Refuge. In the Kenai Mountains are herds of Dall sheep and mountain goats. Black bears share some of the wilder areas with huge brown bears, among the world's largest carnivorous animals. Caribou once roamed the peninsula but became extinct there about 1913. Transplants in the 1960s reestablished the caribou population. Additional caribou were transplanted in 1985–86.

From Soldotna south, the Sterling Highway follows the west coast of the peninsula along Cook Inlet. There are beautiful views on clear days of volcanic peaks on the Alaska Peninsula.

In 1992, watch for road construction on the Sterling Highway from the Moose River bridge west to Soldotna. Expect some road construction and repaving projects along the Seward Highway.

Emergency medical services: Phone 911 on the Seward and Sterling highways, or use CB channels 9, 11 or 19.

SEWARD HIGHWAY

Alaska Routes 1 and 9
(See map, page 412)

Seward Highway Log

ALASKA ROUTE 1
Distance from Seward (S) is followed by distance from Anchorage (A). Physical mileposts show distance from Seward.

S 127 (204.4 km) **A 0** Gambell Street and 10th Avenue in Anchorage. The Seward Highway (Gambell Street) connects with the Glenn Highway in Anchorage via 5th Avenue (westbound) and 6th Avenue (eastbound). (See area map in the ANCHORAGE section.) Follow Seward Highway signs south on Gambell.

S 126.7 (203.9 km) **A 0.3** (0.5 km) 15th Avenue (DeBarr Road).

S 126.6 (203.7 km) **A 0.4** (0.6 km) 16th Avenue; access to Sullivan sports arena and baseball stadium.

S 126 (202.8 km) **A 1** (1.6 km) Fireweed Lane.

S 125.8 (202.4 km) **A 1.2** (1.9 km) Northern Lights Boulevard (1-way westbound). Access to shopping centers.

S 125.7 (202.3 km) **A 1.3** (2.1 km) Benson Boulevard (1-way eastbound).

S 125.4 (201.8 km) **A 1.6** (2.6 km) Southbound access only to Old Seward Highway.

S 125.3 (201.6 km) **A 1.7** (2.7 km) 36th Avenue; hospital to east.

S 125.2 (201.5 km) **A 1.8** (2.9 km) Freeway begins southbound. There are no services or facilities along the new Seward Highway. However, there are several exits in the next 7.5 miles/12.1 km to the Old Seward Highway (which parallels the new Seward Highway) where traveler services are available.

S 124.7 (200.7 km) **A 2.3** (3.7 km) Tudor Road overpass; exits both sides of highway. (Tudor Road is used as a bypass route for northbound travelers, connecting them with the Glenn Highway via Muldoon Road.)

S 124.2 (199.8 km) **A 2.8** (4.5 km) Campbell Creek bridge.

S 123.7 (199.1 km) **A 3.3** (5.3 km) Dowling Road underpass; exits on both sides of highway.

S 122.7 (197.5 km) **A 4.3** (6.9 km) 76th Avenue exit, southbound traffic only.

S 122.2 (196.7 km) **A 4.8** (7.7 km) Dimond Boulevard underpass; exits on both sides of highway.

S 120.8 (194.4 km) **A 6.2** (10 km) O'Malley Road underpass; exits on both sides of highway. Turn east on O'Malley Road and drive 2 miles/3.2 km to reach the Alaska Zoo. Turn west for access to Old Seward Highway and major shopping area on Dimond Boulevard. Views of Chugach Mountains along this stretch.

S 119.7 (192.6 km) **A 7.3** (11.7 km) Huffman Road underpass; exits on both sides of highway.

S 118.5 (190.7 km) **A 8.5** (13.7 km) De Armoun Road overpass, exits both sides of highway.

S 117.8 (189.6 km) **A 9.2** (14.8 km) Overpass: Exits both sides of highway for Old Seward Highway (west); access to Rabbit Creek Road (east). The picturesque Chapel by the Sea overlooks Turnagain Arm. The church is often photographed because of its unique setting and its display of flowers.

S 117.6 (189.3 km) **A 9.4** (15.1 km) View of Turnagain Arm and Mount Spurr.

S 117.4 (188.9 km) **A 9.6** (15.4 km) Rabbit Creek Rifle Range to west. Boardwalk Wildlife Viewing exit leads east to Potter Point State Game Refuge. This is a very popular spot for bird watching. From the parking lot, an extensive boardwalk crosses Potter Marsh, a refuge and nesting area for waterfowl. The marsh was created when railroad construction dammed a small creek in the area. Today, the marsh is visited by arctic terns, Canadian geese, trumpeter swans, many species of ducks and other

Watch for Dall sheep on rocks above Seward Highway. (Nancy Faville)

KENAI PENINSULA

We have it all! Deep-sea, river and lake fishing, glaciers, wildlife, rafting, historic sites, museums, camping, golfing, clamming, RV parks, fine accomodations and more.

Call or write any of these Chambers of Commerce to see why we say.....

It's a Play-full place

Anchor Point Chamber of Commerce
Box 610, Anchor Point, AK 99556 235-2600

Funny River Chamber of Commerce, HC-1, Box 1587, Soldotna, AK 99669 262-7711

Homer Chamber of Commerce
Box 541, Homer, AK 99603 235-7740

Kenai Chamber of Commerce
Box 497, Kenai, AK 99611 283-7989

North Peninsula Chamber
Box 8053, Nikiski, AK 99635 776-8369

Seldovia Chamber of Commerce
Drawer L, Seldovia, AK 99663 234-7890

Seward Chamber of Commerce
Box 749, Seward, AK 99664 224-8051

Soldotna Chamber
Box 236, Soldotna, AK 99669 262-9814

Hope Chamber
Box 89, Hope
AK 99605

Kenai Bicentennial
Box 1991, Kenai
AK 99611 283-1991

Kenai Peninsula Tourism Marketing Council
110 Willow, Suite 106, Kenai, AK 99611 (907) 283-3850

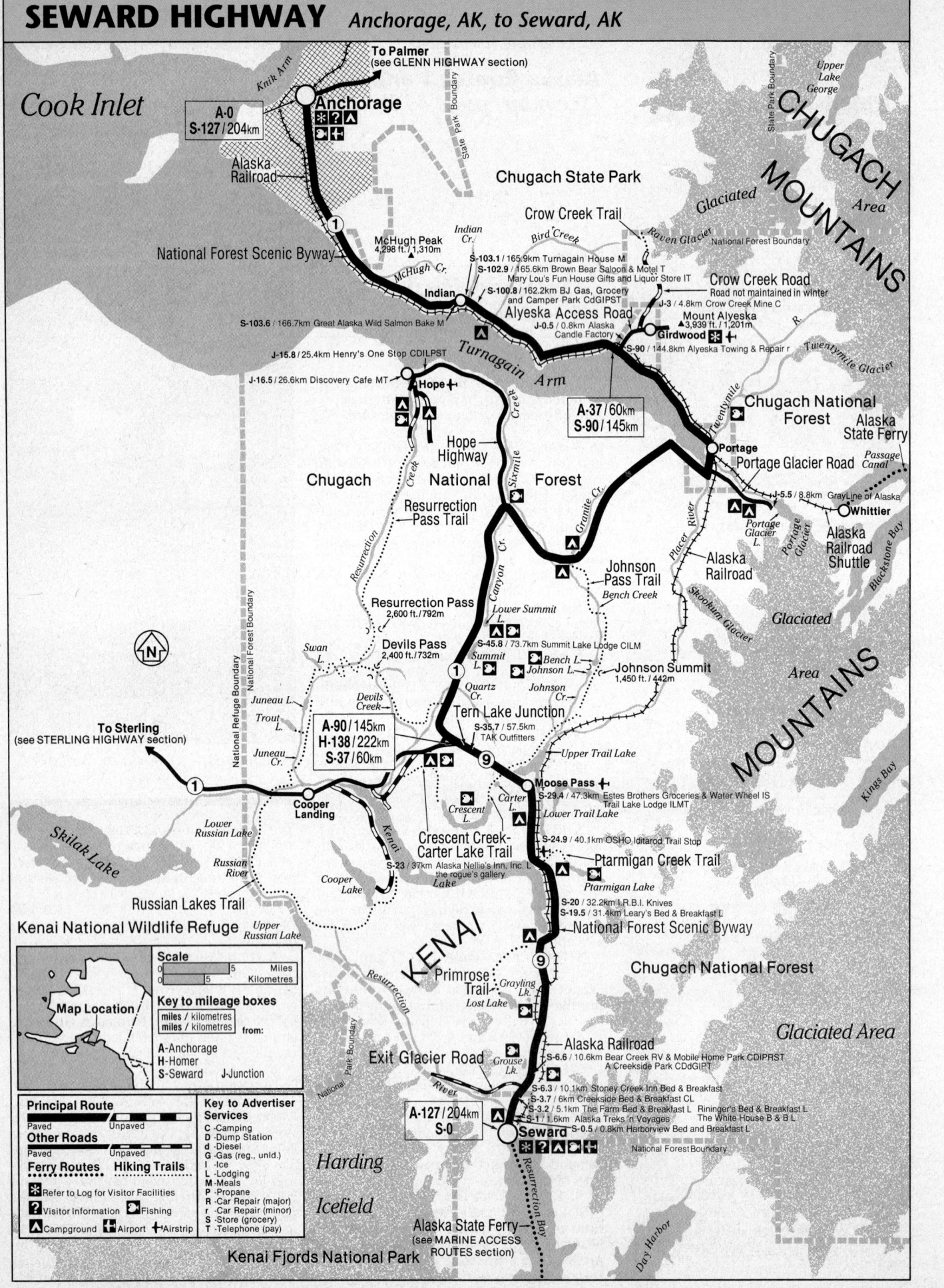

SEWARD HIGHWAY Anchorage, AK, to Seward, AK

water birds. Bring binoculars.

S 116.1 (186.8 km) **A 10.9** (17.5 km) Paved double-ended turnout to east. Highway parallels Alaska Raiload southbound to **Milepost S 90.8**.

S 115.4 (185.7 km) **A 11.6** (18.7 km) **Junction** with Old Seward Highway; access to Potter Valley Road. Old Johnson trail begins 0.5 mile/0.6 km up Potter Valley Road; parking at trailhead. This state park trail is cleared only in the first 10 miles/16 km. Moderate to difficult hike; watch for bears.

The natural gas pipeline from the Kenai Peninsula emerges from beneath Turnagain Arm here and follows the roadway to Anchorage.

WARNING: When the tide is out the sand in Turnagain Arm might look inviting. DO NOT go out on it. Some of it is quicksand. You could become trapped in the mud and not be rescued before the tide comes in, as happened to a victim in 1989.

S 115.3 (185.6 km) **A 11.7** (18.8 km) Entering Chugach State Park southbound. Potter Section House, Chugach State Park Headquarters (phone 345-5014) to west; large parking lot, wheelchair-accessible toilets. Open daily in summer. The renovated Potter Section House, dedicated in October 1986, was home to a small crew of railroad workers who maintained the Alaska Railroad tracks between Seward and Anchorage in the days of coal- and steam-powered locomotives. Displays here include photographs from the National Archives, a vintage snowblower and working model railroad.

S 115.1 (185.2 km) **A 11.9** (19.2 km) Potter Creek trailhead to east.

S 115 (185 km) **A 12** (19.3 km) Watch for rockfalls. Avalanche area and hazardous driving conditions during winter for the next 25 miles/40.2 km.

From here to **Milepost S 90** there are many turnouts on both sides of the highway, some with scenic views of Turnagain Arm.

S 114.7 (184.6 km) **A 12.3** (19.8 km) Weigh station and pay phone to east.

S 114.5 (184.3 km) **A 12.5** (20.1 km) Double-ended gravel turnout to east. From here to **Milepost S 104**, patches of harebells (Bluebells of Scotland) can be seen in late July and early August.

S 113.1 (182 km) **A 13.9** (22.4 km) Small gravel turnout to east at McHugh boulder area. Watch for rock climbers practicing on the steep cliffs alongside the highway. The cliffs are part of the base of McHugh Peak (elev. 4,298 feet/1,310m).

S 111.8 (179.9 km) **A 15.2** (24.5 km) McHugh Creek state wayside to east with 30 picnic sites. A stream and waterfall make this a very refreshing place to stop. *CAUTION: Steep but paved road into this picnic site. Be sure you have plenty of power and good brakes for descent, especially if you are towing a trailer.* There is also a parking area beside the highway. Good berry picking in season near the stream for wild currants, blueberries and watermelon berries. A 1-mile portion of the Old Johnson trail here is wheelchair accessible.

S 111.6 (179.6 km) **A 15.4** (24.8 km) Double-ended gravel turnout to east. There are numerous turnouts southbound to Indian.

S 110.3 (177.5 km) **A 16.7** (26.9 km) Beluga Point scenic viewpoint and photo stop has a commanding view of Turnagain Arm. A good place to see bore tides and beluga whales. Large paved double-ended turnout to west with tables, benches, telescopes and interpretive signs.

WARNING: Do not go out on the mud flats at low tide. The glacial silt and water can create a dangerous quicksand.

S 108.5 (174.6 km) **A 18.5** (29.8 km) Rainbow Road to Rainbow Valley.

S 108.4 (174.4 km) **A 18.6** (29.9 km) Rainbow trailhead and parking; access to Old Johnson trail.

S 107.3 (172.7 km) **A 19.7** (31.7 km) Gravel turnout to east. Rock climbers practice on the cliffs here.

S 107 (172.2 km) **A 20** (32.2 km) From here to Girdwood, in summer when snow is still on the peaks or after heavy rainfall, watch for many small waterfalls tumbling down the mountainsides to Turnagain Arm.

S 106.9 (172 km) **A 20.1** (32.3 km) Scenic viewpoint. Double-ended paved turnout to west; Old Johnson trail access. Watch for Dall sheep near road. *NOTE: DO NOT FEED WILDLIFE.*

S 106.7 (171.7 km) **A 20.3** (32.7 km) Paved turnout to east; Windy trailhead.

S 106.6 (171.5 km) **A 20.4** (32.8 km) Large paved turnout to west; watch for Dall sheep.

S 105.7 (170.1 km) **A 21.3** (34.3 km) Falls Creek trailhead and parking to east; Old Johnson trail access.

S 104 (167.4 km) **A 23** (37 km) Indian Valley Mine National Historic Site.

S 103.9 (167.2 km) **A 23.1** (37.2 km) Indian Road and Indian Valley businesses to east.

S 103.6 (166.7 km) **A 23.4** (37.7 km) **Great Alaska Wild Salmon Bake.** Treat yourself to 2 of nature's wonders—fresh Alaska salmon and Alaska halibut. Grilled to perfection on our outdoor barbecue as you watch, our Alaska salmon and halibut are the freshest in the world! Also featuring New York steaks, reindeer sausage, reindeer burgers, plus our fresh salad bar, and cheesecake smothered in Alaska blueberries for dessert. Top it all off with our spectacular view of Turnagain Arm while you dine!
[ADVERTISEMENT]

S 103.5 (166.6 km) **A 23.5** (37.8 km) **INDIAN.** Pay phone at restaurant.

S 103.1 (165.9 km) **A 23.9** (38.5 km) Bore Tide Road, also called Ocean View Road. Turnagain House restaurant.

Dip-netters fish for hooligan at Twentymile River, Milepost S 81. (Jerrianne Lowther, staff)

FRESH SEAFOOD
FINE STEAKS   **BABY BACK RIBS**

Turnagain House

Indian, Alaska   **Res. 653-7500**
Between Anchorage and Alyeska

KENAI PENINSULA • SEWARD HIGHWAY

Turnagain House, Milepost 103.1 Seward Highway at Indian, AK. Fresh Alaskan seafood, fine steaks and baby back ribs. Located 16 miles south of Anchorage. Excellent view of Turnagain Arm and bore tides. Rustic and casual atmosphere. The Turnagain House is a year-round favorite of Anchorage residents and is considered one of the finest restaurants in the area. Major credit cards accepted. Reservations: (907) 653-7500. [ADVERTISEMENT]

S 103 (165.8 km) **A 24** (38.6 km) Bridge over Indian Creek.

Indian Creek, heavily fished! Pink salmon, sea-run Dolly Varden, few coho (silver) salmon and rainbow, June to September; pink salmon run from latter part of July to mid-August in even-numbered years. **Bird Creek**, same fishing as Indian Creek, except heavier run of pink salmon in July and August.

S 102.9 (165.6 km) **A 24.1** (38.8 km) Indian Creek rest area to west; wheelchair accessible toilets and parking. Bar and liquor store to east.

Brown Bear Saloon & Motel. See display ad this section.

Mary Lou's Fun House Gifts and Liquor Store. See display ad this section.

S 102.1 (164.3 km) **A 24.9** (40.1 km) Bird Ridge trailhead and parking; Old Johnson trail access.

S 101.5 (163.3 km) **A 25.5** (41 km) Bridge over Bird Creek; parking. Watch for pedestrians next mile southbound.

S 101.2 (162.9 km) **A 25.8** (41.5 km) Bird Creek State Recreation Site with picnic sites and 19 campsites, firepits, pay phone, covered picnic tables, toilets and water. Firewood is sometimes available. Camping fee $8/night or annual pass. A pleasant campground densely wooded but cleared along the high banks of Turnagain Arm. Paved bike trail goes through campground (nice ride along Turnagain Arm). Great spot for sunbathing. This campground is full most weekends in the summer. Don't count on coming in late at night and finding a space. Check our advertisers for commercial campgrounds in this area.

WARNING: Do not go out on the mud flats at low tide. The glacial silt and water can create a dangerous quicksand.

S 100.8 (162.2 km) **A 26.2** (42.2 km) **BJ Gas, Grocery and Camper Park.** See display ad this section.

S 100.5 (161.7 km) **A 26.5** (42.6 km) To the east is the Bird House Bar, a local landmark.

S 99.8 (160.6 km) **A 27.2** (43.8 km) Paved turnout to west. Southbound traffic entering avalanche area, northbound traffic leaving avalanche area.

S 99.3 (159.8 km) **A 27.7** (44.6 km) Large gravel turnout to west with view across Turnagain Arm to the cut in the mountains where Sixmile Creek drains into the arm; the old mining settlement of Sunrise was located here. The town of Hope is to the southwest. The peak visible across Turnagain Arm between here and Girdwood is Mount Alpenglow in the Kenai mountain range. Avalanche gates.

S 99.2 (159.6 km) **A 27.8** (44.7 km) Avalanche gun emplacement (motorists will notice several of these along the highway southbound).

S 97.2 (156.4 km) **A 29.8** (48 km) Southbound traffic leaving winter avalanche area, northbound traffic entering avalanche area.

S 96.8 (155.8 km) **A 30.2** (48.6 km) *CAUTION: Narrow winding road from here south to Milepost S 91.5 with pavement breaks, holes and hazardous road edge. Watch for road construction crews doing surveying and slope stability work in 1992.* Winter avalanche area. There are many gravel turnouts the next 5 miles/8 km southbound.

S 95.5 (153.7 km) **A 31.5** (50.7 km) Turnout to west; avalanche gun emplacement.

S 94.4 (151.9 km) **A 32.6** (52.5 km) Large gravel turnout to west; avalanche safety zone.

S 90.8 (146.1 km) **A 36.2** (58.3 km) *CAUTION: Railroad crossing and very bad curve.*

S 90.6 (145.8 km) **A 36.4** (58.6 km) Bridge crosses Tidewater Slough. Avalanche gun emplacement at south end of bridge.

S 90.4 (145.5 km) **A 36.6** (58.9 km) Leaving Chugach State Park southbound. The 1964 Good Friday earthquake caused the subsidence of land in the Turnagain Arm area, particularly apparent from here to **Milepost S 74**. As a result many trees had their root systems invaded by salt water, as seen by the stands of dead spruce trees along here. Good bird watching, including bald eagles, arctic terns, sandhill cranes.

S 90.2 (145.2 km) **A 36.8** (59.2 km) Girdwood highway maintenance station. End avalanche area southbound.

S 90 (144.8 km) **A 37** (59.5 km) **Junction** with 3-mile/4.8-km Alyeska (pronounced al-ee-ES-ka) access road to Crow Creek road and mine, Girdwood and Alyeska Recreation Area. Worth the drive! ALYESKA ACCESS ROAD log starts on opposite page. This intersection is "old" Girdwood; the railroad station, a school, gas station and shopping center are located here. After the 1964 earthquake and tidal wave, Girdwood moved up the access road 2.1 miles/3.4 km.

Alyeska Towing & Repair. See display ad this section.

S 89.8 (144.5 km) **A 37.2** (59.9 km) Glacier Creek bridge.

S 89.1 (143.4 km) **A 37.9** (61 km) Virgin Creek bridge. View of 3 glaciers to east.

S 89 (143.2 km) **A 38** (61 km) Wide straight highway from here to Portage. The Alaska Railroad parallels the highway.

S 88.2 (141.9 km) **A 38.8** (62.4 km) Turnout to east.

S 87.5 (140.8 km) **A 39.5** (63.6 km) Avalanche gun emplacement.

S 86.1 (138.6 km) **A 40.9** (65.8 km) Small gravel turnout by ocean. Chugach National Forest boundary sign.

S 84.1 (135.3 km) **A 42.9** (69 km) Peterson Creek. View of Blueberry Mountain.

S 82.3 (132.4 km) **A 44.7** (71.9 km) Turnout to east.

S 81 (130.4 km) **A 46** (74 km) BLM observation platform with informative plaques on Twentymile River wetlands and wildlife. Watch for dipnetters in the spring fishing for hooligan (also known as eulachon or candlefish), a smelt. Road access east to Twentymile River.

Twentymile River, good hooligan fishing in May. These smelt are taken with long-handled dip nets. Pink, red and silver (coho) salmon 4 to 10 lbs., use attraction lures, best in August. Dolly Varden 4 to 10 lbs., eggs best, good all summer in clear-water tributaries.

S 80.7 (129.9 km) **A 46.3** (74.5 km) Bridge over Twentymile River, which flows out of the Twentymile Glacier and other glaciers through a long green valley at the edge of the highway. Twentymile Glacier can be seen at the end of the valley to the northeast. Twentymile River is a popular windsurfing area in summer. Gravel turnout west side of highway.

S 80.3 (129.2 km) **A 46.7** (75.2 km) Access to the Alaska Railroad loading area for ferry traffic taking the shuttle train to Whittier. Ticket office and pay phone. Connections at Whittier with Alaska Marine Highway; regular ferry service is provided across Prince William Sound past the spectacular Columbia Glacier to Valdez. For details see the ALASKA RAILROAD and PRINCE WILLIAM SOUND sections.

S 80.1 (128.9 km) **A 46.9** (75.5 km) **PORTAGE**. No facilities here; a restaurant is located at **Milepost S 78.8**. Town was destroyed in the 1964 earthquake.

Leaving Game Management Unit 14C, entering unit 7, southbound.

S 80 (128.7 km) **A 47** (75.6 km) Second access to motor vehicle loading ramps and passenger parking for Alaska Railroad shuttle train from Portage to Whittier.

S 79.4 (127.8 km) **A 47.6** (76.6 km)
(Continues on page 418)

Mary Lou Redmond welcomes you
Hardcore Alaskan Gifts™
— Since 1952 ▪ Tourists Welcome —
MARY LOU'S FUN HOUSE GIFTS AND LIQUOR STORE
Mile S 102.9 – Indian Creek
(907) 653-7654 ☎ Pay phone on premises

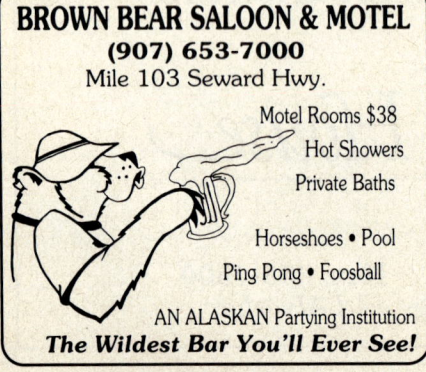

BJ GAS GROCERY and CAMPER PARK
ICE CREAM • ICE
LIQUOR STORE
PAY PHONE
Milepost 100.8 • (907) 653-1144
Write: Box 8500, Bird Creek, AK 99540
GAS • DIESEL PROPANE

BROWN BEAR SALOON & MOTEL
(907) 653-7000
Mile 103 Seward Hwy.
Motel Rooms $38
Hot Showers
Private Baths
Horseshoes • Pool
Ping Pong • Foosball
AN ALASKAN Partying Institution
The Wildest Bar You'll Ever See!

Alyeska Towing & Repair
783-3100
24-Hour Towing
Tire Repair • Welding
Minor Auto Repair
Girdwood, Alaska
MILE 90 Seward Highway

Alyeska Access Road Log

This 3-mile/4.8-km spur road provides access to Crow Creek Road, Girdwood and Alyeska Resort and Skyride. There are numerous restaurants, gift shops, accommodations and attractions in the Girdwood/Alyeska area.

Distance is measured from junction with Seward Highway (J).

J 0.2 (0.3 km) Bridge over Alaska Railroad tracks. Paved bike trail to Alyeska Resort begins.

J 0.4 (0.6 km) Monarch Mine Road. Chugach National Forest Glacier Ranger District office (P.O. Box 129, Girdwood 99587; phone 783-3242). Maps and information on USFS cabins and campgrounds available here.

J 0.5 (0.8 km) **Alaska Candle Factory.** One-half mile off Seward Highway on Alyeska. Home of handcrafted candles made in the form of Alaska wild animals. Hand-dipped tapers and molded candles made daily. All candles have unique individual designs. Open 7 days a week, 10 A.M. to 6 P.M. Visitors welcome. (907) 783-2354. P.O. Box 786, Girdwood, AK 99587. [ADVERTISEMENT]

J 1.9 (3.1 km) **Junction** with Crow Creek Road on left. Restaurant located 0.2 mile/0.3 km up Crow Creek Road. This single-lane dirt road leads 3.1 miles/5 km to Crow Creek Mine, 7 miles/11.3 km to Crow Pass trailhead. In winter, the road is not maintained past Mile 0.6. Crow Creek Mine is a national historic site. The authentic gold mine and 8 other buildings at the mine are open to the public (fee charged).

Crow Creek Mine. Visit this historic 1898 mining camp located in the heart of Chugach National Forest. Drive 3 miles up Crow Creek Road (Old Iditarod trail). Eight original buildings. Pan for gold. Visit our gift shop. Enjoy beautiful grounds, ponds, flowers. Animals and friendly people. Campground for tents and self-contained vehicles. Open May 15-Sept. 15, 9 A.M. to 6 P.M. daily. Phone (907) 278-8060 (messages). [ADVERTISEMENT]

Crow Pass and Old Iditarod trailhead at Mile 7 Crow Creek Road. Crow Pass trail climbs steeply 3 miles/4.8 km to ruins of an old gold mine and a USFS public-use cabin at Crow Pass near Raven Glacier; hiking time approximately 2½ hours. The Old Iditarod trail extends 22.5 miles/36.2 km north from Crow Pass down Raven Creek drainage to the Chugach State Park Visitor Center on Eagle River Road. All of the hiking trail, from Crow Creek Road trailhead to the state park visitor center, is part of the Iditarod National Historic Trail used in the early 1900s. Trail is usually free of snow by mid-June. Closed to motorized vehicles; horses prohibited during early spring due to soft trail conditions.

J 2 (3.2 km) California Creek bridge.

J 2.1 (3.4 km) **GIRDWOOD** (pop. 300), at the junction of Alyeska access road and Hightower Road. **Emergency Services: Alaska State Troopers, EMS** and **Fire Department,** phone 911 or 783-2704 or 269-5711. Located here are a post office, 2 restaurants, vacation rental offices, laundromat, grocery store, small shops and fire hall.

Private Aircraft: Girdwood landing

Golden Eagle Property Rentals
Discover luxury for less in our chalets and condos with fully equipped kitchens and spectacular mountain views.
Nightly / Weekly
P.O. Box 1196, Girdwood, Alaska 99587
(907) 783-2000 • FAX (907) 783-2425

"EDELWEISS" Restaurant
A German Restaurant, at Alyeska Resort in Girdwood, near the Kobuk Jade Shop

Specializing in homecooked beef soup with dumplings, goulash soup, bratwurst, knackwurst, German potato salad and sauerkraut. We also have Weiner Schnitzel, beef rouladen, pork roast and other daily specials. Don't forget the German beers and wines, Espresso, Cappuccino, and of course chocolate cakes and our famous apple strudel.

Summer Hours 10 a.m. - 9 p.m. 7 Days A Week
Fall, Winter & Spring 11 a.m. - 9 p.m.

For information (907) 783-2526 • Volker J. Hruby, Owner

Pan for GOLD at Historic CROW CREEK MINE
National Historic Site
Gorgeous Grounds
Campground • Gift Shop

See log ad Alyeska Access Road

TIMBERLINE BED & BREAKFAST
Host: Ann Sassara
Rooms in a family atmosphere
2nd House-Chalet-off Timberline Dr.
(907) 783-2917
P.O. Box 596, Girdwood, Alaska 99587

Alyeska Access Road Log (continued)

Fresh Pasta, Pizza, Steaks, Seafood
54 Varieties of Beer
MasterCard/VISA/American Express

CHAIR 5 RESTAURANT

OPEN 9 a.m.–Midnight
(907) 783-2500
GIRDWOOD, ALASKA

Alyeska View Bed & Breakfast
Main house guest rooms with shared bath
OPEN YEAR-ROUND
From Alyeska Access Road, right on Timberline, left on Vail
P.O. Box 234, Girdwood, Alaska 99587

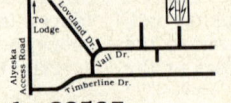

Emmy's Hair Studio
Professional licensed hairstylist
Men • Women • Children
(907) 783-2747

Gifts of Jade
From North of the Arctic Circle

- Located across from the Golden Nugget Hotel at Alyeska Resort in Girdwood.
- Open Daily. Winter: 10 a.m. to 6 p.m. Summer: 9 a.m. to 6 p.m.

We invite you to stop by and have a cup of coffee while you watch our jade being cut. You'll find our artifact collection interesting also. Outside we have a 22-ton jade boulder on display.

Jade Jewelry • Raw Jade
Jade and Ivory Carvings

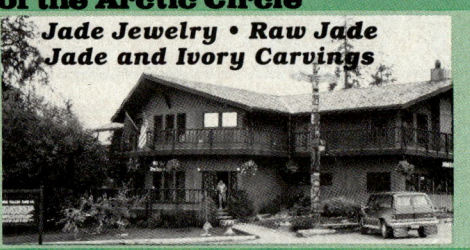

Kobuk Valley Jade Company
Box 516 • Phone (907) 783-2764 • Girdwood, Alaska 99587
Member, Alaska Visitors Association

Vista Alyeska Accommodations
Fully Furnished Cabins • Condos • Chalets
Available by the night at very reasonable rates

P.O. Box 1029
Girdwood
Alaska 99587

(907) 783-2010

Locally Owned & Operated

✱ The Bake Shop ✱ *At Alyeska Resort*

Home of Alyeska Sourdough Bread

Open daily 7 a.m. - 7 p.m.
Saturdays 'til 9 p.m.

✱ Serving Breakfast -
Sourdough Pancakes, Sweet Rolls

Soup ✱ Pizza

✱ Hot & Cold Sandwiches

At Alyeska Ski Resort
Next to Golden Nugget Inn

(907) 783-2831
Werner Egloff, Owner

KENAI PENINSULA • SEWARD HIGHWAY

---

strip; elev. 150 feet/46m; length 2,100 feet/640m; gravel; unattended.

Girdwood Community Center offers tennis courts, pay phone, Kinder Park day-care center and picnic area, and is the site of the Girdwood midsummer crafts fair. The town was named after Col. James Girdwood who established a mining operation near here in 1901.

Chair 5 Restaurant. Searching for that special place that's off the beaten path, is fun and relaxing to dine in? Nestled in the woods of downtown Girdwood is Chair 5 Restaurant. Quality food is served with true Alaskan hospitality. Highlights include fresh pasta, pizza, choice steak and Alaskan seafood dinners, priced from $8 to $15. Breakfast and lunch feature daily specials in the $4 to $8 range. MasterCard, VISA, American Express. Beer and wine served. Hours 9 A.M. to midnight. Turn left Mile 2.4 Alyeska Access Road. [ADVERTISEMENT]

J 2.3 (3.7 km) Glacier Creek bridge.
J 2.4 (3.9 km) Linblad Avenue.
J 2.6 (4.2 km) Airport Road.
J 2.7 (4.3 km) Timberline Drive.

Timberline Bed & Breakfast. Longtime Alaskans (38 years) and travelers Ann and Chuck Sassara welcome our guests. Join us in an evening of conversation around the fireplace. Enjoy a genuine "sourdough" breakfast. Feel free to explore the area via complimentary bicycles or cross-country skis. Inquire about airplane sightseeing. (907) 783-2917 for reservations. [ADVERTISEMENT]

J 3 (4.8 km) RE O ALYESKA Resort and Recreation Area at Mount Alyeska (elev. 3,939 feet/1,201m); jade shop, gift and crafts shops, restaurants, a hotel and the ski resort. Paved bike trail ends.

Alyeska Resort is Alaska's largest ski area. The resort and ski area, owned and operated by Seibu Group of Japan since 1980, are open year-round. Ski season is generally from November through May. Recent improvements include a high-speed detachable quad chair lift and a large day lodge—the Activities Center—with cafeteria. There are 4 double chair lifts, a rope tow and pony lift as well as lighting for night skiing. Complete ski

---

GIRDWOOD / ALYESKA ADVERTISERS

Alyeska Resort ....Ph. (907) 783-2222
Alyeska View Bed & Breakfast ....Vail Dr.
Bake Shop, The.....................Alyeska Resort
Chair 5 Restaurant ....Linblad Ave.
Edelweiss
    Restaurant......Mile 3 Alyeska Access Rd.
Emmy's Hair Studio ....Vail Dr.
Golden Eagle Property
    Rentals................Across from Girdwood post office
Kobuk Valley
    Jade Co...........Mile 3 Alyeska Access Rd.
Timberline Bed &
    Breakfast.......................Timberline Dr.
Vista Alyeska Accommodations ....Mile 3 Alyeska Access Rd.

vacation facilities at the base area include accommodations at the 29-room hotel or in condominiums, restaurants, bars, ski rental, ski school and ski shop. Dogsled rides, helicopter skiing and cross-country ski tours are also available.

Under construction for 1993 is the new Alyeska Prince Hotel. When completed, the hotel will include 311 guest rooms, 4 restaurants, lounge, gift shop, meeting and convention areas, health spa with indoor swimming pool and on-site parking for 950 cars. A chair lift will connect the hotel with lower mountain ski slopes.

Recommended in summer is the scenic chair lift ride to the Skyride Restaurant, 2,000 feet/610m above the valley floor. This 20-minute ride offers a spectacular view of area glaciers and Turnagain Arm. Gift shops and dining facilities at the base area. Hiking, fishing, canoeing, tennis, gold panning, river rafting and sightseeing nearby.

Return to Milepost S 90
Seward Highway

Discover Northland adventures from Alaska Northwest Books™. For a free catalog, including our books about the North Country, call toll free 1-800-343-4567, Ext. 571

Alyeska chair lift operates in summer for views of Turnagain Arm. (Jerrianne Lowther, staff)

KENAI PENINSULA • SEWARD HIGHWAY

Alyeska RESORT

As spectacular in summer as it is in winter.

Alyeska offers an endless variety of beautiful summer scenery and exciting activities. Relax in a mountain meadow, browse through charming shops, and enjoy a delicious lunch at the Nugget Inn Restaurant and outdoor patio . . . all in the same afternoon. Then for dinner, dine at our mountainside BBQ and salmon bake.

Located just 40 miles from Anchorage, Alyeska is only minutes away from beautiful Portage Glacier and Crow Creek Mine. It is a perfect day tour from Anchorage for all Alaskan visitors.

The Nugget Inn, at the foot of Mt. Alyeska, is the perfect place to get away from the bustle of the city for a day or two. You'll find clean comfortable rooms and affordable summer rates.

If you are traveling in a camper or RV, we welcome you. You may park in our lot at no charge; however, RV facilities are not available.

Call **(907) 783-2222** for information and reservations. Recorded visitor information **(907) 783-2121**.

SPECIAL DISCOUNT OFFER
10% Off
Any purchase from our gift shop.

Summer season only.

1992 ■ The MILEPOST® 417

Portage Glacier is a top visitor attraction. (George Wuerthner)

Seward Highway Log

(continued from page 414)
Bridge No. 2 southbound over Portage Creek. Parking and interpretive sign to west at south end of bridge. This gray-colored creek carries the silt-laden glacial meltwater from Portage Glacier and Portage Lake to Turnagain Arm. Mud flats in Turnagain Arm are created by silt from the creek settling close to shore.

S 79 (127.1 km) **A 48** (77.2 km) Bridge No. 1 southbound over Portage Creek.

S 78.9 (127 km) **A 48.1** (77.4 km) **Junction** with Portage Glacier access road. Portage Glacier is one of Alaska's most popular attractions. Cafe and pay phone south side of junction. See PORTAGE GLACIER ROAD log this page. *NOTE: There is no gas or lodging available at the glacier.*

S 78.8 (126.8 km) **A 48.2** (77.5 km) Restaurant/cafe east side of highway.

S 78.4 (126.1 km) **A 48.6** (78.2 km) Bridge over Placer River; boat launch. Second bridge over Placer River at **Milepost S 77.9**. Turnouts next to both bridges. Between Placer River and Ingram Creek there is an excellent view on clear days of Skookum Glacier to the northeast. To the north across Turnagain Arm is Twentymile Glacier. Arctic terns and waterfowl are often seen in the slough here.

Placer River has good hooligan fishing in May. These smelt are taken with long-handled dip nets. Silver salmon may be taken in August and September.

S 77.9 (125.4 km) **A 49.1** (79 km) Bridge over Placer River overflow. Paved turnout to south.

S 77 (123.9 km) **A 50** (80.5 km) Boundary of Chugach National Forest.

S 75.5 (121.5 km) **A 51.5** (82.9 km) Paved double-ended scenic viewpoints both sides of highway.

S 75.2 (121 km) **A 51.8** (83.4 km) Bridge over **Ingram Creek**; pink salmon fishing (even years).

S 75 (120.7 km) **A 52** (83.7 km) Paved turnout to west. Highway begins ascent to Turnagain Pass southbound. Passing lane next 5 miles/8 km southbound.

S 74.5 (119.9 km) **A 52.5** (84.5 km) Double-ended paved turnout to east. Several kinds of blueberries, together with false azalea blossoms, are seen along here during summer months.

S 72.5 (116.7 km) **A 54.5** (87.7 km) Double-ended paved turnout to east.

S 71.5 (115.1 km) **A 55.5** (89.3 km) Double-ended paved turnout to west.

S 71.2 (114.6 km) **A 55.8** (89.8 km) Double-ended paved turnout to west.

S 71 (114.3 km) **A 56** (90.1 km) Paved turnout to east. The many flowers seen in surrounding alpine meadows here include yellow and purple violets, mountain heliotrope, lousewort and paintbrush.

S 69.9 (112.5 km) **A 57.1** (91.9 km) Scenic viewpoint with double-ended parking area to west. The highway traverses an area of mountain meadows and parklike stands of spruce, birch and aspen, interlaced with glacier-fed streams. Lupine and wild geranium grow profusely here in the summer.

S 69.2 (111.4 km) **A 57.8** (93 km) Paved turnout to east.

S 69.1 (111.2 km) **A 57.9** (93.2 km) Passing lane ends southbound.

S 68.9 (110.9 km) **A 58.1** (93.5 km) Divided highway begins southbound, ends northbound.

S 68.5 (110.2 km) **A 58.5** (94.1 km) Turnagain Pass Recreation Area (elev. 988 feet/301m). Parking area and restrooms (southbound lane); emergency call box. U-turn.

Turnagain Pass Recreation Area is a favorite winter recreation area for snowmobilers (west side of highway) and cross-country skiers (east side of highway). Snow depths here frequently exceed 12 feet/4m.

S 68.1 (109.6 km) **A 58.9** (94.8 km) Parking area and restrooms for northbound traffic. U-turn.

S 67.8 (109.1 km) **A 59.2** (95.3 km) Bridge over Lyon Creek.

S 67.6 (108.8 km) **A 59.4** (95.6 km) Divided highway ends southbound,

Portage Glacier Road Log

Distance from the junction with the Seward Highway (J).

J 0 Junction with Seward Highway at **Milepost S 78.9**. *CAUTION: Alaska Railroad tracks.*

J 2 (3.2 km) Portage Glacier Work Center; no services available.

J 2.4 (3.8 km) Paved turnout. Explorer Glacier viewpoint on right.

J 3.1 (5 km) Bridge. Beaver dam visible from road.

J 3.7 (5.9 km) Black Bear USFS campground; 12 sites (2 will accommodate medium-sized trailers), toilets, water, firepits, dumpsters, tables, $6 fee. Pleasant wooded area.

J 4.1 (6.6 km) Bridge over Williwaw Creek. USFS campground, south of road below Middle Glacier; 38 campsites, toilets, dumpsters, water, firepits, tables, $6 fee. Beautiful campground. Spawning red salmon and dog salmon can be viewed (from late July to mid-September) from Williwaw Creek observation deck near campground entrance. Self-guided Williwaw nature trail off the campground loop road goes through moose and beaver habitat.

J 5.2 (8.4 km) Paved road forks at Portage Glacier Lodge; left fork leads to visitor center (description follows). Take right fork 0.8 mile/1.3 km to parking lot; 1.2 miles/1.9 km to Byron Glacier overlook; and 1.5 miles/2.4 km to MV *Ptarmigan* sightseeing boat cruise dock and passenger waiting facility.

J 5.5 (8.8 km) Begich, Boggs Visitor Center at Portage Glacier and Portage Lake. Open daily in summer. Phone the visitor center at 783-2326 or the U.S. Forest Service district office at 783-3242 for current schedule.

Forest Service naturalists are available to answer questions and provide information about Chugach National Forest resources. There are displays on glaciers and on the natural history of the area. The award-winning film *Voices from the Ice* is shown in the theater several times daily in summer. Schedules of hikes and programs led by naturalists are posted at the center. One of the most popular activities is the iceworm hunt. (Often regarded as a hoax, iceworms actually exist; the small, thin, segmented black worms thrive at temperatures just above freezing.) A self-guided moraine trail begins just south of the visitor center.

Large paved parking area provides views of the glacier and floating blue-white icebergs in Portage Lake. There are several excellent spots in the area to observe salmon spawning (August and September) in Portage Creek and its tributaries.

Gray Line of Alaska Portage Glacier Cruise. Don't miss cruising up close to the face of Portage Glacier on Gray Line of Alaska's MV *Ptarmigan*. One-hour-long cruises depart every 90 minutes. Ample RV parking available. Tickets are $19.50 for adults and $9.75 for children under 12. Call the Portage Glacier Cruise Center, phone (907) 783-2983.

[ADVERTISEMENT]

Return to Milepost S 78.9 Seward Highway

begins northbound.

S 66.8 (107.5 km) **A 60.2** (96.9 km) Paved double-ended turnout to east.

S 65.3 (105.1 km) **A 61.7** (99.3 km) Bridge over Bertha Creek. Bertha Creek USFS campground; 12 sites, water, toilets, firepits, table, dumpsters and $6 fee. ▲

S 64.8 (104.3 km) **A 62.2** (100.1 km) Bridge over Spokane Creek.

S 64 (102.9 km) **A 63** (101.3 km) Granite Creek fireguard station.

S 63.7 (102.5 km) **A 63.3** (101.9 km) Johnson Pass north trailhead. This 23-mile-/37-km-long trail is a fairly level good family trail which follows a portion of the Old Iditarod trail which went from Seward to Nome. See **Milepost S 32.6**.

Johnson Pass trail leads to **Bench Lake**, which has arctic grayling, and **Johnson Lake**, which has rainbow trout. Both lakes are about halfway in on trail.

S 63.3 (101.9 km) **A 63.7** (102.5 km) Bridge over Granite Creek. Traditional halfway point on highway between Anchorage and Seward.

S 63 (101.4 km) **A 64** (103 km) Granite Creek USFS campground, 0.8 mile/1.3 km from main highway; 19 sites (most beside creek), water, toilets, dumpsters, tables, firepits and $6 fee. **Granite Creek**, small Dolly Varden.

S 62 (99.8 km) **A 65** (104.6 km) Bridge over the East Fork Sixmile Creek.

S 61 (98.2 km) **A 66** (106.2 km) Bridge over Silvertip Creek.

S 59.7 (96.1 km) **A 67.3** (108.3 km) Gravel turnout next to Granite Creek. Excellent place to photograph this glacial stream. Beaver dam.

S 58.8 (94.6 km) **A 68.2** (109.8 km) Large gravel turnout to west. There are several turnouts along this stretch of highway.

S 57.6 (92.7 km) **A 69.4** (111.7 km) Bridge over Dry Gulch Creek.

S 57 (91.7 km) **A 70** (112.7 km) Bridge over Canyon Creek.

S 56.8 (91.4 km) **A 70.2** (113 km) State wayside with picnic tables, toilets and litter barrels. Travelers sometimes confuse wayside entrance with Hope Highway turnoff.

S 56.7 (91.2 km) **A 70.3** (113.1 km) Southbound **junction** with Hope Highway to historic mining community of Hope. See HOPE HIGHWAY log this page.

NOTE: Southbound travelers may find this junction confusing. Hope Highway veers right; Seward Highway veers left.

S 56.6 (91.1 km) **A 70.4** (113.3 km) Northbound **junction** with Hope Highway. Numerous gravel turnouts next 6 miles/9.7 km southbound.

S 50.1 (80.6 km) **A 76.9** (123.8 km) Begin improved highway southbound with wide shoulders and passing lanes. Winter avalanche area next 1.5 miles/2.4 km southbound.

S 48 (77.2 km) **A 79** (127.1 km) Fresno Creek bridge; turnout to east at south end of bridge.

S 47.6 (76.6 km) **A 79.4** (127.8 km) Double-ended paved turnout to east on lake.

S 47.2 (76 km) **A 79.8** (128.4 km) Paved double-ended turnout to east next to Lower Summit Lake; a favorite photo stop. Extremely picturesque with lush growth of wildflowers in summer.

Upper and Lower Summit lakes, good spring and fall fishing for landlocked Dolly Varden (goldenfins), ranging in size from 6 to 11 inches, flies and single salmon eggs.

S 46 (74 km) **A 81** (130.4 km) Colorado

Hope Highway Log

The paved 17.7-mile/28.5-km Hope Highway leads northwest to the historic community of Hope on the south side of Turnagain Arm and provides access to the Resurrection Creek area.

Distance is measured from junction with the Seward Highway (J).

J 0.1 (0.2 km) Silvertip highway maintenance station.

J 0.6 (1 km) Double-ended paved turnout to east; road access to creek. Highway parallels Sixmile Creek, a glacial stream. There are many paved turnouts along the Hope Highway, some with views of Turnagain Arm.

J 1.4 (2.3 km) Beaver marsh to east.

J 2.3 (3.7 km) Large paved turnout to east. Moose may often be seen in Sixmile Creek valley below. The old gold mining town of Sunrise City, with a population of 5,000, was founded in 1895 at the mouth of Sixmile Creek. The present community of Sunrise has a population of about 20.

J 3.4 (5.5 km) Large paved turnout to east; trail access to creek.

J 3.9 (6.3 km) Large paved turnout to east; trail access to creek.

J 10 (16.1 km) Double-ended paved turnout to east overlooking Turnagain Arm.

J 11.1 (17.9 km) Large paved turnout to east overlooking Turnagain Arm.

J 11.8 (19 km) Double-ended paved turnout to east overlooking Turnagain Arm.

J 15.8 (25.4 km) **Henry's One Stop**. See display ad this section. ▲

J 16.2 (26 km) Turn left (south) for Hope airport; Resurrection Pass trailhead, 4 miles/6.4 km south on Resurrection Creek Road, a privately owned gold mining town at the end of Resurrection Creek Road, 4.6 miles/7.4 km; and Coeur d'Alene Campground on Palmer Creek Road, 7.6 miles/12.2 km. ▲

The 38-mile-/61-km-long Resurrection Pass trail climbs from an elevation of 400 feet/122m at the trailhead to Resurrection Pass (elev. 2,600 feet/792m) and down to the south trailhead at **Milepost S 53.1** on the Sterling Highway. There are 8 cabins on the trail. Parking area at the trailhead.

Coeur d'Alene USFS campground has 5 sites (not recommended for large RVs or trailers); no water, no camping fee. Palmer Creek Road continues past the campground to alpine country above 1,500 feet/457m elevation, and views of Turnagain Arm and Resurrection Creek valley. The road past the campground is rough and narrow and not recommended for low-clearance vehicles.

J 16.5 (26.6 km) Turn on Hope Road for downtown **HOPE** (pop. 224). Hope Road leads past the post office down to the waterfront, a favorite fishing spot near the ocean; motel, cafe, grocery store and gift shop.

This historic mining community was founded in 1896 by gold seekers working Resurrection Creek and its tributary streams. Today, many Anchorage residents have vacation homes here.

Discovery Cafe. See display ad this section.

J 17 (27.3 km) Road to historic Hope townsite. Interpretive sign at intersection. The original townsite of Hope City was founded in 1896. Portions of the town destroyed by the 1964 earthquake are marked with dotted lines on the map sign.

J 17.1 (27.5 km) Resurrection Creek bridge.

J 17.7 (28.4 km) Gas station.

J 17.8 (28.6 km) Hope Highway ends at Porcupine USFS campground; 24 sites, tables, tent spaces, toilets, firepits, dumpster, drinking water and $6 fee. Gull Rock trailhead. ▲

Return to Milepost S 56.7 Seward Highway

Drive to Hope ... where the Gold Miners meet

GOOD FOOD • BEER • WINE

DISCOVERY CAFE

... at HOPE, ALASKA — PH: 782-3274

Intersection of Hope Highway and Hope Road

Henry's ONE STOP

Motel • Grocery • Laundromat • RV Parking • Propane
Water & Electric Hookups • Dump Station • Showers • Phone
Fishing & Hunting Licenses • Fishing Tackle • Ice

OPEN YEAR AROUND
Henry & Sachi Mori   (907) 782-3222
Box 50, Hope, Alaska 99605

MILE 15.8 HOPE HIGHWAY

Creek bridge. Tenderfoot Creek USFS campground 0.6 mile/0.9 km from highway; 28 sites, water, toilets (wheelchair accessible), dumpsters, tables, firepits, boat launch, $6 fee. ▲

S 45.8 (73.7 km) **A** 81.2 (130.7 km) Lodge with restaurant and overnight accommodations; open year-round. Emergency radio. Winter avalanche area begins just south of lodge (avalanche gates).

Summit Lake Lodge. Genuine hospitality on the north shore of Summit Lake in Alaska's most beautiful log lodge. Located in the heart of Chugach National Forest, it is a landmark for many. The view is spectacular and the food excellent. Complete menu from eye-opening omelettes to mouth-watering steaks. Enjoy our cozy motel and relaxing lounge. Open year-round. Fishing, hiking, photography, cross-country skiing, snowmobiling. It's a must stop for every visitor in the last frontier. See display ad this section. [ADVERTISEMENT] ▲

S 45.5 (73.2 km) **A** 81.5 (131.2 km) Upper Summit Lake. Paved turnout to east.

S 44.5 (71.6 km) **A** 82.5 (132.7 km) Large paved double-ended turnout to east at end of Upper Summit Lake.

S 44.3 (71.3 km) **A** 82.7 (133.1 km) Beaver dams.

S 44 (70.8 km) **A** 83 (133.6 km) Gravel turnout to east. Avalanche gun emplacement.

S 43.8 (70.5 km) **A** 83.2 (133.9 km) Winter avalanche area begins northbound. Avalanche gates.

S 43.7 (70.3 km) **A** 83.3 (134.1 km) Paved double-ended turnout to east.

S 42.6 (68.6 km) **A** 84.4 (135.8 km) Summit Creek (not signed).

S 42.2 (67.9 km) **A** 84.8 (136.5 km) Quartz Creek (not signed).

S 41.4 (66.6 km) **A** 85.6 (137.8 km) Passing lane next 1 mile/1.6 km northbound.

S 39.6 (63.7 km) **A** 87.4 (140.7 km) Avalanche gates.

S 39.4 (63.4 km) **A** 87.6 (141 km) Devils Pass trailhead; parking area to west. This USFS trail starts at an elevation of 1,000 feet/305m and follows Devils Creek to Devils Pass (elev. 2,400 feet/732m) continuing on to Devils Pass Lake and Resurrection Pass trail. Hiking time to Devils Pass is about 5 1/2 hours.

S 39 (62.8 km) **A** 88 (141.6 km) Truck lane extends northbound to Milepost S 39.3.

S 38.6 (62.1 km) **A** 88.4 (142.3 km) Paved turnout to west adjacent **Jerome Lake**, rainbow and Dolly Varden to 22 inches, use salmon egg clusters, year-round, still fish. A sign here explains rainbow plant in lake.

S 38.3 (61.6 km) **A** 88.7 (142.7 km) Paved double-ended turnout to west overlooking Jerome Lake. Interpretive sign about sticklebacks.

S 38.2 (61.5 km) **A** 88.8 (42.9 km) Truck lane ends northbound.

S 37.7 (60.7 km) **A** 89.3 (143.7 km) **Junction.** First southbound exit (1-way road) for Sterling Highway (Alaska Route 1) on right. Continue straight ahead on Alaska Route 9 for Seward.

If you are bound for Soldotna, Homer, or other Sterling Highway communities and attractions, turn to the STERLING HIGHWAY section and begin that log. Continue with this log if you are going to Seward.

ALASKA ROUTE 9

S 37.2 (59.9 km) **A** 89.8 (144.5 km) Paved turnout to west overlooking Tern Lake for Seward-bound travelers.

S 37 (59.5 km) **A** 90 (144.8 km) **Tern Lake Junction.** Second southbound turnoff on right (2-way road) for Sterling Highway (Alaska Route 1) and access to Tern Lake USFS campground and salmon spawning channel. To reach campground, drive 0.4 mile/0.6 km around Tern Lake; 25 sites, water, toilets, picnic tables, firepits, canoe launch, $6 fee. Tern Lake is a good spot for bird watching in summer. See STERLING HIGHWAY section. ▲

Continue straight ahead on Alaska Route 9 for Seward.

S 36.7 (59.1 km) **A** 90.3 (145.3 km) Truck lane begins northbound.

S 36.4 (58.6 km) **A** 90.6 (145.8 km) Avalanche gates.

S 35.7 (57.5 km) **A** 91.3 (146.9 km) **TAK Outfitters.** See display ad this section.

S 35.3 (56.8 km) **A** 91.7 (147.6 km) End avalanche area southbound.

S 35 (56.3 km) **A** 92 (148 km) For the next 3 miles/4.8 km many small waterfalls tumble down the brushy slopes. Winter avalanche area between **Milepost S** 35.3 and **34.6**. You are driving through the Kenai mountain range.

S 33.1 (53.3 km) **A** 93.9 (151.1 km) Carter Lake USFS trailhead No. 4 to west; parking and toilets. Trail starts at an elevation of 500 feet/152m and climbs 986 feet/300m to Carter Lake (stocked with rainbow trout). Trail is good, but steep; hiking time about 1 1/2 hours. Good access to sheep and mountain goat country. Excellent snowmobiling area in winter.

S 32.6 (52.5 km) **A** 94.4 (151.9 km) Johnson Pass south trailhead with parking area, toilet. North trailhead at **Milepost S** 63.8.

S 32.5 (52.3 km) **A** 94.5 (152.1 km) Large paved double-ended turnout; USFS information sign on life cycle of salmon, short trail to observation deck on stream where spawning salmon may be seen in August.

S 32.4 (52.1 km) **A** 94.6 (152.2 km) Cook Inlet Aquaculture Assoc. Trail Lake fish hatchery on Moose Creek. Display room and restrooms. Open 8 A.M. to 6 P.M. daily. Tours available June 1 to Sept. 15; phone 288-3688 for more information.

S 31.8 (51.1 km) **A** 95.2 (153.2 km) Paved double-ended rest area to east on Upper Trail Lake; toilets, picnic tables.

S 30 (48.3 km) **A** 97 (156.1 km) Short side road to large undeveloped gravel parking area on Upper Trail Lake; boat launch.

S 29.9 (48.1 km) **A** 97.1 (156.3 km) Gravel turnout by Trail Lake.

SEE ALASKA'S BACK COUNTRY BY HORSE

GUIDED HORSE PACKING TRIPS

TAK OUTFITTERS
P.O. Box 66, Moose Pass,
Alaska 99631   (907)288-3640

See Alaska by horse for the adventure of a lifetime!

Marty and June Arnoldy welcome you to
SUMMIT LAKE LODGE
MILE 45.8 Seward Highway
(907) 595-1520, Ext. 1
Moose Pass, Alaska 99631
Resaurant Lounge Lodging Gifts

ESTES BROTHERS GROCERIES & WATER WHEEL
WATER WHEEL T-SHIRTS
HUNTING AND FISHING LICENSES
Moose Pass is a peaceful town.
If you have an "ax to grind," do it here.
See the water wheel and stop and shoot the bull with Ed Estes — longest resident in Moose Pass.

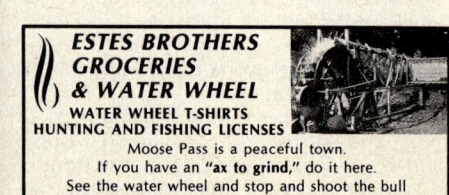

S 29.4 (47.3 km) **A 97.6** (157.1 km) Large working waterwheel, built by Ed Estes, on way into Moose Pass. Parking area and sign at waterwheel which reads: "Moose Pass is a peaceful little town. If you have an ax to grind, do it here."

MOOSE PASS (pop. 145) has a motel, general store, knit shop, restaurant, post office and highway maintenance station. Pay phone outside GTE building. Alaska State Troopers, emergency only phone 911. This mountain village on Upper Trail Lake was a construction camp on the Alaska Railroad in 1912. Local resident Ed Estes attributes the name Moose Pass to a 1904 observation by Nate White of the first moose recorded in this area. Another version holds that "in 1903, a mail carrier driving a team of dogs had considerable trouble gaining the right-of-way from a giant moose." A post office was established in 1928.

Moose Pass has a 1.3-mile-/2.1-km-long paved bike trail which winds along Trail Lake from the Moose Pass ball diamond to the McFadden house on the south. Gravel turnout by lake.

The main street of town is the site of the Annual Moose Pass Summer Festival, a community-sponsored event which takes place the weekend nearest summer solstice (June 21). The festival features a triathlon, arts and crafts booths, a barbecue, auction and other events.

Estes Brothers Groceries & Water Wheel. See display ad this section.

Trail Lake Lodge. See display ad this section.

NOTE: Watch for road construction crews working on slope stability from Moose Pass south to Seward in 1992.

S 26 (41.8 km) **A 101** (162.5 km) Lower Trail Lake. Timbered slopes of Madson Mountain (elev. 5,269 feet/1,605m) to the west. Crescent Lake lies just west of Madson.

S 25.4 (40.9 km) **A 101.6** (163.5 km) Bridge over Trail River.

S 25 (40.2 km) **A 102** (164.1 km) Bridge over Falls Creek.

S 24.9 (40.1 km) **A 102.1** (164.3 km) **OSHO Iditarod Trail Stop,** offers a touch of the past and present history. Located on the actual historic trail, a dog team and sled are waiting for you to jump on and take your picture! The artist/owner welcomes you to her studio. Peruse carvings she makes from fossil whale bone, moose antler, etc., Eskimo dolls, bears, whales, masks, dog teams. As an official finisher of the 1980 Iditarod Sled Dog Race from Anchorage to Nome, she also offers a book on her experiences entitled *Chasing the Northern Lights!* (907) 288-3622. Open year-round. [ADVERTISEMENT]

S 24.2 (38.9 km) **A 102.8** (165.4 km) Side road leads 1.2 miles/1.9 km to Trail River USFS campground; $6 fee, 64 sites, picnic tables, firepits, dumpsters, toilets and volleyball and horseshoe area. Day-use group picnic area. Spacious, wooded campsites in tall spruce on shore of Kenai Lake and Lower Trail River. Pull-through sites available. Campground host may be in residence during summer, providing fishing and hiking information. Good spot for mushrooming and berry picking in August.

Lower Trail River, lake trout, rainbow and Dolly Varden to 25 inches, July, August and September, use salmon eggs, small spinners. Access via Lower Trail River campground road. **Trail River,** Dolly Varden 12 to 20 inches, spring and fall, use fresh eggs; rainbow 12 to 20 inches, spring, use fresh eggs.

S 23.4 (37.7 km) **A 103.6** (166.7 km) *CAUTION: Railroad crossing.* USFS work center (no information services available). Report forest fires here.

Private Aircraft: Lawing landing strip; elev. 475 feet/144m; length 2,300 feet/701m; gravel; unattended.

S 23.1 (37.1 km) **A 103.9** (167.2 km) **Ptarmigan Creek** bridge and USFS picnic area and campground with 16 sites, water, toilets, tables, firepits and dumpsters, $6 fee. Fair to good fishing in creek and in lake outlets at **Ptarmigan Lake** (hike in) for Dolly Varden. Watch for spawning salmon in Ptarmigan Creek in August.

Ptarmigan Creek USFS trail No. 14 begins at campground (elev. 500 feet/152m) and leads 3.5 miles/5.6 km to Ptarmigan Lake (elev. 755 feet/230m). Trail is steep in spots; round-trip hiking time 5 hours. Good chance of seeing sheep, goats, moose and bears. Carry insect repellent. Trail is poor for winter use due to avalanche hazard.

S 23 (37 km) **A 104** (167.3 km) **the rogue's gallery.** If you enjoy browsing you'll be very comfortable in our gallery. We expect that you'll have questions about the artists and their products—don't hold back—just ask! Many "fresh" ideas in soapstone, ivory, pen and ink, prints . . . gifts and keepsakes from all over Alaska. Also please see our display ad in this section. [ADVERTISEMENT]

S 23 (37 km) **A 104** (167.3 km) Turnoff for Alaska Nellie's Homestead. The late Nellie Neal-Lawing arrived in Alaska in 1915. Her colorful life included cooking for the railroad workers and big game hunting and guiding. She converted a roadhouse at Lawing into a museum to house her trophies and souvenirs she and her husband, Billie Lawing, gathered on their travels.

Alaska Nellie's Inn, Inc. See display ad this section.

S 22.9 (36.9 km) **A 104.1** (167.5 km)

Cow parsnip grows on the shore of scenic Summit Lake. (George Wuerthner)

---

the rogue's gallery...

Creative Gifts
Native Crafts
International Boutiques

Fresh ideas in all types of Alaskan art

Lawing-on-Kenai
Star Route • Mile 23
Seward, Alaska 99664
(907) 288-3636

ALASKA NELLIE'S INN, INC.
Bed & Breakfast at Lawing, Alaska, on the bend of beautiful Kenai Lake
Rainbow trout fishing at Ptarmigan Creek
(907) 288-3124 • PO Box 88, Moose Pass, Alaska 99631
Mile 23 Seward Highway

Trail Lake Lodge
A Landmark Lodge in the Midst of All the Fun!

RESTAURANT ■ BAR
LAUNDROMAT ■ SHOWERS
MOTEL – OVER 35 ROOMS

Mile 29.4 Seward Highway
Open Year-Round
(907) 288-3101 ■ 288-3103
Box 69, Moose Pass, Alaska 99631

Viewpoint to west overlooking Kenai Lake. This lake (elev. 436 feet/132m) extends 24 miles/39 km from the head of the Kenai River on the west to the mouth of Snow River on the east. A sign here explains how glacier meltwater gives the lake its distinctive color.

Winter avalanche area next 3 miles/4.8 km southbound.

S 22.5 (36.2 km) **A 104.5** (168.2 km) Rough gravel double-ended turnout to east.

S 21.3 (34.3 km) **A 105.7** (170.1 km) Gravel turnout to east overlooking lake.

S 20.2 (32.5 km) **A 106.8** (171.9 km) Avalanche gun emplacement.

S 20 (32.2 km) **A 107** (172.2 km) Gravel turnout. Avalanche area ends southbound.

S 20 (32.2 km) **A 107** (172.2 km) **I.R.B.I. Knives.** See display ad this section.

S 19.5 (31.4 km) **A 107.5** (173 km) Victor Creek bridge. Victor Creek USFS trail No. 23 begins here. A 2-mile/3.2-km hike with good view of mountains. Turnoff for bed and breakfast.

Leary's Bed & Breakfast. Milepost 19.5 Seward Highway. Just 30 steps south from Victor Creek sits a charming hand-built family home nestled in the Chugach forest. Fashioned from native woods, it features 2 spacious ground-level bedrooms, fully carpeted and furnished with grand old 4-poster beds, warm feather comforters and hand embroidery. Sleep to the gentle babbling of the nearby brook and waken to the smell of good old-fashioned home cooking and the twittering of nesting songbirds. Open May through October. $65/room. Please call as we are usually full. (907) 288-3168. [ADVERTISEMENT]

S 17.7 (28.5 km) **A 109.3** (175.9 km) Bridge over center channel of Snow River. This river has 2 forks that flow into Kenai Lake.

S 17 (27 km) **A 110** (177 km) Turn west for Primrose USFS campground, 1 mile/1.6 km from the highway. (Campground access road leads past private homes: Drive carefully!) The campground, overlooking Kenai Lake, has 10 sites, toilets, dumpsters, tables, firepits, boat ramp, water, $6 fee. Primrose trail (6.5 miles/10.5 km) starts from the campground and connects with Lost Lake trail (7 miles/11.2 km). High alpine hike, trail is posted. ▲

Bridge over south channel of Snow River.

S 16.8 (27 km) **A 110.2** (177.3 km) Gravel turnout to east.

S 16.2 (26.1 km) **A 110.8** (178.3 km) Gravel turnout to east.

S 16 (25.7 km) **A 111** (178.6 km) Snow River hostel.

S 15 (24.1 km) **A 112** (180.2 km) Watch for moose in ponds and meadows in this area.

S 14.9 (24 km) **A 112.1** (180.4 km) Gravel turnout to east.

S 14 (22.5 km) **A 113** (181.9 km) *CAUTION: Railroad crossing.*

S 13.3 (21.4 km) **A 113.7** (183 km) Grayling Lake USFS trailhead to west, large paved parking area to east. Grayling Lake trail No. 20, 1.6 miles/2.6 km, connects with trails to Meridian and Leech lakes. Good spot for photos of Snow River valley. Watch for moose. **Grayling Lake**, 6- to 12-inch grayling, use flies, May to October.

S 12 (19.3 km) **A 115** (185.1 km) Alaska Railroad crosses under highway.

S 11.6 (18.6 km) **A 115.4** (185.7 km) Gravel parking area to east and USFS trail No. 6 to **Golden Fin Lake**, Dolly Varden averaging 8 inches. This is a 0.6-mile/1-km hike on a very wet trail: wear rubber footwear.

S 10.8 (17.4 km) **A 116.2** (187 km) Large gravel turnout to east.

S 8.5 (13.6 km) **A 118.5** (190.7 km) Gravel turnout to east.

S 8.3 (13.4 km) **A 118.7** (191 km) Paved turnout by creek. Leaving Chugach National Forest land southbound.

S 8 (12.9 km) **A 119** (191.5 km) **Grouse Creek** bridge. Dolly Varden fishing.

S 7.4 (11.9 km) **A 119.6** (192.5 km) **Grouse Lake** access road. Good ice fishing for Dolly Varden in winter.

S 6.6 (10.6 km) **A 120.4** (193.7 km) Bear Creek bridge and Bear Lake Road; access to 2 private RV parks and a flying service. Drive in 0.7 mile/1.1 km on Bear Lake Road to see a state-operated fish weir. Silver and red (sockeye) salmon are trapped to provide life-cycle data and also eggs for the state's salmon stocking program.

Bear Creek RV and Mobile Home Park, 0.4 Mile Bear Lake Road. Good Sam Park has full and partial hookups, dump station, restrooms, showers, cable TV, travelers lounge, propane, laundry, convenience store. Excellent water from deep, underground wells. Glacier and fishing trips. Reservations accepted for all activities booked through our office. Fishing and hunting licenses. Auto and RV repair and service. RV and boat storage. High-pressure wash. Leave your trailer/RV with us, have it serviced or repaired in our RV garage while you explore Seward and the beautiful surroundings. Short walk to fish weir. See display ad this section. [ADVERTISEMENT] ▲

A **Creekside Park** opening spring 1992, Bear Lake Road. Full and partial RV hookups, dry camping, tent sites. Dump station, restrooms, showers, laundry. Free shower with hookups, free firewood. Gas, diesel, propane, ice, pay phone. Senior citizen discounts. Family owned and operated. Located on salmon spawning stream. Bring your camera. Fishing for Dolly Varden, rainbow trout and grayling in the park. Fishing charters for salmon and halibut arranged. See display ad this section. ▲

S 6.3 (10.1 km) **A 120.7** (194.2 km) Lake Drive.

Stoney Creek Inn Bed & Breakfast. See display ad this section.

S 5.9 (9.4 km) **A 121.1** (194.8 km) **Salmon Creek** bridge. Good fishing in stream for sea-run Dolly Varden averaging 10 inches, use single salmon eggs, begins about Aug. 1.

S 5.2 (8.4 km) **A 121.8** (196 km) Bear Creek volunteer fire department.

S 3.8 (6.1 km) **A 123.2** (198.3 km) Clear Creek bridge.

S 3.7 (6 km) **A 123.3** (198.4 km) Turnoff for Exit Glacier Road; access to restaurant and bed and breakfasts.

The 9-mile/14.5-km dirt and gravel Exit Glacier Road (open May to mid-October) ends at a parking lot with toilets and picnic area next to Exit Glacier ranger station. Walk-in campground with 10 sites open year-round. Picnic shelter near the ranger station converts to a winter-use cabin; reservations required. Seward Chamber of Commerce operates a visitor center at the ranger

---

BEAR CREEK RV & MOBILE HOME PARK

Bear Lake Air & Guide Service

Exclusive Floatplane Service
Flightseeing
Fly-in Hunting and Fishing

Full Hook-ups
Partial Hook-ups

AUTO & RV REPAIR AND SERVICE
HIGH PRESSURE WASH

Dump Station • Propane
Laundry • Showers • Restrooms
Convenience Store
Glacier and Fishing Trips

Mile 6.6 Seward Highway
Bear Lake Road

(907) 224-5725   CB Channel 17
HCR 64, Box 386
Seward, Alaska 99664

Family Owned and Operated
See log ad at Mile 6.6 Seward Highway

I.R.B.I.

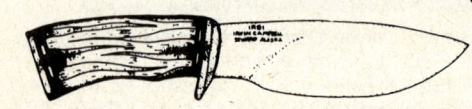

KNIVES HANDCRAFTED BY IRVIN & VIRGIL CAMPBELL

- Hand Forged Carbon Steel
- Fillet Knives
- Sharpening Available
- Most Knives include Sheath
- Open 7 days a week

HCR 64 Box 465   (907) 288-3616
Seward, Alaska 99664   Mile 20 Seward Highway

station (seasonal). The flat, easy 0.8-mile Lower Loop trail (and the longer 1-mile/1.6 km Upper Loop trail) leads to the base of the glacier; the first 0.3 mile of the trail is paved and wheelchair accessible. There is also an easy nature trail. A strenuous 3.5-mile/5.6-km trail leads to Harding Icefield from the parking lot. Summer weekend activities include ranger-led walks to the glaciers and all-day hikes to Harding Icefield. Worth the drive to see an active glacier up close. *(CAUTION: Falling ice at face of glacier, stay behind warning signs.)*

On the drive out, note the finger dikes built along the road to protect it from erosion by the Resurrection River. The trailhead for Resurrection River trail is located just before crossing the Resurrection River bridge on the access road. The 16-mile/25.7-km USFS trail ties in with the Russian Lakes trail. It is part of the 75-mile/121-km Hope-to-Seward route. *CAUTION: Black and brown bears also use this trail.*

S 3.7 (6 km) A 123.3 (198.4 km) **Creekside Bed & Breakfast.** See display ad this section.

S 3.2 (5.1 km) A 123.8 (199.2 km) Nash Road; access to bed and breakfasts. It is a scenic 5-mile/8-km drive out Nash Road to Seward's Marine Industrial Center in the Fourth of July Creek valley. Fine views along the way and from Kertulla Point of Resurrection Bay and the city of Seward. At Mile 2.1 Nash Road is the trailhead for the Iditarod Trail, which begins at the ferry terminal in downtown Seward. Hike to Bear Lake; from north end of lake, trail continues to Mile 12 on the Seward Highway.

The White House B&B. See display ad this section.

The Farm Bed & Breakfast. Turn off Seward Highway on Nash Road, turn left immediately on Salmon Creek Road, and follow the signs to "The Farm." Tranquil country setting on acres of trees and green grass. Elegantly casual rooms, private baths, decks and entrances. Cable TV, barbecues. Delightful continental breakfast. "We are not in the middle of everything." Reservations welcome. VISA and MasterCard accepted. Call (907) 224-5691, fax (907) 224-2300. Your host: Jack Hoogland. Open year-round. See display ad in Seward section. [ADVERTISEMENT]

Rininger's Bed & Breakfast (Mile 1.6 Nash Road) is located on Rabbit Run Road. Open year-round. Large, sunny, private room with bath, kitchenette, loft, and outdoor wood-heated sauna. Hiking and cross-country ski trails nearby. Families welcome. Kent and Lisa Rininger, P.O. Box 548, Seward, AK 99664. (907) 224-5918. [ADVERTISEMENT]

S 3 (4.8 km) A 124 (199.6 km) Resurrection River, 3 channels and 3 highway bridges. This river, formed by snowmelt from the Harding Icefield, empties into Resurrection Bay just northeast of Seward.

Seward city limits.

S 2.7 (4.3 km) A 124.3 (200 km) Turnoff for Seward airport.

S 2.4 (3.9 km) A 124.6 (200.5 km) Forest Acres municipal campground; water, flush toilets, 14-day limit. No tables. ▲

S 2.1 (3.4 km) A 124.9 (201 km) U.S. Air Force and U.S. Army Seward Recreation Area.

S 2 (3.2 km) A 125 (201.1 km) Seward Chamber of Commerce visitor center. Seward High School.

S 1.2 (1.9 km) A 125.8 (202.4 km) Large parking area to west with memorial to Benny Benson, who designed the Alaska state flag.

S 1 (1.6 km) A 126 (202.8 km) Main entrance to boat harbor.

Alaska Treks 'n Voyages. Sea kayak rentals, instruction and tours in Resurrection Bay and Kenai Fjords National Park highlights our Seward-based operations. We offer 1-day to week-long trips as well as kayak drop-offs in Kenai Fjords and in Prince William Sound. Visit us at our Seward Small Boat Harbor location, phone (907) 224-3960, or call our central booking office at (907) 276-8282. Winter mailing address: P.O. Box 210402, Anchorage, AK 99521. [ADVERTISEMENT]

S 0.5 (0.8 km) A 126.5 (203.5 km) **Harborview Bed and Breakfast.** 900 3rd and C Street. Best location in Seward. Just a few minutes walk to tour boats, fishing charters, trolley stop, downtown and the beach. Featuring new rooms with private entrance and private bath, cable color TV. Nestled between beautiful Resurrection Bay and majestic Mount Marathon. (907) 224-3217. Box 1305, Seward, AK 99664. [ADVERTISEMENT]

S 0.3 (0.5 km) A 126.7 (203.9 km) Intersection of 3rd Avenue (Seward Highway) and Jefferson. Post office 1 block east, Information Cache rail car at intersection.

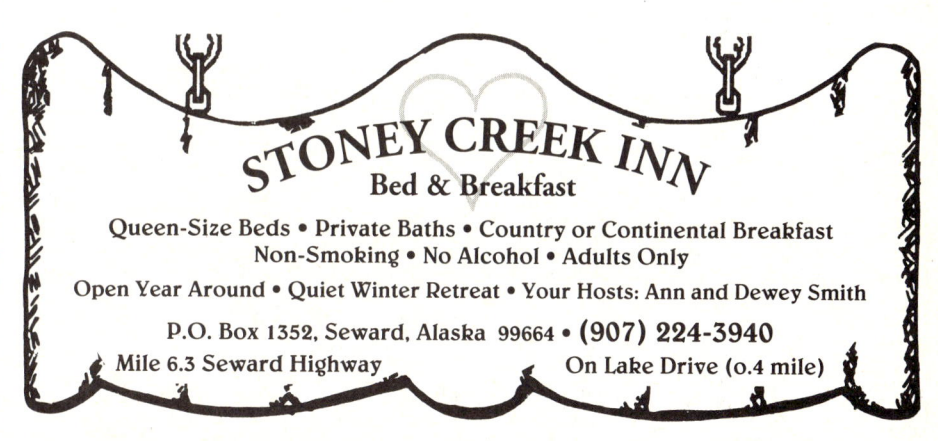

STONEY CREEK INN
Bed & Breakfast

Queen-Size Beds • Private Baths • Country or Continental Breakfast
Non-Smoking • No Alcohol • Adults Only
Open Year Around • Quiet Winter Retreat • Your Hosts: Ann and Dewey Smith

P.O. Box 1352, Seward, Alaska 99664 • **(907) 224-3940**
Mile 6.3 Seward Highway   On Lake Drive (0.4 mile)

OPENING SPRING 1992

A CREEKSIDE PARK

Full and Partial RV Hookups • Dry Camping • Tent Sites
Dump Station • Restrooms • Showers • Laundry
Free Shower with Hookups • Free Firewood

GAS • DIESEL • PROPANE • ICE • PAY PHONE
Fishing Charters • Senior Citizen Discounts
Located on Salmon Spawning Stream   Family Owned and Operated

(907) 224-3647   HCR 64, Box 375, Seward, Alaska 99664

BEAR LAKE ROAD AT MILE 6.6 SEWARD HIGHWAY

CREEKSIDE BED & BREAKFAST
ON THE WAY TO EXIT GLACIER

Cozy Cabins
Tent Sites • Sauna • Showers

See log ad in Seward Accommodations
Mile .5 Exit Glacier Road
Box 1514, Seward, AK 99664
(907) 224-3834

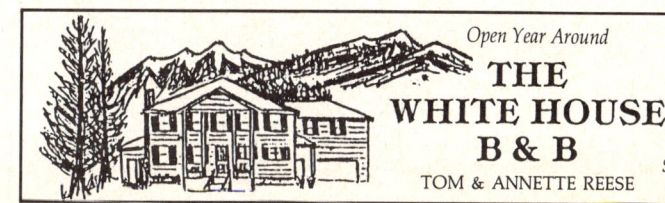

Open Year Around
THE WHITE HOUSE B & B
TOM & ANNETTE REESE

MILE 1.7 NASH ROAD
P.O. Box 1157
Seward, Alaska 99664
(907) 224-3614
-NON-SMOKING-
See log ad in Seward section under accommodations

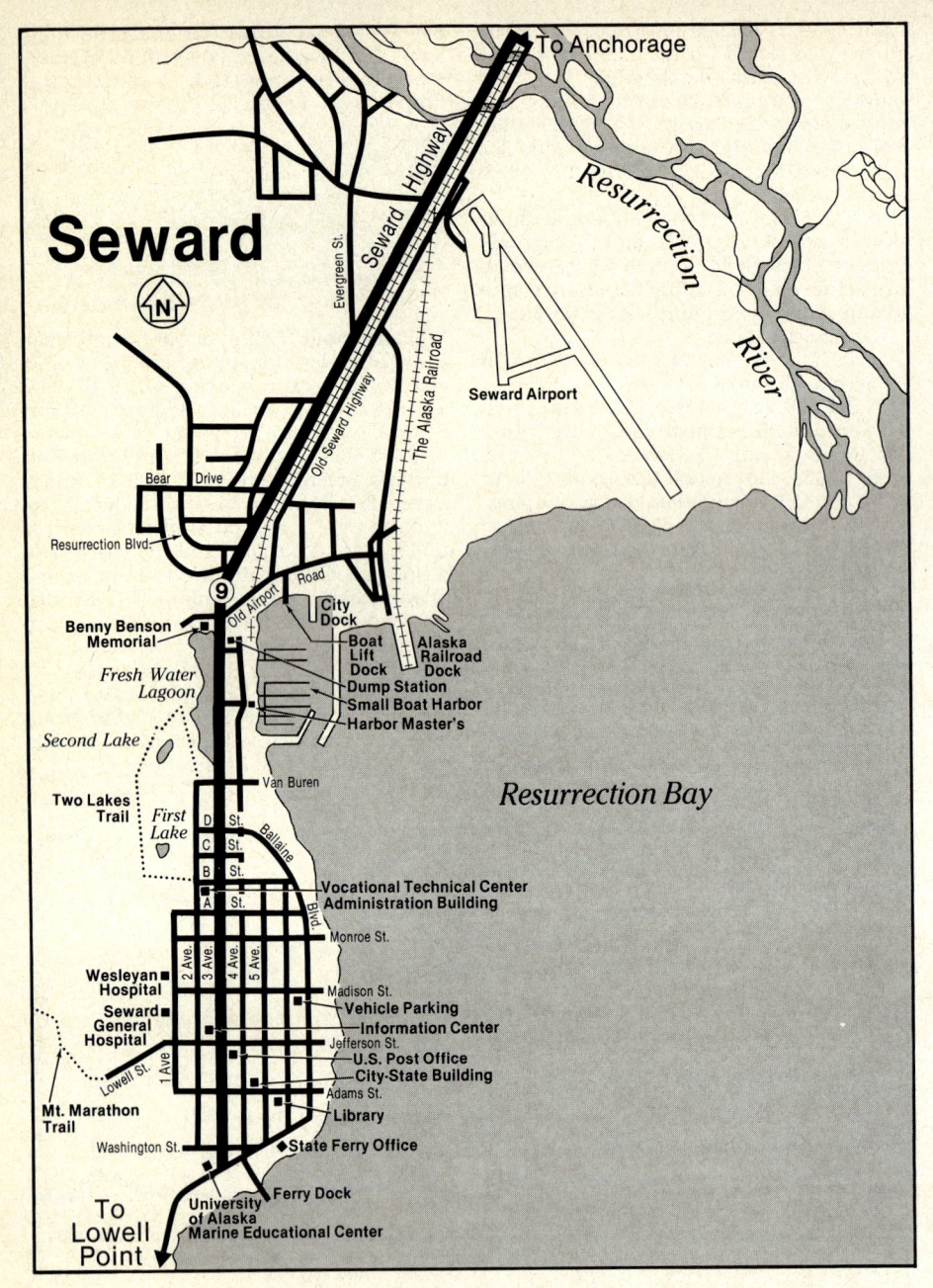

Seward

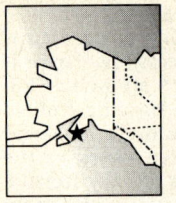

S 0 A 127 (203.2 km) Located on Resurrection Bay, east coast of Kenai Peninsula; 127 miles/203.2 km south of Anchorage by road, or 35 minutes by air. **Population:** 3,000. **Emergency Services: Police, Fire Department** and **Ambulance**, emergency only, phone 911. **State Troopers**, phone 224-3033. **Hospital**, Seward General, 1st Avenue and Jefferson Street, phone 224-5205. **Maritime Search and Rescue**, phone 1-800-478-5555.

Visitor Information: Available at 3 locations, operated by the Seward Chamber of Commerce. The visitor center at Exit Glacier ranger cabin operates seasonally. The visitor center at **Milepost S 2** Seward Highway (2001 Seward Highway) is open 7 days a week from Memorial Day through Labor Day, weekdays the rest of the year; phone 224-8051. The Information Cache, located in the historic railroad car *Seward* at 3rd and Jefferson Street, is open daily from 11 A.M. to 4 P.M., June through August; phone 224-3094, or write Box 749, Seward 99664.

Chugach National Forest, Seward Ranger District office, is located at 334 4th Ave. USFS personnel can provide information on hiking, camping and fishing opportunities on national forest lands. Mailing address: P.O. Box 390, Seward 99664. Phone 224-3374.

Elevation: Sea level. **Climate:** Average daily maximum temperature in July, 62°F/17°C; average daily minimum in January, 18°F/-7°C. Average annual precipitation, 67 inches; average snowfall, 80 inches. **Radio:** KSWD 950, KSKA-FM 92. **Television:** Several channels by cable. **Newspaper:** *Seward Phoenix Log* (weekly).

Private Aircraft: Seward airport, 1.7 miles/2.7 km northeast; elev. 22 feet/7m; length 4,500 feet/1,371m; asphalt; fuel 80, 100, jet.

Seward—known as the "Gateway to Kenai Fjords National Park"—is a picturesque community nestled between high mountain ranges on a small rise stretching from Resurrection Bay to the foot of Mount Marathon. Thick groves of cottonwood and scattered spruce groves are found in the immediate vicinity of the city, with stands of spruce and alder growing on the surrounding mountainsides to the 1,000-foot/305-m level.

Downtown Seward (the main street is 4th Avenue) has a frontier-town atmosphere with some homes and buildings dating back to the early 1900s. The town was established in 1903 by railroad surveyors as an ocean terminal and supply center. The 470-mile/756-km railway connecting Fairbanks in the Interior with Seward, the railroad's southern terminus, was completed in 1923.

The city was named for U.S. Secretary of State William H. Seward, who was instrumental in arranging the purchase of Alaska from Russia in 1867. Resurrection Bay was named in 1791 by Russian fur trader and explorer Alexander Baranof. While sailing from Kodiak to Yakutat he found unexpected shelter in this bay from a storm and named the bay Resurrection because it was the Russian Sunday of the Resurrection.

Resurrection Bay is a year-round ice-free harbor and Seward is an important cargo port and fishing port. Seward's economic

---

BREEZE INN

RESTAURANT - MOTEL - LOUNGE

MODERN MOTEL
- 50 Deluxe Rooms
- Suites Available
- Free Coffee
- Free Local Calls • Cable TV

Located at Small-Boat Harbor —128 scenic miles south of Anchorage—

Beautiful View of Resurrection Bay

PHOTOGRAPHER'S PARADISE

All Major Credit Cards Accepted

RESERVATIONS
Phone (907) 224-5237
FAX (907) 224-7024
Box 2147
Seward, Alaska 99664

base includes tourism, a coal terminal, sawmill, fisheries and government offices.

The Alaska Vocational Technical Center at Seward provides vocational technical training for Alaska's adults in order to meet the needs of Alaskan employers. Classes are given in the building trades, oil technology, mechanics, office occupations, emergency medical training and other trades. Visitors are welcome to tour the center; stop by the Administration Bldg. on 2nd Avenue.

ACCOMMODATIONS

All visitor facilities, including 2 hotels, 3 motels, sevreal bed and breakfasts, many cafes and restaurants, post office, grocery stores, drugstore, travel agencies, gift shops, gas stations, bars, laundromats, churches,

SEWARD ADVERTISERS

Alaska Raiload	Ph. (800) 544-0552
Aurora Charters	Ph. (907) 224-3968
Bardarson Studio	Small Boat Harbor
Bear Lake Air and Guide Service	Ph. (907) 224-5725
Best Western Hotel Seward	Ph. (907) 224-2378
Breeze Inn	Small Boat Harbor
By the Sea Bed & Breakfast	Ph. (907) 224-3401
Command Charters	Ph. (907) 694-2833
Creekside Bed and Breakfast	Mile 3.7 Seward Hwy.
Downtown Lodging	Ph. (907) 224-3939
Farm Bed & Breakfast, The	Ph. (907) 224-5691
Fish House, The	Small Boat Harbor
Harbor Air Service	Seward Airport
Harborview Bed and Breakfast	900 3rd Ave.
House of Diamond Willow	2 locations—See ad
Kenai Coastal Tours, Inc.	Ph. (907) 277-2131
Kenai Fjords RV Park	Small Boat Harbor
Kenai Fjords Tours, Inc.	Ph. (907) 224-8068
Le Barn Appétit Bed and Breakfast	Ph. (907) 224-8706
Le Barn Appétit Restaurant & Bakery	Exit Glacier Rd.
Mackinaw Charters	Ph. (907) 224-3910
Major Marine Tours	Small Boat Harbor
Mariah Charters and Tours	Small Boat Harbor
Marina Motel	Ph. (907) 224-5518
Miller's Landing	Lowell Point Rd.
Mom Clock's Bed and Breakfast	Ph. (907) 224-3195
Murphy's Motel	4th Ave. & D St.
New Seward Hotel & Saloon	Ph. (907) 224-8001
Northern Nights Bed & Breakfast	Ph. (907) 224-5688
Ray's Waterfront	Small Boat Harbor
Select Charters	Ph. (907) 224-8763
Seward Chamber of Commerce	Ph. (907) 224-8051
Seward Fishing Adventures	Ph. (907) 224-8087
Seward Laundry	806 4th Ave.
Seward Trolley	Ph. (907) 224-7373
Seward Waterfront Lodging	Ph. (907) 224-5563
Silver Lining Charters	Ph. (907) 224-3802
Swiss Chalet Bed & Breakfast	Ph. (907) 224-3939
Taroka Inn	Ph. (907) 224-8687
Treasure Chest, The	Small Boat Harbor
Van Gilder Hotel	308 Adams St.
White House B&B, The	Mile 1.7 Nash Rd.

TAROKA INN
(907) 224-8687
9 Cozy Units with Private Bath • Kitchenettes
Families Welcome • Children Free

Brochure: P.O. Box 2448, Seward, Alaska 99664
Downtown — Corner of Third & Adams • *See our log ad under Accommodations*

SWISS CHALET
Bed & Breakfast
Adult Atmosphere
Smoke-free Environment
(907) 224-3939
MILE .1 EXIT GLACIER RD.
P.O. BOX 1734, SEWARD, AK 99664
Hosted by Charlotte Freeman & Stan Jones

DOWNTOWN LODGING
Spacious Suites • Queen Beds
Accommodating Two to Four People
Kitchenettes, Cable TV, Linens

Convenient • One Block from Bay

Reasonable Nightly Rates
(907) 224-3939
P.O. Box 1734, Seward, AK 99664

In The Shadow of Mt. Marathon   (907) 224-8090

murphy's motel   A GREAT PLACE TO STAY!

10 Units • Private Baths • Cable TV • Phones • Courtesy Coffee

4TH AND D STREETS • BOX 736 • SEWARD, ALASKA 99664

Kenai Fjords RV Park

40 Spaces with water & electric hookups
24-hour registration • Propane
Fishing & sightseeing information

Phone (907) 224-8779 • PO Box 2772, Seward, Alaska 99664

Small Boat Harbor • Mile 1 Seward Highway

"SEWARD — ALASKA'S ONE-STOP VACATION SPOT"
—*Anchorage Daily News*

SEWARD CHAMBER OF COMMERCE
VISITOR INFORMATION CENTERS:
Open Year-Round: Mile 2 Seward Hwy.

Open June through August:
- Historic Railcar "Seward"
   3rd & Jefferson
- Exit Glacier
   Mile 9 Exit Glacier Road

Photo by D. Marshall Clark Photography

SEWARD, FAMOUS FOR:
- Annual Polar Bear Jump
- **4th of July Mt. Marathon Race®**
- Annual Halibut Tournament
- Annual **Seward Silver Salmon Derby®**
- Historic Iditarod Trail - Mile "0"
- Birthplace of the Alaska State Flag
- Gateway to Kenai Fjords National Park

Leisurely 2-1/2 hour drive from Anchorage via National Scenic Byway
Convenient day trips

For more information, write:
Seward Chamber of Commerce, P.O. Box 749-MP, Seward, Alaska 99664 • (907) 224-8051

Ray's WATERFRONT

- Spectacular Waterfront Setting
- Overlooking Seward Boat Harbor
- SEAFOOD is our specialty
- Cocktails

VISA • MasterCard • American Express

(907) 224-5606
Over 50 fish on display

Hotel Seward
"Independently owned & operated"

Best Western Independent Worldwide Lodging

(907) 224-BEST • Toll-free in Alaska 1-800-478-4050

AAA ♦♦ rating, highest rating on the Kenai Peninsula

Overlooking Resurrection Bay
Seward's Most Luxurious Hotel

- Queen-size Beds
- Executive Suites
- Free In-room Movies
- Cable TV and VCRs
- Close to Everything
- Downtown Seward

P.O. Box 670-MP, Seward, AK 99664 • FAX (907) 224-3112
See our log ad under Accommodations

NEW SEWARD HOTEL & SALOON
Departure Point for Kenai Fjords Tours
Exceptionally Clean, Well-Furnished Rooms
In the heart of Downtown Seward

Reservations (907) 224-8001 • FAX (907) 224-3112
P.O. Box 670-MP, Seward, Alaska 99664
See our log ad under Accommodations

---

bowling alley and theater.

Best Western Hotel Seward. Enjoy being in the center of activity, yet in a quiet setting overlooking Resurrection Bay. Our 1991 extensive expansion includes breathtaking view rooms with in-room coffee and your own refrigerator. And check this out! For your in-room entertainment, all rooms include (1) remote control TVs with cable-vision, (2) remote control VCRs with videotape rental available and (3) 2 channels of free in-room movies featuring the latest hits! Complimentary scheduled shuttle bus service for our guests to boat harbor, train depot and airport. We accept all major credit cards. Reservations (907) 224-2378 or (800) 478-4050 inside Alaska. Fax (907) 224-3112. See display ad this section. [ADVERTISEMENT]

Creekside Bed and Breakfast. Clean, cozy cabins; tent sites. Heated restrooms with sauna and showers. Located on beautiful Clear Creek, surrounded by tall spruce. Peaceful country setting for a relaxing stay. Mile 0.5 on the road to Exit Glacier. Phone (907) 224-3834. See display ad Mile 3.7 Seward Highway. [ADVERTISEMENT]

The Fish House at the Small Boat Harbor offers complete one-stop service. Charter boats for halibut and salmon fishing. Sightseeing tours to Kenai Fjords National Park. Fishing tackle, bait, licenses, ice, weigh station, film, rain gear, clothing, RV supplies. Public phone. Mechanic on duty. Up-to-date fishing and tourist information. Come and visit our trophy room. See display ad this section. [ADVERTISEMENT]

Le Barn Appétit Bed and Breakfast. Creekside setting in the trees; beautiful views. Nonsmoking, nonalcoholic. Families welcome. Petting park and carousel for small children. Convenient to town. Yvon and Janet Van Driessche, P.O. Box 601, Seward, AK 99664. Phone (907) 224-8706 or 224-3426. Mile 3.7 Seward Highway, off Exit Glacier Road. [ADVERTISEMENT]

Le Barn Appétit Restaurant & Bakery. Breakfast, lunch, dinner. Continental cuisine. Omelettes, crepes, quiches. Delicious homemade soups. Sandwiches on fresh-baked bread. European pastries. Ice cream. European-style coffees and teas. Music (live sometimes) and dancing. Complete health food store. (907) 224-8706 or 224-3426. Mile 3.7 Seward Highway, off Exit Glacier Road. [ADVERTISEMENT]

New Seward Hotel & Saloon. Centrally located in downtown Seward, within walking distance of shops, ferry, bus terminal, boat harbor; 35 rooms featuring TV, phones,

---

Mom Clock's ♥ Bed and Breakfast

Over the river and
through the woods,
to Mom Clock's house today,
Three and one-half miles
north of Seward town,
A warm homey place to stay!

P.O. Box 1382   Seward, AK 99664-1382
Phone (907) 224-3195

KENAI FJORDS TOURS, INC.

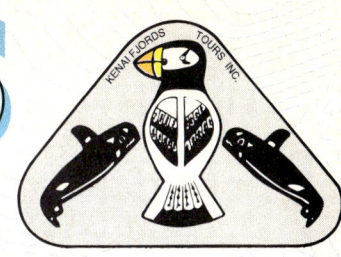

Want to see Kenai Fjords National Park?

Want to see glaciers?

Want to see wildlife?

See us first.

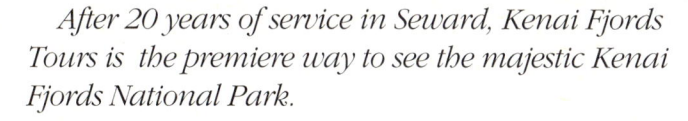

After 20 years of service in Seward, Kenai Fjords Tours is the premiere way to see the majestic Kenai Fjords National Park.

We welcome you aboard our clean, comfortable, and safe marine vessels the Spirit, the Kenai Fjords, and the new FjordLand. Come with us on the ORIGINAL Kenai Fjords National Park tour, where the wildlife watches you!

Kenai Fjords National Park Tour
Daily Departures:
8:00 a.m. and returns at 5:00 p.m.
$80 per person (plus sales tax)
Lunches and beverages are available.

Resurrection Bay Tour
Daily Departures:
8:30 a.m. and returns at 12:30 p.m.
1:00 p.m. and returns at 5:00 p.m.
$50 per person (plus sales tax)

ALL TOURS OPERATE MID MAY - MID SEPTEMBER

For reservations and information:
KENAI FJORDS TOURS, INC.
Box 1889MP, Seward, Alaska 99664
(907) 224-8068 • In Alaska (800) 478-8068

See our log ad under ATTRACTIONS

THE FARM Bed & Breakfast

Host: Jack Hoogland
Open Year Around

Phone (907) 224-5691   FAX (907) 224-2300
3 miles from Seward on Salmon Creek Road • See log ad at Mile 3.2 Seward Highway

---

free videos. Some kitchenettes. Salmon and halibut fishing charters or Kenai Fjords tours available. Year-round service. Brochure. All major credit cards accepted. Reservations (907) 224-8001 or (800) 478-4050 inside Alaska. Fax (907) 224-3112. See display ad this section. [ADVERTISEMENT]

Taroka Inn. Originally built to house officers stationed in Seward during WWII (Taroka is the local Indian name for the coastal brown bear). Taroka Inn has 9 cozy units with private baths and kitchenettes.

Walking distance to downtown attractions and Seward Trolley stop. Fishing charters and sightseeing tours arranged. (907) 224-8687. See display ad this section. [ADVERTISEMENT]

The White House B&B, (nonsmoking) bed-and-breakfast, is nestled in a mountain panorama. Our home's intrigue is country charm. Private or shared bath. Breakfast is

---

HARBORVIEW BED and BREAKFAST

900 3rd and "C" Street
Jerry & Jolene King, Box 1305, Seward, Alaska 99664
(907) 224-3217 (year round)
✻ private bath ✻ private entrance ✻ colored cable TV ✻ $55 - 60
✻ within walking distance of all major attractions
✻ on Seward Trolley route (so park and ride)
(See log ad under Accommodations)

SEWARD WATERFRONT LODGING
Bed and Breakfast
Open Year-Round
Downtown Seward • Adjacent to Ferry Terminal
550 Railway   (907) 224-5563
PO Box 618, Seward, AK 99664

KENAI FJORDS NATIONAL PARK & CHISWELL ISLANDS WILDLIFE REFUGE

Experience an abundance of marine wildlife, fjords, and glaciers in a comfortable one day cruise.
Harding Ice Field • Stellar Sea Lions • Whale Migration Routes • Puffins & Exotic Sea Birds, Friendly, Professional Service • Lunch Included

For Reservations Call:
(907) 277-2131

See Alaska's Best!
Kenai Coastal Tours
KENAI COASTAL TOURS, INC.

The "M/V KENAI COAST" : 82' Stabilized Vessel, Sightseeing Yacht Departs Seward AK., Daily 7 hr, 100 Mile Cruise.
KENAI COASTAL TOURS, INC. 524 W. 4th Ave., Suite 101, Anchorage AK. 99501 Located next to the Log Cabin

self-served in our guest kitchen. We welcome families and groups. Room rates $45 to $75. Open year-round, winter rates. (907) 224-3614. Mile 1.7 Nash Road. (See display ad at Mile 3.2 Seward Highway.) [ADVERTISEMENT]

The Harbormaster Building has public restrooms and pay showers, mailbox and pay phones. Weather information is available here during the summer. Public restrooms on Ballaine Boulevard along the ocean between the boat harbor and town. Dump station and freshwater fill-up at the Small Boat Harbor at the end of 4th Avenue (see city map). There are picnic areas with covered tables along B Street beside the bay and at the corner of Ballaine and Railway.

Seward has made a good effort to provide overnight parking for self-contained RVs. There are designated camping areas along the shore south of Van Buren; camping fee charged. RV parking is marked by signs. (Caravans contact the City Parks and Recreation Dept. for reservations, phone 224-3331.) Forest Acres municipal campground is at **Milepost S 2.4** Seward Highway. Private RV parks at Small Boat Harbor, at **Milepost S 6.6** and on Lowell Point Road. Camping also available on Exit Glacier Road (turnoff at **Milepost S 3.7** Seward Highway). ▲

Miller's Landing. Alaskan family operated fishing and tent/RV campground located on family homestead. Boat and pole rentals, fishing/sightseeing charters (full and half day), water taxi service to remote fishing areas, boat launch, kayak dropoffs to Aialik Glacier, Holgate Arm, Fox Island. Catch king salmon, Dolly Varden, pink, silver, chum salmon from beach, catch halibut from boat rentals or charters. Scenic campground located on Resurrection Bay. See sea otters, eagles, seals from camp. Private beaches. Hiking trail to Caine's Head State Park. Cozy cabin rentals. Country store sells bait, tackle, ice, fishing licenses, T-shirts, hats, gifts. Pull-through RV and large tent sites. Beach sites or forested sites. WWII landmarks, phone. Mike Miller homesteaded here, and is an expert on fishing advice and visitor information. Survived 1964 earthquake. Free coffee. Fishing advice 5¢. Guaranteed effective or your nickel back! Down-home Alaskan atmosphere. Box 81, Seward, AK 99664. (907) 224-5739. [ADVERTISEMENT] ▲

TRANSPORTATION

Air: Seward airport is reached by turning east on Airport Road at **Milepost S 2.9** on the Seward Highway. Scheduled daily service to Anchorage; charters also available.

Highway: Seward is reached via the 127-mile/203.2-km Seward Highway from Anchorage.

Ferry: The offices of the Alaska Marine Highway system in Seward are in the former Alaska Railroad depot, now one of Seward's

Marina Motel

AAA approved

In-room coffee
Cable TV

BOX 1134
SEWARD, ALASKA
99664

Phone: 907 • 224 • 5518

On the Right Coming Into Seward

Overlooking the Bay and Boat Harbor

By the Sea Bed & Breakfast
Located on the Bay — 1 block from Downtown
Open April thru September
(907) 224-3401
P.O. Box 284, Seward, Alaska 99664
Hosted by John and Sandy Taylor

Northern Nights Bed & Breakfast
Downtown Seward, On Resurrection Bay
Hosts: Marilyn & Don Sutherland • Open Year Around
225 Sixth Avenue • (907) 224-5688 • PO Box 491, Seward, AK 99664

Listed in the National Register of Historic Places

VAN GILDER HOTEL
308 Adams Street
LANDMARK HOTEL IN THE HEART OF SEWARD

In our cozy guest lounge you will find the warm friendly atmosphere of old Alaska

Reservations Advised
Phone: (907) 224-3525 • FAX (907) 224-3689
Or write: P.O. Box 2, Seward, Alaska 99664
Attention Deane Nelson

SELECT CHARTERS
for
SEA FUN

Fishing Charters
Sightseeing
1 Day to 1 Week
Halibut ■ Salmon
Bottomfishing
Licensed Skippers

SWIFTY, SNOWBIRD,
LORILEE II, BREAKTIME,
CACHALOT, DIZZY IZZY,
CRAZEES II, FRESH AIRE

Ask us about accommodations
in Seward

In Alaska call:
1-800-478-CFUN (2386)

Office: North Harbor at J-Dock
(907) 224-8763 May-September
(206) 385-1415 October-April

P.O. Box 1568, Seward, AK 99664
See our log ad under Attractions

KENAI PENINSULA • SEWARD

BARDARSON STUDIO Dot's art and gift gallery in the Seward boat harbor.

FLY-IN FISHING • HUNTING • SIGHTSEEING • COMMUTER SERVICE

Air Tours to world famous Kenai Fjords National Park and Harding Ice Cap
Serving Chugach National Forest area
Flights to the U.S. Forest Service Cabins on the Kenai Peninsula

HARBOR AIR SERVICE

Our wheel- and float-equipped aircraft can take you to Alaska's finest kayaking or backpacking country. Hunting, fishing, kayaking or just-to-get-away camps where you can tie into a hungry grayling or hard-running salmon. Air tours of the Kenai Fjords National Park and Harding Ice Cap for some of Alaska's most spectacular attractions. For details, phone, write or drop by our flight office at the Seward Airport.

Daily Scheduled Air Service
Between Seward and Anchorage
Ludwig H. & Linda K. Pfleger
P.O. Box 269
Seward, Alaska 99664 • (907) 224-3133

historic buildings, at the south end of 5th Avenue. The Alaska ferry MV *Tustumena* departs Seward for Kodiak and Valdez. For schedule information see the MARINE ACCESS ROUTES section.

Bus: Scheduled service to Anchorage.
Railroad: The Alaska Railroad connects Seward to Anchorage and Fairbanks. See the ALASKA RAILROAD section.
Taxi: Service available.
Rental cars: Available.

ATTRACTIONS

The Railcar *Seward* houses the chamber of commerce information center and is the best place to begin your visit. Located at 3rd and Jefferson Street, this railcar was the Seward observation car on the Alaska Railroad from 1936 until the early 1960s. Information and detailed map of the city are available.

Walking Tour of Seward encompasses more than 30 attractions including homes and businesses that date back to the early 1900s; some are still being used while others have been restored as historic sites. A brochure containing details on all the attractions of the tour is available at the railcar information center. The complete tour covers about 2 miles/3.2 km and takes about 1 to 2 hours, depending upon how much time you wish to spend browsing.

Marine Educational Center, maintained by the University of Alaska, has laboratories, aquaculture ponds and the vessel *Alpha Helix*, which carries on oceanographic research in Alaskan waters. There is a marine display here. Open 1-5 P.M. weekdays, 8 A.M. to 5 P.M. on Saturday, June through August.

Major Marine Tours 1415 Western Ave., Suite 503, Seattle WA 98101
For year-around information call 206/292-0595

KENAI FJORDS

SCENIC WILDLIFE DINNER CRUISES

Cruise the breathtaking Kenai Fjords aboard the 100 ft. Emerald Sea and enjoy an Alaska crab and shrimp feed with all the trimmings. You'll glide past puffins, sea lions, otters, eagles, whales and the awe-inspiring Bear Glacier. Our memorable 4 1/2-hour trips are perfect for the active traveler.

$65
• Fully narrated 55-mile cruise
• Departs from Seward's Boat Harbor
• Inside heated seating/outside viewing decks
• All-you-can-eat crab and shrimp buffet
• Call for daily sailing times

Major MARINE TOURS

RESERVATIONS / INFORMATION
JUNE - SEPTEMBER
Seward 907/224-8030   Anchorage 907/274-7300

Visit the Small Boat Harbor. This municipal harbor, built after the 1964 earthquake, is home port to fishing boats, charter boats and sightseeing boats. The harbor is also home to sea otters; watch for them! Visitors may notice the great number of sailboats moored here: many are members of the William H. Seward Yacht Club, which sponsors an annual sailboat and yacht show.

Bardarson Studio and House of Diamond Willow. In the Seward boat harbor come sit on the boardwalk and listen to New Age music that is piped outdoors. Wander through 2 shops that complement each other with fine art and gifts that range from sophisticated to down home. Postal package wrap service, too. [ADVERTISEMENT]

Seward Museum, at Jefferson and 3rd Avenue, is operated by the Resurrection Bay Historical Society (Box 871, Seward 99664). The museum features artifacts and photographs from the 1964 earthquake, WWII, the founding days of Seward, and other highlights of Seward's history. Also on display is a collection of Native baskets and ivory carvings. The museum is open June through Labor Day; hours vary. A modest admission fee.

Seward Community Library, across from the City–State Bldg., presents (on request) short slide/sound shows on a variety of subjects and has some informative displays. A program on the 1964 earthquake is shown daily at 2 P.M. (except Sunday) from June 15 through the first Saturday in September. Library hours are 1-8 P.M. Monday through Friday, 1-6 P.M. Saturday.

St. Peter's Episcopal Church is 3 blocks west of the museum at the corner of 2nd Avenue and Adams Street. It was built in 1906 and is the oldest Protestant church on the Kenai Peninsula. A feature is the unique painting of the Resurrection, for which Alaskans were used as models and Resurrection Bay as the background. Well-known Dutch artist Jan Van Emple was commissioned to paint the picture in 1925 when he was living in Seward. Obtain key to church from the Information Cache in season.

Hiking Trails. Two Lakes trail is an easy mile-long loop trail along the base of Mount Marathon. The trail passes through a wooded area and follows what used to be Hemlock Street. Beautiful view of marina below and north end of Resurrection Bay. Start at First Lake, behind the Alaska Vocational and Technical Center Administration Bldg. at 2nd Avenue and B Street.

The National Historic Iditarod Trail begins at the ferry terminal and follows a marked course through town, then north on the Seward Highway. At Mile 2.1 Nash Road (turn off at **Milepost S 3.2** Seward Highway) the trail continues from a gravel parking area on the east side of Sawmill Creek north to Bear Lake. The trail eventually rejoins the Seward Highway at **Milepost S 12**.

Caines Head State Recreation Area, 6 miles/9.6 km south of Seward, is accessible by boat or via a 4.5-mile/7.2-km beach trail (low tide only). The trailhead/parking is located about Mile 2 Lowell Point Road. The Caines Head area has bunkers and gun emplacements that were used to guard the entrance to Resurrection Bay during WWII.

Mount Marathon Race™, Seward's annual Fourth of July endurance race to the top and back of Mount Marathon (elev. 3,022 feet/921m), is a grueling test for athletes. The race is said to have begun in 1909 with a wager between 2 sourdoughs as to how long it would take to run up and back down Mount Marathon. The first year of the official race is uncertain, but records indicate either 1912 or 1915. Fastest recorded time is 43 minutes, 23 seconds set in 1981 by Bill Spencer, who broke his own 1974 record. Racers jump and slide back down the mountain in less than 10 minutes. The race attracts competitors from all over and thousands of spectators line the route each year.

Fourth of July in Seward includes a parade, fireworks and a variety of entertainment. For information contact the Seward Chamber of Commerce.

Annual Seward Silver Salmon Derby™ in August is one of the largest sporting events in Alaska. It is held over 9 days, starting the second Saturday in August through Sunday of the following weekend. 1992 will be the derby's 37th year. Record derby catch to date is a 19-lb., 10 1/4-oz. salmon caught off Caines Head by Doug Popwell II using herring bait.

There are more than $50,000 in prizes for the derby. There is $10,000 in cash for the largest fish. Also part of the derby are the sought-after tagged silvers worth $7,500 and $10,000. Prizes are sponsored by various merchants and the chamber of commerce.

Also held during derby days are a 10K run and a softball tournament.

The town fills up fast during the derby: Make reservations! For more information contact the Seward Chamber of Commerce.

Annual Seward Halibut Jackpot Tournament runs the entire month of July. First, second and third place prizes awarded for heaviest fish. Winners are in the 275-lb. class. Sponsors include the chamber of commerce and Seward Charter Assoc.

Kenai Fjords National Park. Seward is the gateway to this popular 650,000-acre national park. The park encompasses a coastal mountain system on the southeastern side of the Kenai Peninsula. Dominant feature of the park is the Harding Icefield, a 700-square-mile vestige of the last ice age. The mountaintops, called nunataks (an Eskimo word for "lonely peaks"), rise thousands of feet above this snow-covered ice field. Harding Icefield can be reached by a strenuous all-day hike from the base of Exit Glacier or by a charter flightseeing trip out of Seward.

The fjords of the park were formed when glaciers flowed down to the sea from the ice field and then retreated, leaving behind the

Catch the TROLLEY in Seward Town Shuttle CB Ch. 15

SEWARD TROLLEY
A service of the
Seward Chamber of Commerce
(907) 224-7373 (seasonal)
(907) 224-8051 (all year)
Information and Schedule at Visitor Centers

THE TREASURE CHEST
for the finest selection of Alaskan T-shirts

Seward's only locally designed
T-shirts and apparel
• Kenai Fjords National Park
• Seward Polar Bear Jump
• Authentic Russian and Ukrainian Handiwork
• Native Ivory and Bone Carvings
• Delicious Wildberry Jellies and Candies

Small Boat Harbor
(907) 224-8087

SEWARD FISHING ADVENTURES

Discover fishing in beautiful
KENAI FJORDS NATIONAL PARK

• BOTTOM FISHING
  Halibut, Ling Cod, Black Bass, Rockfish
• TROLLING
  Coho, Chinook and Sockeye Salmon

P.O. Box 2746, Seward, AK 99664
(907) 224-8087

MACKINAW CHARTERS

Take fish home!

Halibut, Salmon, Bass, Lingcod

Glen Szymoniak, Capt.
USCG Licensed

Tackle furnished
Safe, seaworthy vessel

(907) 224-3910
P.O. Box 825, Seward, AK 99664

HOUSE OF DIAMOND WILLOW

Diamond Willow Craftwork • Ivory and Gold Nugget Gifts 
Alaskan-made
Handcrafts
and Artwork

(907) 224-3415
P.O. Box 1137, Seward
Alaska 99664

AT SMALL BOAT HARBOR ◀ TWO LOCATIONS ▶ 213 3RD AVENUE

KENAI PENINSULA • SEWARD

deep inlets that characterize the coastline here. Substantial populations of marine mammals inhabit or migrate through the park's coastal waters, including sea otters, Steller sea lions, porpoises and whales. Icebergs from calving glaciers provide ideal refuge for harbor seals, and the rugged coastline provides habitat for more than 100,000 nesting birds. More than 30 species of seabirds have been identified, including tufted and horned puffins, cormorants, kittiwakes, murres and parakeet auklets. The park's spectacular scenery and wildlife may be viewed by daily charter boats or by charter planes.

Exit Glacier is the most accessible of the park's glaciers. Turn at **Milepost S 3.7** on the Seward Highway and follow Exit Glacier Road to the visitor center parking area. The main trail to the glacier is 0.8 mile long, with the first 0.3 mile paved for wheelchair access. There are about 3 miles/4.8 km of nature trails that provide easy access to the glacier. Ranger-led hikes are available at Exit Glacier in summer, where there are a picnic area and walk-in campground. Visitor information is available at the Exit Glacier ranger station and visitor center; open summer only. The picnic shelter near the ranger station converts to the winter-use cabin (reservations required). *CAUTION: Active glacier with unstable ice. Do not walk past warning signs!*

Slide programs, videos, exhibits and information on Kenai Fjords National Park and organized activities at the park are available at the park visitor center on 4th Avenue in the Small Boat Harbor area next to the Harbor Master's office. The center is open daily from Memorial Day to Labor Day; hours are 8 A.M. to 7 P.M. The remainder of the year hours are 8 A.M. to 5 P.M. weekdays. Write the park superintendent, Box 1727, Seward 99664.

CAUTION: The waters in this area can be extremely dangerous due to weather and violent storms that come out of the Gulf of Alaska, almost at a moment's notice. It is advisable to take a charter boat or flightseeing tour; both available out of Seward.

Kenai Fjords Tours, Inc. Treat yourself to a magnificent day in the national park aboard *Kenai Fjords, Fjordland* or *Spirit*. Kenai Fjords Tours, Inc. proudly presents Alaska's finest nature show. See puffins and seabird rookeries. Watch seals frolic in the deep blue waters . . . and hear sea lions bellow lazily from their cliffs. Kenai Fjords Tours will introduce you to the ice age splendor of tidewater glaciers. See and identify over 50 species of birds and marine mammals. You'll never feel rushed or hurried. Take plenty of pictures so family and friends can share your wonderful Alaskan experience. Bring warm clothing, camera, extra film. Lunches and beverages available or bring your own. Complimentary coffee. Mid-May to mid-September. Let us entertain your guests. The Oldows and Scobys—20 years in Seward. Write or call for brochure and reservations. Office at The Landing, Seward Small Boat Harbor. See display ad this section.
[ADVERTISEMENT]

Charter Sightseeing Cruises in Resurrection Bay offer chances to spot whales, porpoises, harbor seals and sea otters swimming about. Steller sea lions are generally spotted sunning themselves on the rocks. Thousands of gulls and other seabirds swarm about the cliffs and small islands at the mouth of the bay. There's also a popular tour of part of the coastline within Kenai Fjords National Park; an unusually large amount of wildlife is seen on this tour. Contact the Seward Chamber of Commerce or stop by the Small Boat Harbor.

Bear Lake Air and Guide Service. Exclusive floatplane service from beautiful Bear Lake. Flightseeing, air charters, fly-in day

---

Mariah Charters and tours
Est. 1981 — Seward, Alaska

- **Kenai Fjords Chiswell Islands Wildlife and Glacier Tour**
- **Fishing**
- **Exclusive and Overnight**

MARIAH CHARTERS and tours, based at Seward since 1981, operates in some of the most beautiful marine environment found in Alaska: Kenai Fjords National Park, the North Gulf Coast and Resurrection Bay.

MARIAH and **MISTY** are comfortable custom-built 43-foot ships.

Daily wildlife and glacier tour to Kenai Fjords National Park and the Chiswell Islands Wildlife Refuge. See them up close and in comfort aboard our 22-passenger vessels, for personalized tours.
Also offering fishing charters for large Pacific Halibut.

FOR PRICES and RESERVATIONS

MARIAH CHARTERS and tours 3812 Katmai Circle Anchorage, AK 99517-1024 *Office at Seward Boat Harbor*	**SEWARD OFFICE -** (907) 224-8623 **ANCHORAGE OFFICE -** (907) 243-1238	April 20-Sept. 30 FAX • (907) 224-8625 Oct. 1-April 20 FAX • (907) 243-1238

See Part of Alaska No One Else Can Show You!

Take a ride on the Alaska Railroad and see the heart of Alaska. From Seward, past majestic Mt. McKinley to Fairbanks, explore the same route as our pioneers onboard the **NEWEST** passenger cars traveling the railroad. Call 800-544-0552 for information and reservations for both independent excursions and package tours. Group rates are also available.

ALASKA RAILROAD CORPORATION
Anchorage, Alaska
Call Toll Free 800-544-0552

fishing. Guiding services for big game hunting. Remote modern lodge. Reservations welcome, (907) 244-5725. Bear Lake Air Service office located at Bear Creek RV Park, Mile 6.6 Seward Highway on Bear Lake Road. [ADVERTISEMENT]

Command Charters. Sportfishing for halibut, silver salmon, rockfish in beautiful Resurrection Bay/Kenai Fjords. Sightseeing is built-in. USCG licensed. Individuals and small parties welcome. All gear provided. May to October. In Alaska phone (907) 694-2833. From outside Alaska call 1-800-874-7834. [ADVERTISEMENT]

Mariah Charters and Tours. Established in 1981 at Seward, Mariah Charters takes pride in offering 2 custom-built 43-foot ships and personalized service. Daily wildlife and glacier tour to Kenai Fjords National Park and the Chiswell Islands Wildlife Refuge. See them up close and in comfort aboard our 22-passenger vessels, featuring 360° walk around deck area for viewing and photography; complimentary hot beverages, and personalized attention from our crew. Also offering fishing charters for large Pacific halibut. Tournament-grade tackle and bait furnished. Popular overnight as well as exclusive charters are offered for that special group or occasion. April 20–Sept. 30. For reservations April 20–Sept. 30 call (907) 224-8623; Oct. 1–April 20 call (907) 243-1238. Office located at Seward Boat Harbor. See display ad this section. [ADVERTISEMENT]

Major Marine Tours. Offering Seward's only wildlife cruise on Resurrection Bay that includes an all-you-can-eat Alaska crab and shrimp buffet. The cruise through Kenai Fjords includes incredible scenery and glaciers, as well as otters, sea lions, puffins, eagles, porpoises and more. The 100-foot *Emerald Sea* features reserved seating in an inside heated cabin with 2 outside decks for wildlife viewing and photography. Our complete 4½-hour tour (including dinner) costs only $65 and departs daily from Seward's Boat Harbor late May to early September. Major Marine Tours also books halibut and salmon fishing trips (full day and half day). Reservations: June–September—Seward (907) 224-8030; Anchorage (907) 274-7300. Year-round reservations/information (206) 292-0595. [ADVERTISEMENT]

Select Charters for fish 'n fun. Fishing and sightseeing charters. Photographers' paradise. Comfortable cruising, specializing in smaller groups for individualized attention. Kenai Fjords National Park day tours. Reasonable rates for overnight and multi-day trips to Pye Island or Prince William Sound. Our halibut and bottomfishing charters are full of surprises: red snapper, ling cod, black bass, Japanese perch and more. Tournament-quality fishing equipment and bait provided. We book for *Swifty, Snowbird, Cachalot, Loralee II, Breaktime, Dizzy Izzy* and others. USCG licensed skippers. Comfortable 32- to 43-foot boats. In Alaska call 1-800-478-2386. Parties of 4 to 20 (combos arranged). See display ad this section. [ADVERTISEMENT]

Silver Lining Charters. Fish or sightsee aboard one of the newest and fastest boats on Resurrection Bay. Halibut, lingcod, rockfish or salmon. Top quality tackle and bait furnished. Personalized service (4-6 per trip). Experienced captain; 5 IGFA world records. Call (907) 224-3802 or write P.O. Box 1654, Seward, AK 99664. [ADVERTISEMENT]

AREA FISHING: Resurrection Bay, coho (silver) salmon to 22 lbs., use herring, troll or cast, July to October; king salmon to 45 lbs., May to Aug.; also bottom fish, flounder, halibut to 300 lbs. and cod, use small weighted spoons and large red spinners by jigging, year-round. Charter fishing boats are available.

View from Kertulla Point of Seward and Mount Marathon in May. (Jerrianne Lowther, staff)

KENAI PENINSULA • SEWARD

Seward Laundry
Dry Cleaning • Coin-op Laundry
Drop-off Laundry • Showers
Attendant on Duty
8 a.m.-10 p.m. — 7 days a week Summers
806 Fourth Ave. (907) 224-5727

Aurora Charters 
- Salmon
- Halibut
- Bottomfish

Full-day and 1/2-day Charters
Carl & Kim Hughes
(907) 224-3968
PO Box 241, Seward, Alaska 99664
Office on the Boardwalk
Seward Small Boat Harbor

The Fish House
Seward Jackpot Halibut Derby
July 1 - 31

SEWARD SILVER SALMON DERBY
9 days, starts second Saturday in August
Alaska's Biggest Salmon Derby • Over $50,000 in Cash Prizes

— See our log ad under Attractions —

Fishing Tackle • Ice • Bait • RV Supplies
Halibut and Salmon Fishing Charters
Fishing and Hunting Licenses and Information

Joan Clemens • Box 1345, Seward, Alaska 99664
Phone: (907) 224-3674 • In Alaska: 1-800-478-8007
FAX (907) 224-7108

1992 ■ The MILEPOST® 433

STERLING HIGHWAY

Junction with Seward Highway to Homer, Alaska
Includes Seldovia
Alaska Route 1
(See maps, pages 435–436)

The Sterling Highway ends at the tip of Homer Spit. (Jerrianne Lowther, staff)

Sterling Highway Log

ALASKA ROUTE 1
Distance from Seward (S) is followed by distance from Anchorage (A) and distance from Homer (H). Physical mileposts show distance from Seward.

S 37.7 (60.7 km) **A 89.3** (143.7 km) **H 141.8** (228.2 km) Junction with Seward Highway. First exit southbound (1-way road) for Sterling Highway.

S 37 (59.5 km) **A 90** (144.8 km) **H 142.5** (229.3 km) Tern Lake Junction. Second southbound exit (2-way road) for Sterling Highway. This exit provides access to Tern Lake Campground (see description next milepost). Gravel turnout beside Tern Lake with interpretive sign on arctic terns.

S 37.4 (60.2 km) **A 90.4** (145.5 km) **H 142.1** (228.7 km) USFS Tern Lake Campground; 25 campsites, toilets, water, picnic tables, firepits, $5 camping fee. USFS spawning channel for king salmon on Daves Creek at outlet of Tern Lake. Short viewing trail with information signs illustrating use of log weirs and stream protection techniques. ▲

S 38 (61.1 km) **A 91** (146.4 km) **H 141.5** (227.7 km) Avalanche gates. Gravel turnouts.

S 38.3 (61.6 km) **A 91.3** (146.9 km) **H 141.2** (227.2 km) Gravel turnout. Emergency call box.

S 39 (62.8 km) **A 92** (148 km) **H 140.5** (226.1 km) Daves Creek, an unusually beautiful mountain stream which flows west into Quartz Creek. Dolly Varden and rainbow averaging 14 inches, June through September. A good place to view spawning salmon in late July and August.

S 40.5 (65.2 km) **A 93.5** (150.5 km) **H 139** (223.7 km) Double-ended gravel turnout to south with interpretive sign about Alaska moose.

S 40.9 (65.8 km) **A 93.9** (151.1 km) **H 138.6** (223 km) Bridge over Quartz Creek. This stream empties into Kenai Lake. You are now entering one of Alaska's best-known lake and river fishing regions, across the center of the Kenai Peninsula. The burn on the hillsides to the south was part of a Forest Service moose habitat improvement program.

S 41.1 (66.1 km) **A 94.1** (151.4 km) **H 138.4** (222.7 km) Cooper Landing Closed Area. This area is closed to the hunting of Dall sheep. The ridges to the north are a lambing ground for Dall sheep.

S 42.8 (68.9 km) **A 95.8** (154.2 km) **H 136.7** (220 km) Gravel turnouts on Quartz Creek.

S 43.1 (69.4 km) **A 96.1** (154.6 km) **H 136.4** (219.5 km) Double-ended gravel turnout to east on Quartz Creek.

S 43.5 (70 km) **A 96.5** (155.3 km) **H 136** (218.9 km) Double-ended gravel turnout to east.

S 44 (70.8 km) **A 97** (156.1 km) **H 135.5** (218.1 km) Gravel turnout on Quartz Creek; dumpster.

S 44.3 (71.3 km) **A 97.3** (156.6 km) **H 135.2** (217.6 km) Small gravel turnout to east; dumpsters.

S 45 (72.4 km) **A 98** (157.7 km) **H 134.5** (216.5 km) Sunrise Inn. See display ad this section.

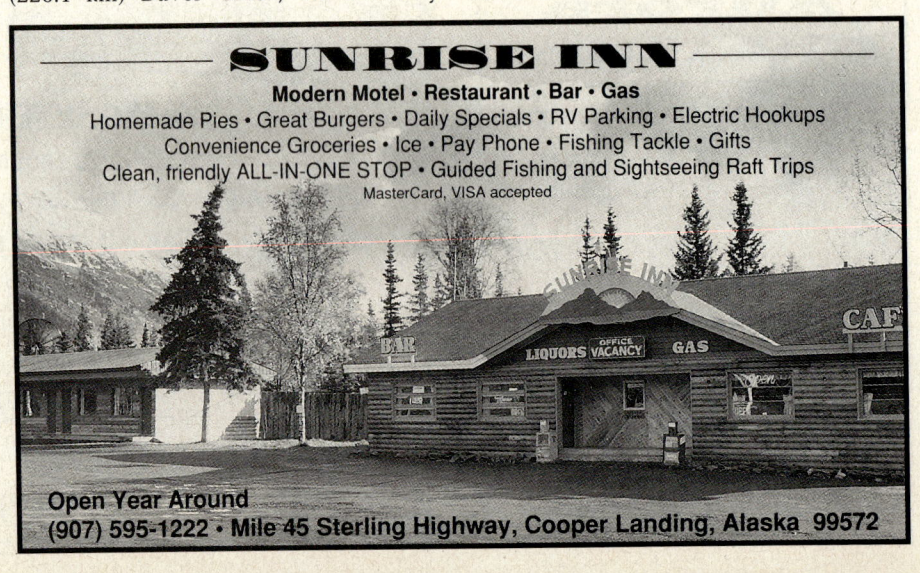

SUNRISE INN
Modern Motel • Restaurant • Bar • Gas
Homemade Pies • Great Burgers • Daily Specials • RV Parking • Electric Hookups
Convenience Groceries • Ice • Pay Phone • Fishing Tackle • Gifts
Clean, friendly ALL-IN-ONE STOP • Guided Fishing and Sightseeing Raft Trips
MasterCard, VISA accepted

Open Year Around
(907) 595-1222 • Mile 45 Sterling Highway, Cooper Landing, Alaska 99572

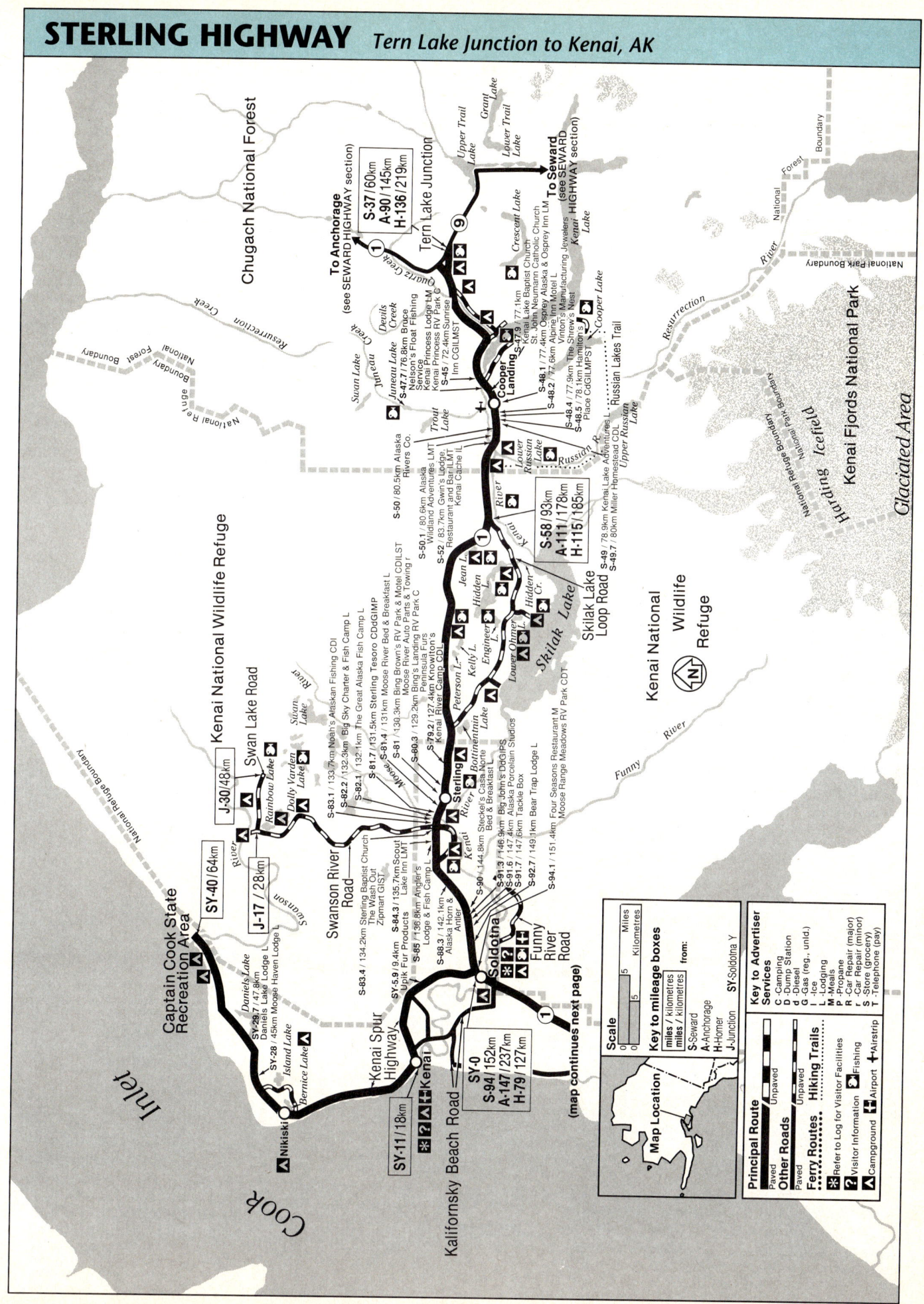

STERLING HIGHWAY Tern Lake Junction to Kenai, AK

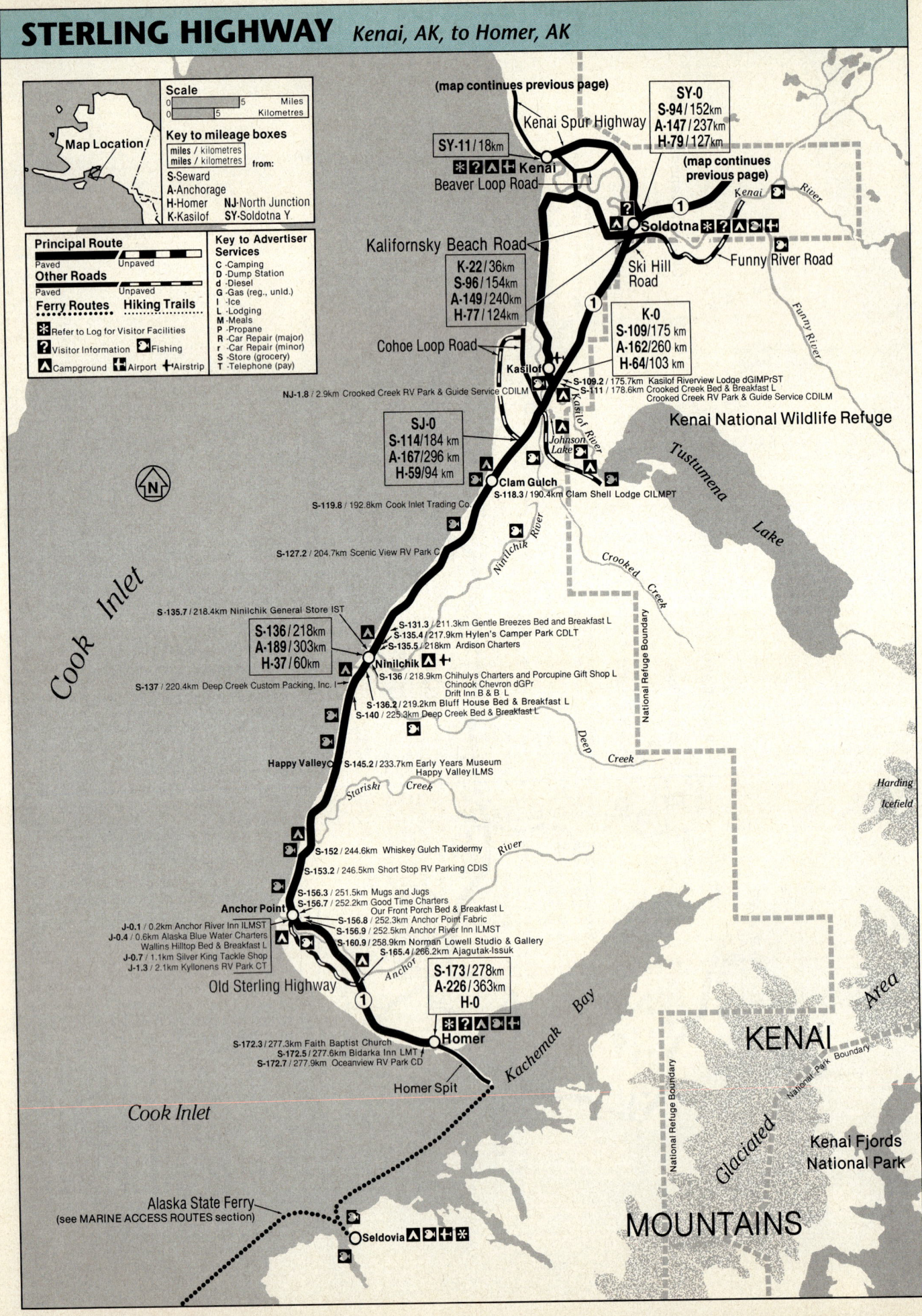

STERLING HIGHWAY — Kenai, AK, to Homer, AK

KENAI PENINSULA • STERLING HIGHWAY

Scale
0 — 5 Miles
0 — 5 Kilometres

Key to mileage boxes
miles / kilometres
miles / kilometres from:
S—Seward
A—Anchorage
H—Homer   NJ—North Junction
K—Kasilof   SY—Soldotna Y

Principal Route — Paved / Unpaved
Other Roads — Paved / Unpaved
Ferry Routes   **Hiking Trails**

✱ Refer to Log for Visitor Facilities
? Visitor Information   🎣 Fishing
▲ Campground   ✈ Airport   ✚ Airstrip

Key to Advertiser Services
C—Camping
D—Dump Station
d—Diesel
G—Gas (reg., unld.)
I—Ice
L—Lodging
M—Meals
P—Propane
R—Car Repair (major)
r—Car Repair (minor)
S—Store (grocery)
T—Telephone (pay)

SY-0
S-94 / 152km
A-147 / 237km
H-79 / 127km

Kenai Spur Highway
(map continues previous page)

SY-11 / 18km
Kenai ✱?▲✚
Beaver Loop Road

Soldotna ✱?▲✚
Kalifornsky Beach Road
Funny River Road
Ski Hill Road

K-22 / 36km
S-96 / 154km
A-149 / 240km
H-77 / 124km

K-0
S-109 / 175 km
A-162 / 260 km
H-64 / 103 km

Cohoe Loop Road
Kasilof ✚
S-109.2 / 175.7km Kasilof Riverview Lodge dGIMPrST
S-111 / 178.6km Crooked Creek Bed & Breakfast L
Crooked Creek RV Park & Guide Service CDILM

NJ-1.8 / 2.9km Crooked Creek RV Park & Guide Service CDILM

SJ-0
S-114 / 184 km
A-167 / 296 km
H-59 / 94 km

Johnson Lake
Kenai National Wildlife Refuge

Clam Gulch
S-118.3 / 190.4km Clam Shell Lodge CILMPT
S-119.8 / 192.8km Cook Inlet Trading Co.
S-127.2 / 204.7km Scenic View RV Park C

Cook Inlet
Ninilchik River
Crooked Creek
Tustumena Lake

S-135.7 / 218.4km Ninilchik General Store IST
S-131.3 / 211.3km Gentle Breezes Bed and Breakfast L
S-135.4 / 217.9km Hylen's Camper Park CDLT
S-135.5 / 218km Ardison Charters

S-136 / 218km
A-189 / 303km
H-37 / 60km

Ninilchik ▲✚
S-136 / 218.9km Chihulys Charters and Porcupine Gift Shop L
Chinook Chevron dGPr
Drift Inn B & B L
S-136.2 / 219.2km Bluff House Bed & Breakfast L
S-137 / 220.4km Deep Creek Custom Packing, Inc.
S-140 / 225.3km Deep Creek Bed & Breakfast L

Happy Valley
S-145.2 / 233.7km Early Years Museum
Happy Valley ILMS

Stariski Creek
Deep Creek
Harding Icefield
National Refuge Boundary

S-152 / 244.6km Whiskey Gulch Taxidermy
S-153.2 / 246.5km Short Stop RV Parking CDIS
S-156.3 / 251.5km Mugs and Jugs
Anchor Point
S-156.7 / 252.2km Good Time Charters
Our Front Porch Bed & Breakfast L
J-0.1 / 0.2km Anchor River Inn ILMST
S-156.8 / 252.4km Anchor Point Fabric
J-0.4 / 0.6km Alaska Blue Water Charters
S-156.9 / 252.5km Anchor River Inn ILMST
Wallins Hilltop Bed & Breakfast L
S-160.9 / 258.9km Norman Lowell Studio & Gallery
J-0.7 / 1.1km Silver King Tackle Shop
S-165.4 / 266.2km Ajagutak-Issuk
J-1.3 / 2.1km Kyllonens RV Park CT

Old Sterling Highway
Anchor River
Kachemak Bay

S-173 / 278km
A-226 / 363km
H-0

Homer ✱?▲✚
S-172.3 / 277.3km Faith Baptist Church
S-172.5 / 277.6km Bidarka Inn LMT
S-172.7 / 277.9km Oceanview RV Park CD

Homer Spit
Cook Inlet

Alaska State Ferry
(see MARINE ACCESS ROUTES section)

Seldovia ▲✚✱

KENAI Glaciated MOUNTAINS Area
Kenai Fjords National Park
National Park Boundary

436   The MILEPOST® ■ 1992

S 45 (72.4 km) **A 98** (157.7 km) **H 134.5** (216.5 km) Quartz Creek Road to Quartz Creek Recreation Area. Quartz Creek Campground, 0.3 mile/0.5 km from the highway, has 31 sites, boat launch, flush toilets, firepits and a $6 camping fee. Crescent Creek Campground, 3 miles/4.8 km from the highway, has 9 sites, tables, water and pit toilets; $6 fee. Crescent Creek USFS trail leads 6.2 miles/10 km to the outlet of Crescent Lake. The trailhead is about 1 mile/1.6 km from Crescent Creek Campground. A public-use cabin is located at the lake; not accessible in winter or early spring due to extreme avalanche danger. ▲

Beautiful views of Kenai Lake next 3 miles/4.8 km westbound. The lake's unusual color is caused by glacial silt.

The Sterling Highway from the junction with the Seward Highway west to Sterling takes the traveler through the heart of some prime fishing country, and provides access to numerous fishing lakes and rivers. *NOTE: The diversity of fishing conditions and frequent regulation changes in all Kenai waters make it advisable to consult locally for fishing news and regulations.*

Quartz Creek, rainbow, midsummer; Dolly Varden to 25 inches, late May through June. **Crescent Lake**, grayling, July 1 to April 14 (2 grayling daily bag and possession limit). **Kenai Lake**, lake trout, May 15 to Sept. 30; trout, May to September; Dolly Varden, May to September. Kenai Lake and tributaries are closed to salmon fishing. 🐟

S 45.6 (73.4 km) **A 98.6** (158.7 km) **H 133.9** (215.5 km) Large turnout; dumpsters. Observation point for Dall sheep on near mountain and mountain goats on Cecil Rhode Mountain (directly across Kenai Lake).

S 46.2 (74.3 km) **A 99.2** (159.6 km) **H 133.3** (214.5 km) Small gravel turnout to east.

S 47 (75.6 km) **A 100** (160.9 km) **H 132.5** (213.2 km) Turnout to east.

S 47.1 (75.8 km) **A 100.1** (161.1 km) **H 132.4** (213.1 km) Kenai Lake Lodge (restaurant).

S 47.3 (76.1 km) **A 100.3** (161.4 km) **H 132.2** (212.7 km) The Landing Restaurant on Kenai Lake.

S 47.7 (76.8 km) **A 100.7** (162 km) **H 131.8** (212.1 km) Bean Creek Road, access to Bruce Nelson's guide service, and the Kenai Princess Lodge and RV Park, on the Kenai River. The lodge, which opened in 1990, has an interesting chandelier in the lobby made from antlers.

Bruce Nelson's Float Fishing Service. See display ad this section.

Kenai Princess Lodge at Cooper Landing. 50 deluxe rooms with sun porches, wood stoves, TVs and phones. Located on the Kenai River with outdoor deck, gift shop, dining room, lounge, hot tubs and tour office. River rafting, flightseeing, fishing and horseback riding. Seasonal service May to October. Meeting space available. Rates from $160. VISA, MasterCard, American Express. Write Princess Tours®, 2815 2nd Ave., Suite #400, Seattle, WA 98121, or call (800) 426-0500 year-round. [ADVERTISEMENT]

Kenai Princess RV Park at Cooper Landing on the Kenai River. Water, power and septic at each site. General store, showers, laundry and hotel services. Hiking, fishing, river rafting. Seasonal service mid-May to late-September. $15 per night; discount for 3-plus nights. VISA, MasterCard, American Express accepted. Write Princess Tours®, 2815 2nd Ave., Suite #400, Seattle, WA 98121, or call (800) 426-0500 year-round. [ADVERTISEMENT] ▲

FLOAT FISHING
Bruce Nelson's SERVICE
907 595-1313

FISHING THE KENAI RIVER SINCE 1968
We specialize in trophy Rainbow Trout and King Salmon, Sockeye Salmon, Arctic Char and Silver Salmon
Licensed and insured Kenai River guide service
P.O. Box 545, Cooper Landing, Alaska 99572
Bean Creek Road • Mile 47.7 Sterling Highway

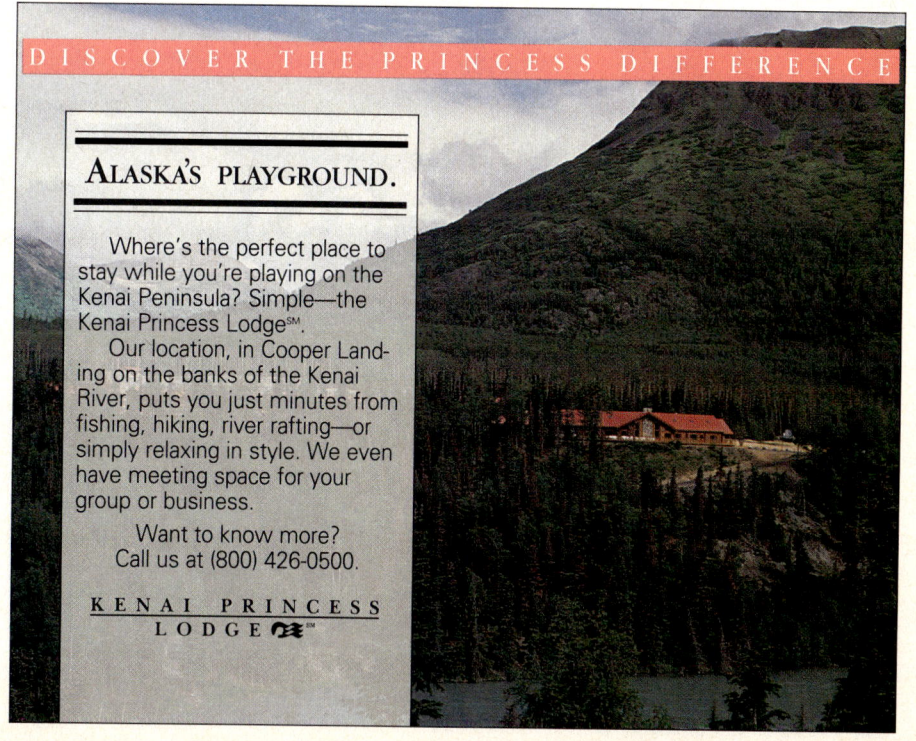

DISCOVER THE PRINCESS DIFFERENCE

RV IN THE HEART OF THE KENAI.

Planning a visit to the Kenai Peninsula with your RV? Then plan to reserve your spot at the Kenai Princess RV Park.

We have 38 deluxe hook-ups with power, water, septic, fire pits, and picnic tables. Plus a general store, showers, and laundry facilities. All located at Cooper Landing in the heart of the Kenai Peninsula, adjacent to the Kenai Princess Lodge℠.

For reservations call: (800) 426-0500.

KENAI PRINCESS RV PARK

DISCOVER THE PRINCESS DIFFERENCE

ALASKA'S PLAYGROUND.

Where's the perfect place to stay while you're playing on the Kenai Peninsula? Simple—the Kenai Princess Lodge℠.

Our location, in Cooper Landing on the banks of the Kenai River, puts you just minutes from fishing, hiking, river rafting—or simply relaxing in style. We even have meeting space for your group or business.

Want to know more? Call us at (800) 426-0500.

KENAI PRINCESS LODGE

KENAI PENINSULA • STERLING HIGHWAY

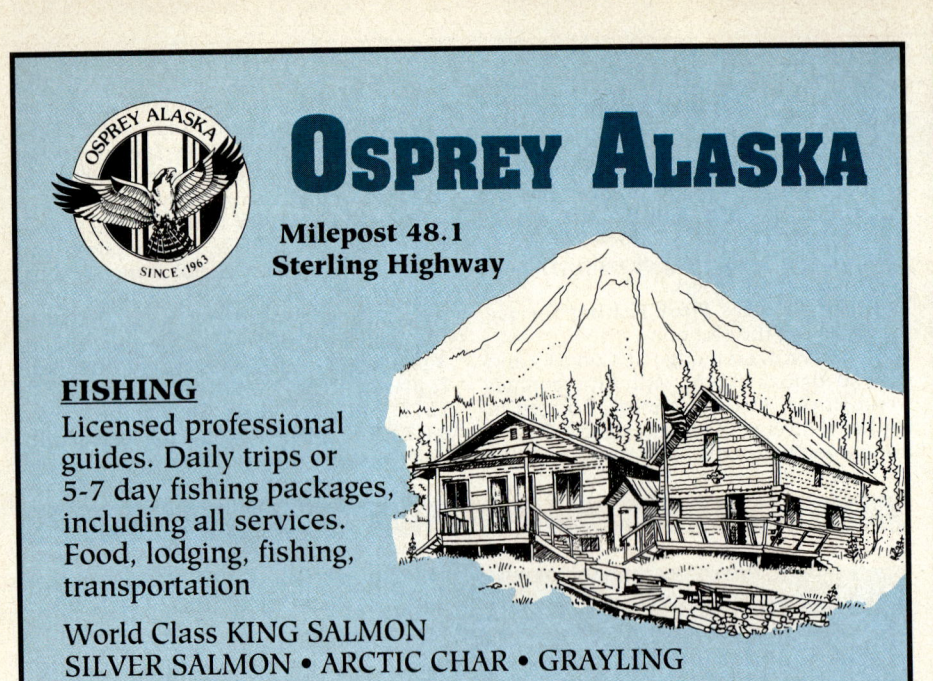

OSPREY ALASKA

Milepost 48.1
Sterling Highway

FISHING
Licensed professional guides. Daily trips or 5-7 day fishing packages, including all services. Food, lodging, fishing, transportation

World Class KING SALMON
SILVER SALMON • ARCTIC CHAR • GRAYLING
RAINBOW TROUT

LODGING
The OSPREY INN — New, modern motel, opened in 1990. Huge suites with mountain views. Groups and families welcome. Bed and Breakfast units also available.

FOOD
Complete restaurant — Steak, seafood, pasta, pizza

RAFT TRIPS
Scenic raft trips through spectacular Kenai River Valley and Kenai Canyon daily.

TACKLE
Up-to-date fishing information from Kenai guides. Complete tackle shop.

"We can outfit you to fish the Kenai effectively!"

VAN TOURS
See Alaska with a small group. Tour Kenai Fjords, Denali National Park, Fairbanks and much more. (Brochure available).

RESERVATIONS and INFORMATION
Outside Alaska call 1-800-533-5364 • In Alaska call 595-1265
Osprey Alaska, P.O. Box 504, Cooper Landing, Alaska 99572

The Sterling Highway winds through the Kenai Mountains. (John W. Warden)

S 47.8 (76.9 km) **A 100.8** (162.2 km) **H 131.7** (211.9 km) Kenai River bridge. Parking at west end of bridge, boat launch at both ends.

The Kenai River flows directly alongside the highway for the next 10 miles/16 km with several gravel turnouts offering good views.

Kenai River from Kenai Lake to Skilak Lake, closed to king salmon fishing. Use artificial lures only. Silver salmon 5 to 15 lbs., August through October; pink salmon 3 to 7 lbs., July and August; red salmon 3 to 12 lbs., late May through mid-August (be familiar with regulations on closed areas); rainbow and Dolly Varden, April to November. Also whitefish.

S 47.9 (77.1 km) **A 100.9** (162.4 km) **H 131.6** (211.8 km) Snug Harbor Road. This side road leads 12 miles/19.3 km to Cooper Lake and trailhead for 23-mile/37-km USFS trail to Russian River Campground (see **Milepost S 52.8**). A Baptist church and the St. John Neuman Catholic Church, named after one of the first American saints, are on Snug Harbor Road.

Kenai Lake Baptist Church. See display ad this section.

St. John Neumann Catholic Church. See display ad this section.

S 48.1 (77.4 km) **A 101.1** (162.7 km) **H 131.4** (211.7 km) **Osprey Alaska & Osprey Inn.** Salmon fishing trips daily. Light tackle specialists. Licensed guides. Complete tackle store, licenses, information.

KENAI LAKE BAPTIST CHURCH
Mile 47.9 Sterling Highway
(at Snug Harbor Road)

Sunday School	9:45 a.m.
Worship	11:00 a.m.
Evening Service	6:00 p.m.

A friendly community church
Member, Conservative Baptist Association

4-hour whitewater raft trips twice daily. Modern motel, huge suites, mountain views. Complete restaurant, steak, seafood, pizza, pasta. 1-800-533-5364. In Alaska, call 595-1265. Brochure available. See display ad.
[ADVERTISEMENT]

S 48.2 (77.6 km) **A 101.2** (162.9 km) **H 131.3** (211.3 km) Motel, grocery and jewelry store.

Alpine Inn Motel. See display ad this section.

Vinton's Manufacturing Jewelers. See display ad this section.

S 48.4 (77.9 km) **A 101.4** (163.2 km) **H 131.1** (211 km) **COOPER LANDING** (pop. 386) stretches along several miles of the highway. All visitor facilities. Cooper Landing ambulance, phone 595-1255.

The Shrew's Nest. See display ad this section.

Private Aircraft: Quartz Creek airstrip, 4 miles/6.4 km west; elev. 450 feet/137m; length 2,700 feet/823m; gravel; unattended.

S 48.5 (78.1 km) **A 101.5** (163.3 km) **H 131** (210.8 km) **Hamilton's Place** river resort, only complete stop on the upper Kenai River. Information center for the famous Russian River and surrounding area. Centrally located for day trips to Seward, Soldotna/Kenai, Homer. Make us your Kenai

KENAI LAKE ADVENTURES
"Fly In"
HUNTING • FISHING • CHARTER
Flightseeing Tours • Air Service
Air Taxi to Forest Service Cabins

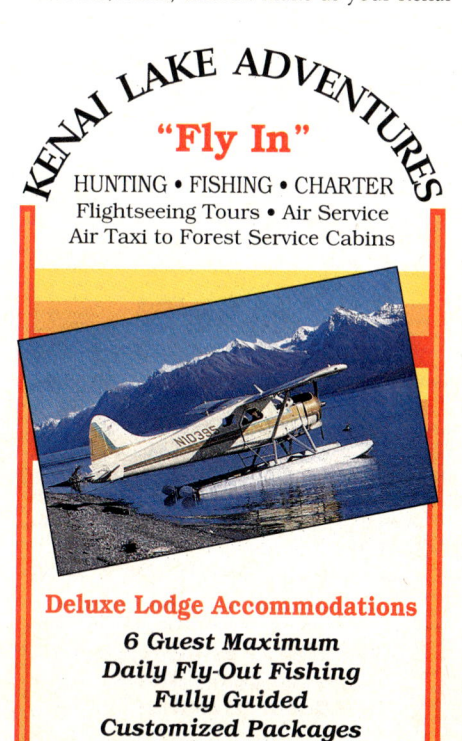

Deluxe Lodge Accommodations
6 Guest Maximum
Daily Fly-Out Fishing
Fully Guided
Customized Packages
Daily & Weekly Rates
Halibut Fishing

BED & BREAKFAST
P.O. Box 830
Cooper Landing, Alaska 99572
Call Ken Bethe (907) 595-1363
Mile 49 Sterling Highway

Skilak Lake Loop Road Log

The 19.1-mile/30.7-km Skilak Lake Loop Road (good gravel) loops south through the Skilak Wildlife Recreation Area to campgrounds, trails and fishing spots.

Distance from east junction (EJ) with Sterling Highway at Milepost S 58 is followed by distance from west junction (WJ) with Sterling Highway at Milepost S 75.2.

EJ 0 WJ 19.1 (30.7 km) **Junction** with Sterling Highway at **Milepost S 58.**

EJ 0.1 (0.2 km) **WJ 19** (30.5 km) Jim's Landing Campground on Kenai River, 0.2 mile/0.3 km from road; 9 sites, toilets, dumpster, tables, firepits, water, boat launch, parking area.

EJ 0.6 (1 km) **WJ 18.5** (29.7 km) Kenai River trail (6.3-mile/10.1-km hike); parking area.

EJ 2.4 (3.9 km) **WJ 16.7** (26.8 km) Kenai River trail (6.3-mile/10.1-km hike); parking area.

EJ 3.6 (5.8 km) **WJ 15.5** (24.9 km) Hidden Lake Campground is an exceptionally nice camping area with 44 sites on paved loop roads. Located 0.5 mile/0.8 km in from the road on the lakeshore, it has a dump station, wheelchair accessible toilets, tables, water, firepits and boat launch. There is an amphitheater for campfire programs and an observation deck for viewing wildlife. Campground hosts in residence. Camping fee $6. Trailer parking area, interpretive exhibits and kitchen shelter with barbecue.

Hidden Lake, lake trout average 16 inches and kokanee 9 inches, year-round, best from May 15 to July 1, use spoon, red-and-white or weighted, by trolling, casting and jigging. This lake is a favorite among local ice fishermen from late December through March.

EJ 4.7 (7.6 km) **WJ 14.4** (23.1 km) Hidden Creek trail (1.5-mile/2.4-km hike); parking area.

EJ 5.5 (8.9 km) **WJ 13.6** (21.8 km) Skilak Lookout trail (2.6-mile/4.2-km hike); parking area.

EJ 6.2 (10 km) **WJ 12.9** (20.7 km) Bear Mountain trail (1-mile/1.6-km hike); parking area with firepit across from lily pond.

EJ 6.9 (11.1 km) **WJ 12.2** (19.6 km) Scenic viewpoint of Skilak Lake.

EJ 8.5 (13.6 km) **WJ 10.6** (17 km) Upper Skilak Lake Campground, drive 2 miles/3.2 km around Lower Ohmer Lake; 0.2-mile/0.3-km loop road through campground. Ten sites, some sites on lakeshore, boat launch, toilets, tables.

Lower Ohmer Lake, rainbow 14 to 16 inches, year-round. **Skilak Lake,** offers rainbow and Dolly Varden. Red (sockeye) salmon enter lake in mid-July.

EJ 8.6 (13.8 km) **WJ 10.5** (16.9 km) Lower Ohmer Lake, short side road to parking area on lakeshore; 3 campsites, toilet, boat launch, firepits and tables.

EJ 9.5 (15.2 km) **WJ 9.6** (15.4 km) Short side road to **Engineer Lake,** boat launch and Seven Lakes trail; turnaround and parking area with firepits. Stocked silver salmon to 15 inches, best in July.

EJ 9.6 (15.4 km) **WJ 9.5** (15.3 km) Engineer Lake wayside; gravel turnout.

EJ 13.8 (22.2 km) **WJ 6.3** (8.5 km) Well-marked 1-mile/1.6-km side road to Lower Skilak Lake Campground; 14 sites, tables, toilets, firepits, boat launch.

CAUTION: Skilak Lake is cold, winds are fierce and unpredictable. Wear life jackets!

EJ 14.2 (22.8 km) **WJ 4.9** (7.8 km) Fire guard station.

EJ 18.7 (30.1 km) **WJ 0.4** (0.6 km) Bottinentnin Lake; well-marked side road leads 0.3 mile/0.5 km to parking area on lakeshore.

EJ 19.1 (30.7 km) **WJ 0** Junction with Sterling Highway at **Milepost S 75.2.**

Return to Milepost S 58 or S 75.2 Sterling Highway

St. John Neumann Catholic Church
Mile 47.9 Sterling Highway
Snug Harbor Rd. (1 mile)
Sunday Mass 12:30 p.m. — *Visitors Welcome*

The Shrews' Nest
General Merchandise, Hardware, Arts & Crafts
Gifts, Video Rentals, Film, Fishing Tackle Fishing, Hunting Licenses Art Gallery
Mile 48.4 Sterling Highway
Joyce Olsen • (907) 595-1257
P.O. Box 797, Cooper Landing, AK 99572

Vinton's Manufacturing Jewelers
Gold Nugget, Jade, Ivory
Specializing in Gold Nugget and Custom Design
— OVER 30 YEARS IN ALASKA — AAA

ALPINE INN MOTEL
Kitchenettes • TV
Raft Trips, Fishing, Air Service Available
Box 801 Phone (907) 595-1212
Cooper Landing, Alaska 99572

Alpine Inn MOTEL
Kitchenettes TV
REASONABLE RATES
595-1212

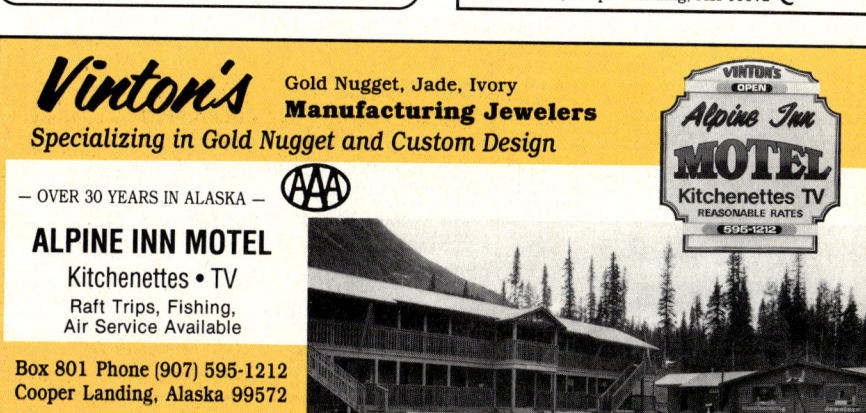

HAMILTON'S PLACE

MILE 48.5 STERLING HIGHWAY
BOX 505, COOPER LANDING, ALASKA 99572
(907) 595-1260
100 MILES SOUTH OF ANCHORAGE

"THE ONLY STOP FOR ALL YOUR TRAVEL NEEDS!"

SHOP
General Store
MUNCHIES, JUNK FOOD, SNACKS
Tackle Shop
LURES, NETS, POLES, HIP BOOTS, CAMP SUPPLIES
"Killer Coho Flies" and "Russian River Riggins"
Public Telephone

FISHING and HUNTING LICENSES
Freezer Storage · Fish Boxes
WE NEVER RUN OUT OF CUBE ICE!

DINE AND RELAX
RESTAURANT & LOUNGE OVERLOOKING THE KENAI RIVER
Cheeseburgers, Juicy Steaks, Seafood, Fries, Homemade Soups, Chili and Pies
SPECIAL — HALIBITS and FRIES
(Beer Battered and Deep Fried Halibut Chunks)
Come see our trophy animal display!

PACKAGE STORE
AUTO SERVICES
CHEVRON GAS STATION AND PRODUCTS
Propane, Tires, Welding, Mechanic On Duty and
24-HOUR EMERGENCY WRECKER SERVICE

STAY OVERNIGHT
Camping Facilities with Full Hookups · Tenting
Picnic Area · River Dock Fishing · Summer Vehicle Storage

MODERN CABINS WITH COOKING FACILITIES ROOMS AT REASONABLE RATES
ONLY LOCAL LAUNDROMAT and PUBLIC SHOWERS!

SIGHTSEE
Take time to Enjoy Cooper Landing's Extensive Recreation Area
Long mountain hikes into the wilderness. A natural wonderland!
Experience massive moose, brown and black bear, dall sheep, mountain goats, colorful salmon, bald eagles, wild birds and assorted Alaskan critters!
DALL SHEEP and GOAT VIEWING AREA 
THE BEST SALMON FISHING IN THE WORLD!
Rainbow, Dolly Varden, etc., fishing

MasterCard · VISA

INQUIRE
WE SPECIALIZE IN UPDATED AREA INFORMATION.
Ask for fish, boating and local "tips".

Peninsula headquarters. Chevron services, 24-hour wrecker service, propane. (Good Sam road service providers.) General store, groceries, licenses, tackle, ice. Restaurant, lounge, liquor store. Hair salon. RV hookups, efficiency cabins, laundromat, phone. Fish freezing, storage, Federal Express shipping. Hamilton's Place, serving the public since 1952, hopes to make your stay enjoyable. See display ad. [ADVERTISEMENT] ▲

S 49 (78.9 km) **A 102** (164.1 km) **H 130.5** (210 km) Cooper Landing post office, located in resort; open 9 A.M. to 5 P.M. weekdays and Saturday morning. Pay phone.

Kenai Lake Adventures. See display ad on page 439.

S 49.4 (79.5 km) **A 102.4** (164.8 km) **H 130.1** (209.4 km) Large paved turnout by Kenai River. The highway winds along the Kenai River. Many spruce trees in this area have died from a spruce bark beetle infestation and are being removed.

S 49.7 (80 km) **A 102.7** (165.3 km) **H 129.8** (208.9 km) **The Miller Homestead,** bed and breakfast and RV park on the Kenai River. Make us your headquarters for Kenai Peninsula guided fishing and float trips. Trophy rainbow, Russian River red salmon, Dolly Varden. Bank fishing available. Salmon charters for Kenai River kings and silvers. Halibut charters arranged. See display ad this section. [ADVERTISEMENT] ▲

S 49.8 (80.1 km) **A 102.8** (165.4 km) **H 129.7** (208.7 km) Haul road used by loggers removing dead spruce trees. Watch for trucks.

S 50 (80.5 km) **A 103** (165.8 km) **H 129.5** (208.4 km) **Alaska Rivers Co.,** right side westbound. Rafting daily on the beautiful Kenai River. Half-day scenic float, or full-day canyon trip with white water. Both trips include homemade picnic lunch, excellent viewing of wildlife, professional guides, all equipment provided. All ages welcome. Personalized guided drift boat fishing for all species of fish. Bed-and-breakfast accommodations available. Family-owned and operated by Cooper Landing residents. Gary Galbraith, owner. (907) 595-1226 for reservations or just stop by. [ADVERTISEMENT]

S 50.1 (80.6 km) **A 103.1** (165.9 km) **H 129.4** (208.2 km) **Alaska Wildland Adventures.** Don't pass up taking a float or fishing trip with Alaska Wildland Adven-

---

The Miller Homestead
on the Kenai River
— Bed & Breakfast —

RV Park · 18 Pull-through Spaces
Electric Hookups · Dump Station · Water
Restrooms and Showers

Guided Fishing and Float Trips
Bank Fishing for Rainbow and Dollies

(907) 595-1406 · **(817) 433-5669**
May 15 - Oct. 1   Oct. 1 - May 15
P.O. Box 693, Cooper Landing, Alaska 99572
See log ad, Mile 49.7 Sterling Highway

tures. You'll enjoy this facility's unique and scenic setting on the Kenai River. They offer daily guided float trips along with a delicious Alaskan picnic lunch served at noon. You can expect to see wildlife and enjoy the scenery of one of the world's most beautiful rivers. If you're seeking a quality fishing experience, ask about their guided fishing trips for salmon and rainbow trout. This company is well known for its professional guides and deluxe drift boats. All tackle, rods and reels are furnished. 2- and 3-day fishing packages are also available here. Operating since 1977. Within Alaska call toll free (800) 478-4100, or outside Alaska (800) 334-8730, for more information or reservations. [ADVERTISEMENT]

S 50.4 (81.1 km) A 103.4 (166.4 km) H 129.1 (207.8 km) Juneau Creek, Dolly Varden and rainbow, mid-June through July.

S 50.5 (81.3 km) A 103.5 (166.6 km) H 129 (207.6 km) Bridge over Cooper Creek. USFS Cooper Creek Campground. Camping area on the river side of highway (second entrance westbound) has 10 sites, several on the riverbank. Camping area on the other side of the highway has 16 sites. Both have tables, water, firepits and wheelchair-accessible toilets. Fee is $6.

S 52 (83.7 km) A 105 (169 km) H 127.5 (205.2 km) Kenai Cache. See display ad this section.

Gwin's Lodge, Restaurant and Bar, left side southbound. The best little eating house in Alaska. Where Alaskans always stop for the best food with the fastest service. Heart of the Kenai Peninsula fishing/hunting area. Package store, modern cabins, restaurant, bar, ice, fishing tackle, shirts, caps, gifts. Your Russian River headquarters. Fishing trips available; local guides. Near Kenai and Russian rivers confluence, Russian Lakes and Resurrection Pass trailheads. Phone (907) 595-1266. [ADVERTISEMENT]

S 52.6 (84.6 km) A 105.6 (169.9 km) H 126.9 (204.2 km) USFS Russian River Campground has 84 sites at the end of a 2-mile/3.2-km road. All have river access, toilets, water, tables and firepits. Fish cleaning stations, covered picnic tables and dump station. The Russian River Campground is often full during the summer, particularly during the Russian River red salmon runs. Arrive early! No reservations are accepted. Fees: $8 single RV occupancy, $16 double RV occupancy, $2 park and fish.

Bears, attracted by the salmon, are frequent visitors to this campground.

Russian Lakes USFS trail, trailhead and parking at Mile 0.9/1.4 km on campground road. Lower Russian Lake at Mile 2.6/4.2 km (elev. 500 feet/152m; hiking time 1½ hours). Good trail to Mile 3/4.8 km. Upper Russian Lake at Mile 12/19.3 km (elev. 690 feet/210m). Trail continues to Cooper Lake at end of Snug Harbor Road (see **Milepost S 47.9**). Public-use cabins along trail (see Cabins in the GENERAL INFORMATION section).

CAUTION: This is brown bear country, USFS recommends carrying a rifle of .30-06 caliber or larger. Winter use; good snowmobiling to lower lake only, avalanche danger beyond.

The **Russian River**. Closed to all fishing April 15 through May 30. No bait area. Check regulations for limits and other restrictions. Red (sockeye) salmon run starts during the first half of June, lasts 2 to 3 weeks. A second run of larger fish in July lasts about 3 weeks, must use flies only (streamer or coho). Silver (coho) salmon to 15 lbs., run begins mid-August, also flies only (streamer or coho). Rainbow (hook and release only), average 15 inches.

S 53 (85.3 km) A 106 (170.6 km) H 126.5 (203.6 km) Bridge over Kenai River.

S 53.2 (85.6 km) A 106.2 (170.9 km) H 126.3 (203.3 km) Well-marked entry point to Resurrection Pass USFS trail; parking at trailhead. This 38-mile-/61-km-long trail climbs to Resurrection Pass (elev. 2,600 feet/792m) and descends to north trailhead near Hope on Turnagain Arm.

S 54.7 (88 km) A 107.7 (173.3 km) H 124.8 (200.8 km) Leaving Chugach National Forest lands westbound. Gravel turnout to east. Many turnouts and access to the Kenai River between here and **Milepost S 58**.

S 55 (88.5 km) A 108 (173.8 km) H 124.5 (200.4 km) Kenai–Russian River recreation area, access to Russian River ferry. During salmon season this USF&WS campground, a favorite with fishermen, is heavily used; toilets, water, dumpsters, interpretive display, pay phone. Fee is $6 for camping or parking. Privately operated 28-person ferry crosses the Kenai River here offering access to good fishing on opposite bank and to the mouth of the Russian River. Ferry fee is $3 adults round-trip, $1.50 children.

Leaving Game Management Unit 7, entering Unit 15 westbound. Entering Kenai National Wildlife Refuge westbound, administered by the USF&WS; contains more than 1.97 million acres of land set aside to preserve the moose, bear, sheep and other wildlife found here.

S 57.1 (91.9 km) A 110.1 (177.2 km) H 122.4 (197 km) Fuller Lake trailhead (well marked), parking. **South Fuller Lake**, arctic grayling; **North Fuller Lake**, Dolly Varden.

S 58 (93.3 km) A 111 (178.6 km) H 121.5 (195.5 km) USF&WS information cabin opposite **junction** with Skilak Lake Loop Road. See SKILAK LAKE LOOP ROAD log page 439. The information cabin is open Memorial Day through Labor Day; brochures and information on Kenai Peninsula attractions including federal, state and local

---

GWIN'S LODGE

Experience the romance and charm of one of the few remaining log roadhouses.
BUILT TRADITIONALLY IN 1952.

Near confluence Kenai and Russian Rivers. Central peninsula location. Outstanding fishing for trophy Rainbow, Salmon, Dolly Varden. Sightseeing, hiking, photography, flightseeing, cross country skiing.

★ Restaurant
★ Bar
★ Liquor Store
★ Tackle
★ Modern Cabins

Let Tony and Kay Watkins share authentic Alaska with you by personalizing your vacation at reasonable rates.

Mile 52 Sterling Hwy. Cooper Landing, AK 99572 (907) 595-1266

Kenai Cache
TACKLE
All Your Fishing Needs!

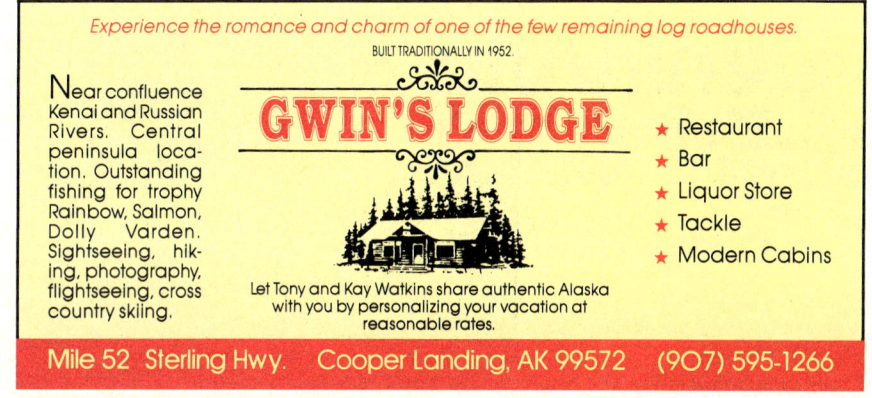

Fishing Information
Hand-tied Flies
Fish Freezing and Shipping
Rental Equipment

Block & Cubed Ice
Free Coffee
Cabin Rentals
Mounted Fish Display

Mile 52, Sterling Highway, Cooper Landing, Alaska 99572 • (907) 595-1401

Why Just Sightsee When You Can... Experience Alaska!

DAILY SCENIC RAFT TRIPS

FLOAT OR FISH THE KENAI RIVER

SALMON AND TROUT FISHING

ALASKA WILDLAND ADVENTURES
800-478-4100 (In Alaska)
800-334-8730 (Outside Alaska)

Milepost 50, Hwy. 1, Cooper Landing, Alaska

EXTENDED ADVENTURE VACATIONS
■ 7-10 Day Natural History Safaris
■ 3-6 Day Sportfishing Packages
For Brochure Call or Write Box 26, Cooper Landing, AK 99572

Showy bloom of the prickly wild rose. Seed pods are edible. (Jerrianne Lowther, staff)

recreation areas, such as Kenai National Wildlife Refuge and Chugach National Forest.

S 59 (94.9 km) A 112 (180.2 km) H 120.5 (193.9 km) **Milepost S 59.** Actual driving distance between here and **Milepost S 61** is 2.6 miles/4.2 km or 0.6 mile/1 km more than the posts indicate.

S 60.6 (97.5 km) A 113.6 (182.8 km) H 118.9 (191.3 km) **Jean Lake**, small campground (3 sites) and picnic area; boat launch, rainbow fishing.

S 61.4 (98.8 km) A 114.4 (184.1 km) H 118.1 (190.1 km) Skyline trail to west; double-ended gravel parking area to east.

S 62.3 (100.3 km) A 115.3 (185.6 km) H 117.2 (188.6 km) Large gravel turnout to west. Mystery Hills to the north and Hideout Hill to the south.

S 64.5 (103.8 km) A 117.5 (189.1 km) H 115 (185.1 km) Gravel turnout to west.

S 68.3 (109.9 km) A 121.3 (195.2 km) H 111.2 (179 km) Turnoff to south for Peterson Lake (0.5 mile/0.8 km) and Kelly Lake (1 mile/1.6 km) public campgrounds. Both have tables and firepits for 4 camping parties, water and boat launch, and parking space for self-contained RVs. **Kelly** and **Peterson lakes** have rainbow population. Access to Seven Lakes trail.

S 70.4 (113.3 km) A 123.4 (198.6 km) H 109.1 (175.6 km) Egumen wayside with large parking area. East Fork Moose River and Seven Lakes trail. Half-mile marshy trail to **Egumen Lake** (lake not visible from highway); good rainbow population.

S 71.3 (114.7 km) A 124.3 (200 km) H 108.2 (174.1 km) Parking area at entrance to Watson Lake public campground; 0.4-mile/0.6-km drive from highway to small campground with 3 sites, toilets, picnic tables, fireplaces, water, dumpsters and steep boat launch (suitable for canoes or hand-carried boats). **Watson Lake**, rainbow. Views of Kenai Mountains next few miles westbound.

S 72.8 (117.2 km) A 125.8 (202.4 km) H 106.7 (171.7 km) Paved double-ended turnout to east, lake to west.

S 75.2 (121 km) A 128.2 (206.3 km) H 104.3 (167.8 km) West **junction** with Skilak Lake Loop Road. See SKILAK LAKE LOOP ROAD log page 439.

Kenai River from Skilak Lake to Soldotna. Consult regulations closely for legal tackle, limits and seasons. King salmon 20 to 80 lbs., use spinners, excellent fishing June to August; red salmon 6 to 12 lbs., many, but hard to catch, use flies, best from July 15 to August 10; pink salmon 4 to 8 lbs., abundant fish on even years Aug.1 to Sept. 1, spoons; silver salmon 6 to 15 lbs., use spoons, Aug. 15 to Nov. 1; rainbow, Dolly Varden 15 to 20 inches, June through September, use spinners, winged bobber, small-weighted spoon.

S 79 (127.1 km) A 132 (212.4 km) H 100.5 (161.7 km) *NOTE: Watch for major road construction westbound to Soldotna in 1992.*

S 79.2 (127.4 km) A 132.2 (212.7 km) H 100.3 (161.4 km) Kenai Keys Road; access to private campground.

Knowlton's Kenai River Camp. Private camp overlooking the beautiful Kenai River. Fish for trophy-sized trout and salmon or just kick back and enjoy the scenery from our comfortable lodge. RV or tent camping, boat rentals, rooms with private baths, restrooms, hot showers, dump station. Caravans welcome. See display ad this section.
[ADVERTISEMENT]

S 80.3 (129.2 km) A 133.3 (214.5 km) H 99.2 (159.6 km) Turnoff for Peninsula Furs, private RV park and for Bing's Landing State Recreation Site with RV and tent camping, picnic area, water, boat launch, toilets (wheelchair accessible), dumpster and access to Kenai River. Camping fee $6/night or annual pass. Boat launch fee $5 or annual boat launch pass.

Peninsula Furs. See display ad this section.

Bing's Landing RV Park. See display ad this section.

S 81 (130.3 km) A 134 (215.6 km) H 98.5 (158.5 km) **STERLING** (pop. 1,732; elev.150 feet/45m). Traveler services include a gas station, a motel, several restaurants and cafes; gift, grocery, hardware, antique, fur and furniture stores, laundromat and a

---

Knowlton's Kenai River Camp
HEART OF FISHING COUNTRY

- ■ **RV CAMPING**
  Dump Station
  Some Electric Hookups
- ■ **Lodging with Continental Breakfast**
- ■ **TENT CAMPING**
  Hot Showers
  Restrooms • Water
- ■ **BOAT RENTALS**
  Pole Rentals
  Tackle

Trout and Salmon Fishing

From Milepost 79.2 Sterling Highway, drive 2.4 miles on Kenai Keys Road.

(907) 262-7765 (summer) • (907) 696-2446 (winter)
P.O. Box 834, Sterling, Alaska 99672

Fully Outfitted
Fishing Guide Available

Peninsula FURS
Fine Selected Dressed FURS

Located 1 mile off Sterling Highway

Turn At Bing's Landing State Park Road

WELCOME TO MY WORLD OF FURS

Owned and operated by obsession — Ed Whitaker   *30 years of fur business in the Sterling area*

The North's largest and only noncompetitive fur house of its kind, offering some of the finest in dressed pelts or beautifully made up furs. From Mexico to Prudhoe, this choice of quantity isn't found anywhere else in dressed furs. The price and place can be the height of any "vacation." For that Special Occasion, for that Special Lady —
THINK FURS... MY LADY DOES!

Open 7 days a week, year-round 10 to 7. After hours, call me. Mail orders guaranteed.

Where beautiful people and place meet.
State Park Road. Lots of convenient turning and parking room.

MILEPOST 80.3 • P.O. Box 68 • Sterling, Alaska 99672 • Phone (907) 262-4695

private camper park. Post office at **Milepost S 81.6**. (Businesses with a Sterling mailing address extend west to **Milepost S 85**.) Nearby recreational opportunities include fishing and the extensive canoe trail system (see description at **Milepost S 82**). Moose River Raft Race and Sterling Days held in July.

Bing Brown's RV Park & Motel. See display ad this section. ▲

Moose River Auto Parts & Towing. See display ad this section.

S 81.1 (130.5 km) **A 134.1** (215.8 km) **H 98.4** (158.4 km) Gift shop and grocery store.

S 81.4 (131 km) **A 134.4** (216.3 km) **H 98.1** (157.9 km) **Moose River Bed & Breakfast.** See display ad this section. ▲

S 81.6 (131.3 km) **A 134.6** (216.6 km) **H 97.9** (157.6 km) Sterling post office (Zip code 99672).

S 81.7 (131.5 km) **A 134.7** (216.8 km) **H 97.8** (157.4 km) **Sterling Tesoro.** See display ad this section.

S 82 (132 km) **A 135** (217.3 km) **H 97.5** (156.9 km) Pay phone on highway just before turnoff for Isaak Walton State Recreation Site, located at the confluence of the Kenai and Moose rivers. Paved access road, 25 campsites, parking, tables, toilets, water and dumpster. Camping fee $6/night or annual pass. Boat launch ($5 fee or annual boat launch pass) and good access to Kenai River. A small log cabin, totem pole and an information sign about Moose River archaeological site. ▲

Bridge over Moose River. CAUTION: *Drive carefully during fishing season when fishermen walk along bridge and highway.*

Canoe rentals and shuttle bus service to the head of the canoe trail system are available by the Moose River bridge. This is the terminus of the Swan Lake canoe trail. There are 2 canoe routes in Kenai National Wildlife Refuge: Swan Lake route, a 60-mile/97-km route connecting 30 lakes; and the Swanson River route, an 80-mile/129-km route linking 40 lakes. Guided canoe tours and fishing charters are available. Portions of the canoe system may be traveled taking anywhere from 1 to 4 days. Contact Kenai National Wildlife Refuge, Box 2139, Soldotna 99669 for details. See SWANSON RIVER AND SWAN LAKE ROADS log page 445.

Moose River, 0.3 mile/0.4 km of fishing down to confluence with Kenai River. Sockeyes here in June. Big summer run of reds follows into August; silvers into October.

Kenai and **Moose rivers** (confluence), Dolly Varden to 25 inches, big rainbow, salmon (red, king, pink and silver). May through October for trout, kings, silvers and pinks. This is a fly-fishing-only area from May 15 through Aug. 15; closed to fishing from boats, May 15 to July 31.

S 82.1 (132.1 km) **A 135.1** (217.4 km) **H 97.4** (156.7 km) **The Great Alaska Fish Camp.** Most complete fishing destination on the Kenai. Charters for king, silver, rainbow and halibut; air taxi for fly-in hunting and fishing. Outfitters for Swan Lake Wilderness Canoe Trail and raft trips, float trips on wild rivers and natural history safaris. Lodge and 1-day fishing trips out of Anchorage. Write HC 01 Box 218, Sterling, AK 99672. Phone (907) 262-4515 or (800) 544-2261.
[ADVERTISEMENT]

S 82.2 (132.3 km) **A 135.2** (217.6 km) **H 97.3** (156.6 km) **Big Sky Charters & Fish Camp.** See display ad this section.

MOOSE RIVER
Log Lodge and Cabin
BED & BREAKFAST
MILE 81.4 STERLING HIGHWAY
(907) 262-5670
P.O. Box 1073, Sterling, AK 99672

Bing Brown's RV Park & Motel
(907) 262-4780
Liquor and Country Store • Ice • Tackle
Full Hookups • Showers • Laundry • Dump Station
Kitchenettes • Bed & Breakfast • Fishing Licenses
Mile 81, Sterling Highway   Write: P.O. Box 235, Sterling, Alaska 99672

MOOSE RIVER AUTO PARTS & TOWING 
— 24-HOUR TOWING SERVICE —
Auto & RV Parts • Minor Repairs
Norm & Joyce, Owners
(907) 262-5333 • MILE 81 STERLING HIGHWAY

Sterling Tesoro
Mile 81.7 Sterling Highway
(907) 262-5969
Open 24 Hours - 7 Days A Week • Starting June 1 through Labor Day 
- Low Gas Prices
- Diesel • Propane • Ice
- Clean Rest Rooms!!
- RV's Free Dump & Water with Fill-up!

Cook's Cafe & Gifts
Open 7 Days a Week
Mile 81.7 Sterling Highway
- Breakfast • Lunch • Dinner Menus • Ice Cream
- Great Burgers • Yummy Cinnamon Rolls • Daily Specials
- Full Size Dining Area • Alaskan Ivory and Gifts

Bing's Landing
RV PARK
Mile 80.3 Sterling Highway
Sterling, Alaska 99672

PARK-LIKE-SETTING • PICNIC TABLES
FIRE PITS • HOOK-UPS
1/2 MILE TO KENAI RIVER BOAT LAUNCH
SHOWERS • LAUNDROMAT UNDERWAY

OPENING MAY, 1992
WRITE: P.O. BOX 246• KENAI, AK 99611
PHONE: (907) 283-7473

BIG SKY CHARTER & FISH CAMP

Kenai River Fishing at its Best
Power & Drift Boats • Cabin Rentals
– Brochure Available –

Summer (907) 262-9496
All Year (907) 345-5760

13120 Saunders Road
Anchorage, Alaska 99516
Mile 82.2 Sterling Highway

STERLING BAPTIST CHURCH

An independent, fundamental, Bible-believing church

SERVICES: SUNDAY 9:45 a.m. - 11:00 a.m. and 6:00 p.m. WEDNESDAY 7:00 p.m.

"WHEN YOU VISIT - BRING YOUR BIBLE ... AT OUR CHURCH YOU WILL USE IT."

Stop and say hello, we'd be so glad to have you in our services

Fishermen Welcome
Mile 83.4 Sterling Hwy. at Swanson River Road

THE WASH OUT
NEW, CLEAN, MODERN

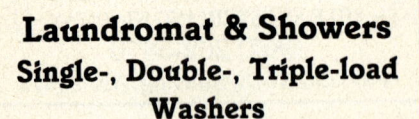

Laundromat & Showers
Single-, Double-, Triple-load Washers

*Friendly Service • Children's Playroom
Complimentary Coffee • TV*

(907) 262-7666

Open Daily in Summer
Large Circle Drive for RVs
Next to Zipmart

MILE 83.4 STERLING HIGHWAY on
ROBINSON LOOP/SWANSON RIVER RD.

NOAH'S ALASKAN FISHING

GUIDED FISHING
- Everything Furnished
- King, Silver, & Red Salmon
- Rainbow Trout
- Fly-Out Fishing
- Scenic Raft Trips

TACKLE SHOP
- Bait • Ice
- Licenses
- Tackle Rentals
- Coho Flies
- Free Coffee

CABIN RENTALS AVAILABLE

NOAH'S ALASKAN FISHING SCHOOL
Learn local techniques and tackle rigging necessary to catch Alaskan Salmon.
SEVERAL 1-HOUR CLASSES DAILY

Stop In And Visit With Our Friendly Staff At
Mile 83.1 Sterling Hwy.
R.V. HOOK-UPS AVAILABLE
SEND FOR OUR FREE BROCHURE
P.O. BOX 3721 • SOLDOTNA, AK 99669
(907) 262-6171 Ask For Senior Discount
"You'll Be Happy You Fished With Noah's"
KENAI & KASILOF RIVERS

S 82.6 (132.9 km) A 135.6 (218.2 km) H 96.9 (155.9 km) Airstrip. Restaurant and bar.

S 83 (133.6 km) A 136 (218.9 km) H 96.5 (155.3 km) Truck weigh station and senior center.

S 83.1 (133.7 km) A 136.1 (219 km) H 96.4 (155.1 km) **Noah's Alaskan Fishing.** See display ad this section.

S 83.4 (134.2 km) A 136.4 (219.5 km)

Mile 84.3
Scout Lake Inn

Phone (907) 262-5898
HOME-STYLE COOKING
Specials Daily
Open 6:00 a.m.-10:00 p.m.
Specializing in Homemade Pies
Steaks & Seafoods
BEER & WINE
Served in our main dining room
ORDERS TO GO
NEW 15-UNIT MOTEL
FISHING CHARTERS ARRANGED
See log ad at Mile 84.3
P.O. Box 493, Sterling, Alaska 99672

H 96.1 (154.7 km) Convenience store with gas, church, laundromat and showers located here.

Sterling Baptist Church. See display ad this section.

The Wash Out. See display ad this section.

ZIPMART. See display ad this section.

S 83.4 (134.2 km) A 136.4 (219.5 km) H 96.1 (154.7 km) Swanson River Road turnoff to north (see SWANSON RIVER AND SWAN LAKE ROADS log opposite page). Scout Lake Loop Road turns off to south and rejoins the Sterling Highway at **Milepost S 85** (see that milepost for description of Scout Lake Loop Road). Sterling elementary school.

S 84.3 (135.7 km) A 137.3 (221 km) H 95.2 (153.2 km) **Scout Lake Inn**, a family-owned and operated restaurant and motel, is located in the heart of the Swanson River canoe system, Kenai and Moose River fishing area. Our restaurant is well known for fine food and has a large seating capacity. Tour buses welcome. See display ad this section.
[ADVERTISEMENT]

S 85 (136.8 km) A 138 (222.1 km) H 94.5 (152.1 km) Scout Lake state recreation site to south on Scout Lake Loop Road; 12 campsites, water, toilets, covered picnic shelter. Camping fee $6/night or annual pass. Scout Lake Loop Road loops south of the Sterling Highway for 7 miles/11.3 km and rejoins the Sterling Highway at **Milepost S 83.4**. Turn here and drive down Scout Lake Loop Road 1.6 miles/2.6 km to turnoff for Morgans Landing: follow side road 2.4 miles/3.9 km to reach Morgans Landing State Recreation Area; 50 campsites, $6 nightly fee or annual pass, toilets and water. The Alaska state parks district headquarters is located here. Good access from here to the **Kenai River**, king salmon from mid-June through July, average 30 lbs. Red (sockeye) salmon average

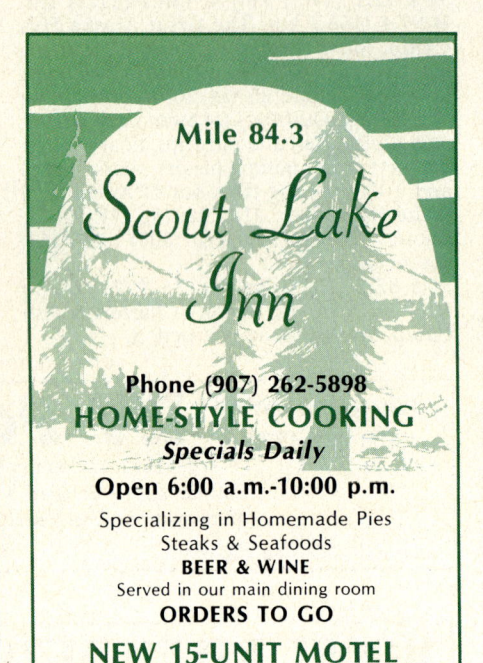

ZIPMART
(907) 262-3988
GAS • GROCERIES • ICE • PAY PHONE
HUNTING and FISHING LICENSES • FISHING TACKLE
COFFEE • PICNIC SUPPLIES • COLD POP

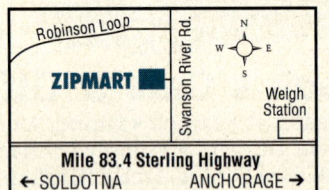

Free cup of coffee with gas fill up

➤ Turn at Mile 83.4 Sterling Highway
(0.4 mile past weigh station)
➤ Turn north on Swanson River Road ➤ Drive 0.3 mile

ANGLER'S LODGE & FISH CAMP
"on the banks of the World Famous Kenai River"

Kenai River
Guided Fishing & Lodging
FOR MORE INFORMATION CALL OR WRITE:
P.O. Box 508, Sterling, Alaska 99672
(907) 262-1747

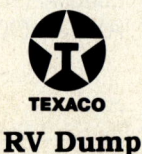

BIG JOHN'S
TEXACO
Gas • Diesel • Propane • Groceries • Liquor • Ice
3 1/2 Acres • 12 Pumps • 6 Islands
"The Nicest & Cleanest Restrooms on the Peninsula"
RV Dump   Mile 91.3 Sterling Highway   Open 24 Hours

Swanson River and Swan Lake Roads Log

Swanson River Road leads north 17.2 miles/27.7 km, where it junctions with Swan Lake Road, which leads east 12.7 miles/20.4 km and dead ends at Paddle Lake. Both roads provide access to fishing, hiking trails and canoe trails. **Distance from junction with the Sterling Highway (J) is shown.**

J 0 Junction with Sterling Highway at **Milepost S 83.4**. Swanson River Road is a good gravel road but can be rough in spots: Slow speeds are advised. There are numerous turnouts suitable for overnight camping in self-contained RVs.

J 0.7 (1.1 km) Robinson Loop Road; rejoins Sterling Highway at **Milepost S 87.5**.

J 1.3 (2.1 km) Airstrip.

J 4.4 (7.1 km) Entering Kenai National Wildlife Refuge.

J 7.9 (12.7 km) **Mosquito Lake**, turnout; 0.5-mile trail to lake. Rainbow trout.

J 9.1 (14.6 km) **Silver Lake** trailhead and parking: 1-mile/1.6-km hike to lake. Rainbow trout and arctic char.

J 9.8 (15.8 km) **Finger Lake** trailhead: 2.3-mile/3.7-km hike to lake. Good arctic char fishing.

J 10.6 (17.1 km) **Forest Lake** wayside, parking: 0.3-mile/0.5-km trail to lake. Rainbow trout; best fished from canoe or raft.

J 13 (20.9 km) **Weed Lake** wayside: small turnout by lake. Rainbow trout.

J 13.3 (21.4 km) **Drake** and **Skookum lakes** trailhead and parking; 2-mile/3.2-km trail. Rainbow trout and arctic char.

J 14 (22.5 km) Access to Breeze Lake.

J 14.2 (22.9 km) **Dolly Varden Lake** Campground; 15 sites, water, toilets, boat launch. Large RVs and trailers note: 0.5-mile/0.8-km access road to campground is narrow and bumpy, check turnaround space before driving in. Fishing for Dolly Varden and rainbow; best in late August and September.

J 14.9 (24 km) Access road to canoe trails to east. Oil field road to west closed to private vehicles. The Swanson River Road was originally built as an access road to the Swanson River oil field. Chevron operated the field from 1958 to 1986; it is currently operated by ARCO.

J 15.7 (25.2 km) **Rainbow Lake** Campground; small 3-unit camping area on lakeshore with toilets, water and boat launch. Fishing for Dolly Varden and rainbow trout.

J 17.2 (27.7 km) **Junction** with Swan Lake Road. Continue north 0.5 mile/0.8 km for Swanson River Landing at end of Swanson River Road; camping area with picnic tables, firepits, water, toilets, boat launch, large gravel parking area. This is the terminus of the Swanson River canoe route, which begins at Paddle Lake at the end of Swan Lake Road. Log now follows Swan Lake Road east.

J 17.3 (27.8 km) Swanson River Outdoor Environmental Education Center.

J 20.2 (32.5 km) **Fish Lake**; 3 sites, tables, firepits, toilets. Fishing for Dolly Varden.

J 21.2 (34 km) **Canoe Lake**, parking. West entrance to Swan Lake canoe route. Fishing for Dolly Varden.

J 21.8 (35.1 km) Sucker Creek wayside; campsite, table, fireplace. **Sucker Lake**, rainbow trout.

J 23.3 (37.5 km) **Merganser Lakes**, 0.5 mile/0.8 km south; rainbow trout.

J 25.4 (40.9 km) Nest Lakes trail, 0.5 mile/0.8 km hike north.

J 26.9 (43.3 km) Large turnout and toilet to west.

J 27 (43.5 km) **Portage Lake**. East entrance to Swan Lake canoe route. Lake is stocked with coho salmon.

J 27.3 (43.9 km) Informal campsite on lake.

J 29.4 (47.3 km) Y in road; bear left.

J 29.9 (48.1 km) End of road. **Paddle Lake** entrance to Swanson River canoe route; parking, picnic table, water and toilet. Fishing for rainbow and Dolly Varden.

Return to Milepost S 83.4 Sterling Highway

KENAI PENINSULA • STERLING HIGHWAY

---

8 lbs., use flies in July and August; silver (coho) salmon to 15 lbs., August and September, use lure; pink salmon average 4 lbs. with lure, best in July, even-numbered years only (1992, 1994, etc.); rainbow and Dolly Varden, use lure, June through August.

Angler's Lodge & Fish Camp. Affordable fresh- and saltwater fishing, bed-and-breakfast lodge on Kenai River. Overnight to 5-day complete packages. Cross-country skiing, snow machines, dogsleds and ice fishing. Big fish, hot tub, great fun, and families welcomed. Host: Roger Byerly, P.O. Box 508, Sterling, AK 99672; (907) 262-1747. [ADVERTISEMENT]

S 87.5 (140.8 km) **A 140.5** (226.1 km) **H 92** (148.1 km) Robinson Loop Road.

S 88 (141.6 km) **A 141** (226.9 km) **H 91.5** (147.3 km) St. Theresa's Drive.

S 88.3 (142.1 km) **A 141.3** (227.4 km) **H 91.2** (146.8 km) **Alaska Horn & Antler.** See display ad this section.

S 90 (144.8 km) **A 143** (230.1 km) **H 89.5** (144 km) **Steckel's Casa Norte Bed and Breakfast and Sportfishing.** Welcome to the Kenai Peninsula, home of the famous Kenai River and its record-breaking king salmon. Come . . . stay with us and settle into one of our private, comfortable rooms and enjoy our sincere hospitality. Licensed guide available. Sportfishing packages—salmon, halibut. Hosts: Capt. John and Marti Steckel (907) 262-1257 or write P.O. Box 2468, Soldotna, AK 99669. See display ad. [ADVERTISEMENT]

S 91.3 (146.9 km) **A 144.3** (232.2 km) **H 88.2** (141.9 km) **Big John's** is the newest facility in this area, offering acres of off-highway area devoted to the needs and

ALASKA HORN & ANTLER
(907) 262-9759

Specializing in Ram Horn Carvings
Also Moose, Caribou, Fossil Ivory and Mastodon
Custom orders welcome

Thomas W Cooper

Tom Cooper
HC 1, Box 156
Soldotna, Alaska 99669

Watch Tom Carve
8 - 6 Monday - Saturday
at Mile 88.3 Sterling Highway
Near Soldotna, Alaska
LARGE CIRCLE DRIVE

Available at Alaska's Finest Gift Shops

Kenai Peninsula Visitor Information Center at Soldotna. (Jerrianne Lowther, staff)

comforts of the traveling public! There is a convenience store, liquor store, "take-out" food, RV dump, potable water, ice, propane, 6 gas station islands (under canopy), 12 pumps, the nicest and cleanest restroom facilities in the area and literally "oodles and oodles" of parking space. Open 24 hours. See our display ad. [ADVERTISEMENT]

S 91.6 (147.4 km) **A 144.6** (232.7 km) **H 87.9** (141.5 km) **Alaska Porcelain Studios.** See display ad this section.

S 91.7 (147.6 km) **A 144.7** (232.9 km) **H 87.8** (141.3 km) **The Tackle Box**, just 2 miles north of Soldotna, has one of the most complete selections of fishing tackle on the peninsula. The coffee is always on. Fishing information is free. Guided fishing trips, boat engine repair, and boat rentals available. Alaska-owned and operated. See display ad this section. [ADVERTISEMENT]

S 92.5 (148.9 km) **A 144.5** (234.2 km) **H 87** (140 km) State Division of Forest, Land and Water Management. Fire danger indicator sign.

S 92.7 (149.1 km) **A 145.7** (234.5 km) **H 86.8** (139.7 km) Mackey Lake Road. Private lodging is available on this side road.

Bear Trap Lodge. See display ad this section.

S 93.1 (149.8 km) **A 146.1** (235.1 km) **H 86.4** (139 km) Loren Lake.

S 94 (151.2 km) **A 147** (236.6 km) **H 85.5** (137.6 km) Four-lane highway begins and leads through Soldotna.

NOTE: Watch for road construction eastbound to **Milepost S 79** *in 1992.*

S 94.1 (151.4 km) **A 147.1** (236.7 km) **H 85.4** (137.4 km) Turn on East Redoubt Street and follow the gravel road 0.5 mile/ 0.8 km for private RV park and Swiftwater Park municipal campground. The city campground has 20 spaces on Kenai River (some pull-throughs), some tables, firepits, firewood, phone, dump station, 2-week limit, litter barrels, toilets, boat landing, fee charged, good fishing. ▲

Moose Range Meadows RV Park, on the beautiful Kenai River, has 49 spaces (some pull-throughs) with picnic tables, firepits, firewood, dump station, clean toilet facilities, potable water, boat launch, pay phone. Tent campers welcome. Full-time attendant. Excellent fishing. Turn on East Redoubt Street. See display ad this section. [ADVERTISEMENT] ▲

Four Seasons Restaurant specializes in fine dining in pleasant surroundings. Open daily for lunch and dinner. Sunday breakfast 9:30 A.M.-1 P.M. Lunch: homemade breads, gourmet soups, sandwiches made with freshly roasted meats. Dinner: seafoods, homemade pasta, steak and nightly specials. Four Seasons cheesecakes. Fine wines and imported beers. See display ad in Soldotna section. [ADVERTISEMENT]

S 94.2 (151.6 km) **A 147.2** (236.9 km) **H 85.3** (137.3 km) **Junction** with Kenai Spur Highway. This junction is called the Soldotna Y.

There are 2 ways to reach the city of Kenai (description of city on page 457): Turn right (westbound) at the Y, physical **Milepost S 94.2**, and continue 11 miles/17.7 km northwest to Kenai, or continue on the Sterling Highway to **Milepost S 96.1** and turn right (southbound) on the Kalifornsky Beach Road and continue 9.3 miles/14.9 km to Kenai via the Warren Ames Memorial Bridge. For details see KENAI SPUR HIGHWAY log on page 456 and KALIFORNSKY BEACH ROAD log on page 462. Description of Soldotna follows; description of Kenai begins on page 457.

S 94.4 (151.6 km) **A 147.4** (236.9 km) **H 85.1** (137 km) Soldotna DOT/PF highway maintenance station. Turn east here for access to Soldotna Creek Park (day use only). Follow road behind restaurant.

S 95 (152.8 km) **A 148** (238.2 km) **H 84.5** (136 km) Soldotna city center; Peninsula Center shopping mall. Turn on Binkley Street for access to fire station, police station and post office. See description of city

---

the Tackle Box

- Boat Rentals
- Fishing Tackle • Fishing Licenses
- King and Silver Salmon Charters
- Saltwater Salmon and Halibut Charters
- Fly-In Fishing Trips
- Certified Scales

Mile 91.7 Sterling Highway
(907) 262-6313

Owned and Operated by Lifetime Alaskans
Mark Torwick, Manager   Roy and Phyllis Torwick, Owners
PO Box 1330, Soldotna, Alaska 99669

American Express, VISA and MasterCard Welcome

Bear Trap Lodge

CABIN RENTALS
2 modern log cabins
Fully carpeted, private bath
Sleeps 2-3 per cabin

GUIDED & OUTFITTED HUNTING TRIPS
Remote fly-in rental cabin across Cook Inlet

GUIDED FLY-OUT FISHING
Trophy rainbow, salmon, halibut, grayling
Spin or fly-fish

(907) 262-7409

Mile 92.7 Sterling Highway • Turn on Mackey Lake Road, drive 2.3 miles   P.O. Box 963, Soldotna, Alaska 99669

ALASKA PORCELAIN STUDIOS

FINE PORCELAIN — Locally Made

"Our Porcelain has been Selected by Discriminating Collectors Worldwide!"

Milepost 91.6
P.O. Box 1550, Soldotna, AK 99669
(907) 262-5682

following. See city map on this page.

Homer-bound travelers continue south across the Kenai River bridge past visitor center then turn west on Kalifornsky Road for Soldotna city campground; turn east off the Sterling Highway on Funny River Road for airport. See descriptions at **Milepost S 96.1** on page 462.

Log of the Sterling Highway continues on page 461.

Soldotna

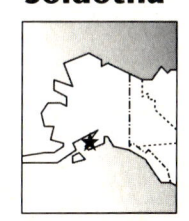

S 95.2 (153.2 km) A 148.2 (238.5 km) H 77.6 (124.9 km) On the western Kenai Peninsula, the city stretches over a mile southwest along the Sterling Highway and northwest along the Kenai Spur Highway. Population: 3,818; Kenai Peninsula Borough 38,919. **Emergency Services:** Phone 911 for all emergency services. **Alaska State Troopers** at Mile 22 Kalifornsky Beach Road just off Sterling Highway, phone 262-4453. **City Police**, phone 262-4455. **Fire Department**, phone 262-4792. **Ambulance**, phone 262-4500. **Hospital**, Central Peninsula General, 1 mile/1.6 km north of Public Safety Bldg. on Marydale Drive, phone 262-4404.

Visitor Information: The Kenai Peninsula Visitor Information Center is located in downtown Soldotna on the Sterling Highway south of the Kenai River bridge. The center is open 7 days a week, mid-May through mid-September, 9 A.M. to 7 P.M. The

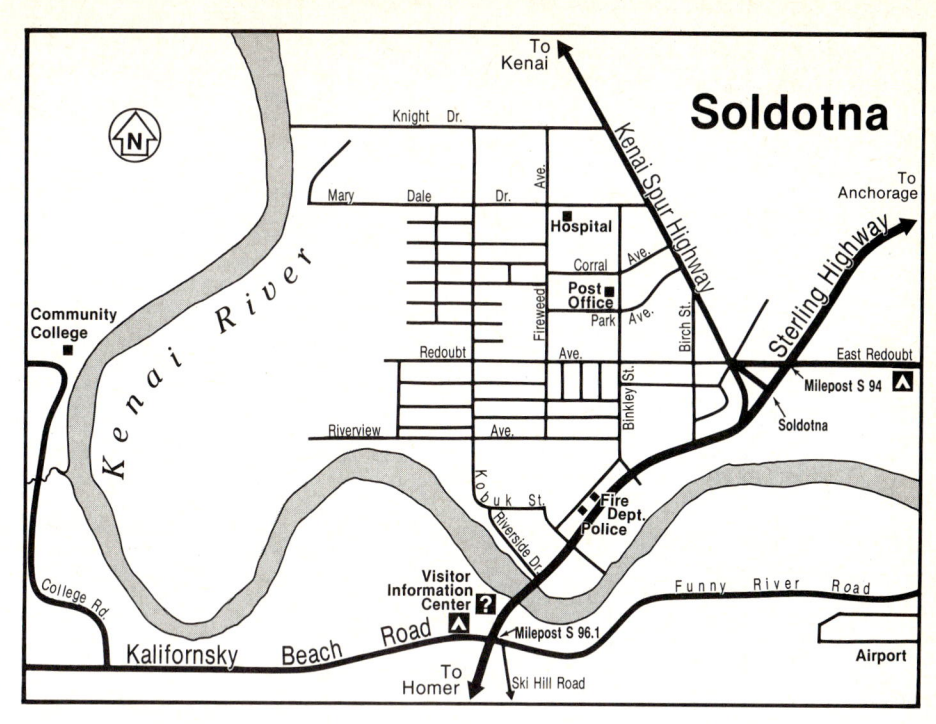

KENAI CUSTOM SEAFOODS
- Processing • Smoking
- Vacuum Packing

Mile 14.4 Kalifornsky Road
(907) 283-9109

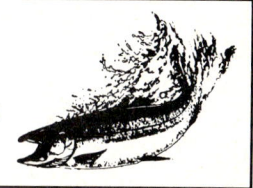

Birch Tree Gallery
ORIGINAL ART
Featuring Alaskan Artists
Pottery • Hand Woven Baskets
Jewelry • Duck Carvings
Siberian Santas

On Funny River Road 1/4 Mile From Soldotna Bridge Traffic Light
(907) 262-4048
Complimentary packaging for mailing

STECKEL'S

CASA NORTE BED & BREAKFAST
- Secluded Panoramic View
- Homey Atmosphere
- Full Alaskan Breakfast
- Horses
- Complimentary Refreshments
- Private Bath
- Convenient Location close to the Kenai River

Hosts: Capt. John & Marti Steckel, P.O. Box 2468, Soldotna, AK 99669

SPORTFISHING
- Licensed Guide Services
- Halibut, Salmon, Touring
- Saltwater - Freshwater

"Join us for a full day of fishing"
(907) 262-1257

FOUR SEASONS RESTAURANT
Lunch 11 - 3 p.m.
HOMEMADE BREADS • GOURMET SOUPS
Sandwiches made with freshly roasted meats
Quiche & Fresh Pasta
Dinner 5:30 - 10:00
Halibut Florentine, Dungeness Crab, Scallops, Homemade Pasta
Teriyaki Chicken, New York Steak • Fine Wines & Imported Beers
Four Seasons Homemade Cheesecakes & Desserts
In season: Local seafood, vegetables and berries from our garden
Sunday Breakfast Buffet $6.95; Children $3.95 • 9:30 am –1 pm
(907) 262-5006 • Open Daily summers
GERRI LITZENBERGER and MARGE MULLEN
Look for our sign on the right just before Soldotna Y.
43960 Sterling Highway, Soldotna, Alaska 99669

KENAI RIVER FAMILY CAMPGROUND
RV Parking • Electric Hookups • Tent Sites • Water

MILE 2.2
Big Eddy Road
(off Kenai Spur Hwy.)

Great Bank Fishing • We book fishing charters - Kings! Silvers!
We also book trail rides for Alaskan Saddle Safaris in Cooper Landing
BOAT RENTALS • BOAT LAUNCH • BOAT MOORING
HC 1 Box 8616, Soldotna, Alaska 99669   (907) 262-2444

SOLDOTNA ADVERTISERS

China Sea Restaurant — BLAZY MALL, SOLDOTNA
Our Customers Are Our Guests
Full Menu of Chinese And American Cuisine
20 ft · All You Can Eat · LONG BUFFET LINE
LUNCH BUFFET 11:30-1:30
DINNER BUFFET 5:00-8:00
OPEN FROM 11AM — 9PM
VISA · MasterCard · Diners Club
ORDERS TO GO **262-5033**

OUR ARCTIC YEAR, by Vivian and Gil Staender, records life in the Arctic tundra. Available from Alaska Northwest Books™.

KING'S KITCHEN Bed and Breakfast
True Alaskan Hospitality
Conveniently located near downtown Soldotna. Minutes from Kenai River.
Salmon & Halibut Charters
Open Year-round
(907) 262-2973
309 Vine Street
Soldotna, AK 99669 
Hosts: Daryl & Elaine Kellum

Alaska Recreational Rentals	Ph. (907) 262-2700
Alaskan Adventure Charters	Ph. (907) 262-7773
Alaskan Rivers & Seas Fishing Guides	Ph. (907) 262-4015
Alpine Laundromat & Showers	Downtown
Beemun's V & S Variety Store	35277 Kenai Spur Hwy.
Birch Tree Gallery	Mile 0.2 Funny River Rd.
Blazy's B & B	Ph. (907) 262-4591
Bo's Fishing Guide Service	Ph. (907) 262-5154
Bunk House Inn	44715 Sterling Hwy.
C & R Charters	Edgewater RV Park
China Sea Restaurant	Blazy Mall
Chinulna Point Lodge	Ph. (907) 283-7799
Denny's Gone Fishin' Guide Service	Ph. (907) 283-9495
Donna's Country & Victorian Gifts	Blazy's Soldotna Mall
Duck Inn	35458 Kaliforsky Beach Rd.
Eagles Roost Bed & Breakfast	Ph. (907) 262-9797
Edgewater RV Park	Ph. (907) 262-7733
Fenton Bros. Guided Sportfishing	Ph. (907) 262-2502
First Baptist Church	Binkley St.
Foto Quick	Between McDonald's and Godfather's Pizza
Four Seasons Restaurant	At the Y
Garden Inn Bed and Breakfast	Ph. (907) 262-2335
Greater Soldotna Chamber of Commerce	Sterling Hwy. & Kenai River Bridge
Harry Gaines Kenai River Fishing Guide	Ph. (907) 262-5097
Homestead Manufacturing Jewelers	Peninsula Center Mall
Irish Lord Charters	Ph. (907) 262-9512
Jim Rusk's Fishing Guide	Ph. (907) 262-4911
John Metcalf's Jughead Salmon Charters	Ph. (907) 277-1218
Johnson Bros. Guides & Outfitters	Downtown
Kenai Custom Seafoods	Mile 14.4 Kalifornsky Beach Rd.
Kenai Peninsula Apts.	Ph. (907) 262-1383
Kenai River Family Campground	Mile 2.2 Big Eddy Rd.
Kenai River Lodge Motor Inn	Kenai River Bridge
Kenai Riverbend Campground	Ciechansky and Kalifornsky Beach Rds.
King of the River	Ph. (907) 262-2897
King's Budget Charters	Ph. (907) 262-4564
King's Kitchen Bed and Breakfast	309 W. Vine Ave.
Kings Sportfishing	Ph. (907) 262-9478
Klondike City	Downtown
Knight Manor Bed & Breakfast	Ph. (907) 262-2438
Moose Range Meadows RV Park	Mile 94 Sterling Hwy.
Nordic Trading Post	Binkley St.
Northcountry Fair	Ph. (907) 262-7715
Northstar	Ph. (800) 869-9418
Orca Lodge	Ph. (907) 262-5649
Peninsula Center Mall	Sterling Hwy.
Posey's Kenai River Hideaway B & B Lodge	Ph. (907) 262-7430
Riverside Auto Supply	Kenai River Bridge
Riverside Resort Bed and Breakfast	355 Riverside Dr.
Rod 'N Real Charters	Ph. (907) 262-6064
Sal's Klondike Diner	Downtown
Silver King Charters	Ph. (907) 262-5489
Soldotna Bed & Breakfast	Ph. (907) 262-4779
Soldotna Inn	Mile 0.2 Kenai Spur Hwy.
Soldotna Wash & Dry	At the Y
Steckel's Casa Norte Bed & Breakfast	Ph. (907) 262-1257
Sunset Park Sports Fishing	Ph. (907) 262-2226
Tim Hiner Professional Fishing	Ph. (907) 262-9729
Windwalkers Trading Post, Inc.	Peninsula Center Mall

Bits and Pieces of Alaskan History, Vol. I (1935–1959) and Vol. II (1960–1974), with hundreds of nostalgic photos. Available from Alaska Northwest Books™.

Eagles Roost Bed & Breakfast 
Elegant rooms with private baths overlooking Kenai River. For reservations call your host - Magga Laber - (907) 262-9797 or write to 319 Riverside Dr., Soldotna, AK 99669.

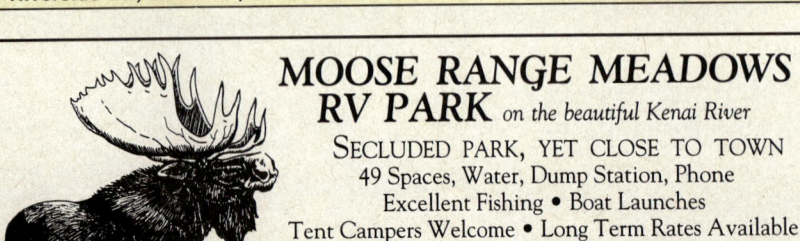

Blazy's B & B
Minutes from the Kenai River
Rates $35 - $65
Box 758, Soldotna, Alaska 99669
(907) 262-4591

MOOSE RANGE MEADOWS RV PARK *on the beautiful Kenai River*
SECLUDED PARK, YET CLOSE TO TOWN
49 Spaces, Water, Dump Station, Phone
Excellent Fishing • Boat Launches
Tent Campers Welcome • Long Term Rates Available
OPEN MEMORIAL DAY – AUGUST
See log ad at Mile 94 Sterling Highway
Turn on East Redoubt Street, drive 3.6 miles
Year-round phone (907) 283-7864 • Summer: 262-6340
Write: SNA, Inc., PO Box 2682, Kenai, Alaska 99611

Posey's Kenai River Hideaway B & B Lodge
Hosts
Ray & June Posey
PO Box 4094
Soldotna, AK 99669
(907) 262-7430
A BEAUTIFUL LODGE...
located on the bank of the Kenai River
Charters for King Salmon, Halibut, Rainbow, Silvers arranged, plus car rental. Call or write for brochures and rates.
— **Open all year.** —
Arrive as guests, leave as friends.
Enjoy our Alaskan hospitality and country breakfasts.

remainder of the year the center is open weekdays from 9 A.M. to 5 P.M. Write: Greater Soldotna Chamber of Commerce, Box 236-MP, Soldotna 99669; phone 262-1337 or 262-9814.

Elevation: 115 feet/35m. **Climate:** Average daily temperature in July, 63°F to 68°F/17°C to 20°C; January, 19°F to 23°F/-7°C to -5°C. Annual precipitation, approximately 18 inches. **Radio:** KGTL 620, KFQD 750, KSRM 920, KGTL-FM 100.9/103.5, KKEN 980, MBN-FM 95.3/97.7, KWHQ-FM 1001, KPEN-FM 101-7, KCSY 1140. **Television:** Channels 4, 9, 12 and 13 via booster line from Anchorage and KANG public education channel. **Newspapers:** *Peninsula Clarion* (daily).

Private Aircraft: Soldotna airstrip, 0.9 mile/1.4 km southeast; elev. 107 feet/32m; length 5,000 feet/152m; asphalt; fuel 80, 100, B; unattended.

The town of Soldotna was established in the 1940s because of its strategic location at the Sterling–Kenai Spur Highway junction. Soldotna was named for a nearby stream (it is a Russian word meaning "soldier," although some believe the name came from an Indian word meaning the "stream fork").

Today, Soldotna is a business center and sportfishing capital of the Kenai Peninsula and a bedroom community for oil-related industry in Cook Inlet.

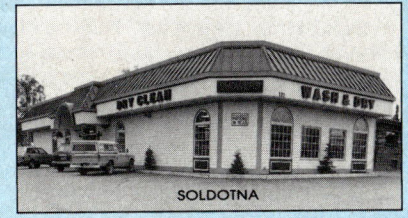

Soldotna was incorporated as a first-class city in 1967. It has a council–manager form of government. Kenai Peninsula Borough headquarters and state offices of the Depts. of Highways, Public Safety, Fish and Game, and Forest, Land and Water Management are located here. Soldotna is also headquarters for the Kenai Peninsula Borough school district. There are 3 elementary schools, a junior high school and 2 high schools here. University of Alaska Kenai Peninsula Community College is also located in Soldotna. The Central Peninsula Sports Center, located on Kalifornsky Beach Road, has facilities for hockey, ice skating and other sports, and convention facilities.

Area terrain is level and forested, with many streams and lakes nearby. Large rivers of the area are the Swanson River, the Moose River, and the Kenai River, which empties into Cook Inlet just south of Kenai. The area affords a majestic view of volcanic mountains across Cook Inlet. Always snow covered, they are Mount Spurr (elev. 11,100 feet/3,383m), which has 3 coequal peaks; Mount Iliamna (elev. 10,016 feet/3,053m) which has 3 smaller peaks to the left of the larger one; and Mount Redoubt (elev. 10,197 feet/3,108m) which was identified by its very regular cone shape until December 1989 when it erupted.

The Soldotna–Kenai area offers a wide variety of recreation and all goods and services. Many fishing guides operate out of Soldotna; write the chamber of commerce for more information.

ACCOMMODATIONS

All modern conveniences and facilities are available, including a 24-hour supermarket, banks, hotels/motels, restaurants and drive-ins, medical and dental clinics, bowling alley, golf course, veterinarians, churches and a library. Two shopping malls are located on the Sterling Highway near the center of town. Bed-and-breakfast accommodations are available.

Soldotna Creek Park (day use only), located behind Hutchings Chevrolet at the Y, has picnic facilities and offers river access for bank fishing.

Chinulna Point Lodge. Cook Inlet's luxurious bed and breakfast, on the bluff overlooking Cook Inlet. Roomy bedrooms, private baths. Hot tub, TV, VCR. No Smoking. Full breakfast. Mile S 8.6 Kalifornsky

---

JOHNSON BROS.
GUIDES & OUTFITTERS

Come See Our VIDEO

**Salmon Fishing Guides
Fishing Tackle Shop
Halibut Charters
Fly-out Fishing
& Hunting Trips**

"Allow us to assist you in making your Alaskan salmon fishing experience a success." — Jim Johnson

**Located on the Sterling Highway
Downtown Soldotna
44526 STERLING HWY.
SOLDOTNA, ALASKA 99669
PHONE: (907) 262-5357**

BUNK HOUSE INN

MOTEL FEATURES
COMFORTABLE ROOMS WITH SATELLITE COLOR TV
RESTAURANT
SPECIALIZING IN STEAKS AND SEAFOOD FOR YOUR DINING PLEASURE
BRAND X LOUNGE
PROVIDES YOU WITH A RELAXING WESTERN ATMOSPHERE
COMPLETE GUIDE SERVICES AVAILABLE
WALK TO THE WORLD-FAMOUS KENAI RIVER KING SALMON FISHING

(907) 262-4584 • SOLDOTNA, ALASKA 9966 • 44715 STERLING HIGHWAY

Soldotna Bed & Breakfast

It is a lovely 16-room European home located on the banks of the Kenai River, yet within walking of downtown Soldotna. All rooms are tastefully decorated and furnished with comfortable beds. Full breakfast.
5% extra for credit cards • Checks accepted

399 LOVER'S LANE • SOLDOTNA, ALASKA 99669 • (907) 262-4779

Free 20-minute video and brochure of **Soldotna Bed & Breakfast** and of **Northstar Adventures Guide Service** available upon request.

1-800-869-9418
Mail: PO Box 3292
Soldotna, Alaska 99669

NORTHSTAR

A day's catch of Kenai Kings
EVERYTHING FURNISHED

Beach Road, 10 minutes from Kenai or Soldotna. Kathy Harris, 36725 Chinulna Dr., Kenai, AK 99611. (907) 283-7799. American Express, VISA, MasterCard, Discover card. [ADVERTISEMENT]

Garden Inn Bed and Breakfast. Located on the banks of the Kenai River. Offering friendly Alaskan hospitality with style. Choose our splendid daily bed-and-breakfast service, or weekly executive gourmet packages designed to accommodate the discriminating Alaskan visitor. Brochures available upon request to 206 Rockwell, Soldotna, AK 99669 or call (907) 262-2335 for reservations. [ADVERTISEMENT]

Orca Lodge. Beautiful, luxurious, hand-crafted Kenai riverfront log cabins. Roomy cabins with loft and full bath accommodate up to 4. Community picnic area for outdoor cooking. Great bank fishing or hire our professional guides and catch the trophy of a lifetime. Ideal base camp for hunters. Hunter booking service. Open year-round. (907) 262-5649. [ADVERTISEMENT]

Riverside Resort Bed and Breakfast. Live the Alaska dream. Stay in a beautiful log home overlooking famous Kenai River. Two rooms overlook river, third has private bath. Provisions: airport/guide service transporta-

JIM RUSK
Fishing Guide
▲ Lifetime resident
▲ Bed & Breakfast available
▲ *Everything* furnished

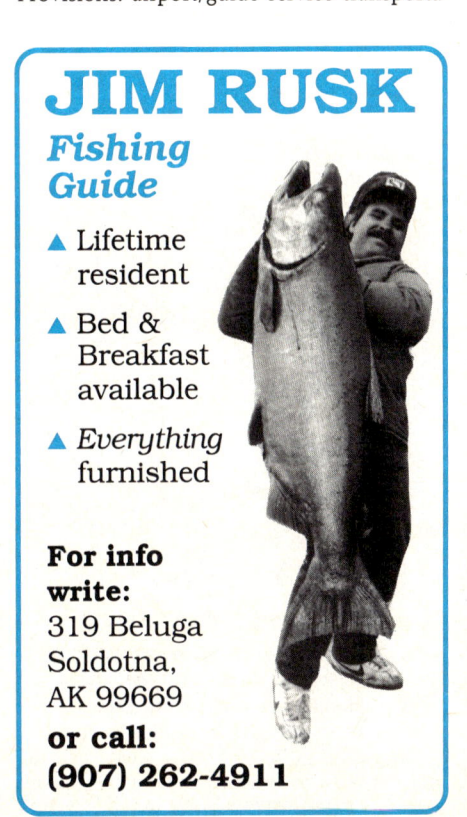

For info write:
319 Beluga
Soldotna,
AK 99669

or call:
(907) 262-4911

KENAI RIVER LODGE MOTOR INN

Deluxe MOTEL UNITS OVERLOOKING KENAI RIVER
GUIDED FISHING TRIPS • PRIVATE DOCKING FACILITIES
At the Bridge in Soldotna (907) 262-4292 • 393 Riverside Dr., Soldotna, AK 99669

STOP LOOKING!

RENT A CONDO FOR LESS THAN A MOTEL!
Sleeps 1-6 — Full Kitchen, Microwave, Washer/Dryer, TV
Spacious, Clean and Private — 5 minutes from Kenai River
ASK FOR YOUR MILEPOST DISCOUNT
(907) 262-1383
Kenai Peninsula Apts.   Box 3416, Soldotna, AK 99669

HARRY GAINES KENAI RIVER FISHING GUIDES

MAY - OCTOBER

Fish with the Kenai River's oldest professional guide service - 20 years

Riverside Cabins • Free RV Parking

**EVERYTHING FURNISHED
BIG TIME FUN GUARANTEED**

Call or Write: Reuben Hanke, Box 624, Kenai, Alaska 99611
(907) 262-5097 - Fish Camp   **(907) 283-4618 - Home**

SOLDOTNA INN   Mykel's Restaurant and Lounge

28 modern units with private baths • Kitchenettes • Color TV
Phones • Courtesy Coffee • Cable TV • Guided Fishing Trips
At Soldotna Y • A few minutes to Kenai • 1 1/2 hours to Homer • Mike & Linda Sipes

35041 Kenai Spur Highway • Soldotna, Alaska 99669 • Phone (907) 262-9169

King's Budget Charters
King and Silver Salmon Fishing on the Kenai River
EVERYTHING FURNISHED • VERY REASONABLE RATES
PERSONABLE SERVICE • QUALITY EQUIPMENT
JEFF KING   Box 2711, Soldotna, Alaska 99669
Professional Guide — Local   (907) 262-4564

Sunset Park Sports Fishing

• *Fish the Famous Kenai River*
• *Fly-in Fishing*
• *Halibut Charters Lower Cook Inlet*

1-800-634-3332 Ext. 26
(907) 262-2226   Soldotna, Alaska

Sunset Park Sports Fishing — RV, Camping Tours, Guides

KENAI PENINSULA • SOLDOTNA

1992 ■ The MILEPOST®   451

KENAI PENINSULA · SOLDOTNA

Denny's Gone Fishin' GUIDE SERVICE

KING SALMON — Mid-May thru July
SILVERS — August thru September
Senior Discount • Quality Gear

An experienced, independent, licensed local guide for personalized service

Addtional 10% discount with this ad

Call or write for brochure
Summer: (907) 283-9495   HC 78 Box 2205
All Year: (907) 688-4321   Chugiak, AK 99567

Cook Inlet halibut draw fishermen to the Kenai Peninsula. (John W. Warden)

IRISH LORD CHARTERS
ALASKAN ADVENTURE FISHING

**Kenai River Kings
Cook Inlet Halibut
Reasonable Rates**

Robbie Carroll
Alaska Resident Guide

Box 545   (907) 262-9512
Kasilof, AK 99610

Trophy Salmon Fishing on Alaska's Kenai River

- Customized weekly packages
- Fish May–November
- Reasonable Rates
- Friendly, First-rate Service
- Advance Reservations

Fenton Bros.
GUIDED SPORTSFISHING

P.O. Box 1716, Soldotna, AK 99669
(907) 262-2502

tion, delicious home-cooked breakfasts (from menu) and/or sack lunches. Laundry facilities. Color cable TV. Boat docking and excellent bank fishing. Walk-ins welcome. Phone/fax (907) 262-5371 or write 355 Riverside Dr., Soldotna, AK 99669.
[ADVERTISEMENT]

Swiftwater Campground, turn on East Redoubt Street at **Milepost S 94.1** Sterling Highway. Soldotna Alaska Purchase Centennial Park Campground is 0.1 mile/0.2 km from the Sterling Highway just south of the Kenai River bridge; turn west at **Milepost S 96.1**. Both campgrounds are operated by the city of Soldotna (fee charged) and you may register for camping at either park at the office at Soldotna Alaska Purchase Centennial Park. Dump stations at both camp-

Silver King Charters *Est. 1978*

World-Class Kenai River Salmon
Cook Inlet Halibut • All Gear and Tackle Provided
Season - May through September

For Brochure and Reservations
Silver King Charters, Bob & JoAnne Saxton
PO Box 2440, Soldotna, Alaska 99669

PLAN YOUR
VACATION
TO FISH
**THE
KENAI RIVER,
ALASKA'S
BEST!**

Specializing in
TROPHY SIZE
King Salmon and
Silver Salmon.
Experience Alaska
with
John Metcalf's

**JUGHEAD
SALMON
CHARTERS**

(907) 277-1218
1218 E Street, Anchorage, AK 99501
Call or write for more information.

ALASKAN ADVENTURE CHARTERS & RV PARK
Located Mile 99.9 Sterling Highway

Fish for Kenai River Kings & Silvers
Saltwater Fishing for Kings & Halibut
➢ Personalized Service   ➢ Affordable Rates
➢ Complete Fishing / Lodging Packages Available
➢ Full Hookup RV Park

Please call or write for information or reservations:
Mike Hopley, Alaskan Adventure Charters
PO Box 4273, Soldotna, Alaska 99669
PHONE: (907) 262-7773

KINGS SPORTFISHING
Established 1978

Magnificent King Salmon
King Salmon in the Kenai River reach over
80 pounds. An exciting and challenging
adventure. Everything furnished.
Limited Bookings • Competitive Rates
Larry and Frani Barnes   Box 4194, Soldotna, AK 99669
(907) 262-9478 (summer)   (907) 688-8315 (winter)

grounds. These campgrounds are heavily used; good idea to check in early. There are several private campgrounds located in and near Soldotna; see ads this section. ▲

Edgewater RV Park. Located on the banks of the Kenai River, across from the visitors center in downtown Soldotna. Full and partial hookups, laundry and shower facilities, grassy sites, picnic tables, boat rental, guide service and fish cleaning facilities available on location. Call (907) 262-7733 for reservations. For information write: 206 Rockwell, Soldotna, AK 99669.
[ADVERTISEMENT] ▲

TRANSPORTATION

Air: Charters available. Soldotna airport is south of Soldotna 2 miles/3.2 km off the Sterling Highway; at **Milepost S 96.1**, just after crossing Kenai River bridge, turn left (east) on Funny River (Airport) Road 2 miles/3.2 km. Scheduled air service to Anchorage. **Local:** Intercity bus service available. Also taxi service, car rentals, vehicle leasing, boat rentals and charters.

ATTRACTIONS

Join in local celebrations. Soldotna has its share of local events. The Peninsula Winter Games take place in January. The Alaska State Championship Sled Dog Races and Dog Weight Pull Contest take place in February.

July's big event is the annual Soldotna Progress Days, held during the fourth weekend of the month. Activities include a parade, 2 days of rodeo, autocross competi-

Alaska Recreational Rentals
Motorhome Rentals
Joe & Barbara Dilley
OWNERS
Box 592 • Soldotna, Alaska 99669
(907) 262-2700
YOUR SAFETY, COMFORT AND ENJOYMENT ARE OUR BUSINESS!

EDGEWATER RV PARK
Full and Partial Hookups • City Water • 30-amp Power
Laundromat • Showers • Jacuzzi • Fish Cleaning Facilities

Home of C&R CHARTERS
See log ad under Attractions
• Salmon and Halibut Fishing at it's best
• 35 years of guiding experience personally takes you fishing
• At the Kenai River, directly across from the Visitor Center in Soldotna
(907) 283-7400

Welcome to **ALPINE LAUNDROMAT & Showers**
262-9129
Norge **DOUBLE LOAD** Washers & Dryers
Spacious Showers... Cleaned after each use
Drop Off Laundry • Attendant on Duty
Lounge • TV • Free Coffee
BEST PRICES IN TOWN
Summer: Open 7 a.m. to midnight 7 days a week
DAIRY QUEEN BLDG. • STERLING HIGHWAY • DOWNTOWN SOLDOTNA

NORDIC TRADING POST
NEW • USED
Furniture • Appliances
Gifts • Glassware
Camping and RV Equipment
Books • Sporting Goods
BUY • SELL
(907) 262-6625
Tourists Welcome   Large parking lot
Binkley Street,
one block off Sterling Highway
behind Safeway

KENAI PENINSULA • SOLDOTNA

TIM HINER
Professional Fishing
Kenai River, Alaska
Monster Chinook
& Huge Coho
My Specialty!!!
We've Landed
**Over 800 Chinook
Over 50 Pounds**
Since 1978
For information and reservations, write:
P.O. Box 2122
Soldotna, Alaska 99669
Phone (907) 262-9729

ALASKAN RIVERS & SEAS FISHING GUIDES
Fish the
Kenai River
with
MEL FORSYTH JR.
King Salmon
Silver Salmon
(907) 262-4015
PO Box 3477
Soldotna, Ak 99669

FISHING ALASKA'S BEST!
Salmon Fishing on the Famous KENAI RIVER
1-800-876-5774 wait for tone 037

Group Rates
Everything Furnished

BO's
Fishing Guide Service
Box 1728
Soldotna, AK 99669
907-262-5154

ROD 'N REAL ALASKAN SPORT FISHING GUIDES & CHARTERS
Kenai River
King & Silver Salmon
Cook Inlet **Halibut**
Trophy Rainbows
Dolly Varden - Char
Sockeye & Pink Salmon

Inquire about our
Fishing/Lodging
Packages
Seasons - May
thru September

Rodney Berg
266 Redwood Ct.
Soldotna, AK 99669
(907) 262-6064
or
Randy Berg
Box 4177
Soldotna, AK 99669
(907) 262-5727

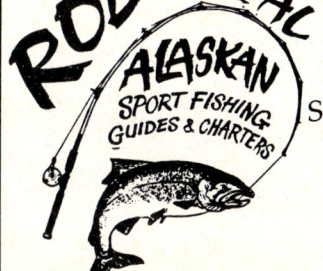

1992 • The MILEPOST® 453

KENAI PENINSULA · SOLDOTNA

WINDWALKERS TRADING POST, INC.

Unique Alaskan-made Gifts

Native-made
Dolls • Masks
Baskets
Sealskin Slippers
Ivory and Whalebone Carvings

LARGE SELECTION
Buckles • Knives
Gold Nugget Jewelry
Salmon Skin Wallets
Antler Carvings

— Visit our *Center Island* —

Alaskan T-Shirts and Sweatshirts
Waterproof Gear
Jackets and Hats
(Quantity Discounts)

10% Senior Citizens Discount
Major Credit Cards

(907) 262-1055

44332 Sterling Highway
Soldotna, Alaska 99669

Peninsula Center *(Safeway)* **Mall**
Next to Pay 'N Save

tion, car show, community barbecue and dance, arts and crafts show, and other events.

During the month of August, the Cook Inlet Professional Sportfishing Assoc. (CIPSA) sponsors the annual Soldotna Silver Salmon Derby. 1992 marks the 6th year for this event. Daily prizes are awarded for the heaviest and smallest silver salmon caught, in addition to other categories. Several thousand dollars in cash and merchandise is awarded in this exciting event.

Donna's Country & Victorian Gifts at Blazy's Soldotna Mall. Specializing in Romantic Victoriana. Dolls, linens, dried and silk flowers, wreaths, wall decor, jewelry, inspirational gifts, glassware. We strive to have the latest gift ideas. Browsers welcome! Coffee shop in mall for bored husbands. Located across from Safeway, 1 block south.

[ADVERTISEMENT]

Fish the Kenai River. Soldotna is one of Alaska's best-known sportfishing headquarters and many claim that some of the world's best fishing is here at the Kenai River, which flows next to town. Many charter boats and fishing guides for Kenai River

---

Northcountry Fair

LOCAL POTTERY, WOODCARVING & FIBRE ART

Many delights... from kaleidoscopes to cookware to Scandinavian furniture!

under blue awning on left coming into town   **262-7715**

HOMESTEAD MANUFACTURING JEWELERS

Custom Manufacturing
Diamond Setting · Repair
Diamonds · Gemstones
· Nugget Jewelry

262·2252

Peninsula Center Mall
Soldotna, Alaska

FIRST BAPTIST CHURCH

Sunday School .... 9:45 a.m.
Worship .... 11:00 a.m.
Discipleship Training .... 5:00 p.m.
Worship .... 6:00 p.m.
Wednesday Service .... 7:00 p.m.

Located one block up from Safeway store on Binkley St.
Soldotna, AK 99669
Pastor Ed Wolfe — (907) 262-4304

Welcome to Soldotna, Alaska

"A place for all seasons"

- Kenai Peninsula Visitor Center (World class photo display of the Peninsula)
- Kenai National Wildlife Refuge (Wildlife Interpretive Center, trail system)
- Sports & Convention Center (Small meetings to large Conventions)
- Year-round Recreational Opportunities
- Located on the World Famous Kenai River

For more information write or call to receive our visitor services directory or relocation packet.

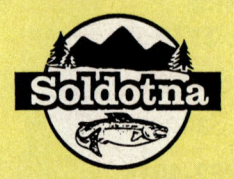

Soldotna

Greater Soldotna Chamber of Commerce
P.O. Box 236-MP, Soldotna, AK 99669
(907) 262-9814

---

peninsula center mall
COMFORTABLE INDOOR SHOPPING - - YEAR AROUND!

In The Heart of Downtown Soldotna
Open Mon.-Fri. 10-9
Sat. 10-6 · Sun. 12-5

A to Zumething
Etc. By Su
Alaskan Gifts and T-shirts
Windwalkers
Card and Book Store
Book Cache
Catalog Store
JCPenney
Florist and Gifts
Kathy's Flowers
Jewelry and Fine Art
Homestead Jewelers

Food To Go / Restaurant
Bull Feathers
I Love Cookies and Creme
Kandy Korner
Subs 'N More
Kitchen Gifts
Concepts Unlimited
Music (Tapes/CDs/Videos)
Toonz
Ready Wear
Jay Jacobs
Water Systems
Culligan

Personal Service
Alaska Travel Cache
First National Bank of Anchorage
Freedom Reality
Glenn's Barber Shop
Hutchings Chev/Olds/Cadillac/Geo
Lynn's Hair Gallery
Peninsula Clarion
Photography Studio
New Generation Photography Studio
Shoes
Foot Locker
Kinney Shoes

By Kenai River Bridge

SINCE 1974
Riverside AUTO SUPPLY INC.
SOLDOTNA · ALASKA

ROLLIN BRADEN
Owner

Foreign and Domestic
(907) 262-5851

fishing are located in the Soldotna area. In May 1985, Les Anderson of Soldotna landed a 97-lb., 4-oz. king salmon, a new world's record. The mounted fish is on display at the Kenai Peninsula Visitor Information Center.

Soldotna gets very busy during fishing season, and for those fishermen who want a more remote fishing spot—or for visitors who want to see wildlife and glaciers—there are fly-in fishing trips for rainbow, grayling, salmon and Dolly Varden, and flightseeing trips to see Tustumena Glacier and wildlife, through local outfitters.

In Soldotna, the early run of kings begins about May 15 with the peak of the run occurring between June 12 and 20. The late run enters the river about July 1, peaking between July 23 and 31; season closes July 31. The first run of red salmon enters the river during early June and is present in small numbers through the month; the second run enters about July 15 and is present through early August. In even years pink salmon are present from early through mid-August. The early silver salmon run arrives about July 25, peaks in mid-August, and is over by the end of the month. Late run silver salmon enter the Kenai in early September, peak in mid- to late September, and continue to enter the river through October. Dolly Varden and rainbow trout can be caught all summer.

C & R Charters. Let Richard and Char Daus's 35 years of guiding experience help you catch those Kenai River king and silver salmon. Hear Richard's daily fishing reports on KSRM radio. Ask Char about bank fishing. Guided fishing for king salmon May, June, July, $225 for 2 people. Silvers in August–September, $79 per person. Call (907) 283-7400. Ask about our super deep-sea fishing camp in Mexico for those winter vacation excursions for tuna, marlin, sailfish and mahi mahi. Summer location: Edgewater RV Park. See display ad this section. [ADVERTISEMENT]

Soldotna Creek Park. This day-use only park on the Kenai River has covered picnic tables, grills, playground and trails. Facilities include parking, wheelchair-accessible toilets and dumpsters. The park is located behind Hutchings Chevrolet at the Y. Turn at highway maintenance station and follow road behind restaurant.

Kenai National Wildlife Refuge Visitor Center, located at the top of Ski Hill Road (see **Milepost S 97.9**) and also accessible from Funny River Road (see **Milepost S 96.1**), hosts some 25,000 visitors annually. This modern center has dioramas containing lifelike mounts of area wildlife in simulated natural settings. There is a free video about the refuge shown on the hour, between noon and 4 P.M., weekdays in summer. Free wildlife films are shown on the hour every weekend from noon to 5 P.M. Information available here on canoeing, backcountry hiking and camping. There is a 1-mile-/1.6-km-long nature trail with an observation platform and spotting scope. The Alaska Natural History Assoc. has a sales outlet here with books, posters and slide sets. Pay phone located in center. Open weekdays, 8 A.M. to 4:30 P.M., and weekends 10 A.M. to 6 P.M. No admission fee.

The refuge was created in 1941 when Pres. Franklin D. Roosevelt set aside 1,730,000 acres of land (then designated the Kenai National Moose Range) to assure that the large numbers of moose, Dall sheep and other wild game would remain for people to enjoy. With the passage of the Alaska National Interest Lands Conservation Act in 1980, the acreage was increased to 1.97 million acres and redesignated Kenai National Wildlife Refuge. The area is managed by the

KING OF THE RIVER
King • Silver • Halibut Charters
Dean Schlehoffer and Michael Marts, Fishing Guides
VISA (907) 262-2897 • T.D.D. MasterCard
PO Box 107, Soldotna, Alaska 99669

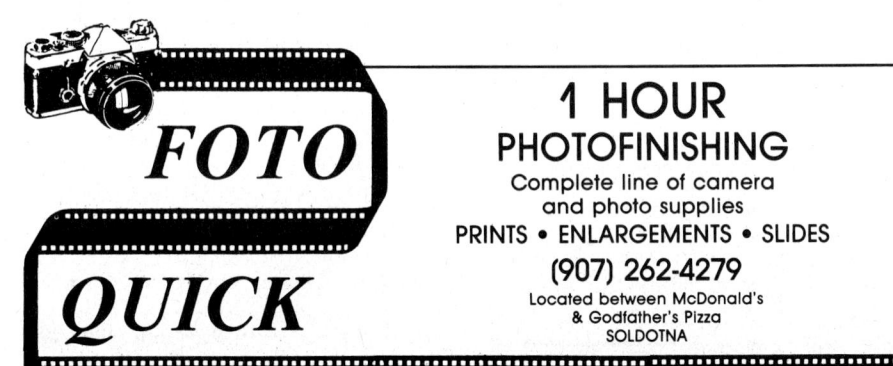

FOTO QUICK
1 HOUR PHOTOFINISHING
Complete line of camera and photo supplies
PRINTS • ENLARGEMENTS • SLIDES
(907) 262-4279
Located between McDonald's & Godfather's Pizza
SOLDOTNA

BEEMUN'S / **V&S. Variety Store**

The unusual as well as everyday needs

ALASKANA GIFTS - SOUVENIRS - ARTS & CRAFTS - CARDS - TOYS
SWEATS - HOUSEWARES - BEDDING - EDUCATIONAL AIDS - BIBLES

——— FREE POPCORN ———

In SOLDOTNA, next to Lamonts   Open 9 - 6 Monday - Saturday
35277 Kenai Spur Highway • Phone (907) 262-5151

KLONDIKE CITY

KSLD RADIO 1140 AM
Summer Fishing Reports
6 Times Daily

DOWNTOWN SOLDOTNA
MILE 95.5 Sterling Highway

SAL'S KLONDIKE DINER

FAMOUS FOR
Alaskan & Yukon *Burgers*

OPEN 24 HOURS

Breakfast Anytime

• ORDERS TO GO •
262-2220

Gold Strike Lanes
262-9065

Sam's Pawn Shop

Gold • Guns • Jewelry
Etc • Etc

Kenai Spur Highway Log

Distance from Soldotna Y (SY). The Kenai Spur Highway branches off the Sterling Highway at the Soldotna Y. Milepost S 94.2.

SY 0 Junction with Sterling Highway at **Milepost S 94.2**.

SY 1.8 (2.8 km) Big Eddy Road to west. Access to Big Eddy state recreational site on Kenai River with wheelchair-accessible toilets, fishing guides, private camping, moorage, boat launches and rental facilities.

SY 2.2 (3.5 km) Big Eddy second access.

SY 2.5 (4 km) Sport Lake Road.

SY 4 (6.4 km) Kenai city limits.

SY 5.9 (9.4 km) Dogwood Street.

Upik Fur Products. See display ad this section.

SY 6.1 (9.8 km) Beaver Creek Park (day use only); parking, toilets, picnic tables, playground, basketball court, covered table, litter barrels.

SY 6.4 (10.3 km) Twin City Raceway. South **junction** with Beaver Loop Road: Drive 2.5 miles/4 km on Beaver Loop Road and turn south (left fork), crossing Warren Ames Memorial Bridge, to connect with Kalifornsky Beach Road. Turn north (right fork) for return to Kenai Spur Highway at Mile 10.9.

SY 8.2 (13.2 km) Mountain View elementary school.

SY 9.3 (14.9 km) Tinker Lane. Access to Peninsula Oilers baseball park, municipal golf course and junior high school.

SY 9.6 (15.4 km) Kenai high school.

SY 10.1 (16.2 km) Marathon Road.

SY 10.2 (16.4 km) Airport Road (right), Walker Road (left). Begin divided 4-lane highway, 35-mph/56-kmph zone, through Kenai business area.

SY 10.5 (16.9 km) Bridge Access Road; north **junction** with Beaver Loop Road. Access south to Bridge Access Road and Port of Kenai; public boat launch with parking and toilets available. Road crosses Warren Ames Bridge and junctions with Kalifornsky Beach Road. Kenai River Flats state recreation site south of bridge has toilets and dumpster. Good spot to see migrating waterfowl.

SY 11 (17.7 km) KENAI (description of city begins on opposite page). Kenai Mall; shopping, supermarket. Willow Street access to Kenai Municipal Airport 1 mile northeast. Continue north for North Kenai and Captain Cook state recreation area.

SY 11.4 (18.3 km) Main Street. Chamber of commerce and Kenai Bicentennial Visitors and Cultural Center. Access to Beluga Point overlook at mouth of Kenai River.

SY 11.5 (18.5 km) Overland Avenue; access to private RV park.

SY 12.1 (19.5 km) Forest Drive. Scenic viewpoint overlooking Cook Inlet. Access to municipal campground located behind the National Guard Armory. ▲

SY 12.4 (20 km) C-Plaza; shopping, pharmacy.

SY 15 (24.1 km) Kenai city limits.

SY 17.8 (28.6 km) Nikiski Fire Station No. 1.

SY 19.3 (31 km) South Miller Loop Road; access to private RV park. ▲

SY 21.3 (34.3 km) Turnoff on Miller Loop Road for Bernice Lake State Recreation Site with 11 campsites and boat launch. Camping fee $6/night or annual pass. Road connects with Island Lake Road. ▲

SY 22.1 (35.5 km) NIKISKI (pop. 5,000). **Emergency Services,** phone 911 for fire and paramedics. Also known as Port Nikiski and Nikishka, this area was homesteaded in the 1940s and grew with the discovery of oil on the Kenai Peninsula in 1957. By 1964, oil-related industries here included Unocal Chemical, Phillips LNG, Chevron and Tesoro. Oil docks servicing offshore drilling platforms today include Rigtenders, Standard Oil, Phillips 66 and Union Collier Chemical. Commercial fishing, hunting and trapping are still a source of income for some residents.

SY 22.5 (36.2 km) Access to Nikiski Rigtenders dock; tankers may be seen next to dock.

SY 23.5 (37.8 km) North Peninsula Recreation Area and Nikiski elementary school. Dome-shaped building in trees near highway is the modern Nikiski swimming pool; visitor observation area at pool. Other facilities include an ice rink, hiking and ski trails, a picnic area and ball fields. Phone 776-8472.

SY 25.8 (41.5 km) Island Lake Road.

SY 26.6 (42.8 km) Nikishka Mall shopping, restaurant, supermarket, gas station, laundromat with showers, and Nikiski branch Kenai post office.

SY 26.7 (43 km) Nikiski Beach Road; views of Nikishka Bay and Cook Inlet. Nikiski Fire Station No. 2.

SY 28 (45 km) Moose Haven Lodge & RV Park. See display ad this section. ▲

SY 29.7 (47.8 km) Halbouty Road.

SY 29.7 (47.8 km) Daniels Lake Lodge. See display ad this section.

SY 30 (48.2 km) Daniels Lake.

SY 32.5 (52.3 km) Turnout west opposite Twin Lakes.

SY 32.7 (52.6 km) Twin Lake Drive.

SY 35.6 (57.3 km) Entering Captain Cook State Recreation Area.

SY 35.9 (57.8 km) Bishop Creek Campground; 15 sites, parking, toilets, water, picnic area and trail to beach. Camping fee $6/night or annual pass. Watch for spawning red salmon in creek in July and August, silvers August to September. Closed to salmon fishing. ▲

SY 36.5 (58.7 km) Access to **Stormy Lake** swimming area, changehouse, toilet, water, parking and rainbow and arctic char fishing.

SY 36.7 (59.1 km) Stormy Lake overlook; large paved turnout to east.

SY 36.9 (59.4 km) Stormy Lake picnic area; water, toilets, covered tables.

SY 37.8 (60.8 km) Stormy Lake boat launch; water, toilets, parking.

SY 38.6 (62.1 km) Swanson River canoe landing; drive 0.6 mile/1 km east to parking and toilets, river access.

SY 38.7 (62.3 km) Clint Starnes Memorial Bridge crosses **Swanson River**; parking, toilets, view of Mount Spurr. Fishing for silver and red salmon, and rainbow.

SY 39 (62.8 km) Pavement ends at T. Take left fork for Discovery Campground; 53 campsites, picnic area, hiking trail, water, beachcombing for agates. Camping fee $6/night or annual pass. ▲

SY 39.6 (63.7 km) Picnic area with tables and toilets, on bluff overlooking ocean at end of Kenai Spur Highway.

Return to Milepost S 94.2 Sterling Highway

Upik Fur Products

Many items in stock.
We also do custom work.
Expert Skin Sewers.
Fur Parkas • Slippers • Coats
Hats • Wholesale • Retail
All types of fur including seal skin.

Violet Mack invites you to visit the shop.

TURN WEST AT MILE 5.9 KENAI SPUR ROAD

Watch for the sign at the house.
P.O. Box 2826   Kenai, AK   PH: (907) 283-4390

Moose Haven Lodge & RV Park

Secluded, Quiet, Comfortable Rooms • TV and Phones
Homecooked Full Breakfasts • *Daily and Weekly Rates*

For Reservations: (907) 776-8535
Box 8597, Nikiski, AK 99635 • Mile 28, Kenai Spur Hwy.

DANIELS LAKE LODGE
Bed & Breakfast
Secluded Lake Setting
Open Year Around
20 miles north of Kenai

View Rooms, Private or Shared Bath, Kitchen, more...
Native Rainbow Trout • Boat and Fishing Poles

Brochure: P.O. Box 1444-MP, Kenai, Alaska 99611 • (907) 776-5578

U.S. Dept. of the Interior's Fish and Wildlife Service. Mailing address: Refuge Manager, Kenai National Wildlife Refuge, P.O. Box 2139, Soldotna 99669-2139; phone 262-7021.

Take a canoe trip on one of several routes available in this part of the Kenai Peninsula. Enjoyment of wildlife in their natural habitat, true wilderness scenery, camping and fishing for trout and salmon are a few highlights of a canoe trip.

Established canoe trails include the Swanson River route (80 miles/129 km) and Swan Lake route (60 miles/97 km). Complete information on Kenai Peninsula canoe trails is available at the Skilak Lake Road and Soldotna USF&WS visitor centers, as well as visitor centers in Kenai and Soldotna.

Kenai

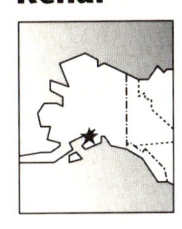

SY 11 (17.7 km). On the western Kenai Peninsula. Reached via the Kenai Spur Highway, or 9.3 miles/14.9 km from Sterling Highway via the Kalifornsky Beach Road, 158.5 miles/255 km from Anchorage, 89.3 miles/143.7 km from Homer. **Population:** 6,730.

Emergency Services: Phone 911 for all emergency services. **Alaska State Troopers** (in Soldotna), phone 262-4453. **Kenai City Police**, phone 283-7879. **Fire Department** and **Ambulance**, phone 911. **Hospital** (in Soldotna), phone 262-4404. **Maritime Search and Rescue**, dial 0 for Zenith 5555, toll free.

Visitor Information: Kenai Bicentennial Visitors and Cultural Center, located at the corner of Main Street and the Kenai Spur Highway. Open 9 A.M. to 5 P.M. weekdays year-round, extended weekend hours during summer. Write P.O. Box 1991, 11471 Kenai Spur Highway, Kenai, AK 99611, phone

KENAI ADVERTISERS

Alaska Guides & Irene's Lodge .... Ph. (907) 283-4501
Altland's Kenai River Guides .... Ph. (907) 283-7466
Beaver Creek Cabin Rentals .... Ph. (907) 283-4262
Brown Bear Gunshop & Museum .... 104 N. Tinker Ln.
Chalet Bed & Breakfast, The .... Ph. (907) 283-4528
Coyle's Landing Bed and Breakfast .... Ph. (907) 283-5378
Hi-Lo Charters & Riverside Lodging .... Ph. (907) 283-9691
Inlet Card & Craft .... C-Plaza
Inlet Pharmacy .... C-Plaza
Katmai Hotel .... Main St. & Kenai Spur Hwy.
Kenai Bicentennial Visitors and Cultural Center .... Ph. (907) 283-1991
Kenai Golf Course .... 1420 Lawton Dr.
Kenai Kings Inn .... Kenai Spur at Airport Way
Kenai Mall .... Mile 11 Kenai Spur Hwy.
Louie's Steak and Seafood Restaurant .... Ph. (800) 777-3650
Overland RV Park .... Mile 11.5 Kenai Spur Hwy.
Peanut Gallery, The .... Carr's Mall
Silver Pines Bed & Breakfast .... Ph. (907) 283-3352
Uptown Motel .... Ph. (800) 777-3650

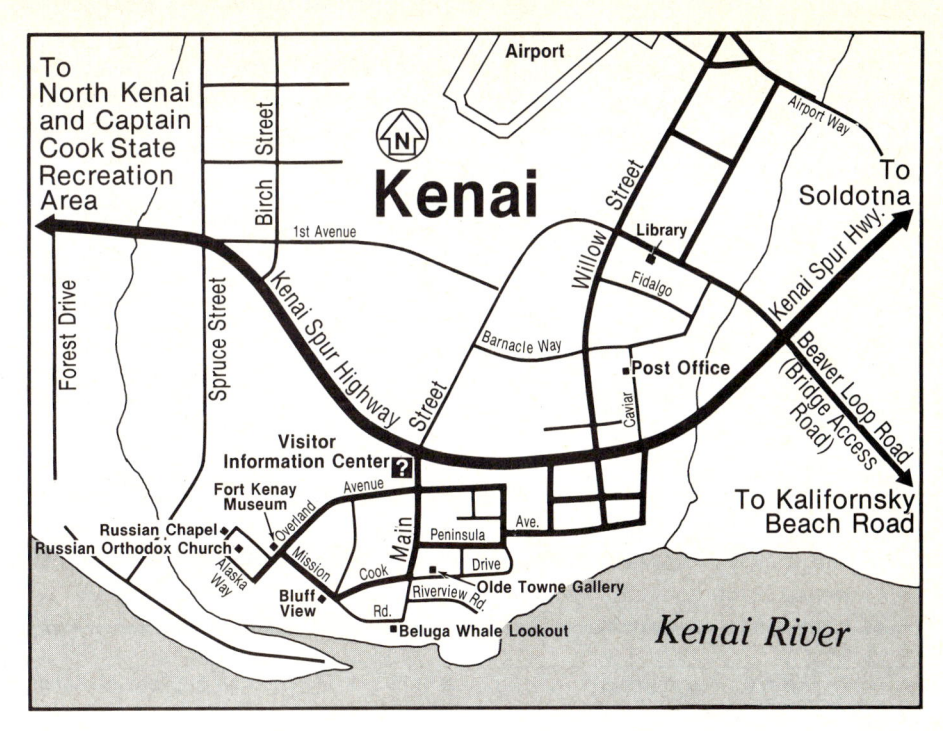

THE CHALET
Bed & Breakfast
(907) 283-4528
A taste of real Alaska
Large rooms, private baths
2-bedroom cottage with kitchen
— QUIET SETTING IN TALL TREES —
Midway between Soldotna and Kenai
Close to KENAI RIVER fishing, guides,
tourist activities, shopping.
No children under 12 • No smoking in rooms
Your Hosts: J.B. and Dolly Johnson
4705 Strawberry Road, Kenai, AK 99611

BEAVER CREEK CABIN RENTALS
"Cabins By The Kenai River"
* Completely furnished cabins
* Off the beaten path in a beautiful creekside pastoral setting
* Sightings of moose, bear, eagles and even caribou are common
* Fishing charters on the Kenai River and boat rentals are available

For Reservations Call or Write:
WILL & BECKY JAHRIG
P.O. Box 51, Kenai, Alaska 99611
(907) 283-4262

UPTOWN MOTEL
52 Clean Modern Rooms · Phones
In-Room Movies · Satellite TV

SEE THE LARGEST COLLECTION OF
ALASKAN TROPHY ANIMALS & FISH

PHONE: (907) 283-3660

WRITE: 47 Spur View Drive
(Downtown) Kenai, Alaska 99611

LOUIE'S STEAK & SEAFOOD
Finest Steaks & Seafood
Great Breakfasts · Room Service

KENAI PENINSULA · KENAI

Three-domed Orthodox church recalls Kenai's Russian heritage. (Jerrianne Lowther, staff)

---

(907) 283-3352 Open all seasons

SILVER PINES
BED AND BREAKFAST
John & Jamie Bemowski
1607 Pine Ave., Kenai, Alaska 99611

Katmai Hotel

HOTEL – Newly Remodeled
Direct Dial Phones – Satellite TV
Room Service
RESTAURANT – Open 24 hours
LOUNGE – Live Music

24 Hour Reservation Phone
Airport & Pick-up Service
283-6101
VISA, MasterCard, & American Express
Walking distance to downtown Kenai

10800 KENAI SPUR HIGHWAY & MAIN

283-1991. Excellent walking tour of Kenai available.

Elevation: Sea level. **Climate:** Average daily maximum temperature in July, 61°F/16°C; January temperatures range from 11° to -19°F/-12° to -28°C. The lowest winter temperature ever recorded in Kenai was -48°F/-44°C. Average annual precipitation, 19.9 inches (68.7 inches of snowfall). **Radio:** KCSY 1140, KENI 550, KGTL 620, KSRM 920, KWVV 105, KGTL-FM 100.9/103.5, MBN-FM 95.3/97.7, KENY 980, KWHQ-FM 100.1, KPEN-FM 101.7. **Television:** Channels 3, 5, 9 and 12 via booster from Anchorage. **Newspaper:** *Peninsula Clarion* (daily).

Private Aircraft: Kenai Municipal Airport, adjacent north; elev. 92 feet/28m; length 7,575 feet/2,309m; asphalt; fuel 80, 100. Transient tie-down fees $2/day. Adjacent floatplane base offers 3,500-foot/1,067-m basin with 35 slips; transient fee $3/day.

Kenai, which celebrated its bicentennial in 1991, is situated on a low rise overlooking the mouth of the Kenai River where it empties into Cook Inlet. It is the largest city on the Kenai Peninsula. Prior to Russian Alaska, Kenai was an Indian community. Indians fished, hunted, trapped, farmed and traded with neighboring tribes here. In 1791 it became the second permanent settlement established by the Russians in Alaska, when a fortified post called Fort St. Nicholas, or St. Nicholas Redoubt, was built near here by Russian traders. In 1869 the U.S. Army established Fort Kenai (Kenay); in 1899 a post office was authorized.

Oil exploration began in the mid-1950s, with the first major discovery in this area, the Swanson River oil reserves, 20 miles/32.2 km northeast of Kenai in 1957. Two years later, natural gas was discovered in the Kalifornsky Beach area 6 miles/9.6 km south of the city of Kenai. Extensive exploration offshore in upper Cook Inlet has established that Cook Inlet's middle-ground shoals contain one of the major oil and gas fields in the world.

The industrial complex on the North Kenai Road is the site of Unocal Chemicals, which produces ammonia and urea for fertilizer. Phillips Petroleum operates a liquid natural gas plant. Tesoro and Chevron have refineries here.

Offshore in Cook Inlet are 15 drilling platforms, all with underwater pipelines bringing the oil to the shipping docks on both sides of Cook Inlet for loading onto tankers.

Federal and state agencies based in and around Kenai contribute to the local economy. Next to oil, tourism, fishing and fish processing are the leading industries.

ACCOMMODATIONS

Kenai has all shopping facilities and conveniences. Medical and dental clinics, banks, laundromats, theaters, pharmacies, supermarkets and numerous gift and specialty shops are located on and off the highway and in the shopping malls. Several motels and hotels and about a dozen restaurants and drive-ins are located in Kenai. Local artists are featured at the Kenai Fine Arts Center on Cook Street. Showers, sauna, hot tub, racquetball courts and gym at Kenai Recreation Center, on Caviar Street. Open 6 A.M. to 10 P.M. Monday through Saturday,

---

Alaska Guides & Irene's Lodge
Fishing Charters   (Bed & Breakfast)

Halibut
King (chinook) Salmon
Red (sockeye) Salmon
Silver (coho) Salmon
Pink Salmon
Coast Guard Licensed & Insured
Home of the World Records!
Salmon 97 1/4 lbs.
Halibut 466 lbs.

First Class
Accommodations
Large Rooms · Private Entrances
Private Baths · Full Breakfast
Airport Transportation
A-1 Recreation Facilities
*Come To A World
of Fun and Beauty!*
Herman & Irene Fandel

702 Lawton Drive, Kenai, Alaska 99611 · (907) 283-4501

Sunday 1-10 P.M. Phone 283-3855. For joggers there's the Bernie Huss Memorial Trail, a 0.5-mile jogging and exercise course located at Wells Fargo Gamefield just off the Kenai Spur Highway on Main Street Loop. Dump stations located at 3 local service stations.

Coyle's Landing Bed and Breakfast. Enjoy old Alaskan stories as told by an old homesteader, Waldo Coyle. Located on the Kenai River, we offer world-class fishing, wildlife viewing and warm hospitality in a comfortable atmosphere. See display ad this section. [ADVERTISEMENT]

Uptown Motel and Louie's Steak and Seafood Restaurant. We pride ourselves in giving you the very cleanest rooms. Famous Alaskan atmosphere. Trophy wildlife and fish displayed in restaurant, lounge. Largest seafood menu on the peninsula. Salmon, halibut, king crab, scallops, prawns, steamers, more. Excellent prime rib and steaks. Toll free, 1-800-777-3650. See display ad. [ADVERTISEMENT]

City of Kenai public boat ramp on Boat Launch Road off Bridge Access Road has 24-hour parking, dump station, restrooms with flush toilets, pay phone.

Kenai City Park has covered picnic tables and fireplaces. Arrangements for caravan camping may be made in advance through the Kenai Bicentennial Visitors and Cultural Center. To reach the city campground, follow Kenai Spur Highway through city center and turn left (northbound) on Forest Drive. The campground is located behind the National Guard Armory. Two private RV parks are located off Overland Street. ▲

TRANSPORTATION

Air: Kenai is served by South Central Air, MarkAir and Era–Alaska. Several firms offer charter service out of Kenai. Kenai Municipal Airport (see description under Private Aircraft) is off the Kenai Spur Highway about a mile from the Kenai Mall. Traveling toward Soldotna from the mall, take the first left

---

kenai mall

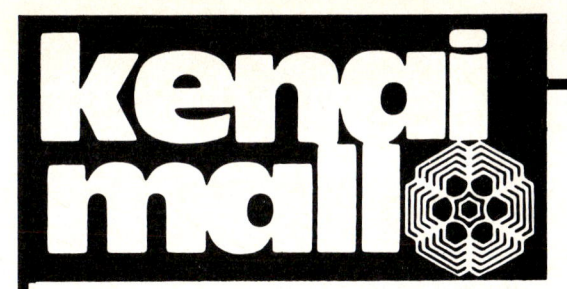

Shopping Convenience in Kenai!
Plenty of parking for R/V's

Fred Meyer Family Apparel and Family Shoes
- Groceries
- Pharmacy
- Fishing Tackle
- Fashions
- Alaskan Gifts
- Books
- Alaskan Art
- Beauty/Barber Shops
- Photo/Film
- Snack Bar
- Keys
- Jewelry

LOOK FOR CARRS QUALITY CENTER ON THE KENAI SPUR

Inlet Card & Craft
Hallmark • Alaska Souvenirs
Art & Craft Supplies • Toys
283-7114
C Plaza (by Moose Lodge)

Inlet Pharmacy
Prescriptions
All Drug Sundry Needs
Drive-up Window • 283-3714
Mile SY 12.4 Kenai Spur Highway

OVERLAND RV PARK

Welcomes you
—Downtown Kenai—
Walking distance to Visitor Information Center, Kenai River bluff view, Fort Kenay, Russian Orthodox Church, restaurants, major shopping mall

Level Spaces • Pull-Throughs
Full & Partial Hookups • 30-amp Power
Clean Restrooms • Showers • Laundry (guests only)

—FISHING CHARTERS—
Daily, Weekly, Monthly Rates - Come stay awhile

(907) 283-4512
(907) 283-4227

P.O. Box 326
Kenai, Alaska 99611

Mile 11.5 Kenai Spur Hwy.
Overland RV Park ★
410 Overland Ave. — Tourist Information Center

We can tell you where to Bank Fish!!
Mile 11.5 Kenai Spur Highway

Coyle's Landing
Bed and Breakfast
on the Kenai River

Magnificent View
World Class Fishing
Full Kitchen and Laundry
Day, Week or Monthly Rates
Clean and Comfortable
Guide Service Available

1412 Barabara
Kenai, Alaska 99611
(907) 283-5378 or
(907) 283-3223
FAX (907) 283-3366

See log ad under Accommodations

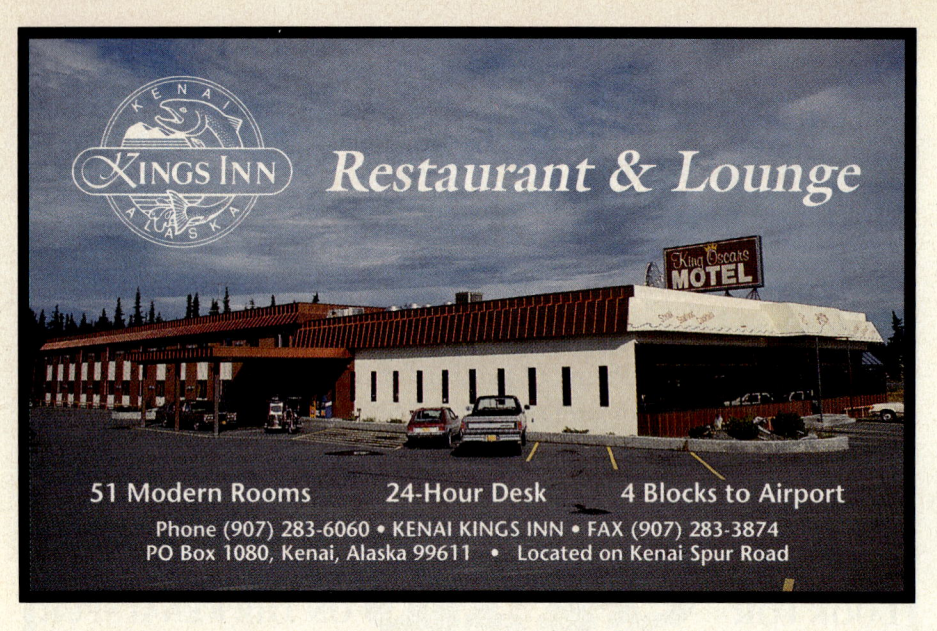

KENAI PENINSULA • KENAI

KENAI KINGS INN Restaurant & Lounge

51 Modern Rooms • 24-Hour Desk • 4 Blocks to Airport
Phone (907) 283-6060 • KENAI KINGS INN • FAX (907) 283-3874
PO Box 1080, Kenai, Alaska 99611 • Located on Kenai Spur Road

---

(Willow Street) and follow it 0.7 mile/1.1 km to the airport. **Local:** Limousine and taxi service is available as well as car rentals, vehicle leasing, boat rentals and charters.

ATTRACTIONS

Get Acquainted. Pick up an Old Kenai tour brochure with map at the Kenai Bicentennial Visitors and Cultural Center. The center, constructed in 1991 to celebrate Kenai's 200th birthday, also houses the Kenai Museum, which has old photos, artifacts and wildlife displays. The center also offers daily showings of films on Alaska.

Brown Bear Gunshop & Museum, 104 N. Tinker Lane, Kenai, AK 99611. Phone (907) 283-3800. Specializing in 98 Mauser rifles. New and used rifles, ammunition,

KENAI
Village with a Past. City with a Future.

Kenai Bicentennial Visitors and Cultural Center

VISITORS & CULTURAL CENTER
Stop by our new Kenai Bicentennial Visitors and Cultural Center and see history come alive from our rich Russian past to our Indian cultural legacy. The center, which was constructed in 1991 to celebrate Kenai's 200th birthday, boasts ancient artifacts, wildlife displays and old photos. It also has various exhibits, visitor information and an audio visual room with daily showings of movies on Alaska.

HISTORY
Two centuries ago, Russian fur traders settled near a Dena'ina Indian village at what is now modern Kenai. The 3-domed Orthodox church built nearly 100 years ago still stands as a reminder of the Russian presence. Across from the church is a little log chapel that covers the grave of Kenai's first resident priest.

RECREATION
The Kenai River boasts the world-record King salmon — 97-1/4 lbs.! Cast your line into these fabled waters or join a halibut charter. You can play golf at Kenai's 18-hole course, exercise at the city recreation center, explore parks and trails, or walk the many miles of sandy beach.

FACILITIES
Kenai is a modern city with hotels, motels, RV and camping parks, restaurants, churches, shopping malls, movie theaters, and a municipal airport, with more than 60 scheduled flights per day, and a float plane basin.

WILDLIFE/SCENERY
Kenai sits on a bluff where the Kenai River meets Cook Inlet, and where some of the greatest tidal ranges occur. Incoming tides actually reverse the flow of the river, influencing the movement of fish and the white beluga whales that follow them. Watch the whales as their arching backs break the water. See other wildlife, including moose, caribou, snow geese, bald eagles, trumpeter swans, cranes, arctic terns and more. Enjoy fiery sunsets and the best view of Alaska's highly active volcano — Mt. Redoubt.

Kenai Bicentennial Visitors and Cultural Center
11471 Kenai Spur Hwy., P.O. Box 1991
Kenai, Alaska 99611
(907) 283-1991

reloading supplies. Unusual Alaska gifts. Museum has numerous Alaska wildlife mounts, artifacts, antique Fairbanks–Morris engines and tools. Open Monday through Saturday 10 A.M. to 6 P.M. [ADVERTISEMENT]

Kenai River Flats is a must stop for birdwatchers. Great numbers of Siberian snow geese and other waterfowl stop to feed on this saltwater marsh in the spring. The state recreation site on Bridge Access Road at Warren Ames Bridge has toilets, parking and interpretive signs. A boardwalk for wildlife-watchers is scheduled to be built. Also watch for caribou on the Kenai Flats.

Beluga Whale Lookout on the Kenai River at west end of Main Street is, as the name implies, a good place to watch for beluga whale. Beluga whales are easy to identify by their distinctive white color. They are the only all-white whale. The Bluff Viewpoint offers a good view of Kenai's fish-processing industry.

Watch Baseball or Play Golf. Some fine semipro baseball is played at the Peninsula Oilers ball park on Tinker Lane. Golfers may try the 18-hole Kenai golf course on Lawton Drive.

Fort Kenay was the first American military installation in the area, established in 1869. More than 100 men were stationed here in the 1½ years it officially served to protect American citizens in the area. A replica of the fort's barracks building was built as an Alaskan Purchase Centennial project by Kenai residents in 1967.

Holy Assumption Russian Orthodox Church is across from Fort Kenay. The original church was founded in 1846 by a Russian monk, Egumen Nicolai. The present church was built some 50 years after the original and with its 3 onion-shaped domes is considered one of the finest examples of a Russian Orthodox church built on a vessel or quadrilateral ground plan. It is the second oldest Russian Orthodox church in Alaska. In 1971 it was designated a national historic landmark. An 1847 edition of the book of the Holy Gospel of 4 evangelists—Matthew, Mark, Luke and John—with 5 enameled icons on the cover, is awaiting restoration (not on display). Regular church services are held here and tours are available; inquire at the Parish House near the church. Donations accepted.

Parish House, north across Mission Street from the Russian church, was built in 1886 and was used as a home for resident priests. The original Galanka fireplace may be seen here.

St. Nicholas Chapel, built in 1906, west of the Russian church, marks the burial location of Father Egumen Nicolai and other Russian Orthodox church workers.

Look for arctic terns on tidal flats, marshes, rivers and lakes. (John W. Warden)

Sterling Highway Log

(continued from page 447)
S 95.9 (154.3 km) A 148.9 (239.6 km) H 83.6 (134.5 km) Kenai River bridge.
Entering Soldotna northbound. Description of city begins on page 447.
S 96 (154.5 km) A 149 (239.8 km) H 83.5 (134.4 km) Soldotna visitor center at south end of Kenai River bridge.

ALTLAND'S GUIDES
97¼ # KING

KINGS SILVERS
KENAI RIVER
• Resident Master Guide
• Former ADF&G Fisheries Biologist

(907) 283-7466
610 Set Net Drive
Kenai, Alaska 99611

Kenai's Souvenir Headquarters
Alaskan Jewelry
Postcards • Carvings
Ivory • Jade • Gold
Coffee Beans

The Peanut Gallery
SPECIAL GIFTS FOR SPECIAL PEOPLE
Alaskan Hospitality • Phone: (907) 283-7458
CARR'S MALL • KENAI

Kenai, Kasilof & Cook Inlet — Kings! Silvers! Halibut!

HI-LO CHARTERS & RIVERSIDE LODGING

• LICENSED, EXPERIENCED ALASKAN GUIDES
• EVERYTHING FURNISHED
• DELUXE RIVERSIDE LODGING & RV PARKING
• BROCHURE AVAILABLE

(907) 283-9691
1105 Angler Drive, Kenai, AK 99611

KENAI GOLF COURSE ALASKA

1420 LAWTON DRIVE
Kenai, Alaska
(907) 283-7500
18-Hole Public Course

Cart and Club Rentals • RV Parking
Pro Shop • Cafe • Driving Range

VISA and MasterCard Accepted

Near Downtown Kenai and Kenai River
Good Golfing at Reasonable Prices

Kalifornsky Beach Road Log

Also called K–Beach Road, Kalifornsky Beach Road leads west and south from the Sterling Highway at Soldotna, following the shore of Cook Inlet to Kasilof. **Distance from the Sterling Highway junction at Milepost S 96.1 at Soldotna (S) is followed by distance from Sterling Highway junction at Milepost S 108.8 at Kasilof (K). Mileposts run south to north.**

S 0 K 22.2 (35.7 km) Junction with Sterling Highway at **Milepost S 96.1.**

S 0.1 (0.2 km) K 22.1 (35.6 km) Soldotna Alaska Purchase Centennial Park campground, operated by the city of Soldotna. Kenai River access for bank fishing, boat launch (fee charged).

S 0.2 (0.3 km) K 22 (35.4 km) Alaska State Troopers.

S 0.4 (0.6 km) K 21.8 (35.1 km) Rodeo grounds.

S 0.6 (1 km) K 21.6 (34.8 km) Central Peninsula Sports Center; hockey, ice skating and other sports available.

S 1.7 (2.7 km) K 20.5 (33 km) Kenai Peninsula Community College access road. Also access to Slikok Creek State Recreation Site, 0.7 mile/1.1 km north; day use only with 12-hour parking, wheelchair accessible toilets, picnic tables, information kiosk and trails. No fires or ATVs.

S 2.9 (4.7 km) K 19.3 (31.1 km) K–Beach center. ADF&G office; stop in here for current sportfishing information.

S 3.5 (5.6 km) K 18.7 (30.1 km) Red Diamond shopping center, Duck Inn Motel and restaurant.

S 4.6 (7.4 km) K 17.6 (28.3 km) Firehouse.

S 4.7 (7.6 km) K 17.5 (28.2 km) Ciechansky Road leads 2.2 miles/3.5 km to Ciechansky State Recreation Site, a day-use only picnic area with tables, toilets, dumpster and Kenai River access. Also access to private campgrounds with RV hookups on the Kenai River.

S 6 (9.7 km) K 16.2 (26.1 km) Turnoff for city of Kenai, 3.1 miles/5 km north via the Warren Ames Memorial Bridge.

S 6.8 (10.9 km) K 15.4 (24.8 km) Magnificent beaver dam and lodge.

S 7.6 (12.2 km) K 14.6 (23.5 km) Robinsons mini-mall.

S 7.9 (12.7 km) K 14.3 (23 km) Kenai Custom Seafoods.

S 8 (12.9 km) K 14.2 (22.9 km) Cafe.

S 13 (20.9 km) K 9.2 (14.8 km) Scenic viewpoint overlooking Cook Inlet.

S 17.4 (28 km) K 4.8 (7.7 km) Kasilof Beach Road.

S 20.1 (32.3 km) K 2.1 (3.4 km) Kasilof Airfield Road.

S 22.1 (35.6 km) K 0.1 (0.2 km) Kasilof post office.

S 22.2 (35.7 km) K 0 Junction with Sterling Highway at **Milepost S 108.8** at Kasilof.

Return to Milepost S 96.1 or S 108.8 Sterling Highway

S 96.1 (154.7 km) A 149.1 (239.9 km) H 83.4 (134.2 km) Junction. Funny River Road to east, Kalifornsky Beach Road to west. Kalifornsky Beach Road rejoins the Sterling Highway at **Milepost S 108.8.** (See KALIFORNSKY BEACH ROAD log this page.)

Soldotna Alaska Purchase Centennial Park campground, 0.1 mile/0.2 km west, on the banks of the Kenai River. There are 126 campsites (some on river), tables, firepits, firewood provided, water, restrooms, dump station, pay phone, 2-week limit. Boat launch and favorite fishing site at far end of campground. Register at campground entrance (you may also register here for camping at Swiftwater Park in Soldotna).

Funny River (Airport) Road leads east 2 miles/3.2 km to Soldotna airport and 11.5 miles/18.5 km to Funny River State Recreation Site; 12 campsites, $6 nightly fee or annual pass, picnic tables, water, toilets, river access. Salmon and trout fishing at the confluence of the **Kenai** and **Funny rivers** at the recreation area. Turn on Funny River Road and take first right (Ski Hill Loop Road) for USF&WS visitor center. Funny River Road dead ends 17.2 miles/27.7 km from the highway.

S 97.9 (157.6 km) A 150.9 (242.8 km) H 81.6 (131.3 km) Sky View High School. Easy-to-miss turnoff for Kenai National Wildlife Refuge headquarters and information center: Turn east off highway and drive 1 mile/1.6 km on Ski Hill Road, which loops back to Funny River Road (see preceding milepost). The center is open 8 A.M. to 4:30 P.M. on weekdays, 10 A.M. to 6 P.M. weekends.

S 99.9 (160.8 km) A 152.9 (246.1 km) H 79.6 (128.1 km) Echo Lake Road to west.

S 108.8 (175 km) A 161.8 (260.4 km) H 70.7 (113.8 km) South **junction** with Kalifornsky Beach Road. (See KALIFORNSKY BEACH ROAD log this page.) Drive west 3.6 miles/5.8 km to Beach Road for access to beach, Kasilof small-boat harbor and Kasilof River. This loop road rejoins Sterling Highway at **Milepost S 96.1.**

KASILOF (kuh-SEE-lawf; pop. about 1,200; elev. 75 feet/23m) was originally a settlement established in 1786 by the Russians as St. George. An Indian fishing village grew up around the site, but no longer exists. Native inhabitants of the peninsula are mostly Kanai Indians, a branch of the great Athabascan family. The population is spread out over the general area which is called Kasilof. The area's income is derived from fishing and fish processing.

Kasilof River. The red salmon dip-net fishery here is open by special announcement for Alaska residents only. Check with the ADF&G for current regulations.

Private Aircraft: Kasilof airstrip, 1.7 miles/2.7 km north; elev. 125 feet/38m; length 2,300 feet/701m; gravel; unattended.

S 109.2 (175.7 km) A 162.2 (261 km) H 70.3 (113.1 km) Kasilof Riverview Lodge. See display ad this section.

S 109.4 (176.1 km) A 162.4 (261.3 km) H 70.1 (112.8 km) Bridge over Kasilof River, which drains Tustumena Lake, one of the largest lakes on the Kenai Peninsula. Kasilof River State Recreation Site; 16 campsites, $6 nightly fee or annual pass, 5 picnic sites on riverbank, picnic tables, toilets and water are on the south side of the bridge. Entering Game Management Subunit 15C southbound, 15B northbound.

S 110 (177 km) A 163 (262.3 km) H 69.5 (111.8 km) Tustumena Elementary School and north end of Tustumena Lake Road. This is the first turnoff southbound for access to Johnson and Tustumena lakes. Also turn off here for picnic area with covered picnic tables, toilets (wheelchair accessible), firepits, water and dumpster. There is a huge metal T at Tustumena Lake Road, just beyond the picnic area: Turn east at the T for Johnson and Tustumena lakes. **Johnson Lake** is 0.3 mile/0.5 km from the highway. Johnson Lake state campground has 50 sites (some double and some pull-throughs), $6 nightly fee or annual pass, water, toilets, boat launch and firewood. Lake is stocked with rainbow. Watch for beaver, moose, and king salmon migrating up Crooked Creek. **Tustumena Lake** is 6.4 miles/10.3 km from the highway; a campground on the Kasilof River near the lake has 10 sites, toilets and boat launch. Fishing for lake trout and salmon. *CAUTION: This lake is 6 miles/10 km wide and 25 miles/40 km long and subject to severe winds.*

S 110.5 (177.8 km) A 163.5 (263.1 km) H 69 (111 km) Double-ended paved parking by Crooked Creek.

S 111 (178.6 km) A 164 (263.9 km) H 68.5 (110.2 km) Cohoe Loop Road north **junction** (turnoff to west) and south end of Tustumena Lake Road (to east) for Johnson

---

KASILOF RIVERVIEW LODGE
Mile 109.2 Sterling Hwy.

In the heart of Kenai Peninsula hunting & fishing

Fine Dining • Beer and Wine available
★ Restaurant overlooks Kasilof River ★
Gas • Diesel • Minor Repair • Phone

Owned & Operated by Jim, Joanne & Joe Browning

Tire Repair • 24-Hour Towing and Road Service • Propane • Ice
Liquor Store • Groceries • Tackle Shop • Gift Shop • Boat Ramp
Great King and Silver Salmon Fishing
Kasilof, Alaska 99610 • Phone (907) 262-1573

and Tustumena lakes (see description at **Milepost S 110.1**). Cohoe Loop Road rejoins the Sterling Highway at **Milepost S 114.3** (see COHOE LOOP ROAD log on page 464).

Just east of the highway on the Johnson and Tustumena lakes access road is Crooked Creek fish hatchery, open 8 A.M. to 4 P.M.; a sign explains the chinook and sockeye salmon operation here. The hatchery-produced salmon create a popular fishery at the confluence of Crooked Creek and the Kasilof River, accessible via the Cohoe Loop Road. Just past the hatchery is Crooked Creek Road (private RV park and bed and breakfast) and just beyond there is a huge metal T at Tustumena Lake Road: Continue past this monument for a picnic area and return to Sterling Highway at **Milepost S 110**, turn at the T for lakes and camping.

Crooked Creek RV Park & Guide Service. See display ad this section.

Crooked Creek Bed & Breakfast. Located south shore of Johnson Lake on Crooked Creek Road, just uphill from fish hatchery. Turn at Youth Ranch Mile 1 Crooked Creek Road. Housekeeping log cabin, private bath, fish cleaning and freezer facilities, canoe, airstrip, RV parking. Also rooms in private home. Clean, quiet, reasonable rates. Harold and Chris Hansen, Box 7, Kasilof, AK 99610. (907) 262-2729. [ADVERTISEMENT]

S 114.3 (183.9 km) **A 167.3** (269.2 km) **H 65.2** (104.9 km) Cohoe Loop Road south **junction** with the Sterling Highway. The 13-mile/21-km road loops north to **Milepost S 111**. See COHOE LOOP ROAD log page 464.

S 117.4 (188.9 km) **A 170.4** (274.2 km) **H 62.1** (99.9 km) Clam Gulch State Recreation Area (watch for easy-to-miss sign) is 0.5 mile/0.8 km from highway; picnic tables, picnic shelter, toilets, water, 116 campsites, $6 nightly fee or annual pass. *CAUTION: High ocean bluffs are dangerous.* Short access road to beach (recommended for 4-wheel-drive vehicles only, limited turnaround space).

Clam digging for razor clams on most of the sandy beaches of the western Kenai Peninsula from Kasilof to Anchor Point can be rewarding. Many thousands of clams are dug each year at Clam Gulch. You must have a sportfishing license to dig, and these are available at most sporting goods stores. The bag limit is 60 clams regardless of size (always check current regulations). There is no legally closed season, but quality of the clams varies with month; check locally. Good clamming and fewer people in March and April, although there may still be ice on the beach. Any tide lower than a minus 1-foot tide is enough to dig clams. Minus 4- to 5-foot tides are best for clamming. The panoramic view of Mount Redoubt, Mount Iliamna and Mount Spurr across Cook Inlet and the expanse of beach are well worth the short side trip even during the off-season.

S 118.2 (190.2 km) **A 171.2** (275.5 km) **H 61.3** (98.7 km) CLAM GULCH (pop. 115) post office, lodge and a sled dog racing outfitters shop.

S 118.3 (190.4 km) **A 171.3** (275.7 km) **H 61.2** (98.5 km) **Clam Shell Lodge.** See display ad this section.

S 119.1 (191.7 km) **A 172.1** (277 km) **H 60.4** (97.2 km) Large double-ended paved turnout with litter barrel to west.

S 119.8 (192.8 km) **A 172.8** (278.1 km) **H 59.7** (96.1 km) **Cook Inlet Trading Co.**

Minus tides bring clam diggers to Clam Gulch, Milepost S 117.4. (Jerrianne Lowther, staff)

on the Bluff at Clam Gulch. Specializing in handmade Alaskan gold nugget jewelry and polished Alaskan rocks. Check out our pipeline pig and pipe display. Open May 1-Sept. 30. Other times by chance or appointment. Dave, Rosie and Ben Peterson, your hosts. [ADVERTISEMENT]

S 122.8 (197.6 km) **A 175.8** (282.9 km) **H 56.7** (91.2 km) Paved, double-ended turnout oceanside (no view).

S 124.8 (200.8 km) **A 177.8** (286.1 km) **H 54.7** (88 km) Paved, double-ended turnout oceanside with view of Cook Inlet.

S 126.8 (204.1 km) **A 179.8** (289.4 km) **H 52.7** (84.8 km) Double-ended paved

---

Clam Shell Lodge
Mile 118.3 Sterling Highway
Clam Gulch   (907) 262-4211

RV Park • Campground • Motel
Restaurant • Liquor Store • Bar
Convenience Store • Gift Shop
Showers • Laundromat • Propane
Charter Service • Clam Shovel Rentals

"Famous Clam Chowder, Razor Clam, Steamers and Halibut Dinners"
PO Box 439, Clam Gulch, Alaska 99568

CROOKED CREEK RV PARK & Guide Service

MILE 111 STERLING HIGHWAY (Drive 1.8 miles on Cohoe Loop Road)
CONFLUENCE OF CROOKED CREEK AND KASILOF RIVER

HIGHEST SUCCESS RATE OF ALL PENINSULA STREAMS

KINGS • SILVERS • STEELHEAD
► This fishery is one of the few open 7 days a week
► Bank fishing — Boats not required
► Guided drift boats on Kasilof River and Guided power boats on Kenai River available

Tackle • Soft Drinks • Snacks

Fully Equipped Travel Trailers for Rent

40' x 50' RV SPACES • Full, Partial or No Hookups
Picnic Tables and Barbecues
Dump Station • Water • Tent Sites • Showers

INFORMATION and RESERVATIONS
(907) 262-1299 May-October
(907) 344-9462 year around
P.O. Box 601, Kasilof, Alaska 99610

See Our Log Ad Mile 13.5 Cohoe Loop Road

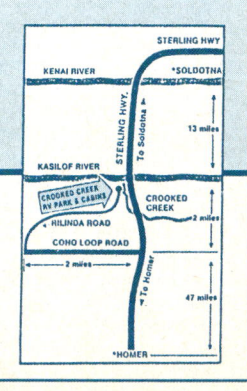

scenic wayside overlooking upper Cook Inlet. Polly Creek, due west across Cook Inlet, is a popular area for clam diggers (fly in). Across the inlet is Mount Iliamna; north of Iliamna is Mount Redoubt.

S 127.2 (204.7 km) A 180.2 (290 km) H 52.3 (84.2 km) Double-ended paved scenic viewpoint to west.

Scenic View RV Park, spectacular view Cook Inlet, Mount Redoubt. Ten minutes to Deep Creek fishing, king salmon, halibut, clamming; 40 minutes to Homer. Stay away from the crowds, return to the peaceful scenic view sunsets. Hookups, tenting, showers, laundry, gifts, food. 27 spaces. Handicap access. Weekly/monthly rates. (907) 567-3909 or 349-7410. Write P.O. Box 202553, Anchorage, AK 99520. [ADVERTISEMENT] ▲

S 131.3 (211.3 km) A 184.3 (296.6 km) H 48.2 (77.6 km) **Gentle Breezes Bed and Breakfast and Charters**. Located 4 miles above 2 fantastic fishing rivers in Ninilchik: Deep Creek and the Ninilchik River. Walking distance to the beach. Private baths. Full Alaskan breakfast. Salmon and halibut charters. Hosts: Mark and Sandy Gower, P.O. Box 487, Ninilchik, AK 99639. Phone (907) 567-1008. [ADVERTISEMENT]

S 132.2 (212.7 km) A 185.2 (298 km) H 47.3 (76.1 km) Pay phone at bar.

S 134.5 (216.4 km) A 187.5 (301.7 km) H 45 (72.4 km) Ninilchik State Recreation Area. Ninilchik Campground has 35 campsites (most will accommodate 2 parties of campers), covered picnic tables, toilets (wheelchair accessible), water, firepits. Trail to **Ninilchik River**; fishing for king and silver salmon, steelhead and Dolly Varden. Camping fee $6/night or annual pass. ⬅▲

S 134.7 (216.8 km) A 187.7 (302 km) H 44.8 (72.1 km) Coal Street; access west to Ninilchik's historic Russian Orthodox church at top of hill; plenty of parking and turnaround space.

S 135.1 (217.4 km) A 188.1 (302.7 km) H 44.4 (71.4 km) Double-ended gravel turnout and dumpsters at north end of Ninilchik River bridge. Side road leads to **NINILCHIK VILLAGE**, the original village of Ninilchik, and to the beach. A short road branches off this side road and leads into the old village of Ninilchik. Continue straight on side road for motel, beach, overnight RV parking, camping and toilets (follow signs). Sea breezes here keep the beach free of mosquitoes. Historic signs near beach and at village entrance tell about Ninilchik Village, which includes several old dovetailed log buildings. A walking tour brochure is available from businesses in the village and along the highway. Present-day Ninilchik is located at **Milepost S 135.5**. A beautiful white Russian Orthodox church sits on a hill overlooking the sea above the historic old village. Trail leads up to it from the road into town (watch for sign just past the old village store). The church and cemetery are still in use. You are welcome to walk up to it but use the well-defined path behind the store (please do not walk through private property), or drive up using the Coal Street access at **Milepost S 134.7**. ▲

S 135.3 (217.7 km) A 188.3 (303 km) H 44.2 (71.1 km) Gravel turnout to west.

S 135.4 (217.9 km) A 188.4 (303.2 km) H 44.1 (71 km) Kingsley Road; access to Ninilchik post office and a private campground. Ninilchik View state campground is across the highway. (Descriptions follow.)

S 135.4 (217.9 km) A 188.4 (303.2 km) H 44.1 (71 km) **Hylen's Camper Park**. Next to post office. Fish Deep Creek and Ninilchik River for kings, silvers and Cook Inlet's record halibut, king salmon, May-September. Great clamming. Fish cleaning tables. Smoker. Local businesses, fishing charter discounts. Housekeeping cabins, showers, laundry, storage, social room. Horseshoes. Pay phone. Clean, friendly, reasonable rates. [ADVERTISEMENT] ▲

Coho Loop Road Log

The Cohoe Loop Road loops south 15.3 miles/24.7 km from **Milepost S 111** on the Sterling Highway. The popular Crooked Creek fishing and camping area is at the top or north end of the loop. The bottom (or south) 10 miles of the Cohoe Loop Road travels through mostly undeveloped parcels of land; no services, views or recreation. Motorists may wish to use the north junction approach.

Distance from north junction with the Sterling Highway (NJ) at Milepost S 111 is followed by distance from south junction (SJ) at Milepost S 114.3. Mileposts run south to north.

NJ 0 SJ 15.3 (24.6 km) **Junction** with Sterling Highway at **Milepost S 111**.

NJ 1.8 (2.9 km) SJ 13.5 (21.7 km) **Crooked Creek RV Park & Guide Service**. Located at the confluence of Crooked Creek and Kasilof River. "The total number of adult king salmon which returned to Crooked Creek (last year) was 12,565. Of these 8,479 were hatchery-produced fish. Sportsmen harvested an estimated 8,146 fish. The total number of adult silver salmon which returned to Crooked Creek (last year) was 8,300. Of these 6,640 were hatchery-produced fish. The success rate of participating fishermen was the highest of all Peninsula salmon sport fisheries." (Excerpt from Alaska Dept. of Fish and Game, Division of Fisheries Rehabilitation, Enhancement and Development [FRED] Annual Report.) See display ad this section. [ADVERTISEMENT] ▲

NJ 1.8 (2.9 km) SJ 13.5 (21.7 km) Crooked Creek/Rilinda Drive; access to private RV park and Crooked Creek State Recreation Site at the confluence of Crooked Creek and the Kasilof River. The recreation site has tables, firepits, water, and overnight parking for 118 vehicles. Camping fee $6/night or annual pass. ▲

Fishing in **Crooked Creek** for coho salmon from Aug. 1, peaks mid-August; steelhead from Aug. 1, bait prohibited after Sept. 15; closed to king salmon fishing and closed to all fishing near hatchery. Fishing access to confluence of Crooked Creek and Kasilof River is through the state recreation site. *NOTE: Fishing access to Crooked Creek frontage above confluence is through a private RV park; fee charged.* Fishing in the **Kasilof River** for king salmon, late May through July, best in mid-June; coho salmon, mid-August to September, use salmon egg clusters, wet flies, assorted spoons and spinners; steelhead in May and September. 🐟

NJ 2.4 (3.9 km) SJ 12.9 (20.7 km) Webb-Ramsell Road. Kasilof River access across private property, fee charged.

NJ 5.3 (8.5 km) SJ 10 (16 km) Turn on Cohoe Spur Road and drive 0.2 mile/0.3 km to the home of Charlie and Elfrida Lewis. The Lewises own and operate the Victor Holm cabin, a national historic site, located in Cohoe. A post office was established at **COHOE**, an agricultural settlement, in 1950. The Victor Holm cabin was built in 1890 using local trees and inside are Mr. Holm's homemade furniture, tools, fishing equipment, dog sled, snowshoes and other belongings. Also housed in the cabin is the private rock and mineral collection of Charlie Lewis.

NJ 5.6 (9 km) SJ 9.7 (15.6 km) T intersection; go west 0.8 mile/1.3 km for beach and boat launch. Cohoe Loop Road continues north. Pavement begins northbound.

NJ 15.3 (24.6 km) SJ 0 **Junction** with Sterling Highway at **Milepost S 114.3**.

Return to Milepost S 114.3 or S 111 Sterling Highway

HYLEN'S CAMPER PARK

Mile S 135.4 Sterling Highway (Ninilchik)

May 1 – September 15
50 Full Hookups

Daily, Weekly, Monthly Rates

Great Fishing for Salmon, Halibut, Dolly Varden and Steelhead in Deep Creek and Ninilchik Rivers and Cook Inlet • Clam Digging

Showers • Laundry • Cabins • Storage

Sheldon Associates, Owners
P.O. Box 39361
Ninilchik, Alaska 99639

(907) 567-3393   See log ad

S 135.4 (217.9 km) **A 188.4** (303.2 km) **H 44.1** (71 km) Ninilchik View state campground overlooking the village and sea; 12 campsites, water, toilets, litter disposal, 2 dump stations, drinking water fill-up, pay phone. Camping fee $6/night or annual pass. Foot trail from campground down to beach and village. DOT/PF road maintenance station. ▲

S 135.5 (218 km) **A 188.5** (303.4 km) **H 44** (70.8 km) Restaurant, lodging and charter service east side of road are part of the community of **NINILCHIK** (pronounced Nin-ILL-chick)). Ninilchik extends roughly from Ninilchik State Recreation Area to the north to Deep Creek to the south, with services (grocery stores, gas stations, campgrounds, etc.) located at intervals along the highway. The original village of Ninilchik (signed Ninilchik Village) is reached by a side road from **Milepost S 135.1**.

Population: 451. **Emergency services:** Phone 911. **Clinic and ambulance**, phone 567-3412. **Visitior Information:** At Ninilchik Library, **Milepost S 135.6**. Local businesses are also very helpful. **Private Aircraft:** Ninilchik airstrip, 6.1 miles/9.8 km southeast; elev. 270 feet/82m; length 2,100 feet/640m; dirt; unattended.

On Memorial Day weekend, Ninilchik is referred to as the third biggest city in Alaska, as thousands of Alaskans arrive for the fishing (see Area Fishing following). The Kenai Peninsula State Fair is held at Ninilchik in late August. Dubbed the "biggest little fair in Alaska," it features a parade, horse show, livestock competition and exhibits ranging from produce to arts and crafts. Pancake breakfasts, bingo and other events, such as the derby fish fry, are held at the fairgrounds throughout the year. The king salmon derby is held from May to June 11. A halibut derby is planned. There is an active senior center offering meals and events. Swimming pool at the high school.

Ardison Charters. See display ad this section.

AREA FISHING: Well-known area for saltwater king salmon fishing and record halibut fishing. Charter services available. Salt water south of the mouth of **Deep Creek** has produced top king salmon fishing in late May, June and July. Kings 50 lbs. and over are frequently caught. "Lunker" king salmon are available 1 mile/1.6 km south of Deep Creek in Cook Inlet from late May through July. Trolling a spinner or a spoon from a boat is the preferred method. Silver, red and pink salmon are available in salt water between Deep Creek and the Ninilchik River during July. **Cook Inlet**, king salmon up to 76 lbs., year-round, although best time is May through July, use #5 and #6 spoons and herring. A major halibut fishery off Ninilchik has produced some of the largest trophy halibut found in Cook Inlet, including a 466-lb. unofficial world record sport-caught halibut.

S 135.6 (218.2 km) **A 188.6** (303.5 km) **H 43.9** (70.6 km) Ninilchik High School. Ninilchik Library and visitor information center. Open 10 A.M. to 4 P.M. daily in the summer.

S 135.7 (218.4 km) **A 188.7** (303.7 km) **H 43.8** (70.5 km) **Ninilchik General Store,**

Picturesque Ninilchik village at Milepost S 135.1. (Jerrianne Lowther, staff)

KENAI PENINSULA • STERLING HIGHWAY

Fish with . . .
ARDISON CHARTERS
P.O. Box 39135   (907) 567-3600
Ninilchik, Alaska 99639

Trophy Size Halibut
World Record King Salmon
1989, 1990 & 1991 1st Place Derby Winners

Mile 135.5 Sterling Highway

NINILCHIK GENERAL STORE
Mile 135.7 Sterling Highway

All your Fishing & Clamming needs
- Licenses
- Bait
- Tackle
- *10% Senior Citizen Discount on most tackle*
- Public Telephone

- Groceries
- Sweatshirts
- T-shirts
- Gifts
- Souvenirs
- Postcards
- Books
- Film • Ice

Large parking lot for RVs – Open Year-Round
Summer Hours: 6 a.m. to Midnight

Duane & Judith Giarratana, Owners
P.O. Box 39434, Ninilchik, AK 99639
(907) 567-3378

Favorite launch area for boaters and fishermen is Deep Creek State Recreation Area at Milepost S 137.3. (Sharon Nault)

open 7 days a week for all your travel needs. We carry groceries, gifts, T-shirts, souvenirs, ice, film, tackle, bait, licenses and the information you need while visiting the Ninilchik area. You'll like our prices and our service. Ask your friends who have met us. We compete for business, we don't just wait for it to happen. See display ad this section.

[ADVERTISEMENT]

S 136 (218.9 km) A 189 (304.1 km) H 43.5 (70 km) **Chinook Chevron.** Between Ninilchik River and Deep Creek. Open year-round. Propane, filtered diesel. Self-serve gasoline, fishing, clamming and visitor information. Chevron, VISA, American Express, Discover, MasterCard and JCB cards welcome. See display ad this section.

[ADVERTISEMENT]

S 136 (218.9 km) A 189 (304.1 km) H 43.5 (70 km) **Chihuly's Charters** and **Porcupine Gift Shop.** See display ad this section.

S 136 (218.9 km) A 189 (304.1 km) H 43.5 (70 km) **Drift-In B&B.** See display ad this section.

S 136.2 (219.2 km) A 189.2 (304.5 km) H 43.3 (69.7 km) Peninsula Fairgrounds.

S 136.2 (219.2 km) A 189.2 (304.5 km) H 43.3 (69.7 km) **Bluff House Bed & Breakfast.** See display ad this section.

S 136.7 (219.9 km) A 189.7 (305.3 km) H 42.8 (68.9 km) Bridge over Deep Creek. Ample parking east side of highway both sides of creek; overnight camping for self-contained vehicles only (no facilities).

Freshwater fishing in **Deep Creek** for king salmon up to 40 lbs., use spinners with red bead lures, May 30 and 3 weekends in June; Dolly Varden in July and August; silver salmon to 15 lbs., August and September; steelhead to 15 lbs., use large red spinners, late September through October. No bait fishing permitted after Sept. 15. Mouth of Deep Creek access from Deep Creek State Recreation Area turnoff at Milepost S 137.3.

S 137 (220.4 km) A 190 (305.8 km) H 42.5 (68.4 km) **Deep Creek Custom Packing, Inc.** See display ad this section.

S 137.3 (220.9 km) A 190.3 (306.2 km) H 42.2 (67.9 km) Deep Creek State Recreation Area on the beach at the mouth of Deep Creek; parking for 300 vehicles, overnight camping, water, tables, dumpsters, toilets and fireplaces. Drive 0.5 mile/0.8 km down gravel road. Camping fee $6/night or annual pass. Favorite area for surf fishing and to launch boats. (Seasonal checks by U.S. Coast Guard for personal flotation devices, boating safety.) Good bird watching in wetlands behind beach; watch for eagles. Good clamming at low tide. The beaches here are lined with coal which falls from the exposed seams of high cliffs.

CAUTION: Rapidly changing tides and weather. Although the mouth of Deep Creek affords boaters good protection, low tides may prevent return; check tide tables.

S 140 (225.3 km) A 193 (310.6 km) H 39.5 (63.5 km) **Deep Creek Bed & Breakfast.** See display ad this section.

S 140.3 (225.8 km) A 193.3 (311.1 km) H 39.2 (63.1 km) Double-ended turnout with scenic view to west.

S 142.7 (229.6 km) A 195.7 (314.9 km) H 36.8 (59.2 km) Double-ended paved turnout, view of Mount Iliamna across the inlet.

CHIHULY'S CHARTERS — **PORCUPINE SHOP**

Alaskan Gifts
Salmon & Halibut
Fishing
Rental Cabins

(907) 567-3374
Box 39294
Ninilchik, Alaska 99639

Drift-In B & B

1 mile from Sterling Highway and Cook Inlet

Quiet • Large Clean Rooms

**Call for Reservations
(907) 567-3448**

PO Box 39068, Ninilchik, Alaska 99639

Your Hosts: Hans and Barbara Pinnow

Mile 136 Sterling Highway

Chevron CHINOOK CHEVRON

MP 136, NINILCHIK

- GASOLINE
- PROPANE • DIESEL
- SNACKS
- CLEAN RESTROOMS
- PAVED PARKING

- Halfway between Deep Creek and Ninilchik Beaches
- Easy Access for Motorhomes, 5th Wheels, and Caravans
- Major Credit Cards and Traveler's Checks Welcome - Same as Cash

---

**BLUFF HOUSE
Bed & Breakfast**

*Comfortable Bedrooms • Deck
Jacuzzi • Sauna • Private Den*

OPEN ALL YEAR

Spectacular view of Cook Inlet and 3 majestic volcanos
—A most popular fishing area—

Cliff and Betty Porter, Hosts
PO Box 39194, Ninilchik, Alaska 99639
(907) 567-3605

Mile 136.2 Sterling Highway

S 143.8 (231.4 km) **A 196.8** (316.7 km) **H 35.7** (57.4 km) Happy Valley Creek. The area surrounding this creek is known locally as the Happy Valley community.

S 145.2 (233.7 km) **A 198.2** (319 km) **H 34.3** (55.2 km) **Early Years Museum.** See display ad this section.

S 145.2 (233.7 km) **A 198.2** (319 km) **H 34.3** (55.2 km) **Happy Valley** was originally named because of the still on a creek now called Happy Valley Creek. Years ago, natives of the area would come down to the still to "get wood" and "get happy." Now Happy Valley boasts a modern bar with Alaskan animal and sea-life mounts. Excellent food, modern rooms with baths, package store, grocery store. Phone (907) 567-3357. [ADVERTISEMENT]

S 148 (238.1 km) **A 201** (323.5 km) **H 31.5** (50.7 km) Scenic viewpoint. Sign here reads: "Looking westerly across Cook Inlet, Mt. Iliamna and Mt. Redoubt in the Chigmit Mountains of the Aleutian Range can be seen rising over 10,000 feet above sea level. This begins a chain of mountains and islands known as the Aleutian Chain extending west over 1,700 miles to Attu beyond the International Date Line to the Bering Sea, separating the Pacific and Arctic oceans. Mt. Redoubt on the right, and Iliamna on the left, were recorded as active volcanoes in the mid-18th century. Mt. Redoubt had a minor eruption in 1966."

Mount Redoubt had a major eruption in December 1989. The eruptions continued through April 1990, then subsided to steam plumes. Mount Redoubt is still considered to be active.

S 150.9 (242.8 km) **A 203.9** (328.1 km) **H 28.6** (46 km) Bridge over Stariski Creek.

S 151.9 (244.4 km) **A 204.9** (329.7 km) **H 27.6** (44.4 km) Stariski Creek State Recreation Site on bluff overlooking Cook Inlet; 13 campsites, $6 nightly fee or annual pass, toilets (wheelchair accessible) and well water. ▲

S 152 (244.6 km) **A 205** (329.9 km) **H 27.5** (44.3 km) **Whiskey Gulch Taxidermy and Fish and Wildlife Museum,** hard to find—too good to miss. Bob and Ann James have specialized in mounting all types of fish since the 1950s. Stop in and see the most complete collection of mounted fish species in Alaska (free). Take your picture with our 400-lb. halibut. We can reproduce any catch-and-release trophy fish from molds in stock. Handcrafted items from our studio. (907) 235-5681. Write: HC 67, Box 292, Anchor Point, AK 99556. See display ad. [ADVERTISEMENT]

S 153.2 (246.5 km) **A 206.2** (331.8 km) **H 26.3/42.3 km** **Short Stop RV Parking.** See display ad this section. ▲

S 156.3 (251.5 km) **A 209.3** (336.8 km) **H 23.2** (37.3 km) **Mugs and Jugs.** See display ad this section.

S 156.7 (252.2 km) **A 209.7** (337.5 km) **H 22.8** (36.7 km) Pay phone and Anchor Point post office at turnoff for North Fork Road which leads east on an 18-mile/29-km loop, rejoining the Sterling Highway at **Milepost S 164.3.** Post office is open 9 A.M. to 5 P.M. weekdays, 9 A.M. to noon on Saturday.

ANCHOR POINT (pop. 1,327) has groceries, gas stations with major repair service, motel, restaurant and fast-food stands, liquor store, clinic, sporting goods, gift shops and ceramic studio. Volunteer fire department and ambulance, phone 911. **Visitor Information:** Located in the log cabin just off the Sterling Highway on Old Sterling Highway. Open 10 A.M. to 4 P.M., Friday through Monday, from Memorial Day weekend through Labor Day. The center is manned by volunteers from Anchor Point Senior Citizens, Inc.

Good Time Charters. See display ad this section.

HAPPY VALLEY
Mile 145.2 Sterling Highway
Grocery Store   Restaurant
Package Store   Motel • Bar
(907) 567-3357

SHORT STOP RV PARKING
Electric Hookups • Dump • Water
Showers • Laundry • Convenience Store
YEAR AROUND LOCKED STORAGE
Resident Owners   (907) 235-5327
MILE 153.2 STERLING HIGHWAY

DEEP CREEK CUSTOM PACKING, Inc.
Custom
Smoking & Canning
Freezing & Shipping
Fresh & Smoked Fish
Vacuum Packing
Ice • Bait
Phone or FAX (907) 567-3395
Mile 137 Sterling Highway

Mugs & Jugs
Original Handpainted Ceramics by Artists in Anchor Point, Alaska
Visitors Welcome...
We Ship Everywhere
Linda Feiler
Box 148
Anchor Point
Alaska 99556
(907) 235-8457
Mile 156.3 STERLING HWY.
ALASKAN GIFTS • CERAMIC STUDIO

Deep Creek Bed & Breakfast
Spectacular area includes views of Mt. Redoubt, bald eagles, whales, and sea otters
Outdoor hot tub and sauna overlooking Cook Inlet.
For reservations call
Tim & Dodi Rebischke
at (907) 567-3567
Mile 140 Sterling Highway
P.O. Box 39544
Ninilchik, Alaska 99639

WHISKEY GULCH TAXIDERMY & FISH & WILDLIFE MUSEUM
See log ad at Mile 152 Sterling Highway

GOOD TIME CHARTERS
Fishing for salmon and halibut on the same trip.
Half day is our specialty
Anchor River departure for less travel time and more fishing time.
Booking Service • Other Charters & Lodging
Office at MILE 156.7 Sterling Highway
TACKLE • GIFTS • T-SHIRTS
For detailed literature, call or write:
(907) 235-8579
P.O. Box 636, Anchor Point, AK 99556

EARLY YEARS MUSEUM
Happy Valley, Alaska 
✓ Histories and information of the area
✓ Beautiful work by local artists
✓ Books about Alaska ...
The historical and true book,
The Pioneers of Happy Valley, Alaska 1944-1964,
by Ella Mae McGann
Rodeo July 4-5, 1992 • 31 years of fun in the sun
ALL OF THIS IN HAPPY VALLEY, ALASKA
MILE 145 Sterling Highway

Anchor River (Beach) Road Log

Turn off the Sterling Highway at **Milepost S 156.9** on to the Old Sterling Highway and continue past the Anchor River Inn to the Anchor River. Just beyond the bridge is the turnoff for Anchor River (Beach) Road, a 1.2-mile/1.9-km spur road providing access to Anchor River recreation area.

Distance from junction (J) is shown.

J 0 Junction of Old Sterling Highway and Sterling Highway at **Milepost S 156.9**.

J 0.1 (0.2 km) School Road. Anchor River visitor information center. A plaque across from the visitor center marks the westernmost point on the contiguous North American Highway system.

Anchor River Inn, overlooking beautiful Anchor River and in business for 20 years, has the finest family restaurant on the peninsula, serving breakfast, lunch and dinner. Smells of fresh-baked bread, cinnamon rolls, delicious pies, etc., fill the dining room from our bakery. Large cocktail lounge has a wide-screen TV, pool tables, dance floor and video games. 20 modern motel units with phones; 10 spacious units with color TV and 2 queen-sized beds, and 10 smaller units overlooking the river. Our new liquor and grocery store serves the Anchor Point area year-round. Both are fully stocked. Write: Box 154, Anchor Point, AK 99556; phone (907) 235-8531. Your hosts: Bob and Simonne Clutts. [ADVERTISEMENT]

J 0.3 (0.5 km) Anchor River bridge, also known as "the erector set bridge."

J 0.4 (0.6 km) Road forks: Old Sterling Highway continues south and rejoins Sterling Highway at **Milepost S 164.9**. Turn right for Anchor River (Beach) Road which follows the Anchor River west and dead ends at Cook Inlet. Viewing platform and plaque at end of road mark the westernmost point you can drive to on the contiguous North American road system.

Silver King state campground (Anchor River State Recreation Area); RV camping, toilets, dumpster, $6 nightly fee or annual pass. Public water source located at the Anchor Angler. At west end of this campground is a special senior/handicapped campground. ▲

Alaska Blue Water Charters. See display ad this section.

Wallin's Hilltop Bed & Breakfast. See display ad this section.

View across Cook Inlet of the Aleutian Range. (Bruce M. Herman)

J 0.6 (1 km) Coho state campground (Anchor River SRA); camping, toilets, $6 nightly fee or annual pass. ▲

J 0.7 (1.1 km) **Silver King Tackle Shop.** See display ad this section.

J 0.8 (1.3 km) Steelhead state campground (Anchor River SRA); camping, toilets, $6 nightly fee or annual pass. ▲

J 1.1 (1.8 km) Slide Hole state campground (Anchor River SRA); camping, toilets, $6 nightly fee or annual pass. ▲

J 1.3 (2.1 km) **Kyllonen's RV Park**, a few steps from famous Anchor River and picturesque Cook Inlet. Providing spring water, electricity and sewer. Additional amenities include fish cleaning station, BBQ pits, free firewood and picnic tables. Showers, restrooms. May through September. Year-round area information center, phone (907) 235-7451. See display ad this section. [ADVERTISEMENT] ▲

J 1.5 (2.4 km) Halibut state campground (Anchor River SRA); camping, toilets, $6 nightly fee or annual pass. ▲

J 1.6 (2.6 km) Road ends on shore of Cook Inlet; beach access, 12-hour parking. Signs here mark the most westerly point on the North American continent accessible by continuous road system and depict outlines of Cook Inlet volcanoes.

The Anchor Point area is noted for seasonal king and silver salmon, steelhead and rainbow fishing. Saltwater trolling for king salmon to 80 lbs., halibut to 200 lbs., spring through fall. **Anchor River**, king salmon fishing permitted only on 5 consecutive weekends, beginning Memorial Day weekend; trout and steelhead from July to October; closed to all fishing December 31 to June 30, except for king salmon weekends. Fishermen report excellent fishing for 12- to 24-inch sea-run Dollies in July and late summer. During the August silver runs, fishing with high tides is usually more productive, because the Anchor River's water level is lower at that time of year.

Anchor River King Salmon Derby is usually held the last weekend in May and the first 3 weekends in June. Prizes for first fish caught and heaviest fish, each weekend, plus a mystery fish special prize. 🐟

Return to Milepost S 156.9 Sterling Highway

GREAT FISHING ON THE ANCHOR RIVER ALL SEASON!
SILVER KING TACKLE SHOP
By Silver King Wayside
Halibut — spring 'til fall • **Kings** from the end of May through June • **Silvers** the middle of August • **Steelhead** fishing all fall • We weigh your fish free • Freezer space available • Drinking water
FREE FISHING INFORMATION
Curly Kelly   Mile S 156.9 Sterling Hwy.

WALLIN'S HILLTOP
BED & BREAKFAST
New Log Home • Spectacular View Sourdough Breakfast
(907) 235-8354 • Mail: P.O. Box 8
Anchor Point, Alaska 99556
Old Sterling Highway and Forest Drive
(Turn at Mile 156.9 Sterling Highway)

KYLLONEN'S RV PARK 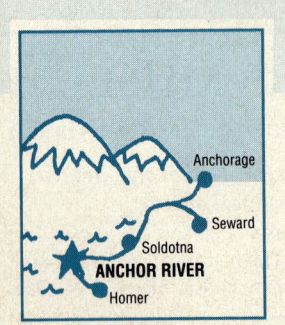
ANCHOR RIVER, ALASKA
★ **AREA INFORMATION CENTER** ★
FULL HOOK-UPS at each site (see log ad)
SPECTACULAR VIEW of COOK INLET, MOUNTAINS & ANCHOR RIVER.
★ The most westerly highway point in North America!
See our log ad at Mile 1.3 Anchor River Road.
P.O. Box 49, Anchor Point, Alaska 99556
Turn on Anchor River Road Mile 156.9 Sterling Highway, drive 1.3 miles. • **(907) 235-7451**

Alaska Blue Water Charters
CUSTOM CHARTERS
Cook Inlet • Kachemak Bay
Explore Alaska's Rich Marine Environments
Halibut and/or Salmon
Sightseeing • Hiking
Captain Roger Watney; USCG Licensed
(907) 235-4063
PO Box 511 • Anchor Point, Alaska 99556

Sterling Highway Log

(continued)

Our Front Porch Bed & Breakfast. See display ad this section.

S 156.8 (252.3 km) A 209.8 (337.6 km) H 22.7 (36.4 km) **Anchor Point Fabric.** See display ad this section.

S 156.9 (252.5 km) A 209.9 (337.8 km) H 22.6 (36.4 km) **Junction** with Old Sterling Highway; access to Anchor River businesses and Anchor River (Beach) Road. See ANCHOR RIVER (BEACH) ROAD log on opposite page.

Anchor River Inn. See display ad this section.

S 157.1 (252.8 km) A 210.1 (338.1 km) H 22.4 (36 km) Anchor River bridge.

S 160.9 (258.9 km) A 213.9 (344.2 km) H 18.6 (29.9 km) Side road to artist Norman Lowell's studio and KWLS radio station.

Norman Lowell Studio & Gallery. See display ad this section.

S 161 (259.1 km) A 214 (344.4 km) H 18.5 (29.8 km) Anchor River bridge.

S 161.5 (259.9 km) A 214.5 (345.2 km) H 18 (29 km) Anchor River State Recreation Site; 9 sites, $6 nightly fee or annual pass, toilets. Large vehicle parking. Large RVs and trailers note: Do not take road to right as you turn in, limited turnaround space. ▲

S 164.3 (264.4 km) A 217.3 (349.7 km) H 15.2 (24.5 km) North Fork Loop Road to Anchor River.

S 164.8 (265.2 km) A 217.8 (350.5 km) H 14.7 (23.7 km) Old Sterling Highway leads 9.4 miles/15.1 km northwest in a loop to Anchor River (Beach) Road, which provides access to Cook Inlet, Anchor River recreation and Anchor Point businesses. See ANCHOR RIVER (BEACH) ROAD log this section and **Milepost S 156.9**.

S 165.4 (266.2 km) A 218.4 (351.5 km) H 14.1 (22.7 km) **Ajagutak–Issuk.** See display ad this section.

S 167.1 (268.9 km) A 220.1 (354.2 km) H 12.4 (20 km) Diamond Ridge Road.

S 168.5 (271.2 km) A 221.5 (356.5 km) H 11 (17.7 km) Alaska State Parks' South

ANCHOR POINT FABRIC
Turn left on Thurmond Drive in Anchor Point
Complete line of Sewing and Quilting Supplies • Quilting Classes
Quilts made to order **(907) 235-8675**
— Fishing Widows Welcome —

VISIT AMERICA'S "LAST" SOUTHERN BAPTIST CHURCH
—Meet the people who live and work in Homer—

ALL DENOMINATIONS WELCOMED
- Come as You Are -

FAITH BAPTIST
Homer, Alaska

▶ *Located on the left of Sterling Highway as you enter Homer*

Sunday School	10:00 A.M.
Worship	11:00 A.M.
Evening Worship	6:00-7:00 P.M.
Wednesday Service	7:00 P.M.

"INFORMAL"
Pastor: **Dr. Greg Pierce**, D. Bible, D. Min.
(907) 235-5319
P.O. Box 2866, Homer, Alaska 99603

Our Front Porch Bed & Breakfast
Rooms - Clean • Quiet - $40 - $50 - $60
3 Miles from Salmon • Halibut • Beaches
In Anchor Point - 3.2 mile North Fork Road
(907) 235-8885
Or write Jim & Donna Toci • PO Box 83, Anchor Point, Alaska 99556

MILE 156.9 STERLING HWY.   *Turn right southbound*   ANCHOR POINT, AK

⚓ ANCHOR RIVER INN ⚓
LARGE PARKING AREA • MAJOR CREDIT CARDS

EXCELLENT RESTAURANT
Breakfast • Lunch • Dinner
FRIENDLY COCKTAIL LOUNGE
Satellite TV • Pool Tables • Video Games
20 MODERN MOTEL UNITS
Large New **LIQUOR STORE**
and **GROCERY STORE**

Bakery • Ice • Film • Telephone
Hosts: Bob & Simonne Clutts
Phone **(907) 235-8531**

Norman Lowell Studio & Gallery

• RESIDENT ARTIST SINCE 1958 •

Alaska's Largest Private Art Gallery

—Also—
Separate Alaska Homestead Museum and Gardens

Mile 160.9, half mile from highway
Large parking area, turnaround

AJAGUTAK-ISSUK
(Rainbow's End)

Beautiful Cottonwood Bark Carvings
Face Masks • Miniatures • Clocks
Custom Knives • Jewelry
All handmade Alaskan art

We invite you to visit our studio – Dave & Dusty Hendren
Milepost S 165.4 Sterling Highway
(halfway between Anchor Point and Homer) • Phone **(907) 235-8881**

BIDARKA INN
Best Western WORLDWIDE LODGING

FINE DINING
COCKTAIL LOUNGE

COLOR TV • PHONES
CONFERENCE FACILITIES
FITNESS CENTER

Phone **(907) 235-8148**
All major Credit Cards accepted

Write: Box 1408, Homer, AK 99603
Located Sterling Highway Mile S 172.5

Bald eagles, often seen in the Homer area, have a wingspan to 8 feet. (Alissa Crandall)

District office is located on the bluff here. A small parking lot is adjacent to the log office where visitors may obtain information on Kachemak Bay state park, as well as other southern Kenai Peninsula state park lands.

S 169 (271.9 km) A 222 (357.2 km) H 10.5 (16.9 km) Homer DOT/PF highway maintenance station.

S 169.6 (272.9 km) A 222.6 (358.2 km) H 9.9 (15.9 km) Two viewpoints overlooking Kachemak Bay.

S 170 (273.6 km) A 223 (358.9 km) H 9.5 (15.3 km) Motel.

S 171.9 (276.6 km) A 224.9 (361.9 km) H 7.6 (12.2 km) West Hill Road.

S 172.3 (277.3 km) A 225.3 (362.6 km) H 7.2 (11.6 km) **Faith Baptist Church.** See display ad on page 469.

S 172.5 (277.6 km) A 225.5 (362.9 km) H 7 (11.3 km) **Bidarka Inn.** See display ad on page 469.

S 172.6 (277.8 km) A 225.6 (363 km) H 6.9 (11.1 km) Homer Junior High School.

S 172.7 (277.9 km) A 225.7 (363.2 km) H 6.8 (10.9 km) **Oceanview RV Park.** See display ad this section. ▲

S 172.8 (278.1 km) A 225.8 (363.4 km) H 6.7 (10.8 km) Exit onto Pioneer Avenue for downtown **HOMER** (description follows). Drive 0.2 mile/0.3 km on Pioneer Avenue and turn left on Bartlett Avenue for the Pratt Museum (see Attractions in the Homer section) and Homer city campground (follow signs). Pioneer Avenue continues through downtown Homer to Lake Street and to East Hill Road. ▲

S 173.1 (278.6 km) A 226.1 (363.9 km) H 6.4 (10.3 km) Main Street, access to food, lodging and other services. Bishop's Beach Park.

S 173.5 (279.2 km) A 226.5 (364.5 km) H 6 (9.7 km) Eagle Quality Center; shopping, groceries.

S 173.7 (279.5 km) A 226.7 (364.8 km) H 5.8 (9.3 km) Heath Street. Post office.

S 173.9 (279.9 km) A 226.9 (365.2 km) H 5.6 (9 km) Lake Street. Access to downtown Homer and Lakeside Center.

S 174 (280 km) A 227 (365.3 km) H 5.5 (8.9 km) Beluga Lake floatplane base.

S 174.4 (280.7 km) A 227.4 (366 km) H 5.1 (8.2 km) Lambert Lane, access to floatplane base.

S 174.7 (281.1 km) A 227.7 (366.4 km) H 4.8 (7.7 km) Alaska Dept. of Fish and Game office.

S 175 (281.6 km) A 228 (366.9 km) H 4.5 (7.2 km) Airport Road. Sterling Highway crosses onto Homer Spit.

A series of boardwalks along the Spit house shops, charter services, food outlets, etc. Also on the Spit: A Chamber of Commerce Visitor Center, private campgrounds, and public camping areas (check-in with camping registration office at visitor center); the harbormaster's office and a boat ramp. ▲

S 179.5 (288.9 km) A 232.5 (374.2 km) H 0 Sterling Highway ends at Land's End Resort and Campground at the tip of Homer Spit.

Homer

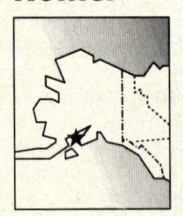

Located on the southwestern Kenai Peninsula on the north shore of Kachemak Bay at the easterly side of the mouth of Cook Inlet; 226 miles/364 km by highway or 40 minutes by jet aircraft from Anchorage. **Population:** 4,000. **Emergency Services:** Phone 911 for all emergency services. **City Police**, phone 235-3150. **Alaska State Troopers**, in the Public Safety Bldg., phone 235-8239. **Fire Department** and **Ambulance**, phone 235-3155. **Coast Guard**, phone Zenith 5555. (Coast Guard Auxiliary, phone 235-7277.) **Hospital**, South Peninsula, phone 235-8101. **Veterinary Clinic**, phone 235-8960.

Visitor Information: Chamber of commerce office is located on Homer Spit. Open from Memorial Day to Labor Day. Contact the Homer Chamber of Commerce, Box 541, Homer 99603; phone during business hours 235-7740 or (summer only) 235-5300.

The Pratt Museum Visitor Information Center is open daily 10 A.M. to 6 P.M. from May through September; open noon to 5 P.M. Tuesday through Sunday from October through April; closed in January. Contact the Pratt Museum, 3779 Bartlett St., Homer 99603. Phone 235-8635.

Elevation: Sea level to 800 feet/244m. **Climate:** Winter temperatures occasionally fall below zero, but seldom colder. The Kenai Mountains north and east protect Homer from severe cold, and Cook Inlet provides warming air currents. The highest temperature recorded is 81°F/27°C. Average annual precipitation is 27.9 inches. Prevailing winds are from the northeast, averaging 6.5 mph/10.5 kmph. **Radio:** KGTL 620, KWAV 103.5/104.9/106.3, MBN-FM 107.1/96.7/95.3, KBBI 890, KPEN-FM 99.3/100.9/102.3, KWHQ-FM 98.3. **Television:** KENI Channel 2, KTVA Channel 4, KAKM Channel 7, KIMO Channel 13. **Newspaper:**

LAKEWOOD INN

- Family Suites • Kitchens
- Private Baths • Phones
- Cable TV • HBO
- Major Credit Cards
- Excellent Restaurant
- Lounge
- Convention / Meeting Rooms

984 Ocean Drive, Homer, Alaska 99603
Call (907) 235-6144 • FAX (907) 235-6774
1-800-478-LAKE in Alaska

Flo's B & B
Full Fishermen's Breakfast
Clean, Quiet Residential Area
Downtown • (907) 235-2516
P.O. Box 1081, Homer, AK 99603

O·C·E·A·N·V·I·E·W R·V P·A·R·K
Spectacular View of Kachemak Bay with Beach Front Setting
Full and Partial Hookups • Pull-thru Spaces • Level
Gift Shop • Visitor Information
Picnic Area • Restrooms • Showers • Laundry
Dump Station • Cable TV • Pay Phone
Walking distance to Downtown
See log ad under Accommodations

Special Charter Rates for RV Park Guests • Caravans Welcome
Phone (907) 235-3951

MILE 172.7 Sterling Highway • P.O. Box 891, Homer, Alaska 99603
VISA, MasterCard Accepted

HALCYON HEIGHTS B & B
61850 Mission Avenue

- Tranquil / Deluxe Rooms
- View of Kachemak Bay and the Kenai Mountain Range
- Royal Continental Breakfast

Life-time Alaskan Hostess
Bob and Gail Ammerman
P.O. Box 3552
Homer, AK 99603 **(907) 235-2148**

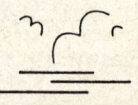

Homer News (weekly).

Private Aircraft: Homer airport, 1.7 miles/2.7 km east; elev. 78 feet/24m; length 7,400 feet/2,255m; asphalt; fuel 80, 100.

In the late 1800s, a coal mine was operating at Homer's Bluff Point and a railroad carried the coal out to the end of Homer Spit. (The railroad was abandoned in 1907.) Gold seekers debarked at Homer, bound for the goldfields at Hope and Sunrise. The community of Homer was established about 1896 and named for Homer Pennock.

Coal mining operations ceased about WWI, but settlers continued to trickle into the area, some to homestead, others to work in the canneries built to process Cook Inlet fish.

Today, Homer's picturesque setting, mild climate and great fishing (especially for halibut) attract thousands of visitors each year. In addition to its tourist industry and role as a trade center, Homer's commercial fishing industry is an important part of its economy. Homer calls itself the "Halibut Fishing Capital of the World." Manufacturing and seafood processing, government offices, trades and construction are other key industries.

Rising behind the townsite are the gently sloping bluffs which level off at about 1,200 feet/366m to form the southern rim of the western plateau of the Kenai. These green slopes are tinted in pastel shades by acres of wildflowers from June to September; fireweed predominates among scattered patches of geranium, paintbrush, lupine, rose and many other species. Two main roads (East Hill Road and West Hill Road) lead from the Homer business section to the "Skyline Drive" along the rim of the bluffs, and other roads connect with many homesteads on the "Hill."

The name *Kachemak* (in Aleut dialect said to mean "smoky bay") was supposedly derived from the smoke which once rose from the smoldering coal seams jutting from the clay bluffs of the upper north shore of Kachemak Bay and the cliffs near Anchor Point. In the early days many of the exposed coal seams were slowly burning from causes unknown. Today the erosion of these bluffs drops huge fragments of lignite and bituminous coal on the beaches, creating a plentiful supply of winter fuel for the residents. There are an estimated 400,000,000 tons of coal deposit in the immediate vicinity of Homer.

Kachemak is a magnificent deep-water bay that reaches inland from Cook Inlet for 30 miles/48.3 km, with an average width of 7 miles/11.3 km. The bay is rich in marine life. The wild timbered coastline of the south shore, across from Homer, is indented with

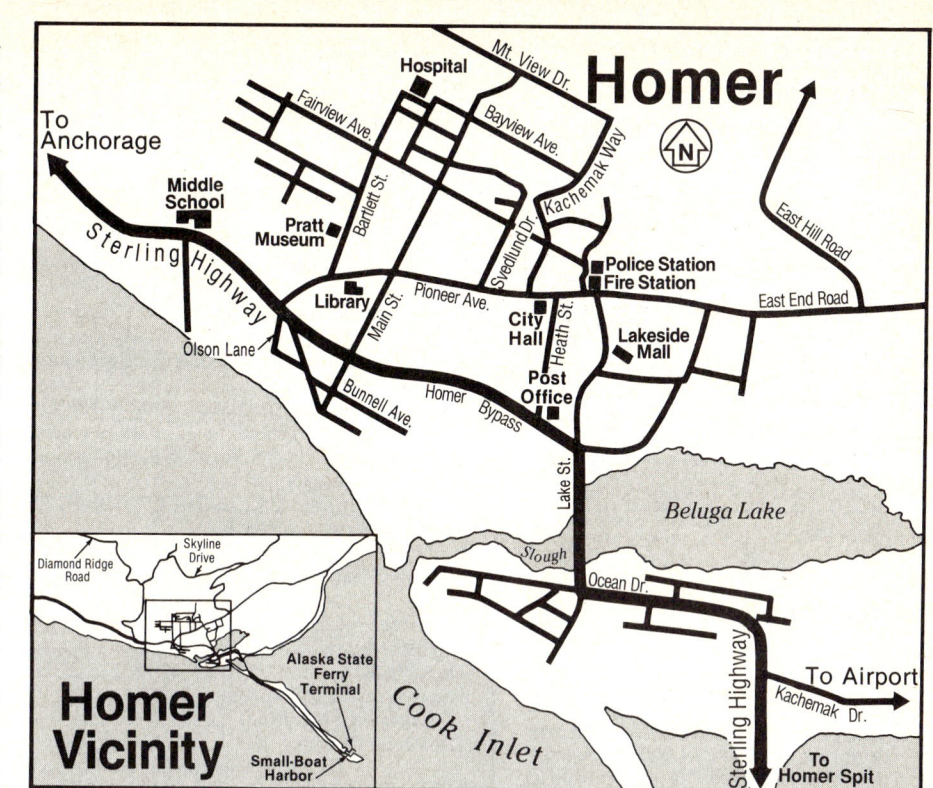

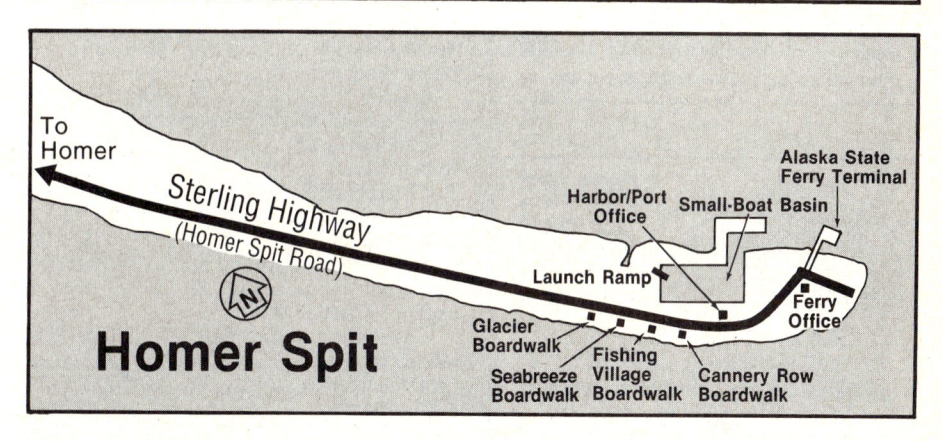

HALIBUT COVE CABINS
Two cozy cabins that sleep four, with kitchens, heat stoves, and a great view. Boat or plane access only. Bring your favorite foods and sleeping bags. Shower and phone available. Ask about Kayaks.
Summer: (907) 296-2214 Winter (808) 322-4110
Agent: (907) 235-7847
or write: **HALIBUT COVE CABINS, Inc.**
P.O. Box 1990, Homer, AK 99603

BAY VIEW INN
HOMER, ALASKA
Spectacular View from Clean, Attractive Rooms
Quiet Setting • Comfortable Beds • Kitchenettes
See our ad under accommodations
Box 804, Homer, Alaska 99603 **235-8485**

Driftwood Inn
Charming, Historic, B&B
Beachfront Hotel/Motel

Color TV, In-Room Movies
Reasonable Rates
Open Year-Round

135 W. Bunnell Ave., MP
Homer, AK 99603
(907) 235-8019
In AK 1-800-478-8019

See Log Ad under Accommodations

KACHEMAK KIANA
Bed and Breakfast

P.O. Box 855, Homer, AK 99603

Phone: (907) 235-8824

MILE 5, East Road   Great View

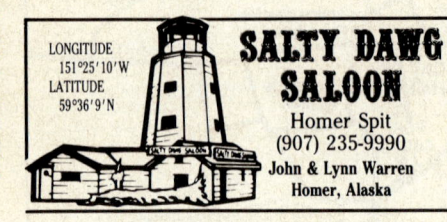

SALTY DAWG SALOON

LONGITUDE 151°25'10"W
LATITUDE 59°36'9"N

Homer Spit
(907) 235-9990

John & Lynn Warren
Homer, Alaska

WOODSIDE
Quiet Nights
300 Woodside, No. 1
Homer, AK 99603

(907) 235-8389

at **WOODSIDE APTS. and B&B**
overlooking Kachemak Bay & Kenai Mountains

Plush, spacious furnished apartments with sparkling kitchens and bathrooms, dishes, pans, linens, phones and cable TV. Bed & breakfast rooms available also. Nestled in a little woods in downtown Homer.

VISA / MasterCard

Affordable Nightly & Weekly Rates   (see log)

SPRUCE ACRES
Bed & Breakfast
Cabins in Homer

Cozy and Comfortable • Private
NO SMOKING or ALCOHOL
Country Decor • Continental Breakfast
Private Baths • Kitchenettes • TV

For more information: John and Joyce Williams

In Town   **(907) 235-8388**
Daily and   910 Sterling Hwy.
Weekly Rates   Homer, AK 99603

HOMER ADVERTISERS

A-1 Charters......................Ph. (907) 235-3929
Alaska Fishing Charters ....Ph. (907) 235-6468
Alaska Maritime
   Tours, Inc. ....Dockside Bldg., Homer Spit
Alaska Wild Berry
   Products ....528 E. Pioneer Ave.
Arctic Wolf Gallery/Snow
   Geese Originals................510 Pioneer Ave.
Bay View Inn ....Mile 170 Sterling Hwy.
Boardwalk Variety ....Cannery Row Boardwalk, Homer Spit
Bookstore, The.................Eagle Quality Center
Brass Ring Bed and
   Breakfast...............................987 Hillfair Ct.
Captain Mike's Charters ....Cannery Row Boardwalk, Homer Spit
Center for Alaskan
   Coastal Studies ....Ph. (907) 235-7272
Central Charters Booking
   Agency ....Ph. (907) 235-7847
Cie' Jae Ocean Charters ....Fishing Village Boardwalk, Homer Spit
Dockside.........................4460 Homer Spit Rd.
Driftwood Inn ....135 W. Bunnell Ave.
Flo's B & B ....Ph. (907) 235-2516
Fresh Sourdough Express
   Bakery & Restaurant ....1316 Ocean Dr.
Greatland Charters ....Fishing Village Boardwalk, Homer Spit
Halcyon Heights B & B .....Ph. (907) 235-2148
Halibut Cove Cabins....................Halibut Cove
Heritage Hotel ....Ph. (907) 235-7787
Homer Bed and
   Breakfast........................Ph. (907) 235-8996
Homer Chamber of Commerce Jackpot
   Halibut Derby ....Ph. (907) 235-7740
Homer Ocean
   Charters, Inc........Cannery Row, Homer Spit
Homer Referral
   Agency ....Ph. (907) 235-8996
Homer Spit Campground ....Homer Spit
Homer Vacations ....Ph. (907) 235-2575
Homer Vacations &
   Conventions.....Dockside Bldg., Homer Spit
Inlet Charters....................Ph. (907) 235-6126
J & D Charters...................Ph. (907) 235-2524
K-Bay Charters...........................Fishing Village Boardwalk, Homer Spit
Kachemak Bay Adventures
   Boat Tours ....Ph. (907) 235-8206

Kachemak Gear
   Shed II........................3815 Homer Spit Rd.
Kachemak Kiana Bed and
   Breakfast......................Ph. (907) 235-8824
Lakewood Inn ....Lake St. & Ocean Dr.
Land's End Resort ....End of Homer Spit
Land's End RV Park ....End of Homer Spit
Lucky Pierre
   Charters ......Glacier Boardwalk, Homer Spit
Mama Bear's
   Loft..................At Sportsman Marine Supply
Mary's Corner Kitchen.................Old Cannery Row Boardwalk, Homer Spit
North Country Halibut Charters ....Cannery Row Boardwalk, Homer Spit
Ocean Shores Motel ....3500 Crittenden Dr.
Oceanview RV Park...........Ph. (907) 235-3951
Picture Alaska ....395 E. Pioneer Ave.
Pier One
   Theatre ....Homer Spit, City Warehouse
Pioneer Bed &
   Breakfast ....243 Pioneer Ave.
Pratt Museum ....3779 Bartlett St.
Ptarmigan Arts ....471 Pioneer Ave.
Quiet Sports ....144 W. Pioneer Ave.
Rainbow Tours ....Cannery Row Boardwalk
Raven Marine Charters..................Homer Spit
Ridgetop Bed and
   Breakfast.......................Ph. (907) 235-7590
Salt Water Charters ....Ph. (907) 235-8337
Salty Dawg Saloon.........................Homer Spit
Samer-I
   Seafoods......Glacier Boardwalk, Homer Spit
Seaside Farm Bed and
   Breakfast....................Mile 4.5 East End Rd.
Silver Fox Charters........................Homer Spit
Sports N Wear ....Mile 2.3 East End Rd.
Sportsman Marine
   Supply Inc. ....Homer Spit
Spruce Acres Bed &
   Breakfast.......................Ph. (907) 235-8338
Stardust Charters..............Ph. (907) 235-6820
Subway ....Lake St. & Pioneer Ave.
Sunny Chevron Service ....Pioneer Ave.
West Hill Bed &
   Breakfast.......................Ph. (907) 235-2406
Wild Rose
   Bed & Breakfast...........Ph. (907) 235-8780
Woodside Apartments and Woodside
   Bed & Breakfast...........Ph. (907) 235-8389

HERITAGE HOTEL — DOWNTOWN HOMER

45 ROOMS • Reasonable Rates • In-Room Movies • Satellite Color TV Phones
Courtesy Coffee and Tea

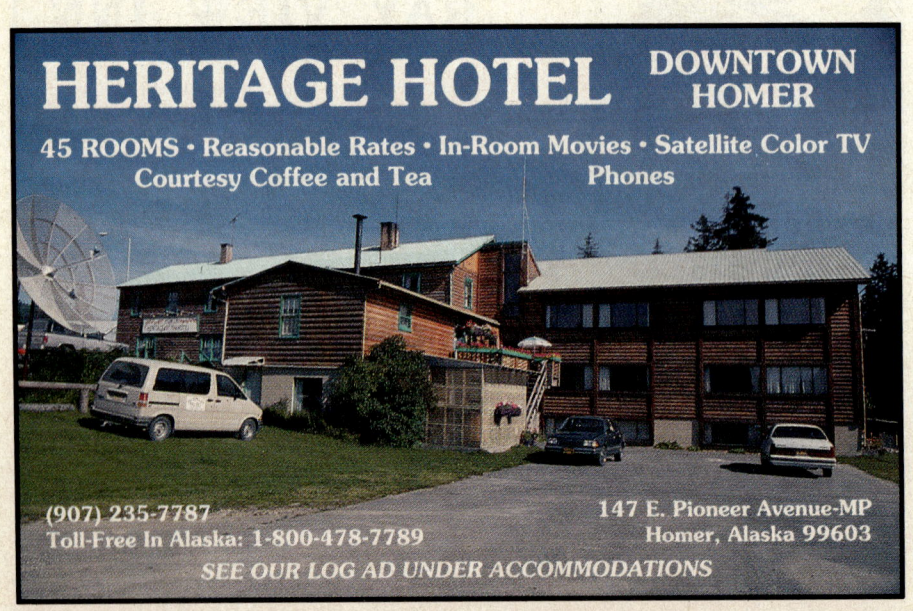

(907) 235-7787
Toll-Free In Alaska: 1-800-478-7789

147 E. Pioneer Avenue-MP
Homer, Alaska 99603

SEE OUR LOG AD UNDER ACCOMMODATIONS

BAG A BIG ONE.

Ask for your favorite Subway sub as a Super Sub and you'll get twice the meat. We'll pile it high on fresh baked bread and stuff it with free fixin's. 6" or footlong, get it on the double at Subway.

235-2782 • Two Locations: 637 East Pioneer and behind The Salty Dawg, Homer Spit

SUBWAY

many fjords and inlets, reaching far into the rugged glacier-capped peaks of the Kenai Mountains.

Jutting out for nearly 5 miles/8 km from the Homer shore is the Homer Spit, a long, narrow bar of gravel. The road along the backbone of the Spit connects with the main road through Homer (all the Sterling Highway). The Spit has had quite a history and it continues to be a center of activity for the town. In 1964, after the earthquake, the Spit sank 4 to 6 feet, requiring several buildings to be moved to higher ground. Today, the Spit is the site of a major dock facility for boat loading, unloading, servicing and refrigerating. The deep-water dock can accommodate up to 2 340-foot vessels with 30-foot drafts at the same time, making it accessible to cruise and cargo ships. The small-boat harbor on the Spit has a 5-lane load/launch ramp. Also in the small-boat harbor area are the harbormaster's office, canneries, parking/camping areas, charter services, small shops, restaurants and a motel.

In summer, Homer Spit bustles with activity: People fish from its shores for king salmon; fishermen come and go in their boats; cars, trucks and trailers line the road; tent camps are set up on the beach; and boat builders and repairers are busy at their craft. Fresh crab, shrimp and halibut, as well as smoked fish, can be purchased from seafood shops on the Spit or sometimes from the fishermen themselves. Seafood processors on Homer Spit offer custom smoking, freezing and air shipping for sport-caught fish. It is also possible to trade your sport-caught fish for similar fish already processed and ready to ship or take with you.

Busy Homer Spit is packed with boats and RVs in summer. (Jerrianne Lowther, staff)

ACCOMMODATIONS

Homer has hundreds of small businesses offering a wide variety of goods and services. There are many hotels, motels and bed and breakfasts for lodging. Nearly 40 restaurants offer meals ranging from fast food to fine dining. Travelers are advised to book overnight accommodations well in advance during the busy summer months. Homer has a post office, library, museum, laundromats, gas stations with propane and dump stations, 4 banks and a hospital. There are many boat charters, boat repair and storage facilities, marine fuel at Homer marina, bait, tackle and sporting goods stores, and also art galleries, gift shops and groceries.

Homer Spit has both long-term parking and camping. Camping and parking areas are well-marked. Camping fees are $7 per night for RVs and $3 per night for tents. Camping permits are available at the Chamber of Commerce Visitor Center on the Spit. There is a 14-day limit; restrooms, water and garbage available. Check with the harbormaster's office or the Chamber of Commerce Visitor Center on the Spit if you have ques-

HOMER
HALIBUT FISHING CAPITAL OF THE WORLD!

HOMER JACKPOT HALIBUT DERBY

MAY 1ST thru LABOR DAY
OVER $60,000 IN PRIZES. (MONTHLY PRIZES, TAGGED FISH & JACKPOT PRIZE!)
Last year's winner: $18,434.

HOMER IS A UNIQUE AND EXCITING FULL SERVICE COMMUNITY

Homer Chamber of Commerce

For additional information, please call or write:
Homer Chamber of Commerce
P.O. Box 541, Homer, AK 99603-0541
(907) 235-7740

Sportsman Marine Supply, Inc.

Follow the Bear Tracks to **MAMA BEAR'S LOFT** upstairs at **SPORTSMAN MARINE SUPPLY, INC.**

The **GENERAL STORE** on Homer Spit

Distributors for **THOMAS SPINNING LURES**
In Alaska Call 1-800-478-LURE

- Groceries • Package Liquor
- Ice • Fishing Licenses
- Sundries • Clothing • T-Shirts
- Marine & Regular Hardware
- Camping Supplies • Souvenirs

HEADQUARTERS FOR FISHING TACKLE & CHARTER SERVICE

Been Halibut Fishing Yet?

Raven Marine Charters
For the discriminating fisherman

SUCCESS is our business
Halibut
(907) 235-8918 • 235-6430
4400 Homer Spit Road
At the **GENERAL STORE** on the spit
See our log ad on Mama Bear's Loft under Attractions

tions on rules and regulations pertaining to camping, campfires, long-term parking, boat launching and moorage. Homer City Campground, on a hill overlooking town, is reached via Bartlett Avenue (follow signs). ▲

Following are paid advertisements for campgrounds, lodging, restaurants, and food, gift, clothing and equipment outlets. A number of other services and stores are listed under Attractions.

Homer Spit Campground, at the end of the Homer Spit. Shore fishing, crabbing, clamming, beachcombing within a minute's walk. Clean restrooms, plenty of hot water for showers. Electrical hookups, dump station and cheerful complete visitor information. Reservations advised. Headquarters for Kachemak Bay Adventures Boat Tours. Ask about puffin-viewing trips to Gull Island and Seldovia aboard our 60-foot MV *Endeavor*. Campground, boat tour packages. Box 1196, Homer, AK 99603; phone (907) 235-8206. [ADVERTISEMENT] ▲

Land's End RV Park. On the water's edge, at the tip of Homer Spit. Truly the most spectacular spot on the Kenai Peninsula. Gorgeous mountain views and sunsets. Minutes from the Spit's boardwalks and small-boat harbor. Electric hookups, laundry, $howers, ice, sundries. Open May through September. (907) 235-2525. P.O. Box 273, Homer, AK 99603. [ADVERTISEMENT] ▲

Oceanview RV Park (Good Sam Park) just past Best Western Bidarka Inn on your right coming into Homer. Spectacular view of Kachemak Bay, beachfront setting. 85 large pull-through spaces in terraced park. Full/partial hookups, restrooms, showers, laundry, pay phone, cable TV, picnic area. Walking distance to downtown Homer. Special halibut charter rates for park guests. Phone (907) 235-3951. See display ad at Mile 172.7 Sterling Highway. [ADVERTISEMENT] ▲

Bay View Inn, top of the hill as you enter Homer. Spectacular panoramic view. Every room overlooking Kachemak Bay and the Kenai Mountains. Clean, attractive rooms with firm, comfortable beds and private bathrooms. Options: kitchenettes, suite with fireplace, and secluded honeymoon cottage. Picturesque, quiet setting with picnic tables and lawn. Friendly, personal service with local tour information and activity recommendations. Fresh morning coffee. Mile 170 Sterling Highway. P.O. Box 804, Homer, AK 99603. Phone (907) 235-8485. See display ad this section. [ADVERTISEMENT]

Brass Ring Bed and Breakfast is a beautiful custom log home nestled in a quiet stand of spruce trees within walking distance of shops and restaurants. Our 7 guest rooms, each with a different theme, are decorated with Norwegian stenciling, antiques and quilts. A large country kitchen is the setting for the sumptuous breakfasts with emphasis on Alaskan entrees and a friendly atmosphere. Enjoy our outdoor spa tub! No smoking or pets, children 6 and older welcome. Rates after May 15, $60 and $65. 987 Hillfair Court, Homer, AK 99603. (907) 235-5450. [ADVERTISEMENT]

Dockside. You'll find it all at Dockside, 4460 Homer Spit Road. Gift shop features made-in-Alaska gifts and souvenirs. Full deli specializes in homemade chowders, fresh baked muffins, charter and picnic lunches. Cook your catch BBQ-style overlooking Homer boat harbor, salad bar provided. Convenient RV parking, pay phone, newsstand.

HOMER REFERRAL AGENCY
Referrals for fishing charters and other Bed & Breakfasts
Land Tours
Bus • Van • Limo
Brochures Available

HOMER BED & BREAKFAST
SEEKINS — Floyd & Gert
Fantastic View — Clean - Quiet
Friendly Alaskan Hospitality
Phone: (907) 235-8996 or 235-8998
Box 1264 • Homer, Alaska 99603
See our log ad

Completely furnished apartments for rent. Daily Rates.

WEST HILL BED & BREAKFAST
Kitchenettes • Private Bath
Satellite TV • Generous Breakfast
Opening June 1, 1992
(907) 235-2406   Hosts: Arn & Kathy Johnson
PO Box 2403, Homer, Alaska 99603

GREATLAND CHARTERS
"Fishin' is The Mission at **GREATLAND CHARTERS**"

Come and join us for a day of fun-filled fishing for the Mighty Halibut

Make Reservations Now
Summer (907) 235-6222
Winter (907) 283-7109

PO Box 3081, Kenai, Alaska 99611

Office: 4025 Homer Spit Road #17
Homer, Alaska 99603

FUN IN HOMER!
at Alaska Wild Berry Products

Delicious JAMS, JELLIES & WILD BERRY CANDIES

No visit to Alaska Wild Berry would be complete without a pause at the taster's stand, where you can dip into savory, free samples of jams and jellies. How about a slice of fresh fudge or Wild Berry candy? (Taster's stand open May - September.)

Watch the action in our kitchen through glassed in observation points.

GIFT SHOP & ALASKAN RELICS

Take some time to browse through our unique gift shop, featuring fine jewelry, souvenirs, and Alaska crafts. Also view the fascinating bits of Alaska's rich heritage collected over our 40 years in business in Homer.

VISIT US SOON!

Alaska Wild Berry Products is located in Homer on Beautiful Kachemak Bay at the southern tip of the Kenai Peninsula. The drive south from Anchorage takes you through some of the most spectacular countryside in America. Once in Homer, turn left onto Pioneer Avenue and look for our log cabin store. We'll be waiting to greet you.

Don't leave Homer without it!!

Alaska Wild Berry Products

Large parking lot. Picnic area. Open year round. Long summer hours. 7 days a week. For more information call 907-235-8858 or for free mail order catalog write Alaska Wild Berry Products, 528 E. Pioneer Ave., Homer, Alaska 99603. And in Anchorage at the Dimond Center Mall, next to Kay-Bee Toys, overlooking the ice rink. 907-349-5984.

KENAI PENINSULA • HOMER

HALIBUT FISHING
WILDLIFE TOURS • LODGING

"Largest Fishing Fleet in Homer"

Enjoy a day of Halibut Fishing on the protected waters of Kachemak Bay and Lower Cook Inlet

Fast, clean, heated cabin cruisers with restrooms Friendly, Professional Captain and Crew to help you Bring In The **"BIG ONE"**

U.S. Coast Guard Licensed and insured boats and crews

Member - Homer Charter Association

Caught on Sea Katch. Homer Jackpot Halibut Derby Winner 312½ lb. Halibut —1990

VISIT OUR STORE
T-SHIRTS
GIFTS
SOUVENIRS
FISHING LICENSE
DERBY TICKETS

ALSO:
WE ARRANGE LODGING IN HOMER
OVER 500 ROOMS
QUAINT, FRIENDLY, FULL SERVICE HOTELS
BED & BREAKFAST HOMES

No Extra Charge For Booking Service

HALIBUT COVE
For a MILEPOST on your Alaskan Adventure Don't miss your trip on the **KACHEMAK BAY FERRY**

"Gateway to Halibut Cove"   Since 1966

Cruise around Gull Island for a thrilling view of the birds and sea life. The Kachemak Bay Ferry is a longtime tradition in Kachemak Bay enjoyed by Alaskans and visitors alike.

While in the cove, stroll the 12 blocks of boardwalk connecting the homes and businesses of local artists. Visit galleries featuring octopus ink paintings, sculptors, pottery and much more.

Take the "Phenomenal tree walk". You may even meet a "mama llama". Get a close-up view of special Alaskan lifestyle.

For a most unique culinary experience Visit **"The Saltry"**
• Seafood • Red Hook Ale on tap
Reservations required

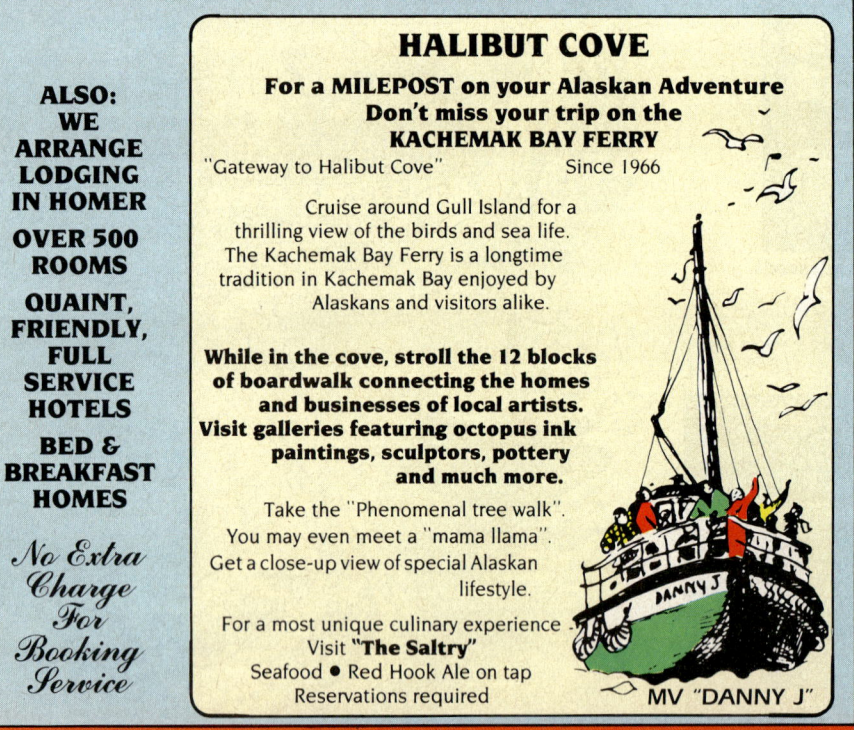

MV "DANNY J"

"THE CENTER OF IT ALL IN HOMER"
LOCALLY OWNED & OPERATED SINCE 1981

CENTRAL CHARTERS
BOOKING AGENCY
MAY through SEPTEMBER
In Alaska Call 1-800-478-7847
or Write 4241 Homer Spit Road, Homer, AK 99603
FOR INFORMATIONS & RESERVATIONS (907) 235-7847

Stop by Dockside for information and reservations on halibut charters, birding and natural history tours of Kachemak Bay. Group rates available. Open May–October. (907) 235-8337. See display ads for Dockside, Alaska Maritime Tours and Homer Vacations and Conventions. [ADVERTISEMENT].

Driftwood Inn. Charming, historic beachfront hotel/motel, B&B, RV parking. Spectacular view overlooking beautiful Kachemak Bay, mountains, glaciers. Quiet downtown location. Completely renovated, color TVs, in-room movies, immaculately clean, unique rooms, reasonable rates. Free coffee, tea, local pickup/delivery, local information center. Comfortable common areas with TV, fireplace, library, microwave, refrigerator, barbecue, shellfish cooker, fish cleaning area, freezer, picnic and laundry facilities. Continental breakfast available. Friendly, knowledgeable staff, specializing in helping make your stay in Homer the best possible. Rates $40-$80 single, $7 per additional person over age 12. Open year-round. Write, call for brochure. 135 W. Bunnell Ave., MP, Homer, AK 99603. (907) 235-8019. In Alaska 1-800-478-8019. [ADVERTISEMENT]

Fresh Sourdough Express Bakery & Restaurant. Come, enjoy our cozy restaurant on the way to Homer Spit. Warm, friendly atmosphere. We grind our flour fresh daily for highest quality. Sourdough breads and bagels. Gourmet full-line bakery. Healthy, hearty breakfast, lunch and dinners specializing in all-you-can-eat seafood barbecue. Fine beer and wine. Charter lunches and special orders. Fresh ground coffee and cappuccino. (907) 235-7571. [ADVERTISEMENT]

Heritage Hotel. One of Alaska's finest log hotels, conveniently located in the heart of Homer. Walking distance to beach, shops, museum. Accommodations: 36 rooms including suite with wet bar. Reasonable rates. In-room movies, satellite TV, phones, courtesy coffee-tea, airport shuttle. Restaurant on premises. Alaskan hospitality and decor greet you in our spacious lobby. Open

Inlet Charters

HALIBUT FISHING
KING SALMON TROLLING
Marine Wildlife Tours
Lodging • Vacation Packages
Reasonalbe rates for any size group

Experienced, professional Coast Guard licensed guides

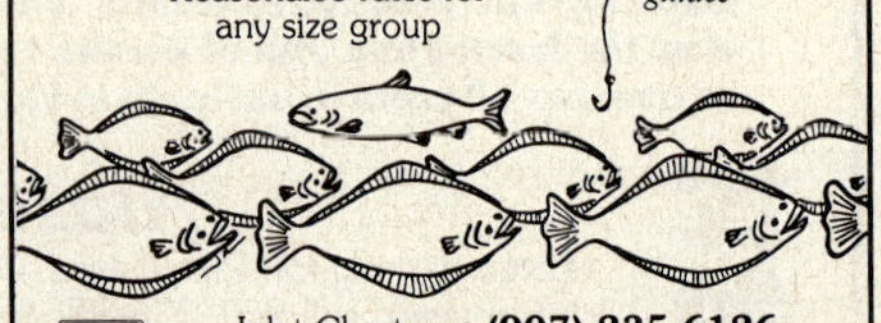

Inlet Charters • **(907) 235-6126**
P.O. Box 2083, Homer, AK 99603
Toll-free In Alaska **1-800-478-0026**

year-round. 147 E. Pioneer Ave., phone (907) 235-7787, toll free in Alaska 1-800-478-7789. See display ad this section. [ADVERTISEMENT]

Homer B&B/Seekins: Located 2 miles up East Hill on Race Road. Spectacular view of Kachemak Bay, glacier, snow-covered mountains. Private bath, color TV. Kitchen completely furnished, coffee, tea, popcorn and popper, dishes. Yummy breakfasts. Wildflowers, occasional moose, outdoor wood-heated sauna. Fishing charters, halibut, salmon, full/half days. Land tours. Reasonable rates, clean, fantastic view, Alaskan hospitality. Your hosts, Floyd and Gert, moved to Homer in 1969 from Wisconsin and Minnesota. Box 1264, Homer, AK 99603. (907) 235-8996 or 235-8998. [ADVERTISEMENT]

Land's End Resort. Homer Spit's only hotel, located on the water's edge, at the end of Homer Spit Road. Breathtaking views of Kachemak Bay and the rugged peaks and glaciers of the Kenai Mountains. Fine dining at reasonable prices in one of Alaska's premier restaurants. Breakfast, lunch or dinner. Homer's favorite Sunday brunch! Rooms from $75. Color TVs, phones, private decks, entertainment. Truly an Alaskan landmark! (907) 235-2500. P.O. Box 273, Homer, AK 99603. [ADVERTISEMENT]

Mama Bear's Loft. Mama Bear has a way of taking care of everyone's needs. From the fisherman to the grandkids, she has it all. Foul weather gear, housewares, camping and RV equipment. Her selection of T-shirts, sweatshirts, souvenirs and gifts is "beary" complete. Mama Bear carries Woolrich, Prentiss and other brand-name clothing, and she doesn't stop there. Her handmade rag dolls and bears will delight every member of the family. See Mama Bear's wares in the loft upstairs at the General Store on Homer Spit. Just follow the bear tracks. (See our display ad under Sportsman Marine Supply.) [ADVERTISEMENT]

Mary's Corner Kitchen. A cozy corner with a great view. Hearty to-go lunches for any of your outdoor adventures. Open early to accommodate the fisherman. Home of Mary's famous giant chocolate chip cookies. Watch for the advertising dog. Open summers, 7 days a week, 5:30 A.M. to 7 P.M. Call (907) 235-6603 or 235-8348. Located in Captain Mike's Charter Building. [ADVERTISEMENT]

Ocean Shores Motel. Beachfront property, 2 blocks to downtown. $40 to $90. Conventional motel rooms, kitchens, also available. Spectacular views, acres of grass, flowers, picnic tables and fenced playground for children. Centrally located for fishing and sightseeing. (907) 235-7775 or 1-800-456-5593. Write: 3500-M Crittenden Dr., Homer, AK 99603. [ADVERTISEMENT]

BOARDWALK VARIETY
GIFTS • SOUVENIRS
GIFTS 'N THINGS
THE BIGGEST LITTLE SHOP ON THE SPIT
Your best bet for a selection at reasonable prices
SOUVENIRS • T-SHIRTS • HATS • CERAMICS
JEWELRY • LOCAL CRAFTS • LOTS MORE!
Stop by and see us on the Cannery Row Boardwalk before you buy Alaskan gifts
HOMER SPIT
SUMMER HOURS: 9 to 9 • PH: (907) 235-8206

HOMER SPIT CAMPGROUND (See our log ad)
...At the harbor...At the beach
Campers • Trailers • Tents
Reservations Accepted • (907) 235-8206
BOX 1196 • HOMER, ALASKA 99603

STARDUST HALIBUT CHARTERS
Bed & Breakfast Retreat
World-Class Halibut Fishing... Overnight Trips
Bed & Breakfast Retreat, MILE 11 Scenic East End Road   Special Package Rates
Spacious Private Rooms • Homecooked Breakfast • Alaskan Hospitality
(907) 235-6820 • P.O. Box 625M, Homer, Alaska 99603 • (907) 235-7077

Wild Rose BED & BREAKFAST
Quiet, restful... • 5010 E. Hill Road •
Just 2 miles from downtown Homer overlooking beautiful Kachemak Bay
Enjoy freshly baked full breakfasts
LONG-TIME ALASKAN HOSTS,   (907) 235-8780
BOB AND ANNE HAYNES   Box 665, Homer, Alaska 99603

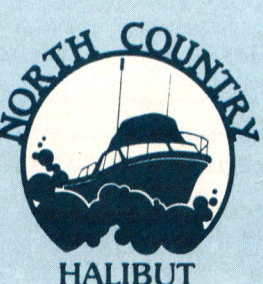

NORTH COUNTRY HALIBUT CHARTERS
Halibut Fishing
Professional Fishing Guides
• 5 Comfortable Boats
• Enclosed Heated Cabins, Full Restroom Facilities
• All Equipment, Bait and Fish Cleaning Included
• 10-12-Hour Fishing Trips

Celebrating Quality Catches Since 1979

RESERVATIONS REQUIRED
PO Box 889-M, Homer, Alaska 99603
(907) 235-7620

Kachemak Bay Adventures Boat Tours

* Marine Life Excursions
* Sightseeing Cruises
* Fishing Charters
* Custom Trips
* Discounts available

Sail aboard the comfortable 60' ENDEAVOR for an exciting journey on beautiful Kachemak Bay. View breathtaking glaciers, mountains, and ocean scenery with abundant waterfowl and sealife. Captain Le Roy, a foremost Kachemak Bay naturalist will guide you through a memorable experience.

* Coast Guard Licensed & Approved
* Binoculars & cameras a must!
* Scheduled departures
* Affordable Prices

For More Information or Reservations Contact:
Homer Spit Campground
P.O. Box 1196
Homer, Alaska 99603
(907) 235-8206

Kachemak Gear Shed II

Tackle – Bait – Licenses

Clothing – Film – Food

Hunting & Camping Needs

Commercial Fishing Supplies

3815 Homer Spit Road
(907) 235-5562

Across from the Fishing Hole

ALASKA FISHING CHARTERS
— Five Derby Prize Winners —
101 fish over 100# 1990-91 ♦ 11 fish over 200# 1990-91

In Alaska: **1-800-478-7777**
Box 2807, Homer, Alaska 99603 • (907) 235-6468

SILVER FOX CHARTERS

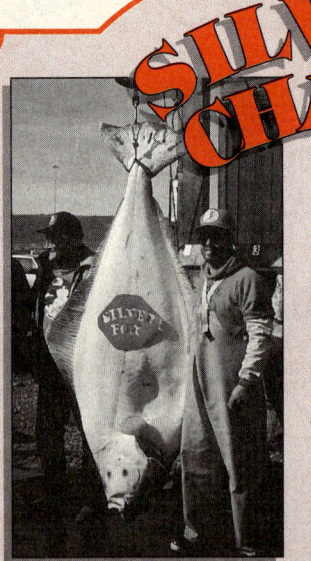

Located on the Homer Spit
behind The Salty Dawg

Reservations Required
(907) 235-8792
PO Box 402, Homer, Alaska 99603

In Business Since 1975

Member of
Homer Charter Association

307 lb. HALIBUT
CAUGHT ON SILVER FOX CHARTERS
JUNE 10, 1991

CIÉ JAE Ocean Charters

- Luxurious 53' vessel
- Single Day Excursions
- Overnight Fishing Tours

Summer (907) 235-5587
Winter (907) 776-8688
HC Rt. 1, Box 1120 MP
Kenai, Alaska 99611

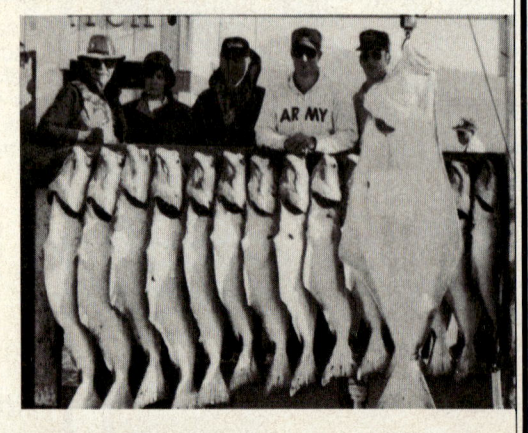

ALL MEALS, TACKLE, BAIT, FILLETING & PACKAGING INCLUDED

Call or Write for Brochure — See log ad under Attractions
Office: Fishing Village Boardwalk, 4025 Homer Spit Rd. #14

Pioneer Bed & Breakfast, 243 Pioneer Ave., in downtown Homer. Comfortable 1-bedroom suites with private baths and furnished kitchens. Sleeps up to 4. Continental breakfast available or prepare your own. Complimentary coffee. Walk-ins welcome. Year-round. Freezer space. Homer's best value. Brochure: P.O. Box 1430, Homer, AK 99603. (907) 235-5670. In Alaska, 1-800-478-8765. [ADVERTISEMENT]

Quiet Sports, located on Pioneer Avenue, offers quality outdoor equipment for the camper, backpacker or nordic skier. Rentals include packs and tents, skis, bikes, sea kayaks. In addition, Quiet Sports is also an excellent source of information and maps for guided and nonguided outdoor activities in the surrounding backcountry. (907) 235-8620. [ADVERTISEMENT]

Ridgetop Bed and Breakfast. Tucked 4 miles above Homer. Panoramic glacier view. Spacious suites with full kitchen and bathroom facilities or comfortable rooms available. Alaskan sourdough breakfasts. Come and share our experiences of Alaskan bush living and flying. Aviation library. Reasonable rates. Children welcome. P.O. Box 4103, Homer, AK 99603. (907) 235-7590. [ADVERTISEMENT]

Seaside Farm Bed and Breakfast. Friendly Alaskan family offers charming, furnished vacation cottages with view and cozy rooms in farmhouse. Private camping and farm hostel. Beachcombing, fishing, horses. Also, guided overnight horsepacking trips along spectacular wilderness beaches. See eagles, glaciers, pioneer homesteads. Brochures available. 58335 East End

---

SALT WATER CHARTERS
Halibut • Salmon - Electric Reels -
Homer Slip Q-38 • Captain Jerry Eidem, USCG
(907) 333-7056 • (907) 338-5905
331 Pamela Place, Anchorage, AK 99504
Homer Booking Agent: Dockside Charters (907) 235-8337

HALIBUT FISHING
K-BAY CHARTERS
HOMER, ALASKA

- Comfortable 6 passenger boats
- All bait and tackle provided
- Experienced USCG licensed skippers
- Locally owned and operated

Located in The Fishing Village
on Homer Spit
Call or write for reservations
(907) 235-8119
P.O. Box 3223
Homer, Alaska 99603

"Let's Go Fishing"

Road, Homer, AK 99603. (907) 235-7850.
[ADVERTISEMENT]

Sports N Wear, Mile 2.3 East End Road, open 10 A.M. to 5 P.M. daily except Sunday year-round; stocks warm clothing, quality lines for outdoor activities. Woolrich, Pendleton, Speedo, Body Glove, Helly-Hansen, Polypropylene underwear, wool pants and shirts, raingear, etc. Warm-up suits. Unique accessories, jewelry and gift items. [ADVERTISEMENT]

Subway. Stop by for the freshest sandwich available. We bake our bread every few hours. Looking for a quick breakfast? Try a breakfast sandwich served on our fresh croissants or a cinnamon roll straight from the oven. Two convenient locations: in town at the corner of Lake and Pioneer, and our Homer Spit store behind the Salty Dawg. Pick up a sandwich on the Spit and enjoy lunch at a picnic table overlooking the harbor, or get a charter lunch for your fishing trip. We're open early as needed to accommodate the charter fleet. (907) 235-2782. [ADVERTISEMENT]

Woodside Apartments and **Woodside Bed & Breakfast.** At Woodside, your warm enthusiastic hosts, Tom and Dale Samples, welcome guests with flowers, hospitality and a wealth of local information. Nightly and weekly rates of these plush apartments are very affordable. From Sterling Highway, turn on to Pioneer then turn left immediately. Woodside is behind Intermediate School (see Homer map). (907) 235-8389. See display ad.
[ADVERTISEMENT]

TRANSPORTATION

Air: Regularly scheduled air service to Anchorage. Several charter services also operate out of Homer.

Ferry: The Alaska State ferry *Tustumena* serves Seldovia, Kodiak, Seward, Port Lions, Valdez and Cordova from Homer with a limited schedule to Sand Point and King Cove. See MARINE ACCESS ROUTES section for details or contact the offices of the Alaska Marine Highway System at the City Dock, phone 235-8449. Tour boats offer passenger service to Seldovia and Halibut Cove.

Local: 2 major rental car agencies and several taxi services.

ATTRACTIONS

The **Pratt Museum**, focusing on the natural history of southcentral Alaska, is located at 3779 Bartlett St. Exhibits include artifacts from the area's earliest human settlers, Dena'ina Indians, to modern inhabitants. Excellent aquariums and a touch-tank feature live Kachemak Bay sea creatures. Also exhibited are Alaskan birds and land and sea mammals, including the complete skeletons of a Bering Sea beaked whale and a beluga whale.

Changing exhibits feature Alaskan artwork and other topics of special interest. Beautiful handmade quilts depict local natural history themes. Summer visitors may take a self-guided tour through the botanical garden for a look at local wild plants. The museum store features books and Alaskan collectibles.

The Pratt Museum is sponsored by the Homer Society of Natural History. All facilities are handicap accessible. Admission fees: $3 adults, $2 seniors, children under 18 years free, members and their guests free. Summer hours (May through September), 10 A.M. to 6 P.M. daily. Winter hours (October through April), noon to 5 P.M., Tuesday through Sunday. Closed in January. Phone (907) 235-8635.

The **U.S. Fish and Wildlife Alaska Maritime National Wildlife Refuge** office and visitor center is open in summer from 8:30 A.M. to 5 P.M. Monday through Friday; 10 A.M. to 5 P.M. Saturday and Sunday. Winter hours are 8:30 A.M. to 5 P.M. weekdays only. The center has nature displays, videos and a small shop selling books and pamphlets. Wildlife programs include guided bird walks on Homer Spit, special slide presentations and a children's nature hour. Join the naturalists at the visitor

---

A-1 HALIBUT FISHING
$90 COUPON
Full Day Charter
235-3929

HOMER, ALASKA
ALASKA FISHING at its BEST

LuckyPierre Charters

Overnight and Custom Charters Available

Lower 48: 800-678-8503
Alaska: 800-478-8903
Homer: 235-8903

Office Located at first boardwalk on the Homer Spit

P. O. Box 2438
Homer, Alaska 99603

VISA • DISCOVER • MasterCard • American Express

Just for the HALIBUT
May - August
J&D Charters
CG Licensed & Insured
(907) 235-2524
or 1-800-478-3140 (In Alaska)
PO Box 1487 • Homer, Alaska 99603-1487

$1000 Derby Winner May 1991

DOCKSIDE
(907) 235-8337
4460 Homer Spit Road
Toll free in Alaska
1-800-478-8338

- Gift shop features "made-in-Alaska" items
- Deli for take-out, charter/picnic lunches
- Convenient RV parking
- "Cook Your Catch" BBQ style
- Fishing licenses and derby tickets
- Visitor information and brochures

- Halibut charters
- Birding tours of Gull Island and the Barren Islands
- Water taxi to state parks
- Natural history tours of Kachemak Bay
- Two daily trips to Seldovia

Overlooking Homer Harbor
P.O. Box 1503, Homer, Alaska 99603

CHARTERS • CRUISES • GIFT SHOP • DELI

KENAI PENINSULA • HOMER

ALASKA'S HALIBUT DERBY WINNERS!!
HOMER OCEAN CHARTERS, INC.
ALASKA'S BEST FISHING

Red Carpet Service
MAKE RESERVATIONS NOW
In Alaska: 1-800-478-6212
(907) 235-6212
P.O. Box 2543, Homer, AK 99603

---

center for an informative day. Phone (907) 235-6546. It is located at 202 Pioneer Ave., Homer 99603.

Fish the Homer Halibut Derby. The annual Jackpot Halibut Derby, sponsored by GCI and the Homer Chamber of Commerce, runs from May 1 to Labor Day. More than $60,000 in cash prizes are awarded for biggest halibut and tagged fish. Tickets are $5 and available at the visitor center or local charter service offices. The 1991 winner was a 304 3/4-lb. halibut (cash prize was $18,434).

Charter boats, operating out of the boat harbor on Homer Spit, offer sightseeing and halibut fishing trips. (Charter salmon fishing trips, clamming, crabbing, and sightseeing charters are also available.) These charter operators provide gear, bait and expert knowledge of the area. Homer is one of Alaska's largest charter fishing areas (most charters are for halibut fishing). Charter boats for halibut fishermen cost about $120 to $155 a day. Several sightseeing boats operate off the Homer Spit, taking visitors to view the bird rookery on Gull Island, to Halibut Cove and to Seldovia. (Most sightseeing trips are available Memorial Day to Labor Day.)

AREA FISHING: The Kachemak Bay and Cook Inlet area is one of Alaska's most popular spots for halibut fishing with catches often weighing 100 to 200 lbs. Guides and charters are available locally. Halibut up to 350 lbs. are fished from June through September, bottom fish with herring. Year-round trolling for king salmon is popular, use small herring; pink salmon 4 to 5 lbs., July and August, use winged bobbers, small weighted spoons and spinners; silver salmon 6 to 8 lbs., August and September. Dolly Varden and rainbow are pulled from nearby streams and Tutka Lagoon from April to October, try candlefish for bait.

Fishermen have had great success in recent years casting from the shore of Homer Spit for king salmon. The Fishin' Lagoon on the Homer Spit supports a large run of hatchery-produced kings beginning in late May and continuing to mid-July. Kings range from 20 to 30 lbs. The fishery is open 7 days a week in season; limit of 2 kings per day from lagoon up to season limit of 5 Cook Inlet kings. (Check current regulations.)

Pink and coho salmon are also released on Homer Spit. Pink salmon return in July and coho provide the best fishing in August and September. The limit for both these species is 6 fish per day.

Take a scenic drive. East End Road, a 20-

Captain Mike's Charters

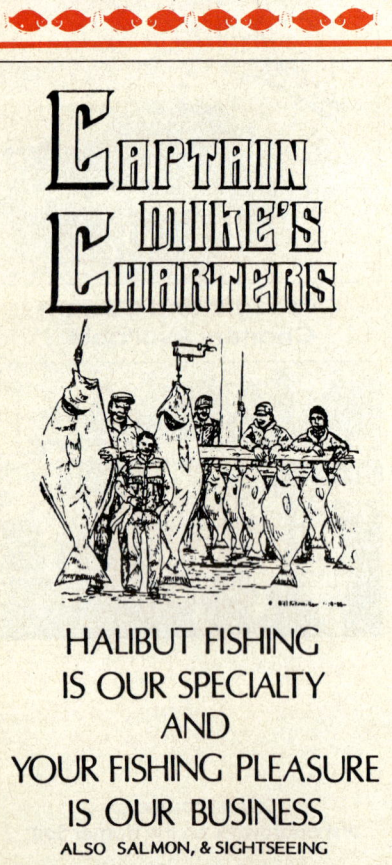

HALIBUT FISHING IS OUR SPECIALTY AND YOUR FISHING PLEASURE IS OUR BUSINESS
ALSO SALMON, & SIGHTSEEING

FOR RESERVATIONS
CALL: (907) 235-8348
WRITE: P.O. BOX 269
HOMER, ALASKA 99603
Location: Cannery Row Boardwalk

Fresh Sourdough Express Bakery & Restaurant
(907) 235-7571   HOMER
Unique Alaskan Flavor
On Ocean Drive 1/2 mile from Homer Spit
See our log ad under Attractions

Visit the PRATT MUSEUM
3779 Bartlett Street, Homer, AK 99603
- Emphasis on natural and cultural diversity of the Kenai Peninsula
- Special exhibits and artwork
- Marine touch tank and aquaria
- Hand-made quilt collection
- Botanical garden
- Museum store

SUMMER HOURS: 10-6 pm daily 907/235-8635

QUALITY ALASKAN Arts & Crafts
featuring over 45 Artists
Open 7 Days a Week
471 Pioneer Avenue
PTARMIGAN ARTS Studios & Gallery

SAMER-I SEAFOODS
**Custom Processing
Retail Seafood Market**
You Catch It – We Do The Rest
3815 HOMER SPIT ROAD, HOMER, AK 99603
See our log ad under Attractions   (907) 235-6767

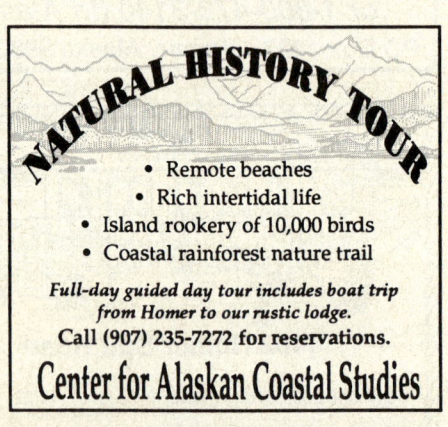

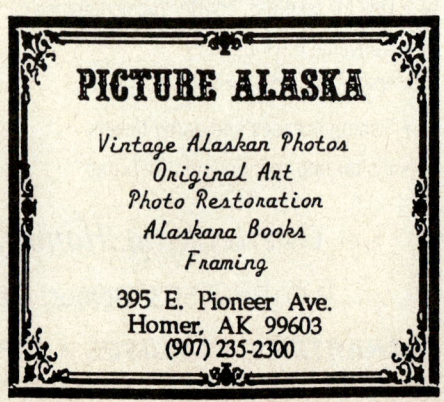

NATURAL HISTORY TOUR
- Remote beaches
- Rich intertidal life
- Island rookery of 10,000 birds
- Coastal rainforest nature trail

Full-day guided day tour includes boat trip from Homer to our rustic lodge.
Call (907) 235-7272 for reservations.
Center for Alaskan Coastal Studies

PICTURE ALASKA
Vintage Alaskan Photos
Original Art
Photo Restoration
Alaskana Books
Framing

395 E. Pioneer Ave.
Homer, AK 99603
(907) 235-2300

mile/32-km drive from downtown Homer, climbs through hills and forests toward the head of Kachemak Bay; pavement ends at Mile 10, beautiful views of the bay. Or turn off East End Road on to East Hill Road and drive up the bluffs to Skyline Drive; beautiful views of the bay and glaciers. Return to town via West Hill Road, which intersects the Sterling Highway at **Milepost S 167.1**.

The glaciers that spill down from the Harding Icefield straddling the Kenai Mountains across the bay create an ever-changing panorama visible from most points in Homer, particularly from the Skyline Drive. The most spectacular and largest of these glaciers is Grewingk Glacier in Kachemak Bay State Park, visible to the east directly across Kachemak Bay from Homer. The glacier was named by Alaska explorer William H. Dall in 1880 for Constantin Grewingk, a German geologist who had published a work on the geology and volcanism of Alaska. The Grewingk Glacier has a long gravel bar at its terminal moraine, behind which the water draining from the ice flows into the bay. This gravel bar, called Glacier Spit, is a popular excursion spot, and may be visited by charter plane or boat. (There are several charter plane operators and charter helicopter services in Homer.) Portlock and Dixon glaciers are also visible directly across from the spit.

Kachemak Bay State Park is located on the south shore of the bay and includes glaciers, alpine tundra, forests, fjords, bays and high-country lakes. The trail system offers hiking from Glacier Spit to China Poot Peak. Crabs, clams, Dolly Varden and salmon abound. Campsites available on Glacier Spit, Halibut Cove Lagoon and China Poot Lake. Inquire locally about transportation to the park. Phone the district office at 235-7024 for more information or stop by the state park office at **Milepost S 168.5**.

McNeil River State Game Sanctuary. Homer is the main base for visitors flying across Cook Inlet to the sanctuary, where the world's largest concentration of bears in a natural area this size is found. Brown bears congregate near the mouth of the river, where a falls slows down migrating salmon, making fishing easy for the bears. Visits to the game sanctuary are on a permit basis; a drawing for the limited number of permits is held in April each year. Permit applications are available from the Alaska Dept. of Fish and Game, Attn: McNeil River, 333 Raspberry Road, Anchorage 99518. Phone 267-2180.

Study Marine Environment. The Center for Alaskan Coastal Studies is located across Kachemak Bay from Homer. Volunteer naturalists lead a day tour which includes Gull Island bird rookery, coastal forest and intertidal areas. Write the Center for Alaskan Coastal Studies, P.O. Box 2225-MP, Homer 99603; phone 235-6667. Reservations,

---

Chevron — Sunny Chevron Service
....A Friendly Place....
Pioneer Avenue, Town Center — Homer
Complete auto repairs and lubrication
Tire sales & repairs
Box 863, Homer   Phone 235-8800

Alaska Travel Packages

Write us for *free* information concerning:
- RV camping
- sightseeing tours
- statewide lodging
- salmon/halibut charters
- tickets/reservations
- Alaska Marine Hwy.
- fishing licenses
- Denali Park

Homer Vacations & Conventions
4460 Homer Spit Rd.
P.O. Box 1050, Homer, AK 99603
907/235-2575

We would love for you to drop by and see us in our office located in the DOCKSIDE.

Homer - Seldovia Wildlife Tour

Homer - Gull Island Bird Rookery - Seldovia

- The ONLY tour departing Homer which includes Gull Island en route to Seldovia.
- 4 1/2 hours wildlife cruise aboard the M/V Tulchina (includes 1 1/2 hours ashore in Seldovia)
- TWO daily departures - 8am and 1:30pm

WEEKLY BARREN ISLANDS TRIPS

WILDLIFE • SCENERY • SIGHTSEEING

ALASKA MARITIME TOURS

BOX 3098-MP • HOMER, AK 99603
Dockside Building Homer Spit Road
(907) 235-2490 • 1-800-478-2490

phone 235-7272.

Alaska Maritime Tours, Inc. Enjoy the only half-day wildlife tour departing Homer which includes Gull Island (summer home of 10,000 seabirds) en route to Seldovia. A fully licensed crew provides top-quality service aboard the 25-passenger 43-foot MV *Tulchina*. Bring camera and extra film for close-up views of puffins, sea otters, occasional sea lions and whales. Warm clothing recommended. 1½ hours onshore in Seldovia included. Morning and afternoon departures. Deli cafe and gift shop on premises. Dockside Building, 4460 Homer Spit Road. Call (907) 235-2490 or 1-800-235-478-2490 for reservations. See display ad this section. [ADVERTISEMENT]

Arctic Wolf Gallery/Snow Geese Originals, 510 Pioneer, Homer. This interesting collection of shops and artists offers the best of made-in-Alaska arts. Lynn Wolf, metal sculptor and jeweler, has created her gallery in one of several old wooden boats being restored on the property. Available are metal sculptures of antique boats and other machines from Alaskan history. Snow Geese Originals is a group of artists who handcraft baskets, porcelain Eskimo dolls, imaginative colorful sweaters, wood carvings, jewelry, leather goods, hand-painted T-shirts, sweatshirts and other fiber arts. Work is usually in progress on the premises, and these cheerful artists will gladly demonstrate their crafts. [ADVERTISEMENT]

The Bookstore, located in Eagle Quality Center, specializes in Alaskan, nature, cooking and children's books. It is acclaimed as one of the nicest bookstores in the state. Besides a great selection of paperback books, it features the most original card selection on the Peninsula (many by local artists) and a very special kids' corner. Browsers invited. Hours 10 A.M. to 7 P.M. 436 Sterling Highway. (907) 235-7496. [ADVERTISEMENT]

Cie' Jae Ocean Charters. Homer halibut fishing on luxurious 53-foot USCG inspected *Shenandoah*. Single-day excursions, overnight 2-day packages available. All meals, tackle, bait, filleting and packaging included. Seasonal service May 15–Sept. 7. Brochure available. VISA, MasterCard accepted. Summers: 4025 Homer Spit Road, Bldg. 14MP, Homer, AK 99603. Winters: HC Route 1, Box 1120MP, Kenai, AK 99611. Phone 1-800-677-5587; summer—(907) 235-5587; winter—(907) 776-8688. See display ad this section. [ADVERTISEMENT]

Homer Vacations. Located in the Dockside on the Homer Spit, this all-year Alaskan business has designed travel packages for visitors coming to Homer and the Kenai Peninsula. Maps, roadside fishing tips, restaurants, camping, charters, tours and local lodging information available. Write or call for information on the "Roadside Fishing and Sights Galore" package. Homer Vacations, Box 1050, Homer, AK 99603. Phone (907) 235-2575. [ADVERTISEMENT]

Kachemak Bay Adventures Boat Tours. Join us on the 60-foot MV *Endeavor* for a memorable experience on beautiful Kachemak Bay. See puffins, murres, kittiwakes and other nesting birds at Gull Island seabird rookery. Sea otters, seabirds, porpoises, seals and even whales are commonly seen on our Seldovia excursions. Headquarters at Homer Spit Campground. Camping and boat tour packages. Scheduled departures daily. Brochure available. P.O. Box 1196, Homer, AK 99603. Reservations and information (907) 235-8206. [ADVERTISEMENT]

North Country Charters, originally owned and operated by Sean and Gerri Martin since 1979, has brought in some of the largest halibut catches ever landed in Homer. Two 50-foot boats for large groups from 16 to 20 passengers. Three 6-passenger boats. All twin-engine, Coast Guard-equipped, heated cabins, full restrooms. See display ad. [ADVERTISEMENT]

Pier One Theatre. Live theatre on summer weekends, celebrating the variety of "end of the road" talent. Comedy, cabarets, drama, dance, barbershop, musicals, a summer symphony, and youth theatre productions. Presented in a come-as-you-are city warehouse on the Homer Spit. More information locally. Phone (907) 235-7333. [ADVERTISEMENT]

Rainbow Tours, Cannery Row Boardwalk, Homer Spit, has been offering affordable daily scheduled sightseeing cruises on Kachemak Bay since 1982. New 100-passenger MV *Rainbow Connection* has a warm comfortable cabin and snack bar. The vessel features a fully automated roll control system for a comfortable ride. See the "Puffins" of Gull Island seabird rookery. Join a guided Natural History Tour to the Center for Alaskan Coastal Studies. Watch for whales on a 5-hour fully narrated cruise to Seldovia. Rainbow Tours also offers Water Taxi Service to Kachemak Bay State Park for campers, hikers, kayakers, mountain bikers. For the salmon fisherman we have boat, guide and gear. For information or reservations phone (907) 235-7272 or write P.O. Box 1526MP, Homer, AK 99603. Adult, junior, senior rates, group discounts, under 5 free. Hope you're having a great trip. See ya in Homer. [ADVERTISEMENT]

Samer-I Seafoods, located at Glacier Boardwalk on Homer Spit, specializes in sport-caught fish. "You catch the fish, we do the rest." Vacuum-packing, freezing, boxing, storing, smoking. We ship anywhere. Enjoy your dream vacation; leave the work to us. Fresh Alaska crab, shrimp, halibut, salmon for sale. See display ad this section. [ADVERTISEMENT]

Seldovia

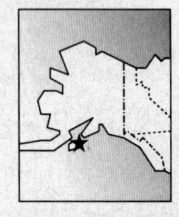

Reached by air or ferry. Located on the southwestern Kenai Peninsula on Seldovia Bay, an arm of Kachemak Bay, 16 miles/25.7 km southwest of Homer. **Population:** 403. **Emergency Services:** City Police, Ambulance, Fire and Rescue, emergency only, phone 911, monitor CB Channel 9. Seldovia Medical Clinic, phone 234-7825. Seldovia has a resident doctor and dentists.

Visitor Information: Seldovia Chamber of Commerce, Drawer F, Seldovia, AK 99663. Information cache at Synergy Art Works on Main Street, across from the boat harbor. You may also stop by the Seldovia Native Assoc. office on Main Street. The office features a small museum with Native artifacts; open 8 A.M. to 5 P.M. weekdays.

Elevation: Sea level. **Climate:** Rather mild for Alaska, with a year-round average temperature of about 39°F/4°C. Annual precipitation, 28 inches. Wind is a small factor due to the protecting shield of the Kenai Mountains. **Radio:** Homer stations. **Television:** KENI Channel 2, KTVA Channel 4, KAKM Channel 7, KIMO Channel 13.

Private Aircraft: Seldovia airport, 0.6 mile/1 km east; elev. 29 feet/9m; length 2,600 feet/792m; gravel; unattended.

Seldovia is a small community connected to Homer by the Alaska Marine Highway Southwest ferry system. Because it is removed from Kenai Peninsula highways, Seldovia has retained much of its old Alaska charm and traditions (its historic boardwalk dates from 1931). There are some areas just outside town, accessible by car, that have been called "Alaska's hidden paradises." A good place to observe bald eagles, seabirds, and sea otters, Seldovia is included as a stop on some tour boat cruises out of Homer.

The name Seldovia is derived from Russian *Seldevoy*, meaning "herring bay." Between 1869 and 1882, a trading station was located here. A post office was established in November 1898.

The economy has long depended on commercial fishing and fish processing, and to a lesser degree on the lumber industry. Lower Cook Inlet oil exploration and tourism are expected to increase in economic importance.

ACCOMMODATIONS

Seldovia has most visitor facilities, including 2 hotels, 3 bed and breakfasts, a lodge, general store, 3 restaurants, sports shop and gift shop. The post office is in the center of town. Public restrooms, showers, and pay phone in front of the boat harbor near town center. Pay phone also at the ferry dock outside ferry office.

Annie McKenzie's Boardwalk Hotel/

SELDOVIA ADVERTISERS

Annie McKenzie's Boardwalk
  Hotel B&B ....Seldovia Harbor
Dancing Eagles Lodge ......Ph. (907) 234-7627
Gerry's Place ....One blk. from harbor
Harmony Point Wilderness
  Lodge............................Ph. (907) 234-7858
Homer Air ....Ph. (907) 235-8591
Jakolof Ferry Service ....Ph. (907) 234-7686
Kachemak Kafe..................................Main St.
Seldovia Native Assoc. ....206 Main St.
Seldovia Rowing Club Inn
  Bed & Breakfast........On the old boardwalk

WATERFRONT/RECREATIONAL LOTS

Kachemak Bay recreation and homesite land for lease. Waterfront lots, easy access or remote sites. For more information contact Seldovia Native Assn. Inc., P.O. Drawer L, Seldovia, AK 99663 or stop by 206 Main St. Phone (907) 234-7625 or 234-7890.

Picturesque Seldovia is a 1½-hour ferry ride from Homer. (Jerrianne Lowther, staff)

B&B. Waterfront view. 14 lovely rooms with private baths. Large harbor view deck. Bicycles. Interior features local art, plants and library. Free airport or harbor pickup. Friendly service. Romantic getaway. 3 restaurants within 3 blocks. P.O. Box 72, Seldovia, AK 99663. (907) 234-7816. [ADVERTISEMENT]

Gerry's Place. Bed and breakfast 1 block from harbor. Convenient for fishermen and divers. Private entrance. Close to everything. Air fills available. Rates for families. Freshly baked continental breakfast. Accommodates 6, share bathroom. Box 74, Seldovia, AK 99663. (907) 234-7471. [ADVERTISEMENT]

Harmony Point Wilderness Lodge. Easily reached by sea or air from Homer. We offer sea kayaking, boating, mountain biking, fishing, hiking, wildlife, sauna and fun. Private guest cabins and local seafood served in a new, handcrafted lodge. Come, explore or relax. Call (907) 234-7858 or write Box 110, Seldovia, AK 99663. [ADVERTISEMENT]

Undeveloped campground for tent camping only at Outside Beach; picnic tables, litter containers, pit toilet. Private RV park nearby. From downtown, drive 1 mile/1.6 km out via Anderson Way to fork in road; turn left and drive 0.9 mile/1.4 km to beach. ▲

TRANSPORTATION

Air: Scheduled and charter service. **Ferry:** Alaska's Southwestern Marine Highway system serves Seldovia, with connections to and from Homer, Port Lions, Kodiak, Valdez, Cordova and Seward. See MARINE ACCESS ROUTES section for schedules. **Charter and Tour Boats:** Available for passenger service; inquire locally and in Homer.

ATTRACTIONS

Special Events. Just about the whole town participates in Seldovia's old-fashioned Fourth of July celebration. The holiday includes a barbecue, parade, games and contests. Seldovia also holds a summer-long fishing derby. Check with the chamber of commerce for details.

Scenic drives. Outside Beach, a beautiful spot with undeveloped tent camping, beachcombing, surf fishing, rockhounding, and a view of Kachemak Bay, Mount Iliamna and Mount Redoubt, is 1.9 miles/3.1 km from town. Drive out Anderson Way from downtown 1 mile/1.6 km to a fork in the road by a gravel pit; turn left and drive 0.9 mile/1.4 km to beach.

Continue on Anderson Way (past the Outside Beach turnoff) to hilly and unpaved Jakalof Bay Road, which offers panoramic views of Kachemak Bay, McDonald Spit, Jakalof Bay and Kasitsna Bay. At Mile 7.5, steps lead down to 1.5-mile-long McDonald Spit, a favorite spot for seabirds and marine life. Spend an afternoon exploring the spit, or continue out to Jakalof Bay, where the road offers many opportunities to get onto the beach. The road becomes impassable to vehicles at Mile 13.

It is a pleasant drive out to Seldovia's refuse dump, with wonderful blueberry picking in the fall. From downtown, cross the bridge over Seldovia Slough; then turn right on North Augustine Avenue, then left on Rocky Street for the dump. This is a 1.4-mile/2.3-km drive.

Inquire locally about hiking trails (Red Mountain, city reservoir, Seldovia Otterbahn trail) and mountain biking opportunities in the area.

Fishing: Kachemak Bay, king salmon, June and July; halibut June through October; Dolly Varden, June through September; silver salmon in August; red salmon, July through August. **Seldovia Bay**, king, silver and red salmon, also halibut, June through September. Excellent bottom fishing.

St. Nicholas Orthodox Church, built in 1891, is open to visitors by prior arrangement. There are some interesting icons here. Donations are welcome.

KODIAK

View of downtown Kodiak and Near Island. (Marion Stirrup)

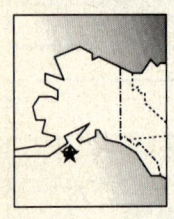

The Kodiak Island group lies in the Gulf of Alaska, south of Cook Inlet and the Kenai Peninsula. The city of Kodiak is located near the northeastern tip of Kodiak Island, at the north end of Chiniak Bay. By air it is 45 minutes from Anchorage and 3 hours and 10 minutes from Seattle.

Population: 15,575 Kodiak Island Borough. **Emergency Services in Kodiak:** Dial 911 for emergencies. **Alaska State Troopers,** phone 486-4121. **Police,** phone 486-8000. **Fire Department,** phone 486-8040. **Hospital,** Kodiak Island Hospital, Rezanof Drive, phone 486-3281. **Coast Guard,** Public Affairs Officer, phone 487-5542. **Crime Stoppers,** phone 486-3113.

Visitor Information: Located at Center Avenue and Marine Way; open weekdays, 8:30 A.M. to 5 P.M., year-round. Knowledgeable local staff will answer your questions and help arrange tours and charters. Free maps, brochures, hunting and fishing information. For information, contact the Kodiak Island Convention & Visitors Bureau, 100 Marine Way, Kodiak 99615; phone 486-4782 or 486-4070 or write the Kodiak Area Chamber of Commerce, Box 1485, Kodiak 99615; phone 486-5557.

Elevation: Sea level. **Climate:** Average daily temperature in July is 54°F/12°C; in January, 30°F/1°C. September, October and May are the wettest months in Kodiak, with each month averaging over 6 inches of rain. **Radio:** KVOK 560, KMXT-FM 100.1, MBN-FM 107.1, KJJZ-FM 101.1, KPEN-FM 102.3, KWAVE-FM 105. **Television:** Via cable and satellite. **Newspapers:** *The Kodiak Daily Mirror* (daily except Saturday and Sunday).

Private Aircraft: Kodiak state airport, 3 miles/4.8 km southwest; elev. 73 feet/22m; length 7,500 feet/2,286m; asphalt, fuel 80, 100, jet A-1. Kodiak Municipal Airport, 2 miles/3.2 km northeast; elev. 139 feet/42m; length 2,883 feet/879m; gravel; fuel 80, 100; attended daylight hours. Kodiak (Lilly Lake) seaplane base, 1 mile/1.6 km northeast; elev. 130 feet/40m. Inner Harbor seaplane base, adjacent north; unattended, docks; watch for boat traffic; no fuel.

Gravel airstrips at Akhiok, length 3,600 feet/1,097m; Karluk, length 2,400 feet/732m; Larsen Bay, length 2,400 feet/732m; Old Harbor, length 2,000 feet/610m; Ouzinkie, length 2,500 feet/762m; and Port Lions, length 2,600 feet/792m.

Kodiak Island, home of the oldest permanent European settlement in Alaska, is about 100 miles/161 km long. Known as "the emerald isle," Kodiak is the largest island in Alaska and the second largest island in the U.S. (after Hawaii), with an area of 3,588 square miles and about 87 miles/140 km of road (see logs this section). The Kodiak Borough includes some 200 islands, the largest being Kodiak, followed in size by Afognak, Sitkalidak, Sitkinak, Raspberry, Tugidak, Shuyak, Uganik, Chirikof, Marmot and Spruce islands. The borough has only 1 unincorporated townsite: **KARLUK** (pop. 107), located on the west coast of Kodiak Island, 75 air miles/121 km from Kodiak.

The 6 incorporated cities in the Kodiak Island Borough are: **KODIAK** (pop. 6,774) on Chiniak Bay, with all visitor services (see Accommodations, Transportation and Attractions this section); **AKHIOK** (pop. 109) at Alitak Bay on the south side of Kodiak Island, 80 miles/129 km southwest of Kodiak; **LARSEN BAY** (pop. 169) on the northwest coast of Kodiak Island, 62 miles/100 km southwest of Kodiak; **OLD HARBOR** (pop. 380) on the southeast side of Kodiak Island, 54 miles/87 km from Kodiak; **OUZINKIE** (pop. 204) on the west coast of Spruce Island; and **PORT LIONS** (pop. 296) on Settler Cove on the northeast coast of Kodiak Island.

Kodiak Island was first discovered by Stephen Glotov, a Russian explorer, in 1763. The name Kodiak, of which there are several variations, was first used in English by Captain Cook in 1778. Kodiak was Russian Alaska's first capital city, until the capital was moved to Sitka in 1804.

Kodiak's turbulent past includes the 1912 eruption of Novarupta Volcano, on the nearby Alaska Peninsula, and the tidal wave of 1964. The Novarupta eruption covered the island with a black cloud of ash. When the cloud finally dissipated, Kodiak was buried under 18 inches of drifting pumice. On Good Friday in 1964 the greatest earthquake ever recorded in North America (9.2 on the Richter scale) shook the Kodiak area. The tidal wave that followed virtually leveled downtown Kodiak, destroying the fishing fleet, processing plants, canneries and 158 homes; in all about $24 million in damage.

Because of its strategic location for defense, military facilities were constructed on Kodiak in 1939. Fort Abercrombie, now a state park and a national historic landmark, was one of the first secret radar installations in Alaska. Cement bunkers still remain for exploration by the curious.

The Coast Guard occupies the old Kodiak Naval Station. Kodiak is the base for the Coast Guard's North Pacific operations; the Coast Guard cutters USCGC *Yocona, Storis, Ironwood* and *Firebush* patrol from Kodiak to seize foreign vessels illegally fishing U.S. waters. (The 200-mile/322-km fishing limit went into effect in March 1977.) A 12-foot star, situated halfway up the side of Old Woman Mountain overlooking the base, was rebuilt and rededicated in 1981 in memory of military personnel who have lost their lives while engaged in operations from Kodiak. Originally erected in the 1950s, the star is lit every year between Thanksgiving and Christmas.

Commercial fishing is the backbone of Kodiak's economy. Kodiak is one of the largest commercial fishing ports in the U.S. Some 2,000 commercial fishing vessels use the harbor each year, delivering salmon, shrimp, herring, halibut and whitefish, plus king, tanner and Dungeness crab to the 15 seafood processing companies in Kodiak. Cannery tours are not available. Kodiak's famous seafood is premarketed, with almost all the commercially caught seafood exported. (Kodiak is the only city in Alaska with more tonnage exported than imported.) A trip through the boat harbor offers the opportunity to talk to local fishermen, see nets being mended, vessels repaired, and—if you're on hand when a fishing boat is unloaded—possibly sample the catch. You can celebrate Kodiak's main industry at the Kodiak Crab Festival, May 21-25, 1992.

Kodiak is also an important cargo port and transshipment center. Container ships stop here to transfer goods to smaller vessels bound for the Aleutians, the Alaska Peninsula and other destinations.

ACCOMMODATIONS

There are several hotels/motels in Kodiak. Bed-and-breakfast accommodations are also available. A variety of restaurants offer a wide range of menus and prices. Shopping is readily available for gifts, general merchandise and sporting goods.

There are 3 state campgrounds: Fort Abercrombie, north of town (see Rezanof–

KODIAK ADVERTISERS

Afognak Wilderness Lodge............Ph. (907) 486-6442
Backcountry Sports..............1314 Mill Bay Rd.
Baranov Museum...................101 Marine Way
Buskin River Inn................Ph. (907) 487-2700
Cy's Sporting Goods....................202 Shelikof
Evangel Media Center.........3201 Bayview Dr.
Inlet Bed & Breakfast........Ph. (907) 486-4004
Kodiak Arts Council..........Ph. (907) 486-5291
Kodiak Bed and Breakfast......................Ph. (907) 486-5367
Kodiak Island Convention & Visitors Bureau ....100 Marine Way
Kodiak Star Motel.............Ph. (907) 486-5657
Kodiak Western Charters .Ph. (907) 486-2200
Mack's Sport Shop, Inc......Ph. (907) 486-4276
Norman's ....On the Mall
Northern Exposure Gallery.....The Bakery Mall
Road's End......................Mile 42.2 Chiniak Rd.
Wintel's Bed & Breakfast..Ph. (907) 486-6935
Wodlinger Drug and Photo..........On the Mall

Kodiak Vicinity

Afognak Wilderness Lodge

in the "enchanted" forest of Afognak Island

Enjoy photographing, at close range, our unique combination of land and sea wildlife from EAGLES to AUKLETS, KODIAK BROWN BEAR to SEA OTTER and excellent salmon/halibut fishing. Elegant log lodge & guest cabins with superb local cuisine for 12 guests. Floatplane access.

Color brochure. International references.

Roy & Shannon Randall
Seal Bay, AK 99697-WMP

Microwave phone:
(907) 486-6442

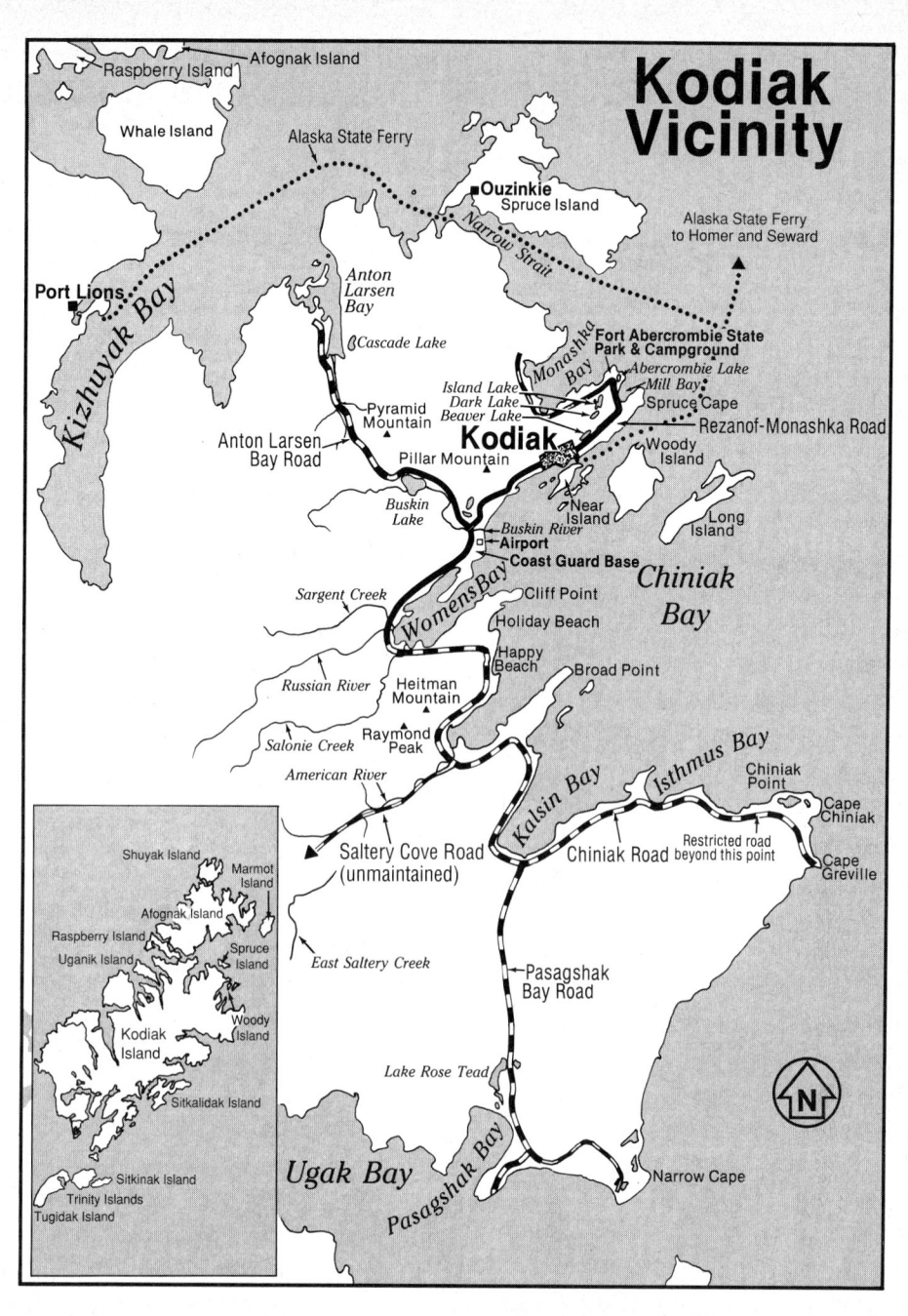

BUSKIN RIVER INN

(907) 487-2700

1395 Airport Way, Kodiak, Alaska 99615

- Brand New Facilities
- 51 Private Rooms
- Cable, Phone
- Corporate Rates Available
- Courtesy Van Available

Restaurant
Lounge

- Banquet & Meeting Facilities
- Next to State Airport Kodiak, Alaska

Wintel's BED & BREAKFAST

"Hospitality is our gift to you"

Ocean view,
pleasant non-smoking rooms

Jacuzzi, full breakfast,
Alaska gift shop.

Open Year-Round • *Brochure Available*

Conveniently located — walking distance to Baranof Museum and Russian Orthodox Church.

(907) 486-6935
P.O. Box 2812, Kodiak, Alaska 99615

Monashka Road log); Buskin River state recreation site, south of town (see Chiniak Road log); and Pasagshak River state recreation site at the end of Pasagshak Bay Road (see log). City campground at Gibson Cove has showers and restrooms, $2 per night camping fee.

Dump stations are located at the Buggy Banya station on Mill Bay Road, at the Union 76 service station in downtown Kodiak, and at Buskin River state recreation site at Mile 4.4 Chiniak Road.

There are several remote fly-in hunting and fishing lodges in the Kodiak area, several roadhouses on the island road system, and recreation cabins available within Kodiak National Wildlife Refuge.

TRANSPORTATION

Air: Scheduled service via MarkAir and Era.

Ferry: The Alaska state ferry MV *Tustumena* serves Kodiak from Homer and Seward. It also stops at Port Lions on the north side of Kodiak Island. Ferry terminal is downtown; phone 486-3800 or toll free in the U.S. 1-800-642-0066. See MARINE ACCESS ROUTES section for details.

Highways: There are 4 roads on Kodiak Island (see logs this section). The 11.4-mile/18.3-km Rezanof–Monashka Road leads from downtown Kodiak north to Fort Abercrombie and Monashka Bay. Chiniak Road leads 47.6 miles/76.6 km south from Kodiak along the island's eastern shore to Cape Greville (it is a beautiful drive!). Anton Larsen Bay Road leads 11.6 miles/18.7 km from junction with Chiniak Road near Kodiak airport to Anton Larsen Bay. Pasagshak Bay Road branches off Chiniak Road and leads 16.4 miles/26.4 km to Fossil Beach at Pasagshak Point.

Car Rental and Taxi: Available.

ATTRACTIONS

See historic drama in Alaska's only outdoor theater. Alaska's longest running play (now in its 26th year), *Cry of the Wild Ram* is presented each August in the Frank Brink Amphitheater on Monashka Bay. It tells the story of the first Russian–American colony in Alaska. Performances in 1992 are scheduled for July 31, Aug. 1, 5-8 and 12-15. Performances begin at 8 P.M. and play rain or shine; dress warmly and bring rain gear (just in case). Seating $12 adults ($15 reserved). For tickets, contact Kodiak Arts Council, Box 1792, Kodiak 99615; phone 486-5291.

State fair and rodeo held Labor Day weekend, at the fairgrounds in Womens Bay, includes all-state competitions in crafts, gardening, 4-H livestock raising and home products. Stock car races are held at the fairgrounds on weekends during the summer.

St. Herman's Day, Aug. 9, is of particular significance to the Kodiak community as Father Herman, the first saint of the Russian Orthodox Church in North America, was canonized in Kodiak in 1970. Father Herman arrived in Kodiak in 1794.

Picnic on the beach. There are some outstandingly beautiful beaches along Chiniak Road (see log this section). These unpopulated beaches are also good for beachcombing. Watch for Sitka deer and foxes.

City Parks and Recreation Department maintains a swimming pool year-round and the school gyms are available on a year-round basis for community use. The town has 8 parks and playgrounds including the 7-acre Baranof Park with 4 tennis courts, Babe Ruth field, track, football field, playgrounds and picnic areas.

Fort Abercrombie State Park. Site of a WWII coastal fortification, bunkers and other evidence of the Aleutian campaign. The park is located north of Kodiak on scenic Miller Point. Picnicking and camping in a setting of lush rain forest, wildflowers, seabirds and eagles.

The Baranov Museum (Erskine House), maintained by the Kodiak Historical Society (101 Marine Way, Kodiak 99615), is open in summer, 10 A.M. to 3 P.M. weekdays, and noon to 4 P.M. Saturday and Sunday. (Open 11 A.M. to 3 P.M. weekdays, except Thursday, and noon to 3 P.M. Saturday in winter.) The building was originally a warehouse built circa 1808 by Aleksandr Andreevich Baranov to store precious sea otter pelts. Purchased by the Alaska Commercial Co. around 1867, the building was sold to W.J. Erskine in 1911, who converted it into a residence; it was then referred to as the Erskine House. In 1962 it was declared a national historic landmark. Many items from the Koniag and Russian era are on display. In the gift shop, Russian samovars, Russian Easter eggs, Alaska Native baskets and other items are for sale. A walking tour map of Kodiak is available here. Donations accepted, $1 per adult, children under 12 free.

Russian Orthodox Church. The oldest parish in Alaska, the church was established in 1794 with the first mission from Russia. Father Herman was one of the original clerics. The church is on the National Register of Historic Places. Inquire at the visitor center about hours. Within the church are

---

Inlet Bed & Breakfast
Comfortable Private Rooms with Private Baths
Room Only $55
Single or Double Room with Breakfast $65
Coffee and TV's in each room
(907) 486-4004
P.O. Box 703, Kodiak, Alaska 99615

Kodiak Bed and Breakfast
Comfortable, gracious hospitality in Kodiak homes
1992 Rates: Single $55 - Double $66
Enjoy the magic of this northern fishing community with its Russian heritage, its stunning physical setting, and its friendly people.
Mary Monroe, Coordinator • (907) 486-5367
308 Cope Street, Kodiak, Alaska 99615

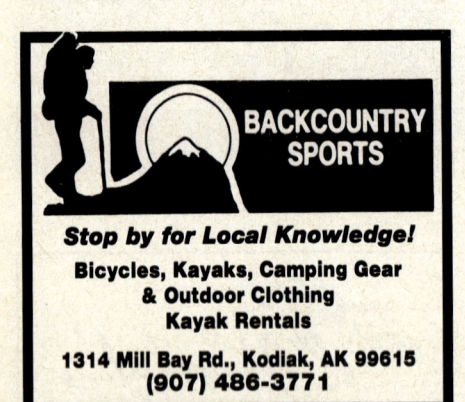

BACKCOUNTRY SPORTS
Stop by for Local Knowledge!
Bicycles, Kayaks, Camping Gear & Outdoor Clothing
Kayak Rentals
1314 Mill Bay Rd., Kodiak, AK 99615
(907) 486-3771

★ Kodiak Star Motel ★
Comfort, Convenience at Reasonable Rates
- 10-Channel TV
- Kitchenettes
- Complimentary Coffee
- Private Entrance
- Laundry Facilities
- Private Telephones
- Downtown Location

119 YUKON, KODIAK, ALASKA 99615
Phone (907) 486-5657

WODLINGER DRUG and PHOTO...All Your Drug and Photo Needs
DRUG SUNDRIES
PRESCRIPTIONS • COSMETICS
CIGARETTES & TOBACCO
Books & Magazines • Souvenirs
Toys • Film & Film Processing
CAMERAS • TVs • RADIOS
Kodiak — downtown on the Mall
Phone 486-4035   Open every day

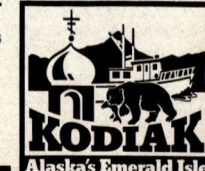

MACK'S Sport Shop Inc.
"The Outfitters of Kodiak"
117 Lower Mill Bay, Kodiak, AK 99615
(Next to McDonald's)
EVERYTHING FOR THE SPORTSMAN
MACK'S has one of the Largest and most Complete selections of Fishing, Camping & Hunting supplies in Alaska. Also a large selection of clothing, boots and shoes.
Hunting & Fishing Licenses, Commercial Crew Licenses
"MACK'S - Much more than just a Sporting Goods Store"
We Accept Credit Cards
Mon. - Sat.: 9-7; Sun.: 10-5
FAX: (907) 486-2928
PH.: (907) 486-4276

KODIAK
RUGGED AND MAJESTIC
An Island of Adventure and Unspoiled Beauty.
Filled with the romantic history of three fascinating cultures.
For Information Write:
Kodiak Island Convention & Visitors Bureau
100 Marine Way, Dept. MP
Kodiak, AK 99615
(907) 486-4782
FAX 907-486-6545
Kodiak — Alaska's Emerald Isle

handmade brass works, rare paintings and several icons dating back to the Czarist period. The hand-rung church bells visitors may hear were a gift of Kodiak residents. St. Herman Theological Seminary, founded in 1973, is a degree-granting institution for the training of orthodox readers, deacons and priests. The seminary is located on Mission Road, north of the church.

The St. Innocent Veniaminov Research Institute Museum at St. Herman's Theological Seminary has Native artifacts, icons and arts and crafts used by Orthodox missionaries on the Yukon River in the 1800s on display. The institute has a bookstore and gift shop. Check with the visitor information center for hours.

Evangel Media Center. By 1-hour appointment, a mini-museum housed in the dry-docked historic Navy/archaeological/Baptist vessel *Evangel* at 3201 Bayview Dr., shows half-hour videos of touristic highlights of Kodiak or a docudrama which traces the intertwined lives of 3 Kodiak Creole families. Call (907) 486-4666 or 486-5516. $7 per person. [ADVERTISEMENT]

Pillar Mountain (elev. 1,270 feet/387m) is behind Kodiak. Visitors may wish to drive up to the scenic overlook. Inquire locally for directions. The short, scenic access road winds around the hill in back of Kodiak, climbing to a point that affords a fine view of the mountains, sea, islands and beaches. Many species of wildflowers grow on the mountain, including some varieties not found on the mainland.

Charter a boat for fishing and hunting trips, sightseeing and photography. There are several marine charter services in Kodiak.

Kodiak National Wildlife Refuge encompasses 1,865,000 acres on Kodiak Island, Uganik Island and Afognak Island. The refuge was established in 1941 to preserve the natural habitat of the famed Kodiak bear and other wildlife. Biologists estimate that more than 2,700 bears inhabit Kodiak Island. Most bears enter dens by December and remain there until April. Bears are readily observable on the refuge in July and August when they congregate along streams to feed on salmon.

Wildlife within the refuge includes the red fox, land otter, black-tailed deer and mountain goat. On Afognak Island, an introduced band of elk share the island with the bears. The coastline on the Kodiak refuge shelters a large population of waterfowl and marine mammals. Bald eagles are common nesting birds on the refuge, along with 215 other bird species which have been seen on the island.

NOTE: The refuge is accessible only by floatplane or boat. There are public-use recreation cabins available for use; application must be made in advance to the refuge manager. For more information contact the Kodiak National Wildlife Refuge Manager, 1390 Buskin River Road, Kodiak, AK 99615; phone 487-2600. You may also stop by the U.S. Fish and Wildlife Service Visitor Center at Mile 4.4 Chiniak Road. The center is open weekdays, 8 A.M. to 4:30 P.M. and weekends noon to 4:30 P.M., year-round. Exhibits and films on Kodiak wildlife are featured.

AREA FISHING: Kodiak Island is in the center of a fine marine and freshwater fishery and possesses some excellent fishing for rainbow, halibut, Dolly Varden and 5 species of Pacific salmon, but visiting fishermen will have to charter a boat or aircraft to reach remote lakes, rivers and bays.

Afognak Island and adjacent Raspberry Island, both approximately 30 air miles/48 km northeast of Kodiak, offer excellent remote hunting and fishing. There is a lodge on Afognak Island with accommodations for 12 people. Both islands are brown bear country. Hikers and fishermen should make noise as they travel and carry a .30-06 or larger rifle. Stay clear of bears. If you take a dog, make sure he is under control. Dogs can create dangerous situations with bears.

Rezanof–Monashka Road Log

Distance is measured from the junction of Rezanof Drive and Marine Way in downtown Kodiak (K).

K 0.1 (0.2 km) Mill Bay Road access to library, post office and Kodiak businesses.

K 0.4 (0.6 km) Entrance to Near Island bridge to St. Herman Harbor and Northend Park.

K 1.5 (2.4 km) Kodiak Island Hospital on left.

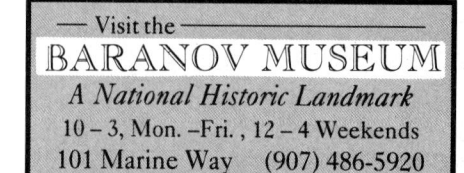

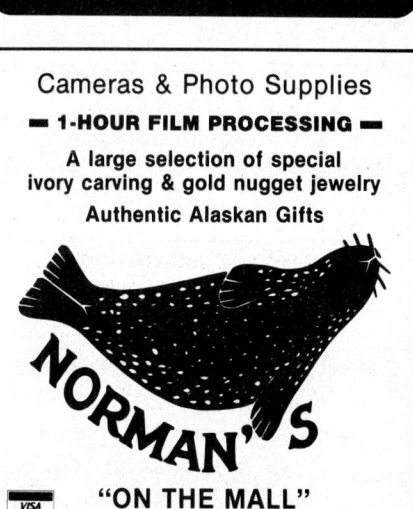

Visit the
BARANOV MUSEUM
A National Historic Landmark
10 – 3, Mon. –Fri., 12 – 4 Weekends
101 Marine Way   (907) 486-5920

Northern Exposure GALLERY
Fine Art & Quality Framing
103 Center Street   Bakery Mall
Kodiak, Alaska 99615   (907) 486-4956

Cameras & Photo Supplies
— 1-HOUR FILM PROCESSING —
A large selection of special ivory carving & gold nugget jewelry
Authentic Alaskan Gifts

NORMAN'S
"ON THE MALL"
Kodiak, Alaska
414 Marine Way
Phone (907) 486-3315
Established 1944

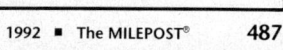

Outdoor Theater and Historic Drama at its best...
Frank Brink's
CRY OF THE WILD RAM
Alaska's longest Running Play - 26th Season - 1992
8 p.m.
July 31, August 1, 5, 6, 7, 8, 12, 13, 14, 15
For Tickets or Information:
The Kodiak Arts Council
P.O. Box 1792, Kodiak, Alaska 99615
(907) 486-5291

CY'S SPORTING GOODS
Open 7 days a week
- Complete Licensed Outfitter
- Hunting, Fishing & Commercial Gear
- Sport & Commercial Licenses

(907) 486-3900
202 Shelikof
(right across from small boat harbor)

BUILDING MEMORIES aboard the *M/V Ten Bears*
- Photography Excursions
- Fishing & Hunting Charters

Kodiak Western Charters, Dept. 10
PO Box 4123 • Kodiak, Alaska • 99615
Phone: 907 • 486 • 2200

K 3.1 (5 km) Turnout with picnic tables by beach, good viewpoint.

K 3.6 (5.8 km) Road on right leads to Fort Abercrombie State Park. Drive in 0.2 mile/ 0.3 km to campground; 18 campsites, water, toilets. View of bay and beach, WWII fortifications. Just beyond the campground entrance is the Alaska State Parks ranger station, open weekdays 9 A.M. to 2 P.M.; pay phone, public restrooms, park information. At the end of the access road, 0.5 mile/ 0.8 km from Monashka Road is the amphitheater where *Cry of the Wild Ram* is performed in August. ▲

K 6.9 (11.1 km) Road on right leads to VFW.

K 8.4 (13.5 km) Road to right leads to Pillar Creek Beach, a fishing and picnicking spot.

K 9.3 (15 km) Viewpoint with beautiful, panoramic view.

K 11.3 (18.2 km) Bridge over Monashka Creek.

K 11.4 (18.3 km) Road end. Paths lead through woods to secluded Monashka beach.

Chiniak Road Log

Distance from Kodiak's U.S. post office building (K) is followed by distance from Cape Greville (CG).

K 0 CG 47.6 (76.6 km) Kodiak U.S. post office building.

K 2.3 (3.7 km) **CG 45.3** (72.9 km) Gibson Cove city campground with showers and restrooms. Fee $2 per night. ▲

K 4.4 (7.1 km) **CG 43.2** (69.5 km) U.S. Fish and Wildlife Service Visitor Center and Kodiak National Wildlife Refuge headquarters; open weekdays year-round, 8 A.M. to 4:30 P.M., weekends, noon to 4:30 P.M. Exhibits and films on Kodiak wildlife. Road on left to Buskin River state recreation site; 18 RV campsites, picnic tables and shelter, water, pit toilets and dump station. Fishing along **Buskin River** and on beach area at river's mouth for red, silver and pink salmon and trout. Parking for fishermen. ⊷▲

K 5 (8 km) **CG 42.6** (68.5 km) Turnoff on right for Anton Larsen Bay Road (see log this section).

K 5.1 (8.2 km) **CG 42.5** (68.4 km) Entrance to Kodiak airport.

K 5.6 (9 km) **CG 42** (67.6 km) CAUTION: Jet blast area at end of runway. Stop here and wait if you see a jet preparing for takeoff.

K 6.7 (10.8 km) **CG 39.9** (64.2 km) Entrance to U.S. Coast Guard station.

K 7.2 (11.6 km) **CG 40.4** (65 km) Road continues around Womens Bay. The drive out to Cape Greville affords excellent views of the extremely rugged coastline of the island.

K 9.5 (15.3 km) **CG 38.1** (61.3 km) Rodeo and fairgrounds.

K 10.1 (16.3 km) **CG 37.5** (60.3 km) Sargent Creek.

K 10.7 (17.2 km) **CG 36.9** (59.5 km) Russian River and Bells Flat Road.

K 11 (17.7 km) **CG 36.6** (58.9 km) Pavement ends, gravel begins.

K 11.1 (17.9 km) **CG 36.5** (58.7 km) Grocery and liquor store, diesel and unleaded gas.

K 11.2 (18 km) **CG 36.4** (58.6 km) View of Bells Flat.

K 11.3 (18.2 km) **CG 36.3** (58.4 km) Store and gas station (diesel and unleaded).

K 12.3 (19.8 km) **CG 35.3** (56.8 km) Saloni Creek.

K 14.1 (22.7 km) **CG 33.5** (53.9 km) Turnout with view of Mary Island and Womens Bay.

K 16.5 (26.6 km) **CG 31.1** (50 km) USCG Holiday Beach radio station. Watch for livestock on road from here on.

K 17.4 (28 km) **CG 30.2** (48.6 km) Road east to Holiday Beach.

K 17.7 (28.5 km) **CG 29.9** (48.1 km) USCG receiving station; emergency phone.

K 19.8 (31.9 km) **CG 27.8** (44.7 km) Undeveloped picnic area in grove of trees along beach of Middle Bay; access to beach. Watch for cattle.

K 20 (32.2 km) **CG 27.6** (44.4 km) Small Creek bridge.

K 20.2 (32.5 km) **CG 27.4** (44.1 km) Salt Creek bridge.

K 21.4 (34.4 km) **CG 26.2** (42.2 km) American River bridge. River empties into Middle Bay.

K 21.8 (35.1 km) **CG 25.8** (41.5 km) Unimproved road on right, suitable only for 4-wheel-drive vehicles, leads toward Saltery Cove. Check road conditions in Kodiak before driving it.

K 24.5 (39.4 km) **CG 23.1** (37.2 km) Mayflower Beach; rock in distance resembling square-rigged vessel is Mayflower Rock.

K 25 (40.2 km) **CG 22.6** (36.4 km) View of Kalsin Bay.

K 26.2 (42.2 km) **CG 21.4** (34.4 km) Turnout.

K 28.3 (45.5 km) **CG 19.3** (31.1 km) Road drops down to head of Kalsin Bay.

K 28.6 (46 km) **CG 19** (30.6 km) Kalsin Inn Ranch; food, bar, gas (no unleaded), camping and lodging. ▲

K 29.6 (47.6 km) **CG 18** (29 km) Olds River.

K 30 (48.3 km) **CG 17.6** (28.3 km) Kalsin River (creek) bridge. Slow down for cattle guard in road just before bridge. Kalsin Inn Ranch; bar, restaurant, gas, camping. ▲

K 30.3 (48.8 km) **CG 17.3** (27.8 km) Road forks: Turn left for Chiniak, right for Pasagshak Bay. Northland Ranch Resort; food, lodging and horseback rides. See Pasagshak Bay Road log this section.

K 31.1 (50 km) **CG 16.5** (26.6 km) Highway maintenance station.

K 32 (51.5 km) **CG 15.6** (25.1 km) Picnic area with tables beside Kalsin Bay.

K 33.2 (53.4 km) **CG 14.4** (23.2 km) Myrtle Creek, picnic site.

K 36 (57.9 km) **CG 11.6** (18.7 km) Brookers Lagoon.

K 36.6 (58.9 km) **CG 11** (17.7 km) Roslyn River. Access to Isthmus Bay beach, a beautiful area with picnic tables.

K 39.2 (63.1 km) **CG 8.4** (13.5 km) Access to a beautiful point overlooking the sea; site of WWII installations. Good place for photos.

K 39.5 (63.6 km) **CG 8.1** (13 km) Beautiful beach on Chiniak Bay with rolling breakers.

K 40 (64.4 km) **CG 7.6** (12.2 km) Twin Creek.

K 40.3 (64.8 km) **CG 7.3** (11.7 km) **Pony Lake** (stocked). ⊷

K 41.1 (66.1 km) **CG 6.5** (10.5 km) Chiniak School and public library.

K 42.2 (67.9 km) **CG 5.4** (8.7 km) Road's End bar and restaurant; phone 486-2885.

K 42.3 (68.1 km) **CG 5.3** (8.5 km) Chiniak Point. State-maintained road ends. Unmaintained road continues as public easement across Leisnoi Native Corp. land.

K 42.4 (68.2 km) **CG 5.2** (8.4 km) Road to Chiniak Lake.

K 47.6 (76.6 km) **CG 0** Cape Greville. Named by Captain Cook in 1778.

Pasagshak Bay Road Log

Distance from junction with Chiniak Road (J) is followed by distance from Fossil Beach (FB).

J 0 FB 16.4 (26.4 km) Turn right for Pasagshak Bay and Fossil Beach at **Milepost K 30.3** Chiniak Road. Road leads up the valley of Kalsin Creek past a dude ranch.

J 6.6 (10.6 km) **FB 9.8** (15.8 km) Road crosses Lake Rose Tead on causeway. Good fishing in river from here to the ocean. ⊷

J 10.9 (17.5 km) **FB 5.5** (8.8 km) View of Pasagshak Bay.

J 14.4 (23.2 km) **FB 2** (3.2 km) Trail leads left toward Narrow Cape. Trail is recommended for 4-wheel-drive vehicles only.

J 16.4 (26.4 km) **FB 0** Road ends at Fossil Beach at Pasagshak Point. Pasagshak River state recreation site: camping, toilets, water. ▲

Anton Larsen Bay Road Log

Distance from the turnoff (T) is followed by distance from the end of the road (E).

T 0 E 11.6 (18.7 km) Turnoff for Anton Larsen Bay Road is on Chiniak Road immediately before crossing the Buskin River bridge; turnoff is unmarked.

T 1.2 (1.9 km) **E 10.4** (16.7 km) USCG communications site Buskin Lake. Road leads through this facility.

T 1.4 (2.2 km) **E 10.3** (16.4 km) Turn on unpaved road to Anton Larsen Bay.

T 2 (3.2 km) **E 9.6** (15.4 km) High hill on right is Pyramid Mountain (elev. 2,420 feet/ 738m).

T 7.3 (11.7 km) **E 4.3** (6.9 km) Red Cloud River bridge. A small, unimproved campsite is adjacent to river on right. ▲

T 8.7 (14 km) **E 2.9** (4.7 km) Cascade Lake trail leads off to the right.

T 9 (14.5 km) **E 2.6** (4.2 km) Head of Anton Larsen Bay. The bay is named for an early Scandinavian settler of this area. Bears are occasionally spotted in the Anton Larsen area.

T 10.1 (16.3 km) **E 1.5** (2.4 km) A public small-boat launch is adjacent to the road. Road continues on left side of bay for approximately 1.5 miles/2.4 km.

T 11.6 (18.7 km) **E 0** Road ends. A footpath continues beyond this point.

Meet Ernest and Dorothy Hopper At...

ROAD'S END

Mile 42 Chiniak Road

Come out and enjoy our lounge and restaurant.

Whale and deer watching
Eagles, otters and birds galore
Fantastic scenery
Wonderful photography

ROOMS • FULL MENU • BAR

Box 5629, Chiniak, Alaska 99615

(907) 486-2885

PRINCE WILLIAM SOUND

Includes Columbia Glacier, Whittier, Valdez and Cordova
(See map, page 543)

Southcentral Alaska's Prince William Sound lies at the north extent of the Gulf of Alaska. It is equally as spectacular as southeastern Alaska's Inside Passage. The area is also rich in wildlife. Visitors may see Dall sheep, mountain goats, sea lions, sea otters, whales, harbor seals, bald eagles and other birds. The waters carry all species of Pacific salmon, king, Dungeness and tanner crab, halibut and rockfish.

This section includes: Columbia Glacier; Whittier; Valdez, start of the Richardson Highway; and Cordova, start of the Copper River Highway.

There are several ways to explore Prince William Sound. From Anchorage, drive south on the Seward Highway 47 miles/75.6 km to Portage and board the Alaska Railroad shuttle train for a 30-minute ride to Whittier (there is no road connection to Whittier), or take the Alaska Railroad train from Anchorage to Whittier. (See the ALASKA RAILROAD section.) You may also start your trip across Prince William Sound from Valdez by driving 304 miles/498.2 km from Anchorage to Valdez via the Glenn and Richardson highways (see GLENN HIGHWAY and RICHARDSON HIGHWAY sections).

From Whittier or Valdez, board the ferry or one of the privately operated excursion boats to tour Prince William Sound. Flightseeing trips are also available. Depending on your itinerary and type of transportation, you may see the glacier and return to Anchorage in a day or have to stay overnight along the way. All-inclusive tours of Prince William Sound are available out of Anchorage.

Plan your trip in advance. Reservations for the ferry or cruise boats are necessary. The Alaska Railroad does not take reservations, although passengers with confirmed ferry reservations are given first priority when loading.

Tour boats offer close-up views of Prince William Sound scenery. (Jerrianne Lowther, staff)

Columbia Glacier

Star attraction of Prince William Sound is Columbia Glacier, one of the largest and most magnificent of the tidewater glaciers along the Alaska coast. The Columbia Glacier has an area of about 440 square miles/1144 square km. The glacier is more than 40 miles/64 km long; its tidewater terminus, which visitors will see on their trip across Prince William Sound, is more than 6 miles/9.7 km across. Columbia Glacier has receded almost a mile in recent years, and scientists are currently studying the glacier's retreat and increased iceberg production, which could pose a hazard to oil tankers from Valdez.

The face of the glacier, which is visible from the bay, varies in height above sea level from 164 to 262 feet/50 to 80m. Columbia Bay teems with life at the face of the glacier. An abundance of plankton (microscopic water plants and animals) thrives here attracting great numbers of fish which in turn attract bald eagles, kittiwakes, gulls and harbor seals. Seals can usually be seen resting on ice floes or swimming about in the icy waters.

The glacier was named by the Harriman Alaska expedition in 1899 for Columbia University in New York City.

The present-day glacier is born in the perpetual snows of Mount Einstein (elev. 11,552 feet/3,521m) in the Chugach Mountains. Near the glacier's source is Mount Witherspoon (elev. 12,012 feet/3,661m). Both peaks are visible from the face of the glacier in clear weather.

By boat you can enjoy close-up views of the glacier face and watch giant icebergs calve (break off) from the ice wall. There are daily and weekly charters by yacht or sailboat. You might also try a flightseeing trip over the glacier. (See the ads in Whittier, Valdez and Cordova in this section for charter boats offering sightseeing trips and flying services offering flightseeing trips.) See the MARINE ACCESS ROUTES section for ferry schedule.

Whittier

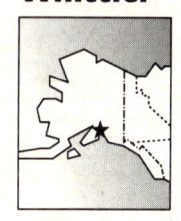

Located at the head of Passage Canal on Prince William Sound, 75 miles/121 km southeast of Anchorage. **Population:** 299. **Emergency Services:** Police, Fire and Medical, phone 472-2340. **Visitor Information:** Information kiosk at the Harbor Triangle.

Elevation: 30 feet/9m. **Climate:** Normal daily temperature for July is 56°F/13°C; for

---

IRMA'S OUTPOST
Delicatessen • Liquor Store
Deli Sandwiches and Pastries
Char-Burgers • Beer and Wine Available
ORDERS TO GO • CHARTER LUNCHES
• At The Harbor Triangle   472-2461

U.S.C.G. Master Licensed & Insured
SEA HUNTER CHARTERS
Prince William Sound ★ Alaska
Specializing in Overnight & Fishing Charters
Call Capt. Don Hanks c/o (907) 694-2229
P.O. Box 621 • Eagle River, Alaska 99577

1992 ■ The MILEPOST®   489

January, 25°F/-4°C. Mean annual precipitation is 174 inches, including 264 inches of snow.

Private Aircraft: Airstrip adjacent northwest; elev. 30 feet/9m; length 1,500 feet/457m; gravel; no fuel; unattended.

Named after the poet John Greenleaf Whittier, Whittier is nestled at the base of mountains that line Passage Canal, a fjord that extends eastward into Prince William Sound. The community is connected to the Seward Highway by railroad and to other Prince William Sound communities by ferry. No roads lead to Whittier.

Whittier was created by the U.S. government during WWII as a port and petroleum delivery center tied to bases farther north by the Alaska Railroad and later a pipeline. The railroad spur from Portage was completed in 1943 and Whittier became the primary debarkation point for cargo, troops and dependents of the Alaska Command. Construction of the huge buildings that dominate Whittier began in 1948 and the Port of Whittier, strategically valuable for its ice-free deep-water port, remained activated until 1960, at which time the population was 1,200. The government tank farm is still located here.

The 14-story Begich Towers, formerly the Hodge Bldg., houses more than half of Whittier's population. Now a condominium, the building was used by the U.S. Army for family housing and civilian bachelor quarters. The building was renamed in honor of U.S. Rep. Nick Begich of Alaska, who along with Rep. Hale Boggs of Louisiana, disappeared in a small plane near here in 1972 while on a campaign tour.

The Buckner Bldg., completed in 1953, was once the largest building in Alaska and was called the "city under one roof." It is now privately owned and is to be renovated.

Whittier Manor was built in the early 1950s by private developers as rental units for civilian employees and soldiers who were ineligible for family housing elsewhere. In early 1964, the building was bought by another group of developers and became a condominium, which now houses the remainder of Whittier's population.

Since military and government activities ceased, the economy of Whittier rests largely on the fishing industry, tourism and the port.

Whittier has 2 inns providing accommodations, several restaurants, 2 bars, gift shops, laundry facilities, 4 general stores, and a camper park for tents and self-contained RVs ($5 nightly fee). There is no bank in Whittier.

WHITTIER ADVERTISERS

Anchor Inn ....Ph. (907) 472-2354
Irma's Outpost ....Ph. (907) 472-2461
Sea Hunter Charters ....Ph. (907) 694-2229
Sportsman's Inn ....Ph. (907) 472-2352

Prince William Sound is home to many marine mammals. (Nancy Faville)

Valdez

Located on Port Valdez (pronounced val-DEEZ), an estuary off Valdez Arm in Prince William Sound. Valdez is 115 air miles/185 km and 304 highway miles/489 km from Anchorage, 368 highway miles/592 km from Fairbanks. Valdez is the southern terminus of the Richardson Highway and the trans-Alaska pipeline. **Population:** 3,271.

Emergency Services: Alaska State Troopers, phone 835-4359 or 835-4350. **City Police, Fire Department** and **Ambulance**, emergency only phone 911. **Hospital**, Valdez Community, phone 835-2249. Report **oil spills** to Dept. of Environmental Conservation, dial 0 and ask for Zenith 9300. **Maritime Search and Rescue**, dial 0 for Zenith 5555, toll free.

Visitor Information: The visitor information center, located opposite city hall at 200 Chenega St., is open 7 days a week from 8 A.M. to 8 P.M. The visitor center features daily films on the earthquake. Write: Valdez Convention and Visitors Bureau, Box 1603-M, Valdez 99686; or phone 835-2984, fax 835-4845. Visitors may also check the community calendar at the Valdez Civic Center for information on local events, or phone 835-4440 with questions about ongoing or special events.

Elevation: Sea level. **Climate:** Record high was 81°F/27°C in August 1977; record

---

⚓ ANCHOR INN

Mountain, Glacier Waterfront Hotel

Satellite TV
Room Phones

Bar and Restaurant

**Grocery Store
Modern Laundromat**

Phone: (907) 472-2354
Box 750, Whittier, Alaska 99693

SPORTSMAN'S INN
WHITTIER ALASKA

— **DINING • BAR** —
Overlooking beautiful Prince William Sound and harbor activity.

— **HOTEL** —
Modern Conveniences, with
Public Laundry, Showers and Sauna

(907) 472-2352   Gary & Woody
P.O. Box 626, Whittier, Alaska 99693

COOPER'S COTTAGE
Bed & Breakfast
(the cozy alternative)
Charming, Clean, Comfortable
3 Bedrooms, 2 Baths
Private Living, Dining area
Continental Breakfast
Homemade bread & jam
Fresh ground coffee
(907) 835-4810
324 Mendeltna Street
(walk to downtown, waterfront)
Dick & Bonnette Cooper
PO Box 563
Valdez, AK 99686

Arctic Tern
Bed & Breakfast

• Home-cooked breakfast
• Three clean, non-smoking rooms
• Comfortable dining and TV area
• Laundry facilities
• Walking distance to town

Rates - $50 Single - $60 Double

(907) 835-5290   724 Copper Drive
                    P.O. Box 1542
VISA MasterCard   Valdez, AK 99686

low -20°F/-29°C in January 1972. Normal daily maximum in January, 30°F/-1°C; daily minimum 21°F/-6°C. Normal daily maximum in July, 61°F/16°C; daily minimum 46°F/8°C. Average snowfall in Valdez from October to May is 303 inches, or about 25 feet. (By comparison, Anchorage averages about 6 feet in that period.) New snowfall records were set in January 1990, with snowfall for 1 day at 47 1/2 inches and snowfall for the month at 134 inches. Record monthly snowfall is 174.5 inches in February 1928. Windy (40 mph/64 kmph) in late fall. **Radio:** KCHU-770, KVAK 1230. **Television:** 7 channels via cable and satellite. **Newspaper:** *Valdez Vanguard* (weekly).

Private Aircraft: Valdez NR 2, 3.5 miles/5.6 km east; elev. 120 feet/37m; length 6,500 feet/1,981m; asphalt; fuel 80, 100, jet A1.

Flanked by the Alp-like Chugach Mountains, Valdez is often called Alaska's "Little Switzerland." The city lies on the north shore of Port Valdez, an estuary named in 1790 by Spanish explorer Don Salvador Fidalgo for Antonio Valdes y Basan, a Spanish naval officer.

Valdez was established in 1897-98 as a port of entry for gold seekers bound for the Klondike goldfields. Thousands of stamped-

---

GUSSIE'S LOWE ST. INN
BED & BREAKFAST
354 Lowe St., P.O. Box 64, Valdez, AK 99686
CLEAN, lovely rooms, private bath, comfortable beds, cable TV, homey-friendly atmosphere. NO stairs.
Complimentary breakfast. Call (907) 835-4448

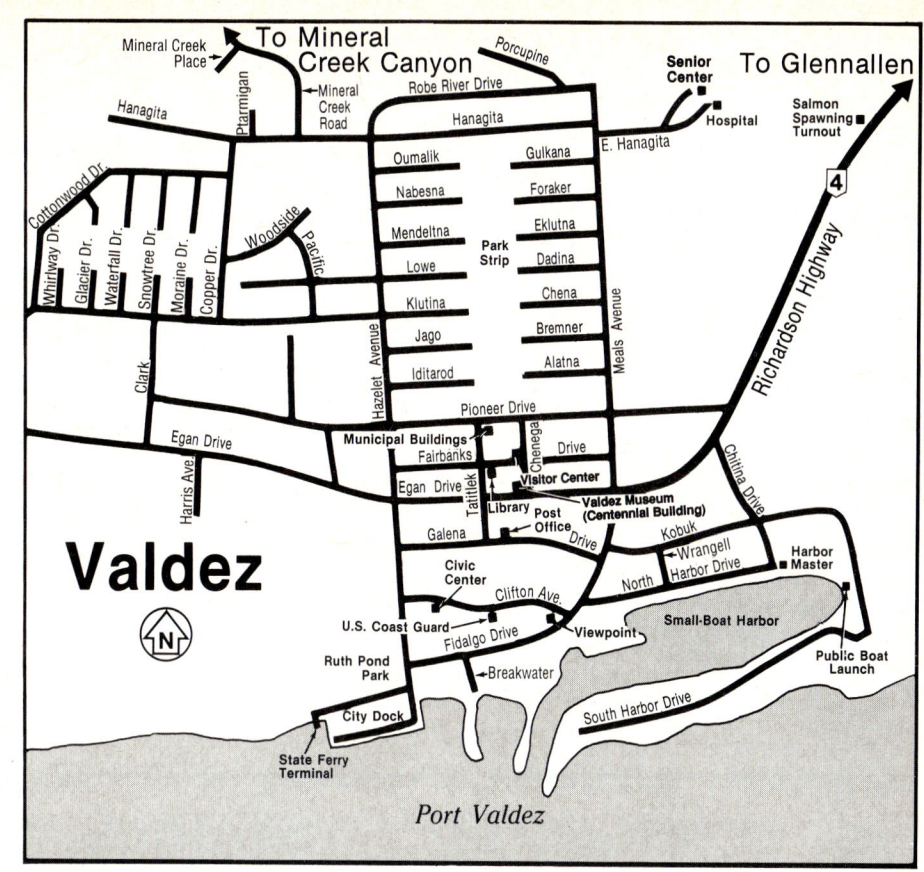

PRINCE WILLIAM SOUND • VALDEZ

Protect the environment—keep the North Country clean—use litter barrels.

Valdez
Don't miss the MAGIC

- Gold Rush Days
- Pipeline Terminus
- Scheduled Charters
- Flightseeing:
  Helicopter & Fixed Wing
- Modern Accommodations
- Glacier Cruises:
  Columbia, Shoup and more
- Fishing Charters & Derbies
- Camping, RV Parks & Services
- Historical Sightseeing & Museum
- Family Town with full range of shopping & health services

For further information contact:
Valdez Convention & Visitors Bureau
Box 1603-M
Valdez, Alaska 99686
(907) 835-2984
Fax: (907) 835-4845

photo by Paul Giraudin III

ers arrived in Valdez to follow the Valdez trail to the Eagle mining district in Alaska's Interior, and from there up the Yukon River to Dawson City and the Klondike. The Valdez trail was an especially deadly route, the first part of it leading over Valdez Glacier, where the early stampeders faced dangerous crevasses, snowblindness and exhaustion.

Copper discoveries in the Wrangell Mountains north of Valdez in the early 1900s brought more development to Valdez, and conflict. A proposed railroad from tidewater to the rich Kennicott copper mines at McCarthy began a bitter rivalry between Valdez and Cordova for the railway line. The Copper River & Northwestern Railway eventually went to Cordova, but not before Valdez had started its own railroad north. The Valdez railroad did not get very far: the only trace of its existence is an old hand-drilled railway tunnel at **Milepost V 14.9** on the Richardson Highway.

The old gold rush trail out of Valdez was developed into a sled and wagon road in the early 1900s, routed through Thompson Pass (rather than over the Valdez Glacier) by Captain Abercrombie of the U.S. Army, who was commissioned with connecting Fort Liscum (a military post established in 1900 near the present-day location of the pipeline terminal) with Fort Egbert in Eagle. Colonel Wilds P. Richardson of the Alaska Road Commission further developed the wagon road, building an automobile road from Valdez to Fairbanks which was completed in the early 1920s.

Old photos of Valdez show Valdez Glacier directly behind the town. This is because until 1964 Valdez was located about 4 miles east of its present location, closer to the glacier. The 1964 Good Friday earthquake, the most destructive earthquake ever to hit southcentral Alaska, virtually destroyed Valdez. The quake measured between 8.4 and 8.6 on the Richter scale (since revised to 9.2) and was centered in Prince William Sound. A tidal wave swept over Valdez wharf and engulfed the downtown area. Afterward, it was decided that Valdez would be rebuilt at a new townsite. By late August 1964, reconstruction projects had been approved for Valdez and relocation was under way. The last residents remaining at "old" Valdez moved to the new town in 1968.

Since its days as a port of entry for gold seekers, Valdez has been an important gate-

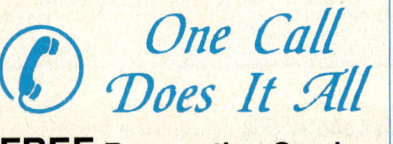

One Call Does It All

FREE Reservation Service
(907) 835-4988

BED & BREAKFAST ACCOMMODATIONS

Columbia Glacier Tours
Sightseeing • Flightseeing • Rafting
Halibut & Salmon Fishing Charters

P.O. Box 2197-MP
Valdez, Alaska 99686

STARR'S COUNTRY INN
Bed & Breakfast

Enjoy a quiet night in the pines in a quaint, 3-story log home

• Smoke-free rooms
• Queen-size beds
• Private baths
• Private entrances
• Homemade treats

(907) 835-2917
P.O. Box 2197-MP
Valdez, Alaska 99686

Snowtree Inn
Bed & Breakfast

• Beautiful Mountain View
• Homey atmosphere, 4 rooms available, each with Country decor
• Continental Breakfast serving Homemade breads & muffins
• Cable T.V. • No Smoking Please

$65 per night, per room

For Information & Reservations
Laura Rust • Owner
(907) 835-4399
P.O. Box 2195   Valdez, Alaska 99686

VALDEZ ADVERTISERS

Alaskan Flower Forget-Me-Not
  Bed and Breakfast ....Ph. (907) 835-2717
Alpine Aviation Adventures ....Valdez airport
Always Inn Bed &
  Breakfast ....Ph. (907) 835-4634
Anadyr Sea Kayaking
  Adventures ....Ph. (907) 835-2814
Arctic Tern Bed
  & Breakfast ....Ph. (907) 835-5290
Barra's Sunshine Inn Bed
  and Breakfast ....Ph. (907) 835-2776
Bear Paw R.V. Park ....Small Boat Harbor
Bear Paw Trading Post........Small Boat Harbor
Bed & Breakfast Valdez ....Ph. (907) 835-4211
Best of All Bed and
  Breakfast ....1104 Mineral Creek Dr.
Birch Tree Bed & Breakfast...........118 Eklutna
Boat House Bed and
  Breakfast, The ....725 N. Snowtree
Casa de LaBellezza Bed
  & Breakfast ....Ph. (907) 835-4489
Chapel of the Sea ....Ph. (907) 835-5141
Cooper's Cottage Bed
  & Breakfast ....324 Mendeltna St.
Downtown B&B Inn..........Ph. (907) 835-2791
Eagle Claw R.V. Park ....630 E. Pioneer Dr.
Easy Living Bed &
  Breakfast ....Ph. (907) 835-4208
Era Helicopters..................Ph. (907) 835-2595
Glacier Charter Service........Behind Totem Inn
Gussie's Lowe St. Inn........Ph. (907) 835-4448
Harbor Landing
  General Store, the ....Harbor Court
Hook Line and Sinker ......Chitina & Kobuk sts.
Ketchum Air
  Service, Inc. ....Ph. (907) 835-3789
Keynotes Bed
  & Breakfast ....Ph. (907) 835-4521
Keystone Raft &
  Kayak Adventures Inc...Ph. (907) 835-2606
Lake House Bed &
  Breakfast, The........Mile 6 Richardson Hwy.
Last Frontier
  Gallery ....Across from city museum
Lu-Lu Belle..........................Ph. (907) 835-5141
MacMurray's Alaska
  Halibut House ....Meals Ave.
Mike's Palace......................201 N. Harbor Dr.
New Town Chevron......................Downtown
One Call Does It All...........Ph. (907) 835-4988
Pat's Place Bed & Breakfast ....733 Copper Dr.
Prospector Apparel &
  Sporting Goods ....Ph. (907) 835-3858
Snowtree Inn Bed
  & Breakfast ....715 N. Snowtree
Stan Stephens Charters ....Westmark Dock
Starr's Country Inn Bed
  & Breakfast ....Ph. (907) 835-4988
Sugar & Spice.....................................Egan Dr.
Totem Inn ....Ph. (907) 835-4443
Valdez Convention and
  Visitors Bureau ....Ph. (907) 835-2984
Valdez Drug & Photo ....321 Fairbanks Dr.
Valdez Red Apple Market ....Egan Dr.
Valdez Tesoro ..Richardson Hwy. & Meals Ave.
Valdez Village Inn...............Ph. (907) 835-4445
Village Pharmacy ......Meals Ave. & Pioneer Dr.
Vintage B&B ....Ph. (907) 835-2092
Wendy's Bed &
  Breakfast ....Ph. (907) 835-4770
Westmark Valdez.............Ph. 1-800-544-0970

Readers of all ages will enjoy *TOKLAT: The Story of an Alaskan Grizzly Bear,* by Elma and Alfred Milotte. From Alaska Northwest Books™.

Pipeline workers sculpture outside the marine terminal. (Jerrianne Lowther, staff)

way to interior Alaska. With its port the most northerly ice-free port in the Western Hemisphere, and the Richardson Highway connecting it to the Alaska highway system, Valdez has evolved into a shipping center, offering the shortest link to much of interior Alaska for seaborne cargo.

Construction of the trans-Alaska pipeline was begun in 1974 and completed in 1977 (the first tanker load of oil shipped out of Valdez on Aug. 1, 1977). The 1,000-acre site at Port Valdez was chosen as the pipeline terminus; tours of the marine terminal are available (see Attractions).

From Prudhoe Bay on the Arctic Ocean, the 48-inch-diameter, 800-mile-/1287-km-long pipeline follows the Sagavanirktok River and Atigun Valley, crossing the Brooks Mountain Range at 4,747-foot/1,447-m Atigun Pass. South of the Brooks Range it passes through Dietrich and Koyukuk valleys and crosses the hills and muskeg of the Yukon–Tanana uplands to the Yukon River. South of the Yukon the line passes through more rolling hills 10 miles/16 km east of Fairbanks, then goes south from Delta Junction to the Alaska Range, where it reaches an elevation of 3,500 feet/1,067m at Isabel Pass before descending into the Copper River basin. It crests the Chugach Mountains at Thompson Pass (elev. 2,500 feet/762m) and descends through the Keystone Canyon to Valdez, where it is fed by gravity into tanks or directly into waiting oil tankers at the marine terminal.

Because of varying soil conditions along its route, the pipeline is both above and below ground. Where the warm oil would cause icy soil to thaw and erode, the pipeline goes above ground to avoid thawing. Where the frozen ground is mostly well-drained gravel or solid rock, and thawing not a problem, the line is underground.

The line has 10 pump stations and numerous large valves to control the flow of oil. The entire system is designed for central computer control from Valdez, or independent local control at each pump station.

National attention was focused on Valdez and the pipeline when the oil tanker *Exxon Valdez* ran aground in March 1989, causing an 11-million-gallon oil spill.

Valdez's economy depends on the oil industry, the Prince William Sound fishery and tourism. The city limits of Valdez comprise an area of 274 square miles/712 square km, including all surrounding mountains to timberline. Valdez has long been known for its beautiful setting, with the Chugach Mountains rising behind the city, and the small-boat harbor in front. The town has wide streets and open spaces, with the central residential district built around a park strip which runs from the business district almost to the base of the mountains behind town.

ACCOMMODATIONS

Services in Valdez include several restaurants and bars, grocery stores, sporting goods stores, 2 drugstores, gift shops, 4 service

WENDY'S BED & BREAKFAST

213 Porcupine, Valdez, Alaska   (907) 835-4770
Queen & Single Rooms ... Shared Bath ... Private Entrance ...
Community Room with TV ... Continental Breakfast ...
Walking Distance to Downtown – Shopping and Dining
QUIET • OPEN YEAR-ROUND
RATES $45–$65   Box 629, Valdez, AK 99686

ALWAYS INN BED & BREAKFAST

Charming, Clean, Comfortable Rooms
Complimentary Continental Breakfast
Convenient Downtown Location • Open Year Around
Families Welcome • Smoking Permitted • Single Rate $50 + tax.
Reservations (907) 835-4634.   See log ad under Accommodations.

Barra's Sunshine Inn Bed and Breakfast
HOME OF AMY LOU CHARTERS

Our sunny Alaskan hospitality includes:
- Alaska Travel Videos and Local Lore With a Smile
- Full Breakfast, Family Style, at Your Leisure
- Cheerful, Nonsmoking Rooms
- Close to Downtown and Ferry • Lots of Conversation and Information

Information (907) 835-2776 — Phil, Mary Lou and Amy Barra
1167 Mineral Creek Dr., P.O. Box 1676, Valdez, Alaska 99686

VALDEZ VILLAGE INN ALASKA

"Big city" comforts and convenience in a warm, friendly atmosphere.

100 Spacious Rooms with Private Baths
Color Television/Cable
Two Extra-Length Double Beds
Limited Room Service
Handicap Access

Our Health Club is a complete fitness center with exercise equipment, whirlpool and sauna. The Sugarloaf Saloon & Restaurant offer excellent dining.

VILLAGE INN HEALTH CLUB

SUGARLOAF SALOON & RESTAURANT

For Reservations Contact Your Travel Agent or

VALDEZ VILLAGE INN
P.O. Box 365
Valdez, Alaska 99686
(907) 835-4445

PRINCE WILLIAM SOUND • VALDEZ

BEAR PAW R.V. PARK
BOX 93, VALDEZ, ALASKA 99686 · PHONE (907) 835-2530

CARAVANS WELCOME

BEAR PAW R.V. PARK
STAN STEPHENS CHARTERS
TURN LEFT AT NEW TOWN CHEVRON
COMPLETE LOCAL & TOUR INFORMATION

ON THE SMALL-BOAT HARBOR IN DOWNTOWN
VALDEZ
A BLOCK OR LESS TO MOST SHOPS AND STORES

- FULL AND PARTIAL HOOKUPS
- Level, crushed gravel pads
- Clean, private restrooms
- Hot unmetered showers
- Coin-operated launderette and dump station for registered guests only
- Two public telephones

Ticket Agent For
Stan Stephens Charters
SEE MAJESTIC COLUMBIA GLACIER

We can ticket:
- Major Columbia Glacier Cruises
- Pipeline Terminal Tours
- Halibut and Salmon Fishing Charters
- Flightseeing

You haven't seen glaciers until you've seen Columbia

494 The MILEPOST® ■ 1992

---

stations, hardware, hair stylists and numerous churches.

Valdez has 7 motel/hotel facilities and numerous bed and breakfasts. You are advised to make reservations well in advance. Summer tourist season is also the peak work season, and accommodations fill up quickly. Expect to pay $90 and up for a double motel room with bath, $50 to $70 for a bed and breakfast.

Bear Paw Trading Post Gift Shop, next to Bear Paw RV Park on Harbor Drive, features fine Alaska Native arts and crafts. Carved walrus ivory, scrimshaw, soapstone carvings, Native masks, fur items. Gold nugget jewelry, jade, hematite. Prints and books by Doug and Patti Lindstrand. Film, postcards, souvenirs, Alaska books.
[ADVERTISEMENT]

One Call Does It All. Free reservation service for bed-and-breakfast accommodations, Columbia Glacier tours, and rafting trips. Halibut and salmon fishing charters. We can find you a place to stay; accommodations at reasonable prices; some with wheelchair access. One call does it all! (907) 835-4988. See display ad this section.
[ADVERTISEMENT]

Alaskan Flower Forget-Me-Not Bed and Breakfast, (907) 835-2717. Prince William

BEAR PAW TRADING POST
Walrus Ivory · Furs · Jade
Art Prints · Gold Nugget Jewelry
Film · Postcards

See log ad

BED & BREAKFAST VALDEZ
• 3346 EAGLE •

Just minutes away from downtown, BED & BREAKFAST - VALDEZ offers you some of the finest accommodations available. Quiet, cozy rooms with private bath, cable television, and beautifully furnished in Turn of the Century antique oak.

All homemade quiches, cheesecakes, coffeecakes and rolls, plus fruit, cereals, coffee and juice are ready when you are.

Valdez hospitality, the wonderful warmth of the decor, the relaxed atmosphere, meeting new friends and sharing your adventures, all combine to truly make this your home away from home.

$65.00 per night

FOR MORE INFORMATION
Ms. Patricia Wilson, Bed & Breakfast-Valdez
BOX 442, VALDEZ, ALASKA 99686
(907) 835-4211 Evenings

VALDEZ, ALASKA

Glacier Day

Glacier Night

Prince William Sound and the mighty Columbia Glacier. Awe-inspiring mountains that plunge into a deep blue ocean. **Spend the day** with us, getting to know this beautiful land and the creatures that inhabit it—sea otters, whales, eagles and seals. Captain Stan Stephens, his family and crew offer their daily 8 to 8½-hour cruise to Columbia Glacier, which includes a seafood feast at Growler Island Wilderness Camp. Cruises depart daily from Valdez, mid-May—mid-September.

$87.50 per adult, $59.50 per child

STAN STEPHENS CHARTERS & CRUISES

Spend the night at Growler Island Wilderness Camp. With almost 24 hours of daylight, the night is full of adventure. Explore the many icebergs beached on our island's shores, or canoe and hike around this wilderness retreat. Tuck into your private tent/cabin for a peaceful night's rest, lulled by the soft rumble of icebergs from nearby Columbia Glacier. Price includes 8 to 8½-hour cruise, overnight accommodations, all meals and activities.

$152.50. per adult, $130. per child
($75. per adult and $55. per child for each additional night)

Call today for reservations 1-800-992-1297
Ask about our special cruises & tours departing from Whittier

Stan Stephens Charters & Cruises • P.O. Box 1297-M92 • Valdez, Alaska 99686 • (907) 835-4731

PRINCE WILLIAM SOUND

Sound hospitality at its best. We know you will enjoy your stay. Relax in one of our luxurious guest rooms with TV and phone. Nonsmoking. Informal breakfast. Downtown Valdez. P.O. Box 1153, Valdez, AK 99686. Also "Ask Us" Alaska Flower Reservation Service for B&Bs, charters, tours; (907) 835-2646. [ADVERTISEMENT]

Always Inn Bed & Breakfast. Charming, clean, comfortable rooms with refrigerators, microwaves, coffee pots and cable TVs with HBO, Cinemax and Disney. Complimentary continental breakfast. Convenient downtown location within walking distance of restaurants, shopping, the museum, etc. Families welcome, infants and toddlers free, smoking permitted, well-behaved pets accepted. Single rate $50 + tax. Group and winter rates available. Hostess: Peggie Coats, P.O. Box 3149, Valdez, AK 99686. Phone (907) 835-4634. See display ad this section. [ADVERTISEMENT]

Birch Tree Bed & Breakfast offers Alaskan hospitality and decor. We provide a suite with a private entrance, bath, bedroom, family room and dining area with microwave and refrigerator. Breakfast is at your convenience with continental service. Call Kandi and David Connor at (907) 835-4254 or write P.O. Box 2500, 118 Eklutna, Valdez, AK 99686. [ADVERTISEMENT]

Casa de LaBellezza Bed & Breakfast in beautiful Valdez. Elegant, first-class accommodations located within the city. Explore, go fishing, take tours to Columbia Glacier and Alyeska pipeline terminus. Evenings: Relax and enjoy Alaskan hospitality with coffee and pizzelles. Late night arrivals or early morning departures (ferry) okay. Hot breakfasts. See display ad. [ADVERTISEMENT]

Downtown B & B Inn and local bed-and-breakfast referral service, 113 Galena Dr. Centrally located near small-boat harbor, museum, ferry terminal, downtown shopping. View rooms, private and shared baths, coin-op laundry, TV available. Serve your own breakfast at your convenience. Reasonable rates. Single, double, family rooms. In Alaska: (800) 478-2791 or (907) 835-2791. See display ad this section. [ADVERTISEMENT]

Totem Inn, downtown Valdez, featuring 23 deluxe rooms and one 2-bedroom suite. Private baths, satellite TV, phones, handicap access. RV parking available. Totem restaurant open 5 A.M. Dinner specialty: Seafood Platter. Our restaurant and lounge are famous for their Alaskan hospitality. Open year-round. Motel reservations suggested. (907) 835-4443. See display ad this section. [ADVERTISEMENT]

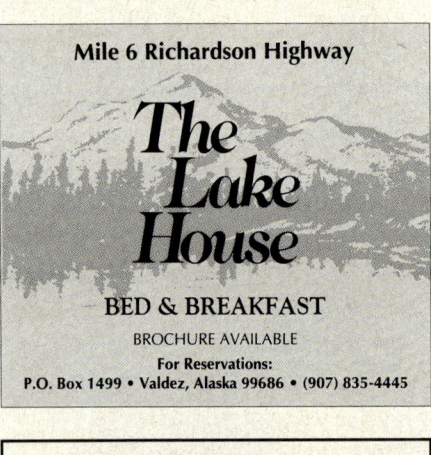

Sound Advice

Located between mountain peaks that pierce the clouds and the splendor of Prince William Sound, Valdez offers the traveler a perfect combination of scenic delights and outdoor activities.

The Westmark Valdez offers guests a splendid view of the boat harbor & port area, comfortable lodging and exceptional food & beverage service.

- 98 Rooms • No-smoking Rooms
- Dining Room and Lounge
- Free Parking

Special Summer Value Rates from $49

Rooms at lower rates are capacity controlled and good on selected rooms & dates only. Call for complete information. Subject to change without notice.

Westmark
VALDEZ

100 Fidalgo Drive
P.O. Box 468,
Valdez Alaska 99686

Central Reservations
1-800-544-0970 (U.S.)
1-800-999-2570 (Canada)

Westmark Hotels covers the north with hotels and inns throughout Alaska and the Yukon. Come be our guest.

VINTAGE B & B
405 W. Mendeltna
(907) 835-2092
Full-size bed • Private hall bath
Continental or full breakfast
No smoking or children

Mile 6 Richardson Highway

The Lake House
BED & BREAKFAST
BROCHURE AVAILABLE
For Reservations:
P.O. Box 1499 • Valdez, Alaska 99686 • (907) 835-4445

KEYNOTES
Bed & Breakfast
at the Note Pad
338 Oumalik Street
Cozy, old fashioned room in the heart of Valdez.
Home baked breads, freshly ground coffee.
— No smoking, please —
Jim and Robin Lindsey
(907) 835-4521
Box 809, Valdez, Alaska 99686

Welcome to Valdez
BEST OF ALL
Bed and Breakfast

Your Home Away From Home

Enjoy Alaskan hospitality with us in our spacious home within walking distance of downtown, restaurants and ferry.

Guests can choose to be alone in their room with TV and VCR or socialize in our cathedral-ceilinged living room which has Asian-Alaskan decor.

Beautiful mountain views from every window

SPECIAL BREAKFASTS
Families Welcome • No Pets
Smoking Outside Please

Bed & Breakfast (907) 835-4524

Write:
P.O. Box 1578, 1104 Mineral Creek Dr.
Valdez, Alaska 99686

CLEAN & COZY
Easy Living Bed & Breakfast

3 large non-smoking Rooms, each with private bath
Separate guest kitchen, dining area and laundry
Guest lounge with cable TV and phone
Continental breakfast • Freezer space for your catch
Wheelchair accessible, handicapped facility • Centrally located
Children welcome • Smoking outside only
Short walk to museum, ferry terminal, downtown shopping
Your Hosts: lifetime Alaskans, Mike & Donna Waller

OPEN YEAR AROUND • (907) 835-4208

551 Woodside Drive, PO Box 2435
Valdez, Alaska 99686

Valdez Village Inn, downtown Valdez: 100 modern rooms. Cable TV, private baths. Cottages with kitchenettes. Handicap access. Fitness center, sauna, jacuzzi. Sugarloaf Restaurant & Saloon. Courtesy van to airport and ferry terminal. Room/Glacier Cruise packages. Phone (907) 835-4445, fax (907) 835-2437. See display ad this section.

[ADVERTISEMENT]

There are 3 private RV parks with hookups in town near the small-boat harbor. The nearest public campground is Valdez Glacier campground, at the end of airport road, about 6 miles/9.7 km from town; turn left at **Milepost NV 3.4** on the Richardson Highway. This city-operated campground has 101 sites, tent camping areas, grassy picnic areas, firepits, tables, litter barrels, water and toilets; 15-day limit, $5 fee charged.   ▲

Municipal dump station and freshwater fill-up on Chitina Drive in the small-boat docking area. Dump station and diesel at Valdez Tesoro. Dump station at Bear Paw R.V. Park for registered guests.

Bear Paw R.V. Park, centrally located on scenic North Harbor Drive overlooking the boat harbor, puts you within easy walking distance of museums, shops, restaurants, entertainment, charter boats—no need to unhook and drive to grocery stores or points of interest. Full, partial or no hookups; immaculate private restrooms with hot showers. Dump station and coin-operated launderette for guests. Tenters welcome. Also available: waterfront full-hookup RV sites for adults only. Fish cleaning table and freezer available. Don't miss the Bear Paw Trading Post Gift Shop. Let us book your glacier tour at the reservations desk in our spacious office lounge, where the coffee pot is always on. Advance reservations recommended: (907) 835-2530. (Bear Paw does fill up!) Let us know if you're coming in on the evening ferry and we'll be there to help you get parked. See our large display ad this section.

[ADVERTISEMENT]

Eagle Claw RV Park, the newest RV park in downtown Valdez offers you service with ▲

Pat's Place Bed & Breakfast
Nicely furnished 2-bedroom apartment with self-serve continental breakfast, washer and dryer and private entry. For a pleasant experience, be our guests while visiting Valdez!   Hosts: Pat, Roger and Heather Holmes

P.O. Box 2328, Valdez, Alaska 99686   •   (907) 835-5078

Alaskan Hospitality with an Italian Flavor

Casa de LaBellezza
Bed & Breakfast
in Valdez, Alaska

(907) 835-4489

Full Breakfast • Quiet
Open Year Around

333 Oumalik Street, P.O. Box 294
Valdez, Alaska 99686

Walking distance to Shopping • Dining • Ferry

SEE OUR AD UNDER ACCOMMODATIONS

THE BOAT HOUSE BED and BREAKFAST
Private or Shared Bath • Laundry • Walking Distance to Downtown

Rates from $50 tax included • 10% Senior Discount

725 North Snowtree   Brochure: P.O. Box 1815, Valdez, Alaska 99686
Your Hosts: Ken, Linda, Helen and David Neslund   (907) 835-4407

DOWNTOWN B&B INN

View Rooms
Private and Shared Baths

Close to Small Boat Harbor,
Ferry Terminal and
Downtown Shopping

Reasonable Rates • Families Welcome • Local Bed & Breakfast Referrals

113 GALENA DR. • P.O. BOX 184, VALDEZ, AK 99686

In Alaska (800) 478-2791   (907) 835-2791

Totem Inn
VALDEZ

RESTAURANT
We *specialize* in the
SEAFOOD PLATTER

LOUNGE & MOTEL
Serving great libations
and
Alaskan tales

*Largest
Wildlife Display
in this area*

PLEASE CALL OR WRITE
TO ENSURE RESERVATIONS
MasterCard, VISA & American Express

P.O. BOX 648MP
VALDEZ, AK 99686

835-4443

PRINCE WILLIAM SOUND • VALDEZ

1992 ■ The MILEPOST®   497

PRINCE WILLIAM SOUND · VALDEZ

The greatest concentration of tidewater-calving glaciers is in Prince William Sound.
(Jerrianne Lowther, staff)

a smile. Let Herb, Jeff or Laura take care of all your bookings on cruises, tours and charters. Enjoy the beautiful panoramic view of our mountains and glaciers right off our front porch! We also can let you know where the hottest fishing spots are or the quietest walking trails! Fish-cleaning table and freezer available. Parking with us puts you within walking distance of our museum, gift shops, banks and even the largest grocery store on our same block! Call us for reservations, (907) 835-2373. Stay with us and leave feeling like family! See display ad this section. [ADVERTISEMENT] ▲

TRANSPORTATION

Air: Daily scheduled service to Anchorage via Alaska Airlines and Mark Air. Air taxi and helicopter services available.

Highway: The Richardson Highway extends north from Valdez to the Glenn Highway and the Alaska Highway. See the RICHARDSON HIGHWAY section.

Ferry: Scheduled state ferry service to Cordova, Whittier and Seward. Phone 835-4436. Reservations are a must! See MARINE ACCESS ROUTES section.

Bus: Regularly scheduled service to Anchorage and Fairbanks.

Taxi: 1 local taxi service.

Car Rental: Available at airport terminal.

Everyone in Alaska has the **"best"** glacier cruise, *however*... there is *only one!*

COLUMBIA GLACIER
Alaska's largest accessible glacier

AND

LU-LU BELLE
The **limousine** of Prince William Sound

Glacier Charter Service

MID-MAY to MID-SEPTEMBER
(907) 835-5141
P.O. Box 1832
Valdez, AK 99686

MID-SEPTEMBER to MID-MAY
(206) 789-2204
P.O. Box 70333
Seattle, WA 98107

SEE OUR LOG AD FOR MORE INFORMATION

ATTRACTIONS

See the Oil Painting: On display at the Church of the Epiphany is a famous artwork representation of the 15th century by Sr. Eugenio Cappilli of Florence, Italy.

Valdez Public Library, on Fairbanks Street, has a half-hour video presentation on Valdez called *Living Here Together,* shown at 11 A.M. and 4 P.M. daily in summer. The library also has a magazine swapbox for travelers: Trade in your well-thumbed magazine for one you haven't read yet. (If you don't have anything to trade in, check with the librarian.) The library also has music listening rooms and a children's program in summer. Wheelchair accessible. Open Monday through Thursday, 10 A.M. to 8 P.M., Friday and Saturday 10 A.M. to 6:30 P.M.

Celebrate Gold Rush Days: Held Aug. 5-9, 1992, this celebration includes a parade, contests and a casino night. During the celebration cancan girls meet the cruise ships and a jail is pulled through town by "deputies" who arrest citizens without beards and other suspects.

Valdez Arm supports the largest sport fishery in Prince William Sound. Important species include pink salmon, coho (silver) salmon, halibut, rockfish and Dolly Varden, with incidental catches of red, king and chum salmon. Charter boats are available in Valdez. A hot fishing spot near Valdez accessible by road is the **Allison Point** fishery (or "Winnebago Point" as it is known locally) created by the Solomon Gulch Hatchery, which produces major pink and silver salmon returns annually. Turn off the Richardson Highway at **Milepost V 2.9**. It is one of the largest pink salmon fisheries in the state. Pink salmon returns are best in odd years, but with hatchery production good pink runs are anticipated every year. Pinks average 3 to 5 lbs., from late June to early August. Silvers from 6 to 10 lbs., late July into September. Use light spinning gear or flies.

Fish a Derby. The Valdez Chamber of Commerce holds a halibut and silver salmon derby every year, with cash prizes awarded to the 1st through 5th place winners for both derbies. The Halibut Derby will be held May 9 through Sept. 6, 1992; the Silver Salmon Derby Aug. 1 through Sept. 6, 1992. For further information contact the Valdez Chamber of Commerce at 835-5109.

Seafood processors in Valdez offer custom smoking, freezing and air shipping for sport-caught fish. You may also trade your sport-caught fish for similar fish already processed and ready to ship or take with you. Salmon Exchange, phone 835-5559.

Take a boat tour to see Columbia Glacier, Shoup Glacier and other Prince William Sound attractions. Columbia Glacier, a tidewater glacier in Columbia Bay 28 miles/45 km southwest of Valdez, has become one of Alaska's best-known attractions. See ads in this section.

Raft and Kayak trips of Prince William Sound, Keystone Canyon and surrounding rivers are available.

Go flightseeing and see Columbia Glacier, spectacular Prince William Sound and the surrounding Chugach Mountains from the air. There are several air charter services and 2 helicopter services in Valdez; see ads in this section.

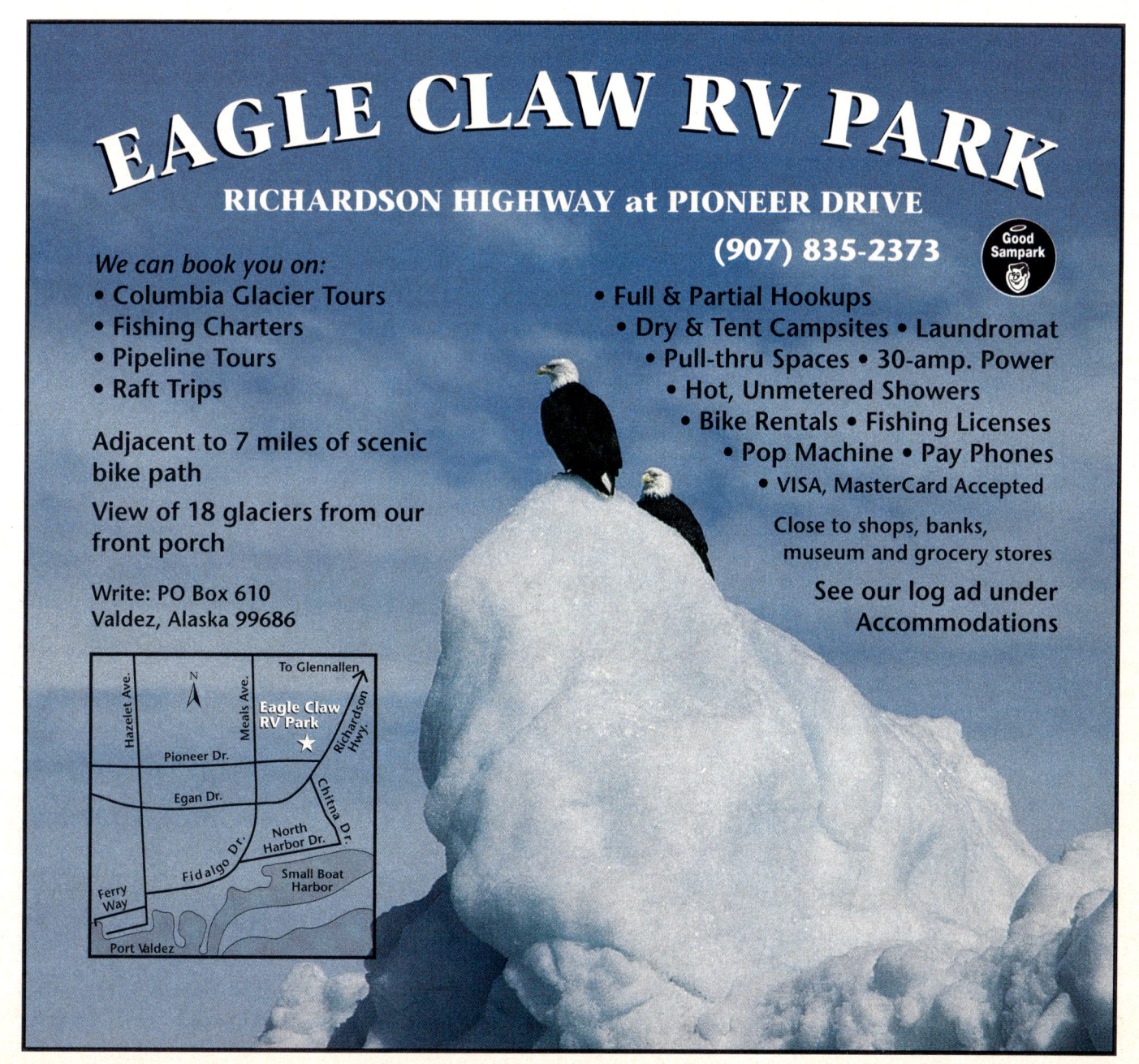

EAGLE CLAW RV PARK

RICHARDSON HIGHWAY at PIONEER DRIVE

(907) 835-2373

Good Sampark

We can book you on:
- Columbia Glacier Tours
- Fishing Charters
- Pipeline Tours
- Raft Trips

Adjacent to 7 miles of scenic bike path

View of 18 glaciers from our front porch

Write: PO Box 610
Valdez, Alaska 99686

- Full & Partial Hookups
- Dry & Tent Campsites • Laundromat
- Pull-thru Spaces • 30-amp. Power
- Hot, Unmetered Showers
- Bike Rentals • Fishing Licenses
- Pop Machine • Pay Phones
- VISA, MasterCard Accepted

Close to shops, banks,
museum and grocery stores

See our log ad under Accommodations

PRINCE WILLIAM SOUND • VALDEZ

Era Helicopters. Fly over Valdez and the Prince William Sound in the comfort and safety of Alaska's oldest and largest helicopter company. Soar over the breathtaking Columbia Glacier. Watch for otters, seals and bald eagles. Land at the face of Shoup Glacier. Phone (907) 835-2595 or outside Alaska (800) 843-1947. Tours also available in Anchorage, Juneau and Mount McKinley. [ADVERTISEMENT]

Ketchum Air Service, Inc. Alaska's outdoor specialists. Floatplane tours/charters into Prince William Sound, Wrangell–St. Elias park. Day fishing/fully equipped. Columbia Glacier tour. Drop-off cabins. Kennecott mine visit! Floatplane tour office located small-boat harbor Valdez. Call or write for brochure. VISA, MasterCard. Phone (907) 835-3789 or (800) 433-9114. Box 670, Valdez, AK 99686. [ADVERTISEMENT]

Visit Valdez Museum, located at 217 Egan Dr. Exhibits depict family lifestyles and workplaces from 1898 to present. Displays include a beautifully restored 1907 Ahrens steam fire engine, the original Cape Hinchinbrook lighthouse lens, a Civil War-era field cannon, and an illuminated model of the Alyeska Marine Terminal. Interpretive exhibits explain the impact of the 1964 earthquake, the construction of the trans-Alaska oil pipeline, and the 1989 *Exxon Valdez* oil spill cleanup. Visitors can touch 10,000-year-old Shoup Glacier ice, play slot machines (for entertainment only!), and sing along with the jukebox in the Pinzon Bar exhibit, and feel the luxurious softness of the sea otter pelt. The museum's new William A. Egan Commons provides a showcase setting for the Ahrens steam fire engine, a Model-T fire truck, antique aircraft models and the lighthouse lens. Outside exhibits include displays of local wildflowers, an oil pipeline "pig" and a unique snow tractor.

A portion of the 800-mile-long trans-Alaska oil pipeline. (Joe Prax)

Valdez Red Apple MARKET

Drive straight into Valdez on the Richardson Highway (Egan Drive) . . . right downtown

GROCERIES • FRESH FRUIT and VEGETABLES • ICE
SUNDRIES • PET SUPPLIES
FILM • MAGAZINES

FAMOUS FOR OUR MEAT COUNTER and FRIENDLY BUTCHERS

DON'T MISS: *The Deli*
• LOCATED IN THE STORE •
Delicious ready-to-eat **HOT FOOD TO GO**
Fancy **FRIED CHICKEN** (crispy or regular)
FRESH SANDWICHES
(roast beef, turkey, ham, corned beef)
Try our special **TANKER SANDWICHES**
Large variety of cheeses – Lunch meats • Salamis
FRESH PIZZA • FRESH SALADS

Need information?
Come in and ask us.

VALDEZ'S FRIENDLY STORE
(907) 835-4496
VISA • MasterCard

KEYSTONE RAFT & KAYAK ADVENTURES Inc.

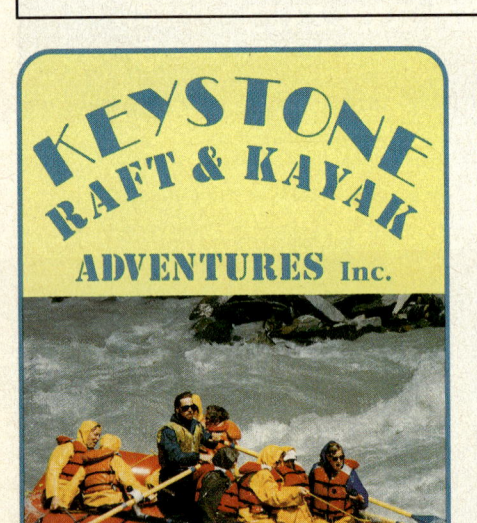

Day Trips
Keystone Canyon White-Water Trip

Extended Expeditions
Fishing and Hunting Charters
Raft Support Kayak Trips

Mike Buck
KEYSTONE ADVENTURES, INC.
P.O. Box 1486, Valdez, Alaska 99686
(907) 835-2606
or contact your local travel agent

Anadyr Sea Kayaking Adventures
Three Hour Nature Trips in Port Valdez
Day trips to Shoup Glacier, Galena Bay and Columbia Glacier
Extended Trips in Prince William Sound
Kayak Rentals   Box 1821, Valdez, AK. 99686   (907) 835-2814

The PROSPECTOR — APPAREL & SPORTING GOODS

Fishing Tackle • Camping and Marine Supplies • Hunting and Fishing Licenses
Guns and Ammunition • Outdoor Clothing and Boots • Rain Gear
T-SHIRTS and Alaskan Souvenirs • Lots More!

OPEN 7 DAYS • (907) 835-3858   *Major Credit Cards*
141 GALENA STREET, BEHIND THE VALDEZ POST OFFICE

VALDEZ TESORO
Welcome Visitors

VISA • MasterCard   GAS • PROPANE • ICE
RICHARDSON HIGHWAY AT MEALS AVE.

500 The MILEPOST® ■ 1992

Valdez Museum is open year-round: daily during summer months (May to September); Tuesday through Saturday during off-season (October to April). Children free; $2 for adults (19 and older). Call (907) 835-2764 for more information.

Tour the oil pipeline terminus. The marine terminal of the Alyeska pipeline is across the bay from the city of Valdez. Bus tours of the pipeline terminal are available in summer from the Alyeska Pipeline Service Co. visitor center at Valdez Airport. Reservations are suggested. Phone Alyeska for details on the tours: 835-2686 or 835-6983.

While entry to the terminal is restricted to authorized bus tours only, the drive out to the terminal is worthwhile. From Meals Avenue drive 6.8 miles/10.9 km out the Richardson Highway and turn right on the terminal access road (Dayville exit). The 5.4-mile/8.7-km road leading to the terminal passes Solomon Gulch dam and a spectacular view of Solomon Gulch Falls. There is also excellent fishing in season at Allison Point for pink and silver salmon. Entrance to the pipeline terminal is at the end of the road.

Outside the marine terminal gate is a bronze sculpture commemorating the efforts of men and women who built the trans-Alaska oil pipeline. Dedicated in September 1980, the sculpture was created by Californian Malcolm Alexander. It is composed of 5 figures representing various crafts and skills employed in the construction project. The work is the focal point of a small park from which visitors can watch tankers loading Alaska crude oil at the terminal. A small parking lot accommodates about 30 cars and a series of signs explain the pipeline and terminal operations.

Our Point of View, an observation platform offering views of the original Valdez townsite, pipeline terminal and the town is located by the Coast Guard office.

Visit Prince William Sound Community College, located at 303 Lowe St. Three huge wooden carvings on campus, by artist Peter Toth, are dedicated to the Indians of America. An Elderhostel is held at Prince William Sound Community College from about mid-May through September. This educational program (college credit given) is available for people over age 60. Subjects include Alaska history, wildlife and literature. Contact Elderhostel, 80 Boylston St., Suite 400, Boston, MA 02116, for more information on their Alaska programs.

View salmon spawning at Crooked Creek. From Meals Avenue drive 0.9 mile/1.4 km out the Richardson Highway to the Crooked Creek salmon spawning area and hatchery. An observation platform gives a close-up look at salmon spawning in mid-summer and fall. This is also a waterfowl sanctuary and an excellent spot for bird

PRINCE WILLIAM SOUND • VALDEZ

Sugar & Spice
The Everything Nice Store

Valdez's largest selection of Alaska and Valdez T-shirts and hats
MUCH MORE!
Clothing for the family
Stop in, browse around

9 a.m. – 10 p.m. daily
MAIL ORDERS WELCOME
P.O. Box 186   (907) 835-4336
Downtown Valdez, Alaska 99686

℞ VILLAGE PHARMACY

Kay Houghton, R.Ph.
(907) 835-3737

For all your health care needs

9-6 Monday-Thursday
9-7 Friday • 11-2 Saturday

at Eagle Quality Center
Entrance on Pioneer

Meals & Pioneer Drive
P.O. Box 248, Valdez, AK 99686

---

watching various migrating birds.

Stan Stephens Charters. Let Alaskans show you Alaska. This family business, operated by year-round Alaskans, offers a variety of cruises to Columbia Glacier, designed to fit any budget. Cruises aboard the 80-foot *Glacier Spirit*, 75-foot *Nautilus* or our new 80-foot vessel include a stop at Growler Island where you will enjoy an Alaskan feast of salmon, halibut, chicken, salads, and all the trimmings. You can explore the beaches and intertidal zone. The longer excursions offer greater opportunity to view the wildlife of the Sound (sea otters, seal, sea lions, porpoise and the possibility of spotting orca, humpback or minke whales). For those who wish to, you can stay overnight in heated tent/cabins at this wilderness camp, in view of the largest tidewater glacier in Prince William Sound. New in '92, Stan Stephens Charters will be offering a Whittier–Valdez schedule. All cruises will be stopping at Growler Island. Please call toll free for schedule information and a brochure. Westmark Dock, Box 1297-M, Valdez, AK 99686. (907) 835-4731 or (800) 992-1297. [ADVERTISEMENT]

Lu-Lu Belle. The motor yacht *Lu-Lu Belle* operates out of Glacier Charter Service. The *Lu-Lu Belle* is probably the cleanest and most

---

THE VIEW FROM ON TOP OF THE WORLD

There is nowhere on earth like Alaska, and there's no better way to see it than from the safety of an Era Helicopter.

Discover Alaska as the eagles see it. With Era Helicopters, the freedom is yours.

Era Helicopters Flightseeing Tours

Anchorage (907) 248-4422
Juneau (907) 586-2030
Mt. McKinley (907) 683-2574
Valdez (907) 835-2595

Chapel of the Sea
"A different church service"

Cruise the Port of Valdez each Sunday morning 8:00 'til 9:00 a.m.

Sponsored by Valdez First Baptist Church
Everyone Welcome

---

the HARBOR LANDING GENERAL STORE
Welcome to Valdez!

Valdez's Largest Gift Shop

REASONABLE PRICES!

We offer the finest in all your gift needs.
Stop in and see us and have a complimentary cup of coffee or spiced tea while you browse.
Located in the beautiful Harbor Court, we are open 7 days a week and evenings.

ALASKAN GIFTS GALORE!

Film • Post Cards • Ulus • Alaskan Dolls
Belt Buckles • Collector's Spoons • Sourdough Products
Original Design T-shirts
Valdez Jackets and Caps
Alaska Wild Berry Candies
Marble Etchings by Kiana of Alaska
Scrimshaw • Ivory • Gold Nugget
Jewelry and MUCH MORE!

This ad entitles you to 10% off any one item of your choice except film. One coupon per family please.

We are happy to wrap and mail your gifts for you!

MacMurray's Alaska Halibut House
Valdez, Alaska
835-2788

FAST FRIENDLY SERVICE

• Homemade Clam Chowder Soup
• Sandwiches   • Fresh salad Bar
• Fresh Local Seafood at Affordable Prices
• Breakfast 6 a.m. – 10:30 a.m.
Memorial Day – Labor Day
• Senior Citizens' Discount

Located at:
Corner of Fairbanks and Meals

plush tour vessel you will ever see. When you come aboard and see all the teak and mahogany, with hand-woven Oriental rugs, you will understand why Captain Rodolf asks you to wipe your feet. The *Lu-Lu Belle* has wide walk-around decks, thus assuring everyone ample opportunity for unobstructed outside viewing. She is equipped with several 110-volt current outlets for your battery chargers. Captain Fred Rodolf has logged over 1,800 Columbia Glacier cruises since 1979, and he will personally guide and narrate each and every cruise that the *Lu-Lu Belle* makes. Come let Captain Rodolf show you why he refers to Switzerland as being the Valdez of Europe. The cruise leaves the tour dock at 2 P.M. each day from Memorial Day through Labor Day. During the busier part of the season, an 8 A.M. cruise may be added. The cost of our cruise is $55 per person. Up to June 15 we have an early-bird special of $50 each. Persons under 3 years of age and over 99 years of age are free. The cruise is approximately 4½ hours long, depending on the wildlife and the amount of ice in Columbia Bay. There is a full service bar on board, with snacks. Friendliness and gracious hospitality on a beautiful yacht, no wonder people refer to the *Lu-Lu Belle* as being the limousine of Prince William Sound. We also have halibut and salmon fishing charters which leave each day starting at 6 A.M. Our phone number in Valdez is (907) 835-5141, our winter phone is (206) 789-2204. For more information stop by our office on Kobuk Street just off Chitna Drive behind the Totem Inn. [ADVERTISEMENT]

Drive Mineral Creek Road. A 5.5-mile/8.9-km drive behind town leading northwest through the breathtaking alpine scenery along Mineral Creek. *Drive carefully!* This is a narrow road; conditions depend on weather and how recently the road has been graded. Bears are frequently sighted here. To reach Mineral Creek Road drive to the end of Hazelet Street toward the mountains and turn left on Hanagita then right on Mineral Creek Road. Excellent view of the city from the water tower hill just to the right at the start of Mineral Creek Road.

Mineral Creek flows out of Mineral Creek Glacier. Mineral Creek Glacier is located approximately 2.5 miles/4 km beyond the end of the Mineral Creek Road. The old Hercules Mine, located at its base, is being mined again. Hike in about 30 minutes beyond the road end to the old stamp mill.

Don't Miss Keystone Canyon and **Bridal Veil** and **Horsetail falls.** The beginning of Keystone Canyon is at **Milepost V 13** Richardson Highway. This spectacular canyon is known for its sheer face and the 2 waterfalls (Horsetail at **Milepost V 13.5** and Bridal Veil, **Milepost V 13.8**) which plunge in a magnificent display down the canyon walls.

Commercial fishing boats in Valdez harbor. (Jim Hunter)

PRINCE WILLIAM SOUND • VALDEZ

LICENSED, INSURED ALASKA AIR TAXI SERVICE
P.O. Box 1909   Valdez, Alaska 99686
VALDEZ AERO SERVICES, INC. dba
Alpine Aviation Adventures
◄ (907) 835-4304 ►
Scenic Tours
• Columbia Glacier
• Wrangell Mountains
• Prince William Sound

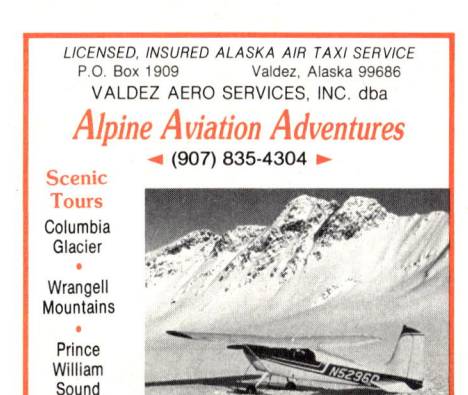

VALDEZ
DRUG & PHOTO
321 FAIRBANKS DRIVE
Under the Rexall sign
FULL LINE PHARMACY — ValuRite
KODAK FILM
ALASKA SOUVENIRS • GIFTS
SUMMER HOURS:
Monday-Friday 9 a.m. to 9 p.m.
Saturday 9 a.m. to 6 p.m.
Open Sunday
Phone: (907) 835-4956

Last Frontier Gallery
Alaskan Art & Ivory
Eskimo & Athabascan Handmade Gifts
Originals & Prints • Framing & Art Supplies
Bob & Helen Wade, Alaskans since territorial days
P.O. Box 587, Valdez, Alaska 99686 • (907) 835-4959
Across from the City Museum

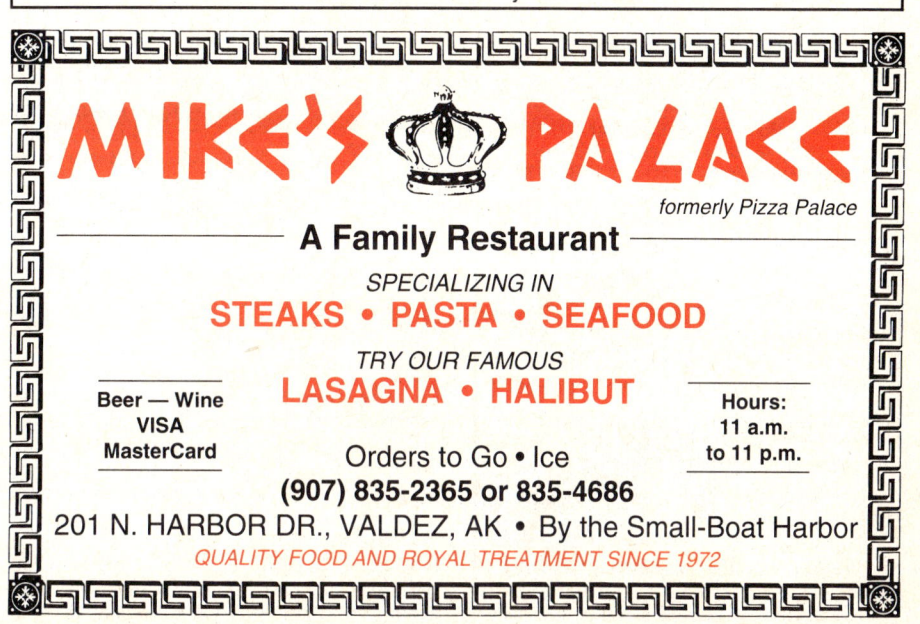

MIKE'S PALACE
formerly Pizza Palace
A Family Restaurant
SPECIALIZING IN
STEAKS • PASTA • SEAFOOD
TRY OUR FAMOUS
LASAGNA • HALIBUT
Beer — Wine
VISA
MasterCard
Orders to Go • Ice
(907) 835-2365 or 835-4686
Hours: 11 a.m. to 11 p.m.
201 N. HARBOR DR., VALDEZ, AK • By the Small-Boat Harbor
QUALITY FOOD AND ROYAL TREATMENT SINCE 1972

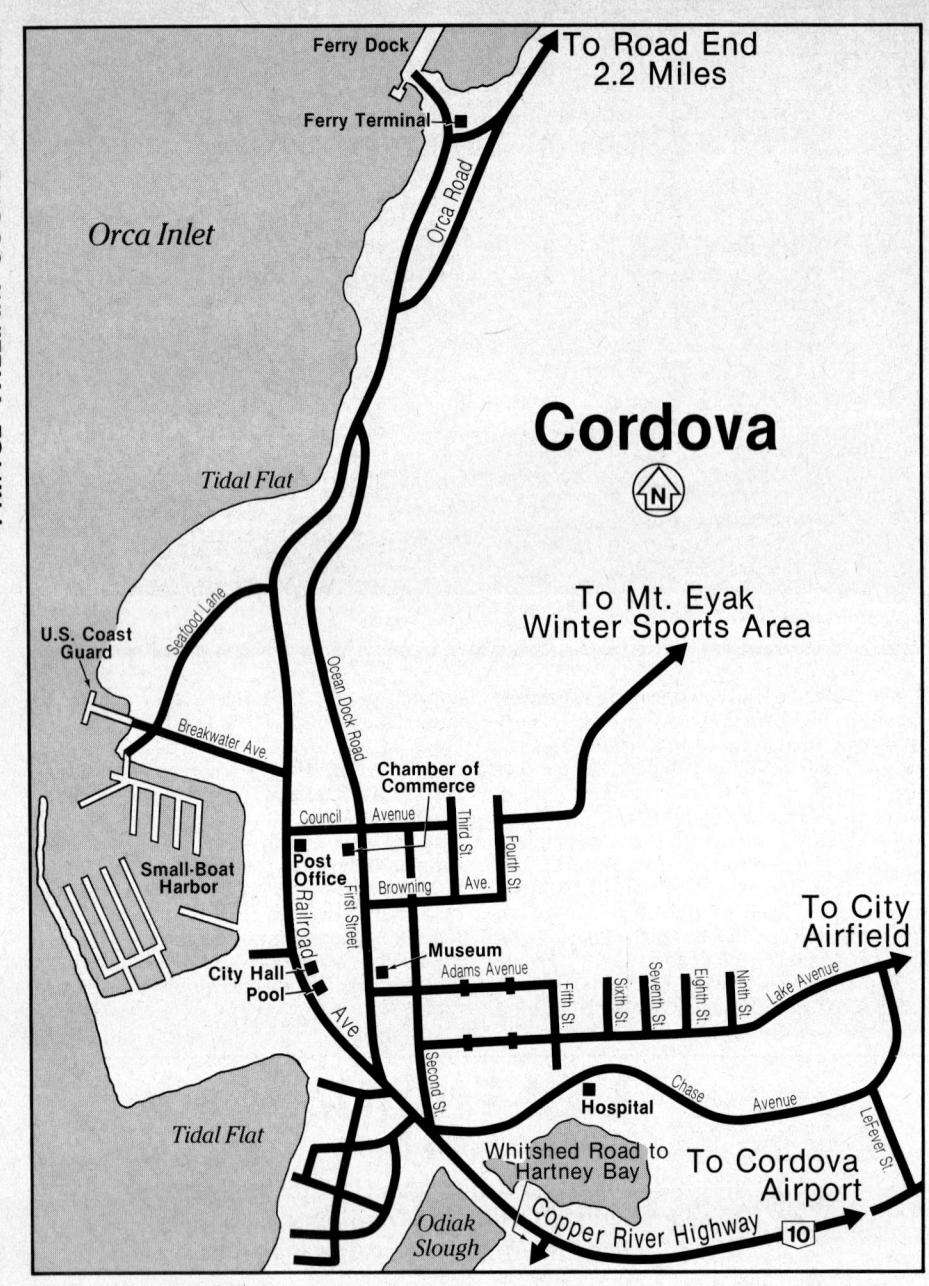

lands. The office is open weekdays from 8 A.M. to 5 P.M. Write P.O. Box 280, Cordova 99574, or phone 424-7661.

Elevation: Sea level to 400 feet/122m.

Climate: Average temperature in July is 54°F/12°C, in January 21°F/-6°C. Average annual precipitation is 167 inches. Prevailing winds are easterly at about 4 knots.

Radio: KLAM-AM, KCHU-FM (National Public Radio). **Television:** Cable. **Newspaper:** *Cordova Times* (weekly).

Private Aircraft: Cordova Mile 13 (Merle K. "Mudhole" Smith Airport), 11.3 miles/18.2 km southeast; elev. 42 feet/13m; length 7,500 feet/2,286m; asphalt; attended. Cordova Municipal (city air field), 0.9 mile/1.4 km east; elev. 12 feet/4m; length 1,900 feet/579m; gravel; unattended. Eyak Lake seaplane base, 0.9 mile/1.4 km east.

Modern-day Cordova owes its origins to Michael J. Heney, builder of the Copper River & Northwestern Railway. A post office with this name was established in 1906. The town was chosen as the railroad terminus and ocean shipping port for copper ore shipped by rail from the Kennecott mines near Kennicott and McCarthy.

The railroad and town prospered until 1938 when the mine closed. Following the end of copper mining activity, fishing became the area's major economic base. One of the first producing oil fields in Alaska was located at Katalla, 47 miles/76 km southeast of Cordova on the Gulf of Alaska. The discovery was made in 1902 and the field produced until 1933.

Supporting the area's economy are the Prince William Sound fishery and fish processing plants. The fishing and canning season for salmon runs from about May to September, with red, king and silver (coho) salmon taken from the Copper River area, chum, red and pink salmon from Prince William Sound. Black cod, crab and shrimp season runs during winter. Dungeness crab season runs during the summer and early fall months. Razor clams, halibut and scallops are also processed.

ACCOMMODATIONS

Cordova has 2 motels and 2 hotels, 5 bed and breakfasts, 8 restaurants, 2 laundromats and a variety of shopping facilities.

There are no commercial campgrounds or RV parks in Cordova. (Odiak Camper Park, the city's gravel camping area on Whitshed Road, is generally full of seasonal workers.)

TRANSPORTATION

Air: Scheduled service via Alaska Airlines and Wilbur's Flight Service. Several air taxi services based at the municipal airport, Mile 13 airport and Eyak Lake offer charter and flightseeing service.

Ferry: The Alaska Marine Highway system ferries connect Cordova with Valdez, Whittier and Seward. Phone 424-7333. See the MARINE ACCESS ROUTES section for details.

Taxi: Local service available.

Car Rental: Available locally.

Highways: The Alaska state highway system does not reach Cordova. The Copper River Highway leads 48 miles/77 km east and north of Cordova, ending at the Million Dollar Bridge. (See the COPPER RIVER HIGHWAY section.)

ATTRACTIONS

Cordova's Museum and Library are connected by a central entryway. "Where

---

Cordova

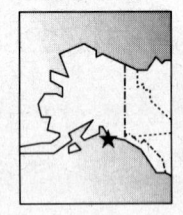

Located on the east side of Prince William Sound on Orca Inlet. **Population:** 2,585. **Emergency Services: Alaska State Troopers,** phone 424-7331, emergency phone 911. **Police, Fire Department, Ambulance,** phone 424-6100, emergency phone 911. **Hospital,** phone 424-8000.

Visitor Information: Information kiosk at the ferry office. Chamber of Commerce on 1st Street next to the National Bank of Alaska. Open 9 A.M. to noon Monday through Thursday; phone 424-7260 or write Box 99, Cordova, AK 99574. There is also a visitor information center at the museum. A self-guided walking tour map of Cordova, prepared by the Cordova Historical Society, points out historic structures of the town.

Chugach National Forest Cordova Ranger District office is located at 612 2nd St. USFS personnel can provide information on trails, cabins and other activities on national forest

---

Mary and John Davis'
Oystercatcher
BED & BREAKFAST
IN CORDOVA
Home-cooked Breakfast
(907) 424-5154 (Teachers' Hours)
2 Blocks From Town   Box 1735

POWDER HOUSE
Bar and Liquor Store
Homemade Soup, Sandwiches and Chili
Seasonal Seafood and Barbecues
Mile 2.1 Copper River Highway
On the Original Site of Copper River R.R. Powder House
Folk, Bluegrass and Country Music
FOOD TO GO • (907) 424-3529
Join us on the deck overlooking Eyak Lake

View of Cordova from Whitshed Road at high tide. (Ruth Fairall)

Cultures Meet" is the theme of the museum, which encompasses displays from various Alaska Native and other cultures. A bronze plaque explains the archaeological significance of *Palugvik,* a national historic site marking the southernmost movement of the Eskimo along the Northwest Pacific coast. The actual site is on Hawkins Island across the inlet from Cordova. The Chugaches, as these Eskimos were called, migrated some 4,000 years ago.

Among the exhibits in the museum are a leatherback turtle, usually found only in tropical waters, which was taken in the Cordova area in 1962, and displays of sea life and fossils. Relics of the history of the area include a fine example of a 3-seater bidarka (kayak-type boat) used by members of the Eyak tribe; samples of copper ore; a Fresnel lighthouse lens from Cape St... lighthouse; a large collection ...tos; Native baskets... and stone...

world. Birders can view up to 31 different species as 15 million shorebirds pass through the delta each spring.

Ketchum Air Service, Inc. Alaska's outdoor specialists. Floatplane tours/charters into Prince William Sound, Wrangell–St. Elias park. Day fishing/fully equipped. Columbia Glacier tour. Drop-off cabins. Kennecott Mine visit! Floatplane tour office located at Eyak Lake, Cordova. Call or write for brochure. VISA, MasterCard. Phone (907) 424-7703 or (800) 433-9114. Box 1669, Cordova, AK 99574. [ADVERTISEMENT]

Swim in Cordova's Olympic-sized swimming pool located on Railroad Avenue below Main Street. Open year-round to the public. Check locally for hours.

Silver Salmon Derby, held the last weekend in August and first weekend in September, offers cash and merchandise prizes. Contact the Chamber of Commerce, Box 99, for details. Tackle, licenses and supplies may be purchased locally. You can fish from the beach (the Fleming Creek area near the ferry terminal is especially popular).

Attend the Iceworm Festival: Held the first full weekend in February, this festival offers a parade, art show, dances, craft show, ski events, survival suit race, beard judging and a King and Queen of Iceworm contest. Highlight is the 100-foot-/30-m-long "iceworm" that winds its way through the streets of Cordova.

Visit the USFS office on the 3rd floor of the USFS Bldg. at 612 2nd St. Erected in 1925, it is the original federal building for the town of Cordova. Natural history display in 2nd floor Interpretive Center. The USFS office is next to the old courtroom and jail. Open weekdays 8 A.M. to 5 P.M.

Ski Hill, located at the end of 6th Street, operates between Dec. 15 and April 30, depending on the weather. Open Wednesday (adults only), Saturday, Sunday and holidays, 9 A.M. to dusk. The single chair lift rises 880 feet/268m up Eyak Peak.

Power Creek Road, from the corner of Lake and Chase avenues, leads out past the municipal airport to Crater Lake trailhead and Skaters' Cabin picnic area (Mile 1.2), Hatchery Creek salmon spawning channel (Mile 5.7), and ends at the Power Creek trailhead (Mile 6.9). The Crater Lake trailhead is directly northwest of the Eyak Lake Skaters Cabin. The 2.4-mile/3.8-km trail climbs to 1,500 feet/457m. Excellent views, alpine lake with fishing for cutthroat trout. Watch for bears. Visitors may view spawning salmon at the Hatchery Creek channel in July and August. Power Creek trail, 5 miles/8 km long, accesses both the Power Creek Basin and a ridge that connects with the Crater Lake trail creating an 12-mile/19.3-km loop. Power Creek trail offers spectacular scenery, with waterfalls, hanging glaciers and views of Power Creek Basin (called "surprise valley" by locals), the Chugach Range and Prince William Sound. Excellent berry picking. Watch for bears.

Area Fishing: Halibut year-round in Orca Inlet. Winter king salmon fishing, January through March. Trolling for silver salmon mid-August through September. **Fleming Creek/lagoon,** near the ferry terminal off Orca Bay Road, is the site of an ADF&G coho enhancement project; excellent fishing in late August. **Eyak Lake,** cutthroat and whitefish; salmon fishing within 200 yards of wier (flies only). See also the COPPER RIVER HIGHWAY section for area fishing.

The Queen's Chair
— Bed and Breakfast —
Panoramic View of Eyak Lake and the Queen's Chair
Single Rooms or Suites
Kitchen and Laundry Facilities
Private Telephone in Each Room
(907) 424-3000

Cordova Outboard, Inc.
SALES and SERVICE
MerCruiser and OMC Stern Drives
Johnson Outboards
Honda Power Equipment • Homelite
BOAT STORAGE FACILITIES
T. Fisher, Pres.   Phone (907) 424-3220
960   Cordova, Alaska 99574

CORDOVA DRUG CO.
"A friendly store in a friendly town"
Since 1908
Cordova, Alaska
GIFT ITEMS
Good Selection Alaskan Books
CAMERAS • FILM SUPPLIES
Phone (907) 424-3246   Len & Sigga Pingatore

Cordova Air Service, Inc.
Charter Service
for
Prince William Sound
Wheels — Skis — Floats
Box 528
Cordova, Alaska 99574
(907) 424-3289

CORDOVA'S FINEST
Fine dining with a harbor view

Restaurant • Lounge
Car Rentals • Curio Shop
Hotel
(907) 424-3272
Travel Agency In Lobby

Reluctant Fisherman Inn
Box 150, Cordova, Alaska 99574

RICHARDSON HIGHWAY

Valdez, Alaska, to Delta Junction, Alaska
Alaska Route 4

View of Worthington Glacier from Milepost V 28.7. (Jerrianne Lowther, staff)

The Richardson Highway extends 368 miles/592 km from Valdez to Fairbanks. This section logs the first 270 miles/434.5 km of the Richardson Highway from Valdez to Delta Junction (the remaining 98 miles/157.7 km from Delta Junction to Fairbanks are logged in the ALASKA HIGHWAY section). Southbound travelers read log back to front.

The Richardson is a wide paved highway in good condition except for sporadic frost heaving. Watch for road construction between **Milepost V 79** and **V 99.7** and between **Milepost V 106.2** and **V 115** in summer of 1992. A new section of highway completed in 1989 bypasses the historic community of Copper Center. *The MILEPOST®* logs the old highway through town. The "new" Richardson Highway (bypass route) is of equal distance—6.5 miles/10.5 km—with no notable features. You must exit the highway (watch for signs) to see Copper Center.

The Richardson Highway is a scenic route through the magnificent scenery of the Chugach Mountains and Alaska Range, leading past spectacular glaciers, through spruce forests and across tundra meadows.

The Richardson Highway was Alaska's first road, known to gold seekers in 1898 as the Valdez to Eagle trail. The gold rush trail led over the treacherous Valdez Glacier, then northeast to Eagle and the Yukon River route to the Klondike goldfields. Captain W.R. Abercrombie of the U.S. Army rerouted the trail in 1899 through Keystone Canyon and over Thompson Pass, thus avoiding the glacier. As the Klondike gold rush waned, the military kept the trail open to connect Fort Liscum in Valdez with Fort Egbert in Eagle. In 1903, the U.S. Army Signal Corps laid the trans-Alaska telegraph line along this route.

Gold stampeders started up the trail again in 1902, this time headed for Fairbanks, site of a big gold strike. The Valdez to Fairbanks trail became an important route to the Interior, and in 1910 the trail was upgraded to a wagon road under the direction of Gen. Wilds P. Richardson, first president of the Alaska Road Commission. The ARC updated the road to automobile standards in the 1920s. The Richardson Highway was hard-surfaced in 1957.

Emergency medical services: Phone 911 anywhere along the highway.

Richardson Highway Log

Mileposts on the Richardson Highway were erected before the 1964 Good Friday earthquake and therefore begin 4 miles/6.4 km from present-day downtown Valdez near the Old Valdez townsite (destroyed during the earthquake).
Distance from New Valdez (NV) is followed by distance from Old Valdez (OV).

NV 0 OV 4 (6.4 km) Intersection of Meals Avenue and the Richardson Highway.
NV 0.4 (0.6 km) **OV 3.6** (5.8 km) Paved doubled-ended turnout to north with Valdez information kiosk, maps, brochures, pay phones.
NV 0.5 (0.8 km) **OV 3.5** (5.6 km) DOT/PF district office.
NV 0.6 (1 km) **OV 3.4** (5.5 km) Valdez highway maintenance station.
NV 0.9 (1.4 km) **OV 3.1** (5 km) Double-ended turnout to north with litter barrels at Crooked Creek salmon spawning area and hatchery. Viewing platform on creek offers close-up look at salmon spawning in mid-summer and fall. There is a small hatchery here open to visitors when manned. Migrating birds such as Canada geese and various ducks are often here. It is a game sanctuary; no shooting is allowed. Good spot for pictures.
NV 1.3 (2.1 km) **OV 2.7** (4.3 km) Paved turnout to south.
NV 2 (3.2 km) **OV 2** (3.2 km) Paved turnout to south.
NV 2.1 (3.4 km) **OV 1.9** (3.1 km) Mineral Creek Loop Road through business and residential area on outskirts of Old Valdez comes out at **Milepost NV 3.4**. Access to Port of Valdez container terminal and grain elevators. The 5 grain elevators were built in 1982 in anticipation of the Port of Valdez receiving Delta barley for shipment.
NV 3.4 (5.5 km) **OV 0.6** (1 km) Road toward mountains leads 0.6 mile/1 km to Valdez Airport, 2 miles/3.2 km to Valdez Glacier campground, and 3.9 miles/6.3 km to a parking area next to the glacial moraine of Valdez Glacier. Good views of the glacier area are *not* available from this spot, nor is Valdez Glacier a very spectacular glacier. Valdez Glacier campground has 101 sites, tent camping, covered picnic area, litter barrels, water, toilets and fireplaces; 15-day limit, camping fee. *CAUTION: Beware of bears.* ▲

Mineral Creek Loop Road (turn toward ocean) leads to the original townsite of Valdez, destroyed during the Good Friday earthquake on March 27, 1964. A few homes and businesses are here now; there is little evidence of the earthquake's destruction.
NV 4 (6.4 km) **OV 0** Former access road to Old Valdez, now blocked off. Milepost 0 of the Richardson Highway is located here.

(Southbound travelers note: Physical mileposts end here, it is 4 miles/6.4 km to downtown Valdez.)

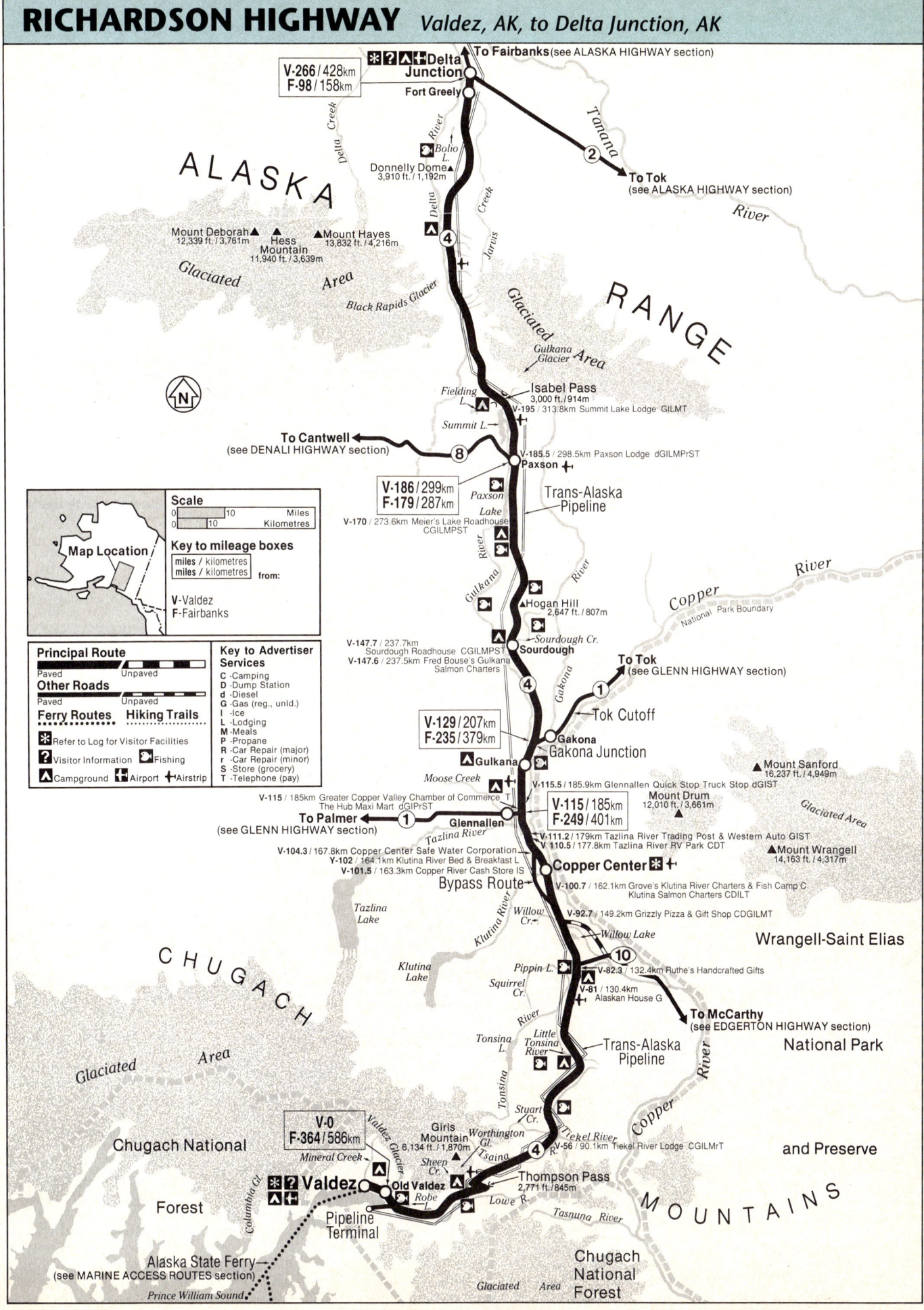

RICHARDSON HIGHWAY — Valdez, AK, to Delta Junction, AK

RICHARDSON HIGHWAY

Distance from Old Valdez (V) is followed by distance from Fairbanks (F). Physical mileposts begin northbound showing distance from Old Valdez.

V 0 F 364 (585.8 km) Milepost 0 of the Richardson Highway is located here at the former access road to Old Valdez.

V 0.3 (0.5 km) **F 363.7** (585.3 km) Large turnout to east.

V 0.9 (1.4 km) **F 363.1** (584.4 km) The highway passes over the terminal moraine of the Valdez Glacier, bridging several channels and streams flowing from the melting ice.

V 1.4 (2.3 km) **F 362.6** (583.5 km) Valdez Trapshooting Range.

V 1.5 (2.4 km) **F 362.5** (583.4 km) City of Valdez Goldfields Recreation Area; trails, ponds, swimming, picnic sites and baseball field.

V 2.2 (3.5 km) **F 361.8** (582.2 km) Dylen Drive.

V 2.4 (3.9 km) **F 361.6** (581.9 km) Paved turnout to west.

V 2.5 (4 km) **F 361.5** (581.8 km) Valdez cemetery to east.

V 2.7 (4.3 km) **F 361.3** (581.5 km) Large paved double-ended turnout to west beside Robe River. During August and early September watch for pink and silver salmon spawning in roadside creeks and sloughs. Please *DO NOT* attempt to catch or otherwise disturb spawning salmon. *CAUTION: Beware of bears.*

V 2.9 (4.7 km) **F 361.1** (581.1 km) Turnoff for Old Dayville Road to Trans-Alaska Pipeline Valdez Marine Terminal and access to Allison Point fishery. This 5.4-mile/8.7-km paved road (open to the public) crosses the Lowe River 4 times. At Mile 2.4/3.9 km the road parallels the bay and there is excellent fishing in season at Allison Point, especially for pink and silver salmon; also watch for sea otters and bald eagles along here. At Mile 4.1/6.6 km is the Solomon Gulch water project and a spectacular view of Solomon Gulch Falls; a fish hatchery is located across from the water project. Entrance to the pipeline terminal is at the end of the road. Supertankers load oil pumped from the North Slope to this facility via the trans-Alaska pipeline. Bus tours of the terminal are available from the Alyeska Pipeline Service Co. visitor center at Valdez Airport. (For more information on the pipeline and terminal tours, see the VALDEZ section.)

V 3 (4.8 km) **F 361** (581 km) Weigh station.

V 3.4 (5.5 km) **F 360.6** (580.3 km) A 0.5-mile/0.8-km gravel road to Robe Lake and floatplane base. Watch for cow parsnip and river beauty (dwarf fireweed). Also watch for bears!

V 4.7 (7.5 km) **F 359.3** (578.2 km) Turnout to east. Access to **Robe River**; Dolly Varden, red salmon (fly-fishing only, mid-May to mid-June).

V 5.3 (8.5 km) **F 358.7** (577.3 km) Salmonberry Ridge ski area road to west.

V 6 (9.7 km) **F 358** (576.1 km) Lake House Bed & Breakfast.

V 7.3 (11.7 km) **F 356.7** (574 km) Lowe River parallels the highway next mile northbound.

V 9.6 (15.4 km) **F 354.4** (570.3 km) Fire station.

V 11.6 (18.7 km) **F 352.4** (567.1 km) Large paved turnout to east.

V 12.8 (20.6 km) **F 351.2** (565.2 km) Here the Lowe River emerges from Keystone Canyon. This is an area of special historic interest dating from the days of the great gold rush and the Copper River exploration of Abercrombie. Captain William Ralph Abercrombie was selected in 1884 to lead an expedition up the Copper River to the Yukon River. Although unsuccessful, he did survey the Copper River Delta and a route to Port Valdez. He returned in 1898 and again in 1899, carrying out further explorations of the area. The canyon was named by Abercrombie presumably for Pennsylvania, the Keystone State. He named the Lowe River for Lt. Percival Lowe, a member of his expedition. Glacier melt imparts the slate-gray color to the river.

V 13.5 (21.7 km) **F 350.5** (564.1 km) Horsetail Falls; large paved turnout to west.

V 13.7 (22 km) **F 350.3** (563.7 km) Goat trail is visible on the west side of the highway; see description of this landmark at **Milepost V 15.2.**

V 13.8 (22.2 km) **F 350.2** (563.6 km) Bridal Veil Falls; large paved turnout to west.

V 14.9 (24 km) **F 349.1** (561.8 km) Lowe River bridge (first of 3 bridges northbound); view of Riddleston Falls. About 175 yards east of this bridge and adjacent to the highway is an abandoned hand-drilled tunnel. Large paved turnout with historical marker. Sign reads: "This tunnel was hand cut into the solid rock of Keystone Canyon and is all that is left of the railroad era when 9 companies fought to take advantage of the short route from the coast to the copper country. However, a feud interrupted progress. A gun battle was fought and the tunnel was never finished."

V 15.2 (24.5 km) **F 348.8** (561.3 km) Small gravel turnout. On the far side just above the water are the remains of the old sled trail used in the early days. This trail was cut out of the rock just wide enough for 2 horses abreast. 200 feet above can be seen "the old goat trail." This road was used until 1945.

V 15.3 (24.6 km) **F 348.7** (561.2 km) Lowe River bridge No. 2, built in 1980, replaced previous highway route through the long tunnel visible beside highway. Turnout at south end of bridge. Traces of the old trail used by horse-drawn sleds can be seen about 200 feet/61m above the river.

V 15.9 (25.6 km) **F 348.1** (560.2 km) Leaving Keystone Canyon northbound, entering Keystone Canyon southbound. Raft trips of Keystone Canyon are available; check with outfitter in Valdez.

V 16.2 (26.1 km) **F 347.8** (559.7 km) Avalanche gun emplacement.

V 16.3 (26.2 km) **F 347.7** (559.6 km) Lowe River bridge No. 3.

V 18 (29 km) **F 346** (556.8 km) Large paved turnouts both sides of road.

V 18.6 (29.9 km) **F 345.4** (555.8 km) Sheep Creek bridge.

Truck lane begins northbound as highway ascends 7.5 miles/12 km to Thompson Pass. This was one of the most difficult sections of pipeline construction, requiring heavy blasting of solid rock for several miles. The pipeline runs under the cleared strip beside the road. Low-flying helicopters often seen along the Richardson Highway are usually monitoring the pipeline.

V 21.6 (34.8 km) **F 342.4** (551 km) Paved turnout to east.

V 23 (37 km) **F 341** (548.8 km) Large gravel turnout to east.

V 23.4 (37.7 km) **F 340.6** (548.1 km) Large paved turnout to east with view.

Horsetail Falls in Keystone Canyon, Milepost V 13.5. (Jerrianne Lowther, staff)

V 23.6 (38 km) **F 340.4** (547.8 km) Loop road past Thompson Lake to Blueberry Lake and state recreation site; see **Milepost V 24.1**

V 23.8 (38.3 km) **F 340.2** (547.5 km) Small paved turnout.

V 24.1 (38.8 km) **F 339.9** (547 km) Loop road to Blueberry Lake State Recreation Site; drive in 1 mile/1.6 km. Tucked into an alpine setting between tall mountain peaks, this is one of Alaska's most beautifully situated campgrounds; 10 campsites, 4 covered picnic tables, toilets, firepits and water. Camping fee $6/night or annual pass. ▲

Blueberry Lake, and **Thompson Lake** (formerly Summit No. 1 Lake). Good grayling and rainbow fishing all summer.

V 24.4 (39.3 km) **F 339.6** (546.5 km) Large paved turnout to west. Bare bone peaks of the Chugach Mountains rise above the highway. Thompson Pass ahead; Marshall Pass is to the east.

During the winter of 1907, the A.J. Meals Co. freighted the 70-ton river steamer *Chitina* (or *Chittyna*) from Valdez over Marshall Pass and down the Tasnuna River to the Copper River. The ship was moved piece by piece on huge horse-drawn freight sleds and assembled at the mouth of the Tasnuna. The 110-foot-/34-m-long ship navigated 170 miles/274 km of the Copper and Chitina rivers above Abercrombie Rapids, moving supplies for construction crews of the Copper River & Northwestern Railway. Much of the equipment for the Kennicott mill and tram was moved by this vessel.

V 25.5 (41 km) **F 338.5** (544.7 km) Large paved turnout to west. Entering Game Management Unit 13D, leaving unit 6D, northbound.

V 25.7 (41.4 km) **F 338.3** (544.4 km) Large paved turnout to west with view; Keystone Glacier to the south.

V 26 (41.8 km) **F 338** (543.9 km) Thompson Pass (elev. 2,678 feet/816m) at head of Ptarmigan Creek. The pass, named by Captain Abercrombie in 1899, is comparatively low elevation but above timberline. A wildflower lover will be well repaid if he rambles over the rocks in this area: tiny alpine plants may be in bloom, such as yellow heather (Aleutian heather) and bluebell (mountain harebell).

According to the National Climatic Center, snowfall extremes in Alaska are all credited to the Thompson Pass station, where record measurements are: 974.5 inches for season (1952-53); 298 inches for month (February 1953); and 62 inches for 24-hour period (December 1955).

Private Aircraft: Thompson Pass airstrip; elev. 2,080 feet/634m; length 1,800 feet/549m; turf; unattended.

V 27 (43.5 km) **F 337** (542.3 km) Thompson Pass highway maintenance station. Truck lane ends northbound; begin 7.5-mile/12-km descent southbound.

V 27.5 (44.3 km) **F 336.5** (541.5 km) Steep turnout to east by **Worthington Lake**; rainbow fishing.

V 27.7 (44.6 km) **F 336.3** (541.2 km) Good viewpoint of 27 Mile Glacier.

V 28 (45.1 km) **F 336** (540.7 km) Paved turnout to east.

V 28.6 (46 km) **F 335.4** (539.8 km) Paved turnout to west.

V 28.7 (46.2 km) **F 335.3** (539.6 km) Worthington Glacier State Recreation Site; glacier viewpoint with large viewing shelter, interpretive displays, toilets, picnic sites and parking. According to state park rangers, this is the most visited site in the Copper River Basin. The glacier, which heads on Girls Mountain (elev. 6,134 feet/1,870m), is accessible via a short road to the left. It is possible to drive almost to the face of the glacier. Care should be exercised when walking on ice because of numerous crevasses.

V 30.2 (48.6 km) **F 333.8** (537.2 km) Large paved turnout both sides of highway. Excellent spot for photos of Worthington Glacier.

V 31.1 (50 km) **F 332.9** (535.7 km) Small turnout to east. Avalanche gun emplacement.

V 32 (51.5 km) **F 332** (534.3 km) Highway parallels Tsaina River. Long climb up to Thompson Pass for southbound motorists.

V 33.6 (54.1 km) **F 330.4** (531.7 km) Tsaina River access to west.

V 34.7 (55.8 km) **F 329.3** (529.9 km) Tsaina Lodge.

V 36.5 (58.7 km) **F 327.5** (527 km) Pipeline runs under highway.

V 37 (59.5 km) **F 327** (526.2 km) Entering BLM public lands northbound.

V 37.3 (60 km) **F 326.7** (525.8 km) Tsaina River bridge, turnout at south end.

V 40.5 (65.2 km) **F 323.5** (520.6 km) Pipeline passes under highway. Avalanche gun emplacement.

V 40.8 (65.7 km) **F 323.2** (520.1 km) Gravel turnout to west.

V 42 (67.6 km) **F 322** (518.2 km) Buried pipeline. View of waterbars (ridges on slope designed to slow runoff and control erosion).

V 43.3 (69.7 km) **F 320.7** (516.1 km) Long double-ended turnout.

V 43.5 (70 km) **F 320.5** (515.8 km) Small turnout to east.

V 45.6 (73.4 km) **F 318.4** (512.4 km) Large paved turnout to east at north end of Stuart Creek bridge.

V 45.8 (73.7 km) **F 318.2** (512.1 km) Watch for moose next 20 miles/32 km northbound.

V 46.9 (75.5 km) **F 317.1** (510.3 km) **Tiekel River** bridge; small Dolly Varden. Small turnout at north end of bridge.

V 47.9 (77.1 km) **F 316.1** (508.7 km) Large paved rest area by Tiekel River; covered picnic sites, toilets, no drinking water. Viewpoint and historical sign for Mount Billy Mitchell (straight ahead if you are headed south for Valdez). Lieutenant William "Billy" Mitchell was a member of the U.S. Army Signal Corps which in 1903 was completing the trans-Alaska telegraph line (Washington–Alaska Military Cable and Telegraph System) which was to connect all the military posts in Alaska. The 2,000 miles/3200 km of telegraph wire included the main line between Fort Egbert in Eagle and Fort Liscum at Valdez, and a branch line down the Tanana River to Fort Gibson and on to Fort St. Michael near the mouth of the Yukon and then to Nome. Mitchell was years later to become the "prophet of American military air power."

V 50.7 (81.6 km) **F 313.3** (504.1 km) Bridge over Tiekel River.

V 53.8 (86.6 km) **F 310.2** (499.2 km) Squaw Creek culvert.

V 54.1 (87.1 km) **F 309.9** (498.7 km) Large paved turnout to east by Tiekel River. Look for lupine in June, dwarf fireweed along river bars in July.

V 54.3 (87.4 km) **F 309.7** (498.4 km) Old beaver lodge. Beaver may inhabit the same site for generations.

V 54.5 (87.7 km) **F 309.5** (498.1 km) Moose often seen here in the evenings.

V 55.1 (88.7 km) **F 308.9** (497.1 km) Large paved turnout to east by Tiekel River.

V 56 (90.1 km) **F 308** (495.7 km) **Tiekel River Lodge.** See display ad this section.

V 56.3 (90.6 km) **F 307.7** (495.2 km) Large paved turnout to east by Tiekel River.

V 57 (91.7 km) **F 307** (494.1 km) Old beaver lodge and dams in pond to east. Tireless and skillful dam builders, beavers construct their houses in the pond created by the dam. Older beaver dams can reach 15 feet in height and may be hundreds of feet long.

V 58.1 (93.5 km) **F 335.9** (540.6 km) Wagon Point Creek culvert.

V 60 (96.6 km) **F 304** (489.2 km) Large paved turnout to east. Highway parallels **Tiekel River**; fishing for small Dolly Varden.

V 61.6 (99.1 km) **F 302.4** (486.6 km) Old beaver lodge to the east. Beaver can sometimes be spotted. The largest rodent in North America, beaver range south from the Brooks Range. They eat a variety of vegetation, including aspen, willow, birch and poplar.

V 62 (99.7 km) **F 302** (486 km) Ernestine Station highway maintenance camp.

V 62.4 (100.4 km) **F 301.6** (485.4 km) Boundary for Sport Fish Management areas. Entering Upper Susitna/Copper River Area N northbound, Prince William Sound southbound.

V 64.7 (104.1 km) **F 229.3** (481.7 km) Pump Station No. 12 to east. Interpretive viewpoint and parking to west. Short walk to viewpoint from parking area.

V 65 (104.6 km) **F 229** (481.2 km) Little Tonsina River.

V 65.1 (104.8 km) **F 298.9** (481 km) **Little Tonsina** River State Recreation Site with 10 campsites, firepits, water, litter barrels and toilets. Camping fee $6/night or annual pass. Dolly Varden fishing. Road to right as you enter wayside dead ends, road to left goes to the river (no turnaround space); follow loop road for easy access. Good berry picking in fall. *CAUTION: Beware of bears!*

Watch for moose next 20 miles/32 km southbound.

V 66.2 (106.5 km) **F 297.8** (479.2 km) Double-ended gravel turnout to west.

V 68.1 (109.6 km) **F 295.9** (476.2 km) Site of former Tonsina Camp (Alyeska Pipeline Service Co.) used during pipeline construction. These camps have been completely removed.

V 70.5 (113.5 km) **F 293.5** (472.3 km) Trans-Alaska pipeline follows base of

MILE 56 RICHARDSON HIGHWAY

TIEKEL RIVER LODGE

PHONE

FISHING LICENSES

GASOLINE

GIFT SHOP

SHOWERS

LODGING

CAFE

**Full Camper Hookups Along The River
Bus Tours Welcome**

Mike and Gail Huntley
Mile 56, SR Box 110
c/o Valdez, Alaska 99686

(907) 822-3259

1992 ■ The MILEPOST® 509

mountains across valley.

V 71.2 (114.6 km) **F 292.8** (471.2 km) Long double-ended paved turnout to east.

V 72 (115.9 km) **F 292** (469.9 km) Double-ended paved turnout to west. Leaving BLM public lands northbound. View of trans-Alaska pipeline across the valley.

V 74.4 (119.7 km) **F 289.6** (466.1 km) Paved double-ended turnout to west. Vehicle access to Little Tonsina River.

V 78.9 (127 km) **F 285.1** (458.8 km) Bernard Creek trail. According to the BLM, this 15-mile loop road—which was originally part of the WAMCATS line (see **Milepost V 101.9**)—provides mountain bikers with an uphill ride on hard-pack dirt to near Kimball Pass.

V 79 (127.1 km) **F 285** (458.7 km) Tonsina Lodge. **Private Aircraft:** (Upper) Tonsina airstrip, adjacent south of lodge; elev. 1,500 feet/457m; length 1,700 feet/518m; turf; fuel 80; unattended.

NOTE: Watch for road construction northbound to **Milepost V 99.7** (Copper Center bypass) in summer 1992.

V 79.2 (127.5 km) **F 284.8** (458.3 km) Bridge over Tonsina River, which rises in Tonsina Lake to the southwest.

V 79.6 (128.1 km) **F 284.4** (457.7 km) Bridge and Squirrel Creek state campground. Pleasant campsites on the bank of Squirrel Creek, some pull-through spaces; $6/night or annual pass; dumpster, boat launch, water, toilets and firepits. Rough access road through campground; low-clearance vehicles use caution. Large vehicles note: Limited turnaround on back loop road. ▲

Mouth of **Squirrel Creek** at Tonsina River. Some grayling and salmon; small, use flies or eggs, all season; salmon, average size, egg clusters and spoons, all season. Also try the gravel pit beside the campground; according to state park rangers, some fishermen have good luck catching rainbow and grayling here using flies, eggs and spinners.

V 79.7 (128.3 km) **F 284.3** (457.5 km) Begin 1.3 mile/2.1 km truck lane northbound up Tonsina Hill. Hill can be slippery in winter. Watch for severe frost heaves.

V 81 (130.4 km) **F 283** (455.4 km) Alaskan House. See display ad this section.

V 82.3 (132.4 km) **F 281.7** (453.33 km) **Ruthe's Handcrafted Gifts.** Stop by our cabin for a visit and see quilts and critters, one-of-a-kind wearing apparel, and many other functional and attractive gifts. I also do fun things with recyclables. For a unique remembrance of Alaska, take home one of my handcrafted treasures. [ADVERTISEMENT]

V 82.6 (132.9 km) **F 281.4** (452.9 km) Junction. Edgerton Highway leads east through the settlement of Kenny Lake to Chitina and the McCarthy Road to McCarthy in Wrangell–St. Elias National Park and Preserve (see EDGERTON HIGHWAY section).

V 83 (133.6 km) **F 281** (452.2 km) Small paved turnout to west beside Pippin Lake.

V 87.7 (141.1 km) **F 276.3** (444.6 km) Paved double-ended turnout to east at Willow Lake. On a clear day this lake mirrors the Wrangell Mountains which lie within Wrangell–St. Elias National Park and Preserve. The park visitor center is at **Milepost V 105.1** and there is a good mountain viewpoint at **V 112.6**.

V 88.5 (142.4 km) **F 275.5** (443.4 km) Pipeline parallels road. Interpretive viewpoint to west on pipeline (1 of 3 Alyeska pipeline displays along this highway). National Park Service plaque with schematic diagram of Wrangell Mountains.

V 90.8 (146.1 km) **F 273.2** (439.7 km) Large paved turnout to west by Willow Creek culvert; thick patches of diamond willow in woods off highway (and thick clouds of mosquitoes!).

V 91.1 (146.6 km) **F 272.9** (439.2 km) Turnoff to east is an 8-mile/12.9-km gravel cutoff that intersects Edgerton Highway at **Milepost J 7.3**. This is a drive through the rolling hills of homestead country and heavy thickets of birch and spruce.

V 92.7 (149.2 km) **F 271.3** (436.6 km) Grizzly Pizza & Gift Shop. See display ad this section.

V 98.1 (157.9 km) **F 265.9** (427.9 km) Microwave tower.

V 99.7 (160.4 km) **F 264.3** (425.3 km) IMPORTANT: South **junction** with Copper Center Bypass (New Richardson Highway). Northbound travelers TURN OFF on to Old Richardson Highway for scenic route through historic Copper Center (log and description follow). The MILEPOST® does not log the bypass route (New Richardson Highway), which is the same distance as the old highway (6.5 miles/10.5 km) with no notable features. Although according to the BLM, there is an old 4-wheel-drive road to Klutina Lake (25 miles/40 km) which is appropriate for mountain bikes. Turn west at Brenwick–Craig Road sign on the bypass and cross under pipeline. The old highway rejoins the bypass route at **Milepost V 106.2**.

NOTE: Watch for road construction south to **Milepost V 79** in summer 1992.

V 100.7 (162.1 km) **F 263.3** (423.7 km) **Grove's Klutina River Charters and Fish Camp.** One of the friendliest places around. Great king and red salmon fishing. Also Dolly Varden, grayling and lake trout. Charter here for August–September silver salmon fishing in Prince William Sound. Camping and RV parking on the south bank of the Klutina River. Electrical hookups and potable water. Headquarters in historic log cabin on premises. Call 1-800-658-0051. See Klutina River Services ad in Copper Center. [ADVERTISEMENT] ▲

V 100.7 (162.1 km) **F 263.3** (423.7 km) **Klutina Salmon Charters.** See display ad this section. ▲

V 100.7 (162.1 km) **F 263.3** (423.7 km) Klutina River bridge. Excellent fishing in the **Klutina River** for king salmon (peaks in August); also grayling, Dolly Varden and red salmon (June through August). Campground and fishing charter services located here.

Copper Center

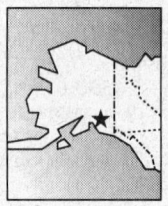

V 100.8 (162.2 km) **F 263.2** (423.6 km) The community of Copper Center extends down the road to the east then north through the trees and along the highway. A loop road leads through Copper Center and rejoins the Richardson Highway at **Milepost V 101.1**. **Population:** 229. **Emergency Services:** Phone 911. **Ambulance** in Glennallen, phone 822-3203. **Elevation:** 1,000 feet/305m.

Private Aircraft: Copper Center NR 1 airstrip, adjacent west; elev. 1,033 feet/315m; length 1,800 feet/549m; turf; unattended. Copper Center NR 2 airstrip, 1 mile/1.6 km south; elev. 1,150 feet/351m; length 2,800 feet/853m; gravel; fuel 100; unattended.

Facilities include lodging, private campgrounds, meals, groceries, gas station, general store, post office, book shop and gift

---

ALASKAN HOUSE — GOLD NUGGETS
Ivory ▪ Jade ▪ Hematite ▪ Furs

Alaskan Gifts ▪ Coffee Stop ▪ Tesoro Gas
Open 8 a.m. – 6 p.m. Daily, May – September

HC 60, Box 146, Copper Center, Alaska 99573
(907) 822-3230 — Mile 81 Richardson Highway

GRIZZLY PIZZA & GIFT SHOP
FOOD ▪ ALASKAN GIFTS ▪ LIQUOR STORE
CAMPGROUND ▪ PUBLIC PHONE ▪ GAS
EST. 1958 — *A little bit of Old Alaska*
LIVE BUFFALO
Mile 92.7, Copper Center, Alaska 99573   Phone: (907) 822-3828

KLUTINA SALMON CHARTERS
GUIDED CHARTERS & CAMPGROUND

COME FISH WITH US!!!
- Fishing Fools and First-timers Welcome
- Complete Charters, Everything Furnished
- We'll Freeze and Ship Your Catch
- RV Park & Campground on the River
- Kings June 15 - August 10 ▪ Reds June 1 - August 30

FRANK & SHIRLEEN HILLS ▪ **(907) 822-3991**
Mile 101 Old Richardson (North side of Bridge) ▪ P.O. Box 78, Cooper Center, Alaska 99573

shops. Fishing charters, tackle, riverboat services, and guides available.

A trading post was established in Copper Center in 1898. With the influx of gold seekers in 1898-99, following the trail from Valdez which joined the Eagle Trail to Forty Mile and Dawson country and later extended to Fairbanks, Copper Center became a mining camp. A telegraph station and post office were established in 1901 and Copper Center became the principal settlement and supply center in the Nelchina–Susitna region.

Copper Center Lodge, selected by the Alaska Centennial Commission as a site of historic importance (a plaque is mounted to the right of the lodge's entrance), had its beginning as the Holman Hotel and was known as the Blix Roadhouse during the gold rush days of 1897-98. It was the first lodging place in the Copper River valley and was replaced by the Copper Center Lodge in 1932.

The George I. Ashby Memorial Museum, operated by the Copper Valley Historical Society, is housed in the bunkhouse annex at the Copper Center Lodge on the loop road. It contains early Russian religious articles, Athabascan baskets, telegraph and mineral displays, copper and gold mining memorabilia and trapping articles from early-day Copper Valley. Hours vary. Donations appreciated.

The Copper River reportedly carries the highest sediment load of all Alaskan rivers. The river cuts through the Chugach Mountains and connects the interior of southcentral Alaska with the sea; it is the only corridor of its kind between Cook Inlet and the Canadian border.

Richardson Highway Log

(continued)

V 101 (162.5 km) **F 263** (423.3 km) A visitor attraction in Copper Center is the log Chapel on the Hill built in 1942 by Rev. Vince Joy with the assistance of U.S. Army volunteers stationed in the area. The chapel is open daily and there is no admission charge. A short slide show on the Copper River area is usually shown to visitors in the chapel during the summer. A highway-level parking lot is connected to the Chapel on the Hill by stairs.

V 101.1 (162.7 km) **F 262.9** (423 km) Turnoff on loop road to historic Copper Center Lodge and other businesses.

V 101.4 (163.2 km) **F 262.6** (422.6 km) Post office to east; outside mailbox.

V 101.5 (163.3 km) **F 262.5** (422.4 km) Old Post Office Gallery.

V 101.5 (163.3 km) **F 262.5** (422.4 km) **Copper River Cash Store**, established in 1896, sits on part of the first farm started in Alaska. The center of the building is the original structure. Behind the store is the old jail, bars still on windows. Open 6 days a week, all year. Complete line of groceries, general merchandise, RV supplies, video rentals. [ADVERTISEMENT]

V 101.9 (164 km) **F 262.1** (421.8 km) Parking area. Historical marker about Copper Center reads: "Founded in 1896 as a government agriculture experiment station, Copper Center was the first white settlement in this area. The Trail of '98 from Valdez over the glaciers came down from the mountains and joined here with the Eagle Trail to Forty Mile and Dawson. 300 miners, destitute and lonely, spent the winter here. Many suffered with scurvy and died. Soon after the turn of the century, the Washington Alaska Military Cable and Telegraph System, known as WAMCATS, the forerunner of the Alaska communications system, operated telegraph service here between Valdez and Fairbanks."

V 102 (164.1 km) **F 262** (421.6 km)

COPPER CENTER ADVERTISERS

Copper Center Lodge & Trading Post .... Mile 101.1 Old Richardson Hwy.
Copper River Cash Store .... Mile 101.5 Old Richardson Hwy.
Klutina River Services .... Mile 100.8 Old Richardson Hwy.

"ASHBY'S"
Copper Center Lodge & Trading Post
HISTORIC ROADHOUSE
One of Alaska's 30 Historic Sites
Mile 101.1 Richardson Highway, on Loop Road

14 Miles South of Glennallen
Comfortable Modern Rooms
Choice of Private or Adjoining Baths
Dining Room — Cocktail Lounge
Excellent Food
District Museum Next Door
Campsites Close By
Ideal Vacation Headquarters
Center of Famed Hunting & Fishing

River trips on the Klutina and Copper rivers available for fishing or ... fish either river from levee.

A FAMILY ORIENTED LODGE
A Place You Will Remember
Mrs. George Ashby   Phone (907) 822-3245
Resident Owner & Manager
Write: Copper Center, Alaska 99573

COPPER RIVER CASH STORE
Mile 101.5 Richardson Highway

Part of the Old Trading Post Established in 1896

— Groceries —
— Fresh Produce —
— Meat — Ice —
— Film — Cold Pop —
— RV Supplies —
— Picnic Supplies —
— Video Rentals —
— General Merchandise —

Open 9-7 Mon.-Sat.   FISHING AND HUNTING LICENSES   **(907) 822-3266**

KLUTINA RIVER SERVICES

GAS & LIQUOR
AND
GROVE'S KLUTINA RIVER CHARTERS

GAS • DIESEL • OIL • PROPANE

Liquor Store • Ice • Snacks
Tackle • Fishing & Hunting Licenses

GREAT KING & RED SALMON FISHING
Riverboat Charters • Raft Trips

Historic log cabin built between 1898-1906.

OLD STYLE FISH CAMP
RV Parking • Electrical Hookups
Potable Water
*One of the friendliest places around.
Right on the river where the action is.*

VISA MasterCard AMERICAN EXPRESS DISCOVER

Your Hosts: Stan, Lona and Rex

Mile 100.8 Old Richardson Hwy.
P.O. Box 236, Copper Center, AK 99573
(907) 822-3243
Charters **(907) 822-5822**
Toll Free: **1-800-658-0051**

Klutina Road.

Klutina River Bed & Breakfast. See display ad this section.

V 102.2 (164.5 km) **F 261.8** (421.3 km) Copper Center Community Chapel and Indian graveyard.

V 102.5 (165 km) **F 261.5** (420.8 km) Fish wheel may sometimes be seen here operating in Copper River to east. The old school is a local landmark.

V 104 (167.4 km) **F 260** (418.4 km) Ahtna building houses Copper River Indian Corp.

V 104.3 (167.8 km) **F 259.7** (417.9 km) **Copper Center Safe Water Corporation.** See display ad this section.

V 104.5 (168.2 km) **F 259.5** (417.6 km) Silver Springs Road. Copper Center school.

V 104.8 (168.7 km) **F 259.2** (417.1 km) Paved turnout to east. Watch for horses.

V 105.1 (169.1 km) **F 258.9** (416.6 km) National Park Service headquarters and visitor center for Wrangell–St. Elias National Park and Preserve. Access to Wrangell–St. Elias National Park and Preserve is via the Edgerton Highway and McCarthy Road (see EDGERTON HIGHWAY section) and the Nabesna Road off the Tok Cutoff (see the GLENN HIGHWAY section). Ranger on duty, general information available. A 10-minute video is shown; additional video programs shown on request. Maps and publications are for sale. Open 9 A.M. to 6 P.M. daily, Memorial Day through Labor Day. Winter hours are 8 A.M. to 5 P.M. weekdays. For more information write P.O. Box 29, Glennallen, AK 99588; or phone 822-5234.

V 106.2 (170.9 km) **F 257.8** (414.9 km) IMPORTANT: North **junction** with Copper Center Bypass (New Richardson Highway). Southbound travelers TURN OFF on to Old Richardson Highway for scenic route through Copper Center (see description this section). *The MILEPOST®* does not log the bypass route (New Richardson Highway), which is the same distance as the old highway (6.5 miles/10.5 km) but without notable features. The old highway rejoins the bypass route at **Milepost V 99.7**.

NOTE: Watch for road construction north to Milepost V 115 (Glenn Highway junction) in summer 1992.

V 110 (177 km) **F 254** (408.8 km) Dept. of Highways Tazlina station and Dept. of Natural Resources office. Report forest fires here.

V 110.5 (177.8 km) **F 253.5** (408 km) Pipeline storage area. Turn west on pipeline storage area road and take second right for private RV park.

V 110.5 (177.8 km) **F 253.5** (408 km) **Tazlina River RV Park.** See display ad this section. ▲

V 110.6 (178 km) **F 253.4** (407.8 km) Rest area to east on banks of Tazlina River; large paved surface, 2 covered picnic tables, water, toilets.

V 110.7 (178.2 km) **F 253.3** (407.6 km) Tazlina River bridge. *Tazlina* is Indian for "swift water." The river flows eastward from the glacier of the same name into the Copper River.

V 111.2 (179 km) **F 252.8** (406.8 km) Community college and trading post.

Tazlina River Trading Post & Western Auto. See display ad this section.

V 111.7 (179.8 km) **F 252.3** (406 km) Copperville access road. Developed during pipeline construction, this area has a church and private homes. Glennallen fire station.

V 112.3 (180.7 km) **F 251.7** (405 km) Steep grade southbound from Tazlina River to the top of the Copper River bluffs.

V 112.6 (181.2 km) **F 251.4** (404.6 km) Paved parking area with historical information sign on the development of transportation in Alaska. Short (0.1 mile) walk to good viewpoint on bluff with schematic diagram of Wrangell Mountains: Mount Sanford (elev. 16,237 feet/4,949m); Mount Drum (elev. 12,010 feet/3,661m); Mount Wrangell (elev. 14,163 feet/4,317m); and Mount Blackburn (elev. 16,237 feet/4,949m).

Sign at viewpoint reads: "Across the Copper River rise the peaks of the Wrangell Mountains. The 4 major peaks of the range can be seen from this point, with Mount Drum directly in front of you. The Wrangell Mountains, along with the St. Elias Mountains to the east, contain the most spectacular array of glaciers and ice fields outside polar regions. The Wrangell Mountains are part of Wrangell–St. Elias National Park and Preserve, the nation's largest national park. Together with Kluane National Park of Canada, the park has been designated a World Heritage site by the United Nations."

Visitor information for Wrangell–St. Elias National Park is available at **Milepost V 105.1** Richardson Highway, or from ranger stations in Chitina and Slana.

V 115 (185 km) **F 249** (400.7 km) **South junction** of Richardson and Glenn highways at Glennallen. Greater Copper Valley Visitor Information Center at junction, open daily in summer; pay phone. Gas station with groceries also located at junction. The town of Glennallen extends west along the Glenn Highway from here, with businesses located at the junction and along the Glenn Highway. Anchorage is 189 miles/ 304 km, Tok 139 miles/224 km, from here.

NOTE: Watch for road construction south to Milepost V 106 in summer 1992.

Greater Copper Valley Chamber of Commerce. See display ad this section.

For the next 14 miles/22.5 km northbound the Richardson and Glenn highways

---

15 miles south of Glennallen on the way to Valdez

KLUTINA RIVER BED & BREAKFAST

Quiet Family Atmosphere
King Salmon Fishing Nearby
Information, Maps, Travel Ideas

Brad & Ramona Henspeter and Family
(907) 822-5858

Tazlina River Trading Post & Western Auto *Chevron Products*
Groceries • Liquor • Ammunition
Fishing Tackle • Hunting & Fishing Licenses
9 a.m. to 8 p.m. • 10 a.m. to 6 p.m. Sunday
Don & Joyce Horrell   Mile 111.2
Box 364 • Glennallen, Alaska 99588

LAUNDROMAT
COPPER CENTER SAFE WATER CORPORATION
Mile 104.3 Richardson Highway   Copper Center, Alaska
OPEN 8 a.m. – 9 p.m. Year-Round
GOOD WATER – Laundry, Showers, Toilets

TAZLINA RIVER RV PARK
Mile 110.5 Richardson Highway

- ELECTRIC and WATER HOOKUPS
- DUMP STATION • SHOWERS
- REST ROOMS   • LAUNDROMAT
- COVERED PICNIC and BARBECUE AREA

Facilities for registered guests only   No tent camping
Close to grocery — Western Auto — gas station
John & Sandy Fillman   Phone **(907) 822-3034**

Visit the Greater Copper Valley!

The Greater Copper Valley Chamber of Commerce invites you to visit our visitor information center at the junction of the Glenn and the Richardson highways in Glennallen. Our log cabin boasts a warm, friendly atmosphere complete with free hot coffee.

The Copper River Valley hosts the nation's largest national park, **Wrangell–St. Elias** — six times the size of Yellowstone National Park. Unlimited recreational activities abound in the valley including fishing, hiking, backpacking, photography, mountain climbing, rafting, bird watching, wild flowers, flightseeing, to name but a few.

For more information, please call:
(907) 822-5555
Write: P.O. Box 469, Glennallen, AK 99588
Or better yet, STOP BY!
Visitor Center open Mid-May through Labor Day

share a common alignment. They separate at **Milepost V 128.6.**

NOTE: Anchorage- or Tok-bound travelers turn to **Milepost A 189** *in the GLENN HIGHWAY section. Valdez- or Fairbanks-bound travelers continue with this log.*

The Hub Maxi Mart. See display ad this section.

V 115.5 (185.9 km) **F 248.5** (399.9 km) **Glennallen Quick Stop Truck Stop.** Stop for friendly family service and gas and diesel prices that are hard to beat. A well-stocked convenience store contains ice, pop, snacks, postcards, ice cream, specialty items, a phone, and free coffee. Several interesting items are on display, including an authentic Native Alaskan fish wheel. [ADVERTISEMENT]

V 118 (189.9 km) **F 246** (395.9 km) Dry Creek State Recreation Site; 51 campsites, walk-in tent camping, water, tables, toilets, firepits, 15-day limit. Camping fee $6/night or annual pass. *Bring mosquito repellent!* Old ore car here was once used to haul gravel to Tonsina.

V 118.1 (190.1 km) **F 245.9** (395.7 km) **Private Aircraft:** Gulkana airport; elev. 1,578 feet/481m; length 4,200 feet/1,280m; asphalt; fuel 80, 100, B.

V 123.2 (198.3 km) **F 240.8** (387.5 km) Large paved turnout to east and well-defined 1.5-mile/2.4-km trail east side of road to the mouth of the **Gulkana River** (see **Milepost V 126.9** for details on access and permits.) Excellent fishing mid-June to mid-July for king salmon to 50 lbs. (average is 30 lbs.), and red salmon to 6 lbs. Use bright colored yarn or flies, half-inch hook. Heavy tackle with 25- to 30-lb.-test line recommended for kings. No spinners or spoons below the Gulkana River bridge.

V 126 (202.8 km) **F 238** (383 km) Paved double-ended turnout to west.

V 126.8 (204.1 km) **F 237.2** (381.7 km) Gulkana River bridge. Entering Game Management Unit 13B, leaving unit 13A, northbound.

V 126.9 (204.2 km) **F 237.2** (381.6 km) Access road to **GULKANA** (pop. 98) on the bank of the Gulkana River. Camping is permitted along the river by the bridge; signs posted tell where to pay camping fee. ▲

NOTE: Gulkana River frontage from 2 miles/3.2 km downstream of Sourdough Roadhouse to the mouth of the Gulkana is owned by Gulkana Village and managed by Ahtna, Inc. There are public easements along the Richardson Highway between Sourdough Roadhouse and the bridge. Access permits to fish on Ahtna lands are sold at the Ahtna Corp. building. In summer, there is often someone selling these permits along the highway. Permits are $10 and good for season. Children under 18 years of age are not required to buy a permit.

V 128.6 (206.9 km) **F 235.4** (378.8 km) **North junction** (Gakona Junction) of the Richardson and Glenn highways, known locally as the Glenn–Rich or Gulkana Junction. Here the Glenn Highway (Tok Cutoff) branches off east to Tok on the Alaska Highway, 125 miles/201 km away. The Richardson Highway crosses the Gulkana River bridge and continues straight ahead north. Lodge.

NOTE: Tok-bound travelers turn to **Milepost A 203** *in the GLENN HIGHWAY section. Valdez- or Fairbanks-bound travelers continue with this log.*

V 129.2 (207.9 km) **F 234.8** (377.9 km) Pond with lily pads and occasionally a floatplane.

V 129.4 (208.2 km) **F 234.6** (377.5 km) Paved turnout to west. Sailor's Pit (gravel pit opposite lake to west); BLM trail across to **Gulkana River.** Fishing for rainbow trout, grayling, king and red salmon. Highway follows the Gulkana River.

V 132.1 (212.6 km) **F 231.9** (373.2 km) Paved turnout to west.

V 134.6 (216.6 km) **F 229.4** (369.2 km) Paved double-ended turnout with view of Gulkana River to west.

V 135.5 (218.1 km) **F 228.5** (367.7 km) Watch for caribou.

V 135.8 (218.5 km) **F 228.2** (367.2 km) Paved turnout to east.

V 136.4 (219.5 km) **F 227.6** (366.3 km) Coleman Creek bridge.

V 136.7 (220 km) **F 227.3** (365.8 km) Side road west to Gulkana River fishing access.

V 138.1 (222.2 km) **F 225.9** (363.5 km) **Poplar Grove Creek** bridge; spring grayling fishing. Paved turnout to west at north end of bridge.

V 139.4 (224.3 km) **F 224.6** (361.4 km) Paved turnout to west with view of Gulkana River.

V 140.6 (226.3 km) **F 223.4** (359.5 km) Paved turnout to east.

V 141.2 (227.2 km) **F 222.8** (358.6 km) Side road west to Gulkana River fishing access.

V 141.4 (227.6 km) **F 222.6** (358.2 km) Paved double-ended scenic viewpoint to west.

V 146 (234.9 km) **F 218** (350.8 km) Little lakes and potholes can be seen the next 9 miles/14.5 km northbound. Lily pads grow thickly. Watch for mallard ducks and other waterfowl.

V 146.4 (235.6 km) **F 217.6** (350.2 km) Entering BLM public lands northbound.

V 147.1 (236.7 km) **F 216.9** (349.1 km) Double-ended paved scenic viewpoint.

V 147.6 (237.5 km) **F 216.4** (348.3 km) **SOURDOUGH.** BLM Sourdough Creek Campground; closed for reconstruction in 1991. Access to Gulkana River, marked trail to Sourdough Creek. Across the bridge (load limit 8 tons) and to the right a road leads to parking, toilets and boat launch on river. Watch for potholes in access roads.

The Sourdough Roadhouse (open to the public year-round) next to the creek was established in 1903, approved as a historical site by the state of Alaska in the spring of

Fish wheels are used for subsistence salmon fishing. (Jerrianne Lowther, staff)

THE HUB MAXI MART
GAS, GIFT SHOP & Tourist Information Center

Largest Gift Selection between Valdez and Fairbanks

FULL LINE GROCERY STORE
Produce • Meat • Ice • Ice Cream
ALASKAN-MADE GIFTS • Jewelry • Furs
Magazines • Drugs • Sundries • Pay Phone
Hot Sandwiches • Coffee
FRESH PASTRIES
Fishing and Hunting Licenses
Fishing Tackle and Local Fishing Information
Maxi Mart Open 24 Hours June 1-Sept. 15
Phone (907) 822-3393

GAS • DIESEL
Propane • Repairs
RV SERVICING
Towing

Phone
(907) 822-3555
Service Station Open
24 Hours Year Around

TEXACO
All Major Credit
Cards Accepted

Located at the JUNCTION of the Glenn & Richardson in Glennallen

RICHARDSON HIGHWAY

1974 and became a national historic landmark in 1979. The old Valdez trail runs 150 yards/46m behind the buildings.

The Gulkana River is part of the National Wild and Scenic Rivers System managed by the BLM. A popular float trip for experienced canoeists begins at Paxson Lake and ends at Sourdough Campground. See description at **Milepost V 175.**

V 147.6 (237.5 km) **F 216.4** (348.3 km) **Fred Bouse's Gulkana Salmon Charters.** See display ad this section.

V 147.7 (237.7 km) **F 216.3** (348.1 km) **Sourdough Roadhouse** is the oldest roadhouse in Alaska still operating in the original building and is listed on the National Register of Historic Places. Come, enjoy our family atmosphere, good home-cooked food. Sourdough hotcakes, homemade pies, and 6 clean cabins, bunkhouse available. Souvenirs, gas, grocery, tackle. Fish smoking and freezing. The Sourdough Saloon welcomes you. Package liquor. Grayling, rainbow and salmon fishing in the Gulkana River. Guide service available. Immediately adjacent to Sourdough BLM Campground. Call (907) 822-3355 for reservations. Jim "Swede" and Marvelee Ruechel, your hosts. Open year-round. See display ad this section.

[ADVERTISEMENT]

Gulkana River above Sourdough Creek, grayling 9 to 21 inches (same as Sourdough Creek below), rainbow 10 to 24 inches, spinners, June through September; red salmon 8 to 25 lbs. and king salmon up to 62 lbs., use streamer flies or spinners, mid-June through mid-July. **Sourdough Creek**, grayling 10 to 20 inches, use single yellow eggs or corn, fish deep early May through first week in June, use spinners or flies mid-June until freezeup.

V 150.7 (242.5 km) **F 213.3** (343.3 km) Large gravel turnout to east.

V 151 (243 km) **F 213** (342.8 km) Double-ended gravel turnout to west by large pond; watch for trumpeter swans in spring.

V 153.8 (247.5 km) **F 210.2** (338.3 km) Highway passes through boggy terrain; watch for caribou. *CAUTION: No turnouts, little shoulder. Watch for dips and rough patches in highway next 10 miles/16 km northbound.*

V 156.4 (251.7 km) **F 207.6** (334.1 km) As the highway winds through the foothills of the Alaska Range, over a crest called Hogan Hill (elev. 2,647 feet/807m), there are magnificent views of 3 mountain ranges: the Alaska Range through which the highway leads, the Wrangell Mountains to the southeast and the Chugach Mountains to the southwest. To the west is a vast wilderness plateau where the headwaters of the big Susitna River converge to flow west and south into Cook Inlet, west of Anchorage.

V 156.7 (252.2 km) **F 207.3** (333.6 km) Good view of pothole lakes to west.

V 157 (252.7 km) **F 207** (333.1 km) Good long-range viewpoints from highway. This is an area of lakes and ponds: moose and other game may be spotted from here (use binoculars).

V 158.9 (255.7 km) **F 205.1** (330.1 km) Sweeping view of the Glennallen area to the south.

V 160.7 (258.6 km) **F 203.3** (327.2 km) **Haggard Creek** BLM trailhead; grayling fishing. Access to Gulkana River.

V 162.2 (261 km) **F 201.8** (324.8 km) Double-ended gravel turnout to east.

V 168.1 (270.5 km) **F 195.9** (315.3 km) **Gillespie Lake** trailhead and parking to west. Walk up creek 0.3 mile to lake; grayling fishing.

V 169.3 (272.5 km) **F 194.7** (313.3 km) Large gravel pit. Turnout to west.

V 169.4 (272.6 km) **F 194.6** (313.2 km) Middle Fork BLM trail to Meier's Lake and Middle Fork Gulkana River.

V 170 (273.6 km) **F 194** (312.2 km) Roadhouse with gas, food, lodging and camping. **Meier's Lake**; parking area, good grayling fishing.

Meier's Lake Roadhouse. See display ad this section.

V 171.6 (276.2 km) **F 192.4** (309.6 km) Gravel turnout by river to west. Long upgrade begins northbound.

V 172.7 (277.9 km) **F 191.3** (307.9 km) Small turnout to west, view of pipeline to east.

V 173.2 (278.7 km) **F 190.8** (307 km) **Dick Lake** to the east via narrow side road (easy to miss); no turnaround space. Good grayling fishing in summer. View of trans-Alaska oil pipeline across the lake. Good spot for photos.

V 175 (281.6 km) **F 189** (304.2 km) BLM Paxson Lake Campground turnoff. Wide gravel road (full of potholes if not recently graded) leads 1.5 miles/2.4 km to large camping area near lakeshore; 50 campsites, some pull-throughs, spaces for all sizes of vehicles but some sites on slope (RVs may need leveling boards); toilets, water, tables, firepits, dump station and concrete boat launch. Parking for 80 vehicles. Bring mosquito repellent. *CAUTION: Watch for bears.* Fishing in **Paxson Lake** for lake trout, grayling, red salmon and burbot.

This is the launch site for floating the Gulkana River to Sourdough Campground at **Milepost V 147.6**. Total distance is about 50 miles and 4 days travel, according to the BLM, which manages this national wild river. While portions of the river are placid, the Gulkana does have Class II and III rapids, with a gradient of 38 feet/mile in one section. Canyon Rapids may be Class IV depending on water levels (there is a portage). Recommended for experienced boaters only. For further information on floating the Gulkana, contact the BLM at Box 147, Glennallen 99588, or phone 822-3217.

V 177.1 (285 km) **F 186.9** (300.8 km) Small gravel turnout to west with view of Paxson Lake.

V 177.5 (285.7 km) **F 186.5** (300.1 km) Turnout to east. Trans-Alaska oil pipeline may be seen on the ridge northwest of the highway.

V 178.7 (287.6 km) **F 185.3** (298.2 km) Small gravel turnout to east.

V 179 (288.1 km) **F 185** (297.7 km) Gravel turnout overlooking Paxson Lake. The lake was named for the owner of the roadhouse (still Paxson Lodge) about 1906.

SOURDOUGH ROADHOUSE
Established 1903

National Register of Historical Places

**Cafe • Bar • Gas
Cabins • Souvenirs
Groceries • Fishing Tackle
Package Liquor
Homecooked Foods
Homemade Pies**
Sourdough Breakfast Anytime

Clean Cabins • Bunkhouse Available
FABULOUS FISHING!
REASONABLE RATES
Owners: Jim "Swede" & Marvelee Ruechel
Open Year around   MasterCard and VISA
Summer hours 6 a.m. to midnight

(907) 822-3355
TESORO
**Mile 147.5 Richardson Hwy.
Gakona, Alaska 99586**

TESORO ALASKA

**GREAT GRAYLING FISHING LICENSES
(907) 822-3151
MEIER'S LAKE ROADHOUSE**

Restaurant • Bar • Lounge
Gas • Groceries • Gifts • Tenting
Hot Showers • Lodging
Housekeeping Cabins • Rustic

MILE 170 Richardson Highway
Delta Junction, Alaska 99737

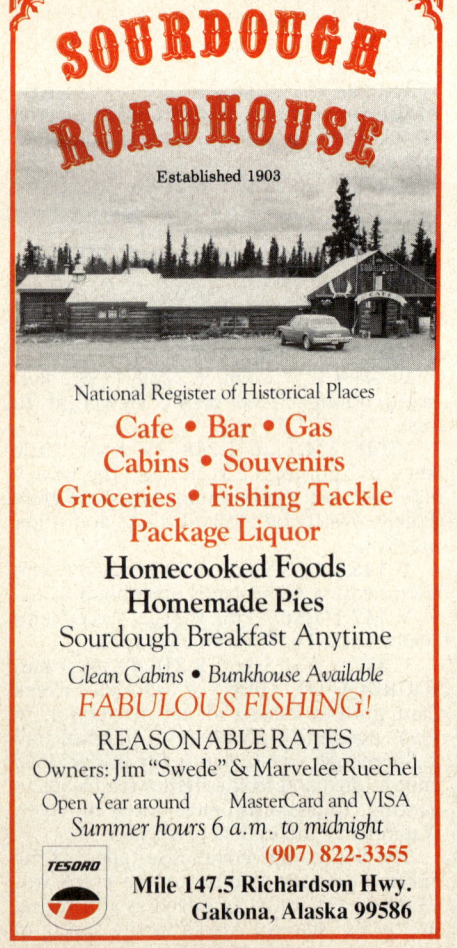

A King Salmon catching experience you'll never forget!

Fred Bouse's GULKANA SALMON CHARTERS

Fred Bouse has 17 years Gulkana River experience! *All gear furnished.*
Based at Sourdough Roadhouse   MILE 147.5 Richardson Highway
For Reservations Call: **(907) 479-2122 • 474-8488 • 822-3355**
Go ahead — treat yourself. You'll be glad you did!

V 179.2 (288.4 km) F 184.8 (297.4 km) Gravel turnout to west overlooking Paxson Lake.

V 179.4 (288.7 km) F 184.6 (297.1 km) Steep gravel road to former BLM wayside on Paxson Lake (elev. 2,553 feet/778m). Road is not regularly maintained. Better access to lake is from Paxson Lake Campground at **Milepost V 175**.

V 182.1 (293 km) F 181.9 (292.7 km) Large gravel turnout at head of Paxson Lake. Rough gravel trail to lake.

V 183.2 (294.8 km) F 180.8 (291 km) Entering Paxson Closed Area northbound (closed to taking of all big game).

V 184.4 (296.8 km) F 179.6 (289 km) Large gravel turnout to west.

V 184.7 (297.2 km) F 179.3 (288.6 km) One Mile Creek bridge.

V 185.5 (298.5 km) F 178.5 (287.3 km) **Junction** with Denali Highway to Denali National Park and George Parks Highway (see DENALI HIGHWAY section for details) at **PAXSON** (pop. 33), site of a lodge with gas station (open year-round), restaurant and small grocery store. Sled dog racing first weekend in April. Paxson Mountain (elev. 5,200 feet/1,585m) is 3 miles/4.8 km west-southwest.

V 185.5 (298.5 km) F 178.5 (287.3 km) **Paxson Lodge**. See display ad this section.

Private Aircraft: Paxson airstrip (Hufman Field), adjacent south; elev. 2,653 feet/809m; length 2,200 feet/671m; gravel; fuel 80, 100, A, B.

V 185.7 (298.9 km) F 178.3 (286.9 km) Site of original Paxson Lodge.

V 185.8 (299 km) F 178.2 (286.8 km) Paxson Station highway maintenance camp.

V 186.4 (300 km) F 177.6 (285.8 km) Leaving BLM public lands northbound.

V 188.3 (303 km) F 175.7 (282.8 km) Large paved double-ended rest area to east across from Gulkana River; tables, fireplaces, toilets, litter barrels and water.

V 189.6 (305.1 km) F 174.4 (280.7 km) Long paved double-ended turnout with dumpster to west.

V 190.4 (306.4 km) F 173.6 (279.4 km) Paved parking area by Gulkana River with picnic tables, dumpster and view of Summit Lake and pipeline. Access to Summit Lake. Interpretive sign about red salmon. Salmon spawning area; fishing for salmon prohibited. Access to **Fish Creek** at north end of turnout; grayling fishing. Access to Fish Lake is via trail paralleling creek for 2 miles/3.2 km, according to the ADF&G.

V 191 (307.4 km) F 172 (278.4 km) Summit Lake to west; turnout at head of stream.

V 191.1 (307.5 km) F 172.9 (278.2 km) Double-ended turnout to west.

V 192.2 (309.3 km) F 171.8 (276.5 km) Turnout with table and boat launch on **Summit Lake**; lake trout, grayling, burbot and red salmon.

V 192.6 (310 km) F 171.4 (275.8 km) Large gravel turnout on Summit Lake.

V 193.3 (311.1 km) F 170.7 (274.7 km) Gravel turnout to west by Summit Lake.

V 194.1 (312.4 km) F 169.9 (273.4 km) Gravel turnout on Summit Lake.

V 195 (313.8 km) F 169 (271.9 km) Large gravel turnout at **Summit Lake** (elev. 3,210 feet/978m). This lake, 7 miles/11.3 km long, is named for its location near the water divide between the Delta and Gulkana rivers. Fishing for lake trout, grayling, red salmon and burbot.

V 195 (313.8 km) F 169 (272 km) **Summit Lake Lodge**. See display ad this section.

V 195 (313.8 km) F 169 (272 km) Private airstrip.

V 196.8 (316.7 km) F 167.2 (269.1 km) Gunn Creek bridge. View of Gulkana Glacier to the northeast. This glacier, perched on 8,000-foot/2,438-m Icefall Peak, feeds through connecting streams and rivers into Prince William Sound.

V 197.6 (318 km) F 166.4 (267.8 km) Large gravel turnout with picnic table and dumpster. Memorial monument honoring Gen. Wilds P. Richardson, for whom the highway is named, at summit of Isabel Pass (elev. 3,000 feet/914m). Sign here reads: "Captain Wilds P. Richardson presented the need for roads to Congress in 1903. His familiarity with Alaska impressed Congress with his knowledge of the country and his ability as an engineer. When the Act of 1905 became a law, he was placed at the head of the Alaska Road Commission in which position he served for more than a decade. The Richardson Highway, from Valdez to Fairbanks, is a fitting monument to the first great road builder of Alaska."

Entering Sport Fish Management Area C southbound.

V 198.5 (319.4 km) F 165.5 (266.3 km) Gravel turnout to west.

V 200.4 (322.5 km) F 163.6 (263.3 km) Gravel side road leads west 1.5 miles/2.4 km to **Fielding Lake** Campground. Pleasant area above tree line; 7 campsites, picnic tables, pit toilets, large parking areas and boat ramp. Good fishing for lake trout, grayling and burbot.

V 201.5 (324.3 km) F 162.5 (261.5 km) Phelan Creek bridge. Buried section of pipeline to west is a large animal crossing.

V 202 (325.1 km) F 162 (260.7 km) Trans-Alaska oil pipeline parallels the highway above ground here. Entering BLM public lands northbound.

V 202.5 (325.9 km) F 161.5 (259.9 km) McCallum Creek bridge, highway follows Phelan Creek northbound. This stream heads in Gulkana Glacier and flows northwest to the Delta River.

V 203.5 (327.5 km) F 160.5 (258.3 km) Watch for beaver ponds (and beaver); lupine in June.

V 204 (328.3 km) F 160 (257.5 km) Spring water piped to east side of highway; paved turnout with litter barrels.

V 204.7 (329.4 km) F 159.3 (256.4 km) Large gravel turnouts both sides of highway.

V 205.3 (330.4 km) F 158.7 (255.4 km) Small gravel turnout by stream. Good place for pictures of the pipeline up a very steep hill.

V 206.4 (332.2 km) F 157.6 (253.6 km) Double-ended turnout with picnic tables, litter barrels and view of mineralized Rainbow Ridge to northeast. Wildflowers include yellow arnica and sweet pea.

V 207 (333.1 km) F 157 (252.7 km) Good

PAXSON LODGE
(Established 1903)

Gateway to the most scenic route to Denali National Park and Preserve

MILEPOST 185.5 RICHARDSON HIGHWAY • AT JUNCTION OF DENALI HIGHWAY

A MODERN RESORT WITH OLD-TIME ALASKAN HOSPITALITY

- ROOMS WITH BATH
- DINING ROOM
- COCKTAIL LOUNGE
- SOUVENIR & GIFT SHOP
- PACKAGE LIQUOR STORE
- GAS & TOWING

— *In famous big game and trout fishing area* —

CHEVRON PRODUCTS and CREDIT CARDS • ADJACENT 3,000 FT. AIRSTRIP

Address: Paxson Lodge
Paxson, Alaska 99737

For Reservations
Phone (907) 822-3330

Stanley F. Brown
Manager

Summit Lake Lodge

Spacious modern rooms with private baths * Fine dining and cocktails with glacier view

* Package liquor
* Gifts
* Gas and oil
* 24-hour laundry
* Fishing charters available
* Boats and motors for rent
* Miscellaneous sundries
* Hiking
* Photography
* Hunting
* Skiing and snowmachining

Open 365 days a year

VISA • MasterCard • American Express Welcome

MILE 195 RICHARDSON HIGHWAY   Phone (907) 822-3969

gravel turnout to west. There are frequent turnouts the next 6 miles/9.6 km northbound.

V 207.8 (334.4 km) **F 156.2** (251.4 km) Turnout. Rock slide and avalanche area next mile northbound; watch for rocks on road.

V 208.1 (334.9 km) **F 155.9** (250.9 km) Turnout to west by river. Look for wild, or Alaskan, rhubarb (*P. alaskanum*), a member of the buckwheat family. Grows to 6 feet with showy clusters of small yellowish white flowers.

V 211.7 (340.7 km) **F 152.3** (245.1 km) Side roads signed APL are Alyeska pipeline access roads and closed to the public.

V 213.2 (343.1 km) **F 150.8** (242.7 km) Gravel turnout to west along Phelan Creek.

V 213.6 (343.7 km) **F 150.4** (242 km) Gravel turnout and road to gravel pit to east. Avalanche area ends northbound.

V 214 (344.4 km) **F 150** (241.4 km) Double-ended paved turnout with picnic tables and litter barrels. Highway follows Delta River northbound, Phelan Creek southbound.

V 215.1 (346.2 km) **F 143.9** (231.6 km) Pipeline crosses Miller Creek right next to bridge. Parking at both ends of bridge, access to creek.

V 215.9 (347.4 km) **F 148.1** (238.3 km) Pipeline interpretive viewpoint with information sign.

V 216.3 (348.1 km) **F 147.7** (237.7 km) Gravel turnout to east.

V 216.7 (348.7 km) **F 147.3** (237 km) Lower Miller Creek. Turnouts at both ends of bridge. This is a pipeline interpretive viewpoint and one of the best spots on the highway to photograph the pipeline.

V 217.2 (349.5 km) **F 146.8** (236.2 km) Castner Creek; parking at both ends of bridge, west side of road.

V 218.2 (351.1 km) **F 145.8** (234.6 km) Trims Station DOT/PF highway maintenance camp.

V 218.8 (352.1 km) **F 145.2** (233.7 km) Bridge over Trims Creek, parking. Watch for caribou on slopes.

V 219.2 (352.8 km) **F 144.8** (233 km) Access to Pipeline Pump Station No. 10.

V 219.3 (352.9 km) **F 144.7** (232.9 km) Small gravel turnout. Note the flood control dikes (also called finger dikes) in stream to slow erosion.

V 219.9 (353.9 km) **F 144.1** (231.9 km) Michael Creek bridge; parking at both ends of bridge. Southbound drivers have a spectacular view of Pump Station No. 10 and the surrounding mountains.

V 220.9 (355.5 km) **F 143.1** (230.3 km) Flood Creek bridge, parking.

V 223 (358.9 km) **F 141** (226.9 km) Whistler Creek bridge; parking. Watch for frost heaves.

V 223.8 (360.2 km) **F 140.2** (225.6 km) Boulder Creek bridge; parking.

V 224.5 (361.3 km) **F 139.5** (224.5 km) Lower Suzy Q Creek bridge; parking.

V 224.8 (361.8 km) **F 139.2** (224 km) Suzy Q Creek bridge. Double-ended gravel turnout.

V 225.2 (362.4 km) **F 138.8** (223.4 km) Large gravel turnout to east.

V 225.4 (362.7 km) **F 138.6** (223.1 km) Double-ended paved turnout with picnic table and litter barrels. Historical marker here identifies the terminal moraine of Black Rapids Glacier to the west. This is a retreating glacier and little ice is visible. But this same glacier was nicknamed the Galloping Glacier when it advanced more than 3 miles/4.8 km during the winter of 1936–37, almost engulfing the Richardson Highway.

Black Rapids Lake trail begins across from historical sign (0.3 mile/0.4 km to the lake). Look for river beauty (dwarf fireweed), wild sweet pea and members of the saxifrage family blooming in June.

Private Aircraft: Black Rapids airstrip, adjacent north; elev. 2,125 feet/648m; length 2,200 feet/671m; gravel.

V 226 (363.7 km) **F 138** (222.1 km) Good gravel turnout by river to west.

V 226.3 (364.2 km) **F 137.7** (221.6 km) Falls Creek bridge.

V 226.7 (364.8 km) **F 137.3** (221 km) Black Rapids U.S. Army training site at Fall Creek. Boundary between Game Management Units 20D and 13.

V 227 (365.3 km) **F 137** (220.5 km) Gunnysack Creek. View of Black Rapids Glacier to west.

V 227.4 (366 km) **F 136.6** (219.8 km) Old Black Rapids Lodge. Dirt airstrip.

V 228.4 (367.6 km) **F 135.6** (218.2 km) Parking beside One Mile Creek bridge.

V 230.4 (370.8 km) **F 133.6** (215 km) Large paved turnout overlooks Delta River. Dips and pavement breaks next 0.2 mile/0.3 km northbound.

V 231 (371.7 km) **F 133** (214 km) Darling Creek. Gravel turnout with litter barrel to east.

V 232.1 (373.5 km) **F 131.9** (212.3 km) Small gravel turnout by creek to west.

V 233.3 (375.5 km) **F 130.7** (210.3 km) Bear Creek bridge; turnouts at either end, access to creek. Wildflowers include pale oxytrope, yellow arnica, fireweed, wild rhubarb and cow parsnip.

V 234.2 (376.9 km) **F 129.8** (208.9 km) Large paved turnout to east.

V 234.5 (377.4 km) **F 129.5** (208.4 km) Paved turnout with litter barrels to west. Pipeline access road. Pipeline comes up out of the ground here and goes through forest.

V 234.8 (377.9 km) **F 129.2** (207.9 km) Ruby Creek bridge; parking.

V 237.9 (382.9 km) **F 126.1** (202.9 km) Loop road (watch for potholes) through Donnelly Creek State Recreation Site; 12 campsites, tables, firepits, toilets and water. Camping fee $6/night or annual pass. ▲

Watch for frost heaves northbound.

V 239.1 (384.8 km) **F 124.9** (201 km) Small gravel turnout to east.

V 241.3 (388.3 km) **F 122.7** (197.5 km) Large paved turnout to west with litter barrel and marker about the bison herd. This is the calving ground for the Delta herd. Sometimes more than 100 bison can be seen across the Delta River.

V 242 (389.5 km) **F 122** (196.3 km) Pipeline parallels highway about 0.3 to 0.5 mile/0.4 to 0.6 km away. View of Donnelly Dome ahead northbound.

V 242.1 (389.6 km) **F 121.9** (196.2 km) Coal Mine Road (4-wheel-drive vehicles only) leads east to fishing lakes; **Last Lake**, arctic char; **Coal Mine No. 5 Lake**, lake trout; **Brodie Lake** and **Pauls Pond**, grayling and lake trout. Check with the ADF&G for details.

V 243.4 (391.7 km) **F 120.6** (194.1 km) Pipeline viewpoint with interpretive signs. Good photo stop.

V 243.9 (392.5 km) **F 120.1** (193.3 km) Paved double-ended turnout with litter barrels to east. The trans-Alaska oil pipeline snakes along the ground and over the horizon. A spectacular view to the southwest of 3 of the highest peaks of the Alaska Range about 40 miles/64.4 km in the distance. From west to south they are: Mount Deborah (elev. 12,339 feet/3,761m); Hess Mountain (elev. 11,940 feet/3,639m), center foreground; and Mount Hayes (elev. 13,832 feet/4,216m).

In spring look for wild sweet pea, chiming bells, lupine, lousewort (the bumblebee flower) and bluebell (mountain harebell) for the next 3 miles/4.8 km.

V 244.3 (393.2 km) **F 119.7** (192.6 km) Gravel turnout to east. Trail to **Donnelly Lake**; king and silver salmon, rainbow trout. View of Donnelly Dome ahead northbound.

V 245 (394.3 km) **F 119** (191.5 km) Gravel turnout to east overlooking lake.

V 245.2 (394.4 km) **F 118.9** (191.3 km) Large gravel turnout to east; ponds.

V 246 (395.9 km) **F 118** (189.9 km) Donnelly Dome immediately to the west (elev. 3,910 feet/1,192m), was first named Delta Dome. For years the mountain has been used to predict the weather: "The first snow on the top of the Donnelly Dome means snow in Delta Junction within 2 weeks."

V 246.9 (397.3 km) **F 117.1** (188.4 km) Gravel turnout to east.

V 247 (397.5 km) **F 117** (188.3 km) Cutoff to Old Richardson Highway loop to west; access to fishing lakes.

V 247.3 (398 km) **F 116.7** (187.8 km) From here northbound the road extends straight-as-an-arrow for 4.8 miles/7.7 km.

V 249.3 (401.2 km) **F 114.7** (184.6 km) Bear Drop Zone. Military games area. Controlled access road: No trespassing.

V 252.8 (406.8 km) **F 111.2** (179 km) Scenic viewpoint to west with picnic tables and litter barrels.

V 253.9 (408.6 km) **F 110.1** (177.2 km) Good view of Pump Station No. 9 if southbound.

V 257.6 (414.6 km) **F 106.4** (171.2 km) Entrance to U.S. Army Cold Regions Test Center at Fort Greely.

Meadows Road (4-wheel-drive vehicles only) leads west to fishing lakes. Access to **Bolio Lake**; grayling, rainbow, lake trout. Rainbow-producing **Mark Lake** is 4.5 miles/7.2 km along this road. Meadows Road junctions with the Old Richardson Highway loop. Check with the ADF&G for details on fishing lakes.

V 258.3 (415.7 km) **F 105.7** (170.1 km) Pump Station No. 9 access road.

V 261.2 (420.3 km) **F 102.8** (165.4 km) **FORT GREELY** (restricted area) main gate. Fort Greely was named for A.W. Greely, arctic explorer and author of *Three Years of Arctic Service*.

V 262.6 (422.6 km) **F 101.4** (163.2 km) Double-ended paved turnout with scenic view. Watch for bison. Wind area next 2 miles/3.2 km northbound.

V 262.7 (422.8 km) **F 101.3** (163 km) FAA buildings. Big Delta.

V 264.7 (426.3 km) **F 99.1** (159.5 km) Jarvis Creek, rises near Butch Lake to the east and flows into the Delta River. Buffalo (bison) may be seen in this area.

V 266 (428 km) **F 98** (157.7 km) **Junction** of the Richardson Highway and the Alaska Highway, **Milepost DC 1422**, at Delta Junction. Visitor center is located at junction. Turn to page 169 for description of Delta Junction services and continuation of highway log to Fairbanks (the remaining 98 miles/157.7 km of the Richardson Highway leading into Fairbanks are logged in the ALASKA HIGHWAY section).

COPPER RIVER HIGHWAY

**Cordova to the Million Dollar Bridge
Alaska Route 10**
(See map, page 518)

The Copper River Highway leads 48.1 miles/77.4 km northeast from Cordova to the Million Dollar Bridge at the Copper River.

Construction of the Copper River Highway began in 1945. Built along the abandoned railbed of the Copper River & Northwestern Railway, the highway was to extend to Chitina (on the Edgerton Highway), thereby linking Cordova to the Richardson Highway.

Construction was halted by the 1964 Good Friday earthquake, which severely damaged the highway's roadbed and bridges. The quake also knocked the north span of the Million Dollar Bridge into the Copper River and distorted the remaining spans. The 48 miles of existing highway have been repaired and upgraded since the earthquake, but repairs to the Million Dollar Bridge remain temporary and travel across the bridge and beyond is not recommended.

Copper River Highway Log

Spring at Alaganik Slough, a distributary of the Copper River. (Ruth Fairall)

Distance is measured from Cordova (C).

C 0 CORDOVA. See description in PRINCE WILLIAM SOUND section. The Copper River Highway starts at the ferry terminal and leads east through town.

C 1.4 (2.3 km) Whitshed Road on right leads 0.5 mile/0.8 km to Odiak municipal camper park (usually filled with seasonal workers), 5.5 miles/8.9 km to **Hartney Bay**. Fishing from Hartney Bay bridge for Dolly Varden from May; pink and chum salmon, mid-July through August; closed for salmon upstream of bridge. Use small weighted spoons, spinners and eggs. Clam digging at low tide (license required).

C 2.1 (3.4 km) Site of CR&NW railway powder house. Restaurant.

C 2.3 (3.7 km) Paved turnout to north by Eyak Lake. View of the Heney Range to the south. Mount Eccles (elev. 2,357 feet/3,793m) is the first large peak. Pointed peak beyond is Heney Peak (elev. 3,151 feet/960m).

C 3.7 (5.9 km) Large paved turnout with litter barrels by Eyak Lake.

C 4.1 (6.6 km) Historical marker on left gives a brief history of the CR&NW railway. Also here is a monument erected by the railroad builder M.J. Heney in memory of those men who lost their lives during construction of the CR&NW. Begun in 1907 and completed in 1911, the CR&NW railway connected the port of Cordova with the Kennecott Copper Mines near Kennicott and McCarthy. The mine and railway ceased operation in 1938.

For the next 2 miles/3.2 km, watch for bears during early morning and late evening (most often seen in June).

C 5.3 (8.5 km) Paved turnout on lake to north.

C 5.4 (8.7 km) Paved turnout at lake to north.

C 5.7 (9.2 km) Bridge over Eyak River, access to Eyak River trail. This is a good spot to see waterfowl feeding near the outlet of Eyak Lake. An estimated 100 trumpeter swans overwinter on Eyak Lake.

Eyak River trailhead is on the west bank of the river. The 2.2-mile/3.5-km trail, much of which is boardwalk over muskeg, is popular with fishermen.

C 6 (9.7 km) **Eyak River**, boat launch. Dolly Varden; red salmon, June–July; silvers, August–September. Also pinks and chums. Use Vibrax spoon, spinner or salmon eggs. Fly-fishing only for salmon within 200 yards of weir.

C 7.4 (11.9 km) Paved turnout with litter barrels. *CAUTION: High winds for next 4 miles/6.4 km.* In January and February, these winds sweep across this flat with such velocity it is safer to pull off and stop.

C 7.6 (12.2 km) Bridge over slough.

C 7.7 (12.4 km) First bridge across Scott River.

C 8.1 (13 km) Bridge over slough waters. Gravel turnout; access to slough.

C 8.4 (13.5 km) Scott River bridge.

C 9 (14.5 km) Between **Mileposts 9** and **10** there are 4 bridges across the Scott River and the slough. Sloughs along here are from the runoff of the Scott Glacier, visible at a distance to the northeast of the highway. Bear and moose are often seen in this area, especially in July and August. In May and August, thousands of dusky Canada geese, a subspecies of the Canada goose, nest here. This is the only known nesting area of the dusky geese, which winter in Oregon's Willamette Valley.

Moose feed in the willow groves on either side of the highway. Moose are not native to Cordova; the mountains and glaciers prevent them from entering the delta country. Today's herd stems from a transplant of 26 animals made between 1949 and 1959.

C 10.4 (16.7 km) Scott River bridge. Watch for old and new beaver dams and lodges beside the highway.

C 10.7 (17.2 km) Large paved turnout with litter barrel to south. Game management area, 330,000 acres. Trumpeter swans and Canada geese. Look for arctic terns here.

C 10.8 (17.4 km) Bridge, beaver dam.

C 11.1 (17.9 km) Elsner River bridge.

C 11.5 (18.5 km) Look for brown bears feeding in the outwash plains of Scott Glacier. Thousands of salmon swim up

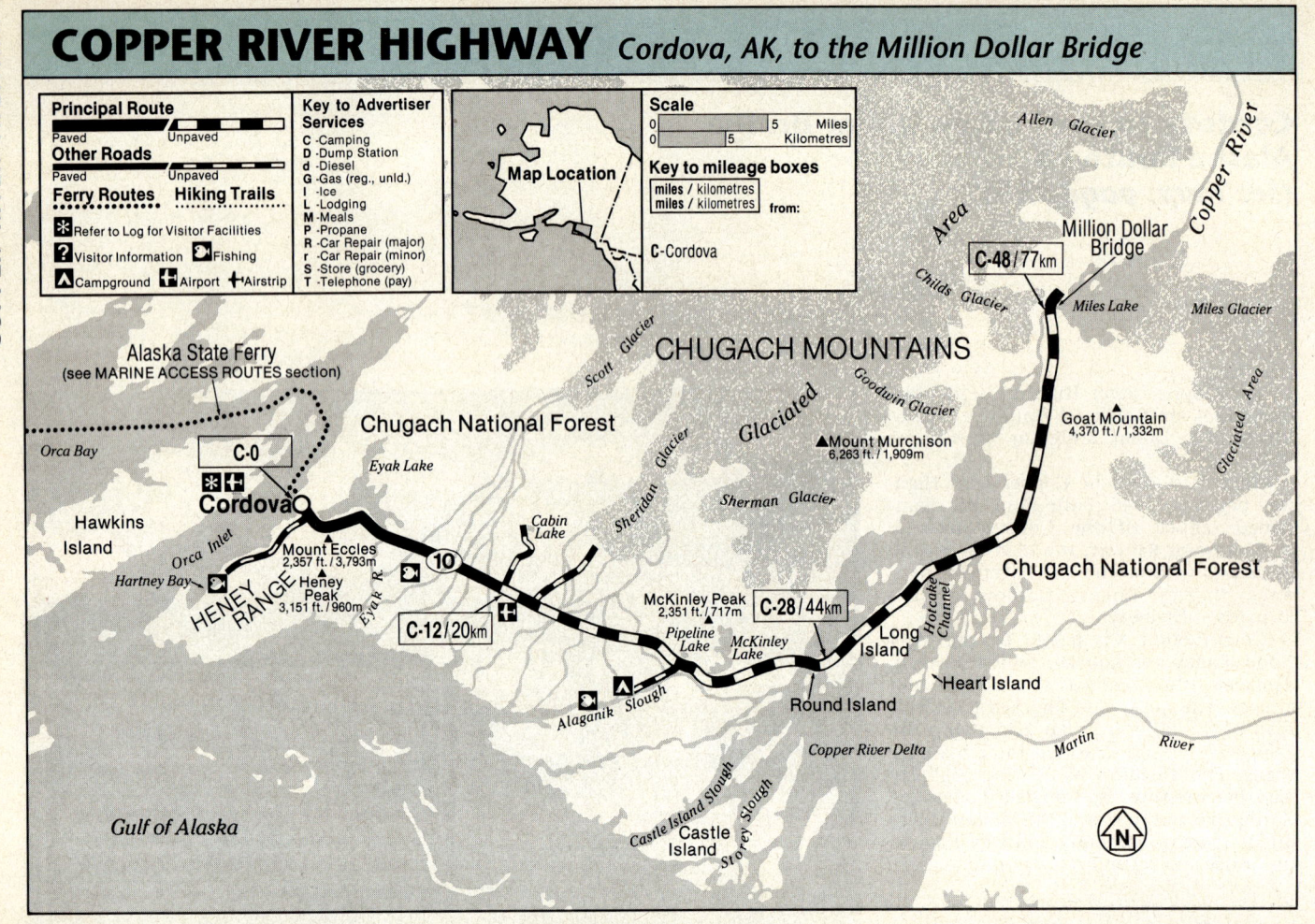

COPPER RIVER HIGHWAY
Cordova, AK, to the Million Dollar Bridge

nearby rivers to spawn. There are numerous beaver lodges on both sides of the highway.

C 11.8 (19 km) State of Alaska Cordova highway maintenance station to northeast. U.S. Coast Guard station.

C 12.1 (19.5 km) Cordova airport and access to Elsner Lake trail and Cabin Lake Recreation Area. Drive north 2.8 miles/4.5 km for trailhead and recreation area (gravel access road forks 0.3 mile/0.5 km in; right fork leads to gravel pit, continue straight ahead for recreation area). CAUTION: Narrow road, watch for logging trucks. Picnic tables, toilets, litter barrels and firepits at **Cabin Lake**; cutthroat fishing. **Elsner Lake** trail is a 4.1-mile/6.6-km loop along several lakes offering fishing for cutthroat. There are many wet muskeg areas: Rubber boots are necessary. CAUTION: Watch for bears.

C 12.4 (20 km) Pavement ends, gravel begins. Watch for potholes.

C 13 (20.9 km) Keep a lookout for snowshoe hare and birds of prey.

C 13.7 (22 km) Sheridan Glacier access road leads 4.3 miles/6.9 km to the terminus of Sheridan Glacier. CAUTION: Narrow road, watch for logging trucks. The glacier was named by U.S. Army explorer Captain Abercrombie for Gen. Philip H. Sheridan of Civil War fame. Sheridan Mountain trailhead, several picnic tables, litter barrels and a partial view of the glacier are available at the end of the access road. It is about a 0.5-mile hike to the dirt-covered glacial moraine.

C 14.8 (23.8 km) Bridge over Sheridan River. View of Sheridan Glacier. To the east of Sheridan Glacier is Sherman Glacier.

Winter moose range next 8 miles/13 km eastbound.

C 15 (24.1 km) Silver salmon spawn during September and October in the stream beside the highway.

C 16 (25.7 km) Beautiful view of Sheridan Glacier to the northeast.

C 16.3 (26.2 km) Second bridge over Sheridan River. Runoff from the Sheridan Glacier is joined upstream from this point by runoff from the Sherman Glacier (hidden from view).

C 16.9 (27.2 km) Turnoff for **Alaganik Slough**, Chugach National Forest Recreation Area. Drive south 3 miles/4.8 km via gravel road; picnic tables, firepits, toilets and boat launch. No water, informal camping. Interpretive plaque on side road reads: "Why are Delta moose the largest and healthiest? This moose herd, first introduced in 1949, maintains its vitality primarily due to its abundant willow supply. As part of a normal cycle, accelerated by the 1964 earthquake, much of the willow is becoming unavailable to moose. As the willow grows tall, the moose can no longer reach the tender new shoots. In the future this could cause a decrease in the numbers of moose on the delta. To slow the cycle down, the Forest Service is experimenting in this area, cutting back the shrubs. This should increase the amount of available willow browse. Biologists will evaluate the response of moose to new willow growth." Fishing in Aaganik Slough for Dolly Varden, sockeye (July) and silver salmon (August and September). Also fishing in pond stocked with grayling at Mile 0.2 on access road.

C 17.4 (28 km) Trumpeter swans often can be seen in the pond beside the highway. One of the largest of all North American waterfowl (with a wingspan of 6 to 8 feet), it faced extinction less than 40 years ago. Almost completely eliminated in the Lower 48 and Canada, Alaska harbors more than 80 percent of breeding trumpeters. More than 10 percent of the Alaska population of trumpeter swans breeds in the Copper River Delta.

C 18 (29 km) For the next mile look for silver salmon spawning in the streams during September. To the left and on the slopes above timberline mountain goats may be seen.

The mountain to the left of the road ahead eastbound is McKinley Peak (elev. 2,351 feet/717m).

C 18.1 (29.1 km) Entering Chugach National Forest eastbound.

C 18.5 (29.8 km) Road narrows. NOTE: Road not maintained in winter (after Nov. 1) beyond this point.

C 18.8 (30.3 km) Trailhead to north for Muskeg Meander cross-country ski trail; length 2.5 miles/4 km. According to the USFS district office, this trail offers a beautiful view of the Copper River Delta.

C 19.2 (30.9 km) Haystack trailhead to north, turnout to south. Easy 0.8-mile/1.2-km trail leads to delta overlook; excellent place to see moose and bear according to the USFS district office in Cordova.

C 21.4 (34.4 km) **Pipeline Lakes** trailhead to north, parking to south. The 1.8-mile/2.9-km trail was originally built as a water pipeline route to supply locomotives on the CR&NW railway. Segments of the pipeline are still visible. Fishing for grayling and cutthroat, fly or bait. Trail joins McKinley Lake trail. Rubber boots are necessary.

C 21.6 (34.8 km) Small turnout to north. **McKinley Lake** trail is an easy 2.1-mile/3.4-km hike with excellent fishing for sockeye, Dolly Varden and cutthroat. Access to USFS public-use cabins: McKinley Trail cabin (100 yards from highway) and McKinley Lake cabin (45-minute walk in from highway; also accessible by boat via Alaganik Slough).

C 22 (35.4 km) Double-ended turnout to north.

C 22.1 (35.5 km) **Alaganik Slough** boat ramp, picnic area, litter barrel and fishing access to south at west side of Alaganik Slough river bridge. Sockeye (red) and coho (silver) salmon, July to September. Also boat access to McKinley Lake.

C 23.7 (38.1 km) Salmon Creek bridge, parking. Beaver lodge.

C 24.5 (39.4 km) Saddlebag Alaganik Canoe Route trailhead and turnout to north. The USFS office in Cordova says this is a 2½-hour paddle downstream with access to McKinley Lake and the takeout point at the bridge at **Milepost 22.1**. Use caution during high-water flow. Not recommended for novice canoeists.

C 24.8 (39.9 km) Channel to beaver pond for spawning salmon. A plaque here reads: "Pathway to salmon rearing grounds. Channel provided access to beaver pond (north side of road) for coho fry. Beaver pond can support up to 25,400 young salmon. Fallen trees and brush provide cover from predators." Side road north around pond leads to woodcutting area.

C 25 (40.2 km) Turnoff to north for 1-mile/1.6-km access road to Saddlebag Glacier trailhead and parking area. According to the USFS office in Cordova, this is an easy 3-mile/4.8-km trail to Saddlebag Lake. View of Saddlebag Glacier; look for goats on surrounding mountains. CAUTION: Watch for bears.

C 25.4 (40.9 km) Small gravel turnout by 2 spawning channels with weirs built in 1987 as part of a USFS stream enhancement project for resident sockeye and coho salmon. Interpretive signs along a short trail here explain the project: "Channel built by USDA Forest Service to provide high quality spawning habitat for coho and sockeye salmon. Before construction, the streambed was muddy and the stream dried up during low flow periods. Fish spawned in the streams but few eggs survived. Improved channel is deeper and ensures a consistent flow. Adjustable weirs control water depth. Clean gravels placed in the channel make better spawning conditions while large rip rap on streambanks prevent erosion.

"Can you see small circles of gravel which appear to have been turned over? These are salmon 'redds,' or nests in which female salmon lay their eggs. Female salmon create the redds by digging with their tails. Environmental conditions and predators take a heavy toll on salmon eggs and small fry. Of the 2,800 eggs which the average female coho salmon lays, only about 14 will survive to adulthood. Most of these will then be caught by commercial, sport or subsistence fishermen. Only 2 salmon from each redd will actually return to spawn and complete their life cycle."

Near here was the cabin of Rex Beach, author of *The Iron Trail*, a classic novel about the building of the CR&NW railway.

C 26.4 (42.5 km) Flag Point. Turnout with view of the Copper River which empties into the Gulf of Alaska. Downriver to the southwest is Castle Island Slough. Storey Slough is visible a little more to the south. Castle Island and a number of small islands lie at the mouth of the Copper River.

C 26.7 (43 km) Two bridges cross the Copper River to Round Island, a small island with sand dunes and a good place to picnic. Monument on the riverbank is dedicated to the men who built these bridges and "especially to the crane crew who lost their lives on July 21, 1971."

In midsummer the Copper River has half a million or more red (sockeye) and king salmon migrating 300 miles/483 km upstream to spawn in the river's clear tributaries. There is no sportfishing in this stretch of the Copper River because of glacial silt.

Candlefish (eulachon) also spawn in the Copper River. Candlefish oil was once a significant trade item of the Coastal Indians. These fish are so oily that when dried they can be burned like candles.

C 27.5 (44.3 km) Bridge from Round Island to Long Island. The 6.2 miles/10 km of road on Long Island pass through a sandy landscape dotted with dunes. Long Island is in the middle of the Copper River.

C 27.9 (44.9 km) Double-ended turnout to north.

C 28.5 (45.9 km) Lake to south is stocked with grayling.

C 30.8 (49.5 km) Watch for nesting swans, other birds and beaver in slough to south of road. *Use extreme caution if you drive off road: sandy terrain.*

C 31 (49.9 km) Lake to south is stocked with grayling.

C 33 (53.1 km) View of 2 glaciers to the northwest; nearest is Goodwin, the other is Childs.

C 33.3 (53.6 km) First bridge leaving Long Island. View to south down Hotcake Channel to Heart Island. Road built on top of a long dike which stretches across the Copper River Delta. From here to **Milepost C 37.7** there are 7 more bridges across the delta. The Copper River channels have changed in recent years, with many bridges now crossing almost dry gulches. The fifth bridge eastbound from here crosses what is now the main channel of the Copper River.

C 34.2 (55 km) Large gravel turnout to north.

C 34.3 (55.2 km) Copper River bridge.

C 35.7 (57.5 km) Large gravel turnout to north.

C 36.8 (59.2 km) Bridge crossing main flow of the Copper River (this is the fifth bridge after leaving Long Island eastbound). Access to river at east end of bridge. The Copper River constantly changes course: previously the main flow was at the 2 bridges at **Milepost C 26.7**. Currently, 40 percent of the river's flow is through this channel. Note the erosion and dying trees along the newer course, and the dry channels of the older course.

C 37.8 (60.8 km) Large gravel turnout to north.

C 38.8 (62.4 km) Childs Glacier directly ahead.

C 39.9 (64.2 km) Milky glacial waters of Sheep Creek pass through large culvert under road.

C 40.9 (65.8 km) **Clear Creek**; Dolly Varden, cutthroat, red salmon (July) and silvers (August–September). Use flies, lures, spinners or eggs. Watch for bears.

C 41.1 (66.1 km) Park on old railroad grade to south for access to Clear Creek.

C 41.7 (67.1 km) Goat Mountain (elev. 4,370 feet/1,332m) rises to the east of the highway. To the west parts of the Sherman and Goodwin glaciers flow down the sides of Mount Murchison (elev. 6,263 feet/1,909m).

C 42.1 (67.7 km) Side road to gravel pit, pond, informal camping and picnic site by Goat Mountain.

C 48 (77.2 km) Access to Childs Glacier Recreation Area with handicap-accessible covered viewing platform, picnic sites, covered tables, toilets, trails and parking. Childs Glacier was named by Capt. W.R. Abercrombie (1884 expedition) for George Washington Childs of Philadelphia. The glacier face is approximately 350 feet/107m high and very active. Calving ice may cause waves to break over the beach. Be prepared to move to higher ground!

C 48.1 (77.4 km) The Million Dollar Bridge; viewing platform. The north span collapsed during the 1964 earthquake. Temporary repairs were made and people have been driving across it, but driving across the bridge and beyond is definitely a "drive at your own risk" venture. Primitive road extends only about 10 miles/16 km beyond the bridge to the Allen River. Proposed extension of the Copper River Highway to Chitina is currently under debate.

From here there is a view of Miles Glacier to the east. This glacier was named by Lieutenant Allen (1885 expedition) for Maj. Gen. Nelson A. Miles.

The Copper River Highway ends at the Million Dollar Bridge. The north span of the bridge collapsed during the 1964 earthquake. (Ruth Fairall)

EDGERTON HIGHWAY

Junction with Richardson Highway, Milepost V 82.6, to Chitina, Alaska
Alaska Route 10
Includes log of McCarthy Road

Known locally as the Edgerton Cutoff, this scenic paved road leads 35.1 miles/56.5 km east through the settlement of Chitina, across the Copper River bridge to the start of the McCarthy Road. The Edgerton Highway is paved with some long, steep grades. The highway follows approximately the route of the old pack trail that once connected Chitina with Copper Center on the Valdez–Fairbanks trail. The Edgerton Highway is named for U.S. Army Maj. Glenn Edgerton of the Alaska Territorial Road Commission.

Beyond Chitina, the gravel McCarthy Road leads 58.3 miles/93.8 km east and dead ends at the Kennicott River, about 1 mile/1.6 km west of the settlement of McCarthy, located within Wrangell–St. Elias National Park and Preserve. The McCarthy Road follows the right-of-way of the old Copper River & Northwestern Railway. Begun in 1907, the CR&NW (also referred to as the "can't run and never will") was built to carry copper ore from the Kennecott Mines to Cordova. It took 4 years to complete the railway. The railway and mine ceased operation in 1938.

Emergency medical services: Between the junction of the Richardson and Edgerton highways and McCarthy contact the Copper River EMS in Glennallen, phone 911 or 822-3203.

View of the Wrangell Mountains near Long Lake on McCarthy Road. (Jennifer Becroft)

---

9 a.m.-8 p.m. 7 days a week
Kenny Lake Mercantile
GROCERIES • GAS • HOT SNACKS
Camper Parking • Propane • Tourist Information
Mile 7.2 Edgerton Highway

Edgerton Highway Log

Distance from junction with Richardson Highway (R) is followed by distance from junction with McCarthy Road (M).

R 0 M 35.1 (56.5 km) Junction. The Edgerton Highway leads off to the east. Begin long downgrade. Watch for horses.

Excellent view of Mount Drum (to the left), a 12,010-foot/3,661-m peak of the Wrangell Mountains. Mount Wrangell (elev. 14,163 feet/4,317m) and Mount Blackburn (elev. 16,390 feet/4,996m) are visible straight ahead.

R 5 (8 km) M 30.1 (48.4 km) Water Well Site Road.

R 5.2 (8.4 km) M 29.9 (48 km) Kenny Lake School.

R 5.3 (8.5 km) M 29.8 (48 km) Paved turnout to north.

R 7.2 (11.6 km) M 27.9 (44.9 km) Kenny Lake Mercantile. See display ad this section.

R 7.3 (11.7 km) M 27.8 (44.7 km) Old Edgerton Loop Road (gravel) leads from here 8 miles/12.9 km through homestead and farm country to the Richardson Highway at **Milepost V 91.1.**

R 7.5 (12.1 km) M 27.6 (44.4 km) Kenny Lake community hall, fairgrounds.

R 7.7 (12.4 km) M 27.4 (44.1 km) Spacious double-ended paved rest area to south with picnic table on shore of Kenny Lake.

R 12.3 (19.8 km) M 22.8 (36.7 km) Paved turnouts to south.

R 13 (20.9 km) M 22.2 (35.7 km) Tonsina River Gift Shop. See display ad this section.

R 18 (29 km) M 17.1 (27.5 km) Steep downhill grade eastbound. Views of the Copper River and bluffs. A buffalo herd in the area can be seen occasionally on the bluffs across the river.

R 19.3 (31 km) M 15.8 (25.4 km) Site of the settlement of Lower Tonsina, formerly a roadhouse for travelers using the Copper River. Tonsina and Copper rivers are visible here. Beyond are the Wrangell Mountains.

The road continues from here east up a steep bluff. Much of the highway has been hewn from solid rock, leaving great cuts on either side. Pockets of pure peat moss are evident in breaks in the rock walls along the road. *CAUTION: Peat fires can be a serious problem; be careful with campfires.*

R 19.4 (31.2 km) M 15.7 (25.3 km) Tonsina River bridge. Former Lower Tonsina

---

Tonsina River Gift Shop

Authentic Native Alaskan gifts sold by the artist herself.
My shop is small but it's all Alaskan produced gifts, mostly my own.

- Baskets
- Fur Hats
- Furs
- Eskimo Masks
- Quill Jewelry
- Kuspuks
- Eskimo Dolls
- Beadwork
- Slippers
- Mukluks
- Seal Products
- Diamond Willow
- Handmade Christmas Ornaments

HC 60, Box 288, Copper Center, Alaska 99573

EDGERTON HIGHWAY
Milepost V 82.6 Richardson Highway to McCarthy, AK

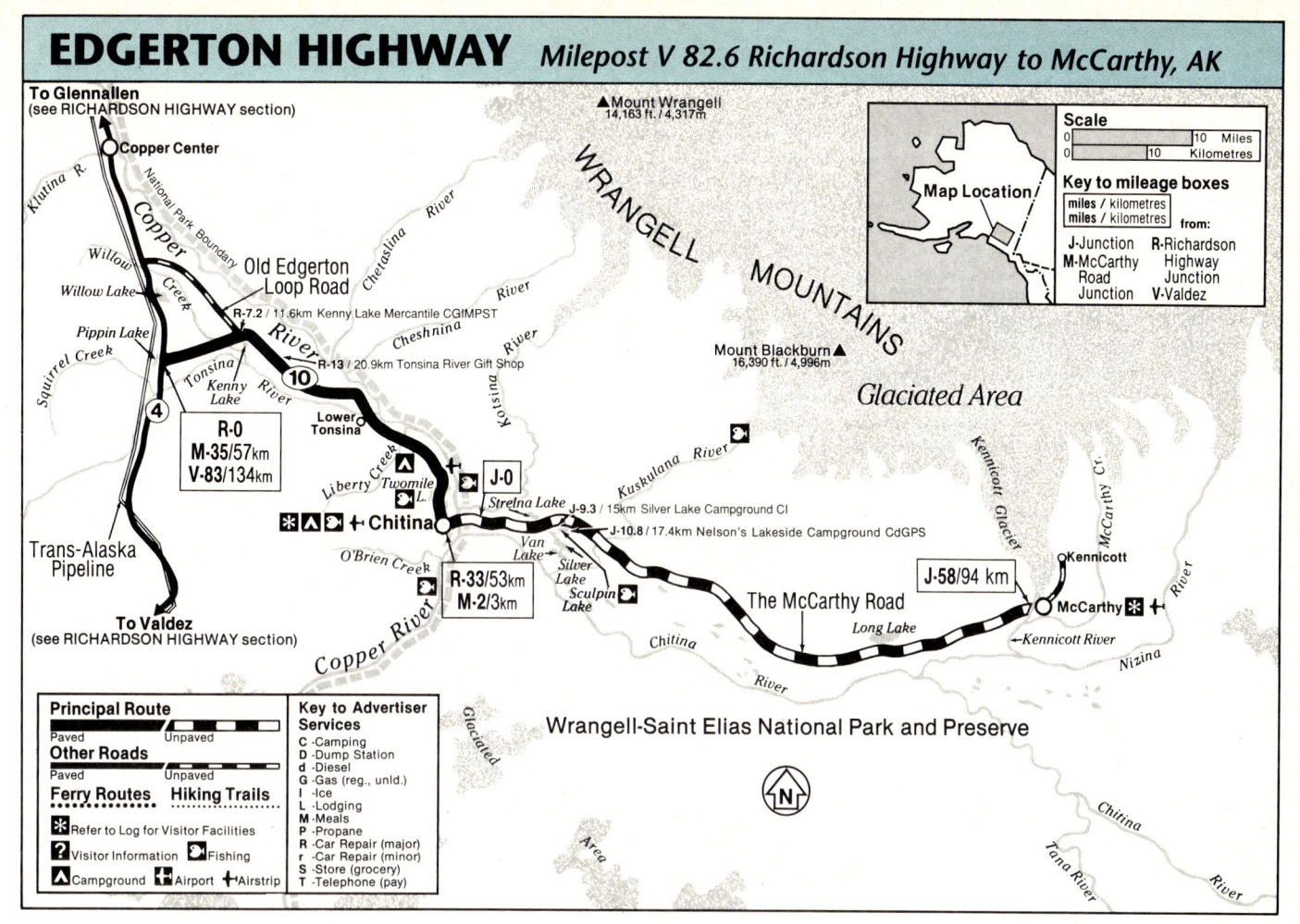

townsite to west of bridge.

R 19.5 (31.4 km) M 15.6 (25.1 km) Turnout to south.

R 19.6 (31.5 km) M 15.5 (24.9 km) Double-ended turnout at lake to north.

R 21 (33.8 km) M 14.2 (22.9 km) Gravel turnout to north overlooking the Copper River.

R 21.6 (34.8 km) M 13.5 (21.7 km) Paved viewpoint to north above Copper River.

R 21.9 (35.2 km) M 13.3 (21.4 km) Small gravel turnout to north.

R 22 (35.4 km) M 13.1 (21.1 km) Top of hill, steep descents both directions.

R 23.5 (37.8 km) M 11.6 (18.7 km) Liberty Falls Creek trailhead to south.

R 23.7 (38.1 km) M 11.4 (18.3 km) Liberty Creek bridge (8-ton load limit) and Liberty Falls State Recreation Site. The campground is just south of the highway on the banks of Liberty Creek, near the foot of the thundering falls. Loop road through campground (large RVs and trailers check road before driving in); 5 sites, no water, no camping fee. Berry picking; watch for bears.

R 28.4 (45.7 km) M 6.7 (10.8 km) Small gravel turnout to north overlooking river.

R 28.5 (45.9 km) M 6.6 (10.6 km) Side road north to Chitina DOT/PF maintenance station and Chitina Municipal Airfield (elev. 556 feet/169m) with a 3,500-foot/1,067-m dirt runway.

R 29.5 (47.5 km) M 5.7 (9.2 km) Small gravel turnout by Threemile Lake.

R 29.7 (47.8 km) M 5.4 (8.7 km) Paved turnout by **Threemile Lake**; good grayling and rainbow trout fishing.

R 30.1 (48.4 km) M 5 (8 km) Small turnout to south by **Twomile Lake**; good grayling and rainbow trout fishing, canoe launch.

R 30.6 (49.2 km) M 4.5 (7.2 km) Large paved turnout at end of Twomile Lake.

R 31.9 (51.3 km) M 3.2 (5.1 km) Onemile Lake (also called First Lake). Access road to boat launch at east end of lake.

Chitina

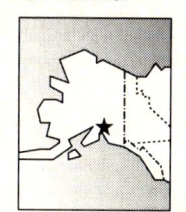

R 33 (53.1 km) M 2.1 (3.4 km). Located about 120 miles/193 km northeast of Valdez, and about 66 miles/106 km southeast of Glennallen. **Population:** 40. **Emergency Services:** Copper River EMS, phone 822-3203.

Visitor Information: National Park Service ranger station for Wrangell–St. Elias National Park and Preserve in Chitina is

Chitina Fuel & Grocery
GAS • Diesel • Propane
Wide Selection of GROCERIES and Sundries
Good Water and Hot Showers • Fishing Licenses
Ice • Cold Pop • Ice Cream Bars • Picnic Supplies

See Fishwheels and Dipnetting at Chitina   Gateway to Wrangell–St. Elias National Park & Preserve
(907) 823-2211 • Open Daily Year Around • Long Summer Hours

Main Street, (Box 22), Chitina, Alaska—(907) 823-2222
SPIRIT MOUNTAIN ARTWORKS
FINE ARTS & QUALITY CRAFTS FROM AROUND ALASKA
Art Koeninger, Custom Jeweler-National Historic Site

CHITINA ADVERTISERS

Chitina Fuel & Grocery .....Ph. (907) 823-2211
Spirit Mountain
  Artworks ....Ph. (907) 823-2222

open 8 A.M. to 5 P.M. daily, Memorial Day to Labor Day. A slide show on the McCarthy Road is available. Write Box 29, Glennallen, AK 99588, or phone 822-5234.

Chitina has a post office, store, gas station, bar, restaurant, tire repair service and phone service. The National Park Service ranger station is housed in a historic cabin. One of the first buildings in Chitina, a hardware and sheet metal shop now on the National Register of Historic Places, houses an art gallery. The public pay phone is located on the outside of the Telephone Bldg. (look for the small building at the end of Chitina's main street as you turn left toward the McCarthy Road).

Chitina (pronounced CHIT-na) was established about 1908 as a railroad stop on the Copper River & Northwestern Railway and as a supply town for the Kennecott Copper Mines at McCarthy. The mine and railroad were abandoned in 1938. The McCarthy Road east of town follows the old railroad bed, which is listed on the National Register of Historic Places.

Inquire locally about informal camping areas: much of the land around Chitina is owned by the Chitina Native Corp. and posted no trespassing. Primitive camping is available along the Edgerton Highway at Onemile and Twomile lakes. There is an 8-site state campground east of Chitina across the Copper River bridge, and 2 private campgrounds on the McCarthy Road. ▲

A big attraction in Chitina for fishermen and spectators is the seasonal salmon run, which draws hundreds of dip-netters to the **Copper River.** The dip-net fishery for salmon runs June through September (depending on harvest levels), and it's worth the trip to see fish wheels and dip nets in action. O'Brien Creek Road provides a state right-of-way access to popular fishing areas on large sandbars along the Copper River. This fishery is open only to Alaska residents with a personal-use permit and residents of the Copper Basin and Tok areas with subsistence permits. Check with the ADF&G office in Chitina for details and current regulations.

Edgerton Highway Log

(continued)

R 33.6 (54.1 km) M 1.6 (2.6 km) Pavement ends eastbound. No road maintenance east of this point between Oct. 15 and May 15.

R 33.8 (54.4 km) M 1.4 (2.3 km) Turnout overlooking the Copper River.

R 34.1 (54.9 km) M 1.1 (1.8 km) Turnout overlooking the Copper River. Access to river.

R 34.7 (55.8 km) M 0.5 (0.8 km) Copper River bridge. Completed in 1971, this 1,378-foot/420-m steel span was designed for year-round use. The $3.5 million bridge reestablished access across the river into the McCarthy–Kennicott area.

R 35.1 (56.5 km) M 0 Junction with McCarthy Road (see McCARTHY ROAD log following). Dept. of Transportation campground on the **Copper River**; 8 sites, picnic tables, fireplaces, toilets, boat launch, no water. Fishing for red and king salmon. Travelers are now within Wrangell–St. Elias National Park and Preserve. ▲

McCarthy Road Log

The road to McCarthy is a 58.3-mile/93.8-km gravel road through virtually untouched Alaskan wilderness. (Although keep in mind that some of the wilderness might be privately owned land.) The road begins where the Edgerton Highway ends and dead ends on the west side of the Kennicott River. The McCarthy Road is recommended for the adventurous traveler and only in the summertime. Allow 3 to 4 hours driving time. Maintained by the state Dept. of Transportation, the road is suitable for most vehicles to **Milepost 15** (Strelna Creek). The road is narrow and unpaved; it may be dusty in dry weather and muddy in wet weather. Beyond Strelna Creek there are turnouts for meeting oncoming vehicles. Motorists with large vehicles or trailers exercise caution, especially in wet weather. Watch for old railroad spikes in roadbed. Unless recently graded, watch for potholes, soft spots and severe washboard. Tire repair available at Silver Lake Campground, Mile 9.3. The National Park Service ranger station in Chitina can provide information on current road conditions and also on backcountry travel in Wrangell–St. Elias National Park and Preserve.

Distance is measured from junction with the Edgerton Highway (J). Traditional mileposts used by local residents are indicated in the log.

J 0 Junction with the Edgerton Highway.

J 3.7 (6 km) Small turnout overlooking the Chitina River.

J 8.3 (13.4 km) **Milepost 10.** Physical mileposts indicate distance from Chitina. Trail opposite homestead leads 0.3 mile/0.5 km north to **Strelna Lake**; rainbow trout and silver salmon. (Private property adjacent trail.)

J 9.3 (15 km) **Milepost 11.** Private campground on **Silver Lake**; rainbow trout fishing, boat rentals, tire repair. Trail access to **Van Lake**, located south of Silver Lake; good rainbow trout fishing.
Silver Lake Campground. See display ad this section.

J 10.8 (17.4 km) **Milepost 12.** Private campground on **Sculpin Lake** (also known as Nelson Lake); rainbow trout fishing and boat launch.
Nelson's Lakeside Campground. See display ad this section.

J 13.3 (21.4 km) **Milepost 15. Strelna Creek** (culvert); fair fishing for Dolly Varden.

J 16 (25.7 km) Kuskulana bridge. This old railroad bridge (built in 1910) is approximately 525 feet/160m long and 385 feet/117m above the river below. It is a narrow 3-span steel railway bridge with wood decking. Before the bridge was rehabilitated in 1988 with new decking and guard rails, the Kuskulana crossing was called the "biggest thrill on the road to McCarthy."

Large gravel turnout at east end of bridge, small turnout at west end.

J 22.3 (35.9 km) Large gravel turnout to south with view of Wrangell Mountains.

There are several turnouts between here and the Kennicott River.

J 23.5 (37.8 km) **Lou's Lake** to north; silver salmon and grayling fishing.

J 25.5 (41 km) Chokosna River bridge.

J 27.7 (44.6 km) One-lane bridge over Gilahina River. Old railroad trestle and parking.

J 40.3 (64.9 km) Crystal Lake.

J 41.4 (66.6 km) Double-ended turnout with view to south.

J 42.9 (69 km) One-lane bridge over Lakina River, access to river at east end.

J 44.1 (71 km) Long Lake Wildlife Refuge next 2.6 miles/4.2 km eastbound.

J 44.2 (71.1 km) Watch for salmon spawning in Long Lake outlet (no fishing at outlet within 300 feet/91m of weir).

J 44.7 (71.9 km) Turnout on **Long Lake**; lake trout, silver salmon, grayling, Dolly Varden and burbot.

J 54.9 (88.4 km) Swift Creek culvert.

J 58.1 (93.5 km) Upper parking lot for visitors crossing Kennicott River to McCarthy (see description next milepost); toilets and dumpsters. Primitive camping. Park here when there is danger of glacial lake breaking out. ▲

J 58.2 (93.7 km) Parking (subject to flooding). Here, 2 hand-pulled cable trams provide the only means of crossing the Kennicott River to reach McCarthy. The trams are small open platforms (built in 1982–83 by local residents and upgraded in 1988) and should be attempted only by travelers strong enough to pull themselves across several hundred feet (part of the distance uphill). It is easier if a friend pulls on the return cable from the riverbank. Wear gloves. *CAUTION: DO NOT attempt to wade across this glacial river; strong currents and cold water make it extremely treacherous.*

A CB radio at the tram has instructions for calling businesses in McCarthy and Kennicott (they monitor Channel 5).

Parking on the lower lot by the riverbank is not recommended in July or early August because of flooding when Hidden

---

SILVER LAKE
Campground

Rainbow Trout Fishing
RV and Tent Camping on beautiful Silver Lake
Boat and Canoe Rental

MILEPOST 11 CHITINA
McCarthy Road Alaska 99566

Nelson's Lakeside Campground
George's Trading Post
FISHING'S GREAT — BOAT RENTAL
Supplies • Groceries • Fuels
MILE 12 MCCARTHY ROAD
P.O. Box 69, Chitina, Alaska 99566

View from Kuskulana bridge at Mile J 16 McCarthy Road. (Ruth Fairall)

J 58.3 (93.8 km) McCarthy Road dead ends at Kennicott River.

McCarthy

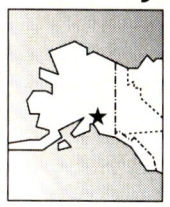

Located within the Wrangell–St. Elias National Park and Preserve 61 miles/98.1 km east of Chitina. **Population: 12 to 16.** There is a store in McCarthy and shuttle service between McCarthy and Kennicott. Lodging is available in McCarthy at McCarthy Wilderness Bed & Breakfast and at the McCarthy Lodge, which also offers food service. There is also Kennicott Glacier Lodge in Kennicott. Check with the lodges about tours and flightseeing.

The town of McCarthy is in a beautiful area of glaciers and mountains. The Kennicott River flows by the west side of town and joins the Nizina River which flows into the Chitina River. The local museum, located in the railway depot, has historical artifacts and photos from the early mining days.

It is 4.5 miles/7.2 km from McCarthy at the end of the CR&NW railroad bed to the old mining town of KENNICOTT (pop. 8 to 15). Perched on the side of a mountain next to Kennicott Glacier, the town was built by Kennecott Copper Corp. between 1910 and 1920. (An early-day misspelling made the mining company Kennecott, while the region and settlement are Kennicott.) The richest copper mine in the world until its closure in 1938, Kennicott's mill processed more than 591,535 tons of copper ore and employed some 800 workers in its heyday. Today, a lodge is located here. The mine buildings are on private land.

McCarthy lies within **WRANGELL–ST. ELIAS NATIONAL PARK AND PRESERVE.** This 12-million-acre park encompasses the southeast corner of the Alaskan mainland, stretching from the Gulf of Alaska to the Copper River basin. Access to the park is by way of the McCarthy Road, the Nabesna Road (off the Tok Cutoff) and out of Yakutat. This vast unspoiled wilderness offers backpacking, mountaineering, river running, hunting and sportfishing. For more information, contact: Superintendent, Wrangell–St. Elias National Park and Preserve, P.O. Box 29, Glennallen, AK 99588; phone (907) 822-5234.

McCARTHY/KENNICOTT ADVERTISERS

Kennicott Glacier
 Lodge.....................Ph. 1-800-582-5128
McCarthy Lodge..........Ph. (907) 333-5402
McCarthy Wilderness Bed
 & Breakfast.............Ph. (907) 277-6867

Lake breaks out from under Kennicott Glacier (usually in July, according to local residents). It is recommended you park just up the road at the upper parking lot.

After exiting the tram, follow the road for about a quarter of a mile to a fork; the right fork leads to McCarthy (less than a mile) and the left fork goes to Kennicott (about 5 miles).

McCarthy Lodge
"IT TAKES YOU BACK"

Home Cooked Food
Famous Sourdough Hamburgers
Relics of Kennicott Copper Days

Located in McCarthy, founded in 1910 at the height of the great Copper Rush

**SUMMER SEASON
MAY 1 – OCTOBER 15**

Saloon — Early 1900's Bar Brags the Largest single plate glass mirror in Alaska

*Hotel Bulit 1916
Modern Baths*

AREA ACTIVITIES
River Rafting • Trail Rides • Cycling
Glacier Treks • Flightseeing
Volleyball & Badminton Court

**4th Annual
TALL TALES CONTEST
JULY 18**

• Special Spring Skiing Packages
• Adventure Packages Arranged

Your Hosts, Gary & Betty Hickling, are lifelong Alaskans
Write: c/o McCarthy Lodge, McCarthy, Alaska 99588
Call (907) 333-5402

McCarthy Wilderness
Bed & Breakfast
*in the heart of the
Wrangell-St. Elias National Park*
Historic Accommodations • Kennicott Tours
Whitewater Rafting • Glacier Hiking
Two Night Minimum
*Bob and Babbie Jacobs • (907) 277-6867
Box 111241, Anchorage, Alaska 99511*

KENNICOTT GLACIER LODGE

GHOST TOWN & GLACIERS

JOIN US on main street Kennicott where miners carved an impossible dream from the heart of North America's most memorable show. Explore a world of soaring peaks, massive rivers of ice, wilderness waterways and the world's largest ghost town — all nestled in the nation's biggest park. At **Kennicott Glacier Lodge**, we offer you the memories of a lifetime at a price you can afford.

Hiking
Glacier Walks
History Tours
Modern Lodge
Excellent Dining
Flightseeing
Photography

Box 103940-5, Anchorage, AK 99510
Outside AK - 1-800-582-5128
Inside AK - 800-478-2350 • FAX - (907) 248-7975

MARINE ACCESS ROUTES

Alaska ports via British Columbia Ferries, Cruise Ships and Alaska State Ferries
Includes: SOUTHEAST ferry system connecting Bellingham, WA, Port Hardy and Prince Rupert, BC, to Ketchikan and other southeastern Alaska ports
(See maps, pages 525-526)
SOUTHWEST ferry system connecting Kenai Peninsula, Kodiak and Prince William Sound ports
(See map, page 543)

The "trusty Tusty" is on the Southwestern ferry system. (Marion Stirrup)

Much of Alaska's southeastern region, with its thousands of islands, bays and steep, mountainous shorelines, prohibits building highways from city to city. The Alaska Marine Highway—which stretches almost 1,000 nautical miles from Bellingham, WA, to Skagway, AK—provides the vital link for people and their vehicles.

Many visitors to Alaska use the Alaska Marine Highway as an alternative route to driving to Alaska. Travelers often drive one direction and take the Marine Highway the other. This option not only eliminates the necessity of driving the road system twice, but affords the traveler the opportunity to take in the magnificent scenery and picturesque communities of Southeast Alaska and the Inside Passage.

The Alaska state ferries depart from Bellingham, WA (85 miles north of Seattle on Interstate 5, Exit 250), or Prince Rupert, BC, for southeastern Alaska communities. Alaska state ferries out of Bellingham do not stop in Canada. The cruise route goes up the famed Inside Passage through several hundred miles of forested islands and deep fjords in Canada and southeastern Alaska. Ferries out of Prince Rupert follow the same route as the ferries out of Bellingham from Chatham Sound north. Ketchikan (the first stop for both) is a 36-hour ferry ride from Bellingham and about 6 hours by ferry from Prince Rupert. There is also ferry service between Ketchikan, AK, and Stewart, BC/Hyder, AK, and feeder service between southern and northern panhandle communities. Descriptions of southeastern Alaska communities start on page 548. Details on the Alaska State Ferry System begin on page 543; schedules begin on page 530.

British Columbia ferries operates between Port Hardy and Prince Rupert, Tsawwassen and Swartz Bay, Horseshoe Bay and Nanaimo, the Queen Charlotte Islands, and also cruise the Gulf Islands and Sunshine Coast.

Cruise ships offer a variety of itineraries from West Coast ports through the Inside Passage and to Southcentral Alaska.

Your...

alaska marine highway

Reservation and Ticketing Center
For Interior Alaska
1-800-448-7181
(907) 456-7888

VISTA TRAVEL, INC.

911 CUSHMAN STREET
FAIRBANKS, ALASKA 99701

AMERICAN EXPRESS® Travel Agency Representative

Member Alaska Visitors Association

524 The MILEPOST® ■ 1992

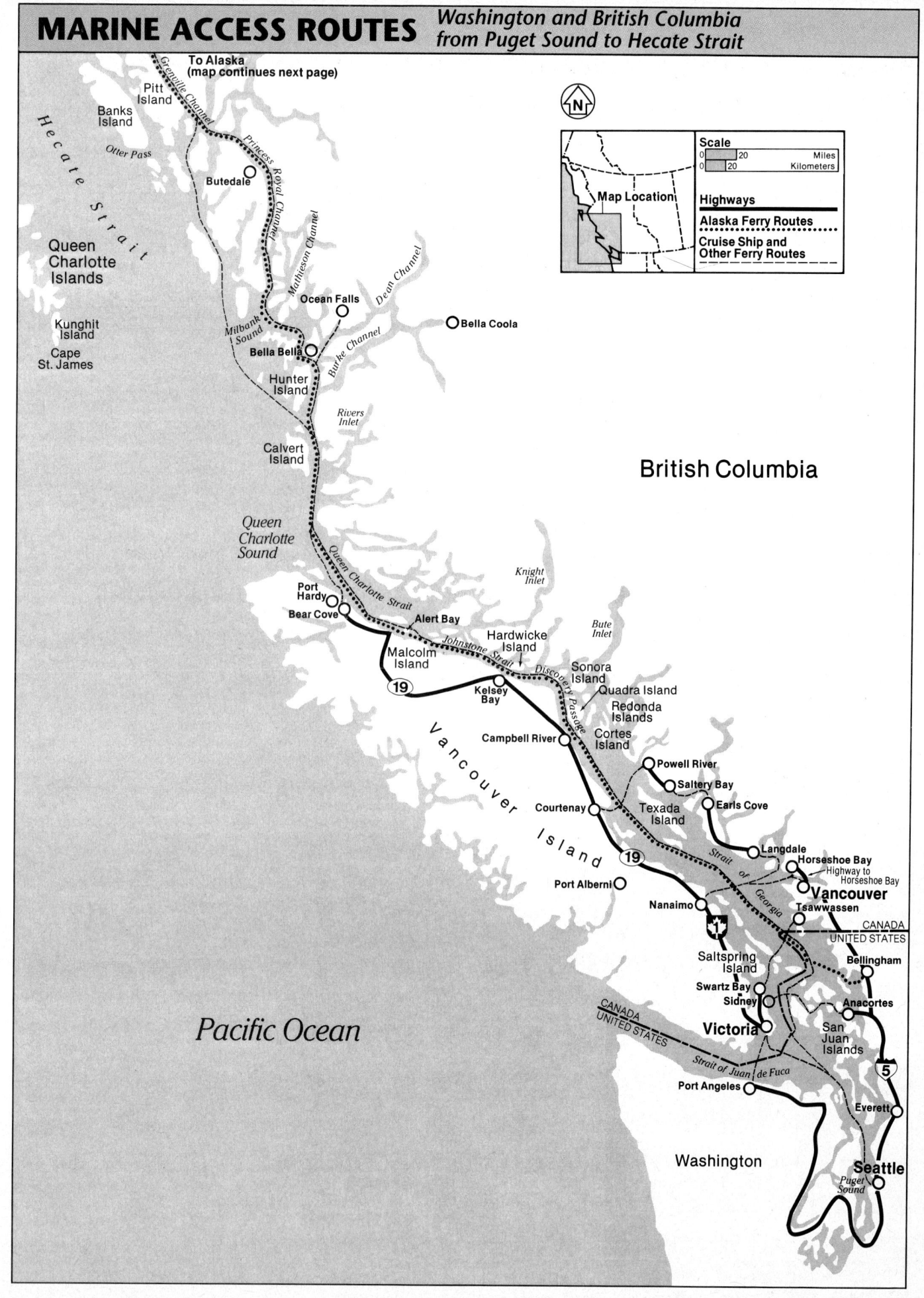

MARINE ACCESS ROUTES
Washington and British Columbia from Puget Sound to Hecate Strait

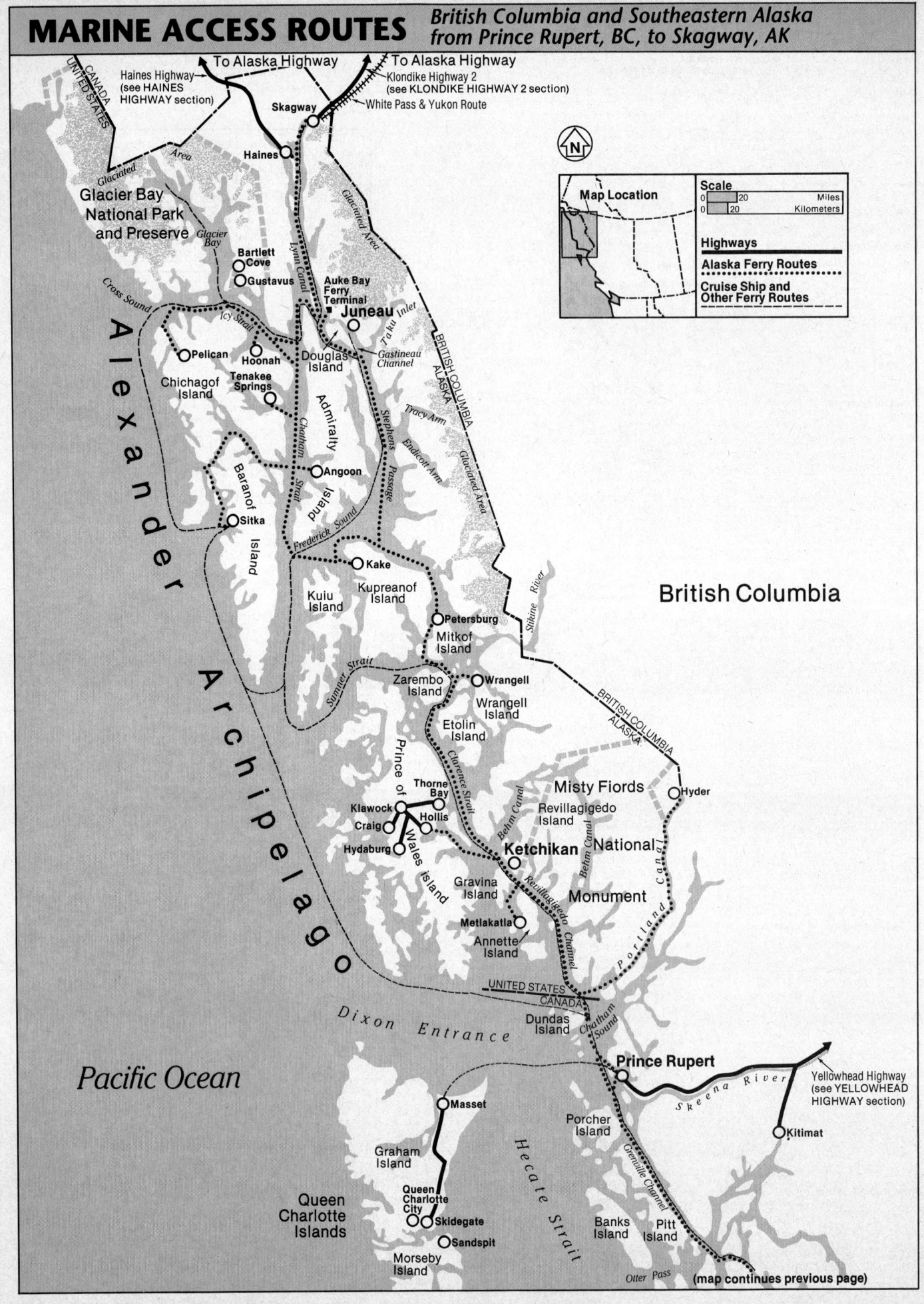

MARINE ACCESS ROUTES
British Columbia and Southeastern Alaska from Prince Rupert, BC, to Skagway, AK

British Columbia Ferries

British Columbia Ferry Corp. operates passenger and vehicle service between Prince Rupert, southern port for most Alaska state ferries, and Port Hardy on the north end of Vancouver Island. BC Ferries also serves 3 major routes between the British Columbia mainland and Vancouver Island: Tsawwassen to Swartz Bay, Tsawwassen to Nanaimo, and Horseshoe Bay to Nanaimo.

Service between Port Hardy and Prince Rupert is aboard the *Queen of the North*, which carries 750 passengers and 157 vehicles. The ferry has a cafeteria, dining room, news/gift shop, licensed lounges, children's playroom, and cabins.

Reservations: Strongly recommended for passengers and vehicles for Port Hardy–Prince Rupert ferry service. Contact BC Ferries, 1112 Fort St., Victoria, BC V8V 4V2, or phone the reservation office in Vancouver (604) 669-1211, in Victoria (604) 386-3431.

Fares and schedules: Following is the 1992 Inside Passage summer sailing schedule (subject to change). At our press time, 1992 fares were not available. Following are 1991 fares; expect fares to be higher in 1992. Adult passenger, $80; child (5 to 11 years), $33.60; car, $165; camper/RV (up to 20 feet in length, over 7 feet in height), $250.

Day cabins may be reserved. Staterooms are available for round-trip passengers. Check-in time for vehicles is 1½ hours before sailing. Cancellations made less than 30 days prior to departure are subject to a cancellation fee.

BC FERRIES SCHEDULE

PORT HARDY TO PRINCE RUPERT
May 26 to Sept. 30, 1992

NORTHBOUND
Departs: Port Hardy 7:30 A.M.
Arrives: Prince Rupert 10:30 P.M.
Dates: May 26, 28, 30
June, July, September (odd-numbered days)
August (even-numbered days)

SOUTHBOUND
Departs: Prince Rupert 7:30 A.M.
Arrives: Port Hardy 10:30 P.M.
Dates: May 27, 29, 31
June, July, September (even-numbered days)
August (odd-numbered days)

Prince Rupert is located 450 miles/724 km west of Prince George via the Yellowhead Highway (see YELLOWHEAD HIGHWAY 16 section). Port Hardy is approximately 307 miles/494 km north of Victoria via Trans-Canada Highway 1 and BC Highway 19. From Nanaimo it is 236 miles/380 km to Port Hardy. Allow at least 8 hours driving time between Victoria and Port Hardy. The route is almost all 2-lane highway and traffic can be particularly heavy between Victoria and Campbell River. Keep in mind that there are limited services between Campbell River and Port Hardy, a distance of 145 miles/233 km. The Port Hardy ferry terminal is located at Bear Cove, 4 miles/7 km from downtown Port Hardy.

To reach Vancouver Island from the lower British Columbia mainland, take BC Ferries from either Tsawwassen or Horseshoe Bay. Follow Highway 99 through Vancouver for the Horseshoe Bay terminal, 13 miles/21 km northwest of the city, and ferry service to Nanaimo. Or turn off Highway 99 approximately 17 miles/27 km north of the U.S. border for the Tsawwassen terminal and service to Swartz Bay near Victoria and to Nanaimo. Both crossings take less than 2 hours and there are a minimum of 16 round-trips daily during summer from each terminal. Reservations are not accepted for passengers or vehicles on these routes.

To reach Vancouver Island from Washington, you can take the Washington state ferry from Anacortes, WA, to Victoria (Sidney), cruising through the San Juan Islands or the MV *Coho* from Port Angeles, WA, to Victoria. Reservations are not accepted for either passengers or vehicles on the ferry out of Port Angeles. For information on Washington state ferries, phone (206) 464-6400 in Seattle or 1-800-542-0810 or 542-7052 toll free in Washington. For information on the MV *Coho* contact Black Ball Transport, 540 Belleville St., Victoria, BC V8V 1W0; phone (206) 822-2222 in Seattle, (206) 457-4491 in Port Angeles, or (604) 386-2202 in Victoria.

Passenger service only between Seattle and Victoria is available on the catamaran *Victoria Clipper*; contact Clipper Navigation Inc. at (206) 448-5000 or 1-800-888-2535. Passenger service only between Port Angeles and Victoria is available on the 120-passenger *Victoria Express*, several times daily in summer.

Bus service is available between Vancouver and Victoria, and between Victoria and Port Hardy from Pacific Coach Lines, 710 Douglas St., Victoria; phone (604) 385-4411 in Victoria, 681-1161 in Vancouver. The bus depot in Victoria is located directly behind the Empress Hotel. Pacific Western Airlines and Air BC have scheduled air service to Port Hardy.

Cruise Ships

From May through September, luxury cruise ships carry visitors to Alaska via the Inside Passage. There are more than 20 ships

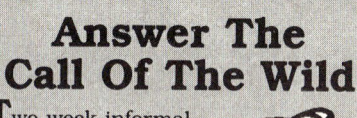

Answer The Call Of The Wild

Two-week informal cruises aboard the **SS Universe**. Excellent lectures on art, history, culture and wildlife. 8 departures visiting 9 ports. Plenty of time to explore on shore. Group or senior rates on selected sailings.

ALASKA NORTHWEST TRAVEL SERVICE, INC.
A Division of Alaska Northwest Publishing Co.
130 2nd Ave. S. - Dept. MP92
Edmonds, WA 98020
206-775-4504 • 1-800-533-7381
FAX 206-672-2824

CRUISE TO VICTORIA & SPEND THE NIGHT
OR
SPEND A DAY IN THE SAN JUAN ISLANDS

Alaska bound? Take a side trip prior to or following your Alaska cruise or road trip. Enjoy a day cruise through the San Juan Islands aboard the 300 passenger "Victoria Star", or cruise to the "British" city of Victoria B.C. for an overnight stay!
(Easy access off I-5; secure R.V. parking available)

GRAY LINE CRUISES
BELLINGHAM CRUISE TERMINAL
355 HARRIS AVE. SUITE 104
BELLINGHAM, WA 98225
1-800-443-4552

NEW! BELLINGHAM TO VICTORIA

MARINE ACCESS ROUTES

MARINE ACCESS ROUTES

Sightseeing boats and some large cruise ships visit Tracy Arm. (Steve Threndyle)

to choose from and almost as many itineraries. There's also a bewildering array of travel options. Both round-trip and 1-way cruises are available, or a cruise may be sold as part of a packaged tour which includes air, rail and/or motorcoach transportation. Various shore excursions may be included in the cruise price or offered to passengers for added cost. Ports of call may depend on length of cruise, which ship you choose, time of sailing or debarkation point. Because of the wide variety of cruise trips available, it is wise to work with your travel agent or contact Alaska Northwest Travel Service, Inc., 130 2nd Ave. S., Edmonds, WA 98020, phone 1-800-533-7381 or (206) 775-4504.

Following is a list of cruise ships serving Alaska in the 1992 season:

Alaska Sightseeing/Cruise West, Suite 700, 4th & Battery Bldg., Seattle, WA 98121; phone 1-800-426-7702 or (206) 441-8687. *Spirit of Glacier Bay* (60 passengers); 3 days from Juneau cruising up Glacier Bay's East and West arms. *Sheltered Seas* (90 passengers); 3- or 4-day daylight cruises between Ketchikan and Juneau. Ports of call: Petersburg, LeConte Glacier, Frederick Sound and Tracy Arm. Overnights in Ketchikan and Juneau. *Spirit of Alaska* and *Spirit of Discovery* (82 passengers); offer 7-night 1-way cruises between Seattle and Juneau. Ports of call: Victoria, Ketchikan, Petersburg, Sitka, Glacier Bay.

Clipper Cruise Lines, 7711 Bonhomme Ave., St. Louis, MO 63105-1965, phone 1-800-325-0010 or (314) 727-2929. Marketing the *Society Explorer* (98 passengers); from Society Expeditions, 14 nights 1 way Aug. 23 between Kodiak and Vancouver, BC. Ports of call: Katmai National Park, Kenai Peninsula, Seward, Prince William Sound, Glacier Bay, Tracy Arm, Wrangell/Petersburg, Misty Fiords, Prince Rupert, Queen Charlotte Islands, Victoria, Gulf Islands. Earlier in the season there are 7-nights between Juneau and Prince Rupert. And 10-nights between Prince Rupert and Kodiak. Ports of call: Misty Fiords, Wrangell/Petersburg, Tracy Arm, Glacier Bay, Prince William Sound, Seward, Kenai Peninsula, Katmai National Park, Kodiak Island.

Costa Cruise Lines N.V., World Trade Center, 80 SW 8th St., Miami, FL 33130-3097; phone 1-800-462-6782 or (305) 358-7325. MTS *Daphne* (420 passengers); 7-night round-trip from Vancouver, BC. Ports of call: Ketchikan, Endicott Arm, Juneau, Skagway, Davidson and Rainbow glaciers, Wrangell.

Cunard Line Ltd., 555 5th Ave., New York, NY 10017-2453, phone 1-800-5-CUNARD or (212) 880-7500. *Sagafjord* (589 passengers); 10- and 11-day cruises from Vancouver, BC, and Anchorage. Ports of call: Ketchikan, Endicott Arm, Juneau, Skagway, Glacier Bay northbound only, Sitka, Yakutat/Hubbard Glacier, Valdez, Columbia Glacier/College Fjords, Seward, Kenai Fjords, Homer.

Glacier Bay Cruises & Tours 520 Pike St., Suite 1610, Seattle, WA 98101, phone 1-800-622-2042 or (206) 623-4245. *Executive Explorer* (49 passengers); 7-day cruises between Ketchikan and Glacier Bay. Ports of call: Misty Fiords, Sitka, Baranof Island, Tracy Arm, Juneau, Haines, Skagway, Glacier Bay. Also 3-day cruises into Glacier Bay's East and West arms. *Spirit of Adventure* (225 passengers); 1-day, fly/cruise up the West Arm of Glacier Bay from Juneau, Skagway and Haines. *Wilderness Explorer* (30 passengers); bunk and quad-occupancy cabins only, 2-, 3- and 4-night cruises in Glacier Bay and 4-night cruises to Admiralty Island, Tracy Arm, Point Adolphus, Inian Island and Althorpe Rock. Kayaking and canoeing are available on these wilderness cruises. Meals are additional.

Hapag–Lloyds, 1640 Hempstead Turnpike, East Meadow, NY 11554, phone 1-800-334-2724 or (516) 794-1253. *Europa* (600 passengers); May 18 sailing 27-day, extensive cruise within Alaska, West Coast, Mexico, Costa Rica and Panama.

Holland America Line, 300 Elliott Ave. W., Seattle, WA 98119; phone 1-800-426-0327 or (206) 281-3535. MS *Noordam* and MS *Nieuw Amsterdam* (1,214 passengers) and MS *Westerdam* (1,494 passengers); 7-night round-trip cruises from Vancouver, BC, and depending upon availability some 3-day northbound and 4-day southbound 1-way may be offered. Ports of call: Ketchikan, Juneau, Glacier Bay, Sitka. SS *Rotterdam* (1,114 passengers); 7-night 1-way cruises between Vancouver, BC, and Seward. Ports of call: Ketchikan, Juneau, Sitka, Hubbard Glacier, Valdez, Columbia Glacier.

Princess Cruises, 10100 Santa Monica Blvd., Suite 1800, Los Angeles, CA 90067; phone 1-800-421-0522 or (213) 553-1770. *Regal Princess* (1,590 passengers); 7-days round-trip from Vancouver, BC. Ports of call: Juneau, Skagway, Glacier Bay, Ketchikan. *Sky Princess* (1,200 passengers); 10-day round-trip from San Francisco. Ports of call: Vancouver, BC, Juneau, Glacier Bay, Sitka, Victoria. *Fair Princess* and *Dawn Princess* (890 passengers) and *Pacific Princess* and *Island Princess* (610 passengers); 7-day 1-way cruises between Vancouver, BC, and Whittier. Ports of call: Ketchikan, Tracy Arm, Juneau, Skagway, Sitka, Columbia Glacier, College Fjords. Some departures cruise into Glacier Bay.

Regency Cruises, 260 Madison Ave., New York, NY 10016, phone 1-800-388-5500 or (212) 972-4499. *Regent Sea* (729 passengers) and *Regent Star* (950 passengers); 7 days between Vancouver, BC, and Whittier, AK. Ports of call: Ketchikan, Juneau, Skagway, Sitka, Columbia Glacier/College Fjords.

(Continues on page 541)

ALASKA STATE FERRY SYSTEM

Reservation and Ticketing Center for All Alaska Marine Highway Vessels.

1-800-526-6731
(907) 486-3800

or write
P.O. Box 703, Kodiak, Alaska 99615

MARINE ACCESS ROUTES

Think of us as a floating highway... that travels through paradise.

We take you to places no ordinary highways go. Between the mainland and Victoria or Nanaimo. To the Gulf Islands and along the Sunshine Coast. Through the Inside Passage, and to the Queen Charlotte Islands.

Like any good highway, we carry vehicles of all shapes and sizes. Our service is year-round and inexpensive, and with typical travel times of a brisk two hours or less, you'll have just enough time to enjoy the trip.

During holiday periods (when we experience our version of the rush hour) the best bet is to plan ahead. Your choice of terminal can also help. On the lower mainland, Tsawwassen is well-equipped to handle travellers going to or from Nanaimo and Victoria during busy times.

Once aboard, our advice is to please yourself. Admire the scenery, smile back at the crew, try one of our good meals, or just think about the wonderful destination you're headed towards.

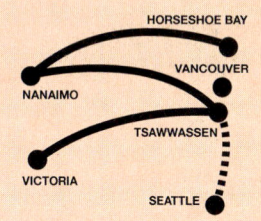

Relax and enjoy. This highway travels through paradise.

FriendShips

BC FERRIES

Dept. MP:2, 1112 Fort Street, Victoria, B.C., Canada V8V 4V2   Vancouver (604) 669-1211   Victoria (604) 386-3431

1992 ■ The MILEPOST® 529

1992 Southeast Ferry Schedules
May 1992 Northbound Schedule

MARINE ACCESS ROUTES

LEAVE BELLINGHAM	LEAVE PRINCE RUPERT	LEAVE STEWART/HYDER	METLAKATLA	KETCHIKAN	HOLLIS	WRANGELL	PETERSBURG	KAKE	ARRIVE SITKA	ANGOON	TENAKEE	HOONAH	JUNEAU/AUKE BAY	HAINES	ARRIVE SKAGWAY
												TH30 5:00A	TH30 9:00P	F1 2:30A	F1 3:30A
	F1 10:30A			F1 5:30P	F1 8:15P					Lv. Pelican S2 10:45A			S2 5:15P		
	F1 9:00A			F1 3:30P		F1 10:15P	S2 2:00A		S2 12:30P				SU3 3:00A	SU3 8:15A	SU3 9:15A
				S2 7:15A	S2 10:00A	S2 12:45P									
				S2 8:45P	S2 11:30P	SU3 2:15P									
F1 8:00P			SU3 11:00A	SU3 9:00A	SU3 4:45P	SU3 3:30P	SU3 7:30P						M4 4:30A	M4 10:00A	M4 11:00A
S2 4:00P		M4 3:15P		M4 10:00A		M4 4:30P	M4 9:30P						T5 7:00A	T5 12:15P	T5 1:15P
				T5 1:45A	T5 4:30A		M4 6:30P	M4 11:45P	T5 10:00A	T5 5:00P	T5 8:30P	W6 12:45A	W6 4:00A		
				T5 10:30A	T5 1:15P								W6 1:00P	W6 4:15P	
	T5 9:00A			T5 3:30P		T5 9:45P	W6 1:30A						W6 10:45A	W6 4:30P	W6 5:30P
	W6 3:30P			W6 10:30P	TH7 1:15A				Lv. Pelican TH7 1:00P				TH7 8:30P	F8 2:00A	F8 3:00A
	TH7 9:00A		TH7 11:30A	TH7 2:15P	TH7 5:00P	TH7 9:45P	F8 1:30A						F8 10:45A	F8 4:30P	F8 5:30P
	F8 10:30A			F8 5:30P	F8 8:15P										
	F8 9:00A			F8 2:00P					Lv. Sitka S9 2:45P	S9 10:00P		SU10 3:00A	SU10 6:15A		
				S9 7:15A	S9 10:00A	S9 12:45P									
	S9 9:00A			S9 3:30P		S9 9:45P	SU10 1:30A						SU10 11:00A	SU10 4:45P	SU10 5:45P
				S9 8:45P	S9 11:30P	SU10 2:15P									
F8 8:00P			SU10 11:00A	SU10 9:00A	SU10 4:45P	SU10 3:30P	SU10 7:30P						M11 4:30A	M11 10:00A	M11 11:00A
	M11 9:00A	M11 3:15P		M11 3:30P		M11 9:45P	T12 1:30A	M11 7:30P	T12 1:00A	T12 11:00A	T12 5:45P	T12 8:45P	W13 1:15A		
				T12 1:45A	T12 4:30A								W13 6:30A	W13 12:15P	W13 1:15P
				T12 10:30A	T12 1:15P										
	T12 9:00A			T12 3:30P		T12 9:45P	W13 1:30A		W13 4:30P				TH14 5:15A	TH14 10:45A	TH14 11:45A
				T12 7:30P	T12 10:15P										
	W13 3:30P			W13 10:30P	TH14 1:15A										
	TH14 9:00A		TH14 11:30A	TH14 2:15P	TH14 5:00P	TH14 9:45P	F15 1:30A						F15 10:45A	F15 4:30P	F15 5:30P
T12 5:45P				TH14 8:00A		TH14 2:30P	TH14 7:00P		F15 5:30A				F15 9:30P	S16 3:45A	S16 4:45A
	F15 10:30A			F15 5:30P	F15 8:15P				Lv. Sitka F15 8:30P	S16 2:30A	S16 5:30A	S16 9:45A	S16 1:00P		
				S16 7:15A	S16 10:00A	S16 12:45P				S16 6:15P			S16 9:30P		
	S16 9:00A			S16 3:30P		S16 9:45P	SU17 1:30A						SU17 11:00A	SU17 4:45P	SU17 5:45P
				S16 8:45P	S16 11:30P	SU17 2:15P									
F15 8:00P			SU17 11:00A	SU17 9:00A	SU17 4:45P	SU17 3:30P	SU17 7:30P						M18 4:30A	M18 10:00A	M18 11:00A
	M18 9:00A	M18 3:15P		M18 3:30P		M18 9:45P	T19 1:30A	M18 6:15P	M18 11:30P	T19 10:00A	T19 5:00P	T19 8:30P	W20 12:45A	W20 6:30A	W20 12:15P	W20 1:15P
				T19 1:45A	T19 4:30A										
				T19 10:30A	T19 1:15P										
	T19 9:00A			T19 5:00P		W20 12:15A	W20 4:30A		W20 3:15P				TH21 4:30A	TH21 10:15A	TH21 11:15A
				T19 7:30P	T19 10:15P										
	W20 3:30P			W20 10:30P	TH21 1:15A										
	*TH21 9:00A		TH21 11:30A	TH21 3:30P	TH21 5:00P	TH21 9:45P	F22 1:30A						F22 10:45A	F22 4:30P	F22 5:30P
T19 5:45P				TH21 7:30A		TH21 1:45P	TH21 5:30P		F22 4:00A				F22 9:30P	S23 3:45A	S23 4:45A
	F22 10:30A			F22 5:30P	F22 8:15P				Lv. Sitka F22 7:30P	S23 1:30A	S23 4:30A	S23 9:00A	S23 12:15P		
				S23 7:15A	S23 10:00A	S23 12:45P									
	*S23 9:00A			S23 3:30P		S23 9:45P	SU24 1:30A			Lv. Pelican S23 9:45P		SU24 4:15A			
				S23 8:45P	S23 11:30P	SU24 2:15P							SU24 11:00A	SU24 4:45P	SU24 5:45P
F22 8:00P			SU24 11:00A	SU24 7:00A	SU24 4:45P	SU24 1:00P	SU24 4:30P						M25 12:30P	M25 5:15A	M25 6:15A
				SU24 2:00P									M25 2:00P	M25 6:30P	M25 7:30P
	M25 9:00A	M25 3:15P		M25 3:30P		M25 9:45P	T26 1:30A	M25 6:15P	M25 11:30P	T26 8:15A	T26 5:00P	T26 8:30P	W27 12:45A	W27 6:30A	W27 12:15P	W27 1:15P
				T26 1:45A	T26 4:30A										
				T26 10:30A	T26 1:15P										
	T26 9:00A			T26 5:00P		W27 12:15A	W27 4:45A		W27 3:15P				TH28 4:30A	TH28 10:15A	TH28 11:15A
				T26 7:30P	T26 10:15P										
	W27 3:30P			W27 10:30P	TH28 1:15A										
	TH28 9:00A		TH28 11:30A	TH28 3:30P	TH28 5:00P	TH28 9:45P	F29 1:30A						F29 10:45A	F29 4:30P	F29 5:30P
T26 5:45P				TH28 8:00A		TH28 2:15P	TH28 6:15P		F29 4:30A				F29 9:30P	S30 3:45A	S30 4:45A
	F29 10:30A			F29 5:30P	F29 8:15P				Lv. Sitka F29 7:15P	S30 1:30A	S30 4:30A	S30 9:00A	S30 12:15P		
				S30 7:15A	S30 10:00A	S30 12:45P					S30 6:15P		S30 9:30P		
	S30 9:00A			S30 3:30P		S30 9:45P	SU31 1:30A						SU31 11:00A	SU31 4:45P	SU31 5:45P
				S30 8:45P	S30 11:30P	SU31 2:15P									
F29 8:00P			SU31 11:00A	SU31 9:00A	SU31 4:45P	SU31 3:30P	SU31 7:30P						M1 4:30A	M1 10:00A	M1 11:00A

*THE FOLLOWING EVENTS MAY AFFECT AVAILABILITY OF SPACE:
MAY 9 - SCHOOL TRACK MEET - ANGOON
MAY 22-23 - REGION V TRACK MEET - JUNEAU

- AURORA (pink)
- COLUMBIA (gray)
- LE CONTE (yellow)
- MALASPINA (blue)
- MATANUSKA (green)
- TAKU (orange)

May 1992 Southbound Schedule

The state reserves the right to revise or cancel schedules and rates without prior notice and assumes no responsibility for delays and/or expenses due to such modifications.

Alaska state ferry schedules reprinted courtesy of Alaska Marine Highway

MARINE ACCESS ROUTES

LEAVE SKAGWAY	HAINES	JUNEAU/ AUKE BAY	HOONAH	TENAKEE	ANGOON	ARRIVE SITKA	KAKE	PETERSBURG	WRANGELL	HOLLIS	KETCHIKAN	METLAKATLA	ARRIVE STEWART/ HYDER	ARRIVE PRINCE RUPERT	ARRIVE BELLINGHAM
F1 4:30A	F1 6:30A	F1 11:15A								F1 10:00P	S2 5:30A	S2 6:45A			
	S2 1:30A	Ar. Pelican	S2 8:00A												
		S2 8:15P	SU3 12:30A	SU3 4:15A	SU3 7:45A	SU3 1:15P	M4 2:45A	M4 7:00A							
SU3 7:30P	SU3 10:00P	M4 3:45A						M4 12:15P	M4 4:00P		M4 11:15P			T5 6:15A	
										S2 2:15P	S2 7:00P	S2 8:15P			
										SU3 5:15P	SU3 9:00A	SU3 10:15P			
M4 3:00P	M4 5:30P	T5 12:15A				T5 8:00A		T5 9:15P	W6 1:15A		W6 10:00A				TH7 10:00P
										SU3 6:30P	SU3 11:00P		M4 10:00A		
T5 6:15P	T5 8:15P	W6 12:15A								T5 6:15A	T5 9:00A				
		W6 8:00A	W6 11:15A												
		TH7 4:00A	Ar. Pelican	TH7 10:30A											
		F8 3:00A				F8 11:30A	F8 3:15P			F8 11:15P			S9 6:15A		
W6 7:30P	W6 10:00P	TH7 3:45A						TH7 12:15P	TH7 4:00P		TH7 11:15P			F8 6:15A	
										W6 1:15A	W6 5:30A			W6 1:00P	
										TH7 5:30A	TH7 9:45A	TH7 11:00A			
*F8 4:00A	F8 5:45A	F8 11:45A	F8 4:00P	F8 8:15P	F8 11:45P	S9 5:30A									
F8 11:30P	S9 2:30A	S9 9:00A				S9 6:15P		SU10 8:00A	SU10 1:30P		SU10 11:15P			M11 6:15A	
										TH7 6:45P	TH7 11:00P			F8 6:30A	
										F8 10:00P	S9 5:30A	S9 6:45A			
		SU10 7:30A			SU10 2:00P	SU10 7:30P	M11 8:15A	M11 12:30P		S9 5:30A					T12 8:00A
										S9 2:15P	S9 7:00P	S9 8:15P			
SU10 7:30P	SU10 10:00P	M11 3:45A						M11 12:15P	M11 4:00P		M11 11:15P			T12 6:15A	
										SU10 5:15A	SU10 9:00A	SU10 10:15A			
M11 3:00P	M11 5:30P	T12 12:15A				T12 9:00A		T12 10:00P	W13 2:00A		W13 10:00A				TH14 10:00P
										SU10 6:30P	SU10 11:00P		M11 10:00A		
T12 7:30P	T12 10:00P	W13 3:45A						W13 12:15P	W13 4:00P		W13 11:15P			TH14 6:15A	
W13 3:15P	W13 5:15P	W13 10:00P								T12 6:15A	T12 9:00A				
		TH14 6:30P	TH14 10:45P	F15 2:45A	F15 6:15A	F15 11:45A									
										T12 3:00P	T12 5:45P				
TH14 6:30P	TH14 9:00P	F15 3:00A				F15 11:30A	F15 3:15P			F15 11:15P			S16 6:15A		
										W13 1:15A	W13 5:30A			W13 1:00P	
										TH14 5:30A	TH14 9:45A	TH14 11:00A			
F15 10:30P	S16 1:30A	S16 9:00A				S16 6:45P		SU17 12:30P	SU17 4:15P		SU17 11:15P			M18 6:15A	
										TH14 6:45P	TH14 11:00P			F15 6:30A	
S16 8:45A	S16 11:45A	S16 6:15P						SU17 3:15P	SU17 7:30A		SU17 5:30P			T19 8:00A	
		S16 2:00P	S16 5:15P							F15 10:00P	S16 6:45A	S16 6:45A			
		SU17 1:15A		SU17 7:45A	SU17 1:15P	M18 2:15A	M18 6:30A			S16 2:15P	S16 7:00P	S16 8:15P			
SU17 7:30P	SU17 10:00P	M18 3:45A						M18 12:15P	M18 4:00P		M18 11:15P			T19 6:15A	
										SU17 5:15A	SU17 9:00A	SU17 10:15A			
M18 3:00P	M18 5:30P	T19 12:15A				T19 8:00A		T19 9:15P	W20 1:15A		W20 10:00A				TH21 10:00P
										SU17 6:30P	SU17 11:00P		M18 10:00A		
T19 7:30P	T19 10:00P	W20 3:45A						W20 12:15P	W20 4:00P		W20 11:15P			TH21 6:15A	
W20 3:15P	W20 5:15P	W20 10:00P								T19 6:15A	T19 9:00A				
		TH21 5:45P	TH21 10:00P	F22 1:45A	F22 5:00A	F22 10:30A									
										T19 3:00P	T19 5:45P				
*TH21 6:30P	TH21 9:00P	F22 3:00A				F22 11:30A	F22 3:15P			F22 11:15P			S23 6:15A		
										W20 1:15A	W20 5:30A			W20 1:00P	
										TH21 5:30A	TH21 9:45A	TH21 11:00A			
F22 10:45P	S23 1:15A	S23 9:00A				S23 5:30P		SU24 7:15A	SU24 11:45A		SU24 11:15P			M25 6:15A	
										TH21 6:45P	TH21 11:00P			F22 6:30A	
*S23 8:45A	S23 11:45A	S23 9:45A						SU24 6:15A	SU24 10:00A		SU24 5:30P			T26 8:00A	
		S23 1:15P	Ar. Pelican	S23 7:45P						F22 10:00P	S23 5:30A	S23 6:45A			
										S23 2:15P	S23 7:00P	S23 8:15P			
SU24 7:30P	SU24 10:00P	M25 3:45A						M25 12:15P	M25 4:00P		M25 11:15P			T26 6:15A	
		SU24 6:15A		SU24 1:00P	SU24 6:30P	M25 8:15A	M25 12:30P			SU24 5:15A	SU24 9:00A	SU24 10:15A			
M25 7:00A	M25 9:00A	M25 1:00P													
										SU24 6:30P	SU24 11:00P		M25 10:00A		
M25 9:30P	M25 11:30P	T26 5:30A				T26 2:00P		W27 3:30A	W27 9:00A		W27 5:45P				F29 8:00A
T26 7:30P	T26 10:00P	W27 3:45A						W27 12:15P	W27 4:00P		W27 11:15P			TH28 6:15A	
W27 2:15P	W27 4:15P	W27 9:00P								T26 6:15A	T26 9:00A				
		TH28 5:30P	TH28 9:45P	F29 1:45A	F29 5:15A	F29 10:45A									
										T26 3:00P	T26 5:45P				
TH28 6:30P	TH28 9:00P	F29 3:00A				F29 11:30A	F29 3:15P			F29 11:15P			S30 6:15A		
										W27 1:15A	W27 5:30A			W27 1:00P	
										TH28 5:30A	TH28 9:45A	TH28 11:00A			
F29 10:45P	S30 1:15A	S30 7:30A				S30 5:30P		SU31 9:45A	SU31 1:45P		SU31 11:15P			M1 6:15A	
										TH28 6:45P	TH28 11:00P			F29 6:30A	
S30 8:45A	S30 11:45A	S30 6:15P						SU31 3:15A	SU31 7:30A		SU31 5:30P			T2 8:00A	
		S30 2:00P	S30 5:15P							F29 10:00P	S30 5:30A	S30 6:45A			
		SU31 12:15A		SU31 6:45A	SU31 12:15P	M1 2:15A	M1 6:30A			S30 2:15P	S30 7:00P	S30 8:15P			
SU31 7:30P	SU31 10:00P	M1 3:45A						M1 12:15P	M1 4:00P		M1 11:15P			T2 6:15A	
										SU31 5:15A	SU31 9:00A	SU31 10:15A			
										SU31 6:30P	SU31 11:00P		M1 10:00A		

ALL TIMES ARE LOCAL TIMES

Each horizontal line represents a ferry sailing and each color a vessel (see color key). The day of the week (M for Monday, etc.), date of month, and time (A.M. or P.M.) of departures and/or arrivals are listed for each port. Read from left to right.

June 1992 Northbound Schedule

LEAVE BELLINGHAM	LEAVE PRINCE RUPERT	LEAVE STEWART/ HYDER	METLAKATLA	KETCHIKAN	HOLLIS	WRANGELL	PETERSBURG	KAKE	ARRIVE SITKA	ANGOON	TENAKEE	HOONAH	JUNEAU/ AUKE BAY	HAINES	ARRIVE SKAGWAY
F29 8:00P				SU31 9:00A		SU31 3:30P	SU31 7:30P						M1 4:30A	M1 10:00A	M1 11:00A
	M1 9:00A			M1 3:30P		M1 9:45P	T2 1:30A						T2 10:45A	T2 4:30P	T2 5:30P
		M1 3:15P		T2 1:45A	T2 4:30A		M1 5:45P	M1 11:00P	T2 7:15A	T2 3:45P	T2 6:45P	T2 11:15P	W3 6:30A	W3 12:15P	W3 1:15P
				T2 10:30A	T2 1:15P										
	T2 9:00A			T2 5:00P		T2 11:45P	W3 3:45A		W3 2:15P				TH4 3:45A	TH4 9:30A	TH4 10:30A
				T2 7:30P	T2 10:15P										
	W3 3:30P			W3 10:30P	TH4 1:15A										
	TH4 9:00A			TH4 3:30P		TH4 9:45P	F5 1:30A						F5 10:45A	F5 4:30P	F5 5:30P
			TH4 11:30A	TH4 2:15P	TH4 5:00P										
T2 5:45P				TH4 8:00A		TH4 3:15P	TH4 7:30P		F5 10:30A				F5 11:15P	S6 5:30A	S6 6:30A
	F5 10:30A			F5 5:30P	F5 8:15P			Lv. Sitka	F5 6:45P	S6 12:45A	S6 3:45A	S6 8:00A	S6 11:15A		
			S6 7:15A	S6 10:00A	S6 12:45P										
	S6 9:00A			S6 3:30P		S6 9:45P	SU7 1:30A						SU7 11:00A	SU7 4:45P	SU7 5:45P
			S6 8:45P	S6 11:30P	SU7 2:15A					Lv. Pelican	S6 9:45P		SU7 4:15A		
F5 8:00P				SU7 9:00A		SU7 3:30P	SU7 7:30P						M8 4:30A	M8 10:00A	M8 11:00A
			SU7 11:00A	SU7 2:00P	SU7 4:45P										
	M8 9:00A			M8 3:30P		M8 9:45P	T9 1:30A						T9 10:45A	T9 4:30P	T9 5:30P
		M8 3:15P		T9 1:45A	T9 4:30A		M8 6:15P	M8 11:30P	T9 9:30A	T9 4:30P	T9 8:00P	W10 12:15A	W10 6:30A	W10 12:15P	W10 1:15P
				T9 10:30A	T9 1:15P										
	T9 9:00A			T9 5:00P		T9 11:45P	W10 3:45A		W10 3:00P				TH11 4:30A	TH11 10:15A	TH11 11:15A
				T9 7:30P	T9 10:15P										
	W10 3:30P			W10 10:30P	TH11 1:15A										
	TH11 9:00A			TH11 3:30P		TH11 9:45P	F12 1:30A						F12 10:45A	F12 4:30P	F12 5:30P
			TH11 11:30A	TH11 2:15P	TH11 5:00P										
T9 5:45P				TH11 8:00A		TH11 2:15P	TH11 6:15P		F12 4:30A				F12 9:30P	S13 3:45A	S13 4:45A
	F12 10:30A			F12 5:30P	F12 8:15P			Lv. Sitka	F12 7:15P	S13 1:30A	S13 4:30A	S13 9:00A	S13 12:15P		
			S13 7:15A	S13 10:00A	S13 12:45P							S13 6:15P	S13 9:30P		
	S13 9:00A			S13 3:30P		S13 9:45P	SU14 1:30A						SU14 11:00A	SU14 4:45P	SU14 5:45P
			S13 8:45P	S13 11:30P	SU14 2:15A										
F12 8:00P				SU14 9:00A		SU14 3:30P	SU14 7:30P						M15 4:30A	M15 10:00A	M15 11:00A
			SU14 11:00A	SU14 2:00P	SU14 4:45P										
	M15 9:00A			M15 3:30P		M15 9:45P	T16 1:30A						T16 10:45A	T16 4:30P	T16 5:30P
		M15 3:15P		T16 1:45A	T16 4:30A		M15 5:45P	M15 11:00P	T16 9:00A	T16 4:00P	T16 7:30P	T16 11:45P	W17 6:30A	W17 12:15P	W17 1:15P
				T16 10:30A	T16 1:15P										
	T16 9:00A			T16 5:00P		T16 11:30P	W17 3:30A		W17 2:15P				TH18 3:45A	TH18 9:30A	TH18 10:30A
				T16 7:30P	T16 10:15P										
	W17 3:30P			W17 10:30P	TH18 1:15A										
	TH18 9:00A			TH18 3:30P		TH18 9:45P	F19 1:30A						F19 10:45A	F19 4:30P	F19 5:30P
			TH18 11:30A	TH18 2:15P	TH18 5:00P										
T16 5:45P				TH18 8:00A		TH18 3:15P	TH18 7:30P		F19 10:00A				F19 10:30P	S20 3:45A	S20 4:45A
	F19 10:30A			F19 5:30P	F19 8:15P			Lv. Sitka	F19 6:00P	S20 12:15A	S20 3:15A	S20 7:30A	S20 10:45A		
			S20 7:15A	S20 10:00A	S20 12:45P										
	S20 9:00A			S20 3:30P		S20 9:45P	SU21 1:30A						SU21 11:00A	SU21 4:45P	SU21 5:45P
			S20 8:45P	S20 11:30P	SU21 2:15A					Lv. Pelican	S20 8:45P		SU21 3:15A		
F19 8:00P				SU21 9:00A		SU21 2:45P	SU21 6:30P						M22 2:30A	M22 7:15A	M22 8:15A
			SU21 11:00A	SU21 2:00P	SU21 4:45P										
													M22 4:30P	M22 9:15P	M22 10:15P
	M22 9:00A			M22 3:30P		M22 9:45P	T23 1:30A						T23 10:45A	T23 4:30P	T23 5:30P
		M22 3:15P		T23 1:45A	T23 4:30A		M22 8:30P	T23 3:30A	T23 12:15P	T23 9:00P	W24 12:15A	W24 4:30A	W24 10:30A	W24 4:15P	W24 5:15P
				T23 10:30A	T23 1:15P										
	T23 9:00A			T23 4:30P		T23 11:00P	W24 3:00A		W24 1:30P				TH25 2:00A	TH25 7:45A	TH25 8:45A
				T23 7:30P	T23 10:15P										
	W24 3:30P			W24 10:30P	TH25 1:15A										
	TH25 9:00A			TH25 3:30P		TH25 9:45P	F26 1:30A						F26 10:45A	F26 4:30P	F26 5:30P
			TH25 11:30A	TH25 2:15P	TH25 5:00P										
T23 5:45P				TH25 8:00A		TH25 3:15P	TH25 7:30P		F26 10:00A				F26 10:30P	S27 4:30A	S27 5:30A
	F26 10:30A			F26 5:30P	F26 8:15P			Lv. Sitka	F26 5:45P	F26 11:45P	S27 3:15A	S27 7:30A	S27 10:45A		
			S27 7:15A	S27 10:00A	S27 12:45P							S27 6:15P	S27 9:30P		
	S27 9:00A			S27 3:30P		S27 9:45P	SU28 1:30A						SU28 11:00A	SU28 4:45P	SU28 5:45P
			S27 8:45P	S27 11:30P	SU28 2:15A										
F26 8:00P				SU28 9:00A		SU28 3:30P	SU28 7:30P						M29 4:30A	M29 10:00A	M29 11:00A
			SU28 11:00A	SU28 2:00P	SU28 4:45P										
	M29 9:00A			M29 3:30P		M29 9:45P	T30 1:30A						T30 10:45A	T30 4:30P	T30 5:30P
		M29 3:15P		T30 1:45A	T30 4:30A		M29 4:45P	M29 10:00P	T30 6:15A	T30 3:15P	T30 6:45P	T30 11:00P	W1 6:30A	W1 12:15P	W1 1:15P
	T30 9:00A			T30 4:30P		T30 10:45P	W1 2:45A		W1 1:15P				TH2 2:45A	TH2 8:30A	TH2 9:30A
				T30 10:30A	T30 1:15P										
				T30 7:30P	T30 10:15P										
T30 5:45P				TH2 8:00A		TH2 3:15P	TH2 7:30P		F3 9:30A				F3 10:00P	S4 4:15A	S4 5:15A

AURORA
COLUMBIA
LE CONTE
MALASPINA
MATANUSKA
TAKU

June 1992 Southbound Schedule

MARINE ACCESS ROUTES

LEAVE SKAGWAY	HAINES	JUNEAU/ AUKE BAY	HOONAH	TENAKEE	ANGOON	ARRIVE SITKA	KAKE	PETERSBURG	WRANGELL	HOLLIS	KETCHIKAN	METLAKATLA	ARRIVE STEWART/ HYDER	ARRIVE PRINCE RUPERT	ARRIVE BELLINGHAM
SU31 7:30P	SU31 10:00P	M1 3:45A						M1 12:15P	M1 4:00P		M1 11:15P			T2 6:15A	
		SU31 12:15A			SU31 6:45A	SU31 12:15P	M1 2:15P	M1 6:30A							
M1 8:00P	M1 11:00P	T2 5:00A				T2 1:15P		W3 2:30A	W3 9:00A		W3 5:45P				F5 8:00A
T2 7:30P	T2 10:00P	W3 3:45A						W3 12:15P	W3 4:00P		W3 11:15P			TH4 6:15A	
W3 2:15P	W3 4:15P	W3 9:00P								T2 6:15P	T2 9:00A				
		TH4 4:15P	TH4 8:30P	F5 12:45A	F5 4:15A	F5 9:45A				T2 3:00P	T2 5:45P				
TH4 7:30P	TH4 10:00P	F5 3:45A						F5 12:15P	F5 4:00P		F5 11:15P			S6 6:15A	
										W3 1:15A	W3 5:30A			W3 1:00P	
										TH4 5:30A	TH4 9:45A	TH4 11:00A			
F5 11:30P	S6 1:30A	S6 7:45A			S6 5:00P			SU7 5:30A	SU7 1:00P		SU7 11:15P			M8 6:15A	
										TH4 6:45P	TH4 11:00P			F5 6:30P	
S6 9:30A	S6 12:30P	S6 7:00P						SU7 3:45A	SU7 7:30A		SU7 5:30P			T9 8:00A	
		S6 1:15P	Ar. Pelican	S6 7:45P						F5 10:00P	S6 5:30A	S6 6:45A			
										S6 2:15P	S6 7:00P	S6 8:15P			
SU7 7:30P	SU7 10:00P	M8 3:45A						M8 12:15P	M8 4:00P		M8 11:15P			T9 6:15A	
		SU7 6:15A			SU7 12:30P	SU7 6:15P	M8 6:30A	M8 10:45A			SU7 5:15P	SU7 9:00A	SU7 10:15A			
M8 3:00P	M8 5:30P	M8 11:30P				T9 7:30A		T9 9:15A	W10 1:15A		W10 10:00A				TH11 10:00P
										SU7 6:30P	SU7 11:00P		M8 10:00A		
T9 7:30P	T9 10:00P	W10 3:45A						W10 12:15P	W10 4:00P		W10 11:15P			TH11 6:15A	
W10 3:15P	W10 5:15P	W10 10:00P								T9 6:15A	T9 9:00A				
		TH11 5:30A	TH11 9:45P	F12 1:45A	F12 5:15A	F12 10:45A				T9 3:00P	T9 5:45P				
TH11 7:30P	TH11 10:00P	F12 3:45A						F12 12:15P	F12 4:00P		F12 11:15P			S13 6:15A	
										W10 1:15A	W10 5:30A			W10 1:00P	
										TH11 5:30A	TH11 9:45A	TH11 11:00A			
F12 10:30P	S13 1:30A	S13 8:30A			S13 5:45P			SU14 12:30P	SU14 4:15P		SU14 11:15P			M15 6:15A	
										TH11 6:45P	TH11 11:00P			F12 6:30P	
S13 8:45A	S13 11:45A	S13 6:15P						SU14 3:15A	SU14 7:30A		SU14 5:30P			T16 8:00A	
		S13 2:00P	S13 5:15P							F12 10:00P	S13 5:30A	S13 6:45A			
		SU14 12:15A			SU14 6:45A	SU14 12:15P	M15 2:15A	M15 6:30A		S13 2:15P	S13 7:00P	S13 8:15P			
SU14 7:30P	SU14 10:00P	M15 3:45A						M15 12:15P	M15 4:00P		M15 11:15P			T16 6:15A	
M15 3:00P	M15 5:30P	M15 11:00P				T16 7:00A		T16 9:15A	W17 1:15A		SU14 5:15P	SU14 9:00A	SU14 10:15A		TH18 10:00P
										W17 10:00A		M15 10:00A			
										SU14 6:30P	SU14 11:00P				
T16 7:30P	T16 10:00P	W17 3:45A						W17 12:15P	W17 4:00P		W17 11:15P			TH18 6:15A	
W17 3:15P	W17 5:15P	W17 10:00P								T16 6:15A	T16 9:00A				
		TH18 3:15P	TH18 8:00P	F19 12:15A	F19 3:45A	F19 9:15A				T16 3:00P	T16 5:45P				
TH18 7:30P	TH18 10:00P	F19 3:45A						F19 12:15P	F19 4:00P		F19 11:15P			S20 6:15A	
										W17 1:15A	W17 5:30A			W17 1:00P	
										TH18 5:30A	TH18 9:45A	TH18 11:00A			
F19 10:00P	S20 12:30A	S20 6:45A			S20 4:00P			SU21 5:30A	SU21 1:00P		SU21 11:15P			M22 6:15A	
										TH18 6:45P	TH18 11:00P			F19 6:30P	
S20 8:45A	S20 11:45A	S20 6:15P						SU21 3:15A	SU21 7:30A		SU21 5:30P			T23 8:00A	
		S20 12:15P	Ar. Pelican	S20 6:45P						F19 10:00P	S20 5:30A	S20 6:45A			
										S20 2:15P	S20 7:00P	S20 8:15P			
SU21 7:30P	SU21 10:00P	M22 3:45A						M22 12:15P	M22 4:00P		M22 11:15P			T23 6:15A	
		SU21 5:00A			SU21 11:15A	SU21 4:45P	M22 5:15A	M22 9:30A			SU21 5:15A	SU21 9:00A	SU21 10:15A			
M22 9:00A	M22 11:00A	M22 3:00P									SU21 6:30P	SU21 11:00P		M22 10:00A	
T23 12:15A	T23 3:15A	T23 9:30A				T23 5:45P		W24 7:15A	W24 11:00A		W24 6:30P				F26 8:00A
T23 7:30P	T23 10:00P	W24 3:45A						W24 12:15P	W24 4:00P		W24 11:15P			TH25 6:15A	
W24 6:45P	W24 8:45P	TH25 1:30A								T23 6:15A	T23 9:00A				
		TH25 3:15P	TH25 8:00P	F26 12:15A	F26 3:45A	F26 9:15A				T23 3:00P	T23 5:45P				
TH25 7:30P	TH25 10:00P	F26 3:45A						F26 12:15P	F26 4:00P		F26 11:15P			S27 6:15A	
										W24 1:15A	W24 5:30A			W24 1:00P	
										TH25 5:30A	TH25 9:45A	TH25 11:00A			
F26 10:15P	S27 12:45A	S27 7:00A			S27 4:15P			SU28 8:15A	SU28 1:00P		SU28 11:15P			M29 6:15A	
										TH25 6:45P	TH25 11:00P			F26 6:30P	
S27 8:45A	S27 11:45A	S27 6:15P						SU28 3:15A	SU28 7:30A		SU28 5:30P			T30 8:00A	
		S27 2:00P	S27 5:15P							F26 10:00P	S27 5:30A	S27 6:45A			
		S27 11:00P			SU28 5:30A	SU28 11:00A	M29 2:15A	M29 6:30A		S27 2:15P	S27 7:00P	S27 8:15P			
SU28 7:30P	SU28 10:00P	M29 3:45A						M29 12:15P	M29 4:00P		M29 11:15P			T30 6:15A	
M29 5:00P	M29 9:00P	T30 3:45A				T30 12:15P		W1 1:30A	W1 5:30A		SU28 5:15A	SU28 9:00A	SU28 10:15A		F3 8:00A
										W1 5:45P					
										SU28 6:30P	SU28 11:00P		M29 10:00A		
T30 7:30P	T30 10:00P	W1 3:45A						W1 12:15P	W1 4:00P		W1 11:15P			TH2 6:15A	
										T30 6:15A	T30 9:00A				
										T30 3:00P	T30 5:45P				

ALL TIMES ARE LOCAL TIMES

Each horizontal line represents a ferry sailing and each color a vessel (see color key). The day of the week (M for Monday, etc.), date of month, and time (A.M. or P.M) of departures and/or arrivals are listed for each port. Read from left to right.

July 1992 Northbound Schedule

MARINE ACCESS ROUTES

LEAVE BELLINGHAM	LEAVE PRINCE RUPERT	LEAVE STEWART/HYDER	METLAKATLA	KETCHIKAN	HOLLIS	WRANGELL	PETERSBURG	KAKE	ARRIVE SITKA	ANGOON	TENAKEE	HOONAH	JUNEAU/AUKE BAY	HAINES	ARRIVE SKAGWAY
							M29 4:45P	M29 10:00P	T30 6:15A	T30 3:15P	T30 6:45P	T30 11:00P	W1 6:30A	W1 12:15P	W1 1:15P
	T30 9:00A			T30 4:30P		T30 10:45P	W1 2:45A		W1 1:15P				TH2 2:45A	TH2 8:30A	TH2 9:30A
	W1 3:30P			W1 10:30P	TH2 1:15A										
	TH2 9:00A			TH2 3:30P		TH2 9:45P	F3 1:30A						F3 10:45A	F3 4:30P	F3 5:30P
			TH2 11:30A	TH2 2:15P	TH2 5:00P										
T30 5:45P				TH2 8:00A		TH2 3:15P	TH2 7:30P		F3 9:30A				F3 10:00P	S4 4:15A	S4 5:15A
	F3 10:30P			F3 5:30P	F3 8:15P			Lv. Sitka	F3 5:30P	F3 11:30P	S4 2:30A	S4 6:45A	S4 10:00A		
			S4 7:15A	S4 10:00A	S4 12:45P										
	S4 9:00A			S4 3:30P		S4 9:45P	SU5 1:30A						SU5 11:00A	SU5 4:45P	SU5 5:45P
			S4 8:45P	S4 11:30P	SU5 2:15A										
F3 8:00P				SU5 9:00A		SU5 2:45P	SU5 6:30P						M6 2:30A	M6 7:15A	M6 8:15A
			SU5 11:00A	SU5 2:00P	SU5 4:45P								M6 4:30P	M6 9:15P	M6 10:15P
	M6 9:00A			M6 3:30P		M6 9:45P	T7 1:30A						T7 10:45A	T7 4:30P	T7 5:30P
		M6 3:15P		T7 1:45A	T7 4:30A		M6 4:30P	M6 9:45P	T7 6:30A	T7 3:00P	T7 6:30P	T7 10:45P	W8 6:30A	W8 12:15P	W8 1:15P
	T7 9:00A			T7 4:30P		T7 11:00P	W8 3:00A		W8 1:30P				TH9 2:30A	TH9 8:15A	TH9 9:15A
				T7 7:30P	T7 10:15P										
	W8 3:30P			W8 10:30P	TH9 1:15A										
	TH9 9:00A			TH9 3:30P		TH9 9:45P	F10 1:30A						F10 10:45A	F10 4:30P	F10 5:30P
			TH9 11:30A	TH9 2:15P	TH9 5:00P										
T7 5:45P				TH9 8:00A		TH9 3:15P	TH9 7:30P		F10 10:15A				F10 11:00P	S11 5:15A	S11 6:15A
	F10 10:30A			F10 5:30P	F10 8:15P			Lv. Sitka	F10 6:15P	S11 12:15A	S11 3:45A	S11 8:00A	S11 11:15A		
			S11 7:15A	S11 10:00A	S11 12:45P							S11 6:15P	S11 9:30P		
	S11 9:00A			S11 3:30P		S11 9:45P	SU12 1:30A						SU12 11:00A	SU12 4:45P	SU12 5:45P
			S11 8:45P	S11 11:30P	SU12 2:15A										
F10 8:00P				SU12 9:00A		SU12 3:30P	SU12 7:30P						M13 4:30A	M13 10:00A	M13 11:00A
			SU12 11:00A	SU12 2:00P	SU12 4:45P										
	M13 9:00A			M13 3:30P		M13 9:45P	T14 1:30A						T14 10:45A	T14 4:30P	T14 5:30P
		M13 3:15P		T14 1:45A	T14 4:30A		M13 4:45P	M13 10:00P	T14 6:30A	T14 3:15P	T14 6:30P	T14 10:45P	W15 6:30A	W15 12:15P	W15 1:15P
	T14 9:00A			T14 4:30P		T14 10:45P	W15 2:45A		W15 1:15P				TH16 2:15A	TH16 8:00A	TH16 9:00A
				T14 7:30P	T14 10:15P										
	W15 3:30P			W15 10:30P	TH16 1:15A										
	TH16 9:00A			TH16 3:30P		TH16 9:45P	F17 1:30A						F17 10:45A	F17 4:30P	F17 5:30P
			TH16 11:30A	TH16 2:15P	TH16 5:00P										
T14 5:45P				TH16 8:00A		TH16 3:15P	TH16 7:30P		F17 9:00A				F17 9:30P	S18 3:45A	S18 4:45A
	F17 10:30A			F17 5:30P	F17 8:15P			Lv. Sitka	F17 5:00P	F17 11:00P	S18 2:30A	S18 6:45A	S18 10:00A		
			S18 7:15A	S18 10:00A	S18 12:45P										
	S18 9:00A			S18 3:30P		S18 9:45P	SU19 1:30A						SU19 11:00A	SU19 4:45P	SU19 5:45P
			S18 8:45P	S18 11:30P	SU19 2:15A						Lv. Pelican	S18 7:45P	SU19 2:15A		
F17 8:00P				SU19 9:00A		SU19 3:30P	SU19 7:30P						M20 4:30A	M20 10:00A	M20 11:00A
			SU19 11:00A	SU19 2:00P	SU19 4:45P										
	M20 9:00A			M20 3:30P		M20 9:45P	T21 1:30A						T21 10:45A	T21 4:30P	T21 5:30P
		M20 3:15P		T21 1:45A	T21 4:30A		M20 3:00P	M20 8:15P	T21 4:15A	T21 1:15P	T21 4:45P	T21 9:00P	W22 6:30A	W22 12:15P	W22 1:15P
	T21 9:00A			T21 6:15P		W22 2:45A	W22 6:45A		W22 5:15P				TH23 8:00A	TH23 1:45P	TH23 2:45P
				T21 7:30P	T21 10:15P										
	W22 3:30P			W22 10:30P	TH23 1:15A										
	TH23 9:00A			TH23 3:30P		TH23 9:45P	F24 1:30A						F24 10:45A	F24 4:30P	F24 5:30P
			TH23 11:30A	TH23 2:15P	TH23 5:00P										
T21 5:45P				TH23 8:00A		TH23 3:15P	TH23 7:30P		F24 8:00A				F24 8:45P	S25 3:00A	S25 4:00A
	*F24 10:30A			F24 5:30P	F24 8:15P			Lv. Sitka	F24 4:00P	F24 10:00P	S25 1:30A	S25 5:45A	S25 9:00A		
			*S25 7:15A	S25 10:00A	S25 12:45P							S25 6:15P	S25 9:30P		
	S25 9:00A			S25 3:30P		S25 9:45P	SU26 1:30A						SU26 11:00A	SU26 4:45P	SU26 5:45P
			*S25 8:45P	S25 11:30P	SU26 2:15A										
F24 8:00P				SU26 9:00A		SU26 3:30P	SU26 7:30P						M27 4:30A	M27 10:00A	M27 11:00A
			SU26 11:00A	SU26 2:00P	SU26 4:45P										
	M27 9:00A			M27 3:30P		M27 9:45P	T28 1:30A						T28 10:45A	T28 4:30P	T28 5:30P
		M27 3:15P		T28 1:45A	T28 4:30A		M27 4:00P	M27 9:15P	T28 5:15A	T28 2:00P	T28 5:15P	T28 9:30P	W29 6:30A	W29 12:15P	W29 1:15P
	T28 9:00A			T28 3:00P		T28 9:15P	W29 1:15A		W29 12:15P				TH30 1:30A	TH30 7:30A	TH30 8:30A
				T28 7:30P	T28 10:15P										
	W29 3:30P			W29 10:30P	TH30 1:15A										
	TH30 9:00A			TH30 3:30P		TH30 9:45P	F31 1:30A						F31 10:45A	F31 4:30P	F31 5:30P
			TH30 11:30A	TH30 2:15P	TH30 5:00P										
T28 5:45P				TH30 8:00A		TH30 3:15P	TH30 7:30P		F31 8:30A				F31 9:00P	S1 3:15A	S1 4:15A
	F31 10:30A			F31 5:30P	F31 8:15P			Lv. Sitka	F31 4:30P	F31 10:30P	S1 2:00A	S1 6:15A	S1 9:30A		
F31 8:00P				SU2 9:00A		SU2 3:30P	SU2 7:30P						M3 4:30A	M3 10:00A	M3 11:00A

*THE FOLLOWING EVENT MAY AFFECT AVAILABILITY OF SPACE:
JULY 25-26 - LOGGING SHOW AND FAIR - HOLLIS

AURORA — MALASPINA
COLUMBIA — MATANUSKA
LE CONTE — TAKU

534 The MILEPOST® ■ 1992

July 1992 Southbound Schedule

MARINE ACCESS ROUTES

LEAVE SKAGWAY	HAINES	JUNEAU/ AUKE BAY	HOONAH	TENAKEE	ANGOON	ARRIVE SITKA	KAKE	PETERSBURG	WRANGELL	HOLLIS	KETCHIKAN	METLAKATLA	ARRIVE STEWART/ HYDER	ARRIVE PRINCE RUPERT	ARRIVE BELLINGHAM
M29 5:00P	M29 9:00P	T30 3:45A				T30 12:15P		W1 1:30A	W1 5:30A		W1 5:45P				F3 8:00A
										W1 1:15P	W1 5:30A			W1 1:00P	
T30 7:30P	T30 10:00P	W1 3:45A						W1 12:15P	W1 4:00P		W1 11:15P			TH2 6:15A	
W1 3:15P	W1 5:15P	W1 10:00P													
		TH2 3:15P	TH2 7:30P	TH2 11:45P	F3 3:15A	F3 8:45A									
TH2 7:30P	TH2 10:00P	F3 3:45A						F3 12:15P	F3 4:00P		F3 11:15P			S4 6:15A	
										TH2 5:30P	TH2 9:45A	TH2 11:00A			
F3 10:15P	S4 12:15A	S4 6:30A				S4 3:45P		SU5 5:30A	SU5 1:00P		SU5 11:15P			M6 6:15A	
										TH2 6:45P	TH2 11:00P			F3 6:30A	
S4 8:45A	S4 11:45A	S4 6:15P						SU5 3:15A	SU5 7:30A		SU5 5:30P				T7 8:00A
	S4 11:15P	Ar. Pelican	S4 5:45P							F3 10:00P	S4 5:30A	S4 6:45A			
										S4 2:15P	S4 7:00P	S4 8:15P			
SU5 7:30P	SU5 10:00P	M6 3:45A						M6 12:15P	M6 4:00P		M6 11:15P			T7 6:15A	
		SU5 4:30A			SU5 11:00A	SU5 4:30P	M6 4:30A	M6 8:45A		SU5 5:15P	SU5 9:00A	SU5 10:15A			
M6 9:00A	M6 11:00A	M6 3:00P								SU5 6:30P	SU5 11:00P		M6 10:00A		
T7 12:15A	T7 3:15A	T7 9:30A				T7 6:15P		W8 7:15A	W8 11:00A		W8 6:30P			F10 8:00A
T7 7:30P	T7 10:00P	W8 3:45A						W8 12:15P	W8 4:00P		W8 11:15P			TH9 6:15A	
W8 3:15P	W8 5:15P	W8 10:00P								T7 6:15A	T7 9:00A				
		TH9 4:15P	TH9 8:30P	F10 12:30A	F10 4:00A	F10 9:30A				T7 3:00P	T7 5:45P				
TH9 7:30P	TH9 10:00P	F10 3:45A						F10 12:15P	F10 4:00P		F10 11:15P			S11 6:15A	
										W8 1:15P	W8 5:30A			W8 1:00P	
F10 10:45P	S11 1:00A	S11 7:15A				S11 4:30P		SU12 8:15A	SU12 1:00P		SU12 11:15P			M13 6:15A	
										TH9 6:45P	TH9 11:00P			F10 6:30A	
S11 9:45A	S11 12:45P	S11 7:15P						SU12 3:45A	SU12 7:30A		SU12 5:30P				T14 8:00A
	S11 2:00P	S11 5:15P			SU12 11:45A	SU12 5:15P	M13 5:00A	M13 9:15A		F10 10:00P	S11 5:30A	S11 6:45A			
	SU12 5:15A									S11 2:15P	S11 7:00P	S11 8:15P			
SU12 7:30P	SU12 10:00P	M13 3:45A						M13 12:15P	M13 4:00P		M13 11:15P			T14 6:15A	
										SU12 5:15A	SU12 9:00A	SU12 10:15A			
M13 5:00P	M13 9:00P	T14 4:00A				T14 12:15P		W15 1:15A	W15 5:30A		W15 5:45P			F17 8:00A
										SU12 6:30P	SU12 11:00P		M13 10:00A		
T14 7:30P	T14 10:00P	W15 3:45A						W15 12:15P	W15 4:00P		W15 11:15P			TH16 6:15A	
W15 3:15P	W15 5:15P	W15 10:00P								T14 6:15A	T14 9:00A				
		TH16 3:00P	TH16 7:15P	TH16 11:15P	F17 2:45A	F17 8:15A				T14 3:00P	T14 5:45P				
TH16 7:30P	TH16 10:00P	F17 3:45A						F17 12:15P	F17 4:00P		F17 11:15P			S18 6:15A	
										W15 1:15A	W15 5:30A			W15 1:00P	
										TH16 5:30A	TH16 9:45A	TH16 11:00A			
F17 8:15P	F17 11:15P	S18 5:30A				S18 2:45P		SU19 5:00A	SU19 1:00P		SU19 11:15P			M20 6:15A	
										TH16 6:45P	TH16 11:00P			F17 6:30A	
S18 8:45A	S18 11:45A	S18 6:15P						SU19 3:15A	SU19 7:30A		SU19 5:30P				T21 8:00A
	S18 11:15P	Ar. Pelican	S18 5:45P							F17 10:00P	S18 5:30A	S18 6:45A			
										S18 2:15P	S18 7:00P	S18 8:15P			
SU19 7:30P	SU19 10:00P	M20 3:45A						M20 12:15P	M20 4:00P		M20 11:15P			T21 6:15A	
		SU19 3:15A			SU19 9:45A	SU19 3:15P	M20 3:30A	M20 7:45A		SU19 5:15P	SU19 9:00A	SU19 10:15A			
M20 3:00P	M20 5:30P	T21 1:30A				T21 10:15A		T21 11:00P	W22 3:00A		W22 11:00A			TH23 11:00P
										SU19 6:30P	SU19 11:00P		M20 10:00A		
T21 7:30P	T21 10:00P	W22 3:45A						W22 12:15P	W22 4:00P		W22 11:15P			TH23 6:15A	
W22 3:15P	W22 5:15P	W22 10:00P								T21 6:15A	T21 9:00A				
		TH23 2:00P	TH23 6:15P	TH23 10:15P	F24 1:45A	F24 7:15A				T21 3:00P	T21 5:45P				
TH23 7:30P	TH23 10:00P	F24 3:45A						F24 12:15P	F24 4:00P		F24 11:15P			S25 6:15A	
										W22 1:15A	W22 5:30A			W22 1:00P	
										TH23 5:30A	TH23 9:45A	TH23 11:00A			
F24 8:45P	F24 11:15P	S25 5:30A				S25 2:45P		SU26 7:15A	SU26 1:00P		SU26 11:15P			M27 6:15A	
										TH23 6:45P	TH23 11:00P			F24 6:30A	
S25 8:45A	S25 11:45A	S25 6:15P						SU26 3:15A	SU26 7:30A		SU26 5:30P				T28 8:00A
		S25 2:00P	S25 5:15P							F24 10:00P	S25 5:30A	S25 6:45A			
		SU26 4:00A			SU26 10:30A	SU26 3:45P	M27 3:30A	M27 7:45A		S25 2:15P	S25 7:00P	S25 8:15P			
SU26 7:30P	SU26 10:00P	M27 3:45A						M27 12:15P	M27 4:00P		M27 11:15P			T28 6:15A	
										SU26 5:15A	SU26 9:00A	SU26 10:15A			
M27 3:00P	M27 5:30P	T28 2:30A				T28 11:15A		W29 2:15A	W29 6:15A		W29 5:45P			F31 8:00A
										*SU26 8:00P	M27 1:00A		M27 12:15P		
T28 7:30P	T28 10:00P	W29 3:45A						W29 12:15P	W29 4:00P		W29 11:15P			TH30 6:15A	
W29 3:15P	W29 5:15P	W29 10:00P								T28 6:15A	T28 9:00A				
		TH30 2:00P	TH30 6:15P	TH30 10:30P	F31 2:00A	F31 7:45A				T28 3:00P	T28 5:45P				
TH30 7:30P	TH30 10:00P	F31 3:45A						F31 12:15P	F31 4:00P		F31 11:15P			S1 6:15A	
										W29 1:15A	W29 5:30A			W29 1:00P	
										TH30 5:30A	TH30 9:45A	TH30 11:00A			
F31 8:30P	F31 11:00P	S1 5:15A				S1 2:30P		SU2 4:45A	SU2 1:00P		SU2 11:15P			M3 6:15A	
										TH30 6:45P	TH30 11:00P			F31 6:30A	
									F31 10:00P	S1 5:30A	S1 6:45A				

ALL TIMES ARE LOCAL TIMES

Each horizontal line represents a ferry sailing and each color a vessel (see color key). The day of the week (M for Monday, etc.), date of month, and time (A.M. or P.M) of departures and/or arrivals are listed for each port. Read from left to right.

1992 ■ The MILEPOST®

August 1992 Northbound Schedule

Ferry schedule table for Alaska Marine Access Routes. Columns: Leave Bellingham, Leave Prince Rupert, Leave Stewart/Hyder, Metlakatla, Ketchikan, Hollis, Wrangell, Petersburg, Kake, Arrive Sitka, Angoon, Tenakee, Hoonah, Juneau/Auke Bay, Haines, Arrive Skagway.

Ships: Aurora (pink), Columbia (gray), Le Conte (yellow), Malaspina (blue), Matanuska (green), Taku (orange).

*THE FOLLOWING EVENT MAY AFFECT AVAILABILITY OF SPACE
AUG 12 – 16 — SOUTHEAST ALASKA STATE FAIR – HAINES

536 The MILEPOST® ■ 1992

August 1992 Southbound Schedule

MARINE ACCESS ROUTES

LEAVE SKAGWAY	HAINES	JUNEAU/ AUKE BAY	HOONAH	TENAKEE	ANGOON	ARRIVE SITKA	KAKE	PETERSBURG	WRANGELL	HOLLIS	KETCHIKAN	METLAKATLA	ARRIVE STEWART/ HYDER	ARRIVE PRINCE RUPERT	ARRIVE BELLINGHAM
F31 8:30P	F31 11:00P	S1 5:15A				S1 2:30P		SU2 4:45A	SU2 1:00P		SU2 11:15A			M3 6:15A	
		S1 11:15A	Ar. Pelican S1 5:45P							S1 2:15P	S1 7:00P	S1 8:15P			T4 8:00A
S1 8:45A	S1 11:45A							SU2 3:15A	SU2 7:30A		SU2 5:30P			T4 6:15A	
SU2 7:30P	SU2 10:00P	M3 3:45A						M3 12:15P	M3 4:00P		M3 11:15P				
		SU2 3:15A			SU2 9:45A	SU2 3:15P	M3 3:15A	M3 7:30A		SU2 5:15P	SU2 9:00A	SU2 10:15A			
M3 5:00P	M3 9:00P	T4 8:00A				T4 4:30P		W5 6:00A	W5 10:00A		W5 6:45P				F7 8:00A
										SU2 6:30P	SU2 11:00P		M3 10:00A		
T4 7:30P	T4 10:00P	W5 3:45A						W5 12:15P	W5 4:00P		W5 11:15P			TH6 6:15A	
W5 3:15P	W5 5:15P	W5 10:00P								T4 6:15A	T4 9:00A				
		TH6 2:15P	TH6 6:30P	TH6 10:45P	F7 2:15A	F7 8:00A				T4 3:00P	T4 5:45P				
TH6 7:30P	TH6 10:00P	F7 3:45A						F7 12:15P	F7 4:00P		F7 11:15P			S8 6:15A	
										W5 1:15P	W5 5:30A			W5 1:00P	
										TH6 5:30A	TH6 9:45A	TH6 11:00A			
F7 9:15P	F7 11:45P	S8 6:00A				S8 3:15P		SU9 5:15A	SU9 1:00P		SU9 11:15P			M10 6:15A	
										TH6 6:45P	TH6 11:00P			F7 6:30P	
S8 8:45A	S8 11:45A	S8 6:15P						SU9 4:15A	SU9 8:00A		SU9 5:30P				T11 8:00A
		S8 2:00P	S8 5:15P							F7 10:00P	S8 5:30A	S8 6:45A			
		SU9 4:15A			SU9 10:45A	SU9 4:15P	M10 4:00A	M10 8:15A		S8 2:15P	S8 7:00P	S8 8:15P			
SU9 7:30P	SU9 10:00P	M10 3:45A						M10 12:15P	M10 4:00P		M10 11:15P			T11 6:15A	
										SU9 5:15A	SU9 9:00A	SU9 10:15A			
M10 3:00P	M10 5:30P	T11 2:30A				T11 11:30A		W12 12:15A	W12 4:00A		W12 11:00A				TH13 11:00P
										SU9 6:30P	SU9 11:00P		M10 10:00A		
T11 7:30P	T11 10:00P	W12 3:45A						W12 12:15P	W12 4:00P		W12 11:15P			TH13 6:15A	
W12 12:15P	W12 2:15P	W12 8:15P	W12 11:30P							T11 6:15A	T11 9:00A				
										T11 3:00P	T11 5:45P				
TH13 7:30P	TH13 10:00P	F14 3:45A						F14 12:15P	F14 4:00P		F14 11:15P			S15 6:15A	
		TH13 12:30P	TH13 8:00P	F14 12:15A	F14 4:15A	F14 7:45A	F14 1:15P			W12 1:15P	W12 5:30A			W12 1:00P	
										TH13 5:30A	TH13 9:45A	TH13 11:00A			
F14 7:45P	F14 10:15P	S15 4:30A				S15 1:45P		SU16 4:45A	SU16 11:45A		SU16 11:15P			M17 6:15A	
										TH13 6:45P	TH13 11:00P			F14 6:30P	
S15 8:45A	S15 11:45A	S15 6:15P						SU16 3:15A	SU16 7:30A		SU16 5:30P				T18 8:00A
*SU16 3:00A	SU16 5:30A	SU16 10:15A								F14 10:00P	S15 5:30A	S15 6:45A			
										S15 2:15P	S15 7:00P	S15 8:15P			
*SU16 7:30P	SU16 10:00P	M17 3:45A						M17 12:15P	M17 4:00P		M17 11:15P			T18 6:15A	
		*SU16 5:30P	M17 1:00A					M17 9:15A		SU16 5:15A	SU16 9:00A	SU16 10:15A			
*M17 7:00A	M17 9:00A	M17 1:00P													
										SU16 6:30P	SU16 11:00P		M17 10:00A		
*M17 10:15P	T18 12:15A	T18 6:15A				T18 2:45P		W19 4:00A	W19 9:00A		W19 5:45P				F21 8:00A
T18 7:30P	T18 10:00P	W19 3:45A						W19 12:15P	W19 4:00P		W19 11:15P			TH20 6:15A	
W19 3:15P	W19 5:15P	W19 10:00P								T18 6:15A	T18 9:00A				
		TH20 5:45P	TH20 10:00P	F21 2:15A	F21 5:45A	F21 11:15A				T18 3:00P	T18 5:45P				
TH20 7:30P	TH20 10:00P	F21 3:45A						F21 12:15P	F21 4:00P		F21 11:15P			S22 6:15A	
										W19 1:15P	W19 5:30A			W19 1:00P	
										TH20 5:30A	TH20 9:45A	TH20 11:00A			
F21 11:45P	S22 2:45A	S22 9:00A				S22 6:45P		SU23 9:15A	SU23 1:00P		SU23 11:15P			M24 6:15A	
										TH20 6:45P	TH20 11:00P			F21 6:30P	
S22 8:45A	S22 11:45A	S22 6:15P						SU23 3:30A	SU23 7:30A		SU23 5:30P				T25 8:00A
		S22 2:45P	Ar. Pelican S22 9:15P							F21 10:00P	S22 5:30A	S22 6:45A			
										S22 2:15P	S22 7:00P	S22 8:15P			
SU23 7:30P	SU23 10:00P	M24 3:45A						M24 12:15P	M24 4:00P		M24 11:15P			T25 6:15A	
		SU23 8:15A			SU23 2:45P	SU23 8:15P	M24 8:45A	M24 1:00P		SU23 5:15A	SU23 9:00A	SU23 10:15A			
M24 3:00P	M24 5:30P	T25 2:30A				T25 10:00A		T25 11:15P	W26 3:00A		W26 10:45A				TH27 10:00P
										SU23 6:30P	SU23 11:00P		M24 10:00A		
T25 7:30P	T25 10:00P	W26 3:45A						W26 12:15P	W26 4:00P		W26 11:15P			TH27 6:15A	
W26 4:45P	W26 6:45P	W26 11:30P								T25 6:15A	T25 9:00A				
		TH27 7:15P	TH27 11:30P	F28 3:45A	F28 7:15A	F28 12:45P				T25 3:00P	T25 5:45P				
TH27 7:30P	TH27 10:00P	F28 3:45A						F28 12:15P	F28 4:00P		F28 11:15P			S29 6:15A	
										W26 1:15P	W26 5:30A			W26 1:00P	
										TH27 5:30A	TH27 9:45A	TH27 11:00A			
F28 10:30P	F29 1:45A	S29 9:00A				S29 7:45P		SU30 12:30P	SU30 4:15P		SU30 11:15P			M31 6:15A	
										TH27 6:45P	TH27 11:00P			F28 6:30P	
S29 8:45A	S29 11:45A	S29 6:15P						SU30 3:15A	SU30 7:30A		SU30 5:30P				T1 8:00A
		S29 3:30P	S29 6:45P							F28 10:00P	S29 5:30A	S29 6:45A			
		SU30			SU30 8:45A	SU30 2:15P	M31 2:00A	M31 6:15A		S29 2:15P	S29 7:00P	S29 8:15P			
SU30 7:30P	SU30 10:00P	M31 3:45A						M31 12:15P	M31 4:00P		M31 11:15P			T1 6:15A	
										SU30 5:15A	SU30 9:00A	SU30 10:15A			
M31 3:00P	M31 5:30P	T1 1:30A				T1 9:15A		W2 1:15A	W2 5:00A		W2 5:45P				F4 8:00A
										SU30 6:30P	SU30 11:00P		M31 10:00A		

ALL TIMES ARE LOCAL TIMES

Each horizontal line represents a ferry sailing and each color a vessel (see color key). The day of the week (M for Monday, etc.), date of month, and time (A.M. or P.M) of departures and/or arrivals are listed for each port. Read from left to right.

1992 ■ The MILEPOST® 537

September 1992 Northbound Schedule

MARINE ACCESS ROUTES

Leave Bellingham	Leave Prince Rupert	Leave Stewart/Hyder	Metlakatla	Ketchikan	Hollis	Wrangell	Petersburg	Kake	Arrive Sitka	Angoon	Tenakee	Hoonah	Juneau/Auke Bay	Haines	Arrive Skagway
	M31 9:00A			M31 3:30P		M31 9:45P	T1 1:30A						T1 10:45A	T1 4:30P	T1 5:30P
		M31 3:15P		T1 1:45A	T1 4:30A		M31 8:00P	T1 1:15A	T1 11:00A	T1 6:15P	T1 9:45P	W2 2:00A	W2 6:30A	W2 12:15P	W2 1:15P
				T1 10:30A	T1 1:15P										
	T1 9:00A			T1 6:15P		W2 1:45A	W2 5:45A		W2 4:15P				TH3 5:30A	TH3 11:15A	TH3 12:15P
				T1 7:30P	T1 10:15P										
	W2 3:30P			W2 10:30P	TH3 1:15A										
	TH3 9:00A			TH3 3:30P		TH3 9:45P	F4 1:30A						F4 10:45A	F4 4:30P	F4 5:30P
			TH3 11:30A	TH3 2:15P	TH3 5:00P										
T1 5:45P				TH3 8:00A		TH3 3:15P	TH3 7:30P		F4 6:15A				F4 8:00P	S5 2:15A	S5 3:15A
	F4 10:30A			F4 5:30P	F4 8:15P			Lv. Sitka	F4 9:45P	S5 3:45A	S5 7:00A	S5 11:15A	S5 2:30P		
			S5 7:15A	S5 10:00A	S5 12:45P										
	S5 9:00A			S5 3:30P		S5 9:45P	SU6 1:30A						SU6 11:00A	SU6 4:45P	SU6 5:45P
			S5 8:45P	S5 11:30P	SU6 2:15A										
F4 8:00P				SU6 9:00A		SU6 2:45P	SU6 6:30P				Lv. Pelican	SU6 12:15A	SU6 6:45A	M7 7:15A	M7 8:15A
			SU6 11:00A	SU6 2:00P	SU6 4:45P								M7 2:30A		
													M7 4:00P	M7 8:45P	M7 9:45P
	M7 9:00A			M7 3:30P		M7 9:45P	T8 1:30A						T8 10:45A	T8 4:30P	T8 5:30P
		M7 3:15P		T8 1:45A	T8 4:30A		M7 9:00P	T8 2:15A	T8 10:30A	T8 7:15P	T8 10:45P	W9 3:00A	W9 7:30A	W9 1:15P	W9 2:15P
				T8 10:30A	T8 1:15P										
	T8 9:00A			T8 6:15P		W9 1:00A	W9 6:45A		W9 5:15P				TH10 6:15A	TH10 11:45A	TH10 12:45P
				T8 7:30P	T8 10:15P										
	W9 3:30P			W9 10:30P	TH10 1:15A										
	TH10 9:00A			TH10 3:30P		TH10 9:45P	F11 1:30A						F11 10:45A	F11 4:30P	F11 5:30P
			TH10 11:30A	TH10 2:15P	TH10 5:00P										
*T8 5:45P				TH10 8:00A		TH10 3:15P	TH10 7:30P		F11 6:15A				F11 10:00P	S12 3:15A	S12 4:15A
	F11 10:30A			F11 5:30P	F11 8:15P			Lv. Sitka	F11 8:00P	S12 3:15A	S12 6:30A	S12 10:45A	S12 2:00P		
											S12 7:15P	S12 10:30P			
			S12 7:15A	S12 10:00A	S12 12:45P										
	S12 9:00A			S12 3:30P		S12 9:45P	SU13 1:30A						SU13 11:00A	SU13 4:45P	SU13 5:45P
			S12 8:45P	S12 11:30P	SU13 2:15A										
F11 8:00P				SU13 9:00A		SU13 3:30P	SU13 7:30P						M14 4:30A	M14 10:00A	M14 11:00A
			SU13 11:00A	SU13 2:00P	SU13 4:45P										
	M14 9:00A			M14 3:30P		M14 9:45P	T15 1:30A						T15 10:45A	T15 4:30P	T15 5:30P
		M14 3:15P		T15 1:45A	T15 4:30A		M14 6:30P	M14 11:45P	T15 9:30A	T15 4:45P	T15 8:00P	W16 12:15A	W16 6:30A	W16 12:15P	W16 1:15P
				T15 10:30A	T15 1:15P										
	T15 9:00A			T15 5:00P		T15 11:15P	W16 3:00A		W16 2:15P				TH17 3:45A	TH17 9:30A	TH17 10:30A
				T15 7:30P	T15 10:15P										
	W16 3:30P			W16 10:30P	TH17 1:15A										
	TH17 9:00A			TH17 3:30P		TH17 9:45P	F18 1:30A						F18 10:45A	F18 4:30P	F18 5:30P
			TH17 11:30A	TH17 2:15P	TH17 5:00P										
T15 5:00P				TH17 7:15A		TH17 1:30P	TH17 5:15P		F18 3:45A				F18 5:00P	F18 11:15P	S19 12:15A
	F18 10:30A			F18 5:30P	F18 8:15P			Lv. Sitka	F18 6:00P	S19 1:15A	S19 4:30A	S19 9:00A	S19 12:15P		
			S19 7:15A	S19 10:00A	S19 12:45P										
	S19 9:00A			S19 3:30P		S19 9:45P	SU20 1:30A						SU20 11:00A	SU20 4:45P	SU20 5:45P
			S19 8:45P	S19 11:30P	SU20 2:15A						Lv. Pelican	S19 10:15P	SU20 4:45A		
F18 8:00P				SU20 9:00A		SU20 3:30P	SU20 7:30P						M21 4:30A	M21 10:00A	M21 11:00A
			SU20 11:00A	SU20 2:00P	SU20 4:45P										
	*M21 9:00A			M21 3:30P		M21 9:45P	T22 1:30A						T22 10:45A	T22 4:30P	T22 5:30P
		M21 3:15P		T22 1:45A	T22 4:30A										
	T22 9:00A			T22 5:30P		T22 11:45P	W23 4:45A		W23 4:15P				TH24 5:00A	TH24 10:45A	TH24 11:45A
			T22 9:00A	T22 11:15A	T22 2:00P										
				T22 10:30A	T22 1:15P										
				T22 7:15P	T22 10:00P										
				W23 4:15P	W23 8:15P	W23 5:45P	TH24 2:30A	TH24 10:45A	TH24 7:30P	TH24 10:45P	F25 3:00P	F25 6:15A			
T22 5:45P				TH24 8:00A		TH24 2:15P	TH24 6:30P		F25 5:30A				F25 9:30P	S26 2:45A	S26 3:45A
	TH24 9:00A			TH24 3:30P		TH24 9:45P	F25 1:30A						F25 10:45A	F25 4:30P	F25 5:30P
	S26 9:00A			S26 3:30P		S26 9:45P	SU27 1:30A		Lv. Sitka	S26 9:15P	SU27 3:15A	SU27 6:30A	SU27 10:45A	SU27 12:30P	
													SU27 11:00A	SU27 4:45P	SU27 5:45P
F25 8:00P				SU27 9:00A		SU27 3:30P	SU27 7:30P						M28 4:30A	M28 10:00A	M28 11:00A
	M28 9:00A			M28 3:30P		M28 9:45P	T29 1:30A						T29 10:45A	T29 4:30P	T29 5:30P
			T29 11:00A	T29 1:15P	T29 4:00P										
	T29 9:00A			T29 3:30P		T29 9:45P	W30 1:30A						W30 11:00A	W30 4:45P	W30 5:45P
			T29 10:30P	W30 4:30A	W30 8:30A	W30 5:45P	TH1 1:45A	TH1 9:45A	TH1 6:15P	TH1 9:30P	F2 1:15A	F2 4:30A			

*THE FOLLOWING EVENTS MAY AFFECT AVAILABILITY OF SPACE:
SEP 12 - 13 - KLONDIKE FUN RUN - SKAGWAY
SEP 23 - 26 - ALASKA STATE FIREFIGHTERS CONVENTION - SKAGWAY

Color Key:
- AURORA (pink)
- MALASPINA (blue)
- COLUMBIA (gray)
- MATANUSKA (green)
- LE CONTE (yellow)
- TAKU (orange)

Each horizontal line represents a ferry sailing and each color a vessel (see color key). The day of the week (M for Monday, etc.), date of month, and time (A.M. or P.M.) of departures and/or arrivals are listed for each port. Read from left to right.

September 1992 Southbound Schedule

MARINE ACCESS ROUTES

LEAVE SKAGWAY	HAINES	JUNEAU/ AUKE BAY	HOONAH	TENAKEE	ANGOON	ARRIVE SITKA	KAKE	PETERSBURG	WRANGELL	HOLLIS	KETCHIKAN	METLAKATLA	Arrive STEWART/ HYDER	Arrive PRINCE RUPERT	ARRIVE BELLINGHAM
M31 3:00P	M31 5:30P	T1 1:30A				T1 9:15A		W2 1:15A	W2 5:00A		W2 5:45P			F4 8:00A	
T1 7:30P	T1 10:00P	W2 3:45A						W2 12:15P	W2 4:00P		W2 11:15P			TH3 6:15A	
W2 3:15P	W2 5:15P	W2 10:00P								T1 6:15A	T1 9:00A				
		TH3 6:45P	TH3 11:00P	F4 3:15A	F4 7:00A	F4 12:30P				T1 3:00P	T1 5:45P				
TH3 7:30P	TH3 10:00P	F4 3:45A						F4 12:15P	F4 4:00P		F4 11:15P			S5 6:15A	
										W2 1:15A	W2 5:30A			W2 1:00P	
										TH3 5:30A	TH3 9:45A	TH3 11:00A			
F4 7:30P	F4 10:00P	S5 4:30A				S5 1:45P		SU6 5:00A	SU6 11:45A		SU6 11:15P			M7 6:15A	
										TH3 6:45P	TH3 11:00P			F4 6:30A	
S5 8:45A	S5 11:45A	S5 6:15P						SU6 3:15A	SU6 7:30A		SU6 5:30P			T8 8:00A	
		S5 3:30P	Ar. Pelican	S5 10:15P						F4 10:00P	S5 5:30A	S5 6:15A			
										S5 2:15P	S5 7:00P	S5 8:15P			
SU6 7:30P	SU6 10:00P	M7 3:45A						M7 12:15P	M7 4:00P		M7 11:15P			T8 6:15A	
		SU6 9:00A		SU6 3:30P	SU6 9:00P	M7 9:00A	M7 1:15P			SU6 5:15A	SU6 9:00A	SU6 10:15A			
M7 9:00A	M7 11:00A	M7 3:00P								SU6 6:30P	SU6 11:00P		M7 10:00A		
M7 11:45P	T8 2:00A	T8 8:00A				T8 4:15P		W9 8:15A	W9 12:15P		W9 8:00P			F11 8:00A	
T8 7:30P	T8 10:00P	W9 3:45A						W9 12:15P	W9 4:00P		W9 11:15P			TH10 6:15A	
W9 4:15P	W9 6:15P	W9 11:00P								T8 6:15A	T8 9:00A				
		TH10 6:45P	TH10 11:00P	F11 3:15A	F11 6:45A	F11 12:15P				T8 3:00P	T8 5:45P				
TH10 7:30P	TH10 10:00P	F11 3:45A						F11 12:15P	F11 4:00P		F11 11:15P			S12 6:15A	
										W9 1:15A	W9 5:30A			W9 1:00P	
										TH10 5:30A	TH10 9:45A	TH10 11:00A			
F11 10:45P	S12 1:45A	S12 9:00A				S12 7:00P		SU13 9:30A	SU13 1:30P		SU13 11:15P			M14 6:15A	
										TH10 6:45P	TH10 11:00P			F11 6:30A	
S12 8:45A	S12 11:45A	S12 6:15P						SU13 3:15A	SU13 7:30A		SU13 5:30P			T15 8:00A	
		S12 3:00P	S12 6:15P							F11 10:00P	S12 5:30A	S12 6:45A			
		SU13 1:15A		SU13 7:45A	SU13 1:15P	M14 2:00A	M14 6:15A			S12 2:15P	S12 7:00P	S12 8:15P			
*SU13 7:30P	SU13 10:00P	M14 3:45A						M14 12:15P	M14 4:00P		M14 11:15P			T15 6:15A	
										SU13 5:15A	SU13 9:00A	SU13 10:15A			
M14 3:00P	M14 5:30P	M14 11:45P				T15 8:00A		T15 11:00P	W16 3:00A		SU13 6:30P	SU13 11:00P		M14 10:00A	TH17 10:00P
T15 7:30P	T15 10:00P	W16 3:45A						W16 12:15P	W16 4:00P		W16 11:15P			TH17 6:15A	
W16 3:15P	W16 5:15P	W16 10:00P								T15 6:15A	T15 9:00A				
		TH17 4:15P	TH17 8:30P	F18 12:45A	F18 4:15A	F18 9:45A				T15 3:00P	T15 5:45P				
TH17 7:30P	TH17 10:00P	F18 3:45A						F18 12:15P	F18 4:00P		F18 11:15P			S19 6:15A	
										W16 1:15A	W16 5:30A			W16 1:00P	
										TH17 5:30A	TH17 9:45A	TH17 11:00A			
F18 10:45P	S19 1:45A	S19 7:45A				S19 5:00P		SU20 7:30A	SU20 1:00P		SU20 11:15P			M21 6:15A	
										TH17 6:45P	TH17 11:00P			F18 6:30A	
S19 8:45A	S19 11:45A	S19 6:15P						SU20 3:15A	SU20 7:30A		SU20 5:30P			T22 8:00A	
		S19 1:45P	Ar. Pelican	S19 8:15P						F18 10:00P	S19 5:30A	S19 6:45A			
										S19 2:15P	S19 7:00P	S19 8:15P			
SU20 7:30P	SU20 10:00P	M21 3:45A						M21 12:15P	M21 4:00P		M21 11:15P			T22 6:15A	
		SU20 6:15A		SU20 1:00P	SU20 6:30P	M21 8:15A	M21 12:30P			SU20 5:15A	SU20 9:00A	SU20 10:15A			
								M21 1:30P		T22 1:00A	T22 7:15A	T22 8:30A			
M21 3:00P	M21 5:30P	T22 12:15A				T22 8:45A		T22 11:00P	W23 3:00A		W23 10:00A		M21 10:00A		TH24 10:00P
T22 7:30P	T22 10:00P	W23 3:45A						W23 12:15P	W23 4:00P		W23 11:15P			TH24 6:15A	
										T22 6:15A	T22 9:00A				
TH24 7:30P	TH24 10:00P	F25 3:45A						F25 12:15P	F25 4:00P		F25 11:15P			S26 6:15A	
										T22 3:30P	T22 6:15P				
										T22 3:00P	T22 5:45P				
										T22 11:30P	W23 2:15A				
		S26 1:00A	S26 5:15A	S26 9:15A	S26 1:00P	S26 6:30P									
S26 8:45A	S26 11:45A	S26 6:15P						SU27 3:15A	SU27 7:30A		SU27 5:30P			T29 8:00A	
F25 9:30P	F25 11:45P	S26 7:00A				S26 6:30P		SU27 9:45A	SU27 1:30P		SU27 11:15P			M28 6:15A	
*SU27 7:30P	SU27 10:00P	M28 3:45A						M28 12:15P	M28 4:00P		M28 11:15P			T29 6:15A	
		SU27 5:00P	SU27 9:15P		M28 2:15A	M28 7:45A	M28 7:00P	T29 12:15A			T29 9:00A	T29 10:15A			
M28 5:00P	M28 9:00P	T29 5:30A				T29 1:45P		W30 3:15A	W30 9:00A		W30 5:45P			F2 8:00A	
T29 7:30P	T29 10:00P	W30 3:45A						W30 12:15P	W30 4:00P		W30 11:15P			TH1 6:15A	
										T29 5:00P	T29 8:45P	T29 10:00P			

ALL TIMES ARE LOCAL TIMES

Approximate Running Times Between Ports

Bellingham to Ketchikan .... 36 hours	Petersburg to Sitka .... 10 hours
Prince Rupert to Ketchikan .... 6 hours	Petersburg to Juneau/Auke Bay .... 7.8 hours
Stewart/Hyder to Ketchikan .... 9.8 hours	Sitka to Juneau/Auke Bay .... 8.8 hours
Ketchikan to Wrangell .... 6 hours	Juneau/Auke Bay to Haines .... 4.5 hours
Wrangell to Petersburg .... 3 hours	Haines to Skagway .... 1 hours

1992 ■ The MILEPOST® 539

MARINE ACCESS ROUTES

Southeast Alaska Passenger and Vehicle Tariffs

Effective May 1, 1992–September 30, 1992

ITEM ADT: ADULT 12 YEARS OR OVER (Meals and Berth NOT included)

BETWEEN AND	BELLINGHAM	PRINCE RUPERT	STEWART/HYDER	KETCHIKAN	METLAKATLA	HOLLIS	WRANGELL	PETERSBURG	KAKE	SITKA	ANGOON	HOONAH	JUNEAU	HAINES	SKAGWAY	PELICAN
KETCHIKAN	154	32	36													
METLAKATLA	158	36	40	12												
HOLLIS	168	46	50	18	20											
WRANGELL	170	50	56	22	26	22										
PETERSBURG	182	62	68	36	40	36	16									
KAKE	192	74	80	46	50	46	32	20								
SITKA	198	80	86	52	56	52	36	24	22							
ANGOON	212	94	98	66	70	66	50	38	26	20						
HOONAH	216	98	104	72	76	72	54	42	36	22	18					
JUNEAU	216	98	104	72	76	72	54	42	42	24	22	18				
HAINES	230	112	118	86	90	86	68	56	56	38	36	32	18			
SKAGWAY	236	118	122	90	94	90	74	62	62	42	40	38	24	12		
PELICAN	238	120	126	94	98	94	76	64	50	38	36	20	30	44	52	
TENAKEE	216	98	104	72	76	72	54	42	30	20	14	14	20	32	38	30

ITEM CHD: CHILD 6 THRU 11 YEARS (Under 6 Transported Free)

BETWEEN AND	BELLINGHAM	PRINCE RUPERT	STEWART/HYDER	KETCHIKAN	METLAKATLA	HOLLIS	WRANGELL	PETERSBURG	KAKE	SITKA	ANGOON	HOONAH	JUNEAU	HAINES	SKAGWAY	PELICAN
KETCHIKAN	78	16	18													
METLAKATLA	80	18	20	6												
HOLLIS	84	24	26	10	10											
WRANGELL	86	26	28	12	14	12										
PETERSBURG	92	32	34	18	20	18	8									
KAKE	96	38	40	24	26	24	16	10								
SITKA	100	40	44	26	28	26	18	12	12							
ANGOON	106	48	50	34	36	34	26	20	14	10						
HOONAH	108	50	52	36	38	36	28	22	18	12	10					
JUNEAU	108	50	52	36	38	36	28	22	22	12	12	10				
HAINES	116	56	60	44	46	44	34	28	28	20	18	16	10			
SKAGWAY	118	60	62	46	48	46	38	32	32	22	20	20	12	6		
PELICAN	120	60	64	48	50	48	38	32	26	20	18	10	16	22	26	
TENAKEE	108	50	52	36	38	36	28	22	16	10	8	8	10	16	20	16

ITEM AMC: ALTERNATE MEANS OF CONVEYANCE (Bicycles, Kayaks and Inflatables)

BETWEEN AND	BELLINGHAM	PRINCE RUPERT	STEWART/HYDER	KETCHIKAN	METLAKATLA	HOLLIS	WRANGELL	PETERSBURG	KAKE	SITKA	ANGOON	HOONAH	JUNEAU	HAINES	SKAGWAY	PELICAN
KETCHIKAN	26	8	9													
METLAKATLA	27	9	10	5												
HOLLIS	28	10	11	6	7											
WRANGELL	29	11	12	7	8	7										
PETERSBURG	30	12	13	9	10	9	6									
KAKE	32	14	15	10	11	10	8	6								
SITKA	33	15	16	11	12	11	9	7	6							
ANGOON	35	17	18	13	14	13	11	9	7	5						
HOONAH	36	18	19	14	15	14	12	10	9	6	6					
JUNEAU	36	18	19	14	15	14	12	10	10	7	7	6				
HAINES	37	20	21	16	17	16	14	12	12	9	8	8	6			
SKAGWAY	38	21	22	17	18	17	15	13	13	10	9	9	7	5		
PELICAN	39	21	22	17	18	17	15	13	11	9	8	6	8	10	11	
TENAKEE	36	18	19	14	15	14	12	10	8	6	5	5	7	8	9	8

ITEM 710: VEHICLES UP TO 10 FEET (Driver NOT Included)

BETWEEN AND	BELLINGHAM	PRINCE RUPERT	STEWART/HYDER	KETCHIKAN	METLAKATLA	HOLLIS	WRANGELL	PETERSBURG	KAKE	SITKA	ANGOON	HOONAH	JUNEAU	HAINES	SKAGWAY	PELICAN
KETCHIKAN	169	35	40													
METLAKATLA	173	41	45	11												
HOLLIS	184	51	57	21	23											
WRANGELL	188	56	61	25	30	25										
PETERSBURG	201	69	75	39	43	39	18									
KAKE	214	82	88	52	57	52	34	22								
SITKA	220	88	94	58	63	58	39	26	24							
ANGOON	235	103	109	73	78	73	55	42	29	21						
HOONAH	241	109	115	79	84	79	60	47	39	24	20					
JUNEAU	241	109	115	79	84	79	60	47	47	26	24	19				
HAINES	256	124	130	94	99	94	75	61	61	41	39	34	20			
SKAGWAY	262	130	136	100	105	100	81	68	68	47	45	41	26	11		
PELICAN	265	133	139	103	107	103	83	69	54	42	39	23	34	50	57	
TENAKEE	241	109	115	79	84	79	60	47	33	22	16	16	22	36	42	34

ITEM 715: VEHICLES UP TO 15 FEET (Driver NOT Included)

BETWEEN AND	BELLINGHAM	PRINCE RUPERT	STEWART/HYDER	KETCHIKAN	METLAKATLA	HOLLIS	WRANGELL	PETERSBURG	KAKE	SITKA	ANGOON	HOONAH	JUNEAU	HAINES	SKAGWAY	PELICAN
KETCHIKAN	363	73	83													
METLAKATLA	372	84	95	21												
HOLLIS	394	107	119	41	46											
WRANGELL	405	117	129	51	61	51										
PETERSBURG	433	145	158	80	90	80	35									
KAKE	460	174	187	109	119	109	70	44								
SITKA	473	187	200	122	132	122	80	52	49							
ANGOON	505	220	233	155	164	155	116	86	60	41						
HOONAH	518	233	246	168	177	168	126	98	82	49	39					
JUNEAU	518	233	246	168	177	168	126	98	98	52	47	38				
HAINES	551	265	278	200	210	200	158	129	129	85	80	71	39			
SKAGWAY	564	278	291	213	224	213	172	143	143	99	94	85	53	21		
PELICAN	570	285	298	220	228	220	176	147	114	86	80	47	70	104	119	

ITEM 719: VEHICLES UP TO 19 FEET (Driver NOT Included)

BETWEEN AND	BELLINGHAM	PRINCE RUPERT	STEWART/HYDER	KETCHIKAN	METLAKATLA	HOLLIS	WRANGELL	PETERSBURG	KAKE	SITKA	ANGOON	HOONAH	JUNEAU	HAINES	SKAGWAY
KETCHIKAN	432	87	99												
METLAKATLA	443	100	113	25											
HOLLIS	470	128	141	49	55										
WRANGELL	482	139	153	61	73	61									
PETERSBURG	515	172	188	95	107	95	42								
KAKE	548	207	223	130	141	130	83	52							
SITKA	563	223	238	145	157	145	96	63	58						
ANGOON	602	261	277	184	196	184	138	103	71	49					
HOONAH	617	277	292	200	211	200	150	117	97	58	47				
JUNEAU	617	277	292	200	211	200	150	117	117	62	56	45			
HAINES	656	316	331	238	250	238	188	154	154	101	95	84	46		
SKAGWAY	672	331	347	254	267	254	205	171	171	117	112	101	63	25	
PELICAN	679	339	354	261	271	261	210	175	136	103	95	56	83	124	141

ITEM 721: VEHICLES UP TO 21 FEET (Driver NOT Included)

BETWEEN AND	BELLINGHAM	PRINCE RUPERT	STEWART/HYDER	KETCHIKAN	METLAKATLA	HOLLIS	WRANGELL	PETERSBURG	KAKE	SITKA	ANGOON	HOONAH	JUNEAU	HAINES	SKAGWAY
KETCHIKAN	557	112	127												
METLAKATLA	572	129	145	31											
HOLLIS	606	164	182	62	70										
WRANGELL	622	179	197	78	93	78									
PETERSBURG	665	222	242	122	137	122	53								
KAKE	707	267	287	167	182	167	107	67							
SITKA	727	287	307	187	202	187	123	80	74						
ANGOON	777	337	357	237	252	237	177	132	91	63					
HOONAH	797	357	377	257	272	257	193	150	125	74	60				
JUNEAU	797	357	377	257	272	257	193	150	150	79	72	57			
HAINES	847	407	427	307	322	307	242	198	198	130	122	108	59		
SKAGWAY	867	427	447	327	344	327	264	220	220	151	144	130	81	31	
PELICAN	877	437	457	337	350	337	270	225	175	132	122	71	107	159	182

ITEM 723: VEHICLES UP TO 23 FEET (Driver NOT Included)

BETWEEN AND	BELLINGHAM	PRINCE RUPERT	STEWART/HYDER	KETCHIKAN	METLAKATLA	HOLLIS	WRANGELL	PETERSBURG	KAKE	SITKA	ANGOON	HOONAH	JUNEAU	HAINES	SKAGWAY
KETCHIKAN	646	130	147												
METLAKATLA	663	150	168	36											
HOLLIS	703	190	211	72	81										
WRANGELL	721	208	228	90	108	90									
PETERSBURG	771	257	281	141	159	141	61								
KAKE	820	310	333	194	211	194	124	78							
SITKA	843	333	356	217	234	217	143	93	86						
ANGOON	901	391	414	275	292	275	205	153	105	73					
HOONAH	924	414	437	298	315	298	224	174	145	86	69				
JUNEAU	924	414	437	298	315	298	224	174	174	92	83	66			
HAINES	982	472	495	356	373	356	281	230	230	151	141	125	68		
SKAGWAY	1006	495	518	379	399	379	306	255	255	175	167	151	94	36	
PELICAN	1017	507	530	391	406	391	313	261	203	153	141	82	124	184	211

ITEM 725: VEHICLES UP TO 25 FEET (Driver NOT Included)

BETWEEN AND	BELLINGHAM	PRINCE RUPERT	STEWART/HYDER	KETCHIKAN	METLAKATLA	HOLLIS	WRANGELL	PETERSBURG	KAKE	SITKA	ANGOON	HOONAH	JUNEAU	HAINES	SKAGWAY
KETCHIKAN	768	154	175												
METLAKATLA	789	177	199	42											
HOLLIS	836	226	251	85	96										
WRANGELL	858	246	271	107	128	107									
PETERSBURG	917	306	333	168	188	168	72								
KAKE	975	368	395	230	251	207	147	92							
SITKA	1003	395	423	257	278	257	169	110	101						
ANGOON	1072	464	492	326	347	326	244	182	125	86					
HOONAH	1099	492	520	354	375	354	266	206	172	101	82				
JUNEAU	1099	492	520	354	375	354	266	206	206	108	99	78			
HAINES	1168	561	589	423	444	423	333	273	273	179	168	148	81		
SKAGWAY	1196	589	616	451	474	451	364	303	303	208	198	179	111	42	
PELICAN	1210	602	630	464	482	464	372	310	241	182	168	97	147	219	251

ITEM 728: VEHICLES UP TO 28 FEET (Driver NOT Included)

BETWEEN AND	BELLINGHAM	PRINCE RUPERT	STEWART/HYDER	KETCHIKAN	METLAKATLA	HOLLIS	WRANGELL	PETERSBURG	KAKE	SITKA	ANGOON	HOONAH	JUNEAU	HAINES	SKAGWAY
KETCHIKAN	912	182	207												
METLAKATLA	937	210	236	49											
HOLLIS	992	267	297	100	113										
WRANGELL	1019	292	322	126	151	126									
PETERSBURG	1089	363	395	199	223	199	85								
KAKE	1158	436	469	272	297	272	174	108							
SITKA	1191	469	502	305	330	305	200	130	120						
ANGOON	1273	551	584	387	412	387	289	215	148	102					
HOONAH	1306	584	617	420	445	420	315	245	204	120	97				
JUNEAU	1306	584	617	420	445	420	315	245	245	128	117	92			
HAINES	1388	666	699	502	527	502	395	323	323	212	199	176	95		
SKAGWAY	1420	699	732	535	563	535	431	359	359	246	235	212	131	49	
PELICAN	1437	715	748	551	573	551	441	368	286	215	199	115	174	259	297

Southeast Alaska Passenger and Vehicle Tariffs (cont.)
Effective May 1, 1992–September 30, 1992

MARINE ACCESS ROUTES

ITEM 731: VEHICLES UP TO 31 FEET (Driver NOT Included)

BETWEEN	AND BELLINGHAM	PRINCE RUPERT	STEWART/HYDER	KETCHIKAN	METLAKATLA	HOLLIS	WRANGELL	PETERSBURG	KAKE	SITKA	ANGOON	HOONAH	JUNEAU	HAINES	SKAGWAY
KETCHIKAN	1024	205	233												
METLAKATLA	1052	236	266	56											
HOLLIS	1114	301	334	113	128										
WRANGELL	1144	328	362	143	170	143									
PETERSBURG	1223	408	444	224	251	224	97								
KAKE	1300	490	527	306	334	306	196	122							
SITKA	1337	527	564	343	371	343	225	146	135						
ANGOON	1429	619	656	435	463	435	325	242	167	115					
HOONAH	1466	656	693	472	500	472	354	275	229	135	110				
JUNEAU	1466	656	693	472	500	472	354	275	275	144	132	104			
HAINES	1558	748	785	564	592	564	444	363	363	238	224	198	108		
SKAGWAY	1594	785	822	601	632	601	485	404	404	277	264	238	148	56	
PELICAN	1613	803	840	619	643	619	496	413	321	242	224	130	196	292	334

ITEM 736: VEHICLES UP TO 36 FEET (Driver NOT Included)

	BELLINGHAM	PR	ST/HY	KET	MET	HOL	WRA	PET	KAK	SIT	ANG	HOO	JUN	HAI	SKA
KETCHIKAN	1213	243	276												
METLAKATLA	1246	280	315	66											
HOLLIS	1320	356	396	134	151										
WRANGELL	1355	389	428	169	201	169									
PETERSBURG	1448	483	526	265	297	265	114								
KAKE	1540	581	624	363	396	363	232	145							
SITKA	1584	624	668	406	439	406	267	173	160						
ANGOON	1693	733	777	515	548	515	385	287	197	136					
HOONAH	1736	777	821	559	592	559	419	326	271	160	130				
JUNEAU	1736	777	821	559	592	559	419	326	326	171	156	123			
HAINES	1845	886	930	668	701	668	526	430	430	282	265	234	127		
SKAGWAY	1889	930	973	712	749	712	574	478	478	328	313	282	175	66	
PELICAN	1911	951	995	733	762	733	587	489	380	287	265	154	232	345	396

ITEM 741: VEHICLES UP TO 41 FEET (Driver NOT Included)

	BELLINGHAM	PR	ST/HY	KET	MET	HOL	WRA	PET	KAK	SIT	ANG	HOO	JUN	HAI	SKA
KETCHIKAN	1386	278	316												
METLAKATLA	1424	321	360	77											
HOLLIS	1508	408	453	154	174										
WRANGELL	1548	445	490	194	181	194									
PETERSBURG	1655	552	602	303	341	303	132								
KAKE	1760	664	714	415	453	415	266	166							
SITKA	1810	714	764	465	503	465	306	199	184						
ANGOON	1934	839	888	590	627	590	440	328	226	156					
HOONAH	1984	888	938	640	677	640	480	373	311	184	149				
JUNEAU	1984	888	938	640	677	640	480	373	373	196	179	142			
HAINES	2108	1013	1063	764	801	764	602	493	493	323	303	268	146		
SKAGWAY	2158	1063	1113	814	856	814	657	547	547	376	358	323	201	77	
PELICAN	2183	1088	1138	839	871	839	672	560	435	328	303	176	266	395	453

ITEM 746: VEHICLES UP TO 46 FEET (Driver NOT Included)

	BELLINGHAM	PR	ST/HY	KET	MET	HOL	WRA	PET	KAK	SIT	ANG	HOO	JUN	HAI	SKA
KETCHIKAN	1573	318	360												
METLAKATLA	1615	366	411	90											
HOLLIS	1711	465	516	177	200										
WRANGELL	1756	507	558	222	265	222									
PETERSBURG	1878	628	685	346	389	346	152								
KAKE	1996	755	812	473	516	473	304	191							
SITKA	2052	812	868	530	572	530	349	228	211						
ANGOON	2193	953	1009	671	713	671	501	375	259	180					
HOONAH	2250	1009	1065	727	769	727	547	425	355	211	171				
JUNEAU	2250	1009	1065	727	769	727	547	425	425	225	205	163			
HAINES	2391	1150	1206	868	910	868	685	561	561	369	346	307	169		
SKAGWAY	2447	1206	1263	924	972	924	747	623	623	428	408	369	231	90	
PELICAN	2475	1235	1291	953	989	953	764	637	496	375	346	202	304	451	516

ITEM 751: VEHICLES UP TO 51 FEET (Driver NOT Included)

	BELLINGHAM	PR	ST/HY	KET	MET	HOL	WRA	PET	KAK	SIT	ANG	HOO	JUN	HAI	SKA
KETCHIKAN	1764	358	405												
METLAKATLA	1811	412	462	102											
HOLLIS	1919	522	579	200	225										
WRANGELL	1969	570	626	250	298	250									
PETERSBURG	2105	705	769	389	437	389	171								
KAKE	2238	848	911	532	579	532	342	216							
SITKA	2301	911	974	595	642	595	393	257	238						
ANGOON	2459	1069	1132	753	800	753	563	421	291	203					
HOONAH	2522	1132	1195	816	863	816	614	478	399	238	193				
JUNEAU	2522	1132	1195	816	863	816	614	478	478	254	231	184			
HAINES	2680	1290	1353	974	1021	974	769	630	630	415	389	345	190		
SKAGWAY	2744	1353	1416	1037	1091	1037	838	699	699	481	459	415	260	102	
PELICAN	2775	1385	1448	1069	1110	1069	857	715	557	421	389	228	342	506	579

ITEM 756: VEHICLES UP TO 56 FEET (Driver NOT Inlcuded)

	BELLINGHAM	PR	ST/HY	KET	MET	HOL	WRA	PET	KAK	SIT	ANG	HOO	JUN	HAI	SKA
KETCHIKAN	1940	395	447												
METLAKATLA	1992	454	510	114											
HOLLIS	2110	576	638	222	250										
WRANGELL	2165	628	690	277	329	277									
PETERSBURG	2314	777	846	430	482	430	191								
KAKE	2460	933	1003	586	638	586	378	239							
SITKA	2529	1003	1072	656	708	656	434	284	263						
ANGOON	2703	1176	1246	829	881	829	621	465	322	225					
HOONAH	2772	1246	1315	899	951	899	676	527	440	263	215				
JUNEAU	2772	1246	1315	899	951	899	676	527	527	281	257	205			
HAINES	2946	1419	1488	1072	1124	1072	846	694	694	458	430	381	211		
SKAGWAY	3015	1488	1558	1141	1200	1141	923	770	770	531	506	458	288	114	
PELICAN	3050	1523	1593	1176	1221	1176	944	787	614	465	430	253	378	558	638

ITEM 760: VEHICLES UP TO 60 FEET (Driver NOT Included)

	BELLINGHAM	PR	ST/HY	KET	MET	HOL	WRA	PET	KAK	SIT	ANG	HOO	JUN	HAI	SKA
KETCHIKAN	2159	441	499												
METLAKATLA	2217	507	569	129											
HOLLIS	2348	642	712	248	279										
WRANGELL	2410	700	769	310	368	310									
PETERSBURG	2576	866	943	480	538	480	214								
KAKE	2738	1040	1117	654	712	654	422	268							
SITKA	2815	1117	1194	731	789	731	484	318	295						
ANGOON	3008	1310	1387	924	982	924	692	519	360	252					
HOONAH	3085	1387	1464	1001	1059	1001	754	588	491	294	241				
JUNEAU	3085	1387	1464	1001	1059	1001	754	588	588	314	287	229			
HAINES	3278	1580	1657	1194	1252	1194	943	773	773	511	480	426	237		
SKAGWAY	3356	1657	1734	1271	1337	1271	1028	858	858	592	565	511	322	129	
PELICAN	3394	1696	1773	1310	1360	1310	1051	877	684	519	480	283	422	623	712

ITEM 770: VEHICLES UP TO 70 FEET (Driver NOT Included)

	BELLINGHAM	PR	ST/HY	KET	MET	HOL	WRA	PET	KAK	SIT	ANG	HOO	JUN	HAI	SKA
KETCHIKAN	3063	633	715												
METLAKATLA	3145	766	813	191											
HOLLIS	3331	917	1016	360	404										
WRANGELL	3418	999	1097	448	530	448									
PETERSBURG	3653	1234	1343	688	770	688	311								
KAKE	3882	1480	1589	934	1016	934	606	388							
SITKA	3991	1589	1698	1043	1125	1043	693	459	426						
ANGOON	4264	1862	1971	1316	1398	1316	988	743	519	366					
HOONAH	4373	1971	2080	1425	1507	1425	1076	841	704	426	349				
JUNEAU	4373	1971	2080	1425	1507	1425	1076	841	841	453	414	333			
HAINES	4646	2244	2353	1698	1780	1698	1343	1103	1103	732	688	611	344		
SKAGWAY	4756	2353	2462	1807	1900	1807	1463	1223	1223	846	808	732	464	191	
PELICAN	4810	2408	2517	1862	1933	1862	1496	1250	977	743	688	409	606	890	1016

(continued from page 528)

Royal Caribbean Cruise Line, 1050 Caribbean Way, Miami, FL 33132, phone 1-800-327-6700. *Sun Viking* (726 passengers); 7-night round-trip from Vancouver, BC. Ports of call: Tracy Arm, Skagway, Haines, Juneau, Ketchikan, Misty Fiords.

Royal Cruise Line, 1 Maritime Plaza, San Francisco, CA 94111, phone 1-800-227-4534 or (415) 956-7200. *Royal Odyssey* (765 passengers); 10-day cruises from Los Angeles and San Francisco, 12-day round-trips from San Francisco (both include Glacier Bay) plus 7-day Vancouver, BC, to Anchorage.

Seven Seas Cruises, 333 Market St., #2600, San Francisco, CA 94105, phone 1-800-285-1835 or (415) 905-6000. *Song of Flower* (172 passengers); 7-days 1-way between Vancouver, BC, and Whittier, AK. Ports of call: Ketchikan, Juneau, Skagway, Haines, Sitka. Also 7-day round-trip from Vancouver, BC. Ports of call: Ketchikan, Tracy Arm, Juneau, Glacier Bay, Petersburg.

Special Expeditions, 720 5th Ave., New York, NY 10019, phone 1-800-762-0003. *Sea Bird* and *Sea Lion* (70 passengers); 11-day wilderness cruises between Prince Rupert, BC, and Sitka. Ports of call: Misty Fiords, Agate Pass, Snow Pass, LeConte Glacier, Petersburg, Admiralty Island, Seymour Canal, Tracy Arm, Glacier Bay, Point Adolphus, Elfin Cove.

World Explorer Cruises, 555 Montgomery St., San Fransico, CA 94111-2544; phone 1-800-854-3835. SS *Universe* (550 passengers); 14-day round-trip from Vancouver, BC. Ports of call: Wrangell, Juneau, Skagway, Glacier Bay, Columbia Glacier, Seward, Sitka, Ketchikan, Victoria.

Southeast Alaska Cabin Tariffs
Effective May 1, 1992–September 30, 1992

MARINE ACCESS ROUTES

BETWEEN AND: BELLINGHAM / PRINCE RUPERT / KETCHIKAN / WRANGELL / PETERSBURG / SITKA / JUNEAU / HAINES

ITEM 4BS: FOUR BERTH CABIN/SITTINGROOM - OUTSIDE/COMPLETE FACILITIES
M/V COLUMBIA - M/V MALASPINA

	BEL	PR	KET	WRA	PET	SIT	JUN	HAI
KETCHIKAN	235	60						
WRANGELL	260	85	58					
PETERSBURG	275	98	71	47				
SITKA	304	122	91	71	60			
JUNEAU	321	138	107	91	78	54		
HAINES	339	156	129	108	97	74	51	
SKAGWAY	339	156	129	108	97	74	51	39

ITEM 4BF: FOUR BERTH CABIN - OUTSIDE/COMPLETE FACILITIES
M/V COLUMBIA - M/V MALASPINA - M/V MATANUSKA - M/V TAKU

	BEL	PR	KET	WRA	PET	SIT	JUN	HAI
KETCHIKAN	214	55						
WRANGELL	237	76	53					
PETERSBURG	250	88	65	41				
SITKA	276	109	84	64	55			
JUNEAU	291	122	100	80	69	48		
HAINES	313	145	121	100	90	67	45	
SKAGWAY	313	145	121	100	90	67	45	35

ITEM 4BI: FOUR BERTH CABIN - INSIDE/COMPLETE FACILITIES
M/V MALASPINA - M/V TAKU

	BEL	PR	KET	WRA	PET	SIT	JUN	HAI
KETCHIKAN	182	48						
WRANGELL	202	66	48					
PETERSBURG	216	76	57	39				
SITKA	238	95	75	56	48			
JUNEAU	252	107	88	69	60	42		
HAINES	270	125	106	88	79	59	39	
SKAGWAY	270	125	106	88	79	59	39	31

ITEM 3BF: THREE BERTH CABIN - OUTSIDE/COMPLETE FACILITIES
M/V COLUMBIA - M/V MATANUSKA

	BEL	PR	KET	WRA	PET	SIT	JUN	HAI
KETCHIKAN	175	43						
WRANGELL	192	60	44					
PETERSBURG	201	69	52	35				
SITKA	220	86	67	52	45			
JUNEAU	234	97	77	62	55	40		
HAINES	254	113	91	74	67	53	37	
SKAGWAY	254	113	91	74	67	53	37	30

ITEM 2BF: TWO BERTH - OUTSIDE/COMPLETE FACILITIES
M/V COLUMBIA - M/V MALASPINA - M/V MATANUSKA - M/V TAKU

	BEL	PR	KET	WRA	PET	SIT	JUN	HAI
KETCHIKAN	153	41						
WRANGELL	167	55	37					
PETERSBURG	176	64	46	33				
SITKA	196	80	61	47	40			
JUNEAU	210	92	72	58	50	37		
HAINES	228	108	84	69	62	48	34	
SKAGWAY	228	108	84	69	62	48	34	27

ITEM 2BI: TWO BERTH CABIN - INSIDE/COMPLETE FACILITIES
M/V COLUMBIA - M/V MALASPINA - M/V MATANUSKA - M/V TAKU

	BEL	PR	KET	WRA	PET	SIT	JUN	HAI
KETCHIKAN	135	36						
WRANGELL	150	50	34					
PETERSBURG	156	57	41	29				
SITKA	172	70	53	41	35			
JUNEAU	183	79	63	51	44	33		
HAINES	196	93	76	63	57	44	31	
SKAGWAY	196	93	76	63	57	44	31	25

ITEM DOM/DOF: DORMITORY ROOMS - RATE PER BERTH
M/V COLUMBIA - M/V MALASPINA - M/V MATANUSKA - M/V TAKU

	BEL	PR	KET	WRA	PET	SIT	JUN	HAI
KETCHIKAN	68	18						
WRANGELL	75	25	17					
PETERSBURG	78	29	21	15				
SITKA	86	35	27	21	18			
JUNEAU	92	40	32	26	22	17		
HAINES	98	47	38	32	29	22	16	
SKAGWAY	98	47	38	32	29	22	16	13

MALE OR FEMALE DORMS ARE AVAILABLE. NO CHILDREN ALLOWED. NO SMOKING ALLOWED.

Southwest System Schedule
M/V BARTLETT

EFFECTIVE MAY 1, 1992 THROUGH MAY 11, 1992

FRI	MAY 1	LV VALDEZ	12:30AM	WED	MAY 6	LV WHITTIER	2:45PM
		AR CORDOVA	6:00AM			LV VALDEZ	11:45PM
FRI	MAY 1	LV CORDOVA	6:30AM	THU	MAY 7	AR CORDOVA	5:15AM
		AR WHITTIER	1:30PM	THU	MAY 7	LV CORDOVA	9:00AM
FRI	MAY 1	LV WHITTIER	2:45PM			AR VALDEZ	2:45PM
		AR CORDOVA	9:45PM	THU	MAY 7	LV VALDEZ	11:45PM
SAT	MAY 2	LV CORDOVA	12:30AM	FRI	MAY 8	AR CORDOVA	5:15AM
		LV VALDEZ	7:15AM	FRI	MAY 8	LV CORDOVA	6:30AM
		AR WHITTIER	2:00PM			AR WHITTIER	1:30PM
SAT	MAY 2	LV WHITTIER	2:45PM	FRI	MAY 8	LV WHITTIER	2:45PM
		AR VALDEZ	9:30PM			AR CORDOVA	9:45PM
SUN	MAY 3	LV VALDEZ	7:15AM	SAT	MAY 9	LV CORDOVA	12:30AM
		AR WHITTIER	2:00PM			LV VALDEZ	7:15AM
SUN	MAY 3	LV WHITTIER	2:45PM			AR WHITTIER	2:00PM
MON	MAY 4	AR CORDOVA	5:15AM	SAT	MAY 9	LV WHITTIER	2:45PM
TUE	MAY 5	LV CORDOVA	9:00AM			AR VALDEZ	9:30PM
		AR VALDEZ	2:45PM	SUN	MAY 10	LV VALDEZ	7:15AM
						AR WHITTIER	2:00PM
WED	MAY 6	LV VALDEZ	7:15AM	SUN	MAY 10	LV WHITTIER	2:45PM
		AR WHITTIER	2:00PM			LV VALDEZ	11:45PM
				MON	MAY 11	AR CORDOVA	5:15AM

MAY 11, 1992 THROUGH SEPTEMBER 15, 1992

MON	LV CORDOVA	6:30AM	FRI	LV CORDOVA	6:30AM
	AR WHITTIER	1:30PM		AR WHITTIER	1:30PM
MON	LV WHITTIER	2:45PM	FRI	LV WHITTIER	2:45PM
	AR CORDOVA	9:45PM		AR CORDOVA	9:45PM
TUE	LV CORDOVA	12:30AM	SAT	LV CORDOVA	12:30AM **
	LV VALDEZ	7:15AM		LV VALDEZ	7:15AM
	AR WHITTIER	2:00PM		AR WHITTIER	2:00PM
TUE	LV WHITTIER	2:45PM	SAT	LV WHITTIER	2:45PM
WED	LV VALDEZ	12:30AM		AR VALDEZ	9:30PM
	AR CORDOVA	6:00AM	SUN	LV VALDEZ	7:15AM
THU	LV CORDOVA	12:30AM		AR WHITTIER	2:00PM
	LV VALDEZ	7:15AM	SUN	LV WHITTIER	2:45PM
	AR WHITTIER	2:00PM		LV VALDEZ	11:45PM
THU	LV WHITTIER	2:45PM	MON	AR CORDOVA	5:15AM
	LV VALDEZ	11:45PM			
FRI	AR CORDOVA	5:15AM			

**PRINCE WILLIAM SOUND ROYAL FLUSH REGATTA ALTERNATE SAILING MAY 16-WHITTIER

**SAT MAY 16	LV CORDOVA	12:30AM	SAT	MAY 16	LV WHITTIER	9:00AM
	AR WHITTIER	7:30AM			AR VALDEZ	6:00PM

DAILY SERVICE BETWEEN VALDEZ-WHITTIER AND RETURN
FROM SEPTEMBER 16, THROUGH SEPTEMBER 22, 1992

LV VALDEZ	7:15AM		AR WHITTIER	2:00PM
LV WHITTIER	2:45PM		AR VALDEZ	9:30PM

The M/V BARTLETT will accept vehicles to a maximum length of 60 feet and a gross weight of 35 tons.

Railway connections required between Portage and Whittier for all Whittier departures and arrivals. Contact the Alaska Railroad at 800-544-0552 (outside Alaska) or (907) 265-2623 for schedules and fares.

SENIOR CITIZENS PASS - HANDICAPPED PERSONS PASS travel will not be allowed on the M/V BARTLETT or M/V TUSTUMENA during May 1 - September 30 period on sailings between Whittier and Valdez or Seward and Valdez

---

M/V TUSTUMENA ALEUTIAN CHAIN TRIPS

CHAIN TRIP #1 MAY 8-MAY 13

FRI	LV	SEWARD	3:30AM	MON	LV	DUTCH HARBOR	7:00AM
FRI	LV	KODIAK	8:00PM	MON	LV	COLD BAY	10:45PM
SAT	LV	CHIGNIK	5:00PM	TUE	LV	KING COVE	1:30AM
SUN	LV	SAND POINT	3:15AM	TUE	LV	SAND POINT	9:30AM
SUN	LV	KING COVE	11:00AM	TUE	LV	CHIGNIK	8:30PM
SUN	LV	COLD BAY	2:00PM	WED	AR	KODIAK	3:30PM
MON	AR	DUTCH HARBOR	4:15AM				

CHAIN TRIP #2 MAY 20-MAY 25

WED	LV	KODIAK	11:30PM	SAT	LV	DUTCH HARBOR	10:30AM
THU	LV	CHIGNIK	8:00PM	SUN	LV	COLD BAY	2:00AM
FRI	LV	SAND POINT	6:15AM	SUN	LV	KING COVE	5:00AM
FRI	LV	KING COVE	2:30PM	SUN	LV	SAND POINT	1:00PM
FRI	LV	COLD BAY	5:15PM	MON	LV	CHIGNIK	12:15AM
SAT	AR	DUTCH HARBOR	7:30AM	MON	AR	KODIAK	7:15PM

CHAIN TRIP #3 JUN 5-JUN 10

FRI	LV	KODIAK	8:00PM	MON	LV	DUTCH HARBOR	7:00AM
SAT	LV	CHIGNIK	5:00PM	MON	LV	COLD BAY	10:45PM
SUN	LV	SAND POINT	3:15AM	TUE	LV	KING COVE	1:30AM
SUN	LV	KING COVE	11:00AM	TUE	LV	SAND POINT	9:30AM
SUN	LV	COLD BAY	2:00PM	TUE	LV	CHIGNIK	8:30PM
MON	AR	DUTCH HARBOR	4:15AM	WED	AR	KODIAK	3:30PM

CHAIN TRIP #4 JUL 3-JUL 8 JUL 31-AUG 5 AUG 28-SEP 2 SEP 11-SEP 16

FRI	LV	KODIAK	8:00AM	SUN	LV	DUTCH HARBOR	7:00PM
SAT	LV	CHIGNIK	5:00AM	MON	LV	COLD BAY	10:45AM
SAT	LV	SAND POINT	3:15PM	TUE	LV	KING COVE	1:30PM
SAT	LV	KING COVE	11:00PM	MON	LV	SAND POINT	9:30PM
SUN	LV	COLD BAY	2:00AM	TUE	LV	CHIGNIK	8:30AM
SUN	AR	DUTCH HARBOR	4:15PM	WED	AR	KODIAK	3:30AM

SOUTHWEST FERRY SYSTEM Southcentral Alaska

Alaska State Ferries

The main office of the Alaska Marine Highway is in Juneau. Write P.O. Box 25535, Juneau, AK 99802-5535; phone (907) 465-3941 or toll free in the U.S. 1-800-642-0066.

The Alaska State Ferry System is divided into 2 different systems serving 2 different areas: Southeast and Southwest. These 2 systems *DO NOT* connect with each other.

If you are headed for Alaska from Bellingham, WA, or Prince Rupert, BC, via the Alaska Marine Highway, you'll take the Southeast system, which stops at southeastern Alaska cities from Ketchikan to Skagway. Keep in mind that only 2 Southeast communities are connected to the Alaska Highway: Haines, via the Haines Highway; and Skagway, via Klondike Highway 2. (See the HAINES HIGHWAY and KLONDIKE HIGHWAY 2 sections.) During the summer months, the system also calls at Stewart/Hyder, located at the end of the Stewart–Cassiar Highway. Other Southeast communities are accessible only by ferry or by air.

The Southwest system services southwestern Alaska cities. Some of these Southwest communities, such as Homer and Seward, are also accessible by highway; others such as Seldovia, Cordova and Kodiak, are accessible only by ferry or air.

Travel on the Alaska state ferries is at a leisurely pace, with observation decks, food service and vehicle decks on all ferries. Cabins are available only on 4 Southeast ferries and 1 Southwest ferry.

Keep in mind that the state ferries are not cruise ships: They do not have beauty salons, gift shops, deck games and the like. The small stores on the larger ferries are open limited hours and sell a limited selection of items. The cafeteria-style food service is open only for meals. Cocktail lounges on board the larger vessels are open from late morning to midnight. It's a good idea to bring your own snacks, books, games and toiletries.

Season: The Alaska Ferry System has 2 seasons—May 1 to Sept. 30, when sailings are most frequent, and Oct. 1 to April 30, when departures are somewhat less frequent. Schedules and information appearing in this section are for the summer season only.

Contact the Alaska Marine Highway office for fall and winter schedules, fares and information. (Fares are normally reduced between Oct. 1 and April 30 and crowds are virtually nonexistent.)

Reservations: Required on all vessels. The Alaska state ferries are very popular in summer and we advise you make reservations as far in advance as possible to get the sailing dates you wish. Cabin space on summer sailings is often sold out by early December on the Bellingham sailings. Requests for space are accepted year-round and held until reservations open. For reservations, write the Alaska Marine Highway, P.O. Box 25535, Juneau, AK 99802-5535, or phone (907) 465-3941 or toll free in the U.S. 1-800-642-0066.

Reservation requests must include departure dates and ports of embarkation/debarkation; full names of all members of the party, and the ages of those under 12 years; width, height, and overall length (including hitch if with trailer) of vehicles; mailing address and phone number; alternate dates in the event cabin or vehicle space is not available on your first choice; and approximate date you will be leaving home.

If you are unable to obtain reservations at the time of advance booking, you may be wait listed. If a cancellation occurs you will be notified of confirmation of space. You may also choose to go standby, which is literally standing by in line until all reserved

(Continues on page 546)

DO THE FERRY SCHEDULES CONFUSE YOU?

Let Us Translate!

... and help you with your itinerary, stopover plans, cabin requirements, reservations and ticketing for:
- Alaska Marine Highway
- British Columbia Ferry
- Camper and Vehicle Rental
- Wilderness Side Trips

ALASKA NORTHWEST TRAVEL SERVICE, INC.
A Division of Alaska Northwest Publishing Co.

130 2nd Ave. S. - Dept. MP92
Edmonds, WA 98020
206-775-4504 • 1-800-533-7381
FAX 206-672-2824

Southwest System Schedule–M/V TUSTUMENA
Effective May 1, 1992–September 30, 1992

MARINE ACCESS ROUTES

MAY EASTBOUND

LEAVE SELDOVIA	LEAVE HOMER	LEAVE PORT LIONS	ARRIVE KODIAK	ARRIVE SEWARD	ARRIVE VALDEZ
S2 12:30A	S2 3:30A		S2 3:30P		
SU3 11:00A	SU3 3:00P		M4 3:00A		
M4 11:30P	T5 3:00A	T5 1:00P	T5 3:15P		
W6 11:00A	W6 3:00P		TH7 6:15A	TH7 7:45P	
*** FROM CHAIN TRIP #1 ***			W13 3:30P		
	TH14 7:00A	TH14 5:00P	TH14 7:00P		
F15 3:00P	F15 8:30P		S16 8:30A		
SU17 4:15A	SU17 6:45A		SU17 6:45P		
	*M18 8:30P		*T19 8:30A	KODIAK KING CRAB FESTIVAL TRAFFIC	
M18 12:30P	W20 1:30P	W20 7:00P	W20 9:00P		
W20 6:30A					
*** FROM CHAIN TRIP #2 ***			M25 7:15P		
T26 3:00P	T26 6:30P		*W27 6:30A		
TH28 10:00A	TH28 2:00P		F29 2:00A		
S30 12:30A	S30 3:30A		S30 3:30P		
SU31 11:00A	SU31 3:00P		M1 3:00A		

MAY WESTBOUND

LEAVE VALDEZ	LEAVE SEWARD	LEAVE KODIAK	LEAVE PORT LIONS	LEAVE HOMER	ARRIVE SELDOVIA
	TH30 4:00P	F1 7:00A		F1 9:00P	F1 10:30P
	S2 6:30P	S2 9:00P	SU3 8:00A	SU3 9:30A	
	M4 6:30A			M4 8:00P	M4 9:30P
	T5 6:30P			W6 8:00A	W6 9:30A
F8 3:30A	F8 8:00P	*** TO CHAIN TRIP #1 ***	TH14 5:30A		
	W13 10:00P	Ar.	F15 12:30P	F15 2:00P	
	TH14 10:00P	S16 11:30A	S16 2:00P	SU17 1:45A	SU17 3:15A
	SU17 8:45P	M18 10:00A	M18 11:30A		
	T19 2:30P	W20 4:00P	W20 5:30A		
	W20 11:30P	*** TO CHAIN TRIP #2 ***			
M25 10:15P		T26 12:15P		T26 1:45P	
W27 1:00P		*TH28 7:00A	TH28 8:30A		
F29 7:00A		F29 9:00P	F29 10:30P		
S30 9:00P	SU31 8:00A	SU31 9:30A			

JUNE EASTBOUND

LEAVE SELDOVIA	LEAVE HOMER	LEAVE PORT LIONS	ARRIVE KODIAK	LEAVE SEWARD	ARRIVE VALDEZ
M1 11:30P	T2 3:00A	T2 1:00P	T2 3:15P		
W3 11:00A	W3 3:00P	Lv.	TH4 6:15A	Ar. TH4 7:45P	
*** FROM CHAIN TRIP #3 ***			W10 3:30P		
	TH11 7:00A	TH11 5:00P	TH11 7:00P		
F12 4:00P	F12 8:30P		S13 8:30A		
SU14 5:00A	SU14 8:30A		SU14 8:30P		
M15 4:45P	M15 8:30P	T16 6:30A	T16 8:45A		
	W17 1:00A	Lv.	W17 3:00P	TH18 10:00A	TH18 9:00P
SU21 5:30A	SU21 8:30A		SU21 8:30P		
	M22 1:30P	M22 11:30P	T23 1:30A		
T23 8:00P	T23 11:00P	Lv.	W24 3:00P	TH25 10:00A	TH25 9:00P
SU28 5:30A	SU28 8:30A		SU28 8:30P		
	M29 1:30P	M29 11:30P	T30 1:30A		
T30 8:00P	T30 11:00P		W1 11:00A		

JUNE WESTBOUND

LEAVE VALDEZ	LEAVE SEWARD	LEAVE KODIAK	LEAVE PORT LIONS	LEAVE HOMER	ARRIVE SELDOVIA
	M1 6:30A			M1 8:00P	M1 9:30P
	T2 6:30P			W3 8:00A	W3 9:30A
F5 3:30A	F5 8:00P	*** TO CHAIN TRIP #3 ***			
	W10 5:30P	Ar.	TH11 5:30A		
	TH11 10:00P			F12 12:30P	F12 2:00P
	S13 11:30A	S13 2:00P	SU14 1:45A	SU14 3:15A	
	SU14 11:30P		M15 1:30P	M15 3:00P	
	T16 11:45A	Ar.	T16 11:45P		
F19 7:00A	F19 8:00P	S20 12:30P	S20 3:00P	SU21 2:30A	SU21 4:00A
	SU21 11:30P	Ar.	M22 11:30A		
	T23 3:30A			T23 5:00P	T23 6:30P
F26 7:00A	F26 8:00P	S27 12:30P	S27 3:00P	SU28 2:30A	SU28 4:00A
	SU28 11:30P	Ar.	M29 11:30A		
	T30 3:30A			T30 5:00P	T30 6:30P

JULY EASTBOUND

LEAVE SELDOVIA	LEAVE HOMER	LEAVE PORT LIONS	ARRIVE KODIAK	LEAVE SEWARD	ARRIVE VALDEZ
TH2 9:00A	TH2 3:00P	F3 1:15A	F3 8:00A	*** TO CHAIN TRIP #4 ***	
		Lv.	W8 3:00P	TH9 10:00A	TH9 9:00P
SU12 5:30A	SU12 8:30A		SU12 8:30P		
	M13 1:30P	M13 11:30P	T14 1:30A		
T14 8:00P	T14 11:00P	Lv.	W15 3:00P	TH16 10:00A	TH16 9:00P
SU19 5:30A	SU19 8:30A		SU19 8:30P		
	M20 1:30P	M20 11:30P	T21 1:30A		
T21 8:00P	T21 11:00P	Lv.	W22 3:00P	TH23 10:00A	TH23 9:00P
SU26 5:30A	SU26 8:30A		SU26 8:30P		
	M27 1:30P	M27 11:30P	T28 1:30A		
T28 8:00P	T28 11:00P		W29 11:00A		
TH30 9:00A	TH30 3:00P	F31 1:15A	Lv. F31 8:00A	*** TO CHAIN TRIP #4 ***	

JULY WESTBOUND

LEAVE VALDEZ	LEAVE SEWARD	LEAVE KODIAK	LEAVE PORT LIONS	LEAVE HOMER	ARRIVE SELDOVIA
	W1 3:00P	W1 5:30P	TH2 5:45A	TH2 7:15A	
*** FROM CHAIN TRIP #4 ***	Ar.	W8 3:30A			
		S11 12:30P	S11 3:00P	SU12 2:30A	SU12 4:00A
F10 7:00A	F10 8:00P	SU12 11:30P	Ar.	M13 11:30A	
		T14 3:30A		T14 5:00P	T14 6:30P
F17 7:00A	F17 8:00P	S18 12:30P	S18 3:00P	SU19 2:30A	SU19 4:00A
		SU19 11:30P	Ar.	M20 11:30A	
		T21 3:30A		T21 5:00P	T21 6:30P
F24 7:00A	F24 8:00P	S25 12:30P	S25 3:00P	SU26 2:30A	SU26 4:00A
		SU26 11:30P	Ar.	M27 11:30A	
		T28 3:30A		T28 5:00P	T28 6:30P
		W29 3:00P	W29 5:30P	TH30 5:45A	TH30 7:15A

AUGUST EASTBOUND

LEAVE SELDOVIA	LEAVE HOMER	LEAVE PORT LIONS	ARRIVE KODIAK	LEAVE SEWARD	ARRIVE VALDEZ
		Lv.	W5 3:00P	TH6 10:00A	TH6 9:00P
SU9 5:30A	SU9 8:30A		SU9 8:30P		
	M10 1:30P	M10 11:30P	T11 1:30A		
T11 8:00P	T11 11:00P	Lv.	W12 3:00P	TH13 10:00A	TH13 9:00P
SU16 5:30A	SU16 8:30A		SU16 8:30P		
	M17 1:30P	M17 11:30P	T18 1:30A		
T18 8:00P	T18 11:00P	Lv.	W19 3:00P	TH20 10:00A	TH20 9:00P
SU23 5:30A	SU23 8:30A		SU23 8:30P		
	M24 1:30P	M24 11:30P	T25 1:30A		
T25 8:00P	T25 11:00P		W26 11:00A		
TH27 9:00A	TH27 3:00P	F28 1:15A	Lv. F28 8:00A	*** TO CHAIN TRIP #4 ***	

AUGUST WESTBOUND

LEAVE VALDEZ	LEAVE SEWARD	LEAVE KODIAK	LEAVE PORT LIONS	LEAVE HOMER	ARRIVE SELDOVIA
*** FROM CHAIN TRIP #4 ***	Ar.	W5 3:30A			
F7 7:00A	F7 8:00P	S8 12:30P	S8 3:00P	SU9 2:30A	SU9 4:00A
		SU9 11:30P	Ar.	M10 11:30A	
		T11 3:30A		T11 5:00P	T11 6:30P
F14 7:00A	F14 8:00P	S15 12:30P	S15 3:00P	SU16 2:30A	SU16 4:00A
		SU16 11:30P	Ar.	M17 11:30A	
		T18 3:30A		T18 5:00P	T18 6:30P
F21 7:00A	F21 8:00P	S22 12:30P	S22 3:00P	SU23 2:30A	SU23 4:00A
		SU23 11:30P	Ar.	M24 11:30A	
		T25 3:30A		T25 5:00P	T25 6:30P
		W26 3:00P	W26 5:30P	TH27 5:45A	TH27 7:15A
*** FROM CHAIN TRIP #4 ***	Ar.	W2 3:30A			

SEPTEMBER EASTBOUND

LEAVE SELDOVIA	LEAVE HOMER	LEAVE PORT LIONS	ARRIVE KODIAK	LEAVE SEWARD	ARRIVE VALDEZ
		Lv.	W2 3:00P	TH3 10:00A	TH3 9:00P
SU6 5:30A	SU6 8:30A		SU6 8:30P		
	M7 1:30P	M7 11:30P	T8 1:30A		
T8 8:00P	T8 11:00P		W9 11:00A		
TH10 9:00A	TH10 3:00P	F11 1:15A	Lv. F11 8:00A	*** TO CHAIN TRIP #4 ***	
		Lv.	W16 3:00P	TH17 10:00A	TH17 9:00P

SEPTEMBER WESTBOUND

LEAVE VALDEZ	LEAVE SEWARD	LEAVE KODIAK	LEAVE PORT LIONS	LEAVE HOMER	ARRIVE SELDOVIA
*** FROM CHAIN TRIP #4 ***	Ar.	W2 3:30A			
F4 7:00A	F4 8:00P	S5 12:30P	S5 3:00P	SU6 2:30A	SU6 4:00A
		SU6 11:30P	Ar.	M7 11:30A	
		T8 3:30A		T8 5:00P	T8 6:30P
		W9 3:00P	W9 5:30P	TH10 5:45A	TH10 7:15A
*** FROM CHAIN TRIP #4 ***	Ar.	W16 3:30A			

SEP 17 - SEP 30

THU	SEP 17	LV VALDEZ	10:00PM	MON	SEP 21	LV SEWARD	6:30AM		
		AR CORDOVA	3:45AM			LV KODIAK	10:15PM		
				TUE	SEP 22	LV PORT LIONS	1:00AM		
FRI	SEP 18	LV CORDOVA	3:00PM			LV HOMER	12:45PM		
		AR VALDEZ	8:45PM			AR SELDOVIA	2:15PM		
SAT	SEP 19	LV VALDEZ	8:30AM	TUE	SEP 22	LV SELDOVIA	3:45PM		
		AR CORDOVA	2:15PM			LV HOMER	7:15PM		
				WED	SEP 23	LV PORT LIONS	5:30AM		
SAT	SEP 19	LV CORDOVA	10:00PM			LV KODIAK	10:30AM		
SUN	SEP 20	LV VALDEZ	8:00AM			AR SEWARD	11:45PM		
		AR SEWARD	7:00PM						
THU	SEP 24	LV SEWARD	8:00AM	MON	SEP 28	LV SEWARD	6:30AM
FRI	SEP 25	LV CORDOVA	9:15PM			LV KODIAK	10:15PM
		AR VALDEZ	3:00AM	TUE	SEP 29	LV PORT LIONS	1:00AM
FRI	SEP 25	LV VALDEZ	5:00AM			LV HOMER	12:45PM
		AR CORDOVA	10:45AM			AR SELDOVIA	2:15PM
FRI	SEP 25	LV KODIAK	10:15PM	TUE	SEP 29	LV SELDOVIA	3:45PM
SAT	SEP 26	AR VALDEZ	4:00AM			LV HOMER	7:15PM
				WED	SEP 30	LV PORT LIONS	5:30AM
SAT	SEP 26	LV VALDEZ	10:00PM			LV KODIAK	10:30AM
SUN	SEP 27	LV CORDOVA	8:00AM			AR SEWARD	11:45PM
		AR SEWARD	7:00PM				

MARINE ACCESS ROUTES

Southwest Alaska Passenger and Vehicle Tariffs

Effective May 1, 1992–September 30, 1992

ITEM ADT: PASSENGER 12 YEARS AND OVER (Meals and Berths NOT included)

BETWEEN / AND	DUTCH HARBOR	COLD BAY	KING COVE	SAND POINT	CHIGNIK	KODIAK	PORT LIONS	SELDOVIA	HOMER	SEWARD	WHITTIER	VALDEZ
COLD BAY	60											
KING COVE	72	16										
SAND POINT	96	40	30									
CHIGNIK	130	74	64	40								
KODIAK	200	144	134	110	74							
PORT LIONS	200	144	134	110	74	18						
SELDOVIA	244	190	178	154	120	50	50					
HOMER	240	186	174	150	116	46	46	16				
SEWARD	248	192	182	158	122	52	52	98	94			
WHITTIER	314	258	248	224	188	118	118	164	160	72		
VALDEZ	290	236	224	200	166	96	96	140	136	56	56	
CORDOVA	290	236	224	200	166	96	96	140	136	56	*56	28

* CORDOVA/WHITTIER DIRECT = $34 (NOT VIA GLACIER or VALDEZ)

ITEM CHD: CHILDREN 6 THROUGH 11 YEARS OLD (Under 6 Transported Free)

BETWEEN / AND	DUTCH HARBOR	COLD BAY	KING COVE	SAND POINT	CHIGNIK	KODIAK	PORT LIONS	SELDOVIA	HOMER	SEWARD	WHITTIER	VALDEZ
COLD BAY	30											
KING COVE	36	8										
SAND POINT	48	20	16									
CHIGNIK	114	38	32	20								
KODIAK	100	72	68	56	38							
PORT LIONS	100	72	68	56	38	10						
SELDOVIA	122	96	90	78	60	26	26					
HOMER	120	94	88	76	58	24	24	8				
SEWARD	124	96	92	80	62	26	26	50	48			
WHITTIER	156	130	124	112	94	60	60	82	80	36		
VALDEZ	146	118	112	100	83	48	48	70	68	28	28	
CORDOVA	146	118	112	100	83	48	48	70	68	28	*28	14

* CORDOVA/WHITTIER DIRECT = $18 (NOT VIA GLACIER or VALDEZ)

ITEM AMC: ALTERNATE MEANS OF CONVEYANCE(Bicycles-Kyaks-Inflatables)

BETWEEN / AND	DUTCH HARBOR	COLD BAY	KING COVE	SAND POINT	CHIGNIK	KODIAK	PORT LIONS	SELDOVIA	HOMER	SEWARD	WHITTIER	VALDEZ
COLD BAY	12											
KING COVE	14	6										
SAND POINT	18	9	8									
CHIGNIK	23	15	13	9								
KODIAK	33	25	23	20	15							
PORT LIONS	33	25	23	20	15	6						
SELDOVIA	40	32	30	26	21	11	11					
HOMER	39	31	29	26	21	10	10	5				
SEWARD	40	32	30	27	22	11	11	18	17			
WHITTIER	50	42	40	37	31	21	21	28	27	14		
VALDEZ	47	38	37	33	28	18	18	24	24	10	8	
CORDOVA	47	38	37	33	28	18	18	24	24	10	*8	8

* CORDOVA/WHITTIER DIRECT = $8 (NOT VIA GLACIER or VALDEZ)

ITEM 710: VEHICLES UP TO 10 FEET (Driver NOT included)

BETWEEN / AND	DUTCH HARBOR	COLD BAY	KING COVE	SAND POINT	CHIGNIK	KODIAK	PORT LIONS	SELDOVIA	HOMER	SEWARD	WHITTIER	VALDEZ
COLD BAY	67											
KING COVE	79	18										
SAND POINT	106	45	33									
CHIGNIK	145	84	72	45								
KODIAK	223	162	150	123	84							
PORT LIONS	223	162	150	123	84	20						
SELDOVIA	273	211	199	172	133	55	55					
HOMER	268	207	195	168	129	51	51	15				
SEWARD	276	214	202	175	136	58	58	109	105			
WHITTIER	349	288	276	249	210	132	132	183	178	79		
VALDEZ	324	262	250	223	184	106	106	157	153	52	38	
CORDOVA	324	262	250	223	184	106	106	157	153	52	*38	31

* CORDOVA/WHITTIER DIRECT = $34 (NOT VIA GLACIER or VALDEZ)

ITEM 715: VEHICLES UP TO 15 FEET (Driver NOT included)

BETWEEN / AND	DUTCH HARBOR	COLD BAY	KING COVE	SAND POINT	CHIGNIK	KODIAK	PORT LIONS	SELDOVIA	HOMER	SEWARD	WHITTIER	VALDEZ
COLD BAY	142											
KING COVE	168	34										
SAND POINT	226	93	67									
CHIGNIK	311	177	151	93								
KODIAK	480	346	320	262	177							
PORT LIONS	480	346	320	262	177	39						
SELDOVIA	587	454	428	369	285	116	116					
HOMER	577	444	418	359	275	106	106	29				
SEWARD	593	460	434	376	291	122	122	233	223			
WHITTIER	753	619	593	535	450	281	281	392	382	168		
VALDEZ	697	564	538	480	395	226	226	337	327	109	70	
CORDOVA	697	564	538	480	395	226	226	337	327	109	*70	64

* CORDOVA/WHITTIER DIRECT = $66 (NOT VIA GLACIER or VALDEZ)

ITEM 719: VEHICLES UP TO 19 FEET (Driver NOT included)

BETWEEN / AND	DUTCH HARBOR	COLD BAY	KING COVE	SAND POINT	CHIGNIK	KODIAK	PORT LIONS	SELDOVIA	HOMER	SEWARD	WHITTIER	VALDEZ
COLD BAY	169											
KING COVE	200	41										
SAND POINT	269	110	80									
CHIGNIK	370	211	180	110								
KODIAK	571	412	381	312	211							
PORT LIONS	571	412	381	312	211	46						
SELDOVIA	699	540	509	439	339	138	138					
HOMER	687	528	497	428	327	126	126	35				
SEWARD	706	548	517	447	347	145	145	277	265			
WHITTIER	896	737	706	637	536	335	335	467	455	200		
VALDEZ	830	672	641	571	470	269	269	401	389	130	83	
CORDOVA	830	672	641	571	470	269	269	401	389	130	*83	76

* CORDOVA/WHITTIER DIRECT = $78 (NOT VIA GLACIER or VALDEZ)

ITEM 721: VEHICLES UP TO 21 FEET (Driver NOT included)

BETWEEN / AND	DUTCH HARBOR	COLD BAY	KING COVE	SAND POINT	CHIGNIK	KODIAK	PORT LIONS	SELDOVIA	HOMER	SEWARD	WHITTIER	VALDEZ
COLD BAY	217											
KING COVE	257	52										
SAND POINT	347	142	102									
CHIGNIK	477	272	232	142								
KODIAK	737	532	492	402	272							
PORT LIONS	737	532	492	402	272	59						
SELDOVIA	902	697	657	567	437	177	177					
HOMER	887	682	642	552	422	162	162	44				
SEWARD	912	707	667	577	447	187	187	357	342			
WHITTIER	1157	952	912	822	692	432	432	602	587	257		
VALDEZ	1072	867	827	737	607	347	347	517	502	167	107	
CORDOVA	1072	867	827	737	607	347	347	517	502	167	*107	97

* CORDOVA/WHITTIER DIRECT = $90 (NOT VIA GLACIER or VALDEZ)

ITEM 723: VEHICLES UP TO 23 FEET (Driver NOT included)

BETWEEN / AND	DUTCH HARBOR	COLD BAY	KING COVE	SAND POINT	CHIGNIK	KODIAK	PORT LIONS	SELDOVIA	HOMER	SEWARD	WHITTIER	VALDEZ
COLD BAY	252											
KING COVE	298	60										
SAND POINT	402	165	118									
CHIGNIK	553	315	269	165								
KODIAK	855	617	571	466	315							
PORT LIONS	855	617	571	466	315	68						
SELDOVIA	1046	808	762	658	507	205	205					
HOMER	1029	791	745	640	489	188	188	51				
SEWARD	1058	820	774	669	518	217	217	414	397			
WHITTIER	1342	1104	1058	953	803	501	501	698	681	298		
VALDEZ	1243	1006	959	855	704	402	402	600	582	194	124	
CORDOVA	1243	1006	959	855	704	402	402	600	582	194	*124	112

* CORDOVA/WHITTIER DIRECT = $114 (NOT VIA GLACIER or VALDEZ)

ITEM 725: VEHICLES UP TO 25 FEET (Driver NOT included)

BETWEEN / AND	DUTCH HARBOR	COLD BAY	KING COVE	SAND POINT	CHIGNIK	KODIAK	PORT LIONS	SELDOVIA	HOMER	SEWARD	WHITTIER	VALDEZ
COLD BAY	299											
KING COVE	354	71										
SAND POINT	478	195	140									
CHIGNIK	658	375	320	195								
KODIAK	1016	734	678	554	375							
PORT LIONS	1016	734	678	554	375	81						
SELDOVIA	1244	961	906	782	602	244	244					
HOMER	1223	941	885	761	582	223	223	60				
SEWARD	1258	975	920	796	616	257	257	492	471			
WHITTIER	1596	1313	1258	1134	954	596	596	830	809	354		
VALDEZ	1479	1196	1141	1016	837	478	478	713	692	230	147	
CORDOVA	1479	1196	1141	1016	837	478	478	713	692	230	*147	133

* CORDOVA/WHITTIER DIRECT = $136 (NOT VIA GLACIER or VALDEZ)

ITEM 728: VEHICLES UP TO 28 FEET (Driver NOT included)

BETWEEN / AND	DUTCH HARBOR	COLD BAY	KING COVE	SAND POINT	CHIGNIK	KODIAK	PORT LIONS	SELDOVIA	HOMER	SEWARD	WHITTIER	VALDEZ
COLD BAY	354											
KING COVE	420	84										
SAND POINT	568	231	166									
CHIGNIK	781	445	379	231								
KODIAK	1207	871	805	658	445							
PORT LIONS	1207	871	805	658	445	95						
SELDOVIA	1478	1142	1076	928	715	289	289					
HOMER	1453	1117	1051	904	691	264	264	71				
SEWARD	1494	1158	1092	945	732	305	305	584	559			
WHITTIER	1896	1560	1494	1347	1133	707	707	986	961	420		
VALDEZ	1757	1420	1355	1207	994	568	568	846	822	272	174	
CORDOVA	1757	1420	1355	1207	994	568	568	846	822	272	*174	158

* CORDOVA/WHITTIER DIRECT = $160 (NOT VIA GLACIER or VALDEZ)

ITEM 731: VEHICLES UP TO 31 FEET (Driver NOT included)

BETWEEN / AND	DUTCH HARBOR	COLD BAY	KING COVE	SAND POINT	CHIGNIK	KODIAK	PORT LIONS	SELDOVIA	HOMER	SEWARD	WHITTIER	VALDEZ
COLD BAY	398											
KING COVE	472	95										
SAND POINT	638	260	187									
CHIGNIK	877	500	426	260								
KODIAK	1355	978	904	739	500							
PORT LIONS	1355	978	904	739	500	108						
SELDOVIA	1659	1282	1208	1042	803	325	325					
HOMER	1631	1254	1180	1015	776	297	297	80				
SEWARD	1677	1300	1226	1061	822	343	343	656	628			
WHITTIER	2128	1751	1677	1512	1272	794	794	1107	1079	472		
VALDEZ	1972	1594	1521	1355	1116	638	638	950	923	306	196	
CORDOVA	1972	1594	1521	1355	1116	638	638	950	923	306	*196	178

* CORDOVA/WHITTIER DIRECT = $182 (NOT VIA GLACIER or VALDEZ)

ITEM 736: VEHICLES UP TO 36 FEET (Driver NOT included)

BETWEEN / AND	DUTCH HARBOR	COLD BAY	KING COVE	SAND POINT	CHIGNIK	KODIAK	PORT LIONS	SELDOVIA	HOMER	SEWARD	WHITTIER	VALDEZ
COLD BAY	472											
KING COVE	559	112										
SAND POINT	755	308	221									
CHIGNIK	1039	592	505	308								
KODIAK	1605	1159	1071	875	592							
PORT LIONS	1605	1159	1071	875	592	127						
SELDOVIA	1965	1518	1431	1235	951	385	385					
HOMER	1932	1486	1398	1202	919	352	352	95				
SEWARD	1987	1540	1453	1257	973	406	406	777	744			
WHITTIER	2521	2074	1987	1791	1507	941	941	1311	1278	559		
VALDEZ	2336	1889	1802	1605	1322	755	755	1126	1093	363	232	
CORDOVA	2336	1889	1802	1605	1322	755	755	1126	1093	363	*232	210

* CORDOVA/WHITTIER DIRECT = $220 (NOT VIA GLACIER or VALDEZ)

MARINE ACCESS ROUTES

Southwest Alaska Passenger and Vehicle Tariffs (cont.)
Effective May 1, 1992–September 30, 1992

ITEM 740: VEHICLES UP TO 40 FEET (Driver NOT included)

BETWEEN AND	DUTCH HARBOR	COLD BAY	KING COVE	SAND POINT	CHIGNIK	KODIAK	PORT LIONS	SELDOVIA	HOMER	SEWARD	WHITTIER	VALDEZ
COLD BAY	540											
KING COVE	640	129										
SAND POINT	864	353	254									
CHIGNIK	1187	677	577	353								
KODIAK	1835	1324	1225	1001	677							
PORT LIONS	1835	1324	1225	1001	677	146						
SELDOVIA	2246	1735	1636	1411	1088	440	440					
HOMER	2208	1698	1598	1374	1050	403	403	109				
SEWARD	2270	1760	1660	1436	1113	465	465	889	851			
WHITTIER	2881	2370	2271	2046	1723	1075	1075	1499	1461	640		
VALDEZ	2669	2158	2059	1835	1511	864	864	1287	1250	415	266	
CORDOVA	2669	2158	2059	1835	1511	864	864	1287	1250	415	*266	241

* CORDOVA/WHITTIER DIRECT = $250 (NOT VIA GLACIER or VALDEZ)

The preceeding ports (with the exception of Whittier) are served by the M/V TUSTUMENA. The M/V TUSTUMENA can transport vehicles to a maximum length of 40 feet. The following ports also receive service from the M/V BARTLETT which can transport vehicles to 60 feet in length.

VALDEZ TO:

VEHICLE FARES (Driver Not Included)

	41'	46'	51'	56'	60'	60'+
WHITTIER	$266	304	342	378	422	660

CORDOVA TO:

VEHICLE FARES (Driver Not Included)

	41'	46'	51'	56'	60'	60'+
WHITTIER	$266	304	342	378	422	660
VALDEZ	$241	276	310	343	383	551

M/V TUSTUMENA–Cabin Rates
Effective May 1, 1992–September 30, 1992

ITEM 4BF: FOUR BERTH CABIN - OUTSIDE/COMPLETE FACILITIES

BETWEEN AND	DUTCH HARBOR	COLD BAY	KING COVE	SAND POINT	CHIGNIK	KODIAK	PORT LIONS	SELDOVIA	HOMER	SEWARD	VALDEZ
COLD BAY	109										
KING COVE	122	43									
SAND POINT	152	79	68								
CHIGNIK	194	124	113	80							
KODIAK	282	209	194	166	124						
PORT LIONS	282	209	194	166	124	43					
SELDOVIA	337	264	250	216	182	96	96				
HOMER	328	256	242	209	175	88	88	43			
SEWARD	349	276	262	228	194	98	98	163	155		
VALDEZ	(NO DIRECT SAILINGS)			164	164	216	209	91			
CORDOVA	(NO DIRECT SAILINGS)			164	164	216	209	91	59		

ITEM 4NO: FOUR BERTH CABIN - INSIDE/NO FACILITIES

COLD BAY	91										
KING COVE	102	36									
SAND POINT	127	66	57								
CHIGNIK	162	103	94	67							
KODIAK	235	174	162	138	103						
PORT LIONS	235	174	162	138	103	36					
SELDOVIA	281	220	208	180	152	80	80				
HOMER	274	213	202	174	146	73	73	36			
SEWARD	291	230	218	190	162	82	82	136	129		
VALDEZ	(NO DIRECT SAILINGS)			137	137	180	174	76			
CORDOVA	(NO DIRECT SAILINGS)			137	137	180	174	76	49		

ITEM 2NO: TWO BERTH CABIN - OUTSIDE/NO FACILITIES

COLD BAY	64										
KING COVE	75	28									
SAND POINT	100	46	40								
CHIGNIK	129	78	68	43							
KODIAK	179	141	130	110	76						
PORT LIONS	179	141	130	110	76	28					
SELDOVIA	213	175	164	140	115	56	56				
HOMER	208	170	159	136	111	52	52	28			
SEWARD	218	179	168	144	119	60	60	101	96		
VALDEZ	(NO DIRECT SAILINGS)			103	103	144	140	54			
CORDOVA	(NO DIRECT SAILINGS)			103	103	144	140	54	38		

(continued from page 543) passengers and vehicles are on board; if there is space, standbys may board. Standbys are subject to off-loading at each port of call!

If cabin space is filled, you may go deck passage. This means you'll be sleeping on lounge chairs or on the deck itself.

Fares and fare payment: See pages 540-541 for Southeast passenger and vehicle, page 542 for cabin rates; see pages 545-546 for Southwest passenger, vehicle and cabin rates. Fares are charged for passengers, vehicles and cabins on a port to port basis. If you are traveling from Ketchikan to Skagway with a stopover at Juneau, you are charged from Ketchikan to Juneau and Juneau to Skagway, with the total ticket cost being slightly higher than if you were not stopping off in Juneau.

Full payment is required as follows: if you are booking 55 or more days in advance, payment is due 30 days after the date you book the reservation; if you are booking less than 55 days prior to departure, payment is due within 10 days after the date you book the reservations; reservations booked 10 days or less prior to departure require payment at time of booking. Failure to meet this requirement may result in the cancellation of reservations. Payment may be made by mail with certified or cashier's check, or money order. Personal checks are not accepted unless written on an Alaska bank. Credit cards (VISA, MasterCard, American Express, Discover and Diners Club) are accepted at all terminals (some restrictions may apply) and by phone.

Cancellation fees are charged if a change or cancellation is made within 14 days of sailing.

Vehicle tariffs depend on the size of vehicle. You are charged by how much space you take up, so a car with trailer is measured from the front of the car to the end of the trailer, including hitch space. (In summer, drivers' fares are not included in the vehicle tariff.)

Bicycles, kayaks and inflatables are charged a surcharge. Check the Alternate Means of Conveyance charges in the tariff section.

Passenger tariffs are charged as follows: adults and children 12 and over, full fare; children 6-11, half fare; children under 6, free. Passenger fares do not include cabins or meals. Special passes and travel rates are available to senior citizens (over 65) and handicapped persons. Check with the Alaska Marine Highway or consult the official Marine Highway schedule for costs and restrictions.

Cabin rates depend on vessel, size of cabin and facilities. Only 5 vessels have cabins available.

Pick up cabin keys from the purser's office when you board. Cabins are sold as a unit, not on a per berth basis. In other words, the cost of the cabin is the same whether 1 person occupies it or 10 people share it.

All cabins on the Southeast system ferries have a toilet and shower. Linens (towels, sheets, blankets) are provided. Restrooms and shower facilities are available for deck-passage (walk-on) passengers.

Surcharges are assessed on pets ($10 to/from Bellingham, $5 to/from Prince Rupert) and unattended vehicles ($30 to/from Bellingham, $10 to/from Prince Rupert). The Marine Highway does not provide for loading and off-loading of unattended vehicles.

Check-in times: Summer check-in times for reserved vehicles prior to departure are: Bellingham and Prince Rupert, 3 hours; Ketchikan, Juneau, Haines, Skagway, Homer, Seward, Kodiak, 2 hours; Petersburg 1½ hours; all other ports, 1 hour. Call the Sitka terminal for check-in time (747-3300). Passengers without vehicles must check in 1 hour prior to departure at all ports except Bellingham, where check-in is 2 hours prior to departure. For MV *Bartlett* departures from Whittier, check-in time at the Portage train loading ramp is noon.

Local times are shown on all Alaska Marine Highway schedules: That is Alaska time for Alaska ports on the Southeast and Southwest schedules, Pacific time for Prince Rupert, BC, and Bellingham, WA, on the Southeast schedules.

Luggage: You are responsible for your own luggage! Foot passengers may bring hand luggage only (not to exceed 100 lbs.). There is no limit on luggage carried in a vehicle. Coin-operated storage lockers are available aboard most ships, and baggage carts are furnished on the car deck. Baggage handling is NOT provided by the Marine Highway. Bicycles, small boats and inflatables are not considered baggage and will be charged a fare.

Stopovers: In-port time on all vessels is only long enough to unload and load. A stopover is getting off at any port between your point of origin and final destination and taking another vessel at a later time. For travelers with vehicles and/or cabins this can be done as long as reservations to do so have been made in advance. For example, travelers with a camper may wish to go from Prince Rupert to Haines but stop over at Petersburg for 2 days before continuing to Haines. As long as reservations for Prince Rupert to Petersburg and Petersburg to Haines are made before leaving Prince Rupert there will be no problems. But you cannot change your mind once you are loaded and under way. Passenger, vehicle and cabin fares are charged on a point-to-point basis, and stopovers will increase the total ticket cost.

NOTE: Check the schedules carefully. Ferries do *NOT* stop at all ports daily, and northbound and southbound routes vary. You may have to wait 3 to 4 days for the next ferry. Also keep in mind that ferries may be late; do not schedule connections too close together.

Vehicles: Reservations are required. Any vehicle that may be driven legally on the highway is acceptable for transport on the 4 larger vessels. There are some vehicle size and weight limits on the *Bartlett* and *Tustumena*, and a load limit of 25 tons to or from Angoon and Pelican, but none which would affect a personal vehicle such as car or camper. Maximum size and weight are noted on schedules.

Motorcycles, motorscooters, bicycles and kayaks are charged.

Hazardous materials may not be transported on the ferries. Bottled gas containers must be turned off. Portable containers of fuel are permitted but must be stored with vessel personnel while en route.

The state assumes no responsibility for the loading and unloading of unattended vehicles. If you ship a vehicle on the ferry you must make your own arrangements for loading and unloading. Unaccompanied vehicles are assessed a surcharge of $30 to or from Bellingham, and $10 to or from Prince Rupert.

Meals: The cost of meals is not included in passenger, cabin or vehicle fares. During the summer season all Southeastern system ferries have cafeteria-style dining rooms plus cocktail lounges. Southwestern system ferries—the *Bartlett* and the *Tustumena*—also have cafeteria dining and bar service.

Vehicle deck restrictions: U.S. Coast Guard regulations prohibit passenger access to the vehicle deck while under way, so plan on bringing up items you will need for the voyage soon after boarding the vessel. Passengers can gain access to their vehicle by applying to the purser's desk for an escort. Regulations prohibit sleeping in your vehicle while the vessel is under way.

Pet policy: Dogs and other pets are not allowed in cabins and must be transported on the vehicle deck only—*NO EXCEPTIONS.* Animals and pets are to be transported inside a vehicle or in suitable containers furnished by the passenger. Animals and pets must be cared for by the owner. Passengers who must visit pets or animals en route should apply to the purser's office for an escort to the vehicle deck. (On long sailings the purser periodically announces "cardeck calls.") You may walk your pet at port stops. Keep in mind that some port stops are very brief and that sailing time between some ports will be as long as 36 hours (Bellingham to Ketchikan).

Dogs, cats, or larger animals are assessed a charge of $10 to or from Bellingham and $5 to or from Prince Rupert. This surcharge applies even if the animal is traveling inside the owner's vehicle.

Deck passage: Because access to the vehicle deck is not permitted and because of the limited number of cabins available, many people ride the ferries overnight without cabin accommodations. This is done by sleeping in one of the reclining lounge chairs or rolling out your sleeping bag in an empty corner or even out on deck. Public washrooms are available.

Cruise ship offers close-up of seracs in Glacier Bay. (Steve Threndyle)

Crossing the U.S.–Canada border: If any part of your trip is to, from or through Canada, you must report to customs at the port of entry. No passport is required for citizens of either country, but you will be required to furnish proof of citizenship, financial responsibility, and vehicle registration, ownership and liability coverage. Special restrictions govern firearms and animals. See Customs Requirements in the GENERAL INFORMATION section.

Information aboard state ferries: There are U.S. Forest Service interpreters on duty in summer aboard most vessels. They provide information about points of interest, lectures, audiovisual presentations and answer questions concerning the area.

ALASKA FERRY SYSTEM

Friendly, Courteous, *Service.*

All Major Credit Cards Accepted.

Information, Reservations & Ticketing For all Alaska State Ferries

1-800-382-9229
(907) 235-8449

or Write Homer Ferry Terminal, P.O. Box 166, Homer, AK 99603

SOUTHEASTERN ALASKA

(See map, page 526)

Ketchikan

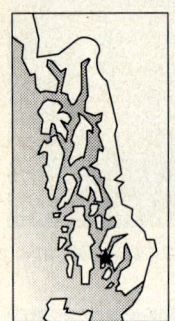

Located on Revillagigedo Island in southeastern Alaska, 235 miles/378 km south of Juneau, AK, 90 miles/145 km north of Prince Rupert, BC, and 600 miles/966 km north of Seattle, WA. **Population:** Ketchikan Gateway Borough 13,828; Ketchikan city 8,263. **Emergency Services:** Alaska State Troopers, phone 225-5118. **City Police**, phone 225-6631, or 911 for all emergency services. **Fire Department**, phone 225-9616. **Ambulance**, phone 225-9616. **Hospital**, Ketchikan General at 3100 Tongass Ave., phone 225-5171. **Ketchikan Volunteer Rescue Squad**, phone 225-9616. **Maritime Search and Rescue:** call the Coast Guard at 225-5666.

Visitor Information: Ketchikan Visitors Bureau office is located on the downtown dock, open during daily business hours and weekends May through September. Write them at 131A Front St., Ketchikan 99901; or phone 225-6166. U.S. Forest Service office for Misty Fiords National Monument is located at 3031 Tongass Ave.; open 8 A.M. to 5 P.M. weekdays; phone 225-2148.

Elevation: Sea level. **Climate:** Rainy. Yearly average rainfall is 162 inches and snowfall is 32 inches. Average daily maximum temperature in July 65°F/18°C; daily minimum 51°F/11°C. Daily maximum in January, 39°F/4°C; daily minimum 29°F/-2°C. **Radio:** KTKN 930, KRBD-FM 105.9, KGTW-FM 106.7. **Television:** CFTK (Prince Rupert, BC) and 27 cable channels. **Newspapers:** *Ketchikan Daily News* (daily); *Southeastern Log* (monthly); *New Alaskan* (monthly).

Private Aircraft: Ketchikan International Airport on Gravina Island; elev. 88 feet/27m; length 7,500 feet/2,286m; asphalt; fuel 80, 100, A. Ketchikan Harbor seaplane base downtown; fuel 80, 100. For more information call the Ketchikan Flight Service Station at 225-3531.

Ketchikan is located on the southwest side of Revillagigedo (ruh-vee-uh-guh-GAY-doh) Island, on Tongass Narrows opposite Gravina Island. The name Ketchikan is derived from a Tlingit name, Kitschk-Hin, meaning the creek of the "thundering wings of an eagle." The creek flows through the town, emptying into Tongass Narrows. Prior to Ketchikan becoming a settlement in 1887, the area at the mouth of Ketchikan Creek was a Tlingit Indian fish camp. Settlement began with interest in both mining and fishing. The first salmon cannery moved here in 1886, operating under the name of Tongass Packing Co. It burned down in August 1889. Gold was discovered nearby in 1898. This, plus residual effects of the gold, silver and copper mines, caused Ketchikan to become a booming little mining town. It was incorporated in 1901.

As mining waned, the fishing industry began to grow. By the 1930s over a dozen salmon canneries had been built and during the peak years of the canned salmon industry, Ketchikan earned the title of "Salmon Capital of the World." By the 1940s overfishing caused a drastic decline in salmon, and today only 4 canneries and a cold storage plant operate. A new industry under development is the commercial harvest of abalone near Ketchikan.

Once the redlight district, Creek Street now has art and gift shops. (John W. Warden)

As fishing reached a low point, the timber industry expanded. The first sawmill was originally built in 1898 at Dolomi on Prince of Wales Island to cut timber for the Dolomi Mine. It was dismantled and moved to Ketchikan and rebuilt in 1903. A large pulp mill was constructed in 1953 at Ward Cove, a few miles northwest of town.

Tourism is also a very important industry; Ketchikan is Alaska's first port of call for cruise ships and Alaska Marine Highway vessels.

Ketchikan is Alaska's southernmost major city and the state's fourth largest (after Anchorage, Fairbanks and Juneau). The

THE LANDING • MOTEL • RESTAURANT • LOUNGE
Best Western Independent Worldwide Lodging

◄ DIRECTLY ACROSS FROM THE FERRY TERMINAL AND AIRPORT

DELUXE ACCOMMODATIONS
All major credit cards accepted

Large spacious double-double and queen size guest rooms all with combination tub-showers, direct dial phones, color TV, exercise room, courtesy van and all amenities. Lots of free parking.

Conference room and two-bedroom suite available on request.

Most popular restaurant in all Ketchikan and beautiful view lounge, *Jeremiah's*.

Contact: **THE LANDING** • 3434 Tongass Avenue, Ketchikan, Alaska 99901
PHONE (907) 225-5166

Alaska Begins In Ketchikan!

GATEWAY TO MISTY FJORDS NAT. MONUMENT
SPORTFISHING • TOTEMS • CONVENTIONS
FLIGHTSEEING • CHARTERS • TOURS

FOR MORE INFORMATION AND BROCHURES WRITE:

Ketchikan Visitors Bureau
131A Front Street
Ketchikan, Alaska 99901

KETCHIKAN VISITORS BUREAU

Or Call:
907-225-6166

closest city in British Columbia is Prince Rupert. Ketchikan is a linear waterfront city with much of its 3-mile-/4.8-km-long business district suspended above water on pilings driven into the bottom of Tongass Narrows. It clings to the steep wooded hillside with many homes perched on cliffs and reached by long wooden staircases or narrow winding streets.

The area supports 4 public grade schools, 4 parochial grade schools, a junior high school, 2 high schools and the University of Alaska Southeast campus.

ACCOMMODATIONS

Ketchikan has 7 hotels/motels. Bed and breakfast and dorm-style accommodations are also available. There are 2 major shopping districts, 1 at each end of the city—downtown and west end.

Ketchikan AYH hostel is located at the First United Methodist Church, Grant and Main streets; write Box 8515, Ketchikan, AK 99901, phone 225-3319 (in summer). Open Memorial Day to Labor Day, the hostel has showers, sleeping pads (bring sleeping bag) and kitchen facilities. Check-in time is 6-11 P.M. Reservations not necessary. Cost is $5 per night for members (AYH membership passes may be purchased at the hostel), $8 for nonmembers.

There are 5 campgrounds (4 public campgrounds and a private resort) north of the city on North Tongass Highway and Ward Lake Road. See highway logs in this section. Dump station located at Ketchikan Public Works office, 2 blocks north of state ferry terminal. Contact the visitor bureau for location of RV parking. ▲

TRANSPORTATION

Air: Daily scheduled jet service is provided from the Ketchikan International Airport by Alaska Airlines to other Southeast cities, Anchorage and Seattle, WA. Trans Provincial has scheduled flights to Prince Rupert, BC. Commuter and charter service to other Southeast communities is available via Ketchikan Air and Taquah Air.

Airport terminal, across Tongass Narrows on Gravina Island, is reached via shuttle ferry (10-minute ride, $2.50) departing from the ferry terminal on North Tongass Avenue at half-hour intervals. Airporter service between downtown and airport is $11 to $12 (includes ferry fare). Taxi service is also available for about $8 from downtown.

Ferry: Alaska Marine Highway vessels connect Ketchikan with all mainline southeastern Alaska port cities, Prince Rupert, BC,

KETCHIKAN ADVERTISERS

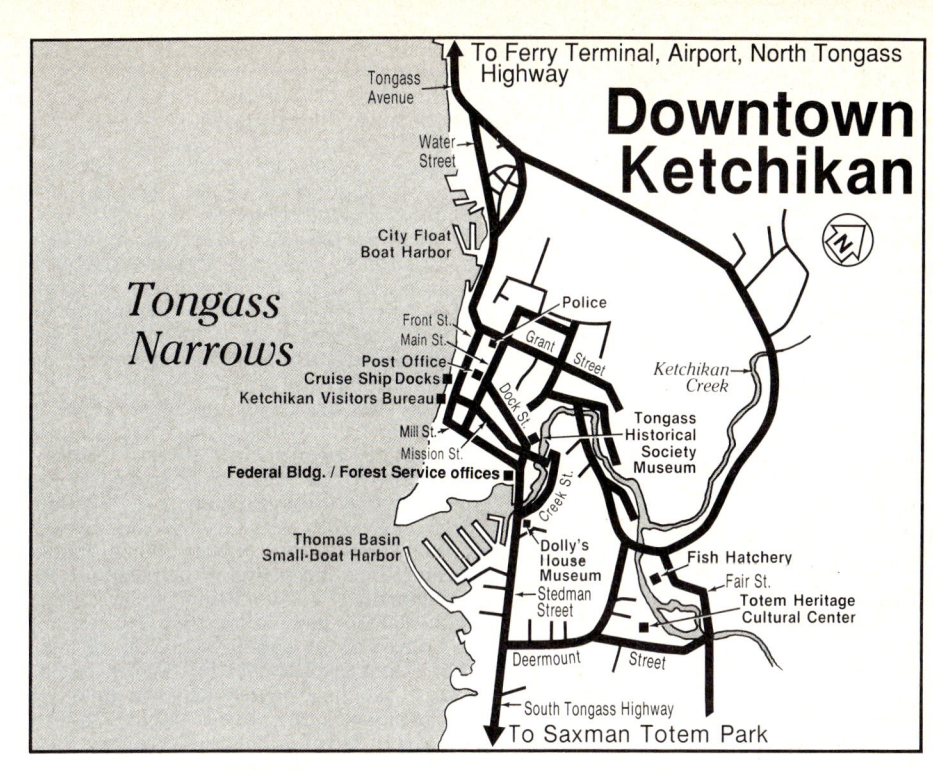

Alaska Fishing Adventures	326 Front St.
Authentic Alaska Craft	318 Dock St.
Dolly's House	No. 24 Creek St.
Grandeli's	Plaza Shopping Center
Ingersoll Hotel, The	303 Mission St.
Ketchikan Visitors Bureau	131A Front St.
Landing, The	3434 North Tongass Hwy.
Newtown Liquors	Plaza Shopping Center
Outdoor Alaska	Ph. (907) 225-6044
Plaza, The	214 Plaza Port W.
Plaza Sports	Plaza Shopping Center
Race Avenue Drug	Tongass Ave.
Salmon Busters Fishing	Ph. (907) 225-2731
Sea Mart Supermarket	2417 Tongass Ave.
Super 8 Motel	Ph. 1-800-800-8000
Trading Post Inc.	201 Main St.

Downtown Ketchikan

[Map of Downtown Ketchikan showing Tongass Narrows, Water Street, City Float Boat Harbor, Front St., Main St., Police, Post Office, Cruise Ship Docks, Ketchikan Visitors Bureau, Grant Street, Dock St., Mill St., Mission St., Federal Bldg./Forest Service offices, Creek St., Ketchikan Creek, Tongass Historical Society Museum, Thomas Basin Small-Boat Harbor, Dolly's House Museum, Stedman Street, Fish Hatchery, Fair St., Totem Heritage Cultural Center, Deermount Street, South Tongass Highway, To Saxman Totem Park, To Ferry Terminal, Airport, North Tongass Highway]

Beautiful Mornings Begin At 8.

SUPER 8 MOTEL

Toll-Free Reservations:
1-800-800-8000

Four Convenient Alaska Locations

KETCHIKAN

Anchorage • Fairbanks • Juneau

Serve Grandeli's For Rave Reviews!
• Meat • Cheese • Catering
• Sandwiches • Pizza • Ice Cream

✕ Newtown Liquor IN THE PLAZA

Ketchikan's Most Convenient Liquor Store

Open 8-midnight daily • 10-10 Sunday
IN THE PLAZA SHOPPING CENTER

PLAZA SPORTS
• Hunting and Fishing Licenses • Fishing Tackle
• Camping Supplies • Guns and Ammo • Rain Gear

IN THE PLAZA SHOPPING CENTER
2417 Tongass Ave. (907) 225-1587

THE INGERSOLL HOTEL

GRACIOUS ALASKAN HOSPITALITY

303 Mission Street, Ketchikan, AK 99901
(907) 225-2124
In State 1-800-478-2124
Or Contact Your Travel Agent

• Courtesy Transportation

• Complimentary Continental Breakfast Each Morning

• Located In The Heart of Historic Downtown Ketchikan, Directly Across From The Visitor Center

• Fishing Packages Available

and Bellingham, WA. There are also state ferry connections from Ketchikan to Metlakatla on Annette Island; to Hollis on Prince of Wales Island; and once-weekly service to Hyder in summer. See MARINE ACCESS ROUTES section for schedules.

Terminal building with waiting room, ticket counter and loading area is on North Tongass Avenue (Highway), 2 miles north of downtown. Phone 225-6181. Foot passengers can walk from the ferry to a post office, restaurant and grocery store if stopover time permits. Taxi service available.

Rental Cars: Available at airport and downtown locations.

Taxi: Available at ferry terminal and airport.

Highways: North Tongass, South Tongass, Ward Lake Road and Harriet Hunt Lake Road. See logs this section.

Cruise Ships: Ketchikan is the first port of call for many cruise ships to Alaska. Cruises depart from U.S. West Coast ports and Vancouver, BC. Two cruise lines depart from Ketchikan.

Private Boats: Two public docks downtown, Thomas Basin and City Float, provide transient moorage. In the West End District, 1 mile from downtown, Bar Harbor has moorage, showers. No gas available. Permits required.

ATTRACTIONS

Ketchikan's waterfront is the center of the city. A narrow city on a mountainside, Ketchikan's waterfront runs for several miles and consists of docks, stores on pilings, seaplane floats, 3 picturesque boat harbors, a seaplane base and ferry terminals. There is constant activity here as seaplanes take off and vessels move in and out of the harbor. Walking tour maps are available at the visitors bureau and at the ferry terminal.

The Plaza. Southeast Alaska's premier shopping center. Thirty fine merchants on 2 comfort-controlled levels feature a variety of retail shops and services for complete one-stop shopping. Plenty of free parking. Less than a mile south of the ferry terminal. Open every day. [ADVERTISEMENT]

Fish Pirate's Daughter, a well-done local musical-comedy melodrama, portrays Ketchikan's early fishing days, with some of the city's spicier history added. Performed 7 P.M. and 8:45 P.M. Fridays during July and August. Contact First City Players, 338 Main St., phone 225-4792 or 225-2211, for more information. Admission fee.

Tongass Historical Museum, in the Centennial Bldg., on Dock Street on Ketchikan Creek in central downtown area, featuring the only history of the timber industry in the state, including a re-created camp bunkhouse; a history of the commercial fishing industry; and an exhibit of Native life before the arrival of outsiders. Open in summer from 8:30 A.M. to 5 P.M. Monday through Saturday; and 1-5 P.M. Sunday. Winter (Oct. to mid-May) hours are 1-5 P.M. Wednesday through Friday, 1-4 P.M. Saturday and Sunday. The Raven Stealing the Sun totem stands just outside the entrance. Salmon viewing platforms. Admission fee is $1 for adults; free admission Sundays. Phone 225-5600 for more information.

Chief Kyan Totem at the top of Main Street is a favorite spot for visitors. Legend says that those who touch this pole will have money in their hands within 24 hours.

Creek Street is Ketchikan's famous "red-light district," where Black Mary, Dolly, Frenchie and others plied their trade for over half a century until 1954. Nearly 20 houses lined the far side of Ketchikan Creek; some have been restored. There are also several art and gift shops. Dolly's House, a former brothel, is open during the summer. Admission charged. Creek Street is a wooden street on pilings that begins just past the bridge on Stedman (South Tongass Highway). Watch for salmon in the creek below the bridge from July to September.

Totem Heritage Center, at 601 Deermount St., houses 33 totem poles and fragments retrieved from deserted Tlingit and Haida Indian villages. This national landmark collection comprises the largest exhibit of original totems in the U.S. Facilities include craft exhibits, craft shops for local artists and reference library. Gift shop, crafts

demonstrations, videos and guided tours during summer months. Summer admission fee $2. No admission charged off-season. Summer hours are 8 A.M. to 5 P.M. Monday through Saturday, 9 A.M. to 5 P.M. Sunday. Winter hours are 1-5 P.M. Tuesday through Friday and 6-9 P.M. Tuesday.

Deer Mountain Hatchery is located in the city park within walking distance of downtown (take the bridge across Ketchikan Creek from the Totem Heritage Center). The hatchery produces about 360,000 king and 360,000 coho fingerlings annually. Observation platforms and information signs provide education on the life cycles of salmon. Open from 8 A.M. to 4:30 P.M. 7 days a week during summer.

The Ketchikan Mural on Stedman Street was created by 21 Native artists in 1978. The 125-by-18-foot/38-by-4-m design is collectively entitled *The Return of the Eagle*.

Fourth of July is a major celebration in Ketchikan. The Timber Carnival takes place over the Fourth of July with events such as ax throwing and chopping, power saw bucking and a tug-of-war. There are also fireworks, the Calamity Race (by canoe or kayak, bicycle and on foot), a parade and other events.

The Blueberry Arts Festival, held the second Saturday in August, features arts and crafts, the performing arts and plenty of homemade blueberry pies, blueberry crêpes, blueberry cheesecakes and other culinary delights. Sponsored and coordinated by the Ketchikan Area Arts and Humanities Council, Inc. (338 Main St., Ketchikan 99901; 225-2211), a juried art show, fun run and dance are also part of the festival.

AREA FISHING: Check with the Alaska Dept. of Fish and Game at 2030 Sea Level Dr., Suite 207, or phone 225-2859 for details on fishing in the Ketchikan area. Good fishing spots range from Mountain Point, a 5-mile/8-km drive from Ketchikan on South Tongass Highway, to lakes, bays and inlets 50 miles/80 km away by boat or by air. Half-day and longer charters available out of Ketchikan. There are fishing resorts at George Inlet, Yes Bay, Clover Pass and at the entrance to Behm Canal (Salmon Falls Resort); and 8 fishing resorts on Prince of Wales Island. Fish include salmon, halibut, steelhead, Dolly Varden, cutthroat and rain-

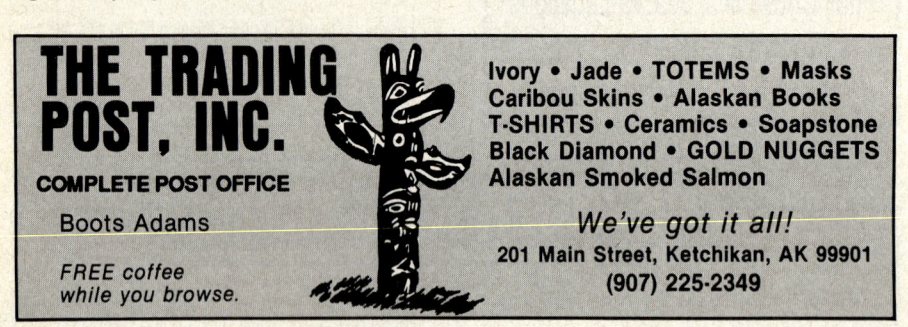

THE TRADING POST, INC.
COMPLETE POST OFFICE
Boots Adams
FREE coffee while you browse.

Ivory • Jade • TOTEMS • Masks
Caribou Skins • Alaskan Books
T-SHIRTS • Ceramics • Soapstone
Black Diamond • GOLD NUGGETS
Alaskan Smoked Salmon

We've got it all!
201 Main Street, Ketchikan, AK 99901
(907) 225-2349

MISTY FJORDS
NATIONAL MONUMENT CRUISES
50' MV *Misty Fjord* Licensed
32 Passengers • Kayak drop, pick-up
Dale Pihlman
Box 7814-MP
Ketchikan, AK 99901
(907) 225-6044
OUTDOOR ALASKA

Sea Mart supermarket
2417 TONGASS AVE.
"Surrounded by Ketchikan's only Shopping Mall"
WE TAKE PRIDE IN SERVING YOU!
✓ USDA Choice Meat ✓ Farm Fresh Produce
✓ Salad Bar ✓ Alaskan Seafood & Gift Pack Items
✓ Children's Play Area for Your Shopping Pleasure
ADJACENT TO KETCHIKAN'S RV PARK

TOURISTS - LOGGERS - CAMPERS
RACE AVENUE DRUG
Open 7 Days a Week
Sub Post Office
Toys • Gifts • Souvenirs
Alaskan Jewelry
**2300 Tongass
225-4151**
Open 9-7 Mon.-Fri.—9-6 Sat.—12-5 Sun.

bow, lingcod and rockfish. Ketchikan has 2 king salmon derbies, a silver salmon derby and a halibut derby in summer.

Saxman Totem Park, at **Milepost 2.5** South Tongass Highway, is included in local sightseeing tours. Open year-round. There is no admission charge, but there is a fee for guided tours. The totem park has 26 totems. The tour includes demonstrations at the Carving Center and performances by the Cape Fox Dancers at the Beaver Tribal House. Guided tours are given from May to September. For more information on hours, tours and events phone the Saxman Visitor Center at 225-8687 or 225-2853.

Totem Bight community house and totem park, **Milepost 9.9** North Tongass Highway, contain an excellent model of a Tlingit community house and a park with 13 totems. Situated on a point overlooking Tongass Narrows, it is reached by a short trail through the forest from parking area. Admission charged.

Misty Fiords National Monument, 30 miles/48.3 km east of Ketchikan, is accessible by boat or floatplane. This 2.2-million-acre wilderness has abundant fishing opportunities and is the home of brown and black bears, mountain goat, wolves, moose and numerous waterfowl and eagles. Whales and porpoises often can be seen in Behm Canal. USFS cabins, mostly on freshwater lakes, are available for rent. Tours to the monument are available via excursion boat or floatplane from Ketchikan. More information is available from the Forest Service and the Ketchikan Visitor Bureau.

Charter boats: About 40 yachts operate out of Ketchikan for half-day, all-day or overnight sightseeing or fishing trips, transport to USFS public-use cabins and outlying communities. See advertisements this section and check with the visitor bureau or at the marinas.

Salmon Busters Fishing. One- or 2-person custom salmon and halibut fishing trips. I furnish poles, bait, tackle, and have extra rain gear. 28 years experience. Write: Salmon Busters, 3222 Tide Ave. S., Ketchikan, AK 99901; phone (907) 225-2731. [ADVERTISEMENT]

Fishing resorts in the area are top quality. There are several, the most distant is an hour by floatplane. One resort is located at an old fish cannery which has been renovated.

Charter planes operate from the airport and from the waterfront on floats and are available for fly-in fishing, flightseeing or service to lodges and smaller communities.

Picnic areas include Settlers Cove by Settlers Cove Campground, **Milepost 18.2** North Tongass Highway; Refuge Cove, **Milepost 8.7** North Tongass Highway; Rotary Beach at **Milepost 3.5** South Tongass Highway; and Grassy Point and Ward Lake, **Milepost 1.1** Ward Lake Road.

Hiking trails include Deer Mountain trail, which begins at the corner of Fair and Deermount streets. The 3-mile/4.8-km, 3,001-foot/915-m ascent gives trekkers an excellent vantage of downtown Ketchikan and Tongass Narrows. Good but steep trail. Access to Deer Mountain cabin, the only USFS public-use cabin accessible by trail from Ketchikan. Perseverance Lake trail, 2.4 miles/3.8 km from Ward Lake to Perseverance Lake. Talbot Lake trail, about 1.5 miles/2.4 km along north shore of Connell Lake, is in poor condition. An easy and informative 1-mile/1.6-km nature trail circles Ward Lake.

Forest Service Exhibition: Tongass Visitor Center, in the Forest Service offices on Stedman Street, offers exhibits and films on Tongass National Forest. Open 8 A.M. to 4:30 P.M., 7 days a week in summer.

USFS public-use cabins are available for $20 a night. There are 52 cabins in the Ketchikan management area of the Tongass National Forest. Most are accessible by floatplane, with some accessible by hiking or on salt water by boat. Reservations may be made at Ketchikan Ranger Station, 3031 Tongass Ave.; office hours are 8 A.M. to 5 P.M. 5 days a week. Phone 225-2148. For additional information see Cabins in the GENERAL INFORMATION section.

North Tongass Highway Log

The North Tongass Highway is 18.4 miles/29.6 km long with 15.2 miles/24.5 km paved. It begins at the corner of Mill Street and Stedman (at the Federal Bldg.) and proceeds north to Ward Lake Road, Totem Bight, Clover Pass and Settlers Cove Campground.

0 Federal Bldg. on left with area information display. Proceeding on Mill Street.

0.2 (0.3 km) Turning right onto Front Street, cruise ship dock on left where passengers disembark from major ships.

0.3 (0.5 km) Tunnel. North of this, Front Street becomes Water Street.

0.5 (0.8 km) City Float on left. Note older vessels, some dating back to the early 1900s.

0.7 (1.1 km) Highway turns left, then right, and becomes Tongass Avenue.

1.2 (1.9 km) West end shopping area begins.

1.7 (2.7 km) Bar Harbor boat basin on left.

Long and narrow, Ketchikan hugs the shore of Tongass Narrows. (Rollo Pool, staff)

ALASKA
Fishing Adventures

Complete Fishing Package
4 Days – 3 Nights All Inclusive $869

KETCHIKAN
The Salmon Capital Of The World

Excellent Accommodations at Affordable Prices

Write: Gilmore Hotel, K. Sims
326 Front St.-MP, Ketchikan, AK 99901
(907) 225-9423

Dolly's House

Antiques – History – Color

A rare opportunity to relive the colorful past of Ketchikan's Redlight District — Creek Street.

Don't Miss
Dolly's House
Museum
Admission Charged
No. 24 Creek Street
3204 S. Tongass
Ketchikan, Alaska 99901

LOCATED IN DOWNTOWN KETCHIKAN

AUTHENTIC ALASKAN CRAFT

Mail Orders & Major Credit Cards Welcome

10% OFF your purchase with this AD!

The Taylors
318 Dock St. • P.O. Box 8616
Ketchikan, AK 99901 • (907) 225-6925

1992 ■ The MILEPOST® 551

2 (3.2 km) Ketchikan General Hospital on right, Ketchikan Ranger Station and Misty Fiords National Monument on left, northbound.

2.3 (3.7 km) Ferry terminals for Alaska Marine Highway.

2.4 (3.9 km) Main branch post office.

2.6 (4.2 km) Carlanna Creek and bridge.

2.7 (4.3 km) Airport shuttle ferry.

3.2 (5.1 km) Almer Wolfe Memorial viewpoint of Tongass Narrows. 24-hour RV parking. Airport terminal is visible across the narrows on Gravina Island.

4 (6.4 km) Hillside on right is a logged area, an example of clear-cut logging method and regrowth.

4.4 (7.1 km) Alaska State Troopers and Highway Dept.

5.5 (8.8 km) Small paved viewpoint overlooking Tongass Narrows and floatplane dock.

6 (9.6 km) Ward Cove Cannery next to road. Cannery Creek and bridge.

6.8 (10.9 km) **Junction** with Ward Lake Road (see log this section).

7 (11.3 km) Ward Creek and bridge, Ketchikan sawmill.

7.3 (11.7 km) **WARD COVE**. Post office, gas station and grocery.

7.8 (12.5 km) Ketchikan Pulp Co. entrance.

8.7 (14 km) Refuge Cove state recreation site with 14 picnic sites.

9.4 (15.1 km) Mud Bight; "float houses" rest on mud at low tide and float during high tide.

9.9 (15.9 km) Totem Bight state historical park; parking area, restrooms and phones. A short trail leads through the woods to Totem Bight community house and totem park. A striking setting. Don't miss this!

10.8 (17.4 km) Grocery store and gas station.

12.9 (20.8 km) Scenic viewpoint overlooking Guard Island lighthouse built in 1903 and manned until 1969 when finally automated.

14.2 (22.9 km) Clover Pass Resort turnoff. Left, North Point Higgins Road leads 0.6 mile/1 km to turnoff to resort; food, lodging, camping.

Left, then immediately right, is Knudson Cove Road which leads 0.4 mile/0.6 km to Knudson Cove Marina with public float, boat launch and boat rentals. Road rejoins North Tongass Highway at **Milepost 14.8**. ▲

14.8 (23.8 km) Knudson Cove Marina to left 0.5 mile/0.6 km.

15.2 (24.5 km) Pavement ends.

16.6 (26.8 km) Salmon Falls Resort; private fishing lodge with restaurant and boat rentals.

18.2 (29.3 km) Settlers Cove state campground, parking area and picnic area; 9 tent spaces and 7 car and trailer pads. Camping fee $6 per night. Tables, water, pit toilets; 11 picnic units along beach to either side of campground. Parking area available for overnight. Good gravel beach for kids and boats. To right is **Lunch Creek** (pink salmon in August) and falls and trail to beach. ⊸▲

18.4 (29.6 km) Road end.

Ward Lake Road Log

An 8.3-mile/13.4-km road leading to Ward Lake Recreation Area and Harriet Hunt Road. Motorists and hikers should be aware of private property boundaries, posted by Cape Fox Corp. (CFC), and logging and trucking activities.

0 Right turn northbound from North Tongass Highway at **Milepost 6.8**.

0.1 (0.2 km) Tongass National Forest boundary.

0.4 (0.6 km) Small scenic turnout on right. Pond with lily pads surrounded by pine in muskeg.

0.7 (1.1 km) Signal Creek USFS campground on left; 24 sites with tables, water and pit toilets. Camping fee. Located among large trees on shore of Ward Lake. One end of nature trail around Ward Lake begins here and encircles lake; a 30- to 50-minute easy walk on well-graveled path. ▲

0.9 (1.4 km) Beginning of Perseverance Lake trail on right, a 2.4-mile/3.9-km boardwalk trail to **Perseverance Lake** (elev. 518 feet/158m); brook trout fishing. ⊸

1 (1.6 km) CCC (or Three C's) USFS campground entrance on right; 4 campsites, camping fee. ▲

1.1 (1.8 km) Ward Creek bridge. Grassy Point USFS picnic area. Several walk-in picnic sites with tables and shelters near road. Footbridge across Ward Creek leads to Ward Lake trail.

Ward Creek and **Ward Lake**, rainbow, cutthroat, Dolly Varden, March to June; steelhead to 16 lbs.; silver salmon to 18 lbs. and pink salmon to 5 lbs., August to October. (Hatchery-raised coho salmon and steelhead; bring head of tagged fish to ADF&G.) ⊸

1.3 (2.1 km) Ward Lake USFS picnic area; beach, parking area and picnic shelters. One end of nature trail around Ward Lake.

2.9 (4.7 km) Right, Last Chance USFS campground; 23 spaces, tables, pit toilets, water, camping fee. ▲

3 (4.8 km) Connell Lake Road, on right, a narrow gravel road extending 0.6 mile/1 km to Connell Lake Reservoir. At Mile 0.4 Connell Lake Road, a bridge passes over large pipe which carries water from the reservoir to the pulp mill at Ward Cove. Talbot Lake trail at Connell Lake.

3.3 (5.3 km) Turnout.

7.1 (11.4 km) **Junction** with Harriet Hunt Lake Road (log follows), turn left.

8.3 (13.4 km) End public road. Private logging road begins.

Harriet Hunt Lake Road Log

Harriet Hunt Lake Road leads 2.4 miles/3.9 km from **Milepost 7.1** Ward Lake Road to Harriet Hunt Lake; road is on CFC lands. Watch for logging trucks.

0 Turn left at **Milepost 7.1** Ward Lake Road.

2 (3.2 km) Turnout, alpine meadows.

2.2 (3.5 km) Left, small scenic waterfall.

2.4 (3.9 km) **Harriet Hunt Lake** Recreation Area; pit toilets. Rainbow to 20 inches, May to November. Road end and parking area. ⊸

South Tongass Highway Log

The South Tongass Highway is a 12.9-mile/20.8-km road (paved for 8.5 miles/13.7 km) leading from the corner of Mill Street and Stedman south to Saxman Totem Park and ending at the power plant.

0 Federal Bldg. on right.

0.1 (0.2 km) Ketchikan Creek and bridge. Beginning of Creek Street boardwalk on left next to bridge.

0.2 (0.3 km) Thomas Street begins on right, a boardwalk street where old-time businesses are located. Thomas Basin boat harbor.

0.5 (0.8 km) Cannery and cold storage plant.

0.9 (1.4 km) U.S Coast Guard base.

2.5 (4 km) **SAXMAN** (pop. 369) was founded in 1894 by Tlingit Indians and named after a Presbyterian missionary who served the Tlingit people. Saxman has a gas station and convenience store and is also the site of Saxman Totem Park. Developed by Cape Fox Corp., this popular attraction has the totem park, a carving center and tribal house. Guided tours available.

2.7 (4.3 km) Gas station.

3.5 (5.6 km) Rotary Beach, public recreation area, contains a shelter and table.

5 (8.1 km) Mountain Point parking area. Good salmon fishing from shore in July and August. ⊸

5.6 (9 km) Boat ramp on right.

8.2 (13.2 km) Herring Cove bridge and sawmill. Private hatchery for chum, king and coho salmon on short road to left; no tours.

8.5 (13.7 km) Pavement ends.

8.8 (14.2 km) Whitman Creek and bridge.

9 (14.5 km) Scenic turnout on right. Note different shades of green on trees across the water. Light green are cedar; medium, hemlock; and the darker are spruce. Species grow intermixed.

10.3 (16.6 km) Left, scenic waterfall.

11 (17.7 km) Scenic turnout.

11.8 (19 km) Lodge.

12.9 (20.8 km) Road end, view of power plant, an experimental sockeye salmon hatchery (no tours) and an abandoned cannery.

Metlakatla

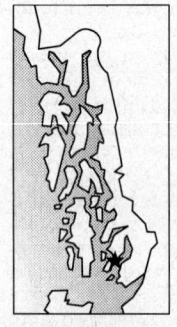

Located on the west coast of Annette Island, 15 miles/24 km south of Ketchikan, southeastern Alaska's southernmost community. **Population:** 1,386. **Emergency Services: Police, fire** and **ambulance,** emergency only phone 911. **Visitor Information:** Contact the tourism department, phone 886-1216, or the mayor's office, phone 886-4868. A permit from the Metlakatla Indian Community is required for long-term visits to Metlakatla.

Elevation: Sea level. **Climate:** Mild and moist. Summer temperatures range from 36°F/12°C to 65°F/18°C; winter temperatures from 28°F/-2°C to 44°F/7°C. Average annual precipitation is 115 inches: October is the wettest month with a maximum of 35 inches of rainfall. Annual snowfall averages 61 inches. **Radio:** KTKN (Ketchikan). **Television:** 20 channels via cable.

Transportation: Air–Charter and air

service. **Ferry**–State ferry from Ketchikan.
Private Aircraft: Floatplane services.

Overnight accommodations, restaurant, groceries and banking services available.

Metlakatla was founded in 1887 by William Duncan, a Scottish-born lay minister, who moved here with several hundred Tsimshian Indians from a settlement in British Columbia after a falling-out with church authorities. Congress granted reservation status and title to the entire island in 1891, and the new settlement prospered under Duncan, who built a salmon cannery and sawmill. Today, fishing and lumber continue to be the main economic base of Metlakatla. The community and island also retain the status of a federal Indian reservation, which is why Metlakatla has the only salmon fish traps in Alaska. (Floating fish traps were outlawed by the state shortly after statehood.)

The well-planned community has a town hall, a recreation center with an Olympic-sized swimming pool, well-maintained wood-frame homes, a post office, the mill and cannery. The Metlakatla Indian Community is the largest employer in town, with retail and service trades the second largest. Many residents also are commercial fishermen. Subsistence activities remain an important source of food for residents, who harvest seaweed, salmon, halibut, cod, clams and waterfowl.

Attractions include the Duncan Museum, the original cottage occupied by Father William Duncan until his death in 1918. A replica of the turn-of-the-century William Duncan Memorial Church, built after the original was destroyed by fire in 1948, is also open to the public.

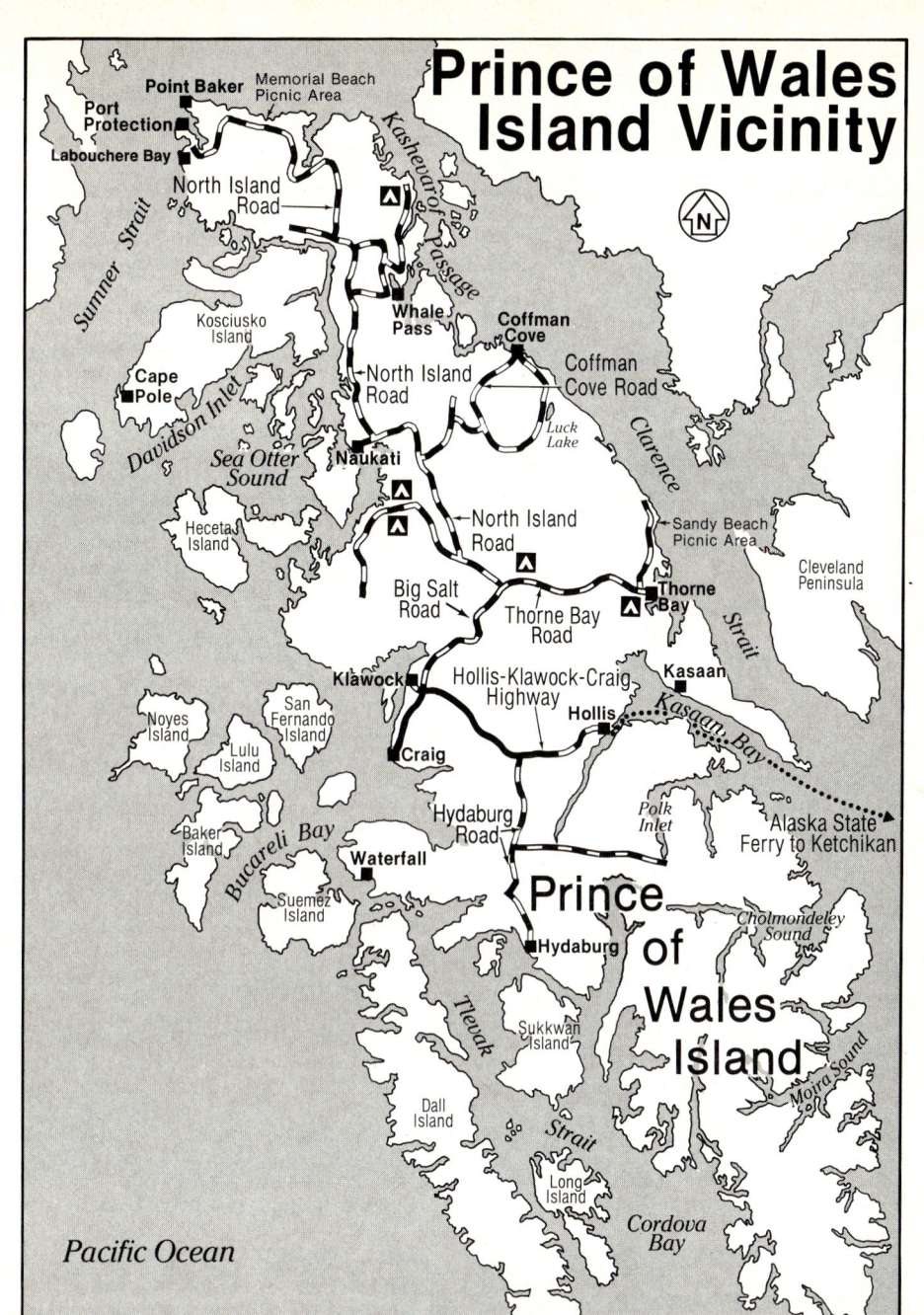

Prince of Wales Island

Includes Craig, Klawock, Hydaburg, Thorne Bay and Hollis

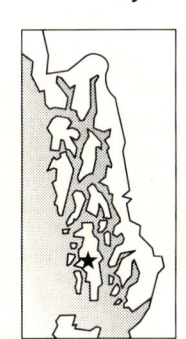

In southern southeastern Alaska, about 45 miles/72 km west of Ketchikan. **Population**: On the island, approximately 3,500. **Emergency Services: Alaska State Troopers**, in Klawock, phone 755-2918. **Police**, in Craig, phone 826-3665; **Village Public Safety Officers** in Thorne Bay, phone 828-3905; in Hydaburg, phone 285-3321. **Ambulance**, Hydaburg emergency response team, phone 285-3111. **Health Clinics**, in Craig, phone 826-3257; in Klawock, phone 755-2900; in Thorne Bay, phone 828-3906; in Hydaburg, phone 285-3462. **Maritime Search and Rescue**, call the Coast Guard at 1-800-478-5555.

Elevation: Sea level to 4,000 feet/1,219m. **Climate**: Mild and moist, but variable due to the island's size and topography. Rainfall in excess of 100 inches per year, with modest snowfall in winter at lower elevations. **Radio**: KRSA 580 (Petersburg), KTKN (Ketchikan), KRBD-FM 90.1 (Ketchikan). **Television**: Via satellite. **Newspaper**: *Island News* (Thorne Bay, weekly).

Private Aircraft: Klawock airstrip, 2 miles/3.2 km northeast; elev. 50 feet/15m; length 5,000 feet/1,524m; paved; fuel 80. Seaplane bases adjacent to all 4 communities and in several bays.

A heavily forested island with low mountains, Prince of Wales Island measures roughly 130 miles/209 km north–south by 30 miles/48 km east–west. The third largest island under the American flag (Kodiak is second, the big island of Hawaii is largest), it is 2,731 square miles/7101 square km. The 4 major communities on the island—Craig (the largest with 1,535 residents), Klawock, Thorne Bay, Hydaburg—and the smaller camps and communities of Coffman Cove, Whale Pass, Labouchere Bay and Naukati are connected by road. Among these small scattered villages not connected by road are **KASAAN**, a small Haida village at the head of Kasaan Bay, and **PORT PROTECTION** and **POINT BAKER**, both at the northwest tip of the island. (See *The ALASKA WILDERNESS MILEPOST* for details on these communities.)

Prince of Wales Island has been the site of several lumbermills and mining camps since the 1800s. But it was the salmon that led to permanent settlement on the island. Klawock was the site of one of Alaska's first canneries, built in 1878. In the following years, some 25 canneries were built on the island to process salmon. Today, logging is prevalent on the island.

Prince of Wales Island offers uncrowded backcountry, fishing for salmon and trout, good canoeing waters, good opportunities

PRINCE OF WALES ISLAND ADVERTISERS

Black Bear Quick Stop	Klawock
Fireweed Lodge	Klawock
Haida Way Lodge	Craig
Island Propane	Craig
Log Cabin R.V. Park & Resort	Klawock

1992 ■ The MILEPOST® 553

Much of Prince of Wales Island is accessible by road. (Rollo Pool, staff)

for viewing wildlife (black bear, Sitka black-tailed deer, bald eagles), adequate visitor facilities and some historical attractions. Most of the island is U.S. Forest Service land, although there are some Native corporation and private land holdings. Respect No Trespassing signs.

There is a city-run trailer park in Klawock for monthly rentals and a private campground at Mile 0.4 Big Salt Road. RV camping also is available at the Eagle's Nest Campground operated by the USFS just east of the Thorne Bay Road near Control Lake; water, chemical toilets, camping fee $5. Altogether, there are 5 USFS campsites on the island (see map this section). There are also more than 20 USFS cabins (accessible by plane, boat or on foot) available for public use; reservations and a fee are required. Contact the USFS office in Ketchikan or the local ranger districts at Craig and Thorne Bay (phone 828-3304). Also see Cabins in the GENERAL INFORMATION section.

There are several good fishing spots along the roads on Prince of Wales Island. See the road logs in this section for details. Lakes and streams support red, pink and silver salmon; cutthroat and rainbow; and Dolly Varden.

TRANSPORTATION

Air: Craig, Klawock, Thorne Bay and Hydaburg are served by floatplane; wheel planes land at Klawock. Daily scheduled service from Ketchikan.

Ferry: Alaska Marine Highway ferry operates from Ketchikan to Hollis. See MARINE ACCESS ROUTES section for rates and schedule. Van taxi service meets ferry at Hollis and offers service to Craig and Klawock.

Car rental in Klawock at Prince of Wales Lodge.

Highways: The island's main roads are the Hollis–Klawock–Craig Highway, Big Salt Road, Thorne Bay Road, Hydaburg Road, Coffman Cove Road and North Island Road (USFS Road No. 20) to Labouchere Bay. See the map and road logs in this section for details.

DRIVER CAUTION: Watch for heavily loaded logging trucks while driving, they have the right of way. Carry a spare tire and spare gas. (Gas is available in Coffman Cove, Hydaburg, Craig, Klawock, Whale Pass and Thorne Bay.) Use turnouts and approach hills and corners on your side of the road. Spur roads are *NOT* recommended for large RVs or cars with trailers. Some side roads may be closed intermittently during logging operations or highway construction. Watch for signs posted when roads are closed and expect delays.

DESCRIPTION AND ACCOMMODATIONS

COFFMAN COVE (pop. approximately 300), 53 miles/85 km north of Klawock. Coffman Cove is a family logging community, one of the largest independent camps in Southeast. Housing is in mobile homes. Recreation includes hunting (deer and bear), good fishing in area lakes and streams, boating, hiking, and also TV and VCRs.

Coffman Cove has a general store, gift shop, cafe and gas pump. There is a dock and a small beach with access to salt water for canoes and cartop boats.

CRAIG (pop. 1,535), 31 miles/50 km from Hollis, is on a small island connected to Prince of Wales Island by a short causeway. Set on a hillside facing the waterfront, it has a boat harbor, seaplane float, fuel dock and an old cannery dock. There are 2 smaller harbors on either side of the causeway. Craig has sidewalks and a paved main street.

Visitor information is available from Craig City Hall, phone 826-3275; open weekdays 8 A.M. to 5 P.M. U.S. Forest Service office, open weekdays 8 A.M. to 4:30 P.M., phone 826-3271.

Craig was once a temporary fish camp for the Tlingit and Haida people of this region. In 1907, with the help of local Haidas, Craig Millar established a saltery at Fish Egg Island. Between 1908 and 1911, a permanent saltery and cold storage facility, along with about 2 dozen homes, were built at the city's present location and the settlement was named for its founder. In 1912, the year the post office was established, E.M. Streeter opened a sawmill and Craig constructed a salmon cannery, both of which peaked during WWI. Craig was incorporated in 1922, and continued to grow throughout the 1930s, with some families from the Dust Bowl relocating to this Prince of Wales Island community. Although the salmon industry has both prospered and foundered over the years, fishing still accounts for about half of the employment in Craig today. In recent years, increased timber harvesting on the island has contributed jobs in logging and timber processing. There is also employment in government and construction.

In front of the old school gym is a totem that was found washed up on the beach then restored and painted by local people. The town has a big Fourth of July celebration and a fishing derby is held in summer.

Craig has a motel and Haida Way Lodge, a post office, 4 restaurants, 2 grocery stores, clothing store and general stores, 2 gas stations, a laundromat, 2 gift shops, 3 liquor stores, 3 bars, beauty shops, a library and 2 banks. Propane available. Towing and auto repair service available. Charter boats are also available.

HOLLIS, 25 road miles/40 km from Klawock, 35 water miles/56 km west of Ketchikan. Hollis was a mining town with a population of 1,000 from about 1900 to 1915. In the 1950s, Hollis became the site of Ketchikan Pulp Co.'s logging camp, and served as the base for timber operations on Prince of Wales Island until 1962, when the camp was moved to Thorne Bay. Recent state land sales have spurred the growth of a small residential community here. The ferry terminal and a school are located here.

HYDABURG (pop. 457), 36 miles/58 km from Hollis, 45 miles/72 km from Craig. Hydaburg was founded in 1911 and combined the populations of 3 Haida villages: Sukkwan, Howkan and Klinkwan. President

---

FIREWEED LODGE

Fishing
Hunting
Canoeing
Hiking

20 Deluxe Rooms • Excellent Meals
Fly In or Drive In • Rental Cars
Fishing Charters • Hunting
STEELHEAD • SALMON • HALIBUT • TROUT

P.O. Box 116 • Klawock, Alaska 99925
(907) 755-2930   Open Year Around

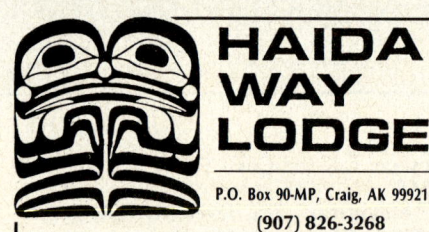

HAIDA WAY LODGE

P.O. Box 90-MP, Craig, AK 99921
(907) 826-3268

LODGE • RESTAURANT • LOUNGE
NEWLY REMODELED ROOMS
16 Units • No Smoking Rooms • Color TV
One of Prince of Wales' Newest
...Located in Downtown Craig
FISHING CHARTERS AVAILABLE

Log Cabin R.V. Park & Resort
Full Hookups on Saltwater Beach

• Cabins • Skiff & Outboards • Free Mooring
• Salmon & Halibut Charters • Fish Freezing – Smoking
• Full Fishing Packages • Apartments • Alaska Gifts

Write: Box 54-MP, Klawock, Alaska 99925
Call 1-800-544-2205

GAS • GROCERIES • LAUNDROMAT
BLACK BEAR QUICK STOP
in Klawock
At start of Big Salt Lake Road
HOURS: Daily 9 a.m. to 9 p.m.

William Howard Taft established an Indian reservation on the surrounding land in 1912, but, at the residents request, most of the land was restored to its former status as part of Tongass National Forest in 1926. Hydaburg was incorporated in 1927, 3 years after its people had become citizens of the United States.

Most of the residents are commercial fishermen, although there are some jobs in construction and the timber industry. Subsistence is also a traditional and necessary part of life here. Hydaburg has an excellent collection of restored Haida totems. The totem park was developed in the 1930s by the Civilian Conservation Corps. There is also good salmon fishing here in the fall.

A boardinghouse provides rooms and meals for visitors. Groceries, hardware and sundry items available locally. There are a gift shop and gas station.

KLAWOCK (pop. 897), 24 miles/39 km from Hollis. Klawock originally was a Tlingit Indian summer fishing village: a trading post and salmon saltery were established here in 1868. Ten years later a salmon cannery was built—the first cannery in Alaska and the first of several cannery operations in the area. Over the years the population of Klawock, like other Southeast communities, grew and then declined with the salmon harvest. The local economy is still dependent on fishing and cannery operations, along with timber cutting and sawmilling. A state fish hatchery is located on Klawock Lake, very near the site of a salmon hatchery that operated from 1897 until 1917. Klawock Lake offers good canoeing and boating.

Recreation here includes good fishing for salmon and steelhead in Klawock River, salmon and halibut fishing, and deer and bear hunting. Klawock's totem park contains 21 totems—both replicas and originals—from the abandoned Indian village of Tuxekan.

Groceries and gas are available in Klawock. Laundromat at Black Bear Quick Stop. Banking service available. Accommodations and meals available at 2 lodges just outside town (Fireweed Lodge and Log Cabin Resort). Log Cabin Resort also offers RV sites. Towing service available. Boat charters and rentals are also available. ▲

THORNE BAY (pop. 614), 59 miles/95 km from Hollis. Thorne Bay was incorporated in 1982, making it one of Alaska's newest cities. The settlement began as a logging camp in 1962, when Ketchikan Pulp Co. (a subsidiary of Louisiana Pacific Corp.) moved its operations from Hollis. Thorne Bay was connected to the island road system in 1974. Camp residents created the community—and gained city status from the state—as private ownership of the land was made possible under the Alaska Statehood Act. Employment here depends mainly on the lumber company and the U.S. Forest Service, with assorted jobs in municipal government and in local trades and services. Thorne Bay is centrally located between 2 popular Forest Service recreation areas: Eagles Nest Campground and Sandy Beach picnic area. The Thorne River offers excellent canoeing and kayaking and the bay offers excellent sailing and waterskiing (wetsuit advised).

There are a snack bar, grocery and hardware stores, gas station, small-boat repair, tackle shop and gift shop. Accommodations available at a floathouse, 3 bed and breakfasts and 4 rental cabins. Propane is available. The gas station here is open Monday through Saturday, 8 A.M. to 5 P.M. Fuel oil is also available. Boat charters and rentals are available. Gas for boats may be purchased at the city harbor (unleaded fuel) and from the gas station float (unleaded and diesel). The harbor gas facility is open Monday and Wednesday through Friday from 1-7 P.M.; Saturday and Sunday 11 A.M. to 4 P.M. City operated RV park with dump station. ▲

There is scheduled floatplane service to Thorne Bay from Ketchikan.

WHALE PASS (pop. approximately 100), accessible by loop road from the North Island Road, was the site of a floating logging camp. The camp moved out in the early 1980s, but new residents moved in with a state land sale. The community has a small grocery store and gas pump. Accommodations at Whale Pass Lodge. Good fishing on the loop road into Whale Pass.

Hollis–Klawock–Craig Highway Log

This highway, 31.5 miles/50.7 km long, begins at the ferry landing at Hollis and heads west through Klawock then south to Craig. It is a wide paved road. Posted speed is 35 to 50 mph/56 to 80 kmph. *CAUTION: Watch for logging trucks.*
Distance from Hollis (H) is followed by distance from Craig (C). Physical mileposts show distance from Craig.

H 0 C 31.5 (50.7 km) **HOLLIS**. Alaska Marine Highway ferry terminal.

H 1.4 (2.3 km) C 30.1 (48.4 km) Stop sign. Turn right for Craig and Klawock; turn left for boat ramp.

H 2 (3.2 km) C 29.5 (47.5 km) **Maybeso Creek** bridge. Scenic viewpoint to left. Cutthroat; Dolly Varden; pink and silver salmon; steelhead run begins in mid-April. Pools offer the best fishing. Walking good along streambed but poor along the bank. Watch for bears.

H 3.2 (5.1 km) C 28.3 (45.5 km) Hollis townsite area. Virtually no ruins of the original townsite remain. Large rotting tree stumps in woods are evidence of logging in the early 1900s. Road continues along Harris River valley.

H 5.2 (8.4 km) C 26.3 (42.3 km) Left, **Harris River** bridge road extends 0.7 mile/ 1.1 km down into the valley to the bridge. Cutthroat; steelhead run mid-April; salmon and Dolly Varden run beginning in mid-July. Easy walking on the gravel bars in the middle of river. Bridge across river passable by foot or trail bike. Watch for bears.

H 7 (11.3 km) C 24.5 (39.4 km) Upper Harris River Road (rough) extends 0.6 mile/ 1 km to Harris River.

H 11 (17.7 km) C 20.5 (33 km) Road crosses Harris River. **Junction** with Hydaburg Road (see log this section).

H 11.8 (19 km) C 19.7 (31.7 km) Harris River bridge.

H 12.4 (20 km) C 19.1 (30.9 km) End of Harris River valley. Island divide is here at 500 feet/152m elevation; streams now flow west.

H 14.1 (22.7 km) C 17.4 (28 km) East end of Klawock Lake on left. Klawock Lake is about 7 miles/11 km long and up to 1 mile/ 1.6 km wide. Lake borders the road on the left at several places. Private property; contact Heenya Corp. in Klawock.

H 19.5 (31.4 km) C 12 (19.3 km) Threemile Creek passes under road through 2 large culverts. Private property; contact Heenya Corp. in Klawock.

H 22.3 (35.9 km) C 9.2 (14.8 km) Turnout on left. Short trail leads to Klawock River and view of rapids and salmon run in season. Private property; contact Heenya Corp. in Klawock.

H 22.5 (36.2 km) C 9 (14.5 km) Klawock Lake Hatchery, operated by the Division of Fisheries Rehabilitation, Enhancement and Development, Alaska Dept. of Fish and Game. The hatchery produces sockeye and coho salmon and steelhead. Visitors welcome Monday through Friday, 8 A.M. to 4:30 P.M.

H 24.1 (38.8 km) C 7.4 (11.9 km) **Junction** with Big Salt Road (see log this section). A state highway maintenance station and a grocery store with gas station are located at this junction.

H 24.3 (39.1 km) C 7.2 (11.6 km) Fireweed Lodge: food and lodging.

H 24.5 (39.4 km) C 7 (11.3 km) Entering village of **KLAWOCK**. State troopers in building on right.

H 24.6 (39.6 km) C 6.9 (11.1 km) **Klawock River** bridge spans tidal estuary where river meets salt water. Fishing from bridge.

H 25.2 (40.6 km) C 6.3 (10.1 km) Alaska Timber Corp. mill (closed 1986).

H 27.3 (43.9 km) C 4.2 (6.8 km) Scenic viewpoint on right overlooking bay.

H 28.3 (45.5 km) C 3.2 (5.1 km) Left, short road to Craig sanitary fill. Bears can usually be seen here.

H 30.5 (49 km) C 1 (1.6 km) Craig school.

H 31.5 (50.7 km) C 0 Downtown **CRAIG**.

Big Salt Road Log

Big Salt Road begins at **Milepost C 7.5** on the Hollis–Klawock–Craig Highway and extends 17.1 miles/27.5 km, ending at its junction with Thorne Bay Road. It is a gravel road with much logging traffic. Top speed for much of the road is about 25 mph/ 40 kmph.
Distance is measured from Klawock.

0 Black Bear Quick Stop: grocery store, laundromat and gas station.

0.1 (0.2 km) Klawock city trailer park on right with some overnighter sites; obtain permits from the city clerk. A camping fee is charged. ▲

0.4 (0.6 km) Log Cabin R.V. Park & Resort: tackle store, skiff rentals, lodging and campground. ▲

0.5 (0.8 km) Lodge and restaurant.

2.3 (3.7 km) Road on left leads 0.7 mile/ 1.1 km to Klawock airport and highway maintenance station.

4 (6.4 km) View of Big Salt Lake and mountains.

8.7 (14 km) Big Salt Lake, actually a salt-

ISLAND PROPANE
For All Your RV and Propane Needs
305 Easy Street, Craig, Alaska
(907) 826-2944

water body protected by small islands but permitting tidal flow in and out, is visible to the left from several spots along road. Waterfowl and bald eagles are often observed here. Wreckage of a military aircraft can be seen across lake. The plane crashed in 1969 en route to Vietnam; all aboard survived the crash.

8.9 (14.3 km) Boat ramp and canoe launching area on Big Salt Lake. If boating on this tidal lake, be aware of strong currents.

9.7 (15.6 km) **Black Bear Creek**, cutthroat; Dolly Varden; red, pink, dog and silver salmon, run mid-July to mid-September. Except for the lower 2 miles/3.2 km, creek can be fished from the bank. Best at the mouth of stream, 200 yards/183m upstream from the bridge or in large meadow 1.5 miles/2.4 km from the mouth. Road on right leads to Black Lake. Watch for heavy equipment.

12.6 (20.3 km) **Steelhead Creek**, cutthroat; Dolly Varden; steelhead; pink, dog and silver salmon. Creek can be reached by boat through south entrance to Big Salt Lake. Lake should only be entered during high and low slack tides due to the strong tidal currents. High tide in lake is delayed 2 hours from outside waters. Bank fishing restricted by undergrowth.

16.6 (26.7 km) Short boardwalk on right leads to **Control Lake**, cutthroat; Dolly Varden; pink and silver salmon; good red salmon stream in August. USFS cabin on other side is available for public use. Skiff docked at end of boardwalk is for registered cabin users.

17.1 (27.5 km) End of Big Salt Road (SR 929), **junction** with Thorne Bay Road (USFS Road No. 30) and North Island Road (USFS Road No. 20). Road to Thorne Bay (log follows) is on the right. Road to Labouchere Bay, with access to Whale Pass and Coffman Cove, is on the left; see North Island Road log this section. Turn right for USFS RV park (no services). ▲

Thorne Bay Road Log

Thorne Bay Road extends 18 miles/29 km to Thorne Bay logging camp.
Physical mileposts show distance from Thorne Bay post office.

18 (29 km) **Junction** with Big Salt Road and North Island Road.

16.6 (26.7 km) Eagles Nest USFS campground; 12 sites, water, toilet and canoe launch. Camping fee $5. **Balls Lake**, cutthroat; Dolly Varden; red, pink and silver salmon.

13 (20.9 km) Bridge. **Rio Roberts** and **Rio Beaver creeks**, cutthroat; pink and silver salmon.

10.7 (17.2 km) Rio Beaver Creek bridge.

6.7 (10.8 km) **Goose Creek**, cutthroat; pink and silver salmon. Excellent spawning stream. Good run of pink salmon in mid-August. Lake Ellen Road on right leads 4.5 miles/7.2 km south to Lake No. 3 USFS campsite; 2 RV sites, pit toilet, 2 fire rings and 2 picnic tables. No water or garbage. Road continues beyond campsite to lake and hiking trail to Salt Chuck. Abandoned Salt Chuck Mine is located here.

6.5 (10.5 km) **Thorne River** runs beside road for the next 0.5 mile/0.8 km. Cutthroat; Dolly Varden; steelhead; rainbow; red, pink, dog and silver salmon. Excellent fishing reported at **Milepost 4.9** to **2.1**.

4.9 (7.9 km) Thorne River bridge. Thorne River now follows road on right.

4.1 (6.6 km) Falls Creek.

4 (6.4 km) Gravelly Creek USFS picnic area; walk in to picnic area on the bank of Thorne River at the mouth of Gravelly Creek; 3 tables, fire rings, vault toilet and open-sided shelter. This site was logged in 1918. Note the large stumps with notches. Notches were used by old-time loggers for spring boards to stand on while sawing or chopping.

3.7 (5.9 km) Gravelly Creek.

2.1 (3.4 km) Right, mouth of Thorne River.

1.7 (2.7 km) Hill on right is an example of a logging cut.

1.3 (2.1 km) Log sorting area. Here different species of logs are sorted for rafting and transporting to mills or for export.

1.2 (1.9 km) Log raft holding area. After logs are sorted and tied into bundles, the bundles are chained together into a raft suitable for towing by tugboat.

0 THORNE BAY. The road extends about 10 miles/16 km beyond the community to Sandy Beach picnic area; 6 tables, fire rings, vault toilet and RV parking. Good view of Clarence Strait.

Hydaburg Road Log

The Hydaburg Road is 24.6 miles/39.6 km long and begins 11 miles/17.7 km west of the Hollis main ferry terminal on the Hollis–Klawock–Craig Highway. Opened in 1983, the road has been much improved. Road construction may be under way. Some sections of the road are heavily used by logging trucks.

0 Junction with Hollis–Klawock–Craig Highway.

0.5 (0.8 km) Harris River bridge.

2 (3.2 km) Trailhead for One Duck trail to alpine area and cabin. Contact the USFS office for more information.

4.1 (6.6 km) Bridge.

9.8 (15.8 km) Fork in road, keep right for Hydaburg.

11 (17.7 km) Road on left leads to Twelvemile Arm. This logging road leads to Polk Inlet. Watch for logging and construction activity.

11.8 (19 km) Fork in road, keep right for Hydaburg.

13.9 (22.4 km) View of South Pass.

16.6 (26.7 km) Construction camp.

16.9 (27.2 km) Bridge. Take right fork just after crossing bridge for Hydaburg.

23.5 (37.8 km) Keep right at junction.

23.9 (38.5 km) Take right at junction for Hydaburg, left for Saltery.

24.6 (39.6 km) **HYDABURG**.

North Island Road Log

Signed as USFS Road No. 20, this narrow 2-lane road leads north 79.5 miles/127.9 km from its junction with Big Salt and Thorne Bay roads near Control Lake to Labouchere Bay on the northwest corner of the island. The road has a fair to excellent gravel surfacing and some steep grades. Slow down for approaching vehicles. Posted speed is 25 mph/40 kmph. Gas is available at Whale Pass and Coffman Cove.

0 Junction with Big Salt and Thorne Bay roads near Control Lake.

4.8 (7.7 km) USFS Road No. 2050 leads west to upper Staney Creek/Horseshoe Hole and loops back to Road No. 20. Access to Staney Bridge campsite. ▲

7.4 (11.9 km) Rock quarry to east.

10.9 (17.5 km) USFS Road No. 2054 leads west to Staney Creek campsite, Staney Creek cabin and access to salt water. ▲

15.5 (24.9 km) **Junction** with Coffman Cove Road (see log this section).

18.4 (29.6 km) Naukati Creek.

19.2 (30.9 km) View to west of Tuxekan Island and Passage.

21 (33.8 km) Logging road leads west to Naukati Bay.

21.4 (34.4 km) Yatuk Creek bridge.

23.3 (37.5 km) **NAUKATI**, a former logging camp, is 3 miles/4.8 km west; no services.

26.5 (42.6 km) **Sarkar Lake** to east. Fishing and boat launch. USFS public-use cabin at east end of lake.

27.9 (44.9 km) Bridge over Sarkar Lake outlet to salt water.

39.7 (63.9 km) USFS Road No. 25 leads east 7 miles/11.3 km) past Neck Lake to small settlement of **WHALE PASS**; groceries and gas available. A side road continues beyond Whale Pass 16 miles/25.7 km to Exchange Cove USFS campsite. Whale Pass Road loops back to the main North Island Road at **Milepost 48.6**. ▲

40 (64.4 km) View of Neck Lake to east.

48.6 (78.2 km) Whale Pass loop road to east. Whale Pass is 8 miles/12.9 km from here; Exchange Cove is 16 miles/25.7 km from here.

50.3 (80.9 km) View of El Capitan Passage and Kosciusko Island to west.

51 (82.1 km) Side road leads west 1 mile/1.6 km to USFS field camp; good place to launch cartop boats at salt water.

55.6 (89.5 km) Summit of the North Island Road (elev. 907 feet/276m).

59.5 (95.8 km) Rough road, heavy truck traffic and 1-lane bridges north from here.

60.6 (97.5 km) Red Creek 1-lane bridge.

61.7 (99.3 km) Big Creek 1-lane bridge.

63.9 (102.8 km) View of Red Bay to north; Red Lake is to the south.

67.6 (108.8 km) Buster Creek 1-lane bridge.

68.3 (109.9 km) Shine Creek 1-lane bridge.

72 (115.9 km) Flicker Creek 1-lane bridge.

72.1 (116 km) Memorial Beach picnic area 1.7 miles/2.7 km north; follow signs to parking area. A short trail leads to picnic tables, pit toilet, memorial plaque and beach. Good view of Sumner Strait and Kupreanof Island. This site is a memorial to 12 victims of a 1978 air crash.

79.5 (127.9 km) **LABOUCHERE BAY**, a small logging camp (no facilities) owned and operated by Louisiana–Pacific Corp. The road continues several miles and dead ends at the base of Mount Calder.

Coffman Cove Road Log

Coffman Cove Road branches off the North Island Road (No. 20) at **Milepost 15.5** and leads east and north 20.5 miles/33 km to the logging camp of Coffman Cove. Watch for heavy truck traffic; 25 mph/40 kmph. Slow down for approaching vehicles.

0 Junction with North Island Road.

4.4 (7.1 km) Side road on left (USFS Road No. 30) leads 5 miles/8 km through clear-cut and dead ends.

4.5 (7.2 km) **Logjam Creek** bridge; cutthroat, Dolly Varden, steelhead, pink, silver and sockeye salmon.

9.1 (14.6 km) **Hatchery Creek** bridge; fishing same as Logjam Creek. Trailhead for canoe route to Thorne Bay.

9.4 (15.1 km) Bumpy road on right leads 13 miles/20.9 km to USFS access site; parking area and canoe launch (no trailers) on Luck Lake. Side road then loops north along Clarence Strait to Coffman Cove.

12.1 (19.5 km) View of Sweetwater Lake to left. USFS access site: parking area for Sweetwater public-use cabin, located 0.5 mile/0.8 km along west shore of lake.

17 (27.4 km) Coffman Creek bridge.

19.5 (31.4 km) Chum Creek bridge.

20.2 (32.5 km) **Junction** with Luck Lake loop road.

20.3 (32.7 km) Chum Creek bridge.

20.5 (33 km) **COFFMAN COVE**, a logging camp; groceries, gas, cafe and gifts.

Wrangell

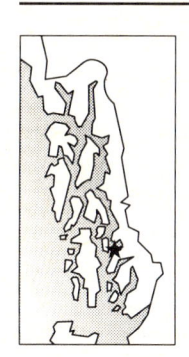

Located at northwest tip of Wrangell Island on Zimovia Strait in central southeastern Alaska; 2.5 miles/4 km south of the Stikine River delta; 3 hours by ferry or 32 air miles/51.5 km southeast of Petersburg, the closest major community; and 6 hours by ferry or 85 air miles/136.8 km north of Ketchikan. **Population:** 2,630. **Emergency Services: Police**, phone 874-3304. **Fire Department** and **Ambulance**, phone 874-2000. **Hospital**, Wrangell General, on Bennett Street just off Zimovia Highway, phone 874-3356. **Maritime Search and Rescue**; contact the Coast Guard at 1-800-478-5555.

Visitor Information: Center located in an A-frame building on the corner of Brueger Street and Outer Drive, next to the city hall; phone 874-3901. Write: Chamber of Commerce, Box 49MP, Wrangell, AK 99929. Or contact the Wrangell Convention and Visitors Bureau, Box 1078-MP, Wrangell, AK 99929; phone 874-3770.

WRANGELL ADVERTISERS

Harding's Old Sourdough
  Lodge............................Ph. (907) 874-3613
Norris Gift Shop................................Front St.
Stikine Inn and
  Dock Side Restaurant...............Stikine Ave.
TH Charters.......................Ph. (907) 874-2085
Thunderbird Hotel and
  Laundromat...................................Front St.
Tyee Travel, Inc..................Ph. (907) 874-3383
Wrangell Chamber of
  Commerce....................Ph. (907) 874-3901
Wrangell Drug.....................................Front St.

Information is also available at the Wrangell Museum, 1 block from the ferry terminal at 122 2nd St.

Elevation: Sea level. **Climate:** Mild and moist with slightly less rain than other Southeast communities. Mean annual precipitation is 79.16 inches, with 63.9 inches of snow. Record monthly precipitation, 20.43 inches in October 1961. Average daily maximum temperature in June is 61°F/16°C; in July 64°F/18°C. Daily minimum in January is 21°F/-6°C. **Radio:** KSTK-FM 101.7. **Television:** Cable and satellite. **Newspaper:** *Wrangell Sentinel* (weekly).

Private Aircraft: Wrangell airport, adjacent northeast; elev. 44 feet/13m; length 6,000 feet/1,829m; paved; fuel 80, 87.

Wrangell is the only Alaskan city to have existed under 4 nations and 3 flags—the Stikine Tlingits, the Russians, British and Americans. Wrangell began in 1834 as a Russian stockade called Redoubt St. Dionysius, built to prevent the Hudson's Bay Co. from fur trading up the rich Stikine River to the east. The Russians, with a change of heart, leased the mainland of southeastern Alaska to Hudson's Bay Co. in 1840. Under the British the stockade was called Fort Stikine.

The post remained under the British flag until Alaska was purchased by the United States in 1867. A year later the Americans established a military post here, naming it Fort Wrangell after the island, which was named by the Russians after Baron von Wrangel, a governor of the Russian–American Co.

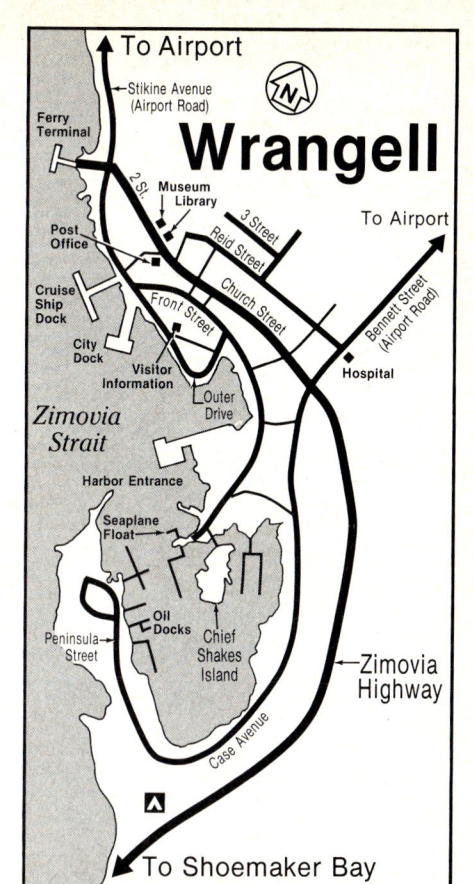

THUNDERBIRD HOTEL and LAUNDROMAT

On Front Street

All Rooms with Bath, TV and Phones

For reservations and information write: Mary Engdahl
Box 110-MP, Wrangell, Alaska 99929 or phone (907) 874-3322

STIKINE INN

Enjoy Modern Comfort with a View of Wrangell

ONE BLOCK FROM FERRY TERMINAL

34 SPACIOUS ROOMS • BATHS • COLOR TV • PHONES • 24-HOUR DESK SERVICE

Phone 874-3388 for Inn Reservations
Box 990, Wrangell, Alaska 99929

Special Weekend Rates

- INN • RESTAURANT
- LOUNGE AND LIQUOR STORE
- TRAVEL AGENCY
- HAIR SALON
- ALL UNDER ONE ROOF

Dock Side Restaurant... *Open 7 days.*

FEATURING LOCAL SEAFOOD, IN SEASON • COMPLETE SALAD BAR
BANQUET FACILITIES • MEALS CHARGEABLE TO ROOMS

WRANGELL
Lodging Bed & Breakfast

Harding's OLD SOURDOUGH LODGE

Fine Dining & Cocktails Sourdough Room
(convention room)
Sauna • Steam Bath • Laundry Facilities
Quiet Lodging   Charters available

P.O. Box 1062-MP
Wrangell, Alaska 99929
Bruce E. Harding

874-3613 *Call upon arrival for courtesy pickup*

TH CHARTERS PRESENTS
JET BOATS NORTHWEST
AND THE MIGHTY STIKINE RIVER

STIKINE RIVER RAT
M/V Stikine Princess Wrangell, Alaska

For Sightseeing Tours,
The M/V Stikine Princess

And For A Thrilling Ride and Fun,
The Wild Side and River's Edge

Chief Shakes Glacier & Hot Tubs
Anan Bear Observatory
U.S. Forest Service Cabins

P.O. Box 934-MP
Wrangell, Alaska 99929
Todd E. Harding, Coast Guard
Licensed Owner-Operator

874-2085

Its strategic location near the mouth of the Stikine River, the fastest free-flowing navigable river in North America, made Wrangell an important supply point not only for fur traders but also for gold seekers following the river route to the goldfields. Today, the Stikine River is a popular hunting and recreation area. It is also under study for its potential for hydroelectric power and as a source for copper and other minerals.

Wrangell serves as a hub for goods, services and transportation for outlying fishing villages and logging and mining camps. Wrangell's economy is also supported by a lumbermill, operated by Alaska Pulp Corp., located 6.2 miles/10 km south of town on the Zimovia Highway. The town depended largely on fishing until Japanese interests arrived in the mid-1950s and established a mill downtown (now closed). Fishing is Wrangell's second largest industry, with salmon the major catch.

ACCOMMODATIONS

Wrangell has 2 motels and 3 restaurants downtown, as well as service stations, hardware and appliance stores, bakery, fast-food outlets, banks, drugstore, laundromat, grocery stores and gift shops. Bed-and-breakfast accommodations are available. Lodges with restaurants are located on Peninsula Street and at Mile 4.4 Zimovia Highway.

RV camping and picnic area at Shoemaker Bay, **Milepost 4.9** Zimovia Highway. Dump stations located at Shoemaker Bay and downtown at the corner of Front Street and Case Avenue. City Park, at **Milepost 1.9** Zimovia Highway, has tent sites, picnic area with tables, flush toilets and shelters and playground. ▲

TRANSPORTATION

Air: Daily scheduled jet service is provided by Alaska Airlines to other Southeast cities with through service to Seattle and Anchorage. Scheduled commuter air service to Petersburg, Kake and Ketchikan. Charter service available.

Airport terminal is 1.1 miles/1.8 km from ferry terminal or 1.1 miles/1.8 km from Zimovia Highway on Bennett Street.

Ferry: Alaska Marine Highway vessels connect Wrangell with all southeastern Alaska ports plus Prince Rupert, BC, and Bellingham, WA. See MARINE ACCESS ROUTES section for details. Ferry terminal is at the north end of town at the end of Zimovia Highway (also named Church or 2nd Street at this point). Terminal facilities include ticket office, waiting room and vehicle waiting area. Phone 874-3711.

Car Rental: Available.
Taxi: Available to and from airport and ferry terminal.
Highways: Zimovia Highway (see log this section). Logging roads have opened up most of Wrangell Island to motorists. Check with the USFS office at 525 Bennett St. for a copy of the Wrangell Island Road Guide map. (Write USDA Forest Service, Wrangell Ranger District, P.O. Box 51, Wrangell, AK 99929; phone 874-2323.)
Cruise Ships: Wrangell is a regular port of call in summer for several cruise lines.
Private Boats: Transient float located downtown. Reliance Float is located near Chief Shakes House.

ATTRACTIONS

Chief Shakes Island and Community House, in Wrangell Harbor, is reached by boardwalk. It is the site of several excellent totem poles and the Chief Shakes Community House, a replica tribal house which contains Indian working tools, an original Chilkat blanket design and other cultural items. It is listed on the National Register of Historic Places. Open irregular hours during summer (May to September) or by appointment; phone 874-3747. Admission fee.

Totem Poles. The last original totems standing in Wrangell were cut down in November 1981 and removed for preservation. A totem restoration project funded by both state and federal agencies was initiated, and replicas of original totems can be found at Kiksadi Totem Park at the corner of Front and Episcopal streets.

Wrangell Museum, at 2nd and Bevier streets, features items of local and Tlingit Indian history and petroglyphs. The building is a former schoolhouse (on the National Register of Historic Buildings). In summer, the museum is open 1-4 P.M., Monday through Saturday, and when cruise ships and most ferries are in port. Open Wednesday in winter 1-4 P.M. and by appointment (phone 874-3770). Admission fee.

Bigelow Museum, located on Stikine Avenue, is a private collection of antiques and Alaska memorabilia. Open when cruise ships and ferries are in port and by special request. Phone 874-3646.

Sightseeing Tours of historic attractions and fish bakes are available upon request. Sightseeing buses meet some ferries. Inquire at the visitor center or Wrangell Museum.

The Stikine River delta lies north of Wrangell within the Stikine–LeConte Wilderness. It is accessible for boat or by plane only. The delta is prime habitat for migrating waterfowl, eagles, moose and bear.

Come enjoy the Adventure and History in
WRANGELL
The Only Alaskan City to be Ruled by Four Nations

Send more information about:
- Stikine River
- LeConte Glacier
- Anan Bear Observatory
- Petroglyph Beach
- Garnet Ledge
- 4th of July/Tent City Festivals
- Fishing, Hunting, Flightseeing
- RV & Tent Camping Facilities
- Other _____

★ Third Oldest City in Alaska
★ Four Gold Rushes
★ Chief Shakes Island & Tribal House
★ Museums
★ Oldest Protestant Church & Catholic Parish in Alaska
★ Oldest Continuously Published Newspaper in Alaska

Wrangell Chamber of Commerce
P.O. Box 49 MP
Wrangell, Alaska 99929
(907) 874-3901

Fishing is Wrangell's second largest industry. (John W. Warden)

Also watch for seals resting on ice floes from LeConte Glacier (the glacier is at the head of LeConte Bay, just north of the delta), the southernmost tidewater glacier in North America.

Anan Bear Observatory, managed by the U.S. Forest Service, is located 35 miles/56 km southeast of Wrangell. During July, August and early September, visitors can watch bears catch pink salmon headed for the salmon spawning grounds. Bald eagles and seals also may be seen feeding on the fish.

AREA FISHING: Boat in or fly in to **Thoms Lake, Long Lake, Marten Lake, Salmon Bay, Virginia Lake, Anan Creek** (on salt water), **Anan Lake** and **Eagle Lake**. (Thoms Lake and Long Lake are also accessible via road and trail.) Black bear and some brown bear viewing at Anan Creek during July-August salmon runs; fish lower creek. **Stikine River** near Wrangell (closed to king salmon fishing), Dolly Varden to 22 inches, and cutthroat to 18 inches, best in August; steelhead to 12 lbs., use bait or lures; coho salmon 10 to 15 lbs., use lures, September and October. Saltwater fishing near Wrangell for king salmon, 20 to 40 lbs. Stop by the Dept. of Fish and Game at 215 Front St. for details.

Wrangell Salmon Derby runs from mid-May to Memorial Day weekend. Kings weighing more than 50 lbs. are not unusual.

Petroglyphs are ancient carvings on rock faces, usually found near the high tide marks on beaches. Petroglyph Beach is located 0.3 mile/0.5 km from the ferry terminal; a boardwalk trail leads to the head of the beach from the left of the road. Turn right as you reach the beach and look for petroglyphs between there and a rock outcrop several hundred feet away; at least 20 can be seen. Petroglyphs are also located on the library lawn and are on display in the museum. Visitors are welcome to make rubbings (bring your own materials).

Garnet Ledge, a rocky outcrop on the right bank of the Stikine River delta at Garnet Creek, is 7.5 miles/12.1 km from Wrangell Harbor, reached at high tide by small boat. Garnet, a semiprecious stone, can be found embedded in the ledge here. The garnet ledge is on land deeded to the Southeast Council of the Boy Scouts of America by the late Fred Hanford (former mayor of Wrangell). The bequest states that the land shall be used for scouting purposes and the children of Wrangell may take garnets in reasonable quantities (garnets are sold by children at the docks when ships and ferries are in port). Contact the Wrangell Museum (Box 1050-MP, Wrangell 99929; phone 874-3770) for information on digging for garnets.

USFS public-use cabins in the Wrangell district are accessible by air or by boat. The 21 USFS cabins are scattered throughout the region. See Cabins in the GENERAL INFORMATION section, and stop by the USFS office at 525 Bennett St.; phone 874-2323. Visitors may also use the white courtesy phone located in the ferry terminal building. Contact the Wrangell Ranger District at Box 51, Wrangell 99929.

Celebrations in Wrangell include a big Fourth of July celebration which begins with a salmon bake. (Candidates for queen of this festival get things started during June by selling tickets to raise funds for the July 4 activities.) The annual Tent City Festival, celebrated the first weekend in February, commemorates Wrangell's gold rush days.

Zimovia Highway Log

Zimovia Highway leads south from the ferry terminal to Pat Creek at Mile 11, where it connects with island logging roads.

0 Alaska Marine Highway ferry terminal, ticket office and waiting area. There is a bike path to Mile 1.9.

0.2 (0.3 km) Wrangell Museum and library on left. Two totems stand in front. Post office and customs station located across from library.

0.3 (0.5 km) St. Rose of Lima Catholic Church, the oldest Roman Catholic parish in Alaska, founded May 2, 1879.

0.4 (0.6 km) First Presbyterian Church has a red-lighted cross, 1 of 2 in the world that serve as navigational aids. This was the first church in Wrangell and is the oldest Protestant church in Alaska (founded in 1877 and built in 1879).

0.6 (1 km) Bennett Street (Airport Road) loops north to the airport and back to the ferry terminal, a distance of 2.2 miles/ 3.5 km.

0.7 (1.1 km) Public Safety Bldg.

1.9 (3.1 km) Picnic area with shelters, firepits, restrooms, litter barrels. Tent camping only allowed; 24-hour limit. ▲

3.6 (5.8 km) Turnout with beach access. Several turnouts along the highway here offer beach access and good spots for bird watching.

4.4 (7.1 km) Lodge on left with restaurant and lounge.

4.9 (7.9 km) Shoemaker Bay small-boat harbor, boat launch, picnic, camping and parking area. Camping area has tent sites, 15 RV sites, water, dump station and restrooms. Tennis court, horseshoe pits and children's playground nearby. Rainbow Falls trailhead; 0.7 mile/1.1 km trail to scenic waterfall. Rainbow Falls trail intersects with Institute Creek trail, which leads 3.5 miles/5.6 km to viewpoint overlooking Shoemaker Bay. ▲

6.5 (10.5 km) Alaska Pulp Corp.

7.3 (11.7 km) **Milepost 7**, scenic turnout.

8 (12.9 km) Turnout.

8.5 (13.7 km) Turnout, beach access (8 Mile Beach undeveloped recreation area).

10.8 (17.4 km) Access road west to Pat Creek Log Transfer Facility. Road east (Pat Creek Road) leads 0.3 mile/0.5 km to Pat's Lake. This single-lane maintained gravel road continues approximately 6 miles/9.7 km northeast through logging area.

Pat Creek and **Pat's Lake**, cutthroat, Dolly Varden, pink and silver salmon; use bait, spinning gear or flies for Dolly Varden and cutthroat, May to October; use herring, spoon for silvers.

11 (17.7 km) Pat Creek camping area (unmaintained, no facilities); parking for self-contained vehicles. ▲

11.1 (17.9 km) State-maintained highway ends. Begin 1-lane Forest Development Road No. 6265 connecting with other Forest Service logging roads (map available from USFS office in Wrangell). Watch for logging trucks.

GOOD NEIGHBOR PHARMACY
WRANGELL DRUG
Robert Fisher — Kathleen C. Fisher
FRONT STREET (907) 874-3422
Beauty, Health & Prescription Center
PHARMACY • SOUVENIRS • FILM
P.O. Box 757, Wrangell, Alaska 99929

NORRIS GIFT SHOP
WRANGELL, ALASKA
REAL ALASKA JEWELRY • NUGGET • JADE
IVORY • PETROGLYPH RUBBING SUPPLIES
ALASKAN BOOKS • ALASKAN KEEPSAKES

Book any custom individual or group itinerary with us!
* AIR * FERRY * ACCOMMODATIONS *
* CHARTERS * TOURS * CRUISES *
TYEE TRAVEL, INC.
BOX 738 - MP
WRANGELL, AK 99929
Fax 907-874-2111
Phone 907-874-3383
• We'll arrange a ride on the Wild Side with JET BOATS NORTHWEST
THE MIGHTY STIKINE RIVER
"The fastest navigable river in North America"
Coast Guard licensed since 1981
• Regular scheduled river trips and charters available •

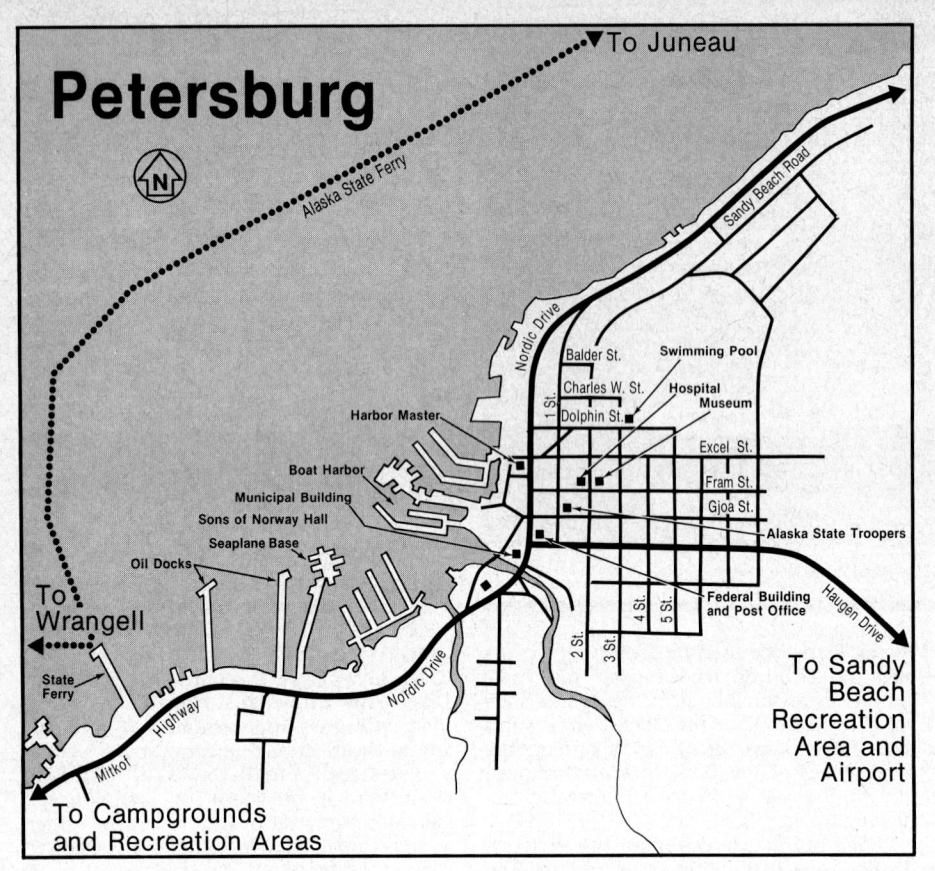

Petersburg

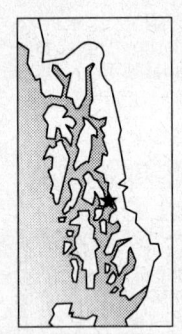

Located on the northwest tip of Mitkof Island at the northern end of Wrangell Narrows, midway between Juneau and Ketchikan. **Population**: 3,576. **Emergency Services**: Phone 911. **Alaska State Troopers**, phone 772-3100. **City Police, Poison Center, Fire Department** and **Ambulance**, phone 772-3838. **Hospital**, Petersburg General, 1st and Excel streets, phone 772-4291. **Maritime Search and Rescue**: contact the Coast Guard at 1-800-478-5555. Harbormaster, phone 772-4688, or CB Channel 9, or VHF Channel 16.

Visitor Information: Chamber of commerce information center located at 1st and Fram streets is open weekdays from 8 A.M. to 5 P.M. spring and summer, limited hours during fall and winter. Write: Petersburg Chamber of Commerce, P.O. Box 649MP, Petersburg 99833, phone 772-3646. Petersburg Museum, 2nd and Fram streets. Summer hours 11 A.M. to 5 P.M., Monday, Tuesday, Wednesday; 1-5 P.M. Thursday, Friday, Saturday; 1-8 P.M. Sunday. Phone 772-3598 for winter hours and other information. Alaska Dept. of Fish and Game, State Office Bldg., Sing Lee Alley; open 8 A.M. to 4:30 P.M., Monday through Friday. U.S. Forest Service, in the Federal Bldg.; phone 772-3871 or write P.O. Box 1328, Petersburg 99833.

Elevation: Sea level. **Climate**: Average daily maximum temperature in July, 64°F/18°C; daily minimum in January, 20°F/-7°C. All-time high, 84°F/29°C in 1933; record low, -19°F/-28°C in 1947. Mean annual precipitation, 105 inches; mean annual snowfall, 119 inches. **Radio**: KFSK-FM 100.9, KRSA 580. **Television**: KTOO (PBS) Channel 9 and cable channels. **Newspaper**: *Petersburg Pilot* (weekly).

Private Aircraft: Petersburg airport, 1 mile/1.6 km southeast; elev. 107 feet/33m; length 6,500 feet/1,981m; asphalt. Seaplane base 0.5 mile/0.8 km from downtown.

Petersburg was named for Peter Buschmann, who selected the present townsite for a salmon cannery and sawmill in 1897. The sawmill and dock were built in 1899 and the cannery was completed in 1900. He was followed by other Norwegian–Americans who came to fish and work in the cannery and sawmill. Since then the cannery has operated continuously (with rebuilding, expansion and different owners) and is now known as Petersburg Fisheries, a division of Icicle Seafoods, Inc.

Today, Petersburg boasts the largest home-based halibut fleet in Alaska and is also well known for its shrimp, crab, salmon, herring and other fish products. Most families depend on the fishing industry for a livelihood.

ACCOMMODATIONS

Petersburg has a hotel, several motels and bed and breakfasts, many restaurants and several fast-food outlets downtown. The 5-block-long commercial area on Main Street (Nordic Drive) has grocery stores, marine and fishing supply stores, hardware, drugstores, travel agency, public showers, banks, gift and variety stores specializing in both Alaskan and Scandinavian items, city hall, post office, gas stations, cocktail bars and a public swimming pool. Petersburg has 14 churches.

In town RV park at Haugen and 4th streets; dump station, hookups, showers, laundry, fee charged. There is a tent campground (known locally as Tent City) on Haugen Drive; it is often filled to capacity in summer with young cannery workers. Public campgrounds and a private RV park are located on Mitkof Highway south of town. ▲

TRANSPORTATION

Air: Daily scheduled jet air service is by Alaska Airlines to major Southeast cities and Seattle, WA, with connections to Anchorage and Fairbanks. Local and charter service available.

The airport, located 1 mile/1.6 km from the Federal Bldg. on Haugen Drive, has a ticket counter and waiting room.

Ferry: Alaska Marine Highway vessels connect Petersburg with all southeastern Alaska cities plus Prince Rupert, BC, and Bellingham, WA. (See MARINE ACCESS ROUTES section for schedules.) Terminal at Milepost 0.9 Mitkof Highway, includes dock,

---

Friendly Alaska Hospitality

Stay at... TIDES INN
Complimentary Continental Breakfast
- Color TV — MOVIE CHANNEL
- Downtown — OFF STREET PARKING
- Mountain Bike Rental
- Visitor Information
- Avis Rental Cars Available

Ask about our LOCAL TOURS
P.O. Box 1048MP   (907) 772-4288
First and Dolphin Street
Petersburg, Alaska 99833

4th and Haugen Drive • One Mile from ferry terminal
• Walking distance to town

Le Conte RV Park
Hookups • Showers • Laundromat   Box 1548
Rest Rooms and Dump Station   Petersburg
Phone (907) 772-4680   Alaska 99833

TWIN CREEK RV PARK
7.5 MILE MITKOF HIGHWAY
Spring Water • Level Spaces
Full & Partial Hookups
Grocery Store • TV • Laundromat
Rest Rooms • Showers • Dump Station
P.O. BOX 90-M, PETERSBURG, ALASKA 99833
PHONE (907) 772-3282 or 772-3244

PETERSBURG ADVERTISERS

Jewell's By The Sea
  Bed & Breakfast............Ph. (907) 772-3620
Le Conte RV Park.................4th & Haugen sts.
Lee's Clothing ....212 Nordic Dr.
Petersburg Chamber of
  Commerce...........................1st & Fram sts.
Petersburg Motors, Inc. ......2nd & Haugen sts.
Tides Inn ....1st & Dolphin sts.
Trading Union, The ....Main St.
Twin Creek RV Park ....Mile 7.5 Mitkof Hwy.

ticket office with waiting room and parking area. Phone 772-3855.

NOTE: RVs arriving late at night are allowed to park free for up to 8 hours at the south boat harbor parking lot just north of the ferry terminal.

Car Rental. Available at downtown hotels.

Taxi: There are 2 taxi companies. Cab service to and from the airport and ferry terminal.

Highways: Mitkof Highway, Sandy Beach Road and Three Lakes Loop Road (see logs this section).

Private Boats: Boaters must check with harbormaster for moorage assignment.

ATTRACTIONS

Clausen Memorial Museum, 203 Fram St., features the world-record king salmon caught commercially (126 1/2 lbs.) and chum salmon (36 lbs.), along with collections of local historical items including a re-creation of the office of colorful local cannery owner Earl Ohmer. Hours are noon-5 P.M. daily from early May to mid-September; call 772-3598 for schedule changes and winter hours.

The Fisk, a 10-foot/3-m bronze sculpture commemorating Petersburg's fishing way of life, stands in a working fountain in front of the museum. It was completed during the Alaska centennial year of 1967 by sculptor Carson Boysen.

Sons of Norway Hall, on the National Register of Historic Places, was built in 1912. Situated on pilings over Hammer Slough (a favorite photography subject), its window shutters are decorated with rosemaling (Norwegian tole painting).

Little Norway Festival is usually scheduled on the weekend closest to Norwegian Independence Day, May 17. This year the annual festival, which celebrates the town's Norwegian heritage, is scheduled for May 15–17, 1992. Pageantry, old-country dress, contests, Vikings, a Viking ship, dancing and a Norwegian "fish feed" for locals and visitors are featured.

LeConte Glacier, in LeConte Bay, 25 miles/40 km east of Petersburg, is the continent's southernmost tidewater glacier. Fast-moving, the glacier continually "calves," creating thunderous ice falls from its face into the bay. Seals and porpoises are common; whales are often seen. Small aircraft and boats may be chartered in Petersburg or Wrangell to see LeConte Glacier.

Salmon migration and spawning are best observed in the Petersburg area during August and September. Falls Creek bridge and fish ladder is a good location (silver and pink) as are Blind Slough and the Blind River Rapids area, Petersburg Creek and Ohmer Creek (silver, pink and chum).

Crystal Lake Fish Hatchery is at Milepost 17.5 Mitkof Highway. This hatchery for coho, king, and steelhead trout is operated by the state of Alaska and used for fish stocking projects in southeastern Alaska. It is open for visits and hatchery personnel will explain the operation, though formal guided tours are not available. Best time to visit is between 8 A.M. and 4 P.M., Monday through Friday.

Falls Creek fish ladder is at **Milepost 10.8** Mitkof Highway. The ladder helps migrating salmon bypass difficult falls on the way to spawning grounds in Falls Creek. It can be observed from the creek bank just off the road side. Best time is late summer and early fall to observe coho and pink salmon.

Petersburg Salmon Derby is scheduled for Memorial Day weekend. Check with the chamber of commerce for details.

Charter a Boat or Plane. There are charter boat services in Petersburg for guided salt- and freshwater fishing trips. Inquire at the chamber of commerce office. Charter floatplanes and helicopters are available for flightseeing, fly-in fishing and transportation.

AREA FISHING: Salmon, steelhead, cutthroat and Dolly Varden at **Falls Creek, Blind Slough** and **Blind River Rapids;** see log of Mitkof Highway this section. Salmon can be caught in the harbor area and **Scow Bay** area. (Rapid tidal currents in front of the town necessitate the use of an outboard motor.) **Petersburg Creek,** directly across Wrangell Narrows from downtown within Petersburg Creek–Duncan Salt Chuck Wilderness Area, also offers good fishing. Dolly Varden can be caught from the beach north of town and from downtown docks.

Wrangell Narrows is a 23-mile-/37-km-long channel between Mitkof and Kupreanof islands. The channel was dredged in the 1940s to a depth of 26 feet/42m. Extremely narrow in places and filled with rocky reefs, islands and strong currents, the narrows is navigated by ships and ferries with the aid of dozens of markers and flashing lights. The 1 1/2-hour run through Wrangell Narrows begins on ferries immediately departing

Petersburg's major industries are fishing and fish processing. (Rollo Pool, staff)

Petersburg southbound or about 1½ hours after departing Wrangell northbound.

Cabins, canoe and hiking trails managed by the USFS are all within reach of Petersburg, which is the administrative center for the Stikine Area of Tongass National Forest. Stop by the USFS office in the Federal Bldg., or phone 772-3871 for detailed information on cabins and trails. Also consult *The ALASKA WILDERNESS MILEPOST*®. See also Cabins in the GENERAL INFORMATION section. Information for canoers and kayakers interested in the Stikine River delta or Tebenkof Bay is also available here or at the USFS office in Wrangell.

Sandy Beach Road Log

From Federal Bldg., drive north through town; road leads to Sandy Beach Recreation Area.

0 Federal Bldg. and post office.
0.1 (0.2 km) Petersburg boat harbor 1 block to left contains one of Alaska's finest fishing fleets.
0.2 (0.3 km) Downtown Petersburg.
0.3 (0.5 km) Petersburg Fisheries, Inc., processing plant, Petersburg's largest.
1.2 (1.9 km) Eagle observation point. Eagles can be seen nesting nearby and fishing in Wrangell Narrows. To the northeast is Frederick Sound and the mainland. Icebergs may be spotted in Frederick Sound in the summer.
2.8 (4.5 km) Sandy Beach Recreation Area on left; picnic tables, shelter, toilets, limited parking, no camping. **Junction** with Haugen Road which loops to airport and back to town.

Mitkof Highway Log

The major road on the island, Mitkof Highway leads 33.8 miles/54.4 km south from the Federal Bldg. to the Stikine River delta at the south end of Mitkof Island. The highway is paved to **Milepost 17.5**; good wide gravel to road end.

0 Federal Bldg. and post office.
0.1 (0.2 km) Bridge over Hammer Slough, an intertidal estuary.
0.5 (0.8 km) Harbor parking and RV staging area (8-hour RV parking).
0.6 (1 km) Pier and floatplane base.
0.8 (1.3 km) Marine Highway ferry terminal, office and waiting area on right.
2.8 (4.5 km) Muskeg meadows on left. Muskeg is a grassy bog, common in Alaska.
2.9 (4.6 km) **Scow Bay**, a wide portion of Wrangell Narrows with king salmon fishing in spring. Scow Bay is noted traditionally as the first election precinct to report its vote in statewide elections. Scow Bay Loop Road rejoins highway at **Milepost 3.1**.
4 (6.4 km) Lodging on right.
4.3 (6.9 km) Turnout on right with view of Wrangell Narrows.
7.5 (12.1 km) Twin Creek RV Park, private campground and phone. ▲
10.7 (17.2 km) North exit to Three Lakes Loop Road (see log this section).
10.8 (17.4 km) **Falls Creek** and fish ladder. Steelhead, April and May; pink salmon below falls in August; coho, August and September; Dolly Varden and cutthroat late summer and fall. No fishing within 300 feet of fish ladder.
11 (17.7 km) Road on right leads 0.5 mile/0.6 km to Papke's Landing; transient boat moorage and boat ramp. USFS Log Transportation Facility.
12.5 (20.1 km) Trailhead.
14.5 (23.3 km) Blind River Rapids turnout and trail. A 0.3-mile/0.4-km boardwalk trail leads through a muskeg meadow to **Blind River Rapids**, hatchery steelhead, mid-April to mid-May; king salmon, June to late July; coho, mid-August to October. Also Dolly Varden and cutthroat.
16.3 (26.2 km) Blind Slough waterfowl viewing area on right. Covered platform with interpretive sign on area waterfowl. Trumpeter swans overwinter in this area.
17.5 (28.2 km) Pavement ends; wide, hard-packed gravel to end of road. Short road leads to Crystal Lake Fish Hatchery and **Blind Slough** Recreation Area with picnic tables, shelter and pit toilets. Hatchery is open for visiting, though no scheduled tours are available. Fishing for steelhead, best in May; cutthroat and Dolly Varden in summer; coho salmon, mid-August to mid-September; king salmon in June and July.
20 (32.2 km) **Manmade Hole** picnic area with tables, firepits, swimming and short trail. Ice-skating in winter. Fishing for cutthroat and Dolly Varden year-round; best in summer and fall.
20.6 (33.1 km) Three Lakes Loop Road begins on left leading to Three Lakes on other side of Mitkof Island, looping back to Mitkof Highway at **Milepost 10.7** near Falls Creek bridge.
21.4 (34.4 km) Woodpecker Cove Road (1-lane) leads about 15 miles/24 km along south Mitkof Island to Woodpecker Cove and beyond. Good views of Sumner Strait. Watch for logging trucks.
21.7 (34.9 km) Ohmer Creek Campground, 15 sites, pit toilets, parking area, picnic tables and firepits. Set in meadow area among trees.
24 (38.6 km) Blind Slough USFS Log Transportation Facility. Excellent fishing from skiff for king salmon in June and July, coho salmon, mid-August to mid-September.
26.1 (42 km) Narrow 0.7-mile/1.1-km road on right to Sumner Strait Campground (undeveloped); parking for a dozen vehicles but no other facilities. ▲
27 (43.4 km) View of city of Wrangell.
28 (45 km) Wilson Creek state recreation area (undeveloped); picnic tables, parking. Good view of Sumner Strait.
28.6 (46 km) Banana Point, boat ramp.
31 (49.9 km) Stikine River mud flats, visible on right at low tide. Part of the Stikine River delta, this is the area where Dry Strait meets Sumner Strait.
33.8 (54.4 km) Road ends with turnaround.

Three Lakes Loop Road Log

Access to this 21.4-mile-/34.4-km-long, 1-lane loop road, is from **Mileposts 10.7** and **20.6** on the Mitkof Highway. *CAUTION: No services, use turnouts.*

0 Junction at **Milepost 10.7** Mitkof Highway; turn east.
1.4 (2.3 km) View of Wrangell Narrows to west. Older clear-cuts; this area was logged between 1964 and 1968.
4.4 (7.1 km) Falls Creek bridge.
7 (11.3 km) Second-growth stand of spruce-hemlock. First growth was destroyed by fire or wind throw more than 180 years ago. This second-growth stand serves as an example of what a logging unit could look like a century after clear-cutting.
9.7 (15.6 km) Directly south is a 384-acre clear-cut logged in 1973 under a contract predating the current policy which usually limits clear-cut tracts to 100 acres.
10.2 (16.4 km) **Big Creek**; steelhead in April and May; coho late August and September; cutthroat and Dolly Varden, best late summer and fall.
12.3 (19.8 km) Muskeg; view of Frederick Sound.
14.2 (22.8 km) Sand Lake trail. Short boardwalk trail leads to each of the Three Lakes. Tennis shoes are ideal for these short walks, but for areas around the lakes it is advisable to wear rubber boots. A 0.7-mile/1.1-km connecting trail to Hill Lake.
14.7 (23.6 km) Hill Lake trail.
15.1 (24.3 km) Crane Lake trail, 1.3 miles/2.1 km to lake; connecting trail to Hill Lake. USFS skiffs and picnic platforms are located at Sand, Hill and Crane lakes.
Sand, **Hill** and **Crane lakes**, cutthroat trout from May through September.
16.4 (26.4 km) Dry Straits Road.
21.4 (34.4 km) Second **junction** with Mitkof Highway, at **Milepost 20.6**.

Sitka

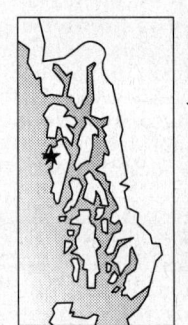

Located on west side of Baranof Island, 95 air miles/153 km southwest of Juneau, 185 air miles/298 km northwest of Ketchikan; 2 hours flying time from Seattle, WA. **Population:** City and Borough, 8,526. **Emergency Services: Alaska State Troopers, City Police, Fire Department**, and **Ambulance**, phone 911. **Hospital**, Sitka Community, phone 747-3241; Mount Edgecumbe, phone 966-2411. **Maritime Search and Rescue;** phone the Coast Guard at 1-800-478-5555.

Visitor Information: Available at the Isabel Miller Museum in the Centennial

SITKA ADVERTISERS

Biorka Bed & Breakfast..............611 Biorka St.
Helga's Bed &
   Breakfast..................2821 Halibut Point Rd.
Karras Bed & Breakfast .....230 Kogwanton St.
Marina Italian and
   Mexican Restaurant............205 Harbor Dr.
Mt. View Bed &
   Breakfast ....201 Cascade Creek Rd.
Potlatch House, The ....713 Katlian St.
Seafish Alaska ....Ph. (907) 747-5497
Sheldon Jackson Museum
   Shop....................................104 College Dr.
Sitka Convention & Visitors
   Bureau ....Ph. (907) 747-5940
Sitka Super 8 Motel ....Ph. 1-800-800-8000
White's Pharmacy ....705 Halibut Point Rd.

Bldg. on Harbor Drive. Museum hours are 8 A.M. to 5 P.M. in summer, extended hours to accommodate ferry passengers; phone 747-6455. Also located in the Centennial Bldg. are the offices of the Sitka Convention and Visitors Bureau and the Greater Sitka Chamber of Commerce. Write the chamber of commerce at Box 638, Sitka 99835. Write the Sitka Convention and Visitors Bureau at Box 1226 or phone 747-5940. For U.S. Forest Service information write the Sitka Ranger District at 204 Siginaka Way, or phone 747-6671. For information on Sitka National Historical Park, write Box 738.

Elevation: Sea level. **Climate:** Average daily temperature in July, 55°F/13°C; in January, 33°F/1°C. Annual precipitation, 95 inches. **Radio:** KIFW 1230, KCAW-FM 104.7. **Television:** Cable channels. **Newspaper:** *Daily Sitka Sentinel.*

Private Aircraft: Sitka airport on Japonski Island; elev. 21 feet/6m; length 6,500 feet/1,981m; asphalt; fuel 100, jet A-50. Sitka seaplane base adjacent west; fuel 80, 100.

One of the most scenic of southeastern Alaskan cities, Sitka rests on the ocean shore protected at the west by a myriad of small islands and Cape Edgecumbe. Mount Edgecumbe, the Fuji-like volcano (dormant), is 3,201 feet/976m high.

The site was originally occupied by Tlingit Indians. Alexander Baranof, chief manager of the Russian–American Company headquartered in Kodiak, built a trading post and fort (St. Michael's Redoubt) north of Sitka in 1799. Indians burned down the fort and looted the warehouses. Baranof returned in 1804, and by 1808 Sitka was capital of Russian Alaska. Baranof was governor from 1790 to 1818. A statue of the Russian governor was unveiled in 1989; it is located outside of the Centennial Bldg. Castle Hill in Sitka is where Alaska changed hands from Russia to the United States in 1867. Salmon was the mainstay of the economy from the late 1800s until the 1950s, when the numbers of salmon decreased. A pulp mill was established at nearby Silver Bay in 1960. Today, tourism, along with the mill, commercial fishing, cold storage plants and government provide most jobs.

ACCOMMODATIONS

Sitka has several hotels/motels, most with adjacent restaurants. Bed and breakfasts are also available.

Sitka Youth Hostel is located at the United Methodist Church, 303 Kimsham St. (1½ blocks north from Peterson Avenue and Halibut Point Road). Open June 1 to Sept. 1; 20 beds, showers, no kitchen facilities. Phone (907) 747-8356.

An array of businesses are clustered in the downtown area, including restaurants, a laundry, drugstore, clothing and grocery stores and gift shops. Shopping and services are also available along Sawmill and Halibut Point roads. Dump stations are located at the City Maintenance Shop at 1410 Halibut Point Road; and at the Wastewater Treatment Plant on Japonski Island.

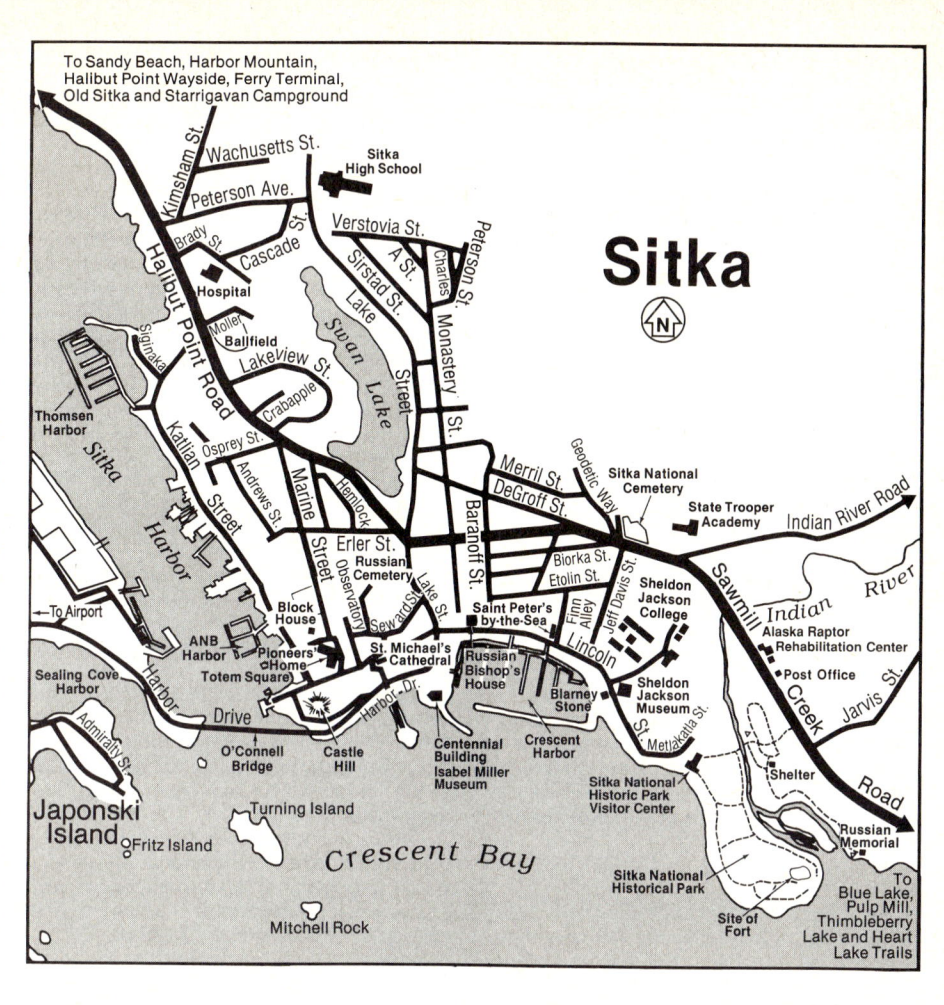

Four campgrounds are available in the Sitka area. From the ferry terminal south they are: the U.S. Forest Service's Starrigavan Campground at **Milepost 7.8** Halibut Point Road, with 30 sites, water, tables, pit toilets, 14-day limit, $5 fee; Sportsman's Campground (operated by Sitka Sportsman's Assoc.), located 1 block south of the ferry terminal on Halibut Point Road, with 8 sites, water and electrical hookups, $10.40 fee, reservations accepted (phone 747-8791); Sealing Cove (operated by the City and Borough of Sitka), located adjacent Sealing Cove Boat Harbor on Japonski Island, has overnight parking for 26 RVs, water and electrical hookups, 15-night limit, $10 fee; and Sawmill Creek Campground (U.S. Forest Service) at **Milepost 5.4** Sawmill Creek Road,

---

MT. VIEW BED & BREAKFAST
201 Cascade Creek Road
P.O. Box 119, Sitka, Alaska 99835
Phone (907) 747-8966
Private & Shared Baths • Furnished Apartments
Laundry Facilities • No Smoking • No Alcohol

HELGA'S BED & BREAKFAST
Located on the beach — Fantastic View
• OPEN YEAR AROUND •
(907) 747-5497
2821 Halibut Point Road
P.O. Box 1885, Sitka, Alaska 99835

SEAFISH ALASKA
Personalized Saltwater Fishing in Spectacular Sitka Sound
HALF-DAY or ALL DAY
(907) 747-5497
P.O. Box 1855, Sitka, Alaska 99835

BIORKA Bed & Breakfast
Conveniently located in town
Private Entrance and Bath
611 Biorka St., Sitka, AK 99835
(907) 747 3111
No Smoking   No Alcohol

---

the POTLATCH house

Six blocks from Downtown
"Call ahead and book the salmon or halibut trip you've only dreamed about"

Large modern rooms
Daily and Weekly Rates

Ample Parking
Courtesy Pickup from Ferry or Airport
Rental Cars starting at $29.95
Car-Room Packages starting at $89.95
(based on availability)

Children under 12 Free
Color Cable TV • Direct dial telephones
Laundry facilities
Lounge & dining room • Room service

713 Katlian Street, Sitka, Alaska 99835
(907) 747-8611 • FAX (907) 747-5810

has 6 sites for self-contained RVs and tenting, boil water, no camping fee.

TRANSPORTATION

Air: Scheduled jet service via Alaska Airlines. Charter and commuter service also available. The airport is on Japonski Island, across O'Connell Bridge, 1.7 miles/2.7 km from downtown via Airport Road. Airport facilities include ticket counters, rental cars, small gift shop, restaurant and lounge. Van service to downtown hotels available.

Ferry: Alaska Marine Highway ferry terminal is located at **Milepost 7** Halibut Point Road; phone 747-8737. Buses for downtown meet all ferries. Van and taxi service also available. Sitka is connected via the Marine Highway to other Southeast ports, Prince Rupert, BC, and Bellingham, WA (see MARINE ACCESS ROUTES section).

Bus: Available to downtown hotels.

Taxi: Local service is available.

Car Rental: At airport.

Highways: Halibut Point Road, 7.9 miles/12.7 km, and Sawmill Creek Road, 7.4 miles/11.9 km; see logs this section.

Cruise Ships: Sitka is a popular port of call for several cruise lines.

Private Boats: Transient moorage available at ANB Harbor, located downtown next to the fuel dock; Thomsen Harbor on Katlian Street, 0.6 mile from city center; and Sealing Cove on Japonski Island. Moorage is limited during the summer.

ATTRACTIONS

St. Michael's Cathedral is the focal point of Sitka's history as the capital of Russian Alaska. Built in 1844–48 by Bishop Innocent Veniaminov of the Russian Orthodox Church, this building stood for 118 years as one of the finest examples of rural Russian church architecture until it was destroyed by fire on Jan. 2, 1966. Priceless icons, some dating back before 1800, were saved by townspeople and are now back in place in the rebuilt cathedral (an exact replica).

St. Michael's is located in the center of Lincoln Street downtown; a donation is requested when entering to view icons. Open daily during summer season (June 1 to Sept. 30), 11 A.M. to 3 P.M. St. Michael's currently serves a Russian Orthodox congregation of about 100 families in Sitka. Visitors are reminded that this is an active parish conducting weekly services.

Castle Hill (Baranof Castle Hill Historic Site) is where Alaska changed hands from Russia to the United States on Oct. 18, 1867. Castle Hill was the site of Baranof's Castle. Walkway to site is located on the south side by the bridge (look for sign).

Sitka Pioneers' Home, near the waterfront at Lincoln and Katlian streets, was built in 1934. Pioneers welcome visitors, and handicrafts made by the residents are sold in the shop in the basement of the home.

The Prospector is a 13½-foot/4-m clay and bronze statue in front of the Pioneers' Home. Done by Alonzo Victor Lewis, the statue was dedicated on Alaska Day in 1949. Lewis's model was a real pioneer, William "Skagway Bill" Fonda.

Totem Square is across Katlian Street from the Pioneers' Home and contains a totem, petroglyphs, Russian cannon and 3 large anchors found in Sitka Harbor and believed to be 18th century English.

Russian Blockhouse beside Pioneers' Home is a replica of the blockhouse that separated Russian and Tlingit sections of Sitka after the Tlingits moved back to the area 20 years after the 1804 battle. (See model of early Sitka in Centennial Bldg.)

New Archangel Russian Dancers, a group of local women, perform authentic Russian dances in authentic costumes. Performances are scheduled to coincide with the arrival of cruise ships. Fee charged. Inquire at the Centennial Bldg. for details.

Old Russian Cemetery is located behind Pioneers' Home and includes graves of such notables as Princess Maksoutoff, wife of Alaska's last Russian governor.

Sitka National Cemetery, at **Milepost 0.5** Sawmill Creek Road, is open 8 A.M. to 5 P.M. daily (maintained by the Veterans Administration). It was known locally as military cemetery. In 1924 Pres. Calvin Coolidge designated the site as Sitka National Cemetery and until WWII it was the only national cemetery west of the Rockies. Civil War veterans, veterans of the Aleutian Campaign in WWII and many notable Alaskans are buried here. One gravestone is dated December 1867, 2 months after the United States purchase of Alaska from Russia.

Alaska Day Celebration, Oct. 14-18, celebrates the transfer of Alaska from Russia to the United States with a reenactment of the event, complete with Sitka's own 9th (Manchu) Infantry, authentic uniforms and working muskets of the period. Period costumes and beards are the order of the day. Events ranging from pageant to costume ball and parade highlight the affair.

Annual Sitka Summer Music Festival (June 5-26, 1992). Concerts on Tuesday, Friday and some Saturday evenings in the Centennial Bldg., praised for its excellent acoustics. Emphasizing chamber music, an international group of professional musicians gathers to give evening concerts during the festival, plus open rehearsals. Advance tickets are a good idea; the concerts are popular. Dress is informal and concert-goers may have the opportunity to talk with the musicians. Children under 6 years not admitted.

Centennial Building, by the boat harbor on Harbor Drive, is used for Russian dance performances, music festivals, banquets and conventions. Its glass-fronted main hall overlooks Sitka Sound. Chamber of commerce and Sitka Visitors Bureau offices are located here. Nearby is a large hand-carved Tlingit canoe made from a single log.

Isabel Miller Museum, located in the Centennial Bldg., has permanent exhibits highlighting the history of Sitka and its people. Russian tools, paintings from all eras, fishing and forestry exhibits, Alaska Purchase exhibit, and an 8-foot-square scale model of Sitka in 1867 are among the displays. Operated by the Sitka Historical Society, hosts are available to answer questions. Open year-round. Hours are 8 A.M. to 5 P.M.

RUSSIA ALASKA

For years, the Russian flag flew over Sitka—next to Tlingit totems. Culturally rich. Strikingly scenic. And waters that yield the world's largest salmon. Sitka is a must for anyone in search of Alaska.

For information, write:

Sitka
Sitka Convention & Visitors Bureau
P.O. Box 1226-MP
Sitka, Alaska 99835
(907) 747-5940

Karras
BED & BREAKFAST
230 Kogwanton Street
Sitka, Alaska 99835
Rates: $43.20 to $59.40
Centrally Located   (907) 747-3978

Sitka Super 8 Motel
Complimentary coffee • Remote control cable TV • Non-smoking rooms & suites available • FAX (907) 747-8804 ext. 103

404 Sawmill Creek Rd. • Sitka, AK 99835
(907) 747-8804 or **1-800-800-8000**

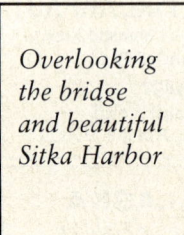

Marina
Italian and Mexican Restaurant

Overlooking the bridge and beautiful Sitka Harbor

205 Harbor Drive
Sitka, Alaska

Lunch & Dinner
Open 7 Days A Week
Credit Cards Accepted

(907) 747-8840

Birds of prey are the featured attraction at the Raptor Center. (John W. Warden)

daily in summer; 10 A.M. to noon and 1-4 P.M. weekdays, and by appointment during the winter.

Sitka Lutheran Church, downtown on Lincoln Street, has a small historical display. This was the first organized Lutheran congregation west of the Rockies and the first protestant church in Alaska.

Sitka National Historical Park reflects both the community's rich Tlingit Indian heritage and its Russian-ruled past. The park consists of 2 units; the Fort Site, located at the end of Lincoln Street, 0.5 mile/0.8 km from town, and the Russian Bishop's House, located on Lincoln Street near Crescent Harbor.

At the Fort Site stood the Tlingit fort, burned to the ground by Russians after the 1804 Battle of Sitka; this was the last major stand by the Tlingits against Russian settlement. For Alexander Baranof, leader of the Russians, the battle was revenge for the 1802 destruction of Redoubt St. Michael by the Tlingits. There is a visitor center here with audiovisual programs and exhibits of Indian artifacts. The Southeast Alaska Indian Cultural Center has contemporary Tlingit artists demonstrate and interpret for visitors various traditional arts.

There is a self-guiding trail through the park to the fort site and battleground of 1804. The National Park Service conducts guided walks; check for schedule. The park's totem pole collection stands near the visitor center and along the trail. The totem pole collection contains both original pieces collected in 1901-03, and copies of originals lost to time and the elements. The pieces, primarily from Prince of Wales Island, were collected by Alaska governor John Brady (now buried in Sitka National Cemetery). The originals were exhibited at the 1904 St. Louis Exposition.

The Russian Bishop's House was built by the Russian-American Co. in 1842 for the first Russian Orthodox Bishop to serve Alaska. It was occupied by the church until 1969, and was added to Sitka National Historical Park in 1972. The house is one of the last major Russian log structures remaining in Sitka, and one of the few remaining in North America.

The park's visitor center is open daily except weekends, 8 A.M. to 5 P.M., October to May; daily, 8 A.M. to 6 P.M., June to September. The park grounds and trails are open daily, 5 A.M. to 10 P.M. in summer, shorter hours in winter. The Russian Bishop's House is open 9 A.M. to 5 P.M. daily in summer; other times by appointment. The visitor center is closed Thanksgiving, Christmas and New Year's. No admission fee. Phone 747-6281 for more information.

Sheldon Jackson Museum, on the Sheldon Jackson College campus, contains some of the finest Native arts and crafts found in Alaska. Much of it was collected by missionary Sheldon Jackson and is now owned by the state of Alaska. Admission $2, children free. Open in summer 8 A.M. to 5 P.M. daily. Winter hours: Tuesday through Saturday, 10 A.M. to 4 P.M.

All-Alaska Logging Championships (June 27-28, 1992) features loggers from Alaska and the Pacific Northwest competing in splicing, stock power saw bucking, double-hand bucking, horizontal and vertical ax chopping, tree topping and choker setting among other events. Women's events include the rolling pin toss and sawing events. While the contestants are all professional and experienced loggers, there are a few events for amateurs and the general public, such as amateur chopping and Jack-and-Jill bucking (2 contestants use a handsaw to cut through a 24-inch spruce).

Alaska Pulp Corporation on Sawmill Creek Road offers a free video presentation of its logging and pulp mill operations. Open Monday through Friday 8 A.M. to 4:30 P.M. in the Administration Building. This company produces dissolving pulp, most of which is sold overseas and converted into rayon.

Blarney Stone, across from Sheldon Jackson College. Believed to originally have been called Baranof's stone and used as a resting stop by Russian-American Co. chief manager Alexander Baranof.

O'Connell Bridge, 1,225 feet/373m long, connecting Sitka with Japonski Island, was the first cable-stayed, girder-span bridge in the United States. It was dedicated Aug. 19, 1972. You'll get a good view of Sitka and the harbors by walking across this bridge.

Old Sitka, at **Milepost 7.5** Halibut Point Road, is a registered national historic landmark and the site of the first Russian settlement in the area in 1799, known then as Fort Archangel Michael. In 1802, in a surprise attack, the Tlingit Indians of the area destroyed the fort and killed most of its occupants, driving the Russians out until Baranof's successful return in 1804.

Visit the Alaska Raptor Rehabilitation Center, located at 1101 Sawmill Creek Road (**Milepost 0.8**) just across Indian River, within easy walking distance of downtown Sitka. This unique facility treats injured eagles, hawks, owls and other birds of prey. Visitors will have the opportunity of seeing American bald eagles and other raptors close up, review case histories of birds treated at the center, observe medical care being administered to current patients, and watch as eagles are exercised in anticipation of their release into the wild. The facility is open several days a week for self-guided tours, or attend one of the center's education programs. The schedule is subject to ferry and cruise ship arrivals. These guided interpretive tours are scheduled frequently during the summer; phone 747-8662 for times. Admission fee charged for guided tours; donations accepted for self-guided tours.

Hiking Trails. The Sitka Ranger District office at 204 Siginaka Way can provide information sheets and maps for area trails. Trails include Harbor Mountain Ridge trail, which begins near the summit of Harbor Mountain and offers some spectacular views; 2.5-mile/4.8-km Gavan Hill trail; 2.5-mile/4-km Mount Verstovia trail; the easy 5-mile/8-km Indian River trail; and the short Beaver Lake trail off Sawmill Creek Road on Blue Lake Road.

AREA FISHING: Sitka holds an annual salmon derby. Saltwater fishing charters available locally. There are also many lakes and rivers on Baranof Island with good fishing; these range from **Katlian River**, 11 miles/17.7 km northeast of Sitka by boat, to more remote waters such as **Rezanof Lake**, which is 40 air miles/64 km southeast of Sitka. USFS public-use cabins at some lakes (see Cabins in the GENERAL INFORMATION section). Stop by the Dept. of Fish and Game office at 304 Lake St. for details on fishing.

Sawmill Creek Road Log

Sawmill Creek Road is a 7.4-mile/11.9-km road, paved for the first 5.4 miles/8.7 km, which begins at Lake Street and ends beyond the pulp mill at Silver Bay.

0 Intersection of Lake Street (Halibut Point Road) and Sawmill Creek Road.
0.5 (0.8 km) Sitka National Cemetery.
0.7 (1.1 km) Indian River bridge.

White's PHARMACY
Open 7 days a week
'til 9 p.m. weekdays

• Prescriptions • First Aid Kits
• Fishing Licenses
• Maps • Charts • Books
• Magazines • Film • Cards
• Next Day Photo Processing
• Jewelry • Gifts

705 HALIBUT POINT ROAD, SITKA, ALASKA 99835 • (907) 747-5755 • LAKESIDE SHOPPING CENTER

Sheldon Jackson Museum Shop
in the Sheldon Jackson Museum
104 College Drive, Sitka, Alaska 99835
(907) 747-6233

• Gifts of fine Native Alaskan arts and crafts
• Ivory
• Baskets
• Silver Jewelry
• Eskimo Dolls
• Beadwork

May 15-Sept 15 8-5 M-F
Sept 15-May 15 10-4 T-Sa

Beginning of Indian River trail on left.
 0.9 (1.4 km) Alaska Raptor Rehabilitation Center.
 1 (1.6 km) Post office.
 1.7 (2.7 km) Mount Verstovia trail on left next to supper club.
 3.6 (5.8 km) Thimbleberry Creek bridge.
 3.7 (6 km) On left past bridge is start of Thimbleberry Lake and Heart Lake trail. Hike in 0.5 mile/0.8 km to **Thimbleberry Lake**, brook trout to 12 inches, use eggs, May to September. Trail continues 1 mile/1.6 km past Thimbleberry Lake to **Heart Lake**, brook trout.
 4.4 (7.1 km) Scenic viewpoint turnout.
 5.3 (8.5 km) Alaska Pulp Corp.
 5.4 (8.7 km) Blue Lake Road on left. Pavement ends on Sawmill Creek Road. Blue Lake Road (narrow dirt) leads 2.2 miles/3.5 km to small parking area and short downhill trail to Blue Lake (no recreational facilities; check with city for information). At Mile 1.5 on right is Sawmill Creek USFS campground (unmaintained). **Blue Lake**, rainbow, May to September, use flies, lure or bait. Lightweight skiff or rubber boat recommended.
 5.7 (9.2 km) Sawmill Creek and bridge.
 7.2 (11.6 km) Public road ends at Herring Cove near mouth of Silver Bay (boat tours of the bay available in Sitka). City road to hydroelectric power plant continues.
 7.4 (11.9 km) Gate marking boundary of city road. Road closed to vehicles beyond this point; access for hikers and bicyclists only. No guardrails or road signs to road end.
 10.5 (16.9 km) Fish hatchery and gate. Steep grades; watch for rocks on road.
 13.7 (22 km) Road end. Green Lake Power Plant.

Halibut Point Road Log

Halibut Point Road (paved) leads northwest from the intersection of Harbor Drive and Lincoln Street past Old Sitka to Starrigavan Creek Campground.

 0 Harbor Drive and Lincoln Street. Proceed northwest (road is now Lake Street).
 0.1 (0.2 km) Fire station. Intersection with Sawmill Creek Road; keep left.
 0.3 (0.5 km) **Swan Lake** to right of road, rainbow from 12 to 14 inches.
 0.6 (1 km) Katlian Street on left leads to boat ramp and then to downtown. Hospital to the right.
 1.8 (2.9 km) Pioneer Park picnic and day-use area with beach access; parking available.
 2.2 (3.5 km) Cascade Creek bridge.
 2.3 (3.7 km) Tongass National Forest work center.
 2.4 (3.9 km) Sandy Beach; good swimming beach, ample parking, view of Mount Edgecumbe. Whales are sometimes sighted from here.
 3.8 (6.1 km) Viewpoint. On a clear day you can see for 50 miles/80 km.
 4.2 (6.8 km) Harbor Mountain Road on right. Steep gravel, accessible to cars. Road leads 5 miles/8 km to road end and Harbor Mountain Ridge trail to lookout at 2,300 feet/701m.
 4.4 (7.1 km) Granite Creek bridge. Just beyond the bridge on left is Halibut Point picnic wayside with swimming beach, shelters, tables, fireplaces and toilets.
 7 (11.3 km) Alaska Marine Highway ferry terminal on left.
 7.3 (11.7 km) Boat ramp, litter barrel and pit toilet to left.
 7.5 (12.1 km) Old Sitka historical site at left, and Starrigavan Creek bridge just ahead. Old Sitka was the site of the Russian Fort Archangel Michael, established in 1799. Commemorative plaque and historical markers. The site is a registered national historic landmark. A narrow road on the right runs along the bank of Starrigavan Creek, where pink salmon spawn in August and September.
 7.6 (12.2 km) Road on right leads several miles along Starrigavan River valley. Off-road vehicles permitted.
 7.8 (12.6 km) Starrigavan Creek camping and picnic areas. Access to beach.
 Starrigavan Bay, Dolly Varden, pink and silver salmon, May to October.
 7.9 (12.7 km) Road ends.

Kake

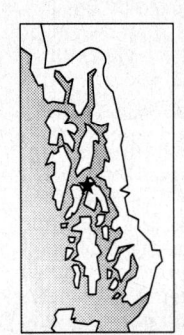

Located on northwest coast of Kupreanof Island in central southeastern Alaska; Petersburg is 40 air miles/64 km or 65 miles/105 km by boat to the southeast; Juneau is 95 air miles/153 km northeast. **Population:** 682 (approximately 85 percent Native). **Emergency Services: Police**, phone 785-3393. **Public Health Center**, phone 785-3333. **Maritime Search and Rescue**, phone the Coast Guard at 1-800-478-5555.

Visitor Information: City of Kake, Box 500, Kake 99830.

Elevation: Sea level. **Climate:** Less than average rainfall for southeastern Alaska, approximately 50 inches annually. Mild temperatures. January average temperatures are around freezing. Slightly warmer than nearby Petersburg.

Private Aircraft: Kake seaplane base, located adjacent southeast; fuel 100. Airstrip 1 mile/1.6 km west; elev. 148 feet/45m; length 4,000 feet/1,219m; gravel; unattended.

Transportation: Air–Scheduled service from Petersburg (25-minute flight), Juneau (1 hour), Wrangell and Sitka. **Ferry**–Alaska Marine Highway vessel from Petersburg and Sitka. See MARINE ACCESS ROUTES section for schedule.

Accommodations at local inn and bed and breakfast. There are several general stores, a cafe and other services. Church groups include Baptist, Salvation Army, Presbyterian and Assembly of God.

The town is permanent village of the Kake (pronounced cake) tribe of the Tlingit Indians. The Tlingits from Kake had a well-earned reputation for aggression in the 18th and 19th centuries. In 1869, the Kakes murdered 2 Sitka traders in revenge for the shooting of a Native by a Sitka sentry. Reprisals taken by the U.S. resulted in the shelling and destruction of 3 Kake villages. The tribe eventually settled at the present-day site of Kake, where the government established a school in 1891. Residents have historicallly drawn ample subsistence from the sea. However, with the advent of a cash economy, the community has come to depend on commercial fishing, fish processing (there is a cannery) and logging. The post office was established in 1904 and the city was incorporated in 1952. The city's claim to fame is its totem, reputedly the world's tallest at 132 feet, 6 inches. It was carved for the 1967 Alaska Purchase Centennial Celebration.

Angoon

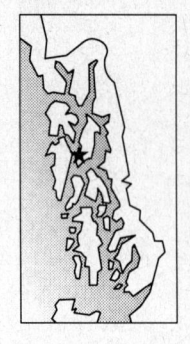

Located on west coast of Admiralty Island on Chatham Strait, at the mouth of Kootznahoo Inlet. The east end of Peril Strait is directly across Chatham Strait from Angoon. Juneau is 60 air miles/96.6 km northeast. Sitka is 41 miles/66 km southwest. **Population:** 685. **Emergency Services: Police**, phone 788-3631. **Clinic**, phone 788-3633.

Visitor Information: Local people are happy to help. You may also contact the U.S. Forest Service's Admiralty Island National Monument office in Angoon (phone 788-3166) or the city of Angoon (phone 788-3653).

Elevation: Sea level. **Climate:** Moderate weather with about 40 inches of annual rainfall and mild temperatures.

Private Aircraft: Angoon seaplane base; 0.9 mile/1.4 km southeast; unattended.

Transportation: Air–Scheduled seaplane service from Juneau. **Ferry**–Alaska Marine Highway service. See MARINE ACCESS ROUTES section for schedule.

Accommodations available at a motel and a bed and breakfast. There is a general store. Fuel service available. There are no RV facilities. Charter fishing boats and canoes are available. Transient moorage for private boats available.

Angoon is a long-established Tlingit Indian settlement at the entrance to Kootznahoo Inlet. It is the only permanent community on Admiralty Island. On Killisnoo Island, across the harbor from the state ferry landing, a community of mostly summer homes has grown up along the island beaches. The lifestyle of this primarily Tlingit community is heavily subsistence: fish, clams, seaweed, berries and venison. Fishing, mostly hand trolling for king and coho salmon, is the principal industry.

The scenery of Admiralty Island draws many visitors to Angoon. All but the northern portion of the island was declared a national monument in December 1980 and is jointly managed by the U.S. Forest Service and Kootznoowoo Inc. Kootznahoo Inlet and Mitchell Bay near Angoon offer a network of small wooded islands, reefs and channels for kayaking. Mitchell Bay and Admiralty Lakes Recreational Area are the 2 major recreational attractions within the monument. Wildlife includes many brown bears (Admiralty Island's Indian name *Kootznoowoo* means "Fortress of Bears"), Sitka black-tailed deer and bald eagles. There are 12 USFS cabins available for public use in the monument; reservations and fee are required. Contact the U.S. Forest Service in Angoon. Also see Cabins in the GENERAL

INFORMATION section.

Local residents can provide directions to the interesting old Killisnoo graveyards, located both on the island and on the Angoon shore of the old Killisnoo settlement, which once was one of the larger communities in southeastern Alaska.

Fishing for salmon is excellent in the Angoon area. (Record kings have been caught in nearby Kelp Bay and in Angoon harbor.) There is also excellent halibut and other bottom fish fishing. Trout (cutthroat and Dolly Varden) fishing in the lakes and streams on Admiralty Island; fair but scattered.

Tenakee Springs

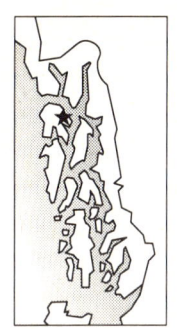

Located on the north shore of Tenakee Inlet on Chichagof Island, 50 miles/80.5 km northeast of Sitka. **Population:** 108. **Visitor Information:** Can be obtained from city hall, phone 736-2221, or from the town's store, phone 736-2205. **Elevation:** Sea level. **Climate:** Average rainfall 63.2 inches annually, with moderate snowfall. **Private Aircraft:** Seaplane base.

Transportation: Air–Scheduled and charter service available. **Ferry**–Alaska Marine Highway service from Sitka and Juneau. See MARINE ACCESS ROUTES section for schedule.

Tenakee Springs has 1 street—Tenakee Avenue—which is about 2 miles/3.2 km long and 4 to 12 feet wide. Many residents use 3-wheel motor bikes for transportation, some ride bicycles, but most walk the short distances between buildings. There are a store, cafe, tavern, clinic with health aide on call, post office, library, senior center and city hall. Accommodations at 7 rental cabins (bring your sleeping bag) are available at Snyder Merchantile, and the Tenakee Inn offers rooms and bunkhouse accommodations. Reservations suggested. Tenakee Springs became a city in 1971 and has a mayor, council and planning commission. The city has limited TV and radio reception.

The word Tenakee comes from the Tlingit word *tinaghu*, meaning "Coppery Shield Bay." This refers to the loss of 3 copper shields, highly prized by the Tlingits, in a storm.

The hot springs (temperature from 106°F to 108°F/41°C to 42°C) brought people to Tenakee at the turn of the century. A bathhouse, completed in 1940, is located on the waterfront and has posted times of use for men and women. The facility is maintained by contributions from residents and visitors.

The major industry at Tenakee might be described as relaxation, as many retirees have chosen to live here, away from the bustle of other Southeast cities. There are many summer homes along Tenakee Avenue. During the summer, watch for whales in Tenakee Inlet, which are sometimes spotted from town.

Some logging is under way in the area around Tenakee. Tenakee Inlet produces salmon, halibut, Dungeness and king crab, red snapper and cod. A small fleet of fishing vessels is home-ported in Tenakee's harbor, located about 0.5 mile/0.8 km east of town. Although many visitors come to Tenakee to hunt and fish, there are no hunting guides or rental boats available locally. There is a fishing charter service.

Hoonah is located on the northeast shore of Chichagof Island. (John W. Warden)

Pelican

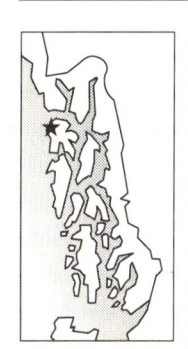

Located on Lisianski Inlet on the northwest coast of Chichagof Island. **Population:** 290. **Emergency Services: Public Safety Officer** and **Fire Department**, phone 735-2212. **Clinic**, phone 735-2250. **Elevation:** Sea level. **Climate:** Average winter temperatures from 21°F/-6°C to 39°F/4°C; summer temperatures from 51°F/11°C to 62°F/17°C. Total average annual precipitation is 127 inches, with 120 inches of snow.

Private Aircraft: Seaplane base; fuel 80, 100.

Transportation: Air–Scheduled air service from Juneau via Glacier Bay Airlines and Wings of Alaska. Also scheduled service from Sitka via Bell Air. **Ferry**–Alaska Marine Highway vessel serves Pelican. See MARINE ACCESS ROUTES section for schedules.

Pelican has 2 bar-and-grills (1 with 4 rooms for rent), a bed and breakfast, a cafe, grocery and dry goods stores, laundromats and 2 liquor stores. There is a small-boat harbor, marine repair and a fuel dock.

Established in 1938 by Kalle (Charley) Raataikainen, and named for Raataikainen's fish packer, *The Pelican,* Pelican relies on commercial fishing and seafood processing. The cold storage plant processes salmon, halibut, crab, herring and black cod, and is the primary year-round employer. Pelican has dubbed itself "closest to the fish," a reference to its close proximity to the rich Fairweather salmon grounds. Nonresident fishermen swell the population during the salmon trolling season, from about June to mid-September, and the king salmon winter season, from October through April. Pelican was incorporated in 1943. Most of Pelican is built on pilings over tidelands. A wooden boardwalk extends the length of the community and there are about 2 miles of gravel road.

Local recreation includes kayaking, hiking, fishing, and watching birds and marine mammals.

Hoonah

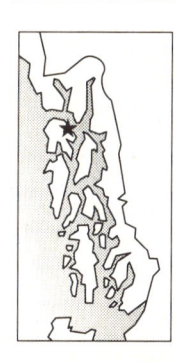

Located on the northeast shore of Chichagof Island, about 40 miles/64 km west of Juneau and 20 miles/32 km south across Icy Strait from the entrance of Glacier Bay. **Population:** 894. **Emergency Services: Alaska State Troopers** and **Hoonah City Police**, phone 945-3655; emergency only phone 911. **Maritime Search and Rescue**, call the Coast Guard at 1-800-478-5555.

Visitor Information: Local business people, city office staff (945-3663, weekdays 8 A.M. to 4:30 P.M.) and the postmaster are happy to help. The U.S. Forest Service office in Hoonah (P.O. Box 135, Hoonah 99829, phone 945-3631) also has visitor information, including a Hoonah area road guide showing forest roads on Chichagof Island.

Elevation: Sea level. **Climate:** Typical southeastern Alaska climate, with considerable rainfall (100 inches annually). Average daily temperature in July, 57°F/13°C; in January, 35°F/1°C. Prevailing winds are southeasterly.

Private Aircraft: Hoonah airport, adjacent southeast; elev. 30 feet/9m; length 3,100 feet/945m; gravel. Seaplane base adjacent.

Transportation: Air–Scheduled and charter service from Juneau. Airport is located about 3 miles from town. **Ferry**–Alaska Marine Highway vessel serves Hoonah. See MARINE ACCESS ROUTES section for schedule.

A lodge offers accommodations. Occasional room rentals and bed-and-breakfast lodging are also available. Hoonah has 3 restaurants, a grocery, 3 general stores, a gift shop, a variety store, bank, 2 marine fuel docks, 2 gas pumps and flying service. The marina here, which has showers and a laundromat, is a popular layover for boaters awaiting permits to enter Glacier Bay.

Hoonah is a small coastal community with a quiet harbor for the seining and trolling fleets. The most prominent structures are a cold storage facility, the lodge, bank, post office and the public school. The village has been occupied since prehistory by the Tlingit people. In the late 1800s, missionaries settled here. Canneries established in the area in the early 1900s spurred the growth of commercial fishing, which remains the mainstay of Hoonah's economy. During the summer fishing season, residents work for nearby Excursion Inlet Packing Co. or Thomson Fishing Co. in town. Halibut season begins in May and salmon season opens in midsummer and runs through September. Logging also contributes to the economy, with employment loading log ships and other industry-related jobs. Subsistence hunting and fishing remain an important lifestyle here, and many families gather food in the traditional way: catching salmon and halibut in summer, shellfish and bottom fish year-round; hunting deer, geese and ducks; berry picking in summer and fall.

Hunting and fishing are the main attractions for visitors. Charter fishing is available locally, with good seasonal king and coho (silver) salmon and halibut fishing as well as crabbing. Guide services are available.

Hoonah is the starting point for an extensive logging and forest road system for northwest Chichagof Island. Island road maps ($2) are available through the USFS in Hoonah, Sitka and Juneau.

Juneau

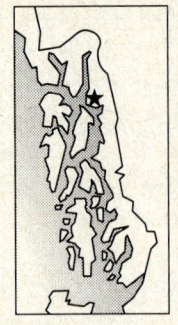

Located in mainland southeastern Alaska on Gastineau Channel opposite Douglas Island; 900 air miles/1448 km (2 hours, 10 minutes flying time) from Seattle, WA, 650 air miles/1046 km (1 hour, 25 minutes by jet) from Anchorage. **Population:** Borough 28,965. **Emergency Services:** Phone 911 for all emergencies. **Police**, phone 586-2780. **Fire Department**, phone 586-5245. **Alaska State Troopers**, phone 789-2161. **Poison Center** and **Hospital**, Bartlett Memorial, phone 586-2611. **Maritime Search and Rescue**, Coast Guard, phone 463-2000 or 1-800-478-5555.

Visitor Information: Juneau Convention & Visitors Bureau, Davis Log Cabin Information Center, 134 3rd St., phone 586-2201 or 586-2284; open year-round 8:30 A.M. to 5 P.M. Monday through Friday; additional hours during the summer, 10 A.M. to 5 P.M. Saturday, Sunday and holidays. To find out about current events in Juneau, phone 586-JUNO for a recorded message. Visitor information kiosk located in Marine Park on waterfront near Merchants Wharf, open daily 8:30 A.M. to 6 P.M., from about June 1 to Sept. 15. Information booth at the airport terminal. Visitor information is also available at the cruise ship terminal on S. Franklin St. when cruise ships are in port, and at the Auke Bay ferry terminal. Large groups contact the Davis Log Cabin Information Center in advance for special assistance.

National Park Service/U.S. Forest Service Information Center at Centennial Hall, 101 Egan Dr.; open 8 A.M. to 5 P.M. daily from Memorial Day to mid-September; 8 A.M. to 5 P.M. Monday through Friday the rest of the year. Phone 586-8751. The center has seasonal exhibits, natural history films and video tapes. USFS cabins may also be reserved here. Juneau Ranger District (USFS), **Milepost 9.4** Glacier Highway (airport area), phone 586-8800, open 8 A.M. to 5 P.M. weekdays. Mendenhall Glacier Visitor Center (USFS), phone 789-0097, open 9 A.M. to 6:30 P.M. daily in summer, weekends only in winter.

Elevation: Sea level. **Climate:** Mild and wet. Average daily maximum temperature in July, 63°F/17°C; daily minimum in January, 20°F/-7°C. Highest recorded temperature was 90°F/32°C in July 1975; the lowest -22°F/-30°C in January 1972. Average annual precipitation, 56.5 inches (airport), 92 inches (downtown); 103 inches of snow annually. Snow on ground intermittently from mid-November to mid-April. Prevailing winds are east-southeasterly. **Radio:** KINY-AM 800, KJNO-AM 630, KTOO-FM 104.3, KTKU-FM 105.1, KSUP-FM 106. **Television:** KJUD Channel 8; JATV cable; KTOO (public television). **Newspaper:** *Juneau Empire* (Monday through Friday).

Private Aircraft: Juneau International Airport, 9 miles/14.5 km northwest; elev. 18 feet/5m; length 8,400 feet/2,560m; asphalt; fuel 80, 100, JP4. Juneau harbor seaplane base, adjacent north; fuel 80, 100, A1. International seaplane base, 7 miles/11.3 km northwest. For more information, phone the Juneau Flight Service Station at 789-6124.

HISTORY AND ECONOMY

In 1880, nearly 20 years before the great gold rushes to the Klondike and to Nome, 2 prospectors named Joe Juneau and Dick Harris found "color" in what is now called Gold Creek, a small, clear stream that runs through the center of present-day Juneau. What they found led to the discovery of one of the largest lodes of gold quartz in the world. Juneau (called Harrisburg the first year) quickly boomed into a gold rush town as claims and mines sprang up in the area.

Jan's View Bed & Breakfast
Offers year-round service, guest kitchen, laundry facilities, on bus line —
1-1/2 miles from downtown
Free pickup on arrival and departure included with a two-day stay
1670 GLACIER HIGHWAY, JUNEAU, ALASKA 99801 • (907) 463-5897

The Driftwood Lodge

**435 Willoughby Avenue W.
Juneau, Alaska 99801**

★ Courtesy Transportation Airport and Ferries
★ Restaurant on premises
★ Free spacious parking area
★ Color TVs and phones in all rooms
★ Glacier tours available
★ Private baths in all rooms
★ Liquor and grocery store on premises
★ Kitchen units up to two-bedroom suites
★ Coffee in rooms

Sixty-two units located downtown next to the Alaska State Museum and Juneau Convention Center. Rooms to accommodate singles or large families. Grocery, restaurant, laundry and liquor store. Handicap rooms available. Year-round service. Rates from $55 – $95. 4 page color Brochure.
VS, AE, MC, DC, CB, SD accepted.

**TOLL-FREE RESERVATIONS
1-800-544-2239
(907) 586-2280**

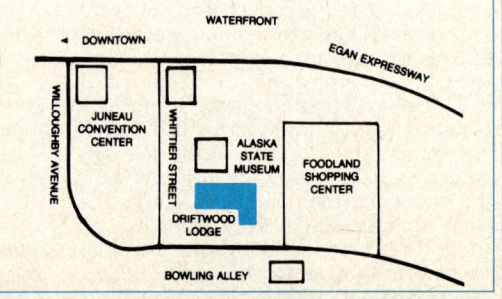

BED & BREAKFAST INN - JUNEAU

Enjoy a full hearty breakfast at our B & B on the outskirts of Juneau.

Bicycles, picnic tables, outdoor grill, and laundry facilities available.

Decorated with Alaskan artwork.

Six rooms with shared baths,
One room with private bath
and a one-bedroom apartment.
Summer rates begin at $48
Fall-Winter rates begin at $40

**1801 Old Glacier Highway
Juneau, Alaska 99801**

RESERVATIONS CALL
(907) 463-5855

Ample Parking for Vehicles

For a time the largest mine was the Treadwell, across Gastineau Channel south of Douglas (which was once a larger town than Juneau), but a cave-in and flood closed the mine in 1917. In 36 years of operation, Treadwell produced $66 million in gold. The Alaska–Gastineau Mine, operated by Bart Thane in 1911, had a 2-mile shaft through Mount Roberts to the Perseverance Mine near Gold Creek. The Alaska–Juneau (A–J) Mine was constructed on a mountain slope south of Juneau and back into the heart of Mount Roberts. It operated until 1944, when it was declared a nonessential wartime activity after producing over $80 milllion in gold. Post–WWII wage and price inflation and the fixed price of gold prevented its reopening.

In 1900, given Juneau's growth, mining activity and location on the water route to Skagway and the Klondike, and the simultaneous decline of Sitka after the Russians left and whaling and fur trade fell off, it was decided to move Alaska's capital to Juneau. Actual transfer of government functions did not occur until 1906.

Congress first provided civil government for Alaska in 1884, and until statehood in 1959 Alaska was governed by a succession of presidential appointees, first as the District of Alaska, then as the Territory of Alaska. Between 1867 (when the U.S. purchased Alaska from Russia) and 1884, the military had jurisdiction over the Dept. of Alaska, except for a 3-year period (1877–79) when Alaska was put under control of the U.S. Treasury Dept. and governed by U.S. Collectors of Customs.

In 1974, Alaskans voted to move the capital from Juneau to a site between Anchorage and Fairbanks, closer to the state's population center. In November 1976 Alaska voters selected a new capital site near Willow, 65 road miles/105 km north of Anchorage on the George Parks Highway. However, in November 1982, voters defeated funding

JUNEAU ADVERTISERS

Alaska Bed & Breakfast
   Association..................Ph. (907) 586-2959
Alaskan Hotel & Bar, The ....167 S. Franklin St.
Bed & Breakfast
   Inn—Juneau ....1801 Old Glacier Hwy.
Blueberry Lodge ....Ph. (907) 463-5886
Dawson's Bed & Breakfast..1941 Glacier Hwy.
Driftwood Lodge, The ....435 Willoughby Ave.
Era Helicopters.................Ph. (907) 586-2030
Fiddlehead Restaurant &
   Bakery, The...........429 W. Willoughby Ave.
Gastineau Salmon
   Hatchery..........................2697 Channel Drive
Glacier Bay Tours
   and Cruises ....(907) 463-5510
Jan's View Bed &
   Breakfast........................1670 Glacier Hwy.
Juneau Convention &
   Visitors Bureau..........................134 3rd St.
Lady Lou Revue..................Ph. (907) 586-3686
Lost Chord, The ....2200 Fritz Cove Rd.
Nina's Originals........................221 Seward St.
Pearson's Pond
   Luxury B & B................Ph. (907) 789-3772
Pot Belly Bed &
   Breakfast.......................Ph. (907) 586-1279
Slovakian House.................Ph. (907) 463-5812
Super 8 Motels................Ph. 1-800-800-8000
Windsock Inn B & B..........Ph. (907) 364-2431
Wings of Alaska.................Juneau Intl. Airport

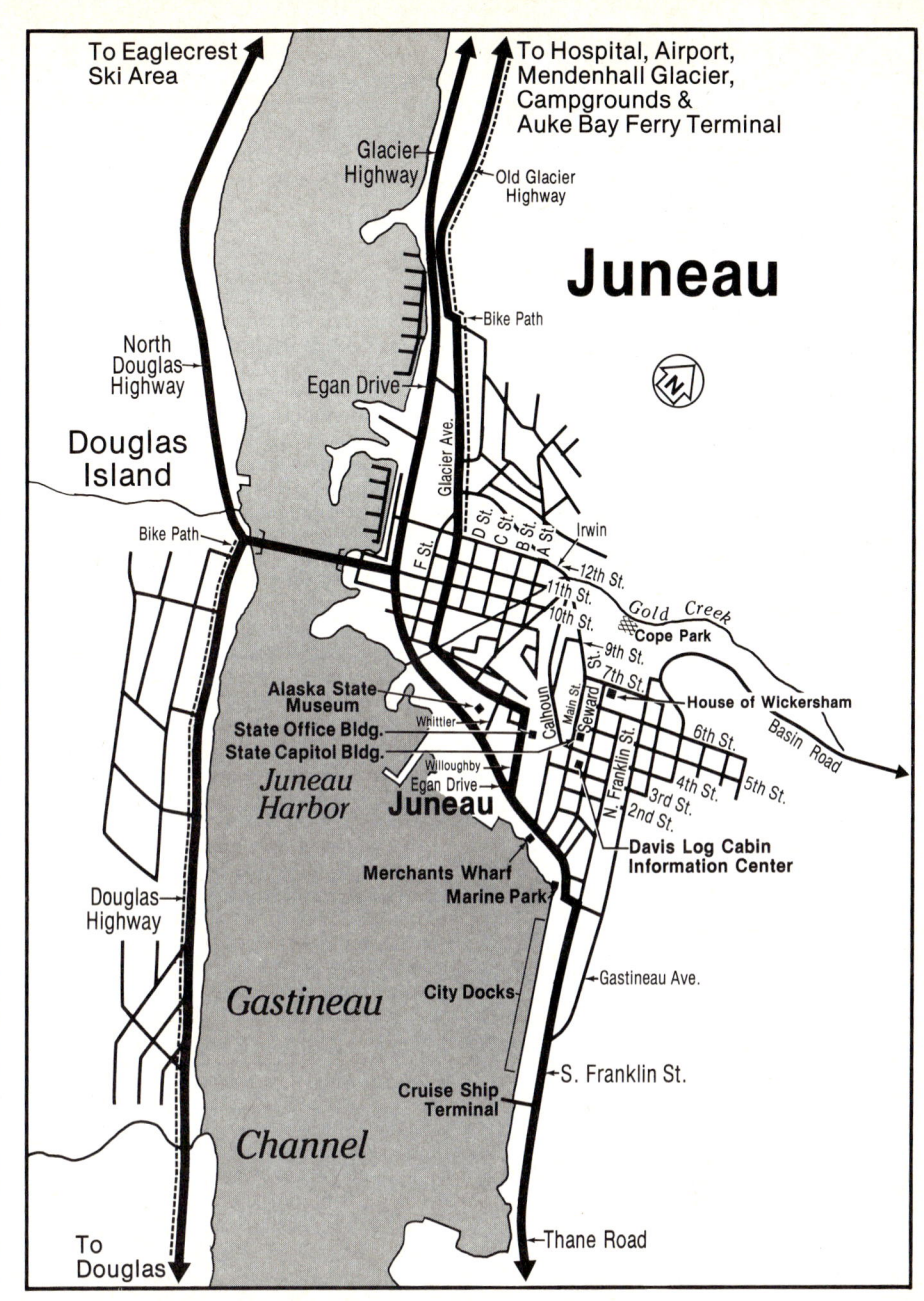

DAWSON'S BED & BREAKFAST

Relax with friendly locals. Comfortable modern home on bus line. 2 miles from downtown. Beautiful view. Full breakfast. Laundry facilities. Parking, transportation, and tours can be arranged.
Year round service. $55-$65 double + tax
Brochure available.   VISA/MasterCard
1941 GLACIER HIGHWAY, JUNEAU, AK 99801
(907) 586-9708

A SLOVAKIAN HOUSE
Bed & Breakfast

Downtown Juneau   Rates $40 - $75
Offering old-world gracious hospitality
Kitchenettes available with laundry facilities
Gladys R. Fory's   Phone (907) 463-5812
127 Behrends Avenue, Juneau, AK 99801

BLUEBERRY LODGE
Bed & Breakfast
HAND-CRAFTED LOG LODGE
- Downhill and Cross-country Skiing
- Fishing, Hiking and Berry Picking
- View of Inland Ocean Waterway, Wetlands, Game Refuge and Eagle's Nest
- Fishing Charters Available
- HOT and HEARTY BREAKFAST
- Families and Groups Welcome ■ Open Year-round ■ No Smoking

9436 N. Douglas Highway, Juneau, Alaska 99801   (907) 463-5886
Your hosts - Jay and Judy Urquhart   Brochure Available

Downtown Juneau is easy to explore on foot. (John W. Warden)

for the capital move.

With the coming of Alaska statehood in 1959, Juneau's governmental role increased even further. Today, government (federal, state and local) comprises an estimated half of the total basic industry. Tourism is the largest employer in the private sector.

DESCRIPTION

Juneau, often called "a little San Francisco," is nestled at the foot and on the side of Mount Juneau (elev. 3,576 feet/1,091m) with Mount Roberts (elev. 3,819 feet/1,164m) rising immediately to the right as you approach up Gastineau Channel. The residential community of Douglas is south of Juneau on Douglas Island; Juneau and Douglas are connected by a bridge. Neighboring residential areas at the airport, Mendenhall Valley and Auke Bay lie north of Juneau on the mainland.

Shopping is in the downtown area and at suburban malls in the airport and Mendenhall Valley areas.

Juneau's skyline is dominated by several government buildings, including the Federal Bldg. (1962), the massive State Office Bldg. (1974), the State Court Bldg. (1975) and the older brick and marble-columned Capitol Bldg. (1931). The modern Sealaska Plaza is headquarters for Sealaska Corp., 1 of the 13 regional Native corporations formed after congressional passage of the Alaska Native Claims Settlement Act in 1971.

To explore downtown Juneau, it is best to park and walk; distances are not great. The streets are narrow and congested with pedestrians and traffic, especially during rush hours, and on-street parking is scarce. Public parking lots are located across from Wharf Mall at Main Street and Egan Drive (2-hour parking) and south of Marine Park at the Marine Park parking garage (3-hour parking).

The Juneau area supports 35 churches, a high school, 2 middle schools, several elementary schools and the University of Alaska–Southeast campus at Auke Lake. There are 3 municipal libraries and the state library.

The area is governed by the unified city and borough of Juneau, which encompasses 3,108 square miles/8060 square km. It is the first unified government in the state, combining the former separate and overlapping jurisdictions of the city of Douglas, city of Juneau and greater Juneau borough.

ACCOMMODATIONS

Juneau has 13 hotels and motels, most of them downtown. There are also several bed and breakfasts. The Juneau International Hostel is located at 614 Harris St. (Juneau 99801), 4 blocks northeast of the Capitol Bldg. All ages are welcome. Check-in time is 5-11 P.M. during summer, 5-10 P.M. the rest of the year. Showers, cooking and laundry facilities are available. Fees from $8 to $11 a night. Open year-round. Phone 586-9559.

More than 60 restaurants offer a wide variety ranging from steaks to hot dogs. Also watch for sidewalk food vendors downtown in summer.

Pearson's Pond Luxury B & B. Affordable, private luxury. Soothe your cares in a steaming spa nestled in the forest on the banks of a scenic pond just steps from your private deck and entrances. Enjoy ample room to live, dine and rest in fully equipped studios or apartment. Behold majestic glaciers, accessible wilderness and wildlife nearby. 3-plus days best; reserve early. (907) 789-3772 evening/weekend. "A definite 10." See display ad this section. [ADVERTISEMENT]

There are 2 U.S. Forest Service campgrounds: Mendenhall Lake (turn off Glacier Highway at **Milepost 9.4** or **12.2** and continue to Montana Creek Road) and Auke Village (**Milepost 15.4** Glacier Highway). Mendenhall Lake has 60 sites (RVs to 22 feet), water, pit toilets, dump station. Auke Village has 11 campsites. There is a private campground with RV hookups located at **Milepost 12.3** Glacier Highway. The City and Borough of Juneau offers limited RV overnight parking spaces at the Juneau Yacht Club for $5 per space, per night, paid at the harbormaster's office (turnoff at **Milepost 1.7** Egan Drive/Glacier Highway), and at Savikko Park/Sandy Beach (**Milepost 2.5** Douglas Highway). Contact the visitor information center (586-2201) for a brochure on RV facilities. Dump stations are located at Mendenhall Lake campground, Valley Chevron at Mendenhall Valley shopping mall, and Savikko Park. ▲

THE ALASKAN HOTEL & BAR
ON NATIONAL REGISTER OF HISTORIC SITES
Established 1913
Antique Oak Bar
Kitchenettes
Hot Tubs
167 South Franklin-MP, Juneau, Alaska 99801
Call toll free for reservations (800) 327-9347

Alaska Bed & Breakfast Association

A personalized reservation service for Alaska and Yukon. Hospitality in unique homes offering rooms, suites, apartments and cabins to meet your needs while experiencing the North lifestyle.
Brochure and Directory at Request:
P.O. Box 21890, Juneau, Alaska 99802
(907) 586-2959 • FAX (907) 463-6788

Pioneer Alaskan Hosts at —
WINDSOCK INN B & B
(5 minutes from downtown Juneau)
Catering to Retirees, Teachers and Foreign Travelers.
Courtesy Airport/Ferry transp. for visits of two nights or more.
Rates: $45 - $50
(907) 364-2431 • P.O. Box 240223-MP
DOUGLAS, ALASKA 99824

Beautiful Mornings Begin At 8.
SUPER 8 MOTEL
Toll-Free Reservations:
1-800-800-8000
Four Convenient Alaska Locations
JUNEAU
Ketchikan • Anchorage • Fairbanks

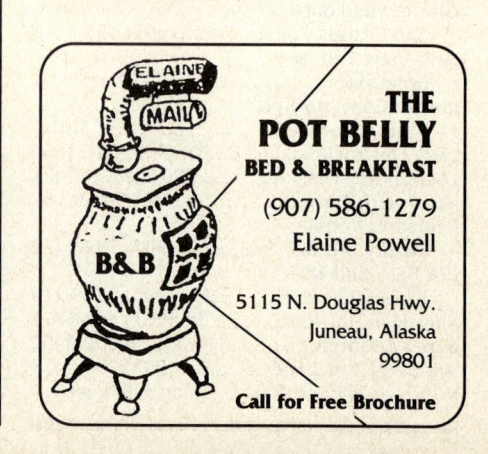

Pearson's Pond
Luxury B & B
4541 Sawa Circle
Juneau, Alaska 99801
(907) 789 - 3772
Always A Safe Landing
• Expansive, quality studios, views
• Pristine ambience, spa, decks, bbq
• Stereo, vcr, kitchen, capuccino
• Sports, laundry, computer, rowboat
• Year-round smoke/pet-free experience
• Near airport/ferry, glacier, trails, shops
• Superb value $64-$94 -10%wk/30%mo
"The Best B & B Ever"

THE POT BELLY BED & BREAKFAST
(907) 586-1279
Elaine Powell
5115 N. Douglas Hwy.
Juneau, Alaska 99801
Call for Free Brochure

TRANSPORTATION

Air: Juneau Municipal Airport turnoff is at **Milepost 8.8** Egan Drive (Glacier Highway). Airport terminal contains ticket counters, lockers, waiting area, gift shop, rental cars, restaurant, lounge and visitor information booth.

The city express bus stops at the airport daily except weekends. Taxi service and van service to downtown are also available. Courtesy vans to some hotels.

Alaska Airlines serves Juneau daily from Seattle, WA, Anchorage, Fairbanks, Ketchikan, Sitka, Yakutat, Cordova, Petersburg and Wrangell. Delta Airlines serves Juneau from Seattle and Fairbanks. Scheduled commuter service to Haines, Skagway, Sitka, Angoon and other points via several air services. Scheduled service between Juneau and Whitehorse, YT, is available in summer.

Charter air service (wheel and floatplanes and helicopters) for hunting, fishing, sightseeing and transportation to other communities (see ads in this section).

Ferry: Juneau is served by Alaska Marine Highway ferries. See MARINE ACCESS ROUTES section for schedule and fares.

Alaska state ferries dock at the Auke Bay terminal at **Milepost 13.9** Glacier Highway; phone 465-3941 or 789-7453. Taxi service and private bus service available from Auke Bay terminal to downtown Juneau.

Bus: Capital Transit system runs from the cruise ship terminal downtown and includes Juneau, Douglas, Auke Bay (the community, which is about 1.5 miles/2.4 km south of the ferry terminal), Mendenhall Valley and airport area. Hourly service Monday through Saturday, year-round, limited service on Sundays. Route map and schedule available at the visitor information center. Flag buses at any corner except in downtown Juneau, where bus uses marked stops only.

Highways: Longest road is Glacier Highway, which begins in downtown Juneau and leads 40.2 miles/64.7 km north to Echo Cove. Other major roads are Mendenhall Loop Road and Douglas and North Douglas highways. See logs this section.

Taxi: 2 companies.

Cruise Ships: Juneau is southeastern Alaska's most frequent port of call. There were 351 port calls by cruise ships in 1991.

The tour boat MV *Fairweather* offers cruises between Juneau and Skagway. Offered on package tours by Gray Line of Alaska, seats are sold on a space available basis to visitors not on a package tour. Contact their Juneau office in the Baranof Hotel lobby, phone 586-3773. The MV *Fairweather* departs from Yankee Cove, **Milepost 33** Glacier Highway.

Car Rental: Available at the airport and downtown. Best to reserve ahead of time because of the great demand for cars.

Private Boats: Transient moorage is available downtown at Harris and Douglas floats and at Auke Bay. Most boaters use Auke Bay. For more information call the Juneau harbormaster at 586-5255 or hail on Channel 16 UHF.

THE LOST CHORD
BED & BREAKFAST
Secluded beach cove on Auke Bay
Jesse & Ellen Jones
2200 Fritz Cove
Juneau, Alaska 99801
(907) 789-7296

FREE BROCHURE

ATTRACTIONS

Juneau walking tour map is available from the Davis Log Cabin Information Center at 134 3rd St. and from other visitor centers and from hotels. See Juneau's many attractions—the Russian church, totems, Capitol Bldg., Governor's Mansion, historic graves, monuments, state museum, city museum, and others.

Charter a Boat for salmon and halibut fishing or sightseeing. The visitor information center can provide a list of charter operators; also see ads in this section.

Charter a Plane for fly-in fishing, hunting, transportation to remote lodges and longer flightseeing trips.

Take a Tour. Tours of Juneau and area attractions—by boat, bus, plane and helicopter—can be arranged. These tours range from sightseeing trips out to Mendenhall Glacier to river trips on the Mendenhall River.

Home of **Nina's Originals**, a unique shop on Seward Street, where distinctive, contemporary high styles are created using finest skins, furs and imported fabrics without use of machines or thread. Coats, hats, purses with an international flavor using patented processes. Owned, operated and designed by Nina and daughter. [ADVERTISEMENT]

Era Helicopters. Soar over the massive Juneau Icefield, viewing 4 unique and distinctive glaciers. Land on a glacier and walk on ice centuries of years old. Fly past historical gold mining areas. Personalized tour with Alaska's oldest and largest helicopter company. Phone (907) 586-2030 or outside Alaska 1-800-843-1947. Tours also available in Anchorage, Mount McKinley and Valdez. [ADVERTISEMENT]

Glacier Bay Tours and Cruises. Special packages, Juneau to Glacier Bay National Park, feature round-trip air, lodging, 1-day and 3-day glacier cruises, sportfishing and more. See Glacier Bay Lodge advertisement in the Glacier Bay section. Contact Glacier Bay Tour Center, 76 Egan Dr., downtown Juneau, 463-5510. For brochure, call toll free 1-800-451-5952. [ADVERTISEMENT]

Visit the Juneau Library. Built on top of the 4-story public parking garage in downtown Juneau, this award-winning designed library by Minch Ritter Voelckers Architects is well worth a visit. Take the elevator to the 5th floor and spend a morning or afternoon reading in this well-lighted and comfortable space with a wonderful view of Juneau, Douglas and Gastineau Channel. Located at South Franklin and Admiralty Way, between Marine Park and the cruise ship terminal.

Juneau–Douglas City Museum, located in the Veteran's Memorial Bldg. next to the State Capitol Bldg. at 4th and Main. Features Juneau's rich gold-mining history with exhibits and video presentations that show the early-day culture, society, politics, commerce, transportation and agriculture. A special display for 1992 is "Images of Glaciers," a nontechnical approach to knowing more about glaciers through photography, paintings, folklore, even a timeless chunk of blue glacier ice. Free walking-tour maps of Juneau are available. Summer hours are 9 A.M. to 5 P.M. weekdays, 11 A.M. to 5 P.M. weekends, May 15 to Sept. 15. Winter hours: noon to 4:30 P.M. Thursday through Saturday, or by appointment at other times; closed in January and February. Admission $1. Phone 586-3572 for more information.

State Capitol Building, at 4th and Main, contains the legislative chambers and the governor's office. Free tours available from capitol lobby; daily on the half-hour from 8:30 A.M. to 5 P.M. in summer. The **State Office Building,** 1 block west, houses the State Historical Library and Kimball theatre

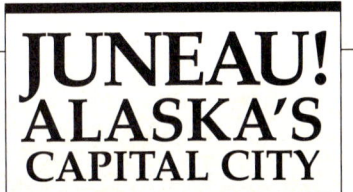

JUNEAU!
ALASKA'S CAPITAL CITY

★ Plenty of RV Parks
★ More than 800 hotel rooms
★ Incredible scenery
★ Drive up to beautiful Mendenhall Glacier
★ Flightseeing
★ Fishing
★ Hiking
★ Alaska State Museum
★ State Capitol & Historic Governor's Mansion
★ Daily ferry service from Haines, Skagway and Prince Rupert

For more information, please write to:
Juneau Convention & Visitors Bureau
134 3rd Street, Dept. 103
Juneau, Alaska 99801

Wings OF ALASKA

PRIVATE CHARTERS
• Glacier Flightseeing
  Glacier Bay
  Tracy Arm Fjord
  Juneau Icefield
• Forest Service Cabins
• Fishing and Camping

DAILY SCHEDULED FLIGHTS
Serving 10 Destinations on the Inside Passage

Repeated Recipient of the Alaska Air Carriers Safety Award

(907) 789-0790
Fax: (907) 789-2021
1873-MP Shell Simmons Dr. • Juneau, AK 99801

organ (free organ concerts at noon Fridays).

Alaska State Museum, on Whittier Street just off Egan Drive, is open weekdays from 9 A.M. to 6 P.M., weekends 10 A.M. to 6 P.M., during summer; open 10 A.M. to 4 P.M. Tuesday through Saturday in winter. Excellent Indian, Athabascan, Eskimo and Aleut cultural displays, wildlife, mining, Russian–American historical exhibits, art and original totems, including the famous Lincoln Totem. Admission $2 adults, children under 18 free. Free Saturday admission during winter.

The **House of Wickersham**, 213 7th St., has an important historical collection dating to the days of the late Judge James Wickersham, one of Alaska's first federal judges, who collected Native artifacts, baskets, many photographs and historical documents during his extensive travels throughout the territory early in the century. Thirty- to 90-minute guided tours, complete with a cup of tea and a sample of sourdough bread, are available from noon to 5 P.M. Sunday through Friday, and 10 A.M. to 2 P.M. Saturday, May through September, or by appointment from October to April. Admission is an optional $1 donation. Phone 586-9001.

The **Governor's Mansion** at 716 Calhoun Ave. has been home to Alaska's chief executives since it was completed in 1913. The 2½-story structure, containing 12,900 square feet of floor space, took nearly a year to build. Group tours by advance arrangement.

Douglas Island Pink and Chum, Inc. opened a new $6.4 million hatchery in 1989. Located on Channel Drive 3 miles from downtown, the Gastineau Salmon Hatchery offers visitors a chance to see 4 of the 5 kinds of Pacific salmon, a fish ladder and incubation areas. The visitors center features interpretive displays, saltwater aquariums with adult salmon and other sea life. Salmon runs return starting in mid-July. Tours are self-guided but hatchery staff is available to answer questions. Open 10 A.M. to 6 P.M. Sunday through Friday, noon to 5 P.M. Saturday, during summer; by appointment during the winter. Admission: $2.25 adults, $1 for children under 12. Phone 463-4810.

See Old Mine Ruins. Remnants from the Treadwell Mine may be seen from Sandy Beach on the Douglas Highway. Ruins from the Alaska–Juneau (A–J) Mine are found along Basin Road. The impressive remains of the A–J mine stamp mill are located on the hillside along Gastineau Channel just south of Juneau; good views from Douglas Island and from the water. Evidence of the Alaska–Gastineau Mine can be seen south of town on Thane Road. Walking tour maps of the Treadwell Mine and Last Chance Basin mining areas are available from Davis Log Cabin Visitor Center and from the city museum.

Marine Park, located at foot of Seward Street, has tables, benches, information kiosk, sculpture of hard-rock miners and lightering facilities for tour ship launches. Free concerts on Friday evenings in summer.

Mount Juneau Waterfall, scenic but difficult to photograph, descends 3,576 feet/1,091m from Mount Juneau to Gold Creek behind the city. Best view is from Basin Road. The waterfall is also visible from Marine Park.

Mount Roberts Trail Observation Point offers an elevated view of Juneau. Though the trail extends to the 3,819-foot/1,164-m summit, an excellent observation point above Juneau is reached by a 20-minute hike from the start of Mount Roberts trail at the top of Starr Hill (6th Street).

Mendenhall Glacier is about 13 miles/21 km from Juneau at the end of Mendenhall Glacier Spur Road. Turn right northbound at **Milepost 9.4** Egan Drive (Glacier Highway) and then drive straight for 3.6 miles/5.8 km to the glacier and visitor center. There is a large parking area and trails lead down to the edge of the lake (a sign warns visitors to stay back; falling ice can create huge waves). The visitor center, a short walk up a paved switchback path (accessible to wheelchairs) from the parking area, is open daily from Memorial Day week through September, 9 A.M. to 6:30 P.M.; weekends only October to May. The visitor center has audiovisual display, glacier view, guided hikes and daily slide and video programs in summer; phone 789-0097 or 586-8800. A 0.5-mile/0.8-km self-guiding nature trail starts behind the visitor center. Trailheads for 2 longer trails—East Glacier and Nugget Creek—are a short walk from the visitor center. Programs and guided hikes with Forest Service interpreters are offered in summer.

Bike Paths. There are designated bike routes to Douglas, to Mendenhall Valley and the glacier and to Auke Bay. The Mendenhall Glacier bike route starts at the intersection of 12th Street and Glacier Avenue; total biking distance is 15 miles/24.1 km. Bikes can be rented downtown.

Juneau Icefield lies immediately to the east of Juneau over the first ridge of mountains, a 1,500-square-mile expanse of mountains and glaciation that is the source of all the glaciers in the area, including Mendenhall, Taku, Eagle and Herbert. Best way to experience and photograph it is via charter flightseeing. Flights usually take 30 to 60 minutes. Helicopter tours, which land on the glacier, are also available. Helicopter tours last from about 45 minutes to 1½ hours.

Ski Eaglecrest, Juneau's downhill and cross-country ski area on Douglas Island. Built and maintained by the city of Juneau, the area features a day lodge, cafeteria, ski rental shop, 2 chair lifts, a tow and runs for experienced, intermediate and beginning skiers. Eight kilometers of maintained cross-country trails available. Open 5 days a week, late November to early April. The view from Eaglecrest alone is worth the visit—Mendenhall Glacier, Juneau Icefield, Lynn Canal, Stephens Passage and more. Drive North Douglas Highway to **Milepost 6.9**, then 5.3 miles/8.5 km up the Eaglecrest access road to the lodge. For more information phone 586-5284, or phone 586-5330 for a recorded message about ski conditions.

Perseverance Theatre presents Duffey and Chapman's *Lady Lou Revue*, a musical based on Robert Service's infamous characters. Performances mid-May to mid-September on the Voices Stage in the Merchants' Wharf Mall. Admission is $14 for adults, $7 for children under 18. Phone 586-3686 for more information. Perseverance Theatre was begun in 1978 by Molly Smith and has established a reputation for artistic

LADY LOU REVUE 
JUNEAU, ALASKA
Mid May—Mid September
A bawdy, rip-roaring musical comedy about the Klondike Goldrush—based on Robert Service's most memorable characters.
Showtimes vary with cruise ship schedule
Downtown Juneau
At Merchants Wharf Mall
FUN FOR ALL AGES
Box office: 586-3686

THE FIDDLEHEAD Restaurant & Bakery
Around the corner from Alaska State Museum
Reservations Welcome. Visa, M/C accepted.
Juneau's Best For Fresh Alaska Seafood
586-3150

World Class GASTINEAU SALMON HATCHERY
Summer hours 10-6 • Winter hours 12-5
View Hatchery Operations, Saltwater Aquariums, Aquaculture Displays and more at our Hatchery Visitor Center. 
Educational Tours Provided
Tour Information (907) 463-4810
Douglas Island Pink & Chum, Inc.
2697 CHANNEL DR.

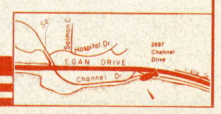

excellence with its production of both classics and original works. Main stage season runs from September through May.

St. Nicholas Russian Orthodox Church, 5th and Gold streets, built in 1894, is a tiny structure of Russian architecture and is now the oldest original Russian church in southeastern Alaska. Visitors are welcome to Sunday services; open daily for summer tours. Phone 586-1023.

Chapel-by-the-Lake (Presbyterian), **Milepost 11.6** Glacier Highway, is a log structure perched above Auke Lake. Its front, entirely of glass, frames the scenic lake, Mendenhall Glacier and mountains. Popular marriage chapel.

Shrine of St. Terese (Catholic), **Milepost 22.8** Glacier Highway, is a natural stone chapel building on its own island connected to shore by a gravel causeway. A 1 P.M. Sunday mass is said during the summer.

Golden North Salmon Derby is a 3-day derby held in early August, offering more than $100,000 in prizes with a $12,000 first prize for the largest king salmon.

Thane Road is a wide, straight paved road beginning just south of downtown Juneau and extending 5.5 miles/8.9 km along Gastineau Channel. Good views of the channel and old mines. Excellent viewpoint for spawning salmon at Sheep Creek bridge and falls, Mile 4.3, in summer.

Hiking Trails. A guide to Juneau trails is widely available in town for $3 per copy. Juneau Parks and Recreation Dept. offers organized hikes; phone 586-5226 for information and schedule.

AREA FISHING: (Several special sportfishing regulations are in effect in the Juneau area; consult current regulations booklet.) Good Dolly Varden fishing available along most saltwater shorelines in Juneau area; pink salmon available about mid-July through August. Good fishing by boat from Juneau, Auke Bay or Tee Harbor in **Favorite** and **Saginaw channels, Chatham Strait** and near mouth of **Taku Inlet,** for salmon, Dolly Varden, halibut and rockfish. Boat in and hike or fly in to **Turner Lake,** 25 miles/40 km east of Juneau, for kokanee and cutthroat; USFS public-use cabins available (see Cabins in the GENERAL INFORMATION section).

For up-to-date angling data for Juneau area, phone 465-4116 for recorded message (April through October). For specific angling information contact the ADF&G, Division of Sport Fish, Area Management Biologist, P.O. Box 20, Douglas 99824; phone 465-4270. A list of charter boats available is maintained at the visitor center.

Egan Drive and Glacier Highway/Juneau Veterans' Memorial Highway Log

Egan Drive from downtown Juneau proceeds north to **Milepost 9.4,** then becomes Glacier Highway. Egan Drive is named for William A. Egan (1914–84), first governor of the state of Alaska. From **Milepost 12.2** to road end, Glacier Highway has been renamed the Juneau Veterans' Memorial Highway. The highway ends 40.5 miles/65.3 km north of Juneau near Echo Cove on Berners Bay. It is a scenic drive northward along Favorite Channel.

Distance from the cruise ship terminal downtown is followed by the distance from road end (RE).

0 RE 40.5 (65.3 km) Cruise ship terminal.

0.3 (0.5 km) **RE 40.2** (64.7 km) Parking garage, 3-hour limit.

0.5 (0.8 km) **RE 40** (64.2 km) Stoplight. Marine Way and Main Street. Egan Drive begins here.

0.7 (1.1 km) **RE 39.8** (63.9 km) Alaska State Museum, exit east onto Whittier Street.

1.2 (1.9 km) **RE 39.3** (63.4 km) Stoplight. Tenth Street exit east. For access to Douglas Highway and North Douglas Highway, turn west across Juneau-Douglas bridge (see logs this section).

1.3 (2.1 km) **RE 39.2** (63.1 km) Harris Harbor for small boats.

1.5 (2.4 km) **RE 39** (62.8 km) Juneau–Douglas High School.

1.7 (2.7 km) **RE 38.8** (62.6 km) Aurora Basin small-boat harbor. Access to Juneau Yacht Club on Harbor Way Road; overnight RV parking.

3.9 (6.3 km) **RE 36.6** (59 km) Stoplight. Picnic tables at Twin Lakes to east. Also exit east for Bartlett Memorial Hospital and Alaska Native Health Center; access to Old Glacier Highway and residential area. Gastineau salmon hatchery to west.

5.5 (8.9 km) **RE 35** (56.4 km) Stoplight. Lemon Creek area.

5.9 (9.5 km) **RE 34.6** (55.8 km) Lemon Creek passes beneath highway.

6.1 (9.8 km) **RE 34.4** (55.5 km) Southbound traffic, view area of tide lands; great place to see eagles and waterfowl.

6.7 (10.7 km) **RE 33.8** (54.5 km) Access to Old Glacier Highway and Switzer Creek; exit east.

8.1 (13 km) **RE 32.4** (52.3 km) Airport access road.

8.2 (13.2 km) **RE 32.3** (52.1 km) Fred Meyer shopping center.

8.8 (14.2 km) **RE 31.7** (51.1 km) Stoplight. Airport turnoff and access to shopping malls; exit west for 0.3-mile/0.5-km loop road to Juneau Municipal Airport. Loop road rejoins Egan Drive at **Milepost 9.4.**

9.4 (15.1 km) **RE 31.1** (50.1 km) Stoplight. **Junction** with Mendenhall Loop Road. Turn west for airport. Turn east for Mendenhall Valley shopping mall (just east of junction) and Mendenhall Glacier and visitor center (3.6 miles/5.8 km from junction).

Mendenhall Loop Road is a paved 6.8-mile/10.9-km loop which rejoins Glacier Highway at **Milepost 12.2.** To reach Mendenhall Glacier from here, drive east 2.2 miles/3.5 km and take spur road another 1.4 miles/2.2 km to the glacier and visitor center. The visitor center is open daily in summer from 9 A.M. to 6:30 P.M.; weekends only in winter.

Continue on Mendenhall Loop Road past glacier spur road turnoff for Montana Creek Road (3.7 miles/6 km from junction) and access to Mendenhall Lake USFS campground, at Mile 0.4 Montana Creek Road. The campground has 60 sites, tables, fireplaces, water, pit toilets and dump station. Reservations not available. Fee charged. Montana Creek Road dead ends 3.5 miles/5.6 km from Mendenhall Loop Road.

9.7 (15.6 km) **RE 30.8** (49.7 km) Airport area access for southbound travelers via Old Glacier Highway.

9.9 (15.9 km) **RE 30.6** (49.4 km) Mendenhall River and Brotherhood Bridge.

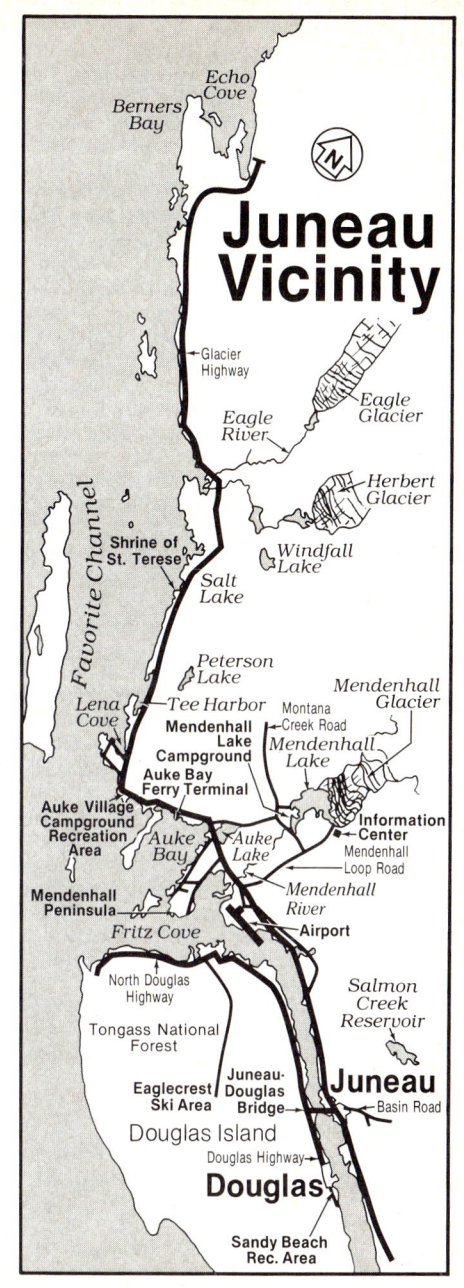

The bridge was named in honor of the Alaska Native Brotherhood and is lined by bronze plaques symbolizing the Raven and Eagle clans.

10 (16.1 km) **RE 30.5** (49.2 km) Mendenhall Glacier viewpoint to east; parking area with sign about Brotherhood Bridge and short walking trail.

10.5 (16.9 km) **RE 30** (48.4 km) State troopers office.

10.8 (17.4 km) **RE 29.7** (47.9 km) The 2.1-mile/3.4-km Mendenhall Peninsula Road, a 2-lane gravel road, to west. About halfway along this road, Engineer's Cutoff leads 0.3 mile/0.5 km to Fritz Cove Road.

11.4 (18.3 km) **RE 29.1** (46.9 km) Auke Lake scenic wayside to east; limited overnight RV parking spaces. Good view of Mendenhall Glacier reflected in the still waters of the lake. This is one of the most photographed spots in Alaska. Red, pink and coho salmon spawn in Auke Lake system July to September. Chum salmon are primarily from Auke Creek hatchery program.

11.5 (18.5 km) **RE 29** (46.8 km) Fritz Cove Road (paved) leads 2.6 miles/4.2 km west and dead ends at Smuggler's Cove;

excellent small-boat anchorage. Scenic viewpoint on Fritz Cove Road at Mile 1.2; Engineer's Cutoff at Mile 1.9 extends 0.3 mile/0.5 km to Mendenhall Peninsula Road.

11.6 (18.7 km) **RE 28.9** (46.6 km) Turnoff to east for Chapel-by-the-Lake and to southeastern branch of University of Alaska.

11.8 (19 km) **RE 28.7** (46.3 km) Short road west to National Marine Fisheries Service biological laboratory (self-guided walking tours can be made between 8 A.M. and 4:30 P.M. Monday through Friday) and University of Alaska–Juneau campus.

12.2 (19.6 km) **RE 28.3** (45.7 km) **Junction** with Mendenhall Loop Road to west. Glacier Highway becomes Juneau Veterans' Memorial Highway and curves around Auke Bay to west. A small-boat harbor with snack shop, skiff and tackle rentals and boat launch located at the head of the bay. Large schools of herring enter the bay to spawn in the spring.

The 6.8-mile/10.9-km Mendenhall Loop Road rejoins Glacier Highway at **Milepost 9.4.** Motorists may turn east here and follow loop road 3.1 miles/5 km to Montana Creek Road and access to Mendenhall Lake USFS campground, or drive 4.6 miles/7.4 km and turn off on Mendenhall Glacier spur road, which leads another 1.4 miles/2.2 km to the glacier and visitor center. Parking area at Mendenhall Glacier, short steep path to visitor center. The center is open daily in summer from 9 A.M. to 6:30 P.M. ▲

12.3 (19.8 km) **RE 28.2** (45.5 km) Private RV park.

12.4 (20 km) **RE 28.1** (45.3 km) Auke Bay post office to west.

12.6 (20.3 km) **RE 27.9** (45 km) Spaulding trailhead to east; 3.5 miles/5.6 km long. Access to John Muir USFS cabin.

12.8 (20.6 km) **RE 27.7** (44.8 km) Waydelich Creek and bridge.

13.8 (22.2 km) **RE 26.7** (43.1 km) Auke Bay ferry terminal exit.

13.9 (22.4 km) **RE 26.6** (42.9 km) Auke Bay ferry terminal entrance. *LeConte* ferry passengers use parking area and terminal on right; all others use parking area and large terminal on left. Visitor information counter staffed during ferry arrival.

15.1 (24.3 km) **RE 25.4** (41 km) Auke Village Recreation Area begins northbound; 14 beachside picnic shelters accessible to west of highway (park on highway shoulder).

15.3 (24.6 km) **RE 25.2** (40.7 km) Auke Village totem pole to east.

15.4 (24.8 km) **RE 25.1** (40.5 km) Auke Village USFS campground; 14 picnic units, 11 campsites, tables, fireplaces, water, flush and pit toilets. Fee charged. Open May 1 to Sept. 30. ▲

16.5 (26.4 km) **RE 24.1** (38.9 km) Lena Point Road, south entrance to loop road.

17 (27.3) **RE 23.5** (37.9 km) Lena Point Road, north entrance to loop road.

17.4 (28.1 km) **RE 23.1** (37.3 km) Lena Beach picnic area.

18.4 (29.6 km) **RE 22.1** (35.7 km) Tee Harbor–Point Stevens Road (gravel) leads 0.3 mile/0.6 km west to public parking area and a private marina and fuel float.

19.2 (30.9 km) **RE 21.3** (34.4 km) Inspiration Point turnout to west with view of the Chilkat Range, and over Tee Harbor and Shelter Island across Favorite Channel. Once a "bread-and-butter" commercial fishing area, particularly for halibut fishermen, it is now a popular sportfishing area.

23.1 (37.3 km) **RE 17.4** (28.1 km) Short road west to Catholic Shrine of St. Terese, located on a small island reached by a causeway.

23.3 (37.5 km) **RE 17.2** (27.8 km) Turnout to west and view of island on which Shrine of St. Terese is situated.

23.9 (38.5 km) **RE 16.6** (26.8 km) Peterson Lake trailhead to east; 4 miles/6.4 km long. Access to Peterson Lake USFS cabin. This trail connects with the Spaulding Trail (see **Milepost 12.6**).

24.2 (39 km) **RE 16.3** (26.3 km) **Peterson Creek** bridge. View spawning salmon here in late summer and early fall. Trout fishing. Black and brown bears in area.

24.8 (40 km) **RE 15.7** (25.3 km) Gravel road leads 0.6 mile/1 km west to Amalga Harbor; dock, boat launch, bait casting area. Fireplace and chimney near end of road are remains of an old trapper's cabin.

27.1 (43.7 km) **RE 13.4** (21.6 km) Windfall Lake trailhead to east; 3 miles/4.8 km long.

27.2 (43.9 km) **RE 13.3** (21.4 km) Herbert River bridge.

27.4 (44.2 km) **RE 13.1** (21.1 km) Herbert Glacier trailhead to east; 5 miles/8 km long.

27.7 (44.7 km) **RE 12.8** (20.6 km) Eagle River bridge. Amalga trailhead just across bridge to east; 4 miles/6.4 km long.

28.4 (45.8 km) **RE 12.1** (20.2 km) Eagle Beach picnic area with 8 units to west. View of Chilkat Range across Lynn Canal. Duck hunting on flats in low tide during open season.

28.7 (46.2 km) **RE 11.8** (19.1 km) Scenic viewpoint to west.

29.3 (47.2 km) **RE 11.2** (18.1 km) Scenic viewpoint to west.

32.7 (52.8 km) **RE 7.8** (12.6 km) Turnout to west with view of Benjamin Island to southwest; just beyond it is Sentinel Island lighthouse. Visible to the northwest is North Island and northwest of it is Vanderbilt Reef, site of a great sea disaster. The SS *Princess Sophia*, carrying 288 passengers and 61 crew, ran aground on the Vanderbilt Reef in the early morning hours of Oct. 24, 1918. All aboard perished when a combination of stormy seas and a high tide forced the *Sophia* off the reef and she sank early in the evening of Oct. 25. The Vanderbilt Reef is now marked by a navigation light.

32.8 (52.9 km) **RE 7.7** (12.5 km) Pavement ends northbound, 2-lane gravel extension of the Glacier Highway begins.

33 (53.1 km) **RE 7.5** (12.1 km) Scenic viewpoint to west. Yankee Cove and beach below this point. The MV *Fairweather* docks at Yankee Cove.

35.4 (57.1 km) **RE 5.1** (8.2 km) Sunshine Cove public beach access.

37.6 (60.7 km) **RE 2.9** (4.7 km) North Bridget Cove trailhead, Point Bridget State Park. The 2,850-acre park offers meadows, forests, rocky beaches, salmon streams and a trail system. Area is popular for cross-country skiing. Fires allowed on beach.

38.8 (61.3 km) **RE 1.7** (2.8 km) Point Bridget trailhead.

39.4 (63.5 km) **RE 1.1** (1.8 km) Kowee Creek bridge. Large parking area to west.

40.4 (65 km) **RE .1** (.3 km) Access left to Echo Cove beach. Park area.

40.5 (65.3 km) **RE 0** Road dead ends near Echo Cove on Berners Bay.

Douglas Highway Log

Douglas Highway is a 3-mile/4.8-km paved road beginning on the Juneau side of the Douglas Bridge, crossing to Douglas Island, turning southeast, passing through the city of Douglas to road end and beginning of Treadwell Mine area.

0 Intersection of Egan Drive and Douglas Bridge.

0.5 (0.8 km) Right, Cordova Street leads to Dan Moller trail.

1.5 (2.4 km) Lawson Creek bridge.

2 (3.2 km) Tlingit Indian cemetery and grave houses.

2.5 (4 km) Turn left to boat harbor; dump station and Savikko Park with 5 overnight RV parking spaces. Short gravel road leads to Juneau Island U.S. Bureau of Mines headquarters. Sandy Beach Recreation Area with water, toilets, play area, tennis courts, track, 2 ball fields, picnic tables, shelters and children's playground. Aptly named, this is one of the few sandy beaches in southeastern Alaska. Highway becomes St. Ann's Avenue. ▲

3 (4.8 km) Road end.

North Douglas Highway Log

North Douglas Highway begins after crossing Douglas Bridge from Juneau and immediate right turn northwest. **Milepost 1** appears at small bridge on this turn.

0 Douglas Bridge.

0.3 (0.5 km) **Junction** of Douglas Highway and North Douglas Highway.

4.4 (7.1 km) Heliport to right.

6.9 (11.1 km) Eaglecrest Ski Area turnoff on left; drive 5.3 miles/8.5 km on gravel road to ski area. Good blueberry picking in August.

8.3 (13.5 km) Fish Creek bridge. Large parking area on right of bridge.

8.6 (13.9 km) Ninemile trail on right; small parking area.

9.5 (15.3 km) Scenic turnout and parking area with excellent view of Mendenhall Glacier; litter barrel. Boat ramp; launch permit required (contact harbormaster before arrival).

10.3 (16.6 km) Small waterfall on left.

11.4 (18.4 km) False Outer Point public beach access. Scenic view of Favorite Channel and Lynn Canal; parking area on right. Near the northern tip of Douglas Island, this is an excellent spot to observe marine activity and eagles.

12.3 (19.8 km) Outer Point trailhead on right.

13.1 (21 km) Road end.

Glacier Bay National Park and Preserve

What Tlingit Indians called "Big ice-mountain bay" in John Muir's day (1879) is today one of southeastern Alaska's most dramatic attractions, Glacier Bay National Park and Preserve. Muir described Glacier Bay as "a picture of icy wildness unspeakably pure and sublime."

There are no roads to Glacier Bay National Park, except for a 10-mile/16-km stretch of gravel road connecting Bartlett Cove with Gustavus. Bartlett Cove is the site of a ranger station and Glacier Bay Lodge. Park naturalists conduct daily hikes and other activities from the lodge and the

Glacier Bay National Park and Preserve

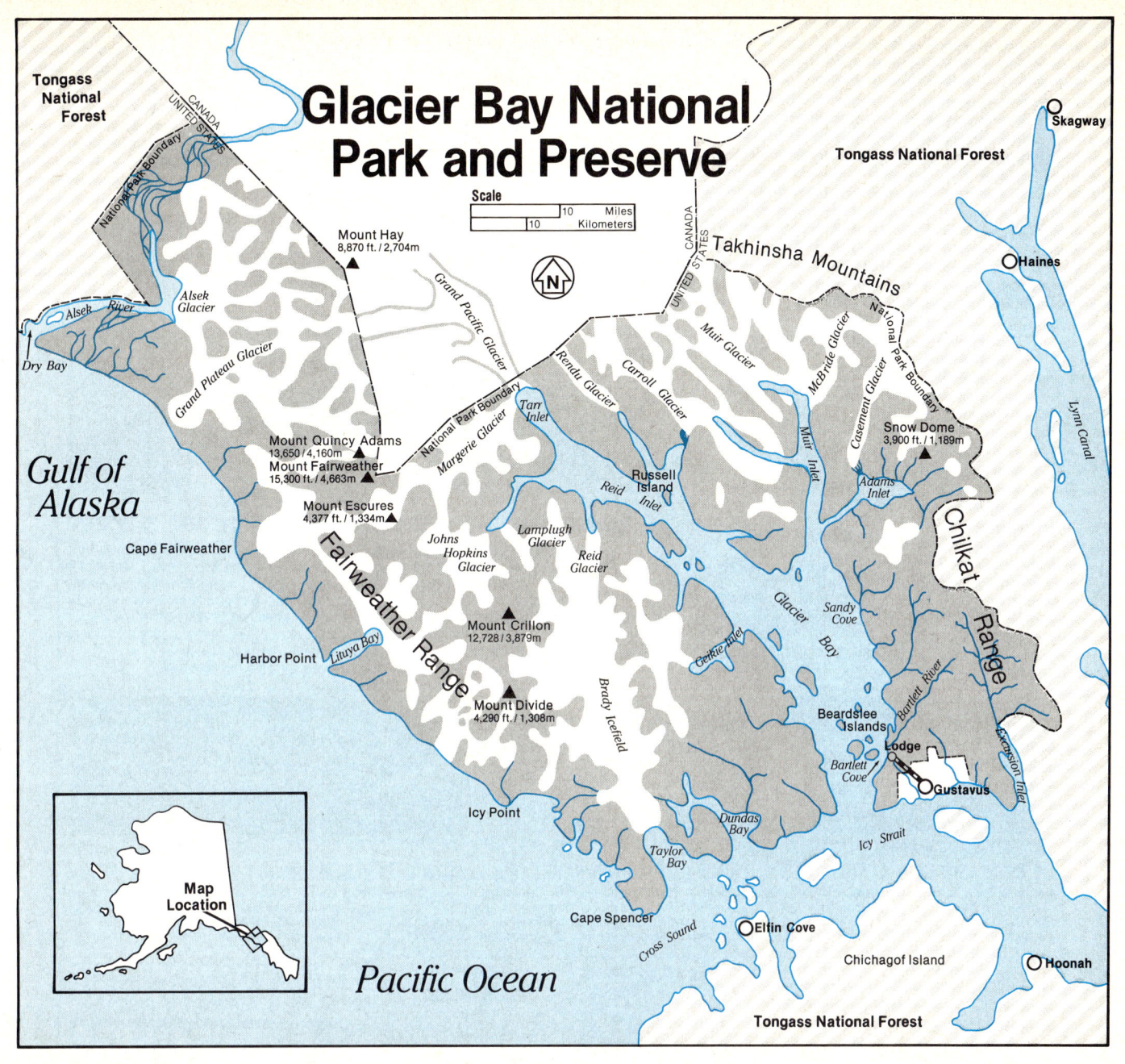

excursion boats depart from there. Airlines land at Gustavus airport. See Accommodations and Transportation under Gustavus in this section.

Visitors should contact the Superintendent, Glacier Bay National Park and Preserve, Gustavus, AK 99826 for more information or check with Glacier Bay tour operators. The national park's headquarters is at Bartlett Cove; phone 697-2230.

Situated at the northwest end of the Alexander Archipelago, Glacier Bay National Park includes not only tidewater glaciers but also Mount Fairweather in the Fairweather Range of the St. Elias Mountains, the highest peak in southeastern Alaska, and also the United States portion of the Alsek River.

With passage of the Alaska National Interest Lands Conservation Act in December 1980, Glacier Bay National Monument, established in 1925 by Pres. Calvin Coolidge, became a national park. Approximately 585,000 acres were added to the park/preserve to protect fish and wildlife habitat and migration routes in Dry Bay and along the lower Alsek River, and to include the northwest slope of Mount Fairweather. Total acreage is 3,328,000 (3,271,000 in park, 57,000 in preserve) with 2,770,000 acres designated wilderness.

When the English naval explorer Capt. George Vancouver sailed through the ice-choked waters of Icy Strait in 1794, Glacier Bay was little more than a dent in the coastline. Across the head of this seemingly minor inlet stood a towering wall of ice marking the seaward terminus of an immense glacier that completely filled the broad, deep basin of what is now Glacier Bay. To the north, ice extended more than 100 miles/160 km into the St. Elias Mountains, covering the intervening valleys with a 4,000-foot-/1,219-m-deep mantle of ice.

During the century following Vancouver's pioneer explorations, the glacier

GLACIER BAY ADVERTISERS

Alaska's Glacier Bay Tours and Cruises	Ph. (800) 451-5952
Annie May Lodge	Ph. (907) 697-2346
Glacier Bay Country Inn	Ph. (907) 697-2288
Glacier Bay Tours and Charters	Ph. (907) 697-2254
Grand Pacific Charters	Ph. (907) 697-2288
Gustavus Inn	Ph. (907) 697-2254
Puffin, The	Ph. (907) 697-2260
Puffin Travel	Ph. (907) 697-2260
W.T. Fugarwe Lodge	Ph. (907) 697-2244

ANNIE MAE LODGE

Peace, comfort, and old fashioned hospitality served Grandma's way

- Meals served with garden vegetables, fresh berries, and local seafood
- Wilderness surroundings
- Easy access to sea kayaking, fishing, and Glacier Bay tours

Write or call for more information
Box 80, Gustavus, AK 99826•(907)697-2346

GLACIER BAY

A MUST—ON YOUR ALASKA VISIT!

ADVENTURE EXCURSIONS TO ALASKA'S MOST FAMOUS ATTRACTION

PRICED FROM: $269

FROM JUNEAU, HAINES OR SKAGWAY — 1 DAY, 2 DAYS OR MORE

Attractively priced and packaged tours, so you can experience and enjoy GLACIER BAY NATIONAL PARK, the very best of what Alaska has to offer. (Prices are plus tax.)

Watch for whales in Glacier Bay. 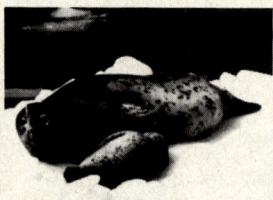   *Mother seal and pup.*    *Majestic Bald Eagle.*

SPIRIT OF ADVENTURE DAY CRUISE TO THE GLACIERS

Our Glacier Bay Tours feature this comfortable, high-speed vessel that takes you from Glacier Bay Lodge to where the massive, highly active glaciers stretch down from mighty mountains, "calving" icebergs into beautiful blue fjords ... where whales, seals and sea lions play ... where bear, moose, mountain goat, eagles and thousands of exotic sea birds congregate for your viewing and enjoyment. With large picture windows all around, and with top-deck viewing, you won't miss a thing. Includes lunch. Packages which include this cruise, plus round-trip air from the gateway cities of Juneau, Haines or Skagway, are priced from **$269**

The SPIRIT OF ADVENTURE Day-Excursion boat gets you close up to the wonders of Glacier Bay. Here, a glacier "calves" an iceberg. Nowhere else in Alaska equals this spectacular National Park & wildlife preserve.

Glacier Bay Lodge, only hotel or lodge within the park, is the home base for your Glacier Bay Adventure, and departure point for cruises.

Try delicious Alaska seafood in our full-service, view dining room.

Deluxe, comfortable accommodations at Glacier Bay Lodge.

Extensive National Park Service Interpretive Exhibits located on the Lodge's Mezzanine enhance your understanding of the Bay.

BE SURE YOU STAY AT GLACIER BAY LODGE WITHIN THE PARK; IT'S ALASKA'S PREMIER LUXURY WILDERNESS LODGE.

Nestled in the lush, green rain forest of Bartlett Cove, this is the only hotel within the Park. This spectacular Lodge is the start of all our Glacier Bay adventures: cruising the Bay; sport fishing; Park Naturalist programs; kayaking; hiking and more. At the end of day, a roaring fire, delicious meals and deluxe accommodations await you. Our 55-room Lodge offers twin, double and family configurations and a full-service restaurant and lounge. Packages which include an overnight at the Lodge, Day-Cruise and round-trip air from Juneau, Haines or Skagway, are priced from **$339**   Packages with TWO nights lodging are priced from **$408**

3-DAY/2-NIGHT CRUISES COMPLETELY *WITHIN* THE PARK, EXPLORING *BOTH* ARMS

This is the premier cruise of Alaska's premier attraction! You cruise from Glacier Bay Lodge and spend more time exploring and sightseeing close up — the fantastic fjords, the tidewater glaciers, and the abundant wildlife — than you would with any other cruise. And you enjoy the luxury, elegance, service, amenities and camaraderie of this small 25-stateroom, 49-passenger, full-service cruiseship. Picture windows and top-deck viewing. Elegant Dining Room with passenger-pleasing meals. View Lounge. Single, twin, queen and family stateroom configurations. Packages which include this 2-night cruise plus round-trip air from Juneau, Haines or Skagway are priced from **$549.** With an extra night at the Lodge included, prices start at **$618.**

Enjoy the best close up viewing of any full-service cruise liner onboard the EXECUTIVE EXPLORER.

DRIVE TO GLACIER BAY?

You cannot drive or ferry to Glacier Bay National Park, so our 1-2- or 3-Day air/tour/cruise packages from Juneau, Haines or Skagway are perfect for you. Security parking is available.

ENJOY *SEE*-LEVEL VIEWING!

Flightseeing isn't enough! Only from water-level, aboard one of our vessels, can you really see, hear and watch the awesome forces of nature, and photograph the abundant wildlife close up. On our packages you fly, *plus* truly experience the majesty of Glacier Bay.

DON'T BE DISAPPOINTED RESERVE SPACE IN ADVANCE IF POSSIBLE

1-800-451-5952

Or stop in at one of the following offices on your arrival in Alaska or Yukon; or at any Travel Agency:

Juneau:	Glacier Bay Tour Center 76 Egan Dr., Suite 110 (907) 463-5510
Haines:	Travel Connection 301 2nd Ave. (907) 766-2681
Skagway:	Gray Line of Alaska Westmark Inn 3rd & Spring (907) 983-2241
Ketchikan:	Gray Line of Alaska 3436 Tongass (907) 225-5930
Sitka:	Sheldon Jackson College Travel 801 Lincoln St. (907) 747-2540
Anchorage:	Gray Line of Alaska 745 W. Fourth Ave. (907) 277-5581
Fairbanks:	Gray Line of Alaska Westmark Hotel 820 Noble St. (907) 452-2843
Whitehorse:	Atlas Tours Westmark-Whitehorse Mall 2nd & Steele (403) 668-3161

GUIDED SPORT-FISHING CHARTERS

Fish for salmon and trophy-size halibut. Charters include: Deluxe cabin cruisers with only 6 persons per boat. Experienced Skipper-Guide. Fishing gear including bait. Cleaning, freezing and wrapping of your catch to take home. Priced from **$125**

Experience the thrill of Glacier Bay Sportfishing.

3½ - HOUR WHALE - WATCHING, NATURAL HISTORY CRUISES

Enhance and expand your sightseeing on our Natural History Day - Boat skippered by an experienced guide. Cruise Icy Strait to Pt. Adolphus, prime whale-watching habitat for Humpback, Minke and Orca Whales, along with other marine mammals. Whales feed on the rich marine life that exists there, allowing for outstanding viewing and photography opportunities. Whale sightings guaranteed!

Priced from **$75**

Glacier Bay Lodge, Inc.
520 PIKE TOWER, Suite 1610, Seattle, WA 98101

NATIONAL PARK SERVICE PROGRAMS

Naturalists lead guided nature walks through the beautiful rain forest and along the beaches and inter-tidal zones. Likewise, interesting educational audiovisual presentations are available, as well as extensive interpretive exhibits in the Lodge.

ALASKA'S Glacier Bay™ TOURS AND CRUISES

The Authorized Concessionaire of the National Park Service

SOUTHEASTERN ALASKA • GLACIER BAY NATIONAL PARK

retreated some 40 miles/64 km back into the bay, permitting a spruce–hemlock forest to gradually colonize the land. By 1916, Tarr Inlet, at one of the heads of Glacier Bay, was free of ice, and the Grand Pacific Glacier, which once had filled the entire bay, had retreated some 65 miles/105 km from the position observed by Captain Vancouver in 1794. Nowhere else in the world have glaciers receded at such a rapid pace in recent time.

Today, few of the many tributary glaciers that once supplied the huge ice sheet extend to the sea. Glacier Bay National Park encloses 16 active tidewater glaciers, including several on the remote and seldom visited western edge of the park along the Gulf of Alaska and Lituya Bay. Icebergs, cracked off from near-vertical ice cliffs, dot the waters of Glacier Bay.

A decline in the number of humpback whales using Glacier Bay for feeding and calf-rearing led the National Park Service to limit the number of boats visiting Glacier Bay between June and September. These regulations affect all motorized vessels. Check with the National Park Service for current regulations.

Glacier Bay is approximately 100 miles/160 km from Juneau by boat. Park rangers at Bartlett Cove are available to assist in advising visitors who wish to tour Glacier Bay in private boats or by kayak. Permits are required for motorized pleasure boats between June 1 and Aug. 31. The permits are free. A limited number are available, but rarely are boaters turned away. Permits must be obtained prior to entry into Glacier Bay and Bartlett Cove. Request permits no more than 2 months in advance by writing the National Park Service, Gustavus, AK 99826. For more information, phone 697-2268.

Glacier Bay Lodge is the only accommodation within the national park, although nearby Gustavus (see description this section) has a number of lodges, inns, bed and breakfasts and rental cabins. Contact the National Park Service for more information on the concessionaire-operated Glacier Bay Lodge and excursion boat cruises offered from the lodge.

Excursion boats depart from Bartlett Cove in Glacier Bay National Park. (Steve Threndyle)

Gasoline and diesel fuel may be purchased at Bartlett Cove, where a good anchorage is available. There are no other public facilities for boats within park bound-

Gustavus Inn AT GLACIER BAY SINCE 1965

For Free Brochure:
Summer: P.O. Box 60-MP
Gustavus, AK 99826
(907) 697-2254
FAX (907) 692-2255

Winter: 7920-MP Outlook
Prairie Village, KS 66208
(913) 649-5220

WEST ARM DAY CRUISE TOUR
Includes all-day Cruise to Glacier Bay, Lodging, Meals, Transfers
2 days/1 night $275 • 3 days/2 nights $395

- Homestead Garden
- Local Gourmet Seafood
- Friendly Host Family
- 6-Stool Bar

CUSTOM & SCHEDULED OVERNIGHT CRUISES
FISHING CHARTERS, local skipper, full service

Glacier Bay COUNTRY INN & GRAND PACIFIC CHARTERS

A peaceful storybook setting for an unforgettable Alaska adventure . . .

- Charming rooms, private baths
- Superb dining
- Fishing, whalewatching, sightseeing
- Glacier Bay boat/plane tours

BOX 5-MP • GUSTAVUS, AK 99826
(907) 697-2288
FAX (907) 697-2289

ALASKA
AT THE GATEWAY TO BEAUTIFUL
GLACIER BAY
NATIONAL PARK

TROPHY
HALIBUT & SALMON FISHING

W.T. FUGARWE LODGE

WHALE WATCHING
Flight-seeing Glacier Bay National Park
Home-cooked Family Style Meals • Congenial Atmosphere

HOME OF THE ALASKA HALIBUT SOCIETY
OPEN June 1st to September 15th

FOR MORE INFORMATION

W.T. Fugarwe Lodge

P.O. Box 280
Gustavus, Alaska 99826

Off-Season: P.O. Box 459
Georgetown, Colorado 80444

(907) 697-2244
FAX (907) 697-2373

(303) 623-7108
FAX (303) 569-2632

Doc and Ruthanne Bailey

aries; Sandy Cove, about 20 miles/32 km from Bartlett Cove, is a popular anchorage. Gustavus has a dock and small-boat harbor.

CAUTION BOATERS: No attempt should be made to navigate Glacier Bay without appropriate charts, tide tables and local knowledge. Floating ice is a special hazard. Because of the danger from waves caused by falling ice, small craft should not approach closer than 0.5 mile/0.8 km from tidewater glacier fronts.

Wildlife in the national park area is protected and hunting is not allowed. Firearms are illegal. *CAUTION: Brown and black bears are present.*

Fishing for silver and king salmon, Dolly Varden and halibut is excellent. A valid Alaska fishing license is required. Charter fishing trips are available.

There is an established campground at Bartlett Cove with 25 sites. Wilderness camping is also available throughout the park.

Gustavus

Gateway to Glacier Bay National Park and Preserve, the small community of Gustavus is located just outside the park boundary at the mouth of the Salmon River on the north shore of Icy Passage, 48 miles northwest of Juneau. It is 10 miles/16 km by road from Gustavus to Bartlett Cove within the park.

Population: approximately 200. **Emergengy Services:** Phone 911. **Visitor Information:** Write the Gustavus Visitors Assoc., Box 167, Gustavus 99826.

Surrounded on 3 sides by the snow-covered peaks of the Chilkat Range and the Fairweather Mountains, Gustavus offers miles of level land with expansive sandy beaches, farmland and forest. Homesteaded in 1914 as a small agricultural community, the area was once named Strawberry Point because of its abundant wild strawberries. Today, most residents maintain gardens and make their living by fishing (commercial and subsistence), fish processing, tourism, arts and crafts, and working for the National Park Service and in various local trades.

Besides its proximity to the national park, Gustavus offers a number of attractions. There is fishing for salmon, halibut and trout; excellent berry picking (strawberries, blueberries, nagoonberries and huckleberries); beachcombing; bird watching; hiking; and kayaking. Charter boats offer trips into Icy Strait and Glacier Bay.

Glacier Bay Tours and Charters. For 20 years we have arranged custom fishing and sightseeing tours of Glacier Bay and northern southeast Alaska. All our charters use local year-round resident guides. Lodging and meals are provided by the Gustavus Inn, famous for their hospitality and food. Please write: Glacier Bay Tours, Box 60-MP, Gustavus, AK 99826. (907) 697-2254. [ADVERTISEMENT]

ACCOMMODATIONS

Accommodations in Gustavus include several inns, lodges, bed and breakfasts, and self-sufficient cabins. The lodges and inns serve meals for guests (drop-in customers check for space-available reservations for meals). Taxi service is available. Businesses in Gustavus include a grocery store, art gallery, cafe, laundromat, gift shop, hardware/building supply store, gas station, auto repair shop and fish processing facilities. Fishing supplies and licenses may be purchased locally.

Annie Mae Lodge. Old-fashioned good food and good company. Three fine family-style meals using home-baked bread and pastries, fresh caught seafood, berries off the bush, and garden vegetables. We offer beautiful comfortable rooms, peace, quiet, abundant wildlife, wilderness, sportfishing, kayak trips, whale watching. Glacier Bay boat/plane tours. Box 80, Gustavus, AK 99826 (907) 697-2346. [ADVERTISEMENT]

Glacier Bay Country Inn and Grand Pacific Charters. Peaceful, storybook accommodations, away from the crowds in a wilderness setting. Cozy comforters, warm flannel sheets, private baths. Superb dining features local seafoods, garden-fresh produce, homebaked breads, spectacular desserts. Fishing, whale-watching, sightseeing. Glacier Bay boat/plane tours. Courtesy van, bikes. Box 5MP, Gustavus, AK 99826. Phone (907) 697-2288, fax (907) 697-2289. [ADVERTISEMENT]

Gustavus Inn. Country living, family-style gourmet local seafood meals, cozy bar, kitchen garden, bikes, trout fishing poles, courtesy van, afternoon park naturalist trip. Family-run since 1965. Custom fishing and Glacier Bay sightseeing packages arranged. For map, brochures, please write: Gustavus Inn, Box 60-MP, Gustavus, AK 99826 or call (907) 697-2254. [ADVERTISEMENT]

The Puffin. See nearby Glacier Bay and Icy Strait. Stay in your own modern, comfortable, attractively decorated cabin with electricity on quiet wooded homestead. Complete country breakfast. Bicycles included. Children, pets welcome. Reservations for all charters, Glacier Bay tours. Qualified captains guide fishing, sightseeing charters. Friendly, personal attention; full travel services! (907) 697-2260 [ADVERTISEMENT]

W.T. Fugarwe Lodge is a family owned and operated lodge featuring outstanding double-entree family-style meals with fresh home-baked bread and pastries. Deluxe accommodations for 24. Fish for halibut or salmon in our new charter boats with the latest safety and electronic gear. We have set more IGFA line-class halibut records than any other Alaskan lodge in the last 7 years. Our private halibut derby lasts all season and offers over $5,000 in prizes. Flightsee beautiful Glacier Bay from our Cessna 206 with a pilot that has been flying Alaska for 49 years! Your hosts, Doc and Ruthanne Bailey. Open June 1-Sept. 15. Call (907) 697-2244, fax (907) 697-2373 or write Box 280, Gustavus, AK 99826. Off-season, write Box 459, Georgetown, CO 80444. Call (303) 623-7108 or fax (303) 569-2632. [ADVERTISEMENT]

TRANSPORTATION

NOTE: There is no state ferry service to Glacier Bay. Closest port of call for state ferries is Hoonah. (Kayakers getting off at Hoonah can expect a 2-day paddle across Icy Strait.)

Air: Glacier Bay may be reached by Alaska Airlines daily jet flights from Juneau and by charter service from Juneau, Sitka, Haines and Skagway to Gustavus airport. Charter air service available in Gustavus. Bus service between the airport and Bartlett Cove is available on jet flights. Taxi service to local facilities and courtesy van service for some lodges are also available.

Private Aircraft: Gustavus airport, adjacent northeast; elev. 36 feet/11m; length 6,800 feet/2,072m; asphalt. Landing within the park is restricted to salt water (Adams Inlet is closed to aircraft landing). Fuel 100.

Boat Service: Excursion boats depart daily from Bartlett Cove. You may also charter a boat in Gustavus for sightseeing or fishing. Cruise tours are available from Juneau and Glacier Bay.

Several cruise ships include Glacier Bay cruising in their itineraries.

Yakutat

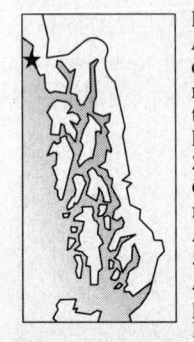

Located on the Gulf of Alaska coast where southeastern Alaska joins the major body of Alaska to the west; 225 miles/362 km northwest of Juneau, 220 miles/354 km southeast of Cordova and 380 miles/611 km southeast of Anchorage. **Population:** 527. **Emergency Services: Alaska State Troopers,** phone 784-3330. **Fire Department:** phone 911. **Yakutat Health Center,** phone 784-3275. **Maritime Search and Rescue,** contact the Coast Guard at 1-800-478-5555.

Visitor Information: Inquire at one of the lodges, at the city office or the USFS office, or write the city manager at P.O. Box 6, Yakutat, AK 99689. For sportfishing information, stop by the ADF&G office at Mile

---

The PUFFIN
GLACIER BAY
ICY STRAIT
GUSTAVUS

GLACIER BAY BOAT DAY AND OVERNIGHT TOURS
YOUR OWN ALASKAN BED AND BREAKFAST CABIN
FISHING • SIGHTSEEING • PHOTOGRAPHY • KAYAK CHARTERS
FREE PICKUP AT GUSTAVUS DOCK OR AIRPORT

FLIGHTSEEING GLACIER BAY and JUNEAU ICE FIELDS
ALASKA MARINE HIGHWAY • AIR • TRAIN • BUS
RESERVATIONS

PACKAGES CUSTOMIZED TO MEET YOUR NEEDS

PUFFIN TRAVEL BOX 3-MP, GUSTAVUS, AK 99826
(907) 697-2260 • IN AK 1-800-478-2258 • FAX (907) 697-2258
Family owned and operated by your hosts: Sandy and Chuck Schroth

SERVING INDEPENDENT TRAVELERS

0.5 Cannon Beach Road, or write Sport Fish Division, P.O. Box 49, Yakutat 99689, phone 784-3222.

Elevation: Sea level. **Climate:** Similar to the rest of coastal southeastern Alaska: mild in summer, winters are moderate. Average annual snowfall is 216 inches. Total (rain and snow) annual precipitation is about 130 inches. Normal daily maximum in August, 60°F/16°C; minimum in January, 17°F/-8°C. Prevailing winds are southeasterly.

Private Aircraft: Yakutat airport, 2.6 miles/4.2 km southeast; elev. 33 feet/10m; length 7,800 feet/2,377m; asphalt; fuel 80, 100. Seaplane base 1 mile/1.6 km northwest. For more information, contact the Yakutat Flight Service Station at 784-3314.

Transportation: Air–Daily jet service from Seattle, Juneau, Anchorage and Cordova. Charter air service available.

Yakutat has 3 lodges, 2 bed and breakfasts, a restaurant, cafe, gift shop, bank, 2 grocery stores, post office, clinic and gas station. Boat rentals, car rentals and cab service are available.

Glacier Bear Lodge. See display ad this section.

Leonard's Landing Lodge, Inc. See display ad this section.

Yakutat Bay is one of the few refuges for vessels along this long stretch of coast in the Gulf of Alaska. The site was originally the principal winter village of the local Tlingit Indian tribe. Sea otter pelts brought Russians to the area in the 19th century. Fur traders were followed by gold seekers, who came to work the black sand beaches. Commercial salmon fishing developed in this century and the first cannery was built here in 1904. Today's economy is based primarily on fishing and fish processing. Salmon and some halibut, crab and black cod make up the fishery. Government and local businesses employ most residents. Timber harvesting is under way in the area. Subsistence activities are primarily fishing (salmon and shellfish), hunting (moose, bear, goats, ducks and small game) and gathering seaweed and berries. The soil is not suitable for agriculture and a vegetable garden requires a great deal of preparation to produce even small quantities.

While hunting and fishing in particular draw visitors to Yakutat, the surge of Hubbard Glacier in June 1986, which sealed off the mouth of Russell Fiord, drew national attention. Malaspina Glacier, largest on the North American continent, is northwest of town. Nearer to town, Cannon Beach has good beachcombing and a picnic area.

AREA FISHING: Yakutat is considered a world-class sportfishing destination. Steelhead fishing is among the finest anywhere. King and silver (coho) salmon run in abundance in Yakutat area salt water, rivers and streams May through September. The area also boasts red and pink (chum) salmon and smelt in season. USFS cabins available on some rivers; check with the Forest Service (586-8751).

Lost River and **Tawah Creek**, 10 miles/16 km south of Yakutat on Lost River Road, silver (coho) salmon to 20 lbs., mid-August through September, spinners and spoons. **Situk River**, 12 miles/19.3 km south of Yakutat on the Lost River Road (also accessible by Forest Highway 10), is one of Alaska's top fishing spots spring and fall for steelhead and silver salmon and has one of the best sockeye (red) salmon runs in the state, late June through August; steelhead averaging 10 lbs., April 1 to May 30 for spring run, October and November for fall run, use salmon roe or yarn; king salmon to 45 lbs., mid-June through July, salmon roe or spinners; silver salmon to 23 lbs., mid-August through September, salmon roe or spinners; pink salmon run in August, yields Dolly Varden also, use spinners. **Yakutat Bay**, king salmon 30 to 50 lbs., May through June, troll with herring; silver salmon to 20 lbs., late August through September, troll with spoons, herring with flashers.

Haines

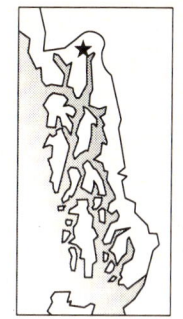

Located on Portage Cove, Chilkoot Inlet, on the upper arm of Lynn Canal, northern southeastern Alaska, 80 air miles/129 km northwest of Juneau; 151 road miles/243 km southeast of Haines Junction, YT. Southern terminus of the Haines Highway. *NOTE: Although Haines is only 13 miles/21 km by water from Skagway, it is 359 miles/578 km by road!*

Population: 1,238. **Emergency Services: Alaska State Troopers,** phone 766-2552. **City Police,** phone 766-2121. **Fire Department** and **Ambulance,** emergency only phone 911. **Doctor,** phone 766-2521. **Maritime Search and Rescue,** contact the Coast Guard at 1-800-478-5555.

Visitor Information: At 2nd and Willard streets. There are free brochures for all of Alaska and the Yukon. Open daily, 8 A.M. to 8 P.M., June through August; hours posted in winter. Phone 766-2202 or toll free 1-800-458-3579. Write the Haines Chamber of Commerce at Box 518-MP, Haines 99827.

Elevation: Sea level. **Climate:** Average daily maximum temperature in July, 66°F/19°C; average daily minimum in January, 17°F/-8°C. Extreme high summer temperature, 90°F/32°C; extreme winter low, -16°F/-27°C; average annual precipitation, 59 inches. **Radio:** KHNS-FM 102.3. **Television:**

GLACIER BEAR LODGE
Year-round lodge on Gulf of Alaska
Fishing-hunting and charter boats arranged
Write for information
BOX 303, YAKUTAT, ALASKA 99689 • (907) 784-3202

Leonard's Landing Lodge, inc.
Saltwater Front • Bay & River Fishing
April through October (907) 784-3245
PO Box 282, Yakutat, Alaska 99689

Captain's Choice MOTEL
44 LUXURIOUS ROOMS & SUITES IN HAINES, ALASKA
Toll Free 1-800-247-7153 or Alaska & Canada 1-800-478-2345
P.O. Box 392M, Haines, Alaska 99827   (907) 766-3111

DESTINATION HAINES

The Haines Chamber of Commerce Welcomes You

in Haines where the beauty of Southeast Alaska is waiting for you. Enjoy unique cultural attractions, spectacular natural surroundings, gold rush historical sites, comfortable lodging, excellent meals, local crafts, plus all the modern services you need for a trouble-free stay.

ACCOMMODATIONS

① **ALASKA THUNDERBIRD MOTEL** Downtown motel, all ground floor. Clean, comfortable, direct dial phones, color TV, some kitchenettes. (907) 766-2131, or 1-800-327-2556.

② **CAPTAIN'S CHOICE MOTEL** Haines' newest, finest & most comfortable lodging. Car rentals; courtesy transfers; centrally located. See our display ad. 766-3111 or 1-800-247-7153 or 1-800-478-2345 Alaska & Yukon. AAA Approved.

③ **EAGLE'S NEST MOTEL & CAR RENTAL** Fully modern, quiet rooms, AAA approved. Car rental available in Haines & Skagway. POB 250, Haines, AK 99827. (907) 766-2891.

④ **FT. SEWARD LODGE & RESTAURANT** Affordable lodging, spectacular ocean view, restaurant-saloon, Alaskan cuisine and decor. (907) 766-2009. See our display ad.

⑤ **FORT SEWARD CONDOS** Completely furnished apartments overlooking the bay. 1 and 2 bedrooms, 3 day minimum. Reasonable. POB 75, Haines, AK 99827. (907) 766-2425.

⑥ **HOTEL HALSINGLAND** Gracious Victorian Hotel. Renowned Seafood Restaurant. Cocktail lounge. Reasonable rates. See our display ad. 1-800-542-6363 or Canada 1-800-478-2525.

⑦ **MOUNTAIN VIEW MOTEL** Modern, quiet, view units. Reasonable rates, kitchenettes, color TV. Located adjacent to Ft. Seward on Second Ave. (907) 766-2900 or 1-800-478-2902 BC, Yukon & AK.

⑧ **SUMMER INN BED & BREAKFAST** Open year round. Full homemade breakfast, centrally located, comfortable rooms. Second Ave. (907) 766-2970.

ART GALLERIES/GIFT SHOPS

⑨ **BELL'S STORE** For the very best Alaskan Gifts and a unique shopping experience. Fresh flowers too. Second Ave.

⑩ **CHILKOOT GARDENS** "Best kept secret" for fine gifts; Alaskan wildflower seeds & plants. FTD florist & nursery. Union St. 766-2703. Mention this ad for 10% off.

⑪ **HELEN'S SHOP** Quality Alaskan Jewelry and Gifts. Open year round. Main Street, POB 284, Haines, AK 99827.

⑫ **J.M. & CO.** For special Alaskan-made T-shirts, Jewelry & Gifts. A special treat on Main Street.

⑬ **KING'S STORE** A browser's paradise ... Necessities & Gifts. "What Alaska was, we still are." Main Street.

⑭ **NORTHERN ARTS GALLERY** Northern Art by Northern Artists. Wide variety of gifts by local artists.

⑮ **WHALE RIDER GALLERY** Artists at work at this fine studio-gallery. Wood carving, prints, jewelry, metal sculpture.

ATTRACTIONS

⑯ **ALASKA INDIAN ARTS/CHILKAT DANCERS** Traditional Northwest Coast totem carvers, silversmiths & printmakers at work. Home of the Chilkat Dancers. At Fort Seward.

⑰ **FORT WILLIAM H. SEWARD** First Army Post built in Alaska. Historic district and arts & cultural center. Walking tours available.

⑱ **SOUTHEAST ALASKA STATE FAIR & ALASKAN BALD EAGLE MUSIC FESTIVAL** August 12–16, 1992. Great music, competitive exhibits, logging show, pig races, food & trade booths.

AUTO SERVICE

⑲ **THE PARTS PLACE** Auto–RV–Marine. If you need it, we have it or will get it. 206 3rd Ave. S. (907) 766-2940.

⑳ **BIGFOOT AUTO SERVICE** Napa Parts, RV Service & Towing; A.S.E. Technicians, Gas, Diesel, Tire Service. 766-2458/2459.

㉑ **SECOND AVENUE SERVICE** For all of your car care needs. 355 Second Ave. 766-3100.

㉒ **WHITE PASS ALASKA'S EAGLE CHEVRON** Providing Gas & Diesel. Free RV Water & Dump; Propane and volume discounts. 766-2338.

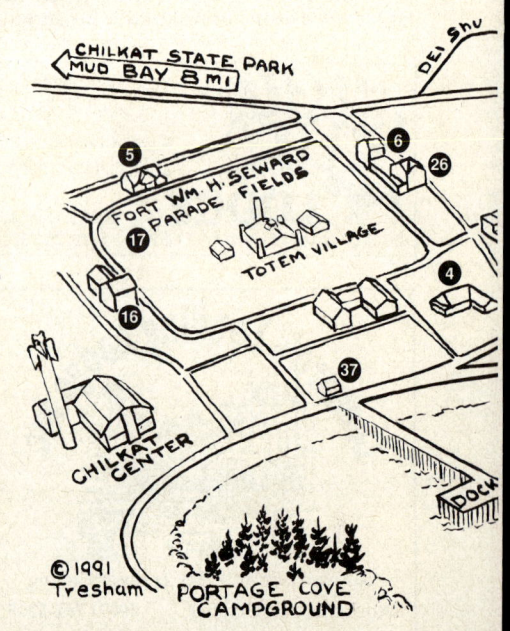

Tours   Wildlife Viewing   Museums   Historical Sites

CAMPER PARKS

㉓ **EAGLE CAMPER PARK** 30 Full Hook-ups w/cable TV. Electric Hook-ups. Tents welcome. Showers, Laundry, Propane. SENIOR DISCOUNTS. (907) 766-2335. FAX 766-2339.

㉔ **HITCH-UP RV PARK** 92 full & partial hook-ups, 20 pull-thrus. Immaculate Showers and Restrooms, Laundromat, Gift Shop, Propane. (907) 766-2882.

㉕ **OCEANSIDE RV PARK** On waterfront. Full service, downtown Haines, adjacent to laundry and showers. 766-2444.

㉖ **PORT CHILKOOT CAMPER PARK** Lovely wooded area; full & partial hook-ups; showers, laundry; tents welcome. 800-542-6363 or 800-478-2525 AK & Yukon.

FISHING CHARTERS

㉗ **GRAY FOX CHARTERS** Sightseeing and exciting wilderness fishing for salmon and halibut; all gear provided. POB 247, Haines, AK 99827. (907) 766-2163.

㉘ **LYNN CANAL FISHING CHARTERS** 25′ Cabin cruiser. Specializing in king salmon & halibut. Experienced historian & fishing guide. All gear provided. POB 341, Haines, AK. (907) 766-2254.

FISHING LODGES

㉙ **DON'S CAMP** Chilkat Lake, where great cutthroat trout fishing and good times are found. All gear provided. POB 74, Haines, AK 99827. (907) 766-2303.

GROCERIES

㉚ **HAINES' QUICK SHOP** Groceries, Deli, Fountain, Ice Cream, Bait, Videos. Open DAILY 8 a.m.–12 p.m. Next to Post Office.

㉛ **HOWSERS SUPERMARKET** One Stop Shopping. Groceries, Meat, Dairy, ICE. Try our Deli & Salad Bar. On Main Street.

RESTAURANTS

㉜ **CHILKAT BAKERY & RESTAURANT** Bakery products fresh daily. Breakfast–Lunch–Dinner. 7 a.m.–9 p.m. Plenty of parking. 5th Avenue.

SERVICES

㉝ **AMERICAN LEGION** Lynn Canal Post No. 12. All Legionnaires welcome. Open all week. BINGO Mon. & Thurs. at 7 p.m. Second Avenue & Dalton St.

㉞ **E.D.&D.** Cable TV, Computers, Video Tapes, Electronic Parts & Service. Radio Shack Dealer. Mile 1 Haines Highway.

㉟ **FIRST NATIONAL BANK OF ANCHORAGE** Friendly people at your service. Member FDIC

SIGHTSEEING/TRANSPORTATION

㊱ **ALASKA NATURE TOURS** Coastal beach to mountain rainforest. Interpretive, bus and walking tours. Bald eagles our specialty. (907) 766-2876.

㊲ **CHILKAT GUIDES** 3½ hour float trips through the world famous Bald Eagle Preserve. Trips daily June to October. (907) 766-2491.

㊳ **CHILKOOT LAKE TOURS** Majestic eagles, colorful red salmon, beautiful waterfalls. Fish, take photos or just relax and enjoy. POB 250, Haines, AK. (907) 766-2891.

㊴ **HAINES AIRWAYS** Flightsee tours from Haines, Juneau & Skagway. Scheduled service to Juneau & Haines. 766-2646 or 789-2336.

㊵ **L.A.B. FLYING SERVICE** Explore Glacier Country. Scheduled Service and Charters. Flightsee Glacier Bay. (907) 766-2222.

㊶ **RIVER ADVENTURES** Exclusive Jet Boat Tours in the heart of Bald Eagle Preserve. Great opportunity for wildlife viewing. 766-2050 or 1-800-478-9827.

㊷ **THE TRAVEL CONNECTION** See us for ferry reservations, sightseeing, Glacier Bay tours, independent trip planning. Across from Visitor Center. (907) 766-2681.

㊸ **WATER TAXI & SCENIC CRUISE** 40 passenger boat serves Haines and Skagway roundtrip twice daily. POB 246, Haines, AK 99827. 766-3395.

㊹ **WINGS OF ALASKA** *Fly* magnificent S.E. Alaska with us! Scheduled, Charter and Flightseeing air service. (800) 478-9464 or (907) 766-2030.

Haines is waiting for you!
CALL (800) 458-3579

Native Crafts   Winter Attractions   Hiking & Camping

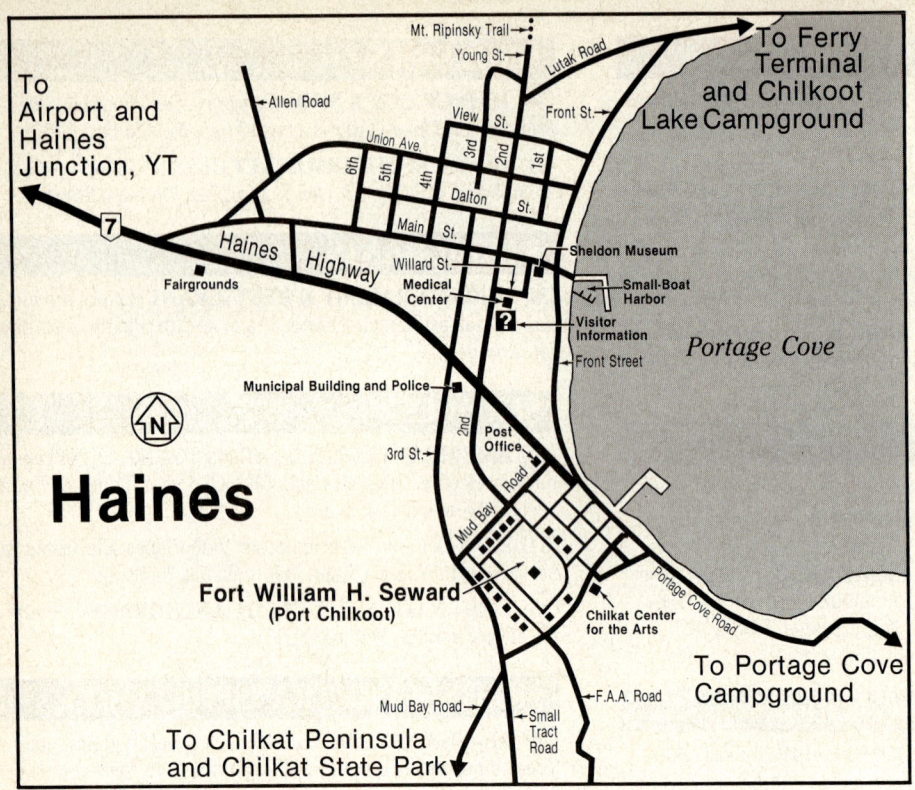

12 cable channels. **Newspaper:** *Chilkat Valley News* (weekly).

Private Aircraft: Haines airport, 3.5 miles/5.6 km west; elev. 16 feet/5m; length 4,200 feet/1,280m; chip seal; unattended.

The original Indian name for Haines was *Dtehshuh*, meaning "end of the trail." It was a trading post for both Chilkat and Interior Indians. The first white man to settle here was George Dickinson who came as an agent for the North West Trading Co.

The following year S. Hall Young, a Presbyterian missionary, came into Chilkat Inlet with his friend, naturalist John Muir. They planned to build a Christian town, offering the Chilkat people a missionary and teacher. The site chosen was on the narrow portage between the Chilkat River and Lynn Canal. By 1881, with financial help from Sheldon Jackson, the mission was established and the town was named for Mrs. F.E. Haines, secretary of the Presbyterian National Committee of Home Missions, which raised funds for the new mission.

In 1884 the Haines post office was established, although the settlement was still known locally as Chilkoot. The town became an important outlet for the Porcupine Mining District, producing thousands of dollars' worth of placer gold at the turn of the century. Haines also marked the beginning of the Dalton Trail, which crossed the Chilkat mountain pass to the Klondike goldfields in the Yukon.

Just to the south of Haines city center is Port Chilkoot on Portage Cove. The U.S. government established a permanent

---

EAGLE'S NEST
Motel and Car Rental

Fully Modern Rooms
with Phones, Cable TV and Ample Parking

Rental Cars Available with offices
in Haines and Skagway
Perfect for the Golden Circle Loop

Call (907) 766-2891
P.O. Box 250, Haines, Alaska 99827

AAA approved

HÄLSINGLAND HOTEL
RESTAURANT • LOUNGE
A NATIONAL REGISTERED HISTORICAL SITE

Charming Rooms • Private Baths • Reasonable Rates

Our Victorian Hotel offers 60 rooms, many with Views and Fireplaces. TVs, Phones, Senior Discounts, Fire Sprinkler System
FORMER OFFICERS' QUARTERS OF HISTORIC FORT SEWARD.

We boast our renowned Seafood Restaurant, and our popular cocktail lounge, with famous wine bar and view of Fort Seward parade grounds. We offer Avis car rentals, courtesy transfers, and area Bus Terminal.

WRITE: P.O. Box 1589-MP, Haines, Alaska 99827 • (907) 766-2000
CALL TOLL FREE: 1-800-542-6363 or in Yukon/BC: 1-800-478-2525

HAINES ADVERTISERS

Alaska Indian Arts Inc.	Fort Seward
Alaska Nature Tours	Ph. (907) 766-2876
Bear Creek Camp & International Hostel	Ph. (907) 766-2259
Captain's Choice Motel	Ph. (907) 766-3111
Chilkat Restaurant and Bakery, The	5th Ave.
Chilkoot Lake Tours	Ph. (907) 766-2891
Don's Camp	Ph. (907) 766-2303
Eagle Camper RV Park	751 Union Ave.
Eagle's Nest Motel and Car Rental	Ph. (907) 766-2891
First Out, Last In Fishing Charters	Ph. (907) 766-2854
Fort Seward Lodge, Inc.	Fort Seward
Haines Chamber of Commerce	Ph. 1-800-458-3579
Haines Hitch-Up RV Park	Ph. (907) 766-2882
Haines Quick Shop	Next to post office
Haines-Skagway Water Taxi	Ph. (907) 766-3395
Hälsingland Hotel, Restaurant and Lounge	Fort Seward
Helen's Shop	Main St.
Howsers Supermarket	Main St.
King's Store	Main St.
L.A.B. Flying Service Inc.	Main St.
Mt. View Motel	Ph. (907) 766-2900
Northern Arts Gallery	2nd & Willard
Oceanside R.V. Park	Front St.
Officers Inn Bed & Breakfast	Fort Seward
Port Chilkoot Camper Park	Fort Seward
Port Chilkoot Potlatch	Fort Seward
Sheldon Museum and Cultural Center, The	25 Main St.
Summer Inn Bed & Breakfast, The	247 2nd Ave.
Thunderbird Motel	242 Dalton St.

military post here in 1904 and called it Fort William H. Seward in honor of the secretary of state who negotiated the purchase of Alaska from Russia in 1867.

In 1922, the fort was renamed Chilkoot Barracks, after the mountain pass and the Indian tribe on the Chilkoot River. (There are 2 tribes in this area: the Chilkat and the Chilkoot.) Until WWII this was the only U.S. Army post in Alaska. Chilkoot Barracks was deactivated in 1946 and sold in 1947 to a group of enterprising U.S. veterans who had designs of creating a business cooperative on the site. Their original plans were never fully realized, but a few stayed on to convert some of the houses on Officers' Row into homes, and to renovate and redecorate the old barracks as a tourist attraction; see Attractions this section.

In 1970, Port Chilkoot merged with Haines to become one municipality, the city of Haines. Two years later, the post was designated a national historic site and became officially known, again, as Fort William H. Seward (although many people still call it Port Chilkoot).

Fishing and gold mining were the initial industries of the Haines area. Haines is also remembered for its famous strawberries, developed by Charles Anway about 1900. His Alaskan hybrid, *Burbank*, was a prize winner at the 1909 Alaska–Yukon–Pacific Exposition in Seattle, WA. A strawberry festival was held annually in Haines for many years, and this local event—with funding from the state—grew into the Southeast Alaska State Fair, which each summer draws thousands of visitors from all over the state. Today, halibut and gill-net salmon fishing, lumbering and tourism are the basis of the economy. Haines is an important port on the Alaska Marine Highway System as the southern terminus of the Haines Highway, one of the 2 year-round roads linking southeastern Alaska with the Interior, the gulf coast and Yukon Territory.

ACCOMMODATIONS

Haines offers travelers comfortable accommodations with 7 hotels/motels and several bed and breakfasts. There is a youth hostel (families welcome) with cabin accommodations on Small Tract Road.

Haines has all traveler facilities, including hardware and grocery stores, gift shops and art galleries, automotive repair, laundry, post office and bank. Gift shops and galleries feature the work of local artisans. There are several restaurants, cafes and taverns.

State campgrounds in the area (all of which charge a $6 nightly fee) include the following: Portage Cove Campground with 9 tent sites (backpackers and bicyclists only), 2 miles/3.2 km from Haines on Portage Cove (take beach road south of Fort William H. Seward), may be reached via a paved bike path. Chilkat State Park with 33 campsites, is about 7 miles/11 km from Haines on Mud Bay Road (from the Haines Highway, bear right at the Y by the Welcome to Haines sign; continue straight ahead past the high school and up the hill, where road bends to the right; follow signs from hill to Chilkat State Park). Chilkoot Lake Campground (32 sites) is approximately 8 miles/13 km from Haines on Lutak Road (5 miles/8 km past the ferry terminal; turn right when exiting the ferry for Chilkoot Lake). There are 5 private campgrounds in Haines. ▲

Eagle Camper RV Park, located at 751 Union St. in beautiful Haines, Alaska. 30 full

Officers Inn
Haines, Alaska

Charming Rooms, Views, Phones, TV, Fireplaces, Private & Shared Baths, Courtesy Transfers, Senior Discount

BED & BREAKFAST
in Historic Fort Seward

Call Toll Free 1-800-542-6363
Or Yukon/BC 1-800-478-2525

(907) 766-2000
Box 1589-MP
Haines, Alaska 99827

DON'S CAMP
In the heart of the CHILKAT BALD EAGLE PRESERVE

Lakeshore cabin with modern facilities at Chilkat Lake

Freshwater fishing
Fly-in or take a Riverboat

P.O. Box 74, Haines, AK 99827
Book early: (907) 766-2303

BEAR CREEK CAMP & INTERNATIONAL HOSTEL

DORMITORY LODGING and FAMILY CABINS

Kitchen Facilities
Laundry • Showers

No prepaid reservations needed

Ferry Shuttle Available
Call from Terminal

Box 1158, Haines, Alaska 99827
(907) 766-2259

Port Chilkoot CAMPER PARK

LAUNDROMAT • ELECTRIC HOOKUPS
SHOWERS • WATER • DUMP STATION

In wooded setting on Mud Bay Road AT FORT SEWARD
Walking distance to Restaurants and Shops
BOX 1589....HAINES, AK 99827...(907) 766-2755

CALL TOLL FREE 1-800-542-6363
or in Yukon/BC 1-800-478-2525

Mt. View Motel

MODERN, QUIET, VIEW UNITS

Reasonable Prices • Family and Winter Rates
KITCHENETTES and CABLE TV

Above Post Office
Adjacent to historic Fort Seward
• *Major credit cards accepted*

Phone (907) 766-2900
2nd Avenue & Mud Bay Road
P.O. Box 62, Haines, Alaska 99827

FORT SEWARD LODGE
In Historic Fort William Seward
MILE 0 HAINES HIGHWAY
Phone: (907) 766-2009

Huge Outdoor Deck with Sweeping View of Lynn Canal

OPEN YEAR-ROUND

• COURTESY VAN
• LODGING - 10 Rooms • Reasonable Rates
• DINING - Fresh Seafood and Steaks
  Salad Bar and Homemade Bread
  Fresh Local Crab - *All-You-Can-Eat* (seasonal)
  Prime Rib - *All-You-Can-Eat*
  (Wednesday & Saturday)

Unique Antique Alaskan Decor

Free Brochure: P.O. Box 307-M, Haines, AK 99827

Fort William H. Seward—Port Chilkoot—south of Haines city center. (John W. Warden)

hookups with cable TV, tents welcome. Lawn with barbecues and picnic tables. Laundromat (for registered guests only). Public showers and propane. This RV park is just blocks from town and is located on 3½ acres with grass and trees. It has a circle drive for easy entrance to all spaces. Senior discounts, 60 years or older. P.O. Box 28, Haines, AK 99827. Phone (907) 766-2335, fax (907) 766-2339. [ADVERTISEMENT] ▲

Haines Hitch-up RV Park. This 5-acre camper park offers easy access to all 92 spaces. 20 pull-throughs, 25-foot-wide lots. Full, partial and no hookups. 30 amps. Level grassy spaces. Immaculate restrooms and showers (for registered guests only). Laundromat, gift shop, propane. Storage of RVs. Within walking distance of town. (907) 766-2882. Box 383, Haines, AK 99827. Half mile west of Main Street. [ADVERTISEMENT] ▲

TRANSPORTATION

Air: Haines is served regularly by L.A.B. Flying Service and Haines Airways.

Haines airport is 3.5 miles/5.6 km from downtown. Commercial airlines provide transportation to and from motels and some motels offer courtesy car pickup.

Ferry: Alaska Marine Highway vessels serve Haines from southeastern Alaska, British Columbia and Bellingham, WA. Alaska state ferries run year-round; phone 766-2111. See MARINE ACCESS ROUTES section for details.

Ferries unload at the terminal on Lutak Road, 3.6 miles/5.8 km from downtown Haines. Bus/van service meets all ferries in summer.

A local company also provides a water-taxi service to and from nearby Skagway twice daily during the summer.

Cruise Ships: 5 cruise ships make Haines a port of call.

Private Boats: Transient moorage is available at Letnikof Cove and at the small boat harbor downtown. Contact the harbormaster.

Bus: Local bus service to ferry terminal and guided sightseeing tours are available. Two companies also offer service to and from Anchorage, Fairbanks and Whitehorse, YT, via the Alaska Highway.

Taxi: 24-hour service to ferry terminal and airport. Some motels offer courtesy car transportation.

Car Rental: Available at Thunderbird Motel, Captain's Choice Motel, Eagle's Nest Motel and Halsingland Hotel.

Highways: The Haines Highway connects Haines, AK, with Haines Junction, YT. It is maintained year-round. See HAINES HIGHWAY section for details.

ATTRACTIONS

Take the walking tour of historic Fort William H. Seward; details and map are available at the visitor information center and at other businesses. Historic buildings of the post include the former cable office; warehouses and barracks; "Soapsuds Alley," the housing for noncommissioned officers whose wives did washing for the soldiers; the former headquarters building, now a residence, fronted by a cannon and a totem depicting a bear and an eagle; Officers' Row at the "Top O' the Hill," restored houses now rented as apartments; the commanding officers' quarters, now the Halsingland Hotel, where Elinor Dusenbury (who later wrote the music for "Alaska's Flag" which became the state song) once lived; the fire hall; the guard house (jail); the former contractor's office, then plumber's quarters, now a motel; the post exchange (now a lodge), gymnasium and movie house; and the mule stables.

Visit the Chilkat Center for the Arts at the auditorium at Fort William H. Seward. Here, the Chilkat Dancers interpret ancient Tlingit Indian legends and the production *Lust for Dust,* a historically based local melodrama, is performed by the Lynn Canal Community Players. Check with the visitor information center or Alaska Indian Arts Inc. for schedule of performances.

Totem Village, on the former post

Oceanside R.V. Park
..."Park by the Sea"

Water • Electrical • Sewer • TV
Downtown, adjacent to groceries, showers, restaurant, bar
P.O. Box 149-MP
HAINES, ALASKA 99827
(907) 766-2444 Office in Harbor Bar

HAINES
THUNDERBIRD MOTEL

"Alaska's Wally Walrus"

DOWNTOWN HAINES
(907) 766-2131
1-800-327-2556

20 DELUXE ROOMS with TV and PHONES

HERTZ Car Rental

Box 589
Haines 99827

MasterCard, VISA, American Express

THE SUMMER INN
BED & BREAKFAST
— OPEN YEAR-ROUND —
Full Breakfast • Convenient Location
Excellent View of Lynn Canal
P.O. Box 1198, Haines, Alaska 99827
(907) 766-2970

247 Second Avenue

EXPERIENCE

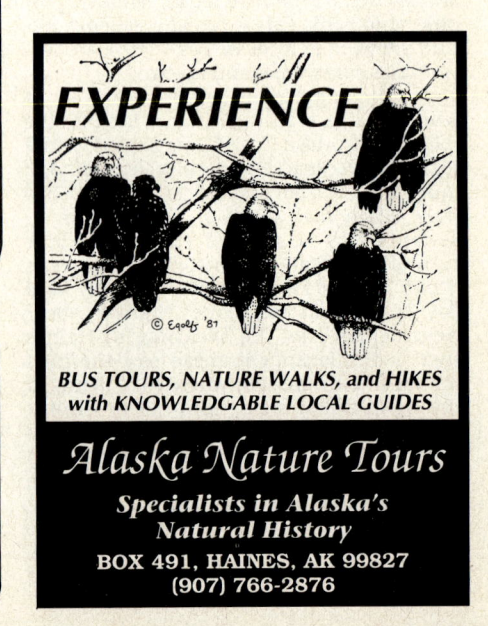

BUS TOURS, NATURE WALKS, and HIKES with KNOWLEDGABLE LOCAL GUIDES

Alaska Nature Tours
Specialists in Alaska's Natural History
BOX 491, HAINES, AK 99827
(907) 766-2876

parade ground, includes a replica of a tribal ceremonial house and a trapper's cabin and cache. There is a salmon bake, the Port Chilkoot Potlatch, held nightly in summer next to the tribal house; reservations recommended. Prior to the establishment of the fort, this area was part of an ancient portage route for Tlingit Indians transporting canoes from the Chilkat River to Lynn Canal.

See the Welcome Totems located at the Y on the Haines Highway. These poles were created by carvers of Alaska Indian Arts Inc. *The Raven* pole is symbolic of Raven, as founder of the world and all his great powers. The second figure is *The Whale*, representing Alaska and its great size. The bottom figure is the head of *The Bear,* which shows great strength. *The Eagle* pole tells of his feeding grounds (the Haines area is noted for its eagles). Top figure is *The Salmon Chief,* who provides the late run of salmon to the feeding grounds. *The Eagle Chief,* head of the Eagle clan, is the third figure, and the bottom figure is *The Brown Bear,* which also feeds on salmon and is a symbol of strength and great size. Inquire at the visitor information center about location of poles.

The Sheldon Museum and Cultural Center, at the end of Main Street near the small-boat harbor, serves Russian tea and has exhibits of Tlingit artifacts, Russian items, Jack Dalton's old sawed-off shotgun and other pioneer items. Children enjoy the fur samples, animal heads and old telephones. Film on eagles. A fascinating history lesson. Open 1-5 P.M. (other hours as posted) daily in summer. Admission fee $2; children free when accompanied by parents.

Enjoy the Fourth of July celebration, which includes the Mad Raft Race and canoe and kayak races on Chilkoot Lake, logging events, bicycle and foot races, contests, parades and performances at the Chilkat Center for the Arts.

The Southeast Alaska State Fair, held at

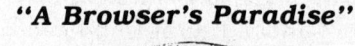

the fairgrounds in Haines (Aug. 12-16, 1992), features agriculture, home arts, and fine arts and crafts. A big event at the fair is the Bald Eagle Music Festival. There are exhibits of flowers, livestock, baked goods, beer and wine, needlework, quilting, woodworking and a dozen other categories. There are also a parade, horse show and other events, including pig racing on the set used for the Disney film *White Fang*. Make reservations early for accommodations and transportation.

Visit the small-boat harbor at the foot of Main Street for a fascinating afternoon outing. Watch gill-net and crab fishermen setting out from here. Good views from Lookout Park and also from the shoreline between Haines and Portage Cove campground.

Visit State Parks. Chilkoot Lake, at the end of Lutak Road, is worth a visit. Beautiful setting with a picnic area, campground and boat launch. Watch for brown bears in nearby waters in the fall, attracted by spawning salmon. (Private boat tours of Chilkoot Lake are available; check in town.) Chilkat State Park out Mud Bay Road is also a scenic spot with hiking trails, beach access, views of glaciers (Rainbow and Davidson), fishing, camping and picnicking. Both parks are within 10 miles/16 km of downtown Haines.

Go Flightseeing. Local air charter operators offer flightseeing trips for spectacular close-up views of glaciers, ice fields, mountain peaks and bald eagles. Glacier Bay is just west of Haines.

Charter boat operators in Haines offer fishing, sightseeing and photography trips.

Watch totem carvers at the Alaska Indian Arts Inc. workshop, located in the restored hospital at Fort William H. Seward. This nonprofit organization is dedicated to the revival of Tlingit Indian art. Craftsmen also work in silver and stone and sew blankets. Visitor hours 9 A.M. to noon and 1-5 P.M. weekdays year-round.

Hike Area Trails. Mount Ripinski trail is a strenuous all-day hike with spectacular views from the summit of mountains and tidal waters. Start at the end of 2nd and Young streets; follow pipeline right-of-way about 1.3 miles/2.1 km to trail, which climbs 3.6 miles/5.8 km to the 3,610-foot/1,100-m summit.

Battery Point trail starts 0.3 mile/0.5 km beyond Portage Cove Campground and leads about 2.4 miles/3.9 km to a primitive camping site on Kelgaya Point overlooking Lynn Canal.

Mount Riley (elev. 1,760 feet/536m) has 3 routes to the summit. The steepest trail starts at Mile 3 Mud Bay Road and climbs 2.1 miles/3.4 km to the summit. A second route starts at the end of F.A.A. Road and leads 2 miles/3.2 km along the city water supply route to connect with the trail from Mud Bay Road to the summit. A third route follows the Battery Point trail for approximately 2 miles/3.2 km, then forks right for a fairly steep climb through underbrush and over Half Dome to summit of Mount Riley.

Seduction Point, at the southern tip of the Chilkat Peninsula, is accessible from Chilkat State Park via a 6-mile/9.7-km trail.

Count eagles when the world's greatest concentration of American bald eagles takes place October through January on Chilkat River flats below Klukwan. The eagle viewing area begins at **Milepost H 17** on the Haines Highway. The 48,000-acre Alaska Chilkat Bald Eagle Preserve was established in 1982. The Chilkat Valley at Haines is the annual gathering site of more than 3,000 bald eagles, which gather to feed on the late run of chum salmon in the Chilkat River.

AREA FISHING: Local charter boat operators offer fishing trips. Good freshwater and saltwater fishing in area lakes, streams, rivers and inlets, for salmon, trout, halibut, shellfish, cod and, occasionally, red snapper.

Mud Bay Road

Mileposts on Mud Bay Road measure distance from its junction with the Haines Highway near Front Street to road end at Mud Bay, a distance of 8 miles/13 km. This paved then wide gravel road leads to Chilkat State Park, following the shoreline of Chilkat Inlet to Mud Bay on Chilkoot Inlet.
Distance is measured from junction with Haines Highway.

0.1 (0.2 km) Hotel on left, motel and private camper park on right.
0.2 (0.3 km) **Junction** with 3rd Street, which leads back to town.
0.5 (0.8 km) Small Tract Road on left, a 1.9-mile/3.1-km loop road which rejoins Mud Bay Road at **Milepost 2.3**. Small Tract Road leads to private residences and to Bear Creek Camp and Youth Hostel (dorms, cabins and tent camping).
Mud Bay Road leads to the right, following the shoreline of Chilkat Inlet, with views of Pyramid Island. Excellent area for eagle pictures.
2.3 (3.7 km) Stop sign at T intersection: go right for state park, left to return to town via Small Tract Road.
3 (4.8 km) Mount Riley trail on left, parking area on right.
3.9 (6.3 km) View of Pyramid Island and Rainbow Glacier across Chilkat Inlet. Rainbow Glacier, so named because someone once saw a rainbow over it, is a hanging glacier. The ice field moved out over a cliff rather than moving down a valley to the sea. Davidson Glacier is about 2 miles/3.2 km south of Rainbow Glacier.
4.9 (7.9 km) Boat dock on right for small boats (summer tie-off only), boat ramp and pit toilets.
5.2 (8.4 km) Pavement ends, gravel begins.
5.3 (8.5 km) Private road on right to cannery on Letnikof Cove.
6.7 (10.8 km) Turn right and drive in 1.2 miles/1.9 km to entrance of Chilkat State Park (camping area 0.5 mile/0.8 km beyond entrance): 32 campsites, $6 nightly fee or annual pass, picnic sites, pit toilets and boat launch. It's a steep and bumpy gravel access road with grades to 11 percent. Drive carefully. Beach access, view of glaciers and hiking trail to Seduction Point at southern tip of Chilkat Peninsula.
7.2 (11.6 km) Blueberries, raspberries and highbush cranberries grow along this section of the road during summer.
8 (12.9 km) Mud Bay Road turns east and crosses Chilkat Peninsula to Flat Bay (commonly called Mud Bay) on Chilkoot Inlet. Road ends at Mud Bay; short walk to rocky beach.

Lutak Road

Lutak Road begins at Front Street, and leads north along Chilkoot Inlet past the Alaska State ferry terminal, then northwest along Lutak Inlet past Chilkoot Lake Campground to road end, a distance of 10 miles/16 km.
Distance is measured from the junction of Front Street with Lutak Road.

0 **Junction**, Front Street and Lutak Road.
0.1 (0.2 km) Turnout on right with view of Fort Seward and Lynn Canal.
1.6 (2.6 km) Turnouts along road from here to Mile 7 allow good view of gill-net fleet, July through September.
2.4 (3.9 km) Government tank farm, petroleum distribution terminal and beginning of an oil pipeline to Fairbanks. No entry.
3.2 (5.1 km) Dock for oil tankers on right.
3.6 (5.8 km) Alaska State ferry terminal on right.
3.8 (6.1 km) City dock on right is used for shipping lumber and also for docking cruise ships and barges.
Pavement ends.
4.4 (7.1 km) Sawmill.
7.8 (12.6 km) Barge on beach sells snacks.
8.3 (13.4 km) Road on left follows a wide stretch of the Chilkoot River for 1 mile/1.6 km to Chilkoot Lake picnic area and boat launch; state campground with 32 sites just beyond picnic area, 7-day limit, $6 nightly fee or annual pass.
8.4 (13.5 km) Bridge over the mouth of the **Chilkoot River**. Good salmon fishing in June, July and August. Watch for bears.
In 1983, the Chilkoot tribe dedicated Deer Rock (on right side of road) as a historic reminder of the original location of their village. Deer Rock is also called Peace Rock.
10 (16 km) Road end. Turnaround.

Crab fishermen work Lynn Canal.
(John W. Warden)

Skagway

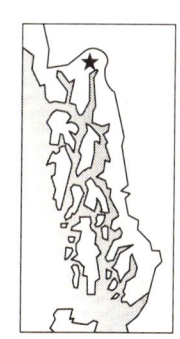

Located on the north end of Taiya Inlet on Lynn Canal, 90 air miles/145 km northwest of Juneau; 108 road miles/174 km south of Whitehorse, YT. The northern terminus of the Alaska Marine Highway Southeast ferry system and southern terminus of Klondike Highway 2 which connects with the Alaska Highway. *NOTE: Although Skagway is only 13 miles/21 km by water from Haines, it is 359 miles/578 km by road!* **Population:** 695. **Emergency Services: Skagway Police Department,** phone 983-2301. **Fire Department** and **Ambulance,** phone 983-2300. **Clinic,** phone 983-2255. **Maritime Search and Rescue;** contact the Coast Guard at 1-800-478-5555.
Visitor Information: Write the Skagway Convention and Visitors Bureau, Box 415MP, Skagway 99840. Phone 983-2854, fax 983-2151. The bureau operates a walk-in

HAINES-SKAGWAY WATER TAXI

$29 Round Trip

TWO ROUND TRIPS DAILY BETWEEN HAINES AND SKAGWAY
Call (907) 766-3395
Write Box 246, Haines, Alaska 99827

GOLD RUSH LODGE

Smoke-free Rooms Available
Complimentary Continental Breakfast
Courtesy Van
Airplane Parking

"The Cleanest Rooms and Most Comfortable Beds in Alaska"

ALL ROOMS HAVE –
• Twin, Full, King/Queen Beds
• Private Bathrooms
• Cable TV and Showtime
• Competitive Rates

VISA, MasterCard, Discounts for Cash, Seniors
JUST THREE BLOCKS FROM DOWNTOWN AT 6TH AVE. AND ALASKA ST.
P.O. Box 514   Skagway, Alaska 99840   Phone (907) 983-2831
OPEN YEAR AROUND   FAX (907) 983-2742

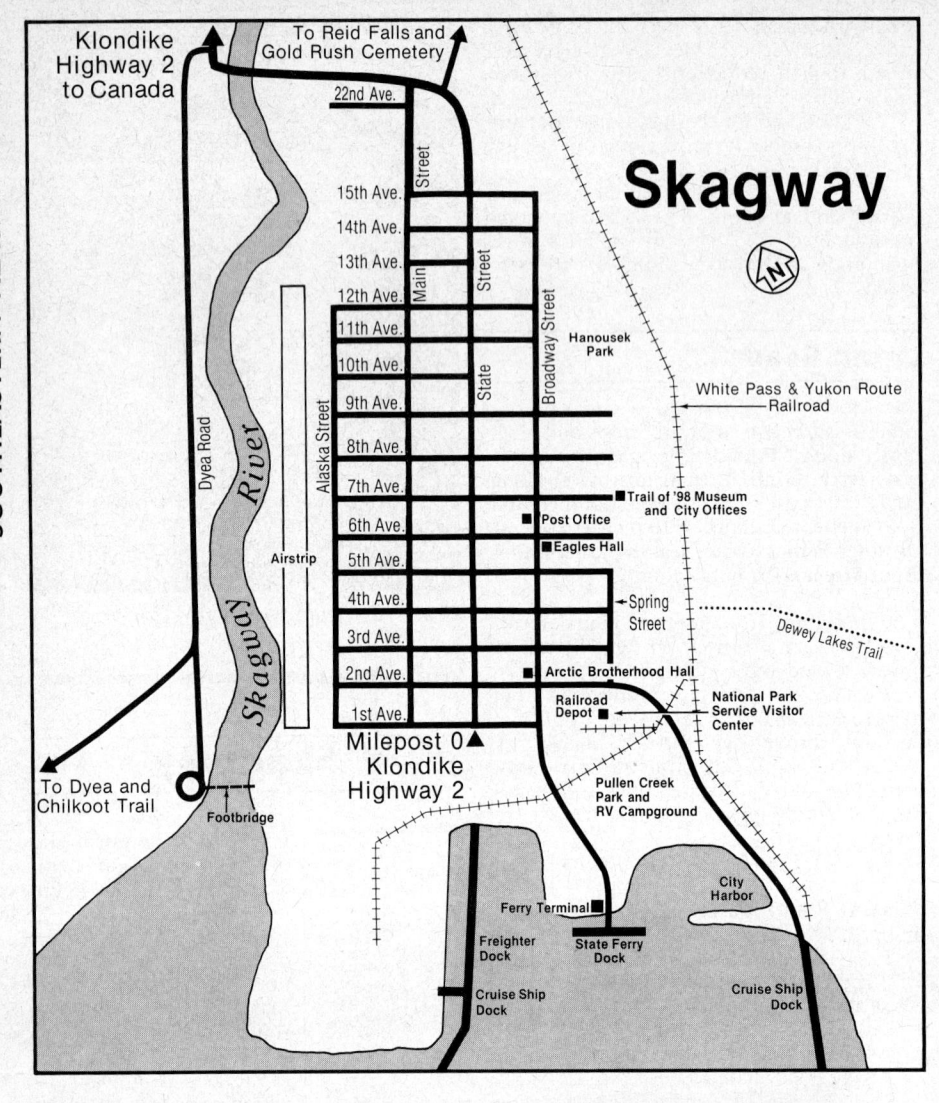

information center from May through September in the historic Arctic Brotherhood Hall on Broadway between 2nd and 3rd. Klondike Gold Rush National Historical Park Visitor Center has exhibits and films on the history of the area and information on hiking the Chilkoot Trail; write Box 517, Skagway 99840; phone 983-2921. Located in the refurbished railroad depot on 2nd Avenue and Broadway, it is open in summer.

Elevation: Sea level. **Climate:** Average daily temperature in summer, 57°F/14°C; in winter, 23°F/-5°C. Average annual precipitation is 29.9 inches. **Radio:** KHNS-FM 91.9. **Newspaper:** *Skagway News* (biweekly).

Private Aircraft: Skagway airport, adjacent west; elev. 44 feet/13m; length 3,500 feet/1,067m; asphalt; fuel 80, 100.

The name Skagway (originally spelled Skaguay) is said to mean "home of the north wind" in the local Tlingit dialect. It is the oldest incorporated city in Alaska (incorporated in 1900). Skagway is also a year-round port and 1 of the 2 gateway cities to the Alaska Highway in southeastern Alaska: Klondike Highway 2 connects Skagway with the Alaska Highway. (The other gateway city is Haines, connected to the Alaska Highway via the Haines Highway.)

The first white residents were Capt. William Moore and his son, J. Bernard, who settled in 1887 on the east side of the Skagway River valley (a small part of the Moore homesite was sold for construction of a Methodist college, now the city hall).

But Skagway owes its birth to the Klondike gold rush. Skagway, and the once-thriving town of Dyea, sprang up as thousands of gold seekers arrived to follow the White Pass and Chilkoot trails to the Yukon goldfields.

In July 1897, the first boatloads of stam-

SKAGWAY ADVERTISERS

Dedman's Photo Shop & Art Gallery	Broadway
Door Knob, The	Broadway
Fairway Market	4th & State
Gold Rush Lodge	6th & Alaska
Gold Rush Productions	Eagles Hall
Golden North Hotel	2nd & Broadway
Hoover's RV Park	4th & Main
Irene's Inn	6th & Broadway
Klondike Mikes	Broadway
Klothes Rush Gifts	5th & Broadway
McFarlane Trading Co. Alaska	Ph. (907) 983-2774
Native Carvings & Gifts	Broadway
Prospector's Sourdough Restaurant	4th & Broadway
Sergeant Preston's Lodge	6th & State St.
Skaguay News Depot	Broadway
Skagway Air Service	4th & Broadway
Skagway Convention & Visitors Bureau	Ph. (907) 983-2854
Skagway Hardware	4th & Broadway
Skagway Inn Bed & Breakfast	7th & Broadway
Skagway RV & Camping Parks	Ph. (907) 983-2768
Skagway Sports Emporium	4th Ave.
Taiya River Jewelry	252 Broadway
Trail Bench, The	2nd & Broadway
Westmark Inn	1-800-544-0970
White Pass & Yukon Route	Ph. (907) 983-2217
Wind Valley Lodge	22nd & State St.

Local merchants help Skagway retain its Klondike atmosphere. (John W. Warden)

Irene's Inn

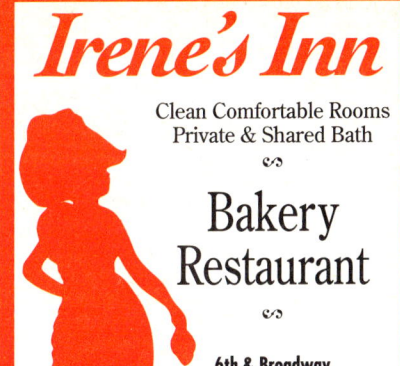

Clean Comfortable Rooms
Private & Shared Bath

Bakery Restaurant

6th & Broadway
Across from Bank and Post Office
The Center of most
Downtown Attractions

(907) 983 2520

PO Box 380 Skagway, AK 99840

Getaway to Skagway

Add Skagway's breathtaking mountains, fjords and the gold rush to your northern adventure. Located on scenic Lynn Canal, Skagway captures the magic of the gold rush in a setting still true to the "Days of 98."

And visit the Westmark Inn Skagway where you'll find comfortable lodging and fine dining in a setting reminiscent of those days gone by.

Special Summer Value Rates from $49

Rooms at lower rates are capacity controlled and good on selected rooms & dates only.
Call for complete information.
Subject to change without notice.

Westmark Inn

SKAGWAY

Third and Spring Streets
P.O. Box 515
Skagway, Alaska 99840

OPEN SEASONALLY

Central Reservations
1-800-544-0970 (U.S.)
1-800-999-2570 (Canada)

Westmark Hotels covers the north with hotels and inns throughout Alaska and the Yukon. Come be our guest.

HOOVER'S

Box 304, Skagway, Alaska 99840
(907) 983-2454

- Propane • Oil
- Gas • Diesel
- RV PARK

Chevron

Corner of 4th & Main

Mechanic
Tire repair
Hot showers

Historic SKAGWAY INN

Bed & Breakfast

Rates Start At **$48.00**

12 clean, comfortable rooms with shared baths

Gene & Emily Zimbrich

Featuring Miss Emily's Tea Room

- Visit our Gift Shop
- Tours Available

(907) 983-2289
PO Box 500-MP
Skagway, Alaska 99840

Northern Wonders

The finest northern gifts & handicrafts at very reasonable prices.

Located at Westmark Hotels

GOLDEN NORTH HOTEL

TRADITIONAL HOST TO ADVENTURERS SINCE THE DAYS OF THE GOLD RUSH

ALASKA'S OLDEST HOTEL
(Built 1898)

On Broadway
SKAGWAY, ALASKA

- DINING ROOM
- • LOUNGE •
- BEAUTY SALON
- TELEPHONES IN ROOMS

Let us assist you with tours of:
HOTEL • SKAGWAY
DYEA • WHITE PASS

FOR RESERVATIONS, WRITE
Box 343, Skagway, Alaska 99840
OR CALL **(907) 983-2451** • **(907) 983-2294**
FAX (907) 983-2755
OPEN YEAR-ROUND (winter rates)

An exciting past comes alive in *The Skagway Story*, Alaska's "Gateway to the Klondike." From Alaska Northwest Books™.

SOUTHEASTERN ALASKA • SKAGWAY

Sergeant Preston's Lodge

- 23 Custom rooms.
- All on street level.
- **TELEPHONES in every room.**
- Cable TV - Courtesy Van.
- Reasonable Rates.
- Open All Year.
- Downtown - 6th & State.
- By the Bank & Post Office.

P.O. Box 538
SKAGWAY, Alaska
99840

(907) 983-2521

SKAGUAY NEWS DEPOT

Come inside the gift shop where we still spell Skaguay with a "U" and do things the old way

Alaska Books & Videos, Latest Newspapers, Magazines & Paperbacks

Personalized Headlines, Skaguay News Press Aprons, Stationery, Calendars & Maps

Situated on Historic Broadway

---

peders bound for the Klondike landed at Skagway and Dyea. By October 1897, according to a North West Mounted Police report, Skagway had grown "from a concourse of tents to a fair-sized town, with well-laid-out streets and numerous frame buildings, stores, saloons, gambling houses, dance houses and a population of about 20,000." Less than a year later it was reported that "Skagway was little better than a hell on earth." Customs office records for 1898 show that in the month of February alone 5,000 people landed at Skagway and Dyea.

By the summer of 1899 the stampede was all but over. The newly built White Pass & Yukon Route railway reached Lake Bennett, supplanting the Chilkoot Trail from Dyea. Dyea became a ghost town. Its post office closed in 1902, and by 1903 its population consisted of 1 settler. Skagway's population—once estimated at 20,000—dwindled to 500. But Skagway persisted, both as a port and as terminus of the White Pass & Yukon Route railway, which connected the town to Whitehorse, YT, in 1900. Cruise ships, and later the Alaska State Ferry System, brought tourism and business to Skagway. Scheduled state ferry service to southeastern Alaska began in 1963.

Today, tourism is Skagway's main economic base, with Klondike Gold Rush National Historical Park Skagway's major visitor attraction. Within Skagway's downtown historical district, false-fronted buildings and boardwalks dating from gold rush times line the streets. The National Park Service, the city of Skagway and local residents have succeeded in retaining Skagway's Klondike atmosphere.

COME TO HISTORIC SKAGWAY

110 MILES TO WHITEHORSE VIA THE KLONDIKE HIGHWAY

NORTHERN TERMINUS OF THE ALASKA MARINE HIGHWAY

WHITE PASS & YUKON RAILROAD (MID MAY-SEPTEMBER)

KLONDIKE GOLD RUSH NATIONAL HISTORICAL PARK

RESTAURANTS, LOUNGES AND ENTERTAINMENT

HISTORIC & MODERN ACCOMMODATIONS

EXCELLENT SHOPPING OPPORTUNITIES

TRAIL OF '98 MUSEUM

SKAGWAY ALASKA — GATEWAY TO THE KLONDIKE — GOLD RUSH OF 1898

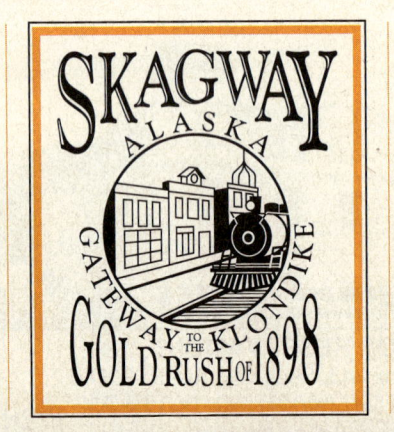

CONTEMPORARY AND TRADITIONAL ART

RV PARKS & SERVICE

GROCERIES, HARDWARE, FUEL AND FACILITIES

THE CHILKOOT TRAIL

WARM, FRIENDLY PEOPLE

∞ SKAGWAY CONVENTION & VISITORS BUREAU • BOX 415MP, SKAGWAY ALASKA 99840 • (907) 983-2854 FAX (907) 983-2151 ∞

Skagway has modern schools, churches, a clinic, bank and post office. A U.S. customs office and branch of the U.S. Immigration and Naturalization Service are located in the White Pass depot. The boat harbor and seaplane base has space for cruisers up to 100 feet/30m. Gas, diesel fuel and water are available.

ACCOMMODATIONS

Skagway offers a variety of sleeping accommodations, from gold rush-style hotels and inns to modern motels (reservations are advised in summer). See ads this section.

Historic Skagway Inn Bed & Breakfast, located at 7th and Broadway, has 12 rooms, 5 rooms are family size. Decorated in Victorian-era, has shared bath, color TV in parlor, continental plus breakfast. Rates start at $48, with 10 percent discount for seniors. Tours of area available. Gift shop. (907) 983-2289. Gene and Emily Zimbrich. [ADVERTISEMENT]

There are several restaurants, cafes and bars, grocery, hardware and clothing stores, and many gift and novelty shops offering Alaska and gold rush souvenirs, photos, books, records, gold nugget jewelry, furs and ivory. Propane, marine and automobile gas are available, as is diesel fuel.

McFarlane Trading Co. Alaska. Just 2 doors from Skagway's incredible ice cream shop, you'll find McFarlane Trading Co. Alaska—a gift shop you must not miss! They have a wide range of genuine Alaskan gifts, usually with printed information to go with them. You'll see a fantastic collection of scrimshaw, refined from the early American whaler's folk art, to today's fine art on Alaskan fossilized walrus or mammoth ivory. Then, there are masks and carvings by Alaskan artists made of ancient whalebone excavated from remote St. Lawrence Island. And don't miss their traditionally created Eskimo dolls, a truly ancient art. Finally, among the Sue Coleman sweatshirts and Northwest Indian cedar plaques, you'll find dog fur sweaters, created by Tagish's Claudia McPhee. McFarlane's store is a definite must! [ADVERTISEMENT]

There is 1 bank in town (National Bank of Alaska), located at 6th and Broadway; open 10 A.M. to 4 P.M. Monday through Friday.

There are 4 RV campgrounds: 1 located adjacent Pullen Creek Park (phone 983-2768) on the waterfront, with hookups, restrooms and showers; Hanousek Park, located east of 14th Avenue (phone 983-2768); an RV park with full hookups at 4th and Main (phone 983-2454); and a private RV park just north of town on the Klondike Highway (phone 983-2061). A campground for backpackers is located at the Chilkoot Trail trailhead near Dyea.

TRANSPORTATION

Air: Daily scheduled service between Skagway and Haines and Juneau via L.A.B. Flying Service and Skagway Air. Charter service also available between towns and for flightseeing via Skagway Air. Temsco provides helicopter tours. Transportation to and from the airport is provided by the flight services and local hotels.

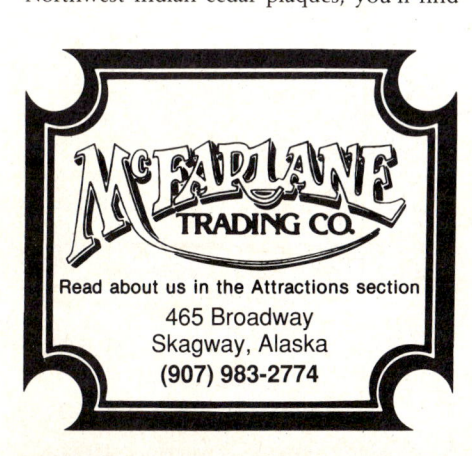

Historic buildings along Skagway's Broadway Street. (Barb Michaels)

SOUTHEASTERN ALASKA • SKAGWAY

THE DAYS OF '98 SHOW
WITH SOAPY SMITH

66th Year

THE HISTORIC MUSICAL COMEDY
OF SKAGUAY AND THE LEGENDARY CON MAN

EAGLES HALL

6th & Broadway ~ Skagway, Alaska

Shows Nightly ~ Matinees for Cruise Ships

Tickets at the Door: $12

Gold Rush Productions, Inc. • P.O. Box 1897-MP • Skagway, AK 99840
907-983-2545

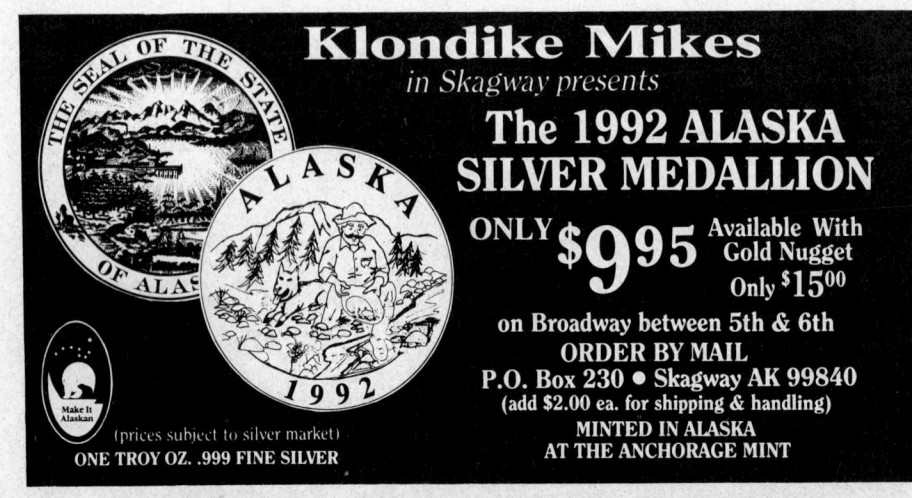

Bus: Daily bus/van service to Anchorage, Fairbanks, Haines and Whitehorse, YT.

Taxi: Operate year-round and also offer sightseeing service and transportation to Chilkoot Trail trailhead.

Car Rental: 2 companies.

Highway: Klondike Highway 2 was completed in 1978 and connects Skagway to the Alaska Highway. It is open year-round. See KLONDIKE HIGHWAY 2 section.

Railroad: White Pass & Yukon Route offers 3-hour excursions from Skagway to White Pass Summit and return. Through rail/bus connections are also available daily between Skagway and Whitehorse, with rail motorcar service to Lake Bennett. See WHITE PASS & YUKON ROUTE section for details.

Ferry: Alaska Marine Highway vessels call regularly year-round, as Skagway is the northern terminus of the Southeast ferry system. See MARINE ACCESS ROUTES section for schedules. The ferry terminal is in the large building on the waterfront (see city map this section); restrooms, pay phone and lockers inside. Ferry terminal office hours vary: opening hours are usually posted at the front door. Phone 983-2941.

Ships: Skagway is a regular port of call for cruise ships from U.S. and Canadian ports.

The excursion boat MV *Fairweather* cruises to Juneau. Operated by Gray Line of Alaska for their package tours, seats may be purchased by the general public on a space-available basis. Contact their Skagway office at the Klondike Hotel (phone 983-2500).

Private Boats: Transient moorage is available at the Skagway small boat harbor.

PROSPECTOR'S SOURDOUGH RESTAURANT

Alaskan Sourdough:
- HOTCAKES & WAFFLES
- CRAB OMELETTES

Open 6 a.m. — 9 p.m.
Serving Breakfast until 3 p.m.
Daily Breakfast, Lunch and Dinner Specials

4th & Broadway
Downtown Skagway

Klondike Mikes
in Skagway presents

The 1992 ALASKA
SILVER MEDALLION

ONLY **$9.95**
Available With Gold Nugget Only **$15.00**

on Broadway between 5th & 6th

ORDER BY MAIL
P.O. Box 230 • Skagway AK 99840
(add $2.00 ea. for shipping & handling)

MINTED IN ALASKA
AT THE ANCHORAGE MINT

(prices subject to silver market)
ONE TROY OZ. .999 FINE SILVER

Make It Alaskan

---

for Skagway Today
shop
THE DOOR KNOB
as exciting as the
'98 GOLD RUSH

NATIVE CARVINGS & GIFTS | "For the Unusual as Well as the Usual" Shop

SKAGWAY, ALASKA

The GIFT CORNER
Skagway's newest and most innovative shop

4th & Broadway Street
We'll look for you!

Contact the harbormaster at 983-2628.

ATTRACTIONS

Trail of '98 Museum, owned and operated by the citizens of Skagway, is located on the second floor of city hall, corner of 7th Avenue and Spring Street; open 8 A.M. to 6 P.M. daily June through August, 9 A.M. to 5 P.M. daily May and September; admission is $2 for adults, $1 for students and children. The building is the first granite building constructed in Alaska. It was built by the Methodist Church as a school in 1899-1900 to be known as McCabe College, but public school laws were passed that made the enterprise impractical and it was sold to the federal government. For decades it was used as U.S. District Court No. 1 of Alaska, but as the population of the town declined, the court was abandoned and in 1956 the building was purchased by the city. Since May 1961, the second floor has been open as a museum; the main floor is occupied by city of Skagway offices. The museum's main interest is to help preserve Alaskan historical material and to display Alaskan pioneer life. The decor of the old courtroom has been preserved, including the judge's bench and chair and some of Soapy Smith's personal items. For more information, phone 983-2420.

Arctic Brotherhood Hall. Located on Broadway between 2nd and 3rd, some 20,000 pieces of driftwood adorn the false front of this 1899 fraternal meeting hall, used as a visitor information center during the summer. Films are shown here. Admission fee charged.

See the show *The Days of 1898 Show With Soapy Smith*. This show, produced by Gold Rush Productions, is put on twice each evening (subject to cruise ship arrivals) in summer in Eagles Hall. Check the billboard in front of the hall for show times. The show relates the history of Skagway, from the days of the notorious Soapy Smith. Phone 983-2545.

This show is good family entertainment; bring your camera, gamble with funny money (during evening show only), and enjoy this well-done historical musical comedy. Admission fee charged.

Klondike Gold Rush National Historical Park was authorized in 1976 to preserve and interpret the history of the Klondike gold rush of 1897–98. The park, managed by the National Park Service, consists of 4 units: a 6-block historical district in Skagway's business area; a 1-mile-/1.6-km-wide, 17-mile-/27.4-km-long corridor of land comprising the Chilkoot Trail; a 1-mile-/1.6-km-wide, 5-mile-/8-km-long corridor of land comprising the White Pass Trail; and a visitor center at 117 S. Main St. in Seattle, WA.

In Skagway, the National Park Service offers a variety of free programs in summer. There are daily guided walking tours of downtown Skagway and ranger talks on a variety of topics. Films are also shown. Check with the Park Service's visitor center in the refurbished railroad depot on 2nd Avenue and Broadway. Summer hours at the center are 8 A.M. to 6 P.M.

Hike the Chilkoot Trail. This 33-mile/53-km trail begins on Dyea Road (see log this section) and climbs Chilkoot Pass (elev. 3,739 feet/1,140m) to Lake Bennett, following the historic route of the gold seekers of '98. The trail is arduous but offers both spectacular scenery and historical relics. There are several campgrounds and shelters along the route. White Pass & Yukon Route offers hiker rail service from Bennett back to Skagway (see WHITE PASS & YUKON ROUTE section). Detailed information and maps of the trail are available from the National Park Service (Box 517, Skagway 99840). *The ALASKA WILDERNESS MILEPOST®* also has details on

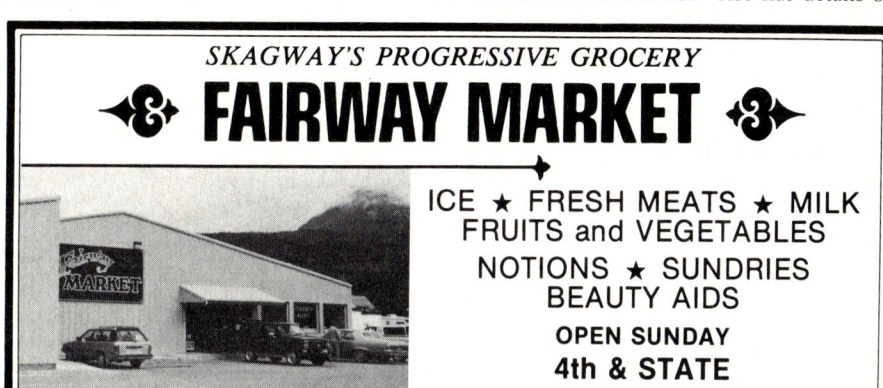

SKAGWAY'S PROGRESSIVE GROCERY

FAIRWAY MARKET

ICE ★ FRESH MEATS ★ MILK
FRUITS and VEGETABLES
NOTIONS ★ SUNDRIES
BEAUTY AIDS

OPEN SUNDAY
4th & STATE

ON THE TRAIL OF '98

RIDE THE RAILWAY BUILT OF GOLD

For gold rush fortune hunters, the trip over White Pass to the Yukon goldfields was hard and bitter. For you, it's a comfortable ride aboard the "Scenic Railway of the World." Past rushing torrents, cascading falls, up craggy mountainsides. All the way to the Summit. Don't miss this Railroad Adventure of a Lifetime!

Round trip excursions from Skagway, and through connections to Whitehorse.

For reservations or information, call
1-800-343-7373, or (907) 983-2217.
1-800-478-7373 — B.C., Y.T. & N.W.T.

WHITE PASS & YUKON ROUTE
GATEWAY TO THE YUKON

The White Pass & Yukon Route
P.O. Box 435   Skagway, Alaska 99840

the Chilkoot Trail, and *Chilkoot Pass* by Archie Satterfield is both a good hiking and history guide to the trail; both available from Alaska Northwest Books™.

Corrington Museum of Alaska History, located at 5th and Broadway, offers a unique record of events from prehistory to the present. Each of the 40 exhibits at the museum features a scene from Alaska history hand-engraved (scrimshawed) on a walrus tusk. The museum is open in summer. Admission fee charged.

Picnic at Pullen Creek Park. This attractive waterfront park has a covered picnic shelter, 2 footbridges and 2 small docks. It is located between the cruise ship and ferry docks, behind the White Pass & Yukon Route depot. Watch for pink salmon in the intertidal waters in August, silver salmon in September.

Helicopter and airplane tours of Skagway and White Pass are available in summer.

Gold Rush Cemetery is 1.5 miles/2.4 km from downtown and makes a nice walk. Go north on State Street to a sign pointing to the cemetery. Follow dirt road across tracks into railroad yard, through a narrow space between a building and the tracks, then about 0.4 mile/0.6 km farther to the cemetery. If you drive in, a circular road around the cemetery eliminates having to back up to get out. A path on left at the end of the road leads to the cemetery where the graves of both "bad guy" Soapy Smith and "good guy" Frank Reid are located (both men died in a gunfight in July 1898). Smith's original gravestone was whittled away by souvenir hunters and the resting place of the feared boss of Skagway is now marked by a metal marker.

Reid Falls are located near Gold Rush Cemetery, and it is only a short hike from Frank Reid's grave to view them.

AREA FISHING: The ADF&G Sport Fish Division recommends the following areas and species. Dolly Varden: Fish the shore of **Skagway Harbor**, **Long Bay** and **Taiya Inlet**, May through June. Try the **Taiya River** by the steel bridge in Dyea in early spring or fall; use red and white spoons or salmon eggs. Salmon: A small local hatchery has good returns of pink salmon. Fish **Skagway Harbor** and **Pullen Creek** in town, July and August; use flashing lures. Coho and chum salmon near the steel bridge on the **Taiya River**, mid-September through October. Trolling in the marine areas is good but often dangerous for small boats. Trout: A steep trail near town will take you to Dewey lakes, which were stocked with Colorado brook trout in the 1920s. **Lower Dewey Lake**, ½- to 1-hour hike; heavily wooded shoreline, use raft. The brook trout are plentiful and grow to 16 inches but are well fed, so fishing can be frustrating. **Upper Dewey Lake**, a steep 2½- to 4-hour hike to above tree line, is full of hungry brook trout to 11 inches. Use salmon eggs or size #10 or #12 artificial flies. **Lost Lake** is reached via a rough trail near Dyea (ask locals for directions). The lake lies at about 1,300 feet elevation and has a good population of rainbow trout. Use small spinners or spoons. For more information, contact the ADF&G office in Haines at 766-2625.

Dyea Road Log

The Dyea Road begins at **Milepost S 2.3** on Klondike Highway 2. It leads southwest toward Yakutania Point, then northwest past Long Bay and the Taiya River to the beginning of the Chilkoot Trail and to a side road leading to the old Dyea townsite and Slide Cemetery. The Dyea Road is a narrow winding gravel road.

Distance is from the junction with Klondike Highway 2.

0 Junction.

0.1 (0.2 km) Old cemetery on right. Gate locked; see mayor, police chief or city clerk for key.

0.4 (0.6 km) View of Reid Falls east across the Skagway River.

0.7 (1.1 km) City dump.

1.4 (2.3 km) A scenic wayside with platform on left southbound affords view of Skagway, Taiya Inlet and the Skagway River.

1.7 (2.7 km) A steep, primitive road on left southbound descends 0.4 mile/0.6 km toward bank of the Skagway River, with a view of the Skagway waterfront and Taiya Inlet.

Drive to parking area and walk 0.2 mile/0.3 km to Yakutania Point; 4-wheel drive only beyond parking area. Bridge at base of hill leads to a short trail back to town. Dyea Road turns northwest along Long Bay at this point.

1.9 (3.1 km) Skyline trailhead (poorly signed). This trail leads to top of AB Mountain (elev. 5,000 feet/1,524m).

2.1 (3.4 km) Head of Long Bay.

4.3 (6.9 km) Taiya Inlet comes into view on left northbound as the road curves away from Long Bay.

5.1 (8.2 km) View of the old pilings in Taiya Inlet. The docks of Dyea used to stretch from the trees out and beyond the pilings that are still visible. These long docks were needed to reach deep water because of the great tidal range in this inlet.

5.7 (9.2 km) Hooligan (smelt) run here in the Taiya River in May and early June. Local swimming hole across the road.

6.5 (10.5 km) Dyea information display.

6.7 (10.8 km) Chilkoot Trail trailhead campground, parking area and ranger station.

7.2 (11.6 km) The Chilkoot Trail begins on right northbound. Bridge over Taiya River.

7.4 (11.9 km) A primitive road on left northbound leads southwest to Slide Cemetery (keep right at forks and follow signs) and old Dyea townsite. The cemetery, reached by a short unmarked path through the woods, contains the graves of men killed in the Palm Sunday avalanche, April 3, 1898, on the Chilkoot Trail. At Dyea townsite, covered with fireweed and lupine in summer, hardly a trace remains of the buildings that housed 8,000 people here during the gold rush. About 30 people live in the valley today.

8.4 (13.5 km) Narrow wooden bridge across West Creek. Four-wheel drive recommended beyond this point.

WHITE PASS & YUKON ROUTE

The White Pass & Yukon Route (WP&YR) is a narrow-gauge (36-inch) privately owned railroad built in 1898 at the height of the Klondike gold rush. Between 1900 and 1982, the WP&YR provided passenger and freight service between Skagway, AK, and Whitehorse, YT. Out of service from late 1982 until the spring of 1988, today the WP&YR offers train service from Skagway to White Pass, Fraser and Bennett, with connecting motorcoach service to Whitehorse.

Construction of the White Pass & Yukon Route began in May 1898. It was the first railroad in Alaska and at the time the most northern of any railroad in North America. The railroad reached White Pass in February 1899 and Whitehorse in July 1900.

The railroad follows the old White Pass trail. The upper section of the old "Deadhorse" trail near the summit (Mile 19 on the WP&YR railway) is visible right beside the tracks. During the Klondike gold rush, thousands of men took the 40-mile White Pass trail from Skagway to Lake Bennett, where they built boats to float down the Yukon River to Dawson City and the goldfields. (The 33-mile Chilkoot Trail from Dyea to Lake Bennett—a popular trail with today's hikers—was also the more popular of the 2 routes from tidewater to the Interior, but was abandoned when the railroad was completed.)

Except for a stint carrying construction materials for the Alaska Highway during the war years, the railroad's major role was supplying the Yukon mining industry and transporting ore to port. In 1982, world metal prices fell and the major mines in the Yukon shut down. WP&YR suspended service in October 1982. While mining resumed, with ore trucked to ports from Yukon mines, the railroad remained mothballed until 1988, when limited excursion service began to accommodate the increasing number of summer visitors interested in riding the historic White Pass & Yukon Route.

The White Pass & Yukon Route has one of the steepest railroad grades in North America. From sea level at Skagway the railroad climbs to 2,885 feet/879m at White Pass in only 20 miles of track. Currently, the railroad offers train service on 28 miles of track between Skagway and Fraser, plus an additional 13 miles for motorcar service to Bennett.

Following are services, schedules and fares available on the White Pass & Yukon Route from mid-May to mid-September 1992. All times indicated in schedules are local times. Children 12 and under are half fare when accompanied by an adult. Children under 2 years ride free if not occupying a seat; half fare for separate seat. Reservations are required. For reservations and information, contact the White Pass & Yukon Route, P.O. Box 435, Skagway, AK 99840. Phone toll free in the U.S. 1-800-343-7373 or (907) 983-2217 in Skagway; phone toll free in western Canada 1-800-478-7373.

Historic WP&YR train on the climb to White Pass. (John W. Warden)

SUMMIT EXCURSION

This approximatey 2-hour-and-45-minute round-trip excursion features the most spectacular part of the WP&YR railway, including the steep climb to White Pass Summit, Bridal Veil Falls, Inspiration Point and Dead Horse Gulch. Offered twice daily, the morning train departs Skagway at 8:45 A.M. and returns at 11:45 A.M.; the afternoon train departs Skagway at 11:45 P.M. and returns at 4:15 P.M. Fares are $72 for adults and $36 for children 12 and under.

THROUGH–SERVICE ("The International")

Through–service between Skagway, AK, and Whitehorse, YT, is offered daily. Through passengers travel by train between Skagway, AK, and Fraser, BC, and by motorcoach between Fraser and Whitehorse, YT. Northbound service departs Skagway at 12:45 P.M., arrives Fraser at 2:30 P.M., and arrives Whitehorse at 6:30 P.M. Southbound service departs Whitehorse at 8:15 A.M., departs Fraser at 10:25 A.M., and arrives Skagway at 12:10 P.M. One-way fares are $92 for adults and $46 for children 12 and under.

LAKE BENNETT HIKER SERVICE

The WP&YR runs a track motorcar between Fraser and Lake Bennett, end of the Chilkoot Trail, for hikers. Connections to Skagway are made at Fraser. Hikers should contact the railroad for dates of operation. The proposed schedule in 1992 calls for departures from Bennett at 8:30 A.M. and 1:15 P.M., and from Fraser at 10:15 A.M. and 3 P.M. One-way fare between Bennett and Fraser is $15. One-way fare between Bennett and Skagway is $72.

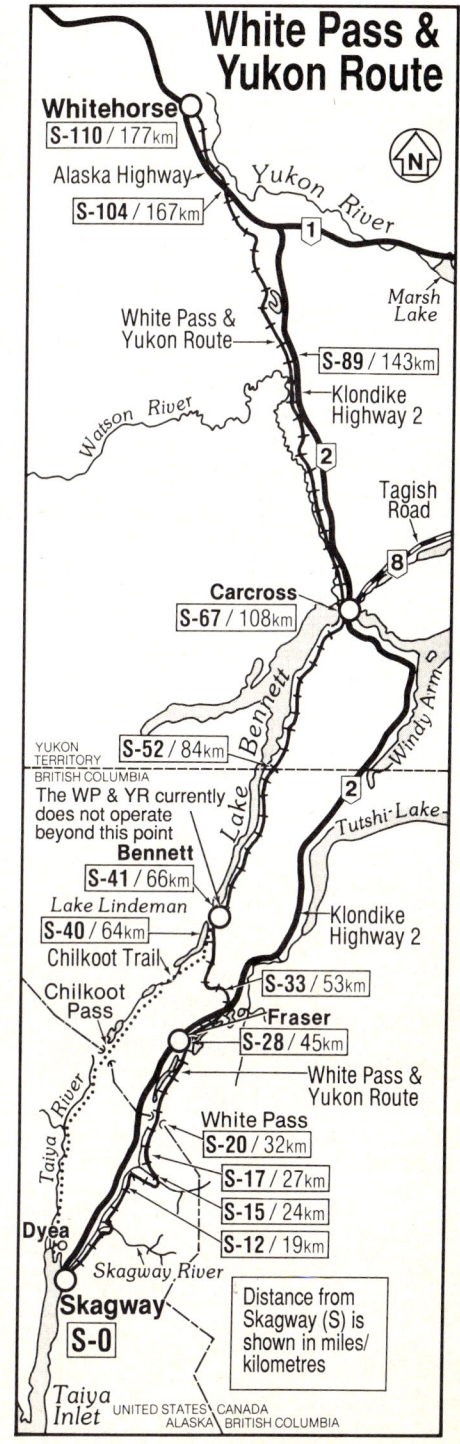

HAINES HIGHWAY

Haines, Alaska, to Haines Junction, Yukon Territory
Alaska Route 7, British Columbia Highway 4 and Yukon Highway 3

Haines Highway winds along 15-mile-long Dezadeash Lake. (Earl L. Brown, staff)

The 151.6-mile-/244-km-long Haines Highway is an all-weather road that connects Haines, AK (on the state ferry route), at the head of Lynn Canal with the Alaska Highway at Haines Junction, YT. The highway is open year-round. Allow about 4 hours' driving time. The highway is paved with some gravel breaks. Watch for logging and fuel trucks. Park only at turnouts!

Noted for the grandeur and variety of its alpine scenery, the highway leads from coastal forests near Haines up over the backbone of the St. Elias Mountains along the western border of Kluane National Park and down into the valleys of the Yukon basin. Information on Kluane National Park is available in Haines Junction, YT.

Part of what is now the Haines Highway was originally a packhorse trail to the Klondike blazed by Jack Dalton in the late 1800s. The present road was built as a military access highway during WWII to provide an alternative route from the Pacific tidewater into Yukon Territory.

NOTE: Between May and October there is no gas service between 33 Mile Roadhouse and Haines Junction, a distance of 118 miles/190 km.

U.S. and Canada customs stations are located about 40 miles/64 km north of Haines. U.S. customs is open from 7 A.M. to 11 P.M. (Alaska time); Canada customs open from 8 A.M. to midnight (Pacific time). *There are no facilities or accommodations at the border.* All travelers must stop at one of the stations.

If you plan to drive the Haines Highway in winter, check road conditions before starting out and carry adequate survival and emergency equipment. In Haines Junction check with the maintenance garage (634-2227) or the RCMP (634-2221). Cold weather, white-outs, and blowing and drifting snow (especially in the summit area) can make the highway treacherous. Watch for fuel trucks and graders.

A valid Alaska fishing license is required for fishing along the highway between Haines and the international border at **Milepost H 40.7**. The highway then crosses the northern tip of British Columbia into Yukon Territory. You must have valid fishing licenses for both British Columbia and Yukon Territory if you fish these areas, and a national park fishing license if you fish waters in Kluane National Park.

Emergency medical services: Between Haines and the U.S.–Canada border at **Milepost H 40.7**, phone 911. Between the U.S.–Canada border and Haines Junction, phone the RCMP at 634-2221.

Haines Highway Log

ALASKA ROUTE 7
Driving distance is measured in miles from Haines, AK. Mileposts are up along the Alaska portion of the highway. The kilometre figures on the Canadian portion of the highway reflect the physical kilometreposts and are not an accurate metric conversion of the mileage figure.

Distance from Haines (H) is followed by distance from Haines Junction (HJ).

H 0 HJ 151.6 (244 km) HAINES. See HAINES section for accommodations and facilities.

H 0.2 (0.3 km) **HJ 151.4** (243.7 km) Front Street.

H 0.4 (0.6 km) **HJ 151.2** (243.4 km) Second Street. Turn right northbound (left southbound) for visitor information center and downtown Haines.

H 0.5 (0.8 km) **HJ 151.1** (243.2 km) Third Street. Turn right northbound (left southbound) for downtown Haines.

H 1 (1.6 km) **HJ 150.6** (242.4 km) Haines Hitch–Up RV Park. ▲

H 1.2 (1.9 km) **HJ 150.4** (242.1 km) Main Street Y. If southbound, turn right to Fort William H. Seward, left to downtown Haines.

H 1.3 (2.1 km) **HJ 150.3** (241.9 km) Eagle's Nest Motel.

H 3.3 (5.3 km) **HJ 148.3** (238.7 km) Indian graveyard on the right northbound.

H 3.5 (5.6 km) **HJ 148.1** (238.3 km) **Private Aircraft:** Haines airport; elev. 16 feet/5m; length 4,200 feet/1,280m; chip seal; unattended.

The Chilkat River estuary, which the highway parallels for the next 15 miles/24 km, flows into Chilkat Inlet of Lynn Canal, a massive fjord about 60 miles/96.5 km long. Lynn Canal was named by English explorer Captain Vancouver for his birthplace (King's Lynn) in England. The yellow signs along the highway indicate mileages on the U.S. Army oil pipeline. The pipeline formerly pumped oil from Haines over the St. Elias Mountains to the Alaska Highway at Haines Junction, YT. These signs were used for aerial checking and monitoring of the line.

H 4.3 (6.9 km) **HJ 147.3** (237 km) Turnout along river.

H 6 (9.6 km) **HJ 145.6** (234.3 km) Picnic spot next to Chilkat River and a clear creek.

H 6.6 (10.6 km) **HJ 145** (233.3 km) Mount Ripinski trailhead.

H 8 (12.8 km) **HJ 143.6** (231.1 km) Watch for subsistence fish camps along the highway in June. Also watch for fish wheels on the river.

H 9.2 (14.8 km) **HJ 142.4** (229.2 km) Entering Alaska Chilkat Bald Eagle Preserve northbound. Established in 1982, the 48,000-acre preserve is the annual home to more than 3,000 bald eagles, which gather to feed on the late run of chum salmon. Eagle-viewing area begins at **Milepost H 19**;

596   The MILEPOST® ■ 1992

HAINES HIGHWAY — Haines, AK to Haines Junction, YT

HAINES HIGHWAY

Watch for bald eagles along the Chilkat River. Best viewing from October to January. (Henry H. Holdsworth)

best viewing is mid-October to January.

H 9.6 (15.4 km) HJ 142 (228.5 km) Magnificent view of Takhinsha Mountains across Chilkat River. This range extends north from the Chilkat Range; Glacier Bay is on the other side. Prominent peaks are Mount Krause and Mount Emmerich (elev. 6,405 feet/1,952m) in the Chilkat Range.

H 10.1 (16.2 km) HJ 141.5 (227.7 km) Ten Mile Steakhouse and Bar.

H 14.7 (23.6 km) HJ 136.9 (220.3 km) Watch for mountain goats on the ridges.

H 17.6 (28.3 km) HJ 134 (215.6 km) Rustic barn and old cabins. Good photo shots.

H 18.8 (30.3 km) HJ 132.8 (213.7 km) Slide area.

H 19 (30.6 km) HJ 132.6 (213.4 km) Begin eagle viewing area (northbound) on Chilkat River flats. Best viewing is mid-October to January. *CAUTION: Eagle watchers use turnouts and park well off highway!*

H 21.4 (34.4 km) HJ 130.2 (209.5 km) Turnoff to Indian village of **KLUKWAN**. Gravel access road dead ends at village. No visitor facilities.

H 22 (35.4 km) HJ 129.6 (208.5 km) Second access northbound to Klukwan (steep grade).

H 23.8 (38.3 km) HJ 127.8 (205.6 km) Chilkat River bridge. Highway now follows Klehini River. Watch for eagles beginning in late summer.

H 26.3 (42.3 km) HJ 125.3 (201.6 km) Road west leads across Klehini River; turn off here for Don's Camp on Chilkat Lake.

H 27.3 (43.9 km) HJ 124.3 (200 km) Mosquito Lake State Recreation Site campground; 10 sites, tables, water, toilets, $6/night or annual pass. Mosquito Lake general store. ▲

H 28.8 (46.3 km) HJ 122.8 (197.6 km) Muncaster Creek bridge.

H 30.9 (49.7 km) HJ 120.7 (194.2 km) Leaving Alaska Chilkat Bald Eagle Preserve northbound.

H 31.6 (50.9 km) HJ 120 (193.1 km) Bridge over Little Boulder Creek.

H 33.2 (53.4 km) HJ 118.4 (190.5 km) Roadhouse with food, gas and phone. Store. *NOTE: Last available gas northbound until Haines Junction, YT. Check your gas tank.*

33 Mile Roadhouse. See display ad this section.

H 33.8 (54.4 km) HJ 117.8 (189.6 km) Bridge over Big Boulder Creek. Watch for salmon swimming upstream during spawning season. Closed to salmon fishing.

H 36.2 (58.3 km) HJ 115.4 (185.7 km) View of Saksaia Glacier.

H 40.4 (65 km) HJ 111.2 (179 km) U.S. customs, Dalton Cache station. All travelers entering United States MUST STOP. Open year-round 7 A.M. to 11 P.M., Alaska time. Restrooms, large parking area.

Jarvis Glacier moraine is visible from the old Dalton Cache (on the National Register of Historic Places), located behind the customs building.

H 40.7 (65.5 km) HJ 110.9 (178.5 km) U.S.–Canada border. Last milepost marker is Mile 40, first kilometrepost marker is Kilometrepost 74, northbound.

TIME ZONE CHANGE: Alaska observes Alaska time, Canada observes Pacific time. See Time Zones in the GENERAL INFORMATION section.

BC HIGHWAY 4

H 40.8 (71.8 km) HJ 110.8 (178.3 km) Canada Customs and Immigration office at Pleasant Camp. All travelers entering Canada MUST STOP. Open year-round 8 A.M. to midnight, Pacific time. No public facilities.

H 44.9 (78.5 km) HJ 106.7 (171.7 km) Bridge over Fivemile Creek.

H 49.7 (86 km) HJ 101.9 (164 km) Highway crosses Seltat Creek. This is eagle country; watch for them soaring over the uplands. Three Guardsmen Mountain (elev. 6,300 feet/1,920m) to the east.

H 53.9 (92 km) HJ 97.7 (157.2 km) Three Guardsmen Lake to the east. Glave Peak, part of Three Guardsmen Mountain, rises directly behind the lake.

H 55.1 (94.6 km) HJ 96.5 (155.3 km) Three Guardsmen Pass to the northeast, hidden by low hummocks along the road. Stonehouse Creek meanders through a pass at the base of Seltat Peak to join the Kelsall River about 6 miles/10 km to the east. To the north is the Kusawak Range; to the south is Three Guardsmen Mountain. The tall poles along the highway indicate the edge of the road for snowplows.

H 55.8 (95.8 km) HJ 95.8 (154.2 km) Stonehouse Creek culvert.

H 56.2 (96.3 km) HJ 95.4 (153.5 km) Clear Creek culvert.

H 59.8 (102.1 km) HJ 91.8 (147.7 km) Double-ended paved turnout on west side of highway at Chilkat Pass, highest summit on this highway (elev. 3,493 feet/1,065m). White Pass Summit on Klondike Highway 2 is 3,290 feet/1,003m. The wind blows almost constantly on the summit and causes drifting snow and road closures in winter. The summit area is a favorite with snow machine and cross-country ski enthusiasts in winter. Snow until late May.

The Chilkat Pass was one of the few mountain passes offering access into the Yukon from the coast. The Chilkat, as well as the Chilkoot Pass, were tenaciously guarded by Tlingit Indians. These southern Yukon Indians did not want their lucrative fur-trading business with the coastal Indians and Russians jeopardized by white strangers. But the gold rush of 1898, which brought thousands of white people inland, finally opened Chilkat Pass, forever altering the lifestyle of the Interior Natives.

From the Chilkat Pass over Glacier Flats to Stanley Creek, the highway crosses silt-laden streams flowing from the Crestline Glacier. Nadahini Mountain (elev. 6,809 feet/2,075m) to the northwest. Three Guardsmen Mountain to the southeast.

H 63 (107 km) HJ 88.6 (142.6 km) Chuck Creek culvert.

H 64.4 (109.3 km) HJ 87.2 (140.3 km) Nadahini River culvert.

H 67.8 (114.7 km) HJ 83.8 (134.8 km) **Private Aircraft:** Mule Creek airstrip; elev. 2,900 feet/884m; length, 4,000 feet/1219m; gravel. No services.

H 68.9 (116.4 km) HJ 82.7 (133 km) Mule Creek.

H 73.6 (124.2 km) HJ 78 (125.5 km) Goat Creek bridge. Watch for horses on road.

H 75.7 (127.3 km) HJ 75.9 (122.1 km) Holum Creek.

H 81.3 (136.3 km) HJ 70.3 (113.1 km) Stanley Creek bridge.

H 86.5 (143.6 km) HJ 65.1 (104.8 km) Blanchard River bridge.

H 87.1 (144.5 km) HJ 64.5 (103.8 km) Welcome to Yukon sign.

H 87.4 (145 km) HJ 64.2 (103.3 km) Entering Kluane Game Sanctuary northbound.

H 87.5 (145.2 km) HJ 64.1 (103.1 km) BC–YT border. Former U.S. Army Alaska–Blanchard River Petroleum pump station, now a highway maintenance camp.

YUKON HIGHWAY 3

H 90.7 (150.7 km) HJ 60.9 (98 km) Blanchard River Gorge to west.

H 96.2 (159.4 km) HJ 55.4 (89.1 km) Yukon government Million Dollar Falls Campground on opposite side of Takhanne River; follow access road 0.7 mile/1.1 km

---

Last Stop in Alaska — NEXT GAS 100 MILES

POP • FOOD • BEER & WINE DINING

33 Mile Roadhouse

Friendly, courteous service

Watch for the new log cabin...

HOURS
Summer: 7 am-8 pm Mon.-Sat.; 8 am-6 pm Sun.
Winter: 7 am-7 pm Mon., Wed.-Sat.; 8 am-6 pm Sun.
Closed Tuesday

Known for delicious **HAMBURGERS**
BREAKFAST served anytime
HOMEMADE PIES
Propane

Chevron

(907) 767-5510
Jerry and Kathi Lapp, your hosts

west. Boardwalk trail and viewing platform of scenic falls. View of the St. Elias Mountains. Two kitchen shelters, tenting and group firepit, 27 campsites, $8 fee, playground and drinking water (boil water). Walk-in tent sites available. ▲

Good fishing below **Takhanne Falls** for grayling, Dolly Varden, rainbow and salmon. **Takhanne River**, excellent king salmon fishing in early July.

CAUTION: The Takhanne, Blanchard, Tatshenshini and Klukshu rivers are grizzly feeding areas. Exercise extreme caution when fishing or exploring in these areas.

H 96.3 (159.5 km) HJ 55.3 (89 km) Takhanne River bridge.

H 96.4 (159.7 km) HJ 55.2 (88.8 km) Parking area at Million Dollar Falls trailhead to west.

H 97.2 (160.8 km) HJ 54.4 (87.5 km) Second Million Dollars Falls trailhead to west.

H 98.3 (162.6 km) HJ 53.3 (85.8 km) Good view of Kluane Range.

H 99.5 (164.5 km) HJ 52.1 (83.8 km) Turnoff to historic Dalton Post, a way point on the Dalton Trail. Steep, narrow, winding access road; 4-wheel drive recommended in wet weather. Road not recommended for large RVs or trailers at any time. Several old abandoned log cabins and buildings are located here. Indians once formed a human barricade at Dalton Post to harvest the Klukshu River's run of coho salmon.

Fishing for chinook, coho, sockeye salmon in **Village Creek**. Grayling, Dolly Varden and salmon in **Klukshu River**. Fishing restrictions posted. *CAUTION: Watch for bears.*

H 103.4 (169.7 km) HJ 48.2 (77.5 km) Viewpoint with information sign to east. Alsek Range to southwest.

H 104 (170.7 km) HJ 47.6 (76.6 km) Motheral Creek culvert.

H 106.1 (174 km) HJ 45.5 (73.2 km) Vand Creek.

H 110.8 (181.6 km) HJ 40.8 (65.6 km) Klukshu Creek.

H 111.6 (183 km) HJ 40 (64.4 km) Turnoff for **KLUKSHU**, an Indian village, located 0.5 mile/0.8 km off the highway via a gravel road. This summer fish camp and village on the banks of the Klukshu River is a handful of log cabins, meat caches and traditional fish traps. Steelhead, king, sockeye and coho salmon are taken here. Each autumn families return for the annual catch. The site is on the old Dalton Trail and offers good photo possibilities. Museum, picnic spot, Indian souvenirs for sale.

Kluane National Park borders the highway to the west from here to Haines Junction (the visitor centre there has information on the park). Watch for signs for hiking trails, which are posted 3.1 miles/5 km before trailheads.

H 112.8 (185 km) HJ 38.8 (62.4 km) Gribbles Gulch.

H 114 (187 km) HJ 37.6 (60.5 km) Parking area at St. Elias Lake trailhead (4-mile/6.4-km round-trip). Novice and intermediate hiking trail winds through subalpine meadow. Watch for mountain goats.

H 117.8 (193 km) HJ 33.8 (54.4 km) Dezadeash Lodge (closed 1991, current status unknown). Historically, this spot was known as Beloud Post and is still noted as such on some maps. Mush Lake trail (13.4 miles/21.6 km long) begins behind lodge. It is an old mining road.

NOTE: Watch for horses on highway.

H 119.3 (195 km) HJ 32.3 (52 km) Turnout along Dezadeash Lake, which parallels the highway for 9 miles/14.5 km northbound, and Dezadeash mountain range. Dezadeash (pronounced DEZ-dee-ash) is said to be the Indian word describing their fishing method. In the spring, the Indians built small fires around the bases of large birch trees, peeled the heat-loosened bark and placed it, shiny white side up, on the bottom of the lake near shore, weighted with stones. From log wharfs built over the white bark Indians waited with spears for lake trout to cross the light area. Another interpretation of Dezadeash relates that Chilkat Indians referred to it as *Dasar-ee-ASH*, meaning "Lake of the Big Winds." One of the earliest known features in the Yukon, entire tribes were annihilated during mid-19th century Indian wars here.

Dezadeash Lake offers good trolling, also fly-fishing along the shore where feeder streams flow into the lake. There are northern pike, lake trout and grayling in Dezadeash Lake. *(CAUTION: This is a mountain lake and storms come up quickly.)*

H 119.7 (195.7 km) HJ 31.9 (51.3 km) Entrance to Yukon government Dezadeash Lake Campground; 20 campsites, $8 fee, kitchen shelter, picnic area, boat launch, no drinking water, pit toilets. ▲

H 123.9 (202.3 km) HJ 27.7 (44.6 km) Rock Glacier trailhead to west; short 0.5-mile/0.8-km self-guiding trail, partially boardwalk. Interesting and easy walk. Parking area and viewpoint.

H 126.2 (206.9 km) HJ 25.4 (40.8 km) Dalton Trail Lodge to east with food, lodging and boat rentals.

H 134.8 (219 km) HJ 16.8 (27 km) Access road west to Kathleen Lake and Kathleen Lake Campground, the only established campground within Kluane National Park. There are 42 sites and a kitchen area at the campground; day-use area with boat launch at lake; campfire programs by park staff. Camping fee $8. The 53-mile/85-km Cottonwood loop trail begins here. ▲

NOTE: National parks fishing license

Day-use area at Kathleen Lake, Milepost H 134.8. Kathleen Lake Campground is the only established campground in Kluane National Park. (Earl L. Brown, staff)

required. **Kathleen Lake**, lake trout average 10 lbs., use lures, June and July; kokanee average 2 lbs., June best; grayling to 18 inches, use flies, June to September. **Kathleen River**, rainbow to 17 inches, June to September; grayling to 18 inches, July and August; lake trout average 2 lbs., best in September.

H 135.2 (220.3 km) HJ 16.4 (26.4 km) Kathleen Lake Lodge (closed 1991, current status unknown).

H 135.8 (220.5 km) HJ 15.8 (25.4 km) **Kathleen River** bridge; a popular spot for rainbow, lake trout and grayling fishing. Some kokanee.

H 139.2 (227 km) HJ 12.4 (20 km) Turnout to west. Good view of Kathleen Lake. Information plaque on Kluane and Wrangell–St. Elias national parks.

H 143.4 (233.5 km) HJ 8.2 (13.2 km) Quill Creek trailhead to west (7-mile/11-km trail).

H 147.1 (239.1 km) HJ 4.5 (7.2 km) Parking area to west at Auriol trailhead (12-mile/19-km loop trail); skiing and hiking.

H 148.8 (241.1 km) HJ 2.8 (4.5 km) Rest stop to east with litter barrels and pit toilets. View of community of Haines Junction and Shakwak Valley.

H 151 (245 km) HJ 0.6 (1 km) Bridges over Dezadeash River. This river is part of the headwaters system of the Alsek River, which flows into the Pacific near Yakutat, AK.

H 151.3 (245.5 km) HJ 0.3 (0.5 km) Weigh station to west.

H 151.6 (246 km) HJ 0 **HAINES JUNCTION**, turn left for Alaska, keep right for Whitehorse. Turn to Haines Junction (page 140) in the ALASKA HIGHWAY section for description of town and highway log. Whitehorse-bound travelers read log back to front, Alaska-bound travelers read log front to back.

Approximate driving distances from Haines Junction are: Whitehorse 100 miles/161 km; Tok 298 miles/480 km; Fairbanks 504 miles/811 km; and Anchorage 626 miles/1008 km.

KLONDIKE HIGHWAY 2

Skagway, Alaska, to Alaska Highway

Emerald Lake, also called Rainbow Lake, at Milepost S 73.5. (Earl L. Brown, staff)

The 98.8-mile-/159-km-long Klondike Highway 2 (also known as the Skagway–Carcross Road and South Klondike Highway) connects Skagway, AK, with the Alaska Highway south of Whitehorse. The highway between Skagway and Carcross (referred to locally as the Skagway Road) was built in 1978 and formally dedicated on May 23, 1981. The highway connecting Carcross with the Alaska Highway (referred to locally as the Carcross Road) was built by the U.S. Army in late 1942 to lay the gas pipeline from Skagway to Whitehorse.

Klondike Highway 2 is a 2-lane, asphalt-surfaced road, open year-round. The road has been improved in recent years and is fairly wide. There is a steep 11.5-mile/18.5-km grade between Skagway and White Pass.

IMPORTANT: *If you plan to cross the border between midnight and 8 A.M., call ahead or inquire locally regarding customs stations hours of operation.*

Klondike Highway 2 is 1 of the 2 highways connecting ferry travelers with the Alaska Highway; the other is the Haines Highway out of Haines. Klondike Highway 2 offers some spectacular scenery and adds only about 55 miles/89 km to the trip for Alaska-bound motorists compared with the Haines Highway. (The distance from Haines to Tok, AK, is approximately 445 miles/716 km; the distance from Skagway to Tok is 500 miles/805 km.) Klondike Highway 2, like the Haines Highway, crosses from Alaska into British Columbia then into Yukon Territory.

Klondike Highway 2 continues north of Whitehorse, turning off the Alaska Highway to Dawson City. See the KLONDIKE LOOP section for the log of Klondike Highway 2 between the Alaska Highway and Dawson City.

CAUTION: Watch for ore trucks. Yukon Alaska Transport trucks, carrying up to 50 tons of lead–zinc concentrates, operate between Faro mine on the Campbell Highway and Skagway. Depending on production levels at the mine, these 8-axle vehicles may travel the highway at the rate of 1 every 40 minutes. The trucks are 8 1/2 feet wide and 85 feet long. Drive carefully, with your headlights on.

Emergency medical services: Between Skagway and the BC–YT border, phone the Skagway Fire Department at (907) 983-2300. Between the border and the Alaska Highway, phone the Whitehorse ambulance at (403) 668-9333. Police monitor CB Channel 9.

Klondike Highway 2 Log

Mileposts in Alaska and kilometreposts in Canada reflect distance from Skagway. The kilometre distance from Skagway in *The MILEPOST* log reflects the location of the physical kilometreposts, and is not necessarily an accurate conversion of the mileage figure.

Distance from Skagway (S) is followed by distance from Alaska Highway (AH).

S 0 AH 98.8 (159 km) Ferry terminal in Skagway. See SKAGWAY section for details.

S 1.6 (2.6 km) **AH 97.2** (156.4 km) Skagway River bridge.

S 2.3 (3.7 km) **AH 96.5** (155.3 km) **Junction** with Dyea Road.

S 2.6 (4.2 km) **AH 96.2** (154.8 km) Highway maintenance camp.

S 2.8 (4.5 km) **AH 96** (154.5 km) Plaque to east honoring men and women of the Klondike gold rush and access to parklike area along Skagway River.

S 2.9 (4.7 km) **AH 95.9** (154.3 km) Access road east to Skagway River. Highway begins steep 11.5-mile/18.5-km ascent northbound from sea level to 3,290 feet/1,003m at White Pass. The massive valleys seen along this stretch of highway were carved by glaciers.

S 4.7 (7.6 km) **AH 94.1** (151.4 km) Turnout to west.

S 5 (8 km) **AH 93.8** (151 km) Turnout to east with view across canyon of White Pass & Yukon Route railway tracks and bridge. The narrow-gauge WP&YR railway was completed in 1900. See the WHITE PASS & YUKON ROUTE section for details on the railway.

S 5.5 (8.8 km) **AH 93.3** (150.1 km) Turnout to west with historical information signs.

S 6 (9.6 km) **AH 92.8** (149.3 km) Turnout to east.

S 6.1 (9.8 km) **AH 92.7** (149.2 km) U.S. customs station; open 24 hours in summer (hours are subject to change). All travelers entering the United States must stop. See Customs Requirements in the GENERAL INFORMATION section.

S 7.4 (11.9 km) **AH 91.4** (147.1 km) View to east of White Pass & Yukon Route railway line.

S 7.7 (12.4 km) **AH 91.1** (146.6 km) Good photo stop for Pitchfork Falls, visible across the canyon. One of Alaska's many spectacular falls, and one of several in this canyon, Pitchfork Falls flows from Goat Lake.

S 8.1 (13 km) **AH 90.7** (146 km) Turnout to east.

S 9.1 (14.6 km) **AH 89.7** (144.4 km) Turnout to east with historical interest signs about the Klondike gold rush trail. Viewpoint looks across the gorge to the White Pass & Yukon Route railway tracks and the canyon leading up to Esk Glacier.

S 9.9 (15.9 km) **AH 88.9** (143.1 km) Truck runout ramp to west for large transport units that may lose air brakes on steep descent southbound.

S 11.1 (17.9 km) **AH 87.7** (141.1 km) Captain William Moore Bridge. This unique cantilever bridge over Moore Creek spans a 110-foot-/34-m-wide gorge. Just north of the bridge to the west is a large waterfall. The

KLONDIKE HIGHWAY 2
Skagway, AK, to Junction with Alaska Highway (includes Tagish and Atlin Roads)

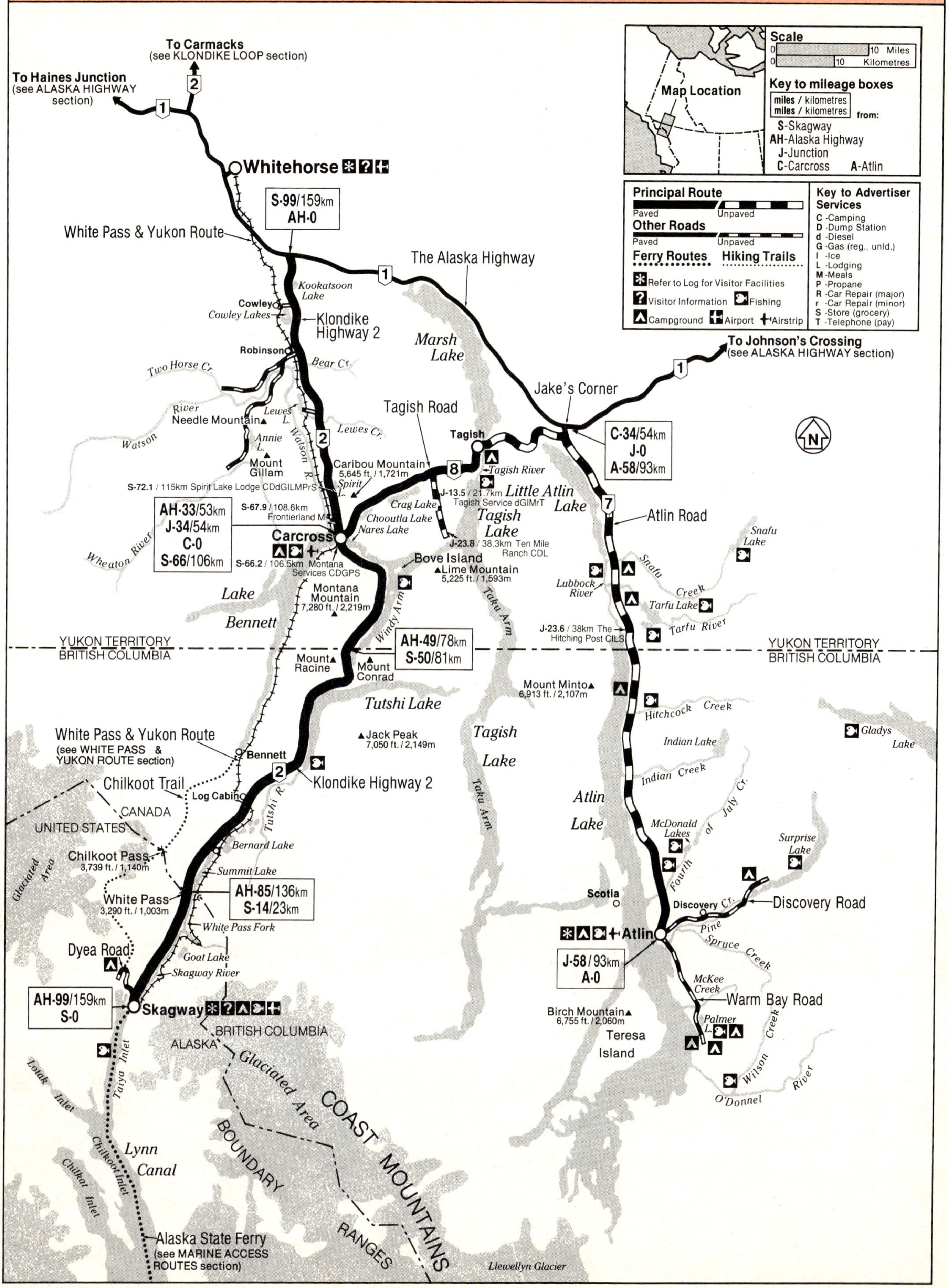

bridge is named for Capt. Billy Moore, a riverboat captain and pilot, prospector, packer and trader, who played an important role in settling the town of Skagway. Moore discovered this route over White Pass into the Yukon and was among the first to realize the potential of a railroad across the pass.

S 11.6 (18.7 km) **AH 87.2** (140.3 km) Turnouts to east with view of Skagway River gorge, Captain William Moore Bridge and waterfalls, next 0.1 mile/0.2 km northbound.

S 12 (19.3 km) **AH 86.8** (139.7 km) Truck runout ramp to west.

S 12.6 (20.3 km) **AH 86.2** (138.7 km) Posts on east side of road mark highway shoulders and guide rails for snowplows.

S 14.4 (23.2 km) **AH 84.4** (135.8 km) White Pass Summit (elev. 3,290 feet/1,003m). Turnout to west.

CAUTION: Southbound traffic begins steep 11.5-mile/18.5-km descent to Skagway.

Many stampeders on their way to the Klondike goldfields in 1898 chose the White Pass route because it was lower in elevation than the famous Chilkoot Pass trail, and the grade was not as steep. But the White Pass route was longer and the final ascent to the summit treacherous. Dead Horse Gulch (visible from the railway line) was named for the thousands of pack animals that died on this route during the gold rush.

The North West Mounted Police were stationed at the summit to meet every stampeder entering Canada and ensure that each carried at least a year's provisions (weighing about a ton).

S 14.5 (23.3 km) **AH 84.3** (135.7 km) Turnout to west.

S 14.9 (24 km) **AH 84** (135.2 km) U.S.–Canada (AK–BC) border. Turnout to west. Monument to east.

TIME ZONE CHANGE: Alaska observes Alaska time; British Columbia and Yukon Territory observe Pacific time. See Time Zones in the GENERAL INFORMATION section.

S 16.2 (26.1 km) **AH 82.6** (133 km) Highway winds through rocky valley of Summit Lake (visible to east).

S 18.1 (29.1 km) **AH 80.7** (129.9 km) Short bridge with 4 red pole markers.

S 18.4 (29.6 km) **AH 80.4** (129.4 km) Summit Lake to east.

S 19.3 (31.1 km) **AH 79.5** (128 km) North end of Summit Lake.

S 21.4 (34.4 km) **AH 77.4** (124.5 km) Creek and railroad bridge to east.

S 22.5 (36.2 km) **AH 76.3** (122.8 km) Canada customs at Fraser, open 24 hours. Pay phone. All travelers entering Canada must stop. See Customs Requirements in the GENERAL INFORMATION section.

Old railroad water tower to east, highway maintenance camp to west.

S 22.6 (36.4 km) **AH 76.2** (122.7 km) Beautiful deep-green Bernard Lake to east.

S 24.2 (38.9 km) **AH 74.6** (120.1 km) Turnout to east.

S 25.1 (40.4 km) **AH 73.7** (118.6 km) Shallow Lake to east.

S 25.5 (41 km) **AH 73.3** (118 km) Old cabins and buildings to east.

S 25.9 (41.7 km) **AH 72.9** (117.3 km) A-frame structure to east.

S 26.6 (42.8 km) **AH 72.2** (116.2 km) Turnout to east. Beautiful view of Tormented Valley, a rocky desolate "moonscape" of stunted trees and small lakes east of the highway.

S 27.3 (43.9 km) **AH 71.5** (115 km) Highway crosses tracks of the White Pass & Yukon Route at Log Cabin. With completion of the railway in 1900, the North West Mounted Police moved their customs checkpoint from the summit to Log Cabin. There is nothing here today.

NOTE: There are numerous turnouts along the highway between here and Carcross. Turnouts may be designated for either commercial ore trucks or passenger vehicles.

S 30.7 (49.4 km) **AH 68.1** (109.6 km) Tutshi (too-shy) River visible to east.

S 31.1 (50 km) **AH 67.7** (108.9 km) **Tutshi Lake.** Highway parallels the lake for several miles northbound. Excellent fishing for lake trout and grayling early in season. Be sure you have a British Columbia fishing license.

S 40.1 (64.5 km) **AH 58.7** (94.5 km) Short narrow gravel access road to picnic area with pit toilet on Tutshi Lake. Large vehicles check turnaround space before driving in.

S 40.7 (65.5 km) **AH 58.1** (93.5 km) Good views of Tutshi Lake along here.

S 43.7 (70.5 km) **AH 55.1** (88.7 km) Turnout to east with view of Tutshi Lake.

S 46.4 (75.1 km) **AH 52.4** (84.3 km) To the east is the Venus Mines concentrator, with a capacity of 150 tons per day. A drop in silver prices caused the Venus mill's closure in October 1981. Venus Mines is owned by United Keno Hill Mines (a Falconbridge Nickel company) which operates the silver mines at Elsa, YT.

S 48.5 (78.1 km) **AH 50.3** (81 km) South end of Windy Arm, an extension of Tagish Lake.

S 49.2 (79.2 km) **AH 49.6** (79.9 km) Viewpoint to east.

S 49.9 (80.5 km) **AH 48.9** (78.7 km) Dall Creek.

S 50.2 (81 km) **AH 48.6** (78.2 km) BC–YT border. Turnout with picnic table and litter barrel to east overlooking Windy Arm.

S 51.9 (83.5 km) **AH 46.9** (75.5 km) Large turnout to east with litter barrel, picnic table and historical information sign about Venus Mines.

The first claim on Montana Mountain was staked by W.R. Young in 1899. By 1904 all of the mountain's gold veins had been claimed. In 1905, New York financier Col. Joseph H. Conrad acquired most of the Montana Mountain claims, formed Conrad Consolidated Mines, and began exploration and mining. A town of about 300 people sprang up along Windy Arm and an aerial tramway was built from the Conrad townsite up the side of Montana Mountain to the Mountain Hero adit. (This tramline, visible from the highway, was completed in 1906 but was never used to ship ore because the Mountain Hero tunnel did not find a vein.) More tramways and a mill were constructed, but by 1911 Conrad was forced into bankruptcy: the ore was not as rich as estimated and only a small quantity of ore was milled before operations ceased.

Small mining operations continued over the years, with unsuccessful startups by various mining interests. United Keno Hill Mines (Venus Division) acquired the mining claims in 1979, constructed a 100-ton-per-day mill and rehabilitated the old mine workings in 1980.

S 52.9 (85.1 km) **AH 45.9** (73.8 km) Pooly Creek and canyon, named for J.M. Pooly who staked the first Venus claims in 1901.

Access road east to Pooly Point and Venus Mines maintenance garage, trailers, and security station. No services, facilities or admittance.

S 54.2 (87.2 km) **AH 44.6** (71.8 km) Venus Mines ore storage bin and foundation of old mill to east. The mill was built in the late 1960s and disassembled and sold about 1970. A sign here warns of arsenic being present: do not pick or eat berries.

S 55.7 (89.6 km) **AH 43.1** (69.4 km) Tramline support just east of highway.

S 59.5 (95.8 km) **AH 39.3** (63.3 km) Turnout with historic information sign about Bove Island. There are magnificent views along here of Windy Arm and its islands (the larger island is Bove Island). Windy Arm is an extension of Tagish Lake. Lime Mountain (elev. 5,225 feet/1,593m) rises to the east beyond Bove Island.

S 63.5 (102.2 km) **AH 35.3** (56.8 km) Sections of the old government wagon roads that once linked Carcross, Conrad, and other mining claims, are visible on either side of the highway.

S 65.3 (105.1 km) **AH 33.5** (53.9 km) Access road west to Indian community, Carcross Indian Band office, and Carcross cemetery. Buried at the cemetery are the famous gold discoverers, Skookum Jim, Dawson (or Tagish) Charlie and Kate

MONTANA SERVICES — Chevron

Grocery Store • Laundromat • RV Park
Electrical Hookups • Water • Dump Station
Gas, Oil, Propane • RV Wash
Yukon Souvenirs • Caravans Welcome

(403) 821-3708
Box 75, Carcross, YT Y0B 1B0
Mile 65 Klondike Highway

SPIRIT LAKE LODGE

GROUP TOURS WELCOME

Our Specialty: Homemade Perogies & Pie
Nightly Dinner Specials • Ice Cream Cones
Fully Licensed Restaurant & Lounge
Accommodations • Campground • Showers
Propane • Welding • Tires & Mechanic

Mile 72.3 Klondike Highway **(403) 821-4337**
6 miles north of Carcross   Souvenirs

Carmack; pioneer missionary Bishop Bompas; and Polly the parrot.

S 65.9 (106 km) AH 32.9 (52.9 km) Access road west to Montana Mountain.

S 66 (106.2 km) AH 32.8 (52.7 km) Nares Bridge crosses the narrows between Lake Bennett to the west and Tagish Lake to the east. Nares Lake remains open most winters, despite air temperatures that drop well below -40°F/-40°C. The larger lakes freeze to an ice depth of more than 3 feet/1m.

Caribou Mountain (elev. 5,645 feet/1,721m) is visible to the east.

S 66.2 (106.5 km) AH 32.6 (52.4 km) Turnoff west for Carcross (description follows).

Montana Services. See display ad this section.

Carcross

On the shore of Lake Bennett, 44 miles/71 km southeast of Whitehorse. **Population:** 350. **Emergency Services: Police,** phone 821-4441. **Fire Department,** phone 821-4461. **Ambulance:** phone 821-3141. **Health Centre:** phone 821-4581.

Visitor Information: Carcross Visitor Reception Centre is located in the old White Pass & Yukon Route train station. The centre operates daily from 8:30 A.M. to 8:30 P.M., mid-May to mid-September; phone 821-4431. Ferry schedules, maps and information on Yukon, British Columbia and Alaska available. Inquire here about free historic town walking tours and special Rendezvous '92 events.

Elevation: 2,175 feet/663m. **Climate:** Average temperature in January, -4.2°F/-20.1°C; in July, 55.4°F/13°C. Annual rainfall 44.7 inches, snowfall 41.5 inches. Driest month is April, wettest month August. **Radio:** CKRW, CBC, CKYN-FM 96.1 visitor information station. **Television:** CBC. **Transportation:** Scheduled bus service.

Private Aircraft: Carcross airstrip, 0.3 mile/0.5 km north of town via highway; elev. 2,161 feet/659m; length 2,000 feet/610m.

There are a general store, gift shops with Native handicrafts, snack bar and RV park. Gas station with gifts, groceries and cafe located on the highway by the airstrip. ▲

Carcross was formerly known as Caribou Crossing because of the herds of caribou that migrated through the narrows here between Bennett and Nares lakes. It became a stopping place for gold stampeders on their way to the Klondike goldfields. Carcross was a major stop on the White Pass & Yukon Route railroad from 1900 until 1982, when the railroad ceased operation. (The WP&YR currently operates a limited excursion service; see WHITE PASS & YUKON ROUTE section for details.) Passengers and freight transferred from rail to stern-wheelers at Carcross. One of these stern-wheelers, the SS *Tutshi* (too-shy), was a historic site here in town until it burned down in July 1990.

A cairn beside the railroad station marks the site where construction crews laying track for the White Pass & Yukon Route from Skagway met the crew from Whitehorse. The golden spike was set in place when the last rail was laid at Carcross on July 29, 1900. The construction project had begun May 27, 1898, during the height of the Klondike gold rush.

Other visitor attractions include St. Saviour's Anglican Church, built in 1902; the Royal Mail Carriage; and the little locomotive *Duchess*, which once hauled coal on Vancouver Island. Frontierland, 2 miles/3.2 km north of town on the highway, is also a popular attraction. On sunny days you may sunbathe and picnic at Sandy Beach on Lake Bennett. Since the water is only a few degrees above freezing, swimming is not recommended. Behind the post office there is a footbridge across Nares Lake. This small body of water joins Lake Bennett and Tagish Lake. Check locally for boat tours and boat service on Bennett Lake.

Fishing in **Lake Bennett** for lake trout, northern pike, arctic grayling, whitefish and cisco.

Klondike Highway 2 Log

(continued)

S 66.4 (106.9 km) AH 32.4 (52.1 km) Gas station with gifts, groceries and cafe, and airstrip to east. Follow airport access road for Carcross community campground; 12 sites, no drinking water. ▲

S 66.5 (107 km) AH 32.3 (52 km) Junction with Yukon Highway 8 which leads east to Tagish, Atlin Road and the Alaska Highway at Jake's Corner (see TAGISH ROAD section). Turn east here for alternate access to Alaska Highway and for Yukon government campground on Tagish Road.

S 67.3 (108.3 km) AH 31.5 (50.7 km) Turnout with point of interest sign about Carcross desert. This unusual desert area of sand dunes, seen east of the highway between Kilometreposts 108 and 110, is the world's smallest desert and an International Biophysical Programme site for ecological studies. The desert is composed of sandy lake-bottom material left behind by a large glacial lake. Strong winds off Lake Bennett have made it difficult for vegetation to take hold here; only lodgepole pine and kinnikinnick survive. (Kinnikinnick is a low trailing evergreen with small leathery leaves; used for tea.)

S 67.9 (108.6 km) AH 30.9 (49.7 km) Frontierland (formerly the Museum of Yukon Natural History) features a Yukon wildlife museum, gift shop and coffee house.

Frontierland. See display ad this section.

S 70.3 (112.3 km) AH 28.5 (45.9 km) Dry Creek.

S 71.2 (113.8 km) AH 27.6 (44.4 km) Carl's Creek.

S 72.1 (115 km) AH 26.7 (43 km) Spirit Lake Lodge east side of road with food, gas, propane, repairs, lodging, camping, and ice cream. Access road east to public use area on Spirit Lake. ▲

Spirit Lake Lodge. See display ad this section.

S 73.2 (116.8 km) AH 25.6 (41.2 km) Spirit Lake is visible to the east.

S 73.5 (117.3 km) AH 25.3 (40.7 km)

Sandy Beach at Lake Bennett. The lake is too cold for swimming. (Rollo Pool, staff)

～ FRONTIERLAND ～
2 miles north of Carcross on the South Klondike Highway

WILDLIFE MUSEUM
The museum has on display many of Yukon's wildlife species. These are set in authentic dioramas with state of the art re-creation of their natural habitat.

GIFT SHOP
The museum gift shop provides an opportunity to shop for locally created works of art. These range from paintings to sculptings from natural products as well as Yukon-made souvenirs.

COFFEE HOUSE
Experience our coffee house specializing in fresh coffee and homemade donuts. Pastries, ice creams, sandwiches and soft drinks are also available.

HERITAGE PARK — *"YUKON IN ONE STOP"*
Journey through time and enjoy replicas of Yukon's past as you stroll the largest map in the world. View live dall sheep and lynx as well as the only mounted saber-toothed tiger in existence.

Box 5449, Whitehorse, Yukon Y1A 5H4

Mention "MILEPOST" and receive 10% Discount on Admissions

ATLIN ROAD

Tagish Road Junction, Yukon Territory, to Atlin, British Columbia, Yukon/BC Highway 7
(See map, page 601)

Turnout with point of interest sign to west overlooking beautiful Emerald Lake (also called Rainbow Lake by Yukoners). The rainbowlike colors of the lake result from blue-green light waves reflecting off the white sediment of the lake bottom. This white sediment, called marl, consists of fragments of decomposed shell mixed with clay; it is usually found in shallow, freshwater lakes that have low oxygen levels during the summer months.

S 75.4 (120.3 km) **AH 23.4** (37.7 km) Highway follows base of Caribou Mountain (elev. 5,645 feet/1,721m). View of Montana Mountain to south, Caribou Mountain to east and Gray Ridge Range to the west between Kilometreposts 122 and 128. Flora consists of jack pines and lodgepole pines.

S 79.8 (127.1 km) **AH 19** (30.6 km) Highway crosses Lewes Creek.

S 85.4 (136.3 km) **AH 13.4** (21.6 km) Access road west leads 1 mile/1.6 km to Lewes Lake.

S 85.6 (136.5 km) **AH 13.2** (21.2 km) Rat Lake to west.

S 86.7 (138.2 km) **AH 12.1** (19.4 km) Bear Creek.

S 87.3 (139.1 km) **AH 11.5** (18.5 km) Access road west to large gravel pull-through with historic information sign about Robinson and view of Robinson. In 1899, the White Pass & Yukon Route built a railroad siding at Robinson (named for Stikine Bill Robinson). Gold was discovered nearby in the early 1900s and a townsite was surveyed. A few buildings were constructed and a post office—manned by Charlie McConnell—operated from 1909 to 1915. Low mineral yields caused Robinson to be abandoned, but postmaster Charlie McConnell stayed and established one of the first ranches in the Yukon. Robinson is accessible from Annie Lake Road (see next milepost).

S 87.5 (139.4 km) **AH 11.3** (18.2 km) Road west to Annie Lake (turn left after crossing the railroad tracks to reach Robinson).

Annie Lake Road (can be rough) leads 0.8 mile/1.4 km to Annie Lake golf course, 1.9 miles/3.1 km to McConnell Lake, and 11 miles/17.7 km to Annie Lake. Beyond Annie Lake the road crosses the Wheaton River. The Wheaton Valley–Mt. Skukum area has seen a surge of mineral exploration by private prospectors and mining companies in recent years. For the adventuresome, this is beautiful and interesting country. There are no facilities along Annie Lake Road. *CAUTION: Annie Lake Road can be very muddy during spring breakup or during rain.*

S 93 (148.5 km) **AH 5.8** (9.4 km) Turnoff west for Cowley, an abandoned WP&YR railway station, and for access to Cowley Lake (1.6 miles/2.6 km).

S 95.5 (154.2 km) **AH 3.3** (5.3 km) Turnoff east for Kookatsoon Lake. There is a Yukon government picnic area at Kookatsoon Lake (day-use only). The lake is shallow and usually warm enough for swimming in summer. Picnic tables, firepits and pit toilets. Canoe launch.

S 98.4 (156.5 km) **AH 0.4** (0.7 km) Rock shop on east side of road.

S 98.8 (157.1 km) **AH 0** **Junction** with the Alaska Highway. Turn left (north) for Whitehorse, right (south) for Watson Lake. Turn to **Milepost DC 874.4** (page 122) in the ALASKA HIGHWAY section: Whitehorse-bound travelers continue with that log; travelers heading south down the Alaska Highway read that log back to front.

This 58-mile/93.3-km all-weather gravel road leads south to the pioneer gold mining town of Atlin. Built in 1949 by the Canadian Army Engineers, Atlin Road is a good road, usually in excellent condition, with some winding sections. The first 50 miles/80 km are gravel, with the remaining 8 miles/13 km into Atlin paved. Watch for construction and further paving in 1992. Watch for slippery spots in wet weather.

To reach Atlin Road, turn south at Jake's Corner on the Alaska Highway and drive 1.1 miles/1.8 km to the junction of Atlin Road (Highway 7) and Tagish Road (Highway 8); turn left (south) for Atlin.

It is about a 2½-hour drive to Atlin from Whitehorse and the view of the lake scenery from the village is well worth the trip.

Atlin Road Log

Physical kilometreposts in Yukon Territory and mileposts in British Columbia show distance from Tagish Road junction.
Distance from Tagish Road junction (J) is followed by distance from Atlin (A).

J 0 A 58 (93.3 km) **Junction** of Tagish and Atlin roads.

J 1.4 (2.3 km) **A 56.6** (91 km) Fish Creek crossing. The road is bordered by many low-lying, boggy areas brilliant green with horsetail *(equisetium)*.

J 1.8 (2.9 km) **A 56.2** (90.4 km) Side road west to Little Atlin Lake. Atlin Road descends along east shoreline of Little Atlin Lake approximately 7.6 miles/12.2 km southbound. During midsummer, the roadsides are ablaze with fireweed and wild roses.

J 2.4 (3.9 km) **A 55.6** (89.4 km) Large turnout to west on Little Atlin Lake; informal boat launch and camping area. Mount Minto (elev. 6,913 feet/2,107m) can be seen to the southwest. Road climbs southbound.

A YUKON WILDERNESS EXPERIENCE

THE HITCHING POST

Mile 23 (Km 38) Atlin Rd.

Cabins ✦ RV and Tent Sites
Boat Rentals ✦ Horseback Riding
Shower ✦ Convenience Store
Great Fishing

VISA   OPEN YEAR ROUND   MasterCard

RR1, Site 20, Comp. 182
Whitehorse, YT Y1A 4Z6
Mobile 2M 5177 White Mtn. Channel

J 2.8 (4.5 km) **A 55.2** (88.8 km) Turnout to west. Watch for bald eagles.

J 5 (8 km) **A 53** (85.3 km) Information sign to east about 1983–84 mountain goat transplant. The 12 goats were brought from Kluane National Park. They may be observed on the mountainsides.

J 8.1 (13 km) **A 49.9** (80.3 km) Haunka Creek. Turnout to west.

J 8.9 (14.3 km) **A 49.1** (79 km) Good view of Mount Minto ahead southbound.

J 13.8 (22.2 km) **A 44.2** (71.1 km) Unmarked side road leads 2.4 miles/3.9 km to **Lubbock River** which connects Little Atlin Lake with Atlin Lake. Excellent for grayling from breakup to mid-September.

J 15.5 (24.9 km) **A 42.5** (68.4 km) Snafu Creek. Turnout to west, north of bridge. According to R. Coutts, author of *Yukon Places & Names*, the creek name is an acronym bestowed by army crews who built the road. It stands for Situation Normal—All Fouled Up. Mr. Coutts resides in Atlin.

J 16.4 (26 km) **A 41.6** (66.9 km) Access road leads 0.7 mile/1.1 km to **Snafu Lake** Yukon government campground; 4 sites, pit toilets, tables, gravel boat ramp, good fishing.

J 18.6 (29.9 km) **A 39.4** (63.4 km) Tarfu Creek. Small turnout to east, north of bridge. Creek name is another army acronym. This one stands for Things Are Really Fouled Up.

J 18.7 (30 km) **A 39.3** (63.2 km) Abandoned cabin and turnout to west.

J 20.4 (32.8 km) **A 37.6** (60.5 km) Turnoff to east for **Tarfu Lake** Yukon government campground via 2.4-mile/3.8-km side road; 6 sites, pit toilets, fishing. Steep grade near campground; not recommended for large RVs or trailers.

J 20.5 (33 km) **A 37.5** (60.3 km) Short narrow side road leads east to Marcella Lake; good lake for canoeing.

J 21.8 (35.1 km) **A 36.2** (58.2 km) Turnout to west with view of Atlin Lake, which covers 307 square miles/798 square km and is the largest natural lake in British Columbia. Coast Mountains to the southwest.

J 23.6 (38 km) **A 34.4** (55.3 km) **The Hitching Post.** Beautiful wilderness setting at mouth of Lubbock River and Atlin Lake. Cabins, RV and tent sites, shower, boat and canoe rentals, guided fishing. Horseback riding, convenience store. Open year-round. Your hosts, Eric and Jane Hitchcock. Mobile 2M 5177 White Mountain Channel. RR#1, Site 20, Comp. 182, Whitehorse, YT Y1A 4Z6. [ADVERTISEMENT]

J 25.8 (41.5 km) **A 32.2** (51.8 km) BC–YT border. Road follows east shoreline of Atlin Lake into Atlin.

J 26.8 (43.1 km) **A 31.2** (50.2 km)

Survival shelter to east.

J 27 (43.5 km) A 31 (49.9 km) Mount Minto to west, Black Mountain to east, and Halcro Peak (elev. 5,856 feet/1,785m) to the southeast.

J 28.5 (45.8 km) A 29.5 (47.5 km) Slow down for sharp curve.

J 32 (51.5 km) A 26 (41.9 km) Excellent views of Coast Mountains, southwest across Atlin Lake, next 6 miles/9.7 km southbound.

J 32.7 (52.6 km) A 25.3 (40.7 km) **Hitchcock Creek**, grayling to 2 lbs. Survival shelter to east.

J 32.8 (52.7 km) A 25.2 (40.5 km) Campground on Atlin Lake; 6 sites, pit toilets, tables, boat ramp for small boats.

J 36.3 (58.4 km) A 21.7 (35 km) Turnout with litter barrel to west, south side of Base Camp Creek.

J 36.8 (59.2 km) A 21.2 (34.1 km) Old Milepost 38.

J 40 (64.4 km) A 18 (29 km) Indian River. Pull-through turnout south of creek.

J 40.2 (64.7 km) A 17.8 (28.7 km) Big-game outfitter to east.

J 45.2 (72.7 km) A 12.8 (20.6 km) Survival shelter to east.

J 45.3 (72.9 km) A 12.7 (20.5 km) Turnout to west.

J 49.8 (80.1 km) A 8.2 (13.2 km) Burnt Creek. Gravel ends, pavement begins, southbound.

J 49.9 (80.3 km) A 8.1 (13.1 km) Davie Hall Lake and turnout to west. Waterfowl are plentiful on lake.

J 51.2 (82.4 km) A 6.8 (11 km) Watch for horses.

J 51.6 (83 km) A 6.4 (10.3 km) Ruffner Mine Road leads east 40 miles/64.4 km. Access to **MacDonald Lake**, 2 miles/3.2 km east; bird watching and lake trout fishing from spit.

J 52.8 (85 km) A 5.2 (8.4 km) Fourth of July Creek.

J 53.4 (85.9 km) A 4.6 (7.4 km) Spruce Mountain (elev. 5,141 feet/1,567m) to west.

J 55.1 (88.7 km) A 2.9 (4.7 km) Road skirts east shore of Como Lake next 0.6 mile/1 km southbound.

J 55.2 (88.8 km) A 2.8 (4.5 km) Turnout with litter barrel to west on Como Lake; good lake for canoeing.

J 55.7 (89.6 km) A 2.3 (3.7 km) South end of Como Lake; boat ramp.

J 57.1 (91.9 km) A 0.9 (1.4 km) Atlin city limits.

J 58 (93.3 km) A 0 Junction of Atlin Road with Discovery Road. Turn right (west) on Discovery Avenue for town of Atlin; description follows. Turn left (east) for Discovery Road and access to Warm Bay Road; both roads are described in Atlin Attractions.

Atlin

The most northwesterly town in British Columbia, located about 112 miles/180 km southeast of Whitehorse, YT. **Population**: 500. **Emergency Services**: **Police**, phone 651-7511. **Fire Department**, phone 651-7666. **Ambulance**, phone 651-7677. Red Cross outpost clinic.

Visitor Information: Atlin Historical Museum, open weekends during June and September, daily July through August. Located in Atlin's original 1-room schoolhouse, the museum has mining artifacts and photo exhibits of the Atlin gold rush; admission fee.

Elevation: 2,240 feet/683m. **Radio**: CBC on FM-band.

Private Aircraft: Peterson Field, 1 mile/1.6 km northeast; elev. 2,348 feet/716m; length 3,950 feet/1,204m; gravel.

Referred to by some visitors as Shangri-la, the village of Atlin overlooks the crystal clear water of 90-mile-/145-km-long Atlin Lake and is surrounded by spectacular mountains. On Teresa Island in Atlin Lake is Birch Mountain (elev. 6,755 feet/2,060m), the highest point in fresh water in the world.

Atlin was founded in 1898. The name was taken from the Indian dialect and means Big Lake. The Atlin Lake area was one of the richest gold strikes made during the great rush to the Klondike in 1897–98. The first claims were registered here on July 30, 1898, by Fritz Miller and Kenneth McLaren.

ACCOMMODATIONS

The village has a hotel, inns, cottages, bed and breakfasts, laundromat (with showers), restaurants, gas stations (propane, diesel and unleaded available), grocery and general

View of Atlin Lake and Teresa Island from Atlin Road. (Earl L. Brown, staff)

stores. Dump station at Mile 2.3 Discovery Road. The museum and several shops feature local gold nugget jewelry, arts and crafts, and other souvenirs. Air charter service for glacier tours and fly-in fishing trips. Charter boats and fishing charters available.

Bus tours are welcome, but phone ahead so this small community can accommodate you.

The Noland House. This historic home has been restored to provide luxurious accommodations for 4 guests. Host residence is next door. Private baths and sitting rooms, complimentary wine and snacks, fully equipped kitchen, lake and mountain views, airport and floatplane dock pickup. $85 double, open May–October. Box 135, Atlin, BC V0W 1A0. (604) 651-7585. [ADVERTISEMENT]

RV park with electric and water hookups downtown on lake. There are several camp-

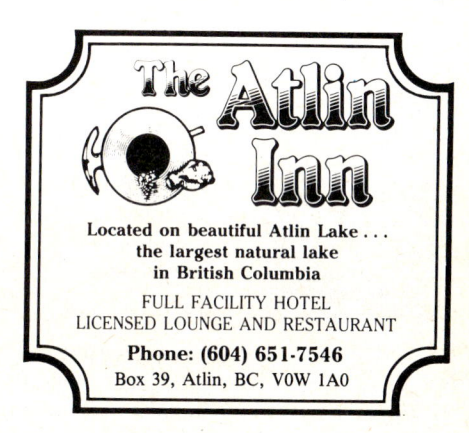

ATLIN ADVERTISERS

Atlin General Store .... Ph. (604) 651-7555
Atlin Inn, The .... Ph. (604) 651-7546
Fireweed Inn, The .... Ph. (604) 651-7729
Hitching Post, The .... Mile 23.6 Atlin Rd.
Kirkwood Cottages .... Ph. (604) 651-7500
Noland House, The .... Ph. (604) 651-7585
Norseman
 Adventures, Ltd. .... Ph. (604) 651-7535
Pine Tree Services .... Ph. (604) 651-7636
Sidka Tours .... Warm Bay Rd.
Simply Gold .... Ph. (604) 651-7708
Studers Restaurant .... Downtown by the clock

THE FIREWEED INN
Bed & Breakfast
Accommodation
Box 316, Atlin, BC V0W 1A0
(604) 651-7729
FAMILIES WELCOME

The Atlin Inn
Located on beautiful Atlin Lake...
the largest natural lake
in British Columbia
FULL FACILITY HOTEL
LICENSED LOUNGE AND RESTAURANT
Phone: (604) 651-7546
Box 39, Atlin, BC V0W 1A0

KIRKWOOD COTTAGES

• 2-Bedroom self-contained log cottages on beautiful Atlin Lake.

For reservations phone (604) 651-7500
Box 123, Atlin, B.C., V0W 1A0

— ATLIN —
Canada's Switzerland of the North

ing areas on Atlin Road (see log); on Discovery Road at Surprise Lake (Mile 12); and on Warm Bay Road at Pine Creek Campground (Mile 1.6), Palmer Lake (Mile 11.9), Warm Bay recreation site (Mile 13.9), Warm Springs camping area (Mile 14.4), and at the Grotto recreation site at Mile 16.3.

ATTRACTIONS

The SS *Tarahne* (Tah-ron) sits on the lakeshore in the middle of town. Built at Atlin in 1916 by White Pass and Yukon Route, she carried passengers and freight from Atlin to Scotia Bay until 1936. (Scotia Bay is across the lake from Atlin and slightly north.) A 2-mile/3.2-km railway connected Scotia Bay on Atlin Lake to Taku Landing on Tagish Lake, where passengers arrived by boat from Carcross, YT. She was the first gas-driven boat in the White Pass fleet and could carry up to 198 passengers. She was lengthened by 30 feet in 1927. In recent years, Atlin residents have launched a drive to restore the boat; they hope to eventually refloat the vessel and offer tours of Atlin Lake.

Visit the mineral springs at the north end of town, where you may have a drink of sparkling cold mineral water. The gazebolike structure over the springs was built by White Pass in 1922. Picnic area nearby.

The Pioneer Cemetery, located at Mile 1.1 Discovery Road, contains the weathered grave markers of early gold seekers, including Fritz Miller and Kenneth McLaren, who made the first gold discovery in the Atlin area in July 1898. Also buried here is Walter Gladstone Sweet, reputed to have been a card dealer for Soapy Smith in Skagway.

Take a Hike. At Mile 2.3 Warm Bay Road are 2 trails: the 2-mile/3.2-km Monarch trail and the short, easy Beach trail. The Monarch trail is a moderately strenuous hike with a steep climb at the end to a bird's-eye view of the area.

Tours and Rentals. Houseboat rentals, boat tours of Atlin and Tagish lakes, guided fishing trips and marine gas are available. Helicopter service, floatplanes for charter hunting and fishing trips and flightseeing trips of Llewellyn Glacier and the Atlin area are also available.

Take a Drive. 13-mile/21-km Discovery Road and 16.5-mile/26.5-km Warm Bay Road are both suitable for passenger cars and RVs and both offer sightseeing and recreation.

A scenic half-hour drive south of Atlin along Warm Bay Road to Mile 14.4. brings you to the warm springs, with a water temperature comparable to that of an indoor swimming pool; grassy camping area, picnic tables. Two miles/3.2 km beyond the warm springs at Mile 16.4 is "The Grotto," where a small creek flows out of an apparently solid rock wall. There are viewpoints along Warm Bay Road for viewing distant Llewellyn Glacier, one of the largest ice fields on the North American continent. Much of this mountainous ice field area is included in Atlin Provincial Park (undeveloped).

Follow Discovery Road approximately 3 miles/4.8 km east from Atlin to reach the Spruce Creek mining area, where $25 million in gold was taken from the creek. Six miles/9.7 km from Atlin is the former townsite of Discovery, once a bustling city of 10,000. There is active gold mining under way along the road; watch for large trucks. Discovery Road ends a mile beyond Surprise Lake.

Atlin Centre for the Arts, located at Mile 2 Warm Bay Road, is a summer school and retreat for artists and students run by Gernot Dick. The centre is designed to allow participants to distance themselves from urban distractions and focus on the creative process. Contact Atlin Centre for the Arts, 19 Elm Grove Ave., Toronto, ON M6K 2H9, for more information.

AREA FISHING: The Atlin area is well known for its good fishing. Fly-in fishing for salmon, steelhead and rainbow, or troll locally for lake trout. Grayling can be caught at the mouths of most creeks and streams or off Atlin docks. Public boat launch on Atlin Lake, south of the SS *Tarahne*. For information on fishing in the area contact local businesses. British Columbia fishing licenses are available from the government agent and local outlets. Fresh and smoked salmon may be available for purchase locally in the summer.

The Noland House
Luxury Bed & Breakfast
Box 135 · Atlin · B.C. V0W 1A0
(604) 651-7585
Let us welcome you to Atlin

Welcome Visitors To Atlin!
Studers Restaurant
Good Food
Ice Cream
Drugstore Goods
"Downtown – By The Clock"

R.V. PARK
POWER & WATER
► On the Lake Shore
Houseboats
Powerboats
Charters
Licenses
(604) 651-7535
NORSEMAN ADVENTURES LTD.
P.O. Box 184, Atlin, BC V0W 1A0

---

sidka tours
7.3 miles/11.7 km Warm Bay Road, past glacier lookout
BEST VIEW IN TOWN
Cabin or Bed And Breakfast • Sauna
Guided Motorcycle and Hiking Tours
Canoes for Rent
— Wir Sprechen Deutsch —
For brochure or reservations write to:
sidka tours, Box 368-M,
Atlin, BC V0W 1A0, Canada

Simply Gold
Handcrafted Jewellery with Atlin Gold Nuggets
Winner of Dawson City International 88/89 Gold Show Jewellery Competition

Kathy Taylor   Box 88
(Goldsmith)   Atlin, BC
(604) 651-7708   V0W 1A0
VISA MasterCard   (located across from the Liquor Store)

PINE TREE SERVICES
CHEVRON
Oils & Gas
Diesel, Propane
Bulk Fuel
Tires
LICENSED DINING ROOM
Home Baked Pies & Pastries — Restaurant Open Daily
Sheldon & Randy Sands • Box 287, Atlin, BC, V0W 1A0 • Phone (604) 651-7636

ATLIN GENERAL STORE
"Northern Supplies for Northern Living"
Hardware • Housewares
Sporting Goods • Souvenirs
BC Hunting & Fishing Licenses
BC Lottery Tickets
Clothing • Books • Gifts

Locally Made
GOLD NUGGET JEWELRY
ATLIN'S FISHING CENTER
On the Boardwalk - 1st & Trainor
(604) 651-7555

TAGISH ROAD

Alaska Highway (Jake's Corner) to Carcross, Yukon Territory
Yukon Highway 8
(See map, page 601)

The Tagish Road was built in 1942 to lay a gas pipeline. It leads south from the Alaska Highway through the settlement of Tagish to Carcross. This 33.8-mile/54.4-km road connects the Alaska Highway with Klondike Highway 2. The road is good gravel from the Alaska Highway junction to Tagish, asphalt-surfaced between Tagish and Carcross.

If you are traveling Klondike Highway 2 between Skagway and Whitehorse, Tagish Road provides access to Atlin Road and also makes a pleasant side trip. Travelers may wish to use Tagish Road as an alternate route if there is road construction on Klondike Highway 2 between Carcross and the Alaska Highway.

Tagish Road Log

Kilometreposts measure east to west from Alaska Highway junction to Carcross turn-off; posts are up about every 2 kilometres. **Distance from the junction (J) is followed by distance from Carcross (C).**

J 0   C 33.8 (54.4 km) **Junction** with the Alaska Highway at Jake's Corner. Drive south 1.1 miles/1.8 km to junction of Tagish Road (Highway 8) and Atlin Road (Highway 7).

J 1.1 (1.8 km) **C 32.7** (52.6 km) **Junction** of Tagish and Atlin roads. Turn southeast for Atlin, BC (see ATLIN ROAD section); head west for Tagish and Carcross.

J 8.8 (14.2 km) **C 25** (40.2 km) For several miles, travelers may see the NorthwesTel microwave tower on Jubilee Mountain (elev. 5,950 feet/1,814m) to the south between Little Atlin Lake and Tagish River.

J 12.8 (20.6 km) **C 21** (33.8 km) Tagish Yukon government campground, on **Six Mile River** between Marsh Lake to the north and Tagish Lake to the south. Good fishing, boat launch, picnic area, playground, kitchen shelter, 28 campsites with firepits and tables, drinking water and toilets. *CAUTION: Watch for black bears.*

J 13.1 (21 km) **C 20.7** (33.3 km) Tagish bridge. Good fishing is a tradition from Tagish bridge, which has an anglers' walkway on the north side. **Tagish River**, lake trout, arctic grayling, northern pike, whitefish and cisco. Marina on north side of road at east end of bridge has bait, tackle, fishing licenses, boat rental, gas and snacks. Pay phone on road.

J 13.1 (21.1 km) **C 20.7** (33.3 km) Gravel ends, pavement begins, westbound.

J 13.5 (21.7 km) **C 20.3** (32.6 km) Improved gravel road leads through parklike area to tiny settlement of **TAGISH** on Tagish River between Marsh and Tagish lakes. Tagish means "fish trap" in the local Indian dialect. It was traditionally an Indian meeting place in the spring on the way to set up fish camps and again in the fall to celebrate the catch. Inquire locally for location of post office.

Tagish Service. See display ad this section.

Two miles/3.2 km south of Tagish on the Tagish River the North West Mounted Police and Canadian customs cleared stampeders on their way to the goldfields in the Klondike. Some days as many as 1,000 boats waited in the bay for clearance.

J 16.3 (26.2 km) **C 17.5** (28.1 km) Side road leads 1.2 miles/2 km to Tagish Lake and homes.

J 23 (37 km) **C 10.8** (17.4 km) Bryden Creek.

J 23.8 (38.3 km) **C 10** (16.1 km) **Ten Mile Ranch**, located 8 miles south on a maintained gravel road, is a wilderness ranch with rustic log cabins and large RV and tent sites right along the shore of Tagish Lake. A variety of activities include wildlife watching, canoeing, boating, fishing, guided adventure tours from 1 to 4 weeks, or just relaxing surrounded by the quiet splendor of mountains and lakes. We look forward to seeing you. Phone (403) 667-1009. [ADVERTISEMENT]

J 24.8 (39.9 km) **C 9** (14.4 km) Crag Lake. Road now enters more mountainous region westbound. Caribou Mountain (elev. 5,645 feet/1,721m) on right.

J 27.2 (43.8 km) **C 6.6** (10.6 km) Porcupine Creek.

J 28.4 (45.7 km) **C 5.4** (8.7 km) Pain Creek.

J 30.2 (48.6 km) **C 3.6** (5.8 km) Side road to Chooutla Lake.

J 31 (49.9 km) **C 2.8** (4.5 km) First glimpse westbound of Montana Mountain (elev. 7,230 feet/2,204m) across narrows at Carcross.

Kayakers find solitude and smooth water on Six Mile River. (Rollo Pool, staff)

J 33.8 (54.4 km) **C 0 Junction** with Klondike Highway 2. Westbound travelers turn left for Carcross, right for Whitehorse. See **Milepost S 66.5** (page 603) in the KLONDIKE HIGHWAY 2 section.

TAGISH SERVICE
(Located at the end of the bridge)

GAS • OIL • DIESEL
Tire Sales and Repairs
Minor Repairs and Welding

Fishing Licenses
Area and Fishing Information
Ice • Post Office • Pay Phone

"FAST FOOD TAKEOUT AT THE GAZEBO"

(403) 399-3663 • Tagish, Yukon Y0B 1T0
Your Hosts: Art and Renie Smith

TEN MILE RANCH
8 miles south of Tagish Road on the shore of Tagish Lake

Secluded Wilderness Guest Ranch
Lakefront Camping and Log Cabins
Canoe and Boat Rental
Guided Adventure Tours

Information and Reservations
Phone (403) 667-1009
P.O. Box 3889-A, Whitehorse, YT Y1A 5M6

SILVER TRAIL

Klondike Highway Junction to Keno City, YT
Yukon Highway 11

The Silver Trail leads northeast from the Klondike Highway (see **Milepost J 214.4** in the KLONDIKE LOOP section) to Mayo, Elsa and Keno City. From its junction with the Klondike Highway (Yukon Highway 2), the Silver Trail (Yukon Highway 11) leads 31.9 miles/51.3 km to Mayo; 60.3 miles/97 km to Elsa; and 69.1 miles/111.2 km to Keno City. The Silver Trail also provides access to Duncan Creek Road, the original Silver Trail. It is approximately 140 miles/225 km round-trip to Keno City and an easy day trip for motorists. The road is asphalt-surfaced to Mayo, hard-packed gravel from Mayo to Keno. Watch for soft shoulders, especially in wet weather. Gas is available only at Mayo and at Stewart Crossing on the Klondike Highway.

There is an information kiosk on the Klondike Highway, at the south end of Stewart River bridge, 0.2 mile/0.3 km south of the Silver Trail junction. Stop at the kiosk for maps and information on the Silver Trail or write Silver Trail Tourism, Mayo, YT Y0B 1M0; phone (in summer) 996-2926.

The Silver Trail to Mayo follows the Stewart River through what has been one of the richest silver mining regions in Canada.

THE SILVER TRAIL TOURISM ASSOCIATION

and the following local businesses invite you to drive the historic Silver Trail.

- Holly's Place Deli
- Conde North Ventures
- Mayo Caselot & Expediting
- St. Mary's Anglican Church
- Mayo Taxi, Bus Service / Charters
- Mayo Variety Store
- Repairs Unlimited
- Stewart River Services (Chevron)
- Bedrock Motel
- Mayo Bed and Breakfast
- North Star Motel, Mayo
- Stewart Valley Enterprises
- Silver Trail Inn
- Duncan Creek Golddusters
- Keno City Hotel
- Stewart Crossing Lodge
- Bleiler Placers
- Whispering Willows RV Park
- Country Charm Bed and Breakfast
- Kalzas Lake Outfitters
- Silver Trail Restaurant

? Silver Trail Information Center Located at Stewart Crossing

- **SEE** the exquisite collection of historic photographs and mining artifacts at the Keno City Mining Museum.
- **VISIT** an operating gold mine at Duncan Creek.
- **ENJOY** spectacular scenery and superb fishing.

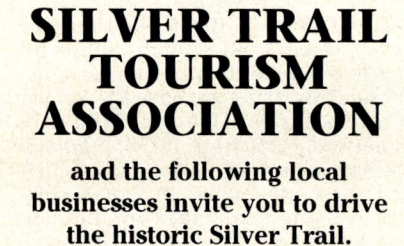

For more information:
Write to Silver Trail Tourism • Mayo, YT, Canada Y0B 1M0
Summer months - Phone (403) 996-2926

Silver Trail Log

Distance is measured from the junction with the Klondike Highway (J).

J 0 Junction of Silver Trail (Yukon Highway 11) and Klondike Highway.

J 0.2 (0.3 km) Marker shows distance to Mayo 51 km, Elsa 97 km, Keno 110 km.

J 1.2 (2 km) Stewart River to the south.

J 3 (4.8 km) Bad curve. Turnout to south.

J 9.6 (15.4 km) Large gravel pit turnout to south.

J 27.4 (44.1 km) Pull-through rest area with outhouses, litter barrel and picnic tables.

J 30.7 (49.5 km) Winding descent for northeast-bound traffic; good view of valley.

J 31.2 (50.2 km) McIntyre Park picnic area to south on banks of the Mayo River.

J 31.3 (50.3 km) **Mayo River** bridge. Good fishing from bridge for grayling.

J 31.9 (51.3 km) **Junction** with access road to Mayo (description follows). Turn right (south) for Mayo, keep left (north) for road to Elsa and Keno City.

Bedrock Motel located 1 mile north of Mayo on the Silver Trail. New facility containing 12 spacious rooms and lounge. Full baths, continental breakfast, laundry facilities, air conditioning, handicap suite. Major credit cards accepted. Rates from $65 up. Automotive and bottle propane available, dump station, shower, camping. Open April 1 to Oct. 31. Darren and Joyce Ronaghan, Box 69, Mayo, YT Y0B 1M0. Phone (403) 996-2290 or fax (403) 996-2728. [ADVERTISEMENT] ▲

Mayo

Located on the bank of the Stewart River near its confluence with the Mayo River. **Population:** 500. **Emergency Services:** RCMP, phone 996-2322. Ambulance, phone 996-2345. **Elevation:** 1,650 feet/503m. **Radio:** CBC 1230. **Television:** CBC Anik, Channel 7.

Climate: Residents claim it the coldest and hottest spot in Yukon. Record low, -80°F/-62.2°C (February 1947); record high, 97°F/36.1°C (June 1969).

Private Aircraft: Mayo airstrip, 4 miles/6.5 km north; elev. 1,653 feet/504m; length, 4,850 feet/1,478m; gravel; fuel 100, Jet B.

Mayo has most traveler facilities including 2 motels, 2 bed and breakfasts, cafe, laundromat, gas station, hardware, grocery and variety stores (closed Sunday). Tire

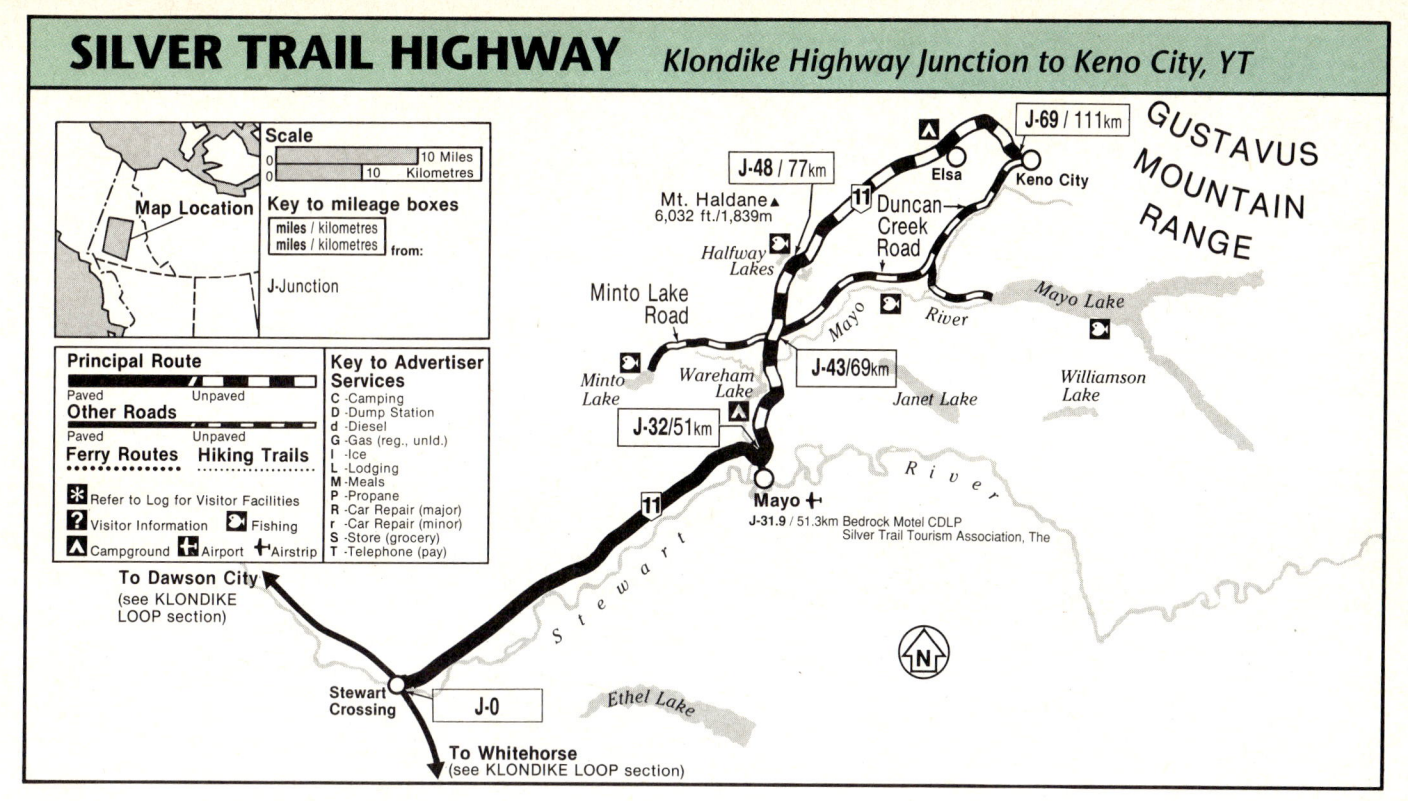

SILVER TRAIL HIGHWAY
Klondike Highway Junction to Keno City, YT

repair and minor vehicle repair are available. Post office, liquor store and library located in the Territorial Bldg. Bank service available 10 A.M. to 1 P.M. Monday, Wednesday and Friday.

Scheduled air service to Whitehorse and Dawson City. Charter floatplane and helicopter service available. Scheduled bus service. Canoeists can put in at Mayo on the Stewart River for a paddle to Stewart Crossing.

Mayo was formerly known as Mayo Landing and began as a river settlement and port for silver ore shipments to Whitehorse. It is now a service centre for mineral exploration in the area. Yukon Electrical Co. Ltd. operates a hydroelectric project here.

The Silver Trail Tourism Association. See display ad this section.

Silver Trail Log

(continued)

J 32.8 (52.8 km) Mayo airport, built in 1928 by the Treadwell Mining Co. Pavement ends, gravel begins, northbound.

J 34.9 (56.2 km) Side road to Mayo hydro dam, built in 1951 and completed in 1952.

J 35.8 (57.6 km) Turnoff to west for Five Mile Lake Yukon government campground; 20 sites, boat launch, picnic tables, firepits. ▲

J 36.1 (58.1 km) Five Mile Lake day-use area.

J 36.2 (58.2 km) Access to small lake to east.

J 37.6 (60.5 km) Wareham Lake to east, created by the Mayo River power project. This lake is not good for fishing.

J 38.2 (61.4 km) Survival shelter to east.

J 40.3 (64.8 km) Minto bridge. Just south of the bridge is the Mease farm (private property), a good example of agriculture in this area.

J 42.9 (69 km) **Junction** of Yukon Highway 11 with Minto Lake Road and Duncan Creek Road. Turn west (left) and drive 12 miles/19 km for **Minto Lake**; good fishing for lake trout and grayling. Also access to Highet Creek.

Turn east (right) at junction for Duncan Creek Road, which leads to Mayo Lake and Keno City. The original Silver Trail, Duncan Creek Road was used by Treadwell Yukon during the 1930s to haul silver ore from Keno into Mayo, where it was loaded onto riverboats. This 25-mile/40-km back road is mostly good hard-packed gravel. Motorists note, however, that the last 10 miles/16 km into Keno City via Duncan Creek Road are narrow and winding, slippery when wet, and not recommended for large vehicles or trailers. Heading northeast on Duncan Creek Road, travelers will see the site of Fields Creek Roadhouse at Mile 5, and Stones Roadhouse at Mile 11. At Mile 14 Duncan Creek Road junctions with a 6-mile/10-km side road which leads to **Mayo Lake**; there is good fishing along the **Mayo River** to the dam at the west end of Mayo Lake. At Mile 14.2 there is a private gold mine, Duncan Creek Golddusters, with guided tours and gold panning (fee charged). At Mile 18 are the remains of the Van Cleaves Roadhouse. At Mile 25 Duncan Creek Road junctions with Highway 11 at Keno City.

J 48 (77.2 km) **Halfway Lakes**; fishing for northern pike. Hike up Mount Haldane (to the west) for view of the area. Mount Haldane (elev. 6,015 feet/1,833m) was named after an early prospector; it is called Lookout Mountain by local residents. Good rockhounding.

J 54.9 (88.3 km) South McQuesten River Road; drive northwest 5 miles/8 km for Silver Centre Campsite, a public campground built by the people of Elsa. ▲

J 60.3 (97 km) **ELSA** (pop. 10) was a company town for United Keno Hill Mines, formerly one of the largest silver mines in North America and one of the Yukon's oldest, continuously operating hardrock mines until its closure in 1989. The Elsa claim is a well-mineralized silver vein, located on Galena Hill, which was named for the sister of prospector Charlie Brefalt, who received $250,000 for Treadwell Yukon's richest mine. A plaque here commemorates American engineer Livingston Wernecke, who came to the Keno Hill area in 1919 to investigate the silver–lead ore discoveries for Treadwell–Yukon Mining Co..

Rock hounds request permission from the mine security office to look for galena, quartz crystals, pyrite and other minerals.

J 63.8 (102.6 km) Side road leads north to Hanson Lakes and McQuesten Lake. Galena Mountains to east. An information sign marks the Wind River trail, a former winter road to oil exploration sites, which leads 300 miles/483 km north to the Bell River. The twin towers are abandoned telephone relays.

J 69.1 (111.2 km) **KENO CITY** (pop. about 50). Originally called Sheep Hill by the early miners, it was renamed Keno—a gambling game—after the Keno mining claim that was staked by Louis Bouvette in July 1919. This enormously rich discovery of silver and galena sparked the interest of 2 large mining companies, the Guggenheims and Treadwell Yukon, who set up camps in the area. During the 1920s, Keno City was a boom town.

Keno has a hotel with a bar (no food service available), a coffee shop, and washers, dryers and showers available for the public. There is a city campground located on Lightning Creek. ▲

Well worth a visit here is the Keno Mining Museum, housed in the 2-story 1920s community hall. Photographs and tools recall the mining history of the area. It is open 10 A.M. to 8 P.M., June through August.

There is a magnificent view of the Wernecke Mountains and McQuesten River valley from 6,200-foot/1,890-m Keno Hill. A milepost sign on the rim gives great circle route distances to points around the globe.

1992 ■ The MILEPOST® 609

CAMPBELL HIGHWAY

Watson Lake, Yukon Territory, to Junction with Klondike Loop Yukon Highway 4

Eagles Nest Bluff, a well-known marker for Yukon River travelers. (Rollo Pool, staff)

Named for Robert Campbell, the first white man to penetrate what is now known as Yukon Territory, this all-weather gravel road leads 367.5 miles/591.4 km northwest from the Alaska Highway at Watson Lake, to junction with the Klondike Highway 2 miles/3.2 km north of Carmacks (see the KLONDIKE LOOP section). Gas is available at Watson Lake, Ross River, Faro and Carmacks.

CAUTION: Watch for large ore trucks on the Campbell Highway between Faro and Carmacks. Drive with your headlights on.

The Campbell Highway is an alternative route to Dawson City. It is about 20 miles/32 km shorter than driving the Alaska Highway through to Whitehorse then driving up the Klondike Highway to Dawson City.

The Robert Campbell Highway was completed in 1968 and closely follows sections of the fur trade route established by Robert Campbell. Campbell was a Hudson's Bay Co. trader who was sent into the region in the 1840s to find a route west into the unexplored regions of central Yukon. Traveling from the southeast, he followed the Liard and Frances rivers, building a chain of posts along the way. His major discovery came in 1843, when he reached the Yukon River, which was to become the major transportation route within the Yukon.

Emergency medical services: In Watson Lake, phone (403) 536-2541; in Ross River, phone (403) 969-2221; and in Carmacks, phone (403) 863-5501.

Campbell Highway Log

YUKON HIGHWAY 4
Distance from Watson Lake (WL) is followed by distance from junction with the Klondike Highway just north of Carmacks (J).

WL 0 J 367.5 (591.4 km) Junction of the Campbell Highway with the Alaska Highway at Watson Lake (see description of Watson Lake in the ALASKA HIGHWAY section). The famous sign forest is located at this junction. In the parking area off the Campbell Highway (also called Airport Road) is a point of interest sign relating the highway's history.

WL 0.6 (1 km) **J 366.9** (590.4 km) Hospital on right northbound.

WL 4.3 (6.9 km) **J 363.2** (584.5 km) Access road on right northbound to Mount Maichen ski hill.

WL 6.3 (10.1 km) **J 361.2** (581.3 km) Airport Road left to Watson Lake airport. Pavement ends, hard-packed gravel begins, northbound.

WL 6.7 (10.8 km) **J 360.8** (580.6 km) Watson Creek. The highway begins to climb to a heavily timbered plateau and then heads north following the east bank of the Frances River. Tamarack is rare in Yukon but this northern type of larch can be seen along here. Although a member of the pine family, it sheds its needles in the fall.

WL 10.4 (16.7 km) **J 357.1** (574.7 km) MacDonald Creek.

WL 22.5 (36.2 km) **J 345** (555.2 km) Tom Creek.

WL 27.3 (44 km) **J 340.2** (547.5 km) Sa Dena Hes Mine access.

WL 36.1 (58.1 km) **J 331.4** (533.3 km) Frances River bridge. Turnout at north end of bridge; picnic spot. The highway crosses to west bank and follows the river northward. Named by Robert Campbell for the wife of Sir George Simpson, governor of the Hudson's Bay Co. for 40 years, the Frances River is a tributary of the Liard River. Robert Campbell ascended the Liard River to the Frances River and then went on to Frances Lake and the Pelly River. The Frances River was part of Hudson's Bay Co.'s route into central Yukon for many years before being abandoned because of its dangerous rapids and canyons.

WL 46.6 (75 km) **J 320.9** (516.4 km) Lucky Creek.

WL 49 (78.8 km) **J 318.5** (512.5 km) Simpson Creek.

WL 51.2 (82.4 km) **J 316.3** (509 km) Access road leads west 1 mile/1.6 km to **Simpson Lake** Yukon government campground: 19 campsites, boat launch, dock, swimming beach, playground, kitchen shelter and drinking water (boil water). Excellent fishing for lake trout, arctic grayling and northern pike.

WL 58.1 (93.5 km) **J 309.4** (497.9 km) Access road west to Simpson Lake.

WL 67.9 (109.3 km) **J 299.6** (482.1 km) **Miner's Junction**, junction with Nahanni Range Road (formerly known as Cantung Junction); status of services unknown. Nahanni Range Road leads 125 miles/201.2 km northeast to Tungsten (see NAHANNI RANGE ROAD section).

WL 69.4 (111.7 km) **J 298.1** (479.7 km) Yukon government Tuchitua River maintenance camp to east.

WL 69.5 (111.8 km) **J 298** (479.5 km) One-lane bridge over Tuchitua River.

WL 90.9 (146.3 km) **J 276.6** (445.1 km) Jules Creek.

WL 105.7 (170.1 km) **J 261.8** (421.3 km) Caesar Creek.

WL 106.2 (171 km) **J 261.3** (420.5 km) View of Frances Lake to east, Campbell Range of the Pelly Mountains to west.

WL 108 (173.8 km) **J 259.5** (417.6 km) Access road leads 0.6 mile/1 km to **Frances Lake** Yukon government campground: 19 campsites, boat launch, kitchen shelter, drinking water (boil water). The solitary peak between the 2 arms of Frances Lake is Simpson Tower (elev. 5,500 feet/

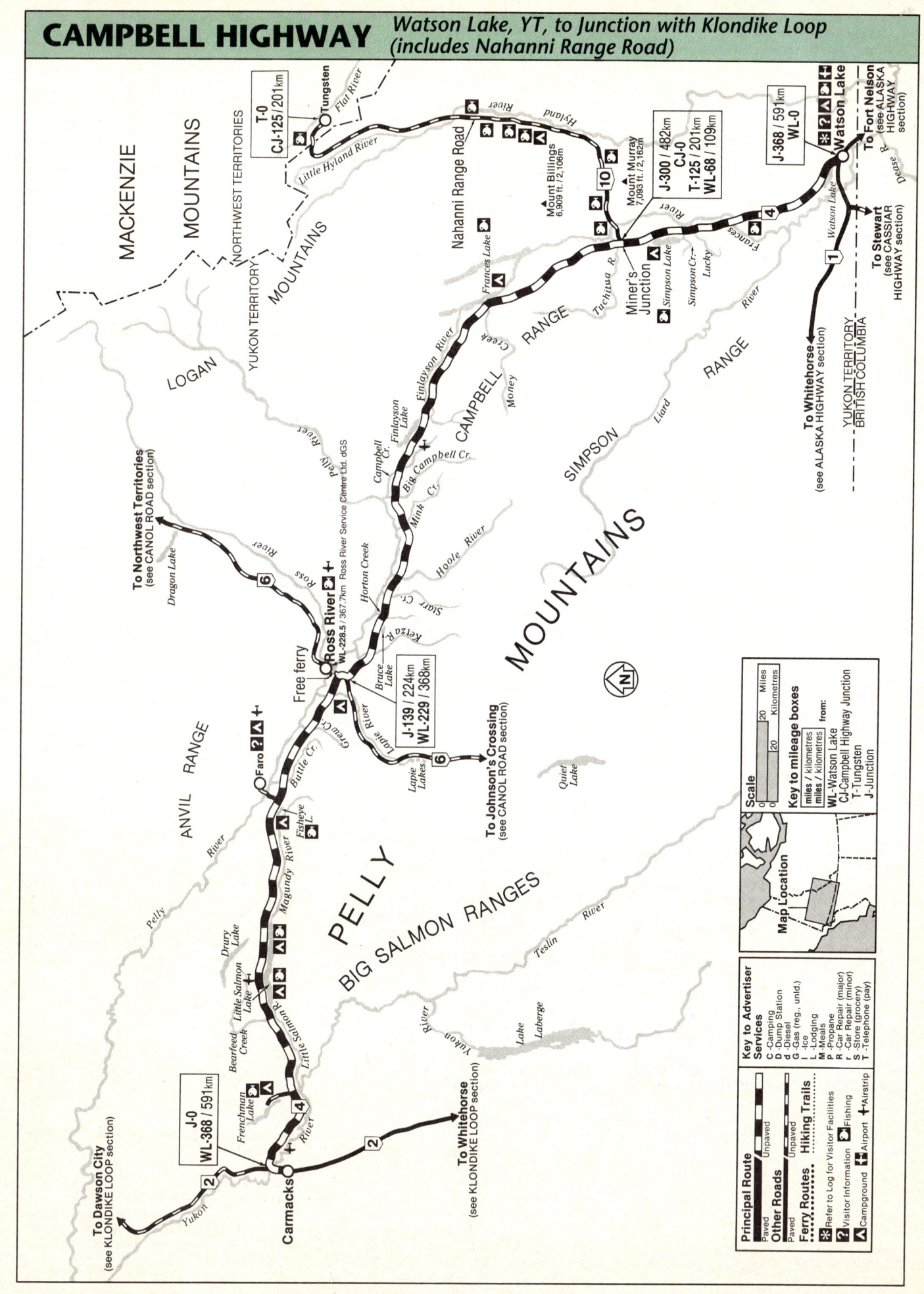

CAMPBELL HIGHWAY
Watson Lake, YT, to Junction with Klondike Loop (includes Nahanni Range Road)

1,676m). It was named by Robert Campbell for Hudson's Bay Co. governor, Sir George Simpson, and the lake after the governor's wife, Frances. Fishing for lake trout, grayling and northern pike.

WL 108.1 (174 km) **J 259.4** (417.4 km) Money Creek, which flows into the west arm of Frances Lake, one of the Yukon's largest lakes. The creek was named for Anton Money, a mining engineer and prospector who found and mined placer gold in this area between 1929–46.

WL 112.6 (181.2 km) **J 254.9** (410.2 km) Dick Creek.

WL 122.6 (197.3 km) **J 244.9** (394.1 km) Highway descends Finlayson River valley, swinging west away from Frances Lake and following the Finlayson River that may be seen occasionally to the east for about the next 20 miles/32 km. Mountains to the west are part of the Campbell Range.

WL 125.3 (201.6 km) **J 242.2** (389.8 km) Light Creek.

WL 144.8 (233 km) **J 222.7** (358.4 km) Finlayson Creek, flows into the river of the same name, drains Finlayson Lake into Frances Lake. Named by Robert Campbell in 1840 for Chief Factor Duncan Finlayson, who later became director of the Hudson's Bay Co. Placer gold mined at the mouth of Finlayson River in 1875 is believed to be some of the first gold mined in the territory. Finlayson Lake (elev. 3,100 feet/945m), on the Continental Divide, separates watersheds of Mackenzie and Yukon rivers.

WL 145.4 (234 km) **J 222.1** (357.4 km) Access road north to Finlayson Lake picnic area. To the southwest are the Pelly Mountains.

WL 155 (249.4 km) **J 212.5** (342 km) **Private Aircraft**: Finlayson Lake airstrip to south; elev. 3,300 feet/ 1,006m; length 2,100 feet/640m; gravel.

WL 162.6 (261.7 km) **J 204.9** (329.7 km) Campbell Creek. Robert Campbell followed this creek to the Pelly River in 1840.

WL 168.6 (271.3 km) **J 198.9** (320.1 km) Bridge over Big Campbell Creek which flows into Pelly River at Pelly Banks. Robert Campbell named the river and banks after Hudson's Bay Co. governor Sir John Henry Pelly. Campbell built a trading post here in 1846; never successful, it burned down in 1849. Isaac Taylor and William S. Drury later operated a trading post at Pelly Banks, one of a string of successful posts established by their firm in remote spots throughout the Yukon from 1899 on.

For the next 90 miles/145 km the highway follows the Pelly River.

WL 176.3 (283.7 km) **J 191.2** (307.7 km) Mink Creek culvert.

WL 190.8 (307 km) **J 176.7** (284.4 km) Bridge over Hoole Canyon; turnout to north. Kilometrepost 312. Confluence of the Hoole and Pelly rivers. Campbell named the Hoole River after his interpreter, Francis Hoole, a half-Iroquois and half-French Canadian employed by the Hudson's Bay Co. Dig out your gold pan—this river once yielded gold.

WL 196.8 (316.7 km) **J 170.7** (274.7 km) Kilometrepost 320. Starr Creek culvert.

WL 203.5 (327.5 km) **J 164** (263.9 km) Horton Creek.

WL 207.8 (334.4 km) **J 159.7** (257 km) Kilometrepost 338. Bruce Lake to south.

WL 208.4 (335.4 km) **J 159.1** (256 km) Bruce Creek.

WL 212.2 (341.5 km) **J 155.3** (249.9 km) Private side road leads south 27.3 miles/44 km to Ketza River Project. The first gold bar was poured at Ketza River mine in 1988. The Ketza River hard-rock gold deposit was first discovered in 1947, but the mine was only recently developed. No visitor facilities.

WL 214.5 (345.2 km) **J 153** (246.2 km) Ketza River. St. Cyr Range to southwest.

WL 215.8 (347.3 km) **J 151.7** (244.1 km) Ketza Creek.

WL 217.9 (350.7 km) **J 149.6** (240.7 km) Beautiful Creek culvert.

WL 221.1 (355.8 km) **J 146.4** (235.6 km) **Coffee Lake** to south; local swimming hole. Kamloops cutthroat, fly or small spoons, summer; picnic tables.

WL 223.6 (359.8 km) **J 143.9** (231.6 km) **Junction** with South Canol Road (see CANOL ROAD section) which leads south 129 miles/207 km to Johnson's Crossing and the Alaska Highway. Floatplane base on Jackfish Lake here.

WL 223.8 (360.2 km) **J 143.7** (231.2 km) Unmaintained side road on right westbound is continuation of Canol Road to Ross River. Use main Ross River access road next milepost.

WL 228.5 (367.7 km) **J 139** (223.7 km) Access road leads 7 miles/11.2 km to Ross River (description follows). Rest area with toilets on highway just north of this turnoff.

Ross River

Located on the southwest bank of the Pelly River. **Population**: 376. **Emergency Services**: RCMP, phone 969-2227. **Hospital**, phone 969-2221. **Radio**: CBC 990, local FM station. **Transportation**: Scheduled air service via Trans North Air.

Private Aircraft: Ross River airstrip; elev. 2,408 feet/734m; length 5,500 feet/1,676m; gravel; fuel 40.

A point of interest sign on the way into Ross River relates that in 1843, Robert Campbell named Ross River for Chief Trader Donald Ross of the Hudson's Bay Co. From 1903, a trading post called Nahanni House (established by Tom Smith and later owned by the Whitehorse firm of Taylor and Drury) located at the confluence of the Ross and Pelly rivers supplied the Indians of the area for nearly 50 years. With the building of the Canol pipeline service road in WWII and the completion of the Robert Campbell Highway in 1968, the community was linked to the rest of the territory by road. Originally situated on the north side of the Pelly River, the town has been in its present location since 1964. Today, Ross River is a supply and communication base for prospectors testing and mining mineral bodies in this region.

Ross River has gas stations with diesel and tire repair, grocery stores and 2 motels with dining. The nearest campground is Lapie Canyon (see **Milepost WL 229.7**). Self-contained RVs may overnight at the gravel parking lot at the end of the pedestrian suspension bridge on the Ross River side.

Ross River is also a jumping-off point for big game hunters and canoeists. There are 2 registered hunting outfitters here. Canoeists traveling the Pelly River can launch just downriver from the ferry crossing. Experienced canoeists recommend camping on the Pelly's many gravel bars and islets to avoid bears, bugs and the danger of accidentally setting tundra fires. The Pelly has many sweepers, sleepers and gravel shallows, some gravel shoals, and extensive channeling. There are 2 sets of rapids between Ross River and the mouth of the Pelly: Fish Hook and Granite Canyon. Water is potable (boil), firewood available and wildlife plentiful. Inquire locally about river conditions before setting out and read pertinent government publications before attempting to navigate any Yukon river.

Rock hounds watch for coal seams on the access road into Ross River. Also check Pelly River gravels for jaspers and the occasional agate.

The suspension footbridge at Ross River leads across the Pelly River to the site of an abandoned Indian village 1 mile/1.6 km upstream at the mouth of the Ross River.

A government ferry crosses the Pelly River daily in summer, from 8 A.M. to noon and 1-5 P.M. Across the river, the North Canol Road leads 144 miles/232 km to Macmillan Pass at the Northwest Territories border. See the CANOL ROAD section for details.

Ross River Service Centre Ltd. See display ad this section.

Campbell Highway Log

(continued)

WL 228.5 (367.7 km) **J 139** (223.7 km) Access road leads 7 miles/11.2 km to Ross River (see preceding description).

WL 228.7 (368 km) **J 138.8** (223.4 km) Rest area with toilets.

WL 229.6 (369.5 km) **J 137.9** (221.9 km) Lapie River bridge crosses deep gorge of Lapie River, which flows into the Pelly River from Lapie Lakes on the South Canol Road. Highway continues to follow the Pelly River and Pelly Mountains.

WL 229.7 (369.6 km) **J 137.8** (221.7 km) Turnoff to left (south) to Lapie Canyon Yukon government campground adjacent Lapie River: short scenic trails, picturesque canyon; kitchen shelters, group firepit and picnic area; walk-in tent sites, 14 campsites, drinking water (boil water).

WL 232.5 (374.2 km) **J 135** (217.2 km) Kilometrepost 380. Danger Creek. In 1905, naturalist Charles Sheldon named this creek after his horse, Danger, supposedly the first horse into this area.

WL 236.1 (380 km) **J 131.4** (211.5 km) Kilometrepost 386. Panoramic view of the Pelly River valley just ahead westbound.

WL 239.7 (385.7 km) **J 127.8** (205.6 km) Kilometrepost 392. Hill and bad corner.

WL 240.5 (387 km) **J 127** (204.4 km)

ROSS RIVER SERVICE CENTRE LTD.

Gas & Diesel
Grocery & Hardware
——— Supplies ———

EXPEDITING SERVICES

Brian & Colleen Hemsley

General Delivery
Ross River   Phone (403) 969-2212
Yukon Y0B 1S0   FAX (403) 969-2108

Highway narrows over Grew Creek, no guide rails. This creek was named for Hudson's Bay Co. trader Jim Grew, who trapped this area for many years before his death in 1906.

WL 247.9 (398.9 km) J 119.6 (192.5 km) Kilometrepost 404. Turnout to north.

WL 256.2 (412.3 km) J 111.3 (179.1 km) Buttle Creek, named for Roy Buttle, a trapper, prospector and trader who lived here in the early 1900s, and at one time owned a trading post at Ross River.

WL 260.6 (419.4 km) J 106.9 (172 km) Kilometrepost 426. Across the wide Pelly River valley to the north is a view of the mining community of Faro.

WL 261.5 (420.8 km) J 106 (170.6 km) Access road on right westbound leads 5.6 miles/9 km to Faro. Point of interest sign about Faro at intersection. Rest area with toilets and litter barrels to south just west of this junction.

Faro

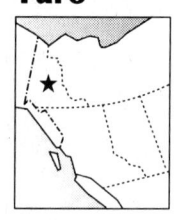

Located in east-central Yukon Territory, 220 road miles/354 km from Whitehorse. **Population:** 1,276. **Emergency Services:** RCMP, phone 994-2444. **Fire Department**, phone 994-2222. **Hospital**, phone 994-2736.

Climate: Temperatures range from -51°F/-46°C in winter to a summer maximum of 84°F/29°C. Freezing conditions from mid-September to early May, with a mean annual precipitation of 14 inches equal parts rain and snow. Maximum snowfall cover in late March up to 50 inches. **Radio:** CBC-FM 100.3, CKRW 97.5, CHON 98.7. **Television:** CBC and 7 cable channels. **Transportation:** Scheduled air service to Whitehorse and Ross River via Alcan Air.

Private Aircraft: Faro airstrip; 1.5 miles 2.4 km south; elev. 2,351 feet/717m; length 3,000 feet/914m; gravel; fuel 100.

Faro is named after the card game. The Cyprus Anvil mining and milling operation began producing lead-silver and zinc concentrates in 1969; operation was shut down in 1982 because of depressed metal price and a poor economic market. A limited waste stripping operation was begun in June 1983. Mothballing of the mine began in the spring of 1985, but the mine was reopened in 1986 by Curragh Resources Inc. The mine ore is trucked to Skagway, AK, via Carmacks and Whitehorse. This mine is one of the biggest lead producers in the world. Five major mineral deposits—Faro, Grum, Vangordo, Dry and Swim—make up the Anvil District. Tours of the mining operation are offered daily in summer; phone 994-2600 for more information.

Faro has a visitor information centre, open June through August. The community also has gas stations, an RV park with dump station, a hotel, motel, restaurants, liquor outlets, groceries, ice, laundromat, sporting goods and gift stores, and postal and banking service (4 days a week).

Campbell Highway Log

(continued)

WL 263.6 (424.3 km) J 103.9 (167.2 km) Johnson Lake Yukon government campground; 15 sites (7 pull-throughs), toilets, water pump, firewood, picnic shelter, boat launch. ▲

The Campbell Highway now follows the valley of the Magundy River. There are several turnouts.

WL 281.4 (452.8 km) J 86.1 (138.5 km) Magundy River airstrip to north; summer use only. Watch for livestock.

WL 283.7 (456.5 km) J 83.8 (134.8 km) Kilometrepost 470. First glimpse of 22-mile-/35-km-long Little Salmon Lake westbound.

WL 294.6 (474.1 km) J 72.9 (117.3 km) East end of Little Salmon Lake. Highway follows north shore.

WL 295.4 (475.4 km) J 72.1 (116 km) Short access road south to Drury Creek Yukon government campground, situated on the creek at the east end of Little Salmon Lake: boat launch, fish filleting table, kitchen shelter, group firepit, 18 campsites, drinking water. Good fishing for northern pike, grayling, whitefish, lake trout 2 to 5 lbs., June 15 through July. ◄▲

WL 295.7 (475.9 km) J 71.8 (115.5 km) Turnout at east end Drury Creek bridge. Yukon government maintenance camp to north.

WL 303.2 (487.9 km) J 64.3 (103.5 km) Turnout overlooking lake.

WL 306.3 (492.9 km) J 61.2 (98.5 km) Slow down for curves. Highway follows lakeshore; no guide rails. Turnouts overlooking Little Salmon Lake next 8.5 miles/13.6 km westbound.

WL 312.4 (502.7 km) J 55.1 (88.7 km) Kilometrepost 510. **Private Aircraft:** Little Salmon airstrip; elev. 2,200 feet/671m; length 1,800 feet/549m; sand and silt.

WL 316.4 (509.2 km) J 51.1 (82.2 km) Steep, narrow, winding road south leads to Yukon government **Little Salmon Lake** campground; boat launch, fishing, 12 campsites, drinking water, picnic tables, outhouses, firepits and kitchen shelter. ◄▲

WL 319.8 (514.6 km) J 47.7 (76.7 km) Bearfeed Creek, a tributary of Little Salmon River, named because of the abundance of bears attracted to the berry patches in this area. Access to creek to north at west end of bridge.

Highway follows Little Salmon River (seen to south) for about 25 miles/40 km westbound.

WL 320.6 (515.9 km) J 46.9 (75.5 km) Begin 4-mile/6.4-km stretch of pavement westbound; watch for gravel patches and potholes. This short stretch of pavement is followed by hard-packed gravel which continues to the junction with the Klondike Loop highway.

FARO ADVERTISERS

Discovery Store, The.........Ph. (403) 994-2470
Rumors Department
    Store ....Ph. (403) 994-2648
SMH Sports......................Ph. (403) 994-3079

SMH Sports

Hunting, Fishing, Camping and Misc. Sporting Supplies

YOUR LOCAL INFORMATION SOURCE

Box 158
Faro, Yukon
Y0B 1K0   (403) 994-3079

RUMORS A Mini Department Store

- Ladies', Men's and Kids' Clothes
- Giftware, Toys and Greeting Cards
- Kitchen and Bathroom Needs
- Souvenirs • Shoes

Box 418, Faro, Yukon Y0B 1K0   Phone (403) 994-2648

THE DISCOVERY STORE

Groceries
Fresh Bakery Products
Fresh Meat
Fresh Produce

Ice
Film
Drug Store Items
FAX Service

— *Your One-Stop Grocery Store* —

P.O. Box 449
Faro, Yukon Y0B 1K0

"DROP IN AND DISCOVER"

Phone (403) 994-2470
FAX (403) 994-3394

CAMPBELL HIGHWAY

WL 335.9 (540.5 km) **J 31.6** (50.8 km) Slow down for hill.

WL 338.7 (545 km) **J 28.8** (46.3 km) Picnic spot on Little Salmon River, which flows into the Yukon River.

WL 339.2 (545.9 km) **J 28.3** (45.5 km) Kilometrepost 554.

WL 342.6 (551.3 km) **J 24.9** (40.1 km) Access road leads 4.9 miles/8 km north to **Frenchman Lake** Yukon government campground (10 sites), 5.6 miles/9 km to photo viewpoint of lake, and 9.3 miles/15 km to Nunatak Yukon government campground (10 sites). Access road narrows and surface deteriorates beyond Frenchman Lake Campground. South end of this 12-mile-/19-km-long lake offers good fishing for trout, pike and grayling.

WL 343 (552 km) **J 24.5** (39.4 km) Kilometrepost 560. Beautiful view coming into Carmacks.

WL 344 (553.6 km) **J 23.5** (37.8 km) Turnoff to south for 0.9-mile/1.4-km gravel road to Little Salmon Indian village near confluence of Little Salmon River and Yukon River. There are some inhabited cabins in the area and some subsistence fishing. Private lands, no trespassing.

WL 350.7 (564.4 km) **J 16.8** (27 km) Turnout with point of interest sign overlooking Eagles Nest Bluff (formerly called Eagle Rock), well-known marker for river travelers. One of the worst steamboat disasters on the Yukon River occurred near here when the paddle-wheeler *Columbian* blew up and burned after a crew member accidentally fired a shot into a cargo of gunpowder.

WL 351.2 (565.2 km) **J 16.3** (26.2 km) View of the Yukon River. At this point Whitehorse is about 160 miles/258 km upstream and Dawson City is about 300 miles/483 km downriver.

WL 355.6 (572.3 km) **J 11.9** (19.2 km) Kilometrepost 580. Northern Canada Power Commission's transmission poles and lines can be seen along highway. Power is transmitted from Aishihik dam site via Whitehorse dam and on to Cyprus Anvil mine and Faro. Orange balls mark lines where they cross river as a hazard to aircraft.

WL 364.5 (586.6 km) **J 3** (4.8 km) **Private Aircraft:** Carmacks airstrip to south; elev. 1,770 feet/539m; length 5,200 feet/1,585m; gravel.

WL 365.2 (587.7 km) **J 2.3** (3.7 km) Tantalus Butte coal mine on hill to north overlooking junction of Campbell and Klondike highways. The butte was named by U.S. Army Lt. Frederick Schwatka in 1883 because of its tantalizing appearance around many bends of the river before reaching it.

The Tantalus coal seam was discovered in 1887 by George Carmack. Yukon Coal Co.'s Tantalus mine was used as the main source of heating material at United Keno Hill mine as well as the communities of Carmacks, Dawson City and Mayo for some 20 years. Cyprus Anvil Mining Corp. reactivated the coal mine in 1969 to feed its one coal-fired kiln used to dry concentrates. In the mid-1970s, Cyprus Anvil began open-pitting the coal mine.

WL 367.5 (591.4 km) **J 0 Junction** with the Klondike Highway (Yukon Highway 2), which leads south 2 miles/3.2 km to **CARMACKS**, 103 miles/166 km to the Alaska Highway, and north 221 miles/355 km to Dawson City. (See the KLONDIKE LOOP section.)

CAUTION: Eastbound travelers watch for ore trucks between here and Faro.

NAHANNI RANGE ROAD

Campbell Highway Junction to Tungsten, NWT
Yukon Highway 10
(See map, page 611)

The Nahanni Range (Tungsten) Road branches off the Campbell Highway 67.9 miles/109.3 km north of Watson Lake and leads 125 miles/201.2 km northeast to the former mining town of Tungsten, NWT.

Nahanni Range Road is maintained by the Yukon government from the Campbell Highway junction to **Milepost CJ 82**. The remaining 43 miles/69 km to Tungsten are unmaintained and not recommended for travel. The road to Mile 82 is gravel surfaced with some small washouts and soft steep shoulders. *NOTE: The Yukon government does not recommend this road for general tourist travel due to lack of services and maintenance.*

Construction of the Nahanni Range Road was begun in 1961 to provide access to the mining property. The road was completed in 1963 with the bridging of the Frances and Hyland rivers.

Nahanni Range Road Log

Distance from Campbell Highway junction (CJ) is followed by distance from Tungsten (T).

CJ 0 T 125 (201.2 km) **Miner's Junction**; formerly known as Cantung Junction.

CJ 5.1 (8.2 km) **T 119.9** (193 km) **Upper Frances River** bridge; good grayling fishing in stream on southeast side.

CJ 7.4 (11.9 km) **T 117.6** (189.2 km) Good grayling fishing at confluence of **Sequence Creek** and **Frances River**.

CJ 11.8 (19 km) **T 113.2** (182.2 km) Queen Creek.

CJ 13.1 (21.1 km) **T 111.9** (180.1 km) King Creek.

CJ 14.2 (22.8 km) **T 110.8** (178.3 km) Road passes between Mount Billings to the north (elev. 6,909 feet/2,106m) and Mount Murray to the south (elev. 7,093 feet/2,162m).

CJ 20.3 (32.7 km) **T 104.7** (168.5 km) Short access road to **Long Lake**, grayling fishing.

CJ 21.5 (34.6 km) **T 103.5** (166.5 km) Long Lake Creek. There are a few private log cabins along here.

CJ 24.1 (38.8 km) **T 100.9** (162.4 km) Dolly Varden Creek.

CJ 28.4 (45.7 km) **T 96.6** (155.4 km) French Creek.

CJ 28.9 (46.5 km) **T 96.1** (154.6 km) Road enters the narrow Hyland River valley between the Logan Mountains.

CJ 32.6 (52.4 km) **T 92.4** (148.7 km) South Bridge Creek.

CJ 33.2 (53.4 km) **T 91.8** (147.7 km) North Bridge Creek.

CJ 38.1 (61.3 km) **T 86.9** (139.8 km) Jackpine Creek.

CJ 40.6 (65.3 km) **T 84.4** (135.8 km) **Spruce Creek**, good glides and broken pools upstream for grayling fishing.

CJ 42.8 (68.9 km) **T 82.2** (132.3 km) Short access road to Hyland River.

CJ 45.8 (73.7 km) **T 79.2** (127.4 km) **Conglomerate Creek**, scenic spot to picnic. Good grayling fishing near small waterfall.

CJ 48 (77.2 km) **T 77** (123.9 km) Mining road to west.

CJ 52.1 (83.8 km) **T 72.9** (117.3 km) South Moose Creek.

CJ 52.2 (84 km) **T 72.8** (117.1 km) Yukon government Nahanni Range Road Campground; 10 sites, kitchen shelter, picnic tables.

CJ 52.5 (84.5 km) **T 72.7** (116.6 km) North Moose Creek.

CJ 62.4 (100.4 km) **T 62.6** (100.7 km) **Flood Creek**, good grayling fishing.

CJ 68.4 (110.1 km) **T 56.6** (91 km) Hyland River bridge; turnout with litter barrel.

CJ 71 (114.2 km) **T 54** (86.9 km) Emergency airstrip to west.

CJ 75.9 (122.1 km) **T 49.1** (79 km) Ostensibility Creek.

CJ 82 (132 km) **T 42.9** (69 km) **Piggott Creek**, good grayling fishing. Outhouse.

NOTE: Yukon government road maintenance ends. Road not recommended for travel beyond this point.

CJ 116.8 (188 km) **T 8.2** (13.2 km) YT–NWT border.

CJ 125 (201.2 km) **T 0 TUNGSTEN** was the company town for one of the richest mines in the world and Canada's only tungsten producer. Originally called Cantung (Canada Tungsten Mining Corp. Ltd.), open-pit mining began here in the early 1960s with the discovery of scheelite in the Flat River area. Scheelite is an ore of tungsten, an oxide used for hardening steel and making white gold. The mine shut down in 1986 and the population of 500 moved out. Only a security staff remains.

Exciting aviation adventure books about flying in the North Country, like Skystruck, *by Herman Lerdahl with Cliff Cernick,* Winging It!, *by Jack Jefford, and* Heroes of the Horizon, *by Gerry Bruder, are available from Alaska Northwest Books™. Call 1-800-343-4567, Ext. 571 to order or request a free catalog of our entire library.*

CANOL ROAD

**Alaska Highway Junction to NWT border
Yukon Highway 6
(See map, page 616)**

The 513-mile-/825-km-long Canol (Canadian Oil) Road was built to provide access to oil fields at Norman Wells, NWT, on the Mackenzie River. Conceived by the U.S. War Dept. to help fuel Alaska and protect it from a Japanese invasion, the road and a 4-inch-diameter pipeline were constructed from Norman Wells, NWT, through Macmillan Pass, past Ross River, to Johnson's Crossing on the Alaska Highway (from there the pipeline carried oil to a refinery at Whitehorse).

Begun in 1942 and completed in 1944, the Canol Project included the road, pipeline, a telephone line, the refinery, airfields, pumping stations, tank farms, wells and camps. Only about 1 million barrels of oil were pumped to Whitehorse before the war ended in 1945 and the $134 million Canol Project was abandoned. (Today, Norman Wells, pop. 757, is a still a major supplier of oil with a pipeline to Zama, AB, built in 1985.)

Since 1958, the Canol Road between Johnson's Crossing on the Alaska Highway and Ross River on the Campbell Highway (referred to as the South Canol Road) and between Ross River and the YT–NWT border (referred to as the North Canol Road) has been rebuilt and is open to summer traffic. The road is maintained to minimum standards.

The 136.8-mile/220.2-km South Canol Road is a narrow winding road which crests the Big Salmon Range and threads its way above Lapie Canyon via a difficult but scenic stretch of road. Construction on the South Canol has replaced many old bridges with culverts, but there are still a few 1-lane wooden bridges. Driving time is about 4 hours one way. Watch for steep hills and bad corners. There are no facilities along the South Canol Road and it is definitely not recommended for large RVs or trailers. Not recommended for any size vehicle in wet weather. Inquiries on current road conditions should be made locally or with the Yukon Dept. of Highways in Whitehorse before driving this road.

The 144.2-mile/232-km North Canol Road is also a narrow, winding road which some motorists have compared to a roller coaster. All bridges on the North Canol are 1-lane, and the road surface can be very slippery when wet. Not recommended during wet weather and not recommended for large RVs or trailers. If mining is under way along the North Canol, watch for large transport trucks.

Our log of the North Canol ends at the YT–NWT border, where vehicles may turn around. Road washouts prohibit travel beyond this point. From the border to Norman Wells it is 230 miles/372 km of unusable road that has been designated the Canol Heritage Trail by the NWT government. Some adventurous travelers have hiked it and report that there are no facilities and river crossings are hazardous, but the route through the Mackenzie Mountains is scenic and there are many relics of the Canol Project.

WARNING: The only facilities on the Canol Road are at Ross River and at Johnson's Crossing on the Alaska Highway.

Emergency medical services: In Ross River, phone (403) 969-2221.

South Canol Road Log

Distance from the junction with the Alaska Highway (J) is followed by distance from the Campbell Highway junction (C).

J 0 C 136.8 (220.2 km) Junction of the Canol Road (Yukon Highway 6) with the Alaska Highway. Food, gas and camping at Johnson's Crossing at the southwest end of the Teslin River bridge, 0.7 mile/1.1 km from Canol Road turnoff.

NOTE: Kilometreposts are up along the South Canol and reflect distance in kilometres from the Alaska Highway.

J 3.9 (6.2 km) C 132.9 (213.8 km) Four-mile Creek. Road begins ascent across the Big Salmon River to the summit (elev. about 4,000 feet/1,219m). Snow possible at summit early October to late spring.

J 6.2 (10 km) C 130.6 (210.1 km) Beaver Creek.

J 13.9 (22.4 km) C 122.9 (197.8 km) Moose Creek.

J 17.2 (27.6 km) C 119.6 (192.4 km) Seventeenmile Creek.

J 19.4 (31.2 km) C 117.4 (188.9 km) Murphy Creek.

J 19.8 (31.8 km) C 117 (188.3 km) Kilometrepost 32. Pelly Mountains can be seen in distance northbound.

J 27 (43.4 km) C 109.8 (176.7 km) One-lane wooden bridge over Evelyn Creek.

J 28.7 (46.2 km) C 108.1 (174 km) Two-lane bridge over Sidney Creek.

J 30.6 (49.2 km) C 106.2 (170.9 km) Access road on right northbound leads to Sidney Lake. Nice little lake and good place to camp.

From here northbound the South Canol follows the Nisutlin River, which is to the east and can be seen from the road the next 30 miles/48 km until the road crosses the Rose River beyond Quiet Lake.

J 30.9 (49.7 km) C 105.9 (170.4 km) Turnout with litter barrel to east.

View of Mount Sheldon from the roller coasterlike North Canol Road.
(Rollo Pool, staff)

J 36.7 (59 km) C 100.1 (161.1 km) Coyote Creek, culverts.

J 39.1 (62.9 km) C 97.7 (157.2 km) Good view of Pelly Mountains ahead. Road crosses Cottonwood Creek.

J 42 (67.6 km) C 94.8 (152.5 km) Access road on right northbound leads to Nisutlin River. Good place to camp with tables and outhouse.

J 47.8 (76.9 km) C 89 (143.2 km) Quiet Lake Yukon government campground; 20 sites, boat launch, picnic tables, kitchen shelter. Watch for steep hills northbound to Quiet Lake. ▲

J 54.7 (88 km) C 82.1 (132.1 km) Lake Creek. Road now follows **Quiet Lake** to west; good fishing for lake trout, northern pike and arctic grayling.

J 56 (90.1 km) C 80.8 (130 km) Turnout with point of interest sign overlooking Quiet Lake. This is the largest of 3 lakes that form the headwaters of the Big Salmon River

CANOL ROAD *Alaska Highway Junction, YT, to NWT Border*

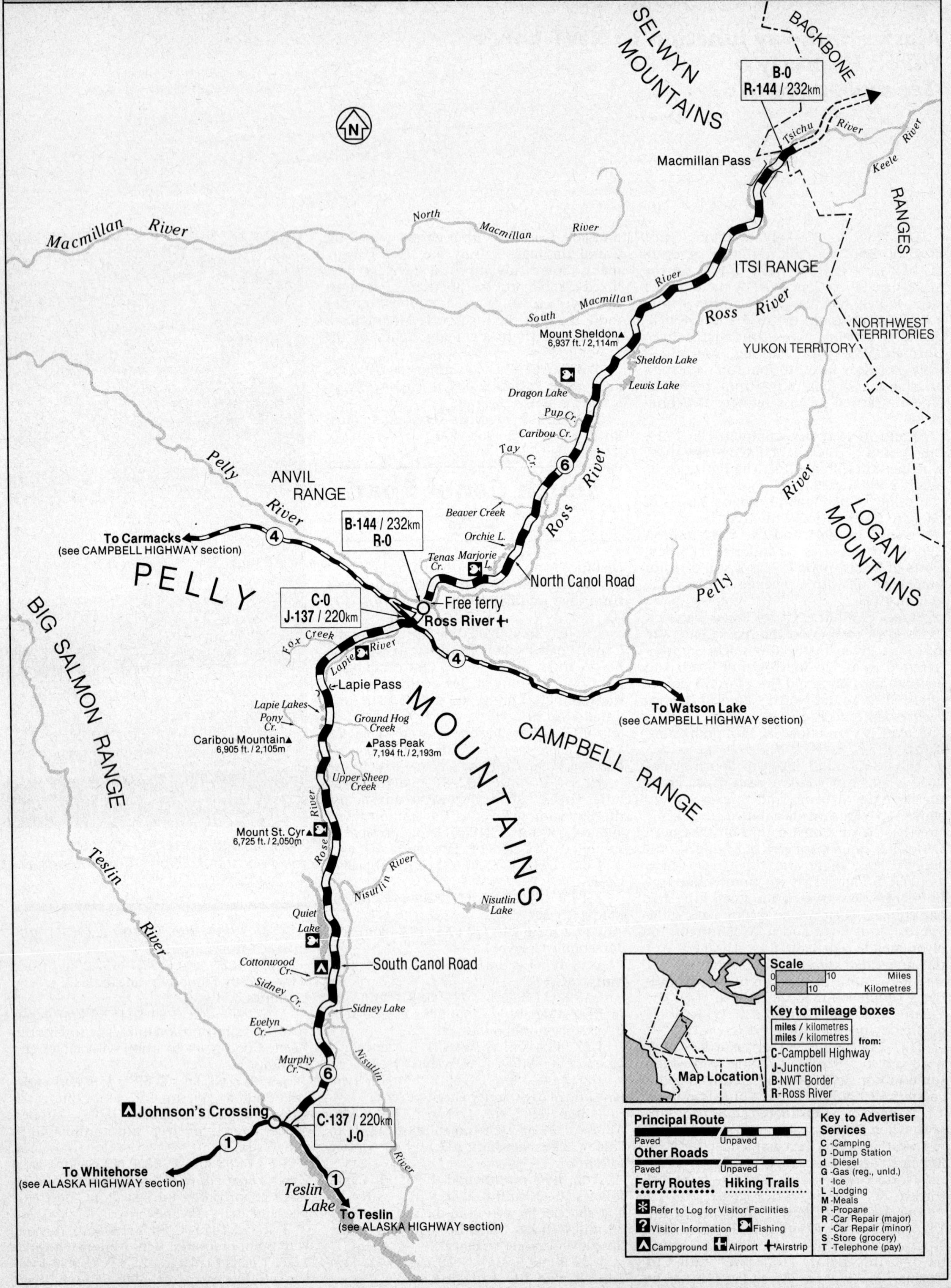

system. The 17-mile-/28-km-long lake was named in 1887 by John McCormack, 1 of 4 miners who prospected the Big Salmon River from its mouth on the Yukon River to its source. Although they did find some gold, the river and lakes have become better known for their good fishing and fine scenery. Until the completion of the South Canol Road in the 1940s, this area was reached mainly by boating and portaging hundreds of miles up the Teslin and Nisutlin rivers.

J 61.2 (98.5 km) **C 75.6** (121.6 km) Turnoff on left northbound (west) for **Quiet Lake**, day-use area with picnic sites, water, boat launch and fishing. Entry point for canoeists on the Big Salmon River.

J 61.5 (99 km) **C 75.3** (121.2 km) Yukon government Quiet Lake maintenance camp on left northbound.

J 62.6 (100.7 km) **C 74.2** (119.4 km) Distance marker indicates Ross River 126 km.

J 63.7 (102.5 km) **C 73.1** (117.6 km) Steep hill and panoramic view of mountains and valley at Kilometrepost 102.

J 65.5 (105.4 km) **C 71.5** (114.7 km) One-lane Bailey bridge across Rose River No. 1. The road now follows the valley of the Rose River into Lapie Pass northbound.

J 70.4 (113.3 km) **C 66.4** (106.8 km) Canol Creek culvert.

J 71.9 (115.7 km) **C 64.9** (104.4 km) Deer Creek.

J 75.7 (121.8 km) **C 61.1** (98.3 km) Gravel Creek culvert.

J 81.1 (130.5 km) **C 55.7** (89.6 km) Road crosses creek (name unknown) in culvert just south of Kilometrepost 130.

J 83.7 (134.7 km) **C 53.1** (85.4 km) Dodge Creek culvert at Kilometrepost 134.

J 87.1 (140.2 km) **C 49.7** (80 km) Rose River No. 2 culvert just south of Kilometrepost 140.

J 89.7 (144.3 km) **C 47.1** (75.8 km) Rose River No. 3 culverts.

J 91.5 (147.2 km) **C 45.3** (72.9 km) Rose River No. 4 culverts.

J 93.8 (151 km) **C 43** (61.2 km) Rose River No. 5 culverts.

J 94.1 (151.4 km) **C 42.7** (68.7 km) Distance marker indicates Ross River 76 km.

J 95.1 (153 km) **C 41.7** (67.1 km) Upper Sheep Creek joins the Rose River here. To the east is Pass Peak (elev. 7,194 feet/2,193m).

J 96.4 (155.1 km) **C 40.4** (65 km) Rose River No. 6.

J 97.1 (156.2 km) **C 39.7** (63.9 km) Rose Lake to east.

J 97.5 (156.5 km) **C 39.3** (63.2 km) Pony Creek. Caribou Mountain (elev. 6,905 feet/2,105m) to west.

J 101.1 (162.7 km) **C 35.7** (57.4 km) Lakes to west are part of Lapie Lakes chain, headwaters of the Lapie River. These features were named by Dr. George M. Dawson of the Geological Survey of Canada in 1887 for Lapie, an Iroquois Indian companion and canoeman of Robert Campbell who was the first to explore the Pelly River area in 1843 for the Hudson's Bay Co.

J 101.2 (162.9 km) **C 35.6** (57.3 km) Ground Hog Creek.

J 102.5 (165 km) **C 34.3** (55.2 km) Access road on left northbound leads west a short distance to Lapie Lakes. Good place to camp.

J 107.4 (172.8 km) **C 29.4** (47.3 km) Lapie River No. 1 culverts. Ponds reported good for grayling fishing.

J 107.5 (173 km) **C 29.3** (47.1 km) Ahead northbound is Barite Mountain (elev. about 6,500 feet/1,981m).

J 110 (177 km) **C 26.8** (43.1 km) Gold Creek.

J 111.4 (179.2 km) **C 25.4** (40.8 km) Bacon Creek.

J 113.4 (182.5 km) **C 23.4** (37.6 km) Boulder Creek.

J 115.6 (186 km) **C 21.2** (34.1 km) Road runs to the east side of Barite Mountain.

J 120.2 (193.4 km) **C 16.6** (26.7 km) Fox Creek culverts.

J 120.7 (194.2 km) **C 16.1** (25.9 km) The road follows the Lapie River Canyon for about the next 11 miles/18 km, climbing to an elevation of about 500 feet/152m above the river. Narrow road, watch for rocks.

J 123.3 (198.4 km) **C 13.5** (21.7 km) Kilometrepost 200. Distance marker indicates Ross River 26 km. Lapie River runs to right side of road northbound.

J 124.7 (200.6 km) **C 12.1** (19.4 km) Glacier Creek.

J 126.3 (203.2 km) **C 10.5** (16.9 km) Turnouts on right side of road northbound overlooking Lapie River Canyon.

J 132.3 (212.9 km) **C 4.5** (7.2 km) Narrow 1-lane bridge over Lapie River No. 2. Point of interest sign on north end of bridge about the Lapie River Canyon. Approximately 100 million years ago, flat horizontal layers of rock were buried several kilometres below the surface of the earth. Movement by rigid plates of the earth's crust subjected the rock to massive compression and strain, and it was deformed into folds. Over millions of years, the rocks rose, exposing the folds in the canyon wall.

J 133 (214 km) **C 3.8** (6.1 km) Erosional features called hoodoos can be seen in the clay banks rising above the road.

J 133.3 (214.5 km) **C 3.5** (5.6 km) Ash layer can be seen in clay bank on right side of road.

J 135.6 (218.2 km) **C 1.2** (1.9 km) Jackfish Lake, below on left northbound, is used for docking floatplanes.

J 136.8 (220 km) **C 0 Junction** of South Canol Road with the Campbell Highway. Approximately straight ahead northbound, across the Campbell Highway, a poorly maintained section of the Canol Road continues to Ross River. Motorists bound for Ross River or the North Canol Road are advised to turn left (west) on the Campbell Highway from the South Canol and drive about 5 miles/8 km to the main Ross River access road (see map).

North Canol Road Log

Distance from Ross River (R) is followed by distance from NWT border (B).

R 0 B 144.2 (232 km) **ROSS RIVER** (see description in the CAMPBELL HIGHWAY section). Yukon government Ross River ferry (free) crosses the Pelly River. Ferry operates from 8 A.M. to noon and 1-5 P.M. daily from late May to mid-October. Those who miss the last ferry crossing of the day may leave their vehicles on the opposite side of the river and use the footbridge to walk into Ross River; vehicles can be brought over in the morning.

R 0.4 (0.6 km) **B 143.8** (231.4 km) Stockpile to west is barite from the Yukon Barite Mine.

R 0.6 (1 km) **B 143.6** (231.1 km) Road to east leads to original site of Ross River and Indian village.

R 0.9 (1.4 km) **B 143.3** (230.6 km) Second access road east to old Ross River and Indian village. Canol Road follows the Ross River.

R 2.1 (3.4 km) **B 142.1** (228.7 km) *CAUTION: Slide area, watch for falling rocks.*

R 3.9 (6.2 km) **B 140.3** (225.8 km) Kilometrepost 236. Kilometreposts on the North Canol reflect distance from the Alaska Highway.

R 4.7 (7.6 km) **B 139.5** (224.5 km) Raspberry patch. Good pickings.

R 6.8 (10.9 km) **B 137.4** (221.1 km) One-lane bridge over Tenas Creek.

R 10.3 (16.5 km) **B 133.9** (215.5 km) Kilometrepost 246.

R 10.6 (17 km) **B 133.6** (215 km) Gravel pit to west.

R 15.5 (24.9 km) **B 128.7** (207.1 km) Kilometrepost 254.

R 17 (27.3 km) **B 127.2** (204.7 km) Deep Creek.

R 20.9 (33.6 km) **B 123.3** (198.4 km) **Marjorie Creek**. Locals report good grayling fishing.

R 21 (33.8 km) **B 123.2** (198.2 km) Access road to west leads to Marjorie Lake. Access road not recommended for large RVs.

R 21.7 (34.9 km) **B 122.5** (197.1 km) Marjorie Lake to west.

R 27 (43.4 km) **B 117.2** (188.6 km) Kilometrepost 272. Unnamed lake to east.

R 28.1 (45.2 km) **B 116.1** (186.8 km) Boat launch on Orchie Lake to west.

R 29.8 (48 km) **B 114.4** (184.1 km) Distance marker indicates NWT border 195 km, Ross River 50 km.

R 30.9 (49.7 km) **B 113.3** (182.3 km) Kilometrepost 278.

R 31.9 (51.3 km) **B 112.3** (180.7 km) One-lane bridge over Gravel Creek. The next 15 miles/24 km are excellent moose country.

R 33.4 (53.7 km) **B 110.8** (178.3 km) One-lane bridge over Flat Creek.

R 34.6 (55.7 km) **B 109.6** (176.3 km) Kilometrepost 284.

R 37 (59.5 km) **B 107.2** (172.5 km) One-lane bridge over Beaver Creek.

R 40.7 (65.5 km) **B 103.5** (166.5 km) Kilometrepost 294.

R 41.8 (67.2 km) **B 102.4** (164.8 km) One-lane bridge over 180 Mile Creek.

R 43.9 (70.6 km) **B 100.3** (161.4 km) One-lane bridge over Tay Creek.

R 44.4 (71.4 km) **B 99.8** (160.6 km) Kilometrepost 300.

R 46.3 (74.5 km) **B 97.9** (157.5 km) One-lane bridge over Blue Creek.

R 48.1 (77.4 km) **B 96.1** (154.6 km) Kilometrepost 306. Flood Creek culvert.

R 57.6 (92.7 km) **B 86.6** (139.3 km) Clifford's Slough to the east.

R 58.6 (94.3 km) **B 85.6** (137.7 km) Steep hill to 1-lane bridge over Caribou Creek.

R 61.1 (98.3 km) **B 83.1** (133.7 km) Distance marker indicates NWT border 145 km, Ross River 100 km.

R 61.8 (99.4 km) **B 82.4** (132.6 km) One-lane bridge over Pup Creek.

R 62.8 (101 km) **B 81.4** (131 km) Kilometrepost 330.

R 64.8 (104.3 km) **B 79.4** (127.7 km) Turnout to west. Steep hill.

R 65.1 (104.7 km) **B 79.1** (127.3 km) Turnout to **Dragon Lake**; overnight parking, litter barrels. Locals report that early spring is an excellent time for pike and trout in the inlet. Rock hounds check roadsides and borrow pits for colourful chert, which can be worked into jewelry.

R 65.4 (105.2 km) **B 78.8** (126.8 km) Kilometrepost 334. Large, level, gravel turnout to west overlooking Dragon Lake; boat launch.

R 68.9 (110.8 km) **B 75.3** (121.2 km) Kilometrepost 340.

R 69.6 (112 km) **B 74.6** (120 km) Wreckage of Twin Pioneer aircraft to west. WWII remnants can be found in this area.

R 69.9 (112.5 km) **B 74.3** (119.5 km) Road to Twin Creek.

R 70.8 (113.9 km) **B 73.4** (118.1 km) Airstrip.

R 71 (114.2 km) **B 73.2** (117.8 km) One-lane bridge over Twin Creek No. 1. Yukon government maintenance camp.

R 71.1 (114.4 km) **B 73.1** (117.6 km) One-lane bridge over Twin Creek No. 2. Good views of Mount Sheldon.

R 75.1 (120.8 km) **B 69.1** (111.2 km) Kilometrepost 350. Mount Sheldon ahead; a very beautiful and distinguishable feature on the Canol Road (elev. 6,937 feet/2,114m). Located 3 miles/4.8 km north of Sheldon Lake, it was named for Charles Sheldon, a well-known sheep hunter and naturalist who came to the area to collect Stone sheep specimens for the Chicago Natural History Museum in 1905.

In 1900, Poole Field and Clement Lewis, who were fans of writer Rudyard Kipling, named this peak Kipling Mountain and the lake at its base Rudyard. In 1907, Joseph Keele of the Geological Survey of Canada renamed them after Charles Sheldon.

R 76.4 (123 km) **B 67.8** (109.1 km) Kilometrepost 352. Of the 3-lake chain, Sheldon Lake is farthest north, then Field Lake and Lewis Lake, which is just visible from here. Lewis Lake is closest to the confluence of the Ross and Prevost rivers.

Field Lake and Lewis Lake were named in 1907 by Joseph Keele of the Geological Survey of Canada after Poole Field and Clement Lewis. The 2 partners, who had prospected this country, ran a trading post called Nahanni House at the mouth of the Ross River in 1905.

R 77.6 (124.9 km) **B 66.6** (107.2 km) Kilometrepost 354. One-lane bridge over Riddell Creek. Tip of Mount Riddell (elev. 6,101 feet/1,859m) can be seen to the west.

R 78.8 (126.8 km) **B 65.4** (105.2 km) View of Sheldon Lake ahead, Field Lake to right northbound.

R 79.8 (128.4 km) **B 64.4** (103.6 km) Access road east to Sheldon Lake.

R 82.7 (133.1 km) **B 61.5** (99 km) One-lane bridge over Sheldon Creek. Road climbs, leaving Ross River valley and entering Macmillan Valley northbound.

R 89.3 (143.7 km) **B 54.9** (88.3 km) Height of land before starting descent northbound into South Macmillan River system.

R 89.7 (144.3 km) **B 54.5** (87.7 km) Steep hill. Road may wash out during heavy rains. Deep ditches along roadside help channel water.

R 91.4 (147.1 km) **B 52.8** (85 km) One-lane bridge over Moose Creek.

R 91.6 (147.4 km) **B 52.6** (84.6 km) **Milepost 230**.

R 92.3 (148.5 km) **B 51.9** (83.5 km) Kilometrepost 378. Peaks of the Itsi Range ahead. Rugged, spectacular scenery northbound.

R 92.7 (149.1 km) **B 51.5** (82.9 km) Distance marker indicates NWT border 95 km, Ross River 150 km.

R 93.5 (150.4 km) **B 50.7** (81.6 km) Kilometrepost 380.

R 93.8 (151 km) **B 50.4** (81.1 km) First of several WWII vehicle dumps to west. To the east is a wannigan, or skid shack, used as living quarters by Canol Road workers during construction of the road. These small buildings were strategically located along the route so the workers had a place to eat and sleep at night because it was too far to return to base camp.

R 94 (151.3 km) **B 50.2** (80.8 km) To east are remains of a maintenance depot where heavy equipment was repaired. Concrete foundations to west. First glimpse of the South Macmillan River northbound.

R 94.7 (152.4 km) **B 49.5** (79.6 km) Kilometrepost 382. Another Canol project equipment dump to explore. Watch ditches for old pieces of pipeline.

R 97.8 (157.4 km) **B 46.4** (74.6 km) One-lane bridge over Boulder Creek.

R 98.4 (158.3 km) **B 45.8** (73.7 km) Kilometrepost 388.

R 98.5 (158.5 km) **B 45.7** (73.5 km) Access road west to South Macmillan River where boats can be launched. Locals advise launching boats here rather than from the bridge at **Milepost R 113.6** which washes out periodically, leaving dangerous debris in the river.

R 100.8 (162.2 km) **B 43.4** (69.8 km) Kilometrepost 392.

R 101 (162.5 km) **B 43.2** (69.5 km) View of Itsi Range ahead northbound. Itsi is said to be an Indian word meaning "wind" and was first given as a name to Itsi Lakes, headwaters of the Ross River. The road dips down and crosses an unnamed creek.

R 102.1 (164.3 km) **B 42.1** (67.7 km) Milepost 240. Kilometrepost 394.

R 104.5 (168.2 km) **B 39.7** (63.9 km) Kilometrepost 398. View of the South Macmillan River from here.

R 105.3 (169.4 km) **B 38.9** (62.6 km) View of Selwyn Mountains, named in 1901 by Joseph Keele of the Geological Survey of Canada for Dr. Alfred Richard Selwyn (1824–1902), a distinguished geologist in England. Dr. Selwyn later became director of the Geological Survey of Australia and then director of the Geological Survey of Canada from 1869 until his retirement in 1895.

R 108.2 (174 km) **B 36** (57.9 km) Kilometrepost 404.

R 111 (178.6 km) **B 33.2** (53.4 km) One-lane bridge over Itsi Creek.

R 112.2 (180.5 km) **B 32** (51.5 km) One-lane bridge over Wagon Creek.

R 113.1 (182 km) **B 31.1** (50 km) Kilometrepost 412.

R 113.6 (182.8 km) **B 30.6** (49.2 km) Turnout to east on South Macmillan River. Good place for a picnic but not recommended as a boat launch. One-lane Bailey bridge over South Macmillan River No. 1.

Robert Campbell, a Hudson's Bay Co. explorer on a journey down the Pelly River in 1843, named this major tributary of the Pelly after Chief Factor James McMillan, who had sponsored Campbell's employment with the company.

R 114.3 (183.9 km) **B 29.9** (48.1 km) Kilometrepost 414.

R 115.1 (185.2 km) **B 29.1** (46.8 km) Access road on left northbound leads about 7 miles/11 km to Yukon Barite Mine. Barite is a soft mineral that requires only crushing and bagging before being shipped over the Dempster Highway to the Beaufort Sea oil and gas wells, where it is used as a lubricant known as drilling mud.

R 115.6 (186 km) **B 28.6** (46 km) Kilometrepost 416.

R 117.2 (188.6 km) **B 27** (43.4 km) Access road on right northbound to gravel pit.

R 118.8 (191.2 km) **B 25.4** (40.8 km) Dept. of Public Works maintenance camp; status unknown.

R 118.9 (191.3 km) **B 25.3** (40.7 km) One-lane bridge over Jeff Creek.

R 121.2 (195 km) **B 23** (37 km) One-lane bridge over Hess Creek. Bears in area.

R 123 (197.9 km) **B 21.2** (34.1 km) Kilometrepost 428.

R 123.2 (198.3 km) **B 21** (33.8 km) Gravel turnout on left northbound with RCMP trailer. Distance marker indicates NWT border 45 km, Ross River 200 km. One-lane bridge over Dewhurst Creek.

R 126.6 (203.7 km) **B 17.6** (28.3 km) Kilometrepost 434.

R 127.5 (205.2 km) **B 16.7** (26.9 km) Entering Macmillan Pass. At "Mac Pass," the road climbs to elevations above 4,480 feet/1,366m.

R 129.4 (208.2 km) **B 14.8** (23.8 km) One-lane bridge over Macmillan River No. 2.

R 129.5 (208.4 km) **B 14.7** (23.6 km) Abandoned Army vehicles from the Canol Project on left northbound.

R 129.6 (208.6 km) **B 14.6** (23.5 km) Abandoned Army vehicles from the Canol Project on right northbound.

R 131.5 (211.6 km) **B 12.7** (20.4 km) Kilometrepost 442.

R 133.6 (215 km) **B 10.6** (17 km) To the west is Cordilleran Engineering camp, managers of the mining development of Ogilvie Joint Venture's Jason Project. The Jason deposit is a zinc, lead, silver, barite property. The deposit's size is still uncertain.

One-lane bridge over Sekie Creek No. 1.

R 133.9 (215.5 km) **B 10.3** (16.6 km) Kilometrepost 446.

R 134.4 (216.3 km) **B 9.8** (15.8 km) Fuel tanks on left northbound.

R 136.3 (219.3 km) **B 7.9** (12.7 km) Sekie Creek No. 2 culvert.

R 136.4 (219.5 km) **B 7.8** (12.5 km) Access to Macmillan airstrip on left northbound. Access road to right to Hudson Bay Mining & Smelting's Tom lead–zinc mineral claims. The Tom is a stratabound silver–lead–zinc deposit and the size is yet to be determined. At one time it was considered to be 9 million tons of 16 percent combined lead–zinc.

R 137.6 (221.4 km) **B 6.6** (10.6 km) Kilometrepost 452.

R 137.7 (221.6 km) **B 6.5** (10.5 km) One-lane bridge over Macmillan River No. 3.

R 141.8 (228.2 km) **B 2.4** (3.8 km) One-lane bridge over Macmillan River No. 4.

R 142.9 (230 km) **B 1.3** (2.1 km) One-lane bridge over Macmillan River No. 5.

R 144.1 (231.9 km) **B 0.1** (0.2 km) One-lane bridge over Macmillan River No. 6.

R 144.2 (232 km) **B 0** YT–NWT border. Sign cautions motorists to proceed at their own risk. The road is not maintained and bridges are not safe beyond this point. Vehicles turn around here.

Ahead is the Tsichu River valley and the Selwyn Mountains. The abandoned North Canol Road continues another 230 miles/372 km from the YT–NWT border to Norman Wells, NWT. Designated the Canol Heritage Trail, it is suitable for hiking, bicycles or motorcycles. There are some river crossings. It is prime grizzly and caribou habitat with exceptional mountain scenery.

DEMPSTER HIGHWAY

Milepost D 25 Klondike Highway 2 to Inuvik, NWT
Yukon Highway 5, NWT Highway 8
(See map, page 620)

The Dempster Highway begins 25 miles/40.2 km east of Dawson City, YT, at its junction with Klondike Highway 2, and leads 460.8 miles/741.5 km northeast to Inuvik, NWT.

The highway is named for Inspector W.J.D. Dempster. Dempster was sent to look for a missing RCMP patrol that had set out for Dawson City by dog team from Fort McPherson in December of 1910. He discovered their frozen bodies on March 22, 1911, only 26 miles from where they had started. Lack of knowledge of the trail, coupled with too few rations, had doomed the 4-man patrol. The "lost patrol" is buried at Fort McPherson.

Construction of the Dempster Highway began in 1959, under the Road to Resources program, and was completed in 1978. A 5-year major reconstruction and surfacing program on the highway concluded in 1988, although freezing weather and heavy truck traffic may erode both road base and surfacing in areas. Calcium chloride is used in some areas to reduce dust and as a bonding agent; wash your vehicle as soon as practical.

The Dempster is a gravel road. There are stretches of clay surface that can be slippery in wet weather. Summer driving conditions on the Dempster vary depending on weather and maintenance. Generally, road conditions range from fair to excellent, with highway speeds attainable on some sections.

Facilities are still few and far between on the Dempster. Full auto services are available at Klondike River Lodge at the Dempster Highway turnoff on Klondike Highway 2. Gas, food and lodging and car repair are also available at Eagle Plains Hotel, located at about the halfway point on the Dempster. Gas is also available in Fort McPherson. Gas up whenever possible.

The Dempster is open year-round. The highway is fairly well-traveled in summer: a driver may not see another car for an hour, and then pass 4 cars in a row. Locals say the highway is smoother and easier to drive in winter, but precautions should be taken against cold weather, high winds and poor visibility; check road conditions before proceeding in winter. DRIVE WITH YOUR HEADLIGHTS ON!

The Dempster Highway also has some magnificent scenery and good opportunities to see wildlife. Watch for moose, foxes, bear, wolves and a variety of birds, including bald and golden eagles, gryfalcons, peregrine falcons, ptarmigan, grouse and owls. The Porcupine caribou herd migrates through the area in October and from March to early April on their way to Alaska.

There are 2 ferry crossings on the Dempster, at **Milepost J 341.7** (Peel River crossing) and **J 384.8** (Arctic Red River crossing). Free government ferry service is available 15 hours a day (9 A.M. to 1 A.M. Northwest Territories time, 8 A.M. to midnight Yukon time) during summer (from about June to mid-October). Cross by ice bridge in winter.

General information on Northwest Territories is available by calling the Arctic Hotline at 1-800-661-0788. For recorded messages on road and weather conditions phone 1-800-661-0750 or 0752. Also stop by the Western Arctic Visitor Information Centre if you are in Dawson City. Located in the B.Y.N. Bldg. on Front Street, across from the Yukon Visitor Centre, the Western Arctic Visitor Centre has information on Northwest Territories and the Dempster Highway. It is open 9 A.M. to 9 P.M., June to September.

The Dempster Highway follows the Ogilvie River through the mountains. (Rollo Pool, staff)

Dempster Highway Log

YUKON HIGHWAY 5
Driving distance is measured in miles. The kilometre figure on the Yukon portion of the highway reflects the physical kilometreposts and is not necessarily an accurate metric conversion of the mileage figure.
Distance from junction with Klondike Highway 2 (J) is followed by distance from Inuvik (I).

J 0 I 460.8 (741.5 km) Junction of Yukon Highways 2 and 5, 25 miles/40.2 km east of Dawson City, also known as Dempster Corner. Lodge with food, gas, lodging, camping and tire repairs; open all year. Vehicle storage.

Klondike River Lodge. See display ad this section.

J 0.1 (0.2 km) **I 460.7** (741.4 km) Dempster Highway monument with information panels.

J 0.2 (0.3 km) **I 460.6** (741.2 km) One-lane wood-planked bridge over Klondike River. The road follows the wooded (spruce and poplar) North Klondike River valley.

J 0.9 (1.4 km) **I 459.9** (740.1 km)

---

25 Miles South of Dawson City At Dempster Corner
MILE 0 DEMPSTER HIGHWAY

Esso **Klondike River Lodge** *Good Sam Club*

(This Business For Sale) (403) 993-6892
Open All Year 7 a.m. to Midnight
Reasonable Prices
Restaurant • Motel • Grocery Store
Gas & Diesel • Propane • Towing
Tires & Repairs • Licensed Mechanic
RV Parking • Dump Station • Car Wash

DEMPSTER HIGHWAY *Klondike Highway Junction to Inuvik, NWT*

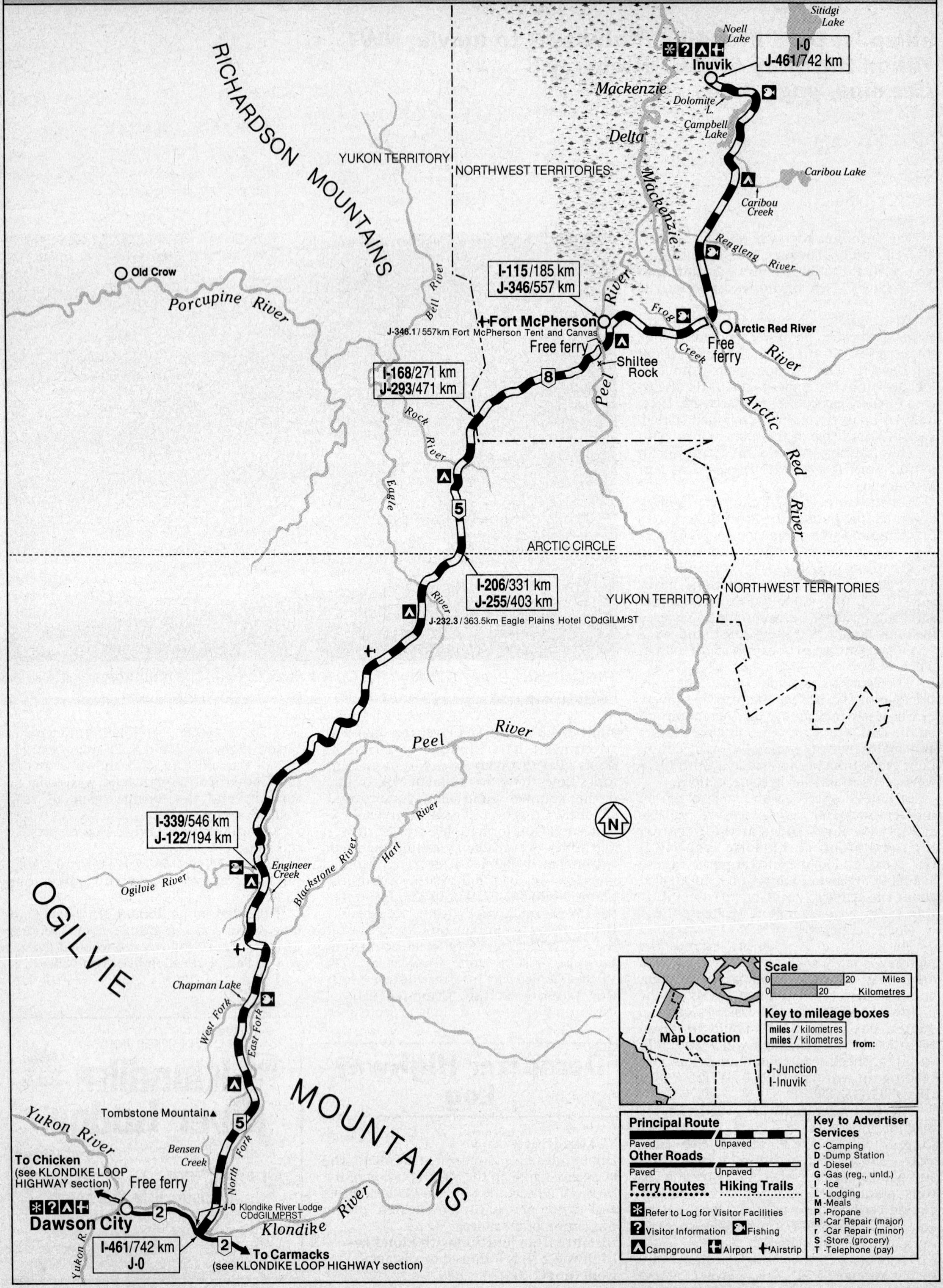

Distance marker shows Eagle Plains 363 km (226 miles), Inuvik 735 km.

J 15.4 (24.5 km) I 445.4 (716.8 km) Glacier Creek.

J 18.1 (29 km) I 442.7 (712.4 km) Bensen Creek.

J 25.6 (41 km) I 435.2 (700.4 km) Pea Soup Creek.

J 29.8 (48 km) I 431 (693.6 km) Scout Car Creek.

J 31.7 (51 km) I 429.1 (690.6 km) Wolf Creek. Trapper's cabin beside creek.

J 34.7 (55.8 km) I 426.1 (685.7 km) Highway follows North Fork Klondike River.

J 36.6 (58.9 km) I 424.2 (682.7 km) Grizzly Creek. Mount Robert Service to right northbound.

J 39.6 (63.7 km) I 421.1 (677.8 km) Mike and Art Creek.

J 40.9 (65.8 km) I 419.9 (675.7 km) Klondike Camp Yukon government highway maintenance station. No services.

J 41.8 (67.3 km) I 419 (674.3 km) First crossing of the North Fork Klondike River. The highway now moves above tree line and on to tundra northbound. At an elevation of approximately 4,003 feet/1,220m, you'll cross the watershed between the Yukon and Mackenzie basins.

J 43 (69.2 km) I 417.8 (672.4 km) Spectacular first view of Tombstone Range northbound.

J 44.9 (72.2 km) I 415.9 (669.3 km) Tombstone Mountain Yukon government campground with 22 sites, shelter, fireplaces, water, tables, pit toilets. Interpretive center located at campground during July and August offers handouts with area information and conducts campfire talks and nature walks. Good hiking trail begins past the outhouses and leads toward the headwaters of the North Fork Klondike River. ▲

J 45.7 (73.5 km) I 415.1 (668 km) Good views of North Fork Pass and river. To the southwest is Tombstone Mountain; to the north is the East Fork Blackstone River valley; on each side are the Ogilvie Mountains, which rise to elevations of 6,890 feet/2,100m.

J 46.5 (74.8 km) I 414.3 (666.7 km) Turnout.

J 48.4 (77.9 km) I 412.4 (663.7 km) Blackstone River culvert.

J 51 (82 km) I 409.8 (659.5 km) Descent to the Blackstone River. Good bird-watching area (eagles, swallows, ravens, robins, jaegers, ptarmigan, short-eared owls).

J 54.2 (87.2 km) I 406.6 (654.3 km) First crossing of East Fork Blackstone River.

J 63.4 (102 km) I 397.4 (639.5 km) Distance marker shows Eagle Plains 261 km (162 miles), Inuvik 633 km, Dawson 142 km (88 miles), Whitehorse 600 km (373 miles).

J 72.3 (116.3 km) I 388.5 (625.2 km) First crossing of West Fork Blackstone River. Good fishing for grayling a short distance downstream where the west and east forks of the Blackstone join to form the **Blackstone River** which the road now follows.

J 72.7 (117 km) I 388.1 (624.5 km) Commemorative road sign about sled dog patrols of the Royal North–West Mounted Police. Also a sign: Watch for horses. View over Chapman Lake, one of the few lakes close to the highway that is large enough to permit floatplane operations.

J 77.9 (125.4 km) I 382.9 (616.2 km) **Private Aircraft:** Government airstrip (road is part of the strip); elev. 3,100 feet/945m; length, 3,000 feet/914m.

J 96 (154.5 km) I 364.8 (587.1 km) Northbound, highway passes through barren gray hills of Windy Pass.

J 106 (169.7 km) I 354.8 (571 km) Creek culvert. Sulfurous smell is from the creek, which is red from iron oxide. Watch for interesting geological features in hills along road.

J 108.1 (173 km) I 352.7 (567.6 km) Views of red-colored Engineer Creek and also erosion pillars and red rock (iron oxide) of nearby hills between here and Kilometrepost 182.

J 121.7 (194 km) I 339.1 (545.7 km) **Engineer Creek** Yukon government campground; 23 sites, fireplaces, water, tables, pit toilets. Grayling fishing.

J 122.9 (195.7 km) I 337.9 (543.8 km) The 360-foot/110-m Jeckell Bridge spans the Ogilvie River here. Built by the Canadian Armed Forces Engineers as a training exercise, it is named in honour of Allan Jeckell, controller of the Yukon from 1932 to 1946.

The Ogilvie River and Ogilvie Mountains were named in honour of William Ogilvie, a highly respected Dominion land surveyor and commissioner of the Yukon during the Klondike gold rush.

J 123 (195.8 km) I 337.8 (543.6 km) Ogilvie grader station, Yukon government maintenance camp is on north side of the river. Emergency-only gas and minor repairs may be available (not guaranteed).

For the next 25 miles/40 km the highway follows the narrow valley of the Ogilvie River. For the first 12 miles/20 km talus slopes edge the road and game trails are evident along their precipitous sides. Dall sheep are sometimes seen at mineral licks.

J 124.3 (197.7 km) I 336.5 (541.5 km) View of castlelike outcroppings of rock on mountaintops to north.

J 131.9 (209.5 km) I 328.9 (529.3 km) Between here and Kilometrepost 216, watch for bird nests in the shale embankments along the highway and unusual rock outcroppings and erosion pillars in surrounding hills. Highway crosses rolling plateau country near Kilometrepost 218.

J 140.7 (223 km) I 320.1 (515.1 km) Good grayling fishing in **Ogilvie River**. Elephant Rock may be viewed from right side of road northbound. Fascinating mountain of broken rock and shale near Kilometrepost 224.

J 149.1 (235.8 km) I 311.7 (501.6 km) Ogilvie airstrip, status unknown.

J 154.4 (244 km) I 306.4 (493.1 km) Highway climbs above and away from the Ogilvie River following a high ridge to the Eagle Plains plateau. One of the few unglaciated areas in Canada, this country is shaped by wind and water erosion rather than by the grinding action of ice. Views of Mount Cronkhite and Mount McCullum to the east.

Seismic lines next 62 miles/100 km provide hiking paths across the tundra. This was the major area of oil and gas exploration activity for which the road was originally built. In season, fields of cotton grass and varieties of tundra plants make good photographic subjects. The road continues to follow a high ridge (elev. 1,969 feet/600m) with broad sweeps and easy grades to give the traveler the feeling of being on top of the world.

J 171.7 (270.6 km) I 289.1 (465.2 km) Highway begins descent northbound and crosses fabulous high rolling country above tree line.

J 175.6 (276.5 km) I 285.2 (459 km) Gravel pit full of old oil drums.

J 204.5 (321 km) I 256.3 (412.5 km) Road widens to become part of an airstrip.

J 232.3 (363.5 km) I 228.5 (367.7 km) **Mile 231.** Eagle Plains Hotel (phone 979-4187); food, gas, diesel and lodging. Open year-round.

Mile 231. Eagle Plains Hotel. Located midway on the Dempster, this year-round facility is an oasis in the wilderness. Modern hotel rooms, plus restaurant and lounge. Full camper services including electrical hook-ups, laundry, store, dump station, minor repairs, tires and road and area information. Check out our historical photos. See display ad this section. [ADVERTISEMENT] ▲

J 237.7 (372.5 km) I 223.1 (359 km) Short side road to picnic site with information sign about Albert Johnson, "The Mad Trapper of Rat River." Something of a mystery man, Johnson wounded a constable who had come to question him about a trapline dispute. The ensuing manhunt became famous in the North, as Johnson eluded Mounties for 48 days during the winter of 1931–32. Johnson was killed in a shoot-out on Feb. 17, 1932. He was buried at Aklavik, a community located 36 miles/58 km by air west of Inuvik.

Dick North, author of 2 books on Johnson (and also author of *The Lost Patrol*), was quoted in the *New York Times* (June 3, 1990) as being 95 percent certain that Johnson, whose true identity has not been known, was a Norwegian–American bank robber named Johnson. Dick North is currently curator of the Jack London exhibit in Dawson City.

J 237.8 (372.7 km) I 223 (358.9 km) Eagle River bridge. Like the Ogilvie bridge, it was built by the Dept. of National Defence as a training exercise. In contrast to the other rivers seen from the Dempster, the Eagle is a more sluggish, silt-laden stream with unstable banks. Canoeists leave here bound for Alaska via the Porcupine and Yukon rivers.

J 242.7 (381.5 km) I 218.1 (351 km) Views of the Richardson Mountains (elev. 3,937 feet/1,200m) ahead. Named for Sir John Richardson, surgeon and naturalist on both of Sir John Franklin's overland expeditions to the Arctic Ocean. These mountains are distinctively smooth and rounded by erosion.

J 245 (385.2 km) I 215.8 (347.3 km) **Private Aircraft:** emergency airstrip; elev. 2,365 feet/721m; length, 2,500 feet/762m; gravel. Used regularly by aircraft hauling freight to Old Crow, a Kutchin Indian settlement (pop. 267) on the Porcupine River and Yukon's most northerly community.

J 255.3 (403.3 km) I 205.5 (330.7 km) Turnout. In summer, 9 A.M. to 5 P.M. weekdays, travelers may receive an Arctic Circle Crossing certificate here. Sign marks Arctic Circle crossing, 66°33'N. The road now

Eagle Plains Hotel
MIDWAY ON THE DEMPSTER
MILE 231
Explore the Land of Legend

MODERN HOTEL • RESTAURANT • LOUNGE • GIFT SHOP
CAMPGROUND • LAUNDRY • SHOWERS
SERVICE STATION
REGULAR • UNLEADED • DIESEL
Bag Service 2735, Whitehorse, Yukon Y1A 3V5
Phone (403) 979-4187

DEMPSTER HIGHWAY

crosses arctic tundra on an elevated berm beside the Richardson Mountains with sweeping views in all directions.

J 280.6 (447 km) **I 180.2** (290 km) Cornwall River Yukon government campground; 20 sites, tables, kitchen shelter, water. ▲

J 283.3 (452 km) **I 177.5** (285.6 km) Turnout. Highway winds toward the Richardson Mountains, crossing them at George's Gap near the YT–NWT border. Good hiking area and excellent photographic possibilities.

J 291.7 (469 km) **I 169.1** (272.1 km) Turnout; good overnight spot for self-contained vehicles.

J 292.2 (470.3 km) **I 168.6** (271.3 km) Plaque about Wright Pass, named for Al Wright, a highway engineer with Public Works Canada who was responsible for the routing of the Dempster Highway.

J 292.7 (471 km) **I 168.1** (270.5 km) YT–NWT border. Historical marker. Continental Divide in the Richardson Mountains: west of here, water flows to the Pacific Ocean; east of here, water flows to the Arctic Ocean.

TIME ZONE CHANGE: Yukon Territory observes Pacific standard time; Northwest Territories is on Mountain time. See Time Zones in GENERAL INFORMATION section for details.

NWT HIGHWAY 8

Kilometreposts northbound indicate distance from YT–NWT border and are indicated at intervals in our log.

J 301.4 (485 km) **I 159.4** (256.5 km) Kilometrepost 14. **James Creek;** good fishing. Highway maintenance camp. Good spot to park overnight.

J 307.4 (494.7 km) **I 153.4** (246.9 km) Wright Pass Summit. From here northbound, the Dempster Highway descends some 2,300 feet/853m to the Peel River crossing, 32 miles/51 km away.

J 320.2 (515.3 km) **I 140.6** (226.3 km) Kilometrepost 44. Side road leads down to Midway Lake. The Midway Lake Music Festival is staged here, July 9-11, 1992.

J 323.4 (520.4 km) **I 137.4** (221.1 km) View of Peel River valley and Fort McPherson to north. Litter barrels.

J 331 (532.7 km) **I 129.8** (208.9 km) **Private Aircraft:** Highway widens to form Midway airstrip; length, 3,000 feet/914m.

J 336.5 (541.5 km) **I 124.3** (200 km) Kilometrepost 70. Highway begins descent northbound to Peel River.

J 339.1 (545.7 km) **I 121.7** (195.8 km) Peel River crossing, called locally Eightmile because it is situated 8 miles/12.8 km south of Fort McPherson. Free government ferry service 15 hours a day during summer (from about early or mid-June to mid-October). Double-ended cable ferry: Drive on, drive off. Light vehicles cross by ice bridge in late November; heavier vehicles cross as ice thickens. *No crossing possible during freezeup or breakup.* Phone (toll free) 1-800-661-0752 for information on ferry crossings, road conditions and weather.

The level of the Peel River changes rapidly in spring and summer in response to meltwater from the mountains and ice jams on the Mackenzie River. The alluvial flood plain is covered by muskeg on the flats and scrubby alder and stunted black spruce on the valley sides.

Indians from Fort McPherson have summer tent camps on the Peel River. They net whitefish and sheefish (inconnu) then dry them on racks or in smokehouses for the winter.

About 4 miles/6.4 km south upstream is a trail leading to Shiltee Rock which gives excellent views of the Peel River and the southern end of the Mackenzie.

J 340.1 (547.3 km) **I 120.7** (194.2 km) Nutuiluie territorial campground with 20 sites. (Campground name is from the Gwich'in term *Noo-til-ee,* meaning "fast flowing waters." Information centre open daily June to September. Camping permits, potable water, firewood, pit toilets available. ▲

J 341.4 (549.4 km) **I 119.4** (192.2 km) Kilometrepost 78.

J 344.7 (554.7 km) **I 116.1** (186.8 km) Access road right to Fort McPherson airport.

J 346.1 (557 km) **I 114.7** (184.6 km) Side road on left to Fort McPherson (description follows).

Fort McPherson

Located on a flat-topped hill about 100 feet/30m above the Peel River, 24 miles/38 km from its junction with the Mackenzie River; 100 miles/160 km southwest of Aklavik by boat along Peel Channel, 31 miles/50 km directly east of the Richardson Mountains. **Population:** 632. **Radio:** CBC 680.

Private Aircraft: Fort McPherson airstrip; 67°24'N 134°51'W; elev. 142 feet/43m; length 3,500 feet/1,067m; gravel.

This Dene Indian settlement has a public phone, cafe, 2 general stores and 2 service stations (1 with tire repair). A co-op hotel here offers 8 rooms and a restaurant. Arts and crafts include beadwork and hide garments.

Aklak Air provides scheduled air service from Inuvik.

Fort McPherson was named in 1848 for Murdoch McPherson, chief trader of the Hudson's Bay Co., which had established its first posts in the area 8 years before. Between 1849 and 1859 there were frequent feuds with neighboring Inuit, who later moved farther north to the Aklavik area where they established a fur trading post.

In addition to subsistence fishing and hunting, income is earned from trapping (mostly muskrat and mink), handicrafts, government employment, and commercial enterprises such as Fort McPherson Tent and Canvas factory, which specializes in nylon bags, tents and teepees. Tours during business hours, 9 A.M. to 5 P.M. weekdays.

Buried in the cemetery outside the Anglican church are Inspector Fitzgerald and 3 other men of the Royal North–West Mounted Police. The 4 men left Fort McPherson by dog team Dec. 21, 1910, on their ill-fated patrol, carrying mail and dispatches from Herschel Island to Dawson City. Corporal W.J.D. Dempster found their bodies on March 22, 1911. A vivid account of their journey is found in Dick North's *Lost Patrol*, available from Alaska Northwest Books™. One of the last entries in Fitzgerald's diary read: "We have now only 10 pounds of flour and 8 pounds of bacon and some dried fish. My last hope is gone... We have been a week looking for a river to take us over the divide, but there are dozens of rivers and I am at a loss."

Photos and artifacts depicting the history and way of life of the community are displayed in the Chief Julius School.

Fort McPherson Tent and Canvas. See display ad this section.

Dempster Highway Log

(continued)

J 346.4 (557.5 km) **I 114.4** (184.1 km) Kilometrepost 86.

J 369.4 (594.5 km) **I 91.4** (147.1 km) **Frog Creek.** Grayling and pike. Road on right northbound leads to picnic area.

J 382 (614.8 km) **I 78.8** (126.8 km) Mackenzie River crossing. Free government ferry service available 15 hours a day during summer (from about early or mid-June to early October). Double-ended ferry: Drive on, drive off. Light vehicles may cross by ice bridge in late November; heavier vehicles can cross as ice thickens. *No crossing possible during freezeup and breakup.*

The ferry travels between landings on either side of the Mackenzie River. If you wish to go to Arctic Red River, you must tell the crewmen. **ARCTIC RED RIVER** (pop. 120) is a Dene Indian settlement situated above the confluence of the Mackenzie and Arctic Red rivers. Limited visitor services available: 2 rooms, gas (not always available), some groceries.

J 403.6 (649.5 km) **I 57.2** (92 km)

VISIT our factory north of the Arctic Circle

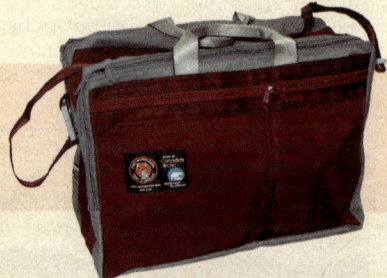

and see our high quality Cordura nylon bags: backpacks, totebags, attaches and Elite Dufflebags.

* Catalogue available

Fort McPherson Tent & Canvas

P.O. Box 58, Fort McPherson, N.W.T., Canada X0E 0J0
Ph. (403) 952-2179   Fax. (403) 952-2718   Toll Free. 1-800-661-0888

---

622   The MILEPOST®   ■   1992

Rengling River, grayling fishing.

J 404.1 (650.3 km) **I 56.7** (91.2 km) Distance marker shows Inuvik 90 km.

J 430.4 (692.6 km) **I 30.4** (48.9 km) Caribou Creek picnic and camping area.

J 436 (701.6 km) **I 24.8** (39.9 km) Campbell Lake and Campbell escarpment ahead northbound. Good place to glass for peregrine falcons.

J 445.1 (716.3 km) **I 15.7** (25.3 km) Cabin Creek picnic spot; pit toilets.

J 447 (719.3 km) **I 13.8** (22.2 km) **Campbell Creek** picnic area; pit toilets. Good fishing for pike and whitefish, some sheefish (inconnu). Creek leads a short distance to Campbell Lake. Boat launch. Bring mosquito repellent.

J 448.2 (721.3 km) **I 12.6** (20.3 km) Distance marker shows Inuvik 20 km.

J 454.7 (731.7 km) **I 6.1** (9.8 km) Airport Road turnoff; pavement begins.

J 456.4 (734.5 km) **I 4.4** (7.1 km) Kilometrepost 262.

J 458.5 (737.9 km) **I 2.3** (3.7 km) Chuk Park territorial campground; 38 campsites, 20 pull-through, electric hookups, firewood, water, showers, $10 fee. Lookout tower.

J 460.8 (741.5 km) **I 0** Turn left northbound for Inuvik town centre (description follows).

Inuvik

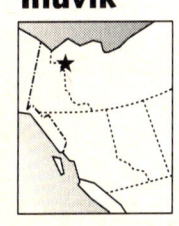

Situated on a flat wooded plateau which runs parallel to the east channel of the Mackenzie River, some 60 air miles/88 km south of the Beaufort Sea, 36 air miles/58 km and 70 water miles/113 km from Aklavik on the western edge of the delta. **Population:** 3,400, Dene, White and Inuit.

Emergency Services: RCMP, phone 979-2935. **Hospital,** Inuvik General, phone 979-2955.

Visitor Information: Tourist booth on Mackenzie Road at stoplight, open May through September. Phone (403) 979-4321, or write Inuvik Visitors Assoc., Box 2667, Inuvik, NT X0E 0T0. Also contact the Western Arctic Visitors Assoc., Box 2759M, Inuvik, NT X0E 0T0, phone 979-4321, fax 979-2434.

Elevation: 224 feet/68m. **Climate:** May 24 marks 57 days of midnight sun. The sun begins to set on July 19; on Dec. 6, the sun sets and does not rise until Jan. 6. Average annual precipitation 4 inches rainfall, 69 inches snowfall. July mean high 67°F/19°C, mean low 45°F/7°C. January mean high -11°F/-24°C, mean low -30°F/-35°C. **Radio** and **Television:** CBC and local. **Newspaper:** *The Drum* (weekly).

Private Aircraft: Inuvik airstrip; elev. 224 feet/68m; length 6,000 feet/1,829m; asphalt; fuel 80, 100. Townsite airstrip; elev. 10 feet/3m; length 1,800 feet/549m; gravel; fuel 80, 100, jet B, F40. High pressure refueling.

Inuvik, meaning "The Place of Man," is the largest Canadian community north of

the Arctic Circle, and the major government, transportation and communication centre for Canada's western arctic. Construction of the town began in 1955 and was completed in 1961. It was the main supply base for the petrochemical exploration of the delta until Tuktoyaktuk took over that role as activity centered in the Beaufort Sea. In Inuvik some hunting, fishing and trapping is done but most people earn wages in government and private enterprises, particularly in transportation and construction. With the delta one of the richest muskrat areas in the world, Inuvik is the western centre for shipping furs south.

The town's official monument says, in part, that Inuvik was "the first community north of the Arctic Circle built to provide the normal facilities of a Canadian town."

TRANSPORTATION

Air: Aklak Air provides scheduled service between Inuvik and Aklavik, Tuktoyaktuk, Sachs Harbour, Fort McPherson and Paulatuk. Scheduled service to Whitehorse and Old Crow, YT, via Alkan Air. Scheduled service to Edmonton, AB, and to Yellowknife, NWT, via NWT Air and Canadian Airlines International. Several air charter services operate out of Inuvik, offering flights to delta communities and charter service for hunting, fishing and camping trips. **Highways:** Dempster Highway from Dawson City. Winter roads (December into April) to Aklavik and Tuktoyaktuk. **Bus:** Service from Dawson City to Inuvik 3 times a week via Arctic Tour Co., phone 979-4100. **Taxi** and **rental cars:** Available.

ACCOMMODATIONS

Visitors will find most facilities available, although accommodations should be reserved in advance, especially during the Inuit Circumpolar Conference and the Great Northern Arts Festival (both in mid-July), and the Northern Games the first week in August 1992. Inuvik has 3 hotels, all with dining lounges, and 2 bed and breakfasts. There are also a laundry, post office, territorial liquor store, banks and churches. There are 3 gas stations and a car wash; auto repair and towing are available. Hardware, grocery and general stores and gift shops are here.

Finto Motor Inn, located on the corner of Bypass Road and Mackenzie Road as you

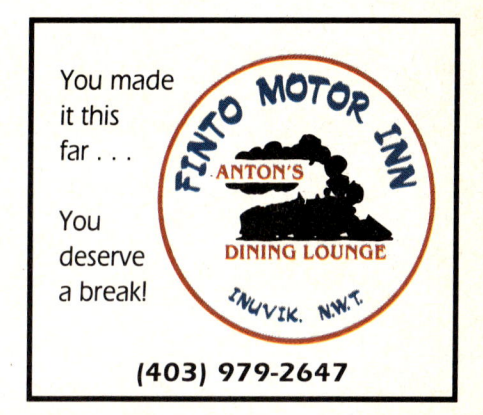

You made it this far... You deserve a break!

FINTO MOTOR INN
ANTON'S DINING LOUNGE
INUVIK, N.W.T.

(403) 979-2647

THE MACKENZIE EXPERIENCE

THE MACKENZIE HOTEL
▼ Inuvik's First Hotel ▼

1st Class Lodging, 2° North of Arctic Circle
Large Rooms & Suites, Cafe, Fine Dining, Pub
Cocktail Lounge, Disco, Entertainment Nightly

Parking: Car / Bus • Box 1618 • Telephone (403) 979-2861

WESTERN ARCTIC
VISITORS ASSOCIATION
IN CANADA'S WESTERN ARCTIC

Travel the Dempster Highway north this summer and experience beautiful scenery, exciting events, and a warm welcome from the people of Canada's northern cultures. For more information or a copy of the Dempster Driving Guide please write WAVA, Box 2759M, Inuvik, Northwest Territories, X0E 0T0, Canada
Phone 1 (403) 979-4321
Fax 1 (403) 979-2434

Highlights 1992

Midway Lake Music Festival
July 9 -11 • Fort McPherson

The Great Northern Arts Festival
July 17 - 26 • Inuvik

Inuit Circumpolar Conference
July 20 - 24 • Inuvik

Northern Games • 1st week in August

INUVIK ADVERTISERS

Finto Motor Inn ....Ph. (403) 979-2647
Mackenzie Hotel, The,.......Ph. (403) 979-2861
Western Arctic
    Visitors Assoc..............Ph. (403) 979-4321

enter town. Modern facilities include: large rooms, laundry services (for guests), satellite TV, kitchenettes, dining room, quiet lounge, crafts, carvings, and local artwork for sale. VISA, Mastercard, En Route accepted. For reservations or more information, call (403)979-2647; fax (403)979-3442. Write Box 1925, Inuvik, NT X0E 0T0. [ADVERTISEMENT]

Happy Valley territorial campground; 20 RV sites, electrical hookups, 10 tent pads, hot showers, firewood, water, dump station, fee. Chuk Park territorial campground; 20 sites, electrical hookups, firewood, water, showers, $10 fee. ▲

ATTRACTIONS

Igloo Church, painted white with lines to simulate snow blocks, is on Mackenzie Road as you drive in to Inuvik. Inside the church is Inuit painter Mona Thrasher's interpretation of the Stations of the Cross. Visitors are welcome.

Ingamo Hall is a 3-story log community hall which serves the social and recreational needs of Native families. The hall was built by Allan Crich over a 3-year period using some 1,020 logs which were cut from white spruce trees in the southern part of the Mackenzie River valley and floated down the river to Inuvik.

Tour Western Arctic Communities: Air charter service is available to AKLAVIK (pop. 800), an important centre for muskrat harvesting; TUKTOYAKTUK (pop. 950), an Inuit village on the Arctic coast and site of oil development; SACHS HARBOUR (pop. 158) on Banks Island, an Inuit settlement supported by trapping and some big game outfitters; PAULATUK (pop. 95), an Inuit settlement supported by hunting, fishing, sealing and trapping; and HOLMAN (pop. 300), an Inuit community on the west coast of Victoria Island, famous for its printmaking. Scheduled air service is also available to OLD CROW, an Indian settlement on the Porcupine River in Yukon Territory.

The **Mackenzie River delta**, one of the largest deltas in North America and an important wildlife corridor to the Arctic, is 40 miles/64 km wide and 60 miles/97 km long. A maze of lakes, channels and islands, the delta supports a variety of bird life, fish and muskrats. Boat tours of the Mackenzie River are available.

Special Events. The annual Northern Games will be held in Inuvik the first week in August 1992. Traditional Inuit and Dene sports, dances, competitions, crafts and Good Woman Contest (where northern women show their talent at animal skinning, bannock baking and other bush skills) are part of the festival. Visitors are welcome to join northerners from Alaska, Yukon Territory, Labrador and the Northwest Territories. For more information, write Northern Games Assoc., Box 1184, Inuvik, NT X0E 0T0.

The 4th annual Great Northern Arts Festival is scheduled for July 17-26, 1992. For more information contact the Arts Festival, Box 2921, Inuvik, NT X0E 0T0; phone 979-3536.

A Whaler & Trader in the Arctic, 1895–1944, by Arthur James Allen, who sailed on the schooners of the 19th century. He tells of icelocked ships, shanghaied crews, baseball games on ice and movie-making in the Arctic. Call Alaska Northwest Books™, 1-800-343-4567.

DALTON HIGHWAY

**(Formerly the North Slope Haul Road)
Milepost F 73.1 Elliott Highway to Deadhorse, Alaska**
(See map, page 626)

The 414-mile/666.3-km Dalton Highway (still referred to as the "Haul Road") begins at **Milepost F 73.1** on the Elliott Highway and ends—for the general public—at Deadhorse, a few miles from Prudhoe Bay and the Arctic Ocean. (Access to Prudhoe Bay, site of oil drilling operations, is restricted by the oil companies.) Maintenance and operation of the state-owned highway is the responsibility of the Dept. of Transportation in Fairbanks, 2301 Peger Road, Fairbanks 99701; phone (907) 451-2209.

The highway is named for James William Dalton, an arctic engineer involved in early oil exploration efforts on the North Slope. It was built as a haul road between the Yukon River and Prudhoe Bay during construction of the trans-Alaska pipeline, and was originally called the North Slope Haul Road. Construction of the road began April 29, 1974, and was completed 5 months later. The road is 28 feet/9m wide with 3 to 6 feet/1 to 2m of gravel surfacing. Some sections of road are underlain with plastic foam insulation to prevent thawing of the permafrost.

Construction of the 800-mile-/1,287-km-long pipeline between Prudhoe Bay and Valdez took place between 1974 and 1977. The 48-inch-diameter pipeline, of which slightly more than half is aboveground, has 10 operating pump stations. The control center is in Valdez. For additional information on the pipeline, contact: Public Affairs Dept., Alyeska Pipeline Service Co., 1835 S. Bragaw St., Anchorage, AK 99512.

The Bureau of Land Management (BLM) manages 2.7 million acres of public land along the Dalton Highway between the Yukon and Pump Station No. 2. For information on BLM lands, contact: Arctic District, BLM, 1150 University Ave., Fairbanks, AK 99709; phone (907) 474-2301.

Public travel on the Dalton Highway was originally restricted to the first 55 miles/89 km of the highway to the Yukon River bridge. In recent years, the public has been able to drive the Dalton Highway 211 miles/340 km to Disaster Creek without a permit. Governor Walter J. Hickel moved to open the Dalton Highway to Deadhorse in July 1991, but the opening was postponed pending the outcome of several issues. Contact the DOT regarding current status of highway beyond Disaster Creek.

Services along the Dalton Highway are limited. Gas, diesel fuel, tire repair, restaurant, motel, phone and emergency communications, and dump station are available at **Milepost J 56**, just past the Yukon River bridge. Gas, tire repair, restaurant, motel and phone are also available at Coldfoot, **Milepost J 175**. (Phones at both locations are for credit card and collect calls only.) Public phone at Wiseman.

Helicopters fly low over the pipeline for both surveillance and to move personnel and equipment for Alyeska Pipeline Service Co. The road is patrolled by Alaska State Troopers. For emergency services contact the Alaska State Troopers via CB radio, Channel 19, or ask that a message be relayed via the Alyeska facility or any state highway maintenance camp. Towing fees by private wrecker service have ranged as high as $5 a mile, each way.

Road conditions vary depending on weather, maintenance and time of year. Watch for dust, soft shoulders and trucks. Watch for road and bridge reconstruction in 1992. There are several steep (10 percent) grades. Drive with your headlights on at all times.

The Dalton Highway is unique in its scenic beauty, wildlife and recreational opportunities. Watch for Dall sheep, bears, moose, wolves, foxes, birds and wildflowers.

All waters between the Yukon River bridge and Dietrich River are part of the Yukon River system and most are tributaries of the Koyukuk River. Fishing for arctic grayling is especially good in rivers accessible by foot from the highway. The larger rivers also support burbot, salmon, pike and whitefish. Small Dolly Varden are at higher elevations in streams north of Coldfoot. According to the Dept. of Fish and Game, anglers should expect high, turbid water conditions throughout much of June as the snowpack melts in the Brooks Range, with the best fishing occurring during July and August.

Dalton Highway Log

Distance from junction with Elliott Highway (J) is followed by distance from Deadhorse (D).

J 0 D 414 (666.3 km) Junction with Elliott Highway at **Milepost F 73.1**.

J 4 (6.4 km) D 410 (659.8 km) Highway descends steeply into the Lost Creek valley. Lost Creek flows into the West Fork Tolovana River. Pipeline is visible stretching across the ridges of the distant hills.

J 5.6 (9 km) D 408.4 (657.2 km) Lost Creek culvert. Steep hills north- and southbound. Pipeline access road; no public admittance. There are many of these access roads along this highway; all are posted that the public is not allowed.

J 9.8 (15.8 km) D 404.2 (650.5 km) Road follows a high ridge with spectacular view of Erickson Creek area and pipeline.

J 12 (19.3 km) D 402 (646.9 km) Small

gravel turnouts.

J 12.1 (19.5 km) D 401.9 (646.8 km) Erickson Creek culvert.

J 20.9 (33.6 km) D 393.1 (632.6 km) Steep double-ended turnout at gravel pit to west.

J 21 (33.8 km) D 393 (632.5 km) Descent to Hess Creek begins northbound.

J 23.6 (38 km) D 390.4 (628.3 km) Pipeline access road, pond.

J 23.8 (38.3 km) D 390.2 (627.9 km) **Hess Creek** bridge. Campsite in trees. Large gravel bar along creek at north end of bridge. *CAUTION: Sandpit at entrance to gravel bar is an easy place to get stuck.* Bring your mosquito repellent. Whitefish and grayling fishing. Hess Creek, known for its colorful mining history, is the largest stream between the junction and the Yukon River bridge.

J 23.9 (38.5 km) D 390.1 (627.8 km) Road to west leads 0.2 mile/0.3 km to pond with parking space adequate for camping.

J 25 (40.2 km) D 389 (626 km) Double-ended rough turnout. Good view of pipeline and remote-operated valve site as the highway crosses Hess Creek and valley.

J 26 (41.8 km) D 388 (624.4 km) Pipeline parallels highway about 250 feet/76m away.

J 26.3 (42.3 km) D 387.7 (623.9 km) Turnout with litter barrel.

J 27 (43.4 km) D 387 (622.8 km) Evidence of 1971 lightning-caused forest fire.

J 28.4 (45.7 km) D 385.6 (620.5 km) Gravel pit road and pipeline access road to west.

J 33.7 (54.2 km) D 380.3 (612 km) Turnout at tributary of Hess Creek.

Sag bends in the oil pipeline allow caribou to cross. (Nancy Faville)

J 35.5 (57.1 km) D 378.5 (609.1 km) Rough turnout at gravel pit.

J 38.1 (61.3 km) D 375.9 (604.9 km) Pipeline goes under road. Evidence of the revegetation project undertaken by the oil companies.

J 40.7 (65.5 km) D 373.3 (600.7 km) Double-ended turnout with litter barrel. Overview of Troublesome and Hess creeks areas. Brush obscures sweeping views.

J 43.1 (69.4 km) D 370.9 (596.9 km) Isom Creek culvert. Steep ascent from valley north- and southbound.

J 44.6 (71.8 km) D 369.4 (594.5 km) Turnout with litter barrel.

J 47.9 (77.1 km) D 366.1 (589.2 km) Highway begins descent to Yukon River.

J 48.5 (78.1 km) D 365.5 (588.2 km)

ARCTIC CIRCLE
ADVENTURE

Original
ARCTIC CIRCLE DRIVE

A one day roundtrip guided journey to the heart of Alaska's northland.

★ Cross over the Arctic Circle & recieve an official Arctic Circle Adventure Certificate.

★ Pass over the mighty Yukon River & enjoy a riverside picnic lunch.

★ Walk out on the delicate arctic tundra & feel the frozen ground beneath the surface.

★ Visit a rural Alaskan homestead.

★ View the 800 mile long Trans-Alaska Pipeline.

Arctic Circle
FLY / DRIVE

The one day Arctic Circle Fly / Drive adventure includes all the highlights of the driving adventure plus:

★ Cruise the Yukon River & enjoy the majestic beauty of the northland's most famous river.

★ Visit a traditional Athabascan Indian summer fish camp. Meet Alaska's Athabascan people & learn how they harvest & preserve salmon for the long winter ahead.

★ Flightsee back to Fairbanks & receive a spectacular aerial view of the vast Alaska wilderness.

Arctic Ocean
PRUDHOE BAY

The first day of your two day Prudhoe Bay adventure includes all the highlights of the fly / drive adventure plus:

★ Overnight in the historic goldmining community of Wiseman. Enjoy a walking tour & sled dog demonstration.

★ Pass through the majestic Brooks Range & cross over the Continental Divide at Atigun Pass.

★ Tour Prudhoe Bay's vast oil fields & feel the frigid Arctic Ocean.

★ Flightsee back to Fairbanks & as an option visit the Inupiat Eskimo village of Anaktuvuk Pass.

Arctic Ocean   Prudhoe Bay
ESKIMO ADVENTURE

A one day flightseeing journey of Alaska's Interior and Arctic regions.

★ Visit the Inupiat Eskimo village of Anaktuvuk Pass nestled in the heart of the Brooks mountain range.

★ Learn of the local Inupiat Eskimo culture with a tour of the village & a memorable visit to the Simon Paneak Memorial Museum.

★ Tour Prudhoe Bay's vast oil fields & feel the frigid waters of the Arctic Ocean.

All tours are lead by an informative, friendly Alaskan guide in the personalized comfort of our custom vans & coaches.

For General Information and Reservations call or write:

NORTHERN ALASKA TOUR COMPANY • 907 / 474-8600 • PO Box 82991-MP Fairbanks AK 99708

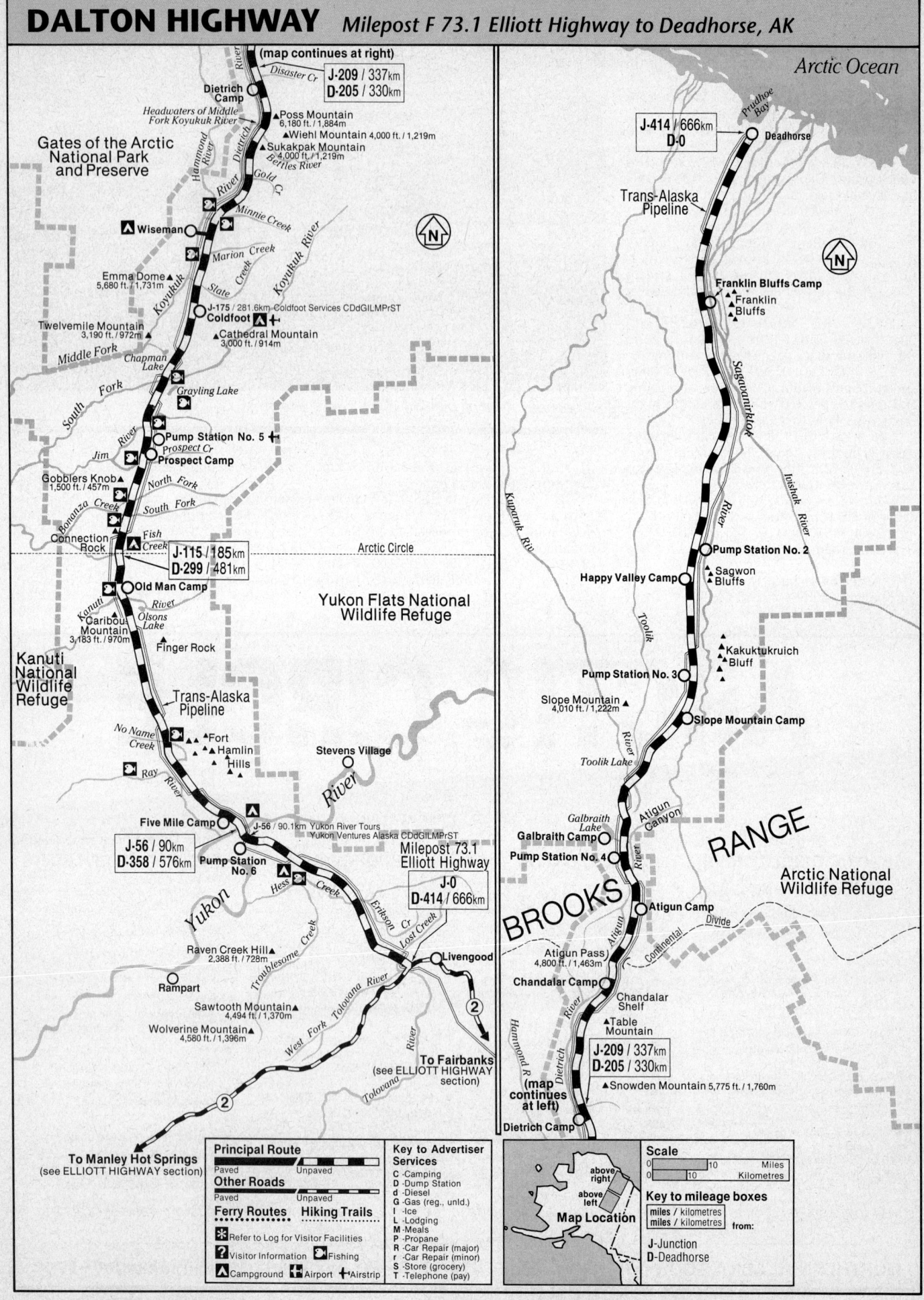

DALTON HIGHWAY
Milepost F 73.1 Elliott Highway to Deadhorse, AK

Pipeline access road. Goalpostlike structures, called "headache bars," guard against vehicles large enough to run into and damage the pipeline.

J 50.1 (80.6 km) D 363.9 (585.6 km) Turnout.

J 53.2 (85.6 km) D 360.8 (580.6 km) First view northbound of the Yukon River. As road drops, you can see the pipeline where it crosses the river. Fort Hamlin Hills are beyond the pipeline.

J 54 (86.9 km) D 360 (579.3 km) **PUMP STATION NO. 6.**

J 54.5 (87.7 km) D 359.5 (578.5 km) Turnout to west.

J 55.6 (89.5 km) D 358.4 (576.8 km) Yukon River bridge (formally the E.L. Patton Bridge, named for the president of the Alyeska Pipeline Service Co. after his death in 1982). This wood-decked bridge, completed in 1975, is 2,290 feet/698m long and has a 6 percent grade.

J 56 (90.1 km) D 358 (576.1 km) Gas, diesel, tire repair, restaurant, motel, phone and emergency communications available at Yukon Ventures Alaska. This is the southern boundary of BLM-managed lands. There is an Alyeska pipeline interpretive display here with information on the Yukon River, pipeline construction and other related subjects. East of the highway is a camping area with dump station and litter barrels. Road closed east of campsite. ▲

Yukon Ventures Alaska. See display ad this section.

Yukon River Tours. Join the Athabascans of Stevens Village on a tour of their homeland! You'll experience the historical "spell of the Yukon," Athabascan culture, an operating Native fish camp, the area's natural history. Summer on the river in Alaska is where it's at! Call (907) 452-7162; 214 2nd Ave., Fairbanks, AK 99701. [ADVERTISEMENT]

J 60.6 (97.5 km) D 353.4 (568.7 km) Site of **FIVE MILE CAMP,** a former pipeline construction camp. No structures remain at these former construction camps. There is an undeveloped campsite here and an outhouse. Water is available from an artesian well. Highway crosses over buried pipeline.

J 60.8 (97.8 km) D 353.2 (568.4 km) Five Mile airstrip (length 3,500 feet/1,067m); controlled by Alyeska Security. *CAUTION: Be prepared to stop at control gates at both ends of airstrip.*

J 61.6 (99.1 km) D 352.4 (567.1 km) View of Fort Hamlin Hills to north, pump station No. 6 to south.

J 61.9 (99.6 km) D 352.1 (566.6 km) Sevenmile DOT/PF highway maintenance camp and Alaska State Trooper.

J 68.4 (110.1 km) D 345.6 (556.2 km) Highway crosses over buried pipeline.

J 69.2 (111.4 km) D 344.8 (554.9 km) Double-ended turnout at crest of hill overlooking the Ray River to the north.

J 70 (112.7 km) D 344 (553.6 km) **Ray River** overlook and turnout. Scenic view of the Ray Mountains to the west. Burbot, grayling and northern pike fishing. ⌦

J 72.6 (116.8 km) D 341.4 (549.4 km) Fort Hamlin Hills Creek bridge and turnout. Winter trail scars are visible here.

J 74.8 (120.4 km) D 339.2 (545.9 km) Steep descent northbound followed by steep ascent; dubbed the Roller Coaster.

J 79.1 (127.3 km) D 334.9 (539 km) **No Name Creek** and turnout; burbot, grayling and whitefish. ⌦

J 81.6 (131.3 km) D 332.4 (534.9 km) Fort Hamlin Hills are visible to the southeast. Tree line on surrounding hills is about 2,000 feet/610m.

J 86.5 (139.2 km) D 327.5 (527 km) Scenic overlook 1 mile/1.6 km west with view of tors to northeast, Yukon Flats Wildlife Refuge to east and Fort Hamlin Hills to southeast. Tors are high, isolated pinnacles of jointed granite jutting up from the tundra and are a residual feature of erosion.

J 88.5 (142.4 km) D 325.5 (523.8 km) Mackey Hill. Entering Game Management Unit 25D northbound, Unit 20F southbound. The high, unnamed hill east of the road is 2,774 feet/846m in elevation.

J 90.2 (145.2 km) D 323.8 (521.1 km) Double-ended turnouts with litter barrels both sides of highway. A good photo opportunity of the road and pipeline to the north. The small green structure over the buried pipe is a radio-controlled valve allowing the pipeline oil flow to be shut down when necessary.

J 91.1 (146.6 km) D 322.9 (519.6 km) Culvert directs water from branch of West Fork of Dall River. Watch for soft spots in road.

J 94 (151.3 km) D 320 (515 km) Turnout at former gravel pit road to west.

J 96 (154.5 km) D 318 (511.8 km) The road lies above tree line for about 5 miles/8 km. Good opportunities for photos, berry picking (blueberries, lowbush cranberries), wildflower viewing and hiking. Northbound, the terrain becomes more rugged and scenic.

J 97.5 (156.9 km) D 316.5 (509.3 km) Finger Rock (signed Finger Mountain), a tor, is visible east of the road and most easily seen to the south. Tors are visible for the next 2 miles/3.2 km.

Prehistoric hunting sites are numerous in this region. Please do not collect or disturb artifacts.

J 98.2 (158 km) D 315.8 (508.2 km) High viewpoint; Caribou Mountain is in the distance to the northwest. Olsens Lake, Kanuti Flats, Kanuti River drainage and site of former Old Man Camp are visible ahead northbound. The road now descends and passes through several miles of valley bottom with an excellent view of the mountains.

J 100.7 (162.1 km) D 313.3 (504.2 km) Pipeline passes under highway.

J 105.8 (170.3 km) D 308.2 (496 km) **Kanuti River,** crossing and turnout; burbot, grayling. Abandoned airstrip. ⌦

J 107 (172.2 km) D 307 (494.1 km) Site of **OLD MAN CAMP,** a former pipeline construction camp.

J 109.1 (175.6 km) D 304.9 (490.7 km) Turnout to west.

J 109.8 (176.7 km) D 304.2 (489.5 km) Turnout at Beaver Slide. *CAUTION: Road descends very steeply northbound. Watch for soft spots. Slippery when wet.*

J 110 (177 km) D 304 (489.2 km) Visible against the hillside to the east are water bars constructed to prevent erosion above the buried pipeline.

J 111.5 (179.4 km) D 302.5 (486.8 km) View of valley and Fish Creek to the north.

J 112.2 (180.6 km) D 301.8 (485.7 km) Turnout at pipeline access road. Moose and bear frequent willow thickets here.

J 113.9 (183.3 km) D 300.1 (483 km) Evidence of old winter trail to Bettles is visible here.

J 114 (183.5 km) D 300 (482.8 km) **Fish**

ENJOY THE BEAUTIFUL YUKON RIVER ...
JUST SOUTH OF THE ARCTIC CIRCLE ...

for a weekend of
fishing • hiking •
boating • relaxation ...

or as a base camp
for hunting
bear • moose •
Dall sheep • caribou •

YUKON RIVER BRIDGE
• **ALASKA** •

THE WARMEST PLACE IN THE COLD ARCTIC

- **40 Motel Rooms**
  Modern Facilities
  Laundry Facilities

- **Restaurant**
  OPEN 6 am - 1 am
  • Homestyle Cooking
  • Homemade Bread & Pies

- **Boat Launch** • **Gift Shop**

- **Fuel**
  • Diesel • Regular
  • Unleaded

- **Shop & Service Station**
  • Tire Repair
  • Wrecker Service

YUKON VENTURES ALASKA
Mi 56 Dalton Hwy.

FOR RESERVATIONS CALL 655-9001
P.O. BOX 60947, Fairbanks, AK 99706

Old cabin at Milepost J 197.
(Jerrianne Lowther, staff)

Creek bridge and turnout; burbot, grayling 12 to 18 inches.

J 115.3 (185.5 km) **D 298.7** (480.7 km) The Arctic Circle, north latitude 66°33'. Wayside with tables, restrooms and sign. Stop and have your picture taken with the sign. This is also a good photo point, with views to the south and to the west. Follow road off turnout 0.6 mile/1 km for undeveloped campsite. If you reach the Alyeska access gate you've gone too far.

J 124.7 (200.7 km) **D 289.3** (465.6 km) Turnout to east at **South Fork Bonanza Creek**; burbot, grayling, whitefish.

J 125.7 (202.3 km) **D 288.3** (464 km) Turnout to east at **North Fork Bonanza Creek**; burbot, grayling, whitefish.

J 127.1 (204.5 km) **D 286.9** (461.7 km) Turnout.

J 127.7 (205.5 km) **D 286.3** (460.7 km) Paradise Hill; blueberries and lowbush cranberries in season.

J 128.9 (207.4 km) **D 285.1** (458.8 km) Gravel pit.

J 129.3 (208.1 km) **D 284.7** (458.2 km) CAUTION: Long ascent northbound with a short stretch that is very steep. Give trucks plenty of room here!

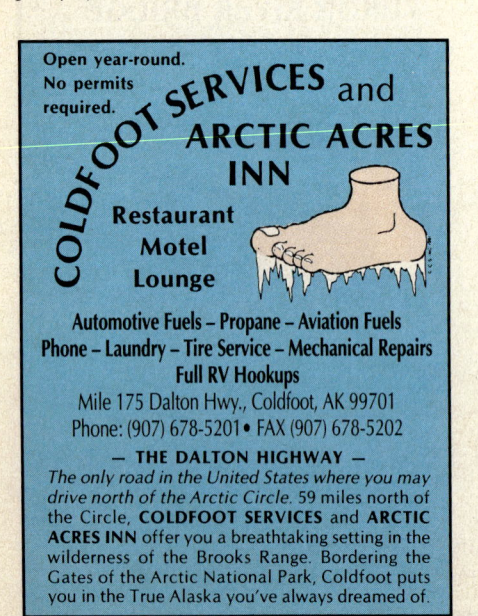

**Open year-round.
No permits required.**

COLDFOOT SERVICES and **ARCTIC ACRES INN**

Restaurant
Motel
Lounge

Automotive Fuels – Propane – Aviation Fuels
Phone – Laundry – Tire Service – Mechanical Repairs
Full RV Hookups

Mile 175 Dalton Hwy., Coldfoot, AK 99701
Phone: (907) 678-5201 • FAX (907) 678-5202

— **THE DALTON HIGHWAY** —
The only road in the United States where you may drive north of the Arctic Circle. 59 miles north of the Circle, **COLDFOOT SERVICES** and **ARCTIC ACRES INN** offer you a breathtaking setting in the wilderness of the Brooks Range. Bordering the Gates of the Arctic National Park, Coldfoot puts you in the True Alaska you've always dreamed of.

J 131.3 (211.3 km) **D 282.7** (454.9 km) Solar-powered communications tower.

J 131.5 (211.6 km) **D 282.5** (454.6 km) View of pump station No. 5 to north.

J 132 (212.4 km) **D 282** (453.8 km) Turnout with litter barrels and toilets at Gobblers Knob (elev. 1,500 feet/457m) overlooking the Jack White Range, Pope Creek Dome (the dominant peak to the northwest), Prospect Creek drainage, Pump Station No. 5, Jim River drainage, South Fork Koyukuk drainage and the Brooks Range on the northern horizon.

J 134.7 (216.8 km) **D 279.3** (449.5 km) Pipeline access road.

J 135.1 (217.4 km) **D 278.9** (448.8 km) **Prospect Creek**; grayling, whitefish and pike. Active gold mining area.

J 135.7 (218.4 km) **D 278.3** (447.9 km) Turnout with outhouse. Old winter road goes up creek to mines. Turn left for site of **PROSPECT CAMP**, which holds the record for lowest recorded temperature in Alaska (-80°F/-62°C, January 23, 1971). Rough road leads 0.5 mile/0.8 km to Claja Pond; beaver, ducks. Undeveloped campsite on Jim River. Old winter road to Bettles crosses river here.

J 137.1 (220.6 km) **D 276.9** (445.6 km) **PUMP STATION NO. 5** (signed incorrectly as Prospect Camp). No public access. Side road leads to well. Pump Station No. 5 is not a pump station, but a "drain down" or pressure relief station.

Private Aircraft: Airstrip; length 5,000 feet/1,524m; lighted runway. This airstrip is used as a BLM fire fighting staging area.

J 138.1 (222.2 km) **D 275.9** (444 km) Jim River DOT/PF highway maintenance camp EMT squad. Site of 1988 burn.

J 139 (223.7 km) **D 275** (442.6 km) Road to gravel pit.

J 140.1 (225.5 km) **D 273.9** (440.8 km) Turnout at **Jim River**, bridge No. 1; burbot, chum and king salmon, grayling, pike, whitefish. CAUTION: *Bears here for fall salmon run.*

J 141 (226.9 km) **D 273** (439.3 km) Turnout to east at Jim River, bridge No. 2.

J 141.8 (228.2 km) **D 272.2** (438.1 km) Douglas Creek; blueberries and lowbush cranberries in season.

J 144.1 (231.9 km) **D 269.9** (434.4 km) Bridge No. 3 across main channel of **Jim River**; turnout to east at south end of bridge. See Milepost J 140.1 for fishing.

J 145 (233.3 km) **D 269** (432.9 km) Road to refuse dump (locked).

J 145.6 (234.3 km) **D 268.4** (431.9 km) Pipeline passes under road. First views northbound of Brooks Range foothills to the north.

J 150.3 (241.9 km) **D 263.7** (424.4 km) **Grayling Lake** to east has good grayling fishing in open water season.

J 150.8 (242.7 km) **D 263.2** (423.6 km) Turnout on Grayling Lake. The road is passing through the foothills of the Brooks Range. There is an active gold mining area behind the hills to the west.

J 155.2 (249.8 km) **D 258.8** (416.5 km) Overlook for the South Fork Koyukuk River valley.

J 156 (251.1 km) **D 258** (415.2 km) Turnout at the **South Fork Koyukuk River** bridge; grayling, whitefish, chum and king salmon.

This large river flows past the villages of Bettles, Allakaket, Hughes and Huslia before draining into the Yukon River near Koyukuk.

J 159.1 (256 km) **D 254.9** (410.2 km) Bridge over pipeline.

J 160 (257.5 km) **D 254** (408.8 km) Good view of Chapman Lake 0.5 mile/0.8 km west of road. Old mine trail, now used in the Coldfoot Classic sled dog race, is visible from the road.

The 2 mountains visible to the north are Twelvemile Mountain (elev. 3,190 feet/972m), left, and Cathedral Mountain (elev. 3,000 feet/914m), on right. The foothills of the Brooks Range are also to the north.

J 163.3 (262.8 km) **D 250.7** (403.5 km) Turnout with litter barrel to west.

J 165.1 (265.7 km) **D 248.9** (400.6 km) Turnout to west with litter barrel and view of pipeline.

J 165.7 (266.7 km) **D 248.3** (399.6 km) Turnout with litter barrel on west side of road overlooking Middle Fork Koyukuk River.

J 167.2 (269.1 km) **D 246.8** (397.2 km) Old winter trail to Tramway Bar.

J 175 (281.6 km) **D 239** (384.6 km) **COLDFOOT**, site of a historic mining camp at the mouth of Slate Creek on the east bank of the Middle Fork Koyukuk River. Food, gas, diesel, phone, lodging, RV park and post office available at Coldfoot Services (phone 678-5201). There is a 3,500-foot/1,067-m runway to west, maintained by the state. BLM camping area on airport access road. An Alaska State Trooper, a Fish and Wildlife officer and BLM field station are located at Coldfoot. A visitor center here, operated by the BLM, USF&WS and National Park Service, offers travel information and nightly presentations on the natural and cultural history of the Arctic. Topographic maps for sale. Coldfoot is home of the 350-mile Coldfoot Classic Sled Dog Race held the first Monday in April.

Originally named Slate Creek, Coldfoot reportedly got its name in 1900 when gold stampeders got as far up the Koyukuk as this point, then got cold feet, turned and departed. The old cemetery still exists. Emma Dome (elev. 5,680 feet/1,731m) is to the west.

Coldfoot Services & Arctic Acres Inn. See display ad this section.

J 184.4 (296.7 km) **D 229.6** (369.5 km) Scenic overlook. Excellent view of Middle Fork Koyukuk River and rock slide on adjacent mountain.

J 186 (299.3 km) **D 228** (366.9 km) The historic mining community of Wiseman can be seen across the Koyukuk River to the west. Access to Wiseman from **Milepost J 188.6**.

J 186.7 (300.5 km) **D 227.3** (365.8 km) Turnouts with litter barrels both sides of highway.

J 187.2 (301.3 km) **D 226.8** (365 km) Turnout with litter barrel to west at **Minnie Creek**; burbot, grayling, whitefish.

J 188.5 (303.4 km) **D 225.5** (362.9 km) Turnout at **Middle Fork Koyukuk River** bridge No. 1; Dolly Varden, grayling, whitefish.

J 188.6 (303.5 km) **D 225.4** (362.7 km) Improved (1991) access road to **WISEMAN**, a historic mining town. The heyday of Wiseman came in about 1910, after gold seekers abandoned Coldfoot. The Wiseman Trading Co. still stands and houses the town's museum, featuring old photos and mining equipment. About 25 residents live here year-round today and the population increases in the summer with the arrival of miners. (Note that this is an active mining area and all buildings are privately owned.)

Wiseman has a general store, public phone and campground.

J 189 (304.2 km) D 225 (362.1 km) Finger dikes keep river away from highway and pipeline.

J 190.5 (306.6 km) D 223.5 (359.7 km) Narrow bridge over Hammond River.

J 190.8 (307.1 km) D 223.2 (359.2 km) Middle Fork Koyukuk River bridge No. 2.

J 192.8 (310.3 km) D 221.2 (356 km) Link Up, where 2 sections of pipeline constructed by different crews were joined.

J 194 (312.2 km) D 220 (354 km) First view northbound of Sukakpak Mountain (elev. 4,000 feet/1,219m) to north. Sukakpak Mountain is believed to mark the traditional boundary between Eskimo and Athabascan Indian territories. Wiehl Mountain (elev. 4,000 feet/1,219m) is east of Sukakpak. The high mountain just to the west of the road is unnamed.

J 197 (317 km) D 217 (349.2 km) Old cabin just west of road is reported to have been constructed in the early 1900s; private property. Gold Creek bridge.

J 197.3 (317.5 km) D 216.7 (348.7 km) Cat trail to gold mining area.

J 197.7 (318.2 km) D 216.3 (348.1 km) Turnout with litter barrel to east and view of Wiehl Mountain.

J 200 (321.9 km) D 214 (344.4 km) View of the Middle Fork Koyukuk River, a typical braided river exhibiting frequent changes of the streambed during high water.

J 203.5 (327.5 km) D 210.5 (338.7 km) Turnout and 0.5-mile/0.8-km footpath to Sukakpak Mountain. The short mounds of earth between the road and Sukakpak are palsas, formed by ice beneath the soil pushing the vegetative mat and soil upward.

J 203.8 (328 km) D 210.2 (338.3 km) Turnouts with litter barrels next 0.6 mile/1 km northbound.

J 204.3 (328.8 km) D 209.7 (337.5 km) Middle Fork Koyukuk River bridge No. 3; turnout with toilets and litter barrels to east.

J 204.5 (329.1 km) D 209.5 (337.1 km) Middle Fork Koyukuk River bridge No. 4.

J 205.3 (330.4 km) D 208.7 (335.9 km) Turnout with litter barrel to west. Good view of north side of Sukakpak Mountain.

J 207 (333.1 km) D 207 (333.1 km) **Dietrich River** bridge, turnout to west at south end; burbot, grayling, whitefish and Dolly Varden.

J 207.5 (333.9 km) D 206.5 (332.3 km) Small, unnamed lake on east side of road with nice view of Sukakpak Mountain. Dillon Mountain (proposed name) is just to the north.

J 209 (336.3 km) D 205 (329.9 km) Drag reducing injection site at pipeline Mile 203. Injected substance facilitates oil flow.

J 209.1 (336.5 km) D 204.9 (329.7 km) Site of **DIETRICH CAMP**, a former pipeline construction camp.

J 211 (339.6 km) D 203 (326.7 km) Disaster Creek. Turnout with litter barrel to east.

J 216 (347.6 km) D 198 (318.6 km) Snowden Creek culvert. Panorama of Dietrich River valley and Brooks Range north and west of the road.

J 217.1 (349.4 km) D 196.9 (316.9 km) Rock spire to east is Snowden Mountain (elev. 5,775 feet/l,760m).

J 221.6 (356.6 km) D 192.4 (309.6 km) Turnout to west is quarry of black marble with white calcite veins.

J 221.8 (356.9 km) D 192.2 (309.3 km) Turnout at gravel pit to east.

J 224 (360.5 km) D 190 (305.8 km) Turnout at gravel pit.

J 226 (363.7 km) D 188 (302.5 km) Pipeline remote valve just west of road. The arch-shaped concrete structures keep pipeline buried in areas of possible flooding.

J 227.3 (365.8 km) D 186.7 (300.5 km) Nutirwik Creek culvert.

J 228 (366.9 km) D 186 (299.3 km) Highway parallels Dietrich River.

J 231.4 (372.4 km) D 182.6 (293.9 km) Small turnouts both sides of highway.

J 234.9 (378 km) D 179.1 (288.2 km) North Slope Borough boundary. Borough offices are located in Barrow.

J 235.3 (378.7 km) D 178.7 (287.6 km) Large turnout with litter barrel at foot of Chandalar Shelf and beginning of a long, steep (10 percent) grade. The farthest north spruce tree along the highway is located just south of the turnout. No trees beyond here.

J 236.3 (380.3 km) D 177.7 (286 km) Turnouts and view of the Dietrich River valley to the south next 0.3 mile/0.5 km.

J 237.1 (381.6 km) D 176.9 (284.7 km) Turnout at top of Chandalar Shelf; DOT/PF checkpoint. Headwaters of the Chandalar River are to the east. Table Mountain (elev. 6,425 feet/1,958m) is to the southeast. Dietrich River valley to south.

J 239 (384.6 km) D 175 (281.6 km) Green net structure west of road is called a Wyoming Gage; it is used to measure precipitation. Sponsored by the Soil and Water Conservation Service.

J 239.2 (384.9 km) D 174.8 (281.3 km) Site of **CHANDALAR CAMP**, a former pipeline construction camp, now used as a BLM field station.

J 239.4 (385.3 km) D 174.6 (281 km) Chandalar highway maintenance station on west side of highway.

J 242.2 (389.8 km) D 171.8 (276.5 km) West Fork Chandalar River bridge.

J 242.5 (390.2 km) D 171.5 (276 km) Begin long, steep climb northbound toward Atigun Pass. Winter avalanche area.

J 244.7 (393.8 km) D 169.3 (272.5 km) Turnout at top of Atigun Pass (elev. 4,800 feet/1,463m), highest highway pass in Alaska; Continental Divide. A Wyoming Gage is located here. Nice example of a cirque, an amphitheater-shaped bowl or depression caused by erosion, in mountain east of road. Endicott Mountains are to the west, Phillip Smith Mountains to the east. James Dalton Mountain is to the left ahead northbound.

Highway descends steeply toward the North Slope. Many mountains in the area exceed 7,000 feet/2,134m in elevation. The pipeline is in a buried, insulated concrete cribbing to the east. Construction in this area was extremely complex, difficult and dangerous.

J 248.4 (399.8 km) D 165.6 (266.5 km) Turnouts both sides of highway. Good spot to view Dall sheep.

J 249.3 (401.2 km) D 164.7 (265.1 km) Bridge over Spike Camp Creek. Highway crosses buried pipeline.

J 249.7 (401.8 km) D 164.3 (264.4 km) Site of **ATIGUN CAMP**, a former pipeline construction camp. Turnouts both sides of highway. View of Atigun River valley. Another Wyoming Gage is located here.

J 251.5 (404.7 km) D 162.5 (261.5 km) Turnouts next 0.3 mile/0.5 km northbound.

J 253.1 (407.3 km) D 160.9 (258.9 km) Atigun River crossing No. 1. Highway crosses buried pipeline. *CAUTION: Grizzly bears in area.*

J 258.4 (415.8 km) D 155.6 (250.4 km) Trevor Creek bridge.

J 258.6 (416.2 km) D 155.4 (250.1 km) Turnout.

J 261.4 (420.7 km) D 152.6 (245.6 km) Turnout.

J 265 (426.5 km) D 149 (239.8 km) Roche Moutonnee Creek bridge.

J 267.5 (430.5 km) D 146.5 (235.8 km) Bridge over Holden Creek.

J 268 (431.3 km) D 146 (235 km) Good view of pump station No. 4.

J 269.3 (433.4 km) D 144.7 (232.9 km) **PUMP STATION NO. 4**. This station has the highest elevation of all the pipeline stations (2,760 feet/841m), and is also a launching and receiving station for special devices called "pigs." A pig consists of spring-mounted scraper blades and/or brushes on a central body which moves through the pipe cleaning accumulated wax from interior walls and monitoring conditions inside the pipe.

J 269.5 (433.7 km) D 144.5 (232.5 km) Highway bridge passes over pipeline.

J 270.9 (436 km) D 143.1 (230.3 km) Atigun River crossing No. 2. The Arctic National Wildlife Refuge boundary is located 3 miles/4.8 km east along the Atigun gorge. Galbraith Lake may be seen to the west. There are a large number of archaeological sites in this vicinity.

J 274 (440.9 km) D 140 (225.3 km) View of Galbraith Lake and Galbraith camp.

J 274.7 (442.1 km) D 139.3 (224.2 km) Road access to **GALBRAITH CAMP**, a construction camp.

J 276.5 (445 km) D 137.5 (221.3 km) Island Lake.

J 284.3 (457.5 km) D 129.7 (208.7 km) Toolik Lake west of road. A former construction camp, Toolik Lake is now the site of a University of Alaska research camp.

J 286.2 (460.6 km) D 127.8 (205.7 km) Turnout with litter barrel to east at high point in road. View of Brooks Range south and east.

J 288.8 (464.8 km) D 125.2 (201.5 km) Kuparuk River bridge.

J 289.3 (465.6 km) D 124.7 (200.7 km) Pipeline crossing. Short, buried section of pipeline to west is called a sag bend and is to allow for wildlife crossing. Watch for caribou northbound.

J 290.4 (467.3 km) D 123.6 (198.9 km) Turnout with litter barrel to east.

J 294.4 (473.8 km) D 119.6 (192.5 km) Second sag bend northbound.

J 297.8 (479.2 km) D 116.2 (187 km) Oxbow Creek culvert. Small turnout to east.

J 301 (484.4 km) D 113 (181.8 km) Turnout. Slope Mountain (elev. 4,010 feet/222m) is just west of road. Watch for Dall sheep.

J 305.7 (492 km) D 108.3 (174.3 km) Site of **SLOPE MOUNTAIN CAMP**, a former pipeline construction camp, now Sag River highway maintenance station.

J 309 (497.3 km) D 105 (169 km) Highway parallels Sagavanirktok River.

J 311.8 (501.8 km) D 102.2 (164.5 km) **PUMP STATION NO. 3**.

J 319.8 (514.7 km) D 94.2 (151.6 km) Turnout to east at Oil Spill Hill.

J 320 (515 km) D 94 (151.3 km) The long range of hills east of the road is the Kakuktukruich Bluff.

J 325.3 (523.5 km) D 88.7 (142.7 km) Turnout with litter barrel to east at the top of a steep grade called Ice Cut.

J 326.2 (525 km) **D 87.8** (141.3 km) Pipeline crossing.

J 330.7 (532.2 km) **D 83.3** (134.1 km) Dan Creek bridge.

J 334.4 (538.1 km) **D 79.6** (128.1 km) Site of **HAPPY VALLEY CAMP**, a former pipeline construction camp. A BLM field station is located here.

J 347.6 (559.4 km) **D 66.4** (106.9 km) Sagwon airstrip. The airstrip is currently not in use in order to protect nesting peregrine falcons in the area.

J 350.5 (564.1 km) **D 63.5** (102.2 km) View of Sagwon Bluffs to the east. The road passes over several low hills that offer views of the surrounding terrain.

J 353 (568 km) **D 61** (98.2 km) Wyoming Gage west of road.

J 355.1 (571.5 km) **D 58.9** (94.8 km) Turnout with litter barrel to east.

J 358.8 (577.4 km) **D 55.2** (88.8 km) **PUMP STATION NO. 2** to the east. This is the northern boundary of BLM-managed land. Land north of here is managed by the state.

NOTE: The worst winter weather conditions on the Dalton Highway are experienced the next 38 miles/61 km northbound. Blowing snow may obscure visibility and block road.

J 364 (585.8 km) **D 50** (80.5 km) Low hills to the north are the Franklin Bluffs. East of the road, the Ivishak River empties into the Sagavanirktok River on its journey to the Arctic Ocean.

J 365.1 (587.6 km) **D 48.9** (78.7 km) Turnout with litter barrel by pond to west; watch for nesting waterfowl.

J 366 (589 km) **D 48** (77.2 km) Large animal crossing in pipeline for caribou.

J 376 (605.1 km) **D 38** (61.2 km) The small hill that rises abruptly on the horizon about 5 miles/8 km west of the road is called a pingo. Pingos often form from the bed of a lake that has been covered by vegetation. Freezing of the water can raise the surface several hundred feet above the surrounding terrain.

J 377.3 (607.2 km) **D 36.7** (59.1 km) Turnout with litter barrel to east at site of **FRANKLIN BLUFFS CAMP**, a former pipeline construction camp. *CAUTION: Watch for loose, coarse gravel on road.*

J 383 (616.4 km) **D 31** (49.9 km) Franklin Bluffs to the east and a pingo to the west.

J 398.7 (641.6 km) **D 15.3** (24.6 km) Underground pipeline crossing.

J 413.3 (665.1 km) **D 0.7** (1.1 km) Turnout at former highway checkpoint. Oil field activity and equipment become visible along the horizon.

J 414 (666.3 km) **D 0** Northern limit of state-owned highway at **DEADHORSE** (description follows). Access to the Arctic Ocean is on roads owned by the oil companies; permission must be obtained. Airport is 2 miles/3.2 km ahead.

Deadhorse was established to accommodate Prudhoe Bay oil operations. The area population, which includes oil and airline-related personnel, varies between 3,500 and 8,600. For security purposes, visitors are not allowed on the docks or on area roads.

Accommodations are available at several camps, but reservations should be made well in advance as increased oil drilling activity will result in a shortage of available rooms.

Scheduled air service from Fairbanks and Anchorage (flying time from Anchorage: 1 hour, 35 minutes). Air taxi service is available at the airport. Packaged tours to the North Slope area are available.

GENERAL INFORMATION

Air Travel

SCHEDULED AIR SERVICE TO ALASKA

Alaska Airlines, MarkAir, Morris Air, Delta Airlines, Northwest Orient Airlines, United Airlines and Hawaiian Air all provide scheduled jet service between Alaska and the Lower 49. Air France, British Airways, China Airlines, Japan Air Lines, KLM Royal Dutch Airlines, Korean Air Lines, Lufthansa, Northwest Orient Airlines (Japan), Sabena Belgian World Airlines, Swissair, and SAS (Scandinavian Airlines System) serve Anchorage from other countries. Contact your travel agent for current schedules and fares.

SCHEDULED AIR SERVICE WITHIN ALASKA

Following are listed many of the carriers offering interstate scheduled air service. Interline service available to most rural Alaska points; check with carriers. Also check local air taxi operators for charter and commuter service to Alaskan communities.

From ANCHORAGE

Alaska Airlines, 4750 International Airport Road, Anchorage 99502—To Fairbanks, Prudhoe Bay, Cordova, Yakutat, Juneau, Sitka, Wrangell, Petersburg, Ketchikan, Nome, Kotzebue and Gustavus/Glacier Bay (summer only).

Delta Airlines—Serves Fairbanks.

Era Aviation (Alaska Airlines commuter), 6160 S. Airpark Dr., Anchorage 99502—To Kenai, Homer, Kodiak, Valdez and Iliamna.

MarkAir, Inc., 4100 W. International Road, Box 196769, Anchorage 99519-6769—To Aniak, Barrow, Bethel, Cold Bay, Dillingham, Fairbanks, Homer, Kenai, Dutch Harbor/Unalaska, Galena, King Salmon/Kodiak, McGrath, Port Heiden, Prudhoe Bay/Deadhorse, St. Mary's, Sand Point, Unalakleet, Valdez.

Reeve Aleutian Airways, 4700 W. International Airport Road, Anchorage 99502—To points on the Alaska Peninsula, on the Aleutian Islands and on the Pribilof Islands.

Southcentral Air, 135 Granite Point Road, Kenai 99611—To Kenai and Homer.

United Airlines, Anchorage International Airport; phone toll free (800) 841-8005—To Fairbanks.

From BARROW

Cape Smythe Air Service, Box 549, Barrow 99723; phone (907) 852-8333—Barrow service to Atqasuk, Wainwright, Point Lay, Point Hope, Nuiqsut, Deadhorse (Prudhoe Bay), and Barter Island. Also offices in Kotzebue with service to Buckland, Deering, Ambler, Kiana, Kivalina, Kobuk, Noatak, Noorvik, Point Hope, Selawik, and Shungnak. Offices in Nome with service to St. Michael, Shishmaref, Stebbins, Teller, Unalakleet, Wales, Shaktoolik, White Mountain, Koyuk, Golovin, Elim, Brevig Mission, Gambell, and Savoonga.

From FAIRBANKS

Frontier Flying Service, 3820 University Ave., Fairbanks 99709—To 16 Interior and Arctic villages including Gates of the Arctic National Park and the Arctic National Wildlife Refuge.

Larry's Flying Service Inc., 3822 University Ave., Fairbanks 99709—To Anaktuvuk Pass, Bettles, Fort Yukon, and 12 more villages.

From GLENNALLEN

Gulkana Air Service, Box 31, Glennallen 99588—Serves McCarthy and May Creek.

From GUSTAVUS (Glacier Bay)

Glacier Bay Airways, Box 1, Gustavus 99826—To Juneau, Hoonah, Excursion Inlet, Skagway, Haines and other Southeast points.

From HAINES

Haines Airways, Box 470, Haines 99827; phone (907) 766-2646—To Juneau and Glacier Bay.

L.A.B. Flying Service (Alaska Airlines commuter), Box 272, Haines 99827—To Juneau, Hoonah, Skagway and Gustavus/Glacier Bay.

From JUNEAU

Air North, Box 4998, Whitehorse, YT

Let us help you arrange a Alaska travel schedule that will get you also "out in the bush." Let us make you a VISITOR... a guest in our land... and not just a rushing through "TOURIST."

There are fly-in hikes, wilderness treks, rafting and kayaking, "little boat" charter cruises... you name it... a lot of extra ways to enjoy Alaska.

Call us. Let us help you.

ALASKA NORTHWEST TRAVEL SERVICE, INC.
A Division of Alaska Northwest Publishing Co.
130 2nd Ave. S. - Dept. MP92
Edmonds, WA 98020
206-775-4504 • 1-800-533-7381
FAX 206-672-2824

Y1A 4S2—To Whitehorse, YT.

L.A.B. Flying Service (Alaska Airlines commuter), Box 2201, Juneau 99803. To Haines, Hoonah, Skagway and Gustavus/Glacier Bay.

Loken Aviation, 8995 Yandukin Dr., Juneau 99801; phone (907) 789-3331—To all Southeast points.

Wings of Alaska/Petersburg Flightseeing and Charters, 1873 Shell Simmons Dr., Juneau 99801—To Haines, Hoonah, Skagway, Pelican, Elfin Cove, Angoon, Tenakee, Kake and Gustavus/Glacier Bay.

From KENAI

Southcentral Air, 125 N. Willow St., Kenai 99611. Serves Anchorage, Homer and Soldotna.

From KETCHIKAN

Ketchikan Air Service, 1600 International Airport, Ketchikan 99901; phone (907) 225-6608—To Stewart, BC, Hyder, Craig and Klawock.

Temsco Airlines (Alaska Airlines commuter), P.O. Box 8015, Ketchikan 99901—Airport and waterfront departures to Craig, Coffman Cove, Hydaburg, Long Island, Klawock, Metlakatla, Petersburg, Thorne Bay, Wrangell, and other Southeast points.

From NOME

Bering Air, Inc., Box 1650, Nome 99762—From Nome and Kotzebue to western Alaska points and Soviet Far East.

From PETERSBURG

Alaska Island Air, Box 508, Petersburg 99833—To Kake and Rowan Bay.

From SKAGWAY

Skagway Air Service, Box 357, Skagway 99840—To Juneau.

From WRANGELL

Ketchikan Air Service, Box 847, Wrangell 99929—To Petersburg, Ketchikan and Kake.

SCHEDULED AIR SERVICE TO/IN YUKON AND WESTERN CANADA

Air North, P.O. Box 4998, Whitehorse, YT Y1A 4S2; phone (403) 668-2228—Between Whitehorse, Dawson, Fairbanks, Juneau, Watson Lake and Old Crow.

AirBC, 4740 Agar Dr., Richmond, BC V7B 1A6; phone (604) 273-2464—Interprovincial service and service from Vancouver to Whitehorse and U.S. destinations of Seattle and Portland.

Alkan Air, P.O. Box 4008, Whitehorse, YT Y1A 3S9; phone (403) 668-6616, fax (403) 668-6486—Between Whitehorse, Dawson City, Mayo, Faro, Ross River, Watson Lake, Old Crow and Inuvik, NWT.

Canadian Airlines International, 1004 W. Georgia St., Vancouver, BC V6E 2Y2; phone (604) 279-6611—To Calgary, Edmonton, Vancouver, Prince George, Prince Rupert, Fort St. John, Fort Nelson, Watson Lake, Whitehorse and other points.

North Coast Air Services, Box 610, Prince Rupert, BC V8J 3R5; phone (604) 627-1351, fax (604) 627-1356—From Prince Rupert to Queen Charlotte Islands. Local and scheduled services.

Alcoholic Beverages

Alaska: Legal drinking age is 21. Packaged liquor, beer and wine are sold by licensed retailers rather than in state liquor stores. The sale and/or importation of alcoholic beverages is prohibited in some 70 Bush communities.

Alberta: Legal age is 18. Packaged liquor, beer and wine are sold in government liquor stores (open daily except Sunday and holidays) and beer (to take out) is also sold in some taverns. On Sunday, liquor is served only with food in licensed dining rooms.

British Columbia: Legal age is 19. Packaged liquor, beer and wine are sold only in government liquor stores (open daily except Sunday and holidays). Sunday serving laws in licensed premises vary from community to community.

Northwest Territories: Legal age is 19. Packaged liquor, beer and wine are sold in government liquor stores at Hay River, Pine Point, Fort Simpson, Fort Smith, Yellowknife, Norman Wells and Inuvik. Beer only agencies are located in some other places. You can purchase liquor in most hotels for consumption on the premises. The sale and possession of alcohol is prohibited in several communities.

Yukon Territory: Legal age is 19. Packaged liquor, beer and wine are sold in government liquor stores at Watson Lake, Whitehorse, Dawson City and Haines Junction. Some licensed premises have beer and wine for take-out sale.

Bicycling in Alaska

Road conditions vary throughout Alaska, from newly paved highways to unimproved dirt roads. In planning your bicycling routes, read the highway logs in *The MILEPOST®* carefully. Abrupt changes in road conditions are generally noted in the log, as are steep grades and whether or not there are shoulders. With the recent popularity of the "mountain bike," additional routes are available to the rider who can travel on unimproved dirt roads and trails. Bicyclists will have to share the highways with vehicles, but you can avoid traffic by riding in the early morning and on weekdays. One advantage of Alaska touring in summer are the long daylight hours.

At press time, there were no laws governing bicyclists other than normal vehicle laws. Helmets are recommended.

Bus Lines

Independent travelers wishing to travel by public bus within Alaska and Yukon Territory will generally find routes and services much more limited than in the Lower 48. Scheduled bus service is available within Alaska and Yukon Territory, but scheduled direct bus service to Alaska from the Lower 48 is not available, unless you wish to join an escorted motorcoach tour. If your schedule allows, you can travel from the Lower 48 to Alaska via public bus service by using several carriers. Most scheduled bus service in the North is seasonal.

Contact the following companies for current schedules:

Alaska–Denali Transit, Box 4557, Anchorage, AK 99510; phone (907) 273-3331. Service from Anchorage to Denali National Park, Fairbanks, Tok, Haines, Kenai and Homer.

Alaska Intercity Line, P.O. Box 230051, Anchorage, AK 99523-0051; phone (907) 279-3221. Service from Anchorage to Portage, Soldotna, Kenai, Homer, Palmer, Wasilla, Valdez, and Denali Park.

Alaska Sightseeing Tours, 4th and Battery Bldg., Suite 700, Seattle, WA 98121; phone (907) 276-1305 (summer) or (800) 426-7701 year-round. Motorcoach trips connect Anchorage and Haines. Motorcoach tours to Anchorage, Denali Park.

Alaska–Yukon Motorcoaches, 349 Wrangell Ave., Anchorage, AK 99501; phone (907) 276-1305 or (800) 637-3334. Routes connecting Anchorage, Valdez, Fairbanks and Haines.

Alaskon Express, 300 Elliott Ave. W., Seattle, WA 98119; phone (800) 544-2206. Scheduled service from Anchorage, Fairbanks, Haines, Skagway and Whitehorse.

Caribou Express–Bus, 501 L St., Anchorage, AK 99501; phone (907) 278-5776. Coach service to Anchorage, Denali Park, Fairbanks, Tok, Alyeska, Portage Glacier, Homer and Seward.

Denali Express, 405 L St., Anchorage, AK 99501; phone (907) 274-8539. Service between Anchorage and Denali Park.

Gray Line of Alaska, 300 Elliott Ave. W., Seattle, WA 98119; phone (800) 544-2206. Scheduled service to Skagway, Whitehorse and Haines. Motorcoach tours to Anchorage, Denali Park, Fairbanks, Prince William Sound, Seward and Portage Glacier.

Norline Coaches (Yukon) Ltd., 2191 2nd Ave., Whitehorse, YT Y1A 4T8; phone (403) 668-3355. Service between Whitehorse and Dawson City.

Princess Tours®, 2815 2nd Ave., Suite 400, Seattle, WA 98121; phone (206) 728-4202. Highway service between major destinations in Alaska and Yukon.

Seward Bus Line, P.O. Box 1338, Seward, AK 99664; phone (907) 224-3608. Service between Anchorage, Homer and Seward.

Cabins

If you've ever wanted to try living in a log cabin in the wilderness, the USDA Forest Service gives you the opportunity for $20 per night per cabin. There are more than 190 of these public-use cabins scattered throughout Tongass and Chugach national forests.

Cabins are accessible by air, boat, or trail. Average size is 12 by 14 feet. Most cabins have wood stoves, some have oil stoves. Check with the Forest Service to determine what type of stove is provided. All cabins have tables and sleeping room for 4 or more

---

ALASKA BICYCLE TOURING GUIDE

Second edition, 1992. By Alys Culhane and Pete Praetorius. Foreword by ex-Governor Cowper. First and only bike guide to Alaska and parts of YT and NWT. Detailed guide divides the route into 50 mile sections and includes extensive info for the cyclist. *Fairbanks Daily News-Miner* called it "comprehensive, reliable and enticing." "The maps and details are specific," noted the *Midwest Book Review*, "making for an essential take-along reference for any devotee of bicycle touring." $17.50 + $2.50/shipping (domestic).

The Denali Press • Box 021535 • Juneau, Alaska 99802 • (907) 586-6014

GENERAL INFORMATION

people. You must supply bedding, cookware, stove oil if necessary, and food. Splitting mauls are provided on site for cutting firewood. There are pit toilets but no garbage dumps (pack garbage out). Skiffs are provided at some cabins.

Permits for use of recreation cabins are issued on either a first-come first-serve basis, or by drawing. Applications for permits may be made in person or by mail up to 180 days in advance. You must have a permit for the specific length of occupancy. There is a 3-day limit May 15 to Aug. 31 on hike-in cabins in the Chugach National Forest. There is a 7-day limit on other cabins in the Tongass National Forest from April 1 to Oct. 31, 10-day limit Nov. 1 through March 31.

For reservations and information on Chugach National Forest cabins, contact: Chugach National Forest, 201 E. 9th Ave., Suite 206, Anchorage 99501; phone 271-2599.

For reservations and information on Tongass National Forest cabins, contact one of the following area offices: Ketchikan Ranger District, Federal Bldg., Ketchikan 99901, phone 225-3101; Petersburg Ranger District, Box 309, Petersburg 99833, phone 772-3871; or Sitka Ranger District, 204 Siginaka Way, Sitka 99835, phone 747-6671.

The Bureau of Land Mangement has public-use cabins in Alaska, all within 75 miles of Fairbanks. Cabins must be reserved prior to use and a fee is required. Contact the Fairbanks Support Center Public Room at 1150 University Ave., Fairbanks 99709, phone 474-2250.

The U.S. Fish & Wildlife Service maintains public-use cabins within Kodiak National Wildlife Refuge. Contact the refuge manager, 1390 Buskin River Road, Kodiak 99615.

The Alaska Division of Parks and Outdoor Recreation maintains several public-use cabins scattered throughout the state. For reservations and information contact the following regional offices: Southcentral, Box 107001, Anchorage 99510, phone 762-2616; Southeast, 400 Willoughby Center, Juneau 99801, phone 465-4563; and Northern Region, 4418 Airport Way, Fairbanks 99709, phone 451-2698.

Calendar of Events—1992

Travelers may wish to take into account some of the North's major celebrations when planning their visit. Following are some of these events listed by month and by place. Additional events are detailed under Attractions under the communities covered in the highway logs. Special events celebrating the 50th anniversary of the Alaska Highway are found in the ALASKA HIGHWAY and FAIRBANKS sections and on pages 5-7.

FEBRUARY
Anchorage—Fur Rendezvous; Iditarod Trail Sled Dog Race. **Cordova**—Iceworm Festival. **Fairbanks**—Yukon Quest Sled Dog Race. **Nenana**—Tripod Raising Festival. **Soldotna**—Peninsula Winter Games; 10-Dog Classic Sled Dog Race. **Whitehorse, YT**—Yukon Quest Sled Dog Race; Sourdough Rendezvous.

MARCH
Fairbanks—Winter Carnival; North American Sled Dog Championships. **Nome**—Bering Sea Ice Classic Golf Tournament; month of Iditarod events. **North Pole**—Winter Carnival.

APRIL
Girdwood—Alyeska Spring Carnival. **Juneau**—Alaska Folk Festival.

MAY
This month is a busy one for fishing derbies for halibut (Homer and Valdez) and salmon (Ketchikan, Petersburg and Sitka).
Delta Junction—Buffalo Wallow Square Dance Jamboree. **Glennallen**—Gulkana Air Show. **Kodiak**—Crab Festival. **Nome**—Polar Bear Swim. **Petersburg**—Little Norway Festival. **Talkeetna**—Miners Day Festival. **Tok**—Tanana 100 Boat Race.

JUNE
Anchorage—Mayor's Midnight Sun Marathon. **Fairbanks**—Midnight Sun Baseball Game; Yukon 800 Marathon Boat Race. **Nenana**—River Daze. **Nome**—Midnight Sun Festival. **Palmer**—Colony Days. **Sitka**—All-Alaska Logging Championships; Summer Music Festival.

JULY
Big Lake—Regatta. **Chugiak–Eagle River**—Bear Paw Festival. **Dawson City, YT**—International Midnight Dome Race; Yukon Gold Panning Championships. **Delta Junction**—Buffalo Barbecue, Deltana Fair. **Fairbanks**—Golden Days; World Eskimo–Indian Olympics. **Seward**—Mount Marathon Race. **Soldotna**—Progress Days. **Talkeetna**—Moose Dropping Festival.

AUGUST
Dawson City, YT—Discovery Days. **Fairbanks**—Tanana Valley State Fair. **Haines**—Southeast Alaska State Fair. **Ketchikan**—Blueberry Arts Festival. **Kodiak**—*Cry of the Wild Ram.* **Ninilchik**—Kenai Peninsula State Fair. **Palmer**—Alaska State Fair. **Seward**—Silver Salmon Derby.

SEPTEMBER
Dawson City, YT—Great Klondike Outhouse Race. **Fairbanks**—Oktoberfest; Tanana Rampart Boat Race. **Kodiak**—State Fair and Rodeo. **Nome**—Golf Tournament; Great Bathtub Race. **Skagway**—Trail of '98 Road Relay to Whitehorse, YT. **Tok**—Tanana 100 Boat Races.

OCTOBER
Haines—Alaska Day Celebration. **Sitka**—Alaska Day Festival.

NOVEMBER
Anchorage—Great Alaska Shootout. **Fairbanks**—Northern Invitational Curling Spiel.

Camping

The MILEPOST® indicates both private and public campgrounds with tent symbols in the highway logs and on the strip maps for Alaska, Yukon Territory, Northwest Territories and parts of Alberta and British Columbia. Federal, state and provincial agencies offering camping areas are listed here. Reservations are not accepted at any provincial, state or federal campgrounds. Keep in mind that government campgrounds do not maintain dump stations (excepting a few British Columbia provincial parks) and few offer electrical hookups. Season dates for most campgrounds in the North depend on weather. Check the highway logs for commercial campgrounds in the North. *NOTE: Campers are urged to use established campgrounds. Overnighting in rest areas and turnouts is illegal unless otherwise posted, and may be unsafe.* ▲

ALASKA
The **Alaska Public Lands Information Centers** in Fairbanks, Anchorage and Tok provide information on all state and federal campgrounds in Alaska, along with state and national park passes and details on wilderness camping. Visit the centers, or contact the Alaska Public Lands Information Center at: 250 Cushman St., Suite 1A, Fairbanks 99701, phone (907) 451-7352, or 605 W. 4th Ave., Suite 105, Anchorage 99501, phone (907) 271-2737.

The **Alaska Division of Parks** maintains an extensive system of roadside campgrounds and waysides. All are available on a first-come, first-served basis. There is a $6 to $8 per night camping fee charged at all developed state campgrounds, except for $10 at Eagle River and $12 Chena River campgrounds. *(NOTE: Rates are subject to change.)* An annual pass, good for unlimited camping in a calendar year, is available for $60 residents, $75 nonresidents. The pass is in the form of a nontransferable windshield decal. Send check or money order payable to State of Alaska to Annual Camping Pass, Division of Parks and Recreation, P.O. Box 107001, Anchorage 99510-7001.

The **USDA Forest Service** provides numerous camping areas in Chugach and Tongass national forests. Most USFS campgrounds charge a fee of from $6 to $8 per night depending on facilities. There is a 14-day limit at most campgrounds; this regulation is enforced. For further information write the Office of Information, USDA Forest Service, Box 1628, Juneau 99802.

The **Bureau of Land Management** maintains about 25 free camping areas in the state. Write to the Bureau of Land Management, Attn: The Public Rooms, 1150 University Ave., Fairbanks 99709; phone 474-2200.

The **National Park Service** maintains 7 campgrounds in Denali National Park and Preserve. There are established hike-in campgrounds at Glacier Bay and Katmai national parks and preserves, wilderness camping in other national parks and preserves in Alaska. For further information contact the Alaska Public Lands Information Center, 605 W. 4th, Suite 105, Anchorage 99501; phone 271-2737.

The **U.S. Fish & Wildlife Service** manages several camping areas within Kenai National Wildlife Refuge. Contact the Refuge Manager, Kenai National Wildlife Refuge, Box 2139, Soldotna 99669.

CANADA
National park campgrounds generally have a per night fee. Per night fees range from $9 for a tent site to $15 for a full-service site with individual water, sewer and electrical hookups. In addition, a park motor license sticker is required for motorists staying overnight in the national parks. Electrical service is standard 60 cycle. Wood for campfires is supplied free to all camping and picnicking grounds. Bring your own ax to split kindling. "Serviced" campgrounds have caretakers.

Alberta has 54 **provincial park campgrounds**, some with limited facilities, others with picnic tables, electrical hookups, flush toilets, barbecues and nature programs. There is a fee for provincial parks. There are no camping fees and limited facilities at roadside campsites provided by Alberta Transportation and at campsites in the **Forest Recreation Areas**.

In British Columbia, **provincial park campgrounds** are indicated 1.2 miles/2 km and 1,312 feet/400m before the entrance along the highways by blue-and-white signs.

They are serviced from spring to early fall (however, they may be used throughout the year). Fees range from $5 to $10 per night. Gates close from 11 P.M. to 6 A.M. in some parks.

In Northwest Territories: **Territorial campground** fees range from $8 to $10 per night in attended campgrounds and parks with facilities. Free firewood is supplied for use in campground.

Yukon Territory has more than 40 **Yukon government campgrounds** located along its road system. There is a per night fee charged for nonresidents. These well-maintained government campgrounds often have kitchen shelters (which may not be used as sleeping accommodations) and free firewood for use at the campground. There is a 14-day limit.

Customs Requirements

Crossing the border into Canada or reentering the United States is a fairly straightforward procedure. However, there are a few items which Alaska-bound travelers should be alerted to.

The first is firearms. Canada has very specific and strict requirements on what firearms may be brought into Canada. If you plan to travel with a firearm, read these requirements carefully.

Certain items, mainly crafts and souvenirs made from parts of wild animals, have caused some problems for travelers to the North in recent years. An item which may be purchased legally in Alaska, for example carved ivory, can be brought back into the Lower 49 but may not be permitted transit through Canada without a permit. Some items which may be purchased legally in parts of Canada may not be allowed into the U.S. For example, a seal fur doll purchased in Inuvik, NWT, would be confiscated by U.S. customs because the import of seal products is restricted except by special permit.

Read through the following information and contact Canadian or U.S. customs offices directly.

ENTRY INTO CANADA FROM THE UNITED STATES

Your best source of general information on this subject is the Canadian Government Office of Tourism's travel information brochure. For further information write Revenue Canada, Customs and Excise, Communications Branch, Ottawa, ON K1A 0L5; phone (613) 957-0275. Here are excerpts from that brochure.

Citizens or permanent residents of the United States can usually cross the U.S.–Canada border either way without difficulty or delay. They do not require passports or visas. However, to assist officers of both countries in speeding the crossing, native-born U.S. citizens should carry some identifying paper that shows their citizenship, just in case they are asked for it. This would include a driver's license, voters registration, passport with photo, or some employment cards with description and photo. Social security cards are not positive identification. Birth certificates of children are sometimes required. Proof of residence may also be required. Permanent residents of the U.S. who are not American citizens are advised to have their Alien Registration Receipt Card (U.S. Form 1-151).

All persons other than U.S. citizens or legal residents, and residents of Greenland, require a valid passport or an acceptable travel document.

Visitors of the U.S. who have a single entry visa to that country should check with an office of the U.S. Immigration and Naturalization Service to make sure that they have all the papers they need to get back into the U.S.

Persons temporarily in the U.S. who would require visas if coming to Canada directly from their countries of origin, should contact the Canadian Embassy, Consulate or Office of Tourism in their home country before departure for the U.S.

Persons under 18 years of age who are not accompanied by an adult should bring a letter with them from a parent or guardian giving them permission to travel into Canada. A divorced parent may find a copy of the divorce/custody papers helpful.

Although there is no set standard for monies required for entrance into Canada, the visitor must have sufficient funds to cover his cost of living per day for the planned length of stay. Consideration in assessing "sufficient funds" includes the locale in which the visitor plans to stay and whether he will be staying with a friend or relative. (Readers report being turned back for lacking $150 in cash.) The visitor must also have return transportation fare to his country of origin.

Vehicles: The entry of vehicles and trailers into Canada for touring purposes, for periods up to 12 months, is generally a quick, routine matter, without payment of a customs assessment, and any necessary permits are issued at the port of entry. Rental trailers of the U-haul luggage variety may be subject to a nominal deposit which is refundable on proof of exportation of trailer. Motor vehicle registration forms should be carried and, if the vehicle is rented from a car rental company, a copy of the rental contract stipulating use in Canada. If a tourist enters Canada using a vehicle not registered in his name, it is suggested that he carry a letter from its registered owner authorizing the use of the vehicle.

U.S. motorists planning to travel in Canada are advised to obtain a Canadian Nonresident Interprovincial Motor Vehicle Liability Insurance Card which provides evidence of financial responsiblity. This card is available only in the U.S. through U.S. insurance agents. All provinces in Canada require visiting motorists to produce evidence of financial responsibility, should they be involved in an accident. Financial responsibility limits vary by province.

All national driver's licenses are valid in Canada.

Trailers: If you plan to leave your vacation trailer in Canada for a season while returning home from time to time, ask Canada customs for a wallet-sized special permit—an E-99. Post the permit inside the trailer so that it can be seen easily from outside. You may not store a vacation trailer in Canada during the off-season.

Entry by private boat: Visitors planning to enter Canada by private boat should contact customs in advance for a list of ports of entry that provide customs facilities and their hours of operation. Immediately upon arrival, visitors must report to customs and complete all documentation. In emergency situations, visitors must report their arrival to the nearest regional customs office or office of the RCMP.

Baggage: The necessary wearing apparel and personal effects in use by the visitor are admitted free of duty. Up to 50 cigars, 200 cigarettes (1 carton) and 2 pounds of manufactured tobacco and up to 40 ounces of spiritous liquor or wine OR 24 12-ounce cans or bottles of beer or ale may be allowed entry in this manner. Additional quantities of alcoholic beverages up to a maximum of 2 gallons may be imported into Canada (except the Northwest Territories) on a payment of duty and taxes plus charges for a provincial permit at port of entry. To import tobacco products a person must be 16 years of age or over and to import alcoholic beverages the importer must have reached the legal age established by authorities of the province or territory into which the alcoholic beverages are being entered.

Recreational Equipment: Visitors may also bring in sporting outfits and other equipment for their own use by declaring them at entry. These can include fishing tackle, portable boats, outboard motors, snowmobiles, equipment for camping, golf, tennis and other games, radios and portable or table-model television sets used for the reception of sound broadcasting and television programs, typewriters and cameras (with a reasonable amount of film and flashbulbs) in their possession on arrival. Although not a requirement, it may facilitate entry if visitors have a list (in duplicate) of each item, including serial numbers when possible. All such articles must be identified and reported when leaving Canada. ▲

Transporting goods through Canada: U.S. citizens from the Lower 49 who wish to transport personally their household or personal effects to Alaska when such goods are not intended for use in Canada, may obtain a temporary admission permit at the border to facilitate the in-transit movements of goods through Canada.

Firearms: Firearms are divided into 3 categories—prohibited, restricted and long guns.

A nonresident importing a "long gun" or moving in transit through Canada with a "long gun" does not require a Firearms Acquisition Certificate nor a Permit to Transport providing the visitor is 16 years of age or older and the firearm is for sporting or competition use. A "long gun" means a regular hunting rifle or shotgun as so described by the manufacturer, and which does not fall into the category of a prohibited or restricted firearm.

A prohibited firearm includes any firearm that is capable of firing bullets in rapid succession during one pressure of the trigger, or any firearm adapted from a rifle or shotgun whether by sawing, cutting or other alteration or modification, that as so adapted, has a barrel that is less than 18 inches/46 cm in length, or that is less than 26 inches/66 cm in overall length. Such weapons are not permitted entry into Canada.

A restricted firearm includes any firearm that is not a prohibited weapon, has a barrel less than 18$^1/_2$ inches/47 cm in length and is capable of discharging center-fire ammunition in a semiautomatic manner, or is designed or adapted to be fired when reduced to a length less than 26 inches/66 cm by folding, telescoping or otherwise. Also included would be any firearm designed, altered or intended to be aimed and fired by the action of one hand, such as revolvers and handguns.

Restricted firearms may only enter Canada when accompanied by a Permit to Transport or a Permit to Carry issued by a Canadian Local Registrar of Firearms. These permits are rarely issued.

The following quantities of explosives may enter Canada for personal use by hunters and competitive marksmen without a permit issued by the Explosives Branch of the Dept. of Energy, Mines and Resources: 2,000 safety cartridges; 1,000 primers for safety cartridges; 500 empty primed safety cartridge cases; 4.4 pounds/2 kg smokeless powder (small-arms nitro compound).

Nonresidents arriving at a Canada Customs port must declare all their firearms. Anyone who illegally carries a firearm into Canada is subject to a number of penalties, including seizure of the weapon and the vehicle in which it is carried.

Plants, fruit and vegetables: House plants may be imported without a permit. Some fruits and vegetables may be restricted entry into Canada and all are subject to inspection at the border.

Animals: Dogs and cats (over 3 months of age) from the U.S. must be accompanied by a certificate issued by a licensed veterinarian of Canada or the U.S. certifying that the animal has been vaccinated against rabies during the preceding 36 months; such a certificate shall describe the animal and date of vaccination and shall be initialed by inspectors and returned to the owner.

Up to 2 pet birds per family may be imported into Canada. Birds of the parrot family and accompanied by the owner, may be admitted if found healthy and if the owner certifies in writing that, upon entering the country, the birds have not been in contact with other birds of the parrot family and have been in his possession for 90 days immediately preceding importation. All birds of the parrot family, except budgies, cockatiels, and Rose-ringed parakeets are on the CITES endangered species list and require at the minimum a U.S. CITES export permit with some species requiring an additional Canadian CITES import permit. The temporary movement of all parrots through Canada requires a CITES Temporary Import Certificate from the Canadian Wildlife Service. Contact Canadian Wildlife Service, Ottawa, ON K1A 0H3, phone (819) 997-1840.

Endangered species: The importation of certain animals and plants that are on the endangered species list is prohibited. This applies to any recognizable by-product made of the fur, skin, feathers, bone, etc., of these creatures. For example, U.S. citizens transporting carved ivory or parts of lynx, otter, brown/grizzly bear or wolf through Canada must first obtain an export and/or transit permit from the U.S. Fish and Wildlife Service. (Permits are available at 1412 Airport Way in Fairbanks or at any U.S. Fish and Wildlife Refuge office.) Many ivory sellers will furnish a permit upon request. To avoid the need for a permit, either mail the items or travel directly back to the Lower 48. Request a list of restricted items from Convention Administrator, Canadian Wildlife Service, Environment Canada, Ottawa, ON K1A 0H3.

Record your trip, expenses and memories in *The Milepost® Souvenir Log Book*—a daily journal that will become a lasting keepsake. To order, call 1-800-343-4567.

REENTRY INTO THE UNITED STATES

It is, of course, the responsibility of the traveler to satisfy U.S. immigration authorities of his right to reenter the U.S.

Canadian immigration officers may caution persons entering from the U.S. if they may have difficulty in returning.

Reentry to the U.S. can be simplified if you list all your purchases before you reach the border, keep sales receipts and invoices handy and pack purchases separately.

Within 48 Hours: Residents of the U.S. visiting Canada for less than 48 hours may take back for personal or household use merchandise to the fair retail value of $25, free of U.S. duty and tax. Any or all of the following may be included, so long as the total value does not exceed $25; 50 cigarettes, 10 cigars (non-Cuban in origin), 4 ounces/150 ml of alcoholic beverage or alcoholic perfume.

If any article brought back is subject to duty or tax, or if the total value of all articles exceeds $25, no article may be exempted from duty or tax. Members of a family household are not permitted to combine the value of their purchases under this exemption.

Persons crossing the International Boundary at one point and reentering the U.S. in order to travel to another part of Canada should inquire at U.S. customs regarding special exemption requirements.

After More Than 48 Hours: U.S. residents returning from Canada may take back, once every 30 days, merchandise for personal or household use to the value of $400 free of U.S. duty and tax, provided they have remained in Canada 48 hours. The exemption will be based on the fair retail value of the article acquired and goods must accompany the resident upon arrival in the U.S. Members of a family household traveling together may combine their personal exemptions—thus a family of 5 could be entitled to a total exemption of $2,000. Up to 100 cigars (non-Cuban in origin) per person may be imported into the U.S. by U.S. residents, and also 1 liter of alcoholic beverages if the resident has attained the age of 21 years, and up to 200 cigarettes.

Federal wildlife laws affect what U.S. citizens may bring back into the U.S. from Canada. The list is extensive, and U.S. visitors to Canada should be particularly aware that the import of the following is restricted except by special permit: products made from sealskin, whalebone and whale and walrus ivory, sea otter, or polar bear, and most wild bird feathers, mounted birds and skins. Thus, an item which may be purchased legally in parts of Canada, such as a seal fur doll, may not be allowed into the U.S. For a complete list of restricted items and information on import permits, contact the nearest U.S. Fish and Wildlife Service office.

Pets: Domestic dogs, including those taken out of the country and being returned, must have a valid rabies vaccination certificate identifying the dog and date of vaccination and bearing the signature of a licensed veterinarian. A date of expiration should be included. If no date of expiration is specified, the certificate is acceptable if the date of vaccination is no more than 12 months before the date of arrival. Vaccination against rabies is not required for cats.

For further information contact the nearest U.S. customs office or write U.S. Customs Service, Washington, DC 20229.

Daylight Hours

SUMMER MAXIMUM

	Sunrise	Sunset	Hrs. of daylight
Barrow	May 10	Aug. 2	84 days continuous
Fairbanks	1:59 A.M.	11:48 P.M.	21:49 hours
Anchorage	3:21 A.M.	10:42 P.M.	19:21 hours
Juneau	3:51 A.M.	10:09 P.M.	18:18 hours
Ketchikan	4:04 A.M.	9:33 P.M.	17:29 hours
Adak	6:27 A.M.	11:10 P.M.	16:43 hours

WINTER MINIMUM

	Sunrise	Sunset	Hrs. of daylight
Barrow	Jan 24 noon	Nov. 18 noon	none
Fairbanks	10:59 A.M.	2:41 P.M.	3:42 hours
Anchorage	10:14 A.M.	3:42 P.M.	5:28 hours
Juneau	9:46 A.M.	4:07 P.M.	6:21 hours
Ketchikan	9:12 A.M.	4:18 P.M.	7:06 hours
Adak	10:52 A.M.	6:38 P.M.	7:46 hours

Driving Information

Driving to the North is no longer the ordeal it was in the early days. Those early images of the Alaska Highway with vehicles sunk in the mud up to their hubcaps are far removed from the asphalt-surfaced Alaska Highway of today.

Highways in the North range from 4-lane paved freeways to 1-lane dirt and gravel roads. Major highways in Alaska are paved with the exception of the following highways which are gravel: Steese Highway (Alaska Route 6), Taylor Highway (Alaska Route 5), Elliott Highway (Alaska Route 2), Dalton Highway and Denali Highway (Alaska Route 8).

In Yukon Territory, all of the Alaska Highway, and most of the Klondike Highway from Skagway to Dawson City, are asphalt-surfaced. All other roads are gravel.

Major routes through Alberta and British Columbia are paved, with the exception of the Cassiar Highway, which has both gravel and asphalt surfacing. The Cassiar Highway (BC Highway 37) is becoming a popular route North.

All highways within Northwest Territories are gravel. Most gravel roads in the North are well-maintained and treated with calcium chloride as a dust-control measure.

Know your vehicle and its limitations. Some Northern roads may not be suitable for a large motorhome or trailer, but most roads will present no problem to a motorist who takes his time and uses common sense.

Auto Preparation: The following recommendations for driving in the North Country in summer are from our MILEPOST field editors. One thing to keep in mind is the variable nature of road conditions: some sections of road may be in poor condition because of construction or weather; other highways—particularly gravel roads closed in winter—may be either very rough or very smooth, depending on when maintenance crews last worked on the road. Another is the wide range of roads in the North, from 4-lane freeway to narrow gravel roads. For example, the Alaska Highway is surfaced almost its entire length and the greatest distance between services is only about 100 miles/160 km. Although there still can be some rough spots on the Alaska Highway, either because of construction or because the surfacing has deteriorated, it is generally a good highway. The more remote roads, such as the Dempster or Dalton highways, are gravel and motorists are much farther from assistance. More preparation is required for these roads.

There are some simple preparations motorists can make for their trip North which can make driving easier. First make sure your vehicle and tires are in good condition before starting out. An inexpensive and widely available item to include are clear plastic headlight covers (or black metal matte screens). These protect your headlights from flying rocks and gravel. You might also consider a wire-mesh screen across the front of your vehicle to protect paint, grill and radiator from flying rocks. The finer the mesh, the more protection from flying gravel. For those of you hauling trailers, a piece of quarter-inch plywood fitted over the front of your trailer offers protection.

There is practically no way to protect the windshield, although some motorists have experimented with screen shields that do not seriously impair their vision. However, these may make you feel like you're driving a hamster cage. These are not recommended nor do you see many of them in the North, but it is, of course, up to the individual motorist whether these are worthwhile.

Many motorists find bug screens a worthwhile investment.

Crankcases are seldom damaged, but gas tanks can be on rough gravel roads. Sometimes rocks work their way in between the plate and gas tank, wearing a hole in the tank. You may wish to insert a rubber mat of some kind between gas tank and securing straps. However, drivers maintaining safe speeds should have no problems with punctured gas tanks. The higher the clearance on your vehicle the better on some of the rougher gravel roads.

Also keep in mind the simple precautions that make driving easier. A visor or tinted glass helps when you're driving into the sun. Good windshield wipers and a full windshield washer (or a bottle of wash and squeegee) make life easier.

Dust and mud are generally not a major problem on Northern roads, though you may run into both. Heavy rains combined with a gravel road or roadbed torn up for construction make mud. Mud flaps are suggested. Many gravel roads in the North (such as the Dalton Highway) are treated with calcium chloride as a dust-control measure. Because calcium chloride tends to eat into paint and metal parts on your vehicle, be sure to thoroughly wash your vehicle. Dust can seep into everything and it's difficult if not impossible to keep it out. Remember to close the windows on your trailer or camper when on a dusty road. It also helps to keep clothes, food and bedding in sealed plastic bags. Also check your air filter periodically.

Driving at slow safe speeds not only keeps down the dust for drivers in back of you, it also helps prevent you from spraying other vehicles with gravel.

Although auto shops in Northern communities are generally well-stocked with parts, do carry the following for emergencies and on-the-spot repairs: flares, first-aid kit; trailer bearings; good bumper jack with lug wrench; a simple set of tools, such as crescent wrenches, socket and/or open-end wrenches, hammer, screwdrivers, pliers, wire, prybar (for changing that fan belt); electrician's tape; small assortment of nuts and bolts; fan belt; and 1 or 2 spare tires (2 spares for remote roads).

If you are driving a vehicle which may require parts not readily available up North, add whatever you think necessary. You may wish to carry an extra few gallons of gas and also water, especially on remote roads. You may also wish to carry a can of fluid for brakes, power steering and automatic transmissions.

If your vehicle should break down on the highway and tow truck service is needed, normally you will be able to flag down a passing motorist. Travelers in the Northland are generally helpful in such situations (traditionally, the etiquette of the country requires one to stop and provide assistance). If you are the only person traveling in the disabled vehicle, be sure to leave a note on your windshield indicating when you left the vehicle and in what direction you planned to travel.

Gasoline: Unleaded gas is widely available in Alaska and is the rule in Canada. Diesel gas is also commonly available. In Alaska, check with the Alaska State Troopers, and in Canada the RCMP, about gas availability. Good advice for Northern travelers: gas up whenever possible.

Gas prices in the North, as elsewhere, vary. Generally, gas prices are slightly higher in Canada and Alaska than the Lower 48, but this is not a hard and fast rule. You may find gas in Anchorage or elsewhere at the same price—or even lower—than at home. A general rule of thumb is the more remote the gas station, the higher the price. And gas prices may vary considerably from service station to service station within the same community.

It is a good idea to carry cash, since some gas stations in Alaska are independents and do not accept credit cards. Most Chevron, Texaco and Tesoro stations will accept VISA or MasterCard. Also watch for posted gas prices that are for *cash*, but not noted as such. Besides double-checking the posted price before filling up, also check with the attendant to make sure you have the correct pump for unleaded, regular or diesel, depending on what you want.

Keep in mind that Canadian gas stations have converted to the metric system; quantity and price are based on liters. There are 3.785 liters per U.S. gallon, 4.5 liters per imperial gallon. See Metric System this section for conversion chart.

Insurance: Auto insurance is mandatory in all Canadian provinces and territories. Drivers should carry adequate car insurance before entering the country. Visiting motorists are required to produce evidence of financial responsibility should they be involved in an accident. There is an automatic fine if visitors are involved in an accident and found to be uninsured, and your car can be impounded. Your insurance company should be able to provide you with proof of insurance coverage (request a Canadian Non-Resident Interprovincial Motor Vehicle Liability Insurance Card) which is accepted as evidence of financial responsibility.

The minimum liability insurance requirement in Canada is $200,000 Canadian, except in the Providence of Quebec where the limit is $50,000 Canadian. Further information regarding automobile insurance in Canada may be obtained from The Insurance Bureau of Canada, 181 University Ave., Toronto, ON M5H 3M7.

Tires: On gravel, the faster you drive, the faster your tires will wear out. So take it easy.

If you take it easy, you should have no problems with your tires, provided you have the right size for your vehicle, with the right pressure, not overloaded, and not already overly worn. Belted bias or radial ply tires are recommended for gravel roads.

Carry 1 good spare. Consider 2 spares if you are traveling remote gravel roads such as the Dempster or Dalton highways. The space-saver doughnut spare tires found in some passenger cars are not adequate for travel on gravel roads.

In Alaska, studded tires are permitted from Sept. 15 to May 1 (Sept. 30 to April 15 south of 60°N).

Emergency Medical Services

Phone numbers of emergency medical services (if available), such as ambulance and hospital, are listed along with police and fire departments at the beginning of each town or city description in *The MILEPOST*®. Emergency medical services along Alaska's highways are listed in the introduction to each highway.

In addition, travelers should note that CB Channels 9 and 11 are monitored for emergencies in most areas, Channels 14 and 19 in some areas. Recommendations for emergency equipment and a list of emergency medical services on Alaska's highways are detailed in a brochure called *Help Along The Way*, available from the Emergency Medical Services Section, Division of Public Health, Dept. of Health & Social Services, P.O. Box H, Juneau 99811-0616.

Fishing

Throughout *The MILEPOST*® you will find this ⤙ friendly little symbol. Wherever you see one, you will find a description of the fishing at that point.

Following is a brief summary of fishing license fees, rules and regulations for Alaska and Canada. It is not possible to list all the latest regulations in *The MILEPOST*®, so we urge you to obtain up-to-date information.

Alaska: A nonresident fishing license, valid for the calendar year issued, costs $50. A special 3-day nonresident fishing license may be purchased for $15. A 14-day nonresident permit is $30. A one day nonresident fishing license may also be purchased for $10. Nonresidents under 16 years of age do not need a fishing license.

Resident sportfishing licenses cost $10. A resident is a person who has maintained a permanent place of abode within the state for the previous 12 consecutive months and has continuously maintained his voting residence in the state, and any member of the military service who has been stationed in the state for the immediately preceding 12 months.

Nearly all sporting goods stores in Alaska sell fishing licenses.

The Alaska Dept. of Fish and Game publishes a variety of materials for fishermen. For a price list and free pamphlets, write the Alaska Dept. of Fish and Game, Public Communications Section, P.O. Box 3-2000,

Juneau 99802-2000; phone 465-4112, or contact any regional office of the Dept. of Fish and Game. Be sure you have the most recent edition of the ADF&G regulations booklet for information on bag limits and special permits.

Canada: A special fishing license is necessary for fishing in Canadian national parks and is good for the entire season in all national parks. These are on sale at park gates.

Alberta: Annual nonresident license (season), $12; limited (3-day) nonresident, $5. Licenses not required for anglers under 16 or residents over 65 years of age.

British Columbia: Annual nonresident, non-Canadian angler's license, $35; nonresident short-term fishing license, valid for 5 consecutive days and not valid for steelhead fishing, $17.50. Licenses not required for anglers under 16 years of age. Special permits required for steelhead and for nonresident fishing lakes and streams classified as "Special Water." Freshwater and saltwater fishing licenses are required of all anglers 16 and older; both are renewable on March 31.

Northwest Territories: Annual nonresident fishing license, $15. Nonresident anglers under 16 years of age do not need a license when accompanied by a licensed angler. Fishing licenses are available from the visitor information center at the Alberta–Northwest Territories border on the Mackenzie Highway and in most communities from hardware and sporting goods stores, fishing lodges, RCMP, and government wildlife offices.

Yukon Territory: Season fishing license fee for a nonresident is $35, or $25 for 3 days. Canadian resident season fee is $30. All persons 16 years of age or over must have a license.

Holidays—1992

The following list of observed holidays in Alaska and Canada can help you plan your trip. Keep in mind that banks and other agencies may be closed on these holidays and traffic may be heavier.

ALASKA

New Year's Day	Jan. 1
Martin Luther King Day	Jan. 20
Presidents' Day	Feb. 17
Seward's Day	March 30
Easter Sunday	April 19
Memorial Day	May 25
Independence Day	July 4
Labor Day	Sept. 7
Columbus Day	Oct. 12
Alaska Day	Oct. 18
Veterans Day	Nov. 11
Thanksgiving Day	Nov. 26
Christmas Day	Dec. 25

CANADA

New Year's Day	Jan. 1
Good Friday	April 17
Easter Monday	April 20
Victoria Day	May 18
Canada Day	July 1
Alberta Heritage Day	Aug. 3
British Columbia Day	Aug. 3
Discovery Day (YT)	Aug. 17
Labour Day	Sept. 7
Thanksgiving Day	Oct. 12
Remembrance Day	Nov. 11
Christmas Day	Dec. 25
Boxing Day	Dec. 26

Hunting

Obtain up-to-date information on fees, licenses, seasons, bag limits and regulations from the following government agencies for Alaska, Alberta, British Columbia, Northwest Territories and Yukon Territory.

Alaska: Alaska Dept. of Fish and Game, Box 2-5525, Juneau, AK 99802. A complete list of registered Alaska guides is available for $5 from the Dept. of Commerce, Guide Licensing and Control Board, Box D, Juneau, AK 99811 or 3601 C St., Anchorage, AK 99503.

Alberta: Alberta Forest, Lands and Wildlife, 9915 108th St., Edmonton, AB T5K 2C9.

British Columbia: Fish and Wildlife Branch, Ministry of Environment, 780 Blanshard St., Victoria, BC V8W 2H1.

Northwest Territories: Department of Economic Development and Tourism, Yellowknife, NT X1A 2L9.

Yukon Territory: Tourism Yukon, Box 2703, Whitehorse, YT Y1A 2C6.

Information Sources

Contact the following state and provincial tourism agencies for free maps and brochures and for travel-related questions.

Alaska: Alaska Division of Tourism, P.O. Box E, Juneau, AK 99811; phone (907) 465-2010.

Alberta: Travel Alberta, 3rd Floor, 10155 102 St., Edmonton, AB T5J 4L6; phone 1-800-661-8888.

British Columbia: Tourism British Columbia, 1117 Wharf Street, Victoria, BC V8W 2Z2; phone 1-800-663-6000.

Northwest Territories: Dept. of Economic Development and Tourism, Yellowknife, NT X1A 2L9; phone 1-800-661-0788.

Yukon Territory: Tourism Yukon, Box 2703, Whitehorse, YT Y1A 2C6; phone (403) 667-5340.

Metric System

Canada has converted to the metric system. Inches have been replaced with centimeters, feet and yards with meters, miles with kilometers and Fahrenheit with Celsius. Miles, feet, yards and temperatures in all sections of *The MILEPOST* are followed by the equivalent metric measure. See conversion table for liters and gallons.

LITERS TO GALLONS CONVERSION TABLE

1	.3	21	5.5	41	10.8
2	.5	22	5.8	42	11.1
3	.8	23	6.1	43	11.4
4	1.1	24	6.3	44	11.6
5	1.3	25	6.6	45	11.9
6	1.6	26	6.9	46	12.2
7	1.8	27	7.1	47	12.4
8	2.1	28	7.4	48	12.7
9	2.4	29	7.7	49	12.9
10	2.6	30	7.9	50	13.2
11	2.9	31	8.2	51	13.5
12	3.2	32	8.5	52	13.7
13	3.4	33	8.7	53	14.0
14	3.7	34	9.0	54	14.3
15	4.0	35	9.2	55	14.5
16	4.2	36	9.5	56	14.8
17	4.5	37	9.8	57	15.0
18	4.8	38	10.0	58	15.3
19	5.0	39	10.3	59	15.6
20	5.3	40	10.6	60	15.9

For more precise conversion: 1 liter equals .2642 gallons; 1 gallon equals 3.785 liters.

Money/Credit Cards

The money system in Canada is based on dollars and cents, but the Canadian dollar and the American dollar are 2 separate currencies and the rate of exchange varies. U.S. currency is accepted as payment in Canada, but the best advice for visitors is: exchange your currency for Canadian funds at a bank in Canada. The visitor is then assured of receiving the rate of exchange prevailing on that day. Although businesses in Canada will accept American dollars, they will often give a lesser rate of exchange than banks or no exchange rate.

As you travel north away from the more populated areas you will find banks located only in the major cities or at best the smaller communities will be served by traveling banks or banks open only 1 to 3 days a week for limited hours. Banks in Whitehorse and Dawson City, YT, Yellowknife, NWT, and major Alaskan cities are open generally 10 A.M. to 3 P.M. weekdays (open until 6 P.M. on Friday). Also, some Canadian holidays differ from U.S. holidays, see list under Holidays in this section.

Major American bank and credit cards, including most oil company cards and those of retailers who do business in both countries, are accepted in Canada, too. Credit card purchases are billed at the U.S. dollar equivalent of the Canadian price.

It is a good idea to carry cash, since some gas stations in Alaska are independents and do not accept oil company credit cards or major bank credit cards.

Tourists to Canada may be eligible for a rebate on Goods and Services Tax (GST) paid on goods and accommodation. Check with tourism or customs authorities for more information.

Mosquitoes

Mosquitoes emerge from hibernation before the snow has entirely disappeared and peak about June but continue active through the fall. Mosquitoes hatch their eggs in water, so the North—with its marshy tundra and many lakes—is a good breeding ground. Mosquitoes are attracted to warmth, moisture, carbon dioxide and dark colors, among other things. Mosquito repellents containing diethyl-meta-toluamide (DEET) are most effective.

National Parks, Preserves and Monuments

The Alaska National Interest Lands Conservation Act, passed in December 1980, placed more than 97 million acres into new or expanded national parks, monuments, preserves and wildlife refuges. Denali and Glacier Bay national parks and preserves are covered in detail in *The MILEPOST*. For general information on all of Alaska's national and state parks, refuges and forests, contact the Alaska Public Lands Information Centers either in Anchorage at 605 W. 4th Ave., Suite 105, Anchorage 99510, phone (907) 271-2737; Fairbanks at 250 Cushman, Suite 1A, Fairbanks 99701, phone (907) 451-7352; or Tok at Box 359, Tok 99780, phone (907) 883-5667.

Postal Rates

Alaska: Rates are the same as for all other U.S. states.

Canada: Rates at press time were 42¢ first class (30 grams, about 1 ounce) within Canada, and 48¢ (30 grams) to the U.S. United States postage stamps may not be used for mailings sent from Canada.

Shipping

Vehicles: Carriers that will ship cars, truck campers, house trailers and motorhomes from Anchorage to Seattle include: Sea–Land Freight Service, Inc., 1717 Tidewater Ave., Anchorage 99501, phone (907) 274-2671; Alaska Railroad, Box 107500, Anchorage 99510, phone (907) 265-2490; and Totem Ocean Trailer Express, 2511 Tidewater, Anchorage 99501, phone (907) 276-5868.

In the Seattle, WA, area, contact Sea–Land Service, Inc., 3600 Port of Tacoma Road, Tacoma 98424, phone (206) 922-3100 or 1-800-426-4512 (outside Washington); Alaska Railroad, 2203 Airport Way S., Suite 215, Seattle, WA 98134, phone (206) 624-4234; Totem Ocean Trailer Express, P.O. Box 24908, Seattle 98124, phone (206) 628-9280 or 1-800-426-0074 (except from Washington, Alaska or Hawaii); or A.A.D.A. Systems, P.O. Box 2323, Auburn 98071, phone (206) 762-7840.

Vehicle shipment between southeastern Alaska and Seattle is provided by Boyer Alaska Barge Line, 7318 4th Ave. S., Seattle 98108, phone (206) 763-8575 (serves Ketchikan and Wrangell); and Alaska Marine Lines, 5615 W. Marginal Way SW, Seattle 98106, phone (206) 763-4244 or toll free (800) 443-4343 (direct service to Ketchikan, Wrangell, Petersburg, Sitka, Juneau, Haines, Skagway, Yakutat, Excursion Inlet and Hawk Inlet).

Persons shipping vehicles between Seattle and Anchorage are advised to shop around for the carrier which offers the services and rates most suited to the shipper's needs. Not all carriers offer year-round service and freight charges vary greatly depending upon the carrier and the length and height of the vehicle. Rates quoted here are only approximate. Sample fares per unit: northbound, Seattle to Anchorage, under 66 inches in height, $1,225; over 66 inches and under 84 inches in height, $1,785; southbound, Anchorage to Seattle, any unit under 84 inches, $640. Over 17 feet to 21 feet, northbound, $2,160; southbound, $65 per foot. Rates increase frequently and the potential shipper is cautioned to call carriers' rate departments for those rates in effect at shipping time.

Not all carriers accept rented moving trucks and trailers, and a few of those that do require authorization from the rental company to carry its equipment to Alaska. Check with the carrier and your rental company before booking service.

Book your reservation at least 2 weeks in advance and 3 weeks during summer months, and prepare to have the vehicle at the carrier's loading facility 2 days prior to sailing. Carriers differ on what nonvehicle items they allow to travel inside, from nothing at all to goods packaged and addressed separately. Coast Guard regulations forbid the transport of vehicles holding more than one-quarter tank of gas, and none of the carriers listed above allow owners to accompany their vehicles in transit. Remember to have fresh antifreeze installed in your car or truck prior to sailing!

You may ship your vehicle aboard a state ferry to southeastern ports (at a lesser rate), however, you must accompany your vehicle or arrange for someone to drive it on and off the ferry at departure and arrival ports. See MARINE ACCESS ROUTES section.

Household Goods and Personal Effects: Most moving van lines have service to and from Alaska through their agency connections in most Alaska and Lower 48 cities. To initiate service contact the van line agents nearest your origin point.

Northbound goods are shipped to Seattle and transferred through a port agent to a water vessel for carriage to Alaska. Few shipments go over the road to Alaska. Southbound shipments are processed in a like manner through Alaska ports to Seattle, then on to destination.

U-Haul provides service into the North Country for those who prefer to move their goods themselves. At press time, there were 53 U-Haul dealerships in Alaska and northwestern Canada for over-the-road service. In Alaska, there were 4 dealerships in Anchorage, 2 in Fairbanks and 1 in each of the following communities: Homer, Juneau, Ketchikan, Delta Junction, Haines, Seward, Soldotna, Tok, Valdez, Wasilla, Eagle River, Sitka, and North Pole. In Canada, there were dealerships and ready stations in Dawson Creek, Fort St. John, Fort Nelson and at other locations along the Alaska Highway.

It's also possible to ship a rented truck or trailer into southeastern Alaska aboard the water carriers that accept privately owned vehicles (see Shipping Vehicles). A few of the water carriers sailing between Seattle and Anchorage also carry rented equipment. However, shop around for this service, for this has not been common practice in the past, and rates can be very high if the carrier does not yet have a specific tariff established for this type of shipment. You will not be allowed to accompany the rented equipment.

Telephone, Telegraph, Money Orders

Alaska: All of Alaska uses the 907 area code.

Telegrams, cablegrams, mailgrams, telex and fax can be sent by telephone from anywhere in Alaska through Western Union. Money transfers can also be sent and received within 15 minutes through Western Union agencies, many with extended hours of operation. Western Union branch offices are located throughout the state and continental U.S. To find the Western Union location nearest you, and for hours of operation, phone 1-800-325-6000.

Alberta: All of the province shares the area code 403.

British Columbia: All of the province shares the area code 604.

Northwest Territories: The territory has 3 area codes. The area code for all communities included in *The MILEPOST®* is 403.

Yukon Territory: All of the territory shares the area code 403 (same as Alberta).

Persons wishing to send telegrams to or from Canada, as well as needing money transfer services, should contact the offices of the Canadian Western Union affiliate, Unitel–Transdollar. To find the location nearest you, phone 1-800-361-1877.

Time Zones

At Alaska's request, the federal government reduced the state's time zones from 4 to 2, effective Oct. 30, 1983. The state now is operating on Alaska time, or 1 hour earlier than Pacific time. The only residents of the state not setting their clocks on Alaska time are in the 4 western Aleutian Island communities of Atka, Adak, Shemya and Attu, which moved from Bering time to Aleutian–Hawaii time.

British Columbia is on Pacific standard time (daylight saving time in summer), the same as Yukon Territory, except for the area around Dawson Creek and Fort St. John and south from Valemount through Cranbrook, which are on mountain time. All of Alberta and western Northwest Territories are on mountain time and both observe daylight saving time.

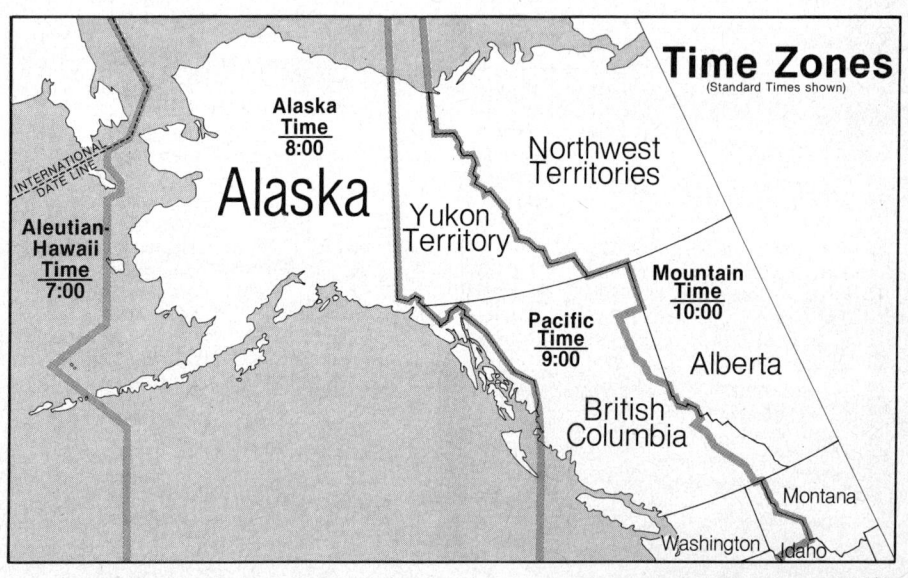

Zip Codes in Alaska

Afognak	99697
Akhiok	99615
Akiachak	99551
Akiak	99552
Akutan	99553
Alakanuk	99554
Aleknagik	99555
Alexander Creek	99695
Alifak	99697
Allakaket	99720
Ambler	99786
Amook	99697
Anaktuvuk Pass	99721
Anchor Point	99556

Anchorage:
General Delivery 99501
See street listings in
official zip code directory.

Anderson	99744
Angoon	99820
Aniak	99557
Anvik	99558
Arctic Village	99722
Atka	99502
Atmautluak	99559
Attu	99502
Auke Bay	99821
Baranof	99850
Barrow	99723
Beaver	99724
Bell Island	99950
Bethel	99559
Bettles Field	99726
Big Lake	99652
Bird Creek	99540
Border	99780
Brevig Mission	99785
Buckland	99727
Cantwell	99729
Cape Pole	99950
Cape Yakataga	99695
Central	99730
Chalkyitsik	99788
Chatham	99850
Chefornak	99561
Chevak	99563
Chickaloon	99674
Chicken	99732
Chignik	99564
Chignik Lagoon	99565
Chignik Lake	99564
Chisana	99790
Chitina	99566
Chuathbaluk	99557
Chugiak	99567
Circle	99733
Clam Gulch	99568
Clarks Point	99569
Clear	99704
Coffman Cove	99950
Cold Bay	99571
Coldfoot	99701
College	99701
P.O. Boxes	99708
Cooper Landing	99572
Copper Center	99573
Cordova	99574
Craig	99921
Crooked Creek	99575
Deep Bay	99950
Deering	99736
Delta Junction	99737
Denali National Park	99755
Dillingham	99576
Dolomi	99950
Dot Lake	99737
Douglas	99824
Driftwood Bay	99695
Dutch Harbor	99692
Eagle	99738
Eagle River	99577
Eek	99578
E...	99579
E...	99695
E...	99702
Ekw...	99580
Elfin Cove	99825
Elim	99739
Elmendorf AFB	99506
Emmonak	99581
English Bay	99603
Ester	99725
Excursion Inlet	99850

Fairbanks:
General Delivery 99701
See street listings in
official zip code directory.

False Pass	99583
Farewell	99695
Fire Cove	99950
Flat	99584
Fort Richardson	99505
Fort Wainwright	99703
Fort Yukon	99740
Fortuna Ledge	99585
Funter Bay	99850
Gakona	99586
Galena	99741
Gambell	99742
Girdwood	99587
Glennallen	99588
Gold Creek	99695
Golovin	99762
GoodnewsBay	99589
Grayling	99590
Gulkana	99695
Gustavus	99826
Haines	99827
Halibut Cove	99603
Happy Harbor	99950
Hawk Inlet	99850
Healy	99743
Holy Cross	99602
Homer	99603
Hoonah	99829
Hooper Bay	99604
Hope	99605
Houston	99694
Hughes	99745
Huslia	99746
Hydaburg	99922
Hyder	99923
Icy Bay	99695
Igiugig	99613
Iliamna	99606
Indian	99540
Ivanoff Bay	99695

Juneau:
General Delivery 99801
See street listings in
official zip code directory

Kake	99830
Kaktovik	99747
Kalskag	99607
Kaltag	99748
Karluk	99608
Kasaan	99950
Kasigluk	99609
Kasilof	99610
Kasitsna Bay	99695
Kenai	99611
Kenny Cove	99695
Ketchikan	99901
Kiana	99749
King Cove	99612
King Salmon	99549
Kipnuk	99614
Kitoi Bay	99697
Kivalina	99750
Klawock	99925
Kobuk	99751
Kodiak	99615
Kokhanok	99606
Koliganek	99576
Kongiganak	99559
Kotlik	99620
Kotzebue	99752
Koyuk	99753
Koyukuk	99754
Kwethluk	99621
Kwigillingok	99622
Lab Bay	99950
Lake Minchumina	99757
Larsen Bay	99624
Levelock	99625
Lime Village	99695
Little Diomede	99762
Long Island	99950
Loring	99950
Lower Kalskag	99626
Manley Hot Springs	99756
Manokotak	99628
May Creek	99695
McCarthy	99695
McGrath	99627
McKinley Park (see Denali National Park)	
Mekoryuk	99630
Mentasta Lake	99780
Metlakatla	99926
Meyers Chuck	99903
Minto	99758
Moose Pass	99631
Moser Bay	99697
Mountain Village	99632
Naknek	99633
Napakiak	99634
Napaskiak	99559
Neets Cove	99950
Nelson Lagoon	99571
Nenana	99760
New Stuyahok	99636
Newtok	99559
Nickolaevsk	99556
Nightmute	99690
Nikiski	99611
Nikolai	99691
Nikolski	99638
Ninilchik	99639
Noatak	99761
Nome	99762
Nondalton	99640
Noorvik	99763
North Pole	99705
Northway	99764
Noyes Island	99950
Nuiqsut	99789
Nulato	99765
Nunapitchuk	99641
Nyac	99642
Old Harbor	99643
Olga Bay	99697
Ophir Bay	99695
Ouzinkie	99644
Palmer	99645
Paxson	99737
Pedro Bay	99647
Pelican	99832
Perryville	99648
Petersburg	99833
Pilot Point	99649
Pilot Station	99650
Platinum	99651
Point Baker	99927
Point Hope	99766
Point Lay	99723
Pope Vancy Landing	99695
Portage Creek	99695
Port Alexander	99836
Port Alice	99950
Port Alsworth	99653
Port Ashton	99695
Port Bailey	99697
Port Clarence	99790
Port Graham	99603
Port Heiden	99549
Port Johnson	99950
Port Lions	99550
Port Moller	99695
Port Protection	99950
Port San Juan	99695
Port Walter	99850
Port Williams	99697
Prudhoe Bay	99734
Quinhagak	99655
Rampart	99767
Red Devil	99656
Red Mountain	99695
Rowan Bay	99850
Ruby	99768
Russian Mission	99657
Saint George Island	99591
Saint Marys	99658
Saint Michael	99659
Saint Paul Island	99660
Salcha	99714
Sand Point	99661
Savoonga	99769
Scammon Bay	99662
Seal Bay	99697
Selawik	99770
Seldovia	99663
Seward	99664
Shageluk	99665
Shaktoolik	99771
Sheldon Point	99666
Shishmaref	99772
Shungnak	99773
Sitka	99835
Skagway	99840
Skwentna	99667
Slana	99586
Sleetmute	99668
Soldotna	99669
Solomon	99790
South Naknek	99670
Sparrevohn	99502
Stebbins	99671
Sterling	99672
Stevens Village	99774
Stony River	99557
Sutton	99674
Takotna	99675
Talkeetna	99676
Tanacross	99776
Tanana	99777
Tatitlek	99677
Telida	99695
Teller	99778
Tenakee Springs	99841
Terror Bay	99697
Tetlin	99779
Thorne Bay	99919
Togiak	99678
Tok	99780
Tokeen	99950
Toksook Bay	99637
Trapper Creek	99683
Tuluksak	99679
Tuntutuliak	99680
Tununak	99681
Twin Hills	99576
Tyonek	99682
Uganik Bay	99697
Ugashik	99695
Unalakleet	99684
Unalaska	99685
Utopia	99790
Uyak	99697
Valdez	99686
Venetie	99781
View Cove	99950
Wainwright	99782
Wales	99783
Ward Cove	99928
Wasilla	99687
Waterfall	99950
West Point	99697
Whale Pass	99950
White Mountain	99784
Whittier	99693
Willow	99688
Wiseman	99790
Wrangell	99929
Yakutat	99689
Yes Bay	99950
Zackar Bay	99697

INDEX OF PLACE NAMES

Communities, Highways, National Parks (NP), National Wildlife Refuges (NWR) and other attractions.

*A detailed map is included.

A

Abbotsford, BC, 42
Airdrie, AB, 26
Akhiok, AK, 484
Aklavik, NT, 624
*Alaska Highway, 68
Alaska Railroad, 397
Alaskaland Pioneer Park, 374
Alyeska Access Road, 415
Alyeska, AK, 416
Anchor Point, AK, 467
Anchor River (Beach) Road, 468
*Anchorage, AK, 285
Anchorage Fur Rendezvous, 314
Anderson, AK, 344
Angoon, AK, 566
Anton Larson Bay Road, 488
Arctic Red River, NT, 622
Ashcroft, BC, 46
Atigun Camp, 629
Atlin, BC, 605
*Atlin Road, 604
Auke Bay, AK, 574

B

Barkerville, BC, 54
Beaver Creek, YT, 149
Beaverlodge, AB, 40
Bezanson, AB, 36
Big Delta, AK, 175
Big Horn Highway, 36
Big Lake, AK, 325
Big Lake Road, 325
Blackfalds, AB, 26
Bodenburg Butte, AK 280
Boston Bar, BC, 46
Boundary, AK, 251
Bowden, AB, 26
Burns Lake, BC, 207
Burwash Landing, YT, 145

C

Cache Creek, BC, 49
Calais, AB, 36
*Calgary, AB, 25
*Campbell Highway, 610
*Canol Road, 615
Cantwell, AK, 339, 396
Carcross, YT, 603
Carmacks, YT, 240
Carrot Creek, AB, 202
Carstairs, AB, 26
Cassiar, BC, 235
*Cassiar Highway, 223
Cedarvale, BC, 215
Central, AK, 404
Centreville, BC, 236
Champagne, YT, 139
Chandalar Camp, 629
Charlie Lake, BC, 91
Chatanika, AK, 402
Chena Hot Springs, AK, 401
Chena Hot Springs Road, AK, 400
Chetwynd, BC, 62
Chicken, AK, 253
Chilkoot Trail, 593
Chistochina, AK, 261
Chiniak Road, 488
Chitina, AK, 521
Chugach State Park, 301, 312
Chugiak, AK, 282
Circle, AK, 405
Circle Hot Springs, AK, 404
Circle Hot Springs Road, AK, 404
Clam Gulch, AK, 463
Claresholm, AB, 25
Clear, AK, 344
Clinton, BC, 49
Coal River, BC, 107
Coffman Cove, AK, 554
Cohoe, AK, 464
Cohoe Loop Road, 464
Coldfoot, AK, 628
Columbia Glacier, AK, 489
Contact Creek, BC, 108
Cooper Landing, AK, 439
Copper Center, AK, 510
*Copper River Highway, 517
*Cordova, AK, 504
Craig, AK, 554
Crooked Creek, AB, 36
Crossfield, AB, 26

D

*Dalton Highway, 624
*Dawson City, YT, 244
*Dawson Creek, BC, 77
Deadhorse, AK, 630
Dease Lake, BC, 233
Debolt, AB, 36
Decker Lake, BC, 208
*Delta Junction, AK, 169
Demmitt, AB, 41
*Dempster Highway, 619
*Denali Highway, 392
*Denali NP, 380
Destruction Bay, YT, 145
Dietrich Camp, 629

Dixonville, AB, 187
Donnelly, AB, 187
Dot Lake, AK, 168
Douglas, AK, 574
Dunvegan, AB, 183
Dyea Road, 594

E

Eagle, AK, 255
Eagle River, AK, 283
*Edgerton Highway, 520
*Edmonton, AB, 27, 187
Edson, AB, 202
Eielson AFB, AK, 177
Eklutna, AK, 281
*Elliott Highway, 406
Elmendorf AFB, AK, 284
Elsa, YT, 609
Endako, BC, 207
Enterprise, NT, 190
Entwistle, AB, 201
Ester, AK, 349

F

*Fairbanks, AK, 350
Fairview, AB, 183
Fallis, AB, 201
Faro, YT, 613
Fireside, BC, 107
Five Mile Camp, 627
Fort Fraser, BC, 205
Fort Greely, AK, 516
Fort Liard, NT, 182
Fort Macleod, AB, 25
Fort McPherson, NT, 622
*Fort Nelson, BC, 96
Fort Providence, NT, 193
Fort Resolution, NT, 196
Fort Richardson, AK, 284
Fort St. James, BC, 206
*Fort St. John, BC, 87
Fort Simpson, NT, 191
Fort Smith, NT, 196
Fort Vermilion, AB, 189
Fox, AK, 401, 406
Fox Creek, AB, 34
Franklin Bluffs Camp, 630
Fraser Lake, BC, 207

G

Gainford, AB, 201
Gakona, AK, 263
Gakona Junction, AK, 263
Galbraith Camp, 629
*George Parks Highway, 316

Girdwood, AK, 415
*Glacier Bay NP, 574
Glacier Highway, 573
*Glenn Highway, 256
Glennallen, AK, 264
Good Hope Lake, BC, 236
Grande Cache, BC, 36
*Grande Prairie, AB, 38
Granisle, BC, 209
Great Falls, MT, 22
Grimshaw, AB, 187
Groundbirch, BC, 64
Gulkana, AK, 263, 513
Gustavus, AK, 578

H

*Haines, AK, 579
*Haines Highway, 596
Haines Junction, YT, 140
Happy Valley Camp, 630
Hatcher Pass Road, 274
Hay River, NT, 190, 192
*Hazelton, BC, 213
Healy, AK, 343
Hells Gate, BC, 46
Heritage Highway, 64
High Level, AB, 189
High River, AB, 25
Highway 26, 54
Highway 37 South, 218
Highway 58 East, 189
Hinton, AB, 202
Hixon, BC, 56
Hollis, AK, 554
Holman, NT, 624
*Homer, AK, 470
Hoonah, AK, 567
Hope, AK, 419
Hope, BC, 45
Hope Highway, 419
Houston, AK, 324
Houston, BC, 209
Hudson's Hope, BC, 66
*Hudson's Hope Loop, 65
Hydaburg, AK, 555
Hyder, AK, 227
Hythe, AB, 41

I

Independence Mine State Hist. Park, 274
Indian, AK, 413
Indian Cabins, AB, 190
Innisfail, AB, 26
Inuvik, NT, 623
Iskut, BC, 232

INDEX

J

Jade City, BC, 235
Jake's Corner, YT, 122
John Hart Highway, 59
Johnson's Crossing, YT, 121
*Juneau, AK, 568
Juneau Veteran's Memorial Highway, 573

K

Kake, AK, 566
Kalifornsky Beach Road, 462
Kantishna, AK, 391
Karluk, AK, 484
Kasaan, AK, 554
Kasilof, AK, 462
Keg River, AB, 189
*Kenai, AK, 457
Kenai Fjords NP, 431
Kenai NWR, 455
Kenai Peninsula, 410
Kenai Spur Highway, 456
Kennicott, AK, 523
Keno City, YT, 609
*Ketchikan, AK, 548
Kispiox, BC, 214
Kitimat, BC, 218
Kitseguecla, BC, 215
Kitsumkalum, BC, 216
Kitwancool, BC, 225
Kitwanga, BC, 225
Klawock, AK, 555
Klondike Gold Rush NP, 593
*Klondike Highway, 600
*Klondike Loop, 237
Kluane NP, YT, 142
Klukshu, YT, 599
Klukwan, AK, 598
Knik, AK, 320
Knik Road, 320
*Kodiak, AK, 484
Kodiak NWR, 487
'Ksan, BC, 214

L

Labouchere Bay, AK, 556
Lac La Hache, BC, 51
Lacombe, AB, 26
La Crete, AB, 189
Lake Louise Road, 270
Larsen Bay, AK, 484
Leduc, AB, 27
Lethbridge, AB, 22
Liard River, BC, 106
*Liard Highway, 180
Little Smoky, AB, 34
Livengood, AK, 408
Lower Post, BC, 109
Lytton, BC, 46

M

MacKay, AB, 201
Mackenzie, BC, 60
*Mackenzie Highway, 183
Manley Hot Springs, AK, 409
Manning, AB, 187
*Marine Access Routes, 524
Matanuska Glacier, 272

Mayerthorpe, AB, 32
Mayo, YT, 608
McBride, BC, 204
McCarthy, AK, 523
*McCarthy Road, 522
McDame Post, BC, 236
McLeese Lake, BC, 53
McNeil River, AK, 481
Meander River, AB, 190
Mendenhall Glacier, AK, 572
Mentasta Lake, AK, 259
Metlakatla, AK, 552
Milk River, AB, 22
Minto, AK, 408
Minto, YT, 241
Mitkof Highway, 562
Moberly Lake, BC, 65
Moose Pass, AK, 421
Moricetown, BC, 213
Mount McKinley, 380
Muncho Lake, BC, 104

N

Nabesna, AK, 261
Nabesna Road, 260
Nahanni NP, 192
*Nahanni Range Road, 614
Nanaimo, BC, 524
Nanton, AB, 25
Naukati, AK, 556
*Nenana, AK, 346
New Hazelton, BC, 213
Nikiski, AK, 456
Ninilchik, AK, 465
Ninilchik Village, AK, 464
Niton Junction, AB, 202
Nojack, AB, 201
North Pole, AK, 178
Northway, AK, 152
Obed, AB, 202
Old Crow, NT, 624
Old Glenn Highway, 280
Old Harbor, AK, 484
Old Man Camp, 627
Olds, AB, 26
100 Mile House, BC, 49
150 Mile House, BC, 51
Onoway, AB, 29
Ouzinkie, AK, 484

P

*Palmer, AK, 276
Pasagshak Bay Road, 488
Paulatuk, NT, 624
Paxson, AK, 392, 515
Peace River, AB, 187
Pelican, AK, 567
Pelly Crossing, YT, 241
Peters Creek, AK, 282
*Petersburg, AK, 560
Petersville Road, AK, 336
Pine Point, NT, 196
Pink Mountain, BC, 92
Pocahontas, AB, 202
Point Baker, AK, 554
Ponoka, AB, 26
Port Alcan, AK, 151
Port Edward, BC, 219
Port Hardy, BC, 524
Port Lions, AK, 484

Port Protection, AK, 554
Portage, AK, 414
Portage Glacier Road, 418
Pouce Coupe, BC, 41
*Prince George, BC, 56
*Prince of Wales Island, AK, 553
*Prince Rupert, BC, 219
Prince William Sound, 489
Prophet River, BC, 95
Prospect Camp, 628
Prudhoe Bay, AK, 630

Q

Quesnel, BC, 53

R

Rae–Edzo, NT, 193
Rainbow Lake, AB, 189
Red Deer, AB, 26
Rezanof–Menashka Road, 487
*Richardson Hwy., 506
Ross River, YT, 612
Rycroft, AB, 183

S

Sachs Harbour, NT, 624
Salcha, AK, 177
Sangudo, AB, 29
Saxman, AK, 552
Seattle, WA, 42
Seldovia, AK, 482
70 Mile House, BC, 49
*Seward, AK, 424
*Seward Highway, 411
Sexsmith, AB, 36, 183
Sikanni Chief, BC, 93
*Silver Trail, 608
*Sitka, AK, 562
*Skagway, AK, 587
Skilak Lake Loop Road, 439
Slana, AK, 260
Slope Mountain Camp, 629
Smithers, BC, 210
*Soldotna, AK, 447
Sourdough, AK, 513
South Hazelton, BC, 215
Southeastern Alaska, 548
Spences Bridge, BC, 46
Spruce Grove, AB, 27, 201
Steamboat, BC, 102
Steen River, AB, 190
*Steese Highway, 398
Sterling, AK, 442
*Sterling Highway, 434
Stewart, BC, 227
Stony Plain, AB, 29, 201
Summit Lake, BC, 103
Sutton, AK, 275
Swan Lake Road, 445
Swanson River Road, 445
Swift River, YT, 117

T

*Tagish Road, 607
Tagish, YT, 607
Talkeetna, AK, 331
Talkeetna Spur Road, 331

Tanacross, AK, 167
Taylor, BC, 87
*Taylor Highway, 252
Telegraph Creek, BC, 234
Telkwa, BC, 210
Tenakee Springs, AK, 567
Terrace, BC, 215
Teslin, YT, 119
Thorne Bay, AK, 555
Toad River, BC, 103
*Tok, AK, 155
Tok Cutoff, 256
Top of the World Highway, 251
Topley, BC, 208
Topley Landing, BC, 208
Totem Bight, 551
Trapper Creek, AK, 336
Trutch Mountain, BC, 94
Tsawwassen, BC, 524
Tuktoyaktuk, NT, 624
Tumbler Ridge, BC, 63
Tungsten, NT, 614
Tupper, BC, 41

U

Upper Liard Village, YT, 114
Usk, BC, 215

V

*Valdez, AK, 490
Valleyview, AB, 35, 187
Vanderhoof, BC, 205
Victoria, BC, 527

W

Ward Cove, AK, 552
Warner, AB, 22
Wasilla, AK, 320
Watson Lake, YT, 109
Wells, BC, 54
Wembley, AB, 40
Whale Pass, AK, 555
White Pass & Yukon Route, 595
Whitecourt, AB, 32
*Whitehorse, YT, 124
Whittier, AK, 489
Wildwood, AB, 201
Williams Lake, BC, 51
Willow, AK, 326
Wiseman, AK, 628
Woking, AB, 183
Wonowon, BC, 92
Wood Buffalo NP, 195
*Wrangell, AK, 557
Wrangell–St. Elias NP, 523

Y

Yakutat, AK, 578
Yale, BC, 45
*Yellowhead Hwy., 197
*Yellowknife, NT, 194
Yukon–Charley Rivers NP, 255

Z

Zama, AB, 190
Zimovia Highway, 559

640   The MILEPOST® ■ 1992

ANCHORAGE

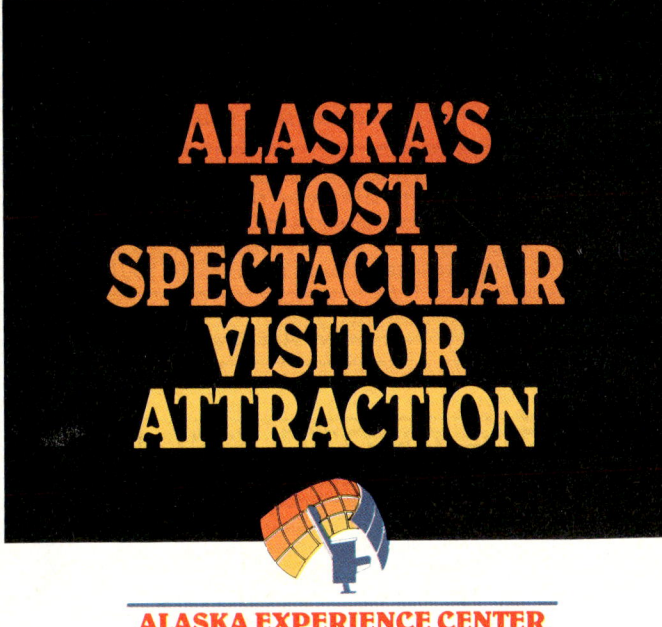

ALASKA'S MOST SPECTACULAR VISITOR ATTRACTION

ALASKA EXPERIENCE CENTER

Two unforgettable Alaskan Attractions

See Alaska come alive on our giant 180° domed screen in the OMNI THEATER and relive the Great Alaska Earthquake in o unique Alaskan Earthquake Exhibit!

Located in Downtown Anchorage
24-hr. recorded message 276-3730

Alaska's Favorite Gift Store

Over 4,000 square feet of Alaskan souvenirs, gifts and friendly service.

Featuring the largest selection of **Alaskana** Sweatshirts and T-shirts.

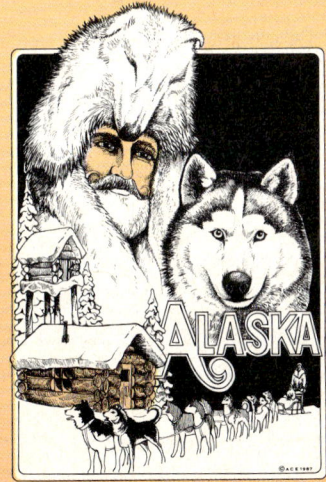

Trapper Jack's TRADING POST

701 West Fourth Avenue
Anchorage, Alaska 99501
(907) 272-6110
WE MAIL

FREE Alaskan Tote Bag

---

longer excursions by motorcoach, rail, ferry and air travel to nearby attractions such as Prince William Sound or remote areas are also available. Inquire at your hotel, see ads this section or contact a travel agent.

The Alaska Public Lands Information Center, located in the historic Federal Bldg. on 4th Avenue and F Street, offers a wide variety of information on all of Alaska's state and federal parks, forests and wildlife refuges. Displays, video programs and computers permit self-help trip-planning. Expert staff provide additional assistance and supply maps, brochures and other aids. Federal passports (Golden Age, Eagle and Access) and state park passes are available. Reservations may be made here (in person or by mail only) for U.S. Forest Service cabins throughout the state. Receive up-to-date public lands news by touch-tone phone by calling 258-PARK for recorded information. The center is open year-round. Summer hours are 9 A.M. to 7 P.M. daily. Open in winter 10 A.M. to 5:30 P.M. Monday through Saturday. Closed holidays. Phone 271-2737

"**RV ALASKA**" with "**THE ORIGINAL**"

ALL RIGS GO! — SINCE 1983

VANS, MOTOR HOMES   TRAILERS, 5TH-WHEELS

"Join us for Rendezvous '92" A 1500-mile long extravaganza!

SPECIAL ALASKAN RV ADVENTURES

- 39 day "ESCORTED" ALASKA TOUR
- FLY / DRIVE / CRUISE TOURS
- INDEPENDENT RV TOURS
- RV RENTALS AVAILABLE
- SPECIAL ADD-ON ADVENTURES
- FISHING / FLIGHTSEEING / RAFTING

FREE 16 PAGE COLOR BROCHURE

1-800-426-9865

CALL TOLL FREE OR WRITE
ALASKA-YUKON RV CARAVANS
400 "D" Street, Suite 210
Anchorage, Alaska 99501

Denny's

ALWAYS OPEN
Three locations in ANCHORAGE
- DeBarr & Bragaw
- Benson & Denali St.
- Dimond Blvd. & New Seward Hwy.

FAIRBANKS - Airport Road

Children's Menu   No Smoking Section

north of the Holiday Inn, between A and C streets. Parking is $5 per space, per day. For more information, phone 276-8970.

Highway: Anchorage can be reached via the Glenn Highway and the Seward Highway.

ATTRACTIONS

Get Acquainted: Start at the Log Cabin Visitor Information Center at 4th Avenue and F Street, open 7:30 A.M. to 7 P.M. June through August; 8:30 A.M. to 6 P.M. in May and September; and 9 A.M. to 4 P.M. the remainder of the year; phone 274-3531. Free visitor guidebooks.

Take a Historic Walking Tour: Start at the Log Cabin Visitor Information Center at 4th Avenue and F Street. The Anchorage Convention and Visitors Bureau's *Anchorage Visitors Guide* has an excellent guide for a downtown walking tour.

Take a Tour: Several tour operators offer local and area sightseeing tours. These range from a 3-hour narrated motorcoach tour of Anchorage to full-day tours of area attractions such as Portage Glacier and Alyeska resort and ski area. Two-day or

---

Sport Fishing Alaska
If you're planning a fishing trip to Alaska, make sure you really PLAN IT!

Call us today at
(907) 344-8674
FAX (907) 349-4330

Russ and Donna Redick
Owners

✓ We're not a guide service: our job is to PLAN YOUR TRIP FOR YOU.
✓ YOU don't need to be an expert on Alaska sportfishing; we've done that for you with 25 years of experience with Alaska Department of Fish & Game.
✓ Guide service or solo; accommodations, connections, advice on gear and optimum times; we do it all for you BEFORE YOU LEAVE FOR ALASKA!

Sport Fishing Alaska — Alaska's only sportfisherman's planning service.
1401-M Shore Drive, Anchorage, Alaska 99515

STEWART'S PHOTO SHOP
ACROSS FROM THE TOURIST LOG CABIN
531 West Fourth Ave. • Anchorage • Phone 272-8581
ALASKA'S LARGEST PHOTO SHOP   Open 9-9 Mon.-Sat., 10-6 Sun.
Photograph our live reindeer!
Over 50 years' collection of Alaska color slides, movies, photos, and postcards.
Alaskan jade for sale by the pound or ton!

PORTAGE GLACIER.
DON'T LEAVE UNTIL YOU'VE SEEN IT.

And unless you see Portage Glacier with us, you'll probably be looking at it from miles away. Because only Gray Line's cruise on the mv Ptarmigan can give you a close-up view of this icy-blue giant. So close you'll want to reach out and touch it. Here is magnificence and antiquity and beauty— seen not from the shore, but from the deck of our vessel that brings you face to face with it. It's truly an experience you'll not forget.

Just an hour's drive from Anchorage, Gray Line has ample RV parking and cruises leaving every ninety minutes. Call or stop by our Anchorage office or the Portage Glacier Cruise Center for information or reservations.

ADULTS $19.50
$9.75 children under 12

Bring this ad to the Portage Glacier Cruise Center to receive $2 off each adult fare.

GRAY LINE   Gray Line of Alaska
745 West 4th Avenue, Anchorage, AK 99501 (907) 277-5581
Portage Glacier Cruise Center at Portage Lake (907) 783-2983

Portage Glacier Cruises operates on National Forest System Lands of the Chugach National Forest and is operated under a special use permit from the U.S.D.A. Forest Service.